THE CATALOG OF CATALOGS V

By Edward L. Palder

The Complete Mail-Order Directory

WOODBINE HOUSE • 1997

Published by Woodbine House, 6510 Bells Mill Road, Bethesda, MD 20817. 800/843-7323.

© 1997 Edward L. Palder

Fifth Edition

All rights reserved under International and Pan-American Copyright Conventions. Published in the United States of America by Woodbine House, Inc.

Library of Congress Cataloging-in-Publication Data

Palder, Edward L.
 The catalog of catalogs V : the complete mail-order directory / Edward L. Palder.—5th ed.
 p. cm.
 Rev. and updated ed. of: The catalog of catalogs IV.
 Includes indexes.
 ISBN 0-933149-88-3 (pbk.)
 1. Commercial catalogs—United States—Directories. 2. Mail-order business—United States—Directories. I. Palder, Edward L. Catalog of catalogs IV. II. Title.
HF5466.P35 1997
381'.142'029473—dc21
96-49762
CIP

Manufactured in the United States of America

Dedicated to everyone who enjoys using this book.

❖ HELP WANTED ❖

Dear Reader:

I am planning to update **The Catalog of Catalogs** periodically. To do this, I need your help.

If you know of a company that you think should be included in the next edition, or if you are dissatisfied, for any reason, with the response you receive from a company, please let me know. I will closely evaluate all your recommendations for the next edition of **The Catalog of Catalogs.**

I would also like to invite merchants or manufacturers who would like to be listed in the next edition, or whose address or telephone number has changed, to send their mailing address and telephone number, along with a copy of their latest catalog(s) to:

> The Catalog of Catalogs
> P.O. Box 6590
> Silver Spring, MD 20916-6590

To those readers of the previous editions who took the time to write me suggesting subjects and companies to be added or deleted—thanks a million. And I thank all of you in advance for your help in making future editions of **The Catalog of Catalogs** as complete as possible.

Happy catalog shopping!

Sincerely,
Edward L. Palder

TABLE OF CONTENTS

INTRODUCTION xxi

AIR COMPRESSORS 1

AIR CONDITIONERS & CONTROLS 1

AIR PURIFIERS 1

AIRCRAFT & AERO ACTIVITIES 1
   Aircraft Kits (Fixed Wing Powered) 1
   Aircraft Kits (Helicopters & Gyroplanes) 2
   Aircraft Kits (Sailplanes & Motorgliders) 2
   Aircraft Recovery Systems & Para-Gear ... 3
   Avionics & Communications Equipment 3
   Hang Gliding & Powered Parachutes 3
   Parts & Tools 4
   Pilot Supplies & Equipment 4

ALARM SYSTEMS, LOCKS & REMOTE CONTROL EQUIPMENT 5

ALL-TERRAIN VEHICLES (ATVs) & SAND BUGGIES 5

ANTIQUES & REPRODUCTIONS 5
   Antique & Art Restoration 5
   Antiques & Reproductions 6

APPLIANCES 7
   Manufacturers 7
   Retailers 7

APPLIQUES 8

ARCHERY & BOW HUNTING 8

ART SUPPLIES & EQUIPMENT 9
   Graphic Art Supplies 9
   Modeling & Casting Supplies 11

ARTHRITIS AIDS 12

ARTWORK 12
   Posters, Paintings, Prints & Other Art Forms 12
   Sculptures, Carvings & Castings 15

ASTROLOGY 16

ASTRONOMY 16
   Astrophotography 16
   Observatories & Planetariums 16
   Radio Astronomy 16
   Software 16
   Telescopes & Accessories 17

AUTOGRAPHS 19

AUTOMOTIVE PARTS & ACCESSORIES .. 21
   Automotive Art & Gifts 21
   Batteries & Chargers 21
   Body Repair Parts 21
   Books & Other Publications 21
   Carriers and Racks 22
   Electricity Conversion 22
   Exhaust Systems & Mufflers 22
   Glass 22
   Headlights & Headlight Covers 22
   License Plates 22
   Locks & Keys 22
   Miscellaneous Repairs 22
   Paint & Touch-Up Supplies 23
   Parts for All Makes & Models 23
   Parts for Specific Makes & Models 25
   Plating 43
   Radar Detectors (Manufacturers) 43
   Radar Detectors (Retailers) 43
   Radiators 43
   Ramps & Lifts 43
   Replica & Conversion Kits 44
   Replica & Conversion Parts & Accessories ... 45

    Rubber Parts & Weatherstripping 45
    Seat & Body Covers 45
    Seats 46
    Security Systems (Manufacturers) 46
    Security Systems (Retailers) 46
    Steering Wheels 46
    Stereo Equipment (Manufacturers) 46
    Stereo Equipment (Retailers) 47
    Tires 47
    Tools 47
    Trailers & Recreational Vehicles 47
    Truck Parts 48
    Upholstery, Carpets & Tops 49
    Wheels & Hubcaps 49

AWARDS & TROPHIES 50

AWNINGS & PATIO COVERS 50

BABY CARE 50

BABY CARE (NURSING SUPPLIES) 51

BADGES & BUTTONS 51

BADMINTON 51

BALLOONS 52

BANKS 52

BARBECUE GRILLS 52

BASEBALL & SOFTBALL 53
    Clothing 53
    Equipment 53

BASKETBALL 54
    Clothing 54
    Equipment 54

BASKETS 55

BATHROOM FIXTURES & ACCESSORIES 56

BATHROOM SCALES 57

BATTERIES & CHARGERS 57

BEAD CRAFTING 58

BEAR MAKING & CLOTHING 60

BEARS 60

BEDDING 61
    Comforters & Bed Coverings 61
    Pillows & Sheets 62

BEEKEEPING 63

BEER CANS & STEINS 64

BELLY DANCING 64

BICYCLES & ACCESSORIES 64
    Bicycles 64
    Clothing 66
    Parts & Accessories 66
    Tricycles 67

BILLIARDS 67

BINOCULARS 68

BIRD FEEDERS & HOUSES 70

BIRTH ANNOUNCEMENTS 71

BLACKSMITHING 71

BLOCK PRINTING 71

BOATS & BOATING 71
    Boating Apparel & Safety Gear 71
    Boat-Building Kits & Plans 72
    Canoes, Kayaks, Shells & Paddles 72
    Catamarans 74
    Inflatable Boats 74
    Life Rafts 75
    Miscellaneous Boats 75
    Rowing Boats & Shells 76
    Sailboats & Supplies 76
    General Supplies & Equipment 76
    Instruments & Electronics 78
    Nautical Books, Videos & Gifts 79

BOCCIE 79

BOOK REPAIR & BINDING 80	**CALCULATORS** 98
BOOK SEARCH SERVICES 80	**CALENDARS** 98
BOOKKEEPING & ACCOUNTING SUPPLIES 80	**CALLIGRAPHY** 98
BOOKPLATES & BOOKMARKS 80	**CAMCORDERS & ACCESSORIES** 99
BOOKS 80	*Manufacturers* 99
Bargain Books 80	*Retailers* 99
Children's Books 80	*Video Editing Equipment* 100
General Books 87	**CAMPING & BACKPACKING** 100
Large-Print & Braille Books 93	*Clothing & Shoes* 100
Religious Books & Software 93	*Equipment* 102
Used Books 94	*Food* 105
BOOKS ON TAPE 94	**CANDLES, CANDLE MAKING & CANDLE HOLDERS** 105
BOOMERANGS 94	**CANDY MAKING & CAKE DECORATING** 106
BOWLING 95	
Clothing 95	**CANES, WALKERS & HIKING STICKS** .. 106
Equipment 95	**CANNING & PRESERVING** 106
BOXING 95	**CARNIVAL SUPPLIES** 107
Clothing 95	**CAROUSEL FIGURES & ART** 107
Equipment 95	**CDs, CASSETTES & RECORDS** 107
BREAD MAKING 96	*Archival Supplies* 107
BRIDGE 96	*Children's Recordings* 107
BRUSHES 96	*Collectible Recordings* 107
BULLETIN & CHALKBOARDS 96	*Current Recordings* 108
BUMPER STICKERS 96	*Radio Recordings* 111
BUSINESS CARDS, ID CARDS & CARD CASES 96	*Soundtracks* 111
	Storage Cabinets 111
BUTTER CHURNS 97	**CERAMIC & POTTERY SUPPLIES** 111
BUTTERFLIES 97	**CHAIR CANING** 114
CABINETS 97	**CHECKS** 114
Bathroom Cabinets 97	**CHEERLEADING** 114
General Purpose Cabinets 97	**CHEESE MAKING** 114
Kitchen Cabinets 97	**CHESS** 115

**CHINA PAINTING &
METAL ENAMELING** 115

CHINA, POTTERY & STONEWARE 115

CHOIR GOWNS 117

**CHRISTMAS DECORATIONS &
OTHER ORNAMENTS** 117

**CHURCH, SYNAGOGUE &
CLERGY SUPPLIES** 118

CIGAR STORE INDIANS 118

CLOCKS & CLOCK MAKING 118

CLOSETS & STORAGE SYSTEMS 119

CLOTHING & ACCESSORIES 119
   Bridal Fashions *119*
   Children's Clothing *119*
   Exercise Clothing *120*
   Full-Figured Women's Clothing *120*
   Lingerie & Underwear *121*
   Maternity Clothing *122*
   Men & Women's Clothing *122*
   Natural Fiber Clothing *125*
   Petite Fashions *125*
   Shirts *126*
   Short Men *126*
   Special-Needs Clothing *126*
   Suspenders, Belts & Buckles *126*
   Sweaters *126*
   Tall & Big Men's Clothing *127*
   Tall Women's Clothing *127*
   T-Shirts & Sweatshirts *127*
   Uniforms *128*
   Western Clothing *128*

CLOWN SUPPLIES 129

COFFEE & ESPRESSO MAKERS 130

COIN-OPERATED MACHINES 130

**COMIC BOOKS & ARCHIVAL
SUPPLIES** 131

COMPASSES 131

COMPUTERS 131
   Components & Peripherals *131*
   Dust Covers & Cases *133*
   Education & Training *133*
   Furniture *134*
   Manufacturers *134*
   Retailers *135*
   Software (Public Domain & Shareware) .. *137*
   *Software Publishers
    (Disks & CD-ROMS)* *138*
   Software & CD-ROM Retailers *144*
   Supplies *145*

COOKIE CUTTERS 146

COPIERS & FAX MACHINES 146

COSMETICS & SKIN CARE 146

**COSTUMES & VINTAGE
CLOTHING** 148

COUNTRY CRAFTS 149

CRAFT SUPPLIES 151

CRICKET 152

CROQUET 152

CRYSTAL & GLASSWARE 152

CURTAINS, DRAPES & BLINDS 153
   Accessories & Controls *153*
   Blinds & Window Shades *153*
   Curtains & Drapes *154*

DANCING 154
   Ballet Barres *154*
   Clothing & Costumes *154*
   Music *155*
   Shoes *155*

DARTS 156

DECALS, EMBLEMS & PATCHES 156

DECORATIVE ITEMS 157

DECOUPAGE 157

DEPARTMENT & GENERAL MERCHANDISE STORES 158

DIABETIC SUPPLIES 158

DISPLAY FIXTURES & PORTABLE EXHIBITS 159

DOLLHOUSES & MINIATURES 160

DOLL MAKING & DOLL CLOTHING ... 163

DOLLS 164

DRAFTING SUPPLIES 166

DUMBWAITERS 166

EGG CRAFTING 166

ELECTRIC GENERATORS & ENGINES 166

ELECTRICAL SUPPLIES 166

ELECTRONICS EQUIPMENT 167
   Components & Equipment 167
   Kits & Plans 168
   Test Equipment 168
   Tools & Accessories 169

ELECTROPLATING 169

ENGRAVING & ETCHING 169

EXERCISE EQUIPMENT 170

FABRIC PAINTING, DYEING & OTHER DECORATING 171

FABRICS & TRIM 171
   Fabrics 171
   Lace & Ribbon 173

FANS 174

FAUCETS & PLUMBING FIXTURES 174

FEATHERS 174

FENCES & GATES 175

FENCING 175

FIRE FIGHTING & POLICE ITEMS 175

FIRE SAFETY 175
   Escape Ladders 175
   Fire Extinguishers 176
   Smoke Detectors 176
   Sprinkler Systems 176

FIREPLACES 176
   Accessories & Tools 176
   Fireplaces & Fireplace Kits 176
   Mantels 177

FIREWORKS 177
   "Backyard" Fireworks 177
   Fireworks Display Specialists 177
   Fireworks Memorabilia 177

FISHING & FLY-TYING 178
   Equipment 178
   Fish-Finding Electronics 181

FLAGS & FLAG POLES 181

FLOWERS & PLANTS 182
   Artificial Flowers 182
   Dried Flowers 182

FOIL CRAFTS 182

FOOD PROCESSORS & DRYERS 183

FOODS 183
   Apple Cider 183
   Breads & Rolls 183
   Cakes, Cookies & Pies 184
   Candy & Dessert Sauces 185
   Caviar 188
   Cheese 188
   Creole & Cajun 189
   Ethnic 189
   Fruits & Vegetables 191
   Gift Assortments & Gourmet Specialties 192
   Gingerbread Houses 195
   Health & Natural 195
   Maple Syrup 196
   Meats 196
   Nuts 199

Popcorn 200
Preserves, Jellies & Honey 200
Salt-free & Low-salt 201
Seafood 201
Seasonings & Condiments 203
Sugar-free & Dietetic 206
Tea, Coffee & Cocoa 206

FOODS, RECIPE MANAGEMENT & COOKBOOK SOFTWARE 207

FOOTBALL 208
Clothing 208
Equipment 208

FOUNTAINS 209

FRAMES & FRAMING SUPPLIES 209

FUND-RAISING 210

FURNACES, HEATING SYSTEMS & CONTROLS 211

FURNITURE 211
Bed 211
Beds, Adjustable 212
Children's Furniture 212
Furniture Kits 212
Home Furnishings 212
Lift Chairs 216
Office Furniture 217
Outdoor Furniture 217
Wicker & Rattan 218

GARAGE DOORS & OPENERS 218

GARDENING EQUIPMENT & SUPPLIES 219
Beneficial Insects, Organisms & Pest Controls 219
Carts 219
Chippers & Shredders 219
Farm Equipment & Supplies 220
Fertilizers & Plant Food 220
Greenhouses 220
Hydroponic Gardening Supplies 221
Indoor Gardening Supplies 222
Landscaping Stone 222

Lawn Ornaments & Statues 222
Markers 223
Mowers, Trimmers & Blowers 223
Organic Gardening Supplies 224
Pots & Planters 224
Software 225
Soil Testing 225
Tillers 225
Tools & Sprayers 225
Topiary Frames & Supplies 227
Tractors 227
Water Gardening Supplies 227
Watering & Irrigation Equipment 227

GARDENING—PLANTS & SEEDS 228
African Violets & Gesneriads 228
Aquatic Plants 228
Azaleas & Rhododendrons 228
Bamboo 229
Banana Plants 229
Begonias 229
Berry Plants 229
Bonsai 230
Cacti & Succulents 231
Carnivorous Plants 231
Chrysanthemums 231
Citrus & Exotic Fruits 231
Daffodils 232
Dahlias 232
Ferns 232
Geraniums 232
Ginseng 233
Gladioli 233
Gourds 233
Grapes 233
Grasses & Ground Covers 233
Herbs 234
Hostas 235
House Plants & Indoor Gardens 235
Hydrangeas 236
Hoyas 236
Ivies & Vines 236
Lilacs 236
Marigolds 236
Mushrooms 236
Nurseries 236
Orchids 236
Palms 237
Peonies, Irises & Daylilies 237

Perennials & Ornamentals 238
Rock Gardens 239
Roses 240
Seeds & Bulbs 240
Shrubs 242
Terrariums 243
Trees 243
Vegetable Plants & Seeds 245
Wildflowers & Native Plants 246

GAZEBOS & OTHER GARDEN STRUCTURES 246

GENEALOGY 247
State Offices & Genealogical Associations 247
Retail Sources & Publishers 250
Software 250

GIFTS & GENERAL MERCHANDISE ... 250
Children's Gifts 250
Miscellaneous Gifts 251
Religious Gifts 258

GLASS COLLECTIBLES & DESIGNER ITEMS 258

GLOBES 258

GO KARTS & MINICARS 258

GOLF 258
Clothing 258
Equipment Manufacturers 259
Equipment Retailers 260
Left-handed Equipment 261

GREETING CARDS & GIFT WRAPPING 261

GUM BALL MACHINES 262

GUNS & AMMUNITION 262
Air Guns & Supplies 262
Ammunition & Ammunition-Loading Equipment 262
Antique, Muzzleloading & Replica Guns 263
Racks, Cases & Holsters 263
Scopes, Mounts & Sights 264

Sportshooting Rifles, Handguns & Shotguns 264
Targets & Range Supplies 265
Trap & Clay Target Shooting 266

GYMNASTICS 266

HAMMOCKS & SWINGS 266

HANDBALL 267

HARDWARE 267

HARMONICAS 268

HATS 268

HEALTH CARE SUPPLIES & AIDS 269
Supplies & Aids 269
Software 270

HEALTH CARE SUPPLIES & AIDS FOR THE DISABLED 271

HEARING & COMMUNICATION AIDS 272

HEAT EXCHANGERS 273

HOCKEY, FIELD 273

HOCKEY, ICE 273
Clothing 273
Equipment 273

HOME BUILDING & IMPROVEMENT .. 273
Ceilings 273
Cupolas 274
Door Chimes 274
Doors 274
Flooring 275
Frames & Beams 276
Paint & Refinishing Supplies 276
Paneling 276
Restoration Materials & Equipment 276
Roofing Materials 277
Salvaged Building Materials 277
Shutters 278
Siding 278

    Stairways 278
    Stucco, Bricks & Stones 278
    Switch Plates 279
    Tile & Linoleum 279
    Trim & Ornamental Materials 279
    Wallcoverings 280
    Window Coverings & Screens 281
    Windows & Skylights 282

HOMES & PREFABS 282
    Conventional & Solar Energy Homes 282
    Domes 283
    Log Homes 283

HORSE & STABLE EQUIPMENT 284
    Health Care & Stable Supplies 284
    Horse Trailers 284
    Saddles & Tack 285

HORSESHOES 286

HOT TUBS, WHIRLPOOLS & SAUNAS 286

HOT WATER HEATERS 286

HOUSEWARES 286

HOVERCRAFT 286

HUMIDIFIERS 286

HUNTING 287
    Clothing & Equipment 287
    Game Calls, Lures & Scents 288

ICE-CREAM MACHINES 289

ICE SKATING 289

INCENSE 289

INCONTINENCE SUPPLIES 289

INDIAN (NATIVE AMERICAN) ARTS & CRAFTS 290

INTERCOMS 294

JET SKIS (PERSONAL WATERCRAFT) .. 295

JEWELRY 295

JEWELRY MAKING 298

JOKES & NOVELTIES 301

JUGGLING 301

JUKEBOXES 301

KALEIDOSCOPES 302

KITCHEN UTENSILS & COOKWARE .. 302

KITES 303

KNITTING 304
    Knitting Machines 304
    Patterns & Accessories 304
    Software 305

KNIVES & KNIFE MAKING 305
    Knives 305
    Sharpeners 306

LABORATORY & SCIENCE EQUIPMENT 306

LACROSSE 307

LADDERS 307

LAMPS & LIGHTING 307
    Chandeliers 307
    Dome Lighting 308
    Lamps & Fixtures 308
    Lamp Shades 311
    Outdoor Lighting 311
    Ultraviolet Light 312

LANGUAGE TRANSLATORS 312

LEATHER CRAFTS 312

LEFT-HANDED MERCHANDISE 312

LOG SPLITTERS 313

Section	Page
LUGGAGE, LUGGAGE-CARRIERS & BRIEFCASES	313
LUMBER	314
MACRAME	315
MAGIC TRICKS & VENTRILOQUISM	315
MAGNETS	316
MAGNIFYING GLASSES	316
MAILBOXES	316
MAILING LISTS	317
MAPS & INFORMATION NAVIGATORS	317
MARBLES	318
MARTIAL ARTS	318
MASSAGE, SALON & SPA EQUIPMENT	319
MATCHBOOK COVERS	319
MEMORABILIA & COLLECTIBLES (MISCELLANEOUS)	319
METAL CRAFTING & SILVERSMITHING	319
METAL DETECTORS	320
MICROSCOPES	321
MILITARY MEMORABILIA	321
General Memorabilia	321
Civil War Collectibles	322
War Medals & Souvenirs	323
MIRRORS	323
MODELS & MODEL BUILDING	323
Aircraft Models	323
Armor & Military Models	325
Automobile Models	325
Dioramas	327
Paper Airplanes	327
Radio Control Equipment	327
Rocket Models	327
Ship Models	328
Steam-Operated Models & Engine Kits	328
Supplies, Hardware & Plans	329
Tools	329
Train Models	330
MOTORCYCLES & MOTOR BIKES	331
Clothing & Helmets	331
Parts & Accessories	332
MOUNTAIN & ICE CLIMBING	333
MOVIE & THEATRICAL MEMORABILIA	334
MOVIE & TV SCRIPTS	336
MOVIE & VIDEO PROJECTION EQUIPMENT	336
MOVIES (FILMS)	336
MUSIC BOOKS & SHEET MUSIC	337
MUSIC BOXES	337
MUSICAL INSTRUMENTS	337
NAMEPLATES	340
NEEDLECRAFTS	340
NEWSPAPERS & MAGAZINES	342
OFFICE & BUSINESS SUPPLIES	343
Business Forms & Booklets	343
General Office Supplies	343
Labels & Tags	344
Receipt Books	344
Shipping Supplies	345

ORIGAMI (PAPER FOLDING) 345

OSTOMY SUPPLIES 345

PADDLEBALL 346

PAGERS 346

PAPER COLLECTIBLES 346

PAPER CRAFTING & SCULPTING 347

PAPERWEIGHTS 347

PARTY DECORATIONS 347

PATIOS & WALKWAYS 347

PENS, PENCILS & DESK SETS 347

PERFUMERY SUPPLIES 348

PERSONALIZED & PROMOTIONAL PRODUCTS 349

PEST CONTROL 349

PETS 349
- *Bird Supplies* 349
- *Dog & Cat Supplies* 350
- *Tropical Fish Supplies* 351
- *Carriers* 352
- *Kennels & Enclosures* 352
- *Pet Doors* 353
- *Reptiles & Amphibians* 353

PHONE CARDS 354

PHONOGRAPHS 354

PHOTOGRAPHY 354
- *Albums & Photo Mounts* 354
- *Backgrounds* 355
- *Bags & Camera Cases* 355
- *Books* 355
- *Camera Manufacturers* 356
- *Darkroom Equipment & Supplies* ... 356
- *Enlargers* 377
- *Exposure Meters & Guides* 377

- *Film (Manufacturers & Distributors)* 357
- *Filters* 357
- *Flash Units & Lighting* 357
- *Photo Processing* 358
- *Photo Restoration* 359
- *Retail Suppliers* 359
- *Slides* 361
- *Storage & Filing Systems* 361
- *Tripods & Monopods* 362
- *Underwater Photography Equipment* 362

PINATAS 362

PINE CONES 362

PINS & PINBACK BUTTONS 362

PLASTICS 363

PLATES, COLLECTIBLE 363

PLATFORM TENNIS 363

PLAYGROUND EQUIPMENT 363

POLITICAL MEMORABILIA 364

PORCELAIN COLLECTIBLES & FIGURINES 364

POSTCARDS 364

POTPOURRI 366

PRINTING PRESSES 366

PROSPECTING & ROCKHOUNDING ... 367

PUPPETS & MARIONETTES 368

PURSES & WALLETS 368

PUZZLES 368

QUILTS & QUILTING 369

RACQUETBALL & SQUASH 369
- *Clothing* 369
- *Equipment* 369

RADIATOR ENCLOSURES & REGISTERS 370

RADIOS 370
   Amateur Radio Equipment 370
   Antique Radios & Repairs 372
   Citizen Band Equipment & Transceivers 372

RADON TESTING 373

RAFTING & WHITEWATER RUNNING 373

RECYCLED & ENVIRONMENTALLY SAFE PRODUCTS 373

ROCKS, MINERALS & FOSSILS 373
   Display Cases & Lights 373
   Fossils 373
   Meteorites 374
   Miscellaneous Varieties & Equipment 374
   Petrified Wood 376

RODEO EQUIPMENT 376

ROLLER & IN-LINE SKATES 376

RUBBER STAMPS & EMBOSSING SUPPLIES 376

RUGBY 378

RUG MAKING 378

RUG & CARPET RESTORATION 378

RUGS & CARPETS 378

RUNNING, JOGGING & WALKING ... 380
   Clothing & Shoes 380
   Pedometers & Stopwatches 380

SAFES 381

SAFETY & EMERGENCY EQUIPMENT 381

SAILBOARDS 381

SCIENCE KITS & PROJECTS 381

SCOOTERS 382

SCOUTING 382

SEASHELLS 382

SEPTIC TANKS 382

SEWING 382
   Dress Forms 382
   Notions & Supplies 382
   Patterns & Kits 384
   Sewing Machines, Pleaters & Sergers 385
   Stuffing & Fill 385
   Tags & Labels 385

SHEDS, BARNS & OTHER BUILDINGS 386

SHOES & BOOTS 386
   Men & Women's Shoes & Boots 386
   Western Boots 387

SHUFFLEBOARD 388

SIGNS & SIGN-MAKING 388

SILK-SCREENING 389

SILVER & FLATWARE 389

SKATEBOARDS 390

SKIING 390
   Clothing 390
   Equipment & Accessories 391
   Goggles 392

SKIN DIVING & SCUBA EQUIPMENT 392

SLEDS, SNOWBOARDS & TOBOGGANS 393

SLIPCOVERS & UPHOLSTERY 393

SNOW BLOWERS 393

SNOWMOBILES 393

SNOWSHOES 393

SOAP MAKING 393

SOCCER 394
    Clothing 394
    Equipment 394

SOLAR & WIND ENERGY 395

SOLARIUMS & SUNROOMS 396

SOUVENIRS 396

SPELEOLOGY (CAVE EXPLORATION) 396

SPINNING WHEELS, LOOMS & CARDERS 396

SPORTS & NON-SPORTS CARDS 397
    Non-Sports Cards 397
    Sports Cards 398

SQUARE DANCING 399
    Amplifiers & Microphones 399
    Badges & Buckles 399
    Books & Videos 400
    Clothing & Shoes 400
    Records & CDs 400

STAINED GLASS CRAFTING 400

STAIRLIFTS & ELEVATORS 401

STATIONERY & ENVELOPES 401

STENCILS 402

STEREOS & CD PLAYERS 403
    Headphones 403
    Home-Theater & Surround Sound Systems 403
    Manufacturers 403
    Retailers 404
    Speakers 405
    Storage Cabinets & Racks 405

STICKERS 405

STOCK CAR RACING (NASCAR) 405

STONE SCULPTING & CARVING 406

STOVES & OVENS 406

SUNDIALS 406

SUNGLASSES & EYE WEAR 407

SURFBOARDS & WINDSURFING 407

SURPLUS & LIQUIDATION MERCHANDISE 407

SURVEILLANCE & PERSONAL PROTECTION EQUIPMENT 408

SWIMMING POOLS & EQUIPMENT .. 408

TABLE TENNIS 409

TABLECLOTHS, PADS & OTHER LINENS 409

TAPESTRIES & WALL HANGINGS 409

TATTOOING SUPPLIES & BODY JEWELRY 409

TAXIDERMY 410

TELEPHONES & ANSWERING MACHINES 410
    Antique Telephones 410
    Cellular Telephones 410
    Telephones & Answering Machines 411

TENNIS 411
    Clothing 411
    Equipment 411

TERM PAPERS 413

TETHERBALL 413	
THEATRICAL SUPPLIES 413	
Make-Up 413	
Plays 414	
Stage Equipment 414	
THERMOMETERS 414	
THIMBLES 414	
TICKETS 414	
TOBACCO, PIPES & CIGARS 415	
TOLE & DECORATIVE PAINTING ... 415	
TOOLS 416	
Clamps 416	
Hand & Power Tools 416	
Paint Sprayers 420	
Welding Equipment 420	
TOWELS 420	
TOY MAKING 420	
TOY SOLDIERS & MINIATURE FIGURES 420	
TOYS & GAMES 421	
Character Toys 421	
Educational Toys & Games 422	
Electronic Toys & Games 423	
General Toys & Games 423	
Special-Needs Toys & Games 424	
Water Toys 424	
TRACK & FIELD SPORTS 424	
Clothing 424	
Equipment 424	
TRAMPOLINES 425	
TRUNK (STORAGE CHEST) REPAIR ... 425	
TVs & VCRs 425	
Manufacturers 425	
Retailers 426	

Cable TV Equipment 427	
Satellite Equipment 427	
TYPEWRITERS & WORD PROCESSORS 427	
UMBRELLAS 428	
VACUUM CLEANERS 428	
VIDEO CASSETTES, TAPES & DISCS ... 428	
VISION IMPAIRMENT AIDS 430	
VITAMINS & NUTRITIONAL SUPPLEMENTS 430	
VOLLEYBALL 431	
Clothing 431	
Equipment 431	
WATER PURIFIERS 431	
WATER SKIING 432	
Clothing 432	
Equipment 432	
WEATHER FORECASTING 433	
WEATHER VANES 433	
WEDDING INVITATIONS & ACCESSORIES 434	
WELDING & FOUNDRY EQUIPMENT ... 435	
WELLS 435	
WHEAT WEAVING 435	
WHEELCHAIRS, TRANSPORTERS & LIFTS 435	
WIGS 436	
WIND CHIMES 436	
WINE, BEER & VINEGAR MAKING ... 437	

WINE CELLARS & RACKS 437

WINES 438

WIRE CRAFTING 438

WOOD FINISHING & RESTORING ... 438

WOODWORKING & WOODCARVING 439
- *Parts, Kits & Supplies* 439
- *Plans* 440
- *Sandpaper* 440

WRESTLING 440

YARN & SPINNING FIBERS 440

YOGA 442

Corporate Index 445

Subject Index 511

❖ INTRODUCTION ❖

Ten years ago, when the **Catalog of Catalogs** was first published, it was the size of an average novel. It is now the size of a hefty phone book. The number of listings has grown by nearly 6000 companies, and the number of product categories has doubled.

Clearly, mail-order shopping is more popular than ever before. And why shouldn't it be? Shopping by mail makes good sense. When you shop by mail, you can:

- ❖ shop when it is convenient for *you*;
- ❖ choose from a wider selection of merchandise than is available in neighborhood stores;
- ❖ shop around for the best deal without being pressured to buy;
- ❖ avoid long lines and parking hassles;
- ❖ return unsatisfactory purchases with no questions asked.

The **Catalog of Catalogs V** is designed to help you locate the companies that sell precisely what you want to buy. This new edition contains listings for about 14,000 different retailers, wholesalers, and manufacturers, grouped into nearly 850 subject areas. As in previous editions, companies that offer a diverse line of products are sometimes listed in more than one category. The number of double listings, however, has been kept to a minimum, so that as many different catalog suppliers as possible could be included. As before, the **Catalog of Catalogs V** also includes companies that will send free or low-cost information about particular brands of merchandise, or lists of nearby dealers who carry those brands.

The **Catalog of Catalogs V** gives you one of the widest possible selections of merchandise to choose from. Retail stores order their inventories from many of the same companies whose catalogs are listed in this book, but stores only have room to display a few items. When you browse through a catalog, you get to see all the possibilities. What's more, you can often save yourself a bundle in the process. First, if you don't live in the state where the mail-order company is based, you might not have to pay sales tax. (A few states have entered into reciprocal arrangements with other states and require that sales tax be paid even on catalog orders.) Second, since mail-order houses don't have to pay for fancy window displays or expensive floor space, they often pass their savings on to you, the catalog shopper.

Making *The Catalog of Catalogs V* Work for You

The **Catalog of Catalogs V** is a directory for obtaining catalogs and information, not an order catalog. The information given is intended to help you determine which catalogs you would like to have and how to get them.

Many of the catalogs, brochures, price lists, and information packets in **The Catalog of Catalogs V** are free. You can request free information simply by calling the phone number in the catalog description or by sending in a postcard. Some mail-order companies ask that a business-size, self-addressed, stamped envelope (SASE) accompany requests for catalogs or other information. When this is the case, you'll find the notation immediately following the address in the catalog listing. If there's a charge for a catalog, you'll also find this information right after the address—with information about how much of the charge, if any, is refundable after you place an order.

No matter what the charge for a catalog is, *never send cash through the mail.* Pay by money order or personal check. That way, if you don't receive the information you requested, you'll have proof of your payment. Not that this is likely to happen. In compiling this new edition of **The Catalog of Catalogs,** I reviewed all of the listings in the fourth edition to verify they were still in business, and that their addresses hadn't changed. I sent at least one letter to each company—whether a repeat or new listing—and requested that they verify the information I had on file. However, merchants do go out of business, change their names, combine with other companies, or move to new addresses without notifying the Post Office. In addition, if you are using this book several years after its publication date, you are bound to run into listings—especially of small businesses--that are no longer accurate. I therefore apologize in advance should any of your requests for information go unanswered.

I'm continually updating the information in **The Catalog of Catalogs V,** so if any of your catalog requests are returned as undeliverable, I invite you to send me the returned correspondence and any other information available. If I have a more recent address, I'll send it to you. Your requests for this information should be sent to: Edward L. Palder, The Catalog of Catalogs, P.O. Box 6590, Silver Spring, MD 20916-6590.

One final note about ordering catalogs: try to be patient. Catalogs are usually mailed fourth class, and delivery can take from two to three weeks. Possible delays can occur when companies are revising or reprinting their catalogs, and some companies process catalog requests only once or twice a month. Remember, too, that some companies *will not send the information requested unless a SASE is enclosed.*

Finding the Catalogs You Need

Catalogs in **The Catalog of Catalogs V** are grouped according to subject matter. For example, all computer catalogs are listed in the *Computer* section, and all food catalogs appear in the *Foods* section. Long sections are further divided into subsections. In the *Computer* section, for example, catalog listings for manufacturers; retailers; components and peripherals; dust covers and cases; education and training materials; software; and supplies are grouped together. In the *Foods* section, catalogs featuring cakes & cookies; maple syrup; meats; and other types of food are grouped together.

Within **The Catalog of Catalogs V,** subjects are listed alphabetically, from *Air Compressors* to *Yoga*. Within each subject area, I've listed catalogs alphabetically by company name. *Silver Eagle Creations* comes before *Silver Nugget*, and so on. Please note that when a company name begins with a personal name, it's alphabetized by last name, instead of first name. For example, *Earl May Seeds & Nursery Company* is alphabetized as though it began with an "M" instead of an "E"; *Walter Drake & Sons* is alphabetized as if it began with a "D." Also, names that include numerals are alphabetized as though the numerals were spelled out.

You can find catalogs within **The Catalog of Catalogs V** two ways: 1) by a company's name, or 2) by the type of product it sells. To locate the catalog of a company whose name you already know, simply turn to the Corporate Index near the end of the book. This index lists the names of every source of product information described in **The Catalog of Catalogs V,** alphabetized according to the rules outlined above. Sometimes a company is listed more than once because it carries several different types of products. To locate catalogs that offer a specific type of product, check the Table of Contents first. Like the book as a whole, the Table of Contents is arranged alphabetically by subject. So if you were looking for catalogs of pet supplies, you'd turn to the "P's" in the Table of Contents to find the page number you needed.

If you can't find exactly what you're looking for in the Table of Contents, turn to the Subject Index at the very back of the book. Here I've listed topics under as many alternate names as I could think of—for example, the words "dishes" and "plates" will refer you to the pages listing suppliers of china. Through cross references ("see also's") the Subject Index can also direct you to related topics you might otherwise overlook. For instance, the listing for *Greeting Cards* instructs you to see also *Birth Announcements* and *Wedding Invitations*.

Your Mail-Order Rights

Although shopping by mail can be fun and adventuresome, it's not entirely without its hassles. Although I made every effort to ensure that **The Catalog of Catalogs V** includes only reputable merchants, sometimes your catalog orders may be damaged in transit, fail to live up to your expectations, take too long to be delivered, or never arrive. Fortunately, in each of these instances, you can take steps to get a refund, repairs, or replacement.

Packages Damaged in Transit

Let's start with the simplest situation. If something you've ordered arrives with obvious damage to the package, write "refused" on the wrapper and return it unopened. Don't sign for it if it arrives insured, registered, certified, or C.O.D., or you'll have to pay the return postage. If you don't discover that your merchandise is damaged until you've opened the package, repackage it with a note describing the problem. Then mail it back by certified or insured mail and wait for the company to send you a free replacement.

Unsatisfactory Merchandise

What if something you ordered breaks soon *after* it arrives, or is unsatisfactory for other reasons (it's the wrong size, shoddily made, or completely different from the description in the catalog)? In this case, your next step depends on the exchange policy of the company you ordered from. Many companies allow you to return unsatisfactory merchandise within thirty days after purchase; others offer unconditional money-back guarantees for the lifetime of their products. Check a company's warranty policies *before you buy*. A bargain is no bargain if it comes without a guarantee. Consult the catalog for the company's return policies and for any special procedures to be followed when returning merchandise for a replacement or refund.

If the company has no stated returns policy, don't give up. Noted consumer activist David Horowitz recommends that you send back the unsatisfactory item with a letter explaining why you're disappointed, a copy of your proof of purchase (cancelled check, money order, or credit card statement), and a copy of the original ad. If you don't receive a reply within two weeks, place a collect call to the president of the company to ask what action he or she intends to take. (Horowitz notes that you may not get through to the president, but should at least find out his or her name.) If your phone call doesn't resolve your problem, write a letter to the president informing him that you'll contact the deputy chief postal inspector in his region if you don't get a refund or replacement in seven days. Then do what you said you would. Bring copies of your letters and proof of purchase to the local post office and fill out a Consumer Service form. Your postmaster will turn the matter over to the postal inspectors and the Post Office Consumer Advocate for investigation of possible fraud.

Delayed or Missing Orders

What if your order never arrives? What if you wait days or weeks longer than the delivery time promised in the catalog and still no package? Under the Mail-Order Rule of the Federal Trade Commission, you can take immediate recourse. The Mail-Order Rule requires a company to ship your order within the time promised in its ad or within thirty days of receiving your order and payment. In case of delay, the merchant must notify you of the new shipment date. If the new date is more than thirty days later than the original date, you can cancel your order (in writing) for a full refund. If the new date is less than thirty days later, you can still cancel for a refund, but if you don't respond, it means that you accept the new date. In either case, it is advisable to send your reply by registered or certified mail so you have a return receipt to show that your letter was delivered.

The merchant must refund your money within ten days of receiving your cancellation (or notify your credit card company within one billing cycle to credit your account). If the merchant does not give you a refund, credit, or the merchandise, take or send a copy of your letter and proof of payment to the: Direct Marketing Association, 1111 19th St. NW, Suite 1100, Washington, DC 20036. If the merchant is a member of the DMA, the Association can pressure the merchant to refund your money.

Preventing and Reducing Problems

I hope you don't run into any of the problems described above, but in the off chance you might, there are several precautions that can make resolution of problems easier. When in doubt about a product, contact the merchant *before you buy* for information about warranties, exchange policies, missing facts, or unbelievable claims. Also make sure you fill out the order form accurately and completely, and enclose all shipping and handling charges requested by the company. And finally, always pay by check, money order, or credit card so you have proof of payment. Keep a record of the name and address of the company, the merchandise ordered, the date you placed the order, the name of the publication in which the merchandise was described, and the number of your money order or check.

Let the World Come to You

Now that you know the ground rules of mail-order shopping **The Catalog of Catalogs** way, why not take a moment to glance through the Table of Contents and Subject Index? I hope you will not only find what you are looking for, but also hundreds of other teasers you'll want to send away for. Don't resist the urge! Ordering by mail is by far the easiest, most convenient, and most cost-effective way I know of to shop. It can also be highly addictive, as the long-suffering civil servant who delivers all my catalogs and packages can attest. But don't worry. In the event you ever want to break the habit of catalog shopping, you can have your name removed from many merchants' mailing lists by contacting the Mail Preference Service, Direct Marketing Association, P.O. Box 9008, Farmingdale, NY 11735-9008. So, sit back and take advantage of all **The Catalog of Catalogs V** has to offer you. Send away for what you want, and let the world come to you.

❖ AIR COMPRESSORS ❖

AIR COMPRESSORS

Campbell Hausfeld, 100 Production Dr., Harrison, OH 45030: Free information ❖ Air compressors, pneumatic tools, and paint sprayers. 800-543-8622; 513-367-4811 (in OH).

Coleman Powermate Compressors, 118 W. Rock St., P.O. Box 206, Springfield, MN 56087: Free information ❖ Air compressors. 800-533-0365.

DeVilbiss Air Power, 213 Industrial Dr., Jackson, TN 38301: Free brochure ❖ Air compressors and air-operated tools. 800-888-2468; 901-423-7000 (in TN).

Stanley-Bostitch Inc., Briggs Dr., East Greenwich, RI 02818: Free information ❖ Air compressors. 800-556-6696.

AIR CONDITIONERS & CONTROLS

Carrier Corporation, 7310 W. Morris, Indianapolis, IN 46231: Free information ❖ Furnaces, heat pumps, and air conditioners. 317-243-0851.

G.E. Appliances, General Electric Company, Appliance Park, Louisville, KY 40225: Free information ❖ Air conditioners and heat pumps. 800-626-2000.

Hunter Fan Company, 2500 Fisco Ave., Memphis, TN 38114: Brochure $1 ❖ Programmable thermostats. 901-745-9222.

Sanyo, 21350 Lassen St., Chatsworth, CA 91311: Free information ❖ Ductless split system air conditioners. 818-998-7322.

Thomas Industries Inc., 1419 Illinois Ave., Sheboygan, WI 53082: Free information ❖ Air conditioners. 414-457-4891.

AIR PURIFIERS

AirXchange Inc., 401 V.F.W. Dr., Rockland, MA 02370: Free information ❖ Energy recovery ventilators. 617-871-4816.

Altech Energy Corporation, 7009 Raywood Rd., Madison, WI 53713: Free information ❖ Air-to-heat exchange ventilators. 608-221-4499.

Carrier Corporation, 7310 W. Morris, Indianapolis, IN 46231: Free information ❖ Electronic air cleaners. 317-243-0851.

✓ **Environtrol Corporation,** 7010 Washington Ave., St. Louis, MO 63130: Free catalog ❖ Air purification systems for use at home, work, or during travel. 800-423-1982; 314-966-6686 (in MO).

Garland Commercial Industries, 185 East South St., Freeland, PA 18224: Free catalog ❖ Kitchen ventilation systems, professional-style ranges, cooktops for the home, and racks for pots and utensils.

Honeywell Inc., Customer Assistance Center, 27-2164, Honeywell Plaza, P.O. Box 524, Minneapolis, MN 55440: Free information ❖ Electronic air cleaners. 800-345-6770.

Nortec Industries, Box 698, Ogdensburg, NY 13669: Free information ❖ Home air filters. 315-425-1255.

Sanyo, 21350 Lassen St., Chatsworth, CA 91311: Free information ❖ Electrostatic air cleaner/ionizer with an automatic smoke sensor. 818-998-7322.

Silos Products Inc., 2139 N. University Dr., Coral Springs, FL 33071: Free brochure ❖ Portable air cleaners, water filtration systems, dental hygienic cleaning systems, and accessories. 800-762-3355.

AIRCRAFT & AERO ACTIVITIES
Aircraft Kits (Fixed Wing Powered)

Adventure Air, P.O. Box 368, Berryville, AR 72616: Information $25 (specify model) ❖ Two or four-place amphibians. 501-423-5350.

Aero Designs Inc., 11910 Radium St., San Antonio, TX 78216: Information $8 ❖ Two-place low-wing aircraft. 210-308-9332.

Avid Aircraft, P.O. Box 728, Caldwell, ID 83606: Information $13 (specify model) ❖ Two-place high-wing aircraft and three-place amphibian. 208-454-2600.

Bounsall Aircraft, P.O. Box 506, Mesquite, NV 89024: Information $5 ❖ One-place high-wing VW-powered bush airplane. 702-346-2171.

Composite Companions Inc., 15425 Dayton Pike, Sale Creek, TN 37373: Free information ❖ Four-place canard airframe in a pre-molded quick-build kit. 423-332-8300.

Europa Aviation, 3400 Airfield Dr. West, Lakeland, FL 33811: Information $20 ❖ Two-place low-wing aircraft. 941-647-5355.

Express Design Inc., P.O. Box 609, Edmond, OR 97756: Information $15 ❖ Low-wing four-place aircraft with optional bellymounted cargo pod. 503-548-2723.

Falconar AVIA, 7739 81st Ave., Edmonton, Alberta, Canada T6C 0V4: Information $10 (specify model) ❖ One- and two-place low-wing aircraft and two-place low-wing amphibian. 403-465-2024.

Fisher Aero Corporation, 7118 SR 335, Portsmouth, OH 45662: Information $8 (specify model) ❖ One and two-place biplanes and two-place side-by-side high-wing aircraft. 614-820-2219.

Fisher Flying Products Inc., P.O. Box 468, Edgeley, ND 58433: Information $5 (specify model) ❖ Two-place biplane and one- and two-place high-wing or one-place low-wing aircraft. 701-493-2286.

Flightstar, Ellington Airport, P.O. Box 760, Ellington, CT 06029: Free brochure ❖ One- and two-place high-wing ultralight aircraft. 203-875-8185.

Hipp's Superbird's Inc., P.O. Box 266, Saluda, NC 28773: Information $5 ❖ One-place high-wing aircraft. 704-749-9134.

Innovation Engineering Inc., Davenport Municipal Airport, 8970 Harrison, Davenport, IA 52804: Information $5 ❖ Pusher-type two-place high-wing aircraft. 319-386-6966.

Keuthan Aircraft Corporation, 910 Airport Rd., Merritt Island, FL 32952: Free information ❖ Two-place side-by-side amphibian. 407-459-3200.

Kolb Company Inc., RD 3, Box 38, Phoenixville, PA 19460: Information $5 ❖ One and two-place high-wing aircraft. 215-948-4136.

Laron Aviation Technologies, P.O. Box 5026, Borger, TX 79008: Information $10 ❖ One- and two-place high-wing aircraft. 806-273-8513.

Leading Edge Air Foils Inc., 8242 Cessna Dr., Peyton, CO 80831: Catalog $6.95 ❖ One and two-place open-cockpit biplane. 719-683-5323.

Light Miniature Aircraft, 19695 NW 80th Dr., Okeechobee, FL 34072: Information $7.50 (specify model) ❖ One- and two-place high-wing aircraft. 813-467-0933.

Lightning Bug Aircraft Corporation, P.O. Box 40, Sheldon, SC 29941: Free information ❖ One-place low-wing aircraft. 803-549-1800.

Lockwood Aircraft Corporation, 280-B Hendricks Way, Sebring, FL 33870: Information $20 ❖ Two-place twin-engine pusher-type utility sport plane. 813-655-4242.

Loehle Aviation Inc., 380 Shipmans Creek Rd., Wartrace, TN 37183: Information $10 (specify model) ❖ One-place low-wing and high-wing aircraft. 615-857-3419.

Merlin Aircraft Inc., 509 Airport Rd., Muskegon, MI 49441: Information $10 (specify model) ❖ Two-place pontoon and two-place high-wing aircraft. 616-798-1622.

Murphy Aircraft Manufacturing Ltd., 8155-K Aitken Rd., Chilliwack, British Columbia, Canada V2R 4H5: Information $20 (specify model) ❖ Two-place biplane, two-place pontoon aircraft, and two and four-place high-wing monoplanes. 604-792-5855.

Neico Aviation Inc., 2244 Airport Way, Redmond, OR 97756: Information $15 (specify model) ❖ Two- and four-place low-wing aircraft. 503-923-2244.

Barney Oldfield Aircraft Company, P.O. Box 228, Needham, MA 02192: Information $10 (specify model) ❖ One- and two-place biplanes. 617-444-5480.

❖ AIRCRAFT & AERO ACTIVITIES ❖

Osprey Aircraft, 3741 El Ricon Way, Sacramento, CA 95864: Information $12 (specify model) ❖ Pusher-type two-place amphibian and two-place low-wing aircraft. 916-483-3004.

Arnet Pereya Aero Design, 490 Barnes Blvd., Rockledge, FL 32955: Free information ❖ One-place high-wing amphibian aircraft. 407-635-8005.

Phantom Sport Airplane, P.O. Box 1684, Carthage, NC 28327: Brochure $2 ❖ One-place high-wing amphibian. 919-947-4744.

Preceptor Aircraft, 1230 Shepard St., Hendersonville, NC 28792: Information $5 ❖ Two-place high-wing airplane with folding wings. 704-697-8284.

Progressive Aerodyne, 520 Clifton St., Orlando, FL 32808: Information $2 ❖ Two-place pusher-type high-wing amphibian. 407-292-3700.

Quad City Ultralight Aircraft, 3610 Coaltown Rd., Moline, IL 61265: Information $5 (specify model) ❖ One- and two-place high-wing aircraft. 309-764-3515.

Questair, 3800 McAree Rd., Waukegan, IL 60087: Information $10 ❖ Two-place low-wing aircraft. 708-244-0005.

Quicksilver Enterprises, P.O. Box 1572, Temecula, CA 92390: Information $6 (specify model) ❖ One and two-place high-wing aircraft with tricycle landing gear. 714-676-6886.

Quikkit, 9002 Summer Glen, Dallas, TX 75243: Information and video $22.50 ❖ Two-place amphibian. 214-349-0462.

Rand-Robinson Engineering Inc., 15641 Product Ln., Huntington Beach, CA 92649: Information $8 (specify model) ❖ One- and two-place low-wing aircraft. 714-898-3811.

Rans Company, 4600 Highway-183 Alternate, Hays, KS 67601: Catalog $15 (specify model) ❖ Two-place low-wing and one and two-place high-wing aircraft. 913-625-6346.

Skystar Aircraft Corporation, 100 N. Kings Rd., Nampa, ID 83687: Information $15 ❖ Two-place high-wing aircraft. 208-466-1711.

Spencer Amphibian Aircraft, P.O. Box 327, Kansas, IL 61933: Information $10 ❖ Four-place amphibian. 217-948-5505.

Stoddard-Hamilton Aircraft Inc., 18701 58th Ave. NE, Arlington, WA 98223: Information $25 (specify model) ❖ Two-place low-wing and high-wing aircraft. 360-435-8533.

Stolp Starduster Corporation, 4301 Twining Flabob Airport, Riverside, CA 95209: Information $5 (specify model) ❖ One and two-place biplanes. 714-686-7943.

TEAM Inc., 10790 Ivy Bluff Rd., Bradyville, TN 37026: Information $5 (specify model) ❖ One-place mid- and high-wing aircraft. 615-765-5397.

Titan Aircraft, 2730 Walter Main Rd., Geneva, OH 44041: Information $10 ❖ Pusher-type one- and two-place high-wing aircraft. 216-466-0602.

Tri-R Technologies, 1114 E. 5th St., Oxnard, CA 93030: Information $10 ❖ Two-place low-wing sport airplane. 805-385-3680.

Ultravia Aero International Inc., 300-D Airport Rd., Mascouche, Quebec, Canada J7K 3C1: Brochure $10 ❖ Two-place high-wing monoplane. 514-953-1491.

Van's Aircraft Inc., P.O. Box 160, North Plains, OR 97133: Information $8 (specify model) ❖ One- and two-place low-wing aircraft. 503-647-5117.

Velocity Aircraft, 200 W. Airport Rd., Sebastian, FL 32958: Information $29.50 ❖ Four-place canard pusher-type airplane. 407-589-1860.

Viking Aircraft Inc., P.O. Box 646, Elkhorn, WI 53121: Information $10 ❖ Two-place low-wing and canard aircraft. 414-723-1048.

Zenith Aircraft Company, P.O. Box 650, Mexico, MO 65265: Information $15 (specify model) ❖ Two-place low- and high-wing aircraft. 314-581-9000.

Aircraft Kits (Helicopters & Gyroplanes)

Air Command International Inc., 702 Cooper Dr., P.O. Box 1345, Wylie, TX 75098: Information $12.50 ❖ Gyroplanes. 214-442-6694.

Barnett Rotorcraft, 4307 Olivehurst Ave., Olivehurst, CA 95961: Information $15 (specify model) ❖ One- and two-place gyroplanes. 916-742-7416.

Ken Brock Manufacturing, 11852 Western Ave., Stanton, CA 90680: Information $7 ❖ One-place gyroplane and parts. 714-898-4366.

Canadian Home Rotors Inc., P.O. Box 370, Ear Falls, Ontario, Canada P0V 1T0: Free information ❖ Two-place helicoper kit. 807-222-2474.

Farrington Aircraft Corporation, 4460 Shemwell Ln., Paducah, KY 42003: Information $25 ❖ Two-place helicopter. 502-898-2403.

Helicraft Inc., P.O. Box 50, Riderwood, MD 21139: Catalog $10 ❖ Helicopter kits. 410-583-6366.

Revolution Helicopter Corporation, 1905 W. Jesse James Rd., Excelsior Springs, MO 64024: Information $15 ❖ Easy-to-assemble one-place helicopter. 800-637-6867.

Robinson Helicopter Company, 2901 Airport Dr., Torrance, CA 90505: Free information ❖ One-place helicopter. 310-539-0508.

Rotary Air Force Inc., Box 1236, Kindersley, Saskatchewan, Canada S0L 1S0: Information $12 ❖ Cross-country gyroplane. 306-463-6030.

RotorWay International, 4140 K.W. Mercury Way, Chandler, AZ 85226: Brochure $15 (specify model) ❖ One- and two-place gyroplanes. 602-961-1001.

SkyPro Inc., 3208 E. Colonial Dr., Orlando, FL 32803: Information $5 ❖ Compact, lighweight, and easy-to-build one-place helicopter. 212-803-5481.

SnoBird Aircraft Inc., P.O. Box 7727, Tacoma, WA 98407: Information $10 (specify model) ❖ One- and two-place gyroplanes. 206-232-9624.

Sport Copter, Scappoose Airport, 34012 N. Honeyman Rd., Scappoose, OR 97056: Information $12 (specify model) ❖ Ultralight one-place and two-place gyroplanes. 503-543-7000.

Star Aviation Inc., 821 Lone Star Dr., New Braunfels, TX 78130: Information $15 ❖ Easy-to-build helicopter kit. 210-608-9001.

Vertical Aviation Technologies Inc., P.O. Box 2527, Sanford, FL 32772: Information $15 ❖ Easy-to-build sport helicopter. 407-322-9488.

Vortech Inc., P.O. Box 511, Fallston, MD 21047: Information $10 ❖ One-place ultra-compact helicopter. 410-692-2692.

Aircraft Kits (Sailplanes & Motorgliders)

Advanced Soaring Concepts, 4730 Calle Quetzal, Camarillo, CA 93012: Free information ❖ One-place sailplane. 805-389-3434.

Aero Dovron Inc., 216 Hibiscus St., Jupiter, FL 33458: Information $5 ❖ One-place motor glider. 407-625-0500.

ARACO, 1121 Lewis Ave., Sarasota, FL 34237: Free information ❖ One-place motor glider. 813-365-3860.

Falconar AVIA, 7739 81st Ave., Edmonton, Alberta, Canada T6C 0V4: Information $10 ❖ One-place sailplane. 403-465-2024.

Group Genesis Inc., 1530 Pole Lake Rd., Marion, OH 43302: Information $10 ❖ One-place sailplane. 614-387-9464.

Higher Planes Inc., Box 4, Dover, KS 66420: Information $10 ❖ One-place motor glider. 913-256-6029.

Marske Aircraft, 975 Loire Valley Dr., Marion, OH 43302: Information $8 (specify model) ❖ One-place high and mid-wing sailplanes. 614-389-3776.

US Aviation, 265 Echo Ln., South St. Paul, MN 55075: Information $5 (specify model) ❖ One-place motor glider and ultralight sailplane. 612-450-0930.

AIRCRAFT & AERO ACTIVITIES

Aircraft Recovery Systems & Para-Gear

Advanced Para-Systems Inc., 113 Hwy. 24, Commerce, TX 75428: Free information ❖ Skydiving parachutes. 903-886-7662.

Aero Store Corporation, 109 High St., Pottsdown, PA 19464: Free catalog ❖ Skydiving gear. 610-327-8555.

Aerodyne Research, P.O. Box 13424, Tampa, FL 33681: Free information ❖ Skydiving parachutes. 813-837-1673.

Altitude Concepts, 4030 Poole Rd., Winston, GA 30187: Free list of retail sources ❖ Digital electronic free-fall altimeter. 404-920-9305.

Body Sport USA, 1621 Oak Ave., St. Helena, CA 94574: Free information ❖ Clothing for skydivers. 800-586-7784.

BRS Parachutes, 1845 Henry Ave., South St. Paul, MN 55075: Free information ❖ Emergency parachutes for sport planes. 203-875-8185.

D.L.T. Designs, P.O. Box 934, Angwin, CA 94508: Free information ❖ Skydiving jump suits. 707-965-1126.

The Drop Zone Gear Store, P.O. Box 3071, Deland, FL 32723: Free information ❖ Altimeters, gear bags, jump suits, videos, and skydiving equipment. 904-738-3539.

Hanson Helmets, Craig Hanson, 8938 Menkar Rd., San Diego, CA 92126: Free information ❖ Camera-fitted helmets and accessories. 619-578-4208.

Para-Gear Equipment Company Inc., 3839 W. Oakton St., Skokie, IL 60076: Free catalog ❖ Sport parachuting equipment. 800-323-0437; 708-679-5905 (in IL). $2

Para-Phernalia Inc., P.O. Box 3468, Arlington, WA 98223: Free information ❖ Parachute gear. 206-435-7220.

The PD Source Inc., P.O. Box 185, Deland, FL 32721: Free information ❖ Instruments, clothing, videos, helmets, and skydiving equipment. 800-222-0482.

Precision Aerodynamics Inc., Hwy. 127 North, P.O. Box 386, Dunlap, TX 37327: Free information ❖ Skydiving equipment. 615-949-4688.

Rigging Innovations Inc., P.O. Box 1398, Romoland, CA 92585: Free information ❖ Skydiving equipment. 909-928-1438.

Skydance Photography, 4518 Granny White Pike, Nashville, TN 37204: Free information ❖ Camera-fitted helmets and accessories. 615-292-8384.

Square One Parachute Sales & Service, 425 W. Rider St., Perris, CA 92571: Free information ❖ Skydiving gear. 800-877-7191.

Sunshine Factory, 38529 5th Ave., Zephyrhills, FL 33540: Free information ❖ Parachuting gear. 800-266-1883; 813-788-9831 (in FL).

Swift Plus Reserve Inc., 5800 Magnolia Ave., Pensauken, NJ 08109: Free information ❖ Skydiving equipment. 609-663-1275.

Avionics & Communications Equipment

Aircraft Spruce & Specialty, 201 W. Truslow Ave., Box 424, Fullerton, CA 92632: Catalog $5 ❖ Avionics equipment. 800-824-1930; 714-870-7551 (in CA).

AirStar Sales, 2251 Shady Willow Ln., Brentwood, CA 94513: Catalog $5 ❖ Avionics and radio equipment. 800-AIRSTAR.

Airwich Avionics Inc., 1611 S. Eisenhower, Wichita, KS 67209: Free brochure ❖ Used and repaired avionics equipment. 316-942-8721.

AlliedSignal General Aviation Avionics, 400 N. Rogers Rd., Olathe, KS 66062: Free information ❖ Instrument displays, flight controls, and communications, navigation, and identification systems. 913-768-3000.

American Avionics Inc., 7675 Perimeter Rd. South, Seattle, WA 98108: Free brochure ❖ New and used avionics equipment. 206-767-9781.

Century Instrument Corporation, 4440 Southeast Blvd., Wichita, KS 67210: Free catalog ❖ Rebuilt avionics equipment. 800-733-0116; 316-683-7571 (in KS).

Chief Aircraft Inc., 1301 Brookside Blvd., Grants Pass, OR 97526: Free information ❖ Avionics, communication, and other equipment. 541-476-6605.

David Clark Company Inc., 360 Franklin St., Box 15054, Worcester, MA 01615: Free information ❖ Aircraft intercom and communications equipment. 508-751-5800.

DayStar Avionics, 1150 Airport Dr., Burlington International Airport, South Burlington, VT 05403: Free information ❖ Avionics equipment. 802-862-8900.

DesignTech Systems, P.O. Box 338, Lombard, IL 60148: Free information ❖ Intercom systems. 708-971-9692.

Electronics International Inc., 12620 SW 231st Pl., Hillsboro, OR 97123: Free information ❖ Avionics instruments. 503-628-9113.

Eventide Avionics, One Alsan Way, Little Ferry, NJ 07643: Free information ❖ Avionics equipment. 201-641-1200.

Flightcom, 7340 SW Durham Rd., Portland, OR 97224: Free information ❖ Communications equipment. 800-432-4342.

Gulf-Coast Avionics Corporation, 4243 N. Westshore Blvd., Tampa International Airport, Tampa, FL 33614: Free catalog ❖ Ready-to-install custom instrument panels for kit planes. Also avionics equipment. 813-879-9714.

Horizon Instruments Inc., 556 S. State College Blvd., Fullerton, CA 92631: Free information ❖ Compact high-visibility engine instruments. 800-541-8128.

ICOM America, 2380 116th Ave. NE, Bellevue, WA 98004: Free list of retail sources ❖ Avionics equipment. 800-999-9877.

IIMorrow, 2345 Turner Rd. South, Salem, OR 97302: Free information ❖ Avionics equipment. 800-525-6726.

J.P. Instruments, P.O. Box 7033, Huntington Beach, CA 92615: Free information ❖ Engine instrumentation with miniature gauges. 714-557-5434.

Leading Edge Air Foils Inc., 8242 Cessna Dr., Peyton, CO 80831: Catalog $6.95 ❖ Avionics instruments. 719-683-5323.

Microflight Products Inc., 16141-6 Pine Ridge Rd., Fort Myers, FL 33980: Catalog $3 ❖ Communication systems, instruments, and avionics equipment. 800-247-6955.

Narco Avionics, 270 Commerce Dr., Fort Washington, PA 19034: Free information ❖ Avionics equipment. 215-643-2900.

Northstar Avionics, 30 Sudbury Rd., Acton, MA 01720: Free information ❖ Avionics equipment. 800-628-4487.

SkySports, Hangar 1, Linden-Price Airport, Linden, MI 48451: Free catalog ❖ Avionics and communications equipment. 800-247-7883.

Vista Aviation Inc., 12653 Osborne St., Pacoima, CA 91331: Free brochure ❖ New and used communications equipment. 800-328-8442; 818-896-6442 (in CA).

Hang Gliding & Powered Parachutes

Buckeye Powered Parachutes Inc., 16111 Linden Rd., Argos, IN 46501: Information $5 ❖ Powered parachutes. 219-892-5566.

EASYUP, 1089 Medford Center, Medford, OR 97504: Free information ❖ Backpack-powered parachutes.

Flytec, P.O. Box 561732, Miami, FL 33156: Free information ❖ Flight instruments. 800-662-2449.

Harmening's High Flyers Inc., Powerized Parachutes, 15487 State Rt. 72, Genoa, IL 60135: Video $15 ❖ One and two-person powered parachutes. 815-784-5876.

Mountain High Equipment & Supply Company, 516 12th Ave., Salt Lake City, UT 84103: Free information ❖ Electronic on-demand oxygen system. 800-468-8185.

4 ❖ AIRCRAFT & AERO ACTIVITIES ❖

New Avionics, 4243 N. Westshore Blvd., Tampa International Airport, Tampa, FL 33614: Free information ❖ Avionics equipment. 813-879-9714.

North American Sports Distributing Inc., Heritage Square, Hwy. 40, Golden, CO 80401: Free information ❖ Communications equipment. 303-278-9566.

Pacific Coast Avionics, Auburn Municipal Airport, 1833 Auburn Way North, Auburn, WA 98002: Free information ❖ Avionics instruments. 206-931-0370.

ParaPlane International, 68 Stacy Haines Rd., Medford, NJ 08055: Free information ❖ Two-person powered parachute. 609-261-1234.

Parascender Technologies Inc., 828 N. Hoagland Blvd., Kissimmee, FL 34741: Free information; video $20 ❖ One-person powered parachute. 407-935-0775.

Personal Flight Inc., 1819 Central Avenue South, Kent, WA 98032: Free information ❖ Backpack-powered parachutes. 800-685-8238.

PS Engineering, 9800 Martel Rd., Lenoir City, TN 37771: Free information ❖ Aircraft intercoms. 423-988-9800.

San-Val Discount, 7444 Valjean Ave., Van Nuys, CA 91406: Free information ❖ Aircraft accessories, avionics equipment, and pilot supplies. 818-786-8274.

Sigtronics, 822 N. Dodsworth Ave., Covina, CA 91724: Free information ❖ Voice-activated panel-mounted intercom with automatic squelch. 818-915-1993.

Six-Chuter Inc., P.O. Box 8331, Yakima, WA 98903: Free information ❖ Sky-riding aero-chute for one and two-persons. 509-966-8211.

Terra Avionics, 3520 Pan American Fwy. NE, Albuquerque, NM 87107: Free information ❖ Avionics instruments. 800-328-1995; 505-884-2321 (in NM).

Vision Microsystems Inc., 5501 East Rd., Bellingham, WA 98226: Free information ❖ Engine monitoring system with easy-to-read graphics and digital readout. 360-398-1833.

Parts & Tools

The Aeroplane Store, Kampel Airport, 8930 Carlisle Rd., Wellsville, PA 17365: Free catalog ❖ Aircraft building supplies. 717-432-9688.

Aircraft Components Inc., P.O. Drawer W, Edwardsburg, MI 49112: Information $5 ❖ Aircraft parts and pilot supplies. 800-253-0800.

Aircraft Spruce & Specialty, 201 W. Truslow Ave., Box 424, Fullerton, CA 92632: Catalog $5 ❖ Tools, construction materials, instruments, engines, pilot supplies, and books. 800-824-1930; 714-870-7551 (in CA).

Aircraft Tool & Supply, 1000 Old US 23, Oscoda, MI 48750: Free information ❖ Test equipment, sheet metal, tools, and fasteners. 800-248-0638; 517-739-1447 (in MI).

✓ **Alexander Aeroplane Company Inc.,** P.O. Box 909, Griffin, GA 30224: Free catalog ❖ Aircraft building supplies. 800-831-2949.

Avery Enterprises, Hicks Airfield, 2290 W. Hicks Rd., Hanger 54-1, Fort Worth, TX 76131: Free catalog ❖ Aircraft sheet metal tools. 817-439-8400.

B & F Aircraft Supply Inc., 9524 W. Gulfstream Rd., Frankfort, IL 60423: Catalog $4 ❖ Supplies for building and maintaining aircraft. 800-345-2558; 815-469-2473 (in IL).

California Power Systems Inc., 790 139th Ave., San Leandro, CA 94578: Catalog $6.95 ❖ Ultralight aircraft parts. 800-247-9653.

Eastside Ultralight Aircraft Inc., 4700 188th St. NE, Arlington, WA 98223: Catalog $7 ❖ Aircraft supplies. 206-435-3737.

Leading Edge Air Foils Inc., 8242 Cessna Dr., Peyton, CO 80831: Catalog $6.95 ❖ Aircraft building materials, hardware, tools, engines and propellers, and books. 719-683-5323.

Wil Neubert Aircraft Supply, 403 3rd Ave., Watervliet, NY 12189: Catalog $5 (refundable) ❖ Avionics equipment, engines, radios and antennas, aircraft components, engine mounts, hardware, and batteries. 518-436-4341.

Poly Fiber Aircraft Coatings, P.O. Box 3129, Riverside, CA 92519: Free information ❖ Fabric for covering aircraft. 800-362-3490.

San-Val Discount, 7444 Valjean Ave., Van Nuys, CA 91406: Free information ❖ Aircraft accessories, avionics equipment, and pilot supplies. 818-786-8274.

Stits Poly-Fiber Aircraft Coatings, P.O. Box 697, 548 Rt. 35, South Amboy, NJ 08879: Free information ❖ Aircraft covering materials. 800-631-5580.

Superfluity Aircraft Supplies, 2149 E. Prate Blvd., Elk Grove Village, IL 60007: Catalog $5 ❖ Aircraft building supplies. 800-323-0611.

U.S. Industrial Tool & Supply Company, 15101 Cleat St., Plymouth, MI 48170: Free information ❖ Aircraft building tools. 313-455-3388.

USATCO Tools, U.S. Airtool International, 60 Fleetwood Ct., Ronkonkoma, NY 11779: Free brochure ❖ Aircraft tools. 516-471-3300.

Wag-Aero Group of Aircraft Services, 1216 North Rd., P.O. Box 181, Lyons, WI 53148: Free information ❖ Avionics equipment, engines, and tools. 800-558-6868.

White Industries Inc., P.O. Box 198, Bates City, MO 64011: Free information ❖ Used aircraft parts. 800-821-7733.

Wicks Aircraft Supply, 410 Pine St., Highland, IL 62249: Catalog $5 ❖ Tools, construction materials, instruments, fabric, engines, and propellers. 800-221-9425; 618-654-7447 (in IL).

Pilot Supplies & Equipment

Aerox Oxygen Systems, 125 Masarik Ave., Stratford, CT 06497: Free brochure ❖ Oxygen systems. 800-237-6902; 800-972-0033 (in CT).

Aircraft Components Inc., P.O. Drawer W, Edwardsburg, MI 49112: Information $5 ❖ Aircraft parts and pilot supplies. 800-253-0800.

Aircraft Spruce & Specialty, 201 W. Truslow Ave., Box 424, Fullerton, CA 92632: Catalog $5 ❖ Tools, construction materials, instruments, engines, fabrics, flight equipment, and books. 800-824-1930; 714-870-7551 (in CA).

✓ **Aviation Book Company,** 7201 Perimeter Rd. S, Ste. C, Seattle, WA 98108: Free catalog ❖ Books, videos, pilot supplies, clothing, and gifts. 800-423-2708.

Butler Parachute Systems Inc., 1820 London Ave. NW, P.O. Box 6098, Reannex, VA 24017: Catalog $2 ❖ Parachute systems. 540-342-2501.

Citizen Watch Company of America, 8506 Osage Ave., Los Angeles, CA 90056: Free information ❖ Professional diving watches and sports, flight, yachting, and windsurfing chronographs.

Flight Products International Inc., P.O. Box 1558, Kalispell, MT 59901: Free information ❖ Cockpit equipment. 800-526-1231.

✓ **Marv Golden Discount Sales Inc.,** 8690 Aero Dr., San Diego, CA 92123: Free catalog ❖ Pilot supplies. 800-348-0014.

National Parachute Industries, 47 E. Main St., Box 1000, Flemington, NJ 08822: Free brochure ❖ Parachute systems. 800-526-5946.

Pilot Supplies, 4243 N. Westshore Blvd., Tampa International Airport, Tampa, FL 33614: Free catalog ❖ Pilot supplies. 813-879-9714.

San-Val Discount, 7444 Valjean Ave., Van Nuys, CA 91406: Free information ❖ Aircraft accessories, avionics equipment, and pilot gear. 818-786-8274.

Schweizer Aircraft Corporation, P.O. Box 147, Elmira, NY 14902: Free list ❖ Glider flight equipment and books. 607-739-3821.

Sporty's Pilot Shop, Clermont Airport, Batavia, OH 45103: Free catalog ❖ Flight equipment. 800-543-8633.

Strong Enterprises, 11236 Satellite Blvd., Orlando, FL 32837: Free catalog ❖ Emergency parachutes. 407-859-9317.

ALARM SYSTEMS, LOCKS, & REMOTE CONTROL EQUIPMENT

ALARM SYSTEMS, LOCKS, & REMOTE CONTROL EQUIPMENT

Active Electronics, 11 Cummings Park, Woburn, MA 01801: Free information ❖ Multi-purpose alarm systems. 800-677-8899.

Ademco, 165 Eileen Way, Syosset, NY 11791: Free information ❖ Multi-purpose alarm systems. 800-573-0154.

ADT Security Systems, 300 Interpace Pkwy., Parsippany, NJ 07054: Free list of retail sources ❖ Burglar alarm systems. 800-ADT-4636.

Advanced Security, 2964 Peachtree Rd., Atlanta, GA 30305: Catalog $1 ❖ Burglar and fire alarm systems. 800-241-0267.

ATV Research Inc., 1301 Broadway, P.O. Box 620, Dakota City, NE 68731: Catalog $3 ❖ Closed circuit surveillance TV systems. 402-987-3771.

CCTV Corporation, 280 Huyler St., South Hackensack, NJ 07606: Free information ❖ Closed circuit cameras for TVs. 800-221-2240.

Dakota Alert Inc., Box 130, Elk Point, SD 57025: Free information ❖ Wireless driveway alarms. 605-356-2772.

DFE Communications Corporation, 1705 W. Main St., Oklahoma City, OK 73106: Free information ❖ "Touch 'n Talk" entry access systems. 800-822-4TNT.

Digi-Key Corporation, 701 Brooks Ave. South, P.O. Box 677, Thief River Falls, MN 56701: Free information ❖ Multi-purpose alarm systems. 800-344-4539.

Doorking, 120 Glasgow Ave., Inglewood, CA 90301: Free information ❖ Telephone entry and access control systems. 800-826-7493.

Fyrnetics Inc., 1055 Stevenson Ct., Roselle, IL 60172: Free information ❖ Burglar and smoke alarm systems with selective control options. 800-654-7665.

Genie, 401 N. Washington St., Rockville, MD 20850: Free information ❖ Multi-purpose alarm systems. 800-638-9636.

Heathkit Educational Systems, P.O. Box 1288, Benton Harbor, MI 49023: Free catalog ❖ Easy-to-install home security, entertainment, and automation equipment. 800-253-0570.

Herbach & Rademan, 401 E. Erie Ave., Philadelphia, PA 19134: Free information ❖ Multi-purpose alarm systems. 215-426-1700.

Home Automation Systems Inc., 151 Kalmus Dr., Costa Mesa, CA 92626: Free catalog ❖ Easy-to-install home automation control and security systems. 800-762-7846.

Home Control Concepts, 7626 Miramar Rd., Ste. 3300, San Diego, CA 92126: Free information ❖ Security and home automation equipment. 800-266-8765.

Interactive Technologies Inc., 2266 N. 2nd St., St. Paul, MN 55109: Free information ❖ Telephone-based home security systems. 612-777-2690.

JDS Technologies, 16750 W. Bernardo Dr., San Diego, CA 92127: Free information ❖ Telephone-based home security systems and remote controls for computers, lights, and other devices. 800-983-5537; 619-487-8787 (in CA).

Lutron Lighting Controls, 7200 Suter Rd., Coopersburg, PA 18036: Free information ❖ Button-operated door jamb and lighting controls. 800-523-9466; 800-222-4509 (in PA).

Makita USA Inc., Drapery Opener Division, 14930 Northam St., La Mirada, CA 90638: Free information ❖ Automatic drapery opener. 800-4-MAKITA.

Mountain West Alarm Supply Company, Alpha Omega Security Group Inc., 9420 E. Doubletree Ranch Rd., Scottsdale, AZ 85258: Catalog $1 ❖ Burglar and fire-protection security systems. 800-528-6169; 602-971-1200 (in AZ).

Mouser Electronics, P.O. Box 699, Mansfield, TX 76063: Free catalog ❖ Multi-purpose alarm systems. 800-992-9943.

National Fire Protection Association, Box 9101, Quincy, MA 02269: Free catalog ❖ Multi-purpose alarm systems. 617-770-3000.

The National Locksmith, 1533 Burgundy Pkwy., Streamwood, IL 60107: Free information ❖ Multi-purpose alarm systems. 708-837-2044.

NuTone Inc., P.O. Box 1580, Cincinnati, OH 45201: Catalog $3 ❖ Video door-answering system with voice transmission over telephones and a wireless security system that can be zone programmed. 800-543-8687.

Oxford Chime Works, P.O. Box 665, Ridgecrest, CA 93555: Catalog $3 ❖ Door bells, chimes, and annunciators. 619-446-1040.

Paladin Electronics, 19425 Soledad Cyn Rd., Ste. 333, Canyon Country, CA 91351: Free information ❖ Talking security systems and motion sensors. 805-251-8725.

Preso-Matic Keyless Locks, 237 Coastline Rd., Sanford, FL 32771: Free information ❖ Keyless entry locks. 800-269-4234.

Radio Shack, Division Tandy Corporation, 1500 One Tandy Center, Fort Worth, TX 76102: Free information ❖ Easy-to-install burglar and fire alarm system for homes. Will work with an automatic message dialer. 817-390-3700.

Sentinel Systems Inc., 2713 Magruder Blvd., Ste. H, Hampton, VA 23666: Free information ❖ Home automation systems. 800-822-2774.

Siemens Solar Industries, P.O. Box 6032, Camarillo, CA 93011: Free information ❖ Solar-powered motion sensor light. 800-272-6765.

Small Parts, P.O. Box 4650, Miami Lakes, FL 33014: Free information ❖ Multi-purpose alarm systems. 800-220-4242.

Stanley Door Systems, 1225 E. Maple Rd., Troy, MI 48083: Free information ❖ Automobile remote control for house lights. 800-355-3515.

Tane Alarm Products, 247-40 Jerico Tnpk., Floral Park, NY 11001: Free information ❖ Multi-purpose alarm systems. 800-852-5050.

Video Surveillance Corporation, 1050 E. 14th St., Brooklyn, NY 11230: Free information ❖ Surveillance TV cameras. 718-258-1310.

Worthington Distribution, 36 Gumbletown Rd., Paupack, PA 18451: Free catalog ❖ Security systems and home automation products for turning household devices off and on. 800-282-8864.

ALL-TERRAIN VEHICLES (ATVS) & SAND BUGGIES

American Honda Motor Company Inc., 1919 Torrance Blvd., Torrance, CA 90501: Free list of retail sources ❖ All-terrain vehicles. 310-783-2000.

DG Performance Specialties Inc., 1220 La Loma Circle, Anaheim, CA 92806: Free catalog ❖ Performance parts and accessories for all-terrain vehicles and personal watercraft. 800-854-9134; 714-630-5471 (in CA).

Intraser Inc., 3580 Wiltshire Blvd., Los Angeles, CA 90010: Free information ❖ New and pre-owned motorcycles, ATVs, snowmobiles, trailers, personal water vehicles, and small boats. 213-365-6030.

Kawasaki Motors Corporation, P.O. Box 25252, Santa Ana, CA 92799: Free list of retail sources ❖ Motorcycles, ATVs, and accessories. 714-770-0400.

Recreatives Industries Inc., 60 Depot St., Buffalo, NY 14206: Free information ❖ Two and 4-passenger six-wheel drive amphibious all-terrain vehicle. 800-255-2511.

Sand Buggy Supply Company, 13055 Rosecrans Ave., Santa Fe Springs, CA 90670: Free list of retail sources ❖ Sand buggies. 310-921-3719.

Weekend Warrior Company, 1614 E. Holt Blvd., Ontario, CA 91761: Free list of retail sources ❖ All-terrain vehicles. 800-500-9914.

Yamaha Motor Corporation, P.O. Box 6555, Cypress, CA 90630: Free list of retail sources ❖ All-terrain vehicles. 800-526-6650.

ANTIQUES & REPRODUCTIONS

Antique & Art Restoration

Antique & Art Restoration by Wiebold, 413 Terrace Pl., Cincinnati, OH 45174: Free brochure ❖ Restoration services for antiques and art objects. 513-831-2541.

ANTIQUES & REPRODUCTIONS

Fredi W. Boese, Master Artist, 96 Rt. 17M, Harriman, NY 10926: Free information ❖ Porcelain and ceramic restoration. 800-755-0417; 914-783-4438.

Igor Edelman, 7466 Beverly Blvd., #205, Los Angeles, CA 90036: Free information ❖ Museum quality poster restoration. 213-934-4219.

Estes-Simmons Silverplating Ltd., 1050 Northside Dr. NW, Atlanta, GA 30318: Free brochure ❖ Silver repair and plating. 800-645-4193.

Fine Art Restoration, RFD 2, Box 1440, Brooks, ME 04921: Free information ❖ Restoration services for paintings. 207-722-3464.

Gone Hollywood, 172 Bella Vista Ave., Belvedere, CA 94920: Free information ❖ Movie poster restoration. 415-435-1929.

Johnson Music Company, P.O. Box 615, Mt. Airy, NC 27030: Brochure $2 ❖ Reed organ restoration and custom bellows recovering. 919-320-2212.

Old World Restorations, 347 Stanley Ave., Cincinnati, OH 45226: Free catalog ❖ Antique and art restoration. 513-321-1911.

Poster Restoration Studio, 7466 Beverly Blvd., Ste. 205, Los Angeles, CA 90036: Free information ❖ Restoration services for posters. 213-934-4219.

VanDyke's, Box 278, Woonsocket, SD 57385: Catalog $1 ❖ Hardware, hardwoods, curved glass, trim, and supplies for restoring antiques. 800-843-3320.

Antiques & Reproductions

Antique Imports Unlimited, P.O. Box 2978, Covington, LA 70434: Catalog $3 ❖ Imported antiques and jewelry. 504-892-0014.

Antiques of Science & Technology, Box 1852, Wakefield, MA 01880: Free catalog ❖ Radio, telegraph, historical instruments, and books. 617-245-2897.

Baker's International Antiques & Collectibles, P.O. Box 558, Oakdale, NY 11769: Catalog $12 ❖ Antique and collectible toys. 516-567-9295.

Bargain John's Antiques, 700 S. Washington, P.O. Box 705, Lexington, NE 68850: Free information ❖ Antique furniture.

Benedikt & Salmon Record Rarities, 3020 Meade Ave., San Diego, CA 92116: Free catalogs: indicate choice of (1) autographs and rare books, (2) classical, (3) jazz, big bands, and blues, and (4) personalities, soundtracks, and country music ❖ Early phonographs and cylinders, autographed memorabilia and rare books in music and the performing arts, and hard-to-find phonograph recordings from 1890 to date. 619-281-3345.

Warren Blake, Old Science Books, 308 Hadley Dr., Trumbull, CT 06611: Catalog $1 ❖ Hard-to-find astronomy books and prints. 203-459-0820.

Joan Bogart, P.O. Box 265, Rockville Centre, NY 11571: Brochure $5 ❖ Authentic antiques. 516-764-5712.

The Brass Lion, 5935 S. Broadway, Tyler, TX 75703: Catalog $5 ❖ English antiques, reproduction 17th and 18th-century fixtures and sconces, and gifts. 903-561-1111.

Chinese Porcelain Company, 475 Park Ave., New York, NY 10022: Free information ❖ Chinese porcelain antiques.

Circa Antiques, 377 Atlantic Ave., Brooklyn, NY 11217: Free information ❖ American furniture from the 19th century. 718-596-1866.

Civil War Antiques, P.O. Box 87, Sylvania, OH 43560: Catalog subscription $8 ❖ Civil War collectibles. 419-882-5547.

Gordon S. Converse & Company, Spread Eagle Village, Stratfords, PA 19087: Catalog subscription $25 ❖ Antique clocks. 800-789-1001.

Dovetail Antiques, 474 White Pine Rd., Columbus, NJ 08022: Catalog $5 ❖ Antique wicker furniture. 609-298-5245.

Dubrow Antiques, P.O. Box 128, Bayside, NY 11361: Free information ❖ American-style 19th-century furniture. 718-767-9758.

Dunbar's Gallery, 76 Haven St., Milford, MA 01757: Catalog $5 (specify interest) ❖ Antiques and Americana collectibles. 508-634-TOYS.

Bill Egleston Inc., 509 Brentwood Rd., Marshalltown, IA 50158: Free price list ❖ Cloisonne, ivory, netsuke, stone, and Oriental collectibles. 800-798-4579.

N. Flayderman & Company Inc., P.O. Box 2446, Fort Lauderdale, FL 33303: Catalog $10 ❖ Antique guns, swords, knives, and western, nautical, and military memorabilia. 305-761-8855.

4x1 Imports Inc., 5873 Day Rd., Cincinnati, OH 45251: Catalog $4 ❖ Nostalgic tin advertising signs. 513-385-8185.

Games People Played, P.O. Box 1540, Pinedale, WY 82941: Catalog $4 ❖ Antique replica game boards. 307-367-2502.

Gasoline Alley, 6501 20th NE, Seattle, WA 98115: Free information with long SASE ❖ Baseball and football collectibles and toys, from 1875 to 1975. 206-524-1606.

The Gemmary, P.O. Box 816, Redondo Beach, CA 90277: Catalog $5 ❖ Rare books and antique scientific instruments. 310-372-5969.

Grace Galleries Inc., Box 2488, Brunswick, ME 04011: Free information (specify items wanted) ❖ Original antique maps, prints, sea charts, and cartographic books. 207-729-1329.

Hake's Americana, P.O. Box 1444, York, PA 17405: Catalog $7.50 ❖ Americana and collectibles. 717-848-1333.

Hoosier-Peddler, Dave Harris, 5400 S. Webster St., Kokomo, IN 46902: Price list $2 ❖ Banks, Walt Disney collectibles, wind-up, character, and other toys. 317-453-6172.

Jacques Noel Jacobsen, 60 Manor Rd., Ste. 300, Staten Island, NY 10310: Catalog $10 ❖ Military insignia, weapons, photos and paintings, band instruments, and Native American and western collectibles. 718-981-0973.

Jukebox Junction, P.O. Box 1081, Des Moines, IA 50311: Catalog $2.50 ❖ Antique jukeboxes. 515-981-4019.

Lake Forest Antiquarians, P.O. Box 841, Lake Forest, IL 60045: Free catalog ❖ English and Continental silver and antiques. 708-234-1990.

Leftover Design Company Inc., P.O. Box 397, Neenah, WI 54956: Catalog $3 (refundable) ❖ Antique American-made heavy steel with porcelain and other signs.

Leonard's Antiques, 600 Taunton Creek, Seekonk, MA 02771: Catalog $4 ❖ Original and reproduction antique beds. 508-336-8585.

Melton's Antiques, 4201 Indian River Rd., Chesapeake, VA 23325: Free information with long SASE ❖ Antique dolls. 804-420-9226.

MidAtlantic Antiques, P.O. Box 691, Mt. Laurel, NJ 08054: Catalog $1 (3 issues) ❖ Antiques, paper collectibles, historical military maps, and autographs. 609-234-2651.

Neon Clock, 246 3rd Ave., New Lenox, IL 60451: Free information ❖ Antique neon clocks to 1890. 815-485-5573.

19th Century America, 3603 Johnson St., Lafayette, LA 70503: Free brochure ❖ American and Victorian furniture and accessories, from 1840 to 1890. 318-988-1020.

Old Friends Antiques, P.O. Box 754, Sparks, MD 21152: Monthly lists $10 (annual subscription) ❖ Steiff bears and stuffed animals in mint condition. 410-472-4632.

Old West Signs, 2887 Industrial Rd., Santa Fe, NM 87505: Catalog $5 ❖ Antique reproductions of old western signs. 505-471-3373.

Philadelphia Print Shop Ltd., 8441 Germantown Ave., Philadelphia, PA 19118: Catalog $4 ❖ Antique maps, prints, and books. 215-242-4750.

Quester Gallery, On the Green, P.O. Box 446, Stonington, CT 06378: Catalog $10 ❖ Marine art and antiques. 203-535-3860.

❖ APPLIANCES ❖

M.S. Rau, 630 Royal St., New Orleans, LA 70130: Free brochure ❖ Antiques from the 19th-century. 504-523-5660.

Eugene & Ellen Reno, Box 191, Lawrence, MA 01842: Free information ❖ Cut and depression glass, other glassware, dolls and toys, miniatures, jewelry, sterling silver, china, and antiques. 603-898-7426 (leave message, will call back).

John F. Rinaldi Nautical Antiques, P.O. Box 785, Kennebunkport, ME 04046: Catalog $3 ❖ American paintings, scrimshaw, and nautical antiques. 207-967-3218.

Rivers Antiques, Joyce & Charles Rivers, Box 297, East Woodstock, CT 06244: Free information ❖ Samplers, coverlets, quilts, and items from the 18th and 19th century. 203-974-3578.

Samurai Antiques, 229 Santa Ynez Ct., Santa Barbara, CA 93103: Price list $1 with long SASE ❖ Japanese antique Samurai, Emperor, and Empress dolls. 805-965-9688.

Setnik's in Time Again, 815 Sutter St., Folsom, CA 95630: Free information ❖ Restored American Victorian furniture, European and American clocks, and accessories. 916-985-2390.

S.J. Shrubsole, 104 E. 57th St., New York, NY 10022: Free information ❖ American and English antique silver, jewelry, art, gold boxes, and collectibles. 212-753-8920.

Southampton Antiques, 172 College Hwy., Rt. 10, Southampton, MA 01073: Video catalog $25 ❖ Antique American oak and Victorian furniture. 413-527-1022.

Spitz Mountain Enterprises, 3013 S. Wolf Rd., Ste. 292, Westchester, IL 60154: Catalog $2.50 ❖ Handcrafted American folk art collectibles. 708-786-8606.

A Summer Place, 37 Boston St., Guilford, CT 06437: Free information ❖ Antique wicker. 203-453-5153.

Dave Taylor Civil War Antiques, Box 87, Sylvania, OH 43560: Catalog $8 ❖ Guns, swords, uniforms, insignia, flags. drums, photographs, letters, diaries, autographs, and antique memorabilia. 419-878-8355.

Tesseract Early Scientific Instruments, Box 151, Hastings-On-Hudson, NY 10706: Catalog $5 ❖ Antique scientific and medical instruments and books. 914-478-2594.

Worldwide Treasure Bureau, P.O. Box 5012, Visalia, CA 93278: Free catalog ❖ Antique coins and collectibles. 800-437-0222.

APPLIANCES
Manufacturers

Amana Refrigeration, Amana, IA 52204: Free information ❖ Refrigerators. 800-843-0304.

Black & Decker, 6 Armstrong Rd., Shelton, CT 06484: Free information ❖ Small appliances. 203-926-3000.

Braun Appliances, 66 Broadway, Rt. 1, Lynnefield, MA 01940: Free information ❖ Small appliances. 800-272-8622.

Dynamic Cooking Systems, 10850 Portal Dr., Los Alamitos, CA 90720: Free catalog ❖ Outdoor gas grills and professional gas ranges. 714-220-9505.

Frigidaire Company, 6000 Perimeter Rd., Dublin, OH 43017: Free information ❖ Refrigerators, freezers, dishwashers, and other appliances. 800-451-7007.

G.E. Appliances, General Electric Company, Appliance Park, Louisville, KY 40225: Free information ❖ Electric cooktop stoves, microwave ovens, dishwashers, refrigerators, freezers, washers and dryers, and small appliances. 800-626-2000.

Garland Commercial Industries, 185 East South St., Freeland, PA 18224: Free catalog ❖ Kitchen ventilation systems, professional-style ranges, cooktops for the home, and racks for pots and utensils.

In-Sink-Erator, Emerson Electric Company, 4700 21st St., Racine, WI 53406: Free information ❖ Dishwashers and appliances. 800-558-5712.

Jenn-Air Company, 3035 Shadeland Ave., Indianapolis, IN 46226: Free information ❖ Cooktop stoves, dishwashers, ranges, and range hoods. 800-536-6247.

Kelvinator, 6000 Perimeter Dr., Dublin, OH 43017: Free information ❖ Appliances. 800-843-0304.

KitchenAid Inc., 2303 Pipestone Rd., Benton Harbor, MI 49022: Free information ❖ Cooktop stoves, dishwashers, range hoods, small appliances, wall ovens, washing machines and dryers, and refrigerators. 800-422-1230.

Magic Chef, 3035 N. Shadeland Ave., Indianapolis, IN 46226: Free information ❖ Electric cooktop stoves, wall ovens, refrigerators, and dishwashers. 800-536-6247.

Mile Appliance Inc., 22D Worlds Fair Dr., Somerset, NJ 08873: Free information ❖ Electric and gas cooktop stoves, dishwashers, ranges, washers and dryers, and wall ovens. 800-843-7231.

Panasonic, Panasonic Way, Secaucus, NJ 07094: Free list of retail sources ❖ Microwave ovens. 201-348-7000.

Regency VSA Appliances Ltd., P.O. Box 3341, Tustin, CA 92681: Free information ❖ Conventional gas and electric ovens. Also cookstoves, electric under-the- counter ovens, and dishwashers. 714-544-3530.

Sanyo, 21350 Lassen St., Chatsworth, CA 91311: Free information ❖ Under-the-counter refrigerators, microwave ovens, portable laundry washers and dryers, and other electronics. 818-998-7322.

Sharp Electronics, Sharp Plaza, Mahwah, NJ 07430: Free information ❖ Microwave ovens. 800-BE-SHARP.

Tappan, 6000 Perimeter Dr., Dublin, OH 43017: Free information ❖ Electric cooktop stoves, ranges, and dishwashers. 800-537-5530.

Thermador/Waste King, 5119 District Blvd., Los Angeles, CA 90040: Free information ❖ Electric and gas cooktop stoves, ranges, wall ovens, and other appliances. 213-562-1133.

Vent-A-Hood Company, P.O. Box 830426, Richardson, TX 75083: Free information ❖ Range hoods. 214-235-5201.

Viking Range Corporation, 111 Front St., Greenwood, MS 38930: Free brochure ❖ Gas ranges, range hoods, and cooktop stoves. 601-455-1200.

Waring Products, 283 Main St., New Hartford, CT 06057: Free information ❖ Small appliances. 203-379-0731.

West Bend, P.O. Box 278, West Bend, WI 53095: Free information ❖ Small appliances. 414-334-6909.

Whirlpool Corporation, 2000 M63 North, Benton Harbor, MI 49022: Free information ❖ Electric cooktop stoves, wall ovens, dishwashers, refrigerators, and freezers. 800-253-1301.

Retailers

Bernie's Discount Center Inc., 821 6th Ave., New York, NY 10001: Catalog $1 (refundable) ❖ Video equipment, telephones and answering machines, and large and small appliances. 212-564-8758.

Bondy Export Corporation, 40 Canal St., New York, NY 10002: Free information with long SASE ❖ Large and small appliances, cameras, video equipment, TVs, office machines and typewriters, and luggage. 212-925-7785.

Dial-A-Brand Inc., 57 S. Main St., Freeport, NY 11520: Free information with long SASE ❖ TVs, large and small appliances, and video equipment. 516-378-9694.

Focus Electronics, 4523 13th Ave., Brooklyn, NY 11219: Free catalog ❖ Appliances, computers, audio and video equipment, and TVs. 718-436-4646.

Foto Electric Supply Company, 31 Essex St., New York, NY 10002: Free information ❖ Appliances. 212-673-5222.

Harry's Discounts & Appliances Corporation, 8701 18th Ave., Brooklyn, NY 11214: Free information with long SASE ❖ Electronics and appliances. 718-236-3507.

Percy's Inc., 19 Glennie St., Worcester, MA 01605: Free information ❖ Appliances and electronics. 508-755-5334.

Richlund Sales, 75695 Hwy. 1053, Kentwood, LA 70444: Free information ❖ Ice-maker, central vacuum system, trash compactor, rear vision camera, electric heating equipment, combination washer and dryer, and other appliances for recreational vehicles. 504-229-4922.

APPLIQUES

Creative Uniques Inc., Rt. 3, Box 390, Linton, IN 47441: Catalog $2 ❖ Easy-to-apply creative appliques. 812-847-7780.

Jehlor Fantasy Fabrics, 730 Andover Park West, Seattle, WA 98188: Catalog $5 ❖ Bridal fabrics, appliques, trim, and jewelry-style decorative sew-on notions. 206-575-8250.

Lace Corner, P.O. Box 1224, Weaverville, CA 96093: Catalog $3 (refundable with $25 order) ❖ Ruffled flat lace, ribbons, and appliques. 916-623-3586.

Laube's Stretch & Sew Fabrics, 521 W. 98th St., Bloomington, MN 55420: Catalog $1 with long SASE ❖ Applique kits. 612-884-7321.

Sonrise Soft Crafts, P.O. Box 5091, Salem, OR 97304: Brochure 50¢ ❖ Patterns and kits for lifelike stuffed animals, puppets, shirt appliques, and wall hangings. 503-362-0027.

ARCHERY & BOW HUNTING

Accra 300, 805 S. 11th St., Broken Arrow, OK 74012: Free information ❖ Archery sights.

Aimpoint, 580 Herndon Pkwy., Herndon, VA 22070: Free brochure ❖ Archery equipment. 703-471-6828.

All Rite Products Inc., 5752 N. Silverstone Circle, Mountain Green, UT 84050: Free information ❖ Bow carrier for mountain bicycles and ATVs. 801-876-3330.

Alpine Archery Inc., P.O. Box 319, Lewiston, ID 83501: Free information ❖ Archery equipment. 208-746-4717.

American Excelsior Company, P.O. Box 5067, Arlington, TX 76005: Free information ❖ Archery targets.

Apple Archery, 1059 Zeigler Rd., Wellsville, PA 17365: Free information ❖ Archery targets.

Archery Dynamics, 2029 S. Elms Rd., Swartz Creek, MI 48473: Free information ❖ Bows.

Arizona Archery Enterprises Inc., P.O. Box 25387, Prescott Valley, AZ 86312: Free information ❖ Arrow-making components. 602-772-9887.

Arrowhead Traditional Archery, P.O. Box 1008, 220 Koch St., Pekin, IL 61555: Free catalog ❖ Archery equipment. 800-773-4373.

Arrows by Kelly, Kelly Peterson, 423 E. 5th St., Rupert, ID 83350: Free price list ❖ Wooden hunting arrows. 208-436-0325.

Assenheimer Bows, 1005 River Rd., Bucyrus, OH 44820: Free brochure ❖ Handmade bows for right or left-handed persons with a choice of lengths. 419-562-7253.

Barnett International, P.O. Box 934, Odessa, FL 33556: Free information ❖ Arrow holders, bow cases, quivers, bows, and sights. 800-237-4507; 813-920-2241 (in FL).

Barry's Custom Leather, 623 S. American St., Ste. 5E, Philadelphia, PA 19147: Free brochure ❖ Handcrafted leather quivers. 215-925-6864.

Bear Archery Inc., 4600 SW 41st Blvd., Gainesville, FL 32608: Free information ❖ Arrows, arrow-making components, bows, sights, and targets. 800-874-4603; 904-376-2327 (in FL).

Besherse Brothers, Rt. 3, Box 142, Ardmore, TN 38449: Catalog $2 ❖ Bowhunting equipment. 615-425-6818.

Bingham Projects Inc., 5739 Monte Verde Dr., Mountain Green, UT 84050: Catalog $2 ❖ Bow and arrow-making supplies. 801-876-2639.

Black Widow Custom Bows, 1201 Eaglecrest, P.O. Box 2100, Nixa, MO 65714: Free information ❖ Bows.

Bohning Company Ltd., 7361 N. Seven Mile Rd., Lake City, MI 49651: Free information ❖ Archery equipment, arrows, and arrow-making components. 800-253-0136.

Bow Works, P.O. Box 1803, Hurst, TX 76053: Free catalog ❖ Bow-making supplies and woodworking tools. 817-285-8000

Bowhunter Supply Inc., 1158 46th St., P.O. Box 5010, Vienna, WV 26105: Free information ❖ Arrows, arrow-making components, bows, sights, targets, game calls, camouflage clothing, and camping equipment. 800-289-2211; 304-295-8511 (in WV).

Bowhunters Discount Warehouse Inc., 1045 Ziegler Rd., Wellsville, PA 17365: Free catalog ❖ Rifles, game calls, targets, camouflage clothing, and equipment for hunting, bow hunting, archery, and camping. 800-735-BOWS.

Bracklyn Archery, 4400 Stillman Blvd., Tuscaloosa, AL 35401: Free information ❖ Archery targets.

Broward Shooter's Exchange, 250 S. 60th Ave., Hollywood, FL 33023: Catalog $8 ❖ Shooting, reloading, muzzle loading, hunting, and archery equipment. 800-554-9002.

Browning Company, Dept. C006, One Browning Pl., Morgan, UT 84050: Catalog $2 ❖ Arm guards, arrow holders, gloves, point sharpeners, scents and lures, quivers, tabs, wax, bows, arrows, arrow-making components, and sights. 800-333-3288.

BSI Sporting Goods, P.O. Box 5010, Vienna, WV 26105: Free catalog ❖ Firearm and muzzle-loading supplies, optics, clothing, and archery, fishing, and hunting equipment. 304-295-8511.

Buckeye Sports Supply, John's Sporting Goods, 2655 Harrison Ave. SW, Canton, OH 44706: Free information ❖ Archery equipment. 800-533-8691.

Butler's Bowhunting, 163 Bear River Dr., Evanston, WY 82930: Free catalog ❖ Bowhunting supplies. 307-789-4982.

Carrt-Lite Inc., 5203 W. Clinton Ave., Milwaukee, WI 53223: Free information ❖ Animal-style 3-D archery targets.

Continental Archery Inc., 210 Railroad Ave., Ambler, PA 19002: Free information ❖ Bows. 215-646-0339.

CRDC Laser System Group, 3972 Barranca Pkwy., Ste. J-484, Irvine, CA 92714: Free information ❖ Laser range finder.

Darton Archery, P.O. Box 68, Hale, MI 48739: Free catalog ❖ Bow hunting equipment. 517-728-4231.

Delta Industries, 117 E. Kenwood St., Reinbeck, IA 50669: Free information ❖ Life-size 3-dimensional archery targets and penetrating arrow heads. 319-345-6476.

Doskocil Manufacturing Company, P.O. Box 1246, Arlington, TX 76004: Free information ❖ Gun and bow cases. 817-467-5116.

Easton, 5040 W. Harold Gatty Dr., Salt Lake City, UT 84116: Free list of retail sources ❖ Arrow shafts. 801-539-1400.

Eatman Archery, 13443 Macadam Rd. South, Tukwila, WA 98168: Free brochure ❖ Hunting bows. 206-433-1167.

F/S Discount Arrows and Supplies, 2852 Walnut, Unit A2, Tustin, CA 92680: Free catalog ❖ Arrow-making supplies and tools. 800-824-8261.

Feather Fletcher, RD 2, Box 2172, Bangor, PA 18013: Catalog $2 (refundable) ❖ Custom-made recurves and longbows, aluminum arrows, leather goods, and accessories. 610-498-4676.

Fine-Line Inc., Sales/Catalog Department, 11220 164th St., East Puyallup, WA 98374: Free information ❖ Quivers. 206-848-4222.

The Footed Shaft, 5510 North Hwy. 63, Rochester, MN 55906: Catalog $1 (refundable) ❖ Archery equipment. 507-288-7581.

Game Tracker, 3476 Eastman Dr., Flushing, MI 48433: Free information ❖ Life-size 3-D animal targets. 810-733-6360.

Gander Mountain Inc., P.O. Box 248, Gander Mountain, Wilmot, WI 53192: Free catalog ❖ Archery equipment. 800-558-9410.

❖ ART SUPPLIES & EQUIPMENT ❖

Golden Eagle Archery, 1111 Corporate Dr., Farmington, NY 14425: Free information ❖ Bows, quivers, scents and lures, slings, and sights. 716-924-1880.

Great Northern Longbow Company, P.O. Box 777, Nashville, MI 49073: Brochure $1 ❖ Archery equipment.

James Greene Archery Products, 2321 Yellow Banks Rd., North Wilkesboro, NC 28659: Free information ❖ Bow cases. 910-670-2186.

High Country Archery, P.O. Box 1269, 312 Industrial Park Rd., Dunlap, TN 37327: Free information ❖ Archery equipment. 615-949-5000.

Howard Hill Archery, Craig & Evie Ekin, 248 Canyon Creek Rd., Hamilton, MT 59840: Free information ❖ Recurves, longbows, and accessories. 406-363-1359.

Horton Manufacturing Company, 484 Tacoma Ave., Tallmadge, OH 44278: Free information ❖ Crossbow hunting equipment. 216-633-0305.

Hoyt USA, 475 N. Neil Armstrong Rd., Salt Lake City, UT 84116: Free information ❖ Bows, cases, stabilizers, strings, quivers, slings, sights, arrows, and arrow-making supplies. 801-363-2990.

Kolpin Manufacturing Inc., 205 Depot St., Fox Lake, WI 53933: Free information ❖ Arm guards, arrow holders, bow cases, gloves, tabs, and arrow-making components. 414-928-3118.

Kota Bows, RR 1, Box 22, Oberon, ND 58357: Brochure $1 ❖ Hunting bows. 701-798-2776.

Kustom King Arrows, 1260 E. 86th Pl., Merrillville, IN 46410: Free catalog ❖ Archery supplies. Includes tapered wooden arrows. 219-769-6640.

Leal's Archery Sights, 62 Liberty St., East Taunton, MA 02718: Free information ❖ Archery hunting sights. 508-824-7274.

Longhorn Archery Systems, P.O. Box 5989, Kingwood, TX 77325: Free information ❖ Life-size 3-D animal archery targets. 800-780-4676.

Martin Archery, Rt. 5, Box 127, Walla Walla, WA 99362: Free information ❖ Bow cases. 509-529-2554.

Mathews Archery, Rt. 4, Box 12, Austin, MN 55912: Free information ❖ Bantam weight bows.

McKenzie Taxidermy Supply, P.O. Box 480, Granite Quarry, NC 28072: Free catalog ❖ Natural-looking 3-D lifelike animal targets. 704-279-7985.

McPherson Archery, P.O. Box 327, Hwy. 31, South Industrial Park, Brewton, AL 36427: Free information ❖ Bows.

Miami Valley Outdoor Products, 800 S. Downing St., Piqua, OH 45356: Free information ❖ Bow and arrow cases. 513-773-9477.

Monarch Longbow Company Inc., P.O. Box 5405, Missoula, MT 59806: Brochure $1 ❖ Handcrafted longbows. 406-251-3224.

Mountaineer Archery Inc., 1312 7th Ave., P.O. Box 2208, Huntington, WV 25722: Free information ❖ Archery equipment. 304-525-9222.

O.H. Mullen Sales Inc., RR 2, Oakwood, OH 45873: Free information ❖ Bows and strings, arm guards, arrow holders, cases, strings, stabilizers, gloves, nock locks, point sharpeners, quivers, racks, scents and lures, slings, tabs, arrows, arrow-making components, sights, and targets. 800-258-6625.

New Archery Products Corporation, 7500 Industrial Dr., Forest Park, IL 60130: Free information ❖ Arrows for bow hunting. 708-488-2500.

New Dawn Outfitters, 1 Quail Run, Mt. Sinai, NY 11766: Catalog $2 (refundable) ❖ Bowhunting and archery supplies. 516-476-1682.

Oneida Labs Inc., P.O. Box 68, Phoenix, NY 13135: Brochure $2 ❖ Bow hunting equipment.

RDS Company, 167 Rt. 33, Englishtown, NJ 07726: Free information ❖ Crossbows. 908-431-4334.

Rhino Crossbows, P.O. Box 934, Odessa, FL 33556: Free list of retail sources ❖ Crossbows. 813-920-4796.

Royal Elk Sewing, 122 E. Main, Belgrade, MT 59714: Free catalog ❖ Burlap 3-D archery targets, fleece hunting packs, tents, tipis, and equipment. 406-388-6850.

Sauk Trail Archery, 13960 S. Kildare, Crestwood, IL 60445: Catalog $2 (refundable) ❖ Handcrafted bows. 708-489-9780.

Saunders Archery Company, P.O. Box 476, Columbus, NE 68601: Free information ❖ Arm guards, arrow holders, cases, strings, stabilizers, gloves, nock locks, point sharpeners, quivers, scents and lures, slings, tools, arrows, arrow-making components, sights, and targets. 800-228-1408; 402-564-7176 (in NE).

Scout Mountain Equipment Inc., 2100 Dana Dr., Pocatello, ID 83201: Free information ❖ Target sights. 208-237-5171.

Screaming Eagle, P.O. Box 4507, Missoula, MT 59806: Free catalog ❖ Bow hunting equipment. 800-458-2017.

Spence's Targets, 3056 Lincoln Hwy., Lynwood, IL 60411: Free information ❖ Multi-layered foam animal targets. 708-758-9277.

Sport Shop of Grifton, Rt. 3, Box 187, Ayden, NC 28513: Free catalog ❖ Archery equipment, cases and racks, lures and cover scents, ladder stands, and targets. 800-334-5778.

Spot Target Decoys, 1637 Westhaven Blvd., Jackson, MS 39209: Free information ❖ Anatomically accurate animal decoy targets. 800-748-8765; 601-922-8212 (in MS).

Stillwater Archery, P.O. Box 992, Harrison, MI 48625: Brochure $1 ❖ Laminated longbows, recurves, and Osage self-bows. 517-539-6333.

Straight'N Arrow, P.O. Box 2125, Salt Lake City, UT 84110: Free brochure ❖ Easy-to-use arrow straightener. 801-363-9856.

Three Rivers Archery Supply, P.O. Box 517, Ashley, IN 46705: Catalog $2 ❖ Archery equipment. 219-587-9501.

Timberline Archery Products, P.O. Box 333, Lewiston, ID 83501: Free catalog ❖ Archery equipment. 208-746-2708.

Tru-Glo Archery Products, P.O. Box 1612, McKinney, TX 75070: Free information ❖ Archery sights.

21st Century Longbows, P.O. Box 8461, Jacksonville, TX 75766: Information $1 ❖ Longbows. 903-586-0715.

Windstorm Archery, 7185 Norfield Rd., Zanesville, OH 43701: Free brochure ❖ Custom-built longbows and flatbows. 614-796-7395.

Xi Compound Bows & Accessories, P.O. Box 889, Evansville, IN 47706: Free catalog ❖ Archery equipment. 812-467-1200.

York Archery, P.O. Box 11804, Fort Smith, AR 72917: Free information ❖ Bows, arm guards, cases, strings, gloves, point sharpeners, quivers, arrows, arrow- making components, sights, and targets. 800-526-5040; 918-436-2432 (in MO).

ART SUPPLIES & EQUIPMENT

Graphic Art Supplies

Aiko's Art Materials Import, 3347 N. Clark St., Chicago, IL 60657: Catalog $1.50 ❖ Japanese handmade paper, Oriental art supplies, and fabric dyes. 312-404-5600.

Alvin & Company Inc., P.O. Box 188, Windsor, CT 06095: Free catalog ❖ Art supplies for artists, drafters, engineers, and surveyors. 800-444-2584; 203-243-8991 (in CT).

Anco Wood Specialties Inc., 71-08 80th St., Glendale, NY 11385: Free information ❖ Easels. 800-262-6963; 718-326-2023 (in NY).

Andy's Art Supplies Inc., 208 W. 23rd St., New York, NY 10011: Free price list ❖ Art supplies and equipment. 800-709-9600; 212-675-9499 (in NY).

❖ ART SUPPLIES & EQUIPMENT ❖

Art Essential of New York Ltd., 3 Cross St., Suffern, NY 10901: Free catalog ❖ Tools, how-to videos, and gold, silver, and other metal leafs in sheets and rolls. 800-283-5323.

Art Express, P.O. Box 21662, Columbia, SC 29221: Catalog $3.50 ❖ Art supplies. 800-535-5908.

The Art Store, 935 Erie Blvd. East, Syracuse, NY 13210: Price list $3 ❖ Fabric dyeing, silk-screening, and marbling supplies. 800-669-2787.

✓ **Art Supply Warehouse Express,** 5325 Departure Dr., Raleigh, NC 37604: Free catalog ❖ Art supplies. 800-243-5038.

Artisan/Santa Fe Inc., 717 Canyon Rd., Santa Fe, NM 87501: Free catalog ❖ Art supplies. 800-331-6375.

Artists' Connection, 600 Rt. 1 South, Iselin, NJ 08830: Free catalog ❖ Art supplies. 800-851-9333.

Artograph Inc., 2838 Vicksburg Ln. North, Minneapolis, MN 55447: Free information ❖ Projector that enlarges and reduces opaque compositions, photographs, drawings, and other illustrations. 800-328-4653.

ASW Express, 360 Main Ave., Norwalk, CT 06851: Free information ❖ Art supplies and equipment. 800-995-6778.

Badger Air-Brush Company, 9128 W. Belmont Ave., Franklin Park, IL 60131: Brochure $1 ❖ Air brushes. 800-247-2787.

Benbow Chemical Packaging Inc., 935 E. Hiawatha Blvd., Syracuse, NY 13208: Free information ❖ Dry pigments. 315-474-8236.

Best Moulding Frames, P.O. Box 10616, Albuquerque, NM 87184: Free information ❖ Wood studio furniture. 505-897-1365.

Binks Manufacturing Company, 9201 Belmont Ave., Franklin Park, IL 60131: Free catalog ❖ Airbrush systems and accessories. 708-671-3000.

Black Market Art Materials, 1925 9th St., Berkeley, CA 94710: Free information ❖ Art supplies and equipment. 800-624-ARTS.

Dick Blick Company, P.O. Box 1267, Galesburg, IL 61402: Catalog $1 ❖ Books, videos, airbrushes, and printing, drafting, and commercial art supplies. 800-447-8192.

Arthur Brown & Bros. Inc., 2 W. 46th St., New York, NY 10036: Free catalog ❖ Art supplies. 800-772-7367.

Stan Brown's Arts & Crafts Inc., 13435 NE Whitaker Way, Portland, OR 97230: Catalog $3.50 ❖ Art supplies and books. 800-547-5531; 503-252-0559 (in OR).

Caran d'Ache of Switzerland Inc., 19 W. 24th St., New York, NY 10010: Free information ❖ Gouache colors. 212-689-3590.

Cartoon Colour, 9024 Lindblade St., Culver City, CA 90232: Start-up kit $3 ❖ Animation supplies. 800-523-3665; 310-838-8467 (in CA).

Chaselle Inc., 9645 Gerwig Ln., Columbia, MD 21046: Catalog $4 ❖ Books, ceramic molds and kilns, sculpture equipment, art, silk-screening, and craft supplies. 800-242-7355.

Chatham Art Distributors, P.O. Box 3851, Frederick, MD 21705: Free information ❖ Art supplies and books. 800-822-4747.

✓ **Cheap Joe's Art Stuff,** 300 Industrial Park Rd., Boone, NC 28607: Free catalog ❖ Art supplies. 800-227-2788.

Chroma, 205 Bucky Dr., Lititz, PA 17543: Free information ❖ Acrylic polymer emulsion-based gesso for fine and decorative art and wildfowl painting. 800-257-8278; 717-626-8866 (in PA).

Co-Op Artists Materials, 205 Armour Dr., Atlanta, GA 30324: Free catalog ❖ Art supplies. 800-877-3242.

Conrad Machine Company, 1525 S. Warner, Whitehall, MI 49461: Free catalog ❖ Etching and lithography presses. 616-893-7455.

Createx Colors, 14 Airport Park Rd., East Granby, CT 06026: Free information ❖ Liquid permanent dyes, pure pigments, and pearlescent, iridescent, acrylic, and other fabric colors. 800-243-2712.

Creative Services, 1327 Park Ave., Emeryville, CA 94608: Free list of retail sources with long SASE ❖ Pastels.

Crown Art Products, 90 Dayton Ave., Passaic, NJ 07055: Free catalog ❖ Silk-screening supplies. 201-777-6010.

D.D. Catalog Corporation, 148 Mercer St., New York, NY 10012: Catalog $3 ❖ Art supplies and equipment. 800-999-8519; 212-343-9040 (in NY).

Decart Inc., P.O. Box 309, Morrisville, VT 05661: Free list of retail sources ❖ Fabric paints and dyes for use with air brushes, water-based enamels and paints for transfer techniques, and glass crafting, silk-screening, and art and craft supplies. 802-888-4217.

Delta Technical Coatings, 2550 Pellissier Pl., Whittier, CA 90601: Free catalog ❖ Acrylics, oils, casein paints, and paint sticks. 800-423-4135; 213-686-0678 (in CA).

Dickerson Press Company, P.O. Box 8, South Haven, MI 49090: Free information ❖ Etching and lithography presses in manual and electric models. Also a press that prints intaglio, relief, lithographs, stone, plate, and other medias. 616-637-4251.

Dixie Art Supplies, 2612 Jefferson Hwy., New Orleans, LA 70121: Free catalog ❖ Airbrush equipment. 800-783-2612.

Gregory D. Dorrance Company, 1063 Oak Hill Ave., Attleboro, MA 02703: Free information ❖ Decoy-making and art supplies, tools, and wood for carving. 508-222-6255.

Dove Brushes, 280 Terrace Rd., Tarpon Springs, FL 34689: Catalog $2.50 ❖ Art supplies. 800-334-3683; 813-934-5283 (in FL).

The Duck Blind, 8709 Gull Rd., Richland, MI 49083: Free catalog ❖ Carving and art supplies, books, and wood. 800-852-7352.

Duncan Enterprises, 5673 E. Shields Ave., Fresno, CA 93727: Free information ❖ Fabric paints, outline writers, and glitter dispensers. 800-438-6226; 209-291-4444 (in CA).

Ebersole Lapidary Supply, 11417 West Hwy. 54, Wichita, KS 67209: Catalog $2 ❖ Shells, lapidary equipment, and supplies for art, calligraphy, and jewelry and clock-making. 316-722-4771.

✓ **Fairgate Rule Company Inc.,** 22 Adams Ave., P.O. Box 278, Cold Spring, NY 10516: Free catalog ❖ Rulers, other measuring devices, stencils, and drawing aids. 800-431-2180; 914-265-3677 (in NY).

The Fine Gold Leaf People, Art Essentials, Three Cross St., Suffern, NY 10901: Free information ❖ Genuine, imitation, and variegated sheets and rolls of metallic foil. Also brushes, supplies, and books. 800-283-5323.

Flax Artist Materials, 240 Valley Dr., Brisbane, CA 94005: Catalog $6 ❖ Supplies for artists, architects, drafters, and sign painters. 800-547-7778.

Fletcher-Lee & Company, P.O. Box 626, Elk Grove Village, IL 60009: Free information ❖ Acrylic paints and art supplies. 800-468-2897; 708-766-8888 (in IL).

Foster Manufacturing Company, 414 N. 13th St., Philadelphia, PA 19108: Free catalog ❖ Equipment and storage cabinets for graphic artists. 800-523-4855; 215-625-0500 (in PA).

A.I. Friedman Art Supplies, 44 W. 18th St., New York, NY 10011: Catalog $5 ❖ Art supplies. 212-243-9000.

Gamblin, P.O. Box 625, Portland, OR 97207: Free list of retail sources ❖ Oil paints, oil painting mediums, and etching inks. 503-228-9763.

Gill Mechanical Company, P.O. Box 7247, Eugene, OR 97401: Free information ❖ Tube wringers. 503-686-1606.

Gold Leaf & Metallic Powders, 74 Trinity Pl., Ste. 1200, New York, NY 10006: Free information ❖ Genuine and composition leaf in rolls, sheets, and books. Also supplies and tools. 800-322-0323; 212-267-4900 (in NY).

Graphic Chemical & Ink Company, P.O. Box 27, Villa Park, IL 60181: Free catalog ❖ Printmaking supplies for etching, block prints, lithography, and other reproduction processes. 708-832-6004.

❖ ART SUPPLIES & EQUIPMENT ❖

J.L. Hammett Company, P.O. Box 9057, Braintree, MA 02184: Free catalog ❖ Art supplies. 617-848-1000.

Russell Harrington Cutlery Inc., 44 Green River St., Southbridge, MA 01550: Free information ❖ Mat cutters. 508-765-0201.

Hearlihy & Company, 714 W. Columbia St., Springfield, OH 45504: Free catalog ❖ Art supplies and drafting furniture. 800-622-1000.

Heritage Brushes, 511 NW Service Rd., Warrenton, MO 63383: Free information ❖ Brushes. 314-456-2500.

Hobby Game Distributors Inc., 3710 W. Tuohy, Skokie, IL 60076: Free information ❖ Art supplies. 800-621-6419.

Hofcraft, P.O. Box 72, Grand Haven, MI 49417: Catalog $4 ❖ How-to art books, brushes, dyes, paints, and handcrafted wooden items. 800-828-0359.

Christian J. Hummul Company, 11001 York Rd., Hunt Valley, MD 21030: Free catalog ❖ Carving tools, art supplies, and how-to-books. 800-762-0235.

The Italian Art Store, 84 Maple Ave., Morristown, NJ 07960: Free catalog ❖ Art supplies. 800-643-6440.

Jerry's Artarama Inc., P.O. Box 58638, Raleigh, NC 27658: Catalog $2 ❖ Art supplies. 800-827-8478.

K & S Tole & Craft Supply, 1556 Florence St., Aurora, CO 80010: Free catalog with long SASE ❖ Art supplies.

Kalish Brushes, 43 Parkside Dr., East Hanover, NJ 07936: Free information ❖ Watercolor brushes. 800-664-2221.

KidsArt, P.O. Box 274, Mt. Shasta, CA 96067: Free catalog ❖ How-to art books and supplies for children from kindergarten up to the 8th grade. 916-926-5076.

Krylon, 31500 Solon Rd., Solon, OH 44139: Free information ❖ Textured paints that make wood, metal, plastic, ceramic, and other surfaces look like stone. 800-797-3332.

Loew-Cornell Inc., 563 Chestnut Ave., Teaneck, NJ 07666: Free brochure ❖ Brushes for all mediums and surfaces. 201-836-7070.

Martin Universal Design, 4444 Lawton Ave., Detroit, MI 48208: Free information ❖ Studio furniture. 800-366-7337.

Marx Brush Manufacturing Company Inc., 130 Beckwith Ave., Paterson, NJ 07503: Catalog $2 ❖ Brushes. 800-654-6279.

Multimedia Artboard, 15727 NE 61st Ct., Redmond, WA 98052: Free information ❖ Archival artboard for all mediums. 800-701-ART1; 206-881-5304 (in WA).

The Napa Valley Art Store, 1041 Lincoln Ave., Napa, CA 94558: Free catalog ❖ Art supplies. 800-648-6696.

Nasco, 901 Janesville Ave., Fort Atkinson, WI 53538: Free catalog ❖ Paints, brushes, airbrushes, pastels and crayons, drawing and drafting equipment, and craft supplies. 800-558-9595.

Naz-Dar Company, 1087 N. North Branch St., Chicago, IL 60622: Free catalog ❖ Graphic art and silk-screening equipment. 312-943-8215.

New York Central Art Supply Company, 62 3rd Ave., New York, NY 10003: Free information ❖ Art supplies.

Nova Color, 5894 Blackwelder St., Culver City, CA 90232: Free price list ❖ Pearls, metallic supplies, and acrylic paints. 213-870-6000.

OAS Art Supplies, P.O. Box 6596, Huntington Beach, CA 92615: Free information ❖ Brushes, rice paper, ink, Chinese colors, books, and supplies for Chinese brush painting. 800-969-4471.

Ott's Art Supplies, 102 Hungate Dr., Greenville, NC 27858: Free catalog ❖ Art, calligraphy, and drawing supplies. 800-356-3289.

Paasche Airbrush Company, 7440 W. Lawrence Ave., Harwood Heights, IL 60656: Free information ❖ Airbrushing and spraying equipment. 708-867-9191.

Pearl Paint, P.O. Box 946, Smithtown, NY 11787: Catalog $1 ❖ Art supplies. 800-451-7327.

Plaid Enterprises, P.O. Box 7600, Norcross, GA 30091: Free information ❖ Acrylic paints and art supplies. 404-923-8200.

Jack Richeson & Company Inc., 557 Marcella Dr., Kimberly, WI 54136: Free list of retail sources ❖ Brushes and studio furniture. 800-233-2404.

Safco Products Company, P.O. Box 195, Minneapolis, MN 55440: Free information ❖ Storage and filing systems and studio furniture. 800-328-3020

Salis International Inc., 4093 N. 28th Way, Hollywood, FL 33020: Free information ❖ Airbrush acrylic and fluorescent colors. 800-843-8293; 305-921-6971 (in FL).

Sargent Art Inc., 100 E. Diamond Ave., Hazleton, PA 18201: Free information ❖ Crayons, powdered and liquid tempera, water colors, and finger paints. 717-454-3596.

Heinz Scharff Brushes, P.O. Box 746, Fayetteville, GA 30214: Free catalog ❖ Brushes for tole, chinaware, and decorative painting. 404-461-2200.

Sepp Leaf Products Inc., 381 Park Ave. South, New York, NY 10016: Free information ❖ Gold and palladium leaf, rolled gold, tools, and kits. 212-683-2840.

Daniel Smith Art Supplies Inc., 4150 1st Ave. South, Seattle, WA 98134: Free catalog ❖ Art and framing supplies, books, and studio equipment and furniture. 800-426-6740.

M. Swift & Sons Inc., 10 Love Ln., Hartford, CT 06141: Free information ❖ Silver, palladium, aluminum, and composite gold leaf for decorating and restoring artwork and surfaces. 800-628-0380.

Technical Papers Corporation, P.O. Box 546, Dedham, MA 02027: Free catalog ❖ Sheets and rolls of handmade rice paper in prints and solids and multi-colors for all types of artistic printing, including block printing, etching, lithography, and silk-screening. 617-461-1111.

Testrite Instrument Company Inc., 135 Monroe St., Newark, NJ 07105: Free catalog ❖ Lightweight aluminum and chrome-steel easels, portable light boxes, photography equipment, and opaque projectors. 201-589-6767.

Texas Art Supply Company, 2001 Montrose Blvd., Houston, TX 77006: Catalog $5 ❖ Furniture for the artist. 800-888-9278.

Thayer & Chandler, 28835 N. Herky Dr., Lake Bluff, IL 60044: Free brochure ❖ Air brushes. 800-548-9307; 708-816-1611 (in IL).

Think Ink, 7526 Olympic View Dr., Edmonds, WA 98026: Catalog $2 ❖ Easy-to-use multiple color machine for printing greeting cards, stationery, ribbons, and T-shirts. 800-778-1935; 206-778-1935 (in WA).

Torrington Brush Works Inc., P.O. Box 56, Torrington, CT 06790: Free catalog ❖ Brushes and accessories.

United Art Supply Company, Box 9219, Fort Wayne, IN 46899: Free catalog ❖ Art supplies. 800-322-3247.

Utrecht Art & Drafting Supply, 33 35th St., Brooklyn, NY 11232: Free catalog ❖ Art, sculpture, and print-making supplies. 718-768-2525.

Visual Systems Company Inc., 1596 Rockville Pike, Rockville, MD 20852: Free catalog ❖ Art and drawing supplies. 800-368-2803; 301-770-0500 (in MD).

Wehrung & Billmeier Company, 1924 Eddy St., Chicago, IL 60657: Free information ❖ Gilding supplies.

Yasutomo & Company, 490 Eccles Ave., South San Francisco, CA 94080: Free list of retail sources ❖ Easy-to-blend and apply oil pastels. 415-737-8888.

Modeling & Casting Supplies

Abatron, 5501 95th Ave., Kenosha, WI 53144: Free information ❖ Mold-making supplies. 800-445-1754; 414-653-2000 (in WI).

Ace Resin, 7481 E. 30th St., Tucson, AZ 85710: Free information ❖ Casting and molding kit. 520-886-8051.

ARTHRITIS AIDS

American Art Clay Company Inc., 4717 W. 16th St., Indianapolis, IN 46222: Free catalog ❖ Modeling and self-hardening clay, paper mache, casting compounds, mold-making materials, acrylics, fabric dyes, fillers and patching compounds, wood stains, and metallic finishes. 800-374-1600; 317-244-6871 (in IN).

Aves Studio, P.O. Box 344, River Falls, WI 54022: Free information ❖ Self-hardening clays, paper mache, and sculpting materials. 715-386-9097.

Bare-Metal Foil Company, P.O. Box 82, Farmington, MI 48332: Catalog $2.50 ❖ Quick-setting molding materials. Also adhesive-backed chrome, black chrome, gold, matte aluminum, and real copper foil sheets.

Belmont Metals Inc., 301 Belmont Ave., Brooklyn, NY 11207: Free information ❖ Non-ferrous metals for making sculptures. 718-342-4900.

Castcraft, Box 17000, Memphis, TN 38187: Free information ❖ How-to information, rubber and plastic materials, and mold-making and casting supplies.

Castolite, 4915 Dean, Woodstock, IL 60098: Catalog $3 ❖ Casting resins, mold-making supplies, and how-to books. 815-338-4670.

Cementex Latex Corporation, 121 Varick St., New York, NY 10013: Free catalog ❖ Molds and liquid rubber. 800-782-9056; 212-741-1770 (in NY).

Chaselle Inc., 9645 Gerwig Ln., Columbia, MD 21046: Catalog $4 ❖ Books, ceramic molds and kilns, sculpture equipment, and art, silk-screening, and craft supplies. 800-242-7355.

Chavant Inc., 42 West St., Red Bank, NJ 07701: Free information ❖ Water-base clay for sculpting at room temperature. 908-842-6272.

The Clay Factory, P.O. Box 460598, Escondido, CA 92046: Free information ❖ Modeling materials. 800-243-3466.

Concrete Machinery Company, P.O. Box 99, Hickory, NC 28603: Information $10 ❖ Supplies and aluminum molds for making ornamental concrete items. 704-322-7710.

Craft Time Catalog, 10940 S. Parker Rd., Ste. 476, Parker, CO 80134: Catalog $2 (refundable) ❖ Ready-to-paint figurines. 303-792-2463.

Creative Paperclay Company, 1800 S. Robertson Blvd., Ste. 907, Los Angeles, CA 90035: Free information ❖ Air hardening sculpting material. 800-899-5952.

Design-Cast Materials Division, 951 Pennsylvania Ave., Trenton, NJ 08638: Free information ❖ Easy-to-use lightweight and weatherized modeling stone that can be ground, colored, or stained. 609-392-1922.

Gerlachs of Lecha, P.O. Box 213, Emmaus, PA 18049: Catalog $2.25 ❖ Paper sculpting kits. 215-965-9181.

Gold's Artworks Inc., 2100 N. Pine St., Lumberton, NC 28358: Free catalog with long SASE ❖ Paper-making pigments and chemicals, pulp materials, kits, and supplies. 800-356-2306; 910-739-9605 (in NC).

Handcraft Designs Inc., 63 E. Broad St., Hatfield, PA 19440: Free information with long SASE ❖ Molds, tools, modeling material, and how-to books for use with polymer and air-drying clays. 800-523-2430; 215-855-3022 (in PA).

L.A. Cave, 360 N. Palm Canyon Dr., Palm Springs, CA 92262: Free information ❖ Minerals, gems, fossils, books, gifts, and soapstone for carving. 619-3420-1672.

Montoya/MAS International Inc., 435 Southern Blvd., West Palm Beach, FL 33405: Catalog $3 ❖ Bronze casting (lost wax process), mold-making, polishing and stone finishing, and alabaster, steatite, soapstone, marble, and onyx carving stones. 800-682-8665.

Nasco, 901 Janesville Ave., Fort Atkinson, WI 53538: Free catalog ❖ Modeling materials, non-firing and firing clays, tools, molds, and craft supplies. 800-558-9595.

Polyform Products Company, 9420 Byron St., Schiller Park, IL 60176: Free information ❖ Shatter and chip-proof ceramic-like sculpting compound, paints, glazes, tools, and modeling sets. 708-678-4836.

Sculpture House, 100 Camp Meeting Ave., Skilman, NJ 08558: Catalog $2 ❖ Sculpting tools, modeling and mold-making accessories, and supplies. 609-466-2986.

Smooth-On, 1000 Valley Rd., Gillette, NJ 07933: Free information ❖ Liquid plastic compounds. 800-766-6841; 908-647-5800 (in NJ).

Sutton Supply Company, Hwy. 64-70 East, Conover, NC 28613: Free information ❖ Casting glue gelatin. 704-464-8297.

United States Gypsum Company, Industrial Products Division, 125 S. Franklin St., Chicago, IL 60680: Free list of retail sources ❖ Plaster for molding. 800-487-4431.

Vacuum Form, 272 Morganhill Dr., Lake Orion, MI 48360: Free catalog ❖ Low-cost vacuum-forming machines, books, and supplies for the hobbyist. 800-391-2974.

Wisconsin Fibrecraft Inc., 516 Madison Ave., P.O. Box 465, Sullivan, WI 53178: Free brochure ❖ Paper mache forms for decoration. 800-645-7857; 414-593-8336 (in WI).

ARTHRITIS AIDS

adaptAbility, P.O. Box 515, Colchester, CT 06415: Free catalog ❖ Mobility, grooming, dressing, bathing, eating and cooking aids, exercise and therapy games, and adaptive home products for arthritis sufferers. 800-288-9941.

Danmar Products Inc., 221 Jackson Industrial Dr., Ann Arbor, MI 48103: Free brochure ❖ Easy-to-hold utensil handles and arthritis aids. 800-783-1998; 313-761-1990 (in MI).

Fashion Ease, Division M & M Health Care, 1541 60th St., Brooklyn, NY 11219: Free catalog ❖ Clothing with Velcro closures, wheelchair attachments, and incontinence supplies. 800-221-8929; 718-853-6376 (in NY).

Miles Kimball Company, 41 W. 8th Ave., Oshkosh, WI 54906: Free catalog ❖ Assistive devices and aids for people with arthritis and physical disabilities. 800-546-2255.

ARTWORK

Posters, Paintings, Prints & Other Art Forms

A & K Historical Art, P.O. Box 6521, Hamden, CT 86517: Free information ❖ Limited edition historical art. 800-286-3884; 283-562-5212 (in CT).

African Corner, 1235 W. Southern Ave., South Williamsport, PA 17701: Catalog $5 (refundable) ❖ Handcrafted African art. 800-499-KUDU.

American Print Gallery, P.O. Box 4477, Gettysburg, PA 17325: Information $1 ❖ Military art prints and note cards. 800-448-1863.

Animation Art Resources, 118 N. 3rd St., Philadelphia, PA 19106: Free information (specify interests) ❖ Disney, Warner Brothers, Hanna Barbera, and other studio cels. 800-269-1009; 215-925-2009 (in PA).

The Animation Celection, 1002 Prospect St., La Jolla, CA 92037: Free catalog ❖ Animation art collectibles. 800-223-5328.

The Animation Company, 19806 N. 4th St., Ste. 63, Phoenix, AZ 85024: Free catalog ❖ Animated artwork from Disney, Warner Brothers, Hanna Barbera, and other studios. 888-222-0332.

Applejack Limited Editions, P.O. Box 1527, Historic Rt. 7A, Manchester Center, VT 05255: Free information ❖ Western, Native American, and other art reproductions. 800-969-1171; 802-362-3662 (in VT).

Around the Corner, P.O. Box 1126, Centerville, VA 20122: Catalog $5 ❖ American, European, Victorian, and traditional posters, prints, and canvas art replicas. 703-257-0821.

Art & Frame Classics, Northlake Square, 4135 LaVista Rd., Ste. 220, Tucker, GA 30084: Catalog $1 ❖ Military and aviation art prints. 404-270-0542.

Art-Toons, P.O. Box 600, Northfield, OH 44067: Free catalog ❖ Animated art for collectors. 216-468-2655.

Artrock Posters, 1153 Mission St., San Francisco, CA 94103: Free catalog ❖ Original rock concert posters, T-shirts, books, and memorabilia. 415-255-7390.

Arts & Designs of Japan, Box 22075, San Francisco, CA 94122: Catalog $6 ❖ Japanese woodblock prints. 415-759-6233.

ARTWORK

Ascalon Studios, 115 Atlantic Ave., Berlin, NJ 08009: Free brochure ❖ Synagogue art. 609-768-3779.

The Astronomical Society of the Pacific, 390 Ashton Ave., San Francisco, CA 94112: Free catalog ❖ Posters of the cosmos. 800-335-2624.

B & R Gallery, 17720 Sierra Hwy., Canyon County, CA 91351: Free brochure ❖ Limited edition western theme prints and other works of art. 800-255-6498; 805-298-2038 (in CA).

Breedlove Enterprises, P.O. Box 538, Bolivar, OH 44612: Free information ❖ Limited edition, numbered, and signed Civil War lithographs. 800-221-1863.

Brush Strokes, 19312 Haviland Dr., South Bend, IN 46637: Brochure $3 ❖ Signed and numbered limited editions of reproduction prints of oil paintings with optional framing. 219-277-5414.

Buchanan Aviation Art, 56 S. Broad St., Milford, CT 06460: Free catalog ❖ Aviation art. 800-659-4174; 203-876-0560 (in CT).

Buck Hill Associates, P.O. Box 4736, Queensbury, NY 12804: Free catalog ❖ Posters, handbills, historical documents, and other Americana.

Matthew Burak Furniture, Box 279, Rt. 2, Danville, VT 05828: Catalog $5 ❖ Reproduction 18th and 19th-century furniture, lighting, and folk art. 802-684-2156.

CA Animation Galleries, 69 Middle Neck Rd., Level 2, Great Neck, NY 11021: Catalog $3 ❖ Vintage and modern animation art. 800-541-2278; 516-487-3556 (in NY).

Cartoon Art Unlimited, 379 Belmont Ave., Haledon, NJ 07508: Free catalog ❖ Animation art. 800-966-TOON; 201-942-1003 (in NJ).

The Cartoon Company, Crown Center Shops, 2nd Floor, 2450 Grand Ave., Kansas City, MO 64108: Free catalog ❖ Vintage cels and drawings from Disney, Warner Brothers, and other major studios. 816-842-3300.

Cel-ebration Animation Art Gallery, P.O. Box 123, Little Silver, NJ 07739: Free catalog ❖ Animation art. 908-842-8489.

Cherokee National Museum Gift Shop, P.O. Box 515, TSA-LA-GI, Tahlequah, OK 74464: Free price list with long SASE ❖ Original paintings, prints, sculptures, and Native American crafts and art. 918-456-6007.

Christian Book Distributors, P.O. Box 7000, Peabody, MA 01961: Free catalog ❖ Religious-theme Christian artwork and books. 508-977-5000.

Cincinnati Art Museum, Eden Park Dr., Cincinnati, OH 45202: Free catalog ❖ Reproductions of posters, postcards, and museum collectibles. 513-721-5204.

Comic Book College, 3151 Hennepin Ave. South, Minneapolis, MN 55408: Catalog $2 ❖ Original art and rock posters. 612-822-2309.

Countryside Prints Inc., 35 W. Prospect Ave., Washington, PA 15301: Free information ❖ Historical prints. 412-228-2461.

Covington Fine Arts Gallery, 6536 E. Tanque Verde Rd., Ste. F, Tucson, AZ 85715: Free catalog ❖ American art, from the 19th and 20th century.

The Craft Room, 584 W. Girard Rd., Union City, MI 49094: Catalog $3 ❖ Our own copyrighted prints framed in oak or barn wood. Sizes from 2 x 3 to 11 x 14. 517-741-5511.

The Cricket Gallery, 5525 Glen Errol Rd., Atlanta, GA 30327: Free catalog ❖ Vintage and contemporary animation cels, drawings, and Disney backgrounds. 800-BUY-CELS.

Laurel D'Agnillo, 148 Robin Ln., West Seneca, NY 14224: Free information ❖ Original oil paintings and limited edition carousel-theme lithographs. 716-674-2807.

The Decoy, P.O. Box 3652, Carmel, CA 93921: Free brochure ❖ Hand-carved wooden birds, antique decoys, limited edition prints, and original art. 800-332-6988.

DeRus Fine Art, 9100 Artesia Blvd., Bellflower, CA 90706: Free list ❖ Art books and 19th and early 20th-century artworks. 310-920-1312.

Filmart's Cartoon World, 362 New York Ave., Huntington, Long Island, NY 11743: Free catalog ❖ Vintage and contemporary animation art from most major studios. 800-ART-CELS.

Wally Findlay Galleries, 814 N. Michigan Ave., Chicago, IL 60602: Free information ❖ Original paintings. 312-649-1500.

Fine Art Impressions, 5115 Excelsior Blvd., #204, Minneapolis, MN 55416: Free catalog ❖ Oil-on-canvas art reproductions of famous masterpiece works. 800-279-4278.

Folio One, 635 C St., Ste. 403, San Diego, CA 92101: Free catalog ❖ Signed limited edition lithographs by theatrical designers. 800-597-2710.

Framing Fox Art Gallery, P.O. Box 679, Lebanon, NJ 08833: Free information with long SASE ❖ Civil War prints. 800-237-6077.

Fredericksburg Historical Prints, 829 Caroline St., Fredericksburg, VA 22401: Free information ❖ Civil War prints with optional custom framing. 540-373-1861.

Galerie Robin, P.O. Box 42275, Cincinnati, OH 45242: Free information ❖ Limited edition art prints. 800-635-8279.

Gallery Lainzberg, 222 3rd St. SE, Ste. 200, Cedar Rapids, IA 52401: Catalog $4.95 ❖ Limited edition, classic, and modern production cels, serigraphs, and other animation art from most major studios. 800-678-4608.

Gallery 247, 814 Merrick Rd., Baldwin, NY 11510: Free brochure ❖ Collectible plates and prints. 516-868-4800.

Gifted Images Gallery, P.O. Box 34, Baldwin, NY 11510: Free catalog ❖ Animation art. 800-726-6708; 516-536-6886 (in NY).

Ari Gradus, 414 7th St., Brooklyn, NY 11215: Free catalog ❖ Original serigraphs, lithographs, and paintings. 718-768-6688.

Graphic Encountering Inc., 15236 Burbank Blvd., Ste. 201, Sherman Oaks, CA 91411: Free information ❖ Hand-cast paper sculptures, hand-painted acrylics, and mixed media serigraphs. 800-472-7445; 818-988-9623 (in CA).

Grayworks/Winterworks, P.O. Box 1150, Hoodsport, WA 98548: Catalog $2 ❖ Greeting cards and art prints. 360-877-479.

The Greatest Scapes, 1613 Hawthorne St., Pittsburgh, PA 15201: Free catalog ❖ Framed art reproductions. 800-786-3022.

The Greenwich Workshop Inc., 30 Lindeman Dr., Trumbull, CT 06611: Free information ❖ Fantasy, wilderness, western, exotic lands, aviation themes, and other limited edition prints. 800-243-4246.

Grunewald Folk Art, P.O. Box 52, Alpen, IL 60001: Catalog $2 ❖ Signed and numbered limited edition lithographs of animals and people in rural American settings. 815-648-4683.

Guarisco Gallery, 2828 Pennsylvania Ave. NW, Washington, DC 20007: Catalog $10 ❖ European, British, and American 19th-century paintings. 202-333-8533.

Halibar Company, P.O. Box 608, Chatfield, MN 55923: Catalog $2 (refundable) ❖ Screen-printed silhouettes. 800-848-0130.

Harvest Gallery Inc., 1527 Beverly Dr., Wichita Falls, TX 76309: Free brochure ❖ Limited edition prints. 800-545-8231.

Harwell Studios, P.O. Box 471, Greensburg, IN 47240: Free information ❖ Historical paintings that reflect Native American culture to Civil War images. 812-591-3951.

Heirloom Editions, Box 520-B, Rt. 4, Carthage, MO 64836: Catalog $4 ❖ Lithographs, greeting cards, stickers, miniatures, stationery, framed prints, turn-of-the-century art, and paper collectibles. 800-725-0725.

Heritage Aviation Art, 12819 SE 38th St., #211, Bellevue, WA 98006: Catalog $5 (refundable) ❖ Paintings, prints, posters, and art by aviation artists. 800-331-9044; 206-747-7429 (in WA).

ARTWORK

F.B. Horowitz Fine Art Ltd., 830 Edgemoor Dr., Hopkins, MN 55343: Free list ❖ Fine art. 612-935-2120.

Intergalactic Trading Company, P.O. Box 521516, Longwood, FL 32752: Free catalog ❖ Movie posters and related material. 800-383-0747.

Kennedy Galleries, 730 5th Ave., New York, NY 10019: Catalog $5 ❖ Prints and other artwork. 212-541-9600.

Leslie Levy Fine Art, 1505 N. Hayden Rd., Ste. J-10, Scottsdale, AZ 85257: Free information ❖ Contemporary American paintings, drawings, and sculptures. 800-765-2787; 602-945-8491 (in AZ).

Liros Gallery Inc., Main St., Blue Hill, ME 04614: Free catalog ❖ Art prints and paintings. 800-287-5370; 207-374-5370 (in ME).

Lisa Mallory, Country Artist, 284 Main St., Weed, CA 96094: Free information ❖ Limited edition western theme prints. 916-938-3545.

Ben Marra Studios, 310 1st Ave. South, Seattle, WA 98104: Free information ❖ Photographs that capture the authentic pride and spirituality of today's Native Americans. 800-624-1940.

Masters' Collection

The Masters' Collection, P.O. Drawer D-1025, Somersville, CT 06072: Catalog $3 ❖ Framed art replicas on canvas of the world's masterpieces. 800-749-2281.

The Masters Gallery, Box 5601, Middletown, CA 95461: Catalog $7.50 (refundable) ❖ Original art in handcrafted period-style frames. 800-642-5537.

Nedra Matteucci Galleries, 1075 Paseo de Peralta, Santa Fe, NM 87501: Free information ❖ Historical American art and contemporary Southwestern paintings and sculpture. 505-982-4631.

Meehan Military Posters, P.O. Box 477, New York, NY 10028: Catalog $10 ❖ Original authentic World War I and II posters. 212-734-5683.

Metropolitan Museum of Art, Special Service Office, Middle Village, NY 11381: Free catalog ❖ Porcelain, ceramics and glass, scarves, shawls, neckties, books, jewelry, and original lithographs, prints, and graphics from around the world. 800-468-7386.

Miscellaneous Man, George Theofiles, Box 1776, New Freedom, PA 17349: Catalogs $5 ❖ Rare posters and vintage graphics. 717-235-4766.

The Moss Portfolio, 1 Poplar Grove Ln., Mathews, VA 23109: Catalog $10 ❖ Collectible prints. 804-725-7378.

Motorhead, 1917 Dumas Circle NE, Takoma, WA 98422: Catalog $5 ❖ Automotive art prints and collectibles. Also scale model cars and kits and books. 206-924-0776.

Moulton Gallery Inc., 12262 SW 131st Ave., Miami, FL 33186: Free brochure ❖ Limited edition contemporary paintings and 3-dimensional art renditions. 703-774-7966.

Mt. Nebo Gallery, 243 Grandma Moses Rd., P.O. Box 94, Eagle Bridge, NY 12057: Free catalog ❖ Limited edition lithographs, prints, serigraphs, and etchings by Will Moses. 800-328-6326.

C.W. Mundy Studio/Gallery, 8609 Manderley Dr., Indianapolis, IN 46240: Free information ❖ American impressionistic paintings. 317-848-1330.

Museum Editions of New York Ltd., 12 Harrison St., 3rd Floor, New York, NY 10013: Catalog $5 ❖ Reproductions of contemporary to modern posters. 212-431-1913.

Mystic Seaport Museum Stores, 39 Greemanville Ave., Mystic, CT 06355: Free catalog ❖ Marine paintings and sculptures. 800-248-1066.

Jeanne Nash Studio, 974 Marlin Dr., Jupiter, FL 33458: Free information ❖ Watercolors, embossings, and limited edition prints. 407-575-2030.

National Archives & Records Administration, National Archives Books, Washington, DC 20408: Free brochure ❖ Historic patriotic posters and postcards. 202-523-3164.

Nostalgia Decorating Company, P.O. Box 370, Drums, PA 18222: Brochure $2 ❖ Framed or unframed turn-of-the-century prints. 717-788-4017.

Novagraphics, P.O. Box 37197, Tucson, AZ 85740: Catalog $3 ❖ Astronomy and space-theme artwork and greeting cards. 800-727-6682.

Old Glory Gallery & Frame Shop, 2966 Park Hill Dr., Fort Worth, TX 76109: Free list ❖ Civil War prints. 800-731-0060; 817-923-5576 (in TX).

Old Grange Graphics, 1590 Reed Rd., Building B, Ste. 101, West Trenton, NJ 08628: Catalog $6 (refundable) ❖ Prints and canvas replicas of folk art in large and miniature sizes. 800-282-7776.

The Old Print Gallery, 1220 31st St. NW, Washington, DC 20007: Catalog $3 ❖ Prints and maps from the 18th and 19th century. 202-965-1818.

Original Print Collectors Group Ltd., 88 Astor Square, Rhinebeck, NY 12572: Free catalog ❖ Numbered, signed, and framed original limited edition prints, serigraphs, etchings, and lithographs. 800-556-6200.

Pendleton Cowgirl Company, P.O. Box 30142, Eugene, OR 97403: Catalog $2 ❖ Classic western theme T-shirts, lithographs, note cards, and calendars. 503-484-9194.

Posters of Santa Fe, 111 E. Palace Ave., Santa Fe, NM 87501: Free catalog ❖ Art posters. 800-827-6745.

Presentations Gallery, 200 Lexington Ave., New York, NY 10016: Free information ❖ Contemporary synagogue art, furniture, memorial renditions, and recognition gifts. 212-481-8181.

Quality Collectables, 71 S. Mast St., Goffstown, NH 03045: Free information ❖ Limited edition figurines and statues, signed plates and lithographs, and sports art. 800-422-6514.

Steven S. Raab, 2033 Walnut St., Philadelphia, PA 19103: Free catalog ❖ Autographs, signed books and photos, old newspapers, World War I posters, and historic memorabilia. 610-446-6193.

Red Fox Fine Art, 7 N. Liberty St., Middleburg, VA 22117: Catalog $5 ❖ Sculptures and 19th-century animal and sports paintings. 540-687-5780.

Red Lancer, P.O. Box 8056, Mesa, AZ 85214: Catalog $6 ❖ Original 19th-century military art, rare books, Victorian campaign medals and helmets, toy soldiers, and other collectibles. 602-964-9667.

Rockabilia Inc., P.O. Box 4206, Hopkins, MN 55343: Free catalog ❖ T-shirts, backstage passes, promotional glossy photographs, imported rare posters from around the world, and other concert collectibles and investibles. 612-942-7895.

The Norman Rockwell Museum, P.O. Box 308, Stockbridge, MA 01262: Catalog $1 ❖ Prints, books about Norman Rockwell, and other reproductions of artwork by Americas's favorite illustrator. 800-742-9450.

Ronin Gallery, 605 Madison Ave., New York, NY 10022: Catalog $6 ❖ Contemporary prints, 19th-century masks, netsuke, wood, and other Japanese art. Also 18th, 19th, and 20th-century woodblock prints. 212-688-0188.

Rosenbaum Fine Art, 5181 NE 12th Ave., Fort Lauderdale, FL 33334: Free information ❖ Limited edition paintings, sculptures, and water colors. 800-344-2787; 305-772-1386 (in FL).

Salzer's, 5801 Valentine Rd., Ventura, CA 93003: Free information ❖ Vintage concert posters.

Scheele Fine Arts, P.O. Box 18869, Cleveland Heights, OH 44118: Free information ❖ Original paintings and drawings of prehistoric and contemporary animals. 216-421-0600.

Connie Seaborn Studio, P.O. Box 23795, Oklahoma City, OK 73132: Free information with long SASE ❖ Original paintings, drawings, and hand-pulled prints. 405-728-3903.

ARTWORK

Philip Sears Disney Collectibles, 24592 Via Carissa, Laguna Niguel, CA 92677: Free catalog ❖ Walt Disney autographs, animation art, and memorabilia. 714-543-1477.

Shadow Box, 655 Saratoga Ave., San Jose, CA 95129: Free catalog ❖ Art reproductions. 800-551-5285.

Sketch 'n' Cel, Starr Ridge Rd., Brewster, NY 10509: Free catalog ❖ Production animation art from Disney, Warner Brothers, Hanna Barbera, and other major studios. 914-278-5360.

Starland Collector's Gallery, P.O. Box 622, Los Olivos, CA 93441: Catalog $2.50 ❖ Sports cards, movie posters, original comic art, and hard-to-find movies. 805-686-5122.

The Stokes Collection, Box 1420, Pebble Beach, CA 93953: Free catalog ❖ Limited edition lithographs and reproductions on canvas of aviation art. 800-359-4644.

Taggart Galleries, 3233 P St. NW, Washington, DC 20007: Free information ❖ American paintings from the 19th and 20th-century and contemporary realism art. 202-298-7676.

Thoroughbred Racing Catalog, Warsaw, VA 22572: Catalog $2 ❖ Calendars and limited edition prints with pictures of famous racing horses and horse-decorated mailboxes, doormats, sweatshirts and T-shirts, mugs and glasses, jewelry, and wall clocks. 800-777-RACE.

True Reproductions, Box 21, 155 Tycos Rd., Toronto, Ontario, Canada M6B 1W6: Catalog $2 ❖ Reproduction World War II posters.

United Communications, 644 Merrick Rd., Lynbrook, NY 11563: Free information ❖ Posters with optional custom framing. 516-593-2206.

Vestal Press Ltd., P.O. Box 97, Vestal, NY 13851: Catalog $2 ❖ Posters, books, and recordings that relate to museum antiquities and the theater. Includes carrousels, music boxes, player pianos and music machines, antique radios and phonographs, theater pipe and reed organs, early movie theater and film stars, and radio personalities. 607-797-4872.

Vintage Animation Gallery, 1404 3rd Street Promenade, Santa Monica, CA 90401: Free information ❖ Original animation art, from the 1940s, 1950s, and 1960s. 310-393-8666.

Vladimir Arts U.S.A. Inc., 5401 Portage Rd., Kalamazoo, MI 49002: Free information ❖ Original oils, acrylics, watercolors, and graphics. 800-676-8523; 616-383-0032 (in MI).

WaterColours, 625 Florida Ave., P.O. Box 2900, Cocoa Beach, FL 32923: Free brochure ❖ Marine art. 800-3-COLOUR.

Thelma Winter, 8260 E. Eden Rd., Eden, NY 14057: Free brochure ❖ Limited edition original paintings in pen, ink, and watercolors. 716-992-4277.

Sculptures, Carvings & Castings

Kurt S. Adler Inc., 1107 Broadway, New York, NY 10010: Free information ❖ Wood carvings. 800-243-9627; 212-924-0900 (in NY).

American Bronze Fine Art Foundry, 1650 E. Lake Mary Blvd., Sanford, FL 32773: Free catalog ❖ Artist bronze and silver castings and reproductions. 800-881-8090; 407-328-8090 (in FL).

Arrow Gems & Minerals Inc., 9827 Cave Creek Rd., Phoenix, AZ 85020: Free catalog ❖ Pewter figurines. 602-997-6373.

Ballard Designs, 1670 DeFoor Ave. NE, Atlanta, GA 30318: Catalog $3 ❖ Sculptured castings, furniture, lamps, decorative and fireplace accessories, garden and landscaping items, frames, and pictures. 800-367-2810.

Henry Bonnard Bronze Company, 1490 S. Hwy. 17-92, Longwood, FL 32750: Free catalog ❖ Bronze statuary with optional marble bases. 800-521-3179.

Cherokee National Museum Gift Shop, P.O. Box 515, TSA-LA-GI, Tahlequah, OK 74464: Free price list with long SASE ❖ Original paintings, prints, sculptures, baskets, and Native American arts and crafts. 918-456-6007.

Churchills, Twelve Oaks Mall, Novi, MI 48377: Free information ❖ Art collectibles and plates. 800-388-1141.

Duncan Royale, 1141 S. Acacia Ave., Fullerton, CA 92631: Free information ❖ Sculptured figurines. 800-366-4646.

Eleganza Ltd., Magnolia Village, 3217 W. Smith, Seattle, WA 98199: Catalog $6 ❖ Sculptures made from oxolyte that resembles Carrara marble. 206-283-0609.

Enesco Corporation, 1 Enesco Plaza, Elk Grove Village, IL 60007: Free list of retail sources ❖ Figurines, sculptures, ornaments, Barbie dolls, and gifts.

European Imports & Gifts, Oak Mill Mall, 7900 N. Milwaukee Ave., Niles, IL 60648: Free information ❖ Art, porcelains, Christmas ornaments, and pewter. 708-967-5253.

Excalibur Bronze Sculpture Foundry, 85 Adams St., Brooklyn, NY 11201: Catalog $10 (refundable) ❖ Bronze sculptures. 718-522-3330.

Bill Glass Studio, Star Route South, Box 39B, Locust Grove, OK 74352: Free information with long SASE ❖ Original stone sculptures, carvings, bronzes, and pottery. 918-479-8884.

Goebel Inc., Goebel Plaza, P.O. Box 10, Pennington, NJ 08534: Free information ❖ Miniature sculptures of characters from Walt Disney's animated film classics. 800-366-4632.

Kelley Haney Art Gallery, Haney Inc., P.O. Box 3817, Shawnee, OK 74802: Free brochure with long SASE ❖ Original Native American paintings and prints, sculptures, jewelry, baskets, and pottery. 405-275-2270.

Historical Sculptures, P.O. Box 141, Cairo, NY 12413: Free brochure ❖ Bronze historical sculptures. 518-622-3508.

Imagine That, 5903 Queens Chapel, Hyattsville, MD 20782: Free information ❖ Sculptures, figurines, and art objects. 800-223-5903.

Imperial Manufacturing, 14502 Resort Ln., Lakewood, WI 54138: Free catalog ❖ Pewter figurines. 715-276-7865.

Judaic Folk Art, Lois Kramer, 8101 Timber Valley Ct., Dunn Loring, VA 22027: Free brochure ❖ Judaic folk art. 703-560-2914.

Will Kirkpatrick Decoys, 124 Forest Ave., Hudson, MA 01749: Catalog $2 ❖ Authentic reproductions of works by early carvers. 800-505-7841.

Leslie Levy Fine Art, 7135 Main St., Scottsdale, AZ 85262: Free information ❖ Contemporary American paintings, drawings, and sculptures. 800-283-ARTS; 602-947-2925 (in AZ).

MAX-CAST, 611 B. Ave., P.O. Box 662, Kalona, IA 52247: Free brochure ❖ Sculptures and custom casting in iron, aluminum, and bronze. 319-656-5365.

Miller Import Company, 300 Mac Ln., Keasbey, NJ 08832: Free list of retail sources ❖ Giuseppe Armani religious figurines. 800-3-ARMANI.

Munyon & Sons, 1119 Waverly Hills Dr., Thousand Oaks, CA 91360: Free catalog ❖ Reproductions of Remington bronzes. 800-289-2850.

Mystic Seaport Museum Stores, 39 Greemanville Ave., Mystic, CT 06355: Free catalog ❖ Marine paintings and sculptures. 800-248-1066.

Navarro Studio, 5231 Squaw Creek Rd., Casper, WY 82604: Free information ❖ Bronze animal castings. 307-234-5547.

Bob Parker's Sports Collectibles, 712 Evergreen Pkwy., Union, NJ 07083: Free information ❖ Sports statuary and plates. 800-543-7794.

Red Fox Fine Art, 7 N. Liberty St., Middleburg, VA 22117: Catalog $5 ❖ Sculptures and 19th-century animal and sports paintings. 540-687-5780.

Renaissance Marketing, P.O. Box 2546, Bonita Springs, FL 33959: Free catalog ❖ Bronze sculptures and collectible art glass. 813-495-6033.

Rostand Fine Jewelers, 8349 Foothill Blvd., Sunland, CA 91040: Free information ❖ Lladro porcelain. 800-222-9208; 818-352-7814 (in CA).

Windy Meadows Pottery Ltd., 1036 Valley Rd., Knoxville, MD 21758: Free brochure ❖ Detailed stonewear buildings. 800-527-6274.

Wolf Chief Graphics, 907 C Ave. NW, Great Falls, MT 59404: Free price list with long SASE ❖ Original watercolor paintings, alabaster and bronze sculptures, hand-pulled serigraphs, bone chokers, and art. 406-452-4449.

Wood Carvings by Ted Nichols, Noah's Ark, 2909 Old Ocean City Rd., Salisbury, MD 21801: Catalog $1 ❖ Hand-carved and painted wood carvings. 410-546-9522.

ASTROLOGY

ACS Publications Inc., 408 Nutmeg St., San Diego, CA 92103: Free information ❖ Books on astrology, Tarot reading, psychic understanding, nutrition, healing, and channeling. 619-297-9203.

Astro Communications Services Inc., 5521 Ruffin Rd., San Diego, CA 92123: Free catalog ❖ Astrology products and services. 619-492-9919.

Aurora Press, P.O. Box 573, Santa Fe, NM 87504: Free catalog ❖ Books on astrology and yoga. 207-363-4393.

Cosmic Patterns, P.O. Box 140790, Gainesville, FL 32614: Catalog $3 ❖ Kepler astrology program. 352-373-1504.

Times Cycles Research, 375 Willets Ave., Waterford, CT 06385: Free information ❖ Astrology software for the Macintosh. 203-444-6641.

ASTRONOMY

Astrophotography

Electrim Corporation, 356 Wall St., Princeton, NJ 08540: Free information ❖ Electronic imaging equipment. 609-683-5546.

SBIG Astronomical Instruments, Santa Barbara Instrument Group, 1482 E. Valley Rd., P.O. Box 50437, Santa Barbara, CA 93150: Free catalog ❖ Color imaging equipment. 805-969-1851.

Sky Scientific, 28578 Hwy. 18, #184, Skyforest, CA 92385: Catalog $1 ❖ Astrophotography equipment and telescopes. 909-337-3440.

Spectra Astronomy, 6631 Wilbur Ave., Ste. 30, Reseda, CA 91335: Free catalog ❖ Astrophotography and telescopic equipment for beginning and advanced astronomers. 800-735-1352.

TAURUS Technologies, P.O. Box 14, Woodstown, NJ 08098: Free information ❖ Astrophotography systems. 609-769-4509.

Observatories & Planetariums

Ash Manufacturing Company Inc., Box 312, Plainfield, IL 60544: Free catalog ❖ Mechanical and electrical-operated observatory domes from 10 to 36 feet in diameter. 815-436-9403.

Astro Haven, 144 E. 19th St., North Vancouver, British Columbia, Canada V7L 2YB: Free information ❖ Easy-to-assemble fiberglass rotating dome for most telescopes. 604-985-2491.

Learning Technologies Inc., 40 Cameron Ave., Somerville, MA 02144: Free catalog ❖ Portable planetarium system. 800-537-8703.

Minolta, 101 Williams Dr., Ramsey, NJ 07446: Free information ❖ Planetariums. 201-825-4000.

Observa-Dome Laboratories Inc., 371 Commerce Park Dr., Jackson, MS 39213: Free information ❖ Domes for amateur astronomers and professional tracking, research, communications, and defense systems. 800-647-5364; 601-982-3333 (in MS).

Seiler Instrument, 170 E. Kirkham Ave., St. Louis, MO 63119: Free information ❖ Planetariums and accessories. 800-726-8805.

Solar Works, HC 30, Box 157, Concho, AZ 85924: Free information ❖ Full-rotating observatory. 520-537-8851.

Stewart Research Enterprises, 1658 Belvoir Dr., Los Altos, CA 94024: Free information ❖ Lightweight fiberglass observatory domes. 415-941-6699.

Technical Innovations Inc., 22500 Old Hundred Rd., Barnesville, MD 20838: Free brochure ❖ Easy-to-assemble observatories for amateur astronomers. 301-972-8040.

Radio Astronomy

Bob's Electronic Service, 7605 Deland Ave., Fort Pierce, FL 34951: Catalog $3 ❖ Radio astronomy equipment. 407-464-2118.

Software

Andromeda Software Inc., P.O. Box 605, Amherst, NY 14226: Free catalog ❖ Astronomy software for PCs. 716-6691-4510.

ARC Science Simulations, P.O. Box 1955S, Loveland, CO 80539: Free information ❖ Astronomy simulation software for PCs. 303-667-1168.

The Astronomical Society of the Pacific, 390 Ashton Ave., San Francisco, CA 94112: Free catalog ❖ Software and CD-ROMs for Macintosh and PC computers. 800-335-2624.

CapellaSoft, P.O. Box 3964, La Mesa, CA 91944: Free information ❖ Views of the sky software for PCs. 619-460-8265.

Carina Software, 12919 Alcosta Blvd., San Ramon, CA 94543: Free information ❖ Astronomy software for Macintosh computers. 510-355-1266.

CEB Metasystems, 1200 Lawrence Dr., Ste. 175, Newbury Park, CA 91320: Free brochure ❖ Astronomy software. 800-232-7830; 805-499-0958 (in CA).

David Chandler Software, P.O. Box 309, La Verne, CA 91750: Free information ❖ Custom star charts for PCs. 909-988-5678.

CompuScope, 3463 State St., Ste. 431, Santa Barbara, CA 93105: Free catalog ❖ Astronomy imaging software and equipment. 805-966-7179.

E.L.B. Software, 8910 Willow Meadow, Houston, TX 77031: Information $2 ❖ Astronomy software. 713-541-9723.

Etion Software, 1936 Quail Circle, Louisville, CO 80027: Free information ❖ Astronomy software. 303-665-3444.

Etlon Software, 2250 Parkview Dr., Longmont, CO 80501: Free information ❖ Macintosh software that shows the planets, stars, moon, and sky summaries. 303-702-9274.

Farpoint Research, 10932 Hasty Ave., Downey, CA 90241: Free information ❖ PC software that shows the stars, planets, and all-known comets and asteroids. 310-861-6606.

Lewis-Michaels Engineering, 48 Delemere Blvd., Fairport, NY 14450: Free catalog ❖ Astronomy software and telescope-making supplies. 716-425-3470.

Logos Software, 110 Bagot St., Kingston, Ontario, Canada K7L 3E5: Free information ❖ Macintosh software that displays many comets, asteroids, and the planets with their moons.

Maris Multimedia Software, 100 Smith Ranch Rd., Ste. 301, San Rafael, CA 94903: Free information ❖ Windows-based PC and Macintosh astronomy software. 800-336-0185.

Maxis Software, 2 Theatre Square, Orinda, CA 94563: Free information ❖ Astronomy software. 510-254-9700.

National Technical Information Service, 5285 Port Royal Rd., Springfield, VA 22161: Free information ❖ Astronomical data for PCs and Macintosh computers. 703-487-4650.

Nova Astronomics, P.O. Box 31013, Halifax, Nova Scotia, Canada B3K 5T9: Free information ❖ Astronomy software for PCs. 902-443-5989.

Pickering Anomalies, P.O. Box 1214, Belmont, CA 94002: Free information ❖ Star location software for PCs. 415-593-7332.

picoScience, 41512 Chadbourne Dr., Fremont, CA 94539: Free information with long SASE ❖ Astronomy software for PCs. 510-498-1095.

Project Pluto Software, Ridge Rd., Box 1607, Bowdoinham, ME 04008: Free information ❖ Star charts for PCs. 207-666-5750.

Software Bisque, 912 12th St., Golden, CO 80401: Free information ❖ Astronomy software. 800-843-7599.

Stellar Software, P.O. Box 10183, Berkeley, CA 94709: Free information ❖ Astronomy software for PCs and the Macintosh. 510-845-8405.

Virtual Reality Labs Inc., 2341 Ganador Ct., San Luis Obispo, CA 93401: Free catalog ❖ Astronomy software for Mac and PC computers. 800-829-8754; 805-545-8515 (in CA).

Willmann-Bell Inc., P.O. Box 35025, Richmond, VA 23235: Catalog $1 ❖ Astronomy software. 804-320-7016.

❖ ASTRONOMY ❖

Zephyr Services, 1900 Murray Ave., Pittsburgh, PA 15217: Free catalog ❖ Astronomy software for PCs and Macintosh computers. 412-422-6600.

Telescopes & Accessories

Adorama, 42 W. 18th St., New York, NY 10011: Catalog $3 ❖ Telescopes, telescope-making supplies, photographic equipment, audiovisual aids, mounts, charts and star maps, books, and binoculars. 212-741-0466.

Analytical Scientific, 11049 Bandera Rd., San Antonio, TX 78250: Catalog $3 (refundable) ❖ Telescopes. 210-684-7373.

The Astronomical Society of the Pacific, 390 Ashton Ave., San Francisco, CA 94112: Free catalog ❖ Astronomy teaching and observing aids. 800-335-2624.

Astronomics, 2401 Tee Circle, Ste. 106, Norman, OK 73069: Free information ❖ Astronomy equipment. 405-364-0858.

The Astronomy Shoppe, 15836 N. Cave Creek Rd., Phoenix, AZ 85032: Free information with long SASE ❖ Telescopes, maps and star charts, and books. 602-971-3170.

AstroSystems Inc., 5348 Ocotillo Ct., Johnstown, CO 80534: Free catalog ❖ Telescope kits, components, and accessories. 970-587-5838.

Ball Photo Supply Company, 85 Tunnel Rd., Asheville, NC 28805: Free information ❖ Telescopes, spotting scopes, camera equipment, binoculars, eyepieces, and accessories. 704-252-2443.

Bausch & Lomb, 9200 Cody, Overland Park, KS 66214: Free list of retail sources ❖ Telescopes. 800-423-3537.

Berger Brothers Camera Exchange, 209 Broadway, Amityville, NY 11701: Free information ❖ Telescopes, telescope-making supplies, audiovisual aids, photographic equipment, mounts, charts and star maps, books, and binoculars. 800-262-4160.

Brite Sky, Rivers Camera Shop, 454 Central Ave., Dover, NH 03820: Free information ❖ Astronomy equipment, accessories, and cleaning fluid for lenses. 800-245-7963.

Byers Company, 29001 W. Hwy. 58, Barstow, CA 92311: Information $2 ❖ Telescope drives, custom-designed instruments, and equipment. 619-256-2377.

California Telescope Company, P.O. Box 1338, Burbank, CA 91507: Catalog $5 ❖ Telescopes, telescope-making supplies, audiovisual aids, photographic equipment, computer software, charts and star maps, books, and binoculars. 818-505-8424.

Camera Bug Ltd., 1799 Briarcliff Rd., Atlanta, GA 3030: Free information ❖ Telescopes, binoculars, spotting scopes, and accessories. 404-873-4513.

Celestron International, 2385 Columbia St., Torrance, CA 90503: Catalog $2 ❖ Telescopes. 310-328-9560.

Ceravolo Optical Systems, P.O. Box 1427, Ogdensburg, NY 13669: Brochure $2 ❖ Astronomy optical systems. 613-258-4480.

City Camera, 15336 W. Warren, Dearborn, MI 48126: Free information ❖ Telescopes. 800-359-5085.

Cosmic Connection Telescopes, 32 Ashgrove Blvd., Brandon, Manitoba, Canada R7B 1C2: Free information ❖ Telescopes. 204-727-3111.

Cosmic Connections Inc., P.O. Box 7, Aurora, IL 60505: Catalog $2 ❖ Telescopes, telescope-making supplies, photographic equipment, charts and star maps, domes, books, and binoculars. 800-634-7702.

Cosmos Ltd., 9215 Waukegan Rd., Morton Grove, IL 60053: Free catalog ❖ Ultra-wide field and equatorial telescopes, binoculars, and microscopes. 708-827-4846.

Coulter Optical Company, P.O. Box K, 54140 Pinecrest Rd., Idyllwild, CA 92549: Free information ❖ Telescopes, mirrors, and mounts. 800-555-4570.

D & G Optical, 6490 Lemon St., East Petersburg, PA 17520: Catalog $2 ❖ Ready-to-use tube assemblies with objective and 2-inch focusing lenses, 50mm finder-scope, dewcap, and dustcover. 717-560-1519.

Davilyn Corporation, 13406 Saticoy St., North Hollywood, CA 91605: Free information ❖ Star drives and declination motors. 800-235-6222; 818-787-3334 (in CA).

Daystar Filter Corporation, P.O. Box 5110, Diamond Bar, CA 91765: Free catalog ❖ Filters. 909-591-4673.

DFM Engineering Inc., 1035 Delaware Ave., Unit D, Longmont, CO 80501: Brochure $4 ❖ Computer-controlled telescopes. 303-678-8143.

Dino Productions, P.O. Box 3004, Englewood, CO 80155: Catalog $2 (refundable) ❖ Fossils, rocks and minerals, ecology and oceanography equipment, and chemistry, general science, astronomy, and biology supplies. 303-741-1587.

Eagle Optics, 716 S. Whitney Way, Madison, WI 53711: Free catalog ❖ Telescopes, photographic equipment, books, and binoculars. 608-271-4751.

Edmund Scientific Company, Edscorp Building, Barrington, NJ 08007: Free catalog ❖ Telescopes, telescope-making supplies, audiovisual aids, photographic equipment, charts and star maps, domes, books, and binoculars. 609-573-6260.

Efstonscience Inc., 3350 Dufferin St., Toronto, Ontario, Canada M6A 3A4: Catalog $6 ❖ Telescopes, telescope-making supplies, audiovisual aids, books, cameras, computers and software, and planetariums. 416-787-4581.

Epoch Instruments, 2331 American Ave., Hayward, CA 94545: Free catalog ❖ Telescope mounts, clock drives, setting circles, telescopes, and photographic systems. 415-784-0391.

Equatorial Platforms, 11065 Peaceful Valley Rd., Nevada City, CA 95969: Brochure $2 ❖ Direct roller-drive equatorial platforms with computer controls. 916-265-3183.

Focus Camera, 4419 13th Ave., Brooklyn, NY 11219: Free information ❖ Telescopes, audiovisual aids, photographic equipment, and binoculars. 718-436-6262.

Galaxy Optics, P.O. Box 2045, Buena Vista, CO 81211: Catalog $2 ❖ Telescope-making supplies and Newtonian optics. 719-395-8242.

Edwin Hirsch, 29 Lakeview Dr., Tomkins Cove, NY 10986: Free brochure ❖ Telescopes. 914-786-3738.

J.M.B. Inc., 20762 Richard, Trenton, MI 48183: Free information ❖ Glass solar filters and other optics. 313-675-3490.

A. Jaegers Optical Supply Company, 11 Roosevelt Ave., Spring Valley, NY 11581: Free catalog ❖ Telescopes, telescope-making supplies, photographic equipment, and binoculars. 516-599-3167.

Jim's Mobile Inc., 810 Quail St., Unit E, Lakewood, CO 80215: Video catalog $10 (refundable with $100 purchase) ❖ Dedicated computers with object databases, telescope-to-PC links, focusing motors, push and snap-on declination motors, drive controls, locking easels, telescopes, software, and astronomy equipment. 303-233-5353.

JSL, P.O. Box 51, Willard, UT 84340: Free catalog ❖ Telescopes and accessories. 801-723-5568.

Khan Scope Center, 3243 Dufferin St., Toronto, Ontario, Canada M6A 2T2: Free price list ❖ Telescopes, telescope-making supplies, binoculars, audiovisual aids, books, photographic equipment, computers and software, and planetariums. 416-783-4140.

La Maison de l'Astronomie, 8056 St. Hubert, Montreal, Quebec, Canada H2H 2P3: Free catalog ❖ Telescopes. 514-279-0063.

Lewis-Michaels Engineering, 48 Delemere Blvd., Fairport, NY 14450: Free catalog ❖ Astronomy software and telescope-making supplies. 716-425-3470.

Light Speed Telescopes Inc., 3991 Weld County Rd. 18, Erie, CO 80516: Brochure $2 ❖ Easy-to-set up car-transportable and clock-driven equatorial mounted telescope. 303-678-9547.

Lire La Nature Inc., 1699 Chemin Chandly, Longueuil, Quebec, Canada J4J 3X7: Free price list ❖ Telescopes, microscopes, and equipment. 514-463-5072.

❖ ASTRONOMY ❖

Los Angeles Optical Company, 4870 Lankershim Blvd., North Hollywood, CA 91601: Free information ❖ Telescopes, books, maps and charts, filters, and photographic equipment. 818-762-2206.

Lumicon, 2111 Research Dr., Livermore, CA 94550: Free catalog ❖ Telescopes, binoculars, eye pieces and filters, mirrors and lenses, mounts, star maps and atlases, computers and software, and photographic equipment. 510-447-9570.

Mardiron Optics, 4 Spartan Circle, Stoneham, MA 02180: Free brochure with two 1st class stamps ❖ Telescopes and binoculars. 617-938-8339.

Meade Instruments Corporation, 16542 Millikan Ave., Irvine, CA 92714: Catalog $3 ❖ Telescopes, spotting scopes, and telephoto lenses. 714-556-2291.

F.C. Meichsner Company, 182 Lincoln St., Boston, MA 02111: Free information ❖ Telescopes, antique instruments, photographic equipment, charts and star maps, books, and binoculars. 800-321-8439.

MMI Corporation, P.O. Box 19907, Baltimore, MD 21211: Catalog $2 ❖ Portable planetariums, 35mm slides, videos, celestial globes, computer software, laser disks, teaching manuals, and telescopes. 410-366-1222.

National Camera Exchange, 9300 Olson Memorial Hwy., Golden Valley, MN 55427: Free information ❖ Telescopes, audiovisual aids, photographic equipment, charts and star maps, books, and binoculars. 800-624-8107; 612-546-6831 (in MN).

New Mexico Astronomical, 834 N. Gabaldon Rd., Belen, NM 87002: Free information ❖ Telescopes. 505-864-2953.

Kenneth F. Novak & Company, Box 69, Ladysmith, WI 54848: Free catalog ❖ Telescopes, mounts, and books. 715-532-5102.

Nurnberg Scientific, 6310 SW Virginia Ave., Portland, OR 97201: Free information ❖ Telescopes. 503-246-8297.

Optec Inc., 199 Smith St., Lowell, MI 49331: Free information ❖ Photometers with easy-to-use controls. 616-897-9351.

Optron Systems, 15840 E. Alta Vista Way, San Jose, CA 95127: Free information ❖ Telescopes, binoculars, and optical equipment. 408-923-6800.

Orion Telescope & Binocular Center, P.O. Box 1815, Santa Cruz, CA 95061: Free catalog ❖ Telescopes, photographic equipment, charts and star maps, books, science supplies, and binoculars. 800-447-1001.

Palomar Optical Supply, P.O. Box 1310, Wildomar, CA 92595: Catalog $2 ❖ Mirror-making kits, pyrex blanks, grinding and polishing compounds, primary and elliptical mirrors, and supplies. 619-631-2835.

Parks Optical Company, 270 Easy St., Simi Valley, CA 93065: Catalog $3 ❖ Telescopes and optical equipment. 805-522-6722.

Pauli's Wholesale Optics, 29 Kingswood Rd., Danbury, CT 06811: Catalog $10 (refundable) ❖ Telescopes, telescope-making supplies, photographic equipment, computer software, science supplies, books, and binoculars. 203-746-3579

Perceptor, Brownsville Junction Plaza, Box 38, Ste. 201, Schomberg, Ontario, Canada L0G 1T0: Free information ❖ Telescopes, telescope-making supplies, mounts, audiovisual aids, books, cameras, computers and software, planetariums, and binoculars. 905-939-2313.

Photon Instrument Ltd., 122 E. Main St., Mesa, AZ 85201: Free information ❖ Telescopes and accessories. 800-574-2589; 602-835-1767 (in AZ).

Pocono Mountain Optics, RR 6, Box 6329, Moscow, PA 18444: Catalog $6 ❖ Astronomy equipment, binoculars, sighting scopes, telescope-making supplies, charts and star maps, photographic supplies, and books. 800-569-4323; 717-842-1500 (in PA).

Quantum Creations, 709 Rt. 206, Ste. 429, Belle Meade, NJ 08502: Catalog $2 ❖ Telescope cleaning kit. 908-359-7057.

Quasar Optics, 3715 51st St. SW, Calgary, Alberta, Canada T3E 6V2: Catalog $4 ❖ Telescopes, telescope-making supplies, photographic equipment, eyepieces, science supplies, books, and binoculars. 403-240-0680.

Questar, Rt. 202, P.O. Box 59, New Hope, PA 18938: Catalog $4 ❖ Telescopes and accessories. 215-862-5277.

R.V.R. Optical, P.O. Box 62, Eastchester, NY 10709: Catalog $5 ❖ Telescopes. 914-337-4085.

Redlich Optical, 711 W. Broad St., Falls Church, VA 22046: Free information with long SASE ❖ Telescopes, telescope-making equipment, binoculars, books, cameras, photographic supplies, computers and software, star maps, and atlases. 703-241-4077.

Royal Optics, 20 Glassco Ave. South, Hamilton, Ontario, Canada L8H 1B3: Free brochure ❖ Eyepieces and binoculars.

Sarasota Camera Exchange & Video Center, 1055 S. Tamiami Trail, Sarasota, FL 34236: Free information ❖ New and used telescopes, binoculars, filters, parts, and software. 941-366-7484.

Scope City, P.O. Box 440, Simi Valley, CA 93065: Catalog $7 (refundable) ❖ Telescopes, telescope-making supplies, photographic equipment, books, & binoculars. 805-522-6646.

Shutan Camera & Video, 312 W. Randolph, Chicago, IL 60606: Free catalog ❖ Telescopes, telescope-making supplies, photographic equipment, charts and star maps, binoculars, video accessories, and other electronics. 800-621-2248; 312-332-2000 (in IL).

Sky Designs, 4100 Felps, Ste. C, Colleyville, TX 76034: Free catalog ❖ Portable telescopes. 817-581-9878.

Sky Scientific, 28578 Hwy. 18, #184, Skyforest, CA 92385: Catalog $1 ❖ Telescopes and astrophotography equipment. 909-337-3440.

Spectra Astronomy, 6631 Wilbur Ave., Ste. 30, Reseda, CA 91335: Free catalog ❖ Astrophotography and telescopic equipment for beginning and advanced astronomers. 800-735-1352.

Stano Components, P.O. Box 2048, Carson City, NV 89702: Catalog $4 ❖ Night-vision optical equipment. 702-246-5281.

Star-Liner Company, 1106 S. Columbus Blvd., Tucson, AZ 85711: Catalog $14 ❖ Telescopes, from a 6-inch amateur unit to 24-inch observatory models. 520-795-3361.

Star Instruments, P.O. Box 597, Flagstaff, AZ 86002: Catalog $2 ❖ Custom optics for amateurs and professionals. 602-774-9177.

Stardrive Systems, 233 Bannock St., Denver, CO 80223: Free information ❖ Newtonian mirror cells. 303-722-4104.

Starsplitter Telescopes, 3228 Rikkard Dr., Thousand Oaks, CA 91362: Free information ❖ Telescopes with optional complete systems or install-your-own optics. 805-493-2489.

Stellar Dynamics Company, P.O. Box 765, Horsham, PA 19044: Free information ❖ Astronomical clock. 215-465-6462.

Swift Instruments Inc., 952 Dorchester Ave., Boston, MA 02125: Free information ❖ Telescopes, weather instruments, binoculars, and other optics. 800-446-1115; 617-436-2960 (in MA).

Tectron Telescopes, 2111 Whitfield Park Dr., Sarasota, FL 34243: Free catalog ❖ Easy-to-set-up Dobsonian telescopes. 941-758-9890.

Tele Vue Optics, 100 Rt. 59, Suffern, NY 10901: Catalog $3 ❖ Telescopes and optical equipment. 914-357-9522.

Texas Nautical Repair Company, 3110 S. Shepherd, Houston, TX 77098: Free catalog ❖ Portable camera mounting and tracking systems, telescopes, science equipment, star maps, and atlases. 713-529-3551.

Thousand Oaks Optical, Box 4813, Thousand Oaks, CA 91359: Free brochure ❖ Solar filters and astronomy equipment. 805-491-3642.

Roger W. Tuthill Inc., 11 Tanglewood Dr., Mountainside, NJ 07092: Free catalog with 9x12 self-addressed envelope and four 1st class stamps ❖ Telescopes, audiovisual aids, telescope-making supplies, photographic equipment, books, and binoculars. 800-223-1063.

Unitron Inc., 170 Wilbur Pl., P.O. Box 469, Bohemia, NY 11716: Free catalog ❖ Telescopes, spotting scopes, binoculars, and other optical instruments. 516-589-6666.

❖ AUTOGRAPHS ❖

University Optics, P.O. Box 1205, Ann Arbor, MI 48106: Free catalog ❖ Telescopes. 800-521-2828.

VERNONscope & Company, 5 Ithaca Rd., Candor, NY 13743: Catalog $3 ❖ Portable telescopes. 607-659-7000.

Vista Instrument Company, P.O. Box 1919, Santa Maria, CA 93454: Catalog $2 ❖ Precision camera tracker with optional accessories. 800-552-9170.

Vogel Enterprises Inc., 38W150 Hickory Ct., Batavia, IL 60510: Free information ❖ Quartz-controlled drive correctors. 800-457-8725; 708-879-8725 (in IL).

Ward's Natural Science, P.O. Box 92912, 5100 W. Henrietta Rd., Rochester, NY 14692: Earth science catalog $10; biology catalog $15; middle school catalog $10 ❖ Telescopes, telescope-making supplies, binoculars, audiovisual aids, books, computers and software, planetariums, meteorites, and other science equipment. 800-962-2660.

Wholesale Optics Division, 20 Kingswood Rd., Danbury, CT 06811: Catalog $15 ❖ Telescopes. 203-746-3579.

Willmann-Bell Inc., P.O. Box 35025, Richmond, VA 23235: Catalog $1 ❖ Telescopes and books. 804-320-7016.

Wonder Works, 280 W. Coleman, Mt. Pleasant, SC 29464: Free information ❖ Telescopes. 800-352-2316.

AUTOGRAPHS

Alfie's Autographs of Hollywood, 1608 N. Cahuenga Blvd., Ste. 510, Hollywood, CA 90028: Catalog $10 ❖ Autographed 8x10 color glossies. 310-652-0909.

Richard Altman, Hollywood Collectibles, 4238 Hollywood Blvd., Hollywood, FL 33021: Free information ❖ Autographs and autographed memorabilia. 305-986-0707.

Michael J. Amenta Autographs, P.O. Box 618, Merrick, NY 11566: Free catalog with long SASE ❖ Autographs by entertainment personalities, sports figures, astronauts, and others. 516-868-9208.

American Historical Guild, 17 Firelight, Ste. 100, Dix Hills, NY 11746: Catalog $2 ❖ Original letters and documents by world leaders, scientists, authors, composers, artists, and others. 800-544-1947; 516-621-3051 (in NY).

Ray Anthony Autograph Company, P.O. Box 687, Elkton, OR 97436: Catalog $8 ❖ Autographed letters, albums, books, photographs, and documents. 800-626-3393; 503-584-2257 (in OR).

Authentic Cinema Collectibles, 7726 Girard St., La Jolla, CA 92037: Free information ❖ Autographs, posters, lobby cards, and memorabilia. 619-551-9886.

Autograph Outlet, Susan Sanders Wadopian, 3 Ellenwood Dr., Asheville, NC 28804: Free catalog with long SASE ❖ Autographs. 704-253-5202.

B & J Collectibles, 999 Airport Rd., Unit 2, Lakewood, NJ 08701: Free information with long SASE ❖ Autographed sports cards, balls, photos, and memorabilia. 908-905-5000.

Benedikt & Salmon Record Rarities, 3020 Meade Ave., San Diego, CA 92116: Free catalogs, indicate choice of (1) autographs and rare books, (2) classical, (3) jazz, big bands, and blues, and (4) personalities, soundtracks, and country music ❖ Autographed memorabilia and rare books in music and the performing arts, hard-to-find rare phonograph recordings, from 1890 to date, and antique phonographs and cylinders for collectors. 619-281-3345.

Walter R. Benjamin, Autographs, P.O. Box 255, Hunter, NY 12442: Catalog subscription $10 ❖ Letters and documents from historical, literature, musical, and scientific areas. 518-263-4133.

John Blumenthal Autographs, 2853 Rikkard Dr., Thousand Oaks, CA 91362: Catalog $2 ❖ Autographs and signed photographs and letters. 805-493-5070.

Broadway Rick's Strike Zone, 1840 N. Federal Hwy., Boynton Beach, FL 33435: Free information with long SASE ❖ Autographed sports memorabilia, sports cards, and collectibles. 800-344-9103; 407-364-0453 (in FL).

Celebrity Gallery, 1840 N. Federal Hwy., Boynton Beach, FL 33435: Catalog $5 ❖ Autographs and vintage sports memorabilia. 800-344-9103; 407-364-0453.

Champion Sports Collectables Inc., 150 E. Santa Clara, Arcadia, CA 91006: Free information ❖ Autographed sports memorabilia, sports and non-sports cards, and collecting supplies. 818-574-5500.

Classic Rarities & Company, P.O. Drawer 29109, Lincoln, NE 68529: Free catalog ❖ Autographed letters and documents. 402-467-2948.

CPG Direct, P.O. Box 1020, Valley Cottage, NY 10989: Free information ❖ Sports and entertainment autographs. 800-382-3075.

The Dance Mart, P.O. Box 994, Teaneck, NJ 07666: Free catalog with long SASE ❖ Rare books, magazines, autograph material, and other dance collectibles. 201-833-4176.

Eileen Delaney Autographs, 1593 Monrovia, Newport Beach, CA 92663: Catalog $10 (refundable) ❖ Autographed rarities by Hollywood stars, presidents, scientists and inventors, and other personalities. 714-645-8566.

Erik L. Dorr, 203 E. Philadelphia St., York, PA 17403: List $1 with long SASE ❖ Entertainment, political, and historical autographs.

A. Lovell Elliott, 940 Crescent Beach Rd., Vero Beach, FL 32963: Free information ❖ Autographed letters, photos, and documents. 508-362-2334.

Elmer's Nostalgia Inc., 3 Putnam St., Sanford, ME 04073: Free catalog with long SASE and two 1st class stamps ❖ Entertainment, political, historical, literary, and pop culture autographs. Also memorabilia. 207-324-2166.

Empire State Sports Memorabilia & Collectibles Inc., 331 Cochran Pl., Valley Stream, NY 11581: Free information ❖ Baseball and other sports cards. Also autographs and memorabilia. 516-791-9091.

Robert Gentry, P.O. Box 850, Many, LA 71449: Free list ❖ Country music albums, 78 and 45 rpm records, autographs, movie posters, books and magazines, press kits, and collectibles.

Gibraltar Trade Center North Inc., 237 N. River Rd., Mt. Clemens, MI 48043: Free information ❖ Autographed sports memorabilia. 810-465-6440.

Golden State Autographs, P.O. Box 14776, Albuquerque, NM 87191: Free information with long SASE ❖ Autographs from all fields. 505-293-7407.

Brian & Maria Green, P.O. Box 1816, Kernersville, NC 27285: Free price list ❖ Civil War autographs, letters, diaries, and collectibles. 910-993-5100.

Roger Gross Ltd., 225 E. 57th St., New York, NY 10022: Free list ❖ Autographs, books, memorabilia, and unsigned photographs of opera stars. 212-759-2892.

Jim Hayes, Box 12560, James Island, SC 29422: Catalog subscription $6 ❖ Autographs from the Civil and Revolutionary war periods. 803-795-0732.

Historical Documents International Inc., P.O. Box 10488, Bedford, NH 03110: Free information ❖ Historical documents, autographs, and manuscripts. 800-225-6233.

History Makers Inc., 4040 E. 82nd St., Indianapolis, IN 46250: Catalog $3 ❖ Original letters and documents, photographs, and rare books signed by famous people from all fields. 800-424-9259.

Hollywood Legends, 6621 Hollywood Blvd., Hollywood, CA 90028: Free information ❖ Celebrity autographs from the early days of Hollywood to the present. 213-962-7411.

Houle Rare Books & Autographs, 7260 Beverly Blvd., Los Angeles, CA 90036: Catalog $5 ❖ Autographs in all fields. 213-937-5858.

Jeanne Hoyt Autographs, P.O. Box 1517, Rohnert Park, CA 94927: Free catalog ❖ Autographs from all areas. 707-584-4077.

Hummerdude's, P.O. Box 4348, Dunellan, NJ 08812: Catalog $4 ❖ Thousands of celebrity photos, autographs, and collectibles. Movie and TV stars, music artists, and more. 908-424-9367.

❖ AUTOGRAPHS ❖

Kaller Historical Documents Inc., P.O. Box 173, Allenhurst, NJ 07711: Free information ❖ Autographs and historical documents. 908-774-0222.

Kohl's Celebrity Gallery, 1840 N. Federal Hwy., Boynton Beach, FL 33435: Catalog $5 ❖ Autographs and vintage sports memorabilia. 800-344-9103; 407-364-0453 (in FL).

Robert A. LeGresley, P.O. Box 1199, Lawrence, KS 66044: Free catalog with long SASE ❖ Autographs, signed letters, photographs, and original comic art. 913-749-5458.

Blake LeVine Autographs, 128 Old East Neck Rd., Melville, NY 11747: Free catalog ❖ Autographs by theatrical performers, political figures, and others. 516-249-7391.

Abraham Lincoln Book Shop, 357 W. Chicago Ave., Chicago, IL 60610: Catalog $10 (2-year subscription) ❖ New and used books, autographed letters, prints, oils, photographs, Lincolniana, and United States Civil War and Presidential documents. 312-944-3085.

William Linehan Autographs, Box 1225, Concord, NH 03301: Catalog $3 ❖ Autographs and costumes of movie stars. 603-224-7226.

Lone Star Autographs, P.O. Box 500, Kaufman, TX 75142: Free catalog ❖ Books signed or owned by Presidents and First Ladies and autographed letters, documents, and photographs, from the Civil War, movie stars, scientific community, authors, musicians, astronauts, military greats, and politicians. 214-932-6050.

Joseph M. Maddalena, 345 N. Maple Dr., Ste. 202, Beverly Hills, CA 90210: Free information ❖ Letters, photos, documents, signed books, and memorabilia from presidents, statesmen, movie stars, scientists, authors, inventors, and others. 800-942-8856.

Main Street Fine Books & Manuscripts, 206 N. Main St., Galena, IL 61036: Free information ❖ American literature and Civil War collectibles. Also Grant, Lincolniana, Illinoisana, and autographed memorabilia. 815-777-3749.

Matthews, 6841 SW 66th Ave., Miami, FL 33143: Free catalog ❖ Rock and roll, sports, and Hollywood collectibles. 305-666-4463.

Menig's Memorabilia, 517 Manor, Peotone, IL 60468: Free catalog ❖ Civil War autographs, newspapers, and documents. 708-258-9487.

Merit Adventures, P.O. Box 66262, Houston, TX 77266: Catalog $3 ❖ Autographed music collectibles. 713-680-2233.

MidAtlantic Antiques, P.O. Box 691, Mt. Laurel, NJ 08054: Catalog $1 (3 issues) ❖ Antiques and memorabilia, paper collectibles, historical military maps, and autographs. 609-234-2651.

J.B. Muns, Bookseller, 1162 Shattuck Ave., Berkeley, CA 94707: Price list $1 ❖ Autographs by classical singers, musicians, and composers. 510-525-2420.

Nate's Autographs, 1015 Gayley Ave., Los Angeles, CA 90024: Catalog subscription (4 issues) $24 ❖ Autographs and memorabilia by entertainers, presidents, and historic, air and space, science, and sports personalities. 213-683-3907.

Odyssey Auctions Inc., 510-A S. Corona Mall, Corona, CA 91719: Catalog $20 ❖ Movie memorabilia and autographed letters, manuscripts, photographs, and documents from the arts and sciences to politics and entertainment stars. 909-371-7137.

Olde Soldier Books Inc., 18779 N. Frederick Ave., Gaithersburg, MD 20879: Free information ❖ Civil War books, documents, autographs, prints, and Americana. 301-963-2929.

The Opera Box, Box 994, Teaneck, NJ 07666: Free catalog ❖ Rare books, magazines, autographs, and opera collectibles. 201-833-4176.

The Pengellys, 502 Madison Ave., Fort Washington, PA 19034: Free catalog ❖ World War II, Civil War, and vintage entertainment autographs. 215-643-5646.

Tom Peper, 32 Shelter Cove Lane, #109, Hilton Head Island, SC 29928: Price list $1 ❖ Autographs, lobby cards and posters, and original comic and animation art. 800-628-7497.

Polo Grounds, 9900 Stirling Rd., Ste. 214, Pembroke Pines, FL 33024: Free information ❖ Vintage collectible sports cards. 305-432-2424.

Profiles in History, 345 N. Maple Dr., Ste. 202, Beverly Hills, CA 90210: Free information ❖ Historical autographs. 800-942-8856.

The Queen's Shilling, 14 Loudoun St. SE, Leesburg, VA 22075: Catalog $3 ❖ Autographs and old, rare, and antiquarian books on military history. 703-779-4669.

R & R Enterprises, 3 Chestnut Dr., Bedford, NH 03110: Free catalog ❖ Autographs of movie, television, sport, music, and history personalities.

Steven S. Raab, 2033 Walnut St., Philadelphia, PA 19102: Free catalog ❖ Autographs, signed books and photos, historic newspapers, World War I posters, and memorabilia. 610-446-6193.

Max Rambod Autographs, 9903 Santa Monica Blvd., Ste. 371, Beverly Hills, CA 90212: Catalog $2 ❖ Signed letters and autographs. 310-475-4535.

Kenneth W. Rendell Inc., 989 Madison Ave., New York, NY 10021: Catalog $5 ❖ Autographs and documents by famous persons, from early American history to the present. 212-717-1776.

Ron's Collectibles, 312 3rd St. SE, Cedar Rapids, IA 52401: Catalog $2 ❖ Autographed sports, entertainment, music, and political items. 319-365-6108.

Safka & Bareis, Autographs, P.O. Box 886, Forest Hills, NY 11375: Free catalog ❖ Signed photos, letters, and autographs by opera, music, and movie entertainers. 718-263-2276.

St. Louis Baseball Cards, 5456 Chatfield, St. Louis, MO 63129: Free information ❖ Sports cards and memorabilia, autographs, uniforms, press pins, and advertising collectibles. 314-892-4737.

H. Drew Sanchez, P.O. Box 2618, Apple Valley, CA 92307: Free catalog ❖ Cartoon art and autographs by entertainers and personalities. 619-242-7523.

The Score Board Inc., 1951 Old Cuthbert Rd., Cherry Hill, NJ 08034: Free information ❖ Autographed sports memorabilia. 800-327-4145; 609-354-8011 (in NJ).

Seaport Autographs, 6 Brandon Ln., Mystic, CT 06355: Free catalog ❖ Autographed letters, manuscripts, and documents. 860-572-8441.

Searle's Autographs, P.O. Box 18509, Asheville, NC 28814: Free list ❖ Autographs of television, movie, and theater personalities. 704-258-8096.

Philip Sears Disney Collectibles, 1457 Avon Terrace, Los Angeles, CA 90026: Free catalog ❖ Walt Disney autographs, animation art, and memorabilia. 213-666-3740.

Fred Senese, P.O. Box 310, Brockton, MA 02403: Free catalog ❖ Entertainment, sports, political, literary, and historical autographs. 508-586-1796.

R.M. Smythe, 26 Broadway, New York, NY 10004: Catalog $15 ❖ Obsolete stocks and bonds, bank notes, and autographs. 800-622-1880; 212-943-1880 (in NY).

SportsCards Plus, 28221 Crown Valley Pkwy., Laguna Niguel, CA 92677: Catalog $1 ❖ Sports cards, autographs, and sports memorabilia. 800-350-2273.

Stampede Investments, 1533 River Rd., Wisconsin Dells, WI 53965: Free catalog ❖ Fine books, autographs, and historical artifacts. 608-254-7751.

Star Shots, 5389 Bearup St., Port Charlotte, FL 33981: Free catalog ❖ Celebrity autographs. 813-697-6935.

Starr Autographs, P.O. Box 686181, Milwaukee, OR 97268: Free catalog ❖ Entertainment and sports celebrity autographs. 503-650-2793.

Jim Stinson Sports Collectibles, P.O. Box 756, St. George, UT 84771: Free information ❖ Autographed sports cards, photos, and sports memorabilia. 801-628-1399.

T.C. Vintage Autographs, 18 Via Aurelia, Ste. B, Palm Beach Gardens, FL 33418: Free catalog with long envelope and four 1st class stamps ❖ Autographed photos of entertainers. 407-624-1909.

AUTOMOTIVE PARTS & ACCESSORIES

Georgia Terry, Autographs, 840 NE Cochran Ave., Gresham, OR 97030: Free catalog ❖ Autographs by entertainment personalities. 503-667-0950.

Mark Vardakis Autographs, Box 1430, Coventry, RI 02816: Catalog $2 ❖ Autographs, paper Americana, pre-1900 stocks, and bonds and checks. 401-823-8440.

Wex Rex Records & Collectibles, 280 Worcester Rd., Framingham, MA 01701: Catalog $3 ❖ Autographs, movie and TV show character toys, and collectibles. 508-620-6181.

AUTOMOTIVE PARTS & ACCESSORIES

Automotive Art & Gifts

Applewood Cards Inc., P.O. Box 1212, Glastonbury, CT 06033: Catalog $2 ❖ Auto-related greeting cards. 860-657-4097.

Auto Cards Inc., P.O. Box 452, Stuart, FL 34995: Brochure and sample card $2 ❖ Color greeting cards for auto enthusiasts, featuring classic Mustangs, Corvettes, and Chevrolets.

Auto Motif Inc., 2941 Atlanta Rd., Smyrna, GA 30080: Catalog $3 ❖ Books, prints, puzzles, models, office accessories, lamps, original art, posters, and other gifts with an automotive theme. 800-367-1161.

Automobilia Collectibles, Division Lustron Industries, 18 Windgate Dr., New City, NY 10956: Catalog $3 ❖ Die-cast and pewter automotive miniatures, car badges, cruise ship models, and toy cars of the 1950s. 914-639-6806.

Automotive Emporium, 280 Preston Forest Village, Dallas, TX 75230: Free information with long SASE ❖ Automotive books and original literature, art and memorabilia, miniatures, and bronze sculptures. 214-361-1969.

Autosaurus, 109 N. Fairfax St., Alexandria, VA 22314: Free information ❖ Automotive art, books, models, clothes, posters, memorabilia, and gifts. 800-269-7221; 703-519-0742.

Benkin & Company, 14 E. Main St., Tipp City, OH 45371: Free information ❖ Automotive collectibles. 513-667-5975.

Car Collectables, 32 White Birch Rd., Madison, CT 06443: Free brochure ❖ Christmas cards, note cards, and gifts with an automotive theme. 203-245-7299.

Marlene Cavanaugh Posters, P.O. Box 988, Las Vegas, NV 89125: Free information ❖ Signed full-color lithographs of 1930s-style fictional automobiles.

Comet Products, 101-B Cherry Parke, Cherry Hill, NJ 08002: Catalog $3 ❖ Car grille emblem badges and car-related gifts. 609-795-4810.

Gee Gee Studios Inc., 6636 S. Apache Dr., Littleton, CO 80120: Catalog $2 (refundable) ❖ Original pen and ink drawings and numbered lithographs of famous cars. 303-794-2788.

Harmony Filling Station, 2024 E. Harmony Rd., Fort Collins, CO 80525: Free information with long SASE ❖ Filling station signs, pumps, cans, maps, and collectibles. 970-226-3830.

International Autosport, Catalog Sales, Rt. 29 North, P.O. Box 9036, Charlottesville, VA 22906: Catalog $1 ❖ Travel and auto accessories, safety items, collectibles, and clothing. 800-726-1199.

Merchandising Incentives Corporation, P.O. Box 877, Troy, MI 48099: Catalog $3 ❖ Chevrolet and Ford-licensed gifts and collectibles.

Motorhead, 1917 Dumas Circle NE, Takoma, WA 98422: Catalog $5 ❖ Automotive art prints and collectibles. Also scale model cars and kits and books. 206-924-0776.

Nostalgia Unlimited, P.O. Box 291563, Port Orange, FL 32129: Catalog $1 ❖ Automotive nostalgia. 800-843-3487.

Past Gas, 308 Willard St., Cocoa, FL 32922: Catalog $1 ❖ Automotive memorabilia. 407-636-0449.

Petro Classics, P.O. Box 201, Payson, UT 84651: Free list ❖ Restored automotive service station collectibles. 801-465-0130.

Pelham Prints, 2819 N. 3rd St., Clinton, IA 52732: Free information ❖ Note cards, antique and classic automotive art, and pen and ink drawings. 319-242-0280.

Universal Tire Company, 987 Stony Battery Rd., Lancaster, PA 17601: Free catalog ❖ Lucas electric parts, wheel hardware, moldings, antique and classic tires, and other automotive memorabilia. 800-233-3827.

Weber's Nostalgia Supermarket, 6611 Anglin Dr., Fort Worth, TX 76119: Catalog $4 (refundable) ❖ Gas globes, gas pump restoration supplies, car models, photographs, posters, and automotive gifts. 817-534-6611.

Batteries & Chargers

The Antique Auto Battery Manufacturing Company, 2320 Old Mill Rd., Hudson, OH 44236: Free information ❖ Automotive batteries. 800-426-7580; 216-425-2395 (in OH).

Becker Battery Sales, Rear 519 Wyoming Ave., West Pittston, PA 18643: Free information ❖ Batteries, cables, and master switches. 800-272-2682.

Deltran Corporation, 801 US Hwy. 92 East., Deland, FL 32724: Free information ❖ Battery chargers. 904-736-7900.

Walnut Grove Auto Parts, 5614 Hwy. 138, Oxford, GA 30267: Free information ❖ Battery and charging system tester. 800-992-9550.

Body Repair Parts

Auto Body Specialties Inc., Rt. 66, P.O. Box 455, Middlefield, CT 06455: Catalog $5 ❖ Reproduction and original quarter panels, fenders, repair panels, grilles, bumpers, and carpets for 1950 to 1986 American and foreign cars, pickups, and vans. 203-346-4989.

Bill's Speed Shop, 13951 Millersburg Rd., Navarre, OH 44662: Free information ❖ Hard-to-find panels for older cars and current models. 216-832-9403.

Made-Rite Auto Body Products Inc., 869 E. 140th St., Cleveland, OH 44110: Free information ❖ Steel replacement panels for cars, pickups, and vans. 216-681-2535.

Mill Supply, 3241 Superior Ave., Cleveland, OH 44114: Catalog $4 ❖ Steel replacement panels, tools, and body shop equipment for most United States cars, vans, pickups, and foreign cars. 800-888-5072; 216-241-5072 (in OH).

Rootlieb Inc., P.O. Box 1829, Turlock, CA 95381: Free catalog ❖ Hoods, fenders, running boards, splash aprons, and other parts for older Ford and Chevrolet cars. 209-632-2203.

Scarborough Faire, 1151 Main St., Pawtucket, RI 02860: Catalog $3 (specify year and car) ❖ Body repair panels for most cars. 401-724-4200.

Books & Other Publications

ADP Hollander Inc., 14800 28th Ave. North, Ste. 190, Plymouth, MN 55447: Free information ❖ Reference parts interchange manuals, from the 1920s and later. 800-825-0644.

Applegate & Applegate, Box 1, Annville, PA 17003: Free information ❖ Sales literature, owner manuals, tune-up charts, and photographs. 717-964-2350.

Auto Literature Shoppe, Box 328, HC 75, Fort Littleton, PA 17223: Catalog $2 ❖ Shop and owner manuals, showroom literature, and memorabilia. 717-987-3702.

The Auto Review, P.O. Box 510, Florissant, MO 63032: Free information ❖ Books and information on antique and classic car history and restoration. 314-355-3609.

Auto World Books, P.O. Box 562, Camarillo, CA 93011: Free information with long SASE ❖ Automobile, truck, and motorcycle books, service manuals, and back issues of magazines. 805-987-5570.

Automotive Information Clearinghouse, P.O. Box 1746, La Mesa, CA 92041: Free information with long SASE ❖ Original domestic and foreign automobile shop and parts manuals. 619-447-7200.

Aztex Corporation, P.O. Box 50046, Tucson, AZ 85703: Free list with long SASE ❖ Books on transportation and how-to automotive subjects. 520-882-4656.

AUTOMOTIVE PARTS & ACCESSORIES

Car Books, 1660 93rd Ln. NE, Minneapolis, MN 55449: Free information ❖ Automotive books and manuals. 800-642-3289.

Chewning's Auto Literature Ltd., 2011 Elm Tree Terrace, Bufford, GA 30518: Free information (specify year and car) ❖ Shop and owner automotive manuals, parts, and sales catalogs. 404-945-9795.

Chilton Book Company, One Chilton Way, Radnor, PA 19089: Free catalog ❖ Books on automotive mechanics and repair. 215-964-4000.

Dragich Auto Literature, 1660 93rd Ln. NE, Minneapolis, MN 55434: Free catalog ❖ Original and reproduction automotive books and manuals. 612-786-3925.

The Evergreen Press, 3380 Vincent Rd., Pleasant Hill, CA 94523: Free information with long SASE ❖ Reference books on Fords (Model A, T, and pre-war V-8), Chevrolet, Volkswagen, Thunderbird, Mustang, Falcon, Corvette, and Camaro. 510-933-9700.

Faxon Auto Literature, 1655 E. 6th St., Corona, CA 91719: Free information ❖ Automotive factory manuals and literature. 800-458-2734.

Bob Johnson's Auto Literature, 21 Blandin Ave., Framingham, MA 01701: Free information ❖ Automotive shop and interchange manuals and literature. 800-334-0688.

Lloyds Literature, P.O. Box 491, Newbury, OH 44065: Free information with long SASE ❖ Shop and owner manuals, parts and data books, dealer albums, sales brochures, service bulletins, and other publications. 800-292-2665; 216-338-1527 (in OH).

Ken McGee Holdings Inc., 232 Britannia Rd. West, Goderich, Ontario, Canada N7A 2B9: Free information with long SASE ❖ Factory original manuals, brochures, dealer books, and other publications, 519-524-5821.

Walter Miller, 6710 Brooklawn Pkwy., Syracuse, NY 13211: Free information ❖ Original repair and owner manuals, sales brochures, and parts books for domestic and foreign cars. 315-432-8282.

Motorbooks International, 729 Prospect Ave., P.O. Box 1, Osceola, WI 54020: Free catalog ❖ Automotive books. 800-458-0454.

Portrayal Press, P.O. Box 1190, Andover, NJ 07821: Catalog $3 ❖ Books and manuals for early Jeeps, military vehicles, and trucks. 201-579-5781.

Schiff European Automotive Literature Inc., 373 Richmond St., Providence, RI 02903: Free information with long SASE ❖ European and Japanese automotive publications. 401-453-5370.

Carriers & Racks

Allsop, P.O. Box 23, Bellingham, WA 98227: Free information ❖ Nordic skis and poles and carriers. 800-426-4303; 206-734-9090 (in WA).

Collins Ski Products Inc., P.O. Box 11, Bergenfield, NJ 07621: Free brochure ❖ Ski carriers, goggles, and ski poles and locks. 800-526-0369; 201-384-6060 (in NJ).

Cycle Goods, 2801 Hennepin Ave. South, Minneapolis, MN 55408: Catalog $4 (refundable) ❖ Parts, tools, bicycles, clothing, books, carriers, and safety gear. 612-872-7600.

Cycle Products Company, 2900 Rightview Dr., Memphis, TN 38116: Free information ❖ Car-mounted bicycle carriers and other cycling products. 800-842-2472; 901-345-5090 (in TN).

D & R Industries, 7111 Capitol Dr., Lincolnwood, IL 60645: Free information ❖ Car-mounted bicycle racks and other cycling products. 800-323-2852; 708-677-3200 (in IL).

Graber, 5253 Verona Rd., Madison, WI 53711: Free list of retail sources ❖ Bicycle, ski, and snowboard carriers. Also cargo containers and accessories. 800-783-7257.

Hike-A-Bike Inc., 2706 S. Willow Ave., Fresno, CA 93725: Free information ❖ Easy-to-install automobile-mounted carrier for up to four bicycles. 800-541-4453.

Primex of California, P.O. Box 505, Benicia, CA 94510: Catalog $5 ❖ Kayak and canoe carrier. 800-422-2482.

Technic Tool Corporation, P.O. Box 1406, Lewiston, ID 83501: Free list of retail sources ❖ Car carrier rack system for sports equipment and canoes, kayaks, surfboards, sailboards, or rubber rafts. 800-243-9592.

Tip Top Mobility, Box 5009, Minot, ND 58702: Free information ❖ Battery-operated car-top wheelchair carrier. 800-735-5958.

Worldwide Engineering Inc., 3240 N. Delaware St., Chandler, AZ 85225: Free information ❖ Automatic and semi-automatic fold-up wheelchair and scooter carrier for automotive vehicles. 800-848-3433.

Yakima, 1385 8th, Arcata, CA 95521: Free catalog ❖ Racks for bicycles, skis, and other equipment. Also luggage carriers. 707-826-8000.

Electricity Conversion

Electro Automotive, P.O. Box 1113, Felton, CA 95018: Catalog $5 ❖ Conversion components and books.

Exhaust Systems & Mufflers

Vetus Denouden Inc., P.O. Box 8712, Baltimore, MD 21240: Free information ❖ Exhaust system parts and accessories. 410-712-0760.

Kanter Auto Parts, 76 Monroe St., Boonton, NJ 07005: Free catalog ❖ Heavy-duty replacement exhaust systems for most cars, from 1909 to 1970. 201-334-9575.

John Kepich, 17370 Allco Center Rd., Fort Myers, FL 33912: Free information ❖ Heavy-duty stainless steel exhaust systems. 813-267-2550.

King & Queen Mufflers, Box 423, Plumsteadville, PA 18949: Free information ❖ NOS exhaust system parts for cars and trucks, 1926 and later. 215-766-8699.

Glass

Buchingers, P.O. Box 66114, Chicago, IL 60666: Free information ❖ Windshields and side and back windows, for 1940 to 1970 cars. 800-892-8636; 815-246-7221 (in IL).

Iowa Glass, P.O. Box 122, Cedar Rapids, IA 52406: Free information ❖ Hard-to-find windshields for most pre-1960 cars. 800-553-8134; 800-332-5402 (in IA).

Lo-Can Glass International, 693 McGrath Hwy., P.O. Box 45248, Somerville, MA 02145: Free information ❖ Hard-to-find glass for old and new cars. 800-345-9595; 617-396-9595 (in MA).

Headlights & Headlight Covers

Donald I. Axelrod, 354 Timson St., Lynn, MA 01902: Catalog $2 ❖ Headlights, headlight lenses, and parts. 617-598-0523.

Headlight Headquarters, Donald I. Axelrod, 35 Timson St., Lynn, MA 01902: Catalog $2 ❖ Headlight units, lenses, and parts for 1914 to 1939 American cars (except Fords). 617-598-0523.

High Performance Bulbs, 7057 Driftwood, Fenton, MI 48430: Free information ❖ Headlights. 800-414-BULB.

Innovative Products, P.O. Box 952793, Lake Mary, FL 32795: Free information ❖ Ultrabright headlights. 800-477-4490.

License Plates

Richard Diehl, 5965 W. Colgate Pl., Denver, CO 80227: Free list with long SASE ❖ License plates from most states, Canada, and foreign countries.

Eurosign Metalwerke Inc., 1469 Bank Rd., Margate, FL 33063: Free information ❖ Antique license plate replicas. 305-979-1448.

Bob Lint Motor Shop, P.O. Box 87, Danville, KS 67036: Inventory list $2 ❖ Old license plates. 316-962-5247.

Locks & Keys

Jesser's Classic Keys, 26 West St., Akron, OH 44303: Free information ❖ NOS keys. 216-376-8181.

Mito Corporation, 54847 County Rd. 17, Elkhart, IN 46516: Free information ❖ Electronic rear view mirror and remote keyless entry systems. 800-433-6486.

Miscellaneous Repairs

Instrument Services Inc., 11765 Main St., Roscoe, IL 61073: Free information ❖ Auto clock repairs. 800-558-BORG; 815-623-2993 (in IL).

❖ AUTOMOTIVE PARTS & ACCESSORIES ❖ 23

Vintage Radio Restorations, 900 Crestview Dr., Newberg, OR 97132: Free information ❖ Automobile radios restored to factory specifications. 503-538-2392.

Paint & Touch-Up Supplies

Bill Hirsch, 396 Littleton Ave., Newark, NJ 07103: Free information ❖ High-temperature engine enamels for spray or brush application. 800-828-2061; 201-642-2404 (in NJ).

Parts for All Makes & Models

A-1 Auto Wrecking, 13818 Pacific Ave., Tacoma, WA 98444: Free information ❖ Brake drums, axles, transmission parts, wheels, and parts for old cars. 206-537-3445.

All Auto Acres, W3862 Hwy. 16, Rio, WI 53960: Free information ❖ Parts for most cars, from 1955 to 1985. 414-992-5362.

Alley Auto Parts, Rt. 2, Box 551, Immokalee, FL 33934: Inventory list $4 ❖ Parts for cars and trucks, from 1948 to 1975. 813-657-3541.

American Performance Products, 675 S. Industry Rd., Cocoa, FL 32926: Catalog $6 ❖ New, used, NOS, and reproduction parts for AMX, Javelin, Jeep, Wagoneer, and other AMC cars. 407-632-8299.

Antique Auto Parts, P.O. Box 64, Elkview, WV 25071: Parts for most cars, from 1935 to 1969. 304-965-1821.

Antique Auto Parts Cellar, P.O. Box 3, South Weymouth, MA 02190: Free information with long SASE ❖ NOS and reproduction mechanical parts for most cars, from 1909 to 1965. 617-335-1579.

Arnold's Auto Parts, 1484 Crandall Rd., Tiverton, RI 02878: Free information ❖ Parts for American cars and trucks, from 1930 to 1970. 401-624-6936.

Auto Body Specialties Inc., Rt. 66, P.O. Box 455, Middlefield, CT 06455: Catalog $5 ❖ Reproduction and original quarter panels, fenders, repair panels, grilles, bumpers, and carpets for 1950 to 1986 American and foreign cars, pickups, and vans. 203-346-4989.

B.C. Automotive Inc., 2809 Damascus, Zion, IL 60099: Free information ❖ Parts for 1960 to 1982 domestic cars and 1970 to 1984 foreign cars. 708-746-8056.

Bartnik Sales & Service, 6524 Van Dyke, Cass City, MI 48726: Free information ❖ Parts for cars and trucks, from 1960 to 1970. 517-872-3541.

Beckers Auto Salvage, Hwy. 30 West, Atkins, IA 52206: Free information ❖ Parts for AMC, Ford, Studebaker, Edsel, Chevrolet, and other cars. 319-446-7141.

Big Ben's Used Cars & Salvage, Hwy. 79 East, Fordyce, AR 71742: Free information ❖ Used parts for 1975 and older cars. 501-352-7423.

Bob & Art's Auto Parts, 2641 Reno Rd., Schodack Center, Castleton, NY 12033: Free information ❖ Parts for the Rambler, Hudson, Studebaker, Ford, and other cars, from late 1940 to 1980. 518-477-9183.

Bob's Auto Parts, 6390 N. Lapeer Rd., Fostoria, MI 48435: Free information with long SASE ❖ Parts for most 1930 to 1970 cars. 810-793-7500.

Bradley Auto Inc., 2026 Hwy. A, West Bend, WI 53095: Free information ❖ Parts for American cars, imports, and light duty trucks, 1975 and later. 414-334-4653.

Bryant's Auto Parts, RR 1, Westville, IL 61883: Free information with long SASE ❖ Parts for most 1939 to 1988 cars. 217-267-2124.

Burlington Foreign Car Parts Inc., 863 Shelburne Rd., Shelburne, VT 05482: Free information ❖ Parts for imported and domestic cars. 800-343-3033.

Canfield Motors, 22-24 Main, New Waverly, IN 46961: Free information ❖ Parts for American cars, 1940 and later. 219-722-3230.

Cedar Auto Parts, 1100 Syndicate St., Jordan, MN 55352: Free information ❖ Parts for cars, from 1949 to current models. 800-755-3266.

Cherry Auto Parts, 5650 N. Detroit Ave., Toledo, OH 43612: Free brochure ❖ Used and rebuilt parts for foreign cars. 419-476-7222.

Chuck's Used Auto Parts, 4722 St. Barnabas Rd., Marlow Heights, MD 20748: Free information ❖ Parts for General Motors early and late model cars and trucks. 301-423-0007.

City Wrecking Company, P.O. Box 1188, Waco, TX 76703: Free information ❖ Parts for most cars. 817-829-1665.

Classic Auto Air Mfg. Company, 2020 W. Kennedy Blvd., Tampa, FL 33606: Free catalog ❖ Air-conditioning systems and parts for pre-1973 General Motor auto temperature control systems. 813-251-4994.

Classic Tube, 80 Rotech Dr., Lancaster, NY 14086: Catalog $1 ❖ Brake, fuel, and transmission lines for collector cars and trucks. 800-TUBES-1; 716-759-1800 (in NY).

Del-Car Auto Wrecking, 6650 Harlem Rd., P.O. Box 157, Westerville, OH 43081: Free information ❖ Parts for cars and trucks, from 1965 to 1992. 614-882-0220.

Doc's Auto Parts, 38708 Fisk Lake Rd., Paw Paw, MI 49079: Free information ❖ Parts for most cars, from 1930 to 1970. 616-657-5268.

E & J Used Auto & Truck Parts, 315 31st Ave., P.O. Box 6007, Rock Island, IL 61204: Free information ❖ Parts for 1940 to 1987 American and foreign cars and trucks. 800-728-7686; 309-788-7686 (in IL).

East End Auto Parts, 75 10th Ave. East, Box 183, Dickinson, ND 58601: Inventory list $5 ❖ Parts for 1940 to 1980 Chevrolets, Fords, Dodges, and foreign cars. 701-225-4206.

Eastern Nebraska Auto Recyclers, Mile Marker 351 on Hwy. 34, P.O. Box 266, Elmwood, NE 68349: Free information ❖ Parts for cars, from late 1940 to 1980. 402-994-4555.

Easy Jack & Sons Auto Parts, 2725 S. Milford Lake Rd., Junction City, KS 66441: Free information ❖ Used parts, from 1912 to 1982. 913-238-7541.

Eaton Detroit Spring, 1555 Michigan, Detroit, MI 48216: Free information ❖ Springs, U-bolts, shackles, and parts for most American cars and trucks. 313-963-3839.

Egge Machine Company, 8403 Allport, Santa Fe Springs, CA 90670: Catalog $2 ❖ Parts for older American cars. 800-866-EGGE; 310-945-3419 (in CA).

Ferrill's Auto Parts Inc., 18306 Hwy. 99, Lynwood, WA 98037: Free information ❖ Parts for American cars, from 1970 to 1985. 206-778-3147.

Fitz Auto Parts, 24000 Hwy. 9, Woodinville, WA 98072: Free information ❖ Parts for Ford, General Motors, Chrysler, AMC, and some European and Japanese cars. 206-483-1212.

Flathead Salvage & Storage, 495 Hwy. 82, Box 128, Somers, MT 59932: Free information ❖ Parts for most cars, from 1932 to 1950 and 1970 to current year. 406-857-3791.

Fleetline Automotive, P.O. Box 291, Highland, NY 12528: Free information ❖ Parts for Chevrolet cars and trucks, Corvairs, Novas, Camaros, Chevelles, Buicks, Pontiacs, Cadillacs, and Oldsmobiles. 914-895-2381.

Fort Auto Parts, P.O. Box 4528, Huachuca City, AZ 85616: Free information ❖ Parts for most cars, from 1923 to 1973. 602-456-9082.

Golden Sands Salvage, 501 Airport Rd., Boscobel, WI 53805: Free information ❖ Parts for most cars, from the 1930s to 1970s. 608-375-5353.

Hidden Valley Auto Parts, 21046 N. Rio Bravo Rd., Maricopa, AZ 85239: Free information with long SASE (specify parts wanted) ❖ Used antique and classic parts for older American and foreign cars. 602-568-2945.

J & B Auto Parts Inc., 17105 E. Hwy. 50, Orlando, FL 32820: Free information with long SASE ❖ Parts for most makes and models of American and foreign cars and trucks. 305-568-2131.

J & M Vintage Auto, P.O. Box 297, Goodman, MO 64843: Free information ❖ Parts for 1930 to 1968 cars. 417-364-7203.

Joblot Automotive Inc., 98-11 211th St., Queens Village, NY 11429: Catalog $2 ❖ Parts for 1928 to 1948 Ford cars and trucks. 800-221-0172; 718-468-8585 (in NY).

AUTOMOTIVE PARTS & ACCESSORIES

Kalend's Auto Wrecking, 8237 East Hwy. 26, Stockton, CA 95215: Free information with long SASE ❖ Parts for 1978 to 1988 foreign and domestic cars. 209-931-0929.

Kanter Auto Parts, 76 Monroe St., Boonton, NJ 07005: Free catalog ❖ Automotive parts. 201-334-9575.

Kelsey Auto Salvage, Rt. 2, Iowa Falls, IA 50126: Free information ❖ Parts for 1948 to 1981 American cars. 515-648-3066.

M.A.T.S. Auto Parts, 701 Straugh Rd., Rio Linda, CA 95673: Free information ❖ Parts for most cars up to 1975. 916-991-3033.

W.L. Wally Mansfield, P.O. Box 237, 526 E. 2nd, Blue Springs, NE 68318: Free information ❖ Parts for Ford Models A and T,; prewar V-8s; Chevrolets, from 1925 to 1948; Dodges, from 1929 to 1926; and cars up to 1952. 402-645-3546.

McCoy's Auto & Truck Wrecking, 80820 Pacific Hwy. 99N, Cresswell, OR 97426: Free information ❖ Parts for most cars, from 1950 to 1985. 503-942-0804.

Meier Auto Salvage, RR 1, Box 6L, Sioux City, IA 51108: Free information ❖ Automotive parts, from 1935 to 1988. 712-239-1344.

Memory Lane Collector Car Dismantlers, 1131 Pendleton, Sun Valley, CA 91352: Free information ❖ Pre-1974 American-made used car parts. 818-504-3341; 800-AT-YARD (in CA).

Gus Miller, Box 634, Heyworth, IL 61745: Free information with long SASE ❖ Parts for 1940 to 1950 cars. 309-473-2979.

Minot Wrecking & Salvage Company, 1215 Valley St., Minot, ND 58701: Free information ❖ Parts for most domestic and foreign cars, from 1925 to the present. 800-533-5904.

Morgan Auto Parts, 722 Kennie Rd., Pueblo, CO 81001: Free information ❖ Parts for most cars. 303-545-1702.

Art Morrison Enterprises, 5301 8th St. East, Fife, WA 98424: Catalog $5 (refundable) ❖ Drag car racing suspension components. 206-922-7188.

Nash Auto Parts, Pump Rd., Weedsport, NY 13166: Free information ❖ NOS and 1920 to 1975 parts. 800-526-6334.

North End Wrecking Inc., 55 W. 32nd St., Dubuque, IA 52001: Free information with long SASE ❖ Parts for late model cars. 319-556-0044.

Northern Tire & Auto Sales, N. 8219 Hwy. 51, Irma, WI 54442: Free information with long SASE ❖ Parts for most cars, from the 1920s to the 1970s. 715-453-5050.

Old Car City USA, 3098 Hwy. 411 NE, White, GA 30184: Video catalog $19.95 ❖ Parts for cars, from 1969 and later. 404-382-6141.

Old Gold Cars & Parts, Rt. 2, Box 1133, Old Town, FL 32680: Free information ❖ Parts for American cars, from 1948 to 1978. 904-542-8085.

Pacific Auto Accessories, 5882 Machine Dr., Huntington Beach, CA 92649: Brochure $3 ❖ Easy-to-install ground effect styling parts for most cars, trucks, and sport utility vehicles. 714-891-3669.

Pearson's Auto Dismantling & Used Cars, 2343 Hwy. 49, Mariposa, CA 95338: Free information ❖ Parts for 1940 to 1960 cars. 209-742-7442.

Performance Automotive Warehouse, 8966 Mason Ave., Chatsworth, CA 91311: Catalog $5 ❖ Stock, performance, and racing engine parts. 818-998-6000.

Performance Corner, 150 Engineers Rd., Hauppage, NY 11788: Catalog $3 ❖ High-performance automotive and truck parts and accessories.

Petry's Junk Yard Inc., 800 Gorsuch Rd., Westminster, MD 21157: Free information with long SASE ❖ Parts for most cars, from 1940 to 1970. 410-876-3233.

Philbates Auto Wrecking Inc., Hwy. 249, P.O. Box 28, New Kent, VA 23124: Free information ❖ Parts for most cars, from 1940 to 1982. 804-843-9787.

Pine River Salvage, Hwy. 371 North, Pine River, MN 56474: Free information with long SASE ❖ Parts for cars, from 1940 to 1980. 218-587-2700.

Porter Auto Repair & Salvage, Rt. 1, Box 180, Park River, ND 58270: Free information ❖ Parts for Ford, Chevrolet, Dodge, Oldsmobile, Buick, Pontiac cars, pickups, and trucks, from 1950 to 1975. 701-284-6517.

Restoration Specialties & Supply Inc., P.O. Box 328, Windber, PA 15963: Catalog $3.50 ❖ Restoration parts and accessories, from the 1920s to 1970. 814-467-9282.

Richard's Auto Sales & Salvage, 7638 NC Hwy. 49 South, Denton, NC 27239: Free information with long SASE ❖ Parts for 1950 to 1970 cars. 919-857-2222.

Ron's Auto Salvage, RR 2, Box 54, Allison, IA 50602: Free information ❖ Parts for most cars, from 1949 to 1977. 319-267-2871.

Wm. Sanders Company of New England, 141 S. Main St., Beacon Falls, CT 06403: Free information ❖ Motoring accessories ❖ 203-723-6907.

Seward Auto Salvage Inc., 2506 Vincent Rd., Milton, WI 53563: Free information with long SASE ❖ Parts for American and foreign cars, from 1946 to 1986. 608-752-5166.

Bill Shank Auto Parts, 14648 Promise Rd., Noblesville, IN 46060: Free information with long SASE ❖ Parts for 1948 to 1988 cars. 317-776-0080.

Sherman & Associates Inc., 28460 Groesbeck, Roseville, MI 48066: Catalog $5 ❖ Reproduction parts and panels for classic car and truck restorations. 810-774-8297.

Sil's Foreign Auto Parts Inc., 1498 Spur Dr. South, Islip, NY 11751: Free information with long SASE ❖ Parts for late model European and Japanese cars. 516-581-7624.

Sleepy Eye Salvage Company, RR 4, Box 60, Sleepy Eye, MN 56085: Free information ❖ Parts for 1937 to 1977 cars. 507-794-6673.

Gale Smyth Antique Auto, 8316 East A.J. Hwy., Whitesburg, TN 37891: Free information ❖ Parts for 1935 to 1972 American cars. 615-235-5221.

Speedway Motors, P.O. Box 81906, Lincoln, NE 68501: Catalog $5 ❖ Restoration and performance parts. 402-474-4411.

Lynn H. Steele Rubber Products, 1601 Hwy. 150 East, Denver, NC 28037: Catalog $2 (specify car) ❖ Reproduction rubber parts for Cadillacs, Pontiacs, Buicks, Chevrolets, Chryslers, Oldsmobiles, Packards, and GM trucks. 800-544-8665; 704-483-9343 (in NC).

Stevens Auto Wrecking, 160 Freeman Rd., Charlton, MA 01507: Free information with long SASE ❖ Parts for early and late model cars and trucks. 508-832-6380.

Summit Racing Equipment, P.O. Box 909, Akron, OH 44309: Catalog $3 ❖ Performance automobile parts. 216-630-0230.

Sunrise Auto Sales & Salvage, Rt. 3, Box 6, Aero Ave., Lake City, FL 32055: Free information ❖ Parts for most cars, from the 1950s through early 1970s. 904-755-1810.

Umatilla Auto Salvage, 19714 Saltsdale Rd., Umatilla, FL 32784: Free information ❖ Parts for most cars, from the 1950s to 1970s. 904-669-6363.

Van's Auto Salvage, Rt. 2, Box 164, Waupun, WI 53963: Free information with long SASE ❖ Parts for most cars, from 1947 to 1976. 414-324-2481.

Vintage Automotive, P.O. Box 958, 2290 N. 18th East, Mountain Home, ID 83647: Parts for most cars prior to 1970. 208-587-3743.

Vogt's Inc., 2239 Old Westminster Rd., Finksburg, MD 21048: Free information ❖ Parts for most cars, from 1935 to 1990.

West 29th Auto Inc., 3200 W. 29th St., Pueblo, CO 81003: Free information ❖ Old and new parts for most cars. 719-543-4247.

J.C. Whitney & Company, 1917-19 Archer Ave., P.O. Box 8410, Chicago, IL 60680: Free catalog ❖ Automotive parts, tools, and specialized equipment. 312-431-6102.

Wiese Auto Recycling Inc., Rt. 1, Box 32, Hwy. T.W., Theresa, WI 53091: Free information ❖ Parts for most cars, from the 1960s to the present. 414-488-3030.

❖ AUTOMOTIVE PARTS & ACCESSORIES ❖ 25

Leo Winakor & Sons Inc., 470 Forsyth Rd., Salem, CT 06420: Free information ❖ Parts for most cars, from 1930 through 1981. 203-859-0471.

Windy Hill Auto Parts, 9200 240th Ave. NE, New London, MN 56273: Free information ❖ Parts for American cars and trucks, from 1915 to 1990. Most parts pre-1968. 612-354-2201.

Winnicks Auto Sales & Parts, Rt. 61, P.O. Box 476, Shamokin, PA 17872: Free information with long SASE ❖ Parts for American and imported cars and trucks. Also Ford and Chevrolet engines. 717-648-6857.

Wiseman's Auto Salvage, 900 W. Cottonwood Ln., Casa Grande, AZ 85222: Free information with long SASE ❖ Parts for 1930 to 1970 cars. 602-836-7960.

Woller Auto Parts Inc., 8227 Rd. South, Lamar, CO 81052: Free information ❖ Parts for 1955 to 1984 domestic cars and pickups. 719-336-2108.

Zeb's Salvage, 2426 Bernitt Rd., Tigerton, WI 54486: Free information ❖ Parts for most cars, from the 1930s to 1970s.

Parts for Specific Makes & Models
ACURA

Alpharetta Auto Parts Inc., 5770 Hwy. 9 North, Alpharetta, GA 30201: Free information ❖ Used Acura parts. 800-494-PART; 404-475-1929 (in GA).

HKS USA Inc., 20312 Gramercy Pl., Torrance, CA 90501: Catalog $8 ❖ Performance parts. 310-328-8100.

King Motorsports, 105 E. Main St., Sullivan, WI 53178: Catalog $5 ❖ Acura parts and accessories. 414-593-2800.

MSO Parts, 1543 Easton Rd., Roslyn, PA 19001: Free information ❖ Acura factory parts. 800-500-PART; 215-657-8423 (in PA).

Options Auto Salon, 4523 San Fernando Rd., Ste. 1, Glendale, CA 91204: Catalog $5 ❖ Dress-up and restoration parts and accessories. 818-545-8218.

ALFA-ROMEO

Algar Enterprises Inc., 1234 Lancaster Ave., P.O. Box 167, Rosemont, PA 19010: Free information ❖ Alfa-Romeo parts. 800-441-9824; 215-527-1100 (in PA).

Beach Imports, 30 Auto Center Dr., Tustin, CA 92680: Free information ❖ Alfa-Romeo parts. 800-777-4895.

Bobcor Motors, 243 W. Passaic St., Maywood, NJ 07607: Catalog $6 ❖ Alfa-Romeo performance parts. 800-526-0337.

Ereminas Imports Inc., P.O. Box 1214, Torrington, CT 06790: Catalog $3 ❖ Alfa-Romeo parts. 203-496-9800.

International Autosport, Catalog Sales, Rt. 29 North, P.O. Box 9036, Charlottesville, VA 22906: Catalog $1 ❖ Replacement, restoration, and performance parts for the Alfa-Romeo. 800-726-1199.

Momentum Alfa-Romeo, 7300 Southwest Freeway, Houston, TX 77074: Free information ❖ Alfa-Romeo parts and accessories. 800-234-1063.

Prestige Imports, 14800 Biscayne Blvd., North Miami Beach, FL 33181: Free information ❖ Alfa-Romeo parts. 305-944-1800.

AMX

American Parts Depot, 409 N. Main St., West Manchester, OH 45382: Catalog $5 ❖ New, used, reproduction, and NOS parts. 513-678-7249.

American Performance Products Inc., 681 S. Industry Rd., Cocoa, FL 32926: Catalog $6 ❖ AMX parts. 407-632-8299.

Year One Inc., P.O. Box 129, Tucker, GA 30085: Catalog $5 ❖ New, used, and reproduction AMX restoration parts. 800-950-9503.

ANTIQUE & CLASSIC CARS

A-1 Auto Wrecking, 13818 Pacific Ave., Tacoma, WA 98444: Free information ❖ Parts for old cars. 206-537-3445.

B & W Antique Auto, 4653 Guide Meridian Rd., Bellingham, WA 98226: Catalog $5 (specify year and model) ❖ Antique Ford automotive parts. 800-561-4622.

Burchill Antique Auto Parts, P.O. Box 610637, Port Huron, MI 48061: Catalog $5 ❖ Parts for early vintage passenger and commercial vehicles. 313-385-3838.

Egge Machine Company, 8403 Allport, Santa Fe Springs, CA 90670: Catalog $2 ❖ Parts for old cars. 800-866-EGGE; 213-945-3419 (in CA).

Bob Lint Motor Shop, P.O. Box 87, Danville, KS 67036: Inventory list $2 ❖ Collectible license plates and parts for early Fords, Chevrolets, Pontiacs, Plymouths, Dodges, and Buicks. 316-962-5247.

OlCar Bearing Company, 455 Lakes Edge Dr., Oxford, MI 48371: Free information ❖ Bearings and seals for antique, classic, and special interest cars. Also for trucks and tractors. 810-969-2628.

PRO Antique Auto Parts, 50 King Spring Rd., Windsor Locks, CT 06096: Catalog $3 ❖ Restoration parts for antique cars. 203-623-0070.

ASTON MARTIN

Aston Martin of Cincinnati, 220 Mill St., Milford, OH 45150: Free information ❖ Aston Martin parts. 513-831-7100.

AUBURN

W.H. Lucarelli, 14 Hawthorne Ct., Wheeling, WV 26003: Free information ❖ Parts for 1931 to 1933 and 1935 to 1936 Auburns. 304-232-8906.

AUDI

Euromeister, 19507 Yuma St., Castro Valley, CA 94546: Catalog $4.95 ❖ Audi parts and accessories. 800-581-3327.

O.E.M. Parts Distributor, P.O. Box 25312, San Mateo, CA 94402: Free information ❖ Audi parts. 415-802-8125.

Parts Hotline, 10385 Central Ave., Montclair, CA 91763: Free information with long SASE ❖ Audi parts. 800-637-4662; 714-625-4888 (in CA).

Sonnen Motors, 601 Francisco Blvd. East, San Rafael, CA 94901: Free information ❖ Genuine factory parts and accessories. 800-543-7626; 800-SONNEN-1 (in CA).

Valley Motors, 3203 Bragg Blvd., Fayetteville, NC 28303: Free information ❖ Audi parts. 800-264-3203.

AUSTIN HEALEY

British Miles, 222 Grove, Morrisville, PA 19067: Free information ❖ Austin Healey parts. 215-736-9300.

English Car Spares Ltd., 345 Branch Rd SW, Alpharetta, GA 30201: Free information ❖ Austin Healey parts. 800-241-1916; 404-475-2662 (in GA).

Hemphill's Healey Haven, 4-B Winters Ln., Baltimore, MD 21228: Free information ❖ New and used parts. 800-9-HEALEY.

Moss Motors Ltd., 7200 Hollister Rd., P.O. Box 847, Goleta, CA 93116: Free catalog (specify model) ❖ Hard-to-find Austin Healey parts. 800-235-6954.

Sports & Classics, 512 Boston Post Rd., Darien, CT 06820: Catalog $4 ❖ Restoration, engine, electrical, and body parts for the Austin Healey. 203-655-8731.

AVANTI

Expressly Avanti, 1068 Elwood St., Narvon, PA 17555: Catalog $3 ❖ Avanti parts, from 1963 to 1991. 717-354-8847.

Newman & Altman Inc., P.O. Box 4276, South Bend, IN 46634: Catalog $5 ❖ Avanti parts. 800-722-4295.

Nostalgic Motor Cars, 47400 Avante Dr., Wixom, MI 48393: Free information ❖ NOS, new original, and new replacement parts, from 1963 to 1985. 800-AVANTI-X.

Penn Auto Sales, Dr. Roger Penn, 7115 Leesburg Pike, #113, Falls Church, VA 22043: Free information ❖ Avanti parts, from 1963 to 1991. 703-538-4388.

Southwest Avanti, 21824 N. 19th Ave., Phoenix, AZ 85027: Free information with long SASE ❖ Avanti parts, from 1963 to 1989. 602-581-7389.

BENTLEY

Carriage House Motor Cars Ltd., 25 Railroad Ave., Greenwich, CT 06830: Free information ❖ Rolls-Royce and Bentley parts. 800-883-2462.

Classic Auto Air Mfg. Company, 2020 W. Kennedy Blvd., Tampa, FL 33606: Free catalog ❖ Air-conditioning systems and parts for 1949 to 1969 Bentleys. 813-251-4994.

Foreign Motors West, 253 N. Main St., Natick, MA 01760: Free information ❖ Factory-new parts for the Silver Shadow and all postwar Rolls-Royces and Bentleys. 800-338-3198.

George Haug Company Inc., 517 E. 73rd St., New York, NY 10021: Free information ❖ Bentley parts. 212-288-0176.

Orlando's Classic & Sports Car Specialists, 412 Smith St., Keasbey, NJ 08832: Free information ❖ New, used, and remanufactured parts. 800-317-6557.

Replacement Parts Company, P.O. Box 152, Villa Rica, GA 30180: Free information ❖ Rolls-Royce and Bentley replacement parts. 404-459-0040.

Rolls-Royce Obsolete Parts Inc., P.O. Box 796, Ann Maria, FL 34216: Free information with long SASE ❖ Bentley and Rolls-Royce parts and literature. 813-778-7270.

BMW

Alpharetta Auto Parts Inc., 5770 Hwy. 9 North, Alpharetta, GA 30201: Free information ❖ Used BMW parts. 800-494-PART; 404-475-1929 (in GA).

The Auto Works, 846 NW 8th Ave., Fort Lauderdale, FL 33311: Free information ❖ Used BMW parts. 800-377-2520.

Bavarian Auto Service Inc., 44 Exeter St., Newmarket, NH 03857: Catalog $3 ❖ BMW parts. 800-535-2002.

The Best Source Inc., 389 Fort Salonga Rd., Northport, NY 11768: Catalog $5 (refundable) ❖ BMW parts. 800-537-8248.

BMP Design, 3208 Park Center Dr., Tyler, TX 75701: Catalog $5 ❖ BMW parts. 800-648-7278.

Electrodyne Inc., 4750 Eisenhower Ave., P.O. Box 9670, Alexandria, VA 22304: Catalog $3 ❖ BMW parts. 800-658-8850; 703-823-0202 (in VA).

Euromeister, 19507 Yuma St., Castro Valley, CA 94546: Catalog $4.95 ❖ BMW parts and accessories. 800-581-3327.

Greenfield Imported Car Parts, 335 High St., Greenfield, MA 01301: Free information ❖ BMW parts and accessories. 413-774-2819.

Hoffman BMW Parts, 425 Bloomfield Ave., Bloomfield, NJ 07003: Free information ❖ BMW parts. 800-238-8373.

Maximillian Importing Company, 606 Maiden Choice, Baltimore, MD 21228: Free information ❖ BMW parts. 410-744-2697.

MSO Parts, 1543 Easton Rd., Roslyn, PA 19001: Free information ❖ BMW factory parts. 800-500-PART; 215-657-8423 (in PA).

O.E.M. Parts Distributor, P.O. Box 25312, San Mateo, CA 94402: Free information ❖ BMW parts. 415-802-8125.

Perfect Plastics Industries Inc., 14th St., Building 201, New Kensington, PA 15068: Free information ❖ BMW body parts. 800-229-3568; 412-339-3568 (in PA).

BRITISH SPORTS CARS

British Car Specialists, 2060 N. Wilson Way, Stockton, CA 95205: Catalog $2 ❖ MG, Jaguar, Triumph, and Austin Healey parts. 209-948-8767.

British Miles, 222 Grove, Morrisville, PA 19067: Free information ❖ MG, Triumph, Austin Healey, and Jaguar parts. 215-736-9300.

FASPEC British Parts, 1036 SE Stark St., Portland, OR 97214: Free catalog (specify MGA/MGB, Sprite-Midget, or Austin Healey) ❖ New and used parts. 800-547-8788; 503-232-1232 (in OR).

Mini Mania, 31 Winsor St., Milpitas, CA 95035: Catalog $5 ❖ Parts for the Morris Minor, Mini Cooper, Austin Sprite, and MG Midget. 408-942-5595.

Moss Motors Ltd., 7200 Hollister Rd., P.O. Box 847, Goleta, CA 93116: Free catalog (specify model) ❖ Hard-to-find parts for British sports cars. 800-235-6954.

Perfect Plastics Industries Inc., 14th St., Building 201, New Kensington, PA 15068: Free information ❖ Body parts for MGA, MGB, Midget, Austin Healey, and Triumph TR-4 and TR-6. 800-229-3568; 412-339-3568 (in PA).

Scarborough Faire, 1151 Main St., Pawtucket, RI 02860: Catalog $3 (specify year and car) ❖ Parts for the MGB, MGA, Austin Healey, and Sprite. 401-724-4200.

Sports & Classics, 512 Boston Post Rd., Darien, CT 06820: Catalog $4 ❖ Restoration, engine, electrical, and body parts. 203-655-8731.

TS Imported Automotive, Pandora, OH 45877: Catalog $2 (refundable) ❖ New, used, and NOS parts for British cars. 800-543-6648.

Victoria British Ltd., P.O. Box 14991, Lenexa, KS 66215: Free catalog ❖ Original and reproduction Austin Healey and British sports car parts. 800-255-0088.

BRONCO

Auto Krafters Inc., P.O. Box 8, Broadway, VA 22815: Catalog $1 (specify year) ❖ New, used, and reproduction parts, from 1966 to 1977. 703-896-5910.

Bronco Parts, 8169-A Alpine Ave., Sacramento, CA 95826: Catalog $2 ❖ New and used Bronco parts, accessories, and restoration supplies, from 1966 to 1977.

Midland Automotive Products, Rt. 1, Box 27, Midland City, AL 36350: Free information ❖ Reproduction and new Bronco products. 205-983-1212.

New England Mustang, 1830 Barnum Ave., Bridgeport, CT 06610: Catalog $3 ❖ Bronco parts, from 1966 to 1977. 203-333-7454.

Obsolete Ford Parts Company, 311 E. Washington Ave., Nashville, GA 31639: Catalog $3 ❖ Parts for 1948 to 1977 Broncos. 912-686-2470.

Obsolete Ford Parts Inc. (Oklahoma City), 8701 South I-35, Oklahoma City, OK 73149: Catalog $3 (specify year) ❖ Parts for 1948 to 1972 Broncos. 405-631-3933.

BUICK

Bob's Automobilia, Box 2119, Atascadero, CA 93423: Catalog $4 ❖ Parts, rubber, literature, upholstery fabrics, and hardware for 1919 to 1953 Buicks. 805-434-2963.

The Buick Farm, 4143 W. Hwy. 166, Carrollton, GA 30116: Catalog $2 ❖ Parts for postwar Buicks, 1950 to 1975. 404-214-0145.

Buick Specialist, P.O. Box 5368, Kent, WA 98064: Catalog $4 ❖ Buick parts, from 1946 to 1963. 206-852-0584.

Cars Inc., Pearl St., Neshanic Station, NJ 08853: Catalog $3 (specify year) ❖ New, used, and reproduction parts for 1935 to 1975 Buicks. 201-369-3666.

Classic Buicks Inc., 4632 Riverside Dr., Chino, CA 91710: Catalog $5 ❖ New, used, and reproduction parts for 1946 to 1975 Buicks. 909-591-0283.

Cooper's Vintage Auto Parts, 121 E. Linden Ave., Burbank, CA 91502: Free information ❖ Vintage parts for Buicks. 818-567-4140.

Fannaly's Auto Exchange, 701 Range Rd., P.O. Box 23, Ponchatoula, LA 70454: Free information ❖ Parts for 1939 to 1975 Buicks. 504-386-3714.

GM Muscle Car Parts Inc., 10345 75th Ave., Palos Hills, IL 60465: Free information ❖ Buick parts, from 1964 to 1987. 708-599-2277.

Kanter Auto Parts, 76 Monroe St., Boonton, NJ 07005: Free catalog ❖ Parts for Buicks. 201-334-9575.

❖ AUTOMOTIVE PARTS & ACCESSORIES ❖

LaMance Autoworks, P.O. Box 449, 914 Old Mill Rd., Wartburg, TN 37887: Free information ❖ Buick parts. 615-346-7350.

Poston Enterprises, 206 N. Main St., Atmore, AL 36502: Catalog $2 ❖ Buick Skylark performance and restoration parts. 205-368-8577.

PRO Antique Auto Parts, 50 King Spring Rd., Windsor Locks, CT 06096: Catalog $3 ❖ New parts for 1929 to 1964 Buicks. 203-623-0070.

Speedway Automotive, 2300 W. Broadway, Phoenix, AZ 85041: Free information with long SASE ❖ Buick parts, from 1961 to 1987. 602-276-0090.

Swanson's, 3574 Western Ave., Sacramento, CA 95838: Free information ❖ Vintage parts and accessories, from 1938 to 1948. 916-646-0430.

Terrill Machine Inc., Rt. 2, Box 61, DeLeon, TX 76444: Free information with long SASE ❖ Engine overhaul parts for Buicks, from 1937 to 1958. 817-893-2610.

Terry's Auto Parts, Box 131, Granville, IA 51022: Free information with long SASE ❖ Parts for 1940 to 1984 Buicks and 1963 to 1984 Rivieras. 712-727-3273.

Year One Inc., P.O. Box 129, Tucker, GA 30085: Catalog $5 ❖ New, used, and reproduction Skylark restoration parts. 800-950-9503.

CADILLAC

Aabar's Cadillac & Lincoln Salvage, 9700 NE 23rd, Oklahoma City, OK 73141: Free information with long SASE ❖ Cadillac and Lincoln parts, from 1939 and later. 405-769-3318.

Akerman Old Cadillac Parts, 19 Gulf Rd., Box 107, Sanbornton, NH 03269: Free information with long SASE ❖ NOS and used Cadillac parts, from the 1930s to the 1970s. 800-487-3903.

All Cadillacs of the 40's, 12811 Foothill Blvd., Sylmar, CA 91342: Catalog $2 ❖ Used and reproduction parts, from 1940 to 1950. 818-361-1147.

Cadillac King Inc., 9840 San Fernando Rd., Pacoima, CA 91331: Free information with long SASE ❖ New, used, and rebuilt Cadillac parts. 818-890-0621.

Cadillac USA Parts Supply, 8505 Euclid Ave., Manassas, VA 22111: Free catalog ❖ Cadillac parts, from 1949 to 1985. 703-335-1935.

Continental Enterprises, 1673 Cary Rd., Kelowna, British Columbia, Canada V1X 2C1: Information $12 ❖ Cadillac dress-up accessory kits, from 1949 to 1993. 604-763-7727.

Cooper's Vintage Auto Parts, 121 E. Linden Ave., Burbank, CA 91502: Free information ❖ Vintage parts for Cadillacs. 818-567-4140.

F.E.N. Enterprises, P.O. Box 1559, Wappingers Falls, NY 12590: Free catalog (specify year and model) ❖ New, used, and reproduction parts. 914-462-5094.

Fannaly's Auto Exchange, 701 Range Rd., P.O. Box 23, Ponchatoula, LA 70454: Free information ❖ Parts for 1939 to 1974 Cadillacs. 504-386-3714.

Ted M. Holcombe Cadillac Parts, 2933 Century Ln., Bensalem, PA 19020: Free information ❖ Cadillac parts. 215-245-4560.

Honest John's Caddy Corner, P.O. Box 741, Justin, TX 76247: Free information ❖ NOS, rebuilt, and reproduction Cadillac parts, from 1941 to 1981. 817-648-3330.

Kanter Auto Parts, 76 Monroe St., Boonton, NJ 07005: Free catalog ❖ Parts for Cadillacs. 201-334-9575.

McVey's, 5040 Antioch, Merriam, KS 66203: Catalog $4 ❖ Cadillac parts and accessories, from 1936 to 1970. 913-722-0707.

PRO Antique Auto Parts, 50 King Spring Rd., Windsor Locks, CT 06096: Catalog $3 ❖ New parts for 1929 to 1964 Cadillacs. 203-623-0070.

Robinson's Auto Sales, 200 New York Ave., New Castle, IN 47362: Free information ❖ Parts for 1960 to 1970 models. 317-529-7603.

Silverstate Cadillac Parts, P.O. Box 2161, Sparks, NV 89432: Free information ❖ NOS Cadillac parts, from 1932 to 1982. 702-331-7252.

Lynn H. Steele Rubber Products, 1601 Hwy. 150 East, Denver, NC 28037: Catalog $2 (specify car) ❖ Reproduction rubber parts for Cadillacs and LaSalles. 800-544-8665; 704-483-9343 (in NC).

Terrill Machine Inc., Rt. 2, Box 61, DeLeon, TX 76444: Free information with long SASE ❖ Engine overhaul parts for Cadillacs, from 1936 to 1962. 817-893-2610.

Vintage Tin Auto Parts, 4550 Scotty Ln., Hutchinson, KS 67502: Free information with long SASE ❖ Cadillac parts, from 1940 to 1970. 316-669-8449.

CAMARO

Auto Heaven, 103 W. Allen St., Bloomington, IN 47401: Free information ❖ Parts for 1967 to 1969 models. 800-777-0297; 812-332-9401 (in IN).

Camaro Connection, 139 Cortland St., Lindenhurst, NY 11757: Free information with long SASE ❖ NOS and reproduction parts for 1967 to 1988 Camaros. Also sheet metal, interiors, electrical items, and decals. 800-835-8301.

Camaro Specialties, 900 E. Fillmore Ave., East Aurora, NY 14052: Catalog $1 ❖ New, used, NOS, and reproduction parts for 1967 to 1972 Camaros. 716-652-7086.

Chevy Parts Warehouse, 13545 Sycamore Ave., San Martin, CA 95046: Catalog $3 ❖ Camaro restoration parts. 800-408-2438; 408-683-2438 in CA).

Chevyland, 3667 Recycle Rd., Rancho Cordova, CA 95742: Catalog $4 ❖ Camaro parts and accessories. 800-624-6490; 800-624-8756 (in CA).

Chicago Muscle Car Parts, 912 E. Burnett Rd., Island Lake, IL 60042: Catalog $5 (refundable) ❖ New and used Camaro parts, from 1967 to 1969. 708-526-2200.

Classic Industries, 17832 Gothard St., Huntington Beach, CA 92647: Catalog $5 ❖ Camaro parts and accessories. 800-854-1280.

Competition Automotive Inc., 2095 West Shore Dr., Warwick, RI 02886: Free information ❖ Restoration supplies. 401-739-6262.

Dick's Chevy Parts, 1821 Columbus Ave., Springfield, OH 45503: Catalog $3 ❖ Rubber, chrome, moldings, interiors, emblems, and parts, from 1928 to 1972. 513-325-7861.

Harmon's Inc., P.O. Box 6, Hwy. 27 North, Geneva, IN 46740: Free catalog ❖ Camaro restoration parts, from 1967 to 1980. 219-368-7221.

J & M Auto Parts, RFD 5, Box 170, Pelham, NH 03076: Price list $1 (specify year) ❖ NOS, new, and reproduction 1967 to 1972 Camaro parts. 603-635-3866.

Kanter Auto Parts, 76 Monroe St., Boonton, NJ 07005: Free catalog ❖ Camaro parts. 201-334-9575.

Luttys Chevys, 2385 Saxonburg Blvd., Cheswick, PA 15024: Catalog $3 ❖ Camaro restoration parts, from 1967 to 1981. 412-265-2988.

Martz Classic Chevy Parts, RD 1, Box 199 B, Thomasville, PA 17364: Free catalog (specify year) ❖ NOS and reproduction parts, from 1955 to 1975. 717-225-1655.

National Parts Depot, 3101 SW 40th Blvd., Gainesville, FL 32608: Free catalog ❖ Camaro parts and accessories, from 1967 to 1981. 904-378-9000.

Obsolete Chevrolet Parts Company, P.O. Box 68, Nashville, GA 31639: Catalog $3 (specify year) ❖ Camaro reproduction parts, from 1962 to 1972. 912-686-7230.

Ole Chevy Store, 2509 S. Cannon Blvd., Kannapolis, NC 28083: Free list ❖ Parts for Camaros. 704-938-2923.

The Paddock Inc., 221 W. Main, Knightstown, IN 46148: Catalog $1 ❖ Camaro parts. 317-345-2131.

Rick's First Generation, 120 Commerce Blvd., Bogart, GA 30622: Catalog $3 ❖ Used, rare, and discontinued parts for 1967 to 1969 Camaros. 800-359-9717.

AUTOMOTIVE PARTS & ACCESSORIES

Southwestern Classics, 1230 Dan Gould Dr., Arlington. TX 76017: Free catalog ❖ New, used, remanufactured, and hard-to-find parts and accessories for 1967 to 1973 Camaros. 800-346-7362; 817-477-1322 (in TX).

Super Sport Restoration Parts Inc., 7138 Maddox Rd., Lithonia, GA 30058: Free information ❖ Camaro, Chevy II, Nova, and Chevelle parts. 404-482-9219.

Tamraz's Parts Discount Warehouse, 10022 S. Bode Rd., Plainfield, IL 60544: Free information ❖ Camaro parts. 708-904-4500.

Tom's Obsolete Chevy Parts, 14 Delta Dr., Pawtucket, RI 02860: Catalog $1 ❖ Camaro parts, from 1955 to 1972. 401-723-7580.

Valley View Automotive Products, 1646 Valley View Ave., Lewistown, PA 17044: Free information ❖ Camaro parts and accessories. 717-248-6447.

Volunteer State Obsolete Chevy Parts, Hwy. 41 South, Greenbrier, TN 37073: Catalog $5 (specify year) ❖ Camaro parts. 615-643-4583.

Year One Inc., P.O. Box 129, Tucker, GA 30085: Catalog $5 ❖ New, used, and reproduction Camaro restoration parts. 800-950-9503.

CAPRI

Dobi Capri Catalog, 320 Thor Pl., Brea, CA 92621: Catalog $2 ❖ Capri parts. 714-529-1977.

Racer Walsh Company, 1849 Forster Dr., Jacksonville, FL 32211: Catalog $3 ❖ Engines, suspensions, and parts for the Capri. 800-334-0151.

CAPRICE

Old Car Parts, 109 N. 15th St., Box 184, Clear Lake, IA 50428: Catalog $3.75 (specify year) ❖ NOS, new, and reproduction Caprice parts, from 1965 to 1970. 515-357-5510.

CHECKER

Blackheart Enterprises Ltd., 65 S. Service Rd., Plainview, NY 11803: Free information with long SASE (specify parts wanted) ❖ NOS Checker taxicab parts. 516-752-6065.

Pollard Company, Joe Pollard, 9331 Johnell Rd., Chatsworth, CA 91311: Free information with long SASE (specify parts wanted) ❖ Parts for Checker sedans and station wagons, from 1960 to 1982. 818-999-1485

CHEVELLE

Chevelle Classics, 17892 Gothard St., Huntington Beach, CA 92647: Catalog $4 ❖ Chevelle parts. 800-CHEVELLE; 714-841-5363 (in CA).

D & R Classic Automotive, 31 W. 280 Diehly Rd., Naperville, IL 60563: Free price list ❖ Chevelle parts. 800-472-6952.

Danchuk Manufacturing Inc., 3201 S. Standard Ave., Santa Ana, CA 92705: Catalog $4 ❖ Parts for 1964 to 1972 Chevelles. 800-854-6911; 714-751-1957 (in CA).

Dick's Chevy Parts, 1821 Columbus Ave., Springfield, OH 45503: Catalog $3 ❖ Rubber, chrome, moldings, interiors, emblems, and Chevelle parts, from 1928 to 1972. 513-325-7861.

Harmon's Inc., P.O. Box 6, Hwy. 27 North, Geneva, IN 46740: Free catalog ❖ Chevelle restoration parts, from 1947 to 1980. 219-368-7221.

J & M Auto Parts, RFD 5, Box 170, Pelham, NH 03076: Price list $1 (specify year) ❖ NOS, new, and reproduction 1964 to 1972 Chevelle parts. 603-635-3866.

Kanter Auto Parts, 76 Monroe St., Boonton, NJ 07005: Free catalog ❖ Chevelle parts. 201-334-9575.

Luttys Chevys, 2385 Saxonburg Blvd., Cheswick, PA 15024: Catalog $3 ❖ Chevelle restoration parts, from 1964 to 1972. 412-265-2988.

Martz Classic Chevy Parts, RD 1, Box 199 B, Thomasville, PA 17364: Free catalog (specify year) ❖ Chevelle NOS and reproduction parts, from 1955 to 1975. 717-225-1655.

Muscle Factory, 2031 D Via Burton, Anaheim, CA 92806: Free catalog ❖ Chevelle parts, from 1964 to 1972. 800-762-0317; 714-635-2314 (in CA).

National Parts Depot, 3101 SW 40th Blvd., Gainesville, FL 32608: Free catalog ❖ Chevelle parts and accessories, from 1964 to 1972. 904-378-9000.

Obsolete Chevrolet Parts Company, P.O. Box 68, Nashville, GA 31639: Catalog $3 (specify year) ❖ Chevelle reproduction parts, from 1962 to 1972. 912-686-7230.

Ole Chevy Store, 2509 S. Cannon Blvd., Kannapolis, NC 28083: Free list ❖ Parts for Chevelles. 704-938-2923.

Original Parts Group Inc., 17892 Gothard St., Huntington Beach, CA 92647: Catalog $4 ❖ Chevelle parts. 800-243-8355.

The Paddock Inc., 221 W. Main, Knightstown, IN 46148: Catalog $1 ❖ Chevelle parts. 317-345-2131.

Southwestern Classics, 1230 Dan Gould Dr., Arlington. TX 76017: Free catalog ❖ New, used, remanufactured, and hard-to-find parts and accessories for 1964 to 1972 Chevelles. 800-346-7362; 817-477-1322 (in TX).

Super Sport Restoration Parts Inc., 7138 Maddox Rd., Lithonia, GA 30058: Free information ❖ Parts for the Chevelle, Chevy II, Nova, and Camaro. 404-482-9219.

Tamraz's Parts Discount Warehouse, 10022 S. Bode Rd., Plainfield, IL 60544: Free information ❖ Chevelle parts. 708-904-4500.

Tom's Obsolete Chevy Parts, 14 Delta Dr., Pawtucket, RI 02860: Catalog $1 ❖ Chevelle parts, from 1955 to 1972. 401-723-7580.

True Connections, P.O. Box 4397, 8829 Pembroke, Riverside, CA 92504: Free information ❖ NOS, reproduction, and previously installed parts for 1964 to 1972 Chevelles. 909-688-6040.

Valley View Automotive Products, 1646 Valley View Ave., Lewistown, PA 17044: Free information ❖ Chevelle parts and accessories. 717-248-6447.

Volunteer State Obsolete Chevy Parts, Hwy. 41 South, Greenbrier, TN 37073: Catalog $5 (specify year) ❖ Chevelle parts. 615-643-4583.

Ted Williams, 5615 Rt. 45, Box A, Lisbon, OH 44432: Free catalog ❖ Restoration parts for 1964 to 1972 Chevelles. 216-424-9413.

Year One Inc., P.O. Box 129, Tucker, GA 30085: Catalog $5 ❖ New, used, and reproduction Chevelle restoration parts. 800-950-9503.

CHEVETTE

Year One Inc., P.O. Box 129, Tucker, GA 30085: Catalog $5 ❖ New, used, and reproduction Chevette restoration parts. 800-950-9503.

CHEVROLET

Adler's Antique Autos Inc., 801 New York 43, Stephentown, NY 12168: Free information ❖ Parts for Chevrolet cars and trucks, from 1930 to 1970. 518-733-5749.

Allchevy Auto Parts, 4999 Vanden Rd., Vacaville, CA 95667: Free information ❖ Parts for 1955 to 1993 Chevrolet cars and trucks. 707-437-5466.

American Classic Automotive, P.O. Box 50286, Denton, TX 76206: Free catalog (specify year) ❖ Chevrolet car and GMC truck parts, from 1936 to 1959 and 1960 to 1972. 817-497-2456.

C & P Chevy Parts, Box 348, Kulpsville, PA 19443: Catalog $3 ❖ New and restoration parts for 1955 to 1957 Chevrolet cars. 800-235-2475.

C.A.R.S. Inc., 1964 W. 11 Mile Rd., Berkley, MI 48072: Catalog $4 ❖ Parts for the 1955 to 1972 Bel-Air, Impala, Camaro, Nova, and Chevelle. 800-521-2194.

C.A.R.S. Inc., West, 525 S. Raymond Ave., Fullerton, CA 92631: Catalog $4 ❖ Parts for the 1955 to 1972 Bel-Air, Impala, Camaro, Nova, and Chevelle. 800-451-1955.

Car Shop, 420 W. Chapman Ave., Orange, CA 92666: Catalog $3 ❖ Chevrolet parts, from 1955 to 1957. 714-771-6432.

John Chambers Vintage Chevrolet, P.O. Box 35068, Phoenix, AZ 85069: Catalog $2 ❖ Chevrolet parts, from 1955 to 1957. 602-934-CHEV.

Chev's of the 40's, 2027 B St., Washougal, WA 98671: Catalog $3.75 ❖ Chevrolet parts, from 1937 to 1954. 800-999-2438.

AUTOMOTIVE PARTS & ACCESSORIES

Ciadella, 3757 E. Broadway, Phoenix, AZ 85040: Free information ❖ Reproduction Chevrolet interiors. 800-528-1342.

Classic Auto Parts Inc. (Chevrolet), 8723 S. Interstate 35, Oklahoma City, OK 73149: Catalog $2 ❖ Chevrolet parts, from 1932 to 1972. 405-631-4400.

Cliff's Classic Chevrolet Parts Company, 619 SE 202nd, P.O. Box 16739, Portland, OR 97216: Catalog $4 ❖ Used, new, and reproduction parts for 1955 to 1957 Chevrolets. 503-667-4329.

Continental Enterprises, 1673 Cary Rd., Kelowna, British Columbia, Canada V1X 2C1: Information $12 ❖ Chevrolet dress-up accessory kits, from 1949 to 1993. 604-763-7727.

Danchuk Manufacturing Inc., 3201 S. Standard Ave., Santa Ana, CA 92705: Catalog $4 ❖ Parts for 1955 to 1957 Chevrolets. 800-854-6911; 714-751-1957 (in CA).

Doug's Auto Parts, Hwy. 59 North, Box 811, Marshall, MN 56258: Free information ❖ Chevrolet parts, from 1955 to 1961. 507-537-1487.

Mike Drago Chevrolet Parts, 141 E. Saint Joseph St., Easton, PA 18042: Catalog $3 ❖ NOS, reproduction, and used Chevrolet parts, from 1955 to 1957. 215-252-5701.

Edmonds Old Car Parts, 307 E. Pearl, P.O. Box 303, McLouth, KS 66054: Free information ❖ Chevrolet parts, from 1928 to 1957. 913-796-6415.

Fiberglass & Wood Company, Rt. 3, Box 385, Nashville, GA 31639: Catalog $4 (specify year) ❖ Chevrolet parts, from 1927 to 1957. 912-686-3838.

The Filling Station, 990 S. 2nd St., Lebanon, OR 97355: Catalog $5 ❖ Reproduction parts for the 1929 to 1954 Chevrolet and 1929 to 1972 trucks. 800-841-6622.

Fleetline Automotive, P.O. Box 291, Highland, NY 12528: Free information ❖ Parts for 1935 to 1975 Chevrolet cars and trucks. 914-895-2381.

Garton's Auto, 5th & Vine, Millville, NJ 08332: Free information with long SASE (specify car) ❖ Fenders, grilles, trim, ornaments, and mechanical, chassis, and other 1929 to 1960 Chevrolet parts. 609-825-3618.

GM Muscle Car Parts Inc., 10345 75th Ave., Palos Hills, IL 60465: Free information ❖ Chevrolet parts, from 1964 to 1987. 708-599-2277.

H & H Classic Parts, 12325 Hwy. 72 West, Bentonville, AR 72712: Catalog $4 ❖ Parts for 1955 to 1957 Chevrolets. 501-787-5575.

Harmon's Inc., P.O. Box 6, Hwy. 27 North, Geneva, IN 46740: Free catalog ❖ Chevrolet restoration parts, from 1955 to 1972. 219-368-7221.

J & M Auto Parts, RFD 5, Box 170, Pelham, NH 03076: Price list $1 (specify year) ❖ NOS, new, and reproduction 1955 to 1972 Chevrolet parts. 603-635-3866.

J.R.'S Chevy Parts, 478 Moe Rd., Box 2, Clifton Park, NY 12065: Catalog $2 (specify car) ❖ NOS parts for the Caprice, Bel Air, and Biscayne. 518-383-5512.

Kanter Auto Parts, 76 Monroe St., Boonton, NJ 07005: Free catalog ❖ Parts for 1955 to 1986 Chevrolets. 201-334-9575.

Martz Classic Chevy Parts, RD 1, Box 199 B, Thomasville, PA 17364: Free catalog (specify year) ❖ NOS and reproduction 1955 to 1975 Chevrolet parts. 717-225-1655.

Modern Performance Classics, 1127 W. Collins, Orange, CA 92667: Free information ❖ NOS, reproduction, and used Nova and Chevy II parts. 800-457-NOVA.

Dick Moffit's Chevy Parts, 1821 Columbus Ave., Springfield, OH 45503: Catalog $4 (specify year) ❖ Chevrolet parts, from 1928 to 1972. 513-325-7861.

North Yale Auto Parts, Rt. 1, Box 707, Sperry, OK 74073: Free information ❖ Chevrolet parts, from the 1960s to 1980s. 800-256-6927; 918-288-7218 (in OK).

Obsolete Chevrolet Parts Company, P.O. Box 68, Nashville, GA 31639: Catalog $3 (specify year) ❖ Reproduction parts for 1929 to 1954, 1955 to 1957, and 1958 to 1970 cars. 912-686-7230.

Ol' 55 Chevy Parts, 4154-A Skyron Dr., Doylestown, PA 18901: Catalog $4 ❖ Chevrolet parts, from 1955, 1956, and 1957. 215-348-5568.

Old Car Parts, 109 N. 15th St., Box 184, Clear Lake, IA 50428: Catalog $3.75 (specify year) ❖ NOS, new, and reproduction Chevrolet parts, from 1930 to 1970. 515-357-5510.

Ole Chevy Store, 2509 S. Cannon Blvd., Kannapolis, NC 28083: Free list ❖ Parts for 1937 to 1958 Chevrolets. 704-938-2923.

Out of the Past Parts, 3720 SW 23rd St., Gainesville, FL 32601: Free information ❖ Chevrolet parts, 1935 and later. 904-377-4079.

Pioneer Classic Auto Inc., 2111 W. Deer Valley Rd., Phoenix, AZ 85027: Catalog $4 (specify year) ❖ New and used parts for 1955 to 1972 Chevrolets. 602-993-5999.

PRO Antique Auto Parts, 50 King Spring Rd., Windsor Locks, CT 06096: Catalog $3 ❖ New parts for 1929 to 1964 Chevrolets. 203-623-0070.

SC Automotive, 409 Super Sport Ln., Rt. 3, Box 9, New Ulm, MN 56073: Free catalog ❖ Chevrolet parts. 800-62-SS-409.

Southwestern Classics, 1230 Dan Gould Dr., Arlington, TX 76017: Free catalog ❖ New, used, and re-manufactured parts and accessories for 1961 to 1970 Chevrolets. 800-346-7362; 817-477-1322 (in TX).

Super Sport Restoration Parts Inc., 7138 Maddox Rd., Lithonia, GA 30058: Free information ❖ Parts for the Chevy II, Nova, Chevelle, and Camaro. 404-482-9219.

Terrill Machine Inc., Rt. 2, Box 61, DeLeon, TX 76444: Free information with long SASE ❖ Engine overhaul parts for Chevrolets, from 1929 to 1951. 817-893-2610.

Tom's Obsolete Chevy Parts, 14 Delta Dr., Pawtucket, RI 02860: Catalog $1 ❖ Chevrolet parts, from 1955 to 1972. 401-723-7580.

Volunteer State Obsolete Chevy Parts, Hwy. 41 South, Greenbrier, TN 37073: Catalog $5 (specify year) ❖ Chevrolet parts, from 1955 to 1957. 615-643-4583.

Winnicks Auto Sales & Parts, Rt. 61, P.O. Box 476, Shamokin, PA 17872: Free information with long SASE ❖ Ford and Chevrolet engines and parts for American and imported cars and trucks. 717-648-6857.

Year One Inc., P.O. Box 129, Tucker, GA 30085: Catalog $5 ❖ New, used, and reproduction Nova and Chevy II restoration parts. 800-950-9503.

CHRYSLER

Andy Bernbaum Auto Parts, 315 Franklin St., Newton, MA 02158: Catalog $4 ❖ Chrysler parts. 617-244-1118.

Vin Devers of Sylvania, 5570 Monroe St., Sylvania, OH 43560: Catalog $5 (refundable) ❖ MOPAR accessories. 800-887-5921.

Hardens Muscle Car World, P.O. Box 306, Lexington, MO 64067: Catalog $4 ❖ NOS, reproduction, and used Chrysler parts. 800-633-4690.

Mid-South Auto Sales, 2700 Neiman Ind. Dr., Winston-Salem, NC 27103: Free information ❖ Chrysler parts and accessories. 910-768-6251.

Mike's Auto Parts, Box 358, Ridgeland, MS 39157: Free information with long SASE ❖ Chrysler parts. 601-856-7214.

Mitchell Motor Parts Inc., 2467 Jackson Pike, Columbia, OH 43223: Free information with long SASE ❖ Chrysler parts, from 1928 to the present. 614-875-4919.

North Yale Auto Parts, Rt. 1, Box 707, Sperry, OK 74073: Free information ❖ Parts for Chrysler cars, 1977 and later. 800-256-6927; 918-288-7218 (in OK).

PRO Antique Auto Parts, 50 King Spring Rd., Windsor Locks, CT 06096: Catalog $3 ❖ New parts for 1929 to 1964 Chrysler cars. 203-623-0070.

Roberts Motor Parts, 17 Prospect St., West Newbury, MA 01985: Catalog $4 ❖ Parts for Chrysler cars. 508-363-5407.

Terrill Machine Inc., Rt. 2, Box 61, DeLeon, TX 76444: Free information with long SASE ❖ Engine overhaul parts for Chryslers, from 1937 to 1954. 817-893-2610.

Vintage Tin Auto Parts, 4550 Scotty Ln., Hutchinson, KS 67502: Free information with long SASE ❖ Chrysler parts, from 1940 to 1970. 316-669-8449.

CITROEN

B & B Used Auto Parts, Rt. 7, Box 691, Big Pine Key, FL 33043: Free information ❖ Parts for Citroens, 1968 and later. 305-872-9761.

COBRA

Cobra Restorers, 3099 Carter, Kenesaw, GA 30144: Catalog $5 ❖ Parts for Cobra cars. 404-427-0020.

Contemporary Classic Motor Car Company, 115 Hoyt Ave., Mamaroneck, NY 10543: Catalog $5 ❖ Cobra parts. 914-381-5678.

COMET

Dennis Carpenter Reproductions, P.O. Box 26398, Charlotte, NC 28221: Catalog $3 (specify year) ❖ Rubber parts for 1960 to 1970 Comets. 219-335-2425.

Bob Cook Classic Auto Parts, North 3rd St., Hazel, KY 42049: Catalog $6 (specify year) ❖ Reproduction parts for the 1956 to 1972 Comet. 502-492-8166.

Highway Classics, 949 N. Cataract Ave., San Dimas, CA 91773: Catalog $3 ❖ Comet parts and accessories, from 1960 to 1970. 909-592-5160.

Dale King Obsolete Parts Inc., P.O. Box A, Courthouse Square, Liberty, KY 42539: Free information ❖ NOS and reproduction Comet parts. 606-787-5031.

Northwest Classic Falcons, 1964 NW Pettygrove, Portland, OR 97209: Parts list $2 ❖ Used, new, reproduction, and NOS Comet parts, from 1960 to 1970. 503-241-9454.

Obsolete Ford Parts Inc. (Oklahoma City), 8701 South I-35, Oklahoma City, OK 73149: Catalog $3 (specify year) ❖ Parts for 1949 to 1972 Comets. 405-631-3933.

CORVAIR

Clark's Corvair Parts Inc., Rt. 2, Shelburne Falls, MA 01370: Catalog $5 ❖ Corvair parts. 510-625-9776.

Corvair Underground, P.O. Box 339, Dundee, OR 97115: Catalog $5 ❖ New, used, reproduction, and rebuilt Corvair parts. 800-825-VAIR.

Robinson's Auto Sales, 200 New York Ave., New Castle, IN 47362: Free information ❖ Parts for 1960 to 1970 models. 317-529-7603.

CORVETTE

Andover Corvette, P.O. Box 3143, Laurel, MD 20709: Free catalog (specify year) ❖ Parts for 1963 to 1967, 1968 to 1972, 1973 to 1977, and 1978 to 1982 Corvettes. 410-381-6700.

Auto Accessories of America, Rt. 322, Box 427, Boalsburg, PA 16827: Catalog $5 ❖ Corvette accessories and parts. 800-458-3475.

Blue Ribbon Products Ltd., 4965 Old House Trail NE, Atlanta, GA 30342: Free catalog ❖ Corvette parts, from 1956 to 1967. 404-843-8414.

Central Corvette, 5865 Sawyer Rd., Sawyer, MI 49125: Catalog $4 (specify catalog wanted) ❖ Corvette parts, from 1953 to 1982 and 1984 to 1995. Also 1953 to 1995 accessories. 616-426-3342.

Chevyland, 3667 Recycle Rd., Rancho Cordova, CA 95742: Catalog $4 ❖ Corvette parts and accessories. 800-624-6490; 800-624-8756 (in CA).

Chicago Corvette Supply, 7322 S. Archer Ave., Justice, IL 60458: Catalog $3 ❖ New and reproduction parts for 1953 to 1982 Corvettes. 800-872-2446; 708-458-2500 (in IL).

Contemporary Corvette, 2705 Old Rogers Rd., Bristol, PA 19007: Free information ❖ Used Corvette parts, from 1968 to 1992. 215-788-8693.

Corvette Central, 5865 Sawyer Rd., Sawyer, MI 49125: Catalog $4 ❖ New, used, and reproduction parts for 1953 to 1982 Corvettes. 616-426-3342.

Corvette Rubber Company, 10640 W. Cadillac Rd., Cadillac, MI 49601: Free catalog (specify year) ❖ Rubber parts and weatherstripping for 1953 to 1993 Corvettes. 616-779-2888.

Corvette Specialties of MD, 1912 Liberty St., Eldersburg, MD 21784: Free information ❖ New, used, and reproduction Corvette parts. 410-795-3180.

Eckler's, P.O. Box 5637, Titusville, FL 32783: Catalog (1953 to 1982) $4.95; (1984 to 1992) $3.95 ❖ Corvette restoration parts and accessories. 800-327-4868.

Howard's Corvettes, RR 3, Box 162, Sioux Falls, SD 57106: Free inventory list ❖ Parts for 1968 to 1986 Corvettes. 605-743-5233.

J.B.'s Corvette Supplies, 1992 White Plains Rd., Bronx, NY 10462: Catalog $5 ❖ Corvette parts. 800-874-6019; 718-823-3100 (in NY).

John's Corvette Cars, 23954 Kean St., Dearborn, MI 48124: Catalog $2 ❖ Corvette parts and weatherstripping for 1956 to 1995 Corvettes. 800-521-4774.

Kanter Auto Parts, 76 Monroe St., Boonton, NJ 07005: Free catalog ❖ Corvette parts, from 1963 to 1982. 201-334-9575.

Keen Parts Inc., 6048 SR 128, Cleves, OH 45002: Catalog $5 ❖ Restoration parts for Corvettes, from 1953 to 1982. 513-353-3997.

Long Island Corvette Supply Inc., 1445 Strong Ave., Copiague, NY 11726: Catalog $3 ❖ Corvette parts, from 1963 to 1967. 516-225-3000.

Mid America Designs Inc., P.O. Box 1368, Effingham, IL 62401: Catalog $5 ❖ Corvette replacement and performance parts. 800-500-8388.

Paragon Reproductions Inc., 8040 S. Jennings Rd., Swartz Creek, MI 48473: Free information ❖ Corvette restoration parts. 810-655-4641.

Rik's Unlimited, 3758 Hwy. 18 South, Morganton, NC 28655: Catalog $2 ❖ Corvette parts and accessories, from 1963 to 1982. 704-433-6506.

Stoudt Auto Sales, 1350 Carbon St., Reading, PA 19601: Catalog $3 ❖ Corvette parts, from 1953 to 1994. 610-374-4856.

Western Corvette Supply, P.O. Box 1262, Bothell, WA 98041: Catalog $2.50 (refundable) ❖ Corvette parts, interiors, and literature. 206-481-0206.

Zip Products, 1250 Commercial Centre, Mechanicsville, VA 23111: Catalog $3 ❖ Corvette restoration parts. 804-746-2290.

COUGAR

Auto Krafters Inc., P.O. Box 8, Broadway, VA 22815: Catalog $1 (specify year) ❖ New, used, and reproduction parts, from 1967 to 1973. 703-896-5910.

Bob Cook Classic Auto Parts, North 3rd St., Hazel, KY 42049: Catalog $6 (specify year) ❖ Reproduction parts for 1965 to 1973 Cougars. 502-492-8166.

Highway Classics, 949 N. Cataract Ave., San Dimas, CA 91773: Catalog $3 ❖ Cougar parts and accessories, from 1967 to 1973. 909-592-5160.

Dale King Obsolete Parts Inc., P.O. Box A, Courthouse Square, Liberty, KY 42539: Free information ❖ NOS and reproduction Cougar parts. 606-787-5031.

Midland Automotive Products, Rt. 1, Box 27, Midland City, AL 36350: Free information ❖ Reproduction and new Cougar products. 205-983-1212.

Mustangs Unlimited, 185 Adams St., Manchester, CT 06040: Catalog $3 (specify year) ❖ Cougar parts. 800-243-7278.

CROSLEY

Edwards Crosley Parts, P.O. Box 632, Mansfield, OH 44901: Free information with long SASE (specify parts wanted) ❖ Crosley parts. 419-589-5767.

AUTOMOTIVE PARTS & ACCESSORIES

CUTLASS

Tamraz's Parts Discount Warehouse, 10 South 123 Normantown Rd., Naperville, IL 60564: Free information ❖ Cutlass parts. 708-851-4500.

Year One Inc., P.O. Box 129, Tucker, GA 30085: Catalog $5 ❖ New, used, and reproduction Cutlass restoration parts. 800-950-9503.

DATSUN (NISSAN)

Autoshow, 8148 Woodland Dr., Indianapolis, IN 46278: Catalog $3 (refundable) ❖ Parts for the Datsun Z and other models. 800-428-2200; 317-875-0076 (in IN).

Dobi Datsun Catalog, 320 Thor Pl., Brea, CA 92621: Catalog $2 ❖ Replacement parts for the Datsun Z, 200SX, and 510. 714-529-1977.

HKS USA Inc., 20312 Gramercy Pl., Torrance, CA 90501: Catalog $8 ❖ Performance accessories for the Datsun. 310-328-8100.

Motorsport, 1139 W. Collins Ave., Orange, CA 92667: Free catalog ❖ Parts for the Datsun Z and ZX. 800-633-6331.

Options Auto Salon, 4523 San Fernando Rd., Ste. 1, Glendale, CA 91204: Catalog $5 ❖ Dress-up and restoration parts and accessories. 818-545-8218.

Perfect Plastics Industries Inc., 14th St., Building 201, New Kensington, PA 15068: Free information ❖ Body parts for the Datsun Z. 800-229-3568; 412-339-3568 (in PA).

DELOREAN

Delorean One, 20229 Nordhoff St., Chatsworth, CA 91311: Free information ❖ Delorean parts. 818-341-1796.

P.J. Grady Delorean, 118 Montauk Hwy., West Sayville, NY 11796: Free information ❖ DeLorean parts. 516-589-6224.

Specialty Automotive, 1510 Lakemoor Loop Ct., Olympia, WA 98512: Free information with long SASE (specify parts wanted) ❖ DeLorean parts and accessories. 206-943-2497.

DESOTO

Andy Bernbaum Auto Parts, 315 Franklin St., Newton, MA 02158: Catalog $4 ❖ Parts for the DeSoto. 617-244-1118.

Mike's Auto Parts, Box 358, Ridgeland, MS 39157: Free information with long SASE ❖ DeSoto parts. 601-856-7214.

Mitchell Motor Parts Inc., 2467 Jackson Pike, Columbia, OH 43223: Free information with long SASE ❖ Desoto parts, from 1928 to the present. 614-875-4919.

PRO Antique Auto Parts, 50 King Spring Rd., Windsor Locks, CT 06096: Catalog $3 ❖ New parts for 1929 to 1964 DeSotos. 203-623-0070.

Roberts Motor Parts, 17 Prospect St., West Newbury, MA 01985: Catalog $4 ❖ Parts for DeSotos. 508-363-5407.

Terrill Machine Inc., Rt. 2, Box 61, DeLeon, TX 76444: Free information with long SASE ❖ Engine overhaul parts for DeSotos, from 1937 to 1954. 817-893-2610.

Vintage Tin Auto Parts, 4550 Scotty Ln., Hutchinson, KS 67502: Free information with long SASE ❖ DeSoto parts. 316-669-8449.

DODGE

Andy Bernbaum Auto Parts, 315 Franklin St., Newton, MA 02158: Catalog $4 ❖ Parts for Dodge cars. 617-244-1118.

Hardens Muscle Car World, P.O. Box 306, Lexington, MO 64067: Catalog $4 ❖ NOS, reproduction, and used Dodge parts. 800-633-4690.

Koller Dodge, 1565 W. Ogden Ave., Naperville, IL 60540: Catalog $7 ❖ Dodge restoration parts. 708-355-3411.

LaMance Autoworks, P.O. Box 449, 914 Old Mill Rd., Wartburg, TN 37887: Free information ❖ Dodge parts. 615-346-7350.

Mid-South Auto Sales, 2700 Neiman Ind. Dr., Winston-Salem, NC 27103: Free information ❖ Dodge parts and accessories. 910-768-6251.

Mike's Auto Parts, Box 358, Ridgeland, MS 39157: Free information with long SASE ❖ Dodge parts. 601-856-7214.

Mitchell Motor Parts Inc., 2467 Jackson Pike, Columbia, OH 43223: Free information with long SASE ❖ Dodge parts, from 1928 to the present. 614-875-4919.

Out of the Past Parts, 3720 SW 23rd St., Gainesville, FL 32601: Free information ❖ Dodge parts, 1935 and later. 904-377-4079.

PRO Antique Auto Parts, 50 King Spring Rd., Windsor Locks, CT 06096: Catalog $3 ❖ New parts for 1929 to 1964 Dodge cars. 203-623-0070.

Roberts Motor Parts, 17 Prospect St., West Newbury, MA 01985: Catalog $4 ❖ Dodge parts. 508-363-5407.

Terrill Machine Inc., Rt. 2, Box 61, DeLeon, TX 76444: Free information with long SASE ❖ Engine overhaul parts for Dodges, from 1937 to 1954. 817-893-2610.

Vintage Tin Auto Parts, 4550 Scotty Ln., Hutchinson, KS 67502: Free information with long SASE ❖ Dodge parts, from 1940 to 1970. 316-669-8449.

Year One Inc., P.O. Box 129, Tucker, GA 30085: Catalog $5 ❖ New, used, and reproduction Dodge restoration parts. 800-950-9503.

EDSEL

B & W Antique Auto, 4653 Guide Meridian Rd., Bellingham, WA 98226: Catalog $5 (specify year and model) ❖ Edsel automotive parts, 1958 to 1960. 360-647-4574.

Beckers Auto Salvage, Hwy. 30 West, Atkins, IA 52206: Free information ❖ Parts for Edsel cars. 319-446-7141.

Bob Cook Classic Auto Parts, North 3rd St., Hazel, KY 42049: Catalog $6 (specify year) ❖ Reproduction parts for 1958 to 1960 Edsels. 502-492-8166.

LaMance Autoworks, P.O. Box 449, 914 Old Mill Rd., Wartburg, TN 37887: Free information ❖ Edsel parts, from 1958 to 1959. 615-346-7350.

EL CAMINO

Chevelle Classics, 17892 Gothard St., Huntington Beach, CA 92647: Catalog $4 ❖ El Camino parts. 800-CHEVELLE; 714-841-5363 (in CA).

Chevyland, 3667 Recycle Rd., Rancho Cordova, CA 95742: Catalog $4 ❖ El Camino parts and accessories. 800-624-6490; 800-624-8756 (in CA).

Danchuk Manufacturing Inc., 3201 S. Standard Ave., Santa Ana, CA 92705: Catalog $4 ❖ Parts for the 1964 to 1972 El Camino. 800-854-6911; 714-751-1957 (in CA).

Muscle Factory, 2031 D Via Burton, Anaheim, CA 92806: Free catalog ❖ El Camino parts, from 1964 to 1972. 800-762-0317; 714-635-2314 (in CA).

Original Parts Group Inc., 17892 Gothard St., Huntington Beach, CA 92647: Catalog $4 ❖ El Camino parts. 800-243-8355.

Southwestern Classics, 1230 Dan Gould Dr., Arlington, TX 76017: Free catalog ❖ New, used, remanufactured, and hard-to-find parts and accessories for 1964 to 1972 El Caminos. 800-346-7362; 817-477-1322 (in TX).

Ted Williams, 5615 Rt. 45, Box A, Lisbon, OH 44432: Free catalog ❖ Restoration parts for 1964 to 1972 El Caminos. 216-424-9413.

Year One Inc., P.O. Box 129, Tucker, GA 30085: Catalog $5 ❖ New, used, and reproduction El Camino restoration parts. 800-950-9503.

ENGLISH FORD

Anglia Obsolete, 1311 York Dr., Vista, CA 92084: Free information ❖ New, used, and reproduction parts for English Fords. 619-630-3136.

Dave Bean Engineering Inc., 636 E. Saint Charles St., San Andreas, CA 95249: Catalog $6 ❖ Parts for the English Ford. 209-754-5802.

ESCORT

Racer Walsh Company, 1849 Forster Dr., Jacksonville, FL 32211: Catalog $3 ❖ Engines, suspensions, and parts for Escorts. 800-334-0151.

ESSEX

K-Gap Automotive Parts, P.O. Box 3065, Santa Fe Springs, CA 90670: Catalog $2 (refundable) ❖ Reproduction Hudson and Essex parts. 714-523-0403.

Kenneth Fogarty, Anson Valley Rd., New Vineyard, ME 04956: Free information with long SASE (specify parts wanted) ❖ Essex parts, from 1919 to 1933. 207-652-2210.

FAIRLANE

Auto Krafters Inc., P.O. Box 8, Broadway, VA 22815: Catalog $1 (specify year) ❖ New, used, and reproduction parts for 1962 to 1971 Fairlanes. 703-896-5910.

B & W Antique Auto, 4653 Guide Meridian Rd., Bellingham, WA 98226: Catalog $5 (specify year and model) ❖ Fairlane automotive parts, 1955 to 1971. 360-647-4574.

Dennis Carpenter Reproductions, P.O. Box 26398, Charlotte, NC 28221: Catalog $3 (specify year) ❖ Rubber parts for 1962 to 1971 Fairlanes. 219-335-2425.

Bob Cook Classic Auto Parts, North 3rd St., Hazel, KY 42049: Catalog $6 (specify year) ❖ Reproduction parts for 1960 to 1972 Fairlanes. 502-492-8166.

Dearborn Classics, P.O. Box 1248, Sunset Beach, CA 90742: Catalog $3 ❖ Fairlane parts and accessories. 714-372-3175.

Ford Parts Specialists, 98-11 211th St., Queens Village, NY 11429: Catalog $2 (specify year) ❖ Parts for 1949 to 1969 Fairlanes. 212-468-8585.

Ford Parts Store, P.O. Box 226, Bryan, OH 43506: Catalog $2 ❖ Fairlane parts. 419-636-2475.

Highway Classics, 949 N. Cataract Ave., San Dimas, CA 91773: Catalog $3 ❖ Fairlane parts and accessories, from 1962. 909-592-5160.

Joblot Automotive, ASpecialists, 98-11 211th St., Queens Village, NY 11429: Catalog $2 ❖ Parts for 1949 to 1969 Fairlanes. 800-221-0172; 718-468-8585 (in NY).

Dale King Obsolete Parts Inc., P.O. Box A, Courthouse Square, Liberty, KY 42539: Free information ❖ NOS and reproduction Fairlane parts. 606-787-5031.

Midland Automotive Products, Rt. 1, Box 27, Midland City, AL 36350: Free information ❖ Reproduction and new Fairlane products. 205-983-1212.

Obsolete Ford Parts Company, 311 E. Washington Ave., Nashville, GA 31639: Catalog $3 (specify year) ❖ Parts for 1962 to 1972 Fairlanes. 912-686-2470.

Obsolete Ford Parts Inc. (Oklahoma City), 8701 South I-35, Oklahoma City, OK 73149: Catalog $3 (specify year) ❖ Parts for 1960 to 1972 Fairlanes. 405-631-3933.

Sixties Ford Parts, 639 Glanker St., Memphis, TN 38112: Catalog $4 ❖ Fairlane parts, from 1960 to 1968.

Thunderbird, Falcon & Fairlane Connection, 728 E. Dunlap, Phoenix, AZ 85020: Catalog $2 (specify year) ❖ New and used Fairlane parts. 602-997-9285.

FALCON

Auto Krafters Inc., P.O. Box 8, Broadway, VA 22815: Catalog $1 (specify year) ❖ New, used, and reproduction parts for 1960 to 1970 Falcons. 703-896-5910.

B & W Antique Auto, 4653 Guide Meridian Rd., Bellingham, WA 98226: Catalog $5 (specify year and model) ❖ Falcon automotive parts, 1960 to 1970. 360-647-4574.

Dennis Carpenter Reproductions, P.O. Box 26398, Charlotte, NC 28221: Catalog $3 (specify year) ❖ Rubber parts for 1960 to 1970 Falcons. 219-335-2425.

Bob Cook Classic Auto Parts, North 3rd St., Hazel, KY 42049: Catalog $6 (specify year) ❖ Reproduction parts for 1960 to 1972 Falcons. 502-492-8166.

Dearborn Classics, P.O. Box 1248, Sunset Beach, CA 90742: Catalog $3 ❖ Falcon parts. 714-372-3175.

Ford Parts Specialists, 98-11 211th St., Queens Village, NY 11429: Catalog $2 (specify year) ❖ Falcon parts, 1949 to 1969. 212-468-8585.

Highway Classics, 949 N. Cataract Ave., San Dimas, CA 91773: Catalog $3 ❖ Falcon parts and accessories, from 1960 to 1970. 909-592-5160.

Joblot Automotive, Ford Parts Specialists, 98-11 211th St., Queens Village, NY 11429: Catalog $2 ❖ Parts for 1949 to 1969 Falcons. 800-221-0172; 718-468-8585 (in NY).

Dale King Obsolete Parts Inc., P.O. Box A, Courthouse Square, Liberty, KY 42539: Free information ❖ NOS and reproduction Falcon parts. 606-787-5031.

Midland Automotive Products, Rt. 1, Box 27, Midland City, AL 36350: Free information ❖ Reproduction and new Falcon products. 205-983-1212.

Northwest Classic Falcons, 1964 NW Pettygrove, Portland, OR 97209: Parts list $2 ❖ Hard-to-find new, used, and reproduction 1960 to 1970 Falcon parts. 503-241-9454.

Obsolete Ford Parts Company, 311 E. Washington Ave., Nashville, GA 31639: Catalog $2.50 (specify year) ❖ NOS and reproduction parts for 1960 to 1970 Falcons. 912-686-2470.

Obsolete Ford Parts Inc. (Oklahoma City), 8701 South I-35, Oklahoma City, OK 73149: Catalog $3 (specify year) ❖ Parts for 1960 to 1972 Falcons. 405-631-3933.

Sixties Ford Parts, 639 Glanker St., Memphis, TN 38112: Catalog $4 ❖ Falcon parts, from 1960 to 1968.

Thunderbird, Falcon & Fairlane Connection, 728 E. Dunlap, Phoenix, AZ 85020: Catalog $2 (specify year) ❖ New and used Falcon parts. 602-997-9285.

FERRARI

Alfa Ricambi, 6644 San Fernando Rd., Glendale, CA 91201: Free information ❖ Parts for the Ferrari. 818-956-7933.

Algar Enterprises Inc., 1234 Lancaster Ave., P.O. Box 167, Rosemont, PA 19010: Free information ❖ Ferrari parts. 800-441-9824; 215-527-1100 (in PA).

International Auto Parts Inc., Rt. 29 North, P.O. Box 9036, Charlottesville, VA 22906: Free catalog ❖ Ferrari parts. 804-973-0555.

Shelton Sports Cars, 5750 N. Federal Hwy., Fort Lauderdale, FL 33308: Free information ❖ Ferrari parts and accessories. 800-448-6777.

FIAT

Bayless Inc., 1111 Via Bayless, Marietta, GA 30066: Catalog $4 ❖ High-performance replacement parts. 404-928-1446.

Caribou Imports Inc., 231541-A3 Alcade Dr., Laguna Hills, CA 92653: Catalog $5 ❖ Fiat parts. 714-770-3136.

International Auto Parts Inc., Rt. 29 North, P.O. Box 9036, Charlottesville, VA 22906: Free catalog ❖ Replacement and restoration parts and performance accessories. 804-973-0555.

Orion Motors Inc., 10722 Jones Rd., Houston, TX 77065: Free information ❖ Fiat parts. 800-736-6410; 713-894-1982 (in TX).

Perfect Plastics Industries Inc., 14th St., Building 201, New Kensington, PA 15068: Free information ❖ Body parts for the Fiat. 800-229-3568; 412-339-3568 (in PA).

FIERO

The Fiero Store, 219 Buff Cap Rd., Tolland, CT 06084: Catalog $4 ❖ Fiero parts. 203-870-7167.

FIREBIRD

Ames Performance Engineering, Bonney Rd., Marlborough, NH 03455: Free catalog ❖ Firebird parts. 800-421-2637.

Auto Heaven, 103 W. Allen St., Bloomington, IN 47401: Free information ❖ Firebird 1967 to 1969 parts. 800-777-0297; 812-332-9401 (in IN).

Camaro Specialties, 900 E. Fillmore Ave., East Aurora, NY 14052: Catalog $1 ❖ New, used, NOS, and reproduction parts for 1967 to 1972 Firebirds. 716-652-7086.

Chicago Muscle Car Parts, 912 E. Burnett Rd., Island Lake, IL 60042: Catalog $5 (refundable) ❖ New and used Firebird parts, from 1967 to 1969. 708-526-2200.

Classic Industries, 17832 Gothard St., Huntington Beach, CA 92647: Catalog $5 ❖ Firebird and Trans-AM parts and accessories. 800-854-1280.

AUTOMOTIVE PARTS & ACCESSORIES

Competition Automotive Inc., 2095 West Shore Dr., Warwick, RI 02886: Free information ❖ Restoration supplies. 401-739-6262.

D & R Classic Automotive, 31 W. 280 Diehly Rd., Naperville, IL 60563: Free price list ❖ Firebird parts. 800-472-6952.

Firebird/Trans Am America, Rt. 322, Box 427, Boalsburg, PA 16827: Free information with long SASE ❖ Parts for 1967 to 1987 Firebirds. 800-458-3475.

The Paddock Inc., 221 W. Main, Knightstown, IN 46148: Catalog $1 ❖ Firebird parts. 317-345-2131.

Triangle Automotive, P.O. Box 2293, Arcadia, CA 91077: Free information ❖ Restoration parts and accessories. 818-357-2377.

Valley View Automotive Products, 1646 Valley View Ave., Lewistown, PA 17044: Free information ❖ Firebird parts and accessories. 717-248-6447.

Year One Inc., P.O. Box 129, Tucker, GA 30085: Catalog $5 ❖ New, used, and reproduction Firebird restoration parts. 800-950-9503.

FORD

Auto Krafters Inc., P.O. Box 8, Broadway, VA 22815: Catalog $1 (specify year) ❖ Ford new, used, and reproduction parts, from 1960 to 1970. 703-896-5910.

B & B Used Auto Parts, Rt. 1, Box 691, Big Pine Key, FL 33043: Free information ❖ Ford parts, from 1950 and later. 305-872-9761.

B & W Antique Auto, 4653 Guide Meridian Rd., Bellingham, WA 98226: Catalog $5 (specify year and model) ❖ Antique Ford automotive parts, 1928 to 1953. 360-647-4574.

C & G Early Ford Parts, 1941 Commercial St., Escondido, CA 92029: Catalog $6 ❖ Reproduction parts for 1932 to 1956 Ford cars and trucks. 619-740-2400.

Dennis Carpenter Reproductions, P.O. Box 26398, Charlotte, NC 28221: Catalog $3 (specify year) ❖ Rubber parts for 1932 to 1964 Fords. 219-335-2425.

Concours Parts & Accessories, 3563 Numancia St., P.O. Box 1210, Santa Ynez, CA 93460: Catalog $4 ❖ Ford parts, from 1949 to 1966. 805-688-7795.

Continental Enterprises, 1673 Cary Rd., Kelowna, British Columbia, Canada V1X 2C1: Information $12 ❖ Ford dress-up accessory kits, from 1949 to 1993. 604-763-7727.

Bob Cook Classic Auto Parts, North 3rd St., Hazel, KY 42049: Catalog $6 ❖ Carpet, sheet metal, and new, obsolete, and reproduction parts for 1960 to 1972 Fords. 502-492-8166.

Crossroads Auto Dismantling, 12421 Riverside Ave., Mira Loma, CA 91752: Free catalog ❖ Ford, Lincoln, and Mercury parts. 909-986-6789.

Doug's Auto Parts, Hwy. 59 North, Box 811, Marshall, MN 56258: Free information ❖ Ford parts, from 1932 to 1948. 507-537-1487.

Bob Drake Reproductions Inc., 1819 NW Washington Blvd., Grants Pass, OR 97526: Catalog $5 (specify model) ❖ Reproduction Ford car and pickup parts. 800-221-3673.

Early Ford Parts, 2948 Summer Ave., Memphis, TN 38112: Catalog $4 ❖ New parts for 1928 to 1969 Ford cars and 1928 to 1972 Ford pickup trucks. 901-323-2179.

Find-A-Part, Box 358, Ridgeland, MS 39158: Free information with long SASE ❖ Ford NOS parts, automotive literature, signs, and collectible calendars. 601-856-7214.

Ford Parts Store, P.O. Box 226, Bryan, OH 43506: Catalog $2 ❖ Ford parts. 419-636-2475.

Lou Fusz Toyota, 10725 Manchester, St. Louis, MO 63122: Catalog $4 ❖ Ford parts and accessories. 800-325-9581.

Garton's Auto, 5th & Vine, Millville, NJ 08332: Free information with long SASE (specify car) ❖ Fenders, grilles, trim, ornaments, and mechanical, chassis, and other 1932 to 1975 Ford parts. 609-825-3618.

Joblot Automotive, Ford Parts Specialists, 98-11 211th St., Queens Village, NY 11429: Catalog $2 ❖ Parts for cars and trucks, from 1949 to 1969. 800-221-0172; 718-468-8585 (in NY).

Kanter Auto Parts, 76 Monroe St., Boonton, NJ 07005: Free catalog ❖ Parts for Fords, from 1932 to 1953. 201-334-9575.

Dale King Obsolete Parts Inc., P.O. Box A, Courthouse Square, Liberty, KY 42539: Free information ❖ NOS and reproduction Ford parts. 606-787-5031.

Lakeview Vintage Ford Parts, 1410 E. Genesee, Skaneateles, NY 13152: Free information ❖ Reproduction parts for 1928 to 1948 Ford cars. 315-685-7414.

Mac's Antique Auto Parts, P.O. Box 238, Lockport, NY 14095: Free catalog ❖ Parts for 1928 to 1931 Model A; 1909 to 1927 Model T; and early Ford V-8s, from 1932 to 1948. 800-777-0948; 716-433-1500 (in NY).

Medicine Bow Motors Inc., 5120 Hwy. 93 South, Missoula, MT 59801: Free information ❖ Parts for 1928 to 1948 Fords. 406-251-2244.

Midland Automotive Products, Rt. 1, Box 27, Midland City, AL 36350: Free information ❖ Reproduction and new Ford products. 205-983-1212.

Mustangs Unlimited, 185 Adams St., Manchester, CT 06040: Catalog $3 (specify year) ❖ Ford performance parts, from 1965 to 1973. 800-243-7278.

North Yale Auto Parts, Rt. 1, Box 707, Sperry, OK 74073: Free information ❖ Parts for 1977 and later Fords. 800-256-6927; 918-288-7218 (in OK).

Obsolete Ford Parts Company, 311 E. Washington Ave., Nashville, GA 31639: Catalog $3 (specify year) ❖ NOS and reproduction parts for 1949 to 1964 Fords. 912-686-2470.

Obsolete Ford Parts Inc. (Oklahoma City), 8701 South I-35, Oklahoma City, OK 73149: Catalog $3 (specify year) ❖ Ford parts, from 1928 to 1932. 405-631-3933.

Out of the Past Parts, 3720 SW 23rd St., Gainesville, FL 32601: Free information ❖ Ford parts, 1935 and later. 904-377-4079.

Papke Enterprises, 17202 Gothard St., Huntington Beach, CA 92647: Catalog $4 ❖ Parts for 1949 to 1951 Fords. Some 1952 to 1953 parts available. 714-843-6969.

PRO Antique Auto Parts, 50 King Spring Rd., Windsor Locks, CT 06096: Catalog $3 ❖ New parts for 1928 to 1964 Fords. 203-623-0070.

Sixties Ford Parts, 639 Glanker St., Memphis, TN 38112: Catalog $4 ❖ Ford parts, from 1960 to 1968.

Dick Spadaro Early Ford Reproductions, 124 Maple Ave., Altamont, NY 12009: Catalog $4 ❖ Ford parts, from 1932 to 1948. 518-861-5367.

T-Bird Nest, 2550 E. Southlake Rd., Southlake, TX 76092: Free information ❖ New parts for 1928 to 1959 Fords. 817-481-1776.

Tee-Bird Products Inc., P.O. Box 728, Exton, PA 19341: Catalog $3 ❖ Ford car parts, from 1955 to 1956. 610-363-1725.

Valley Ford Parts, 11610 Van Owen St., North Hollywood, CA 91605: Free information ❖ New and used parts for 1928 to 1970 Fords.

Vintage Tin Auto Parts, 4550 Scotty Ln., Hutchinson, KS 67502: Free information with long SASE ❖ Ford parts, from 1940 to 1970. 316-669-8449.

Winnicks Auto Sales & Parts, Rt. 61, P.O. Box 476, Shamokin, PA 17872: Free information with long SASE ❖ Ford and Chevrolet engines and parts for American and imported cars and trucks. 717-648-6857.

FRAZER

Wayne's Auto Salvage, RR 3, Box 41, Winner, SD 57580: Free information ❖ Frazer parts. 605-842-2054.

GALAXIE

B & W Antique Auto, 4653 Guide Meridian Rd., Bellingham, WA 98226: Catalog $5 (specify year and model) ❖ Galaxie automotive parts, 1960 to 1964. 360-647-4574.

Dennis Carpenter Reproductions, P.O. Box 26398, Charlotte, NC 28221: Catalog $3 (specify year) ❖ Rubber parts for 1960 to 1964 Galaxies. 219-335-2425.

Bob Cook Classic Auto Parts, North 3rd St., Hazel, KY 42049: Catalog $6 (specify year) ❖ Reproduction parts for 1960 to 1972 Galaxies. 502-492-8166.

Greg Donahue, 12900 S. Betty Point, Floral City, FL 34436: Catalog $5 ❖ Reproduction and NOS Galaxie parts, from 1963 to 1964. 904-344-4329.

Joblot Automotive, Ford Parts Specialists, 98-11 211th St., Queens Village, NY 11429: Catalog $2 ❖ Parts for 1949 to 1969 Galaxies. 800-221-0172; 718-468-8585 (in NY).

GTO

Ames Performance Engineering, Bonney Rd., Marlborough, NH 03455: Free catalog ❖ GTO parts. 800-421-2637.

Obsolete Ford Parts Inc. (Oklahoma City), 8701 South I-35, Oklahoma City, OK 73149: Catalog $3 (specify year) ❖ Ford parts, from 1928 to 1932. 405-631-3933.

Original Parts Group Inc., 17892 Gothard St., Huntington Beach, CA 92647: Catalog $4 ❖ Chevelle parts. 800-243-8355.

The Paddock Inc., 221 W. Main, Knightstown IN 46148: Catalog $1 ❖ GTO parts. 317-345-2131.

Triangle Automotive, P.O. Box 2293, Arcadia, CA 91077: Free information ❖ Restoration parts and accessories. 818-357-2377.

Valley View Automotive Products, 1646 Valley View Ave., Lewistown, PA 17044: Free information ❖ GTO parts and accessories. 717-248-6447.

Year One Inc., P.O. Box 129, Tucker, GA 30085: Catalog $5 ❖ New, used, and reproduction GTO restoration parts. 800-950-9503.

HONDA

Alpharetta Auto Parts Inc., 5770 Hwy. 9 North, Alpharetta, GA 30201: Free information ❖ Used Honda parts. 800-494-PART; 404-475-1929 (in GA).

Dobi Honda Catalog, 320 Thor Pl., Brea, CA 92621: Catalog $2 ❖ Honda parts. 714-529-1977.

HKS USA Inc., 20312 Gramercy Pl., Torrance, CA 90501: Catalog $8 ❖ Performance parts for the Honda. 310-328-8100.

Ide Honda, 875 Panoma, Rochester, NY 14625: Free information ❖ Factory parts. 800-362-9012.

King Motorsports, 105 E. Main St., Sullivan, WI 53178: Catalog $5 ❖ Acura parts and accessories. 414-593-2800.

MSO Parts, 1543 Easton Rd., Roslyn, PA 19001: Free information ❖ Genuine factory parts for the Honda. 800-500-PART; 215-657-8423 (in PA).

Options Auto Salon, 4523 San Fernando Rd., Ste. 1, Glendale, CA 91204: Catalog $5 ❖ Dress-up and restoration parts and accessories. 818-545-8218.

HUDSON

Wm. Albright's Vintage Coach, 16593 Arrow Blvd., Fontana, CA 92335: Free information with long SASE (specify parts wanted) ❖ N.O.S. and reproduction parts. 909-823-9168.

K-Gap Automotive Parts, P.O. Box 3065, Santa Fe Springs, CA 90670: Catalog $2 (refundable) ❖ Reproduction Hudson and Essex parts. 714-523-0403.

Vintage Tin Auto Parts, 4550 Scotty Ln., Hutchinson, KS 67502: Free information with long SASE ❖ Hudson parts. 316-669-8449.

Wayne's Auto Salvage, RR 3, Box 41, Winner, SD 57580: Free information ❖ Hudson parts. 605-842-2054.

IMPALA

Hubbard's Impala, 813 Kenwood Dr., Burlington, NC 27215: Catalog $3 ❖ Impala parts. 919-227-1589.

Impala Bob's, 9006 E. Fannin, Mesa, AZ 85207: Catalog $6 ❖ Restoration parts for 1958 to 1975 Impalas. 800-209-0678.

Luttys Chevys, 2385 Saxonburg Blvd., Cheswick, PA 15024: Catalog $3 ❖ Impala restoration parts, from 1958 to 1970. 412-265-2988.

Old Car Parts, 109 N. 15th St., Box 184, Clear Lake, IA 50428: Catalog $3.75 (specify year) ❖ NOS, new, and reproduction Impala parts, from 1965 to 1970. 515-357-5510.

Tom's Obsolete Chevy Parts, 14 Delta Dr., Pawtucket, RI 02860: Catalog $1 ❖ Impala parts, from 1955 to 1972. 401-723-7580.

Valley View Automotive Products, 1646 Valley View Ave., Lewistown, PA 17044: Free information ❖ Impala parts and accessories. 717-248-6447.

JAGUAR

G.W. Bartlett Company, 1912 Granville Ave., Muncie, IN 47303: Free catalog ❖ Interior restoration parts. 800-338-8034.

Bassett's Jaguar Inc., P.O. Box 245, Wyoming, RI 02898: Free catalog ❖ Jaguar parts. 401-539-3010.

Bluff City British Cars, 1810 Getwell, Memphis, TN 38111: Free information ❖ Parts for Jaguars. 800-621-0227; 901-743-4422 (in TN).

British Auto/USA, 92 Londonberry Tnpk., Manchester, NH 03104: Catalog $4 ❖ Jaguar upholstery and hard-to-find chrome, electrical, mechanical, and brake system parts. 603-622-1050.

British Parts International, 8101 Hempstead, Houston, TX 77008: Free information ❖ Jaguar parts. 800-231-6563.

British Parts Northwest, 4105 SE Lafayette Hwy., Dayton, OR 97114: Catalog $2.50 ❖ Jaguar parts. 503-864-2001.

British Vintages Inc., 1115-A Toro St., San Luis Obispo, CA 93401: Catalog $3 ❖ New, used, and reproduction Jaguar parts, from 1948 and later. 800-350-JAGS.

Classic Automobiles, 1974 Charles St., Costa Mesa, CA 92627: Catalog $5 ❖ Jaguar parts, maintenance aids, books, and owner manuals. 714-646-6293.

English Car Spares Ltd., 345 Branch Rd SW, Alpharetta, GA 30201: Free information ❖ Jaguar parts. 800-241-1916; 404-475-2662 (in GA).

Exotic Car Parts, 923 N. Central Ave., Upland, CA 91786: Free information ❖ Parts for Jaguar XK120 and MKVII to XJ6 and XJS. 800-231-3588.

George Haug Company Inc., 517 E. 73rd St., New York, NY 10021: Free information ❖ Jaguar parts. 212-288-0176.

Jaguar & SAAB of Troy, 1815 Maplelawn, Troy, MI 48084: Free catalog ❖ Parts for the Jaguar. 800-832-5839; 313-643-7894 (in MI).

Jaguar Heaven, 1433 Tillie Lewis Dr., Stockton, CA 95206: Free information ❖ Used Jaguar parts. 209-942-4524.

Jaguar Motor Works, 3701 Longview Dr., Atlanta, GA 30341: Free information ❖ New, used, and rebuilt parts for XJ6 and XJS Jaguars. 800-331-2193; 404-451-3839 (in GA).

Moore Jaguar, 14116 Manchester, St. Louis, MO 63011: Free information ❖ Jaguar parts. 800-JAG-PART; 314-394-0900 (in MO).

Moss Motors Ltd., 7200 Hollister Rd., P.O. Box 847, Goleta, CA 93116: Free catalog (specify model) ❖ Hard-to-find parts for Jaguars. 800-235-6954.

Motorcars Ltd., 8101 Hempstead, Houston, TX 77008: Free information ❖ Used Jaguar parts. 800-338-5238.

Peninsula Import Auto Parts, 3749 Harlem, Buffalo, NY 14215: Free catalog ❖ Jaguar parts. 905-827-9407.

Special Interest Car Parts, 1340 Hartford Ave., Johnston, RI 02919: Free catalog ❖ Parts for 1948 to 1988 Jaguars. 800-556-7496.

Terry's Jaguar Parts, 117 E. Smith St., Benton, IL 62812: Free catalog ❖ High-performance Jaguar parts. 800-851-9438.

Vicarage, c/o Gables Cats, 220 Granello Ave., Coral Gables, FL 33146: Free information (specify part wanted) ❖ Hard-to-find parts for E-type and Mark II Jaguars. 305-444-8759.

Welsh Jaguar Enterprises Inc., 223 N. 5th St., P.O. Box 4130, Steubenville, OH 43952: Free catalog ❖ New and used parts for XX-120 to XJ40 Jaguars. 800-875-5247; 614-282-8649 (in OH).

AUTOMOTIVE PARTS & ACCESSORIES

Ed West, 1941 Jan Marie Pl., Tustin, CA 92680: Parts list $2 (specify year and car) ❖ New, used, and reproduction XK120, 140, 150 and Mark I, II, VII, VIII, and IX Jaguar parts. 714-832-2688.

XK's Unlimited, 850 Fiero Ln., San Luis Obispo, CA 93401: Catalog $6 ❖ Parts for Jaguars, from 1948 to 1994. 800-445-JAGS.

JAVELIN

American Parts Depot, 409 N. Main St., West Manchester, OH 45382: Catalog $5 ❖ New, used, reproduction, and NOS parts. 513-678-7249.

American Performance Products Inc., 681 S. Industry Rd., Cocoa, FL 32926: Catalog $6 ❖ Javelin parts. 407-632-8299.

Eddie Stakes' Planet Houston AMX, 3400 OCEE, #1601, Houston, TX 77063: Catalog $6 ❖ AMX and Javelin parts, from 1968 to 1974. 713-785-1375.

Webb's Classic Auto Parts, 5084 W. State Rd. 114, Huntington, IN 46750: Free information with long SASE ❖ AMX and Javelin parts. 219-344-1714.

JEEP

American Performance Products Inc., 681 S. Industry Rd., Cocoa, FL 32926: Catalog $6 ❖ Jeep parts. 407-632-8299.

Army Jeep Parts, P.O. Box 1006, Bristol, PA 19007: Free information ❖ Military Jeep parts. 215-788-6012.

Paul Barry, 6152 Cazadero Hwy., P.O. Box 364, Cazadero, CA 95421: Free information ❖ Parts for Willys Overland Jeeps and trucks. 707-632-5258.

Daryl Bensinger, 2442 Main St., Narvon, PA 17555: Free information ❖ Parts for military jeeps and trucks. 215-788-6012.

Find-A-Part, Box 358, Ridgeland, MS 39158: Free information with long SASE ❖ NOS parts and automotive literature. 601-856-7214.

JD's Off-Road & Performance, 740 N. Bedford Rd., Bedford Hills, NY 10507: Free information ❖ Jeep accessories. 800-884-JEEP; 914-666-5337 (in NY).

Obsolete Jeep & Willys Parts, 6110 17th St. East, Bradenton, FL 34203: Free information ❖ New, used, rebuilt, and NOS parts. 813-756-7844.

Quadratec, 5125 West Chester Pike, Newtown Square, PA 19073: Catalog $3 ❖ Mechanical and performance parts for Jeep Wranglers. 800-745-5337.

Leon Rosser Jeep/Eagle, P.O. Box 1185, Bessemer, AL 35021: Free information ❖ Jeep parts. 800-633-4724.

Sports & Classics, 512 Boston Post Rd., Darien, CT 06820: Catalog $4 ❖ Restoration, engine, electrical, and body parts. 203-655-8731.

Walck's Four Wheel Dr., 700 Cedar St., Bowmanstown, PA 18030: Free information ❖ Jeep parts. 610-852-3110.

Willy's Jeep Parts, P.O. Box 11468, Yuma, AZ 85366: Free information ❖ Jeep parts, owner manuals, parts lists, and shop manuals. 800-4-WILLYS.

JENSEN

Dave Bean Engineering Inc., 636 E. Saint Charles St., San Andreas, CA 95249: Catalog $6 ❖ Jensen parts. 209-754-5802.

Delta Motorsports Inc., 2724 E. Bell Rd., Phoenix, AZ 85032: Free catalog ❖ Jensen factory parts. 602-265-8026.

KAISER-FRAZER

Fannaly's Auto Exchange, 701 Range Rd., P.O. Box 23, Ponchatoula, LA 70454: Free information ❖ A limited selection of Kaiser-Fraser parts. 504-386-3714.

LaMance Autoworks, P.O. Box 449, 914 Old Mill Rd., Wartburg, TN 37887: Free information ❖ Kaiser parts. 615-346-7350.

Wayne's Auto Salvage, RR 3, Box 41, Winner, SD 57580: Free information ❖ Kaiser parts. 605-842-2054.

Zeug's K-F Parts, 1435 Moreno Dr., Simi Valley, CA 93063: Parts list $2 ❖ NOS and used Kaiser-Frazer, Henry J, and Kaiser-Darrin parts. 818-718-7722.

LAMBORGHINI

Prestige Imports, 14800 Biscayne Blvd., North Miami Beach, FL 33181: Free information ❖ Lamborghini parts. 305-944-1800.

LANCIA

Alfa Ricambi, 6644 San Fernando Rd., Glendale, CA 91201: Free information ❖ Parts for the Lancia. 818-956-7933.

Bayless Inc., 1111 Via Bayless, Marietta, GA 30066: Catalog $4 ❖ Replacement parts. 404-928-1446.

Caribou Imports Inc., 231541-A3 Alcade Dr., Laguna Hills, CA 92653: Catalog $5 ❖ Lancia parts. 714-770-3136.

Celiberti Motors, 615 Oak St., Santa Rosa, CA 95404: Free information ❖ Lancia parts. 800-USA-FIAT.

International Autosport, Catalog Sales, Rt. 29 North, P.O. Box 9036, Charlottesville, VA 22906: Catalog $1 ❖ Replacement, restoration, and performance parts for the Lancia. 800-726-1199.

LASALLE

Classic Auto Parts, 550 Industrial Dr., Carmel, IN 46032: Free information ❖ Genuine classic LaSalle parts, from 1928 to 1941. 317-844-8154.

McVey's, 5040 Antioch, Merriam, KS 66203: Catalog $4 ❖ LaSalle parts and accessories, from 1936 to 1970. 913-722-0707.

Out of the Past Parts, 3720 SW 23rd St., Gainesville, FL 32601: Free information ❖ Parts for 1935 and later LaSalles. 904-377-4079.

LE MANS

Ames Performance Engineering, Bonney Rd., Marlborough, NH 03455: Free catalog ❖ Le Mans parts, 1964 to 1977. 800-421-2637.

Chicago Muscle Car Parts, 912 E. Burnett Rd., Island Lake, IL 60042: Catalog $5 (refundable) ❖ New and used Le Mans parts, from 1964 to 1972. 708-526-2200.

Original Parts Group Inc., 17892 Gothard St., Huntington Beach, CA 92647: Catalog $4 ❖ Le Mans parts. 800-243-8355.

Triangle Automotive, P.O. Box 2293, Arcadia, CA 91077: Free information ❖ Restoration parts and accessories. 818-357-2377.

Year One Inc., P.O. Box 129, Tucker, GA 30085: Catalog $5 ❖ New, used, and reproduction Firebird restoration parts. 800-950-9503.

LINCOLN

Aabar's Cadillac & Lincoln Salvage, 9700 NE 23rd, Oklahoma City, OK 73141: Free information with long SASE ❖ Lincoln and Cadillac parts, from 1939 and later. 405-769-3318.

Baker's Auto Inc., Rt. 44, Putnam, CT 06260: Free information ❖ Lincoln parts, from 1961 to 1979. 203-928-7614.

Classic Cars Unlimited, P.O. Box 249, Lakeshore, MS 39558: Catalog $3 (specify year) ❖ Lincoln parts, from 1960 to 1976. 800-543-8691; 601-467-9633 (in MS).

Classique Cars Unlimited, P.O. Box 249, Lakeshore, MS 39558: Parts list $4 ❖ Lincoln parts, from 1958 to 1988. 601-467-9633.

Continental Enterprises, 1673 Cary Rd., Kelowna, British Columbia, Canada V1X 2C1: Information $12 ❖ Lincoln dress-up accessory kits, from 1949 to 1993. 604-763-7727.

Bob Cook Classic Auto Parts, North 3rd St., Hazel, KY 42049: Catalog $6 (specify year) ❖ Reproduction parts for 1960 to 1972 Lincolns. 502-492-8166.

Crossroads Auto Dismantling, 12421 Riverside Ave., Mira Loma, CA 91752: Free catalog ❖ Ford, Lincoln, and Mercury parts. 909-986-6789.

Fannaly's Auto Exchange, 701 Range Rd., P.O. Box 23, Ponchatoula, LA 70454: Free information ❖ Parts for 1946 to 1956 Lincolns. 504-386-3714.

Lincoln Land Inc., 1928 Sherwood St., Clearwater, FL 34625: Free information ❖ Lincoln parts. 813-531-5351; 813-446-2193 (in FL).

Lincoln Parts International, 707 E. 4th St., Building G, Perris, CA 92570: Free catalog ❖ Lincoln 1961 to 1980 parts. 909-657-5588.

Narragansett Reproductions, 107 Woodville Rd., P.O. Box 51, Wood River Junction, RI 02894: Catalog $2 (specify car) ❖ Parts for 1936 to 1948 Lincolns, 1956 to 1957 Lincoln Continentals, and the Lincoln Zephyr. 401-364-3839.

Jack Rosen, 5525 Canyon Crest Dr., Riverside, CA 92507: Catalog $2 ❖ New, reproduction, rebuilt, and used Mark II and Lincoln parts, after 1965. 909-686-2752.

LOTUS

Dave Bean Engineering Inc., 636 E. Saint Charles St., San Andreas, CA 95249: Catalog $6 ❖ Lotus parts. 209-754-5802.

Prestige Imports, 14800 Biscayne Blvd., North Miami Beach, FL 33181: Free information ❖ Lotus parts. 305-944-1800.

MASERATI

Algar Enterprises Inc., 1234 Lancaster Ave., P.O. Box 167, Rosemont, PA 19010: Free information ❖ Maserati parts. 800-441-9824; 215-527-1100 (in PA).

Beach Imports, 30 Auto Center Dr., Tustin, CA 92680: Free information ❖ Maserati parts. 800-777-4895.

Caribou Imports Inc., 231541-A3 Alcade Dr., Laguna Hills, CA 92653: Catalog $5 ❖ Maserati parts. 714-770-3136.

Celiberti Motors, 615 Oak St., Santa Rosa, CA 95404: Free information ❖ Maserati parts. 800-USA-FIAT.

International Autosport, Catalog Sales, Rt. 29 North, P.O. Box 9036, Charlottesville, VA 22906: Catalog $1 ❖ Replacement, restoration, and performance parts for the Maserati. 800-726-1199.

Maserati Automobiles Inc., 1501 Caton Ave., Baltimore, MD 21227: Free information ❖ Maserati parts. 410-646-6400.

MAVERICK

Auto Krafters Inc., P.O. Box 8, Broadway, VA 22815: Catalog $1 (specify year) ❖ New, used, and reproduction parts, from 1970 to 1977. 703-896-5910.

MAZDA

Autoshow, 8148 Woodland Dr., Indianapolis, IN 46278: Catalog $3 (refundable) ❖ Parts for the Mazda Rx-7. 800-428-2200; 317-875-0076 (in IN).

Dobi Mazda Catalog, 320 Thor Pl., Brea, CA 92621: Catalog $2 ❖ Parts for the Mazda Rx7 and GLC. 714-529-1977.

HKS USA Inc., 20312 Gramercy Pl., Torrance, CA 90501: Catalog $8 ❖ Performance parts for the Mazda. 310-328-8100.

MSO Parts, 1543 Easton Rd., Roslyn, PA 19001: Free information ❖ Genuine factory parts for the Mazda. 800-500-PART; 215-657-8423 (in PA).

Options Auto Salon, 4523 San Fernando Rd., Ste. 1, Glendale, CA 91204: Catalog $5 ❖ Dress-up and restoration parts and accessories. 818-545-8218.

MERCEDES-BENZ

Aase Brothers Inc., 701 E. Cypress St., Anaheim, CA 92805: Free information ❖ Mercedes-Benz parts. 800-444-7444; 714-956-2419 (in CA).

Adsit Company Inc., 12440 S. Old Rd., Muncie, IN 47303: Free information ❖ New parts for the Mercedes-Benz. 800-521-7656.

Atlanta Stuttgart Auto Parts, 1200 Menlo Dr., Atlanta, GA 30318: Free information ❖ Used Mercedes-Benz parts. 404-351-4811.

ATVM Automotive Parts, 97 Mount Royal Ave., Aberdeen, MD 21001: Free information with long SASE ❖ Mercedes-Benz parts, from 1934 to 1972. 410-272-2252.

Embee Parts, 4000 Lee Rd., Smyrna, GA 30080: Free information ❖ Parts for 1934 to 1988 Mercedes-Benz. 404-434-5686.

Euromeister, 19507 Yuma St., Castro Valley, CA 94546: Catalog $4.95 ❖ Mercedes-Benz parts and accessories. 800-581-3327.

European Parts Specialists Ltd., 4141 State St., Santa Barbara, CA 93110: Free information ❖ Parts and accessories for the Mercedes-Benz. 805-683-4020.

Fletcher-Jones Motor Cars, 1001 Quail St., Newport Beach, CA 92660: Free information ❖ Replacement parts for the Mercedes-Benz. 800-328-3095; 714-832-4421 (in CA).

IMPCO Inc., 5300 Glenmont Dr., Houston, TX 77081: Free catalog ❖ Original 1977 to 1985 Mercedes-Benz parts. 800-243-1220.

IPCO Inc., 2171 W. Park Ct., Stone Mountain, GA 30087: Free information ❖ Original Mercedes-Benz parts. 800-635-8590; 404-498-5328 (in Atlanta).

John Marshall Inc., Box 10036, Olympia, WA 98502: Free information ❖ Mercedes-Benz parts and accessories. 360-754-7717.

Metro Motors, 9377 Autoplex Dr., Montclair, CA 91763: Free information ❖ Parts and accessories for the Mercedes-Benz. 800-446-5703.

Midwestern Motors & Dismantlers, 19785 W. Twelve Mile Rd., Building 404, Southfield, MI 48076: Free information ❖ Mercedes-Benz parts and accessories. 810-559-8848.

Miller's Incorporated, 7412 Count Circle, Huntington Beach, CA 92647: Catalog $5 ❖ Replacement parts for the 1950s, 1960s, and 1970s. 800-538-4222.

O.E.M. Parts Distributor, P.O. Box 25312, San Mateo, CA 94402: Free information ❖ Mercedes-Benz parts. 415-802-8125.

Signature Line Accessories, 1610 S. La Cienega Blvd., Ste. 104, Los Angeles, CA 90035: Free catalog ❖ Parts and accessories for the Mercedes-Benz. 800-346-3040.

Star Quality, One Alley Rd., LaGrangeville, NY 12540: Free catalog ❖ Parts for 190SL, 230SL, 250SL, and 280SL Mercedes-Benz. 914-223-5385.

Thoroughbred Coach Builders, P.O. Box 171, Mount Dora, FL 32757: Information package $10 ❖ Mercedes-Benz reproduction parts. 904-735-4607.

Valley Motors, 3203 Bragg Blvd., Fayetteville, NC 28303: Free information ❖ Mercedes-Benz parts. 800-264-3203.

MERCURY

B & W Antique Auto, 4653 Guide Meridian Rd., Bellingham, WA 98226: Catalog $5 (specify year and model) ❖ Antique Mercury automotive parts, 1928 to 1953. 360-647-4574.

Continental Enterprises, 1673 Cary Rd., Kelowna, British Columbia, Canada V1X 2C1: Information $12 ❖ Mercury dress-up accessory kits, from 1949 to 1993. 604-763-7727.

Bob Cook Classic Auto Parts, North 34th St., Hazel, KY 42049: Catalog $6 (specify year) ❖ Reproduction parts for the 1956 to 1972 Mercury. 502-492-8166.

Crossroads Auto Dismantling, 12421 Riverside Ave., Mira Loma, CA 91752: Free catalog ❖ Ford, Lincoln, and Mercury parts. 909-986-6789.

Garton's Auto, 5th & Vine, Millville, NJ 08332: Free information with long SASE (specify car) ❖ Fenders, grilles, trim, ornaments, and mechanical, chassis, and other 1932 to 1975 Mercury parts. 609-825-3618.

Dale King Obsolete Parts Inc., P.O. Box A, Courthouse Square, Liberty, KY 42539: Free information ❖ NOS and reproduction Mercury parts. 606-787-5031.

Mercury Research Company, 639 Glankler St., Memphis, TN 38112: Catalog $4 ❖ New parts for 1949 to 1959 Mercury cars.

Mustangs Unlimited, 185 Adams St., Manchester, CT 06040: Catalog $3 (specify year) ❖ Cougar reproduction and original restoration parts, from 1965 to 1973. 800-243-7278.

Obsolete Ford Parts (Oklahoma City), 8701 South I-35, Oklahoma City, OK 73149: Catalog $3 (specify year) ❖ Parts for 1949 to 1972 Mercury cars. 405-631-3933.

Papke Enterprises, 17202 Gothard St., Huntington Beach, CA 92647: Catalog $4 ❖ Parts for 1949 to 1951 Mercury cars. 714-843-6969.

AUTOMOTIVE PARTS & ACCESSORIES

PRO Antique Auto Parts, 50 King Spring Rd., Windsor Locks, CT 06096: Catalog $3 ❖ New parts for the 1928 to 1964 Mercury. 203-623-0070.

METEOR

Bob Cook Classic Auto Parts, North 3rd St., Hazel, KY 42049: Catalog $6 (specify year) ❖ Reproduction parts for the 1956 to 1964 Meteor. 502-492-8166.

MG

Abingdon Spares Ltd., South St., P.O. Box 37, Walpole, NH 03608: Catalog $6 ❖ MG parts. 800-225-0251.

Aurora Auto Wrecking Inc., 9217 Aurora Avenue North, Seattle, WA 98103: Free information ❖ New, used, and rebuilt MG parts. 800-426-6464.

British Miles, 222 Grove, Morrisville, PA 19067: Free information ❖ Reconditioned and new MG parts. 215-736-9300.

Dobi MGB Catalog, 320 Thor Pl., Brea, CA 92621: Catalog $2 ❖ Parts for MGB cars. 714-529-1977.

English Car Spares Ltd., 345 Branch Rd SW, Alpharetta, GA 30201: Free information ❖ MG parts. 800-241-1916; 404-475-2662 (in GA).

George Haug Company Inc., 517 E. 73rd St., New York, NY 10021: Free information ❖ MG parts. 212-288-0176.

M & G Vintage Auto, 265 Rt. 17, Box 226, Tuxedo Park, NY 10987: Free information ❖ Parts for the MGA, MGB, and MGT. 914-753-5900.

Moss Motors Ltd., 7200 Hollister Rd., P.O. Box 847, Goleta, CA 93116: Free catalog (specify model) ❖ MG parts. 800-235-6954.

Northwest Import Parts, 10915 SW 64th Ave., Portland, OR 97219: Information $1 ❖ Parts for the MGB, MGA, and Midget. 503-245-3806.

Peninsula Import Auto Parts, 3749 Harlem, Buffalo, NY 14215: Free catalog ❖ MG parts. 800-999-1209.

Scarborough Faire, 1151 Main St., Pawtucket, RI 02860: Catalog $3 (specify year) ❖ MGB body repair parts and panels. 401-724-4200.

Special Interest Car Parts, 1340 Hartford Ave., Johnston, RI 02919: Free catalog ❖ MG parts. 800-556-7496.

Sports & Classics, 512 Boston Post Rd., Darien, CT 06820: Catalog $4 ❖ Restoration, engine, electrical, and body parts. 203-655-8731.

Victoria British Ltd., P.O. Box 14991, Lenexa, KS 66215: Free catalog ❖ Original, replacement, and reproduction parts for the MG and British sports cars. 800-255-0088.

MITSUBISHI

HKS USA Inc., 20312 Gramercy Pl., Torrance, CA 90501: Catalog $8 ❖ Performance parts for the Mitsubishi. 310-328-8100.

Options Auto Salon, 4523 San Fernando Rd., Ste. 1, Glendale, CA 91204: Catalog $5 ❖ Dress-up and restoration parts and accessories. 818-545-8218.

MODEL A & MODEL T FORDS

Bob's Antique Auto Parts, 7826 Forest Hills Rd., P.O. Box 2523, Rockford, IL 61132: Catalog $2 ❖ Ford Model T parts. 815-633-7244.

Bratton's Antique Ford Parts, 9410 Watkins Rd., Gaithersburg, MD 20879: Free catalog ❖ Parts for the Model A Ford. 301-253-1929.

BSIA Mustang Supply, 278 S. 700 East, Mill Creek, IN 46365: Free information ❖ Ford Model A parts. 219-326-9300.

Car-Line Manufacturing & Distributor Inc., 1250 Gulf St., P.O. Box 1192, Beaumont, TX 77701: Catalog $2 ❖ Wood, sheet metal, seat springs, and engine and chassis parts for Ford Model T, A, and V8 cars. 409-833-9757.

Cars & Parts, Rt. 1, Dyer, TN 38330: Free information ❖ Parts for Ford Model A and T cars. 901-643-6448.

Classic Wood Manufacturing, 1006 N. Raleigh St., Greensboro, NC 27405: Free information ❖ Kiln-dried ash wood kits. 910-691-1344.

Chuck & Judy Cubel, P.O. Box N, Superior, AZ 83273: Free information (specify year) ❖ Wood replacement parts. 520-689-2734.

Ford Parts Specialists, 98-11 211th St., Queens Village, NY 11419: Free catalog (specify year) ❖ Ford Model A and T parts. 718-468-8585.

Funk's Antique Auto Parts, 330 Industry Dr., P.O. Box 8208, Carlisle, OH 45005: Catalog $3 ❖ Parts for Ford Model A and early V8 cars. 513-746-1113.

Gaslight Auto Parts Inc., P.O. Box 291, Urbana, OH 43078: Catalog $2 ❖ Replacement parts for the Ford Model A and T. 513-652-2145.

Lang's Old Car Parts, 202 School St., Winchedon, MA 01475: Catalog $1 ❖ Ford Model T reproduction parts, from 1909 to 1927. 800-872-7871.

LeBaron Bonney Company, 8 Chestnut St., Amesbury, MA 01913: Catalog $1 ❖ Interiors and tops, seat upholstery, panels and headlining, top kits and assemblies for 1928 to 1931 Fords. 508-388-3811.

Mac's Antique Auto Parts, P.O. Box 238, Lockport, NY 14094: Free catalog ❖ Parts for 1928 to 1931 Model A, 1909 to 1927 Model T, and early Ford V-8s, from 1932 to 1948. 800-777-0948; 716-433-1500 (in NY).

Obsolete Ford Parts Inc. (Oklahoma City), 8701 South I-35, Oklahoma City, OK 73149: Catalog $3 (specify year and car) ❖ Model A and T parts. 405-631-3933.

Rootlieb Inc., P.O. Box 1829, Turlock, CA 95381: Free catalog ❖ Sheet metal parts for early vintage Ford cars. 209-632-2203.

Sacramento Vintage Ford Parts Inc., 4675 Aldona Ln., Sacramento, CA 95841: Catalog $5 ❖ Model T parts, from 1909 to 1927 and Model A parts, from 1928 to 1931. 916-489-3444.

Smith & Jones Antique Parts, 1 Biloxi Square, Columbia Airport, West Columbia, SC 29170: Catalog $2.50 ❖ Reproduction Model A and T Ford parts. 803-822-8502.

Snyder's Antique Auto Parts, 12925 Woodworth Rd., New Springfield, OH 44443: Catalog $1 ❖ Model T parts, 1909 to 1927 and Model A parts, 1928 to 1931. 216-519-5313.

Tin Lizzie Antique Auto Parts, 1549 Ellinwood, Des Plaines, IL 60016: Catalog $3 ❖ Antique Ford parts, from 1928 to 1931. 708-298-7889.

MONTE CARLO

Harmon's Inc., P.O. Box 6, Hwy. 27 North, Geneva, IN 46740: Free catalog ❖ Monte Carlo restoration parts, from 1970 to 1977. 219-368-7221.

Original Parts Group Inc., 17892 Gothard St., Huntington Beach, CA 92647: Catalog $4 ❖ Monte Carlo parts. 800-243-8355.

The Parts Place, 950 Paramount Pkwy., Batavia, IL 60510: Free information ❖ Monte Carlo parts, from 1963 to 1977. 708-879-1600.

Tamraz's Parts Discount Warehouse, 10 South 123 Normantown Rd., Naperville, IL 60564: Free information ❖ Monte Carlo parts. 708-851-4500.

Year One Inc., P.O. Box 129, Tucker, GA 30085: Catalog $5 ❖ New, used, and reproduction Monte Carlo restoration parts. 800-950-9503.

MONTEGO

Bob Cook Classic Auto Parts, North 3rd St., Hazel, KY 42049: Catalog $6 (specify year) ❖ Reproduction parts for the 1965 to 1972 Montego. 502-492-8166.

MORRIS MINOR

Greystone Automotive, 6555 San Fernando Rd., Glendale, CA 91021: Free information ❖ New and used parts for Morris Minor and other British cars. 818-240-5780.

MUSTANG

Auto Krafters Inc., P.O. Box 8, Broadway, VA 22815: Catalog $1 (specify year) ❖ New, used, and reproduction parts for 1965 to 1973 Mustangs. 703-896-5910.

AUTOMOTIVE PARTS & ACCESSORIES

B & W Antique Auto, 4653 Guide Meridian Rd., Bellingham, WA 98226: Catalog $5 (specify year and model) ❖ Mustang automotive parts, from 1964 to 1973. 360-647-4574.

Branda Shelby & Mustang Parts, 1434 E. Pleasant Valley Blvd., Altoona, PA 16602: Catalog $3 ❖ Mustang parts. 800-458-3477.

BSIA Mustang Supply, 278 S. 700 East, Mill Creek, IN 46365: Free information ❖ Mustang parts, from mid-1964 to 1973. 219-326-9300.

California Mustang, 19400 San Jose Ave., City of Industry, CA 91748: Catalog $5 (refundable with $25 purchase) ❖ Mustang parts and accessories, from 1965 to 1973. 800-775-0101.

Canadian Mustang, 1844 78th Ave., Surrey, British Columbia, Canada V3W 8E7: Catalog $3 ❖ Mustang parts, from 1965 to 1973. 604-594-2425.

CJ Pony Parts Inc., 7441-B Rd., Allentown Blvd., PA 17112: Free information ❖ Mustang parts, from 1964 to 1973. 800-888-6473.

Classic Auto Air Mfg. Company, 2020 W. Kennedy Blvd., Tampa, FL 33606: Free catalog ❖ Air-conditioning systems and parts for 1965 to 1973 Mustangs. 813-251-4994.

Classic Mustang, 24 Robert Porter Rd., Southington, CT 06489: Catalog $3 ❖ Mustang parts, from 1965 to 1973. 203-276-9704.

Classic Mustang Parts of Oklahoma, 8801 S. I-35, Oklahoma City, OK 73149: Catalog $5 ❖ Mid-1964 to 1973 Mustang parts. 405-631-1400.

Bob Cook Classic Auto Parts, North 3rd St., Hazel, KY 42049: Catalog $6 (specify year) ❖ Reproduction parts for 1964 to 1973 Mustangs. 502-492-8166.

Dallas Mustang Parts, 10720 Sandhill Rd., Dallas, TX 75238: Free catalog ❖ Mustang parts. 800-527-1223.

Florida Mustang Inc., 1219 Dixie Cutoff Rd., Stuart, FL 34994: Catalog $3 ❖ NOS, reproduction, new, and used 1964 to 1997 Mustang parts and accessories. 561-288-4068.

Glazier's Mustang Farm, 531 Wambold Rd., Souderton, PA 18964: Free catalog ❖ Mustang parts. 800-523-6708.

Highway Classics, 949 N. Cataract Ave., San Dimas, CA 91773: Catalog $3 ❖ Mustang parts and accessories, from 1965 to 1973. 909-592-5160.

Joblot Automotive, Ford Parts Specialists, 98-11 211th St., Queens Village, NY 11429: Catalog $2 ❖ Parts for 1949 to 1969 Mustangs. 800-221-0172; 718-468-8585 (in NY).

John's Mustang, 5234 Glenmont Dr., Houston, TX 77081: Free catalog ❖ Mustang parts and accessories, from 1965 to 1973. 713-668-5646.

Dale King Obsolete Parts Inc., P.O. Box A, Courthouse Square, Liberty, KY 42539: Free information ❖ NOS and reproduction Mustang parts. 606-787-5031.

Larry's Thunderbird & Mustang Parts, 511 S. Raymond Ave., Fullerton, CA 92631: Catalog $2 ❖ New and used parts for 1958 to 1956 Mustangs. 714-871-6432.

Midland Automotive Products, Rt. 1, Box 27, Midland City, AL 36350: Free information ❖ Reproduction and new Mustang products. 205-983-1212.

Mostly Mustang's Inc., 55 Alling St., Hamden, CT 06517: Free catalog ❖ New, used, and reproduction Mustang parts. 203-562-8804.

MPC Classics, Inc., 2100 E. Main, Ste. 4A, Grand Prairie, TX 75050: Free catalog ❖ Mustang parts, from 1964 to 1973. 800-888-1672.

Mustang Corral, Rt. 6, Box 242, Edwardsville, IL 62065: Free information with long SASE ❖ New and used parts for 1965 to 1973 Mustangs. 800-327-2897.

Mustang Headquarters, 1080 Detroit Ave., Concord, CA 94518: Free catalog ❖ Parts, upholstery, and interior fittings for 1965 to 1969 Mustangs. 800-227-2174.

Mustang of Chicago, 1321 W. Irving Park Rd., Bensenville, IL 60106: Catalog $4 ❖ New and used Mustang parts, from 1965 to 1991. 708-860-7077.

Mustang Specialties, 308 Washington Ave., Nutley, NJ 07110: Free information ❖ Reproduction and Ford parts for mid-1964 to 1973 Mustangs. 201-667-1475.

Mustangs & More, 2065 Sperry Ave., Ventura, CA 93003: Free catalog ❖ New and reproduction parts, from mid-1964 to 1973. 800-356-6573.

Mustangs Unlimited, 185 Adams St., Manchester, CT 06040: Catalog $3 (specify year) ❖ Performance parts for Mustang and Shelby, 1965 to 1973 and Mustang parts, 1974 to present. 800-243-7278.

National Parts Depot, 3101 SW 40th Blvd., Gainesville, FL 32608: Free catalog ❖ Mustang parts and accessories, from 1965 to 1973. 904-378-9000.

Obsolete Ford Parts Company, 311 E. Washington Ave., Nashville, GA 31639: Catalog $3 (specify year) ❖ NOS and reproduction parts for 1960 to 1970 Mustangs. 912-686-2470.

The Paddock Inc., 221 W. Main, Knightstown, IN 46148: Catalog $1 ❖ Mustang parts. 317-345-2131.

Racer Walsh Company, 1849 Forster Dr., Jacksonville, FL 32211: Catalog $3 ❖ Engines, suspensions, and Mustang parts. 800-334-0151.

Stilwell's Obsolete Car Parts, 1617 Wedeking Ave., Evansville, IN 47711: Catalog $3 ❖ New and reproduction Mustang parts. 812-425-4794.

Texas Mustang Parts, Rt. 6, Box 996, Waco, TX 76706: Free catalog ❖ New and reproduction parts for 1965 to 1973 Mustangs. 817-662-2893.

Treasure Chest Sales, 413 Montgomery, Jackson, MI 49202: Free information ❖ Used and NOS parts. 517-787-1475.

Valley Ford Parts, 11610 Van Owen St., North Hollywood, CA 91605: Free information ❖ New and used parts for 1965 to 1973 Mustangs.

Virginia Classic Mustang Inc., P.O. Box 487, Broadway, VA 22815: Catalog $3 ❖ Mustang parts, from mid-1964 to 1973. 703-896-2695.

NASH

Blaser's Auto, 3200 48th Ave., Moline, IL 61265: Free information ❖ Nash parts. 309-764-3571.

Charles Chambers Parts, Box 60, HC 64, Goldthwaite, TX 76844: Free information with long SASE ❖ Nash parts.

LaMance Autoworks, P.O. Box 449, 914 Old Mill Rd., Wartburg, TN 37887: Free information ❖ Nash parts. 615-346-7350.

Vintage Tin Auto Parts, 4550 Scotty Ln., Hutchinson, KS 67502: Free information with long SASE ❖ Nash parts. 316-669-8449.

Wayne's Auto Salvage, RR 3, Box 41, Winner, SD 57580: Free information ❖ Nash parts. 605-842-2054.

NOVA & CHEVY II

Chevyland, 3667 Recycle Rd., Rancho Cordova, CA 95742: Catalog $4 ❖ Nova parts and accessories. 800-624-6490; 800-624-8756 (in CA).

Classic Industries, 17832 Gothard St., Huntington Beach, CA 92647: Catalog $5 ❖ Nova parts and accessories. 800-854-1280.

D & R Classic Automotive, 31 W. 280 Diehly Rd., Naperville, IL 60563: Free price list ❖ Nova parts. 800-472-6952.

Dick's Chevy Parts, 1821 Columbus Ave., Springfield, OH 45503: Catalog $3 ❖ Rubber, chrome, moldings, interiors, emblems, and Nova parts, from 1938 to 1972. 513-325-7861.

Harmon's Inc., P.O. Box 6, Hwy. 27 North, Geneva, IN 46740: Free catalog ❖ Nova restoration parts, from 1962 to 1972. 219-368-7221.

J & M Auto Parts, RFD 5, Box 170, Pelham, NH 03076: Price list $1 (specify year) ❖ NOS, new, and reproduction 1962 to 1972 Nova parts. 603-635-3866.

❖ AUTOMOTIVE PARTS & ACCESSORIES ❖

Kanter Auto Parts, 76 Monroe St., Boonton, NJ 07005: Free catalog ❖ Nova and Chevy II parts. 201-334-9575.

Luttys Chevys, 2385 Saxonburg Blvd., Cheswick, PA 15024: Catalog $3 ❖ Nova restoration parts, from 1962 to 1974. 412-265-2988.

Martz Classic Chevy Parts, RD 1, Box 199 B, Thomasville, PA 17364: Free catalog (specify year) ❖ NOS and reproduction parts, from 1955 to 1975. 717-225-1655.

Modern Performance Classics, 1127 W. Collins, Orange, CA 92667: Free information ❖ NOS, reproduction, and used Nova and Chevy II parts. 800-457-NOVA.

Ole Chevy Store, 2509 S. Cannon Blvd., Kannapolis, NC 28083: Free list ❖ Parts for the Chevy II and Nova. 704-938-2923.

The Parts Place, 950 Paramount Pkwy., Batavia, IL 60510: Free information ❖ Nova parts, from 1963 to 1977. 708-879-1600.

SC Automotive, 409 Super Sport Ln., Rt. 3, Box 9, New Ulm, MN 56073: Free catalog ❖ Nova parts. 800-62-SS-409.

Southwestern Classics, 1230 Dan Gould Dr., Arlington, TX 76017: Free catalog ❖ New, used, remanufactured, and hard-to-find parts and accessories for 1962 to 1974 Novas and Chevy II. 800-346-7362; 817-477-1322 (in TX).

Super Sport Restoration Parts Inc., 7138 Maddox Rd., Lithonia, GA 30058: Free information ❖ Parts for the Nova, Chevy II, Chevelle, and Camaro. 404-482-9219.

Tom's Obsolete Chevy Parts, 14 Delta Dr., Pawtucket, RI 02860: Catalog $1 ❖ Nova parts, from 1955 to 1972. 401-723-7580.

Valley View Automotive Products, 1646 Valley View Ave., Lewistown, PA 17044: Free information ❖ Nova parts and accessories. 717-248-6447.

Volunteer State Obsolete Chevy Parts, Hwy. 41 South, Greenbrier, TN 37073: Catalog $5 (specify year) ❖ Chevy II parts. 615-643-4583.

Ted Williams, 5615 Rt. 45, Box A, Lisbon, OH 44432: Free catalog ❖ Chevy II and Nova restoration parts, from 1962 to 1972. 216-424-9413.

Year One Inc., P.O. Box 129, Tucker, GA 30085: Catalog $5 ❖ New, used, and reproduction Nova and Chevy II restoration parts. 800-950-9503.

OLDSMOBILE

Cooper's Vintage Auto Parts, 121 E. Linden Ave., Burbank, CA 91502: Free information ❖ Vintage Oldsmobile parts. 818-567-4140.

Fusick Automotive Products, P.O. Box 655, East Windsor, CT 06088: Catalog $3 (specify car) ❖ Parts for Oldsmobiles, from 1935 to 1960 and 1961-1975. Also Cutlass 1961 to 1977 parts. 203-623-1589.

GM Muscle Car Parts Inc., 10345 75th Ave., Palos Hills, IL 60465: Free information ❖ Oldsmobile parts, from 1964 to 1987. 708-599-2277.

Oldsmobile USA Parts Supply, 8505 Euclid Ave., Manassas, VA 22111: Free catalog ❖ New, rebuilt, and reproduction parts for 1941 to 1975 Oldsmobiles. 703-335-1935.

Out of the Past Parts, 3720 SW 23rd St., Gainesville, FL 32601: Free information ❖ Oldsmobile parts, 1935 and later. 904-377-4079.

The Parts Place, 950 Paramount Pkwy., Batavia, IL 60510: Free information ❖ Cutlass parts and accessories. 708-879-1600.

PRO Antique Auto Parts, 50 King Spring Rd., Windsor Locks, CT 06096: Catalog $3 ❖ New parts for 1929 to 1964 Oldsmobiles. 203-623-0070.

Tamraz's Parts Discount Warehouse, 10022 S. Bode Rd., Plainfield, IL 60544: Free information ❖ Oldsmobile parts. 708-904-4500.

Terrill Machine Inc., Rt. 2, Box 61, DeLeon, TX 76444: Free information with long SASE ❖ Engine overhaul parts for Oldsmobiles, from 1937 to 1960. 817-893-2610.

Vintage Tin Auto Parts, 4550 Scotty Ln., Hutchinson, KS 67502: Free information with long SASE ❖ Oldsmobile parts, from 1940 to 1970. 316-669-8449.

OPEL

Opel GT Source, 8030 Remmet Ave., Canoga Park, CA 91304: Catalog $4 ❖ Opel parts, from 1968 to 1973. 818-992-7776.

Opels Unlimited, 801 E. Lambert Rd., La Habre, CA 90631: Free information ❖ Opel parts, from 1960 to current models. 310-690-1051.

PACKARD

Gary Brinton's Antique Auto Parts, 6826 SW McVey Ave., Redmond, OR 97756: Free information ❖ Packard parts, from 1920 to 1940. 503-548-3483.

Classic Auto Parts, 550 Industrial Dr., Carmel, IN 46032: Free information ❖ Genuine Packard parts, from 1928 to 1941. 317-844-8154.

Fannaly's Auto Exchange, 701 Range Rd., P.O. Box 23, Ponchatoula, LA 70454: Free information ❖ Parts for 1946 to 1956 Packards. 504-386-3714.

Kanter Auto Parts, 76 Monroe St., Boonton, NJ 07005: Free catalog ❖ Used and reproduction parts for rebuilding Packards. 201-334-9575.

Packard Farm, 97 N. 150 West, Greenfield, IN 46140: Free information ❖ Engine and transmission parts and exhaust systems. 317-462-3124.

Patrician Industries Inc., 22644 Nona, Dearborn, MI 48124: Free information (specify parts wanted) ❖ New and used parts. 313-565-3573.

Steve's Studebaker-Packard, 2287 2nd St., Napa, CA 94559: Free information with long SASE ❖ Packard parts, from 1951 to 1956. 707-255-8945.

Terrill Machine Inc., Rt. 2, Box 61, DeLeon, TX 76444: Free information with long SASE ❖ Engine overhaul parts for 1935 to 1956 Packards. 817-893-2610.

Vintage Tin Auto Parts, 4550 Scotty Ln., Hutchinson, KS 67502: Free information with long SASE ❖ Packard parts, from 1940 to 1970. 316-669-8449.

PANTERA

Mostly Mustang's Inc., 55 Alling St., Hamden, CT 06517: Free catalog ❖ New, used, and reproduction Pantera parts. 203-562-8804.

PEUGEOT

Stamford Peugeot, 107 Myrtle Ave., Stamford, CT 06902: Free information ❖ Peugeot parts. 800-281-8658; 203-359-2266 (in CT).

PIERCE ARROW

Classic Auto Parts, 550 Industrial Dr., Carmel, IN 46032: Free information ❖ Genuine classic Pierce Arrow parts, from 1928 to 1941. 317-844-8154.

PINTO

Racer Walsh Company, 1849 Forster Dr., Jacksonville, FL 32211: Catalog $3 ❖ Engines, suspensions, and parts. 800-334-0151.

PLYMOUTH

Andy Bernbaum Auto Parts, 315 Franklin St., Newton, MA 02158: Catalog $4 ❖ Parts for Plymouth cars. 617-244-1118.

Hardens Muscle Car World, P.O. Box 306, Lexington, MO 64067: Catalog $4 ❖ NOS, reproduction, and used Plymouth parts. 800-633-4690.

Mid-South Auto Sales, 2700 Neiman Ind. Dr., Winston-Salem, NC 27103: Free information ❖ Plymouth parts and accessories. 910-768-6251.

Mike's Auto Parts, Box 358, Ridgeland, MS 39157: Free information with long SASE ❖ Plymouth parts. 601-856-7214.

Mitchell Motor Parts Inc., 2467 Jackson Pike, Columbia, OH 43223: Free information with long SASE ❖ Plymouth parts, from 1928 to the present. 614-875-4919.

Out of the Past Parts, 3720 SW 23rd St., Gainesville, FL 32601: Free information ❖ Plymouth parts, 1935 and later. 904-377-4079.

PRO Antique Auto Parts, 50 King Spring Rd., Windsor Locks, CT 06906: Catalog $3 ❖ New parts for 1929 to 1934 Plymouths. 203-623-0070.

Roberts Motor Parts, 17 Prospect St., West Newbury, MA 01985: Catalog $4 ❖ Parts for Plymouth cars. 508-363-5407.

Terrill Machine Inc., Rt. 2, Box 61, DeLeon, TX 76444: Free information with long SASE ❖ Engine overhaul parts for Plymouths, from 1933 to 1952. 817-893-2610.

Vintage Tin Auto Parts, 4550 Scotty Ln., Hutchinson, KS 67502: Free information with long SASE ❖ Parts for 1940 to 1970 Plymouths. 316-669-8449.

Year One Inc., P.O. Box 129, Tucker, GA 30085: Catalog $5 ❖ New, used, and reproduction Plymouth restoration parts. 800-950-9503.

PONTIAC

Ames Performance Engineering, Bonney Rd., Marlborough, NH 03455: Free catalog ❖ Pontiac parts, from 1955 to 1977. 800-421-2637.

Bill's Birds, 1021 Commack Rd., Dix Hills, NY 11746: Catalog $3 ❖ Pontiac parts and accessories. 516-667-3853.

Continental Enterprises, 1673 Cary Rd., Kelowna, British Columbia, Canada V1X 2C1: Information $12 ❖ Dress-up accessory kits for Pontiacs, from 1949 to 1993. 604-763-7727.

GM Muscle Car Parts Inc., 10345 75th Ave., Palos Hills, IL 60465: Free information ❖ Pontiac parts, from 1964 to 1987. 708-599-2277.

Kurt Kelsey, RR 2, Iowa Falls, IA 50126: Free information ❖ Antique Pontiac parts and accessories. 515-648-9086.

Original Parts Group Inc., 17892 Gothard St., Huntington Beach, CA 92647: Catalog $4 ❖ Parts for the LeMans and Tempest. 800-243-8355.

Out of the Past Parts, 3720 SW 23rd St., Gainesville, FL 32601: Free information ❖ Parts for 1935 and later Pontiacs. 904-377-4079.

PRO Antique Auto Parts, 50 King Spring Rd., Windsor Locks, CT 06096: Catalog $3 ❖ New parts for 1929 to 1964 Pontiacs. 203-623-0070.

Terrill Machine Inc., Rt. 2, Box 61, DeLeon, TX 76444: Free information with long SASE ❖ Engine overhaul parts for Pontiacs, from 1937 to 1956. 817-893-2610.

Vintage Tin Auto Parts, 4550 Scotty Ln., Hutchinson, KS 67502: Free information with long SASE ❖ Pontiac parts, from 1940 to 1970. 316-669-8449.

PORSCHE

Aase Brothers Inc., 701 E. Cypress St., Anaheim, CA 92805: Free information ❖ Porsche parts. 800-444-7444; 714-956-2419 (in CA).

Automotion, 193 Commercial St., Sunnyvale, CA 94086: Catalog $4 (refundable) ❖ Porsche parts and accessories. 800-777-8881.

Best Deal Porsche, 8171 Monroe, Stanton, CA 90680: Free information ❖ New, used, and reproduction parts for 1953 to 1986 models. 714-995-0081.

Euromeister, 19507 Yuma St., Castro Valley, CA 94546: Catalog $4.95 ❖ Porsche parts and accessories. 800-581-3327.

International, 2900 E. Miraloma Ave., Anaheim, CA 92806: Free brochure ❖ New and used Porsche parts. 714-632-9288.

928 International, 2900 E. Miraloma Ave., Anaheim, CA 92806: Free brochure ❖ Parts and accessories. 714-632-9288.

O.E.M. Parts Distributor, P.O. Box 25312, San Mateo, CA 94402: Free information ❖ Porsche parts. 415-802-8125.

Par-Porsche Specialists, 310 Main St., New Rochelle, NY 10801: Free information ❖ New and used Porsche parts and accessories. 914-637-8800.

Parts Hotline, 10385 Central Ave., Montclair, CA 91763: Free information with long SASE ❖ Porsche parts. 800-637-4662; 714-625-4888 (in CA).

Performance Products, 16129 Leadwell, Van Nuys, CA 91406: Catalog $4 ❖ Parts and tools for Porsche cars. 800-423-3173; 818-787-7500 (in CA).

Stoddard Imported Cars Inc., 38845 Mentor Ave., Willoughby, OH 44094: Catalog $5 ❖ Restoration parts for the Porsche. 800-342-1414; 216-951-1040 (in OH).

Valley Motors, 3203 Bragg Blvd., Fayetteville, NC 28303: Free information ❖ Porsche parts. 800-264-3203.

RAMBLER

American Parts Depot, 409 N. Main St., West Manchester, OH 45382: Catalog $5 ❖ Rambler and AMC parts. 513-678-7249.

Blaser's Auto, 3200 48th Ave., Moline, IL 61265: Free information ❖ Rambler parts. 309-764-3571.

Bob & Art's Auto Parts, 2641 Reno Rd., Schodack Center, Castleton, NY 12033: Free information ❖ Rambler parts. 518-477-9183.

LaMance Autoworks, P.O. Box 449, 914 Old Mill Rd., Wartburg, TN 37887: Free information ❖ Rambler parts, from 1963 to 1964. 615-346-7350.

Vintage Tin Auto Parts, 4550 Scotty Ln., Hutchinson, KS 67502: Free information with long SASE ❖ Rambler parts. 316-669-8449.

Webb's Classic Auto Parts, 5084 W. State Rd. 114, Huntington, IN 46750: Free information with long SASE ❖ Parts for Rambler and AMC cars, 1950 and later. 219-344-1714.

RANCHERO

Dearborn Classics, P.O. Box 1248, Sunset Beach, CA 90742: Catalog $3 ❖ Ranchero parts. 714-372-3175.

Highway Classics, 949 N. Cataract Ave., San Dimas, CA 91773: Catalog $3 ❖ Ranchero parts and accessories, from 1960 to 1979. 909-592-5160.

RENAULT

4-CV Service, 3301 Shetland Rd., Beavercreek, OH 45434: Free information with long SASE ❖ NOS and used parts and accessories.

Patton Orphan Spares, 28 Simon St., Babylon, NY 11702: Free information with long SASE ❖ Renault parts and accessories. 516-669-2598.

PF Engineering, P.O. Box 39472, Los Angeles, CA 90039: Free information with long SASE ❖ Renault parts and accessories. 818-244-2498.

ROLLS-ROYCE

Albers Rolls-Royce, 360 S. 1st St., Zionsville, IN 46077: Free information ❖ Rolls-Royce parts. 317-873-2360.

Carriage House Motor Cars Ltd., 25 Railroad Ave., Greenwich, CT 06830: Free information ❖ Rolls-Royce and Bentley parts. 800-883-2462.

Classic Auto Air Mfg. Company, 2020 W. Kennedy Blvd., Tampa, FL 33606: Free catalog ❖ Air-conditioning systems and parts for 1949 to 1969 Rolls-Royces. 813-251-4994.

Foreign Motors West, 253 N. Main St., Natick, MA 01760: Free information ❖ Factory-new parts for the Silver Shadow and all postwar Rolls-Royces and Bentleys. 800-338-3198.

George Haug Company Inc., 517 E. 73rd St., New York, NY 10021: Free information ❖ Rolls-Royce parts. 212-288-0176.

Orlando's Classic & Sports Car Specialists, 412 Smith St., Keasbey, NJ 08832: Free information ❖ New, used, and remanufactured parts. 800-317-6557.

Replacement Parts Company, P.O. Box 152, Villa Rica, GA 30180: Free information ❖ Rolls-Royce and Bentley replacement parts. 404-459-0040.

Rolls-Royce Obsolete Parts Inc., P.O. Box 796, Anna Maria, FL 34216: Free information with long SASE ❖ Rolls-Royce and Bentley parts and literature. 813-778-7270.

The Vintage Garage, North Brookfield, MA 01535: Free information ❖ Hard-to-find parts for the Rolls-Royce. 508-867-2892.

ROVER

Atlantic British Parts, P.O. Box 110, Mechanicsville, NY 12118: Free catalog ❖ Parts for the Rover. 800-533-2210.

AUTOMOTIVE PARTS & ACCESSORIES

Bluff City British Cars, 1810 Getwell, Memphis, TN 38111: Free information ❖ Parts for the Range Rover. 800-621-0227; 901-743-4422 (in TN).

The British Northwest Land-Rover Company, 1043 Kaiser Rd. SW, Olympia, WA 98512: Free information ❖ New, rebuilt, and used parts for Land-Rovers. 360-866-2254.

British Pacific Ltd., 3317 Burton Ave., Burbank, CA 91504: Free information ❖ Land Rover parts. 818-841-8945.

Rovers West, 4060 E. Michigan, Tucson, AZ 85714: Free information ❖ Parts for the Rover Sedan, Range Rover, and Land Rover. 520-748-8115.

Roverworks, 307 Ruskey Ln., Hyde Park, NY 12538: Free information ❖ Remanufactured parts for Land Rovers. 800-4A-ROVER.

Spectral Kinetics, 17 Church St., Garnerville, NY 10923: Free information ❖ Range Rover parts. 914-947-3126.

SAAB

European Automotive Specialists, 4080 E. Michigan St., Tucson, AZ 85714: Free information ❖ SAAB parts and accessories. 602-747-1097.

Jaguar & SAAB of Troy, 1815 Maplelawn, Troy, MI 48084: Free catalog ❖ Parts for the SAAB. 800-832-5839; 313-643-7894 (in MI).

O.E.M. Parts Distributor, P.O. Box 25312, San Mateo, CA 94402: Free information ❖ SAAB parts. 415-802-8125.

SHELBY

Branda Shelby & Mustang Parts, 1434 E. Pleasant Valley Blvd., Altoona, PA 16602: Catalog $3 ❖ Shelby parts. 800-458-3477.

Cobra Restorers, 3099 Carter, Kenesaw, GA 30144: Catalog $5 ❖ Parts for the Shelby. 404-427-0020.

Mostly Mustang's Inc., 55 Alling St., Hamden, CT 06517: Free catalog ❖ New, used, and reproduction Shelby parts. 203-562-8804.

Mustangs Unlimited, 185 Adams St., Manchester, CT 06040: Catalog $3 (specify year) ❖ Shelby parts. 800-243-7278.

Valley Ford Parts, 11610 Van Owen St., North Hollywood, CA 91605: Free information ❖ New and used parts for the 1965 to 1973 Shelby.

SPITFIRE

British Parts Northwest, 4105 SE Lafayette Hwy., Dayton, OR 97114: Catalog $2.50 ❖ Spitfire parts. 503-864-2001.

STANLEY

Stanley Sales & Service by Amsley, 4885 Lincoln Way West, St. Thomas, PA 17252: Free information with long SASE (specify parts wanted) ❖ Parts mostly for steam cars. 717-369-2151.

STEARNS-KNIGHT

Arthur W. Aseltine, 18215 Challenge Cut-Off Rd., Forbestown, CA 95941: Free information with long SASE (specify parts wanted) ❖ Parts. 916-675-2773.

STERLING

Bluff City British Cars, 1810 Getwell, Memphis, TN 38111: Free information ❖ Parts for the Sterling. 800-621-0227; 901-743-4422 (in TN).

Classic Enterprises, Box 92, Barron, WI 54812: Catalog $3 ❖ Studebaker parts. 715-537-5422.

Jaguar & SAAB of Troy, 1815 Maplelawn, Troy, MI 48084: Free catalog ❖ Parts for the Sterling. 800-832-5839; 313-643-7894 (in MI).

Special Interest Autos of St. Louis Inc., P.O. Box 944, St. Charles, MO 63302: Specify catalog wanted ❖ NOS and reproduction parts for 1947 to 1952 cars ($3.50); 1941 to 1964 pickups ($4.50); 1953 to 1964 coupes and Hawks ($3.50); 1959 to 1966 Larks, Daytonas, and Commanders ($4.50). 800-433-1257.

STUDEBAKER

Beckers Auto Salvage, Hwy. 30 West, Atkins, IA 52206: Free information ❖ Parts for Studebakers. 319-446-7141.

Jim's Auto Sales, Rt. 2, Inman, KS 67546: Free information ❖ Studebaker parts, from 1935 to 1966. 316-585-6648.

Newman & Altman Inc., P.O. Box 4276, South Bend, IN 46634: Catalog $5 ❖ Studebaker parts and accessories, for 1947 to 1966 cars and trucks. 800-722-4295.

Packard Farm, 97 N 150 West, Greenfield, IN 46140: Free information ❖ Studebaker engine and transmission parts and exhaust systems. 317-462-3124.

Parmer Studebaker Sales, 408 S. Lincoln, Van Wert, IA 50262: Free information ❖ Parts for Studebakers, from 1947 to 1966. 515-445-5692.

Steve's Studebaker-Packard, 2287 2nd St., Napa, CA 94559: Free information with long SASE ❖ Studebaker parts, from 1953 to 1966. 707-255-8945.

Tucker's Auto Salvage, RD 1, Box 170, Burke, NY 12917: Free information ❖ Studebaker, NOS and used parts. 518-483-5478.

Wayne's Auto Salvage, RR 3, Box 41, Winner, SD 57580: Free information ❖ Studebaker parts. 605-842-2054.

SUBARU

Parts Hotline, 10385 Central Ave., Montclair, CA 91763: Free information with long SASE ❖ Subaru parts. 800-637-4662; 714-625-4888 (in CA).

Stamford Subaru, 107 Myrtle Ave., Stamford, CT 06902: Free information ❖ Subaru parts and accessories. 800-281-8658; 203-359-2266 (in CT).

SUNBEAM

Moss Motors Ltd., 7200 Hollister Rd., P.O. Box 847, Goleta, CA 93116: Free catalog (specify model) ❖ Parts for the Sunbeam. 800-235-6954.

Sunbeam Specialties, 765 McGlincey Ln., Campbell, CA 95008: Free catalog ❖ Parts for 1959 to 1968 Tigers and Alpines. 408-371-1642.

Victoria British Ltd., P.O. Box 14991, Lenexa, KS 66285: Free catalog ❖ Sunbeam parts. 800-255-0088.

TEMPEST

Original Parts Group Inc., 17892 Gothard St., Huntington Beach, CA 92647: Catalog $4 ❖ Tempest parts. 800-243-8355.

THUNDERBIRD

Auto Krafters Inc., P.O. Box 8, Broadway, VA 22815: Catalog $1 (specify year) ❖ New, used, and reproduction parts, from 1958 to 1976. 703-896-5910.

B & W Antique Auto, 4653 Guide Meridian Rd., Bellingham, WA 98226: Catalog $5 (specify year and model) ❖ Thunderbird parts, 1955 to 1966. 360-647-4574.

Bob's T-Birds, 5397 NE 14th Ave., Fort Lauderdale, FL 33334: Free information with long SASE ❖ New and used parts. 305-491-6652.

Dennis Carpenter Reproductions, P.O. Box 26398, Charlotte, NC 28221: Catalog $3 (specify year) ❖ Rubber parts for 1958 to 1966 Thunderbirds. 219-335-2425.

Classic Auto Supply Company Inc., 795 High St., P.O. Box 850, Coshocton, OH 43812: Catalog $1 ❖ Parts for 1955 to 1957 Thunderbird cars. 800-374-0914.

Classique Cars Unlimited, P.O. Box 249, Lakeshore, MS 39558: Parts list $4 ❖ Thunderbird parts, from 1958 to 1988. 601-467-9633.

Concours Parts & Accessories, 3563 Numancia St., P.O. Box 1210, Santa Ynez, CA 93460: Catalog $4 ❖ Thunderbird 1955 to 1957 parts. 805-688-7795.

Continental Enterprises, 1673 Cary Rd., Kelowna, British Columbia, Canada V1X 2C1: Information $12 ❖ Thunderbird dress-up accessory kits, from 1949 to 1993. 604-763-7727.

Bob Cook Classic Auto Parts, North 3rd St., Hazel, KY 42049: Catalog $6 (specify year) ❖ Reproduction parts for 1958 to 1960, 1961 to 1964, 1965 to 1966, and 1967 to 1972 Thunderbirds. 502-492-8166.

Ford Parts Specialists, 98-11 211th St., Queens Village, NY 11429: Free catalog (specify year) ❖ Thunderbird parts, 1949 to 1969. 718-468-8585.

Hollywood Classic Motorcars Inc., 363 Ansin Blvd., Hallandale, FL 33009: Free information ❖ Used Thunderbird parts, from 1958 to 1966. 800-235-2444; 954-454-4641 (in FL).

Joblot Automotive, Ford Parts Specialists, 98-11 211th St., Queens Village, NY 11429: Catalog $2 ❖ Parts for 1949 to 1969 Thunderbirds. 800-221-0172; 718-468-8585 (in NY).

Larry's Thunderbird & Mustang Parts, 511 S. Raymond Ave., Fullerton, CA 92631: Catalog $2 ❖ New and used parts for 1955 to 1957 Thunderbirds. 714-871-6432.

LeBaron Bonney Company, 8 Chestnut St., Amesbury, MA 01913: Catalog $1 ❖ Thunderbird parts. 508-388-3811.

Lincoln Parts International, 707 E. 4th St., Building G, Perris, CA 92570: Free information ❖ Thunderbird parts, from 1972 to 1979. 909-657-5588.

Midland Automotive Products, Rt. 1, Box 27, Midland City, AL 36350: Free information ❖ Reproduction and new Thunderbird products. 205-983-1212.

Muck Motor Sales, 10 Campbell Blvd., Buffalo, NY 14068: Free information ❖ Thunderbird parts and accessories. 800-228-6825.

National Parts Depot, 3101 SW 40th Blvd., Gainesville, FL 32608: Free catalog ❖ Thunderbird parts and accessories, from 1955 to 1957. 904-378-9000.

Obsolete Ford Parts Inc. (Oklahoma City), 8701 South I-35, Oklahoma City, OK 73149: Catalog $3 (specify year) ❖ Parts for 1949 to 1959 and 1960 to 1972 Thunderbirds. 405-631-3933.

Prestige Thunderbird Inc., 10215 Greenleaf Ave., Santa Fe Springs, CA 90670: Catalog $1 ❖ Parts and upholstery. 310-944-6237.

Sixties Ford Parts, 639 Glanker St., Memphis, TN 38112: Catalog $4 ❖ Thunderbird parts, from 1960 to 1968.

T-Bird Connection, 728 E. Dunlap, Phoenix, AZ 85020: Free information ❖ Thunderbird parts, from 1958 to 1972. 602-997-9285.

T-Bird Nest, 2550 E. Southlake Rd., Southlake, TX 76092: Free information ❖ Thunderbird parts, from 1958 to 1966. 817-481-1776.

The T-Bird Sanctuary, 9997 SW Avery, Tualatin, OR 97062: Catalog $5 ❖ Parts for 1958 to 1976 Thunderbirds. 503-692-9848.

Tee-Bird Products Inc., Box 153, Exton, PA 19341: Catalog $2 ❖ Parts for 1955 to 1957 Thunderbirds. 610-363-1725.

Thunderbird Bar, 2919 Elkin Hwy. 268, North Wilkesboro, NC 28659: Free information ❖ Thunderbird parts, from 1958 to 1969. 910-667-0837.

Thunderbird, Falcon & Fairlane Connection, 728 E. Dunlap, Phoenix, AZ 85020: Catalog $2 (specify year) ❖ New and used parts for 1958 to 1971 Thunderbirds. 602-997-9285.

Thunderbird Center, 23610 John R., Hazel Park, MI 48030: Free catalog ❖ Upholstery, sheet metal, weatherstripping, and new, used, NOS, and reproduction parts for 1956 to 1957 Thunderbirds. 810-548-1721.

Thunderbird Headquarters, 1080 Detroit Ave., Concord, CA 94518: Free catalog ❖ Thunderbird parts, from 1955 to 1957. 800-227-2174; 800-642-2405 (in CA).

Thunderbird Parts & Restoration, 5844 Goodrich Rd., Clarence Center, NY 14032: Free information ❖ NOS, reproduction, used, and re-manufactured parts. 800-289-2473; 716-741-2866 (in NY).

Thunderbirds One, P.O. Box 1091, Gastonia, NC 28053: Free catalog ❖ Thunderbird parts, from 1955 to 1957. 704-867-5557.

Thunderbirds USA Parts Supply, 3621 Resource Dr., Tuscaloosa, AL 35401: Free catalog ❖ 1955 to 1957 Thunderbird upholstery, decals, radios, books, and NOS, used, and reproduction parts. 800-842-5557; 205-758-5557 (in AL).

TORINO

Auto Krafters Inc., P.O. Box 8, Broadway, VA 22815: Catalog $1 (specify year) ❖ New, used, and reproduction parts for 1962 to 1971 Torinos. 703-896-5910.

Dennis Carpenter Reproductions, P.O. Box 26398, Charlotte, NC 28221: Catalog $3 ❖ Rubber parts for 1962 to 1971 Torinos. 219-335-2425.

Bob Cook Classic Auto Parts, North 3rd St., Hazel, KY 42049: Catalog $6 (specify year) ❖ Reproduction parts for 1960 to 1972 Torino cars. 502-492-8166.

Dearborn Classics, P.O. Box 1248, Sunset Beach, CA 90742: Catalog $3 ❖ Torino parts and accessories. 714-372-3175.

Ford Parts Store, P.O. Box 226, Bryan, OH 43506: Catalog $2 ❖ Torino parts. 419-636-2475.

Highway Classics, 949 N. Cataract Ave., San Dimas, CA 91773: Catalog $3 ❖ Torino parts and accessories. 909-592-5160.

Obsolete Ford Parts Company, 311 E. Washington Ave., Nashville, GA 31639: Catalog $3 (specify year) ❖ NOS and reproduction parts for 1949 to 1964 Torino cars. 912-686-2470.

Obsolete Ford Parts Inc. (Oklahoma City), 8701 South I-35, Oklahoma City, OK 73149: Catalog $3 (specify year) ❖ Parts and accessories for 1962 to 1972 Torinos. 405-631-3933.

TOYOTA

Dobi Toyota Catalog, 320 Thor Pl., Brea, CA 92621: Catalog $2 ❖ Replacement parts for the Toyota Celica and Corolla. 714-529-1977.

Lou Fusz Toyota, 10725 Manchester, St. Louis, MO 63122: Catalog $4 ❖ Toyota parts and accessories. 800-325-9581.

HKS USA Inc., 20312 Gramercy Pl., Torrance, CA 90501: Catalog $8 ❖ Toyota performance parts. 310-328-8100.

Impact Parts, Glen Wild Rd., Glen Wild, NY 12738: Catalog $1 ❖ Parts for the Toyota. 914-434-3338.

Jaguar & SAAB of Troy, 1815 Maplelawn, Troy, MI 48084: Free catalog ❖ Parts for the Toyota. 800-832-5839; 313-643-7894 (in MI).

Options Auto Salon, 4523 San Fernando Rd., Ste. 1, Glendale, CA 91204: Catalog $5 ❖ Dress-up and restoration parts and accessories. 818-545-8218.

Price Toyota Newark, 1344 Marrows Rd., Newark, DE 19711: Catalog $4 ❖ Toyota parts. 800-537-4510.

TRANS AM

Firebird/Trans Am America, Rt. 322, Box 427, Boalsburg, PA 16827: Free information with long SASE ❖ Trans Am parts, from 1967 to 1987. 800-458-3475.

TRIUMPH

Aurora Auto Wrecking Inc., 9217 Aurora Avenue North, Seattle, WA 98103: Free information ❖ New, used, and rebuilt Triumph parts. 800-426-6464.

British Miles, 222 Grove, Morrisville, PA 19067: Free information ❖ Reconditioned and new Triumph parts. 215-736-9300.

British Parts Northwest, 4105 SE Lafayette Hwy., Dayton, OR 97114: Catalog $2.50 ❖ Triumph parts. 503-864-2001.

EightParts, 4060 E. Michigan, Tucson, AZ 85714: Free information ❖ Parts for 8-cylinder Triumphs. 520-748-8115.

English Car Spares Ltd., 345 Branch Rd SW, Alpharetta, GA 30201: Free information ❖ Triumph parts. 800-241-1916; 404-475-2662 (in GA).

George Haug Company Inc., 517 E. 73rd St., New York, NY 10021: Free information ❖ Triumph parts. 212-288-0176.

Moss Motors Ltd., 7200 Hollister Rd., P.O. Box 847, Goleta, CA 93116: Free catalog (specify model) ❖ Triumph parts. 800-235-6954.

Peninsula Imports, 3749 Harlem, Buffalo, NY 14215: Free catalog ❖ Triumph parts. 800-999-1209.

AUTOMOTIVE PARTS & ACCESSORIES

Roadster Factory, P.O. Box 332, Armagh, PA 15920: Free catalog ❖ Parts for the Triumph, TR2 through TR8, Spitfire, and GT6. 800-283-3723.

Special Interest Car Parts, 1340 Hartford Ave., Johnston, RI 02919: Free catalog ❖ Parts and accessories for Triumphs. 800-556-7496.

Sports & Classics, 512 Boston Post Rd., Darien, CT 06820: Catalog $4 ❖ Restoration, engine, electrical, and body parts. 203-655-8731.

Victoria British Ltd., P.O. Box 14991, Lenexa, KS 66215: Free catalog ❖ Original, replacement, and reproduction parts for the Triumph and British sports cars. 800-255-0088.

VENTURA

Ames Performance Engineering, Bonney Rd., Marlborough, NH 03455: Free catalog ❖ Ventura parts, from 1971 to 1974. 800-421-2637.

VOLKSWAGEN

Electro Automotive, P.O. Box 1113, Felton, CA 95018: Catalog $5 ❖ Bolt-in kit for converting a gas or diesel Rabbit to electricity. 408-429-1989.

O.E.M. Parts Distributor, P.O. Box 25312, San Mateo, CA 94402: Free information ❖ Volkswagon parts. 415-802-8125.

Rocky Mountain Motorworks, 1003 Tamarac Pkwy., Woodland Park, CO 80863: Free catalog ❖ Restoration parts. 800-544-1066.

Sonnen Motors, 601 Francisco Blvd. East, San Rafael, CA 94901: Free information ❖ Genuine factory parts and accessories. 800-543-7626; 800-SONNEN-1 (in CA).

VOLVO

B & B Used Auto Parts, Rt. 1, Box 691, Big Pine Key, FL 33043: Free information ❖ Parts for the Volvo, 1968 and later. 305-872-9761.

Beechmont Volvo, 8639 Beechmont Ave., Cincinnati, OH 45255: Free catalog ❖ Volvo parts. 800-255-3601.

Brentwood Volvo, 7700 Manchester Rd., St. Louis, MO 63143: Free information ❖ Volvo parts. 800-844-9502.

Euromeister, 19507 Yuma St., Castro Valley, CA 94546: Catalog $4.95 ❖ Volvo parts and accessories. 800-581-3327.

Foreign Autotech, 3225 Sunset Ln., Hatboro, PA 19040: Free information ❖ Volvo 1800 parts. 215-441-4421.

Impact Parts, Glen Wild Rd., Glen Wild, NY 12738: Catalog $1 ❖ Parts for the Volvo. 800-431-3400.

O.E.M. Parts Distributor, P.O. Box 25312, San Mateo, CA 94402: Free information ❖ Volvo parts. 415-802-8125.

Stamford Volvo, 107 Myrtle Ave., Stamford, CT 06902: Free information ❖ Genuine Volvo parts. 800-281-8658; 203-359-2266 (in CT).

Swedish Classics, P.O. Box 557, Oxford, MD 21654: Catalog $5 (specify model) ❖ Original and original Volvo parts and accessories. 410-226-5542.

Voluparts, 751 Trabert Ave., Atlanta, GA 30318: Free information ❖ New and used Volvo parts. 404-352-3402.

WILLYS

Obsolete Jeep & Willys Parts, 6110 17th St. East, Bradenton, FL 34203: Free information ❖ New, used, rebuilt, and NOS parts. 813-756-7844.

YUGO

Orion Motors Inc., 10722 Jones Rd., Houston, TX 77065: Free information ❖ Yugo parts and accessories. 800-736-6410; 713-894-1982 (in TX).

Plating

A & A Plating, 9400 E. Wilson Rd., Independence, MO 64053: Free information ❖ Custom plating. 800-747-9914.

Arizona Chrome Plastic, 118 W. Hatcher Rd., Phoenix, AZ 85021: Free information ❖ Custom plating. 602-331-4187.

Burns Binnert Plating Inc., 412 Clifford Ave., Rochester, NY 14621: Free information ❖ Custom chrome plating. 716-342-5180.

Castle Metal Finishing, Ron McGilvray, 15 Broad St., Hudson, MA 01749: Free information ❖ Chrome restoration plating. 508-562-7294.

Chrome Brite Plating, Box 915, Thompson Cove Rd., Clyde, NC 28721: Free information ❖ Chrome plating. 800-849-3813.

Custom Chrome Inc., 117 Elk St., Rock Springs, WY 82901: Free information ❖ Restoration plating. 307-362-1504.

Custom Chrome Plating, 963 Mechanic St., P.O. Box 125, Grafton, OH 44044: Free information ❖ Chrome, nickel, and copper plating. 216-926-3116.

Custom Plating, 3030 Alta Ridge Way, Snellville, GA 30278: Free information ❖ Chrome plating. 404-736-1118.

Eagle Plating Inc., 124 Smathers St., Waynesville, NC 28786: Free information ❖ Chrome, nickel, cadmium, copper, and brass plating. 704-456-4858.

Graves Plating Company, Industrial Park, P.O. Box 1052, Florence, AL 35631: Free information ❖ Chrome, nickel, brass, and gold plating. 205-764-9487.

International Chromium Plating Company, 2 Addison Pl., Providence, RI 02909: Free information ❖ Custom chrome plating of marine, motorcycle, and auto hardware. Also nickel, zinc, and cadmium plating for antique automobile and motorcycle parts. 401-421-0205.

J & P Custom Plating, Box 16, 807 N. Meridian St., Portland, IN 47371: Free information ❖ Copper, nickel, chrome, and brass plating. 219-726-9696.

King's Bumper Company Inc., 1 Ontario Ave., New Hanford, NY 13413: Free information ❖ Chrome plating. 315-732-8988.

Ron Monte Inc., 25 Roseland Ave., Caldwell, NJ 07006: Free information ❖ Copper, nickel, chrome, brass, and silver plating. 201-226-6184.

Palm City Metal Finishing, 3520 SW Armellini Ave., Palm City, FL 34990: Free information ❖ Chrome, nickel, and copper plating. 407-221-8999.

Paul's Chrome Plating Inc., 341 Mars-Valencia Rd., Mars, PA 16046: Free information ❖ Plating and pot metal restoration. 800-245-8679; 412-625-3135 (in PA).

Plating Service, N3503 Hwy. 55, Chilton, WI 53014: Free information with long SASE ❖ Antique car and cycle custom plating and polishing. 414-989-1901.

Speed & Sport Chrome Plating, 404 Broadway, Houston, TX 77012: Free information ❖ Chrome plating, specializing in antique automobile parts. 713-921-0235.

Verne's Chrome Plating, 1559 El Segundo Blvd., Gardena, CA 90249: Free information ❖ Chrome plating and polishing. 213-754-4126.

Radar Detectors (Manufacturers)

Audiovox, 185 Oser Ave., Hauppage, NY 11788: Free information ❖ Mini and standard-size radar detectors. 516-233-3300.

Cincinnati Microwave, One Microwave Plaza, Cincinnati, OH 45249: Free information ❖ Micro and standard-size radar detectors. 800-543-1608.

Cobra, 6500 W. Cortland St., Chicago, IL 60635: Free information ❖ Micro, remote, and standard-size radar detectors. 800-COBRA-22.

Escort Detectors, 5200 Fields-Ertel Rd., Cincinnati, OH 45249: Free information ❖ Radar and laser detectors. 800-433-3487.

K-40 Electronics, 1500 Executive Dr., Elgin, IL 60123: Free brochure ❖ Radar detectors. 800-323-5608.

Radar U.S.A., 1749 Golf Rd., Mt. Prospect, IL 60056: Free information ❖ Radar units and accessories. 800-777-6570; 708-350-0201 (in IL).

Radio Shack, Division Tandy Corporation, One Tandy Center, Fort Worth, TX 76102: Free information ❖ Mini, remote, and standard-size radar detectors. 817-390-3011.

Radar Detectors (Retailers)

ComputAbility Consumer Electronics, P.O. Box 17882, Milwaukee, WI 53217: Free catalog ❖ Radar detectors. 800-554-9949.

Executive Photo & Electronics, 120 W. 31st St., New York, NY 10001: Free information ❖ Radar detectors and electronics. 800-882-2802.

Radar City, 67-38 Myrtle Ave., Glendale, NY 11385: Free information ❖ Radar detectors and electronics. 800-419-2323.

Radar U.S.A., 1749 Golf Rd., Mt. Prospect, IL 60056: Free information ❖ Radar detectors. 800-777-6570; 708-350-0201 (in IL).

S.B.H. Enterprises, 1678 53rd St., Brooklyn, NY 11204: Free information ❖ Radar detectors. 800-451-5851; 718-438-1027 (in NY).

Radiators

Brassworks, 289 Prado Rd., San Luis Obispo, CA 93401: Free information ❖ Handcrafted rebuilt and duplicated radiators, from the 1890s and later. 805-544-8841.

Ramps & Lifts

Backyard Buddy Corporation, P.O. Box 5104, Niles, OH 44446: Free information ❖ Hydraulic-powered lifts for standard wheelbase cars and trucks. 800-837-9353.

RhinoRamps, 99 S. Cameron St., Harrisburg, PA 17101: Free information ❖ Compact weight-bearing ramps. 800-400-6642.

Stinger Inc., 2080 E. Kansas Ave., McPherson, KS 67460: Free information ❖ Lifts for commercial parking and residential use. 800-854-4850; 316-241-5580 (in KS).

Replica & Conversion Kits

ALLARD

Hardy Motors, P.O. Box 1302, Bonita, CA 91908: Brochure $5 ❖ Reproduction car kits. 619-421-5920.

AUBURN

The Classic Factory, 1454 E. 9th St., Pomona, CA 91766: Information $3 ❖ Replica car kits. 714-629-5968.

Elegant Motors Inc., P.O. Box 30188, Indianapolis, IN 46230: Catalog $5 ❖ Sports car reproduction kits. 317-253-9898.

BRADLEY GT

Sun Ray, Products Corporation, 8017 Ranchers Rd., Fridley, MN 55432: Free brochure ❖ Replica car kits. 612-780-0774.

CHEETAH

Elegant Motors Inc., P.O. Box 30188, Indianapolis, IN 46230: Free information ❖ Reproduction car kits. 317-253-9898.

COBRA

Antique & Collectible Autos Inc., 35 Dole St., Buffalo, NY 14210: Brochure $1 ❖ Replica car kits. 800-245-1310.

Bennett Automotive, 3385 Enterprise, Hayward, CA 94545: Free brochure ❖ Reproduction car kits. 510-782-0705.

Butler Racing Inc., 103 Santa Felicia Dr., Goleta, CA 93117: Free brochure ❖ Replica car kits. 805-685-3535.

Classic Roadsters, 1617 Main Ave., Fargo, ND 58103: Free brochure ❖ Easy-to-assemble Cobra kit. 800-373-9000.

Contemporary Classic Motor Car Company, 115 Hoyt Ave., Mamaroneck, NY 10543: Catalog $5 ❖ Replica car kits. 914-381-5678.

Elegant Motors Inc., P.O. Box 30188, Indianapolis, IN 46230: Free information ❖ Reproduction car kits. 317-253-9898.

ERA Replica Automobiles, 608 E. Main St., New Britain, CT 06051: Brochure $10 ❖ Replica car kits. 203-229-7968.

Everett-Morrison Motorcars, 5137 W. Clifton St., Tampa, FL 33634: Brochure $5 ❖ Replica car kits. 813-887-5885.

T. Green Enterprises, 5621 E. Bonna, Indianapolis, IN 46219: Information $5 ❖ Cobra body kits. 317-352-8248.

Hi-Tech Motorsports, 2204 W. Southern Ave., Tempe, AZ 85282: Free catalog ❖ Cobra kits. 602-431-9400.

LA Exotics, 6900 Knott Ave., Unit E, Buena Park, CA 90621: Information $10 ❖ Replica car kits. 714-523-8464.

MidStates Classic Cars, 835 W. Grant, P.O. Box 427, Hooper, NE 68031: Catalog $5 ❖ Replica car kits. 402-654-2772.

Shell Valley Motors, Rt. 1, Box 69, Platte Center, NE 68653: Free information ❖ Replica car kits. 402-246-2355.

Unique Motorcars Inc., 230 E. Broad St., Gadsden, AL 35903: Brochure $5 ❖ Reproduction car kits. 205-546-3708.

West Coast Cobra, 6785 16 Mile Rd., Sterling Heights, MI 48077: Information $5 ❖ Replica car kits. 519-736-7274.

CORD

Elegant Motors Inc., P.O. Box 30188, Indianapolis, IN 46230: Free information ❖ Reproduction car kits. 317-253-9898.

CORVETTE

Beck Development, 1531 W. 13th St., Upland, CA 91786: Free information ❖ Replica car kits. 909-981-3840.

Central Industries, 5865 Sawyer Rd., Sawyer, MI 49125: Catalog $4 ❖ Factory assembled 1957 Corvette body and parts. 616-426-3342.

D & D Corvette, 1985 Manchester Rd., Akron, OH 44314: Information $5 ❖ Replica car kits. 216-745-2544.

DATSUN

Blue Ray G.T. Engineering, 416 Woodline Dr., The Woodlands, TX 77386: Information package $5 (specify car) ❖ Body conversion kits for the 1970 to 1978 Datsun 240/260/280Z and 1979 to 1983 Datsun 280ZX. 713-363-2000.

California Mustang, 19400 San Jose Ave., City of Industry, CA 91748: Catalog $5 (refundable with $25 purchase) ❖ Mustang parts and accessories, from 1965 to 1973. 800-775-0101.

FERRARI

Corson Motorcars Ltd., P.O. Box 41396, Phoenix, AZ 85080: Brochure $5 ❖ Replica car kits. 602-375-2544.

FIERO

American Fiberbodies International, P.O. Box 726, Xenia, OH 45385: Information $10 ❖ Body package for any stock Fiero. 513-372-5938.

Fiero Conversions Inc., 3410 Walker Rd., Windsor, Ontario, Canada N8W 3S3: Information $5 ❖ Body and aerodynamic conversion accessories. 519-972-4989.

Fiero Plus, 12 Banner Rd., Nepean, Ontario, Canada K2H 5T2: Catalog $7 ❖ Body conversion kits. 613-596-6269.

Mac's Auto Body, 4427 Maygog Rd., Sarasota, FL 34233: Information $5 ❖ Body kits. 813-921-4420.

PISA Corporation, P.O. Box 15088, Phoenix, AZ 85060: Free information ❖ Bolt-on body kit for the Fiero. 602-376-1550.

FORD

Antique & Collectible Autos Inc., 35 Dole St., Buffalo, NY 14210: Brochure $1 ❖ Replica car kits. 800-245-1310.

JAGUAR

Antique & Collectible Autos Inc., 35 Dole St., Buffalo, NY 14210: Brochure $1 ❖ Replica car kits. 800-245-1310.

Braden River Engineering, 1620 Palma Sola Blvd., Bradenton, FL 34209: Free information ❖ Body conversion kits. 813-747-6146.

Eagle Coach Works Inc., 760 Northland Ave., Buffalo, NY 14211: Brochure $3 ❖ Replica car kits. 716-897-4292.

Predator Performance Inc., 12280 7th St. North, Largo, FL 34643: Free information ❖ Replica car kits. 813-539-0218.

MAZDA

Design Energy Inc., 414 N. Salsipuedes, Santa Barbara, CA 93103: Information $5 ❖ Body conversion kits. 805-965-5115.

AUTOMOTIVE PARTS & ACCESSORIES   45

MG

Classic Auto Replicar, P.O. Box 10, Miami, FL 33354: Free brochure ❖ Replica car kits. 800-328-5671.

PORSCHE

Beck Development, 1531 W. 13th St., Upland, CA 91786: Free information ❖ Reproduction car kits. 909-981-3840.

Classic Auto Replicar, P.O. Box 10, Miami, FL 33354: Free brochure ❖ Replica car kits. 800-328-5671.

Vintage Speedsters, 12112 Centralia Rd., Hawaiian Gardens, CA 90716: Information $5 ❖ Replica car kits. 310-402-4334.

SEBRING MX

Classic Roadsters, 1617 Main Ave., Fargo, ND 58103: Free brochure ❖ Easy-to-assemble kit. 800-373-9000.

SPECIALTY CARS

Classic Auto Replicar, P.O. Box 10, Miami, FL 33354: Free brochure ❖ Replica car kits. 800-328-5671.

D & R Replicars Inc., 525 Haycock Run Rd., Kintnersville, PA 18930: Catalog $5 ❖ Conversion body kits. 610-847-2188.

Euro-Works, 3771 Eileen Rd., Dayton, OH 45429: Information $5 ❖ Sports car kit. 513-293-6834.

Exotic Automotive Designs, 1460 S. Vineyard, Ontario, CA 91761: Information $5 with long SASE ❖ Coupe and convertible body and accessory packages. 909-923-6727.

Exotic Illusions, Rear 347 Main St., Dickson City, PA 18519: Information $5 ❖ Replica kits. 717-383-1206.

I.F.G. Cars, 15740 El Prado Rd., Chino, CA 91710: Information $3 with long SASE ❖ Sports car kits. 909-597-4110.

Legendary Motorworks, 4 Arch St., Canonsburg, PA 15312: Free brochure ❖ Replica classic American sports cars. 800-858-0436; 412-745-7785 (in PA).

Lucas Group International, P.O. Box 14052 NE Plaza, Sarasota, FL 34278: Catalog $5 ❖ Exotic kit cars. 813-365-0678.

Mirror Image Motorworks, 616 Wagon Wheel, Round Rock, TX 78681: Information $5 ❖ Sports car kit. 512-218-8290.

PISA Corporation, P.O. Box 15088, Phoenix, AZ 85060: Free information ❖ Conversion car kits for the Fiero chassis. 602-376-1550.

Spartan Motorcar Company, 1655 S. Rancho Santa Fe Rd., San Marcos, CA 92069: Free information ❖ Sports car conversion kit for Nissan 300ZX. 619-744-3565.

Warlock Designs, 15740 El Prado Rd., Unit B, Chino, CA 91710: Free information ❖ Phantom VT car kit. 909-597-3621.

Westfield Components Inc., 17 Knight St., Watertown, CT 06795: Free information ❖ Sports car kits. 203-274-1935.

TOYOTA

Aeroform, 6300 St. John Ave., Kansas City, MO 64123: Information $5 ❖ Reproduction car kits. 800-345-2376.

VOLKSWAGEN

Archway Import Auto Parts Inc., 1900 Telegraph Rd., St. Louis, MO 63125: Catalog $3.95 ❖ Parts for Volkswagen-based kit cars. 314-638-7700.

Innovations in Fiberglass, P.O. Box 55301, Phoenix, AZ 85078: Brochure $4 ❖ Conversion car kits. 602-377-0104.

WILLYS

Antique & Collectible Autos Inc., 35 Dole St., Buffalo, NY 14210: Brochure $1 ❖ Replica car kits. 800-245-1310.

Replica & Conversion Parts & Accessories

CB Performance Parts, 1715 N. Farmersville, Farmersville, CA 93223: Catalog $5 ❖ Kit car accessories and high-tech parts. 800-274-8337; 209-733-8222 (in CA).

Heidt's, 1345 N. Old Rand Rd., Wauconda, FL 60084: Free catalog ❖ Front suspension kits. 800-841-8188; 708-487-0150 (in IL).

Hi-Tech Motorsports, 2204 W. Southern Ave., Tempe, AZ 85282: Free catalog ❖ Cobra accessories. 602-431-9400.

Moto-Lita Inc., 503 Corporate Square, 1500 NW 62nd St., Fort Lauderdale, FL 33309: Free brochure ❖ Parts and steering wheels for most custom and kit cars. 305-776-2748.

Speedway Motors, P.O. Box 81906, Lincoln, NE 68501: Catalog $5 ❖ Kit car parts and accessories. 402-474-4411.

Tilton Engineering, 25 Easy St., Box 1787, Buelton, CA 93427: Free information ❖ Kit car parts. 805-688-2353.

Rubber Parts & Weatherstripping

A & M Soffseal Inc., 104 May Dr., Harrison, OH 45030: Catalog $3 (request list of retail sources) ❖ Weatherstripping and rubber detail parts for 1955 and later General Motors cars and 1962 to 1974 Chrysler Performance A, B, and E bodies. 800-426-0902.

Dennis Carpenter Reproductions, P.O. Box 26398, Charlotte, NC 28221: Catalog $3 (specify year) ❖ Rubber parts for 1932 to 1964 Fords, 1958 to 1966 Thunderbirds, and 1960 to 1965 Falcons. 219-335-2425.

John's Corvette Cars, 23954 Kean St., Dearborn, MI 48124: Catalog $2 ❖ Corvette parts and weatherstripping for 1956 to 1995 Corvettes. 800-521-4774.

Kari Rubber Manufacturing, 133 Lolita St., El Segundo, CA 90245: Catalog $5 ❖ Reproduction rubber extrusions. 310-322-1993.

Metro Moulded Parts Inc., 11610 Jay St., P.O. Box 33130, Minneapolis, MN 55433: Catalog $3 ❖ Rubber reproduction parts for most American and foreign cars and trucks, from 1929 to 1970. 800-878-2237.

Lynn H. Steele Rubber Products, 1601 Hwy. 150 East, Denver, NC 28037: Catalog $2 (specify car) ❖ Reproduction rubber parts for Cadillac, Packard, Chrysler, Chevrolet, Buick, Oldsmobile, and Pontiac cars and Chevrolet trucks. 800-544-8665; 704-483-9343 (in NC).

Seat & Body Covers

A-Cover, Mark Savran, 965 W. River St., Milford, CT 06460: Free information ❖ Instant car storage garage with double zipper front and solid back panel. 800-426-8004.

Anything Car Covers Ltd., 11431 Santa Monica, West Los Angeles, CA 90025: Free information ❖ Car covers for small, medium, and large cars. Also for most vans and trucks. 800-445-4048.

Auto Stand Fine Motoring Gifts & Accessories, 505 S. Beverly Dr., Beverly Hills, CA 90212: Free information ❖ Ready-fit and custom car covers with cable and lock options. 800-334-4196.

Beverly Hills Motoring Accessories, 200 S. Robertson Blvd., Beverly Hills, CA 90211: Free catalog ❖ Car covers. 800-FOR-BHMA; 310-657-4800 (in CA).

Boulevard Motoring Accessories, 7033 Topanga Canyon Blvd., Canoga Park, CA 91303: Catalog $3 ❖ Sheepskin seat covers, car covers, and automotive accessories. 800-325-0022; 818-883-9696 (in CA).

Canvas Shoppe Inc., 3198½ S. Dye Rd., Flint, MI 48507: Free catalog ❖ Lightweight water-resistant car covers. 800-345-3670.

Car Cover Pros, 1624 Wilshire Blvd., Santa Monica, CA 90403: Free brochure ❖ Car covers. 800-221-9872.

CarCovers USA, 1015 Galey Ave., Building 1208, Los Angeles, CA 90024: Free information ❖ Car covers. 800-872-6837.

Classic Motoring Accessories, 146 W. Pomona Ave., Monrovia, CA 91016: Catalog $3 ❖ Car covers. 800-327-3045.

Cover-Up Enterprises, 1444 Manor Ln., Blue Bell, PA 19422: Free information ❖ Car covers for all cars, trucks, vans, classics, and limousines. 800-268-3757.

Fleetfoot Industries, 2680 Blake St., Denver, CO 80205: Catalog $3.50 (refundable) ❖ Front end covers for cars and trucks. 800-503-2727.

46 ❖ AUTOMOTIVE PARTS & ACCESSORIES ❖

Bill Hirsch, 396 Littleton Ave., Newark, NJ 07103: Free information ❖ Car covers and convertible tops. 800-828-2061; 201-642-2404 (in NJ).

Jean Seat International, P.O. Box 7798, Hollywood, FL 33021: Free information ❖ Seat covers. 800-881-0509.

Kanter Auto Parts, 76 Monroe St., Boonton, NJ 07005: Free catalog ❖ Fitted seat cover and upholstery kits for most American cars, from 1932 to 1980. 201-334-9575.

Mac Neil Automotive Products Ltd., 2435 Wisconsin St., Downers Grove, IL 60515: Free information ❖ Seat covers and floor mats. 800-441-6287.

McCullough's Automotive Products, 15532 Computer Ln., Huntington Beach, CA 92649: Free information ❖ Car covers, convertible tops, carpets, and upholstery sets. 800-395-9624; 714-897-9768 (in CA).

Multisheep, 646 S. Hauser Blvd., Los Angeles, CA 90036: Free information ❖ Sheepskin seat covers for most cars. 800-532-1222.

New England Auto Accessories Inc., 2984 E. Main St., Waterbury, CT 06705: Catalog $3 ❖ Car and sheepskin seat covers and accessories. 800-732-2761; 203-573-1504 (in CT).

Quality Sheepskin, 5643 Sale Ave., Woodland Hills, CA 91367: Free brochure ❖ Sheepskin seat covers, floor mats, and car covers. 800-852-4293.

Superior Seat Covers, 2954 NW 72nd Ave., Miami, FL 33122: Free information ❖ Easy-to-install seat covers. 800-2-COVERS.

J.C. Whitney & Company, 1917-19 Archer Ave., P.O. Box 8410, Chicago, IL 60680: Free catalog ❖ Car covers for American and imported models. 312-431-6102.

Seats

Keiper-Recaro Inc., 905 W. Maple Rd., Clawson, MI 48017: Free information ❖ Orthopaedically designed car seats. 800-873-2276.

PAR Seating Specialists, 310 Main St., New Rochelle, NY 10802: Free catalog ❖ Office chairs and automotive seats. 800-367-7270.

ProAm, The Seat Warehouse, 6125 Richmond, Houston, TX 77057: Free catalog ❖ Car seats. 800-847-5712.

Relaxo-Back Inc., P.O. Box 48580, Fort Worth, TX 76148: Free information ❖ Form-fitting auxiliary seat that can be used to relieve lower back pain. 800-527-5496.

Security Systems (Manufacturers)

Alpine Electronics of America, 19145 Gramercy Pl., Torrance, CA 90505: Free information ❖ Automotive security systems. 213-326-8000.

Audiovox, 185 Oser Ave., Hauppage, NY 11788: Free information ❖ Automotive security systems. 516-233-3300.

Auto Page, 1815 W. 205th St., Ste. 101, Torrance, CA 90501: Free information ❖ Automotive security systems. 800-423-6687.

Fultron, P.O. Box 177, Memphis, TN 38101: Free information ❖ Automotive security systems. 901-525-5711.

Kenwood, P.O. Box 22745, Long Beach, CA 90801: Free information ❖ Automotive security systems. 800-536-9663.

Radio Shack, Division Tandy Corporation, One Tandy Center, Fort Worth, TX 76102: Free information ❖ Automotive security systems. 817-390-3011.

Sansui USA, 210 Clay Ave. West, P.O. Box 625, Lyndhurst, NJ 07071: Free information ❖ Automotive security systems. 201-460-9710.

Spyder Lock, 17800 S. Main St., Ste. 402, Gardena, CA 90248: Free brochure ❖ Anti-theft tire boot.

Wolo Manufacturing Corporation, 1 Saxwood St., Deer Park, NY 11729: Free list of retail sources ❖ Electronically-operated security/alarm system with a key-lock. 800-991-9656.

Security Systems (Retailers)

Spectre Security Systems, 843 Dumont Pl., #22, Rochester Hills, MI 48307: Free information ❖ Home and automotive security systems. 810-652-8117.

Steering Wheels

Bighorn Sheepskin Company, 4810 Hwy. 90 East, San Antonio, TX 78219: Free informnation ❖ Sheepskin steering wheel covers. 800-992-1650.

Moto-Lita Inc., 503 Corporate Square, 1500 NW 62nd St., Fort Lauderdale, FL 33309: Free brochure ❖ Steering wheels for most American, European, Japanese, custom and kit cars, and sport trucks. 305-776-2748.

Stereo Equipment (Manufacturers)

Aiwa America Inc., 800 Corporate Dr., Mahwah, NJ 07430: Free information ❖ Stereo receivers. 800-289-2492.

Alpine Electronics of America, 19145 Gramercy Pl., Torrance, CA 90501: Free information ❖ Sound systems. 213-326-8000.

Audiovox, 185 Oser Ave., Hauppage, NY 11788: Free information ❖ Stereo receivers. 516-233-3300.

Blaupunkt, 2800 S. 25th Ave., Broadview, IL 60153: Free information ❖ Stereo receivers. 708-865-5200.

Clarion Corporation of America, 661 W. Redondo Beach Blvd., Gardena, CA 90247: Free information ❖ Sound systems. 800-487-9007.

Denon America, 222 New Rd., Parsippany, NJ 07054: Free information ❖ Stereo receivers. 201-575-7810.

Fujitsu America, 2801 Telecom Pkwy., Richardson, TX 75082: Free information ❖ Stereo receivers. 800-955-9926.

Harmon/Kardon, 80 Crossways Park West, Woodbury, NY 11797: Free information ❖ Audio and stereo in-dash receivers and cassette tuners, amplifiers, and equipment. 800-422-8027.

Hitachi Sales Corporation, Customer Service, 675 Old Peachtree Rd., Suwanee, GA 30174: Free information ❖ Stereo receivers. 800-241-6558.

Jensen, 25 Tri-State International, Office Center, Lincolnshire, IL 60069: Free information ❖ Stereo receivers. 800-323-0707.

JVC, 41 Slater Dr., Elmwood Park, NJ 07407: Free information ❖ Stereo receivers. 201-794-3900.

Kenwood, P.O. Box 22745, Long Beach, CA 90801: Free information ❖ Audio and stereo sound systems. 800-536-9663.

LKB Enterprises, 1014 S. 2nd St., Elkhart, IN 46516: Free information ❖ Custom sound systems for classic cars and trucks. 800-552-1005.

Marantz America Inc., 440 Medinah Rd., Roselle, IL 60172: Free information ❖ Stereo receivers. 708-307-3100.

Mitsubishi Electronics, 5665 Plaza Dr., Cypress, CA 90630: Free information ❖ Stereo receivers. 800-843-2515.

Panasonic, Panasonic Way, Secaucus, NJ 07094: Free information ❖ Stereo receivers. 201-348-7000.

Pioneer New Media Technologies, 2265 E. 220th St., Long Beach, CA 90810: Free information ❖ Stereo receivers. 800-444-OPTI.

Proton Corporation, 13855 Struikman Rd., Cerritos, CA 90703: Free information ❖ Stereo and cassette receivers that play the sound from television shows. 310-404-2222.

Radio Shack, Division Tandy Corporation, One Tandy Center, Fort Worth, TX 76102: Free information ❖ Stereo receivers. 817-390-3011.

Sansui Electronics, 1290 Wall St. West, Lyndhurst, NJ 07071: Free information ❖ Audio and stereo sound systems and removable cassette receivers. 201-460-9710.

Sanyo, 21350 Lassen St., Chatsworth, CA 91311: Free information ❖ Stereo receivers. 818-998-7322.

Sharp Electronics, Sharp Plaza, Mahwah, NJ 07430: Free information ❖ Stereo receivers. 800-BE-SHARP.

AUTOMOTIVE PARTS & ACCESSORIES

Sherwood, 14830 Alondra Blvd., La Mirada, CA 90638: Free information ❖ Stereo receivers. 800-962-3203.

Sony Consumer Products, 1 Sony Dr., Park Ridge, NJ 07656: Free information with long SASE ❖ Stereo receivers. 201-930-1000.

Technics, One Panasonic Way, Secaucus, NJ 07094: Free information ❖ Stereo receivers. 201-348-7000.

Toshiba, 82 Totowa Rd., Wayne, NJ 07470: Free information ❖ Stereo receivers. 201-628-8000.

Yamaha, P.O. Box 6660, Buena Park, CA 90620: Free information ❖ Audio and stereo receivers. 800-492-6242.

Stereo Equipment (Retailers)

Crutchfield, 1 Crutchfield Park, Charlottesville, VA 22906: Free catalog ❖ Stereo equipment. 800-955-9009.

Crystal Sonics, 1638 S. Central Ave., Glendale, CA 91204: Catalog $2 ❖ Stereo equipment. 800-545-7310; 818-240-7310 (in CA).

Custom Autosound, 808 W. Vermont Ave., Anaheim, CA 92805: Free catalog ❖ Custom radios for classic cars and trucks with no modifications to original dash opening. 800-888-8637.

Haven Industries, 2950 Lake Emma Rd., Lake Mary, FL 32746: Free information ❖ Computers, cellular telephones, audio and video equipment, and electronic accessories. 800-231-0031.

S.B.H. Enterprises, 1678 53rd St., Brooklyn, NY 11204: Free information ❖ Radar detectors and car stereo systems. 800-451-5851; 718-438-1027 (in NY).

Tires

Antique Automotive Accessories, 889 S. Rainbow Blvd., Las Vegas, NV 89128: Free information ❖ Radial tires for classic cars. 800-742-6777.

Classic Tires of America Inc., 435 Rear Newberry Rd., Middletown, PA 17057: Free information ❖ Tires. 800-347-4251.

Coker Tires, 1317 Chestnut St., Chattanooga, TN 37402: Free catalog ❖ Original tires. 800-251-6336; 615-265-6368 (in TN).

Euro-Tire Inc., 500 Rt. 46, Fairfield, NJ 07004: Free catalog ❖ European tires, light alloy wheels, and shock absorbers. 800-631-0080; 201-575-0080 (in NJ).

Exotic Tires International, P.O. Box 88564, Atlanta, GA 30356: Free information ❖ Tires. 800-729-0367.

Kelsey Tire Inc., Box 564, Camdenton, MO 65020: Free information ❖ Tires and tubes for vintage automobiles. 800-325-0091.

Lucas Automotive, 2850 Temple Ave., Long Beach, CA 90806: Free catalog ❖ Antique and classic tires. 800-952-4333.

Snyder's Antique Auto Parts, 12925 Woodworth Rd., New Springfield, OH 44443: Catalog $1 ❖ Tires. 216-519-5313.

Teletire, 17622 Armstrong Ave., Irvine, CA 92714: Free catalog ❖ Performance-rated steel-belted and other tires. 800-835-8473; 714-250-9141 (in CA).

Ken Thorpe, P.O. Box 230244, Portland, OR 97233: Free information ❖ Tires. 503-590-8550.

Tire Rack, 771 W. Chippewa Ave., South Bend, IN 46614: Brochure $3 (specify car) ❖ Tires and wheels for most domestic and imported cars. 800-428-8355; 219-287-2316 (in IN).

Universal Tire Company, 987 Stony Battery Rd., Lancaster, PA 17601: Free list of retail sources ❖ Antique and classic car tires and wheel hardware. 800-233-3827.

Vintage Tire, 25700 Solan Rd., Bedford Heights, OH 44146: Free information ❖ Tires. 800-225-8473.

Wallace W. Wade Wholesale Tires, 4303 Irving Blvd., Dallas, TX 75247: Free information ❖ Antique and classic automobile tires. 800-666-TYRE; 214-688-0091 (in TX).

Willies Antique Tires, 5257 W. Diversey Ave., Chicago, IL 60639: Free price list ❖ Tires for antique cars. 312-622-4037.

Tools

A & I Supply, 405 Radio City Dr., North Pekin, IL 61554: Free information ❖ Electric and air-operated tools. Also special-purpose tools, welders, and compressors. 309-353-3002.

Daytona Manufacturing, 1821 Holsonback Dr., Daytona Beach, FL 32117: Free information ❖ Welding equipment. 800-331-9353.

Eastwood Company, 580 Lancaster Ave., Box 3014, Malvern, PA 19355: Free catalog ❖ Welding tools, rust removers, sand blasting equipment, body repair tools, pin striping equipment, and buffing supplies. 800-345-1178.

Griot's Garage, 3500-A 20th St. East, Tacoma, WA 98424: Free catalog ❖ Automotive tools, storage cabinets, workbenches, and diagnostic equipment. 800-345-5789.

HTP America Inc., 261 Woodwork Ln., Palatine, IL 60067: Free information ❖ Welding equipment. 800-USA-WELD.

RhinoRamps, 99 S. Cameron St., Harrisburg, PA 17101: Free information ❖ Easy-to-use ramps. 800-400-6642.

Tip Tools & Equipment, P.O. Box 649, Canfield, OH 44406: Free catalog ❖ Automotive power tools. 800-321-9260.

Trailers & Recreational Vehicles

Atwood Mobile Products, 4750 Hiawatha Dr., Rockford, IL 61103: Free information ❖ Trailers, appliances, engineered components, and systems for recreational vehicles and boats. 815-877-5700.

Camper's Choice, 502 4th St. NW, P.O. Box 1546, Red Bay, AL 35582: Free catalog ❖ Trailer accessories. 800-833-6713; 205-356-2810 (in AL).

Casita Travel Trailers, 3030 S. McKinney, Rice, TX 75155: Free brochure ❖ All-fiberglass self-contained trailers. 800-442-9986.

Chinook Motorhomes, 1100 E. Lincoln Ave., Yakima, WA 98901: Free list of retail sources ❖ Motorhomes. 800-552-8886.

Coachmen Recreational Vehicle Company, P.O. Box 30, Middlebury, IN 46540: Free information ❖ Fifth wheels and travel trailers.

Correct Craft, 6100 S. Orange Ave., Orlando, FL 32809: Free information ❖ Boat trailers. 800-346-2092; 407-855-4141 (in FL).

Fleetwood Enterprises Inc., P.O. Box 92919, Milwaukee, WI 53202: Free list of retail sources ❖ Mini-vans and recreational vehicles. 800-444-4905.

Glen-L Trailers, 9152 Rosecrans, Box 1804, Bellflower, CA 90706: Catalog $1 ❖ Plans and kits for campers and travel trailers. 310-630-6258.

Grove Boat-Lift, P.O. Box 8095, Fresno, CA 93727: Free information ❖ Easy-to-use boat lift for cars. 800-447-5115; 209-251-5115 (in CA).

Hi-Lo Trailer Company, 145 Elm St., Butler, OH 44822: Free information ❖ Folding travel trailers. 800-321-6402; 419-883-3000 (in OH).

Holiday Rambler Corporation, P.O. Box 465, Wakarusa, IN 46573: Free information ❖ Motor homes. 219-862-7211.

Intraser Inc., 3580 Wilshire Blvd., Los Angeles, CA 90010: Free information ❖ New and pre-owned motorcycles, ATVs, snowmobiles, trailers, personal water vehicles, and small boats. 213-365-6030.

Lazy B Trailer Sales Inc., 6040 State Rt. 45, Bristoville, OH 44402: Free information ❖ Automotive trailers. 800-424-5110; 216-889-2353 (in OH).

MO Trailers, P.O. Box 486, Goshen, IN 46527: Free information ❖ Canoe trailers. 219-533-0824.

MSI Structures Inc., 2405 Cassopolis St., Elkhart, IN 46514: Free information ❖ Concession, car, and display trailers. 800-348-8541.

47

Omnifac Corporation, 1700 W. Whipp Rd., Dayton, OH 45440: Free information ❖ Battery and AC monitors and polarity indicators, bilge pump monitors, and electronic digital clocks for recreational vehicles and on-board boat electrical systems. 513-434-8400.

Pierce Sales, Rt. 1, Box 3A, Henrietta, TX 76365: Catalog $1 ❖ Cargo carriers, runabouts, horse and stock trailers, and truck beds. 817-538-5646.

Play-Mor Trailers Inc., P.O. Box 128, Hwy. 63 South, Westphalia, MO 65085: Free information ❖ Multi-purpose recreational vehicles. 314-455-2322.

Richlund Sales, 75695 Hwy. 1053, Kentwood, LA 70444: Free information ❖ Icemaker, central vacuum system, trash compactor, rear vision camera, electric heat equipment, combination washer-dryer, and other recreational vehicle appliances. 504-229-4922.

S & H Trailer Manufacturing Company, 800 Industrial Dr., Madill, OK 73446: Free information ❖ Recreational vehicles and horse, cargo, utility, and carryall trailers with optional features. 405-795-5577.

Scamp Eveland's Inc., Box 2, Backus, MN 56435: Free brochure ❖ Trailers. 800-346-4962; 800-432-3749 (in MN).

Sunnybrook RV Inc., 11756 C.R. 14, Middlebury, IN 46540: Free information ❖ Recreational vehicles. 219-825-5250.

Teton Homes, P.O. Box 2349, Mills, WY 82644: Free information ❖ Fifth wheel motorhomes. 307-235-1525.

Trailer World, P.O. Box 1687, Bowling Green, KY 42102: Free catalog ❖ Enclosed and open car trailers, vendor trailers, and parts. 502-843-4587.

Trailers of New England, Rt. 20, Palmer, MA 01069: Free information ❖ Wells Cargo and open car trailers. 800-628-9982; 413-289-1211 (in MA).

Trailex, 60 Industrial Park Dr., P.O. Box 553, Canfield, OH 44406: Free brochure ❖ Boat trailers. 800-282-5042.

Veri-Lite Inc., 22540 Pine Creek Rd., P.O. Box 339, Elkhart, IN 46515: Free information ❖ Truck campers. 219-295-8313.

Wells Cargo Inc., P.O. Box 728-1178, Elkhart, IN 46514: Free information ❖ Concession, car, and display trailers. 800-348-7553.

Truck Parts

All Chevy Auto Parts, 4999 Vanden Rd., Vacaville, CA 95687: Free information ❖ Parts for Chevrolet cars and trucks, from 1955 to 1990. 707-437-5466.

Alley Auto Parts, Rt. 2, Box 551, Immokalee, FL 33934: Inventory list $4 ❖ Parts for cars and trucks, from 1948 to 1975. 813-657-3541.

American Classic Truck Parts Inc., P.O. Box 50286, Denton, TX 76206: Catalog $4 (specify year) ❖ GMC truck parts, from 1936 to 1959 and 1960 to 1972. 817-497-2456.

Arnold's Auto Parts, 1484 Crandall Rd., Tiverton, RI 02878: Free information ❖ Parts for American cars and trucks, from 1930 to 1970. 401-624-6936.

Auto Body Specialties Inc., Rt. 66, P.O. Box 455, Middlefield, CT 06455: Catalog $5 ❖ Ford, Chevrolet, and Dodge truck body parts, from 1949 to 1992. 203-346-4989.

B & T Truck Parts, P.O. Box 799, Siloam Springs, AR 72761: Catalog $3 ❖ Chevrolet and GMC truck parts, from 1960 to 1966. 501-524-5959.

Paul Barry, 6152 Cazadero Hwy., P.O. Box 364, Cazadero, CA 95421: Free information ❖ Parts for Willys Overland Jeeps and trucks. 707-632-5258.

Bartnik Sales & Service, 6524 Van Dyke, Cass City, MI 48726: Free information ❖ Parts for trucks and cars, from 1960 to 1970. 517-872-3541.

Daryl Bensinger, 2442 Main St., Narvon, PA 17555: Free information ❖ Parts for military jeeps and trucks. 215-788-6012.

Andy Bernbaum Auto Parts, 315 Franklin St., Newton, MA 02158: Catalog $4 ❖ Parts for Dodge and Plymouth trucks. 617-244-1118.

Brothers Truck Parts, 5670 Schaefer Ave., Unit G, Chino, CA 91708: Catalog $4 ❖ Chevrolet and GMC truck parts, from 1947 to 1972. 800-977-2767.

C & P Chevy Parts, Box 348, Kulpsville, PA 19443: Catalog $3 ❖ Restoration supplies for 1955 to 1959 Chevrolet trucks. 800-235-2475.

Carolina Classics, 624 E. Geer St., Durham, NC 27701: Catalog $3 ❖ Ford truck parts, from 1948 to 1966. 919-682-4211.

Dennis Carpenter Reproductions, P.O. Box 26398, Charlotte, NC 28221: Catalog $3 (specify year) ❖ Parts for Ford pickups. 219-335-2425.

Jim Carter Antique Truck Parts, 1500 E. Alton, Independence, MO 64055: Catalog $2.50 ❖ Chevrolet and GMC truck parts, from 1934 to 1972. 800-336-1913.

Chev's of the 40's, 2027 B St., Washougal, WA 98671: Catalog $3.75 ❖ Parts for Chevrolet trucks, from 1937 to 1954. 800-999-2438.

Chevy Duty Pickup Parts, 4319 NW Gateway, Kansas City, MO 64150: Catalog $3 ❖ Restoration supplies for 1947 to 1972 Chevy and GMC pickups. 816-741-8029.

Chevyland, 3667 Recycle Rd., Rancho Cordova, CA 95742: Catalog $4 ❖ Chevrolet truck parts and accessories, from 1967 to 1972. 800-624-6490; 800-624-8756 (in CA).

Cheyenne Pick Up Parts, Box 959, Noble, OK 73068: Catalog $4 ❖ Chevrolet pickup truck parts, from 1960 to 1987. 405-364-3334.

Classic Tube, 80 Rotech Dr., Lancaster, NY 14086: Catalog $1 ❖ Brake, fuel, and transmission lines for collector cars and trucks. 800-TUBES-1; 716-759-1800 (in NY).

Cliff's Classic Chevrolet Parts Company, 619 SE 202nd, P.O. Box 16739, Portland, OR 97216: Catalog $4 ❖ Used, new, and reproduction parts for 1955 to 1959 Chevrolet trucks. 503-667-4329.

Concours Parts & Accessories, 3563 Numancia St., P.O. Box 1210, Santa Ynez, CA 93460: Catalog $4 ❖ Parts for 1948 to 1966 Ford trucks. 805-688-7795.

Dearborn Classics, P.O. Box 1248, Sunset Beach, CA 90742: Catalog $3 ❖ Ford Ranchero parts and accessories. 714-372-3175.

E & J Used Auto & Truck Parts, 315 31st Ave., P.O. Box 6007, Rock Island, IL 61204: Free information ❖ Parts for most American and foreign cars and trucks, from 1940 to 1987. 800-728-7686; 309-788-7686 (in IL).

Eaton Detroit Spring, 1555 Michigan, Detroit, MI 48216: Free information ❖ Springs, U-bolts, shackles, and parts for most American cars and trucks. 313-963-3839.

Fiberglass & Wood Company, Rt. 3, Box 810, Nashville, GA 31639: Catalog $4 (specify year) ❖ Chevrolet and GMC truck parts, from 1934 to 1984. 912-686-3838.

Gilbert's Early Chevy Pickup Parts, 470 RD 1 North, P.O. Box 1316, Chino Valley, AZ 86323: Catalog $2 (specify year) ❖ Chevrolet and GMC pickup parts, from 1947 to 1966. 602-636-5337.

Golden State Pickup Parts, P.O. Box 1019, Santa Ynez, CA 93460: Catalog $8.95 (specify year) ❖ Chevy and GMC truck parts, from 1947 to 1954, 1955 to 1966, 1967 to 1972, and 1973 to 1987. 805-564-2020.

Harmon's Inc., P.O. Box 6, Hwy. 27 North, Geneva, IN 46740: Free catalog ❖ Chevrolet truck restoration parts, from 1947 to 1980. 219-368-7221.

Heavy Chevy Truck Parts, P.O. Box 650, Siloam Springs, AR 72761: Catalog $2 ❖ Parts for 1948 to 1959 GMC and Chevrolet trucks. 501-524-9575.

Bruce Horkey Cabinetry, Rt. 4, Box 188, Windom, MN 56101: Catalog $2 ❖ Wood and other parts for 1934 to 1992 Chevrolet, 1939 to 1985 Dodge, and 1928 to 1992 Ford pickups. 507-831-5625.

Joblot Automotive Inc., 98-11 211th St., Queens Village, NY 11429: Catalog $2 ❖ Parts for 1928 to 1948 Ford cars and trucks. 800-221-0172; 718-468-8585 (in NY).

AUTOMOTIVE PARTS & ACCESSORIES

Dale King Obsolete Parts Inc., P.O. Box A, Courthouse Square, Liberty, KY 42539: Free information ❖ NOS and reproduction Ford truck parts. 606-787-5031.

Lakeview Vintage Ford Parts, 1410 E. Genesee, Skaneateles, NY 13152: Free information ❖ Reproduction parts for 1928 to 1960 Ford pickups. 315-685-7414.

M.A.T.S. Auto Parts, 701 Straugh Rd., Rio Linda, CA 95673: Free information ❖ Parts for most pickups, from 1948 to 1985. 916-991-3033.

Midland Automotive Products, Rt. 1, Box 27, Midland City, AL 36350: Free information ❖ Reproduction and new Ford truck products. 205-983-1212.

Obsolete Chevrolet Parts Company, P.O. Box 68, Nashville, GA 31639: Catalog $3 (specify year) ❖ Reproduction Chevrolet truck parts, from 1929 to 1959 and 1960 to 1972. 912-686-7230.

Obsolete Ford Parts Company, P.O. Box 68, Nashville, GA 31639: Catalog $3 (specify year) ❖ Ford pickup parts for 1948 to 1956 and 1957 to 1972. 912-686-5812.

Ole Chevy Store, 2509 S. Cannon Blvd., Kannapolis, NC 28083: Free list ❖ Parts for 1947 to 1972 Chevrolet trucks. 704-938-2923.

Performance Corner, 150 Engineers Rd., Hauppauge, NY 11788: Catalog $3 ❖ High performance automotive parts and truck accessories.

Pioneer Classic Auto Inc., 2111 W. Deer Valley Rd., Phoenix, AZ 85027: Catalog $4 (specify year) ❖ New and used parts for 1947 to 1972 Chevrolet pickups. 602-993-5999.

Roberts Motor Parts, 17 Prospect St., West Newbury, MA 01985: Catalog $4 ❖ Chevrolet and GMC truck parts. 508-363-5407.

Sherman & Associates Inc., 28460 Groesbeck, Roseville, MI 48066: Catalog $5 ❖ Reproduction parts and panels for classic car and truck restorations. 810-774-8297.

O.B. Smith Chevy Parts, P.O. Box 11703, Lexington, KY 40577: Catalog $3 ❖ Parts for 1947 to 1972 Chevrolet trucks. 606-254-1957.

Special Interest Autos of St. Louis Inc., P.O. Box 944, St. Charles, MO 63302: Catalog $4.50 ❖ NOS and reproduction parts for 1941 to 1964 Studebaker pickups. 800-433-1257.

The Truck Shop, 104 W. Marion Ave., P.O. Box 5035, Nashville, GA 31639: Catalog $5 ❖ Parts for 1927 to 1972 Chevrolet and GMC trucks. 912-686-3833.

Truck Shop Parts, 424 W. Chapman Ave., Orange, CA 92666: Catalog $3 (specify years) ❖ Parts for Chevrolet trucks, from 1947 to 1954, 1955 to 1966, and 1967 to 1972. 714-771-7871.

Vander Haag's Inc., Box 550, Sanborn, IA 51248: Free information ❖ Truck parts. 712-729-3268.

Vintage Ford & Chevrolet Parts of AZ, 3427 E. McDowell, Phoenix, AZ 85008: Ford catalog $2; Free Chevrolet price sheet ❖ Parts for 1948 to 1966 Fords and 1947 to 1972 Chevrolet trucks. 602-275-7990.

Upholstery, Carpets & Tops

ABC Auto Upholstery & Top Company, 1634 Church St., Philadelphia, PA 19124: Free information ❖ Upholstery kits for 1954 to 1959 Fords. 215-289-0555.

Auto Custom Carpets Inc., P.O. Box 1167, Anniston, AL 36202: Free information ❖ Original-style carpets for General Motors, Chrysler, and Ford cars and trucks. 800-633-2358.

G.W. Bartlett Company, 1912 Granville Ave., Muncie, IN 47303: Free catalog ❖ Interior restoration parts. 800-338-8034.

Carpet King, P.O. Box 16303, Columbus, OH 43216: Free information ❖ Reproduction molded carpets. 800-826-4279.

Denning Automotive, P.O. Box 28, Springfield, NJ 07081: Catalog $5 ❖ Convertible top and carpet sets. 201-379-2335.

Hampton Coach, 6 Chestnut St., P.O. Box 6, Amesbury, MA 01913: Free information ❖ Upholstery and top kits. 508-388-8047.

Bill Hirsch, 396 Littleton Ave., Newark, NJ 07103: Free information ❖ Car covers and convertible tops. 800-828-2061; 201-642-2404 (in NJ).

Kanter Auto Products, 76 Monroe St., Boonton, NJ 07005: Free catalog ❖ Interior products. 201-334-9575.

LeBaron Bonney Company, 8 Chestnut St., Amesbury, MA 01913: Catalog $1 ❖ Upholstery materials for antique, classic, and special interest cars. 508-388-3811.

Legendary Auto Interiors Ltd., 121 W. Shore Blvd., Newark, NJ 14513: Catalog $4 ❖ Reproduction seat upholstery, door panels, and interior and exterior trim for 1957 to 1980 Chrysler, Dodge, and Plymouth cars. 800-363-8804.

Midland Automotive Products, Rt. 1, Box 27, Midland City, AL 36350: Free information ❖ Chevrolet carpeting, truck mats, landau tops, and convertible top pads. 205-983-1212.

McCullough's Automotive Products, 15532 Computer Ln., Huntington Beach, CA 92649: Free information ❖ Car covers, convertible tops, carpets, and upholstery sets. 800-395-9624; 714-897-9768 (in CA).

Original Auto Interiors, 7869 Trumble Rd., Columbus, MI 48063: Free information (specify year) ❖ Upholstery fabrics and original molded carpet sets. 810-727-2486.

Smart Buy, 4027 Rucker Ave., #C803, Everett, WA 98201: Free information ❖ Carpets and convertible tops.

SMS Auto Fabrics, 2325 SE 10th Ave., Portland, OR 97214: Free information ❖ Auto upholstery fabrics. 503-234-1175.

Winross Restorations Upholstery Shop, 2060 O'Neil Rd., Macedon, NY 14502: Free information ❖ Upholstery for antique automobiles. 315-986-7368.

World Upholstery & Trim, P.O. Box 4857, Thousand Oaks, CA 91359: Free information (specify model and year) ❖ Head liners, seat upholstery, and carpets for European cars. 800-222-9577.

Wheels & Hubcaps

Agape Auto, 2825 Selzer, Evansville, IN 47712: Free information ❖ Wheel covers from 1949 to 1980 and fender skirts from 1935 to 1972. 812-423-7332.

Dayton Wheel Products, 1147 S. Broadway St., Dayton, OH 45408: Free information ❖ Wire wheels. 800-862-6000; 513-461-1707 (in OH).

Early Wheel Company, P.O. Box 1438, Santa Ynez, CA 93460: Free information ❖ Hubcaps and chromed or ready-to-paint wheels. 805-688-1187.

Freedom Design Wheels, 4750 Eisenhower Ave., Alexandria, VA 22034: Brochure $1 ❖ Special-designed wheels. 800-296-1792; 703-823-5606 (in VA).

House of Hubcaps, 20034 Pacific Hwy. South, Seattle, WA 98198: Free information ❖ New and used hubcaps. 800-825-9715; 206-824-5040 (in WA).

Hubcap Mike, 26242 Dimension, Ste. 150, Lake Forest, CA 92630: Free information with long SASE (specify items wanted) ❖ Hubcaps and wheelcovers. 714-597-8120.

Motorsport Specialties Inc., 435A W. 4th St., Quarryville, PA 17566: Free information ❖ Wheels. 800-621-8408.

Tire Rack, 771 W. Chippewa Ave., South Bend, IN 46614: Brochure $3 (specify car) ❖ Tires and wheels for most domestic and imported cars. 800-428-8355; 219-287-2316 (in IN).

Wheel Repair Service Inc., 317 Southbridge St., Auburn, MA 01501: Free information ❖ Hubcaps and wheel covers for most cars, street rods, and replicas. Also wire spoke, alloy, and steel disc wheels. 508-832-4949.

Wheel Vintiques, 5468 E. Lamona, Fresno, CA 93727: Free information ❖ Wheels. 209-251-6957.

Wheelcovers - Robinson's Auto Sales, 200 New York Ave., New Castle, IN 47362: Free information ❖ Hubcaps, wheel covers, hub cap sets, and NOS and used parts. 317-529-7603.

AWARDS & TROPHIES

Award Company of America, P.O. Box 2029, Tuscaloosa, AL 35403: Free brochure ❖ Plaques, acrylic awards, recognition certificates, badges, and awards. 800-633-2021.

Bale Company, 222 Public St., Box 6400, Providence, RI 02940: Free catalog ❖ Pins, class and club school rings, academic and scholastic medals, athletic medals, novelties and charms, and other awards. 800-822-5350.

W. & E. Baum Bronze Tablet Corporation, 200 60th St., Brooklyn, NY 11220: Free catalog ❖ Donor walls, trees of life, yahrzeit tablets, plaques and awards, and other Judaic tablets. 800-922-7377; 718-439-3311 (in NY).

Captain's Emporium, 7855 Gross Point Rd., Smokie, IL 60077: Free information ❖ Trophies and gifts. 708-675-5411.

Chicago Trophy & Awards Company, 3255 N. Milwaukee Ave., Chicago, IL 60618: Free catalog ❖ Trophies and plaques. 800-621-8826; 312-685-8200 (in IL).

Classic Medallics, 2-15 Borden Ave., Long Island City, NY 11101: Free information ❖ Letters, ribbons, cups, medals, emblems, pins, plaques, and other awards. 800-221-1348; 718-392-5410 (in NY).

Cornette Ribbon & Trophy Company, 850 Dunbar Ave., Oldsmar, FL 34677: Free catalog ❖ Ribbons, awards, and trophies. 800-869-0234; 813-855-5520 (in FL).

Crown Trophy, 1 Odell Plaza, Yonkers, NY 10701: Free information ❖ Letters, ribbons, cups, emblems, pins, plaques, and other awards. 800-227-1557; 914-963-0005 (in NY).

Dern Trophy Corporation, 267 Broad St., Westerville, OH 43081: Free catalog ❖ Trophies and plaques. 800-848-3988.

Dinn Brothers Inc., 68 Winter St., P.O. Box 111, Holyoke, MA 01040: Free catalog ❖ Trophies, plaques, ribbons, silverware, medals, and desk sets. 800-628-9657.

Emblem & Badge Inc., P.O. Box 6226, Providence, RI 02940: Free information ❖ Trophies, trophy cases, plaques, medals, pins, and ribbons. 800-875-5444; 401-331-5444 (in RI).

Hodges Badge Company Inc., 1170 E. Main, Portsmouth, RI 02871: Free catalog ❖ Brass medals with gold, silver and copper/bronze finish. Also award certificates. 800-556-2440.

Music Stand, 1 Music Stand Plaza, 66 Benning St., West Lebanon, OH 03784: Free catalog ❖ Trophies, plaques, and certificates. 800-717-7010.

Successories Inc., 919 Springer Dr., Lombard, IL 60148: Free catalog ❖ Awards for promotion of individual and team excellence. 800-535-2773.

Sun State Trophy Supply, 1090 Rainer Dr., Altamonte Springs, FL 32714: Free catalog ❖ Trophies and plaques. 800-327-2020; 800-432-1058 (in FL).

Trophy Supply, 1 Odell Plaza, Yonkers, NY 10701: Free information ❖ Trophies, plaques, medals, club awards, around-the-neck medals, pins, and badges. 800-227-1557; 914-237-9500 (in NY).

Trophyland USA Inc., 7001 W. 20th Ave., Hialeah, FL 33014: Free catalog ❖ Awards for incentive programs, athletic events, and other competitions. 800-432-3528; 305-823-4830 (in FL).

Volk Corporation, 23936 Industrial Park Dr., Farmington Hills, MI 48024: Free information ❖ Award ribbons. 800-521-6799; 810-477-6700 (in MI).

Whippoorwill Crafts, North Market Building, 6 Fanueil Hall Marketplace, Boston, MA 02109: Free information ❖ Imaginative crafts customized for awards. 800-487-5937; 617-248-0671 (in MA).

AWNINGS & PATIO COVERS

Inter Trade Inc., 3175 Fujita St., Torrance, CA 90505: Free information ❖ Indoor-operated patio covers and awnings for protection from heat, sun, cold, rain, and noise. 310-515-7177.

International E-Z UP Inc., 1601 Iowa Ave., Riverside, CA 92507: Free information ❖ Easy-to-set-up spring-loaded center pole shelter/canopy. 909-781-0843.

JIL Industries Inc., 184 Charles St., Malden, MA 02148: Free brochure ❖ Retractable deck and patio awnings. 800-876-2340.

Pease Industries Inc., P.O. Box 14-8001, Fairfield, OH 45014: Information $1 ❖ Retractable-arm awning with optional wind sensor for automatic closing and sun sensor that opens the awning. 800-543-1180.

Somfy/Sunbrella, P.O. Box 3900, Peoria, IL 61614: Free information ❖ Retractable awnings. 800-441-5118.

The Sunsetter Awning, JIL Industries, 184 Charles St., Malden, MA 02148: Free information ❖ Retractable awnings for decks and patios. 800-876-8060.

BABY CARE

After the Stork, 1501 12th St. NW, Albuquerque, NM 87104: Free catalog ❖ Natural fiber clothing, records, tapes, books, and toys for children, from birth to age 7. 800-333-5437.

Audio-Therapy Innovations Inc., P.O. Box 550, Colorado Springs, CO 80901: Free brochure ❖ Music therapy tapes to help babies sleep. 800-537-7748.

Baby Basics, Box 224, East Rockaway, NY 11518: Free catalog ❖ Cotton wear and diapers, health essentials, items for nursing mothers, and travel accessories. 800-778-3887.

Baby Biz Products Inc., P.O. Box 370182, Denver, CO 80237: Free list of retail sources ❖ Diaper covers, diapers, and combination diaper bag/purse. 303-368-8436.

Baby Bunz & Company, P.O. Box 113, Lynden, WA 98264: Catalog $1 ❖ Diapering and layette supplies. 800-676-4559.

Babyworks, 11725 NW West Rd. #2, Portland, OR 97229: Free catalog ❖ Diapers, diaper covers and bags, blankets, pads, and other supplies. 800-422-2910.

Biobottoms, P.O. Box 6009, Petaluma, CA 04953: Free catalog ❖ Cotton diapers and wool covers; cotton clothing for infants and children. 800-766-1254; 707-778-7152 (in CA).

Caring Products International Inc., 200 1st Ave. West, Ste. 200, Seattle, WA 98119: Free information ❖ Toilet training products. 800-333-5379; 206-282-6040 (in WA).

COMBI, 1471 N. Wood Dale Rd., Wood Dale, IL 60191: Free list of retail sources ❖ Lightweight and easy-to-operate strollers. 800-992-6624.

Diaperaps, 9760 Owensmouth Ave., Chatsworth, CA 91311: Free brochure ❖ Cotton outer layer and polyfoam-protected diaper covers. 800-477-3424.

Double Trouble, P.O. Box 464, Midway City, CA 92655: Free catalog ❖ Baby care items, birth announcements, party accessories, and other items for twins. 800-966-TWIN.

Hand in Hand, Catalogue Center, 891 Main St., Oxford, ME 04270: Free catalog ❖ Books, toys and games, car seat time occupiers, furniture, bathroom accessories, car seats, housewares and hardware, health aids, and other products that help nurture, teach, and protect children. 800-872-9745.

Mother-ease, 6391 Walmore Rd., Niagara Falls, NY 14304: Free information ❖ Fitted cotton diapers and accessories. 800-416-1475.

Mother's Wear Diapers, P.O. Box 114, Northampton, MA 01061: Free brochure ❖ Contour-shaped diapers and covers. 800-633-0303; 413-586-3488 (in MA).

The Natural Baby Company Inc., 816 Silvia St., Trenton, NJ 08628: Free information ❖ Diapering and medical products, wood toys, cotton clothes, and alternative products. 800-388-BABY.

The Natural Bedroom, Jantz Design, 175 N. Main St., Sebastopol, CA 95472: Free information ❖ Natural fiber baby's bedding. 800-365-6563.

BABY CARE (NURSING SUPPLIES)

The Nurtured Baby, Rt. 1, Box 112-C, Grimesland, NC 27837: Free catalog ❖ Cloth diapers and accessories. 800-462-2293.

One Step Ahead, P.O. 517, Lake Bluff, IL 60044: Free catalog ❖ Baby items for use when traveling, feeding, at bath time, and for security. 800-950-5120.

J.C. Penney Company Inc., Catalog Division, Atlanta, GA 30390: Free information ❖ Nursery furniture, bedding, strollers, car seats, and other baby care items. 800-222-6161.

Peg Perego U.S.A. Inc., 3625 Independence Dr., Fort Wayne, IN 46818: Free list of retail sources ❖ Baby strollers with easy-to-handle maneuverability. Also nursery furniture, high chairs, and walk 'n play walkers. 219-482-8191.

Perfectly Safe, 7245 Whipple Ave. NW, North Canton, OH 44720: Free catalog ❖ Safety items for children age 3 to 6. 216-494-2323.

Pettersen Infant Products, 189 Dadson Row, Flin Flon, Manitoba, Canada R8A 0C8: Free information ❖ Baby carrier with 4 positions. 800-665-3957.

Pleasant Company, P.O. Box 620190, Middleton, WI 53562: Free catalog ❖ Bassinets, diaper bags, bunting, and knits for newborns and infants. 800-845-0005.

Racing Strollers Inc., P.O. Box 2189, Yakima, WA 98902: Free brochure ❖ Baby joggers for exercise fun. 800-241-1848.

Walter Rau & Company, P.O. Box 407, Wyoming, RI 02898: Free catalog ❖ Natural skin care products. 800-499-7037.

Right Start Catalog, Right Start Plaza, 5334 Sterling Center Dr., Westlake Village, CA 91361: Catalog $2 ❖ Car seats, clothing, educational toys, and shopping carts that convert into strollers. 800-548-8531.

Rubens & Marble Inc., P.O. Box 14900, Chicago, IL 60614: Free brochure with long SASE ❖ Stretch stay-up diapers with elastic ends. 312-348-6200.

Snugglebundle, 444 A N. Main St., #165, East Longmeadow, MA 01028: Free catalog ❖ Diapers and other layette and baby care supplies. Includes organic cotton products. 413-525-1972.

Tot Tenders Inc., 9030 Kenamar Dr., Ste. 309, San Diego, CA 92121: Free information ❖ Baby carrier for twins. 800-634-6870.

Tough Traveler, 1012 State St., Schenectady, NY 12307: Free catalog ❖ Baby carriers. 800-468-6844.

Twincerely Yours, 748 Lake Ave., Clermont, FL 34711: Free catalog with long SASE ❖ Gifts, novelties, and T-shirts for twins and their families. 904-394-5493.

BABY CARE (NURSING SUPPLIES)

Bosom Buddies, P.O. Box 6138, Kingston, NY 12402: Free catalog ❖ Maternity bras and clothing for fashion-conscious women. Also accessories. 914-338-2038.

Bravado Designs, 69 Broadview Ave., Ste. 405, Toronto, Ontario, Canada M4M 2E6: Free information ❖ Maternity and nursing bra. 800-590-7802.

C.D.M., P.O. Box 635, San Clemente, CA 92674: Free catalog ❖ Dresses, tops, pants, skirts, shorts, nighties, breast pumps and pads, milk coolers, books, and other supplies. 800-637-9246; 714-361-1089 (in CA).

Decent Exposures, P.O. Box 27206, Seattle, WA 98125: Free information ❖ Pregnancy and nursing bras. 800-505-4949; 206-364-4540 (in WA).

Lady Grace Stores, P.O. Box 128, Malden, MA 02148: Free catalog ❖ Intimate apparel for everyday wear, nursing and maternity, and post-breast surgery. 800-922-0504.

Maturna, P.O. Box 3500, Milford, CT 06460: Free information ❖ Adjustable maternity bra for use during and after pregnancy. 800-944-4006.

Motherwear, P.O. Box 927, Northampton, MA 01061: Free catalog ❖ Easy-access clothing for nursing mothers. 800-950-2500.

The Zaks Company, 12905 Alderleaf Dr., Germantown, MD 20874: Free information ❖ Nursing tops, jogging sets, and jumpers. 301-972-5936.

BADGES & BUTTONS

AABCO Printing, 628 W. Mitchell St., Milwaukee, WI 53204: Free information ❖ Custom buttons. 414-643-1894.

B & K Buttons, 16 S. Detroit St., Xenia, OH 45385: Free information ❖ Custom buttons. 800-223-4392.

Badge-A-Minit Ltd., Box 800, LaSalle, IL 61301: Free catalog ❖ Badge-making machine, supplies, and beginner's starter kit for making badges and pin-back buttons. 800-223-4103.

H & R Badge & Stamp Company, 2585 Mock Rd., Columbus, OH 43219: Free catalog ❖ In-stock and custom badges and rubber stamps. 614-471-3735.

KA-MO Engravers, P.O. Box 30337, Albuquerque, NM 87190: Free catalog ❖ Badges for square and round dancers. 800-352-5266; 505-883-4963 (in NM).

J.R. Kush & Company, 7623 Hesperia St., Reseda, CA 91335: Free information ❖ Handcrafted belt buckles for round and square dancers. 818-344-9671.

Lifton Studio Inc., 121 S. 6th St., Stillwater, MN 55082: Catalog $5 ❖ Authentic reproduction of Old West and nickel-plated badges from America's history. 612-439-7208.

Micro Plastics, Box 847, Rifle, CO 81650: Free information ❖ Custom club badges. 303-625-1718.

Nasco, 901 Janesville Ave., Fort Atkinson, WI 53538: Free catalog ❖ Badge-making equipment and supplies. 800-558-9595.

N.G. Slater Corporation, 220 W. 19th St., New York, NY 10011: Free catalog ❖ Equipment for making buttons. 212-924-3133.

BADMINTON

Buckeye Sports Supply, John's Sporting Goods, 2655 Harrison Ave. SW, Canton, OH 44706: Free information ❖ Nets, posts, presses, racquets, sets, shuttlecocks, and strings. 800-533-8691.

Cannon Sports Inc., P.O. Box 797, Greenland, NH 03840: Free list of retail sources ❖ Nets, posts, racquets, strings, shuttlecocks, and sets. 800-362-3146.

Century Sports Inc., Lakewood Industrial Park, 1995 Rutgers University Blvd., Box 2035, Lakewood, NJ 08701: Free information ❖ Nets, posts, shuttlecocks, and racquets. 800-526-7548; 908-905-4422 (in NJ).

Douglas Sport Nets & Equipment Company, 3441 S. 11th Ave., P.O. Box 393, Eldridge, IA 52748: Free information ❖ Nets, posts, and sets. 800-553-8907; 319-285-4162 (in IA).

Fischer Tennis, 2412 Logan Rd., Owings Mills, MD 21117: Free information ❖ Racquets and shuttlecocks. 410-356-0196.

Franklin Sports Industries Inc., 17 Campanelli Pkwy., P.O. Box 508, Stoughton, MA 02072: Free information ❖ Nets, posts, racquets, strings, shuttlecocks, and sets. 800-426-7700.

General Sportcraft Company, 140 Woodbine Rd., Bergenfield, NJ 07621: Free information ❖ Nets, posts, sets, racquets, strings, and shuttlecocks. 201-384-4242.

Indian Industries Inc., P.O. Box 889, Evansville, IN 47706: Free catalog ❖ Nets, posts, racquets, strings, shuttlecocks, and sets. 800-457-3373; 812-467-1200 (in IN).

Dick Martin Sports Inc., 181 E. Union Ave., P.O. Box 7381, East Rutherford, NJ 07073: Free information ❖ Nets, posts, racquets, strings, and sets. 800-221-1993; 201-438-5255 (in NJ).

Olympia Sports, 745 State Circle, Ann Arbor, MI 48106: Free information ❖ Shuttlecocks, racquets, and sets. 800-521-2832.

BALLOONS

Park & Sun Inc., 2150 17th St. South, Englewood, CO 80110: Free information ❖ Nets, posts, and sets. 800-776-7275.

Porter Athletic Equipment Company, 2500 S. 25th Ave., Broadview, IL 60153: Free information ❖ Nets, posts, racquets, sets, and shuttlecocks. 708-338-2000.

Rackets International, 24572 La Cienega St., Laguna Hills, CA 92653: Free information ❖ Badminton rackets. 800-726-8913.

Spalding Sports Worldwide, 425 Meadow St., P.O. Box 901, Chicopee, MA 01201: Free list of retail sources ❖ Nets, posts, racquets, strings, shuttlecocks, cases, covers, grips, presses, and sets. 800-225-6601.

Sport Fun Inc., 4621 Sperry St., Los Angeles, CA 90039: Free information ❖ Nets, posts, racquets, strings, shuttlecocks, and sets. 800-423-2597; 818-240-6700 (in CA).

Sportime, Customer Service, 1 Sportime Way, Atlanta, GA 30340: Free information ❖ Nets, posts, shuttlecocks, racquets, and sets. 800-444-5700; 770-449-5700 (in GA).

Yonex Corporation, 350 Challenger St., Torrance, CA 90503: Free list of retail sources ❖ Racquets, strings, and shuttlecocks. 800-44-YONEX.

BALLOONS

Anagram International Inc., 7700 Anagram Dr., Minneapolis, MN 55344: Free list of retail sources ❖ Balloons with birthday messages and one-of-a-kind designs. 800-554-4711; 612-949-5600 (in MN).

Balloon Printing Company, P.O. Box 150, Rankin, PA 15104: Free information ❖ Imprinted balloons. 800-533-5221.

Balloons For You, 2152 Chennault, Carrollton, TX 75006: Free information ❖ Balloons. 800-636-4887.

Clown City, 6 Salem Market Pl., CT 06420: Catalog $2 ❖ Balloons and clown supplies. 860-889-1000.

Clown Heaven, 4792 Old State Rd. 37 South, Martinsville, IN 46152: Catalog $3 ❖ Balloons, make-up, puppets, wigs, ministry and gospel items, novelties, magic, clown props, and books. 317-342-6888.

Dewey's Good News Balloons, 1202 Wildwood, Deer Park, TX 77536: Free catalog ❖ Gospel clown supplies and balloon books. 713-479-2759.

The Entertainers Supermarket, 21 Carol Pl., Staten Island, NY 10303: Free brochure ❖ Supplies for balloon sculptors, clowns, magicians, jugglers, face painters, stilt walkers, and other entertainers. 718-494-6232.

Flowers & Balloons Inc., 325 Cleveland Rd., Bogart, GA 30622: Free catalog ❖ Balloons and gifts. 800-241-2094; 706-548-1588 (in GA).

Gayla Balloons, P.O. Box 920800, Houston, TX 77292: Free catalog ❖ Balloons for the balloon artist. 800-327-9513.

La Rock's Fun & Magic Outlet, 3847 Rosehaven Dr., Charlotte, NC 28205: Catalog $3 ❖ Clown and balloon how-to books, balloons, balloon sculpture kits, juggling supplies, and magic equipment. 704-563-9300.

Mecca Magic Inc., 49 Dodd St., Bloomfield, NJ 07003: Catalog $10 ❖ Balloons, theatrical make-up, clown equipment, magic, costumes and wigs, puppets, ventriloquism equipment, and juggling supplies. 201-429-7597.

More Than Balloons Inc., 2409 Ravendale Ct., Kissimmee, FL 34758: Free information ❖ Regular balloons, balloons for making sculptures, how-to books, balloon accessories, and magic. 800-BALUNES.

Morris Costumes, 3108 Monroe Rd., Charlotte, NC 28205: Catalog $20 ❖ Balloons, costumes, clown props, masks, joke items, magic tricks, special effects, novelties, and books. 704-332-3304.

T. Myers Magic Inc., 1509 Parker Bend, Austin, TX 78734: Free catalog ❖ Balloons and balloon-sculpting supplies. 800-648-6221.

Novelties Unlimited, 410 W. 21st St., Norfolk, VA 23517: Catalog $5 ❖ Balloons, magic tricks, party decorations, make-up, clown supplies, props, and gags. 804-622-0344.

Ed Rohr Company, 3323 Darlington Rd., Toledo, OH 43606: Free information ❖ Compact self-contained balloon inflator in an ultra-lightweight shoulder pack.

Sparkle's Entertainment Express, Jan Lovell, 152 N. Water St., Gallatin, TN 37066: Product list $1 ❖ Make-up, costumes and clown shoes, balloons, juggling and magic equipment, puppets, books, and other supplies. 615-452-9755.

Suburban Balloon & Helium, 31535 Vine St., Willowick, OH 44094: Free information ❖ Remote and stationary helium or nitrogen filling stations with hose, connectors, and crimping tool. 800-572-0100.

Wyco Props, 8344 Yecker Ave., Kansas City, KS 66109: Free information ❖ Battery-operated balloon pump. Comes with a charger and car lighter adapter. 913-788-9338.

BANKS

American Classics Unlimited, Frank Groll-Karen Groll, P.O. Box 192, Oak Lawn, IL 60454: Free information ❖ Promotional model cars and banks, other automobilia, and kits. 708-424-9223.

Domino Ent. Co., P.O. Box 847, Wheatley Heights, NY 11798: Free information ❖ Reproduction Wizard of OZ banks. 516-467-5043.

G & J Toys & Clocks, 28780 Front St., Temecula, CA 92590: Free information with long SASE ❖ ERTL coin banks. 714-676-5508.

Gateway Toys, Ron & Nancy Russell, 2290 Riverbluff, Arnold, MO 63010: Free price list with long SASE ❖ ERTL banks. 314-282-2827.

Homestead Collectibles, P.O. Box 173, Mill Hall, PA 17751: Information $1 ❖ Die-cast metal, Ertle, and airplane banks. 717-726-3597.

JPE Enterprises, 11319 W. Jayhawk, Houston, TX 77044: Free information ❖ Banks. 713-456-8181.

Midwest Toys, P.O. Box 56, Kimmswick, MO 63053: Free list with long SASE ❖ Banks. 314-464-1685.

RP & Company, P.O. Box 3030, Boscawen, NH 03303: Catalog $2 ❖ Country-style oak banks with original United States brass and bronzed mail doors. 603-796-2200.

Toys Plus, 2353 N. Wilson Way, Stockton, CA 95205: Free price list with long SASE and two 1st class stamps ❖ Automobile, airplane, and oil company banks. 209-944-9977.

Valley Crafts & Collectibles, 3620 Shelby Way, Sevierville, TN 37862: Free information with long SASE and two 1st class stamps ❖ Die-cast banks and replicas. 615-428-6881.

BARBECUE GRILLS

B-WEST Outdoor Specialties, 2425 N. Huachuca, Tucson, AZ 85745: Free information ❖ Outdoor cookware and BBQ accessories. 800-293-7855; 520-628-1990 (in AZ).

Bradley's, P.O. Box 1300, Columbus, GA 31993: Free catalog ❖ Gas and charcoal barbecue grills. 800-252-8248.

Char-Broil, Grill Lovers Catalog, 1037 Front Ave., Columbus, GA 31902: Free catalog ❖ Grills, outdoor furniture, barbecue cookers, and seasonings, spices, and condiments. 800-241-8981.

The Compleat Company Inc., 35 Donaldson Center, P.O. Box 6161, Greenville, SC 29606: Free information ❖ Electric and gas-operated slow pit-style outdoor grills. 800-889-9237; 803-235-0238 (in SC).

Exclusively Bar-B-Q, P.O. Box 3048, Concord, NH 28025: Free catalog ❖ Everything for grilling and barbecuing. 800-948-1009.

Grill Parts Distributors, 6150 49th Street North, St. Petersburg, FL 33709: Free catalog ❖ Parts and accessories, smoking chips, cookbooks, and rotisserie kits. 800-447-4557; 800-282-4513 (in FL).

❖ BASEBALL & SOFTBALL ❖

Hart-Bake Charcoal Ovens, 7656 E. 46th St., Tulsa, OK 74145: Free brochure ❖ Multi-purpose outdoor charcoal ovens. 800-426-6836; 918-665-8220 (in OK).

Hasty-Bake, P.O. Box 471285, Tulsa, OK 74147: Free catalog ❖ Gourmet foods, charcoal ovens, and grill accessories. 800-426-6836.

Klose Bar-B-Que Pits, 2214-1/2 W. 34th St., Houston, TX 77018: Free catalog ❖ Adjustable grills with firebox. 800-487-7487.

Morrone Company, 465 Albert St., Macon, GA 31206: Free information ❖ Portable cooker with cast-iron gas burner. 800-826-8863.

Weber-Stephen Products, Customer Service Center, 250 S. Hicks Rd., Palatine, IL 60067: Free information ❖ Permanent-mounted gas barbecues with cooking chambers, side burners, and warmers. 800-446-1071.

BASEBALL & SOFTBALL

Clothing

Don Alleson Athletic, 2921 Brighton-Henrietta Town Line Rd., Rochester, NY 14623: Free information ❖ Uniforms. 800-641-0041; 716-272-0606 (in NY).

Alpha Shirt Company, 401 E. Hunting Park Ave., Philadelphia, PA 19124: Free information ❖ Caps, jackets, and shorts. 800-523-4585; 215-291-0300 (in PA).

Athletes Wear Company, 145 Market Ave., Winnipeg, Manitoba, Canada R3B 1C5: Free catalog ❖ Clothing for baseball players. 204-949-1885.

Austin Sportsgear, 621 Liberty St., Jackson, MI 49203: Free information ❖ Caps, pants, shorts, and uniforms. 800-999-7543; 517-784-1120 (in MI).

Betlin Manufacturing, 1445 Marion Rd., Columbus, OH 43207: Free information ❖ Uniforms and undershirts. 614-443-0248.

Bike Athletic Company, P.O. Box 666, Knoxville, TN 37901: Free information ❖ Uniforms and undershirts. 800-251-9230.

Bomark Sportswear, P.O. Box 2068, Belair, TX 77402: Free information ❖ Caps and uniforms. 800-231-3351.

Capco Sportswear Inc., 252 Beinoris Dr., Wood Dale, IL 60191: Free information ❖ Caps. 800-833-5856; 708-766-6000 (in IL).

Champion Products Inc., 475 Corporate Square Dr., Winston-Salem, NC 27105: Free information ❖ Uniforms, undershirts, and footwear.

DeLong, 733 Broad St., P.O. Box 189, Grinnell, IA 50112: Free information ❖ Uniforms, caps, and undershirts. 800-733-5664; 515-236-3106 (in IA).

Diamond Sports Company, P.O. Box 830, Los Alamitos, CA 90720: Free information ❖ Baseballs and softballs, bats, gloves and mitts, and bags for balls, bats, and uniforms. 800-366-2999; 310-598-9717 (in CA).

Empire Sporting Goods Manufacturing Company, 443 Broadway, New York, NY 10013: Free information ❖ Uniforms, undershirts, caps, and socks. 800-221-3455; 212-966-0880 (in NY).

Everitt Knitting Company, 234 W. Florida St., Milwaukee, WI 53204: Free information ❖ Ragwool and natural wool caps. 414-276-4647.

Fab Knit Manufacturing, Division Anderson Industries, 1415 N. 4th St., Waco, TX 76707: Free information ❖ Caps, uniforms, and undershirts. 800-333-4111; 817-752-2511 (in TX).

Georgia Tees Inc., 4200 McEver Industrial Dr., Box Tee, Achworth, GA 30101: Free information ❖ Caps. 800-553-0021; 404-974-0040 (in GA).

Jewel & Company Inc., 9601 Apollo Dr., Landover, MD 20705: Free information ❖ Caps and jackets. 800-638-8583; 301-925-6200 (in MD).

Majestic Athletic Wear, 636 Pen Argyl St., Pen Argyl, PA 18072: Free information ❖ Uniforms, caps, and undershirts. 800-955-8555; 215-863-6161 (in PA).

Manny's Baseball, 3000 SW 42nd Ave., Palm City, FL 34990: Catalog $2 ❖ Clothing for baseball players. 800-PRO-TEAM.

Markwort Sporting Goods, 4300 Forest Park Ave., St. Louis, MO 63108: Catalog $8 (request list of retail sources) ❖ Clothing and equipment. 800-669-6626; 314-652-3757 (in MO).

Matrix Group Ltd., 1536 S. Missouri Ave., Clearwater, FL 34616: Free information ❖ Caps. 800-370-9300.

Mitchell & Ness Nostalgia Company, 1229 Walnut St., Philadelphia, PA 19107: Free information ❖ Vintage major league team uniforms. 800-483-6377; 215-592-6512 (in PA).

Movin USA, 7411 W. Boston, Ste. 1, Chandler, AZ 85225: Free information ❖ Caps and shorts. 800-445-6684.

New South Athletic Company Inc., 301 E. Main, P.O. Box 604, Dallas, NC 28034: Free information ❖ Shoes, uniforms, caps, undershirts, and socks. 800-438-9934; 704-922-1557 (in NC).

J.C. Penney Company Inc., Catalog Division, Atlanta, GA 30390: Free information ❖ Atlanta, GA 30390: Free information ❖ Athletic clothing and accessories. 800-222-6161.

Puma USA Inc., 147 Centre St., Brockton, MA 02403: Free information with long SASE ❖ Shoes and other athletic clothing. 508-583-9100.

Saucony/Hyde, 13 Centennial Dr., Peabody, MA 01961: Free list of retail sources ❖ Shoes. 800-365-7282.

Sportsprint Inc., 252 S. Florisant Rd., St. Louis, MO 63135: Free information ❖ Uniforms, caps, and socks. 800-325-4858.

Venus Knitting Mills Inc., 140 Spring St., Murray Hill, NJ 07974: Free information ❖ Uniforms, caps, socks, and undershirts. 800-955-4200; 908-464-2400 (in NJ).

Wilson Sporting Goods, 8700 Bryn Mawr, Chicago, IL 60631: Free information ❖ Caps and socks. 800-443-0011.

Equipment

ATEC, 10 Greg St., Sparks, NV 89431: Free information ❖ Baseballs and softballs, field equipment, pitching machines, training aids, and bags for balls, bats, and uniforms. 800-755-5100; 702-352-2800 (in NV).

The Athletic Connection, 1901 Diplomat, Dallas, TX 75234: Free information ❖ Bat and ball bags, bats, baseballs and softballs, field equipment, protective gear, helmets, and pitching machines. 800-527-0871; 214-243-1446 (in TX).

Bolco Athletic Company, P.O. Box 489, Cooksville, TN 38501: Free information ❖ Bases, home plates, pitchers plates, and other field equipment. 800-423-4321; 615-526-2109 (in TN).

Cannon Sports, P.O. Box 797, Greenland, NH 03840: Free list of retail sources ❖ Softballs and baseballs, bats, field equipment, mitts and gloves, protective gear, and bags for bats, balls, and uniforms. 800-362-3146.

Continental Sports Supply, P.O. Box 1251, Englewood, CO 80150: Free information ❖ Bats. 303-934-5657.

Dalco Athletic, P.O. Box 550220, Dallas, TX 75355: Free information ❖ Baseballs and softballs, bats, batting gloves and helmets, catcher masks, chest protectors, and gloves and mitts. 800-288-3252; 214-494-1455 (in TX).

Douglas Sport Nets & Equipment, 3441 S. 11th Ave., P.O. Box 393, Eldridge, IA 52748: Free information ❖ Baseball equipment and supplies. 800-553-8907; 319-285-4162 (in IA).

Dudley Sports Company, 521 Meadow St., Chicopee, MA 01021: Free information ❖ Baseballs and softballs. 800-523-5387; 413-536-1200 (in MA).

Easton Sports Inc., 577 Airport Blvd., Burlingame, CA 94010: Free information ❖ Baseballs and softballs, bats, gloves and mitts. 800-347-3901; 415-347-4727 (in CA).

BASKETBALL

Flaghouse, 150 N. MacQuesten Pkwy., Mt. Vernon, NY 10550: Free catalog ❖ Baseball equipment. 800-793-7900.

Gared Sports Inc., 1107 Mullanphy St., St. Louis, MO 63106: Free information ❖ Baseball equipment. 800-325-2682.

Hillerich & Bradsby Company Inc., P.O. Box 35700, Louisville, KY 40232: Free list of retail sources ❖ Baseball and softball bats, gloves, and other equipment. 800-282-2287.

Jayfro Corporation Inc., Unified Sports Inc., 976 Hartford Tnpk., P.O. Box 400, Waterford, CT 06385: Free catalog ❖ Safety protectors, batting tees, mats, baseball and softball practice cages, batting cubicles, and backstops. 860-447-3001.

Markwort Sporting Goods, 4300 Forest Park Ave., St. Louis, MO 63108: Catalog $8 (request list of retail sources) ❖ Baseballs and softballs, bats, batting gloves and helmets, catcher masks, chest protectors, and gloves and mitts. 800-669-6626; 314-652-3757 (in MO).

Dick Martin Sports Inc., 181 E. Union Ave., P.O. Box 7381, East Rutherford, NJ 07073: Free information ❖ Bat bags, baseballs and softballs, gloves, and protective gear. 800-221-1993; 201-438-5255 (in NJ).

Rawlings Sporting Goods Company, P.O. Box 22000, St. Louis, MO 63126: Free information ❖ Baseballs, bats, mitts and gloves, protective gear, and bags for balls, bats, and uniforms. 314-349-3500.

Riddell Inc., 3670 N. Milwaukee Ave., Chicago, IL 60641: Free information ❖ Baseballs and softballs, gloves and mitts, and protective gear. 800-445-7344; 312-794-1994 (in IL).

Sportime, Customer Service, 1 Sporting Way, Atlanta, GA 30340: Free information ❖ Bats and bags for balls and bats, protective gear, and helmets. 800-444-5700; 770-449-5700 (in GA).

SSK Sports, SSK Corporation Japan, 21136 S. Wilmington Ave., Ste. 220, Long Beach, CA 90810: Free information ❖ Bats, gloves, and score books. 800-421-2674; 310-549-2762 (in CA).

Steele's Sports Company, 5223 W. 137th, Brook Park, OH 44142: Free information ❖ Softball and baseball equipment. 800-367-7114; 216-267-5300 (in OH).

Tennessee Sports Company, P.O. Box 310, 2102 N. Jackson St., Tullahoma, TN 37388: Free information ❖ Softball and baseball bats for youths and adults. 615-455-7765.

Wolvering Sports, 745 State Circle, Box 1941, Ann Arbor, MI 48106: Catalog $1 ❖ Baseball, basketball, field hockey, soccer, football, and other athletic and recreation equipment. 313-761-5691.

BASKETBALL

Clothing

Don Alleson Athletic, 2921 Brighton-Henrietta Town Line Rd., Rochester, NY 14623: Free information ❖ Uniforms and warm-up clothing. 800-641-0041; 716-272-0606 (in NY).

Athletes Wear Company, 145 Market Ave., Winnipeg, Manitoba, Canada R3B 1C5: Free catalog ❖ Clothing for basketball players. 204-949-1885.

Austin Sportsgear Inc., 621 Liberty St., Jackson, MI 49203: Free information ❖ Uniforms. 800-999-7543; 517-784-1120 (in MI).

AVIA Group International Inc., 9605 SW Nimbus Ave., Beaverton, OR 97005: Free information ❖ Shoes. 800-345-2842.

Betlin Manufacturing, 1445 Marion Rd., Columbus, OH 43207: Free information ❖ Uniforms, warm-up jackets, and pants. 614-443-0248.

Boast Inc., Box 10176, Riviera Beach, FL 33419: Free information ❖ Uniforms and warm-up clothing. 800-327-7666; 407-848-1096 (in FL).

Champion Products Inc., 475 Corporate Square Dr., Winston Salem, NC 27105: Free information ❖ Uniforms, warm-up jackets, pants, socks, and shoes.

Empire Sporting Goods Manufacturing Company, 443 Broadway, New York, NY 10013: Free information ❖ Uniforms, warm-up jackets, pants, socks, and wristbands. 800-221-3455; 212-966-0880 (in NY).

GeorGI-Sports, P.O. Box 1107, Lancaster, PA 17603: Free information ❖ Uniforms, warm-up jackets, pants, and socks. 800-338-2527; 717-291-8924 (in PA).

Letrell Sports, 3004 Industrial Pkwy. West, Knoxville, TN 37921: Free information ❖ Uniforms and warm-up clothing. 800-325-3975; 615-546-8070 (in TN).

Lotto Sports, 1900 Surveyor Blvd., Carrollton, TX 75006: Free information ❖ Shoes. 800-527-5126; 214-416-4003 (in TX).

Majestic Athletic Wear, 636 Pen Argyl St., Pen Argyl, PA 18072: Free information ❖ Uniforms and warm-up clothing. 800-955-8555; 215-863-6161 (in PA).

J.C. Penney Company Inc., Catalog Division, Atlanta, GA 30390: Free information ❖ Atlanta, GA 30390: Free information ❖ Athletic clothing and accessories. 800-222-6161.

Pony USA Inc., 2801 Red Dot Ln., Knoxville, TN 37914: Free information ❖ Shoes, socks, and sweat bands.

Puma USA Inc., 147 Centre St., Brockton, MA 02403: Free information with long SASE ❖ Warm-up jackets, pants, wristbands, shoes, and socks. 508-583-9100.

Purcells Activewear, 5733 San Leandro St., Oakland, CA 94621: Free information ❖ Uniforms and warm-up clothing. 800-641-6868; 510-536-7770 (in CA).

Shaffer Sportswear, 224 N. Washington, Neosho, MO 64850: Free information ❖ Uniforms and warm-up clothing. 417-451-9444.

Southland Athletic, P.O. Box 280, Terrell, TX 75160: Free list of retail sources ❖ Uniforms, warm-up jackets, and pants. 800-527-7637; 214-563-3321 (in TX).

Spalding Sports Worldwide, 425 Meadow St., P.O. Box 901, Chicopee, MA 01021: Free list of retail sources ❖ Uniforms, warm-up jackets, pants, wristbands, socks, shoes, and equipment. 800-225-6601.

Equipment

Alchester Mills Company Inc., 1160 Wright Ave., Camden, NJ 08103: Free information ❖ Pads and guards, supporters, and knee braces. 609-964-9700.

Amko Inc., P.O. Box 5809, Huntsville, AL 35814: Free information ❖ Basketballs. 800-289-2656; 205-851-7080 (in AL).

The Athletic Connection, 1901 Diplomat, Dallas, TX 75234: Free information ❖ Backboards, basketballs, and nets. 800-527-0871; 214-243-1446 (in TX).

Bike Athletic Company, P.O. Box 666, Knoxville, TN 37901: Free information ❖ Pads and guards, supporters, and knee braces. 800-251-9230.

Cannon Sports Inc., P.O. Box 797, Greenland, NH 03840: Free list of retail sources ❖ Basketballs, ball carriers, goals, nets, knee braces, pads and guards, supporters, and whistles. 800-223-0064.

Carron Net Company, 1623 17th St., P.O. Box 177, Two Rivers, WI 54241: Free information ❖ Portable and stationary backboards, ball carriers, goals and nets, and whistles. 800-558-7768; 414-793-2217 (in WI).

Cramer Products Inc., P.O. Box 1001, Gardner, KS 66030: Free information ❖ Knee braces, pads, and guards. 800-345-2231; 913-884-7511 (in KS).

Escalade Sports, P.O. Box 889, Evansville, IN 47706: Free catalog ❖ Backboards and nets. 800-457-3373; 812-467-1200 (in IN).

Flaghouse, 150 N. MacQuesten Pkwy., Mt. Vernon, NY 10550: Free catalog ❖ Basketball equipment. 800-793-7900.

BASKETS

Franklin Sports Industries Inc., 17 Campanelli Pkwy., P.O. Box 508, Stoughton, MA 02072: Free information ❖ Pads, guards, miscellaneous equipment, and basketballs. 800-426-7700.

Gared Sports Inc., 1107 Mullanphy St., St. Louis, MO 63106: Free information ❖ Basketball equipment. 800-325-2682.

Grid Inc., NDL Products, 4031 NE 12th Terrace, Oakland Park, FL 33334: Free information ❖ Supporters, knee braces, pads, and guards. 800-843-3021.

Holabird Sports Discounters, 9220 Pulaski Hwy., Baltimore, MD 21220: Free catalog ❖ Equipment and clothing for basketball, tennis, running and jogging, golf, exercising, and racquetball. 410-687-6400.

Huffy Sports, 2021 MacArthur Rd., Waukesha, WI 53188: Free information ❖ Portable and stationary backboards, goals and nets, whistles, and other equipment. 800-558-5234; 414-548-0440 (in WI).

Hutch Sports USA, 1835 Airport Exchange Blvd., Erlanger, KY 41018: Free information ❖ Backboards, basketballs, and nets. 800-727-4511; 606-282-9000 (in KY).

Indian Industries Inc., P.O. Box 889, Evansville, IN 47706: Free catalog ❖ Backboards, nets, and poles. 800-457-3373; 812-467-1200 (in IN).

Jayfro Corporation Inc., Unified Sports Inc., 976 Hartford Tnpk., P.O. Box 400, Waterford, CT 06385: Free catalog ❖ Backboards, post and portable standards, and goals. 860-447-3001.

M.W. Kasch Company, 5401 W. Donges Bay Rd., Mequon, WI 53092: Free information ❖ Basketballs, backboards, goals, nets, and basketball sets. 414-242-5000.

Porter Athletic Equipment Company, 2500 S. 25th Ave., Broadview, IL 60153: Free information ❖ Backboards, basketballs, goals, and nets. 708-338-2000.

Rawlings Sporting Goods Company, P.O. Box 22000, St. Louis, MO 63126: Free information ❖ Basketballs, nets, and score books. 314-349-3500.

Riddell Inc., 3670 N. Milwaukee Ave., Chicago, IL 60641: Free information ❖ Basketballs and nets. 800-445-7344; 312-794-1994 (in IL).

Spalding Sports Worldwide, 425 Meadow St., P.O. Box 901, Chicopee, MA 01021: Free list of retail sources ❖ Basketballs, other equipment, uniforms, warm-up jackets and pants, wristbands, socks, and shoes. 800-225-6601.

Sportline of Hilton Head Ltd., 816 Friendly Center Rd., Greensboro, NC 27408: Free information ❖ Basketballs. 800-438-6021.

Sportime, Customer Service, 1 Sporting Way, Atlanta, GA 30340: Free information ❖ Backboards, basketballs, and nets. 800-444-5700; 770-449-5700 (in GA).

TC Sports, 7251 Ford Hwy., Tecumseh, MI 49286: Free information ❖ Backboards and nets. 800-523-1498; 517-451-5221 (in MI).

Venus Knitting Mills Inc., 140 Spring St., Murray Hill, NJ 07974: Free information ❖ Basketballs, nets, and score books. 800-955-4200; 908-464-2400 (in NJ).

Wolvering Sports, 745 State Circle, Box 1941, Ann Arbor, MI 48106: Catalog $1 ❖ Baseball, basketball, field hockey, soccer, football, and other athletic and recreation equipment. 313-761-5691.

BASKETS

Abebros Company, 999 Criss Circle Dr., Elk Grove Village, IL 60007: Catalog $1 ❖ Wreaths, twig wreaths, seagrass items, and wall, hanging, mini, and other baskets. 708-593-6703.

Allen's Basketworks, P.O Box 82638, Portland, OR 97282: Catalog $2 ❖ Basket-making supplies. 503-238-6384.

Rhonda N. Anderson, 49 Ramsdell Rd., Gray, ME 04039: Free information ❖ Maine Abenaki sweetgrass baskets. 207-657-2218.

Karen & Darryl Arawjo, P.O. Box 477, Bushkill, PA 18324: Brochure $1 ❖ White oak Shaker, Nantucket, and Appalachian baskets. 717-588-6957.

Ashwood Basket Corporation, 375 Union St., Peterborough, NH 03458: Free catalog ❖ Handcrafted baskets. 800-463-6233.

Bamboo & Rattan Works Inc., 470 Oberlin Ave. South, Lakewood, NJ 08701: Free information ❖ Rattan, cords, chair cane, matting, and bamboo, flat, and round reeds. 800-4-BAMBOO.

Basket Beginnings, 25 W. Tioga St., Tunkhannock, PA 18657: Free price list ❖ Basket-making and fiber art supplies. 800-82-FIBER.

Basket Hollow, 1641 Etta Kable Dr., Beavercreek, OH 45432: Free brochure with long SASE ❖ Hand-woven round and flat reed baskets with an optional black walnut finish. 937-429-3937.

The Basket Works, P.O. Box 65062, Baltimore, MD 21228: Catalog $1 ❖ Basket-making supplies.

Basketville Inc., Main St., P.O. Box 710, Putney, VT 05364: Catalog $2 ❖ Ready-to-finish baskets. 802-387-5509.

Basquetrie, 810 Rangeline, Columbia, MO 65201: Catalog $3 ❖ Victorian picnic baskets and accessories, bed trays, and cameos and other keepsakes for bridesmaids. 800-342-7278.

Braid-Aid, 466 Washington St., Pembroke, MA 02359: Catalog $4 ❖ Braided rug kits and braiding accessories, wool by the pound or yard, and hooking, basket-making, shirret, spinning, and weaving supplies. 617-826-2560.

Cane & Basket Supply Company, 1283 S. Cochran, Los Angeles, CA 90019: Catalog $2 ❖ Fiber and genuine rush, Danish seat cord, raffia, rattan, sea grass, hoops and handles, other supplies, and flat, oval, and round reeds. 800-468-3966.

Caning Shop, 926 Gilman St., Berkeley, CA 94710: Catalog $1 (refundable) ❖ Supplies and how-to books for basket-making and chair-weaving. 800-544-3373.

Carib-America Inc., 10160 Fisher Ave., Tampa, FL 33619: Free brochure ❖ Baskets. 800-783-0812; 813-653-1012 (in FL).

Carolina Basketry, 2703 Hwy. 70 East, New Bern, NC 28560: Free information ❖ Basketry supplies. 919-637-6290.

Connecticut Cane & Reed Company, P.O. Box 762, Manchester, CT 06040: Catalog 50¢ ❖ Caning and basket-making supplies. 860-646-6586.

Country Basket Weaving, Atkinson's Country House, 2775 Riniel Rd., Lennon, MI 48449: Free catalog ❖ Basket-making supplies. 800-832-3071.

Country Seat, RD 2, Box 24A, Kempton, PA 19529: Price list with three 1st class stamps ❖ How-to books and basket-making and chair-caning supplies. 610-756-6124.

English Basketry Willows, RFD 1, Box 124A, South New Berlin, NY 13843: Brochure $1 ❖ Imported basket-making willows, tools, and books. 607-847-8264.

Family Heritage Baskets, 51 Mechanic St., Berlin Heights, OH 44814: Free information ❖ Handmade domestic decorative wood baskets. 800-877-7721.

Finger Lakes Basketry Supply, 2450 County House Rd., Penn Yan, NY 14527: Free catalog with two 1st class stamps ❖ Basket-making supplies and tools. 315-536-7521.

Frank's Cane & Rush Supply, 7252 Heil Ave., Huntington Beach, CA 92647: Free information ❖ Wood parts, tools, cane and rush, and other basket-making and seat-weaving supplies. 714-847-0707.

Jeffrey E. Gale, Basketmaker, RFD 1, Box 124A, South New Berlin, NY 13843: Brochure $1 with long SASE ❖ Handmade white ash baskets. 607-847-8264.

GH Productions, 521 E. Walnut St., Scottsville, KY 42164: Catalog $1 (refundable) ❖ Basket-making supplies. 800-447-7008.

Gundula's & Peerless Rattan & Reed, 624 S. Burnett Rd., Springfield, OH 45505: Catalog 50¢ ❖ Caning supplies. 513-323-7353.

Debra Paulson Johnson, P.O. Box 75, Chester, CT 06412: Brochure $1 with long SASE ❖ Handmade knitting, wool-drying, gathering, and other baskets.

Jonathan Kline Black Ash Baskets, 5066 Mott Evans Rd., Trumansburg, NY 14886: Brochure $2 ❖ Traditional handmade black ash baskets. 607-387-5718.

John E. McGuire Basketry Supplies, 398 S. Main St., Geneva, NY 14456: Free price list with two 1st class stamps ❖ Basket-making supplies and tools. 315-781-1251.

Michigan Cane Supply, 5348 N. Riverview Dr., Kalamazoo, MI 49004: List $1 ❖ Chair cane, rush, and basket-weaving supplies. 616-282-5461.

Nantucket Wholesaler, Box 171, Eastman Hill Rd., Sanbornton, NH 03269: Catalog $1 ❖ Basket-making supplies and kits. 603-286-8927.

Nasco, 901 Janesville Ave., Fort Atkinson, WI 53538: Free catalog ❖ Basket-making supplies. 800-558-9595.

New England Basket Company, P.O. Box 1335, North Falmouth, MA 02556: Catalog $3 ❖ Bamboo trays, picnic hampers, and rustic rattan, country-style, and willow baskets. 800-524-4484; 508-759-2000 (in MA).

Susi Nussbaum, Basketmaker, 5 Steele Crossing Rd., Bolton, CT 06043: Brochure $2 ❖ Handmade reproduction 19th-century baskets. 203-646-3876.

Alice Ogden, 48 Old Hillsboro Rd., Henniker, NH 032142: Free brochure with long SASE ❖ Black ash baskets. 603-428-7849.

Ozark Basketry Supply, P.O. Box 599, Fayetteville, AR 72702: Catalog $1 ❖ Books, basket-making kits, chair cane, dyes, hoops, and handles. 501-442-9292.

J. Page Basketry, 820 Albee Rd. West, Nokomis, FL 34275: Catalog $2 (refundable) ❖ Basket-making, wheat-weaving, and pine needle crafting supplies, and tools, books, dried and preserved flowers, and herbs. 813-485-6730.

Peacock Crate Factory, 1511 S. Jackson St., Jacksonville, TX 75766: Catalog $2 ❖ Ready-to-finish and use baskets. 800-666-5647.

H.H. Perkins Company, 10 S. Bradley Rd., Woodbridge, CT 06525: Free catalog ❖ Basket-making, seat-weaving, and macrame supplies. Also books and how-to instructions. 800-462-6660.

Plymouth Reed & Cane, 1200 W. Ann Arbor Rd., Plymouth, MI 48170: Brochure $1 ❖ Reed, cane, fiber rush, handles, hoops, kits, dyes, tools, books, and other basket-making and chair-caning materials. 313-455-2150.

Royalwood Ltd., 517 Woodville Rd., Mansfield, OH 44907: Catalog $1 ❖ Basket-weaving and chair-caning supplies. 419-526-1630.

Snapvent Company, 147 W. Baxter Ave., Knoxville, TN 37917: Free price list with long SASE ❖ Basket-making and chair-caning supplies. 615-523-6784.

Splintworks, P.O. Box 858, Cave Junction, OR 97523: Brochure $1 ❖ Hand-woven baskets. 503-592-2311.

V.I. Reed & Cane, Rt. 5, Box 632, Rogers, AR 72756: Free catalog ❖ Flat and round reeds, smoked reed, cane, hoops, handles, raffia, dyes, and basket-weaving kits. 800-852-0025.

Weaving Works, 4717 Brooklyn Ave. NE, Seattle, WA 98105: Catalog $4.50 ❖ Basket-making supplies, looms, spinning wheels, yarns and fibers, hand and machine-knitting supplies, dyes, and how-to books. 206-524-1221.

West Rindge Baskets Inc., 47 W. Main St., Rindge, NH 03461: Free brochure ❖ Hand-woven New England-style baskets. 603-899-2231.

Martha Wetherbee Basket Shop, 171 Eastman Hill Rd., Sanbornton, NH 03269: Catalog $3 ❖ Hand-woven and pounded brown ash Shaker basket reproductions. 603-286-8927.

Wood-Knot Crafts, 36 Chateau Dr., Monorville, NY 11949: Catalog $2 (refundable) ❖ Reproduction Shaker baskets.

Stephen Zeh, Basketmaker, P.O. Box 381, Temple, ME 04984: Catalog $2 ❖ Hand-split and woven traditional brown ash baskets in Native American, Shaker, and other styles. 207-778-2351.

BATHROOM FIXTURES & ACCESSORIES

The Adaptive Design Shop, 12847 P Pleasant Dr., Fairfax, VA 22033: Free brochure ❖ Toilet supports and combination bath and shower chairs for children and adults. 800-351-2327.

Alumax, P.O. Box 40, Magnolia, AR 71753: Free information ❖ Bathroom fixtures and shower enclosures. 800-643-1514.

American China, 3618 E. LaSalle St., Phoenix, AZ 85040: Free brochure ❖ China and marble drop-in and pedestal bathroom lavatories. 800-470-1005.

American Standard Inc., P.O. Box 18411, Kansas City, MO 04133: Free information ❖ Whirlpool tubs with molded headrest and grab bars, toilets, and other fixtures. 800-524-9797.

Antique Baths & Kitchens, 2220 Carlton Way, Santa Barbara, CA 93109: Catalog $2 ❖ Reproduction sinks, toilets, tank toilets, pedestal basins, marble vanity tops, faucets, medicine chests, and cast-iron tubs. 805-962-8598.

Antique Hardware Store, 1 Matthews Ct., Hilton Head Island, SC 29926: Catalog $3 ❖ Antique pedestal sinks, faucets, high-tank toilets, and cabinet hardware. 800-422-9982.

AquaGlass Corporation, P.O. Box 412, Industrial Park, Adamsville, TN 38310: Free information ❖ Whirlpool baths, combination steam showers, lavatories, wall surrounds, and shower floors. 800-238-3940; 901-632-0911 (in TN).

Automatic Steam Products, 43-20 34th St., Long Island City, NY 11101: Free information ❖ Equipment to convert shower stalls into steam rooms. 800-238-3535.

Baldwin Hardware Corporation, P.O. Box 15048, Reading, PA 19612: Bathroom accessories brochure 75¢, fixtures brochure $3, door hardware brochure 75¢, hardware brochure 75¢ ❖ Brass dead bolts and door hardware, bathroom accessories, and fixtures. 800-346-5128.

Bathroom Machineries, 495 Main St., P.O. Box 1020, Murphys, CA 95247: Catalog $3 ❖ Early American and Victorian-style antique and reproduction bathroom fixtures. 209-728-2031.

Baths from the Past, 83 E. Water St., Rockland, MA 02370: Catalog $5 ❖ Designer Victorian and traditional bathroom fixtures and plumbing accessories. 800-697-3871; 617-871-8530 (in MA).

Biolet Composting Toilet, Damonmill Square, Concord, MA 01742: Free list of retail sources ❖ Plumbing-free and self-contained biological toilet system. 800-5-BIOLET.

Bona Decorative Hardware, 3073 Madison Rd., Cincinnati, OH 45209: Price list $2 ❖ English and French-style bathroom fittings and accessories, cabinet and door hardware, and fireplace tools. 513-321-7877.

Brass Menagerie, 524 St. Louis St., New Orleans, LA 70130: Free information with long SASE (specify items wanted) ❖ Plumbing, bathroom fixtures, and hardware. 504-524-0921.

Briggs Industries, 4350 W. Cypress, Ste. 800, Tampa, FL 33607: Free information ❖ Acrylic one-piece tub-shower combination units and multi-jet whirlpool tubs. 813-878-0178.

Country Plumbing, 5042 7th St., Carpinteria, CA 93013: Free information ❖ Antique and new plumbing supplies. 805-684-8685.

Dimestore Cowboys, 614 2nd St. SW, Albuquerque, NM 87102: Catalog $7 ❖ Door sets, cabinet pulls, shutters, bathroom accessories, curtain rods and rings, and hardware. 505-244-1493.

Eljer Plumbingware, 17120 Dallas Pkwy., Ste. 205, Dallas, TX 75248: Free information ❖ Bathroom accessories in chrome and polished brass, frame-free shower doors, and designer tubs with multi jets. 800-435-5372.

❖ BATHROOM SCALES ❖

Equiparts, 817 Main St., Pittsburgh, PA 15215: Free information ❖ Vintage plumbing, heating, and electrical parts. 800-442-6622.

The Faucet Factory, 19 Thompson St., Winchester, MA 01890: Free catalog ❖ Designer solid cast brass fixtures in polished, untreated brass, and other optional finishes. 800-270-0028.

Fiat Tubs, Showers & Steam Baths, 1235 Hartrey Ave., Evanston, IL 60202: Free information ❖ Multi-jet tubs, showers, whirlpools, and steam baths. 847-864-7600.

Granite Lake Pottery Inc., Rt. 9, P.O. Box 236, Munsonville, NH 03457: Free catalog ❖ Handcrafted stoneware sinks, accessories, and tile. 800-443-9908.

Häfele America Company, 3901 Cheyenne Dr., Archdale, NC 27263: Free information ❖ Folding shower seat and textured grab bars. 919-889-2322.

Hansgrohe Inc., 1465 Ventura Dr., Cumming, GA 30130: Catalog $3 ❖ Faucets, massaging and hand showers, make-up/shaving mirrors, and other accessories.

Home Decorators Collection, 2025 Concourse Dr., St. Louis, MO 63146: Free catalog ❖ Oak, high-glazed porcelain, chrome and brass, and wicker bathroom accessories. 800-240-6047; 314-993-6045 (in MO).

Interbath Inc., 665 N. Baldwin Park Blvd., City of Industry, CA 91748: Free list of retail sources ❖ Shower head attachments. 800-800-2132.

InWall Creations, Box 3699, Santa Rosa, CA 95402: Free brochure ❖ Handcrafted solid oak towel hangers, magazine racks, recessed bathroom cabinets, paper holders, and other accessories. 800-888-5044.

Kohler Company, 444 Highland Dr., Kohler, WI 53044: Catalog $3 ❖ Solid brass faucets and other plumbing fixtures, bathroom tubs and toilets, and low threshold shower stalls for wheelchair accessibility. 800-220-2291.

Lyons Industries, P.O. Box 88, Dowagiac, MI 49047: Free information ❖ Whirlpools for space-saving corner installation with optional walls and shatter-proof folding shower stall doors. 800-458-9036.

MAC the Antique Plumber, 6325 Elvas Ave., Sacramento, CA 95819: Catalog $6 (refundable) ❖ Antique plumbing fixtures. 916-454-4507.

Nexton Industries Inc., 51 S. 1st St., Brooklyn, NY 11211: Free information ❖ Brass decorative hardware and bathroom accessories. 718-599-3837.

Ole Fashion Things, 402 SW Evangeline, Lafayette, LA 70501: Catalog $5 ❖ Clawfoot bathtubs, pedestal lavatories, china bowls, high-tank commodes, faucets, and traditional plumbing supplies. 800-228-4967.

Paragon Products, P.O. Box 14914, Scottsdale, AZ 85267: Catalog $4.50 ❖ Faucets and fixtures, sinks, pedestals, whirlpools, and other bathroom accessories. 800-A-FAUCET.

Plastic Creations, 1023 S. Hamilton St., Dalton, GA 30720: Free brochure ❖ Acrylic whirlpool baths. 800-868-0254.

Potterton-Myson, Myson Inc., 20 Lincoln St., Essex Junction, VT 05452: Free list of retail sources ❖ Towel warmers. 802-879-1170.

Remodelers & Renovators Supplies, P.O. Box 45478, Boise, ID 83711: Catalog $3 ❖ Vintage hardware and plumbing fixtures. 800-456-2135.

Reon Shower, 5010 Shoreham Pl., Ste. 300, San Diego, CA 92122: Free brochure ❖ Kitchen and bathroom accessories from around the world. 800-776-7366.

Research Products, 2639 Andjon, Dallas, TX 75220: Free information ❖ Self-contained INCINOLET electric, non-polluting, and water-less toilet that incinerates waste to clean ash.

The Restoration Place, 305 20th St., Rock Island, IL 61201: Free brochure ❖ Plumbing, hardware, architectural and decorative accessories, and fixtures. 309-786-0004.

Restoration Works Inc., P.O. Box 486, Buffalo, NY 14205: Catalog $3 ❖ Plumbing fixtures, bathroom accessories, ceiling medallions and trims, furniture, and hardware. 716-856-6400.

Robern Inc., 1648 Winchester Rd., Bensalem, PA 19020: Free list of retail sources ❖ Bathroom mirrors and cabinets. 215-245-6550.

Roy Electric Company Inc., 1054 Coney Island Ave., Brooklyn, NY 11230: Catalog $6 ❖ Antique plumbing fixtures. 800-366-3347; 718-434-7002 (in NY).

Seagull Creations, 222 Calais, Tijeras, NM 87059: Brochure $2 ❖ Western lifestyle ceramic bathroom accessories. 505-286-1253.

Showerlux, P.O. Box 20202, Atlanta, GA 30325: Free information ❖ Shower enclosures. 404-355-3550.

The Sink Factory, 2140 San Pablo Ave., Berkeley, CA 94702: Catalog $3 ❖ Traditional oval and round porcelain basins, from the classic styles of 1880 to the 1930s. 510-540-8193.

Sonoma Woodworks Inc., 1285 S. Cloverdale Blvd., Cloverdale, CA 95425: Brochure $1 ❖ High-tank pull-chain toilets, solid oak cabinets, and medicine and vanity cabinets. 800-659-9003.

Sterling Plumbing Group, 2900 W. Golf Rd., Rolling Meadows, IL 60008: Free information ❖ Faucets in fired-on epoxy colors, chrome, and polished brass. 800-895-4774.

Studio Workshop, 2808 Tucker St., Omaha, NE 68112: Catalog $2 ❖ Solid oak bathroom accessories. 800-383-7072.

Sunflower Showerhead Company, P.O. Box 4218, Seattle, WA 98104: Free information ❖ Traditional big face showerheads and custom shower arms. All rustproof materials with copper, nickel, chrome, brass, and gold finishes. 206-722-1232.

Sunrise Specialty Company, 5540 Doyle St., Emeryville, CA 94608: Catalog $2 ❖ Reproduction Victorian-style bathroom fixtures. 510-654-1794.

Swan Corporation, 1 City Centre, St. Louis, MO 63101: Free information ❖ Shower enclosures. 314-231-8148.

Touch of Class Catalog, 1905 N. Van Buren St., Huntingburg, IN 47542: Free catalog ❖ Bathroom accessories, comforters, pillows and shams, window treatments, towels and rugs, and nightwear and robes for men, women, and children. 800-457-7456.

BATHROOM SCALES

Attitudes, 1213 Elko Dr., Sunnyvale, CA 94088: Free catalog ❖ Decor accessories, bathroom scales and personal care, travel, bathroom, and kitchen aids. 800-241-1107.

Frontgate, 2800 Henkle Dr., Lebanon, OH 45036: Free catalog ❖ Bathroom scales, housewares, and kitchen accessories. 800-626-6488.

One Step Ahead, P.O. 517, Lake Bluff, IL 60044: Free catalog ❖ Bathroom scales and baby items for use when travelling, feeding, and at bath time. 800-950-5120.

J.C. Penney Company Inc., Catalog Division, Atlanta, GA 30390: Free information ❖ Bathroom scales. 800-222-6161.

Spiegel, P.O. Box 182556, Columbus, OH 43218: Free information ❖ Bathroom scales. 800-345-4500.

BATTERIES & CHARGERS

Aerocell, 407 Commerce Way, Jupiter, FL 33458: Free information ❖ Flight pack batteries and charger for model airplanes. 407-575-0422.

B & P Associates, P.O. Box 22054, Waco, TX 76702: Free information ❖ Starter batteries for model airplanes. 817-662-5587.

58 ❖ BEAD CRAFTING ❖

Battery Biz, 31352 Via Colinas, Ste. 104, Westlake Village, CA 91362: Free catalog ❖ Batteries. 800-848-6782.

Battery Specialists, 74 W. 38th St., 2nd Floor, New York, NY 10018: Free information ❖ Batteries, chargers, and battery belts. 800-275-2879; 212-768-7595 (in NY).

Battery-Tech Inc., 28-25 215th Pl., Bayside, NY 11360: Free information ❖ Replacement batteries. 800-442-4275.

Cunard Associates, RD 6, Box 104, Bedford, PA 15522: Free catalog ❖ Batteries, battery packs, and battery rebuilding services. 814-623-7000.

Digital Distributors, 1274 49th St., Ste. 129, Brooklyn, NY 11219: Free information ❖ Video cameras, editing equipment, batteries and chargers, and other electronics. 718-768-0609.

MK Model Products, 7209 Balboa Blvd., Van Nuys, CA 91406: Free information ❖ Off-road and on-road car models, chargers, speed controls, and batteries. 800-446-6335; 818-787-5851 (in CA).

Motorcycle Accessory Warehouse, 925 E. Fillmore St., Colorado Springs, CO 80907: Free information ❖ Tires, helmets, batteries, seats, saddlebags, and sportswear. 800-241-2222.

SR Batteries Inc., Box 287, Bellport, NY 11713: Information $3 ❖ Batteries for model airplanes. 516-286-0079.

Sunshine Computers, 22191 Powerline Rd., Boca Raton, FL 33433: Free information ❖ Portable computers, memory upgrades, fax modems, carrying cases, mouse devices, and batteries. 800-828-2992.

Thrifty Distributors, 641 W. Lancaster Ave., Frazer, PA 19355: Free catalog ❖ Video cameras, editing equipment, batteries, wireless microphones, lights, and accessories. 800-342-3610.

W & W Associates, 800 S. Broadway, Hicksville, NY 11801: Free information ❖ Batteries and chargers. 800-221-0732; 516-942-0011 (in NY).

E.H. Yost & Company, 2211-D Parview Rd., Middleton, WI 53562: Free catalog ❖ Batteries for radios, computers, and other equipment. 608-631-3443.

BEAD CRAFTING

Aardvark Adventures, P.O. Box 2449, Livermore, CA 94551: Catalog $2 (refundable) ❖ Beads and bead-crafting supplies. 510-443-2687.

Abeada Corporation, 1205 N. Main St., Royal Oak, MI 48067: Free information ❖ Beads, bead-stringing kits, and findings. 800-521-6326; 313-399-6642 (in MI).

Alpha Supply, P.O. Box 2133, Bremerton, WA 98310: Catalog $3 ❖ Beads, engraving and jewelry-making tools, and supplies. 360-373-3302.

ARA Imports, P.O. Box 41054, Brecksville, OH 44141: Catalog $1 ❖ Semi-precious beads, fresh water pearls, precious metal beads, and findings. 216-838-1372.

Arizona Gems & Minerals Inc., 22025 N. Black Canyon Hwy., Phoenix, AZ 85027: Catalog $4 ❖ Chip and other beads, findings, geodes, silversmithing and lapidary tools, and jewelry-making supplies.

Art to Wear, 5 Crescent Pl. South, St. Petersburg, FL 33711: Catalog $1 ❖ Beads, bead-stringing supplies, findings, and tools. 813-867-3711.

Artgems Exporters Inc., P.O. Box 12610, Scottsdale, AZ 85267: Free catalog ❖ Beads, gemstones, and other supplies. 602-951-0032.

B & J Rock Shop, 14744 Manchester Rd., Ballwin, MO 63011: Catalog $3 ❖ Rockhounding equipment, beads, quartz crystals, imported and domestic gemstones, and jewelry-making and bead-stringing supplies. 314-394-4567.

Bally Bead Company, 2304 Ridge Rd., Rockwall TX 75087: Catalog $4.95 (refundable) ❖ Beads and findings. 214-771-4515.

Banasch, 2810 Highland Ave., Cincinnati, OH 45212: Free catalog ❖ Beads, pearls, sewing notions, and buttons. 800-543-0355; 513-731-2040 (in OH).

Baubanbea Enterprises, P.O. Box 1205, Smithtown, NY 11787: Catalog $1 ❖ Rhinestones, sequins, beads, semi-precious and precious gemstones, and craft supplies. 516-724-4661.

Bead Boppers, 11224 Meridian, East Puyallup, WA 98373: Catalog $2.50 (refundable) ❖ Beads and findings, tools, charms, seed beads, leather, supplies, and books. 206-848-3880.

The Bead Dreamer, P.O. Box 16, Newport News, VA 23607: Catalog $2 ❖ Beads, charms, findings, and craft supplies. 804-245-5844.

The Bead Fairy, 178 Ramona Dr., San Luis Obispo, CA 93405: Catalog $3 (refundable) ❖ Beads. 805-541-5475.

Bead Source, 7047 Reseda Blvd., Reseda, CA 91335: Catalog $11 ❖ Beads, Austrian crystals, Peruvian beads, findings, and appliques. 818-708-0972.

Bead Warehouse, 55 San Remo Dr., South Burlington, VT 05403: Free catalog ❖ Beads, books, tools, clay, and other craft items. 802-658-0013.

Bead World, 4923 Prospect NE, Albuquerque, NM 87110: Catalog $2 ❖ Beads, findings and supplies, and leather cord. 505-884-3133.

Beada Beada, 4262 N. Woodward Ave., Royal Oak, MI 48073: Free catalog ❖ Beads, bead-stringing supplies, and findings. 810-549-1005.

Beadbox Inc., 10135 E. Via Linda, Scottsdale, AZ 85258: Catalog $5 ❖ Beads from worldwide sources and jewelry kits. 800-232-3269.

Beadniks, 1104 E. 200 South, Salt Lake City, UT 84102: Catalog $2 (refundable) ❖ Beads, beading supplies, and kits.

Beads Galore International Inc., 2123 S. Priest, Tempe, AZ 85282: Free information ❖ Beads and bead-stringing supplies. 800-424-9577.

Beadtrader, 3435 S. Broadway, Englewood, CO 80110: Free catalog ❖ Beads from Africa, India, Europe, the Orient, and North and South America. 800-805-BEAD.

Beadworks, 149 Water St., Norwalk, CT 06854: Catalog $7.95 ❖ Thousands of beads. 800-232-3761.

BeadZip, 2316 Sarah Ln., Falls Church, VA 22043: Free catalog ❖ Beads from around the world. 703-849-8463.

Beyond Beadery, 54 Tinker St., Woodstock, NY 12498: Catalog $1 ❖ Looms, findings, needles and thread, and Czechoslovakian, Japanese, and Austrian crystal beads. 800-840-5548.

Bourget Bros., 1636 11th St., Santa Monica, CA 90404: Catalog $5 ❖ Beads, bead-stringing and jewelry-making supplies, and tools. 310-450-6556.

Libby Brink, RR 1, Box 165B, Hunlock Creek, PA 18621: Catalog $3 ❖ Bead jewelry-making kits.

Bucks County Classic, 73 Coventry Lane, Longhorn, PA 19047: Catalog $2 ❖ Cabochons, fresh water pearls, findings, and gemstone, Chinese cloisonne, Austrian crystal, stone, and metal beads. 800-942-GEMS.

Carol Chapman, 218 Willow Ave., Hoboken, NJ 07030: Price list $1 with long SASE ❖ Bead-stringing supplies. 201-420-9560.

Charlie's Rock Shop, P.O. Box 399, Penrose, CO 81240: Free catalog ❖ Beads, bead-stringing and jewelry-making supplies, jewelry boxes, and faceted gemstones. 719-372-0117.

The Cracker Box, Solebury, PA 18963: Catalog $4.50 ❖ Bead-crafting kits. 215-862-2100.

Creative Castle, 2321 Michael Dr., Newbury Park, CA 91320: Free catalog ❖ Bead-making jewelry kits. 805-499-1377.

Discount Bead House, P.O. Box 186, The Plains, OH 45780: Catalog $5 ❖ Seed beads, findings, and tools. 800-793-7592.

❖ BEAD CRAFTING ❖

E & W Imports Inc., P.O. Box 15703, Tampa, FL 33684: Price list $1 ❖ Gemstone, cloisonne, and Austrian crystal beads and 14K findings. 813-885-1138.

Eagle Feather Trading Post, 168 W. 12th St., Ogden, UT 84404: Catalog $3.50 ❖ Beading and Native American craft supplies, beads and bead-stringing kits, and how-to beading and craft books.

Ebersole Lapidary Supply Inc., 11417 West Hwy. 54, Wichita, KS 67209: Catalog $2 ❖ Beads, bead-stringing supplies, carving materials, tools, findings, mountings, cabochons and rocks, and jewelry kits. 316-722-4771.

Enterprise Art, P.O. Box 2918, Largo, FL 33771: Free catalog ❖ Beads from around the world, bead and jewelry-making kits, and craft and jewelry-making supplies. 800-366-2218.

Fire Mountain Gems, 28195 Redwood Hwy., Cave Junction, OR 97523: Catalog $3 ❖ Beads, findings, jewelry-making supplies, Japanese seed beads. 800-423-2319.

Frantz Bead Company, E. 1222 Sunset Hill Rd., Shelton, WA 98584: Catalog $6 ❖ Glass bead-making supplies, handmade glass beads from India and Thailand, other beads, and findings. 360-426-6712.

Garden of Beadin', 752 Redwood Dr., Garberville, CA 95542: Catalog $2 ❖ Seed beads, crystals, semi-precious gemstones, books, and bead-stringing supplies. 800-232-3588.

Gem-O-Rama Inc., 150 Recreation Park Dr., Hingham, MA 02043: Free catalog ❖ Beads and bead-stringing supplies. 617-749-8250.

Hardies, P.O. Box 1920, Quartzsite, AZ 85346: Free catalog ❖ Czech, seed, hand-made glass, and other beads. Also findings, buckles, bolas, Native American jewelry, gems, rocks, and books. 800-962-2775; 602-927-6381 (in AZ).

Hedgehog Handworks, P.O. Box 45384, Westchester, CA 90045: Catalog $5 (refundable with $30 order) ❖ Semi-precious beads, sewing notions, gold and silver threads, and needlecraft, embroidery, and other craft supplies. 310-670-6040.

International Bead Trader, 3435 S. Broadway, Englewood, CO 80110: Free catalog ❖ Beads, findings, books, and supplies. 303-781-8335.

Jay's of Tucson Inc., 6637 S. 12th Ave., Tucson, AZ 85706: Catalog $5 (refundable) ❖ Findings, crafts, gifts, Navajo rugs, sandpaintings, Taos moccasins, drums, and Navajo, Hopi, and Zuni jewelry. Also Czech, seed, pony, Peruvian, and other beads. 602-294-3397.

Jeanne's Rock & Jewelry, 5420 Bissonet, Bellaire, TX 77401: Price list $1 ❖ Beads, bead-stringing and lapidary supplies, seashells, and petrified wood products. 713-664-2988.

Kikico Beads, P.O. Box 8353, Scottsdale, AZ 85252: Catalog $2 ❖ Beads for jewelry designing. 800-484-9565.

KUMA Beads, P.O. Box 25049, Glenville, NY 12325: Catalog $2 ❖ Beads, bead-stringing supplies, semi-precious gemstones, tools, findings, and craft kits. 518-384-0110.

Victor H. Levy Inc., 1355 S. Flower St., Los Angeles, CA 90015: Catalog $5 ❖ Rocailles, shells, jewelry-making supplies, and seed, bone, fancy, and other beads. 800-421-8021; 213-749-8247 (in CA).

Mangum's Beads, P.O. Box 362, Blackfoot, ID 83221: Catalog $1 ❖ Beads and bead-crafting supplies. 208-785-1838.

Morning Light Emporium, Roxy Grinnell, P.O. Box 1155, Paronia, CO 81428: Free catalog ❖ Beads from worldwide sources, stringing supplies, looms, and other accessories. 970-527-4493.

New England International Gems, 188 Pollard St., Billerica, MA 01862: Free catalog ❖ Beads and beading supplies. 617-863-8331.

Optional Extras, P.O. Box 8550, Burlington, VT 05402: Catalog $2 ❖ Jewelry findings and beads from worldwide sources. 800-736-0781.

Out On A Whim, 121 E. Cotan Ave., Cotati, CA 94931: Free information ❖ Imported beads, glass beads, semi-precious stones, jewelry findings and supplies, and beading accessories. 707-664-8343.

Peninsula Bead & Supply, 5166 Moorpark Ave., San Jose, CA 95129: Catalog $5 ❖ Glass and Austrian crystal, horn, metal, and bone beads. 408-253-1928.

Pennylane Beads, P.O. Box 327, Sulsun City, CA 94585: Catalog $2 ❖ Beads. 707-864-3515.

The Peruvian Bead Company, 1601 Callens Rd., Ventura, CA 93003: Catalog $2 ❖ Hand-painted ceramic and porcelain beads. 805-642-0952.

Promenade Le Bead Shop, 1970 13th St., Boulder, CO 80302: Catalog $2.50 (refundable) ❖ Beads, bead-crafting kits, and books. 303-440-4807.

Red & Green Minerals Inc., 7595 W. Florida Ave., Lakewood, CO 80226: Free information ❖ Beads, bead-stringing supplies, petrified wood products, clocks, clock movements and parts, and rock and mineral specimens. 303-985-5559.

River Gems & Findings, 6901 Washington NE, Albuquerque, NM 87109: Free catalog ❖ Beads, beading and craft supplies, and sewing notions. 800-396-9895.

Riviera Lapidary Supply, 30595 Mesquite, Riviera, TX 78379: Catalog $3 ❖ Beads, bead-stringing supplies and kits, shells, petrified wood products, cabochons, slabs, cabbing rough, gemstones, and crystals. 512-296-3958.

Elvee Rosenberg, 21 W. 38th St., New York, NY 10018: Free catalog ❖ Beads, acrylic gemstones, pearls, and high-fashion jewelry. 212-575-0767.

S.E.A.T. Publication, P.O. Box 2593, Longmont, CO 80502: Information $4 ❖ Mineral specimens, jewelry, and beads. 303-678-9930.

Marvin Schwab, 2740 Garfield Ave., Silver Spring, MD 20910: Catalog $3.50 ❖ Beads, bead-crafting supplies, and findings. 301-565-0487.

Shipwreck Beads Inc., 2727 Westmoor Ct., Olympia, WA 98502: Catalog $4 ❖ Beads, bead-stringing supplies, and findings. 360-754-2323.

Simara's Bead World, 215 1st St., Liverpool, NY 13088: Catalog $3.95 (refundable) ❖ Beads from worldwide sources, beaded jewelry kits, beading supplies, and books. 315-451-3784.

Sioux Trading Post Inc., 415 6th St., Rapid City, SD 57701: Catalog $2 ❖ Beads and beadwork. 800-456-3394.

Soho South, P.O. Box 1324, Cullman, AL 35056: Catalog $2.50 (refundable) ❖ Beads and findings, fabric dyes and paints, silk scarves and fabrics, and marbling supplies. 205-739-6114.

South Pacific Wholesale Company, Rt. 2, P.O. Box 249, East Montpelier, VT 05651: Free price list ❖ Beads, findings, semi-precious gemstone settings, gold and silver bracelets, necklaces, and earrings. 800-338-2162.

Terre Celeste, Box 4125, Kenmore, NY 14217: Free catalog ❖ Swarovski, Austrian crystal, carved, heart, and other beads.

Trader Rose, P.O. Box 429, Alachua, FL 32615: Information $10 ❖ Bead crafting supplies and beads from Indonesia, China, and Thailand. 904-462-7580.

TSI Jewelry Supply, 101 Nickerson St., Seattle, WA 98109: Free catalog ❖ Jewelry-making tools and supplies, beads, findings, and gemstones. 800-426-9984.

Veon Creations, 3565 State Rd. V, DeSoto, MO 63020: Catalog $4 ❖ Beads, gemstones, pearls, findings, and jewelry-making supplies. 314-586-5377.

Wale Apparatus Company Inc., 400 Front St., P.O. Box D, Hellertown, PA 18055: Catalog $5 ❖ Beadmaking and artistic glassworking equipment and supplies. 800-334-WALE; 610-838-7047 (in PA).

Westbrook Bead Company, 16641 Spring Gulch Dr., Anderson, CA 96007: Catalog $2 ❖ Bead-stringing supplies, gemstones, beads, and jewelry-making accessories. 916-357-3143.

BEAR MAKING & CLOTHING

Animal Crackers Patterns, 5824 Isleta SW, Albuquerque, NM 87105: Catalog $2.50 ❖ Bear-making supplies. 505-873-2806.

Bear Clawset, 27 Palermo Walk, Long Beach, CA 90803: Catalog $2 ❖ Bear-making supplies. 310-434-8077.

Carver's Eye Company, P.O. Box 16692, Portland, OR 97216: Catalog $1 ❖ Glass and plastic eyes, noses, joints, growlers, and eye glasses for bears and dolls. 503-666-5680.

CR's Crafts, Box 8, Leland, IA 50453: Catalog $2 ❖ Doll and bear-making supplies, new jointed bears, electronic melody units, kits, patterns, and crafting items. 515-567-3652.

Edinburgh Imports Inc., P.O. Box 722, Woodland Hills, CA 91365: Free catalog with two 1st class stamps ❖ Bear-making supplies. 800-EDINBRG; 818-591-3800 (in CA).

Emily Farmer, P.O. Box 2911, Sanford, NC 27330: Catalog $3 ❖ Miniature teddy bear kits. 919-775-5365.

Intercal, 1760 Monrovia, Ste. A-17, Costa Mesa, CA 92627: Free information with two 1st class stamps ❖ Imported mohair, alpaca, woven synthetics, glass eyes, wool felt, and other bear-making supplies. 714-645-9396.

Miniature Teddy Bear Kits, Emily Farmer, P.O. Box 2911, Sanford, NC 27330: Catalog $3 ❖ Miniature teddy bear kits.

Monterey Inc., 1725 E. Delavan Dr., Janesville, WI 53545: Free information ❖ Knitted deep pile fur fabrics. 800-432-9959; 608-754-8309 (in WI).

Patterns by Diane, 1126 Ivon Ave., Endicott, NY 13760: Catalog $3 ❖ Furs and mohair, growlers, squeakers, music boxes, noses, eyes, joint sets, and patterns for bears, soft toys, and puppets. 607-754-0391.

A. Roosevelt Bear Company, 1016 Nandina Way, Sunnyvale, CA 94086: Brochure $3 ❖ Bear-making patterns and kits. 408-739-4659.

Spare Bear Parts, P.O. Box 56, Interlochen, MI 49643: Catalog $1 ❖ Bear-making supplies, patterns, and kits. 616-275-6993.

Teddies N' Tole, Earlene Vaughn, 16324 Langfield Ave., Cerritos, CA 90701: Price list $1 with long SASE ❖ Supplies for miniature bears. 310-926-0778.

The Teddy Tailor, P.O. Box 234, Sutherlin, OR 97479: Pattern brochure $3 ❖ Original patterns and kits. 503-459-9517.

Teddys by Tracy, 32 Pikehall Pl., Baltimore, MD 21236: Catalog $5 (refundable with first $10 order) ❖ Bear fabrics, eyes, kits, silk and organdy ribbons, and other supplies. 410-529-2418.

Tender Heart Treasures Ltd., P.O. Box 2310, Omaha, NE 68103: Free catalog ❖ Clothing and accessories for bears and dolls. 800-443-1367.

Unicorn Studios, Box 370, Seymour, TN 37865: Catalog $1 ❖ Wind-up and electronic music box movements, voices for dolls and bears, winking units, and other craft supplies. 615-984-0145.

BEARS

Animal Haus Ltd., 7784 Montgomery Rd., Cincinnati, OH 45236: Free catalog with four 1st class stamps ❖ Bears. 513-984-9955.

Anything Goes Inc., 9801 Gulf Dr., Anna Maria, FL 34216: Quarterly newsletter $2 ❖ Antique and collectible bears. 813-778-4456.

Bear Hugs, 7 Cooper Ave., Marlton, NJ 08053: Free information ❖ Bears and bear clothing. 800-MR-BEARS.

Bear Hugs & Baby Dolls, 1184 Lexington Ave., New York, NY 10028: Free information ❖ Artist bears. 212-717-1514.

Bear In Mind Inc., 53 Bradford St., Concord, MA 01742: Catalog $1 ❖ Exclusive handcrafted bears and other collectibles. 508-369-1167.

Bear Pawse, 502 S. Montezuma, Prescott, AZ 86303: Catalog $6 ❖ Bears. 520-445-3800.

Beardeaux Farm, 8907 Warner Ave., Ste. 166, Huntington Beach, CA 92647: Catalog $4 (specify patterns or bears) ❖ Artist bears, bear-related items, and bear-making supplies. 714-842-4460.

The Bears' Den, Cedar Hill Plaza, 525 Cedar Hill Ave., Wyckoff, NJ 07481: Free information ❖ Collectible and retired bears. 201-449-9133.

Bears in the Attic, 227 Main St., Reisterstown, MD 21136: Free information ❖ Manufactured and artist bears. 800-232-8842.

The Bears of Bruton Street, 107 S. Bruton St., Wilson, NC 27893: Free information with long SASE ❖ Bears. 800-488-BEAR.

Bears 'N Things, 1491 Bacon Rd., Albion, NY 14411: Monthly list (annual subscription) $10 ❖ Artist bears. 716-589-4066.

Bears 'n Wares, 312 Bridge St., New Cumberland, PA 17070: Brochure $2 ❖ Bears. 717-774-1261.

Campbell's Collectibles, 10971 Four Seasons Pl., Crown Point, IN 46307: Free information with long SASE ❖ Collectible bears. 219-988-3615.

Laura Caruso, The Country Bear, 10465 Big Hand Rd., Columbus Twp., MI 48063: Catalog $5 ❖ Artist bears. 810-727-1737.

Christy's Bears, Buckingham Green, #202, Buckingham, PA 18912: Free information with long SASE ❖ Bears. 215-794-5840.

Collector's Corner Bears, P.O. Box 816, Grand Haven, MI 49417: Newsletter $20 (annual subscription) ❖ New and retired collectible bears. 616-846-0876.

CR's Crafts, Box 8, Leland, IA 50453: Catalog $2 ❖ Doll and bear-making supplies, new jointed bears, electronic melody units, kits, patterns, and crafting items. 515-567-3652.

Cynthia's Country Store, The Wellington Mall, 12794 W. First Hill Blvd., Ste. 15A, West Palm Beach, FL 33414: Catalog $15 ❖ Collectible bears. 407-793-0554.

Divine Little Delights, P.O. Box 167, Grant, FL 32949: Free brochure with long SASE ❖ Miniature teddy bears and stuffed animals.

The Doll House, 18 S. Broadway, Edmond, OK 73034: Free information ❖ Limited edition bears. 800-428-1719.

dolls 'n bearland, 15001 N. Hayden Rd., Ste. 104, Scottsdale, AZ 85260: Catalog $3.50 ❖ Bears. 800-359-9541; 602-596-9947 (in AZ).

Dollsville Dolls & Bearsville Bears, 461 N. Palm Canyon Dr., Palm Springs, CA 92262: Catalog $2 ❖ Bears. 619-325-2241.

Enchanted Doll House, Rt. 7A, RR 1, Box 2535, Manchester Center, VT 05255: Catalog $2 ❖ Bears, toys, and dolls. 802-362-1327.

Ernie's Toyland, 1012 6th St., Ste. 120, Yuba City, CA 95901: Free information ❖ Manufactured, limited edition, and discontinued bears. 800-367-1233.

European Artist Dolls & Bears, 11632 Busy St., Richmond, VA 23236: Free information ❖ German Schuco bears. 804-379-8595.

FairyTales Inc., 3 S. Park Ave., Lombard, IL 60148: Catalog $2 ❖ Artist and other bears and plush toys. 800-495-6973.

The Fantasy Den, 25 Morehouse Ave., Stratford, CT 06497: Catalog $2 ❖ Bears, bear-making supplies, bearaphenalia, and art prints. 203-377-2968.

Gift World, 2392 Locust St., Portage, IN 46368: Brochure $2 ❖ Registered limited edition collector bears. 800-847-4450; 219-763-2408 (in IN).

GiGi's Dolls & Sherry's Teddy Bears Inc., 6029 N. Northwest Hwy., Chicago, IL 60631: Free catalog ❖ Bears, dolls, plush toys, and miniatures. 312-594-1540.

Golden Rule Bears, 1103 Main St., Sumner, WA 98390: Free price list with long SASE ❖ Collectible artist bears. 206-863-0280.

Groves Quality Collectibles, 343 S. Jameson Ave., Lima, OH 45805: Catalog $4 (refundable) ❖ Bears from the United States and international sources. 419-229-7177.

Gund Bears, P.O. Box H, Edison, NJ 08818: Free brochure ❖ Collectible bears.

Johanna Haida Bears USA, 11632 Busy St., Richmond, VA 23236: Free catalog ❖ Johanna Haida bears. 804-379-8639.

Harper General Store, RD 2, Box 512, Annville, PA 17003: Bi-monthly newsletter $10 per year ❖ Antique bears. 717-865-3456.

Hug A Bear, Seaport Village, 849 W. Harbor Dr., Ste. A, San Diego, CA 92101: Free information ❖ Handmade bears. 619-230-1362.

It's A Zoo, 3009 W. Magnolia Blvd., Burbank, CA 91505: Free information ❖ Artist and manufactured bears. 818-842-5534.

Jona Originals, 4458 Augusta Rd., #1-C, Lexington, SC 29073: Free catalog ❖ Original bears and stationery, Christmas cards, bookmarks, T-shirts, sweatshirts, pillows, totes, wall hangings, afghans, and teddy bear-related gifts. 800-838-5662.

Lanes & Gifts, 720 Realtor Ave., Texarkana, AR 75502: Free catalog ❖ Collectible bears. 800-421-8697.

Lexin Inc., Nice Stuff, 148 W. 132nd St., #D, Los Angeles, CA 90061: Free brochure ❖ Bears. 310-329-7568.

Littlethings, 129 Main St., Irvington, NY 10533: Free list with long SASE ❖ Bears, dollhouses, miniatures, furniture, miniature paintings, and other collectibles. 914-591-9150.

Marj's Doll Sanctuary, 5238 Plainfield Ave. NE, Grand Rapids, MI 49505: Free catalog with three 1st class stamps ❖ Bears and dolls. 616-361-0054.

Mary D's Dolls & Bears & Such, 8407 W. Broadway, Brooklyn Park, MN 55445: Catalog $1 ❖ Collectible bears. 612-424-4375.

Moore Bears, Rt. 896, P.O. Box 232, Strasburg, PA 17579: Catalog $4 ❖ Bears and collectibles. 717-687-6954.

My Kind of Bear, Kathy Nearing, 38 Montague St., Binghamton, NY 13901: Free brochure with long SASE ❖ Limited edition artist bears. 607-648-6122.

Kathy Nearing, 38 Montague St., Binghamton, NY 13901: Free brochure with long SASE ❖ Artist bears. 607-648-6122.

North American Bear Company, 401 N. Wabash, Ste. 500, Chicago, IL 60610: Free information with long SASE ❖ Bears. 312-329-0020.

Old Friends Antiques, P.O. Box 754, Sparks, MD 21152: Monthly lists $10 (annual subscription) ❖ Steiff and antique bears and plush animals. 410-472-4632.

The Old Game Store, Rt. 11/30, Manchester, VT 05254: Free information with long SASE ❖ Games, puzzles, collectible teddy bears, and toys. 802-362-2756.

Old-Timers Antiques, 3717 S. Dixie Hwy., West Palm Beach, FL 33405: Free list with long SASE ❖ New and older Steiff bears. Also discontinued and limited editions. 407-832-5141.

The Paper Place & Doll Place, 212 S. River, Holland, MI 49423: Catalog $3 (refundable) ❖ Collectible bears and dolls. 616-392-7776.

The Park Bears, 5467 Greenvillage Rd., Chambersburg, PA 17201: Catalog $2 ❖ Handpainted and hand-carved wood jointed teddy bears.

Parlor Bears, 1423 NW Hwy. 101, Lincoln City, OR 97367: Free information ❖ Artist bears. 503-994-2082.

Playhouse, Mary Radbill, 4512 Eden St., Philadelphia, PA 19114: Free catalog ❖ Artist dolls, bears, and accessories. 215-632-4606.

Romerhaus Creations, 951 S. Alvord Blvd., Evansville, IN 47714: Catalog $10 ❖ Miniature bears. 812-473-7277.

Rose's Doll House Store, 2241 116th St., Milwaukee, WI 53227: Free catalog ❖ Bears, dolls, and dollhouse furnishings. 414-321-0680.

Sara's Bears & Gifts, 173 S. Yonge St., Ormond Beach, FL 32174: Free video catalog ❖ Current and retired bears. 800-988-4073.

Shirley's Doll House, 20509 North Hwy. 21, P.O. Box 99A, Wheeling, IL 60090: Free information with long SASE ❖ Bears and dolls, doll-making supplies, dollhouse furniture, and collectibles. 708-537-1632.

Stuf'd 'N Stuff, 10001 Westheimer, Houston, TX 77042: Catalog $1 (refundable) ❖ Collectible bears and plush animals. 713-266-4352.

Swan's Nest, RR 1, Box 21, East Lebanon, ME 04027: Catalog $5 (refundable) ❖ Imported handmade bears from Scotland, England, Wales, Australia, and New Zealand. 207-457-1845.

T-BRRRs, West 3227 Enoch, Deer Park, WA 99006: Price list $2 ❖ Artist bears. 800-368-5227.

Ted E. Bear's Shoppe, 2120 N. 9th St., Naples, FL 33940: Free information ❖ Handcrafted bears, original bear art, bear clothing, books, miniatures, and novelties. 813-261-2225.

The Teddy Bear Emporium, 51 N. Broad St., Lititz, PA 17543: Free information with long SASE ❖ Bears. 800-598-6853; 717-626-TEDI (in PA).

Teddy Bear Ranch, W.R. Enterprises, P.O. Box 364, Lowell, MI 49331: Catalog $5 ❖ Collectible bears from Germany and United States. 616-897-8073.

Teddytown U.S.A., 73 White Bridge Rd., Nashville, TN 37205: Free information ❖ Bears. 615-356-2484.

Tide-Rider Inc., P.O. Box 429, Oakdale, CA 95361: Free information ❖ Handmade bears and stuffed animals from Merrythought Iron Bridge in Great Britain. 209-848-4420.

Today's Treasures, 655 73rd St., Niagara Falls, NY 14304: Catalog $3 (refundable) ❖ Collector dolls and bears. 716-283-1726.

Toy Shoppe, 11632 Busy St., Richmond, VA 23236: Free information ❖ Collectible dolls and bears. 800-447-7995.

Toy Village, 3105 W. Saginaw, Lansing, MI 48917: Free information ❖ Toys, dolls, bears, and collectibles. 517-323-1145.

Vermont Teddy Bear Company, US Rt. 7, Shelburne Rd., Shelburne, VT 05482: Free information with long SASE ❖ Bears. 800-829-BEAR; 802-985-1322 (in VT).

Pamela Wooley Bears, 5021 Stringtown Rd., Evansville, IN 47711: Catalog $7.50 ❖ Bears. 812-464-2521.

Worldly Bear Company, P.O. Box 430, Greenfield, MA 01302: Catalog $3 ❖ Collectible bears. 413-774-4590.

BEDDING

Comforters & Bed Coverings

Alden Comfort Mills, P.O. Box 55, Plano, TX 75086: Catalog $2 (refundable) ❖ Down-filled comforters. 800-822-5336; 214-423-4000 (in TX).

Ambiance Quilt Company, P.O. Box 305, Walnut, IA 51577: Catalog $2.50 (refundable) ❖ Handmade quilts. 800-704-3362.

Antique Quilt Source, 385 Springview Rd., Carlisle, PA 17013: Catalog $7 ❖ Antique quilts. 717-245-2054.

Barton-Sharpe Ltd., 119 Spring St., New York, NY 10012: Free information ❖ Reproduction 18th and 19th-century furniture, lighting, bedding, stoneware, and decorative items. 212-925-9562.

The Bed Rizer, Division A-1 Manufacturing Corporation, 736 Davenport, IA 52803: Free information ❖ Bed elevating legs, bed ruffles, and matching accessories. 800-321-9447.

Betsy Bourdon, Weaver, Scribner Hill, Wolcott, VT 05680: Catalog $3 ❖ Hand-woven blankets, rugs, and linens. 802-472-6508.

Carter Canopies, P.O. Box 808, Troutman, NC 28166: Brochure $1 ❖ Hand-tied cotton fishnet canopies, dust ruffles, coverlets, and other country-style bedroom furnishings. 800-538-4071.

Chambers, Mail Order Department, P.O. Box 7841, San Francisco, CA 94120: Free catalog ❖ Bed and bath furnishings. 800-334-1254.

❖ BEDDING ❖

Choices, 1000 Lake St., Oak Park, IL 60301: Brochure $2 ❖ Hand quilted 100 percent cotton yarn quilts with bonded cotton batting. Also quilted tote bags and pillow shams. 708-386-6555.

The Company Store, 500 Company Store Rd., LaCrosse, WI 54601: Free catalog ❖ Linens, mattress pads, and down-filled pillows, comforters, and outerwear. 800-289-8508.

Laura Copenhaver Industries Inc., P.O. Box 149, Marion, VA 24354: Free brochure ❖ Handmade quilts, coverlets, hand-tied canopies, and curtains. 800-227-6797.

Cuddledown of Maine, 312 Canco Rd., Portland, ME 04103: Free catalog ❖ Down and feather/down comforters, sheets, sleepwear, mattress pads, throw pillows, flannel bedding, and nursery items. 800-323-6793.

Curtains & Home, 1600 Old Country Rd., Plainview, NY 11803: Free catalog ❖ Curtains and other window treatments, bedspreads and quilts, table cloths, bathroom ensembles, and rugs. 800-228-7824.

Designer Secrets, P.O. Box 529, Fremont, NE 68025: Free catalog ❖ Bedspreads, comforters, window treatments, and decorative pillows. 800-955-2559.

Domestications, P.O. Box 40, Hanover, PA 17333: Free catalog ❖ Bedding and bath ensembles. 717-633-3333.

Dona Designs, 1611 Bent Tree, Seagoville, TX 75159: Free information ❖ Cotton bedding.

Donna's Custom Canopies, 255 Chapel Hills Rd., Boone, NC 28607: Brochure $1 with long SASE ❖ Cotton hand-tied canopies, throw pillows, and down-filled comforters. 704-262-1631.

Down Home Comforts, P.O. Box 2281, West Brattleboro, VT 05303: Brochure $1 ❖ New and re-made down comforters, pillows, and featherbeds. 203-688-3780.

Down Home Factory Outlet, 85 Rt. 46 West, Totowa, NJ 07512: Free catalog ❖ Comforters, pillows, and other bedding. 800-ALL-DOWN.

Eldridge Textile Company, 277 Grand St., New York, NY 10002: Catalog $3 (refundable) ❖ Blankets, sheets, towels, comforters, bedspreads, rugs, and pillows. 212-925-1523.

Family Heirloom Weavers, 775 Meadowview Dr., Red Lion, PA 17356: Catalog $4 ❖ Coverlets woven in the tradition of Pennsylvania German weavers in the early 1800s. Also other coverlets. 717-246-2431.

Feathered Friends Mail Order, 1415 10th Ave., Seattle, WA 98122: Free information ❖ Down comforters and robes, slip covers, pillows, shams, dust ruffles, and flannel sheets. 206-328-0887.

Freedom Quilting Bee, Rt. 1, P.O. Box 72, Alberta, AL 36720: Free information ❖ Handmade quilts. 205-573-2225.

G & K Enterprises, 1408 Glenwood Ave., Greensboro, NC 27403: Free information ❖ Throws and pillows with a western motif. 910-632-9899.

Garnet Hill, 262 Main St., Franconia, NH 03580: Free catalog ❖ Natural fiber linens and sheets, blankets, comforters, and clothing. 800-622-6216.

Gazebo of New York, 127 E. 57th St., New York, NY 10022: Catalog $6 ❖ Patchwork quilts and hand-woven rag, hooked, and braided rugs. 212-832-7077.

Hale House, 4208 Malden Dr., Malden, WV 25306: Free catalog ❖ Patchwork quilts. 304-925-9499.

Home Etc., Palo Verde at 34th St., P.O. Box 28806, Tucson, AZ 85726: Free catalog ❖ Bedding ensembles, curtains, bedspreads and comforters, rugs, linens and pillows, and towels. 800-362-8415.

Homecraft Services, 340 W. 5th St., Kansas City, MO 64105: Catalog $3 ❖ Pre-cut quilt kits.

The Horchow Collection, P.O. Box 620048, Dallas, TX 75262: Free catalog ❖ Linens, bed coverings, and home accessories. 800-395-5397.

JANICE Corporation, 198 Rt. 46, Budd Lake, NJ 07828: Free catalog ❖ Allergy-free women and men's clothing, towels, bathroom accessories, quilts, linens, personal grooming aids, hats, gloves, and scarves. 800-JANICES.

Lakota Collection, St. Joseph Lakota Development Council, St. Joseph Indian School, Chamberlain, SD 57326: Free catalog ❖ Sioux star quilts and other Native American crafts and gifts. 605-734-6021.

Lancaster Towne Quilts, 600 Olde Hickory Rd., Ste. 100, Strasburg, PA 17601: Catalog $5 ❖ Custom-made quilts and wall hangings. 717-5871-9100.

Landau Woolens, 114 Nassau St., Princeton, NJ 08542: Free catalog ❖ Machine washable wool blankets. 800-257-9445.

Leron, 750 Madison Ave., New York, NY 10021: Free catalog ❖ Linens, towels, pillows and covers, and imported handkerchiefs with optional monogramming for men and women. 212-753-6700.

Linen & Lace, 4 Lafayette, Washington, MO 63090: Catalog $2 ❖ Bed ruffles, canopies, and curtains. 800-332-5223.

The Linen Source, 5401 Hangar Ct., P.O. Box 31151, Tampa, FL 33631: Free catalog ❖ Bedroom ensembles, linens, pillows, and curtains. 800-431-2620.

Missouri Breaks Industries, Quilt Brochure, HCR 64, Box 52, Timber Lake, SD 57656: Free brochure ❖ Original Sioux Native American star quilt patterns. 605-865-3418.

Oak Tree Furniture Company, 828 S. Main St., St. Charles, MO 63301: Free information ❖ Afghans.

Quilted Treasures, P.O. Box 96, Indore, WV 25111: Free information ❖ Handmade quilts, pillows, wall hangings, and other items. 304-587-8313.

Quilts Unlimited, 1023 Emmet St., Charlottesville, VA 22903: Catalog $6 ❖ Antique and new crib quilts. 804-979-8110.

Rocky Mountain Tanners Inc., 2331 W. Hampden Ave., #146, Englewood, CO 80110: Brochure $2 ❖ Elk and deer leather throws for beds, couches, and chairs. 303-761-1049.

J. Schachter Corporation, 5 Cook St., Brooklyn, NY 11206: Catalog $1 (refundable) ❖ Shams, ruffles, table covers, and draperies. 718-384-2100.

Sherry Street, 9141 Walworth Rd., Bancroft, MI 48414: Free information ❖ Heirloom family throws with optional monogramming. 517-634-5596.

The Village Weaver, P.O. Box 71, Dillard, GA 30537: Brochure $2 ❖ Hand-woven Tartan blankets. 706-746-2287.

Warm Things, 180 Paul Dr., San Rafael, CA 94903: Free catalog ❖ Down quilts, pillows, and quilt covers. 415-472-2154.

Western Trading Post, P.O. Box 9070, Denver, CO 80209: Catalog $3 ❖ Blankets, Navajo wool rugs, and Eagle-design bed throws. 303-777-7750.

Yankee Pride, 29 Parkside Circle, Braintree, MA 02184: Catalog $3 (refundable) ❖ Handcrafted quilts, comforters, bedspreads, and hand-braided, hooked wool, and rag rugs. 617-848-7610.

Pillows & Sheets

Bedroom Secrets, P.O. Box 529, Fremont, NE 68025: Catalog $2 ❖ Linens for the bath and bed. 800-955-2559; 402-727-4004 (in NE).

Betsy Bourdon, Weaver, Scribner Hill, Wolcott, VT 05680: Brochure $3 ❖ Linens, hand-woven blankets, and rugs. 802-472-6508.

Celestial Silks, P.O. Box 824, Fairfield, IA 52556: Free information ❖ In-stock and custom-made silk sheets, pillowcases, and silk-filled comforters. Also silk lingerie. 515-472-9062.

The Company Store, 500 Company Store Rd., LaCrosse, WI 54601: Free catalog ❖ Down-filled pillows and comforters, linens, mattress pads, and down-filled outerwear. 800-289-8508.

Cuddledown of Maine, 312 Canco Rd., Portland, ME 04103: Free catalog ❖ Down and feather/down comforters, sheets, sleepwear, mattress pads, throw pillows, flannel bedding, and nursery items. 800-323-6793.

Domestications, P.O. Box 40, Hanover, PA 17333: Free catalog ❖ Comforters, sheets, pillows, blankets, bedspreads, throws, solid and lace tablecloths, mini blinds, shower curtains, and bathroom accessories. 717-633-3313.

Dona Designs, 1611 Bent Tree, Seagoville, TX 75159: Free information ❖ Cotton bedding.

Down Home Comforts, P.O. Box 2281, West Brattleboro, VT 05303: Brochure $1 ❖ Down comforters and pillows. 203-688-3780.

Down Home Factory Outlet, 85 Rt. 46 West, Totowa, NJ 07512: Free catalog ❖ Comforters, pillows, and other bedding. 800-ALL-DOWN.

Eldridge Textile Company, 277 Grand St., New York, NY 10002: Catalog $3 (refundable) ❖ Blankets, sheets, towels, comforters, bedspreads, rugs, and pillows. 212-925-1523.

Feathered Friends Mail Order, 1415 10th Ave., Seattle, WA 9812: Free information ❖ Down comforters and robes, slip covers, pillows, shams, dust ruffles, and flannel sheets. 206-328-0887.

G & K Enterprises, 1408 Glenwood Ave., Greensboro, NC 27403: Free information ❖ Throws and pillows with a western motif. 910-632-9899.

Garnet Hill, 262 Main St., Franconia, NH 03580: Free catalog ❖ Natural fiber linens and sheets, blankets, and comforters. 800-622-6216.

The Horchow Collection, P.O. Box 620048, Dallas, TX 75262: Free catalog ❖ Linens, bed coverings, and accessories. 800-395-5397.

JANICE Corporation, 198 Rt. 46, Budd Lake, NJ 07828: Free catalog ❖ Allergy-free women and men's clothing, towels, bathroom accessories, quilts, linens, personal grooming aids, hats, gloves, and scarves. 800-JANICES.

Johnsen Woolen Mills Inc., Rt. 15, Johnson, VT 05656: Free brochure ❖ Woolen outerwear for men, women, and children. Also blankets, underwear, and sweaters. 802-635-2271.

Just for You, Doris Gianni Scruggs, P.O. Box 4818, Laguna Beach, CA 92652: Brochure $3 ❖ Hand-stenciled and painted pillows. 714-494-9670.

Leron, 750 Madison Ave., New York, NY 10021: Free catalog ❖ Linens, towels, pillows and covers, and imported handkerchiefs with optional monogramming for men and women. 212-753-6700.

Harris Levy, 278 Grand St., New York, NY 10002: Free catalog ❖ Linens for tables, beds, and bathrooms. 800-221-7750; 212-226-3102 (in NY).

The Linen Source, 5401 Hangar Ct., P.O. Box 31151, Tampa, FL 33631: Free catalog ❖ Linens, pillows, curtains, and bedroom ensembles. 800-431-2620.

M.C. Ltd., P.O. Box 17696, Whitefish Bay, WI 53217: Free information ❖ Pillows and steerhide rugs. 800-236-5224; 414-263-5422 (in WI).

The Natural Bedroom, Jantz Design, 175 N. Main St., Sebastopol, CA 95472: Free information ❖ Natural fiber baby's bedding. 800-365-6563.

Palmetto Linen Company, 50 Palmetto Bay Rd., Hilton Head, SC 29928: Free information ❖ Sheets and matching dust ruffles, bath towels, blankets, comforters, pillows, tablecloths, place mats, and shower curtains. 800-972-7442.

Primarily Pillows, P.O. Box 601, Conrwall, NY 12518: Free catalog ❖ Designer pillows. 914-534-5296.

Rubin & Green, 290 Grand St., New York, NY 10002: Free information with long SASE ❖ Bed, bathroom, and table linens. 212-226-0313.

Rue de France, 28 Jacome Way, Middletown, RI 02842: Catalog $3 ❖ Pillows, tablecloths and runners, and lace curtains. 800-777-0998.

Warm Things, 180 Paul Dr., San Rafael, CA 94903: Free catalog ❖ Down quilts, pillows, and quilt covers. 415-472-2154.

BEEKEEPING

Archia's Floral & Plants, 712 S. Ohio, Sedalia, MO 65301: Free catalog ❖ Vegetable and flower seeds, gardening supplies, nursery stock, and beekeeping equipment. 816-826-4000.

B & B Honey Farm, Rt. 2, Box 245, Houston, MN 55943: Free catalog ❖ Beekeeping and candle-making supplies. 507-896-3955.

Betterbee-Meadery Inc., RR 4, Box 4070, Greenwich, NY 12834: Free information ❖ Beekeeping supplies. 518-692-9669.

Bob Brandi Honey, 1518 Paradise Ln., Los Banos, CA 93635: Free information ❖ Package bees, queens, bulk bees, and nucs. 209-826-0921.

Brushy Mountain Bee Farm, 610 Bethany Church Rd., Moravian Falls, NC 28654: Free catalog ❖ Gloves and protective clothing, equipment for processing honey, books, video tapes, and other beekeeping supplies. 800-BEESWAX.

Cowen Manufacturing Company, P.O. Box 399, Parowan, UT 84761: Free information ❖ Extracting equipment. 800-257-2894; 801-477-8902 (in UT).

Dadant & Sons Inc., 51 S. 2nd St., Hamilton, IL 62341: Free catalog ❖ Honey extracting equipment, honey containers, beeswax foundation and plasticell, woodenware, and queen and package bees. 217-847-3324.

Friesen Honey Farms Inc., 8099 Rd. 29, Glenn, CA 95943: Free information ❖ Italian package bees and queens. 916-934-4944.

Glenn Apiaries, P.O. Box 2737, Fallbrook, CA 92088: Free information ❖ Italian and Carnolian queen bees. 619-728-3731.

Glorybee Honey & Supplies, P.O. Box 2744, Eugene, OR 97402: Catalog 50¢ ❖ Beekeeping and honey processing supplies, honey, honey-prepared foods, and gift assortments. 800-456-7923; 503-689-0913 (in OR).

Hardeman Apiaries, P.O. Box 214, Mt. Vernon, GA 30445: Free price list ❖ Italian packages and queen bees. 912-583-2710.

Harrell & Sons Inc., P.O. Box 215, Haynesville, AL 36040: Free information ❖ Italian package bees and queens. 205-548-2313.

Hawaiian Queen Company, HC1 Box 21-A, Captain Cook, HI 96704: Free information ❖ Bees. 808-328-2656.

Heitkam's Honey Bees, 25815 Post Ave., Orland, CA 95963: Free price list ❖ Queen bees. 916-865-9562.

Holder Homan & Sons Apiaries, Rt. 2, Box 123, Shannon, MS 38868: Free price list ❖ Queen and package bees. 601-767-3880.

F.W. Jones & Son Ltd., 68 Tycos Dr., Toronto, Ontario, Canada M6B 1V9: Catalog $2 ❖ Wood, metalwares, and other beekeeping supplies. 416-783-2818.

The Walter T. Kelley Company Inc., P.O. Box 240, Clarkson, KY 42726: Free catalog ❖ Beekeeping supplies. 502-242-2012.

C.F. Koehnen & Sons Inc., 3131 Hwy. 45, Glenn, CA 95943: Free brochure ❖ Italian packages and queen bees. 916-891-5216.

Kona Queen Company, P.O. Box 768, Captain Cook, HI 96704: Free information ❖ Italian queen bees. 808-328-9016.

Lapp's Bee Supply Center, Box 460, 500 S. Main St., Reeseville, WI 53579: Free information ❖ Package bees, fructose, beeswax, glass accessories, honey, and woodenware. 800-321-1960; 414-927-3848 (in WI).

Mann Lake Supply, County Rd. 40 & 1st St., Hackensack, MN 56452: Free catalog ❖ Beekeeping and honey production equipment, protective clothing, and candle molds. 800-233-6663.

Maxant Industries Inc., P.O. Box 454, Ayer, MA 01432: Catalog $1 ❖ Honey processing equipment. 508-772-0576.

Mid-Continent Agrimarketing Inc., 8883 Lenexa Dr., Overland Park, KS 66215: Free catalog ❖ Beekeeping and candle-making supplies. 800-547-1392.

Miksa Honey Farm, David & Linda Miksa, 13404 Honeycomb Rd., Groveland, FL 34736: Free information ❖ Queens, cells, and nucs. 904-429-3447.

Miller Wood Products, P.O. Box 2414, White City, OH 97503: Free information ❖ Woodenware. 800-827-9266.

Millry Bee Company, Rt. 2, Box 90, Millry, AL 36558: Free information ❖ Three-banded Italian queens and package bees. 205-846-2662.

Palmetto Apiaries, P.O. Box 1241, Lexington, SC 29071: Free information ❖ Queens. 800-458-8591.

Homer E. Park, P.O. Box 38, Palo Cedro, CA 96073: Free price list ❖ Italian queen bees. 916-547-3391.

Pendell Apiaries, Frank & Sheri Pendell, P.O. Box 148, Stonyford, CA 95979: Free information ❖ Italian queens and package bees. 916-963-3062.

Plantation Bee Company, P.O. Box 24559, St. Simon's Island, GA 31522: Free information ❖ Bees. 912-634-1884.

Powell Apiaries, 4140 County Rd. KK, Orland, CA 95963: Free information ❖ Italian package bees and queens, hives, and beekeeping supplies. 916-865-3346.

A.I. Root Company, P.O. Box 706, Medina, OH 44258: Free catalog ❖ Hives, protective clothing and gloves, tools, honey-processing equipment, books, video tapes, smokers, and beekeeping supplies. 800-289-7668.

Rossman Apiaries Inc., P.O. Box 905, Moultrie, GA 31768: Free catalog ❖ Package bees and queens, beekeeping supplies, and starter kit for beginners. 800-333-7677.

Jerry Shumans Apiaries, Rt. 4, Box 1710, Baxley, GA 31513: Free information ❖ Italian queen and package bees. 800-368-7195; 912-367-2243 (in GA).

Southwestern Ohio Hive Parts Company, 52 Marco Ln., Centerville, OH 45458: Free information ❖ Beekeeping supplies. 800-765-5112; 513-435-5112 (in OH).

Spell Bee Company, Rt. 7, Box 1895, Baxley, GA 31513: Free information ❖ Italian queens. 912-367-9352.

Strachan Apiaries Inc., 2522 Tierra Buena Rd., Yuba City, CA 95993: Free information ❖ Queen bees. 916-674-3881.

Swords Apiaries, 5 28th Ave. NW, Moultrie, GA 31768: Free information ❖ Package bees and queens. 912-985-9725.

Taber's Honey Bee Genetics, P.O. Box 1672, Vacaville, CA 95696: Free brochure ❖ Queens and package bees. 707-449-0440.

Tollett Apiaries, 8700 Honey Lane, Millville, CA 96062: Free information ❖ Italian package bees and queens. 916-547-3387.

Howard Weaver Apiaries Inc., Rt. 1, Box 256, Navasota, TX 77868: Free information ❖ Buckfast and Weaver All-American queens and package bees. 409-825-2312.

The Wilbanks Apiaries, P.O. Box 12, Claxton, GA 30417: Free information ❖ Package bees and queens. 912-739-4820.

York Bee Company, P.O. Box 307, Jesup, GA 31545: Free information ❖ Starline, midnight, Italian, package, and queen bees. 912-427-7311.

BEER CANS & STEINS

Anheuser-Busch Inc., 2700 S. Broadway, St. Louis, MO 63150: Free catalog ❖ Heirloom Budweiser and other collectible plates and steins. 800-PICK-BUD.

Classic Carolina Collection, 1502 N. 23rd St., Wilmington, NC 28405: Free catalog ❖ Limited edition steins and tankards with history, sports, entertainment, notable individuals, and anniversary themes. 800-457-9700.

Flash Collectables, 560 N. Moorpark Rd., Thousand Oaks, CA 91360: Free brochure ❖ Collectible American steins. 800-266-BEER.

Gene's Can Shop, 27 State Rt. 34, Martville, NY 13111: Free catalog with one 1st class stamp ❖ Hard-to-find United States, Canadian, and foreign beer cans. 315-564-6699.

Charlie Golden Jr., 345 S. Sterley St., Shillington, PA 19607: United States list $2, foreign list $3, both lists $4.50 ❖ Beer cans from the United States and foreign countries. 610-777-7078.

House of Tyrol, P.O. Box 909, Alpenland Center, Helen Highway/75 North, Cleveland, GA 30528: Free catalog ❖ Musical cuckoo clocks, steins, crystal, porcelain, lamps, music boxes, pillows, knitted items, decor accessories, bar accessories, collector plates, pewter, tapestries, cards, Alpine hat pins, Christmas decorations, and folk music videos. 800-241-5404.

Chester J. Kilanowicz, 5446 Rockwood Rd., Columbus, OH 43229: List $1 ❖ Beer cans. 614-888-0917.

Les Paul, Steinologist, 568 Country Isle, Alameda, CA 94501: Free information ❖ Antique steins. 510-523-7480.

Sam's Steins & Collectables, 2207 Lincoln Hwy East, Lancaster, PA 17602: Free catalog with two 1st class stamps ❖ Beer steins. 800-608-BREW.

Sellek Industries Inc., 9547 Brenda Dr., P.O. Box 290, Roscoe, IL 61073: Free brochure ❖ Sports and professional-theme beer steins for collectors. 800-369-7287.

Soda Mart-Can World, 1055 Ridgecrest Dr., Millersville, TN 37072: Free catalog ❖ Beer and soda cans, signs, trays, glasses, steins, bottle caps, and other reproduction and original nostalgic collectibles. 615-859-5236.

BELLY DANCING

Distant Caravans, P.O. Box 5254, Reno, NV 89513: Catalog $1 ❖ Belly dancing jewelry, music, clothing, drums, lanterns, and other accessories. 702-746-0416.

BICYCLES & ACCESSORIES

Bicycles

AngleTech Cycles, 318 N. Hwy. 67, P.O. Box 1893, Woodland Park, CO 80863: Catalog $2 ❖ Recumbent, special needs, and women's bicycles. 800-793-3038.

Matthew Assenmacher Bikes, 8053 Miller Rd., Swartz Creek, MI 48473: Free information ❖ Mountain and tandem bicycles. 313-635-7844.

Avon Marine, 1851 McGaw Ave., Irvine, CA 92714: Free catalog ❖ Folding bicycles. 800-854-7595; 714-250-0880 (in CA).

Balance Bicycles, 27712 Ave. Mentry, Santa Clarita, CA 91355: Free information ❖ Mountain bicycles. 805-257-2020.

Barracuda, 463 Turner Dr., Durango, CO 81301: Free list of retail sources ❖ Mountain bicycles. 303-259-2622.

Bianchi USA, 2371 Cabot Blvd., Hayward, CA 94545: Free information ❖ Racing, mountain, and city bicycles. 800-431-0006; 510-264-1001 (in CA).

Bicycle Corporation of America, 2811 Brodhead Rd., Bethlehem, PA 18017: Free information ❖ Mountain bicycles. 800-225-2453.

Bike Empire, 12630 Poway Rd., Poway, CA 92064: Free catalog ❖ Bicycles, components, and accessories. 619-679-0306.

Bike Nashbar, 4111 Simon Rd., P.O. Box 3449, Youngstown OH 44512: Free catalog ❖ Racing, sport-touring, touring, and mountain bicycles. 800-627-4227.

Bike Pro, 1599 Cleveland Ave., Santa Rosa, CA 95401: Free information ❖ Bicycles, components, accessories, and clothing.

Bike Rack Inc., 11 Constance Ct., Hauppauge, NY 11788: Free information ❖ Racing and mountain bicycles. 800-645-5477.

Bilenky Cycle Works, 5319 N. 2nd St., Philadelphia, PA 19120: Free information ❖ Tandem bicycles. 800-213-6388.

❖ BICYCLES & ACCESSORIES ❖ 65

BMC Racing, 3620 SE 18th Ct., Renton, WA 98058: Free information ❖ Racing, tandem, and other bicycles. 206-575-2440.

Jeffrey Bock, 929 N. 4th, Ames, IA 50010: Free information ❖ Racing, touring, sport-touring, hybrid, track, and tandem bicycle frames. 515-232-9593.

Boulder Bikes, P.O. Box 1400, Lyons, CO 80540: Free information ❖ Frames and bicycles. 303-823-5021.

Burley Design Cooperative, 4080 Stewart Rd., Eugene, OR 97402: Free list of retail sources ❖ Tandems, other bicycles, and folding bike trailers for children. 503-687-1644.

Cannondale Corporation, P.O. Box 122, Georgetown, CT 06829: Free list of retail sources ❖ Racing, sport-touring, and touring bicycles. 800-245-3872; 203-544-9800 (in CT). [handwritten: FOR CANNONDALE PRODUCTS?]

The Colorado Cyclist, 3970 E. Bijou St., Colorado Springs, CO 80909: Free catalog ❖ Bicycles, bicycle components, tools and accessories, and men and women's clothing. 719-591-4040. [✓]

Curtio Cycles, P.O. Box 896, Santa Clarita, CA 91322: Free information ❖ Frames and bicycles. 805-251-9582.

Dahon California, 633 Meridian St., Duarte, CA 91010: Free information ❖ Folding bicycles. 818-305-5264.

Davidson Cycle, 2116 Western Ave., Seattle, WA 98121: Free information ❖ Mountain, tandem, and women's bicycles. 800-292-5374.

Dean Ultimate Bicycles, 2525 Arapahoe, Ste. E-4, Boulder, CO 80302: Free information ❖ Full-suspension bicycles. 303-530-3091.

Diamond Back Bicycles, 4030 Via Pescador, Camarillo, CA 93012: Free list of retail sources ❖ Off-road and mountain bicycles. 800-776-7641.

Albert Eisentraut, Bicycle Ensemble Corporation, 543 E. 11th St., Oakland, CA 94606: Free information ❖ Racing, touring, sport-touring, hybrid, track, mountain, and tandem bicycle frames. 510-452-4485.

Erickson Cycles, 6119 Brooklyn NE, Seattle, WA 98115: Free information ❖ Mountain, tandem, women's, track, and touring bicycles. 206-527-5259.

Excel Sports Boulder, 2045 32nd St., Boulder, CO 80301: Free catalog ❖ Bicycle computers, off-road equipment, bicycle frame sets, tires, and tubes. 800-627-6664. [✓]

Fat City Cycles, P.O. Box 1439, South Glens Falls, NY 12803: Free information ❖ Mountain and racing bicycles.

Gary Fisher, 801 W. Madison, Waterloo, WI 53594: Free information ❖ Mountain bicycles. 414-478-3532.

FOES Racing, 2660 Deodor Circle, Pasadena, CA 91107: Free information ❖ Mountain bicycles. 818-683-8368.

Fuji America, 118 Bauer Dr., Oakland, NJ 07436: Free information ❖ Racing, sport-touring, touring, mountain, and city bicycles. 800-631-8474; 201-337-1700 (in NJ).

Steve Garn, Brew Racing Frames, 1733 Sutherland Rd., Creston, NC 28615: Free information ❖ Racing, touring, sport-touring, hybrid, track, and mountain bicycle frames.

Giant Bicycle Company, 475 Apra St., Rancho Dominguez, CA 90220: Free information ❖ Racing, mountain, and city bicycles. 800-874-4268; 310-609-3340 (in CA). [✓]

Gita Sporting Goods, 12600 Steele Creek Rd., Charlotte, NC 28273: Free information ❖ Racing and track bicycles. 800-366-4482; 704-588-7550 (in NC).

Bruce Gordon Cycles, 613 2nd St., Petaluma, CA 94952: Free information ❖ Frames and bicycles. 707-762-5601.

GT Bicycles, 3100 W. Segerstrom Ave., Santa Ana, CA 92704: Free information ❖ Mountain bicycles. 800-RID-EAGT; 714-513-7100 (in CA).

Haro Designs Inc., 5922 Farnsworth Ct., Ste. 102B, Carlsbad, CA 92008: Free information ❖ Mountain and racing bicycles. 619-438-4812.

HH Racing Group, 1901 S. 13th St., Philadelphia, PA 19148: Free information ❖ Racing, touring, tandem, and track bicycles. 215-334-8500.

High Zoot/ViaTech Inc., 1700 W. Drake Dr., Ste. 4, Tempe, AZ 85283: Free list of retail sources ❖ Carbon fiber bicycles and components. 602-730-4300.

Holland Cycles, 3735 Kenora Dr., Spring Valley, CA 91977: Free information ❖ Racing, track, tandem, triathlon, and time-trial bicycle frames. 619-469-1772.

Ibis Cycles, P.O. Box 275, Sebastopol, CA 95473: Free information ❖ Mountain and tandem bicycles. 707-829-5615. [✓] [handwritten: HAVE LIST OF RETAIL SOURCES?]

Intense Cycles, 18273 Grand Ave., Lake Elsinore, CA 92530: Free list of retail sources ❖ Mountain bicycles. 909-678-4576.

Iron Horse Bicycles, 1 Constance Ct., Hauppage, NY 11788: Free information ❖ Mountain bicycles. 516-348-6900.

Jamis Bicycles, 151 Ludlow Ave., Northvale, NJ 07647: Free information ❖ Off-road and mountain bicycles.

Joannou Cycle, 151 Ludlow Ave., Northvale, NJ 07647: Free list of retail sources ❖ Mountain bicycles. 201-768-9050.

Kestrel, 120 Lee Rd., Watsonville, CA 95076: Free list of retail sources ❖ Mountain bicycles. 408-724-9079.

KHS Bicycles, 1264 E. Walnut St., Carson, CA 90746: Free information ❖ Mountain and hybrid bicycles. 310-632-7173.

Klein Bicycle Corporation, 801 W. Madison St., P.O. Box 183, Waterloo, WI 53594: Free list of retail sources ❖ Mountain, road, sport-touring, and women's bicycles. 800-52-KLEIN.

Kona Mountain Bikes, 2455 Salashan, Ferndale, WA 98248: Free information ❖ Mountain bicycles. 360-366-2254.

Lippy Bikes, 60265 Fuagarwee Circle, Bend, OR 97702: Free information ❖ Tandem bicycles. 503-389-2503.

Living Extreme, 104 E. Main St., Vermillion, SD 57069: Free information ❖ Mountain bicycles. 605-624-3220.

Mantis Bicycle, 719 W. Woodbury Rd., Altadena, CA 91001: Free list of retail sources ❖ Mountain bicycles. 818-296-1051.

Marble Associates Inc., 1819 Timberlake Dr., Delaware, OH 43015: Free information ❖ Folding motor bike. 614-548-5561.

Marin Mountain Bikes, 16 Mary St., San Rafael, CA 94901: Free information ❖ Mountain bicycles. 800-222-7557; 415-485-5100 (in CA).

Marinoni USA Inc., P.O. Box 187, Bakersfield, VT 05441: Free information ❖ Racing bicycles. 802-827-3647.

McMahon Racing Components, 4195 Carpinteria Ave., Carpinteria, CA 93013: Free information ❖ Bicycle frames and components. 805-684-7398. [✓]

Mongoose Bicycles, 3400 Kashiwa St., Torrance, CA 90505: Free information ❖ Lightweight fitness and mountain bicycles. 310-539-8860.

Montague Bicycle Company, P.O. Box 1118, Cambridge, MA 02238: Free information ❖ Mountain, hybrid, and tandem folding bicycles. 800-736-5348.

Morgan's Cycle & Fitness, 2509 Sunset Ave., Rocky Mount, NC 27804: Free information ❖ Recumbent bicycles. 919-443-4480.

Mountain Goat Cycles, 2145 Park Ave., Chico, CA 95927: Free information ❖ Mountain, hybrid, and tandem bicycles. 916-342-4628. [✓] [handwritten: ? of WHAT?]

New Sense, 5504 Chapel Hill Blvd., Durham, NC 27707: Free information ❖ Mountain bicycles. 800-775-4424.

Nobilette Cycles, 1616 S. Horseshoe Circle, Longmont, CO 80501: Free information ❖ Custom bicycle frames. 303-772-8139.

BICYCLES & ACCESSORIES

Norco Products USA Inc., 7950 Enterprise St., Burnaby, British Columbia, Canada V5A 1V7: Free information ❖ Racing, sport-touring, mountain, and city bicycles. 206-251-9370.

Nytro Bicycles, 940 1st St., Encinatas, CA 92024: Free information ❖ Bicycles and accessories. 619-632-0006.

Ochsner International, 246 Marquardt Dr., Wheeling, IL 60090: Free information ❖ Racing, mountain, and trail bicycles. 312-286-3111.

One-Off Titanium, 221 Pine St., Florence, MA 01060: Free information ❖ Racing, touring, sport-touring, hybrid, track, mountain, tandem, and recumbent bicycle frames. 413-585-5913.

Panasonic Bicycle Division, Panasonic Way, Secaucus, NJ 07094: Free information ❖ Racing, sport-touring, touring, and mountain bicycles. 201-348-5375.

R & A Cycles Inc., 105 5th Ave., Brooklyn, NY 11217: Free information with long SASE ❖ Bicycles and frames. 718-636-5242.

Raleigh Cycle Company of America, 22710 72nd Ave. South, Kent, WA 98032: Free information ❖ Racing, sport-touring, and mountain bicycles. 800-222-5527; 206-395-1100 (in WA).

Rhoades Car, 125 Rhoades Ln., Hendersonville, TN 37075: Free information ❖ Easy-to-pedal 4-wheel bicycles for 1, 2, and 4-persons. 615-822-2737.

Riedel Cycles, 2893 Railroad St., Graton, CA 95444: Free list of retail sources ❖ Mountain bicycles. 707-823-0263.

Ritchey Design, 1326 Hancock St., Redwood City, CA 94063: Free information ❖ Mountain, racing, and tandem bicycles. 415-368-4018.

Rock Lobster Cycles, 219 Trescony St., Santa Cruz, CA 95060: Free information ❖ Mountain, track, and hybrid bicycles. 408-429-1356.

Rock N' Roll Marketing Inc., P.O. Box 1558, Levelland, TX 79336: Free information ❖ Single riders, tandems, and hand-and-foot-powered cycles with optional seat configurations and custom-fitting for individual needs. 800-894-5700.

Rocky Mountain Bicycle Company, 414-5940 No. 6 Rd., Richmond, British Columbia, Canada V6V 1Z1: Free information ❖ Mountain bicycles. 604-270-2710.

Romic Cycle Company, 4434 Steffani Ln., Houston, TX 77041: Free information ❖ Custom racing, touring, and sport-touring bicycles. 713-466-7806.

Ross Bicycles USA, 51 Executive Blvd., Farmingdale, NY 11735: Free information ❖ Mountain and hybrid bicycles. 800-338-7677; 516-249-6000 (in NY).

Ryan Recumbent Cycles, One Chestnut St., 4th Floor, Nashua, NH 03060: Free information ❖ Recumbent bicycles and tandems. 603-598-1711.

Richard Sachs Cycles, No. 1 Main St., Box 194, Chester, CT 06412: Free information ❖ Road racing bicycles. 203-526-2059.

Salsa Bicycles, 6112 2nd St., Petaluma, CA 94952: Free information ❖ Bicycle frames, components, and clothing. 707-762-8191.

Santana Cycles Inc., P.O. Box 206, La Verne, CA 91750: Free information ❖ Tandem bicycles. 909-596-7570.

Schwinn Bicycle Company, 1690 38th St., Boulder, CO 80301: Free information with long SASE ❖ Racing, mountain, tandem, and city bicycles. 303-545-1638.

Scott USA, 1690 38th St., Boulder, CO 80301: Free information ❖ Mountain bicycles. 800-292-5875.

Scorpio Bikes, 17230 S. Avalon Blvd., Carson, CA 90746: Free information ❖ Bicycles. 310-538-8355.

Specialized Bicycle Components, 15130 Concord Circle, Morgan Hill, CA 95037: Free information ❖ Racing and mountain bicycles. 800-245-3462; 408-779-6229 (in CA).

Spectrum Cycles, 1190 Donney Rd., Breinigsville, PA 18031: Free information ❖ Frames and bicycles. 215-398-1986.

Supergo Bike Shops, 501 Broadway, Santa Monica, CA 90401: Free information ❖ Used bicycles. 310-451-9977.

Tandems Limited, Jack & Susan Goertz, 2220 Vanessa Dr., Birmingham, AL 35242: Free information ❖ Tandems, parts, and accessories. 205-991-5519.

Terry Precision Bicycles, 1704 Wayneport Rd., Macedon, NY 14502: Free information ❖ Racing, sport-touring, touring, and mountain bicycles. 800-289-8379; 315-986-2103 (in NY).

Torelli Imports, 1181 Calle Suerte, Camarillo, CA 93012: Free list of retail sources ❖ Racing bicycles. 805-484-8705.

Trek Bicycle Corporation, 801 W. Madison St., P.O. Box 183, Waterloo, WI 53594: Free information ❖ Racing, sport-touring, touring, mountain, city bicycles, and accessories. 800-369-TREK.

UNIVEGA, 3030 Walnut Ave., Long Beach, CA 90807: Free information ❖ Mountain, road, and tandem bicycles. 310-426-0474.

Veltec Sports Inc., 1793 Catalina St., Sand City, CA 93955: Free information ❖ Racing bicycles. 408-394-7114.

Ted Wojcik, 4 Poplar St., Amesbury, MA 01913: Free information ❖ Mountain, road, sport, hybrid, tandem, and track bicycles. 508-388-4150.

Zaskar Bicycles, 3100 W. Segerstrom Ave., Santa Ana, CA 92704: Free information ❖ Mountain bicycles. 714-513-7171.

Clothing

Bike Pro, 1599 Cleveland Ave., Santa Rosa, CA 95401: Free information ❖ Bicycles, components, accessories, and clothing.

Branford Bike, 1074 Main St., Branford, CT 06405: Free catalog ❖ Frames, parts and accessories, tires and tubes, team clothing, cycling gloves, socks, caps, and headbands. 203-488-0482.

Canari Cycle Wear, 10025 Huennekens St., San Diego, CA 92121: Free information ❖ Winter apparel for bikers. 800-929-2925; 619-455-8245 (in CA).

Cannondale Corporation, P.O. Box 122, Georgetown, CT 06821: Free list of retail sources ❖ Jackets and tights for women. Also frame and saddle bags. 800-245-3872; 203-544-9800 (in CT).

Dyno Safety Gear, P.O. Box 25253, Santa Ana, CA 92799: Free information ❖ Safety gear.

The Finals, 1466 Broadway, Ste. 500, New York, NY 10036: Free catalog ❖ Bicycling, aerobic, swimming, running, and exercise clothing. 800-SWIM-816; 212-302-1308 (in NY).

Kucharik Bicycle Clothing, 1745 W. 182nd St., Gardena, CA 90248: Free information ❖ Winter clothing. 310-538-4611.

Pearl Izumi, 2300 Central Ave., Boulder, CO 80301: Free information ❖ Wind-resistant tights and jerseys with zippers for easy removal of the front panel. 800-328-8488; 303-938-1700 (in CO).

Performance Bicycle Shop, P.O. Box 2741, Chapel Hill, NC 27514: Free catalog ❖ Clothing, frames, bicycles and parts, and frame and saddle bags. 800-727-2433.

Puma USA Inc., 147 Centre St., Brockton, MA 02403: Free information with long SASE ❖ Clothing, shoes, and gloves. 508-583-9100.

Salsa Bicycles, 6112 2nd St., Petaluma, CA 94952: Free information ❖ Bicycle frames, components, and clothing. 707-762-8191.

Parts & Accessories

Antique Cycle Supply, P.O. Box 600, Rockford, MI 49341: Catalog $5 ❖ Bicycle parts, books and literature, and antique, classic, and balloon tires. 616-636-8200.

Avocet Inc., P.O. Box 120, Palo Alto, CA 94302: Free information with long SASE ❖ Bike computer that measures speed, distance, and time. 800-227-8346; 415-321-8501 (in CA).

Bell Sports Inc., Rt. 136 East, Rantoul, IL 61866: Free catalog ❖ Bicycle racks, cages, pumps, workstands, trainers, and cycling bags.

❖ BILLIARDS ❖

Bike Nashbar, 4111 Simon Rd., P.O. Box 3449, Youngstown OH 44512: Free catalog ❖ Bicycles, components, and saddlebags. 800-627-4227.

Bike Pro, 1599 Cleveland Ave., Santa Rosa, CA 95401: Free information ❖ Bicycles, components, accessories, and clothing.

The Bike Source, 17801 Main St., Irvine, CA 92714: Free information ❖ Mountain bicycles, parts, and accessories. 714-622-8103.

Bike Tight, P.O. Box 3242, Paso Robles, CA 93447: Free information ❖ Bicycles transporter for cars. 805-238-2976.

Bikecentennial, P.O. Box 8308, 150 E. Pine St., Missoula, MT 59807: Free catalog ❖ Bicycling maps. 406-721-1776.

Branford Bike, 1074 Main St., Branford, CT 06405: Free catalog ❖ Frames, parts and accessories, tires and tubes, team clothing, cycling gloves, socks, caps, and headbands. 203-488-0482.

Burley Design Cooperative, 4080 Stewart Rd., Eugene, OR 97402: Free brochure ❖ Bike trailers for children. Comes with chest harness, seat belt, and roll bar. 503-687-1644.

Cosmopolitan Motors Inc., 301 Jacksonville Rd., Hatboro, PA 19040: Free information ❖ Bicycle locks, packs and bags, and tires. 800-523-2522; 215-672-9100 (in PA).

CyclePro, Derbie Cycle, 22710 72nd Ave. South, Kent, WA 98032: Free information ❖ Frame and saddle bags. 800-222-5527.

D & R Industries, 7111 Capitol Dr., Lincolnwood, IL 60645: Free information ❖ Car-mounted bicycle carriers and child carriers, horns, lamps, locks, packs and bags, racks, reflectors, speedometers, tires and tubes, and helmets. 800-323-2852; 708-677-3200 (in IL).

Eastpak, 50 Rogers Rd., P.O. Box 8232, Ward Hill, MA 01835: Free list of retail sources ❖ Frame and saddle bags. 508-373-1581.

Excel Sports Boulder, 2045 32nd St., Boulder, CO 80301: Free catalog ❖ Bicycle computers, off-road equipment, bicycle frame sets, tires, and tubes. 800-627-6664.

Fairfield Processing Corporation, P.O. Box 1130, Danbury, CT 06813: Free information ❖ Lightweight folding bicycle fairing. 800-442-2271; 203-371-1901 (in CT).

FOES Racing, 2660 Deodor Circle, Pasadena, CA 91107: Free information ❖ Mountain bicycles. 818-683-8368.

Frankford Bicycle Company, 964 N. State St., Girard, OH 44420: Free catalog ❖ Bicycle components and accessories. 800-621-3593; 216-545-0392 (in OH).

Giro Sport Designs, 380 Encinal, Santa Cruz, CA 95060: Free information ❖ Lightweight foam helmets. 800-969-4476.

Lone Peak, 3474 S. 2300 East, Salt Lake City, UT 84109: Free information ❖ Frame and saddle bags. 800-777-7679.

Loose Screws, 12225 Hwy. 66, Ashland, OR 97520: Catalog $3 ❖ Small parts for bicycles. 541-488-4800.

Madden Mountaineering, 2400 Central Ave., Boulder, CO 80301: Free catalog ❖ Frame and saddle bags. 303-442-5828.

Nightsun Performance Lighting, 396 W. Washington Blvd., Ste 600, Pasadena, CA 91103: Free list of retail sources ❖ Dual-beam lighting systems. 818-791-0457.

Overland Equipment, 2145 Park Ave., Ste. 4, Chico, CA 95928: Free catalog ❖ Frame and saddle bags and backpacks. 800-487-8851.

Park Tool Brochure, 3535 International Dr., St. Paul, MN 55110: Free brochure ❖ Mini tool kits.

Pedal Pusher Ski & Sport, 658 Easton Rd., Rt. 611, Horsham, PA 19044: Free catalog ❖ Bicycles, frames, components, tools, clothing, and car carry-all racks. 215-672-0202.

Performance Bicycle Shop, P.O. Box 2741, Chapel Hill, NC 27514: Free catalog ❖ Clothing, frames, bicycles and parts, and frame and saddle bags. 800-727-2433.

Phat Tire, 405 N. Bowser, Richardson, TX 75081: Free information ❖ Tires, wheels, frames, and parts and accessories. 214-437-1020.

REI Recreational Equipment Company, Sumner, WA 98352: Free catalog ❖ Frame and saddle bags. 800-426-4840.

Sachs Bicycle Components, 22445 E. LaPalma Ave., Ste. J, Yorba Linda, CA 92687: Catalog $2 ❖ Bicycle components.

Schwinn Bicycle Company, 1690 38th St., Boulder, CO 80301: Free information with long SASE ❖ Bicycle computer that measures current and maximum speeds, trip distance, odometer readings, and cadence. 303-545-1638.

Malcom Smith Products, 252 Granite St., Corona, CA 91719: Free information ❖ Ultralight bicycle helmet that meets ANSI standards. 800-854-4742; 909-340-3301 (in CA).

Specialized Bicycle Components, 15130 Concord Circle, Morgan Hill, CA 95037: Free information ❖ Frame and saddle bags. 800-245-3462; 408-779-6229 (in CA).

Third Hand, 12225 Hwy. 66, Ashland, OR 97520: Free catalog ❖ Bicycle repair tools, repair stands, parts, and how-to books. 503-488-4800.

Thule Car Rack Systems, 42 Silvermine Rd., Seymour, CT 06483: Free catalog ❖ Automobile multi-purpose storage box systems. 800-783-4160.

Ultimate Bicycle Support, 2506 Zurich Dr., Fort Collins, CO 80522: Free information ❖ Bicycle storage and repair stands. 303-493-4488.

Vetta/Orleander USA, 13659 Victory Blvd, Ste. 264, Van Nuys, CA 91401: Free information with a long SASE ❖ Bicycle computers. 818-780-8808.

VistaLite, 160 Knowles Dr., Los Gatos, CA 95030: Free information ❖ Easy-to-install halogen lights. 800-776-5677.

Wheel World, 22718 Ventura Blvd., Woodland Hills, CA 91364: Free information ❖ Bicycle components and accessories. 818-224-2044.

Zzip Designs, P.O. Box 14, Davenport, CA 95017: Catalog $1 ❖ Bicycle fairings. 408-425-8650.

Tricycles

Mary Arnold Toys, 962 Lexington Ave., New York, NY 10021: Free catalog ❖ Tricycles. 212-744-8510.

Back to Basics Toys, 4315 Walney Rd., Chantilly, VA 22021: Free catalog ❖ Tricycles. 800-356-5360.

Childcraft, 250 College Park, P.O. Box 1811, Peoria, IL 61656: Free catalog ❖ Tricycles. 800-631-5657.

One Step Ahead, P.O. 517, Lake Bluff, IL 60044: Free catalog ❖ Tricycles. 800-950-5120.

BILLIARDS

Adam Custom Cues, 25 Hutcheson Pl., Lynbrook, NY 11563: Free information ❖ Pool cues. 800-645-2162; 516-593-5050 (in NY).

Ajay Leisure Products Inc., 1501 E. Wisconsin St., Delavan, WI 53115: Free list of retail sources ❖ Billiard balls, bridges, chalk, cues and cases, and racks. 800-558-3276; 414-728-5521 (in WI).

Beach Manufacturing, 624 Poinsettia, Santa Ana, CA 92701: Free information ❖ Billiard tables. 800-443-5570.

Billiard Pro Shop, 3673 Mendenhall South, Memphis, TN 38115: Free information ❖ Cues, cases, and billiard tables. 800-365-4776; 901-366-1124 (in TN).

Black Boar, 5110 College Ave., College Park, MD 20740: Free information ❖ Handcrafted pool cues. 301-277-3236.

Bruns Manufacturing Ltd., 10110 State Rt. 13, Huron, OH 44839: Free information ❖ Billiard tables, cue racks, and accessories. 419-433 6137.

Connelly Billiard Manufacturing, 2540 E. Grant Rd., Tucson, AZ 85716: Free information ❖ Billiard tables. 520-881-5503.

Creative Inventions, 7745 Alabama, Unit 1, Canoga Park, CA 91303: Free information ❖ Cues and cases. 800-388-5132; 818-883-5131 (in CA).

The Cuetender Company, P.O. Box 924, Ojai, CA 93024: Free information ❖ Handcrafted wood cue holder that attaches to tables. 805-646-7508.

D & R Industries, 7111 Capitol Dr., Lincolnwood, IL 60645: Free information ❖ Billiard balls, bridges, chalk, cues and cases, and racks. 800-323-2852; 708-677-3200 (in IL).

Dufferin Inc., 1514 St. Paul Ave., Gurnee, IL 60031: Free information ❖ Pool cues. 708-244-4762.

Elephant Balls Ltd., 7723 Southwick Dr., Dublin, OH 43017: Free information ❖ Balls. 614-799-2677.

Elite Custom Cues Inc., P.O. Box 4224, Lincoln, NE 68504: Free information ❖ Cues. 402-464-8401.

Escalade Sports, P.O. Box 889, Evansville, IN 47706: Free catalog ❖ Pool tables. 800-457-3373; 812-467-1200 (in IN).

Giuseppe, 6920 Knott Ave., Buena Park, CA 90620: Free information ❖ Custom cue cases. 800-432-4382.

Huebler Industries Inc., P.O. Box 644, Linn, MO 65051: Free list of retail sources ❖ Pool cues. 314-897-3692.

Indian Industries Inc., P.O. Box 889, Evansville, IN 47706: Free catalog ❖ Racks and cues. 800-457-3373; 812-467-1200 (in IN).

International Billiards Inc., 2311 Washington Ave., Houston, TX 77007: Free information ❖ Billiard balls, bridges, chalk, cues and cases, and racks. 800-255-6386; 713-869-3237 (in TX).

It's George, 403 Lake St., Shrevesport, LA 71101: Free information ❖ Pool cue cases. 800-343-6743.

J-S Sales Company Inc., 5 S. Fulton Ave., Mt. Vernon, NY 10550: Free information ❖ Billiard balls, bridges, chalk, cues and cases, non-slate and slate tables, and racks. 800-431-2944; 914-668-8051 (in NY).

Karella Corporation, 25 Hutcheson Pl., Lynbrook, NY 11563: Free information ❖ Custom cues and cases. 800-645-2162; 516-593-5050 (in NY).

Kasson Game Tables, 11 Commerce Rd., Babbitt, MN 55706: Free information ❖ Billiard tables. 218-827-3701.

The Henry W.T. Mali & Company, 257 Park Ave. South, New York, NY 10010: Free information ❖ Cues. 800-223-6468; 212-475-4960 (in NY).

Mueller Sporting Goods Inc., 4825 S. 16th, Lincoln, NE 68512: Free catalog ❖ Billiard and dart supplies. 800-627-8888.

Murrey & Sons Company Inc., Billiard & Recreation Manufacturing Division, 14150 S. Figueroa St., Los Angeles, CA 90061: Free information ❖ Tables, cues and cases, and accessories. 310-323-1752.

National Merchandise of Virginia, 143 Riverview Ave., Danville, VA 24541: Free catalog ❖ Cues and cases. 800-843-3483.

Owl Darts, 1001 SW Adams, Peoria, IL 61602: Free catalog ❖ Billiards supplies and darts. 800-832-7871.

Papa's Gameroom, 121 Lakeside Dr., Mayfield, NY 12117: Free catalog ❖ Everything for your home gameroom. Darts, billiards, foosball, table tennis, jukeboxes, home casino equipment, and gifts. 888-321-PAPA.

Pennray Billiard & Recreational Products, 6400 W. Gross Point Rd., Niles, IL 60714: Free catalog ❖ Dart, billiard, and soccer equipment. 800-523-8934.

Prathers Custom Cue Parts Inc., P.O. Box 7, Mooreland, OK 73852: Free information ❖ Cue building components. 405-994-2414.

Saunier-Wilhem Company, 3216 5th Ave., Pittsburgh, PA 15213: Free catalog ❖ Equipment and accessories for bowling, billiards, darts, table tennis, shuffleboard, and board games. 412-621-4350.

Schmelke Manufacturing Company, 1879 28th Ave., Rice Lake, WI 54868: Free information ❖ Pool cue cases. 715-234-6553.

Showcase Custom Cues, Division Showcase Billiards, 12031 N. Tejon St., Westminster, CO 80234: Free information ❖ Custom-made cues. 800-783-7849; 303-457-2501 (in CO).

Sporty's Preferred Living Catalog, Clermont Airport, Batavia, OH 45103: Free catalog ❖ Billiard tables complete with balls, rack, bridge, and cues. 800-543-8633.

Tom's Q Stix, 4111 Dudley, Lincoln, NE 68503: Free information ❖ Cues, cases, tips, and accessories. 402-466-6078.

Trusty Enterprises Inc., 2453 Rosemead, South El Monte, CA 91733: Free catalog ❖ Cues and cases. 800-222-2174.

Universal Bowling, Golf & Billiard Supplies, 619 S. Wabash Ave., Chicago, IL 60605: Free catalog ❖ Billiard supplies. 800-523-3037.

Valley Recreation Products Inc., P.O. Box 656, Bay City, MI 48707: Free information ❖ Cues. 800-248-2837; 517-892-4536 (in MI).

Wa-Mac Inc., Highskore Products, P.O. Box 128, Carlstadt, NJ 07410: Free information ❖ Billiard balls, bridges, chalk, cues and cases, and racks. 800-447-5673; 201-438-7200 (in NJ).

World of Leisure Manufacturing Company, 13504 Phantom St., Victorville, CA 92394: Free list of retail sources ❖ Billiard balls, bridges, chalk, cues and cases, and racks. 619-246-3790.

BINOCULARS

Adorama, 42 W. 18th St., New York, NY 10011: Catalog $3 ❖ Binoculars and telescope equipment. 212-741-0466.

Advance Camera Corporation, 15 W. 46th St., New York, NY 10036: Free information ❖ Binoculars. 212-944-1410.

Armchair Sailor Bookstore, 543 Thames St., Newport, RI 02840: Free information ❖ Binoculars. 800-292-4278; 401-847-4252 (in RI).

Astronomics, 2401 Tee Circle, Ste. 106, Norman, OK 73069: Free information ❖ Binoculars. 405-364-0858.

Ball Photo Supply Company, 85 Tunnel Rd., Asheville, NC 28805: Free information ❖ Telescopes, spotting scopes, camera equipment, binoculars, eyepieces, and accessories. 704-252-2443.

Bausch & Lomb, 9200 Cody, Overland Park, KS 66214: Free list of retail sources ❖ Binoculars. 800-423-3537.

Beckson Marine, 165 Holland Ave., Bridgeport, CT 06605: Free catalog ❖ Binoculars. 203-333-1412.

Berger Brothers Camera Exchange, 209 Broadway, Amityville, NY 11701: Free information ❖ Binoculars. 800-262-4160.

The Bushnell Corporation, Customer Service, 9200 Cody, Overland Park, KS 66214: Free information ❖ Binoculars for eyeglass wearers. 800-423-3537.

California Telescope Company, P.O. Box 1338, Burbank, CA 91507: Catalog $5 ❖ Binoculars. 818-505-8424.

Camera Bug Ltd., 1799 Briarcliff Rd., Atlanta, GA 3030: Free information ❖ Telescopes, binoculars, spotting scopes, and accessories. 404-873-4513.

❖ BINOCULARS ❖

Camera Corner of Iowa, 3523 Eastern Ave., Davenport, IA 52807: Free information ❖ Camera equipment and binoculars. 319-391-6851.

Canon Binoculars, C.S.B. 3192A, Melville, NY 11747: Free list of retail sources ❖ Lightweight, compact, or waterproof binoculars.

Celestron International, 2835 Columbia St., Torrance, CA 90503: Catalog $2 ❖ Binoculars. 310-328-9560.

The Chartroom, Chase, Leavitt & Company, 10 Dana St., Portland, ME 04112: Free information ❖ Marine binoculars. 800-638-8906; 207-772-3751 (in ME).

Chinon America Inc., 1065 Bristol Rd., Mountainside, NJ 07092: Free information ❖ Binoculars. 908-654-0404.

Christophers Ltd., 2401 Tee Circle, Ste. 106, Norman, OK 73069: Free information ❖ Binoculars. 800-356-6603.

City Camera, 15336 W. Warren, Dearborn, MI 46126: Free information ❖ Binoculars and spotting scopes. 800-359-5085.

Compass Industries, 104 E. 25th St., New York, NY 10010: Free information ❖ Binoculars. 800-221-9904.

Cosmic Connections Inc., P.O. Box 7, Aurora, IL 60505: Catalog $2 ❖ Binoculars. 800-634-7702.

Cosmos Ltd., 9215 Waukegan Rd., Morton Grove, IL 60053: Free catalog ❖ Binoculars. 800-643-2351.

Eagle Optics, 716 S. Whitney Way, Madison, WI 53711: Free catalog ❖ Binoculars. 608-271-4751.

Edmund Scientific Company, Edscorp Building, Barrington, NJ 08007: Free catalog ❖ Binoculars, telescopes, and other educational and science equipment. 609-573-6260.

Europtik Ltd., P.O. Box 319, Dunmore, PA 18509: Free information ❖ Binoculars and rifle scopes. 717-347-6049.

Eye-1 Optics, 1525 Xenia Ave., Yellow Springs, OH 45387: Free information ❖ Binoculars and spotting scopes. 800-800-EYE-1.

Focus Camera, 4419 13th Ave., Brooklyn, NY 11219: Free information ❖ Binoculars. 718-436-6262.

Fujinon, 10 High Point Dr., Wayne, NJ 07470: Free information ❖ Binoculars. 201-633-5600.

Garden State Camera, 101 Kuller Rd., Clifton, NJ 07015: Free information ❖ Photographic equipment, camcorders, video and audio accessories, binoculars, and other optical equipment. 201-742-5777.

Helix, 310 S. Racine, Chicago, IL 60607: Free catalog ❖ Binoculars. 800-33-HELIX; 312-421-6000 (in IL).

HP Marketing Group, 16 Chapin Rd., Pine Brook, NJ 07058: Free information ❖ Binoculars. 201-808-9010.

InteliOptics, Division Brunton Company, 620 E. Monroe, Riverton, WY 82501: Free brochure ❖ Binoculars with an integrated microprocessor for precision rangefinding and data interpretation. 307-856-6559.

ITT Night Vision, 7671 Enon Dr., Roanoke, VA 24019: Free list of retail sources ❖ Night vision optical viewer. 800-448-8678.

A. Jaegers Optical Supply Company, 11 Roosevelt Ave., Spring Valley, NY 11581: Free catalog ❖ Surplus binoculars, telescopes, lenses, and prisms. 516-599-3167.

Khan Scope Center, 3243 Dufferin St., Toronto, Ontario, Canada M6A 2T2: Free price list ❖ Binoculars. 416-783-4140.

Leica USA Inc., 156 Ludlow St., Northvale, NJ 07647: Free information ❖ Binoculars and camera equipment. 201-767-7500.

Leupold & Stevens Inc., P.O. Box 688, Beaverton, OR 97075: Free list of retail sources ❖ Binoculars. 503-526-1491.

Lumicon, 2111 Research Dr., Livermore, CA 94550: Free catalog ❖ Binoculars. 510-447-9570.

Mardiron Optics, 4 Spartan Circle, Stoneham, MA 02180: Free brochure with two 1st class stamps ❖ Binoculars and astronomy equipment. 617-938-8339.

Meade Instruments Corporation, 16542 Millikan Ave., Irvine, CA 92714: Catalog $3 ❖ Binoculars. 714-556-2291.

F.C. Meichsner Company, 182 Lincoln St., Boston, MA 02111: Free information ❖ Binoculars. 800-321-8439.

Minolta, 101 Williams Dr., Ramsey, NJ 07446: Free information ❖ Binoculars. 201-825-4000.

Mirador Optical, P.O. Box 11614, Marina Del Rey, CA 90295: Free information ❖ Binoculars. 213-821-5587.

National Camera Exchange, 9300 Olson Memorial Hwy., Golden Valley, MN 55427: Free information ❖ Binoculars and spotting scopes. 800-624-8107; 612-546-6831 (in MN).

Nikon Photo, Customer Relations, 19601 Hamilton Ave., Torrance, CA 90502: Free information ❖ Binoculars. 800-645-6687.

Optron Systems, 15840 E. Alta Vista Way, San Jose, CA 95127: Free information ❖ Binoculars. 408-923-6800.

Orion Telescope & Binocular Center, P.O. Box 1815, Santa Cruz, CA 95061: Free catalog ❖ Telescopes, photographic equipment, charts and star maps, books, science supplies, and binoculars. 800-447-1001.

Parks Optical Company, 270 Easy St., Simi Valley, CA 93065: Catalog $3 ❖ Binoculars. 805-522-6722.

Pauli's Wholesale Optics, 29 Kingswood Rd., Danbury, CT 06811: Catalog $10 (refundable) ❖ Binoculars. 203-748-3579.

Pentax Corporation, 35 Inverness Dr. East, Englewood, CO 80112: Free information ❖ Binoculars, cameras, lenses, and other optical equipment. 303-799-8000.

Perceptor, Brownsville Junction Plaza, Box 38, Ste. 201, Schomberg, Ontario, Canada L0G 1T0: Free information ❖ Binoculars. 905-939-2313.

Pioneer Research, 216 Haddon Ave., Westmont, NJ 08108: Free information ❖ Binoculars. 800-257-7742; 609-854-2424 (in NJ).

Pocono Mountain Optics, RR 6, Box 6329, Moscow, PA 18444: Catalog $6 ❖ Binoculars, spotting scopes, and astronomy equipment. 800-569-4323; 717-842-1500 (in PA).

Quasar Optics, 3715 51st St. SW, Calgary, Alberta, Canada T3E 6V2: Catalog $4 ❖ Binoculars. 403-240-0680.

Redlich Optical, 711 W. Broad St., Falls Church, VA 22046: Free information with long SASE ❖ Binoculars, spotting scopes, and telescopes. 703-241-4077.

Ricoh Consumer Products Group, 475 Lillard Dr., Sparks, NV 89434: Free brochure ❖ Binoculars. 800-225-1899.

Royal Optics, 20 Glassco Ave. South, Hamilton, Ontario, Canada L8H 1B3: Free brochure ❖ Eyepieces and binoculars.

Sarasota Camera Exchange & Video Center, 1055 S. Tamiami Trail, Sarasota, FL 34236: Free information ❖ New and used telescopes, binoculars, filters, parts, and software. 941-366-7484.

Scope City, P.O. Box 440, Simi Valley, CA 93065: Catalog $7 (refundable) ❖ Binoculars. 805-522-6646.

Selsi Binoculars, P.O. Box 10, Midland Park, NJ 07432: Free information ❖ Binoculars.

Shutan Camera & Video, 312 W. Randolph, Chicago, IL 60606: Free catalog ❖ Binoculars. 800-621-2248; 312-332-2000 (in IL).

Simmons Outdoor Company, 2120 Killearney Way, Tallahassee, FL 32308: Catalog $2 ❖ Binoculars. 904-878-5100.

Stano Components, P.O. Box 2048, Carson City, NV 89702: Catalog $4 ❖ Night-vision optical equipment. 702-246-5281.

Steiner Binoculars, c/o Pioneer Research Inc., 216 Haddon Ave., Westmont, NJ 08108: Free information ❖ Binoculars. 609-854-2424.

Swarovski Optik, One Wholesale Way, Cranston, RI 02920: Free information ❖ Binoculars. 800-426-3089.

Swift Instruments Inc., 952 Dorchester Ave., Boston, MA 02125: Free list of retail sources ❖ Binoculars and cases, and spotting scopes that can be used on cameras. 800-446-1115; 617-436-2960 (in MA).

Tamron Industries Inc., P.O. Box 388, Port Washington, NY 11050: Free brochure ❖ Binoculars and spotting scopes that can be adapted for camera use as an ultra-telescopic zoom lens. 800-827-8880.

Tasco Sales Inc., P.O. Box 520080, Miami, FL 33152: Free information ❖ Binoculars and other optical equipment. 305-591-3670.

Tokina Optical Corporation, 1512 Kona Dr., Compton, CA 90220: Free information ❖ Binoculars. 310-537-9380.

Roger W. Tuthill Inc., 11 Tanglewood Ln., Mountainside, NJ 07092: Free catalog with 9x12 self-addressed envelope and four 1st class stamps ❖ Binoculars. 800-223-1063.

Unitron Inc., 170 Wilbur Pl., P.O. Box 469, Bohemia, NY 11716: Free catalog ❖ Binoculars. 516-589-6666.

University Optics, P.O. Box 1205, Ann Arbor, MI 48106: Free catalog ❖ Binoculars. 800-521-2828.

Vivitar Corporation, 1280 Rancho Conejo Blvd., P.O. Box 2559, Newbury Park, CA 91319: Free brochure ❖ Binoculars. 805-498-7008.

Ward's Natural Science, P.O. Box 92912, 5100 W. Henrietta Rd., Rochester, NY 14692: Earth science catalog $10; biology catalog $15; middle school catalog $10 ❖ Binoculars and other optical science equipment. Also other laboratory equipment and supplies. 800-962-2660.

Zeiss Optical Inc., 1015 Commerce St., Petersburg, VA 23803: Free brochure ❖ Binoculars. 800-338-2984.

BIRD FEEDERS & HOUSES

American Pie Company, P.O. Box 1317, Castleton, VT 05735: Free information ❖ Weatherproof bird feeders.

Animal Environments, 2270 Camino Vida Roble, Ste. 1, Carlsbad, CA 92009: Free information ❖ Environmentally-designed cages. 619-438-4442.

Anyone Can Whistle, P.O. Box 4407, Kingston, NY 12401: Free catalog ❖ Bird feeders, wind chimes, and other musical gifts. 800-435-8863.

Audubon Naturalist, 8940 Jones Mill Rd., Silver Spring, MD 20815: Free information with long SASE ❖ Birdhouses, feeders, baths, handcrafted jewelry, binoculars, puppets, and other gifts. 800-699-BIRD; 301-652-3606 (in MD).

Avian Accents, P.O. Box 109, Troy, IL 62294: Free information ❖ Hardwood bird cages. 618-667-2243.

The Backyard Sanctuary Company, 550 Warren St., P.O. Box 307, Hudson, NY 12534: Free information ❖ Handcrafted copper bird feeders. 800-247-3735.

Beck's Feeders, P.O. Box 103, Williamsburg, IN 47393: Free information ❖ Feeder for chickadees, titmice, nuthatches, and gold-finches. 317-874-1496.

Best Feeders Inc., P.O. Box 998, Poteet, TX 78065: Free list of retail sources ❖ Hummingbird feeders and accessories. 800-772-3604.

Birding Concepts, P.O. Box 296, Appleton, WI 54912: Free information ❖ Wild bird feeders and seed. 800-269-4450.

The Brewster Birdhouse, P.O. Box 620073, Newton Lower Falls, MA 02162: Free information with long SASE ❖ Antique reproduction of an English roost house. 617-235-9552.

The Brown Company, Yawgoo Pond Rd., West Kingston, RI 02892: Free information ❖ Hummingbird and butterfly feeders. 800-556-7670.

Brushy Mountain Bee Farm, 610 Bethany Church Rd., Moravian Falls, NC 28654: Free catalog ❖ Birdhouses, feeders, and beekeeping supplies. 800-BEESWAX.

C & S Products Company Inc., Box 848, Fort Dodge, IA 50501: Free catalog ❖ Suet products and feeders. 515-955-5605.

California Cage Company, 705 Soscol Ave., Napa, CA 94559: Free information ❖ Wrought-iron bird cages with optional feeders. 800-90-FEATHER; 707-257-8815 (in CA).

California Cageworks Corporation, 3314 Burton Ave., Burbank, CA 91504: Free information ❖ Breeding cages with custom options. 813-843-MATE.

The Clarion Martin House, RR 1, Box 130, Winfield, MO 63389: Free information ❖ Purple martin house with telescoping pole. 800-845-9178.

Droll Yankees Inc., 27 Mill Rd., Foster, RI 02825: Free catalog ❖ Bird feeders. 800-352-9164.

Duncraft, 102 Fisherville Rd., Concord, NH 03303: Free catalog ❖ Wild bird supplies, squirrel-proof feeders, birdhouses, bird baths, and books. 800-763-7878.

The Edisonville Woodshop, 1916 Edisonville Rd., Strasburg, PA 17579: Brochure $1 ❖ Handcrafted all-wood mailboxes and bird feeders. 717-687-0116.

1891 Originals, P.O. Box 9505, Canton, OH 44711: Brochure $1 (refundable) ❖ Antique reproduction nesting boxes. 800-381-BIRD.

The Gathering Place, 868 15th St., P.O. Box 163, Otsego, MI 49078: Free information ❖ Hiking and walking sticks, bamboo and cedar birdhouses, and feeders. 616-694-4477.

Hammer's Wire & Wood, P.O. Box 205, Judson, TX 75660: Free information ❖ Handcrafted birdhouses. 800-227-8841; 903-663-1145 (in TX).

Hyde Bird Feeder Company, 56 Felton St., P.O. Box 168, Waltham, MA 02254: Free catalog ❖ Bird feeders and wild bird food. 617-893-6780.

Inglebrook Forges, 151 N. San Dimas Canyon Rd., San Dimas, CA 91773: Free information ❖ Bird cages. 909-599-0933.

The Kinsman Company, River Rd., Point Pleasant, PA 18950: Free catalog ❖ Thatched English birdhouses. 800-733-4146.

Lady Slipper Designs, Rt. 3, Box 556, Bemidji, MN 56601: Free information with long SASE ❖ Birdhouses. 800-950-5903.

Lazy Hill Farm Designs, P.O. Box 197, Charlotte, NC 28204: Free information ❖ Handcrafted garden accessories and birdhouses. 800-396-7706.

Lexacon Pet Products, P.O. Box 1091, Kent, OH 44240: Free information ❖ Cage-top play gyms. 800-752-4589.

Los Angeles Audubon Society Bookstore, 7377 Santa Monica Blvd., West Hollywood, CA 90046: Free catalog ❖ Bird and nature books, bookmarks, and feeders. 213-876-0202.

Mac Industries, 8125 South I-35, Oklahoma City, OK 73149: Brochure $1 ❖ Traditional and colonial-style Martin houses with galvanized steel telescoping and perch poles, stops, and weather vanes. 800-654-4970.

McCoy's Arts & Crafts, 706 E. Sprague, Spokane, WA 99202: Brochure $2 ❖ Decorated or undecorated wooden birdhouses. 800-456-5005.

Meadowlark Manufacturing Ltd., 916 Birmingham Rd., Liberty, MO 64068: Free information ❖ Bird and bluebird houses, winter roosting boxes, and feeders for birds, bluebirds, squirrels, and bats.

Nature's Nest, 1551 Barwise, Wichita, KS 67214: Free information ❖ Gazebo bird feeder. 800-268-9240.

Peters Feeders, Division Peter's Products, P.O. Box 337, Chetek, WI 54728: Catalog $1 ❖ Hummingbird and oriole feeders and supplies. 800-775-0124.

Plow & Hearth, P.O. Box 5000, Madison, VA 22727: Free catalog ❖ Outdoor furniture, birdhouses and feeders, bird baths, and gardening tools. 800-627-1712.

Poise N' Ivy, 120 Maine Ave. North, Twin Falls, ID 83301: Free catalog ❖ Natural birch birdhouse kits. 208-733-1907.

Safeguard Products Inc., P.O. Box 8, New Holland, PA 17557: Free catalog ❖ Exotic bird and parrot breeding and flight cages. 800-433-1819.

❖ BIRTH ANNOUNCEMENTS ❖

Spirit of the Wood, P.O. Box 647, Lake Placid, NY 12946: Free brochure ❖ Cedar birdhouses and bird feeders. 518-523-8113.

UPCO, P.O. Box 969, St. Joseph, MO 64502: Free catalog ❖ Cages, birdseed, books, toys, and remedies for birds. 800-444-8651.

Vermont Nature Creations, P.O. Box 1317, Castleton, VT 05735: Free brochure ❖ Handcrafted bird feeders.

Wild Bird Supplies, 4815 Oak St., Crystal Lake, IL 60012: Free catalog ❖ Feeders, birdhouses and baths, birdseed mixes, and books on bird care. 815-455-4020.

Wings of Wausau, P.O. Box 178, Wausau, WI 54482: Free catalog ❖ Bird feeders. 800-799-7005.

Woodcrest Ltd., 7675 Lawndale Ln. North, Maple Grove, MN 55311: Free brochure ❖ Vintage-style bird houses. 612-420-2978.

Zachariasen Studio, N659 Drumm Rd., Denmark, WI 54208: Catalog $3 ❖ Handmade ceramic birdbaths, fountains, and other garden ornaments. 414-776-1778.

BIRTH ANNOUNCEMENTS

Baby Face, P.O. Box 12410, Portland, OR 97212: Free brochure ❖ Personalized birth announcements. 800-553-1412.

Babygram Service Center, 201 Main St., Ste. 1955, Fort Worth, TX 76102: Free brochure ❖ Photographic birth announcements. 800-345-BABY.

Birth-O-Gram Company, P.O. Box 144782, Coral Gables, FL 33114: Catalog $1 (refundable) ❖ Birth announcements with work-related, sport, and hobby themes. 305-267-1479.

Grapevine Graphics, 4231 Knollview Dr., Danville, CA 94506: Free brochure ❖ Birth announcements. 510-736-3871.

H & F Announcements, 3734 W. 95th, Leawood, KS 66206: Free catalog ❖ Birth announcements and invitations. 800-964-4002.

Heart Thoughts Cards, 6200 E. Central, Ste. 100, Wichita, KS 67208: Free brochure ❖ Birth announcements and thank-you notes. 800-670-4224.

The Personal Touch, 19 Forest Dr., Flemington, NJ 08822: Free information ❖ Personalized birth announcements. 800-488-8404.

Pride & Joy Announcements, 5415 Kendall St., Boise, ID 83706: Free catalog ❖ Birth announcements. 800-657-6404.

BLACKSMITHING

Centaur Forge Ltd., 117 N. Spring St., P.O. Box 340, Burlington, WI 53105: Catalog $5 (refundable) ❖ Blacksmithing equipment. 414-763-9175.

Cumberland General Store, Rt. 3, Box 81, Crossville, TN 38555: Catalog $3 ❖ Blacksmithing equipment, hand pumps, windmills, wood cooking ranges, gardening tools, cast-iron wares, farm bells, buggies, harnesses, and other equipment. 800-334-4640.

Mankel Blacksmith Shop, P.O. Box 29, Cannonsburg, MI 49317: Free information ❖ Forging equipment. 616-874-6955.

NC Tool Company, 6568 Hunt Dr., Pleasant Garden, NC 27313: Free information ❖ Equipment for blacksmiths and farriers. 800-446-6498.

BLOCK PRINTING

Cutbill & Company, 274 Sherman Ave. North, Unit 213, Hamilton, Ontario, Canada L8I 6N6: Free catalog ❖ Block printing supplies and kits. 800-960-3592.

Graphic Chemical & Ink Company, P.O. Box 27, Villa Park, IL 60181: Free catalog ❖ Print-making supplies for etching, block prints, lithography, and other reproduction processes. 708-832-6004.

Technical Papers Corporation, P.O. Box 546, Dedham, MA 02027: Free catalog ❖ Sheets and rolls of handmade rice paper in prints and solids and multi-colors for all types of artistic printing, including block printing, etching, lithography, and silk-screening. 617-461-1111.

BOATS & BOATING

Boating Apparel & Safety Gear

ACR Electronics, 5757 Ravenswood Rd., Fort Lauderdale, FL 33312: Free information ❖ Safety and survival equipment. 305-981-3333.

Atlantis, 30 Barnet Blvd., New Bedford, MA 02745: Free catalog ❖ Foul weather gear and clothing for yachtsmen and fishermen. 508-995-7000.

L.L. Bean, Freeport, ME 04033: Free catalog ❖ Safety apparel, foul weather gear, and deck shoes. 800-483-2326.

Cal-June, P.O. Box 9551, North Hollywood, CA 91609: Free information ❖ Safety apparel and equipment. 818-761-3516.

Colorado Kayak, P.O. Box 3059, Buena Vista, CO 81211: Free catalog ❖ Men and women's clothing. 800-535-3565.

Commodore Uniform & Nautical Supplies, 335 Lower County Rd., Harwichport, MA 02646: Free information ❖ Boating uniforms, insignia, and flags. 800-438-8643; 508-430-7877 (in MA).

Datrex, P.O. Box 1150, Kinder, LA 70648: Free information ❖ Safety and survival gear. 800-828-1131.

Defender Industries Inc., 25542 Great Neck Rd., Waterford, CT 06385: Free catalog ❖ Clothing, life vests, foul weather gear, and marine supplies. 800-701-3400.

Fireboy Halon Systems, P.O. Box 152, Grand Rapids, MI 49502: Free information ❖ Fire extinguishers for boats. 616-454-8337.

Fletcher-Barnhardt & White, 1211 S. Tyron St., Charlotte, NC 28203: Free catalog ❖ Sportswear. 800-543-5453.

Givens Ocean Survival Systems, 35 Lagoon Rd., Portsmouth, RI 02871: Free information ❖ Safety and survival gear. 800-328-8050; 401-683-7400 (in RI).

Halotech Inc., P.O. Box 5102, Center Square, PA 19422: Free information ❖ Emergency radio beacons. 610-275-8359.

Hellamarine, 201 Kelly Dr., P.O. Box 2665, Peachtree City, GA 30269: Free information ❖ Hand-held searchlights, navigation and interior lamps, halogen floodlights, and other lamps. 404-631-7500.

High Seas Foul Weather Gear, 880 Corporate Woods Pkwy., Vernon Hills, IL 60061: Free list of retail sources ❖ Clothing for the outdoors. 708-913-1100.

Kokatat, 5350 Ericson Way, Arcata, CA 95521: Free information ❖ Waterproof and breathable water sportswear. 800-225-9749; 707-822-7621 (in CA).

Life Raft & Survival Equipment, 1 Maritime Dr., Portsmouth, RI 02871: Free information ❖ Inflatable life jackets. 800-451-2127; 401-683-0307 (in RI).

Maximum Whitewater Performance, 6211 Ridge Dr., Bethesda, MD 20816: Free catalog ❖ Boats, paddles, clothing, and safety gear. 301-229-4304.

MRC (Mariner Resource), 86 Orchard Beach Blvd., Port Washington, NY 11050: Free information ❖ Safety harnesses and flotation coats. 800-645-6516.

Mustang Survival, 3870 Mustang Way, Bellingham, WA 98226: Free information ❖ Survival flotation clothing for protection against hypothermia and overboard accidents. 800-526-0532; 206-676-1782 (in WA).

Northwest Outdoor Center, 2100 Westlake Ave. North, Seattle, WA 98109: Free catalog ❖ Kayak equipment, safety and rescue equipment, clothing, and books. 800-683-0637.

O-S Systems, The Drysuit People, 33550 SE Santosh, P.O. Box 864, Scappoose, OR 97056: Free information ❖ Men and women's clothing. 503-543-3126.

Patagonia Mail Order, P.O. Box 8900, Bozeman, MT 59715: Free catalog ❖ Sportswear and foul weather clothing. 800-336-9090.

Peconic Paddler, 89 Peconic Ave., Riverhead, NY 11901: Free information ❖ Canoes, kayaks, rowing shells, sea kayaks, paddles, life jackets, and dry suits. 516-727-9895.

❖ BOATS & BOATING ❖

Port Supply/Lifesling, 500 Westridge Dr., Watsonville, CA 95076: Free information ❖ Overboard rescue system. 800-621-6885; 408-728-4417 (in CA).

Rainbow Designs, Box 3155, Boulder, CO 80307: Free information ❖ White water equipment, paddle jackets, and neoprene products. 303-444-8495.

Safety Flag Company of America, P.O. Box 1088, 390 Pine St., Pawtucket, RI 02862: Free catalog ❖ Flags, vests, belts, and marine safety equipment. 401-722-0900.

The Sailor's Source, P.O. Box 20926, St. Petersburg, FL 33742: Free information ❖ Overboard rescue system, safety harnesses, emergency position indicating beacons, and other equipment. 813-577-3220.

Seda Products, 926 Coolidge Ave., National City, CA 91950: Free catalog ❖ Kayaks and canoes, life vests, and paddles. 619-336-2444.

Smallwoods Yachtwear, 1001 SE 17th St., Fort Lauderdale, FL 33316: Free catalog ❖ Uniforms and casual boating attire. 800-771-2283.

SMR Technologies Inc., 1420 Wolf Creek Trail, P.O. Box 326, Sharon Center, OH 44274: Free list of retail sources ❖ Life rafts with emergency equipment. 216-239-1000.

Survival Products Inc., 5614 SW 25th St., Hollywood, FL 33023: Free information ❖ Emergency life rafts. 305-966-7329.

Survival Technologies Group, 6418 US Hwy. 41 North, Ste. 266, Apollo Beach, FL 33572: Free information ❖ Safety and survival gear. 800-525-2747; 813-645-5586 (in FL).

Switlik Parachute, 1325 E. State St., Trenton, NJ 08609: Free information ❖ Safety and survival products. 609-587-3300.

Boat-Building Kits & Plans

Benford Design Group, P.O. Box 447, St. Michaels, MD 21663: Catalog $10 ❖ Catboats, yachts, other boat kits, and plans. 410-745-3235.

Boat Plans International, P.O. Box 18000, Boulder, CO 80308: Catalog $24.95 ❖ Boat plans. 604-932-6874.

Boucher Kayak Company, 1907 Ludington Ave., Wauwatosa, WI 53226: Brochure $2 with long SASE ❖ Kayak kits. 414-476-3787.

Chesapeake Light Craft, 1805 George Avenue, Annapolis, MD 21401: Free brochure ❖ Kits, plans, and finished wood kayaks. 410-267-0137; 301-858-6335 (in DC Metro area).

Clark Craft Boat Company, 16 Aqualane, Tonawanda, NY 14150: Catalog $3 ❖ Power and sailboat kits, plans, and hardware. 716-873-2640.

Norman Cross Boat Plans, 4326 Ashton, San Diego, CA 92110: Free information ❖ Boat plans. 619-276-0910.

Bruce Farr & Associates, 613 3rd St., P.O. Box 4964, Annapolis, MD 21403: Free information ❖ Sailboat plans for amateur and professional construction. 410-267-0780.

Feather Canoes Inc., 3080 N. Washington Blvd., Sarasota, FL 34234: Free information ❖ Boat kits. 813-953-7660.

J. Gengler Boat Design, Rt. 2, Box 209, Plainfield, WI 54966: Free information ❖ Fishing skiffs.

Glen-L Marine Designs, 9152 Rosecrans, Box 1804, Bellflower, CA 90706: Catalog $5 ❖ Marine hardware, boat-building supplies, and kits for canoes, kayaks, dinghies, and plywood and fiberglass boats. 310-630-6258.

Great Lakes Boat Building Company, 7066 103rd Ave., South Haven, MI 49090: Free information ❖ Boat kits. 616-637-6805.

Ken Hankinson Associates, P.O. Box 272, Hayden Lake, ID 83835: Free information ❖ Boat plans, patterns, kits, and supplies. 208-772-5547.

Jordan Wood Boats, P.O. Box 194, South Beach, OR 97366: Information $3 ❖ Tenders and skiffs.

King Boat Works, P.O. Box 234, Putney, VT 05346: Information $5 ❖ Shells for 1, 2, 4, and 6-persons. 802-387-5373.

Laughing Loon, Rob Macks, 833 W. Colrain Rd., Greenfield, MA 01301: Catalog $5 ❖ Custom canoes and kayaks and building plans. 413-773-5375.

MDS Designs, Orlando Business Center, 2200 Forsyth Rd., Orlando, FL 32807: Brochure $2 ❖ Paddle, sail, and motor-powered canoes.

Merryman Boats, 4915 Delta River Dr., Lansing, MI 48906: Free information ❖ Boat kit complete with sails, oars, brass hardware, ropes, and tools. 517-482-9333.

Monfort Associates, Division Aladdin Products, RR 2, Box 416, Wiscasset, ME 04878: Catalog $5.95 ❖ Boat plans and kits. 207-882-5504.

The Newfound Woodworks Inc., RFD 2, Box 850, Bristol, NH 03222: Free information ❖ Canoe kits, books, plans, supplies, and accessories. 603-744-6872.

Old Wooden Boatworks, 106 8th St. East, Bradenton, FL 33508: Free information ❖ Dinghy kit. 813-747-8898.

David Pecci Carpentry, 4 Patricia Dr., Topsham, ME 04086: Free information ❖ Dinghy kit. 207-442-8581.

Bruce Roberts Designs, P.O. Box 1086, Severna Park, MD 21146: Catalog $5 ❖ Sail and power boat plans. 410-544-4311.

Stimson Marine Inc., RR 1, Box 524, River Rd., Boothbay, ME 04537: Brochure $2 ❖ Boat lumber and building plans. 207-633-7252.

Tri-Star Trimarans, P.O. Box 286, Venice, CA 90291: Free information ❖ Boat plans. 310-396-6154.

Wayland Marine Ltd., Ron Mueller, P.O. Box 4330, Bellingham, WA 98227: Free catalog ❖ Boat kits. 360-738-8059.

Windward Designs, 794 Creekview Rd., Severna Park, MD 21146: Plans catalog $10 ❖ Easy-to-build skiffs, daysailers, shallow-draft sharpies, and cruisers. 800-376-3152.

The Wooden Boat Shop, 1007 NE Boat St., Seattle, WA 98105: Catalog $3 ❖ Easy-to-build skiff kit. 800-933-3600; 206-634-3600 (in WA).

WoodenBoat Books, Naskeag Rd., P.O. Box 78, Brooklin, ME 04616: Free information ❖ Wood racing shell kit. 800-225-5205; 207-359-4647 (in ME).

Canoes, Kayaks, Shells & Paddles

Aire, P.O. Box 3412, Boise, ID 83703: Free catalog ❖ Self-bailing, inflatable touring kayaks. 208-344-7506.

Alden Ocean Shells Inc., P.O. Box 368, Eliot, ME 03903: Free catalog ❖ Shells and rowing accessories. 800-626-1536.

Alder Creek Boat Works, RFD 3, Box 78, Remsen, NY 13438: Catalog $3 (refundable) ❖ Wood canoes. 315-831-5321.

Alumacraft Boat Company, 315 W. Julien St., St. Peter, MN 56082: Free information ❖ Aluminum canoes. 507-931-1050.

American Traders Classic Canoes, 627 Barton Rd., Greenfield, MA 01301: Free catalog ❖ Wood canoes. 800-782-7816.

Aqua-Bound Technology Ltd., 8938 192nd St., Surrey, British Columbia, Canada V4N 3W8: Free information ❖ Sea cruising and touring kayak paddles. 604-882-2052.

Aquaterra, P.O. Box 8002, Easley, SC 29641: Free information ❖ Touring kayaks. 803-859-7518.

Baidarka Boats, Box 6001, Sitka, AK 99835: Free catalog ❖ Folding kayaks. 907-747-8996.

Baldwin Boat Company, RFD 2, Box 268, Orrington, ME 04474: Free information ❖ Kayaks. 207-825-4439.

Barton Paddle Company, 402 NW 9th St., Grand Rapids, MI 55744: Free information ❖ Lightweight carbon-fiber canoe paddles. 218-326-8757.

Bear Creek Canoe, RR Box 163, Rt. 11, Limerick, ME 04048: Free information ❖ Handbuilt recreational canoes. 207-793-2005.

❖ BOATS & BOATING ❖

Betsie Bay Kayak, P.O. Box 1706, Frankfort, MI 49635: Free information ❖ Fiberglass and wood/epoxy kayaks. 616-352-7774.

L.L. Bean, Freeport, ME 04033: Free catalog ❖ Canoes and boating and outdoor equipment. 800-483-2326.

Bell Canoe Works, 25355 Hwy. 169 South, Zimmerman, MN 55398: Information $1 ❖ Kevylar, fiberglass, and graphite canoes. 612-856-2231.

Bending Branches Paddles, 812 Prospect Ct., Osceola, WI 54020: Free information ❖ Straight shaft, bent shaft, and kayak paddles. 715-755-3405.

Black Bart Paddles, 5830 US 45 South, Bruce Crossing, MI 49912: Free information ❖ Ultralight graphite paddles for racing, cruising, and whitewater. 906-927-3405.

Camp Canoe & Paddle Manufacturing, P.O. Box 192, Otego, NY 13825: Free information ❖ Kayak and canoe paddles. 607-988-6842.

Carlisle Paddles, P.O. Box 488, Grayling, MI 49738: Free information ❖ Kayak paddles. 800-258-0290.

Caviness Woodworking Company, P.O. Box 710, Calhoun City, MS 38916: Free information ❖ Paddles and oars. 800-626-5195; 601-628-5195 (in MS).

Chesapeake Light Craft, 1805 George Avenue, Annapolis, MD 21401: Free brochure ❖ Kits, plans, and finished wood kayaks. 410-267-0137; 301-858-6335 (in DC Metro area).

William Clements, Boat Builder, P.O. Box 87, North Billerica, MA 01862: Catalog $3 ❖ Classic cruising boats, double-paddle and decked sailing canoes, and canoe yawls. 508-663-3103.

Cricket Paddles, 7196 Apen Meadow Dr., Evergreen, CO 80439: Free brochure ❖ Whitewater and canoe touring paddles. 800-243-0586.

Current Adventures, 1800 Twitchell Rd., Placerville, CA 95667: Free information ❖ Surf kayaks. 916-642-9755.

Current Designs, 10124 McDonald Park Rd., Sidney, British Columbia, Canada V8L 5X9: Free catalog ❖ Touring kayaks. 604-655-1822.

Dagger Canoe Company, P.O. Box 1500, Harriman, TN 37748: Free catalog ❖ Canoes and kayaks. 615-882-0404.

Down River Equipment Company, 12100 W. 52nd Ave., Wheat Ridge, CO 80033: Free catalog ❖ Canoes and inflatable boats. 303-467-9489.

Easy Rider Canoe & Kayak Company, P.O. Box 88108, Seattle, WA 98138: Catalog $5 ❖ Single and double-seating sea kayaks and canoes, rowing trainers, and paddles. 206-228-3633.

Ecomarine Ocean Kayak Center, 1668 Duranleau St., Vancouver, British Columbia, Canada V6H 3S4: Free brochure ❖ Folding kayaks and kits. 604-689-7575.

Eddyline Kayak Works, 1344 Ashten Rd., Burlington, WA 98223: Free catalog ❖ Kayaks and paddles. 800-788-3634.

Englehart Products Inc., 10420 Kinsman Rd., P.O. Box 377, Newbury, OH 44065: Free information ❖ Sea and touring kayaks. 216-564-5565.

Essex Industries, Box 374, Mineville, NY 12956: Free catalog ❖ Portable and easy-to-store canoe seats and accessories. 518-942-6671.

Feathercraft Kayaks, 1244 Cartwright St., Granville Island, Vancouver, British Columbia, Canada V6H 3R8: Free brochure ❖ Lightweight folding kayaks. 604-681-8437.

Gillies Canoes & Kayaks, Margaretville, Nova Scotia, Canada B0S 1N0: Free information ❖ High-performance canoes and kayaks. 902-825-3725.

Gillespie Paddles, 1283 Harris Rd., Webster, NY 14580: Free information ❖ Kayak and canoe paddles. 716-872-1723.

Great Canadian Canoe Company, 64 Worcester Providence Tnpk., Sutton, MA 01590: Free catalog ❖ Handmade canoes. 508-865-0010.

Great River Outfitters, 4180 Elizabeth Lake Rd., Waterford, MI 48328: Catalog $1 (request list of retail sources) ❖ Sea and white water kayaks. 810-683-4770.

Grey Owl Paddle Company, 62 Cowansview Rd., Cambridge, Ontario, Canada N1R 7N3: Free catalog ❖ Paddles. 519-622-0001.

Headwaters, P.O. Box 1356, Harriman, TN 37748: Free information ❖ Kayak and canoe equipment for flat or whitewater use. 615-882-8757.

Hydra Tuf Lite Kayaks, 5061 S. National Dr., Knoxville, TN 37914: Catalog $5 ❖ Touring kayaks for lakes, rivers, and the open sea. 800-537-8888.

Hyside Inflatables, P.O. Box Z, Kernville, CA 93238: Free information ❖ Kayaks, catarafts, and rafts. 619-376-3723.

Impex International Inc., 1107 Station Rd., Bellport, NY 11713: Free information ❖ Kayaks. 516-286-1988.

Island Falls Canoe, Jerry Stelmok, RFD 3, Box 76, Dover-Foxcroft, ME 04426: Free catalog ❖ Custom-built canoes. 207-564-7612.

Jersey Paddler, Rt. 88 West, Brick, NJ 08724: Free information ❖ Canoes and kayaks. 908-458-5777.

Keel Haulers Outfitters, 30940 Lorain Rd., North Olmsted, OH 44070: Free catalog ❖ Canoes, kayaks, safety gear, clothing and wet suits, and outdoor equipment. 216-779-4545.

Ketter Canoeing, 101 79th Ave. North, Minneapolis, MN 55444: Free information ❖ Canoes and paddles. 612-561-2208.

Kiwi Kayak Company, P.O. Box 1140, Windsor, CA 95492: Free information ❖ Two-seat kayaks and other models. 800-K-4-KAYAK.

Klepper America, 168 Kinderkamack Rd., Park Ridge, NJ 07656: Free list of retail sources ❖ Folding boats and kayaks. 800-323-3525.

Lee's Value Right Inc., P.O. Box 19346, Minneapolis, MN 55419: Free information ❖ Touring kayak paddles. 800-758-1720.

Lightning Paddles, 22800 S. Unger Rd., Colton, OR 97017: Free information ❖ Lightweight custom kayak and canoe paddles. 503-824-2938.

Mad River Canoe Inc., P.O. Box 610, Waitsfield, VT 05673: Free catalog ❖ Canoes for navigating rivers, rapids, and pleasure boating. 800-843-8985.

Marine Technologies International Inc., P.O. Box 1045, Watertown, MA 02272: Free catalog ❖ Kayaks. 800-783-4684.

Mariner Kayaks, 2134 Westlake North, Seattle, WA 98109: Free information ❖ Kayaks. 206-284-8404.

Kevin Martin Boatbuilder, Box 441, RFD 1, Epping, NH 03042: Free information ❖ Solo and sailing canoes, runabouts, lobster boats, daysailers, and other small boats.

Maximum Whitewater Performance, 6211 Ridge Dr., Bethesda, MD 20816: Free catalog ❖ Racing and other boats, paddles, clothing, and safety gear. 301-229-4304.

Merrimack Canoe Company, 202 Harper Ave., Crossville, TN 38555: Free information ❖ Fiberglass canoes. 615-484-4556.

Mitchell Paddles Inc., RD 2, P.O. Box 922, Canaan, NH 03741: Free information ❖ Canoe and kayak paddles and dry suits. 603-523-7004.

Mohawk Canoes, 963 North Hwy. 427, Longwood, FL 32750: Free information ❖ Solo and tandem canoes. 407-834-3233.

Navarro Canoe Company, 17901 Van Arsdale, Potter Valley, CA 95469: Free information ❖ Lightweight canoes. 707-743-1255.

Necky Kayaks Ltd., 1100 Riverside Rd., Abbotsford, British Columbia, Canada V2S 4N2: Free information ❖ Touring kayaks. 604-850-1206.

New Wave Kayak Products, 2535 Roundtop Rd., Middletown, PA 17057: Free catalog ❖ Cruising and racing kayaks, paddles, and helmets. 717-944-6320.

The Newfound Woodworks Inc., RFD 2, Box 850, Bristol, NH 03222: Free information ❖ Canoe kits, books, plans, supplies, and accessories. 603-744-6872.

Nimbus Paddles, 2330 Tyner St., Unit 6, Port Coquilam, British Columbia, Canada V3C 2Z1: Free information ❖ Touring, whitewater kayak, and recreational canoe paddles. 604-941-8138.

Northwest Design Works Inc., 12322 Hwy. 99 South, #100, Everett, WA 98204: Free list of retail sources ❖ Handcrafted kayak and canoe paddles. 800-275-3311.

Northwest Kayaks, 15145 NE 90th, Redmond, WA 98052: Free information ❖ Handcrafted kayaks. 800-648-8908; 206-869-1107 (in WA).

Northwest Outdoor Center, 2100 Westlake Ave. North, Seattle, WA 98109: Free catalog ❖ Kayak equipment, safety and rescue equipment, clothing, and books. 800-683-0637.

Nova Craft Canoe, 235-A Exeter Rd., London, Ontario, Canada N6L 1A4: Free catalog ❖ Whitewater kayaks. 519-652-3649.

Oak Orchard Canoe, 2133 Eagle Harbor Rd., Waterport, NY 14571: Catalog $2 (specify canoes, kayaks, or accessories) ❖ Canoes, kayaks, and accessories. 716-682-4849.

Ocean Kayak Inc., 1920 Main St., Ferndale, WA 98248: Free list of retail sources ❖ Ocean kayaks and clothing. 800-8-KAYAKS.

Old Town Canoe Company, 58 Middle St., Old Town, ME 04468: Free catalog ❖ Canoes. 800-595-4400.

Osagian, Rt. 7, Box 506, Lebanon, MO 65536: Free brochure ❖ Canoes, trailers and haulers, and accessories. 417-532-7288.

Pacific Water Sports, 16055 Pacific Hwy. South, Seattle, WA 98188: Brochure $2 ❖ Kayaks and paddles. 206-246-9385.

Paddle & Pack Outfitters Inc., P.O. Box 50299, Nashville, TN 37205: Free catalog ❖ Canoeing, kayaking, and backpacking equipment. 800-786-5565.

Pakboats, P.O. Box 700, Enfield, NH 03748: Free information ❖ Folding canoes. 603-632-7654.

Peconic Paddler, 89 Peconic Ave., Riverhead, NY 11901: Free information ❖ Canoes, kayaks, rowing shells, sea kayaks, paddles, life jackets, and dry suits. 516-727-9895.

Perception, 111 Kayaker Way, Easley, SC 29642: Free information ❖ Kayaks for river running. 803-859-7518.

Piragis Northwoods Company, 105 N. Central Ave., Ely, MN 55731: Catalog $2 ❖ Canoes, boating gear, boats, videos and tapes, and trail foods. 800-223-6565.

Primex of California, P.O. Box 505, Benicia, CA 94510: Catalog $5 ❖ Kayak and canoe carriers, helmets, gloves, face-savers, sailing rigs, and repair supplies. 800-422-2482.

Pygmy Boat Company, P.O. Box 1529, Port Townsend, WA 98368: Catalog $3 ❖ Kayak and rowing skiff kits. 206-385-6143.

Quimby's Paddle Designs, P.O. Box 677, Mellen, WI 54546: Free information ❖ Recreational and tripping canoes and touring kayak paddles. 715-274-3416.

RGP Composites, 9628 153rd Ave. NE, Redmond, WA 98052: Free information ❖ Whitewater, slalom, touring, canoe, racing, and recreation paddles. 206-969-7272.

Rutabaga, 220 W. Broadway, Madison, WI 53716: Free information ❖ Canoes and kayaks. 800-I-PADDLE.

Sawbill Canoe Outfitters, Box 2127, Tofte, MN 55615: Free information ❖ Ultralite canoes. 218-387-1360.

Sawyer Paddles & Oars, 299 Rogue River Pkwy., Talent, OR 97540: Free information ❖ Wood paddles and oars with solid fiberglass tips. 503-535-3606.

Seavivor, 576 Arlington Ave., Des Plaines, IL 60016: Catalog $3 ❖ Folding kayaks. 847-297-5953.

Seda Products, 926 Coolidge Ave., National City, CA 91950: Free catalog ❖ Kayaks and canoes, life vests, and paddles. 619-336-2444.

Sevylor USA, 6651 E. 26th St., Los Angeles, CA 90040: Free information ❖ Inflatable boats, canoes, kayaks, dinghies, paddles, and oars. 213-727-6013.

Shaw & Tenney, P.O. Box 213, Orono, ME 04473: Free catalog ❖ Oars and paddles. 207-866-4867.

SOAR Inflatable, 3152 Cherokee St., St. Louis, MO 63118: Free information ❖ Solo and tandem inflatable canoes. 314-776-6994.

Southern Exposure Sea Kayaks, P.O. Box 4530, Tequesta, FL 33469: Free information ❖ Sea kayaks. 407-575-4530.

Stowe Canoe & Snowshoe Company, River Rd., Box 207, Stowe, VT 05672: Free information ❖ Lightweight fiberglass canoes. 802-253-7398.

Valhalla Products, 4724 Renex Pl., San Diego, CA 92117: Free information ❖ Easy handling kayaks. 619-569-1395.

We-No-Nah Canoes, Box 247, Winona, MN 55987: Free catalog ❖ Canoes for whitewater and flatwater boating and racing. 507-454-5430.

Western Canoeing Inc., Box 115, Abbotsford, British Columbia, Canada V2S 4N8: Information $1 ❖ Kayaking and canoeing equipment. 604-853-9320.

Wilderness House, 1048 Commonwealth Ave., Boston, MA 02215: Free information ❖ Small boats, sea kayaks, canoes, lightweight sleeping bags, tents, packs, shoes and boots, and clothing. 617-277-5858.

Wilderness Systems, 1110 Surrett Dr., High Point, NC 27260: Free list of retail sources ❖ Kayaks, accessories, and sail rigs for kayaks. 910-883-7410.

Wildwasser Sport USA Inc., P.O. Box 4617, Boulder, CO 80306: Free information ❖ Kayaks for whitewater, river, and lake touring and ocean paddling; kayaking accessories. 303-444-2336.

Windspeed Designs, Giant Slide, Mt. Desert, ME 04660: Free information ❖ Single and double-quick reefing spinnakers for kayaks. 207-276-5612.

Catamarans

Murrays Catamarans, P.O. Box 490, Carpinteria, CA 93014: Free list of retail sources ❖ Catamarans, factory parts, books, and videos. 800-788-8964.

Inflatable Boats

Access Inflatable Boats, Thompson Creek Rd., P.O. Box 400, Stevensville, MD 21666: Free information ❖ Semi-rigid inflatable boats and accessories. 410-643-4141.

Achilles Inflatable Craft, 355 Murray Hill Pkwy., East Rutherford, NJ 07073: Free information ❖ Inflatable boats. 201-438-6400.

Aire, P.O. Box 3412, Boise, ID 83703: Free catalog ❖ Self-bailing inflatable touring kayaks. 208-344-7506.

Altco Trading International, 6 Macaulay St. East, Hamilton, Ontario, Canada L8L 8B1: Free information ❖ Soft and rigid bottom inflatable dinghies. 905-521-1061.

APEX Inflatable, 919 Bay Ridge Rd., Annapolis, MD 21403: Free catalog ❖ Inflatable boats. 800-422-5977; 410-267-0850 (in MD).

Avon Marine, 1851 McGaw Ave., Irvine, CA 92714: Free catalog ❖ Inflatable boats. 800-854-7595; 714-250-0880 (in CA).

Berry Scuba Company, 6674 Northwest Hwy., Chicago, IL 60631: Free catalog ❖ Inflatable boats, watches, clothing, skin diving and scuba equipment, diving lights, and underwater cameras. 800-621-6019; 312-763-1626 (in IL).

Bombard, Thompson Creek Rd., P.O. Box 400, Stevensville, MD 21666: Free information ❖ Inflatable boats. 410-643-4141.

❖ BOATS & BOATING ❖

Caribe Inflatable USA, 14372 SW 139th Ct., #7, Miami, FL 33186: Free list of retail sources ❖ Inflatable boats. 305-667-2997.

Coleman Outdoor Products Inc., 250 N. Saint Francis, Wichita, KS 67202: Free catalog ❖ Inflatable boats, canoes, and dinghies. 800-835-3278.

Down River Equipment Company, 12100 W. 52nd Ave., Wheat Ridge, CO 80033: Free catalog ❖ Canoes and inflatable boats. 303-467-9489.

Eric Manufacturing Inc., P.O. Box 279, Arcata, CA 95521: Free information ❖ Catarafts, self-bailing white water rafts, and custom inflatable boats. 707-826-2887.

Kirby Kraft, Box 582, Seachelt, British Columbia, Canada V0N 3A0: Free information ❖ Folding fiberglass rigid bottom inflatable. 614-885-2695.

Nautica International, 6135 NW 167th St., Miami, FL 33015: Free information ❖ Rigid inflatable boats. 305-556-5554.

Northwest River Supplies Inc., 2009 S. Maine, Moscow, ID 83843: Free catalog ❖ Inflatable boats. 800-635-5202.

Novurania Inflatable Boats, 4775 NW 132nd St., Miami, FL 33054: Free information ❖ Inflatable boats. 305-685-2464.

Quicksilver Inflatable, Attn: Quicksilver Consumer Services, P.O. Box 1939, Fond du Lac, WI 54936: Free catalog ❖ Easy-to-tow and stow inflatable boats. 414-929-5000.

Sea Eagle, 200 Wilson St., Port Jefferson Station, NY 11776: Free brochure ❖ Inflatable boats that can be used as fishing platforms, motor runabouts, or yacht tenders. 800-852-0925.

Sevylor USA, 6651 E. 26th St., Los Angeles, CA 90040: Free information ❖ Inflatable boats, canoes, kayaks, dinghies, paddles, and oars. 213-727-6013.

SOAR Inflatable, 3152 Cherokee St., St. Louis, MO 63118: Free information ❖ Solo and tandem inflatable canoes. 314-776-6994.

West Marine Products, P.O. Box 1020, Watsonville, CA 95077: Free catalog ❖ Inflatable boats and boating supplies. 800-463-0775.

Zodiac of North America Inflatable Boats, Thompson Creek Rd., P.O. Box 400, Stevensville, MD 21666: Free information ❖ Inflatable boats. 410-643-4141.

Life Rafts

Dunlop-Beaufort, P.O. Box 1599, Blaine, WA 98230: Free list of retail sources ❖ Life rafts. 206-762-2710.

Givens Ocean Survival Systems Company Inc., 35 Lagoon Rd., Portsmouth, RI 02871: Free information ❖ Life rafts. 800-328-8050; 401-683-7400 (in RI).

Miscellaneous Boats

The Anchorage, 65 Miller St., Warren, RI 02885: Free information ❖ Rigid dinghies. 410-245-3300.

BayCraft Inc., 17525 Industrial Park West, Citronelle, AL 36522: Free information ❖ Wood boats. 334-866-5996.

Brooklin Boat Yard, Brooklin, ME 04616: Free information ❖ Custom boats. 207-359-2236.

William Clements, Boat Builder, P.O. Box 87, North Billerica, MA 01862: Catalog $3 ❖ Classic cruising boats, double-paddle and decked sailing canoes, and canoe yawls. 508-663-3103.

Clinton Cloarec Custom Wooden Boats, Penetanguishe, Ontario, Canada L0K 1P0: Free information ❖ Custom wood boats. 705-549-4780.

Covey Island Boatworks, Petite Riviere, Lunenburg County, Nova Scotia, Canada B0J 2P0: Free information ❖ Wood and epoxy power and sailing yachts. 902-688-2843.

Dayton Marine Products, 2101 N. Lapeer Rd., Lapeer, MI 48446: Free information ❖ Rigid dinghies. 313-664-0850.

Eric Manufacturing Inc., P.O. Box 279, Arcata, CA 95521: Free information ❖ Catarafts, self-bailing white water rafts, and custom inflatable boats. 707-826-2887.

Fletcher Boats Inc., 292 Wellman Rd., Port Angeles, WA 98363: Free information ❖ Inboard and outboard mahogany runabouts. 360-452-8430.

Folbot Inc., P.O. Box 70877, Charleston, SC 29415: Free catalog ❖ Boat kits and sail, power, paddle wheel, and folding boats. 800-533-5099.

Freedom Boatworks, P.O. Box 511, Baraboo, WI 53913: Free information ❖ Mahogany runabouts. 608-356-5861.

Futura Surf Skis, 730 W. 19th St., National City, CA 92050: Free brochure ❖ Surfing skis. 619-474-8382.

GarWood Boat Company Inc., 329 Broadway, Watervliet, NY 12189: Free information ❖ Mahogany runabouts. 518-273-2654.

Grand-Craft, 430 W. 21st St., Holland, MI 49423: Free information ❖ Mahogany runabouts. 616-396-5450.

Hill's Boat Yard, Little Cranberry Island, Islesford, ME 04646: Free information ❖ Skiffs and tenders for oars and sails. 207-244-7150.

Hyde Drift Boats, 1520 Pancheri Dr., Idaho Falls, ID 83402: Free brochure ❖ Drift boats for fishermen. 800-444-4933; 208-529-4343 (in ID).

Intraser Inc., 3580 Wilshire Blvd., Los Angeles, CA 90010: Free information ❖ New and pre-owned motorcycles, ATVs, snowmobiles, trailers, personal water vehicles, and small boats. 213-365-6030.

JW Outfitters, 169 Balboa, San Marcos, CA 92069: Free information ❖ Pontoon boats with optional operating systems. 619-471-2171.

Lowell's Boat Shop, 457 Main St., Amesbury, MA 01913: Brochure $2 ❖ Wood boats. 508-388-0162.

Marshall Marine Corporation, Box P-266, South Dartmouth, MA 02748: Free information ❖ Catboats. 508-994-0414.

Kevin Martin Boatbuilder, Box 441, RFD 1, Epping, NH 03042: Free information ❖ Solo and sailing canoes, runabouts, lobster boats, daysailers, and other small boats.

Maximum Whitewater Performance, 6211 Ridge Dr., Bethesda, MD 20816: Free catalog ❖ Racing and other boats, paddles, clothing, and safety gear. 301-229-4304.

Damian McLaughlin Jr. Corporation, Box 538, North Falmouth, MA 02556: Free information ❖ Sailing dinghy, canoe yawl, and rowing dory. 508-563-3075.

Nexus Marine Corporation, 3816 Railway Ave., Everett, WA 98201: Brochure $3 ❖ Custom power and sailboats. 206-252-8330.

North River Boatworks, 6 Elm St., Albany, NY 12202: Brochure $4 ❖ River skiffs and other boats for sails, oars, or engines. 518-434-4414.

Norton Boat Works, 535 Commercial, Green Lake, WI 54941: Free information ❖ Ready-to-use ice boats, parts, kits, and plans. 414-294-6813.

Ostercraft Inc., 609 SE 134th, Portland, OR 97233: Free information ❖ All-mahogany runabouts. 503-255-5419.

Pakboats, P.O. Box 700, Enfield, NH 03748: Free information ❖ General boating and whitewater boats that fold and can be carried in one bag. 603-632-7654.

Porta-Bote International, 1074 Independence Ave., Mountain View, CA 94043: Free information ❖ Folding dinghies. 800-227-8882; 415-961-5334 (in CA).

Sarnia Wooden Boats, 807 Michigan Ave., Pt. Edward, Ontario, Canada N7V 1H1: Free information ❖ Wood runabouts. 519-337-0436.

Sea Rhoades, 125-6071 Rhoades Ln., Hendersonville, TN 37075: Free information ❖ Pedal, gas, or electric-operated small boats for fishing and sport fun. 615-822-2737.

Stauter Boat Works, 4549 Clearview Dr., Mobile, AL 36619: Free information ❖ Wood boats. 334-666-1152.

Greg Tatman Wooden Boats, 1075 Clearwater Ln., Springfield, OR 97478: Free catalog ❖ Easy-to-assemble drift boats for fishermen. 503-746-5287.

Van Dam Wood Craft, 970 E. Division St., Boyne City, MI 49712: Free information ❖ Custom wood boats. 616-582-2323.

Chris White Designs Inc., 5 Smith's Way, South Dartmouth, MA 02748: Design Portfolio $10 ❖ Cruising catamarans. 508-636-6111.

Rowing Boats & Shells

F.M. Barretta Rowing Boats, P.O. Box 57, Cold Spring Harbor, NY 11742: Free brochure ❖ Long-cockpit open water rowing shell with extra storage space and oars. 516-365-4932.

Durham Boat Company, 220 Newmarket Rd., Durham, NH 03824: Free information ❖ Rowing equipment and hardware, wood and composite shells, oars, clothes, books, and videos. 603-659-7575.

Johannsen Boat Works, P.O. Box 7048, Vero Beach, FL 32961: Free information ❖ Rowing and sailing dinghies. 800-869-0773.

Little River Marine, P.O. Box 986, Gainesville, FL 32602: Free information ❖ Rowing shells. 800-247-4591; 904-378-5025 (in FL).

MAAS Rowing Shells, 1319 Canal Blvd., Richmond, CA 94804: Free brochure ❖ Open water rowing shells. 510-232-1612.

Martin Marine Company, 671-1/2 Main St., Eliot, ME 03903: Free catalog ❖ Rowing boats, single hull ocean shells, and a sliding seat rowing skiff kit. 800-477-1507.

Pygmy Boat Company, P.O. Box 1529, Port Townsend, WA 98368: Catalog $3 ❖ Kayak and rowing skiff kits. 206-385-6143.

Sailboats & Supplies

Bacon & Associates, 116 Legion Ave., Annapolis, MD 21401: Free information ❖ Sailboat hardware and equipment. 410-263-4880.

Bainbridge/Aquabatten, 255 Revere St., Canton, MA 02021: Free information ❖ Sail cloth. 800-422-5684; 617-821-2600 (in MA).

Benjamin River Marine Inc., Rt. 175, Brooklin, ME 04616: Free information ❖ Handcrafted classic sailing boats. 207-359-2244.

James Bliss Marine Company, 201 Meadow Rd., Edison, NJ 08818: Free catalog ❖ Power and sailboat equipment. 908-819-7400.

Bohndell Sails, Commercial St., Rockport, ME 04856: Free information ❖ Sails, rigging, life lines, and canvas. 207-236-3549.

Canvas Crafts, 501 N. Fort Harrison Ave., Clearwater, FL 34615: Catalog $2 ❖ Marine fabrics and accessories for the do-it-yourselfer. 813-447-0189.

Dwyer Aluminum Mast Company Inc., 2 Commerce Dr., North Branford, CT 06471: Free information ❖ Sailboat masts, booms, rigging, and hardware. 203-484-0419.

E & B Discount Marine, 201 Meadow Rd., P.O. Box 3138, Edison, NJ 08818: Free catalog ❖ Power and sailboat equipment and accessories. 800-634-6382.

Forespar, 22322 Gilberto, Rancho Santa Margarita, CA 92688: Free catalog ❖ Rigging and hardware. 714-858-8820.

Gambell & Hunter Sailmakers, 16 Limerock St., Camden, ME 04843: Free information ❖ Sails and furling systems. 800-736-7981.

Goldbergs' Marine, 201 Meadow Rd., Edison, NJ 08818: Free catalog ❖ Power and sailboat equipment. 800-BOA-TING.

Hacker Boat Company, P.O. Box 2576, Silver Bay, NY 12874: Free information ❖ Custom-built boats with seating and size options. 518-543-6666.

Hild Sails, 225 Fordham St., P.O. Box 207, City Island, NY 10464: Free catalog ❖ Sails. 718-885-2255.

Hill's Boat Yard, Little Cranberry Island, Islesford, ME 04646: Free information ❖ Skiffs and tenders for oars and sails. 207-244-7150.

Johannsen Boat Works, P.O. Box 7048, Vero Beach, FL 32961: Free information ❖ Rowing and sailing dinghies. 800-869-0773.

Ludlow Boat Works, RR 4, Becketts Landing, Kempville, Ontario, Canada K0G 1J0: Free information ❖ Ready-to-sail boats. 613-258-4270.

M & E Marine Supply Company, P.O. Box 601, Camden, NJ 08101: Catalog $2 ❖ Power and sailboat equipment. 800-541-6501.

Kevin Martin Boatbuilder, Box 441, RFD 1, Epping, NH 03042: Free information ❖ Solo and sailing canoes, runabouts, lobster boats, daysailers, and other small boats.

Damian McLaughlin Jr. Corporation, Box 538, North Falmouth, MA 02556: Free information ❖ Sailing dinghy, canoe yawl, and rowing dory. 508-563-3075.

Nexus Marine Corporation, 3816 Railway Ave., Everett, WA 98201: Brochure $3 ❖ Custom power and sailboats. 206-252-8330.

Pease Boatworks, 50 Great Western Rd., North Harwich, MA 02645: Free information ❖ Handcrafted classic sailboats. 508-432-8112.

The Rigging Company, 1 Maritime Dr., Portsmouth, RI 02871: Catalog $2 ❖ Sailboat rigging and tools. 800-322-1525; 401-683-1525 (in RI).

Sailrite Kits, 305 W. Van Buren, P.O. Box 987, Columbia City, IN 46725: Free catalog ❖ Sail-making supplies. 800-348-2769; 219-244-6715 (in IN).

Skipper Marine Electronics Inc., 3170 Commercial Ave., Northbrook, IL 60062: Free catalog ❖ Sailboat instruments. 800-SKIPPER; 708-272-4700 (in IL).

Ralph W. Stanley Inc., Southwest Harbor, ME 04679: Free information ❖ Day-sailers. 207-244-3795.

Sumner Boat, 334 S. Bayview Ave., Amityville, NY 11701: Free information ❖ Sailing and rowing dinghies. 516-264-1830.

West Marine Products, P.O. Box 50050, Watsonville, CA 95077: Free catalog ❖ Power and sailboat equipment. 800-463-0775.

Whitehall Reproductions, Box 1141, St. East Victoria, British Columbia, Canada V8W 2T6: Free brochure ❖ Handcrafted classic rowing and sailboats. 800-663-7481.

Nathaniel S. Wilson, Sailmaker, Lincoln St., P.O. Box 71, East Boothbay, ME 04544: Free information ❖ Hand-finished sails. 207-633-5071.

General Supplies & Equipment

A & B Industries Inc., 1160-A Industrial Ave., Petaluma, CA 94952: Free list of retail sources ❖ Marine hardware for power and sailboats. 707-765-6200.

Aamstrand Corporation, 629 Grove, Manteno, IL 60950: Free information ❖ Anchor, winch, and general rigging ropes. 800-338-0557; 312-458-8550 (in IL).

Adventure 16 Inc., 11161 W. Pico Blvd., West Los Angeles, CA 90064: Free information ❖ Compasses, boat bags, water purifiers, and rigging ropes. 619-283-6314.

Atwood Mobile Products, 4750 Hiawatha Dr., Rockford, IL 61103: Free information ❖ Appliances and engineered components and systems for recreational vehicles and boats. 815-877-5700.

Avon Seagull Marine, 1851 McGaw Ave., Irvine, CA 92714: Free catalog ❖ Anchors, barometers, bilge pumps, ropes, and other equipment. 800-854-7595; 714-250-0880 (in CA).

Barkley Sound Marine, 3073 Vanhorne Rd., Qualicum Beach, British Columbia, Canada V9K 1X3: Free information ❖ Custom-made and in-stock solid or laminated straight and spoon blade oars. 604-752-5115.

Basic Designs, 5815 Bennett Valley Rd., Santa Rosa, CA 95404: Free information ❖ Plastic collapsible boarding ladders. 707-575-1220.

Beckson Marine, 165 Holland Ave., Bridgeport, CT 06605: Catalog $3.25 ❖ Marine equipment and accessories. 203-333-1412.

Berkeley Inc., One Berkeley Dr., Spirit Lake, IA 51360: Free catalog ❖ Bilge pumps, compasses, boating cables, and rigging, anchor, winch, and other ropes. 800-237-5539; 712-336-1520 (in IA).

❖ BOATS & BOATING ❖

James Bliss Marine Company, 201 Meadow Rd., Edison, NJ 08818: Free catalog ❖ Power and sailboat equipment. 908-819-7400.

Boat Owners Association of the United States, Washington National Headquarters, 880 S. Pickett St., Alexandria, VA 22304: Free catalog ❖ Boating equipment. 800-937-2628.

Boulter Plywood Corporation, 24 Broadway, Somerville, MA 02145: Free catalog ❖ Plywood and hardwood lumber for building boats. 617-666-1340.

L.S. Brown Company, Pawley Industries Corporation, 3610 Atlanta Industrial Dr. NW, Atlanta, GA 30331: Free information ❖ Anchors, bumpers, cables, deck chairs, compasses, paddles, ropes, and other equipment. 404-691-8200.

Canor Plarex, P.O. Box 33765, Seattle, WA 98133: Free information ❖ Folding anchors. 206-365-3006.

Classic Canoes, 627 Baron Rd., Greenfield, MA 01301: Free information ❖ Easy-to-use folding boat walker. 800-782-7816; 413-773-9631 (in MA).

William Clements, Boat Builder, P.O. Box 87, North Billerica, MA 01862: Catalog $3 ❖ Wood boat and canoe restoration supplies. 508-663-3103.

Maurice L. Condon Company, 252 Ferris Ave., White Plains, NY 10603: Catalog $2 ❖ Boat-building lumber. 914-946-4111.

Crook & Crook, 2795 SW 27th Ave., P.O. Box 109, Miami, FL 33133: Free catalog ❖ Boating gear. 305-854-0005.

Cruising Equipment, 6315 Seaview Ave. NW, Seattle, WA 98107: Free information ❖ Battery monitors. 206-782-8100.

Davis Anchors, 1609 S. Central Ave., Kent, WA 98032: Free information ❖ Galvanized carbon-manganese or stainless steel anchors. 800-328-4770; 206-852-6833 (in WA).

Durham Boat Company, 220 Newmarket Rd., Durham, NH 03824: Free information ❖ Rowing equipment, marine hardware, wood and composite shells, oars, clothes, books, and videos. 603-659-7575.

E & B Discount Marine, 201 Meadow Rd., P.O. Box 3138, Edison, NJ 08818: Free catalog ❖ Power and sailboat equipment and accessories. 800-634-6382.

Edensaw Woods Ltd., 211 Seton Rd., Port Townsend, WA 98368: Free information ❖ Boat lumber and marine plywood. 800-745-3336; 206-385-7878 (in WA).

Edson International, 146 Duchaine Blvd., New Bedford, MA 02745: Free catalog ❖ Power and sail marine steering systems and accessories, boat davits, radar towers, and marine pumps. 508-995-9711.

Electra Marine, 610 Merrick Rd., Lynnbrook, NY 11563: Catalog $2 ❖ Marine equipment. 516-599-3003.

Essex Industries, Box 374, Mineville, NY 12956: Free catalog ❖ Portable and easy-to-store canoe seats and accessories. 518-942-6671.

Fiberglass Coatings Inc., 3201 28th St., North, St. Petersburg, FL 33713: Free catalog ❖ Composite materials and supplies. Resins, glass, fillers, hard-to-find products, and information bulletins. 800-272-7890.

Flounder Bay Boatbuilding, 1019 3rd St., Anacortes, WA 98221: Free information ❖ Imported hardwood, marine plywood, epoxies, fasteners, paint, and varnish for boat-building and repairs. 800-228-4691.

Frabill Inc., 536 Main St., P.O. Box 499, Allentown, WI 53002: Free information ❖ Anchors, bilge pumps, convenience and comfort aids, lighting equipment, and ropes. 414-629-5506.

Gander Mountain Inc., P.O. Box 248, Gander Mountain, Wilmot, WI 53192: Free catalog ❖ Boating equipment. 800-558-9410.

Glenwood Marine, 1627 W. El Segundo Blvd., Gardena, CA 90249: Catalog $3 ❖ Marine hardware. 213-757-3141.

Goldbergs' Marine, 201 Meadow Rd., Edison, NJ 08818: Free catalog ❖ Power and sailboat equipment. 800-BOA-TING.

Grove Boat-Lift, P.O. Box 8095, Fresno, CA 93727: Free information ❖ Easy-to-use boat lift. 800-447-5115; 209-251-5115 (in CA).

Hamilton Marine Inc., Box 227, Rt. 1, Searsport, ME 04974: Free catalog ❖ Marine hardware, accessories, navigation equipment, safety gear, and other equipment. 800-639-2715.

Ken Hankinson Associates, P.O. Box 272, Hayden Lake, ID 83835: Free information ❖ Boat plans, patterns, kits, and supplies. 208-772-5547.

The Harbor Sales Company Inc., 1401 Russell St., Baltimore, MD 21230: Information $1 ❖ Boat-building lumber. 800-345-1712.

Hudson Marine Plywoods, P.O. Box 1184, Elkhart, IN 46515: Free information ❖ Flooring, decking boards, marine plywood, and other lumber. 219-262-3666.

Idea Development Company, 83 Idea Pl., Sequim, WA 98382: Free catalog ❖ Trolling equipment, water ski storage holders, launching wheels, small boat dollies, bumpers and line shock absorbers, and other accessories. 800-994-4677.

Imperial Marine Equipment, 600 Ansin Blvd., Hallandale, FL 33009: Free catalog ❖ Windshields, windows, and other accessories. 305-456-7755.

Imtra, 30 Barnet Blvd., New Bedford, MA 02745: Free information ❖ Anchors. 508-995-7000.

Jamestown Distributors, P.O. Box 348, Jamestown, RI 02835: Free catalog ❖ Boat-building supplies, marine fasteners, and tools. 800-423-0030.

Johnson Sails Inc., P.O. Box 20926, St. Petersburg, FL 33742: Free catalog ❖ Sails, electronics, rigging gear, and other equipment. 800-234-3220.

M & E Marine Supply Company, P.O. Box 601, Camden, NJ 08101: Catalog $2 ❖ Power and sailboat equipment. 800-541-6501.

Marinetics Corporation, 3901 Brioso Dr., #101, Costa Mesa CA 92627: Free information ❖ Electrical power systems, distribution panels, alert and alarm systems, and other equipment. 800-762-1414.

Maritime Wood Products Corporation, The Teak Connection, 3361 SE Slater St., Stuart, FL 34997: Free catalog ❖ Teak furnishings and boat-building supplies.

Matrix Desalination Inc., 3295 SW 11th Ave., Fort Lauderdale, FL 33315: Free information ❖ Desalination equipment. 305-524-5120.

Nautica International, 6135 NW 167th St., Miami, FL 33015: Free information ❖ Safety and survival gear. 305-556-5554.

New England Ropes, 848 Airport Rd., Fall River, MA 02720: Free information ❖ High-strength and easy-to-splice polyester ropes. 508-678-8200.

New Found Metals Inc., 240 Airport Rd., Port Townsend, WA 98368: Catalog $3 ❖ Silicon and manganese-bronze marine hardware. 206-385-3315.

Offshore Marine Products Inc., 510 Long Meadow Dr., Salisbury, NC 28144: Free brochure ❖ Davits for inflatable boats and dinghies. 704-636-6558.

Overton's Sports Center Inc., P.O. Box 8228, Greenville, NC 27835: Free catalog ❖ Boating accessories. 800-334-6541.

Peconic Paddler, 89 Peconic Ave., Riverhead, NY 11901: Free information ❖ Canoes, kayaks, rowing shells, sea kayaks, paddles, life jackets, and dry suits. 516-727-9895.

❖ BOATS & BOATING ❖

Piragis Northwoods Company, 105 N. Central Ave., Ely, MN 55731: Catalog $2 ❖ Canoes, boating gear, boats, videos and tapes, and trail foods. 800-223-6565.

C. Plath, 222 Severn Ave., Annapolis, MD 21403: Free list of retail sources ❖ Marine instruments, other electronics, navigation gear, books, and other accessories. 410-263-6700.

Roloff Manufacturing, P.O. Box 7002, Kaukauna, WI 54130: Free information ❖ Anchors. 414-766-3501.

Rule Industries Inc., 70 Blanchard Rd., Burlington, MA 01803: Free information ❖ Compasses, anchors, pumps, and other equipment. 617-272-7400.

Sawyer Paddles & Oars, 299 Rogue River Pkwy., Talent, OR 97540: Free information ❖ Wood paddles and oars with solid fiberglass tips. 503-535-3606.

Sea Mate Products, P.O. Box 2, West Pittston, PA 18643: Free catalog ❖ Transom platforms, anchor pulpits, and swimming ladders. 800-SEA-MATE.

Seitech Marine Products Inc., P.O. Box 514, Portsmouth, RI 02871: Free information ❖ Launching dolly for any kind of dinghy. 401-683-6898.

Shaw & Tenney, P.O. Box 213, Orono, ME 04473: Free catalog ❖ Handcrafted paddles and oars. 207-866-4867.

Solo Loader, 3260 W. Highview Dr., Appleton, WI 54914: Free information ❖ Easy-to-use canoe and kayak loader for automobiles. 800-394-1744.

Spring Creek Outfitters Inc., P.O. Box 246, 5714 Mineral Ave., Mt. Iron, MN 55768: Free catalog ❖ Canoe accessories. 800-937-8881.

SPS Marine, P.O. Box 2418, Farmington Hills, MI 48333: Free information ❖ Instantaneous tank-free marine water heaters. 810-476-0531.

SSI Boating Accessories, P.O. Box 99, Hollywood, MD 20636: Free catalog ❖ Boating and sport fishing equipment. 301-373-2372.

Stimson Marine Inc., RR1, Box 524, River Rd., Boothbay, ME 04537: Brochure $2 ❖ Boat lumber and building plans. 207-633-7252.

John Stortz & Son Inc., 210 Vine St., Philadelphia, PA 19106: Catalog $4 ❖ Ship-building tools. 215-627-3855.

Suncor Marine & Industrial, 440 Corporate Park, Pembroke, MA 02359: Free information ❖ Anchors. 800-394-2222; 617-829-8899 (in MA).

Super Dock Products, RR 2, Box 37, Center Harbor, NH 03228: Free catalog ❖ Dock rafts and docks, hardware, and accessories. 603-253-4000.

Fred Tebb & Sons Inc., 1906 Marc St., P.O. Box 2235, Tacoma, WA 98401: Free information ❖ Sitka spruce for masts and spars, canoes, and oars. 206-272-4107.

Travaco Labs/ITW Philadelphia Resins, 130 Commerce Dr., Montgomeryville, PA 18936: Free catalog ❖ Boat repair supplies. 215-855-8450.

Value Carpets Inc., Marine Division, 1802 Murray Ave., Dalton, GA 30721: Free information ❖ Do-it-yourself replacement carpet kits for boats. 800-634-3702.

Vetus-Denouden Inc., P.O. Box 8712, Baltimore, MD 21240: Free catalog ❖ Boating accessories and equipment. 410-712-0740.

Voyageur, P.O. Box 207, Waitsfield, VT 05673: Free catalog ❖ Waterproof bags, packs, camera bags, storage and flotation systems, and other performance canoe and kayak gear. 800-843-8985.

West Marine Products, P.O. Box 50050, Watsonville, CA 95077: Free catalog ❖ Power and sailboat equipment. 800-463-0775.

The Wooden Boat Shop, 1007 NE Boat St., Seattle, WA 98105: Catalog $3 ❖ Tools, building supplies, and accessories. 800-933-3600; 206-634-3600 (in WA).

Instruments & Electronics

Alpha Marine Systems, 1235 Columbia Hill Rd., Reno, NV 89506: Free information ❖ Autopilots and compasses. 800-257-4225.

Apelco Marine Electronics, 676 Island Pond Rd., Manchester, NH 03109: Free information ❖ Communication equipment, navigation gear, marine instruments, and other electronics. 800-539-5539.

Aqua Meter Instrument Corporation, Rule Industries, 70 Blanchard Rd., Burlington, MA 01803: Free catalog ❖ Navigation gear and other electronics. 508-281-0440.

Armchair Sailor Bookstore, 543 Thames St., Newport, RI 02840: Free information ❖ Navigation aids. 800-292-4278; 401-847-4252 (in RI).

Autohelm, 676 Island Pond Rd., Manchester, NH 03109: Free information ❖ Weather and marine instruments, compasses and autopilots, and navigation and electronic gear. 800-539-5539.

Baker, Lyman & Company, 3220 South I-10 Service Rd., Metairie, LA 70001: Free information ❖ Navigation aids. 800-535-6956; 504-831-3685 (in LA).

Cassens & Plath of U.S. Inc., 3220 S. I-10 Service Rd., Metairie, LA 70001: Free brochure ❖ Sextants. 800-535-6956; 504-831-3685 (in LA).

Celestaire, 416 S. Pershing, Wichita, KS 67218: Free information ❖ Navigation instruments and books. 800-727-9785.

Citizen Watch Company of America, 8506 Osage Ave., Los Angeles, CA 90056: Free information ❖ Diving watches and sports, flight, boating, and windsurfing chronographs.

Davis Instruments, 3465 Diablo Ave., Hayward, CA 94545: Free information ❖ Weather and marine instruments, compasses, and navigation and electronic gear. 800-678-3669.

Eagle Electronics, P.O. Box 669, Catoosa, OK 74015: Free information ❖ Navigation gear and other marine instruments. 800-324-1354.

Furuno USA, P.O. Box 2343, South San Francisco, CA 94083: Free information ❖ Marine instruments, communications equipment, navigation and electronic gear, compasses, and alarm systems. 415-873-9393.

Garmin, 9875 Widmer Rd., Lenexa, KS 66215: Free information ❖ Communications, navigation equipment, hand-held plotter, and other electronics. 800-800-1020; 913-599-1515 (in KS).

ICOM America, 2380 116th Ave. NE, Bellevue, WA 98004: Free list of retail sources ❖ Marine instruments, compasses, navigation and electronic gear, and communications equipment. 800-999-9877.

InfoCenter Inc., P.O. Box 47175, Forestville, MD 20753: Free catalog ❖ Sextants and accessories, hand-held computers, and PC software. 800-852-0649; 301-420-2468 (in MD).

KVH Industries Inc., 110 Enterprise Center, Middletown, RI 02842: Brochure $1 ❖ Hand-held pocket-size compasses, weather and marine instruments, navigation equipment, and electronics gear. 401-847-3327.

Leica Navigation & Positioning Division, 23868 Hawthorne Blvd., Torrance, CA 90505: Free information ❖ Navigation instruments.

Lowrance Electronics, 12000 E. Skelly Dr., Tulsa, OK 74070: Free information ❖ Marine instruments and electronics. 800-324-4737.

Magellan Systems Corporation, 960 Overland Ct., San Dimas, CA 91773: Free information ❖ Navigation equipment, compasses, communications equipment, and other electronics. 909-394-5000.

Marine Electronics, Rt. 33, Box 160, Hartfield, VA 23071: Free information ❖ Marine electronics. 800-654-9251; 804-776-9251 (in VA).

Marisystems Inc., 77 Tosca Dr., Stoughton, MA 02072: Free information ❖ Battery-operated tide and current information indicator. 617-341-3611.

Maryland Nautical Sales Inc., 400 E. Clement St., Baltimore, MD 21230: Free information ❖ Nautical books and videos, clocks, barometers, binoculars, sextants, compasses, and other equipment. 800-596-SAIL.

Maximum Inc., 30 Barnet Blvd., New Bedford, MA 02745: Free catalog ❖ Weather and marine instruments. 508-995-2200.

Micrologic, 9174 Deering, Chatsworth, CA 91311: Free information ❖ Navigation, electronics, and communications equipment. 818-998-1216.

Morad Electronics, 1125 NW 46th St., Seattle, WA 98107: Free information ❖ Antennas. 206-789-2525.

Nautical Software, 14657 SW Teal Blvd., Ste. 132, Beaverton, OR 97007: Free information ❖ Windows-based tides and currents software for PCs. 800-946-2877.

Navico Inc., 10701 Belcher Rd., Ste. 128, Largo, FL 34643: Free information ❖ Weather and marine instruments, compasses and autopilots, and communications equipment. 813-524-1555.

Netcraft Company, P.O. Box 5510, Toledo, OH 43613: Free catalog ❖ Marine electronics, fishing rods, reels, rod and lure-building components, and fly-tying supplies. 419-472-9826.

No Compromise Communications, The SGC Building, 13737 SE 26th St., Box 3526, Bellevue, WA 98009: Free information ❖ Marine communications equipment with Weatherfax connections. 206-746-6310.

Ockam Instruments, 26 Higgins Dr., Milford, CT 06460: Free information ❖ Weather and marine instruments and navigation gear. 203-877-7453.

Omnifac Corporation, 1700 W. Whipp Rd., Dayton, OH 45440: Free information ❖ Battery and AC monitors and polarity indicators, bilge pump monitors, electronic digital clocks, and on-board boat electrical systems. 513-434-8400.

Plastimo USA Inc., Airguide Instruments, 2210 W. Wabansa, Chicago, IL 60647: Free information ❖ Weather and marine instruments, autopilots, and navigation and electronic gear. 708-215-7888.

C. Plath, 222 Severn Ave., Annapolis, MD 21403: Free list of retail sources ❖ Marine instruments, other electronics, navigation gear, books, and other accessories. 410-263-6700.

Radio-Holland Group, 8943 Gulf Freeway, Houston, TX 77017: Free information ❖ Alarm systems, other electronics, marine instruments, and communications equipment. 713-943-3325.

Raytheon Marine Company, 676 Island Pond Rd., Manchester, NH 03109: Free information ❖ Navigation and electronic gear, communications equipment, and alarm systems. 800-539-5539.

Resolution Mapping Inc., 35 Hartwell Ave., Lexington, MA 02173: Free information ❖ Nautical mapping and chart software for PCs. 617-860-0430.

Ritchie Compasses, 243 Oak St., Pembroke, MA 02359: Free catalog ❖ Compasses. 617-826-5131.

Si-Tex Marine Electronics, 11001 Roosevelt Blvd., Ste. 800, St. Petersburg, FL 34716: Free information ❖ Autopilots, navigation and electronic gear, communications equipment, and alarm systems. 813-576-5734.

Signet Marine, 505 Van Ness Ave., Torrance, CA 90501: Free information ❖ Analog and digital instruments. 310-320-4349.

Simerl Instruments, 528 Epping Forest Rd., Annapolis, MD 21401: Free brochure ❖ Weather instruments. 410-849-8667.

Skipper Marine Electronics Inc., 3170 Commercial Ave., Northbrook, IL 60062: Free information ❖ Navigation systems, radar, autopilots, and marine electronics. 800-SKIPPER; 708-272-4700 (in IL).

Somerset Publishing Company Inc., 307 Bradford Pkwy., Syracuse, NY 13224: Free information ❖ Celestial navigation software. 315-446-0614.

Sperry Marine, 1070 Seminole Trail, Charlottesville, VA 22901: Free information ❖ Weather and marine instruments, compasses and autopilots, and navigation and electronic gear. 804-974-2000.

SR Instruments, 600 Young St., Tonawanda, NY 14150: Free information ❖ Weather and marine instruments. 800-654-6360; 716-693-5977 (in NY).

Trimble Navigation Limited, Marine Products, 2800 Wells Branch Pkwy., Austin, TX 78728: Free information ❖ Navigation and communications equipment and other electronics. 800-827-2424.

Vetus-Denouden Inc., P.O. Box 8712, Baltimore, MD 21230: Free information ❖ Wind/weather forecasting equipment for boats. 410-712-0740.

W-H Autopilots, 655 NE Northlake Pl., Seattle, WA 98105: Free information ❖ Autopilots for power and sailboats. 206-633-1830.

Yazaki-VDO, 188 Brooke Rd., Winchester, VA 22603: Free information ❖ Weather and marine instruments, compasses, and navigation and electronic gear. 703-665-0100.

Nautical Books, Videos, & Gifts

Captain's Emporium, 7855 Gross Point Rd., Smokie, IL 60077: Free information ❖ Trophies and gifts. 708-675-5411.

International Marine, Division McGraw Hill, 13311 Montrey Ln., Blue Ridge Summit, PA 17294: Free catalog ❖ Nautical books. 800-822-8158.

The Maritime Store, 2905 Hyde St. Pier, San Francisco, CA 94109: Free catalog ❖ Maritime maps, greeting cards, boat models, children's and maritime books, and gifts. 415-775-BOOK.

Maryland Nautical Sales Inc., 400 E. Clement St., Baltimore, MD 21230: Free information ❖ Nautical books and videos, clocks, barometers, binoculars, sextants, compasses, and other equipment. 800-596-SAIL.

Moby Dick Marine Specialties, 27 William St., New Bedford, MA 02740: Catalog $5 ❖ Nautical gifts, accessories, and scrimshaw. 800-343-8044.

Mystic Seaport Museum Stores, 39 Greemanville Ave., Mystic, CT 06355: Free catalog ❖ Books about American maritime history and gifts with a nautical and historical theme. 800-248-1066.

Nauticode Inc., 274 Harkers Island Rd., Beaufort, NC 28516: Free catalog ❖ Clothing and gifts for boating enthusiasts. 800-628-8263.

Naval Institute Press, Customer Service, 2062 Generals Hwy., Annapolis, MD 21401: Free catalog ❖ Books on navigation, seamanship, naval history, ships, and aircraft. 800-233-8764.

Preston's, Main Street Wharf, Greenport, NY 11944: Free catalog ❖ Ship's wheels, clocks and bells, tavern signs, harpoons, binoculars, nautical lamps, caps and sweaters, antique maps, glassware, and marine paintings. 800-836-1165.

John F. Rinaldi Nautical Antiques, P.O. Box 785, Kennebunkport, ME 04046: Catalog $3 ❖ American paintings, scrimshaw, and nautical antiques. 207-967-3218.

The Sailor's Source, P.O. Box 20926, St. Petersburg, FL 33742: Free information ❖ Nautical gifts. 813-577-3220.

Ship's Hatch, 10376 Main St., Fairfax, VA 22030: Brochure $1 ❖ Military patches, pins and insignia, official USN ship ball caps, ship's clocks, military and hatch cover tables, nautical and military gifts, jewelry, lamps, lanterns, ship's wheels, jewelry boxes, and plaques. 703-691-1670.

Wind in the Rigging, 125 E. Main St., P.O. Box 323, Port Washington, WI 53074: Free catalog ❖ Nautical gifts and gear. 800-236-7444; 414-284-3494 (in WI).

WoodenBoat Books, Naskeag Rd., P.O. Box 78, Brooklin, ME 04616: Free catalog ❖ Books about boats. 800-225-5205; 207-359-4647 (in ME).

BOCCIE

Sport Fun Inc., 4621 Sperry St., Los Angeles, CA 90039: Free information ❖ Boccie sets. 800-423-2597; 818-240-6700 (in CA).

Venus Knitting Mills Inc., 140 Spring St., Murray Hill, NJ 07974: Free information ❖ Boccie sets. 800-955-4200; 908-464-2400 (in NJ).

BOOK REPAIR & BINDING

Associated Book & Document Restoration Company, M. Clyde Murray, 222 Seneca St., Ste. 231, Oil City, PA 16301: Free information ❖ Bookbinding and restoration services for rare books. 814-676-5377.

The Bookbinder's Warehouse, 31 Division St., Keyport, NJ 07735: Free catalog ❖ Bookbinding supplies and equipment. 908-264-0306.

BookMakers, 6001 66th Ave., Ste. 101, Riverdale, MD 20737: Free catalog ❖ Supplies and equipment for hand bookbinding, book and paper conservation, and book arts. 301-459-3384.

Colophon Book Arts Supply, 3046 Hogum Bay Rd. NE, Olympia, WA 98506: Free information ❖ Bookbinding and marbling supplies. 360-459-2940.

Library Binding Company, 2900 Franklin Ave., Waco, TX 76710: Free price list ❖ Bookbinding and restoration services for rare books. 800-792-3352.

John Neal, Bookseller, 1833 Spring Garden St., Greensboro, NC 27403: Free information ❖ Calligraphy and marbling supplies, books, and bookbinding services. 800-369-9598.

TALAS, 568 Broadway, New York, NY 10012: Catalog $5 ❖ Bookbinding supplies. 212-219-0770.

BOOK SEARCH SERVICES

American Indian Books & Relics, P.O. Box 16175, Huntsville, AL 35802: Free information with long SASE ❖ Search service for books about Native Americans. 205-881-6727.

Avonlea Books, P.O. Box 74, White Plains, NY 10602: Free information ❖ Search service for hard-to-find and out-of-print books. 800-423-0622; 914-946-5923 (in NY).

M.F. Adler Books, Box 627, Stockbridge, MA 01262: Free information ❖ Book search services for out-of-print children's books. 413-298-3559.

K.S. Alden Books, 511 W. Fairmount Ave., State College, PA 16801: Free information ❖ Book search services. 800-359-8848.

Allen's Book Shop, 416 E. 31st St., 2nd Floor, Baltimore, MD 21218: Free information ❖ Book search services.

Barner Books, 220 E. 73rd St., Ste. 10, New York, NY 10021: Free information ❖ Book search services. 914-255-2635.

Fritz T. Brown-Books, P.O. Box 652, Newburyport, MA 01950: Free information ❖ Book search services. 508-462-2294.

R. Chalfrin, 310 Riverside Dr., #10A, New York, NY 10025: Free information ❖ Book search service for out-of-print hard covers. 212-316-5634.

Michael Dennis Cohan, Bookseller, 502 W. Alder St., Missoula, MT 59802: Free catalog ❖ Search service for books on geology, mining, and related subjects. 406-721-7379.

Hard-to-Find Needlework Books, 96 Roundwood, Newton, MA 02164: Catalog $1 ❖ Search services for hard-to-find and rare books on needle crafts. 617-969-0942.

Richard A. LaPosta, 154 Robindale Dr., Kensington, CT 06037: Information $1 ❖ Searches for out-of-print, first editions, and other Civil War books. 203-828-0921.

The Military Bookman, 29 E. 93rd St., New York, NY 10128: Free information ❖ Search service for military, naval, and aviation out-of-print and rare books. 212-348-1280.

NightinGale Resources, P.O. Box 322, Cold Spring, NY 10516: Catalog $3 ❖ Search service for out-of-print and rare cookbooks.

Fran Palminteri, 61-04 78th St., Middle Village, NY 11379: Free information ❖ Book search services for all editions and categories. 718-672-0104.

R.H. Pettit, Viewpoint Gallery, Zeckendorf Towers, 111 E. 14th St., New York, NY 10003: Free information ❖ Book search services. 212-242-5478.

Reed Books, 2323 1st Ave. North, Birmingham, AL 35203: Free information ❖ Book search services. 205-326-4460.

The Wayward Bookman, 3 Main St., Wales, MA 01081: Free information ❖ Book search services. 413-245-3706.

Wilhite Collectible Bookstore, 425 Cleveland St., Clearwater, FL 34615: Free newsletter ❖ Rare books and current publications. Also a search service. 813-447-5722.

BOOKKEEPING & ACCOUNTING SUPPLIES

Accountants Supply House, 3012 Grove Rd., Thorofare, NJ 08086: Free catalog ❖ Stationery and envelopes, forms and labels, adding machines, shipping materials, disk storage cabinets, typewriter and data processing ribbons, office furniture, and other supplies. 800-342-5274.

HG Professional Forms Company, 2020 California St., Omaha, NE 68102: Free catalog ❖ Pre-printed forms, accounting and office supplies, record-keeping systems, and computer paper. 800-228-1493.

Medical Arts Press, 8500 Wyoming Ave. North, Minneapolis, MN 55445: Free catalog ❖ Forms for medical and dental professions.

BOOKPLATES & BOOKMARKS

Bookplate Ink, P.O. Box 558, Yellow Springs, OH 45387: Free brochure ❖ Self-adhesive bookplates with optional custom imprinting. 513-767-2042.

Creations by Elaine, 6253 W. 74th St., Box 2001, Bedford Park, IL 60499: Free catalog ❖ Art motif bookmarks. 800-323-2717.

Walter Drake & Sons, Drake Building, Colorado Springs, CO 80940: Free catalog ❖ Bookmarks, personalized stationery, toys, household items, clothing, decor and office accessories, and other items. 800-525-9291.

David Howell & Company, 405 Adams St., Bedford Hills, NY 10507: Free catalog ❖ Bookmarks inspired by museum collections. 800-648-5455; 914-666-4080 (in NY).

Lixx Labelsz, 2619 14th St. SW, P.O. Box 32055CC4, Calgary, Alberta, Canada T2T 5X0: Catalog $4 ❖ Labels and bookmarks that combine wildlife designs, calligraphy, eco-action, and recycling. 403-245-2331.

Los Angeles Audubon Society Bookstore, 7377 Santa Monica Blvd., West Hollywood, CA 90046: Free catalog ❖ Bird and nature books, bookmarks, and feeders. 213-876-0202.

My Own Bookplate, P.O. Box 558, Yellow Springs, OH 45387: Free information ❖ Personalized bookplates. 513-767-2042.

World Wildlife Fund Catalog, P.O. Box 224, Peru, IN 46970: Free catalog ❖ Wildlife theme bookmarks. 800-833-1600.

BOOKS

Bargain Books

The Bargain Book Warehouse, P.O. Box 8515, Ukiah, CA 95482: Free catalog ❖ Popular fiction paperbacks and hardcovers. 800-301-7567.

Barnes & Noble, 126 5th Ave., New York, NY 10011: Free catalog ❖ Books, records, and tapes. 800-242-6657.

Critics' Choice Video, P.O. Box 749, Itasca, IL 60143: Free catalog ❖ Books, records, and video cassettes. 800-544-9852.

Daedalus Books Inc., 4601 Decatur St., Hyattsville, MD 20781: Free information ❖ Publisher overstocks and remainders. 800-944-8879.

Edward R. Hamilton, Bookseller, 5014 Oak, Falls Village, CT 06031: Free catalog ❖ Overstocks, remainders, imports, and reprints from major publishers.

Children's Books

Advocacy Press, P.O. Box 236, Santa Barbara, CA 93102: Free information ❖ Books for children and young adults on gender equity, career planning, problem solving, personal planning, life skills, self-esteem, and self-awareness. 800-676-1480.

Aladdin/Collier Books, MacMillan Publishing, 1230 Avenue of Americas, New York, NY 10020: Free information ❖ Board books, pop-ups, and paperbacks for children, from age 3 to 16.

❖ BOOKS ❖

Astor Books, 62 Cooper Square, New York, NY 10003: Free catalog ❖ Children's books. 212-777-3700.

Bellerophon Books, 36 Anacapa St., Santa Barbara, CA 93101: Free catalog ❖ Art books for children of all ages. 800-253-9943.

Beyond Beadery, 54 Tinker St., Woodstock, NY 12498: Catalog $1 ❖ Books on how to work with beads. 800-840-5548.

✓ **Boyds Mill Press,** 815 Church St., Honesdale, PA 18431: Free catalog ❖ Books for children. 800-949-7777.

Charington House

Charington House, P.O. Box 9661, Bradenton, FL 34206: Catalog $2 ❖ The best new children's books from all publishers. Picture books, multi-cultural, special needs, and multimedia. 941-746-3326.

Cheshire Cat Children's Books, 5512 Connecticut Ave. NW, Washington, DC 20015: Free information ❖ Books, records, and tapes. 202-244-3956.

Children's Book Press, 6400 Hollis St., Ste. 4, Emeryville, CA 94608: Free information ❖ Multi-cultural and bilingual picture books and audio cassettes for children. 510-655-3395.

✓ **Chinaberry Book Service,** 2780 Via Orange Way, Ste. B, Spring Valley, CA 91978: Free catalog ❖ Books from a variety of publishers for children and adults. Also music. 800-776-2242.

✓ **Christian Book Distributors,** P.O. Box 7000, Peabody, MA 01961: Free catalog ❖ Christian books. 508-977-5000.

✓ **Dover Publications Inc.,** 31 East 2nd St., Mineola, NY 11501: Free catalog ❖ Children's classics, cut-and-assemble and coloring books, paper dolls and stickers, and other educational activity books. 516-294-7000.

✓ **Essential Learning Products,** 2300 W. 5th Ave., P.O. Box 2590, Columbus, OH 43272: Free catalog ❖ Supplementary materials for kindergarten through grade 8. Includes aids for guided practice in basic skills, reading and handwriting, literature-based education, arts and crafts, enrichment goals, learning fun, and motivation. 614-486-0633.

The Evergreen Press, 3380 Vincent Rd., Pleasant Hill, CA 94523: Free information with long SASE ❖ Adult and children's books, greeting cards, book marks and bookplates, wedding certificates, calendars, ornaments, paper dolls, postcards, and 19th and early 20th-century paper memorabilia. 510-933-9700.

Free Spirit Publishing Inc., 400 1st Ave. North, Ste. 616, Minneapolis, MN 55401: Free information ❖ Nonfiction, psychology and self-help materials for and about gifted, talented, and creative young people, their parents, and teachers. 800-735-7323.

W.H. Freeman & Company, 41 Madison Ave., New York, NY 10010: Free information ❖ Adult and children's books on science, computers, and other subjects. 212-576-9400.

Kar-Ben Copies Inc., 6800 Tildenwood Ln., Rockville, MD 20852: Free catalog ❖ Judaic books and cassettes. 800-452-7236.

KidsArt, P.O. Box 274, Mt. Shasta, CA 96067: Free catalog ❖ How-to art books and supplies for children from kindergarten up to the 8th grade. 916-926-5076.

Klutz Press, 2121 Staunton Ct., Palo Alto, CA 94306: Free information ❖ How-to, fun, and song books for children. 415-424-0739.

✓ **The Maritime Store,** 2905 Hyde St. Pier, San Francisco, CA 94109: Free catalog ❖ Maritime maps, greeting cards, boat models, children's and maritime books, and gifts. 415-775-BOOK.

✓ **Metacom Inc.,** 5353 Nathan Ln., Plymouth, MN 55442: Free catalog ❖ Golden Age Radio programs, comedy super stars of past years, famous radio plays, foreign language cassettes, coloring books with stories, and read-along books and cassettes for teaching children to read. 800-328-0108.

✓ **The Mind's Eye,** P.O. Box 6547, Chelmsford, MA 01824: Free catalog ❖ Children's favorites and classics, military intrigue, mystery, horror, science fiction, adventure, drama, history, comedy, poetry, and self-improvement. Also audio cassettes and compact disks. 800-949-3333.

Music for Little People, P.O. Box 1720, Lawndale, CA 90260: Free catalog ❖ Music books, musical instruments, cassettes, and videos. 800-727-2233.

Nerman's Books & Collectibles, 410-63 Albert St., Winnipeg, Manitoba, Canada R3B 1G4: Catalog $3 ❖ Books for children and juveniles.

✓ **Positive Books,** Division Aton International Inc., 7654 Benassi Dr., Gilroy, CA 95020: Free catalog ❖ A family resource for books for all ages and interests. 800-833-0835.

Silver Burdett Press, P.O. Box 2649, Columbus, OH 43216: Free information ❖ Beginning-to-read books and others about nature and animals, science, holiday fun, and teen issues. 800-321-3106.

✓ **Warren Publishing House Inc.,** P.O. Box 2250, Everett, WA 98203: Free catalog ❖ Children's story books and resources with activities for teachers, parents, and librarians. 800-773-7240.

General Books

A.R.C. Books, P.O. Box 2, Carlisle, MA 01741: Free information ❖ Books for collectors of antique radios. 508-371-0512.

A & C Books, P.O. Box 706, Mt. Morris, IL 61054: Free information ❖ Reference books for collectors. 800-445-4154.

Abenaki Publishers, 126 North St., P.O. Box 4100, Bennington, VT 05201: Free information ❖ Books on fishing. 802-447-2471.

Harry N. Abrams Inc., 100 5th Ave., New York, NY 10011: Free information ❖ Art, how-to craft, food and wine, architecture, science, folk art, and pictorial non-fiction books. 212-206-7715.

Academic Press Inc., Order Fulfillment Dept. DM17915, 6277 Sea Harbor Dr., Orlando, FL 32887: Free catalog ❖ Scientific and technical books. 800-321-5068.

Adamas Publishers, P.O. Box 1991, York, PA 17405: Free information ❖ Lapidary books.

Addison-Wesley Publishing Company, One Jacob Way, Reading, MA 01867: Free catalog ❖ Books about computers, child care and health, biographies, children's activities, psychology, current affairs, and business. 617-944-3700.

Advanced Vivarium Systems, 10728 Prospect Ave., Ste. G, Santee, CA 92071: Free information ❖ Books on reptiles. 619-258-2629.

Advanstar Marketing Service, 7500 Old Oak Blvd., Cleveland, OH 44130: Free information ❖ PC graphics and video books. 800-598-6008.

Adventures in Crime & Space Books, 609-A W. 6th St., Austin, TX 78701: Free information ❖ New, used, and rare science fiction, mystery, and horror books. 512-473-2665.

✓ **Adventurous Traveler Bookstore,** P.O. Box 577, Hinesburg, VT 05461: Free catalog ❖ Books and maps for hiking, climbing, kayaking, diving, and travel. 800-282-3963.

✓ **Jamey Aebersold Jazz Inc.,** P.O. Box 1244, New Albany, IN 47151: Free catalog ❖ Books on music and musical instruments.

Air Age Mail Order Service, P.O. Box 280, 251 Danbury Rd., Wilton, CT 06897: Free information ❖ Books on model boating. 800-243-6685; 203-834-2329 (in CT).

Alcott Press, 6325 NE 7th Ave., Portland, OR 97211: Free catalog with long SASE ❖ Books on fabric painting and plus and supersize clothing for women. 503-287-3140.

AlpenBooks, 3616 South Rd., Mukilteo, WA 98275: Free information ❖ Books on the outdoors. 206-290-8587.

Alpine Publications, P.O. Box 7027, Loveland, CO 80537: Free catalog ❖ Books on horses, dogs, mules, and llamas. 800-777-7257.

BOOKS

Amadeus Press, 133 SW 2nd Ave., Ste. 450, Portland, OR 97204: Free catalog ❖ Books on classical music and opera. 800-327-5680.

American Botanical Council, P.O. Box 201660, Austin, TX 78720: Free information ❖ Books on herbs and herbal medicine. 800-373-7105.

American Council for an Energy-Efficient Economy, 2140 Shattuck Ave., Ste. 202, Berkeley, CA 94704: Free catalog ❖ Books on energy efficiency. 510-549-9914.

American Diabetes Association, 1970 Chain Bridge Rd., Arlington, VA 22213: Free catalog ❖ Books for professionals and people with diabetes. Includes nutrition and cooking.

American Homeowners Foundation, 5776 Little Falls Rd., Arlington, VA 22213: Free catalog ❖ Books on real estate, home improvement, and new home construction. 703-536-7776.

American Indian Books & Relics, P.O. Box 16175, Huntsville, AL 35802: List $3 (10 issues) ❖ Books on Native Americans and their relics. 205-881-6727.

The American Institute of Architects Press, 1735 New York Ave. NW, Washington, DC 20006: Free information ❖ Books on architecture and design. 202-626-7498.

American Map Corporation, 46-35 54th Rd., Maspeth, NY 11378: Free information ❖ Bilingual dictionaries, travel guides and atlases, travel language aids, maps, and other educational publications. 718-784-0055.

American Psychiatric Press Inc., 1400 K St. NW, Washington, DC 20005: Free information ❖ Books on psychiatry and mental illness. 202-682-6262.

American Radio Relay League, 225 Main St., Newington, CT 06111: Free information ❖ Books on how to become a HAM radio operator, get a license, learn Morse code, organize equipment, how to operate and set up equipment, and other topics. 800-326-3942.

American Regional Cookbooks, Lion House Distributors, Box 91283, Pittsburgh, PA 15221: Free catalog ❖ Cookbooks. 800-786-6235.

Andy's Front Hall, P.O. Box 307, Voorheesville, NY 12186: Free catalog ❖ Books and music for and about folk, traditional, and acoustic sounds. 800-759-1775; 518-765-4193 (in NY).

The Anglers Art, P.O. Box 148, Plainfield, PA 17081: Free catalog ❖ Books on fishing. 800-848-1020.

Antheil Booksellers, 2177 Isabelle Ct., North Bellmore, NY 11710: Catalog $6 (4 issues) ❖ Books about the navy, maritime, aviation, and military. 516-826-2094.

Antique Collectors Club, Market Street Industrial Park, Wappingers Falls, NY 12590: Free brochure ❖ Books on fine and decorative art, architecture, and gardening. 800-252-5231.

Aperture, 20 E. 23rd St., New York, NY 10010: Free information ❖ Fine art and photography books. 800-929-2323.

Apollo Books, 151 Tremont St., Boston, MA 02111: Free catalog ❖ Reference books and price guides for fine art, antiques, and gardening. 800-431-5003.

Appalachian Mountain Club Books, 5 Joy Street, Boston, MA 02108: Free catalog ❖ Maps and hiking, river, and recreation guides. 617-523-0636.

Art Book Services, P.O. Box 360, Hughsonville, NY 12537: Free information ❖ Books on art and antiques. 914-297-1312.

The Artist Magazine Bookshelf, 1507 Dana Ave., Cincinnati, OH 45207: Free information ❖ Books for artists. 800-289-0963.

Asian World of Martial Arts, 11601 Caroline Rd., Philadelphia, PA 19154: Catalog $5 ❖ Martial arts books. 800-345-2962.

The Astragal Press, Box 239, Mendham, NJ 07945: Free catalog ❖ Books on early tools, technology, and trades. 201-543-3045.

Astronomical League Sales, 1901 S. 10th St., Burlington, IA 52601: Free price list ❖ Books and manuals on astronomy. Also astronomy-theme T-shirts, sweatshirts, and logo items. 319-753-1442.

Audel Library, MacMillan Publishing, 1633 Broadway, New York, NY 10019: Free catalog ❖ Books about vocational trades and crafts.

Audio-Forum, 96 Broad St., Guilford, CT 06437: Free catalog ❖ Self-instruction foreign language courses. 800-448-7671; 203-453-9794 (in CT).

Audubon Naturalist, 8940 Jones Mill Rd., Silver Spring, MD 20815: Free information with long SASE ❖ Natural history books and field guides. 800-699-BIRD; 301-652-3606 (in MD).

August House Publishers Inc., P.O. Box 3223, Little Rock, AR 72203: Free information ❖ Story teller books. 501-372-5450.

Aunt Clowney's Warehouse, P.O. Box 1444, Corona, CA 91718: Free catalog with two 1st class stamps ❖ Books on clowning.

Aurora Press, P.O. Box 573, Santa Fe, NM 87504: Free catalog ❖ Books on astrology and yoga. 207-363-4393.

Australian Catalogue Company, 7412 Wingfoot Dr., Raleigh, NC 27615: Free catalog ❖ Books about Australia. 919-878-8266.

Autograph Collector, 510-A S. Corona Mall, Corona, CA 91720: Free information ❖ Books on autographs and autograph collecting. 800-395-1359.

Aviation Book Company, 7201 Perimeter Rd. S, Ste. C, Seattle, WA 98108: Free catalog ❖ Books, videos, pilot supplies, clothing, and gifts. 800-423-2708.

B & B Honey Farm, Rt. 2, Box 245, Houston, MN 55943: Free catalog ❖ Beekeeping books. 507-896-3955.

Backcountry Bookstore, P.O. Box 6235, Lynnwood, WA 98036: Catalog $1 ❖ Books, maps, and videos on backpacking, skiing, biking, paddle sports, trekking, and climbing. 206-290-7652.

Bailey Craftsman Supply, P.O. Box 276, Fulton, MO 65251: Free information ❖ How-to books on metal-working and fabrication. 314-642-5998.

Bantam Doubleday Dell Publishing Group Inc., 1540 Broadway, New York, NY 10036: Free catalog ❖ Fiction and non-fiction books. 212-354-6500.

Bantam Doubleday Dell Travel Books, 1540 Broadway, New York, NY 10036: Free information ❖ Travel guidebooks, atlases, and other books. 212-354-6500.

Bantam Electronic Publishing, 1540 Broadway, New York, NY 10036: Free information ❖ Computer books. 212-354-6500.

Barney's Ginseng Patch, Rt. 2, Box 43, Montgomery City, MO 63361: Free brochure ❖ Books on ginseng. 573-564-575.

Barron's Educational Series, 250 Wireless Blvd., Hauppage, NY 11788: Free catalog ❖ Educational books. 800-645-3476.

Basic Books Inc., Division HarperCollins, 10 E. 53rd St., New York, NY 10022: Free catalog ❖ Books on psychology, business, history, science, political science, women's studies, and other subjects. 212-207-7000.

Bel Bay Publications Inc., 4 Industrial Dr., Pacific, MO 63069: Free information ❖ How-to books on musical instruments. 800-863-5229.

Berkshire House Publishers, P.O. Box 297, Stockbridge, MA 01262: Free information ❖ Travel, recreation, self-help, crafts, psychology, and cooking books. 800-321-8526.

Better Homes & Gardens Books, 1716 Locust St., Des Moines, IA 50336: Free information with long SASE ❖ Books on cooking, gardening, how-to, crafts, and other subjects. 800-678-8091.

Betterway Books, 1507 Dana Ave., Cincinnati, OH 45207: Free catalog ❖ Woodworking books. 800-289-0963.

BOOKS

Bibliomania, 195 W. 200 North, Logan, UT 84321: Free price list ❖ Herpetological books, cage and field supplies, and collectibles.

Bicycle Books Inc., 1282 7th Ave., San Francisco, CA 94122: Free information ❖ Books about bicycles, touring guides, health and fitness, mountain biking, racing, and other topics. 415-665-8214.

Bird Watcher's Digest, P.O. Box 110, Marietta, OH 45750: Free information ❖ Books on birds. 800-879-2473.

Black Moon Company, Mail Order Specialty Books, P.O. Box 12510, Baltimore, MD 21217: Free catalog ❖ Hard-to-find books. 410-792-9601.

Warren Blake, Old Science Books, 308 Hadley Dr., Trumbull, CT 06611: Catalog $1 ❖ Hard-to-find old-to-early astronomy books and prints. 203-459-0820.

Anny Blatt Boutique, 6728 Lowell Ave., McLean, VA 22101: Catalog $2 ❖ Kits, how-to knitting books, and accessories. 800-767-4036.

Bloomington Wholesale Garden Supply, 3151 S. Hwy. 446, Bloomington, IN 47401: Free information ❖ Books on hydroponic gardening. 800-274-9676.

Blystone's Books, 2132 Delaware Ave., Ottsburgh, PA 15218: Free information ❖ Hard-to-find books for toy collectors. 412-371-3511.

The Bold Strummer Ltd., 20 Turkey Hill Circle, P.O. Box 2037, Westport, CT 06880: Catalog $1 (refundable) ❖ Books on music and musical instruments. 203-259-3021.

The Book Corner, 728 W. Lumsden Rd., Brandon, FL 33511: Free catalog ❖ General out-of-print and used books. Also books on pirates and treasure hunting. 800-781-6060.

Book Publishing Company, P.O. Box 99, Summertown, TN 38483: Free brochure ❖ Books on cooking, pest control, natural birth control, midwifery, fertility, and spiritual teachings. 615-964-3571.

Book Sales Inc., 114 Northfield Ave., Edison, NJ 08818: Free catalog ❖ Books on Americana, Civil War, fine arts, military, photography, religion, travel, humor, health, cooking, and crafts. 908-225-0530.

BookBound, Box 2376, East Hampton, NY 11937: Free information ❖ Can supply any book in print, from new releases to classics. 800-859-READ.

Books for Cooks, 231 W. 256th St., Riverdale, NY 10471: Free catalog ❖ Cookbooks and books on wine. 800-355-CHEF.

The Bookshelf, P.O. Box 6925, Ventura, CA 93006: Free information ❖ Books on metalsmithing.

Bookworm & Silverfish, P.O. Box 639, Wytheville, VA 24382: Free catalog ❖ Out-of-print and other books on Americana, technology, Civil War, and miscellaneous subjects. 540-686-5813.

Bowling's Bookstore, Tech-Ed Publishing Company, P.O. Box 4, Deerfield, IL 60015: Free information ❖ Books and videos on bowling. 800-521-BOWL.

Brandy Station Bookshelf, P.O. Box 1863, Harrah, OK 73045: Free catalog ❖ New, rare, and out-of-print Civil War books. 405-964-5730.

Brew Pot, 13031 11th St., Old Bowie, MD 20715: Free catalog ❖ Books on homebrewing and wine-making. 301-805-6799.

Broadfoot Publishing Company, 1907 Buena Vista Circle, Wilmington, NC 28405: Free catalog ❖ Books about the Civil War. 919-686-4816.

Broadway Press, P.O. Box 1037, Shelter Island, NY 11964: Free catalog ❖ Books on theatrical production, scenery construction, and backstage direction. 800-869-6372.

Brooklyn Botanic Garden, Attention: Plants & Gardens, 1000 Washington Ave., Brooklyn, NY 11225: Free brochure ❖ Gardening books and videos. 718-622-4433.

Brudy's Exotics, Box 820874, Houston, TX 77282: Free catalog ❖ Exotic plants and seeds, butterfly egg/caterpillar kits, and books on butterflies. 800-926-7333.

The Business Reader, P.O. Box 41268, Brecksville, OH 44141: Free catalog ❖ Business, professional, technical, and computer books. 216-838-8653.

C & T Publishing/Fox Hill Workshop, P.O. Box 1456, Lafayette, CA 94549: Free catalog ❖ Books on quilting, color, dollmaking, dying, embroidery, ethnic textiles, fabric painting, wearable art, and quilt gift cards. 800-284-1114.

Caboose Hobbies, 500 S. Broadway, Denver, CO 80209: Free information ❖ Fiction, nonfiction, and how-to books on model trains. 303-777-6766.

T. Cadman, 2029 Meadow Valley Terrace, Los Angeles, CA 90039: Free catalog ❖ World War II and other military history books.

Gretchen Cagle Publications, 403 W. 4th St., Claremore, OK 74017: Free information ❖ Books on designing and decorative art. 918-342-1080.

Calibre Press Inc., 666 Dundee Rd., Ste. 1607, Northbrook, IL 60062: Free catalog ❖ Law enforcement videos, books, and survival products. 800-323-0037; 847-498-5680 (in IL).

Cambridge University Press, 40 W. 20th St., New York, NY 10011: Free catalog ❖ Reference and academic books. 212-924-3900.

Camper's Library, P.O. Box 1142, Park Ridge, IL 60068: Free catalog ❖ How-to and where-to-go books for hikers and backpackers.

Capability's Books, 2379 Hwy. 46, Deer Park, WI 54007: Catalog $1 ❖ Books for gardeners. 800-247-8154.

Cascadia Company, 375 Candalaria Blvd. South, Ste. 15, Salem, OR 97302: Catalog $1 ❖ Books on garden design, shade and water gardening, ornamentals, grass, and other topics.

Tony Chachere's Creole Foods, P.O. Box 1687, Opelousas, LA 70571: Free brochure ❖ Cajun country specialties and Cajun and Creole cookbooks. 800-551-9066.

Charlesbridge Publishing, 85 Main St., Watertown, MA 02172: Free catalog ❖ Nature, science, and multi-cultural books. 617-926-0329.

Chautauqua Inc., 1627 Marion Ave., Durham, NC 27705: Free information ❖ Books about beer. 800-977-BEER.

Chessler Books, P.O. Box 399, Kittredge, CO 80457: Free catalog ❖ New, used, and rare books on mountaineering. 800-654-8502; 303-670-0093 (in CO).

Chilton Book Company, One Chilton Way, Radnor, PA 19089: Free catalog ❖ Books about automobiles, crafts, antiques, technical, and businesses. 610-964-4000.

China Books & Periodicals Inc., 2929 24th St., San Francisco, CA 94110: Free catalog ❖ Imported books and periodicals (in English) about China. 415-282-2994.

The China Decorator Library, P.O. Box 575, Shingle Springs, CA 95682: Free catalog ❖ Books on china decorating. 916-677-1455.

Chronicle Books, 275 5th St., San Francisco, CA 94103: Free information ❖ Books about cooking and food, art and photography, architecture, nature, travel, and history. 800-722-6657.

Chronicles Bookshop, 322 S. Shelby, Shelbina, MO 63468: Free catalog ❖ Science fiction, fantasy, horror, mystery, and suspense books. 573-588-4573.

Stan Clark Military Books, 915 Fairview Ave., Gettysburg, PA 17325: Catalog $2 ❖ Civil War books. 717-337-1728.

Classical Numismatic Group Inc., P.O. Box 479, Lancaster, PA 17608: Free list ❖ Numismatic books. 717-390-9194.

Cliff's Notes Inc., P.O. Box 80728, Lincoln, NE 68501: Free information ❖ Study aids, test preparation guides, and complete study editions. 800-228-4078; 402-423-5050 (in NE).

Coin World Books, P.O. Box 150, Sidney, OH 45365: Free information ❖ Books on coin collecting. 800-253-4555.

BOOKS

Collector Books, P.O. Box 3009, Paducah, KY 42002: Free catalog ❖ Books on antiques, depression glassware, pottery, toys, dolls, teddy bears, thimbles, and other collectibles. 800-626-5420.

The Collector's Book Source, 1 Corporate Dr., Grantsville, MD 21536: Free catalog ❖ Books on dolls and teddy bears. 800-554-1447.

Collector's Guide Publishing Inc., P.O. Box 62034, Burlington, Ontario, Canada L7R 4K2: Free information ❖ Books for the music collector.

The College Board, 45 Columbus Ave., New York, NY 10023: Free information ❖ Books that help students and their families in the transition from high school to college and college to work. 212-713-8165.

William H. Collins Gardens, Box 48, Viola, IA 52350: Free information ❖ How-to and about books on ginseng and other medicinal plants.

Columbia Gifts, 6135 Good Hunters Ride, Columbia, MD 21045: Free catalog ❖ Self-improvement books.

Columbia Trading Company, 1 Barnstable Rd., Hyannis, MA 02601: Free catalog ❖ Used and rare nautical antiques, marine art, books, and gifts. 508-778-2929.

Columbia University Press, 562 W. 113th St., New York, NY 10025: Free catalog ❖ Scholarly and general interest books. 212-666-1000.

The Complete Traveler of Overland Park, 7321 W. 80th St., Overland Park, KS 66204: Free catalog ❖ Maps, travel books, travel accessories, and luggage. 888-862-0888.

Congressional Quarterly Inc., 1414 22nd St. NW, Washington, DC 20037: Free information ❖ Books on government, political science, current affairs, and the Congress. 202-887-8501.

Consumer Information Center, Pueblo, CO 81003: Free catalog ❖ United States Government books and pamphlets for consumers. 719-948-4000.

Consumer Reports Books, 101 Truman Ave., Yonkers, NY 10703: Free catalog ❖ Books on consumer information and advice on goods, services, health, and personal finances. 914-378-2000.

Cookbook Cellar, 1455 Page Industrial Blvd., St. Louis, MO 63132: Free catalog ❖ Cookbooks. 800-791-4438.

The Cotton Patch, 1025 Brown Ave., Lafayette, CA 94549: Catalog $8 ($5 refundable) ❖ Quilting books. 510-284-1177.

Cowboy Cuisine, P.O. Box 2441, Cupertino, CA 95015: Free information ❖ Recipes from around the world for cowboys. 800-95-CUISINE.

CQ Communications Inc., 76 N. Broadway, Hicksville, NY 11801: Free information ❖ Books and videos for radio amateurs. 800-853-9797.

John S. Craig, 111 Edward Ave., P.O. Box 1637, Torrington, CT 06790: Free information ❖ Hard-to-find instruction books for photography equipment. Also other photographic literature. 203-496-9791.

Creative Homeowner Press, 24 Park Way, Upper Saddle River, NJ 07458: Free information ❖ How-to books on home improvement and repair. 800-631-7795.

Creative Stitches, P.O. Box 89, Bountiful, UT 84011: Free information ❖ How-to books on machine embroidery, quilting, and other related crafts. 801-292-9111.

Culinary Arts Ltd., Publishers of Unique Specialty Books, P.O. Box 2157, Lake Oswego, OR 97035: Free brochure ❖ Books on cooking, liqueurs and wines, parties for children, microwave preserving, how to make and cook with gourmet vinegars and mustards, and other topics. 503-639-4549.

Curriculum Associates, P.O. Box 2001, North Billerica, MA 01862: Free catalog ❖ Assessment and instruction books for teachers, test-prep/study skills aids, student books and teacher guides, and other educational materials. 800-225-0248;m 508-667-8000 (in MA).

Cygnus-Quasar Books, P.O. Box 85, Powell, OH 43065: Free brochure ❖ Books on radio antennas, electromagnetics, and radio astronomy. 614-548-7895.

Da Capo Press, 233 Spring St., New York, NY 10013: Free information ❖ Classic military paperbacks. 800-321-0050.

Q.M. Dabney & Company, P.O. Box 42026, Washington, DC 20015: Catalog $1 ❖ Old and rare aviation, World War II, and military history books.

The Dance Mart, P.O. Box 994, Teaneck, NJ 07666: Free catalog with long SASE ❖ Rare books, magazines, autograph material, and dance collectibles. 201-833-4176.

Darrow Production Company, P.O. Box 1457, El Reno, OK 73036: Free information ❖ Decorative painting books. 405-422-5727.

The Dartmouth Bookstore, 33 S. Main St., Hanover, NH 03755: Free catalog ❖ Classic books on philosophy, psychology, history, fiction, poetry, and other subjects. 800-624-8800; 800-675-3616 (in NH).

Charles Davis, Box 547, Wenham, MA 01984: Free price list ❖ United States, ancient, and British numismatic books, catalogs, and periodicals. 508-468-2933.

Daw Books Inc., 375 Hudson St., New York, NY 10014: Free catalog ❖ Science fiction, fantasy, and horror books. 800-253-6476.

Cy Decosse Incorporated, 5900 Green Oak Dr., Minnetonka, MN 55343: Free information ❖ How-to books on cooking, sewing, hunting, and fishing. 612-936-4700.

Defender Industries Inc., 25542 Great Neck Rd., Waterford, CT 06385: Free catalog ❖ Clothing, life vests, foul weather gear, books, and marine supplies. 800-701-3400.

Deltiologists of America, P.O. Box 8, Norwoods, PA 19074: Price list $1 ❖ Postcard reference books.

Demos Publications, 386 Park Ave. South, New York, NY 10016: Free catalog ❖ Health resources for people with disabilities and chronic disease. 800-532-8663; 212-683-0072 (in NY).

Dorothy Dent, 108 W. Hwy. 174, Republic, MO 65738: Free information ❖ Instructional books and videos on painting and supplies. 417-732-2076.

DeRus Fine Art, 9100 Artesia Blvd., Bellflower, CA 90706: Free list ❖ Art from the 19th and early 20th century. Also fine art books. 310-920-1312.

Design Originals, 2425 Cullen St., Fort Worth, TX 76107: Free information ❖ How-to books on making rag rugs, baskets, wood and fabric items, cross stitching, and other crafts. 800-877-7820.

Direct Book Service, P.O. Box 2778, Wenatchee, WA 98807: Free catalog ❖ Dog and cat books and videos. 800-776-2665.

Dos Tejedoras, Fiber Arts Publications, P.O. Box 14238, St. Paul, MN 55114: Catalog $2.50 ❖ Books for knitters, weavers, and ethnic textile lovers.

Dover Publications Inc., 31 E. 2nd St., Mineola, NY 11501: Free catalog ❖ Books on arts and crafts, business, hobbies, architecture, science, juvenile interests, health, fiction, and other subjects. 516-294-7000.

John Dromgoode's Natural Gardener's Catalog, 8648 Old Bee Caves Rd., Austin, TX 78735: Free catalog ❖ Books on organic gardening. 800-320-0724.

Dubrow Antiques, P.O. Box 128, Bayside, NY 11361: Free information ❖ Out-of-print books on decorative arts and furniture. 718-767-9758.

Gameroom Antiques, 909 26th St. NW, Washington, DC 20037: Catalog $2 ❖ Jukebox service manuals and books on coin-operated machines. 202-338-1342.

Eagle Feather Trading Post, 168 W. 12th St., Ogden, UT 84404: Catalog $3.50 ❖ Beading and Indian craft supplies, beads, and how-to beading and craft books.

Eagle Golf, P.O. Box 2022, Bellevue, WA 98009: Free catalog ❖ Golf instructional videos, books, and training aids. 800-752-3149.

BOOKS

East Coast Prospecting & Mining Supplies, Rt. 3, Box 321-J, Ellijay, GA 30540: Catalog $3 ❖ How-to books on mining and prospecting. 706-276-4433.

East Earth Trade Winds, P.O. Box 493151, 1620 E. Cypress Ave., Ste. 8, Redding, CA 96049: Free catalog ❖ Books on Chinese herbs. 800-258-6878.

Eastman Kodak Company, Information Center, 343 State St., Rochester, NY 14650: Free information ❖ Photography books. 800-462-6495.

Effective Learning Systems Inc., 5255 Edina Industrial Blvd., Edina, MN 55439: Free catalog ❖ Self-improvement books on weight control, stress relief, health and healing, and inner peace and happiness. 800-966-5683.

Eisers, 360 Kiwanis Blvd., P.O. Box T, Hazleton, PA 18201: Free list of retail sources ❖ Books and manuals on horses. 800-526-6987.

Electronic Technology Today Inc., P.O. Box 240, Massapequa Park, NY 11762: Free information ❖ Books on electronics.

Empire Publishing, Box 717, Madison, NC 27025: Catalog $3 ❖ Comedy, action, western, drama, glamour, and classic TV star and movie books. 919-427-5850.

Alan Ende, 40 Morrow Ave., Scarsdale, NY 10583: List $3 ❖ Ventriloquist figures, accessories, and vintage magic books.

Enterprising Solutions, 6 Harbor Way, Santa Barbara, CA 93109: Free catalog ❖ How-to books for home-based businesses. 800-219-4203.

Eureka! Daylily Reference Guide, Ken Gregory, Editor, 5586 Quail Creek Dr., Granite Falls, NC 28630: Free information ❖ How-to books on daylilies. 704-396-6107.

The Evergreen Press, Box 306, Avalon, CA 90704: Free information with long SASE ❖ Adult and children's books, greeting cards, book marks and bookplates, wedding certificates, calendars, ornaments, paper dolls, postcards, and 19th and early 20th-century paper memorabilia. 310-510-1700.

Fabricators & Manufacturers Association International, Attn: Books, P.O. Box 626, Rockford, IL 61105: Free information ❖ How-to books on metal-working and fabrication. 815-399-8799.

Falcon, P.O. Box 1718, Helena, MT 59624: Free catalog ❖ Cookbooks and books on western adventure and lifestyles, human interest, and cowboy poetry. 800-582-2665.

The Family Travel Guides Catalog, P.O. Box 6061, Albany, CA 94706: Catalog $1 ❖ Family travel guides and items to keep children happy in the car. 510-527-5849.

Farmer's Books, P.O. Box 2111, Mission Viejo, CA 92690: Catalog $2 ❖ Books on German military history of World War I and II.

Fascinating Folds, P.O. Box 2820-235, Torrance, CA 90509: Catalog $1 ❖ Supplies, kits, and how-to books on origami (paper folding). 801-968-2418.

Farnsworth Military Gallery, 401 Baltimore St., Gettysburg, PA 17325: Free information ❖ Art prints and new, used, and rare Civil War books. 717-334-8838.

Fatwise, 1130 E. Linden Ave., Colina, NJ 07036: Free catalog ❖ Books on good health for dessert-lovers who are dieting, fat-free baking books, and other related areas. 908-862-3886.

The Feminist Press, The City University of New York, 311 E. 94th St., New York, NY 10128: Free information ❖ Books by and about women. 212-360-5794.

Fielding Worldwide Inc., 308 S. Catalina Ave., Radiant Beach, CA 90277: Free information ❖ Travel guides. 800-FEW-2-GUIDE.

Firefighters Bookstore, 18281 Gothard St., #105, Huntington Beach, CA 92648: Free catalog ❖ Books, software, and videos for firefighters. 714-375-4888.

Fireside Classics, 17 Berk Rd., Roosevelt, WA 99356: Free catalog ❖ Classic books in hardcover, softcover, and audio and video form. 800-757-3891.

Fiskars Corporation, P.O. Box 8027, Wausau, WI 54402: Free information ❖ Paper crafting project books.

The Fly Box, 1293 NE 3rd St., Bend, OR 97701: Catalog $1 ❖ Books on fly fishing. 503-388-3330.

Focal Press, 313 Washington St., Newton, MA 02158: Free catalog ❖ Books on photography, cinematography, broadcasting, and the theater. 617-928-2500.

Fodor's Travel Publications Inc., 201 E. 50th St., New York, NY 10022: Free information ❖ Travel books. 212-572-8756.

For the People Bookstore, Tefford Hotel, 3 River St., White Springs, FL 32096: Free catalog ❖ Books for everyone. 800-888-9999.

Forsooth Travel Library Inc., P.O. Box 2975, Shawnee Mission, KS 66201: Free brochure ❖ Travel books, maps, and other publications. 800-367-7984; 913-384-3440 (in KS).

Forum Publishing Company, 383 E. Main St., Centerport, NY 11721: Catalog $1 ❖ Business start-up, expansion, diversification, mail order, legal, and other books for business activities. 800-635-7654.

Franklin, Beedle & Associates Inc., 814 N. Franklin St., Chicago, IL 60610: Free catalog ❖ Books for the computer sciences. 312-337-0747.

W.H. Freeman & Company, 41 Madison Ave., New York, NY 10010: Free information ❖ Adult and children's books on science and computers. 212-576-9400.

Freeperson Press, 1516 Grant Ave., #212, Novato, CA 94945: Free information ❖ Yoga books. 415-892-0617.

Samuel French Catalog, 45 W. 25th St., New York, NY 10010: Catalog $4.50 ❖ Scripts for plays and other theatrical productions. 212-206-8990.

Samuel French Trade, 7623 Sunset Blvd., Hollywood CA 90046: Free catalog ❖ Books about the film industry. 213-876-0570.

Fulcrum Publishing, 350 Indiana St., Ste. 350, Golden, CO 80401: Free catalog ❖ Books on a variety of subjects. 800-992-2908.

Fun Publishing Company, 2121 Alpine Pl., Cincinnati, OH 45206: Free information ❖ Soft toys for children ages 1 to 3, books for children in kindergarten and 1st grade, and ages 2 to 4, 5 to 6, and 7 to 8. Also music items for children age 3 to adults and special books for teachers. 513-533-3636.

Gallaudet University Press, 800 Florida Ave. NE, Washington, DC 20002: Free catalog ❖ Books for children and adults about deafness, hard-of-hearing, and sign language. 800-451-1073.

Gambler's Book Shop, 630 S. 11th, Las Vegas, NV 89101: Free catalog ❖ Books and computer software on gambling. 800-522-1777.

Gateways, P.O. Box 1706, Ojai, CA 93024: Free catalog ❖ Books on self-improvement, relaxation, health and healing, creativity, stress reduction, and other life-style self-improvement subjects. 800-477-8908.

Paul Gaudette Books, 2050 E. 17th St., Tucson, AZ 85719: Catalog $2 ❖ Military aircraft books. 800-874-3097.

Robert Gavora Bookseller, 4514 E. Burnside St., Portland, OR 97215: Free catalog ❖ First edition science fiction, horror, and mystery books. 503-231-7338.

The Gemmary, P.O. Box 816, Redondo Beach, CA 90277: Catalog $5 ❖ Rare books and antique scientific instruments. 310-372-5969.

Gemstone Press, Rt. 4, Sunset Farm Offices, P.O. Box 237, Woodstock, VT 05091: Free catalog ❖ Books for the consumer, hobbyist, investor, and retail trade on buying, identifying, selling, and enjoying jewelry and gems. 802-457-4000.

Genealogical Publishing Company, 1001 N. Calvert St., Baltimore, MD 21202: Free catalog ❖ Books on genealogy. 800-296-6687.

The General's Books, Blue & Gray Magazine, 522 Norton Rd., Columbus, OH 43228: Free catalog ❖ Civil War books. 614-870-1861.

❖ **BOOKS** ❖

Robert Gentry, P.O. Box 850, Many, LA 71449: Free list ❖ Country music albums, 78 and 45 rpm records, autographs, movie posters, books and magazines, press kits, and other collectibles.

David Ginn Magic, 4387 St. Michaels Dr., Lilburn, GA 30247: Catalog $10 ❖ Books, props, and how-to magic on video tapes for magicians and clowns.

Glass Crafters, 398 Interstate Ct., Sarasota, FL 34240: Catalog $3 ❖ Stained glass crafting books. 800-422-4552.

Globe Pequot Press, P.O. Box 833, 6 Business Park Rd., Old Saybrook, CT 06475: Free catalog ❖ Travel guides, cookbooks, outdoor recreation, how-to, and nature books. 800-243-0495.

Gluten-Free Pantry, P.O. Box 881, Glastonbury, CT 06033: Free information ❖ Gluten-free cooking. 203-633-3826.

✓ **Golden West Publishers,** 4113 N. Longview, Phoenix, AZ 85024: Free catalog ❖ Cookbooks and books on western adventure and lifestyles, western humor, and human interest. 800-658-5830.

Gotham Book Mart, 41 W. 47th St., New York, NY 10036: Free information ❖ Postcard reference books. 212-719-4448.

Orville J. Grady, 6602 Military Ave., Omaha, NE 68104: Free information ❖ New and out-of-print numismatic literature. 800-295-4846; 402-558-6782 (in NE).

Graywolf Press, 2402 University Ave., Ste. 203, St. Paul, MN 55114: Free catalog ❖ New books and reprints of poetry, fiction, and nonfiction. 612-641-0077.

Great Chefs Television, P.O. Box 56757, New Orleans, LA 70156: Free information ❖ Great Chef cookbooks. 800-321-1499.

✓ **Great Christian Books,** 229 S. Bridge St., P.O. Box 8000, Elkton, MD 21922: Free catalog ❖ Bibles, commentaries, language tools, cookbooks, home schooling books, bible study software, and bible video games. 800-775-5422.

Green Horizons, 145 Scenic Hill Rd., Kerrville, TX 78028: Free brochure ❖ Books on wildflowers, herbs, grasses, fruits and vegetables, trees, shrubs, and woody vines. 210-257-5141.

✓ **Gryphon House Books,** 10726 Tucker St., Beltsville, MD 20704: Free catalog ❖ Books for parents, children, and teachers. 301-779-6200.

Gulf Publishing Company, Book Division, P.O. Box 2608, Houston, TX 77252: Free information ❖ Camping guides, cookbooks, and books on travel, snorkeling, gardening, business, and other subjects. 713-520-4444.

H & R Magic Books, 3702 Cyril Dr., Humble, TX 77396: Catalog $3 ❖ Old and new magic books and magazines. 713-454-7219.

Half Halt Press, 6416 Burkittsville Rd., Middletown, MD 21769: Free catalog ❖ Books on western adventure, training horses, and general equine subjects. 301-371-9110.

Hamilton Books, P.O. Box 450, Moorpark, CA 93021: Catalog $3 ❖ How-to craft books. 805-529-5900.

Hammond Incorporated, 515 Valley St., Maplewood, NJ 07040: Free information ❖ Maps and prints, travel guides, road atlases, adult and juvenile references, and books on business. 201-763-6000.

Hard-to-Find Needlework Books, 96 Roundwood, Newton, MA 02164: Catalog $1 ❖ Search services for hard-to-find and rare books on needle crafts. 617-969-0942.

Harmonica Music Publishing, P.O. Box 2101, Huntington Beach, CA 92647: Free information ❖ Harmonicas, how-to books, videos, audio cassettes, and instructional tapes on the harmonica. 800-950-7664.

HarperCollins, 10 E. 53rd St., New York, NY 10022: Free catalog ❖ Books for preschool children through young adult, fiction and nonfiction for adults, cookbooks, business titles, religion, and other subjects. 212-207-7000.

Have Book, Will Travel Inc., 124 Deer Run Rd., Wilton, CT 06897: Free information (specify information wanted) ❖ Travel and outdoor recreation books. 203-761-0604.

The Haworth Press Inc., 10 Alice St., Binghamton, NY 13904: Free catalog ❖ Books and journals on psychotherapy and mental health. 800-342-9678.

Hays Electronics, P.O. Box 26848, Prescott Valley, AZ 86312: Free catalog ❖ Metal detectors and books and maps on prospecting, mining, and relic hunting. 800-699-2624.

Hazelden Publishing Group, P.O. Box 176, Center City, MN 55012: Free catalog ❖ Psychology, self-help, chemical dependency, gambling addiction, self-esteem, compulsive eating disorders, and spirituality books. 800-328-0098.

Heimburger House Publishing Company, 7236 W. Madison St., Forest Park, IL 60130: Free information with long SASE ❖ Books on model and prototype railroads, cooking, history, humor, and Walt Disney. 708-366-1973.

Hemmings Bookshelf, P.O. Box 76-S14945, Bennington, VT 05201: Free information ❖ Automotive books.

Herb Products Company, P.O. Box 898, 11012 Magnolia Blvd., North Hollywood, CA 91601: Free price list ❖ Books on herbs and their uses. 818-984-3141.

Herzinger & Company, 2821 NE 65th Ave., Vancouver, WA 98661: Free catalog ❖ Books on antiques, collectibles, and art.

Hey Enterprises, 2100 Hwy. 35, Old Mill Plaza, Sea Girt, NJ 08750: Free catalog ❖ Postcards, rare books, and other collectibles. 908-974-8855.

Higginson Books, 14 Derby Square, Salem, MA 01970: Catalog $3 ❖ Genealogies, how-to guides, and local histories.

High-Grade Publications, P.O. Box 20904, Cheyenne, WY 82003: Catalog $1 ❖ Books and maps on treasure hunting, gold locations, lost mines, ghost towns, gems and minerals, and geology. 307-634-8835.

High-Lonesome Books, P.O. Box 878, Silver City, NM 88062: Free catalog ❖ New, used, rare, and out-of-print books on the outdoors, homesteading, hunting, fishing, and other subjects. 505-388-3763.

High View Publications, P.O. Box 51967, Pacific Grove, CA 93950: Free catalog ❖ Chinese martial arts books and videos. 408-655-2990.

Highsmith Multicultural Bookstore, P.O. Box 800, W5527 Hwy. 106, Fort Atkinson, WI 53538: Free information ❖ Multi-cultural books about Native and Afro-Americans. 800-558-2110.

HighText Publications Inc., P.O. Box 1489, Solana Beach, CA 92075: Free catalog ❖ Books about radios, scanners, antennas, and shortwave listening.

Highwood Bookshop, P.O. Box 1246, Traverse City, MI 49685: Free catalog with two 1st class stamps (specify area of interest) ❖ Books on collecting duck and fish decoy carvings and fishing tackle. Also books on wildlife and fish. 616-271-3898.

Himalayan International Institute of Yoga Science, RR 1, Box 405, Honesdale, PA 18431: Free information ❖ Holistic health, yoga, preventive medicine, meditation, diet and health, and self-development books. 800-822-4547.

Historic Aviation, 1401 Kings Wood Rd., Eagan, MN 55122: Free catalog ❖ History, biography, classic, humor, and aviation books and videos. 800-225-5575.

Hobby House Press Inc., 1 Corporate Dr., Grantsville, MD 21536: Free information ❖ Books on dolls, teddy bears, postcards, costumes, and crafts. 800-554-1447.

Peter M. Holmes Books, 3112 Fremont Ave. South, Minneapolis, MN 55408: Catalog $2 ❖ Rare and out-of-print books. 612-827-0461.

Home Buyer Publications Inc., 4451 Brookfield Corporate Dr., Ste. 101, P.O. Box 220039, Chantilly, VA 22022: Free information ❖ Books on how-to-build log homes. 800-826-3893; 703-222-9411 (in VA).

Home Planners Inc., 3275 W. Ina Rd., Ste. 110, Tucson, AZ 85741: Catalog $2 ❖ Books on home planning, architectural design, landscaping, and remodeling. 800-848-2550.

BOOKS

The Home Shop Machinist Magazine, P.O. Box 1810, Traverse City, MI 49685: Free information ❖ Home shop how-to books on metalworking. 800-447-7367.

Honda Martial Arts Supply, 61 W. 23rd St., New York, NY 10010: Free catalog ❖ Books about martial arts. 212-620-4050.

Horse Prints, 9030 W. Sahara Ave., Ste. 103, Las Vegas, NV 89117: Free catalog ❖ Books for and about horses and for horse lovers. 800-311-6795.

Howell Book House Inc., MacMillan Publishing, 1633 Broadway, New York, NY 10019: Free information ❖ Books about dogs, cats, birds, horses, and other animals. 212-698-7000.

Hudson Hills Press, 230 5th Ave., Ste. 1308, New York, NY 10001: Free information ❖ Books on photography and fine art. 212-889-3090.

Human Kinetics, P.O. Box 5076, Champaign, IL 61825: Free information ❖ Sport and physical fitness books. 800-747-4457.

Humanities Press International Inc., 165 1st Ave., Atlantic Highlands, NJ 07716: Free catalog ❖ Books that focus on radical social and political theory, European history, and the history and philosophy of science. 908-872-1441.

Hunter Publishing Inc., 300 Raritan Center Pkwy., Edison, NJ 08818: Free information ❖ Travel guides, language cassette courses, and maps. 908-225-1900.

ICS Books Inc., P.O. Box 10767, Merrillville, IN 46411: Free list ❖ Books on outdoor lifestyles, narratives, how-to, medical care, humor, and other activities. 800-541-7323.

IDG Books Worldwide Inc., 7260 Shadeland Station, Ste. 100, Indianapolis, IN 46256: Free information ❖ Computer books. 800-762-2974.

Image Club Graphics Inc., U.S. Catalog Fulfillment Center, c/o Publisher's Mail Service, 10545 W. Donges Ct., Milwaukee, WI 53224: Free catalog ❖ How-to books and training materials for hands-on graphics manipulation and computer-designing. 800-387-9193.

Imagiknit Ltd., 2586 Yonge St., Toronto, Ontario, Canada M4P 2J3: Catalog $4.50 ❖ Yarns, how-to books on knitting, and kits. 800-318-9426.

Impact Publishers, P.O. Box 1094, San Luis Obispo, CA 93406: Free catalog ❖ Self-help books. 805-543-5911.

In One Ear Publications, 29481 Manzanita Dr., Campo, CA 91906: Catalog $1 ❖ Books and audio tapes for easy foreign language learning. 619-478-5619.

Independent Publishers Group, 814 N. Franklin St., Chicago, IL 60610: Free catalog ❖ Adult, young adult, and children's books. 312-337-0747.

Innovative & Quaint, P.O. Box 4873, West Hills, CA 91308: Free catalog ❖ Books on nutrition, herbs, and educational products. 818-884-4651.

Intel Corporation, 2200 Mission College Blvd., Santa Clara, CA 95052: Free catalog ❖ Computer books. 408-765-1709.

International Center of Photography, 1133 Avenue of Americas, New York, NY 10036: Free catalog ❖ Photography books. 800-688-8171.

International Fabric Collection, 3445 W. Lake Rd., Erie, PA 16505: Catalog $3 ❖ Quilting and embroidery books and fabrics from Italy, India, Japan, Holland, Africa, and other worldwide sources. 800-462-3891; 814-838-0740 (in PA).

International Marine, Division McGraw Hill, 13311 Montrey Ln., Blue Ridge Summit, PA 17294: Free catalog ❖ Nautical books. 800-822-8158.

International Universities Press Inc., 59 Boston Post Rd., Box 1524, Madison, CT 06443: Free catalog ❖ Books for mental health professionals. 800-835-3487.

Interweave Press, 201 E. 4th St., Loveland, CO 80537: Free catalog ❖ Books on basket-making, weaving and spinning, sweater designing, hand and machine knitting, rug-weaving, tapestry-making, fabric-designing and sewing, and spinning wheels. 800-645-3675.

Iranbooks Inc., 6831 Wisconsin Ave., Bethesda, MD 20814: Catalog $3 ❖ Books about Iran in Persian and English. 301-986-0079.

Janus Books, P.O. Box 40787, Tucson, AZ 85717: Free catalog ❖ Fine and first editions of detective, mystery, and suspense fiction. 520-881-8192.

Jerboa-Redcap Books, P.O. Box 1058, Highstown, NJ 08520: Catalog $2 ❖ British military books. 609-443-3817.

Jessica's Biscuit, The Cookook People, P.O. Box 301, Newtonville, MA 02160: Free catalog ❖ Cookbooks. 800-878-4264.

Johns Hopkins University Press, 2715 N. Charles St., Baltimore, MD 21218: Free catalog ❖ Books on a variety of subjects. 410-516-6936.

Johnson Publishing Company Inc., Book Division, 820 S. Michigan Ave., Chicago, IL 60605: Free information ❖ Books by and about Afro-Americans. 312-322-9248.

Jope's Bonsai Nursery, P.O. Box 594, Wenham, MA 01984: Catalog $2 ❖ Books on bonsai. 508-468-2249.

JTG of Nashville, P.O. Boix 158116, Nashville, TN 37215: Catalog $1.50 ❖ Professional and educational books and music products. Also publications for children. 615-254-2441.

Kaufman Supply, Rt. 1., Centertown, MO 65023: Free catalog ❖ How-to home study courses on sign painting techniques. 314-893-2124.

Kedco Homebrew & Wine Supply, 564 Smith St., Farmingdale, NY 11735: Free brochure ❖ Wine accessories, beer and wine making supplies, books and videos, and wine racks, cellars and cabinets. 516-454-7800.

Keepsake Quilting, Rt. 25B, P.O. Box 1618, Centre Harbor, NH 03226: Free catalog ❖ Quilting books and accessories, patterns, notions, fabrics, scrap bags, and batting. 800-865-9458.

Kennel Vet Corporation, P.O. Box 4092, Farmingdale, NY 11735   Refundable: Catalog $1 (refundable) ❖ Books about dogs, cats, birds, and horses. 800-782-0627.

Paul E. Kisselburg, 665 Wildwood, Stillwater, MN 55082: Free catalog ❖ Military history World War II books. 612-430-9223.

Knollwood Books, P.O. Box 197, Oregon, WI 53575: Free catalog ❖ Rare, hard-to-find, and out-of-print books on astronomy, meteorology, space exploration, rocketry, and related fields. 608-835-8861.

Kodansha America Inc., 114 5th Ave., New York, NY 10011: Free information ❖ Books in English from and about Japan. 800-788-6262.

Krause Publications, 700 E. State St., Iola, WI 54990: Free information ❖ Books on hobbies, records, collectibles, and the outdoors. 800-258-0929.

Krieger Publishing Company, P.O. Box 9542, Melbourne, FL 32902: Free information ❖ Books on reptiles and other exotic pets. 407-724-9542.

Owen D. Kubik Fine Books, 3474 Clar-Von Dr., Dayton, OH 45430: Catalog $3 ❖ Rare and out-of-print books on American, British, French, and European military history. 513-294-0253.

LA Bookstore, P.O. Box 753, Waldorf, MD 20604: Free information ❖ Books on landscaping.

La Rock's Fun & Magic Outlet, 3847 Rosehaven Dr., Charlotte, NC 28205: Catalog $3 ❖ Clown and balloon how-to books, balloons, balloon sculpture kits, juggling supplies, and magic equipment. 704-563-9300.

Lacis, 3163 Adeline St., Berkeley, CA 94703: Catalog $4 ❖ Books on fabrics, costumes, needle crafts, and beading. 510-843-7178.

LadyBug Art Center, 1901 E. Bennett, Springfield, MO 65808: Catalog $2 ❖ Craft painting books. 417-883-4708.

BOOKS

Lancer Militaria, P.O. Box 886, Mt. Ida, AR 71957: Free brochure ❖ Military books. 501-867-2232.

Langenscheidt Publishers, 46-35 54th Rd., Maspeth, NY 11378: Free catalog ❖ Foreign language dictionaries, skills building texts, children's books. language phrase cards, and electronic translators. 718-784-0055.

Lapidary Journal Book & Video Sellers, 60 Chestnut Ave., Ste. 201, Devon, PA 19333: Free information ❖ Lapidary and jewelry-making books. 800-676-4367.

Lark Books, 50 College St., Asheville, NC 28801: Free catalog ❖ Kits, books on arts and crafts, and gifts. 800-284-3388.

Lark in the Morning, P.O. Box 1176, Mendocino, CA 95460: Free catalog ❖ Hard-to-find musical instruments, books about music, CDs and cassettes, and videos. 707-964-5569.

The Las Vegas Insider, P.O. Box 1185, Chino Valley, AZ 86323: Free information ❖ How-to books on Las Vegas casinos. 520-636-1649.

Guy Lautard, 2570 Rosebery Ave., West Vancouver, British Columbia, Canada V7V 2Z9: Free information ❖ How-to books on metal-working and fabrication. 604-922-4909.

Leisure Arts, Attn.: Consumer Service, P.O. Box 5595, Little Rock, AR 72215: Catalog $2 ❖ Cookbooks. 501-868-8800.

Alan Levine Movie & Book Collectibles, P.O. Box 1577, Bloomfield, NJ 07003: Catalog $5 ❖ Books on old-time movie posters, lobby cards, and old radio, television, and movie magazines. 201-743-5288.

Light Impressions, 439 Monroe Ave., P.O. Box 940, Rochester, NY 14607: Free catalog ❖ Books on photography and supplies for archival storage of negatives and prints. 800-828-6216.

Linden Books, Box 352, Interlaken, NY 14847: Free information ❖ How-to books on beekeeping.

Linden Publishing Company Inc., 336 W. Bedford, Ste. 107, Fresno, CA 93711: Catalog $1 ❖ New and out-of-print books and videos on woodworking. 800-345-4447.

Lindsay Publications Inc., P.O. Box 538, Bradley, IL 60915: Catalog $1 ❖ Metal working books. 815-935-5353.

Live Steam Magazine, P.O. Box 629, Traverse City, MI 49685: Free information ❖ Books on machine shop practice and live steam train models. 800-447-7367.

Log Homes Books, 65 Commerce Rd., Stanford, CT 06902: Free information ❖ Books on log home building. 800-439-6154.

Lonely Planet Publications, 155 Filbert St., Ste. 251, Oakland, CA 94607: Free booklist ❖ Guidebooks for worldwide destinations. 800-275-8555.

Los Angeles Audubon Society Bookstore, 7377 Santa Monica Blvd., West Hollywood, CA 90046: Free catalog ❖ Bird and nature books, bookmarks, and bird feeders. 213-876-0202.

Louisiana State University Press, 102 French House, Baton Rouge, LA 70893: Free catalog ❖ Books about the Civil War and scholarly subjects. 504-388-6666.

Lucidity Institute, 2555 Park Blvd., Ste 2, Palo Alto, CA 94306: Free catalog ❖ Yoga books, tapes, and biofeedback devices. 800-GO-LUCID.

Herbert A. Luft, Box 684, West Acton, MA 01720: Free list ❖ Rare and current astronomy books. 508-264-0017.

J.K. Lutherie Guitars, 11115 Sand Run, Harrison, OH 45030: Free catalog ❖ Vintage guitar parts, new and vintage accessories, catalogs and other literature, guitar magazines, and out-of-print guitar books. 800-344-8880; 513-353-3320 (in OH).

MacMillan Computer Publishing, MacMillan Publishing Company, 1633 Broadway, New York, NY 10019: Free catalog ❖ Computer books. 212-698-7000.

MacMillan Publishing Company, 1633 Broadway, New York, NY 10019: Free catalog ❖ Fiction and nonfiction books for children and adults. 212-698-7000.

The Mail Order Catalog, P.O. Box 180, Summertown, TN 38483: Free catalog ❖ Books on vegetarian cooking, other health food cookbooks, nutrition, health care, Native American traditions, animal issues, and odds and ends. 800-695-2241.

Mainly Shades, One Hundred Gray Rd., Falmouth, ME 04105: Catalog $3 ❖ Lampshade crafting supplies and how-to books. 207-797-7568.

Mallery Press, 4206 Sheraton Dr., Flint, MI 48532: Free information ❖ How-to quilt-making books. 800-A-STITCH.

Man at Arms Bookshelf, P.O. Box 460, Lincoln, RI 02865: Free information ❖ Books on antique and other famous guns, Civil War, other major military conflicts, and infantry weapons. 800-999-4697.

Manny's Woodworkers Place, 555 S. Broadway, Lexington, KY 40508: Free information ❖ Woodworking books and videos. 800-243-0713.

The Maritime Store, 2905 Hyde St. Pier, San Francisco, CA 94109: Free catalog ❖ Maritime maps, greeting cards, boat models, children's and maritime books, and gifts. 415-775-BOOK.

Maryland Reptile Farm, 109 W. Cherry Hill Rd., Reisterstown, MD 21136: Free catalog with long SASE ❖ Books on reptiles and related herps supplies. 410-526-4184.

Bill Mason Books, 104 N. 7th St., Morehead City, NC 28557: Free catalog ❖ Rare, new, and used books. Also prints and Civil War, Western Americana, and other military and nautical collectibles. 919-247-6161.

Merriam-Webster Inc., P.O. Box 281, Springfield, MA 01102: Free brochure ❖ Dictionaries and reference books. 800-828-1880.

Meyerbooks Publisher, 235 W. Main St., P.O. Box 427, Glenwood, IL 60425: Free catalog ❖ Books on stage magic history, herbs, health, cooking, and Americana. 708-757-4950.

Microsoft Press, One Microsoft Way, Redmond, WA 98052: Free information ❖ Books on computers. 800-227-4679.

The Military Bookman, 29 E. 93rd St., New York, NY 10128: Free information with long SASE ❖ Military, naval, and aviation out-of-print and rare books. 212-348-1280.

The Mind's Eye, P.O. Box 6547, Chelmsford, MA 01824: Free catalog ❖ Children's favorites and classics, military intrigue, mystery, horror, science fiction, adventure, drama, history, comedy, poetry, and self-improvement. Also audio cassettes and compact disks. 800-949-3333.

Minnesota Clay USA, 8001 Grand Ave. South, Bloomington, MN 55420: Free catalog ❖ Books on ceramic and pottery crafts. 800-252-9872; 612-884-9101 (in MN).

The MIT Press, 55 Hayward St., Cambridge, MA 02142: Free catalog ❖ Books on a variety of subjects. 800-356-0343.

Morningside Bookshop, P.O. Box 1087, Dayton, OH 45401: Catalog $3 ❖ Reprints and original Civil War books and other memorabilia. 800-648-0710.

Mother Earth News, P.O. Box 10941, Des Moines, IA 50340: Free information ❖ Books on homebuilding and making repairs, log homes, gardening and farming, home workshops, solar energy, and other topics. 800-888-9098.

Motorbooks International, 729 Prospect Ave., P.O. Box 1, Osceola, WI 54020: Free catalog ❖ Automotive, motorcycle, aviation, and other books. 800-458-0454.

Mt. Eden Books & Bindery, P.O. Box 1014, Cedar Ridge, CA 95924: Free catalog ❖ Out-of-print and rare geology books. 916-274-BOOK.

Mountain Musicrafts, Jeanalee Schilling Inc., 267 South Hwy. 32, P.O. Box 8, Cosby, TN 37722: Free catalog ❖ Hammered dulcimer playing instructions, building books, and songs. 615-487-5543.

Mountain Press Publishing Company, P.O. Box 2399, Missoula, MT 59806: Free catalog ❖ Geology books, outdoor guides, and history titles. 800-234-5308.

❖ BOOKS ❖

The Mountaineers Books, 300 3rd Ave. West, Seattle, WA 98119: Free information ❖ Books about the outdoors, hiking, bicycling, skiing, mountaineering, nature, and conservation. 800-284-8554.

Murrays Catamarans, P.O. Box 490, Carpinteria, CA 93014: Free list of retail sources ❖ Catamarans, factory parts, books, and videos. 800-788-8964.

Music Dispatch, P.O. Box 13920, Milwaukee, WI 53213: Free catalog ❖ Books, cassettes, CDs, and videos for guitars, percussionists, and other instruments. 800-637-2852.

Mysteries by Mail, Division Soda Creek Press, P.O. Box 8515, Ukiah, CA 95482: Free catalog ❖ Mystery books. 800-722-0726.

Mystic Seaport Museum Stores, 39 Greemanville Ave., Mystic, CT 06355: Free catalog ❖ Books about American maritime history and gifts with a nautical and historical theme. 800-248-1066.

Nancy's Specialty Market, P.O. Box 530, Newmarket, NH 03857: Free catalog ❖ Wild mushroom caviar, exotic Mexican spices, pasta, extracts and flavorings, other international specialties, books, and kitchenware. 800-688-2433.

National Geographic Society, 1145 17th St. NW, Washington, DC 20036: Free catalog ❖ Books on geography, history, archeology, science, and industry. 800-447-0647.

National Rifle Association, Sales Department, P.O. Box 5000, Kearneysville, WV 25430: Free information ❖ Books on guns and shooting.

National Wildlife Federation, P.O. Box 8925, Vienna, VA 22183: Free catalog ❖ Books, holiday cards, and gifts. 800-432-6564.

Nautical Book Catalog, P.O. Box F, Ringoes, NJ 08551: Free catalog ❖ Marine, educational, and technical books. 800-297-7617.

Naval Institute Press, Customer Service, 2062 Generals Hwy., Annapolis, MD 21401: Free catalog ❖ Books on navigation, seamanship, naval history, ships, and aircraft. 800-233-8764.

John Neal, Bookseller, 1833 Spring Garden St., Greensboro, NC 27403: Free information ❖ Calligraphy and marbling supplies, books, and bookbinding services. 800-369-9598.

The Needlework Attic, 4706 Bethesda Ave., Bethesda, MD 20814: Free information ❖ How-to books on knitting and yarns. 301-652-8688.

Nevada Mineral & Book Company, P.O. Box 44230, Las Vegas, NV 89116: Free book list with three 1st class stamps ❖ Books on minerals, gems, and fossils. 702-453-5718.

New England Wildflower Society, Garden in the Woods, 180 Hemenway Rd., Framingham, MA 01701: Free catalog with two 1st class stamps ❖ Books on wildflowers and their propagation. 508-877-7630.

New Harbinger Publications, 5674 Shattuck Ave., Oakland, CA 94609: Free catalog ❖ Self-help books on psychology. 800-748-6273.

New Moon Gardening Books, P.O. Box 1027, Corvallis, OR 97339: Free list ❖ Indoor and outdoor gardening books. 800-888-6785.

The New Orleans School of Cooking and Louisiana General Store, The Jackson Brewery, 620 Decatur St., New Orleans, LA 70130: Free catalog ❖ New Orleans specialties and cookbooks. 800-237-4841.

New Wireless Pioneers, Jim & Felicia Kreuzer, P.O. Box 398, Elma, NY 14059: Free information ❖ Books, magazines, and other literature on antique radios. 716-681-3186.

Nicholson's Trading Post, P.O. Box 291, Burley, WA 98322: Free catalog ❖ Books and maps on prospecting and mining. 206-876-0716.

Nolo Press, 950 Parker St., Berkeley, CA 94710: Free catalog ❖ Self-help law books and computer software. 800-992-6656.

The Noontide Press, P.O. Box 2739, Newport Beach, CA 92659: Free catalog ❖ Books, audiotapes, and videos on the social, political, economic, and historical taboos of the modern age. 714-631-1490.

North Light Books, 1507 Dana Ave., Cincinnati, OH 45207: Free information ❖ Art and graphic design books. 800-289-0963.

North Star Gardens, 19060 Manning Trail North, Marine on St. Croix, MN 55047: Free catalog ❖ Culture and how-to books on berry plants. 612-227-9842.

Northland Publishing, P.O. Box 1389, Flagstaff, AZ 86002: Free catalog ❖ Cookbooks and books on western adventure and lifestyles, general equine subjects, and cowboy poetry. 800-346-3257; 602-774-5251 (in AZ).

Numismatic Arts of Santa Fe, P.O. Box 9712, Santa Fe, NM 87504: Free information ❖ Out-of-print and other numismatic and philatelic books. 505-982-8792.

O'Reilly & Associates, 101 Morris St., Sebastopol, CA 95472: Free information ❖ How-to books on using E-mail and other computer areas. 800-998-9938.

Ohara Publications Inc., P.O. Box 918, Santa Clarita, CA 91380: Free information ❖ Books on martial arts. 805-257-4066.

Old Tech-Books & Things, John V. Terrey, P.O. Box 803, Carlisle, MA 01741: Free information (specify subject areas) ❖ Early technical books and apparatus.

Olde Soldier Books Inc., 18779 N. Frederick Ave., Gaithersburg, MD 20879: Free information ❖ Civil War books, documents, autographs, prints, manuscripts, photographs, and other Americana. 301-963-2929.

Olsson's Books & Records, 1239 Wisconsin Ave. NW, Washington, DC 20007: Free catalog ❖ Compact disks, cassettes, and books on fiction, poetry, history, biography, the classics, philosophy, children's stories, humor, travel, mystery, art, photography, cooking, interior design, antiques, and collecting. 202-338-9544 (books); 202-338-6712 (music).

Online Press Inc., Quick Course Books, 14320 NE 21st St., Bellevue, WA 98007: Free information ❖ Quick-course computer training books. 206-641-3434.

The Opera Box, P.O. Box 994, Teaneck, NJ 07666: Free catalog ❖ Rare books about the opera. 201-833-4176.

Ortho Books, 1160 Research Blvd., St. Louis, MO 63132: Free information ❖ Books about gardening, nature, and home improvement. 800-822-6349.

Outdoor Publications, P.O. Box 355, Ithaca, NY 14851: Free brochure ❖ New York maps, guides, and books. 607-273-0061.

The Overlook Connection, P.O. Box 526, Woodstock, GA 30188: Catalog $1 ❖ Books, audio cassettes, and magazines on horror, science fiction, fantasy, and mystery. 770-926-1762.

Oxfam Publishing, c/o Humanities Press, 1st Ave., Atlantic Highlands, NJ 07716: Free catalog ❖ Books and resource materials to educate and empower the world's poor in their struggle against hunger and exploitation. 908-872-1441.

Oxford Paperbacks, Oxford University Press, 200 Madison Ave., New York, NY 10016: Free information ❖ Historical and contemporary books on the arts and other subjects.

Oxmoor House, P.O. Box 2463, Birmingham, AL 35201: Free catalog ❖ Books for everyone. 205-877-6000.

Pachart Publishing House, 1130 San Lucas Circle, P.O. Box 35549, Tucson, AZ 85704: Free catalog ❖ Astronomy and astrophysics books.

Pacific Motorbooks, 1880 E. Main St., Ventura, CA 93001: Free information ❖ Antique, vintage, and classic motorcycle literature. 805-641-9545.

Paladin Press, P.O. Box 1307, Boulder, CO 80306: Catalog $2 ❖ Books on self defense, how to establish privacy and personal security, history of weapons, locksmithing, military and police science, and martial arts. 303-443-7250.

Panorama Camera, P.O. Box 463, Williston Park, NY 11596: Free list with long SASE ❖ Photocopies of instruction manuals.

Peri Lithon Books, Box 9996, San Diego, CA 92169: Catalog $2 ❖ Out-of-print, rare, and other books about gemstones, minerals, fossils, jewelry, and geology. 619-488-6904.

BOOKS

Pet Bookshop, P.O. Box 507, Oyster Bay, NY 11771: Free catalog ❖ Books on birds, dogs, cats, fish, reptiles, and other pets. 516-922-1169.

A Photographer's Place, P.O. Box 274, Prince St., New York, NY 10012: Free catalog ❖ Books on photography. 212-431-9358.

Pieces of History, P.O. Box 4470, Cave Creek, AZ 85331: Catalog $2 ❖ Military history books. 602-488-1377.

Pig Out Publications, 4245 Walnut St., Kansas City, MO 64111: Free catalog ❖ Books on barbecuing and grilling. 800-877-3119.

Pioneer Press, P.O. Box 684, Union City, TN 38281: Free catalog ❖ Books on the American Frontier, technical books on muzzleloading and black powder arms, cookbooks, and other subjects. 901-885-0374.

The Planetary Society, 65 N. Catalina Ave., Pasadena, CA 91106: Free brochure ❖ Astronomy books, videos, and slide sets. 818-793-1675.

Planetree Health Resource Center, California Pacific Medical Center, 2040 Webster St., San Francisco, CA 94115: Free catalog ❖ Books and tapes on aging, animal health, and various medical conditions. 415-923-3681.

Bud Plant Comic Art, P.O. Box 1886, Grass Valley, CA 95945: Free catalog ❖ Graphic novels, comic strip collections, history of comics and comic creators, limited editions, prints, and other comic book-related material. 916-273-2166.

Popular Topics Publications, 741 N. Countyline St., Fostoria, OH 44830: Free brochure ❖ Books on computer fundamentals, Windows, MS-DOS, and networking. 419-435-6868.

Portrayal Press, P.O. Box 1190, Andover, NJ 07821: Catalog $3 ❖ Hard-to-find books on 20th-century subjects. 201-579-5781.

The Potters Shop, 31 Thorpe Rd., Needham Heights, MA 02194: Free catalog ❖ Books on pottery and ceramics. 617-449-7687.

Practitioners Publishing Company, P.O. Box 966, Fort Worth, TX 76101: Free brochure ❖ Books on financial management and planning. 800-323-8724.

Print Books, 3200 Tower Oaks Blvd., Rockville, MD 20852: Free catalog ❖ Books on graphic design. 800-222-2654.

Pro-Mack South, 940 W. Apache Trail, Apache Junction, AZ 85220: Catalog $3 ❖ How-to books on metal detecting and prospecting. 800-722-6463.

Pruett Publishing Company, 2928 Pearl St., Boulder, CO 80301: Free catalog ❖ Books about the history and people of the American West, outdoor adventures, railroads, cooking, and horticulture. 303-449-4919.

Publications International Ltd., Customer Service, 7373 N. Cicero Ave., Lincolnwood, IL 60646: Free catalog ❖ Cookbooks and books on automobiles, sports, lifestyles, entertainment, consumer information, crafts and hobbies, and health. 708-676-3502.

Purchase for Less, 231 Floresta, Portola Valley, CA 94028: Catalog $2 ❖ Books on quilting, sewing, and fiber arts.

Que Corporation (Books), 201 W. 103rd St., Indianapolis, IN 46290: Free information ❖ Computer books. 317-581-3500.

The Queen's Shilling, 14 Loudoun St. SE, Leesburg, VA 22075: Catalog $3 ❖ Autographs and old and rare books on military history. 703-779-4669.

Quest for Rare Books, 774 Santa Ynez, Stanford, CA 94305: Catalog $3 ❖ Antiquarian, scarce, and out-of-print books on landscape and garden design, history, and other horticulture subjects. 415-324-3119.

R & R Books, 3020 E. Lake Rd., Livonia, NY 14487: Free information ❖ Books on Civil War weapons. 716-346-2577.

Radio Bookstore, P.O. Box 209, Rindge, NH 03461: Free catalog ❖ Books about radios and shortwave listening. 800-457-7373.

Rainbow Gardens Bookshop, 1444 E. Taylor St., Vista, CA 92084: Catalog $2 ❖ Books on gardening, plants, greenhouse propagation, and related subjects. 619-758-4290.

Rainy Day Books, P.O. Box 775, Fitzwilliam, NH 03447: Free list ❖ Books on radio and related technologies. 603-585-3448.

Ranco Deluxe Design Books, 4054 Del Ray Ave., Ste. 202, Marina Del Rey, CA 90292: Free information ❖ Books on western collectibles. 310-822-0788.

Random House, 201 E. 50th St., New York, NY 10022: Free catalog ❖ Calendars, travel guides, books for children and adults, and other publications. 212-751-2600.

Reader's Digest, P.O. Box 107, Pleasantville, NY 10571: Free catalog ❖ Books on gardening, crafts and hobbies, travel, science and nature, cooking, health, history, geography, religion, and archeology. 914-241-7445.

Reel World, 10 Depot Plaza, Scarsdale, NY 10583: Catalog $3 ❖ Rare books. 914-722-4333.

Research Unlimited, P.O. Box 448, Fremont, NE 68025: Free catalog ❖ Books about the Civil War, gems, ghost towns, history, maps and mining, Old West, self-help subjects, treasure how-to's, and other topics. 402-721-8588.

Roberts Rinehart Publishers, 5455 Spine Rd., Mezzanine West, Boulder, CO 80301: Free information ❖ Books about natural history, Native Americans, the west, and Irish history and culture. 800-352-1985.

Robinson's Harp Shop, P.O. Box 161, 33908 Mount Laguna Dr., Mount Laguna, CA 91948: Free catalog ❖ How-to books on harps. 619-473-8556.

The Rock Barrell, 13650 Floyd Rd., Ste. 209, Dallas, TX 75243: Free catalog ❖ How-to books on jewelry making and design. 214-231-4809.

The Norman Rockwell Museum, P.O. Box 308, Stockbridge, MA 01262: Free catalog ❖ Prints, books about Norman Rockwell, and reproductions of artworks by America's favorite illustrator. 800-742-9450.

Rodale Books, Box 8, Emmaus, PA 18099: Free information ❖ Gardening books.

Mark E. Rogers Minerals, P.O. Box 806, Minden, NV 89423: Free information ❖ Rare, used, and new books on minerals.

Ryon's Saddle & Ranch Supplies, 2601 N. Main, Fort Worth, TX 76106: Free catalog ❖ Books on training horses and general equine subjects. 800-725-7966.

Ryukyu Imports Inc., P.O. Box 535, Olathe, KS 66051: Free price list ❖ Books on martial arts. 913-782-3920.

S.A.E. Historical Book Series, 400 Commonwealth Dr., Warrendale, PA 15096: Free brochure ❖ Books on automotive history. 412-772-7118.

Sampler Publications, P.O. Box 228, St. Charles, IL 60174: Free information ❖ How-to books on crafts and home decor. 708-377-8399.

J.M. Santarelli, 226 Paxson Ave., Glenside, PA 19038: Free information with two 1st class stamps ❖ Antique, reprints, and out-of-print Civil War books. 215-576-5358.

Saratoga Soldier Shop & Military Bookstore, 831 Rt. 67, Ste. 40, Ballston Spa, NY 12020: Catalog $6 ❖ Civil War miniatures and books. 518-885-1497.

Susan Scheewe Publications Inc., 13435 NE Whittaker Way, Portland, OR 97230: Catalog $2 ❖ Instructional painting books. 503-254-9100.

The Scholar's Bookshelf, 110 Melrich Rd., Cranbury, NJ 08512: Free catalog ❖ Old and new World War II books. 800-817-9993.

Schoolhouse Press, 6899 Cary Bluff, Pittsville, WI 54466: Catalog $3 ❖ Lace knitting books, wool samples, how-to videos, kits, and knitting tools. 715-884-2799.

Scott Publications, 30595 Eight Mile, Livonia, MI 48152: Free catalog ❖ Books for the ceramist, china painter, and doll-maker. 800-477-6650; 810-477-6650 (in MI).

Self-Help Warehouse, P.O. Box 683, Ashland, OR 97520: Free catalog ❖ Self-help books, tapes, and other products. 818-587-6013.

BOOKS

Sentimental Times Inc., 234 5th Ave., New York, NY 10001: Free brochure ❖ Books about rare and vintage postcards. 800-845-1451.

Sharon & Gayle Publications, P.O. Box 15394, Covington, KY 41015: Catalog $2 (refundable) ❖ How-to books on decorative art and tole painting. Also pattern packets.

Jackie Shaw Studio Inc., The Old Stone Mill, 13306 Edgemont Rd., Smithsburg, MD 21783: Catalog $1 ❖ Craft books. 301-824-7592.

Ship to Shore Inc., 10500 Mount Holly Rd., Charlotte, NC 28214: Free brochure ❖ Cookbooks that contain Caribbean-style recipes. 704-392-4740.

Shootin' Accessories Ltd., P.O. Box 6810, Auburn, CA 95604: Free information ❖ Books on target shooting, shotshell reloading, shotguns, shotgun ballistics, trapshooting, sporting clays, skeet shooting, and hunting. 916-889-9106.

Show-Biz Services, 1735 E. 26th St., Brooklyn, NY 11229: Free list ❖ Books for magicians. 718-336-0605.

Shutterbug Store, 5211 S. Washington Ave., Titusville, FL 32780: Free information ❖ Books on photography. 800-677-5212.

Sierra Books, P.O. Box 2504, Martinez, CA 94553: Free catalog ❖ Out-of-print mining books. 510-228-1849.

Sierra Club Books, 100 Bush St., 13th Floor, San Francisco, CA 94104: Free catalog ❖ Books about ecology, natural history, environment, wildlife, outdoor activities, and nature photography. 415-291-1600.

Silvercat Publications, 4070 Goldfinch St., Ste. C, San Diego, CA 92103: Free brochure ❖ Non-fiction and quality of life books. 619-299-6774.

Skipjack Press Inc., 637 Drexel Ave., Drexel Hill, PA 19026: Free information ❖ Books on blacksmithing. 610-284-7693.

Sky Publishing Corporation, P.O. Box 9111, Belmont, MA 02178: Free information ❖ Astronomy books, posters, and videos. 800-253-0245.

Small Press Distribution Inc., 1814 San Pablo Ave., Berkeley, CA 94702: Free catalog ❖ Poetry, fiction, and critical-cultural studies. 510-549-3336.

Samuel Patrick Smith, P.O. Box 769, Tavares, FL 32778: Free information ❖ How-to books on theatrical marketing, writing letters, entertaining children, performing better on the stage, advertising, and other topics. 904-343-3274.

Smith, Gibbs Publisher, P.O. Box 667, Layton, UT 84041: Free catalog ❖ Cookbooks and books on western adventure and lifestyles, human interest, western humor, cowboy poetry, and western and equine art. 800-421-8714; 801-544-9800 (in UT).

Sokolow Music, P.O. Box 491264, Los Angeles, CA 90049: Free catalog ❖ Blues guitar books and tapes and other books and cassettes. 310-838-4215.

Specialty Books Company, P.O. Box 616, Croton-on-Hudson, NY 10520: Catalog $1 ❖ Books on wine, wine regions, wine and travel, wine and food, and other wine-related subjects. 800-274-4816.

Spoken Arts, 801 94th Ave. North, St. Petersburg, FL 33702: Free catalog ❖ Literature-based audiovisual products for libraries, schools, or use at home. 800-326-4090.

Sporting Clays Books & Videos, 5211 S. Washington Ave., Titusville, FL 32780: Free information ❖ Sporting clays books and videos. 407-268-5010.

Sporty's Pilot Shop, Clermont Airport, Batavia, OH 45103: Free catalog ❖ Aircraft pilot training books. 800-543-8633.

Springer-Verlag New York, 175 5th Ave., New York, NY 10010: Free information ❖ Books on medicine and science. 212-460-1500.

Springhouse Direct, P.O. Box 10613, Des Moines, IA 50336: Free catalog ❖ Books on nursing and health. 800-666-5597.

Stackpole Books, 5067 Ritter Rd., Mechanicsburg, PA 17055: Free catalog ❖ Outdoor and adventure books. 800-732-3669.

Stage Step, P.O. Box 328, Philadelphia, PA 19105: Free catalog ❖ Dance, theater, film, music, and fitness books, videos, and CDs. 800-523-0960.

Stampede Investments, 1533 River Rd., Wisconsin Dells, WI 53965: Free catalog ❖ Fine books, autographs, and other historical artifacts. 608-254-7751.

State House Press, P.O. Box 15247, Austin, TX 78761: Free information ❖ Books on the Civil War. 800-421-3378.

STB Books Inc., P.O. Box 7020, Brick, NJ 08723: Free information ❖ Books about log homes. 800-477-4114.

Sterling Publishing Company Inc., 387 Park Ave. South, New York, NY 10016: Free catalog ❖ Books on body building, hobbies, crafts, occult, herbs and gardening, science, cooking, health, sports, music, theater, and self-defense. Also books for children. 212-532-7160.

The Stonebrier, 7900 E. Princess Ave., Scottsdale, AZ 85255: Price list $3 ❖ Designer yarns and accessories. 602-502-0800.

Storey's How-To Books for Country Living, Schoolhouse Rd., Pownal, VT 05261: Free information ❖ How-to books on crafts, gardening, animals, woodworking and building, cooking, nature, beer and wine, and the outdoors. 800-441-5700.

Straw into Gold, 3006 San Pablo Ave., Berkeley, CA 94702: Catalog $2 with long SASE and two 1st class stamps ❖ Ready-to-spin alpaca and books for spinners, weavers, and knitters. 510-548-5243.

Studio Limestone, 253 College St., Box 316, Toronto, Ontario, Canada M5T 1R5: Price list $2 ❖ Yarns, kits, and how-to knitting books. 416-864-0984.

Sylvan Publications, P.O. Box 1315, Hamilton, MT 59840: Free information ❖ Books on archery. 406-363-7688.

Tab Books Inc., Division McGraw Hill, 13311 Montrey Ln., Blue Ridge Summit, PA 17294: Free catalog ❖ How-to books on electronics, computers, aviation, science, hobbies, automobiles, crafts, and other subjects. 800-233-1128.

The Taunton Press, 63 S. Main St., P.O. Box 5506, Newtown, CT 06470: Free information ❖ Books, videos, and magazines on sewing, fabrics and patterns, gardening, woodworking, and other crafts. 800-888-8286.

Taxidermy Today Magazine, 119 Gadsden St., Chester, SC 29706: Free information ❖ Taxidermy books. 800-851-7955.

Technical Analysis Inc., 4757 California Ave. SW, Seattle, WA 98116: Free information ❖ How to understand books on stocks and commodities. 800-832-4642.

The Textile Museum Shop, 2320 S St. NW, Washington, DC 20008: Free catalog ❖ Books on rugs, textiles, and related craft techniques. 202-667-0441.

That Patchwork Place, P.O. Box 118, Bothell, WA 98041: Free information ❖ Quilting books. 800-426-3126.

Timber Press, 133 SW 2nd Ave., Ste. 450, Portland, OR 97204: Free catalog ❖ Books for gardeners, horticulturists, and botanists. 800-327-5680.

Timeless Books, P.O. Box 3543, Spokane, WA 99220: Free catalog ❖ Books, audiotapes, and videos on yoga, Buddhism, and Eastern philosophy. 509-838-6652.

TKD Enterprises Inc., 1423 18th St., Bettendorf, IA 52722: Free information ❖ Martial arts books and videos. 800-388-5966.

The Tool Chest, 45 Emerson Plaza East, Emerson, NJ 07630: Catalog $2 (refundable) ❖ Books for the home craftsman. 201-261-8665.

Tools for Exploration, 47 Paul Dr., San Rafael, CA 94903: Free catalog ❖ Self-improvement books, tapes, machines, and other products. 415-499-9050.

Top of the World Books, 20 Westview Circle, Williston, VT 05495: Free catalog ❖ New and used books on mountaineering. 802-878-8737.

❖ BOOKS ❖

TOPAZ-Mineral Exploration, 1605 Hillcrest, Grand Haven, MI 49417: Catalog $1 ❖ Pseudomorphs, rare and unusual specimens, and books on minerals. 616-842-3506.

James Townsend & Son Inc., 133 N. 1st St., P.O. Box 415, Pierceton, IN 46562: Catalog $2 ❖ Costuming, textile, cooking, music, and other books. 800-338-1665.

Trafalgar Square Publishing, P.O. Box 257, North Pomfret, VT 05053: Free catalog ❖ Books on gardening, crafts, and equestrian how-to. 800-423-4525.

Travel Keys Books, Order Desk, P.O. Box 160691, Sacramento, CA 95816: Free information ❖ Travel guides. 916-452-5200.

Travelers Bookstore, 22 W. 52nd St., New York, NY 10019: Catalog $2 ❖ Maps and books on travel, adventure, student opportunities, trekking, hiking, biking, kayaking, and mountaineering. 800-755-8728; 212-664-0995 (in NY).

Turtle Press, P.O. Box 290206, Wethersfield, CT 06129: Free catalog ❖ Books on martial arts. 800-778-8785.

U.S. Chess Federation, 186 Rt. 9W, Newburgh, NY 12550: Free catalog ❖ How-to books on chess. 800-388-KING.

U.S. Government Printing Office, Free Business Catalog, Stop SM, Washington, DC 20401: Free catalog ❖ Best-selling Federal government publications.

Unicorn Books & Crafts Inc., 1338 Ross St., Petaluma, CA 94954: Catalog $3 ❖ Books on basketry, color, costumes, dolls, dyeing, embroidery, fabric decoration, historic and ethnic textiles, jewelry, knitting and crochet, lace, machine knitting, paper-crafting, rug hooking, sewing, weaving, and spinning. 800-289-9276; 707-762-3362 (in CA).

Uniquity, P.O. Box 10, Galt, CA 95632: Free catalog ❖ Books on mental health, aggression release, child abuse, play therapy, sexuality, and other subjects. 209-745-2111.

United Ostomy Association, 36 Executive Park, Ste. 120, Irvine, CA 92714: Free information ❖ Books that dispel anxiety and encourage positive approaches to healing and coping with ostomies. 800-826-0826; 714-660-8624 (in CA).

United States Holocaust Memorial Museum Shop, P.O. Box 92420, Washington, DC 20090: Free catalog ❖ Books, memoirs, and Holocaust studies for adults and younger readers. 800-259-9998.

United Synagogue Book Service, 155 5th Ave., New York, NY 10010: Free information ❖ Books on Judaism. 212-533-7800.

Vacations with Children, P.O. Box 67, Suffern, NY 10901: Free catalog ❖ How to keep children occupied books and other travel-related publications. 800-606-4892; 914-352-4476 (in NY).

VCH Publishers Inc., 333 7th Ave., New York, NY 10001: Free catalog ❖ Science books. 800-367-8249.

Vestal Press Ltd., P.O. Box 97, Vestal, NY 13851: Catalog $2 ❖ Posters, recordings, and books on carousels, music boxes, player pianos and other music machines, antique radios and phonographs, early movie stars, and radio personalities. 607-797-4872.

Viking Folk Art Publications Inc., 301 16th Ave. SE, Waseca, MN 56093: Free information ❖ Decorative painting books. 507-835-8009.

Vintage '45 Press, P.O. Box 266, Orinda, CA 94563: Free brochure ❖ Books about older women and mid-life problems. 510-254-7266.

Wagon Wheel Records & Books, 17191 Cornina Ln., #203, Huntington Beach, CA 92649: Free catalog ❖ Square dancing records and books. 714-846-8169.

Warner-Crivellaro, 1855 Weaversville Rd., Allentown, PA 18103: Free information ❖ How-to books on stained glass crafting and supplies. 800-523-4242; 610-264-1100 (in PA).

T.E. Warth Esq., Automotive Books, 15 Lumberyard Shops, Marine on St. Croix, MN 55047: Free information ❖ Rare and out-of-print automotive books. 612-433-5744.

Watson-Guptill Publications, 1515 Broadway, New York, NY 10036: Free information ❖ How-to books on decorative painting, silk painting, and marbling techniques. 800-ART-TIPS.

Gary Wayner Books, 1002 Glenn Blvd. SW, Fort Payne, AL 35967: Free catalog ❖ Natural history books. 205-845-7828.

The Weaver's Place, 75 Mellor Ave., Baltimore, MD 21228: Free information ❖ Japanese braiding equipment and books. 410-788-7262.

Web-sters Handspinners, Weavers & Knitters, 11 N. Main St., Ashland, OR 97520: Free catalog ❖ Designer yarns, books, and tools. 800-482-9801.

Barbara Weindling, 69 Ball Pond Rd., Danbury, CT 06811: Catalog $2 ❖ Out-of-print cookbooks.

Wennawoods Publishing, RR 2, Box 529C, Lewisburg, PA 17837: Free catalog: Reprints of books and maps on 17th and 18th-century Eastern Frontier Indian history. 717-524-4820.

Western Horseman Books, P.O. Box 7980, Colorado Springs, CO 80933: Free information ❖ Books on horsemanship and training, barrel racing, team and calf roping, reining, cutting, health problems, and horse breaking and shoeing. 800-874-6774.

Western Publishing Company Inc., 850 3rd Ave., New York, NY 10022: Free catalog ❖ Golden Field Guides on birds, reptiles, rocks and minerals, seashells, astronomy, trees, insects, fishes, fossils, and weather.

Ivan Whillock Studio, 122 NE 1st Ave., Faribault, MN 55021: Free catalog ❖ Woodcarving tools, supplies, how-to books, and kits. 800-882-9379.

Whitehorse Press, P.O. Box 60, North Conway, NH 03860: Free information ❖ Books and videos on motorcycle touring, maintenance, history, performance, restoration, and riding techniques. 800-531-1133.

The Whole Mirth Catalog, 1034 Page St., San Francisco, CA 94117: Free brochure ❖ Humor and joke books. 415-431-1913.

Whole Person Associates, 210 W. Michigan, Duluth, MN 55802: Free catalog ❖ Self-improvement books and videos on wellness promotion, stress management, and relaxation. 800-247-6789.

The Whole Work Catalog, P.O. Box 339, Boulder, CO 80306: Free catalog ❖ Books on alternative careers, new work options, home business opportunities, self-employment, and job hunting. 303-447-1087.

Wicwas Press, P.O. Box 817, Cheshire, CT 06410: Free information ❖ Beekeeping books. 303-250-7575.

Wiegand & Company, Box 563, Glastonbury, CT 06033: Free catalog ❖ Out-of-print books on maritime subjects.

Wilderness Press, 2440 Bancroft Way, Berkeley, CA 94704: Free catalog ❖ Over 100 hiking guides to the West and beyond. Also how-to, nature, and literature. 800-443-7227.

Wilhite Collectible Bookstore, 425 Cleveland St., Clearwater, FL 34615: Free newsletter ❖ Rare books and current publications. Also a search service. 813-447-5722.

Willmann-Bell Inc., P.O. Box 35025, Richmond, VA 23235: Catalog $1 ❖ Astronomy books. 804-320-7016.

Windmill Publishing Company, 2147 Windmill View Rd., El Cajon, CA 92020: Free information ❖ Books on antiques, Victorian items, and other collectibles.

Windsurfing Express, 6043 NW 167th St., Miami, FL 33015: Free brochure ❖ Books and videos on windsurfing. 800-843-7873.

BOOKS

Wine Appreciation Guild, 155 Connecticut St., San Francisco, CA 94107: Free information ❖ Wine cellars, racks, accessories, and books. 800-231-9463.

Wine Art, 5890 N. Keystone Ave., Indianapolis, IN 46220: Free catalog ❖ How-to books on wine, beer, and liqueur-making at home. 800-255-5090; 317-546-9940 (in IN).

Wolfe Publishing Company, 6471 Airpark Dr., Prescott, AZ 86301: Free catalog ❖ Sporting books. 800-899-7810.

Woodbine House, 6510 Bells Mill Rd., Bethesda, MD 20817: Free catalog ❖ Consumer reference books and The Special Needs Collection on disabilities for parents, educators, and medical professionals. 800-843-7323; 301-897-3570 (in MD).

Wooden Porch Books, Rt. 1, Box 262, Middlebourne, WV 26149: Catalog $2 ❖ Books on fiber arts and related subjects. 304-386-4434.

WoodenBoat Books, Naskeag Rd., P.O. Box 78, Brooklin, ME 04616: Free information ❖ Calendars, posters, prints, and books about wooden boats. 800-225-5205; 207-359-4647 (in ME).

Woodland Books, 1044 NE Sunrise Ln., Hillsboro, OR 97124: Free catalog ❖ Logging, lumber, and related books. 503-648-6530.

Sylvia Woods Harp Center, P.O. Box 816, Montrose, CA 91021: Free catalog ❖ Harps, recordings, books, harp-theme jewelry, and gifts. 818-956-1363.

Woodworkers' Discount Books & Videos, 1649 Turn Point Rd., Friday Harbor, WA 98250: Free catalog ❖ How-to books and videos on woodworking. 800-378-4060.

The Woolery, RD 1, Genoa, NY 13071: Catalog $2 ❖ Books on spinning, weaving, knitting, and dyeing. 315-497-1542.

Workman Publishing Company Inc., 708 Broadway, New York, NY 10003: Free catalog ❖ Cooking, food and wine, travel, homes and gardens, space, humor, exercise and health, pregnancy and babies, sports and television, games, hobbies and handicrafts, computers, and children's books. 800-722-7202; 212-254-5900 (in NY).

Write Stuff Syndicate Inc., 1515 SE 4th Ave., Fort Lauderdale, FL 33316: Free brochure ❖ Hardbound coffee table books and classic boat calendars. 954-462-6657.

Writer's Digest Books, 1507 Dana Ave., Cincinnati, OH 45207: Free catalog ❖ Self-help and how-to books for writers, fine and graphic artists, songwriters, musicians, photographers, homemakers, and children. 800-289-0963.

Yarn Barn, 918 Massachusetts, Box 334, Lawrence, KS 66044: Free catalog ❖ Fiber books and yarns. 800-468-0035.

YMAA Publication Center, 38 Hyde Park Ave., Jamaica Plain, MA 02130: Free catalog ❖ Martial arts books, videos, clothing, and music. 800-669-8892.

Yoga Journal's Book & Tape Source, 2054 University Ave., Berkeley, CA 94704: Free information ❖ Books and audio and video tapes on yoga. 800-359-YOGA.

Zed Books, c/o Humanities Press, 1st Ave., Atlantic Highlands, NJ 07716: Free catalog ❖ Books on Third World sustainable development, environmental issues, self-empowerment, gender, and cultural studies. 908-872-1441.

Zenith Books, 1000 Milwaukee Ave., Glenview, IL 60025: Free catalog ❖ Books about ragwings, supersonic spy planes, and other aircraft. Also calendars and video tapes on military aircraft, plastic and radio control modeling, warplanes, and aviation history. 708-391-7000.

Zephyr Press, P.O. Box 66006, 3316 N. Chapel Ave., Tucson, AZ 85728: Free catalog ❖ Innovative teaching methods for all ways of learning. 520-322-5090.

Zon International Publishing Company, P.O. Box 6459, Santa Fe, NM 87502: Catalog $2.50 ❖ Guides and books about carousels, cowboy antiques, and other collectibles. 800-266-5767.

Large-Print & Braille Books

American Printing House for the Blind, 1839 Frankfort Ave., P.O. Box 6085, Louisville, KY 40206: Free catalog ❖ Accessible large-print and braille books for people who are visually impaired. 800-223-1839; 502-895-2405 (in KY).

The William A. Thomas Braille Bookstore, Division Braille International Inc., 3290 SE Slater St., Stuart, FL 34997: Free catalog ❖ Books in braille and large-print. 800-336-3142.

Thorndike Press, P.O. Box 159, Thorndike, ME 04986: Free catalog ❖ Large-print books. 800-223-6121.

Religious Books & Software

American Bible Sales, 870 S. Anaheim Blvd., Anaheim, CA 92805: Free information ❖ King James, New International, and New American Standard Bible software for the Macintosh. 800-535-5131.

Augsburg Fortress Publishers, 426 S. 5th St., Box 1209, Minneapolis, MN 55440: Free catalog ❖ Books, curriculum materials, music, gifts, audiovisuals, and ecclesiastical arts items. 800-328-4648; 612-330-3300 (in MN).

Baker Book House, P.O. Box 6287, Grand Rapids, MI 49546: Free catalog ❖ Religious books for the home, church, and school. 616-676-9185.

Behrman House Publishers Inc., 235 Watchung Ave., West Orange, NJ 07052: Free information ❖ Books on Jewish subjects for children and adults. 800-221-2755.

Bible Research Systems, 2013 Wells Branch Pkwy., Ste. 304, Austin, TX 78728: Free brochure ❖ Bible education software for PCs and Macintosh computers. 800-423-1228.

BibleSoft, 22014 7th Ave. South, Seattle, WA 98198: Free information ❖ Windows and DOS-based bible-study software. 800-995-9058.

Christian Book Distributors, P.O. Box 7000, Peabody, MA 01961: Free catalog ❖ Books, bibles, videos, computer software, music items for children and adults, and artwork. 508-977-5000.

Cokesbury, Division United Methodist Publishing House, 201 8th Ave. South, P.O. Box 801, Nashville, TN 37202: Free information ❖ Bibles and bible reference books, bible study and Christian education books, fund-raising programs, gifts and casual clothing, choir apparel, church and clergy supplies, and church furniture and equipment. 800-672-1789.

Dharma Publishing, 2910 San Pablo Ave., Berkeley, CA 94702: Free information ❖ Books and art reproductions on Tibet meditation. 800-873-4276.

Eborn Books, P.O. Box 2093, Peoria, AZ 85380: Free catalog ❖ Rare and out-of-print Mormon books. 602-979-0707.

God's World Books, P.O. Box 2330, Asheville, NC 28802: Free catalog ❖ Selected books from Christian and secular publishers. 800-951-2665.

Gospel Advocate Bookstores, Order Department, 1006 Elm Hill Pike, Nashville, TN 37210: Free catalog ❖ Bibles and Christian books and magazines. 800-251-8446.

Great Christian Books, 229 S. Bridge St., P.O. Box 8000, Elkton, MD 21922: Free catalog ❖ Bibles, commentaries, language tools, cookbooks, home schooling books, bible study software, and bible video games. 800-775-5422.

Immaculata Bookstore, P.O. Box 159, St. Mary's, KS 66536: Catalog $4 ❖ Educational books, and music tapes, compact disks, full score music books of great composers, and other Catholic books and publications. 913-437-2409.

Jewish Publication Society, 1930 Chestnut St., Philadelphia, PA 19103: Free information ❖ Books about Judaica. 800-234-3151.

Lion Publishing, 20 Lincoln Ave., Elgin, IL 60120: Free information ❖ Christian books for children and adults. 800-447-5466.

The Liturgical Press, St. John's Abbey, Box 7500, Collegville, MN 56321: Free information ❖ Catholic and general Christian books on scripture, theology, and liturgy. 800-858-5450.

Melton Book Company, P.O. Box 140990, Nashville, TN 37214: Free catalog ❖ Christian books, bibles, audio and video recordings, and music. 800-441-0511.

The Neumann Press, Rt. 2, Box 30, Long Prairie, MN 56347: Free catalog ❖ Catholic reading for children young people, and adults. 612-732-6358.

1-800-Judaism, America's Jewish Bookstore, 2028 Murray Ave., Pittsburgh, PA 15217: Free catalog ❖ Current and classic Jewish books for adults and children. 1-JUDAISM.

Orbis Books, Box 302, Maryknoll, NY 10545: Free catalog ❖ Religious books. 914-941-7636.

Precept Ministries, P.O. Box 182218, Chattanooga, TN 37422: Free catalog ❖ Religious books, audio cassettes, and videos. 615-894-3277.

Riverside-World, P.O. Box 370, Iowa Falls, IA 50126: Free catalog ❖ Adult and children's religious books, bibles, and other audio products. 800-247-5111.

Torah Educational Software, Developers of ArtScroll's Multimedia Educational, 750 Chestnut Ridge Rd., Spring Valley, NY 10977: Free information ❖ Judaic educational software on CD-ROMs for PCs and Macintosh computers. 914-356-1485.

Zondervan DirectSource, P.O. Box 668, Holmes, PA 19043: Free information ❖ Bibles and religious books. 800-876-7335.

Used Books

Adventures in Crime & Space Books, 609-A W. 6th St., Austin, TX 78701: Free information ❖ New, used, and rare science fiction, mystery, and horror books. 512-473-2665.

Benedikt & Salmon Record Rarities, 3020 Meade Ave., San Diego, CA 92116: Free catalogs: indicate choice of (1) rare books and autographs, (2) classical, (3) jazz, big bands, and blues, and (4) personalities, soundtracks, and country music ❖ Autographed memorabilia and rare books on music and the performing arts, antique phonographs and cylinders, and rare recordings from the 1890s to date. 619-281-3345.

Michael Dennis Cohan Bookseller, 502 W. Alder St., Missoula, MT 59802: Free catalog ❖ Out-of-print and rare books on geology, mining, and related subjects. 406-721-7379.

David E. Doremus Books, 100 Hillside Ave., Arlington, MA 02174: Catalog subscription $2 ❖ Used and rare Civil War books. 617-646-0892.

Editions, Boiceville, NY 12412: Catalog $2 ❖ Used, old, and rare books. 914-657-7000.

John W. Knott, Bookseller, 8453 Early Bud Way, Laurel, MD 20723: Free information ❖ First edition science fiction, fantasy, and horror books. 301-317-8427.

Herbert A. Luft, Box 684, West Acton, MA 01720: Free list ❖ Rare and current astronomy books. 508-264-0017.

Robert A. Madle, 4406 Bestor Dr., Rockville, MD 20853: Catalog $3 ❖ Science fiction and fantasy magazines and books, from 1900 to present. 301-460-4712.

McGowan Book Company, P.O. Box 16325, Chapel Hill, NC 27516: Catalog $3 ❖ Rare and out-of-print Civil War books. 919-968-1121.

David Meyer Magic Books, P.O. Box 427, Glenwood, IL 60425: Catalog $2 ❖ New and old books on magic. 708-757-4950.

Old Hickory Bookshop Ltd., 20225 New Hampshire Ave., Brinklow, MD 20862: Free catalog ❖ Used medical books. 301-924-2225.

Bud Plant Illustrated Books, P.O. Box 1886, Grass Valley, CA 95945: Free catalog ❖ Rare and out-of-print children's books, art monographs, and history of book illustrating. Also books about comics, comic strips, and their creators. 916-273-2166.

Wallace D. Pratt, Bookseller, 1801 Gough St., Ste. 304, San Francisco, CA 94109: Free catalog ❖ Out-of-print and rare books about the Civil War, Indian Wars, American Revolution, World War I and II, and miscellaneous military history. 415-673-0178.

Red Lancer, P.O. Box 8056, Mesa, AZ 85214: Catalog $6 ❖ Rare books, Victorian-era campaign medals and helmets, toy soldiers, and original 19th-century military art. 602-964-9667.

Unicorn Books & Crafts Inc., 1338 Ross St., Petaluma, CA 94954: Catalog $3 ❖ Books on basketry, color, costumes, dolls, dyeing, fabric decoration, historic and ethnic textiles, jewelry, knitting and crochet, lace, machine knitting, paper-crafting, rug hooking, sewing, weaving, and spinning. 800-289-9276; 707-762-3362 (in CA).

BOOKS ON TAPE

Audio-Depot, 7916 NW 23rd., Ste. 114, Bethany, OK 73008: Free catalog ❖ Abridged and unabridged books on cassettes. 800-745-4830.

Audio Diversions, 6639 Madison-McLean Dr., McLean, VA 22101: Catalog $2 ❖ Best selling books on tape. 800-628-6145.

Audio Editions, Books on Cassette, P.O. Box 6930, Auburn, CA 95604: Free catalog ❖ Best sellers and all-time favorites, books for young people, classics, drama and poetry, languages, books on cassettes, and personal growth, business, and management titles. 800-231-4261.

Blackstone Audio Books, P.O. Box 969, Ashland, OR 97520: Free catalog ❖ Unabridged books on audio cassettes. 800-729-2665.

Bookcassette Sales, 1704 Eaton Dr., P.O. Box 481, Grand Haven, MI 49417: Free catalog ❖ Best selling titles in unabridged and abridged format for adults and children. 800-222-3225.

Books on Tape Inc., P.O. Box 7900, Newport Beach, CA 92658: Free catalog ❖ Books recorded on cassettes. 800-626-3333.

Listening Library Inc., One Park Ave., Old Greenwich, CT 06970: Free catalog ❖ Literature-based listening books (cassettes) for adults and children. 203-637-3616.

Recorded Books Inc., 270 Skipjack Rd., Prince Frederick, MD 20678: Free catalog ❖ Unabridged books on cassettes. 800-638-1304.

Frank Schaffer, P.O. Box 2179, Basalt, CO 81621: Free information ❖ Children's books on tape. 800-937-7771.

Sounds True Audio, 735 Walnut St., Boulder, CO 80302: Free catalog ❖ Audios and videos on personal discovery, relationships, sacred music of the world, homeopathy, psychology and the spirit, health and healing, and other life-related recordings. 800-333-9185.

Trenna Productions, P.O. Box 2179, Basalt, CO 81621: Free information ❖ Children's books on tape. 800-937-7771.

BOOMERANGS

Boomerang Man, 1806 N. 3rd St., Monroe, LA 71201: Free catalog ❖ Quality returning boomerangs. The leading boomerang source since 1975. Fast, personal service. 318-325-8157.

Colonel Gerrish Boomerangs, 4885 SW 78th Ave., Portland, OR 97225: Free information ❖ Boomerangs. 503-292-5697.

Colorad Boomerangs, 407 W. Tomichi Ave., Gunnison, CO 81230: Free catalog ❖ Boomerangs. 970-641-2344.

Into the Wind/Kites, 1408 Pearl St., Boulder, CO 80302: Free catalog ❖ Boomerangs and kites. 800-541-0314.

What's Up Kites, 4500 Chagrin River Rd., Chagrin Falls, OH 44022: Free list of retail sources ❖ Boomerangs, kites, air toys, and books. 216-247-4222.

BOWLING

Clothing

Converse Inc., 1 Fordham Rd., North Reading, MA 01864: Free information ❖ Shoes. 800-428-2667; 508-664-1100 (in MA).

Eastern Bowling/Hy-Line Inc., 4717 Stenton Ave., Philadelphia, PA 19144: Free information ❖ Shoes. 800-523-0140; 215-438-9000 (in PA).

King Louie International, 13500 15th St., Grandview, MO 64030: Free information ❖ Jackets, shirts, and blouses. 800-521-5212; 816-765-5212 (in MO).

National Sporting Goods Corporation, 25 Brighton Ave., Passaic, NJ 07055: Free information ❖ Shoes. 201-779-2323.

Nike Footwear Inc., One Bowerman Dr., Beaverton, OR 97005: Free list of retail sources ❖ Shoes, shirts, blouses, and bowling ball bags. 800-344-6453.

Saucony/Hyde, 13 Centennial Dr., Peabody, MA 01961: Free list of retail sources ❖ Shoes. 800-365-7282.

Shaffer Sportswear, 224 N. Washington, Neosho, MO 64850: Free information ❖ Jackets and shirts. 417-451-9444.

Universal Bowling, Golf & Billiard Supplies, 619 S. Wabash Ave., Chicago, IL 60605: Free catalog ❖ Shirts, one and two-ball bags, and women's shoes. 800-523-3037.

Wa-Mac Inc., Highskore Products, P.O. Box 128, Carlstadt, NJ 07410: Free information ❖ Shoes, gloves, bowling ball and shoe bags, grips, novelties, and towels. 800-447-5673; 201-438-7200 (in NJ).

Windjammer, 525 N. Main St., Bangor, PA 18013: Free information ❖ Jackets, shirts, T-shirts, sweat suits, and other sportswear. 800-441-6958.

Wolverine Boots & Shoes, 9341 Courtland Dr., Rockford, MI 49351: Free list of retail sources ❖ Shoes. 800-543-2668.

Equipment

Ajay Leisure Products Inc., 1501 E. Wisconsin St., Delavan, WI 53115: Free list of retail sources ❖ Bowling ball bags, grips, novelties, and towels. 800-558-3276; 414-728-5521 (in WI).

Bowling's Bookstore, Tech-Ed Publishing Company, P.O. Box 4, Deerfield, IL 60015: Free information ❖ Books and videos on bowling. 800-521-BOWL.

Ebonite International Inc., 1813 W. 7th St., Box 746, Hopkinsville, KY 42240: Free information ❖ Bags, balls, and wrist supports. 800-626-8350; 502-886-5261 (in KY).

J-S Sales Company Inc., 5 S. Fulton Ave., Mt. Vernon, NY 10550: Free information ❖ Bowling ball bags, grips, towels, and novelties. 800-431-2944; 914-668-8051 (in NY).

KR Industries Inc., 1200 S. 54th Ave., Cicero, IL 60650: Free information ❖ Bags. 800-621-6097.

Master Industries Inc., 17222 Von Karman Ave., Irvine, CA 92713: Free information ❖ Bags, balls, grips, novelties, and towels. 800-854-3794; 714-660-0644 (in CA).

Nike Footwear Inc., One Bowerman Dr., Beaverton, OR 97005: Free list of retail sources ❖ Bowling ball bags, shoes, shirts, and blouses. 800-344-6453.

Pin Breaker Inc., 300 S. Calhoun, Fairbury, IL 61739: Catalog $1 (refundable) ❖ Bowling balls and other equipment. 800-442-2903.

Saunier-Wilhem Company, 3216 5th Ave., Pittsburgh, PA 15213: Free catalog ❖ Equipment and accessories for bowling, billiards, darts, table tennis, shuffleboard, and board games. 412-621-4350.

Sports Technologies Inc., 2923 Industrial Dr., Sanford, NC 27330: Free information ❖ Bags, balls, and accessories. 800-322-3962; 919-776-9544 (in NC).

Universal Bowling, Golf & Billiard Supplies, 619 S. Wabash Ave., Chicago, IL 60605: Free catalog ❖ Bowling equipment. 800-523-3037.

Universal Trav-Ler, 359 Wales Ave., Bronx, NY 10454: Free information ❖ Bowling ball and shoe bags. 800-833-3026; 212-993-7100 (in NY).

Wa-Mac Inc., Highskore Products, P.O. Box 128, Carlstadt, NJ 07410: Free information ❖ Bowling ball and shoe bags, grips, novelties, towels, shoes, and gloves. 800-447-5673; 201-438-7200 (in NJ).

BOXING

Clothing

Adidas USA, 5675 N. Blackstock Rd., Spartanburg, SC 29303: Free list of retail sources ❖ Shoes. 800-423-4327.

Butwin Sportswear Company, 3401 Spring St. NE, Minneapolis, MN 55413: Free information ❖ Robes. 800-328-1445.

Converse Inc., 1 Fordham Rd., North Reading, MA 01864: Free information ❖ Shoes. 800-428-2667; 508-664-1100 (in MA).

Eisner Brothers, 75 Essex St., New York, NY 10002: Free information ❖ Trunks. 800-426-7800.

Faber Brothers, 4141 S. Pulaski Rd., Chicago, IL 60632: Free information ❖ Bags, gloves, and head guards. 312-376-9300.

Franklin Sports Industries Inc., 17 Campanelli Parkway, P.O. Box 508, Stoughton, MA 02072: Free information ❖ Bags and gloves. 800-426-7700.

G & S Sporting Goods, 43 Essex St., New York, NY 10002: Free price list ❖ Trunks, robes, gloves, training equipment, and protective gear. 212-777-7590.

Genesport Industries Ltd., Hokkaido Karate Equipment Manufacturing Company, 150 King St., Montreal, Quebec, Canada H3C 2P3: Free information ❖ Robes, shoes, trunks, punching bags, skip ropes, and boxing rings. 514-861-1856.

Markwort Sporting Goods, 4300 Forest Park Ave., St. Louis, MO 63108: Catalog $8 (request list of retail sources) ❖ Bags, gloves, and head guards. 800-669-6626; 314-652-3757 (in MO).

Otomix, 431 N. Oak St., Inglewood, CA 90302: Free information ❖ Fitness clothing, shoes, and martial arts equipment. 800-597-5425.

Pony USA Inc., 2801 Red Dot Ln., Knoxville, TN 37914: Free information ❖ Shoes, socks, and sweat bands.

Tuf-Wear USA, P.O. Box 239, Sidney, NE 69162: Free information ❖ Robes, shoes, and trunks. 800-445-5210; 308-254-4011 (in NE).

Equipment

Betlin Manufacturing, 1445 Marion Rd., Columbus OH 43207: Free information ❖ Robes and trunks. 614-443-0248.

Cannon Sports, P.O. Box 797, Greenland, NH 03840: Free list of retail sources ❖ Punching bags and skip ropes. 800-362-3146.

Everlast Sports Manufacturing Corporation, 750 E. 132nd St., Bronx, NY 10454: Free information ❖ Punching bags, boxing rings, skip ropes, gloves, head guards, helmets, and tooth and mouth protectors. 800-221-8777; 718-993-0100 (in NY).

Faber Brothers, 4141 S. Pulaski Rd., Chicago, IL 60632: Free information ❖ Clothing for boxers. 312-376-9300.

G & S Sporting Goods, 43 Essex St., New York, NY 10002: Free price list ❖ Trunks, robes, gloves, training equipment, and protective gear. 212-777-7590.

Genesport Industries Ltd., Hokkaido Karate Equipment Manufacturing Company, 150 King St., Montreal, Quebec, Canada H3C 2P3: Free information ❖ Punching bags, skip ropes, boxing rings, robes, shoes, trunks, gloves, head guards, helmets, and tooth and mouth protectors. 514-861-1856.

Gladiator Sports, 3499 Cowes Mewes, Woodbridge, VA 22193: Free information ❖ Gloves, protective gear, punching bags, and dummies. 703-878-9284.

Ivanko Barbell Company, P.O. Box 1470, San Pedro, CA 90731: Free list of retail sources ❖ Punching bags and skip ropes. 800-247-9044; 310-514-1155 (in CA).

Macho Products Inc., 10045 102nd Terrace, Sebastian, FL 32958: Free catalog ❖ Equipment and clothing. 800-327-6812; 407-388-9892 (in FL).

NDL Products Inc., 4031 NE 12th Terrace, Oakland Park, FL 33334: Free information ❖ Punching bags and skip ropes. 800-843-3021.

Ringside, P.O. Box 14171, Lenexa, KS 66285: Free catalog ❖ Boxing equipment, clothing, and training aids. 800-KARATE-1; 913-888-1719 (in KS).

T.F. Wear USA, P.O. Box 239, Sidney, NE 69162: Free information ❖ Punching bags, skip ropes, boxing rings, robes, shoes, trunks, gloves, head guards, helmets, and tooth and mouth protectors. 800-445-5210; 308-254-4011 (in NE).

BREAD MAKING

Burnt Cabins Grist Mill, P.O. Box 65, Burnt Cabins, PA 17215: Free brochure ❖ Old-fashioned buckwheat and wheat flours, roasted and regular cornmeal, and pancake and muffin mixes. 800-BRT-MILL.

Genie's Kitchen, 150 Magic Ln., Box 456, Wibaux, MT 59353: Free list of retail sources ❖ Low-fat and no cholesterol muffin mixes. 406-795-2228.

The Gluten-Free Pantry, P.O. Box 881, Glastonbury, CT 06033: Free catalog ❖ Easy-to-make wheat-free and gluten-free gourmet bread and cake baking mixes. 203-633-3826.

HeartyMix Company, 1231 Madison Hill Rd., Rahway, NJ 07065: Free catalog ❖ Mixes for bread machines. 908-382-3010.

The J.B. Dough Company, P.O. Box 557, St. Joseph, MI 49085: Free price list ❖ Mixes for automatic bread machines. 800-528-6222; 616-933-1025 (in MI).

The King Arthur Flour Baker's Catalog, P.O. Box 876, Norwich, VT 05055: Free information ❖ Sourdough starter for bread, pancakes, biscuits, and cakes. 800-827-6836.

Native Grains Inc., 101 1st St. West, Fosston, MN 56542: Free information ❖ Mixes for easy-to-make natural organic bread. 800-845-2486.

R.F. Nature Farm Foods Inc., 850 NBC Center, Lincoln, NE 68508: Free list of retail sources ❖ All-natural bread mixes for bread machines and oven-baking. 800-222-FARM; 402-474-7576 (in NE).

Spent Grain Baking Company, 1530 Eastlake Ave. East, Ste. 307, Seattle, WA 98103: Free list of retail sources ❖ Fat-free bread mixes and pancake/waffle mix. 800-860-4533; 206-860-4110 (in WA).

Wanda's Nature Farm Foods, 850 NBC Center, Lincoln, NE 68508: Free catalog ❖ All-natural bread, muffin, pancake, waffle, and double-chocolate cake mixes. 800-222-FARM.

BRIDGE

Baron/Barclay Bridge Supplies, 3600 Chamberlain Ln., Ste. 230, Louisville, KY 40201: Free catalog ❖ Bridge supplies and books. 800-274-2221; 502-426-0410.

BRUSHES

Ace Wire Brush Company Inc., 30 Henry St., Brooklyn, NY 11201: Free brochure ❖ Brushes and brooms. 718-624-8032.

Fuller Direct, One Fuller Way, Great Band, KS 67530: Free catalog ❖ Brooms and brushes, space-saving organizers, and other home aids. 800-522-0499.

BULLETIN & CHALKBOARDS

Bangor Cork Company Inc., William & D Streets, Pen Argyl, PA 18072: Free catalog ❖ Cork bulletin, marker, and chalkboards. 215-863-9041.

Business & Institutional Furniture Company, P.O. Box 92039, Milwaukee, WI 53202: Free catalog ❖ Office and institutional furniture. 800-558-8662.

Flaghouse Furniture Express, 150 N. MacQuesten Pkwy., Mt. Vernon, NY 10550: Free catalog ❖ Bulletin and chalkboards, and other office furnishings. 800-793-7900.

Memindex Inc., 149 Carter St., P.O. Box 20566, Rochester, NY 14602: Free catalog ❖ Organizational tools for scheduling, planning, and controlling time. 716-342-7740.

Office Depot Inc., 2200 Old Germantown Rd., Delray Beach, FL 33445: Free catalog ❖ Bulletin and chalkboards, office supplies, and furniture. 800-685-8800.

Staples Inc., Attention: Marketing Services, P.O. Box 9328, Framingham, MA 01701: Free catalog ❖ Office furniture, drafting equipment, fax machines, typewriters, and supplies. 800-333-3330.

BUMPER STICKERS

Communication Graphics, 14560 Manchester, Ballwin, MO 63011: Free information ❖ Bumper stickers, matchbooks, magnets, and cassette and mailing labels. 800-966-2545.

Lancer Label, 301 S. 74th St., Omaha, NE 68114: Free catalog ❖ Bumper stickers and labels in rolls, sheets, and pinfeed for computers. 800-228-7074.

Magic Systems Inc., P.O. Box 23888, Tampa, FL 33623: Free information ❖ Easy-to-use portable bumper sticker printing machine and supplies. 813-886-5495.

Prestige Promotions, 4875 White Bear Pkwy., White Bear Lake, MN 55110: Free information ❖ Pens, coffee mugs, calendars, and bumper stickers. 800-328-9351.

Royal Graphics Inc., 3117 N. Front St., Philadelphia, PA 19133: Free information ❖ Bumper stickers, posters, and show cards. 215-739-8282.

N.G. Slater Corporation, 220 W. 19th St., New York, NY 10011: Free catalog ❖ Advertising novelties, T-shirts, clips and pins, ID cards, bumper stickers, and equipment for making imprinted buttons. 212-924-3133.

BUSINESS CARDS, ID CARDS & CARD CASES

Advanced Products, 11201 Hindry Ave., Los Angeles, CA 90045: Free catalog ❖ Plastic ID cards, calendars, and Rolodex cards. 800-421-2858; 213-410-9965 (in CA).

Artistic Greetings Catalog, The Personal Touch, P.O. Box 1623, Elmira, NY 14902: Free catalog ❖ Business cards, memo and informal note cards, and personalized stationery. 800-733-6313.

Arthur Blank & Company Inc., 225 Rivermoor St., Boston, MA 02132: Free information ❖ Plastic credit, ID, membership, and other cards. 800-776-7333; 617-325-9600 (in MA).

The Business Book, P.O. Box 8465, Mankato, MN 56002: Free catalog ❖ Pressure sensitive labels, stampers, personalized business envelopes and stationery, speed letters, memo pads, business cards and forms, greeting cards, books, and other office supplies. 800-558-0220.

Business Envelope Manufacturers, 900 Grand Blvd., Deer Park, NY 11729: Free catalog ❖ Business cards, imprinted envelopes, forms, stationery, and labels. 516-667-8500.

Color Tree, 11726 Westgate Rd., P.O. Box 1603, Eau Claire, WI 54703. Free information ❖ Full-color photo business cards. 800-873-9102.

Colorfast, 9522 Canyon Blvd., Chatsworth, CA 91311: Catalog $3 ❖ Full-color photo business cards. 818-407-1881.

Comprehensive Identification Products Inc., 209 Middlesex Tnpk., Burlington, MA 01803: Free catalog ❖ Instant photo ID cameras, equipment for making photo ID cards, and badges, badge holders, and luggage tags. 617-229-8780.

Cowens, 215 NE 59th St., Miami, FL 33137: Free information ❖ Vinyl card cases. 800-442-0244.

Custom Business Cards, 656 Axminister Dr., St. Louis, MO 63026: Free information ❖ Full-color photo business cards. 800-325-9541; 314-343-0178 (in MO).

Day-Timers, One Day-Timer Plaza, Allentown, PA 18195: Free catalog ❖ Business cards, stationery, forms, and office supplies. 800-225-5005.

Discovery Products, 4141 Ball Rd., Ste. 288, Cypress, CA 90630: Free information ❖ Thermographed business cards. 310-429-4931.

Enfield Stationers, 215 Moody Rd., Enfield, CT 06082: Free catalog ❖ Business cards, calendars, and gifts. 203-763-3980.

Grayarc, P.O. Box 2944, Hartford, CT 06104: Free catalog ❖ Stationery, business cards, forms, labels, and envelopes. 800-562-5468.

Heirloom Editions, Box 520-B, Rt. 4, Carthage, MO 64836: Catalog $4 ❖ Victorian-style calling cards. 800-725-0725.

Hodgins Engraving, P.O. Box 597, Batavia, NY 14021: Free catalog ❖ Thermographed business cards. 800-666-8950.

Jackson Marketing Products, Brownsville Rd., Mt. Vernon, IL 62864: Free information ❖ Business cards and supplies for making rubber stamps. 800-STAMP-CALL.

L & D Press, Box 641, 78 Randall St., Rockville Center, NY 11570: Free price list ❖ Business cards, letterheads, and envelopes. 516-593-5058.

Lee's Company Inc., 1717 N. Bayshore Dr., Unit 4145, Miami, FL 33132: Free information ❖ Photo business cards. 800-LEES-023.

Mid-South Business Cards, P.O. Box 2183, Jackson, TN 38302: Free catalog ❖ Thermographed business cards.

Photo Card Specialists Inc., 1726 Westgate Rd., Eau Claire, WI 54703: Free information ❖ Full-color photo business cards. 800-727-4488; 715-839-9102 (in WI).

Photo Images, 554 Park Dr., Jackson, MS 39208: Free information ❖ Photo business cards. 800-637-1440.

Pictures Plus Marketing Corporation, P.O. Box 3009, Teaneck, NJ 07666: Free information ❖ Color photo business cards. 800-262-4921.

Prolitho Inc., 630 New Ludlow Rd., South Hadley, MA 01075: Free information ❖ Thermographed business cards and stationery and envelopes with flat and raised printing. 413-532-9473.

Pronto Business Cards, Box 548, Safety Harbor, FL 34695: Free catalog ❖ Raised business cards. 813-726-8120.

Supreme Cards Inc., 14000 63rd Way, Clearwater, FL 34620: Free catalog ❖ Business cards. 800-771-5273.

ZIP Business Cards, P.O. Box 935, Norwalk, OH 44857: Free information ❖ Thermographed business cards in wholesale quantities. 800-882-6757.

BUTTERCHURNS

Lehman Hardware & Appliances Inc., P.O. Box 41, Kidron, OH 44636: Catalog $2 ❖ Butter churns. 216-857-5757.

Mills River Industries, 713 Old Orchard Rd., Hendersonville, NC 28739: Catalog $1 ❖ Butter churns and other decorative accents for the home. 704-687-9778.

Zimmerman Handcrafts, 254 E. Main St., Leola, PA 17540: Brochure $1 ❖ Butter churns, country-style decorative items, and traditional crafts. 800-267-5689.

BUTTERFLIES

American Butterfly Company, 3609 Glen Ave., Baltimore, MD 21215: Free information ❖ Imported and domestic butterfly specimens.

The Brown Company, Yawgoo Pond Rd., West Kingston, RI 02892: Free information ❖ Hummingbird and butterfly feeders. 800-556-7670.

Brown's Edgewood Gardens, 2611 Corrine Dr., Orlando, FL 32803: Catalog $3 ❖ Butterfly-attracting plants, herbs, and organic gardening products. 407-896-3203.

Brudy's Exotics, Box 820874, Houston, TX 77282: Free catalog ❖ Exotic plants and seeds, butterfly egg and caterpillar kits, and books on butterflies. 800-926-7333.

Insect Lore, P.O. Box 1535, Shafter, CA 93263: Free brochure ❖ Live butterflies. 805-746-6047.

Scientific, P.O. Box 307, Round Lake, IL 60073: Catalog $1 ❖ Exotic moths, butterflies, and other insects. 708-546-3350.

CABINETS

Bathroom Cabinets

Decorá, P.O. Box 420, Jasper, IN 47546: Free information ❖ Bathroom cabinets, knobs, and pulls. 812-634-2288.

NuTone Inc., P.O. Box 1580, Cincinnati, OH 45201: Catalog $3 ❖ Bathroom cabinets, other fixtures, and accessories. 800-543-8687.

Sonoma Woodworks Inc., 1285 S. Cloverdale Blvd., Cloverdale, CA 95425: Brochure $1 ❖ Medicine and vanity cabinets, high-tank pull chain toilets, and bathroom furniture. 800-659-9003.

General Purpose Cabinets

Campbell Cabinets, 39 Wall St., Bethlehem, PA 18018: Brochure $1. 610-835-7775.

Craftsmen in Wood, 5441 W. Hadley St., Phoenix, AZ 85043: Catalog $8. 602-278-8054.

Iberia Millwork, P.O. Box 12139, New Iberia, LA 70562: Free information. 318-365-8129.

The Kennebec Company, One Front St., Bath, ME 04530: Portfolio $10. 207-443-2131.

La Pointe Cabinetmaker, 41 Gulf Rd., Pelham, MA 01002: Free information. 413-256-1558.

Specialty Woodworks, P.O. Box 1450, Hamilton, MT 59840: Catalog $7. 406-363-6353.

Kitchen Cabinets

Aristokraft, P.O. Box 3513, Evansville, IN 47734: Planning kit $7.95.

CrownPoint Cabinetry, 153 Charlestown Rd., P.O. Box 1560, Claremont, NH 03743: Free information. 800-999-4994.

Crystal Cabinet Works Inc., 1100 Crystal Dr., Princeton, MN 55371: Free list of retail sources. 612-389-4187.

Decorá, P.O. Box 420, Jasper, IN 47546: Free information. 812-634-2288.

Fieldstone Cabinetry Inc., P.O. Box 109, Northwood, IA 50459: Free information. 515-324-2114.

Haas Cabinet Company Inc., 625 W. Utica St., Sellersburg, IN 47172: Free information. 800-457-6458.

Heritage Custom Kitchens, 215 Diller Ave., New Holland, PA 17557: Free information. 717-354-4011.

Hirsh Company, 8051 Central Ave., Skokie, IL 60076: Free information. 708-673-6610.

HomeCrest Corporation, P.O. Box 595, Goshen, IN 46526: Free information. 219-533-9571.

J & M Custom Cabinets & Millworks, 2750 North Bauer Rd., St. Johns, MI 48879: Catalog $2. 517-593-2244.

The Kennebec Company, One Front St., Bath, ME 04530: Portfolio $10. 207-443-2131.

Kitchen Kompact Inc., P.O. Box 868, Jeffersonville, IN 47131: Free information. 812-282-6681.

KraftMaid Cabinetry Inc., 16052 Industrial Pkwy., P.O. Box 1055, Middlefield, OH 44062: Catalog $4. 800-654-3008.

Merillat Industries Inc., P.O. Box 1946, Adrian, MI 49221: Free information. 800-624-1250.

Plain 'n Fancy Kitchens, P.O. Box 519, Schaefferstown, PA 17088: Free information. 800-447-9006.

98 ❖ CALCULATORS ❖

Quaker Maid, Rt. 61, Leesport, PA 19533: Free information. 610-926-3011.

Rutt Custom Cabinetry, P.O. Box 129, Goodville, PA 17528: Catalog $15 (request list of retail sources). 800-420-7888.

SieMatic Corporation, Feasterville, PA 19047: Information $12 (request list of retail sources).

Southwest Door Company, 219 N. 3rd Ave., Tucson, AZ 85705: Free list of retail sources ❖ Traditional, contemporary, and country-style doors, windows, hardware, cabinets, and flooring. 602-624-1434.

Triangle Pacific Corporation, 16803 Dallas Pkwy., Dallas, TX 75266: Free information. 214-931-3000.

Wellborn Cabinet Inc., P.O. Box 1210, Rt. 1, Hwy. 77 South, Ashland, AL 36251: Free list of retail sources. 800-336-8040.

Wilsonart, 600 General Bruce Dr., Temple, TX 76504: Free information. 800-322-3222.

Wood-Hu Kitchens Inc., 343 Manly St., West Bridgewater, MA 02379: Free information. 800-343-7919; 800-344-8777 (in MA).

Wood-Mode Cabinets, 1 Second St., Kreamer, PA 17833: Free information. 717-374-2711.

CALCULATORS

Elek-Tek, 7530 N. Linder Ave., Skokie, IL 60077: Free catalog ❖ Calculators, computers and accessories, and office supplies. 800-395-1000; 708-677-7660 (in IL).

Fidelity Products Company, P.O. Box 155, Minneapolis, MN 55440: Free catalog ❖ Calculators, equipment, and office supplies. 800-328-3034; 612-526-6500 (in MN).

47th Street Photo, Mail Order Department, 455 Smith St., Brooklyn, NY 11231: Catalog $2 ❖ Calculators, other electronics, and photography and video equipment. 718-722-4750.

Office Depot Inc., 2200 Old Germantown Rd., Delray Beach, FL 33445: Free catalog ❖ Calculators, equipment, and other office supplies. 800-685-8800.

Quill Office Supplies, 100 Schelter Rd., Lincolnshire, IL 60197: Free catalog ❖ Calculators, computers and accessories, and office supplies and equipment. 708-634-4800.

Reliable Home Office, P.O. Box 1501, Ottawa, IL 61350: Catalog $2 ❖ Calculators, computer accessories and furniture, filing and storage systems, fax machines, and office supplies. 800-869-6000. (Attention: Address Correction, P.O. Box 1020, Westboro, MA 01581.)

Staples Inc., Attention: Marketing Services, P.O. Box 9328, Framingham, MA 01701: Free catalog ❖ Calculators, office supplies, furniture, computer accessories, drafting equipment, fax machines, and typewriters. 800-333-3330.

Viking Office Products, 13809 S. Figueroa St., P.O. Box 61144, Los Angeles, CA 90061: Free catalog ❖ Office supplies, calculators, and equipment. 800-421-1222.

CALENDARS

Angler's, P.O. Box 161, Twin Falls, ID 83303: Free catalog ❖ Fishing gifts and calendars. 800-657-8040.

Bookmark, P.O. Box 335, Delafield, WI 53018: Catalog $1 ❖ Fine art calendars and boxed note cards. 414-646-4499.

Cedco Publishing Company, 2955 Kerner Blvd., San Rafael, CA 94901: Free catalog ❖ Calendars and date and other memorandum-style books. 800-233-2624.

Christian Book Distributors, P.O. Box 7000, Peabody, MA 01961: Free catalog ❖ Religious-theme calendars. 508-977-5000.

Down East Books & Gifts, P.O. Box 679, Camden, ME 04843: Free catalog ❖ Calendars, books, and crafts from Maine and New England. 800-766-1670.

Enfield Stationers, 215 Moody Rd., Enfield, CT 06082: Free catalog ❖ Business cards, calendars, and gifts. 203-763-3980.

G & K Enterprises, 1408 Glenwood Ave., Greensboro, NC 27403: Free information ❖ Calendars and all-occasion and Christmas greeting cards with a western theme. 910-632-9899.

Heirloom Editions, Box 520-B, Rt. 4, Carthage, MO 64836: Catalog $4 ❖ Lithographs, greeting cards, stickers, miniatures, stationery, framed prints, and turn-of-the-century art and paper collectibles. 800-725-0725.

Kar-Ben Copies Inc., 6800 Tildenwood Ln., Rockville, MD 20852: Free catalog ❖ Calendars. 800-452-7236.

Lang Companies, P.O. Box 1, Delafield, WI 53018: Catalog $1 ❖ Country-style calendars, boxed note cards, and greeting cards. 800-967-3399.

Main Street Press, P.O. Box 126, Delafield, WI 53018: Catalog $1 ❖ Wall calendars, boxed greeting cards, note cards and pads, and stationery products. 414-646-8511.

Naval Institute Press, Customer Service, 2062 Generals Hwy., Annapolis, MD 21401: Free catalog ❖ Calendars. 800-233-8764.

Pomegranate Calendars & Books, Box 6099, Rohnert Park, CA 94927: Free catalog ❖ Wall, mini, pocket, wallet, and poster calendars. 800-227-1428; 707-586-5500 (in CA).

Posty Cards, 1600 Olive St., Kansas City, MO 64127: Free catalog ❖ Calendars and greeting and birthday cards. 800-554-5018.

Sormani Calendars Inc., P.O. Box 6059, Chelsea, MA 02150: Free catalog ❖ Photo illustrated calendars. 800-321-9327; 617-387-7300 (in MA).

Thoroughbred Racing Catalog, Warsaw, VA 22572: Catalog $2 ❖ Calendars and limited edition prints with pictures of famous racing horses and horse-decorated mailboxes, doormats, sweatshirts and T-shirts, mugs and glasses, jewelry, and wall clocks. 800-777-RACE.

Tide-Mark Press Ltd., P.O. Box 280311, East Hartford, CT 06128: Catalog $2 ❖ Calendars and desk diaries. 800-338-2508.

Write Stuff Syndicate Inc., 1515 SE 4th Ave., Fort Lauderdale, FL 33316: Free brochure ❖ Hardbound coffee table books and classic boat calendars. 954-462-6657.

Zenith Books, 1000 Milwaukee Ave., Glenview, IL 60025: Free catalog ❖ Calendars, books, and video tapes about aviation. 708-391-7000.

CALLIGRAPHY

American Stationery Company, 100 Park Ave., Peru, IN 46970: Free catalog ❖ Regular and calligraphy stationery, wedding invitations, note cards and personal memos, envelopes, and postcards. 800-822-2577.

Ken Brown Studio, P.O. Box 22, McKinney, TX 75069: Free information with long SASE ❖ Calligraphy supplies. 800-654-6100; 214-562-0605 (in TX).

The Calligraphy Shoppe, 7296 Coolidge Rd., Fort Myers, FL 33912: Catalog $3 ❖ Calligraphy supplies. 800-592-3887.

Creative Calligraphy, 1600 E. Lincoln Hwy., P.O. Box 943, DeKalb, IL 60115: Catalog $2 ❖ Framed personal remembrances and family heirloom collectibles. 800-545-3928; 815-756-6900 (in IL).

Ebersole Arts & Crafts Supply, 11417 West Hwy. 54, Wichita, KS 67209: Catalog $2 ❖ Calligraphy and art supplies. 316-722-4771.

Hunt Manufacturing Company, 2005 Market St., Philadelphia, PA 19103: Free information ❖ Fountain pens and sets, nibs, inks, and calligraphy papers, markers, and kits. 800-765-5669.

J & N Creations, 48 1st St. North, Sauk Centre, MN 56378: Brochure $2 ❖ Framed verses with optional personalization. 612-352-6260.

Literary Calligraphy, Rt. 1, Box 56A, Moneta, VA 24121: Catalog $2 ❖ Framed art and stationery. 800-261-6325.

Nasco, 901 Janesville Ave., Fort Atkinson, WI 53538: Free catalog ❖ Calligraphy supplies and greeting cards. 800-558-9595.

CAMCORDERS & ACCESSORIES

John Neal, Bookseller, 1833 Spring Garden St., Greensboro, NC 27403: Free information ❖ Calligraphy and marbling supplies, books, and bookbinding services. 800-369-9598.

Ott's Art Supplies, 102 Hungate Dr., Greenville, NC 27858: Free catalog ❖ Art, calligraphy, and drawing supplies. 800-356-3289.

Paper & Ink Books, 15309A Sixes Bridge Rd., Emmitsburg, MD 21727: Free catalog ❖ Calligraphy books and supplies. 301-447-6487.

Pendragon, P.O. Box 1995, Arlington Heights, IL 60006: Catalog $2 ❖ Calligraphy supplies. 800-775-7367.

CAMCORDERS & ACCESSORIES
Manufacturers

Allsop, P.O. Box 23, Bellingham, WA 98227: Free information ❖ Camcorders. 800-426-4303; 206-734-9090 (in WA).

AMI Corporation, P.O. Box 27682, Denver, CO 80227: Free information ❖ Camcorders and accessories. Also computer accessories and other audio and video equipment. 800-325-0853.

Azden Corporation, 147 New Hyde Park Rd., Franklin Square, NY 11016: Free information ❖ Camcorders, headphones, and other electronics. 516-328-7500.

Canon, One Canon Plaza, Lake Success, NY 11042: Free information ❖ Cassette players, camcorders, and other electronics. 516-488-6700.

Casio, 570 Mount Pleasant Ave., P.O. Box 7000, Dover, NJ 07801: Free information ❖ Camcorders. 201-361-5400.

Chinon America Inc., 1065 Bristol Rd., Mountainside, NJ 07092: Free information ❖ Camcorders. 908-654-0404.

Discwasher, 2950 Lake Emma Rd., Lake Mary, FL 32746: Free information ❖ Camcorders. 800-325-0573.

Eastman Kodak Company, Kodak Information Center, 343 State St., Rochester, NY 14650: Free information ❖ Camcorders. 800-462-6495.

Emerson Radio Corporation, 9 Entin Rd., Parsippany, NJ 07054: Free information ❖ Camcorders, monitors, receivers, cassette and CD players, and TVs. 201-884-5800.

Fisher, 21350 Lassen St., Chatsworth, CA 91311: Free information ❖ Speakers, cassette and CD players, camcorders, TVs, and other electronics. 818-998-7322.

Hitachi Sales Corporation, Customer Service, 675 Old Peachtree Rd., Suwanee, GA 30174: Free information ❖ Cassette and CD players, camcorders, TVs, and other electronics. 800-241-6558.

Instant Replay, 8290 NW 27th St., Ste. 605, Miami, FL 33122: Free information ❖ Camcorders and cassette players. 305-854-6777.

JVC, 41 Slater Dr., Elmwood Park, NJ 07407: Free information ❖ CD and cassette players, camcorders, receivers, amplifiers, TVs, and headphones. 201-794-3900.

Memorex, 1600 II Tandy Center, Fort Worth, TX 76102: Free information ❖ Camcorders. 800-548-8308.

Minolta, 101 Williams Dr., Ramsey, NJ 07446: Free information ❖ Cassette players and camcorders. 201-825-4000.

Mitsubishi Electronics, 5665 Plaza Dr., Cypress, CA 90630: Free information ❖ Audio and video systems, cassette and CD players, camcorders, and TVs. 800-843-2515.

NEC Home Electronics, 1255 Michael Dr., Wood Dale, IL 60191: Free information ❖ Speakers, CD and cassette players, receivers, amplifiers, TVs, camcorders, and other electronics. 708-860-9500.

Olympus Corporation, 145 Crossways Park, Woodbury, NY 11797: Free information ❖ Camcorders. 800-221-3000.

Panasonic, Panasonic Way, Secaucus, NJ 07094: Free list of retail sources ❖ Audio and video systems, cassette and CD players, TVs, camcorders, headphones, and other electronics. 201-348-7000.

Pentax Corporation, 35 Inverness Dr. East, Englewood, CO 80112: Free information ❖ Cassette players, camcorders, and other electronics. 303-799-8000.

Quasar, One Panasonic Way, Secaucus, NJ 07094: Free list of retail sources ❖ Audio and video systems, CD and cassette players, camcorders, and TVs. 201-348-7000.

Radio Shack, Division Tandy Corporation, One Tandy Center, Fort Worth, TX 76102: Free information ❖ Cassette and CD players, camcorders, universal remotes, computers, and other electronics. 817-390-3011.

RCA Sales Corporation, Thomson Consumer Electronics, P.O. Box 1976, Indianapolis, IN 46206: Free information ❖ Audio and video systems, cassette and CD players, TVs, camcorders, and other electronics. 800-336-1900.

Ricoh Consumer Products Group, 180 Passaic Ave., Fairfield, NJ 07004: Free brochure ❖ Camcorders. 800-225-1899.

Sanyo, 21350 Lassen St., Chatsworth, CA 91311: Free information ❖ Cassette and CD players, camcorders, TVs, and other electronics. 818-998-7322.

Sharp Electronics, Sharp Plaza, Mahwah, NJ 07430: Free information ❖ Cassette and CD players, camcorders, TVs, and other electronics. 800-BE-SHARP.

Sony Consumer Products, 1 Sony Dr., Park Ridge, NJ 07656: Free information with long SASE ❖ Camcorders, speakers, CD and cassette players, headphones, and other electronics. 201-930-1000.

Retailers

Abe's of Maine Camera & Electronics, 1957 Coney Island Ave., Brooklyn, NY 11223: Free information ❖ Video and photography equipment, camcorders, and accessories. 800-531-2237.

B & H Photo-Video, 119 W. 17th St., New York, NY 10011: Catalog $3.95 ❖ Photographic and video equipment and camcorders. 212-807-7474.

Beach Photo & Video Inc., 604 Main St., Daytona Beach, FL 32118: Free information ❖ Video equipment and camcorders. 904-252-0577.

Bel Air Camera & Video, 1025 Westwood Blvd., Los Angeles, CA 90024: Free information ❖ Photographic equipment and video cameras. 310-208-5150.

Berger Brothers Camera Exchange, 209 Broadway, Amityville, NY 11701: Free information ❖ Camcorders and accessories. 800-262-4160.

Camera Sound of Pennsylvania, 1104 Chestnut St., Philadelphia, PA 19107: Free information ❖ Camcorders, VCRs, editing equipment, and other electronics. 800-477-1003.

Camera World, 1809 Commonwealth Ave., Charlotte, NC 28205: Catalog $1 ❖ Video equipment, camcorders, and photography equipment. 800-868-3686; 704-375-8453 (in NC).

Camera World of Oregon, Camera World Building, 500 SW 5th Ave., Portland, OR 97204: Free information ❖ Camcorders and tapes. 503-227-6008.

Colonel Video & Audio, 16451 Space Center Blvd., Houston, TX 77058: Free information ❖ Video and audio editing equipment, camcorders, and accessories. 713-486-8866.

Coast to Coast, 2570 86th St., Brooklyn, NY 11214: Free information ❖ Camcorders, video editing equipment, receivers, CD and cassette players, and other equipment. 718-265-1723.

Data Vision, 445 5th Ave., New York, NY 10016: Free information ❖ Video cameras and editing equipment. 800-482-7466; 212-689-1111 (in NY).

The Electronic Mailbox, 10-12 Charles St., Glen Cove, NY 11542: Free information ❖ Video editing and lighting equipment. 800-323-2325.

Electronic Wholesalers, 1166 Hamburg Tnpk., Wayne, NJ 07470: Free information ❖ Camcorders, TVs, cassette players, audio and video receivers, CD and laser players, and telephones. 201-696-6531.

Electronics Depot, 22 Rt. 22 West, Springfield, NJ 07081: Free information ❖ Video equipment, camcorders, and accessories. 800-500-1553.

Executive Photo & Electronics, 120 W. 31st St., New York, NY 10001: Free information ❖ Photography and video equipment, camcorders, and other electronics. 800-882-2802.

Gabriel Video & Camera, 260 W. Swedesford Rd., Berwyn, PA 19312: Free information ❖ Camcorders and accessories. 800-420-5050.

Garden State Camera, 101 Kuller Rd., Clifton, NJ 07015: Free information ❖ Photographic and other optical equipment, camcorders, video and audio accessories, and binoculars. 201-742-5777.

Genesis Camera Inc., 814 W. Lancaster Ave., Bryn Mawr, PA 19010: Free information ❖ Audio, video, and photographic equipment. 800-575-9977; 610-527-5261 (in PA).

Global Video, 260 W. Swedesford Rd., Berwyn, PA 19312: Free information ❖ Video cameras and editing equipment. 800-420-5050.

Haven Electronics, 46-23 Crane St., Long Island City, NY 11101: Free information ❖ Video equipment and camcorders. 800-231-0031.

Haven Industries, 2950 Lake Emma Rd., Lake Mary, FL 32746: Free information ❖ Camcorders and accessories, car audio equipment, video games, and other electronics. 800-231-0031.

Hunt's Photo & Video, 100 Main St., Melrose, MA 02176: Free information ❖ Camcorders and accessories. 617-662-8822.

Marine Park Camera & Video Inc., 3126 Avenue U, Brooklyn, NY 11229: Free information ❖ Video equipment and VCRs. 800-448-8811; 718-891-1878 (in NY).

Markertek Video Supply, 4 High St., Saugerties, NY 12477: Free catalog ❖ Video equipment. 800-522-2025.

Mission Service Supply, 4565 Cypress St., West Monroe, LA 71291: Free catalog ❖ Camcorders, video systems, and accessories. 800-352-7222; 318-397-2755 (in LA).

New West Electronics, 4120 Meridian, Bellingham, WA 98226: Free information ❖ VCRs, Camcorders, TVs and monitors, disk players, audio components and speakers, and other electronics. 800-488-8877.

Newtech Video & Computers, 350 7th Ave., New York, NY 10001: Free information ❖ Video equipment, computers and peripherals, software, cellular phones, fax machines, and office equipment. 800-554-9747.

Peach State Photo, 1706 Chantilly Dr., Atlanta, GA 30324: Free information ❖ Camcorders, electronic imaging and video editing equipment, and accessories. 800-766-9653.

Philly's Camera, 27 S. 11th St., Philadelphia, PA 19107: Free information ❖ Camcorders and accessories. 215-922-5130.

PowerVideo, 6808 Hornwood Dr., Houston, TX 77074: Free information ❖ Camcorders, TVs, cassette players, and video equipment. 713-772-4400.

Prime Time Video & Cameras, 1104 Chestnut St., Philadelphia, PA 19107: Free information ❖ Video cameras and editing equipment. 800-477-8445.

Profeel Video, 42 Main St., Monsey, NY 10952: Free information ❖ Video cameras and editing equipment. 914-425-2070.

Professional Video Warehouse, 575 SE Ashley Pl., Grants Pass, OR 97526: Free information ❖ Video equipment. 800-736-6677.

Samman's Electronics, 1166 Hamburg Tnpk., Wayne, NJ 07470: Free information ❖ Camcorders, home theater systems, and accessories. 800-AUDIO-93.

Sixth Avenue Electronics, Rt. 22 West, Springfield, NJ 07081: Free information ❖ Video and audio equipment, TVs, monitors, camcorders, laser players, and other electronics. 201-467-0100.

Sunshine Video & Computers, 22191 Powerline Rd., Boca Raton, FL 33433: Free information ❖ Video cameras. 407-394-3742.

Supreme Camera & Video, 1562 Coney Island Ave., Brooklyn, NY 11230: Free information ❖ Video editing equipment. 800-332-2661; 718-692-4110 (in NY).

Thrifty Distributors, 641 W. Lancaster Ave., Frazer, PA 19355: Free catalog ❖ Video cameras, editing equipment, batteries, wireless microphones, lights, and accessories. 800-342-3610.

Tri-State Camera, 650 6th Ave., New York, NY 10011: Free information ❖ Audio and video equipment, camcorders, video cassettes, fax machines, and accessories. 800-221-1926; 212-633-2290 (in NY).

Universal Video & Camera, P.O. Box 54269, Southeastern, PA 19105: Free information ❖ Video cameras and editing equipment. 800-477-1003.

Video Direct Distributors, 116 Production Dr., Yorktown, VA 23693: Free catalog ❖ Video and audio equipment, TVs, monitors, camcorders, microphones, carrying cases, and other electronics. 800-368-5020.

Video Discount Warehouse, 295 Greenwich St., Ste. 360, New York, NY 10007: Free information ❖ Camcorders and accessories. 800-301-0028; 212-432-6104 (in NY).

Video Innovators, P.O. Box 4130, Frisco, CO 80443: Free information ❖ Camcorders and equipment. 800-832-6840.

Videonics, 1370 Dell Ave., Campbell, CA 95008: Free information ❖ Video editing equipment. 408-866-8300.

Vidicomp Inc., 10988 Wilcrest, Houston, TX 77099: Free information ❖ Video cameras and editing equipment. 800-263-8211; 305-265-9339 (in south FL).

Westcoast Discount Video, 5201 Eastern Ave., Baltimore, MD 21224: Catalog $5 ❖ Camcorders. 800-344-7123; 410-633-0508 (in MD).

World Trade Video, 295 Greenwich St., Ste. 360, New York, NY 10007: Free information ❖ Camcorders and accessories. 800-253-2639.

Video Editing Equipment

Colonel Video & Audio, 16451 Space Center Blvd., Houston, TX 77058: Free information ❖ Video and audio editing equipment. 713-486-8866.

CrystalGraphics, 3110 Patrick Henry Dr., Santa Clara, CA 95054: Free information ❖ Windows-based 3-D animation titling software. 800-TOPAS-3D.

Energetic Music, P.O. Box 84583, Seattle, WA 98124: Free catalog ❖ Royalty-free production music on CD or cassette. 800-323-2972.

Fast Electronic U.S. Inc., 393 Vintage Park Dr., Foster City, CA 94404: Free information ❖ Desktop video production software for PCs. 800-249-FAST.

FutureVideo, 28 Argonaut, Aliso Viejo, CA 92656: Free information ❖ Windows-based video editing software. 800-346-5254; 714-770-4416 (in CA).

Planet Electronics, 8418 Lilley, Canton, MI 48187: Free information ❖ Computer-controlled editing software for PCs. 800-247-4663; 313-453-4750 (in MI).

Videonics, 1370 Dell Ave., Campbell, CA 95008: Free information ❖ Editing controller. 408-866-8300.

CAMPING & BACKPACKING
Clothing & Shoes

Adidas USA, 5675 N. Blackstock Rd., Spartanburg, SC 29303: Free list of retail sources ❖ Hiking and climbing shoes. 800-423-4327.

Alpina Sports Corporation, P.O. Box 23, Hanover, NH 03755: Free list of retail sources ❖ Hiking and climbing shoes. 603-448-3101.

Alpine Adventures, P.O. Box 921262, Sylmar, CA 91392: Free catalog ❖ Outdoor apparel and gear. 800-717-1919.

❖ CAMPING & BACKPACKING ❖

Asolo Boots, 139 Harvest Ln., Williston, VT 05495: Free list of retail sources ❖ Outdoor footwear. 802-879-4644.

B-West Outdoor Specialties, 2425 N. Huachuca, Tucson, AZ 85745: Free catalog ❖ Backpacks, shoes and boots, and outdoor accessories. 800-293-7855; 520-628-1990 (in AZ).

Eddie Bauer, P.O. Box 3700, Seattle, WA 98124: Free catalog ❖ Men and women's active and casual clothes, footwear, and goose down outerwear. 800-426-8020.

L.L. Bean, Freeport, ME 04033: Free catalog ❖ Clothing for hiking, camping, fishing, sports, and other outdoor activities. 800-221-4221.

Bowhunter Supply Inc., 1158 46th St., P.O. Box 5010, Vienna, WV 26105: Free information ❖ Rainwear and hiking shoes. 800-289-2211; 304-295-8511 (in WV).

Brigade Quartermasters Inc., 1025 Cobb International Blvd., Kenesaw, GA 30144: Free catalog ❖ Clothing and rainwear. 404-428-1234.

Browning Company, Dept. C006, One Browning Pl., Morgan, UT 84050: Catalog $2 ❖ Clothing, rainwear, and hiking shoes. 800-333-3288.

Camp 7 Inc., 3701 W. Carriage Dr., Santa Ana, CA 92704: Catalog $1 ❖ Sleeping and duffel bags, backpacks, outdoor clothing, and accessories. 714-545-2204.

Campmor, P.O. Box 700, Saddle River, NJ 07458: Free catalog ❖ Outdoor clothing and equipment for climbing, camping, hiking, backpacking, and biking. 800-226-7667.

Climb High Inc., 60 Northside Dr., Shelburne, VT 05482: Free catalog ❖ Boots and clothing, carabiners, ropes, backpacks, sleeping bags, and other equipment. 802-985-5056.

Coleman Outdoor Products Inc., 250 N. Saint Francis, Wichita, KS 67202: Free catalog ❖ Clothing, hiking and climbing shoes, and equipment. 800-835-3278.

Damart, 3 Front St., Rollinsford, NH 03805: Free information ❖ Thermal underwear for men and women. 800-258-7300.

Danner Shoe Manufacturing Company, 12722 NE Airport Way, Portland, OR 97230: Free catalog ❖ Climbing and hiking boots. 800-345-0430.

Dorfman-Pacific, P.O. Box 213005, Stockton, CA 95213: Free information ❖ Clothing and rainwear. 800-367-3626; 209-982-1400 (in CA).

Ex Officio Outdoor Sport, 1419 Elliott Ave. West, Seattle, WA 98119: Free information ❖ Outdoor clothing.

Fabiano Shoe Company, 850 Summer St., South Boston, MA 02127: Free information with long SASE ❖ Insulated hiking and climbing shoes. 617-268-5625.

Garmont, Customer Service, One 2nd St., Peabody, MA 01960: Free information ❖ Boots, backpacks, and hiking poles. 800-556-8246.

Gorilla & Sons, P.O. Box 2309, Bellingham, WA 98227: Free catalog ❖ Outdoor apparel and equipment. 800-246-7455.

Hi-Tec Sports USA Inc., 4801 Stoddard Rd., Modesto, CA 95356: Free list of retail sources ❖ Hiking and climbing boots. 800-521-1698.

Hiker's Hut, 126 Main St., Box 542, Littleton, NH 03561: Free information ❖ Boots and other footwear. 603-444-6532.

Integral Designs, P.O. Box 40023, Highfield Postal Outlet, Calgary, Alberta, Canada T2G 5G5: Free catalog ❖ Sleeping bags, tents, and outerwear. 403-640-1445.

La Sportiva USA, 3235 Prairie Ave., Boulder, CO 80304: Free list of retail sources ❖ Climbing and hiking boots. 303-443-8710.

Legends Footwear, 14450 Chambers Rd., Tustin, CA 92680: Free catalog ❖ Climbing and hiking boots. 714-731-5707.

Leisure Outlet, 421 Soquel Ave., Santa Cruz, CA 95062: Free catalog ❖ Camping equipment and clothing. 800-322-1460.

Leisure Unlimited, P.O. Box 308, Cedarburg, WI 53012: Free information ❖ Clothing and rainwear. 800-323-5118; 414-377-7454 (in WI).

Lowe Alpine, P.O. Box 1449, Broomfield, CO 80038: Free list of retail sources ❖ Outdoor clothing, mountaineering fleecewear, and backpacks. 303-465-0522.

Orvis Manchester, 1711 Blue Hills Dr., P.O. Box 12000, Roanoke, VA 24022: Free catalog ❖ Outdoor clothing and equipment. 800-541-3541.

Martin Archery Inc., Rt. 5, Box 127, Walla Walla, WA 99362: Free information ❖ Hiking shoes. 509-529-2554.

Merrell Footwear, P.O. Box 4249, South Burlington, VT 05406: Free list of retail sources ❖ Outdoor footwear. 800-869-3348.

Mont-Bell, Catalog Customer Service, 940 1st Ave., Santa Cruz, CA 95062: Free catalog ❖ Outerwear, sleeping bags, backpacks, trekking packs, waterproof shell protection, and travel accessories. 800-683-2002.

Moonstone Factory Store, 1563 G St., Arcata, CA 95521: Free information ❖ Clothing. 707-826-0851.

H. Mullen Sales Inc., RR 2, Oakwood, OH 45873: Free information ❖ Clothing and rainwear. 800-258-6625.

New Balance Athletic Shoe Inc., 38 Everett St., Boston, MA 02134: Free list of retail sources ❖ Hiking shoes. 800-622-1218.

Nike Footwear Inc., One Bowerman Dr., Beaverton, OR 97005: Free list of retail sources ❖ Climbing shoes. 800-344-6453.

North by Northeast, 181 Conant St., Pawtucket, RI 02862: Free information ❖ Clothing and rainwear. 800-556-7262.

North Face, 999 Harrison St., Berkeley, CA 94710: Free list of retail sources ❖ Clothing and rainwear. 800-447-2333.

One Sport Outdoor Footwear, 1003 6th Ave. South, Seattle WA 98134: Free list of retail sources ❖ Outdoor footwear. 206-621-9303.

Only the Lightest Camping Equipment, P.O. Box 266, Troutdale, OR 97060: Catalog $1 ❖ Lightweight clothing and camping equipment. 503-666-9365.

Out There Gear, P.O. Box 3394, Idylwild, CA 92549: Free catalog ❖ T-shirts, fleece jackets and vests, wool and denim clothing, travel bags, sweatshirts, and outdoor apparel. 909-659-7006.

Pachmayr Ltd., 831 N. Rosemead Blvd., South El Monte, CA 91733: Free catalog ❖ Shooting and hunting accessories, clothing, camping equipment, books, and video tapes. 800-350-7408.

Patagonia, 8550 White Fir St., Reno, NV 89523: Free catalog ❖ Outdoor clothing for children and adults. 800-638-6464.

Quest Outfitters, 2590 17th St., Sarasota, FL 34234: Free catalog ❖ Clothing, outdoor fabrics, patterns, fasteners, and zippers. 813-378-1620.

Raichle Molitor USA, Geneva Rd., Brewster, NY 10509: Free list of retail sources ❖ Climbing and hiking boots. 914-279-5121.

Rainshed Outdoor Fabrics, 707 NW 11th, Corvallis, OR 97330: Catalog $1 ❖ Outdoor fabrics, hardware, webbing, patterns, and supplies. 541-753-8900.

Ramsey Outdoor Store, 226 Rt. 17, P.O. Box 1689, Paramus, NJ 07653: Free catalog ❖ Outdoor apparel and equipment. 800-526-7436; 201-261-5000 (in NJ).

REI Recreational Equipment Company, Sumner, WA 98352: Free catalog ❖ Outdoor equipment and clothing, exercise and walking shoes, rainwear, packs that convert to tents, ski equipment, knives, cooking utensils, sunglasses, and foods. 800-426-4840.

Rocky Shoes & Boots Inc., Nelsonville, OH 45764: Free list of retail sources ❖ Outdoor shoes and boots. 614-753-1951.

The Royal Robbins Company, 1314 Coldwell Ave., Modesto, CA 954350: Free information ❖ Outdoor clothing. 800-587-9044.

❖ CAMPING & BACKPACKING ❖

Salomon/North America, 400 E. Main St., Georgetown, MA 01833: Free list of retail sources ❖ Outdoor shoes and boots. 800-225-6850.

Search Gear, 882 Bruce Ln., Chico, CA 95928: Free catalog ❖ Backpacking accessories and clothing, safety and first aid gear, and rescue equipment. 800-474-2612; 916-899-2612 (in CA).

Sequel, Box 409, Durango, CO 81302: Free catalog ❖ Outdoor clothing. 970-385-4660.

Sierra Trading Post, 5025 Campstool Rd., Cheyenne, WY 82007: Free catalog ❖ Outdoor clothing and equipment. 307-775-8000.

Solstice, 2120 NE Oregon St., Portland, OR 97232: Free list of retail sources ❖ Outdoor clothing. 503-239-6991.

Sportif USA, 1415 Greg St., Sparks, NV 89431: Free information ❖ Outdoor clothing. 800-776-7843.

Sportiva, 3235 Prairie Ave., Boulder, CO 80301: Free list of retail sources ❖ Hiking boots. 303-443-8710.

Tecnica USA, 19 Technology Dr., West Lebanon, NH 03784: Free list of retail sources ❖ Outdoor footwear. 603-298-8032.

Thousand Mile Outdoor Wear, 1894 Alta Vista Dr., Vista, CA 92084: Free catalog ❖ Men and women's outdoor clothing. 800-786-7577; 619-945-1609 (in CA).

TrailPrints, 14450 Chambers Rd., Tustin, CA 92680: Free information ❖ Shoes. 800-948-7245.

Vasque Boots, 314 Main St., Red Wing, MN 55066: Free list of retail sources ❖ Hiking and climbing boots. 612-388-8211.

Jack Wolfskin, P.O. Box 2487, Binghamton, NY 13902: Free list of retail sources ❖ Outerwear, backpacks, sleeping bags, tents, travel luggage, and outdoor equipment. 800-572-8822.

Wyoming River Raiders, P.O. Box 50490, Casper, WY 82605: Free catalog ❖ Outdoor clothing, camping and river expedition equipment, fishing gear, hiking equipment, books, and supplies. 800-247-6068.

Equipment

Alpine Adventures, P.O. Box 921262, Sylmar, CA 91392: Free catalog ❖ Outdoor apparel and gear. 800-717-1919.

Appalachian Mountain Supply, 731 Highland Ave. NE, Studio C, Atlanta, GA 30312: Free brochure ❖ Self-inflating sleeping pads, hydration systems, and accessories. 800-569-4110.

Arc Teryx Backpacks, 170 Harbour Ave., North Vancouver, British Columbia, Canada V7J 2E6: Free information ❖ Backpacks. 604-985-6681.

B-West Outdoor Specialties, 2425 N. Huachuca, Tucson, AZ 85745: Free catalog ❖ Backpacks, shoes and boots, and outdoor accessories. 800-293-7855; 520-628-1990 (in AZ).

Bass Pro Shops, 1935 S. Campbell, Springfield, MO 65898: Free information ❖ Camping and backpacking equipment. 800-227-7776.

Bay Archery Sales, 2713 Center Ave., Essexville, MI 48732: Free catalog ❖ Camping and backpacking equipment and survival supplies.

L.L. Bean, Freeport, ME 04033: Free catalog ❖ Tents, backpacks, bicycles, boats, and outdoor equipment. 800-221-4221.

Bear Archery Inc., 4600 SW 41st Blvd., Gainesville, FL 32608: Free information ❖ Backpacks, eating utensils, knives, camping tools, lanterns and flashlights, and other equipment. 800-874-4603; 904-376-2327 (in FL).

Bibler Tents, 5441 Western, Boulder, CO 80301: Catalog $1 ❖ Easy-to-set-up tents. 303-449-7351.

Blue Star Inc., 6980 US Hwy. 10 East, Missoula, MT 59802: Free catalog ❖ Tipis, tents, and trail gear.

The Boundary Waters Catalog, 105 N. Central Ave., Ely, MN 55731: Free catalog ❖ Canoe and camping gear. 800-223-6565.

Bowhunter Supply Inc., 1158 46th St., P.O. Box 5010, Vienna, WV 26105: Free information ❖ Backpacks and equipment. 800-289-2211; 304-295-8511 (in WV).

Brunton, 620 E. Monroe, Riverton, WY 82501: Free brochure ❖ Pocket transits, compasses and accessories, binoculars, pocket field vests, and handcrafted knives. 800-443-4871.

Buck Knives, P.O. Box 1267, El Cajon, CA 92022: Free list of retail sources ❖ Knives. 800-215-2825.

Buffalo Tipi Pole Company, 3355 Upper Gold Creek, Sandpoint, ID 83864: Catalog $2 ❖ Tipis, tipi poles, and accessories. 208-263-6953.

Bumjo's, 1700 E. 18th St., Ste. 100, Tucson, AZ 85719: Free catalog ❖ Caving, climbing, backpacking, and mountaineering equipment. 800-649-0318.

Cabela's, 812 13th Ave., Sidney, NE 69162: Free catalog ❖ Tents, sleeping bags, outdoor clothing, footwear, and hunting equipment. 800-588-7512.

Camel Outdoor Products, 5988 Peachtree Corners East, Norcross, GA 30071: Free list of retail sources ❖ Camping equipment and easy-to-set-up dome tents. 800-251-9412.

Camp 7 Inc., 3701 W. Carriage Dr., Santa Ana, CA 92704: Catalog $1 ❖ Sleeping and duffel bags, backpacks, outdoor clothing, and accessories. 714-545-2204.

Camp Trails/Johnson Worldwide Associates, 1326 Willow Rd., Sturtevant, WI 53177: Free list of retail sources ❖ Backpacks, eating utensils, sleeping bags, and other equipment. 800-848-3673.

Camping World, P.O. Box 90017, Bowling Green, KY 42102: Free information ❖ Accessories and supplies for recreational vehicles. 800-626-5944.

Campmor, P.O. Box 700, Saddle River, NJ 07458: Free catalog ❖ Clothing and equipment for climbing, camping, hiking, backpacking, and biking. 800-226-7667.

Caribou Mountaineering, P.O. Box 3696, Chico, CA 95927: Free catalog ❖ Backpacks, sleeping and shoulder bags, tents, travel packs, and soft luggage. 800-824-4153.

CarTop Tent, 1039 W. Bridge St., Phoenixville, PA 19460: Free brochure ❖ Easy-to-assemble tent that mounts on top of a car roof rack. 610-935-7848.

Climb High Inc., 1861 Shelburne Rd., Shelburne, VT 05482: Free catalog ❖ Boots and clothing, carabiners, ropes, backpacks, sleeping bags, and other equipment. 802-985-5056.

Coghlan's, The Outdoor Accessory People, 121 Irene St., Winnipeg, Manitoba, Canada R3T 4C7: Free information ❖ Camping, fishing, hunting, backpacking, trailering, and boating equipment. 204-284-9550.

Coleman Outdoor Products Inc., 250 N. Saint Francis, Wichita, KS 67202: Free catalog ❖ Backpacks, dining utensils, knives, camping tools, lanterns and flashlights, sleeping bags, and other equipment. 800-835-3278.

Colorado Saddlery Company, 1631 15th Street, Denver, CO 80202: Free catalog ❖ Tents and accessories, sleeping bags, stoves, tack and pack equipment, and supplies. 800-521-2465; 303-572-8350 (in CO).

Colorado Tent Company, 2228 Blake St., Denver, CO 80205: Free information ❖ Tents and sleeping bags. 800-354-TENT.

Comtrad Industries, 2820 Waterford Lake Dr., Ste. 106, Midlothian, VA 23113: Free information ❖ Portable refrigerator with optional built-in food warmer. 800-704-1211.

Crazy Creek Products Inc., P.O. Box 1050, 1401 S. Broadway, Red Lodge, MT 59068: Free list of retail sources ❖ Folding transportable chairs for backpacking, mountaineering, and other outdoor activities. 800-331-0304.

Dana Designs, 333 Simmental Way, Bozeman, MT 59715: Free list of retail sources ❖ Backpacks and external frames for men and women. 406-587-4188.

CAMPING & BACKPACKING

Design Salt, P.O. Box 1220, Redway, CA 95560: Free catalog ❖ Sleeping bags. 800-254-7258.

Diamond Brand Canvas Products, P.O. Box 249, Naples, NC 28760: Free list of retail sources ❖ Two and four-person tents. Also backpacks for men, women, and children. 800-258-9811.

Eagle Creek, 1740 La Costa Meadows Dr., San Marcos, CA 92069: Free list of retail sources ❖ Backpacks. 800-874-9925.

Early Winters, P.O. Box 4333, Portland, OR 97208: Free catalog ❖ Camping and backpacking clothing and equipment. 800-458-4438.

Eastern Mountain Sports Inc., One Vose Farm Rd., Peterborough, NH 03458: Free list of retail sources ❖ Camping equipment and outdoor clothing. 603-924-6154.

Eastpak, 50 Rogers Rd., P.O. Box 8232, Ward Hill, MA 01835: Free list of retail sources ❖ Backpacks that convert to a suitcase. 508-373-1581.

Ecotrek, P.O. Box 9638, Amherst, MA 01059: Free catalog ❖ Backpacks and apparel. 800-958-1383.

Envirogear Ltd., 127 Elm St., Cortland, NY 13045: Free catalog ❖ All-weather and all-terrain sleeping enclosures. 607-753-8801.

Eureka Tents, Johnson Worldwide Associates, Camping Division, P.O. Box 966, Binghamton, NY 13902: Free list of retail sources ❖ Backpacks and self-supporting tents. 800-848-3673.

EXQ Catalog, P.O. Box 50137, Colorado Springs, CO 80949: Free catalog ❖ Outdoor apparel and gear. 800-229-0945.

Feathered Friends Mail Order, 1415 10th Ave., Seattle, WA 98122: Free information ❖ Sleeping bags in short, regular, and long sizes. Options include Gore-Tex, down collar, overfill, and underfill. 206-328-0887.

Fieldline, 1919 Vineburn Ave., Los Angeles, CA 90032: Free brochure ❖ Backpacks. 213-226-0830.

Fiskars Incorporated, Gerber Legendary Blades Division, Customer Service, P.O. Box 23088, Portland, OR 97281: Free catalog ❖ Outdoor recreational products, knives, sheaths, pocket tools, and accessories. 503-639-6161.

Flaghouse Camping Equipment, 150 Macquesten Pkwy., Mt. Vernon, NY 10550: Free catalog ❖ Outdoor equipment. 800-221-5185.

Four Rivers, 244 Mid Rivers Center, Ste. 230, St. Peters, MO 63376: Catalog $3 ❖ Outdoor gear for campers, hunters, and fishermen.

Four Seasons Tentmasters, 4221 Livesay Rd., Sand Creek, MI 49279: Catalog $2 ❖ Tipis, wall and wedge tents, and marquees. Also camping equipment. 517-436-6245.

Frank's Center Inc., P.O. Box 530, Nevada, MO 64772: Catalog $2 ❖ Backpacking, camping, rescue/rappelling equipment, and sportshooting guns. 417-667-9190.

Gander Mountain Inc., P.O. Box 248, Gander Mountain, Wilmot, WI 53192: Free catalog ❖ Camping and other outdoor equipment, boats, archery supplies, knives, rifle reloading equipment and scopes, and hunting and fishing videos. 800-558-9410.

Garmont, Customer Service, One 2nd St., Peabody, MA 01960: Free information ❖ Boots, backpacks, and hiking poles. 800-556-8246.

Garuda Mountaineering, P.O. Box 24804, Seattle, WA 98124: Free catalog ❖ One, two, and three-person tents. 206-763-2989.

The Gearfitter Inc., 1520 Kensington Rd., Ste. 104, Oakbrook, IL 60521: Free information ❖ Outdoor equipment and accessories. 800-340-7077.

Don Gleason's Camping Supply Inc., 9 Pearl St., Northampton, MA 01060: Free catalog ❖ Camping and backpacking equipment. 413-584-4895.

Gold-Eck of Austria, 6313 Seaview Ave. NW, Seattle, WA 98107: Free catalog ❖ Sleeping bags. 206-781-0886.

Gorilla & Sons, P.O. Box 2309, Bellingham, WA 98227: Free catalog ❖ Outdoor apparel and equipment. 800-246-7455.

Gregory Mountain Products, 100 Calle Cortez, Temecula, CA 92390: Free list of retail sources ❖ External frame backpacks. 800-477-3420.

Henderson Camp Products Inc., Raleigh Rd., Box 867, Henderson, NC 27536: Free information ❖ Tents and sleeping bags. 800-547-4605; 919-492-6061 (in NC).

High Sierra, H. Bernbaum Import Export, 880 Corporate Woods, Vernon Hills, IL 60061: Free information ❖ Backpacks, dining utensils, sleeping bags, and other equipment. 800-323-9590; 708-913-1100 (in IL).

Integral Designs, P.O. Box 40023, Highfield Postal Outlet, Calgary, Alberta, Canada T2G 5G5: Free catalog ❖ Sleeping bags, tents, and outerwear. 403-640-1445.

James Kits, P.O. Box 933, 164 E. Deloney, Jackson, WY 83001: Free information ❖ Pocket survival kits. 800-396-KITS.

JanSport Inc., 10411 Airport Rd., Everett, WA 98204: Free list of retail sources ❖ Backpacks and sleeping bags. 800-552-6776.

Kelly's Camping, P.O. Box 602, Lindsay, CA 93247: Free catalog ❖ Backpacking, camping, and optical equipment. 800-69-KELLY.

Kelty Packs Inc., 1224 Fern Ridge Pkwy., St. Louis, MO 63141: Free list of retail sources ❖ Tents, sleeping bags, and backpacks that convert to luggage. 314-576-8069.

Lafuma Camping Equipment, 7034 Sofia Ave., Van Nuys, CA 91406: Free information ❖ Sleeping bags, backpacks, and two, three, and four-person tents. 800-514-4807.

Leatherman Tool Group Inc., P.O. Box 20595, Portland, OR 97220: Free information ❖ Compact folding multi-purpose tools for campers. 503-253-7826.

Leisure Outlet, 421 Soquel Ave., Santa Cruz, CA 95062: Free catalog ❖ Camping equipment and clothing. 800-322-1460.

❖ Leisure Pro ❖

Leisure Pro, 42 W. 18th St., 3rd Floor, New York, NY 10011: Free information ❖ Expedition and day packs, tents, sleeping bags, and accessories. Also scuba and tennis equipment. 212-645-1234.

Leki Sport USA, 60 Earhart Dr., Williamsville, NY 14221: Free information ❖ Trekking poles. 716-633-8062.

Lowe Alpine, P.O. Box 1449, Broomfield, CO 80038: Free list of retail sources ❖ Outdoor clothing, mountaineering fleecewear, and backpacks. 303-465-0522.

Madden Mountaineering, 2400 Central Ave., Boulder, CO 80301: Free catalog ❖ Backpacks and other equipment. 303-442-5828.

Mark One Distributors, 627 N. Morton, Bloomington, IN 47404: Free catalog ❖ Camping equipment, sporting goods, hardware and outdoor maintenance products, and safety aids. 800-869-9058.

Marmot Mountain Works, 827 Bellevue Way NE, Bellevue, WA 98004: Free catalog ❖ Sleeping bags. 800-254-6246.

McHale & Company, 29 Dravus St., Seattle, WA 98109: Catalog $2 ❖ Backpacks. 206-281-7861.

Mont-Bell, Catalog Customer Service, 940 1st Ave., Santa Cruz, CA 95062: Free catalog ❖ Outerwear, sleeping bags, backpacks, trekking packs, waterproof shell protection, and accessories. 800-683-2002.

Moonstone Factory Store, 1563 G St., Arcata, CA 95521: Free information ❖ Sleeping bags. 707-826-0851.

Moss Tents Inc., P.O. Box 248, Belfast, ME 04915: Free list of retail sources ❖ One, two, three, and four-person tents.

Mountain Equipment Inc., 4776 E. Jensen, Fresno, CA 93725: Free list of retail sources ❖ Adjustable backpacks. 209-486-8211.

Mountain Hardware, 950 Gilman St., Berkeley, CA 94710: Free list of retail sources ❖ Sleeping bags. 510-559-6700.

CAMPING & BACKPACKING

Mountainsmith, 18301 W. Colfax Ave., Heritage Square, Building P, Golden, CO 80401: Free catalog ❖ Backpacks, external frames, and two, four, and eight-person tents. 800-426-4075.

O.H. Mullen Sales Inc., RR 2, Oakwood, OH 45873: Free information ❖ Backpacks, dining utensils, knives, camping tools, sleeping bags, and other equipment. 800-258-6625.

Natural Balance, 503 S. Main, Fairfield, IA 52556: Catalog $2 ❖ Internal frame backpacks. 515-472-7918.

Nelson Weather-Rite Clothing, 14760 Santa Fe Trail Dr., Lenexa, KS 66215: Free list of retail sources ❖ Camouflage clothing and backpacks. 800-315-2267.

Nexco, Box 13081, Ogden, UT 84412: Free catalog ❖ Backpacking equipment. 800-597-4743.

Norland Trading Company, Box 10, Norland, Ontario, Canada K0M 2L0: Video catalog $5 (refundable) ❖ Hunting, fishing, and outdoor products. 800-318-0717.

North Face, 999 Harrison St., Berkeley, CA 94710: Free list of retail sources ❖ Backpacks, camping equipment, and sleeping bags. 800-447-2333.

Northwest River Supplies Inc., 2009 S. Main, Moscow, ID 83843: Free catalog ❖ Backpacks and equipment. 800-635-5202.

Only the Lightest Camping Equipment, P.O. Box 266, Troutdale, OR 97060: Catalog $1 ❖ Lightweight clothing and camping equipment. 503-666-9365.

OSI Direct, P.O. Box 4421, Burlingame, CA 94011: Free information ❖ Digital compass, altimeter, barometer, and thermometer watch. 800-533-0314.

Osprey Packs, P.O. Box 539, Dolores, CO 81323: Free catalog ❖ External frame backpacks. 303-882-2221.

Outbound Products, Box 56148, Hayward, CA 94546: Free list of retail sources ❖ Backpacks, sleeping bags, and two, three, and four-person tents. 800-866-9880.

Outdoor Outlet, 1062 E. Tabernacle, St. George, UT 84770: Free catalog ❖ Tents, backpacks, and sleeping bags. 800-726-8106.

Overland Equipment, 2145 Park Ave., Ste. 4, Chico, CA 95928: Free catalog ❖ Frame and saddle bags and backpacks. 800-487-8851.

Pachmayr Ltd., 831 N. Rosemead Blvd., South El Monte, CA 91733: Free catalog ❖ Shooting and hunting accessories, clothing, camping equipment, books, and video tapes. 800-350-7408.

Paddle & Pack Outfitters Inc., P.O. Box 50299, Nashville, TN 37205: Free catalog ❖ Canoeing, kayaking, and backpacking equipment. 800-786-5565.

Pop Tent, 8800 NW 23rd St., Miami, FL 33172: Free catalog ❖ Easy-to-open folding tents. 395-592-5600.

Premier International Inc., 901 N. Stuart St., Ste. 804, Arlington, VA 22203: Free catalog ❖ Backpacks with built-in rain covers. 800-354-5420.

Pyramid Cooking Equipment, American Innovation Marketing Inc., 3292 S. Hwy. 97, Redmond, OR 96656: Free brochure ❖ Outdoor cooking systems. 800-824-4288.

Ramsey Outdoor Store, 226 Rt. 17, P.O. Box 1689, Paramus, NJ 07653: Free catalog ❖ Camping and backpacking equipment. 800-526-7436; 201-261-5000 (in NJ).

Ranger Manufacturing Company Inc., P.O. Box 14069, Augusta, GA 30919: Free information ❖ Camouflage clothing. 800-847-3469.

REI Recreational Equipment Company, Sumner, WA 98352: Free catalog ❖ Exercise and walking shoes, Gore-Tex rain gear, day packs that convert to tents, ski equipment, gifts, knives and utensils, sunglasses, and camping foods. 800-426-4840.

Remington Outdoor Products, c/o Nelson/Weather-Rite, P.O. Box 14488, Lenexa, KS 66285: Free list of retail sources ❖ Backpacks, sleeping bags, and two, three, and four-person tents. 913-492-3200.

Royal Elk Sewing, 122 E. Main, Belgrade, MT 59714: Free catalog ❖ Fleece hunting packs, 3-D burlap archery targets, tents, tipis, and other equipment. 406-388-6850.

A.G. Russell Knife Company, 1705 Hwy. 71 B North, Springdale, AR 72764: Free catalog ❖ Knives and cutlery. 800-255-9034.

Safesport Outdoor Gear, 786 Wilson Rd., Newberry, SC 29108: Free catalog ❖ Knives, camping and hunter safety equipment, first aid supplies, snowshoes, and other gear. 800-433-6506.

Search Gear, 882 Bruce Ln., Chico, CA 95928: Free catalog ❖ Backpacking equipment and clothing, safety and first aid gear, and rescue equipment. 800-474-2612; 916-899-2612 (in CA).

Siemens Solar Industries, P.O. Box 6032, Camarillo, CA 93010: Free information ❖ Rechargeable solar-operated lantern. 800-272-6765.

Sierra Designs, 1255 Powell St., Emeryville, CA 94608: Free list of retail sources ❖ Lightweight two-person free-standing tent. 800-736-8551.

Sierra Trading Post, 5025 Campstool Rd., Cheyenne, WY 82007: Free catalog ❖ Outdoor clothing and equipment. 307-775-8000.

Sims Stoves, P.O. Box 21405, Billings, MT 59104: Free information ❖ Folding camp stoves, tents, pack saddles, books, and other equipment. 800-736-5259.

Slumberjack Inc., P.O. Box 7048, St. Louis, MO 63177: Free information ❖ Insulated sleeping bags. 800-233-6283.

The Sportsman's Guide, 411 Farwell Ave., South St. Paul, MN 55075: Free catalog ❖ Camping gear. 800-888-3006.

The Sportsman's Kitchen Inc., 3038 John Young Pkwy., Orlando, FL 32804: Free information ❖ Refrigerators, cooking equipment, tables, and knives. 800-435-9787.

Stephensons-Warmlite, 22 Hook Rd., Gilford, NH 03246: Catalog $1 ❖ Sleeping bags and two, three and four-person tents. 603-293-8526.

SunDog, 6700 S. Glacier St., Seattle, WA 98188: Free catalog ❖ Packs, bags, and cases for sports, travel, and photography. 800-634-0005.

Swallow's Nest, 2308 6th Ave., Seattle, WA 98121: Free catalog ❖ Backpacking, climbing, and mountaineering equipment. 800-676-4041; 206-441-4100 (in WA).

Tents & Trails, 21 Park Pl., New York, NY 10007: Free information ❖ Camping and mountaineering equipment and clothing. 800-237-1760; 212-227-1760 (in NY).

Texsport, P.O. Box 55326, Houston, TX 77255: Free information ❖ Backpacks, dining utensils, knives, camping tools, lanterns and flashlights, sleeping bags, and other equipment. 800-231-1402; 713-464-5551 (in TX).

Tough Traveler, 1012 State St., Schenectady, NY 12307: Free catalog ❖ Backpacks. 800-468-6844.

Trail Ridge Traders, 334 E. Mountain, Fort Collins, CO 80524: Free catalog ❖ New and used backpacking, climbing, and mountaineering equipment; operates trade-in program. 970-484-8895.

Traveling Light, Outback Oven, 1563 Solano Ave., Ste. 284, Berkeley, CA 94707: Free list of retail sources ❖ Fuel-efficient compact oven for outdoor use. 800-594-9154.

Trigon, 306 Westlake Ave. North, #313, Seattle, WA 98109: Free catalog ❖ Backpacks. 206-624-4453.

U.S. Cavalry, 2855 Centennial Ave., Radcliff, KY 40160: Free catalog ❖ Camping equipment. 800-908-9455.

Variety International, 1977 O'Toole Ave., San Jose, CA 95131: Free information ❖ Camping furniture. 800-700-1666.

Volcano Corporation, 3450 W. 8550 South, West Jordan, UT 84084: Free information ❖ All-purpose outdoor cook stove. 800-454-8304; 801-566-5496 (in UT).

Walrus Inc., 4225 2nd Ave. South, Seattle, WA 98134: Free information ❖ One, two, three, and four-person tents. 800-550-TENT.

CANDLES, CANDLE MAKING & CANDLE HOLDERS

Wenzel, P.O. Box 7048A, St. Louis, MO 63177: Free list of retail sources ❖ Padded shoulder strap-adjustable frame back pack, sleeping bags, tents, and accessories. 800-325-4121.

Wiggy's Inc., P.O. Box 2124, Grand Junction, CO 81502: Free information ❖ Sleeping bags and insulated clothing. 303-241-6465.

Wild Country USA, 230 E. Conway Rd., Center Conway, NH 03813: Free catalog ❖ Two, three, and four-person tents. 603-356-5590.

Wild Things, P.O. Box 400, North Conway, NH 03800: Free catalog ❖ Backpacks. 603-356-6907.

The Wilderness Wanderer, P.O. Box 2070, Kamloops, British Columbia, Canada V2B 7K6: Free information ❖ Modular backpack system. 604-376-9505.

Jack Wolfskin, P.O. Box 2487, Binghamton, NY 13902: Free list of retail sources ❖ Outerwear, backpacks, sleeping bags, tents, travel luggage, and outdoor equipment. 800-572-8822.

Wyoming River Raiders, P.O. Box 50490, Casper, WY 82605: Free catalog ❖ Outdoor clothing, camping and river expedition equipment, fishing gear, hiking equipment, books, and supplies. 800-247-6068.

ZZ Corporation, 10806 Kaylor St., Los Alamitos, CA 90720: Free information ❖ Woodburning backpacker stove. 800-594-9046.

Food

Adventure Foods, 481 Banjo Ln., Whittier, NC 28789: Free brochure ❖ Freeze-dried and dehydrated entree specialties. Also individual food items in bulk and vegetarian packaging. 704-497-4113.

AlpineAire, P.O. Box 926, Nevada City, CA 95959: Free information ❖ Freeze-dried and concentrated foods. 800-322-6325.

Full Circle Foods Inc., P.O. Box 451, North Conway, NH 03860: Free catalog ❖ Trail mixes, granola, and organic dried fruit.

Hardee, 579 Speers Rd., Oakville, Ontario, Canada L6K 2G4: Free price list ❖ Freeze-dried foods. 905-844-1471.

L.D.P. Foods, 1101 NW Evangeline, Lafayette, LA 70501: Free price list ❖ Freeze-dried foods. 800-826-5767.

Myers Meats, Rt. 1, Box 132, Parshall, ND 58770: Free information ❖ Original or peppered beef jerky and beef stick. 800-635-3759.

Nitro-Pak Preparedness Center, 151 N. Main St., Heber City, UT 84032: Catalog $3 ❖ Survival equipment and other supplies, **freeze-dried** and dehydrated foods, books, and **videos. 800-866-4876.**

Outdoor Kitchen, Box 1600, Nevada City, CA 95959: Free catalog ❖ Additive-free freeze-dried foods. 800-322-MEAL.

Piragis Northwoods Company, 105 N. Central Ave., Ely, MN 55731: Catalog $2 ❖ Canoes, boating gear, boats, videos and tapes, and trail foods. 800-223-6565.

REI Recreational Equipment Company, Sumner, WA 98352: Free catalog ❖ Exercise and walking shoes, Gore-Tex rain gear, day packs that convert to tents, shoes, ski equipment, gifts, knives and other utensils, sunglasses, and camping foods. 800-426-4840.

Richmoor Corporation, P.O. Box 8092, Van Nuys, CA 91409: Free information ❖ Freeze-dried and concentrated foods. 800-423-3170; 818-787-2510 (in CA).

Trail Foods Company, 12455 Branford St., Arleta, CA 91331: Free catalog ❖ Two and four-person meal pouches. 818-897-4370.

Uncle John's Foods, P.O. Box 489, Fairplay, CO 80440: Free information ❖ Freeze-dried foods. 800-530-8733.

Wee-Pak, Knightsbridge International, P.O. Box 6189, Sun Valley, ID 83354: Free information ❖ Freeze-dried foods. 800-622-8519.

CANDLES, CANDLE MAKING & CANDLE HOLDERS

American Candle Classics, 19 E. Martin St., Allentown, PA 18103: Free brochure ❖ Classic-style candles with a choice of scents and colors. 610-791-7768.

Amigos, P.O. Box 720024, McAllen, TX 78504: Free brochure ❖ Italian mosaic illuminating candle holders. 800-752-0046.

Angel's Earth, 1633 Scheffer Ave., St. Paul, MN 55116: Catalog $2 ❖ Soaps, candles, cosmetics, incense, skin care preparations, essential oils, and other aromatherapy items. 612-698-3601.

B & B Honey Farm, Rt. 2, Box 245, Houston, MN 55943: Free catalog ❖ Beekeeping and candle-making supplies. 507-896-3955.

Barker Enterprises Inc., 15106 10th Ave. SW, Seattle, WA 98166: Catalog $2 ❖ Candle-making supplies and molds. 800-543-0601.

Jack Brubaker Designs, 2900 Shepherd Rd., Nashville, IN 47448: Free catalog ❖ Forged metal candle holders and wine racks. 812-988-7830.

Busy Bee Products, P.O. Box 143, Horseheads, NY 14845: Free information ❖ Beeswax candles in a choice of colored tapers or pillars. 607-796-2432.

The Candle Factory, 4411 South IH 35, Georgetown, TX 78626: Free catalog ❖ Hand-dipped tapers, dinner and novelty candles, machine-made and molded decorative pillars, and wax potpourri chips. 512-863-6025.

Candlechem Products, 32 Thayer Circle, P.O. Box 705, Randolph, MA 02368: Catalog $1 ❖ Oils, perfume oils, dyes, and other scents for making candles and perfumery items. 508-586-0844.

Country Charm Inc., 322 S. Main St., Plymouth, MI 48170: Catalog $2 ❖ Long-burning candles and decorative country craft accessories. 800-288-5699; 313-455-9292 (in MI).

D'lights Candles & Scents, RR 1, Box 148-C, Oak Hill, WV 25901: Free information ❖ Hand-rolled beeswax candles.

Gardens Past, P.O. Box 1846, Estes Park, CO 80517: Catalog $1 ❖ Soaps and soap-making supplies, dried flowers, potpourri, herbs, candles, and aromatherapy items. 303-823-5565.

The Glowing Candle Factory, 131 W. 33rd, National City, CA 91950: Free information ❖ Handcrafted decorated candles. 800-622-6353.

K & L Candles, 12 Barden Ln., P.O. Box 322, Warren, RI 02885: Catalog $3 (refundable) ❖ In-stock and custom-made candles. 800-886-5338; 401-245-4460 (in RI).

The Keeping Room, P.O. Box 1573, Beaver Falls, PA 15010: Brochure $2 ❖ Heavy metal, Amish-made lantern-like votive holders. 412-843-2459.

Mann Lake Supply, County Rd. 40 & 1st St., Hackensack, MN 56452: Free catalog ❖ Beekeeping and honey production equipment, protective clothing, candle molds and kits, and how-to books. 800-233-6663.

Mid-Continent Agrimarketing Inc., 8883 Lenexa Dr., Overland Park, KS 66215: Free catalog ❖ Beekeeping and candle-making supplies. 800-547-1392.

MoonAcre IronWorks, 62 Chambersburg St., Gettysburg, PA 17325: Catalog $2 ❖ Simulated pewter candle holders. 800-966-4766.

Moonlight Lane Inc., P.O. Box 20747, Bradenton, FL 34203: Brochure $1 (refundable) ❖ Environmentally safe handcrafted beeswax candles. 941-755-5719.

Nasco, 901 Janesville Ave., Fort Atkinson, WI 53538: Free catalog ❖ Candle-making supplies. 800-558-9595.

Nelson Candle & Beeswax Co., 506 Blarney St., Havelock, NC 28532: Catalog $2 ❖ Precious fragrances blended with Carolina beeswax and pureed into decorative containers. 919-447-0969.

North Country Crafts, P.O. Box 500, Marinette, WI 54143: Free information ❖ Fragrance candles in collectible tins. 800-637-7989.

Pourette Manufacturing, P.O. Box 17056, Seattle, WA 98107: Catalog $2 ❖ Soap and candle-making supplies.

CANDY MAKING & CAKE DECORATING

Soap Saloon, 7309 Sage Oak Ct., Citrus Heights, CA 95621: Catalog $2 ❖ Soap and candle-making supplies. 916-723-6859.

Teasel, 46 Main St., Middlebury, VT 05753: Free information ❖ Lingerie, fine soaps and toiletries, potpourri, and candles. 800-300-1204.

Traditional Country Crafts, Box 66, Mount Joy, PA 17552: Brochure $1 ❖ Pennsylvania Amish-dipped candles in old-fashioned colors and sizes. 717-653-5969.

CANDY MAKING & CAKE DECORATING

Assouline & Ting Inc., 314 Brown St., Philadelphia, PA 19123: Free information ❖ Cocoa powder and chocolate couverture. 800-521-4491; 215-627-3000 (in PA).

Epicurean Traders, P.O. Box 5107, Newport Beach, CA 92662: Free information ❖ Fat and cholesterol-free meringue mix. 800-490-6509.

Holcraft Collection, 211 El Cajon Ave., P.O. Box 792, Davis, CA 95616: Catalog $2 ❖ Molds for making chocolate candy. 916-756-3023.

Josey B. (U.S.A.) Corporation, 823 Asbury Ct., San Jose, CA 95126: Free information ❖ Imported pure German chocolate. 408-297-8225.

Kitchen Krafts, Box 442, Waukon, IA 52172: Free catalog ❖ Cake decorating, candy-making, and bread and pie baking supplies. 800-776-0575.

Lorann Oils, P.O. Box 22009, Lansing, MI 48909: Free information ❖ Supplies for making suckers and other hard candies. 800-862-8620.

Meadow's Chocolate & Cake Supplies, P.O. Box 448, Richmond Hill, NY 11419: Catalog $2 ❖ Candy-making and cake-decorating supplies. 718-835-3600.

Paradigm Foodworks, 5775 SW Jean Rd., Ste. 106A, Lake Oswego, OR 97034: Catalog $1 (refundable) ❖ Chocolate for bakers and candy makers. 800-234-0250.

Parrish's Cake Decorating, 225 W. 146th St., Gardena, CA 90248: Tools and equipment catalog $3, cake novelties and wedding decorations catalog $3, candy mold catalog $1 ❖ Cake decorating and candy-making supplies.

Albert Uster Imports Inc., 9211 Gaither Rd., Gaithersburg, MD 20877: Free catalog ❖ Chocolate couverture, cocoa powder, disposable pastry bags, and candy boxes. 800-231-8154; 301-258-7350 (in MD).

Wilton Enterprise Inc., 2240 W. 75th St., Woodbridge, IL 60517: Catalog $6 (refundable) ❖ Supplies for making candy, cookies, and cakes. 708-963-7100.

CANES, WALKERS & HIKING STICKS

American Foundation for the Blind Inc., Product Center, 3342 Melrose Ave., Roanoke, VA 24017: Free catalog ❖ Canes, watches, and clocks, household and personal care supplies, and other aids for visually impaired persons. 800-829-0500.

American Walker Inc., 900 Market St., Oregon, WI 53575: Free information ❖ Wheeled walkers and walk-a-cycles. 800-828-6808.

Cascade Designs Inc., 4000 1st Ave. South, Seattle, WA 98134: Free information ❖ Adjustable walking staffs. 800-531-9531.

DutchGuard, P.O. Box 411687, Kansas City, MO 64141: Free catalog ❖ Gadget and flask canes and secrecy sticks in lustrous hardwoods and exotics with optional silver, brass, gold, and wooden heads. 800-821-5157.

ETAC USA, 2325 Parklawn Dr., Ste. J, Waukesha, WI 53186: Free brochure ❖ Walking aids, bath safety equipment, wheelchairs, and accessories that make daily living easier. 800-678-3822.

Garmont, Customer Service, One 2nd St., Peabody, MA 01960: Free information ❖ Boots, backpacks, and hiking poles. 800-556-8246.

The Gathering Place, 868 15th St., P.O. Box 163, Otsego, MI 49078: Free information ❖ Hardwood walking, hiking, and jogging sticks. Also gourd art. 616-694-4477.

Guardian Products Inc., 4175 Guardian St., Simi Valley, CA 93063: Free catalog ❖ Walkers, crutches, canes, home activity aids, beds, lifters, ramps, and transporting equipment. 800-255-5022.

House of Canes, P.O. Box 574, Wilderville, OR 97543: Catalog $1 ❖ Walking sticks and staffs in wrist, elbow, and shoulder lengths. 800-458-5920.

Miles Kimball Company, 41 W. 8th Ave., Oshkosh, WI 54906: Free catalog ❖ Canes and aids for people with physical disabilities. 800-546-2255.

Leki Sport USA, 60 Earhart Dr., Williamsville, NY 14221: Free brochure ❖ Hiking and trekking poles. 716-633-8062.

Momentum, Medical Corporation, 964 S. 200 West, Ste. 3, Salt Lake City, UT 84101: Free information ❖ Canes and quads with extra-leverage handles for easier standing up from a seated position. 800-644-2263.

NobleMotion Inc., P.O. Box 5366, Pittsburgh, PA 15206: Free information ❖ Adjustable and folding rolling walker with seat, basket, and optional tray. 800-234-9255.

Poestenkill Hiking Staff, P.O. Box 300, Poestenkill, NY 12140: Catalog $1 ❖ Victorian-style cane replicas. 518-279-3011.

Tracks Walking Staffs, 4000 1st Ave. South, Seattle, WA 98134: Free information ❖ Telescoping walking staffs. 800-527-1527.

The Umbrella Shop, 233 E. Wacker Dr., Apt. 1112, Chicago, IL 60601: Catalog $2 ❖ Umbrellas and walking sticks.

Uncle Sam Umbrella Shop, 161 W. 57th St., New York, NY 10019: Free catalog ❖ Umbrellas, canes, and walking sticks. 212-247-7163.

Walk Easy Inc., 2915 S. Congress Ave., Delray Beach, FL 33445: Free brochure ❖ Crutches, walkers, commode chairs, and regular, tripod, and quad canes. 800-441-2904.

Whistle Creek, 4576 Claire Chennault, Dallas, TX 75248: Free information ❖ Handcrafted hardwood hiking and walking sticks. 214-931-1917.

CANNING & PRESERVING

Alltrista Corporation, P.O. Box 2005, Muncie, IN 47307: Free catalog ❖ Home canning and easy-to-make jams and jellies supplies. 800-240-3340.

Berry-Hill Limited, 75 Burwell Rd., St. Thomas, Ontario, Canada N5P 3R5: Catalog $2 ❖ Canning supplies, weather vanes, cider press, and garden tools. 519-631-0480.

Farmer Seed & Nursery Company, 818 NW 4th St., Faribault, MN 55021: Free catalog ❖ Canning supplies. 507-334-1623.

Gardener's Supply Company, 128 Intervale Rd., Burlington, VT 05401: Free catalog ❖ Garden carts, composters, sprayers, watering systems, weeding and cultivating tools, organic fertilizers and other chemical preparations, leaf mulchers, canning and preserving supplies, and furniture. 800-688-5510.

Gurney Seed & Nursery Company, 110 Capitol St., Yankton, SD 57079: Free catalog ❖ Canning supplies. 605-665-1671.

Heritage Home Canning, P.O. Box 722722, San Diego, CA 92172: Free catalog ❖ Home canning supplies.

Home Canning Supply, P.O. Box 1158, Ramona, CA 92065: Catalog $1 ❖ Canning supplies and equipment.

Kitchen Krafts, Box 442, Waukon, IA 52172: Free information ❖ Canning and food preservation supplies. 800-776-0575.

❖ CARNIVAL SUPPLIES ❖

Earl May Seeds & Nursery Company, N. Elm St., Shenandoah, IA 51603: Free catalog ❖ Canning supplies. 712-246-1020.

Mellinger's Inc., 2310 W. South Range Rd., North Lima, OH 44452: Free catalog ❖ Canning supplies. 330-549-9861.

Modern Homesteader, 1825 Big Horn Ave., Cody, WY 82414: Free catalog ❖ Canning supplies. 800-443-4934; 307-587-5946 (in WY).

CARNIVAL SUPPLIES

Allen-Lewis Manufacturing Company, Division TCC Industries Inc., P.O. Box 16546, 5601 Logan, Denver, CO 80216: Free catalog ❖ Souvenirs, carnival and party supplies, fund-raising merchandise, toys and games, T-shirts and sweatshirts, and craft supplies. 303-295-0196.

Oriental Trading Company Inc., P.O. Box 3407, Omaha, NE 68103: Free catalog ❖ Toys, gifts, novelties, fund raisers, holiday and seasonal items, and other carnival supplies. 800-327-9678.

B. Palmer Sales Company Inc., 3510 Wyw. 80 East, P.O. Box 850247, Mesquite, TX 75185: Free catalog ❖ Carnival, fund-raising, and party supplies. 800-888-3087; 214-288-1026 (in TX).

U.S. Toy Company Inc., 1227 E. 119th St., Grandview, MO 64030: Catalog $3 ❖ Carnival supplies, prizes, and games. 800-448-7830; 816-761-5900 (in MO).

CAROUSEL FIGURES & ART

Americana Antiques, Rusty & Emmy Donohue, P.O. Box 650, Oxford, MD 21654: Catalog $7.50 ❖ Antique wooden carousel horses and menagerie figures. 410-226-5677.

Americana Carousel Collection, 3645 NW 67th St., Miami, FL 33147: Catalog $5 ❖ Authentic reproductions of carousel horses, from 1915 to 1927. 800-852-0494.

Amusement Arts, P.O. Box 1158, Burlington, CT 06013: Free price list with long SASE ❖ Antique carousel figures. 860-675-7653.

Stuart & Mel Bond, HCR 60, Box 1092, Seaside, OR 97138: Free information ❖ Hand-carved carousel animals. 503-755-2905.

Dave Boyle, 150 Andrews Trace, New Castle, PA 16102: Free brochure ❖ Carousel animals. 412-657-8181.

The Carousel at Casino Pier, Boardwalk & Sherman Ave., Seaside Heights, NJ 08751: Free brochure ❖ Carousel reproductions, music boxes, books, T-shirts, cotton throws, miniatures, and jewelry. 908-830-4183.

The Carousel Lady, 1350 Vista Way, Red Bluff, CA 96080: Brochure $3 (refundable) ❖ Carousel posters. 916-347-6985.

Carousel Shopper, Box 6459, Santa Fe, NM 87502: Catalog $2.50 ❖ Carousel collectibles, restoration supplies, books, posters, and other hsrd-to-find items.

Carousel Workshop, 218 S. High St., DeLand, FL. 32720: Catalog $3 ❖ Reproduction and antique carousel collectibles. 904-738-4229.

Carrousel Magic, P.O. Box 1466, Mansfield, OH 44901: Catalog $1 ❖ Hand-carved carousel horses and menagerie figures. Also carving kits and accessories. 419-526-4009.

Steve Crescenze, 8480 Gunston Rd., Welcome, MD 20693: Free list with long SASE ❖ Restored and reproduction carousel figures. 301-932-2734.

Frederick & Sons Custom Wood Carving, 1248 W. Bridge St., Spring City, PA 19475: Free brochure ❖ Carved wooden carousel animals. 610-948-2254.

Bill Gagne, 8 N. Munroe Terr., Dorchester, MA 02122: Free information ❖ Accessories and miniature carousel components. 617-265-6132.

Ken Gross, 7232 Steam Corners Rd., Steam Corners, OH 44904: Free information ❖ Carousel restoration services.

Marlene Irvin, P.O. Box 771331, Wichita, KS 67277: Free information ❖ One-of-a-kind hand-carved carousel horses. 316-722-1872.

J & M Carousel, Jack & Meg Hurt, 1711 Calavaras Dr., Santa Rosa, CA 95405: Free list with long SASE ❖ Restoration supplies. 800-789-1026.

Layton Studios, Joyce A. Hughes, 115 N. Marsh Rd., Savannah, GA 31410: Free information ❖ Restored carousel horses. 912-897-1901.

Merry-Go-Art, 2606 Jefferson, Joplin, MO 64804: Free list with long SASE ❖ Antique and restored carousel figures. 417-624-7281.

Merry-Go-Round Antiques, Al Rappaport, 29541 Roan Dr., Warren, MI 48093: Free information with long SASE ❖ Antique carousel figures. 810-751-8078.

Miniature Carousel Components, 8 N. Munroe Terrace, Dorchester, MA 02122: Free brochure with long SASE ❖ Drive mechanisms and parts. 617-265-6132.

Rader's Horse House, 2277 Ogden Rd., Wilmington, OH 45177: Free list with long SASE ❖ Antique carousel horses. 513-382-3266 (evenings).

Shriver's Carving Kits, 502 Barclay, Dewey, OK 74029: Free catalog with long SASE ❖ Kits for carving carousel miniatures with base and hardware for mounting. 918-534-2730.

The Spirited Steeds, 3001 S. 45th St., Phoenix, AZ 85040: Catalog $3 ❖ Carousel art. 602-894-0494.

Vestal Press Ltd., P.O. Box 97, Vestal, NY 13851: Catalog $2 ❖ Posters, recordings, and books about carousels. 607-797-4872.

Wonder Products Inc., 465 Hamilton Rd., Bossier City, LA 71111: Free catalog ❖ Unpainted carousel and western-style horses for crafters. 318-742-1100.

Zon International Publishing Company, P.O. Box 6459, Santa Fe, NM 87502: Catalog $2.50 ❖ Blueprints for carving your own carousel figures. 800-266-5767.

CDS, CASSETTES & RECORDS

Archival Supplies

Andy's Record Supplies, 48 Colonial Rd., Providence, RI 02906: Free information with two 1st class stamps ❖ Album cardboard jackets, blister packs, storage boxes, record sleeves, and other archival supplies. 401-421-9453.

Bags Unlimited Inc., 7 Canal St., Rochester, NY 14608: Free information ❖ Collection Protection. Storage boxes, poly bags, divider cards, acid free boards, mailers for comics, LPs, CDs, posters, and magazines. 800-767-BAGS.

Something Special Enterprises, P.O. Box 74, Allison Park, PA 15101: Free information ❖ Archival supplies. 412-487-2626.

Children's Recordings

Music for Little People, P.O. Box 1720, Lawndale, CA 90260: Free catalog ❖ Musical cassettes and videos of famous stories, favorite songs, lullabies, nature stories, and folk and classical music. 800-727-2233.

Collectible Recordings

Ace Video & Music, 285 Caillavet St., P.O. Box 1934, Biloxi, MS 39530: Catalog $5 ❖ Collectible vinyl records in all categories. 601-374-0777.

The Album Hunter, P.O. Box 510, Maple Shade, NJ 08052: Catalog $5 ❖ Rare LPs, 45s, and 76s. 609-482-2273.

Axe Wound Records, 872 S. Broadway, Hicksville, NY 11801: Free information (specify interest) ❖ Collectible records and imports. 516-942-1733.

Benedikt & Salmon Record Rarities, 3020 Meade Ave., San Diego, CA 92116: Free catalogs (indicate choice of (1) classical, (2) jazz, big-bands, and blues, (3) personalities, soundtracks, and country music) ❖ Hard-to-find rare records from 1890 to date, early phonographs, cylinders, autographed memorabilia, and rare books on music and the performing arts. 619-281-3345.

C.D.I. Imports, P.O. Box 471, Lincoln, MA 01773: Catalog $5 ❖ Imported live concert CDs and videos. 617-259-9155.

❖ CDS, CASSETTES & RECORDS ❖

California Albums, P.O. Box 3426, Hollywood, CA 90078: Free information ❖ Collectible records. 213-461-9806.

Carousel Records, P.O. Box 427, Sun Prairie, WI 53500: Free information ❖ Western and cowboy songs. 800-424-4445.

CD Wherehouse, 4779 Transit Rd., Apt. 11-172, Depew, NY 14043: Catalog $1 ❖ Rare CDs.

Collectables Records, Box 35, Narberth, PA 19072: Free catalog ❖ Rhythm and blues records from the 1970s.

Coronet Books, CDs & Cassettes, 311 Bainbridge St., Philadelphia, PA 19147: Catalog $2 ❖ Rhythm, classical, blues, big-band, soundtracks, Broadway musicals, rock, and other recordings. 215-925-2762.

Don Records, 27 Grand Ave., Farmingdale, NY 11735: Catalog $2 ❖ Current and hard-to-find 45rpm records. 516-752-1770.

Encore Records, P.O. Box 410126, St. Louis, MO 63141: Catalog $1 (refundable) ❖ 45rpm records. 314-434-4121.

Flipside Records, 215 Arch St., Meadville, PA 16335: Free information ❖ Music and other vintage sounds from the 1920s to the 1980s, and later.

45's, Box 358, Lemoyne, PA 17043: Catalog $2 with long SASE ❖ Hard-to-find 45rpm records.

Fox Music, 127 N. Main St., Oconomowoc, WI 53066: Free information ❖ Rare and collectible LPs and 45s. Also new and used domestic and imported CDs. 414-567-2997.

Bob Getreuer, P.O. Box 582, Nanuet, NY 10954: Catalog $1 ❖ Long-playing records, 45s, compact disks, and tapes, from the 1940s to the 1980s. 914-352-5259.

Golden Oldies, Music Exchange, 2297 Peachtree Rd., Atlanta, GA 30309: Free catalog ❖ Records, CDs, and tapes. Also specializes in 45rpm records for jukeboxes. 404-352-1311.

Good As Any...Better 'n Some, P.O. Box 88, Franklin, PA 16323: Catalog $1 ❖ Vinyl and CD collectibles. 814-437-5154.

Graceland Records, 2036 Dixie Garden Loop, Holiday, FL 34690: Free price list with long SASE ❖ Elvis records, tapes, compact disks, and memorabilia. 813-942-1935.

Granny's Turntable, P.O. Box 1585, Hendersonville, TN 37077: Catalog $3 ❖ Country and western record albums and cassette tapes.

Larry's Records, 25 S. State Rd. 7, Plantation, FL 33317: Free information ❖ Rare and collectible 45s, LPs, 12-inch singles, and imported CDs. 800-551-9070.

Mainly Music, 36 Main St., Brattleboro, VT 05301: Catalog $3 ❖ CDs, tapes and new, used, and rare records. Also vintage sheet music and other memorabilia and collectibles. 802-257-0881.

Manchester/Manchester, 1711 S. Willow St., Manchester, NH 03103: Catalog $2 ❖ Out-of-print and used records, compact disks, and tapes. 603-644-0199.

Metro Music, P.O. Box 10004, Silver Spring, MD 20904: Free catalog with two 1st class stamps ❖ Collectible records, LPs, and CDs. 301-622-2473.

Mountain Musicrafts, Jeanalee Schilling Inc., 267 South Hwy. 32, P.O. Box 8, Cosby, TN 37722: Free catalog ❖ Dulcimer CDs and cassettes. 615-487-5543.

Music Box Melodies, Panchronia Antiquities, P.O. Box 210, Whitehall, NY 12887: Catalog $1 ❖ Popular, classical, waltz, marches, and show tunes, from the 1850s to 1990s. Includes carousel band organs, calliopes, street organs, European fair organs, orchestrions, street pianos, disk and cylinder musical boxes, and monkey organs. 518-282-9770.

Oldies Unlimited, 5913 Main St., Williamsville, NY 14221: Free information ❖ Hard-to-find records. 716-631-0257.

Pack Central Inc., 6745 Denny Ave., North Hollywood, CA 91606: Catalog $2 ❖ Records and cassettes from the 1950s, 1960s, 1970s, and 1980s. 818-760-2828.

Park Avenue Record Planet, 532 Queen Anne Avenue North, Seattle, WA 98109: Free information ❖ Out-of-print records, rare LPs, CDs, and imports. 206-283-4446.

Right Hemisphere, 19 S. Jackson St., Media, PA 19063: Free information ❖ Records, tapes, compact disks, imports, and independents, from the 1960s and 1970s. Also out-of-print collectibles. 215-566-1322.

Roanoke's Record Room, P.O. Box 2445, Roanoke, VA 24010: Free price list ❖ Out-of-print 10 and 12-inch rock and pop long-playing records, from 1949 to 1992. 540-343-9570.

Rock Classics, 1511 E. Babydoll Rd., Port Orchard, WA 98366: Catalog $1 ❖ Rock classics on compact disks, from the 1950s, 1960s, and 1970s. 360-769-0456.

Rock Island, 114 W. Fletcher Ave., Tampa, FL 33612: Free information ❖ Collectible recordings. 813-933-2823.

The Soar Corporation, P.O. Box 8606, Albuquerque, NM 87198: Free catalog ❖ Contemporary and traditional Native American music. 505-268-6110.

John Tefteller, P.O. Box 1727, Grants Pass, OR 97526: Free information ❖ Rhythm and blues, rockabilly, rock-and-roll, country music, and other rare 45s, 78s, and a few long-playing records. 503-476-1326.

Time Machine Music & Video, P.O. Box 6961, Metairie, LA 70009: Free information ❖ Hard-to-find music and video recordings.

Unique Record Club, Flaming Star Ranch, 10933 E. Elmwood St., Apache Junction, AZ 85220: Catalog $10 ❖ Elvis rarities. 602-984-5026.

Current Recordings

Acoustic Sounds, P.O. Box 1905, Salina, KS 67402: Catalog $3 ❖ Classical, waltzes, rhythm, Latin American, and other recordings. Includes compact disks. 800-525-1630; 913-825-8609 (in KS).

Alligator Records, P.O. Box 60234, Chicago, IL 60660: Free catalog ❖ Blues and rock CDs, cassettes, and LPs. 800-344-5609.

❖ AMI Music ❖

AMI Music, P.O. Box 72124, Marietta, GA 30007: Two free catalogs (specify interest) ❖ (1) "Classic & Contemporary Jazz & Blues" (traditional jazz blues and Big Band hits prior to 1980); (2) "New World of Music" (new age, jazz fusion, smooth jazz, and others). 770-977-4172.

Andy's Front Hall, P.O. Box 307, Voorheesville, NY 12186: Free catalog ❖ Domestic and imported cassettes and CDs. 518-765-4193.

June Appal Recordings, 306 Madison St., Whitesburg, KY 41858: Free brochure ❖ Traditional and folk music cassettes and CDs. 606-633-0108.

Arhoolie Records, 10341 San Pablo Ave., El Cerrito, CA 94530: Catalog $1 ❖ Old-time folk lyric blues and classics, specializing in regional music. 510-525-7471.

Audio-Forum, 96 Broad St., Guilford, CT 06437: Free catalog ❖ Full-length courses for teaching yourself a foreign language. 800-448-7671; 203-453-9794 (in CT).

Audio House Compact Disk Club, 4304 Brayan Dr., Swartz Creek, MI 48473: Catalog $2 (refundable) ❖ Used compact disks. 810-655-8639.

Axe Wound Records, 872 S. Broadway, Hicksville, NY 11801: Free information (specify interest) ❖ Collectible records and imports. 516-942-1733.

Rediscover Music Catalogue, 705 S. Washington St., Naperville, IL 60540: Catalog $3 ❖ Hard-to-find CDs from the 1950s and 1960s. 800-232-7328.

Barnes & Noble, 126 5th Ave., New York, NY 10011: Free catalog ❖ Records, cassettes, and books. 800-242-6657.

CDS, CASSETTES & RECORDS

The Beautiful Music Company, 320 Main St., Northport, NY 11768: Free catalog ❖ Bluegrass and country, marches, instrumentals, jazz, gospel, big bands and favorite artists, classics and opera, and barbershop quartet recordings.

Berkshire Record Outlet Inc., RR 1, Lee, MA 01238: Catalog $2 ❖ Classical recordings. 413-243-4080.

Bernel Music Ltd., 798 Pressley Creek Rd., P.O. Box 2438, Cullowhee, NC 28723: Free catalog ❖ Brass band compact disks. 704-293-9312.

Blind Pig Records, P.O. Box 2344, San Francisco, CA 94126: Free catalog ❖ Blues records, CDs, and cassettes. 415-550-6484.

Boogie Music, P.O. Box 2054, San Mateo, CA 94401: Free list ❖ LPs and 45s from 1950 to 1990.

C.D.I. Imports, P.O. Box 471, Lincoln, MA 01773: Catalog $5 ❖ Imported live concert CDs and videos. 617-259-4371.

CD Research, Mail Order Department, 407 G St., Davis, CA 95616: Catalog $3 ❖ New and used CDs. 916-756-9499.

Classic Recordings, 2954 28th St. SE, Southridge Center, Grand Rapids, MI 49512: Free information ❖ Compact and laser disks. 800-433-8979; 616-957-3614 (in MI).

Coin Machine Trader, P.O. Box 602, Huron, SD 57350: Information $4 ❖ 45rpm records for most jukeboxes. 605-352-7590.

Collectors' Choice Music, P.O. Box 838, Itasca, IL 60143: Free catalog ❖ Popular and hard-to-find music recordings. 800-494-2211.

Concord Records Inc., P.O. Box 845, Concord, CA 94522: Free catalog ❖ Classical recordings on compact disks. 800-551-5299.

Coronet Books, CDs & Cassettes, 311 Bainbridge St., Philadelphia, PA 19147: Catalog $2 ❖ Compact disks and cassettes. 215-925-2762.

Country Music Hall of Fame, 4 Music Square East, Nashville, TN 37203: Catalog $2 ❖ Cajun, bluegrass, old-time and early country classics, country fiddling, western swing and cowboy, Elvis Presley and rock, gospel, and Christmas albums, cassettes, compact disks, books about country music, and song books. 800-255-2357; 615-256-1639 (in TN).

Ken Crane's, 15251 Beach Blvd., Westminster, CA 92683: Free catalog ❖ Laser disks. 800-624-3078; 800-626-1768 (in CA).

Critics' Choice Video, P.O. Box 749, Itasca, IL 60143: Free catalog ❖ Records, tapes, video cassettes, and books. 800-544-9852.

Diamond Needle Enterprises, 3550 Wilshire Blvd., Ste. 1500, Los Angeles, CA 90010: Free catalog ❖ Audiophiles, imports, and domestic recordings. 800-296-DISC.

DISCollection, P.O. Box 501832, Indianapolis, IN 46250: Free catalog ❖ Classical, soundtrack, and vocal CDs. 800-551-3472; 317-845-9212 (in IN).

Double-Time Jazz, Jamey & Julia Aebersold, P.O. Box 1244, New Albany, IN 47151: Free catalog ❖ Jazz records and videos.

Earwig Music Company Inc., 1818 W. Pratt Blvd., Chicago, IL 60626: Catalog $1 ❖ Traditional and modern blues recordings. 312-262-0278.

Effective Learning Systems Inc., 5255 Edina Industrial Blvd., Edina, MN 55439: Free catalog ❖ Self-improvement tapes. 800-966-5683.

Evidence Music Inc., 1100 E. Hector St., Ste. 392, Conshohocken, PA 19428: Free catalog ❖ Blues and jazz CDs. 610-832-0844.

Express Trax Accompaniment Tapes, P.O. Box 382945, Franklin, TN 37068: Free catalog ❖ Sound-alike sing-along professional accompaniment cassettes. 800-844-8273.

Fishbite Recordings, Box 280632, San Francisco, CA 94128: Free catalog ❖ Hammered and mountain dulcimer, Celtic, old-time, and other traditional recordings. Also dulcimers and how-to information.

Folk-Legacy Records Inc., Box 1148, 85 Sharon Mountain Rd., Sharon, CT 06069: Free information ❖ Country folk music on records, compact disks, and cassettes. 800-836-0901; 860-364-5661 (in CT).

Fort Brooke Quartermaster, Brandon B. Barszcz, P.O. Box 1628, Brandon, FL 33509: Catalog $2 ❖ Native American, square dancing, and other cassettes and CDs. 813-621-7256.

Four BAR B Records Inc., Box 7-11, Macks Creek, MO 65786: Free list ❖ Square dancing records. 314-363-5432.

Fox Music, 127 N. Main St., Oconomowoc, WI 53066: Free information ❖ Rare and collectible LPs and 45s. Also new and used domestic and imported CDs. 414-567-2997.

Full Circle Records, 279 Road 41, Blackwood, NJ 08012: Free information ❖ New and used CDs, imported recordings, other records, and videos. 609-227-0662.

Gambler's Book Shop, 630 S. 11th, Las Vegas, NV 89101: Free catalog ❖ Cassettes on how to achieve personal success, succeed in the stock market, business, finance and how to win at sports betting, poker, blackjack, keno, baccarat, craps, and roulette. 800-522-1777.

Robert Gentry, P.O. Box 850, Many, LA 71449: Free list ❖ Country music albums, 78 and 45 rpm records, autographs, movie posters, books and magazines, press kits, and other collectibles.

Golden Gallery, P.O. Box 267, Strausstown, PA 19559: Free information ❖ Imported and domestic CDs. 717-933-5361.

Good As Any...Better 'n Some, P.O. Box 88, Franklin, PA 16323: Free catalog ❖ Vinyl records and CDs. 814-437-5154.

Good Music Record Company, P.O. Box 1935, Ridgely, MD 21681: Free catalog ❖ CDs, cassettes, and videos.

Granny's Turntable, P.O. Box 1585, Hendersonville, TN 37077: Catalog $3 ❖ Country and western record albums and cassette tapes. 615-822-8675.

H & B Recordings, 12037 Starcrest, San Antonio, TX 78247: Free catalog ❖ Classical and jazz CDs and video cassettes. 800-222-6872.

Heartland Music, 605 S. Douglas St., Box 1034, El Segundo, CA 90245: Free catalog ❖ Big-band, nostalgic, patriotic, romantic, inspirational, gospel, rock-and-roll, country, and easy listening music. 800-788-2400.

High Water Recording Company, c/o Dr. David Evans, Dept. of Music, Memphis State University, Memphis, TN 38152: Free catalog ❖ Deep South blues on LPs and 45s.

Homespun Tapes, Box 694, Woodstock, NY 12498: Free catalog ❖ Blues video and audio cassettes. 800-33-TAPES.

The House of Music, 2057 W. 95th St., Chicago, IL 60643: Free information ❖ Hard-to-find records, tapes, CDs, and videos. 312-239-4114.

Infinity Records Ltd., 3852 Sunrise Hwy., Seaford, NY 11783: Free information ❖ Jazz, soul, doo-wop, and other records.

J & R Music World, 59-50 Queens-Midtown Expwy., Maspeth, NY 11378: Free catalog ❖ Records, cassettes, and video tapes. 800-221-8180.

Jay Distributors, Box 191332, Dallas, TX 75219: Free information ❖ Ballet, tap, and jazz videos and records, tapes, CDs, and cassettes. 800-793-6843.

Johnny Average Records, 151 1st Ave., Room 151, New York, NY 10003: Catalog $3 ❖ Jukebox records from the 1940s to the 1990s and current hits. 212-674-2049.

Kimbo Educational, P.O. Box 477, Long Branch, NJ 07740: Free catalog ❖ Cassettes, CDs, records, videos, read-alongs, and filmstrips for children. 800-631-2187.

Ladyslipper Inc., P.O. Box 3124-R, Durham, NC 27715: Free catalog ❖ Music by women. 919-644-1942.

Lark in the Morning, P.O. Box 1176, Mendocino, CA 95460: Catalog $3 ❖ Hard-to-find musical instruments, books about music, and CDs, cassettes, and videos. 707-964-5569.

Laserdisc Fan Club Inc., 1058 E. 230th St., Carson, CA 90745: Free catalog ❖ New and recent CDs. 800-801-3472.

❖ CDS, CASSETTES & RECORDS ❖

Lasertown Video Discs, 50 School House Rd., Box 348, Kulpsville, PA 19443: Free catalog ❖ Laser disks. 800-893-0390.

Last Vestige Music Shop, 173 Quail St., Albany, NY 12203: Free information ❖ Used, rare, and other hard-to-find out-of-print records, tapes, and CDs. 518-432-7736.

Mainly Music, 32 Main St., Brattleboro, VT 05301: Catalog $3 ❖ New, used, and rare records, CDs, and tapes. Also vintage sheet music and other memorabilia. 802-257-0881.

Melton Book Company, P.O. Box 140990, Nashville, TN 37214: Free catalog ❖ Christian books, bibles, audio and video recordings, and music. 800-441-0511.

Metro Music, P.O. Box 10004, Silver Spring, MD 20904: Free catalog with two 1st class stamps ❖ Long-playing records and CDs. 301-622-2473.

Metropolitan Opera Guild, 835 Madison Ave., New York, NY 10021: Free information ❖ Classical, concert, operatic, and documentary videos, records, CDs, and books. 212-634-8406.

Midnight Records, Box 390, Old Chelsea Station, New York, NY 10011: Free catalog ❖ Rock and roll, blues, and other hard-to-find records. 212-675-2768.

Craig Moerer Records, P.O. Box 42546, Portland, OR 97242: Free list (specify interests) ❖ Rock, soul, jazz, folk, pop, and country records. 503-232-1735.

Mosaic Records, 35 Melrose Pl., Stamford, CT 06902: Free catalog ❖ Jazz records and CDs. 203-327-7111.

Motoring Music, P.O. Box 1096, Manhasset, NY 11030: Catalog $2 (refundable) ❖ Live concert CDs from all countries. 212-979-2299.

Music By Mail, P.O. Box 090424, Fort Hamilton Station, Brooklyn, NY 11209: Catalog $2 ❖ Cassettes and CDs.

Music Connection, 430 Market St., Elmwood Park, NJ 07407: Free information ❖ New and used CDs, imported recordings, and videos. 201-797-5212.

Music Dispatch, P.O. Box 13920, Milwaukee, WI 53213: Free catalog ❖ Books, cassettes, CDs, and videos for guitars, percussionists, and other instruments. 800-637-2852.

Music Hunter, 347 5th Ave., Ste. 201, New York, NY 10016: Free information (specify items wanted) ❖ CDs, audio and video cassettes, laser discs, blank tapes, and accessories. 212-685-0819.

Music Lovers Recording Society, P.O. Box 2222, Doylestown, PA 18901: Free catalog ❖ Instrumental musical recordings. 215-348-0707.

The Noontide Press, P.O. Box 2739, Newport Beach, CA 92659: Free catalog ❖ Books, audio tapes, and videos on the social, political, economic, and historical taboos of the modern age. 714-631-1490.

Pack Central Inc., 6745 Denny Ave., North Hollywood, CA 91606: Catalog $2 ❖ Records and cassettes from the 1950s, 1960s, 1970s, and 1980s. 818-760-2828.

Park Avenue Record Planet, 532 Queen Anne Avenue North, Seattle, WA 98109: Free information ❖ Out-of-print records, rare LPs, CDs, and imports. 206-283-4446.

Pocket Songs, 50 Executive Blvd., Elmsford, NY 10523: Catalog $3.98 ❖ Broadway shows, pop to rock, big band, country music, gospel, and other CDs and cassettes. 800-NOW-SING.

Precept Ministries, P.O. Box 182218, Chattanooga, TN 37422: Free catalog ❖ Religious books, audio cassettes, and videos. 615-894-3277.

Price-Music Sales, P.O. Box 441348, Somerville, MA 02144: Free catalog ❖ Factory overstocked and discontinued rock, pop, jazz, and other records and CDs. 800-388-1386.

Radio Library, Box 200725, Arlington, TX 76006: Free catalog ❖ Old radio shows on cassettes. 817-261-8745.

Razor & Tie Music, 214 Sullivan St., New York, NY 10012: Free catalog ❖ Re-issues, anthologies, and new recordings. 212-473-9173.

Reach Out, 7324 Noah Reid Rd., Chattanooga, TN 37421: Free catalog ❖ Recordings with a Christian theme. 615-892-6814.

Rego Irish Records & Tapes Inc., 64 New Hyde Park Rd., Garden City, NY 11530: Catalog $2 ❖ Irish records and tapes. 800-854-3746.

Revolution Records, 1620 Alton Rd., Miami Beach, FL 33139: Free information (specify items wanted) ❖ New and used CDs and records. 305-673-6464.

Rhythm Recordings, P.O. Box 22372, San Francisco, CA 94116: Free catalog ❖ Rare and obscure originals, reproductions, and imports, from the 1940s to the present. 415-753-3480.

Rizzetta Music, P.O. Box 510, Inwood, WV 25428: Free brochure ❖ Standard, compact standard, and extended range dulcimers. Also tapes and CDs.

RJC Records, P.O. Box 661, Somersworth, NH 03878: Catalog $1 ❖ Country music recordings. 207-698-1862.

Robbie Music, Scherzer Rare Records Inc., P.O. Box 222, Pueblo, CO 81002: Free catalog ❖ Records, CDs, books, and other memorabilia. 719-543-6858.

Rockin' Robin, 1800 S. Robertson Blvd., Los Angeles, CA 90035: Catalog $3.50 (specify interest) ❖ LPs, CDs, vinyl records, and other collectible recordings.

Marion Roehl Recordings, 3533 Stratford Dr., Vestal, NY 13850: Free catalog ❖ Carousel organ, player piano, music box, and calliope music cassettes and CDs. 607-797-9062.

Roots & Rhythm Inc., P.O. Box 2216, San Leandro, CA 94577: Catalog $5 (specify blues, country, or vintage rock-and-roll) ❖ Records, tapes, compact disks, music books, and videos. 510-614-5353.

Rose Records, 214 S. Wabash Ave., Chicago, IL 60604: Free catalog ❖ New releases, imports, and overstocks of classical, folk, blues, pop, jazz, soul, and country music records. 800-955-ROSE.

Rounder Roundup Records, 1 Camp St., Cambridge, MA 02140: Catalog $1 ❖ Blues, rock, jazz, and folk CDs, LPs, and cassettes. Includes instrumental and vocal recordings. 617-661-6308.

Samra Promotions, P.O. Box 2221, Redondo Beach, CA 90278: Catalog $3 ❖ Imported CDs, sheet music, books, and videos. 310-318-3949.

SilverDisc Music Company, 19425 Saledad Ctn. Rd., Ste. 272, Canyon Country, CA 91351: Catalog $1 ❖ Imported CDs.

Sonic Recollections, 2701 SE Belmont St., Portland, OR 97214: Free catalog with long SASE ❖ Specializes in weird and other recordings. 503-236-3050.

Sound Delivery, P.O. Box 2213, Davis, CA 95617: Catalog $7.50 ❖ CDs, cassettes, and music videos. Includes rock and pop music, classical, jazz, soundtracks, opera, new age, and world-famous performers. 800-888-8574.

Sound Exchange, 45 N. Industry Ct., Deer Park, NY 11729: Free catalog ❖ Music, gifts, and collectibles. 800-841-3059.

Soundmind, P.O. Box 1386, Montpelier, VT 05601: Catalog $3 (refundable) ❖ Blues and jazz CDs.

Sounds True Audio, 735 Walnut St., Boulder, CO 80302: Free catalog ❖ Audio and video recordings on personal discovery, relationships, sacred music of the world, homeopathy, psychology and the spirit, health and healing, and other life-related subjects. 800-333-9185.

Stage Step, P.O. Box 328, Philadelphia, PA 19105: Free catalog ❖ Dance, theater, film, music, and fitness books, videos, and CDs. 800-523-0960.

Starship Industries, 605 Utterback Store Rd., Great Falls, VA 22066: Free catalog ❖ Laser and CD video disks. 703-430-8692.

Time Warner Viewer's Edge, P.O. Box 85098, Richmond, VA 23285: Free catalog ❖ One hundred years of movies on video cassettes, from 1895 to 1995. 800-305-1989.

Toneup Music, P.O. Box 631, Hinsdale, IL 60522: Free information ❖ Motivating music for exercise walkers. 800-519-9999.

Tower Records Mailorder, 22 E. 4th St., 3rd Floor, New York, NY 10003: Free information ❖ Classical and opera recordings. 800-648-4844

VAI Direct, 158 Linwood Plaza, Ste. 301, Fort Lee, NJ 07024: Free catalog ❖ Classical music video cassettes and CDs. Includes recordings of historic performances and rare repertoire. 201-944-0099.

Vinylmaniac, Bill Jurof, 1829 SW 14th St., Miami, FL 33145: Catalog $5 ❖ LPs. 305-854-5903.

Wagon Wheel Records & Books, 17191 Cornina Ln., #203, Huntington Beach, CA 92649: Free catalog ❖ Rhythm, movement, and folk records for education and recreation. 714-846-8169.

Waterloo Records & Video, 600 N. Lamar Blvd., Austin, TX 78703: Free information ❖ Imports, dance music, and Texas favorites. 512-474-2500.

The Wireless Music Source, P.O. Box 64422, St. Paul, MN 55164: Free catalog ❖ Records, CDs, and cassettes. 800-726-8742.

Sylvia Woods Harp Center, P.O. Box 816, Montrose, CA 91021: Free catalog ❖ Harps and recordings, books, harp-theme jewelry, and other gifts. 818-956-1363.

Radio Recordings

Adventures in Cassettes, 5353 Nathan Ln., Plymouth, MN 55442: Free information ❖ Old radio shows on cassettes as aired in the 1930s and 1940s. 800-328-0108.

Erstwhile Radio, P.O. Box 2284, Peabody, MA 01960: Catalog $2 ❖ Old-time radio broadcasts on cassettes.

Hello Again, Radio, 10280 Gunpowder Rd., Florence, KY 41042: Free catalog ❖ Old-time radio shows on cassettes. 606-282-0333.

Radio Library, Box 200725, Arlington, TX 76006: Free catalog ❖ Old radio shows on cassettes. 817-261-8745.

Radio Showcase, P.O. Box 4357, Santa Rose, CA 95402: Catalog $10; free sample list ❖ Programs from radio's golden era on cassettes. 707-525-0825.

Tucker-Barry, P.O. Box 1914, Lawrence, KS 66044: Free information ❖ Radio shows.

The Video Finder, Box 25066, Portland, OR 97298: Catalog $2 ❖ Hard-to-find and rare TV shows and serials on video. Also old radio shows.

Soundtracks

Coronet Books, CDs & Cassettes, 311 Bainbridge St., Philadelphia, PA 19147: ❖ Rhythm, classical, blues, big-band, soundtracks, Broadway musicals, rock, and other recordings. 215-925-2762.

Star Soundtracks, P.O. Box 487, New Holland, PA 17557: Free catalog ❖ Soundtracks with original casts.

Storage Cabinets & Supplies

AGM Woodworking, 870 Capitolio Way, San Luis Obispo, CA 93401: Free brochure ❖ Storage cabinets for audio and video recordings. 800-858-9005.

Allen Products Company, 2454 Rosemead Blvd., El Monte, CA 91733: Free information ❖ Storage cabinets for compact disks and audio and video equipment. 800-729-1251.

Leslie Dame Enterprises Ltd., 111-20 73rd Ave., Forest Hills, NY 11375: Free information ❖ CD, video cassette, and audio cassette storage cabinets. 718-261-4919.

Door County Design & Woodworking, 142 S. Madison Ave., Sturgeon Bay, WI 54235: Free information ❖ Audio storage systems. 800-746-0881.

Hills Products Inc., P.O. Box 55, Candia, NH 03034: Free information ❖ Compact disk storage cabinets. 800-247-2018.

HY-Q Enterprises, 14040 Mead St., Longmont, CO 80504: Free information ❖ Storage cabinets for CDs, video cassettes, and audio tapes. 800-878-7458.

Lorentz Design Inc., P.O. Box 277, Lanesboro, MN 55949: Free catalog ❖ Storage cabinets for CDs, video cassettes, and video game cartridges. 800-933-0403.

Per Madsen Design, P.O. Box 882464, San Francisco, CA 94188: Free brochure ❖ Stackable portable units for storing disks, tapes, and components. 415-822-4883.

Soricé, P.O. Box 747, Nutley, NJ 07110: Free information ❖ Audio and video disk and cassette storage cabinets. 800-432-8005.

CERAMIC & POTTERY SUPPLIES

A.R.T. Studio Clay Company, 1555 Louis Ave., Elk Grove Village, IL 60007: Catalog $5 ❖ Ceramic supplies. 800-323-0212; 708-593-6060 (in IL).

Aardvark Clay & Supplies, 1400 E. Pomoma St., Santa Ana, CA 92705: Price list $1 ❖ Ceramic supplies. 714-541-4157.

Adventure in Ceramics, 1421 Ellis St., Waukeesha, WI 53186: Catalog $4 ❖ Ready-to-paint kiln-fired ceramic bisque projects.

Aegean Sponge Company Inc., 4722 Memphis Ave., Cleveland, OH 44144: Free catalog ❖ Ceramic supplies. 216-749-1927.

Africana Colors, Batavia, OH 45103: Free information ❖ Textured stains. 513-625-9486.

Aftosa, 1034 Ohio Ave., Richmond, CA 94804: Free catalog ❖ Pottery-making supplies. 800-231-0397.

Aim Kiln, 350 SW Wake Robin, Corvallis, OR 97333: Free information ❖ Electric kilns. 800-647-1624.

Alberta's Molds Inc., P.O. Box 2018, Atascadero, CA 93423: Catalog $6 ❖ Ceramic molds. 805-466-9255.

AMACO, 4717 W. 16th St., Indianapolis, IN 46222: Free catalog ❖ Underglaze colors for brush application on bisque or greenware. 800-374-1600; 317-244-6871 (in IN).

American Art Clay Company Inc., 4717 W. 16th St., Indianapolis, IN 46222: Free catalog ❖ Clays, kilns, pottery-making equipment, glazes, tools, coloring materials, and metal enameling supplies. 800-374-1600; 317-244-6871 (in IN).

Art Decal Company, 1145 Loma Ave., Long Beach, CA 90804: Free information ❖ Ceramic decals. 800-742-0270; 310-434-2711 (in CA).

Astro Artcraft Supply, 1026 W. 44th St., Norfolk, VA 23508: Free information ❖ Ceramic supplies. 800-USA-COST; 804-440-1373 (in VA).

Atlantic Mold Corporation, 55 Main St., Trenton, NJ 08620: Catalog $6.50 ❖ Ceramic molds. 609-581-0880.

Badger Air-Brush Company, 9128 W. Belmont Ave., Franklin Park, IL 60131: Brochure $1 ❖ Air brushes. 800-247-2787.

Bailey Ceramic Supply, Box 1577, Kingston, NY 12401: Free catalog ❖ Ceramic supplies. 800-431-6067.

Bennett's Pottery & Ceramic Supplies, 431 Enterprise St., Ocoee, FL 34761: Free information ❖ Kilns, glazes, potter wheels, clay, slip, tools, and supplies for ceramics and pottery. 407-877-6311.

Black Magic Cleaners, P.O. Box 404, Burlington, WI 53105: Free information ❖ Greenware cleaner. 414-642-7121.

Blue Diamond Kiln Company, P.O. Box 172, Metarie, LA 70004: Information $1 ❖ Automatic kilns. 800-USA-KILN; 504-835-2035 (in LA).

Bluebird Manufacturing Inc., P.O. Box 2307, Fort Collins, CO 80522: Free information ❖ Potter wheels and clay-working equipment. 970-484-3243.

Boothe Mold Company, 9 Boothe Plaza, Dupo, IL 62239: Catalog $7 ❖ Ceramic molds. 800-782-0512.

❖ CERAMIC & POTTERY SUPPLIES ❖

Brickyard House of Ceramics, 4721 W. 16th St., Speedway, IN 46222: Free information ❖ Glazes, stains, under-glazes, brushes, tools, molds, kiln and potter wheel repair parts, and kilns. 800-677-3289.

Byrne Ceramic Supply Company Inc., 95 Bartley Rd., Flanders, NJ 07836: Free information ❖ White and colored, stoneware, and firebird porcelain slips. Also wheel and modeling clays and liquid silk one-coat clear glaze. 201-584-7492.

C & F Wholesale Ceramics, 3241 E. 11th Ave., Hialeah, FL 33013: Catalog $4 ❖ Ceramic supplies, stains and glazes, brushes, tools, music boxes, clock works, and airbrushes. 305-835-8200.

Campbell Pump Company Inc., P.O. Box 26326, Fresno, CA 93729: Free information ❖ Slip pump. 800-869-7867.

Cedar Heights Clay Company Inc., P.O. Box 295, Oak Hill, OH 45656: Free information ❖ Foundry and ceramic clay. 614-682-7794.

Cer Cal Decals Inc., 626 N. San Gabriel Ave., Azusa, CA 91702: Free brochure ❖ Ceramic decals. 818-969-1456.

Cerami Corner, P.O. Box 1206, Grants Pass, OR 97526: Catalog $8 ❖ Ceramic molds, decals, china paints, and brushes. 800-423-8543.

Ceramic Supply of NY/NJ, 7 Rt. 46 West, Lodi, NJ 07644: Catalog $4 ❖ Electric and gas kilns, clays, colors, slip casting and sculpting equipment, potter wheels, and glazes. 800-7-CERAMIC; 201-340-3005 (in NJ).

Ceramichrome, P.O. Box 327, Stanford, KY 40484: Catalog $6.50 ❖ Ceramic molds, colors, and supplies. 800-544-0764.

Chaselle Inc., 9645 Gerwig Ln., Columbia, MD 21046: Catalog $4 ❖ Art software and books, brushes and paints, tempera colors, acrylics, pastels, ceramic molds and kilns, sculpture equipment, silk-screening supplies, and other art and craft supplies. 800-242-7355.

Clay Magic Ceramic Products Inc., 21201 Russell Dr., P.O. Box 148, Rockwood, MI 48173: Catalog $8 ❖ Ceramic molds. 313-379-4944.

Continental Clay Company, 1101 Stinson Blvd., Minneapolis, MN 55413: Catalog $4 ❖ Ceramic supplies. 800-432-CLAY.

Creative Ceramics, 1259 Trinity Dr., Carol Stream, IL 60188: Free brochure ❖ Paints, brushes, molds, and supplies. Also ceramic accessories. 708-289-4343.

Creative Hobbies, 900 Creek Rd., Bellmawr, NJ 08031: Free catalog ❖ Ceramic supplies. 800-THE-KILN; 609-933-2540 (in NJ).

Cress Manufacturing Company Inc., 1718 Floradale Ave., South El Monte, CA 91733: Free catalog ❖ Automatic and manual operated kilns for ceramics, porcelain crafts, stoneware, china painting, and lost wax process. 800-423-4584.

Cridge Inc., Box 210, Morrisville, PA 19067: Catalog $2 ❖ Jewelry supplies for decorating ceramics. 215-295-3667.

Crusader Kilns, American Art Clay Company Inc., 4717 W. 16th St., Indianapolis, IN 46222: Free information with long SASE ❖ Energy-saving kilns. 800-374-1600; 317-244-6871 (in IN).

D & R Molds, 4815 E. Main St., Ste. 2, Mesa, AZ 85205: Catalog $3 ❖ Ceramic molds.

Debcor Inc., 513 W. Taft Dr., South Holland, IL 60573: Free list of retail sources ❖ Furniture for art and ceramic-working and industrial and graphic arts.

Doc Holliday Molds Inc., 125 MacArthur Ct., Nicholasville, KY 40356: Catalog $7.50 ❖ Ceramic molds. 606-887-1427.

Dona's Molds Inc., P.O. Box 145, West Milton, OH 45383: Catalog $7.50 ❖ Ceramic molds and coloring materials. 513-947-1333.

Dove Brushes, 280 Terrace Rd., Tarpon Springs, FL 34689: Catalog $2.50 ❖ Brushes. 800-334-3683; 813-934-5283 (in FL).

Duncan Enterprises, 5673 E. Shields Ave., Fresno, CA 93727: Free list of retail sources ❖ Molds, surface-texture products, and other supplies. 800-438-6226; 209-291-4444 (in CA).

Evenheat Kiln Inc., 6949 Legion Rd., Caseville, MI 48725: Free information ❖ Kilns. 517-856-2281.

Ex-Cel Inc., 1011 N. Hollywood, Memphis, TN 38108: Free information ❖ Slip for ceramic-casting. 800-238-7270; 901-324-3851 (in TN).

Fash-en-Hues, 118 Bridge St., Piqua, OH 45356: Free information ❖ Translucent colors for staining ceramic and porcelain crafts. 513-778-8500.

G & J Enterprises, 4199 State Road 144, Mooresville, IN 46158: Catalog $2 (refundable) ❖ Ceramic and electrical supplies. 317-831-1452.

Gare Incorporated, 165 Rosemont St., P.O. Box 1686, Haverhill, MA 01830: Catalog $9 ❖ Ceramic molds, fired colors, stains, stone washed glazes, brushes, tools, and kilns. 508-373-9131.

Georgies Ceramic & Clay Company, 756 NE Lombard, Portland, OR 97211: Supplies catalog $5.50, mold catalog $5 ❖ Ceramic supplies and molds. 800-999-2529.

Heritage Brushes, 511 NW Service Rd., Warrenton, MO 63383: Free information ❖ Brushes. 314-456-2500.

Highlands Ceramic Supply, 465 Oak Circle, Sebring, FL 33872: Free information ❖ Ceramic molds, kilns and kiln parts, pouring equipment, slip, clay, and greenware. 813-385-6656.

Hill Decal Company, 5746 Schutz St., Houston, TX 77032: Catalog $2 ❖ Floral decals for ceramics and glass. 713-449-1942.

Holland Mold Inc., 1040 Pennsylvania Ave., P.O. Box 5021, Trenton, NJ 08638: Catalog $7 ❖ Ceramic molds. 609-392-7032.

House of Caron, 10111 Larrylyn Dr., Whittier, CA 90603: Price list $2.50 ❖ Molds and supplies for miniature dolls. 310-947-6753.

House of Ceramics Inc., 1011 N. Hollywood, Memphis, TN 38108: Free catalog ❖ Molds for ceramics and chinaware-crafting. 901-324-3851.

Iandola Mold Company, P.O. Box 5507, Trenton, NJ 08638: Catalog $6 ❖ Ceramic molds. 609-396-8832.

Indiana Hobby Molds, 3844 Hwy. 62 West, Boonville, IN 47601: Catalog $4 ❖ Ceramic molds. 812-897-4467.

International Technical Ceramics Inc., P.O. Box 1726, Ponte Vedra, FL 32004: Free information ❖ Kilns and repair parts. 904-285-0200.

Jay-Kay Molds, P.O. Box 2307, Quinlan, TX 75474: Catalog $5 ❖ Ceramic molds. 903-356-3416.

Jaygot Products, 1585 Beverly Dr., Clearwater, FL 34624: Brochure 50¢ ❖ Luster paste and metallic wax. 813-535-9605.

Jones Mold Company, 919 4th Ave. South, Nashville, TN 37210: Ceramics catalog $6.25, doll catalog $6.75 ❖ Molds for ceramics and dolls. 615-251-8989.

K-Ceramic Imports, 732 Ballough Rd., Daytona Beach, FL 32114: Catalog $10 ❖ European decals, sponges, and brushes. 904-252-6530.

Kelly's Ceramics Inc., 3016 Union Ave., Merchantville, NJ 08109: Free information ❖ Ceramic supplies and molds. 609-665-4181.

Kemper Tools & Doll Supplies Inc., 13595 12th St., Chino, CA 91710: Free catalog ❖ Pottery, sculpting, craft, and art tools. Also doll-making supplies. 800-388-5367.

Kerry Specialties, P.O. Box 5129, Deltona, FL 32728: Free information ❖ Brushes and cleaning tools. 407-574-6209.

Kimple Mold Corporation, 415 Industrial, P.O. Box 734, Goddard, KS 67052: Catalog $7 (plus $2 shipping/handling) ❖ Ceramic molds. 316-794-8621.

L & L Kiln, Kiln Manufacturing Inc., P.O. Box 2409, Aston, PA 19014: Free information ❖ Kilns. 610-558-3899.

CERAMIC & POTTERY SUPPLIES

L & R Specialties, 202 E. Mount Vernon St., P.O. Box 309, Nixa, MO 65714: Free price list ❖ Basic and moist clays, other chemicals, glazes, stains, accessories, and equipment. 417-725-2606.

Laguna Clay Company, 14400 Lomitas Ave., City of Industry, CA 91746: Free information ❖ Clays, glazes, tools, and supplies. 800-4-LAGUNA.

Lamp Specialties Inc., Box 240, Westville, NJ 08093: Catalog $5 (refundable) ❖ Electrical supplies for ceramic-crafting. 800-225-5526.

Lee's Ceramic Supply, P.O. Box 337, La Feria, TX 78559: Catalog $2 (refundable) ❖ Ceramic supplies, molds, decals, and kits. 800-424-LEES.

Lehman Manufacturing Company Inc., P.O. Box 46, Kentland, IN 47951: Free information ❖ Casting and mixing machines, parts, and slip. 800-348-5196.

Lily Pond Products, 351 W. Cromwell, Ste. 105, Fresno, CA 93711: Free information ❖ Easy-to-store portable drain table. 209-431-5003.

Marx Brush Manufacturing Company Inc., 130 Beckwith Ave., Paterson, NJ 07503: Catalog $2 ❖ Ceramic adhesive for mending greenware, bisque, fastening greenware to bisque, adding pieces, mending hairline cracks, and repairing broken stilts and hard spots. 800-654-6279.

Mayco Molds, 4077 Weaver Ct. South, Hilliard, OH 43026: Catalog $6.95 ❖ Ceramic molds, tools, brushes, colors, and other supplies. 614-876-1171.

McRon Ceramic Molds, 2660 NE 7th Ave., Pompano Beach, FL 33064: Catalog $8 ❖ Ceramic molds. 954-784-7707.

Med-Mar Metals, P.O. Box 6453, Anaheim, CA 92816: Free information ❖ Lusters, enamels, and paints. 714-533-6280.

Miami Clay Company, 270 NE 183rd St., North Miami, FL 33179: Catalog $2 ❖ Pottery supplies. 305-651-4695.

Mike's Ceramic Molds Inc., 5217 8th Ave. South, St. Petersburg, FL 33707: Catalog $6 ❖ Ceramic molds. 813-321-3725.

Mile Hi Ceramics Inc., 77 Lipan, Denver, CO 80223: Free catalog ❖ Clays and ceramic supplies. 303-825-4570.

Minnesota Ceramic Supply, 962 Arcade St., St. Paul, MN 55106: Free catalog ❖ Ceramic molds and supplies. 800-652-9724.

Minnesota Clay USA, 8001 Grand Ave. South, Bloomington, MN 55420: Free catalog ❖ Equipment, clays, glazes, tools, and books on ceramic and pottery crafts. 800-252-9872; 612-884-9101 (in MN).

Mr. & Mrs. of Dallas, 1301 Ave. K, Plano, TX 75074: Free catalog ❖ Ceramics and china painting supplies. 214-881-1699.

Mug Merchant, 982 N. Batavia St., Ste. B-11, Orange, CA 92667: Free information ❖ Decals for ceramics and glass. 714-532-2298.

Nasco, 901 Janesville Ave., Fort Atkinson, WI 53538: Free catalog ❖ Ceramic supplies, potter's tools, glazes, and kilns. 800-558-9595.

National Artcraft Company, 7996 Darrow Rd., Twinsburg, OH 44087: Catalog $1 ❖ Ceramic supplies. 800-793-0152.

Nowell's Molds, 1532-C Pointer Ridge Place, Bowie, MD 20716: Catalog $6 ❖ Ceramic molds. 301-249-0846.

Ohio Ceramic Supply Inc., 2881 State Rt. 59, P.O. Box 630, Kent, OH 44240: Free information ❖ Ceramic supplies. 800-899-4627.

Olympic Enterprises, P.O. Box 321, Campbell, OH 44405: Catalog $5 ❖ Ceramic supplies, decals, chinaware, sponges, and brushes. 216-755-2726.

Olympic Kilns, Division Haugen Manufacturing Inc., 6301 Button Gwinnett Dr., Atlanta, GA 30340: Free catalog ❖ Kilns. 770-441-5550.

Orton, 6991 Old 3C Hwy., Westerville, OH 43082: Free information ❖ Down-draft accessories for kilns. 614-895-2663.

Paragon Industries, 2011 S. Town East Blvd., Mesquite, TX 75149: Free catalog ❖ Kilns. 800-876-4328; 214-288-7557 (in TX).

Pierce Tools, 1610 Parkdale Dr., Grants Pass, OR 97527: Free catalog ❖ Ceramic, pottery, doll, and sculpting tools. 503-476-1778.

Pine Tree Molds, P.O. Box 33, Mill Village, PA 16427: Catalog $6.50 ❖ Ceramic molds. 800-346-4428.

Provincial Ceramic Products, 140 Parker Ct., Chardon, OH 44024: Brochure $6 (plus $3 shipping/handling) ❖ Ceramic supplies and molds. 216-286-1277.

R-Molds, 18711 St. Clair Ave., Cleveland, OH 44110: Catalog $7.50 ❖ Ceramic molds. 216-531-9185.

Red Barn Ceramics Inc., RD 5, Rt. 13 South, Cortland, NY 13045: Catalog $3 (refundable) ❖ Ceramic equipment and electrical supplies. 607-756-2039.

Riverview Molds Inc., 2141 P Ave., Williamsburg, IA 52361: Catalog $7 ❖ Ceramic molds. 319-668-9800.

Schafer's Wholesale, 1219 N. Jesse James Rd., Excelsior Springs, MO 64024: Free information ❖ Ceramic supplies. 800-747-6375.

Heinz Scharff Brushes, P.O. Box 746, Fayetteville, GA 30214: Free catalog ❖ Brushes for ceramic and tole painting, china decoration, and decorative crafts. 404-461-2200.

Scioto Ceramic Products Inc., 2455 Harrisburg Pike, Grove City, OH 43123: Catalog $5.95 ❖ Ceramic molds. 614-871-0090.

Scott Publications, 30595 W. 8 Mile Rd., Livonia, MI 48152: Free catalog ❖ Books for the ceramist, china painter, and doll maker. 800-477-6650; 810-477-6650 (in MI).

Sheffield Pottery Inc., US Rt. 7, P.O. Box 399, Sheffield, MA 01257: Free catalog ❖ Kilns, stains, other equipment and supplies, and moist, screened fire, and slip clays. 413-229-7700.

Skutt Ceramic Products, 2618 SE Steele St., Portland, OR 97202: Free brochure ❖ Electric kilns. 503-231-7726.

Southern Oregon Pottery & Supply, 111 Talent Ave., P.O. Box 158, Talent, OR 97540: Catalog $4 ❖ Manual, automatic, and electronic 110 and 240-volt kilns. Also tools, plasters, glazes, clays, books, and other supplies. 541-535-6700.

Star Stilts, P.O. Box 367, Feasterville, PA 19053: Free catalog ❖ Stilts and other supports. 215-357-1893.

Stewart's of California Inc., 16055 Heron Ave., La Mirada, CA 90638: Catalog $2 ❖ Ceramic supplies. 800-252-2603; 714-523-2603 (in CA).

Sugar Creek Industries Inc., P.O. Box 354, Linden, IN 47955: Free catalog ❖ Ceramic equipment. 317-339-4641.

Tampa Bay Mold Company, 2724 22nd St. North, St. Petersburg, FL 33713: Catalog $5 ❖ Ceramic molds. 800-359-0534.

Tari Tan Ceramic & Craft Supply, 3919 N. Greenbrooke SE, Grand Rapids, MI 49512: Free information ❖ Ceramic molds and supplies. 616-698-2460.

Trenton Mold Boutique, 329 Whitehead Rd., Trenton, NJ 08619: Catalog $5 ❖ Ceramic molds. 609-890-0606.

Truebite Inc., 2590 Glenwood Rd., Vestal, NY 13850: Free catalog ❖ Cutting, grinding, drilling, and clean-up aids for porcelain and ceramics. 800-676-8907.

V.I.P. Molds Inc., 1819 German St., Erie, PA 16503: Catalog $8 ❖ Ceramic molds. 814-455-3396.

Vitrex Ceramics Ltd., P.O. Box 888, Tonawanda, NY 14150: Catalog $7 ❖ Ceramic molds. 905-333-1988.

Weaver's Ceramic Mold Inc., 684 W. Main St., New Holland, PA 17557: Catalog $2 ❖ Ceramic molds. 717-354-4491.

Weidlich Ceramics Inc., 2230 W. Camplain Rd., Somerville, NJ 08876: Free information ❖ Greenware, kilns, and fired and non-fired colors. 908-725-8554.

114 ❖ CHAIR CANING ❖

Wise Screenprint Inc., 1011 Valley St., Dayton, OH 45404: Free information ❖ Decals for ceramics and glass. 513-223-1573.

The Wishing Well, 221 W. 8th, Box 226, Cozad, NE 69130: Free information ❖ Liquid suede kits and non-toxic water soluble ceramic paints. 308-784-3100.

Yozie Molds Inc., Rt. 1, Box 415, Dunbar, PA 15431: Catalog $12 ❖ Ceramic molds. 412-628-3693.

Zembillas Sponge Company Inc., P.O. Box 24, Campbell, OH 44405: Catalog $3.50 ❖ Decals, brushes, and tools. 216-755-1644.

CHAIR CANING

A & H Brass & Supply, 126 W. Main St., Johnson City, TN 37604: Catalog $1 ❖ Chair-caning restoration materials. 800-638-4252; 615-928-8220 (in TN).

Al Con Enterprises, P.O. Box 429, Hickory, NC 28603: Free catalog ❖ Macrame, chair-weaving, and crochet supplies. 800-523-4371.

Bamboo & Rattan Works Inc., 470 Oberlin Ave. South, Lakewood, NJ 08701: Free information ❖ Rattan, cords, chair canes, matting, and bamboo, flat, and round reeds. 800-4-BAMBOO.

Barap Specialties, 835 Bellows Ave., Frankfort, MI 49635: Catalog $1 ❖ Caning and craft supplies, tools, lamp parts, and turned wooden part. 800-3-BARAP-3.

Cane & Basket Supply Company, 1283 S. Cochran, Los Angeles, CA 90019: Catalog $2 ❖ Reeds, fiber and rush, Danish seat cord, raffia, rattan sea grass, and caning and basket-making accessories. 800-468-3966.

Caning Shop, 926 Gilman St., Berkeley, CA 94710: Catalog $2 (refundable) ❖ Caning and basket-making supplies and tools. 800-544-3373.

Connecticut Cane & Reed Company, P.O. Box 762, Manchester, CT 06040: Catalog 50¢ ❖ Caning and basket-making supplies. 860-646-6586.

Country Seat, RD 2, Box 24A, Kempton, PA 19529: Free catalog with three 1st class stamps ❖ How-to books and basket-making and chair-caning supplies. 610-756-6124.

Frank's Cane & Rush Supply, 7252 Heil Ave., Huntington Beach, CA 92647: Free information ❖ Cane, rush, other basket-making supplies, and wooden parts. 714-847-0707.

Gundula's & Peerless Rattan & Reed, 624 S. Burnett Rd., Springfield, OH 45505: Catalog 50¢ ❖ Caning supplies. 513-323-7353.

Michigan Cane Supply, 5348 N. Riverview Dr., Kalamazoo, MI 49004: List $1 ❖ Chair cane, rush, and basket-weaving supplies. 616-282-5461.

Ozark Basketry Supply, P.O. Box 599, Fayetteville, AR 72702: Catalog $1 ❖ Books, basket-making kits, chair cane, dyes, hoops, and handles. 501-442-9292.

H.H. Perkins Company, 10 S. Bradley Rd., Woodbridge, CT 06525: Free catalog ❖ Seat-weaving and basket-making supplies, macrame supplies, and how-to books. 800-462-6660.

Royalwood Ltd., 517 Woodville Rd., Mansfield, OH 44907: Catalog $1 ❖ Caning and basket-making supplies, tools, kits, and dyes. 419-526-1630.

Snapvent Company, 147 W. Baxter Ave., Knoxville, TN 37917: Free price list with long SASE ❖ Basket and chair-caning supplies. 615-523-6784.

V.I. Reed & Cane, Rt. 5, Box 632, Rogers, AR 72756: Free catalog ❖ Flat and round reeds, smoked reed, cane, hoops, handles, raffia, dyes, and basket-weaving kits. 800-852-0025.

Veterans Caning Shop, 442 10th Ave., New York, NY 10001: Free catalog ❖ Caning supplies. 212-868-3244.

CHECKS

Business Envelopes, Mid Atlantic Industrial Park, P.O. Box 517, Thorofare, NJ 08086: Free catalog ❖ Business envelopes, checks, pens, and other office supplies. 800-275-4400.

Checks in the Mail, P.O. Box 7802, Irwindale, CA 91706: Free brochure ❖ Personalized checks with optional designs and colors. 800-733-4443.

Current Inc., Express Processing Center, Colorado Springs, CO 80941: Free catalog ❖ Personalized checks with optional designs and colors, greeting cards, stationery, gift wrapping, holiday and special occasion decorations, toys, calendars, and gifts. 800-848-2848.

NEBS Inc., 500 Main St., Groton, MA 01471: Free catalog ❖ Business forms, stationery, labels, checks, business cards, and other supplies.

Viking Office Products, 13809 S. Figueroa St., P.O. Box 61144, Los Angeles, CA 90061: Free catalog ❖ Personalized checks and office supplies. 800-421-1222.

CHEERLEADING

Asics Tiger Corporation, 10540 Talbert Ave., West Building, Fountain Valley, CA 92708: Free information ❖ Shoes. 800-678-9435.

Betlin Manufacturing, 1445 Marion Rd., Columbus, OH 43207: Free information ❖ Jackets, skirts, and uniforms. 614-443-0248.

Butwin Sportswear Company, 3401 Spring St. NE, Minneapolis, MN 55413: Free information ❖ Jackets. 800-328-1445.

CAMBER Universal Sportswear, 2 Dekalb, Norristown, PA 19401: Free information ❖ Jackets, skirts, and uniforms. 800-345-7518.

Danskin, 111 W. 40th St., 18th Floor, New York, NY 10018: Free information ❖ Uniforms. 800-288-6749; 212-764-4630 (in NY).

Dodger Industries, 1702 21st St., Eldora, IA 50627: Free information ❖ Sweaters. 800-247-7879; 515-858-5464 (in IA).

Fancy Pants, 3360 Sports Arena Blvd., Ste. G, San Diego, CA 92110: Free information ❖ Skirts and uniforms. 800-755-9565; 619-222-1104 (in CA).

Wm. Getz Corporation, 1024 S. Linwood Ave., Santa Ana, CA 92705: Free information ❖ Pom poms and megaphones. 800-854-7447; 714-835-0100 (in CA).

Hatchers Manufacturing Inc., 130 Condor St., Box 424, East Boston, MA 02128: Free information ❖ Megaphones, pom poms, and sweaters. 800-225-6842; 617-568-1262 (in MA).

Johnny Jones Jr. Company, 6633 Hamilton Ave., Pittsburgh, PA 15206: Free information ❖ Pom poms. 800-245-4252; 412-363-4600 (in CA).

Markwort Sporting Goods, 4300 Forest Park Ave., St. Louis, MO 63108: Catalog $8 (request list of retail sources) ❖ Pom poms. 800-669-6626; 314-652-3757 (in MO).

Dick Martin Sports Inc., 181 E. Union Ave., P.O. Box 7381, East Rutherford, NJ 07073: Free information ❖ Megaphones. 800-221-1993; 201-438-5255 (in NJ).

Pepco Poms, 9611 Hwy. 60 South, Lane City, TX 77453: Free information ❖ Megaphones and pom poms. 800-527-1150.

Recreonics Corporation, 4200 Schmitt Ave., Louisville, KY 40213: Free information ❖ Megaphones. 800-428-3254.

Shaffer Sportswear, 224 N. Washington, Neosho, MO 64850: Free information ❖ Jackets and uniforms. 417-451-9444.

Sportime, Customer Service, 1 Sporting Way, Atlanta, GA 30340: Free information ❖ Megaphones. 800-444-5700; 770-449-5700 (in GA).

CHEESE MAKING

Caprine Supply Company, P.O. Box Y, De Soto, KS 66018: Free information ❖ Mesophilic culture for making cheese. 913-585-1191.

Cheesemaking Supply Outlet, 9155 Madison Rd., Montville, OH 44064: Free catalog ❖ Cheese-making supplies. 216-968-3770.

Lehman Hardware & Appliances Inc., P.O. Box 41, Kidron, OH 44636: Catalog $2 ❖ Vegetable rennet and mesophilic culture for making cheese. 216-857-5757.

New England Cheesemaking Supply Company, P.O. Box 85, Ashfield, MA 01330: Catalog $1 ❖ Supplies for making cheese, butter, yogurt, and buttermilk. 413-628-3808.

CHESS

Bookup Inc., 2763 Kensington Pl. West, Columbus, OH 43202: Free information ❖ Lessons by Bobby Fischer on how to play chess on a Windows-based CD-ROM. 800-949-5445; 614-263-1434 (in OH).

Expert Software, 800 Douglas Rd., Executive Tower, 7th Floor, Coral Cables, FL 33134: Free information ❖ Windows-based how-to-play chess software. 800-759-2562; 305-567-9990 (in FL).

ICD/Your Move, 21 Walt Whitman Rd., Huntington Station, NY 11746: Free information ❖ Computerized chess games, playing pieces, books, supplies, and accessories. 800-645-4710.

International Chess Enterprises Inc., P.O. Box 19457, Seattle, WA 98109: Free information ❖ Chess games on CD-ROM. 800-26-CHESS.

U.S. Chess Federation, 186 Rt. 9W, Newburgh, NY 12550: Free catalog ❖ Conventional and computer chess sets, books, and competition supplies. 800-388-KING.

CHINA PAINTING & METAL ENAMELING

Allcraft Tool & Supply Company, 666 Pacific St., Brooklyn, NY 11207: Catalog $5 ❖ Metal enameling tools and supplies. 800-645-7124; 718-789-2800 (in NY).

American Art Clay Company Inc., 4717 W. 16th St., Indianapolis, IN 46222: Free catalog ❖ Clays, kilns, pottery-making equipment, glazes, tools, coloring materials, and metal enameling supplies. 800-374-1600; 317-244-6871 (in IN).

Cerami Corner, P.O. Box 1206, Grants Pass, OR 97526: Catalog $8 ❖ Ceramic molds, decals, china paints, and brushes. 800-423-8543.

Charlie's Rock Shop, P.O. Box 399, Penrose, CO 81240: Free catalog ❖ Metal enameling tools and supplies. 719-372-0117.

Chaselle Inc., 9645 Gerwig Ln., Columbia, MD 21046: Catalog $4 ❖ Art software and books, brushes and paints, tempera colors, acrylics and sets, pastels, ceramic molds and kilns, sculpture equipment, and screen-printing supplies. 800-242-7355.

Cridge Inc., Box 210, Morrisville, PA 19067: Catalog $2 ❖ Gold and silver settings, bisque and glazed porcelain insets, and china painting supplies. 215-295-3667.

Evenheat Kiln Inc., 6949 Legion Rd., Caseville, MI 48725: Free information ❖ Kilns. 517-856-2281.

Firemountain Gems, 28195 Redwood Highway, Cave Junction, OR 97523: Catalog $3 ❖ Metal enameling tools and supplies. 800-423-2319.

T.B. Hagstoz & Son Inc., 709 Sansom St., Philadelphia, PA 19106: Catalog $5 (refundable with $25 order) ❖ Metal enameling tools and supplies. 800-922-1006; 215-922-1627 (in PA).

Maryland China Company, 54 Main St., Reisterstown, MD 21136: Free catalog ❖ China painting supplies. 800-638-3880.

Mr. & Mrs. of Dallas, 1301 Ave. K, Plano, TX 75074: Free catalog ❖ Ceramics and china painting supplies. 214-881-1699.

Nasco, 901 Janesville Ave., Fort Atkinson, WI 53538: Free catalog ❖ Metal enameling supplies. 800-558-9595.

National Artcraft Company, 23456 Mercantile Rd., Beachwood, OH 44122: Catalog $4 ❖ Tiles, china, paints and other coloring preparations, and brushes. 800-793-0152.

Paragon Industries, 2011 S. Town East Blvd., Mesquite, TX 75149: Free catalog ❖ Kilns. 800-876-4328; 214-288-7557 (in TX).

Rynne China Company, 222 W. 8 Mile Rd., Hazel Park, MI 48030: Free information ❖ Decals, books, china and glass paints, overglaze, kilns, brushes, and supplies. 800-468-1987.

Southern Oregon Pottery & Supply, 111 Talent Ave., Box 158, Talent, OR 97540: Catalog $4 ❖ Manual, automatic, and electronic 110 and 240-volt kilns. Also supplies. 503-535-6700.

CHINA, POTTERY & STONEWARE

Alice's Past & Presents Replacements, P.O. Box 465, Merrick, NY 11566: Free information ❖ Replacement crystal, china, and flatware. 516-379-1352.

William Ashley, 50 Boor St. West, Toronto, Ontario, Canada M4W 3L8: Free information ❖ China, crystal, and silver. 800-268-1122.

Baccarat, 625 Madison Ave., New York, NY 10022: Brochure $3 ❖ Crystal and china Baccarat. 800-777-0100.

Barefoot Pottery, 7539 Oak Ridge Hwy., Knoxville, TN 37931: Free brochure ❖ Decorated hand-thrown pottery pieces. 423-694-7740.

Barrons, P.O. Box 994, Novi, MI 48376: Free information ❖ China, crystal, and silver. 800-538-6340.

Barton-Sharpe Ltd., 119 Spring St., New York, NY 10012: Free information ❖ Reproduction 18th and 19th-century furniture, lighting, bedding, stoneware, and decorative items. 212-925-9562.

Bennington Potters, P.O. Box 199, 324 County St., Bennington, VT 05201: Free catalog ❖ Pottery. 802-447-7531.

Mildred Brumback, P.O. Box 132, Middletown, VA 22645: Free information ❖ Discontinued china and crystal. 703-869-1261.

Cattle Company Cowboy Exchange, P.O. Box 27, Elfrida, AZ 85610: Catalog $2 ❖ Western-style china and stainless steel flatware. 520-824-3540.

Cee Cee China, 3904 Parsons, Chevy Chase, MD 20815: Free information ❖ Discontinued china. 800-619-6226.

China & Crystal Cabinet Inc., 24 Washington St., Tenafly, NJ 07670: Free information with long SASE ❖ China, crystal, flatware, and gifts. 201-567-2711.

The China & Crystal Closet, P.O. Box 426, Clearwater, SC 29822: Free information with long SASE ❖ China and crystal. 803-593-9655.

China & Crystal Matchers Inc., 2379 John Glenn Dr., Chamblee, GA 30341: Free information ❖ Discontinued china and crystal. 404-455-1162.

China, Crystal & Flatware Replacements, P.O. Box 508, High Ridge, MO 63049: Free information ❖ China, crystal, and flatware. 800-562-2655.

The China Connection, Box 972, Pineville, NC 28134: Free information ❖ Inactive fine and everyday china. 800-421-9719; 704-889-8198 (in NC).

The China Hutch, 1333 Ivey Dr., Charlotte, NC 28205: Free information ❖ Discontinued china. 800-524-4397.

China Marketing, Box 33, Cheltenham, PA 19012: Free information ❖ Discontinued china and crystal. 800-599-3569.

China Replacements, 2263 Williams Creek Rd., High Ridge, MO 63049: Free information with long SASE ❖ Discontinued china and crystal. 800-562-2655; 677-5577 (in St. Louis).

The China Warehouse, Box 21797, Cleveland, OH 44121: Free information ❖ China, crystal, and flatware. 800-321-3212.

Classic China, 870 N. Coit Rd., Richardson, TX 75080: Free information with long SASE ❖ China, flatware, and other table setting accessories.

Clay Craftsman, Willis & Denise Myers, 686 Barts Church Rd., Hanover, PA 17331: Brochure $1 ❖ Handmade pottery. 717-359-9458.

Clay Creations, 505 Norway St., Silverton, OR 97381: Brochure $2 (refundable) ❖ Hand-painted country-style mixing bowls. 503-873-2025.

❖ CHINA, POTTERY & STONEWARE ❖

Clay in Motion Inc., Rt. 3, Reser Rd., Box 120-A, Walla Walla, WA 99362: Free brochure ❖ Handmade dinnerware. 509-529-6146.

Clintsman International, 20855 Watertown Rd., Waukesha, WI 53186: Free information ❖ Discontinued china, crystal, and flatware. 800-781-8900.

Collectible Outlet Inc., 6925 Oakland Mills Rd., Columbia, MD 21045: Free price guide with long SASE ❖ China and accessories. 800-555-6022.

Creative Ceramics, 1259 Trinity Dr., Carol Stream, IL 60188: Free brochure ❖ Handcrafted ceramic kitchen accessories. 708-289-4343.

Crystal Lalique, 680 Madison Ave., New York, NY 10021: Free information ❖ Crystal and china Lalique. 800-214-2738; 212-355-6550 (in NY).

Dansk, 108 Corporate Park Dr., White Plains, NY 10604: Free list of retail sources ❖ Dinnerware, stemware, flatware, kitchenware, and serving pieces. 914-697-6400.

Designs in the Home, 417-B W. Foothill Blvd., #525, Glendora, CA 91741: Brochure $2 ❖ Hand-decorated oven-proof stoneware. 818-334-3438.

East Knoll North, P.O. Box 163, Becket, MA 01223: Brochure $2 (refundable) ❖ Hand-turned and decorated yellowware reproductions. 413-623-5633.

Eastside Gifts & Dinnerware, 351 Grand St., New York, NY 10002: Free information ❖ China, crystal, flatware, and gifts. 800-443-8711; 212-982-7200 (in NY).

Eldreth Pottery, 902 Hart Rd., Oxford, PA 19363: Catalog $2 ❖ Salt-glazed stoneware and Pennsylvania redware. 717-529-6241.

Felissimo, 10 W. 56th South, New York, NY 10019: Free catalog ❖ Porcelain dinnerware and handcrafted silver serving pieces and accessories. 800-565-6785.

Michael C. Find, 580 5th Ave., New York, NY 10036: Free catalog ❖ Sterling serving pieces, tea sets, crystal stemware, bone china, and pewter. 800-BUY-FINA; 718-937-8484 (in NY).

Fitz & Floyd Consumer Relations, P.O. Box 516125, Dallas, TX 75251: Free list of retail sources ❖ China.

The Five Seasons Corporation, 1901 Rt. 332, Canandaigua, NY 14425: Free information ❖ Hand-painted personalized stoneware crocks. 800-724-4064; 716-396-2021 (in NY).

Flat Earth Clay Works Inc., 5760 N. Broadway, Wichita, KS 67219: Brochure $2 ❖ Lead-free microwave and oven-safe earthenware pottery. 800-654-8695.

Fortunoff Fine Jewelry, P.O. Box 1550, Westbury, NY 11590: Free catalog ❖ China, silver plate and stainless steel serving pieces, and sterling flatware. 800-937-4376.

Gorham, 100 Lenox Dr., Lawrenceville, NJ 08648: Free list of retail sources ❖ Fine china dinnerware, crystal, and silver. 800-635-3669.

Granite Lake Pottery Inc., Rt. 9, P.O. Box 236, Munsonville, NH 03457: Free catalog ❖ Handcrafted oven, microwave, and dishwasher-safe stoneware. 800-443-9908.

Jacquelyn Hall, 10629 Baxter, Los Altos, CA 94022: Free information ❖ Lenox china and crystal. 408-739-4876.

Hartstone Inc., P.O. Box 2626, Zanesville, OH 43702: Free information ❖ Hand-decorated dinnerware and accessories. 614-452-9000.

House of 1776, 3110 S. Jupiter, Garland, TX 75041: Free information ❖ China place settings and open stock, tableware, and gifts. 800-989-1776; 214-864-1776 (in TX).

Jacquelynn's China Matching Service, 219 N. Milwaukee St., Milwaukee, WI 53202: Free information with long SASE ❖ Discontinued American and English china. 414-272-8880.

Jepson Studios Inc., P.O. Box 36, Harveyville, KS 66431: Brochure $2 (refundable) ❖ Country ceramics. 913-589-2481.

Karlin Pottery, P.O. Box 180836, Utica, MI 48318: Brochure $1 ❖ Country pottery and stoneware. 810-997-0575.

Kindred Spirits, Rt. 3, Box 263, Grand Island, NE 68801: Free information ❖ Hand-painted personalized crocks. 308-384-0177.

Kitchen Etc., 32 Industrial Dr., Exeter, NH 03833: Catalog $2 ❖ Dinnerware, stemware, flatware, cookware, and cutlery. Over 120 pages of brand names at everyday low prices. 800-232-4070.

Lanac Sales, 73 Canal St., New York, NY 10002: Free catalog ❖ China, crystal, sterling, and gifts. 212-925-6422.

Le Fanion, ZED International Ltd., 299 W. 4th St., Greenwich Village, New York, NY 10014: Free catalog ❖ French country antique and contemporary pottery. 212-463-8760.

Lenox Collections, P.O. Box 3020, Langhorne, PA 19047: Free catalog ❖ China, crystal, and porcelain sculptures. 800-225-1779.

Locators Inc., 908 Rock St., Little Rock, AR 72202: Free information ❖ Discontinued china, crystal, and silver. 800-367-9690.

Marks China, Crystal & Silverware, 315 Franklin Ave., Wyckoff, NJ 07481: Free information ❖ China, stainless, crystal, and silverware. 800-862-7578.

Martin's Herend Imports Inc., P.O. Box 1178, Sterling, VA 20167: Free list of retail sources ❖ Hand-painted porcelain decorative pieces and dinner service. 800-643-7363; 703-450-1601 (in VA).

Midas China & Silver, 4315 Walney Rd., Chantilly, VA 22021: Free catalog ❖ Silverware, table settings, gifts, and china. 800-368-3153.

Mikasa, One Mikasa Dr., P.O. Box 1549, Secaucus, NJ 07096: Free catalog ❖ Designer china, stoneware, crystal, and flatware. 800-833-4681; 201-392-2501 (in NJ).

Mountain Meadows Pottery, P.O. Box 163, South Ryegate, VT 05069: Free catalog ❖ Functional stoneware and humorous and sentimental plaques. 800-639-6790.

MS China, P.O. Box 229, Monterey, CA 93940: Free information ❖ Newly discontinued and pre-war Noritake patterns. 800-688-6807.

Teresita Naranjo, Santa Clara Pueblo, Rt. 1, Box 455, Espanola, NM 87532: Free information with long SASE ❖ Ceremonial and melon bowls, wedding vases, and other traditional Santa Clara black and red pottery. 505-753-9655.

Noël Pie Plate Company, 771 Hwy 7N, Tonasket, WA 98855: Free information ❖ Personalized platters, bowls, canister sets, and pottery accessories for the kitchen. 509-486-4372.

Noritake China Replacements, 35 Clearbrook Dr., Arlington Heights, IL 60005: Free information ❖ Noritake china replacements. 800-562-1991.

Olympus Cove Antiques, 179 E. 300 South, Salt Lake City, UT 84111: Free information ❖ Discontinued china. 800-564-8253.

Pfaltzgraff Factory Outlet, 2900 Whiteford Rd., York, PA 17402: Catalog $1 (refundable) ❖ Dinnerware, baking and serving pieces, decorative accessories, and stoneware irregulars. 800-999-2811; 717-757-2200 (in PA).

The Pottery Place, 3739 S. Main Rd., Lebanon, OR 97355: Catalog $4 (refundable) ❖ Stoneware serving pieces. 503-451-2965.

Replacement Service, 1415 Michigan, Saint Cloud, FL 34769: Free information ❖ Discontinued china. 800-222-7357; 407-957-1719 (in FL).

Replacements Ltd., 1089 Knox Rd., P.O. Box 26029, Greensboro, NC 27420: Free information with long SASE ❖ Discontinued china, earthenware, and crystal. 800-562-4462.

Rogers & Rosenthal, 22 W. 48th St., Room 1102, New York, NY 10036: Free information with long SASE ❖ China, crystal, and stainless steel. 212-827-0115.

Ross-Simons Jewelers, 9 Ross Simons Dr., Cranston, RI 02920: Free information ❖ Sterling and china. 800-556-7376, 800-553-7370 (in RI).

Rowe Pottery Works, 404 England St., Cambridge, WI 53523: Free catalog ❖ Salt-glazed stoneware in early authentic folk designs. 800-356-5003.

Royal Worcester, The Royal China & Porcelain Companies Inc., 1265 Glen Ave., Moorestown, NJ 08057: Free list of retail sources ❖ Place settings, cookware, glasses and goblets, and accessories. 800-257-7189.

Rudi's Pottery, Silver & China, 176 Rt. 17, Paramus, NJ 07652: Free information with long SASE ❖ Glass stemware, china, and gifts. 201-265-6096.

Nat Schwartz & Company, 549 Broadway, Bayonne, NJ 07002: Free catalog ❖ Crystal, sterling, and china. 800-526-1440; 201-437-4443 (in NJ).

Shannon, 3772 Richmond Ave., Houston, TX 77027: Free information ❖ China. 800-742-7766.

Greg & Mary Shooner, 1772 Jeffery Rd., Oregonia, OH 45054: Free brochure ❖ Redware reproductions. 800-452-7058.

Silver Lane, P.O. Box 322, San Leandro, CA 94577: Free information ❖ Discontinued crystal and china. Also current and obsolete silver. 510-483-0632.

Spode, The Royal China & Porcelain Companies Inc., 1265 Glen Ave., Moorestown, NJ 08057: Free list of retail sources ❖ China and accessories Spode. 800-257-7189.

Stebner Pottery, 1532 Rt. 43, Suffield, OH 44260: Catalog $2 ❖ Salt-glazed stoneware for the home. 216-628-0114.

Stegall's Stoneware, 379 Chandler Cove, Erwin, TN 37650: Free information ❖ Stoneware mugs for grandparents and pottery for baking, serving, and organizing in the kitchen. 800-788-POTS.

Thurber's, 2256 Dabney Rd., Richmond, VA 23230: Free information ❖ China and sterling. 800-848-7237.

Treadwell's Western Mercantile, 201 W. Main, Stroud, OK 74079: Free brochure ❖ Western-style flatware, enamelware, and dinnerware. 918-587-5526.

Van Ness China Company, 601 Shenandoah Village Dr., Waynesboro, VA 22980: Free information ❖ Discontinued and current English bone china. 703-942-2827.

Carol Vigil, P.O. Box 443, Jemez Pueblo, NM 87024: Free information with long SASE ❖ Carved and painted Jemez pottery.

Waterford Crystal Inc., 41 Madison Ave., New York, NY 10010: Free brochure ❖ Crystal and china.

Wedgwood, 41 Madison Ave., New York, NY 10010: Brochure $2 ❖ Fine china serving pieces, dinnerware, and gifts.

White's Collectables & Fine China, P.O. Box 680, Newborg, OR 97132: Free information ❖ Collectible plates and new and discontinued china patterns. 800-618-2782.

Wisconsin Pottery, W3199 Hwy. 16, Columbus, WI 53925: Free catalog ❖ Handcrafted and hand-decorated salt-glazed stoneware and redware pottery. 800-669-5196.

Workshops of David T. Smith, 3600 Shawhan Rd., Morrow, OH 45152: Catalog $5 ❖ Reproduction furniture, pottery, lamps, and chandeliers. 513-932-2472.

CHOIR GOWNS

Cokesbury, Division United Methodist Publishing House, 201 8th Ave. South, P.O. Box 801, Nashville, TN 37202: Free information ❖ Bibles and bible reference books, bible study and Christian education books, fund-raising programs, gifts and casual wear, choir apparel, church and clergy supplies, and church furniture and equipment. 800-672-1789.

Lyric Choir Gown Company, P.O. Box 16954, Jacksonville, FL 32245: Free catalog ❖ Professionally tailored choir gowns.

Regency Cap & Gown Company, P.O. Box 8988, Jacksonville, FL 32211: Free catalog ❖ Choir robes. 800-826-8612.

CHRISTMAS DECORATIONS & OTHER ORNAMENTS

D. Blümchen & Company Inc., P.O. Box 1210, Ridgewood, NJ 07451: Free catalog ❖ Christmas ornaments and decorative items. 201-652-5595.

Christmas Treasures, P.O. Box 53, Dewitt, NY 13214: Catalog $3 ❖ Reproductions of old Christmas decorations.

Christmastime Traditions, Rt. 2, Box 574, Pounding Mill, VA 24637: Free catalog ❖ Mini ornaments, fabric mache figures, music boxes, stocking hangers, ribbons and bows, door posters, and Christmas decorations. 540-964-5479.

The Cookie Tree, 271 Western Ave., Lynn, MA 01904: Free catalog ❖ Handcrafted non-edible dough ornaments. 617-593-3746.

The Cracker Box, Solebury, PA 18963: Catalog $4.50 ❖ Christmas ornament kits. 215-862-2100.

European Imports & Gifts, Oak Mill Mall, 7900 N. Milwaukee Ave., Niles, IL 60648: Free information ❖ Art collectibles, porcelain, Christmas ornaments, pewter, and gifts. 708-967-5253.

The Faith Mountain Company, P.O. Box 199, Sperryville, VA 22740: Free catalog ❖ Kitchen utensils, folk art reproductions, toys and dolls, handmade Appalachian baskets, and Christmas decorations. 800-588-2548.

Fingerhut, P.O. Box 800, St. Cloud, MN 56395: Free catalog ❖ Greeting cards, gift wrapping, stationery, holiday decorative items, organizers, and gifts. 800-322-2226.

Friends, 109 Shawnee, Eldridge, IA 52748: Brochure $2 ❖ Country-style Christmas decorative accessories. 319-285-7354.

Global Shakeup Snowdomes, 2265 Westwood Blvd., Ste. 618, Los Angeles, CA 90064: Catalog $2 (refundable) ❖ Unusual and hard-to-find plastic and glass snowdomes, snowdome books, and more. 213-259-8988.

Hand & Hammer Silversmiths, 2610 Morse Ln., Woodbridge, VA 22192: Free information ❖ Handcrafted sterling silver and vermeil jewelry. Also Christmas ornaments. 800-SIL-VERY.

Holiday Treasures Catalog, P.O. Box 53, Dewitt, NY 13214: Catalog $3 ❖ Collectible holiday decorative items and reproduction antique ornaments.

Kaye's Holiday, 6N021 Meredith, Maple Park, IL 60151: Catalog $1 (2 issues) ❖ Handmade ornaments of blown glass for Christmas, Easter, Halloween, other holidays, and special occasions. 708-365-2224.

The Lady Bug Company, P.O. Box 613054, Dallas, TX 75261: Brochure $2 ❖ Handcrafted ceramic ornaments with a sports theme. 214-991-6586.

Select Artificials Inc., 701 N. 15th St., St. Louis, MO 63103: Catalog $10 (refundable) ❖ Silk flowers, large plants, and Christmas decorative items. 800-666-6999; 314-621-3050 (in MO).

Sterling & Collectables Inc., P.O. Box 1665, Mansfield, OH 44901: Free list ❖ Current and obsolete sterling silver patterns, sterling Christmas ornaments, stainless, and serving pieces. 419-756-8817.

Tilearts, P.O. Box 1560, Santa Ynez, CA 93460: Brochure $1 (refundable) ❖ Handcrafted ceramic ornaments. 805-688-4296.

Truly Victorian Mercantile, P.O. Box 88231, Black Forest, CO 88231: Catalog $3 ❖ Hard-to-find Victorian-style Christmas decorations. 719-495-2651.

CHURCH, SYNAGOGUE & CLERGY SUPPLIES

Wooden Soldier, P.O. Box 800, North Conway, NH 03860: Free catalog ❖ Christmas decorations and ornaments and designer clothing for children. 800-375-6002.

CHURCH, SYNAGOGUE & CLERGY SUPPLIES

Ascalon Studios, 115 Atlantic Ave., Berlin, NJ 08009: Free brochure ❖ Synagogue art. 609-768-3779.

W. & E. Baum Bronze Tablet Corporation, 200 60th St., Brooklyn, NY 11220: Free catalog ❖ Donor walls, trees of life, yahrzeit tablets, plaques and awards, and other Judaic tablets. 800-922-7377; 718-439-3311 (in NY).

Cokesbury, Division United Methodist Publishing House, 201 8th Ave. South, P.O. Box 801, Nashville, TN 37202: Free information ❖ Bibles and bible reference books, bible study and Christian education books, fund-raising programs, gifts and casual wear, choir apparel, church and clergy supplies, and church furniture and equipment. 800-672-1789.

Emanuel Milstein, Syagogue Art, 29 Wyncrest Rd., Marlboro, NJ 07746: Free information ❖ Synagogue memorials, sculptures, trees of life, and other interior design art. 908-946-8604.

Presentations Gallery, 200 Lexington Ave., New York, NY 10016: Free information ❖ Contemporary synagogue art, furniture, memorial renditions, and recognition gifts. 212-481-8181.

Sanctuary Design Corporation, 14 Broadway, Malverne, NY 11565: Free information ❖ Eternal lights, holocaust memorials, other memorial systems, Torah ornaments, bimahs, and other sanctuary design components. 516-599-3173.

The Source for Everything Jewish, P.O. Box 48836, Niles, IL 60714: Free catalog ❖ Ritual and ceremonial objects, books, fine art, Kosher gourmet food, and audio and video cassettes. 800-426-2567.

David Strauss Designs Inc., 16 Braeland Ave., Newton Centre, MA 02159: Free information ❖ Synagogue art and furnishings. 617-527-0010.

U.S. Bronze Sign Company, 811 2nd Ave., New Hyde Park, NY 11040: Free catalog ❖ Donor recognition signs. 800-872-5155; 516-352-5155 (in NY).

CIGAR STORE INDIANS

Darren Hussey, P.O. Box 5, Newark, DE 19715: Free information with long SASE ❖ Handmade life-size solid wooden cigar store Indians and other wood carvings. 302-738-1888.

CLOCKS & CLOCK MAKING

Alpha Supply, P.O. Box 2133, Bremerton, WA 98310: Catalog $7 ❖ Clocks, clock movements, parts, and engraving tools. 800-257-4211.

The American Clock Maker, Division Woodland Products Inc., 71 S. Main St., P.O. Box 326, Clintonville, WI 54929: Free information ❖ Clock-making kits.

Armor Products, P.O. Box 445, East Northport, NY 11731: Free catalog ❖ Replacement movements for mantel, banjo, and grandfather clocks. 800-292-8296.

B & J Rock Shop, 14744 Manchester Rd., Ballwin, MO 63011: Catalog $3 ❖ Quartz clock movements and kits. 314-394-4567.

Charlie's Rock Shop, P.O. Box 399, Penrose, CO 81240: Free catalog ❖ Clocks, movements and parts, beads, display boxes, jewelry-making supplies, and faceted gemstones. 719-372-0117.

Circadian Clock Company, P.O. Box 7806, Dallas, TX 75209: Free brochure ❖ Analogue and dual-digit clocks. 800-637-8583.

Clock Repair Center, 33 Boyd Dr., Westbury, NY 11590: Catalog $6 ❖ Clock movements, repair parts, supplies, and tools. 516-997-4810.

Clocks Etc., 3401 Mt. Diablo Blvd., Lafayette, CA 94549: Brochure $1 ❖ Old and new clocks, antique furniture, and other gifts. 510-284-4720.

Gordon S. Converse & Company, Spread Eagle Village, 503 W. Lancaster Ave., Stratford, PA 19087: Catalog subscription $25 ❖ Antique clocks. 800-789-1001.

Craftsman Wood Service, 1735 W. Cortland Ct., Addison, IL 60101: Catalog $2 ❖ Kiln-dried and imported rare woods, veneers, hand and power tools, hardware, finishing materials, clock movements and kits, and lamp parts. 708-629-3100.

Ebersole Lapidary Supply, 11417 West Hwy. 54, Wichita, KS 67209: Catalog $2 ❖ Clocks, clock-making parts, tools, findings and mountings, cabochons and rocks, and jewelry kits. 316-722-4771.

Ed's House of Gems, 7712 NE Sandy Blvd., Portland, OR 97211: Free information with long SASE ❖ Clocks, clock-making parts, crystals, minerals, gemstones, and lapidary equipment. 503-284-8990.

Eloxite Corporation, Dept. 51, P.O. Box 729, Wheatland, WY 82201: Catalog $1 ❖ Clock-making parts, tools, gemstones, belt buckles, mountings, equipment for rock hounds, and craft supplies. 307-322-3050.

Emperor Clock Company, Emperor Industrial Park, P.O. Box 1089, Fairhope, AL 36533: Catalog $1 ❖ Grandfather clocks, kits, and parts. 800-642-0011; 334-928-2316 (in AL).

R. Engels & Company, 4031 Chicago Dr., P.O. Box 235, Grandville, MI 49418: Catalog $5 ❖ Wall, mantel, and grandfather clocks. 800-637-1118.

Gallery of Time, P.O. Box 1030, South Orleans, MA 02662: Free information ❖ Grandfather, wall, mantel, and table clocks. 800-325-6259.

Haskell's Handcraft, 40 College Ave., Waterville, ME 04901: Catalog $6 ❖ Quartz clock movements, parts, kits and assembled clocks, and electrical supplies. 207-873-5070.

House of Tyrol, P.O. Box 909, Alpenland Center, Helen Highway/75 North, Cleveland, GA 30528: Free catalog ❖ Musical cuckoo clocks. 800-241-5404.

Innovation Clock-Making Specialties, 11869 Teale St., Culver City, CA 90230: Free catalog ❖ Clock-making components and weather instruments. 800-421-4445; 310-398-8116 (in CA).

It's About Time, 7151 Ortonville Rd., Clarkston, MI 48016: Catalog $5 (refundable) ❖ Grandfather, wall, self-chiming, and other clocks. 800-423-4225.

Klockit, P.O. Box 636, Lake Geneva, WI 53147: Free catalog ❖ Grandfather and other clock kits, quartz and mechanical movements, parts, wood-finishing supplies, and tools. 800-556-2548.

Kuempel Chime, 21195 Minnetonka Blvd., Excelsior, MN 55331: Catalog $3 ❖ Kits and plans for grandfather clocks with bells or chimes, hand-painted moon wheels, and handcrafted pendulums. 800-328-6445.

S. LaRose Inc., 3223 Yanceyville St., P.O. Box 21208, Greensboro, NC 27420: Catalog $2.50 ❖ Clock replacement movements, motors, parts, and tools. 910-621-1936.

Little Big Horn Replica Company, P.O. Box 415, Crow Agency, MT 59022: Brochure $2 ❖ Wagon wheel clocks and chandeliers. 406-638-4458.

Merritt's Antiques Inc., P.O. Box 277, Douglassville, PA 19518: Catalog $3 ❖ Clock repair supplies and reproduction antique grandfather, wall, and shelf clocks. 215-689-9541.

Howard Miller Clock Company, 860 E. Main St., Zeeland, MI 49464: Catalog $5 ❖ Parts for building and repairing clocks. 616-772-9131.

Neon Clock, 246 3rd Ave., New Lenox, IL 60451: Free information ❖ Antique neon clocks. 815-485-5573.

Oregon Scientific, 18383 SW Boones Ferry Rd., Portland, OR 97224: Free brochure ❖ Liquid crystal display clocks. 800-863-8883.

Precision Movements, P.O. Box 689, Emmaus, PA 18049: Free catalog ❖ Clock kits, quartz movements, and parts. 215-967-3156.

Red & Green Minerals Inc., 7595 W. Florida Ave., Lakewood, CO 80226: Free information ❖ Clocks, movements, parts, and rock specimens from worldwide sources. 303-985-5559.

❖ CLOSETS & STORAGE SYSTEMS ❖

Richardson's Recreational Ranch Ltd., Gateway Route, Box 440, Madras, OR 97741: Free information ❖ Clocks, parts, movements, and rock specimens from worldwide sources. 503-475-2680.

Simply Country Furniture, HC 69, Box 147, Rover, AR 72860: Brochure $3 ❖ Grandfather clocks. 501-272-4794.

Steebar, P.O. Box 980, Andover, NJ 07821: Catalog $3 ❖ Clock kits, quartz clock and music box movements, and parts. 201-383-1026.

Terry Clocks, Patrick J. Terry, 2669 N. Lakeview Dr., Warsaw, IN 46580: Free brochure with long SASE ❖ Shelf clocks with a 19th-century-style. 219-858-2404.

Time Gallery, 3121 Battleground Ave., Greensboro, NC 28603: Free information ❖ Grandfather clocks. 910-282-5132.

Turncraft Clocks Inc., P.O. Box 100, Mound, MN 55364: Catalog $2 ❖ Clock kits and parts. 800-544-1711.

Whippoorwill Crafts, North Market Building, 6 Fanueil Hall Marketplace, Boston, MA 02109: Free information ❖ Kaleidoscopes, wooden boxes and chests, chimes, toys and games, clocks, and other crafts. 800-487-5937; 617-248-0671 (in MA).

Yankee Ingenuity, P.O. Box 113, Rt. 3, Box 164, Altus, OR 93521: Brochure $1 ❖ Clocks and clock-making parts. 800-537-0464.

CLOSETS & STORAGE SYSTEMS

Closetmaid, 720 SW 17th St., Ocala, FL 34478: Free information ❖ Wire basket caddies and shelving accessories. 800-874-0008.

Elfa Closet Storage Accessories, 300-3A Rt. 17 South, Lodi, NJ 07644: Free information ❖ Epoxy-covered steel shelves, bins, and accessories for storage rooms and closets. 201-777-1554.

Consolidated Plastics Company Inc., 8181 Darrow Rd., Twinsburg, OH 44087: Free information ❖ Closet and storage room accessories. 800-362-1000.

Hirsh Company, 8051 Central Ave., Skokie, IL 60076: Free information ❖ Easy-to-install closet organizers and shelf units. 708-673-6610.

Journeyman Products Ltd., 303 Najoles Rd., Millersville, MD 21108: Free information ❖ Stackable tray and box storage system. 800-248-8707.

Kasten Inc., 5080 N. Ocean Dr., Singer Island, FL 33404: Free information ❖ Bedside, foot-end, and under-the-bed slide-and-hide support for heavy luggage and TVs. 407-845-1087.

Knape & Vogt, 2700 Oak Industrial Dr. NE, Grand Rapids, MI 49505: Free catalog ❖ Shelving, storage, and work systems. Also drawer slides. 616-459-3311.

Laminations Inc., 3311 Windquest Dr., Holland, MI 49424: Free information ❖ Easy-to-install storage units, shelves, and rods. 800-562-4257.

Lean-2 Racks, Jack Murray Company, P.O. Box 1776, Cedar Ridge, CA 95924: Free brochure ❖ Sport and home utility storage racks for bicycles, skis, fishing poles, flower pots, books and video tapes, towels and quilts, and collector plates. 916-274-3710.

Lifestyle Systems, P.O. Box 5031, Huntington Beach, CA 92615: Free information with long SASE ❖ Easy-to-assemble any-size drawer compartment organizers. 800-955-3383.

Material Control Inc., 338 Sullivan Rd. East, Aurora, IL 60504: Free catalog ❖ Industrial storage bins and accessories for home use. 800-926-0376; 708-892-4274 (in IL).

Rubbermaid, 1147 Akron Rd., Wooster, OH 44691: Free information ❖ Closet and storage room accessories. 216-264-6464.

Rutt Custom Cabinetry, P.O. Box 129, Goodville, PA 17528: Catalog $7 ❖ Storage room and closet cabinets. 800-420-7888.

Schulte Corporation, 12115 Ellington Ct., Cincinnati, OH 45249: Free information ❖ Closet and room storage organizers. 800-669-3225.

The SICO Room Makers, 5000 Beltline Rd., #250, Dallas, TX 75240: Free information ❖ Wall beds, home office furniture, and wall systems. 800-659-8634; 214-960-1315 (in TX).

White Home Products, P.O. Box 340, Smyrna, GA 30081: Free information ❖ Automatic revolving carousels for closets. 404-431-0900.

CLOTHING & ACCESSORIES

Bridal Fashions

Bridal Slips, 65 Hope St., #FL6, Brooklyn, NY 11211: Free information ❖ Bridal slips and lingerie.

Country Elegance, 7353 Greenbush Ave., North Hollywood, CA 91605: Catalog $4.50 ❖ Bridal fashions and accessories. 818-765-1551.

Peter Fox Bridal Shoes, 806 Madison Ave., New York, NY 10021: Catalog $3 ❖ Bridal boots and shoes. 800-338-3430.

Illusions of Grandeur, P.O. Box 735, Cloverdale, CA 95425: Free catalog ❖ Make-them-yourself kits for headpieces, veils, and other bridal accessories.

Impression Bridal, 10850 Wilcrest, Houston, TX 77099: Free information ❖ Wedding gowns, headpieces, and veils. 800-274-3251; 713-530-6695 (in TX).

Jessica McClintock Bridal, Mail Order Department, 1400 16th St., San Francisco, CA 94103: Catalog $6 ❖ Bridal fashions and bridesmaid dresses. 415-495-3030.

J.C. Penney Company Inc., Catalog Division, Milwaukee, WI 53263 (west of Mississippi River), Atlanta, GA 30390 (east of Mississippi River): Free information ❖ Fashions and accessories for the bride and attendants. Includes petite and misses clothing. 800-222-6161.

P.C. Mary's Inc., 10520 Kinghurst Dr., Houston, TX 77099: Free catalog ❖ Wedding gowns. 713-933-9678.

Children's Clothing

After the Stork, 1501 12th St. NW, Albuquerque, NM 87104: Free catalog ❖ Natural fiber clothing for infants and children up to age 7. 800-333-5437.

Hanna Anderson, 1010 NW Flanders, Portland, OR 97209: Free catalog ❖ Children's clothing. 800-222-0544.

Baby Clothes Wholesale, 70 Ethel Rd. West, Piscataway, NJ 08854: Catalog $3 (3 issues) ❖ Clothing for babies and children. 908-572-9520.

Bemidji Woolen Mills, P.O. Box 277, Bemidji, MN 56601: Free brochure ❖ Woolen outerwear for men, women, and children. 218-751-5166.

Big Dog Sportswear, Mail Order, 3112 A Seaborg Ave., Ventura, CA 93003: Free catalog ❖ T-shirts and clothing for children. 800-642-3647.

Biobottoms, P.O. Box 6009, Petaluma, CA 94953: Free catalog ❖ Cotton outerwear and dress-up clothing for infants, toddlers, and older children. 800-766-1254; 707-778-7152 (in CA).

Cherry Tree Clothing, 166 Valley St., Providence, RI 02909: Free information ❖ Children's outerwear. 800-869-7742.

Childcraft, 250 College Park, P.O. Box 1811, Peoria, IL 61656: Free catalog ❖ Play clothes for boys, sizes 4 to 16 and girls, sizes 4 to 6X and 7 to 14. 800-631-5657.

Children's Wear Digest, 3607 Mayland Ct., Richmond, VA 23233: Free catalog ❖ Children's clothing for school, playtime, dressing-up, and keeping warm. 800-433-1895.

Croning Angels, 3450 Palmer Dr., Ste. 7153, Cameron Park, CA 95682: Catalog $2.50 ❖ One-stop shopping for tuxedos, slips and socks, sportswear, party dresses, jewelry, hats, crown boxes, and pageant needs for infants through teens. 800-295-8031.

Esprit Outlet, 499 Illinois St., San Francisco, CA 94107: Free catalog ❖ Fashionable clothing for children and their mothers. 415-957-2540.

Exclusive Appeal, 90-05 213th St., Queens, NY 11428: Catalog $4.50 ❖ Denim sportswear for men, women, and children. Includes jumpsuits, dresses, blouses, and items in sizes small to extra-large. 718-468-2534.

CLOTHING & ACCESSORIES

Garnet Hill, 262 Main St., Franconia, NH 03580: Free catalog ❖ Adult sleepwear, maternity clothing, natural fiber underwear, and sleepwear and outerwear for children. 800-622-6216.

Hand Painted Clothing, Main Street, P.O. Box 522, Phoenicia, NY 12464: Free price list ❖ Machine-washable, tumble-dry, and 100 percent pre-shrunk cotton hand-painted clothing. 914-688-7922.

Kid Sport, 122 E. Meadow Dr., Vail, CO 81657: Free catalog ❖ Winterwear and skiwear for children, from newborn through young adult. 800-833-1729.

Kids West, 18924 Hopfe St., Hockley, TX 77447: Catalog $2 ❖ Western fashions and gear, boots, accessories, and gifts for infants to young teens. 713-255-9775.

Laughing Bear, P.O. Box 233, Woodstock, NY 12498: Free brochure ❖ Clothing and T-shirts for infants, toddlers, and older children. 914-246-3810.

Mothertime, 4245 Kanox Ave., Chicago, IL 60641: Free list of retail sources ❖ Maternity, newborn, and infant apparel. 800-888-8281.

The Natural Baby Company, 816 Silvia St., Trenton, NJ 08628: Free information ❖ Children's clothing. 800-388-BABY.

Oshkosh Direct, Division Oshkosh B'Gosh Inc., P.O. Box 2222, Monroe, WI 53566: Free catalog ❖ Oshkosh clothing for babies and older children. 800-MY-BGOSH.

Patagonia, 8550 White Fir St., Reno, NV 89523: Free catalog ❖ Outdoor clothing for children and adults. 800-638-6464.

J.C. Penney Company Inc., Catalog Division, Atlanta, GA 30390: Free information ❖ Children's clothing in large sizes. 800-222-6161.

Playclothes, P.O. Box 29137, Overland Park, KS 66201: Free catalog ❖ Children's clothing for dressing up and playtime. 800-362-7529.

Pleasant Company, P.O. Box 620190, Middleton, WI 53562: Free catalog ❖ Classic clothing for little girls. 800-845-0005.

Rubens & Marble Inc., P.O. Box 14900, Chicago, IL 60614: Free brochure with long SASE ❖ Clothing and bedding for infants. 312-348-6200.

Simply Divine-All Cotton Clothing, 606 S. Congress, Austin, TX 78704: Free brochure ❖ All-cotton clothing for women, infants, and children. 512-444-5546.

Special Clothes, P.O. Box 333, East Harwich, MA 02645: Free catalog ❖ Adaptive clothing for children with disabilities, size 2 toddler through young adult. 508-430-5172.

Spencer's Inc., P.O. Box 988, Mt. Airy, NC 27030: Free information ❖ Infant and children's clothing. 910-789-9111.

Spiegel, P.O. Box 182563, Columbus, OH 43218: Free information ❖ Children's clothing, shoes, and toys. 800-345-4500.

Storybook Heirlooms, 333 Hatch Dr., Foster City, CA 94404: Free catalog ❖ Children's clothing and gifts. 800-899-7666.

Talbots for Kids, 175 Beal St., Hingham, MA 02043: Free catalog ❖ Clothing for boys, sizes 4 to 12 and sizes 4 to 14 for girls. 800-543-7123.

Tortellini, P.O. Box 2515, Sag Harbor, NY 11963: Free catalog ❖ Children's dressing-up and fun-to-wear clothing. 800-527-8725; 516-725-9285 (in NY).

Twincerely Yours, 748 Lake Ave., Clermont, FL 34711: Free catalog with long SASE ❖ Gifts, novelties, and T-shirts for twins and their families. 904-394-5493.

Wooden Soldier, P.O. Box 800, North Conway, NH 03860: Free catalog ❖ Children's designer clothing. 800-375-6002.

Yellow Turtle, Mt. Road, Stowe, VT 05672: Free catalog ❖ Clothing, skiwear, and accessories for children. 800-439-4435; 802-253-4434 (in VT).

Exercise Clothing

Adidas USA, 5675 N. Blackstock Rd., Spartanburg, SC 29303: Free information ❖ Men and women's shorts and singlets, aerobic and workout shoes, socks, and warm-up suits. 800-423-4327.

Austad's, 4500 E 10th St., P.O. Box 5428, Sioux Falls, SD 57196: Free catalog ❖ Equipment and clothing for most major sports. 800-444-1234.

Body Wrappers, Attitudes in Dressing Inc., 1350 Broadway, Ste. 304, New York, NY 10018: Free information ❖ Exercise suits, leotards, headbands, leg warmers, women's shorts, and warm-up suits. 800-323-0786; 212-279-3492 (in NY).

California Best, 970 Broadway, Ste. 104, Chula Vista, CA 91911: Free catalog ❖ Men and women's exercise and fitness clothing. 800-438-9327.

Champion Products Inc., 475 Corporate Square Dr., Winston-Salem, NC 27105: Free information ❖ Exercise clothing, leotards, shorts, and singlets for men and women.

Danmar Products Inc., 221 Jackson Industrial Dr., Ann Arbor, MI 48103: Free catalog ❖ Hydro-fitness products and soft swim boots for sensitive feet. 800-783-1998; 313-761-1990 (in MI).

Danskin, 111 W. 40th St., 18th Floor, New York, NY 10018: Free information ❖ Exercise suits, headbands, leg warmers, leotards, singlets for women, warm-up suits, and wrist bands. 800-288-6749; 212-764-4630 (in NY).

Freed of London Inc., 922 7th Ave., New York, NY 10019: Free price list ❖ Exercise clothing and gym shoes and footwear for women and men. 212-489-1055.

Gold's Gym, 360 Hampton Dr., Venice, CA 90291: Free information ❖ Gloves, headbands, leotards, aerobic and workout shoes, shorts, singlets, and warm-up suits. 800-457-5375; 213-392-3005 (in CA).

Hind Sportswear, P.O. Box 12609, San Luis Obispo, CA 93406: Free information ❖ Exercise suits, gloves, leotards, shorts, socks, and singlets for men and women. 800-426-4463.

Jazzertogs, 1050 Joshua Way, Vista, CA 92083: Free catalog ❖ Exercise clothing. 800-FIT-ISIT.

Jet Trends, 5555 W. 36th Ave., Hialeah, FL 33016: Free information ❖ Men and women's clothing for jet skiing and other water activities. 800-486-7547; 305-637-4020 (in FL).

Leo's Dancewear Inc., 1900 N. Narragansett Ave., Chicago, IL 60639: Free catalog with request on school stationery ❖ Leg warmers, leotards, workout shoes, and headbands. 312-889-7700.

Gilda Marx Industries, 5340 Allard Rd., Los Angeles, CA 90066: Free information ❖ Exercise suits, leotards, headbands, leg warmers, shorts, and warm-up suits. 800-876-6279; 310-578-6279 (in CA).

New Balance Athletic Shoe Inc., 38 Everett St., Boston, MA 02134: Free information ❖ Exercise suits, leotards, workout shoes, shorts and singlets for men and women, and warm-up suits. 800-622-1218.

Pony USA Inc., 2801 Red Dot Ln., Knoxville, TN 37914: Free information ❖ Exercise suits, headbands, leotards, aerobic and workout shoes, shorts, singlets, and warm-up suits.

Puma USA Inc., 147 Centre St., Brockton, MA 02403: Free information with long SASE ❖ Exercise suits, headbands, leg warmers, leotards, shorts, socks, aerobic and workout shoes, singlets, and warm-up suits. 508-583-9100.

Royal Textile Mills Inc., P.O. Box 250, Yanceyville, NC 27379: Free information ❖ Exercise suits, head and wrist bands, leg warmers, leotards, socks, and warm-up suits. 800-334-9361; 910-694-4121 (in NC).

Spalding Sports Worldwide, 425 Meadow St., P.O. Box 901, Chicopee, MA 01201: Free list of retail sources ❖ Exercise suits, headbands, leotards, shorts and singlets for men and women, and warm-up suits. 800-225-6601.

Full-Figured Women's Clothing

Sue Brett, P.O. Box 8384, Indianapolis, IN 46283: Free catalog ❖ Women's clothing in sizes 8 to 24. Also in petite and tall sizes. 800-784-8001.

CLOTHING & ACCESSORIES

Brownstone Woman, 685 3rd Ave., New York, NY 10017: Free catalog ❖ Clothing, sizes 14W to 28W. 800-322-2991.

Lane Bryant, P.O. Box 8320, Indianapolis, IN 46283: Free catalog ❖ Misses clothing in size 14 to 20, half sizes 12-1/2 to 34-1/2, and size 36 to 60. Also shoes, size 6 to 12, AA to EEE. 800-477-7030.

Dion-Jones Ltd., 555 W. Roosevelt Rd., #7, Chicago, IL 60607: Free catalog ❖ Skirts, dresses, pants, jackets, and coats for full-figured women. 312-243-4333.

Essence by Mail, 2515 E. 43rd St., P.O. Box 182204: Free catalog ❖ Fashions for women in sizes 8 to 20 for Misses and 16W to 24W for the full-figured person. 88-6-ESSENCE.

FSA Plus Woman, 85 Laurel Haven, Fairview, NC 28730: Free catalog ❖ Separates, jackets, dresses, pants, sweaters, and other fashions. 800-628-5525.

Just My Size, P.O. Box 748, Rural Hall, NC 27098: Free catalog ❖ Lingerie for full-figured women, size 14 and up. 800-522-9567.

Just Right Clothing, 30 Tozer Rd., Beverly, MA 01915: Free catalog ❖ Clothing, size 14 and up. 800-767-6666.

Lerner New York, Midwest Distribution Center, P.O. Box 8380, Indianapolis, IN 46283: Free catalog ❖ Clothing in half sizes, 12-1/2 to 34-1/2; women's sizes 34 to 54; misses sizes 12 to 24. Also shoes, size 6 to 12, AA to EEE. 800-288-4009.

Old Pueblo Traders, Palo Verde at 34th, P.O. Box 27800, Tucson, AZ 85726: Free catalog ❖ Women's clothing in misses, full-figured, and half sizes. 520-748-8600.

J.C. Penney Company Inc., Catalog Division, Atlanta, GA 30390: Free information ❖ Clothing for full-figured and tall women, in sizes up to 32W. 800-222-6161.

Regalia, Palo Verde at 34th, P.O. Box 27800, Tucson, AZ 85726: Free catalog ❖ Fashions and intimate apparel in large sizes. Also shoes in hard-to-find sizes and narrow to wide-wide widths. 520-747-5000.

Roaman's, P.O. Box 8360, Indianapolis, IN 46283: Free catalog ❖ Clothing for full-figured women. Includes sizes 12 to 26 for misses, 34 to 56 for full-figured women, and half sizes. Also shoes and boots in hard-to-fit sizes. 800-274-7130.

Silhouettes, Five Avery Row, Roanoke, VA 24012: Free catalog ❖ Women's sportswear and casual clothing, size 14W to 26W. 800-704-3322.

Spiegel, P.O. Box 182563, Columbus, OH 43218: Free information ❖ Sportswear and casual clothing in large sizes. 800-345-4500.

Nicole Summers, Winterbrook Way, P.O. 3003, Meredith, NH 03253: Free catalog ❖ Clothing for women, sizes 10 to 20. 800-642-6786.

Lingerie & Underwear

Beauty by Spector Inc., McKeesport, PA 15134: Free catalog ❖ Women's wigs and hairpieces, men's toupees, jewelry, and exotic lingerie. 412-673-3259.

Sue Brett, P.O. Box 8384, Indianapolis, IN 46283: Free catalog ❖ Women's lingerie and nighttime wear. 800-784-8001.

Lane Bryant, P.O. Box 8320, Indianapolis, IN 46283: Free catalog ❖ Intimate clothing, outerwear, dresses, blouses, coordinates, sweaters, and footwear. 800-477-7030.

Celestial Silks, P.O. Box 824, Fairfield, IA 52556: Free information ❖ In-stock and custom-made silk sheets, pillowcases, and silk-filled comforters. Also silk lingerie. 515-472-9062.

Chock Catalog Corporation, 74 Orchard St., New York, NY 10002: Catalog $2 ❖ Lingerie, hosiery, and underwear for women, men, and children. 800-222-0020; 212-473-1929 (in NY).

Damart, 3 Front St., Rollinsford, NH 03805: Free information ❖ Thermal underwear for men and women. 800-258-7300.

Decent Exposures, P.O. Box 27206, Seattle, WA 98125: Free information ❖ Women's underwear in 100 percent cotton. 800-524-4949; 206-364-4540 (in WA).

Frederick's of Hollywood, P.O. Box 229, Hollywood, CA 90099: Free catalog ❖ Intimate clothing and lingerie, casual clothing, swimwear, jewelry, and shoes. 310-637-7770.

Genie Products, 843 W. Adams St., Chicago, IL 60607: Free brochure ❖ Slimming lingerie and underwear for men and women.

Gohn Brothers, 105 S. Main, P.O. Box 111, Middlebury, IN 46540: Free information with long SASE ❖ Men and women's Amish clothing, underwear, and hosiery. 219-825-2400.

Green Pond Company, 12 Piedmont Center, Atlanta, GA 30305: Free brochure ❖ Men's boxer shorts. 800-827-POND.

Intimate Appeal, Palo Verde at 34th, P.O. Box 27800, Tucson, AZ 85726: Free catalog ❖ Intimate clothing for women who have had mastectomies. 520-748-8600.

Johnsen Woolen Mills Inc., Rt. 15, Johnson, VT 05656: Free brochure ❖ Woolen outerwear for men, women, and children. Also blankets, underwear, and sweaters. 802-635-2271.

Just My Size, P.O. Box 748, Rural Hall, NC 27098: Free catalog ❖ Lingerie for full-figured women, size 14 and up. 800-522-9567.

L'eggs Brands Inc., Outlet Catalog, P.O. Box 748, Rural Hall, NC 27098: Free catalog ❖ L'eggs, Hanes, Bali, and Playtex lingerie and hosiery. 800-522-1151.

Lady Grace Stores, P.O. Box 128, Malden, MA 02148: Free catalog ❖ Intimate apparel for everyday wear, nursing and maternity, and post-breast surgery. 800-922-0504.

Manshape, P.O. Box 453, Mill Valley, CA 94942: Free brochure ❖ Men's support underwear. 888-MANSHAPE; 415-435-5588 (in CA).

Mont-Bell, Catalog Customer Service, 940 1st Ave., Santa Cruz, CA 95062: Free catalog ❖ All-weather shells, long underwear, skiwear, clothing for outdoors, and travel and outdoor accessories. 800-683-2002.

National Wholesale Company Inc., 400 National Blvd., Lexington, NC 27294: Free catalog ❖ Hosiery and lingerie. 704-249-4202.

Newport News Fashions, Avon Ln., Hampton, VA 23630: Free catalog ❖ Daytime and nighttime intimate clothing. 800-688-2830.

No Nonsense Direct, P.O. Box 26095, Greensboro, NC 27420: Free catalog ❖ Hosiery. 800-677-5995.

One Hanes Place, Outlet Catalog, P.O. Box 748, Rural Hall, NC 27098: Free catalog ❖ Hosiery, lingerie, and women's clothing. 800-300-2600.

Petticoat Express, 1500 Hudson St., Hoboken, NJ 07030: Free information ❖ Lingerie. 201-798-9077.

Primary Layer, P.O. Box 6697, Portland, OR 97228: Free catalog ❖ Undergarments for men and women, in sizes to fit almost everyone. 800-282-8206.

Regalia, Palo Verde at 34th, P.O. Box 27800, Tucson, AZ 85726: Free catalog ❖ Fashions and intimate apparel in large sizes. Also shoes in hard-to-find sizes and narrow to wide-wide widths. 520-747-5000.

Roby's Intimates, 386 Cedar Ln., Teaneck, NJ 07666: Catalog $1 ❖ Bras, lingerie, and hosiery. 800-8788-BRA; 201-836-0630 (in NJ).

The Smart Saver, P.O. Box 105, Wasco, IL 60183: Free catalog ❖ Women's intimate apparel. 800-554-4453.

Teasel, 46 Main St., Middlebury, VT 05753: Free information ❖ Lingerie, fine soaps and toiletries, potpourri, and candles. 800-300-1204.

Undergear, Order Processing Center, Hanover, PA 17333: Free catalog ❖ Men's clothing and underwear. 800-853-8555.

Victoria's Secret, North American Office, P.O. Box 16589, Columbus, OH 43216: Free catalog ❖ Women's lingerie, other intimate wear, formal and casual clothing, and outerwear. 800-888-1500.

Mendell Weiss Inc., 91 Orchard St., New York, NY 10002: Free brochure ❖ Women's lingerie and lounging clothing. 212-925-6815.

CLOTHING & ACCESSORIES

Maternity Clothing

Bosom Buddies, P.O. Box 6138, Kingston, NY 12402: Free catalog ❖ Maternity bras and clothing for fashion-conscious women. Also accessories. 914-338-2038.

Bravado Designs, 69 Broadview Ave., Ste. 405, Toronto, Ontario, Canada M4M 2E6: Free information ❖ Maternity/nursing bra. 800-590-7802.

Caring Products International Inc., 200 1st Ave. West, Ste. 200, Seattle, WA 98119: Free information ❖ Incontinence supplies and maternity and special-needs clothing. 800-333-5379; 206-282-6040 (in WA).

Decent Exposures, P.O. Box 27206, Seattle, WA 98125: Free information ❖ Pregnancy and nursing bras. 800-524-4949; 206-364-4540 (in WA).

Garnet Hill, 262 Main St., Franconia, NH 03580: Free catalog ❖ Natural fiber maternity clothing, sleepwear, underwear, and outerwear. 800-622-6216.

Dan Howard's Maternity Factory Outlet, 4245 N. Knof Ave., Chicago, IL 60641: Free catalog ❖ Sportswear, casual and informal fashions, career wear, coordinates, sweaters, intimate wear, and maternity fashions. 800-9-MONTHS.

Lady Grace Stores, P.O. Box 128, Malden, MA 02148: Free catalog ❖ Intimate apparel for everyday wear, nursing and maternity, and post-breast surgery. 800-922-0504.

Maternity Blues, 920 S. Olive St., Los Angeles, CA 90015: Free information ❖ Maternity jeans, pants, tops, dresses, and underwear. 213-624-6488.

Maturna, P.O. Box 3500, Milford, CT 06460: Free information ❖ Adjustable maternity bra for use during and after pregnancy. 800-944-4006.

Mother's Place, P.O. Box 94512, Cleveland, OH 44101: Free catalog ❖ Casual, active, dress-up, and sleepwear for mothers-to-be. 800-829-0080; 216-826-1712 (in OH).

Mothers Work, 1309 Noble St., 6th Floor, Philadelphia, PA 19123: Catalog $3 ❖ Maternity suits and dresses. 215-625-9259.

Mothertime, 4245 Kanox Ave., Chicago, IL 60641: Free list of retail sources ❖ Maternity, newborn, and infant apparel. 800-888-8281.

Motherwear, P.O. Box 927, Northampton, MA 01061: Free catalog ❖ Easy access clothing for nursing mothers. 800-950-2500.

Holly Nicolas Nursing Collection, P.O. Box 7121, Orange, CA 92613: Catalog $1 ❖ Clothing for mothers-to-be and after the baby is born. 714-639-5933.

J.C. Penney Company Inc., Catalog Division, Atlanta, GA 30390: Free information ❖ Career and casual maternity clothing in petite, misses, tall, and regular sizes. 800-222-6161.

Men & Women's Clothing

Allen Allen USA, Attention: Catalog Order, 20003 S. Rancho Way, Rancho Dominguez, CA 90220: Free catalog ❖ Women's sportswear, casual clothing, and swimwear. 800-422-0466.

Andover Shop, 127 Main St., P.O. Box 5127, Andover, MA 01810: Free catalog ❖ Silk ties and clothing for men. 508-475-2252.

Appleseed's, 30 Tozer Rd., P.O. Box 1020, Beverly, MA 01915: Free catalog ❖ Clothing for women, size 4 to 18. 800-767-6666.

Armoire, 408 Pasadena Ave., Ste. 5, Pasadena, CA 91105: Free catalog ❖ Women's casual clothing. 800-528-3131.

Artist's Collar Neckties, P.O. Box 330315, Miami, FL 33233: Free catalog ❖ Provocative and unique neckties designed by internationally acclaimed artists. 800-434-8700.

Athletic Supply, 10850 Sanden Dr., Dallas, TX 75238: Free catalog ❖ Men and women's sportswear, jackets, T-shirts, memorabilia, figurines, and gifts. 214-348-7200.

Atlantis, 30 Barnet Blvd., New Bedford, MA 02745: Free catalog ❖ Foul weather gear and clothing for yachtsmen and fishermen. 508-995-7000.

Australian Connection, 1716 E. Brundage Ln., Sheridan, WY 82801: Free information ❖ Outback coats for men and women. 800-248-8355.

Bachrach Clothing Catalog, P.O. Box 8740, Decatur, IL 62524: Free catalog ❖ Men's clothing. 800-637-5840.

Eddie Bauer, P.O. Box 3700, Seattle, WA 98124: Free catalog ❖ Active and casual clothing for men and women. 800-426-8020.

L.L. Bean, Freeport, ME 04033: Free catalog ❖ Outdoor clothing, footwear, and sporting accessories for men and women. 800-221-4221.

Beau Ties Ltd. of Vermont, 19 Gorham Ln., Middlebury, VT 05753: Free brochure ❖ Hand-stitched 100 percent silk free-style bow ties. 800-488-TIES.

Bedford Fair, 421 Landmark Dr., Wilmington, NC 28410: Free catalog ❖ Women's casual and career clothing and swimwear. 800-964-9030.

Bemidji Woolen Mills, P.O. Box 277, Bemidji, MN 56601: Free brochure ❖ Woolen outerwear for men, women, and children. 218-751-5166.

Atelier Biamón, P.O. Box 55-7848, Miami, FL 33255: Catalog $4 ❖ Designer haute couture clothing, sizes 6 to 14. 305-663-1577.

Big Dog Sportswear, Mail Order, 3112 A Seaborg Ave., Ventura, CA 93003: Free catalog ❖ Lounge wear for women, boxer shorts for men, and men and women's outerwear. Also T-shirts and sweatshirts. 800-642-3647.

Bila of California, 2340 E. Olympic Blvd., Los Angeles, CA 90021: Free catalog ❖ Women's casual clothing and jewelry. 800-824-3541; 213-746-4190 (in CA).

Blair, Warren, PA 16367: Free catalog ❖ Men and women's clothing.

Boston Proper, 6500 Park of Commerce Blvds. NW, P.O. Box 3048, Boca Raton, FL 33431: Free catalog ❖ Designer women's sportswear. 800-243-4300.

The Bow Tie Club, P.O. Box 20420, Baltimore, MD 21284: Free catalog ❖ Handmade bow ties. 888-BOW-TIES.

Sue Brett, P.O. Box 8384, Indianapolis, IN 46283: Free catalog ❖ Women's clothing in sizes 8 to 24. 800-784-8001.

Brooks Brothers, 350 Campus Plaza, P.O. Box 4016, Edison, NJ 08818: Free catalog ❖ Men and women's sportswear, casual clothing, and shoes. 800-274-1815.

Brownstone Studio, 685 3rd Ave., New York, NY 10017: Free catalog ❖ Women's sportswear, lounging attire, casual and career clothing, and sleepwear. 800-322-2991.

Lane Bryant, P.O. Box 8320, Indianapolis, IN 46283: Free catalog ❖ Women's outerwear, dresses and blouses, sweaters, intimate clothing, and footwear. 800-477-7030.

Bullock & Jones, P.O. Box 883124, San Francisco, CA 94188: Free catalog ❖ Men and women's clothing. 800-227-3050.

Cable Car Clothiers, 246 Sutter St., San Francisco, CA 94108: Catalog $3 ❖ Men's clothing. 415-397-4740.

Cahall's Brown Duck, P.O. Box 450, Mount Orab, OH 45154: Free catalog ❖ Outdoor work and sports clothing. 800-445-9675.

Canari Cycle Wear, 10025 Huennekens St., San Diego, CA 92121: Free information ❖ Winter apparel for bikers. 800-929-2925; 619-455-8245 (in CA).

Carabella Collection, 1852 McGaw Ave., Irvine, CA 92714: Catalog $3 ❖ Women's swimwear, evening and career wear, party dresses, and other clothing. 800-227-2235.

Casco Bay Fine Woolens, 192 Stevens Ave., Portland, ME 04102: Free brochure ❖ Handcrafted wool capes. 800-788-9842.

Cashmeres Etc., 1160 Kane Concourse, Bay Harbour, FL 33154: Free catalog ❖ Men and women's cashmere, silk, and cotton clothing. 800-441-7743.

Chadwick's of Boston, One Chadwick Pl., Box 1600, Brockton, MA 02403: Free catalog ❖ Casual and career clothing for women. 800-525-4420.

City Spirit, 2025 Concourse Dr., St. Louis, MO 63146: Free catalog ❖ Women's clothing. 800-443-1516; 314-993-1516 (in St. Louis).

❖ CLOTHING & ACCESSORIES ❖

The Classic Outfitters, 1880 Mountain Rd., Stowe, VT 05672: Free catalog ❖ Outdoor clothing. 800-353-3963.

Clifford & Wills, One Clifford Way, Asheville, NC 28810: Free catalog ❖ Career and casual clothing for women. 800-922-0114.

The Cockpit, 595 Broadway, New York, NY 10310: Free catalog ❖ Leather bombers, motorcycle jackets, varsities, jeans, and accessories. 212-925-5455.

Collections, P.O. Box 882883, San Francisco, CA 94188: Free catalog ❖ Men's shirts, sweaters, slacks, shoes, and belts. 800-762-7036.

Columbia Sportswear Company, 6600 N. Baltimore, Portland, OR 97203: Free list of retail sources ❖ Men's sportswear for fishing and other outdoor activities. 800-MA-BOYLE.

Joan Cook, 119 Foster St., P.O. Box 6008, Peabody, MA 01961: Free catalog ❖ Women's classic clothing. 800-935-0971.

J. Crew Outfitters, One Ivy Crescent, Lynchburg, VA 24513: Free catalog ❖ Casual clothing for men and women. 800-932-0043.

Mark Cross, 645 5th Ave., New York, NY 10022: Catalog $2 ❖ Men and women's clothing. 212-421-3000.

Deerskin Place, 283 Akron Rd., Ephrata, PA 17522: Catalog $1 ❖ Cowhide, sheepskin, and deerskin clothing. 717-733-7624.

DEVA Lifewear Inc., P.O. Box CCV, Westhope, ND 58793: Free catalog ❖ Comfortable cotton clothing for women and men, crafted at home. 800-222-8024.

Doneckers at Home, 409 N. State St., Ephrata, PA 17522: Free catalog ❖ Classic fashions for women and men. 800-377-2205.

Draper's & Damon's, 17911 Mitchell Ave. South, Irvine, CA 92714: Free catalog ❖ Women's fashions for misses, petites, and regular sizes. 800-843-1174.

Dress Fore the 9's, 613 1st St., Ste. 19, Brentwood, CA 94513: Free catalog ❖ Sportswear and mix-and-match action wear for women. Also shoes and jewelry. 800-306-FORE.

Early Winters, P.O. Box 4333, Portland, OR 97208: Free catalog ❖ Ski clothing, leisure separates, and outdoor clothing for men and women. 800-458-4438.

Essence by Mail, 2515 E. 43rd St., P.O. Box 182204: Free catalog ❖ Fashions for women in sizes 8 to 20 for Misses and 16W to 24W for the full-figured person. 88-6-ESSENCE.

Exclusive Appeal, 90-05 213th St., Queens, NY 11428: Catalog $7 ❖ Denim sportswear for men, women, and children. Includes jumpsuits, dresses, blouses, and items in sizes small to extra-large. 718-468-2534.

Extrasport Inc., 5305 NW 35th Ct., Miami, FL 33142: Free catalog ❖ All-terrain clothing and sportswear. 800-633-0837.

Faith Mountain Company, 42 Main St., P.O. Box 199, Sperryville, VA 22740: Free catalog ❖ Classic country-style gifts and clothing. 800-588-2548.

Filson, P.O. Box 34020, Seattle, WA 98124: Free information ❖ Outdoor clothing. 800-624-0201.

The Finals, 1466 Broadway, Ste. 500, New York, NY 10036: Free catalog ❖ Bicycling, aerobic, swimming, running, sweats, and exercise clothing. 800-SWIM-816; 212-302-1308 (in NY).

Forever Leather, 25130 County Road F-2, Cortez, CO 81321: Catalog $10 ❖ Elk, deer, horse, cow, and lambskin leather vests with optional decorative styling, lining, and other accents. 970-565-3575.

Frederick's of Hollywood, P.O. Box 229, Hollywood, CA 90099: Free catalog ❖ Intimate clothing and lingerie, casual fashions, swimwear, jewelry, and shoes. 310-637-7770.

FTC Ski & Sports, 1586 Bush St., San Francisco, CA 94109: Free catalog ❖ Skateboards and parts, snowboards, T-shirts, and clothing. 415-673-8363.

Garnet Hill, 262 Main St., Franconia, NH 03580: Free catalog ❖ Natural fiber adult sleepwear, maternity clothing, and underwear. Also sleepwear and outerwear for children. 800-622-6216.

The Gentlemen's Store, Jim Tatum, 5318 Normandy Blvd., P.O. Box 37559, Jacksonville, FL 32205: Free brochure ❖ Men's clothing. 800-874-5200.

Georgetown Leather Design/Tannery West, 400 S. Hwy. 169, Ste. 600, Minneapolis, MN 55426: Free list of retail sources ❖ Outerwear for men and women, purses, brief cases, and other accessories.

Gerry Sportswear, 1051 1st Ave. South, Seattle, WA 98134: Free information ❖ Men and women's outerwear. 800-934-3779.

Gohn Brothers, 105 S. Main, P.O. Box 111, Middlebury, IN 46540: Free information with long SASE ❖ Men and women's Amish clothing, underwear, and hosiery. 219-825-2400.

Green Mountain Mercantile, P.O. Box 3100, Manchester Center, VT 05255: Free catalog ❖ Men and women's clothing. 802-362-2528.

Haband for Her, 100 Fairview Ave., Prospect Park, NJ 07530: Free information ❖ Women's fashions. 800-742-2263.

Haband for Men, 100 Fairview Ave., Prospect Park, NJ 07530: Free information ❖ Men's shoes and wash-and-wear clothing. 800-742-2263.

Harold's, 765 Asp Ave., Norman, OK 73069: Free catalog ❖ Men and women's clothing and accessories. 800-676-5373.

Hermes of Paris Inc., 745 5th Ave., Ste. 800, New York, NY 10151: Free catalog ❖ Hermes scarves from France. 800-441-4488.

High Seas Foul Weather Gear, 880 Corporate Woods Pkwy., Vernon Hills, IL 60061: Free list of retail sources ❖ Clothing for the outdoors. 708-913-1100.

The Horchow Collection, P.O. Box 620048, Dallas, TX 75262: Free catalog ❖ Women's casual clothing. 800-395-5397.

Huntington Clothiers, 1285 Alum Creek Dr., Columbus, OH 43209: Free catalog ❖ Traditional fashions for men and women. 800-848-6203.

International Male, Order Processing Center, Hanover, PA 17333-0075: Free catalog ❖ Men's clothing. 800-293-9333.

James River Traders, James River Landing, Hampton, VA 23631: Free catalog ❖ Casual clothing for men and women. 804-827-6000.

Johnsen Woolen Mills Inc., Rt. 15, Johnson, VT 05656: Free brochure ❖ Woolen outerwear for men, women, and children. Also blankets, underwear, and sweaters. 802-635-2271.

Johnston & Murphy, Mail Order Shop, 1415 Murfreesboro Rd., Ste. 190, Nashville, TN 37217: Free catalog ❖ Men's shoes, socks, belts, and accessories. 800-424-2854.

Charles Keath Ltd., P.O. Box 48800, Atlanta, GA 30362: Free catalog ❖ Women's casual clothing and jewelry. 800-388-6565; 449-3100 (in Atlanta).

Ruth Kishline's Country Clothes, 9201 Old Petersburgh Rd., Evansville, IN 47711: Catalog $3 ❖ Women's clothing. 800-343-3062.

Knights Ltd. Catalog, 2025 Concourse Dr., St. Louis, MO 63146: Free catalog ❖ Women's casual and formal fashions and shoes. 800-240-7052.

La Costa Products International, 2875 Laker Ave. East, Carlsbad, CA 92009: Free catalog ❖ Men and women's clothing and spa essentials. 800-LA-COSTA.

Landau Woolens, 114 Nassau St., Princeton, NJ 08542: Free catalog ❖ Hand-knitted sweaters, Icelandic wool coats and jackets, blanket throws, sportswear, cotton knits, sleepwear, and shirts. 800-257-9445.

❖ CLOTHING & ACCESSORIES ❖

Lee-McClain Company Inc., 1857 Midland Trail, Shelbyville, KY 40065: Free brochure ❖ Men's suits, jackets, coats, and blazers. 502-633-3823.

Lerner New York, Midwest Distribution Center, P.O. Box 8380, Indianapolis, IN 46283: Free catalog ❖ Women's sportswear, casual clothing, sweaters, lingerie, jewelry, shoes and boots, and outerwear. 800-288-4009.

Lewis Creek Company, 2065 Shelburne Rd., Shelburne, VT 05482: Free information ❖ Outerwear. 800-336-4884.

Lion's Pride Catalog, P.O. Box 342, Little Chute, WI 54140: Free catalog ❖ Denim shirts, cotton knit sweaters, robes, and other clothing for men and women. 414-731-4242.

Madeleine Fashions Inc., 1112 7th Ave., Monroe, WI 53566: Catalog $3 ❖ Women's sportswear, sweaters, shoes, and separates. 800-344-1994.

Lew Magram, 414 Alfred Ave., P.O. Box 7696, Teaneck, NJ 07666: Free catalog ❖ Casual, career, coordinates, and formal fashions for women. 201-833-8500.

Orvis Manchester, 1711 Blue Hills Dr., P.O. Box 12000, Roanoke, VA 24022: Free catalog ❖ Outdoor clothing, sportswear, lingerie, sweaters, and shoes. 800-541-3541.

Mary Orvis Marbury, 1711 Blue Hills Dr., P.O. Box 12000, Roanoke, VA 24022: Free catalog ❖ Women's career, casual, and evening wear. 800-541-3541.

Philippe Marcel, 6836 Engle Rd., Cleveland, OH 44101: Free catalog ❖ Women's designer fashions. 800-869-9901.

Mark, Fore & Strike, 6500 Park of Commerce Blvd. NW, P.O. Box 5056, Boca Raton, FL 33431: Free catalog ❖ Classic, casual, and sportswear for men and women. 800-327-3627.

Mast General Store, Hwy. 194, Valle Crucis, NC 28691: Free information ❖ Hammocks and porch swings, housewares, boots, and traditional clothing. 704-963-6511.

Midwest Trade Imports, 1555 Sherman Ave., Ste. 236, Evanston, IL 60201: Information $2 ❖ Authentic hand-woven Ashanti Kente cloth stoles and fabrics from Ghana. 800-64-KENTE.

Midwestern Sport Togs, P.O. Box 230, Berlin, WI 54923: Free catalog ❖ Deerskin gloves, jackets and coats for men and women, footwear, handbags, and accessories. 414-361-5050.

Mont-Bell, Catalog Customer Service, 940 1st Ave., Santa Cruz, CA 95062: Free catalog ❖ All-weather shells, long underwear, skiwear, clothing for outdoors, and travel and outdoor accessories. 800-683-2002.

David Morgan, 11812 Northcreek Pkwy., Ste. 103, Bothell, WA 98011: Free catalog ❖ Hand-braided belts, fur hats, and wool and sheepskin clothing. 800-324-4934.

National Wholesale Company Inc., 400 National Blvd., Lexington, NC 27294: Free catalog ❖ Women's hosiery, panty hose, lingerie, sleepwear, and gowns. 704-249-4202.

Nauticode Inc., 274 Harkers Island Rd., Beaufort, NC 28516: Free catalog ❖ Clothing and gifts for boating enthusiasts. 800-628-8263.

Newport News Fashions, Avon Ln., Hampton, VA 23630: Free catalog ❖ Women's swimwear, casual coordinates, shoes, lingerie, sweaters, and sportswear. 800-688-2830.

North Beach Leather, 1335 Columbus Ave., San Francisco, CA 94133: Catalog $3 ❖ Leather clothing and jackets for men and women. 415-346-1113.

Olsen's Mill Direct, 1641 S. Main St., Oshkosh, WI 54901: Catalog $2 ❖ Clothing for men, women, and children. 800-537-4979.

One 212, 11 Avery Row, Roanoke, VA 24012: Free catalog ❖ Women's fashions. 800-216-2221.

Oomingmak Musk Ox Producers' Co-operative, 604 H St., Anchorage, AK 99501: Free information with long SASE ❖ Traditional hand-knitted clothing from rare wools of the domestic Arctic Musk Ox. 907-272-9225.

Orvis Travel, 1711 Blue Hills Dr., P.O. Box 12000, Roanoke, VA 24022: Free catalog ❖ Luggage, travel accessories, and men and women's clothing. 800-541-3541.

Otsuka, 122 Kentucky St., Petaluma, CA 94952: Free catalog ❖ Classic silk blouses for women. 800-769-4260.

Out of Control Swimwear Inc., 101 1st St., Ste. 602, Los Altos, CA 94022: Catalog $2 ❖ Resort wear, sports wear, and swimwear. 415-948-3390.

Barrie Pace Ltd., 100 Enterprise Pl., P.O. Box 7020, Dover, DE 19903: Free catalog ❖ Women's fashions. 800-441-6011.

Pant Warehouse, 6230 N. Oracle Rd., Tucson, AZ 85704: Catalog $1 (refundable) ❖ Jeans and shirts.

Papillon, 2025 Concourse Dr., St. Louis, MO 63146: Free catalog ❖ Sportswear and coordinates for women. 800-336-5112.

Passport International Ltd., 1007 Johnnie Dodds Blvd., Mt. Pleasant, SC 29464: Free catalog ❖ Men and women's clothing and accessories. 800-533-6904.

Pastille, P.O. Box 650503, Dallas, TX 75265: Free catalog ❖ Classic women's fashions for relaxed and formal occasions. 800-727-3900.

Pearl Izumi, 2300 Central Ave., Boulder, CO 80301: Free information ❖ Wind-resistant tights and jerseys with zippers for easy removal of the front panel. 303-938-1700.

Pendleton Shop, Jordan Rd., P.O. Box 233, Sedona, AZ 86336: Catalog $1 ❖ Men and women's sweaters and sportswear. 602-282-3671.

J.C. Penney Company Inc., Catalog Division, Atlanta, GA 30390: Free information ❖ Women's work clothing in full-figured and extra-tall sizes. Also career and casual fashions. 800-222-6161.

Penthouse Gallery, Priority Order Processing, 194 Barton St., Pawtucket, RI 02860: Free catalog ❖ Dresses for women. 800-221-7611.

J. Peterman Company, 1318 Russell Cave Rd., Lexington, KY 40505: Free catalog ❖ Men and women's apparel, accessories, home furnishings, garden items, gifts, footwear, and luggage. 800-231-7341.

Carroll Reed, P.O. Box 3008, Winterbrook Way, Meredith, NH 03253: Free catalog ❖ Women's sportswear and casual clothing. 800-343-5770.

Reflections Organic Inc., Rt. 1, Box 348, Trinity, TX 75862: Free catalog ❖ Organic cotton clothing for the entire family. 800-852-9273; 409-594-9019 (in TX).

Anthony Richards, 6836 Engle Rd., P.O. Box 94503, Cleveland, OH 44101: Free catalog ❖ Women's fashions. 216-826-1712.

Roaman's, P.O. Box 8360, Indianapolis, IN 46283: Free catalog ❖ Women's casual and career clothing, intimate wear, knits, shoes and boots, sleepwear, and coordinates. 800-274-7130.

Samuel Robert Direct, 414 River St., Haverhill, MA 01832: Free catalog ❖ Women's ultrasuede fashions. 800-288-2556.

Saint Laurie Ltd., 897 Broadway, New York, NY 10003: Catalog $2 ❖ Hand-tailored clothing. 212-473-0100.

Sarah Glove Company Inc., P.O. Box 1940, Waterbury, CT 06722: Catalog $1 ❖ Work clothes and jeans, shoes and boots, shirts, jackets, and gloves. 203-574-4090.

Scotland by the Yard, Rt. 4, Quechee, VT 05059: Free brochure ❖ Classic clothing, sweaters, gifts and jewelry, ties, and scarves from Scotland. 802-295-5351.

Serendipity, Palo Verde at 34th, P.O. Box 27800, Tucson, AZ 85726: Free catalog ❖ Women's formal and casual fashions, sweaters, and shoes. 520-748-8600.

Serengeti, P.O. Box 3349, Serengeti Park, Chelmsford, MA 01824: Free catalog ❖ Wildlife-theme apparel and gifts. 800-426-2852.

CLOTHING & ACCESSORIES

Sickafus Sheepskins, Rt. 78, Exit 7, Strausstown, PA 19559: Free catalog ❖ Sheepskin clothing. 215-488-1782.

Sidney's, P.O. Box 21138, Roanoke, VA 24018: Free catalog ❖ Casual and contemporary fashions for women.

Silk Collection, P.O. Box 620825, Middleton, WI 53562: Free catalog : Free catalog ❖ Silk clothing for women. 800-248-0804.

Ben Silver, 149 King St., Charleston, SC 29401: Free catalog ❖ Blazer buttons with school designs and monograms, cuff links, suspenders, breast patches, blazers, cotton sweats, neckties, shirts, and trousers. 800-BEN-SILVER.

Simply Divine-All Cotton Clothing, 606 S. Congress, Austin, TX 78704: Free brochure ❖ All-cotton clothing for women, infants, and children. 512-444-5546.

Simply Tops, 7 Avery Row, Roanoke, VA 24012: Free catalog ❖ Tops, casuals, sweaters, jackets, evening attire, lingerie, and other women's fashions. 800-624-5636.

Smith & Hawken, P.O. Box 6907, Florence, KY 41022: Free catalog ❖ Casual clothing for men and women. 800-776-3336.

Spike Nashbar Outlet Store, 4111 Simon Rd., Youngstown, OH 44512: Free catalog ❖ Sports clothing and equipment, bags, books and videos, and protective wear. 800-SPIKE-IT.

George Stafford & Sons, P.O. Box 2055, Thomasville, GA 31799: Free catalog ❖ Men and women's sportswear, casual fashions, and shoes. 800-826-0948.

Stage Clothes U.S.A., Division Superman U.S.A., 13 South 7th St., Minneapolis, MN 55402: Catalog $2 ❖ Leather jackets for men. 800-328-0965.

Paul Stuart, Madison Ave. at 45th St., New York, NY 10017: Catalog $3 ❖ Men and women's casual, career, and formal clothing. 800-678-8278.

Talbots, 175 Beal St., Hingham, MA 02043: Free catalog ❖ Women's clothing and coordinates. 800-992-9010.

Ann Taylor, P.O. Box 1304, New Haven, CT 06505: Free catalog ❖ Women's career, casual, and dress-up fashions. 800-825-6250.

Thai Silks, 252 State St., Los Altos, CA 94022: Free brochure ❖ Silk clothing. 800-722-SILK; 800-221-SILK (in CA).

Norm Thompson, P.O. Box 3999, Portland, OR 97208: Free catalog ❖ Men and women's clothing and gifts. 800-821-1287.

Thousand Mile Outdoor Wear, 1894 Alta Vista Dr., Vista, CA 92084: Free catalog ❖ Men and women's outdoor clothing. 800-786-7577; 619-945-1609 (in CA).

Tilley Endurables, 300 Lagner Rd., West Seneca, NY 14224: Free catalog ❖ Clothing for travelers with security and secret pockets for theft protection. 800-338-2797.

The Tog Shop, Lester Square, Americus, GA 31710: Free catalog ❖ Women's jump suits, shirts, outerwear, skirts and blouses, sleepwear, swimwear, and shoes and sandals. 800-342-6789.

Touch of Class Catalog, 1905 N. Van Buren St., Huntingburg, IN 47542: Free catalog ❖ Bathroom accessories, comforters, pillows, shams, window treatments, towels, rugs, and sleepwear for men, women, and children. 800-457-7456.

Travel Smith, 3140 Kerner Blvd., San Rafel, CA 94901: Free catalog ❖ Outdoor clothing and accessories for men and women. 800-950-1600.

Trifles, P.O. Box 620048, Dallas, TX 75262: Free catalog ❖ Clothing and jewelry for men, women, and children. 800-456-7019.

Tuttle Golf Collection, P.O. Box 888, Wallingford, CT 06492: Free catalog ❖ Sportswear for men and women. 800-882-7511.

Tweeds, One Avery Row, Roanoke, VA 24012: Free catalog ❖ Casual fashions for women. 800-999-7997.

The Ujena Company, 1135 Kern Ave., Sunnyvale, CA 94086: Catalog $2 ❖ Women's swimwear and sportswear. 800-227-8318.

Undergear, Order Processing Center, Hanover, PA 17333: Free catalog ❖ Men's clothing and underwear. 800-853-8555.

The Very Thing, Winterbrook Way, P.O. Box 3005, Meredith, NH 03253: Free catalog ❖ Women's clothing. 800-448-4988.

Victoria's Secret, North American Office, P.O. Box 16589, Columbus, OH 43216: Free catalog ❖ Women's clothing, lingerie, sleepwear, slippers, and gifts. 800-888-1500.

Walrus Inc., 4225 2nd Ave. South, Seattle, WA 98134: Free information ❖ Outerwear. 800-550-TENT.

Wathne Corporation, 1095 Cranbury South River Rd., Ste. 8, Jamesburg, NJ 08831: Free catalog ❖ Sportswear and outer clothing for men and women. Also accessories. 800-942-1166.

WearGuard Corporation, 141 Longwater Dr., Norwell, MA 02061: Free catalog ❖ Clothing for the working man and woman. 800-388-3300.

What on Earth, 2451 Enterprise East Pkwy., Twinsburg, OH 44087: Free catalog ❖ Fun wear and gifts for men, women, and children. 216-425-4600.

Whipp Trading Company, RR 1, Arrasmith Trail, Ames, IA 50010: Free catalog ❖ Sheepskin rugs, slippers, mittens, and hats. 800-533-9447.

Willow Ridge, 421 Landmark Dr., Wilmington, NC 28410: Free catalog ❖ Women's career, dress-up, and casual clothing. 800-388-2012.

Windjammer, 525 N. Main St., Bangor, PA 18013: Free information ❖ Jackets, shirts, T-shirts, sweatsuits, and other sportswear. 800-441-6958.

WinterSilks, 2700 Laura Ln., P.O. Box 620130, Middleton, WI 53562: Free catalog ❖ Silk turtlenecks, socks and glove liners, long johns, and ski clothing. 800-621-3229.

Wissota Trader, 1313 1st Ave., Chippewa Falls, WI 54729: Free catalog ❖ Women and men's clothing and shoes in hard-to-fit sizes. 800-962-0160.

WorkAbles for Women, Deborah Evans Crawford, Oak Valley, Clinton, PA 15026: Free catalog ❖ Gloves, hats, T-shirts, socks, outdoor clothing, rain gear, and personal safety items for women. 800-862-9317.

Worldwide Aquatics, 10500 University Center Dr., Ste. 250, Tampa, FL 33612: Free catalog ❖ Swimwear and accessories for men and women. 800-726-1530.

Natural Fiber Clothing

Garnet Hill, 262 Main St., Franconia, NH 03580: Free catalog ❖ Clothing, bed linens, comforters, blankets, pillows, pillow shams, and towels. 800-622-6216.

JANICE Corporation, 198 Rt. 46, Budd Lake, NJ 07828: Free catalog ❖ Allergy-free clothing, exercise wear, sleepwear, robes, towels, bath and personal grooming aids, and mattresses, pads, quilts, and linens. 800-JANICES.

Red Rose Collection, P.O. Box 280140, San Francisco, CA 94128: Free catalog ❖ Natural fiber clothing, books and tapes, art works, jewelry, tools, games, decorative accessories, and toiletries. 800-374-5505.

Vermont Country Store, Mail Order Office, P.O. Box 3000, Manchester Center, VT 05255: Free catalog ❖ Clothing and household items. 802-362-2400.

Petite Fashions

Sue Brett, P.O. Box 8384, Indianapolis, IN 46283: Free catalog ❖ Women's clothing in sizes 8 to 24. Also in petite and tall sizes. 800-784-8001.

Draper's & Damon's, 17911 Mitchell Ave. South, Irvine, CA 92714: Free catalog ❖ Women's fashions for misses, petites, and regular sizes. 800-843-1174.

Jean Grayson's Brownstone Studio Collection, 685 3rd Ave., New York, NY 10017: Free catalog ❖ Fashions for misses and petites. 800-221-2468.

The Horchow Collection, P.O. Box 620048, Dallas, TX 75262: Free catalog ❖ Petite women's clothing. 800-395-5397.

Old Pueblo Traders, Palo Verde at 34th, P.O. Box 27800, Tucson, AZ 85726: Free catalog ❖ Dresses, casual fashions, coordinates, outerwear, shoes, lingerie, and sweaters, for women 5'4" and under. 520-748-8600.

J.C. Penney Company Inc., Catalog Division, Atlanta, GA 30390: Free information ❖ Sportswear, casual fashions, and petite and misses clothing for brides and attendants. 800-222-6161.

Petite Ms, 555 Perkins Extd., Memphis, TN 38117: Catalog $2 ❖ Clothing for women 5'4" and under, sizes 2 to 16. 901-685-8362.

Spiegel, P.O. Box 182563, Columbus, OH 43218: Free information ❖ Career and weekend fashions for women under 5'4". 800-345-4500.

Talbots, 175 Beal St., Hingham, MA 02043: Free catalog ❖ Clothing for petite women. 800-992-9010.

Unique Petite, Palo Verde at 34th, P.O. Box 27800, Tucson, AZ 85726: Free catalog ❖ Sweaters, jeans, swimwear, and other fashions for women 5'4" and under. Also shoes in hard-to-fit sizes. 520-748-8600.

Shirts

Ascot Chang, A Gentlemen's Shirtmaker, 7 W. 57th St., New York, NY 10019: Free information ❖ Custom-made shirts. 800-486-9966.

Burberry's Limited, 9 E. 57th St., New York, NY 10022: Free list of retail sources ❖ Burberry's classic cotton shirts. 212-371-5010.

Paul Frederick Shirt Company, 223 W. Poplar St., Fleetwood, PA 19522: Free catalog ❖ Men's shirts, with French cut, button-down, tab, or straight collars, and French or button cuffs. 800-247-1417.

Huntington Clothiers, 1285 Alum Creek Dr., Columbus, OH 43209: Free catalog ❖ Men's shirts with optional monograms. 800-848-6203.

James River Traders, James River Landing, Hampton, VA 23631: Free catalog ❖ Men and women's casual clothes, beach attire, shirts, shoes, ties, robes, sweaters, and socks. 804-827-6000.

J.C. Penney Company Inc., Catalog Division, Milwaukee, WI 53263 (west of Mississippi River), Atlanta, GA 30390 (east of Mississippi River): Free information ❖ Shirts for men in regular, extra tall, and large sizes. Also ties and accessories. 800-222-6161.

The Queensboro Shirt Company, 1400 Marstellar St., Wilmington, NC 28401: Free brochure ❖ Custom-embroidered clothing in 100 percent cotton. 800-847-4478; 910-251-1251 (in NC).

Tilley Endurables, 300 Lagner Rd., West Seneca, NY 14224: Free catalog ❖ Cotton hooded shirts. 800-338-2797.

Treadwell Shirt Company, P.O. Box 667, Hartwell, GA 30643: Free brochure ❖ Cotton shirts for men. 800-367-7158.

Short Men

Harry Rothman Clothing, 200 Park Ave. South, New York, NY 10003: Free information with long SASE ❖ Extra-long and extra-short clothing in sizes 36 to 56. 212-777-7400.

The Short Shop, 49 Kearny St., San Francisco, CA 94108: Free information ❖ Short men's clothing. 800-233-9522; 415-321-5991 (in CA).

Short Sizes Inc., Southgate Shopping Center, 5385 Warrensville Center Rd., Cleveland, OH 44137: Free information ❖ Short men's clothing. 216-475-2515.

Bob Stern's Short Sizes Inc., 5385 Warrensville Center Rd., Cleveland, OH 44137: Free information ❖ Clothing for men under 5'8". 216-475-2515.

Special-Needs Clothing

Danmar Products Inc., 221 Jackson Industrial Dr., Ann Arbor, MI 48103: Free catalog ❖ Special-needs clothing. 800-783-1998; 313-761-1990 (in MI).

Fashion Ease, Division M & M Health Care, 1541 60th St., Brooklyn, NY 11219: Free catalog ❖ Special-needs clothing and accessories. 800-221-8929; 718-853-6376 (in NY).

The Fullington Corporation, 22186 W. Hwy. 176, Mundelein, IL 60060: Free brochure ❖ Men's easy-dressing clothes for independent living.

M.F. Geriatrics, P.O. Box 320, Ellis, KS 67637: Free catalog ❖ Easy-on and easy-off clothing and accessories for the elderly and disabled. 913-726-4807.

Support Plus, Box 500, Medfield, MA 02052: Free catalog ❖ Medically acceptable support hosiery, personal hygiene and home health care aids, bath safety accessories, and walking shoes. 508-359-2910.

Wardrobe Wagon, 555 Valley Rd., West Orange, NJ 07052: Free catalog ❖ Special-needs clothing. 800-992-2737.

Worldwide Home Health Center Inc., 926 E. Tallmadge Ave., Akron, OH 44310: Free catalog ❖ Ostomy appliances, mastectomy breast forms, special-needs clothing, and skin care products. 800-223-5938; 216-633-0366 (in OH).

Suspenders, Belts & Buckles

Caballo, 727 Canyon Rd., Santa Fe, NM 87501: Catalog $1 (refundable) ❖ Handmade leather belts. 800-359-4174.

Comstock Heritage Collection, 2300 Lockheed Way, Carson City, NV 89706: Free list of retail sources ❖ Silver belt buckles, pins, and jewelry. 702-246-3835.

Eloxite Corporation, Dept. 51, P.O. Box 729, Wheatland, WY 82201: Catalog $1 ❖ Belt buckles, tools, gemstones, jewelry mountings, and clock-making, rockhounding, and jewelry-making supplies. 307-322-3050.

Hay Charlie, 541 Historic Main St., Park City, UT 84060: Free information ❖ Handcrafted western-style boots, buckles and belts, hats, jewelry, clothing, and accessories.

Johnston & Murphy, Mail Order Shop, 1415 Murfreesboro Rd., Ste. 190, Nashville, TN 37217: Free catalog ❖ Men's shoes, socks, belts, and accessories. 800-424-2854.

Lifton Studio Inc., 121 S. 6th St., Stillwater, MN 55082: Catalog $5 ❖ Buckles, leather belts, trophy buckles, and reproductions of Old West badges in sterling silver. 612-439-7208.

David Morgan, 11812 Northcreek Pkwy., Ste. 103, Bothell, WA 98011: Free catalog ❖ Hand-braided belts, wool and sheepskin clothing, and hats. 800-324-4934.

Naples Creek Leather, 188 S. Main St., Naples, NY 14512: Free catalog ❖ Leather moccasins, slippers, belts, gloves, casual footwear, and deerskin handbags. 800-836-0616.

Sweaters

Henri Bendel, 712 5th Ave., New York, NY 10019: Free information ❖ Casual, outdoor, and dress sweaters for women. 212-247-1100.

J. Crew Outfitters, One Ivy Crescent, Lynchburg, VA 24513: Free catalog ❖ Mock turtlenecks, cardigans, button-down, and other sweaters for men and women. 800-932-0043.

Garnet Hill, 262 Main St., Franconia, NH 03580: Free catalog ❖ Cashmere sweaters. 800-622-6216.

James River Traders, James River Landing, Hampton, VA 23631: Free catalog ❖ Men and women's sweaters. 804-827-6000.

Johnsen Woolen Mills Inc., Rt. 15, Johnson, VT 05656: Free brochure ❖ Woolen outerwear for men, women, and children. Also blankets, underwear, and sweaters. 802-635-2271.

Landau Woolens, 114 Nassau St., Princeton, NJ 08542: Free catalog ❖ Men and women's hand-knitted wool sweaters, Icelandic wool coats and jackets, blanket throws, wool sportswear, shirts, and cotton knits. 800-257-9445.

Lion's Pride Catalog, P.O. Box 342, Little Chute, WI 54140: Free catalog ❖ Cotton knit sweaters and clothing for big and tall men. 414-731-4242.

Pendleton Shop, Jordan Rd., P.O. Box 233, Sedona, AZ 86336: Catalog $1 ❖ Men and women's sweaters and sportswear. 602-282-3671.

❖ CLOTHING & ACCESSORIES ❖ 127

Peruvian Connection, Canaan Farm, Box 990, Tonganoxie, KS 66086: Free catalog ❖ Handmade Pima cotton and Alpaca wool sweaters. 800-221-8520.

Scotland by the Yard, Rt. 4, Quechee, VT 05059: Free brochure ❖ Classic clothing, sweaters, gifts and jewelry, ties, and scarves from Scotland. 802-295-5351.

Wanderings Inc., P.O. Box 4344, Warren, NJ 07059: Free catalog ❖ Hand-knitted wool sweaters and special occasion gifts. 800-456-KNIT.

WinterSilks, 2700 Laura Ln., P.O. Box 620130, Middleton, WI 53562: Free catalog ❖ Turtlenecks, sweaters, silk long johns, and other fashions. 800-621-3229.

Tall & Big Men's Clothing

L.L. Bean, Freeport, ME 04033: Free catalog ❖ Outdoor clothing and sportswear for tall men. 800-221-4221.

Casual Male Big & Tall, c/o Brigar Data Services, 5 Sandcreek Rd., Albany, NY 12205: Free list of retail sources ❖ Clothing for big and tall men. 800-THINK-BIG.

King Size Company, P.O. Box 9115, Hingham, MA 02043: Free catalog ❖ Tall and big men's clothing. 800-846-1600.

Lion's Pride Catalog, P.O. Box 342, Little Chute, WI 54140: Free catalog ❖ Recycled cotton knit sweaters and other clothing for big and tall men. 414-731-4242.

J.C. Penney Company Inc., Catalog Division, Atlanta, GA 30390: Free information ❖ Shirts, pants, and other clothing. 800-222-6161.

Phoenix Big & Tall, 1492 Bluegrass Lakes Pkwy., Alpharetta, GA 30201: Free catalog ❖ Casual, informal, sportswear, outerwear, sleepwear, and other large-size clothing. 800-251-8067.

Repp Big & Tall, Bluegrass Lakes Pkwy., Alpharetta, GA 30201: Free catalog ❖ Tall and big men's clothing. 800-690-7377.

Rochester Big & Tall, 1301 Avenue of Americas, New York, NY 10019: Free catalog ❖ Tall and big men's clothing. 800-282-8200.

Sheplers, P.O. Box 7702, Wichita, KS 67277: Free catalog ❖ Western clothing for tall men. 800-242-6540.

I. Spiewak & Sons Inc., 505 8th Ave., New York, NY 10018: Free brochure ❖ Outerwear for men, sizes 6X to XXXXLT. 800-223-6850; 212-695-1620 (in NY).

Tall Women's Clothing

L.L. Bean, Freeport, ME 04033: Free catalog ❖ Outdoor clothing and sportswear for tall women. 800-221-4221.

Sue Brett, P.O. Box 8384, Indianapolis, IN 46283: Free catalog ❖ Women's clothing in sizes 8 to 24. Also petite and tall sizes. 800-784-8001.

Lane Bryant, P.O. Box 8320, Indianapolis, IN 46283: Free catalog ❖ Clothing for tall women. 800-777-7030.

Gander Mountain Inc., P.O. Box 248, Gander Mountain, Wilmot, WI 53192: Free catalog ❖ Clothing for tall women. 800-558-9410.

Long Elegant Legs, 2-1 Homestead Rd., Belle Mead, NJ 08502: Free brochure ❖ Fashionable clothing for tall women. 800-344-2235.

Newport News Fashions, Avon Ln., Newport News, VA 23630: Free catalog ❖ Fashions for tall women. 800-688-2830.

Old Pueblo Traders, Palo Verde at 34th, P.O. Box 27800, Tucson, AZ 85726: Free catalog ❖ Fashions for women, 5'7" and taller. 520-748-8600.

J.C. Penney Company Inc., Catalog Division, Atlanta, GA 30390: Free information ❖ Sportswear and casual fashions. 800-222-6161.

Spiegel, P.O. Box 182563, Columbus, OH 43218: Free information ❖ Clothing for tall women. 800-345-4500.

Tallclassics, 12680 Shawnee Mission Pkwy., Shawnee Mission, KS 66216: Free catalog ❖ Clothing for women 5'10" and taller. 800-345-1958.

T-Shirts & Sweatshirts

Allen-Lewis Manufacturing Company, Division TCC Industries Inc., P.O. Box 16546, 5601 Logan, Denver, CO 80216: Free catalog ❖ Souvenirs, carnival and party supplies, fund-raising merchandise, toys and games, T-shirts and sweatshirts, and craft supplies. 303-295-0196.

Ande Inc., 1310 53rd St., West Palm Beach, FL 33407: Free brochure ❖ T-shirts for fishing enthusiasts. 407-842-2474.

Art-Wear, P.O. Box 691, New Cumberland, PA 17070: Free brochure ❖ Comical T-shirts and sweatshirts. 800-543-0431; 717-774-7080 (in PA).

Astronomical League Sales, 1901 S. 10th St., Burlington, IA 52601: Free price list ❖ Books and manuals on astronomy. Also astronomy-theme T-shirts, sweatshirts, and other logo items. 319-753-1442.

Aussie Connection, 135 NE 3rd Ave., Hillsboro, OR 97124: Free catalog ❖ "Down Under" T-shirts in medium, large, extra-large, and extra-extra-large. 800-950-2668.

Big Dog Sportswear, Mail Order, 3112 A Seaborg Ave., Ventura, CA 93003: Free catalog ❖ Lounge wear for women, boxer shorts for men, and men and women's outerwear. Also T-shirts and sweatshirts. 800-642-3647.

Brass Ring Graphics, Phil & Molly Rader, 2277 Ogden Rd., Wilmington, OH 45177: Free information with long SASE ❖ Carousel art T-shirts and sweatshirts. 513-382-3266.

Caledonian Graphics, 117 W. Alexander St., Ste. 343, Plant City, FL 33566: Free catalog ❖ Skydiving-theme T-shirts. 813-752-0300.

CCS Skateboards, 2701 McMillan Ave., San Luis Obispo, CA 93401: Free catalog ❖ T-shirts, shoes, stickers, skateboards and parts, and safety gear. 800-477-9283.

Christian Book Distributors, P.O. Box 7000, Peabody, MA 01961: Free catalog ❖ Religious-theme T-shirts in small, medium, large, extra-large, and extra-extra-large. 508-977-5000.

Close Range Combat Academy, 5826 N. Wayne, Chicago, IL 60660: Free information ❖ Small, medium, large, extra-large, and extra-extra-large T-shirts, sweatshirts, sweatpants, and satin jackets.

Cotten Concept, P.O. Box 23632, Federal Way, WA 98093: Free brochure ❖ T-shirts with rock climbing designs. 206-926-1553.

Dallas Alice, 8001 Cessna Ave., Ste. 203, Gaithersburg, MD 20879: Free catalog ❖ Silk-screened T-shirts. 301-948-0400.

Daydreams Stencil Company, P.O. Box 65, Oregon, WI 53575: Catalog $3 ❖ Heavyweight T-shirts with a choice of folk art designs. 608-873-3399.

Eastern Emblem, Box 828, Union City, NJ 07087: Free catalog ❖ T-shirts, jackets, patches, cloisonne pins, decals, and stickers. 800-344-5112.

Eisner Brothers, 75 Essex St., New York, NY 10002: Free catalog ❖ American-made T-shirts, sweatshirts, caps, jackets with novelty and licensed prints.

Falling Cloud Farms, 6200 Tony Ave., Woodland Hills, CA 91367: Free information with long SASE ❖ Nature-theme T-shirts in medium, large, and extra-large. 800-6-CLOUDS.

Frosty Little, 222 E. 8th St., Burley, ID 83318: Free information ❖ Sweatshirts, T-shirts, pins, and patches with clown graphics. 208-678-0005.

FTC Ski & Sports, 1586 Bush St., San Francisco, CA 94109: Free catalog ❖ Skateboards and parts, snowboards, T-shirts, and clothing. 415-673-8363.

Goose & Gander Country Gift Shop, 6483 E. Seneca Tnpk., Jamesville, NY 13078: Free information ❖ Women's Battenburg-inlay and collar T-shirts, applique sweatshirts, and Battenburg lace collar cardigans. 315-492-1266.

Wade Green Advertising Inc., 133 Washington St., Ste. 3, Camden, AR 71701: Free information with long SASE ❖ T-shirts with whimsical or social commentary art. 800-887-8461.

CLOTHING & ACCESSORIES

The Green Thumb Collection, 42 Digital Dr., #10, Novato, CA 94949: Free catalog ❖ T-shirts with cooking and medicinal herbs printed on front, back, and sleeves. 800-284-2899.

Hard Times Cafe, 310 Commerce St., Alexandria, VA 22314: Free brochure ❖ Aprons, T-shirts, and sweatshirts. 703-836-7449.

Hound Dog Fashions, Box 2525, Winnipeg, Manitoba, Canada R3C 4A7: Catalog $1 ❖ T-shirts and sweatshirts of up to 70 different breeds of dogs and cats. 800-667-4957.

Hugger-Mugger Yoga Products, 31 W. Gregson Ave., Salt Lake City, UT 84115: Free catalog ❖ Yoga-inspired T-shirts and sweatshirts in medium, large, and extra-large. 800-473-4888.

Jamaican Style, 4-771 Kuhio Hwy., #C-7, Kapaa, HI 96746: Catalog $3 ❖ Jamaican-style T-shirts. 808-823-6100.

Laughing Bear, Box 233, Woodstock, NY 12498: Free brochure ❖ Clothing and T-shirts for infants, toddlers, and older children. 914-246-3810.

Leo T-Shirts, P.O. Box 7701444, Cleveland, OH 44107: Free brochure with long SASE ❖ Original reptile art on T-shirts and sweatshirts. 216-529-0811.

Jim Morris Environmental T-Shirts, P.O. Box 18270, Boulder, CO 80308: Free catalog ❖ T-shirts and sweatshirts with environmental and nature graphics. 800-788-5411.

The Nature Company, Catalog Division, P.O. Box 188, Florence, KY 41022: Free catalog ❖ T-shirts with pictures of African animals. 800-227-1114.

Pedigrees Pet Catalog, P.O. Box 905, Brockport, NY 14559: Free catalog ❖ Carriers, books, pet clothing, collars, toys, and T-shirts with pictures of pets. 800-548-4786.

Pendleton Cowgirl Company, P.O. Box 30142, Eugene, OR 97403: Catalog $2 ❖ Classic western theme T-shirts, lithographs, note cards, and calendars. 503-484-9194.

PiDiDDLE's T-Shirt Factory, P.O. Box 656, Gwynedd Valley, PA 19437: Free information ❖ T-shirts with clown graphics. 215-699-6198.

Privateer Sportswear, 1762 N. Neville St., Orange, CA 92665: Free information ❖ Body heat color-changing T-shirts in medium, large, extra-large, and extra-extra-large.

Reptiles Products, P.O. Box 52864, Boulder, CO 80322: Free information ❖ One-size fits all T-shirts with reptile art. 800-365-4421.

Rockabilia Inc., P.O. Box 4206, Hopkins, MN 55343: Free catalog ❖ T-shirts, backstage passes, promotional glossy photographs, imported rare posters from around the world, and other concert collectibles and investibles. 612-942-7895.

Scene 1 T-Shirts, 6450 Merriman Rd. SW, Roanoke, VA 24018: Brochure $1 ❖ Wildlife T-shirts. 800-690-0238; 703-772-9373 (in VA).

Snake Wear Apparel Company, 24 E. Main St., Fleetwood, PA 19522: Free catalog ❖ T-shirts and caps with embroidered reptile art. 610-944-0274.

Soho Design, 10 Main St., P.O. Box 418, Dobbs Ferry, NY 10522: Free catalog ❖ Sweatshirts with a choice of graphics and designs. 914-478-7953.

US Aviator, 3000 21st St. NW, Winter Haven, FL 33881: Free information ❖ Aviator-theme T-shirts and caps. 800-356-7767.

USA SportWear, 4901 W. Van Buren, Ste. 1, Phoenix, AZ 85043: Catalog $2 ❖ Motorcycle art T-shirts. 800-323-7734.

Vantage Communications Inc., Box 546, Nyack, NY 10960: Free information ❖ T-shirts for adults. 800-872-0068; 914-358-0147 (in NY).

Warner Brothers Catalog, P.O. Box 60048, Tampa, FL 32735: Catalog $3 ❖ Bugs Bunny, Looney Tunes, and other T-shirts and sweatshirts, for children and adults. 800-223-6524.

Wireless, P.O. Box 64422, St. Paul, MN 55164: Free catalog ❖ T-shirts, sweatshirts, boxer shorts, toy banks, coffee mugs, and other gifts. 800-669-9999.

WorkAbles for Women, Deborah Evans Crawford, Oak Valley, Clinton, PA 15026: Free catalog ❖ Gloves, hats, T-shirts, socks, outdoor clothing, rain gear, and personal safety items for women. 800-862-9317.

Yoga Togs, 14 Brookwood Rd., Asheville, NC 28804: Free information ❖ Yoga-theme cotton T-shirts in medium, large, and extra-large. 800-366-4541.

Uniforms

Chef Revival, 12 Dyatt Pl., Hackensack, NJ 07601: Free information ❖ Professional clothing and equipment for chefs. 800-352-2433.

Commodore Uniform & Nautical Supplies, 335 Lower County Rd., Harwichport, MA 02646: Free information ❖ Boating uniforms, insignia, and flags. 800-438-8643; 508-430-7877 (in MA).

Dornan Uniforms, 653 11th Ave., New York, NY 10036: Free catalog ❖ Uniforms. 212-247-0937.

Industrial Uniforms, 906 E. Waterman, Wichita, KS 67202: Catalog $1.50 ❖ Uniforms and work clothing for men and women. 800-333-3666; 316-264-2871 (in KS).

Joseph Krasow, Big Ben Workn P.O. Box 784, Waterbury, CT 06720: Catalog $2 ❖ Uniforms and work clothing. 203-574-0667.

J.C. Penney Company Inc., Catalog Division, Atlanta, GA 30390: Free information ❖ Women's clothing for health care personnel, in petite, misses, tall, and regular sizes. 800-222-6161.

Smallwoods Yachtwear, 1001 SE 17th St., Fort Lauderdale, FL 33316: Free catalog ❖ Uniforms and casual boating attire. 800-771-2283.

Tafford Manufacturing Inc., P.O. Box 1006, Montgomeryville, PA 18936: Free catalog ❖ Nurse uniforms. 800-283-0065.

Todd Uniform Inc., P.O. Box 29107, St. Louis, MO 63126: Free catalog ❖ Work clothing and uniforms. 800-458-3402.

Wasserman Uniform Company, 1082 W. Mound St., Columbus, OH 43223: Free catalog ❖ Uniforms and shoes for men and women. 800-848-3576.

Western Clothing

America's Western Stores, P.O. Box 9200, Springfield, MO 65801: Free catalog ❖ Western-style clothing, shoes and boots, and gifts. 800-284-8191.

Back at the Ranch, 235 Don Gaspar, Santa Fe, NM 87501: Free information ❖ Vintage western clothing, boots, and hats. 505-989-8110.

Buckaroo Bobbins, P.O. Box 95314, Las Vegas, NV 89193: Catalog $1 ❖ Authentic vintage western clothing sewing patterns. 801-865-7922.

Cattle Kate, Box 572, Wilson, WY 83014: Catalog $3 ❖ Contemporary western-style clothing for men, women, and children. 307-733-7414.

Cheyenne Outfitters, P.O. Box 12022, Cheyenne, WY 82003: Free catalog ❖ Western-style clothing, jewelry, and gifts. 800-775-7511.

Creations in Leather, 1212 Sheridan Ave., Cody, WY 82414: Brochure $5 ❖ Leather coats, shirts, vests, chaps, chinks, and jackets. 307-587-6461.

GJ's Wild West, P.O. Box 6202, San Carlos St., Carmel, CA 93921: Free catalog ❖ Contemporary western apparel. 800-613-2762.

Gorlics' Trading Inc., P.O. Box 50, Warwick, NY 10990: Free information ❖ Leather outdoor hunting jackets, cowboy vests, and fur jackets. 914-986-8484.

Hay Charlie, 541 Historic Main St., Park City, UT 84060: Free information ❖ Handcrafted western-style boots, buckles and belts, hats, jewelry, clothing, and accessories.

Hobby Horse Clothing Company Inc., 13775 Stockton Ave., Chino, CA 91710: Catalog $2 (no phone orders for catalogs) ❖ Western clothing and tack, show apparel, and accessories for horseback riders. 909-613-1686.

Jackson Originals, Box 1049, Mission, SD 57555: Catalog $2 ❖ Indian artistry and Western style buckskin clothing. Also custom-made vests, jackets, and other clothing with beadwork. 605-856-2541.

Kids West, 18924 Hopfe St., Hockley, TX 77447: Catalog $2 ❖ Western fashions and gear, boots, accessories, and gifts for infants to young teens. 713-255-9775.

The Last Best Place, Catalog Company, P.O. Box 2807, Monroe, WI 53566: Free catalog ❖ Men and women's western-style clothing and accessories. 800-252-4766.

Luskey/Ryan's Western Stores Inc., 2601 N. Main, Fort Worth, TX 76106: Free catalog ❖ Western fashions, boots, and hats. Also saddles and tack. 800-725-7966.

Main-ly Country Western Wear, 166 Yarmouth Rd., Gray, ME 04039: Catalog $1 (refundable) ❖ Western-style clothing for men and women. 207-657-3412.

Maverick Fine Western Wear, 100 E. Exchange in the Stockyards, Fort Worth, TX 76106: Video catalog $5 ❖ Western apparel, accessories, and gifts. 800-282-1315.

Miller-Stockman Western Wear, P.O. Box 5127, Denver, CO 80217: Free catalog ❖ Men and women's western wear. 800-688-9888.

The Old Frontier Clothing Company, P.O. Box 691836, Los Angeles, CA 90069: Catalog $3 ❖ Men and women's western clothing. 310-246-WEST.

Red River Frontier Outfitters, P.O. Box 241, Tujunga, CA 91043: Catalog $3 ❖ Reproduction western clothing. 818-821-3167.

Rod's Western Palace, 3099 Silver Dr., Columbus, OH 43224: Free catalog ❖ Western-style clothing and tack. 800-325-8508.

Roemers, 1920 N. Broadway, Santa Maria, CA 93455: Free catalog ❖ Western-style clothing and gifts for men and women. 800-242-1890.

Sheplers, P.O. Box 7702, Wichita, KS 67277: Free catalog ❖ Western clothing. 800-242-6540.

Soda Creek Western Outfitters, P.O. Box 4343, 335 Lincoln Ave., Steamboat Springs, CO 80477: Free catalog ❖ Western clothing, hats, and dusters for men and women. 800-824-8426.

Spirit of the West Clothing, Coldwater Creek, One Coldwater Dr., Sandpoint, ID 83864: Free catalog ❖ Western-style women's fashions, jewelry, and accessories. 800-262-0040.

The Territory Ahead, PFI Western Stores, P.O. Box 9200, Springfield, MO 65801: Free catalog ❖ Men and women's western-style clothing. 800-284-8191.

Wild Bills Leather, P.O. Box 13037, Burton, WA 98013: Brochure $3 ❖ Original and authentic frontier leather goods and historical western items. 206-463-5738.

CLOWN SUPPLIES

Abracadabra Magic Shop, 125 Lincoln Blvd., Middlesex, NJ 08846: Catalog $5 ❖ Magic and juggling equipment, balloons, clown props, costumes, and make-up. 908-805-0200.

Apples & Company, 414 Conant Ave., Union, NJ 07083: Free information ❖ Clown-white make-up. 908-353-2193.

Aunt Clowney's Warehouse, P.O. Box 1444, Corona, CA 91718: Free catalog with two 1st class stamps ❖ Books on clowning.

Axtell Expressions, 230 Glencrest Circle, Ventura, CA 93003: Catalog $2 ❖ Clown supplies. 805-642-7282.

Best Magic Gags & Costumes, 625 S. Magnolia Ave., Anaheim, CA 92804: Free information ❖ Magic, juggling equipment, costumes, gags and gifts, dancewear, and clown items. 714-827-MGIC.

Bigfoot Stilt Company, 18064 1st Ave., Orlando, FL 32820: Free information ❖ Custom stilts. 407-568-3121.

Mike Bornstein Clowns, 319 W. 48th St., New York, NY 10036: Free information with long SASE ❖ Clown props.

Bubba's Clown Supplies, P.O. Box 2939, Orange Park, FL 32067: Catalog $2.50 ❖ Clown supplies. 904-272-5878.

Burpo Duh Clown, P.O. Box 160190, Cupertino, CA 95016: Free information ❖ Face-painting rubber stamps and supplies. 408-446-9314.

Chazpro Magic Company, 603 E. 13th, Eugene, OR 97401: Catalog $3 ❖ Clown props, books, juggling equipment, jokes, and novelties. 503-345-0032.

Cherri-Oats & Company, Cheri Venturi, P.O. Box 723, North Olmsted, OH 44070: Free information ❖ Wigs and accessories, stickers, puppets, and face-painting supplies. 216-979-9971.

Circus Clowns, 3556 Nicollet Ave., Minneapolis, MN 55408: Catalog $3 ❖ Clown costumes and props. 612-822-4243.

Clown City, 6 Salem Market Place, Salem, CT 06420: Catalog $2 ❖ Balloons and clown supplies. 860-889-1000.

The Clown Factory, 5724 N. Meridian, Wichita, KS 67204: Catalog $1 (refundable) ❖ Balloons, magic, and clown comedy props, gags, and supplies. 316-838-0818.

Clown Heaven, 4792 Old State Rd. 37 South, Martinsville, IN 46152: Catalog $3 ❖ Balloons, make-up, puppets, wigs, ministry and gospel items, novelties, magic, clown props, and books. 317-342-6888.

Comanche Clown Shoes Mfg., P.O. Box 551, Mountain View, OK 73062: Free information ❖ Clown shoes. 800-832-3424; 405-347-2817 (in OK).

Costumes by Betty, 2181 Edgerton St., St. Paul, MN 55117: Catalog $5 (refundable) ❖ Clown costumes, make-up, wigs, and shoes. 612-771-8734.

Steve Dawson's Magic Touch Catalog, 144 N. Milpitas Blvd., Milpitas, CA 95035: Catalog $3 ❖ Magic effects, books, videos, accessories, clown and juggling supplies, and make-up. 408-263-9404.

The Designer of Smiles, Gary & Nicki Zwerin, 4125 Stagwood Dr., Raleigh, NC 27613: Free information ❖ Wigs, custom-made hats, make-up, and other supplies and accessories. 919-782-8841.

Dewey's Good News Balloons, 1202 Wildwood, Deer Park, TX 77536: Free catalog ❖ Gospel clown supplies and balloons. 713-479-2759.

Eddie's Trick Shop, 70 S. Park Square, Marietta, GA 30060: Free information ❖ Magic and clown supplies. 800-429-4314.

Freckles Clown Supplies, 5509 Roosevelt Blvd., Jacksonville, FL 32244: Catalog $6 ❖ Costumes, make-up, clown supplies, puppets, how-to books on clowning and ballooning, and theatrical supplies. 904-388-5541.

Fun Technicians Inc., P.O. Box 160, Syracuse, NY 13215: Free information ❖ Clown props. 315-492-4523.

Funny Feet Fashions, 5047 W. Chase Ave., Skokie, IL 60077: Free brochure ❖ Custom-made clown shoes. 708-251-4545.

Bob Gibbon's Fun Technicians Inc., P.O. Box 160, Syracuse, NY 13215: Free information ❖ Clown props. 315-492-4523.

David Ginn Magic, 4387 St. Michaels Dr., Lilburn, GA 30247: Catalog $10 ❖ Books, props, and how-to-do magic on video tapes for magicians and clowns.

Graftobian Ltd., 510 Tasman St., Madison, WI 53714: Free information ❖ Face-painting supplies. 800-255-0584.

Happy & Pappy's Clown Bicycles & Handcrafted Shoes, P.O. Box 42, Franklin, IN 46131: Free brochure ❖ Handcrafted footwear, walking stilts, magic tricks, and rodeo bicycles. 317-736-7863.

Holly Sales, 9926 Beach Blvd., Ste. 114, Jacksonville, FL 32246: Free information ❖ Clown stickers. 904-223-5828.

La Rock's Fun & Magic Outlet, 3847 Rosehaven Dr., Charlotte, NC 28205: Catalog $3 ❖ Clown and balloon how-to books, balloon sculpture kits, and magic equipment. 704-563-9300.

Laflin's Magic & Silks, P.O. Box 228, Sterling, CO 80751: Free information ❖ Entertaining and educational magic on video tapes for clowns and magicians. 303-522-2589.

Lynch's Clown Supplies, 939 Howard, Dearborn, MI 48124: Catalog $5 ❖ Wigs, shoes, noses, novelty items, make-up, and costume accessories. 313-565-3425.

Mecca Magic Inc., 49 Dodd St., Bloomfield, NJ 07003: Catalog $10 ❖ Clown equipment, make-up, balloons, magic, costumes and wigs, puppets, ventriloquism and clown props, and juggling supplies. 201-429-7597.

Pricilla Mooseburger Originals, P.O. Box 700, Maple Lake, MN 55358: Catalog $2 ❖ Clown hats and clothing. 800-973-6277.

Morris Costumes, 3108 Monroe Rd., Charlotte, NC 28205: Catalog $20 ❖ Costumes, clown props, masks, joke items, magic and special effects, novelties, balloons, and books. 704-332-3304.

Novelties Unlimited, 410 W. 21st St., Norfolk, VA 23517: Catalog $5 ❖ Clown supplies, props and gags, magic, balloons, make-up, and party decorations. 804-622-0344.

Ben Nye Makeup, 5935 Bowcroft St., Los Angeles, CA 90016: Catalog $2.50 ❖ Clown make-up. 310-839-1984.

M.E. Persson, 17 Chesley Dr., Barrington, NH 03825: Catalog $1 ❖ Clown supplies. 603-664-5111.

Potsy & Blimpo Clown Supplies, P.O. Box 2075, Huntington Beach, CA 92647: Free catalog ❖ Clown make-up, wigs, and supplies. 800-897-0749; 714-897-0749 (in CA).

Sparkle's Entertainment Express, Jan Lovell, 152 N. Water St., Gallatin, TN 37066: Product list $1 ❖ Make-up, costumes and clown shoes, balloons, juggling and magic equipment, puppets, books, and supplies. 615-452-9755.

Spear's Specialty Shoe Company, 12 Orlando St., Springfield, MA 01108: Brochure $2 ❖ Clown shoes.

Under the Big Top, P.O. Box 807, Placentia, CA 92670: Catalog $4 ❖ Clown props, costumes, make-up, juggling equipment, balloons, and party supplies. 800-995-7727.

Up, Up & Away, P.O. Box 159, Beallsville, PA 15313: Catalog $3 ❖ Clown make-up and props. 412-769-5447.

COFFEE & ESPRESSO MAKERS

Chef's Catalog, 3215 Commercial Ave., Northbrook, IL 60062: Free catalog ❖ Calphalon cookware, Cuisinart accessories, Henckels cutlery, coffee-making equipment, and professional restaurant equipment for the home chef. 800-338-3232.

Community Kitchens, The Art of Foods Plaza, Ridgely, MD 21685: Free catalog ❖ Krups coffee makers and presses. 800-535-9901.

A Cook's Wares, 211 37th St., Beaver's Falls, PA 15010: Catalog $2 ❖ Coffee makers, cutlery and cookware, bakeware, French copper pans, and food processors. 412-846-9490.

Mazzoli Coffee Inc., 236 Ave. U, Brooklyn, NY 11223: Catalog 50¢ ❖ Coffee brewers and grinders. 718-449-0909.

Pannikin Mail Order, 1205 J St., San Diego, CA 92101: Free brochure ❖ Gourmet spices, tea, hot chocolate, espresso machines, and coffee makers. 800-232-6482.

Zabar's & Company, 2245 Broadway, New York, NY 10024: Free catalog ❖ Coffee makers, cookware, food processors, microwave ovens, kitchen tools, gourmet foods, and gift baskets. 212-787-2000.

COIN-OPERATED MACHINES

Amusementica Americana, 414 N. Prospect Manor Ave., Mt. Prospect, IL 60056: Free list with seven 1st class stamps ❖ Old saloon artifacts, coin-operated machines, advertising collectibles, paper memorabilia, and other antique artifacts. 847-253-0791.

Antique Slot Machine Part Company, 140 N. Western Ave., Carpentersville, IL 60110: Free catalog ❖ Books and manuals, slot stands and pads, and parts for slot machines, jukeboxes, and pinballs. 847-428-8476.

Ken Arnold, 640 Devonshire Blvd., Longwood, FL 32750: Free information ❖ Jukeboxes and other coin-operated machines. 407-332-6133.

Bernie Berten, 9420 S. Trumbull Ave., Evergreen Park, IL 60642: Free catalog with three 1st class stamps ❖ Slot machines and parts. 708-499-0688.

Howard J. Fink, 174 Main St., Acton, MA 01720: Free information ❖ Vintage pinball and slot machines. 508-263-6480.

Fun-Tronics Inc., P.O. Box 448, Middletown, MD 21769: Catalog $3 ❖ Restoration supplies for Coca-Cola machines, from the 1920s to the 1960s.

GameRoom Antiques, 909 26th St. NW, Washington, DC 20037: Catalog $2 ❖ Antique coin-operated vending and arcade machines, pinballs, counter-top games, and books. 202-338-1342.

Home Arcade Corporation, 1108 Front St., Kisle, IL 60532: Catalog $3 ❖ Restored Coca-Cola machines, reproduction parts, and books and manuals. 708-964-2555.

Illinois Antique Slot Machine Company, P.O. Box 542, Westmont, IL 60559: Free information ❖ Wurlitzer jukeboxes, slot machines, nickelodeons, music boxes, and other coin-operated devices. 708-985-2742.

Norman Johnson, Drop Coin in Slot, 13820 County Home Rd., Bowling Green, OH 43402: Free list with long SASE ❖ Antique coin-operated machines before the 1950s. 419-352-3041.

Jukebox City, 1950 1st Ave. South, Seattle, WA 98134: Free photos with long SASE ❖ Jukeboxes and coin-operated machines. 206-625-1950.

Jukebox Classics & Vintage Slot Machines Inc., 6742 5th Ave., Brooklyn, NY 11220: Free information ❖ Antique coin-operated machines and jukeboxes. 718-833-8455.

Marco Specialties, 5290 Platt Springs, Lexington, SC 29073: Catalog $2 ❖ Pinball machines, parts, and books. 803-957-5500.

National Jukebox Exchange, 121 Lakeside Dr., Mayfield, NY 12117: Free catalog ❖ Antique jukeboxes, slot machines, arcade machines, and parts. 888-321-PAPA.

Bob Nelson's Gameroom Warehouse, 826 W. Douglas, Wichita, KS 67203: Free information ❖ Antique coin-operated machines and parts. 316-263-1848.

Orange Trading Company, 57 S. Main St., Orange, MA 01364: Free list with long SASE ❖ Antique jukeboxes, pinballs, and coin-operated machines. 508-544-6683.

R & J Slots, 249 Blue Ridge Dr., Orange, VA 22960: Free list ❖ Used slot machines. 703-672-4500.

Remember When Collectibles Inc., 6570 Memorial Dr., Stone Mountain, GA 30083: Free brochure ❖ Vintage Coca-Cola machines and jukeboxes. 404-879-7878.

Royal Bell Ltd., 5815 W 52nd Ave., Denver, CO 80212: Catalog $5 ❖ Slot machines and other mechanical memorabilia. 303-431-9266.

St. Louis Slot Machine Company, 9400 Manchester Rd., St. Louis, MO 63119: Catalog $3 ❖ Common to rare Coca-Cola and coin-operated machines. 314-961-4612.

Zielbauer, 2210 Miramonte, Tucson, AZ 85713: Free list ❖ Slot machines.

Zygmunt & Associates, P.O. Box 542, Westmont, IL 60559: Free brochure ❖ Jukeboxes and slot machines. 708-985-2742.

COMIC BOOKS & ARCHIVAL SUPPLIES

Avalon Comics, P.O. Box 821, Medford, MA 02155: Catalog $2 ❖ Pre-1965 comic books.

Bags Unlimited Inc., 7 Canal St., Rochester, NY 14608: Free information ❖ Collection Protection. Storage boxes, poly bags, divider cards, acid free boards, mailers for comics, LPs, CDs, posters, and magazines. 800-767-BAGS.

BEA Comics, P.O. Box 8118, Temple City, CA 91780: Catalog $1 (refundable) ❖ Old to recent comic books.

Best Comics Distribution Center, 252-01 Northern Blvd., Little Neck, NY 11362: Free information ❖ Comic books, original comic art, action figures, and trading cards. 800-966-2099; 718-279-2099 (in NY).

Bill Cole Enterprises Inc., P.O. Box 60, Randolph, MA 02368: Free information ❖ Comic book archival supplies. 617-986-2653.

Comic Conservation Company, P.O. Box 44803, Madison, WI 53744: Free information ❖ Archival supplies. 608-277-8775.

Comic Heaven, 24 W. Main St., Alhambra, CA 91801: Free catalog ❖ Comic books. 818-289-3945.

Discount Comics, P.O. Box 112, Cottage Grove, WI 53527: Free catalog ❖ Hard-to-find comic books. 608-764-8410.

Gary Dolgoff Comics, Brooklyn Navy Yard, Building 280, Ste. 608/609, Brooklyn, NY 11205: Catalog $1 ❖ Collector comic books. 718-596-5719.

Dover Cards & Comics, 11 Main St., Dover, NH 03820: Free catalog ❖ Gold and Silver Age comic books. 603-749-6862.

Fantasy Distribution Company, 2831 Miller St., San Leandro, CA 94577: Free information ❖ Back issue comic books. 510-352-5832.

Geppi's Comic World Inc., 1966 Greenspring Dr., Ste. 300, Timonium, MD 21093: Free information with long SASE ❖ Comic books and science fiction magazines. 800-783-2981.

A Good Time Charlie's, 114 W. Knox, Ennis, TX 75119: Free information with long SASE (specify items wanted) ❖ New and back issue comic books. 214-875-9337.

Will Gorges Civil War Antiques, 2100 Trent Blvd., New Bern, NC 28560: Catalog $10 ❖ Authentic Civil War uniforms, weapons, photographs, and pre-1964 comic books. 919-636-3039.

John M. Hauser, P.O. Box 51673, New Berlin, WI 53151: Price list $1 ❖ Comic books for collectors. 414-789-1863.

High-Quality Comics, 1106 2nd St., Ste. 110, Encinatas, CA 92024: Catalog $1 ❖ Hard-to-find comic books. 619-723-7269.

Gregory Johnson/Game Traders, 1327 Andover Dr., Aurora, IL 60504: Free catalog ❖ Comics. 614-523-2711.

Joseph Koch, 206 41st St., Brooklyn, NY 11232: Catalog $3 ❖ Old and new comic books. 718-768-8571.

Metropolis, 7 W. 18th St., New York, NY 10011: Free information ❖ Vintage comic books and movie posters. 800-229-6387; 212-627-9691 (in NY).

Mint Condition Comic Books & Baseball Cards Inc., 664 Port Washington Blvd., Port Washington, NY 11050: Free information with long SASE ❖ Current and back issue comic books and sports cards. 516-883-0631.

Moondog's Comics, 130 W. Prospect Ave., Mt. Prospect, IL 60056: Free information ❖ Comic book archival supplies. 708-398-6060.

New England Comics, FAST New Comic Service, P.O. Box 310, Quincy, MA 02269: Catalog $1 ❖ Comic book subscription service. 617-774-1218.

Paul & Judy's Coins & Cards, P.O. Box 409, Arthur, IL 61911: Free information ❖ Collectible comic books. 217-543-3366.

Bud Plant Comic Art, P.O. Box 1886, Grass Valley, CA 95945: Free catalog ❖ Comic books, comic strip collections, books about the history of comics and their creators, limited edition books, and prints. 916-273-2166.

Pulps, Richard Meli, 3121 NE 51st St., Apt. 303, Fort Lauderdale, FL 33308: Free list with long SASE and two 1st class stamps ❖ Comics and magazines. 305-351-9944.

Stand-Up Comics, 10020 San Pablo Ave., El Cerrito, CA 94530: Free information with long SASE (specify items wanted) ❖ Collectible comic books. 510-525-3223.

T.J.'s Comics & Cards & Supplies, Lloyds Shopping Center, 330 Rt. 211 East, Middletown, NY 10940: Free information ❖ Comic books, sports and non-sports cards, and hobby supplies. 800-848-1482.

Lee Tennant Enterprises Inc., 6963 W. 111th St., Worth, IL 60482: Free information ❖ New issues and collector comic books and archival supplies. 800-356-6401; 708-532-1771 (in IL).

Time Capsule Comics, 2737 Post Rd., Warwick, RI 02886: Catalog $2 ❖ Back issue comic books from 1970 to the present. 401-732-8007.

Tomorrow Is Yesterday, 5600 N. 2nd St., Rockford, IL 61111: Free information with long SASE ❖ New and back issue comic books, games, and collectibles. 815-633-0330.

Unique Dist., 110 Denton Ave., New Hyde Park, NY 11040: Free information ❖ Sports and non-sports cards and comics. 800-294-5901; 516-294-5900 (in NY).

Westfield Comics, 8608 University Green, P.O. Box 620470, Middleton, WI 53562: Free catalog ❖ Comics and collectibles. 800-WESTFIELD.

COMPASSES

Edmund Scientific Company, Edscorp Building, Barrington, NJ 08007: Free catalog ❖ Compasses, binoculars, telescopes, and educational and science equipment. 609-573-6260.

Goldbergs' Marine, 201 Meadow Rd., Edison, NJ 08818: Free catalog ❖ Compasses and power and sail boat equipment. 800-BOA-TING.

Haverhills, Customer Service, 185 Berry St., San Francisco, CA 94107: Free information ❖ Digital electronic car compass. 415-543-6675.

Magellan's, Box 5485, Santa Barbara, CA 93150: Free catalog ❖ Compasses. 800-962-4943.

Sporty's Preferred Living Catalog, Clermont Airport, Batavia, OH 45103: Free catalog ❖ Compasses. 800-543-8633.

Skipper Marine Electronics Inc., 3170 Commercial Ave., Northbrook, IL 60062: Free catalog ❖ Compasses and marine electronics. 800-SKIPPER; 708-272-4700 (in IL).

COMPUTERS

Components & Peripherals

Agfa, Agfa Division, Miles Inc., 200 Ballardvale St., M.S. 200-3-EDS, Wilmington, MA 01887: Free list of retail sources ❖ Scanners, accessories, and scanning and color-management software. 800-685-4271.

Alltech Electronics Company Inc., 2618 Temple Heights, Oceanside, CA 92056: Free catalog ❖ Computer components and surplus electronics. 619-724-2404.

American Power Conversion, 132 Fairgrounds Rd. West, Kingston, RI 02893: Free information ❖ Power backup and surge protector for PCs. 401-789-5735.

Amicon Technology, 6057 Maple St., Omaha, NE 68104: Free information ❖ Amiga hardware and accessories. 402-556-6160.

Best Power Technology Inc., P.O. Box 280, Necedah, WI 54646: Free information ❖ Uninterruptible power systems. 800-356-5794.

❖ COMPUTERS ❖

Better Concepts Inc., 10 Mandon Terr., New City, NY 10956: Free information ❖ Amiga software and hardware. 914-639-5095.

BISME Computers Inc., 1298 Reamwood Ave., Sunnydale, CA 94089: Free information ❖ Computer components and accessories. 800-899-6430.

Brother International Corporation, 200 Cottontail Ln., Somerset, NJ 08875: Free information ❖ Laser printers. 908-356-8880.

Canon Computer Systems, 2995 Redhill Ave., Costa Mesa, CA 92628: Free information ❖ Laser printers. 714-438-3000.

CD Technology Inc., 764 San Aleso Ave., Sunnyvale, CA 94086: Free information ❖ Portable CD-ROM drive for PCs. 408-752-8500.

Chip Factory, 151 S. Pfingsten Rd., Unit M, Deerfield, IL 60015: Free information ❖ Memory expansion boards. 708-205-0111.

Citizen America Corporation, P.O. Box 4003, 2450 Broadway, Ste. 600, Santa Monica, CA 90411: Free information ❖ Laser printers. 310-453-0614.

Commodore Country, 1420 County Rd. 914, Burleson, TX 76028: Free information ❖ Amiga software and accessories. 817-295-7658.

Communications Data Corporation, 1051 Main St., St. Joseph, MI 49085: Free information ❖ Amateur radio and computer equipment. 800-382-2562; 616-982-0404 (in MI).

Computer Peripherals Inc., 7 Whatney, Irvine, CA 92718: Free information ❖ External fax-modem. 714-454-2441.

Computer Products Corporation, 1431 S. Cherryvale Rd., Boulder, CO 80303: Free information ❖ Hard, tape, and CD-ROM drives. Also multi-media equipment, modems, PS/2 kits, and other accessories. 800-338-4273.

Copperhead Technologies Inc., 106 Jay St., Schenectady, NY 12305: Free information ❖ Amiga accessories and used hardware. 518-346-3894.

Corporate Systems Center, 1294 Hammerwood Ave., Sunnyvale, CA 94089: Free information ❖ Hard drives, optical disks, and memory upgrade accessories. 408-734-3475.

CPA Computers, 2608 NW 72nd Ave., Miami, FL 33122: Free information ❖ Multi-media kits, fax/modems, controller/video cards, monitors, electronic components, storage devices and drives, keyboards, and other accessories. 305-591-5988.

Creative Labs Inc., 1901 McCarthy Blvd., Milpitas, CA 95035: Free catalog ❖ Sound cards, multi-media kits, video products, and accessories for PCs. 408-428-6600.

Diamond Multimedia Systems Inc., 2880 Junction Ave., San Jose, CA 95134: Free brochure ❖ Multi-media kits, desktop communications systems, and multi-media accelerators. 800-4-MULTIMEDIA.

Digital Equipment Corporation, Personal Computer Group, 111 Powdermill Rd., Maynard, MA 01754: Free information ❖ Laser printers. 800-722-9332.

Dirt Cheap Drives, 3716 Timber Dr., Dickinson, TX 77539: Free information ❖ Disk and tape drives, controllers, CD-ROMs, and optical devices. 800-473-0960; 713-534-6292 (in TX).

Dynapoint Inc., 1016-B Lawson St., City of Industry, CA 91748: Free information ❖ Trackballs. 818-854-6440.

Eclipse International, 516 Walt Whitman Rd., Melville, NY 11797: Free information ❖ Dual speed CD-ROM drive with PC card interface. 516-423-6800.

Elek-Tek, 7350 N. Linder Ave., Skokie, IL 60077: Free catalog ❖ Computers, networking systems, software, accessories, and supplies for PCs. Printers, monitors, modems, scanners, peripherals, and accessories for the Macintosh. 800-395-1000; 708-677-7660 (in IL).

Ensoniq, 155 Great Valley Pkwy., P.O. Box 3035, Malvern, PA 19335: Free list of retail sources) ❖ Keyboards. 800-553-5151.

Epson Accessories Inc., 20770 Madrona Ave., P.O. Box 2903, Torrance, CA 90509: Free information ❖ PC desktops, portables, and dot matrix and laser printers. 800-873-7766.

Genovation Inc., 17741 Mitchell North, Irvine, CA 92714: Free information ❖ Universal DOS and Windows compatible keypad for portable computers. 800-822-4333; 714-833-3355 (in CA).

Glyph Technologies Inc., 605 W. State St., Ithaca, NY 14850: Free information ❖ Dual-speed CD-ROM drive with optional multi-media capability and CD audio playback. 800-335-0345; 607-275-9464 (in NY).

Great Lakes Technology, 229 N. Lafayette Blvd., South Bend, IN 46601: Free information ❖ Scanners for Macintosh and PC computers. 800-229-3095.

Hello Direct, 5884 Eden Park Pl., San Jose, CA 95138: Free catalog ❖ Modems and other computer-telephone accessories. 800-444-3556.

Hewlett-Packard Company, Direct Marketing Organization, 5301 Stevens Creek Blvd., P.O. Box 58059, MS 51LSJ, Santa Clara, CA 95052: Free information ❖ PC portables, laser and inkjet printers, and accessories. 800-752-0900.

Info Products, 541 Division St., Campbell, CA 95008: Free information ❖ Trackballs. 408-374-7290.

Infogrip Inc., 1141 E. Main St., Ventura, CA 93001: Free information ❖ Ergonomic keyboard for Macintosh and PC computers. 800-397-0921.

Integrated Technologies, 1101 Chestnut St., Roselle, NJ 07203: Free information ❖ Amiga accessories. 908-245-1313.

The Iomega Corporation, 1821 W. 4000 South, Roy, UT 84067: Free information ❖ Hard drives for PCs and the Macintosh. 800-MY-STUFF; 800-456-5522; 801-778-3450 (in UT).

IPC Technologies Inc., 10300 Metric Blvd., Austin, TX 78758: Free information ❖ Quad-speed multi-media or upgrade kit with CD-ROM capabilities for PCs. 800-624-8654.

J & J Surface, 1110 Dundee Ave., Ben Lomond, CA 95005: Free information ❖ General purpose and specialized components.

Krex Computers, 9320-22 Waukegan Rd., Morton Grove, IL 60053: Free information ❖ Networking and multi-media kits. 800-377-KREX; 708-967-0200 (in IL).

Lexmark International, 740 New Circle Rd. NW, Lexington, KY 40511: Free list of retail sources ❖ Laser, inkjet, and color printers. Also plain-paper fax, scanner, and copier. 800-358-5835.

Lyco Computer, P.O. Box 5088, Jersey Shore, PA 17740: Free information ❖ Storage devices, tape back-ups, monitors, printers, scanners, computer systems, multi-media kits, and other accessories. 800-233-8760; 717-494-1030 (in PA).

MegaHaus, 2201 Pine Dr., Dickinson, TX 77539: Free information ❖ Hard and optical drives, affordable CD recorders, and other accessories. 800-962-0862.

Memory Plus Inc., 22 Water St., Westboro, MA 01581: Free information ❖ Upgrade components for PCs and the Macintosh. 800-388-7587; 508-366-2240 (in MA).

Micro Design International Inc., 6985 University Blvd., Winter Park, FL 32792: Free information ❖ Quad-speed CD-ROM drive for PCs. 407-677-8333.

MicroSolutions, 132 W. Lincoln Hwy., DeKalb, IL 60115: Free list of retail sources ❖ Plug-and-play CD-ROM and disk and hard drives. 800-890-7227; 815-756-3411 (in IL).

Microtek Lab Inc., 3715 Doolittle Dr., Redondo Beach, CA 90278: Free information ❖ Lightweight scanner for use with portable computers. 310-297-5000.

Mind Path Technologies, 12700 Park Central Dr., #1707, Dallas, TX 75251: Free information ❖ Computer remote control. 800-736-6830; 214-233-9296 (in TX).

❖ COMPUTERS ❖

Miramar Systems, 121 Gray Ave., Ste. 200B, Santa Barbara, CA 93101: Free information ❖ Macintosh integration software for use with PCs running Windows-based software. 800-862-2526; 805-966-2432 (in CA).

Motherboard Discount Center, 3701 E. Baseline, #107, Gilbert, AZ 85234: Free information ❖ Motherboards. 800-420-8511.

Motorola Modems, 5000 Bradford Dr., Huntsville, AL 35805: Free information ❖ Fax-modems with security protection. 205-430-8000.

Multi-Tech Systems Inc., 2205 Woodale Dr., Mounds View, MN 55112: Free information ❖ Multi-function modems. 612-785-3500.

NEC Technologies, 1414 Massachusetts Ave., Boxboro, MA 01719: Free information ❖ Laser printers. 800-374-8000.

NETIS Technology Inc., 1606 Centre Point Dr., Milpitas, CA 95035: Free information ❖ Computer components, add-on cards, multi-media products, software, bare-bone systems, network stations, and custom-configured PC systems.

New Media Corporation, One Technology, Building A, Irvine, CA 92718: Free brochure ❖ Fax/modems, stereo sound cards, fast SCSI II adapter cards, and ethernet lan adapters. 800-CARDS-4-U; 714-453-0100 (in CA).

New MMI Corporation, 2400 Reach Rd., Williamsport, PA 17701: Free catalog ❖ Desktop and portable PCs, printers, multi-media products, scanners, and other accessories. 800-221-4283.

Norton-Lambert Corporation, P.O. Box 4085, Santa Barbara, CA 93140: Free brochure ❖ Modem remote communications for accessing a distant PC or network. Also remote, automated, and general communications controls. 805-964-6767.

Notebook Supply Warehouse, 13700 Alton Pkwy., Ste. 154-281, Irvine, CA 92718: Free information ❖ Multi-media accessories for portable computers. 714-753-8810.

Okidata, 532 Fellowship Rd., Mt. Laurel, NJ 08054: Free information ❖ Laser and color ink jet printers. 800-OKIDATA.

Paxtron, 28 Grove St., Spring Valley, NY 10977: Free information ❖ Amiga accessories. 914-578-6522.

Philips Laser Magnetic Storage, 4425 Arrows West Dr., Colorado Springs, CO 80907: Free information ❖ Quad-speed CD-ROM drive for PCs. 719-593-7900.

Pioneer New Media Technologies, 2265 E. 220th St., Long Beach, CA 90810: Free information ❖ Quad-speed six-disk changer. 800-444-OPTI.

Play Incorporated, 2890 Kilgore Rd., Rancho Cordova, CA 95670: Free information ❖ Video image-capture aid for PCs. 916-851-0800.

Plextor, 4255 Burton Dr., Santa Clara, CA 95054: Free list of retail sources ❖ CD-ROM drives for PCs and Macintosh computers. 408-980-1838.

Practical Peripherals, P.O. Box 921789, Norcross, GA 30092: Free information ❖ Modems. 404-840-9966.

Primax Electronics, 521 Almanor Ave., Sunnyvale, CA 94086: Free information ❖ Scanners for PCs. 800-774-6291.

QMS Inc., One Magnum Pass, Mobile, AL 36618: Free information ❖ Color laser printers. 800-392-7559.

Silicon Sports Inc., 127 Independence Dr., Menlo Park, CA 94025: Free catalog ❖ Ergonomic wrist and back pads, protective carrying cases, backpacks for portable computers, and mouse pads. 800-243-2972.

Smart Modular Technologies, 45531 Northport Loop West, Fremont, CA 94538: Free information ❖ Fax-modem for mobile computers. 800-536-1231.

Star Micronics America Inc., 70-D Ethel Rd. West, Piscataway, NJ 08854: Free information ❖ Laser printers. 908-572-5550.

Team America, 16104 Covello St., Van Nuys, CA 91406: Free information ❖ Multi-media kits, controller and other cards, and accessories. 818-787-1920.

Texas Instruments Inc., Literature Response Center, P.O. Box 172228, Denver, CO 80217: Free information ❖ Laser printers. 800-527-3500; 817-771-5856 (in TX).

Timeline Inc., 23605 TELO Ave., Torrance, CA 90505: Free information ❖ Components and accessories. 310-784-5488.

Tripp Lite, 500 N. Orleans, Chicago, IL 60610: Free information ❖ Battery backup systems for computers. 312-755-8741.

Turtle Beach Systems, 52 Grumbacher Rd., York, PA 17402: Free information ❖ Multi-media upgrade kit. 800-645-5640; 717-767-0200 (in PA).

UMAX Technologies Inc., 3353 Gateway Blvd., Fremont, CA 94538: Free information ❖ Flatbed scanner for the Macintosh. 510-651-8883.

U.S. Robotics, 7770 N. Frontage Rd., Skokie, IL 60077: Free information ❖ Fax-modems. 708-676-7010.

USA Flex Inc., 444 Scott Dr., Bloomingdale, IL 60108: Free catalog ❖ Components, PC desktops and portables, upgrade kits, and other peripherals. 800-568-3539.

ValueExpre$$, 635 E. Remington Rd., Unit B, Schaumburg, IL 60173: Free information ❖ Color ink jet plotter. 708-885-4548.

Ven-Tel Inc., 2121 Zanker Rd., San Jose, CA 95131: Free information ❖ Modem with voice, fax, and communications capabilities. 408-436-7400.

Viking Components, 11 Columbia, Laguna Hills, CA 92656: Free information ❖ Expansion boards, add-on modules, and other accessories. 800-643-3255.

VisionSoft, P.O. Box 4398, Carmel, CA 93921: Free information ❖ Amiga peripherals and accessories. 800-735-2633.

Waveco, P.O. Box 1331, Palmetto, FL 34220: Free information ❖ Wrist rest pads. 813-723-2229.

Wearnes Technology Corporation, 2210 O'Toole Ave., #B, San Jose, CA 95131: Free information ❖ Internal CD-ROM drive for PCs. 408-456-8838.

Western Digital Corporation, 8105 Irvine Center Dr., Irvine, CA 92718: Free list of retail sources ❖ Hard drives and multi-media, I/O, and battery management products. 800-832-478; 714-932-4900 (in CA).

Wurlitzer Digital, 422 Wards Corner Rd., Loveland, OH 45140: Free information ❖ Digital keyboards. 800-876-02976.

XANTÉ Corporation, 2559 Emogene St., Mobile, AL 36606: Free information ❖ Laser printers. 800-926-8839.

Dust Covers & Cases

Co-Du-Co Computer Dust Covers, 4802 W. Wisconsin Ave., Milwaukee, WI 53208: Free catalog ❖ Dust covers. 800-735-1584.

Targus Inc., 6180 Valley View, Buena Park, CA 90620: Free catalog ❖ Carrying cases for computers and scientific equipment. 714-523-5429.

Education & Training

Allegro New Media, 16 Passaic Ave., Fairfield, NJ 07004: Free information ❖ Interactive tutorial for Windows 95. 800-424-1992.

Class Act Multi-media, 1121 S. Orem Blvd., Orem, UT 84058: Free information ❖ Interactive Windows-based software training on CD-ROM. 800-CD-LEARN.

The Economics Press Inc., 12 Daniel Rd., Fairfield, NJ 07004: Free information ❖ Windows training on CD-ROM. 800-526-2554.

LearnKey Inc., 1845 W. Sunset Blvd., Room 50-5, St. George, UT 84770: Free catalog ❖ Computer training videos and CD-ROMs. 800-865-0165.

WEKA Publishing Inc., 1077 Bridgeport Ave., P.O. Box 886, Shelton, CT 06484: Free information ❖ Easy-to-follow references and hardware questions for PCs on disk. 800-222-WEKA.

❖ COMPUTERS ❖

Furniture

Anthro Corporation, 10450 SW Manhasset Dr., Tualatin, OR 97062: Free catalog ❖ Computer furniture. 800-325-3841.

ATD-American Company, 135 Greenwood Rd., Wyncote, PA 19095: Free catalog ❖ Office and computer furniture, display cases, and storage and filing cabinets. 800-523-2300; 576-1000 (in area code 215).

Computer Furniture Direct, 2251 St. John's Bluff Rd. South, Jacksonville, FL 32246: Free catalog ❖ Wooden furniture. 800-555-6126.

Factory Direct Furniture, P.O. Box 92967, Milwaukee, WI 53202: Free catalog ❖ Office and computer furniture. 800-972-6570; 289-9770 (in Milwaukee).

Global Computer Supplies, 1050 Northbrook Pkwy., Suwanee, GA 30174: Free catalog ❖ Furniture and work stations, hardware, software, peripherals, and printing supplies. 800-845-6225.

Inmac, 2300 Valley View Ln., Irving, TX 75062: Free catalog ❖ Computer supplies, furniture, cables, disks and tapes, and networking and data communications equipment. 800-547-5444.

K-Log Inc., P.O. Box 5, Zion, IL 60099: Free catalog ❖ Computer and office furniture. 800-872-6611.

The PC Zone, 15815 SE 37th St., City of Bellevue, WA 98660: Free catalog ❖ Computer systems, furniture, software, disks, and networking and communications equipment. 800-258-2088.

ScanCo, P.O. Box 3217, Redmond, WA 98073: Free catalog ❖ Computer furniture. 800-722-6263.

Scandinavian Computer Furniture Inc., P.O. Box 3217, Redmond, WA 98073: Free catalog ❖ Modular computer furniture. 800-722-6263.

Wright-Line, Attention: Marketing Dept., Box 15028, Worcester, MA 01615. Free brochure ❖ Modular furniture for multi-media environments. 800-225-7348.

Manufacturers

Acer America Corporation, 2641 Orchard Pkwy., San Jose, CA 95134: Free information ❖ PC desktops and portables. 408-432-6200.

Advance Computer Source, 101-20 Queens Blvd., Forest Hills, NY 11375: Free information ❖ PC desktops. 718-275-1086.

Advanced Logic Research Inc., 9401 Jeronimo, Irvine, CA 92718: Free information ❖ PC desktops and portables. 800-444-4ALR; 714-581-6770 (in CA).

Ager Portable Computers, 18005 Cortney Ct., City of Industry, CA 91748: Free information ❖ PC portables. 800-669-1624.

Altima Systems Inc., 2440 Stanwell Dr., Ste. 1050, Concord, CA 94520: Free information ❖ PC portables. 800-356-9990.

American Research Corporation, 602 Monterey Pass Rd., Monterey Park, CA 91754: Free information ❖ PC portables. 800-346-3272; 213-265-0835 (in CA).

Amrel Technology Inc., 11801 Goldring Rd., Arcadia, CA 91006: Free information ❖ PC portables. 800-882-6735.

Apple Computer Inc., 1 Infinite Loop, Cupertino, CA 95014: Free information ❖ Macintosh computers and portables, printers, and other peripherals. 800-776-2333.

Aspen Computer Inc., 5550 Main St., P.O. Box 346, Buffalo, NY 14231: Free information ❖ Multimedia accessories for portable and other computer systems. 800-472-3273.

AST Research Inc., 16215 Alton Pkwy., Irvine, CA 92713: Free information ❖ PC desktops and portables. 800-876-4AST.

AT&T Capital Corporation, 1830 W. Airfield Dr., P.O. Box 619260, DFW Airport, TX 75261: Free information ❖ PC desktops, portables, and components. 800-874-7123.

Atari Computer, 455 S., Mathilda Ave., Sunnyvale, CA 94088: Free catalog ❖ Atari computers and portables. 408-745-2000.

Atronics International Inc., 45635 Northport Loop E., Fremont, CA 94538: Free information ❖ PC desktops. 510-656-8400.

Austin Direct, 2121 Energy Dr., Austin, TX 78758: Free catalog ❖ PC portables, desktops, and accessories. 800-952-9816.

Autotech/Viktron Group, 343 St. Paul Blvd., Carol Stream, IL 60188: Free information ❖ PC portables. 800-527-2841; 708-668-3355 (in IL).

Blackship Computer Systems Inc., 2031 O'Toole Ave., San Jose, CA 95131: Free information ❖ PC desktops. 800-531-SHIP; 408-432-7500 (in CA).

Canon Computer Systems, 2995 Redhill Ave., Costa Mesa, CA 92628: Free list of retail sources ❖ PC portables. 714-438-3000.

Commax Technologies, 2031 Concourse Dr., San Jose, CA 95131: Free information ❖ PC portables. 800-526-6629; 408-435-5000 (in CA).

Compaq Computer Corporation, P.O. Box 692000, Houston, TX 77269: Free information ❖ PC desktops and portables. 800-345-1518.

Compass Computer Products Corporation, 17 Harrison Ave., Garfield, NJ 07026: Free information ❖ PC desktops. 201-340-8855.

Computer Free America, 2856 Upper Valley Pike, Springfield, OH 45504: Free information ❖ Custom multi-media PC desktops. 800-995-3733.

Comtrade Electronics USA Inc., 15314 E. Valley Blvd., City of Industry, CA 91748: Free information ❖ PC portables. 800-969-2123.

Data General Corporation, 4400 Computer Dr., Westborough, MA 01580: Free information ❖ PC portables and dot matrix printers. 800-328-2436; 508-366-8911 (in MA).

Dell Computer Corporation, 2214 W. Braker Ln., Austin, TX 78758: Free catalog ❖ PC desktops and portables. 800-819-3355.

Digital Equipment Corporation, Personal Computer Group, 111 Powdermill Rd., Maynard, MA 01754: Free information ❖ PC desktops. 800-722-9332.

Dolch Computer Systems, 3178 Laurel View Ct., Fremont, CA 94538: Free information ❖ PC portables. 800-538-7506.

Epson Accessories Inc., 20770 Madrona Ave., P.O. Box 2903, Torrance, CA 90509: Free information ❖ PC desktops, portables, and dot matrix and laser printers. 800-873-7766.

Ergo Computing, One Intercontinental Way, Peabody, MA 01960: Free information ❖ PC portables. 800-80-1909.

Everex Systems Inc., 5020 Brandin Ct., Fremont, CA 94538: Free information ❖ PC desktops. 800-821-0806.

Falcon Northwest Computer Systems, 263 S. Bayshore, Dr., Coos Bay, OR 97420: Free information ❖ PC desktops. 800-258-6778; 503-269-0775 (in OR).

Fujitsu Personal Systems, 5200 Patrick Henry Dr., Santa Clara, CA 95054: Free information ❖ PC portable computers. 800-831-3183.

FutureTech Systems Inc., 6 Bridge St., Hackensack, NJ 07601: Free information ❖ PC desktops and portables. 201-488-4414.

Gateway 2000 Computers, 610 Gateway, North Sioux City, SD 57049: Free information ❖ PC desktops and portables. 800-523-2000; 605-232-2000 (in SD).

Goldstar, 1000 Sylvan Ave., Englewood, NJ 07632: Free information ❖ PC portables. 201-816-2200.

The Hewlett-Packard Company, Direct Marketing Organization, 5301 Stevens Creek Blvd., P.O. Box 58059, MS 51LSJ, Santa Clara, CA 95052: Free information ❖ PC portables, laser and inkjet printers, and accessories. 800-752-0900.

HyperData, 809 S. Lemon Ave., Walnut, CA 91789: Free information ❖ PC portables. 909-468-2950.

Hyundai Electronics America, 510 Cottonwood Dr., Milpitas, CA 95035: Free information ❖ PC desktops and portables. 800-568-0060.

❖ COMPUTERS ❖

IBM Personal Computer Company, Rt. 100, Somers, NY 10589: Free information ❖ IBM desktop computers, portables, dot matrix and laser printers, and peripherals. 800-IBM-2YOU.

Infostar Inc., 175 Main St., Mount Kisco, NY 10549: Free information ❖ PC desktops. 914-666-2358.

IPC Technologies Inc., 10300 Metric Blvd., Austin, TX 78758: Free information ❖ PC desktops. 800-624-8654.

Keydata International, 111 Corporate Blvd., South Plainfield, NJ 07080: Free information ❖ PC portables. 908-755-0350.

Kris Technologies Inc., 100 San Lucar Ct., Sunnyvale, CA 94086: Free information ❖ PC portables. 800-282-5747.

Leading Edge Products Inc., 117 Flanders Rd., Westborough, MA 01581: Free information ❖ PC desktops and portables. 800-874-3340; 508-836-4800 (in MA).

Mega Computer Systems, 10840 Thornhill Rd., San Diego, CA 92127: Free information ❖ PC desktops. 619-487-8888.

Micro Express, 1801 Carnegie Ave., Santa Ana, CA 92705: Free information ❖ PC desktops, portables, and multimedia upgrade kits. 800-642-7621; 714-852-1400 (in CA).

Micro Professionals Inc., 19261 Burnham, Ste. 100, Lansing, IL 60438: Free information ❖ PC desktops. 800-776-4500.

Midern Computer Inc., 18005 Courtney Ct., City of Industry, CA 91748: Free information ❖ PC portables. 800-669-1624; 818-964-8682 (in CA).

Midwest Micro, 6910 US Rt. 36 East, Fletcher, OH 45326: Free information ❖ PC computers, power protection equipment, and peripherals. 800-728-8584.

Mitra, 20504 Earlgate St., Walnut, CA 91789: Free information ❖ PC desktops and portable computers. 800-324-1441.

Mitsuba Computers, 1925 Wright Ave., La Verne, CA 91750: Free information ❖ PC portables. 800-648-7822; 909-392-2000 (in CA).

NEC Technologies Inc., 1414 Massachusetts Ave., Boxboro, MA 01719: Free information ❖ PC desktops, portables, and printers. 800-374-8000.

NETiS Technology Inc., 1606 Centre Point Dr., Milpitas, CA 95035: Free information ❖ Computer components, add-on cards, multi-media products, software, bare-bone systems, network stations, and custom-configured PC systems.

Olivetti North America Inc., 22425 E. Appleway Ave., Liberty Lake, WA 99019: Free information ❖ PC desktops and portables. 800-633-9909; 509-927-5600 (in WA).

Packard Bell, 8350 Fruitridge Rd., Sacramento, CA 95826: Free information ❖ PC portables and desktops. 415-583-7222.

Panasonic, Panasonic Way, Secaucus, NJ 07094: Free list of retail sources ❖ PC portables, desktop systems, and peripherals. 201-348-7000.

PC Brand Inc., 542 State St., Racine, WI 53402: Free information ❖ PC desktops and portables. 800-PC-BRAND.

Philips Consumer Electronics, One Philips Dr., P.O. Box 14810, Knoxville, TN 37914: Free information ❖ PC portables. 800-822-4788.

Polywell Computers Inc., 1461-1 San Mateo Ave., South San Francisco, CA 94080: Free information ❖ PC desktops. 415-583-7222.

Professional Technologies, 21038 Commerce Pointe Dr., Walnut, CA 91789: Free information ❖ PC desktops. 800-949-5018.

Random Inc., 1035 N. McQueen, Gilbert, AZ 85233: Free information ❖ Custom built computer systems and motherboard upgrades. 602-813-6547.

Samsung, 105 Challenger Rd., Ridgefield Park, NJ 07662: Free information ❖ PC portable computers. 800-446-0262; 201-229-4000 (in NJ).

Seanix Technology Inc., Unit 140-6631 Elmbridge Way, Richmond, British Columbia, Canada V7C 4N1: Free information ❖ PC desktops. 604-273-3692.

Sharp Electronics, Sharp Plaza, Mahwah, NJ 07430: Free information ❖ PC desktops and portables. 800-BE-SHARP.

Source One Business Systems, 3480 S. Broadmont, Ste. 110, Tucson, AZ 85713: Free information ❖ PC desktops. 800-826-9577; 602-792-0100 (in AZ).

Swan Technologies, 313 Boston Post Rd., Ste. 200, Marlborough, MA 01752: Free information ❖ PC desktops and portables. 800-446-2497.

Tempest Micro, 375 N. Citrus Ave., Ste. 611, Azusa, CA 91702: Free information ❖ PC desktops. 818-858-5163.

Texas Instruments Inc., Literature Response Center, P.O. Box 172228, Denver, CO 80217: Free information ❖ PC portables. 800-527-3500; 817-771-5856 (in TX).

Toshiba America, P.O. Box 19724, Irvine, CA 92713: Free information ❖ Portable PC computers.

Tri-Star Computer Corporation, 2424 W. 14th St., Tempe, AZ 95281: Free information ❖ PC desktops. 800-800-1929.

Twinhead Corporation, 1537 Centre Point Dr., Milpitas, CA 95035: Free information ❖ PC portable computers. 408-945-0808.

Ultra-Comp Computers, 3801 Ultra-Comp Dr., Earth City, MO 63045: Free information ❖ PC desktops. 314-298-1998.

USA Flex Inc., 444 Scott Dr., Bloomingdale, IL 60108: Free catalog ❖ Components, PC desktops and portables, upgrade kits, and other peripherals. 800-568-3539.

WinBook Computer Corporation, 1160 Steelwood Rd., Columbus, OH 43212: Free information ❖ PC portable computers. 800-468-7502.

Zenith Data Systems, 2150 E. Lake Cook Rd., Buffalo Grove, IL 60089: Free information ❖ PC desktops, portables, and monitors. 800-582-0524.

Zeos International Ltd., 1301 Industrial Blvd., Minneapolis, MN 55413: Free information ❖ PC desktops and portables. 800-423-5891.

Retailers

Access 90's, 2440 Stanwell Dr., Ste. 200, Concord, CA 94520: Free information ❖ Portable computers and accessories. 800-824-4950.

Acecad, P.O. Box 431, Monterey, CA 93942: Free information ❖ Stylus and touch-sensitive input screen. 800-676-4ACE.

Alltech Electronics Company Inc., 2618 Temple Heights, Oceanside, CA 92056: Free catalog ❖ Computer components and surplus electronics. 619-724-2404.

Aplus Computer Inc., 21038 Commerce Pointe Dr., Walnut, CA 91789: Free information ❖ Disk and hard drives, portables, peripheral boards, and monitors. 800-745-0880.

Apple Computer Inc., 1 Infinite Loop, Cupertino, CA 95014: Free information ❖ Flatbed scanner. 800-776-2333.

APS Technologies, 6131 Deramus, Kansas City, MO 64120: Free information ❖ Macintosh storage devices, disk drives, scanners, modems, and other peripherals. 800-418-6401.

Arlington Computer Products Inc., 851 Commerce Ct., Buffalo Grove, IL 60089: Free information ❖ Computer systems, peripherals, and software. 800-548-5105.

Barnett's Photo Inc., 475 5th Ave., New York, NY 10017: Free information ❖ Desktop systems, portables, and accessories. 800-931-7070; 212-447-1407 (in NY).

BayTech, Data Communications Products Division, 200 N. 2nd St., P.O. Box 387, Bay St. Louis, MS 38520: Free information ❖ Printer sharing equipment. 800-523-2702; 601-467-8231 (in MS).

Blitz Computer, 313 S. 2nd St., Laramie, WY 82070: Free information ❖ PC computers, printers, and other peripherals. 800-927-1429.

❖ COMPUTERS ❖

Broadway Computer & Video, 1623 Broadway, New York, NY 10019: Free information ❖ Desktop systems, portables, and accessories. 212-582-6684.

Bottom Line Distribution, 4544 S. Lamar Blvd., Ste. 100, Austin, TX 78745: Free information ❖ Macintosh storage devices, disk drives, scanners, modems, and other peripherals. 800-990-5795.

Buffalo Products Inc., 2805 19th St. SE, Salem, OR 97302: Free information ❖ Printer-sharing control units. 800-345-2356.

Bulldog Computer Products, 3241-E Washington Rd., Martinez, GA 30907: Free information ❖ Cards and peripherals, disk drives, monitors, mouse devices, modems, software, and portables PCs. 800-438-6039.

Canon Computer Systems, 2995 Redhill Ave., Costa Mesa, CA 92628: Free information ❖ Portable printers. 714-438-3000.

CD-ROM Warehouse, 1720 Oak St., P.O. Box 3031, Lakewood, NJ 08701: Free information ❖ CD-ROMs and accessories. 800-925-6227.

CDW Computer Centers Inc., 1020 E. Lake Cook Rd., Buffalo Grove, IL 60089: Free information ❖ Hardware, software, and peripherals. 800-218-4CDW.

Chinon America Inc., 1065 Bristol Rd., Mountainside, NJ 07092: Free information ❖ CD-ROM drives for the Macintosh. 908-654-0404.

ClubMac, 7 Hammond, Irvine, CA 92718: Free catalog ❖ Macintosh hardware, add-on components, software, and peripherals. 714-768-8130.

CMO Superstore, 101 Reighard Ave., Williamsport, PA 17701: Free information ❖ Computer systems, peripherals, and software. 800-233-8950.

CompuServe, P.O. Box 20212, Columbus, OH 43220: Free information ❖ PC/AT emulator for the Amiga. 800-848-8990.

ComputAbility Consumer Electronics, P.O. Box 17882, Milwaukee, WI 53217: Free information ❖ Computer systems, peripherals, other electronics, and software. 800-554-9949.

Computer City Direct Catalog, P.O. Box 2526, Tempe, AZ 85280: Free catalog ❖ Desktop PCs, portables, accessories, software and CD-ROMs, books, and supplies. 800-843-2489.

Computer Friends Inc., 14250 NW Science Park Dr., Portland, OR 97229: Free information ❖ Ribbon inkers and inks. 800-547-3303.

Control Memory Factory, 1155 Chess Dr., Foster City, CA 94404: Free information ❖ Portable computers. 800-9-LAPTOP.

Creative Computers' PC Mall, Attention: Order Department, 2645 Maricopa St., Torrance, CA 90503: Free catalog ❖ Desktop PCs, portables, accessories, and supplies. 800-555-6255.

Data Comm Warehouse, 1720 Oak St., P.O. Box 3031, Lakewood, NJ 08701: Free information ❖ Networking products. 800-925-6227.

Data Vision, 445 5th Ave., New York, NY 10016: Free information ❖ Computers and accessories. 800-482-7466; 212-689-1111.

DataCal Corporation, 531 E. Elliot Rd., Chandler, AZ 85225: Free catalog ❖ Computer productivity enhancements, software, and keyboard overlays and templates. 800-251-3368.

Daystar Digital, 5556 Atlanta Hwy., Flowery Branch, GA 30542: Free brochure ❖ Peripheral upgrades for the Macintosh. 800-942-2077.

DigiCore Inc., 15500 Erwin St., Van Nuys, CA 91411: Free information ❖ Macintosh hardware, add-on accessories, software, and peripherals. 800-858-4622.

Digital Vision Inc., 270 Bridge St., Dedham, MA 02026: Free information ❖ Video equipment for PC desktops and Macintosh computers. 617-329-5400.

DirectTech Systems Inc., 7615 Golden Triangle Dr., Eden Prairie, MN 55344: Free information ❖ Hard drives, tape backups, and optical drives for the Macintosh. 612-941-2616.

Dirt Cheap Drives, 3716 Timber Dr., Dickinson, TX 77539: Free information ❖ Disk and tape drives, controllers, CD-ROMs, and optical devices. 800-473-0960; 713-534-6292 (in TX).

Eastern Camera & Computer Company, 425 Madison Ave., New York, NY 10017: Free information ❖ Desktop PCs, portables, accessories, and supplies. 800-742-3060.

Educational Resources, 1550 Executive Dr., Elgin, IL 60123: Free catalog ❖ Software, diskettes, peripherals, and computers. 800-860-2009; 708-888-8300 (in IL.

Envisions Solutions Technology Inc., 822 Mahler Rd., Burlingame, CA 94010: Free information ❖ Hand-held scanners for PC desktops. 800-365-7226.

Epson America Inc., 20770 Madrona Ave., P.O. Box 2903, Torrance, CA 90509: Free information ❖ High-resolution color scanners for Amiga computers. 800-873-7766.

Express Direct, 2720 N. Paulina, Chicago, IL 60614: Free information ❖ Macintosh systems and peripherals. 800-535-3252.

GCC Technologies, 209 Burlington Rd., Bedford, MA 01730: Free catalog ❖ Computer peripherals. 800-422-7777.

Global Computer Supplies, 1050 Northbrook Pkwy., Suwanee, GA 30174: Free catalog ❖ Furniture and work stations, hardware, software, peripherals, and printer supplies. 800-845-6225.

Harmony Computers, 1801 Flatbush Ave., Brooklyn, NY 11210: Free information ❖ Computer systems, portables, peripherals, and software. 718-692-2828.

Haven Industries, 2950 Lake Emma Rd., Lake Mary, FL 32746: Free information ❖ Computers, cellular telephones, audio and video equipment for homes and cars, and other electronics. 800-231-0031.

Insight Computers, 1912 W. 4th St., Tempe, AZ 85281: Free information ❖ Computers, hardware, and software. 800-494-8888.

The Iomega Corporation, 1821 W. 4000 South, Roy, UT 84067: Free information ❖ Hard disk drive with removable disk. 800-456-5522; 801-778-3450 (in UT).

K-12 MicroMedia Publishing, 16 McKee Dr., Mahwah, NJ 07430: Free catalog ❖ Teaching aids, software, and accessories for PC desktops and Macintosh computers. 800-292-1997.

Kenosha Computer Center, 2133 91st St., Kenosha, WI 53140: Free information ❖ Computers, cards, peripherals, and software. 800-255-2989.

Lyben Computer Systems, 5545 Bridgewood, P.O. Box 130, Sterling Heights, MI 48311: Free catalog ❖ Computer supplies and accessories. 810-268-8100.

Mac Bargains, 15815 SE 37th St., Bellevue, WA 98006: Free information ❖ Macintosh hardware, add-on accessories, software, and peripherals. 800-619-9091.

Mac Warehouse, P.O. Box 3031, Lakewood, NJ 08701: Free information ❖ Macintosh accessories and software. 800-255-6227.

MacConnection, 14 Mill St., Marlow, NH 03456: Free information ❖ Macintosh accessories and software. 800-800-2222.

MacDirect, 5198 W. 76th St., Edina, MN 55439: Free information ❖ Macintosh data storage devices, scanners, monitors, and other peripherals. 800-759-2133.

MacMail Order Department, 2645 Maricopa St., Torrance, CA 90503: Free catalog ❖ Macintosh hardware, add-on accessories, software, and peripherals. 800-560-6800.

Macronix Inc., 1338 Ridder Park Dr., San Jose, CA 95131: Free information ❖ Voice and fax mail box accessories. 800-858-5311.

Magellan's, Box 5485, Santa Barbara, CA 93150: Free catalog ❖ Voltage converters, electrical adaptor plugs, modular phone jacks, and other accessories for portable computers. 800-962-4943.

COMPUTERS

MicroSYSTEMS Warehouse, 1720 Oak St., P.O. Box 3014, Lakewood, NJ 08701: Free catalog ❖ PCs, peripherals, software, and supplies. 800-660-3222.

Network Express, 1611 Northgate Blvd., Sarasota, FL 34234: Free information ❖ Computer systems, portables, software, peripherals, and CD-ROMs. 800-333-9899.

New MMI Corporation, 2400 Reach Rd., Williamsport, PA 17701: Free catalog ❖ Desktop and portable PCs, printers, multi-media, scanners, and other accessories. 800-221-4283.

Newtech Video & Computers, 350 7th Ave., New York, NY 10001: Free information ❖ Video equipment, computers and peripherals, software, cellular phones, fax machines, and office equipment. 800-554-9747.

Olivetti North America Inc., 22425 E. Appleway Ave., Liberty Lake, WA 99019: Free information ❖ Scanners and dot matrix printers. 800-633-9909; 509-927-5600 (in WA).

Panasonic, Panasonic Way, Seacaucus, NJ 07094: Free list of retail sources ❖ Monitors and printers. 201-348-7000.

Para Systems Inc., 1455 LeMay Dr., Carrollton, TX 75007: Free information ❖ Un-interruptible power supplies. 800-238-7272.

PC Solutions, 100 Plaza Dr., Secaucus, NJ 07094: Free catalog ❖ Software, hardware, peripherals, and accessories. 800-765-8312.

PCs Compleat, 34 St. Martin Dr., Marlborough, MA 01752: Free catalog ❖ Portable computers and accessories, desktop systems, multi-media equipment, scanners, printers, other peripherals, and software. 800-385-4622.

Pinnacle Micro, 19 Technology Dr., Irvine, CA 92718: Free information ❖ Recordable CD-ROM, portable optical, and optical drives and optical library systems. 800-553-7070.

Publishing Perfection, P.O. Box 307, Menomonee Falls, WI 53052: Free catalog ❖ Publishing, graphics, and video computer products. 800-852-2348.

Quill Computers, 100 Schelter Rd., Lincolnshire, IL 60197: Free catalog ❖ Calculators, computers and accessories, and other office supplies and equipment. 800-789-1331.

Radio Shack, Division Tandy Corporation, One Tandy Center, Fort Worth, TX 76102: Free catalog ❖ PC desktops, portables, monitors, dot matrix and laser printers, and supplies. 817-390-3011.

River Computer Inc., P.O. Box 600, Marlow, NH 03456: Free information ❖ Macintosh systems, software, and books. 800-998-0090.

Rose Electronics, P.O. Box 742571, Houston, TX 77274: Free information ❖ Printer-sharing control units. 800-333-9343.

Seiko Instruments USA Inc., Graphic Devices and Systems Division, 1130 Ringwood Ct., San Jose, CA 95131: Free information ❖ Thermal-transfer printer. 800-888-0817.

Shreve Systems, 1200 Marshall, Shreveport, LA 71101: Free information ❖ Macintosh computers, add-ons, and peripherals. 800-227-3971.

Software House International, 2 Riverview Dr., Somerset, NJ 08873: Free information ❖ Software and peripherals for PC desktops. 800-777-5014.

Sunshine Video & Computers, 22191 Powerline Rd., Boca Raton, FL 33433: Free information ❖ Portable computers, memory upgrades, fax modems, carrying cases, mouse devices, and batteries. 800-828-2992.

Supra Corporation, 312 SE Stonemill Dr., Ste. 150, Vancouver, WA 98684: Free information ❖ FAX-modem, disk and hard drives, RAM expansion cards, and other accessories. 360-604-1400.

Tatung Company of America Inc., 2850 El Presidio St., Long Beach, CA 90801: Free information ❖ Monitors. 800-829-2850.

Tri-State Computer, 650 6th Ave., New York, NY 10011: Free information ❖ Amiga computers, monitors, expansion systems, drives, other peripherals, and software. 800-221-1926; 212-633-2290 (in NY).

USA Flex Inc., 444 Scott Dr., Bloomingdale, IL 60108: Free catalog ❖ Components, PC desktops and portables, upgrade kits, and other peripherals. 800-568-3539.

Vektron International Inc., 2100 North Hwy. 360, Ste. 1904, Grand Prairie, TX 75050: Free information ❖ Computer systems, peripherals, and other electronics. 800-725-0063.

Wholesalers Inc., P.O. Box 450, Orchard Park, NY 14127: Free information ❖ Peripherals and upgrades for PC desktops. 800-752-9512.

Z-RAM, 22 Morgan, Irvine, CA 92718: Free information ❖ Memory chips. 800-368-4RAM; 714-454-1500 (in CA).

Software (Public Domain & Shareware)

The Amish Outlaw Shareware Company, 3705 Richmond Ave., Staten Island, NY 10312: Free catalog ❖ Shareware for PCs. 800-947-4346.

Banana Productions, P.O. Box 13492, Overland Park, KS 66282: Free information ❖ PC Windows-based shareware. 913-362-0644.

Big Red Computer Club, 423 Norfolk Ave., Norfolk, NE 68701: Free catalog ❖ Software for Apple computers. 402-379-4680.

CompuServe, P.O. Box 20212, Columbus, OH 43220: Free information ❖ Public domain software and shareware for PCs. 800-848-8990.

Crazy Bob's Software, 50 New Salem St., Wakefield, MA 01880: Free information ❖ Public domain software, shareware, and CD-ROMs for PCs. 800-776-5865.

Donnux Shareware, P.O. Box 410, Milford, VA 22514: Free catalog ❖ Shareware for the Macintosh and PCs. 800-352-3878.

Educorp Computer Services, 7434 Trade St., San Diego, CA 92121: Free information ❖ Public domain software and multi-media CD-ROMS for the Macintosh and PCs. 800-843-9497; 619-536-9999 (in CA).

Excel-nt Software, P.O. Box 2004, Midland, MI 48641: Free catalog ❖ DOS and Windows-based shareware for PCs. 800-839-7190.

Kamyan Software, 1228 Narragansett Dr., Carol Stream, IL 60188: Free information ❖ PC Windows-based shareware games. 708-372-6134.

Micro Star, Crystal Vision Software, 2245 Camino Vida Roble, Carlsbad, CA 92009: Free information ❖ Public domain software for PCs. 800-444-1343.

Northwest Public Domain, P.O. Box 1617, Auburn, WA 98071: Free information ❖ Public domain software for the Amiga. 206-351-9502.

Oregon Software Outlet, 1908-D Ashland St., Ashland, OR 97520: Free catalog ❖ DOS and Windows-based software for PCs. 800-346-2842.

Pendragon Software Library, 75 Meadowbrook Rd., East Greenwich, RI 02818: Free catalog ❖ Public domain and shareware for PCs. 800-828-DISK.

Reasonable Solutions, 1221 Disk Dr., Medford, OR 97501: Free information ❖ User-supported software for PCs. 800-876-3475.

Silicon Commander Games, P.O. Box A-3407, Chicago, IL 60690: Free information ❖ PC Windows-based shareware games.

The Software Labs, Mail Order Department, 100 Corporate Pointe, Ste. 195, Culver City, CA 90231: Free catalog ❖ Public domain software and shareware for PCs. 800-569-7900.

The SoftwareLabs, 8700 148th Ave. NE, Redmond, WA 98052: Free catalog ❖ Software for PCs. 800-569-7900.

Tallon Software, P.O. Box 27823, Seattle, WA 98125: Free catalog ❖ Shareware for PCs. 800-346-0139.

Turtle Lightning Amiga Domain, P.O. Box 30499, Midland, TX 79712: Free information ❖ Public domain software for the Amiga. 915-563-4925.

Walnut Creek Software, 4041 Pike Ln., Ste. D, Concord, CA 94520: Free information ❖ Music education for PCs on CD-ROMs that includes how-to create, play, mix, and change music. Also other CD-ROMs and public domain software and shareware for PCs. 800-786-9907.

Software Publishers (Disks & CD-ROMs)

The following are examples of some of the publishers that one can choose from to find software. They are intended to illustrate the many types and formats of software available. For anyone looking for a specific application, or a larger selection of software publishers, there are several excellent magazines and other publications that can be consulted.

Aatrix Software, P.O. Box 5359, Grand Forks, ND 58201: Free information ❖ Business and home management software for the Macintosh. 800-426-0854.

Abacus Software, 5370 52nd St. SE, Grand Rapids, MI 49508: Free information ❖ Home and business applications and utilities for PCs. 800-451-4319.

Ability Plus Software, 6816 Morrison Blvd., Charlotte, NC 28211: Free information ❖ Software tools that organize and find files in a clear and intuitive way. Also DOS management software for homes and offices and Windows-based integrated word processing, spreadsheet, charting, database, forms, drawing, and communications software. 704-364-3346.

Abra Software Inc., 888 Executive Center Dr. West, Ste. 300, St. Petersburg, FL 33702: Free information ❖ Business, financial management, and employee tracking software for PCs. 800-847-2272.

Abracadata, P.O. Box 2440, Eugene, OR 97402: Free catalog ❖ Graphics software for PCs and Macintosh computers. 800-451-4871.

Access Software Inc., 4750 Wiley Post Way, Building 1, Ste. 200, Salt Lake City, UT 84116: Free information ❖ Games software for PCs. 800-793-0073; 801-359-2900 (in UT).

Accolade Inc., 5300 Stevens Creek Blvd., San Jose, CA 95128: Free information ❖ Software for Amiga, Atari, PCs, and Macintosh computers. 800-245-7744.

Activision, 11601 Wilshire Blvd., Ste. 1000, Los Angeles, CA 90025: Free information ❖ Games software for PCs. 310-473-9200.

Adept Computer Solutions Inc., 10951 Sorrento Valley Rd., Ste. 1G, San Diego, CA 92121: Free brochure ❖ Windows-based mapping software on CD-ROMs. 619-597-1776.

Adobe Systems Inc., P.O. Box 7900, Mountain View, CA 94039: Free information ❖ Desktop publishing and graphics software for PCs. Desktop publishing, graphics, home and business applications, and productivity software for the Macintosh. 800-833-6687.

Adobie Corporation, 411 1st Ave., Seattle, WA 98104: Free information ❖ Desktop publishing software for PCs. Desktop publishing, education, graphics, home and business applications, and utilities software for the Macintosh. 800-333-2538.

Advanced Computer Innovations Inc., 30 Burncoat Way, Pittsford, NY 14534: Free information ❖ Word processing and communications software for PCs. 716-383-1939.

AEC Software Inc., 22611 Markey Ct., Building 113, Sterling, VA 20166: Free information ❖ Scheduling software for the Macintosh. 703-450-1980.

Afterimages, P.O. Box 4803, Cave Creek, AZ 85331: Free information ❖ Western-theme clip art for the Macintosh and PCs.

Agfa, Agfa Division, Miles Inc., 200 Ballardvale St., M.S. 200-3-EDS, Wilmington, MA 01887: Free list of retail sources ❖ Scanners, scanning and color management software, typeface packs, and font management software for PCs. 800-685-4271.

The Aldridge Company, 2500 City West Blvd., Ste. 575, Houston, TX 77042: Free information ❖ Disk cache program for DOS and Windows. 800-548-5019.

AllMicro Inc., 18820 US Hwy. 19 North, Ste. 215, Clearwater, FL 34624: Free information ❖ Data recovery software. 800-653-4933.

Alpha Software Corporation, 168 Middlesex Tnpk., Burlington, MA 01803: Free brochure ❖ DOS, Windows, and Windows 95-based database software. 800-858-4411.

America Online Inc., 8619 Westwood Center Dr., Vienna, VA 22182: Free start-up kit and trial membership ❖ Consumer on-line information system. 800-504-5577.

American Business Information, 5711 S. 86th Circle, P.O. Box 27347, Omaha, NE 68127: Free information ❖ Windows-based CD-ROM telephone directories. 800-555-5666.

American Education Publishing, 150 E. Wilson Bridge Rd., Columbus, OH 43085: Free information ❖ Windows-based mathematics educational software for young children. 800-542-7833; 614-848-8866 (in OH).

American Megatrends, 6145-F Northbelt Pkwy., Norcross, GA 30071: Free information ❖ Diagnostic software for PCs. 800-828-9264.

American Microsystems Inc., 2190 Regal Pkwy., Euless, TX 76040: Free information ❖ Windows-based label design and bar coding software. 800-648-4452.

American Training International, 12638 Beatrice St., Los Angeles, CA 90066: Free information ❖ Educational and entertainment programs for PCs. 310-823-1129.

Andromeda Software Inc., P.O. Box 605, Amherst, NY 14226: Free catalog ❖ Scientific software for PCs. 716-691-4510.

Apple Computer Inc., 1 Infinite Loop, Cupertino, CA 95014: Free information ❖ Software for Macintosh computers. 800-776-2333.

Applied Optical Media Corporation, 1450 Boot Rd., Building 400, West Chester, PA 19380: Free information ❖ American Vista Atlas (atlas of the United States) on CD-ROM for PCs. 800-321-7259.

Archive Arts, P.O. Box 2455, Fallbrook, CA 92088: Free catalog ❖ Civil War clip art. 619-723-2119.

AskSam Systems, 119 S. Washington St., P.O. Box 1428, Perry, FL 32347: Free information ❖ PC information manager that includes word processing, text retrieval, and a database. 800-800-1997.

Athnena Design, 332 Congress St., Boston, MA 02110: Free information ❖ OS/2-based spreadsheet software for PCs. 617-426-6372.

Avalan Technology Inc., P.O. Box 6888, Holliston, MA 01746: Free information ❖ Windows-based remote communications software for PCs. 800-441-2281.

Baler Software Corporation, 1400 Hicks Rd., Rolling Meadows, IL 60008: Free information ❖ Spreadsheet software for PCs. 800-327-6108.

Barron's Educational Series, 250 Wireless Blvd., Hauppage, NY 11788: Free catalog ❖ DOS and Windows-based SAT preparation and other educational software for PCs. 800-645-3476.

Berkeley Systems, 2095 Rose St., Berkeley, CA 94709: Free information ❖ Entertainment and games software for PCs and Macintosh computers. 510-549-2300.

Best Ware, 300 Roundill Dr., Rockaway, NJ 07866: Free information ❖ Windows-based bookkeeping and accounting software for PCs. 800-322-6962.

Bible Research Systems, 2013 Wells Branch Pkwy., Ste. 304, Austin, TX 78728: Free brochure ❖ Bible education software for PCs and Macintosh computers. 800-423-1228.

BibleSoft, 22014 7th Ave. South, Seattle, WA 98198: Free information ❖ Windows and DOS-based bible-study software. 800-995-9058.

Big Red Computer Club, 423 Norfolk Ave., Norfolk, NE 68701: Free catalog ❖ Entertainment, games, utilities, education, productivity, graphics, and programming tools software for Apple computers. 402-379-4680.

❖ COMPUTERS ❖

Bilingual Software Inc., P.O. Box 292700, Davie, FL 33329: Free information ❖ DOS-based Spanish conversion program for PCs. 800-633-4652.

Bit Software Inc., 47987 Fremont Blvd., Fremont, CA 94538: Free information ❖ Windows-based fax and communications software for PCs. 510-490-2928.

BitBrain Software, P.O. Box 355, Allentown, PA 18105: Free information ❖ Windows-based mortgage tracking software for PCs. 800-944-4248; 610-882-2341 (in PA).

Bitstream Inc., Althenaeum House, 215 1st St., Cambridge, MA 02142: Free information ❖ Windows fonts and font management software for PCs. 800-522-3668.

Block Financial Software, 55 Walls Dr., P.O. Box 912, Fairfield, CT 06430: Free information ❖ DOS and Windows-based financial management and tax preparation software for PCs. 800-288-6322.

Blyth Software, 989 E. Hillsdale Blvd., Ste. 400, Foster City, CA 94404: Free information ❖ Database and productivity software for the Macintosh. 800-346-6647; 415-571-0222 (in CA).

Borland International, 1800 Green Hills Rd., Scotts Valley, CA 95066: Free information ❖ Debugger and assembly software for PCs. Database, desktop publishing, education, programming tools, and utilities software for the Macintosh. 800-331-0877.

Brainstorm Concepts, 2609 Windmere Dr., Norcross, GA 30071: Free information ❖ DOS-based integrated accounting system for PCs. 800-240-6257.

Broderbund Software Inc., P.O. Box 6125, Novato, CA 94948: Free catalog ❖ Entertainment and games software and CD-ROMs for PCs and Macintosh computers. 800-521-6263.

Bureau of Electronic Publishing, 141 New Rd., Parsippany, NJ 07054: Free information ❖ Education, Windows, and DOS-based multi-media CD-ROMs for PCs and Macintosh computers. 800-828-4766.

Caere Corporation, 100 Cooper St., Los Gantos, CA 95030: Free brochure ❖ Windows-based forms management and design software. 800-535-SCAN.

J.O. Camp, 1501 34th St. NW, Winter Haven, FL 33881: Free information ❖ Double-entry bookkeeping system for PCs. 813-967-8752.

CaneFire Software, 261 Kekuanaoa St., Hilo, HI 96720: Free information ❖ DOS-based inventory control and retail point-of-sale software. 808-969-1166.

Capstone/Intracorp Inc., 501 Brickell Key Dr., 6th Floor, Miami, FL 33131: Free information ❖ Entertainment and games software and a graphical art program for PCs. 800-468-7226.

Carlisle Development Corporation, P.O. Box 291, Carlisle, MA 01741: Free information ❖ Windows-based inventory control system for coin collectors. 800-219-0257.

CARSoft, RD 1, Box 3694, Rutland, VT 05701: Free information ❖ Automotive-related clip art. 802-773-3526.

CE Software Inc., P.O. Box 65580, West Des Moines, IA 50265: Free information ❖ Macintosh communications, graphics, home and business applications, and utilities software. 800-523-7638.

The Church of Jesus Christ of Latter-day Saints, Salt Lake Distribution Center, 1999 W. 1700 South, Salt Lake City, UT 84104: Free information ❖ DOS-based Macintosh and PC genealogy software. 800-537-5950; 801-240-2584 (in UT).

Claris Corporation, 5201 Patrick Henry Dr., P.O. Box 58168, Santa Clara, CA 95052: Free information ❖ Word processing and art software for Macintosh computers. 800-3-CLARIS.

Clear Software Inc., 199 Wells Ave., Newton, MA 02159: Free information ❖ Flow charting software. 800-338-1759.

Cliff's Notes Inc., P.O. Box 80728, Lincoln, NE 68501: Free information ❖ DOS-based SAT study guide software for the Macintosh. 800-228-4078; 402-423-5050 (in NE).

Cochenille Design Studio, P.O. Box 4276, Ecinas, CA 92023: Free information ❖ Knitting design software for PC, Macintosh, and Amiga computers. 619-259-1698.

Compton's NewMedia, 2320 Camino Vida Roble, Carlsbad, CA 92009: Free information ❖ Windows-based Compton's Interactive Encyclopedia for PCs. 800-862-2206.

CompuServe, P.O. Box 20212, Columbus, OH 43220: Free start-up kit and trial membership ❖ Consumer on-line information system. 800-848-8990.

Computer Associates International Inc., One Computer Associates Plaza, Islandia, NY 11788: Free information ❖ Windows-based business and financial management and graphics paint software for PCs. 800-225-5224.

Computer Support Corporation, 15926 Midway Rd., Dallas, TX 75244: Free information ❖ Windows-based drawing program for PCs. 214-661-8960.

Connectix Corporation, 2600 Campus Dr., San Mateo, CA 94403: Free information ❖ RAM doubler software for the Macintosh. Also Windows-based software for PCs. 800-950-5880; 415-571-5100 (in CA).

ConnectSoft Inc., 11130 NE 33rd Pl., Ste. 250, Bellevue, WA 98004: Free information ❖ Windows-based E-mail software. 800-234-9497.

Corel Corporation, Order Center, P.O. Box 3595, Salinas, CA 93912: Free information ❖ Graphics, drawing, and image-editing software for PCs and Macintosh computers. 800-772-6735.

Corex Technologies, 130 Prospect St., Ste. 201, Cambridge, MA 02139: Free information ❖ Easy-to-use database for business location and organization. 617-492-4200.

COSMI Corporation, 2600 Homestead Pl., Rancho Dominguez, CA 90220: Free information ❖ Screen saver for Windows. Also fonts, forms-maker, spreadsheet, word processor, and other programs for PCs. 310-833-2000.

Cougar Mountain Software, P.O. Box 6886, Boise, ID 83707: Free information ❖ Accounting and other business and financial management software. 800-388-3038.

Creative Wonders, P.O. Box 7532, San Mateo, CA 94403: Free information ❖ Educational alphabet-learning software for children, ages 3 to 6. 800-245-4525; 415-573-7111 (in CA).

CyberMedia, 2029 Century Park East, Ste. 810, Los Angeles, CA 90067: Free information ❖ PC diagnostic software.

DacEasy Inc., 17950 Preston Rd., Ste. 800, Dallas, TX 75252: Free information ❖ Windows-based business and financial management software for PCs. 800-322-3279.

Data Pro Accounting Software Inc., 5439 Beaumont Center Blvd., Ste. 1050, Tampa, FL 33634: Free information ❖ Financial management software for PCs. 800-237-6377.

DATASTORM, 2401 Lemone Blvd., P.O. Box 1471, Columbia, MO 65205: Free information ❖ DOS and Windows-based communications, fax, and networking software for PCs. 314-443-3282.

DataViz Inc., 55 Corporate Dr., Trumbull, CT 06611: Free information ❖ Software for converting PC files for use with the Macintosh. 203-268-0030.

Davidson & Associates, P.O. Box 2961, Torrance, CA 90509: Free catalog ❖ Education software for PC and Macintosh computers. 800-545-7677.

Davka Corporation, 7074 N. Western Ave., Chicago, IL 60645: Free information ❖ Hebrew and Judaic software for PCs and Macintosh computers. 800-621-8227; 312-465-4070 (in IL).

Decathlon Corporation, 4100 Executive Park Dr., Cincinnati, OH 45241: Free information ❖ Logo design software for Macintosh and PCs. 800-648-5646; 513-421-1938 (in OH).

❖ COMPUTERS ❖

Deep River Publishing Inc., P.O. Box 0715-975, Portland, ME 04104: Free brochure ❖ DOS and Windows-based travel guides and other where-to-eat, what-to-see, house designing, and fractal patterns software on CD-ROMs. 800-643-5630; 207-871-1684 (in ME).

DeLorme Mapping, P.O. Box 298, Freeport, ME 04032: Free information ❖ Windows-based atlas information and telephone number software. 800-253-5082.

Delrina Corporation, 6830 Via Del Oro, Ste. 240, San Jose, CA 95119: Free information ❖ Fax management software for PCs. 800-268-6082.

DeltaPoint, 2 Harris Ct., Ste. B-1, Monterey, CA 93940: Free information ❖ Word processing software for PCs and charting software for PCs and the Macintosh. 800-446-6955.

Deneba Software, 7400 SW 87th Ave., Miami, FL 33173: Free information ❖ Macintosh productivity, utilities, and graphics software. Graphics software for PCs. 305-596-5644.

Digital Communications Associates Inc., 1000 Alderman Dr., Alpharetta, GA 30202: Free information ❖ DOS and Windows-based communications programs for PCs. 800-348-3221.

Digital Directory Assistance, 6931 Arlington Rd., Ste. 405, Bethesda, MD 20814: Free information ❖ Windows-based CD-ROM telephone directory. 800-284-8353; 617-639-2900 (in MD).

Digital Impact, 6506 S. Lewis, Ste. 250, Tulsa, OK 74136: Free brochure ❖ Software libraries on CD-ROMs. 800-775-4232.

Disk Technician Corporation, 1940 Garnet Ave., San Diego, CA 92109: Free information ❖ Hard drive diagnostic and repair utility for PCs. 619-274-5000.

Disney Interactive, 500 S. Buena Vista St., Burbank, CA 91521: Free information ❖ Entertainment, games, and educational software for PCs. 800-228-0988.

Domark Software, 1900 S. Norfolk St., Ste. 110, San Mateo, CA 94403: Free information ❖ Games software for PCs.

Dor L'Dor Software, 7103 Mill Run Dr., Rockville, MD 20855: Free brochure ❖ Interactive Judaic learning software for PCs and the Macintosh. 301-963-9303.

Dow Jones & Company Inc., Business Information Services, P.O. Box 300, Princeton, NJ 08540: Free information ❖ Stock and investment management programs for PCs. 800-815-5100.

Dr. Schueler's Health Informatics Inc., P.O. Drawer 410129, Melbourne, FL 32941: Free information ❖ Multi-media health reference database. 800-788-2099.

Dream Maker Software, 925 W. Kenyon Ave., Ste. 16, Englewood, CO 80110: Free information ❖ Clip-art for PCs and Macintosh computers. 303-762-1001.

DSR Software Inc., 5 Park Plaza, Ste. 770, Irvine, CA 92714: Free information ❖ Clip art software on CD-ROM. 714-553-6575.

Dubl-Click Software Inc., 20310 Empire Ave., Ste. A102, Bend, OR 97701: Free information ❖ Macintosh graphics, fonts, and utilities. 503-317-0355.

Edmark Software, P.O. Box 97021, Redmond, WA 98073: Free information ❖ DOS-based Macintosh mathematics and other educational software for young children. 206-556-8400.

Electronic Arts, 1450 Fashion Island Blvd., San Mateo, CA 94404: Free information ❖ Software for Amiga, PCs, and Macintosh computers. 800-245-4525.

Encyclopedia Britannica Inc., Britannica Centre, 310 S. Michigan Ave., Chicago, IL 60604: Free information ❖ Windows-based Encyclopedia Britannica on CD-ROM. 800-323-1229.

ESD USA Inc., 3000 N. Atlantic Ave., Ste. 207, Cocoa Beach, FL 32931: Free information ❖ Russian for beginners. 407-783-6332.

ESF Computer Services Inc., 104-70 Queens Blvd., Forest Hills, NY 11375: Free information ❖ Membership management, accounting, and record-keeping system for organizations. 718-261-9797.

Expert Software Inc., 800 Douglas Rd., Executive Tower, 7th Floor, Coral Gables, FL 33134: Free information ❖ Clip art, educational astronomy, creating legal documents, games, entertainment, fonts, art and drawing, home design, and other software for PCs. 800-759-2562; 305-567-9990 (in FL).

Fineware Systems, P.O. Box 75776, Oklahoma City, OK 73147: Free information ❖ Windows-based disk manager software for PCs. 800-544-1740.

1st Desk Systems Inc., 55-57 Cape Rd., Mendon, MA 01756: Free information ❖ Database software for the Macintosh. 800-522-2286.

FormalSoft, P.O. Box 495, Springville, UT 84663: Free information ❖ Spreadsheet software for PCs. 801-489-3102.

4-Home Productions, Division Computer Associates International Inc., One Computer Associates Plaza, Islandia, NY 11788: Free information ❖ Financial management, accounting, and tax preparation software for PCs. 800-773-5445.

Fractal Design Corporation, 335 Spreckels Dr., Aptos, CA 95003: Free information ❖ Painting and drawing program for the Macintosh. 800-297-2665; 408-688-8836 (in CA).

Frame Technology Corporation, 1010 Rincon Circle, San Jose, CA 95131: Free information ❖ Desktop publishing software for PCs. 40-8-975-6000.

Fujitsu Networks Industry Inc., 1266 E. Main St., Stamford, CT 06902: Free information ❖ Windows-based communications program. 800-446-4736.

Fusion Software, 9337 Katy Fwy., Ste. 444, Houston, TX 77024: Free information ❖ Inventory management control and consumer-oriented software for PCs. 800-856-8566; 713-465-6363 (in TX).

Gamma Productions Inc., 12625 High Bluff Dr., Ste. 218, San Diego, CA 92130: Free information ❖ Windows-based multi-language word processing program. 800-974-2662.

GDT Softworks Inc., 4664 Lougheed Hwy., Ste. 188, Burnaby, British Columbia, Canada V5C 6B7: Free information ❖ Linkage software for Macintosh printing with PC-compatible printers. 604-291-9121.

Geoban Engineering Company, P.O. Box 658, Ridgecrest, CA 93556: Free information ❖ Professional electronic engineering software for PCs. 619-384-3042.

Gibson Research Corporation, 35 Journey, Aliso Viejo, CA 92656: Free information ❖ Hard disk diagnostic and repair program. 800-736-0637.

Global Village Communications Inc., 1144 E. Arques Ave., Sunnyvale, CA 94086: Free information ❖ DOS and Windows-based fax software. 800-FAX-WORK; 408-523-1000 (in CA).

Globalink Inc., 9302 Lee Hwy., 12th Floor, Fairfax, VA 22031: Free information ❖ DOS and Windows based foreign language translation programs for PCs. 800-255-5660.

Golfstats, Box 366, Long Valley, NJ 07853: Free information ❖ Windows and DOS-based golf score-keeping software. 908-850-5262.

Great Bear Technology/HealthSoft, 1100 Moraga Way, Ste. 200, Moraga, CA 94556: Free catalog ❖ Windows-based software for guide to prescription and non-prescription drugs, symptoms and illnesses, and other health-related programs for PCs. Also interactive multi-media software for homes, schools, and offices. 510-631-6800.

Grolier Electronic Publishing Inc., Sherman Tnpk., Danbury, CT 06816: Free information ❖ The New Grolier Multimedia Encyclopedia for PCs. 800-285-4534.

GT Interactive Software, 16 E. 40th St., New York, NY 10016: Free information ❖ PC games software.

Lance Haffner Games, P.O. Box 100594, Nashville, TN 37224: Free brochure ❖ Strategy and simulation football, full-count baseball, and TKO pro-boxing computer games for PCs. 800-477-7032.

❖ COMPUTERS ❖

Harmonic Vision, 906 University Pl., Evanston, IL 60201: Free information ❖ Music education software for PCs. 800-644-4994.

Hayes Microcomputer Products Inc., 5835 Peachtree Corners East, Norcross, GA 30092: Free information ❖ Communications software for PCs and Macintosh computers. 404-840-9200.

Heizer Software, P.O. Box 232019, Pleasant Hill, CA 94523: Free information ❖ Business management, graphics, communications, computer management, programming tools, spreadsheets, utilities, education, word processing, and home management software for the Macintosh. 800-888-7667.

Heritage Graphics, P.O. Box 139, Blauvelt, NY 10913: Free catalog ❖ Judaic clip art. 914-359-9761.

Hi-Tech Expressions, 184 Rivervale Rd., River Vale, NJ 07675: Free information ❖ Entertainment, games, and drawing programs for PCs.

Human Code Inc., 1411 West Ave., Ste. 100, Austin, TX 78701: Free information ❖ Multi-media history stories, cartoons, and interactive games on CD-ROMs. 512-477-5455.

HyperCompleat Angler, 998 Centre St., Ste. 1, Boston, MA 02130: Free information ❖ Windows-based software for outdoor sports. 800-HCA-7698.

HyperGlot Software Company, P.O. Box 10746, 5108-D Kingston Pike, Knoxville, TN 37939: Free information ❖ Spanish-teaching program for PCs. 800-800-8270.

Ibis Software Inc., 4104 24th St., Ste. 523, San Francisco, CA 94114: Free information ❖ Music education software for PCs. 415-546-1917.

Image Club Graphics Inc., U.S. Catalog Fulfillment Center, c/o Publisher's Mail Service, 10545 W. Donges Ct., Milwaukee, WI 53224: Free catalog ❖ PCs and Macintosh clip-art, fonts, photographs, on disk and CD-ROM. 800-387-9193.

IMC Software, 7318 Harrison St., Omaha, NE 68128: Free information ❖ Account management and scheduling system for PCs. 800-704-9009.

Impresario Software, 2055 Dahlia, Denver, CO 80207: Free information ❖ Hand and machine-knitting software for PCs and the Macintosh. 303-333-3871.

Impressions Software, 222 3rd St., Ste. 0234, Cambridge, MA 92142: Free information ❖ Game software for PCs. 800-545-7677.

Informix Software Inc., 4100 Bohannan Dr., Menlo Park, CA 94025: Free information ❖ Spreadsheet software for the Macintosh. 800-331-1763.

Innovation Advertising & Design, 41 Mansfield Ave., Essex Junction, VT 05452: Free information ❖ PC and Macintosh clip-art. 800-255-0562.

Inset Systems Inc., 71 Commerce Rd., Brookfield, CT 06804: Free information ❖ DOS-based graphics capture and conversion utility for PCs. 800-374-6738.

Insight Software Solutions, P.O. Box 354, Bountiful, UT 84011: Free information ❖ Windows-based educational games, management-tracking, financial management, and other software for PCs. 801-295-1890.

Interactive Image Technologies Inc., 908 Niagara Falls Blvd., North Tonawanda, NY 14120: Free information ❖ Design and verification software for electric circuits. 800-263-5552.

International Chess Enterprises Inc., P.O. Box 19457, Seattle, WA 98109: Free information ❖ Chess games on CD-ROM. 800-26-CHESS.

Internet, PSI 510 Huntmar Park Dr., Herndon, VA 22071: Free start-up kit and trial membership ❖ Consumer on-line information system. 800-827-7482.

Intuit, 2650 E. Elvira Rd., Ste. 100, Tucson, AZ 85706: Free information ❖ Home and business applications and tax preparation software for PCs and Macintosh computers. 800-544-1365.

IVI Publishing, 7500 Flying Cloud Dr., Eden Prairie, MN 55344: Free information ❖ Windows-based human anatomy CD-ROM. 800-432-1332; 612-996-6000 (in MN).

Ivydene Software, P.O. Box 1665, Santa Maria, CA 93456: Free information ❖ Windows-based music-cataloging software for 78s, 45s, LPs, tapes, CDs, and music videos.

JetForm Corporation, 800 South St., Ste. 305, Waltham, MA 02154: Free information ❖ Windows-based forms design program. 800-FORM-DSK.

Kitty Hawk Software Inc., 60 Leveroni Ct., Novato, CA 94949: Free information ❖ How to build a paper airplane software for PCs. 415-883-3000.

Knowledge Adventure Inc., 4502 Dyer St., La Crescenta, CA 81214: Free information ❖ United States geography and other educational and multi-media programs for PCs. 800-542-4240; 818-542-4200 (in CA).

Dave Koch Sports, P.O. Box 656, Stevens Point, WI 54481: Free information ❖ PC football. 715-344-0610.

Landmark Research International Corporation, 703 Grand Central St., Clearwater, FL 34616: Free information ❖ Windows-based compression software. 800-683-6696.

Lattice Inc., 3010 Woodcreek Dr., Ste. A, Downers Grove, IL 60515: Free information ❖ Productivity software and home and business applications for Amiga computers. 800-444-4309.

Laureate Learning Systems, 110 E. Spring St., Winooski, VT 05404: Free information ❖ Talking software programs for children 6 months to 8 years of age. Includes language intervention, cognitive processing, reading, and instructional games. 802-655-4755.

Lawrence Productions, 1800 S. 35th St., Galesburg, MI 49053: Free information ❖ Entertainment and games for Amiga computers. 800-421-4157; 616-665-7075 (in MI).

The Learning Company, 6493 Kaiser Dr., Fremont, CA 94555: Free information ❖ Education and games for PCs and Macintosh computers. 800-852-2255.

Leister Productions, P.O. Box 289, Mechanicsburg, PA 17055: Free information ❖ Genealogy family tree software for the Macintosh. 717-697-4373.

Lionheart Press Inc., P.O. Box 20756, Mesa, AZ 85277: Free information ❖ Macintosh home and business applications, productivity, and database management software. 602-396-0899.

LogSat Software Corporation, 425 S. Chickasaw Tr., Ste. 103, Orlando, FL 32825: Free information ❖ Windows-based satellite tracking software. 800-350-3871; 407-275-0780 (in FL).

Lotus Development Corporation, 800 El Camino Real West, Mountain View, CA 94040: Free information ❖ Communications, desktop publishing, education, graphics, home and business applications, productivity, utilities, and word processing software for PCs. 800-205-9933.

Lyriq International Corporation, 1701 Highland Ave., Cheshire, CT 06410: Free information ❖ Golf games software on CD-ROM for PCs.

M-USA Business Systems, 15806 Midway Rd., Dallas, TX 75244: Free information ❖ Easy-to-use DOS-based double-entry accounting system. 800-933-6872.

M & R Technologies Inc., P.O. Box 9403, Wright Brothers Branch, Dayton, OH 45409: Free information ❖ Windows-based software for cross stitch pattern design for PCs. 800-800-8517.

Manhattan Analytics Inc., 912 Manhattan Ave., 2nd Floor, Manhattan Beach, CA 90266: Free information ❖ Mutual funds management system. 800-251-3863.

Maris Multimedia Software, 100 Smith Ranch Rd., Ste. 301, San Rafael, CA 94903: Free information ❖ Windows-based PC and Macintosh astronomy software. 800-336-0185.

❖ COMPUTERS ❖

Maxis Software, 2 Theatre Square, Orinda, CA 94563: Free information ❖ DOS-based games for PCs. 510-254-9700.

MECC Software, 6160 Summit Dr. North, Minneapolis, MN 55430: Free information ❖ Education software for PCs. 800-685-6322.

Media Cybernetics L.P., 8484 Georgia Ave., Ste. 200, Silver Spring, MD 20910: Free information ❖ Windows-based desktop imaging utility for adding graphics to documents. 800-992-4256.

MentorPlus Software Inc., Box 356, 22781 Airport Rd. NE, Aurora, OR 97002: Free information ❖ Flight planning and training, logging and record-keeping, and moving map software programs. 800-628-4640.

Merit Studios, 13707 Gamma Rd., Dallas, TX 75244: Free information ❖ Games software for PCs. 214-385-2957.

Metro ImageBase Inc., 18623 Ventura Blvd., Ste. 210, Tarzana, CA 91356: Free information ❖ Disk and CD-ROM clip-art for PCs and Macintosh computers. 800-525-1552.

MiBAC Music Software, P.O. Box 468, Northfield, MN 55057: Free information ❖ How to read and understand music software for PCs. 800-645-3945.

Micro Perfect Corporation, 225 W. 34th St., Ste. 1001, New York, NY 10122: Free information ❖ DOS-based accounting and business management software for PCs. 212-629-6082.

Micro Sports Inc., P.O. Box 1178, Hixson, TN 37343: Free information ❖ Pro league baseball software for PCs. 800-937-7737.

Micro 2000 Inc., 1100 E. Broadway, Ste. 301, Glendale, CA 91205: Free information ❖ DOS-based data recovery program for PCs. 800-864-8008.

Micro Vision Software Inc., 368 Veterans Memorial Hwy., Commack, NY 11725: Free information ❖ DOS and Windows-based tax preparation and other DOS-based tax software for PCs. 800-829-7354.

MicroBiz, 300 Corporate Dr., Mahwah, NJ 07430: Free brochure ❖ Easy-to-use computerized business control system for sales and inventory management and general overall control. 800-637-8268.

MicroCode Engineering, 573 W. 1830 N., Ste. 4, Orem, UT 84057: Free information ❖ Software for designing electronic circuits. 800-419-4242.

Microforum, 1 Woodborough Ave., Toronto, Ontario, Canada M6M 5A1: Free information ❖ Voice-operated Windows-based game on CD-ROM. 800-465-2323.

MicroLogic Software, 1351 Ocean Ave., Emeryville, CA 94608: Free information ❖ Windows and DOS-based true-type fonts. 800-888-9078.

Microlytics Inc., Two Tobey Village Office Park, Pittsford, NY 14534: Free information ❖ Information and education, language translation, and grammar and writing style-checking programs for PCs. 800-828-6293.

MicroPrecision Software Inc., 65 Washington St., Ste. 202, Santa Clara, CA 95050: Free information ❖ Wedding planning software for Windows (PCs) and the Macintosh. 800-258-2088 (Windows); 800-248-0800 (Macintosh).

MicroProse Software Inc., 180 Lakefront Dr., Hunt Valley, MD 21030: Free information ❖ Entertainment and games for PCs, Amiga, and Atari computers. 800-879-7529.

Microsoft Corporation, One Microsoft Way, Redmond, WA 98052: Free information ❖ Productivity software for the Amiga, Macintosh, and PCs. Database, entertainment, games, graphics, home and business applications, productivity and programming tools, and spreadsheet software for the Macintosh. 800-426-9400; 206-882-8080 (in WA). ✓

MicroStar Research & Trading Inc., 8302 S. Tamiami Trail, Sarasota, FL 34238: Free information ❖ How to track and invest in the bond market for PCs. 800-315-5635; 941-918-8068 (in FL).

Midisoft, 1605 NW Sammamish Rd., Ste. 205, Issaquah, WA 98027: Free information ❖ Windows-based music education software.

Mindscape Inc., 60 Leveroni Ct., Novato, CA 94949: Free information ❖ Windows-based graphics, DOS-based games, and educational programs for PCs. 800-283-8499.

MKS Inc., 35 King St. North, Waterloo, Ontario, Canada N2J 2W9: Free information ❖ Internet and other programs for PCs. 800-884-8861.

My Software Company, 1259 El Camino Real, Ste. 167, Menlo Park, CA 94025: Free catalog ❖ Business and office management software for PCs. 415-325-9383.

Nautical Software, 14657 SW Teal Blvd., Ste. 132, Beaverton, OR 97007: Free information ❖ Windows-based tides and currents software for PCs. 800-946-2877.

Neosoft Corporation, 354 NorthEast Greenwood Ave., Ste. 108, Bend, OR 97702: Free information ❖ Easy-to-use publishing software. 503-389-5489.

Nolo Press, 950 Parker St., Berkeley, CA 94710: Free catalog ❖ Home, business, and productivity software for PCs and Macintosh computers. 800-992-6656.

North Systems, 6821 Lemongrass Loop SE, Salem, OR 97306: Free information ❖ Investment indicator software for PCs. 503-364-3829.

NowWhat Software, 2303 Sacramento, San Francisco, CA 94115: Free information ❖ CD-ROM astronomy software for PCs and the Macintosh. 800-322-1954; 415-885-1689 (in CA).

Odyssey Development, The Denver Technology Center, 8775 E. Orchard Rd., Ste. B11, Englewood, CO 80111: Free information ❖ Windows and DOS-based information retrieval software for WordPerfect and other word processing programs. 800-992-4797.

Omega Research, 9200 Sunset Dr., Miami, FL 33173: Free information ❖ Windows-based stock charting software for investors. 800-422-3410.

Open Systems Computing Corporation, 45 Whitney Rd., Ste. B8, Mahwah, NJ 07430: Free information ❖ DOS-based word processing program and database for PCs. 800-445-9292.

Orange Cherry, New Media Schoolhouse, Box 390, Pound Ridge, NY 10576: Free catalog ❖ Educational software on disks and CD-ROMs for the Macintosh and PCs. 800-672-6002.

Origin Systems Inc., 5918 W. Courtyard Dr., Austin, TX 78730: Free information ❖ Entertainment and games for PCs. 800-245-4525; 512-434-4263 (in TX).

Owl Software Corporation, 13741 Foothill Blvd., Sylmar, CA 91342: Free information ❖ Typeface software and conversion program for PCs.

Oxford Craft Software, P.O. Box 208, Bonsall, CA 92003: Free information with long SASE ❖ Cross-stitch designer software for Macintosh and Amiga computers. Also similar DOS and Windows-based software for PCs. 800-995-0420.

Pangaea Scientific, RR 5, Brockville, Ontario, Canada K6V 5T5: Free catalog ❖ Geological software. 613-342-1513.

Papyrus Design Group, 35 Medford St., Ste. 305, Somerville, MA 02143: Free information ❖ Simulated Indianapolis car racing software for PCs. 617-868-3103.

Parsons Technology, One Parsons Dr., P.O. Box 100, Hiawatha, IA 52233: Free information ❖ Virus detection, business and financial management, entertainment, games, and educational software. 800-223-6925.

Peachtree Software, 1505 Pavilion Pl., Norcross, GA 30093: Free information ❖ Windows-based business and financial management software for PCs. 800-247-3224.

Penelope Craft Programs Inc., P.O. Box 1204, Maywood, NJ 07607: Free information ❖ PC and Macintosh software for knitters. 201-368-8379.

❖ COMPUTERS ❖

PG Music Inc., 266 Elmwood Ave., Ste. 111, Buffalo, NY 14222: Free information ❖ Windows-based and Macintosh software for automatic accompaniment of bass, drums, piano, guitar, and strings in a wide variety of styles. Also other Macintosh and Windows and DOS-based music software. 800-268-6272; 604-475-2874 (in NY).

Pinnacle Publishing Inc., 1800 72nd Ave. South, Ste. 217, Kent, WA 98032: Free information ❖ Windows-based graphics, charts, and presentation software for PCs. 800-788-1900.

Power Up Software, One MISCO Plaza, Holmdel, NJ 07733: Free catalog ❖ Communications, database, desktop publishing, education, graphics, home and business applications, productivity, programming tools, spreadsheets, word processing, and utilities software for PCs. 800-647-2699.

PRODIGY Service, 445 Hamilton Ave., White Plains, NY 10601: Free information ❖ Start-up kit for interactive on-line personal information-getting services for computer systems. 800-776-3449.

Quarterdeck Office Systems, 150 Pico Blvd., Santa Monica, CA 90405: Free information ❖ Memory manager software for PCs. 800-354-3222.

Raima Corporation, 1605 NW Sammamish Rd., Ste. 200, Issaquah, WA 98027: Free information ❖ Database program for PCs. 800-327-2462.

Rand McNally New Media, 8255 N. Central Park Ave., Skokie, IL 60076: Free information ❖ Trip planning, street-finding, and reference atlas software. 800-671-5006; 716-871-6715 (in IL).

Relay Technology Inc., 1604 Spring Hill Rd., Ste. 400, Vienna, VA 22182: Free information ❖ General-purpose Windows and DOS-based relay operating and control program for PCs. 800-795-8674.

Resolution Mapping Inc., 35 Hartwell Ave., Lexington, MA 02173: Free information ❖ Nautical mapping and chart software for PCs. 617-860-0430.

RMS Technology Inc., 124 Berkley, P.O. Box 24, Molalla, OR 97038: Free information ❖ Flight planning and moving map software programs. 800-533-3211.

Rockware Inc., The Rockware Building, 2221 East St., Golden, CO 80401: Free catalog ❖ Earth science software. 800-775-6745.

RT Computer Graphics Inc., 602 San Juan De Rio, Rio Rancho, NM 87124: Free information ❖ Native America and southwest-style clip-art for PCs and the Macintosh. 505-891-1600.

Rupp Technology Corporation, 3228 E. Indian School Rd., Phoenix, AZ 85018: Free information ❖ Hard drive locking program for PCs that prevents booting from a floppy. 800-852-7877.

Safe Harbor Computers, 2120 E. Moreland Blvd., Waukesha, WI 53186: Free information ❖ Amiga software and hardware. 800-544-6599.

Scholastic Software, 555 Broadway, New York, NY 10012: Free information ❖ Education, utilities, programming tools, and word processing software for PCs and the Macintosh. 800-541-5513; 212-505-6006 (in NY).

Serif Inc., P.O. Box 803, Nashua, NH 03061: Free information ❖ Windows-based desktop publishing program for PCs. 800-697-3743.

Sierra Direct, P.O. Box 3404, Salinas, CA 93916: Free information ❖ Software for PC and Macintosh computers. 800-757-7707.

Sir-Tech Software, P.O. Box 245, Ogdensburg, NY 13669: Free information ❖ Game software for PCs. 315-393-6633.

Tom Snyder Productions, 80 Coolidge Rd., Watertown, MA 02172: Free information ❖ Education software for PCs and Macintosh computers. 800-342-0236.

SofNet Inc., 1110 Northchase Pkwy., Ste. 150, Marietta, GA 30067: Free information ❖ Fax management software for PCs. 800-329-9675.

Softdisk Publishing, P.O. Box 30008, Shrevesport, LA 71130: Free catalog ❖ Software for PCs and Macintosh computers. 800-831-2694.

Softkey International Inc., 1 Athenaeum St., Cambridge, MA 023142: Free information ❖ Windows-based CD-ROM road atlas and street map, label-making, and graphics-photograph manipulation software. 800-227-5609; 617-494-1200 (in MA).

Solution Technology, 1101 S. Rogers Circle, Building 14, Boca Raton, FL 33487: Free information ❖ OS/2-based graphics software for PCs. 407-241-3210.

Soundtrek, 3408 Howell St., Ste. F, Duluth, GA 30136: Free information ❖ Windows-based song writing software. 404-623-0879.

Soundware Corporation, 1048 El Camino Real, Redwood City, CA 94063: Free catalog ❖ Music software for PCs and the Macintosh. 800-333-4554.

Spectrum Holobyte, 2490 Mariner Square Loop, Alameda, CA 94501: Free information ❖ Software for the Amiga, PCs, and Macintosh computers. 510-522-3584.

SPG Software, 15505 Bull Run Rd., Ste. 303, Miami Lakes, FL 33014: Free information ❖ OS/2-based graphics software for PCs. 305-362-6602.

Spinnaker Software Corporation, 201 Broadway, 6th Floor, Cambridge, MA 02139: Free catalog ❖ Software for PCs and Macintosh. 617-494-1200.

Sports Software Inc., 949 Sherwood Ave., Ste. 201, Los Altos, CA 94022: Free information ❖ Tennis improvement program. 800-733-6363; 415-941-6363 (in CA).

SPSS Software Inc., 444 N. Michigan Ave., Chicago, IL 60611: Free information ❖ Spreadsheet software with statistics, graphs, and report-writing capability. 800-543-5837.

SSI, 675 Almanor Ave., Ste. 201, Sunnyvale, CA 94086: Free information ❖ Game software for PCs. 408-737-6800.

Starboard Software, Box 1462, Royal Oak, MI 48068: Free information ❖ Boat navigation software for PCs and the Macintosh. 810-545-9928.

StatSoft, 2300 E. 14th St., Tulsa, OK 74104: Free information ❖ Statistical data management and graphic illustration program for the Macintosh. 918-749-1119.

Strata Inc., 2 W. St. George Blvd., St. George, UT 84770: Free information ❖ Graphics modeling, and animation software for the Macintosh. 801-628-5218.

Strategic Gaming Designs, 659 Cary Towne Blvd., #176, Cary, NC 27511: Free information ❖ Pro league basketball software for PCs. 919-552-1807.

Strategic Simulations Inc., c/o Electronic Arts, P.O. Box 7530, San Mateo, CA 94403: Free information ❖ Entertainment and game software for PCs. 800-245-4525.

Streetwise Software, 2216 Wilshire Blvd., Ste. 230, Santa Monica, CA 90403: Free brochure ❖ Add-on desktop publishing programs for WordPerfect and MS-Word. 800-743-6765.

Sumeria Inc., 329 Bryant St., Ste. 3D, San Francisco, CA 94107: Free information ❖ Educational information CD-ROMs for PCs. 800-478-6374.

Suncom Technologies Inc., 6400 W. Gross Point Rd., Niles, IL 60714: Free information ❖ Simulated car racing software for PCs. 708-647-4040.

SWFTE International Ltd., 722 Yorklyn Rd., Hockessin, DE 19707: Free information ❖ Windows-based fonts and font management software for PCs. 800-237-9383.

Symantec Corporation, 10201 Torre Ave., Cupertino, CA 95014: Free information ❖ Graphics, productivity, communications, and utilities software for the Macintosh. 800-441-7234.

SynApps Software Inc., 2208 NW Market, Ste. 500, Seattle, WA 98107: Free information ❖ Windows-based utilities for PCs. 206-784-7085.

T/Maker Company, 1390 Villa St., Mountain View, CA 94041: Free catalog ❖ Macintosh and Windows-based clickart and fonts on CD-ROMs. 800-986-2537.

Target Software Group Inc., 2901 58th Ave. North, St. Petersburg, FL 33714: Free information ❖ Software modules to computerize a small business for PCs. 800-872-4381.

TechPool Studios, 1463 Warrensville Rd., Cleveland, OH 44121: Free catalog ❖ Anatomy, dental, and emergency medical clip-art for the Macintosh and PCs. 800-543-3278.

Theatrix Interactive, 1250 45th St., Emeryville, CA 94608: Free brochure ❖ Windows-based or Macintosh CD-ROM interactive science, math, writing and creativity, and music software for children. 800-955-TRIX.

3G Graphics, 114 2nd Ave. South, Ste. 104, Edmonds, WA 98020: Free information ❖ Clip-art for the Macintosh and PCs. 800-456-0234; 206-774-3518 (in WA).

Time Savers Inc./Timeworks International, 70 W. Madison St., Ste. 2300, Chicago, IL 60062: Free information ❖ Windows-based desktop publisher, database, and information retrieval-storage system for PCs. 800-323-7744.

Torah Educational Software, Developers of ArtScroll's Multi-media Educational, 750 Chestnut Ridge Rd., Spring Valley, NY 10977: Free information ❖ Judaic educational software on CD-ROMs for PCs and Macintosh computers. 914-356-1485.

Totem Graphics Inc., 6200-F Capitol Blvd., Tumwater, WA 98501: Free information ❖ Clip-art for PCs and the Macintosh. 206-352-1851.

TransLanguage Inc., P.O. Box 18024, Anaheim Hills, CA 92807: Free catalog ❖ Foreign language software and fonts for PCs. 714-998-1293.

Transparent Language Inc., P.O. Box 575, Hollis, NH 03049: Free brochure ❖ Spanish, French, German, Italian, Russian, and Latin language-learning diskette and CD-ROMs for Windows (PCs) or the Macintosh. 800-332-8851.

Transparent Software Systems, 2639 N. Adoline Ave., Fresno, CA 93705: Free information ❖ DOS and Windows-based Judaic organization management software. 209-226-5147.

TRIUS Software, 231 Sutton St., P.O. Box 249, North Andover, MA 01845: Free information ❖ Spreadsheet programs for PCs. 800-468-7487.

Tropich Software Inc., 529 Central Ave., Scarsdale, NY 10583: Free information ❖ Windows-based filing system for photographs. 914-472-0278.

Trove Software, P.O. Box 218, Olathe, KS 66051: Free information ❖ Windows and DOS-based and Macintosh inventory control software for coin collectors. 800-548-8901.

True BASIC Inc., 12 Commerce Ave., West Lebanon, NH 03784: Free information ❖ Communications, desktop publishing, education, graphics, programming tools, and productivity software for the Macintosh. Amiga education and programming tools. 800-436-2111.

Twelve Tone Systems, P.O. Box 760, Watertown, MA 02272: Free information ❖ Easy-to-use Windows-based music software for PCs. 800-234-1171.

Ulead Systems, 970 W. 190th St., Ste. 520, Torrance, CA 90502: Free brochure ❖ Multi-media editing and information-management software. 800-858-5323.

Unicorn Software Company, 6000 S. Eastern Ave., Building 9, Ste. A, Las Vegas, NV 89119: Free information ❖ Education software for PCs and the Macintosh. Entertainment and games for the Macintosh. 702-597-0818.

Unitrol Data Protection Systems Inc., 2108-1177 W. Hastings St., Vancouver, British Columbia, Canada V6E 2K3: Free information ❖ DOS and Windows-based disk mirroring software. 800-665-2212.

Upstill Software, 1442-A Walnut, Berkeley, CA 94709: Free information ❖ Cooking and recipe management software for the Macintosh. 800-568-3696; 510-526-0178 (in CA).

UsrEZ Software Inc., 18881 Von Karman Ave., Ste. 1200, Irvine, CA 92715: Free information ❖ Security and privacy management software. 714-756-5140.

Vertisoft Systems, 153-B Grace Dr., Easley, SC 29640: Free information ❖ Memory-management software for PCs. 800-627-6139.

Viacom New Media, 1515 Broadway, New York, NY 10036: Free information ❖ Windows-based graphics software for PCs. 800-469-2539.

Virtual Entertainment, 200 Highland Ave., Needham, MA 02194: Free information ❖ Entertainment and educational software for PCs. 617-449-7567.

The Voyager Company, 578 Broadway, Ste. 406, New York, NY 10012: Free information ❖ Programming tools, utilities, and education software for the Macintosh. 800-446-2001.

Walnut Creek Software, 4041 Pike Ln., Ste. D, Concord, CA 94520: Free information ❖ Music education for PCs on CD-ROM that includes how to create, play, mix, and change music. Also other CD-ROMs and public domain software and shareware for PCs. 800-786-9907.

Wayzata Technology, 2515 East Hwy. 2, Grand Rapids, MI 55744: Free information ❖ World facts and information about 266 countries on CD-ROMs. 800-735-7321.

Wilson WindowWare Inc., 2701 California Ave. SW, Ste. 212, Seattle, WA 98116: Free information ❖ Windows-based on-screen address book, notepad, and other utility-related programs for PCs. 800-762-8383.

Wind & Power, 102 Columbia Dr., Ste. 210, Cape Canaveral, FL 32920: Free catalog ❖ Marine electrical equipment and accessories. 800-282-1003.

WinWay Corporation, 5431 Auburn Blvd., Ste. 398, Sacramento, CA 95841: Free information ❖ Resume and letter writing software. 800-4-WINWAY.

Wizard Games of Scotland Ltd., P.O. Box 498, Wilmington, MA 01887: Free information ❖ Sports management, software simulations, and other software games. 800-ITS-GOAL.

Wizardware Ltd., 918 Delaware Ave., Bethlehem, PA 18015: Free information ❖ Clip art graphics. 800-548-7969; 215-866-9613 (in PA).

Worden Brothers, 4905 Pine Cone Dr., Ste. 12, Durham, NC 27707: Free information ❖ Stock and mutual fund analysis system for PCs. 800-776-4940.

WordPerfect, Division Corel Corporation, Order Center, P.O. Box 3595, Salinas, CA 93912: Free information ❖ Word processing software. 800-772-6735.

World Book Educational Products, 101 Northwest Point Blvd., Elk Grove Village, IL 60007: Free information ❖ Windows-based World Book multi-media encyclopedia on CD-ROM. 800-WORLD-BK; 312-876-2200 (in IL).

World Software Corporation, 124 Prospect St., Ridgewood, NJ 07450: Free brochure ❖ Windows-based document profiling and retrieval system for PCs. 201-444-3228.

WritePro, 43 S. Highland, Ossining, NY 10562: Free information ❖ Writer's software. 800-755-1124.

Zedcor Publishing, 4500 E. Speedway Blvd., Ste. 22, Tucson, AZ 85775: Free information ❖ Clip art for PCs. 602-881-8101.

Software & CD-ROM Retailers

Better Concepts Inc., 10 Mandon Terr., New City, NY 10956: Free information ❖ Amiga software and hardware. 914-639-5095.

Chips & Bits, P.O. Box 234, Rochester, VT 05767: Free information ❖ Software, CD-ROMs, and hardware for PCs. 800-699-4263.

Christian Book Distributors, P.O. Box 7000, Peabody, MA 01961: Free catalog ❖ Windows, DOS-based, and Macintosh religious computer software. Also CD-ROMs. 508-977-5000.

❖ COMPUTERS ❖

Club Kidsoft, 718 University Ave., Ste. 112, Los Gatos, CA 95030: Free catalog ❖ Educational software for DOS, Windows, and the Macintosh, for ages 4 to 12. 800-354-6150.

Commodore Country, 1420 County Rd. 914, Burleson, TX 76028: Free information ❖ Amiga software and accessories. 817-295-7658.

ComputAbility Consumer Electronics, P.O. Box 17882, Milwaukee, WI 53217: Free information ❖ Software and CD-ROM disks. 800-554-9949.

Computer City Direct Catalog, P.O. Box 2526, Tempe, AZ 85280: Free catalog ❖ Desktop PCs, portables, accessories, software and CD-ROMs, books, and supplies. 800-843-2489.

Computer Express, 31 Union Ave., Sudbury, MA 01776: Free information ❖ Sports and other entertainment and games software for PCs. 800-228-7449.

DataCal Corporation, 531 E. Elliot Rd., Chandler, AZ 85225: Free catalog ❖ Computer productivity enhancements, CD-ROM disks, and software. 800-251-3368.

Dell Computer Corporation, 2214 W. Braker Ln., Austin, TX 7875: Free catalog ❖ Software and peripherals for PCs. 800-819-3355.

Educational Resources, 1550 Executive Dr., Elgin, IL 60123: Free catalog ❖ Software, diskettes, peripherals, cards, and computers. 800-860-2009; 708-888-8300 (in IL).

Egghead Software, 22011 SE 51st St., Issaquah, WA 98027: Free information ❖ DOS, Windows-based, and Macintosh software. Also CD-ROMs. 800-EGGHEAD.

Gamer's Gold, 1008 W. 41st St., Sioux Falls, SD 57105: Free price list ❖ Used games and hint books for PCs. 800-377-8578.

Global Computer Supplies, 1050 Northbrook Pkwy., Suwanee, GA 30174: Free catalog ❖ Work stations and furniture, hardware, software, peripherals, and printing supplies. 800-845-6225.

Great Christian Books, 229 S. Bridge St., P.O. Box 8000, Elkton, MD 21922: Free catalog ❖ Bible study software. 800-775-5422.

Hearlihy & Company, 714 W. Columbia St., Springfield, OH 45504: Free catalog ❖ Software for education, computer-aided designing, and drawing and drafting. Also drafting and graphics equipment, instructional aids and how-to information, plotters, furniture, and other supplies and accessories. 800-622-1000.

Legendary Design Technologies Inc., 25 Frantenac Ave., Brantford, Ontario, Canada N3R 3B7: Free information ❖ Amiga software. 519-753-6120.

Mac Warehouse, P.O. Box 3013, Lakewood, NJ 08701: Free catalog ❖ Macintosh software. 800-255-6227.

The Mac Zone, 15815 SE 37th St., Bellevue, WA 98006: Free information ❖ Macintosh software. 800-248-0800.

MacConnection, 14 Mill St., Marlow, NH 03456: Free information ❖ Macintosh accessories and software. 800-800-3333.

National CD-ROM, 11005 Indian Trail, Ste. 101-A, Dallas, TX 75229: Free information ❖ CD-ROMs. 800-237-6613.

Newtech Video & Computers, 350 7th Ave., New York, NY 10001: Free information ❖ Video equipment, computers and peripherals, software, cellular phones, fax machines, and office equipment. 800-554-9747.

PC Connection, 6 Mill St., Marlow, NH 03456: Free information ❖ Software for PCs. 800-800-5555.

PC Solutions, 100 Plaza Dr., Secaucus, NJ 07094: Free catalog ❖ Software, hardware, peripherals, and accessories. 800-765-8312.

Peripherals Plus, 5016 Rt. 9 South, Howell, NJ 07731: Free information ❖ Software for PCs and Macintosh computers. 800-444-7369.

Precision Type, 47 Mall Dr., Commack, NY 11725: Free information ❖ Software fonts. 800-248-3668.

The Programmer's Shop, 90 Industrial Park Rd., Hingham, MA 02043: Free information ❖ Software for PCs. 800-421-8006; 617-740-2510 (in MA).

Publisher's Toolbox, 8845 S. Greenview Dr., Ste. 8, Middleton, WI 53562: Free information ❖ Software and hardware for the Macintosh and PCs. 800-233-3898.

Software House International, 2 Riverview Dr., Somerset, NJ 08873: Free information ❖ Software and peripherals for PCs. 800-777-5014.

Software Hut, Folcroft East Business Park, 313 Henderson Dr., Sharon Hill, PA 19079: Free information ❖ Amiga software and accessories. 800-932-6442.

Surplus Software Inc., 489 N. 8th St., Hood River, OR 97031: Free information ❖ Clearinghouse specials of overstocked, over-produced, and distressed software inventories. 800-753-7877; 503-386-1375 (in OR).

Tiger Direct Inc., P.O. Box 569005, Miami, FL 33256: Free catalog ❖ Software and CD-ROM disks for the Macintosh and PCs. 800-335-4054.

Titan Games, One W. Seminary St., Brandon, VT 05733: Free catalog ❖ Games on disks and CD-ROMs for PCs. 800-247-5447.

Wright-Line, Attention: Marketing Dept., Box 15028, Worcester, MA 01615: Free brochure ❖ CD-ROMS for the Macintosh. 800-225-7348.

Zipperware, 76 S. Main St., Seattle, WA 98104: Catalog $5 ❖ Computers, hardware, and software and discount prices. 206-223-1107.

Supplies

American Ribbon Company, 2895 W. Prospect Rd., Fort Lauderdale, FL 33309: Free information ❖ Printer ribbons, laser toner cartridges, and ink-jet refills. 800-327-1013.

Chenesko Products Inc., 2221 5th Ave., Ste. 4, Ronkonkoma, NY 11779: Free catalog ❖ Recharge kits for laser printer and copier toner cartridges. 800-221-3516; 516-467-3205 (in NY).

Dayton Computer Supply, 6501 State Rt. 123 North, Franklin, OH 45005: Free information ❖ Printer ribbons. 800-735-3272.

Function One, 13641 John Glenn Rd., Apple Valley, CA 92307: Free information ❖ Printer ribbons, ink-jet refills, and formatted disks. 619-247-4755.

Global Computer Supplies, 1050 Northbrook Pkwy., Suwanee, GA 30174: Free catalog ❖ Work stations and furniture, hardware, software, peripherals, and printing supplies. 800-845-6225.

Idea Art, P.O. Box 291505, Nashville, TN 37229: Free catalog ❖ Preprinted laser/copier/offset paper with ready-to-use designs. 800-433-2278.

Image Papers by DataCal, 531 E. Elliot Rd., Chandler, AZ 85225: Free catalog ❖ Paper for flyers, greeting cards, professional brochures, and letterheads. 800-251-3372.

Inmac, 2300 Valley View Ln., Irving, TX 75062: Free catalog ❖ Computer supplies, furniture, cables, disks and tapes, and networking and data communications equipment. 800-547-5444.

International Ribbons, 7707 E. Acoma Dr., Scottsdale, AZ 85260: Free information ❖ Printer ribbons. 800-292-6272.

Island Computer Supply, 305 Grand Blvd., Massapequa Park, NY 11762: Catalog $2 (refundable) ❖ Printer ribbons and diskettes. 516-798-6500.

MEI/Micro Center, 1100 Steelwood Rd., Columbus, OH 43212: Free information ❖ Disks, disk cases, ribbons, surge protectors, and accessories. 800-634-3478.

Paper Access, 23 W. 18th St., New York, NY 10011: Free information ❖ Over 500 choices of paper for laser printers. 800-PAPER-01.

Paper Direct Inc., 100 Plaza Dr., Secaucus, NJ 07094: Free catalog ❖ Pre-designed papers and other supplies. 800-A-PAPERS.

146 ❖ COOKIE CUTTERS ❖

Pendle Company Inc., 1825B Dolphin Dr., Waukesha, WI 53186: Free information ❖ Toner cartridges. 800-869-7973; 414-691-5858 (in WI).

Quality Recharge Company, 3965 Park Ave., St. Louis, MO 63110: Free information ❖ Recycled cartridges for laser printers and copiers. 800-238-2333; 314-865-0929 (in MO).

RAMCO Computer Supplies, P.O. Box 475, Manteno, IL 60950: Free information ❖ Printer and heat transfer ribbons, printer paper, and other supplies. 800-522-6922.

Ultimage Image Inc., 304 S. Price Rd., Ste. 102, Tempe, AZ 85281: Free information ❖ Re-manufactured cartridges for laser printers and copiers. 800-459-9876.

Visible, Subsidiary Wallace Computer Services Inc., 1750 Wallace Ave., St. Charles, IL 60174: Free catalog ❖ Computer and office supplies. 800-323-0628.

COOKIE CUTTERS

Bayberry Farm Peddlers, P.O. Box 447, Perkasie, PA 18944: Catalog $2 ❖ Cookie cutters.

Carol's Heirloom Cookies, Division Dillon Marketing, 850 Meadow Ln., Camp Hill, PA 17011: Free information ❖ Cookie and shortbread molds and hand-carved wall hangings. 717-761-6895.

D.D. Dillon, 850 Meadow Ln., Camp Hill, PA 17011: Free information ❖ Hand-carved cookie and shortbread molds. 717-761-6895.

The House-on-the-Hill, P.O. Box 7003-C, Villa Park, IL 60181: Brochure $2 (refundable) ❖ Over 175 replicas of antique European cookie molds for baking and crafts.

The Little Fox Factory, Ed & Mary Fox, 931 Marion Rd., Bucyrus, OH 44820: Brochure $1 ❖ Handcrafted cookie cutters. 419-562-5420.

The Lyphon & Gryphon, 3779 Schindler Rd., Fallon, NV 89406: Catalog $4 (refundable) ❖ Cookie cutters. 702-867-4574.

Off the Beaten Path, 3837 N. Elmwood, #1, Kansas City, MO 64117: Brochure $3 ❖ Cookie cutters. 816-455-6348.

Sur La Table, Catalog Division, 410 Terry Ave. North, Seattle, WA 98109: Free information ❖ Hand-carved thistle-pattern wooden shortbread molds and other cooking and baking equipment. 800-243-0852.

Wilton Enterprise Inc., 2240 W. 75th St., Woodridge, IL 60517: Catalog $6 (refundable) ❖ Supplies for making cookies, candies, and cakes. 708-963-7100.

COPIERS & FAX MACHINES

AV Distributors, 10765 Kingspoint, Houston, TX 77075: Free information ❖ Fax machines and audio, video, stereo, and TV equipment. 800-843-3697.

Cellular World, Corporate Headquarters, 5025 Arapaho Rd., Ste. 330, Dallas, TX 75248: Free information ❖ Fax machines for homes, offices, or cars. Also cellular phones, modems, and accessories. 800-825-5669.

Computability Consumer Electronics, P.O. Box 17882, Milwaukee, WI 53217: Free catalog ❖ Fax machines and copiers. 800-554-9949.

Computerlane, 7500 Topanga Canyon Blvd., Canoga Park, CA 91304: Free information ❖ Fax machines, computers, and software. 800-526-3482; 818-884-8644 (in CA).

Crutchfield, 1 Crutchfield Park, Charlottesville, VA 22906: Free catalog ❖ Fax machines, telephones and answering machines, word processors, personal copiers, and software. 800-955-9009.

Factory Direct, 35 W. 35th St., New York, NY 10001: Free information ❖ Fax machines and audio, video, stereo, and TV equipment. 212-564-4399.

Fax City Inc., P.O. Box 38182, Greensboro, NC 27438: Free catalog ❖ Fax machines and copiers. 800-426-6499.

Newtech Video & Computers, 350 7th Ave., New York, NY 10001: Free information ❖ Video equipment, computers and peripherals, software, cellular phones, fax machines, and office equipment. 800-554-9747.

Olden Video, 1265 Broadway, New York, NY 10001: Free information ❖ Telephones, copiers, and photographic equipment. 212-725-1234.

Reliable Home Office, P.O. Box 1501, Ottawa, IL 61350: Catalog $2 ❖ Computer accessories and furniture, filing and storage systems, and fax machines. 800-869-6000. (Attention: Address Correction, P.O. Box 1020, Westboro, MA 01581.)

Sound City, Meadtown Shopping Center, Rt. 23, Kinnelon, NJ 07405: Free information ❖ Audio and video equipment, cassette and CD players, camcorders, TVs, fax machines, processors, telephones, and other electronics. 800-542-7283.

Staples Inc., Attention: Marketing Services, P.O. Box 1020, Westboro, MA 01581: Free catalog ❖ Fax machines, typewriters, word processors, office supplies and furniture, computer supplies, and drafting equipment. 800-333-3330.

Tri-State Camera, 650 6th Ave., New York, NY 10011: Free information ❖ Fax machines, copiers, audio and video equipment, camcorders, and photography equipment. 800-221-1926; 212-633-2290 (in NY).

COSMETICS & SKIN CARE

Angel's Earth, 1633 Scheffer Ave., St. Paul, MN 55116: Catalog $2 ❖ Soaps, candles, cosmetics, incense, skin care preparations, essential oils, and other aromatherapy items. 612-698-3601.

Arizona-Sun Products Inc., P.O. Box 1786, Scottsdale, AZ 85252: Free catalog ❖ PABA-free lotions and oil-free sun screens. 800-442-4786.

Aroma De Terra, 401 Euclid Ave., #155, Cleveland, OH 44114: Free catalog ❖ Botanical products for massage, bathing, and skin care. 216-566-8234.

Avon Beauty & Fashion by Mail, One Pine St., Ridgely, MD 21685: Free catalog ❖ Moisturizers, sun protection and special treatments, bath preparations, fragrances, and other cosmetics and skin care aids. 800-453-7460.

B & B Honey Farm, Rt. 2, Box 245, Houston, MN 55943: Free catalog ❖ Natural products for hair, skin, hygiene, and health care. 507-896-3955.

Ella Baché Beauty Products, 8 W. 36th St., New York, NY 10018: Free brochure ❖ Cosmetics and skin care products. 212-279-9411.

Barth Vitamins, 3890 Park Central Blvd. North, Pompano Beach, FL 33064: Free catalog ❖ Natural vitamins, health foods, mineral supplements, cosmetics, and home health aids. 800-645-2328.

Bath Indulgences, 1 Dupont St., Plainview, NY 11803: Free brochure with one 1st class stamp ❖ Bath and shower products.

Baudelaire Fine Imported Cosmetics Inc., Forest Rd., Marlow, NH 03456: Free information ❖ Imported European therapeutic bath oils rich in herbal extracts and essential oils. 800-327-2324.

Beautiful Visions, 1233 Montauk Hwy., P.O. Box 9000, Oakdale, NY 11769: Free catalog ❖ Women and men's nationally advertised cosmetics and toiletries. 800-645-1030.

Beauty Boutique, 6836 Engle Rd., P.O. Box 94519, Cleveland, OH 44101: Free catalog ❖ Cosmetics, toiletries, skin care items, costume jewelry, and women's fashions. 216-826-3008.

Beehive Botanicals Inc., Rt. 8, Box 8257, Hayward, WI 54843: Free brochure ❖ Skin care products made with natural ingredients and propolis produced by honeybees. 800-283-4483.

COSMETICS & SKIN CARE

Bioenergy Nutrients, 6565 Odell Pl., Boulder, CO 80301: Catalog $1 ❖ Nutritional supplements, homeopathic medicines, antioxidants, and all-natural skin care products. 800-627-7775.

Black Pearl Gardens, Herbal General Store, 220 Maple St., Franklin, OH 45005: Catalog $1 ❖ Herb plants, aromatherapy products, potpourri and supplies, culinary and medicinal herbs, herbal bath and body products, and dried florals. 800-891-0142.

Body & Soul, 300 W. Grand Ave., Chicago, IL 60610: Free information ❖ Shampoos, bath care items, and essence and fragrance oils. 800-272-7085; 312-664-9878 (in IL).

The Body Shop Inc., Attention: Catalog Department, 45 Horsehill Rd., Cedar Knolls, NJ 07927: Free catalog ❖ Toiletries, cosmetics, and hair care products. 800-426-3922.

Caswell-Massey Company Ltd., Catalog Division, 100 Enterprise Place, Dover, DE 19901: Catalog $1 ❖ Toiletries, cosmetics, and personal care products. 800-326-0500.

Mary Chess Inc., P.O. Box 754, FDR Station, New York, NY 10150: Free information ❖ Skin care and fragrance products. 800-225-3235.

Classique Perfumes Inc., 139-01 Archer Ave., Jamaica, NY 11435: Free catalog ❖ Designer fragrances for women and men. 718-657-8200.

Common Scents, 3920 A-24th St., San Francisco, CA 94114: Free catalog ❖ Bath and skin care products and essential oils. 800-850-6519.

Crabtree & Evelyn Limited, P.O. Box 158, Woodstock Hill, CT 06281: Catalog $3.50 ❖ Soaps and shampoos, bath gels and oils, colognes and toilet waters, creams, lotions, talcum powders, sponges, brushes, combs from England, France, and Switzerland. 800-624-5211.

Dabney Herbs, P.O. Box 22061, Louisville, KY 40222: Catalog $2 ❖ Natural health and beauty items, aromatherapy products, and oils. 502-893-5198.

Dry Creek Herb Farm, 13935 Dry Creek Rd., Auburn, CA 95602: Free information ❖ Skin care products and herbal teas. 916-878-2441.

Earth Science Inc., P.O. Box 1925, Corona, CA 91718: Free catalog ❖ Skin and hair care preparations, vitamins, and nutrients. 714-692-7190.

East End Import Company, Essex St., Box 107, Montauk, NY 11954: Free brochure with long SASE ❖ Essential oils, absolutes, concretes, creams, lotions, and floral waters. 516-668-4158.

Essential Products Company Inc., 90 Water St., New York, NY 10005: Free catalog ❖ Copies of fragrances for men and women. 212-344-4288.

Famous Smoke Shop Inc., 55 W. 39th St., New York, NY 10018: Free catalog ❖ Women and men's cosmetic fragrances. 800-672-5544.

Floris of London, 703 Madison Ave., New York, NY 10021: Free catalog ❖ English flower perfumes and toiletries. 212-935-9100.

The Florist Shop, 703 Madison Ave., New York, NY 10021: Free catalog ❖ Hand-milled soaps, bath oils, body milk, talc, room fragrances, and potpourris. 800-J-FLORIS.

Fragrance International, 398 East Raven Ave., Youngstown, OH 44505: Free price list ❖ Body lotions, dusting powders, perfumes and colognes, soap and bath products, and health and beauty items. 216-747-3341.

Fredericksburg Herb Farm, P.O. Drawer 927, Fredericksburg, TX 78624: Catalog $2 ❖ Herb plants, seeds, flowers, toiletries, oils, and seasonings. 800-259-4372.

Frontier Cooperative Herbs, 3021 78th St., P.O. Box 299, Norway, IA 52318: Free information ❖ Essential and fragrance oils and herbal extracts. 319-227-7991.

Gabrieana's Herbal & Organic Products, P.O. Box 215322, Sacramento, CA 95821: Free catalog ❖ Skin care and bath care items, essential oils, dried herbs, and organic products. 800-684-4372.

Garden Botanika, 8624 154th Ave. NE, Redmond, WA 98052: Free catalog ❖ Skin, hair, and body care cosmetics. 800-968-7842.

General Nutrition Catalog, Puritan's Pride, 105 Orville Dr., Bohemia, NY 11716: Free catalog ❖ Vitamins, health foods, natural cosmetics, books, and gifts. 800-645-1030.

Gold Medal Hair Products Inc., 1 Bennington Ave., Freeport, Long Island, NY 11520: Free catalog ❖ Wigs for black men and women, hair and beauty preparations, hair styling supplies, eye glasses, and jewelry. 800-535-8101.

Green Cedar Needle Sachets, Box 551, State Rd. 165, Placitas, NM 87043: Free brochure ❖ Sachets, incense cones, and other fragrance products. 800-557-3463.

The Guerlain Boutique by Mail, Rt. 138, Somers, NY 10589: Free catalog ❖ Women and men's fragrance and skin care products. 800-882-8820.

Gayle Hayman Beverly Hills, 750 Lexington Ave., 16th Floor, New York, NY 10026: Free catalog ❖ Cosmetics and jewelry. 800-682-9932.

Ole Henriksen of Denmark, 8601 W. Sunset Blvd., Los Angeles, CA 90069: Free information ❖ Face and body care treatments. 800-327-0331; 310-854-7700 (in CA).

Herb & Spice Collection, P.O. Box 299, Norway, IA 52318: Free catalog ❖ Natural herbal body care products, potpourris, culinary herbs and spices, other herbs, and teas. 800-786-1388.

Herbal Accents, P.O. Box 12303, El Cajon, CA 92022: Catalog $1 ❖ Aromatherapy skin care products. 619-440-4380.

Herbs for Healthy Living, RR 2, Box 128, Saegertown, PA 16433: Free information ❖ Skin care and bath products and herbal soaps. 814-763-2309.

Holbrook Wholesalers, 255 5th Ave., 3rd Floor, New York, NY 10016: Free information ❖ Designer perfumes.

Holzman & Stephanie Perfumes Inc., P.O. Box 921, Lake Forest, IL 60045: Catalog $4.50 (refundable) ❖ Copies of world-famous perfumes. 708-234-7667.

House of Fragrances, 1012 Homeland Ave., Ste. 11, Greensboro, NC 27405: Free catalog ❖ Designer fragrances and personal care products. 910-379-7271.

House of International Fragrances, 4711 Blanco Rd., San Antonio, TX 78212: Free information ❖ Long-lasting perfumes and colognes. 512-341-2283.

Indiana Botanic Gardens, 3401 W. 317th Ave., Hobart, IN 46342: Free catalog ❖ Vitamins, herbs, spices, and personal care products.

Island Tan, 125A Maunalua Ave., Honolulu, HI 96821: Free information ❖ Sunscreens, fragrances, and skin care products with natural ingredients. 800-926-5800.

Victoria Jackson Cosmetics Inc., National Distribution Center, 16 Paoli Corporate Center, Paoli, PA 19301: Free catalog ❖ Body, bath, hair care, and other cosmetics. 800-392-9250.

Jay Design, 365 N. Craig St., Pittsburgh, PA 15213: Free brochure ❖ All-natural handmade and cosmetic soaps. 412-683-1184.

Just America Inc., 100 Log Rd., Harrisville, RI 02830: Free information ❖ Bath care products. 401-765-2495.

Key West Aloe Inc., P.O. Box 1079, Key West, FL 33041: Free catalog ❖ Men's personal care products and toiletries. Also cosmetics and skin care products for women. 800-445-2563.

Kneipp Corporation of America, Valmont Industrial Park, 675 Jaycee Dr., West Hazleton, PA 18201: Free information ❖ Herbal baths and shower gels.

La Costa Products International, 2875 Laker Ave. East, Carlsbad, CA 92009: Free catalog ❖ Hair, skin, and body care products for men and women. 800-LA-COSTA.

Legacy Herbs, Sue Lukens Herbalist/Potter, Box 442, Mountain View, AR 72560: Catalog 50¢ ❖ Herbs, wildflowers, perennial plants, soaps, bath and body care products, oils and fragrances, incense, potpourri, herbal food products, and other scented iems. 501-269-4051.

COSTUMES & VINTAGE CLOTHING

Lucky Heart Cosmetics, 138 Huling Ave., Memphis, TN 38103: Free catalog ❖ Cosmetics and skin care products. 800-526-5825.

Katherine March Ltd., P.O. Box 51844, Durham, NC 27717: Free price list ❖ European soaps and luxuries for the bath. 800-87-MARCH.

Miracle of Aloe, 480 San Juan St., P.O. Box 5230, Pagosa Springs, CO 81147: Free information ❖ Aloe-based skin treatments and insect repellants. Also foot care, relief from muscle pain, hair and scalp, and health care products. 800-966-2563.

Mountain Rose Herbs, P.O. Box 2000, Redway, CA 95560: Catalog $1 ❖ Natural herbal body care products. 800-879-3337.

New Life Systems, 2853 Hedberg Dr., Minneapolis, MN 55305: Free catalog ❖ Health and wellness products, including massage tables, Panasonic massages, loungers, and air purifiers. 800-852-3082.

Nutrition Headquarters, One Nutrition Plaza, Carbondale, IL 62901: Free catalog ❖ Vitamins and mineral supplements, health and beauty aids, and herbal formulas.

Oleda & Company Inc., 6467 Southwest Blvd., Fort Worth, TX 76132: Free catalog ❖ Nutrition, health, and beauty aids. 817-731-1147.

Perfect Skin by Buddy Maurice, 4831 N. Dixie Hwy., Boca Raton, FL 33431: Brochure $2 ❖ Skin care products. 800-642-7546; 407-367-0882 (in FL).

Perfumes for Less, P.O. Box 1527, Salt Lake City, UT 84020: Catalog $2 ❖ Designer fragrances at discount prices. 800-374-5377.

Planta Dei Medicinal Herb Farm, Millville, New Brunswick, Canada E0H 1M0: Catalog $2 (refundable) ❖ Biologically grown teas, medicinal herbs, healing tea mixtures, cosmetics, natural ointments, and massage oils. 506-463-8169.

Puritan's Pride, 1233 Montauk Hwy., P.O. Box 9001, Oakdale, NY 11769: Free catalog ❖ Natural vitamins and health and beauty aids. 800-645-1030.

Sharper Image SPA, 650 Davis St., San Francisco, CA 94111: Free catalog ❖ Skin care products, SPA essentials, and health aids. 800-344-3440.

Simmons Handcrafts, 42295 Hwy. 36, Bridgeville, CA 95526: Catalog $1 ❖ Natural products for home and personal care. 707-777-1920.

Syd Simons Cosmetics, 2 E. Oak St., Chicago, IL 60611: Free price list ❖ Women's cosmetics and make-up. 312-943-2333.

Smith & Hawken, P.O. Box 6907, Florence, KY 41022: Free catalog ❖ Skin care preparations derived from herbs, flowers, and plants. 800-776-3336.

Soap Opera, 319 State St., Madison, WI 55703: Free price list ❖ Scented glycerin soaps, body lotions and creams, eye care cream, lip balms, suntan lotions, bubble baths and oils, essential oils, designer fragrances, herbs, and perfume bases. 800-251-SOAP.

Star Pharmaceuticals Inc., 1500 New Horizons Blvd., Amityville, NY 11701: Free catalog ❖ Vitamin products, nutritional supplements, toiletries, health care products, and pet supplies. 800-274-6400.

Sun Feather Handcrafted Herbal Soap Company, 1551 State Hwy. 72, Potsdam, NY 13676: Catalog $2 ❖ Herbal soaps, shampoos, and candles. Also how-to soap-making books, videos, kits, molds, and supplies. 800-771-7627.

Sunburst Biorganics, 832 Merrick Rd., Baldwin, NY 11510: Free catalog ❖ Nutritional supplements and toiletries. 800-645-8448.

Teasel, 46 Main St., Middlebury, VT 05753: Free information ❖ Lingerie, fine soaps and toiletries, potpourri, and candles. 800-300-1204.

The Uncommon Herb, P.O. Box 2908, Seal Beach, CA 90740: Catalog $1 ❖ Essential oils, handmade soaps, skin care products, teas, and seasonings. 800-845-0008.

Village Herb Shop Catalogue, 152 S. Main St., Chagrin Falls, OH 44022: Catalog and herbal handbook $4 ❖ Books, potpourri, soaps, cosmetics, oils, herbal food products, and other items.

The Vitamin Shoppe, 4700 Westside Ave., North Bergen, NJ 07047: Free catalog ❖ Vitamins, herbs, homeopathic medicines, and pure and natural cosmetics. 800-223-1216.

Woods of Windsor, Traditional English Perfumes, 9-C Brick Plant Rd., South River, NJ 08882: Free brochure ❖ Personal toiletries, traditional herbal and glycerine soaps, and fragrances for men and women. 908-613-1770.

Wynnewood Pharmacy, Wynnewood Shopping Center, Wynnewood, PA 19096: Free catalog ❖ Perfumes and colognes. 800-966-9999; 215-878-4999 (in PA).

ZIA Cosmetics, 410 Townsend Pl., San Francisco, CA 94107: Free brochure ❖ Skin care cosmetics. 800-334-7546.

COSTUMES & VINTAGE CLOTHING

Abracadabra Magic Shop, 125 Lincoln Blvd., Middlesex, NJ 08846: Catalog $5 ❖ Close-up and stage magic, juggling equipment, balloons, clown props, costumes, and theatrical supplies. 908-805-0200.

American Stitches, 28 Forest St., Danvers, MA 01923: Catalog $1 ❖ Reproduction military and civilian clothing of the 1860s for men, women, and children. 508-777-5257.

Best Magic Gags & Costumes, 625 S. Magnolia Ave., Anaheim, CA 92804: Free information ❖ Magic, juggling equipment, costumes, gags and gifts, dancewear, and clown items. 714-827-MGIC.

Cattle Kate, Box 572, Wilson, WY 83014: Catalog $3 ❖ Contemporary western-style clothing for men, women, and children. 307-733-7414.

Cavalry Regimental Supply, Box 64394, Lubbock, TX 79464: Catalog $2 with long SASE (refundable) ❖ Yesteryear western-style clothing.

Circus Clowns, 3556 Nicollet Ave., Minneapolis, MN 55408: Catalog $3 ❖ Clown costumes and props. 612-822-4243.

Clown Heaven, 4792 Old State Rd. 37 South, Martinsville, IN 46152: Catalog $3 ❖ Balloons, make-up, puppets, wigs, ministry and gospel items, novelties, magic, clown props, and books. 317-342-6888.

Confederate Yankee, P.O. Box 192, Guilford, CT 06437: Catalog $3 ❖ Men, women, and children's reproduction Revolutionary to Civil War clothing. 203-453-9900.

The Costume Connection, P.O. Box 4518, Falls Church, VA 22044: Free catalog ❖ Character costumes. 703-237-1373.

Costumes by Betty, 2181 Edgerton St., St. Paul, MN 55117: Catalog $5 (refundable) ❖ Clown costumes, make-up, wigs, and shoes. 612-771-8734.

Eastern Costume Company, 510 N. Elm St., Greensboro, NC 27401: Free information ❖ Theatrical and masquerade costumes and make-up. 800-968-8461; 919-379-1026 (in NC).

Harriet A. Engler, P.O. Box 1363, Winchester, VA 22604: Adult catalog $7, children's catalog $3 ❖ Military and civilian reproduction costumes, uniforms, patterns, and crinolines. 703-667-2541.

Freckles Clown Supplies, 5509 Roosevelt Blvd., Jacksonville, FL 32244: Catalog $6 ❖ Costumes, make-up, clown supplies, puppets, clowning and ballooning how-to books, and theatrical supplies. 904-388-5541.

Lacey Costume Wig, 505 8th Ave., 11th Floor, New York, NY 10018: Free catalog ❖ Wigs, mustaches, beards, and other supplies. 800-562-9911.

Laidlacker Historical Garments, RD 2, Box 989, Milton, PA 17847: Catalog $3 ❖ Reproduction 18th, 19th, and 20th-century clothing for men, women, and children. 717-437-9174.

Lynch's Clown Supplies, 939 Howard, Dearborn, MI 48124: Catalog $5 ❖ Clown wigs, shoes, noses, novelties, make-up, and costumes. 313-565-3425.

COUNTRY CRAFTS

Heidi Marsh Patterns, 3494 N. Valley Rd., Greenville, CA 95947: Catalog $3 ❖ Civil War clothing patterns for adults and children.

Martin's Mercantile & Millinery, 4566 Oakhurst Dr., Sylvania, OH 43560: Catalog $4.50 ❖ Women's underpinnings, work dresses to ball gowns, and accessories. 419-474-2093.

Mary Ellen & Company, 100 N. Main St., North Liberty, IN 46554: Catalog $3 ❖ Victorian-style clothing, lace-up shoes, hats, fans, parasols, books, and patterns. 800-669-1860.

Mecca Magic Inc., 49 Dodd St., Bloomfield, NJ 07003: Catalog $10 ❖ Costumes, wigs, and make-up. 201-429-7597.

Morris Costumes, 3108 Monroe Rd., Charlotte, NC 28205: Catalog $20 ❖ Costumes, clown props, masks, joke items, magic tricks and special effects, novelties, and books. 704-332-3304.

The 1909 Company, 63 Thompson St., New York, NY 10012: Catalog $2 ❖ Reproduction vintage clothing. 800-331-1909.

Northwest Traders Inc., 5055 W. Jackson Rd., Enon, OH 45323: Catalog $1 ❖ Frontier clothing and related items. 513-767-9244.

The Old Frontier Clothing Company, P.O. Box 691836, Los Angeles, CA 90069: Catalog $3 ❖ Old western-style clothing. 310-246-WEST.

Quartermaster Shop, Jeff O'Donnell, 5565 Griswold Rd., Kimball, MI 48074: Catalog $4 ❖ Reproduction Union, Confederate, and civilian Civil War-period clothing. 810-367-6702.

Raiments, P.O. Box 93095, Pasadena, CA 91109: Catalog $5 ❖ Books, under- pinnings, and patterns for historical costumes, from the middle ages to the 1950s. 818-797-2723.

Reflections of the Past, P.O. Box 40361, Bay Village, OH 44140: Catalog $5 ❖ Men, women, and children's American and European fashions, from the 17th to 19th-century. 216-835-6924.

Ronjo's Magic & Costumes Inc., 4600 Nesconset Hwy., Unit 4, Port Jefferson Station, NY 11776: Catalog $2.50 ❖ Magic for amateur and professional magicians, costumes, and make-up and theatrical effects. 516-928-5005.

Rubie's Costume Company, National Sales Office, 999 Gould St., New Hyde Park, NY 11040: Free information ❖ Costumes, make-up, hair goods, and special effects. 516-326-1500.

Salt Lake Costume Company, 1701 S. 1100 East, Salt Lake City, UT 84105: Free catalog ❖ Historical costumes and make-up. 801-467-9494.

Servant & Company, Centennial General Store, 230 Steinwehr Ave., Gettysburg, PA 17325: Pattern catalog $2; men's uniform and accouterment catalog $2 ❖ Civil War period accessories and accouterments for men and women, clothing patterns, and kepis, hats, and leather goods. 717-334-9712.

Star Styled Dancewear, P.O. Box 119029, Hialeah, FL 33011: Free information ❖ Bodywear, shoes, and costumes for dancers. 800-532-6237.

James Townsend & Son Inc., 133 N. 1st St., P.O. Box 415, Pierceton, IN 46562: Catalog $2 ❖ Historical clothing, hats, lanterns, tomahawks, knives, tents, guns, and blankets. 800-338-1665.

Under the Big Top, P.O. Box 807, Placentia, CA 92670: Catalog $4 ❖ Costumes, clown props, make-up, juggling equipment, and party supplies. 800-995-7727.

White Water Creek Trading Company, P.O. Box 272, Tyrone, GA 30290: Free information ❖ Old-style western clothing. 404-969-1607.

COUNTRY CRAFTS

AC Originals, Rt. 2, Box 478, Claremore, OK 74017: Free information ❖ Country-style pine bookcases, plate racks, and baker's rack with a choice of finishes. 918-341-1604.

Adirondack Store & Gallery, 109 Saranac Ave., Lake Placid, NY 12946: Free information ❖ Country-style twig furniture, stoneware and pottery, rugs, fire boards, outdoor lawn and wood furniture, baskets, and pillows. 518-523-2646.

Amish Country Collection, Sunset Valley Rd., RD 5, Box 271, New Castle, PA 16105: Catalog $5 ❖ Amish-style pillows, quilts, wall hangings, rugs, cribs and beds, and household items. 412-458-4811.

Bayou Country Store, 823 E. Jackson St., Pensacola, FL 32501: Free catalog ❖ Country crafts and decorative accessories. 800-262-5403; 904-432-5697 (in FL).

Dennis & CeCe Bork, 715 Genesee St., Delafield, WI 53018: Catalog $5 ❖ Custom furniture, folk art, period lighting, Colonial Williamsburg reproductions, Windsor chairs and settees, and accessories. 414-646-4911.

Brown's Country Creations, Rt. 1, Box 1228, Dunnegan, MO 65640: Catalog $2.50 ❖ Handcrafted bathroom ensembles and hanging towel and matching table sets. 800-338-7696; 417-326-4880 (in MO).

Brush Strokes, 19312 Haviland Dr., South Bend, IN 46637: Brochure $3 ❖ Signed and numbered limited edition prints reproduced from original oil paintings with a choice of mats and frames. 219-277-5414.

Chriswill Forge, 2255 Manchester Rd., North Lawrence, OH 44666: Catalog $2 ❖ Country-style floor lamps with a heavy-duty steel plate base and a choice of designs for the top. 216-832-9136.

Classics by Simply Country, P.O. Drawer 656, Wytheville, VA 24382: Brochure $2 (refundable) ❖ Wall hangings, throws, pillows, clothing, and afghans. 800-537-8911.

Colonial Casting Company Inc., 68 Liberty St., Haverhill, MA 01832: Catalog $3 ❖ Handcrafted lead-free pewter miniature castings. 508-374-8783.

Colonial Collections of New England Inc., 202 Idlewood Dr., Stamford, CT 06905: Catalog $2 ❖ Weather vanes, cupolas, sundials, mailboxes, door knockers, personalized and date plaques, lanterns, and home and garden decorative items. 203-322-0078.

Conewago Junction, 1255 Oxford Rd., New Oxford, PA 17350: Catalog $2 ❖ Colonial chests, cupboards, wooden buckets, tools, afghans, tinware, and household items. 717-624-4786.

The Cotton Gin Inc., Deep Creek Farm, P.O. Box 414, Jarvisburg, NC 27947: Free catalog ❖ Country collectibles, southern-style clothing, and antiques. 800-637-2446.

Country Accents, P.O. Box 437, Montoursville, PA 17754: Catalog $5 ❖ Museum tin replicas and accent pieces. 717-478-4127.

Country Bouquet, P.O. Box 200, Kellogg, MN 55945: Brochure $2 ❖ Candle holders and sconces, Raggedy Ann and Andy dolls, folk items, stenciled aprons, ornaments, and shelves, pegboards, and wall cupboards. 800-328-5598.

Country Charm Inc., 322 S. Main St., Plymouth, MI 48170: Catalog $2 ❖ Long-burning candles and country folk art accessories. 800-288-5699; 313-455-9292 (in MI).

Country Manor, Mail Order Dept., Rt. 211, P.O. Box 520, Sperryville, VA 22740: Catalog $3 ❖ Hand-woven cotton rugs, kitchen utensils, craft items, and decorative accessories. 800-344-8354.

Country Punchin', 14757 Glenn Dr., Whittier, CA 90604: Brochure $1 ❖ Hand-punched and tarnish-proof name signs and plaques in solid copper or pewter-like metal. 310-944-1038.

The Country Store, 28 James St., Geneva, IL 60134: Catalog $2 ❖ Punched tin and turned wooden chandeliers, ceiling lights, outlet covers, country-style decorative accessories, braided rugs, and stoneware. 708-879-0098.

Country Store Crafts, 5925 Country Ln., P.O. Box 990, Greendale, WI 53129: Free catalog ❖ Country gifts for men, women, and children. 800-558-1013.

Craft Village Inc., 8275 Cooley Lake Rd., Commerce, MI 48382: Free information ❖ Country-style crafts for the home. 800-950-4900.

COUNTRY CRAFTS

Crafts 'N Clutter, 670 S. Coast Hwy., Laguna Beach, CA 92651: Free information ❖ Country folk art gifts and accessories. 714-376-8388.

Gregan T. Crawford, Cabinetmaker, Rt. 2, Box 6040, Oakland, MD 21550: Catalog $2 ❖ Shaker-inspired furniture and home accessories. 800-531-4109.

Creations by Cranford, P.O. Box 9007, Hickory, NC 28603: Brochure $2 ❖ Victorian-style country crafts. 704-326-9707.

Creative Crafts, 308 S. Todd, McComb, OH 45858: Brochure $2 ❖ Handcrafted earthenware pottery. 419-293-3838.

Custom Country Wood Products, Rt. 2, Box 108, Greenville, TX 75402: Free information ❖ Country-style furniture with a whitewash stain or unfinished. 903-455-0542.

Darowood Farms, 4614 School Rd., P.O. Box 470, Egg Harbor, WI 54209: Brochure $2 ❖ Handcrafted country wood items. 800-228-3908.

D.D. Dillon, 850 Meadow Ln., Camp Hill, PA 17011: Free information ❖ Wall hangings and hand-carved cookie and shortbread molds. 717-761-6895.

Everything Ewenique, RR 1, Box 73, Mt. Pleasant Mills, PA 17853: Free catalog ❖ Country accents for the home. 800-528-9382.

The Faith Mountain Company, P.O. Box 199, Sperryville, VA 22740: Free catalog ❖ Kitchen utensils, country-style gifts, folk art reproductions, toys and dolls, handmade Appalachian baskets, and Christmas decorations. 800-588-2548.

Friends, 109 Shawnee, Eldridge, IA 52748: Brochure $2 ❖ Country-style Christmas decorative accessories. 319-285-7354.

Frye's Measure Mill, 12 Frye Mill Rd., Wilton, NH 03086: Catalog $3.75 ❖ Early American woodenware. 603-654-6581.

Gard Woodworking, 121 N. Walnut, Colfax, IA 50054: Brochure $1 ❖ Wooden country crafts and decorative accessories. 515-674-3060.

Grandpa's Crafts, 577 Hwy. 70 West, Havelock, NC 28532: Brochure $1 ❖ Country craft decorative accessories. 919-444-1603.

Green Mountain Studios, Rt. 10 North, Box 158, Lyme, NH 03768: Catalog $2 ❖ Country crafts.

Grunewald Folk Art, P.O. Box 52, Alpen, IL 60001: Catalog $2 ❖ Signed and numbered limited edition lithographs of pen and ink drawings of animals and people in rural American settings. 815-648-4683.

Handcrafted Wood Products, 11280 US Hwy. 90, Daphne, AL 36526: Free information ❖ Wood-crafted spool and bobbin organizer and wall rack for serger cones. 334-633-4570.

Heart of the Woods Inc., P.O. Box 210, Ely, MN 55731: Catalog $1 (refundable) ❖ Wooden country-style decorative accessories. 800-852-2075.

Independence Forge, Rt. 1, Box 1, Whitakers, NC 27891: Brochure $1 ❖ Furniture, chandeliers, floor lamps, table and wall lamps, and country-style handcrafted iron pieces. 919-437-2931.

Jepson Studios Inc., P.O. Box 36, Harveyville, KS 66431: Brochure $2 (refundable) ❖ Country ceramics. 913-589-2481.

Karlin Pottery, P.O. Box 180836, Utica, MI 48318: Brochure $1 ❖ Country pottery and stoneware. 810-997-0575.

Lambs Farm, P.O. Box 520, Jct. I-94 & Rt. 176, Libertyville, IL 60048: Free catalog ❖ Country crafts, specialty foods, nuts, candies, and gifts for pets. 800-52-LAMBS.

McVay's Limited, P.O. Box 553, Leslie, MI 49251: Brochure $2 ❖ Wall accent pieces, game boards, weather vanes, and handcrafted household and gift items. 517-589-5312.

MoonAcre IronWorks, 62 Chambersburg St., Gettysburg, PA 17325: Catalog $2 ❖ Country-style iron trellises for climbing plants. 800-966-4766.

North Country Crafts, P.O. Box 500, Marinette, WI 54143: Free information ❖ Country-style upholstered storage ottomans. 800-637-7989.

Orleans Carpenters, P.O. Box 217, Orleans, MA 02653: Catalog $3 ❖ Shaker-style oval bentwood boxes and small wooden crafts. 508-255-2646.

Plain Folk, 21 School St., Box 265, Riverton, CT 06065: Free catalog ❖ Early New England wrought-iron, tinware, pottery, and folk art. 203-379-0492.

Charles Putt, RR 1, Box 144, Robesonia, PA 19551: Catalog $2 ❖ Authentic reproductions, folk art paintings, and other woodwork in an 18th and 19th-century style. 610-488-0543.

Raindrops on Roses Rubber Stamp Company, 4808 Winterwood Dr., Raleigh, NC 27613: Catalog $3 ❖ Country-style rubber stamp sets with brush markers. 800-245-8617; 919-846-8617 (in NC).

Red Feather Arts & Crafts, P.O. Box 341, Pennville, IN 47369: Catalog $2 ❖ Country-style crafts and decorative accessories for the home. 219-731-7562.

Redwood Unlimited, P.O. Box 2344, Valley Center, CA 92082: Brochure $2 ❖ Wall and post-mounted mailboxes with ornamental scrolls, posts, and weather vanes. 800-283-1717.

Rob 'N' Wood, 171 W. Craig Ave., Lake Helen, FL 32744: Catalog $2 ❖ Cabinets, furniture, birdfeeders, and decorative crafts. 904-228-0908.

The Rocking Horse Country Store, RR 3, Box 7343, Rutland, VT 05701: Free brochure ❖ Vermont maple syrup, cheese, crafts, and country collectibles. 802-773-7882.

Shaker Shops West, P.O. Box 487, Inverness, CA 94937: Catalog $3 ❖ Reproductions of traditional music boxes, country-style furniture, candles, accessories for the home, teas and herbs, and books on the lifestyles, traditions, and history of the Shakers. 415-669-7256.

Simply Country Furniture, HC 69, Box 147, Rover, AR 72860: Brochure $2 ❖ Grandfather clocks. 501-272-4794.

South Prairie Crafts, Rt. 3, Box 237, Minot, ND 58701: Free information ❖ Shaker wall clock with combination wall cabinet for displaying collectibles. 701-722-3520.

Studio Workshop Inc., 2808 Tucker St., Omaha, NE 68112: Catalog $2 ❖ Country-style bathroom accessories, oak shelves, shadow boxes, and furniture. 800-383-7072.

Sutter Creek Antiques, 28 Main St., Box 699, Sutter Creek, CA 95685: Free brochure with long SASE ❖ Antique country-style lamps, pottery, and carved wooden items. 209-267-0230.

Sweet Antiques Galleries, RR 2, Box 3435, Montpelier, VT 05602: Free brochure ❖ Reproduction antique-style tin signs, recycled glass bottles, wooden items, oven and dishwasher-safe enamelware, and toys.

The Symmetree Company, P.O. Drawer E, West Rockport, ME 04865: Free brochure ❖ Country crafts, decorative accessories, and country-style gifts. 800-824-2402.

Three Rivers Pottery Productions Inc., 125 N. 2nd St., P.O. Box 462, Coshocton, OH 43812: Free information ❖ Oven, microwave, and dishwasher-safe pottery. 614-622-4154.

Tidy's Storehouse, 1102 Hopewell Rd., Oxford, PA 19363: Catalog $3 ❖ Books and reproduction 18th-century pottery, glass, tinware, clothing, patterns, and shoes.

Tin Bin, 20 Valley Rd., Neffsville, PA 17601: Catalog $2.50 ❖ Handcrafted antiqued copper and brass country-style chandeliers. 717-569-6210.

A Touch of Country, P.O. Box 653, Palos Heights, IL 60463: Catalog $2 ❖ Country-style hand-painted wood ceiling fan, and lighting pulls. 708-361-0142.

Vermont FurnitureWorks, P.O. Box 1496, Stowe, VT 05672: Free catalog ❖ Handcrafted 18th and 19th-century reproduction New England furniture, traditional folk art, and Americana accessories. 802-253-5094.

Westwinds, 3540 76th St. SE, Caledonias, MI 49316: Free brochure ❖ Weather vanes, signs, sundials, and birdbaths. 800-635-5262.

CRAFT SUPPLIES

Wink's Woods, 1225 W. US 2, Crystal Falls, MI 49920: Free information with long SASE ❖ Country-style wooden decorative accessories. 906-875-3750.

Wood Concepts, 23565 Reedy Dr., Elkhart, IN 46514: Free information with long SASE ❖ Easy-to-assemble solid oak country-style furniture and decorative accessories. 219-262-3457.

Woodworks Unlimited, 208 Breckenridge Dr., West Monroe, LA 71292: Catalog $3 ❖ Pine furniture, accent pieces, and lamps. 318-325-2350.

Zimmerman Handcrafts, 254 E. Main St., Leola, PA 17540: Brochure $1 ❖ Country-style decorative items and traditional crafts. 800-267-5689.

CRAFT SUPPLIES

Activa Products, P.O. Box 1296, Marshall, TX 75670: Free information ❖ Non-toxic scenic-crafting sand in permanent approved colors.

Adventure in Ceramics, 1421 Ellis St., Waukeesha, WI 53186: Catalog $4 ❖ Ready-to-paint kiln-fired ceramic bisque projects.

Allen-Lewis Manufacturing Company, Division TCC Industries Inc., P.O. Box 16546, 5601 Logan, Denver, CO 80216: Free catalog ❖ Souvenirs, carnival and party supplies, fund-raising merchandise, toys and games, T-shirts and sweatshirts, and craft supplies. 303-295-0196.

Arrow Fastener Company Inc., 271 Mayhill St., Saddle Brook, NJ 07662: Free information ❖ Hot melt glue guns.

The Art Store, 935 Erie Blvd. East, Syracuse, NY 13210: Price list $3 ❖ Supplies for fabric dyeing, screen-printing, marbling, and other crafts. 800-669-2787.

Atlas Art & Stained Glass, P.O. Box 76084, Oklahoma City, OK 73147: Catalog $3 ❖ Kaleidoscopes, frames, lamp bases, and art and craft, stained glass, jewelry-making, and foil-crafting supplies. 405-946-1230.

Barap Specialties, 835 Bellows Ave., Frankfort, MI 49635: Catalog $1 ❖ Caning and craft supplies, tools, lamp parts, and turned wooden parts. 800-3-BARAP-3.

Baubanbea Enterprises, P.O. Box 1205, Smithtown, NY 11787: Catalog $1 ❖ Rhinestones, sequins, beads, jewels, lace, appliques, fringe, trim, feathers, imported and domestic fabrics, and silk flowers. 516-724-4661.

Brian's Crafts Unlimited, 1421 S. Dixie Freeway, New Smyrna, FL 32168: Catalog $1 (refundable) ❖ Craft supplies. 904-672-2726.

Caldwell Craft Supply, 3853 Goodnight Ave., Pueblo, CO 81005: Free catalog ❖ Craft supplies. 800-441-2279.

Carolan Craft Supplies, P.O. Box 9920, Cleveland, OH 44142: Catalog $3 ❖ Darice beads, plastic canvas, craft books, stencils, basket-making supplies, jewelry, quilts and needle crafts, pom poms, bears, dolls, and wire crafts. 216-362-0340.

Chaselle Inc., 9645 Gerwig Ln., Columbia, MD 21046: Catalog $4 ❖ Ceramic and pottery-making equipment, and supplies for art, sculpting, stained glass, weaving, leather-crafting, etching, and other crafts. 800-242-7355.

Circle Craft Supply, P.O. Box 3000, Dover, FL 33527: Catalog $1 ❖ Art and craft supplies. 813-659-0992.

Columbia Arts, 1515 E. Burnside St., Portland, OR 97214: Free information ❖ Art and craft supplies. 800-547-9750.

Craft Catalog, 6095 McNaughten Centre, Columbus, OH 43232: Catalog $2 ❖ Art and craft supplies.

Craft King Mail Order Dept., P.O. Box 90637, Lakeland, FL 33804: Catalog $2 ❖ Craft, needlework, and macrame supplies. 888-CRAFTY-1.

Craft Kits, 936 E. Green St., Ste. 113, Pasadena, CA 91106: Free information ❖ Educational and cultural craft kits. 818-568-0400.

Craft Makers, 3958 Linden Ave., Dayton, OH 45432: Catalog $2 ❖ Craft supplies. 800-CRAFTS-5.

Craft Resources Inc., Box 828, Fairfield, CT 06430: Catalog $1 ❖ String art, basket-making, metal and wood-crafting, stained glass, and other craft supplies. Also needlework kits for latch hooking, needlepoint, cross-stitching, and crewel. 800-243-2874; 203-254-7702 (in CT).

Craft Time Catalog, 10940 S. Parker Rd., Ste. 476, Parker, CO 80134: Catalog $2 (refundable) ❖ Ready-to-paint figurines. 303-792-2463.

Crafty's Featherworks, P.O. Box 370, Overton, NV 89040: Free information ❖ Feathers for floral arrangements, Native American and other crafts, millinery, fly-tying, and accent pieces. 702-397-8211.

Creative Craft House, Box 2567, Bullhead City, AZ 86430: Catalog $2 (refundable) ❖ Sea shells, pine cones, and craft supplies.

Crysbi Crafts Inc., 17514 South Ave., #4E, Yuma, AZ 85365: Catalog $2 ❖ Craft supplies and accessories.

Lou Davis Wholesale Ceramics & Crafts, N3211 Hwy. H North, Lake Geneva, WI 53147: Free catalog ❖ Craft supplies. 800-748-7991.

Discount Bead House, P.O. Box 186, The Plains, OH 45780: Catalog $5 ❖ Leather, seed beads, findings, wooden items, tools, and modeling supplies. 800-793-7592.

Eagle Feather Trading, 168 W. 12th St., Ogden, UT 84404: Catalog $3.50 ❖ Beads, bead crafting accessories, kits, books, and Native American craft supplies.

Earth Guild, 33 Haywood St., Asheville, NC 28801: Free catalog ❖ Basket-making, weaving, spinning, dyeing, pottery, wood carving, hand and machine knitting, rug-making, netting, and chair-caning supplies. 800-327-8448.

Eastern Art Glass, P.O. Box 341, Wyckoff, NJ 07481: Catalog $2 (refundable) ❖ Stained glass kits, glass-etching equipment, glass coloring materials, fabric dyes, mirror-removing and wood-burning supplies, and how-to videos. 201-847-0001.

Eastman Corporation, P.O. Box 247, Roselle, NJ 07203: Catalog $2 ❖ Stains for metal, glass, shells, bone, plastic, ceramics, and leather. 908-232-1212.

Enterprise Art, P.O. Box 2918, Largo, FL 34649: Free catalog ❖ Beads from around the world, bead and jewelry-making kits, and craft and jewelry-making supplies. 800-366-2218.

Evening Star Designs, 69 Coolidge Ave., Haverhill, MA 01832: Catalog $3 ❖ Craft and jewelry-making supplies. 800-666-3562.

Factory Direct Craft Supplies, 440 Conover Dr., P.O. Box 16, Franklin, OH 45005: Catalog $2 ❖ Art and craft supplies. 513-743-5855.

Fairfield Processing Corporation, P.O. Box 1130, Danbury, CT 06813: Free information ❖ Fiberfill and batting products. 800-442-2271; 203-371-1901 (in CT).

Freudenberg/Pellon, 1040 Avenue of Americas, New York, NY 10018: Free information ❖ Supplies for bonding fabrics to fabric, cardboard, wood, and other porous surfaces. 800-223-5275; 212-391-6308 (in NY).

G & J Enterprises, 4199 State Rd. 144, Moorseville, IN 46158: Free catalog ❖ Craft and electrical supplies. 317-831-1452.

Rolf Gille Import Ltd., P.O. Box 42047, San Francisco, CA 94142: Free catalog ❖ Craft supplies from nature. 800-448-9988.

Green Mountain Studios, Rt. 10 North, Box 158, Lyme, NH 03768: Catalog $2 ❖ Craft supplies.

Guildcraft Company, 100 Firetower Dr., Tonawanda, NY 14150: Free catalog ❖ Supplies for fabric dyeing and foil, chair-caning, basket-making, plaster, candle, wood, leather, and egg-crafting. 716-743-8336.

Homestead Designs Gourds, 2826 Old Street Rd. 67, West Martinsville, IN 46151: Free information ❖ Ready-to-paint gourds. 317-342-8097.

JoyFul Art, P.O. Box 60206, King of Prussia, PA 19406: Free catalog ❖ Craft kits. 800-358-4581.

Kenco, 2531 N. 85th St., Omaha, NE 68134: Free information ❖ Fabrics and supplies, tools, patterns, and how-to books on rag crochet crafting. 800-228-6633.

Kirchen Brothers, Box 1016, Skokie, IL 60076: Catalog $2 ❖ Art and craft supplies. 708-647-6747.

Kitty Korner Designs, 625 Constitution Ln., Madison, WI 53711: Free information with long SASE ❖ Stenciled fabric patches for making wall hangings and decorative accessories.

Lark Books, 50 College St., Asheville, NC 28801: Free catalog ❖ Kits, books, and gifts. 800-284-3388.

Luv 'n Stuff, P.O. Box 85, Poway, CA 92074: Catalog $2 ❖ Sewing supplies, rubber stamps, and patterns for dolls, stuffed animals, holiday decorations, and ornaments. 619-748-8060.

Maplewood Crafts, Humboldt Industrial Park, 1 Maplewood Dr., Hazleton, PA 18201: Free catalog ❖ Beading and needlecraft supplies, other craft materials, kits, tools, and books. 800-899-0134.

MPR Associates, A Specialty Ribbon Company, P.O. Box 7343, High Point, NC 27264: Free catalog ❖ Paper ribbons, twists, kits, and finishing products. 800-454-3331.

Nasco, 901 Janesville Ave., Fort Atkinson, WI 53538: Free catalog ❖ Supplies for art projects, calligraphy, leather-crafting, metal enameling, ceramics, photography, and needle crafts. 800-558-9595.

National Artcraft Company, 23456 Mercantile Rd., Beachwood, OH 44122: Catalog $4 ❖ Tools and supplies for floral-crafting and for making clocks, lamps, dolls, candles, and jewelry. 800-793-0152.

Oppenheim's, P.O. Box 52, North Manchester, IN 46962: Catalog $1 ❖ Sewing notions, fabrics, and craft supplies. 800-461-6728.

Oxmoor House, P.O. Box 2463, Birmingham, AL 35282: Free catalog ❖ Creative craft glues and how-to information. 205-877-6000.

Purr-sonality Plus Kit Company, P.O. Box 1363, Arcadia, CA 91077: Catalog $2 ❖ Original craft kits.

Red Hill Corporation, P.O. Box 4234, Gettysburg, PA 17325: Free catalog ❖ Hot melt glue sticks, glue guns, and sandpaper belts, sheets, and disks. 800-822-4003.

Sax Arts & Crafts, P.O. Box 51710, New Berlin, WI 51710: Free catalog ❖ Art and craft supplies. 800-558-6696; 414-784-6880 (in WI).

Suncoast Discount Arts & Crafts Warehouse, 10601 47th St. North, Clearwater, FL 34622: Catalog $2 ❖ Art and craft supplies. 813-572-1600.

Taylor's Cutaways & Stuff, 2802 E. Washington St., Urbana, IL 61801: Brochure $1 ❖ Satins, lace, velvet, cottons, felt, calico, trim, polyester squares, sewing notions, craft supplies, books, and soft toy and crochet patterns.

United Supply Company Inc., P.O. Box 9219, Fort Wayne, IN 46899: Free catalog ❖ Art and craft supplies, books, and tools. 800-322-3247.

Vanguard Crafts Inc., P.O. Box 340170, Brooklyn, NY 11234: Free catalog ❖ Art and craft supplies. 800-662-7238; 718-377-5188 (in NY).

Warscokins, 7561 Center Ave., #40, Huntington Beach, CA 92647: Catalog $3.50 ❖ Art and craft supplies. 800-225-6356.

Weaving Works, 4717 Brooklyn Ave. NE, Seattle, WA 98105: Catalog $4.50 ❖ Supplies for making baskets, dyeing, weaving, spinning, and knitting. 206-524-1221.

West Mountain Gourd Farm, P.O. Drawer 1049, Gilmer, TX 75644: Information $3 ❖ Ready-to-paint gourds. 903-734-5204.

Wood-N-Crafts Inc., P.O. Box 140, Lakeview, MI 48850: Free catalog ❖ Craft supplies. 800-444-8075.

Zim's, 4370 S. 3rd West, Salt Lake City, UT 84107: Catalog $10 (refundable) ❖ Craft supplies. 801-268-2505.

CRICKET

American Sports Inc., P.O. Box 36662, Los Angeles, CA 90036: Free list of retail sources ❖ Bats, balls, and gloves. 800-922-8939.

General Sportcraft Company, 140 Woodbine Rd., Bergenfield, NJ 07621: Free information ❖ Bats, balls, and gloves. 201-384-4242.

Genesport Industries Ltd., Hokkaido Karate Equipment Manufacturing Company, 150 King St., Montreal, Quebec, Canada H3C 2P3: Free information ❖ Bats, balls, and gloves. 514-861-1856.

Don Jagoda Associates Inc., 100 Marcus Dr., Melville, NY 117476: Free information ❖ Bats, balls, and gloves. 516-454-1800.

CROQUET

Cannon Sports, P.O. Box 797, Greenland, NH 03840: Free list of retail sources ❖ Croquet sets. 800-362-3146.

Clarkpoint Croquet Company, P.O. Box 457, Southwest Harbor, ME 04679: Free information with long SASE ❖ Croquet sets and mallets. 207-244-9284.

Croquet International Ltd., 7100-42 Fairway Dr., Palm Beach Gardens, FL 33418: Free catalog ❖ Croquet and tennis sets. 800-533-9061; 407-627-4009 (in FL).

Escalade Sports, P.O. Box 889, Evansville, IN 47706: Free information ❖ Croquet accessories. 800-457-3373; 812-467-1200 (in IN).

Indian Industries Inc., P.O. Box 889, Evansville, IN 47706: Free catalog ❖ Sets. 800-457-3373; 812-467-1200 (in IN).

Olympia Sports, 745 State Circle, Ann Arbor, MI 48106: Free information ❖ Croquet sets. 800-521-2832.

Porter Athletic Equipment Company, 2500 S. 25th Ave., Broadview, IL 60153: Free information ❖ Croquet sets. 708-338-2000.

Russell Corporation, Russell Athletic Division, P.O. Box 272, Alexander City, AL 35010: Free information ❖ Croquet sets. 205-329-4000.

Spalding Sports Worldwide, 425 Meadow St., P.O. Box 901, Chicopee, MA 01201: Free list of retail sources ❖ Croquet accessories. 800-225-6601.

Sportime, Customer Service, 1 Sporting Way, Atlanta, GA 30340: Free information ❖ Croquet accessories. 800-444-5700; 770-449-5700 (in GA).

CRYSTAL & GLASSWARE

Alberene Crystal, 435 5th Ave., New York, NY 10016: Free information ❖ Edinburgh and Thomas Webb crystal and Perthshire paperweights. Includes discontinued items. 800-843-9078.

Alice's Past & Presents Replacements, P.O. Box 465, Merrick, NY 11566: Free information ❖ Replacement crystal, china, and flatware. 516-379-1352.

Baccarat, 625 Madison Ave., New York, NY 10022: Brochure $3 ❖ Crystal and china Baccarat. 800-777-0100.

Barrons, P.O. Box 994, Novi, MI 48376: Free information ❖ China, crystal, and silver. 800-538-6340.

Mildred Brumback, P.O. Box 132, Middletown, VA 22645: Free information ❖ Discontinued china and crystal. 703-869-1261.

China, Crystal & Flatware Replacements, P.O. Box 508, High Ridge, MO 63049: Free information ❖ China, crystal, and flatware. 800-562-2655.

The China Cabinet (South Carolina), P.O. Box 426, Clearwater, SC 29822: Free information with long SASE ❖ China and crystal. 803-593-9655.

China Marketing, Box 33, Cheltenham, PA 19012: Free information ❖ Discontinued china and crystal. 800-599-3569.

China Replacements, 2263 Williams Creek Rd., High Ridge, MO 63049: Free information with long SASE ❖ Discontinued china and crystal. 800-562-2655; 677-5577 (in St. Louis).

The China Warehouse, Box 21797, Cleveland, OH 44121: Free information ❖ China, crystal, and flatware. 800-321-3212.

❖ CURTAINS, DRAPES & BLINDS ❖

Clintsman International, 20855 Watertown Rd., Waukesha, WI 53186: Free information ❖ Discontinued china, crystal, and flatware. 414-798-0440.

Crystal d'Arques, Durand International, P.O. Box 5001, Millville, NJ 08332: Free information ❖ Crystal d'Arques from France. 800-334-5014.

Crystal Lalique, 680 Madison Ave., New York, NY 10021: Free information ❖ Crystal and china Lalique. 800-214-2738; 212-355-6550 (in NY).

Dansk, 108 Corporate Park Dr., White Plains, NY 10604: Free list of retail sources ❖ Dinnerware, stemware, flatware, kitchenware, and serving pieces. 914-697-6400.

Dartington Crystal, 225 5th Ave., Ste. 1200, New York, NY 10010: Free information ❖ Crystal Dartington. 212-447-7437.

Gorham, 100 Lenox Dr., Lawrenceville, NJ 08648: Free list of retail sources ❖ Fine china dinnerware, crystal, and silver. 800-635-3669.

Jacquelyn Hall, 10629 Baxter, Los Altos, CA 94022: Free information ❖ Lenox china and crystal replacements. 408-739-4876.

Hoya Crystal Gallery, 450 Park Ave., New York, NY 10022: Catalog $5 ❖ Art sculptures, vases, bowls, glass stemware, ornamental pieces, and crystal clocks. 800-462-HOYA.

Kitchen Etc., 32 Industrial Dr., Exeter, NH 03833: Catalog $2 ❖ Cookware, cutlery, flatware, crystal, and dinnerware. 800-232-4070.

Lanac Sales, 73 Canal St., New York, NY 10002: Free catalog ❖ Crystal, china, and sterling. 212-925-6422.

✓ **Lenox Collections,** P.O. Box 3020, Langhorne, PA 19047: Free catalog ❖ China, crystal, and porcelain sculptures. 800-225-1779.

Locators Inc., 908 Rock St., Little Rock, AR 72202: Free information ❖ Discontinued china, crystal, and silver. 800-367-9690.

Luigi Crystal, 7332 Frankford Ave., Philadelphia, PA 19136: Catalog $2 ❖ Table lamps, cut crystal chandeliers, hurricane lamps, sconces, other crystal accessories, and decorative pieces. 215-338-2978.

Marks China, Crystal & Silverware, 315 Franklin Ave., Wyckoff, NJ 07481: Free information ❖ China, stainless, crystal, and silverware. 800-862-7578.

✓ **Mikasa,** One Mikasa Dr., P.O. Box 1549, Secaucus, NJ 07096: Free catalog ❖ Designer china, stoneware, crystal, and flatware. 800-833-4681; 201-392-2501 (in NJ).

Miki's Crystal Registry, 100 Bridge Ave., P.O. Box 320, Delano, MN 55328: Free information ❖ Fostoria crystal matching service. 800-628-9394.

Orrefors Kosta Boda USA, 58 E. 57th St., New York, NY 10022: Free information ❖ Orrefors crystal. 800-351-9842; 212-753-3442 (in NY).

Replacements Ltd., 1089 Knox Rd., P.O. Box 26029, Greensboro, NC 27420: Free information with long SASE ❖ Discontinued bone china, earthenware, and crystal. 800-562-4462.

Rogers & Rosenthal, 22 W. 48th St., Room 1102, New York, NY 10036: Free information with long SASE ❖ Crystal, china, silver, silver plate, and stainless steel. 212-827-0115.

Royal Worcester, The Royal China & Porcelain Companies Inc., 1265 Glen Ave., Moorestown, NJ 08057: Free list of retail sources ❖ Place settings, cookware, glasses and goblets, and other accessories. 800-257-7189.

Rudi's Pottery, Silver & China, 176 Rt. 17, Paramus, NJ 07652: Free information with long SASE ❖ Glass stemware, china, and gifts. 201-265-6096.

Steuben Glass, Customer Relations, Corning Glass Center, Corning, NY 14831: Catalog $8 ❖ Steuben crystal and gifts. 800-424-4240.

Waterford Crystal Inc., 41 Madison Ave., New York, NY 10010: Free brochure ❖ Crystal and china.

Zucker's Fine Gifts, 151 W. 26th St., New York, NY 10001: Free catalog ❖ Hummel, Swarovski silver and crystal, Waterford crystal, Lladro porcelain, and gifts. 212-989-1450.

CURTAINS, DRAPES & BLINDS
Accessories & Controls

Connecticut Curtain Company, Commerce Plaza, Rt. 6, Danbury, CT 06810: Catalog $2 ❖ Drapery hardware. 800-732-4549; 203-798-1850 (in CT).

Country Craftmasters, Rt, 1, Box 211, Carrollton, MO 64633: Brochure $3 ❖ Solid-oak over-the-window curtain shelves. 816-542-2766.

DrapeBoss, 3135 Osgood Ct., Fremont, CA 94539: Free information ❖ Automatic drapery and vertical blind opener system. 800-318-7307.

Makita USA Inc., Drapery Opener Division, 14930 Northam St., La Mirada, CA 90638: Free information ❖ Automatic drapery opener. 800-4-MAKITA.

Nation Wide Outlet, P.O. Box 135, Flanders, NJ 07836: Free information ❖ Wallcoverings and blinds. 800-537-WALL.

SMAutomatic, 10301 Jefferson Blvd., Culver City, CA 90232: Free list of retail sources ❖ Motor and remote controls for draperies, blinds, and other window coverings. 310-559-6405.

Blinds & Window Shades

All States Decorating Network, 810 Main St., Toms River, NJ 08753: Free information ❖ Blinds and verticals. 800-334-8590.

American Blind, Wallpaper & Carpet Factory, 909 N. Sheldon Rd., Plymouth, MI 48170: Free information ❖ Wood, micro, mini, and vertical blinds. Also roller and pleated shades, wallpaper, and carpet. 800-889-2631 (for blinds and wallpaper); 800-346-0608 (for carpet).

Best Blinds, 8026 FM 1960 East, Humble, TX 77346: Free information ❖ Mini blinds, duettes, and other window coverings. 800-548-4840.

Blind Center USA, 7013 3rd Ave., Brooklyn, NY 11209: Free information ❖ Vertical, mini, micro, duettes, and wooden blinds. 800-676-5029.

Colorel Blinds, 8200 E. Park Meadows Dr., Littleton, CO 80124: Free information ❖ Window treatments. 800-877-4800.

Custom Windows & Walls, 32525 Stephenson Hwy., Madison Heights, MI 48071: Free information ❖ Mini blinds. 800-772-1947.

Devenco Products Inc., Box 700, Decatur, GA 30031: Free brochure ❖ Period reproductions of wood blinds and plantation-style, traditional, and movable shutters. Also exterior shutters. 800-888-4597; 404-378-4597 (in GA).

Headquarters Windows & Walls, 8 Clinton Pl., Morristown, NJ 07960: Free information ❖ Wall coverings and micro, mini, verticals, and pleated blinds. 800-338-4882.

Hunter Douglas Window Fashions, 1 Duette Way, Broomfield, CO 80020: Free information ❖ Window coverings. 800-437-4233.

Kestrel Manufacturing, P.O. Box 12, Saint Peters, PA 19470: Information $2 ❖ Knock-down and ready-to-hang folding screens and interior and exterior shutters. 610-469-6444.

MDC Direct Inc., P.O. Box 569, Marietta, GA 30061: Free information ❖ Wooden blinds, cellular shades, and area rugs. 800-892-2083.

National Blind & Wallpaper Factory, 400 Galleria, Southfield, MI 48034: Free information ❖ Window blinds. 800-477-8000.

Peerless Wallpaper & Blind Depot, 39500 14 Mile Rd., Walled Lake, MI 48390: Free information ❖ Wall coverings and blinds. 800-999-0898.

The Shutter Depot, Rt. 2, Box 157, Greenville, GA 30222: Free brochure ❖ Interior and exterior raised panel and fixed louver shutters. 706-672-1214.

❖ CURTAINS, DRAPES & BLINDS ❖

Shuttercraft, 282 Stepstone Hill Rd., Guilford, CT 06437: Free brochure ❖ Moveable door fixed louver and raised panel shutters. 203-453-1973.

Silver's Wholesale Club, 3001-15 Kensington Ave., Philadelphia, PA 19134: Free information ❖ Wall coverings, blinds, and verticals. 800-426-6600.

3 Day Blinds, Attention: Mail Order, 2220 E. Cerritos Ave., Anaheim, CA 92806: Free information ❖ Pleated shades and vertical, mini, and wooden blinds. 800-966-3DAY.

USA Blind Factory, 1312 Live Oak, Houston, TX 77003: Free information ❖ Vertical, pleated, mini, micro, and wooden blinds. 800-275-3219.

Wallpaper & Blinds Connection, P.O. Box 492, Budd Lake, NJ 07828: Free information ❖ Wallpaper, fabrics, and blinds. 800-488-WALL.

Wells Interiors, 7171 Amador Valley Plaza Rd., Dublin, CA 95468: Free catalog ❖ Kits for energy-efficient Roman shades or adding fabric to existing decorative arrangements and mini, wood, vertical, pleated, and woven wooden blinds. 800-547-8982.

Wholesale Verticals, P.O. Box 305, Baldwin, NY 11510: Free information ❖ Minis, verticals, pleated shades, duettes, wooden blinds, and drapery hardware. 800-762-2748.

Worldwide Wallcoverings & Blinds Inc., 333 Skokie Blvd., Northbrook, IL 60062: Free information with long SASE ❖ Wallcoverings and blinds. 800-322-5400.

Yankee Wallpaper & Blind Mart, 6689 Orchard Lake Rd., Ste. 314, West Bloomfield, MI 48322: Free information ❖ Wallpaper and blinds. 800-529-2663.

Curtains & Drapes

Bucks Trading Post, 930 Old Bethlehem Pike, Sellersville, PA 18960: Catalog $2 ❖ European lace curtains and matching tablecloths and doilies. 800-242-0738; 610-453-0623 (in PA).

Caroline's Country Ruffles, 420 W. Franklin Blvd., Gastona, NC 28052: Catalog $2 ❖ Curtains. 800-426-1039.

Country Curtains, Red Lion Inn, Stockbridge, MA 01262: Free catalog ❖ Cotton muslin and permanent-press country-style curtains. 413-243-1474.

Curtains & Home, 1600 Old Country Rd., Plainview, NY 11803: Free catalog ❖ Curtains and other window treatments, bedspreads and quilts, table cloths, bathroom ensembles, and rugs. 800-228-7824.

Curtains Up, 2709 S. Park Rd., Louisville, KY 40219: Free information ❖ Drapery accessories. 502-969-1464.

Designer Secrets, P.O. Box 529, Fremont, NE 68025: Catalog $2 (refundable) ❖ Window treatments, wallcoverings, fabrics, bedspreads, and furniture. 800-955-2559.

Dianthus Ltd., P.O. Box 870, Plymouth, MA 02362: Catalog $6 ❖ Curtains with a country look. 508-747-4179.

Dimestore Cowboys, 614 2nd St. SW, Albuquerque, NM 87102: Catalog $7 ❖ Door sets, cabinet pulls, shutters, bathroom accessories, curtain rods and rings, and handcrafted hardware. 505-244-1493.

Dorothy's Ruffled Originals Inc., 6721 Market St., Wilmington, NC 28405: Catalog $4 ❖ Ruffled curtains and other window treatments. 800-367-6849.

Especially Lace, 202 5th St., West Des Moines, IA 50265: Catalog $4.50 ❖ European lace curtains and ready-to-hang valances. 515-277-8778.

Fabric Shop, 120 N. Seneca St., Shippensburg, PA 17257: Free information with long SASE ❖ Draperies, antique satins, and fabrics for slipcovers and upholstery. 800-233-7012; 717-532-4150 (in PA).

Fabrics by Phone, P.O. Box 234, Walnut Bottom, PA 17266: Brochure and samples $3 ❖ Draperies, antique satins, and slipcover and upholstery fabrics. 800-233-7012; 717-532-4150 (in PA).

Virginia Goodwin, Rt. 2, Box 770, Boone, NC 28607: Information $1 ❖ Window valances, hand-tied fishnet bed canopies, dust ruffles, and bedspreads. 800-735-5191.

Harding's Custom Sheers, 807 S. Auburn, Grass Valley, CA 95945: Free brochure ❖ Pleated seamless sheers. 800-228-0825.

Heritage Lace, 309 South St., P.O. Box 328, Pella, IA 50219: Free brochure ❖ Lace curtains. 800-354-0668.

Linen & Lace, 4 Lafayette, Washington, MO 63090: Catalog $2 ❖ Linen and imported Bavarian lace curtains, runners, and accent pillows. 800-332-5223.

London Lace, 167 Newbury St., Boston, MA 02116: Catalog $2.50 ❖ Lace window coverings. 800-926-LACE.

Mather's Department Store, 31 E. Main St., Westminster, MD 21157: Free catalog ❖ Country-style curtains and other window treatments. 410-848-6410.

Rue de France, 28 Jacome Way, Middletown, RI 02842: Catalog $3 ❖ Lace curtains, tablecloths, runners, and pillows. 800-777-0998.

The Seraph, P.O. Box 500, 420 Main St., Sturbridge, MA 01566: Catalog $3 ❖ Bed hangings and window treatments with coordinating rugs and accessories. 508-347-2241.

South Bound Millworks, P.O. Box 349, Sandwich, MA 02563: Catalog $1 (refundable) ❖ Wooden curtain rods and brackets and wrought-iron accessories. 508-477-9355.

Spring Lace Two, 221 Morris Ave., Spring Lake, NJ 07762: Free brochure ❖ Lace curtains. 800-945-4800.

Vintage Valances, P.O. Box 43326, Cincinnati, OH 45243: Catalog $12 ❖ Ready-to-hang period-style drapes, bed hangings, and window shades, from 1800 to 1930. 513-561-8665.

Ann Wallace & Friends, 767 Linwood Ave., St. Paul, MN 55105: Catalog $5 (refundable) ❖ Natural fiber curtains. 612-228-9611.

Window Quilt, P.O. Box 975, Brattleboro, VT 05301: Information $1 ❖ Insulating window shades. 800-257-4501.

DANCING

Ballet Barres

Alvas Ballet Barres, 1417 W. 8th St., San Pedro, CA 90732: Free brochure ❖ Wall-mounted and free-standing ballet barres. 213-519-1314.

Ballet Barres Inc., P.O. Box 261206, Tampa, FL 33685: Free catalog ❖ Dance shoes, bodywear, legwear, and ballet barres. 800-767-1199.

Victoria's Dance-Theatrical Supply, 1331 Lincoln Ave., San Jose, CA 95125: Catalog $2 ❖ Wall-mounted ballet barres, dance shoes, dancewear, costume accessories, and make-up. 800-626-9258.

Clothing & Costumes

Apparel Warehouse, 6010 Yolanda St., Tarzana, CA 91356: Free catalog ❖ Briefs, leotards, leg warmer socks, and spandex tights. 800-245-8434; 818-344-3224 (in CA).

Ballet Barres Inc., P.O. Box 261206, Tampa, FL 33685: Free catalog ❖ Dance shoes, bodywear, legwear, and ballet barres. 800-767-1199.

Ballet Etc., 106 W. Main St., Mechanicsburg, PA 17055: Free information ❖ Dance and gymnastic wear, shoes, and clothing for ice skaters. 800-DANCE-25.

Baum's Inc., 106 S. 11th St., Philadelphia, PA 19107: Free catalog with request on school stationery ❖ Costumes, leotards, shoes, fabrics, and majorette items. 215-923-2244.

Best Magic Gags & Costumes, 625 S. Magnolia Ave., Anaheim, CA 92804: Free information ❖ Magic, juggling equipment, costumes, gags and gifts, dancewear, and clown items. 714-827-MGIC.

Carushka Inc., 7716 Kester Ave., Van Nuys, CA 91405: Catalog $3 ❖ Women's bodywear, leotards, tank tops, trunks, and bike tights. 800-247-5113; 818-904-0574 (in CA).

❖ DANCING ❖

Chatila Dance & Gymnastic Fashions, P.O. Box 508, Staten Island, NY 10304: Free catalog with request on school stationery ❖ Bodywear, lyrical dresses, and tap, ballet, and jazz shoes. 718-720-3632.

Costume Gallery, 1604 South Rt. 130, Burlington, NJ 08016: Free catalog with request on school stationery ❖ Costumes and dancewear.

The Costume Shop, 253 Broad St., P.O. Box 1497, Manchester, CT 06045: Free catalog with request on school stationery ❖ Dance costumes. 203-646-5758.

Curtain Call Costumes, 333 E. 7th Ave., P.O. Box 709, York, PA 17405: Free catalog with request on school stationery ❖ Dancing attire. 717-852-6910.

Dance Shop, 2485 Forest Park Blvd., Fort Worth, TX 76110: Free catalog ❖ Shoes and bodywear. 800-22-DANCE.

Dansant Boutique, 6623 Old Dominion Dr., McLean, VA 22101: Free catalog ❖ Dancewear, leotards, tights, and shoes. 800-DANSANT; 703-847-9162 (in VA).

Danskin, 111 W. 40th St., 18th Floor, New York, NY 10018: Free information ❖ Leotards, tights, costumes, ballet shoes, swimsuits, lingerie, and hosiery. 800-288-6749; 212-764-4630 (in NY).

Freed of London Inc., 922 7th Ave., New York, NY 10019: Free price list ❖ Soft ballet slippers, leotards and ballroom attire, exercise wear, and pointe, jazz, character, and gym shoes. 212-489-1055.

Hoctor Products, P.O. Box 38, Waldwick, NJ 07463: Free catalog ❖ Costumes, records, dance routines, videos, cassettes, phonographs and cassette players, and video recorders. 800-HOCTOR-9.

Illinois Theatrical, P.O. Box 34284, Chicago, IL 60634: Free catalog with request on school stationery ❖ Costumes. 800-745-3777.

Instructor's Choice, Oakbrook Sales Corporation, 1750 Merrick Ave., Merrick, NY 11566: Free information ❖ Tights, leotards, and other attire. 800-622-7667.

Kling's Theatrical Shoe Company, 218 S. Wabash Ave., Chicago, IL 60604: Catalog 50¢ ❖ Shoes and dancewear. 312-427-2028.

Lebo's of Charlotte Inc., 4118 E. Independence Blvd., Charlotte, NC 28205: Free catalog with request on school stationery ❖ Costumes, footwear, leotards, tights, fabrics, record players, tapes, and records. 704-535-5000.

Leo's Dancewear Inc., 1900 N. Narragansett Ave., Chicago, IL 60639: Free catalog with request on school stationery ❖ Dance costumes. 312-889-7700.

Loshin's Dancewear, 5141 Kennedy Ave., Cincinnati, OH 45213: Free catalog with request on school stationery ❖ Costumes, leotards, tights, sequin trimmings, tiaras, hats, and shoes. 513-531-5800.

Lynch's Clown Supplies, 939 Howard, Dearborn, MI 48124: Catalog $5 ❖ Dancewear, shoes, super tone taps, sequin appliques and fabrics, trim, rhinestones, hats, and make-up. 800-24-LYNCH.

New York Dancewear Company, 188-06 Union Tnpk., Flushing, NY 11366: Free catalog ❖ Dancewear. 800-775-DANCE.

Physical Fashions, 289 Allwood Rd., Clifton, NJ 07012: Free information ❖ Dancewear for children and adults. 800-24-DANCE; 201-773-3887 (in NJ).

Repetto Dance Shoes, 30 Lincoln Plaza, New York, NY 10023: Free information ❖ Classical ballet and contemporary dancewear and shoes. 212-582-3900.

Sadé Bodywear, 516 W. 34th St., New York, NY 10001: Free information ❖ Dancer's clothing. 800-563-9384; 212-563-9383 (in NY).

H.W. Shaw Inc., P.O. Box 4034, Hollywood, FL 33083: Free catalog ❖ Dancewear. 800-327-9548; 305-989-1300 (in FL).

Star Styled Dancewear, P.O. Box 119029, Hialeah, FL 33011: Free information ❖ Bodywear, shoes, and costumes for dancers. 800-532-6237.

Art Stone Dancewear, 1795 Express Dr. North, Smithtown, NY 11787: Free catalog with request on school stationery ❖ Bodywear and footwear for dancers. 516-582-9500.

Victoria's Dance-Theatrical Supply, 1331 Lincoln Ave., San Jose, CA 95125: Catalog $2 ❖ Wall-mounted ballet barres, dance shoes, dancewear, costume accessories, and make-up. 800-626-9258.

Weissman's Designs for Dance, 1600 Macklind Ave., St. Louis, MO 63110: Free catalog with request on school stationery ❖ Dancewear and footwear. 800-477-5410.

R.B. Williams Company Inc., 157 6th Ave. NE, St. Petersburg, FL 33701: Free information ❖ Sweatpants in small, medium, and large. 800-843-7346.

Music

Dansounds, P.O. Box 27618, Philadelphia, PA 19118: Free information ❖ Music for ballet dance classes.

Hoctor Products, P.O. Box 38, Waldwick, NJ 07463: Free catalog ❖ Records, cassettes, dance routines, cassette players, video recorders, phonographs, and books. 800-HOCTOR-9.

Jay Distributors, Box 191332, Dallas, TX 75219: Free information ❖ Ballet, tap, and jazz videos and records, tapes, CDs, and cassettes. 800-793-6843.

Lebo's of Charlotte Inc., 4118 E. Independence Blvd., Charlotte, NC 28205: Free catalog with request on school stationery ❖ Costumes, dancewear, footwear, leotards and tights, fabrics, record players, tapes, and records. 704-535-5000.

Patzius Performing Arts, 754 New Ballas Rd., Creve Coeur, MO 63141: Free brochure ❖ Instrumental music for tap, ballet, jazz, modern, and ballroom dancing. 314-432-3890.

Roper Records, 45-15 21st St., Long Island City, NY 11101: Free catalog ❖ Ballet and ballroom dance music. 718-786-2401.

Tiffany Records, Box 8147, Essex, VT 05451: Free information ❖ Ballet music on CDs and cassettes. 802-8778-2941.

Shoes

Capezio/Ballet Makers Inc., 1411 Broadway, New York, NY 10018: Free information with long SASE ❖ Shoes. 800-234-4858.

Chatila Dance & Gymnastic Fashions, P.O. Box 508, Staten Island, NY 10304: Free catalog with request on school stationery ❖ Bodywear, lyrical dresses, and tap, ballet, and jazz shoes. 718-720-3632.

Coast Shoes Inc., 13401 Saticoy, North Hollywood, CA 91605: Free list of retail sources ❖ Tap, jazz, ballet, and character dance shoes. 800-262-7851.

Dance Shop, 2485 Forest Park Blvd., Fort Worth, TX 76110: Free catalog ❖ Shoes and bodywear. 800-22-DANCE.

Danskin, 111 W. 40th St., 18th Floor, New York, NY 10018: Free information ❖ Ballet shoes, costumes, leotards, tights, swimsuits, lingerie, and hosiery. 800-288-6749; 212-764-4630 (in NY).

Freed of London Inc., 922 7th Ave., New York, NY 10019: Free price list ❖ Pointe shoes, soft ballet slippers, jazz and character shoes, ballet accessories, and leotards. 212-489-1055.

Gaynor Minden, 140 W. 16th St., New York, NY 10011: Free brochure ❖ Ballet shoes. 212-929-0087.

Grishko, 1655 Mt. Pleasant Rd., Villanova, PA 19085: Free information ❖ Dancing shoes. 610-527-9553.

Kling's Theatrical Shoe Company, 218 S. Wabash Ave., Chicago, IL 60604: Catalog 50¢ ❖ Shoes and dancewear. 312-427-2028.

La Mendola, 1795 Express Dr. North, Smithtown, NY 11787: Free list of retail sources ❖ Lyrical/ballet shoes and dance sneakers for jazz, hip-hop, street dance, and kickline. 516-582-3230.

La Ray, 633 Alacci Way, River Vale, NJ 07675: Free information ❖ Toe shoes and ballet slippers. 201-664-5882.

Loshin's Dancewear, 5141 Kennedy Ave., Cincinnati, OH 45213: Free catalog with request on school stationery ❖ Costumes, leotards, tights, sequin trimmings, tiaras, hats, and shoes. 513-531-5800.

Lynch's Clown Supplies, 939 Howard, Dearborn, MI 48124: Catalog $5 ❖ Dancewear, shoes, super tone taps, sequin appliques and fabrics, trim, rhinestones, hats, and make-up. 313-565-3425.

Miquelito's Dancewear, 7315 San Pedro Ave., San Antonio, TX 78216: Free information ❖ Ballet shoes, flamenco boots, and gymnastic wear. 210-349-2573.

Repetto Dance Shoes, 30 Lincoln Plaza, New York, NY 10023: Free information ❖ Classical ballet and contemporary dancewear and shoes. 212-582-3900.

Soloist Corporation, 95 Horatio St., Ste. 2S, New York, NY 10014: Free information ❖ Pointe shoes. 212-645-5858.

Star Styled Dancewear, P.O. Box 119029, Hialeah, FL 33011: Free information ❖ Bodywear, shoes, and costumes for dancers. 800-532-6237.

Art Stone Dancewear, 1795 Express Dr. North, Smithtown, NY 11787: Free catalog with request on school stationery ❖ Bodywear and footwear for dancers. 516-582-9500.

Victoria's Dance-Theatrical Supply, 1331 Lincoln Ave., San Jose, CA 95125: Catalog $2 ❖ Portable wall-mounted ballet barres, dance shoes, dancewear, costume accessories, and make-up. 800-626-9258.

Weissman's Designs for Dance, 1600 Macklind Ave., St. Louis, MO 63110: Free catalog with request on school stationery ❖ Dancewear and footwear. 800-477-5410.

DARTS

Accudart, 160 E. Union Ave., East Rutherford, NJ 07073: Free catalog ❖ Darts and dart boards. 800-526-0451; 201-438-9000 (in NJ).

Bottelsen Dart Company Inc., 945 W. McCoy Ln., Santa Maria, CA 93455: Free list of retail sources ❖ Darts and accessories. 805-922-4519.

Buck Knives, P.O. Box 1267, El Cajon, CA 92022: Free list of retail sources ❖ Darts and dart boards. 800-215-2825.

Custom Manufacturing Inc., 1248 Shappert Dr., Rockford, IL 61115: Free information ❖ Electronic multiple game dart board. 815-654-9876.

Dart Mart Inc., 2255 Computer Ave., Willow Grove, PA 19090: Free information ❖ Dart boards, cabinets, dart-making supplies, and sets. 800-423-3220; 215-830-0501 (in PA).

Dart World Inc., P.O. Box 845, Lynn, MA 01904: Free information ❖ Dart boards, cabinets, dart-making supplies, and sets. 800-225-2558; 617-581-6035 (in MA).

Darts Unlimited, 282 N. Henry St., Brooklyn, NY 11222: Free information ❖ Dart boards, cabinets, dart-making supplies, and sets. 718-389-7755.

Escalade Sports, P.O. Box 889, Evansville, IN 47706: Free catalog ❖ Dart boards, darts, and cabinets. 800-457-3373; 812-467-1200 (in IN).

Franklin Sports Industries Inc., 17 Campanelli Pkwy., P.O. Box 508, Stoughton, MA 02072: Free information ❖ Dart boards, cabinets, and sets. 800-426-7700.

General Sportcraft Company, 140 Woodbine Rd., Bergenfield, NJ 07621: Free information ❖ Dart boards, cabinets, dart-making supplies, and sets. 201-384-4242.

Great Lakes Dart Distributors Inc., S84W 19093 Enterprise Dr., Muskego, WI 52150: Free information ❖ Darts. 800-225-7593.

Horizon Dart Supply, 2415 S. 50th St., Kansas City, MO 66106: Free information ❖ Darts and dart boards. 800-732-7864.

Indian Industries Inc., P.O. Box 889, Evansville, IN 47706: Free catalog ❖ Dart boards, cabinets, dart-making supplies, and sets. 800-457-3373; 812-467-1200 (in IN).

Don Jagoda Associates Inc., 100 Marcus Dr., Melville, NY 117476: Free information ❖ Boards, cases, darts, and dart-making supplies. 516-454-1800.

Marksman Products, 5482 Argosy Dr., Huntington Beach, CA 92649: Free information ❖ Dart boards, cabinets, dart-making supplies, and sets. 714-898-7535.

Mueller Sporting Goods Inc., 4825 S. 16th, Lincoln, NE 68512: Free catalog ❖ Billiard and dart supplies. 800-627-8888.

Owl Darts, 1001 SW Adams, Peoria, IL 61602: Free catalog ❖ Billiard supplies and darts. 800-832-7871.

Papa's Gameroom, 121 Lakeside Dr., Mayfield, NY 12117: Free catalog ❖ Table tennis, football games, air hockey, billiards, darts, records, CDs, collectibles from the 1950s, slot machine, and other gameroom accessories and decorator items. 888-321-PAPA.

Pennray Billiard & Recreational Products, 6400 W. Gross Point Rd., Niles, IL 60714: Free catalog ❖ Darts, billiards, and soccer equipment. 800-523-8934.

Saunier-Wilhem Company, 3216 5th Ave., Pittsburgh, PA 15213: Free catalog ❖ Equipment for bowling, billiards, darts, table tennis, and shuffleboard. Also board games. 412-621-4350.

Spalding Sports Worldwide, 425 Meadow St., P.O. Box 901, Chicopee, MA 01021: Free list of retail sources ❖ Dart boards, cabinets, darts, dart-making supplies, and sets. 800-225-6601.

Sportime, Customer Service, 1 Sportime Way, Atlanta, GA 30340: Free information ❖ Darts and dart boards. 800-444-5700; 770-449-5700 (in GA).

Tide-Rider Inc., P.O. Box 429, Oakdale, CA 95361: Free information ❖ Dart boards, cabinets, dart-making supplies, and sets. 209-848-4420.

Valley Recreation Products Inc., P.O. Box 656, Bay City, MI 48707: Free information ❖ Dart boards, cabinets, dart-making supplies, and sets. 800-248-2837; 517-892-4536 (in MI).

DECALS, EMBLEMS & PATCHES

Adhatters, Box 667, Effingham, IL 62401: Free information ❖ Patches, pins, and decals. 800-225-7642.

Conrad Industries, AB Emblems & Caps, P.O. Box 695, Weaverville, NC 28787: Free catalog ❖ Embroidered emblems and caps. 704-645-3015.

Decorcal Inc., 165 Marine St., Farmingdale, NY 11735: Free catalog ❖ Decorative decals, letter and number stencils, and graphic accessories. 800-645-9868; 516-752-0076 (in NY).

Eagel EMS Specialties, 68 Canterbury, Aurora, IL 60506: Free catalog ❖ Embroidered emblems and reflective/vinyl decals. 708-897-9068.

Eastern Emblem, Box 828, Union City, NJ 07087: Free catalog ❖ Patches, cloisonne pins, decals, stickers, T-shirts, caps, and jackets. 800-344-5112.

Frosty Little, 222 E. 8th St., Burley, ID 83318: Free information ❖ Sweatshirts, T-shirts, pins, and patches with clown graphics. 208-678-0005.

Hoover's Manufacturing Company, 4015 Progress Blvd., Peru, IL 61354: Free catalog ❖ Dog tag key rings, beer and coffee mugs, belt buckles, patches, flags, and Vietnam, Korea, and World War II hat pins. 815-223-1159.

Microscale Industries Inc., P.O. Box 11950, Costa Mesa, CA 92627: Catalog $4 ❖ Micro-scale decals for decorating miniatures.

Namark Cap & Emblem Company, 6325 Harrison Dr., Las Vegas, NV 89120: Free information ❖ Screen-printed emblems, caps, T-shirts, and jackets. 800-634-6271.

Recco Maid Embroidery Company, 4626 W. Cornelia Ave., Chicago, IL 60641: Free catalog ❖ Embroidered emblems. 800-345-3458; 312-286-6333 (in IL).

Southern Emblem, P.O. Box 8, Toast, NC 27049: Free catalog ❖ Embroidered emblems, emblematic jewelry, badges, flags, and screen-printing supplies. 910-789-3348.

❖ DECORATIVE ITEMS ❖

Stadri Emblems, 71 Tinker St., Woodstock, NY 12498: Free catalog ❖ Embroidered emblems, pins, and decals. 914-679-6600.

DECORATIVE ITEMS

Amish Country Collection, Sunset Valley Rd., RD 5, Box 271, New Castle, PA 16105: Catalog $5 ❖ Amish-style pillows, quilts, wall hangings, rugs, beds and cribs, and crafts. 412-458-4811.

Antler Designs for Sale, Jim & Goldie Mason, 15 Curtis Hill Rd., West Paris, ME 04289: Free information ❖ Antlers crafted into chandeliers, sconces, coffee tables, chairs, and novelties. 207-674-2655 (no Friday night or Saturday calls).

Antler Furnishings by Jay "Bird" Jones, 520 Pine Oaks Rd., #4, Colorado Springs, CO 80926: Catalog $10 ❖ Antler chairs, lamps, chandeliers, and carvings. 719-527-1845.

Baldwin Hardware Corporation, P.O. Box 15048, Reading, PA 19612: Bathroom accessories brochure 75¢, lighting fixtures brochure $3, door hardware brochure 75¢, hardware brochure 75¢ ❖ Brass dead bolts and door hardware, bathroom accessories, and lighting fixtures. 800-346-5128.

Ballard Designs, 1670 DeFoor Ave. NE, Atlanta, GA 30318: Catalog $3 ❖ Furniture, pillows, prints, and accessories for indoor room arrangements and outdoor landscaping. 800-367-2810.

The Bean House, 49 Hartford St., Dover, MA 02030: Free information ❖ Decorative fabric picture accessories. 508-785-2731.

Betsy's Place, 323 Arch St., Philadelphia, PA 19106: Brochure $4.50 ❖ Sundials and stands, trivets, and brass reproduction door knockers. 800-452-3524; 215-922-3536 (in PA).

Dennis & CeCe Bork, 715 Genesee St., Delafield, WI 53018: Catalog $5 ❖ Custom furniture, folk art, period lighting, Colonial Williamsburg reproductions, decorative accessories, and Windsor chairs and settees. 414-646-4911.

Bregstone Associates Inc., 500 S. Wabash, Chicago, IL 60605: Free catalog ❖ Seasonal decorations all year. 312-939-5130.

Celestial, P.O. Box 6734, Edison, NJ 08818: Free catalog ❖ Home furnishings and decorative accessories. 800-808-2353.

Country Cousins, 2075 Bellmead Dr., Altoona, PA 16602: Free catalog ❖ Country-style decorative items. 814-946-4611.

Country Manor, Mail Order Dept., Rt. 211, P.O. Box 520, Sperryville, VA 22740: Catalog $3 ❖ Kitchen utensils and accessories, rugs, and carpets. 703-987-8372.

Country Charm Inc., 322 S. Main St., Plymouth, MI 48170: Catalog $2 ❖ Long-burning candles and country craft decorative accessories. 800-288-5699; 313-455-9292 (in MI).

Cowboy Country General Store, P.O. Box 1464, Laporte, CO 80535: Free information ❖ Western-style decorative accessories for the home. 303-482-5960.

Craft Cottage, P.O. Box 99, Vonore, TN 37885: Free information ❖ Decorative accessories for the kitchen. 615-884-6260.

The Craft Room, 584 W. Girard Rd., Union City, MI 49094: Catalog $3 ❖ Original pictures framed in oak or barn wood. 517-741-5511.

Deena'd Li'l Country Nook, 6922 Liverpool Ct. NE, Bremerton, WA 98311: Brochure $1 (refundable) ❖ Decorative country-style wall accessories. 360-698-0803.

Everything Ewenique, RR 1, Box 73, Mt. Pleasant Mills, PA 17853: Free catalog ❖ Country accents for the home. 800-528-9382.

Fabric Hutch, Main St., Box 201, Croghan, NY 13327: Free price list ❖ Napkins, place mats, pads for chairs, appliance covers, towels, and fabric accessories. 315-346-6360.

Fire & Shadow Creations, 6021 Redondo Ct. NW, Albuquerque, NM 87107: Brochure $3 ❖ Antique rust-finished or copper-plated Southwestern art. 505-343-9639.

Garbe's, 4137 S. 72nd East Ave., Tulsa, OK 74145: Free catalog ❖ Home and office accessories. 800-735-2241; 918-627-0284 (in OK).

Gift & Wicker Import Inc., 12770 Moore St., Cerritos, CA 90701: Catalog $5 ❖ Wickerware, hobby craft supplies, basket planters, home decorative accessories, and furniture. 800-622-6209; 310-407-3319 (in CA).

Good Catalog Company, 5456 SE International Way, Portland, OR 97222: Free catalog ❖ Kitchen gadgets and dining, gardening, and decorative accessories. 800-225-3870.

Grandpa's Crafts, 577 Hwy. 70 West, Havelock, NC 28532: Brochure $1 ❖ Country craft decorative accessories. 919-444-1603.

Great American Log, Box 3360, Ketchum, ID 83340: Catalog $4 ❖ Western-style decorative items for the home. 800-624-5779.

Great City Traders, 537 Stevenson St., San Francisco, CA 94103: Free list of retail sources ❖ Decorative accessories and gifts for the home.

Heath Sedgwick, P.O. Box 1305, Stony Brook, NY 11790: Catalog $4 ❖ Victorian-style decorative accessories.

Here's My Heart, 53 Kings Hwy. East, Haddonfield, NJ 08033: Free brochure ❖ Country-style decorative accessories. 609-354-2064.

Historic Housefitters Company, Farm to Market Rd., Brewster, NY 10509: Catalog $3 ❖ Hand-forged ironwork for 18th-century settings. 914-278-2427.

Home Decorators Collection, 2025 Concourse Dr., St. Louis, MO 63146: Free catalog ❖ Hardware, switch plates, mail boxes, weather vanes, plant stands, furniture, clocks, fixtures, chandeliers, bathroom accessories, and wicker items. 800-240-6047; 314-993-6045 (in MO).

Hoya Crystal Gallery, 450 Park Ave., New York, NY 10022: Catalog $5 ❖ Art sculptures, vases, bowls, glasses, ornamental pieces, and crystal clocks. 800-462-HOYA.

Inter-Tribal Traders, 3207 E. Washington St., Phoenix, AZ 85034: Free information ❖ Western and Native American-style decorative accessories. 800-766-4431.

Interiors, 320 Washington St., Mt. Vernon, NY 10553: Free catalog ❖ Art and furnishings for the home. 800-228-5215.

Just Between Us, 41 W. 8th Ave., Oshkosh, WI 54906: Free catalog ❖ Decorative accessories for the home. 800-258-3750.

Just Horsin' A-Round, 210 Dayton Ct., San Ramon, CA 94583: Free information ❖ Decorative wall accessories. 510-829-1746.

Just Quackers, 811 E. Plano Pkwy., Ste. 109, Plano, TX 75074: Brochure $2 with long SASE ❖ Wood-framed stained glass art pictures for window treatments. 214-0423-2736.

LTD Commodities Inc., 2800 Lakeside Dr., Bannockburn, IL 60015: Free catalog ❖ Decorative accessories with a dramatic flair. 708-295-6058.

Marble Arch, Box 833, High Point, NC 27261: Catalog $4 ❖ Brass and crystal finials and accessories. 800-723-1328.

J. Michael's Catalog Company, 152 E. Main St., Rigby, ID 83442: Free catalog ❖ Home decorative and gift items. 208-745-7714.

Mills River Industries, 713 Old Orchard Rd., Hendersonville, NC 28739: Catalog $1 ❖ Butter churns and decorative accents for the home. 704-687-9778.

A.J. Munzinger & Company, 2010 S. Shady Hill Rd., Springfield, MO 65809: Brochure $1 ❖ Antique housewares. 417-886-9184.

Museum Collections, 340 Poplar St., Building 20, Hanover, PA 17333: Free catalog ❖ Decorative glass accessories. 800-442-2460.

Museum of Modern Art New York, Mail Order Department, 11 W. 53rd St., New York, NY 10019: Free catalog ❖ Contemporary items for homes, offices, or gifts. 800-447-6662.

Nature's Gifts Wreath Company, HC 35, Box 1044, St. George, ME 04857: Free catalog ❖ Decorated balsam fir wreaths for beautifying office interiors and exteriors and homes. 800-348-0824.

Ragged Mountain Antler Chandeliers, 897 Bourne Ln., Victor, MT 59875: Free brochure ❖ Western-style home decorative items. 406-961-2400.

Reed Brothers, 5000 Turner Rd., Sebastopol, CA 95472: Catalog $10 ❖ Wall plaques. 707-795-6261.

The Renovator's Supply, P.O. Box 2515, Conway, NH 03818: Free catalog ❖ Reproduction antique hardware, lighting and plumbing fixtures, curtains, and accessories. 800-659-0203.

Shelly's Dolls & Crafts, 11344 S. Hawkwood Dr., Sandy, UT 84094: Brochure $2 ❖ Country doll decorative accessories. 801-572-5731.

Toni's Victorian Creations, 4617 John Day Hwy., Vale, OR 97918: Brochure $5 (refundable) ❖ Victorian-style frame and wall decorative items.

Touch of Class Catalog, 1905 N. Van Buren St., Huntingburg, IN 47542: Free catalog ❖ Bedroom furnishings, bathroom accessories, and draperies. 800-457-7456.

Trumble Greetings, P.O. Box 9800, Boulder, CO 80301: Catalog $1 ❖ Western-style decorative items for the home. 800-525-0656.

Uwchlan Farm, 303 Greenridge Rd., Glenmoore, PA 19343: Free catalog ❖ Wrought-iron accessories for the home and garden. 800-900-IRON.

Vermont Industries, P.O. Box 301, Rt. 103, Cuttingsville, VT 05738: Catalog $3 ❖ Hand-forged wrought iron-wood racks, lamps, fireplace tools, candle holders, pot holders, and more. 800-639-1715; 802-492-3451 (in VT).

Wild Wings, P.O. Box 451, Lake City, MN 55041: Free catalog ❖ Home furnishings and accessories with a wildlife theme. 800-445-4833.

Willow Creek & Company, 3634 Thomasville Rd., Winston-Salem, NC 27107: Free information ❖ Country-style decorative crafts.

Worthington Silks, 6781 Vera Cruz Rd. South, Zionsville, PA 18092: Free information ❖ Easy-to-assemble kits for making silk wild flower wall hangings. 610-967-4889.

Yield House, P.O. Box 2525, Conway, NH 03818: Free catalog ❖ Furniture and accessories in a Shaker tradition. 800-258-0376.

Zimmerman Handcrafts, 254 E. Main St., Leola, PA 17540: Brochure $1 ❖ Country-style accessories. 800-267-5689.

DECOUPAGE

Adventures in Crafts, P.O. Box 6058, Yorkville Station, New York, NY 10128: Catalog $3.50 ❖ Decoupage supplies and projects. 212-410-9793.

DECOYS

Beaver Dam Decoys, 3311 State Rt. 305, P.O. Box 40, Cortland, OH 44410: Catalog $2 ❖ Decoys and carving supplies. 216-637-4007.

Birds in Wood, P.O. Box 2649, Meriden, CT 06450: Catalog $2 (refundable) ❖ Decoy carving kits.

Blue Ribbon Bases, 24 Dewey St., Sayville, NY 11782: Free catalog ❖ Walnut and hardwood bases for mounting projects. 516-589-0707.

The Decoy, P.O. Box 3652, Carmel, CA 93921: Free brochure ❖ Hand-carved wooden birds, antique decoys, limited edition prints, and original art. 800-332-6988.

Decoy Den Galleries, P.O. Box 412, Columbia, IL 62236: Free brochure ❖ Hand-carved wooden geese, ducks, swans, shorebirds, and other decoys. 800-255-0551.

Decoys, I.N.C., P.O. Box 1874, Clinton, IA 52732: Catalog $1 ❖ Decoy kits. 319-289-3224.

Dux' Dekes Decoy Company, RD 2, Box 66, Greenwich, NY 12834: Free information ❖ Goose, duck, loon, shorebird, and carving blanks. 800-553-4725; 518-692-7703 (in NY).

Herter's, 2800 Southcross Dr. West, P.O. Box 1819, Burnsville, MN 55337: Free information ❖ Flexible plastic or mahogany decoys. Available mounted on steel stakes for easy penetration in frozen ground. 800-654-3825.

Jennings Decoy Company, 601 Franklin Ave. NE, St. Cloud, MN 56304: Catalog $1 ❖ Decoy and carving supplies. Also finished decoys and figurines. 800-331-5613.

Will Kirkpatrick Decoys, 124 Forest Ave., Hudson, MA 01749: Catalog $2 ❖ Hand-carved and hand-painted shorebird decoy reproductions. 800-505-7841.

Penn's Woods Products Inc., 19 W. Pittsburgh St., Delmont, PA 15626: Free information ❖ Decoys. 412-468-8311.

Wonderduck Decoys, 505 N. Price St., Marshall, TX 75670: Free information ❖ Moving decoys. 800-876-1697.

DEPARTMENT & GENERAL MERCHANDISE STORES

The department stores listed below publish special edition general merchandise and seasonal specialty catalogs. In some instances there may be a small charge for these catalogs. However, the price may be waived or refunded if you satisfy minimum purchase requirements. For information on how to obtain these catalogs, write or call the stores directly.

Bennett Brothers Inc., 30 E. Adams St., Chicago, IL 60603. 800-621-2626.

Bergdorf Goodman, 754 5th Ave., New York, NY 10019. 800-662-5455.

Bloomingdales's by Mail Ltd., 475 Knotter Dr., Cheshire, CT 06410. 800-777-0000.

Burdines, T.O.B. Office, 7303 SW 88th St., Miami, FL 33156. 305-577-2311.

Filene's, 426 Washington St., Boston, MA 02101. 800-345-3637.

Hecht's, 685 N. Glebe Rd., Arlington, VA 22203. 703-558-1200.

Lord & Taylor, 424 5th Ave., New York, NY 10018. 800-223-7440.

Macy's, Herald Square, New York, NY 10001. 212-695-4400.

Marshall Field, 5505 36th St. SE, Grand Rapids, MI 49512. 800-631-9659.

Neiman-Marcus, 221 E. Walnut Hill Ln., Irving, TX 75039. 800-825-8000.

Nordstrom Mail Order, P.O. Box 91018, Seattle, WA 98111. Free catalog. 800-285-5800.

J.C. Penney Company Inc., Catalog Division, Atlanta, GA 30390. 800-222-6161.

Saks Fifth Ave., SFA Folio Collections Inc., 557 Tuckahoe Rd., Yonkers, NY 10710. 800-322-7257.

Service Merchandise Catalog, Mail Order, P.O. Box 25130, Nashville, TN 37202. 800-251-1212.

Spiegel, P.O. Box 182563, Columbus, OH 43218. 800-345-4500.

Whole Earth Access, 822 Anthony St., Berkeley, CA 94710. 800-829-6300.

DIABETIC SUPPLIES

AD-RX Pharmacy, 6256 Wilshire Blvd., Los Angeles, CA 90048: Free information ❖ Diabetic supplies. 800-435-1992.

❖ DISPLAY FIXTURES & PORTABLE EXHIBITS ❖   159

American Diabetes Association, 1970 Chain Bridge Rd., McLean, VA 22109: Free information ❖ Recipe books for diabetics.

American Ostomy Supplies, P.O. Box 13396, Milwaukee, WI 53213: Free catalog ❖ Urological, diabetic, and incontinence supplies. Also blood pressure, wound-care, and assisted living aids. 800-958-5858.

Atwater-Carey Ltd., 5505 Central Ave., Boulder, CO 80301: Free information ❖ Purse-size and belt-pack carry-all cases for diabetic supplies. 800-359-1646.

Boehringer Mannheim Corporation, Patient Care Systems, 9115 Hague Rd., P.O. Box 50100, Indianapolis, IN 46250: Free information ❖ Glucose monitoring system. 800-858-8072.

Bruce Medical Supply, 411 Waverly Oaks Rd., P.O. Box 9166, Waltham, MA 02154: Free catalog ❖ Health supplies for diabetics, ostomy patients, sick rooms, and first aid. 800-225-8446.

Cascade Medical Inc., 10180 Viking Dr., Eden Prairie, MN 55344: Free information ❖ Blood glucose test strips and monitoring system. 800-525-6718.

Cases Plus, 7757 Bell Rd., Windsor, CA 95492: Free information ❖ Organizer cases for diabetic supplies. 800-982-1880.

DERATA Corporation, 1840 Berkshire Ln., Minneapolis, MN 55441: Free information ❖ Medi-Jector EZ needle-free insulin injection system. 800-328-3074; 612-553-1102 (in MN).

Diabetes Supplies, 6505 Rockside Rd., Ste. 325, Independence, OH 44131: Free catalog ❖ Insulin, blood glucose monitoring equipment, test strips, and health care supplies. 800-622-5587.

Diabetic Express, 2406 W. Tuscarawas, Canton, OH 44708: Free information ❖ Insulin, blood glucose monitoring equipment, test strips, and health care supplies. 800-338-4656.

Diabetic Promotions, P.O. Box 5400, Willowick, OH 44095: Free catalog ❖ Insulin, blood glucose monitoring equipment, test strips, and health care supplies. 800-433-1477; 216-943-6185 (in OH).

Disetronic Medical Systems Inc., 5201 E. River Rd., Ste. 312, Minneapolis, MN 55421: Free information ❖ Insulin pumps. 800-280-7801.

Gainor Medical U.S.A. Inc., P.O. Box 353, McDonough, GA 30253: Free information ❖ Easy-to-use lancets that provide protection from accidental puncture and risks associated with cross-infection of blood-borne illnesses. 800-825-8282; 404-474-0474 (in GA).

GEM Edwards Inc., P.O. Box 429, Hudson, OH 44236: Free information ❖ Diabetic supplies. 800-793-1995.

Generation Software Corporation, P.O. Box 363, Bloomingdale, IL 60108: Free information ❖ Window-based diabetes tracking and data management software. 800-455-4GSC.

Glucoware Company, P.O. Box 43369, Cleveland, OH 44143: Free information ❖ Diabetes database for PCs. 800-774-4448.

H-S Medical Supplies, P.O. Box 42, Whitehall, PA 18052: Free information ❖ Blood glucose meters, test strips, and other supplies for diabetics. 800-344-7633.

Hospital Center Pharmacy, 433 Brookline Ave., Boston, MA 02215: Free information ❖ Insulin, blood glucose monitoring equipment, test strips, and health care supplies. 800-824-2401.

Liberty Medical Supply, P.O. Box 1966, Palm City, FL 34990: Free information ❖ Blood glucose meters, test strips, lancets, monolets, and diabetic supplies. 800-762-8026.

Medicool Inc., 23761 Madison St., Torrance, CA 90505: Free information ❖ Insulin protector for use while traveling. 800-433-2469.

MediSense Inc., 266 2nd Ave., Waltham, MA 02154: Free information ❖ Blood glucose monitoring systems. 800-316-7952.

Miles Inc., Diagnostics Division, P.O. Box 2001, Mishawaka, IN 46544: Free information ❖ Glucometer blood glucose monitoring system. 800-445-5901.

MiniMed Technologies, 12744 San Fernando Rd., Sylmar, CA 91342: Free information ❖ MiniMed pumps for insulin therapy control. 800-933-3322.

Moms Catalog, 24700 Avenue Rockefeller, Valencia, CA 91355: Free catalog ❖ Medical supplies for incontinence, urological aids for daily living, ostomy, wound and skin care, and diabetes. 800-232-7443.

National Diabetic Pharmacies, 2157 Apperson Dr., Salem, VA 24513: Free information ❖ Diabetic supplies. 800-467-8546; 703-776-5572 (in VA).

National Medical Consumables Inc., P.O. Box 102495, Denver, CO 80250: Free information ❖ Ostomy and diabetic supplies and urological, wound care, and incontinence products. 800-797-7107.

Penny Saver Medical Supply, 1851 W. 52nd Ave., Denver, CO 80221: Free catalog ❖ Blood glucose monitors and test strips, syringes, lancets, insulin, and health care supplies. 800-748-1909.

Preferred Rx of Ohio, 34208 Aurora Rd., Ste. 132, Solon, OH 44139: Free information ❖ Diabetic supplies. 800-843-7038.

Suncoast Pharmacy & Surgical Supplies, 9060 Kimberly Blvd., Boca Raton, FL 33434: Free information ❖ Diabetic supplies. 800-799-1991.

Terumo Medical Corporation, Consumer Products Division, 2100 Cottontail Ln., Somerset, NJ 08873: Free information ❖ Insulin syringes. 800-252-6782.

Ulster Scientific Inc., P.O. Box 819, New Paltz, NY 12561: Free information ❖ Autojector which inserts the needle and injects insulin automatically and almost without pain. 800-431-8233.

Vitajet Corporation, 27075 Cabot Rd., #102, Laguna Hills, CA 92653: Free information ❖ Needle-free injector. 800-848-2538.

DISPLAY FIXTURES & PORTABLE EXHIBITS

Abex Display Systems Inc., 7101 Fair Ave., North Hollywood, CA 91605: Free list of retail sources ❖ Transportable display systems. 800-537-0231.

Aftosa, 1034 Ohio Ave., Richmond, CA 94804: Free catalog ❖ Clear acrylic plate stands and bowl holders. 800-231-0397.

Bluegrass Case Company, 272 Airport Rd., Box 386, Stanton, KY 40380: Free information ❖ Collector and display frames. 606-663-9871.

Cabinets by Vector, 25736 Schrader Rd., Sturgis, MI 49091: Free catalog ❖ Specimen storage cabinets. 616-651-3823.

Dave Cohen & Associates Inc., P.O. Box 6517, Freehold, NJ 07728: Free information ❖ Showcases, shelving, and custom woodwork.

Collector Case Company, 194 Woodlark Rd., Versailles, KY 40383: Free information ❖ Display cases. 800-553-5294; 606-873-3569 (in KY).

Columbus Show Case Company, 850 5th Ave., Columbus, OH 43212: Free information ❖ Display fixtures. 800-848-3573; 614-299-3161 (in OH).

Continental Showcase Inc., 128 49th St., Lindenhurst, NY 11757: Catalog $2 (refundable) ❖ Custom showcases. 516-957-1246.

Display Fixtures Company, P.O. Box 7245, Charlotte, NC 28241: Free catalog ❖ Display fixtures. 800-737-0880; 704-588-0880 (in NC).

Emerson Wood Works Inc., 2640 E. 43rd Ave., Denver, CO 80216: Free brochure ❖ Drawers and cases for collectors. 303-295-1360.

ESV Lighting Inc., 525 Court St., Pekin, IL 61554: Free information ❖ Lighting systems for displays. 800-225-5378.

The Fixture Factory, 835 NE 8th St., Gresham, OR 97030: Free information ❖ Display fixtures. 503-661-6525.

❖ DOLLHOUSES & MINIATURES ❖

Franklin Fixtures Inc., 59 Commerce Park Rd., Brewster, MA 02631: Free catalog ❖ Display fixtures. 508-896-3713.

Global Fixtures Inc., 4121 Rushton St., Florence, AL 35631: Free catalog ❖ Display fixtures. 205-767-5200.

Graphic Display Systems, 1243 Lafayette St., Lebanon, PA 17042: Free information ❖ Easy-to-set-up lightweight display system. Comes with base, leg adjusters, and clips. 800-848-3020.

Handy Store Fixtures, 337 Sherman Ave., Newark, NJ 07114: Free catalog ❖ Display fixtures. 888-HANDYSF.

JAMAR Company, 5015 State Rd., Medina, OH 44256: Information $2 (refundable) ❖ Acrylic display cases.

Model Display & Fixture Company Inc., 1405 E. McDowell Rd., Phoenix, AZ 85006: Free information ❖ Display fixtures. 800-528-5306; 800-876-6335 (in AZ).

Neustadt Studios Collectables, 100 Paper Mill Rd., Lawrenceville, GA 30245: Catalog $4 (refundable) ❖ Country-style cabinets for collections. 800-876-5739.

Nomadic Instand, Exhibitor Service Center, 7400 Fullerton Rd., Springfield, VA 22153: Free information ❖ Easy-to-use portable and folding display unit. 800-732-9395.

Pennzoni Wood Products, 1182 White St., Sturgis, MI 49091: Free information ❖ Display showcases. 800-206-6852; 616-659-1093 (in MI).

Melvin S. Roos & Company Inc., 4465 Commerce Dr. SW, Atlanta, GA 30336: Free information ❖ Display fixtures. 800-241-6897; 800-282-9110 (in GA).

Ruddles Mills Products, 19 S. Main St., Cynthiana, KY 41031: Free information ❖ Handcrafted hardwood display cases. 800-825-6951; 606-234-9224 (in KY).

Schacht Lighting, 5214 Burleson Rd., Austin, TX 78744: Free brochure ❖ Track lighting supplies, replacement bulbs, show lights. 800-256-7114.

Showbest Fixture Corporation, P.O. Box 25336, Richmond, VA 23260: Free catalog ❖ Display fixtures. 804-643-3600.

Siegel Display Products, P.O. Box 95, Minneapolis, MN 55440: Free catalog ❖ Display racks. 612-340-9235.

DOLLHOUSES & MINIATURES

A-C's Emporium of Miniatures, 100 E. McMurray Rd., McMurray, PA 15317: Catalog $15 ❖ Handcrafted miniatures and dollhouses. 412-942-4120.

Acquisto Silver Company, 8901 Osuna Rd. NE, Albuquerque, NM 87111: Free brochure with long SASE ❖ Sterling silver miniatures. 505-292-0910.

Angel Children, 4977 Sparr Rd., Gaylord, MI 49735: Catalog $2 (refundable) ❖ Miniature porcelain dolls. 517-732-1931.

Angela's Miniature World, 2237 Ventura Blvd., Camarillo, CA 93010: Free information with long SASE ❖ Miniatures, dollhouses, building materials, and collectibles. 805-482-2219.

Architectural Etcetera, 888 Tower Rd., Mundelein, IL 60060: Catalog $6 ❖ Bookshelves, fireplaces, doors, windows, and architectural details. 708-949-0041.

B.H. Miniatures, 1831 Rose Garden Ln., Ste. 1, Phoenix, AZ 85027: Catalog $3 with long SASE ❖ Pre-pasted wallpaper, coordinated print and solid color fabrics, velvet carpeting, and furniture in kits or assembled. 602-582-3385.

Bauder-Pine Ltd., P.O. Box 518, Langhorne, PA 19047: Catalog $5 ❖ Furniture and kits. 215-355-2033.

Beauvais Castle, 141 Union St., P.O. Box 4060, Manchester, NH 03108: Catalog $5 ❖ Miniatures. 800-282-8944.

Botanicals Etc., 446 Old Falls Blvd., North Tonawanda, NY 14120: Price list $1 with long SASE ❖ Plants, wicker furniture, and miniature landscaping accessories.

Cecil Boyd's Miniatures, 16007 Scenic Oak Tr., Buda, TX 78610: Free information with long SASE and two 1st class stamps ❖ Realistic human figures with a choice of scale. 512-295-2294.

Brodnax Prints, 3870 W. Beverly Dr., Dallas, TX 75209: Catalog $1 ❖ Wallpapers for dollhouses. 214-528-7773.

Bufton's Collectable Miniatures, 1333 S. Avenida Sirio, Tucson, AZ 85710: Free price sheet with long SASE ❖ Miniatures.

C & J Gallery, 109 S. Elmwood, Ste. 18, Oak Park, IL 60302: Catalog $2 ❖ Museum-quality miniature art. 708-383-3634.

Cape May Miniatures, 219 Jackson St., Cape May, NJ 08204: Catalog $25 ❖ Dollhouses, furniture and accessories, lighting, and building supplies. 609-884-7999.

Cardinal Incorporated, 400 Markley St., Port Reading, NJ 07064: Catalog $7.50 (refundable) ❖ Miniature dollhouse furniture and porcelain collectible dolls. 800-888-0936.

Carradus Gifts, 1138 160th St., Dundee, IA 52038: Catalog $3 with long SASE (refundable) ❖ Miniatures. 319-924-2748.

Catworkz...and DOGS' too Inc., P.O. Box 1789, New York, NY 10163: Free brochure with long SASE and two 1st class stamps ❖ Miniature cats, dogs, and accessories.

Cir-Kit Concepts Inc., 32 Woodlake Dr. SE, Rochester, MN 55904: Catalog $4 ❖ Electrical miniatures and wiring kits for dollhouses. 800-676-4252.

CJ Originals, P.O. Box 538, Bridgeville, PA 15017: Catalog $4 ❖ Miniature needlework cross-stitch kits. 412-221-5797.

Crystal Brook Gift & Miniature Shop, Rt. 20, Brimfield, MA 01010: Free information ❖ Furniture, doll houses, log cabins, accessories and kits, books, and building materials. 413-245-7647.

Helen David Miniatures, IGMS Artisan, 8602 Rivercross, Houston, TX 77064: Information $3.75 with long SASE (refundable) ❖ Miniature floral arrangements.

DD's Dollhouse, 1527 Upper Ottawa St., Hamilton, Ontario, Canada L8V 3J4: Catalog $10 ❖ Dollhouses and accessories. 905-574-2942.

Debbie's Dollhouses, 150 Airport Dr., Westminster, MD 21157: Catalog $20 (refundable) ❖ Dollhouses, furniture, and decorating accessories. 410-876-9235.

Diamond M Brand Mold Company, 15W081 91st St., Hinsdale, IL 60521: Catalog $3 ❖ Molds for making miniatures. 708-323-5691.

Doll Faire Miniatures, 2310 Monument Blvd., Pleasant Hill, CA 94523: Catalog $4 ❖ Miniature Victorian trim and lace. 510-680-1993.

The Dollhouse, 6107 N. Scottsdale Rd., Scottsdale, AZ 85253: Free information with long SASE ❖ Miniatures and dollhouses. 800-398-3981.

The Dollhouse Factory, 157 Main St., P.O. Box 456, Lebanon, NJ 08833: Catalog $5.50 ❖ Dollhouses, miniatures, tools, books, and plans. 908-236-6404.

Dollhouses & Miniatures of Myrtle Beach, 10824 Shoppers Walk, The Colonial Shops, Myrtle Beach, SC 29572: Free information with long SASE ❖ Dollhouses, furnishings, and other miniatures. 803-497-9722.

Donna's Dollhouses of Frankfort, 51 W. Clinton St., Ste. 102, Frankfort, IN 46041: Information $1 with long SASE ❖ Everything for dollhouses. 317-654-9075.

Dwyer's Doll House, 1944 Warwick Ave., Warwick, RI 02889: Catalog $25 ❖ Dollhouses, building supplies, and miniatures. 401-738-3248.

Elect-a-Lite, P.O. Box 865, West End, NC 27376: Free information ❖ Miniature lighting accessories for dollhouses.

Elena's Dollhouses & Miniatures, 5565 Schueller Crescent, Burlington, Ontario, Canada L7L 3T1: Free information ❖ Dollhouses and miniatures. 905-333-3402.

Enchanted Doll House, Rt. 7A, RR 1, Box 2535, Manchester Center, VT 05255: Catalog $2 ❖ Dollhouses and kits, furniture, dolls, stuffed animals, and toys. 802-362-1327.

DOLLHOUSES & MINIATURES

England Things, 15 Sullivan Farm, New Milford, CT 06776: Brochure $4 ❖ Miniatures by English artisans.

Fantasy Craft, 933 Carson Ln., Pomona, CA 91766: Catalog $5 (refundable with $50 order) ❖ Traditional, contemporary, and southwest-style dollhouse kits. Also diorama, room box, and furniture kits. 909-591-8252.

Favorite Things, York & Monton Rd., Hereford, MD 21111: Catalog $1 ❖ Alexander dolls and dollhouse miniatures. 800-343-0407.

Fred's Dollhouse & Miniature Center, Rt. 7, Pittsford, VT 05763: Catalog $5 ❖ Dollhouses and kits, building supplies, and furniture. 802-483-6362.

Freda's Fancy, 295 Fairview Ave., Bayport, NY 11705: Catalog $5 ❖ Dollhouse miniatures. 800-451-0078.

G.E.L. Products Inc., 19 Grove St., Vernon, CT 06066: Free list of retail sources ❖ Dollhouse kits. 203-872-6539.

Ginsburg Company, 112 N. May St., Chicago, IL 60607: Free list of retail sources ❖ Dollhouse furniture and decorative items. 312-243-2734.

Grandt Line Products, 1040 Shary Ct., Concord, CA 94518: Catalog $4.75 ❖ Small scale structural items and accessories. 510-671-0143.

Greenhouse Miniature Shop, 6616 Monroe St., Sylvania, OH 43560: Catalog $3 ❖ Miniatures. 419-882-8259.

Handcraft Designs Inc., 63 E. Broad St., Hatfield, PA 19440: Free information with long SASE ❖ Miniature upholstered furniture. 800-523-2430; 215-855-3022 (in PA).

Happy House Miniatures, 135 N. Main St., Mocksville, NC 27028: Catalog $5 (refundable) ❖ Dollhouses and accessories. 704-634-1424.

Haslam's Doll Houses, 7208 S. Tamiami Trail, Sarasota, FL 34231: Free information with long SASE ❖ Dollhouses, miniatures, and building supplies. 941-922-8337.

Hearth Song, Mail Processing Center, 6519 N. Galena Rd., P.O. Box 1773, Peoria, IL 61656: Free catalog ❖ Dollhouse miniatures, books for children, toiletries for babies, cuddly dolls, party decorations, art supplies, and games. 800-325-2502.

Heritage Miniatures, 44 Mountain Base Rd., Goffstown, NH 03045: Catalog $4 ❖ Authentic 18th and 19th-century English kitchenware and porcelains.

J. Hermes, P.O. Box 4023, El Monte, CA 91734: Catalog $3 ❖ Dollhouse kits.

Hobby Builders Supply, P.O. Box 921012, Norcross, GA 30092: Free catalog ❖ Dollhouses, furniture, building supplies, and lighting, landscaping, and accessories. 800-223-7171.

Hobby Craft, 6632 Odama Rd., Madison, WI 53719: Free information (specify item wanted) ❖ Dollhouses, furniture and furniture kits, wallpaper, lighting, and building materials. 608-833-4944.

Hobby World Miniatures, 5450 Sherbrooke St. West, Montreal, Quebec, Canada H4A 1V9: Free catalog ❖ Dollhouses and miniatures. 514-481-5434.

Hopestar Enterprises, P.O. Box 391405, Solon, OH 44139: Free brochure ❖ Dollhouse furniture and miniatures.

House of Caron, 10111 Larrylyn Dr., Whittier, CA 90603: Price list $2.50 ❖ Molds and supplies for making miniature dolls. 310-947-6753.

House of Miniatures, 107 Pine St., East Aurora, NY 14052: Free list with long SASE ❖ Miniature books. 716-655-1476.

Houseworks, 2388 Pleasantdale Rd., Atlanta, GA 30340: Catalog $4 (request list of retail sources) ❖ Dollhouse building components, hardware, lighting, flooring, and furniture. 404-448-6596.

Innovative Photography, 1724 NW 36th, Lincoln City, OR 97367: Catalog $2.50 ❖ Miniature photographs and framed Victorian-style prints, from the 1920s to 1930s. 503-994-9421.

Itty Bitty Builder, 405 Kirby Ct., Walnut Creek, CA 94598: Brochure $1 (refundable) ❖ Accessories and furniture kits.

Jackie & Pat's Dollhouses Inc., 3050 Wade Hampton Blvd., Taylors, SC 29687: Catalog $30 ❖ Dollhouses, building materials, accessories, and furniture. 864-292-2877.

Jan's Dollhouse, 6600 Dixie Hwy., Diplomat Village, Fairfield, OH 45014: Catalog $18.95 ❖ Miniatures, dolls, bears, and dollhouses. 800-528-9135.

Jeepers Miniatures, 1315 S. Rangeline Rd., Carmel, IN 46032: Catalog $21 ❖ Miniatures and finished or ready-to-wire and paint dollhouses. 317-846-6708.

Janna Joseph, P.O. Box 1262, Dunedin, FL 34697: Catalog $5 ❖ Miniature doll molds. 813-784-1877.

Judy's Little Gems, P.O. Box 32396, Tucson, AZ 85751: Pamphlet $2 with long SASE ❖ Easy-to-assemble miniature flower kits.

K & J Miniature Metal Works, 329 Los Cabos Ln., Ventura, CA 93001: Free brochure ❖ Miniature kitchen appliances and accessories. 805-653-2427.

Karen's Miniatures, 6020 Doniphan, Ste. B1, El Paso, TX 79932: Catalog $6 ❖ Architectural moldings and cast metal miniature kits. 508-589-2371.

Kasey's Quilts, 31 Shepherd St., Raleigh, NC 27607: Free brochure with long SASE ❖ Kits for miniature doll house quilts.

The Lawbre Company, 888 Tower Rd., Mundelein, IL 60060: Catalog $4 ❖ Reproduction period-designed dollhouses and miniatures. 800-253-0491.

Lilliput Art, 2693 Bloomfield Rd., Sebastopol, CA 95472: Catalog $2 ❖ Miniatures.

Lilliput Land, 89 Lisa Dr., Northport, NY 11768: Brochure $6.50 ❖ English, French, and American handcrafted miniatures. 516-754-5511.

Little Goodies, P.O. Box 1004, Lewisville, TX 75067: Catalog $2 ❖ Miniature pre-cut paper flowers in kits.

Little House of Miniatures on Chelsea Lane, 615 Sycamore St., Waterloo, IA 50703: Catalog $18 (refundable) ❖ Dollhouses, furniture, dolls, wallpaper, carpets, electric wiring, and building supplies. 319-233-6585.

A Little Something for Everyone, 6203 S. Dover St., Littleton, CO 80123: Catalog $2 ❖ Kits and accessories.

Littlethings, 129 Main St., Irvington, NY 10533: Free list with long SASE ❖ Miniature paintings, dollhouses, furniture, bears, and collectibles. 914-591-9150.

Lolly's, 1054 Dundee Ave., Elgin, IL 60120: Catalog $21.50 (refundable with $50 order) ❖ Dollhouses and miniatures. 708-697-4040.

Lookingglass Miniatures, 635 NE Chestnut, Roseburg, OR 97470: Catalog $4 ❖ Miniature furniture kits. 503-673-5445.

MacDoc Designs, 405 Tarrytown Rd., White Plains, NY 10607: Free list of retail sources ❖ Miniature rugs. 914-376-2156.

Maison des Maisons, 460 S. Marion Pkwy., Denver, CO 80209: Price list $5 ❖ Southwest Indian-style furniture and miniatures. 303-871-0731.

Marilyn's Mini Studio, P.O. Box 34717, Los Angeles, CA 90034: Free price list with long SASE ❖ Miniatures.

Mary Elizabeth Miniatures, 49-04 39th Ave., Woodside, NY 11377: Free information with long SASE ❖ Handcrafted circa 1900 miniature ice cream parlor rooms and accessories. 718-429-4114.

Marydolls Molds, Mary Gukich, 1335 S. Oakland St., Aurora, CO 80012: Free brochure with long SASE ❖ Miniature dolls. 303-752-0468.

Microscale Industries Inc., P.O. Box 11950, Costa Mesa, CA 92627: Catalog $4 ❖ Micro-scale decals for decorating miniatures.

Mini Creations By Judy, 8721 Rt. 380, Brocton, NY 14716: Catalog $1 ❖ Landscaping miniatures. 716-792-9781.

Mini Splendid Things, 626 Main St., Covington, KY 41011: Catalog $25 ❖ Dollhouses and miniatures. 606-261-5500.

❖ DOLLHOUSES & MINIATURES ❖

Mini Temptations, 3633 W. 95th, Overland Park, KS 66206: Catalog $7 ❖ Dollhouse accessories, miniatures, and collectibles. 913-648-2050.

Mini-tiques, P.O. Box 683, 140 S. Main St., Thiensville, MN 53092: Catalog $3 ❖ Miniatures and accessories. 414-242-8053.

Miniature Crafters, P.O. Box 600331, San Diego, CA 92160: Catalog $2 ❖ Miniature furniture kits.

The Miniature Kingdom of River Row, 182 Front St., P.O. Box 39, Oswego, NY 13827: Catalog $2 ❖ Dollhouses and handcrafted miniatures. 607-687-5601.

Miniature Makers' Workshop, 4515 N. Woodward Ave., Royal Oak, MI 48073: Catalog $10 ❖ Furniture, dolls, and dollhouses. 313-549-0633.

Miniature MINIATURES, 7 Madison St., Port Washington, NY 11050: Catalog $3 ❖ Miniatures and dollhouses.

Miniature Rugs by Adams, Joan Adams, 2706 Sheridan Dr., Sarasota, FL 34239: Catalog $2.75 ❖ Miniature rugs.

Miniature Village, 1725 50th St., Kenosha, WI 53140: Catalog $20 (refundable with $50 order) ❖ Dollhouses, furniture, and electrical accessories. 800-383-0188.

Miniatures In-Your-Mailbox, P.O. Box 135, Schnecksville, PA 18078: Catalog $20 ❖ Dollhouses, furniture, building and electrical supplies, wall and floor coverings, and tools. 800-283-8191.

Miniatures Plus, P.O. Box 160, Place Bonaventure, Montreal, Quebec, Canada H5A 1A7: Catalog $1.50 ❖ Dollhouse furniture and accessories. 514-393-8742.

Mother Muck's Minis, 755 Lacey Way, North Salt Lake, UT 84954: Catalog $3 ❖ Miniatures.

Mott Miniatures & Doll House Shop, 7942 La Palma Ave., Ste. 8, Buena Park, CA 90621: Catalog $30 ❖ Furniture, dolls, dollhouses and kits, and building materials. 800-874-6222.

My Dollhouse, 7 S. Broadway, Nyack, NY 10960: Free information with long SASE ❖ Dolls, dollhouses, and miniatures. 914-358-4185.

My Sister's Shoppe Inc., 1671 Penfield Rd., Rochester, NY 14625: Catalog $3 (refundable) ❖ Victorian furniture miniatures. 800-821-0097.

Nola's Miniature Shop, 2351 A Rosewall Crescent, Courtenay, British Columbia, Canada V9N 8R9: Catalog $5 ❖ Furniture, books, supplies, collectibles, and other handcrafted accessories. 604-338-8700.

North Country Gardens, P.O. Box 277, Northport, MI 49670: Catalog $7 ❖ Miniatures. 616-386-5031.

Northeastern Scale Models Inc., P.O. Box 727, Methuen, MA 01844: Catalog $1 ❖ Materials for constructing dollhouses. 508-688-6019.

The Oakridge Corporation, P.O. Box 247, Lemont, IL 60439: Catalog $4 (specify 1/8, 1/4, 1/2, or 1-inch scale) ❖ Dollhouse kits, building supplies, and furniture. 708-739-4554.

Old World Craftsmen Dollhouses Inc., 643 Industrial Dr., Hartland, WI 53029: Brochure $2 ❖ Custom-made or in-stock dollhouses. 800-234-4748; 414-367-2753 (in WI).

Omniarts of Colorado, 498 S. High St., Denver, CO 80209: Catalog $4 ❖ Miniatures.

Once Upon A Time, 120 Church St. NE, Vienna, VA 22180: Free information ❖ Miniature wire wicker furniture. 703-255-3285.

Opening Scene Replicas, 4356 Falcon Crest Dr., Flowery Branch, GA 30542: Catalog $5 ❖ Dollhouses and room boxes.

P.J.'s Miniatures, 5818 Hwy. 74 West, Monroe, NC 28110: Catalog $14.95 ❖ Miniatures. 704-821-9144.

Pat's Miniatures, 515 Highland Ave., Carrollton, KY 41008: Catalog $30 ❖ Miniatures and dollhouse accessories. 800-644-6857; 502-732-6440 (in KY).

Peg's Dollhouse, 4019 Sebastopol Rd., Santa Rosa, CA 95407: Information $1 (refundable) ❖ Miniatures and dollhouses. 707-546-6137.

Penguin in Paradise Miniatures, 2641 NE 7th Terrace, Pompano Beach, FL 33064: Catalog $3 ❖ Dollhouse furniture and accessories. 954-786-0403.

Petite Innovations, 243 High St., Burlington, NJ 08016: Catalog $25 (refundable) ❖ Dollhouses and furnishings, lighting supplies, building materials, and miniatures. 609-386-7476.

Pinocchio's Miniatures, 465 S. Main St., Frankenmuth, MI 48734: Catalog $19.50 ❖ Handmade miniatures. 517-652-2751.

PJ Distributors Inc., 1498 Reistertown Rd., Ste. 216, Pikesville, MD 21208: Catalog $8 ❖ Miniatures, gifts, and collectibles.

Posy Patch Originals, Box 52173, Atlanta, GA 30355: Free price list with long SASE ❖ Plant and flower kits.

Precious Little Things, The Fieldwood Company, P.O. Box 6, Chester, VT 05143: Catalog $3.50 ❖ Handcrafted miniature furnishings. 802-875-4127.

Pricille's Stencils, P.O. Box 633, North Chelmsford, MA 01863: Catalog $6 ❖ Miniature stencils for use on dollhouse furniture and miniatures. Also stencils and accessories. 508-667-8760.

Enrique Quintanar, 210 Post St., Studio 813, San Francisco, CA 94108: Brochure $1 ❖ Sterling silver miniatures. 415-398-5678.

R & N Miniatures, 458 Wythe Creek Rd., Poquoson, VA 23662: Price list $2 ❖ Everything to finish and furnish dollhouses. 804-868-7103.

Real Good Toys, 10 Quarry Hill, Barre, VT 05641: Catalog $3 (request list of retail sources) ❖ Dollhouse kits with easy-to-follow instructions. 802-479-2217.

Riverwood Creations, 806 E. Hill Dr., New Kensington, PA 15068: Free price list with long SASE ❖ Miniatures.

Rose's Doll House Store, 2241 116th St., Milwaukee, WI 53227: Free catalog ❖ Dolls and dollhouse miniatures. 414-321-0680.

Scientific Models Inc., 340 Snyder Ave., Berkeley Heights, NJ 07922: Catalog $1 ❖ Easy-to-assemble museum-quality dollhouse furniture.

Sew What, 45 Green Valley Ct., Howard, OH 43028: Brochure and yarn samples $2 ❖ Miniature braided oval rugs.

Shaker Workshops, Box 8001, Ashburnham, MA 01430: Catalog $1 ❖ Furniture and dolls and Shaker furniture in kits or assembled. 800-840-9121.

Sir Thomas Thumb, P.O. Box 1093, Anna Maria, FL 34216: Catalog $3 ❖ Handcrafted miniatures.

Skycrest Ceramics, 149 W. Oak, Ste. 8, Fort Collins, CO 80524: Free information ❖ Ceramic miniatures. 970-493-3113.

Small Houses, 8064 Columbia Rd., Olmsted Falls, OH 44138: Catalog $6 ❖ Dollhouse kits, furniture, wallpaper, and building supplies. 216-235-5051.

The Squirrel's Nest Miniatures, 401 Buckingham Rd., Pittsburgh, PA 15125: Free information with long SASE ❖ Sterling silver miniatures, Early American accessories, and dollhouse building supplies. 800-852-3156.

Teri's Mini Workshop, P.O. Box 387, Goldenrod, FL 32733: Catalog $1 with long SASE ❖ Miniatures for dollhouses and other settings.

Tiny Colonies, P.O. Box 1505, North Baldwin, NY 11510: Catalog $2 ❖ Miniature Early American furniture and accessories.

Marie Toner Lighting Designs Inc., 725 Inverness Dr., Horsham, PA 19044: Catalog $1 with long SASE ❖ Easy-to-install miniature ceiling and wall fixtures.

The Toy Box, 4657 South US 1, Rockledge, FL 32955: Catalog $4 ❖ Dollhouses and kits, building and electrical supplies, furniture, and books. 407-632-2411.

DOLL MAKING & DOLL CLOTHING

Treasures by Paula K, Village Plaza, Rt. 202 & Lovell St., Lincolndale, NY 10540: Catalog $12 (refundable) ❖ Everything to fully furnish a dollhouse from start to finish. 914-248-7262.

Vernon Pottery, 441 Bethune Dr., Virginia Beach, VA 23452: Catalog $2 ❖ Reproduction 19th-century salt-glazed stoneware miniatures. 804-486-5147.

Vicki's Miniatures, 406 E. Cranford Ave., Valdosta, GA 31602: Free information: Brochure $1 ❖ Handcrafted miniatures, kits, and assembled doll houses. 912-244-4558.

The Victorian Craftsman Ltd., P.O. Box 234, New York, NY 10276: Catalog $6 (refundable with $30 order) ❖ Kits for miniature reproductions in petit point or cross stitch. 212-673-0369.

Victorian Times Houses, 2310 Monument Blvd., Pleasant Hill, CA 94523: Catalog $3 ❖ Dollhouses. 510-680-1993.

Jeffrey W. Vigeant, P.O. Box 414, Williamsburg, VA 23187: Brochure $4 ❖ Miniature Victorian lamps. 804-258-0425.

Walmer Dollhouses, 2100 Jefferson Davis Hwy., Alexandria, VA 22301: Free list of retail sources ❖ Dollhouses. 800-336-0285.

Warling Miniatures, 22453 Covello St., West Hills, CA 91307: Brochure $1 with long SASE and two 1st class stamps ❖ Victorian to modern wicker furniture kits. 818-340-9855.

Donna Wolf, 1200 E. 21st, Hutchinson, KS 67502: Information $1 with long SASE ❖ Handcrafted counted cross-stitch samplers, pillows, quilts, table runners, and comforter sets.

DOLL MAKING & DOLL CLOTHING

All About Dolls, 49 Lakeside Blvd., Hopatcong, NJ 07843: Free price list with long SASE ❖ Porcelain for making dolls. Also kilns, eyes, wigs, and other supplies. 201-770-3228.

Angel's Attic, 3321 W. Cinnamon Dr., Tucson, AZ 85741: Brochure $1.50 ❖ Turn-of-the-century-style doll patterns. 520-797-8212.

Ann's Doll Patterns, P.O. Box 16946, Portland, OR 97216: Catalog $3 ❖ Patterns for doll clothing. 503-829-2603.

Apple Valley Doll Works, P.O. Box 170, Midland, MI 48640: Free information ❖ Vinyl doll kits. 800-635-7933.

BB Doll Supplies, 800 Glenda Dr., Bedford, TX 76022: Catalog $5 (refundable) ❖ Supplies to start, finish, and dress a doll. 817-268-DOLL.

Bell Ceramics, P.O. Box 120127, Clermont, FL 34712: Catalog $8 ❖ Antique reproduction and modern doll molds and supplies. 904-394-2175.

Gina C. Bellows, 3629 Helms Ave., Culver City, CA 90232: Catalog $3 with long SASE ❖ Portrait dolls, porcelain blanks, painted doll kits, and supplies. 310-836-8065.

Broadview Dolls, 5247 State Rd., Parma, OH 44134: Catalog $4 ❖ Doll bisque kits and doll-making supplies. 216-661-4856.

Brown House Dolls, 3200 N. Sand Lake Rd., Allen, MI 49227: Catalog $2 ❖ Easy-to-sew patterns for doll clothing. 517-849-2833.

Carver's Eye Company, P.O. Box 16692, Portland, OR 97216: Catalog $1 ❖ Glass and plastic eyes, noses, joints, growlers, and eye glasses for dolls and bears. 503-666-5680.

Collectible Doll Company, 1421 N. 34th, Seattle, WA 98103: Free information ❖ Doll clothes, molds, and supplies for making dolls. 206-634-3131.

CR's Crafts, Box 8, Leland, IA 50453: Catalog $2 ❖ Doll and bear-making supplies, kits, and patterns for jointed bears. 515-567-3652.

Creative Paperclay Company, 1800 S. Robertson Blvd., Ste. 907, Los Angeles, CA 90035: Free information ❖ Air-hardening sculpting material for doll artists. 800-899-5952.

D & L Doll Supply, 224-228 Admiral St., Providence, RI 02908: Free information ❖ Soft-fired greenware, wigs, eyes, shoes, patterns, and supplies. 401-421-7558.

Lou Davis Doll Supply, N3211 Hwy. H North, Lake Geneva, WI 53147: Free catalog ❖ Doll-making supplies. 800-748-7991.

Dee's Place of Dolls, 140 E. College St., Covina, CA 91723: Free information ❖ Doll-making supplies and dolls. 818-915-1005.

Doll Gallery Supplies, 1137 Susan St., Columbia, SC 29210: Free information with long SASE ❖ Doll-making supplies. 803-798-7044.

Doll Works Etc., 1915 Peters Rd., Ste. 201, Irving, TX 75061: Free price list with long SASE ❖ Doll-making supplies. 214-721-0819.

Dolls Galore, 2008 E. Sandalwood Dr. North, Plant City, FL 33566: Free list with long SASE ❖ Painted doll-making kits with wigs, lashes, and preset eyes. 800-535-DOLL.

Dollspart Supply Company, 8000 Cooper Ave., Building 28, Glendale, NY 11385: Free catalog ❖ Wigs, glass eyes, doll stands, shoes, doll parts and bodies, ceramic supplies, clothing, patterns, and books. 718-326-4587.

Down Memory Lane, 715 Carroll St., Boone, IA 50036: Catalog $2.75 ❖ Patterns for doll clothing. 515-432-3222.

Angela Eoriatti, Custom Doll Fahions, 8511 NW Beaver Dr., Johnston, IA 50131: Catalog $6.50 ❖ Patterns for doll clothing. 515-276-3234.

Fun Stuff, P.O. Box 999, Yuma, AZ 85366: Free list with long SASE ❖ Artist vinyl and porcelain doll kits. 602-726-1513.

Global Dolls Corporation, 1903 Aviation Blvd., Lincoln, CA 95648: Catalog $5 ❖ Doll wigs. 916-645-3000.

Haskell's Handcraft, 40 College Ave., Waterville, ME 04901: Catalog $6 ❖ Doll-making and clock-building supplies. 207-873-5070.

Heartcraft Kids, 5301 Pluto Dr., Rapid City, SD 57701: Catalog $4 ❖ Bisque doll kits. 605-393-0345.

Heavenly Made Seasons, P.O. Box 1311, Cheyenne, WY 82001: Brochure $1 ❖ Original doll patterns; six faces, six costumes, iron-on transfers. 307-635-7899.

Hello Dolly, 6550 Mobile Hwy., Pensacola, FL 32526: Catalog $5 ❖ Doll-making supplies. 800-438-7227.

Herb's Porcelain Doll Studio, 1208 E. 15th St., Plano, TX 75074: Price list $2 (refundable) ❖ Bisque kits for making dolls. 800-628-4696; 214-578-1128 (in TX).

Heritage Miniatures, 44 Mountain Base Rd., Goffstown, NH 03045: Catalog $4 ❖ European lace and trim for doll clothing.

Hickory Dickory Dolls, 124 E. Aurora Rd., Northfield, OH 44067: Free price list ❖ Dolls, clothing, and shoes. 800-468-2085.

House of Caron, 10111 Larrylyn Dr., Whittier, CA 90603: Price list $2.50 ❖ Miniature doll molds and doll-making supplies. 310-947-6753.

Joyce Houston Products, 246 S. Cleveland, Loveland, CO 80537: Free brochure ❖ Supplies, brushes, paints, and mediums for porcelain doll creators. 970-663-3009.

Huston Dolls, 7960 US Rt. 23, Chillicothe, OH 45601: Catalog $2 ❖ Handmade porcelain dolls and make-them-yourself kits. 614-663-2881.

Jennell's Doll House, P.O. Box 43735, Seven Points, TX 75143: Catalog $4 ❖ Doll kits, supplies, pre-sewn bodies, and clothes. 903-432-4894.

Jo's Dolls-N-Fine Porcelain, 7508 SW 12th, Des Moines, IA 50315: Catalog $7.95 ❖ Doll-making supplies. 800-323-4689.

Jomac Dolls & Supplies, 702 Crenshaw, Pasadena, TX 77504: Free information ❖ Doll-making supplies, bisque and wax kits, and greenware. 713-944-8221.

Jones Mold Company, 919 4th Ave. South, Nashville, TN 37210: Ceramics catalog $6.25; doll catalog $6.75 ❖ Molds for making ceramics and dolls. 615-251-8989.

Janna Joseph, P.O. Box 1262, Dunedin, FL 34697: Catalog $4.95 ❖ Miniature doll molds. 813-784-1877.

❖ DOLLS ❖

Joyce's Doll House, 20188 Williamson, Clinton Township, MI 48035: Catalog $1 ❖ Doll parts, wigs, natural straw hats, eyes, and sewing supplies.

Judi's Dolls, P.O. Box 6165, Aloha, OR 97007: Catalog $2 ❖ Patterns and supplies for cloth dolls. 503-848-8361.

Kari & Judy's Creations, 2591 Mercantile Dr., Ste. B, Rancho Cordova, CA 95742: Free price list with long SASE ❖ Finished and unfinished composition doll bodies. 916-858-0150.

✓ **Kemper Tools & Doll Supplies Inc.,** 13595 12th St., Chino, CA 91710: Free catalog ❖ Pottery, sculpting, craft, and art tools. Also doll-making supplies. 800-388-5367.

Kirchen Brothers, Box 1016, Skokie, IL 60076: Catalog $2 ❖ Doll-making supplies and kits, ready-to-wear and ready-to-sew clothing, shoes and socks, and craft supplies. 708-647-6747.

Ledgewood Studio, 6000 Ledgewood Dr., Forest Park, GA 30050: Catalog $2 with long SASE and three 1st class stamps ❖ Dress patterns, period clothing, fabrics, supplies for antique dolls, and sewing notions. 404-361-6098.

Victor H. Levy Inc., 1355 S. Flower St., Los Angeles, CA 90015: Catalog $5 ❖ Doll and jewelry-making supplies. 800-421-8021; 213-749-8247 (in CA).

LH Studio, Louise Hedrick, 1280 Orchard Ln., Elm Grove, WI 53122: Catalog $3 ❖ Costuming kits in 1:12 scale.

Magic Cabin Dolls, P.O. Box 64, Iroqua, WI 54665: Free information ❖ Doll-making supplies, kits and patterns, cotton knits, yarns, and handmade dolls. 608-634-2848.

Marl & Barbie, 10301 Braden Run, Bradenton, FL 34202: Catalog $5 ❖ Barbie doll fashions and dolls, from 1959 to the present. 941-751-6275.

Maybelle's Doll Works, 140 Space Park Dr., Nashville, TN 37211: Catalog $6 ❖ Doll-making supplies and molds. 615-831-0661.

Mini World Doll Supplies, 5899 Raytown Rd., Raytown, MO 64133: Catalog $3 ❖ Doll-making supplies. 816-353-5988.

Minnie's Doll House, Knight Rd., Rt. 3, Box 527, Lake Providence, LA 71254: Brochure $1.50 ❖ Original doll clothes. 318-559-2857.

Monique Trading Corporation, 270 Oyster Point Blvd., South San Francisco, CA 94080: Catalog $3 ❖ Doll wigs and accessories. 800-621-4338; 415-266-6863 (in CA).

Originals By Elaine Inc., 901 Oak Hollow Pl., Brandon, FL 33510: Catalog $6 ❖ Molds for miniature dolls. 813-654-0335.

✓ **Pierce Tools,** 1610 Parkdale Dr., Grants Pass, OR 97527: Free catalog ❖ Tools for the dollmaker, ceramist, potter, and sculptor. 503-476-1778.

Porcelain by Marilyn, 3687 W. US 40, Greenfield, IN 46140: Free list with long SASE ❖ Porcelain doll kits. 317-462-5063.

Mary Radbill Doll Supplies, 4512 Eden St., Philadelphia, PA 19114: Catalog $3 ❖ Doll-making supplies. 215-632-4606.

Thelma Resch, 89 Purple Martin Dr., Murrells Inlet, SC 29576: Brochure $2 ❖ Original doll molds. 803-651-0596.

Rivendell Inc., 8209 Proctor Rd., Painesville, OH 44077: Catalog $4 ❖ Supplies for porcelain dolls. 216-254-4088.

Jennie Rose Creations, 1310 Baylor Dr., Colorado Springs, CO 80909: Catalog $5 ❖ Miniature historic clothing patterns, kits, and ready-to-use garments.

Sandcastle Creations, 124 SE 1st St., Newport, OR 97365: Free information ❖ Wig-making supplies and kits, doll dresses, and accessories. 541-574-1901.

Seeley's, P.O. Box 669, Oneonta, NY 13820: Free catalog ❖ Doll-making supplies.

Sew Sweet Dolls, 787 Industrial Dr., Elmhurst, IL 60126: Catalog $2 ❖ Paper patterns for cloth dolls and accessories. Also hair materials, yarns, books, and supplies. 708-530-7175.

Doreen Sinnett, Box 789, Paso Robles, CA 93447: Catalog $3 ❖ Molds for miniature dolls.

Standard Doll Company, 23-83 31st St., Long Island City, NY 11105: Catalog $3 ❖ Supplies for making and repairing dolls, clothing, doll stands, shoes and socks, buttons, wigs, books, and sewing notions. 800-543-6557.

Sterling Mold Company, 351 Magnolia Pl., Debary, FL 32713: Catalog $7 ❖ Antique reproductions and artist doll molds. 407-668-8379.

✓ **Sugar Creek Industries Inc.,** P.O. Box 354, Linden, IN 47955: Free catalog ❖ Porcelain pouring equipment and supplies. 317 339-4641.

Syndee's, P.O. Box 94978, Las Vegas, NV 89193: Catalog $3 ❖ Accessories for making all types of dolls. 702-564-8118.

Tallina's Doll Supplies Inc., 15790 Southeast Hwy. 224, Clackamas, OR 97015: Catalog $1 ❖ Doll-making supplies. 503-658-6148.

✓ **Tender Heart Treasures Ltd.,** P.O. Box 2310, Omaha, NE 68103: Free catalog ❖ Clothing and accessories for bears and dolls. 800-443-1367.

Theriault's Doll, P.O. Box 151, Annapolis, MD 21404: Free information ❖ Antique, collectible, and other dolls. 410-224-3655.

TM Ceramic Service, Division T.M. Porcelain, 108 N. Henry, Bay City, MI 48706: Catalog $7.50 ❖ Doll-making supplies and molds. 517-893-3526.

Unicorn Studios, Box 370, Seymour, TN 37865: Catalog $1 ❖ Easy-to-install windup and electronic music box movements, winking light units, and voices for dolls and bears. 615-984-0145.

Kate Webster Company, 83 Granite St., Rockport, MA 01966: Catalog $3 ❖ Doll costuming supplies and jewelry. 508-546-6462.

DOLLS

All God's Children Collectors Club, P.O. Box 5038, Glencoe, AL 35905: Free list of retail sources ❖ Historical-theme dolls. 205-492-0221.

Angel Children, 4977 Sparr Rd., Gaylord, MI 49735: Catalog $2 (refundable) ❖ Miniature porcelain dolls. 517-732-1931.

Anything Goes Inc., 9801 Gulf Dr., Anna Maria, FL 34216: Quarterly newsletter $2 ❖ Current Barbie dolls. 813-778-4456.

✓ **The Ashton-Drake Galleries,** 9200 N. Maryland, Niles, IL 60714: Free catalog ❖ Collectible dolls. 800-346-2460.

Aurelia's World of Dolls Inc., 2025 Merrick Rd., Merrick, NY 11566: Free newsletter ❖ United States and international artist dolls. 516-378-3556.

Baby Me, 730 Boston Rd., Rt. 3A, Billerica, MA 01821: Free information ❖ Dolls. 508-667-1187.

Bébé House of Dolls, 282 3rd Ave., Chula Vista, CA 91910: Free information with long SASE ❖ Dolls. 619-476-0680.

Dee Benisek Studio, 2210 Williamsburg, Arlington Heights, IL 60004: Catalog $2 ❖ Antique reproduction dolls. 708-394-8910.

Best of Everything, 199 Main St., Hackettstown, NJ 07840: Free information ❖ Dolls. 908-850-4858.

Biggs Limited Editions, 5517 Lakeside Ave., Richmond, VA 23228: Free information with long SASE ❖ Limited edition artist and other dolls. 800-637-0704.

Bodzer's Collectibles, White Marsh Mall, Baltimore, MD 21236: Free catalog ❖ Ashton-Drake and collectible dolls. 410-931-9222.

Cambri Enterprises, P.O. Box 85, Darlington, SC 29532: Free brochure ❖ Collectible African heritage dolls.

Cardinal Incorporated, 400 Markley St., Port Reading, NJ 07064: Catalog $7.50 (refundable) ❖ Miniature dollhouse furniture and porcelain collectible dolls. 800-888-0936.

Celia's & Susan's Dolls & Collectibles, 800 E. Hallandale Beach Blvd., Hallandale, FL 33009: Catalog $5 ❖ Dolls. 305-458-0661.

❖ DOLLS ❖

CJ's Dolls & Dreams, 5 Plaistow Rd., Rt. 125, Plaistow, NH 03865: Free information ❖ Artist dolls. 603-382-3449.

Corbett's Collectable Dolls, 120 Kings Hwy., Maple Shade, NJ 08052: Catalog $5 ❖ Artist and manufacturer dolls. 609-866-9787.

Marl Davidson Dolls, 10301 Braden Run, Bradenton, FL 34202: Catalog $7.50 ❖ Barbie dolls and clothing, from 1959 to the present. 941-751-6275.

Doll Centre, 665 Placerville Dr., Placerville, CA 95667: Free catalog ❖ Limited edition dolls. 916-621-2889.

Doll City USA, 2080 S. Harbor Blvd., Anaheim, CA 92802: Price list $2 ❖ Dolls. 714-750-3585.

The Doll Gallery, 81 Glasgow St., Clyde, NY 14433: Free price list with long SASE ❖ Dolls. 315-923-9897.

The Doll House, 18 S. Broadway, Edmond, OK 73034: Free information ❖ Collectible dolls. 800-428-1719.

Doll Parlor, 7 Church Street, Allentown, NJ 08501: Free information with long SASE ❖ Dolls. 609-259-8118.

Doll Showcase, 104 Front St., Marietta, OH 45750: Free price list with long SASE ❖ Artist and manufacturer dolls. 800-93-DOLLS.

Dolls of Yesterday & Today, 1014 S. Broadway, Ste. 108, Carrollton, TX 75006: Free list with 1st class stamp ❖ Special occasion dolls. 214-242-8281.

Dolls Plus, 1941 W. Guadalupe, Mesa, AZ 85202: Brochure $3 ❖ Collectible dolls. 602-897-8606.

Dollsville Dolls & Bearsville Bears, 461 N. Palm Canyon Dr., Palm Springs, CA 92262: Catalog $2 ❖ Dolls. 619-325-2241.

Dwyer's Doll House, 1944 Warwick Ave., Warwick, RI 02889: Catalog $25 (refundable) ❖ Dolls, dollhouses, miniatures, and dollhouse building supplies. 401-738-3248.

Barbara Elster's Miniature Corner, German Importers Inc., 1001 Lowry Ave., Jeannette, PA 15644: Information $1 ❖ Handmade German porcelain face dolls with detailed Victorian costumes. 412-527-3003.

Enchanted Doll House, Rt. 7A, RR 1, Box 2535, Manchester Center, VT 05255: Catalog $2 ❖ Dolls, miniatures, bears, stuffed animals, and toys. 802-362-1327.

Enesco Corporation, 1 Enesco Plaza, Elk Grove Village, IL 60007: Free list of retail sources ❖ Figurines, sculptures, ornaments, Barbie dolls, and gifts.

Ernie's Toyland, 1012 6th St., Ste. 120, Yuba City, CA 95901: Free information ❖ Barbies and other dolls. 800-367-1233.

Fabric Creations, Rt. 3, Box 96, Crocker, MO 65452: Free brochure with long SASE ❖ Fabric dolls. 314-736-5733.

Forever Young, P.O. Box 4447, Ithaca, NY 14852: Catalog and other offers with six 1st class stamps ❖ Collectible dolls of yesterday and today. 607-273-5393.

Gepetto's Dolls N' More, P.O. Box 524, Hwy. 441 North, Cherokee, NC 28719: Free information with long SASE ❖ Collector dolls. 704-497-7995.

GiGi's Dolls & Sherry's Teddy Bears Inc., 6029 N. Northwest Hwy., Chicago, IL 60631: Free catalog ❖ Bears, dolls, plush toys, and miniatures. 312-594-1540.

Grandma's Attic, Joyce Kekatos, 3132 Ampere Ave., Bronx, NY 10465: Free information with long SASE ❖ Antique French and German bisque dolls. 718-863-0373.

Mary Gukich, 1335 S. Oakland St., Aurora, CO 80012: Free brochure with long SASE ❖ Miniature doll molds. 303-752-0468.

Jan Hagara Collectors Club, 40114 Industrial Park North, Georgetown, TX 78626: Free information ❖ Jan Hagara porcelain dolls. 512-863-9499.

David Hammon Dolls & Toys, 117 E. 1st St., Long Beach, CA 90802: List $1 ❖ Japanese fashion dolls. 310-436-6444.

Hickory Dickory Dolls, 124 E. Aurora Rd., Northfield, OH 44067: Free price list ❖ Dolls, clothing, and shoes. 800-468-2085.

The Hobby Gallery Miniature Loft, 1810 Meriden Rd., Wolcott, CT 06716: Free information with long SASE ❖ Dolls, dollhouses, miniatures, and plush animals. 203-879-2316.

Iron Horse Gifts, Rt. 9, Latham, NY 12110: Free information ❖ Designer dolls. 800-237-3735.

Jan Dolls, 5204 Godfrey Rd., Godfrey, IL 62035: Free newsletter ❖ Artist dolls. 618-466-0080.

Lane's Toyland & Gifts, 720 Realtor Ave., Texarkana, TX 75502: Free catalog ❖ Barbies and other dolls. 800-421-8697.

Le Allala's Doll Shop, 88 N. Paint St., Chillicothe, OH 45601: Catalog $3 ❖ Collector dolls. 800-577-3655; 614-775-5960 (in OH).

Lee's Collectibles, P.O. Box 19133, Sacramento, CA 95819: Free information with long SASE ❖ Wood, cloth, and contemporary artist dolls. 916-457-4308.

Lynn's Lil' Darlings, 209 N. 13th St., Griffin, GA 30223: Free list with long SASE ❖ New and old Barbie dolls. 404-228-5918.

Seymour Mann, 225 5th Ave., New York, NY 10010: Catalog $7.50 ❖ Dolls. 212-683-7262.

Marj's Doll Sanctuary, 5238 Plainfield Ave. NE, Grand Rapids, MI 49505: Free catalog with three 1st class stamps ❖ Dolls and bears. 616-361-0054.

Marl & Barbie, 10301 Braden Run, Bradenton, FL 34202: Catalog $5 ❖ Barbie doll fashions and dolls, from 1959 to the present. 941-751-6275.

Mary D's Dolls & Bears & Such, 8407 W. Broadway, Brooklyn Park, MN 55445: Catalog $1 ❖ Dolls. 612-424-4375.

Melton's Antiques, 4201 Indian River Rd., Chesapeake, VA 23325: Free information with long SASE ❖ Antique dolls. 804-420-9226.

Monarch Collectibles, 2121 NW Military Hwy., San Antonio, TX 78213: Free information ❖ Dolls. 800-648-3655.

Not Just Dolls, 2447 Gus Thomasson Rd., Dallas, TX 75228: Price list $2 ❖ Artist and manufacturer dolls. 214-321-0412.

Old Towne Doll Shoppe, 227 Main St., P.O. Box 78, Wethersfield, CT 06109: Free information ❖ Collectible dolls. 203-563-3049.

Original Appalachian Artworks Inc., P.O. Box 714, Cleveland, GA 30528: Free information ❖ Cabbage Patch dolls. 706-865-2171.

Originals By Elaine Inc., 901 Oak Hollow Pl., Brandon, FL 33510: Catalog $6 ❖ Molds for miniature dolls. 813-654-0335.

The Paper Place & Doll Place, 212 S. River, Holland, MI 49423: Catalog $3 (refundable) ❖ Collectible bears and dolls. 616-392-7776.

J. Parker, Box 34, Midland, Ontario, Canada L4R 4K6: Catalog $3 (refundable) ❖ Porcelain doll kits.

Pewter Classics, 3635 28th St. SE, Eastbrook Mall, Grand Rapids, MI 49512: Catalog $2 ❖ Dolls, bears, and collectibles. 800-833-3655.

Playhouse, Mary Radbill, 4512 Eden St., Philadelphia, PA 19114: Free catalog ❖ Artist dolls and bears and accessories. 215-632-4606.

Pleasant Company, P.O. Box 620190, Middleton, WI 53562: Free catalog ❖ Dolls. 800-845-0005.

Porter Emporium, P.O. Box 5, Rt. 25, Porter, ME 04068: Free list with long SASE ❖ Barbie dolls. 207-625-8989.

Rainbow Factory, 131 W. Vienna St., Clio, MI 48420: Free information with long SASE ❖ Dolls, miniatures, carrousels, music boxes, and bears. 313-687-1351.

Rose's Doll House Store, 2241 116th St., Milwaukee, WI 53227: Free catalog ❖ Bears, dolls, and dollhouse furnishings. 414-321-0680.

Samurai Antiques, 229 Santa Ynez Ct., Santa Barbara, CA 93103: Price list $1 with long SASE ❖ Japanese antique dolls by Samurai, Emperor, and Empress. 805-965-9688.

Sandy's Dolls & Collectables Inc., 7221 W. College Dr., Palos Heights, IL 60463: Price list $1 ❖ Artist and limited edition dolls. 708-423-0070.

Shirley's Doll House, 20509 North Hwy. 21, P.O. Box 99A, Wheeling, IL 60090: Free information with long SASE ❖ Dolls, bears, antiques, doll house furniture, wigs, clothing, shoes, and socks. 708-537-1632.

Simply Lovely Gift Shoppe, 572 New Brunswick Ave., Fords, NJ 08863: Free price list with long SASE ❖ Dolls. 908-738-4181.

Society's Child, 28686 W. Northwest Hwy., Barrington, IL 60010: Free information with long SASE ❖ Artist and limited edition dolls. 708-381-9559.

Sophia's Heritage Collection, 8 Shepherd Rd., Malvern, PA 19355: Free brochure ❖ German, Irish, and English immigrant dolls, clothing, furniture, and accessories. 610-647-2118.

Mary Stolz Doll Shop, RD 6, Box 6767, East Stroudsburg, PA 18301: Free catalog ❖ Barbies and collectible dolls. 717-588-7566.

Sutter Street Emporium, 731 Sutter St., Folsom, CA 95630: Free information ❖ Limited edition, original artist, and other dolls. 916-985-4647.

Tide-Rider Inc., P.O. Box 429, Oakdale, CA 95361: Free information ❖ Handcrafted felt dolls with detailed facial features and costuming. 209-848-4420.

Today's Treasures, 655 73rd St., Niagara Falls, NY 14304: Catalog $3 (refundable) ❖ Collector dolls and bears. 716-283-1726.

Toni Ann's Doll House, 213 S. 213 S. Caroline St., Herkimer, NY 13350: Free catalog ❖ Collectible dolls. 315-866-3655.

Toy Shoppe, 11632 Busy St., Richmond, VA 23236: Free information ❖ Collectible dolls and bears. 800-447-7995.

Toy Village, 3105 W. Saginaw, Lansing, MI 48917: Free information ❖ Toys, dolls, bears, and collectibles. 517-323-1145.

Ryan Twist Gallery, 430 Teaneck Rd., Ridgefield Park, NJ 07660: Free information with long SASE ❖ Dolls. 800-421-0171.

Wagonhill Dolls, 225 S. Broad St., Grove City, PA 16127: Free list with long SASE ❖ Collector artist dolls. 800-874-6229; 412-458-4711 (in PA).

Your Old Friends Doll Shop, Carmen & Mike Tickal, 21 5th St. SW, Mason City, IA 50401: Catalog $5 ❖ Barbie dolls, clothing, and accessories. 515-424-0984.

DRAFTING SUPPLIES

Alvin & Company, P.O. Box 188, Windsor, CT 06095: Free catalog ❖ Drafting, engineering, and graphic art supplies. 800-444-ALVIN; 203-243-8991 (in CT).

Dick Blick Company, P.O. Box 1267, Galesburg, IL 61402: Catalog $1 ❖ Books, videos, airbrushes, printing and drafting equipment, and commercial art supplies. 800-447-8192.

Co-Op Artists' Materials, 205 Armour Dr., Atlanta, GA 30324: Free catalog ❖ Painting, drafting, drawing, airbrushing, and graphic art supplies. 800-877-3242.

Fairgate Rule Company Inc., 22 Adams Ave., P.O. Box 278, Cold Spring, NY 10516: Free catalog ❖ Rulers, other measuring devices, stencils, and drawing aids. 800-431-2180; 914-265-3677 (in NY).

Hearlihy & Company, 714 W. Columbia St., Springfield, OH 45504: Free catalog ❖ Drafting and graphics equipment, software for education and computer-aided designing, drawing and drafting aids, videos, plotters, and furniture. 800-622-1000.

Nasco, 901 Janesville Ave., Fort Atkinson, WI 53538: Free catalog ❖ Drawing and drafting supplies. 800-558-9595.

Norton Products, 271 North Ave., New Rochelle, NY 10801: Free information ❖ Craft projector that projects an image onto most surfaces. 800-453-3326.

Office Depot Inc., 2200 Old Germantown Rd., Delray Beach, FL 33445: Free catalog ❖ Drafting equipment, office supplies, and accessories. 800-685-8800.

Daniel Smith Art Supplies Inc., 4150 1st Ave. South, Seattle, WA 98134: Free catalog ❖ Art and framing supplies, books, studio and drafting equipment, and furniture. 800-426-6740.

Staples Inc., 8 Technology Dr., P.O. Box 1020, Westborough, MA 01581: Free catalog ❖ Office and computer supplies, drafting equipment, furniture, fax machines, and typewriters. 800-333-3330.

DUMBWAITERS

Econol Lift Corporation, 2513 Center St., Box 854, Cedar Falls, IA 50613: Free information ❖ Dumbwaiters, residential elevators, and vertical, wheelchair, and stair-riding lifts. 319-277-4777.

Inclinator Company of America, P.O. Box 1557, Harrisburg, PA 17105: Free information ❖ Dumbwaiters. 717-234-8065.

Miller Manufacturing Inc., 165 Cascade Ct., Rohnert Park, CA 94928: Free information ❖ Commercial and residential manually operated dumbwaiters. 800-232-2177.

Whitco/Vincent Whitney Company, 60 Liberty Ship Way, Sausalito, CA 94966: Free information ❖ Residential and commercial hand-operated dumbwaiters. 800-332-3286.

EGG CRAFTING

Eggs by Byrd, Rt. 2, Box 2030, Wappapello, MO 63966: Catalog $4.50 ❖ Egg decorating supplies. 800-235-3447.

Olesky Enterprises, W6742 #12 Rd., Wallace, MI 49803: Information $2 with long SASE ❖ Chicken and goose eggs for decorating. 906-227-3051.

Schiltz Goose Farm, 7 Oak St. West, P.O. Box 267, Sisseton, SD 57262: Free information ❖ Decorating supplies, tools, egg stands, and blown goose eggs in jumbo, X-large, large, and regular sizes. 605-698-7651.

Surma Egg Crafting, 11 E. 7th St., New York, NY 10003: Free catalog ❖ Dyes, tools, supplies, and kits for Ukrainian Easter egg decorating. 212-477-0729.

Woods of the World Inc., 897 North Bend Rd., Cincinnati, OH 45224: Brochure $1 ❖ Egg-shaped woods from worldwide sources.

ELECTRIC GENERATORS & ENGINES

Apollo Diesel Generators, 833 W. 17th St., #3, Costa, Mesa, CA 92627: Free information ❖ Lightweight high-performance diesel generators. 714-650-1240.

China Diesel Imports, 15749 Lyons Valley Rd., Jamul, CA 92035: Free catalog ❖ Diesel generators and parts for an economical power source. 619-699-1995.

Engine Mart, 2642 Newfound, Merritt Island, FL 32952: Catalog $2 ❖ Engines.

Generac Corporation, Box 8, Waukesha, WI 53187: Free information ❖ Emergency electricity-generating source. 414-544-4811.

MTS Power Products, 4501 NW 27th Ave., Miami, FL 33142: Free information ❖ Ready-to-work diesel generators. 800-541-7677.

ELECTRICAL SUPPLIES

Ericson Manufacturing Company, 4215 Hamann Pkwy., P.O. Box 800, Willoughby, OH 44094: Free list of retail sources ❖ Safety electrical specialties. 800-ERICSON.

Marlin P. Jones & Associates, P.O. Box 12685, Lake Park, FL 33403: Free catalog ❖ Electrical and electronic components. 407-848-8236.

Wiremold Company, 60 Woodlawn St., West Hartford, CT 06110: Free information ❖ Fixtures, switches, controls, and grounding outlets for installation without having to break into walls or ceilings. 800-621-0049.

ELECTRONICS EQUIPMENT
Components & Equipment

Accord Electronic Systems Inc., 2946 NW 60th St., Fort Lauderdale, FL 33309: Free information ❖ Electronic components. 800-998-2242; 305-968-1026 (in FL).

Ace Communications, 8030 E. 47th St., Indianapolis, IN 46226: Free information ❖ Electronic equipment. 800-445-7717.

All Electronics Corporation, P.O. Box 567, Van Nuys, CA 91408: Free catalog ❖ New and surplus electronic parts and supplies. 800-826-5432; 818-904-0524 (in CA).

Allied Electronics, 7134 Columbia Gateway Dr., Ste. 200, Columbia, MD 21046: Free catalog ❖ Electronic parts, tools, and books. 800-433-8700.

Alltronics, 2300 Zanker Rd., San Jose, CA 95131: Free catalog ❖ Electronic components and test equipment. 408-943-9773.

American Design Components, 6 Pearl Ct., Allendale, NJ 07401: Free catalog ❖ New, reconditioned, and used electrical-mechanical and electronic equipment. 800-776-3800.

American Electronics Inc., 164 Southpark Blvd., P.O. Box 301, Greenwood, IN 46142: Free information ❖ Electronic components. 800-872-1373.

AP Circuits, 1112 40th Ave. NE, Calgary, Alberta, Canada T2E 5T8: Free information ❖ Prototype plated-through circuit boards. 403-291-9342.

ARS Electronics, 7110 de Celis Pl., Van Nuys, CA 91409: Catalog $2.50 ❖ Electronics equipment and tubes. 800-422-4250.

Brigar Electronics, 7-9 Alice St., Binghamton, NY 13904: Free information ❖ Electronic parts. 607-723-3111.

Calcera, P.O. Box 489, Belmont, CA 94002: Free information ❖ Surplus electronic components. 800-257-5549.

Capital Electronics Inc., 852 Foster Ave., Bensenville, IL 60106: Free information ❖ Printed circuit boards and LEDS. 708-350-9510.

Circuit Specialists Inc., 220 S. Country Club Dr., Mesa, AZ 85210: Free catalog ❖ Electronic equipment. 800-528-1417.

Communication Concepts Inc., 508 Millstone Dr., Beavercreek, OH 45434: Free catalog ❖ Amplifiers and hard-to-find parts. 513-426-8600.

Communications Electronics Inc., P.O. Box 1045, Ann Arbor, MI 48106: Free information ❖ Scanners, transceivers, and emergency broadcast, weather station, monitoring, and other electronics. 313-996-8888.

Consolidated Electronics Inc., 705 Watervliet Ave., Dayton, OH 45420: Catalog $5 ❖ Semiconductors, tools, solder equipment, wire, and test equipment. 800-543-3568.

Contact East, 335 Willow St. South, North Andover, MA 01845: Free catalog ❖ Tools and equipment for testing, repairing, and assembling electronic equipment. 800-225-5370; 508-682-2000 (in MA).

Dalbani Electronics, 4225 NW 72nd Ave., Miami, FL 33166: Free catalog ❖ Electronic components. 800-325-2264; 305-716-1016 (in FL).

Debco Electronics, 4025 Edwards Rd., Cincinnati, OH 45209: Free information ❖ Components and tools. 800-423-4499.

Derf Electronics, 1 Biehn St., New Rochelle, NY 10801: Free information ❖ Surplus electronic components. 800-431-2912.

Digi-Key Corporation, 701 Brooks Ave. South, P.O. Box 677, Thief River Falls, MN 56701: Free catalog ❖ Electronic components. 800-344-4539.

The Electronic Goldmine, P.O. Box 5408, Scottsdale, AZ 85261: Free catalog ❖ Electronic components. 602-451-7454.

Fair Radio Sales Company Inc., P.O. Box 1105, Lima, OH 45802: Free information ❖ Surplus electronic parts. 419-227-6573.

Gateway Products Corporation, P.O. Box 93-6397, Margate, FL 33093: Free information ❖ Electronic components. 305-974-6864.

H & R Company, P.O. Box 122, Bristol, PA 19007: Free catalog ❖ Electronic components, tools, computer equipment, power supplies, test equipment, and meters. 800-848-8001.

Halted Electronic Supply, 3500 Ryder St., Santa Clara, CA 95051: Catalog $1 ❖ Electronic equipment. 800-442-5833.

Haltek Electronics, 1062 Linda Vista Ave., Mountain View, CA 94043: Free information ❖ New, used, and surplus electronic equipment. 408-744-1333.

Hosfelt Electronics Inc., 2700 Sunset Blvd., Steubenville, OH 43952: Free catalog ❖ Electronic components. 800-524-6464; 614-264-6464 (in OH).

International Microelectronics, P.O. Box 170415, Arlington, TX 76003: Free catalog ❖ Overstocked, surplus, and discontinued electronic components. 800-999-0463.

Jan Crystals, P.O. Box 60017, Fort Myers, FL 33906: Free catalog ❖ Crystals for radio operation and experimenters. 800-JAN-XTAL; 813-936-2397 (in FL).

Javanco, 501 12th Ave. South, Nashville, TN 37203: Free catalog ❖ Electronic components. 615-244-4444.

JDR Microdevices, 1850 S. 10th St., San Jose, CA 95112: Free information ❖ Electronic components, micro-devices, tools, chips, and computer equipment. 800-538-5000.

Marlin P. Jones & Associates, P.O. Box 12685, Lake Park, FL 33403: Free catalog ❖ Electrical and electronic components. 407-848-8236.

Joseph Electronics, 8830 N. Milwaukee Ave., Niles, IL 60648: Free catalog ❖ Electronic components, test instruments, tools, and soldering equipment. 800-323-5925; 708-297-4200 (in IL).

K & F Electronics Inc., 33041 Groesbeck, Fraser, MI 48026: Free information ❖ Printed circuit boards. 810-294-8720.

K & K Electronics, 170 E. Market St., Alliance, OH 44601: Free information ❖ Printed circuit boards. 800-356-6238.

Kelvin Electronics, 10 Hub Dr., Melville, NY 11747: Free information ❖ Electronic components and test equipment. 800-645-9212; 516-756-1750 (in NY).

MAJ Enterprises Inc., P.O. Box 494, Mississippi State, MS 39762: Free catalog ❖ Equipment for electronic experimenters and amateur radio operators. 800-647-1800.

MCM Electronics, 650 E. Congress Park Dr., Centerville, OH 45459: Free catalog ❖ Test equipment, computer and telephone accessories, TV and electronic components, and speakers. 800-824-TECH.

MECI, 340 E. 1st St., Dayton, OH 45404: Free catalog ❖ Electronic components.

Mendelson Electronics Company Inc., 340 E. 1st St., Dayton, OH 45402: Free catalog ❖ Electronic components. 800-422-3525; 513-461-3525 (in OH).

Mouser Electronics, P.O. Box 699, Mansfield, TX 76063: Free catalog ❖ Electronic components. 800-992-9943.

New England Circuit Sales, 24 Technology Dr., Peabody, MA 01960: Free information ❖ Surplus electronic components. 800-922-NECS.

Ocean State Electronics, P.O. Box 1458, 6 Industrial Dr., Westerly, RI 02891: Free catalog ❖ Electronic components, kits, test equipment, and books. 800-866-6626.

Parts Express, 340 E. 1st St., Dayton, OH 45042: Free catalog ❖ Parts for electronic projects, repair, experimentation, and research. 800-338-0531; 513-222-0173 (in OH).

PCBoards, 2110 14th Ave. South, Birmingham, AL 35205: Free information ❖ Printed circuit design software and supplies. 800-473-7227; 205-933-1122 (in AL).

PolyPhaser Corporation, P.O. Box 9000, 2225 Park Pl., Minden, NV 89423: Free information ❖ Grounding and lightning protection equipment. 800-325-7170; 702-782-2511 (in NV).

Prime Electronic Components Inc., 150 W. Industry Ct., Deer Park, NY 11729: Free information ❖ Electronic components. 516-254-0101.

❖ ELECTRONICS EQUIPMENT ❖

R.A. Enterprises, 2260 De La Cruz Blvd., Santa Clara, CA 95050: Free information ❖ Surplus and new test equipment, electrical-mechanical devices, and other electronics. 408-986-8286.

Radio Shack, Division Tandy Corporation, One Tandy Center, Fort Worth, TX 76102: Free information ❖ Electronic components, science kits, computers, stereo equipment, and toys and games. 817-390-3011.

RF Parts, 435 S. Pacific St., San Marcos, CA 92069: Free information ❖ Power transistors and parts for amateur, marine, and commercial radio operation. 619-744-0900.

Scanner World USA, 10 New Scotland Ave., Albany, NY 12208: Free information ❖ Scanners. 518-436-9606.

Sescom Inc., 2100 Ward Dr., Henderson, NV 89015: Free information ❖ Sheet metal boxes for electronics construction. 702-565-3400.

3M Electronic Specialty Products, Attention: Electronics Dept., 6801 River Place Blvd., Austin, TX 78769: Free information ❖ Solder-less breadboards. 800-328-0411.

Tucker Electronics, 1717 Reserve St., Garland, TX 75042: Free information ❖ Surplus electronic equipment. 800-527-4642; 214-348-8800 (in TX).

Unicorn Electronics, 1142 State Rt. 18, Aliquippa, PA 15001: Free information ❖ Electronic components, tools and vises, soldering products, batteries, robotic kits, and fiber optics training aids. 412-495-1230.

Visitect Inc., P.O. Box 14156, Fremont, CA 94539: Free information ❖ Miniature transmitters and receivers. 510-651-1425.

Kits & Plans

Agrelo Engineering, 1145 Catalyn St., Schenectady, NY 12303: Free information ❖ Electronic kits. 800-588-4300.

Amazing Concepts, Box 716, Amherst, NH 03031: Catalog $1 ❖ Easy-to-assemble sub-miniature FM transmitters for voice transmission over telephones. 603-673-4730.

Black Feather Electronics, 645 Temple, Long Beach, CA 90814: Free information ❖ Electronic kits. 800-526-3717; 310-434-5641 (in CA).

Cal West Supply Inc., 31320 Via Colinas, #105, Westlake Village, CA 91362: Free information ❖ Electronic kits. 800-892-8000.

Consumertronics, 2011 Crescent Dr., P.O. Drawer 537, Alamogordo, NM 88310: Catalog $2 ❖ Electronic kits and parts. 505-439-1776.

DC Electronics, P.O. Box 3203, Scottsdale, AZ 85271: Free information ❖ Electronic kits. 800-423-0070.

Edlie Electronics, 2700 Hempstead Tnpk., Levittown, NY 11756: Free catalog ❖ Electronic kits, parts, and test equipment. 516-735-3330.

The Electronic Goldmine, P.O. Box 5408, Scottsdale, AZ 85261: Free catalog ❖ Easy-to-assemble kits. 602-451-7454.

Electronic Rainbow, 6254 LaPas Trail, Indianapolis, IN 46268: Free information ❖ Easy-to-assemble kits. 317-291-7262.

EUR-AM Electronics, P.O. Box 990, Meredith, NH 03253: Free catalog ❖ Amateur radio equipment and electronic kits. 603-279-1394.

Graymark, P.O. Box 2015, Tustin, CA 92681: Free catalog ❖ Easy-to-build robotic kits. 800-854-7393.

Heathkit Educational Systems, P.O. Box 1288, Benton Harbor, MI 49023: Free catalog ❖ Electronic kits. 800-253-0570.

Information Unlimited, P.O. Box 716, Amherst, NH 03031: Catalog $1 ❖ Lasers, communication equipment, Tesla coils and experiments, mini radios, rocket equipment, flying saucers, and other kits. 603-673-4730.

LNS Technologies, 20993 Foothill Blvd., Ste. 307, Hayward, CA 94541: Catalog $1 ❖ Fun and educational electronic kits for teachers, students, and hobbyists. 800-886-7150.

Mark V Electronics Inc., 8019 E. Slauson Ave., Montebello, CA 90640: Free catalog ❖ Electronic kits for beginning, intermediate, and advanced experimenters. 213-888-8988.

MD Electronics, 875 S. 72nd St., Omaha, NE 68114: Free catalog ❖ Cable TV equipment kits. 800-624-1150.

Meredith Instruments, P.O. Box 1724, Glendale, AZ 85301: Free catalog ❖ Lasers and optical equipment, parts, and accessories. 602-934-9387.

Micro Kits, 177 Telegraph Rd., Ste. 680, Bellingham, WA 98226: Free information ❖ Educational kits. 800-474-7644.

Midwest Laser Products, P.O. Box 2187, Bridgeview, IL 60455: Free catalog ❖ Laser equipment. 708-460-9595.

Mondo-tronics, 524 San Anselmo Ave., San Anselmo, CA 94960: Free brochure ❖ Miniature robotics kits. 800-374-5764.

MWK Industries, 1269 W. Pomona Rd., Building 112, Corona, CA 91720: Free catalog ❖ Laser equipment, power supplies, optics and light shows, and books. 800-356-7714.

Ocean State Electronics, P.O. Box 1458, 6 Industrial Dr., Westerly, RI 02891: Free catalog ❖ Electronic components, kits, test equipment, and books. 800-866-6626.

Radio Adventures Inc., Main St., Seneca, PA 16346: Free information ❖ High-frequency receiver, transmitter kit, and test equipment kits. Also classic radio accessories. 814-677-7221.

Radio Shack, Division Tandy Corporation, One Tandy Center, Fort Worth, TX 76102: Free information ❖ Electronic components, science kits, computers, stereo equipment, and toys and games. 817-390-3011.

Ramsey Electronics Inc., 793 Canning Pkwy., Victor, NY 14564: Free information ❖ Test equipment and easy-to-assemble electronic kits. 716-924-4560.

Silicon Valley Surplus, 1273 Industrial Pkwy., Ste. 460, P.O. Box 55125, Hayward, CA 94544: Free information ❖ Light and motion projects, laser applications, computer interface equipment, and other kits. 510-582-6602.

Unicorn Electronics, 1142 State Rt. 18, Aliquippa, PA 15001: Free information ❖ Electronic components, tools and vises, soldering products, batteries, robotic kits, and fiber optics training aids. 412-495-1230.

Weeder Technologies, P.O. Box 421, Batavia, OH 45103: Free information ❖ Educational kits for electronic hobbyists. 513-752-0279.

Xandi Electronics, 1270 E. Broadway, Tempe, AZ 85282: Free catalog ❖ Satellite TV receiver, voice disguise, FM bug, telephone transmitter, phone snoop, and other easy-to-build kits. 800-336-7389.

Zagros Software, P.O. Box 460342, St. Louis, MO 63146: Free information ❖ Home robotic and artificial intelligence kits. 314-768-1328.

Test Equipment

Advantage Instruments Corporation, 3579 Hwy 50 East, Carson City, NV 89701: Free catalog ❖ Test equipment. 702-885-0234.

Ala Electronics, 741 Alexander Rd., Princeton, NJ 08540: Free catalog ❖ Multi-purpose test equipment. 800-526-2532; 609-520-2002 (in NJ).

Wm. B. Allen Supply Company, 301-99 N. Rampart St., New Orleans, LA 70112: Free information ❖ Multi-purpose test equipment, replacement probes, and electronic components. 800-535-9593.

Alltronics, 2300 Zanker Rd., San Jose, CA 95131: Free catalog ❖ Test equipment and electronic components. 408-943-9773.

Amprobe Test Equipment, Box 329, Lynbrook, NY 11563: Free list of retail sources ❖ Multi-meters, volt-amp-ohmmeters, and other test equipment. 516-593-5600.

❖ ELECTROPLATING ❖

AT&T Capital Corporation, 1830 W. Airfield Dr., P.O. Box 619260, DFW Airport, TX 75261: Free information ❖ Test and measuring instruments. 800-874-7123.

B.C. Electronics, 20 Highpoint, Dove Canyon, CA 92630: Free catalog ❖ Test equipment. 800-532-3221.

C & H Sales Company, 2176 E. Colorado Blvd., Pasadena, CA 91107: Free catalog ❖ Test equipment. 800-325-9465.

C & S Sales Inc., 150 W. Carpenter Ave., Wheeling, IL 60090: Free catalog ❖ Test equipment. 800-292-7711; 708-541-0710 (in IL).

Contact East, 335 Willow St. South, North Andover, MA 01845: Free catalog ❖ Tools for testing, repairing, and assembling electronic equipment. 800-225-5370; 508-682-2000 (in MA).

Danbar Sales Company, 14455 N. 79th St., Scottsdale, AZ 85260: Free catalog ❖ Test equipment. 602-483-6202.

Davilyn Corporation, 13406 Saticoy St., North Hollywood, CA 91605: Free information ❖ Multi-purpose test equipment. 800-235-6222; 818-787-3334 (in CA).

Electro Tool Inc., 9103 Gillman, Livonia, MI 48150: Free information ❖ Tools and electronic test equipment. 313-422-1221.

Fotronic Corporation, P.O. Box 708, Medford, MA 02155: Free information ❖ New and pre-owned test equipment. 800-996-3837.

Global Specialties, 70 Fulton Terrace, New Haven, CT 06512: Free information ❖ Compact multi-meters that measure AC and DC voltage, current, resistance, and check diodes and continuity. 800-572-1028.

GoldStar Precision, 13013 E. 166th St., Cerritos, CA 90701: Free information ❖ Test equipment. 310-404-0101.

Instek, 741 Alexander Rd., Princeton, NJ 08540: Free catalog ❖ Test and measuring equipment. 800-526-2532; 609-520-2002 (in NJ).

JDR Microdevices, 1850 S. 10th St., San Jose, CA 95112: Free information ❖ Multi-purpose test equipment. 800-538-5000.

Joseph Electronics, 8830 N. Milwaukee Ave., Niles, IL 60648: Free catalog ❖ Multi-purpose test equipment. 800-323-5925; 708-297-4200 (in IL).

Kelvin Electronics, 10 Hub Dr., Melville, NY 11747: Free information ❖ Electronic components and test equipment. 800-645-9212; 516-756-1750 (in NY).

MCM Electronics, 650 E. Congress Park Dr., Centerville, OH 45459: Free catalog ❖ Test equipment, computer and telephone accessories, speakers, and parts. 800-824-TECH.

Metric Equipment Sales Inc., 351A Foster City Blvd., Foster City, CA 94401: Free information ❖ Refurbished test and measuring equipment. 800-432-3424.

Ocean State Electronics, P.O. Box 1458, 6 Industrial Dr., Westerly, RI 02891: Free catalog ❖ Electronic components, kits, test equipment, and books. 800-866-6626.

R & S Surplus, 1050 E. Cypress St., Covina, CA 91724: Free information ❖ Surplus test equipment. 818-967-0846.

Tech-Systems, 1309 Why. 71, Belmar, NJ 07719: Free information ❖ Used electronic test equipment. 800-435-1516.

Techni-Tool, 5 Apollo Rd., P.O. Box 368, Plymouth Meeting, PA 19462: Free catalog ❖ Hand tools, production aids, test instruments, and accessories. 610-941-2400.

Toronto Surplus & Scientific, 608 Gordon Baker Rd., Willowdale, Ontario, Canada M2H 3B4: Free information ❖ Test equipment, experimental accessories, and electronics. 416-490-8865.

Westcon Inc., 5101 N. Interstate Ave., Portland, OR 97217: Free catalog ❖ Test probes. 800-547-4515.

Western Test Systems, 530 Compton St., Unit C, Broomfield, CO 80020: Free information ❖ New and used test equipment. 303-438-9662.

Tools & Accessories

Electro Tool Inc., 9103 Gillman, Livonia, MI 48150: Free information ❖ Tools and electronic test equipment. 313-422-1221.

W.S. Jenks & Son, 1933 Montana Ave. NE, Washington, DC 20002: Free catalog ❖ Hand and power tools for electronics. 202-529-6020.

Jensen Tools Inc., 7815 S. 46th St., Phoenix, AZ 85044: Free catalog ❖ Precision tools for electronics. 800-426-1194; 602-968-6231 (in AZ).

Joseph Electronics, 8830 N. Milwaukee Ave., Niles, IL 60648: Free catalog ❖ Electronic components, test instruments, tools, and soldering equipment. 800-323-5925; 708-297-4200 (in IL).

Techni-Tool, 5 Apollo Rd., P.O. Box 368, Plymouth Meeting, PA 19462: Free catalog ❖ Hand tools, production aids, test instruments, and accessories. 610-941-2400.

ELECTROPLATING

American Bronzing Company, 1313 Alum Creek Dr., Columbus, OH 43209: Free information ❖ Bronzing and two-tone antique finish for baby's shoes. 614-252-0967.

Caswell Electroplating in Miniature, 4336 Rt. 31, Palmyra, NY 14522: Free information ❖ Electroplating kits for nickel, chrome, and copper. 315-597-5140.

Edmund Scientific Company, Edscorp Building, Barrington, NJ 08007: Free catalog ❖ Electroplating kits. 609-573-6260.

EFS Company, P.O. Box 770344, Ocala, FL 34477: Free information ❖ Starter kits, rectifiers, electroplating and electrical-forming accessories, and plating solutions. 904-873-0089.

Estes-Simmons Silverplating Ltd., 1050 Northside Dr. NW, Atlanta, GA 30318: Free brochure ❖ Silver repair and plating. 800-645-4193.

New England International Gems, 188 Pollard St., Billerica, MA 01862: Free catalog ❖ Casting and plating equipment. 508-667-7394. (978)

Plating Service, N3503 Hwy. 55, Chilton, WI 53014: Free information with long SASE ❖ Electroplating services. 414-989-1901.

Strassen Plating Company, 3619 Walton Ave., Cleveland, OH 44113: Free information ❖ Metal polishing and brass, nickel, and chrome plating. 216-961-1525.

Texas Platers Supply, 2453 W. Five Mile Pkwy., Dallas, TX 75233: Free information ❖ Electroplating kits. 214-330-7168.

University Publishing, P.O. Box 1071, Provo, UT 84602: Free catalog ❖ Books, videos, kits, and chemicals for gold, silver, chrome, copper, and nickel plating. 801-377-5367.

ENGRAVING & ETCHING

Alpha Supply, P.O. Box 2133, Bremerton, WA 98310: Catalog $7 ❖ Engraving and jewelry-making tools and supplies, and casting, faceting, and lapidary equipment. 800-257-4211.

B. Rush Apple Company, 3855 W. Kennedy Blvd., Tampa, FL 33609: Free price list ❖ Engraving tools. 813-870-3180.

B & B Etching Products Inc., 18700 N. 107th Ave., Sun City, AZ 85373: Free catalog ❖ Etching creme and supplies for glass and mirrors. 602-933-2962.

Brownells Inc., 200 S. Front St., Montezuma, IA 50171: Free catalog ❖ Engraving tools. 515-623-5401.

Eastern Art Glass, P.O. Box 341, Wyckoff, NJ 07481: Catalog $2 (refundable) ❖ Stained glass kits and glass etching, engraving, and crafting supplies. 201-847-0001.

Gamblin, P.O. Box 625, Portland, OR 97207: Free list of retail sources ❖ Oil paints, oil painting mediums, and etching inks. 503-228-9763.

Graphic Chemical & Ink Company, P.O. Box 27, Villa Park, IL 60181: Free catalog ❖ Print-making supplies for etching, block prints, lithography, and other reproduction processes. 708-832-6004.

GRS Tools, 900 Overlander Rd., P.O. Box 1153, Emporia, KS 66801: Free catalog ❖ Engraving tools. 800-835-3519.

Hand Engravers Supply Company, 601 Springfield Dr., Albany, GA 31707: Free catalog ❖ Engraving tools. 912-432-9683.

Indian Jewelers Supply Company, P.O. Box 1774, Gallup, NM 87305: Catalog $6 ❖ Precious and base metals, findings, metal-working equipment, lapidary and engraving tools and supplies, semiprecious stones, shells, and coral. 505-722-4451.

Ken Jantz Supply, P.O. Box 584, Davis, OK 73030: Catalog $4 ❖ Engraving tools. 405-369-2316.

Neycraft, Division of Ney, Ney Industrial Park, Bloomfield, CT 06002: Free information ❖ Engraving tools. 800-538-4593.

Technical Papers Corporation, P.O. Box 546, Dedham, MA 02027: Free catalog ❖ Sheets and rolls of handmade rice paper in prints and solid and multi-colors for all types of artistic printing. Includes block printing, etching, lithography, and silk screening. 617-461-1111.

EXERCISE EQUIPMENT

Ajay Leisure Products Inc., 1501 E. Wisconsin St., Delavan, WI 53115: Free list of retail sources ❖ Monitoring aids and weight training, body building, and exercise equipment. 800-558-3276; 414-728-5521 (in WI).

All Pro Exercise Products, 135 Hazelwood Dr., Jericho, NY 11753: Free list of retail sources ❖ Home exercise equipment. 800-735-9287; 516-938-9287 (in NY).

American Athletic Inc., 200 American Ave., Jefferson, IA 50129: Free information ❖ Monitoring aids, home gymnasiums, and weight training, body building, and exercise equipment. 800-247-3978; 515-386-3125 (in IA).

American Sports Inc., P.O. Box 36662, Los Angeles, CA 90036: Free list of retail sources ❖ Home exercise equipment. 800-922-8939.

Austin Athletic Equipment Corporation, 705 Bedford Ave., Box 423, Bellmore, NY 11710: Free information ❖ Monitoring aids, home gymnasiums, and weight training, body building, and exercise equipment. 516-785-0100.

Better Health Fitness, 5302 New Utrecht Ave., Brooklyn, NY 11219: Free information with long SASE ❖ Home gymnasium, exercise and weight lifting equipment, and other body building systems. 718-436-4801.

BioTech Corporation, P.O. Box 949, Rocky Hill, CT 06067: Free information ❖ Home fitness equipment. 800-774-3664.

Body Masters Sports Industries Inc., Box 259, Rayne, LA 70578: Free information ❖ Home exercise equipment. 800-325-8964; 318-334-9611 (in LA).

Bollinger Fitness Products, 222 W. Airport Freeway, Irving, TX 75062: Free information ❖ Home gymnasiums, trampolines, monitoring aids, and weight training, body building, and exercise equipment. 800-527-1166; 214-445-0386 (in TX).

California Gym Equipment Company, 14829 Salt Lake Ave., City of Industry, CA 91748: Free list of retail sources ❖ Home gymnasiums, monitoring aids, and weight training, body building, and exercise equipment. 800-824-5210; 818-961-6564 (in CA).

Cannon Sports, P.O. Box 797, Greenland, NH 03840: Free list of retail sources ❖ Monitoring aids, home gymnasiums, trampolines, and weight lifting and exercise equipment. 800-362-3146.

Concept II Inc., RR 1, Box 1100, Morrisville, VT 05661: Free list of retail sources ❖ Total body exercise machine. 800-245-5676.

Creative Health Products Inc., 1000 Saddle Ridge Rd., Plymouth, MI 48170: Free catalog ❖ Exercise bicycles, rowing machines, stethoscopes, thermometers, digital blood pressure units, scales, lung capacity testers, and pulse monitors. 800-742-4478.

Dynamic Classics Ltd., 58 2nd Ave., Brooklyn, NY 11215: Free information ❖ Gymnastic bars, home gymnasiums, and weight training, body building, and exercise equipment. 718-369-4160.

Escalade Sports, P.O. Box 889, Evansville, IN 47706: Free catalog ❖ Home fitness equipment. 800-457-3373; 812-467-1200 (in IN).

EverHealth Inc., 1276 S. 500 West, Salt Lake City, UT 84101: Free information ❖ Total body fitness machine. 800-806-3615.

Everlast Sports Manufacturing Corporation, 750 E. 132nd St., Bronx, NY 10454: Free information ❖ Home exercise equipment. 800-221-8777; 718-993-0100 (in NY).

Fitness Master Inc., 504 Industrial Blvd., Waconia, MN 55387: Free list of retail sources ❖ Cardiovascular fitness and body tone exerciser. 800-328-8995.

Fitness To Go Inc., 4251 NE Port Dr., Lee Summit, MO 64064: Free information ❖ Motorized and mechanical isokinetic treadmills. 800-821-3126.

Flaghouse, 150 N. MacQuesten Pkwy., Mt. Vernon, NY 10550: Free catalog ❖ Physical fitness and gymnastic equipment. Also equipment for camping, playgrounds, and other outdoor activities. 800-793-7900.

GameTime, P.O. Box 121, Fort Payne, AL 35967: Free information ❖ Playground and backyard play systems and outdoor fitness equipment. 800-235-2440.

Gold's Gym, 360 Hampton Dr., Venice, CA 90291: Free information ❖ Home exercise equipment. 800-457-5375; 213-392-3005 (in CA).

Gravity Plus, P.O. Box 2182, La Jolla, CA 92038: Free brochure ❖ Inversion therapy exercise equipment. 800-383-8056.

HealthMax, 47 Richards Ave., Norwalk, CT 06857: Free list of retail sources ❖ Total body fitness systems. 800-458-4652.

Heart-Rate Inc., 3188 Airway Ave., Ste. E, Costa Mesa, CA 92626: Free brochure ❖ Total body aerobic exercise machine. 800-237-2271.

Hoist Fitness Systems, 9990 Empire St., Ste. 130, San Diego, CA 92126: Free list of retail sources ❖ Home exercise equipment. 800-548-5438; 619-578-7676 (in CA).

Holabird Sports Discounters, 9220 Pulaski Hwy., Baltimore, MD 21220: Free catalog ❖ Exercise equipment and clothing for basketball, tennis, running and jogging, golf, racquetball, and other sports. 410-687-6400.

Icon Health & Fitness Inc., P.O. Box 313, Logan, UT 84323: Free brochure ❖ Total body low-impact exercise machine with display that shows speed, time, distance, and calories burned. 800-727-9777.

IMC Products Corporation, 100A Tec St., Hicksville, NY 11801: Free list of retail sources ❖ Gripmaster system that exercises each finger individually. 800-752-0164.

Ivanko Barbell Company, P.O. Box 1470, San Pedro, CA 90731: Free list of retail sources ❖ Weight lifting equipment. 800-247-9044; 310-514-1155 (in CA).

Jayfro Corporation, Unified Sports Inc., 976 Hartford Tnpk., P.O. Box 400, Waterford, CT 06385: Free catalog ❖ Wall-mounted gyms and physical fitness and exercise equipment. 860-447-3001.

M.W. Kasch Company, 5401 W. Donges Bay Rd., Mequon, WI 53092: Free information ❖ Home gymnasiums and weight training, body building, and exercise equipment. 414-242-5000.

LifeFitness Inc., 10601 W. Belmont Ave., Franklin Park, IL 60131: Free list of retail sources ❖ Home fitness equipment. 800-877-3867.

Lifegear Inc., 300 Round Hill Dr., Rockaway, NJ 07876: Free brochure ❖ Home exercise equipment. 800-882-1113; 201-627-3065 (in NJ).

Mongoose Bicycles, 3400 Kashiwa St., Torrance, CA 90505: Free information ❖ Lightweight fitness bicycles. 310-539-8860.

Nautilus Direct, One Nautilus Way, Huntersville, NC 28078: Free information ❖ Multi-station gym and exercise machines. 800-628-8458.

New York Barbell, P.O. Box 3473, Elmira, NY 14905: Free information ❖ Home gymnasium and exercise equipment. 800-446-1833; 607-733-8038 (in NY).

FABRIC PAINTING, DYEING & OTHER DECORATING

NordicTrack, 104 Peavey Rd., Chaska, MN 55318: Free brochure ❖ Total body exercisers and other equipment. 800-441-7512.

Olympia Sports, 745 State Circle, Ann Arbor, MI 48106: Free information ❖ Home exercise equipment. 313-761-5135.

PCA Industries Inc., 5642 Natural Bridge, St. Louis, MO 63120: Free information ❖ Gymnastic bars and floor equipment. 800-727-8180.

J.C. Penney Company Inc., Catalog Division, Atlanta, GA 30390: Free information ❖ Atlanta, GA 30390: Free information ❖ Athletic clothing and equipment. 800-222-6161.

Precor USA, P.O. Box 3004, Bothell, WA 98041: Free list of retail sources ❖ Off-snow cross-country skier exercise machine. 800-477-3267.

Pro-Form, Icon Health & Fitness Inc., P.O. Box 313, Logan, UT 84323: Free brochure ❖ Walking exerciser with easy-to-read motivational electrics for constant feedback. 800-514-4554.

Professional Gym Inc., P.O. Box 188, Marshall, MO 65340: Free brochure ❖ Weight training, body building, and exercise equipment. 800-821-7665.

Racing Strollers Inc., P.O. Box 2189, Yakima, WA 98902: Free brochure ❖ Baby Joggers for exercise fun. 800-241-1848.

Ross Bicycles USA, 51 Executive Blvd., Farmingdale, NY 11735: Free information ❖ Home exercise equipment. 800-338-7677; 516-249-6000 (in NY).

Sharper Image SPA, 650 Davis St., San Francisco, CA 94120: Free catalog ❖ Aerobic non-impact fitness machines, treadmills, massagers, and other equipment. 800-344-3440.

Spalding Sports Worldwide, 425 Meadow St., P.O. Box 901, Chicopee, MA 01021: Free list of retail sources ❖ Home gymnasiums, trampolines, monitoring aids, and weight training, body building, and exercise equipment. 800-225-6601.

StairMaster Sports/Medical Products Inc., 12421 Willows Rd. NE, Ste. 100, Kirkland, WA 98034: Free information ❖ Exercise equipment. 800-666-9336.

SuperLife, Zygon International, 18368 Redmond Way, Redmond, WA 98052: Free catalog ❖ Physical fitness and exercise equipment. 800-526-2177.

T & M Enterprises Inc., Box 1527, Council Bluffs, IA 51502: Free information ❖ Portable (fits in a 16-inch carrying case) full-body workout equipment. 800-643-1966.

Trimax, 20 S. Main St., Janesville, WI 53545: Free brochure ❖ Fitness and exercise machine. 800-866-5676.

True Fitness Technology Inc., 865 Hoff Rd., O'Fallon, MO 63366: Free list of retail sources ❖ Home fitness equipment. 314-272-7100.

Universal Gym Equipment, P.O. Box 1270, Cedar Rapids, IA 52406: Free catalog ❖ Weight and exercise equipment, treadmills, computerized aerobic and exercise machines, and gymnastic bars. 800-553-3906; 319-365-7561 (in IA).

Vectra Fitness Inc., 15135 NE 90th St., Edmond, WA 98052: Free list of retail sources ❖ Home gymnasium equipment. 800-2-VECTRA; 206-867-1500 (in WA).

WaterRower Inc., 453 Cottage St., Pawtucket, RI 02861: Free list of retail sources ❖ Water resistance-operated exercise rowing machine. 401-728-1966.

FABRIC PAINTING, DYEING & OTHER DECORATING

Aljo Dyes, 81 Franklin St., New York, NY 10013: Free catalog ❖ Fabric dyes. 212-226-2878.

The Art Store, 935 Erie Blvd. East, Syracuse, NY 13210: Price list $3 ❖ Fabric dyeing, screen-printing, marbling, and other craft supplies. 800-669-2787.

Atelier De Paris, 1543 S. Robertson Blvd., Los Angeles, CA 90035: Free information ❖ Silk painting and fabric decorating supplies. 310-553-6636.

Badger Air-Brush Company, 9128 W. Belmont Ave., Franklin Park, IL 60131: Brochure $1 ❖ Airbrushes and fabric paints. 800-247-2787.

Blueprint-Printables, 1504 Industrial Way, Belmont, CA 94002: Catalog $3 ❖ Fabrics, T-shirts, and blueprinting kits. 800-356-0445.

Createx Colors, 14 Airport Park Rd., East Granby, CT 06026: Free information ❖ Fabric dyes. 800-243-2712.

Decart Inc., P.O. Box 309, Morrisville, VT 05661: Free list of retail sources ❖ Permanent machine-washable and dry-cleanable fabric paints. Also airbrushing paints and water-based enamels. 802-888-4217.

DecoArt, P.O. Box 370, Stanford, KY 40484: Information $1 with long SASE ❖ Easy-to-apply acrylics for fabric decorating.

Dharma Trading Company, P.O. Box 150916, San Rafael, CA 94902: Free catalog ❖ Dyes and fabric paints. 800-542-5227.

Duncan Enterprises, 5673 E. Shields Ave., Fresno, CA 93727: Free list of retail sources ❖ Easy-to-apply iron-on-patterns, foil transfers, and glitter. 800-438-6226; 209-291-4444 (in CA).

Eastern Art Glass, P.O. Box 341, Wyckoff, NJ 07481: Catalog $2 (refundable) ❖ Fabric painting kits and supplies. 201-847-0001.

Gramma's Graphics Inc., 20 Birling Gap, Fairport, NY 14450: Information $1 with long SASE ❖ Sun-printing kits for fabrics and paper. 716-223-4309.

Ivy Crafts Imports, 12213 Distribution Way, Beltsville, MD 20705: Catalog $3.95 ❖ Fabric paints, resists, and applicators. 301-595-0550.

Nasco, 901 Janesville Ave., Fort Atkinson, WI 53538: Free catalog ❖ Fabric and silk painting supplies and textile dyes. 800-558-9595.

Photographers Formulary, P.O. Box 950, Condon, MT 59826: Free catalog ❖ Supplies for blueprinting on fabric. 800-922-5255.

PRO Chemical & Dye Inc., P.O. Box 14, Somerset, MA 02726: Free information ❖ Fabric dyes. 508-676-3838.

Qualin International, P.O. Box 31145, San Francisco, CA 94131: Free catalog with long SASE and two 1st class stamps ❖ Silk fabrics, scarf blanks, and silk painting supplies. 415-647-1329.

Rupert, Gibbon & Spider Inc., P.O. Box 425, Healdsburg, CA 95448: Free catalog ❖ Textile dyes and paints, brushes, resists, and silk and cotton fabrics for printing and dyeing. 800-442-0455.

Silkpaint Corporation, P.O. Box 18, Waldron, MO 64092: Free information ❖ Fabric dyes. 816-891-7774.

Soho South, P.O. Box 1324, Cullman, AL 35056: Catalog $2.50 (refundable) ❖ Beads and findings, fabric dyes and paints, silk scarves and fabrics, and marbling supplies. 205-739-6114.

Texicolor Corporation, Eric Hoyer, 444 Castro St., Ste. 425, Mountain View, CA 94041: Free information ❖ Water-based textile screen-printing inks and fabric paints. 415-968-8183.

FABRICS & TRIM

Fabrics

ABC Decorative Fabrics, 2410 298th Ave. North, Clearwater, FL 34621: Free information ❖ Decorator fabrics. 800-500-9022.

AK Sew & Serge, 1602 6th St. SE, Winter Haven FL 33880: Catalog $5 ❖ Designer and other fabrics, smocking, Battenberg lace, and sewing notions. 800-299-8096; 813-299-3080 (in FL).

Alexandra's Homespun Textile & Seraph Textile Collection, P.O. Box 500, Sturbridge, MA 01566: Catalog $2 ❖ Hand-woven homespun and reproduction museum fabrics for household furnishings and upholstery. 508-347-2241.

Aurora Silk, 5806 N. Vancouver Ave., Portland, OR 97217: Brochure and color chart $15 ❖ Naturally dyed silk fabrics. 503-286-4149.

FABRICS & TRIM

Baltazor's, 3262 Severen Ave., Metairie, LA 70002: Catalog $3 ❖ Lace and lace-making supplies, fabrics, smocking, and bridal fashion-making supplies. 800-532-5223.

Barbeau Fine Fabrics, 1308 Birch St., Fort Collins, CO 80521: Information $12 ❖ Silks, wools, cottons, and other fabrics. 800-766-5588; 303-221-9697 (in CO).

Philips Boyne Corporation, 1646 New Hwy., Farmingdale, NY 11735: Information $3 ❖ Imported and domestic cotton fabrics. 800-292-2830.

Bridal By The Yard, P.O. Box 2492, Springfield, OH 45501: Free information ❖ Re-embroidered Alencon, Schiffli lace, imported Chantilly and Venice lace, satins, taffeta, and organza. Also millinery supplies, trim, and notions. 513-325-2847.

Bridals International, 45 Albany St., Cazenovia, NY 13035: Catalog $9.50 ❖ Imported fabrics and lace for bridal fashions. 800-752-1171.

Calico House, Rt. 4, Box 16, Scottsville, VA 24590: Catalog $6 ❖ French and English lace, Swiss eyelets, and embroideries.

California Bridal Fabrics, Hyman Hendler & Sons Inc., 729 E. Temple St., Los Angeles, CA 90012: Catalog $10 ❖ Satin, taffeta, lace, and metallic fabrics. 800-421-8963; 213-626-5123 (in CA).

Carolina Mills Factory Outlet, Hwy. 76 West, Box V, Branson, MO 65615: Free brochure ❖ Designer fabrics. 417-334-2291.

Cherrywood Fabrics Inc., P.O. Box 486, Brainerd, MN 56401: Information $7 ❖ Solid color gradations and suede-look cotton fabrics. 218-829-0967.

Classic Cloth, 34930 US 19 North, Fountain Shopping Center, Palm Harbor, FL 34684: Swatches $5 ❖ Cotton fabrics. 800-237-7739; 813-785-6593 (in FL).

Clearbrook Woolen Shop, P.O. Box 8, Clearbrook, VA 22624: Free information with long SASE ❖ Wool fabrics. 703-662-3442.

Cotton Express, P.O. Box 221, Apex, NC 27502: Information $4 ❖ Jersey, interlock, cotton mesh, and 100 percent cotton fabrics. 919-387-1650.

The Cotton Shoppe of Key Largo, P.O. Box 3168, Key Largo, FL 33037: Sample swatches $7 ❖ Quilting fabrics. 305-453-0789.

D'Anton Leathers, 3079 NE Oasis Rd., West Branch, IA 52358: Catalog $1.50 with a long SASE ❖ Garment leathers and suede. 319-643-2568.

Delectable Mountain Cloth, 125 Main St., Brattleboro, VT 05301: Brochure $1 with long SASE ❖ Buttons and natural fabrics from worldwide sources.

Denham Fabrics, P.O. Box 241275, Memphis, TN 38124: Fabric portfolio $8 ❖ Polyester and cotton fabrics. 901-683-4574.

Designer Home Fabrics, P.O. Box 2560, Cinnaminson, NJ 08077: Catalog $2 (refundable) ❖ Traditional and contemporary cotton prints, chintzes, damasks, tapestries, solids, and other fabrics. 800-666-4202.

Dharma Trading Company, P.O. Box 150916, San Rafael, CA 94902: Free catalog ❖ Clothing blanks and silk, cotton, and rayon fabrics. 800-542-5227.

DK Sports, Division Daisy Kingdom, 3720 NW Yeon Ave., Portland, OR 97210: Free information ❖ Rainwear and outerwear fabrics and sewing notions. 800-234-6688.

Exotic Silks, 1959 Leghorn St., Mountain View, CA 94043: Brochure 25¢ ❖ Natural silks and scarves in white, solid colors, and patterns. 800-845-SILK; 415-965-7760 (in CA).

Exotic/Thai Silk, 252 State St., Los Altos, CA 94022: Free catalog ❖ Silk fabrics and linen/cotton and wool gabardine. 800-722-SILK; 800-221-SILK (in CA).

Fabric Center, P.O. Box 8212, Fitchburg, MA 01420: Catalog $2 ❖ Decorator fabrics. 508-343-4402.

Fabric Gallery, 146 W. Grand River, Williamson, MI 48895: Information $4 ❖ Imported and domestic silks, wools, cottons, blends, and synthetics. 517-655-4573.

The Fabric Outlet, 30 Airport Rd., West Lebanon, NH 03784: Free information ❖ Decorator fabrics. 800-635-9715.

Fabric Shop, 120 N. Seneca St., Shippensburg, PA 17257: Free information with long SASE ❖ Antique satins and drapery, slipcover, and upholstery fabrics. 800-233-7012; 717-532-4150 (in PA).

Fabrics by Phone, P.O. Box 234, Walnut Bottom, PA 17266: Brochure and samples $3 ❖ Antique satins and drapery, slipcover, and upholstery fabrics. 800-233-7012; 717-532-4150 (in PA).

Fabrics First, 600 Maryland NE, Grand Rapids, MI 49501: Catalog $2 ❖ Decorator and other fabrics. 800-627-2526.

Fabrics Unlimited, 5015 Columbia Pike, Arlington, VA 22204: Free information ❖ Fabrics from designer cutting rooms, ultrasuede, and imported silks, wools, and cottons. 703-671-0324.

Felt People, Box 135, Bloomingdale, NJ 07403: Information $2 (refundable) ❖ Wool felt. 800-631-8968; 201-838-1100 (in NJ).

Fishman's Fabrics, 1101-43 S. Desplaines St., Chicago, IL 60607: Free information ❖ Designer wool, silk, cotton, and linen fabrics. 800-648-5161.

G Street Fabrics, Mail Order Service, 12240 Wilkins Ave., Rockville, MD 20852: Free catalog ❖ Decorator, clothing, and drapery fabrics. 800-333-9191.

Green Pepper, 1285 River Rd., Eugene, OR 97404: Catalog $2 ❖ Rainwear and outerwear fabrics, spandex fabrics, sewing notions, and patterns.

Gutcheon Patchworks Inc., 917 Pacific Ave., #305, Tacoma, WA 98402: Information and fabric samples $3 ❖ Coordinating plain color fabrics and 100 percent cotton prints. 206-383-3047.

Hambrick's Fabrics, 820 Regal Dr., Huntsville, AL 35801: Information $3 ❖ Fabrics. 205-534-4704.

Hancock Fabrics, 3841 Hinkleville Rd., Paducah, KY 42001: Free information ❖ Quilting supplies, fabrics, and sewing notions. 800-845-8723.

Heirloom Creations, 431 Rena Dr., Lafayette, LA 70503: Free information ❖ Swiss and silk batiste, linen, velveteen, cotton corduroy, and lace. 318-984-8949.

Home Fabric Mills Inc., 882 S. Main St., Cheshire, CT 06410: Free brochure ❖ Velvets, upholstery and drapery fabrics, prints, sheers, antique satins, and thermal fabrics. 203-272-3529.

Homespun Fabrics & Draperies, P.O. Box 4315, Thousand Oaks, CA 91359: Catalog $2 ❖ Cotton fabrics. 800-251-0858.

Homespun Weavers, 55 S. 7th St., Emmaus, PA 18049: Brochure 50¢ ❖ Cotton fabrics. 800-290-4550; 610-967-4550 (in PA).

House of Laird, Box 246, Wilson, NC 37893: Free information ❖ Silk and blends, wool, and rayon suiting. 800-338-4618.

International Fabric Collection, 3445 W. Lake Rd., Erie, PA 16505: Catalog $3 ❖ Fabrics from Italy, India, Japan, Holland, Africa, and other worldwide sources. Also quilting and embroidery books. 800-462-3891; 814-838-0740 (in PA).

Jehlor Fantasy Fabrics, 730 Andover Park West, Seattle, WA 98188: Catalog $5 ❖ Bridal fabrics, appliques, trims, and jewelry sew-on notions. 206-575-8250.

Kieffer's Lingerie, P.O. Box 7500, Jersey City, NJ 07307: Free catalog ❖ Tricot fabric with elastic and matching lace. 201-798-2266.

Kunin Felt, P.O. Box 5000, Hampton, NH 03842: Free information ❖ Felt. 800-292-7900.

Lace Heaven, P.O. Box 50150, Mobile, AL 36605: Catalog $3 (refundable) ❖ Lingerie fabrics, ribbons and trim, stretch lace, elastic, and notions. 205-478-5644.

Landau Woolen Company Inc., 561 7th Ave., New York, NY 10018: Free information ❖ Worsted wools, merino jerseys, luxury fibers, rayons, and cottons. 800-553-2292; 212-391-8371 (in NY).

❖ FABRICS & TRIM ❖

Lauratex Fabrics Inc., 153 W. 27th St., New York, NY 10001: Free information ❖ Sateen, ottoman, batiste, canvas, polished cotton, and 100 percent cotton fabrics. 212-645-7800.

Ledgewood Studio, 6000 Ledgewood Dr., Forest Park, GA 30050: Catalog $2 with long SASE and three 1st class stamps ❖ Dress patterns for antique dolls, supplies for recreating period costumes, braids, French lace, silk ribbons and taffeta, China silk, Swiss batiste, trims, and notions. 404-361-6098.

Donna Lee's Sewing Center, 25234 Pacific Hwy. South, Kent, WA 98032: Catalog $4 ❖ Swiss and imperial batiste, China silk, silk charmeuse, French val lace, English lace, Swiss embroideries, trims and yardage, silk ribbon, ribbons, smocking, doll patterns, books, and sewing notions. 206-941-9466.

Samuel Lehrer & Company Inc., 7 Depinedo Ave., Stamford, CT 06902: Free information ❖ Wool flannels, gabardines, linen blends, pinstripes, and plaids for men and women's clothing. 800-221-2433.

Linen & Lace, 4 Lafayette, Washington, MO 63090: Catalog $2 ❖ Linen and lace fabrics. 800-332-5223.

The Linen Fabric World, 1246 Bird Rd., Miami, FL 33146: Information $5 ❖ Imported linen fabrics. 305-663-1577.

Marlene's Decorator Fabrics, 301 Beech St., Hackensack, NJ 07601: Free brochure with long SASE ❖ Decorator and upholstery fabrics. 800-992-7325.

Midwest Trade Imports, 1555 Sherman Ave., Ste. 236, Evanston, IL 60201: Information $2 ❖ Authentic hand-woven Ashanti Kente cloth stoles and fabrics from Ghana, West Africa. 800-64-KENTE.

Mill End Store, 9701 SE McLoughlin, Milwaukee, OR 97222: Free information ❖ Silk fabrics from designers' back rooms. 503-786-1234.

Monterey Outlet Store, P.O. Box 271, 1725 E. Delavan Dr., Janesville, WI 53545: Brochure $4 ❖ Deep pile fabrics (fake furs). 800-432-9959; 608-754-8309 (in WI).

Nancy's Notions, P.O. Box 683, Beaver Dam, WI 53916: Free catalog ❖ Sewing notions, threads, books, patterns, how-to videos, and interlock knits, fleece, gabardines, sweater knits, challis, and other fabrics. 800-833-0690.

Oppenheim's, P.O. Box 52, North Manchester, IN 46962: Catalog $1 ❖ Sewing notions, fabrics, and craft supplies. 800-461-6728.

Outdoor Wilderness Fabrics, 16195 Latah Dr., Nampa, ID 83651: Free price list ❖ Coated and non-coated nylon fabrics, fleece and blends in coat weights, waterproof fabrics, webbing, patterns, and sewing notions. 208-466-1602.

The Patchworks, 6676 Amsterdam Rd., Manhattan, MT 59741: Catalog $1 ❖ Reproduction cotton fabrics for quilts and clothing.

Martha Pullen Company Inc., 518 Madison St., Huntsville, AL 35801: Catalog $2 ❖ Fabrics and trims. 800-547-4176.

Qualin International, P.O. Box 31145, San Francisco, CA 94131: Free catalog with long SASE and two 1st class stamps ❖ Silk fabrics, scarf blanks, and silk painting supplies. 415-647-1329.

Quest Outfitters, 2590 17th St., Sarasota, FL 34234: Free catalog ❖ Clothing, outdoor fabrics, patterns, fasteners, and zippers. 813-378-1620.

Rainshed Outdoor Fabrics, 707 NW 11th, Corvallis, OR 97330: Catalog $1 ❖ Outdoor fabrics, hardware, webbing, and patterns. 541-753-8900.

Salt Box Plaids, 23030 State Rd. 37, Grabill, IN 46741: Brochure $3.75 ❖ Homespun, primitive folk art, reproduction prints, and 100 percent wool flannel fabrics. 800-44-PLAID.

Donna Salyers' Fabulous-Furs, 700 Madison Ave., Covington, KY 41011: Catalog $1 ❖ Alternatives to natural furs and leather, kits, and patterns. 800-848-4650.

Sawyer Brook Fabrics, P.O. Box 1800, Clinton, MA 01510: Catalog $7.50 (annual subscription) ❖ Natural fiber fabrics, polyesters and blends, wools, silks, and cotton prints.

Seattle Fabrics, 8702 Aurora Ave. North Seattle, WA 98103: Price list $3 (refundable) ❖ Outdoor and recreation fabrics. 206-525-0670.

The Seraph, P.O. Box 500, 420 Main St., Sturbridge, MA 01566: Catalog $6 ❖ Fabrics. 508-347-2241.

Sew Sassy Lingerie, 9009 S. Memorial Pkwy., Huntsville, AL 35802: Catalog $2 (refundable) ❖ Lingerie fabrics and supplies. 205-883-1209.

Sew Special, 777 E. Vista Way, Ste. 20, Vista, CA 92084: Free information ❖ Fabrics and lace. 619-940-0363.

Shama Imports, P.O. Box 2900, Farmington Hills, MI 48018: Free brochure ❖ Hand-embroidered crewel fabrics. 810-478-7740.

Slipcovers of America, 58 W. 40th St., New York, NY 10018: Free catalog ❖ Slipcovers, matching draperies, and fabrics.

Smocking Bonnet, P.O. Box 53, Lisbon, MD 21765: Catalog $3 ❖ English smocking, French hand-sewing, fabrics, and lace. 800-524-1678.

Smocking Etceteras, P.O. Box 637, Moab, UT 84532: Catalog $4 ❖ Fabrics, lace, and trims. 512-928-3217.

Soho South, P.O. Box 1324, Cullman, AL 35056: Catalog $2.50 (refundable) ❖ Beads and findings, fabric dyes and paints, silk scarves and fabrics, and marbling supplies. 205-739-6114.

Specialties, Pat Timms, 4425 Cotton Hanlon Rd., Montour Falls, NY 14865: Catalog $2 ❖ Lingerie fabrics, notions, and patterns. 607-594-2021.

Stretch & Sew, 8697 La Mesa Blvd., La Mesa, CA 91941: Catalog $3 ❖ Fabrics, patterns, and notions. 619-589-8880.

Taylor's Cutaways & Stuff, 2802 E. Washington St., Urbana, IL 61801: Brochure $1 ❖ Satins, lace, velvet, cottons, felt, calico, trims, polyester squares, sewing notions, craft supplies, books, and patterns.

Terran Fabrics, P.O. Box 11122, College Station, TX 77845: Brochure $3 with long SASE ❖ Tools, supplies, and imported cotton fabrics for sewing and quilting.

Testfabrics Inc., P.O. Box 420, Middlesex, NJ 08846: Free catalog ❖ Cotton, linen, silk, wool, blends, synthetics, muslin, satin, twill, and other fabrics. 201-469-6446.

Threads at Gingerbread Hill, 356 E. Garfield, Aurora, OH 44202: Information and samples $10 ❖ Imported and domestic silks, wools, cottons, synthetics, and other fabrics. 216-562-7100.

L.P. Thur Fabrics, 126 W. 23rd St., New York, NY 10011: Free information ❖ Costume, designer, craft, theatrical, and other fabrics. 212-243-4913.

Tioga Mill Outlet, 200 S. Hartman St., York, PA 17403: Free brochure ❖ Upholstery and drapery fabrics. 717-843-5139.

Treadle Yard Goods, 1338 Grand Ave., St. Paul, MN 55105: Free information ❖ Natural fiber fabrics. 612-698-9690.

Ultramouse Ltd., 3433 Bennington Ct., Bloomfield Hills, MI 48301: Catalog $2 ❖ Sewing notions, ultrasuede, and fabric scraps. 800-225-1887.

The Unique Needle, 539 Blossom Way, Hayward, CA 94541: Brochure $1.50 ❖ Imported Swiss fabrics and embroideries, French lace, other fabrics, trims, patterns, books, and supplies. 415-727-9130.

Utex Trading, 710 9th St., Ste. 5, Niagara Falls, NY 14301: Free brochure with long SASE ❖ Imported silk fabrics and sewing supplies. 416-596-7565.

Victorian Treasures, 12148 Madison St. NE, Blaine, MN 55434: Catalog $3.50 (refundable) ❖ Imported lace, fabrics, Swiss embroideries, and notions. 612-755-6302.

Lace & Ribbon

Baltazor's, 3262 Severen Ave., Metairie, LA 70002: Catalog $3 ❖ Lace and lace-making supplies, fabrics, smocking, and bridal fashion-making supplies. 800-532-5223.

Beggars' Lace, P.O. Box 481223, Denver, CO 80248: Catalog $2 (refundable) ❖ Lace-making materials and kits. 303-233-2600.

Cache Junction, 2701 W. 1800 South, Logan, UT 84321: Brochure $2 ❖ Iron-on lace. 800-999-1989.

Cindy's Stitches, 1449 Glencoe Ave., Highland Park, IL 60035: Catalog $2 ❖ Lace-making and needlework equipment and books.

Denham Fabrics, P.O. Box 241275, Memphis, TN 38124: Fabric portfolio $8 ❖ Lace. 901-683-4574.

Elsie's Exquisiques, 208 State St., P.O. Box 260, St. Joseph, MI 49085: Free information and list of retail sources ❖ Silk and novelty ribbons, trims, and ribbon roses. 616-982-0449.

Fabric Barn, 3121 E. Anaheim St., Long Beach, CA 90804: Free catalog ❖ Ribbon and lace. 800-544-9374; 310-498-0285 (in CA).

Famous Trading Company, 237 W. 37th St., New York, NY 10018: Free catalog ❖ Lace and trims, elastic, zippers, ribbons, plastic scarves and doilies, Velcro hooks and loop tape, sequins, and notions. 800-326-6878; 212-768-9647 (in NY).

Ginsco Trims, 242 W. 38th, New York, NY 10018: Catalog $6 (refundable) ❖ Fashion trims and braids. 800-929-2529.

Glimakra Looms & Yarns Inc., 1338 Ross St., Petaluma, CA 94954: Catalog $2.50 ❖ Weaving equipment, looms, yarns, and lace-making equipment. 800-289-9276; 707-762-3362 (in CA).

Heirloom Creations, 431 Rena Dr., Lafayette, LA 70503: Free information ❖ Lace, Swiss and silk batiste, linen, velveteen, and cotton corduroy. 318-984-8949.

Heritage Miniatures, 44 Mountain Base Rd., Goffstown, NH 03045: Catalog $4 ❖ European lace and trim for miniature doll dressmakers.

Kagan Trim Center, 750 Towne Ave., Los Angeles, CA 90021: Catalog $14 (refundable) ❖ Trim, lace, braids, cords, and general apparel supplies. 800-437-8746.

Lace Corner, Box 1224, Weaverville, CA 96093: Catalog $3 (refundable with $25 order) ❖ Ruffled flat lace, ribbons, and appliques. 916-623-3586.

Lace Heaven, P.O. Box 50150, Mobile, AL 36605: Catalog $3 (refundable) ❖ Lingerie fabrics, ribbons, trim, stretch lace, elastic, and notions. 205-478-5644.

Lacis, 3163 Adeline St., Berkeley, CA 94703: Catalog $4 ❖ Hairpin lace looms. 510-843-7178.

Mimi's Fabrications, 502 Balsam Rd., Hazelwood, NC 28738: Catalog $3 ❖ Silk ribbon and embroidery supplies. 704-452-3455.

New Scotland Lace Company, P.O. Box 181, Dartmouth, Nova Scotia, Canada B2Y 3Y3: Catalog $3 (refundable) ❖ Scottish Victorian lace window panels and yardage. 902-462-4212.

The Ribbon Factory Outlet, P.O. Box 405, Titusville, PA 16354: Catalog $2 ❖ Ribbons. 814-827-6431.

Sew Fine, 18399 Ventura Blvd., Tarzana, CA 91356: Free information with long SASE ❖ Smocking and sewing supplies, French and English lace, buttons, ribbons, and Swiss embroideries. 818-886-1108.

Sew Special, 777 E. Vista Way, Ste. 20, Vista, CA 92084: Free information ❖ Fabrics and lace. 619-940-0363.

Smocking Etceteras, P.O. Box 637, Moab, UT 84532: Catalog $4 ❖ Fabrics, lace, and trims. 512-928-3217.

Van Sciver Bobbin Lace, 130 Cascadilla Park, Ithaca, NY 14850: Catalog $2 ❖ Lace-making supplies. 607-277-0498.

Viking Design, 11 Schaaf Rd., Bloomsbury, NJ 08804: Free brochure ❖ Lace knitting supplies. 908-479-4959.

Warscokins, 7561 Center Ave., #40, Huntington Beach, CA 92647: Catalog $3.50 ❖ Lace, ribbon, and sewing notions. 800-225-6356.

YLI Corporation, 482 N. Freedom Blvd., Provo, UT 84601: Catalog $2.50 ❖ Silk, spark organdy, synthetic silk, ribbons, silk thread, and craft supplies. 800-854-1932; 801-377-3900 (in UT)

FANS

Casablanca Fan Company, 450 N. Baldwin Park Blvd., City of Industry, CA 91746: Free information ❖ Ceiling fans. 800-759-3267.

Fan Fair, 2251 Wisconsin Ave. NW, Washington, DC 20007: Free information ❖ Fans. 202-342-6290.

The Fan Man Inc., 1914 Abrams Pkwy., Dallas, TX 75214: Brochure $2 ❖ Fans. 214-826-7700.

The Fan Man (Oklahoma City), 2721 NW 109th Terrace, Oklahoma City, OK 73120: Free information ❖ New and restored antique fans. 405-751-0933.

Hunter Fan Company, 2500 Fisco Ave., Memphis, TN 38114: Catalog $1 ❖ Ceiling fans, remote control units, fixtures, and electronic thermostats. 901-745-9222.

Lamp Warehouse, 1073 39th St., Brooklyn, NY 11219: Free information with long SASE ❖ Ceiling fans and fixtures. 800-52-LITES; 718-436-8500 (in NY).

FAUCETS & PLUMBING FIXTURES

Antique Baths & Kitchens, 2220 Carlton Way, Santa Barbara, CA 93109: Catalog $2 ❖ Reproduction Victorian-style plumbing fixtures. 805-962-8598.

Chicago Faucet Company, 2100 S. Clearwater Dr., Des Plaines, IL 60018: Free list of retail sources ❖ Bathroom plumbing fixtures. 708-803-5000.

Delta Faucet Company, 55 E. 111th St., Indianapolis, IN 46280: Free information ❖ Solid brass plumbing fixtures. 317-848-1812.

Elkay Manufacturing Company, 2222 Camden Ct., Oak Brook, IL 60521: Free information ❖ Faucets with retractable nozzles. 708-574-8484.

The Fixture Exchange, 109 S. Broad, Bainbridge, GA 31717: Catalog $1 (refundable) ❖ Plumbing fixtures and faucets. 800-326-2694.

Grohe America Inc., 241 Covington Dr., Bloomingdale, IL 60108: Information $3 ❖ Kitchen faucets and attachments. 708-582-7711.

Kohler Company, 444 Highland Dr., Kohler, WI 53044: Catalog $3 ❖ Solid brass faucets and plumbing fixtures. 800-220-2291.

MAC the Antique Plumber, 6325 Elvas Ave, Sacramento, CA 95819: Catalog $6 (refundable) ❖ Plumbing fixtures in a 1900s style. 916-454-4507.

Moen Inc., 25300 Al Moen Dr., North Olmsted, OH 44070: Free information ❖ Single and double-handle faucets for bathrooms and kitchens. 800-533-6636.

The Renovator's Supply, P.O. Box 2515, Conway, NH 03818: Free catalog ❖ Plumbing fixtures and hardware. 800-659-0203.

FEATHERS

Baubanbea Enterprises, P.O. Box 1205, Smithtown, NY 11787: Catalog $1 ❖ Rhinestones, sequins, beads, jewels, lace, appliques, fringes, trim, feathers, imported and domestic fabrics, and silk flowers. 516-724-4661.

Crafty's Featherworks, P.O. Box 370, Overton, NV 89040: Free information ❖ Feathers for making floral arrangements, Native American crafts, millinery, fly-tying, and accent pieces. 702-397-8211.

Gettinger Feather Corporation, 16 W. 36th St., New York, NY 10033: Price list $2 ❖ Raw or dyed ostrich, marabou, turkey, and feathers from other birds. 212-695-9470.

White Buffalo, 418 E. Beale, Kingman, AZ 86401: Catalog $1 ❖ Exotic feathers. 520-753-7800.

FENCES & GATES

Abode Lumber Corporation, 11212 Bradley Ave., Pacoima, CA 91331: Free list of retail sources ❖ Polyethylene coated wooden fencing. 800-521-3633.

Alcan Pipe/Kroy Industries, P.O. Box 309, York, NE 68467: Free information ❖ White vinyl rail fencing. 402-362-6651.

Architectural Iron Company, P.O. Box 126, Milford, PA 18337: Catalog $4 ❖ Reproduction cast-iron 18th and 19th-century gates, fences, and fountains. 800-442-4766.

Bamboo & Rattan Works Inc., 470 Oberlin Ave. South, Lakewood, NJ 08701: Free information ❖ Custom bamboo fencing. 800-4-BAMBOO.

Bamboo Fencer, 31 Germania St., Jamaica Plain, MA 02130: Catalog $3 ❖ Fences, gates, and construction materials. 617-524-6137.

Benner's Gardens, P.O. Box 875, Bala Cynwyd, PA 19004: Free information ❖ Easily attached mesh barrier for garden and property protection. 800-753-4660.

Bufftech Inc., 2525 Walden Ave., Buffalo, NY 14225: Free brochure ❖ Maintenance-free vinyl fence. 800-333-0569.

California Redwood Association, 405 Enfrente Dr., Ste. 200, Novato, CA 94949: Free information ❖ Redwood fences. 415-382-0662.

Centaur Fencing Systems Inc., 2802 E. Avalon Dr., Muscle Shoals, AL 35661: Free information ❖ Flexible fencing with rails that return to their original shape after being struck. 800-368-7635.

Central Tractor Farm & Family Center, 3915 Delaware, Des Moines, IA 50313: Free catalog ❖ Fencing supplies. 800-247-1760; 515-266-3101 (in IA).

Color Guard Fence Company, P.O. Box 28, Sheboygan Falls, WI 53085: Free information ❖ Vinyl fencing. 800-832-8914.

Comtrad Industries, 2820 Waterford Lake Dr., Ste. 106, Midlothian, VA 23113: Free information ❖ Electric invisible pet containment systems. 800-704-1211.

Custom Ironwork Inc., P.O. Box 180, Union, KY 41091: Catalog $2 ❖ Reproduction cast and wrought-iron fencing in Victorian and other styles. 606-384-4122.

Delgard Fence, 8600 River Rd., Delair, NJ 08110: Free information ❖ Weather-resistant aluminum fences. 800-235-0185.

Elite Aluminum Fence Products, 6675 Burroughs, Sterling Heights, MI 48314: Free information ❖ Aluminum fencing with a baked-on enamel finish. 313-731-1331.

Furman Lumber Inc., P.O. Box 130, Nutting Lake, MA 01865: Free information ❖ Factory-assembled picket fences. 800-843-9663.

Heritage Fence Company, P.O. Box 121, Skippack, PA 19464: Catalog $2 ❖ Reproduction wooden colonial and Victorian-style fences. 215-584-6710.

Innotek Pet Products Inc., One Innoway Dr., Garrett, IN 46738: Free list of retail sources ❖ Pet containment system and remote training equipment. 800-826-5527.

Invisible Fence Company Inc., 355 Phoenixville Pike, Malvern, PA 19355: Free information ❖ Invisible electronic pet containment fence. 800-538-DOGS.

Jerith Manufacturing Company Inc., 3901 G St., Philadelphia, PA 19124: Free brochure ❖ Rust-proof high-strength aluminum alloy fences with a baked on enamel finish. 800-344-2242.

LouveRail, P.O. Box 507, Concordville, PA 19331: Free information ❖ Adjustable louver panels for fences. 215-558-3515.

Moultrie Manufacturing, P.O. Drawer 1179, Moultrie, GA 31776: Catalog $3 ❖ Reproduction "Old South" gates and fences. 800-841-8674.

OuterSpace Landscape Furnishings Inc., 7533 Draper Ave., La Jolla, CA 92037: Free information ❖ Steel fences, gates, and modular components for trellis and garden structures. 800-338-2499.

Pool Fence Company, 1791-907 Blount Rd., Pompano Beach, FL 33069: Free brochure ❖ Swimming pool protection-against-entry fences. 800-992-2206.

Post Fence Company, 105 NE 69th St., Des Moines, IA 50317: Free information ❖ Plastic ornamental fencing that looks like wrought-iron. 515-264-0234.

Radio Fence, 230 E. Russell St., Fayetteville, NC 28301: Free information ❖ Easy-to-install electronic invisible pet containment systems. 800-775-8404.

Southeastern Wood Products Company, P.O. Box 113, Griffin, GA 30224: Free brochure ❖ Wire and wood fences, plant supports, and cold frames. 800-722-7486; 770-227-7486 (in GA).

Stewart Iron Works Company, P.O. Box 2612, Covington, KY 41012: Catalog $3 ❖ Victorian-style fences and gates. 606-431-1985.

Texas Standard Picket Company, P.O. Box 12345, Austin, TX 78711: Free brochure ❖ Reproduction Victorian-style fence pickets. 512-472-1101.

The Timeless Garden, P.O. Box 500998, Atlanta, GA 31150: Free information ❖ Handcrafted authentically reproduced historic garden gates. 404-518-9127.

Triple Crown Fence, P.O. Box 2000, Milford, IN 46542: Free list of retail sources ❖ Vinyl fences. 800-365-3625; 219-658-9442 (in IN).

UltraGuard Fence, 201 E. Palm Dr., Syracuse, NY 46567: Free information ❖ Vinyl post and rail fences. 800-457-4342.

West Virginia Fence Corporation, US Rt. 219, Lindside, WV 24951: Free catalog ❖ Permanent and portable electric pet containment fences. 800-356-5458; 304-753-4387 (in WV).

FENCING

American Fencers Supply Company, 1180 Folsom St., San Francisco, CA 94103: Free information ❖ Gloves, masks, shoes, uniforms, blades, epees, foils, rapiers, and sabers. 415-863-7911.

Blade Fencing Equipment Inc., 212 W. 15th St., New York, NY 10011: Free information ❖ Gloves, masks, shoes, uniforms, blades, epees, foils, rapiers, and sabers. 800-828-5661; 212-620-0114 (in NY/NJ/CT).

Genesport Industries Ltd., Hokkaido Karate Equipment Manufacturing Company, 150 King St., Montreal, Quebec, Canada H3C 2P3: Free information ❖ Gloves, masks, uniforms, blades, and sabers. 514-861-1856.

George Santelli, 465 S. Dean St., Englewood, NJ 07631: Free catalog ❖ Fencing equipment. 201-871-3105.

Sportime, Customer Service, 1 Sportime Way, Atlanta, GA 30340: Free information ❖ Fencing equipment. 800-444-5700; 770-449-5700 (in GA).

FIRE FIGHTING & POLICE ITEMS

Firefighters Bookstore, 18281 Gothard St., #105, Huntington Beach, CA 92648: Free catalog ❖ Books, software, and videos for firefighters. 714-375-4888.

International Logistics Systems Inc., Defense Assistance Research Corporation, 234 McLean Blvd., Paterson, NJ 07504: Free brochure ❖ Law enforcement and intelligence equipment. 201-881-0001.

Mountain Sales, 163 E. Main St., Little Falls, NJ 07424: Free brochure ❖ Audio tapes on fire fighting activities. 800-575-1075; 201-256-3669 (in NJ).

FIRE SAFETY

Escape Ladders

Jomy Safety Ladder Company, 1728 16th St., Ste. 201, Boulder, CO 80302: Free information ❖ Collapsible fire escape ladder. 800-255-2591.

Walter Kidde, Division Kidde Inc., 1394 S. 3rd St., Mebane, NC 27302: Free information ❖ Escape ladders, smoke and fire alarms, and fire extinguishers. 800-654-9677.

Ladder Man Inc., 3025 Silver Dr., Columbus, OH 43224: Free catalog ❖ Safety and attic and fire escape equipment. Also specialty, articulating, and stairwell ladders. 800-783-8887.

Fire Extinguishers

Black & Decker, 6 Armstrong Rd., Shelton, CT 06484: Free information ❖ Fire extinguishers. 203-926-3000.

Fireboy Halon Systems, P.O. Box 152, Grand Rapids, MI 49502: Free information ❖ Fire extinguishers for boats. 616-454-8337.

First Alert, 780 McClure Rd., Aurora, IL 60404: Free information ❖ Fire extinguishers. 800-323-9005.

Walter Kidde, Division Kidde Inc., 1394 S. 3rd St., Mebane, NC 27302: Free information ❖ Escape ladders, smoke and fire alarms, and fire extinguishers. 800-654-9677.

Smoke Detectors

Black & Decker, 6 Armstrong Rd., Shelton, CT 06484: Free information ❖ Smoke alarms. 203-926-3000.

First Alert, 780 McClure Rd., Aurora, IL 60404: Free information ❖ Smoke alarms. 800-323-9005.

Walter Kidde, Division Kidde Inc., 1394 S. 3rd St., Mebane, NC 27302: Free information ❖ Escape ladders, smoke and fire alarms, and fire extinguishers. 800-654-9677.

Radio Shack, Division Tandy Corporation, One Tandy Center, Fort Worth, TX 76102: Free information ❖ Smoke alarms. 817-390-3011.

Sanyo Electric, 200 Riser Rd., Little Ferry, NJ 07643: Free information with long SASE ❖ Electrostatic air cleaner/ionizer with a smoke sensor. 201-641-2333.

Silent Call, P.O. Box 868, Clarkston, MI 48016: Free information ❖ Smoke detectors.

Sprinkler Systems

Central Fire Sprinkler Corporation, 451 N. Cannon Ave., Lansdale, PA 19446: Free information ❖ Residential sprinkler systems. 215-362-0700.

The Reliable Automatic Sprinkler Company, 525 N. MacQuestern Pkwy., Mount Vernon, NY 10552: Free information ❖ Residential sprinkler systems. 800-431-1588; 914-592-1414 (in NY).

FIREPLACES
Accessories & Tools

The Adams Company, 100 E. 4th St., Dubuque, IA 52001: Free list of retail sources ❖ Solid brass and black cast-iron fireplace tool sets, baskets, screens, firebacks, lighters, and fenders. 800-553-3012.

Danny Alessandro, Edwin Jackson Inc., 146 E. 57th St., New York, NY 10022: Catalog $5 ❖ Antique and reproduction fireplace accessories and 18th-century limestone, wood, and marble mantels. 212-759-8210.

Art Marble & Stone, 5862 Peachtree Industrial Blvd., Atlanta, GA 30341: Free brochure ❖ Glass doors, tools, mantels, and gas logs with glowing embers for natural or LP gas. 800-476-0298.

Bona Decorative Hardware, 3073 Madison Rd., Cincinnati, OH 45209: Price list $2 ❖ Solid brass hardware for fireplaces, bathrooms, doors, cabinets, furniture, and kitchens. 513-321-7877.

Coppersmiths, Custom Copper & Brass Works, P.O. Box 2675, Oakhurst, CA 93644: Free brochure ❖ Fireplace hoods, cupolas, mailboxes, and dormers. 209-658-8909.

Country Iron Foundry, P.O. Box 600, Paoli, PA 19301: Catalog $2 ❖ Handcrafted colonial-style and other firebacks. 610-353-5542.

Craft Inc., 94 Bethlehem Pike, Philadelphia, PA 19118: Free brochure ❖ Reproduction fireplace accessories. 610-242-8818.

Fireside Distributors Inc., 4013 Atlantic Ave., Raleigh, NC 27604: Free information ❖ Fireplace accessories. 800-333-3473; 919-872-4434 (in NC).

Gas Logs Direct, 2105 Greentree Rd., Pittsburgh, PA 15220: Free information ❖ Simulated logs ready-to-use with available gas sources. 800-564-4569.

Grate Fires, P.O. Box 351, Athens, GA 30603: Free brochure ❖ Authentic English gas coal fires. 706-353-8281.

Halides America Inc., P.O. Box 731, Sparta, NJ 07871: Free information ❖ Fireplace accessories, hand-carved mantels, and wooden moldings. 201-729-8876.

Hargrove Manufacturing Corporation, 207 Wellston Park Rd., Sand Springs, OK 74063: Free information ❖ Gas log sets. 800-725-4166.

Iron Craft, Old Rt. 28, P.O. Box 351, Ossipee, NH 03864: Free catalog ❖ Kettles and grates, enameled cookware, butcher aprons, bellows, heating systems for fireplaces, weather vanes, signs, and cast-iron items, and gifts. 603-539-2807.

William H. Jackson Company, 210 E. 58th St., New York, NY 10022: Brochure $5 ❖ Antique fireplace accessories and mantels. 212-753-9400.

Kayne & Son Custom Hardware, 100 Daniel Ridge Rd., Candler, NC 28715: Catalog $4.50 ❖ Fireplace tools and hand-forged hardware. 704-667-8868.

Lemee's Fireplace Equipment, 815 Bedford St., Bridgewater, MA 02324: Catalog $2 ❖ Fireplace equipment. 508-697-2672.

Jim Leonard Antique Hardware, 509 Tangle Dr., Jamestown, NC 27282: Catalog $2 ❖ Wrought-iron 18th and 19th-century fireplace equipment. 910-454-3583.

Liberty Forge, 40128 Industrial Park North, Georgetown, TX 78626: Free information ❖ Fireplace screens. 512-869-2830.

New England Fire-backs, 161 Main St., P.O. Box 268, Woodbury, CT 06798: Catalog $5 ❖ Solid hand-cast iron fireback reproductions. 203-263-5737.

Robert H. Peterson Company, 530 N. Baldwin Park Blvd., City of Industry, CA 91744: Free catalog ❖ Stone built-in and outdoor barbecues, handcrafted fireplace accessories, and ceramic radiant heat gas logs. 818-369-5085.

Plow & Hearth, P.O. Box 5000, Madison, VA 22727: Free catalog ❖ Gardening tools, birdhouses and feeders, porch and lawn furniture, fireplace accessories, and gifts for pets. 800-627-1712.

Portland Willamette, Byers Industries Inc., P.O. Box 13097, Portland, OR 97213: Free list of retail sources ❖ Fireplace screens and radiant heat ceramic gas logs. 503-288-7511.

Seymour Manufacturing Company Inc., 500 N. Broadway, P.O. Box 248, Seymour, IN 47274: Free list of retail sources ❖ Fireplace tools, stove and fireplace repair accessories, brooms, bellows, and fire-starting supplies. 812-522-2900.

Vermont Industries, P.O. Box 301, Rt. 103, Cuttingsville, VT 05738: Catalog $3 ❖ Hand-forged wrought iron wood racks, lamps, fireplace tools, candle holders, pot holders, and more. 800-639-1715; 802-492-3451 (in VT).

Fireplaces & Fireplace Kits

Acucraft Inc., 20100 W. Hwy. 10, Big Lake, MN 55309: Free information ❖ Log home fireplace systems. 612-263-3156.

Century Fireplace Furnishings Inc., 1606 E. 20th St., Joplin, MO 64804: Free information ❖ Fireplace furnaces. 800-284-4328.

Charmaster Products Inc., 2307 Hwy. 2 West, Grand Rapids, MN 55744: Free brochure ❖ Fireplaces and wood-burning, wood-gas, and wood-oil furnaces and conversion units. 218-326-6786.

Grate Fires, P.O. Box 351, Athens, GA 30603: Free brochure ❖ Authentic English gas-coal fireplace unit. 706-353-8281.

Heat-N-Glo, 6665 W. Hwy. 13, Savage, MN 55378: Free brochure ❖ Fireplaces and accessories. 800-669-4328.

Heatilator Inc., 1915 W. Saunders St., Mt. Pleasant, IA 52641: Free information ❖ Wood-burning stoves and fireplace inserts. 800-843-2848.

Jotul USA, P.O. Box 1157, Portland, ME 04104: Free list of retail sources ❖ Stoves and fireplaces. 800-797-5912.

FIREWORKS

Lopi International Ltd., Travis Industries, 10850 117th Pl. NE, Kirkland, WA 98033: Free information ❖ Fireplace inserts. 800-654-1177.

Majestic, 1000 E. Market St., Huntington, IN 46750: Free information ❖ Fireplaces and accessories. 800-525-1898.

Napoleon Fireplaces, RR 1, Barrie, Ontario, Canada L4M 4Y8: Free information ❖ Gas and wood-fired fireplaces. 705-721-1212.

Nu-Tec Incorporated, P.O. Box 908, East Greenwich, RI 02818: Free brochure ❖ Wood-burning stoves and fireplace inserts. 800-822-0600.

Rüegg Fireplaces, 216 US Hwy. 206, Ste. 12, Somerville, NJ 08876: Free information ❖ Fireplaces. 800-347-3843.

Superior Fireplace, 4325 Artesia Ave., Fullerton, CA 92633: Free information ❖ Fireplaces and accessories. 714-521-7302.

Tulikivi U.S. Inc., 225 Ridge McIntire Rd., Charlottesville, VA 22902: Planning guide $4.95 ❖ Baking ovens, cook-stoves, and natural stone fireplaces. 804-977-5500.

Vermont Castings Inc., Rt. 107, P.O. Box 501, Bethel, VT 05032: Free information ❖ Easy-to-install energy-efficient fireplaces. 800-227-8683.

Mantels

A.D.I. Corporation, 5000 Nicholson Ct., North Bethesda, MD 20895: Free information ❖ Wood mantels. 301-564-1550.

Danny Alessandro, Edwin Jackson Inc., 146 E. 57th St., New York, NY 10022: Catalog $5 ❖ Antique and reproduction fireplace accessories and 18th-century limestone, wood, and marble mantels. 212-759-8210.

Antiquity Millworks, 205 N. Mannheim Ave., Egg Harbor, NJ 08215: Free information ❖ Handcrafted mantels. 609-965-5046.

Architectural Paneling Inc., 979 3rd Ave., New York, NY 10022: Catalog $10 (refundable) ❖ Hand-carved wooden mantels and moldings. 212-371-9632.

Bradley Custom Mantels & Woodworking, 103 West Chester Pike, Chadds Ford, PA 19317: Free brochure ❖ Mantels and millwork.

Bryant Stove Inc., Box 2048, Thorndike, ME 04986: Free brochure ❖ Wooden mantels and ornamental trim. 207-568-3665.

By-Gone Days Antiques Inc., 3100 South Blvd., Charlotte, NC 28209: Free information ❖ Mantels, restored door hardware, and architectural antiques. 704-527-8717.

Decorators Supply Corporation, 3610 S. Morgan St., Chicago, IL 60609: Free list of retail sources ❖ Wooden mantels, capitals, brackets, medallions, plaster cornices, wood moldings, and composition and wooden fiber ornaments. 312-847-6300.

Art Di Rico, 4109 E. Parkway, Gatlinburg, TN 37738: Free information ❖ Custom-sculpted oak and mahogany wooden doors and mantels. 800-434-5427.

Driwood Ornamental Wood Moulding, P.O. Box 1729, Florence, SC 29503: Catalog $6 (refundable) ❖ Mantels, embossed wooden molding, raised paneling, curved stairs, and doors. 803-669-2478.

Halides America Inc., P.O. Box 731, Sparta, NJ 07871: Free information ❖ Fireplace accessories, hand-carved mantels, and wooden moldings. 201-729-8876.

Hazelmere Mantel Company, P.O. Box 337, Blaine, WA 98231: Catalog $2 ❖ Traditional country and city-style mantels.

Heritage Mantels Inc., P.O. Box 240, Bridgeport, CT 06490: Catalog $3 ❖ Reproduction antique marble composition mantels. 203-335-0552.

House of Moulding, 15202 Oxnard St., Van Nuys, CA 91411: Catalog $5 ❖ Fireplaces, mantels, wooden moldings and trim, and ceiling medallions. 818-781-5300.

William H. Jackson Company, 210 E. 58th St., New York, NY 10022: Brochure $5 ❖ Antique fireplace accessories and mantels. 212-753-9400.

The Maizefield Company, P.O. Box 336, Port Townsend, WA 98368: Free brochure ❖ Mantels, turnings, staircases, and moldings. 360-385-6789.

Mantels of Yesteryear Inc., P.O. Box 908, 70 W. Tennessee Ave., McCaysville, GA 30555: Catalog $4 ❖ Antique, custom, and reproduction mantels. The South's largest antique mantel dealer. 706-492-5534.

Nevers Oak Fireplace Mantels, 933 Rancheros Dr., Ste. B, San Marcos, CA 92069: Catalog $7.50 ❖ Hand-carved mantels. 619-745-8841.

Piedmont Mantel & Millwork, 4320 Interstate Dr., Macon, GA 31210: Catalog $3 ❖ Colonial-style mantels and salvaged heart-pine flooring. 912-477-7536.

Readybuilt Products Company, P.O. Box 4425, Baltimore, MD 21223: Catalog $2 ❖ Hand-carved wooden mantels in American and English-styles, electric/gas fireplace logs, facings, and fireplaces. 410-233-5833.

Stone Magic, 5400 Miller, Dallas, TX 75206: Free brochure ❖ Classic to contemporary cast stone mantels. Also interior and exterior cast stone. 214-826-3606.

Urban Artifacts, 4700 Wissahickon Ave., Philadelphia, PA 19144: Free information ❖ Carved antique wood and marble mantels. 800-621-1962.

The Wood Factory, 111 Railroad St., Navasota, TX 77868: Catalog $2 ❖ Ornamental trim, mantels, doors, and reproduction millwork. 409-825-7233.

FIREWORKS

Because regulations governing the purchase and use of fireworks vary from state to state, consumers should read applicable regulations before ordering them from the companies listed below. Consumers should also make certain that they buy fireworks only from licensed or certified vendors who meet the requirements governing their sale and manufacture. Using fireworks illegally can result in substantial fines and possible jail sentences.

"Backyard" Fireworks

Bethany Sales Company, P.O. Box 248, Bethany, IL 61914: Catalog $10 ❖ Class C "backyard" fireworks. 217-665-3396.

Fireworks of America, 8550 Rt. 224, Deerfield, OH 44411: Free catalog ❖ Class C "backyard" fireworks. 800-423-1776.

Neptune Fireworks Company Inc., 768 E. Dania Beach Blvd., P.O. Box 398, Dania, FL 33004: Free catalog ❖ Class C "backyard" fireworks. 800-456-2264; 305-920-6770 (in FL).

Olde Glory Marketing, P.O. Box 9378, Fargo, ND 58106: Free catalog ❖ Class C "backyard" fireworks. 800-843-8758.

Phantom Fireworks, B.J. Alan Company, 555 Martin Luther King Blvd., Youngstown, OH 44502: Free information ❖ Class C "backyard" fireworks. 800-777-1699; 216-746-1064 (in OH).

Fireworks Display Specialists

Fireworks by Grucci, One Grucci Ln., Brookhaven, NY 11719: Free information ❖ Class B display fireworks. 800-227-0088; 516-286-0088 (in NY).

Zambelli Internationale, P.O. Box 1463, New Castle, PA 16103: Free information ❖ Class B display fireworks. 800-245-0397.

Fireworks Memorabilia

American Fireworks News, HC67, Box 30, Dingmans Ferry, PA 18328: Free brochure ❖ Books, manuals, and information for people who collect and research fireworks and fireworks memorabilia. 717-828-8417.

Dennis C. Manochio, Curator, 4th of July Americana & Fireworks Museum, P.O. Box 2010, Saratoga, CA 95070: Free information ❖ Old fireworks catalogs, literature, toys, and fireworks memorabilia. 408-996-1963.

FISHING & FLY-TYING

Equipment

A.K.'s Fly Tying Tools, P.O. Box 6250, Annapolis, MD 21401: Free brochure ❖ Fly-tying tools. 410-573-0287.

Abby Precision Manufacturing, 70 Industrial Dr., Cloverdale, CA 95425: Free list of retail sources ❖ Fly-tying vises. 800-DYNA-KING; 707-894-5566 (in CA).

Abel Reels, 165 Avlador St., Camarillo, CA 93010: Free information ❖ Precision-engineered fly reels. 805-484-8789.

Acme Tackle Company, P.O. Box 2771, Providence, RI 02907: Catalog $2 ❖ Lures for casting, jigging, and trolling.

Adams Reels, 1 Fairfax St., West Haven, CT 06516: Free information ❖ Trout reels. 203-937-6509.

All Star Graphite Rods Inc., 9750 Whithorn, Houston, TX 77095: Free catalog ❖ Plug and bait casting rods. 713-855-9603.

American Angling Supplies, 23 Main St., Salem, NH 03079: Free information ❖ Fly-fishing equipment and supplies. 603-893-3333.

Ande Inc., 1310 53rd St., West Palm Beach, FL 33407: Free brochure ❖ Monofilament fishing line, T-shirts, bags, hats, and accessories. 407-842-2474.

George Anderson's Yellowstone Angler, Hwy. 89 South, P.O. Box 660, Livingston, MT 59047: Free catalog ❖ Tackle, fly-fishing supplies, and fishing and hunting videos. 406-222-7130.

Angler's Workshop, P.O. Box 1044, Woodland, WA 98674: Free information ❖ Fishing and hunting videos and rods, tackle, reels, and other equipment. 206-225-9445.

Fred Arbogast Company, 313 W. North St., Akron, OH 44303: Free information ❖ Multi-purpose lures for pike, muskie, and large and small-mouth bass. 800-252-5873; 216-253-2177 (in OH).

Area Rule Engineering, 931-E Calle Negocio, San Clemente, CA 92673: Free information ❖ Big-game fishing tackle and accessories. 714-366-1333.

Atlantis, 30 Barnet Blvd., New Bedford, MA 02745: Free catalog ❖ Foul weather gear and clothing for yachtsmen and fishermen. 508-995-7000.

B'n'M Pole Company, Box 231, West Point, MS 39773: Free information ❖ Graphite and fiberglass poles and rods for crappie fishing. 800-647-6363; 601-494-5092 (in MS).

Bagley Baits, P.O. Box 810, Winter Haven, FL 33880: Free information ❖ Lures. 813-294-4271.

Dan Bailey's Fly Shop, P.O. Box 1019, Livingston, MT 59047: Free catalog ❖ Tackle, fly-tying supplies, and fishing and hunting videos. 800-356-4052.

Barlow's Tackle Shop, Box 830369, Richardson, TX 75083: Free catalog ❖ Tackle and rod-building supplies, lure components, plastic lures, and fishing and hunting videos. 214-231-5982.

The Bass Pond, P.O. Box 82, Littleton, CO 80160: Catalog $1 ❖ Flies, fly-tying components, fly rods, reels, lines, leaders, floats, and clothing.

Bass Pro Shops, 1935 S. Campbell, Springfield, MO 65898: Free information ❖ Float fishing and outdoor equipment. 800-227-7776.

Bead Tackle, 600 Main St., Monroe, CT 06468: Catalog $1 ❖ Rod caddies, swivels, bait and eel rigs, sinkers, jigs, and lures. 203-459-1213.

L.L. Bean, Freeport, ME 04033: Free catalog ❖ Fly-tying supplies, fishing and hunting videos, and fly, bass, and saltwater fishing equipment. 800-483-2326.

Berkeley Inc., One Berkeley Dr., Spirit Lake, IA 51360: Free catalog ❖ Fishing and fly lines, fly leaders, and spinning, plug and bait casting, and saltwater rods. 800-237-5539; 712-336-1520 (in IA).

Best American Duffel, 2601 Elliot Ave., Ste. 4317, Seattle, WA 98121: Free information ❖ Tackle bags. 800-424-BAGS.

Blue Ribbon Flies, Box 1037, West Yellowstone, MT 59758: Free catalog ❖ Flies and fly-tying materials. 406-646-7642.

Blue Ridge Rod Company, P.O. Box 6268, Annapolis, MD 21401: Free catalog ❖ Rod-building blanks and components, tools, and finishing supplies. 410-224-4072.

Boardman Flyfisherman, 5667 Mahoning Ave., Youngstown, OH 44515: Free information ❖ Fresh and saltwater fly-fishing and fly-tying equipment.

Braid Products Inc., 616 E. Avenue P, Palmdale, CA 93550: Free information ❖ Trolling lures. 805-266-9791.

Charlie Brewer's Slider Company, P.O. Box 130, Lawrenceburg, TN 38464: Free information ❖ Soft plastic crawfish lures. 800-762-4701; 615-762-4700 (in TN).

Brightwater, P.O. Box 3040, Montrose, CO 81402: Free brochure ❖ Fly rods. 303-728-5788.

Browning Company, Dept. C006, One Browning Pl., Morgan, UT 84050: Catalog $2 ❖ Saltwater spinning reels, spinning rods, and plug and bait casting reels and rods. 800-333-3288.

BSI Sporting Goods, P.O. Box 5010, Vienna, WV 26105: Free catalog ❖ Firearm and muzzle-loading supplies, optics, clothing, and archery, fishing, and hunting equipment. 304-295-8511.

Burke Flex-O Products, P.O. Box 6658, Tyler, TX 75711: Free information ❖ Lures. 903-561-0522.

C & H Lures Custom Lures, 142 Mill Creek Rd., Jacksonville, FL 32211: Free information ❖ Lures and custom rods. 904-724-7469.

Cabela's, 812 13th Ave., Sidney, NE 69162: Free catalog ❖ Float fishing supplies and hunting and outdoor equipment. 800-588-7512.

Capt. Harry's Fishing Supplies, 100 NE 11th St., Miami, FL 33132: Catalog $3 ❖ Fly and saltwater fishing, bass fishing, and fly-tying supplies. 800-327-4088; 305-374-4661 (in FL).

Dale Clemens Custom Tackle, 444 Schantz Spring Rd., Allentown, PA 18104: Catalog $2 ❖ Rod-building and fly-tying materials and tools. 610-395-5119.

Cold Spring Anglers, P.O. Box 129, Carlisle, PA 17013: Catalog $3 ❖ Flies, tackle, and fly-tying supplies. 717-245-2646.

Compleat Angler Inc., 1320 Marshall Ln., Helena, MT 59601: Free information ❖ Fly-fishing accessories.

Cortland Line Company, P.O. Box 5588, Cortland, NY 13045: Free information ❖ Fly reels, lines, and leaders. 607-756-2851.

Creme Lure Company, P.O. Box 6162, Tyler, TX 75711: Free information ❖ Lures. 903-561-0522.

D.O.A. Lures, 3461-B Palm City School Ave., Palm City, FL 34990: Free information ❖ Soft plastic lures filled with shrimp and bait-fish particles. 407-287-5001.

D & T Enterprises, 20518 Meadow Lake Rd., Snohomish, WA 98290: Free information ❖ Handcrafted fishing tackle chest. 360-805-9231.

Daiwa Corporation, 7421 Chapman Ave., Garden Grove, CA 92641: Catalog $1 ❖ Plug and bait casting reels and rods, saltwater reels and rods, and spin casting reels. 714-895-6645.

Atelier De Pêche, Richard Verret, 104 Proulx Ave., Vanier, Québec, Canada G1M 1W4: Free catalog ❖ Fly-tying supplies and equipment. 418-688-7590.

Defender Industries Inc., 255 Main St., P.O. Box 820, New Rochelle, NY 10801: Free catalog ❖ Fishing and tackle equipment. 800-435-7180; 914-632-3001 (in NY).

Diamondback, Rt. 100 South, P.O. Box 308, Stowe, VT 05672: Free catalog ❖ Fishing rods. 800-626-2970.

❖ FISHING & FLY-TYING ❖

Eagle Claw Fishing Tackle, P.O. Box 16011, Denver, CO 80216: Catalog 50¢ ❖ Reels, rods, and fishing hooks. 303-321-1481.

Eagle River Fly Shop, P.O. Box 12859, Drawer 8, Rochester, NY 14580: Free catalog ❖ Fly-fishing equipment. 716-265-3593.

EdgeWater Fishing Products, 35 N. 1000 West, Clearfield, UT 84015: Catalog $5 ❖ Handmade flies and fly-tying supplies. 800-584-7647.

Egger's, P.O. Box 1344, Cumming, GA 30130: Free catalog ❖ Fly-tying supplies, tools, and net kits.

Eldredge Brothers Fly Shop, P.O. Box 69, Rt. 1, Cape Neddick, ME 03902: Free information ❖ Fly-tying materials, salt and freshwater flies, rods and reels, and supplies. 207-363-2004.

Elkhorn Rod Company, P.O. Box 2525, Loveland, CO 80539: Free information ❖ Rod-building kits. 303-227-4707.

English Angling Trappings, P.O. Box 8885, New Fairfield, CT 06812: Catalog $1 (refundable) ❖ Fly-tying materials, tools, and accessories. 203-746-4121.

Eppinger Manufacturing Company, 6340 Schaefer Hwy., Dearborn, MI 48126: Free brochure ❖ Fishing lures. 313-582-3205.

Feather-Craft Fly-fishing, 8307 Manchester Rd., P.O. Box 19904, St. Louis, MO 63144: Free catalog ❖ Fly-tying supplies and accessories. 800-659-1707.

Fenwick Corporation, 5242 Argosy Ave., Huntington Beach, CA 92649: Catalog $1 ❖ Saltwater spinning reels and spinning, plug and bait casting, and fly rods. 800-642-7637.

Fish Creek Rod Company, P.O. Box 638, Windsor, CO 80550: Free information ❖ Fly-fishing rods. 303-227-8128.

Fishing Creek Outfitters, RD 1, Box 310-1, Benton, PA 17814: Free catalog ❖ Fishing tackle, fly-tying accessories, and outdoor clothing. 717-925-2225.

Flies Only, 78 North Rt. 303, Congers, NY 10920: Free catalog ❖ Flies for cold and warm water fishing.

Fly & Field, 560 Crescent Blvd., Glen Ellyn, IL 60137: Free catalog ❖ Fly-tying accessories and videos. 800-328-9753.

The Fly Box, 1293 NE 3rd St., Bend, OR 97701: Catalog $1 ❖ Rods and blanks, reels, rod-building components, fly-lines, cases, wading boots and clothing, float tubes and pontoon boats, custom-tied flies, fishing accessories, and books. 503-388-3330.

Fly-Rite Inc., 7421 S. Beyer, Frankenmouth, MI 48734: Catalog $1 (refundable) ❖ Dubbing materials, fly-tying tools, fly boxes, and accessories. 517-652-9869.

The Fly Shop, 4140 Churn Creek Rd., Redding, CA 96002: Free information ❖ Fly-fishing supplies, tackle, and fishing and hunting videos. 800-669-3474.

Four Rivers, 244 Mid Rivers Center, Ste. 230, St. Peters, MO 63376: Catalog $3 ❖ Outdoor gear for campers, hunters, and fishermen.

Frabill Inc., 536 Main St., P.O. Box 499, Allentown, WI 53002: Free information ❖ Habitat and insulated containers, live bait buckets, traps and cages, and nets. 414-629-5506.

Frontier Anglers, 680 N. Montana St., Dillon, MT 59725: Free catalog ❖ Fly-fishing equipment and supplies. 800-228-5263.

Ganakatsu, P.O. Box 1797, Tacoma, WA 98401: Free catalog ❖ Stiletto-sharp salmon and steelhead fly hooks. 206-922-8373.

Gander Mountain Inc., P.O. Box 248, Gander Mountain, Wilmot, WI 53192: Free catalog ❖ Outdoor sports equipment and clothing for fishing, hunting, and camping. 800-558-9410.

J. Garman, 316 Hartford Rd., Manchester, CT 06040: Free information ❖ Flies, fly-tying tools, and equipment.

The Global Flyfisher, 2849 W. Dundee Rd., Ste. 132, Northbrook, IL 60062: Catalog $2 ❖ Fly-fishing equipment. 800-531-1106.

Ted Godfrey, 3509 Pleasant Plains Dr., Reisterstown, MD 21136: Free information ❖ Tackle for trout, Atlantic salmon, and saltwater fishing. 410-239-8468.

The Golden Hackle Fly Shop, 329 Crescent Pl., Flushing, MI 48433: Catalog $2 (refundable) ❖ Fly-tying tools, supplies, hooks, flies, and accessories. 810-659-0018.

Green River Rodmakers, Box 817, Rural Route 4, Green River, VT 05301: Free list of retail sources ❖ Bamboo and graphite fly rods. 802-257-4553.

Griffin Enterprises Inc., P.O. Box 754, Bonner, MT 59823: Free list of retail sources ❖ Fly-tying tools and vises. 406-244-5407.

Gorilla & Sons, P.O. Box 2309, Bellingham, WA 98227: Free catalog ❖ Fishing equipment. 800-246-7455.

Gudebrod, P.O. Box 357, Pottsdown, PA 19464: Free list of retail sources ❖ Braided fishing line. 215-327-4050.

Harrison-Hoge Industries Inc., Panther Martin, 200 Wilson St., Port Jefferson Station, NY 11776: Free catalog ❖ Fishing lures. 800-852-0925.

Ari T. Hart, 435 S. Guadalupe, Santa Fe, NM 87501: Free information ❖ Fishing reels. 505-983-2141.

Hart Tackle Company Inc., P.O. Box 898, 300 W. Main St., Stratford, OK 74872: Free information ❖ Bass lures. 405-759-2391.

Hodgson Hook Company, 7116 W. Rowland Ave., Littleton, CO 80123: Free catalog ❖ Hooks. 303-979-5206.

Hook & Hackle Company, 7 Kaycee Loop Rd., Plattsburgh, NY 12901: Free catalog ❖ Fly-fishing tackle, fly-tying and fly rod-building supplies, hand-tied flies, clothing, and wading boots. 518-561-5893.

Hopkins Fishing Tackle, Box 11587, Norfolk, VA 23517: Free information ❖ Saltwater lures.

Hunter's Angling Supplies, 2 Central Square Box 300, New Boston, NH 03070: Catalog $3 ❖ Fly-fishing, bass and saltwater fishing, and fly-tying supplies. 800-331-8558; 603-487-3388 (in NH).

Islander Reels, 6771 Kirkpatrick Crescent, Sanichton, British Columbia, Canada V8M 1Z8: Free information ❖ Direct drive or anti-reverse reels. 604-544-1440.

J & J Tackle, P.O. Box 718, Belmar, NJ 07719: Catalog $1.50 ❖ Lures for fresh and saltwater fishing. 908-280-0200.

Jann's Sportsman's Supplies, P.O. Box 89, Maumee, OH 43537: Free catalog ❖ Lures, rods, and fly-tying supplies. 800-346-6590.

The C.W. Jenkins Fly Rod, 5735 S. Jericho Way, Aurora, CO 80015: Brochure $1 ❖ Fishing rods. 303-699-9128.

Jerry's Tackle, 604 12th St., Highland, IL 62249: Free catalog ❖ Fly-fishing and fly-tying supplies, tackle, and fishing and hunting videos. 800-500-6585.

Johnson Fishing Inc., 1531 E. Madison Ave., Mankato, MN 56002: Free information ❖ Lures for large and small mouth bass. 507-345-4623.

Just Reels, S 82 W22820, Packwood Trail, P.O. Box 156, Big Bend, WI 53103: Free information ❖ Fly reels and cases. 414-662-3626.

K & K Flyfishers' Supply, 8643 Grant, Overland Park, KS 66212: Free catalog ❖ Fly-fishing equipment. 800-795-8118.

Kane Klassics, P.O. Box 8124, Fremont, CA 94537: Catalog $3 ❖ Bamboo fishing rods. 510-487-8545.

Kaufmann's Streamborn, P.O. Box 23032, Portland, OR 97281: Free catalog ❖ Fly and bass fishing, saltwater fishing, and fly-tying supplies. 800-442-4FLY.

Bud Lilly's Trout Shop, P.O. Box 698, West Yellowstone, MT 59758: Catalog $2 ❖ Rods, reels, flies, and fly-fishing tackle. 800-854-9539.

G. Loomis Company, 1359 Down River Dr., Woodland, WA 98674: Catalog $1 ❖ Spinning, fly, and plug and bait casting rods. 206-225-6516.

❖ FISHING & FLY-TYING ❖

Loon Outdoors, 7737 W. Mossy Cup St., Boise, ID 83709: Free brochure ❖ Rod-building components, fly-fishing accessories, fly-tying supplies, and fly-dressing caddies. 800-580-3811.

Lure-Craft Industries Inc., 2295-B N. Shadeland Ave., Indianapolis, IN 46219: Catalog $2 ❖ Plastic worm and lure-making components. 800-925-9088; 317-357-7555 (in IN).

Maxwell MacPherson Jr., P.O. Box 141, Bristol, NH 03222: Free brochure ❖ Salmon flies. 603-744-3313.

Madison River 18th Company, Box 627, Ennis, MT 59729: Free catalog ❖ Fresh and saltwater fly tackle, fly-tying materials, rod-building supplies, and books. 406-682-4293.

Orvis Manchester, 1711 Blue Hills Dr., P.O. Box 12000, Roanoke, VA 24022: Free catalog ❖ Fly-fishing rods, reels, leaders, neoprene waders, tackle boxes, and lures. 800-541-3541.

Manhattan Custom Tackle Ltd., 913 Broadway, New York, NY 10010: Catalog $2 (refundable) ❖ Hard-to-find rod-building components. 212-505-6690.

Mann's Bait Company, 604 State Docks Rd., Eufaula, AL 36027: Free information ❖ Lures. 334-687-5716.

Marriott's Fly Store, 2700 W. Orangethorpe, Fullerton, CA 92633: Catalog $3 ❖ Fly-tying and fly, bass, and saltwater fishing supplies. 714-525-1827.

Martin Reel Company, P.O. Box 6554, Yorkville Station, New York, NY 10128: Free information ❖ Fly reels. 315-866-1690.

Mason Tackle Company, 11273 Center St., P.O. Box 56, Otisville, MI 48463: Free list of retail sources ❖ Fishing lines. 810-631-4571.

Merco Products, 1525 Norland Dr., Sunnyvale, CA 94087: Free catalog ❖ Fly-tying cord and thread. 408-245-7803.

Midland Tackle Company, 66 Rt. 17, Sloatsburg, NY 10974: Free catalog ❖ Molds, lures, and rod-building materials. 800-521-0146.

Mikes Fly Desk, 2395 S. 150 East, Bountiful, UT 84010: Free catalog ❖ Fly-tying materials. 801-292-4736.

Mister Twister Inc., P.O. Drawer 1152, Minden, LA 71058: Free information ❖ Lures. 318-377-8818.

Mustad, P.O. Box 838, Auburn, NY 13021: Free list of retail sources ❖ Fly hooks.

Netcraft Company, P.O. Box 5510, Toledo, OH 43613: Free catalog ❖ Rods, reels, marine electronics, rod and lure building components, and fly-tying supplies. 419-472-9826.

Norland Trading Company, Box 10, Norland, Ontario, Canada K0M 2L0: Video catalog $5 (refundable) ❖ Hunting, fishing, and outdoor products. 800-318-0717.

The Norlander Company, P.O. Box 926, Kelso, WA 98626: Free information ❖ Rotary vises and tools for fly-tying. 360-636-2525.

Normark, 10395 Yellow Circle Dr., Minneapolis, MN 55343: Free information ❖ Lures, knives, and accessories.

On the Fly, 3628 Sage Dr., Rockford, IL 61111: Free catalog ❖ Fly-fishing and fly-tying supplies. 815-877-0090.

Patrick's Fly Shop, 2237 Eastlake Ave., Seattle, WA 98102: Free information ❖ Fly rod-building supplies. 206-323-3302.

Peerless Reel Company, 427-3 Amherst St., Ste. 177, Nashua, NH 03063: Free information ❖ Fishing reels. 603-595-2458.

Penn Fishing Tackle, 3028 W. Hunting Park Ave., Philadelphia, PA 19132: Catalog $2 ❖ Saltwater spinning reels, spinning rods, and plug and bait casting reels. 215-229-9415.

Phone Flies, 24 Blades Run Dr., Shrewsbury, NJ 07702: Free catalog ❖ Fishing flies. 800-329-3543.

Powell, P.O. Box 4000, Chico, CA 95927: Free brochure ❖ Fishing rods. 800-228-0615.

PRADCO, P.O. Box 1587, Fort Smith, AR 72902: Free information ❖ Fishing line, lures, and fish attractants. 800-422-FISH.

R.J. Tackle Inc., 5719 Corporation Circle, Unit 1, Fort Meyers, FL 33905: Free information ❖ Lures. 813-693-7070.

Rainy's Flies & Supplies, 690 N. 100 East, Logan, UT 84321: Free information ❖ Fly-tying supplies. 801-753-6766.

Ramsey Outdoor Store, 226 Rt. 17, P.O. Box 1689, Paramus, NJ 07653: Free catalog ❖ Fly-tying and fishing equipment. Also fishing and hunting videos. 800-526-7436; 201-261-5000 (in NJ).

Readco Corporation, P.O. Box 421, Cameron, MO 64429: Free information ❖ Lighted fishing floats. 800-477-1534.

Regal Engineering Inc., RFD 2, Tully Rd., Orange, MA 01364: Free brochure ❖ Big game fly reels, fly-tying vises, and accessories. 508-575-0488.

Renzetti Inc., 6080 Grisson Pkwy., Titusville, FL 32780: Free list of retail sources ❖ Fly-tying tools and vises.

RIO Products, P.O. Box 684, Blackfoot, ID 83221: Free information ❖ Saltwater tapered leaders, hand-tied leaders, and supplies. 208-785-1244.

Robichaud Reels, P.O. Box 119, Hudson, NH 03051: Free information ❖ Fishing reels. 603-880-6484.

Ryobi America Corporation, P.O. Box 1207, Anderson, SC 29622: Free information ❖ Plug and bait casting reels and rods, saltwater reels and rods, and spin casting reels. 800-525-2579.

Sadu Blue Water Inc., 4660 122nd Dr. North, Royal Palm Beach, FL 33411: Free information ❖ Trolling lures. 407-795-9516.

St. Croix Rod, P.O. Box 279, Park Falls, WI 54552: Free list of retail sources ❖ Saltwater and freshwater fly rods. 715-762-3226.

The Saltwater Angler, Capt. Jeffrey Cardenas, 219 Simonton, Key West, FL 33040: Free catalog ❖ Saltwater fly rods. 800-223-1629.

Scientific Anglers, 3M Center, Building 225-3N-04, St. Paul, MN 55144: Free information ❖ Reels, fly lines, fishing accessories, and how-to cassettes on bass and fly-fishing and deer, waterfowl, and turkey hunting. 800-430-5000.

Scintilla, 615 MacGregor Rd., Belgrade, MT 59714: Free information ❖ Fly fishing and tying accessories. 406-388-7169.

Senco Inc., 520 8th St., Gwinn, MI 49841: Free information ❖ Recreational shelters, portable hunting blinds, ice fishing houses, and greenhouses. 906-346-4116.

Sespe Supplies, 925 A Calle Puerto Vallarta, Santa Barbara, CA 93103: Free information ❖ Fly-tying chests, boxes, cases, and accessories. 805-966-7263.

Shakespeare Company, 3801 Westmore Dr., Columbia, SC 29223: Catalog $1 ❖ Plug and bait casting reels and rods, spin casting reels, and fishing lines. 800-334-9103.

Shannon's Fancy Hackle, Rt. 2, Lamar, AR 72846: Free list of retail sources ❖ Fishing supplies.

Sheldon's Inc., 626 Center St., Antigo, WI 54409: Free information ❖ Freshwater lures. 715-623-2382.

Shimano American Corporation, 1 Holland Dr., Irvine, CA 92718: Catalog $1 ❖ Plug and bait casting reels and rods, saltwater reels and rods, and accessories. 714-951-5003.

Silstar America Corporation, P.O., Box 6505, West Columbia, SC 29171: Catalog $2 ❖ Saltwater spinning reels and rods, plug and bait casting reels and rods, and accessories. 803-794-8521.

Snag Proof, 11387 Deerfield Rd., Cincinnati, OH 45232: Free information ❖ Bass and northern pike lures. 800-762-4773.

South Bend Sporting Goods, 1950 Stanley St., Northbrook, IL 60065: Catalog $2 ❖ Rods, reels, and tackle. 708-564-1900.

South Creek Ltd., P.O. Box 981, Lyons, CO 80540: Catalog $1 ❖ Fishing accessories and one, two, and three-piece bamboo rods. 800-354-5050.

FLAGS & FLAG POLES

Storm Manufacturing Company, Box 720265, Norman, OK 73070: Free information ❖ Lures. 405-329-5894.

Stren Fishing Lines, Division Remington Arms Company, 1007 Market St., Wilmington, DE 19898: Free information ❖ Fishing lines. 302-773-5291.

Tackle Craft, P.O. Box 280, Chippewa Falls, WI 54729: Free catalog ❖ Tools and materials for making flies, jigs, spinning lures, and musky lures. 715-723-3645.

R.D. Taylor Rodmakers, P.O. Box 54, Turners Falls, MA 01376: Free brochure ❖ Handcrafted bamboo fly rods. 413-863-8608.

Thomas & Thomas, 2 Avenue A, Turner Falls, MA 01376: Catalog $3 (refundable) ❖ Fly-tying equipment. 413-863-9727.

Tournament Tackle Inc., P.O. Box 372820, Satellite Beach, FL 32937: Free information ❖ Trolling lures. 407-259-1903.

Triple Fish Fishing Line, 321 Enterprise Dr., Ocoee, FL 34761: Free information ❖ Fishing line. 407-656-7834.

Jack Ulrich, 9167 S. Hill Rd., Boston, NY 14025: Free information ❖ Custom fishing rods with a choice of woods. 800-255-RODS; 716-941-5310 (in NY).

Umpqua Feather Merchants, P.O. Box 700, Glide, OR 97443: Free list of retail sources ❖ Fly-fishing hooks. 800-322-3218.

Universal Vise Corporation, 16 Union Ave., Westfield, MA 01085: Free list of retail sources ❖ Fly-tying kits.

Urban Angler, 118 E. 25th St., New York, NY 10010: Catalog $4 ❖ Fly-fishing equipment. 800-255-5488; 212-979-7600 (in NY).

Versitex of America Ltd., 3545 Schuylkill Rd., Spring City, PA 19475: Free catalog ❖ Fresh and saltwater fly rods and braided fishing line. 610-948-4442.

Wapsi Fly Inc., 27 CR 458, Mountain Home, AR 72653: Free list of retail sources ❖ Fly-tying supplies.

Westbank Anglers, P.O. Box 523, Teton Village, WY 83025: Free catalog ❖ Fly-fishing supplies. 800-922-3474.

Whitetail Fly Tieing Supplies, 7060 Whitetail Ct., Toledo, OH 43613: Catalog $2 (refundable) ❖ Fly-tying supplies. 419-474-2348.

R.L. Winston Rod Company, 500 S. Main St., Drawer T, Twin Bridges, MT 59754: Free list of retail sources ❖ Salt water salmon rods and handcrafted bamboo, glass, and graphite fly rods. 406-684-5674.

Wyoming River Raiders, P.O. Box 50490, Casper, WY 82605: Free catalog ❖ Outdoor clothing, books, fishing gear, and camping, river expedition, and hiking equipment. 800-247-6068.

Yakima Bait Company, P.O. Box 310, Granger, WA 98932: Free information ❖ High-speed trolling lures. 509-854-1311.

Fish-Finding Electronics

Computrol Inc., 499 E. Corporate Dr., Meridian, ID 83642: Free information ❖ Electronic fish-finding equipment and accessories. 800-456-5432.

Defender Industries Inc., 255 Main St., P.O. Box 820, New Rochelle, NY 10801: Free catalog ❖ Electronic fish-finding equipment. 800-435-7180; 914-632-3001 (in NY).

Eagle Electronics Inc., P.O. Box 669, Catoosa, OK 74015: Free information ❖ Electronic fish-finding equipment. 800-324-1354.

Furuno USA, P.O. Box 2343, South San Francisco, CA 94083: Free information ❖ Electronic fish-finding equipment. 415-873-9393.

Interphase Technologies Inc., 1201 Shaffer Rd., Santa Cruz, CA 95060: Free information ❖ Electronic fish-finding equipment. 408-426-2007.

Lowrance Electronics, 12000 E. Skelly Dr., Tulsa, OK 74070: Free information ❖ Electronic fish-finding equipment. 800-324-4737.

Magellan Systems Corporation, P.O. Box 5485, Santa Barbara, CA 93150: Free information ❖ Electronic fish-finding equipment. 800-962-4943.

Si-Tex Marine Electronics, 11001 Roosevelt Blvd., Ste. 800, St. Petersburg, FL 34716: Free information ❖ Electronic fish-finding equipment. 813-576-5734.

Skipper Marine Electronics Inc., 3170 Commercial Ave., Northbrook, IL 60062: Free catalog ❖ Electronic fish-finding equipment. 800-SKIPPER; 708-272-4700 (in IL).

Techsonic Industries Inc., 3 Hummingbird Ln., Eufaula, AL 36027: Free information ❖ Electronic fish-finding equipment. 205-687-6613.

FLAGS & FLAG POLES

American Flag & Gift, 737 Manuela Way, Arroyo Grande, CA 93420: Catalog $2 ❖ Flags, banners, bunting, and flag poles. 800-448-3524; 805-473-0395 (in CA).

American Flagpoles & Flags, 109-F Lumber Ln., Goose Creek, SC 29445: Free catalog ❖ Flagpoles and United States, state, international, nautical, and historical flags. 800-777-1706.

Banner Fabric, Kite Studio, 5555 Hamilton Blvd., Wescosville, PA 18106: Catalog $1 ❖ Fabrics, notions, and hardware for kites, flags, banners, and windsocks. 610-395-3560.

Banner Ideas, 1811 Huguenot Rd., Ste. 101, Midlothian, VA 23113: Catalog $2 (refundable) ❖ Special occasion decorating flags. 804-379-0335.

Carrot-Top Industries Inc., P.O. Box 820, Hillsborough, NC 27278: Free catalog ❖ Ready-made and made-to-order flags, banners, and decorations. 800-628-3524.

Central Discount Flag & Banner, Division Central Mass. Flag, 66 West St., Leominster, MA 01463: Free catalog ❖ United States, religious, military, and flags of the world. Also accessories. 800-356-4232; 800-534-5090 (in MA).

Classic Memorials Inc., P.O. Box 4843, Fort Walton Beach, FL 32549: Free information ❖ Memorial flag cases. Available in mahogany, cherry, walnut, traditional oak, or pickled oak. 800-752-0503.

Festival Flags, 322 W. Broad Street, Richmond, VA 23220: Free catalog ❖ Original decorative flags and accessories. 804-643-3419.

Flag America Company, 2708 Long Beach Blvd., Ship Bottom, NJ 08008: Free information ❖ Flags, banners, windsocks, and flag poles. 609-494-2626.

Flag Fables Inc., 880 Sumner Ave., Springfield, MA 01108: Free catalog ❖ All-occasion decorative flags. 800-257-1025.

Flags & Flagpoles, Division Associated Builders Specialties, 7106 Mapleridge, Houston, TX 77081: Free information ❖ Flags and fiberglass flagpoles. 713-666-2371.

Frenchtown Flags Inc., 700 N. 5th St., St. Charles, MO 63301: Free brochure with long SASE ❖ Decorative double-appliqued, weatherproof nylon garden flags. 314-724-0404.

Frontier Flags, 1761 Owl Creek Rt., Thermopolis, WY 82443: Catalog $3 ❖ Hand-sewn historic flag reproductions from all eras. Also accessories. 307-867-2551.

Glory Flag & Pole Company, 1873 Kountry Ln., Fort Dodge, IA 50501: Free catalog ❖ Flag poles and United States, state, foreign, religious, military, and banners. 515-576-7948.

Good Time Flags, Rt. 4, Box 211, Abbeville, SC 29620: Brochure $1 ❖ Handcrafted nylon appliqued flags designed to fit standard lamp posts. 800-372-0220.

FLOWERS & PLANTS

Hennessy House, P.O. Box 57, Sierra City, CA 96125: Free brochure ❖ Handmade wooden flag poles and flags. 800-285-2122.

House of Flags, P.O. Box 4707, East Providence, RI 02916: Catalog $3 ❖ Flagpoles, weather vanes, eagles, and United States, historical, state, foreign, holiday, seasonal, nautical, and flags. 800-45-FLAGS.

Hudson Valley Flags & Banners, 282 Grand Ave., Englewood, NJ 07631: Free catalog ❖ Festive flags and banners. 800-349-3524.

B.J. Lindsy Flag & Banner Company, 28 Munson St., Greenfield, MA 01302: Catalog $3 (refundable) ❖ Flags, banners, and accessories. 800-360-6512; 413-774-5807 (in MA).

Martin's Flag Company, P.O. Box 1118, Fort Dodge, IA 50501: Free catalog ❖ Flags and accessories. 800-992-3524; 800-248-3524 (in IA).

Marvin Display, 322 Boston Post Rd., Milford, CT 06460: Free information ❖ Flagpoles, hardware, and United States, historical, state, foreign, nautical, and fun flags. 800-322-8587.

Master Bisgrove Designs (Flagmakers), P.O. Box 708, Newburyport, MA 01950: Free catalog ❖ All types and custom-made holiday and hospitality flags and banners. 508-462-6746.

Montpelier Stove Works, 178 River St., Montpelier, VT 05601: Free information ❖ Flags for civic, business, religious, and social ceremonies. 800-287-0150.

Patriots Plus, Box 35414, Canton, OH 44735: Catalog $2 ❖ United States, other countries, historic, celebrations, and custom flags. Also flagpoles. 330-493-4030.

Chris Reid Company Inc., P.O. Box 1827, Midlothian, VA 23113: Free catalog ❖ Ethnic, special occasion, state, country, religious, decorative, and other flags. Also flag poles and accessories. 804-744-5862.

Safety Flag Company of America, P.O. Box 1088, Pawtucket, RI 02862: Free catalog ❖ Flags and safety equipment for boats. 401-722-0900.

U.S. Flag Service, 5741 Elmer Derr Rd., Frederick, MD 21701: Free information ❖ Flags and accessories. 800-USA-FLAG.

Vaughn Display & Flag, 1700 Freeway Blvd., Minneapolis, MN 55430: Free catalog ❖ Flagpoles, floor stands, holders, brackets, bunting, pennants, banners, and religious, United States, foreign, state, territorial, and other flags. 800-328-6120.

Windborne Kites, 585 Cannery Row, Monterey, CA 93940: Free catalog ❖ Kites and accessories, windsocks, and flags. 408-373-7422.

FLOWERS & PLANTS

Artificial Flowers

Bailey's Wholesale Floral Supply, P.O. Box 591, Arcadia, IN 46030: Catalog $3 (refundable) ❖ Silk flowers. 317-984-3663.

Baubanbea Enterprises, P.O. Box 1205, Smithtown, NY 11787: Catalog $1 ❖ Rhinestones, sequins, beads, jewels, lace, appliques, fringes, trim, feathers, imported and domestic fabrics, and silk flowers. 516-724-4661.

Fine Design, P.O. Box 310704, New Braunfels, TX 78131: Free information ❖ Silk rose arrangements. 800-200-2224.

May Silk, 16202 Distribution Way, Cerritos, CA 90703: Free catalog ❖ Silk plants, trees, and flowers. 800-282-7455.

Petals, 300 Central Ave., White Plains, NY 10606: Free catalog ❖ Silk floral arrangements, flowers, plants, and trees. 800-431-2464.

Select Artificials Inc., 701 N. 15th St., St. Louis, MO 63103: Catalog $10 (refundable) ❖ Silk flowers, large plants, and Christmas decorative items. 800-666-6999; 314-621-3050 (in MO).

VIVA Crafts, 14246 E. Marshall, Tulsa, OK 74116: Catalog $3 ❖ Silk flowers, baskets, and flower-arranging supplies.

Dried Flowers

Black Pearl Gardens, Herbal General Store, 220 Maple St., Franklin, OH 45005: Catalog $1 ❖ Herb plants, aromatherapy products, potpourri and supplies, culinary and medicinal herbs, herbal bath and body products, and dried florals. 800-891-0142.

Caswell-Massey Company Ltd., Catalog Division, 100 Enterprise Pl., Dover, DE 19901: Catalog $1 ❖ Potpourri and pomander mixes, dried flowers, herb plants, essential oils, and perfumery supplies. 800-326-0500.

Chalmers-Gabrych Plantasia, 3282 Constitution Dr., Yuba City, CA 95933: Free information ❖ Preserved pest-free miniature show roses. 916-673-8494.

Doering Company, 3531 Niles Rd., St. Joseph, MI 49085: Free catalog ❖ Dried floral products, floral arranging supplies, basketry materials, and how-to videos. 616-429-3961.

Gardens Past, P.O. Box 1846, Estes Park, CO 80517: Catalog $1 ❖ Soaps and soap-making supplies, potpourri, dried flowers, herbs, candles, and aromatherapy items. 303-823-5565.

The Gathered Herb & Greenhouse, 12114 N. State Rd., Otisville, MI 48463: Catalog $2 ❖ Dried flowers, herbs, herb tea, perennials, and potpourri supplies. 810-631-6572.

Goodwin Creek Gardens, P.O. Box 83, Williams, OR 97544: Catalog $1 ❖ Dried floral arrangements, seeds and plants, trees, shrubs, and perennial flowers. 541-846-7357.

Hartman's Herb Farm, Old Dana Rd., Barre, MA 01005: Catalog $2 ❖ Herbs and herb products, dried flowers and potpourri, and essential oils. 508-355-2015.

Herb Shady Acres Farm, 7815 Hwy. 212, Chaska, MN 55318: Free information ❖ Dried flowers and herbs. 612-466-3391.

Herbs-Liscious, 1702 S. 6th St., Marshalltown, IA 50158: Catalog $2 (refundable) ❖ Dried flowers, herbs and spices, oils and fragrances, and potpourri.

Meadow Everlastings, 16464 Shabbona Rd., Malta, IL 60150: Catalog $2 (refundable) ❖ Dried flowers, wreath kits, and potpourri.

Meadows Direct, 13805 Hwy. 136, Onslow, IA 52321: Free list ❖ Dried and preserved leaves and flowers. 800-542-9771.

Mountain Farms Inc., 307 Number 9 Rd., Fairview, NC 28730: Free catalog ❖ Dried floral products and herbs. 704-628-4709.

J. Page Basketry, 820 Albee Rd. West, Nokomis, FL 34275: Catalog $2 (refundable) ❖ Dried flowers and herbs, books, and pine needle, wheat weaving, and basket-making supplies and tools. 813-485-6730.

Rasland Farm, Rt. 1, Box 65 HC, Godwin, NC 28344: Catalog $2.50 ❖ Herb plants, scented geraniums, and dried flowers. 910-567-2705.

Riverside Gardens, 300 E. Riverside, Timberville, VA 22853: Free price list ❖ Dried flowers and plants. 800-847-6449; 703-896-9859 (in VA).

Shady Acres Herb Farm, 7815 Hwy. 212, Chaska, MN 55318: Free list with long SASE ❖ Dried plants. 612-466-3391.

Something's Blooming, Rt. 1, Box 3A, Alba, TX 75410: Free price list ❖ Organically grown and air-dried everlasting herbs and flowers.

Tom Thumb Workshops, Rt. 13, P.O. Box 357, Mappsville, VA 23407: Catalog $1 ❖ Potpourri, herbs, spices, essential oils, dried flowers, and art and craft supplies. 804-824-3507.

Well-Sweep Herb Farm, 205 Mt. Bethel Rd., Port Murray, NJ 07865: Catalog $2 ❖ Potpourri and pomander mixes, dried flowers, and herbs. 908-852-5390.

FOIL CRAFTS

Atlas Art & Stained Glass, P.O. Box 76084, Oklahoma City, OK 73147: Catalog $3 ❖ Kaleidoscopes, frames, lamp bases, and art and craft, stained glass, jewelry-making, and foil-crafting supplies. 405-946-1230.

Bare-Metal Foil Company, P.O. Box 82, Farmington, MI 48332: Catalog $2.50 ❖ Adhesive-backed chrome, black chrome, gold, matte aluminum, and real copper foil sheets. Also quick-setting molding materials.

❖ FOOD PROCESSORS & DRYERS ❖

Guildcraft Company, 100 Firetower Dr., Tonawanda, NY 14150: Free catalog ❖ Colored metal foils and supplies. 716-743-8336.

FOOD PROCESSORS & DRYERS

American Harvest, 4064 Peavey Rd., Chaska, MN 55318: Free information ❖ Food dehydrators. 800-288-4545.

A Cook's Wares, 211 37th St., Beaver Falls, PA 15010: Catalog $2 ❖ Food processors, cutlery, bake-ware, porcelain, French copper pans, and kitchen aids. 412-846-9490.

Environmental Solar Systems, 119 West St., Methuen, MA 01844: Free information ❖ Solar food dryers. 800-934-3848.

Excalibur Dehydrator, 6083 Power Inn Rd., Sacramento, CA 95824: Free information ❖ Food dehydrator. 800-875-4254.

Kitchen Krafts, Box 442, Waukon, IA 52172: Free catalog ❖ Food dryers and preservation supplies. 800-776-0575.

Oreck Corporation, 100 Plantation Rd., New Orleans, LA 70123: Free catalog ❖ Small kitchen appliances and food processors. 800-989-4200.

Vita-Mix Corporation, 8615 Usher Rd., Cleveland, OH 44138: Free information ❖ Vita-Mix food processor. 800-848-2649.

Zabar's & Company, 2245 Broadway, New York, NY 10024: Free catalog ❖ Cookware, food processors, microwave ovens, kitchen tools, and coffee makers. 212-787-2000.

FOODS

Apple Cider

Berry-Hill Limited, 75 Burwell Rd., St. Thomas, Ontario, Canada N5P 3R5: Catalog $2 ❖ Cider press, canning equipment, weather vanes, and garden equipment. 519-631-0480.

Happy Valley Ranch, 16577 W. 327th, Paola, KS 66071: Catalog $1 ❖ Cider and wine presses. 913-849-3103.

Jaffrey Manufacturing Company, Box 23527, Shawnee Mission, KS 66223: Brochure $1 ❖ Apple cider and wine presses, assembled or as a kit. 913-849-3139.

Breads & Rolls

Bagelicious, 1864 Front St., East Meadow, NY 11554: Free information ❖ Fresh-baked bagels and gift packages. 800-55-BAGEL; 516-794-0552 (in NY).

Balducci's, Shop from Home Service, 42-25 12th St., Long Island City, NY 11101: Catalog $3 ❖ Bread and food specialties. 800-225-3822.

Baldwin Hill Bakery, 15 Baldwin Hill Rd., Phillipston, MA 01331: Free brochure ❖ Organic sourdough bread. 508-249-4691.

Barn Stream Natural Foods, P.O. Box 760, Walpole, NH 03608: Free brochure ❖ Handmade low-fat and additive, preservative, and cholesterol-free Yankee sourdough, salt-free garlic whole wheat, and hearty multi-grain breads. 800-654-2882.

Boudin Gifts, P.O. Box 885421, San Francisco, CA 94188: Free information ❖ San Francisco sourdough French bread. 800-992-1855.

Bread Alone, Rt. 28, Boiceville, NY 12412: Free information ❖ Hearth-baked bread made with organic grains. 914-657-3328.

Burnt Cabins Grist Mill, P.O. Box 65, Burnt Cabins, PA 17215: Free brochure ❖ Old-fashioned buckwheat and wheat flour, roasted and regular cornmeal, and pancake and muffin mixes. 800-278-6455.

C'est Croissant Inc., 22138 S. Vermont Ave., Unit A, Torrance, CA 90502: Free brochure ❖ Plain, fluffy French almond, chocolate, and all-butter croissants. 800-633-2767.

Dean & DeLuca Mail-Order, Attention: Catalog Department, 560 Broadway, New York, NY 10012: Free information ❖ Bread. 800-221-7714.

Deborah's Country French Bread, 954 W. Washington Blvd., Chicago, IL 60607: Free brochure ❖ Overnight delivery of bread from the Poilane bakery in Paris. 800-952-1400; 312-633-4004.

DiCamillo Bakery, 811 Linwood Ave., Niagara Falls, NY 14305: Free catalog ❖ Italian bread and specialties. 800-634-4363; 716-282-2341 (in NY).

French Meadow Bakery, 2610 Lyndale Ave. South, Minneapolis, MN 55408: Free information ❖ Yeast and wheat-free organic sourdough bread. 612-870-4740.

Genie's Kitchen, 150 Magic Ln., Box 456, Wibaux, MT 59353: Free list of retail sources ❖ Low-fat and no cholesterol muffin mixes. 406-795-2228.

The Gluten-Free Pantry, P.O. Box 881, Glastonbury, CT 06033: Free catalog ❖ Easy-to-make wheat and gluten-free gourmet bread and cake mixes. 203-633-3826.

H & H Bagels, 46th & 12th Ave., New York, NY 10024: Free catalog ❖ Bagels. 800-NY-BAGEL.

HeartyMix Company, 1231 Madison Hill Rd., Rahway, NJ 07065: Free catalog ❖ Mixes for bread machines. 908-382-3010.

The J.B. Dough Company, 5600 E. Napier, Beviton Harbor, MI 49022: Free information ❖ Gourmet mixes for automatic bread machines. 800-528-6222; 616-933-1025 (in MI).

The King Arthur Flour Baker's Catalog, P.O. Box 876, Norwich, VT 05055: Free information ❖ Sourdough starter for bread, pancakes, biscuits, and cakes. Also pizza dough supplies. 800-827-6836.

Manhattan Bagel Company, P.O. Box 580, New York, NY 10014: Free price list ❖ Bagels. 212-691-3041.

Moishe's Homemade Kosher Bakery, 181 E. Houston St., New York, NY 10002: Free information ❖ Corn bread, challah, and bagels. 212-475-9624.

Native Grains Inc., 101 1st St. West, Fosston, MN 56542: Free information ❖ Mixes for easy-to-make natural organic bread. 800-845-2486.

The Pletzel Company, 2660 Walnut St., Denver, CO 80205: Free information ❖ Bagel chips in a variety of flavors. 800-765-4243; 303-296-4132 (in CO).

R.F. Nature Farm Foods Inc., 850 NBC Center, Lincoln, NE 68508: Free list of retail sources ❖ All-natural mixes for bread machines and oven-baking. 800-222-FARM; 402-474-7576 (in NE).

Rock Hill Bakehouse, 21 Saratoga Rd., Gansevort, NY 12831: Free information ❖ Italian peasant, sourdough, cinnamon-raisin, and naturally leavened hearth-baked breads. 518-743-1627.

Rubschlager Baking Corporation, 3320 W. Grand Ave., Chicago, IL 60651: Free information ❖ European-style whole rye and stone-ground wheat bread. 312-826-1245.

Sherwood Brands Inc., 6110 Executive Blvd., Ste. 1080, Rockville, MD 20852: Free list of retail sources ❖ Kosher, all-natural, and cholesterol-free bagel chips. 301-881-9340.

Spent Grain Baking Company, 1530 Eastlake Ave. East, Ste. 307, Seattle, WA 98103: Free list of retail sources ❖ Fat-free bread and pancake-waffle mix. 800-860-4533; 206-860-4110 (in WA).

Sunberry Baking Company, 757 Kohn St., Norristown, PA 19401: Free information ❖ Fresh-baked sourdough bread. 800-833-4090.

Sunrise Gourmet Foods & Gifts, 1813 3rd Ave. East, Hibbing, MN 55746: Free information ❖ Bread and specialties. 800-782-6736.

Vermont Country Maple Mixes, 76 Ethan Allen Dr., South Burlington, VT 05403: Free information ❖ Maple sugar and syrup, maple sugar sprinkles, and maple-sweetened cake, bread, and frosting mixes. 800-528-7021.

Wanda's Nature Farm Foods, 850 NBC Center, Lincoln, NE 68508: Free catalog ❖ All-natural bread, muffin, pancake, waffle, and double-chocolate cake mixes. 800-222-FARM.

Wolferman's, One Muffin Ln., P.O. Box 15913, Lenexa, KS 66215: Free catalog ❖ English muffins, crumpets, scones, and bagels. 800-999-0169.

Ye Olde Sweet Shoppe Bakery, P.O. Box 1672, Shepherdstown, WV 25443: Free information ❖ Home-baked bread, strudels, German stollen, and specialties. 800-922-5379.

Cakes, Cookies & Pies

The Antique Mall & Crown Restaurant, P.O. Box 540, Indianola, MS 38751: Free information ❖ Catfish paté and gourmet pie mixes. 800-833-7731; 601-887-2522 (in MS).

Ariola Foods Inc., 218-38 97th Ave., Queens Village, NY 11429: Free information ❖ Cannoli shells, cheesecakes, and Italian pastries. 800-443-0777.

The Baker's Catalogue, P.O. Box 876, Norwich, VT 05055: Free catalog ❖ Baking equipment and recipe ingredients. 800-827-6836.

Beth's Fine Desserts, 1201 Andersen Dr., San Rafael, CA 94901: Free information ❖ Gourmet cookies. 800-425-BETH.

Bette's Oceanview Diner, 4240 Hollis St., Emeryville, CA 94608: Free information ❖ Scone and pancake mixes. 510-601-6980.

Bittersweet Pastries, 17 S. Greenbush Rd., Orangeburg, NY 10962: Free list of retail sources ❖ All-natural bittersweet chocolate truffle cakes, tarts, and other pastries. 800-537-7791.

Boca Bons Inc., 8080 Mizner Ln., Boca Raton, FL 33433: Free list of retail sources ❖ Handmade truffles, fudge, and brownies. 800-314-2835; 305-346-0494 (in FL).

Boston Coffee Cake Company, 4 Henshaw St., Woburn, MA 01801: Free information ❖ Coffee cakes. 800-434-0500.

Brass Ladle Products, 14 Olde Ridge Village, Chadds Ford, PA 19317: Free list of retail sources ❖ Cholesterol-free, low-fat, and fat-free cake mixes. 610-558-4171.

Brownies on Tour, P.O. Box 1277, Cutchogue, NY 11935: Free brochure ❖ Brownies and cookies inspired by flavors from around the world. 800-736-4069.

Byrd Cookie Company, P.O. Box 13086, Savannah, GA 31406: Free brochure ❖ Preservative-free Southern-style cookies and confections by Savannah's cookie maker, Benjamin "Cookie" Byrd. 800-291-2973.

Cafe Beaujolais, Box 730, Mendocino, CA 95460: Free catalog ❖ Pastries and desserts, candy assortments, hot chocolate mix, and gourmet specialties. 800-930-0443.

Carol's Heirloom Cookies, Division Dillon Marketing, 850 Meadow Ln., Camp Hill, PA 17011: Free information ❖ Springerle cookies. 717-761-6895.

Celia's Sweets Inc., P.O. Box 424, Grand Ledge, MI 48837: Free brochure ❖ Italian wafer cookies and gourmet candy. 517-627-1910.

Charleston Cake Lady, 774 Woodward Rd., Charleston, SC 29407: Free catalog ❖ Cakes made with fresh and natural ingredients. 800-488-0830.

Cheesecake Lady, P.O. Box 584, Hopland, CA 95449: Free brochure ❖ Cheesecakes and a low-fat and low-cholesterol lemon cake. 800-225-3523.

Cheesecake Royale, 9016 Garland Rd., Dallas, TX 75218: Free information with long SASE ❖ Cheesecakes. 800-328-9102; 214-328-9102 (in TX).

Chocolate Catalogue, 3983 Gratiot, St. Louis, MO 63110: Free catalog ❖ Petit fours double-dipped in chocolate with a choice of fillings. 800-325-8881; 314-534-2402 (in MO).

Collin Street Bakery, P.O. Box 79, Corsicana, TX 75151: Free brochure ❖ Fruitcakes, cheesecakes, pecan pies, and other bakery favorites. 903-872-8111.

Crabtree & Evelyn Limited, P.O. Box 158, Woodstock Hill, CT 06281: Catalog $3.50 ❖ English biscuits and cookies, gingerbread, ginger and butter-ginger cookies, Scottish shortbread, Belgian chocolates, cheese wafers and biscuits from Holland, Italian biscuits, preserves, marmalades, jellies, honey, English sauces, spices and condiments, herbs, tea, and candy. 800-624-5211.

Cryer Creek Kitchens, P.O. Box 9003, Corsicana, TX 75151: Free catalog ❖ Homemade cakes, pies, and cookies. 800-353-7437.

Delancey Dessert Company, 573 Grand St., New York, NY 10002: Free information ❖ All-natural kosher rugelach and other baked goods. 800-254-5254; 212-254-5254 (in NY).

DiCamillo Bakery, 811 Linwood Ave., Niagara Falls, NY 14305: Free catalog ❖ Almond macaroons, sesame-coated red wine and finger biscuits, butter cookies, cakes, and bread. 800-634-4363; 716-282-2341 (in NY).

Divine Delights Bakery & Cafe, 24 Digital, Ste. 10, Novato, CA 94949: Free information ❖ Triple-chocolate petit fours and fudge brownies, gourmet cakes, truffles, and tea cakes. 800-4-HEAVEN.

Duo Delights, 1515 S. Fairgrounds Rd., Midland, TX 79705: Free information ❖ Lemon crunch cookies and other favorites. 915-684-6166.

Eilenberger's Bakery, P.O. Box 710, Palestine, TX 75802: Free brochure ❖ Cakes, brownies, cookies, and other pastries. 903-729-2253.

Elegant Sweets, 3916 E. Pine, Seattle, WA 98122: Free list of retail sources ❖ Biscotti, chocolates, toffee, gourmet-flavored white barks, and specialties. 206-443-8633.

Erica's Rugelach & Baking Company Inc., 389 4th St., Brooklyn, NY 11215: Free list of retail sources ❖ Certified kosher bakery specialties. 718-965-3657.

Essentially Chocolate, 6129 Executive Blvd., Rockville, MD 20852: Free information ❖ Chocolate candy and gourmet food gifts. 301-770-5660.

The Estee Corporation, 169 Lackawanna Ave., Parsippany, NJ 07054: Free catalog ❖ Sugarless candy and cookies. 201-335-1000.

Europa Foods Ltd., 170 Commerce Dr., Hauppage, NY 11788: Free list of retail sources ❖ All-natural butter shortbread. 800-521-0141; 516-273-0011 (in NY).

The Famous Pacific Dessert Company, 2414 SW Andover St., Seattle, WA 98106: Free information ❖ Tortes, cheesecakes, and baked goods. 800-666-1950; 206-935-1999 (in WA).

Fancy Fortune Cookies, 6265 Coffman Rd., Indianapolis, IN 46268: Free information ❖ Gourmet fortune cookies in twelve flavors and brilliant colors. Individually wrapped and with custom messages, they are available in tins or loose by the case. 317-299-8900.

Four Oaks Farm Inc., P.O. Box 987, Lexington, SC 29071: Free brochure ❖ Country-style ham and bacon, jams, jellies, pickles, relishes, salad dressings, cakes, and other favorites. 800-858-5006; 803-356-3194 (in SC).

Fralinger's Inc., 1325 Boardwalk, Atlantic City, NJ 08401: Free brochure ❖ Saltwater taffy, sugar-free low-sodium salt water taffy, fudge, almond and coconut macaroons, chocolates, and other candy. 609-345-2177.

Gloria's Kitchen, P.O. Box 1415, Guilford, CT 06437: Free price list ❖ Almond marzipan tea cake mixes. 800-680-9944.

The Gluten-Free Pantry, P.O. Box 881, Glastonbury, CT 06033: Free catalog ❖ Easy-to-make wheat and gluten-free gourmet bread and cake mixes. 203-633-3826.

Godiva Direct, P.O. Box 945, Clinton, CT 06413: Free catalog ❖ Cakes, pastries, and chocolate candy. 800-643-7551.

Golden Walnut Specialty Foods, 3200 16th St., Zion, IL 60099: Free catalog ❖ Packaged all-kosher cookies, cakes, and candies. 800-445-3957.

Grandma's Fruit Cake, Division Metz Baking Company, Box 457, Beatrice, NE 68310: Free brochure ❖ Fruitcake. 800-228-4030; 402-223-2358 (in NE).

Grandma's Recipe Rugelach, 415 W. 15th St., New York, NY 10011: Free information ❖ Low-calorie whole wheat rugelach with natural fruit spreads and other flavors. 800-538-5055.

William Greenberg Desserts Inc., 1100 Madison Ave., New York, NY 10028: Free catalog ❖ Brownies, butter cookies, cheese straws, pound cake, schnecken, Danish pastries, kugelhopf, coffee and chocolate yeast loaves, muffins, pecan rings, and angel food and carrot cakes. 800-255-8278.

Mrs. Hanes' Moravian Cookies, Moravian Sugar Crisp Company, 4643 Friedberg Church Rd., Clemmons, NC 27012: Free brochure ❖ Moravian butterscotch cookies and sugar, lemon, and chocolate crisps. 910-764-1402.

❖ FOODS ❖

Harry & David, P.O. Box 712, Medford, OR 97501: Free catalog ❖ Cakes, baklava, cinnamon pastries, tortes, candy, preserves, fresh and dried fruits, and specialties. 800-345-5655.

HeartyMix Company, 1231 Madison Hill Rd., Rahway, NJ 07065: Free catalog ❖ Salt-free bread and wheat-free products. Also preservative, cholesterol, and saturated fat-free baking mixes for cookies and cakes. 908-382-3010.

Hermitage Bakery, Immaculate Heart Hermitage, Big Sur, CA 93920: Free brochure ❖ Date-nut cake and fruitcakes. 408-667-2456.

MONASTERY Fruit Cake

Holy Cross Abbey, RR 2, Box 3870, Berryville, VA 22611: Free information ❖ Traditional fruitcakes, made of choice fruits and nut meats, in a brandy-laced batter.

Home Baked Group Inc., 1004 S. Rogers Circle, Boca Raton, FL 33487: Free list of retail sources ❖ Kosher fat-free and low-fat brownies. 800-683-3467; 407-995-0767 (in FL).

Hunt Country Foods Inc., P.O. Box 876, Middleburg, VA 22117: Free information ❖ Shortbread cookies. 540-364-2622.

Indian Hill Farms, 213 Old Indian Rd., Milton, NY 12547: Free catalog ❖ Smoked whole turkey and turkey breast, kosher turkey, smoked ham, Norwegian smoked salmon, and brandied fruitcake. 914-795-2700.

Koinonia Partners Inc., 1324 Georgia Hwy. 49 South, Americus, GA 31709: Free catalog ❖ Pecan and peanut candy and baked goods, shelled pecan halves, and pecans in the shell. Also raw-shelled peanuts. 800-569-4128.

Lady Dianne Gourmet Desserts, 410 W. Industrial St., Lecenter, MN 56057: Free information ❖ Gourmet baked desserts.

Linda's Best for the True Brownie Lover, 5699-B SE International Way, Milwaukie, OR 97222: Brochure $2 (refundable) ❖ Fudgy brownies, chocolate tortes, and dessert bars. 800-888-1487.

Linn's Fruit Bin, 2485 Village Ln., Cambria, CA 93428: Free catalog ❖ Fresh-fruit pies, fruit-filled muffins, and cookies. 800-676-1670.

The Magic of Chef Paul Prudhomme, P.O. Box 23342, New Orleans, LA 70183: Free catalog ❖ New Orleans cinnamon-flavored coffee cake and sweet potato pecan pie. 800-457-2857.

Mary of Puddin Hill, P.O. Box 241, Greenville, TX 75403: Free catalog ❖ Fruitcakes, other cakes, pies, and candy. 800-545-8889.

Matthews 1812 House, 250 Kent Rd., P.O. Box 15, Cornwall Bridge, CT 06754: Free brochure ❖ Original fruit, holiday, and special occasion cakes. 800-662-1812.

Mom's Apple Pie Company, 296 Sunset Park, Herndon, VA 22070: Free brochure ❖ Low-sugar fruit pies. 800-221-3897.

Mother Myrick's Confectionary, P.O. Box 1142, Manchester Center, VT 05255: Free brochure ❖ Hot fudge sauce, maple cheesecake, linzer torte, stollen, fudge, butter crunch, truffles, and caramels. 802-362-1560.

My Grandma's of New England Coffee Cake, 231 Bussey St., Dedham, MA 02026: Free brochure ❖ Regular and low-fat coffee cakes. 800-847-2636.

Nanco, P.O. Box 100549, Terra Bedlla, CA 93270: Free list of retail sources ❖ Roasted pistachios and shortbread cookies. 209-535-1030.

Northwest Specialty Baking Mixes, P.O. Box 25240, Portland, OR 97225: Free information ❖ Baking mixes. 800-666-1727.

One Cookie Place, P.O. Box 160756, Altamonte Springs, FL 32716: Free brochure ❖ Chocolate and white-chocolate chip, peanut butter, oatmeal raisin, chocolate crunch, and raspberry white cookies. 800-992-6654; 407-774-9433 (in FL).

Paradigm Foodworks, 5775 SW Jean Rd., Ste. 106A, Lake Oswego, OR 97034: Catalog $1 (refundable) ❖ Scone and Belgian waffle mixes, fruit spreads, and dessert sauces. 800-234-0250.

Pennysticks, 5200 6th Ave., Altoona, PA 16602: Free information ❖ Lightly salted or unsalted cholesterol and sugar-free oat bran pretzel nuggets. 800-344-GIFT.

Pittman & Davis, P.O. Box 532227, Harlingen, TX 78553: Catalog $1 ❖ Fruitcakes, cheese, smoked ham, turkey, ruby-red grapefruit, oranges, citrus fruit packs, and pecans. 210-423-2154.

Real Cookies Inc., 2123 Wantagh Ave., Wantagh, NY 11793: Free list of retail sources ❖ Gourmet cookie mixes. 800-822-5113.

Rhino Foods Inc., 79 Industrial Pkwy., Burlington, VT 05401: Free information ❖ Creamy cheesecakes and cheesecake cookies. 800-639-3350; 802-862-0252 (in VT).

Rowena's, 758 W. 22nd, Norfolk, VA 23517: Free information ❖ Gourmet cakes, preserves and jams, and cooking sauces. 800-980-2253.

Santa Fe Cookie Company, 3905 San Mateo NE, Albuquerque, NM 87110: Free brochure ❖ Gourmet and sugar-free cookies, spicy snacks, pretzels, crackers, and nut mixes. 800-873-5589.

Shaffer, Clarke & Company Inc., 3 Parklands Dr., Darien, CT 06820: Free list of retail sources ❖ All-butter shortbread biscuits and crunchy cookies dipped in chocolate. 203-655-3555.

Slim Waist Foods, 2914 Coney Island Ave., Brooklyn, NY 11235: Free brochure ❖ Weight control and fat-free cookies. 718-769-5700.

Steve's Mom Inc., 113 16th St., Brooklyn, NY 11215: Free list of retail sources ❖ Kosher strudel, rugelach, and bakery specialties. 718-832-6300.

Sugar Spoon All Natural Cheesecake, 451 N. 66th St., Lincoln, NE 68505: Free catalog ❖ Gourmet cheesecakes. 800-228-0052; 402-464-2829 (in NE).

Things of Good Taste, P.O. Box 455, Waynesboro, VA 22980: Free list of retail sources ❖ Cakes, fruit butters, candy, nuts, and dip and seasoning mixes. 800-248-2591.

Turf Cheesecake Corporation, 158 S. 12th Ave., Mt. Vernon, NY 10550: Free information ❖ Cheesecakes. 800-221-8873.

Albert Uster Imports Inc., 9211 Gaither Rd., Gaithersburg, MD 20877: Free catalog ❖ Ready-to-serve petite-size pastries. 800-231-8154; 301-258-7350 (in MD).

Vermont Country Maple Mixes, 76 Ethan Allen Dr., South Burlington, VT 05403: Free information ❖ Maple sugar and syrup, maple sugar sprinkles, and maple sweetened cake, bread, and frosting mixes. 800-528-7021

Walkers Shortbread Ltd., P.O. Box 1328, Hauppauge, NY 11788: Free list of retail sources ❖ Shortbread cookies, Scottish biscuits, fruitcakes, and dessert meringues. 800-521-0141; 516-273-0011 (in NY).

Ye Olde Sweet Shoppe Bakery, P.O. Box 1672, Shepherdstown, WV 25443: Free information ❖ Home-baked bread, strudels, German stollen, and specialties. 800-922-5379.

YZ Enterprises Inc., 377 W. Dussell Dr., Maumee, OH 43537: Free information ❖ Parve kosher cookies. 800-736-8779.

Candy & Dessert Sauces

Angell & Phelps, 154 S. Beach St., Daytona Beach, FL 32114: Free brochure ❖ Handmade gourmet chocolate candy favorites. 800-969-2634.

Aplets & Cotlets Factory, P.O. Box C, Cashmere, WA 98815: Free catalog ❖ Aplets and Cotlets, Washington's famous fruit and nut confection. 800-888-5696.

Arkansas Blue Heron Farms, Rt. 2, Box 323, Lowell, AR 72745: Free catalog ❖ Blueberry jam and marmalades, Amaretto dessert sauce, and specialties. 800-225-6849.

❖ FOODS ❖

Astor Chocolate Corporation, 48-25 Metropolitan Ave., Glendale, NY 11385: Free brochure ❖ Chocolate dessert shells, mocha and liqueur cups, dinner mints, truffles, chocolate greeting cards, and specialties. 718-386-7400.

Aunt Leah's Fudge, P.O. Box 981, Nantucket, MA 02554: Free brochure ❖ Homemade fudge and other candy. 800-824-6330.

Karl Bissinger's French Confections, 3983 Gratiot, St. Louis, MO 63110: Free catalog ❖ Chocolates, fruit and nut bars, jellies, jams, cheese, meat, and tea. 800-325-8881.

Black Hound New York, 149 1st Ave., New York, NY 10003: Free information ❖ Belgian chocolate truffles and gourmet favorites. 212-979-9505.

Boca Bons Inc., 8080 Mizner Ln., Boca Raton, FL 33433: Free list of retail sources ❖ Handmade truffles, fudge, and brownies. 800-314-2835; 305-346-0494 (in FL).

Andre Bollier Ltd., 5018 Main St., Kansas City, MO 64112: Free brochure ❖ Gourmet chocolate candy and gift packages. 800-892-1234; 816-561-3440 (in MO).

Maude Borup, World Trade Center, 30 E. 7th St., St. Paul, MN 55103: Free brochure ❖ Gourmet chocolates and confectionary favorites. 612-293-0530.

Bouchard L'Escaut USA Inc., 811 W. 7th St., Ste. 200, Los Angeles, CA 90017: Free list of retail sources ❖ Belgian chocolates. 213-614-0616.

Cafe Beaujolais, Box 730, Mendocino, CA 95460: Free catalog ❖ Pastries and desserts, candy assortments, hot chocolate mix, and gourmet specialties. 800-930-0443.

Carp River Trading Company, 6005 E. Traverse Hwy., Traverse City, MI 49864: Free catalog ❖ Sugar-free hot fudge and other dessert sauces. Also preserves and condiments. 800-526-9876.

Chapin's Fudge & Chocolates, P.O. Box 285, Beaverton, OR 97075: Free brochure ❖ Assorted chocolate covered fudge. 800-359-3911.

Choco-Logo, 159 Broadway, Buffalo, NY 14201: Free information ❖ Molded chocolate specialties. 716-855-3500.

Chocoholics Divine Desserts, 3765 N. Wilcox Rd., Stockton, CA 95215: Catalog $5 ❖ Traditional semi-sweet chocolate, fat-free and reduced calorie semi-sweet, and fruit-source sweetened chocolate syrups. 800-760-CHOC; 209-931-5188 (in CA).

The Chocolate Barn, Historic Rt. 7A, Shaftsbury, VT 05262: Free information ❖ Hand-dipped chocolates, fudge, molded solid chocolate, and other favorites. 802-375-6928.

Chocolate Catalogue, 3983 Gratiot, St. Louis, MO 63110: Free catalog ❖ Handmade chocolates and petit fours double dipped in chocolate. 800-325-8881; 314-534-2402 (in MO).

The Chocolate Lady Inc., 1455 Page Industrial Blvd., St. Louis, MO 63132: Free information ❖ Handmade chocolate specialties. 314-427-8999.

Chocolate Photos, 7 Bixley Heath, Lynbrook, NY 11563: Free catalog ❖ Custom-molded chocolate novelties. 516-887-4445.

Chukar Cherries, P.O. Box 510, Prosser, WV 99350: Free catalog ❖ Cherry preserves and chocolate candy. 800-624-9544.

Clearbrook Farms, 5514 Fair Ln., Fairfax, OH 45227: Free brochure ❖ Semi-sweet chocolate sauces, marmalades, and preserves. 800-222-9966; 513-271-2053 (in OH).

Cocoa-Mill Chocolate Company, 121 W. Nelson St., Lexington, VA 24450: Free information ❖ Gourmet truffles, turtles, and other favorites. 800-421-6220; 540-464-8400 (in VA).

Community Products Inc., RD 2, Box 1950, Montpelier, VT 05602: Free list of retail sources ❖ Dairy-free chocolate bars. 800-927-2695; 802-229-5702 (in VT).

Coon's Mill Farm, P.O. Box 1097, Woodville, MS 39669: Free information ❖ Gourmet candy. 800-472-5134.

Da Vinci Fine Chocolates Inc., P.O. Box 9787, Seattle, WA 98109: Free information ❖ Syrups for baked goods, beverages, desserts, and pancake toppings. 800-640-6779; 206-682-4682 (in WA).

Richard H. Donnelly Fine Chocolates, 1509 Mission St., Santa Cruz, CA 95060: Free information ❖ Chocolate candy specialties. 408-458-4214.

Elegant Sweets, 3916 E. Pine, Seattle, WA 98122: Free list of retail sources ❖ Biscotti, chocolates, toffee, gourmet-flavored white bark, and specialties. 206-443-8633.

Essentially Chocolate, 6129 Executive Blvd., Rockville, MD 20852: Free information ❖ Chocolate candy and brownies. 301-770-5660.

The Estee Corporation, 169 Lackawanna Ave., Parsippany, NJ 07054: Free catalog ❖ Sugarless candy and cookies. 201-335-1000.

Ethel-M Chocolates Mail-order, P.O. Box 98505, Las Vegas, NV 89193: Free catalog ❖ Milk and dark chocolate truffles, butter creams, nuts, and other candy. 800-4-ETHEL-M.

Evans Creole Candy Company, 848 Decatur St., New Orleans, LA 70116: Free information ❖ Nut clusters, turtles, Creole hash, and old-fashioned favorites. 800-637-6675; 504-522-7111 (in LA).

Fannie May Candies, Attention: Mail Order Department, 1137 W. Jackson, Chicago, IL 60607: Free brochure ❖ Chocolates, nuts and nut candy, hard candy, and other favorites. 800-333-3629.

Figi's, 3200 S. Maple, Marshfield, WI 54404: Free catalog ❖ Candy and specialties. 715-387-6311.

Fralinger's Inc., 1325 Boardwalk, Atlantic City, NJ 08401: Free brochure ❖ Saltwater and sugar-free, low-sodium salt water taffy. Also fudge, almond and coconut macaroons, chocolates, and other candy. 609-345-2177.

Fran's Chocolates, 2805 E. Madison St., Seattle, WA 98112: Free information ❖ Homemade caramel favorites, gourmet dessert sauces, and candy specialties. 206-322-6511.

Godiva Direct, P.O. Box 945, Clinton, CT 06413: Free catalog ❖ Chocolate candy and pastries. 800-643-7551.

Golden Walnut Specialty Foods, 3200 16th St., Zion, IL 60099: Free catalog ❖ Packaged all-kosher cookies, cakes, and candies. 800-445-3957.

Green Mountain Chocolate Company, RR 2, Box 1447, Waterbury, VT 05676: Free brochure ❖ Handmade truffles. 800-686-8783.

Harbor Candy Shop, P.O. Box 498, Ogunquit, ME 03907: Free catalog ❖ Chocolate-covered fruit and dark or milk-chocolate pecan or cashew-caramel turtles. 207-646-8078.

Harbor Sweets Inc., Palmer Cove, 85 Leavitt St., Salem, MA 01970: Free catalog ❖ Handmade chocolates. Includes sugar-free candy, seasonal favorites, gift assortments, chunks for ice cream, and selections for special occasions, weddings, and stocking stuffers. 800-234-4860; 508-745-7648 (in MA).

Harry & David, P.O. Box 712, Medford, OR 97501: Free catalog ❖ Candy, cakes, baklava, cinnamon pastries, tortes, preserves, fresh and dried fruits, and specialties. 800-345-5655.

Hershey's Mailorder, P.O. Box 801, Hershey, PA 17033: Free catalog ❖ Hershey specialties and novelties. 800-544-1347.

Huckleberry Haven, P.O. Box 190523, Hungry Horse, MT 59919: Free brochure ❖ Jams, jellies, syrups, toppings, and flavored honeys. 406-387-5731.

Indian Wells Date Gardens & Chocolatier, 74-774 Hwy. 111, Indian Wells, CA 92210: Free catalog ❖ Candy, nuts, dates, and date specialties. 619-346-2914.

Jinil Au Chocolat, 414 Central Ave., Cedarhurst, NY 11516: Free information ❖ Custom-molded chocolate and gift baskets. 800-646-4645.

The King's Cupboard, P.O. Box 27, Red Lodge, MT 59068: Free information ❖ Bittersweet chocolate, espresso, and orange-flavored dessert sauces. 406-446-3060.

FOODS

Knudsen's Candy & Nut Company, 25067 Viking St., Hayward, CA 94545: Free catalog ❖ Butter cream caramels, triple-chocolate truffles, and dessert sauces. 800-736-6887; 510-293-6887 (in CA).

Koinonia Partners Inc., 1324 Georgia Hwy. 49 South, Americus, GA 31709: Free catalog ❖ Pecan and peanut candy, baked goods, shelled pecan halves, pecans in the shell. Also raw-shelled peanuts. 800-569-4128.

Koppers Chocolate Specialty Company Inc., 39 Clarkson St., New York, NY 10014: Free list of retail sources ❖ Cordials, chocolate-covered fruits and nuts, and gourmet candy. 800-325-0026; 212-243-0220 (in NY).

La Maison du Chocolat, 25 E. 73rd St., New York, NY 10021: Free information ❖ Imported chocolates from Paris, France. 212-744-7117.

Lake Champlain Chocolates, 431 Pine St., Burlington, VT 05401: Free brochure ❖ Fresh-made chocolate candy. 802-864-1807.

Lammes Candy, P.O. Box 1885, Austin, TX 78767: Free catalog ❖ Pecan pralines. 800-252-1885; 512-835-6791 (in TX).

Liberty Orchards Company Inc., P.O. Box 179, Cashmere, WA 98815: Free catalog ❖ Aplets and Cotlets and handmade all-natural candy and fruit specialties. 800-888-5696.

Harry London Candies Inc., 1281 S. Main St., North Canton, OH 44720: Free list of retail sources ❖ Milk chocolate specialties, mocha confections, fondue dessert and dipping sauce, confection snacks, and gourmet candy. 800-321-0444.

Mrs. London's Confections, P.O. Box 529, Lexington, MA 02173: Free price list ❖ Preservative-free handmade toffee. 800-452-8162; 508-371-3074 (in MA).

Maggie Lyon Chocolatiers, 6000 Peachtree Industrial Blvd., Norcross, GA 30071: Free list of retail sources ❖ Regular and sugar-free truffles. 800-969-3500.

Margaret's Superior Desserts, P.O. Box 908, Marquette, MI 49855: Free information ❖ Truffles and truffle cake, baklava, and cheesecakes. 906-226-9001.

Marshall's Inc., 308 E. Central Ave., Mackinaw City, MI 49701: Free catalog ❖ Fresh cream fudge, fine handmade and sugar-free candies. Mail orders year round. 616-436-5082.

Mary of Puddin Hill, P.O. Box 241, Greenville, TX 75403: Free catalog ❖ Candy, fruitcakes, pies, and other baked goods. 800-545-8889.

Matthews 1812 House, 250 Kent Rd., P.O. Box 15, Cornwall Bridge, CT 06754: Free brochure ❖ Candy, dessert sauces, maple syrup, nuts and snacks, and gourmet specialties. 800-662-1812.

May's Candy Shop, Box 483, Mackinac Island, MI 49757: Free brochure ❖ Mackinac fudge, pecans in caramel and hand-dipped in milk chocolate, and English toffee.

MoonShine Trading Company, P.O. Box 896, Winters, CA 95694: Free catalog ❖ Semi-sweet chocolate crunch, white chocolate cashew creme, white chocolate almond, and milk chocolate almond crunch nut spreads. Also fruit spreads, almond and gourmet butters, and sweet clover, yellow star thistle, sunflower, and eucalyptus honey. 800-678-1226; 916-753-0601 (in CA).

Moonstruck Chocolatier, 608 Southwest Alder St., Portland, OR 97205: Free information ❖ Gourmet chocolate specialties. 800-557-6666; 503-241-0955 (in OR).

Moore's Candies Inc., 3004 Pinewood Ave., Baltimore, MD 21214: Free brochure ❖ Homemade candy. 410-426-2705.

Mother Myrick's Confectionary, P.O. Box 1142, Manchester Center, VT 05255: Free brochure ❖ Hot fudge sauce, maple cheesecake, linzer torte, stollen, fudge, butter crunch, truffles, and caramels. 802-362-1560.

Neuhaus USA Inc., 2 Secatoag Ave., Port Washington, NY 11050: Free list of retail sources ❖ Gourmet Belgium chocolates. 516-883-7400.

New Canaan Farms, P.O. Box 386, Dripping Springs, TX 78620: Free brochure ❖ Ice cream toppings, jellies, and mustard. 800-727-5267.

Nunes Farms Almonds, 4012 Pete Miller Rd., P.O. Box 311, Newman, CA 95360: Free information ❖ Fresh, roasted and salted, honey-glazed, and Cheddar cheese almonds. Also almond candy and English toffee. 800-255-1641.

C.J. Olson Cherries, Rt. 1, Box 140, El Camino Real, Sunnyvale, CA 94087: Free brochure ❖ Dried fruit packs, chocolate covered fruits and nuts, and gift assortments. 800-738-2464.

Palais du Chocolat, 3309 Connecticut Ave. NW, Washington, DC 20008: Free information ❖ Gourmet candy inspired by French and Belgian favorites. 202-723-4280.

Paradigm Foodworks, 5775 SW Jean Rd., Ste. 106A, Lake Oswego, OR 97034: Catalog $1 (refundable) ❖ Scone and Belgian waffle mixes, fruit spreads, and dessert sauces. 800-234-0250.

Pecan Producers International, Primera Pecans, P.O. Box 1301, Corsicana, TX 75151: Free information ❖ Chocolate covered pecans. 800-732-2648.

Perugina Chocolates, 520 Madison Ave. (at 54th St.), New York, NY 10022: Free information ❖ Gourmet chocolate candy specialties. 800-272-0500.

Plimoth Lollipop Company, 286 Court St., Plymouth, MA 02360: Free information ❖ Old-fashioned hand-poured lollipops. 800-777-0115.

Ann Raskas Candies, P.O. Box 13367, Kansas City, KS 66113: Free information ❖ Candy for dieters. 913-422-7230.

RoCocoa's Faerie Queene Chocolates, 415 Castro St., San Francisco, CA 94114: Catalog $2 ❖ Imported gourmet candy specialties. 415-252-5814.

Sarris Candies, 511 Adams Ave., Canonsburg, PA 15317: Free catalog ❖ Candy made with all-natural ingredients. 800-255-7771.

See's Candies, P.O. Box S, Culver City, CA 90231: Free catalog ❖ Chocolate candy, seasonal and holiday specialties, lollipops, and assortments. 800-347-7337.

Select Origins, P.O. Box 1748, Mansfield, OH 44901: Free catalog ❖ Dessert sauces, oils, vinegars, sauces, marinades, relishes and condiments, herbs and spices, coffee, tea, and preserves.

Señor Murphy, Candymaker, P.O. Box 2505, Santa Fe, NM 87504: Free catalog ❖ Sugar-free and gourmet chocolate favorites. 505-988-4311.

Seroogy's Chocolates, P.O. Box 143, De Pere, WI 54115: Free catalog ❖ Candy and nut assortments. 800-776-0377; 414-336-1383 (in WI).

Society Hill Snacks, 2121 Gillingham St., Philadelphia, PA 19124: Free list of retail sources ❖ Gourmet chocolate confections. 800-595-0050; 215-288-2888 (in PA).

Splurge Inc., 1204 3rd Ave., Ste. 163, New York, NY 10021: Free information ❖ Low-calorie gourmet specialties. 212-439-6181.

Standard Candy Company, Mail Order Service, P.O. Box 697, Eastman, GA 31023: Free catalog ❖ Goo Goo Clusters, an original combination of chewy caramel, creamy marshmallow, roasted peanuts, and milk chocolate. Also old-fashioned stick candy and southern-style foods. 800-231-3402.

Steel's Sauces, 425 E. Hector St., Conshohocken, PA 19428: Free list of retail sources ❖ Classic and reduced-calorie sugar-free fudge sauces, chocolate syrup, pie fillings, fruit sauce and spreads, and gourmet sweets. 800-6-STEELS; 610-828-9430 (in PA).

FOODS

The Sugar Shack, Rt. 7A, Arlington, VT 05250: Free information ❖ Vermont maple syrup, cream, and candy. Also homemade fudge, cheese, Vermont food products, and gifts. 802-375-6747.

Teuscher Chocolates of Switzerland, 620 5th Ave. at Rockefeller Center, New York, NY 10020: Free catalog ❖ Swiss chocolates. 212-246-4416.

Things of Good Taste, P.O. Box 455, Waynesboro, VA 22980: Free list of retail sources ❖ Cakes, fruit butters, candy, nuts, and dip and seasoning mixes. 800-248-2591.

Top Hat Company, Box 66, Wilmette, IL 60091: Free brochure ❖ Dessert sauces. 847-756-6565.

Trappistine Creamy Caramels, 8325 Abbey Hill, Dubuque, IA 52003: Free brochure ❖ Caramels and creamy mints. 319-556-6330.

Trappistine Quality Candy, Mount Saint Mary's Abbey, 300 Arnold St., Wrentham, MA 02093: Free brochure ❖ Butternut munch, caramels, chocolate fudge, and penuche. 617-528-1282.

Vermont Confectionary, Historic Rt. 7A at the Iron Kettle, Shaftsbury, VT 05262: Free information with long SASE ❖ Chocolates, handmade lollipops, novelty chocolates, and other confections. 802-447-2610.

World of Chantilly, 4302 Farragut Rd., Brooklyn, NY 11203: Free list of retail sources ❖ Certified kosher French pastries. Also chocolate candy and gift baskets. 718-859-1110.

Young Pecans, c/o Pecan Plantations, P.O. Drawer 6709, Florence, SC 29502: Free catalog ❖ Butter-roasted and salted pecans and cashews, double-dipped chocolate pecan halves, butter-toffee pecan popcorn, pecan divinity logs, and praline, sugar and orange, sugar and spiced, and Cheddar cheese pecans. 800-729-8004.

Caviar

Assouline & Ting Inc., 314 Brown St., Philadelphia, PA 19123: Free information ❖ Imported and domestic caviar, smoked fish, snails, and specialties. 800-521-4491; 215-627-3000 (in PA).

Caviar & Caviar, 12307 Washington Ave., Rockville, MD 20852: Free information ❖ American sturgeon and Russian Beluga caviar. 800-472-4456; 301-231-0700 (in MD).

Caviarteria Inc., 502 Park Ave., New York, NY 10022: Free catalog ❖ Smoked fish and American whitefish, sturgeon, salmon, Beluga, and Sevruga caviar. 800-422-8427; 212-759-7410 (in NY).

Hansen Caviar Company, 93D S. Railroad Ave., Bergenfield, NJ 07621: Free information ❖ American sturgeon and Russian Beluga caviar. 800-735-0441; 201-385-6221 (in NJ).

Petrossian Shop, 3342 Melrose Ave. NW, Roanoke, VA 24017: Free catalog ❖ Caviar, foie gras, truffles, and smoked salmon. 800-828-9241.

Poriloff Caviar, Purepak Foods Inc., 47-39 49th St., Woodside, NY 11377: Free information ❖ American sturgeon and Russian Beluga caviar. 718-784-3344.

Cheese

Bandon Cheese Inc., P.O. Box 1668, Bandon, OR 97411: Free brochure ❖ Jalapeno and Monterey Jack, medium and aged sharp Baja, sharp, garlic, onion Cheddar, and Cajun Cheddar cheese. 800-548-8961.

Bel Canto Fancy Foods Ltd., 555 2nd Ave., New York, NY 10016: Free list of retail sources ❖ Italian sheep's milk cheese. 212-689-4433.

Brier Run Farm, HC 32, Box 73, Birch River, WV 26610: Free information ❖ Certified fresh organic goat cheese. 304-649-2975.

The British Shoppe, 45 Wall St., Madison, CT 06443: Free catalog ❖ Traditional British foods and cheese. 203-245-4521.

Cabot Annex, Rt. 100, Waterbury Center, VT 05677: Free information with long SASE ❖ Vermont cheese and specialty foods. 802-244-6334.

Cabot Creamery, P.O. Box 128, Cabot, VT 05647: Free information ❖ All-natural cheese with half the fat and cholesterol and 33 percent fewer calories than Cheddar. 800-639-3198.

Calef's Country Store, P.O. Box 57, Barrington, NH 03825: Free brochure ❖ Homemade cheese, maple syrup, and candy. 800-462-2118.

Chicory Farm, P.O. Box 25, Mount Hermon, LA 70450: Free information ❖ European-style goat, cow, and sheep's milk cheese. 504-877-4550.

Coach Dairy Goat Farm, 105 Mill Hill Rd., Pine Plains, NY 12567: Free list of retail sources ❖ Goat cheese and yogurt. 518-398-5325.

Crowley Cheese, Healdville Rd., Healdville VT 05758: Free brochure ❖ Mild, medium, and sharp cheese and smoked or spiced with garlic, hot pepper, caraway, or dill varieties. 800-683-2606.

Figi's, 3200 S. Maple, Marshfield, WI 54404: Free catalog ❖ Gourmet cheese. 715-387-6311.

Formagg, Galaxy Foods, 2441 Viscount Row, Orlando, FL 32809: Free list of retail sources ❖ Low-fat and low-cholesterol cheese. 800-441-9419.

Fortuna's Sausage Company, 975 Greenville Ave., Greenville, RI 02828: Free catalog ❖ All-natural dry cured Italian sausages, sausage-making kit, pasta, imported Italian cheese, gift baskets, and natural New England specialties. 800-427-6879.

Fromagerie Belle Chèvre, 26910 Bethel Rd., Elkmont, AL 35620: Free information ❖ Fresh goat cheese. 205-423-2238.

Fruit Ranch-West, 7520 W. Bluemound Rd., Milwaukee, WI 53213: Free catalog ❖ Fruit gift baskets, assorted nuts, and Wisconsin cheese variety packages. 800-433-3289.

G & G Foods, 1012 Revere St., San Francisco, CA 94124: Free list of retail sources ❖ Cheese spreads. 415-715-2250.

Gibbsville Cheese Sales, W2663 CTH OO, Sheboygan Falls, WI 53085: Free price list ❖ Natural rindless and flavored processed cheese. Also cheese spreads in bulk and gift assortments. 414-564-3242.

Gourm-E-Co Imports, 405 Glenn Dr., Sterling, VA 20164: Free information ❖ Imported cheese. 800-899-5616.

Grafton Village Cheese Company, P.O. Box 87, Grafton, VT 05146: Free brochure ❖ Cheddar cheese. 800-472-3866.

The Granville Country Store, P.O. Box 141, Granville, MA 01034: Free information ❖ Aged Cheddar cheese. 800-356-3141.

Harlow's Sugar House, RD 1, Box 395, Putney, VT 05346: Free brochure ❖ Maple syrup and specialties, jams, jellies, and Vermont cheese. 802-387-5852.

Heluva Good Cheese Inc., 6152 Barclay Rd., P.O. Box C, Sodus, NY 14551: Free catalog ❖ Gourmet cheese specialties. 800-445-0269.

Hickory Farms, P.O. Box 75, Maumee, OH 43537: Free brochure ❖ Cheese, smoked meat, and specialties. 800-222-4438.

Ideal Cheese Shop, 1205 2nd Ave., New York, NY 10021: Catalog $2 ❖ Imported and domestic cheese. 800-382-0109.

Imperia Foods, 234 St. Nicholas Ave., South Plainfield, NJ 07080: Free list of retail sources ❖ Imported regular, reduced fat, and low-cholesterol grated Romano and Parmesan cheese. 908-756-7333.

Lynn Dairy Inc., W1929 US Hwy. 10, Granton, WI 54436: Free catalog ❖ Gourmet cheese. 715-238-7129.

Mackenzie Limited, 2900-D Whittington Ave., Baltimore, MD 21230: Free brochure ❖ Imported seafood specialties and English cheese. 800-858-7100.

Mahogany Smoked Meats, P.O. Box 1387, Bishop, CA 93515: Free brochure ❖ Smoked jerky, Cheddar cheese, chileno peppers, stuffed olives, smoked trout, and specialties. 619-873-5311.

Marin French Cheese Company, P.O. Box 99, Petaluma, CA 94953: Free brochure ❖ French Camembert, Schloss, Breakfast, and Fromage De Brie cheese. 707-762-6001.

❖ FOODS ❖

Maytag Dairy Farms Inc., P.O. Box 806, Newton, IA 50208: Free catalog ❖ Cheddar cheese spreads, blue cheese, natural white Cheddar, brick, baby Swiss, Edam, and other gourmet cheeses. 800-247-2458; 515-792-1133 (in IA).

Mozzarella Company, 2944 Elm St., Dallas, TX 75226: Free brochure ❖ Queso fresco, a crumbly cheese that resembles farmer's cheese and rindless crescenza, semisoft herb-like caciotta, creamy mascarpone, and cheese made from cow, goat, and sheep's milk. 214-741-4072.

Plymouth Cheese Corporation, P.O. Box 1, Plymouth, VT 05056: Free catalog ❖ Mild or medium-sharp sage, garlic, and caraway cheese. Also aged and naturally cured Vermont granular curd cheese. 802-672-3650.

Rock Cheese Company, 540 Tasman St., Madison, WI 53714: Free brochure ❖ Cheese favorites, honey products, seasonings, and condiments. Also gift assortments. 608-223-6272.

The Rocking Horse Country Store, RR 3, Box 7343, Rutland, VT 05701: Free brochure ❖ Vermont maple syrup, cheese, crafts, and country collectibles. 802-773-7882.

Smith's Country Cheese, 20 Otter River Rd., Winchendon, MA 01475: Free information ❖ Gouda and Cheddar cheese. 508-939-5738.

Sonoma Cheese Factory, 2 Spain St., Sonoma, CA 95476: Free brochure ❖ Light garlic, hot pepper, and Jack cheese with reduced fat, cholesterol, calories, and salt. 800-535-2855.

Soyco Foods, Galaxy Foods, 2441 Viscount Row, Orlando, FL 32809: Free list of retail sources ❖ Casein-free cheese alternative. 800-441-9419.

Split Creek Farm, 3806 Centerville Rd., Anderson, SC 29625: Free information ❖ Fresh goat cheese. 803-287-3921.

The Sugar Shack, Rt. 7A, Arlington, VT 05250: Free information ❖ Vermont maple syrup, cream, and candy. Also homemade fudge, cheese, Vermont food products, and gifts. 802-375-6747.

Sugarbush Farm, RR1, Box 568, Woodstock, VT 05091: Free information with long SASE ❖ Maple syrup and cheese. 802-457-1757.

Sweet Home Farm, 27107 Schoen Rd., Elberta, AL 36530: Free information ❖ Fresh and aged goat and cow's milk cheese. 334-986-5663.

Swiss Colony, Catalog Request Department, P.O. Box 8994, Madison, WI 53794: Free catalog ❖ Cheese, meat, sausage, pastries, nuts, candy, and snacks. 608-324-5050.

Washington State University Creamery, 101 Food Quality Building, Pullman, WA 99164: Free brochure ❖ Cougar Gold, American, smoky Cheddar, sweet basil, dill garlic, hot pepper, and other cheese. 800-457-5442.

Wisconsin Cheeseman, P.O. Box 1, Madison, WI 53701: Free catalog ❖ Aged Wisconsin natural cheese, sausage, cookies and pastries, fruits, nuts, and specialties. 608-837-4100.

Creole & Cajun

Comeaux's Grocery & Market, 118 Canaan Dr., Lafayette, LA 70508: Free information ❖ Andouille, boudin (regular, crawfish, and seafood), tasso, and Cajun specialties. 800-323-2492; 318-989-1528 (in LA).

Community Kitchens, The Art of Foods Plaza, Ridgely, MD 21685: Free catalog ❖ Cajun spices, Creole seasonings, French Quarter Binet and Louisiana corn bread mixes, jambalaya seasoning, tea, and coffee. 800-535-9901.

Creole Delicacies, 533 Saint Ann St., New Orleans, LA 70116: Free brochure ❖ Pecan pralines, remoulade sauce, hot pepper jellies, Creole seasonings, and specialties from Brennan's restaurant. 800-523-6425.

Ethnic

AH! LASKA Products, P.O. Box 940, Homer, AK 99603: Free list of retail sources ❖ Low-fat kosher instant cocoa. 907-235-7561; 708-342-8842 (in continental United States).

Don Alfonso Foods, P.O. Box 201988, Austin, TX 78720: Catalog $1 ❖ Salsa, sauces, seasonings, and chilies. 800-456-6100.

All Cajun Food Company, 1019 Delcambre Rd., Breaux Bridge, LA 70503: Free information ❖ Barbecue sauce, Cajun cayenne juice, chow chow, Cajun powder, and other condiments. 800-467-3613; 318-332-3613 (in LA).

The Amishman, P.O. Box 128, Mount Holly Springs, PA 17065: Free brochure ❖ Candy, apple butter, chow chow, nuts, pretzels, and other snacks. 800-233-7082.

Anjo's Imports, P.O. Box 4031, Cerritos, CA 90703: Free information ❖ Jamaican hot sauces, jerk seasonings, and mango and papaya chutney.

Anzen Oriental Foods & Imports, 736 NE MLK Jr. Blvd., Portland, OR 97232: Free price list ❖ Imported Japanese, Chinese, Korean, and Thai foods. 503-233-5111.

B & L Specialty Foods Inc., P.O. Box 80068, Seattle, WA 98108: Free catalog ❖ Imported pasta, oils, and Italian specialties. 800-EAT-PASTA.

Bangkok Produce, 966 San Julian St., Los Angeles, CA 90015: Free information ❖ Oriental fruits and vegetables. 213-689-7933.

Bayou to Go Seafood Inc., P.O. Box 20104, New Orleans, LA 70141: Free catalog ❖ Cajun food, spices, gumbo, sausage, and seafood. 800-541-6610.

The Brown Adobe, The New Mexican Connection, 200 Lincoln Ave., Ste. 130, Phoenixville, PA 19460: Free brochure ❖ Soups and chili, spices and spicy specialties, Mexican specialties, salsa, and barbecue and pasta sauces. 800-392-2041.

Tony Chachere's Creole Foods, P.O. Box 1687, Opelousas, LA 70571: Free brochure ❖ Cajun country specialties and cookbooks. 800-551-9066.

Chile La Isla, P.O. Box 1379, Fabens, TX 79838: Free information ❖ Roasted and individually quick-frozen chili peppers. 800-895-4603.

CMC Company, P.O. Box 322, Avalon, NJ 08202: Free catalog ❖ Mexican, Thai-Indonesian, and Szechuan-Chinese cooking ingredients. 800-CMC-2780.

Corti Brothers, 5810 Folsom Blvd., Sacramento, CA 95819: Free newsletter ❖ Single garden Chinese teas, regional olive oils, vintage cognac, and food and drink specialties. 916-736-3800.

Coyote Cafe General Store, 132 W. Water St., Santa Fe, NM 87501: Free catalog ❖ Hot sauces, salsa, sweet and spicy products, coffee and teas, and gift baskets. 800-866-4695.

Cuisine Perel, 3100 Kerner Blvd., San Rafael, CA 94901: Free catalog ❖ Flavored and colored pasta. 800-88-PEREL; 415-456-4406 (in CA).

Delancey Dessert Company, 573 Grand St., New York, NY 10002: Free information ❖ All-natural kosher rugelach and other baked goods. 800-254-5254; 212-254-5254 (in NY).

Gaston Dupre Inc., 7904 Hopi Pl., Tampa, FL 33634: Free information ❖ Beet, tomato and basil, lemon and pepper, tarragon and chives, chocolate, wild mushroom, saffron, squid ink, and curry-flavored rolled fettucine and angel hair pasta. 800-937-9445.

El Paso Chili Company, 909 Texas Ave., El Paso, TX 79901: Free information ❖ Medium-hot cactus salsa made from vine-ripened tomatillos, onions, fresh cilantro, mild chilies, fiery jalapeno, vinegar, spices, and nopalitos. 915-544-3434.

Elena's by Houlihan's, Culinary Traditions Ltd., 70 S. Squirrel Rd., Ste. H, Auburn Hills, MI 48326: Free list of retail sources ❖ Low-fat pasta sauces. 800-72-ELENA.

Epicurean International, 155 Filbert, Ste. 252, Oakland, CA 94607: Free information ❖ Authentic Thai food specialties. 800-967-THAI.

Erica's Rugelach & Baking Company Inc., 389 4th St., Brooklyn, NY 11215: Free list of retail sources ❖ Certified kosher bakery specialties. 718-965-3657.

Ferrara Foods & Confections Inc., 195 Grand St., New York, NY 10013: Free brochure ❖ Coffee, candy, syrups, sauces, bread sticks, vegetables, pasta, baked goods, and Italian specialties. 212-226-6150.

FOODS

Fortuna's Sausage Company, 975 Greenville Ave., Greenville, RI 02828: Free catalog ❖ All-natural dry cured Italian sausages, sausage-making kit, pasta, imported Italian cheese, gift baskets, and natural New England specialties. 800-427-6879.

Frieda's by Mail, P.O. Box 58488, Los Angeles, CA 90058: Free catalog ❖ Habaneros and fresh and dried chilies. 800-241-1771; 714-826-6100 (in CA).

Gallina Canyon Ranch, P.O. Box 706, Albuquerque, NM 87510: Free information ❖ Smoked pasillas and chilies. 505-685-4888.

GNS Spices, P.O. Box 90, Walnut, CA 91788: Free information ❖ Dried, flaked, pureed, brined, ground, and fresh Habaneros. 909-594-9505.

Grandma's Recipe Rugelach, 415 W. 15th St., New York, NY 10011, Gracie Station, New York, NY 10028: Free information ❖ Low-calorie whole wheat rugelach with natural fruit spreads and other flavors. 800-538-5055.

The Great Valley Mills, 1774 County Line Rd., Bartow, PA 19504: Free brochure ❖ Pennsylvania Dutch country cheese, ham, bacon, sausage, beef, preserves, fruitcakes, stollen, flour, and cereals. 800-688-6455.

Hard Times Chili, 310 Commerce St., Alexandria, VA 22314: Free brochure ❖ Texas Roadhouse and Cincinnati Chili mixes. 703-836-7449.

Home Baked Group Inc., 1004 S. Rogers Circle, Boca Raton, FL 33487: Free list of retail sources ❖ Kosher fat-free and low-fat brownies. 800-683-3467; 407-995-0767 (in FL).

House of Fire, 1108 Spruce St., Boulder, CO 80302: Free information ❖ Hot and spicy foods from around the world. 800-717-5787; 303-440-0929 (in CO).

Jardine's Texas Foods, 1 Chisholm Trail, Buda, TX 78610: Free catalog ❖ Chili fixings, salsa, hand-stuffed olives, and spicy Bloody Mary mix. 800-544-1880.

Katagiri & Company, 224 E. 59th St., New York, NY 10022: Free information ❖ Japanese foods, sundries, and magazines. 212-755-3566.

KDI Specialty Foods Inc., 15 W. Jefryn Blvd., Deer Park, NY 11729: Free list of retail sources ❖ Salsa. 516-595-2525.

Kosher Cornucopia, P.O. Box 326, Jeffersonville, NY 12748: Free catalog ❖ Gourmet foods and gifts. 800-756-7437; 914-482-3118 (in NY).

Lanvino, P.O. Box 6724, Whitneyville, CT 06517: Free list of retail sources ❖ All-natural sauces and pesto for pasta, seafood, meat, and poultry. 203-230-9362.

Lioni Bufala Corporation, 78-19 15th Ave., Brooklyn, NY 11228: Free information ❖ Italian specialty products. 718-234-3373.

Locus Foods Inc., P.O. Box 1531, Findlay, OH 45840: Free information ❖ Caribbean black bean soup and Italian beans and pasta. 800-295-7777.

Manganaro Foods, 488 9th Ave., New York, NY 10018: Free information ❖ Italian salami, prosciutto ham, cheese, panettone, amaretto, colomba, torrone desserts, and specialties. 800-472-5264.

Mrs. Mazzula's Foods, 240 Carter Dr., Edison, NJ 08817: Free information ❖ All-natural Italian sun-dried tomatoes.

Millie's Pierogi, 129 Broadway, Chicopee Falls, MA 01020: Free information ❖ Cabbage, potato and cheese, farmer's cheese, and prune-filled pierogi. 800-743-7641.

Morisi's Pasta, 647 5th Ave., Brooklyn, NY 11215: Catalog $2.50 (refundable) ❖ All-natural pasta. 800-253-6044.

Old Southwest Trading Company, P.O. Box 7545, Albuquerque, NM 87194: Free catalog ❖ Habanero and exotic and domestic chilies. 505-836-0168.

The Oriental Pantry, 423 Great Rd., Acton, MA 01720: Free catalog ❖ Oriental foods, exotic spices, sauces, and specialties. 800-828-0368.

Pasta Fresca, P.O. Box 243, 112 S. Main St., New Lexington, OH 43764: Free list of retail sources ❖ Flavored dried pasta in a variety of shapes. 800-343-5266.

Pasta Mama's, 1270 Lee Blvd., Richland, WA 99352: Free list of retail sources ❖ Kosher parve egg and cholesterol-free pasta and low-fat sauces. 800-456-4045; 509-946-8282 (in WA).

Patsy's Italian Restaurant, 236 W. 56th St., New York, NY 10019: Free information ❖ Marinara sauce. 800-3-PATSYS; 212-247-3491 (in NY).

Pendery's Inc., 1221 Manufacturing St., Dallas, TX 75207: Catalog $2 ❖ Mexican spices, seasonings, flavorings, and specialties. 800-533-1870; 214-741-1870 (in TX).

Petra Foods International Inc., 1350 Beverly Rd., McLean, VA 22101: Free information ❖ All-natural imported Japanese, kosher, Middle East, Greek, and other international foods. 800-356-1807.

Rossi Pasta, P.O. Box 759, Marietta, OH 45750: Free brochure ❖ Handmade black olive, linguine, garlic fettucine, saffron linguine, and other pasta. 800-227-6774.

Sanctuary Much Inc., Gallina Canyon Ranch, P.O. Box 706, Albuquerque, NM 87510: Free information ❖ Jamaican hot sauce, papaya chutney, and all-natural hot marinade for grilling, roasting, baking, or stir-frying. 505-685-4888.

Schaller & Weber Inc., 22-35 46th St., Long Island City, NY 11105: Free catalog ❖ Sausage, liverwurst, cold cuts, salami and cervelats, Westphalian-style smoked ham, roast beef, bacon, and other gourmet meat. 800-847-4115; 212-721-5480 (in NY).

2nd Avenue Deli, 156 2nd Ave., New York, NY 10003: Free catalog ❖ Delicatessen favorites and baked goods. 800-692-3354.

Sinai Kosher Foods Corporation, 1000 W. Pershing Rd., Chicago, IL 60609: Free information ❖ Kosher beef, lamb, veal, roasts, steaks, chops, and ground beef. 800-823-7746; 312-650-6339 (in IL).

Sorrenti Family Farms, 1630 Main St., Escalon, CA 95320: Free information ❖ California wild rice and pasta combinations. 209-838-1127.

Start Fresh Weight Control Program, 4813 12th Ave., Brooklyn, NY 11219: Free catalog ❖ Prepared kosher meals for weight loss. 800-226-5000.

Sultan's Delight Inc., 59 88th St., Brooklyn, NY 11209: Free catalog ❖ Mideast specialties, grains and beans, spices, flower water, Turkish coffee and tea, olives and specialty oils, cheese, and foods from all over the world. 718-745-2121.

Swahaa Spices Inc., P.O. Box 529, Lexington, MA 02173: Free brochure ❖ Specialty spice blends, basic spices, and culinary items imported from India. 617-862-1444.

Taos Mesa Gourmet, 2400 Rio Grande Blvd. NW, Ste. 234, Albuquerque, NM 87104: Free information ❖ Blue corn bread and pancakes, bean dip, salsa, soups, chile jam, beer bread, and gourmet foods from the southwest. 800-494-0069.

Teitel Brothers, 2372 Arthur Ave., Bronx, NY 10458: Free catalog ❖ Aged cheese, extra virgin cold pressed olive oil, porcini mushrooms, pasta, and Italian specialties. 800-850-7055.

Tryson House, 15635 Alton Pkwy., Ste. 260, Irvine, CA 92718: Free list of retail sources ❖ Preservative-free, low-fat parve, and kosher seasoning sprays. 800-672-7929; 714-453-8820 (in CA).

VIVANDE'S Italian Pantry, 2125 Fillmore St., San Francisco, CA 94115: Free information ❖ Extra virgin olive oils, vinegars, flours, grains, legumes, condiments, honey, dolci, and other specialties. 415-346-4430.

Volpi Foods, 5254 Daggett Ave., St. Louis, MO 63110: Free information ❖ Sliced prosciutto and filsette, sopressata, calabrese, and napoli salami. Also gift assortments. 800-288-3439.

Wolsk's Gourmet Confections, 81 Ludlow St., New York, NY 10002: Free information ❖ Low-calorie sugar-free kosher cookies. Also crackers, biscuits, gourmet confections, dried fruits, nuts, coffee and tea, and international specialties. 800-692-6887.

❖ FOODS ❖

World of Chantilly, 4302 Farragut Rd., Brooklyn, NY 11203: Free list of retail sources ❖ Certified kosher French pastries. Also chocolate candy and gift baskets. 718-859-1110.

Worldwide Thai-Forschner, 645 Madison Ave., #1900, New York, NY 10022: Free information ❖ Thai food specialties.

YZ Enterprises Inc., 377 W. Dussell Dr., Maumee, OH 43537: Free information ❖ Kosher parve cookies. 800-736-8779.

Fruits & Vegetables

Apricot Farm Inc., 2620 Buena Vista Rd., Hollister, CA 95023: Free catalog ❖ Dried fruit. 800-233-4413.

Atkinson's Vidalia Onions, Box 121, Garfield, GA 30425: Free information ❖ Vidalia onions. 800-241-3408; 912-763-2149 (in GA).

Bangkok Produce, 966 San Julian St., Los Angeles, CA 90015: Free information ❖ Oriental fruits and vegetables. 213-689-7933.

Bess' Beans, P.O. Box 1542, Charleston, SC 29402: Free brochure with long SASE ❖ Bean soups and other Southern favorites. 800-233-2326.

Bilgore Groves, 807A Court St., P.O. Box 1958, Clearwater, FL 34617: Free catalog ❖ Fruit gift assortments and specialties. 813-442-2171.

Bland Farms, P.O. Box 506, Glennville, GA 30427: Free catalog ❖ Vidalia onions, marinated mushrooms, relishes, sauces, pickled items, salad dressings, meat, peanuts, nut candy and fudge, and pecans. 800-843-2542.

Blue Heron Fruit Shippers, P.O. Box 936, Sarasota, FL 34234: Free brochure ❖ Tree-ripened citrus fruit, candy, marmalades, pecans, gourmet Southern foods, stone crab claws, and honey. 800-237-3920; 941-954-1605 (in FL).

Chile La Isla, P.O. Box 1379, Fabens, TX 79838: Free information ❖ Roasted and individually quick-frozen chili peppers. 800-895-4603.

Chukar Cherries, P.O. Box 510, Prosser, WV 99350: Free catalog ❖ Preservative and sulfite-free dried cherries and cherry specialties. 800-624-9544.

Crayton Cove Gourmet Shop Inc., 800 12th Ave. South, Naples, FL 33950: Free brochure ❖ Florida fruit assortments. 800-678-4362; 813-262-4362 (in FL).

Crockett Farms, P.O. Box 1150, Harlingen, TX 78551: Free catalog ❖ Ruby red grapefruit and sun-ripened oranges. 800-580-1900.

Cushman's, 3325 Forest Hill Blvd., West Palm Beach, FL 33406: Free catalog ❖ Florida-fresh citrus fruits. 407-965-3535.

Delegeane Garlic Farms, P.O. Box 2561, Yountville, Napa Valley, CA 94599: Free brochure ❖ Fresh garlic, chili ristras, salt-free herb seasonings, wildflower honey, berry jams, gourmet dessert sauces, and specialties. 800-726-6692.

Delftree Farm, 234 Union St., North Adams, MA 01247: Free price list ❖ Fresh and wild dried mushrooms, books, soups, sauces, and other specialties. 800-243-3742.

Desert Glory, P.O. Box 453, Devine, TX 78016: Free information ❖ Cocktail tomatoes. 800-44-SALAD.

Dundee Orchards, P.O. Box 327, Dundee, OR 97115: Free information ❖ Oregon hazelnut butter and hazelnut products. Also Oregon cherries. 503-538-8105.

Fruit Ranch-West, 7520 W. Bluemound Rd., Milwaukee, WI 53213: Free catalog ❖ Fruit gift baskets, assorted nuts, and Wisconsin cheese variety packages. 800-433-3289.

G.I.M.M. Dry Yard, P.O. Box 1016, Winters, CA 95964: Free catalog ❖ Dried fruit. 916-795-2919.

Georgia "Sweets" Brand Inc., 1606 W. North St., Vidalia, GA 30474: Free information ❖ Jumbo and sandwich-size Vidalia onions. 800-552-9902.

Giant Artichoke Company, 11241 Merritt St., Castroville, CA 95012: Free price list ❖ Fresh artichokes and artichoke specialties. 408-633-2778.

Gracewood Fruit Company, 9075 17th Pl., P.O. Box 2590, Vero Beach, FL 32961: Free information ❖ Navel oranges and ruby red grapefruit. 800-678-1154.

Susan Green's California Cuisine, Catalog Order Center, P.O. Box 596, Maumee, OH 43537: Free catalog ❖ Dried and fresh fruit, nuts, delicatessen favorites, baked goods, ham, and candy. 800-753-8558.

Hadley Fruit Orchards, P.O. Box 246, Cabazon, CA 92230: Free catalog ❖ Dried fruit, nuts, candy, honey, and jellies. 800-854-5655.

Harry & David, P.O. Box 712, Medford, OR 97501: Free catalog ❖ Oregold peaches, Alphonse LaValle grapes, Royal Riviera pears, Crisp Mountain apples, other fruits, and gift assortments. 800-345-5655.

Harry's Crestview Groves, 9030 17th Pl., Vero Beach, FL 32966: Free catalog ❖ Tree-ripened ruby red grapefruit, oranges, and gifts. 800-285-8488.

Hart's Crestview Groves, 9030 17th Pl., Vero Beach, FL 32966: Free information ❖ Oranges and tree-ripened ruby red grapefruit. 800-285-8488.

Hendrix Farms, P.O. Box 175, Metter, GA 30439: Free information ❖ Vidalia onions. 800-221-5050.

Indian River Groves, P.O. Box 3689, Seminole, FL 34645: Free brochure ❖ Valencia oranges and ruby red grapefruit from Florida. 800-289-4253.

Jaffe Brothers Natural Foods, P.O. Box 636, Valley Center, CA 92082: Free catalog ❖ Grains and grain products, nuts, fruit, honey, and other natural foods. 619-749-1133.

Kelly & Sons, 3086 Co. Rt. 176, Oswego, NY 13126: Free brochure ❖ Gourmet braided onions and shallots. 800-496-3363.

Kingsfield Gardens, Blue Mounds, WI 53517: Free information ❖ Red Cipollini onions. 608-924-9341.

Frank Lewis' Alamo Fruit, 100 N. Tower Rd., Alamo, TX 78516: Free brochure ❖ Farm-fresh tomatoes, tangelos, apples, persimmons, cheesecake, smoked turkey breast, and gourmet specialties. 800-477-4773.

Lone Star Farms, P.O. Box 685, Mercedes, TX 78570: Free information ❖ Sweet onions. 800-552-1015.

Maples Fruit Farm, P.O. Box 167, Chewsville, MD 21721: Free catalog ❖ Dried fruit, nuts, coffee, other specialties, and gift baskets. 301-733-0777.

Mariani Nut Company, 709 Dutton St., P.O. Box 808, Winters, CA 95694: Free information ❖ Almonds, pistachios, walnuts, and dried tomatoes. 916-795-3311.

Mrs. Mazzula's Foods, 240 Carter Dr., Edison, NJ 08817: Free information ❖ All-natural Italian sun-dried tomatoes.

Mission Orchards, Mail Processing Center, P.O. Box 546, Maumee, OH 43537: Free catalog ❖ Comice pears, red dessert grapes, navel oranges, red grapefruit, cherries, plums, tangelos, pineapples, and kiwi fruit. Also cheese, candy, dried fruit, nuts, truffles, fruitcakes and pastries, and smoked meat and seafood. 419-893-5149.

Mushroom Man, Box 321, Eugene, OR 97140: Free information ❖ Italian dried porcini mushrooms and exotic wild mushroom cooking powders. 800-945-3404.

Neill's Farm, 2709 McNeill Rd., Fort Pierce, FL 34981: Free catalog ❖ Fresh-picked tomatoes. 800-441-6740.

FOODS

New Penny Farm, P.O. Box 448, Presque Isle, ME 04769: Free catalog ❖ Organic-grown potatoes. 800-827-7551.

Newbern Groves Gift Shop, 15315 N. Nebraska Ave., Tampa, FL 33682: Free information ❖ Navel oranges, tangelos, and sweet red grapefruit. 800-486-0441; 971-0440 (in Tampa).

North West Mushroom Company Inc., P.O. Box 2997, LaGrande, OR 97850: Free brochure ❖ Dried mushrooms and freshly harvested morels, chanterelles, crepes, and other varieties. 800-569-6101.

Oasis Date Gardens, P.O. Box 757, Thermal, CA 92274: Free information ❖ Medjool and Noor dates, dried figs, and candied apricots. 800-827-8017.

Old Southwest Trading Company, P.O. Box 7545, Albuquerque, NM 87194: Free catalog ❖ Habanero and exotic and domestic chilies. 505-836-0168.

Pezzini Farms, P.O. Box 1276, Castroville, CA 95012: Free information ❖ Artichokes and artichoke dipping and pasta sauces. 800-347-6118.

Phillips Exotic Mushrooms, 909 E. Baltimore Pike, Kennet Square, PA 19348: Free catalog ❖ Crimini, shitake, oyster, and portabella mushrooms. 800-243-8644.

Phipps Ranch, P.O. Box 349, Pescadero, CA 94060: Free price list ❖ Herbicide and pesticide-free hand-harvested beans. Also bean soup mixes, herb vinegars, cereals and grains, and jams.

Pinnacle Orchards, 1505 Holland Rd., Maumee, OH 43537: Free catalog ❖ Comice pears and other specialties. 800-879-7327.

Pittman & Davis, P.O. Box 532227, Harlingen, TX 78553: Catalog $1 ❖ Ruby red grapefruit, oranges, pecans, fruitcakes, cheese, smoked ham, and turkey. 210-423-2154.

Red Cooper, Rt. 3, Box 10, Alamo, TX 78516: Free catalog ❖ Grapefruit, oranges, pineapples, avocados, apples, persimmons, tangelos, dates, pears, and dried fruit. 800-876-4733.

Sphinx Date Ranch, 3039 N. Scottsdale Rd., Scottsdale, AZ 85251: Free brochure ❖ Date-pecan loaves, trail mixes, fruitcakes, jellies, nuts, and Medjool dates pitted and hand-dipped in creamy milk chocolate, stuffed with walnuts, rolled in powdered sugar, or for cooking. 800-482-3283; 602-941-2261 (in AZ).

Spyke's Grove, 7250 Griffin Rd., Davie, FL 33314: Free catalog ❖ Florida oranges, mangos, avocados, and grapefruit. 800-327-9713; 305-583-0426 (in FL).

Sullivan Victory Groves, P.O. Box 10, Cocoa, FL 32923: Free brochure ❖ Navel oranges. 800-ORANGE-1.

Sweet Energy, 4 Acorn Ln., Colchester, VT 05446: Free brochure ❖ Apricots and other high-fiber fruit. 800-9-SWEETO.

Timber Crest Farms, 4791 Dry Creek Rd., Healdsburg, CA 95448: Free catalog ❖ Dried fruit, dried tomato products, fruit butters, nuts, and trail mixes. 707-433-8251.

Todaro Brothers, 555 2nd Ave., New York, NY 10016: Catalog $1 ❖ Cheese, pasta, dried mushrooms, olives and olive oil, legumes, truffles and porcini, grains, vinegars, and other specialties. 212-679-7766.

Tom Vorbeck, AppleSource, 1716 Apples Rd., Chapin, IL 62628: Free brochure ❖ Mail-order source for apple specialties. 800-588-4854.

Walla Walla Gardener's Association, 210 N. 11th Ave., Walla Walla, WA 99362: Free information ❖ Sweet Walla Walla onions. 800-553-5014; 509-525-7070 (in WA).

Wicklund Farms, 3959 Maple Island Farm Rd., Springfield, OR 97477: Free price list ❖ Spiced green beans. 503-747-5998.

Gift Assortments & Gourmet Specialties

Ace Specialty Foods, 281 West 83rd St., Burr Ridge, IL 60521: Free catalog ❖ Cakes, fruit gifts, candy, and nuts. 800-323-9754; 708-325-9700 (in IL).

AllServe Inc., P.O. Box 43209, Cleveland, OH 44143: Free brochure ❖ Fresh food bases for making sauces and gravy for meat, poultry, seafood, and vegetables. 800-827-8328.

The Antique Mall & Crown Restaurant, P.O. Box 540, Indianola, MS 38751: Free catalog ❖ Smoked catfish specialties and gourmet favorites. 800-833-7731; 601-887-2522 (in MS).

The Art of Food, Kajun Kitchens Way, Ridgely, MD 21685: Free catalog ❖ Foods with a flavor of New Orleans. 800-535-9901.

Ash Enterprises Inc., P.O. Box 40113, Tucson, AZ 85717: Free information ❖ Gift assortments. 800-597-8259.

Australian Catalogue Company, 7412 Wingfoot Dr., Raleigh, NC 27615: Free catalog ❖ Australian cakes, puddings, chocolates, and biscuits. 919-878-8266.

Balducci's, Shop from Home Service, 42-25 12th St., Long Island City, NY 11101: Catalog $3 ❖ Bread and food specialties. 800-225-3822.

Baskets Galore, P.O. Box 7292, Beaverton, OR 97007: Free brochure ❖ Fruit and specialty gift baskets. 503-591-7170.

Basse's Choice Plantation, P.O. Box 1, Smithfield, VA 23431: Free information ❖ Virginia gourmet foods from the coast, Piedmont, and the mountains. 800-292-2773.

Bean Appetit, 818 Jefferson St., Oakland, CA 94607: Free catalog ❖ Bean flour mixes, spices and seasonings, specialty rices, rice blends, and gourmet favorites. 510-839-8988.

Bean Bag Mail Order Company, 818 Jefferson St., Oakland, CA 94607: Catalog $1 ❖ Gourmet seasonings and bean specialties. 800-845-2326.

Black Shield Inc., 5356 Pan American Freeway NE, Albuquerque, NM 87109: Free information ❖ Gourmet flavored popcorn. 800-653-9357.

Bland Farms, P.O. Box 506, Glennville, GA 30427: Free catalog ❖ Vidalia onions, marinated mushrooms, relishes, sauces, pickled items, salad dressings, meat, peanuts, nut candy, fudge, and Georgia pecans. 800-843-2542.

Blue Heron Fruit Shippers, P.O. Box 936, Sarasota, FL 34234: Free brochure ❖ Tree-ripened citrus fruit, candy, marmalades, pecans, gourmet Southern foods, stone crab claws, and honey. 800-237-3920; 941-954-1605 (in FL).

Bogland Inc., 770 Corporate Park, Pembroke, MA 02359: Free information ❖ Cranberry salsa, grilling sauce, catsup, and specialties. 800-BOGLAND.

The British Shoppe, 45 Wall St., Madison, CT 06443: Free catalog ❖ Traditional British foods and cheese. 203-245-4521.

Brittigan's Specialty Soups, 74 Tracey Rd., Huntington Valley, PA 19006: Free brochure ❖ Gourmet clam chowder, mushroom soup, bean and leek soup, and soup sampler packages. 215-830-0942.

Burberry's Limited, 9 E. 57th St., New York, NY 10022: Free list of retail sources ❖ International tea, preserves and marmalades, chutney, mustards, horseradish sauces, cakes, and shortbread biscuits. 212-371-5010.

Burnt Cabins Grist Mill, P.O. Box 65, Burnt Cabins, PA 17215: Free brochure ❖ Old-fashioned buckwheat and wheat flour, roasted and regular cornmeal, and pancake and muffin mixes. 800-278-6455.

Callaway Gardens Country Store, US Hwy. 27 South, Pine Mountain, GA 31822: Free catalog ❖ Southern-style bacon, ham, other meat, and jellies. 800-282-8181.

Cavanaugh Lakeview Farms Ltd., 2000 Thorn Apple Valley Dr., Ponca City, OK 74601: Free information ❖ Honey-cured and smoked poultry, smoked ham and bacon, fresh-frozen poultry, steaks, game, smoked seafood, desserts, and popcorn. 800-243-4438.

Chalet Suzanne Country Inn & Restaurant, 3800 Chalet Suzanne Dr., Lake Wales, FL 33853: Free brochure ❖ Gourmet soups and sauces. 800-686-6012.

❖ FOODS ❖

Chukar Cherries, P.O. Box 510, Prosser, WV 99350: Free catalog ❖ Cherry trail mixes. 800-624-9544.

Coastal Express Food & Spirits, 6129 Executive Blvd., Rockville, MD 20852: Free catalog ❖ Fruit, chocolates, cakes, spirits and wines, and other favorites. 800-243-7466; 301-770-5660 (in MD).

Cold Hollow Cider Mill, Rt. 100 North, Waterbury Center, VT 05677: Free information ❖ Vermont foods, apple cider, and gifts. 800-3-APPLES.

Colonial Williamsburg, P.O. Box 3532, Williamsburg, VA 23187: Free information ❖ Traditional favorites served in Williamsburg's colonial museum restaurants and taverns. 804-220-7378.

Community Kitchens, The Art of Foods Plaza, Ridgely, MD 21685: Free catalog ❖ Imported coffee and tea, Cajun spices, Creole seasonings, French Quarter Binet and Louisiana corn bread mixes, jambalaya seasoning, and candy. 800-535-9901.

Cook in the Kitchen, P.O. Box 3, Post Mills, VT 05058: Free brochure ❖ Mixes for pancakes, sauces, soups, and baked goods. Also gift assortments. 802-333-4141.

Country Herbs, P.O. Box 2007, Wayne, NJ 07474: Free catalog ❖ All-natural low-salt mixes for party dips. 800-823-5230.

Dakin Farm, Rt. 7, Ferrisburg, VT 05456: Free catalog ❖ Vermont smoked ham and bacon, maple syrup, and aged Cheddar cheese. 800-993-2546.

Delegeane Garlic Farms, P.O. Box 2561, Yountville, Napa Valley, CA 94599: Free brochure ❖ Fresh garlic, chili ristras, salt-free herb seasonings, wildflower honeys, berry jams, gourmet dessert sauces, and specialties. 800-726-6692.

Deli Direct, 416 Diens, Wheeling, IL 60090: Free brochure ❖ Delicatessen meat, aged Wisconsin cheese spreads, barbecue sauce, and condiments. 800-321-3354.

Discovery Kitchen, P.O. Box 6325, Woodland Hills, CA 91365: Free brochure ❖ Cheese, apple butter, honey, smoked fish, jams, mustard, and spices. 800-367-6865.

Dufour Pastry Kitchens Inc., 808 Washington St., New York, NY 10014: Free information ❖ Gourmet hors d'oeuvres. 212-929-2800.

S. Wallace Edwards & Sons Inc., P.O. Box 25, Surry, VA 23883: Free catalog ❖ Virginia meat, seafood selections, candy and nuts, and gourmet baked specialties. 800-222-4267.

Epicurean Traders, P.O. Box 5107, Newport Beach, CA 92662: Free information ❖ Mix-and-bake fat and cholesterol-free meringue. 800-490-6509.

Essentially Chocolate, 6129 Executive Blvd., Rockville, MD 20852: Free information ❖ Chocolate candy and gourmet food gifts. 301-770-5660.

Fancy Foods Gourmet Club, 330-E N. Stonestreet Ave., Rockville, MD 20850: Free information ❖ Gourmet foods. 800-576-3548.

Figi's, 3200 S. Maple, Marshfield, WI 54404: Free catalog ❖ Baked goods, meat, cheese, candy, jams and jellies, and nuts. 715-387-6311.

Fin 'n Feather, P.O. Box 487, Smithfield, VA 23430: Free catalog ❖ Smoked meat, poultry, pastries, candy, and regional specialties. 800-628-2242.

Fortuna's Sausage Company, 975 Greenville Ave., Greenville, RI 02828: Free catalog ❖ All-natural dry cured Italian sausages, sausage-making kit, pasta, imported Italian cheese, gift baskets, and natural New England specialties. 800-427-6879.

Frieda's By Mail, P.O. Box 58488, Los Angeles, CA 90058: Free catalog ❖ Gift baskets of exotic fruits and vegetables. 800-241-1771; 714-826-6100 (in CA).

Gazin's Cajun Creole Foods, 2910 Toulouse St., P.O. Box 19221, New Orleans, LA 70179: Catalog $2 ❖ Specialties from New Orleans. 800-262-6410; 504-482-0302 (in LA).

Maggie Gin's Inc., 127 10th Ave., San Francisco, CA 94118: Free list of retail sources ❖ Stir-fry sauces. 415-221-6080.

Good Wives Inc., 86 Sanderson Ave., Lynn, MA 01902: Free list of retail sources ❖ Overnight shipment of frozen hors d'oeuvres. 617-596-0070.

Goodies from Goodman, 13390 Grissom Ln., Dallas, TX 75229: Free catalog ❖ Fruit, cheese, nuts, candy, popcorn specialties, and smoked meat and fish. 800-535-3136.

The Great Valley Mills, 1774 County Line Rd., Bartow, PA 19504: Free brochure ❖ Pennsylvania Dutch country cheese, ham, bacon, sausage, beef, preserves, fruitcakes, stollen, flour, and cereals. 800-688-6455.

Susan Green's California Cuisine, Catalog Order Center, P.O. Box 596, Maumee, OH 43537: Free catalog ❖ Candy, dried fruits, sourdough bread, nuts, seasonings and condiments, farm-fresh crops, cheese, meat, seafood, and pastries. 800-753-8558.

Barney Greengrass, 541 Amsterdam Ave., New York, NY 10024: Free brochure ❖ Smoked fish, pickled goods, caviar, bagels and breads, spreadables, and gourmet specialties. 212-724-4707.

Hagensborg Foods U.S.A. Inc., P.O. Box 6058, Kent, WA 98064: Free information ❖ Smoked salmon, shrimp, and ready-to-spread salmon and shrimp pates. 800-851-1771; 206-622-8025 (in WA).

Hale House, 4208 Malden Dr., Malden, WV 25306: Free catalog ❖ Coffee, tea, jams and jellies, soup mixes, biscuit and dessert mixes, pasta, sauces, honey, herbal vinegars, and gourmet delights. 304-925-9499.

Hard Times Cafe, 310 Commerce St., Alexandria, VA 22314: Free brochure ❖ Chili spice mixes. 703-836-7449.

Harman's Cheese & Country Store, Main St., Box H624, Sugar Hill, NH 03585: Free catalog ❖ Cheddar cheese, maple syrup, fruit preserves, salad dressings, plain and smoked salmon, crab meat, honey, smoked herring fillets, pancake mixes, maple butter, and candy. 603-823-8000.

Harrington Ham Company, Main St., Richmond, VT 05477: Free information ❖ Spiral-sliced and cob-smoked maple-glazed ham. Also smoked bacon, turkey breast, pheasant, cheese, maple syrup, pastries, plum pudding, fruitcakes, and dried fruit. 802-434-4444.

Harrington's of Vermont, Rt. 7, Shelburne, VT 05482: Free information ❖ Ham and specialty foods from Vermont. 802-985-2000.

Harry & David, P.O. Box 712, Medford, OR 97501: Free catalog ❖ Fruit, cakes, baklava, cinnamon pastries, tortes, candy, preserves, and gift assortments. 800-345-5655.

Hasty-Bake, P.O. Box 471285, Tulsa, OK 74147: Free catalog ❖ Gourmet foods, charcoal ovens, and grilling accessories. 800-426-6836.

Hickin's Mountain Mowings Farm, Black Mountain Rd., RR 1, Box 293, Brattleboro, VT 05301: Free catalog ❖ Jams and jellies, pickles, fruit syrups, maple syrup, fruitcakes, candy, and cheese. 802-254-2146.

Hickory Farms, P.O. Box 75, Maumee, OH 43537: Free brochure ❖ Cheese, meat, candy, pastries, deli specialties, seafood, nuts, truffles, fruit and liqueur cakes, tea and coffee, dried fruit, jellies and preserves, fresh fruit, and popcorn. 800-222-4438.

House of Webster, P.O. Box 1988, Rogers, AR 72757: Catalog $2 ❖ Preserves and jellies, cheese, country cured and smoked bacon, biscuit and pancake mixes, candy, syrups, wild honey, and country sorghum. 501-636-4640.

Jasper's Sugar Bush, W1867 Co. Rd. 374, Carney, MI 49812: Free information ❖ Maple syrup, maple cream, maple sugar candy, chocolate maple cream, and gift baskets. 800-646-2753.

Knott's Berry Farm, P.O. Box 1989, Placentia, CA 92670: Free catalog ❖ Jellies and preserves, cheese, sausage, candy, cakes, cookies, and dried fruit. 800-877-6887.

Kozlowski Farms, 5566 Gravenstein Hwy. North, Forestville, CA 95436: Free brochure ❖ Marmalades, jams, preserves, honey, mustards, barbecue sauce, fruit butters, sugar-free berry vinegars, conserves, and chutney. 707-887-1587.

❖ FOODS ❖

Lambs Farm, P.O. Box 520, Jct. I-94 & Rt. 176, Libertyville, IL 60048: Free catalog ❖ Country crafts, specialty foods, nuts, candy, and gifts for pets. 800-52-LAMBS.

Lee Century Farms, John & Deborah Lee, Rt. 3, Box 11, Milton-Freewater, OR 97862: Free brochure ❖ Wheat berry "Caviars" and premium marinated vegetables. 800-645-3663; 503-938-6532 (in OR).

Stew Leonard's, 100 Westport Ave., Norwalk, CT 06851: Free catalog ❖ Fruit, cakes and cookies, cheese, breads, candy, nuts, and meat. 800-729-7839.

Les Trois Petits Cochons Company, 453 Greenwich St., New York, NY 10013: Free information ❖ Terrines, pates, and mousses. 800-LES-PATES; 212-219-1230 (in NY).

Mackinlay Teas, P.O. Box 6, Saline, MI 48176: Catalog $1 ❖ Gourmet teas, premium rice, lentils, beans, soup mixes, and Italian syrups. 313-930-2007.

Maison Glass Delicacies, 111 E. 58th St., New York, NY 10022: Catalog $5 ❖ Smoked meat and fish. 800-822-5564; 212-755-3317 (in NY).

Maples Fruit Farm, P.O. Box 167, Chewsville, MD 21721: Free catalog ❖ Dried fruit, nuts, coffee, other specialties, and gift baskets. 301-733-0777.

Matthews 1812 House, 250 Kent Rd., P.O. Box 15, Cornwall Bridge, CT 06754: Free brochure ❖ Cakes, nuts, chocolates, jams, tea, condiments, and smoked meat. 800-662-1812.

Mikdash Foods Inc., 75 St. Alphonsus St., Ste. D, Boston, MA 02120: Free list of retail sources ❖ Certified Kosher, all-natural gourmet international foods. 800-645-3274.

Mississippi Product Sales Inc., 301 Howard St., Greenwood, MS 38930: Free catalog ❖ Gourmet gift baskets and unique Southern gifts. 800-467-7763.

Nancy's Specialty Market, P.O. Box 530, Newmarket, NH 03857: Free catalog ❖ Wild mushroom caviars, exotic Mexican spices, pasta, extracts and flavorings, international specialties, books, and kitchenware. 800-688-2433.

Nauvoo Mill & Bakery, 1530 Mulholland, Nauvoo, IL 62354: Free brochure ❖ Gourmet food gift assortments. 217-453-6734.

The New Orleans School of Cooking and Louisiana General Store, The Jackson Brewery, 620 Decatur St., New Orleans, LA 70130: Free catalog ❖ New Orleans specialties and cookbooks. 800-237-4841.

Northern Lakes Wild Rice Company, 321 W. Grandview Dr., Teton Village, WY 83452: Free information ❖ Certified hand-harvested wild rice. 208-456-2306.

OH'Brines Pickling Inc., 4103 E. Mission Ave., Spokane, WA 99202: Free list of retail sources ❖ Pickled vegetables. 800-264-1264; 509-534-7255 (in WA).

Oregon Territory Company, 8065 SW Cirrus Dr., Beaverton, OR 97005: Catalog $1 (refundable) ❖ Gourmet foods, gift assortments and baskets, and Northwest specialties. 800-247-0727.

The Peanut Shop of Williamsburg, P.O. Box GN, Williamsburg, VA 23187: Free brochure ❖ Peanut specialties, Virginia country ham, Williamsburg soups, salad dressings, sauces, and gourmet food items. 800-637-3268.

Pepperidge Farm, P.O. Box 917, Clinton, CT 06413: Free catalog ❖ Soups, cookies and other pastries, crackers, candy, cheese, sausage, popcorn, and breakfast mixes. 800-243-9314.

Petrossian Shop, 3342 Melrose Ave. NW, Roanoke, VA 24017: Free catalog ❖ Caviar, foie gras, truffles, and smoked salmon. 800-828-9241.

Pfaelzer Brothers, Catalog Order Department, P.O. Box 1015, Maumee, OH 43537: Free catalog ❖ Gourmet food specialties and gift baskets. 800-621-0226.

Phipps Ranch, P.O. Box 349, Pescadero, CA 94060: Free price list ❖ Herbicide and pesticide-free hand-harvested beans. Also bean soup mixes, herb vinegars, cereals and grains, and jams.

Pinnacle Orchards, 1505 Holland Rd., Maumee, OH 43537: Free catalog ❖ Comice pears and other specialties. 800-879-7327.

Pueblo to People, P.O. Box 2545, Houston, TX 77252: Free catalog ❖ Nuts, dried fruit, ceramics, jewelry, coffee, and gift baskets. 800-843-5257.

Purely American, 1060 W. 35th St., Norfolk, VA 23508: Free list of retail sources ❖ Gift packaged food mixes. 800-359-7873.

RoseMary's Gifts, West Rd., Bennington, VT 05201: Free information with long SASE ❖ Corn cob-smoked meats, cheese, poultry, fish, Vermont Cheddar cheese, and maple syrup. Also gift baskets. 802-447-0373.

Rossi Pasta, P.O. Box 759, Marietta, OH 45750: Free brochure ❖ Handmade black olive, linguine, garlic fettuccine saffron linguine, and other pasta. 800-227-6774.

Salsa Express, P.O. Box 3985, Albuquerque, NM 87190: Free catalog ❖ Salsa, dips, condiments, nuts, snack foods, chili peppers, and spicy food specialties. 800-437-2572.

San Antonio River Mill, 129 E. Gunther, San Antonio, TX 78204: Free catalog ❖ Chili, biscuit and other baking mixes, preserves, jellies, and cooking equipment. 800-235-8186.

Santa Fe Select, 410 Old Santa Fe Trail, Santa Fe, NM 87501: Free information ❖ Southwest salsa, hot chiles, soups, breads, and cookies. Also gift baskets. 800-243-0353.

Sea Island Mercantile, 928 Bay St., P.O. Box 100, Beaufort, SC 29901: Free information ❖ She-crab soup and Carolina low-country foods and gifts. 800-735-3215.

The Secret Garden, P.O. Box 544, Park Rapids, MN 56470: Free catalog ❖ Wild rice, gourmet soup mixes, and gift baskets. 800-950-4409.

Seyco Fine Foods, 970 E. Santa Clara St., Ventura, CA 93001: Catalog $2 ❖ Old-fashioned pure American gourmet food specialties. 800-423-2942.

Simpson & Vail Inc., P.O. Box 309, Pleasantville, NY 10570: Free catalog ❖ Coffee and flavored teas, preserves and syrups, honey, confections and baked specialties, Indian foods and spices, hot sauces, spices and condiments, and gourmet products. 800-282TEAS; 914-747-1336 (in NY).

A Southern Season, Eastgate, Chapel Hill, NC 27514: Free catalog ❖ Irish whiskey cake, shortbread, imported coffee, nuts, candy, fruitcakes and other baked goods, condiments, preserves, and pasta. 800-253-3663; 919-929-7133 (in NC).

Splurge Inc., 1204 3rd Ave., Ste. 163, New York, NY 10021: Free information ❖ Low-fat and no-guilt snacks and confections. 212-439-6181.

The Squire's Choice, Mail Order Department, 2250 W. Cabot Blvd., Langhorne, PA 19047: Free catalog ❖ Food gifts. 800-523-6163.

Standard Candy Company, Mail Order Service, P.O. Box 697, Eastman, GA 31023: Free catalog ❖ Goo Goo Clusters, an original combination of chewy caramel, creamy marshmallow, roasted peanuts, and milk chocolate. Also old-fashioned stick candy and southern-style foods. 800-231-3402.

Stonehill Farm, Box 158, Schwenksville, PA 19473: Free catalog ❖ All-natural low-fat food gift assortments. 800-776-7155.

Sunnyland Farms Inc., P.O. Box 8200, Albany, GA 31706: Free catalog ❖ Pecans, nuts, candy, baked specialties, dried fruits, maple syrup, honey, jellies, and gift assortments. 800-999-2488; 912-883-3085 (in GA).

Sutton Place Gourmet, 10323 Old Georgetown Rd., Bethesda, MD 20814: Free catalog ❖ International and domestic seafood, coffee and tea, fruit, caviar, foie gras, champagnes, nuts, wild rices, condiments, meat, dried fruit, cheese, deli specialties, sauces, candy, and wines. 800-346-8763.

Swiss Colony, Catalog Request Department, P.O. Box 8994, Madison, WI 53794: Free catalog ❖ Cheese, meat, sausage, pastries, nuts, candy, and snacks. 608-324-5050.

FOODS

Swissco Foods, 2025 W. Park Ave., Ste. H, Redlands, CA 92373: Free information ❖ Gourmet dessert mixes.

Thunder Bay Gourmet Foods, 2620 Elmhurst Ln., Portsmouth, VA 23701: Free list of retail sources ❖ Preservative-free dessert sauces, marinades, pancake and brownie mixes, fruit cooler concentrates, and specialties made with natural ingredients. 804-465-7235.

Tillamook Cheese, P.O. Box 313, Tillamook, OR 97141: Free catalog ❖ Cheese, exotic delicacies, candy, meat and fowl, smoked fish, jellies, and preserves. 800-542-7290.

Todaro Brothers, 555 2nd Ave., New York, NY 10016: Catalog $1 ❖ Cheese, pasta, dried mushrooms, olives and olive oil, legumes, truffles, grains, vinegars, and specialties. 212-679-7766.

Traphagen Honey, Rt. 23A West, P.O. Box J, Hunter, NY 12442: Free brochure ❖ Gourmet honey spreads, baked goods, candy, preserves and jams, and condiments. 800-838-9194.

Whet Your Appetite, P.O. Box 2069, Dublin, CA 94568: Free catalog ❖ Gift assortments from around the world. 800-228-9438.

Whitley's Peanut Factory, P.O. Box 647, Hayes, VA 23072: Free catalog ❖ Peanuts, peanut candy and soup, peanut-carrot cake, peanut butter cookie mixes, and other peanut products. Also cured uncooked country ham and gift assortments. 800-470-2244.

Wild Game Inc., 2315 W. Huron, Chicago, IL 60612: Free information ❖ Venison, buffalo, boar and other exotic meat. Also turkey breast, pates and terrines. Also mushrooms and truffles, smoked seafood, cheese, and gourmet foods. 312-278-1661.

Wileswood Country Store, Mail Order Department, P.O. Box 328, Huron, OH 44839: Free brochure ❖ Old-fashioned candy, popcorn and popping oil, cooking accessories, gifts, and gadgets. 419-433-3355.

Wolsk's Gourmet Confections, 81 Ludlow St., New York, NY 10002: Free information ❖ Low-calorie sugar-free kosher cookies. Also crackers, biscuits, gourmet confections, dried fruits, nuts, coffee and tea, and international specialties. 800-692-6887.

World of Chantilly, 4302 Farragut Rd., Brooklyn, NY 11203: Free list of retail sources ❖ Certified kosher French pastries. Also chocolate candy and gift baskets. 718-859-1110.

Yoders Country Market, 61 Locker Ln., Grantsville, MD 21536: Free catalog ❖ Gourmet food specialties, seasonings and spices, candy, popcorn, baked goods, breads, and favorites. 800-321-5148.

Zabar's & Company, 2245 Broadway, New York, NY 10024: Free catalog ❖ Smoked fish, condiments and spices, candy, crackers, and specialties. Also cookware, food processors, microwave ovens, kitchen tools, and coffee makers. 212-787-2000.

Zingerman's Delicatessen, 422 Detroit St., Ann Arbor, MI 48104: Free catalog ❖ Domestic and imported cheese, ethnic and low-fat specialties, condiments, baked goods, pasta, and traditional Jewish foods. 313-663-3400.

Gingerbread Houses

Creative Cakes, 8814 Brookville Rd., Silver Spring, MD 20910: Free information ❖ Gingerbread house kits. 301-587-1599.

Health & Natural

Allergy Resources Inc., P.O. Box 444, Guffey, CO 80820: Free catalog ❖ Wheat and gluten-free products and alternative foods. 800-873-3529; 719-689-2969 (in CO).

The Alternative Food Cooperative, 3362 Kingstown Rd., West Kingston, RI 02892: Free information ❖ Organic fruits and vegetables, spices, and herbs. 401-789-2240.

American Health Food, 3994 N. Oracle, Tucson, AZ 85705: Free catalog ❖ Health foods and nutritional supplements. 800-858-2143.

American Spoon Foods, 1668 Clarion Ave., P.O. Box 566, Petoskey, MI 49770: Free information ❖ Pancake and waffle mix made with organic-grown Indian blue corn. Also wild rice, wild berry preserves, and wild pecans. 800-222-5886.

Barn Stream Natural Foods, P.O. Box 760, Walpole, NH 03608: Free brochure ❖ Additive, preservative, and cholesterol-free Yankee sourdough, salt-free garlic whole wheat, and hearty multi-grain breads. 800-654-2882.

Blue Heron Farm, P.O. Box 68, Rumsey, CA 95679: Free information ❖ Oranges, other citrus fruits, and nuts. 916-796-3799.

Brownville Mills, Box 145, Brownville, NE 68321: Free price list ❖ Fresh natural foods and vitamins. 800-305-7990; 402-825-4131 (in NE).

Cabot Creamery, P.O. Box 128, Cabot, VT 05647: Free information ❖ All-natural cheese with half the fat and cholesterol and 33 percent fewer calories than Cheddar. 800-639-3198.

Cascadian Farm, 719 Metcalf St., Cedro Wooley, WA 98284: Free information ❖ Canned fruit juices, vegetables, and other foods. 206-855-0100.

Community Products Inc., RD 2, Box 1950, Montpelier, VT 05602: Free list of retail sources ❖ Dairy-free chocolate bars. 800-927-2695; 802-229-5702 (in VT).

Deer Valley Farm, RD 1, Box 173, Guilford, NY 13780: Catalog 50¢ ❖ Natural and organic foods. 607-764-8556.

Diamond Organics, P.O. Box 2159, Freedom, CA 95019: Free information ❖ Lettuce, greens, roots, herbs, and fruits. 800-922-2396.

Eden Foods, 701 Tecumseh Rd., Clinton, MI 49236: Free information ❖ Low-sodium and organic soy sauces. 800-654-7521.

Elena's by Houlihan's, Culinary Traditions Ltd., 70 S. Squirrel Rd., Ste. H, Auburn Hills, MI 48326: Free list of retail sources ❖ Low-fat pasta sauces. 800-72-ELENA.

Epicurean Traders, P.O. Box 5107, Newport Beach, CA 92662: Free information ❖ Fat and cholesterol-free meringue mix. 800-490-6509.

Fatwise, 1130 E. Linden Ave., Colina, NJ 07036: Free catalog ❖ Fat-free foods and snacks. 908-862-3886.

Fiddler's Green Farm, P.O. Box 254, Belfast, ME 04915: Free information ❖ Pancake, muffin, and spice cake mixes, and a breakfast gift package that includes pancake and muffin mixes, maple syrup, and honey. 800-729-7935.

Garden Spot Distributor, 438 White Oak Rd., New Holland, PA 17557: Free information ❖ Apples, apple cider vinegar, and apple juice. 800-829-5100.

The Gluten-Free Pantry, P.O. Box 881, Glastonbury, CT 06033: Free catalog ❖ Easy-to-make wheat and gluten-free gourmet bread, cake mixes, and specialties. 203-633-3826.

Gold Mine Natural Food Company, 3419 Hancock St., San Diego, CA 92110: Free information ❖ Organic brown rice and beans. 800-475-FOOD.

Golden Angels Apiary, P.O. Box 2, Singers Glen, VA 22850: Free information ❖ Apples, apple cider vinegar, and apple juice. 540-636-9611.

Harvest Direct Inc., P.O. Box 988, Knoxville, TN 37901: Free catalog ❖ All-natural products for vegetarians. 800-835-2867.

Healthy Kitchen Mail Order Company, 181 Park St., Montclair, NJ 07042: Free information ❖ Low-fat, no-fat, and no-sugar food specialties. 800-776-7155.

Healthy Trader, 31921 Camino Capistrano, #411, San Juan Capistrano, CA 92675: Free catalog ❖ Health foods and gift baskets for all appetites. 800-636-2584.

Hilyard & Hilquist, P.O. Box 5175, Modesto, CA 95352: Free information ❖ Natural gourmet foods. 800-933-2672.

International Yogurt Company, 628 N. Doheny Dr., Los Angeles, CA 90069: Free catalog ❖ Yogurt tablets, acidophilus capsules, yogurt culture, acidophilus milk culture, cheese culture, and Kefir grains and culture. 310-274-9917.

Jaffe Brothers Natural Foods, P.O. Box 636, Valley Center, CA 92082: Free catalog ❖ Preservative and chemical additive-free dried foods. 619-749-1133.

❖ FOODS ❖

Karen's Kitchen, 43 Randolph Rd., Ste. 757, Silver Spring, MD 20904: Free catalog ❖ Organic foods. 301-236-5992.

Living Farms, Box 50, Tracey, MN 56175: Free information ❖ Grains, beans, rice, wheat, sunflowers, and alfalfa, clover, and radish sprouting seeds. 800-533-5320.

The Mail Order Catalog, P.O. Box 180, Summertown, TN 38483: Free catalog ❖ Regular, beef-style, and organic textured vegetable protein products. 800-695-2241.

Maverick Sugarbush Inc., P.O. Box 99, Sharon, VT 05065: Free brochure ❖ Certified organic Vermont maple syrup, organic cornmeal, and multi-grain pancake mixes. 802-763-8680.

Middlesex Farm Food Products, P.O. Box 2470, Darien, CT 06820: Free catalog ❖ All-natural low-fat condiments. 800-779-FARM.

Morgan's Mills, RD 2, Box 4602, Union, ME 04862: Free information ❖ Salt-free mixes for pancakes, waffles, and bran muffins. 800-373-2756.

Mountain Ark Trading Company, P.O. Box 3170, Fayetteville, AR 72702: Free information ❖ Vegetables, miso, seasonings, rice, pasta, fruit, spreads, oils, beans, and soups. 800-643-8909.

Natural Resources, 6680 Harvard Dr., Sebastopol, CA 95472: Free information ❖ All-natural gourmet and dairy-free chocolate candy and chocolate chips, organic chocolate bars, and other natural foods. 800-747-0390; 707-823-4340 (in CA).

Osaanyin Herb Cooperative, 112 Main St., Montpelier, VT 05602: Catalog $1 ❖ Medicinal, exotic, and ayurvedic herbs and other botanicals. Also extracts and oils, ginseng, and books. 802-223-0888.

River Bend Country Store, 2363 Tucker Rd., Hood River, OR 97031: Free catalog ❖ Hand-packed organic fruit and select specialties. 503-386-8766.

Slim Waist Foods, 2914 Coney Island Ave., Brooklyn, NY 11235: Free brochure ❖ Fat-free cookies. 718-769-5700.

Southern Brown Rice, P.O. Box 185, Weiner, AR 72479: Free catalog ❖ Rice products fresh from the farm. 800-421-7423.

Soyco Foods, Galaxy Foods, 2441 Viscount Row, Orlando, Fl 32809: Free list of retail sources ❖ Casein-free cheese alternative. 800-441-9419.

Stonehill Farm, Box 158, Schwenksville, PA 19473: Free catalog ❖ All-natural low-fat foods. 800-776-7155.

Timber Crest Farms, 4791 Dry Creek Rd., Healdsburg, CA 95448: Free catalog ❖ Dried fruit, dried tomato products, fruit butters, nuts, and trail mixes. 707-433-8251.

Transpacific Health Products, 3924 Central Ave., St. Petersburg, FL 33711: Free catalog ❖ Herb teas for health-related conditions. 800-336-9636.

Walnut Acres Organic Farms, Penns Creek, PA 17862: Free catalog ❖ Fresh and canned vegetables, canned and dried fruit, grains, baked goods, natural cheese, fruit and vegetable juices, nuts, jams, preserves, and other specialties. 800-433-3998.

Wanda's Nature Farm Foods, 850 NBC Center, Lincoln, NE 68508: Free catalog ❖ All-natural bread, muffin, pancake, waffle, and double-chocolate cake mixes. 800-222-FARM.

War Eagle Mill, Rt. 5, Box 411, Rogers, AR 72756: Free catalog ❖ Whole grain meals and flours. 501-789-5343.

Wax Orchards, 22744 Wax Orchards Rd. SW, Vashon, WA 98070: Free list of retail sources ❖ Conserves, fruit butters and syrups, dessert toppings, and other food products sweetened with concentrated natural fruit juices. 800-634-6132.

Maple Syrup

Auger's Sugarmill Farm, Rt. 16, Box 26, Barton, VT 05822: Free catalog ❖ Vermont maple syrup. 800-688-7978.

Bascom Maple Farms Inc., RR 1, Box 137, Mount Kingsbury Rd., Alstead, NH 03602: Free brochure ❖ Maple syrup and candy. 800-835-6361.

Bragg Farm, Rt. 14 North, East Montpelier, VT 05651: Free brochure ❖ Maple syrup. 800-376-5757; 802-223-5757 (in VT).

Butternut Mountain Farm, P.O. Box 381, Johnson, VT 05656: Free information ❖ Maple syrup and sugar. 800-828-2376.

Danforth's Sugarhouse, US Rt. 2, East Montpelier, VT 05651: Free information ❖ Maple syrup. 802-229-9536.

Grafton Village Apple Company, 703 Main St., Weston, VT 05161: Free catalog ❖ Maple syrup and sugar. 800-843-4822.

Green Mountain Sugar House, Rt. 100N, Box 820, Ludlow, VT 05149: Free catalog ❖ Maple syrup, maple sugar candy, nut brittle, cheese, smoked slab bacon, candy and fudge, pancake mix, mincemeat, homemade jams, and Vermont specialties. 800-643-9338; 802-228-7151 (in VT).

Hagelberg Farm, 185 Lost Lake Rd., Arlington, VT 05250: Free catalog ❖ Vermont maple syrup.

Harlow's Sugar House, RD 1, Box 395, Putney, VT 05346: Free brochure ❖ Maple syrup and specialties, jams, jellies, and Vermont cheese. 802-387-5852.

Jasper's Sugar Bush, W1867 Co. Rd. 374, Carney, MI 49812: Free information ❖ Maple syrup, maple cream, maple sugar candy, chocolate maple cream, and gift baskets. 800-646-2753.

Maple Grove Farms of Vermont, 167 Portland St., St. Johnsbury, VT 05819: Free information ❖ Maple sugar and syrup. 800-525-2540; 802-748-5141 (in VT).

Maverick Sugarbush Inc., P.O. Box 99, Sharon, VT 05065: Free brochure ❖ Certified organic Vermont maple syrup, organic cornmeal, and multi-grain pancake mixes. 802-763-8680.

Morse Farm, County Rd., HCR 32, Box 870, Montpelier, VT 05602: Free information ❖ Maple syrup and specialties. 800-223-2740.

New England Maple Museum, Gift Shop, P.O. Box 1615, Rutland, 05701: Free brochure ❖ Maple syrup and specialties.

Palmer's Maple Syrup, P.O. Box 240 RD, Waitsfield, VT 05673: Free brochure ❖ Maple syrup, cream, jelly, and candy. 802-496-3696.

The Rocking Horse Country Store, RR 3, Box 7343, Rutland, VT 05701: Free brochure ❖ Vermont maple syrup, cheese, crafts, and country collectibles. 802-773-7882.

RoseMary's Gifts, West Rd., Bennington, VT 05201: Free information with long SASE ❖ Corn cob-smoked meats, cheese, poultry, fish, Vermont Cheddar cheese, and maple syrup. Also gift baskets. 802-447-0373.

Spring Tree Corporation, P.O. Box 1160, Brattleboro, VT 05302: Free list of retail sources ❖ Additive and preservative-free, 100 percent pure maple syrup. 802-254-8784.

The Sugar Shack, Rt. 7A, Arlington, VT 05250: Free information ❖ Vermont maple syrup, cream, and candy. Also homemade fudge, cheese, Vermont food products, and gifts. 802-375-6747.

Sugarbush Farm, RR1, Box 568, Woodstock, VT 05091: Free information with long SASE ❖ Maple syrup and cheese. 802-457-1757.

The Sugarmill Farm, Rt. 16 South, Barton, VT 05822: Free brochure ❖ Maple syrup and specialties. 800-688-7978.

Eldridge C. Thomas, RR 4, Box 336, Chester, VT 05143: Free brochure ❖ Vermont maple syrup. 802-263-5419.

Vermont Country Maple Mixes, 76 Ethan Allen Dr., South Burlington, VT 05403: Free information ❖ Maple sugar and syrup, maple sugar sprinkles, and maple sweetened cake, bread, and frosting mixes. 800-528-7021.

Wood's Cider Mill, RFD 2, Box 477, Springfield, VT 05156: Free catalog with long SASE ❖ Maple syrup, cider jelly and syrup, and boiled cider. 802-263-5547.

Meats

Aidells Sausage Company, Mail Order Department, 1625 Alvarado St., San Leandro, CA 94577: Free catalog ❖ Filler, MSG, and binder-free sausage. 800-546-5795.

❖ FOODS ❖

Allen Brothers, 3737 S. Halsted St., Chicago, IL 60609: Free catalog ❖ Steakhouse steaks, veal, and lamb chops. 800-957-0111.

Amana Meat Shop & Smokehouse, P.O. Box 158, Amana, IA 52203: Free brochure ❖ Ham, bacon, sausage, cheese, and specialties. 800-373-MEAT; 319-622-3111 (in IA).

B3R Country Meats Inc., 2100 W. Hwy. 287, P.O. Box 374, Childress, TX 79201: Free information ❖ All-natural premium beef. 817-937-3668.

Basse's Choice Plantation, P.O. Box 1, Smithfield, VA 23431: Free information ❖ Cured, smoked, aged, low-salt, country, and honey-cured ham. 800-292-2773.

Becky's Country Meats Inc., P.O. Box 955, Columbia Station, OH 44028: Free information ❖ Low-salt and no sugar-added apple-cured whole turkeys, Canadian and slab bacon, and boneless hams. 800-555-0480.

Boyle Meat Packing Company, 500 E. 3rd St., Kansas City, MO 64106: Free brochure ❖ Hand-carved rib eye steaks and other meats. 800-821-3626; 842-5852 (in Kansas City).

Broadbent's B & B Food Products, 6321 Hopkinsville Rd., Cadiz, KY 42211: Free catalog ❖ Jams, jellies, cheese, smoked and hand-cured country ham, bacon, and sausage. 800-841-2202; 502-235-5294 (in KY).

Broadleaf Venison USA, 11030 Randall St., Sun Valley, CA 91352: Free information ❖ Farm-raised venison, buffalo, lamb, and pheasant. 800-336-3844.

Broken Arrow Ranch, P.O. Box 530, Ingram, TX 78025: Free brochure ❖ Venison, smoked wild boar, antelope, emu, and other exotic meat. 800-962-4263.

Burgers' Ozark Country Cured Hams Inc., Rt. 3, Box 3248, California, MO 65018: Free catalog ❖ Barbecued chickens, sausage, cheese, and hickory-smoked and sugar-cured ham, ham steaks, bacon, and turkey. 800-624-5426; 314-796-4111 (in MO).

Cavanaugh Lakeview Farms Ltd., 2000 Thorn Apple Valley Dr., Ponca City, OK 74601: Free information ❖ Honey-cured and smoked poultry, smoked ham and bacon, fresh-frozen poultry, steaks, game, and smoked seafood. 800-243-4438.

Certified Prime, 9139 Francisco, Aberdeen Park, IL 60642: Free information ❖ Gourmet meat. 800-257-2977.

Classic Country Rabbit Company, P.O. Box 1412, Hillsboro, OR 97123: Free catalog ❖ Rabbit specialties. 800-821-7426.

Classic Steaks, 4430 S. 110th St., Omaha, NE 68137: Free catalog ❖ USDA choice steaks. 800-288-2783.

Clifty Farm, P.O. Box 1146, South Paris, TN 38242: Free brochure ❖ Country-cooked hams, baby back pork ribs, slab bacon, hickory-smoked turkey, and gift packages. 800-486-HAMS.

Critchfield Meat, 2254 Vandale Center, Lexington, KY 40503: Free catalog ❖ Old-fashioned sugar-cured country ham and other meat. 800-86-MEATS; 606-276-4965 (in KY).

D'Artagnan, 399 St. Paul Ave., Jersey City, NJ 07306: Free catalog ❖ Foie gras, pates, Muscovy duck, fresh game, and organic poultry. 800-DARTAGN.

Dakin Farm, Rt. 7, Ferrisburg, VT 05456: Free catalog ❖ Smoked ham and bacon, maple syrup, and Cheddar cheese. 800-993-2546.

Denver Buffalo Company, 1120 Lincoln St., Ste. 905, Denver, CO 80203: Free catalog ❖ All-natural buffalo meat and smoked sausage. 800-289-2833; 303-831-1299 (in CO).

Early's, 5087 Colombia Pike, Springhill, TN 37174: Free catalog ❖ Honey-glazed hams, whole smoked turkey, country favorites, and gift assortments. 800-523-2015.

Edes Custom Meats Inc., 6700 W. McCormick Rd., Amarillo, TX 79118: Free information with long SASE ❖ Sausage, ham, bacon, beef jerky, grain fed and aged USA choice beef, lamb, and turkey. 800-537-5902; 806-622-0205 (in TX).

S. Wallace Edwards & Sons Inc., P.O. Box 25, Surry, VA 23883: Free catalog ❖ Preserves from the Blue Ridge Mountains, seafood from the Eastern Shore, and hickory-smoked Virginia ham, bacon, and sausage. 800-222-4267.

Faire Game, P.O. Box 7026, Loveland, CO 80537: Free information ❖ Farm-raised exotic game meat. 800-889-6328.

Fiddler's Creek Farm, Hunter Rd., RD 2, Box 188, Titusville, NJ 08560: Free information ❖ Country-cured smoked turkey and breasts, chicken breasts, capons, bacon, and pork tenderloin. 609-737-0685.

Folk's Folly Prime Cut Shoppe, 551 S. Mendenhall, Memphis, TN 38117: Free catalog ❖ Prime veal, lamb loin chops, steaks, and gourmet meat. 800-467-0245.

Fortuna's Sausage Company, 975 Greenville Ave., Greenville, RI 02828: Free catalog ❖ Fresh and dry-cured sausage and Italian specialties. 800-427-6879.

Four Oaks Farm Inc., P.O. Box 987, Lexington, SC 29071: Free brochure ❖ Country-style ham and bacon, jams, jellies, pickles, relishes, salad dressings, cakes, and other favorites. 800-858-5006; 803-356-3194 (in SC).

Game Sales International, 444 Washington St., Loveland, CO 80538: Free brochure ❖ Venison, buffalo, pheasant, and other exotic meats. 800-729-2090.

Gaspar's Sausage Company, 384 Faunce Corner Rd., North Dartmouth, MA 02747: Free information ❖ Hot and mild Portuguese-style sausage, sweet breads, and sliced meat. 800-542-2038; 508-998-2012 (in MA).

Genuine Canadian Food Products, 3184 Dovetail Mews, Mississauga, Ontario, Canada L5L 5K4: Free information ❖ Canadian bacon. 800-800-6481.

Gerhard's Sausage, 901 Enterprise Way, Napa, CA 94558: Free list of retail sources ❖ MSG and filler-free smoked and fresh sausage. 707-252-4116.

Giuseppe's Original Sausage Company, 181 Cumberland, Memphis, TN 38112: Free brochure ❖ Gourmet sausages. 800-893-3497; 901-323-3068 (in TN).

Golden Trophy, 1101 Perimeter Dr., Ste. 210, Schaumberg, IL 60173: Free catalog ❖ Gourmet meat. 800-835-6607.

Great Plains Meats, P.O. Box 630, Wisner, NE 8791: Free information ❖ Aged steaks. 800-871-6328.

The Great Valley Mills, 1774 County Line Rd., Bartow, PA 19504: Free brochure ❖ Pennsylvania Dutch country cheese, ham, bacon, sausage, beef, preserves, fruitcakes, stollen, flour, and cereals. 800-688-6455.

Greenberg Smoked Turkey Inc., P.O. Box 4818, Tyler, TX 75712: Free information ❖ Smoked turkey. 903-595-0725.

Guadelupe Pit Smoked Meats, 754 Rock St., New Braunfels, TX 78130: Free list of retail sources ❖ Cornish game hens, pit-smoked pork, and beef specialties. 210-625-4036.

Harrington Ham Company, Main St., Richmond, VT 05477: Free information ❖ Spiral-sliced and cob-smoked maple-glazed ham. Also smoked bacon, turkey breast, pheasant, cheese, maple syrup, pastries, plum pudding, fruitcakes, and dried fruit. 802-434-4444.

Harrington's of Vermont, Route 7, Shelburne, VT 05482: Free information ❖ Ham and Vermont specialty foods. 802-985-2000.

Hawaii's Jungle Jerky, P.O. Box 31062, Honolulu, HI 96820: Free brochure ❖ Low-sodium beef jungle jerky. 800-87-ALOHA; 800-540-1793 (in Hawaiian Islands).

Hoffman's Quality Meats, 13225 Cearfoss Pike, Hagerstown, MD 21740: Free brochure ❖ Country ham and bacon, Delmonico and boneless New York strip steaks, and country sausage. 800-356-3193.

The Ideal Sausage Company, 245 W. 38th St., New York, NY 10018: Free catalog ❖ Low-fat spicy poultry sausage. 212-719-0850.

Indian Hill Farms, 213 Old Indian Rd., Milton, NY 12547: Free catalog ❖ Smoked whole turkey and turkey breast, kosher turkey, smoked ham, Norwegian smoked salmon, and brandied fruitcake. 914-795-2700.

❖ FOODS ❖

Inman Wild Game, Box 616, Aberdeen, SD 57401: Free brochure ❖ Fresh, frozen, and smoked pheasant and wild turkey. Also buffalo sausage, quail, and partridge. 800-843-1962.

International Home Cooking, 305 Mallory St., Rocky Mount, NC 27801: Free catalog ❖ Exotic fresh meats. 919-972-7423.

Jamison Farm, 171 Jamison Ln., Latrobe, PA 15650: Free brochure ❖ Lamb. 800-237-5262.

Kansas City Steak Company, 2501 Guinotte, P.O. Box 33442, Kansas City, MO 64120: Free catalog ❖ Corn-fed aged beef. 800-987-8325.

Klement Sausage Company, 207 E. Lincoln Ave., Milwaukee, WI 53207: Free catalog ❖ Gourmet sausage. 800-KLEMENT; 414-744-5554 (in WI).

R. Lefebvre & Son Smokehouse Meats, P.O. Box 278, South Barre, VT 05670: Free information ❖ Maple-cured smoked ham and smoked bacon. 800-457-6066.

Frank Lewis' Alamo Fruit, 100 N. Tower Rd., Alamo, TX 78516: Free brochure ❖ Farm-fresh tomatoes, tangelos, apples, persimmons, cheesecake, smoked turkey breast, and gourmet specialties. 800-477-4773.

Mahogany Smoked Meats, P.O. Box 1387, Bishop, CA 93515: Free brochure ❖ Smoked jerky, Cheddar cheese, chileno peppers and stuffed olives, smoked trout, and other specialties. 619-873-5311.

Jody Maroni's Sausage Kingdom, 2011 Ocean Front Walk, Venice, CA 90291: Free information ❖ Low-fat and nitrate, MSG, and preservative-free all-natural gourmet sausage. 800-HAUTDOG.

Maurice's Flying Pig, P.O. Box 6847, West Columbia, SC 29171: Free catalog ❖ Hickory pit-cooked all-ham barbecue and barbecue sauce. 800-MAURICE.

Myers Meats, Rt. 1, Box 132, Parshall, ND 58770: Free information ❖ Country-style sausage, beef jerky, country-cured dried beef, beef sticks, and other specialties. 800-635-3759; 201-437-4443 (in NJ).

New Braunfels Smokehouse, P.O. Box 311159, New Braunfels, TX 78131: Free catalog ❖ Bin-cured and hickory-smoked turkey, ham, sausage, bacon, chicken, and beef. 800-537-6932.

New Skete Farms, P.O. Box 128, Cambridge, NY 12816: Catalog $1 ❖ Smoked whole ducks and chickens. Also turkey and chicken breasts, bacon, ham, sausage, Cheddar cheese, and cheese spreads. 518-677-3928.

Colonel Bill Newsom's Hams, 127 N. Highland Ave., Princeton, KY 42445: Free information ❖ Hickory-smoked ham, sorghum, hickory-smoked meat, relishes, and preserves. 502-365-2482.

Noble Farms Inc., P.O. Box 1612, Sedalia, MO 65301: Free information ❖ Whole-smoked pheasant and smoked pheasant breast. 800-827-5907.

North Country Smokehouse, P.O. Box 1415, Claremont, NH 03743: Free brochure ❖ All-natural old-fashioned cob-smoked meat, ham, slab and Canadian bacon, pork chops, sausage, spareribs, boneless lamb, whole turkey and turkey breasts, duck, pheasant, and sharp Vermont and mozzarella cheese. 800-258-4304.

Nueske's Hillcrest Farm Meats, RR 2, Wittenberg, WI 54499: Free brochure ❖ Smoked ham, sausage, bacon, smoked shanks, pork loins, pork chops, duck, turkey and turkey breasts, chicken and chicken breasts, and Cornish game hens. 800-382-2266.

The O.K. Market, 542 N. Linden St., Wahoo, NE 68066: Free information ❖ Polish sausage, bologna, beef jerky, wieners, and other meat products. 800-847-6328; 402-443-3015 (in NE).

Oak Grove Smokehouse Inc., 17618 Old Jefferson Hwy., Prairieville, LA 70769: Free catalog ❖ Slow-smoked ham, turkey, and other meat. Also gumbo and jambalaya kits, Creole mixes, and other Louisiana favorites. 504-673-6857.

Oakridge Smokehouse Restaurant, P.O. Box 146, Schulenburg, TX 78956: Free information ❖ Peppered beef tenderloins, smoked pork tenderloins, and baby-back smoked pork spare ribs. 800-548-6325.

Omaha Steaks International, P.O. Box 3300, Omaha, NE 68103: Free catalog ❖ Aged steaks and beef. 800-228-9055.

Ozark Mountain Smoke House Inc., P.O. Box 37, Farmington, AR 72730: Free catalog ❖ Smoked poultry and meat. 800-643-3437; 800-632-0155 (in AR).

Pfaelzer Brothers, Catalog Order Department, P.O. Box 1015, Maumee, OH 43537: Free catalog ❖ Gourmet meat, fruit and gift baskets, desserts, and other specialties. 800-621-0226.

Pittman & Davis, P.O. Box 532227, Harlingen, TX 78553: Catalog $1 ❖ Ruby red grapefruit, oranges, pecans, fruitcakes, cheese, smoked ham, and turkey. 210-423-2154.

Premium Image, 16135 Preston St., Ste. 100, Dallas, TX 75248: Free information ❖ Jalapeno-smoked turkey and spicy foods. 800-894-6225.

Prime Access, P.O. Box 8187, White Plains, NY 10602: Free information ❖ Gourmet meats. 800-314-2875.

Prime Meat Express, P.O. Box 12343, El Paso, TX 79913: Free information ❖ Hand-selected USDA prime meats. 800-761-9666.

RoseMary's Gifts, West Rd., Bennington, VT 05201: Free information with long SASE ❖ Corn cob-smoked meats, cheese, poultry, fish, Vermont Cheddar cheese, and maple syrup. Also gift baskets. 802-447-0373.

The Sausage Maker Inc., 26 Military Rd., Buffalo, NY 14207: Free catalog ❖ Equipment and supplies for making sausage at home. 716-876-5521.

Schaller & Weber Inc., 22-35 46th St., Long Island City, NY 11105: Free catalog ❖ Sausage, liverwurst, cold cuts, salami and cervelats, Westphalian-style smoked ham, roast beef, bacon, and other gourmet meat. 800-847-4115; 212-721-5480 (in NY).

Schiltz Goose Farm, 7 Oak St. West, P.O. Box 267, Sisseton, SD 57262: Free information ❖ Geese, shipped early October through the holidays, packaged for the freezer. Also goose eggs. 605-698-7651.

Scott Hams, 1301 Scott Rd., Greenville, KY 42345: Free information ❖ Hickory-smoked country ham, bacon, and sausage. 502-338-3402.

Semplex, P.O. Box 11476, Minneapolis, MN 55411: Free catalog ❖ Sausage-making equipment and ingredients. 800-488-5444.

Sinai Kosher Foods Corporation, 1000 W. Pershing Rd., Chicago, IL 60609: Free information ❖ Kosher beef, lamb, veal, roasts, steaks, chops, and ground beef. 800-823-7746; 312-650-6339 (in IL).

Smithfield Ham & Products Company, P.O. Box 487, Smithfield, VA 23430: Free catalog ❖ Country-style Red Eye and Amber Smithfield ham, smoked game birds, ham and other meat, cheese, jellies, jams, and cookies. 800-628-2242; 804-357-2121 (in VA).

Stock Yards Packing Company, 340 N. Oakley Blvd., Chicago, IL 60612: Free catalog ❖ Foods and meat specialties. 800-621-3687.

Summerfield Farm, 10044 James Monroe Hwy., Culpeper, VA 22701: Free brochure ❖ Veal, venison, lamb, sausage, prime beef, game birds, and smoked salmon halves. 703-547-9600.

Texas Wild Game Cooperative, P.O. Box 530, Ingram, TX 78025: Free catalog ❖ Venison, antelope, wild boar, and other exotic meat. 800-962-4263.

Thundering Herd Buffalo Products, P.O. Box 1051, Reno, NV 89504: Free catalog ❖ Ranch-raised buffalo meat. 800-525-9730.

Usinger's Famous Sausage, 1030 N. Old World 3rd St., Milwaukee, WI 53203: Free catalog ❖ Over 75 varieties of sausage. 800-558-9998; 414-276-9105 (in WI).

Virginia Diner, P.O. 1030, Wakefield, VA 23888: Free catalog ❖ Virginia bacon and ham, fudge, homemade jellies and jams, peanuts, and peanut specialties. 800-642-6887.

❖ FOODS ❖

Volpi Foods, 5254 Daggett Ave., St. Louis, MO 63110: Free information ❖ Sliced prosciutto and filsette, sopressata, calabrese, and napoli salami. Also Italian meat and gift assortments. 800-288-3439.

The Daniel Weaver Company, P.O. Box 525, Lebanon, PA 17042: Free catalog ❖ Lebanon bologna, smoked meat, and specialties. 800-932-8377; 717-274-6100 (in PA).

Wild Game Inc., 2315 W. Huron, Chicago, IL 60612: Free information ❖ Venison, buffalo, boar and other exotic meat. Also turkey breast, pates and terrines. Also mushrooms and truffles, smoked seafood, cheese, and gourmet foods. 312-278-1661.

Wimmer's Meat Products, 126 W. Grant, West Point, NE 68788: Free catalog ❖ Ham, sausage, bacon, and meat cured using old-world spice recipes. 800-358-0761.

Wolfe's Neck Farm, 10 Burnett Rd., Freeport, ME 04032: Free catalog ❖ All-natural Angus beef. 207-865-4469.

Nuts

A & B Milling Company Inc., Box 327, Enfield, NC 27823: Free information ❖ Shelled and fried peanuts, chocolate peanut clusters, and other nut favorites. 800-843-0105.

Ace Pecan Company, 281 W. 83rd St., Burr Ridge, IL 60521: Free catalog ❖ Pecans and pecan candy. 800-323-9754.

Almond Plaza, Catalog Order Center, P.O. Box 426, Maumee, OH 43537: Free catalog ❖ Almonds, candy, and herbs. 800-225-6887.

Assouline & Ting Inc., 314 Brown St., Philadelphia, PA 19123: Free information ❖ Gourmet nut specialties. 800-521-4491; 215-627-3000 (in PA).

Azar Nut Company, 1800 Northwestern Dr., El Paso, TX 79912: Free information ❖ Mixed nuts, jumbo and honey-roasted cashews and peanuts, pistachios, roasted pecans, and macadamias. 800-351-8178; 915-877-4079 (in TX).

Bates Nut Farm Inc., 15954 Woods Valley Rd., Valley Center, CA 92082: Free price list ❖ Walnuts, pecans, cashews, macadamias, pistachios, fresh apricots, prunes, dates, candy, granolas, dried fruit, preserves, and honey. 800-642-0348; 619-749-3333 (in CA).

Buchanan Hollow Nut Company, 6510 Minturn, Le Grand, CA 95333: Free information ❖ Fresh-roasted pistachios. 800-532-1500; 209-389-4594 (in CA).

Carolyn's Pecans, P.O. Box 1221, Concord, MA 01742: Free brochure ❖ Sweet, salt-flavored, salt-free, and chocolate covered pecans. 800-656-2940; 508-369-2940 (in MA).

Country Estate Pecans, P.O. Box 7, Sahuarita, AZ 85629: Free information ❖ Pecans. 800-327-3226.

Dasher Pecan Company, P.O. Box 5366, Valdosta, GA 31603: Free information ❖ Pecans, cashews, mixed nuts, and nut specialties. 800-992-2688.

Dundee Orchards, P.O. Box 327, Dundee, OR 97115: Free information ❖ Hazelnut butter and hazelnut products. Also Oregon cherries. 503-538-8105.

Durey-Libby Nuts Inc., P.O. Box 345, Carlstadt, NJ 07072: Free brochure ❖ Walnuts, cashews, pecans, macadamias, almonds, and pistachios. 201-939-2775.

Fran's Pecans, P.O. Box 98, Harlem, GA 30814: Free brochure ❖ Honey-roasted and cinnamon-sugar pecan specialties, pralines, and roasted and salted pecan halves. 800-476-6887.

Fruit Ranch-West, 7520 W. Bluemound Rd., Milwaukee, WI 53213: Free catalog ❖ Fruit gift baskets, assorted nuts, and Wisconsin cheese variety packages. 800-433-3289.

Golden Kernel Pecan Company Inc., Box 613, Cameron, SC 29030: Free brochure ❖ Pecans and pecan specialties. 800-845-2448; 803-823-2311 (in SC).

House of Almonds, 5634 River Rd., Oakdale, CA 95361: Free catalog ❖ A wide variety of nuts, chocolates, and assorted munchies. Treat yourself or send to a friend. 800-225-6663.

Houston's Peanut Outlet, P.O. Box 160, Dublin, NC 28332: Free brochure ❖ Raw, blanched, oil-roasted, and salted-in-the-shell peanuts. 800-334-8383.

Huntley-Moore Farms, P.O. Box 332, Fresno, CA 93708: Free catalog ❖ Pistachios, macadamias, nut candy, and other specialties. 800-700-5779.

J.H. Sherard, P.O. Box 75, Sherard, MS 38669: Free brochure ❖ Shelled and unshelled pecans, pistachios, and other nuts. 800-647-5518; 205-627-7211 (in MS).

Lane Pecans, P.O. Box 716, Fort Valley, GA 31030: Free brochure ❖ Shelled and unshelled pecans. 800-277-3224.

Maples Fruit Farm, P.O. Box 167, Chewsville, MD 21721: Free catalog ❖ Dried fruit, nuts, coffee, other specialties, and gift baskets. 301-733-0777.

Mariani Nut Company, 709 Dutton St., P.O. Box 808, Winters, CA 95694: Free information ❖ Almonds, pistachios, walnuts, and dried tomatoes. 916-795-3311.

Mashuga Nuts Inc., 169 Paulin Dr., San Rafael, CA 94903: Free list of retail sources ❖ Thai-flavored hot and sweet spiced pecans. 800-Mashuga.

Mauna Loa Macadamia Nut Corporation, Mainland Expediting Center, 6523 N. Galena Rd., P.O. Box 1772, Peoria, IL 61656: Free catalog ❖ Milk and dark chocolate-coated, honey-roasted, salted and unsalted macadamias, truffles, other candy, and Kona coffee. 800-832-9993.

Missouri Dandy Pantry, P.O. Box A, Stockton, MO 65785: Free brochure ❖ Cashews, pistachios, black walnuts, other nuts, and candy. 800-872-6879.

Nanco, P.O. Box 100549, Terra Bedlla, CA 93270: Free list of retail sources ❖ Pistachios and hand-dipped pistachio/milk chocolate/caramel candy. 209-535-1030.

Nunes Farms Almonds, 4012 Pete Miller Rd., P.O. Box 311, Newman, CA 95360: Free information ❖ Fresh, roasted and salted, honey-glazed, and Cheddar cheese almonds. 800-255-1641.

Nuts D'Vine, P.O. Box 589, Edenton, NC 27932: Free catalog ❖ Peanut brittle and farm-fresh in the shell, roasted, salted, unsalted, and red skin peanuts. 800-334-0492.

Peanut Patch Inc., P.O. Box 186, Courtland, VA 23837: Free brochure ❖ Peanuts, peanut candy assortments, and raw peanuts in bulk. 800-544-0896.

The Peanut Shop of Williamsburg, P.O. Box GN, Williamsburg, VA 23187: Free brochure ❖ Peanut specialties, Virginia country ham, Williamsburg soups, salad dressings, sauces, and gourmet food items. 800-637-3268.

Pecan Producers International, Primera Pecans, P.O. Box 1301, Corsicana, TX 75151: Free information ❖ Pecans and pecan candy. 800-732-2648.

Priester's Pecans, 227 Old Fort Dr., Fort Deposit, AL 36032: Free catalog ❖ Nut brittle, pecan candy, pecan brownies and pie, sugar-free pecan clusters, and roasted, salted, and salt-free pecans. 800-277-3226.

Pueblo to People, P.O. Box 2545, Houston, TX 77252: Free catalog ❖ Nuts, dried fruit, gift baskets, and coffees. Also ceramics, jewelry, and gifts. 800-843-5257.

Ross-Smith Pecan Company Inc., 700 Oak St., McRae, GA 31055: Free brochure ❖ Pecans. 800-841-5503; 912-868-5693 (in GA).

Santa Fe Cookie Company, 3905 San Mateo NE, Albuquerque, NM 87110: Free brochure ❖ Gourmet and sugar-free cookies, spicy snacks, pretzels, crackers, and nut mixes. 800-873-5589.

Senor Pistachio, P.O. Box 10179, Terra Bella, CA 93270: Free information ❖ Salted and unsalted roasted pistachios. 800-468-1319.

FOODS

Society Hill Snacks, 2121 Gillingham St., Philadelphia, PA 19124: Free list of retail sources ❖ Butter-toasted pecans, cashews, almonds, peanuts, mixed nuts, and pistachios. 800-595-0050; 215-288-2888 (in PA).

The Squire's Choice, Mail Order Department, 2250 W. Cabot Blvd., Langhorne, PA 19047: Free catalog ❖ Nuts, coffee, and other specialties. 800-523-6163.

Sun Burst Farms, 352 Paul Sumner Rd., Omega, GA 31775: Free brochure ❖ Pecans and peanuts. 800-358-9412.

Sunnyland Farms Inc., P.O. Box 8200, Albany, GA 31706: Free catalog ❖ Pecans, other nuts, candy, baked specialties, dried fruits, maple syrup, honey, jellies, and gift assortments. 800-999-2488; 912-883-3085 (in GA).

Sun River Packing Company, 1329 Hazeldean Rd., Waterford, CA 95386: Free information ❖ Fresh, blanched, and hickory-smoked almonds. 800-334-NUTS.

Tanner Pecan Company, 10 Springdale Blvd., Mobile, AL 36606: Free catalog ❖ Pecans and pecan confections. 800-635-3651.

H.M. Thames Pecan Company, P.O. Box 2206, Mobile, AL 36652: Free catalog ❖ Nuts and nut specialties, pralines, candy, baked goods, and fruitcake. 800-633-1306.

Things of Good Taste, P.O. Box 455, Waynesboro, VA 22980: Free list of retail sources ❖ Cakes, candy, nuts, dip and seasoning mixes, and fruit butters. 800-248-2591.

Virginia Diner, P.O. 1030, Wakefield, VA 23888: Free catalog ❖ Peanuts, peanut specialties and pie, homemade jellies and jams, Virginia bacon and ham, and fudge. 800-642-6887.

Waterford Nut Company, P.O. Box 37, Waterford, CA 95386: Free information ❖ Natural fresh shelled almonds and almond butter. 209-874-2317.

Whitley's Peanut Factory, P.O. Box 647, Hayes, VA 23072: Free catalog ❖ Mouth-watering gourmet extra-large Virginia peanuts, peanut candy, and other peanut products. Like no other peanut you've ever tasted! 800-470-2244.

Joe C. Williams, P.O. Box 640, Camden, AL 36726: Free brochure ❖ Fresh-shelled pecans. 800-967-3226.

Young Pecans, c/o Pecan Plantations, P.O. Drawer 6709, Florence, SC 29502: Free catalog ❖ Butter-roasted and salted pecans and cashews, double-dipped chocolate pecan halves, butter-toffee pecan popcorn, pecan divinity logs, and praline, sugar and orange, sugar and spiced, and Cheddar cheese pecans. 800-729-8004.

Popcorn

Black Shield Inc., 5356 Pan American Freeway NE, Albuquerque, NM 87109: Free information ❖ Gourmet flavored popcorn. 800-653-9357.

Fisher's Popcorn, 200 S. Boardwalk, Ocean City, MD 21842: Free brochure ❖ Caramel popcorn. 410-289-5638.

Myers Gourmet Popcorn, 8025 W. Hwy. 24, Cascade, CO 80809: Free brochure ❖ Gourmet popcorn gifts. 800-684-1155.

Popcorn Factory, Mail Order Dept., P.O. Box 4530, Lake Bluff, IL 60044: Free catalog ❖ Butter-flavored, Cheddar cheese, homemade caramel, and other popcorn favorites. 800-541-2676.

Popcorn World Inc., 2303 Princeton Rd., P.O. Box 507, Trenton, MO 64683: Free brochure ❖ Butter, caramel, cheese, cinnamon, cinnamon with almonds and pecans, vanilla-butter with almonds, and popcorn with pecans. 800-443-8226.

Preserves, Jellies & Honey

American Spoon Foods, 1668 Clarion Ave., P.O. Box 566, Petoskey, MI 49770: Free information ❖ Fruit preserves and jellies, pumpkin butter, rhubarb marmalade, and fruit conserves. 800-222-5886.

Arkansas Blue Heron Farms, Rt. 2, Box 323, Lowell, AR 72745: Free catalog ❖ Blueberry jam and marmalades and Amaretto dessert sauce. 800-225-6849.

Baranof Berry Patch, P.O. Box 452, Sitka, AK 99835: Free information ❖ Wild berry jellies and jams. 907-747-3031.

Beth's Farm Kitchen, P.O. Box 113, Stuyvesant Falls, NY 12174: Free catalog ❖ Jams, preserves, spreads, chutneys, mustards, and vinegars. 800-331-JAMS.

Blackberry Patch, Rt. 7, Box 918C, Tallahassee, FL 32308: Free list of retail sources ❖ Jellies, fresh fruit jams, syrups, honey, and salad dressings. 800-8-JELLY-8; 904-893-3183 (in FL).

Carp River Trading Company, 6005 E. Traverse Hwy., Traverse City, MI 49864: Free catalog ❖ Fruit preserves. 800-526-9876.

Cascade Conserves Inc., P.O. Box 8306, Portland, OR 97207: Free brochure ❖ All-natural low-sugar conserves and fruit syrups. 800-846-7396; 503-243-3608 (in OR).

Cheri's Desert Harvest, 1840 E. Winsett St., Tucson, AZ 85719: Free information ❖ Cholesterol and fat-free all-natural Southwestern preserves and syrups. 800-743-1141; 520-623-4141 (in AZ).

Chukar Cherries, P.O. Box 510, Prosser, WV 99350: Free catalog ❖ Cherry preserves and sauces. 800-624-9544.

Clairine's Tropica USA Inc., 388 Market St., Ste. 400, San Francisco, CA 94111: Free list of retail sources ❖ Gourmet jams made from tropical fruits. 415-403-1520.

Clearbrook Farms, 5514 Fair Ln., Fairfax, OH 45227: Free brochure ❖ Semi-sweet chocolate sauce, fruit sauces, and marmalades. 800-222-9966; 513-271-2053 (in OH).

Crabtree & Evelyn Limited, P.O. Box 167, Woodstock Hill, CT 06281: Catalog $3.50 ❖ English biscuits and cookies, gingerbread, ginger and butter-ginger cookies, Scottish shortbread, Belgian chocolates, cheese wafers and biscuits from Holland, Italian biscuits, preserves, marmalades, jellies, honey, English sauces, spices and condiments, herbs, tea, and candy. 800-624-5211.

Dutch Gold Honey Inc., 2220 Dutch Gold Dr., Lancaster, PA 17601: Free list of retail sources ❖ All-natural honey spreads. 717-393-1716.

Four Oaks Farm Inc., P.O. Box 987, Lexington, SC 29071: Free brochure ❖ Country-style ham and bacon, jams, jellies, pickles, relishes, salad dressings, cakes, and other favorites. 800-858-5006; 803-356-3194 (in SC).

Glorybee Honey & Supplies, P.O. Box 2744, Eugene, OR 97402: Catalog 50¢ ❖ Beekeeping and honey processing supplies, honey, honey-prepared foods, and gift assortments. 800-456-7923; 503-689-0913 (in OR).

Grandma's Spice Shop, HC 62, Box 65D, Upper Tract, WV 26866: Free catalog ❖ Teas, coffees, cocoa, spices, and herbs. 304-358-2346.

Graves-Mountain Lodge, Syria, VA 22743. Free brochure ❖ Apple butter, fruit preserves, and jellies.

Hadley Fruit Orchards, P.O. Box 246, Cabazon, CA 92230: Free catalog ❖ Jams and jellies, dried fruits, nuts, candy, and honey. 800-854-5655.

Harlow's Sugar House, RD 1, Box 395, Putney, VT 05346: Free brochure ❖ Maple syrup and specialties, jams, jellies, and Vermont cheese. 802-387-5852.

Harry & David, P.O. Box 712, Medford, OR 97501: Free catalog ❖ Fruit preserves, fruits, baked specialties, desserts, and gift assortments. 800-345-5655.

Honey Acres, Hwy. 67, Ashippun, WI 53003: Free information ❖ Honey, honey-fruit spreads, candy, beeswax candles, mustards, gifts, and cookbooks. 800-558-7745.

❖ FOODS ❖

Huckleberry Haven, P.O. Box 190523, Hungry Horse, MT 59919: Free brochure ❖ Jams, jellies, syrups, toppings, and flavored honeys. 406-387-5731.

Johnson Orchards Mail Order, P.O. Box 1144, Athens, AL 35611: Free price list ❖ Jams, jellies, preserves, fruit butters, ciders and syrups, mustards, relishes, pickles, marinades, sauces, and dressings. 205-233-8350.

Knott's Berry Farm, P.O. Box 1989, Placentia, CA 92670: Free catalog ❖ Jellies and preserves, cheese, sausage, candy, cakes, cookies, and dried fruit. 800-877-6887.

Kozlowski Farms, 5566 Gravenstein Hwy. North, Forestville, CA 95436: Free brochure ❖ Marmalades, jams, preserves, honey, mustards, barbecue sauce, fruit butters, sugar-free berry vinegars, conserves, and chutney. 707-887-1587.

Limited Edition Presents, 604 S. Marienfeld, Midland, TX 79701: Free list of retail sources ❖ Honey butters. 800-926-8188; 915-686-2008 (in TX).

✓ **Linn's Fruit Bin,** 2485 Village Ln., Cambria, CA 93428: Free catalog ❖ Low-sugar preserves and sugar-free fruit spreads. 800-676-1670.

Lollipop Tree Inc., 319 Vaughan St., Portsmouth, NH 03801: Free list of retail sources ❖ All-natural preserves, condiments, and baking mixes. 603-436-8196.

Maury Island Farm, P.O. Box L, Vashon, WA 98070: Free brochure ❖ Preserves. 800-356-5880.

The Mayhaw Tree, P.O. Box 3430, Peachtree City, GA 30269: Free information ❖ Sauces, mustard, preserves, and Mayhaw berry jelly, sauce, and syrup. 800-262-9429.

McCutcheon Apple Products Inc., P.O. Box 243, Frederick, MD 21705: Free information ❖ Apple butter, preserves, relishes, dessert toppings, salad dressings, honey, hot sauces, and specialties. 800-875-3451.

Midway Plantation, HC-62, Box 77, Waterproof, LA 71375: Free information ❖ Country-fresh jams and jellies. 800-336-JAMS.

Millicent's Preserves, 2028 Primrose Ave., South Pasadena, CA 91030: Free list of retail sources ❖ Gourmet all-natural jams, jellies, marmalades, and butters. 213-682-1233.

✓ **MoonShine Trading Company,** P.O. Box 896, Winters, CA 95694: Free catalog ❖ Semi-sweet chocolate crunch, white chocolate cashew creme, white chocolate almond, and milk chocolate almond crunch nut spreads. Also fruit spreads, almond and gourmet butters, and sweet clover, yellow star thistle, sunflower, and eucalyptus honey. 800-678-1226; 916-753-0601 (in CA).

Muirhead of Ringoes, 43 Hwy. 202/31, Ringoes, NJ 08551: Free catalog ❖ Dressings and vinaigrettes, mustards, jellies, marmalade, dessert sauces, and chutney mustards, jellies, marmalade, and chutney. 800-782-7803.

New Canaan Farms, P.O. Box 386, Dripping Springs, TX 78620: Free brochure ❖ Ice cream toppings, jellies and jams, mustard, and specialties. 800-727-5267.

Colonel Bill Newsom's Hams, 127 N. Highland Ave., Princeton, KY 42445: Free information ❖ Fruit preserves, fruit-sweetened spreads, relishes, sorghum, hickory-smoked ham, and other meats. 502-365-2482.

Oregon Apiaries, P.O. Box 1078, Newberg, OR 97132: Free information ❖ Gourmet honey, honey cream spreads, and fruit-honey syrups. 800-676-1078.

Oregon Hill Farms Inc., 32861 Pittsburgh Rd., St. Helens, OR 97051: Free information ❖ Naturally sweetened fruit spreads. 800-243-4541.

Pan Handler Products Inc., 1799 Mountain Rd., Stowe, VT 05672: Free brochure ❖ Speciality conserves, jams, jellies, chutneys, and mustards. 800-338-5354.

Penelope's of Evergreen Ltd., P.O. Box 2863, Evergreen, CO 80439: Free list of retail sources ❖ Artificial color and additive-free wine jellies and sauces. 800-748-3443.

Pine Ridge Country Honey, 15533 South Hwy. 385, Chabron, NE 69337: Free brochure ❖ Natural creamed honey flavored with lemon and spices. 800-658-3285.

Rock Cheese Company, 540 Tasman St., Madison, WI 53714: Free brochure ❖ Cheese favorites, honey products, and seasonings and condiments. Also gift assortments. 608-223-6272.

Rocky Top Farms, RR 1, Essex Rd., Ellsworth, MI 49729: Free information ❖ All-natural additive-free preserves and fruit butters. 800-862-9303.

Rowena's, 758 W. 22nd, Norfolk, VA 23517: Free information ❖ Gourmet cakes, preserves and jams, and cooking sauces. 800-980-2253.

St. Dalfour Conserves, 2180 Oakdale Dr., Philadelphia, PA 19125: Free information ❖ No-sugar added, all-natural conserves imported from France. 800-523-3811.

Sarabeth's Kitchen, 169 W. 78th St., New York, NY 10024: Free brochure ❖ Marmalades, preserves, additive and preservative-free fruit butters, chunky apple butter, and cranberry relish. 800-552-JAMS; 212-580-8335 (in NY).

This Blooming Island, P.O. Box 44, Orcas Island, WA 98280: Free information ❖ Homemade marmalades and jams. 360-376-5861.

Traphagen Honey, Rt. 23A West, P.O. Box J, Hunter, NY 12442: Free brochure ❖ Gourmet honey spreads, baked goods, candy, preserves and jams, and condiments. 800-838-9194.

Trillium International, 310 Willow Ln., New Holland, PA 17557: Free information ❖ Specialty honeys and honey products. 717-354-4503.

✓ **Virginia Diner,** P.O. 1030, Wakefield, VA 23888: Free catalog ❖ Homemade jellies and jams, Virginia bacon and ham, fudge, peanuts, and peanut specialties. 800-642-6887.

Wood's Cider Mill, RFD 2, Box 477, Springfield, VT 05156: Free catalog with long SASE ❖ Maple syrup, cider jelly and syrup, and boiled cider. 802-263-5547.

Salt-free & Low-salt

Country Herbs, P.O. Box 2007, Wayne, NJ 07474: Free catalog ❖ Low-salt all-natural mixes for dips. 800-823-5230.

Ener-G Foods, P.O. Box 84487, Seattle, WA 98124: Free information ❖ Low-sodium, gluten-free, low-protein, and non-allergenic foods. 800-331-5222.

HeartyMix Company, 1231 Madison Hill Rd., Rahway, NJ 07065: Free catalog ❖ Salt-free bread and wheat-free products. Also preservative, cholesterol, and saturated fat-free baking mixes for cookies and cakes. 908-382-3010.

Seafood

✓ **Alaskan Harvest Seafood,** 329 Katlian St., Sitka, AK 99835: Free catalog ❖ Crab, salmon, halibut, scallops, shrimp, and smoked fish. 800-824-6389.

Annapolis Seafood Market, 1300 Forest Dr., Annapolis, MD 21403: Free information ❖ Next-day air shipment of soft-shell crabs. 410-263-7787.

The Antique Mall & Crown Restaurant, P.O. Box 540, Indianola, MS 38751: Free information ❖ Catfish paté and gourmet pie mixes. 800-833-7731; 601-887-2522 (in MS).

Assouline & Ting Inc., 314 Brown St., Philadelphia, PA 19123: Free information ❖ Imported and domestic caviar, smoked fish, snails, and specialties. 800-521-4491; 215-627-3000 (in PA).

Baycliff Company Inc., 242 E. 72nd St., New York, NY 10021: Free information ❖ Sushi-making products and equipment. 212-772-6078.

✓ **Beach Seafood Market,** 1100 Shrimpbot Ln., P.O. Box 2490, Fort Myers Beach, FL 33932: Free catalog ❖ Fresh-frozen shrimp, crab, and spiny lobster. 800-771-5050.

Blue Heron Fruit Shippers, P.O. Box 936, Sarasota, FL 34234: Free brochure ❖ Tree-ripened citrus fruit, candy, marmalades, pecans, gourmet Southern foods, stone crab claws, and honey. 800-237-3920; 941-954-1605 (in FL).

❖ FOODS ❖

Captain's Choice, HCR 78, Box 464, Naselle, WA 98638: Free information ❖ Smoked sturgeon. 206-484-3805.

Carolina Mountain, 9 Industrial Park Blvd., Andrews, NC 28901: Free information ❖ Fresh and smoked salmon and trout. 800-722-9477.

Carolina Smoked Specialties Inc., 118 S. Cypress, Mullins, SC 29574: Free information ❖ Oak-apple-smoked trout fillets. 800-776-8731.

Caviar House Inc., 687 NE 79th St., Miami, FL 33138: Free catalog ❖ Imported fresh Russian caviar. Also smoked Scottish salmon, foie gras, and truffles. 800-522-8427.

Chesapeake Bay Gourmet, P.O. Box 456, Chester, MD 21619: Free information ❖ Crab cakes, crab imperial, crab quiche, crab soup, and other gourmet seafood specialties. 800-432-CRAB.

Chesapeake Express, 1129 Hope Rd., Centreville, MD 21617: Free brochure ❖ Maryland's Eastern Shore backfin meat crab cakes, oysters, and soft shell crabs. Delivered ready to heat and serve. 800-282-CRAB.

Chief Seattle Seafood, 672 S. Orcas, Seattle, WA 98108: Free information ❖ Native American-style smoked Pacific Northwest salmon. 800-426-0001; 206-762-4165 (in WA).

Clambake Celebrations, 9 West Rd., Skaket Corners, Orleans, MA 02653: Free information ❖ Cape Cod seafood dinners with live lobsters, shellfish, and fresh corn. Ready to cook, they are shipped air direct to your door. 800-423-4038.

Cotuit Oyster Company, P.O. Box 563, Little River Rd., Cotuit, MA 02635: Free catalog ❖ New England oysters and cherrystone clams. 508-428-6747.

Denzer's Food Products, P.O. Box 5632, Baltimore, MD 21210: Free list of retail sources ❖ Queen conch and spicy Carolina conch chowders. 800-224-2811; 410-889-1500 (in MD).

Down East Direct, 77 Atlantic Ave., Boothbay Harbor, ME 04538: Free information ❖ Fresh live lobsters shipped overnight. 800-972-1454.

Downeast Seafood Express, Rt. 176, Box 138, Brooksville, ME 04617: Free brochure ❖ Live Maine lobsters, ocean-fresh lobster meat, and fresh Maine crab meat, sea scallops, and Maine steamer clams (when available). 800-556-2326.

Ducktrap River Fish Farm Inc., RR 2, Box 378, Lincolnville, ME 04849: Free brochure ❖ Preservative and additive-free smoked salmon, rainbow trout, and a seafood sampler of mussels and scallops. 800-828-3825.

S. Wallace Edwards & Sons Inc., P.O. Box 25, Surry, VA 23883: Free catalog ❖ Preserves from the Blue Ridge Mountains, seafood from the Eastern Shore, and hickory-smoked Virginia ham, bacon, and sausage. 800-222-4267.

Francesca's Favorites, Mail Order Department, 2046 McKinley St., Hollywood, FL 33020: Free catalog ❖ Florida-fresh stone crabs and gourmet seafood. 800-865-2722.

Gerard & Dominique Seafood, 15022 Juanita Dr. NE, Bothell, WA 98011: Free brochure ❖ Smoked salmon. 800-858-0449.

Graffam Brothers, Box 340, Rockport, ME 04856: Free information ❖ Live Maine lobsters. 207-236-3396.

Great Northern Trading Company, P.O. Box 662, Monroe, WA 98272: Free list of retail sources ❖ Smoked salmon fillets. 800-707-8606; 206-794-8606 (in WA).

Green Turtle Cannery, P.O. Box 585, Islamorada, FL 33036: Free information ❖ Turtle and conch chowder, spicy soup stocks, and other seafood. 305-664-4918.

Grossman's Seafood Inc., P.O. Box 205, West Mystic, CT 06388: Free information ❖ Steamers, mussels, shelled sea scallops, oysters (in the shell), seafood dinners, and clambakes. Features next day shipping. 800-742-5511.

Gulf Harvest Gourmet Inc., 548 Mary Esther Cutoff, #207, Fort Walton Beach, FL 32548: Free brochure ❖ Gourmet fresh seafood from Florida's Gulf Coast shipped overnight. 800-976-8742.

Hagensborg Foods U.S.A. Inc., P.O. Box 6058, Kent, WA 98064: Free information ❖ Smoked salmon, shrimp, and ready-to-spread salmon and shrimp pates. 800-851-1771; 206-622-8025 (in WA).

Handy Softshell Crawfish, P.O. Box 309, Crisfield, MD 21817: Free brochure ❖ Softshell crabs and crawfish. 800-426-3977.

Hegg & Hegg, 801 Marine Dr., Port Angeles, WA 98362: Free information ❖ Pacific Northwest smoked salmon, nova smoked salmon, Puget Sound red sockeye salmon steaks, sturgeon, shrimp, baby clams, tuna, smoked shad, and dungeness crab meat seafood. 800-435-3474; 206-457-3344 (in WA).

Homarus Inc., 76 Kisco Ave., Mount Kisco, NY 10549: Free brochure ❖ Cured salmon smoked in pastrami spices, smoked trout, and Norwegian smoked salmon. 800-23-SALMON.

Horton's Seafood, P.O. Box 430, Waterboro, ME 04087: Free catalog ❖ Naturally smoked Maine salmon, mussels, trout, shrimp, mackerel, and blue fish. 800-346-6066.

Houston Seafood Corporation, 6115 Skyline, Houston, TX 77257: Free information ❖ Seafood delicacies from around the world. 800-953-1472.

Indian Hill Farms, 213 Old Indian Rd., Milton, NY 12547: Free catalog ❖ Smoked whole turkey and turkey breast, kosher turkey, smoked ham, Norwegian smoked salmon, and brandied fruitcake. 914-795-2700.

Josephson's Smokehouse, 106 Marine Dr., Astoria, OR 97103: Free catalog ❖ Smoked salmon and oysters, scallops, boneless trout and sturgeon, salmon steaks, and sturgeon caviar. 800-772-3474.

Katch Seafoods, P.O. Box 2677, Homer, AK 99603: Free information ❖ Halibut and red salmon steaks. 800-368-7400; 235-7953 (in AK).

Kirkland Custom Seafood, P.O. Box 2040, Kirkland, WA 98083: Free brochure ❖ Smoked and canned salmon, oysters, sturgeon, trout, and pates. 800-321-3474.

Legal Sea Foods, 33 Everett St., Allston, MA 02134: Free brochure ❖ Smoked salmon from Ireland and smoked bluefish pate. 800-477-LEGAL.

Mackenzie Limited, 2900-D Whittington Ave., Baltimore, MD 21230: Free brochure ❖ Imported seafood specialties and English cheese. 800-858-7100.

Mahogany Smoked Meats, P.O. Box 1387, Bishop, CA 93515: Free brochure ❖ Smoked jerky, Cheddar cheese, chileno peppers and stuffed olives, smoked trout, and other specialties. 619-873-5311.

Naturally Irish, 29 S. High St., West Chester, PA 19382: Free information ❖ Wild Irish smoked salmon. 800-472-5660.

Nelson Crab Inc., 3088 Kindred Ave., P.O. Box 520, Tokeland, WA 98590: Free brochure ❖ Dungeness crab, smoked sturgeon and shad, albacore tuna, chinook and blueback salmon, minced razor clams, and Pacific shrimp. 800-262-0069; 206-267-2911 (in WA).

Northern Discovery Seafoods, 8305 128th St., Surrey, British Columbia, Canada V3W 4G1: Free list of retail sources ❖ Alder wood-smoked salmon fillets. 604-591-3361.

Persona Farms Food Specialties, 350 Andover Sparta Rd., Andover, NJ 07821: Free information ❖ Smoked Atlantic salmon. 800-762-8569; 201-729-6161 (in NJ).

Petrossian Shop, 3342 Melrose Ave. NW, Roanoke, VA 24017: Free catalog ❖ Smoked salmon, caviar, foie gras, truffles, and other specialties. 800-828-9241.

Port Chatham Smoked Seafood, 632 NW 46th St., Seattle, WA 98107: Free brochure ❖ Hand-packed smoked Sockeye and Coho and kipper-smoked salmon. Also salmon pate, smoked rainbow trout and rainbow trout pate, smoked sturgeon, Pacific Northwest oysters, and Dungeness crab. 800-872-5666; 206-783-8200 (in Seattle area).

FOODS

Rent Mother Nature, P.O. Box 380193, 52 New St., Cambridge, MA 02238: Free catalog ❖ Clam, lobster, mussels, cod, onion, potato, and corn (when in season) seafood dinners for two and four-persons in a reusable enameled pot. 800-296-9445.

RoseMary's Gifts, West Rd., Bennington, VT 05201: Free information with long SASE ❖ Corn cob-smoked meats, cheese, poultry, fish, Vermont Cheddar cheese, and maple syrup. Also gift baskets. 802-447-0373.

Scottish Crown Ltd., 1704 Thomasville Rd., Ste. 115, Tallahassee, FL 32303: Free information ❖ Scottish smoked salmon. 800-331-3001.

Sea Island Mercantile, 928 Bay St., P.O. Box 100, Beaufort, SC 29901: Free information ❖ She-Crab soup and Carolina Low-country foods. 800-735-3215.

SeaBear, 605 30th St., P.O. Box 591, Anacortes, WA 98221: Free catalog ❖ Alderwood-smoked Pacific Northwest sockeye salmon and oysters. 800-634-3474.

Seafood Direct, P.O. Box 1836, Woodinville, WA 98072: Free brochure ❖ Canned fresh sockeye salmon, kippered salmon, trout pate, smoked trout and oysters, and salmon pate. 800-732-1836.

Silver Lining Seafood, Box 6092, Ketchikan, AK 99901: Free brochure ❖ Smoked salmon specialties and other seafood. 907-225-9865.

Simply Shrimp, 7794 NW 44th St., Fort Lauderdale, FL 33351: Free information ❖ Seafood from the Gulf and around the world. Also Florida stone-crab claws (when in season). 800-833-0888.

Sullivan Harbor Farms, US Rt. 1, P.O. Box 96, Sullivan Harbor, ME 04664: Free information ❖ Maine smoked salmon. 207-422-3735.

Summerfield Farm, 10044 James Monroe Hwy., Culpepper, VA 22701: Free brochure ❖ Veal, venison, lamb, sausage, prime beef, game birds, and smoked salmon halves. 703-547-9600.

10th & M Seafoods, 1020 M St., Anchorage, AK 99501: Free catalog ❖ Prawns, scallops, lox, king crab, halibut, shrimp, smoked and fresh salmon, and seafood. 907-272-3474.

Totem Smokehouse, 1906 Pike Place Market, Seattle, WA 98101: Free brochure ❖ Alderwood-smoked salmon and other seafood. 800-9-SALMON; 206-443-1710 (in WA).

Villa Tatra Colorado, 729 Pinewood Dr., Lyons, CO 80540: Free information ❖ Preservative-free all-natural smoked salmon, trout, and sausage. 800-430-4003.

Weathervane Seafood, Public Landing, Belfast, ME 04915: Free information ❖ Maine lobsters, steaming clams, fantail shrimp, scallops, and other seafood specialties. 800-914-1774.

Wisconsin Fishing Company, P.O. Box 965, Green Bay, WI 54305: Free catalog ❖ Shrimp, lobster, crab, herring, smoked fish, and other seafood. 800-527-3590.

Seasonings & Condiments

Alfa Casa Company, 1925 Borneman St., Elkhart, IN 46517: Free list of retail sources ❖ Dressings and marinades for fish, poultry, beef, and pork. 800-293-5070.

Almond Plaza, Catalog Order Center, P.O. Box 426, Maumee, OH 43537: Free catalog ❖ Herbs, almonds, and candy. 800-225-6887.

The Alternative Food Cooperative, 3362 Kingstown Rd., West Kingston, RI 02892: Free information ❖ Organic fruits and vegetables, spices, and herbs. 401-789-2240.

Arden's Gardens, 4603 Berkshire, Detroit, MI 48224: Free catalog ❖ Gourmet vinegars, mustards, salsa, herb blends, and specialties. 313-882-2222.

Arizona Champagne Sauces, P.O. Box 41886, Tucson, AZ 85717: Free brochure ❖ Seasoning sauces to highlight a wide variety of foods. 800-327-3226; 602-624-3360 (in AZ).

Ashman Manufacturing & Distributing Company, P.O. Box 1068, Sea Pines Station, Virginia Beach, VA 23451: Free list of retail sources ❖ Marinades for fresh vegetables, beef, and fresh tuna steaks. 800-641-9924; 804-428-6734 (in VA).

Assouline & Ting Inc., 314 Brown St., Philadelphia, PA 19123: Free information ❖ Fruit and nut extracts, vinegars, and olive, nut, and specialty oils. 800-521-4491; 215-627-3000 (in PA).

Charles Baldwin & Sons, 1 Center St., West Stockbridge, MA 01266: Free price list with long SASE ❖ Pure vanilla extract, imitation vanilla, other flavors and extracts, spices, Dutch process cocoa, and walnut pieces. 413-232-7785.

Bean Bag Mail Order Company, 818 Jefferson St., Oakland, CA 94607: Catalog $1 ❖ Gourmet seasonings and bean specialties. 800-845-2326.

Beth's Farm Kitchen, P.O. Box 113, Stuyvesant Falls, NY 12174: Free catalog ❖ Jams, preserves, spreads, chutneys, mustards, and vinegars. 800-331-JAMS.

Bickford Flavors, 19007 St. Clair Ave., Cleveland, OH 44117: Free list ❖ Flavorings, extracts, oils, and syrups. 800-283-8322; 216-531-6006 (in OH).

Norman Bishop, 1655 Newport Ave., San Jose, CA 95125: Free brochure ❖ Low-sodium preservative-free mustards and mayonnaise.

Blackberry Patch, Rt. 7, Box 918C, Tallahassee, FL 32308: Free list of retail sources ❖ Jellies, fresh fruit jams, syrups, honey, and salad dressings. 800-8-JELLY-8; 904-893-3183 (in FL).

Blanchard & Blanchard Ltd., P.O. Box 1080, Norwich, VT 05055: Free information ❖ Preservative-free natural salad dressings, dessert sauces, mustards, glazes, and marinades. 802-295-9200.

Blue Crab Bay Company, P.O. Box 180, 108 Market St., Onancock, VA 23417: Free catalog ❖ All-natural seafood seasonings, seafood marinade, and clam pasta sauces. 800-221-2722; 804-787-3602 (in VA).

Boetje's Foods Inc., 2736 12th St., Rock Island, IL 61201: Free information ❖ Stone-ground Dutch mustard. 309-788-4352.

Bootlegger & Buckaroo Foods, P.O. Box 636, Bartlesville, OK 74005: Free information ❖ Peach salsa and food specialties. 800-972-1119.

Brugger Brothers, 3868 NE 169th St., Ste. 401, North Miami Beach, FL 33160: Free information ❖ Organically grown Talamanca black peppercorns. 800-949-2264.

Cafe Companies Inc., P.O. Box 80386, Baton Rouge, LA 70816: Free information ❖ Cafe Louisiana hot sauce. Same recipe also available in a dry form for use as a shake. 800-223-3495.

Campagna Distinctive Flavors, 40759 McDowell Creek Dr., Lebanon, OR 97355: Free information ❖ Herb and pepper jellies and chive, dill, and peppercorn vinegars. 800-959-4372; 503-258-6806 (in OR).

Canadian Herb & Spice Company, Rt. 78, East Ultraport, Box 714, Swanton, VT 05488: Free list of retail sources ❖ All-natural herbs and spices, pasta, salad seasonings, and other specialties. 882-868-7244.

Carp River Trading Company, 6005 E. Traverse Hwy., Traverse City, MI 49864: Free catalog ❖ Vegetable dips, salsa, vinaigrettes, mustards, and other condiments. 800-526-9876.

Century Sauce Kitchens, P.O. Box 4057, Copley, OH 44321: Free information ❖ Habanero and Thai pepper sauces with fresh garlic, herbs, and spices. 800-831-4687; 216-666-2578 (in OH).

Chile Head-Mouthsurfing by Mail, 23 Banks St., Somerville, MA 02144: Free catalog ❖ Chile peppers and related products. 800-4-WE-BURN.

Chile La Isla, P.O. Box 1379, Fabena, TX 79838: Free information ❖ Quick-frozen gourmet chile peppers. 800-895-4603.

Chukar Cherries, P.O. Box 510, Prosser, WV 99350: Free catalog ❖ Cherry sauces, salsa, and relishes. 800-624-9544.

Colorado Spice Company, 5030 Nome St., Unit A, Denver, CO 80239: Free catalog ❖ Culinary spices and herbs, hot sauces, spice blends, chilies, salsa, and specialty sauces. 303-373-0141; 393-373-2844 (TDD).

Commissariat Imports Inc., P.O. Box 64271, Los Angeles, CA 90064: Free list of retail sources ❖ Authentic Indian chutneys and other specialties. 310-475-5628.

Crabtree & Evelyn Limited, P.O. Box 167, Woodstock Hill, CT 06281: Catalog $3.50 ❖ English mustards and chutney, herbs and spices, French mustard and mustard sauces, oils and vinegars, fruit vinegars and syrups, preserves, biscuits and cookies, and candy. 800-624-5211.

Crazy Cajun Enterprises Inc., P.O. Box 426, Petaluma, CA 94954: Free information ❖ Authentic Cajun sauces. 707-769-8515.

Dat'l Do-It World Headquarters, 3255 Parker Dr., St. Augustine, FL 32095: Free catalog ❖ Hot sauces. 800-468-3285.

Delegeane Garlic Farms, P.O. Box 2561, Yountville, Napa Valley, CA 94599: Free brochure ❖ Fresh garlic, chili ristras, salt-free herb seasonings, and California wildflower honey. 800-726-6692.

Desert Rose Foods Inc., P.O. Box 5391, Tucson, AZ 85703: Free brochure ❖ Salsa, spicy mesquite honey-based barbecue sauce, spicy Italian peppers, and tortilla chips. 800-937-2572.

East Earth Trade Winds, P.O. Box 493151, 1620 E. Cypress Ave., Ste. 8, Redding, CA 96049: Free catalog ❖ Chinese herbs and herb products. 800-258-6878.

Eden Foods, 701 Tecumseh Rd., Clinton, MI 49236: Free information ❖ Low-sodium and organic soy sauces. 800-654-7521.

El Paso Chile Company, 909 Texas Ave., El Paso, TX 79901: Free information ❖ Chili and spice blends. 915-544-3434.

Essex Street Pickle Corporation, 35 Essex St., New York, NY 10002: Free information ❖ Sauerkraut, horseradish, tomatoes and hot peppers, olives, herring, and sour, half-sour, and hot pickles. 800-252-GUSS.

Fitzgerald Fairfield Inc., P.O. Box 3151, Palm Beach, FL 33480: Free information ❖ Herb blends and seasonings. 800-955-4372.

Four Oaks Farm Inc., P.O. Box 987, Lexington, SC 29071: Free brochure ❖ Country-style ham and bacon, jams, jellies, pickles, relishes, salad dressings, cakes, and other favorites. 800-858-5006; 803-356-3194 (in SC).

Fox Hollow Farm, 10 Old Lyme Rd., Hanover, NH 03755: Free information ❖ Gourmet mustard. 603-643-6002.

Fox's Fine Foods, 1847 Port Taggart Pl., Newport Beach, CA 92660: Free list of retail sources ❖ Relishes and sauces with no added fat or preservatives. 714-723-5738.

Fredericksburg Herb Farm, P.O. Drawer 927, Fredericksburg, TX 78624: Catalog $2 ❖ Herb seeds, flowers, toiletries, oils, and seasonings. 800-259-4372.

F.P. Garrettson Inc., 230 Main St., Chatham, NJ 07928: Free brochure ❖ Rare teas, coffees, cocoas, spices, and legumes. 800-821-2549; 201-635-7264 (in NJ).

Gil's Gourmet Gallery, 577 Ortiz, Sand City, CA 93955: Free brochure ❖ Award-winning gourmet foods made with wine, "killer" hot and spicy sauces, condiments, and olives. 800-438-7480.

GNS Spices, P.O. Box 90, Walnut, CA 91788: Free information ❖ Dried, flaked, pureed, brined, ground, and fresh Habaneros. 909-594-9505.

Gorilla Gardens, 10153-1/2 Riverside Dr., Toluca Lake, CA 91602: Free information ❖ Additive and preservative-free all-natural herb-infused vinegars and oils. 818-752-3455.

Grandma's Spice Shop, HC 62, Box 65D, Upper Tract, WV 26866: Free catalog ❖ Teas, coffees, cocoa, spices, and herbs. 304-358-2346.

Great Southern Sauce Company, 5705 Kavanaugh, Little Rock, AR 72207: Free information ❖ Sauces, salsa, marinades, and other specialties. 800-437-2823.

Gunpowder Foods, P.O. Box 293, Texas, MD 21030: Free list of retail sources ❖ Chili mix, seasonings, and spices. 410-879-4280.

Gunsmoke Bar-B-Que Foods, P.O. Box 100, Beaumont, CA 92223: Free information ❖ Barbecue sauce, chili mixes, and ready-to-use barbecue spice rub.

Carol Hall, 330 N. Main St., Fort Bragg, CA 95437: Free list of retail sources ❖ Jams, pepper jellies, syrups, chutneys, mustards, salsa, and other favorites. 707-961-1422.

Hall Mock Productions, 212 S. Main, Colfax, WA 99111: Free information ❖ Sweet red pepper sauce, sweet red bell pepper mustard, smokey red bell pepper glaze, and gift packages. 509-397-2137.

Heaven's Garden, 10103 Rd. #263, Carriere, MS 39426: Free information ❖ Herb vinegars. 601-799-3259.

Helen's Tropical Exotics, 1017 Lees Mill Rd., College Park, GA 30349: Free brochure ❖ Dips, marinades, sauces, Jamaican pimentos, tropical spices, and hot peppers. 800-544-JERK.

Henderson's Heritage Herbs, Rt. 1, Box 44, Burlington, WV 26710: Free information ❖ Fruit and herb vinegars. 304-289-5100.

Herb & Spice Collection, P.O. Box 299, Norway, IA 52318: Free catalog ❖ Culinary herbs and spices, herbs and tea, natural herbal body care products, and potpourris. 800-786-1388.

Herb 'n' Lore, 11 Nadine Ct., Thousand Oaks, CA 91320: Free catalog with long SASE ❖ Spice blends, herbal teas, and specialty items. 805-499-7505.

Herbs-Licious, 1702 S. 6th St., Marshalltown, IA 50158: Catalog $2 (refundable) ❖ Herb plants, dried herbs, spices, and oils.

Huy Fong Foods Inc., 5001 Earle Ave., Rosemead, CA 91770: Free information ❖ Hot chili sauces with a choice of flavors. 818-286-8328.

Johnson Orchards Mail Order, P.O. Box 1144, Athens, AL 35611: Free price list ❖ Jams, jellies, preserves, fruit butters, ciders and syrups, mustards, relishes, pickles, marinades, sauces, and dressings. 205-233-8350.

Jones Barbecue Sauce Inc., P.O. Box 331220, Coconut Grove, FL 33233: Free list of retail sources ❖ Hot and spicy or mildly-sweetened barbecue sauces that are fat-free and low in sodium and calories. 800-DJ-SAUCE; 305-445-1814 (in FL).

The Juarez Chile Company, P.O. Box 29162, Shrevesport, LA 71149: Free catalog ❖ All-natural salsa, sauces, and condiments. 800-221-3578.

Kelchner's, Box 245, Dublin, PA 18917: Free information ❖ Horseradish cocktail, horseradish tartar, tartar, and hot mustard with horseradish sauces. 800-424-1952; 215-249-3439 (in PA).

Kim's Gourmet Products Inc., 7433 Temby Ct., Castle Rock, CO 80104: Free list of retail sources ❖ Low-fat and low-sodium gourmet sauces for use in stir-frying, as dipping sauces, or salad dressings. 800-7-SAUCES.

Kozlowski Farms, 5566 Gravenstein Hwy. North, Forestville, CA 95436: Free brochure ❖ Condiments and mustards, sugar-free berry vinegars, barbecue sauce, conserves, chutney, jams, marmalades, honey, and salad dressings. 707-887-1857.

Legacy Herbs, Sue Lukens Herbalist/Potter, Box 442, Mountain View, AR 72560: Catalog 50¢ ❖ Herbs, wildflowers, perennial plants, soaps, bath and body care products, oils and fragrances, incense, potpourri, herbal food products, and other scented iems. 501-269-4051.

Loriva Supreme Foods, 20 Oser Ave., Hauppage, NY 11788: Free information ❖ Specialty oils. 800-94-LORIVA.

Lots of Hots & Fiery Foods, 39 Pebble Hill Rd., P.O. Box 14450, Fairport, NY 14450: Free catalog ❖ Hot salsa, sauces, condiments, and spices. 800-836-1677; 716-425-7556 (in NY).

❖ FOODS ❖

The Magic of Chef Paul Prudhomme, P.O. Box 23342, New Orleans, LA 70183: Free catalog ❖ All-natural MSG and preservative-free Habanero and cayenne pepper sauce and seasonings. 800-457-2857.

Mahogany Smoked Meats, P.O. Box 1387, Bishop, CA 93515: Free brochure ❖ Smoked jerky, Cheddar cheese, chileno peppers and stuffed olives, smoked trout, and other specialties. 619-873-5311.

Mannon's Foods, 8250 S. Nogales Hwy., Tucson, AZ 85706: Free information ❖ Herb and spice blends and specialty products. 800-622-7178; 520-889-4698 (in AZ).

Maui Jelly Factory, 1464 Lower Main St., Wailuku, Maui, HI 96793: Free information ❖ Onion jelly, mustard, and gourmet food products. 800-803-8343.

The Mayhaw Tree, P.O. Box 3430, Peachtree City, GA 30269: Free information ❖ Sauces, mustard, preserves, and Mayhaw berry jelly, sauce, and syrup. 800-262-9429.

McCutcheon Apple Products Inc., P.O. Box 243, Frederick, MD 21705: Free information ❖ Apple butter, preserves, relishes, salad dressings, honey, hot sauces, and specialties. 800-875-3451.

McIlhenny Company, Avery Island, LA 70513: Free information ❖ Tabasco and barbecue sauces and other Louisiana seasonings and spices. 800-634-9599.

Mendocino Mustard, 1260 N. Main, Fort Bragg, CA 95437: Free brochure ❖ Sodium and fat-free gourmet mustard. 707-964-2250.

Middlesex Farm Food Products, P.O. Box 2470, Darien, CT 06820: Free catalog ❖ All-natural low-fat condiments. 800-779-FARM.

Midwest Pepper Trading Company, 3 Swannanoa, Rochester, IL 62563: Free catalog ❖ Hot sauces and salsa. 217-498-9233.

Mo Hotta-Mo Betta, P.O. Box 4136, San Luis Obispo, CA 93403: Free catalog ❖ Chili pepper and hot pepper sauces, pickled products, spicy condiments, barbecue sauces, seasonings and spices to shake on, curries and chutney, soups, dried chilies, cooking sauces and pastes, and snacks. 800-462-3220.

Morris Farms, Rt. 1, Hwy. 56 East, Uvalda, GA 30473: Free catalog ❖ Vidalia onion relish, relish with mustard, barbecue sauce, onion pickles, and sweet onion vinaigrette. 800-447-9338.

Mount Horeb Mustard Museum, 109 E. Main St., Mount Horeb, WI 53572: Free catalog ❖ Mustards from around the world. 800-438-6878.

Muirhead of Ringoes, 43 Hwy. 202/31, Ringoes, NJ 08551: Free catalog ❖ Dressings and vinaigrettes, mustards, jellies, marmalade, dessert sauces, and chutney. 800-782-7803.

Mushroom Man, Box 321, Eugene, OR 97140: Free information ❖ Dried Italian porcini mushrooms and exotic wild mushroom cooking powders. 800-945-3404.

Nantucket Off-Shore Seasonings Inc., P.O. Box 1437, Nantucket, MA 02554: Free information ❖ Salt and preservative-free seasonings for grilled or broiled fish, meat, and poultry. 508-228-9292.

Napa Valley Kitchens, 910 Enterprise Way, Napa, CA 94558: Free list of retail sources ❖ Seasoning vinegars, mustards, flavored olive oils and vinaigrettes, garlic and pepper spreads, and gourmet specialties. 800-288-1089; 707-967-1107 (in CA).

New Canaan Farms, P.O. Box 386, Dripping Springs, TX 78620: Free brochure ❖ Ice cream toppings, jellies and jams, mustard, and other specialties. 800-727-5267.

Colonel Bill Newsom's Hams, 127 N. Highland Ave., Princeton, KY 42445: Free information ❖ Vidalia onion salad dressing, corn relish, mild or hot chow chow, preserves, and hickory-smoked ham, sorghum, and other smoked meats. 502-365-2482.

No-Salt-Salt, P.O. Box 3151, Palm Beach, FL 33480: Free list of retail sources ❖ All-natural sauces and herb dips. 800-955-4372.

Old Southwest Trading Company, P.O. Box 7545, Albuquerque, NM 87194: Free catalog ❖ Habanero and exotic and domestic chilies. 505-836-0168.

The Olive Company, 11746 Rt. 108, Clarksville, MD 21029: Free list of retail sources ❖ Olive specialties. 410-531-5332.

The Tony Packo Food Company, 1902 Front St., Toledo, OH 43605: Free catalog ❖ Pickles, relishes, salsa, sauces, and other condiments. 800-366-4218; 419-691-1953 (in OH).

Panola Pepper Corporation, Rt. 2, Box 148, Lake Province, LA 71254: Free price list ❖ Gourmet pepper sauces, stuffed olives, green Tabasco peppers, other hot sauces, and boil for crab, shrimp, and crawfish. 800-256-3013; 318-559-17674 (in LA).

Pendery's Inc., 1221 Manufacturing St., Dallas, TX 75207: Catalog $2 ❖ Spices, seasonings, and flavorings for Mexican cooking. 800-533-1870; 214-741-1870 (in TX).

Penzey's Spice House, P.O. Box 1448, Waukesha, WI 53187: Free information ❖ Fresh-ground spices. 414-574-0277.

The Pepper Plant, P.O. Box 1119, Atascadero, CA 93423: Free brochure ❖ Spices, hot pepper sauce with garlic, barbecue sauces, and other seasonings. 800-64-SPICY.

Pezzini Farms, P.O. Box 1276, Castroville, CA 95012: Free information ❖ Artichokes and artichoke dipping and pasta sauces. 800-347-6118.

Phamous Phloyd's Inc., 2998 S. Steele St., Denver, CO 80210: Free information ❖ Barbecue sauce, marinade, and dry rub-on condiments. 303-757-3285.

Pikled Garlik Company, P.O. Box 846, Pacific Grove, CA 93950: Free information ❖ Jalapeno, red chili, lemon dill, smoke-flavored, and mild marinated garlic specialties. 800-775-9788.

Popie's Brands Inc., P.O. Box 80386, Baton Rouge, LA 70898: Free information ❖ Cajun sauces. 800-223-3495.

Porter's Pick-A-Dilly, P.O. Box 1166, Quechee, VT 05059: Free list of retail sources ❖ Oil, preservative, and additive-free pickles. 802-295-1888.

Rafal Spice Company, 2521 Russell, Detroit, MI 48207: Free catalog ❖ Spices, decaffeinated coffee beans, tea, and flavoring extracts. 800-228-4276.

Rapazzini Winery, P.O. Box 247, Gilroy, CA 95021: Free information ❖ Mustard and spices, cooking wines, bordelaise sauce, olives, and garlic-flavored specialties. 800-842-MAMA; 408-842-5649 (in CA).

Rex Pure Foods Inc., 4200 Poche Court West, New Orleans, LA 70129: Free list of retail sources ❖ Spices, seasoning blends, Creole mustards, sauces, crab boil, olives, vinegars, and fish fry. 504-254-9903.

Rock Cheese Company, 540 Tasman St., Madison, WI 53714: Free brochure ❖ Cheese favorites, honey products, seasonings, and condiments. Also gift assortments. 608-223-6272.

Rock Creek Vinegar, P.O. Box 533, Sugar Grove, IL 60554: Catalog $1 ❖ Herbal wine vinegars. 708-552-8323.

The Rosemary House, 120 S. Market St., Mechanicsburg, PA 17055: Catalog $2 ❖ Spices. 717-697-5111.

Rowena's, 758 W. 22nd, Norfolk, VA 23517: Free information ❖ Gourmet cakes, preserves and jams, and cooking sauces. 800-980-2253.

The Royers' Round Top Cafe, 1313 Energy Dr., Kilgore, TX 75662: Free list of retail sources ❖ Pepper sauce and herbal vinegars. 800-86-ROYERS.

San Francisco Herb Company, 250 14th St., San Francisco, CA 94103: Free catalog ❖ Cooking herbs and spices. 800-227-4530; 415-861-7174 (in CA).

San Francisco Mustard Company, 4049 Petaluma Blvd. North, Petaluma, CA 94952: Free information ❖ All-natural salt-free whole seed mustards. 707-769-0866.

Santa Barbara Olive Company, P.O. Box 1570, Santa Ynez, CA 93460: Free information ❖ Hand-picked olives, olive oil, salad dressings, garlic nectar, and other condiments. 800-624-4896; 805-688-9917 (in CA).

Santa Cruz Chili & Spice Company, P.O. Box 177, Tumacacori, AZ 85640: Free information ❖ Chili paste for flavoring meat and chicken, chili powder, and hot picante, picante, chili-barbecue, and green chili salsa. 602-398-2591.

Sauces & Salsas Ltd., 1892 Rear Oakland Park Ave., Columbus, OH 43224: Free brochure ❖ Hot sauces. 614-268-7330.

Scott's Food Products, 122 S. Guadalupe Ave., Ste. 4, Redondo Beach, CA 90277: Free list of retail sources ❖ Sauces, marinades, and spice blends. 800-376-6995; 310-374-1900 (in CA).

Select Origins, P.O. Box 1748, Mansfield, OH 44901: Free catalog ❖ Kitchen-tested vanilla, dessert sauces, oils, vinegars, sauces, marinades, relishes and condiments, herbs and spices, coffee and tea, and preserves.

Shady Acres Herb Farm, 7815 Hwy. 212, Chaska, MN 55318: Free list with long SASE ❖ Dried plants and herbal vinegars. 612-466-3391.

South Side Pepper Company, 320 N. Walnut St., Mechanicsburg, PA 17055: Free catalog ❖ Hot sauces and hot pepper products. 717-691-7132.

Specialty Sauces, 444 Lake Cook Rd., Ste. 2, Deerfield, IL 60015: Free brochure ❖ Gourmet salsa and barbecue sauces. 800-SAUCES-1.

Spice Merchant, P.O. Box 524, Jackson Hole, WY 83001: Free catalog ❖ Spices, herbs, and flavoring condiments from China, Japan, Indonesia, Thailand, and other countries. 800-551-5999.

Spices Etc, P.O. Box 5266, Charlottesville, VA 22905: Free catalog ❖ Herbs and spices, seasoning blends, flavors and extracts, grinders, and gifts. 800-827-6373.

Stonehill Farm, Box 158, Schwenksville, PA 19473: Free information ❖ Fat-free condiments. 800-776-7155.

Stonewall Chili Pepper Company, Hwy. 290 East, Stonewall, TX 78671: Free price list ❖ Chili pepper products. 800-232-2995.

Stony Mountain Natural Foods & Herbs, P.O. Box 27, 3062 SR 3, Loudonville, OH 44842: Free information ❖ Nutritional supplements, spices, teas, and herbs. 419-994-4857.

Talk O'Texas, 1610 Roosevelt St., San Angelo, TX 76905: Free information ❖ Hot and mild crisp okra pickles. 800-749-6572.

Things of Good Taste, P.O. Box 455, Waynesboro, VA 22980: Free list of retail sources ❖ Cakes, fruit butters, candy, nuts, and dip and seasoning mixes. 800-248-2591.

Tutino's, 123 Elm St., P.O. Box 635, Old Saybrook, CT 06475: Free information ❖ Garlic, lemon, and hot pepper-flavored olive oils. 800-388-1919.

The Uncommon Herb, P.O. Box 2908, Seal Beach, CA 90740: Catalog $1 ❖ Essential oils, handmade soaps, skin care products, teas, and seasonings. 800-845-0008.

Victoria's Vinegars, P.O. Box 127, Freehold, NY 12431: Free information ❖ Gourmet flavored vinegars. 800-646-2059.

Victorian Cupboard, P.O. Box 1852, Chelsea Station, New York, NY 10113: Free catalog ❖ Flower and herb vinegars, preserves and jellies, fruits in liqueur, and scone mixes. 800-653-8033.

Village Herb Shop Catalogue, 152 S. Main St., Chagrin Falls, OH 44022: Catalog and herbal handbook $4 ❖ Books, potpourri, soaps, cosmetics, oils, herbal food products, and other items.

Wild Thyme Farm, Medussa, NY 12120: Free information ❖ Herb, berry, and other vinegars, and herb, fruit, and spice mustards. Also virgin olive oils and condiments. 800-724-2877.

World Variety Produce Inc., Customer Service, P.O. Box 21127, Los Angeles, CA 90029: Free catalog ❖ Herbs, spices, and exotic produce from around the world. 800-588-0151.

Sugar-free & Dietetic

Calco Food Company Inc., 3540 W. Jarvis, Skokie, IL 60076: Free catalog ❖ Sugar-free gourmet diet foods. 800-325-5409.

The Estee Corporation, 169 Lackawanna Ave., Parsippany, NJ 07054: Free catalog ❖ Sugarless candy and cookies. 201-335-1000.

Hearty Mix Company, 1231 Madison Hill Rd., Rahway, NJ 07065: Free catalog ❖ Preservative, cholesterol, and saturated fat-free baking mixes for cookies, cakes and other pastries. Also salt-free bread and wheat-free items. 908-382-3010.

Ann Raskas Candies, P.O. Box 13367, Kansas City, KS 66113: Free information ❖ Candy for dieters. 913-422-7230.

Señor Murphy, Candymaker, P.O. Box 2505, Santa Fe, NM 87504: Free catalog ❖ Sugar-free and gourmet chocolates. 505-988-4311.

Tea, Coffee & Cocoa

AH!LASKA Products, P.O. Box 940, Homer, AK 99603: Free list of retail sources ❖ Low-fat kosher instant cocoa. 907-235-7561; 708-342-8842 (in continental United States).

Alaska Herb Tea Company, P.O. Box 110289, Anchorage, AK 99520: Free information ❖ Dried fruit and wild herb tea. 800-654-2664.

Amazon Gourmet Coffee, Division Amazon's Gourmet Foods, P.O. Box 530156, Miami Shores, FL 33153: Free information ❖ Fresh-roasted coffees from around the world. 800-335-JAVA.

American Coffee Company, French Market, 800 Magazine St., New Orleans, LA 70130: Free catalog ❖ Gourmet coffees. 800-554-7234.

Assouline & Ting Inc., 314 Brown St., Philadelphia, PA 19123: Free information ❖ Whole bean gourmet coffees. 800-521-4491; 215-627-3000 (in PA).

Atlanta Coffee Roastery Inc., P.O. Box 1638, Woodstock, GA 30188: Free list of retail sources ❖ Instant cocoa mixes. 800-929-7035.

Baronet Gourmet Coffee, P.O. Box 987, Hartford, CT 06143: Free catalog ❖ Coffee and brewing equipment. 800-253-7374.

Bean Bag, 10400 Old Georgetown Rd., Bethesda, MD 20814: Free catalog ❖ Exotic blends of coffee and tea. 301-530-8090.

Berres Brothers Coffee, 101 Western Ave., Watertown, WI 53094: Free catalog ❖ Regular and decaffeinated flavored coffees. 800-233-5443.

The Beverly Hills Coffee Company, 369 S. Doheny Dr., Beverly Hills, CA 90211: Free catalog ❖ Imported and domestic coffee. 800-576-1674.

Boyd Coffee Company, P.O. Box 20547, Portland, OR 97220: Free catalog ❖ Gourmet coffees. 800-221-8211.

Brothers Coffee, 101 Western Ave., Watertown, WI 53094: Free catalog ❖ Flavored and non-flavored, caffeinated and decaffeinated coffees. Also espresso makers, grinders, filters, thermal carafes, and gift baskets. 800-284-5776.

Cafe Beaujolais, Box 730, Mendocino, CA 95460: Free catalog ❖ Pastries and desserts, candy assortments, hot chocolate mix, and gourmet specialties. 800-930-0443.

Café La Semeuse, 55 Nassau Ave., Brooklyn, NY 11222: Free brochure ❖ Regular or water-processed whole bean decaffeinated coffee. 718-387-9696.

Caffeinds, 4407 N. Saddlebag Trail, Scottsdale, AZ 85251: Free list of retail sources ❖ Gourmet coffees and hand-blended teas.

Cocoa Beach Coffee, P.O. Box 112516, Tacoma, WA 98141: Free catalog ❖ Gourmet coffees. 800-755-9497.

Coffee Caboodle, 525 Maple Ave. West, Vienna, VA 22180: Free price list ❖ Coffee and tea from worldwide sources. 800-541-2469; 703-281-5599 (in VA).

Country Coffee Company Inc., 13081 State Hwy. 64 West, Tyler, TX 75704: Free list of retail sources ❖ Old-fashioned cocoa mixes. 713-871-3182.

Dean & DeLuca Mail-Order, Attention: Catalog Department, 560 Broadway, New York, NY 10012: Free information ❖ Bensdorp and Droste cocoa for chocolate and dessert creations. 800-221-7714.

FOODS, RECIPE MANAGEMENT & COOKBOOK SOFTWARE

Dry Creek Herb Farm, 13935 Dry Creek Rd., Auburn, CA 95602: Free information ❖ Skin care products and herbal teas. 916-878-2441.

Fanci' Premium Tea Company, 58 Prado Rd., San Luis Obispo, CA 93401: Free list of retail sources ❖ Fruit and spice-flavored teas. 805-543-8200.

Fireside Coffee Company, 3239 S. Elms Rd., Swartz Creek, MI 48473: Free information ❖ Cinnamon chocolate, chocolate raspberry, orange-spice mocha, butter rum, and gourmet flavored coffees. 800-344-5282.

First Colony Coffee & Tea Company, P.O. Box 11005, Norfolk, VA 23517: Free catalog ❖ Gourmet coffees, fruit-flavored teas, and hot chocolate. 800-523-1983.

Don Francisco Coffee Traders, P.O. Box 58271, Los Angeles, CA 90058: Free catalog ❖ Coffee from worldwide sources. 800-697-5282.

F.P. Garrettson Inc., 230 Main St., Chatham, NJ 07928: Free brochure ❖ Teas, coffees, cocoa, spices, and legumes. 800-821-2549; 201-635-7264 (in NJ).

Gevalia Kaffe, P.O. Box 11034, Des Moines, IA 50381: Free catalog ❖ Gourmet coffees from around the world. 800-438-4438.

Gilette's Coffee, 9885 Georgetown Pike, Great Falls, VA 22066: Free information ❖ Imported coffees and teas from worldwide sources. 800-221-3030.

Gillies Coffee Company, 150 19th St., Brooklyn, NY 11232: Free brochure ❖ Imported coffee and tea from around the world. 800-344-5526.

The Gilway Company Ltd., 17 Arcadian Ave., Paramus, NJ 07652: Free list of retail sources ❖ Decaffeinated herbal and fruit teas. 201-843-8152.

Golden Walnut Specialty Foods, 3200 16th St., Zion, IL 60099: Free catalog ❖ Packaged all-kosher cookies, cakes, and candies. 800-445-3957.

Grace Tea Company, 50 W. 17th St., New York, NY 10011: Free information ❖ Imported teas. 212-255-2935.

Grandma's Spice Shop, HC 62, Box 65D, Upper Tract, WV 26866: Free catalog ❖ Teas, coffees, cocoa, spices, and herbs. 304-358-2346.

Green Mountain Coffee Roasters, 33 Coffee Ln., Waterbury, VT 05676: Free catalog ❖ Fresh-roasted Colombian coffee. 800-223-6768.

Harney & Sons Tea Company, P.O. Box 676, Salisbury, CT 06068: Free price list ❖ Tea that is available loose, in tea bags, gift canisters, and hotel-style packaging. 800-TEA-TIME; 203-435-9218 (in CT).

The Herb Patch Ltd., P.O. Box 1111, 471 South St., Middletown Springs, VT 05757: Free brochure ❖ All-natural cocoa in several flavors. 800-235-2466.

Kobricks Coffee Company, 693 Henderson St., Jersey City, NJ 07302: Free catalog ❖ Flavored specialty and espresso coffees. 201-656-6313.

Liberty Richter, 400 Lyster Ave., Saddle Brook, NJ 07662: Free list of retail sources ❖ Unsweetened and caffeine-free packets of ready-to-use cappuccino. 201-843-8900.

Lion Coffee, 894 Queen St., Honolulu, HI 96813: Free catalog ❖ Gourmet coffees. 800-338-8353.

Mackinlay Teas, P.O. Box 6, Saline, MI 48176: Catalog $1 ❖ Gourmet teas, premium rice, lentils, beans, soup mixes, and Italian syrups. 313-930-2007.

McNultys Tea & Coffee Company, 109 Christopher St., New York, NY 10014: Free brochure ❖ Imported tea and coffee from around the world. Also brewing equipment. 800-356-5200; 212-242-5351 (in NY).

Mt. Vernon Coffee & Tea Traders, 4202 Mt. Vernon Memorial Hwy., Alexandria, VA 22309: Free catalog ❖ Gourmet coffees and teas. 800-846-1947.

Northwestern Coffee Mills, Middle Rd., Box 370, La Pointe, WI 54850: Free brochure ❖ Imported and domestic coffee and tea, and herb teas. Also coffee syrup. 800-243-5283.

O'Mona International Tea Company, 9 Pine Ridge Rd., Rye Brook, NY 10573: Catalog $1 ❖ Tea from worldwide sources. 914-937-8858.

Pannikin Mail Order, 1205 J St., San Diego, CA 92101: Free brochure ❖ Gourmet spices, tea, hot chocolate, espresso machines, and coffee makers. 800-232-6482.

Rafal Spice Company, 2521 Russell, Detroit, MI 48207: Free catalog ❖ Coffee, coffee beans, tea, spices, and flavoring extracts. 800-228-4276.

The Republic of Tea, P.O. Box 1175, Mill Valley, CA 94942: Free information ❖ Tea. 800-298-4TEA.

Simpson & Vail Inc., P.O. Box 309, Pleasantville, NY 10570: Free catalog ❖ Coffee and flavored teas, preserves and syrups, honey, confections and baked specialties, Indian foods and spices, hot sauces, spices and condiments, and gourmet products. 800-282-TEAS; 914-747-1336 (in NY).

Starbucks Coffee, 2203 Airport Way South, P.O. Box 34510, Seattle, WA 98124: Free catalog ❖ Gourmet coffees. 800-782-7282.

Stash Tea, 9040 SW Burnham, Tigard, OR 97223: Free catalog ❖ Traditional, herb, decaffeinated, and spiced tea. Also tea-making accessories and gifts. 800-826-4218.

Stony Mountain Natural Foods & Herbs, P.O. Box 27, 3062 SR 3, Loudonville, OH 44842: Free information ❖ Nutritional supplements, spices, teas, and herbs. 419-994-4857.

Torrefazione Italia Inc., 1321 2nd Ave., Ste. 200, Seattle, WA 98111: Free information ❖ Coffee. 800-827-2333.

The Uncommon Herb, P.O. Box 2908, Seal Beach, CA 90740: Catalog $1 ❖ Essential oils, handmade soaps, skin care products, teas, and seasonings. 800-845-0008.

Upton Tea Imports, 231 South St., Hopkinton, MA 01748: Free information ❖ Tea. 800-234-TEAS.

Mark T. Wendell, P.O. Box 1312, West Concord, MA 01742: Free information ❖ Regular and decaffeinated imported gourmet teas and coffees. 508-369-3709.

The White Coffee Corporation, 18-35 Steinway Pl., Long Island City, NY 11105: Free list of retail sources ❖ Flavored and decaffeinated green teas. 800-221-0140; 718-204-7900 (in NY).

Williams-Sonoma, Mail Order Department, P.O. Box 7456, San Francisco, CA 94120: Free catalog ❖ Pernigotti and Dark Jersey cocoa for chocolate and dessert creations. 415-541-1262.

Willoughby's Coffee, 550 E. Main St., Branford, CT 06405: Free catalog ❖ Gourmet coffees. 800-388-8400.

FOODS, RECIPE MANAGEMENT & COOKBOOK SOFTWARE

Alos Software, 118 Bracken Rd., Montgomery, NY 12549: Free information ❖ Recipe management software for PCs. 914-457-4400.

Arion Software, 3300 Bee Cave Rd., Austin, TX 78746: Free information ❖ Cooking and recipe management software for the Macintosh and PCs. 512-327-9573.

Books-On-Disk, 311 Harvard St., Brookline, MA 02146: Free information ❖ Windows-based and Macintosh cookbooks. 800-717-4478; 617-734-9700 (in MA).

East Hampton Industries Inc., 81 Newtown Ln., Box 5069, East Hampton, NY 11937: Free brochure ❖ Software for recipe-collecting, cookbook organizing, and meal planning. 800-645-1188; 516-324-2224 (in NY).

Lifestyle Software Group, 63 Orange St., St. Augustine, FL 32084: Free information ❖ Windows-based Betty Crocker's cookbook on CD-ROM. 800-289-1157; 904-825-0220 (in FL).

Microsoft Corporation, One Microsoft Way, Redmond, WA 98052: Free information ❖ Julia Child's Home Cooking with Master Chefs on Windows-based CD-ROM. 800-426-9400; 206-882-8080 (in WA).

Multi-com Publishing Inc., 1100 Olive Way, Ste. 1250, Seattle, WA 98101: Free information ❖ Windows-based and Macintosh Better Homes and Gardens recipes. 800-850-7272; 206-622-5530 (in WA).

Odyssey Computing, 1515 S. Melrose Dr., Ste. 90, Vista, CA 92083: Free brochure ❖ Windows-based software for recipe, cookbook, and meal planning. 619-599-0823.

Pinpoint Publishing, P.O. Box 7329, Santa Rosa, CA 95407: Free information ❖ Cooking and recipe management software for the PC. 800-788-5236.

Sierra On-Line Inc., P.O. Box 3404, Salinas, CA 93916: Free information ❖ Windows-based and Macintosh recipe storage and meal-management software. 800-757-7707.

Upstill Software, 1442-A Walnut St., Berkeley, CA 94709: Free information ❖ Windows-based and Macintosh recipe storage and meal-management software. 800-568-3696; 510-526-0178 (in CA).

FOOTBALL

Clothing

Athletes Wear Company, 145 Market Ave., Winnipeg, Manitoba, Canada R3B 1C5: Free catalog ❖ Clothing for football players. 204-949-1885.

Betlin Manufacturing, 1445 Marion Rd., Columbus, OH 43207: Free information ❖ Clothing for players and coaches. 614-443-0248.

Bomark Sportswear, P.O. Box 2068, Belair, TX 77402: Free information ❖ Clothing for players and coaches. 800-231-3351.

DeLong, 733 Broad St., P.O. Box 189, Grinnell, IA 50112: Free information ❖ Clothing for players and coaches. 800-733-5664; 515-236-3106 (in IA).

Empire Sporting Goods Manufacturing Company, 443 Broadway, New York, NY 10013: Free information ❖ Clothing for players and coaches. 800-221-3455; 212-966-0880 (in NY).

Fab Knit Manufacturing, Division Anderson Industries, 1415 N. 4th St., Waco, TX 76707: Free information ❖ Clothing for players and coaches. 800-333-4111; 817-752-2511 (in TX).

Manny's Baseball, 3000 SW 42nd Ave., Palm City, FL 34990: Catalog $2 ❖ Clothing for football players. 800-PRO-TEAM.

J.C. Penney Company Inc., Catalog Division, Atlanta, GA 30390: Free information ❖ Atlanta, GA 30390: Free information ❖ Athletic clothing and accessories. 800-222-6161.

Shaffer Sportswear, 224 N. Washington, Neosho, MO 64850: Free information ❖ Jackets, pants, and uniforms. 417-451-9444.

Southland Athletic, P.O. Box 280, Terrell, TX 75160: Free list of retail sources ❖ Jackets and uniforms. 800-527-7637; 214-563-3321 (in TX).

Venus Knitting Mills Inc., 140 Spring St., Murray Hill, NJ 07974: Free information ❖ Clothing for players and coaches. 800-955-4200; 908-464-2400 (in NJ).

Wilson Sporting Goods, 8700 Bryn Mawr, Chicago, IL 60631: Free information ❖ Clothing for players and coaches. 800-443-0011.

Equipment

Adams USA, 810 S. Jefferson, P.O. Box 489, Cookeville, TN 38501: Free information ❖ Protective gear. 800-251-6857; 615-526-2109 (in TN).

Alchester Mills Company Inc., 1160 Wright Ave., Camden, NJ 08103: Free information ❖ Protective gear. 609-964-9700.

Ampac Enterprises Inc., All Star Division, Box 1356, Shirley, MA 01464: Free information ❖ Field and playing equipment and protective gear. 800-777-3810; 508-425-6266 (in MA).

The Athletic Connection, 1901 Diplomat, Dallas, TX 75234: Free information ❖ Footballs, goal posts, kicking tees, and equipment. 800-527-0871; 214-243-1446 (in TX).

Austin Athletic Equipment Corporation, 705 Bedford Ave., Box 423, Bellmore, NY 11710: Free information ❖ Goal posts, markers, and marking machines. 516-785-0100.

Baden Sports Inc., 34114 21st Ave. South, Federal Way, WA 98003: Free information ❖ Leather, rubber-covered, synthetic, and juvenile footballs. 800-544-2998; 206-925-0500 (in WA).

Bike Athletic Company, P.O. Box 666, Knoxville, TN 37901: Free information ❖ Protective gear. 800-251-9230.

Body Glove International, 530 6th St., Hermosa Beach, CA 90254: Free information ❖ Protective gear. 800-678-7873; 310-374-4074 (in CA).

H.D. Brown Enterprise Ltd., 23 Beverly St. East, St. George, Ontario, Canada N0E 1N0: Free information ❖ Footballs. 519-448-1381.

Cannon Sports, P.O. Box 797, Greenland, NH 03840: Free list of retail sources ❖ Protective gear. 800-362-3146.

Gerry Cosby & Company, 3 Pennsylvania Plaza, Madison Square Garden, New York, NY 10001: Free information ❖ Protective gear. 800-548-4003; 212-563-6464 (in NY).

Cougar Sports, 6667 W. Old Shakotee Rd., Wilmington, MN 55438: Free information ❖ Protective gear. 800-445-2664.

Cramer Products Inc., P.O. Box 1001, Gardner, KS 66030: Free information ❖ Protective gear. 800-345-2231; 913-884-7511 (in KS).

Flaghouse, 150 N. MacQuesten Pkwy., Mt. Vernon, NY 10550: Free catalog ❖ Football equipment. 800-793-7900.

Franklin Sports Industries Inc., 17 Campanelli Pkwy., P.O. Box 508, Stoughton, MA 02072: Free information ❖ Leather, rubber-covered, synthetic, and juvenile footballs. 800-426-7700.

Gared Sports Inc., 1107 Mullanphy St., St. Louis, MO 63106: Free information ❖ Goal posts, markers, and marking machines. 800-325-2682.

GeorGI-Sports, P.O. Box 1107, Lancaster, PA 17603: Free information ❖ Leather, rubber-covered, synthetic, and juvenile footballs, and protective gear. 800-338-2527; 717-291-8924 (in PA).

Marty Gilman Inc., P.O. Box 97, Gilman, CT 06336: Free information ❖ Blockers and chargers, charging and blocking sleds, kicking cages, and tackling dummies. 800-243-0398; 203-889-7334 (in CT).

Grid Inc., NDL Products, 4031 NE 12th Terrace, Oakland Park, FL 33334: Free information ❖ Protective gear. 800-843-3021.

Hutch Sports USA, 1835 Airport Exchange Blvd., Erlanger, KY 41018: Free information ❖ Footballs, helmets, and shoulder guards. 800-727-4511; 606-282-9000 (in KY).

Jayfro Corporation, Unified Sports Inc., 976 Hartford Tnpk., P.O. Box 400, Waterford, CT 06385: Free catalog ❖ Goals, training equipment, and field markers. 860-447-3001.

Leisure Marketing Inc., 2204 Morris Ave., Ste. 202, Union, NJ 07083: Free information ❖ Leather, rubber-covered, synthetic, and juvenile footballs. 908-851-9494.

Markwort Sporting Goods, 4300 Forest Park Ave., St. Louis, MO 63108: Catalog $8 (request list of retail sources) ❖ Footballs, face masks, gloves, helmets, and shoulder guards. 800-669-6626; 314-652-3757 (in MO).

Dick Martin Sports Inc., 181 E. Union Ave., P.O. Box 7384, East Rutherford, NJ 07073: Free information ❖ Footballs. 800-221-1993; 201-438-5255 (in NJ).

McDavid Sports Medical Products, 5420 W. Roosevelt Rd., Chicago, IL 60650: Free information ❖ Protective gear. 800-237-8254; 312-626-7100 (in IL).

Molten USA Inc., 1095 Spice Island Dr., Sparks, NV 89431: Free information ❖ Leather, rubber-covered, synthetic, and juvenile footballs. 800-666-5836; 702-353-4000 (in NV).

Mueller Sports Medicine Inc., One Quench Dr., Prairie du Sac, WI 53578: Free information ❖ Protective gear. 800-356-9522; 608-643-8530 (in WI).

New South Athletic Company Inc., 301 E. Main, P.O. Box 604, Dallas, NC 28034: Free information ❖ Protective gear. 800-438-9934; 704-922-1557 (in NC).

Olympia Sports, 745 State Circle, Ann Arbor, MI 48106: Free information ❖ Blockers and chargers, charging and blocking sleds, kicking cages, and tackling dummies. 800-521-2832.

Rawlings Sporting Goods Company, P.O. Box 22000, St. Louis, MO 63126: Free information ❖ Leather, rubber-covered, synthetic, and juvenile footballs, and protective gear. 314-349-3500.

Reda Sports Express, 44 N. 2nd St., P.O. Box 68, Easton, PA 18044: Free information ❖ Footballs and protective equipment. 800-444-REDA; 215-258-5271 (in PA).

Riddell Inc., 3670 N. Milwaukee Ave., Chicago, IL 60641: Free information ❖ Helmets, kicking tees, protective gear, footballs, and equipment. 800-445-7344; 312-794-1994 (in IL).

Royal Textile Mills Inc., P.O. Box 250, Yanceyville, NC 27379: Free information ❖ Protective gear. 800-334-9361; 910-694-4121 (in NC).

Spalding Sports Worldwide, 425 Meadow St., P.O. Box 901, Chicopee, MA 01021: Free list of retail sources ❖ Leather, rubber-covered, synthetic, and juvenile footballs. 800-225-6601.

Venus Knitting Mills Inc., 140 Spring St., Murray Hill, NJ 07974: Free information ❖ Clothing for players and coaches and protective gear. 800-955-4200; 908-464-2400 (in NJ).

Wilson Sporting Goods, 8700 Bryn Mawr, Chicago, IL 60631: Free information ❖ Clothing for players and coaches and leather, rubber-covered, synthetic, and juvenile footballs. 800-443-0011.

Wolvering Sports, 745 State Circle, Box 1941, Ann Arbor, MI 48106: Catalog $1 ❖ Baseball, basketball, field hockey, soccer, football, and athletic and recreation equipment. 313-761-5691.

FOUNTAINS

The BB Brass, 10151 Pacific Mesa Blvd., San Diego, CA 92121: Free catalog ❖ Brass fountains and sculptures. 800-536-0987.

Cast Aluminum Reproductions, P.O. Box 1060, San Elizario, TX 79849: Catalog $2 ❖ Cast-aluminum and brass furniture, street lights, outdoor furniture, fountains, mail boxes, and plant stands. 915-764-3793.

Robert Compton Ltd., RD 3, Box 3600, Bristol, VT 05443: Brochure $2 ❖ Original stone fountains. 802-453-3778.

Florentine Craftsmen, 46-24 28th St., Long Island City, NY 11101: Catalog $5 ❖ Ornamental sculptures, fountains, birdbaths, and outdoor furniture. 718-937-7632.

Garden Ornaments Stone, P.O. Box 1451, Roswell, GA 30077: Catalog $10 ❖ Statues, fountains, benches, tables, and ornamentals. 404-475-2127.

Hermitage Gardens, P.O. Box 361, Canastota, NY 13032: Catalog $1 ❖ Fiberglass rocks and waterfalls, redwood water wheels, wooden bridges, garden pools, and bubbling fantasias. 315-697-9093.

Moultrie Manufacturing, P.O. Drawer 1179, Moultrie, GA 31776: Catalog $3 ❖ Cast-aluminum tables, chairs, settees, planters, urns, fountains, chaises, and fixtures. 800-841-8674.

Stone Forest, P.O. Box 2840, Santa Fe, NM 87504: Catalog $3 ❖ Fountains, lanterns, water basins, birdbaths, pedestals, and hand-carved granite statuary. 505-986-8883.

Strassacker Bronze America Inc., P.O. Box 931, Spartanburg, SC 29304: Catalog $15 ❖ Contemporary and abstract bronze sculptures, fountains, and lighting equipment. 803-573-7438.

Zachariasen Studio, N659 Drumm Rd., Denmark, WI 54208: Catalog $3 ❖ Handmade ceramic birdbaths, fountains, and garden ornaments. 414-776-1778.

FRAMES & FRAMING SUPPLIES

American Frame Corporation, 400 Tomahawk Dr., Maumee, OH 43537: Free information ❖ Metal picture frames. 800-537-0944.

Atlas Art & Stained Glass, P.O. Box 76084, Oklahoma City, OK 73147: Catalog $3 ❖ Kaleidoscopes, frames, lamp bases, and art and craft, stained glass, jewelry-making, and foil-crafting supplies. 405-946-1230.

Chris' Craft Supplies, Rt. 4, Box 458, Carthage, MO 64836: Catalog $1 (refundable) ❖ Cross-stitching and framing supplies. 417-358-1900.

Colorado Frame Manufacturing, 1230 Blue Spruce Dr., Fort Collins, CO 80524: Free information ❖ Wholesale supplier of frames and framing materials. 303-493-5966; 970-493-5966 (in CO).

Contemporary Frame Company, 346 Scott Swamp Rd., P.O. Box 514, Farmington, CT 06032: Free information ❖ Aluminum section frames. 800-243-0386; 203-677-7787 (in CT).

Creative Dimensions, 3359 North Federal Hwy., Pompano Beach, FL 33064: Free brochure ❖ Make-them-yourself frames from kits. 305-941-0326.

Creative House Frames, 1200 N. Palafox St., Pensacola, FL 32501: Free information ❖ Ready-to-assemble wood frame kits. 800-521-6023.

Crown Art Products, 90 Dayton Ave., Passaic, NJ 07055: Free catalog ❖ Metal section frames and framing supplies. 201-777-6010.

Cupid's Bow, Box 489, Saline, MI 48176: Catalog $3 (refundable) ❖ Antique replica picture frames. 313-429-7894.

DAB Studio, 31 N. Terrace, P.O. Box 96, Maplewood, NJ 07040: Free catalog ❖ Stained glass picture frames. 800-682-6151.

Decor Frame Company, 4307 Metzger Rd., Fort Pierce, FL 34947: Free catalog ❖ Aluminum section frames with hardware, optional springs, and hangers. 800-826-7969.

Discount Framesource USA Inc., Graphik Dimensions Ltd., 2103 Brentwood St., High Point, NC 27263: Free information ❖ Frames. 800-221-0262.

Documounts, 3709 W. 1st Ave., Eugene, OR 97402: Free information ❖ Wooden picture frames and beveled edge mats. 800-769-5639.

Exposures, 1 Memory Ln., P.O. Box 3615, Oshkosh, WI 54903: Free catalog ❖ Albums and frames. 800-572-5750.

Fletcher-Terry Company, 65 Spring Ln., Farmington, CT 06032: Free information ❖ Easy-to-use picture framing tool that won't tear or dent backing materials or cause frames to split. 800-THE-FTCO; 203-677-7331 (in CT).

Frame Factory, 1909 W. Diversey Pkwy., Chicago, IL 60614: Free catalog ❖ Frames and framing supplies. 800-621-6570.

Frame Fit Company, P.O. Box 8926, Philadelphia, PA 19135: Free information ❖ Aluminum picture frames and hangers. 800-523-3693.

Franken Frames, 609 W. Walnut, Johnson City, TN 37604: Free catalog ❖ Frames and moldings. 800-322-5899.

G-M Marketing, 960 Melaleuca Ave., Carlsbad, CA 92009: Brochure $1 ❖ Reproduction museum-quality gold leaf baroque-style antique frames. 619-929-9164.

Gold Leaf Studios, P.O. Box 50156, Washington, DC 20091: Free brochure with long SASE ❖ Frames. 202-638-4660.

Graphik Dimensions Ltd., 2103 Brentwood St., High Point, NC 27263: Free information ❖ Frames and framing supplies. 800-221-0262.

Russell Harrington Cutlery Inc., 44 Green River St., Southbridge, MA 01550: Free information ❖ Mat cutters. 508-765-0201.

David Howell & Company, 405 Adams St., Bedford Hills, NY 10507: Free catalog ❖ Frames inspired by museum collections. 800-648-5455; 914-666-4080 (in NY).

Imperial Picture Frames, P.O. Box 598, Imperial Beach, CA 91933: Free catalog ❖ Oak, pine, and acrylic frames and framing supplies. 800-423-2620.

Lee House, P.O. Box 35148, Charlotte, NC 28235: Free information ❖ Framing supplies. 800-532-0461; 704-375-0644 (in NC).

Light Impressions, 439 Monroe Ave., Rochester, NY 14607: Free catalog ❖ Custom-cut frames. 800-828-6216.

M & M Distributors, Rt. 522, P.O. Box 189, Tennent, NJ 07763: Free catalog ❖ Glass and framing products. 800-526-2302.

Magnetic Imaginations, 5122 Romohr Rd., Cincinnati, OH 45208: Free brochure ❖ Magnetic picture frames. 513-248-2377.

The Mettle Company, P.O. Box 525, Fanwood, NJ 07023: Free information ❖ Aluminum frames. 800-621-1329.

Abe Munn Picture Frames Inc., 51-02 21st St., Long Island City, NY 11101: Free information ❖ Antique reproduction picture frames. 718-361-1373.

Old Tyme Picture Frames, 32055 Corte Algete, Temecula, CA 92592: Catalog $1 ❖ Reproduction antique frames. 909-699-4321.

Plaid Enterprises, P.O. Box 7600, Norcross, GA 30091: Free information ❖ Frame-making supplies and accessories. 404-923-8200.

Pootatuck, P.O. Box 24, Windsor, VT 05089: Free information ❖ Framing accessories. 802-674-5984.

Press-On-Products, 1020 S. Westgate, Addison, IL 60101: Free catalog ❖ Framing accessories and mat boards. 800-323-1745.

Putnum Distributors, P.O. Box 477, Westfield, NJ 07091: Free catalog ❖ Frames. 800-631-7330; 908-232-9200 (in NJ).

S & W Framing Supplies Inc., Garden City Park, New York, NY 11040: Free catalog ❖ Framing supplies and tools. 800-645-3399; 516-746-1000 (in NY).

Sawdust & Stitches, 9 Timber Ln., New Cumberland, PA 17070: Free information ❖ Shadowbox frames and display cases. 717-774-5280.

Daniel Smith Art Supplies, 4150 1st Ave. South, Seattle, WA 98134: Free catalog ❖ Framing supplies. 800-426-6740.

Stu-Art Supplies, 2045 Grand Ave., Baldwin, NY 11510: Free catalog ❖ Mats, plastic and glass, pre-assembled frames, aluminum and wood frame-making components, shrink wrap, plastic picture saver panels, and framing supplies. 516-546-5151.

Tennessee Moulding & Frame Company, 1188 Antioch, Nashville, TN 37211: Catalog $5 ❖ Mats, framing equipment, and tools, and metal, wood, laminates, and Formica frames. 800-821-5483.

United Mfrs. Supplies Inc., 80 Gordon Dr., Syosset, NY 11791: Free catalog ❖ Frames and framing supplies. 800-645-7260.

Wayne Frame Products Inc., 5832 Lakeside Ave., Toledo, OH 43611: Free information ❖ Horizontal and vertical-style frames. 800-331-5265; 419-729-4006 (in OH).

Wholesale Frame Service-USA, P.O. Box 11047, High Point, NC 27265: Free catalog ❖ Wooden frames in colorful rustics, traditional wood tones, weathered driftwood, gold, and silver. 800-522-3726.

FUND-RAISING

Ace Pecan Company, 281 W. 83rd St., Burr Ridge, IL 60521: Free catalog ❖ Fund-raising programs selling nuts and nut specialties. 800-323-9754.

Acme Premium Supply Corporation, 3815 S. Ashland, Chicago, IL 60609: Free catalog ❖ Specialty merchandise for fund-raising, carnival premium programs, and bingo. 800-325-7888.

Allen-Lewis Manufacturing Company, Division TCC Industries Inc., P.O. Box 16546, 5601 Logan, Denver, CO 80216: Free catalog ❖ Souvenirs, carnival and party supplies, fund-raising merchandise, toys and games, T-shirts and sweatshirts, and craft supplies. 303-295-0196.

Bale Company, 22 Public St., P.O. Box 6400, Providence, RI 02940: Free catalog ❖ Awards for students, teachers, and volunteers. 800-822-5350.

Calico Kitchen Press, Drawer 606, Hartwell, GA 30643: Free information ❖ Fund-raising cookbook plan. 706-376-5711.

Cards USA, A & E Blackwell, 5057 Three Points Blvd., Mound, MN 55364: Free list of retail sources ❖ Custom printed cards and calendars for fund-raising programs. 888-227-3787.

Carriage Trade Publishing II Inc., P.O. Box 1296, Richmond Hill, GA 31324: Free information ❖ Historic scene note cards for educational fund-raising programs. 800-727-3323.

Classic American Fund Raisers, Cookbook Plan, 11184 Antioch, Ste. 415, Overland Park, KS 66210: Free information with long SASE ❖ Custom cookbooks for fund-raising. 800-821-5745.

Cokesbury, Division United Methodist Publishing House, 201 8th Ave. South, P.O. Box 801, Nashville, TN 37202: Free information ❖ Bibles and bible reference books, bible study and Christian education books, fund-raising programs, gifts and casual wear, choir apparel, church and clergy supplies, and church furniture and equipment. 800-672-1789.

Cookbook Publishers Inc., P.O. Box 15920, Lenexa, KS 66285: Free information ❖ Custom cookbooks for fund-raising. 800-227-7282.

Cookbooks by Morris Press, P.O. Box 2110, Kearney, NE 68848: Free information ❖ Custom cookbooks for fund-raising. 800-445-6621.

Crunch Time, 137A Sutherland Rd., Boston, MA 02135: Free brochure ❖ Environmental education fund raisers. 800-2-CRUNCH.

Fancy Fortune Cookies, 6265 Coffman Rd., Indianapolis, IN 46268: Free information ❖ Individually wrapped fortune cookies in twelve flavors and brilliant colors. Enclosed messages can be customized for the occasion. 317-299-8900.

Fundcraft, P.O. Box 340, Collierville, TN 38027: Free information ❖ Fund-raising programs. 800-853-1364; 901-853-7070 (in TN).

G & R Publishing Company, 507 Industrial St., Waverly, IA 50677: Free information ❖ Custom cookbooks for fund-raising. 800-383-1679.

Genevieve's Gift Wrap Sales, P.O. Box 147, West Springfield, MA 01090: Free catalog ❖ Fund-raising programs with distinctive gift wraps, gifts, and food products. 800-842-6656.

Hale Indian River Groves, Indian River Plaza, P.O. Box 217, Wabasso, FL 32970: Free catalog ❖ Fund-raising program with oranges and grapefruit. 800-289-4253.

Krum's Chocolatier, 4 Dexter Plaza, Pearl River, NY 10965: Free catalog ❖ Fund-raising program with kosher chocolates. 800-ME-CANDY.

Mascot Pecan Company, P.O. Box 765, Glennville, GA 30427: Free information ❖ Fund-raising program with pecans and pecan candy. 800-841-3985; 912-654-2195 (in GA).

Nagle Forge & Foundry, 2 Farvue Rd., Novato, CA 94947: Catalog $2 ❖ Jewelry fund-raising program. 415-897-1732.

Nestle-Beich, P.O. Box 2914, Bloomington, IL 61702: Free information ❖ Fund-raising program with boxed chocolates and candy. 800-431-1248.

Oriental Trading Company Inc., P.O. Box 3407, Omaha, NE 68103: Free catalog ❖ Fund raising merchandise, toys, gifts, novelties, carnival supplies, and holiday and seasonal items. 800-327-9678.

B. Palmer Sales Company Inc., 3510 Wyw. 80 East, P.O. Box 850247, Mesquite, TX 75185: Free catalog ❖ Carnival, fund-raising, and party supplies. 800-888-3087; 214-288-1026 (in TX).

The Peanut Shop of Williamsburg, P.O. Box GN, Williamsburg, VA 23187: Free brochure ❖ Peanut specialties, Virginia country ham, Williamsburg soups, salad dressings, sauces, and gourmet food items for fund-raising. 800-637-3268.

❖ FURNACES, HEATING SYSTEMS & CONTROLS ❖

Profit Potentials, 451 Black Forest Rd., Hull, IA 51239: Free catalog ❖ Fund-raising programs. 800-543-5480.

Red Rhino, 4502 Dyer St., La Crescenta, CA 91214: Free starter kit ❖ Fund-raising programs with T-shirts, posters, note cards and stationery, stickers, puppetsm caps, and other items. 800-733-6602.

Revere Company, P.O. Box 751, Montgomery, AL 36101: Free catalog ❖ Fund-raising program with household items. 800-876-9967.

Spirit of America Fund Raisers, P.O. Box 621, Montgomery, AL 36101: Sample $2 ❖ Fund-raising program featuring daily planners with memo pads. 800-628-3671.

Treasure Chest Fund Raising, Division Enesco Corporation, P.O. Box 295, Elk Grove Village, IL 60009: Free catalog ❖ Fund-raising programs. 800-438-3203.

U.S. Pen Fund Raising Company, P.O. Box 1027, Montgomery, AL 36101: Free information ❖ Fund-raising programs for schools, churches, and organizations selling home, office, and school products. 800-633-8738.

Walter's Cookbooks, 215 5th Ave. SE, Waseca, MN 56093: Free information ❖ Custom cookbooks for fund-raising. 800-447-3274.

FURNACES, HEATING SYSTEMS & CONTROLS

AGA Cookers, 17 Towne Farm Ln., Stowe, VT 05672: Brochure $2 ❖ Radiant heating systems. 802-253-9727.

Atlantic Solar Products, 9351 Philadelphia Rd., P.O. Box 70060, Baltimore, MD 21237: Free catalog ❖ Solar energy power systems for the home. 410-686-2500.

Carrier Corporation, 7310 W. Morris, Indianapolis, IN 46231: Free information ❖ Combination gas and electric heating and cooling system, gas and electric furnaces, heat pumps, and air conditioners. 317-243-0851.

Central Boiler Inc., Rt. 1, Box 220, Greenbrush, MN 56726: Free brochure ❖ Outdoor wood furnaces. 800-248-4681.

Charmaster Products Inc., 2307 Hwy. 2 West, Grand Rapids, MN 55744: Free brochure ❖ Fireplaces and wood-burning, wood-gas, and wood-oil furnaces and conversion units. 800-542-6360.

Edwards Engineering Corporation, 101 Alexander Ave., Pompton Plains, NJ 07444: Free information ❖ Blower and fan-free hydronic cooling and heating system. 800-526-5201; 201-835-2800 (in NJ).

Enerzone Systems Corporation, 4103 Pecan Orchard, Parker, TX 75002: Free information ❖ Heating and air conditioning controls. 214-424-9808.

G.E. Appliances, General Electric Company, Appliance Park, Louisville, KY 40225: Free information ❖ Air conditioners and heat pumps. 800-626-2000.

Heatway Radiant Floors & Snowmelting, 3131 W. Chestnut Expwy., Springfield, MO 65802: Free information ❖ Heating systems for installation under frame or slab floors. 800-255-1996.

Hydr-Sil, P.O. Box 662, Fort Mill, SC 29715: Free information ❖ Zone heating systems. 800-627-9276.

Hunter Fan Company, 2500 Fisco Ave., Memphis, TN 38114: Catalog $1 ❖ Electronically programmable thermostats, ceiling fans, fixtures, air conditioners, and dehumidifiers. 901-745-9222.

Maxxon Corporation, 920 Hamel Rd., Hamel, MN 55340: Free list of retail sources ❖ In-floor hot water and electric radiant heating systems. Includes do-it-yourself floor warming kits. 612-478-6072.

Orbit Manufacturing Company, 1507 Park Ave., Perkasie, PA 18944: Free information ❖ Residential electric heating equipment. 215-257-0727.

Panelectric, 1100 Winchester Rd., Irvine, KY 40336: Free information ❖ In-ceiling radiant heating systems. 800-228-9022.

Radiant Technology Inc., 11 Farber Dr., Bellport, NY 11713: Free list of retail sources ❖ Hot water baseboard heating equipment. 516-286-0900.

Radiantec, Box 1111, Lyndonville, VT 05851: Free information ❖ Under-the-floor heating systems. 800-451-7593; 802-626-8045 (in VT).

Rinnai, 1662 Lukken Industrial Dr., West LaGrange, GA 30240: Free information ❖ Energy-saving gas furnaces. 800-621-9419.

Russo Products Inc., 61 Pleasant St., Randolph, MA 02368: Free brochure ❖ Free-standing and fireplace insert models of wood and coal-fired stoves. 617-963-1182.

Street Level Supply, 4728 Bryant Ave. South, Minneapolis, MN 55409: Free information ❖ Steam and hot water radiators, hot air registers, and baseboard heating units. 612-824-7655.

Sunquest Inc., 1555 Rankin Ave., Newton, NC 28658: Free information ❖ Solar energy and radiant floor heating systems. 704-465-6805.

Tarm USA, 5 Main St., Lyme, NH 03768: Free information ❖ Wood-burning furnace with automatic oil or gas back-up. 800-782-9927.

Taylor Manufacturing, P.O. Box 518, Elizabethtown, NC 28337: Free information ❖ Outdoor wood heating systems. 800-545-2293.

TEMP-CAST Enviroheat Ltd., 3332 Yonge St., P.O. Box 94059, Toronto, Ontario, Canada M4N 3R1: Free brochure ❖ Gas/propane or wood-fired masonry heaters. 800-561-8594.

FURNITURE

Beds

American Starbuck, P.O. Box 15376, Lenexa, KS 66215: Free catalog ❖ Pencil-post beds and bedroom furniture. 800-245-7188.

Amish Country Collection, Sunset Valley Rd., RD 5, Box 271, New Castle, PA 16105: Catalog $5 ❖ Early American rustic bedroom furniture. 412-458-4811.

Bartley Collection Ltd., 65 Engerman Ave., Denton, MD 21629: Free catalog ❖ Antique reproduction furniture kits. 800-787-2800.

The Bed Factory, P.O. Box 791, Westerville, OH 43086: Catalog $3 ❖ Heirloom wood, iron, and brass beds. 614-299-4454.

Bedlam Brass, 530 River Dr., Garfield, NJ 07026: Free catalog ❖ Brass beds and mirrors, tables, coat racks, and quilt and blanket racks. 201-546-5000.

Brass Bed Shoppe, 12421 Cedar Rd., Cleveland, OH 44106: Catalog $1 ❖ Brass beds. 216-229-4900.

Brass Beds Direct, 4866 W. Jefferson Blvd., Los Angeles, CA 90016: Free catalog ❖ Brass beds. 800-727-6865.

Carpenter's Brothers Furniture, Box 425, Sunderland, MA 01375: Free information ❖ Desks, dressers, bookcases, furniture, and bunk, twin, full, and queen-size beds. 800-777-BUNK.

Cohasset Colonials, 10 Churchill Rd., Hingham, MA 02043: Catalog $3 ❖ Kits for Early American, Shaker, Queen Anne, and Chippendale beds. Also other furniture. 800-288-2389.

Country Bed Shop, Richardson Rd., RR 1, Box 65, Ashby, MA 01431: Catalog $4 ❖ Handcrafted reproductions of 17th and 18th-century American beds, chairs, tables, and other furniture. 508-386-7550.

Create-A-Bed, 5100 Preston Hwy., Louisville, KY 40213: Free catalog ❖ Easy-to-install wallbed mechanisms. 502-584-8307.

Dreambeds, P.O. Box 205, Rockport, MA 01966: Free information ❖ Pencil post canopy bed frames, netted canopies, and bed curtains. 508-546-5808.

Hollingsworth Furniture, P.O. Box 2592, Wilmington, NC 28402: Free brochure ❖ Hand-painted, stained, or unfinished American, country-style reproduction pencil post and sleigh beds and other furniture. 910-251-0280.

Iron Design Center, 83 Yesler Way, Seattle, WA 98104: Catalog $5 ❖ Metal beds and accessories. 800-971-IRON.

❖ FURNITURE ❖

Leonard's Antiques, 600 Taunton Creek, Seekonk, MA 02771: Catalog $4 ❖ Original and reproduction antique beds. 508-336-8585.

Murphy Bed Company Inc., 42 Central Ave., Farmingdale, NY 11735: Free information ❖ Wall beds. 800-845-2337.

Osborne Wood Products, 8116 Hwy. 123 North, Toccoa, GA 30577: Free information ❖ Easy-to-assemble pencil-post beds. Also turned legs in different styles and wood types. 800-849-8876; 706-886-1065 (in GA).

Rainbow Woodworks, P.O. Box 308, Henderson, MN 56044: Brochure $3 ❖ Solid oak bedroom, other furniture, and cornices. 800-937-2462.

Charles P. Rogers Beds, 899 1st Ave., New York, NY 10022: Catalog $1 ❖ Original 19th and 20th-century brass and iron beds, headboards, canopy beds, and daybeds. 800-272-7726; 212-935-6900 (in NY).

Room & Board, 4800 Olson Memorial Hwy., Minneapolis, MN 55422: Free information ❖ Handcrafted steel beds and tables. 800-486-6554.

SFW Company, P.O. Box 771, Gatesville, TX 76528: Catalog $2 ❖ Handcrafted pencil-post bed and bed steps. 800-460-8677.

The SICO Room Makers, 5000 Beltline Rd., #250, Dallas, TX 75240: Free information ❖ Wall beds, home office furniture, and wall systems. 800-659-8634; 214-960-1315 (in TX).

Thomasville Furniture, P.O. Box 339, Thomasville, NC 27360: Catalog $3.50 ❖ Early American-style beds and other furniture. 800-225-0265.

A Touch of Brass, 9052 Chevrolet Dr., Ellicott City, MD 21042: Catalog $3 ❖ Reproduction iron and solid brass beds. 410-461-8585.

Lisa Victoria Brass Beds, 17106 S. Crater Rd., Petersburg, VA 23805: Catalog $4 ❖ Brass beds. 804-862-1491.

Beds, Adjustable

Craftmatic Beds, 2500 Interplex Dr., Trevose, PA 19047: Free information ❖ Adjustable beds with electric hand controls. 800-677-8200.

Electric Mobility Corporation, 1 Mobility Plaza, P.O. Box 156, Sewell, NJ 08080: Free brochure ❖ Adjustable beds with electric hand controls. 800-662-4548.

Flex-A-Bed, P.O. Box 568, Lafayette, GA 30728: Free information ❖ Electrically-adjustable bed. 800-787-1337.

Ultimate Home Care Company, 3250 E. 19th St., Long Beach, CA 90804: Free information ❖ Regular and adjustable beds for unassisted transfers from wheel chairs. 800-475-8122.

Wonderbed Manufacturing Company, 100 Peachtree St., #1450, Atlanta, GA 30303: Free price list ❖ Adjustable beds with electric hand controls. 800-543-0600.

Children's Furniture

Boston & Winthrop, 2 E. 93rd St., New York, NY 10128: Free catalog ❖ Hand-painted furniture. 212-410-6388.

Little Colorado Inc., 15866 W. 7th Ave., Golden, CO 80401: Catalog $2 ❖ Handcrafted children's furniture and accessories. 303-278-2451.

Reed Brothers, 5000 Turner Rd., Sebastopol, CA 95472: Catalog $10 ❖ Children's furniture. 707-795-6261.

Furniture Kits

Adams Wood Products Inc., 974 Forest Dr., Morristown, TN 37814: Free catalog ❖ Ready-to-assemble furniture. 615-587-2942.

Andover Wood Products, P.O. Box 38, Andover, ME 04216: Free information ❖ Ready-to-assemble Windsor and Shaker-style chairs. 207-392-2101.

Available Plastic Inc., P.O. Box 924, Huntsville, AL 35804: Free price list ❖ PVC components for making your own furniture. 800-633-7212.

Bartley Collection Ltd., 65 Engerman Ave., Denton, MD 21629: Free catalog ❖ Antique reproduction furniture kits. 800-787-2800.

Cohasset Colonials, 10 Churchill Rd., Hingham, MA 02043: Catalog $3 ❖ Kits for Early American, Shaker, Queen Anne, and Chippendale beds. Also other furniture. 800-288-2389.

Cypress Street Center, 350 Cypress St., Fort Bragg, CA 95437: Free catalog ❖ Easy-to-assemble outdoor chairs with matching love seats, foot rests, side carts, and tables. 800-222-0343.

Emperor Clock Company, Emperor Industrial Park, P.O. Box 1089, Fairhope, AL 36533: Catalog $1 ❖ Build-it-yourself grandfather clocks and furniture kits. 800-642-0011; 334-928-2316 (in AL).

ETA Wood Concepts Inc., 23565 Reedy Dr., Elkhart, IN 46514: Catalog $1 ❖ Easy-to-assemble oak and birch veneer furniture. 219-262-3457.

Grand River Workshop, 1955 NW 92nd Ct., Clive, IA 50325: Free catalog ❖ Furniture kits. 800-373-1101.

K Kraft Furniture, 617 Lynne Ave., Ypsilanti, MI 48198: Free information ❖ Ready-to-assemble contemporary-style country furniture. 313-484-0830.

S & S Woodworks, P.O. Box 786, Hays, KS 67601: Free brochure ❖ Furniture kits. 913-628-3120.

Shaker Workshops, Box 8001, Ashburnham, MA 01430: Catalog $1 ❖ Shaker furniture in kits or assembled. Also needle crafts, dolls, and dollhouse furniture. 800-840-9121.

Wood Classics, Osprey Ln., Gardner, NY 12525: Catalog $2 ❖ Teak and mahogany outdoor furniture in kits or assembled. 914-255-7871.

Yield House, P.O. Box 2525, Conway, NH 03818: Free catalog ❖ Pre-sanded furniture kits. 800-258-0376.

Home Furnishings

AC Originals, Rt. 2, Box 478, Claremore, OK 74017: Free information ❖ Country-style pine bookcases, plate racks, and baker's rack with a choice of finishes. 918-341-1604.

Stephen Adams, Furnituremaker, P.O. Box 130, Rt. 160, Denmark, ME 04022: Catalog $5 ❖ Period furniture reproductions. 207-452-2378.

Adriance Furniture Makers, 288 Gulf Rd., South Dartmouth, MA 02748: Catalog $3 ❖ Classic New England designed furniture. 508-993-4800.

American Furniture Galleries, P.O. Box 60, Montgomery, AL 36101: Brochure $1 ❖ Handcrafted reproduction Victorian-style furniture. 800-547-5240.

American Log Furniture Designs, 163 N. Woodward Ave., Birmingham, MI 48660: Free information ❖ Bedroom, family room, and dining room contemporary log furniture. 800-435-LOGS.

Amish Country Collection, Sunset Valley Rd., RD 5, Box 271, New Castle, PA 16105: Catalog $5 ❖ Amish-style oak and hickory twig furniture, rugs, quilts, and wall hangings. 412-458-4811.

Antiquarian Traders, 399 LaFayette St., New York, NY 10003: Catalog $25 ❖ American Renaissance, revival Victorian, American oak, country French and English-style, and other furniture. 212-260-1200.

Antiquity, 715 Genesee St., Delafield, WI 53018: Catalog $5 ❖ Handcrafted reproduction 18th-century furniture. 414-646-4911.

Antler Designs for Sale, Jim & Goldie Mason, 15 Curtis Hill Rd., West Paris, ME 04289: Free information ❖ Antlers crafted into chandeliers, sconces, coffee tables, chairs, and novelties. 207-674-2655 (no Friday night or Saturday calls).

Antler Furnishings by Jay "Bird" Jones, 520 Pine Oaks Rd., #4, Colorado Springs, CO 80926: Brochure $10 ❖ Antler chairs, lamps, chandeliers, and carvings. 719-527-1845.

Art De Mexico, 5356 Riverton Rd., North Hollywood, CA 91601: Free catalog ❖ Hand-assembled furniture and lighting from naturally shed antlers. 818-508-0993.

❖ FURNITURE ❖

Artisan's Choice, P.O. Box 1058, Albany, LA 70711: Catalog $8 (refundable) ❖ Home furnishings. 800-834-0553.

Arts By Alexander, 701 Greensboro Rd., High Point, NC 27260: Free information ❖ Home furnishings. 910-884-8062.

V. Michael Ashford, 6543 Alpine Dr. SW, Olympia, WA 98512: Catalog $8 ❖ Reproduction furniture and lighting. 360-352-0694.

The Atrium, 430 S. Main St., High Point, NC 27260: Free information ❖ Home furnishings in wood. 800-527-2570.

Backwoods Furnishings, Box 161, Indian Lake, NY 12842: Free brochure ❖ Rustic-style tables and chairs, rocking chairs, four-poster beds, and desks. 518-251-3327.

Bargain John's Antiques, 700 S. Washington, P.O. Box 705, Lexington, NE 68850: Free information ❖ Antique furniture.

Barn Again Furniture Company, 800 Wisconsin Ave., Eau Claire, WI 54703: Free information ❖ Country-style furniture. 715-835-5962.

Barnes & Barnes Fine Furniture, 190 Commerce Ave., Southern Pines, NC 28387: Free brochure ❖ Home furnishings. 800-334-8174.

Barton-Sharpe Ltd., 119 Spring St., New York, NY 10012: Free information ❖ Reproduction 18th and 19th-century furniture, lighting, bedding, stoneware, and decorative items. 212-925-9562.

C.H. Becksvoort, Box 12, New Gloucester, ME 04260: Catalog $5 ❖ Cherry furniture and accessories. 207-926-4608.

Bekan Rustic Furniture, P.O. Box 323, Belleville, KS 66935: Free information ❖ Rustic furniture. 913-527-2427.

Bentwood Building, 241 Addison Square, Kalispell, MT 59901: Catalog $4 ❖ Log spiral stairways and furniture. 406-257-4161.

Big Sky Log Furniture, Creative Resources International, Box 7261, Missoula, MT 59807: Free information ❖ Log furniture. 406-729-6320.

Blackwelder's, 294 Turnersburg Hwy., Statesville, NC 28677: Free information with long SASE ❖ Home furnishings. 800-438-0201.

Blake Industries, P.O. Box 155, Abington, MA 02351: Free information ❖ Outdoor and indoor teak furniture, ornamental cast-iron pole lights, and fixtures. 617-337-8772.

Blue Ridge Log Works, 3910 Lynda Ln., Fort Collins, CO 80526: Free brochure ❖ Handcrafted log furniture and hand railings. 800-313-0431.

Bombay Company, P.O. Box 161009, Fort Worth, TX 76161: Free catalog ❖ Antique furniture reproductions. 800-829-7789.

Bonita Furniture Galleries, P.O. Box 9143, Hickory, NC 28603: Free information with long SASE ❖ Home furnishings. 704-324-1992.

Dennis & CeCe Bork, 715 Genesee St., Delafield, WI 53018: Catalog $5 ❖ Custom furniture, folk art, period lighting, Colonial Williamsburg reproductions, Windsor chairs and settees, and accessories. 414-646-4911.

Brentwood Manor Furnishings, 316 Virginia Ave., Clarksville, VA 23927: Free brochure ❖ Home furnishings, clocks, draperies, and mirrors. 800-225-6105.

Curtis Buchanan, Windsor Chairmaker, 208 E. Main St., Jonesborough, TN 37659: Brochure $2 with long SASE ❖ Windsor chairs. 615-753-5160.

Matthew Burak Furniture, Box 279, Rt. 2, Danville, VT 05828: Catalog $5 ❖ Reproduction 18th and 19th-century furniture, lighting, and folk art. 802-684-2156.

Michael Camp, Cabinetmaker, 495 Amelia, Plymouth, MI 48170: Catalog $4 ❖ Reproduction 18th and 19th-century furniture. 313-459-1190.

Candlertown Chairworks, P.O. Box 5159, Mills River, NC 28742: Catalog $2 ❖ Hand-built country-style adult and children's chairs, benches, bar stools, and other furniture. 800-282-0406.

Carolina Interiors, 115 Oak Ave., Kannapolis, NC 28081: Free brochure ❖ Home furnishings. 704-933-1888.

Carpenter's Brothers Furniture, Box 425, Sunderland, MA 01375: Free information ❖ Desks, dressers, bookcases, other furniture, and bunk, twin, full, and queen-size beds. 800-777-BUNK.

Cast Aluminum Reproductions, P.O. Box 1060, San Elizario, TX 79849: Catalog $2 ❖ Cast aluminum and brass furniture, street lights, outdoor furniture, fountains, mail boxes, and plant stands. 915-764-3793.

CCSI Furniture, 13509 Method St., Dallas, TX 75243: Free information with long SASE ❖ Deacon's benches and rustic country-style furniture. 214-231-7178.

Cedar Rock Furniture, P.O. Box 515-0321, Hudson, NC 28638: Free information ❖ Home furnishings. 704-396-2361.

Celestial, P.O. Box 6734, Edison, NJ 08818: Free catalog ❖ Home furnishings and decorative accessories. 800-808-2353.

Chapman, 481 W. Main St., Avon, MA 02322: Brochure $4 (request list of retail sources) ❖ Lighting, furniture, and accessories.

Michael Charles Cabinetmakers, 3 Taber Rd., Sherman, CT 06784: Portfolio $5 ❖ Handcrafted furniture. 203-350-0230.

Cherry Hill Furniture, Box 7405, Furnitureland Station, High Point, NC 27264: Information $5 ❖ Home furnishings. 800-888-0933.

Cherry Pond Designs, P.O. Box 6, Jefferson, NH 03583: Catalog $10 ❖ Shaker furniture. 800-643-7384; 603-586-7795 (in NH).

Chestnut Hill Furniture, 511 W. King St., East Berlin, PA 17316: Free information ❖ Upholstered home furnishings. 717-259-7502.

Clear Lake Furniture, 250 Whipple Rd., Tewksbury, MA 01876: Free information ❖ Handcrafted furniture. 800-758-8767.

Coeur d'Alene Bed Outlet, 213 W. Appleway, Log Cabin Plaza, Coeur d'Alene, ID 83814: Free brochure ❖ Log furniture. 208-664-8502.

Coffey Furniture Galleries, Box 141, Granite Falls, NC 28630: Free information ❖ Home furnishings. 704-396-2900.

Cohasset Colonials, 10 Churchill Rd., Hingham, MA 02043: Catalog $3 ❖ Reproduction furniture in kits or assembled, fabrics, paints and stains, brass and pewter items, and fixtures. 800-288-2389.

Cole's Appliance & Furniture Company, 4026 Lincoln Ave., Chicago, IL 60618: Free information with long SASE ❖ Home furnishings, audio and video equipment, TVs, and kitchen appliances. 312-525-1797.

Colonial Williamsburg Furniture, P.O. Box 3532, Williamsburg, VA 23187: Catalog $14.65 ❖ Williamsburg-style furniture reproductions. 804-220-7378.

The Colorado Log Furniture Company, P.O. Box 996, 40781 US Hwy. 160, Mancos, CO 81328: Free catalog ❖ Log furniture. 303-533-7265.

Conrad Furniture, P.O. Box 1411, Wausau, WI 54402: Free information ❖ Assembled and ready-to-finish solid oak paddle back side chairs. 715-842-8022.

Cornucopia, P.O. Box 1, Harvard, MA 01451: Catalog $2 ❖ Early American and primitive-style rocking and Windsor chairs, settees, tables, and hutches. 508-772-0023.

Countree Living, 18002 County Line Rd., Elkhart Lake, IN 53020: Catalog $9.95 (refundable) ❖ Log, twig, antlers, trestle, and other styles of furniture. 414-894-7985.

Country Bed Shop, Richardson Rd., RR 1, Box 65, Ashby, MA 01431: Catalog $4 ❖ Handcrafted reproductions of 17th and 18th-century American beds, chairs, and tables. 508-386-7550.

❖ FURNITURE ❖

Gregan T. Crawford, Cabinetmaker, Rt. 2, Box 6040, Oakland, MD 21550: Catalog $2 ❖ Shaker inspired furniture and home accessories. 800-531-4109.

Crossroads Rustic Furniture, 10102 Rd. 263, Carriere, MS 38426: Free information with long SASE ❖ Handmade bentwood furniture. Options include exotic woods and styles. 601-799-3259.

Gerald Curry, Cabinetmaker, Pound Hill Rd., Union, ME 04862: Free brochure ❖ Reproduction 18th-century furniture. 207-785-4633.

Custom Country Wood Products, Rt. 2, Box 108, Greenville, TX 75402: Free information ❖ Country-style furniture with a whitewash stain or unfinished. 903-455-0542.

Frederick Duckloe & Bros. Inc., P.O. Box 427, Portland, PA 18351: Catalog $6 ❖ Handcrafted Windsor chairs, rockers, benches, and bar stools. 717-897-6172.

Davis Cabinet Company, P.O. Box 60444, Nashville, TN 37206: Free information with long SASE ❖ Bedroom and custom-built furniture. 800-578-5426.

The Deep River Trading Company, 2436 Willard Rd., High Point, NC 27265: Free information ❖ Reproduction 18th-century furniture. 910-885-2436.

Deer Creek Furniture Company, 50 High Meadow Rd., Guilford, CT 06437: Catalog $5 (refundable) ❖ Hickory country-style furniture.

Designer Secrets, P.O. Box 529, Fremont, NE 68025: Catalog $2 (refundable) ❖ Home furnishings, wall coverings, fabrics, bedspreads, and window treatments. 800-955-2559.

Dovetail Wood Works, 114 W. Boylston St., Worcester, MA 01606: Catalog $3 (refundable) ❖ Handcrafted hardwood furniture. 508-853-3151.

Dubrow Antiques, P.O. Box 128, Bayside, NY 11361: Free information ❖ American-style 19th-century furniture. 718-767-9758.

Charles Durfee Cabinetmaker, RD 1, Box 1132, Woolwich, ME 04579: Brochure $1 ❖ Shaker and Early American-style solid wood furniture. 207-442-7049.

E.P. Woodworks, Lance & Vicki Munn, P.O. Box 271, Bloomfield, IN 47424: Free information with long SASE ❖ Handcrafted hardwood furniture in red oak, black walnut, and wild cherry. 812-384-4806.

Edgar B Furniture, Box 849, Clemmons, NC 27012: Catalog $25 (refundable with $500 order) ❖ Home furnishings. 800-255-6589; 910-766-7321 (in NC).

European Furniture Importers, 2145 W. Grand Ave., Chicago, IL 60612: Catalog $3 ❖ Imported Italian furniture. 800-283-1955; 312-243-1955 (in IL).

Farmhouse Furniture, Thomas H. Kramer Inc., 805 Depot St., Commerce Park, Columbus, IN 47201: Free catalog ❖ Country-style furniture. 800-258-4097; 812-379-4097 (in IN).

Finish-It Furniture, 6 Town Market Place, Susie Wilson Rd., Essex Junction, VT 05452: Free information with long SASE ❖ Unfinished and custom-finished reproduction and contemporary-style furniture. 800-310-1311.

Fireside Reproductions, 4727 Winterset Dr., Columbus, OH 43220: Catalog $5 ❖ Handcrafted reproduction 18th and early 19th-century furniture. 614-451-7695.

Frontier Furniture, 815 Montana Hwy. 82, Somers, MT 59932: Catalog $4 ❖ Handcrafted log furniture. 406-857-3525.

Furniture Connection of Carolina, P.O. Box 21497, Hilton Head, SC 29925: Free information ❖ Home furnishings. 800-869-5664.

The Furniture Patch of Calabash Inc., P.O. Box 4970, Calabash, NC 28467: Free brochure ❖ Home furnishings. 910-579-2001.

Gardner's Farm & Wood Products, HCR 01, Box 1193, Eagle Rock, MO 65641: Free information ❖ Country-style rockers, tables, swings, and other furniture. 417-271-3999.

Genada Imports, P.O. Box 204, Teaneck, NJ 07666: Catalog $1 ❖ Danish-style furniture. 201-790-7522.

Gertz Seating & Upholstery, 642 State St. Rear, New Albany, IN 47150: Free catalog ❖ Upholstered headboards, cedar storage chests, and bedroom accessories. 800-652-6233.

Great American Log, Box 3360, Ketchum, ID 83340: Catalog $4 ❖ Handcrafted log furniture. 800-624-5779.

Great Meadows Joinery, 234 Boston Post Rd., Rt. 20, Wayland, MA 01778: Catalog $4 ❖ Handmade reproduction Shaker-style furniture. 508-358-4370.

Green Design Furniture Company, 267 Commercial St., Portland, ME 04101: Free brochure ❖ Home furnishings. 207-775-4234.

Jeffrey P. Greene, Furniture Maker, 1 W. Main St., Wickford, RI 02852: Catalog $5 ❖ Handcrafted 18th-century style furniture. 401-295-1200.

Habersham Plantation, P.O. Box 1209, Toccoa, GA 30577: Catalog $12 ❖ Reproduction 17th and 18th-century country and contemporary furniture. 800-241-0716.

Handcrafted Log Furnishings, 11372 Ave. 272, Visalia, CA 93278: Information package $10 ❖ Custom log furniture and railings. 209-687-0744.

Harden Furniture, Mill Pond Way, McConnellsville, NY 13401: Catalogs $20 ❖ Handcrafted chairs and upholstered and solid wood furniture.

Harvest House Furniture, P.O. Box 1440, Denton, NC 27239: Free information: Free information with long SASE ❖ Home furnishings. 704-869-5181.

Heirloom Reproductions, 1834 W. 5th St., Montgomery, AL 36106: Catalog $4 ❖ Victorian and French-style period furniture reproductions. 800-288-1513.

Hendricks Furniture Inc., P.O. Box 828, I-40 & Farmington Rd., Mocksville, NC 27028: Free information ❖ Home furnishings. 910-998-7712.

Hickory Furniture Mart, 2220 Highway 70E, Hickory, NC 28602: Free information ❖ Traditional and contemporary furniture. 800-462-MART.

Warren Hile Studio, 89 E. Montecito Ave., Sierra Madre, CA 91024: Catalog $1 ❖ Handcrafted mission furniture. 818-355-4382.

Historic Charleston Reproductions, 105 Broad St., P.O. Box 622, Charleston, SC 29402: Catalog $10 ❖ Reproduction furniture.

Hollingsworth Furniture, P.O. Box 2592, Wilmington, NC 28402: Free brochure ❖ American country furniture reproductions. 910-251-0280.

Holton Furniture Company, P.O. Box 280, Thomasville, NC 27360: Free information ❖ Home furnishings. 800-334-3183; 919-472-0400 (in NC).

Homeway Furniture Company, 121 W. Lebanon St., Mt. Airy, NC 27030: Free information ❖ Home furnishings. 800-334-9094.

Martha M. House, 1022 S. Decatur St., Montgomery, AL 36104: Catalog $3 ❖ Victorian-style sofas, chairs, tables, dining room, and bedroom furniture. 205-264-3558.

House Dressing Furniture, 3608 W. Wendover, Greensboro, NC 27407: Free information ❖ Home furnishings. 800-322-5850.

Hudson's Discount Furniture, P.O. Box 2547, Hickory, NC 28603: Free information ❖ Home furnishings. 704-322-4996.

Hunt Galleries Inc., P.O. Box 2324, Hickory, NC 28603: Catalog $5 ❖ Sofas, upholstered chairs, ottomans, benches, lounges, headboards, and other furniture. 800-248-3876.

IKEA Catalog Department, 185 Discovery Dr., Colmar, PA 18915: Free catalog ❖ Functional furniture.

Ian Ingersoll, Cabinetmakers, Main St., West Cornwall, CT 06796: Brochure $3 ❖ Reproduction Shaker furniture and chairs. 800-237-4926.

Interior Furnishings Ltd., P.O. Box 1644, Hickory, NC 28603: Free brochure ❖ Home furnishings. 704-328-5683.

❖ FURNITURE ❖

Irion Company Furniture Makers, 1 S. Bridge St., Christiana, PA 17509: Free brochure ❖ Handmade 18th-century furniture reproductions. 215-593-2153.

Iverson Snowshoe Company, Maple St., P.O. Box 85, Shingleton, MI 49884: Free information ❖ Handcrafted white ash furniture. 906-452-6370.

Jackson's Cabinet Shop, 2879 Wildwood Rd. Extension, Allison Park, PA 15101: Free information ❖ Reproduction 18th and 19th-century furniture. 412-487-1291.

Jennifer's Trunk Antiques & General Store, 201 N. Riverside, Dr., St. Clair, MI 48079: Free brochure ❖ Victorian-style antique furniture, books, jewelry, lamps and shades, and gifts. 810-329-2032.

John-Michael Furniture, P.O. Box 2901, Hickory, NC 28603: Free information ❖ Home furnishings.

Jungle Zoo Furniture, P.O. Box 809, Tucson, AZ 85702: Free information ❖ Indoor and outdoor furniture with a Mexican and southwestern theme. 800-99-JUNGLE; 520-887-8645 (in AZ).

The Karges Furniture Company Inc., P.O. Box 6517, Evansville, IN 47719: Brochure $10 ❖ Home furnishings. 800-252-7437.

Kestrel Manufacturing, P.O. Box 12, Saint Peters, PA 19470: Information $2 ❖ Knock-down and ready-to-hang folding screens and interior and exterior shutters. 610-469-6444.

Klein Design Inc., 99 Sadler St., Gloucester, MA 01930: Free brochure ❖ Rockers, chairs, love-seats, sofas, and side tables. 800-451-7247.

Knight Galleries, P.O. Box 1254, Lenoir, NC 28645: Free information ❖ Home furnishings. 800-334-4721.

Lanier Furniture Company, P.O. Box 3576, Wilmington, NC 28406: Catalog $3 ❖ Handcrafted reproduction Shaker furniture. 800-453-1362.

Leather Interiors, Box 9305, Hickory, NC 28603: Free information ❖ Traditional and contemporary leather furniture. 800-627-4526.

Lenoir Furniture Market Inc., 2034 Hickory Blvd. SW, Lenoir, NC 28645: Free information with long SASE ❖ Indoor and outdoor furniture, beds, and bedding. 704-728-2946.

Levenger, P.O. Box 1256, Delray Beach, FL 33447: Free catalog ❖ Books, furniture, pens, briefcases, and other gifts for serious readers. 800-545-0242.

Loftin-Black Furniture Company, 111 Sedgehill Dr., Thomasville, NC 27360: Free catalog ❖ Home furnishings. 800-334-7398; 910-472-6117 (in NC).

Luv Those Rugs, 103 N. Main, Box 236, Elkton, KY 42220: Free information ❖ Braided rugs and country-style furniture. 502-265-5550.

Mack & Rodel Cabinet Makers, 44 Leighton Rd., Pownal, ME 04069: Catalog $5 ❖ Home furnishings. 207-688-4483.

Daniel Mack Rustic Furnishings, 14 Welling Ave., Warwick, NY 10990: Free information ❖ Rustic-style furniture from branches, saplings, and logs. 914-986-7293.

Magnolia Hall, 726 Andover, Atlanta, GA 30327: Catalog $3 ❖ Carved furniture. 404-237-9725.

Mallory's Furniture, P.O. Box 1150, Jacksonville, NC 28546: Free brochure ❖ Home furnishings. 919-353-1828.

Marks Sales Company, 609 E. 81st St., Brooklyn, NY 11236: Catalog $3.25 ❖ Ready-to-paint or stain hand-carved country French, Italian, and French Provincial chairs. 718-763-2591.

Mayfield Leather, 340 9th St. SE, Hickory, NC 28603: Free brochure ❖ Heirloom and classic reproducts in leather. 800-342-7729.

Maynard House Antiques, 11 Maynard St., Westborough, MA 01581: Brochure $2 ❖ Handcrafted American country sofas and wing chairs, from the 1780s to 1820s. 508-366-2073.

MidAmerica Furniture, P.O. Box 112, Hamburg, AR 71646: Free brochure ❖ Home furnishings. 800-259-7897.

Miya Shoji & Interiors Inc., 109 W. 17th St., New York, NY 10011: Free brochure ❖ Japanese Shoji screens. 212-243-6774.

Modern Classics, P.O. Box 20023, New York, NY 10021: Free catalog ❖ Classic, modern, and other styles of wood and leather furniture. 800-853-2030.

Thos. Moser Cabinetmakers, 72 Wright's Landing, Auburn, ME 04211: Catalog $10 ❖ Handcrafted furniture for homes and offices. 800-862-1973.

Moultrie Manufacturing, P.O. Drawer 1179, Moultrie, GA 31776: Catalog $3 ❖ Southern-style furniture reproductions for homes and gardens. 800-841-8674.

Mountainman Woodshop, Rt. 2, Box 37A, Eagle Rock, VA 24085: Free brochure ❖ Handcrafted traditional Appalachian slot-back chairs and wooden farming tools. 540-884-2197.

Murrow Furniture Galleries, P.O. Box 4337, Wilmington, NC 28406: Free brochure ❖ Home furnishings. 910-799-4010.

Naylor Furnituremakers, 1660 Camp Betty Wash. Rd., York, PA 17402: Free information ❖ Handcrafted reproduction 18th and 19th-century American-style furniture. 717-755-8884.

Lawrence P. Neal, 212 Old Hebron Rd., Colchester, CT 06415: Catalog $5 (refundable) ❖ Shaker reproductions. 203-537-4007.

Neustadt Studios Collecttables, 100 Paper Mill Rd., Lawrenceville, GA 30245: Catalog $4 (refundable) ❖ Country-style cabinets for collectors. 800-876-5739.

North Branch Trading Company, 914 E. Main St., Rt. 9 East, Bennington, VT 05201: Free catalog ❖ Country-style and traditional furniture. 800-595-1205; 802-447-1205 (in VT).

North Carolina Discount Furniture, 3302 Clarendon Blvd., Hwy. 17 South, New Bern, NC 28652: Catalog $7.50 ❖ Home furnishings. 919-638-9164.

North Country Crafts, P.O. Box 500, Marinette, WI 54143: Free information ❖ Country-style upholstered storage ottomans. 800-637-7989.

North Woods Chair Shop, 237 Old Tilton Rd., Canterbury, NH 03224: Catalog $3 ❖ Handcrafted Shaker furniture. 603-783-4595.

Northwestern Exposure Furniture, 39027 Shelburn Dr., Scio, OR 97374: Catalog $3 ❖ Stick furniture. 800-448-3434; 503-394-2463 (in OR).

O'Donnell Elegant Americana, Walnut Grove Rd., Bloomfield, IN 47424: Free brochure with long SASE ❖ Museum-quality 18th-century furniture. 812-384-8780.

Old Wagon Factory, P.O. Box 1427, Clarksville, VA 23927: Catalog $2 ❖ Chippendale furniture, Victorian-style railings and brackets, and Victorian-style and Chippendale storm screen doors. 804-374-5787.

Orleans Carpenters, P.O. Box 217, Orleans, MA 02653: Catalog $3 ❖ Shaker and colonial furniture reproductions. 508-255-2646.

Plaza Furniture Inc., P.O. Box 1150, North Myrtle Beach, SC 29598: Free brochure ❖ Home furnishings. 800-262-9898.

Plexi-Craft Quality Products, 514 W. 24th St., New York, NY 10011: Catalog $2 ❖ Lucite and Plexiglas furniture. 212-924-3244.

Priba Furniture Sales & Interiors, 210 Stage Coach Trail, Greensboro, NC 27415: Free information ❖ Home furnishings. 910-855-9034.

Rhoney Furniture House, 2401 Hwy. 70 SW, Hickory, NC 28602: Free information ❖ Traditional and contemporary furniture. 704-328-2034.

Richmond's Woodworks Inc., 1577 SR 39, New Philadelphia, OH 44663: Free information ❖ Amish-style furniture. 216-343-8184.

Dana Robes Wood Craftsmen, Lower Shaker Village, P.O. Box 707, Enfield, NH 03748: Catalog $5 ❖ Shaker reproduction furniture. 800-722-5036.

FURNITURE

Mario Rodriguez Cabinetmaker, 1 E. Ridge Rd., Warwick, NY 10990: Catalog $3.50 ❖ Handcrafted reproduction 18th-century furniture. 914-986-6636.

Jace Romick's into the West Gallery, P.O. Box 880767, Steamboat Springs, CO 80488: Free brochure ❖ Western-style furniture. 800-351-8377.

Rose Furniture Company, 916 Finch Ave., P.O. Box 1829, High Point, NC 27261: Free information ❖ Home furnishings. 910-886-6050.

Salem Furnishings, P.O. Box 10340, Winston-Salem, NC 27108: Free information ❖ Home furnishings. 800-226-8755.

David Sawyer, RD 1, East Calais, VT 05650: Brochure $1 ❖ Windsor chairs. 802-456-8836.

Woody Scoville, RR 1, Box 65, East Calais, VT 05650: Brochure $2 ❖ Windsor chairs. 802-456-8179.

The Seraph, P.O. Box 500, 420 Main St., Sturbridge, MA 01566: Catalog $6 ❖ 18th-century-style home furnishings and accessories. 508-347-2241.

Shaker Workshops, Box 8001, Ashburnham, MA 01430: Catalog $1 ❖ Shaker furniture in kits or assembled, needle crafts, dolls, and dollhouse furniture. 800-840-9121.

Shaw Furniture Galleries, P.O. Box 576, Randleman, NC 27317: Free brochure ❖ Home furnishings. 910-498-2628.

The Shop Woodcrafters Inc., P.O. Box 1450, Quitman, TX 75783: Catalog $4 ❖ Stained white pine furniture. 903-763-5491.

The SICO Room Makers, 5000 Beltline Rd., #250, Dallas, TX 75240: Free information ❖ Wall beds, home office furniture, and wall systems. 800-659-8634; 214-960-1315 (in TX).

Simply Country Furniture, HC 69, Box 147, Rover, AR 72860: Brochure $3 ❖ Country-style furniture. 501-272-4794.

George Smith Sofas & Chairs Inc., 73 Spring St., New York, NY 10012: Catalog $5 ❖ Traditionally-made English furniture, fabrics, and kilims. 212-226-4747.

Sobol House of Furnishings, Richardson Blvd., Black Mountain, NC 28711: Free brochure ❖ Home and office furnishings. 704-669-8031.

Southampton Antiques, 172 College Way, Rt. 10, Southampton, MA 01073: Video catalog $25 ❖ Antique American oak and Victorian-style furniture. 413-527-1022.

Spirit of the West, Tomoka Center, 1095 N. US Hwy 1, Ormond Beach, FL 32174: Free information with long SASE ❖ Southwest furniture, art, and decorative accessories. 800-831-9663; 904-673-9402 (in FL).

M. Star Antler Designs, P.O. Box 3093, Lake Isabella, CA 93240: Catalog $5 ❖ Antler-designed chandeliers, lamps, furniture, mirrors, and accessories. 619-379-5777.

Stevens Furniture, 1258 Hickory Blvd. SW, P.O. Box 270, Lenoir, NC 28645: Free information ❖ Home furnishings. 704-728-5511.

Stickley Furniture, Stickley Dr., P.O. Box 480, Manlius, NY 13104: Catalog $5 (request list of retail sources) ❖ Cherry and mahogany 18th-century furniture. 315-682-5500.

Straw Hill Chairs, West Unity, NH 03743: Catalog $3 ❖ Antique Windsor chair reproductions. 603-542-4367.

Stuckey Brothers Furniture, Rt. 1, Box 527, Stuckey, SC 29554: Free information with long SASE ❖ Indoor and outdoor furniture. 803-558-2591.

Sutton-Council Furniture, P.O. Box 3288, Wilmington, NC 28406: Catalog $5 ❖ Home furnishings. 910-799-1990.

Sweet Water Ranch, P.O. Drawer 398, Cody, WY 82414: Free information ❖ Western-style home furnishings and accessories. 800-357-CODY.

T-M Cowboy Classics, 364 Main St., Longmont, CO 80501: Brochure $3 ❖ Western-style furniture. 303-776-3394.

Ernest Thompson, 4531 Osuna NE, Albuquerque, NM 87109: Catalog $8 ❖ Home furnishings. 800-568-2344.

Timberline Furniture, 4040 Heeb Rd., Manhattan, MT 59741: Brochure $3 ❖ Rustic-looking log furniture. 406-282-7152.

Marion Travis, P.O. Box 1041, Statesville, NC 28677: Catalog $1 ❖ Hand-woven fiber rush seats on native hardwood chairs. 704-528-4424.

Turner-Tolson Inc., 3302 Clarendon Blvd., Hwy. 17 South, New Bern, NC 28560: Catalog $10 ❖ Home furnishings. 919-638-2121.

Valley Furniture Shop, 20 Stirling Rd., Watchung, NJ 07060: Catalog $5 ❖ Reproduction 18th-century furniture. 908-756-7623.

Vermont FurnitureWorks, P.O. Box 1496, Stowe, VT 05672: Free catalog ❖ Handcrafted 18th and 19th-century reproduction New England furniture, traditional folk art, and Americana accessories. 802-253-5094.

Victorian Replicas, 251 Rhode Island, San Francisco, CA 94103: Catalog $10 ❖ Antique furniture reproductions. 415-552-6367.

Village Furniture House, 146 West Ave., Kannapolis, NC 28081: Free brochure ❖ Home furnishings. 704-938-9171.

Walpole Woodworkers, 767 East St., Walpole, MA 02081: Catalog $6 ❖ Handcrafted natural cedar New England-style furniture. 800-343-6948.

Charles Webb, Six Story St., Harvard Square, Cambridge, MA 02138: Catalog $4 ❖ Designer furniture. 617-547-2100.

Wellington's Furniture, P.O. Box 1849, Blowing Rock, NC 28605: Free catalog ❖ Leather furniture. 800-262-1049.

Eddy West, A Collection of Hampton Hall, P.O. Box 786, Clarkesville, GA 30523: Catalog $5 ❖ Handcrafted solid pine furniture. 800-829-9037.

Eldred Wheeler, 60 Sharp St., Hingham, MA 02043: Catalog $5 ❖ Reproduction 18th-century furniture. 617-337-5311.

Wilcox Cabinet Works, Rt. 3, Box 94, Marion, KS 66861: Brochure $2 ❖ Handcrafted table reproductions. 316-382-2717.

R.S. Wilkinson, 177 Scotland Rd., Baltic, CT 06330: Free brochure ❖ American-style furniture. 203-822-6790.

Willsboro Wood Products, South Ausable St., Keeseville, NY 12944: Free brochure ❖ Folding Adirondack chairs, rocking chairs, and country-style furniture. 800-342-3373.

Wood-Armfield Furniture Company, P.O. Box C, 460 S. Main St., High Point, NC 27261: Free brochure ❖ Home furnishings. 910-889-6522.

Wood Concepts, 23565 Reedy Dr., Elkhart, IN 46514: Free information with long SASE ❖ Easy-to-assemble solid oak country-style furniture. 219-262-3457.

Workshops of David T. Smith, 3600 Shawhan Rd., Morrow, OH 45152: Catalog $5 ❖ Reproduction furniture, pottery, lamps, and chandeliers. 513-932-2472.

York Leather Collection of Hickory, P.O. Box 785, Hickory, NC 28603: Catalog $5 (refundable) ❖ Handcrafted leather furniture. 704-459-2879.

Lift Chairs

American Stair-Glide Corporation, 4001 E. 138th St., Grandview, MO 64030: Free brochure ❖ Cushioned chairs that rise to a standing position. 800-383-3100.

Ortho-Kinetics, The Independence Company, 1 Mobility Centre, P.O. Box 1647, Waukesha, WI 53187: Free information ❖ Combination power recliner/lounger/lift chair. 800-446-4522.

Whitakers, 1 Odell Plaza, Yonkers, NY 10703: Free catalog ❖ Lifts for transporting people with physical disabilities up and down and into the bathtub. 800-44-LIFTS; 800-924-LIFT (in NY).

FURNITURE

Office Furniture

Abbott Office Systems, 5012 Asbury Ave., P.O. Box 688, Farmingdale, NJ 07727: Free catalog ❖ Stacking storage drawers. 908-938-6000.

Alfax Wholesale Furniture, 370 7th Ave., Ste. 1101, New York, NY 10001: Free catalog ❖ Office furniture. 800-221-5710: 212-947-9560 (in NY).

American Security Products Company, 11925 Pacific Ave., Fontana, CA 92335: Free information ❖ Gun and other safes for homes and offices. 800-421-6142.

Arrow Star, 3-1 Park Plaza, Dept. 15, Glen Head, NY 11546: Free catalog ❖ Storage and shelving, tables, chairs, desks, filing cabinets, lockers, and accessories. 800-645-2833; 516-484-3100 (in NY).

ATD-American Company, 135 Greenwood Rd., Wyncote, PA 19095: Free catalog ❖ Office and computer furniture, display cases, and storage and filing cabinets. 800-523-2300; 576-1000 (in area code 215).

Basil & Jones Cabinetmakers, 2712 36th St. NW, Washington, DC 20007: Free brochure ❖ Wood and leather-finished stand-up desks in period and contemporary styles. 202-337-4369.

Business & Institutional Furniture Company, P.O. Box 92039, Milwaukee, WI 53202: Free catalog ❖ Office and institutional furniture. 800-558-8662.

Frank Eastern Company, 599 Broadway, New York, NY 10012: Catalog $1 ❖ Office furniture. 800-221-4914; 212-219-0007 (in NY).

Factory Direct Furniture, P.O. Box 92967, Milwaukee, WI 53202: Free catalog ❖ Office and computer furniture. 800-972-6570; 289-9770 (in Milwaukee).

K-Log Inc., P.O. Box 5, Zion, IL 60099: Free catalog ❖ Computer and office furniture. 800-872-6611.

Lyon Metal Products Inc., P.O. Box 671, Aurora, IL 60507: Free catalog ❖ Shelving, cabinets, racks, lockers, and shop furniture. 800-323-0096.

❖ NATIONAL BUSINESS FURNITURE ❖

National Business Furniture Inc., 735 N. Water St., Milwaukee, WI 53202: Free catalog ❖ Office furniture. 800-626-6060.

Office Depot Inc., 2200 Old Germantown Rd., Delray Beach, FL 33445: Free catalog ❖ Office supplies and furniture. 800-685-8800.

PAR Seating Specialists, 310 Main St., New Rochelle, NY 10802: Free catalog ❖ Office chairs and automotive seats. 800-367-7270.

Reliable Home Office, P.O. Box 1501, Ottawa, IL 61350: Catalog $2 ❖ Office furniture. 800-869-6000. (Attention: Address Correction, P.O. Box 1020, Westboro, MA 01581.)

Safe Specialties Inc., 10932 Murdock & Lovell Rd., Knoxville, TN 37932: Catalog $2 ❖ Office and home safes. 800-695-2815.

The Stand-Up Desk Company, 5207 Baltimore Ave., Bethesda, MD 20816: Free brochure ❖ Handcrafted stand-up desks and stools. 301-657-3630.

Staples Inc., Attention: Marketing Services, P.O. Box 1020, Westboro, MA 01581: Free catalog ❖ Office furniture, drafting equipment, fax machines, typewriters, and supplies. 800-333-3330.

Stuart-Townsend-Carr Furniture, P.O. Box 373, Limington, ME 04049: Free information ❖ Classic furniture for offices and dens. 800-637-2344.

Outdoor Furniture

Adirondack Designs, 350 Cypress St., Fort Bragg, CA 95437: Free catalog ❖ Redwood chairs, love seats, swings, and tables. 800-222-0343.

Adirondack Store & Gallery, 109 Saranac Ave., Lake Placid, NY 12946: Free information ❖ Oak and maple outdoor furniture. 518-523-2646.

AK Exteriors, 298 Leisure Ln., Clint, TX 79836: Catalog $4 ❖ Cast-aluminum furniture, lighting fixtures, and mail boxes. 915-851-2594.

Amish Country Collection, Sunset Valley Rd., RD 5, Box 271, New Castle, PA 16105: Catalog $5 ❖ Amish-style twig furniture, rugs, quilts, and wall hangings. 412-458-4811.

Barlow Tyrie, 1263 Glen Ave., Ste. 230, Morristown, NJ 08057: Free brochure and list of retail sources ❖ English-style teak outdoor furniture. 609-273-7878.

The BenchSmith, P.O. Box 86, Warrington, PA 18976: Free catalog ❖ Benches, rockers, tables, and planters. 800-482-3327.

Blake Industries, P.O. Box 155, Abington, MA 02351: Free information ❖ Outdoor and indoor teak furniture, ornamental cast-iron pole lights, and fixtures. 617-337-8772.

Brown-Jordan, P.O. Box 5688, El Monte, CA 91734: Free information ❖ Aluminum furniture. 818-443-8971.

Charleston Battery Bench, 191 King St., Charleston, SC 29401: Catalog $1 ❖ Reproduction cast-iron and cypress benches from the 1880s. 803-722-3842.

Charleston Gardens, 61 Queen St., Charleston, SC 29401: Catalog $3 ❖ Outdoor furniture and garden furnishings. 803-723-0252.

Clapper's, P.O. Box 2278, West Newton, MA 02165: Free catalog ❖ Teak furniture for gardens, patios, and breezeways. 617-244-7900.

Columbia Cascade, 1975 SW 5th Ave., Portland, OR 97201: Free catalog ❖ Outdoor furniture. 800-547-1940.

Coppa Woodworking Inc., 1231 Paraiso Ave., San Pedro, CA 90731: Catalog $1 ❖ Adirondack chairs, screen doors, and furniture. 310-548-5332.

Country Casual, 17317 Germantown Rd., Germantown, MD 20874: Catalog $5 ❖ Teak benches, swings, chairs, tables, and planters. 301-540-0040.

Cypress Street Center, 350 Cypress St., Fort Bragg, CA 95437: Free catalog ❖ Easy-to-assemble outdoor chairs with matching love seats, foot rests, side carts, and tables. 800-222-0343.

Diversified Overseas Marketing, 200 Main St., Coraopolis, PA 15108: Free information ❖ Cast-aluminum furniture with all-weather cushions. 412-269-2690.

DuMor Inc., P.O. Box 142, Mifflintown, PA 17059: Free catalog ❖ Outdoor furniture. 800-598-4018.

Fib-Con Corporation, Box 3387, Silver Spring, MD 20918: Free catalog ❖ Reinforced fiberglass planters, benches, waste receptacles, and patio furniture. 301-572-5333.

Flanders Industries Inc., P.O. Box 1788, Fort Smith, AR 72902: Free brochure ❖ Casual and outdoor pool furniture. 800-843-7532.

Gardenside Ltd., 999 Andersen Dr., Ste. 140, San Rafael, CA 94901: Free catalog ❖ Teak garden furniture. 415-455-4500.

Kelly Grayson, Woodcarving & Design, 5111 Todd Rd., Sebastopol, CA 95472: Brochure $1 ❖ Custom redwood garden furniture and accessories. 707-829-7764.

Green Enterprises, 43 S. Rogers St., Hamilton, VA 22068: Brochure $1 ❖ Swings, gliders, tables, and benches. 703-338-3606.

Kingsley-Bate Ltd., 5587 Guinea Rd., Fairfax, VA 22032: Catalog $2 ❖ Teak planters, window boxes, and garden furniture. 703-978-7200.

Kramer Brothers, P.O. Box 255, Dayton, OH 45404: Free catalog ❖ Garden furniture and ornaments. 513-228-4194.

Landscape Forms Inc., 431 Lawndale Ave., Kalamazoo, MI 49001: Free information ❖ Outdoor furniture and garden planters. 800-521-2546; 616-381-0396 (in MI).

Lenoir Furniture Market Inc., 2034 Hickory Blvd., Lenoir, NC 28645: Free information with long SASE ❖ Indoor and outdoor furniture, beds, and bedding. 704-728-2946.

Lloyd/Flanders, 3010 10th St., P.O. Box 550, Menominee, MI 49858: Free information ❖ Aluminum outdoor furniture and umbrella sets. 906-863-4491.

Kenneth Lynch & Sons, 84 Danbury Rd., Wilton, CT 06897: Catalog $4 ❖ Outdoor benches, gates, fountains, and pools. 203-762-8363.

MacMillan-Bloedel, 5895 Windward Pkwy., Ste. 200, Alpharetta, GA 30201: Free information ❖ Unfinished Western red cedar outdoor furniture. 800-432-6226.

Mel-Nor Industries, 303 Gulf Bank, Houston, TX 77037: Information $1 ❖ Hanging lawn and porch swings, park benches, and old-time lamp posts. 713-445-3485.

Moultrie Manufacturing, P.O. Drawer 1179, Moultrie, GA 31776: Catalog $3 ❖ Indoor and outdoor aluminum furniture. 800-841-8674.

Nebraska Plastics Inc., P.O. Box 45, Cozad, NE 69130: Free information ❖ Rose trellises, garden arbors, picnic tables, and outdoor furniture and accessories. 800-445-2887.

Old Hickory Furniture Company, 403 S. Noble St., Shelbyville, IN 46176: Free list of retail sources ❖ Casual and outdoor furniture. 800-232-2275.

The Patio, P.O. Box 1042, Murrieta, CA 92564: Catalog $2 ❖ Outdoor patio furniture. 800-81-PATIO.

Pittman & Davis, P.O. Box 532227, Harlingen, TX 78553: Catalog $1 ❖ Folding tables and outdoor furniture. 210-423-2154.

Plow & Hearth, P.O. Box 5000, Madison, VA 22727: Free catalog ❖ Gardening tools, birdhouses and feeders, porch and lawn furniture, fireplace accessories, and gifts for pets. 800-627-1712.

Pompeian Studios, 90 Rockledge Rd., Bronxville, NY 10708: Catalog $10 ❖ Original sculptures, ornaments, and forged furniture for patio or garden. 800-457-5595.

Reed Brothers, 5000 Turner Rd., Sebastopol, CA 95472: Catalog $10 ❖ Hand-carved wooden furniture for the home and garden. 707-795-6261.

Roberts Furniture, 65 Commerce Rd., Stamford, CT 06902: Free catalog ❖ Brown Jordan, Tropitone, Barlow Tyrie, and Lloyd Flanders furniture. 800-899-4610.

Robinson Iron Corporation, P.O. Box 1119, Alexander City, AL 35010: Catalog $5 ❖ Cast-iron benches. 205-329-8486.

Smith & Hawken, P.O. Box 6907, Florence, KY 41022: Free catalog ❖ Garden furniture. 800-776-3336.

Southerlands for Leisure Living, 10 Biltmore Ave., Asheville, NC 28801: Free catalog ❖ Outdoor furniture and garden accessories. 800-968-5596.

Victor Stanley Inc., P.O. Box 330, Dunkirk, MD 20754: Free information ❖ Indoor and outdoor furniture. 800-368-2573; 301-855-8300 (in MD).

Stuckey Brothers Furniture, Rt. 1, Box 527, Stuckey, SC 29554: Free information with long SASE ❖ Indoor and outdoor furniture. 803-558-2591.

Sun Designs, P.O. Box 6, Oconomowoc, WI 53066: Plan book $9.95 plus $3.95 postage ❖ Gazebos and garden structures. 414-567-4255.

Telescope Casual Furniture, P.O. Box 299, Granville, NY 12832: Free information ❖ Outdoor furniture. 518-642-1100.

Thetford Chair Company, Tucker Hill Rd., Thetford Center, VT 05075: Catalog $4 ❖ Handcrafted steel furniture for the home and garden. 802-785-4034.

Tidewater Workshop, Rt. 9, Oceanville, NJ 08231: Free information ❖ Outdoor furniture. 800-666-TIDE.

Vermont Outdoor Furniture, East Barre, VT 05649: Free catalog ❖ Outdoor furniture in white cedar. 800-588-8834.

Walpole Woodworkers, 767 East St., Walpole, MA 02081: Catalog $6 ❖ Porch and children's swings and handcrafted lawn and garden cedar furniture. 800-343-6948.

Wicker Works, 267 8th St., San Francisco, CA 94103: Free information ❖ Outdoor furniture. 415-626-6730.

Wood Classics, Osprey Ln., Gardner, NY 12525: Catalog $2 ❖ Teak and mahogany outdoor furniture in kits or assembled. 914-255-7871.

Wicker & Rattan

Deutsch Inc., 31 E. 32nd St., New York, NY 10016: Catalog $3 ❖ Rattan furniture. 800-223-4550; 212-683-8746 (in NY).

Dovetail Antiques, 474 White Pine Rd., Columbus, NJ 08022: Catalog $5 ❖ Antique wicker furniture. 609-298-5245.

Ellenburg's Furniture, P.O. Box 5638, Statesville, NC 28687: Catalog $6 ❖ Wicker and rattan furniture with optional upholstered cushions, padding, and covers. 800-841-1420.

Fran's Basket House, 295 Rt. 10, Succasunna, NJ 07876: Catalog $2 ❖ Wicker and rattan furniture. 800-FRANS-99; 201-584-2230 (in NJ).

Gift & Wicker Import Inc., 12770 Moore St., Cerritos, CA 90701: Catalog $5 ❖ Wickerware, hobby craft supplies, basket planters, home decorative accessories, and furniture. 800-622-6209; 310-407-3319 (in CA).

Hopewood Farm, General Delivery, 5997 Carversville Rd., Carversville, PA 18913: Catalog $5 ❖ Antique wicker furniture, from 1870 to 1930. 215-297-0968.

Lloyd/Flanders, 3010 10th St., P.O. Box 550, Menominee, MI 49858: Free information ❖ All-weather wicker furniture. 906-863-4491.

Masterworks, P.O. Box M, Marietta, GA 30061: Catalog $2.50 ❖ Indoor, outdoor, children's, and bent-willow furniture. 404-423-9000.

Out & In Furnishings, P.O. Box 13055, San Luis Obispo, CA 93406: Free catalog ❖ All-weather wicker furniture. 805-995-2770.

Wicker Warehouse Inc., 195 S. River St., Hackensack, NJ 07601: Catalog $5 (refundable) ❖ Wicker and rattan furniture. 800-274-8602.

Wicker Works, 267 8th St., San Francisco, CA 94103: Free information ❖ Outdoor furniture. 415-626-6730.

Wicker Works of High Point, 274 Eastchester Dr., Ste. 117-156, High Point, NC 27262: Catalog $3 ❖ Country, Victorian, contemporary, and traditional wicker furniture. 800-745-7455.

GARAGE DOORS & OPENERS

Atlas Roll-Lite Door, 10407 Rocket Blvd., Orlando, FL 32824: Free information ❖ Insulated raised panel garage doors.

Clopay Corporation, Consumer Affairs Department, 312 Walnut St., Ste. 1600, Cincinnati, OH 45202: Free information ❖ Garage doors with raised panels. 800-225-6729.

Overhead Door, P.O. Box 809046, Dallas, TX 75380: Free information ❖ Insulated steel overhead garage doors and opener with a microprocessor controller program to detect obstructions. 800-543-2269.

Philips Home Products, 22790 Lake Park Blvd., Alliance, OH 44601: Free information ❖ Garage door openers with an option for controlling house lights. 800-654-3643.

Raynor Garage Doors, P.O. Box 448, Dixon, IL 61021: Free information ❖ Wood-grained steel garage doors with raised panels. 800-545-0455.

❖ GARDENING EQUIPMENT & SUPPLIES ❖

Ridge Doors, New Rd., Monmouth, NJ 08852: Free information ❖ Solid wooden garage doors with carved or plain panels and optional trim and glass. 800-631-5656; 800-872-4980 (in NJ).

Stanley Door Systems, 1225 E. Maple Ave., Troy, MI 48084: Free information ❖ Garage door opener transmitter. 800-521-5262.

Wayne-Dalton Corporation, P.O. Box 67, Mount Hope, OH 44660: Free information ❖ Insulated steel garage doors. 216-674-7015.

GARDENING EQUIPMENT & SUPPLIES

Beneficial Insects, Organisms & Pest Controls

Applied Bionomics, 11074 W. Saanich Rd., Sidney, British Columbia, Canada V8L 3X0: Free brochure ❖ Beneficial insects. 604-656-2123.

Arbico Inc., P.O. Box 4247, Tucson, AZ 85738: Free catalog ❖ Beneficial insects. 800-767-2847.

Beatrice Farms, Dawson, GA 31742: Free information ❖ Red worms for soil improvement and composting. 912-995-4654.

Bozeman Bio-Tech, P.O. Box 3146, 1612 Gold Ave., Bozeman, MT 59772: Free catalog ❖ Beneficial insects and pest control products. 800-289-6656.

W. Atlee Burpee & Company, 300 Park Ave., Warminster, PA 18974: Free catalog ❖ Beneficial insects. 215-674-1793.

Cape Cod Worm Farm, 30 Center Ave., Buzzards Bay, MA 02532: Free information ❖ Red worms for soil improvement and composting. 508-759-5664.

John Dromgoode's Natural Gardener's Catalog, 8648 Old Bee Caves Rd., Austin, TX 78735: Free catalog ❖ Organic fertilizers, growth stimulants, composting equipment, books on organic gardening, tools, pest controls, and pet products. 800-320-0724.

Farmer Seed & Nursery Company, 818 NW 4th St., Faribault, MN 55021: Free catalog ❖ Beneficial organisms. 507-334-1623.

Henry Field's Seed & Nursery, 415 N. Burnett, Shenandoah, IA 51602: Free catalog ❖ Beneficial organisms. 605-665-4491.

Garden-Ville, 8648 Old Bee Caves Rd., Austin, TX 78735: Free catalog ❖ Organic gardening supplies, beneficial insects, pest controls, and tools. 800-320-0724.

Gardener's Supply Company, 128 Intervale Rd., Burlington, VT 05401: Free catalog ❖ Beneficial insects. 800-863-1700.

Gardens Alive, 5100 Schenley Pl., Lawrenceburg, IN 47025: Free catalog ❖ Beneficial insects and organisms. 812-537-8650.

The Green Spot Ltd., 93 Priest Rd., Barrington, NH 03825: Catalog $4 ❖ Beneficial insects and other pest control agents. 603-942-8925.

Harmony Farm Supply & Nursery, P.O. Box 460, Graton, CA 95444: Catalog $2 (refundable) ❖ Beneficial insects. 707-823-9125.

IPM Laboratories, P.O. Box 300, Locke, NY 13092: Free catalog ❖ Beneficial insects. 315-497-2063.

M & R Durango Inc., P.O. Box 886, Bayfield, CO 81122: Free catalog ❖ Beneficial insects. 800-526-4075; 303-259-3521 (in CO).

Mellinger's, 2310 W. South Range Rd., North Lima, OH 44452: Free catalog ❖ Beneficial organisms. 330-549-9861.

Natural Gardening Company, 217 San Anselmo Ave., San Anselmo, CA 94960: Free catalog ❖ Beneficial insects, organic gardening supplies, pest controls, drip irrigation equipment, and wildflower seeds. 707-766-9303.

Nature's Control, P.O. Box 35, Medford, OR 97501: Free catalog ❖ Beneficial insects and organisms. 503-899-8318.

Necessary Trading Company, One Natures Way, New Castle, VA 24127: Free catalog ❖ Beneficial insects. 800-447-5354.

Orcon, P.O. Box 781147R, Los Angeles, CA 90016: Free list of retail sources ❖ Packaged natural pest controls, live insects, and earth worm castings.

Peaceful Valley Farm Supply, P.O. Box 2209, Grass Valley, CA 95945: Catalog $2 (refundable) ❖ Beneficial organisms. 916-272-4769.

Rincon-Vitova Insectaries Inc., P.O. Box 1555, Ventura, CA 93002: Free catalog ❖ Beneficial insects. 800-643-5407.

Season Extenders, 971 Nichols Ave., Stratford, CT 06497: Free catalog ❖ Propagation supplies, pots and baskets, lights, greenhouses, pest control and hydroponic growing aids, fertilizers, and tools. 203-375-1317.

Territorial Seed Company, P.O. Box 157, Cottage Grove, OR 97424: Free catalog ❖ Organic fertilizers, natural insecticides, biological pest controls, and vegetable, herb, and flower seeds. 503-942-9547.

Unique Insect Control, 5504 Sperry Dr., Citrus Heights, CA 95621: Free brochure ❖ Beneficial insects. 916-961-7945.

Carts

Ames Lawn & Garden Tools, P.O. Box 1774, Parkersburg, WV 26102: Free information ❖ Easy-to-roll lawn cart. 800-624-2654.

BCS America, P.O. Box 7162, Charlotte, NC 28241: Free catalog ❖ Garden carts, chippers and shredders, tillers, sprayers, mowers, and tractors. 800-227-8791.

Carts Vermont, 1890 Airport Pkwy., South Burlington, VT 05403: Free information ❖ Garden carts. 800-732-7417.

Country Manufacturing, P.O. Box 104, Fredericktown, OH 43019: Free catalog ❖ Quick-dump carts, lawn brooms, pressure sprayers, turf spreaders, wagons, and trailers. 614-694-9926.

Garden Way, 9th Ave. & 102nd St., Troy, NY 12180: Free information ❖ Carts, tillers, clippers, sickle bar mowers, garden composters, and other equipment. 800-828-5500.

Gardener's Supply Company, 128 Intervale Rd., Burlington, VT 05401: Free catalog ❖ Garden carts, composters, sprayers, watering systems, weeding and cultivating tools, organic fertilizers and chemical preparations, leaf mulchers, and canning and preserving supplies. 800-863-1700.

Homestead Carts, 2396 Perkins St. NE, Salem, OR 97303: Free brochure ❖ Garden carts and composters. 800-825-1925; 503-393-3973 (in OR).

Norway Industries, 26 E. 9237 Hwy. O, Sauk City, WI 53583: Free brochure ❖ Garden carts. 608-544-5000.

True Engineering Inc., 999 Roosevelt Trail, Windham, ME 04962: Free list of retail sources ❖ Utility garden cart with snap-out container. 207-892-0200.

WheelAround Corporation, 241 Grandview Ave., Bellevue, KY 41073: Free brochure ❖ Lawn and garden cart. 800-335-CART.

Chippers & Shredders

Amerind MacKissic Inc., P.O. Box 111, Parker Ford, PA 19457: Free information ❖ Gasoline-operated chipper-shredder. 610-495-7181.

Crary Bear Cat, P.O. Box 849, West Fargo, ND 58078: Free list of retail sources ❖ Chippers, chipper-shredders, and stump grinders. 701-282-5520.

Flowtron Outdoor Products, 2 Main St., Melrose, MA 02176: Free information ❖ Electric chipper-shredder. 617-321-2300.

Garden Way, 9th Ave. & 102nd St., Troy, NY 12180: Free information ❖ Compact chipper-shredder. 800-828-5500.

Gardener's Supply Company, 128 Intervale Rd., Burlington, VT 05401: Free catalog ❖ Gasoline-powered chipper-shredder. 800-863-1700.

The Kinsman Company, River Rd., Point Pleasant, PA 18950: Free catalog ❖ Electric chipper-shredder. 800-733-4146.

Mantis Manufacturing Company, 1028 Street Rd., Southampton, PA 18966: Free information ❖ Gasoline and electric-powered chipper-shredders. 800-366-6268.

Mighty Mac, Mackissic Inc., P.O. Box 111, Parker Ford, PA 19457: Free information ❖ Chippers, tillers, blowers, and sprayers. 610-495-7181.

The Patriot Company, 944 N. 45th St., Milwaukee, WI 53208: Free information ❖ Compact chipper-shredder vacuum. 800-798-CHIP.

Snapper Power Equipment, P.O. Box 777, McDonough, GA 30253: Free list of retail sources ❖ Shredder. 404-954-2500.

White Outdoor Products Company, P.O. Box 361131, Cleveland, OH 44136: Free list of retail sources ❖ Gasoline-powered chipper-shredder.

Farm Equipment & Supplies

Sutton AG Enterprises Inc., 746 Vertin Ave., Salinas, CA 93901: Free brochure ❖ Seed planters, measuring devices, field supplies, and bird control products. 408-422-9693.

Fertilizers & Plant Food

Bozeman Bio-Tech, P.O. Box 3146, 1612 Gold Ave., Bozeman, MT 59772: Free catalog ❖ Organic fertilizers, weed and plant disease control aids, and pesticides. 800-289-6656.

John Dromgoode's Natural Gardener's Catalog, 8648 Old Bee Caves Rd., Austin, TX 78735: Free catalog ❖ Organic fertilizers, growth stimulants, composting equipment, books on organic gardening, tools, pest controls, and pet products. 800-320-0724.

Garden-Ville, 8648 Old Bee Caves Rd., Austin, TX 78735: Free catalog ❖ Organic gardening supplies, beneficial insects, pest controls, and tools. 800-320-0724.

Garden City Seeds, 778 Hwy. 93 North, Hamilton, MT 59840: Free catalog ❖ Fertilizers. 406-961-4837.

Gardener's Supply Company, 128 Intervale Rd., Burlington, VT 05401: Free catalog ❖ Garden carts, composters, sprayers, watering systems, weeding and cultivating tools, organic fertilizers and chemical preparations, leaf mulchers, and canning and preserving supplies. 800-863-1700.

Harmony Farm Supply & Nursery, P.O. Box 460, Graton, CA 95444: Catalog $2 (refundable) ❖ Organic fertilizers. 707-823-9125.

Ohio Earth Food, 5488 Swamp St. SE, Hartville, OH 44362: Free information ❖ Organic fertilizers and natural farming and gardening products. 216-877-9356.

Ringer, 9959 Valley View Rd., Eden Prairie, MN 55344: Free catalog ❖ Chemical treatments and fertilizers, tools, growing and propagation aids, and pest control preparations. 800-654-1047.

Rush Industries Inc., 75 Albertson Ave., Albertson, NY 11507: Free information ❖ Plant growth hormone.

Season Extenders, 971 Nichols Ave., Stratford, CT 06497: Free catalog ❖ Propagation supplies, pots and baskets, lights, greenhouses, pest control and hydroponic growing aids, fertilizers, and tools. 203-375-1317.

Territorial Seed Company, P.O. Box 157, Cottage Grove, OR 97424: Free catalog ❖ Organic fertilizers, natural insecticides, biological pest controls, and vegetable, herb, and flower seeds. 503-942-9547.

Greenhouses

Cascade Greenhouse Supply, 4441 26th Ave. West, Seattle, WA 98199: Free catalog ❖ Hobby greenhouses and fans, heaters, misting, other equipment, and supplies. 800-353-0264.

Creative Structures, 1765 Walnut Ln., Quakerstown, PA 18951: Catalog $1 ❖ Sun room and greenhouse kits. 215-538-2426.

Cropking Inc., 5050 Greenwich Rd., Seville, OH 44273: Catalog $3 ❖ Greenhouses. 800-321-5656.

Dixie Greenhouse Manufacturing Company, Rt. 1, Box 558, Alapaha, GA 31622: Free information ❖ Build-it-yourself greenhouse kits. 800-346-9902; 912-532-4600 (in GA).

Elite Greenhouses Ltd., P.O. Box 22960, Rochester, NY 14962: Free information ❖ Aluminum frame greenhouses. 800-514-4441.

Farm Wholesale Inc., 2396 Perkins St. NE, Salem, OR 97303: Free catalog ❖ Easy-to-assemble greenhouses. 800-825-1925.

Florian Greenhouse, 64 Airport Rd., West Milford, NJ 07480: Information $3 ❖ Greenhouses. 800-FLORIAN.

Florist Products Inc., 570 Rock Rd., Unit E, East Dundee, IL 60118: Catalog $3 ❖ Greenhouse equipment and supplies. 800-828-2242.

Four Seasons Solar Products, 5005 Veterans Memorial Hwy., Holbrook, NY 11741: Free information ❖ Greenhouses. 800-368-7732.

Gardener's Supply Company, 128 Intervale Rd., Burlington, VT 05401: Free catalog ❖ Greenhouses. 800-863-1700.

GardenStyles, P.O. Box 50670, Minneapolis, MN 55405: Free brochure ❖ Greenhouses. 800-356-8890.

Gothic Arch Greenhouses, P.O. Box 1564, Mobile, AL 36633: Free brochure ❖ Redwood fiberglass greenhouse kits. 800-628-4974.

GreenTech, 1201 Minters Chapel Rd., Building A-1, Grapevine, TX 76051: Free information ❖ Indoor greenhouses. 800-844-3665.

Grow-It Instant Greenhouses, P.O. Box 26037, West Haven CT 06515: Free brochure ❖ Greenhouse kits. 800-932-9344.

Jacobs Greenhouse Manufacturing, 371 Talbot Rd., Delhi, Ontario, Canada N4B 2A1: Catalog $2 ❖ Greenhouses with tempered glass and automatic roof vents. 519-582-2880.

Janco Greenhouses, 9390 Davis Ave., Laurel, MD 20707: Brochure $5 ❖ Greenhouses. 800-323-6933.

Lindal Cedar Homes, P.O. Box 24426, Seattle, WA 98124: Catalog $15 ❖ Greenhouses and sun rooms. 800-426-0536.

Mellinger's, 2310 W. South Range Rd., North Lima, OH 44452: Free catalog ❖ Greenhouses for the backyard gardener and commercial grower. 330-549-9861.

National Greenhouse Company, P.O. Box 100, Pana, IL 62557: Free catalog ❖ Greenhouses. 800-826-9314; 217-562-9333 (in IL).

Powell & Powell Supply Company, 1206 Broad St., Fuquay-Varina, NC 27526: Free brochure ❖ Greenhouses. 919-552-9708.

Private Garden Greenhouses, 10 Allen St., Box 403, Hampden, MA 01036: Free brochure ❖ Greenhouses. 800-287-4769; 413-566-0277 (in MA).

Progressive Building Products, 1678 Shattuck Ave., Ste. 173, Berkeley, CA 94709: Catalog $5.95 ❖ Greenhouse and solarium components. 800-776-2534.

Rain or Shine, 13126 NE Airport Way, Portland, OR 97230: Free catalog ❖ Hobby greenhouses and supplies. 800-248-1981.

Santa Barbara Greenhouses, 721 Richmond Ave., Oxnard, CA 93030: Free catalog ❖ Redwood greenhouses. 800-544-5276.

Season Extenders, 971 Nichols Ave., Stratford, CT 06497: Free catalog ❖ Propagation supplies, pots and baskets, lights, greenhouses, pest control and hydroponic growing aids, fertilizers, and tools. 203-375-1317.

Senco Inc., 520 8th St., Gwinn, MI 49841: Free information ❖ Recreational shelters, portable hunting blinds and ice fishing houses, and greenhouses. 906-346-4116.

Shelter Systems, P.O. Box 1294, Capitola, CA 95010: Catalog $1 ❖ Easy-to-setup portable domes and greenhouses. 415-323-6202.

Simpson Strong-Tie Company Inc., Box 10789, Pleasanton, CA 94588: Free list of retail sources ❖ Easy-to-assemble greenhouse kits. 800-937-7922.

Solar Components Corporation, 121 Valley St., Manchester, NH 03103: Brochure $1 ❖ Lean-to and free-standing build-it-yourself greenhouse kits and solar energy equipment. 603-668-8186.

Southeastern Insulated Glass, 6477-B Peachtree Industrial Blvd., Atlanta, GA 30360: Free information ❖ Greenhouse and sun room kits, sliding glass doors, and skylights. 800-841-9842; 404-455-8838 (in GA).

GARDENING EQUIPMENT & SUPPLIES

Sturdi-Built Manufacturing Company, 11304 SW Boones Ferry Rd., Portland, OR 97219: Free catalog ❖ Greenhouses, cold frames, and sun rooms. 503-244-4100.

Sun 'N Rain Greenhouses, 45 Dixon Ave., Amityville, NY 11701: Free information ❖ Easy-to-assemble greenhouses. 800-999-9459.

Sundance Supply, 1678 Shattuck Ave., Ste. 173, Berkeley, CA 94709: Catalog $2 ❖ Building components for greenhouses, sun rooms, pool enclosures, and skylights. 800-776-2534.

Sun-Porch Structures, P.O. Box 1353, Stamford, CT 06904: Catalog $2 ❖ Solar greenhouses. 203-324-0010.

Sundome Greenhouses, 42125 Blackhawk Plaza Circle, Danville, CA 94506: Free brochure ❖ Portable greenhouses. 800-252-5346.

Sunglo Solar Greenhouses, 4441 26th Ave. West, Seattle, WA 98199: Free brochure ❖ Solar greenhouses and solariums. 800-647-0606; 206-284-8900 (in WA).

Sunroom Company, P.O. Box 301, Leola, PA 17540: Free information ❖ Window and free-standing greenhouses and solariums. 800-426-2737.

Sunspot Inc., 5030 40th Ave., Hudsonville, MI 49426: Free information ❖ Solariums, greenhouses, and conservatories. 800-635-4786.

Texas Greenhouse Company, 2524 White Settlement Rd., Fort Worth, TX 76107: Catalog $4 ❖ Greenhouse kits. 800-227-5447.

Troy-Bilt Manufacturing Company, 9th Ave & 102nd St., Troy, NY 12180: Free information ❖ Greenhouses. 800-828-5500.

Turner Greenhouses, P.O. Box 1260, Goldsboro, NC 27533: Free catalog ❖ Free-standing and lean-to greenhouses. 800-672-4770.

Under Glass Manufacturing Corporation, P.O. Box 323, Wappingers Falls, NY 12590: Catalog $3 ❖ Indoor window greenhouses, other greenhouses, and solariums. 914-298-0645.

Hydroponic Gardening Supplies

Albuquerque Hydroponics & Lighting, 5030 Southern Ave. SE, Albuquerque, NM 87108: Free catalog ❖ Hydroponic supplies and lighting equipment. 505-255-3677.

Alternative Garden Supply Inc., P.O. Box 662, Cary, IL 60113: Free catalog ❖ Hydroponic supplies. 800-444-2837.

American Agriculture, 9220 SE Stark, Portland, OR 97216: Free catalog ❖ Hydroponic fertilizers, lighting controls, and accessories. 800-433-6805.

American Hydroponics, 286 South G St., Arcata, CA 95521: Free brochure ❖ Hydroponic supplies and kits for beginners. 800-458-6543.

Applied Hydroponics, 3135 Kerner Blvd., San Rafael, CA 94901: Free catalog ❖ Hydroponic equipment. 800-634-9999; 415-459-7898 (in CA).

Aqua Culture Inc., 700 1st St., Tempe, AZ 85281: Free catalog ❖ Hydroponic systems, lights, and plant food. 800-633-2137.

Aqua-Ponics International, 121 North Harbor Blvd., Fullerton, CA 92632: Free catalog ❖ Hydroponic supplies. 800-426-1261.

Bloomington Wholesale Garden Supply, 3151 S. Hwy. 446, Bloomington, IN 47401: Free information ❖ Hydroponic systems, growing supplies, equipment, and books. 800-274-9676.

Brew & Grow, 1824 N. Besly Ct., Chicago, IL 60622: Free information ❖ Home brewing supplies for making beer. Also hydroponic gardening equipment. 312-395-1500.

Cropking Inc., 5050 Greenwich Rd., Seville, OH 44273: Catalog $3 ❖ Hydroponic supplies. 800-321-5656.

Diamond Lights, 628 Lindaro St., San Rafael, CA 94901: Free catalog ❖ Hydroponic nutrients and supplies. Also horticultural lighting. 800-331-3994.

Discount Garden Supply Inc., 14109 E. Sprague, Spokane, WA 99216: Free catalog ❖ Hydroponic systems, lights, nutrients and fertilizers, and propagation aids. 509-924-8333.

East Coast Hydroponics, 439 Castleton Ave., Staten Island, NY 10301: Free catalog ❖ Hydroponic and outdoor gardening supplies. 718-727-9300.

Eco Enterprises, 1240 NE 175th St., Seattle, WA 98155: Free catalog ❖ Hydroponic equipment. 800-426-6937.

FMCI Hydroponics, 480 Guelph Kined, Burlington, Ontario, Canada L7R 3M1: Free information ❖ Hydroponic lighting and growing systems. 905-333-3282.

Foothill Hydroponics, 10705 Burbank Blvd., North Hollywood, CA 91601: Free catalog ❖ Nutrients, grow-lights, climate control and test and irrigation equipment, rock wool, and other supplies. 818-760-0688.

Frank's Magic Crops, 2402 Edith Ave., Burlington, Ontario, Canada L7R 1N8: Free information ❖ Hydroponic systems. 416-333-3282.

Gold Coast Greenhouse, 7390 Bird Rd., Miami, FL 33155: Free information ❖ Hydroponic supplies and lighting equipment. 800-780-6805.

Green Fire, 347 Nord Ave., Chico, CA 95926: Free brochure ❖ Natural liquid fertilizers and hydroponic equipment. 916-895-8301.

Green Gardens, 12748 Bel Red Rd., Bellevue, WA 98005: Free catalog ❖ Hydroponic and indoor garden supplies. 800-217-1233.

Green Grower Supply, P.O. Box 3168, Framingham, MA 01701: Free information ❖ Light fixtures.

The Growing Experience, 1901 NW 18th St., Building E, Pompano Beach, FL 33069: Free information ❖ Hydroponic supplies and equipment. 800-273-6092; 305-960-0822 (in FL).

Mrs. Greenjeans Hydroponic & Garden Supplies, 5020 S. Federal, Englewood, CO 80110: Free catalog ❖ Hydroponic and garden supplies. 303-738-0202.

Halide of Oregon, 9220 SE Stark, Portland, OR 97216: Free information ❖ Hydroponic systems. 800-433-6805; 503-256-2400 (in OR).

Hamilton Technology Corporation, 14902 S. Figueroa St., Gardena, CA 90248: Free catalog ❖ Lights, hydroponic systems, and gardening supplies. 800-447-9797.

Harvest Moon Hydroponics Inc., Airport Plaza, 4214 Union Rd., Cheektowaga, NY 14225: Free catalog ❖ Hydroponic supplies. 800-635-1383.

Heartland Hydroponics, Vernon Plaza, 115 Townline Rd., Vernon Hills, IL 60061: Free catalog ❖ Hydroponic supplies. 800-354-GROW.

Hydrofarm, 3135 Kerner Blvd., San Rafael, CA 94901: Free catalog and list of retail sources ❖ Lights and hydroponic supplies. 800-634-9999.

Higher Yield, 29211 NE Wylie Rd., Camas, WA 98607: Free catalog ❖ Lights, growing equipment, and supplies. 800-451-1952; 360-834-6962 (in WA).

Light Manufacturing Company, 1634 SE Brooklyn, Portland, OR 97202: Free catalog ❖ Hydroponic systems, lights, and nutrient controls. 800-NOW-LITE.

Light Source, P.O. Box 38, Carlsbad, CA 92018: Free information ❖ Horticultural light sources. 800-889-9009; 619-598-6487 (in CA).

MAH Nursery, 115 Commerce Dr., Hauppage, NY 11788: Free information ❖ Hydroponic equipment. 516-434-6872.

New Earth Inc., 9810 Taylorsville Rd., Louisville, KY 40299: Free catalog ❖ Hydroponic and outdoor gardening supplies. 800-462-5953; 502-261-0005 (in KY).

222 ❖ GARDENING EQUIPMENT & SUPPLIES ❖

Season Extenders, 971 Nichols Ave., Stratford, CT 06497: Free catalog ❖ Propagation supplies, pots and baskets, lights, greenhouses, pest control and hydroponic growing aids, fertilizers, and tools. 203-375-1317.

SHIVA Environmental Systems, 26 Fitzwilliam Rd., Jaffrey, NH 03452: Free information ❖ All-in-one indoor climate controller for temperature, humidity, and carbon dioxide. 800-507-8587.

Superior Growers Supply, 4870 Dawn Ave., East Lansing, MI 48823: Free catalog ❖ Hydroponic supplies. 800-227-0027.

Virginia Hydroponics, 368 Newtown Rd., Ste. 105, Virginia Beach, VA 23462: Free information ❖ Hydroponic supplies. 800-490-5425.

Wilder Agriculture Products Company Inc., 4188 Bethel New Wilmington Rd., New Wilmington, PA 16142: Free catalog ❖ Hydroponic nutrients for cloning, seed modification, and tissue culture preparation. 800-462-8102.

Worm's Way, 3151 South Hwy. 446, Bloomington, IN 47401: Free catalog ❖ Hydroponic and organic gardening supplies. 800-274-9676.

Indoor Gardening Supplies

Alternative Garden Supply Inc., P.O. Box 662, Cary, IL 60113: Free catalog ❖ Indoor lighting systems, growing kits, and biological pest controls. 800-444-2837.

Floralight, 6-620 Supertest Rd., North York, Ontario, Canada M3J 2M5: Free information ❖ Indoor lights and garden supplies. 416-665-4000.

Florist Products Inc., 570 Rock Rd., Unit E, East Dundee, IL 60118: Catalog $3 ❖ Greenhouse equipment and supplies. 800-828-2242.

Indoor Gardening Supplies, P.O. Box 40567, Detroit, MI 48240: Free catalog ❖ Indoor gardening supplies, stands, lights, and books. 313-426-9080.

Plant Collectibles, 103 Kenview Ave., Buffalo, NY 14217: Free catalog with two 1st class stamps ❖ Garden and greenhouse supplies and light stands. 716-875-1221.

Landscaping Stone

Allan Block, 7400 Metro Blvd., Ste. 185, Edina, MN 55435: Free list of retail sources ❖ Mortar-less concrete blocks for retaining walls, curves, corners, stairways, and terraces. 800-899-5309; 612-835-5309 (in MN).

Eurocobble, 4265 Lemp Ave., Studio City, CA 91604: Free information ❖ Cobblestone in modules and single sets. 213-877-5012.

Stone Company Inc., W4520 Lime Rd., Eden, WI 53019: Free information ❖ Natural building and landscaping cobblers, granite boulders, and stone for building walls, steppers, and flagstone walks. 414-477-2521.

Urdl's Waterfall Creations Inc., 2010 NW 1st St., Delray Beach, FL 33445: Free information ❖ Manufactured hollow concrete rocks for landscaping and waterfall settings. 407-278-3320.

Lawn Ornaments & Statues

Anderson Design, P.O. Box 4057, Bellingham, WA 98227: Brochure $2 (refundable) ❖ Hand-built arbors and trellises. 800-947-7697.

Architectural Brick Paving Ltd., 1187 Wilmette Ave., Wilmette, IL 60091: Free information ❖ Handmade copper trellises with adaptations from antiquity to Renaissance styles. 708-256-8432.

Armchair Shopper, P.O. Box 419464, Kansas City, MO 64141: Free catalog ❖ Classic old world-style sundials, wind chimes, and lawn ornaments. 816-767-3200.

Ballard Designs, 1670 DeFoor Ave. NE, Atlanta, GA 30318: Catalog $3 ❖ Castings for indoor and outdoor settings, furniture, lamps, fireplace accessories, pillows, and art prints. 800-367-2810.

The BB Brass, 10151 Pacific Mesa Blvd., San Diego, CA 92121: Free catalog ❖ Brass fountains and sculptures. 800-536-0987.

BowBends, P.O. Box 900, Bolton, MA 01740: Catalog $3 ❖ Arbors, bridges, gazebos, and other garden structures. 800-518-6471.

Carruth Studio Inc., 1178 Farnsworth Rd., Waterville, OH 43566: Free catalog ❖ Hand-cast limestone garden art. 800-225-1178.

Robert Compton Ltd., RD 3, Box 3600, Bristol, VT 05443: Brochure $2 ❖ Stone fountains and water sculptures. 802-453-3778.

Continental Bridge, Rt. 5, Box 178, Alexandria, MN 56308: Free information ❖ Pre-fabricated bridges for garden settings. 800-328-2047.

Country Casual, 17317 Germantown Rd., Germantown, MD 20874: Catalog $5 ❖ Garden furnishings. 301-540-0040.

Cross Vinyl Lattice, 3174 Marjan Dr., Atlanta, GA 30340: Free information ❖ Trellises, arbors, and fencing. 800-521-9878.

Design Toscano, 17 E. Campbell St., Arlington Heights, IL 60005: Catalog $5 ❖ Historical garden sculptures. 800-525-1733.

English Arbor Company, 2509 Thousand Oaks Blvd., Thousand Oaks, CA 91362: Free information ❖ Wooden arbors, trellises, benches, and storage sheds. 805-379-3873.

Excel Bridge Manufacturer, 12001 Shoemaker Ave., Santa Fe Springs, CA 90670: Free information ❖ Easy-to-install pre-fabricated bridges. 800-548-0054; 310-944-0701 (in CA).

Flora Fauna, P.O. Box 578, Gualala, CA 95445: Free information ❖ Lattice panels, columns, arches, and sundials. 800-358-9120.

Florentine Craftsmen, 46-24 28th St., Long Island City, NY 11101: Catalog $5 ❖ Sculptures, fountains, birdbaths, and furniture. 718-937-7632.

FrenchWyres, P.O. Box 131655, Tyler, TX 75713: Catalog $3 ❖ Trellises, topiary frames, urns, plant stands, cache pots, window boxes, and arches. 903-597-8322.

Garden Accents, 4 Union Hill Rd., West Conshohocken, PA 19428: Video catalog $15 ❖ Antique and contemporary garden sculptures and ornaments. 610-825-5525.

Garden Architecture, 719 S. 17th St., Philadelphia, PA 19146: Free catalog ❖ Easy-to-assemble trellis structures. 215-545-5442.

Garden Concepts Collection, P.O. Box 241233, Memphis, TN 38124: Catalog $5 ❖ Handcrafted furniture and trellises. 901-756-1649.

The Garden Gate, 5122 Morningside Dr., Houston, TX 77005: Catalog $10 ❖ Imported classical English cast-stone statuary. 800-861-8141; 713-528-2654 (in TX).

Garden Highlights, P.O. Box 8, Cozad, NE 69130: Free catalog ❖ Polyvinyl garden and landscaping accessories. 800-691-6221.

Garden Ornaments Stone, P.O. Box 1451, Roswell, GA 30077: Catalog $10 ❖ Statues, mantlepieces, fountains, benches, tables, and ornamentals. 404-475-2127.

Garden Tools of Maine, RR 2, Box 2208, East Holden, ME 04429: Free information ❖ Trellises, obelisks, supports, planters, arches, and gazebos. 207-843-6271.

Gingerbread Man Woodworks, Factory Outlet Store, P.O. Box 59, Noel, MO 64854: Catalog $5 ❖ Gazebos, garden structures, and ornamental trim. 417-775-2553.

Good Catalog Company, 5456 SE International Way, Portland, OR 97222: Free catalog ❖ Kitchen, dining, gardening, and decorative accessories. 800-225-3870.

Haddonstone (USA) Ltd., 201 Heller Pl., Bellmawr, NJ 08031: Catalog $10 ❖ English garden ornaments and architectural stonework. 609-931-7011.

Hen-Feathers & Company Inc., 250 King Manor Dr., King of Prussia, PA 19406: Free catalog ❖ Hand-cast architectural and garden accents. 800-282-1910.

Irontiques, P.O. Box 268, LeRoy, NY 14482: Free brochure ❖ Wrought-iron garden and lawn accessories. 716-768-8159.

Ironwood, 3435 Junction Rd., Egg Harbor, WI 54209: Free catalog ❖ Handcrafted metal items and original sculptures. 800-823-4769.

GARDENING EQUIPMENT & SUPPLIES

Island Arbors, 732 Sunrise Hwy., West Babylon, NY 11704: Free information ❖ Arbors. 516-669-3886.

Kestrel Manufacturing, P.O. Box 12, Saint Peters, PA 19470: Information $2 ❖ American and English garden accessories. 610-469-6370.

Kramer Brothers, P.O. Box 255, Dayton, OH 45404: Free catalog ❖ Garden furniture and ornaments. 513-228-4194.

Lazy Hill Farm Designs, P.O. Box 197, Charlotte, NC 28204: Free information ❖ Handcrafted garden accessories and bird houses. 800-396-7706.

Legendary Lighting by Copper Sculptures, 1016 N. Flowood Dr., Jackson, MS 39208: Free brochure ❖ Handcrafted gas lanterns and architectural accent pieces. 601-936-4200.

Machin Designs by Amdega, P.O. Box 7, Glenview, IL 60025: Catalog $10 ❖ English-style conservatories constructed in either western red cedar or aluminum. Also garden ornaments. 800-922-0110.

Mister Boardwalk, P.O. Box 789, Pt. Pleasant, NJ 08742: Free information ❖ Do-it-yourself wood walkway kits. 908-341-4800.

Nebraska Plastics Inc., P.O. Box 45, Cozad, NE 69130: Free information ❖ Rose trellises, garden arbors, picnic tables, outdoor furniture, and accessories. 800-445-2887.

New England Garden Ornaments, P.O. Box 235, North Brookfield, MA 01535: Free catalog ❖ Garden ornaments and furniture. 508-867-4474.

OuterSpace Landscape Furnishings Inc., 7533 Draper Ave., La Jolla, CA 92037: Free information ❖ Steel fences, gates, and modular components for trellises and garden structures. 800-338-2499.

Park Place, 2251 Wisconsin Ave. NW, Washington, DC 20007: Catalog $2 ❖ Classic outdoor furnishings and architectural products. 202-342-6294.

Pompeian Studios, 90 Rockledge Rd., Bronxville, NY 10708: Catalog $10 ❖ Original sculptures, ornaments, and forged furniture for patios and gardens. 800-457-5595.

Gary Price Studio, 1307 E. 1200 South, Springville, UT 84663: Free information with long SASE ❖ Garden sculptures. 801-489-6852.

Rivertown Products, 3812 River Rd., P.O. Box 5174, St. Joseph, MO 64505: Brochure $1 ❖ Handcrafted arbors and outdoor products. 816-232-8822.

Sculpture Placement Ltd., P.O. Box 9709, Washington, DC 20016: Free catalog ❖ Bronze life-size sculptures. 202-362-9310.

Southerlands for Leisure Living, 10 Biltmore Ave., Asheville, NC 28801: Free catalog ❖ Outdoor furniture and garden accessories. 800-968-5596.

Southern Statuary & Stone, 901 33rd St. North, Birmingham, AL 35222: Catalog $5 ❖ Stone castings for garden landscaping. 205-322-0379.

Stickney's Garden Houses, One Thompson Square, P.O. Box 34, Boston, MA 02129: Catalog $3 ❖ Handcrafted garden houses with optional seats. 617-242-1711.

Stone Forest, P.O. Box 2840, Santa Fe, NM 87504: Catalog $3 ❖ Fountains, lanterns, water basins, birdbaths, pedestals, and hand-carved granite statuary. 505-986-8883.

Strassacker Bronze America Inc., P.O. Box 931, Spartanburg, SC 29304: Catalog $15 ❖ Contemporary and abstract bronze sculptures, fountains, and lighting equipment. 803-573-7438.

Sun Garden Specialties, P.O. Box 52382, Tulsa, OK 74152: Free information ❖ Wooden landscaping items for gardens. 800-468-1638.

Sun Source Inc., P.O. Box 4191A, Metuchen, NJ 08840: Catalog $2 (refundable) ❖ Modular fan trellises and arbor systems.

Tejas Fountain Designs, 517 Barfknecht Ln., Lewisville, TX 75056: Brochure $3 ❖ Wall fountains, bird feeders, and decorative accessories.

Tom Torrens Sculpture Design Inc., P.O. Box 1819, Gig Harbor, WA 98335: Catalog $2 ❖ Sculptures, fountains, birdbaths, and other accessories for the home and garden. 206-857-5831.

Toscano Design, 17 E. Campbell St., Arlington Heights, IL 60005: Catalog $5 ❖ Hand-cast replica artifacts and sculptures. 800-525-1733.

Trellis Structures, P.O. Box 380, Beverly, MA 01915: Catalog $2 ❖ Trellis sculptures and furniture. 508-921-1235.

Unit Structures, 5724 McCrimmon Pkwy., Morrisville, NC 27560: Free information ❖ Easy-to-assemble prefabricated pedestrian and vehicular shelters and bridges. 800-777-UNIT.

Uwchlan Farm, 303 Greenridge Rd., Glenmoore, PA 19343: Free catalog ❖ Wrought-iron accessories for the home and garden. 800-900-IRON.

Samuel Welch Sculpture Inc., P.O. Box 55, Cincinnati, OH 45201: Catalog $10 ❖ Large-scale sculptures in bronze, aluminum, steel, concrete, marble, and granite. 513-321-8882.

Wind & Weather, P.O. Box 2320, Mendocino, CA 95460: Free catalog ❖ Garden ornaments. 707-964-1284.

Zachariasen Studio, N659 Drumm Rd., Denmark, WI 54208: Catalog $3 ❖ Handmade ceramic birdbaths, fountains, and garden ornaments. 414-776-1778.

Markers

Beason Engraving, 731 Springhill Ave., Spartanburg, SC 29303: Free information ❖ Weather and rust resistant custom-engraved plant markers. 803-583-8913.

Eon Industries, P.O. Box 11, Liberty Center, OH 43532: Free brochure ❖ Metal flower and garden markers.

Evergreen Garden Plant Labels, P.O. Box 922, Cloverdale, CA 95425: Free brochure with first class stamp ❖ Engraved name plates, metal plant markers, and holders.

Frog Pond Nursery, 873 E. Baltimore Pike, Kennett Square, PA 19348: Free brochure with long SASE ❖ Stoneware herb garden markers.

Herb N' Ewe, 11755 National Rd. SE, Thornville, OH 43076: Catalog $1 ❖ Copper garden markers. 614-323-2264.

Paw Paw Everlast Label Company, P.O. Box 93, Paw Paw, MI 49079: Free information with long SASE ❖ Permanent metal garden labels.

Mowers, Trimmers & Blowers

Agri-Fab Inc., 303 W. Raymond St., Sullivan, IL 61951: Free list of retail sources ❖ Walk-behind mowers. Also spreaders, sprayers, rollers, and other equipment. 217-728-8388.

American Lawn Mower Company, P.O. Box 369, Shelbyville, IN 46176: Free information ❖ Push-type lawn mowers. 800-633-1501.

Ariens Company, 655 W. Ryan St., P.O. Box 157, Brillion, WI 54110: Free information ❖ Self-propelled and riding mowers with electric start engines. 414-756-2141.

BCS America, P.O. Box 7162, Charlotte, NC 28241: Free catalog ❖ Garden carts, chippers and shredders, tillers, sprayers, lawn and garden tractors, and mowers. 800-227-8791.

Black & Decker Garden Tools, Consumer Services, P.O. Box 618, Hampstead, MD 21074: Free information ❖ Portable vacuums and blowers in gasoline-powered and cordless electric models. Also electric hedge trimmers and lawn mowers. 800-762-6672.

Country Home Products, Meigs Rd., Box 25, Vergennes, VT 05491: Free information ❖ Power trimmer on wheels. 800-635-4848.

Dixon Industries Inc., P.O. Box 1569, Coffeyville, KS 67337: Free information ❖ Riding mowers. 316-251-2000.

Echo Inc., 400 Oakwood Rd., Lake Zurich, IL 60047: Free catalog ❖ Trimmers, blowers, hedge clippers, sprayers, chain saws, and shredders. 800-432-3246.

Excel Industries Inc., P.O. Box 7000, Hesston, KS 67062: Free information ❖ Riding mowers that mow, shred, edge, and vacuum. 316-327-4911.

GARDENING EQUIPMENT & SUPPLIES

Garden Way, 9th Ave. & 102nd St., Troy, NY 12180: Free information ❖ Carts, tillers, clippers, sickle bar mowers, garden composter, and other equipment. 800-828-5500.

The Grasshopper Company, P.O. Box 637, Moundridge, KS 67107: Free list of retail sources ❖ Riding mowers. 316-345-8621.

Homelite Sales, Box 7047, Charlotte, NC 28273: Free information with long SASE ❖ Push and riding mowers, lawn tractors, electric and gasoline-operated trimmers, hedge trimmers, gasoline-powered blowers, vacuums, sprayers, cut-off saws, and snow removal equipment. 800-242-4672.

Husqvarna Power Products, Perimeter Woods Dr., Charlotte, NC 28216: Free information ❖ Walk-behind and riding mowers. 800-438-7297.

Kubota Tractor Corporation, 3401 Del Amo Blvd., Torrance, CA 90503: Free information ❖ Walk-behind mowers. 310-370-3370.

Lawn-Boy, Lyndale Ave. South, Bloomington, MN 55420: Free information ❖ Walk-behind and riding mowers, lawn and garden tractors, and power-operated tillers. 800-526-6937.

Mainline of North America, P.O. Box 526, London, OH 43140: Free information ❖ All-gear driven tiller with optional sickle bar and no belts or chains. Also hydraulic log splitters, carts, and snow throwers. 800-837-2097.

MTD Products Inc., P.O. Box 360900, Cleveland, OH 44136: Free information ❖ Walk-behind mowers with optional mulching and bagging attachments. 216-225-2600.

Poulan, 5020 Flournoy-Lucas Rd., Shrevesport, LA 71129: Free information ❖ Hand-held gasoline-powered blowers and lawn trimmers. 318-683-3546.

Ryobi America Corporation, P.O. Box 1207, Anderson, SC 29622: Free information ❖ Combination self-propelled mower and mulcher. 800-525-2579.

Simplicity Manufacturing Inc., P.O. Box 997, Port Washington, WI 53074: Free information ❖ Walk-behind and riding mowers. 800-945-0235.

Snapper Power Equipment, P.O. Box 777, McDonough, GA 30253: Free list of retail sources ❖ Walk-behind and riding mowers. 404-954-2500.

Toro Company, 8111 Lyndale Ave., Bloomington, MN 55420: Free information ❖ Riding trimmers. 800-321-8676.

Walker Manufacturing Company, 5925 E. Harmony Rd., Fort Collins, CO 80525: Free information ❖ Riding mowers with a vacuum collection system. 800-279-8537.

White Outdoor Products Company, P.O. Box 361131, Cleveland, OH 44136: Free list of retail sources ❖ Walk-behind and riding mowers.

Organic Gardening Supplies

Bountiful Gardens, 18001 Shafer Ranch Rd., Willits, CA 95490: Free catalog ❖ Seeds for vegetables, compost crops, herbs, and flowers. Also books and organic gardening supplies. 707-459-6410.

Brown's Edgewood Gardens, 2611 Corrine Dr., Orlando, FL 32803: Catalog $3 ❖ Butterfly-attracting plants, herbs, and organic gardening products. 407-896-3203.

John Dromgoode's Natural Gardener's Catalog, 8648 Old Bee Caves Rd., Austin, TX 78735: Free catalog ❖ Organic fertilizers, growth stimulants, composting equipment, books on organic gardening, tools, pest controls, and pet products. 800-320-0724.

Garden-Ville, 8648 Old Bee Caves Rd., Austin, TX 78735: Free catalog ❖ Organic gardening supplies, beneficial insects, pest controls, and tools. 800-320-0724.

Gardens Alive, 5100 Schenley Pl., Lawrenceburg, IN 47025: Free catalog ❖ Organic gardening supplies. 812-537-8650.

Green Earth Organics, c/o Soil Conditioning, P.O. Box 206, 90 W. 1st St., Zillah, WA 98953: Free information ❖ Environmentally-safe fertilizers and nutrients for grasses, shrubs, flowers, and vegetables. 509-829-5733.

Harmony Farm Supply & Nursery, P.O. Box 460, Graton, CA 95444: Catalog $2 (refundable) ❖ Organic fertilizers. 707-823-9125.

A High Country Garden, 2902 Rufina St., Santa Fe, NM 87501: Free catalog ❖ Organic gardening products and flowering plants. 800-925-9387.

Koos Inc., 4500 13th Ct., Kenosha, WI 53140: Free information ❖ Fertilizers, herbicides, insecticides, and organic plant foods. 800-558-5667; 414-654-5301 (in WI).

Natural Gardening Company, 217 San Anselmo Ave., San Anselmo, CA 94960: Free catalog ❖ Beneficial insects, organic gardening supplies, pest controls, drip irrigation equipment, and wildflower seeds. 707-766-9303.

Nitron Industries Inc., P.O. Box 1447, Fayetteville, AR 72702: Free catalog ❖ Organic fertilizers, enzyme soil conditioners, natural pest controls, and pet care products. 800-835-0123.

Peaceful Valley Farm Supply, P.O. Box 2209, Grass Valley, CA 95945: Catalog $2 (refundable) ❖ Organic gardening supplies. 916-272-4769.

Raintree Nursery, 391 Butts Rd., Morton, WA 98356: Free information ❖ Organic gardening supplies. 206-496-6400.

Season Extenders, 971 Nichols Ave., Stratford, CT 06497: Free catalog ❖ Propagation supplies, pots and baskets, lights, greenhouses, pest control and hydroponic growing aids, fertilizers, and tools. 203-375-1317.

Pots & Planters

Cambridge Designs, P.O. Box 765, Hillsdale, MI 49242: Free catalog ❖ Landscaping benches, planters, receptacles, fountains, and pedestrian control screens. 800-477-7320.

The Carpenter's Shop, 1573 Princeton, Berley, MI 48072: Brochure $1 ❖ Handcrafted redwood boxes for homes, decks, patios, or gardens. 810-414-9060.

Cast Aluminum Reproductions, P.O. Box 1060, San Elizario, TX 79849: Catalog $2 ❖ Cast-aluminum and brass furniture, street lights, fountains, mail boxes, and plant stands. 915-764-3793.

Claycraft, 807 Avenue of Americas, New York, NY 10001: Catalog $2 ❖ Indoor and outdoor fiberglass planters. 212-242-2903.

Gift & Wicker Import Inc., 12770 Moore St., Cerritos, CA 90701: Catalog $5 ❖ Wickerware, hobby craft supplies, basket planters, home decorative accessories, and furniture. 800-622-6209; 310-407-3319 (in CA).

Kingsley-Bate Ltd., 5587 Guinea Rd., Fairfax, VA 22032: Catalog $2 ❖ Hand-carved and traditional teak planters, window boxes, and garden furniture. 703-978-7200.

Landscape Forms Inc., 431 Lawndale Ave., Kalamazoo, MI 49001: Free information ❖ Outdoor furniture and garden planters. 800-521-2546; 616-381-0396 (in MI).

MoonAcre IronWorks, 62 Chambersburg St., Gettysburg, PA 17325: Catalog $2 ❖ Country-style iron trellises for climbing plants. 800-966-4766.

Plant Collectibles, 103 Kenview Ave., Buffalo, NY 14217: Free catalog with two 1st class stamps ❖ Plastic pots, hanging baskets, starter trays, watering equipment, plant foods, insecticide sprays, and lighting units. 716-875-1221.

Planters International, 2635 Noble Rd., Cleveland, OH 44121: Free information ❖ Easy-to-use no assembly self-watering planters. 800-341-2673; 216-382-3539 (in OH).

Season Extenders, 971 Nichols Ave., Stratford, CT 06497: Free catalog ❖ Propagation supplies, pots and baskets, lights, greenhouses, pest control and hydroponic growing aids, fertilizers, and tools. 203-375-1317.

Seibert & Rice, P.O. Box 365, Short Hills, NJ 07078: Catalog $2 ❖ Terra cotta planters. 201-467-8266.

❖ GARDENING EQUIPMENT & SUPPLIES ❖

TerraCast, 4700 Mitchell St. North, Las Vegas, NV 89031: Free information ❖ Unbreakable lightweight planters for indoor and outdoor gardens. 800-423-8539; 702-643-2644 (in NV).

Vermont Nature Creations, P.O. Box 1317, Castleton, VT 05735: Free brochure ❖ Handcrafted plant hangers.

The Village Blacksmith, 7756 Main St., Fabius, NY 13063: Brochure $2 (refundable) ❖ Hand-forged planters. 315-683-5589.

Violet House, P.O. Box 1274, Gainesville, FL 32601: Free catalog ❖ Indoor and outdoor plastic pots, hanging baskets, African violet seeds, insecticides, potting soils, fertilizers, perlite, vermiculite, books, and trays. 904-377-8465.

Software

Abracadata, P.O. Box 2440, Eugene, OR 97402: Free catalog ❖ Gardening DOS and Windows-based and Macintosh gardening software. 800-451-4871.

Books that Work, 2300 Geng Rd., Building 3, Ste. 100, Palo Alto, CA 94303: Free information ❖ Gardening software. 800-242-4546.

Capstan Distributing, P.O. Box 245, Manchester, IA 52057: Free information ❖ Software for gardeners and landscape designers. 319-927-5948.

Expert Software, 800 Douglas Rd., Executive Tower, 7th Floor, Coral Gables, FL 33134: Free information ❖ Landscaping design software. 800-759-2562; 305-567-9990 (in FL).

Green Thumb Software Inc., 75 Manhattan Dr., Ste. 100, Boulder, CO 80303: Free catalog ❖ Landscape and garden design software. 800-336-3127.

Multicom Publishing Inc., 1100 Olive Way, Ste. 1250, Seattle, WA 98101: Free information ❖ Better Homes & Garden guide to gardening. 800-850-7272; 206-622-5530 (in WA).

Soil Testing

Cook's Consulting, RD 2, Box 13, Lowville, NY 13367: Free information ❖ Soil testing services. 315-376-3002.

Necessary Trading Company, One Natures Way, New Castle, VA 24127: Free catalog ❖ Soil and garden testing services, testing supplies and equipment, plant nutrients, fertilizers, and pest control preparations. 800-447-5354.

Tillers

Ariens Company, 655 W. Ryan St., P.O. Box 157, Brillon, WI 54110: Free information ❖ Power-operated tillers. 414-756-2141.

BCS America, P.O. Box 7162, Charlotte, NC 28241: Free catalog ❖ Garden carts, chippers and shredders, tillers, sprayers, lawn and garden tractors, and mowers. 800-227-8791.

Black & Decker Garden Tools, Consumer Services, P.O. Box 618, Hampstead, MD 21074: Free information ❖ Power-operated tillers. 800-762-6672.

Garden Way, 9th Ave. & 102nd St., Troy, NY 12180: Free information ❖ Power-operated tiller and composter for small gardens. 800-828-5500.

Hoffco, 358 NW F St., Richmond, IN 47374: Free information ❖ Mini tillers. 800-999-8161.

Husqvarna Power Products, Perimeter Woods Dr., Charlotte, NC 28216: Free information ❖ Power-operated tillers. 800-438-7297.

Kubota Tractor Corporation, 3401 Del Amo Blvd., Torrance, CA 90503: Free information ❖ Power-operated tillers. 310-370-3370.

Lawn-Boy, Lyndale Ave. South, Bloomington, MN 55420: Free information ❖ Walk-behind and riding mowers, lawn and garden tractors, and power-operated tillers. 800-526-6937.

Mainline of North America, P.O. Box 526, London, OH 43140: Free information ❖ All-gear driven tiller with optional sickle bar and no belts or chains. Also hydraulic log splitters, carts, and snow throwers. 800-837-2097.

Mantis Manufacturing Company, 1028 Street Rd., Southampton, PA 18966: Free information ❖ Electric-powered tiller with optional border edger, planter furrower, lawn aerator, and thatch remover. 800-366-6268.

Mighty Mac, Mackissic Inc., P.O. Box 111, Parker Ford, PA 19457: Free information ❖ Chippers, tillers, blowers, and sprayers. 610-495-7181.

New Holland North America Inc., P.O. Box 1895, New Holland, PA 17557: Free list of retail sources ❖ Lawn and garden tractors with optional attachments. 717-355-1121.

Poulan, 5020 Flournoy-Lucas Rd., Shrevesport, LA 71129: Free information ❖ Hand-held gasoline-powered blowers and lawn trimmers. 318-683-3546.

Roto-Hoe, P.O. Box 792, 345 15th St. NW, Barberton, OH 44203: Free list of retail sources ❖ Easy-handling tillers. 216-753-2288.

White Outdoor Products Company, P.O. Box 361131, Cleveland, OH 44136: Free list of retail sources ❖ Power-operated tillers.

Tools & Sprayers

Alsto Company, P.O. Box 1267, Galesburg, IL 61401: Catalog $1 ❖ Tools, pet products, kitchen aids, and convenience items. 800-447-0048.

American Arborist Supplies Inc., 882 S. Matlack St., West Chester, PA 19382: Catalog $4 ❖ Supplies for tree care needs and landscaping. 800-441-8381.

Amerind MacKissic Inc., P.O. Box 111, Parker Ford, PA 19457: Free information ❖ Sprayers for fruit trees, shrubs, gardens, and lawns. 610-495-7181.

Ames Lawn & Garden Tools, P.O. Box 1774, Parkersburg, WV 26102: Free information ❖ Hand garden tools. 800-624-2654.

W. Atlee Burpee & Company, 300 Park Ave., Warminster, PA 18974: Free catalog ❖ Tools, equipment, and growing aids. 215-674-1793.

Brookstone Company, Order Processing Center, 1655 Bassford Dr., Mexico, MO 65265: Free catalog ❖ House and garden tools. 800-926-7000.

Carter Heirlooms, 15383 Nixon Rd., Mt. Vernon, OH 43050: Free information ❖ Red cedar potting bench. 614-892-3883.

Charley's Greenhouse Supply, 1569 Memorial Hwy., Mt. Vernon, WA 98273: Catalog $2 ❖ Shading materials, fans, watering and misting equipment, and propagating aids. 206-428-2626.

Clapper's, P.O. Box 2278, West Newton, MA 02165: Free catalog ❖ Spreaders, sprayers, sprinkling and full-flow watering systems, outdoor furniture, landscaping ornaments, and outdoor lighting. 617-244-7900.

Creative Enterprises Inc., P.O. Box 3452, Idaho Falls, ID 83403: Free information ❖ Weeding tools. 208-523-0526.

Carts Vermont, 1890 Airport Pkwy., South Burlington, VT 05403: Free information ❖ Garden carts. 800-732-7417.

Denman & Company, 1202 E. Pine St., Placentia, CA 92870: Free information ❖ Pruning and other gardening tools. 714-524-0668.

John Dromgoode's Natural Gardener's Catalog, 8648 Old Bee Caves Rd., Austin, TX 78735: Free catalog ❖ Organic fertilizers, growth stimulants, composting equipment, books on organic gardening, tools, pest controls, and pet products. 800-320-0724.

Duraco Products, 1109 E. Lake St., Streamwood, IL 60103: Free information ❖ Garden accessories. 800-888-POTS.

Environmental Concepts, 710 NW 57th St., Fort Lauderdale, FL 33309: Free brochure ❖ Meters that measure soil temperature, pH, light intensity, and the need for fertilizer. 954-491-4490.

Environmental R & D, 137 Bridlewood Trail, Horse Shoe, NC 28742: Free information ❖ Plant care meters.

Florian Gardening Tools, 157 Water St., Southington, CT 06489: Free information ❖ Ratchet-cut pruning tools. 800-275-3618.

Four Seasons Nursery, 1706 Morrisey Dr., Bloomington, IL 61704: Free catalog ❖ Tools, plants, seeds, and growing stock. 309-663-9551.

GARDENING EQUIPMENT & SUPPLIES

Garden Tools of Maine, RR 2, Box 2208, East Holden, ME 04429: Free information ❖ Hand garden tools. 207-843-6271.

Gardener's Supply Company, 128 Intervale Rd., Burlington, VT 05401: Free catalog ❖ Composter, pest control sprayers, watering systems and controls, weeding and cultivating tools, organic fertilizers, garden carts, leaf mulchers, canning and preserving supplies, and furniture. 800-863-1700.

Gardeners Eden, P.O. Box 7307, San Francisco, CA 94133: Free catalog ❖ Tools, landscaping accessories, growing and transplanting aids, and furniture. 800-822-1214.

E.C. Geiger, Rt. 63, Box 285, Harleysville, PA 19438: Free catalog ❖ Greenhouses, gardening supplies, and tools. 800-4-GEIGER.

Gro-Tek, 518 Rt. 81, Killingworth, CT 06417: Catalog 50¢ ❖ Seedling starter kits, tools, and supplies for greenhouses, solariums, and home gardening.

Harmony Farm Supply & Nursery, P.O. Box 460, Graton, CA 95444: Catalog $2 (refundable) ❖ Tools and horticultural supplies. 707-823-9125.

Harris Seeds, P.O. Box 22960, Rochester, NY 14692: Free catalog ❖ Gardening equipment, seeds, and plants. 716-442-0410.

Home Gardener Manufacturing Company, 30 Wright Ave., Lades, PA 17543: Free information ❖ Easy-to-use compost-makers. 800-880-2345.

Indoor Gardening Supplies, P.O. Box 40567, Detroit, MI 48240: Free catalog ❖ Supplies, lights, and books. 313-426-9080.

Johnny's Selected Seeds, 150 Floss Hill Rd., Albion, ME 04910: Free catalog ❖ Tools, growing aids, and gardening supplies. 207-437-4301.

K & G Manufacturing Inc., P.O. Box 350, Duke, OK 73532: Free catalog ❖ Easy-to-use on-wheels lawn and garden power sprayer. 405-679-3955.

The Kinsman Company, River Rd., Point Pleasant, PA 18950: Free catalog ❖ Composters, compost bins, chipper-shredders, rose arbors, garden arches, plant supports, and tools. 800-733-4146.

Langenbach Fine Tool Company, P.O. Box 1140, El Segundo, CA 90245: Free catalog ❖ Tools. 800-362-1991.

Lee Valley Tools Inc., 12 E. River St., Ogdensburg, NY 13669: Free catalog ❖ Hard-to-find garden tools and other work-saving products. 800-513-7885.

A.M. Leonard Inc., P.O. Box 816, Piqua, OH 45356: Free catalog ❖ Tools, sprayers, and gardening supplies. 800-543-8955.

MacKenzie Nursery Supply Inc., P.O. Box 322, Perry, OH 44081: Free brochure ❖ Tools and supplies. 800-777-5030.

Mainline of North America, P.O. Box 526, London, OH 43140: Free information ❖ All-gear driven tiller with optional sickle bar and no belts or chains. Also hydraulic log splitters, carts, and snow throwers. 800-837-2097.

Mantis Manufacturing Company, 1028 Street Rd., Southampton, PA 18966: Free information ❖ Portable sprayer for gardens, washing windows and outside walls, and other uses. 800-366-6268.

Mellinger's, 2310 W. South Range Rd., North Lima, OH 44452: Free catalog ❖ Tools, plants and seeds, and growing aids. 330-549-9861.

Mighty Mac, Mackissic Inc., P.O. Box 111, Parker Ford, PA 19457: Free information ❖ Chippers, tillers, blowers, and sprayers. 610-495-7181.

Modern Homesteader, 1825 Big Horn Ave., Cody, WY 82414: Free catalog ❖ Gardening equipment, clothing and hats, tools, truck and automotive accessories, and canning equipment. 800-443-4934; 307-587-5946 (in WY).

Morco Products, P.O. Box 160, Dundas, MN 55019: Free brochure ❖ Easy-to-use composter. 507-645-4277.

Mountainman Woodshop, Rt. 2, Box 37A, Eagle Rock, VA 24085: Free brochure ❖ Handcrafted traditional Appalachian slot-back chairs and wooden farming tools. 540-884-2197.

Natural Gardening Company, 217 San Anselmo Ave., San Anselmo, CA 94960: Free catalog ❖ Tools, seeds, fertilizers, pest controls, birdhouses, and books. 707-766-9303.

Nature's Backyard Inc., 241 Duchaine Blvd., New Bedford, MA 02745: Free brochure ❖ Easy-to-assemble and use composter. 800-853-2525.

Walt Nicke Company, P.O. Box 433, Topsfield, MA 01983: Free information ❖ Garden tools. 508-887-3388.

Niwa Tool, 1333 San Pablo Ave., Berkeley, CA 94702: Catalog $2 ❖ Handcrafted Japanese garden and bonsai tools. 800-443-5512.

L.L. Olds Seed Company, P.O. Box 7790, Madison, WI 53707: Catalog $2.50 ❖ Tools, growing aids, seeds, and plants. 608-249-9291.

Park Seed Company, Cokesbury Rd., P.O. Box 46, Greenwood, SC 29648: Free catalog ❖ Tools, plants and seeds, and growing aids. 800-845-3369.

PeCo Inc., P.O. Box 1197, Arden, NC 28704: Free information ❖ Battery-powered sprayer with charger and wand. 800-438-5823; 704-684-1234 (in NC).

Pinetree Garden Seeds, Box 300, New Gloucester, ME 04260: Free catalog ❖ Sprayers. 207-926-3400.

Plow & Hearth, P.O. Box 5000, Madison, VA 22727: Free catalog ❖ Tools, outdoor furniture, bird houses and feeders, and birdbaths. 800-627-1712.

Poulan, 5020 Flournoy-Lucas Rd., Shrevesport, LA 71129: Free information ❖ Gasoline-powered hand-held blowers and lawn trimmer. 318-683-3546.

Primus-Sievert Inc., 1462 US Rt. 20, P.O. Box 186, Cherry Valley, IL 61016: Free information ❖ Weed destroyer. 815-332-5504.

Ringer, 9959 Valley View Rd., Eden Prairie, MN 55344: Free catalog ❖ Tools, chemical treatments and fertilizers, growing aids, propagation aids, compost-making equipment, lawn care supplies, and planters. 800-654-1047.

S.A.N. Associates Inc., P.O. Box 88, Greendell, NJ 07839: Free information ❖ Rolling tool carrier. 908-852-4612.

Season Extenders, 971 Nichols Ave., Stratford, CT 06497: Free catalog ❖ Propagation supplies, pots and baskets, lights, greenhouses, pest control and hydroponic growing aids, fertilizers, and tools. 203-375-1317.

Shape Plastics Corporation, P.O. Box 538, Sharon, WI 53585: Free information ❖ Easy-to-use backyard composter. 414-736-8888.

Smith & Hawken, P.O. Box 6907, Florence, KY 41022: Free catalog ❖ Tools, sprayers, and greenhouse supplies. 800-776-3336.

Stillbrook Horticultural Supplies, P.O. Box 600, Bantam, CT 06750: Free information ❖ Garden tools and accessories. 800-414-4468.

Stokes Seeds Inc., Box 548, Buffalo, NY 14240: Free catalog ❖ Greenhouse tools and supplies. 716-695-6980.

Technic Tool Corporation, P.O. Box 1406, Lewiston, ID 83501: Free list of retail sources ❖ Easy-to-use gasoline-powered telescoping pruner. 800-243-9592.

V & B Manufacturing, P.O. Box 268, Walnut Ridge, AR 72476: Free information ❖ Landscaping tools. 800-443-1987.

Vermont Garden Shed, RR 2, Box 180, East St., Wallingford, VT 05773: Free catalog ❖ Garden tools, supplies, and home accents. 800-288-SHED.

Yazoo Manufacturing Company, 3650 Bay St., Jackson, MS 39206: Free information ❖ Lawn care equipment. 800-354-6562.

Topiary Frames & Supplies

Cliff Finch's Zoo, P.O. Box 54, Friant, CA 93626: Free brochure with long SASE ❖ Topiary frames. 209-822-2315.

FrenchWyres, P.O. Box 131655, Tyler, TX 75713: Catalog $3 ❖ Trellises, topiary frames, urns, plant stands, cache pots, window boxes, and arches. 903-597-8322.

✓ **The Kinsman Company,** River Rd., Point Pleasant, PA 18950: Free catalog ❖ Topiary forms. 800-733-4146.

Rabbit Shadow Farm, 2880 E. Hwy. 402, Loveland, CO 80537: Free information ❖ Herbs, roses, topiary supplies, and scented geraniums. 303-667-5531.

Dr. TLC Greenthumb, HC 61, Box 1193, Dewey, AZ 66327: Catalog $1 (refundable) ❖ Easy-care topiaries.

Topiary Inc., 41 Bering, Tampa, FL 33606: Free brochure ❖ Geometric and animal topiary shapes. 813-837-2841.

Tractors

Ariens Company, 655 W. Ryan St., P.O. Box 157, Brillon, WI 54110: Free information ❖ Lawn and garden tractors. 414-756-2141.

✓ **BCS America,** P.O. Box 7162, Charlotte, NC 28241: Free catalog ❖ Lawn and garden tractors, garden carts, chippers and shredders, tillers, sprayers, and mowers. 800-227-8791.

Cub Cadet Corporation, P.O. Box 368023, Cleveland, OH 44136: Free information ❖ Easy-to-operate tractor with optional snow thrower and bagging attachment. 216-273-4550.

Ford New Holland Inc., 500 Diller Ave., Holland, PA 17557: Free information ❖ Lawn and garden tractors. 717-355-1371.

Garden Way, 9th Ave. & 102nd St., Troy, NY 12180: Free information ❖ Lawn and garden tractors. 800-828-5500.

Husqvarna Power Products, Perimeter Woods Dr., Charlotte, NC 28216: Free information ❖ Lawn and garden tractors. 800-438-7297.

Kubota Tractor Corporation, 3401 Del Amo Blvd., Torrance, CA 90503: Free information ❖ Lawn and garden tractors. 310-370-3370.

Lawn-Boy, Lyndale Ave. South, Bloomington, MN 55420: Free information ❖ Walk-behind and riding mowers, lawn and garden tractors, and power-operated tillers. 800-526-6937.

Poulan, 5020 Flournoy-Lucas Rd., Shrevesport, LA 71129: Free information ❖ Lawn and garden tractors. 318-683-3546.

Power-King, 1100 Green Valley Rd., Beaver Dam, WI 53916: Free list of retail sources ❖ Garden and lawn tractors with optional custom attachments. 800-262-1191.

Simplicity Manufacturing Inc., P.O. Box 997, Port Washington, WI 53074: Free information ❖ Lawn and garden tractors. 800-945-0235.

Snapper Power Equipment, P.O. Box 777, McDonough, GA 30253: Free list of retail sources ❖ Lawn and garden tractors. 404-954-2500.

White Outdoor Products Company, P.O. Box 361131, Cleveland, OH 44136: Free information ❖ Lawn and garden tractors.

Yamaha Outdoor Power Equipment Division, 6555 Katella Ave., Cypress, CA 90630: Free information ❖ Lawn and garden tractors.

Water Gardening Supplies

Aquarium Pharmaceuticals Inc., P.O. Box 218, Chalfont, PA 18914: Information $2 ❖ Water garden products for fish, plants, and pond maintenance.

Beckett Corporation, 2521 Willowbrook Rd., Dallas, TX 75220: Free list of retail sources ❖ Water gardening accessories.

✓ **Cambridge Designs,** P.O. Box 765, Hillsdale, MI 49242: Free catalog ❖ Landscaping benches, planters, receptacles, fountains, and pedestrian control screens. 800-477-7320.

Discount Pond Supplies, P.O. Box 423371, Kissimmee, FL 34741: Free catalog ❖ Water gardening supplies and equipment. 407-847-7937.

Dolphin Inc., Dolphin Pet Village, 90 N. San Tomas Aquino Rd., Campbell, CA 95008: Free brochure with long SASE ❖ Fiberglass ponds for water gardens. Also filters, plants, and fish.

Grovhac Inc., 4310 N. 126th St., Brookfield, WI 53005: Free information ❖ Power-operated aerating equipment for water gardens. 414-781-5020.

Hardwicke Gardens, 254-A Turnpike Rd., Westborough, MA 01581: Catalog $2 ❖ Water garden essentials. 508-366-5478.

Lilypons Water Gardens, P.O. Box 10, Buckeystown, MD 21717: Catalog $5 ❖ Supplies for aquatic gardens. 800-723-7667.

Maryland Aquatic Nurseries, 3427 N. Furnace Rd., Jarrettsville, MD 21084: Catalog $5 (refundable) ❖ Plants for water garden settings, ornamental grasses, and Japanese irises. 410-557-7615.

Paradise Water Gardens, 14 May St., Whitman, MA 02382: Catalog $3 (refundable) ❖ Fountains, pools, pumps, goldfish, aquatic plants, and books. 617-447-4711.

Patio Garden Ponds, 7919 S. Shields, Oklahoma City, OK 73149: Catalog $3 ❖ Patio garden pond liners, pumps, filters and filter media, water lilies, nitrifying aids, and bacteria. 405-634-7663.

Pets Unlimited, 1888 Drew, Clearwater, FL 34625: Information $2 ❖ Water pond supplies. 813-442-2197.

S. Scherer & Sons, 104 Waterside Rd., Northport, NY 11768: Free price list ❖ Water lilies, aquatic plants, pools, pumps, waterfalls, and fish. 516-261-7432.

Slocum Water Gardens, 1101 Cypress Gardens Rd., Winter Haven, FL 33884: Catalog $3 ❖ Water garden supplies. 941-293-7151.

Tetra Pond, 3001 Commerce St., Blacksburg, VA 24060: Free brochure ❖ Pool liners, plants, fish and food, and water treatments. 800-526-0650.

Urdl's Waterfall Creations Inc., 2010 NW 1st St., Delray Beach, FL 33445: Free information ❖ Manufactured hollow concrete rocks for landscaping and waterfall settings. 407-278-3320.

Van Ness Water Gardens, 2460 N. Euclid, Upland, CA 91786: Catalog $4 ❖ Water lilies, aquatic plants, waterfalls, and garden supplies. 800-205-2425.

Waterford Gardens, 74 E. Allendale Rd., Saddle River, NJ 07458: Catalog $5 ❖ Water lilies, lotus and bog plants, pools, and fish. 201-327-0721.

Windy Oaks, W377 S10677 Betts Rd., Eagle, WI 53119: Catalog $1 ❖ Water garden supplies. 414-594-3033.

Watering & Irrigation Equipment

Acu-Drip Water System, Wade Manufacturing Company, P.O. Box 23666, Portland, OR 97281: Free brochure ❖ Easy-to-install drip watering systems. 800-222-7246.

Harmony Farm Supply & Nursery, P.O. Box 460, Graton, CA 95444: Catalog $2 (refundable) ❖ Watering system kits, outdoor drip and sprinkler irrigation equipment, and soaker hoses. 707-823-9125.

Hunter Irrigation Products, 1940 Diamond St., San Marcos, CA 92069: Free information ❖ Water-efficient sprinkler systems. 619-744-5240.

International Aeration Systems (Irrigro), P.O. Box 360, Niagara Falls, NY 14304: Free information ❖ Micro-porous irrigation systems for home gardeners and commercial growers. 905-688-4093.

International Aeration Systems (Oxyflo), P.O. Box 360, Niagara Falls, NY 14304: Free information ❖ Micro-porous aeration systems for fish farming and general aeration applications. 905-688-4093.

Irrigro, P.O. Box 360, Niagara Falls, NY 14304: Free information ❖ Drip irrigation systems. 905-688-4090.

Jamar Distributing, 1292 Montclair Dr., Pasadena, MD 21122: Catalog $3 (refundable) ❖ Garden and container water systems, pop-up lawn sprinklers, and equipment. 800-477-4181.

Kourik Drip, 217 San Anselmo Ave., San Anselmo, CA 94960: Free catalog ❖ Easy-to-install maintenance-free drip irrigation system. 707-766-9303.

Mel-Nor Industries, 303 Gulf Bank, Houston, TX 77037: Information $1 ❖ Time controlled sprinklers, hose reel carts, hanging lawn and porch swings, park benches, and old-time lamp posts. 713-445-3485.

Natural Gardening Company, 217 San Anselmo Ave., San Anselmo, CA 94960: Free catalog ❖ Beneficial insects, organic gardening supplies, pest controls, drip irrigation equipment, and wildflower seeds. 707-766-9303.

Rain Bird, 7590 Britannia Ct., San Diego, CA 92173: Free catalog ❖ Drip-watering, irrigation, and conventional do-it-yourself watering systems. 619-661-4200.

Rain Control, P.O. Box 662, Adrian, MI 49221: Free brochure ❖ Easy-to-install garden watering system. Available in a choice of three kits. 800-536-RAIN.

Raindrip Inc., 2250 Agate Ct., Simi Valley, CA 93065: Free catalog ❖ Watering system kits, outdoor irrigation supplies, and soaker hoses. 800-225-3747.

Ramsey Irrigation Systems, 7711 Knoxville Dr., Lubbock, TX 79423: Free information ❖ Drip irrigation equipment. 800-477-2347.

Salco Products Inc., 4463 W. Rosecrans Ave., Hawthorne, CA 90250: Free information ❖ Drip irrigation systems. 310-973-2400.

Submatic Irrigation Systems, P.O. Box 3965, Lubbock, TX 79452: Free catalog ❖ Irrigation systems. 800-692-4100.

Toro Irrigation Division, P.O. Box 489, Riverside, CA 92502: Free information ❖ Irrigation systems.

Urban Farmer Store, 2833 Vicente St., San Francisco, CA 94116: Catalog $2 ❖ Watering system kits, outdoor irrigation supplies, and soaker hoses. 800-753-3747; 415-661-2204 (in CA).

Weiss Brothers Nursery, 11690 Colfax Hwy., Grass Valley, CA 95945: Free catalog ❖ Drip irrigation supplies. 916-272-7657.

GARDENING—PLANTS & SEEDS

African Violets & Gesneriads

Alice's Violet Room, 129 Zeigenbein Rd., Waynesville, MO 65583: Catalog $1 (refundable) ❖ African violets. 314-336-4763.

Florals of Fredericks, 155 Spartan Dr., Maitland, FL 32751: Catalog $2 ❖ African violets and growing supplies. 800-771-0899.

JoS Violets, 2205 College Dr., Victoria, TX 77901: Free list ❖ Standard and miniature African violets. 800-295-1344; 512-575-1344 (in TX).

Judy's Violets, 9 Graeler Dr., Creve Coeur, MO 63146: Catalog $1 ❖ African violets. 314-997-2859.

Kartuz Greenhouses, 1408 Sunset Dr., Vista, CA 92083: Catalog $2 ❖ Gesneriads, begonias, miniature terrarium, and unusual tropical plants. 619-941-3613.

Lauray of Salisbury, 432 Undermountain Rd., Salisbury, CT 06068: Catalog $2 ❖ Gesneriads, begonias, orchids, cacti and succulents, and other plants. 203-435-2263.

Lyndon Lyon Greenhouses Inc., 14 Mutchler St., Dolgeville, NY 13329: Catalog $3 ❖ African violets and exotic house plants. 315-429-8291.

Tinari Greenhouses, 2325 Valley Rd., Huntingdon Valley, PA 19006: Catalog $1 ❖ Standard, miniature, trailer, and variegated African violets. 215-947-0144.

Travis Violets, P.O. Box 42, Ochlochnee, GA 31773: Catalog $1 (refundable) ❖ Hybrid African violets, growing supplies, and pots. 912-574-5167.

Violet Express, 1440-41 Everett Rd., Eagle River, WI 54521: Catalog $2.75 ❖ African violet leaf cuttings.

Violet Showcase, 3147 S. Broadway, Englewood, CO 80110: Catalog $1 ❖ Standards, trailers, pinwheels, miniatures, other African violet plants, and growing supplies. 303-761-1770.

Violets by Appointment, Bill & Kathryn Paauwe, 45 3rd St., West Sayville, NY 11796: List $1.50 (refundable) ❖ African violets. 516-589-2724.

Volkmann Bros. Greenhouses, 2714 Minert St., Dallas, TX 75219: Catalog $1 ❖ African violets and growing supplies. 214-526-3484.

Aquatic Plants

Griffey Nursery, 1670 Hwy. 25/70, Marshall, NC 28753: Free catalog ❖ Aquatic plants. 704-656-2334.

Kester's Birdseed Inc., P.O. Box 516, Omro, WI 54963: Catalog $3 ❖ Aquatic plants. 800-558-8815; 414-685-2929 (in WI).

Maryland Aquatic Nurseries, 3427 N. Furnace Rd., Jarrettsville, MD 21084: Catalog $5 (refundable) ❖ Marginal and bog plants for aquatic gardens. 410-557-7615.

Meadow View Farms, 3360 N. Pacific Hwy., Medford, OR 97501: Catalog $3 ❖ Perennials, grasses, herbs, vines, and aquatic plants.

Nursery & Water Garden Supply, 7767 Fernvale Rd., P.O. Box 658, Fairview, TN 37062: Free information ❖ Aquatic plants. 615-799-0708.

S. Scherer & Sons, 104 Waterside Rd., Northport, NY 11768: Free price list ❖ Water lilies, aquatic plants, pools, pumps, waterfalls, fish, pool liners, and supplies. 516-261-7432.

William Tricker Inc., 7125 Tanglewood Dr., Independence, OH 44131: Catalog $2 ❖ Water lilies, aquatic plants, exotic fish for indoor and outdoor water gardens, and pumps, pool liners, and supplies. 800-524-3492.

Waterford Gardens, 74 E. Allendale Rd., Saddle River, NJ 07458: Catalog $5 ❖ Water lilies, lotus and bog plants, and pools. 201-327-0721.

Wicklein's Aquatic Farm & Nursery Inc., 1820 Cromwell Bridge Rd., Baltimore, MD 21234: Catalog $1 ❖ Water lilies, aquatic plants, and perennials. 410-823-1335.

Azaleas & Rhododendrons

Briarwood Gardens, 14 Gully Ln., East Sandwich, MA 02537: Free catalog ❖ Rhododendrons. 508-888-2146.

Carlson's Gardens, Box 305, South Salem, NY 10590: Catalog $3 ❖ Dwarf rhododendrons and landscape-size azaleas. 914-763-5958.

Crownsville Nursery, P.O. Box 797, Crownsville, MD 21032: Catalog $2 (minimum order $25) ❖ Ferns, wildflowers, azaleas, ornamental grasses, and perennials. 410-923-2212.

Cummins Garden, 22 Robertsville Rd., Marlboro, NJ 07746: Free information ❖ Dwarf rhododendrons, evergreens and deciduous azaleas, dwarf conifers, and companion plants. 908-536-2591.

Eastern Plant Specialties, P.O. Box 226, Georgetown, ME 04548: Catalog $3 ❖ Shrubs, rhododendrons, and wildflowers.

Flora Lan Nursery, 7940 NW Kansas City Rd., Forest Grove, OR 97116: Free catalog ❖ Azaleas and rhododendron hybrids. 503-357-8386.

Girard Nurseries, P.O. Box 428, Geneva, OH 44041: Free catalog ❖ Azaleas and rhododendrons. 216-466-2881.

Greer Gardens, 1280 Goodpasture Island Rd., Eugene, OR 97401: Catalog $3 ❖ Azaleas and rhododendrons, trees, shrubs, Japanese maples, and bonsai. 800-548-0111.

Kelleygreen Rhododendron Nursery, 6924 Hwy. 38, Drain, OR 97435: Free catalog ❖ Rhododendrons. 800-477-5676.

Pen Y Bryn, RR 1, Box 1313, Forksville, PA 18616: Catalog $2 ❖ Azaleas.

GARDENING—PLANTS & SEEDS

Roslyn Nursery, 211 Burrs Ln., Dix Hills, NY 11746: Catalog $3 ❖ Rhododendrons, hardy shrubs, trees, and perennials. 516-643-9347.

Schild Azalea Gardens & Nursery, 1705 Longview St., Hixson, TN 37343: Catalog $1 (refundable) ❖ Nursery-propagated azaleas.

Bamboo

David C. Andrews, P.O. Box 358, Oxon Hill, MD 20750: Free price list ❖ Bamboo plants.

Bamboo Sourcery, 666 Wagnon Rd., Sebastopol, CA 95472: Catalog $2 ❖ Bamboo plants. 707-823-5866.

Kurt Bluemel Inc., 2740 Greene Ln., Baldwin, MD 21013: Catalog $3 ❖ Bamboo plants, perennials, ferns, and ornamental grasses. 410-557-7229.

Burt Associates, P.O. Box 719, Westford, MA 01886: Catalog $2 ❖ Bamboo plants. 508-692-3240.

Colvos Creek Nursery, P.O. Box 1512, Vashon Island, WA 98070: Catalog $2 (refundable) ❖ Trees, shrubs, and bamboo and rare and unusual plants. 206-441-1509.

Endangered Species, P.O. Box 1830, Tustin, CA 92681: Catalog $6 ❖ Giant, medium-sized, dwarf-green, and variegated bamboo and other rare plants. 714-544-9505.

Floribunda Palms, Box 635, Mt. View, HI 96771: Free information with long SASE ❖ Bamboo plants.

Gardens of the Blue Ridge, P.O. Box 10, Pineola, NC 28662: Catalog $3 (refundable) ❖ Bamboo plants. 704-733-2417.

Louisiana Nursery, Rt. 7, Box 43, Opelousas, LA 70570: Catalog $6 ❖ Bamboo, rare, unusual, and other hard-to-find plants. Also books. 318-948-3696.

New England Bamboo Company, P.O. Box 358, Rockport, MA 01966: Catalog $5 ❖ Bamboo plants. 508-546-3581.

Pen Y Bryn, RR 1, Box 1313, Forksville, PA 18616: Catalog $2 ❖ Bamboo plants.

Steve Ray's Bamboo Gardens, 250 Cedar Cliff Rd., Springville, AL 35146: Catalog $3 ❖ Bamboo plants. 205-594-3438.

Tornello Landscape Corporation, P.O. Box 788, Ruskin, FL 33570: Free information ❖ Bamboo plants. 813-645-5445.

Tradewinds Bamboo Nursery, 28446 Hunter Creek Loop, Gold Beach, OR 97444: Catalog $2 ❖ Bamboo plants and books. 503-247-0835.

Tripple Brook Farm, 37 Middle Rd., Southampton, MA 01073: Catalog 50¢ ❖ Bamboo plants, exotic fruits, trees, perennials, and shrubs. 413-527-4626.

Banana Plants

The Banana Tree, 715 Northampton St., Easton, PA 18042: Catalog $3 ❖ Banana and tropical plants and seeds. 610-253-9589.

Brudy's Exotics, Box 820874, Houston, TX 77282: Free catalog ❖ Easy-to-grow container banana corms. 800-926-7333.

Going Bananas, 24401 SW 197th Ave., Homestead, FL 33031: Catalog $1 ❖ Bananas and plantains. 305-247-0397.

Begonias

Antonelli Brothers, 2545 Capitola Rd., Santa Cruz, CA 95062: Catalog $1 ❖ Tuberous and miniature begonias. 408-475-5222.

Davidson-Wilson Greenhouses, Rt. 2, Box 168, Crawfordsville, IN 47933: Catalog $3 ❖ Geraniums, house plants, begonias, impatiens, herbs, and succulents. 317-364-0556.

Fairyland Begonia Garden, Winkey & Leslie Woodriff, 1100 Griffith Rd., McKinleyville, CA 95521: Price list 50¢ ❖ Rex, fibrous, and hybrid begonias. Also garden lilies. 707-839-3034.

Glasshouse Works Greenhouses, P.O. Box 97, Stewart, OH 45778: Catalog $3 ❖ Begonias and rare tropical plants. 614-662-2142.

Kartuz Greenhouses, 1408 Sunset Dr., Vista, CA 92083: Catalog $2 ❖ Gesneriads, begonias, miniature terrarium, and unusual tropical plants. 619-941-3613.

Kay's Greenhouses, 207 W. Southcross Blvd., San Antonio, TX 78221: Price list $2 ❖ Begonias.

Lauray of Salisbury, 432 Undermountain Rd., Salisbury, CT 06068: Catalog $2 ❖ Begonias, gesneriads, orchids, cacti and succulents, and other plants. 203-435-2263.

Berry Plants

Allen Plant Company, P.O. Box 310, Fruitland, MD 21826: Free catalog ❖ Registered virus-free strawberry plants and blueberries, raspberries, thornless blackberries, and asparagus. 410-742-7122.

Vernon Barnes & Son Nursery, P.O. Box 250, McMinnville, TN 37110: Free catalog ❖ Berry plants, shrubs, hedges, vines, wildflowers, and flowering, shade, fruit, and nut trees. 615-668-8576.

Bear Creek Nursery, P.O. Box 4112, Northport, WA 99157: Catalog $1 ❖ Blueberry plants. 509-732-6219.

Blueberry Hill, RR 1, Maynooth, Ontario, Canada K0L 2S0: Free catalog ❖ Hardy native low-bush blueberry plants for cold climates.

Boston Mountain Nurseries, 20189 N. Hwy. 71, Mountainburg, AR 72946: Catalog 50¢ ❖ Berry plants and grapes. 501-369-2007.

Brittingham Plant Farms, P.O. Box 2538, Salisbury, MD 21802: Free catalog ❖ Strawberry, blueberry, raspberry, thornless blackberry, grape, and asparagus plants. 410-749-5153.

W. Atlee Burpee & Company, 300 Park Ave., Warminster, PA 18974: Free catalog ❖ Berry plants, seeds, bulbs, and gardening supplies. 215-674-1793.

Cooley's Strawberry Nursery, P.O. Box 472, Augusta, AR 72006: Free catalog ❖ Strawberry plants. 501-347-2026.

DeGrandchamp's Blueberry Farm, 15575 77th St., Drawer R, South Haven, MI 49060: Free catalog ❖ Blueberry plants. 616-637-3915.

Dyke Blueberry Farm & Nursery Inc., Rt. 1, Box 251, Vincent, OH 45758: Free catalog with long SASE ❖ Blueberry growing stock. 614-678-2192.

Emlong Nurseries, 2671 Marquette Woods Rd., Stevensville, MI 49127: Free catalog ❖ Thornless blackberries and other berry plants. Also shrubs, flowers, landscaping plants, roses, and dwarf and standard fruit, nut, and ornamental trees. 616-429-3431.

Enoch's Berry Farm, Rt. 2, Box 227, Fouke, AR 71837: Free price list ❖ Blackberry plants and root cuttings. 501-653-2806.

Farmer Seed & Nursery Company, 818 NW 4th St., Faribault, MN 55021: Free catalog ❖ Berry plants, vegetable seeds, flowering bulbs, fruit and shade trees, ornamental shrubs and hedges, and roses. 507-334-1623.

Henry Field's Seed & Nursery, 415 N. Burnett, Shenandoah, IA 51602: Free catalog ❖ Strawberry and other berry plants, vegetable and flower seeds, hedges, ornamental shrubs, roses, and fruit, nut, and shade trees. 605-665-4491.

Fig Tree Nursery, P.O. Box 124, Gulf Hammock, FL 32639: Catalog $1 ❖ Berry plants, ornamentals, and grapes for southern climates. 904-486-2930.

Finch Blueberry Nursery, P.O. Box 699, Bailey, NC 27807: Free information with long SASE ❖ Blueberry cultivars. 919-235-4662.

Harris Seeds Inc., P.O. Box 22960, Rochester, NY 14692: Free catalog ❖ Berry plants and seeds. 716-442-0410.

Hartmann's Plantation, P.O. Box E, Grand Junction, MI 49056: Catalog $2.25 (refundable) ❖ Blueberry plants. 616-253-4281.

Highlander Nursery, P.O. Box 177, Pettigrew, AR 72752: Free catalog ❖ Hardy low-chill blueberry plants. 501-677-2300.

Ison's Nursery, P.O. Box 190, Brooks, GA 30205: Free catalog ❖ Fruit and nut trees, muscadine grapevines, and blackberry, blueberry, raspberry, and strawberry plants. 800-733-0324.

Johnny's Selected Seeds, 150 Foss Hill Rd., Albion, ME 04910: Free catalog ❖ Strawberry plants, flower and vegetable seeds for northern climates, gardening tools, and growing supplies. 207-437-4301.

Johnson Nursery, Rt. 5, Ellijay, GA 30540: Free catalog ❖ Strawberry plants, grapevines, and apple, plum, pear, cherry, apricot, and walnut and almond nut trees. Also orchard supplies, tools and accessories, and books. 706-276-3187.

Kelly Nurseries, 1708 Morrissey Dr., Bloomington, IL 61704: Free catalog ❖ Berry plants, grapevines, heavily rooted fruit and nut trees, landscaping trees, shrubs, ornamentals, and flowers. 507-334-1623.

Krohne Plant Farms, 64110 94th Ave., Dowagiac, MI 49047: Free information ❖ Strawberry plants. 616-424-5423.

Lewis Strawberry Nursery Inc., P.O. Box 24, Rocky Point, NC 28457: Free catalog ❖ Strawberry plants. 800-453-5346.

Earl May Seeds & Nursery Company, N. Elm St., Shenandoah, IA 51603: Free catalog ❖ Vegetable and flower seeds, bulbs, fruit and nut trees, roses, berry plants, grapevines, shade and ornamental trees, flowering shrubs, plants, and gardening supplies. 712-246-1020.

Mellinger's, 2310 W. South Range Rd., North Lima, OH 44452: Free catalog ❖ Fruit and nut trees, ornamental and shade trees, flowering shrubs and hedges, perennials, wildflowers, berry plants, and gardening supplies. 330-549-9861.

J.E. Miller Nurseries, 5060 West Lake Rd., Canandaigua, NY 14424: Free catalog ❖ Berry plants, fruit trees, and grapevines. 800-836-9630.

Nichols Garden Nursery, 1190 SW Pacific, Albany, OR 97321: Free catalog ❖ Vegetable and herb seeds, strawberry plants, and saffron crocus, garlic, and shallot growing stock. 541-928-9280.

North Star Gardens, 19060 Manning Trail North, Marine on St. Croix, MN 55047: Free catalog ❖ Raspberries, blueberries, and blackberries. Also books, tools, and equipment. 612-227-9842.

Nourse Farms, 41 River Rd., South Deerfield, MA 01373: Free information ❖ Raspberry, strawberry, asparagus, and rhubarb plants. 413-665-2568.

The Nursery, Hwy. 82, Box 130, Ty Ty, GA 31795: Free catalog ❖ Berries, grapes, trees, and shrubs. 800-972-2101.

Park Seed Company, Cokesbury Rd., P.O. Box 46, Greenwood, SC 29648: Free catalog ❖ Strawberry plants, seeds and bulbs, tools, and gardening supplies. 800-845-3369.

Patrick's Nursery, P.O. Box 130, Ty Ty, GA 31795: Free catalog ❖ Vegetable seeds, fruit and nut trees, berry plants and grapevines. 800-972-2101.

Peaceful Valley Farm Supply, P.O. Box 2209, Grass Valley, CA 95945: Catalog $2 (refundable) ❖ Berry plants. 916-272-4769.

Pense Nursery, 16518 Marie Ln., Mountainburg, AR 72946: Free brochure ❖ Berry plants and grapevines. 501-369-2494.

Raintree Nursery, 391 Butts Rd., Morton, WA 98356: Free information ❖ Berry plants. 206-496-6400.

Savage Nursery Center, 6255 Beersheba Hwy., McMinnville, TN 37110: Free catalog ❖ Berry plants, evergreens, gardening supplies, shrubs, and fruit, shade, and flowering trees. 615-668-8902.

R.H. Shumway Seedsman, P.O. Box 1, Graniteville, SC 29829: Free catalog ❖ Berry plants, fruit trees, roses, seeds and bulbs, ornamental shrubs and plants, and gardening supplies. 413-737-0399.

Stark Brothers, Nurseries & Orchards Company, P.O. Box 10, Louisiana, MO 63353: Free catalog ❖ Fruit trees, berry and landscaping plants, and garden supplies. 800-775-6415.

Thompson & Morgan Inc., P.O. Box 1308, Jackson, NJ 08527: Free catalog ❖ Strawberry plants and vegetable and flower seeds. 800-274-7333.

Bob Wells Nursery, P.O. Box 606, Lindale, TX 75771: Free catalog ❖ Fruit, nut, and shade trees. Also berries, grapes, muscadines, roses, ornamentals, and flowering shrubs. 903-882-3550.

White Flower Farm, Rt. 63, Litchfield, CT 06759: Free catalog ❖ Bulbs, perennials, shrubs, strawberry plants, seeds and plants, books, tools, and gardening supplies. 800-888-7756.

Bonsai

Avid Gardener, Box 200, Hamburg, IL 62045: Catalog $3 ❖ Dwarf conifers, companion shrubs, ground covers, and potential bonsai.

Bonsai Associates Inc., 3000 Chestnut Ave., Baltimore, MD 21211: Catalog $2 ❖ Books, plants, tools, soil components, and wire. 410-235-5336.

Bonsai by the Monastery, 2625 Hwy. 212 SW, Conyers, GA 30208: Catalog $5 ❖ Japanese and Chinese pots, tools, wire, books, videos, and clay figurines. 707-918-9661.

Bonsai Boy of N.Y., 7 Format Ln., Smithtown, NY 11787: Free catalog ❖ Bonsai trees. 516-265-2763.

Bonsai Farm, P.O. Box 130, Lavernia, TX 78121: Catalog $1 ❖ Bonsai trees, indoor and outdoor bonsai plants, books, tools, and pots. 512-649-2109.

Bonsai of Brooklyn, 2443 McDonald Ave., Brooklyn, NY 11223: Free price list ❖ Potted and established bonsai, trained and semi-trained pre-bonsai stock, tools, books, pottery, and supplies. 800-8-BONSAI; 718-339-8252 (in NY).

The Bonsai Shop, P.O. Box 76, Nesconsett, NY 11767: Catalog $3 ❖ Bonsai, growing supplies, tools, and books.

Dallas Bonsai Garden, P.O. Box 801565, Dallas, TX 75380: Free catalog ❖ Bonsai and supplies. 800-982-1223.

Flowertown Bonsai, 207 E. Luke St., Summerville, SC 29483: Free price list ❖ Bonsai and pottery. 800-774-0003.

Forestfarm, 990 Tetherow Rd., Williams, OR 97544: Catalog $3 ❖ Plants, ornamental trees, shrubs, and perennials for bonsai. 541-846-7269.

Girard Nurseries, P.O. Box 428, Geneva, OH 44041: Free catalog ❖ Bonsai and ornamental trees, shrubs, and evergreen seeds and trees. 216-466-2881.

Greer Gardens, 1280 Goodpasture Island Rd., Eugene, OR 97401: Catalog $3 ❖ Bonsai, azaleas and rhododendrons, trees, shrubs, Japanese maples, and succulents. 800-548-0111.

Jope's Bonsai Nursery, P.O. Box 594, Wenham, MA 01984: Catalog $2 ❖ Japanese maples, five-needle pines, pre-bonsai, imported and domestic bonsai, tools, pots, books and supplies. 508-468-2249.

Marrs Tree Farm, P.O. Box 375, Puyallup, WA 98371: Catalog $1 (refundable) ❖ Bonsai plants. 253-848-5755.

Miniature Plant Kingdom, 4125 Harrison Grade Rd., Sebastopol, CA 95472: Catalog $2.50 ❖ Japanese maples, conifers, and other bonsai plants. Also miniature roses. 707-874-2233.

Mt. Si Bonsai, 43321 SE Mt. Si Rd. North, Bend, WA 98045: Catalog $1 ❖ Indoor and outdoor bonsai, pots, tools, and bonsai starters. 206-888-0350.

Mountain Maples, P.O. Box 1329, Laytonville, CA 95454: Catalog $1 ❖ Japanese maples for bonsai. 707-984-6522.

New British Bonsai Magazine, Dallas Bonsai Garden, Dallas, TX 75380: Free catalog ❖ Imported and domestic bonsai and growing supplies. 800-982-1223.

New England Bonsai, 914 S. Main St., Bellingham, MA 02019: Free information ❖ Tropical, sub-tropical, and juniper bonsai in ceramic bonsai pots. Also empty pots, tools, and supplies. 800-457-5445.

Northland Gardens, 423 West Mountain Rd., Queensbury, NY 12804: Information $2 ❖ Bonsai, starter stock, books, pottery, tools, and growing aids. 800-4-BONSAI.

Northridge Gardens Nursery, 9821 White Oak Ave., Northridge, CA 91325: Catalog $1 (refundable) ❖ Cacti, bonsai, and rare and unusual plants. 818-349-9798.

GARDENING—PLANTS & SEEDS

Pen Y Bryn, RR 1, Box 1313, Forksville, PA 18616: Catalog $2 ❖ Pre-bonsai trees and growing supplies.

Pine Garden Bonsai, 20331 SR 530 NE, Arlington, WA 98223: Catalog $2 ❖ Stoneware bonsai containers and finished bonsai. 206-435-5995.

Riverside Bonsai, P.O. Box 633, Columbus, NC 28722: Catalog $1.50 ❖ Bonsai supplies. 704-894-3735.

Spring Hill Nurseries, 6523 N. Galena Rd., P.O. Box 1758, Peoria, IL 61632: Free catalog ❖ Bonsai, perennials, roses, annuals, ground covers, small fruits, house plants, seeds and plants, and gardening supplies. 800-582-8527.

Tom's Tiny Trees & Supplies, 14318 State Rd., North Royalton, OH 44133: Free catalog ❖ Imported bonsai supplies, tools, and pots. 216-582-9411.

Wildwood Gardens, 14488 Rock Creek Rd., Chardon, OH 44024: Catalog $1 ❖ Imported and domestic bonsai, pre-bonsai plants, and tools. 216-286-3714.

Cacti & Succulents

Abbey Garden Nursery, P.O. Box 2249, La Habra, CA 90632: Catalog $2 (refundable) ❖ Cacti and succulents. 310-905-3520.

Aztekakti Seeds, 11306 Gateway East, El Paso, TX 79927: Catalog $1 ❖ Seeds for cacti and succulents. 915-838-1130.

Brudy's Exotics, Box 820874, Houston, TX 77282: Free catalog ❖ Exotic plants and seeds, butterfly kits, and books. 800-926-7333.

Cactus by Mueller, 10411 Rosedale Hwy., Bakersfield, CA 93312: Catalog $2 ❖ Cacti and succulents. 805-589-2674.

Desert Nursery, 1301 S. Copper, Deming, NM 88030: Free list with 1st class stamp ❖ Cacti and succulents. 505-546-6264.

Epi World, 10607 Glenview Ave., Cupertino, CA 95014: Catalog $2 ❖ Orchid cacti. 408-865-0566.

Grigsby Cactus Gardens, 2354 Bella Vista, Vista, CA 92084: Catalog $2 ❖ Rare cacti and succulents. 619-727-1323.

Henrietta's Nursery, 1345 N. Brawley, Fresno, CA 93722: Catalog 50¢ ❖ Cacti and succulents. 209-275-2166.

Highland Succulents, 1446 Bear Run Rd., Gallipolis, OH 45631: Catalog $2 ❖ Succulents. 614-256-1428.

Intermountain Cactus, 1478 N. 750 East, Kaysville, UT 84037: Price list $1 ❖ Winter-hardy cacti. 801-546-2006.

Joe's Nursery, P.O. Box 1867, Vista, CA 92085: Catalog $1 ❖ Palms, cacti, succulents, rare plants, bromeliads, and other garden species.

K & L Cactus/Succulent Nursery, 9500 Brook Branch Rd. East, Ione, CA 95640: Catalog $3 ❖ Cacti and succulents.

Lauray of Salisbury, 432 Undermountain Rd., Salisbury, CT 06068: Catalog $2 ❖ Cacti and succulents, begonias, gesneriads, and orchids. 203-435-2263.

Loehman's Cactus, Box 871, Paramount, CA 90723: List $1 (refundable) ❖ Rare, unusual, and common cacti plants.

Mesa Garden, Box 72, Belen, NM 87002: Catalog $1 ❖ Cacti and succulent seeds and plants. 505-864-3131.

Northridge Gardens Nursery, 9821 White Oak Ave., Northridge, CA 91325: Catalog $1 (refundable) ❖ Cacti, bonsai, and rare and unusual plants. 818-349-9798.

Rainbow Gardens Bookshop, 1444 E. Taylor St., Vista, CA 92084: Catalog $2 ❖ Cacti, hoyas, and books on cacti. 619-758-4290.

Shein's Cactus, 3360 Drew St., Marina, CA 93933: Free information ❖ Cacti plants. 408-384-7765.

Succulenta, P.O. Box 480325, Los Angeles, CA 90048: Catalog $1 ❖ Rare and unusual cacti and succulents. 213-933-8676.

Tropiflora, 3530 Tallevast Rd., Sarasota, FL 34243: Free information ❖ Rare succulents, caudiciforms, and other unusual exotic flora. 800-631-7520.

Carnivorous Plants

Black Copper Kits, 111 Rigwood Ave., Pompton Lakes, NJ 07442: Catalog 50¢ ❖ Carnivorous plants and supplies.

Carolina Exotic Gardens, Rt. 5, Box 283-A, Greenville, NC 27834: Catalog $1 ❖ Carnivorous plants and seeds and terrarium plant groupings. 919-758-2600.

Lee's Botanical Gardens, P.O. Box 669, LaBelle, FL 33975: Free catalog ❖ Carnivorous plants, orchids, and ferns. 813-675-8728.

Orgel's Orchids, 18950 SW 136th St., Miami, FL 33196: Free catalog ❖ Carnivorous plants and orchids. 305-233-7168.

Peter Pauls Nurseries, 4665 Chapin Rd., Canandaigua, NY 14424: Free catalog ❖ Carnivorous and woodland terrarium plants. 716-394-7397.

Chrysanthemums

Dooley Mum Gardens, 210 N. High St., Hutchinson, MN 55350: Free catalog ❖ New and old chrysanthemums. 612-587-3050.

Huff's Garden Mums, 710 Juniatta, Burlington, KS 66839: Catalog $1 (refundable) ❖ Chrysanthemums. 800-279-4675.

King's Chrysanthemums, P.O. Box 368, Clements, CA 94227: Catalog $2 (refundable) ❖ Rooted cuttings. 209-759-3571.

Citrus & Exotic Fruits

Alberts & Merkel Brothers Inc., 2210 S. Federal Hwy., Boynton Beach, FL 33435: Catalog $1 ❖ Citrus and exotic fruits. 407-732-2071.

Aloha Tropicals, 1247 Browning Ct., Vista, CA 92083: Catalog $2 ❖ Heliconias, gingers, bananas, plumeria, and other plants. 512-259-0807.

The Banana Tree, 715 Northampton St., Easton, PA 18042: Catalog $3 ❖ Citrus and exotic fruits. 610-253-9589.

W. Atlee Burpee & Company, 300 Park Ave., Warminster, PA 18974: Free catalog ❖ Exotic fruits. 215-674-1793.

Crockett's Tropical Plants, P.O. Box 1150, Harlingen, TX 78551: Free catalog ❖ Container-grown ornamentals, citrus plants, and palms. 800-580-1900.

Edible Landscaping, P.O. Box 77, Afton, VA 22920: Catalog $1 ❖ Exotic fruits. 800-524-4156.

Henry Field's Seed & Nursery, 415 N. Burnett, Shenandoah, IA 51602: Free catalog ❖ Exotic fruits. 605-665-4491.

Fig Tree Nursery, P.O. Box 124, Gulf Hammock, FL 32639: Catalog $1 ❖ Exotic fruits. 904-486-2930.

Four Seasons Nursery, 1706 Morrisey Dr., Bloomington, IL 61704: Free catalog ❖ Citrus and exotic fruits. 309-663-9551.

Garden of Delights, 14560 SW 14th St., Davie, FL 33325: Catalog $2 (refundable) ❖ Tropical fruits and nuts. 954-370-9004.

Glasshouse Works Greenhouses, P.O. Box 97, Stewart, OH 45778: Catalog $3 ❖ Citrus and exotic fruits. 614-662-2142.

Gurney Seed & Nursery Company, 110 Capitol St., Yankton, SD 57079: Free catalog ❖ Citrus and exotic fruits. 605-665-1671.

Kartuz Greenhouses, 1408 Sunset Dr., Vista, CA 92083: Catalog $2 ❖ Citrus and exotic fruits. 619-941-3613.

Logee's Greenhouses, 141 North St., Danielson, CT 06239: Catalog $3 (refundable) ❖ Citrus and exotic fruits. 860-774-8038.

Mellinger's, 2310 W. South Range Rd., North Lima, OH 44452: Free catalog ❖ Citrus and exotic fruits. 330-549-9861.

Northwoods Retail Nursery, 27635 S. Oglesby Rd., Canby, OR 97013: Free catalog ❖ Citrus and exotic fruits. 503-266-5432.

Pacific Tree Farms, 4301 Lynnwood Dr., Chula Vista, CA 92010: Catalog $2 ❖ Citrus and exotic fruits. 619-422-2400.

Peaceful Valley Farm Supply, P.O. Box 2209, Grass Valley, CA 95945: Catalog $2 (refundable) ❖ Citrus fruits. 916-272-4769.

Raintree Nursery, 391 Butts Rd., Morton, WA 98356: Free information ❖ Citrus and exotic fruits. 206-496-6400.

Richland, P.O. Box 9008, Solvang, CA 93464: Brochure $1 ❖ Hawaiian pineapple, sugar cane, flowers, cacti, and edibles.

Tripple Brook Farm, 37 Middle Rd., Southampton, MA 01073: Catalog 50¢ ❖ Bamboo plants, exotic fruits, trees, perennials, and shrubs. 413-527-4626.

Daffodils

Bonnie Brae Gardens, 1105 SE Christensen Rd., Corbett, OR 97019: Free list with long SASE ❖ Daffodil bulbs.

Breck's Dutch Bulbs, Mail Order Reservation Center, 6523 N. Galena Rd., P.O. Box 1757, Peoria, IL 61656: Free catalog ❖ Daffodil bulbs. 309-691-4616.

Cascade Daffodils, P.O. Box 10626, White Bear Lake, MN 55110: Catalog $2 ❖ Standard, miniature, and show daffodils. 612-426-9616.

The Daffodil Mart, 7463 Heath Trail, Gloucester, VA 23061: Free catalog ❖ Novelty, miniature, hybridized, and species daffodils. 800-255-2852.

Degroot Inc., P.O. Box 934, Caloma, MI 49038: Free catalog ❖ Daffodil bulbs.

Mad River Imports, P.O. Box 1685, Moretown, VT 05660: Free catalog ❖ Daffodil bulbs.

McClure & Zimmerman, P.O. Box 368, Friesland, WI 53935: Free catalog ❖ Daffodil bulbs.

Messelaar Bulb Company, Rt. 1A, P.O. Box 269, Ipswich, MA 01938: Free catalog ❖ Daffodil bulbs.

Grant Mitsch Novelty Daffodils, P.O. Box 218, Hubbard, OR 97032: Catalog $3 (refundable) ❖ Exhibition and garden varieties of pink and hybrid daffodils. 503-651-2742.

Quality Dutch Bulbs, P.O. Box 434, Stockertown, PA 18083: Free catalog ❖ 18083: Free catalog ❖ Daffodils, irises, tulips, and other bulbs. 800-755-2852.

Van Dyck's Flower Farms, P.O. Box 430, Brightwater, NY 11718: Free catalog ❖ Daffodil bulbs. 800-248-2852.

Veldheer Tulip Gardens, 12755 Quincy St., Holland, MI 49424: Free catalog ❖ Daffodil bulbs.

Dahlias

BJ's Dahlias, 130 Taylor Loop Rd., Selah, WA 98942: Free catalog with two 1st class stamps ❖ Dahlias. 509-697-6089.

Connell's, 10216 40th Ave., Tacoma, WA 98446: Catalog $2 ❖ Exhibition and garden varieties of dahlias from worldwide sources. 206-531-0292.

Ferncliff Gardens, Box 66, Sumas, WA 98295: Free catalog ❖ Dahlias. 604-826-2447.

Garden Valley Dahlias, 406 Lower Garden Valley, Roseburg, OR 97470: Free catalog ❖ Dahlias. 503-673-8521.

Swan Island Dahlias, P.O. Box 700, Canby, OR 97013: Catalog $3 (refundable) ❖ Dahlias. 503-266-7711.

Ferns

Kurt Bluemel Inc., 2740 Greene Ln., Baldwin, MD 21013: Catalog $3 ❖ Ferns, perennials, bamboo plants, and ornamental grasses. 410-557-7229.

Busse Gardens, P.O. Box N, Cokato, MN 55321: Catalog $2 ❖ Ferns, seeds and plants, and Siberian irises. 612-286-2654.

Crownsville Nursery, P.O. Box 797, Crownsville, MD 21032: Catalog $2 (minimum order $25) ❖ Ferns, wildflowers, azaleas, ornamental grasses, and perennials. 410-923-2212.

Cycad Gardens, 4524 Toland Way, Los Angeles, CA 90041: Free catalog with long SASE ❖ Cycads.

Foliage Gardens, 2003 128th Ave. SE, Bellevue, WA 98005: Catalog $2 ❖ Indoor and outdoor ferns. 206-747-2998.

Gardens of the Blue Ridge, P.O. Box 10, Pineola, NC 28662: Catalog $3 (refundable) ❖ Wildflower seeds, ferns, trees, plants, shrubs, and bulbs. 704-733-2417.

Gilson Gardens Inc., 3059 US Rt. 20, P.O. Box 277, Perry, OH 44081: Free catalog ❖ Ground covers, perennials, and ferns. 216-259-5252.

Griffey Nursery, 1670 Hwy. 25/70, Marshall, NC 28753: Free catalog ❖ Appalachian wildflowers, ferns and vines, rock and bog plants, and orchids. 704-656-2334.

Growers Service Company, P.O. Box 445, Hartland, MI 48353: Catalog $1 (refundable) ❖ Ferns, perennials, lilies, Dutch and rare bulbs, and other plants.

Jerry Horne, Rare Plants Nursery, 10195 SW 70th St., Miami, FL 33173: Free list with long SASE ❖ Ferns, platyceriums, palms and cycads, and rare and unusual plants. 305-270-1235.

Lee's Botanical Gardens, P.O. Box 669, LaBelle, FL 33975: Free catalog ❖ Carnivorous plants, orchids, and ferns. 813-675-8728.

Limerock Ornamental Grasses Inc., RD 1, Box 111, Port Matilda, PA 16870: Catalog $3 ❖ Ornamental and native grasses, companion perennials, and nursery-grown hardy ferns. 814-692-2272.

Oakridge Nurseries, P.O. Box 182, East Kingston, NH 03827: Catalog $1 (refundable) ❖ Ferns and native wildflowers.

Orchid Gardens, 2232 139th Ave. NW, Andover, MN 55304: Catalog $1 ❖ Wildflowers, native trees, shrubs, and ferns. 612-755-0205.

Pen Y Bryn, RR 1, Box 1313, Forksville, PA 18616: Catalog $2 ❖ Ferns.

Shady Oaks Nursery, 112 10th Ave. SE, Waseca, MN 56093: Information $1 ❖ Ferns, shrubs, perennials, and wildflowers. 507-835-5033.

Squaw Mountain Gardens, 36212 SE Squaw Mountain, Estacada, OR 97023: Catalog $2 (refundable) ❖ Ferns and companion rock garden plants.

Sunlight Gardens, 174 Golden Ln., Andersonville, TN 37705: Catalog $3 ❖ Hardy ferns and perennials. 615-494-8237.

Varga's Nursery, 2631 Pickertown Rd., Warrington, PA 18976: Price list $1 ❖ Ferns. 215-343-0646.

Wildflower Nursery, 1680 Hwy. 25-70, Marshall, NC 28753: Free catalog ❖ Ferns. 704-656-2723.

Geraniums

Clark's Greenhouse & Herbal Country, 2580 100th Ave., San Jose, IL 62682: Catalog $2 ❖ Herbs, everlasting plants, and scented geraniums. 309-247-3679.

Dabney Herbs, P.O. Box 22061, Louisville, KY 40222: Catalog $2 ❖ Ginseng, herbs, scented geraniums, perennials, and wildflowers. 502-893-5198.

Davidson-Wilson Greenhouses, Rt. 2, Box 168, Crawfordsville, IN 47933: Catalog $3 ❖ Geraniums, house plants, begonias, impatiens, herbs, and succulents. 317-364-0556.

Good Hollow Greenhouse & Herbarium, 50 Slaterock Mill Rd., Taft, TN 38488. Catalog $1 ❖ Herb plants and dried herbs, perennials, wildflowers, scented geraniums, essential oils and potpourris, teas, and spices. 615-433-7640.

Lily of the Valley Herb Farm, 3969 Fox Ave., Minerva, OH 44657: Price list $1 (refundable) ❖ Herbs and herbal products, everlastings, perennials, and scented geranium plants. 216-862-3920.

Rabbit Shadow Farm, 2880 E. Hwy. 402, Loveland, CO 80537: Free information ❖ Herbs, roses, topiary supplies, and scented geraniums. 303-667-5531.

Rasland Farm, Rt. 1, Box 65 HC, Godwin, NC 28344: Catalog $2.50 ❖ Herb plants, scented geraniums, and dried flowers. 910-567-2705.

❖ GARDENING—PLANTS & SEEDS ❖

Sandy Mush Herb Nursery, 316 Surret Cove Rd., Leicester, NC 28748: Catalog $4 ❖ Geraniums. 704-683-2014.

Sunnybrook Farms Nursery, P.O. Box 6, Chesterland, OH 44026: Catalog $1 (refundable) ❖ Hostas, herb plants, scented geraniums, perennials, and ivies. 216-729-7232.

Well-Sweep Herb Farm, 205 Mt. Bethel Rd., Port Murray, NJ 07865: Catalog $2 ❖ Geraniums. 908-852-5390.

Williamette Valley Garden, Box 285, Lake Oswego, OR 97034: Catalog $1 ❖ Geraniums and perennials.

Ginseng

American Ginseng Gardens, 404 Mountain Meadow Ln., Flag Pond, TN 37657: Information $1 ❖ Ginseng and goldenseal roots and seeds.

Barney's Ginseng Patch, Rt. 2, Box 43, Montgomery City, MO 63361: Catalog $2 ❖ Ginseng seed and roots and books. 573-564-2575.

Buckhorn Ginseng, Richland Center, WI 53581: Free information with long SASE ❖ Ginseng seed.

William H. Collins Gardens, Box 48, Viola, IA 52350: Free information ❖ Ginseng seed roots.

Dabney Herbs, P.O. Box 22061, Louisville, KY 40222: Catalog $2 ❖ Ginseng, herbs, scented geraniums, perennials, and wildflowers. 502-893-5198.

Ginseng, Flag Pond, TN 37657: Information $1 ❖ Stratified seed and 1st year roots.

The Homestead, 72799 Old 21 Rd., Kimbolton, OH 43749: Free information ❖ Ginseng planting stock.

HSU's Ginseng Enterprises Inc., P.O. Box 509, Wausau, WI 54402: Free information ❖ American and Canadian stratified ginseng seed, rootlets, and ginseng health products and extracts. 800-826-1577; 715-675-2325 (in WI).

Leeland's Ginseng, 5712 Cooper Rd., Indianapolis, IN 46208: Free information with long SASE ❖ Ginseng growing supplies.

Osaanyin Herb Cooperative, 112 Main St., Montpelier, VT 05602: Catalog $1 ❖ Medicinal, exotic, and other herbs and botanicals. Also extracts and oils, ginseng, and books. 802-223-0888.

The Thyme Garden, 20546 Alsea Hwy., Alsea, OR 97324: Catalog $2 (refundable) ❖ Herb seeds, plants, hops, ginseng, dried herbs, and teas. 503-487-8671.

Gladioli

Connell's, 10216 40th Ave., Tacoma, WA 98446: Catalog $2 ❖ Gladioli bulbs. 206-531-0292.

Kingfisher Glads, 11734 Road 33-1/2, Madera, CA 93638: Free catalog ❖ New gladioli and older cultivars. 209-645-5329.

Mellinger's, 2310 W. South Range Rd., North Lima, OH 44452: Free catalog ❖ Fruit and nut, shade, and ornamental trees. Also gladioli, flowering shrubs, hedges, irises, wildflowers, and gardening equipment. 330-549-9861.

Skolaski's Glads & Flowers, 4821 County Trunk Hwy. Q, Waunakee, WI 53597: Catalog $1 ❖ Gladioli bulbs, lilies, and perennials. 608-836-4822.

Waushara Gardens, 5491 5th Dr., Plainfield, WI 54966: Free catalog ❖ Gladioli. 715-335-4462.

Gourds

Alfrey Seeds, P.O. Box 415, Knoxville, TN 37901: Free list with long SASE ❖ Gourds and seeds for chili peppers and vegetables.

H. Bankhead Gourds, Rt. 2, Box 60, Roscoe, TX 79545: Free information with long SASE ❖ Seeds for large luffa gourds.

J.L. Hudson, Seedsman, Box 1058, Redwood City, CA 94064: Catalog $1 ❖ Gourd seeds.

Nichols Garden Nursery, 1190 SW Pacific, Albany, OR 97321: Free catalog ❖ Gourd seeds. 541-928-9280.

West Mountain Gourd Farm, P.O. Drawer 1049, Gilmer, TX 75644: Information $3 ❖ Ready-to-paint gourds in all shapes and sizes. 903-734-5204.

Grapes

Concord Nurseries Inc., 10175 Mile Block Rd., North Collins, NY 14111: Catalog $1 ❖ Grapevines.

Fig Tree Nursery, P.O. Box 124, Gulf Hammock, FL 32639: Catalog $1 ❖ Berry plants, ornamentals, and grapes for southern climates. 904-486-2930.

Ison's Nursery, P.O. Box 190, Brooks, GA 30205: Free catalog ❖ Muscadine grapevines, berries, and fruit and nut trees. 800-733-0324.

Earl May Seeds & Nursery Company, N. Elm St., Shenandoah, IA 51603: Free catalog ❖ Grapevines, berry plants, roses, flowering shrubs, gardening supplies, and fruit, nut, shade, and ornamental trees. 712-246-1020.

J.E. Miller Nurseries, 5060 West Lake Rd., Canandaigua, NY 14424: Free catalog ❖ Grapevines, berry plants, and fruit trees. 800-836-9630.

W.K. Morss & Son, RFD 2, Lakeshore Rd., Boxford, MA 01921: Free brochure ❖ Grapevines and rhubarb, strawberry, and raspberry plants. 508-352-2633.

The Nursery, Hwy. 82, Box 130, Ty Ty, GA 31795: Free catalog ❖ Berries, grapes, trees, and shrubs. 800-972-2101.

Patrick's Nursery, P.O. Box 130, Ty Ty, GA 31795: Free catalog ❖ Grapevines, vegetable seeds, berry plants, and fruit and nut trees. 800-972-2101.

Lon J. Rombough, P.O. Box 365, Aurora, OR 97002: Free catalog with long SASE ❖ Grapevine cuttings. 503-678-1410.

Bob Wells Nursery, P.O. Box 606, Lindale, TX 75771: Free catalog ❖ Fruit, nut, and shade trees. Also berries, grapes, muscadines, roses, ornamentals, and flowering shrubs. 903-882-3550.

Grasses & Ground Covers

Ambergate Gardens, 8015 Krey Ave., Waconia, MN 55387: Catalog $2 ❖ Grasses and perennial flowers. 612-443-2248.

Avid Gardener, Box 200, Hamburg, IL 62045: Catalog $3 ❖ Dwarf conifers, companion shrubs, ground covers, and potential bonsai.

Kurt Bluemel Inc., 2740 Greene Ln., Baldwin, MD 21013: Catalog $3 ❖ Ornamental grasses, water garden plants, and perennials. 410-557-7229.

Bluestone Perennials, 7211 Middle Ridge Rd., Madison, OH 44057: Free catalog ❖ Ground covers. 800-852-5243.

W. Atlee Burpee & Company, 300 Park Ave., Warminster, PA 18974: Free catalog ❖ Ornamental grasses. 215-674-1793.

Classic Groundcovers Inc., 405 Belmont Rd., Athens, GA 30605: Free catalog ❖ Ground covers. 800-248-8424; 404-543-0145 (in GA).

Crownsville Nursery, P.O. Box 797, Crownsville, MD 21032: Catalog $2 (minimum order $25) ❖ Ferns, wildflowers, azaleas, ornamental grasses, and perennials. 410-923-2212.

Czarnick Nursery, RR 2, Genola, NE 68640: Catalog $1 ❖ Perennials, grasses, and wildflowers.

Digging Dog Nursery, P.O. Box 471, Albion, CA 95410: Catalog $3 ❖ Grasses, vines, trees, perennials, and shrubs. 707-937-1130.

Evergreen Nursery, 1220 Dowdy Rd., Athens, GA 30606: Free catalog ❖ Bare root and potted ground covers. 800-521-7267; 404-548-7781 (in GA).

Fieldstone Gardens Inc., 620 Quaker Ln., Vassalboro, ME 04989: Catalog $2 ❖ Mature plants for sun, shade, rock gardens, and ground covers. 207-923-3836.

Gilson Gardens Inc., 3059 US Rt. 20, P.O. Box 277, Perry, OH 44081: Free catalog ❖ Ground covers, perennials, and ferns. 216-259-5252.

GARDENING—PLANTS & SEEDS

Greenlee Nursery, 301-1/2 E. Franklin Ave., Pomona, CA 91766: Catalog $5 ❖ Ornamental grasses. 909-629-9045.

Limerock Ornamental Grasses Inc., RD 1, Box 111, Port Matilda, PA 16870: Catalog $3 ❖ Ornamental and native grasses, companion perennials, and nursery-grown hardy ferns. 814-692-2272.

Maryland Aquatic Nurseries, 3427 N. Furnace Rd., Jarrettsville, MD 21084: Catalog $5 (refundable) ❖ Water garden plants, ornamental grasses, and Louisiana and Japanese irises. 410-557-7615.

Meadow View Farms, 3360 N. Pacific Hwy., Medford, OR 97501: Catalog $3 ❖ Perennials, grasses, herbs, vines, and aquatic plants.

J.E. Miller Nurseries, 5060 W. Lake Rd., Canandaigua, NY 14424: Free catalog ❖ Fruit and nut trees, vines, ornamentals, and ground covers. 800-836-9630.

Park Seed Company, Cokesbury Rd., P.O. Box 46, Greenwood, SC 29648: Free catalog ❖ Ornamental grasses. 800-845-3369.

Peekskill Nurseries, P.O. Box 428, Shrub Oak, NY 10588: Free catalog ❖ Ground covers. 914-245-5595.

Plants of the Southwest, Rt. 6, Box 11A, Santa Fe, NM 87501: Catalog $3.50 ❖ Native trees, grasses, wildflowers, shrubs, and plants. 505-471-2212.

Prairie State Commodities, P.O. Box 6, Trilla, IL 62469: Catalog $1 ❖ Seeds for annuals, perennial rye grass and Park Kentucky bluegrass, corn, clover, and alfalfa. 217-235-4322.

Prentiss Court Ground Covers, P.O. Box 8662, Greenville, SC 29604: Catalog $1 ❖ Ground covers. 864-277-4037.

Stoecklein's Nursery, 135 Critchow Rd., Renfrew, PA 16053: Catalog $1 ❖ Ground covers. 412-586-7882.

Thompson & Morgan Inc., P.O. Box 1308, Jackson, NJ 08527: Free catalog ❖ Ornamental grasses. 800-274-7333.

Zoysia Farm Nurseries, General Offices & Store, 3617 Old Taneytown Rd., Taneytown, MD 21787: Free information ❖ Zoysia plugs. 410-756-2311.

Herbs

Aphrodesia Products, 264 Bleeker St., New York, NY 10014: Catalog $3 ❖ Dried herbs, herb products, and books. 800-221-6898; 212-989-6440 (in NY).

Black Pearl Gardens, Herbal General Store, 425 Main St., Franklin, OH 45005: Catalog $1 ❖ Herb plants, aromatherapy products, potpourri and supplies, culinary and medicinal herbs, herbal bath and body products, and dried florals. 513-746-0004.

Bountiful Gardens, 18001 Shafer Ranch Rd., Willits, CA 95490: Free catalog ❖ Seeds for vegetables, compost crops, herbs, and flowers. Also books and organic gardening supplies. 707-459-6410.

Brown's Edgewood Gardens, 2611 Corrine Dr., Orlando, FL 32803: Catalog $3 ❖ Butterfly-attracting plants, herbs, and organic gardening products. 407-896-3203.

Caprilands Herb Farm, 534 Silver St., Coventry, CT 06238: Free catalog with long SASE ❖ Plants, seeds, books, and potpourris. 203-742-7244.

Clark's Greenhouse & Herbal Country, 2580 100th Ave., San Jose, IL 62682: Catalog $2 ❖ Herbs, everlasting plants, and scented geraniums. 309-247-3679.

Companion Plants, 7247 N. Coolville Ridge, Athens, OH 45701: Catalog $3 ❖ Seeds for exotic, herb, and native plants. 614-592-4643.

Comstock, Ferre & Company, 263 Main St., Wethersfield, CT 06109: Catalog $2 ❖ Vegetable, flower, and herb seeds. 860-571-6590.

Dabney Herbs, P.O. Box 22061, Louisville, KY 40222: Catalog $2 ❖ Ginseng, herbs, scented geraniums, perennials, and wildflowers. 502-893-5198.

Davidson-Wilson Greenhouses, Rt. 2, Box 168, Crawfordsville, IN 47933: Catalog $3 ❖ Geraniums, house plants, begonias, impatiens, herbs, and succulents. 317-364-0556.

Flowery Branch, P.O. Box 1330, Flowery Branch, GA 30542: Catalog $3 ❖ Rare and exotic herb seeds. 404-536-8380.

The Gathered Herb & Greenhouse, 12114 N. State Rd., Otisville, MI 48463: Catalog $2 ❖ Herbs, herb teas, perennials, dried flowers, and potpourri supplies. 810-631-6572.

Good Hollow Greenhouse & Herbarium, 50 Slaterock Mill Rd., Taft, TN 38488: Catalog $1 ❖ Herb plants and dried herbs, perennials, wildflowers, scented geraniums, essential oils and potpourri, teas, and spices. 615-433-7640.

Goodwin Creek Gardens, P.O. Box 83, Williams, OR 97544: Catalog $1 ❖ Dried floral arrangements, herb plants, container-grown native American trees, shrubs, and perennial flowers. 541-846-7357.

The Gourmet Gardener, 8650 College Blvd., Overland Park, KS 66210: Catalog $2 ❖ Herb, vegetable, and edible flower seeds from around the world. 913-345-0490.

Greenfield Herb Garden, P.O. Box 9, Shipshewana, IN 46565: Catalog $1.50 ❖ Herb books and plants. 800-831-0504.

Hartman's Herb Farm, 1026 Old Dana Rd., Barre, MA 01005: Catalog $2 ❖ Herbs and herb products, potpourris, essential oils, and wreaths. 508-355-2015.

Harvest Health Inc., 1944 Eastern Ave. SE, Grand Rapids, MI 49507: Free catalog ❖ Herbs, spices, and essential and perfume oils. 616-245-6268.

Herb Products Company, P.O. Box 898, 11012 Magnolia Blvd., North Hollywood, CA 91601: Free price list ❖ Botanicals, oils and fragrances, extracts and tinctures, and books. 818-984-3141.

Herban Garden, 5002 2nd St., Rainbow, CA 92028: Catalog $1 ❖ Herbs, vegetables, and everlastings. 619-723-2967.

The Herbfarm, 32804 Issaquah-Fall City Rd., Fall City, WA 98024: Information $1 ❖ Herb plants, seed, and herbal items. 800-866-4372.

Herbs-Liscious, 1702 S. 6th St., Marshalltown, IA 50158: Catalog $2 (refundable) ❖ Herb plants, dried herbs, spices, and oils.

Hillary's Garden, P.O. Box 430, Warwick, NY 10990: Catalog $2 ❖ Perennials and organically grown herbs.

Indiana Botanic Gardens, 3401 W. 317th Ave., Hobart, IN 46342: Free catalog ❖ Herbs, herb seeds, and essential oils.

Le Jardin du Gourmet, P.O. Box 75, St. Johnsbury Center, VT 05863: Catalog $1 ❖ Herb plants and seeds. Also vegetable seeds. 802-748-1446.

Lily of the Valley Herb Farm, 3969 Fox Ave., Minerva, OH 44657: Price list $1 (refundable) ❖ Herb plants, everlastings, perennials, scented geraniums, and herbal products. 216-862-3920.

Meadow View Farms, 3360 N. Pacific Hwy., Medford, OR 97501: Catalog $3 ❖ Perennials, grasses, herbs, vines, and aquatic plants.

Meadowbrook Herb Gardens, 93 Kingstown Rd., Wyoming, RI 02898: Catalog $1 ❖ Herb seeds. 401-539-7603.

Nichols Garden Nursery, 1190 SW Pacific, Albany, OR 97321: Free catalog ❖ Seeds, plants, and herbal products. 541-928-9280.

Perennial Pleasures Nursery, P.O. Box 147, East Hardwick, VT 05836: Catalog $3 ❖ Heirloom herbs and flowers. 802-472-5104.

Planta Dei Medicinal Herb Farm, Millville, New Brunswick, Canada E0H 1M0: Catalog $2 (refundable) ❖ Biologically grown teas, medicinal herbs, healing tea mixtures, cosmetics, natural ointments, and massage oils. 506-463-8169.

Rabbit Shadow Farm, 2880 E. Hwy. 402, Loveland, CO 80537: Free information ❖ Herbs, roses, topiary supplies, and scented geraniums. 303-667-5531.

Rasland Farm, Rt. 1, Box 65 HC, Godwin, NC 28344: Catalog $2.50 ❖ Herb plants, scented geraniums, dried flowers, and herbal products. 910-567-2705.

GARDENING—PLANTS & SEEDS

Redwood City Seed Company, P.O. Box 361, Redwood City, CA 94064: Catalog $1 ❖ Herb and vegetable seeds from worldwide sources. 415-325-7333.

The Rosemary House, 120 S. Market St., Mechanicsburg, PA 17055: Catalog $2 ❖ Plants, seeds, herb products, and books. 717-697-5111.

Sandy Mush Herb Nursery, 316 Surret Cove Rd., Leicester, NC 28748: Catalog $4 ❖ Culinary and tea herbs, other herbs, scented geraniums, and flowering perennials. 704-683-2014.

Seeds of Change, Box 15700, Santa Fe, NM 87506: Free information ❖ Organic and open-pollinated hard-to-find vegetable, herb, and flower seeds. 800-957-3337.

Shady Acres Herb Farm, 7815 Hwy. 212, Chaska, MN 55318: Free list with long SASE ❖ Herbs, wildflowers, everlastings, and vegetables. 612-466-3391.

Spice Discounters, P.O. Box 6061, Aberdeen, SD 57401: Free catalog ❖ Herbs, spices, oils, extracts, and vitamins. 800-610-5950.

Story House Herb Farm, Rt. 7, Box 246, Murray, KY 42071: Catalog $2 (refundable) ❖ Organically-grown herb plants. 502-753-4158.

Sunnybrook Farms Nursery, P.O. Box 6, Chesterland, OH 44026: Catalog $1 (refundable) ❖ Hostas, herb plants, scented geraniums, perennials, and ivies. 216-729-7232.

The Thyme Garden, 20546 Alsea Hwy., Alsea, OR 97324: Catalog $2 (refundable) ❖ Herb seeds, plants, hops, ginseng, dried herbs, and teas. 503-487-8671.

Tinmouth Channel Farm, Box 428B, Tinmouth, VT 05773: Catalog $2 ❖ Vermont-certified organic plants and seeds. 802-446-2812.

Vermont Bean Seed Company, 95 Garden Ln., Fair Haven, VT 05743: Free catalog ❖ Bean seeds, heirloom plants, and herbs. 802-273-3400.

Well-Sweep Herb Farm, 205 Mt. Bethel Rd., Port Murray, NJ 07865: Catalog $2 ❖ Seeds for herbs, plants, and perennials. 908-852-5390.

Woodside Gardens, 1191 Egg & I Rd., Chimacum, WA 98325: Catalog $2 ❖ Perennials & herb plants. 360-732-4754.

Hostas

American Daylily & Perennials, P.O. Box 210, Grain Valley, MO 64029: Catalog $5 (refundable) ❖ Hostas, dwarf cannas, and daylilies. 800-770-2777.

Brookwood Gardens Inc., 600 E. 9th St., Michigan City, IN 46360: Catalog $2.98 ❖ Daylilies and hostas. 800-628-0110.

Caprice Farm Nursery, 15425 SW Pleasant Hill Rd., Sherwood, OR 97140: Catalog $2 ❖ Peonies, irises, daylilies, and hostas. 503-625-7241.

Carroll Gardens, 444 E. Main St., P.O. Box 310, Westminster, MD 21157: Catalog $3 (refundable) ❖ Hostas plants and cultivars. 800-638-6334.

Crownsville Nursery, P.O. Box 797, Crownsville, MD 21032: Catalog $2 (minimum order $25) ❖ Hosta plants and cultivars. 410-849-2212.

Daylily Farms & Nursery, Rt. 1, Box 89A, Bakersville, NC 28705: Catalog $2 ❖ Hostas and daylilies.

Good's Nursery, 51225 Ann Arbor Rd., Canton, MI 48187: List $2 with long SASE ❖ Hostas.

Klehm Nursery, 4210 N. Duncan Rd., Champaign, IL, 61821: Catalog $4 ❖ Peonies, irises, daylilies, hostas, and perennials. 800-553-3715.

Savory's Gardens Inc., 5300 Whiting Ave., Edina, MN 55439: Catalog $2 ❖ Hostas. 612-941-8755.

Shady Oaks Nursery, 112 10th Ave. SE, Waseca, MN 56093: Information $1 ❖ Hostas and shade-loving plants. 507-835-5033.

Sunnybrook Farms Nursery, P.O. Box 6, Chesterland, OH 44026: Catalog $1 (refundable) ❖ Hostas, herb plants, scented geraniums, perennials, and ivies. 216-729-7232.

Andre Viette Nurseries, Rt. 1, Box 16, Fisherville, VA 22929: Catalog $3 ❖ Hosta plants and cultivars. 703-942-2118.

Wayside Gardens, 1 Garden Ln., Hodges, SC 29695: Free catalog ❖ Hosta plants and cultivars. 800-845-1124.

White Oak Nursery, 6145 Oak Point Ct., Peoria, IL 61614: Free price list with long SASE ❖ Field-grown hostas.

House Plants & Indoor Gardens

Appalachian Gardens, Box 82, Waynesboro, PA 17268: Free catalog ❖ Hardy native plants, old favorites, and rare and unusual plants. 717-762-4312.

Avid Gardener, Box 200, Hamburg, IL 62045: Catalog $3 ❖ Dwarf conifers, companion shrubs, ground covers, and potential bonsai.

Belisle's Violet House, P.O. Box 111, Radisson, WI 54867: Catalog $2 ❖ Miniature sinninglas tubers and plants. 715-945-2687.

Brudy's Exotics, Box 820874, Houston, TX 77282: Free catalog ❖ Exotic seeds, plumerias, gingers, ornamental bananas, bougainvillea, hibiscus, and dwarf cannas. 800-926-7333.

The Compleat Garden Clematis Nursery, 217 Argilla Rd., Ipswich, MA 01938: Descriptive listing $2 ❖ Unusual and hard-to-find flowering clematis varieties in small and large pots.

Crockett's Tropical Plants, P.O. Box 1150, Harlingen, TX 78551: Catalog $3 ❖ Container-grown ornamentals, citrus plants, and palms. 800-580-1900.

Davidson-Wilson Greenhouses, Rt. 2, Box 168, Crawfordsville, IN 47933: Catalog $3 ❖ Geraniums, house plants, begonias, impatiens, herbs, and succulents. 317-364-0556.

Gardeners' Choice, 81961 Country Rd. 687, P.O. Box 8000, Hartford, MI 49057: Free catalog ❖ House plants, vegetables, flowers, and trees. 616-621-2481.

Glasshouse Works Greenhouses, P.O. Box 97, Stewart, OH 45778: Catalog $3 ❖ Windowsill jasmine plants. 614-662-2142.

Golden Lake Greenhouses, 10782 Citrus Dr., Moorpark, CA 93021: Catalog $2 ❖ Bromeliads, tillandsias, ephyliums, hoyas, and other plants.

Holladay Jungle, P.O. Box 5727, Fresno, CA 93755: Free information ❖ Tillandsias. 209-229-9858.

Lauray of Salisbury, 432 Undermountain Rd., Rt. 41, Salisbury, CT 06068: Catalog $2 ❖ Begonias, orchids, cacti, and succulents. 203-435-2263.

Logee's Greenhouses, 141 North St., Danielson, CT 06239: Catalog $3 (refundable) ❖ Begonias, geraniums, exotics, herbs, and other house plants. 860-774-8038.

Lyndon Lyon Greenhouses Inc., 14 Mutchler St., Dolgeville, NY 13329: Catalog $3 ❖ African violets and exotic house plants. 315-429-8291.

Merry Gardens, P.O. Box 595, Camden, ME 04843: Catalog $2 ❖ House and flowering plants, herbs, ivies, gesneriads, ferns and mosses, impatiens, jasmines, and geraniums. 207-236-9064.

Michael's Bromeliads, 1365 Canterbury Rd. North, St. Petersburg, FL 33710: Free catalog ❖ Species and hybrid bromeliads. 813-347-0349.

Oak Hill Gardens, P.O. Box 25, West Dundee, IL 60118: Catalog $1 ❖ Orchids, bromeliads, and tropical house plants. 708-428-8500.

The Plumeria People, 910 Leander Dr., Leander, TX 78641: Catalog $3 (refundable) ❖ Flowering tropical house plants. 512-259-0807.

Rhapis Palm Growers, 31350 Alta Vista, P.O. Box 84, Redlands, CA 92373: Catalog $2 with long SASE ❖ Rhapis palms. 909-794-3823.

❖ GARDENING—PLANTS & SEEDS ❖

Spring Hill Nurseries, 6523 N. Galena Rd., P.O. Box 1758, Peoria, IL 61632: Free catalog ❖ House plants, perennials, roses, annuals, ground covers, and bonsai. 800-582-8527.

Teas Nursery Company, P.O. Box 1603, Bellaire, TX 77401: Catalog $1 (refundable) ❖ Orchid and exotic plant supplies. 800-446-7723.

Trans-Pacific Nursery, 16065 Oldsville Rd., McMinnville, OR 97128: Catalog $2 (refundable) ❖ Rare, unique, and unusual plants. 503-472-6215.

Well-Sweep Herb Farm, 205 Mt. Bethel Rd., Port Murray, NJ 07865: Catalog $2 ❖ Windowsill jasmine plants. 908-852-5390.

Hoyas

Golden Lake Greenhouses, 10782 Citrus Dr., Moorpark, CA 93021: Catalog $2 ❖ Bromeliads, tillandsias, ephylliums, and hoyas.

Rainbow Gardens Bookshop, 1444 E. Taylor St., Vista, CA 92084: Catalog $2 ❖ Cacti, hoyas, and books on cacti. 619-758-4290.

Hydrangeas

Bell Family Nursery, 6543 S. Zimmerman Rd., Aurora, OR 97002: Catalog $3.50 (refundable) ❖ Rare and unusual hydrangeas. 503-651-2887.

Ivies & Vines

Bluestone Perennials, 7211 Middle Ridge Rd., Madison, OH 44057: Free catalog ❖ Ivies and vines, perennial flowers, and ground covers. 800-852-5243.

Burnt Ridge Nursery & Orchards, 432 Burnt Ridge Rd., Onalaska, WA 98570: Free brochure ❖ Trees, shrubs, and vines that produce edible nuts or fruits.

Garden Scapes, 1840 W. 48th St., Davenport, IA 52806: Information $3 ❖ Winter hardy flowering clematis vines. 800-690-9858.

Griffey Nursery, 1670 Hwy. 25/70, Marshall, NC 28753: Free catalog ❖ Native vines and creepers. 704-656-2334.

Meadow View Farms, 3360 N. Pacific Hwy., Medford, OR 97501: Catalog $3 ❖ Perennials, grasses, herbs, vines, and aquatic plants.

Park Seed Company, Cokesbury Rd., P.O. Box 46, Greenwood, SC 29648: Free catalog ❖ Vines, strawberry plants, seeds, bulbs, and gardening tools. 800-845-3369.

Sunnybrook Farms Nursery, P.O. Box 6, Chesterland, OH 44026: Catalog $1 (refundable) ❖ Hostas, herb plants, scented geraniums, perennials, and ivies. 216-729-7232.

Lilacs

Wildflower Nursery, 1680 Hwy. 25-70, Marshall, NC 28753: Free catalog ❖ Vines. 704-656-2723.

Marigolds

W. Atlee Burpee & Company, 300 Park Ave., Warminster, PA 18974: Free catalog ❖ Marigolds. 215-674-1793.

Park Seed Company, Cokesbury Rd., P.O. Box 46, Greenwood, SC 29648: Free catalog ❖ Marigolds. 800-845-3369.

Stokes Seeds Inc., Box 548, Buffalo, NY 14240: Free catalog ❖ Marigolds. 716-695-6980.

Thompson & Morgan Inc., P.O. Box 1308, Jackson, NJ 08527: Free catalog ❖ Marigolds. 800-274-7333.

Mushrooms

Field & Forest Products Inc., N3296 Kuzuzek Rd., Peshtigo, WI 54157: Catalog $2 (refundable) ❖ Mushroom-growing supplies. 715-582-4997.

Fungi Perfecti, P.O. Box 7634, Olympia, WA 98507: Catalog $4.50 ❖ Mushroom-growing supplies, kits, and spawn. 800-780-9126.

Fungus Foods Inc., P.O. Box 6035, St. Louis, MO 63139: Free brochure ❖ Shitake, portabella, oyster, and reishi mushroom-growing terrarium for the home. 800-299-1352.

Gourmet Mushrooms, P.O. Box 515, Graton, CA 95444: Free information ❖ Morel mushroom spawn for garden-growing. 707-829-7301.

Hardscrabble Enterprises Inc., Box 42, Cherry Grove, WV 26804: Catalog $3 (refundable) ❖ Grow-your-own Shiitake mushroom kits. Also mushroom-growing supplies and spawn. 304-567-2727.

MushroomPeople, P.O. Box 220, 560 Farm Rd., Summertown TN 38483: Free catalog ❖ Mushroom-growing kits, spawns, supplies, and how-to books. 800-FUNGI-95.

Mycelium Fruits, P.O. Box 552, Iron Station, NC 28080: Catalog $2 ❖ Mushroom-growing supplies.

Sohn's Forest Mushrooms, 610 S. Main St., Westfield, WI 53964: Free brochure ❖ Shiitake and oyster spawn, inoculation supplies, and books. 608-296-2456.

Spectrum Garden Supply, Box 18, Southeastern, PA 19399: Catalog $3 ❖ Growing supplies and equipment.

Western Biologicals, Box 283, Aldergrove, British Columbia, Canada V0X 1A0: Catalog $3 ❖ Spawn, cultures, kits, books, and cultivation supplies.

Nurseries

The companies in this section offer a wide variety of seeds and plants, gardening supplies, tools, and equipment.

W. Atlee Burpee & Company, 300 Park Ave., Warminster, PA 18974: Free catalog ❖ 215-674-1793.

Ferry-Morse Seed Company, P.O. Box 488, Fulton, KY 42041: Free catalog. 800-283-3400.

Henry Field's Seed & Nursery, 415 N. Burnett, Shenandoah, IA 51602: Free catalog ❖ 605-665-4491.

Harmony Farm Supply & Nursery, P.O. Box 460, Graton, CA 95444: Catalog $2 (refundable). 707-823-9125.

Harris Seeds Inc., P.O. Box 22960, Rochester, NY 14692: Free catalog ❖ 716-442-0410.

J.W. Jung Seed Company, 335 High St., Randolph, WI 53957: Free catalog ❖ 414-326-4100.

Orol Ledden & Sons, P.O. Box 7, Sewell, NJ 08080: Free catalog ❖ 800-783-SEED.

Earl May Seeds & Nursery Company, N. Elm St., Shenandoah, IA 51603: Free catalog ❖ 712-246-1020.

Mellinger's, 2310 W. South Range Rd., North Lima, OH 44452: Free catalog ❖ 330-549-9861.

Miller Nurseries, 5060 W. Lake Rd., Canandaigua, NY 14424: Free catalog. 800-836-9630.

Nichols Garden Nursery, 1190 SW Pacific, Albany, OR 97321: Free catalog ❖ 541-928-9280.

L.L. Olds Seed Company, P.O. Box 7790, Madison, WI 53707: Catalog $2.50 ❖ 608-249-9291.

Richard Owen Nursery, 2300 E. Lincoln St., Bloomington, IL 61701: Free catalog. 309-663-9551.

Park Seed Company, Cokesbury Rd., P.O. Box 46, Greenwood, SC 29648: Free catalog. 800-845-3369.

Shady Oaks Nursery, 112 10th Ave. SE, Waseca, MN 56093: Information $1 ❖ 507-835-5033.

R.H. Shumway Seedsman, P.O. Box 1, Graniteville, SC 29829: Free catalog. 413-737-0399.

Stark Brothers, Nurseries & Orchards Company, P.O. Box 10, Louisiana, MO 63353: Free catalog ❖ 800-775-6415.

Otis Twilley Seed Company, P.O. Box 65, Trevose, PA 19047: Catalog $1 ❖ 800-622-7333.

Orchids

Adagent Acres, 2245 Floral Way, Santa Rosa, CA 95403: Catalog 50¢ ❖ Orchid species and hybrids. 707-575-4459.

GARDENING—PLANTS & SEEDS

Alberts & Merkel Brothers Inc., 2210 S. Federal Hwy., Boynton Beach, FL 33435: Catalog $1 ❖ Orchid plants and growing supplies. 407-732-2071.

Carter & Holmes Inc., P.O. Box 668, Newberry, SC 29108: Catalog $1.50 (refundable) ❖ Unusual hybrids and orchid-growing supplies. 803-276-0579.

Clargreen Gardens, 814 Southdown Rd., Mississauga, Ontario, Canada L5J 2Y4: Catalog $2 (refundable) ❖ Orchids.

Epi World, 10607 Glenview Ave., Cupertino, CA 95014: Catalog $2 ❖ Orchid cactus starter collections and hybrids. 408-865-0566.

John Ewing Orchids Inc., P.O. Box 1318, Soquel, CA 95073: Catalog 50¢ ❖ Easy-to-grow Phalaenopsis seedlings and plants. 408-684-1111.

Fennell's Orchid Company, 2650 SW 27th Ave., Miami, FL 33133: Free catalog ❖ Easy-to-grow orchids for indoors or outside. 800-344-2457.

G & B Orchid Laboratory & Nursery, 2426 Cherimoya Dr., Vista, CA 92084: Free catalog ❖ Growing supplies, flasking media, chemical supplies, laboratory glassware, fertilizers, seedlings, and orchid species. 619-727-2611.

Huronview Nurseries, RR 1, Bright's Grove, Ontario, Canada N0N 1C0: Free catalog ❖ Easy-to-grow orchids.

J & L Orchids, 20 Sherwood Rd., Easton, CT 06612: Catalog $1 ❖ Hybrid orchids, rare and unusual species, and easy-to-grow miniatures. 203-261-3772.

Kensington Orchids, 3301 Plyers Mill Rd., Kensington, MD 20895: Price list $1 (refundable) ❖ Orchid plants. 301-933-0036.

Krull-Smith Orchids, 2815 Ponkan Rd., Apopka, FL 32712: Free catalog ❖ Easy-to-grow orchids. 407-886-0915.

Lauray of Salisbury, 432 Undermountain Rd., Salisbury, CT 06068: Catalog $2 ❖ Orchids, begonias, gesneriads, cacti, and succulents. 203-435-2263.

Lee's Botanical Gardens, P.O. Box 669, LaBelle, FL 33975: Free catalog ❖ Carnivorous plants, orchids, and ferns. 813-675-8728.

Lenette Greenhouses, 1440 Pom Orchid Ln., Kannapolis, NC 28081: Free catalog ❖ Orchids and growing supplies. 704-938-2042.

Rod McLellan Company, 1450 El Camino Real, South San Francisco, CA 94080: Catalog $2 ❖ Orchid plants and growing supplies. 415-871-5655.

Mellinger's, 2310 W. South Range Rd., North Lima, OH 44452: Free catalog ❖ Fruit, nut, shade, and ornamental trees. Also gladioli, flowering shrubs, hedges, irises, wildflowers, and gardening equipment. 330-549-9861.

Oak Hill Gardens, P.O. Box 25, West Dundee, IL 60118: Catalog $1 ❖ Orchids, bromeliads, and tropical house plants. 708-428-8500.

The Orchid Club, Box 463, Baldwinsville, NY 13027: Free brochure ❖ Club members receive a different plant each month with instructions for care. 800-822-9411.

Orchid Thoroughbreds, 731 W. Siddonsburg Rd., Dillsburg, PA 17019: Catalog $2 ❖ A wide variety of species and hybrids of different genera. 717-432-8100.

Orchids by Hauserman Inc., 2N134 Addison Rd., Villa Park, IL 60181: Catalog $1.25 ❖ Orchid plants and growing supplies. 708-543-6855.

Orgel's Orchids, 18950 SW 136th St., Miami, FL 33196: Free catalog ❖ Orchids and carnivorous plants. 305-233-7168.

Palestine Orchids Inc., Rt. 1, Box 312, Palestine, WV 26160: Free information ❖ Easy-to-grow orchids. 304-275-4781.

Seagulls Landing Orchids, P.O. Box 388, Glen Head, NY 11545: Free price list ❖ Orchid growing supplies. 516-759-5865.

Stewart Orchids, P.O. Box 550, Carpinteria, CA 93014: Free catalog ❖ Orchid-growing supplies. 800-621-2450; 800-831-9765 (in CA).

Sunswept Laboratories, P.O. Box 1913, Studio City, CA 91614: Catalog $2 ❖ Rare and endangered orchid species. 818-506-7271.

Teas Nursery Company, P.O. Box 1603, Bellaire, TX 77401: Catalog $1 (refundable) ❖ Orchid and exotic plant supplies. 800-446-7723.

Palms

Crockett's Tropical Plants, P.O. Box 1150, Harlingen, TX 78551: Catalog $3 ❖ Container-grown ornamentals, citrus plants, and palms. 800-580-1900.

Floribunda Palms, Box 635, Mt. View, HI 96771: Free information with long SASE ❖ Palms from worldwide sources.

The Green Escape, P.O. Box 1417, Palm Harbor, FL 34682: Catalog $6 (refundable) ❖ Indoor, cold-hardy, and tropical palm species.

Jerry Horne, Rare Plants Nursery, 10195 SW 70th St., Miami, FL 33173: Free list with long SASE ❖ Ferns, platyceriums, palms and cycads, and rare and unusual plants. 305-270-1235.

Joe's Nursery, P.O. Box 1867, Vista, CA 92085: Catalog $1 ❖ Palms, cacti, succulents, rare plants, bromeliads, and other garden varieties.

Pen Y Bryn, RR 1, Box 1313, Forksville, PA 18616: Catalog $2 ❖ Palm trees.

Rhapis Gardens, P.O. Drawer 287, Gregory, TX 78359: Catalog $2 ❖ Green, variegated, and other dwarf indoor rhapis excella plants. 512-643-2061.

Rhapis Palm Growers, 31350 Alta Vista, P.O. Box 84, Redlands, CA 92373: Catalog $2 with long SASE ❖ Rhapis palms. 909-794-3823.

Peonies, Irises & Daylilies

Aitken's Salmon Creek Garden, 608 NW 119th St., Vancouver, WA 98685: Catalog $2 ❖ Tall-bearded, medians, Japanese, Siberian, and other irises. 360-573-4472.

Amberway Gardens, 5803 Amberway Dr., St. Louis, MO 63128: Catalog $1 (refundable) ❖ Bearded and beardless irises. 314-842-6103.

American Daylily & Perennials, P.O. Box 210, Grain Valley, MO 64029: Catalog $5 (refundable) ❖ Daylilies, hostas, and dwarf cannas. 800-770-2777.

Anderson Iris Gardens, 22179 Keather Ave. North, Forest Lake, MN 55025: Catalog $1 ❖ Peonies, daylilies, and irises. 612-433-5268.

B & D Lilies, 330 P St., Port Townsend, WA 98368: Catalog $3 ❖ Species and hybrid lilies and special heirloom collections. 206-385-1738.

Big Tree Daylily Garden, 777 General Hutchinson Pkwy., Longwood, FL 32750: Catalog $1 ❖ Daylilies. 407-831-5430.

Borbeleta Gardens, 15980 Canby Ave., Faribault, MN 55021: Catalog $3 ❖ Hardy lilies, daylilies, intermediate/dwarf bearded iris, Siberian irises, and peonies. 507-334-2807.

Lee Bristol, Bloomingfields Farm, Gaylordsville, CT 06755: Free catalog ❖ Daylilies. 203-354-6951.

Brookwood Gardens Inc., 600 E. 9th St., Michigan City, IN 46360: Catalog $2.98 ❖ Daylilies and hostas. 800-628-0110.

The Bulb Crate, 2560 Deerfield Rd., Riverwoods, IL 60015: Catalog $1 (refundable) ❖ Peonies, daylilies, and irises. 708-317-1414.

Busse Gardens, P.O. Box N, Cokato, MN 55321: Catalog $2 ❖ Siberian irises and ferns. 612-286-2654.

Caprice Farm Nursery, 15425 SW Pleasant Hill Rd., Sherwood, OR 97140: Catalog $2 ❖ Peonies, irises, daylilies, and hostas. 503-625-7241.

Comanche Acres Iris Gardens, Rt. 1, Box 258, Gower, MO 64454: Catalog $3 ❖ Tall-bearded and intermediate irises. 816-424-6436.

Cooley's Gardens, 11553 Silverton Rd. NE, P.O. Box 126, Silverton, OR 97381: Catalog $2 (refundable) ❖ Irises. 800-225-5391.

Cooper's Garden, 2345 Decatur Ave., North Golden Valley, MN 55427: Catalog $1 (refundable) ❖ Perennials and irises.

Cordon Bleu Daylilies, P.O. Box 2033, San Marcos, CA 92079: Catalog $1 ❖ Daylilies and irises. 619-744-8367.

Cricket Hill Garden, 670 Walnut Hill Rd., Thomaston, CT 06787: Free catalog ❖ Chinese tree peonies. 860-283-1042.

Daylily Discounters, One Daylily Plaza, Alachua, FL 32615: Catalog $2 ❖ Award winning daylilies. 904-462-1539.

Daylily Farms & Nursery, Rt. 1, Box 89A, Bakersville, NC 28705: Catalog $2 ❖ Hostas and daylilies.

Daylily World, P.O. Box 1612, Sanford, FL 32772: Catalog $5 (refundable) ❖ Daylilies. 407-322-4034.

Ensata Gardens, 9823 E. Michigan Ave., Galesburg, MI 49053: Catalog $2 ❖ Japanese irises. 616-665-7500.

Fairyland Begonia Garden, Winkey & Leslie Woodriff, 1100 Griffith Rd., McKinleyville, CA 95521: Price list 50¢ ❖ Rex, fibrous, and hybrid begonias. Also garden lilies. 707-839-3034.

Growers Service Company, P.O. Box 445, Hartland, MI 48353: Catalog $1 (refundable) ❖ Ferns, perennials, lilies, Dutch and rare bulbs, and other plants.

The Iris Pond, 7311 Churchill Rd., McLean, VA 22101: Price list $1 ❖ Tall-bearded, Japanese, Siberians, table irises, and other species.

Johnson Daylily Garden, 70 Lark Ave., Brooksville, FL 34601: Free price list with 1st class stamp ❖ Daylilies. 352-544-1319.

Klehm Nursery, 4210 N. Duncan Rd., Champaign, IL, 61821: Catalog $4 ❖ Peonies, irises, hostas, daylilies, and perennials. 800-553-3715.

The Lily Garden, P.O. Box 407, La Center, OR 98629: Free catalog ❖ Hybrid lilies exclusively for the garden. 360-263-8588.

Long's Gardens, P.O. Box 19, Boulder, CO 80306: Free catalog ❖ Tall, intermediate, and dwarf irises. 303-442-2353.

Louisiana Nursery, Rt. 7, Box 43, Opelousas, LA 70570: Catalog $3 ❖ Daylily and iris cultivars. 318-948-3696.

Marietta Gardens, P.O. Box 70, Marietta, NC 28362: Catalog $1 ❖ Daylilies. 910-628-8425.

Maryland Aquatic Nurseries, 3427 N. Furnace Rd., Jarrettsville, MD 21084: Catalog $5 (refundable) ❖ Water garden plants, ornamental grasses, and Louisiana and Japanese irises. 410-557-7615.

Mellinger's, 2310 W. South Range Rd., North Lima, OH 44452: Free catalog ❖ Fruit, nut, shade, and ornamental trees. Also gladioli, flowering shrubs, hedges, irises, wildflowers, and gardening equipment. 330-549-9861.

Oakes Daylilies, 8204 Monday Rd., Corryton, TN 37721: Free catalog ❖ Daylily cultivars. 800-532-9545.

Quality Dutch Bulbs, P.O. Box 434, Stockertown, PA 18083: Free catalog ❖ Daffodils, irises, tulips, and other bulbs. 800-755-2852.

Roris Gardens, 8195 Bradshaw Rd., Sacramento, CA 95829: Catalog $3 (refundable) ❖ Irises. 916-689-7460.

Schreiner's Gardens, 3653 Quinaby Rd. NE, Salem, OR 97303: Catalog $4 ❖ Dwarf and tall-bearded irises. 800-525-2367.

Serendipity Gardens, 3210 Upper Bellbrook Rd., Bellbrook, OH 45305: Free catalog ❖ Daylilies. 513-426-6596.

Skolaski's Glads & Flowers, 4821 County Trunk Hwy. Q, Waunakee, WI 53597: Catalog $1 ❖ Gladioli bulbs, lilies, and perennials. 608-836-4822.

Tischler Peony Gardens, 1021 E. Division St., Faribault, MN 55021: Free catalog ❖ Herbaceous peonies. 507-334-7242.

Tranquil Lake Nursery, 45 River St., Rehoboth, MA 02769: Catalog $1 ❖ Daylilies and irises. 508-252-4002.

Van Bourgondien Bros., 245 Farmingdale Rd., P.O. Box 1000, Babylon, NY 11702: Free catalog ❖ Lilies. 800-622-9959.

Wayside Gardens, 1 Garden Ln., Hodges, SC 29695: Free catalog ❖ Siberian irises. 800-845-1124.

White Flower Farm, Rt. 63, Litchfield, CT 06759: Free catalog ❖ Daylilies. 800-888-7756.

Gilbert H. Wild & Son Inc., P.O. Box 338, Sarcoxie, MO 64862: Catalog $3 (refundable) ❖ Peonies, irises, and daylilies. 417-548-3514.

Windmill Gardens, P.O. Box 351, Luverne, AL 36049: Catalog $2 ❖ Daylilies. 334-335-5568.

Perennials & Ornamentals

Ambergate Gardens, 8015 Krey Ave., Waconia, MN 55387: Catalog $2 ❖ Perennial flowers and grasses. 612-443-2248.

Agua Fria Nursery, 1409 Agua Fria St., Santa Fe, NM 87501: Free catalog ❖ Containerized western wildflowers, perennials, and shrubs.

Autumn Glade Botanical, 46857 Ann Arbor Trail, Plymouth, MI 48170: Free catalog ❖ Perennials and bulbs. 800-331-7969.

Kurt Bluemel Inc., 2740 Greene Ln., Baldwin, MD 21013: Catalog $3 ❖ Perennials, ferns, bamboo plants, and ornamental grasses. 410-557-7229.

Bluestone Perennials, 7211 Middle Ridge Rd., Madison, OH 44057: Free catalog ❖ Perennial flowers, ground covers, ivies, and vines. 800-852-5243.

Canyon Creek Nursery, 3527 Dry Creek Rd., Oroville, CA 95965: Catalog $2 ❖ Perennials. 916-533-2166.

Carleybrook Gardens, RD 4, Box 4708, Mohnton, PA 19540: Free catalog ❖ Perennials. 800-856-7394.

Cooper's Garden, 2345 Decatur Ave., North Golden Valley, MN 55427: Catalog $1 (refundable) ❖ Perennials and irises.

Crownsville Nursery, P.O. Box 797, Crownsville, MD 21032: Catalog $2 (minimum order $25) ❖ Ferns, wildflowers, azaleas, ornamental grasses, and perennials. 410-923-2212.

Czarnick Nursery, RR 2, Genola, NE 68640: Catalog $1 ❖ Perennials, grasses, and wildflowers.

Daisy Fields, 12635 SW Brighton Ln., Hillsboro, OR 97123: Catalog $1 ❖ Old-fashioned perennials.

Digging Dog Nursery, P.O. Box 471, Albion, CA 95410: Catalog $3 ❖ Grasses, vines, trees, perennials, and shrubs. 707-937-1130.

Fieldstone Gardens Inc., 620 Quaker Ln., Vassalboro, ME 04989: Catalog $2 ❖ Nursery-propagated perennials. 207-923-3836.

Flowerplace Plant Farm, Box 4865, Meridian, MS 39304: Free catalog ❖ Perennials. 800-482-5686.

Garden Place, 6780 Heisley Rd., P.O. Box 388, Mentor, OH 44061: Catalog $1 ❖ Perennials. 216-255-3705.

Gilson Gardens Inc., 3059 US Rt. 20, P.O. Box 277, Perry, OH 44081: Free catalog ❖ Ground covers, perennials, and ferns. 216-259-5252.

Good Hollow Greenhouse & Herbarium, 50 Slaterock Mill Rd., Taft, TN 38488: Catalog $1 ❖ Herb plants and dried herbs, perennials, wildflowers, scented geraniums, essential oils and potpourris, teas, and spices. 615-433-7640.

The Gourmet Gardener, 8650 College Blvd., Overland Park, KS 66210: Catalog $2 ❖ Herb, vegetable, and edible flower seeds from around the world. 913-345-0490.

❖ GARDENING—PLANTS & SEEDS ❖

Griffey Nursery, 1670 Hwy. 25/70, Marshall, NC 28753: Free catalog ❖ Wild native perennials. 704-656-2334.

Growers Service Company, P.O. Box 445, Hartland, MI 48353: Catalog $1 (refundable) ❖ Ferns, perennials, lilies, Dutch and rare bulbs, and other plants.

Heaths & Heathers, E. 502 Haskell Hill Rd., Shelton, WA 98584: Catalog $1 ❖ Easy-to-grow heathers. 360-427-5318.

Heronswood Nursery, 7530 NE 288th St., Kingston, WA 98346: Catalog $3 ❖ Perennials.

A High Country Garden, 2902 Rufina St., Santa Fe, NM 875054: Free catalog ❖ Perennials. 800-925-9387.

Hillary's Garden, P.O. Box 430, Warwick, NY 10990: Catalog $2 ❖ Perennials and organically grown herbs.

Jerry Horne, Rare Plants Nursery, 10195 SW 70th St., Miami, FL 33173: Free list with long SASE ❖ Ferns, platyceriums, palms and cycads, and rare and unusual plants. 305-270-1235.

Joe's Nursery, P.O. Box 1867, Vista, CA 92085: Catalog $1 ❖ Palms, cacti, succulents, rare plants, bromeliads, and other garden varieties.

Joy Creek Nursery, 20300 NW Watson Rd., Scappoose, OR 97056: Catalog $2 (refundable) ❖ Unique and unusual perennials and native plants.

Klehm Nursery, 4210 N. Duncan Rd., Champaign, IL 61821: Catalog $4 ❖ Peonies, irises, daylilies, hostas, and perennials. 800-553-3715.

Lily of the Valley Herb Farm, 3969 Fox Ave., Minerva, OH 44657: Price list $1 (refundable) ❖ Herb, everlasting, perennial, and scented geranium plants. 216-862-3920.

Limerock Ornamental Grasses Inc., RD 1, Box 111, Port Matilda, PA 16870: Catalog $3 ❖ Ornamental and native grasses, companion perennials, and nursery-grown hardy ferns. 814-692-2272.

Meadow View Farms, 3360 N. Pacific Hwy., Medford, OR 97501: Catalog $3 ❖ Perennials, grasses, herbs, vines, and aquatic plants.

Mellinger's, 2310 W. South Range Rd., North Lima, OH 44452: Free catalog ❖ Fruit, nut, shade, and ornamental trees. Also gladioli, flowering shrubs, hedges, irises, wildflowers, and gardening equipment. 330-549-9861.

Milaeger's Gardens, 4838 Douglas Ave., Racine, WI 53402: Catalog $1 ❖ Perennials. 800-669-9956.

J.E. Miller Nurseries, 5060 W. Lake Rd., Canandaigua, NY 14424: Free catalog ❖ Fruit and nut trees, vines, ornamentals, and ground covers. 800-836-9630.

Mohns Nursery, P.O. Box 2301, Atascadero, CA 93423: Free catalog with two 1st class stamps ❖ Perennial poppies. 805-466-4362.

Niche Gardens, 1111 Dawson Rd., Chapel Hill, NC 27516: Catalog $3 ❖ Nursery-propagated wildflowers, perennials, trees, and shrubs. 919-967-0078.

Patrick's Nursery, P.O. Box 130, Ty Ty, GA 31795: Free catalog ❖ Perennials, vegetables, fruit and nut trees, berry plants, and grapevines. 800-972-2101.

Pen Y Bryn, RR 1, Box 1313, Forksville, PA 18616: Catalog $2 ❖ Oriental plants.

Perennial Pleasures Nursery, P.O. Box 147, East Hardwick, VT 05836: Catalog $3 ❖ Heirloom herbs and flowers. 802-472-5104.

Perpetual Perennials, 1111 Upper Valley Pike, Springfield, OH 45504: Catalog $2 ❖ Perennials. 513-325-2451.

Plant Delights Nursery, 9241 Sauls Rd., Raleigh, NC 27603: Free catalog with ten 1st class stamps ❖ Perennials. 919-772-4794.

Plantation Bulb Company, Box 159, Ty Ty, GA 31795: Free catalog ❖ Bulbs and perennials. 800-972-2101.

Plumeria People, 910 Leander Dr., Leander, TX 78641: Catalog $3 (refundable) ❖ Easy-to-grow flowering, fragrant, and unusual tropical plants. 512-259-0807.

Riverhead Perennials, 5 Riverhead Ln., East Lyme, CT 06333: Catalog $2 (refundable) ❖ Perennials. 203-437-7828.

Shady Oaks Nursery, 112 10th Ave. SE, Waseca, MN 56093: Information $1 ❖ Ferns, shrubs, perennials, and wildflowers. 507-835-5033.

Skolaski's Glads & Flowers, 4821 County Trunk Hwy. Q, Waunakee, WI 53597: Catalog $1 ❖ Gladioli bulbs, lilies, and perennials. 608-836-4822.

Spring Hill Nurseries, 6523 N. Galena Rd., P.O. Box 1758, Peoria, IL 61632: Free catalog ❖ Perennials, roses, annuals, ground covers, bonsai, and house plants. 800-582-8527.

Sun, Wind & Rain Inc., P.O. Box 505, Silverton, OR 97381: Free catalog ❖ Hardy northwest ornamentals. 503-873-5541.

Sunlight Gardens, 174 Golden Ln., Andersonville, TN 37705: Catalog $3 ❖ Hardy ferns and perennials. 615-494-8237.

Sunnybrook Farms Nursery, P.O. Box 6, Chesterland, OH 44026: Catalog $1 (refundable) ❖ Hostas, herb plants, scented geraniums, perennials, and ivies. 216-729-7232.

Surry Gardens, P.O. Box 145, Rt. 172, Surry, ME 04684: Free information ❖ Border, wild garden, and rock garden perennials. 207-667-5589.

Twombly Nursery, 163 Barn Hill Rd., Monroe, CT 06468: Catalog $4 ❖ Dwarf conifer miniatures, rare and unusual plants, and trees. 203-261-2133.

Van Bourgondien Bros., 245 Farmingdale Rd., Babylon, NY 11702: Free catalog ❖ Perennials. 800-622-9959.

Vandenberg, 1 Black Meadow Rd., Chester, NY 10918: Free catalog ❖ Perennials, hybrid lilies, seeds, and bulbs. 800-221-6017.

Andre Viette Nurseries, Rt. 1, Box 16, Fisherville, VA 22939: Catalog $3 ❖ Flowering and rock garden perennials, woodland plants, and daylilies. 703-942-2118.

Wayside Gardens, 1 Garden Ln., Hodges, SC 29695: Free catalog ❖ Perennials, trees, shrubs, ground covers, and gardening supplies. 800-845-1124.

Weiss Brothers Nursery, 11690 Colfax Hwy., Grass Valley, CA 95945: Free catalog ❖ Perennials and drip irrigation supplies. 916-272-7657.

Wildflower Nursery, 1680 Hwy. 25-70, Marshall, NC 28753: Free catalog ❖ Perennials. 704-656-2723.

Williamette Valley Garden, Box 285, Lake Oswego, OR 97034: Catalog $1 ❖ Geraniums and perennials.

Woodside Gardens, 1191 Egg & I Rd., Chimacum, WA 98325: Catalog $2 ❖ Perennials and herb plants. 360-732-4754.

Rock Gardens

Carroll Gardens, 444 E. Main St., P.O. Box 310, Westminster, MD 21157: Catalog $3 (refundable) ❖ Rock garden and alpine plants. 800-638-6334.

Endangered Species, P.O. Box 1830, Tustin, CA 92681: Catalog $6 ❖ Rare and unusual rock garden plants. 714-544-9505.

Fieldstone Gardens Inc., 620 Quaker Ln., Vassalboro, ME 04989: Catalog $2 ❖ Mature plants for sun, shade, rock gardens, and ground covers. 207-923-3836.

The Primrose Path, RD 2, Box 110, Scottsdale, PA 15683: Catalog $2 ❖ Rock garden plants. 412-887-6756.

Siskiyou Rare Plant Nursery, 2825 Cummings Rd., Medford, OR 97501: Catalog $2 ❖ Dwarf and other plants for rock gardens and woodland and alpine settings. 503-772-6846.

Squaw Mountain Gardens, 36212 SE Squaw Mountain, Estacada, OR 97023: Catalog $2 (refundable) ❖ Ferns and companion rock garden plants.

Twombly Nursery, 163 Barn Hill Rd., Monroe, CT 06468: Catalog $4 ❖ Dwarf conifer miniatures, rare and unusual plants, and trees for water gardens. 203-261-2133.

We-Du Nursery, Rt. 5, Box 724, Marion, NC 28752: Catalog $2 ❖ Plants and rock garden supplies. 704-738-8300.

Roses

Antique Rose Emporium, Rt. 5, Box 143, Brenham, TX 77833: Catalog $5 ❖ Antique roses for southern climates. 800-441-0002.

Bridges Roses, 2734 Toney Rd., Lawndale, NC 28090: Free catalog ❖ Miniature roses. 704-538-9412.

Carlton Rose Nurseries, P.O. Box 366, Carlton, OR 97111: Free brochure ❖ Rose plants. 503-852-7135.

Edmunds Roses, 6235 SW Kahle Rd., Wilsonville, OR 97070: Free catalog ❖ Exhibition and European roses. 503-682-1476.

Heirloom Old Garden Roses, 24062 NE Riverside Dr., St. Paul, OR 97137: Catalog $5 ❖ Old garden, English, and winter-hardy roses. 503-538-1576.

Heritage Rose Gardens, 16831 Mitchell Creek Dr., Fort Bragg, CA 95437: Catalog $1.50 ❖ Heritage, antique, and old garden roses. 707-964-3748.

Hidden Garden Nursery Inc., 13515 SE Briggs, Milwaukee, OR 97222: Catalog 50¢ (refundable) ❖ Miniature roses.

High Country Roses, P.O. Box 148, Jensen, UT 84035: Catalog $1 ❖ Old garden, hardy shrub, and species roses. 303-832-4026.

Jackson & Perkins, P.O. Box 1028, Medford, OR 97501: Free catalog ❖ Roses. 800-872-7673.

Lowe's Own Root Roses, 6 Sheffield Rd., Nashua, NH 03062: Catalog $2 ❖ Custom-grown 17th, 18th, and 19th-century roses. 603-888-2214.

Earl May Seeds & Nursery Company, N. Elm St., Shenandoah, IA 51603: Free catalog ❖ Roses, shade and ornamental trees, flowering shrubs, vegetable and flower seeds, bulbs, and gardening supplies. 712-246-1020.

The Mini Rose Garden, P.O. Box 203, Cross Hill, SC 29332: Free catalog ❖ Miniature roses for indoor and outdoor growing. 800-996-4647.

Miniature Plant Kingdom, 4125 Harrison Grade Rd., Sebastopol, CA 95472: Catalog $2.50 ❖ Miniature roses and Japanese maples, conifers, and bonsai plants. 707-874-2233.

Nor'East Miniature Roses Inc., P.O. Box 307, Rowley, MA 01969: Free catalog ❖ Miniature roses. 508-948-7964.

Oregon Miniature Roses, 8285 SW 185th Ave., Beaverton, OR 97007: Catalog $1 ❖ Micro-mini, climbing miniature, and miniature tree roses. 503-649-4482.

Rabbit Shadow Farm, 2880 E. Hwy. 402, Loveland, CO 80537: Free information ❖ Herbs, roses, topiary supplies, and scented geraniums. 303-667-5531.

Rosehill Farm, P.O. Box 188, Galena, MD 21635: Free catalog ❖ Roses. 410-648-5538.

Roses by Fred Edmunds, 6235 SW Kahle Rd., Wilsonville, OR 97070: Free catalog ❖ Roses. 503-682-1476.

Roses of Yesterday & Today, 803 Brown's Valley Rd., Watsonville, CA 95076: Catalog $3 ❖ Old, rare, and unusual roses. 408-724-3537.

Royall River Roses, 70 New Gloucester Rd., North Yarmouth, ME 04097: Catalog $2 ❖ Old-fashioned, uncommon, and hardy roses. 207-829-5830.

Savage Nursery Center, 6255 Beersheba Hwy., McMinnville, TN 37110: Free catalog ❖ Roses. 615-668-8902.

Sequoia Nursery/Moore Miniature Roses, 2519 E. Noble Ave., Visalia, CA 93277: Catalog $1 ❖ Tree roses, climbing miniatures, and roses for hanging baskets. 209-732-0190.

R.H. Shumway Seedsman, P.O. Box 1, Graniteville, SC 29829: Free catalog ❖ Roses, berry plants, fruit trees, seeds and bulbs, ornamental shrubs and plants, and gardening supplies. 413-737-0399.

Spring Hill Nurseries, 6523 N. Galena Rd., P.O. Box 1758, Peoria, IL 61632: Free catalog ❖ Perennials and annuals, trees, shrubs, ground covers, bonsai, house plants, and old, miniature, and other roses. 800-582-8527.

Vintage Gardens, 2227 Gravenstein Hwy. South, Sebastopol, CA 95472: Catalog $4 ❖ Antique and extraordinary roses. 707-829-2035.

Bob Wells Nursery, P.O. Box 606, Lindale, TX 75771: Free catalog ❖ Fruit, nut, and shade trees. Also berries, grapes, muscadines, roses, ornamentals, and flowering shrubs. 903-882-3550.

Womack's Nursery Company, Rt. 1, Box 80, De Leon, TX 76444: Free catalog ❖ Roses and fruit, nut, shade, and flowering trees. 817-893-6497.

Seeds & Bulbs

Abundant Life Seed Foundation, P.O. Box 772, Port Townsend, WA 98368: Catalog $2 ❖ Organic and untreated vegetable, grain, herb, wildflower, and seeds. 360-385-5660.

Alfrey Seeds, P.O. Box 415, Knoxville, TN 37901: Free list with long SASE ❖ Seeds for chili peppers, vegetables, and gourds.

Allen, Sterling & Lothrop Seeds, 191 US Rt. 1, Falmouth, ME 04105: Catalog $1 (refundable) ❖ Vegetable and flower seeds.

Jacques Amand, P.O. Box 59001, Potomac, MD 20859: Free catalog ❖ Imported rare and unusual bulbs from England. 800-452-5414.

Amaryllis Inc., P.O. Box 318, Baton Rouge, LA 70821: Catalog $1 ❖ Amaryllis bulbs. 504-924-5560.

American Horticultural Society, 7931 East Blvd. Dr., Alexandria, VA 22308: Free list for members ❖ Heirloom and hard-to-find seeds. 703-768-5700.

Agua Viva Seed Ranch, Rt. 1, Box 8, Taos, NM 87571: Free catalog ❖ Perennials, bulbs, and wildflowers. 800-248-9080.

Archia's Floral & Plants, 712 S. Ohio, Sedalia, MO 65301: Free catalog ❖ Vegetable and flower seeds, gardening supplies, nursery stock, and beekeeping equipment. 816-826-4000.

Archia's Seed Store, P.O. Box 356, Buckner, MO 64016: Free catalog ❖ Beekeeping equipment, vegetable and flower seeds, and gardening supplies. 816-826-1330.

Autumn Glade Botanical, 46857 Ann Arbor Trail, Plymouth, MI 48170: Free catalog ❖ Perennials and bulbs. 800-331-7969.

The Banana Tree, 715 Northampton St., Easton, PA 18042: Catalog $3 ❖ Seeds from temperate and tropical climates. 610-253-9589.

Berlin Seeds, 5371 County Rd. 77, Millersbury, OH 44654: Free catalog ❖ Vegetable and flower seeds.

Bountiful Gardens, 18001 Shafer Ranch Rd., Willits, CA 95490: Free catalog ❖ Seeds for vegetables, compost crops, herbs, and flowers. Also books and organic gardening supplies. 707-459-6410.

Breck's Dutch Bulbs, Mail Order Reservation Center, 6523 N. Galena Rd., P.O. Box 1757, Peoria, IL 61656: Free catalog ❖ Spring flowering bulbs. 309-691-4616.

John Brudy Exotics, Box 820874, Houston, TX 77280: Catalog $2 (refundable) ❖ Seeds for the rare Adenium plant, trees, and shrubs. 800-926-7333.

Bundles of Bulbs, 112 Greenspring Valley Rd., Owings Mills, MD 21117: Catalog $2 ❖ Spring-flowering bulbs. 410-363-1371.

W. Atlee Burpee & Company, 300 Park Ave., Warminster, PA 18974: Free catalog ❖ Seeds and bulbs. 215-674-1793.

D.V. Burrell Seed Company, P.O. Box 150, Rocky Ford, CO 81067: Free catalog ❖ Seeds, gardening supplies, and tools. 719-254-3318.

Butterbrooke Farm, 78 Barry Rd., Oxford, CT 06478: Free catalog ❖ Chemically untreated and open-pollinated rapidly maturing vegetable seeds. 203-888-2000.

GARDENING—PLANTS & SEEDS

Caladium World, P.O. Drawer 629, Sebring, FL 33872: Free catalog ❖ Caladium bulbs. 941-385-7661.

Comstock, Ferre & Company, 263 Main St., Wethersfield, CT 06109: Catalog $2 ❖ Vegetable, flower, and herb seeds. 860-571-6590.

The Cook's Garden, P.O. Box 535, Londonderry, VT 05148: Catalog $1 ❖ Seeds for baby and Italian-style vegetables. 802-824-3400.

Cruickshank's, 1015 Mount Pleasant Rd., Toronto, Ontario, Canada M4P 2M1: Catalog $3 ❖ Tulip bulbs.

The Daffodil Mart, 7463 Heath Trail, Gloucester, VA 23061: Free catalog ❖ Daffodils, tulips, autumn flowering and forcing bulbs, other bulbs, and growing supplies. 800-255-2852.

Dan's Garden Shop, 5821 Woodwinds Circle, Frederick, MD 21701: Free catalog ❖ Seeds for annuals, perennials, and vegetables. 301-695-5966.

DeGiorgi Seed Company Inc., 6011 N St., Omaha, NE 68117: Catalog $2 ❖ Seeds. 402-731-3901.

Peter de Jager Bulb Company, 188 Asbury St., South Hamilton, MA 01982: Free catalog ❖ Dutch bulbs. 508-468-4707.

Dutch Gardens Inc., P.O. Box 200, Adelphia, NJ 07710: Free information ❖ Tulip, hyacinth, crocus, iris, amaryllis, and other bulbs. 800-818-3861.

Evergreen Y.H. Enterprises, P.O. Box 17538, Anaheim, CA 92817: Catalog $2 (refundable) ❖ Gardening tools, cookbooks, and vegetable seeds from China, Japan, and other countries. 714-637-5769.

Fancy Plants Farms, P.O. Box 989, Lake Placid, FL 33862: Free information ❖ Caladium bulbs. 800-869-0953.

Far North Gardens, P.O. Box 126, New Hudson, MI 48165: Catalog $2 (refundable) ❖ Rare flower seeds from worldwide sources.

Farmer Seed & Nursery Company, 818 NW 4th St., Faribault, MN 55021: Free catalog ❖ Vegetable seeds, flowering bulbs, fruit and shade trees, ornamental shrubs and hedges, berry plants, and roses. 507-334-1623.

Henry Field's Seed & Nursery, 415 N. Burnett, Shenandoah, IA 51602: Free catalog ❖ Strawberry and other berry plants, vegetable and flower seeds, hedges, ornamental shrubs, roses, and fruit, nut, and shade trees. 605-665-4491.

Fisher's Garden Store, P.O. Box 236, Belgrade, MT 59714: Free catalog ❖ Vegetable and flower seeds for high altitude gardening and short growing seasons. 406-388-6052.

Flowery Branch, P.O. Box 1330, Flowery Branch, GA 30542: Catalog $3 ❖ Seeds for rare and exotic herbs. Also everlasting and fragrant flowers, rare and unusual annuals, perennials from worldwide sources, and chili peppers. 404-536-8380.

Four Seasons Nursery, 1706 Morrisey Dr., Bloomington, IL 61704: Free catalog ❖ Citrus and exotic fruits. 309-663-9551.

The Fragrant Path, P.O. Box 328, Fort Calhoun, NE 68023: Catalog $2 ❖ Seeds for prairie wildflowers. Also grasses, ferns, trees, shrubs, and climbing plants.

Garden City Seeds, 778 Hwy. 93 North, Hamilton, MT 59840: Free catalog ❖ Herb and flower seeds for short growing seasons. 406-961-4837.

Gardeners' Choice, 81961 Country Rd. 687, P.O. Box 8000, Hartford, MI 49057: Free catalog ❖ Seeds for house plants, vegetables, flowers, and trees. 616-621-2481.

Growers Service Company, P.O. Box 445, Hartland, MI 48353: Catalog $1 (refundable) ❖ Ferns, perennials, lilies, Dutch and rare bulbs, and plants.

Gurney Seed & Nursery Company, 110 Capitol St., Yankton, SD 57079: Free catalog ❖ Seeds, bulbs, and semi-dwarf and standard varieties of apple trees. 605-665-1671.

Happiness Farms, Fancy Leaf Caladiums, 704 CR 621 East, Lake Placid, FL 33852: Free catalog ❖ Caladium bulbs. 813-465-0044.

Harris Seeds, P.O. Box 22960, Rochester, NY 14692: Free catalog ❖ Seeds and gardening supplies. 716-442-0410.

Heirloom Gardens, P.O. Box 138, Guerneville, CA 95446: Free catalog ❖ Unusual seed varieties for easy growing.

Heirloom Seeds, P.O. Box 245, West Elizabeth, PA 15088: Catalog $1 (refundable) ❖ Heirloom flower and vegetable seeds.

Holland Bulb Farms, P.O. Box 220, Tatamy, PA 18085: Free catalog ❖ Imported bulbs from Holland. 800-283-5082.

J.L. Hudson, Seedsman, Box 1058, Redwood City, CA 94064: Catalog $1 ❖ Seeds from around the world.

Imported Dutch Bulbs, P.O. Box 32, Cavendish, VT 05142: Free catalog ❖ Daffodils, tulips, and other bulbs. 802-226-7653.

Jackson & Perkins, P.O. Box 1028, Medford, OR 97501: Free catalog ❖ Seeds, plants, and roses. 800-872-7673.

Joe's Nursery, P.O. Box 1867, Vista, CA 92085: Catalog $1 ❖ Palms, cacti, succulents, rare plants, bromeliads, and other garden varieties.

Johnny's Selected Seeds, 150 Foss Hill Rd., Albion, ME 04910: Free catalog ❖ Strawberry plants and flower and vegetable seeds for cool northern climates. 207-437-4301.

J.W. Jung Seed Company, 335 High St., Randolph, WI 53957: Free catalog ❖ Seeds and gardening supplies. 414-326-4100.

Kitazawa Seed Company, 1111 Chapman St., San Jose, CA 95126: Free price list ❖ Chinese and Japanese vegetable seeds.

D. Landreth Seed Company, P.O. Box 6398, Baltimore, MD 21230: Catalog $2 ❖ Vegetable and flower seeds. 800-654-2407.

Le Jardin du Gourmet, P.O. Box 75, St. Johnsbury Center, VT 05863: Catalog $1 ❖ Seeds for vegetables and herb plants. 802-748-1446.

Orol Ledden & Sons, P.O. Box 7, Sewell, NJ 08080: Free catalog ❖ Seeds for cantaloupes, corn, and tomatoes. 800-783-SEED.

Liberty Seed Company, P.O. Box 806, New Philadelphia, OH 44663: Free catalog ❖ Flower and vegetable seeds. 216-364-1611.

Lindenberg Seeds Ltd., 803 Princess Ave., Brandon, Manitoba, Canada R7A 0P5: Catalog $1 ❖ Vegetable and flower seeds and gardening supplies.

Earl May Seeds & Nursery Company, N. Elm St., Shenandoah, IA 51603: Free catalog ❖ Vegetable and flower seeds, bulbs, fruit and nut trees, roses, grapes, and flowering shrubs. 712-246-1020.

McClure & Zimmerman, P.O. Box 368, Friesland, WI 53935: Free catalog ❖ Tulip bulbs.

Mellinger's, 2310 W. South Range Rd., North Lima, OH 44452: Free catalog ❖ Fruit, nut, shade, and ornamental trees. Also gladioli, flowering shrubs, hedges, irises, wildflowers, and gardening equipment. 330-549-9861.

Michigan Bulb Company, 1950 Waldorf NW, Grand Rapids, MI 49550: Free catalog ❖ Bulbs, perennials, foliage plants, trees, shrubs, exotic house plants, hedges and climbers, and roses. 616-771-9500.

Moon Mountain Wildflowers, P.O. Box 725, Carpinteria, CA 93014: Catalog $3 ❖ Wildflower seeds. 805-684-2565.

Charles H. Mueller Company, 7091 N. River Rd., New Hope, PA 18938: Free catalog ❖ Old favorites and new bulbs. 215-862-2033.

Netherland Bulb Company, 13 McFadden Rd., Easton, PA 18045: Free catalog ❖ Imported Holland bulbs. 800-755-2852.

Nichols Garden Nursery, 1190 SW Pacific, Albany, OR 97321: Free catalog ❖ Vegetable seeds, herb seeds and plants, saffron crocus, garlic and shallots, and strawberry plants. 541-928-9280.

❖ GARDENING—PLANTS & SEEDS ❖

Old House Gardens, 536 3rd St., Ann Arbor, MI 48103: Catalog $2 ❖ Antique flowering bulbs.

The Old Sturbridge Village Museum Gift Shop, 1 Old Sturbridge Village Rd., Sturbridge, MA 01566: Catalog $1 (refundable) ❖ 19th-century varieties of flower and vegetable seeds.

L.L. Olds Seed Company, P.O. Box 7790, Madison, WI 53707: Catalog $2.50 ❖ Vegetable, herb, and flower seeds. 608-249-9291.

Palos Verdes Begonia Farm, 4111 242nd St., Torrance, CA 90505: Free information ❖ Tuberous begonia and nerine bulbs. 800-349-9299; 310-373-9299 (in CA).

Park Seed Company, Cokesbury Rd., P.O. Box 46, Greenwood, SC 29648: Free catalog ❖ Bulbs, vegetable and flower seeds, gardening tools, and supplies. 800-845-3369.

Patrick's Nursery, P.O. Box 130, Ty Ty, GA 31795: Free catalog ❖ Vegetable and flower seeds, fruit and nut trees, berry plants, and grapevines. 800-972-2101.

Pepper Gal, P.O. Box 23006, Fort Lauderdale, FL 33307: Price list $1 ❖ Seeds for peppers. 305-537-5540.

Pinetree Garden Seeds, Box 300, New Gloucester, ME 04260: Free catalog ❖ Seeds for vegetables, herbs, flowers, house plants, and perennials. 207-926-3400.

Plantation Bulb Company, Box 159, Ty Ty, GA 31795: Free catalog ❖ Bulbs and perennials. 800-972-2101.

Pleasant Valley Glads, P.O. Box 494, Agawam, MA 01001: Free catalog ❖ Gladioli bulbs. 413-789-0307.

Quality Dutch Bulbs, P.O. Box 434, Stockertown, PA 18083: Free catalog ❖ Daffodils, irises, tulips, and other bulbs. 800-755-2852.

Richters, 357 Hwy. 47, Goodwood, Ontario, Canada L0C 1A0: Catalog $2 ❖ Seeds for allium shade plants. Also other garden growing stock.

John Scheepers Inc., 23 Tulip Dr., Bantam, CT 06750: Free catalog ❖ Flowering bulbs. 860-567-0838.

Schipper & Company USA, Box 7584, Greenwich, CT 06836: Free catalog with five 1st class stamps ❖ Tulip bulbs. 800-877-8637.

F.W. Schumacher Company, 36 Spring Hill Rd., Sandwich, MA 02563: Free catalog ❖ Seeds for nurserymen, foresters, and horticulturists. 508-888-0659.

Seeds Blüm, Idaho City Stage, Boise, ID 83706: Catalog $3 ❖ Hybrid and heirloom vegetable seeds. 208-343-2202.

Seeds of Change, Box 15700, Santa Fe, NM 87506: Free information ❖ Organic and open-pollinated hard-to-find vegetable, herbs, and flower seeds. 800-957-3337.

Seedway Inc., 1225 Zeager Rd., Elizabethtown, PA 17022: Free catalog ❖ Vegetable seeds. 800-952-7333.

Select Seeds, 180 Stickney Hill Rd., Union, CT 06076: Catalog $3 ❖ Seeds for foxgloves, mignonetta, balloon flowers, hollyhocks, sweet peas, nicotiana, and other old-fashioned flowers. 203-689-9310.

Seymour's Selected Seeds, P.O. Box 1346, Sussex, VA 23884: Free catalog ❖ Rare and familiar flower seed varieties. Includes many imported from England. 803-663-9771.

Shepherd's Garden Seeds, 30 Irene St., Torrington, CT 06790: Catalog $1 ❖ Seeds for baby, Mexican, Italian, Oriental, and French vegetables. 203-482-3638.

R.H. Shumway Seedsman, P.O. Box 1, Graniteville, SC 29829: Free catalog ❖ Seeds and bulbs, berry plants, fruit trees, roses, ornamental shrubs and plants, and gardening supplies. 413-737-0399.

Southern Exposure Seed Exchange, P.O. Box 170, Earlysville, VA 22936: Catalog $2 (refundable) ❖ Seeds for vegetables, flowers, herbs, and plants. 804-973-4703.

Southern Oregon Organics, 1130 Tetherow Rd., Williams, OR 97544: Free catalog ❖ Organic garden seeds.

Southern Seeds, P.O. Box 2091, Melbourne, FL 32902: Catalog $1 ❖ Seeds for bananas, passion fruit, papaya, and other edible exotics. 407-727-3662.

Stark Brothers, Nurseries & Orchards Company, P.O. Box 10, Louisiana, MO 63353: Free catalog ❖ Fruit trees, berry and landscaping plants, and garden supplies. 800-775-6415.

Stokes Seeds Inc., Box 548, Buffalo, NY 14240: Free catalog ❖ Vegetable and flower seeds. 716-695-6980.

Territorial Seed Company, P.O. Box 157, Cottage Grove, OR 97424: Free catalog ❖ Organic fertilizers, natural insecticides, biological pest controls, and vegetable, herb, and flower seeds. 503-942-9547.

Thompson & Morgan Inc., P.O. Box 1308, Jackson, NJ 08527: Free catalog ❖ Vegetable and flower seeds. 800-274-7333.

Tierra Verde, 6039 Cypress Garden Blvd., #314, Winter Haven, FL 33884: Free list with long SASE ❖ Seeds for exotic vegetables and fruits.

Otis Twilley Seed Company, P.O. Box 65, Trevose, PA 19047: Catalog $1 ❖ Seeds for fruits, vegetables, and flowers. 800-622-7333.

Van Bourgondien Bros., 245 Farmingdale Rd., Babylon, NY 11702: Free catalog ❖ Holland flower bulbs. 800-622-9959.

Van Engelen Inc., 23 Tulip Dr., Boonton, CT 06750: Free catalog ❖ Tulips, daffodils, narcissi, crocuses, hyacinths, irises, muscari, and other imported Dutch bulbs. 860-567-8734.

Mary Mattison Van Schaik, P.O. Box 32, Cavendish, VT 05142: Catalog $1 ❖ Novelty and miniature tulip, daffodil, and hyacinth bulbs. 802-226-7653.

Vandenberg, 1 Black Meadow Rd., Chester, NY 10918: Free catalog ❖ Perennials, hybrid lilies, seeds, and imported bulbs. 800-221-6017.

Vermont Bean Seed Company, 95 Garden Ln., Fair Haven, VT 05743: Free catalog ❖ Bean seeds, heirloom plants, and herbs. 802-273-3400.

Vesey Seeds Ltd., P.O. Box 9000, Charlottetown, Prince Edward Island, Canada C0A 1P0: Free catalog ❖ Early maturing vegetable and flower seeds.

Wayside Gardens, 1 Garden Ln., Hodges, SC 29695: Free catalog ❖ Bulbs. 800-845-1124.

White Flower Farm, Rt. 63, Litchfield, CT 06759: Free catalog ❖ Bulbs, shrubs, strawberry plants, books, tools, and gardening supplies. 800-888-7756.

Willhite Seed Company, P.O. Box 23, Poolville, TX 76076: Free catalog ❖ Seeds. 817-599-8656.

Wyatt-Quarles Seed Company, P.O. Box 739, Garner, NC 27529: Free catalog ❖ Seeds. 919-832-0551.

Shrubs

Agua Fria Nursery, 1409 Agua Fria St., Santa Fe, NM 87501: Free catalog ❖ Containerized western wildflowers, perennials, and shrubs.

Arbor Vitae Farm Inc., 8376 Meadow Rd., Warrenton, VA 22186: Free catalog ❖ Rare flowering trees and shrubs. 800-349-8950.

Arborvillage Farm Nursery, P.O. Box 227, Holt, MO 64048: Catalog $1 ❖ Trees and shrubs. 816-264-3911.

Barber Nursery, Rt. 3, Box 205, Willis, TX 77378: Free catalog ❖ Shrub and tree seedlings. 409-856-8074.

Vernon Barnes & Son Nursery, P.O. Box 250, McMinnville, TN 37110: Free catalog ❖ Wildflowers, hedges and shrubs, vines, berry plants, and sassafras. Also flowering, shade, fruit, and nut trees. 615-668-8576.

Colvos Creek Nursery, P.O. Box 1512, Vashon Island, WA 98070: Catalog $2 (refundable) ❖ Trees, shrubs, and bamboo and rare and unusual plants. 206-441-1509.

GARDENING—PLANTS & SEEDS

Eastern Plant Specialties, P.O. Box 226, Georgetown, ME 04548: Catalog $3 ❖ Shrubs, rhododendrons, and wildflowers.

Eco-Gardens, P.O. Box 1227, Decatur, GA 30031: Price list $1 ❖ Water garden plants, perennials, wildflowers, ferns, daylilies, trees, and shrubs. 404-294-6468.

Emlong Nurseries, 2671 Marquette Woods Rd., Stevensville, MI 49127: Free catalog ❖ Thornless blackberries, other berry plants, shrubs, flowers, landscaping plants, roses, and dwarf and standard fruit, nut, and ornamental trees. 616-429-3431.

Farmer Seed & Nursery Company, 818 NW 4th St., Faribault, MN 55021: Free catalog ❖ Ornamental shrubs and hedges, vegetable seeds, flowering bulbs, fruit and shade trees, berry plants, and roses. 507-334-1623.

Henry Field's Seed & Nursery, 415 N. Burnett, Shenandoah, IA 51602: Free catalog ❖ Strawberry and other berry plants, vegetable and flower seeds, hedges, ornamental shrubs, roses, and fruit, nut, and shade trees. 605-665-4491.

Girard Nurseries, P.O. Box 428, Geneva, OH 44041: Free catalog ❖ Baby evergreen seeds and seedlings, shade trees, and flowering shrubs. 216-466-2881.

Goodwin Creek Gardens, P.O. Box 83, Williams, OR 97544: Catalog $1 ❖ Container-grown native American trees, shrubs, and perennial flowers. 541-846-7357.

Gossler Farms Nursery, 1200 Weaver Rd., Springfield, OR 97478: Catalog $2 ❖ Magnolias and new, rare, and unusual trees and shrubs that include maples, stewartias, and styrax. 503-746-3922.

Greer Gardens, 1280 Goodpasture Island Rd., Eugene, OR 97401: Catalog $3 ❖ Azaleas and rhododendrons, trees, shrubs, Japanese maples, and bonsai. 800-548-0111.

Griffey Nursery, 1670 Hwy. 25/70, Marshall, NC 28753: Free catalog ❖ Native evergreen shrubs and trees. 704-656-2334.

Kelly Nurseries, 1708 Morrissey Dr., Bloomington, IL 61704: Free catalog ❖ Heavily rooted fruit and nut trees. Also landscaping trees, shrubs, ornamentals, berry plants, grapevines, and flowers. 507-334-1623.

Mellinger's, 2310 W. South Range Rd., North Lima, OH 44452: Free catalog ❖ Fruit, nut, shade, and ornamental trees. Also gladioli, flowering shrubs, hedges, irises, wildflowers, and gardening equipment. 330-549-9861.

Musser Forests, P.O. Box 340, Indiana, PA 15701: Free catalog ❖ Evergreen hardwood seedlings and transplants, other trees and shrubs, and ground covers. 800-643-8319.

National Arbor Day Foundation, 100 Arbor Ave., Nebraska City, NE 68410: Free catalog ❖ Berry plants, flowering shrubs and trees, evergreens, flowering bulbs, and nut and standard and dwarf fruit trees. 402-474-5655.

Niche Gardens, 1111 Dawson Rd., Chapel Hill, NC 27516: Catalog $3 ❖ Nursery-propagated wildflowers, trees, shrubs, and perennials. 919-967-0078.

Northwoods Retail Nursery, 27635 S. Oglesvy Rd., Canby, OR 97013: Free catalog ❖ Shrubs, vines, and ornamental trees. 503-651-5432.

The Nursery, Hwy. 82, Box 130, Ty Ty, GA 31795: Free catalog ❖ Berries, grapes, trees, and shrubs. 800-972-2101.

Orchid Gardens, 2232 139th Ave. NW, Andover, MN 55304: Catalog $1 ❖ Wildflowers, native trees, shrubs, and ferns. 612-755-0205.

Savage Farms Nursery, P.O. Box 125, McMinnville, TN 37110: Free catalog ❖ Flowering trees and shrubs, evergreens, berry plants, and gardening supplies. Also fruit and shade trees. 615-668-8902.

R.H. Shumway Seedsman, P.O. Box 1, Graniteville, SC 29829: Free catalog ❖ Ornamental shrubs and plants, berry plants, fruit trees, roses, seeds and bulbs, and gardening supplies. 413-737-0399.

Stark Brothers, Nurseries & Orchards Company, P.O. Box 10, Louisiana, MO 63353: Free catalog ❖ Fruit trees, berry and landscaping plants, shrubs, and garden supplies. 800-775-6415.

Tripple Brook Farm, 37 Middle Rd., Southampton, MA 01073: Catalog 50¢ ❖ Bamboo plants, exotic fruits, trees, perennials, and shrubs. 413-527-4626.

Wildflower Nursery, 1680 Hwy. 25-70, Marshall, NC 28753: Free catalog ❖ Shrubs. 704-656-2723.

Windrose, 1093 Mill Rd., Pen Argyl, PA 18072: Catalog $2 (refundable) ❖ Rare and unusual trees and shrubs. 610-588-1037.

Terrariums

Carolina Exotic Gardens, Rt. 5, Box 283-A, Greenville, NC 27834: Catalog $1 ❖ Carnivorous plants, seeds, terrarium plants, and soil. 919-758-2600.

Kartuz Greenhouses, 1408 Sunset Dr., Vista, CA 92083: Catalog $2 ❖ Gesneriads, begonias, miniature terrarium, and unusual tropical plants. 619-941-3613.

Peter Pauls Nurseries, 4665 Chapin Rd., Canandaigua, NY 14424: Free catalog ❖ Woodland terrarium and carnivorous plants. 716-394-7397.

Trees

Ames Orchard & Nursery, 18292 Wildlife Rd., Rt. 5, Box 194, Fayetteville, AR 72701: Free information ❖ Apple, pear, and peach trees. 501-443-0282.

Arbor Vitae Farm Inc., 8376 Meadow Rd., Warrenton, VA 22186: Free catalog ❖ Rare flowering trees and shrubs. 800-349-8950.

Arborvillage Farm Nursery, P.O. Box 227, Holt, MO 64048: Catalog $1 ❖ Trees and shrubs. 816-264-3911.

Arrowhead Retail Nursery, 5030 Watta Rd., Bryson City, NC 25713: Free catalog ❖ Rare flowering trees and shrubs, stewartias, and native plants. 704-488-8731.

Barber Nursery, Rt. 3, Box 205, Willis, TX 77378: Free catalog ❖ Shrub and tree seedlings. 409-856-8074.

Vernon Barnes & Son Nursery, P.O. Box 250, McMinnville, TN 37110: Free catalog ❖ Wildflowers, hedges and shrubs, vines, berry plants, and sassafras, flowering, shade, fruit, and nut trees. 615-668-8576.

Bear Creek Nursery, P.O. Box 41175, Northport, WA 99157: Catalog $1 ❖ Fruits, nuts, and old apples. 509-732-6219.

Burford Brothers, Rt. 1, Nursery, Monroe, VA 24574: Catalog $2 ❖ Modern and antique apples. 804-929-4950.

Burnt Ridge Nursery & Orchards, 432 Burnt Ridge Rd., Onalaska, WA 98570: Free brochure ❖ Trees, shrubs, and vines that produce edible nuts and fruits.

Carino Nurseries, P.O. Box 538, Indiana, PA 15701: Free catalog ❖ Christmas trees, seedlings, and transplants. 800-223-7075.

Chestnut Hill Nursery Inc., Rt. 1, Box 341, Alachua, FL 32615: Free information ❖ Oriental persimmons, hybrid American-Chinese chestnuts, and other nut and fruit trees. 800-669-2067.

Classical Fruit, 8831 AL Hwy. 157, Moulton, AL 35650: Free catalog ❖ Antique and new varieties of fruit trees from local and worldwide sources. 205-974-8813.

Colvos Creek Nursery, P.O. Box 1512, Vashon Island, WA 98070: Catalog $2 (refundable) ❖ Trees, shrubs, and bamboo and rare and unusual plants. 206-441-1509.

Cumberland Valley Nurseries Inc., P.O. Box 471, McMinnville, TN 37110: Free catalog ❖ Fruit trees. 800-492-0022; 615-668-4153 (in TN).

Digging Dog Nursery, P.O. Box 471, Albion, CA 95410: Catalog $3 ❖ Grasses, vines, trees, perennials, and shrubs. 707-937-1130.

Edible Landscaping, P.O. Box 77, Afton, VA 22920: Catalog $1 ❖ Dwarf citrus trees. 800-524-4156.

Emlong Nurseries, 2671 Marquette Woods Rd., Stevensville, MI 49127: Free catalog ❖ Thornless blackberries and other berry plants. Also shrubs, flowers, landscaping plants, roses, and dwarf and standard fruit, nut, and ornamental trees. 616-429-3431.

❖ GARDENING—PLANTS & SEEDS ❖

Fairweather Gardens, Box 330, Greenwich, NJ 08323: Catalog $3 ❖ Trees and shrubs. 609-451-6261.

Farmer Seed & Nursery Company, 818 NW 4th St., Faribault, MN 55021: Free catalog ❖ Fruit and shade trees, vegetable seeds, flowering bulbs, ornamental shrubs and hedges, berry plants, and roses. 507-334-1623.

Henry Field's Seed & Nursery, 415 N. Burnett, Shenandoah, IA 51602: Free catalog ❖ Berry plants, hedges and ornamental shrubs, and roses. Also dwarf, standard, and seedling apple trees and fruit, nut, and shade trees. 605-665-4491.

Flickingers' Nursery, P.O. Box 245, Sagamore, PA 16250: Free catalog ❖ Seedlings and transplants. 800-368-7381.

Forestfarm, 990 Tetherow Rd., Williams, OR 97544: Catalog $3 ❖ Sassafras trees. 541-846-7269.

Frysville Farms, 300 Frysville Rd., Ephrata, PA 17522: Free catalog ❖ Trees. 800-422-FRYS.

Gardener's Choice, Country Rd. 687, P.O. Box 8000, Hartford, MI 49057: Free catalog ❖ Seeds for vegetables, flowers, house plants, and trees. 800-274-4096.

Girard Nurseries, P.O. Box 428, Geneva, OH 44041: Free catalog ❖ Baby evergreen seeds and seedlings, shade trees, and flowering shrubs. 216-466-2881.

Gleckler Seedmen, Metamora, OH 43540: Free catalog ❖ Unusual seed varieties.

Griffey Nursery, 1670 Hwy. 25/70, Marshall, NC 28753: Free catalog ❖ Native evergreen shrubs and trees. 704-656-2334.

Goodwin Creek Gardens, P.O. Box 83, Williams, OR 97544: Catalog $1 ❖ Container-grown native American trees, shrubs, and perennial flowers. 541-846-7357.

Gossler Farms Nursery, 1200 Weaver Rd., Springfield, OR 97478: Catalog $2 ❖ Magnolias and new, rare, and unusual trees and shrubs that include maples, stewartias, and styrax. 503-746-3922.

Greer Gardens, 1280 Goodpasture Island Rd., Eugene, OR 97401: Catalog $3 ❖ Azaleas and rhododendrons, trees, shrubs, Japanese maples, and bonsai. 800-548-0111.

Grimo Nut Nursery, RR 3, Niagara-on-the-Lake, Ontario, Canada L0S 1J0: Catalog $2 (refundable) ❖ Grafted and seed varieties of nut trees.

Gurney Seed & Nursery Company, 110 Capitol St., Yankton, SD 57079: Free catalog ❖ Seeds, bulbs, and semi-dwarf and standard varieties of apple trees. 605-665-1671.

Harmony Farm Supply & Nursery, P.O. Box 460, Graton, CA 95444: Catalog $2 (refundable) ❖ Miniature and standard size fruit and nut trees. 707-823-9125.

Hollydale Nursery, P.O. Box 69, Pelham, TN 37366: Free list ❖ Fruit trees. 800-222-3026; 615-467-3600 (in TN).

Hughes Nursery, P.O. Box 7705, Olympia, WA 98507: Catalog $1.60 (refundable) ❖ Container-grown dwarf Japanese maples. 360-352-4725.

Ison's Nursery, P.O. Box 190, Brooks, GA 30205: Free catalog ❖ Muscadine grapevines, berry plants, and apple, pear, fig, peach, walnut and pecan trees. 800-733-0324.

Johnson Nursery, Rt. 5, Ellijay, GA 30540: Free catalog ❖ Strawberry plants, grapevines, and apple, plum, pear, cherry, apricot, and walnut and almond nut trees. Also orchard supplies, tools and accessories, and books. 706-276-3187.

Kelly Nurseries, 1708 Morrissey Dr., Bloomington, IL 61704: Free catalog ❖ Heavily rooted fruit and nut trees, landscaping trees and shrubs, ornamentals, berry plants, grapevines, and flowers. 507-334-1623.

Lawson's Nursery, 2730 Yellow Creek Rd., Ball Ground, GA 30107: Free list ❖ Antique apple trees. 770-893-2141.

Henry Leuthardt Nurseries, Box 666, East Moriches, NY 11940: Free catalog ❖ Dwarf fruit trees that grow full-size fruit. 516-878-1387.

Louisiana Nursery, Rt. 7, Box 43, Opelousas, LA 70570: Catalog $6 ❖ Sassafras trees and rare, unusual, and hard-to-find plants. 318-948-3696.

Earl May Seeds & Nursery Company, N. Elm St., Shenandoah, IA 51603: Free catalog ❖ Flowering shrubs, berry plants, roses, seeds for vegetables and fruit, and fruit, nut, shade, and ornamental trees. 712-246-1020.

Mellinger's, 2310 W. South Range Rd., North Lima, OH 44452: Free catalog ❖ Fruit, nut, shade, and ornamental trees. Also gladioli, flowering shrubs, hedges, irises, wildflowers, and gardening equipment. 330-549-9861.

J.E. Miller Nurseries, 5060 W. Lake Rd., Canandaigua, NY 14424: Free catalog ❖ Berry plants, grapevines, spring and fall varieties of semi-dwarf hybrid antique apples, and other fruit and nut trees. 800-836-9630.

Musser Forests, P.O. Box 340, Indiana, PA 15701: Free catalog ❖ Evergreen hardwood seedlings and transplants, other trees and shrubs, and ground covers. 800-643-8319.

National Arbor Day Foundation, 100 Arbor Ave., Nebraska City, NE 68410: Free catalog ❖ Flowering trees and shrubs, shade and ornamental trees, evergreens, and fruit trees. (Note: This is an optional membership organization that offers savings to its members.) 402-474-5655.

Niche Gardens, 1111 Dawson Rd., Chapel Hill, NC 27516: Catalog $3 ❖ Nursery-propagated wildflowers, trees, shrubs, and perennials. 919-967-0078.

Nolin River Nut Tree Nursery, 797 Port Wooden Rd., Upton, KY 42784: Free price list ❖ Grafted or budded Black and Persian walnut, pecan, chestnut, heartnut, and butternut trees. 502-369-8551.

Northwoods Retail Nursery, 27635 S. Oglesby Rd., Canby, OR 97013: Free catalog ❖ Growing stock for figs, persimmons, kiwis, Asian pears, passion fruit, and pomegranates. 503-651-5432.

The Nursery, Hwy. 82, Box 130, Ty Ty, GA 31795: Free catalog ❖ Berries, grapes, trees, and shrubs. 800-972-2101.

Oikos Tree Crops, P.O. Box 19425, Kalamazoo, MI 49019: Free information ❖ Trees and growing stock for nuts and native fruits. Also exotic plants. 616-624-6233.

Orchid Gardens, 2232 139th Ave. NW, Andover, MN 55304: Catalog $1 ❖ Wildflowers, native trees, shrubs, and ferns. 612-755-0205.

Pacific Tree Farms, 4301 Lynnwood Dr., Chula Vista, CA 92010: Catalog $2 ❖ Miniature trees, genetic dwarf avocados, and exotic ornamentals. 619-402-2400.

Patrick's Nursery, P.O. Box 130, Ty Ty, GA 31795: Free catalog ❖ Vegetable seeds, fruit and nut trees, berry plants, and grapevines. 800-972-2101.

Peaceful Valley Farm Supply, P.O. Box 2209, Grass Valley, CA 95945: Catalog $2 (refundable) ❖ Miniature fruit and nut trees, tools, propagation supplies, seeds, and farming equipment. 916-272-4769.

Pikes Peak Nurseries, Box 75, Penn Run, PA 15765: Free catalog ❖ Evergreen and deciduous seedlings, transplants, and nut trees.

Raintree Nursery, 391 Butts Rd., Morton, WA 98356: Free information ❖ Asian pear trees. 206-496-6400.

Rocky Meadow Nursery, 360 Rocky Meadow Rd., New Salisbury, IN 47161: Catalog $1 ❖ Dwarf and semi-dwarf apple, pear, and plum trees. Also grafting supplies. 812-347-2213.

Savage Nursery Center, 6255 Beersheba Hwy., McMinnville, TN 37110: Free catalog ❖ Berry plants, evergreens, gardening supplies, shrubs, and fruit, shade, and flowering trees. 615-668-8902.

Shady Oaks Nursery, 112 10th Ave. SE, Waseca, MN 56093: Information $1 ❖ Ferns, trees and shrubs, perennials, and wildflowers. 507-835-5033.

Sonoma Antique Apple Nursery, 4395 Westside Rd., Healdsburg, CA 95448: Catalog $2 ❖ Old-time apple and pear trees on semi-dwarf root stocks. 707-433-6420.

❖ GARDENING—PLANTS & SEEDS ❖

Southmeadow Fruit Gardens, 10603 Cleveland Ave., Baroda, MI 49101: Catalog $9 ❖ Apples, rare grapes and gooseberries, mediars, nectarines, pears, peaches, cherries, plums, apricots, currants, quince, other trees, and shrubs. 616-422-2411.

Spring Valley Nursery, 11097 Spring Valley Ln., Delaplane, VA 22025: Free catalog ❖ Antique apple trees. 703-364-3160.

Stark Brothers, Nurseries & Orchards Company, P.O. Box 10, Louisiana, MO 63353: Free catalog ❖ Fruit trees, berry and landscaping plants, and garden supplies. 800-775-6415.

TEC Trees, P.O. Box 539, Osseo, MN 55369: Free catalog ❖ Seedlings and transplants.

Toole's Bend Nursery, 3530 Toole's Bend Rd., Knoxville, TN 37922: Catalog $2 (refundable) ❖ Rare and unusual trees and shrubs.

Trees on the Move Inc., P.O. Box 462, Cranbury, NJ 08512: Free information ❖ Rare, unusual, native, and exotic trees and shrubs. 609-395-1366.

Tripple Brook Farm, 37 Middle Rd., Southampton, MA 01073: Catalog 50¢ ❖ Bamboo plants, exotic fruits, trees, perennials, and shrubs. 413-527-4626.

Twombly Nursery, 163 Barn Hill Rd., Monroe, CT 06468: Catalog $4 ❖ Dwarf conifer miniatures, rare and unusual plants, and trees. 203-261-2133.

Waynesboro Nurseries, P.O. Box 987, Waynesboro, VA 22980: Free list of retail sources ❖ Ornamentals and dwarf and standard antique apple, fruit and nut, flowering, and shade trees. 800-868-8676; 703-942-4141 (in VA).

Wayside Gardens, 1 Garden Ln., Hodges, SC 29695: Free catalog ❖ Container-grown trees ready for transplanting. 800-845-1124.

Bob Wells Nursery, P.O. Box 606, Lindale, TX 75771: Free catalog ❖ Fruit, nut, and shade trees. Also berries, grapes, muscadines, roses, ornamentals, and flowering shrubs. 903-882-3550.

Western Maine Nurseries, One Evergreen Dr., Fryeburg, ME 04037: Free catalog ❖ Evergreen trees. 800-447-4745; 207-935-2161 (in ME).

Wildflower Nursery, 1680 Hwy. 25-70, Marshall, NC 28753: Free catalog ❖ Evergreens. 704-656-2723.

Windrose, 1093 Mill Rd., Pen Argyl, PA 18072: Catalog $2 (refundable) ❖ Rare and unusual trees and shrubs. 610-588-1037.

Womack's Nursery Company, Rt. 1, Box 80, De Leon, TX 76444: Free catalog ❖ Fruit, nut, and shade and flowering trees. Also roses and nursery stock for planting in southern states. 817-893-6497.

Vegetable Plants

Alfrey Seeds, P.O. Box 415, Knoxville, TN 37901: Free catalog with long SASE ❖ Pepper seeds.

Archia's Seed Store, P.O. Box 356, Buckner, MO 64016: Free catalog ❖ Beekeeping equipment, vegetable and flower seeds, and gardening supplies. 816-826-1330.

Brown's Omaha Plant Farms Inc., P.O. Box 787, Omaha, TX 75571: Catalog 25¢ ❖ Onion, cauliflower, cabbage, broccoli, and brussel sprouts plants. 903-884-2421.

Delegeane Garlic Farms, P.O. Box 2561, Yountville, Napa Valley, CA 94599: Free brochure ❖ Garlic cloves for planting. 800-726-6692.

Dixondale Farms, P.O. Box 127, Carrizo Springs, TX 78834: Free information ❖ Onion plants. 210-876-2430.

Elephant Garlic Seeds, P.O. Box 10742, Scottsdale, AZ 85271: Information $2 with long SASE ❖ Seeds and planting information.

Enchanted Seeds, P.O. Box 6087, Las Cruces, NM 88006: Free information ❖ Seeds for all types of peppers. 505-523-6058.

Evergreen Y.H. Enterprises, P.O. Box 17538, Anaheim, CA 92817: Catalog $2 (refundable) ❖ Oriental vegetable seeds. 714-637-5769.

Fedco Seeds, P.O. Box 520, Waterville, ME 04903: Catalog $2 ❖ Heirloom hybrid vegetable and herb seeds. 207-873-7333.

Filaree Farm, Rt. 2, Box 162, Okanogan, WA 98840: Catalog $2 ❖ Garlic varieties. 509-422-6940.

Fisher's Garden Store, P.O. Box 236, Belgrade, MT 59714: Free catalog ❖ Vegetable and flower seeds for high altitude gardening and short growing seasons. 406-388-6052.

Fred's Plant Farm, P.O. Box 707, Dresden, TN 38225: Free information ❖ Sweet potato seeds and plants. 800-243-9377.

The Gourmet Gardener, 8650 College Blvd., Overland Park, KS 66210: Catalog $2 ❖ Herb, vegetable, and edible flower seeds from around the world. 913-345-0490.

Hardscrabble Enterprises Inc., Box 42, Cherry Grove, WV 26804: Catalog $3 (refundable) ❖ Grow-your-own Shiitake mushroom kits. Also mushroom-growing supplies and spawn. 304-567-2727.

Herban Garden, 5002 2nd St., Rainbow, CA 92028: Catalog $1 ❖ Herbs, vegetables, and everlastings. 619-723-2967.

Heritage Seed Company, Rt. 4, Box 187, Star City, AR 71667: Free catalog ❖ Onion sets. 501-628-4820.

Horticultural Enterprises, P.O. Box 810082, Dallas, TX 75381: Free catalog ❖ Hot and sweet peppers, jicama, and herbs for Mexican cooking.

Illinois Foundation Seeds, Box 722, Champaign, IL 61824: Free price list ❖ Seeds for sweet corn. 217-485-6260.

Kalmia Farm, P.O. Box 3881, Charlottesville, VA 22903: Free catalog ❖ Shallots, multiplier onions, and garlic varieties.

Lockhart Seeds Inc., P.O. Box 1361, Stockton, CA 92505: Free catalog ❖ Asparagus cultivars and hybrids and vegetables. 209-466-4401.

Manhattan Farms, 3088 Salmon River Rd., Salmon Arm, British Columbia, Canada V1E 4M1: Catalog $2 (refundable) ❖ Tomato seed packets.

Piedmont Plant Company, P.O. Box 424, Albany, GA 31703: Free catalog ❖ Field-grown vegetable plants. 912-883-7029.

Redwood City Seed Company, P.O. Box 361, Redwood City, CA 94064: Catalog $1 ❖ Herb and vegetable seeds from worldwide sources. 415-325-7333.

Ronniger's Seed Potatoes, Star Rt. 55, Moyie Springs, ID 83845: Catalog $1 ❖ Heirloom and European varieties of seed potatoes.

Roswell Seed Company Inc., P.O. Box 725, Roswell, NM 88202: Free price list with long SASE ❖ Chili pepper seed.

Seeds Blüm, Idaho City Stage, Boise, ID 83706: Catalog $3 ❖ Seed potatoes. 208-343-2202.

Seedway Inc., 1225 Zeager Rd., Elizabethtown, PA 17022: Free catalog ❖ Vegetable seeds. 800-952-7333.

Shady Acres Herb Farm, 7815 Hwy. 212, Chaska, MN 55318: Free list with long SASE ❖ Seeds for herbs, wildflowers, everlastings, and vegetables. 612-466-3391.

R.H. Shumway Seedsman, P.O. Box 1, Graniteville, SC 29829: Free catalog ❖ Non-hybrid vegetable seeds. 413-737-0399.

Steele Plant Company, Gleason, TN 38229: Free catalog with two 1st class stamps ❖ Sweet potato, brussel sprouts, onion, cabbage, cauliflower, and broccoli plants. 901-648-5476.

Tomato Growers Supply Company, P.O. Box 2237, Fort Myers, FL 33902: Free catalog ❖ Tomatoes, peppers, books, and gardening supplies. 813-768-1119.

The Tomato Seed Company Inc., P.O. Box 1400, Tryon, NC 28782: Free catalog ❖ Tomato seeds and heirloom vegetables.

Totally Tomatoes, P.O. Box 1626, Augusta, GA 30903: Free catalog ❖ Tomato seeds. 803-663-0016.

Twilley Seed Company, P.O. Box 65, Trevose, PA 19055: Free catalog ❖ Vegetable and flower seeds.

Wood Prairie Farm, Jim & Megan Gerrisen, RR 4, Box 164, Bridgewater, ME 04735: Free catalog ❖ Maine certified seed potatoes. 800-829-9765.

Wildflowers & Native Plants

Agua Viva Seed Ranch, Rt. 1, Box 8, Taos, NM 87571: Free catalog ❖ Wildflowers, bulbs, and perennials. 800-248-9080.

Applewood Seed Company, P.O. Box 10761, Edgemont Station, Golden, CO 80401: Free catalog ❖ Wildflower seeds and mixture packets.

Vernon Barnes & Son Nursery, P.O. Box 250, McMinnville, TN 37110: Free catalog ❖ Wildflowers, nut and sassafras trees, hedges, vines, and berry plants. 615-668-8576.

Blossom Farm, Johnny Cake Ln., Greenville, NY 12083: Free information ❖ Assorted wildflower seeds and individual seed packets. 518-966-5722.

Boothe Hill Wildflowers, 23 B Boothe Hill, Chapel Hill, NC 27514: Free catalog ❖ Wildflower seeds and plants. 919-967-4091.

Crownsville Nursery, P.O. Box 797, Crownsville, MD 21032: Catalog $2 (minimum order $25) ❖ Ferns, wildflowers, azaleas, ornamental grasses, and perennials. 410-923-2212.

Czarnick Nursery, RR 2, Genola, NE 68640: Catalog $1 ❖ Perennials, grasses, and wildflowers.

Dabney Herbs, P.O. Box 22061, Louisville, KY 40222: Catalog $2 ❖ Ginseng, herbs, scented geraniums, perennials, and wildflowers. 502-893-5198.

Eastern Plant Specialties, P.O. Box 226, Georgetown, ME 04548: Catalog $3 ❖ Shrubs, rhododendrons, and wildflowers.

Far North Gardens, P.O. Box 126, New Hudson, MI 48165: Catalog $2 (refundable) ❖ Rare plants, herbs, ornamentals, and plants for woodland settings, and rock gardens.

Forestfarm, 990 Tetherow Rd., Williams, OR 97544: Catalog $3 ❖ Native and unusual ornamental American plants, shrubs, and trees. 541-846-7269.

The Fragrant Path, P.O. Box 328, Fort Calhoun, NE 68023: Catalog $2 ❖ Seeds for prairie wildflowers. Also grasses, ferns, trees, shrubs, and climbing plants.

Gardens of the Blue Ridge, P.O. Box 10, Pineola, NC 28662: Catalog $3 (refundable) ❖ Wildflower seeds, ferns, trees, plants, shrubs, and bulbs. 704-733-2417.

Good Hollow Greenhouse & Herbarium, 50 Slaterock Mill Rd., Taft, TN 38488: Catalog $1 ❖ Herb plants and dried herbs, perennials, wildflowers, scented geraniums, essential oils and potpourris, teas, and spices. 615-433-7640.

Green Horizons, 145 Scenic Hill Rd., Kerrville, TX 78028: Free brochure ❖ Texas wildflower seeds and books. 210-257-5141.

Griffey Nursery, 1670 Hwy. 25/70, Marshall, NC 28753: Free catalog ❖ Appalachian wildflowers, rock and bog plants, ferns, and vines. 704-656-2334.

Las Pilitas Nursery, Las Pilitas Rd., Santa Margarita, CA 93453: Catalog $6 ❖ Native plants and seeds from California.

Mellinger's, 2310 W. South Range Rd., North Lima, OH 44452: Free catalog ❖ Fruit, nut, shade, and ornamental trees. Also gladioli, flowering shrubs, hedges, irises, wildflowers, and gardening equipment. 330-549-9861.

Midwest Wildflowers, P.O. Box 64, Rockton, IL 61072: Catalog $1 ❖ Woodland wildflowers.

Moon Mountain Wildflowers, P.O. Box 725, Carpinteria, CA 93014: Catalog $3 ❖ Wildflower seeds. 805-684-2565.

Native Gardens, 5737 Fisher Ln., Greenback, TN 37742: Catalog $2 ❖ Native wildflower, fern, tree, shrub, and vine plants and seeds. Nursery propagated since 1983. 423-856-0220.

Natural Gardening Company, 217 San Anselmo Ave., San Anselmo, CA 94960: Free catalog ❖ Beneficial insects, organic gardening supplies, pest controls, drip irrigation equipment, and wildflower seeds. 707-766-9303.

New England Wildflower Society, Garden in the Woods, 180 Hemenway Rd., Framingham, MA 01701: Free catalog with long SASE and two 1st class stamps ❖ Wildflower seeds native to New England. 508-877-7630.

Niche Gardens, 1111 Dawson Rd., Chapel Hill, NC 27516: Catalog $3 ❖ Nursery-propagated wildflowers, perennials, trees, and shrubs. 919-967-0078.

Oakridge Nurseries, P.O. Box 182, East Kingston, NH 03827: Catalog $1 (refundable) ❖ Ferns and native wildflowers.

Orchid Gardens, 2232 139th Ave. NW, Andover, MN 55304: Catalog $1 ❖ Wildflowers, native trees, shrubs, and ferns. 612-755-0205.

Plants of the Southwest, Rt. 6, Box 11A, Santa Fe, NM 87501: Catalog $3.50 ❖ Wildflowers and native plants from the southwest. 505-471-2212.

Prairie Moon Nursery, Rt. 3, Box 163, Winona, MN 55987: Catalog $2 ❖ Plants and seeds for prairie wildflowers and grasses. 507-452-1362.

Prairie Nursery, P.O. Box 306, Westfield, WI 53964: Catalog $3 ❖ Plants and seeds for prairie wildflowers and grasses. 608-296-3679.

Prairie Ridge Nursery, 9738 Overland Rd., Mount Horeb, WI 53572: Catalog $3 (refundable) ❖ Wildflowers. 608-437-5245.

The Primrose Path, RD 2, Box 110, Scottsdale, PA 15683: Catalog $2 ❖ Alpine and woodland plants. 412-887-6756.

Putney Nursery Inc., Rt. 5, Putney, VT 05346: Catalog $1 (refundable) ❖ Wildflowers, ferns, herbs, perennials, orchids, and gardening supplies. 802-387-5577.

Clyde Robin Seed Catalog, P.O. Box 2366, Castro Valley, CA 94546: Catalog $2 ❖ Wildflower seeds, trees, and shrubs. 510-785-0425.

Shady Acres Herb Farm, 7815 Hwy. 212, Chaska, MN 55318: Free list with long SASE ❖ Herbs, wildflowers, everlastings, and vegetables. 612-466-3391.

Shady Oaks Nursery, 112 10th Ave. SE, Waseca, MN 56093: Information $1 ❖ Ferns, shrubs, perennials, and wildflowers. 507-835-5033.

Sunlight Gardens, 174 Golden Ln., Andersonville, TN 37705: Catalog $3 ❖ Nursery-grown wildflowers for the north and south, planting in the sun or shade, or for wet and dry locations. 615-494-8237.

Vermont Wildflower Farm, Rt. 7, P.O. Box 5, Charlotte, VT 05455: Free catalog ❖ Seeds for wildflowers, annuals, and perennial flowers. 802-425-3500.

We-Du Nursery, Rt. 5, Box 724, Marion, NC 28752: Catalog $2 ❖ Japanese and American wildflowers, woodland and rock garden plants, unusual perennials, and irises. 704-738-8300.

Wildflower Nursery, 1680 Hwy. 25-70, Marshall, NC 28753: Free catalog ❖ Wild native flowering plants.

Wildseed Farms, P.O. Box 308, 1101 Campo Rosa Rd., Eagle Lake, TX 77434: Catalog $2 ❖ Wildflower seeds. 800-848-0078.

Woodlanders Inc., 1128 Collerton Ave., Aiken, SC 29801: Free information with long SASE ❖ Native and wildlife-attracting plants. 803-648-7522.

GAZEBOS & OTHER GARDEN STRUCTURES

BowBends, P.O. Box 900, Bolton, MA 01740: Brochure $3 ❖ Easy-to-assemble gazebos, bridges, and arbors. 800-518-6471.

❖ GENEALOGY ❖

Caldera Spas, 1080 W. Bradley Ave., El Cajon, CA 92020: Free information ❖ Build-it-yourself gazebo kits. 800-669-1881.

California Redwood Association, 405 Enfrente Dr., Ste. 200, Novato, CA 94949: Free information ❖ Easy-to-build redwood gazebos. 415-382-0662.

Cumberland Woodcraft Company Inc., P.O. Drawer 609, Carlisle, PA 17013: Catalog $5 ❖ Gazebo kits in 10, 12, and 16-foot diameters. 717-243-0063.

Dalton Pavilions Inc., 20 Commerce Dr., Telford, PA 18969: Catalog $5 ❖ Western red cedar gazebos. 800-532-5866; 215-721-1492 (in PA).

Gazebos Ltd., 140 W. Summit St., Milford, MI 48381: Free information ❖ Build-it-yourself gazebo and outdoor enclosure kits. 800-701-6767.

Gazebo Woodcrafters, P.O. Box 187, Bellingham, WA 98227: Free brochure ❖ Easy-to-assemble gazebo kits. 800-634-0463.

Gingerbread Man Woodworks, Factory Outlet Store, P.O. Box 59, Noel, MO 64854: Catalog $5 ❖ Gazebos, garden structures, and ornamental trim. 417-775-2553.

Hand-y Home Products, 6400 E. 11 Mile Rd., Warren, MI 48091: Free information ❖ Build-it-yourself gazebo kits. 800-221-1849.

Kloter Farms Inc., 216 West Rd., Ellington, CT 06029: Brochure $3 ❖ Handcrafted gazebos. 800-289-3463; 203-871-1048 in CT).

Leisure Woods Inc., P.O. Box 177, Genoa, IL 60135: Free information ❖ Colonial and Victorian-style gazebos. 815-784-2497.

Litchfield Industries Inc., 4 Industrial Dr., Litchfield, MI 49252: Free catalog ❖ Garden shelters. 800-542-5282.

The Redwood Shop, 3329 Fitzgerald Rd., Ste. 6, Rancho Cordova, CA 95742: Free catalog ❖ Easy-to-assemble red wood gazebo kits. 800-600-0299; 916-852-0299 (in CA).

Sun Designs, P.O. Box 6, Oconomowoc, WI 53066: Plan book $9.95 plus $3.95 postage ❖ Gazebos and garden structures. 414-567-4255.

Thaxted Cottage, Gardener, 121 Driscoll Way, Gaithersburg, MD 20878: Catalog $2 ❖ Redwood cottage with trellis sides and built-in seat, Amish-style wheelbarrows, and porch swings. 301-330-6211.

Vintage Wood Works, Hwy. 34 South, Box R, Quinlan, TX 75474: Catalog $2 ❖ Pre-assembled gazebos with bolt-together solid wooden panels. 903-356-2158.

Vixen Hill, Main St., P.O. Box 389, Elverson, PA 19520: Catalog $4 ❖ Pre-engineered gazebos for easy assembly by non-carpenters. 800-423-2766.

GENEALOGY
State Offices & Genealogical Associations

ALABAMA

State of Alabama Archives & History, 624 Washington Ave., Montgomery, AL 36130. 205-242-4435.

State of Alabama Genealogical Society, Samford University Library, American Genealogical Society Depository & Headquarters, 800 Lakeshore Dr., Birmingham, AL 35229. 205-870-2749.

State of Alabama Historical Association, P.O. Box 870380, Tuscaloosa, AL 35487.

ALASKA

State of Alaska Archives & Records Management, Division of Libraries & Archives, Department of Education, 141 Willoughby, Juneau, AK 99801. 907-465-2275.

State of Alaska Genealogical Society, 7030 Dickerson Dr., Anchorage, AK 99504.

State of Alaska Historical Society, P.O. Box 100299, Anchorage, AK 99510. 907-276-1596.

ARIZONA

Arizona Archives & Public Records, Arizona Library Department, State Capitol, 1700 W. Washington, Phoenix, AZ 85007. 602-542-3942.

State of Arizona Genealogical Society, P.O. Box 42075, Tucson, AZ 85733.

State of Arizona Historical Society, 949 E. 2nd St., Tucson, AZ 85719. 520-628-5774.

ARKANSAS

History Commission of Arkansas, 1 Capitol Mall, Little Rock, AR 72201. 501-682-6900.

State of Arkansas Genealogical Society, P.O. Box 908, Hot Springs, AR 71902.

State of Arkansas Historical Society, University of Arkansas, Department of History, Old Main 416, Fayetteville, AR 72701. 501-575-5884.

CALIFORNIA

State of California Archives, Office of the Secretary of State, 1020 O St., Room 130, Sacramento, CA 95814.

State Library of California, California Section, P.O. Box 942837, Sacramento, CA 94237. 916-654-0176.

State of California Genealogical Society, P.O. Box 77105, San Francisco, CA 94107. 415-777-9936.

State of California Historical Society, 2099 Pacific Ave., San Francisco, CA 94109. 415-567-1848.

COLORADO

Colorado Division of Archives & Public Records, Department of Administration, 1313 Sherman St., Denver, CO 80203. 303-866-2358.

State Library of Colorado, 201 E. Colfax Ave., Denver, CO 80203. 303-866-6728.

State of Colorado Genealogical Society, P.O. Box 9218, Denver, CO 80209.

State of Colorado Historical Society, Stephen H. Hart Library, 1300 Broadway, Denver, CO 80203. 303-866-2305.

CONNECTICUT

Connecticut State Archives, 231 Capitol Ave., Hartford, CT 06106. 203-566-5650.

State Library of Connecticut, History & Genealogy Unit, 231 Capitol Ave., Hartford, CT 06106. 302-566-3690.

State of Connecticut Historical Society, 1 Elizabeth St., Hartford, CT 06105. 203-236-5621.

State of Connecticut Society of Genealogists, P.O. Box 435, Glastonbury, CT 06433. 203-569-0002.

DELAWARE

Delaware Historical Society, 505 Market St., Wilmington, DE 19801. 302-655-7161.

Delaware State Genealogical Society, 505 Market St., Wilmington, DE 19801.

State of Delaware Archives, Hall of Records, Dover, DE 19901. 302-739-5318.

DISTRICT OF COLUMBIA

The Columbia Historical Society, 1307 New Hampshire Ave. NW, Washington, DC 20036. 202-785-2068.

District of Columbia Archives, 1300 Naylor Ct. NW, Washington, DC 20001. 202-727-2054.

FLORIDA

Florida Genealogical Society, P.O. Box 18624, Tampa, FL 33679.

State Archives of Florida, Bureau of Archives & Records Management, Division of Library & Information Services, Public Services Section, R.A. Gray Building, 500 S. Bronough St., Tallahassee, FL 32399. 904-487-2073.

State of Florida Genealogical Society, P.O. Box 10249, Tallahassee, FL 32302.

State of Florida Historical Society, University of South Florida Library, P.O. Box 3645, University Station, Gainesville, FL 32601. 813-974-3815.

GEORGIA

Georgia Department of Archives & History, Secretary of State, 330 Capitol Ave. SE, Atlanta, GA 30334. 404-656-2350.

❖ GENEALOGY ❖

State of Georgia Genealogical Society, P.O. Box 54575, Atlanta, GA 30308. 404-475-4404.

State of Georgia Historical Society, 501 Whittaker St., Savannah, GA 31499. 912-651-2128.

HAWAII

Sandwich Islands Genealogy Society, Hawaii State Library, 478 S. King St., Honolulu, HI 96813.

State of Hawaii Archives, Dept. of Accounting & General Services, Iolani Palace Grounds, 478 S. King St., Honolulu, HI 96813. 808-586-0329.

State of Hawaii Historical Society, 560 Kawaiahao St., Honolulu, HI 96813. 808-537-6271.

IDAHO

State of Idaho Historical Society, Genealogical Library, 450 N. 4th St., Boise, ID 83702. 208-334-2441.

State of Idaho Historical Society, Library and Archives Division, 450 N. 4th St., Boise, ID 83702. 208-334-2305.

State of Idaho Genealogical Society, 4620 Overland Rd., Boise, ID 83705. 208-384-0542.

ILLINOIS

State of Illinois Archives Division, Secretary of State, Archives Building, Capitol Complex, Springfield, IL 62756. 217-782-4682.

State of Illinois Genealogical Society, P.O. Box 2225, Springfield, IL 62791. 217-789-1968.

State of Illinois Historical Society, Illinois State Historical Library, Old State Capitol, Springfield, IL 62701. 217-782-4836.

INDIANA

State of Indiana Archives, 140 N. Senate Ave., Indianapolis, IN 46204.

State of Indiana Genealogical Society, P.O. Box 10507, Fort Wayne, IN 46852.

State of Indiana Historical Society, Indiana State Library & Historical Building, P.O. Box 88255, Indianapolis, IN 46202. 317-232-1879.

State of Indiana Library, Indiana Division, 140 N. Senate Ave., Indianapolis, IN 46204. 317-232-2537.

IOWA

Historical Iowa State Society, Library-Archives Bureau, Iowa State Historical Building, 600 E. Locust, Des Moines, IA 50319. 515-281-3007.

State of Iowa Archives, Iowa Historical Building, 600 E. Locust, Capitol Complex, Des Moines, IA 50319. 515-281-3007.

State of Iowa Genealogical Society, P.O. Box 7735, Des Moines, IA 50322.

KANSAS

Kansas State Genealogical Society, P.O. Box 103, Dodge City, KS 67801. 316-225-1951.

State Library of Kansas, Statehouse, 3rd Floor, Topeka, KS 66612. 913-296-3296.

State of Kansas Historical Society, Reference Services, 120 W. 10th St., Topeka, KS 66612. 913-296-4776.

KENTUCKY

Kentucky Historical Society, 300 Broadway, P.O. Box H, Frankfort, KY 40602. 502-564-3016.

State Archives of Kentucky, Kentucky Department of Archives & Library, Division of Public Records, 300 Coffee Tree Rd., P.O. Box 537, Frankfort, KY 40602. 502-875-7000.

State of Kentucky Genealogical Society, P.O. Box 153, Frankfort, KY 40602. 502-875-4452.

LOUISIANA

Genealogical & Historical Society of Louisiana, P.O. Box 3454, Baton Rouge, LA 70821.

Le Comité des Archives de la Louisiane, P.O. Box 44370, Capitol Station, Baton Rouge, LA 70804. 504-355-9906.

State of Louisiana Archives & Records, Office of the Secretary of State, P.O. Box 94125, Baton Rouge, LA 70804. 504-922-1206.

MAINE

Historical Society of Maine, L.M.A. Building, 485 Congress St., No. 84, Portland, ME 04111. 207-774-1822.

Maine State Archives, State House Station, Augusta, ME 04333. 207-289-5795.

State of Maine Genealogical Society, P.O. Box 221, Farmington, ME 04938.

MARYLAND

Maryland Historical Society, 201 W. Monument St., Baltimore, MD 21201. 410-685-3750.

Maryland State Genealogy Society, 201 W. Monument St., Baltimore, MD 21201. 410-685-3750.

State Archives of Maryland, Hall of Records Building, 350 Rowe Blvd., Annapolis, MD 21401. 410-974-3914.

MASSACHUSETTS

Commonwealth of Massachusetts Archives, Reference Desk, 220 Morrissey Blvd., Boston, MA 02125. 617-727-2816.

The Massachusetts Society of Genealogists, P.O. Box 215, Ashland, MA 01721.

State of Massachusetts Historical Society, 1154 Boylston St., Boston, MA 02215. 617-536-1608.

MICHIGAN

Michigan Genealogical Council, P.O. Box 80953, Lansing, MI 48908.

Michigan Historical Society, 2117 Washtenaw Ave., Ann Arbor, MI 48104. 313-769-1828.

Michigan State Archives, Bureau of History, State Department, 717 W. Allegan, Lansing, MI 48918. 517-373-1408.

MINNESOTA

Minnesota Historical Society Research Center, 345 Kellogg Blvd. West, St. Paul, MN 55102. 612-296-2143.

State of Minnesota Genealogical Society, P.O. Box 16069, St. Paul, MN 55116. 612-645-3671.

State of Minnesota Historical Society, 345 Kellogg Blvd. West, St. Paul, MN 55102. 612-296-2143.

MISSISSIPPI

Genealogical Society of Mississippi, P.O. Box 5301, Jackson, MS 39296.

Mississippi Archives & History Department, Archives & Library Division, P.O. Box 571, Jackson, MS 39205. 601-359-6876.

Mississippi History and Genealogy Association, 618 Avalon Rd., Jackson, MS 39206. 601-362-3079.

MISSOURI

Historical Society of Missouri, 1020 Lowry St., Columbia, MO 65201. 314-882-7083.

Missouri State Archives, P.O. Box 778, Jefferson City, MO 65102. 314-751-3280.

Missouri State Genealogical Association, P.O. Box 833, Columbia, MO 65205.

MONTANA

Genealogical Society of Montana, P.O. Box 555, Chester, MT 59522.

Montana Historical Society, Memorial Building, 225 N. Roberts St., Helena, MT 59620. 406-444-2716.

State Library of Montana, 1515 E. 6th Ave., Helena, MT 59620. 406-444-3004.

State of Montana Archives, Montana Historical Society, Memorial Building, 225 N. Roberts St., Helena, MT 59620.

NEBRASKA

Nebraska State Genealogical Society, P.O. Box 5608, Lincoln, NE 68505. 402-266-8881.

❖ GENEALOGY ❖

State Historical Society of Nebraska, Archives Division, P.O. Box 82554, Lincoln, NE 68501. 402-471-4771.

NEVADA

Nevada Genealogical State Society, P.O. Box 20666, Reno, NV 89515.

State of Nevada Historical Society, 1650 N. Virginia St., Reno, NV 89503. 702-688-1190.

State of Nevada Library & Archives, Archives & Records Division, 100 Stewart St., Carson City, NV 89710. 702-687-5210.

NEW HAMPSHIRE

New Hampshire Division of Records Management & Archives, New Hampshire Department of State, 71 S. Fruit St., Concord, NH 03301. 603-271-2236.

New Hampshire Historical Society, 30 Park St., Concord, NH 03301. 603-225-3381.

New Hampshire Society of Genealogists, P.O. Box 633, Exeter, NH 03833. 603-432-8137.

NEW JERSEY

New Jersey Genealogical Society, P.O. Box 1291, New Brunswick, NJ 08903. 201-356-6920.

New Jersey State Department of Archives, CN 307, Trenton, NJ 08625. 609-292-6260.

New Jersey State Library, Genealogy Section, CN 520, Trenton, NJ 08625. 609-292-6274.

NEW MEXICO

New Mexico Archives & Records Center, 404 Montezuma St., Santa Fe, NM 87501. 505-827-7332.

New Mexico Historical Society, P.O. Box 1912, Santa Fe, NM 87504.

New Mexico State Genealogical Society, P.O. Box 8283, Albuquerque, NM 87198. 505-256-3217.

NEW YORK

New York State Archives, Department of Education, Cultural Education Center, Room 11D40, Albany, NY 12230. 518-474-8955.

State of New York Genealogical & Biographical Society, 122 E. 58th St., New York, NY 10022. 212-755-8532.

State of New York Historical Association, Fenimore House, West Lake Rd., P.O. Box 800, Cooperstown, NY 13326. 607-547-2533.

NORTH CAROLINA

Federation of North Carolina Historical Society, 109 E. Jones St., Raleigh, NC 27601. 919-733-7305.

North Carolina State Archives, Department of Cultural Resources, Archives & History Division, State Library Building, 109 E. Jones St., Raleigh, NC 27601. 919-733-3952.

State of North Carolina Genealogical Society, P.O. Box 1492, Raleigh, NC 27602.

NORTH DAKOTA

North Dakota State Historical Society, State Archives & Historical Research Library, North Dakota Heritage Center, 612 E. Boulevard Ave., Bismark, ND 58505. 701-224-2091.

State Library of North Dakota, Liberty Memorial Building, Capital Grounds, Bismark, ND 58505. 701-224-2091.

OHIO

Ohio Historical Society, Archives & Library Division, Interstate Rt. 71 & 17th Ave., 1982 Velma Ave., Columbus, OH 43211. 614-297-2510.

State Genealogical Society of Ohio, Library Section, P.O. Box 2625, Mansfield, OH 44906. 419-522-9077.

State Library of Ohio, 65 S. Front St., Columbus, OH 43266. 614-644-6966.

OKLAHOMA

Federation of Oklahoma Genealogical Societies, P.O. Box 26151, Oklahoma City, OK 73157.

Oklahoma Department of Libraries, Office of Archives & Records, 200 NE 18th St., Oklahoma City, OK 73105. 405-521-2502.

Oklahoma Historical Society, Division of Library Resources, Wiley Post Historical Building, 2100 N. Lincoln Blvd., Oklahoma City, OK 73105. 405-521-2491.

OREGON

Archives Division of Oregon, Secretary of State, 800 Summer St. NE, Salem, OR 97310. 503-373-0701.

Genealogical Forum of Oregon, Headquarters & Library, 1410 SW Morrison St., Room 812, Portland, OR 97205. 503-227-2398.

Oregon Historical Society, 1230 SW Park Ave., Portland, OR 97205. 503-222-1741.

PENNSYLVANIA

Pennsylvania Heritage Society, P.O. Box 146, Laughlintown, PA 15655.

Pennsylvania Historical & Genealogy Society, 1300 Locust St., Philadelphia, PA 19107. 215-545-0391.

Pennsylvania State Archives, Reference Division, P.O. Box 1206, Harrisburg, PA 17108. 717-783-3281.

RHODE ISLAND

Rhode Island State Archives, 337 Westminster St., Providence, RI 02903. 401-277-2353.

Rhode Island State Genealogical Society, 13 Countryside Dr., Cumberland, RI 02864.

State of Rhode Island Historical Society, 110 Benevolent St., Providence, RI 02906. 401-331-8575.

SOUTH CAROLINA

South Carolina Department of Archives & History, P.O. Box 11669, Columbia, SC 29211. 803-734-8577.

South Carolina Historical Society, 100 Meeting St., Charleston, SC 29401. 803-723-3225.

State of South Carolina Genealogy Society, P.O. Box 16355, Greenville, SC 29606.

SOUTH DAKOTA

South Dakota Archives, Cultural Heritage Center, 900 Governors Dr., Pierre, SD 57501. 605-773-3804.

South Dakota Genealogical Society, Rt. 2, Box 10, Burke, SD 57523. 605-835-9364.

State of South Dakota Historical Society, Cultural Heritage Center, South Dakota Archives, 900 Governors Dr., Pierre, SD 57501. 605-773-3804.

TENNESSEE

Tennessee Genealogical Society, P.O. Box 111249, Memphis, TN 38111. 901-327-3273.

Tennessee Historical Commission, Department of Environment & Conservation, 701 Broadway, B-30, Nashville, TN 37243. 615-532-1550.

Tennessee State Archives & Library, 403 7th Ave. North, Nashville, TN 37243. 615-741-2764.

TEXAS

Historical Association of Texas, 2.306 SRH, University Station, Austin, TX 78712. 512-471-1525.

State of Texas Genealogy Society, 2507 Tannehill, Houston, TX 77008. 713-864-6862.

Texas State Library, P.O. Box 12927, Capital Station, Austin, TX 78711. 512-463-5463.

UTAH

Family History Library of The Church of Jesus Christ of Latter-day Saints, Genealogical Society of Utah, 35 N. West Temple, Salt Lake City, UT 84150. 801-240-2331.

Utah Archives & Record Services, Archives Building, State Capitol, Salt Lake City, UT 84114. 801-538-3013.

Utah Genealogical Association, P.O. Box 1144, Salt Lake City, UT 84110. 801-262-7263.

Utah State Historical Society, 300 Rio Grande, Salt Lake City, UT 84101. 801-533-5808.

VERMONT

Genealogy Society of Vermont, P.O. Box 422, Pittsford, VT 05763. 802-483-2957.

Historical Society of Vermont, Pavilion Office Building, 109 State St., Montpelier, VT 05609. 802-828-2291.

State of Vermont Archives, Office of the Secretary of State, 26 Terrace St., Redstone Building, Montpelier, VT 05609. 802-828-2308.

VIRGINIA

Historical Society of Virginia, P.O. Box 7311, Richmond, VA 23211. 804-342-9677.

Virginia Genealogical Society, 5001 W. Broad St., Ste. 115, Richmond, VA 23230. 804-285-8954.

Virginia State Library & Archives, Genealogy & Archives Section, 11th Street at Capitol Square, Richmond, VA 23219. 804-786-2306.

WASHINGTON

State of Washington Historical Society, Special Collections Division, 315 N. Stadium Way, Tacoma, WA 98403. 206-593-2830.

Washington State Archives, Main Office, Division of Archives & Records Management, Office of the Secretary of State, State Archives & Records Center Building, 1120 Washington St SE, EA-11, Olympia, WA 98504. 360-586-1492.

Washington State Genealogical Society, P.O. Box 1422, Olympia, WA 98507. 360-352-0595.

WEST VIRGINIA

Archives & History Division of West Virginia, The Cultural Center, Capitol Complex, Charleston, WV 25305. 304-348-2277.

State of West Virginia Genealogy Society, P.O. Box 249, Elkview, WV 25071.

West Virginia Genealogical Society, 5238 Elk River Rd. North, P.O. Box 249, Elkview, WV 25071.

WISCONSIN

Genealogy Society of Wisconsin, P.O. Box 5106, Madison, WI 53705. 378-3006-9405.

Wisconsin State Historical Society, 816 State St., Madison, WI 53706. 608-264-6535.

WYOMING

Wyoming State Archives, Research Division, Barrett State Office Building, 2301 Capitol Ave., Cheyenne, WY 82002. 307-777-7826.

Wyoming State Library, Supreme Court Building, 2301 Capitol Ave., Cheyenne, WY 82002. 307-777-7281.

Retail Sources & Publishers

Civil War Genealogy, T.L. Murphy, P.O. Box 3542, Gettysburg, PA 17325: Free brochure with long SASE ❖ Confederate, Union Pension, and prisoner of war and military service records. Also capsule unit histories.

Consumer Information Center, Pueblo, CO 81009: Free catalog ❖ Offers publications that contain genealogy information: Military Service Records in the National Archives (50¢), Using Records in the National Archives for Genealogical Research (50¢), Where to Write for Vital Records ($2.25), and Your Right to Federal Records (50¢). 719-948-4000.

Genealogical Publishing Company Inc., 1001 N. Calvert St., Baltimore, MD 21202: Free catalog ❖ General reference and how-to books, manuals, directories and finding aids, and state guides. 800-296-6687.

The Genealogical Research Library, 100 Adelaide St. West, 5th Floor, Toronto, Ontario, Canada M5H 1S3: Free catalog ❖ Reference books, family tree kits, and other information resources about Canadians. 416-360-3929.

Heritage Books Inc., 1540 E. Pointer Ridge Place, Ste. 207, Bowie, MD 20716: Free catalog ❖ Books and periodicals arranged by state and subject. 301-390-7709.

Higginson Books, 14 Derby Square, Salem, MA 01970: Catalog $3 ❖ Genealogies, how-to guides, and local histories.

Jayna James Designs, 1107 Elizabeth Dr., Hamilton, OH 45013: Free brochure with long SASE ❖ Hand-painted, matted, and ready-for-framing family trees. 513-868-9452.

David Morgan, 11812 Northcreek Pkwy., Ste. 103, Bothell, WA 98011: Free catalog ❖ Maps of Great Britain for travel or genealogy research. 800-324-4934.

National Archives & Records Administration, National Archives Books, Washington, DC 20408: Paper bound book $19 ❖ Guide to Genealogical Research in the National Archives that describes census records, military service information, passenger ship arrival lists, and other information for genealogy research. 202-523-3164.

The Ships Chandler, Wilmington, VT 05363: Free catalog ❖ Thousands of names from 32 countries in report form, genealogical paintings, plaques, coats of arms, and needlepoints. 305-375-9469.

Software

Broderbund Software, P.O. Box 6125, Novato, CA 94948: Free information ❖ Windows 3.1 and Windows 95-based genealogy family tree-maker software. 800-521-6263.

The Church of Jesus Christ of Latter-Day Saints, Salt Lake Distribution Center, 1999 W. 1700 South, Salt Lake City, UT 84104: Free information ❖ DOS-based and Macintosh and PC genealogy software. 800-537-5950; 801-240-2584 (in UT).

Expert Software, 800 Douglas Rd., Executive Tower, 7th Floor, Coral Cables, FL 33134: Free information ❖ DOS and Windows-based genealogy software. 800-759-2562; 305-567-9990 (in FL).

Family History Library, 35 NW Temple St., Salt Lake City, UT 84150: Free information ❖ DOS-based personal ancestral file software. 800-346-6044; 801-240-2584 (in UT).

Individual Software Inc., 5870 Stoneridge Dr., #1, Pleasanton, CA 94588: Free information ❖ Windows-based family organizer software. 800-822-3522; 510-734-6767 (in CA).

Leister Productions, P.O. Box 289, Mechanicsburg, PA 17055: Free information ❖ Genealogy family tree software for the Macintosh. 717-697-4373.

Parsons Technology, One Parsons Dr., P.O. Box 100, Hiawatha, IA 52233: Free information ❖ Windows-based family origins software. 800-223-6925.

GIFTS & GENERAL MERCHANDISE

Children's Gifts

Daisy Kingdom Inc., 3720 NW Yeon Ave., Portland, OR 97210: Catalog $2 ❖ Apparel, bedding, and ready-to-wear clothing or sew-it-yourself kits. 800-234-6688.

Hand in Hand, Catalogue Center, 891 Main St., Oxford, ME 04270: Free catalog ❖ Teaching toys, travel items, videos, and nursery room furniture that helps nurture, teach, and protect children. 800-872-9745.

Hearth Song, Mail Processing Center, 6519 N. Galena Rd., P.O. Box 1773, Peoria, IL 61656: Free catalog ❖ Books for children, dollhouse miniatures, toiletries for babies, dolls, party decorations, backyard play structures, art supplies, kites, games, and musical instruments. 800-325-2502.

Lilly's Kids, Lillian Vernon Corporation, Virginia Beach, VA 23479: Free catalog ❖ Games, science sets, art, backyard and outdoor toys, dolls, animal toys, and fun things to do on rainy days and while traveling. 800-285-5555.

Metropolitan Museum of Art, Special Service Office, Middle Village, NY 11381: Free catalog ❖ Books, cassettes, records, cards, games, and toys. 800-468-7386.

Out of the Woodwork, 437 Robert E. Lee Dr., Wilmington, NC 28412: Free brochure ❖ Personalized educational gifts for children. 910-792-6882.

Right Start Catalog, Right Start Plaza, 5334 Sterling Center Dr., Westlake Village, CA 91361: Catalog $2 ❖ Music and videos, strollers and car seats, swings, crib sets, personal care aids, clothing, bathtime aids, highchairs, and infant, toddler, and pre-school toys and games. 800-548-8531.

❖ GIFTS & GENERAL MERCHANDISE ❖

Storybook Heirlooms, 333 Hatch Dr., Foster City, CA 94404: Free catalog ❖ Clothing and gifts. 800-899-7666.

Twincerely Yours, 748 Lake Ave., Clermont, FL 34711: Free catalog with long SASE ❖ Gifts, novelties, and T-shirts for twins and their families. 904-394-5493.

Miscellaneous Gifts

Ace Leather Products, 2211 Avenue U, Brooklyn, NY 11229: Free catalog ❖ Desk sets, leather attache cases, luggage, wallets, handbags, and gifts. 800-342-5223.

Amazon Drygoods, 2218 E. 11th St., Davenport, IA 52803: Catalog $7 ❖ Victorian-style clothing, toiletries, books, toys, hats, fans, and garden and home accessories. 800-798-7979.

Ambassador, Palo Verde at 34th St., P.O. Box 28807, Tucson, AZ 85726: Free catalog ❖ Women's clothing and jewelry. 520-748-8600.

America's Western Stores, P.O. Box 9200, Springfield, MO 65801: Free catalog ❖ Western-style clothing, shoes and boots, and gifts. 800-284-8191.

American National Parks, 1100 Hector St., Ste. 105, Conshohocken, PA 19428: Free catalog ❖ Gifts that commemorate American history. 800-821-2903.

American Originals, P.O. Box 85098, Richmond, VA 23285: Free catalog ❖ Clothing, gifts, and accessories. 800-757-6735.

Angler's, P.O. Box 161, Twin Falls, ID 83303: Free catalog ❖ Fishing gifts and calendars. 800-657-8040.

Anheuser-Busch Inc., 2700 S. Broadway, St. Louis, MO 63150: Free catalog ❖ All-occasion gifts. 800-PICK-BUD.

Anticipations by Ross Simons, 9 Ross Simons Dr., Cranston, RI 02920: Free catalog ❖ Decorative accessories, jewelry, rugs, sterling silver flatware, crystal, furniture, artwork, china, gifts for babies, quilts, and porcelain dinnerware. 800-556-7376; 401-463-3100 (in RI).

Anyone Can Whistle, P.O. Box 4407, Kingston, NY 12401: Free catalog ❖ Bird feeders, wind chimes, and musical gifts. 800-435-8863.

Armchair Shopper, P.O. Box 419464, Kansas City, MO 64141: Free catalog ❖ Classic old world-style sundials, wind chimes, and lawn ornaments. 816-767-3200.

Art & Artifact, 2451 E. Enterprise Pkwy., P.O. Box 8021, Twinsburg, OH 44087: Free catalog ❖ Oriental amenities, exotic luxuries, celtic inspirations, contemporary accessories, crafts, comfort items for the home, products from foreign countries, impressionist objects, and gifts. 800-950-9540.

Art Institute of Chicago, Fulfillment Center, 125 Armstrong Rd., Des Plaines, IL 60019: Free catalog ❖ Museum reproductions and publications that relate to the Institute's collections. 800-637-9110.

Artistic Greetings Catalog, The Personal Touch, P.O. Box 1623, Elmira, NY 14902: Free catalog ❖ Personalized stationery, memo and informal note cards, toys and puzzles, kitchen accessories, and gifts for pets. 800-733-6313.

Athletic Supply, 10850 Sanden Dr., Dallas, TX 75238: Free catalog ❖ Men and women's sportswear, jackets, T-shirts, memorabilia, and figurines. 214-348-7200.

Attitudes, 1213 Elko Dr., Sunnyvale, CA 94089: Free catalog ❖ Decorative accessories, high-tech electronics, sporting equipment, bicycle gadgets, barbecue accessories, telescopes, toys, computer games, and personal care, travel, bathroom, and kitchen aids. 800-241-1107.

Audubon Naturalist, 8940 Jones Mill Rd., Silver Spring, MD 20815: Free information with long SASE ❖ Birdhouses, feeders, baths, handcrafted jewelry, binoculars, puppets, and gifts. 800-699-BIRD; 301-652-3606 (in MD).

Australian Catalogue Company, 7412 Wingfoot Dr., Raleigh, NC 27615: Free catalog ❖ Glass, stoneware, and pewter collectibles. Also memorabilia, stationery, books and travel videos, crafts, and gifts from Australia. 919-878-8266.

Auto Motif Inc., 2968 Atlanta Rd., Smyrna, GA 30080: Catalog $3 ❖ Car models, gifts and collectibles with an automotive theme, books, prints, puzzles, office accessories, lamps, original art, and posters. 800-367-1161.

Aviation Book Company, 7201 Perimeter Rd. S, Ste. C, Seattle, WA 98108: Free catalog ❖ Books, videos, pilot supplies, clothing, and gifts. 800-423-2708.

William Barthman Jewelers, 174 Broadway, New York, NY 10038: Free information ❖ Jewelry, watches, porcelain, crystal, and sterling. 800-727-9782; 212-227-3524 (in NY).

Basketfull Inc., 1133 Broadway, New York, NY 10010: Free catalog ❖ Gift baskets for all occasions. 212-255-6800.

Belle & Blade, 124 Penn Ave., Dover, NJ 07801: Catalog $3 ❖ Videos, war books, toys, swords, knives, and gifts.

Bennett Brothers Inc., 30 E. Adams St., Chicago, IL 60603: Free catalog ❖ Rings, pins and bracelets, pearls, semi-precious and precious stones, lockets, charms, electronic gifts, toys, cameras, and leather goods. 800-621-2626.

Jody Bergsma Galleries Inc., 1344 King St., Bellingham, WA 98226: Catalog $4 ❖ Statuary and figurines, plates and porcelain collectibles, dolls, and gifts. 800-237-4762; 360-733-1101 (in WA).

Better Living, 411 Waverly Oaks Rd., P.O. Box 9199, Waltham, MA 02254: Free catalog ❖ Gifts with a better living theme. 800-424-6848.

Big Dog Sportswear, Mail Order, 121 Gray Ave., Santa Barbara, CA 93101: Free catalog ❖ Gifts for pets and their owners. 800-642-3647.

Biggs Limited Editions, 5517 Lakeside Ave., Richmond, VA 23228: Free information with long SASE ❖ Statuary and figurines, plates, dolls, and other porcelain collectibles. 800-637-0704.

Biltmore Estate Direct Inc., One Biltmore Plaza, Asheville, NC 28803: Free catalog ❖ Reproduction items from George Vanderbilt's original collection. Also exclusive items. 800-968-0558.

Bits & Pieces, Stevens Point, WI 54481-7199: Free catalog ❖ Jigsaw puzzles, books, games, and gifts for adults and children. 800-884-2637.

The Blarney Gift Catalogue, Blarney Woollen Mills Inc., 373D Rt. 46 West, Fairfield, NJ 07004: Free catalog ❖ Waterford crystal, Belleek china, jewelry, and Irish gifts. 800-451-8720.

The Blue Willow Branch, Rt. 3, Box 58, Hawley, MN 56549: Catalog $2 ❖ Ceramic pieces. 218-937-5420.

Bruce Bolind, P.O. Box 9751, Boulder, CO 80301: Free catalog ❖ Novelty and gift merchandise for adults, children, and pets. 303-443-9688.

Bombay Company, P.O. Box 161009, Fort Worth, TX 76161: Free catalog ❖ Antique furniture reproductions, mirrors, prints, lamps, and decorative accents. 800-829-7789.

Booker's Specialty Gifts, 2111 Sterne Ave., Palestine, TX 75801: Free catalog ❖ Gifts for the holidays and other occasions. 903-723-3766.

Brainstorms, Division Anatomical Chart Company, 8221 Kimball, Skokie, IL 60076: Catalog $3 ❖ Mind-boggling and creative gift ideas and fun items. 800-621-7500; 708-679-4700 (in IL).

Brielle Galleries, P.O. Box 475, Brielle, NJ 08730: Free catalog ❖ Watches, jewelry, paperweights, and crystal, silver, bronze, pewter, and porcelain gifts. 800-542-7435.

Bright-Life, Box 3703, Hicksville, NY 11855: Free catalog ❖ Novelty gifts and accessories. 516-334-1356.

Brookstone Company, Order Processing Center, 1655 Bassford Dr., Mexico, MO 65265: Free catalog ❖ Homewares, tools, travel aids, and gifts. 800-926-7000.

Buffalo Bill Historical Center, Museum Selections Gift Shop, P.O. Box 2630, Cody, WY 82414: Free catalog ❖ Western frontier-style decorative accessories. 800-533-3838.

❖ GIFTS & GENERAL MERCHANDISE ❖

Burberry's Limited, 9 E. 57th St., New York, NY 10022: Free list of retail sources ❖ Clothing, handbags, luggage, silk scarves and shawls, belts, hats, shoes, and toiletries. 212-371-5010.

Camellia & Main, P.O. Box 1709, Fort Valley, GA 31030: Free catalog ❖ All-occasion gifts and room accessories. 800-920-9494.

Harriet Carter, Dept. 16, North Wales, PA 19455: Free catalog ❖ Distinctive gifts. 215-361-5122.

Cash's of Ireland, Mail Order Courier Center, P.O. Box 158, Plainview, NY 11803: Catalog $3 ❖ China, crystal, walking sticks, wool stoles and cardigans, pottery, frames, serving pieces, lamps and chandeliers, and gifts from Ireland. 800-223-8100.

The Castriota Collection, P.O. Box 12631, Pittsburgh, PA 15241: Free catalog ❖ Gifts for golfers. 800-344-8640.

Casual Collections, P.O. Box 61160, Seattle, WA 98121: Free catalog ❖ All-occasion gifts. 800-886-6878.

Casual Living, 5401 Hangar Ct., P.O. Box 32173, Tampa, FL 33631: Free catalog ❖ Toys, books, furniture, watches and clocks, puzzles, kitchen accessories, hand-painted portraits made from photographs, lamps, mailboxes, music boxes, model construction kits, and computer games. 800-843-1881.

Cat Claws, 1004 W. Broadway, P.O. Box 1001, Morrilton, AR 72110: Free catalog ❖ Gifts for cats. 800-783-0977.

Cats, Cats & More Cats, Rt. 17M, P.O. Box 270, Monroe, NY 10950: Free catalog ❖ Gifts for cat lovers. 914-782-4141.

The Celebration Fantastic, 1620 Montgomery St., Ste. 250, San Francisco, CA 94111: Free catalog ❖ Romantic, whimsical, and imaginative gifts for special occasions. 800-235-3272.

Ann Chapman, 246 N. Main St., Galena, IL 61036: Free catalog ❖ Equestrian gifts. 815-777-3322.

Chef Revival, 12 Dyatt Pl., Hackensack, NJ 07601: Free catalog ❖ Kitchen wear and accessories for cooks. 800-352-2433.

Chiasso, 303 W. Madison St., Chicago, IL 60606: Free catalog ❖ Housewares, jewelry, toys, telephones, clocks, and home office items. 800-654-3570.

Clocks Etc., 3401 Mt. Diablo Blvd., Lafayette, CA 94549: Brochure $1 ❖ Old and new clocks, antique furniture, and gifts. 510-284-4720.

CM Specialties, 504 Normandy, Ste. 2-C, Houston, TX 77015: Free catalog ❖ Gifts, toys, jewelry, miniatures, and collectibles. 713-451-5856.

Coach Leatherware Company, 410 Commerce Blvd., Carlstadt, NJ 07072: Free catalog ❖ Leather bags, belts, wallets, briefcases, and accessories. 201-460-4716.

The Coca-Cola Catalog, 2515 E. 43rd St., P.O. Box 182264, Chattanooga, TN 37422: Free catalog ❖ Coca-Cola theme gifts for men, women, and children. 800-872-6531.

Cokesbury, Division United Methodist Publishing House, 201 8th Ave. South, P.O. Box 801, Nashville, TN 37202: Free information ❖ Bibles and bible reference books, bible study and Christian education books, fund-raising programs, gifts and casual wear, choir apparel, church and clergy supplies, and church furniture. 800-672-1789.

Cold Hollow Cider Mill, Rt. 100 North, Waterbury Center, VT 05677: Free information ❖ Vermont foods, apple cider, and gifts. 800-3-APPLES.

Coldwater Creek, One Coldwater Creek Dr., Sandpoint, ID 83864: Free catalog ❖ Nature-related and Native American jewelry, clothing, decorative accessories, art, pottery, wind chimes, and gifts. 800-262-0040.

Collector's Armoury, 800 Slaters Ln., P.O. Box 59, Alexandria, VA 22313: Free catalog ❖ Western and Civil War collectibles and gifts. 800-544-3456.

Colonial Casting Company Inc., 68 Liberty St., Haverhill, MA 01832: Catalog $3 ❖ Handcrafted lead-free pewter miniature castings. 508-374-8783.

Colonial Williamsburg, P.O. Box 3532, Williamsburg, VA 23187: Catalog $14.65 ❖ Reproduction colonial furnishings and decorative accessories. 804-220-7378.

Colorful Images, 1401 S. Sunset St., Longmont, CO 80501: Free catalog ❖ Decorative accessories, watches and jewelry, pens, note cards, cookie jars, wind chimes, desk accessories, novelty telephones, fancy kitchen mugs, calculators, and paperweights. 800-458-7999.

Columbia Gifts, 6135 Good Hunters Ride, Columbia, MD 21045: Free catalog ❖ Gifts and novelties.

Country Store Gifts, 5925 Country Ln., P.O. Box 990, Greendale, WI 53129: Free catalog ❖ Country-style gifts and crafts. 800-558-1013.

Crate & Barrel, P.O. Box 9059, Wheeling, IL 60090: Free catalog ❖ Personalized stationery, kitchen aids, storage systems, sound equipment, and decorative accessories. 800-323-5461.

The Crow's Nest Birding Shop, Cornell Laboratory of Ornithology, 159 Sapsucker Woods Rd., Ithaca, NY 14850: Free catalog ❖ Books and gifts for bird enthusiasts. 607-254-2400.

Cumberland General Store, Rt. 3, Box 81, Crossville, TN 38555: Catalog $3 ❖ Cooking ranges, gardening tools, cast-iron ware, farm bells, buggies, blacksmithing equipment, harnesses, and old-fashioned gifts. 800-334-4640.

D-Mail U.S.A. Inc., 91 Market St., Wappinger Falls, NY 12590: Free catalog ❖ Gifts and novelties. 800-227-4051.

The Daily Planet, P.O. Box 64411, St. Paul, MN 55164: Free catalog ❖ Novelties, gifts, stationery, musical instruments, T-shirts, jewelry, reproduction memorabilia from the past, toys, and items from worldwide locations. 800-324-5950.

Dancing Dragon, P.O. Box 1106, Arcata, CA 95521: Free catalog ❖ Dragon-theme decorative items and gifts. 800-322-6041.

The Disney Catalog, One Disney Dr., P.O. Box 29144, Shawnee Mission, KS 66201: Free catalog ❖ Disney-theme gifts, collectibles, home furnishings, and clothing for men, women, and children. 800-247-8996.

Dollmasters, P.O. Box 2319, Annapolis, MD 21404: Free catalog ❖ Grown-up gifts and collectibles that celebrate yesterday's childhood. 800-966-3655; 410-224-4386 (in MD).

Down East Books & Gifts, P.O. Box 679, Camden, ME 04843: Free catalog ❖ Calendars, books, and crafts from Maine and New England. 800-766-1670.

DR Marketing Enterprises, P.O. Box 251, Stratford, CT 06497: Free catalog ❖ Distinctive gifts, jewelry, and household accessories.

Walter Drake & Sons, Drake Building, Colorado Springs, CO 80940: Free catalog ❖ Personalized stationery, toys, household items, clothing, decorative and office accessories, and other items. 800-525-9291.

The Early West, Box 9292, College Station, TX 77842: Free catalog ❖ Western-style gifts, books, and videos. 409-775-6047.

Early Winters, P.O. Box 4333, Portland, OR 97208: Free catalog ❖ Men and women's outdoor equipment, ski wear and accessories, other clothing, and gifts. 800-458-4438.

Earth Care, 555 Leslie St., Ukiah, CA 95482: Free catalog ❖ Recycled paper products, environmental gifts, and household goods. 800-992-7747.

Earthmade Products, P.O. Box 609, Jasper, IN 47547: Free catalog ❖ Gifts for the garden and gardener that enhance garden decor and backyard living. 800-843-1819.

Eastside Gifts & Dinnerware, 351 Grand St., New York, NY 10002: Free information ❖ China, crystal, flatware, and gifts. 800-443-8711; 212-982-7200 (in NY).

❖ GIFTS & GENERAL MERCHANDISE ❖

The Emerald Collection, 280 Summer Street, Boston, MA 02210: Free catalog ❖ Gifts from Ireland. 800-345-6686.

Enesco Corporation, 1 Enesco Plaza, Elk Grove Village, IL 60007: Free list of retail sources ❖ Figurines, sculptures, ornaments, Barbie dolls, and gifts.

European Imports & Gifts, Oak Mill Mall, 7900 N. Milwaukee Ave., Niles, IL 60714: Free catalog ❖ Imported and other gifts and collectibles. 708-967-5253.

Eximious, 201 Northfield Rd., Northfield, IL 60093: Free catalog ❖ Travel aids, desk and office accessories, garden aids, and American crafts. 800-446-9454.

Expressions from Potpourri, 120 N. Meadows Rd., Medfield, MA 02052: Free catalog ❖ Toys and puzzles for children and adults, jewelry and watches, note cards and stationery, and decorative accessories. 800-688-8051.

The Faith Mountain Company, P.O. Box 199, Sperryville, VA 22740: Free catalog ❖ Herbs and flowers, clothing, home furnishings, garden accessories, and American crafts. 800-588-2548.

Falcon, P.O. Box 1718, Helena, MT 59624: Free catalog ❖ Outdoor gifts, books, and gear. 800-582-2665.

Fingerhut, P.O. Box 800, St. Cloud, MN 56395: Free catalog ❖ Greeting cards, gift wraps, stationery, holiday decorations, organizers, and gifts. 800-322-2226.

Flax Artist Materials, P.O. Box 7216, San Francisco, CA 94120: Catalog $6 ❖ Gifts. 800-547-7778.

Flibbertigibbet, 6 Home Croft Ct., Durham, NC 27703: Free catalog ❖ Antique miniatures, porcelain sculptures, statuary, tools, music boxes, toys. Miniature furniture, wall masks, jewelry, and other gifts. 919-598-0858.

Fox Ridge Outfitters Inc., 400 N. Main St., P.O. Box 1700, Rochester, NH 03867: Free catalog ❖ Clothing, guns, solid pine carvings, cookware, knives and cutlery, and equipment and supplies for outdoor sportsmen. 800-243-4570.

The Franklin Mint, Franklin Center, PA 19092: Free catalog ❖ Distinctive gifts for family and friends. 800-843-6468.

Frontgate, 2800 Henkle Dr., Lebanon, OH 45036: Free catalog ❖ Housewares, mailboxes, kitchen accessories, outdoor furniture, gardening tools, barbecue and charcoal ovens, gifts for pets, intercoms, scales, dart boards, automobile gadgets, sports equipment, heaters, and floor registers. 800-626-6488.

G & R Publishing Company, 507 Industrial St., Waverly, IA 50677: Free catalog ❖ Perpetual calendars, miniature cookbooks, memory journals, and inspirational gift items. 800-383-1679.

Gatherings, Kaiser Crow Inc., 3545 G South Platte River Dr., Englewood, CO 80110: Free catalog ❖ Gifts for the home and garden, children, and pets. 800-468-2769.

Gavilan's, Gavilan Hills, CA 92599: Free catalog ❖ Jewelry, furniture, decorative kitchen accessories, Lladro and porcelain collectibles, and gifts for men and women.

Geary's, 351 N. Beverly Dr., Beverly Hills, CA 90210: Free catalog ❖ Silver sculptures, Lladro porcelain, Christofle French silver plate, Halcyon enamels, tapestries, dinnerware, desk accessories, and Waterford, Baccarat and Lalique crystal. 800-243-2797; 310-273-3344 (in CA).

Gift Ahoy, P.O. Box 149, Monkton, MD 21111: Free information ❖ Maryland and Chesapeake Bay gifts. 410-771-1242.

Gift World, 2392 Locust St., Portage, IN 46368: Free brochure ❖ Cloth dolls, miniatures, florals, and gifts. 800-847-4450; 219-763-2408 (in IN).

Gifts for All Occasions, 128 Conant St., Concord, MA 01742: Free catalog ❖ Assorted brass engravable gifts. Also baby gifts, various personalized leather goods, lunch bags, personalized tote bags, and auto and home repair guides. 508-371-0826.

Good Catalog Company, 5456 SE International Way, Portland, OR 97222: Free catalog ❖ All-occasion gifts. 800-225-3870.

Good Idea, P.O. Box 955, Vail, CO 81658: Free catalog ❖ All-occasion gifts. 800-538-6690.

Graceland Gifts Mail Order, 3734 Elvis Presley Blvd., Memphis, TN 38116: Free catalog ❖ Elvis Presley-theme gifts. 800-238-2000.

Grand Finale, P.O. Box 620049, Dallas, TX 75262: Free catalog ❖ Household accessories, decorative items, bedroom ensembles, women's clothing, and fine gifts. 800-955-9595.

Great Gadgets, 809 Virginia Ave., Martinsburg, WV 25401: Free catalog ❖ Unusual gifts and gadgets. 304-267-2673.

W.M. Green & Company, P.O. Box 426, Greenville, NC 27835: Free catalog ❖ Gifts for adults and children. 800-482-5050.

Gumps by Mail, 30 Maiden Ln., San Francisco, CA 94108: Free catalog ❖ Rare, unique, and imaginative gifts. 800-436-4311.

Haitian Art Company, 600 Frances St., Key West, FL 33040: Free information with long SASE ❖ Paintings, wood sculptures, steel cut-outs, paper mache crafts, and gifts. 305-296-8932.

Hallmark at Home Inc., 100 Enterprise Pl., Dover, DE 19901: Free catalog ❖ Gifts for special relationships and occasions. 800-983-4663.

Hammacher Schlemmer, 9180 LeSaint Dr., Fairfield, OH 45014: Free catalog ❖ Gifts for the entire family. 800-233-4800.

Handsome Rewards, 19465 Brennan Ave., Perris, CA 92599: Free catalog ❖ Household accessories, tools, games, and all-occasion gifts. 909-943-2023.

Hanover House, Hanover Direct Pennsylvania Inc., Hanover, PA 17333-0002: Free catalog ❖ Clothing, gardening supplies, household aids, jewelry, and novelties. 717-633-3333.

Hansen Planetarium, 1845 S. 300 West, #A, Salt Lake City, UT 84115: Catalog $1 ❖ Gifts for astronomy buffs.

Heartland America, 6978 Shady Oak Rd., Eden Prairie, MN 55344: Free catalog ❖ High-tech electronics, household accessories, telephones, computers, tools, leather goods and luggage, games, office and home furniture, and audio and stereo, optics and astronomy, and exercise equipment. 800-229-2901.

Herrington, 3 Symmes Dr., Londonderry, NH 03053: Free catalog ❖ Automotive gadgets and tools, photographic and video equipment, compact disks, disk and cassette storage cabinets, gifts for music lovers, and astronomy equipment. 800-903-2878.

Hitching Post Supply, 10312 210th St. SE, Snohomish, WA 98290: Free catalog ❖ Gifts for horse owners. 360-668-2349.

Holland Boone Polished Pewter, 3116 E. Shea Blvd., Ste. 236, Phoenix, AZ 85028: Brochure $2 ❖ Polished pewter items, handcrafted jewelry boxes, candlesticks, picture frames, serving trays, and other gifts. 800-973-9837.

Home Silvo Hardware Company, 3201 Tollview Rd., Rolling Meadows, IL 60008: Free catalog ❖ Household accessories, tools, games, and all-occasion gifts. 800-331-1261.

Home Trends, 1450 Lyell Ave., Rochester, NY 14606: Free catalog ❖ Personalized stationery, toys, household items, clothing, decorative office accessories, and gifts. 716-254-6520.

The Horchow Collection, P.O. Box 620048, Dallas, TX 72262: Free catalog ❖ Home furnishings and accessories, dishes and serving pieces, rugs, bedroom linens, and lamps. 800-395-5397.

House of Tyrol, P.O. Box 909, Alpenland Center, Helen Highway/75 North, Cleveland, GA 30528: Free catalog ❖ Musical cuckoo clocks, crystal, porcelain, lamps, music boxes, pillows, knitted items, decorative accessories, bar accessories, collector plates, pewter, tapestries, cards, Alpine hat pins, Christmas decorations, and folk music videos. 800-241-5404.

In the Company of Dogs, P.O. Box 3934, Milford, CT 06460: Free catalog ❖ Gifts and gear for dogs and the people who share their lives. 800-964-3647.

❖ GIFTS & GENERAL MERCHANDISE ❖

Irvin's, RD 1, Box 73, Mt. Pleasant Mills, PA 17853: Free catalog ❖ Handcrafted colonial tinware gifts and lighting. 717-539-8200.

Island Dreams, P.O. Box 1363, Mountainside, NJ 07092: Free catalog ❖ Jewelry, art, T-shirts, books, cosmetic fragrances, and gifts from the Carribean. 908-233-1475.

Iva Mae's Treasures, 780 Webster St., Bakersfield, CA 93307: Free catalog ❖ Household accessories and all-occasion gifts. 800-959-3487.

Thomas Jefferson Memorial Foundation Inc., Monticello Catalog, P.O. Box 318, Charlottesville, VA 22902: Free catalog ❖ Gifts and select items that reflect Thomas Jefferson's varied interests. 800-243-0743.

Jennifer's Trunk Antiques & General Store, 201 N. Riverside, Dr., St. Clair, MI 48079: Free brochure ❖ Victorian-style antique furniture, books, jewelry, lamps and shades, and gifts. 810-329-2032.

Jona Originals, 4458 Augusta Rd., #1-C, Lexington, SC 29073: Free catalog ❖ Original bears and stationery, Christmas cards, bookmarks, T-shirts, sweatshirts, pillows, totes, wall hangings, afghans, and teddy bear-related gifts. 800-838-5662.

Just Between Us, 41 W. 8th Ave., Oshkosh, WI 54906: Free catalog ❖ Decorative items for the home and gifts for family members and friends. 800-258-3750.

Kansas Industries for the Blind, State Department of Social & Rehabilitation Services, 2700 W. 6th, 1st Floor, Biddle Building, Topeka, KS 66606: Free price list ❖ Blind and handicapped person-made products. 913-296-3211.

David Kay Inc., One Jenni Ln., Peoria, IL 61614: Free catalog ❖ Planters, bird houses, furniture, swimming pool and backyard toys, fireplace accessories, games, sculptures, and wind chimes. 800-535-9917.

Charles Keath Ltd., P.O. Box 48800, Atlanta, GA 30362: Free catalog ❖ Women's clothing, jewelry, watches, decorative and fireplace accessories, luggage, and purses. 800-388-6565; 449-3100 (in Atlanta).

Miles Kimball Company, 41 W. 8th Ave., Oshkosh, WI 54906: Free catalog ❖ Gifts and gadgets from around the world. 800-546-2255.

Lakeside Products Company, 6646 N. Western Ave., Chicago, IL 60645: Catalog $1 (refundable) ❖ Housewares, novelties, and gifts. 773-761-5495.

Lane Luggage, 1146 Connecticut Ave. NW, Washington, DC 20036: Free catalog ❖ Luggage, electronic gadgets, toys and games, and desk and decorative accessories. 202-452-1146.

The Last Best Place, Catalog Company, P.O. Box 2807, Monroe, WI 53566: Free catalog ❖ Gifts for all occasions. 800-252-4766.

Lefthanders International, P.O. Box 8249, Topeka, KS 66608: Catalog $2 ❖ Items for lefties. 913-234-2177.

Lehman Hardware & Appliances Inc., P.O. Box 41, Kidron, OH 44636: Catalog $2 ❖ Kitchen accessories, housewares, stoves for heating and cooking, farming and homesteading equipment, non-electric appliances, woodworking and log-smithing tools, and old-time gifts. 216-857-5757.

Leisure Living, 19465 Brennan Ave., Perris, CA 92599: Free catalog ❖ Household accessories, tools, games, and all-occasion gifts. 909-943-2023.

Levenger, P.O. Box 1256, Delray Beach, FL 33447: Free catalog ❖ Books, furniture, pens, briefcases, and gifts for serious readers. 800-545-0242.

Lifestyle Fascination Gifts, 1935 Swarthmore Ave., CN 3023, Lakewood, NJ 08701: Free catalog ❖ High-tech and unusual gifts. 800-669-8875.

Lifton Studio Inc., 121 S. 6th St., Stillwater, MN 55082: Catalog $5 ❖ Harley Davidson-theme money clips, belt buckles, badges, desk accessories, and gifts. 612-439-7208.

Lighter Side Company, 4514 19th St. Court East, P.O. Box 25600, Bradenton, FL 34206: Free catalog ❖ Lighthearted surprises and all-occasion gifts. 813-747-2356.

The Limited of Michigan Ltd., 10861 Paw Paw Dr., Holland, MI 49424: Free catalog ❖ Old and new Hummel figurines, back-issue plates, bells, and gifts. 800-355-6363.

Literary Calligraphy, Rt. 1, Box 56A, Moneta, VA 24121: Catalog $2 ❖ Literary calligraphy gifts. 800-261-6325.

Lynchburg Hardware & General Store, Lynchburg, TN 37352: Catalog $1 ❖ Gifts, novelty items, housewares, tools, and gardening supplies. 615-759-4200.

Maplewood Crafts, Humboldt Industrial Park, 1 Maplewood Dr., Hazleton, PA 18201: Free catalog ❖ Decorative accessories, mini models, embroidery and needle crafts, craft supplies and kits, candy molds, and family fun items. 800-899-0134.

J. Marco Galleries, 4098 E. 71st St., Cleveland, OH 44105: Free catalog ❖ Handmade pottery, jewelry, and gifts that reflect Native American culture. 800-948-3100.

The Maritime Store, 2905 Hyde St. Pier, San Francisco, CA 94109: Free catalog ❖ Maritime maps, greeting cards, boat models, children's and maritime books, and gifts. 415-775-BOOK.

Mathews Wire, 654 W. Morrison, Frankfort, IN 46041: Catalog $2 ❖ Wire-formed giftwares for the home. 800-826-9650.

May Silk, 16202 Distribution Way, Cerritos, CA 90703: Free catalog ❖ Silk plants, gifts, housewares, and jewelry. 800-282-7455.

Metropolitan Museum of Art, Special Service Office, Middle Village, NY 11381: Free catalog ❖ Greeting and note cards, ornaments, books, jewelry, ties, frames, calendars, and reproductions from museum collections. 800-468-7386.

J. Michael's Catalog Company, 152 E. Main St., Rigby, ID 83442: Free catalog ❖ Home decorative gifts. 208-745-7714.

The Mind's Eye, Memory Ln., P.O. Box 6547, Chelmsford, MA 01824: Free catalog ❖ Remember when imaginative gifts for men, women, and children. 800-949-3333.

Minnesota State Parks Nature Store, P.O. Box 5098, Burnsville, MN 55337: Free catalog ❖ Gifts from Minnesota state parks. 800-987-8877.

Moby Dick Marine Specialties, 27 William St., New Bedford, MA 02740: Catalog $5 ❖ Nautical gifts, decorative accessories, and scrimshaw. 800-343-8044.

Modern Farm, P.O. Box 1420, Cody, WY 82414: Free catalog ❖ Items for the field and farm, home and family products, auto accessories and tools, and clothing. 800-443-4934.

Montgomery Ward Direct, 710 Anderson Ave., St. Cloud, MN 56395: Free catalog ❖ Household and kitchen accessories, furniture, bedding, decorative items, audio and TV equipment, rugs and curtains, and all-occasion gifts. 800-852-2711.

Claire Murray Inc., P.O. Box 390, Ascutney, VT 05030: Catalog $5 (refundable) ❖ Hand-painted ceramics, quilts, and hand-hooked rugs. 800-252-4733.

Museum Collections, 340 Poplar St., Building 20, Hanover, PA 17333: Free catalog ❖ Museum replicas and gifts. 800-442-2460.

Museum of Fine Arts, Boston, Catalog Sales Dept., P.O. Box 244, Avon, MA 02322: Free catalog ❖ Museum replicas. 800-225-5592.

Museum of Modern Art New York, Mail Order Department, 11 W. 53rd St., New York, NY 10019: Free catalog ❖ Museum replicas. 800-447-6662.

Museum Replicas Limited, P.O. Box 840, Conyers, GA 30207: Catalog $1 (refundable) ❖ Reproductions of historic weapons and period battle wear.

Music Stand, 1 Music Stand Plaza, 66 Benning St., West Lebanon, OH 03784: Free catalog ❖ Gifts with a music theme, candy, gift baskets, trophies, plaques, and certificates. 800-717-7010.

❖ GIFTS & GENERAL MERCHANDISE ❖ 255

Mystic Seaport Museum Stores, 39 Greemanville Ave., Mystic, CT 06355: Free catalog ❖ Gifts with a seafaring theme. 800-248-1066.

National Geographic Society, 1145 17th St. NW, Washington, DC 20036: Free catalog ❖ Books, games, videos, maps and globes, travel aids, and magazine subscriptions. 800-447-0647.

The National Museum of Women in the Arts, P.O. Box 96049, Washington, DC 20077: Free catalog ❖ All-occasion gifts by and about women. 800-222-7270.

The Nature Company, Catalog Division, P.O. Box 188, Florence, KY 41022: Free catalog ❖ Jewelry made from natural materials, high-tech devices, science gadgets, T-shirts, books, sculptures, optics, clocks, garden accessories, puzzles and toys, and archaeological reproductions. 800-227-1114.

Nauticode Inc., 274 Harkers Island Rd., Beaufort, NC 28516: Free catalog ❖ Clothing and gifts for boating enthusiasts. 800-628-8263.

Naval Academy Gift Shop, Halsey Field House, Annapolis, MD 21402: Free catalog ❖ Gifts from the United States Naval Academy. 410-268-3355.

New Mexico Catalog, 1700 Shalem Colony Trail, P.O. Box 261, Fairacres, NM 88033: Free catalog ❖ Native American, Hispanic, and Anglo-American arts and crafts, gifts, and foods. 800-678-0585; 1-525-0585 (in NM).

Northstyle Gifts, P.O. Box 1360, Minocqua, WI 54548: Free catalog ❖ Nature-influenced gifts. 800-336-5666.

Northwest Passages, By Harry & David, P.O. Box 1548, Medford, OR 97501: Free catalog ❖ Gifts and clothing for men and women. Also for pet dogs and cats. 800-727-7243.

Northystyle, Northwoods Trail, P.O. Box 6529, Chelmsford, MA 01824: Free catalog ❖ Gifts with a Native American and western-theme. 800-336-5666.

O'Grady Presents, 150 E. Huron St., Ste. 1200, Chicago, IL 60611: Free catalog ❖ Gifts for the holidays, young at heart, and adults. 800-548-5759; 312-642-2000 (in IL).

1-800-FLOWERS, 1600 Stewart Avenue, Westbury, NY 11590: Free catalog ❖ Flower and fruit gift assortments and baskets. 800-356-9377.

Orchids etc!, 1 Orchid Ln., Medford, OR 97501: Free catalog ❖ Plants, fresh flowers, and floral gifts. 800-525-7510.

Oriental Trading Company Inc., P.O. Box 3407, Omaha, NE 68103: Free catalog ❖ Toys, gifts, novelties, carnival supplies, and holiday and seasonal items. 800-327-9678.

Orvis Manchester, 1711 Blue Hills Dr., P.O. Box 12000, Roanoke, VA 24022: Free catalog ❖ Men and women's clothing, country gifts, rugs, fireplace and kitchen accessories, gifts for the family pet, luggage, lamps, and fishing equipment. 800-541-3541.

Orvis Travel, 1711 Blue Hills Dr., P.O. Box 12000, Roanoke, VA 24022: Free catalog ❖ Men and women's clothing and outerwear. Also luggage and gifts and accessories for the traveler. 800-541-3541.

Out of the Woodwork, 437 Robert E. Lee Dr., Wilmington, NC 28412: Free brochure ❖ Personalized educational gifts for children. 910-792-6882.

The Outhouse, 2853 Lincoln Hwy. East, Ronks, PA 17572: Free catalog ❖ Gifts and unusual items. 800-346-7678; 717-687-9580 (in PA).

Pandora's Box Mail Order, 1820 S. West Ave., Ste. 150A, Freeport, IL 61032: Catalog $5 (refundable) ❖ Radar and laser detectors and items for the home office and car. 800-360-4047.

ParaFURnalia Pet Products, 5115 Excelsior Blvd., Ste. 306, Minneapolis, MN 55416: Free catalog ❖ Handcrafted gifts for pet lovers. 612-920-1150.

The Paragon Gifts, 89 Tom Harvey Rd., Westerly, RI 02891: Free catalog ❖ Casual clothing, housewares, decorative accessories, games and toys, and bathroom items. 800-343-3095.

Past Times, 280 Summer St., Boston, MA 02210: Free catalog ❖ Fine gifts from Great Britain inspired by the past. 800-242-1020.

Personal Creations, 530 Executive Dr., Burr Ridge, IL 60521: Free catalog ❖ Frames, office and desk accessories, leather goods, and gifts. 800-326-6626.

The Personal Touch Stationery, One Artistic Plaza, P.O. Box 1623, Elmira, NY 14902: Catalog $2 ❖ Personalized stationery and gifts. 800-733-6313.

Petals, 300 Central Ave., White Plains, NY 10606: Free catalog ❖ All-occasion floral arrangements and gifts. 800-431-2464.

J. Peterman Company, 1318 Russell Cave Rd., Lexington, KY 40505: Free catalog ❖ Men and women's apparel, accessories, home furnishings, garden items, gifts, footwear, and luggage. 800-231-7341.

Pitt Petri, 378 Delaware Ave., Buffalo, NY 14202: Free catalog ❖ Crystal, silverware and silver serving pieces, Lladro porcelain, porcelain and china, ceramics, children's clothing, dolls, home and bar accessories, and personal care aids. 800-345-0053.

PJ Distributors Inc., 1498 Reisterstown Rd., Ste. 216, Pikesville, MD 21208: Catalog $8 ❖ Miniatures, gifts, and collectibles.

Playboy, P.O. Box 809, Itasca, IL 60143: Free catalog ❖ Gifts for men and women. 800-423-9494.

Plow & Hearth, P.O. Box 5000, Madison, VA 22727: Free catalog ❖ Gardening tools, birdhouses and feeders, porch and lawn furniture, fireplace accessories, and gifts for pets. 800-627-1712.

Plummer-McCutcheon, A Hammacher Schlemmer Company, 9180 LeSaint Dr., Fairfield, OH 45014: Free catalog ❖ Distinctive and unusual gifts. 800-233-4800.

Post Scripts from Joan Cook, 119 Foster St., P.O. Box 6008, Peabody, MA 01961: Free catalog ❖ Women and children's clothing, toys, home accessories, luggage, personal care items, and electronic gadgets. 508-532-4040.

Potpourri, 120 N. Meadows Rd., Medfield, MA 02052: Free catalog ❖ Jewelry, clothing, party items, games, and decorative accessories. 800-688-8051.

Pottery Barn, Mail Order Dept., P.O. Box 7044, San Francisco, CA 94120: Free catalog ❖ Gifts for the home. 800-922-5507.

Preferred Living, A Catalog from Sporty's, Clermont Century Airport, Batavia, OH 45103: Free catalog ❖ Household accessories, tools, games, and all-occasion gifts. 800-543-8633.

Presentations Gallery, 200 Lexington Ave., New York, NY 10016: Free information ❖ Contemporary synagogue art, furniture, memorial renditions, and recognition gifts. 212-481-8181.

Pressley's, 141 E. Meadow Dr., Vail, CO 81657: Free catalog ❖ Gifts, toys, and accessories. 800-934-0314.

Pueblo to People, P.O. Box 2545, Houston, TX 77252: Free catalog ❖ Nuts, dried fruit, ceramics, jewelry, coffee, and gift baskets. 800-843-5257.

Rand McNally & Company, Catalog Operations Center, 2515 E. 43rd St., P.O. Box 182257, Chattanooga, TN 37422: Free catalog ❖ Gifts for sports enthusiasts, health and exercise equipment, maps, world globes, books, videos, clocks, prints, travel aids, and watches. 800-234-0679.

Real Goods, 555 Leslie St., Ukiah, CA 95482: Free catalog ❖ Solar energy components and educational toys, environmental books and games, and alternative energy-related gifts. 800-762-7325.

Recap Universal, 283 Rhode Island, Buffalo, NY 14213: Free catalog ❖ Gifts, jewelry, leather goods, luggage, kitchen tools, toys, handmade originals. miniatures, porcelain collectibles, and wood, brass, and stone items. 800-292-6338.

Red Cross Gifts, 122 Walnut St., Spooner, WI 54801: Free information ❖ Collectible plates, Ashton-Drake dolls, gifts, and collectibles. 800-344-9958.

GIFTS & GENERAL MERCHANDISE

Red Rose Collection, P.O. Box 280140, San Francisco, CA 94128: Free catalog ❖ Books and tapes, art works, jewelry, tools, games, natural fiber clothing, decorative accessories, and toiletries. 800-374-5505.

Rent Mother Nature, P.O. Box 380193, 52 New St., Cambridge, MA 02238: Free catalog ❖ Food-related gifts. 800-296-9445.

Rodco Products, 2565 16th Ave., Columbus, NE 68601: Catalog 50¢ ❖ High-tech equipment for the home and office. 800-323-2799.

The Rosemary House, 120 S. Market St., Mechanicsburg, PA 17055: Catalog $2 ❖ Herbs, oils, and spices. Also candles, soaps, teas, books, potpourris, and gifts. 717-697-5111.

RoughOut, Box 2667, Missoula, MT 59806: Free catalog ❖ Riding equipment, clothing, and gifts. 800-428-1098.

Leonard Rue Enterprises, 138 Millbrook Rd., Blairstown, NJ 07825: Free catalog ❖ Books, video tapes, and equipment and gifts for photographers and outdoor enthusiasts. 908-362-6616.

Russian Collection, Rt 16A, Box 5, Intervale, NH 03845: Free catalog ❖ Russian lacquer boxes, artistic nesting dolls, and gifts. 603-356-7832.

Sanctuary, P.O. Box 641129, West Los Angeles, CA 90025: Free catalog ❖ Replicas of historical treasures that defy the mysteries of the ages. 800-726-2882.

The Scandinavian Country Shop, Warm Brook Rd., Arlington, VT 05250: Free information with long SASE ❖ Scandinavian gifts and handcrafts. 802-375-6666.

Schrader's Railroad Catalog, 230 S. Abbe Rd., Fairview, MI 48621: Catalog $1 ❖ Gifts for the railroad enthusiast. 517-848-2225.

Scotland by the Yard, Rt. 4, Quechee, VT 05059: Free brochure ❖ Classic clothing, sweaters, gifts and jewelry, and ties and scarves from Scotland. 802-295-5351.

Scottish Lion Import Shop, P.O. Box 1700, Rt. 16, North Conway, NH 03860: Free catalog ❖ Imported gifts from Scotland. 603-356-2942.

Scotty's Gifts & Accessories, 1500 Dixie Hwy., Park Hills, KY 41011: Free catalog ❖ Jewelry, art, collectibles, clothing, stationery, and gifts. 800-638-2338.

Scully & Scully Inc., 504 Park Ave., New York, NY 10126: Free catalog ❖ Handcrafted reproductions of 18th-century enamels by English artisans, figurines, furniture, books and games, men's clothing, crystal, and home office aids. 800-223-3717; 212-755-2590 (in NY).

Seagull Pewter, P.O. Box 370, Pugwash, Nova Scotia, Canada B0K 1L0: Free information ❖ Pewter giftware, holiday and home decorative merchandise, and jewelry. 902-243-2526.

Seacraft Classics, 7850 E. Evans Rd., Ste. 109, Scottsdale, AZ 85260: Free information ❖ Handmade detailed models of 19th-century ships and boats with hardwood display stands and brass name plates. 800-356-1987; 602-998-4988 (in AZ).

Seasons, P.O. Box 64545, St. Paul, MN 55164: Free catalog ❖ All-occasion gifts. 800-776-9677.

Serengeti, P.O. Box 3349, Serengeti Park, Chelmsford, MA 01824: Free catalog ❖ Wildlife apparel and gifts. 800-426-2852.

Service Merchandise Catalog, Mail Order, P.O. Box 25130, Nashville, TN 37202: Free catalog ❖ Homewares, toys and games, hobby supplies, and jewelry. 800-251-1212.

SGF Gifts & Furnishings Catalog, P.O. Box 620047, Dallas, TX 75262: Catalog $3 ❖ Serving pieces, linens, furniture, luggage and attache cases, children's gifts, and jewelry. 214-484-1517.

Shannon Duty Free Mail Order, c/o Aer Lingus-Irish Airlines, Building 87 Cargo PLZ, Jamaica, NY 11430: Free catalog ❖ Imported gifts from Ireland and Europe. 800-448-4988.

Sharper Image, 650 Davis St., San Francisco, CA 94111: Free catalog ❖ Health and exercise equipment, toys, watches and clocks, pet products, calculators, telephones, sunglasses, electronics, and gifts. 800-344-5555.

Ship's Hatch, 10376 Main St., Fairfax, VA 22030: Brochure $1 ❖ Military patches, pins and insignia, official USN ship ball caps, ship's clocks, hatch cover tables, nautical and military gifts, jewelry, lamps and lanterns, ship's wheels, and gifts. 703-691-1670.

Signals Catalog, P.O. Box 64428, St. Paul, MN 55114: Free catalog ❖ Books, T-shirts and sweat shirts, video and cassette tapes, and gifts. 800-669-5225.

Signatures, 19465 Brennan Ave., Perris, CA 92599: Free catalog ❖ All-occasion gifts. 909-943-2021.

Ben Silver, 149 King St., Charleston, SC 29401: Free catalog ❖ Seasonal and graduation gifts for men. 800-BEN-SILVER.

Simcha Designs, P.O. Box 6562, Fresh Meadows Station, 192-04 Horace Harding Expwy., Flushing, NY 11365: Free catalog ❖ Judaic artware and jewelry. 718-776-6688.

Smithsonian Catalogue, 7955 Angus Ct., Springfield, VA 22153: Free catalog ❖ Gifts, toys, games, books, puzzles, and replicas from the Smithsonian Institution's collections. 800-322-0344.

Soccer International Inc., P.O. Box 7222, Arlington, VA 22207: Catalog $2 ❖ Gifts and novelties with a soccer motif. 703-524-4333.

Solutions, P.O. Box 6878, Portland, OR 97228: Free catalog ❖ Home accessories, tableware, jewelry, exercise equipment, and travel aids. 800-342-9988.

Sophisticats Catalog, P.O. Box 4564, North Hollywood, CA 91607: Catalog $1 ❖ Gifts for cat lovers. 818-879-0339.

Sound Exchange, 45 N. Industry Ct., Deer Park, NY 11729: Free catalog ❖ Music, gifts, and collectibles. 800-841-3059.

Sportsman's Guide, 411 Farwell Ave., South St. Paul, MN 55075: Free catalog ❖ Gifts for sports enthusiasts. 800-888-5222.

Sporty's Preferred Living Catalog, Clermont Airport, Batavia, OH 45103: Free catalog ❖ Garden aids, outdoor furniture, sundials, mailboxes, gourmet meat smokers, portable refrigerators, kitchen aids and cutlery, embroidered shirts, automotive aids, sports equipment, games and toys, optics, gifts for pets, and weather forecasting equipment. 800-543-8633.

George Stafford & Sons, P.O. Box 2055, Thomasville, GA 31799: Free catalog ❖ Jewelry, luggage, books on the outdoors, mugs and dishes, men and women's clothing, and shoes. 800-826-0948.

Starcrest of California, 19465 Brennan Ave., Perris, CA 92599: Free catalog ❖ Gifts and novelties. 909-657-2793.

Stik-EES, 1165 Joshua Way, P.O. Box 9630, Vista, CA 92085: Free catalog ❖ Re-usable static cling pre-cut vinyl stickers for decorating gifts, windows, and other surfaces. 800-441-0041.

Sturbridge Yankee Workshop, P.O. Box 9797, Portland, ME 04104: Free catalog ❖ Home furnishings, Victorian and Shaker-style items, kitchen and bathroom accessories, and country crafts. 800-343-1144.

Sugar Hill, 1037 Front Ave., Columbus, GA 31902: Free catalog ❖ Bedroom linens, furniture, mirrors, lamps, and gifts. 800-344-6125.

The Sugar Shack, Rt. 7A, Arlington, VT 05250: Free information ❖ Vermont maple syrup, cream, and candy. Also homemade fudge, cheese, Vermont food products, and gifts. 802 375 6747.

Sundance Catalog, Customer Service Center, 1909 S. 4250 West, Salt Lake City, UT 84106: Free catalog ❖ Sculptures, lamps, stoneware, jewelry, decorative accessories, and Western and Native American gifts. 800-422-2770.

Sunset Catalog, Good Catalog Company, 5456 SE International Way, Portland, OR 97222: Free catalog ❖ Gifts and decorative items. 800-225-3870.

Super Locomotion Inc., 1213 Elko Dr., Sunnyvale, CA 94708: Free catalog ❖ High-tech and children's gifts, automotive accessories, travel aids, and games. 800-525-2468.

A Tale of Two Kitties, 11054 Ventura Blvd., Ste. 13, Studio City, CA 91604: Free catalog ❖ Gifts for cat lovers. 818-509-8415.

❖ GIFTS & GENERAL MERCHANDISE ❖

Tapestry, P.O. Box 46, Hanover, PA 17333: Free catalog ❖ Decorative accessories and home furnishings, Americana, imported gifts, fun and fantasy items, and holiday specials. 717-633-3333.

Taylor Gifts, 355 E. Conestoga Rd., P.O. Box 7705, Wayne, PA 19087: Free catalog ❖ Gifts and novelties. 610-293-3613.

Tender Heart Treasures Ltd., P.O. Box 2310, Omaha, NE 68103: Free catalog ❖ Gifts for homes, offices, friends, and family. 800-443-1367.

Terry's Village, P.O. Box 2309, Omaha, NE 68103: Free catalog ❖ Gifts and decorative items. 800-200-4400.

Norm Thompson, P.O. Box 3999, Portland, OR 97208: Free catalog ❖ Kitchen and bathroom aids, automotive accessories, storage and closet organizers, clothing, shoes and boots, and high-tech gadgets. 800-821-1287.

Thompson Cigar Company, 5401 Hangar Ct., P.O. Box 30303, Tampa, FL 33630: Free catalog ❖ Gifts for friends that smoke. 800-237-2559.

Thoroughbred Racing Catalog, Warsaw, VA 22572: Catalog $2 ❖ Calendars and limited edition prints with pictures of famous racing horses and horse-decorated mailboxes, doormats, sweatshirts and T-shirts, mugs and glasses, jewelry, and wall clocks. 800-777-RACE.

Tidewater Specialties, Box 158, Wye Mills, MD 21679: Free catalog ❖ Gifts for wildlife enthusiasts, dog owners and trainers, golfers, and other outdoor sports persons. 800-535-1314.

Tiffany & Company, Customer Service, 801 Jefferson Rd., Parsippany, NJ 07054: Catalog $1 ❖ Jewelry, crystal, watches, cultured pearls and settings, serving pieces, pens and pencils, and desk accessories. 800-452-9146.

Time Warner Viewer's Edge, P.O. Box 85098, Richmond, VA 23285: Free catalog ❖ Gifts for movie and TV lovers. 800-305-1989.

Touchstone, Order Processing Center, 3589 Broad St., Atlanta, GA 30341: Free catalog ❖ Decorative and desk accessories, furniture and lamps, and traditional American-style gifts. 800-962-6890.

Trifles, P.O. Box 620048, Dallas, TX 75262: Free catalog ❖ Jewelry, coffee and tea service sets, stationery, porcelain and bone china, linens, toys, fireplace accessories, crystal, luggage, furniture, and clothing for men, women, and children. 800-456-7019.

Troll Family Gift Catalog, 100 Corporate Dr., Mahwah, NJ 07430: Free catalog ❖ Clocks, electronic baby sitters, photo albums, stationery, kitchen gadgets, toys, books, cassettes, and gifts. 800-247-6106.

TYROL International, 66 E. Kytle St., P.O. Box 909, Cleveland, GA 30528: Free catalog ❖ Figurines and limited edition collectibles, gifts for holidays, steins, bears, dolls, music videos, CDs, cassettes, and items from worldwide sources. 800-241-5404.

Uncle Bernie's Warehouse Club, 2428 Patterson Ave. SW, Roanoke, VA 24016: Free catalog ❖ Toys, puzzles, decorative items, household accessories, gadgets, and gifts.

Unicef, P.O. Box 182233, Chattanooga, TN 37422: Free catalog ❖ Greeting and note cards, toys, limited edition plates, postcards, and gifts. 800-553-1200.

United States Purchasing Exchange, United States Purchasing Exchange Building, North Hollywood, CA 91611: Free catalog ❖ Household aids, novelties and toys, personal care items, clothing and lingerie, telephones, clocks, kitchen accessories, jewelry, automotive aids, tools, and bathroom furnishings.

Velo, 1830 N. 55th St., Boulder, CO 80301: Free catalog ❖ Gifts for bicycle riders.

Vermont Country Store, Mail Order Office, P.O. Box 3000, Manchester Center, VT 05255: Free catalog ❖ Clothing, shoes, purses, watches, pillows and linens, bed coverings, travel aids, throw rugs, stove top potpourris, cleaning aids, kitchen accessories, and gifts from New England. 802-362-2400.

Vermont Industries, P.O. Box 301, Rt. 103, Cuttingsville, VT 05738: Catalog $3 ❖ Hand-forged wrought iron wood racks, lamps, fireplace tools, candle holders, pot holders, and more. 800-639-1715; 802-492-3451 (in VT).

Lillian Vernon, Virginia Beach, VA 23479: Free catalog ❖ Holiday specialties, clothing, electronic gadgets, jewelry, closet organizers, toys, baby care items, kitchen and cooking accessories, luggage, and leather accessories. 800-285-5555.

Wanderings Inc., P.O. Box 4344, Warren, NJ 07059: Free catalog ❖ Hand-knitted wool sweaters and special occasion gifts. 800-456-KNIT.

War Eagle Mill, Rt. 5, Box 411, Rogers, AR 72756: Free catalog ❖ Arts and crafts, enamelware dishes, foods, specialty items, and gifts. 501-789-5343.

Waterfront Living, P.O. Box 504, Lake Oswego, OR 97034: Free catalog ❖ Gifts for persons who enjoy the water and waterfront living. 800-341-5280.

The Westbury Collection, Good Catalog Company, 5456 SE International Way, Portland, OR 97222: Free catalog ❖ All-occasion gifts. 800-225-3870.

Weston Bowl Mill, P.O. Box 218, Weston, VT 05161: Catalog $1 ❖ Wooden bowls, crafts, and kitchen and dining room accessories. 800-824-6219.

What on Earth, 2451 Enterprise East Pkwy., Twinsburg, OH 44087: Free catalog ❖ Gifts for men, women, and children. 216-425-4600.

Whole Life Products, 1334 Pacific Ave., Forest Grove, OR 97116: Free catalog ❖ Yoga and religious-inspired gifts. 800-634-9056.

Wild Wings, P.O. Box 451, Lake City, MN 55041: Free catalog ❖ Art prints, gun cabinets, solid oak wall clocks, gifts for fishermen and animal lovers, and note cards. 800-445-4833.

Williams-Sonoma, Mail Order Dept., P.O. Box 7456, San Francisco, CA 94120: Free catalog ❖ Kitchenware, gourmet foods, and gifts. 800-541-1262.

Winterthur Museum & Gardens, Catalog Division, 100 Enterprise Pl., Dover, DE 19901: Free catalog ❖ American art, jewelry, playing cards, lamps, dinnerware, clocks, planters, wind chimes, garden sculptures, and reproductions from the Henry Francis du Pont Winterthur Museum. 800-767-0500.

Wireless, P.O. Box 64422, St. Paul, MN 55164: Free catalog ❖ T-shirts and sweatshirts, old time radio broadcasts, toy banks, coffee mugs, Disney cartoons on video cassettes, books, wind chimes, and electronics. 800-669-9999.

Woodbury Pewterers Inc., 860 Main St. South, P.O. Box 482, Woodbury, CT 06798: Free catalog ❖ Handmade pewter gifts. 800-648-2014.

World Wildlife Fund Catalog, P.O. Box 224, Peru, IN 46970: Free catalog ❖ Wildlife-theme clothing, books, games, coasters, coffee mugs, puzzles, note pads, kitchen accents, carryall bags, candlesticks, sculptures, wind chimes, bird feeders, place mats, and umbrellas. 800-833-1600.

Worldwide Collectibles & Gifts, P.O. Box 158, 2 Lakeside Ave., Berwyn, PA 19312: Free catalog ❖ Fine gifts and jewelry, porcelain collectibles, crystal, and items by famous artists. 800-644-2442.

Carol Wright Gifts, 340 Applecreek Rd., P.O. Box 8503, Lincoln, NE 68544: Free catalog ❖ Gifts for homes, offices, friends, and family. 402-474-5174.

The Write Touch, The Rytex Company, 5850 W. 80th St., P.O. Box 68188, Indianapolis, IN 46268: Free catalog ❖ Stationery, writing aids, and gifts. 800-288-6824.

Writewell Company, P.O. Box 68186, Indianapolis, IN 46268: Free catalog ❖ Decorative accessories, household items, stationery, books, home office supplies, games, rubber stamps, videos, business cards, and gifts. 800-968-5850.

258 ❖ **GLASS COLLECTIBLES & DESIGNER ITEMS** ❖

Yankee Barn Catalog, 1120 W. Maple, Hartville, OH 44632: Free catalog ❖ One-of-a-kind decorative pieces, exclusive designer apparel, and handcrafted items. 800-794-8394.

The Yankee Catalog, Good Catalog Company, 5456 SE International Way, Portland, OR 97222: Free catalog ❖ Unique gifts and decorative items. 800-828-1334.

Your Exceptional Home, W.M. Green & Company, P.O. Box 426, Greenville, NC 27835: Free catalog ❖ Home accessories and gifts. 800-482-5050.

Zucker's Fine Gifts, 151 W. 26th St., New York, NY 10001: Free catalog ❖ Hummel items, Swarovski silver and crystal, Waterford crystal, Lladro porcelain, and gifts. 212-989-1450.

Religious Gifts

Abbey Press, 123 Hill Dr., St. Meinrad, IN 47577: Free catalog ❖ Religious gifts for people of Christian faith. 800-962-4760.

Alleon Design Company, 414 41st St., Oakland, CA 94609: Free catalog ❖ Hardwood, semi-precious stone, and art glass mezuzahs. 510-654-8486.

Augsburg Fortress Publishers, 426 S. 5th St., Box 1209, Minneapolis, MN 55440: Free catalog ❖ Books, educational materials, music, gifts, audiovisuals, and ecclesiastical arts items. 800-328-4648; 612-330-3300 (in MN).

California Stitchery, 6015 Sunnyslope Ave., Van Nuys, CA 91401: Free catalog ❖ Judaic-design needlepoint, embroidery, and latch-hook kits. 800-345-3332.

Ergo Media, 668 Front St., P.O. Box 2037, Teaneck, NJ 07666: Free catalog ❖ Award-winning videos on all aspects of Jewish life. 800-695-3746.

Galerie Robin, P.O. Box 42275, Cincinnati, OH 45242: Free information ❖ Judaic art, graphics, and handcrafted gifts. 800-635-8279.

Hamakor Judaica Inc., Mail Order Department, P.O. Box 48836, Niles, IL 60714: Free catalog ❖ Kosher foods, kitchen accessories, Jewish art, watches and pendants, Seder dishes, mezuzahs, candelabras, and other items. 800-426-2567.

Judaic Folk Art, Lois Kramer, 8101 Timber Valley Ct., Dunn Loring, VA 22027: Free brochure ❖ Judaic folk art. 703-560-2914.

Judaica Occasions, 55 Union Rd. 203, Spring Valley NY 10977: Free catalog ❖ Gifts for Bar and Bat Mitzvahs, weddings, and other occasions. 800-336-2291.

Red Rose Collection, P.O. Box 280140, San Francisco, CA 94128: Free catalog ❖ Religious gifts. 800-374-5505.

Shasta Abbey Buddhist Supplies, P.O. Box 199, Mt. Shasta, CA 96067: Catalog $2 ❖ Buddhist meditation supplies and gifts. 800-653-3315.

The Source for Everything Jewish, P.O. Box 48836, Niles, IL 60714: Free catalog ❖ Ritual and ceremonial objects, books, fine art, Kosher gourmet food, and audio and video cassettes. 800-426-2567.

GLASS COLLECTIBLES & DESIGNER ITEMS

Blenko Glass Company Inc., P.O. Box 67, Milton, WV 25541: Free catalog ❖ Hand-blown and finished decorative glass designer items. 304-743-9081.

Ruth E. Jordan, Rt. 28, Meridale, NY 13806: Free list with long SASE ❖ American brilliant period cut glass. 607-746-2082.

Renaissance Marketing, P.O. Box 2546, Bonita Springs, FL 33959: Free catalog ❖ Bronze sculptures and collectible art glass. 813-495-6033.

GLOBES

George F. Cram Company Inc., 301 S. LaSalle St., Indianapolis, IN 46201: Free catalog ❖ Maps, atlases, globes, and charts. 800-227-4199; 317-635-5564 (in IN).

Creative Imaginations, 10879 Portal Dr., Los Alamitos, CA 90720: Free information ❖ Inflatable globes. 800-942-6487.

First State Map & Globe, 12 Mary Ella Dr., Wilmington, DE 19805: Free catalog ❖ Globes and map-related items. 800-327-7992.

Murray Hudson, 109 S. Church St., P.O. Box 163, Halls, TN 38840: Catalog $10 (refundable) ❖ Antique maps, books with maps, world globes, and historical prints. 800-748-9946; 901-836-9057 (in TN).

National Geographic Society, 1145 17th St. NW, Washington, DC 20036: Free catalog ❖ Books, games, videos, maps and globes, travel aids, and magazine subscriptions. 800-447-0647.

Omni Resources, 1004 S. Mebane St., P.O. Box 2096, Burlington, NC 27216: Free catalog ❖ Fossils, rocks, hiking and topography maps, and globes. 800-742-2677.

Rand McNally & Company, Catalog Operations Center, 2515 E. 43rd St., P.O. Box 182257, Chattanooga, TN 37422: Free catalog ❖ Gifts for sports enthusiasts, health and exercise equipment, maps, world globes, books, videos, clocks, prints, travel aids, and watches. 800-234-0679.

Replogle Globes Inc., 2801 S. 25th Ave., Broadview, IL 60153: Free catalog ❖ Earth and space globes in desk and floor models. 708-343-0900.

Trippensee Transparent Globes, 301 Cass St., Saginaw, MI 48602: Free catalog ❖ World globes in desk and floor models. 517-799-8102.

GO KARTS & MINICARS

Kart World, 1488 Mentor Ave., Painesville, OH 44077: Catalog $3 ❖ Go karts and minicars, engines, kits, and parts. 216-357-5569.

Performance Speedway, 2810-C Algonquin Ave., Jacksonville, FL 32210: Catalog $5 ❖ Electric cars, golf carts, mopeds, parts, how-to manuals, and books.

GOLF

Clothing

A.B. Emblem Corporation, P.O. Box 695, Weaverville, NC 28787: Free information ❖ Caps, hats, shirts, and sweaters. 800-438-4285; 704-645-3015 (in NC).

All Star Pro Golf Company Inc., 120 9th St. SW, Clarion, IA 50525: Free information ❖ Caps, hats, gloves, jackets, visors, sweaters, and shirts. 800-247-4830; 515-532-2864 (in IA).

Tommy Armour Golf Company, 8350 N. Lehigh Ave., Morton Grove, IL 60053: Free information ❖ Gloves, shirts, skirts, slacks, sweaters, and visors. 800-723-4653.

Bogner of America, Bogner Dr., Newport, VT 05855: Free information ❖ Caps, hats, gloves, jackets, shirts, skirts, slacks, sweaters, and visors. 800-451-4417; 802-334-6507 (in VT).

Broder Brothers, 45555 Port St., Plymouth, MI 48170: Free information ❖ Jackets, shirts, sweaters, and visors. 800-521-0850.

M. Handelsman Company, 1323 S. Michigan Ave., Chicago, IL 60605: Free information ❖ Caps, hats, shirts, socks, sweaters, and visors. 800-621-4454; 312-427-0784 (in IL).

King Louie International, 13500 15th St., Grandview, MO 64030: Free information ❖ Caps, hats, jackets, shirts, sweaters, and visors. 800-521-5212; 816-765-5212 (in MO).

Le Coq Sportif, 5675 N. Blackstock Rd., Spartanburg, SC 29303: Free information ❖ Caps, hats, shoes, shirts, skirts, slacks, socks, and sweaters. 800-524-2377.

Lily's, 4910-B W. Rosecrans Ave., Hawthorne, CA 90250: Free information ❖ Caps, hats, shoes, shirts, skirts, slacks, socks, sweaters, and visors. 800-421-4474.

MacGregor Golf Clubs, 1601 S. Slappey Blvd., Albany, GA 31708: Free information ❖ Caps, hats, shoes, gloves, shirts, skirts, slacks, socks, sweaters, and visors. 800-841-4358; 912-888-0001 (in GA).

GOLF

Marcia Originals, 18324-3 Oxnard St., Tarzana, CA 91356: Free information ❖ Jackets, shirts, skirts, slacks, and sweaters. 800-423-5208; 818-881-3588 (in CA).

Odyssey Golf, 1945 Camino Vida Roble, Ste. J, Carlsbad, CA 92008: Free brochure ❖ Bags, hats, shirts, and left-handed putters. 800-487-5664.

Ortho-Vent Inc., 11851 30th Ct. North, St. Petersburg, FL 33716: Free catalog ❖ Shoes. 813-573-3730.

Spalding Sports Worldwide, 425 Meadow St., P.O. Box 901, Chicopee, MA 01021: Free list of retail sources ❖ Caps, hats, gloves, jackets, shirts, skirts, slacks, socks, sweaters, and vests. 800-225-6601.

T-Shirt City, 4501 W. Mitchell Ave., Cincinnati, OH 45232: Free information ❖ Caps, hats, jackets, shirts, sweaters, socks, and visors. 800-543-7230.

Tuttle Golf Collection, P.O. Box 888, Wallingford, CT 06492: Free catalog ❖ Sportswear for men and women. 800-882-7511.

The Women's Golf Catalog, P.O. Box 1249, Sagamore Beach, MA 02562: Free catalog ❖ Accessories, jewelry, footwear, gift and novelty items, and equipment. 800-984-7324.

Equipment Manufacturers

Accuform Golf Clubs, 6380 Viscount Rd., Mississaugua, Toronto, Ontario, Canada L4B 1H3: Free information. 800-668-7873.

Aldila, 15822 Bernardo Center Dr., San Diego, CA 92127: Free list of retail sources ❖ Graphite shafts for woods, irons, and putters.

Alien Sport Inc., 2085 Landing Dr., Mountain View, CA 94043: Free information ❖ Matched clubs. 800-229-4882.

Tommy Armour Golf Company, 8350 N. Lehigh Ave., Morton Grove, IL 60053: Free information. 800-723-4653.

Atlas Tee Company, P.O. Box 600, Hollywood, FL 33022: Free information ❖ Personalized golf tees.

Bridgestone Golf Clubs, 15320 Industrial Park Blvd. NE, Covington, GA 30209: Free information. 800-358-6310; 404-787-7400 (in GA).

Browning Golf Clubs, 2346 W. 1000 South, Salt Lake City, UT 84104: Free information. 800-666-6033.

Callaway Golf Clubs, 2285 Rutherford Rd., Carlsbad, CA 92008: Free information. 800-228-2767; 619-931-1771 (in CA).

Carbite Golf Company, 6370 Nancy Ridge Dr., #110, San Diego, CA 92121: Free information. 800-272-4325.

Cobra Golf Clubs, 1812 Ashton Ave., Carlsbad, CA 92008: Free information. 800-BAFFLER.

Components Plus, 7550 Sterns Rd., Ottawa Lake, MI 49267: Free catalog ❖ Woods, irons, putters, putter shafts, graphite components, and assembled irons. 313-854-3214.

Jan Craig Headcovers, 1000 N. Milwaukee, Ste. 203, Chicago, IL 60622: Free information ❖ Headcovers. 312-278-8366.

Cubic Balance Golf Technology, 30231 Tomas Rd., Santa Margarita, CA 92668: Free information. 800-727-7775.

Daiwa Corporation, 7421 Chapman Ave., Garden Grove, CA 92641: Catalog $1. 714-895-6645.

Dalee Imports, P.O. Box 2075, Revelstroke, British Columbia, Canada V0E 2S0: Free information ❖ Electronic golf score calculator. 800-705-9991.

Duffix Golf Products, 5340 South Ave., Youngstown, OH 44512: Free brochure ❖ A swing trainer that teaches how to eliminate slice and hooking problems. 800-972-2947.

Dynacraft, 71 Maholm St., Newark, OH 43055: Free information. 800-321-4833.

Echelon Golf, 1016 Lawson St., City of Industry, CA 91748: Free list of retail sources ❖ State-of-the-art golf clubs. 800-964-4899; 818-964-4799 (in CA).

Founders Club, 1780 La Costa Meadows Dr., San Marcos, CA 92069: Free information. 800-654-9295.

Goldentouch Golf Inc., 1116 E. Valencia Dr., Fullerton, CA 92631: Free information. 800-423-2220.

Goldwin Golf Inc., 2460 Impala Dr., Carlsbad, CA 92008: Free information ❖ Milled metal-wood clubs. 800-609-4653.

Head Golf, 9189 Red Branch Rd., Columbia, MD 21045: Free information.

Hillerich & Bradsby Company Inc., P.O. Box 35700, Louisville, KY 40232: Free list of retail sources. 800-282-2287.

House of Tees, P.O. Box 5000, Dover, NJ 07801: Free information ❖ Personalized golf tees. 800-832-5457.

Hurricane Sports Inc., 1130 Commerce Blvd. North, Sarasota, FL 34243: Free information. 800-749-8848.

La Jolla Golf Club Company, 2440 La Mirada Dr., Ste. A, Vista, CA 92083: Free brochure ❖ Golf clubs for children and adults. 800-468-7700; 619-599-9400 (in CA).

Lynx Golf Clubs, 16017 E. Valley Blvd., City of Industry, CA 91749: Free information. 800-233-5969; 818-961-0222 (in CA).

MacGregor Golf Clubs, 1601 S. Slappey Blvd., Albany, GA 31708: Free information. 800-841-4358; 912-888-0001 (in GA).

Makser, 848 Brickell Ave., Miami, FL 33131: Free information ❖ Putters and metal-wood drivers. 800-925-0477.

Mizuno Corporation, 651 Gateway Blvd., Ste. 300, South San Francisco, CA 94080: Free information. 800-966-1211.

Nassau Investment Casting Company, 99 Russell Pl., Freeport, NY 11620: Free brochure ❖ Custom irons with matched steel shafts, club-building supplies, and golf balls. 800-783-7775; 516-867-8018 (in NY).

Odyssey Golf, 1945 Camino Vida Roble, Ste. J, Carlsbad, CA 92008: Free brochure ❖ Bags, hats, shirts, and left-handed putters. 800-487-5664.

One-Up Health & Sport Inc., 14 Inverness Dr. East, Englewood, CO 80112: Free catalog ❖ Back supports, pain-relieving elbow band, wrap-around knee stabilizer, wrist compression wraps, and fitness accessories. 800-997-6789; 303-790-7249 (in CO).

PING, Karsten Manufacturing Corporation, P.O. Box 9990, Phoenix, AZ 85068: Free information ❖ Putters, irons, and metal-wood drivers. 800-474-6434.

Pinseeker Golf Clubs, 3502 S. Susan St., Santa Ana, CA 92704: Free information. 714-979-4500.

PLOP, 2794 Loker Ave. West, #100, Carlsbad, CA 92008: Free brochure ❖ Personalized computer-fitted putters and accessories.

Joe Powell Golf Inc., 1781 Barber Rd., Sarasota, FL 34240: Free information. 800-237-4660.

Ram Golf Clubs, 2020 Indian Boundary Dr., Melrose Park, IL 60160: Free information. 800-833-4653.

Ryobi-Toski Golf Clubs, 160 Essex St., Box 576, Newark, OH 43055: Free information. 800-848-2075.

Sasse Golf Inc., 2101 Sandhills Blvd., Southern Pines, NC 28387: Free information. 800-334-3451; 910-692-2205 (in NC).

Kenneth Smith Golf Clubs, P.O. Box 419041, Kansas City, MO 64141: Free catalog ❖ Custom handmade golf clubs. 913-631-5100.

Solo Golf Company, 220 N. California Ave., City of Industry, CA 91744: Free information ❖ Matched irons. 800-6-SOLO-44.

Spalding Sports Worldwide, 425 Meadow St., P.O. Box 901, Chicopee, MA 01021: Free list of retail sources. 800-225-6601.

Taylor Made Golf Clubs, 2271 Cosmos Ct., Carlsbad, CA 92009: Free information. 800-888-CLUB.

Titleist Golf Equipment, P.O. Box 965, Fairhaven, MA 02719: Free list of retail sources. 508-979-2000.

Traxx Golf Company, P.O. Box 190445, Dallas, TX 75219: Free information ❖ Putters.

Wood Wand Putters, 2101 Sandhills Blvd., Southern Pines, NC 28387: Free information. 800-334-3451; 910-692-2205 (in NC).

Yamaha Sporting Goods Division, 6600 Orangethorpe Ave., Buena Park, CA 90620: Free information. 800-541-6514; 714-522-9011 (in CA).

Yonex Corporation, 350 Challenger St., Torrance, CA 90503: Free list of retail sources. 800-44-YONEX.

Equipment Retailers

All Star Pro Golf Company Inc., 120 9th St. SW, Clarion, IA 50525: Free information ❖ Grips, head covers, clubs, bags, and bag covers. 800-247-4830; 515-532-2864 (in IA).

Austad's, 4500 E. 10th St., P.O. Box 5428, Sioux Falls, SD 57196: Free catalog ❖ Golf, other sports equipment, and clothing. 800-444-1234.

Clarke Distributing Company, 9233 Bryant St., Houston, TX 77075: Catalog $2 ❖ Tennis, golf, soccer equipment, novelties, and gifts. 800-777-3444.

Custom Golf Clubs Inc., 11000 N. Interstate Hwy. 35; Austin, TX 78753: Free catalog ❖ Repair supplies, clothing, gloves, bags, and other equipment. 800-456-3344; 512-837-4810 (in TX).

D.B. Enterprises, 425 Maplewood Dr., Norristown, PA 19401: Free information ❖ Indoor and outdoor golf net kits. 610-272-1228.

Dimmock Hill Golf Course, Binghamton, NY 13905: Free information ❖ Golf equipment and accessories. 800-727-5511.

Dorson Sports Inc., 1 Roebling Ct., Ronkonkona, NY 51779: Free information ❖ Bags and bag covers, grips, head covers, tubes, and other equipment. 800-645-7215; 516-585-5440 (in NY).

Dynacraft, 71 Maholm St., Newark, OH 43055: Free information ❖ Club heads, shafts, and other components for custom club building. 800-321-4833.

Eagle Golf, P.O. Box 2022, Bellevue, WA 98009: Free catalog ❖ Golf instructional videos, books, and training aids. 800-752-3149.

Essex Manufacturing, 330 5th Ave., New York, NY 10001: Free information ❖ Golf umbrellas. 800-648-6010; 212-239-0080 (in NY).

Global Golf, 59 S. State St., Westerville, OH 43081: Free catalog ❖ Heads, shafts, grips, and other golf club components. 614-523-7402.

Golf Day, 135 American Legion Hwy., Revere, MA 02151: Free catalog ❖ Bags and bag covers, clubs, shoes, gloves, clothing, grips, head covers, tubes, and other equipment. 800-669-8600.

Golf Haus, 700 N. Pennsylvania, Lansing, MI 48854: Free catalog ❖ Clubs, bags, clothing, umbrellas, and score keepers. 517-482-8842.

Golf Sellers Direct, 3165 Estates Pl. North, St. Joseph, MI 49085: Free information ❖ Motorized golf carts. 800-337-7692.

Golfer's Image, 301 S. Summit Ave., Sioux Falls, SD 57104: Free catalog ❖ Equipment and accessories, how-to books and videos, clothing, and gifts for golfers. 800-482-6805; 605-335-6014 (in SD).

Golfsmith, 11000 N. Interstate Hwy. 35, Austin, TX 78753: Free catalog ❖ Golf club-making supplies. 800-925-7709.

The Golfworks, P.O. Box 3008, Newark, OH 43055: Free catalog ❖ Supplies for customizing and assembling golf clubs, how-to books, and video and audio tapes. 800-848-8358.

Harris International Inc., 9999 NE Glisan St., Portland, OR 97220: Free information ❖ Head covers, clubs, bags, and bag covers, and other equipment. 800-547-2880; 503-256-2302 (in OR).

Holabird Sports Discounters, 9220 Pulaski Hwy., Baltimore, MD 21220: Free catalog ❖ Equipment and clothing for golf, basketball, tennis, running and jogging, racquetball, and other sports. 410-687-6400.

Jayfro Corporation, Unified Sports Inc., 976 Hartford Tnpk., P.O. Box 400, Waterford, CT 06385: Free catalog ❖ Outdoor practice cages, chipping and driving mats, and target baffles. 860-447-3001.

Kangaroo Motorcaddies, 5407 Mill Spring Rd., Columbus, NC 28722: Free information ❖ Motorized caddies for golf bags. 800-882-9492 (Mountain/Pacific); 800-438-3011 (Eastern/Central).

Las Vegas Discount Golf & Tennis, 5325 S. Valley View Blvd., Ste. 10, Las Vegas, NV 89118: Free catalog ❖ Equipment, clothing, and shoes for golf, tennis, racquetball, walking and jogging, and other sports. 702-798-7777.

Ralph Maltby Enterprises Inc., P.O. Box 3008, Newark, OH 43055: Free catalog ❖ Golf supplies for repair shops, club makers, manufacturers, and do-it-yourselfers. 800-848-8358.

Masters Golf, 591 Main St., Bayshore, NY 11706: Free catalog ❖ Golf clubs, other equipment, and shoes. 800-825-9025.

McCann Precision Golf Inc., 6511 Proprietors Rd., Worthington, OH 43085: Free catalog ❖ Heads, shafts, grips, and components. 800-969-2525.

Richard Metz Golf Studio Inc., 425 Madison Ave., 3rd Floor, New York, NY 10017: Free information ❖ Golf equipment, antique and collectible clubs, video tapes, and books. 212-759-6940.

Mizuno Corporation, 651 Gateway Blvd., Ste. 300, South San Francisco, CA 94080: Free information ❖ Clubs and lightweight waterproof full-grain leather golf shoes. 800-966-1211.

New York Golf Center, 131 W. 35th St., New York, NY 10001: Free information ❖ Golf equipment. 212-564-2255.

Outbound Golf Inc., Customer Relations Manager, 12043 Blondo St., Omaha, NE 68164: Free catalog ❖ Golf clubs and accessories, club-making supplies, shoes, carts, and AccuSYSTEM golf products. 402-492-9677.

Performance Golf Company, 5405 NW 102nd Ave., Ste. 230, Sunrise, FL 33351: Free catalog ❖ Golf equipment. 305-742-8528.

Polar Golf, 3877 Pacific Hwy., San Diego, CA 92110: Free information ❖ Golf equipment and accessories. 800-334-7741.

Prima, 5380 S. Valley View Blvd., Las Vegas, NV 89118: Free information ❖ Golf clubs for women. 800-932-1622; 702-736-8801 (in NV).

Pro Shop World of Golf, 8130 N. Lincoln Ave., Skokie, IL 60077: Free catalog ❖ Golf equipment and shoes. 800-323-4047; 708-675-5286 (in IL).

Professional Golf & Tennis Suppliers, 7825 Hollywood Blvd., Pembroke Pines, FL 33024: Free catalog with long SASE ❖ Golf, tennis, and racquetball equipment. 305-981-7283.

Professional Golf Factory, 3054 N. Union Rd., Manteca, CA 95337: Free information ❖ Golf equipment, accessories, and clothing. 800-445-4657.

SGD Company Inc., P.O. Box 8410, Akron, OH 44320: Free information ❖ Golf balls, ball retrievers, ball washers, and golf course equipment. 216-239-2828.

Southeast Discount Golf, 1900 N. Kings Hwy., Girardeau, MO 63701: Free information ❖ Golf equipment and accessories. 800-462-4516.

Taylor Made Golf Clubs, 2271 Cosmos Ct., Carlsbad, CA 92009: Free information ❖ Leather and all-weather gloves, ultra-lightweight bags, and golf clubs. 800-888-CLUB.

Telepro Golf Shops, 17642 Armstrong Ave., Irvine, CA 92714: Free information ❖ Golf clubs, shoes, carts, and equipment. 800-333-9903.

UT Golf, 2346 W. 1500 South, Salt Lake City, UT 84104: Free information ❖ Golf club components. 800-509-7767.

Wa-Mac Inc., Highskore Products Inc., P.O. Box 128, Carlstadt, NJ 07410: Free information ❖ Golf balls and ball washers, and golf course equipment. 800-447-5673; 201-438-7200 (in NJ).

Edwin Watts Golf Shops, 20 Hill Ave., Walton Beach, FL 32548: Free catalog ❖ Golf clubs, carts, bags, and equipment. 800-874-0146.

Tom Wells Golf Company, 7806 Aurora Ave. North, Seattle, WA 98103: Free catalog ❖ Custom-made computer-fitted clubs and components. 800-800-5417.

Wittek Golf Supply Company Inc., 3650 N. Avondale, Chicago, IL 60618: Free information ❖ Golf course equipment, grips, head covers, tubes, and clubs, bags, and bag covers. 312-463-2636.

The Women's Golf Catalog, P.O. Box 1249, Sagamore Beach, MA 02562: Free catalog ❖ Accessories, jewelry, footwear, gift and novelty items, and equipment. 800-984-7324.

World of Golf, 147 E. 47th St., New York, NY 10017: Free catalog ❖ Equipment for men and women. 212-755-9398.

World of Golf Equipment, 8130 N. Lincoln Ave., Skokie, IL 60077: Free information ❖ Equipment for men, women, and juniors. 800-323-4047.

Left-handed Equipment

Lefties Only, 1972 Williston Rd., S. Burlington, VT 05403: Free price list ❖ Golf equipment for left-handed persons. 800-533-8437.

Odyssey Golf, 1945 Camino Vida Roble, Ste. J, Carlsbad, CA 92008: Free brochure ❖ Bags, hats, shirts, and left-handed putters. 800-487-5664.

GREETING CARDS & GIFT WRAPPING

Applewood Cards Inc., P.O. Box 1212, Glastonbury, CT 06033: Catalog $2 ❖ Auto-related greeting cards. 860-657-4097.

Auto Cards Inc., P.O. Box 452, Stuart, FL 34995: Brochure and sample card $2 ❖ Color greeting cards for auto enthusiasts, featuring classic Mustangs, Corvettes, and Chevrolets.

Associated Photo Company, Box 817, Florence, KY 41022: Free information ❖ Imprinted photo Christmas cards. 606-282-0011.

Anita Beck Collection, 555 W. 78th St., Ste. P, Edina, MN 55439: Free catalog ❖ Seasonal and special occasion greeting cards. 800-328-3894.

BowMasters, P.O. Box 26, Kingston, MA 02364: Free information ❖ Easy-to-use bow-making kit. 800-335-8312.

Car Collectables, 32 White Birch Rd., Madison, CT 06443: Free brochure ❖ Christmas cards, note cards, and gifts with an automotive theme. 203-245-7299.

Current Inc., Express Processing Center, Colorado Springs, CO 80941: Free catalog ❖ Greeting cards, stationery, gift wrapping, decorations, toys, calendars, and gifts. 800-848-2848.

Walter Drake & Sons, Drake Building, Colorado Springs, CO 80940: Free catalog ❖ Christmas cards. 800-525-9291.

Kristin Elliott Inc., 6 Opportunity Way, Newburyport, MA 01950: Free catalog ❖ Boxed notes, gift enclosures, Christmas and other greeting cards, desk memos, memo pads, postcards, correspondence cards, and gift wrapping. 800-922-1899; 508-465-1899 (in MA).

Enfield Stationers, 215 Moody Rd., Enfield, CT 06082: Free catalog ❖ Greeting cards, calendars, and gifts. 203-763-3980.

Faded Rose, P.O. Box 19575, Portland, OR 97219: Brochure $1 ❖ Recycled paper greeting cards. 503-245-2694.

Fatwise, 1130 E. Linden Ave., Colina, NJ 07036: Free catalog ❖ Greeting cards for diet-conscious persons. 908-862-3886.

Fingerhut, P.O. Box 800, St. Cloud, MN 56395: Free catalog ❖ Greeting cards, gift wraps, stationery, holiday decorations, organizers, and gifts. 800-322-2226.

G & K Enterprises, 1408 Glenwood Ave., Greensboro, NC 27403: Free information ❖ Calendars and all-occasion and Christmas cards with a western-theme. 910-632-9899.

Graphics Inc., 1400 Indiantown Rd., P.O. Box 937, Jupiter, FL 33468: Free brochure ❖ Pop-up Christmas and all-occasion greeting cards. 407-746-6746.

Grayworks/Winterworks, P.O. Box 1150, Hoodsport, WA 98548: Catalog $2 ❖ Greeting cards and art prints. 360-877-6479.

Handshake Greeting Cards, P.O. Box 9027, Columbus, GA 31908: Free catalog ❖ Personalized greeting cards. 800-634-2134.

Heirloom Editions, Box 520-B, Rt. 4, Carthage, MO 64836: Catalog $4 ❖ Lithographs, greeting cards, stickers, miniatures, stationery, framed prints, turn-of-the-century art, and paper collectibles. 800-725-0725.

House-Mouse Designs, P.O. Box 48, Williston, VT 05495: Free catalog ❖ Christmas cards, note and recipe cards, magnets, and stickers. 800-242-6423.

Miles Kimball Company, Christmas Cards, 41 W. 8th Ave., Oshkosh, WI 54906: Free catalog ❖ Christmas cards with optional personalization. 800-546-2255.

Kimmeric Studio, P.O. Box 3586, Napa, CA 94558: Catalog $2 ❖ Craft hang tags. 707-255-8734.

Lang Companies, P.O. Box 1, Delafield, WI 53018: Catalog $1 ❖ Country-style calendars, boxed note cards, and greeting cards. 800-967-3399.

Literary Calligraphy, Rt. 1., Box 56A, Moneta, VA 24121: Catalog $2 ❖ Calligraphy-decorated note cards, Christmas cards, and holiday prints. 800-261-6325.

Main Street Press, P.O. Box 126, Delafield, WI 53018: Catalog $1 ❖ Wall calendars, boxed greeting cards, note cards and pads, and stationery products. 414-646-8511.

The Maritime Store, 2905 Hyde St. Pier, San Francisco, CA 94109: Free catalog ❖ Maritime maps, greeting cards, boat models, children's and maritime books, and gifts. 415-775-BOOK.

Nasco, 901 Janesville Ave., Fort Atkinson, WI 53538: Free catalog ❖ Calligraphy supplies and greeting cards. 800-558-9595.

National Wildlife Federation, P.O. Box 8925, Vienna, VA 22183: Free catalog ❖ Holiday cards and gifts. 800-432-6564.

New England Card Company, Rt. 41, Box 228, West Ossipee, NH 03890: Free brochure ❖ Greeting cards with scenes of New England. 800-762-5562; 603-539-5200 (in NH).

Novagraphics, P.O. Box 37197, Tucson, AZ 85740: Catalog $3 ❖ Astronomy and space-decorative artwork and greeting cards. 800-727-6682.

Posty Cards, 1600 Olive St., Kansas City, MO 64127: Free catalog ❖ Calendars and greeting and birthday cards. 800-554-5018.

The Printery House, Conception Abbey, Conception, MO 64433: Free information ❖ Folk art and religious greeting cards. 800-322-2737.

Prudent Publishing, 65 Challenger Rd., Ridgefield Park, NJ 07660: Free brochure ❖ Special occasion greeting cards for business and personal use. 201-641-8996.

Renaissance Greeting Cards Inc., P.O. Box 845, Springvale, ME 04038: Catalog $1 ❖ Greeting cards. 800-688-9998.

That's A Wrap Inc., 47 W. Division, #371, Chicago, IL 60610: Free brochure ❖ Easy-to-make bows for wrapping gifts. 800-354-0512; 312-440-9741 (in IL).

Trumble Greetings, P.O. Box 9800, Boulder, CO 80301: Catalog $1 ❖ Greeting cards with country and wildlife scenes that depict America's heritage. 800-525-0656.

Unicef, P.O. Box 182233, Chattanooga, TN 37422: Free catalog ❖ Greeting and note cards, toys, limited edition plates, gifts, and postcards. 800-553-1200.

Victorian Papers, P.O. Box 411332, Kansas City, MO 61141: Catalog $2 ❖ Greeting and note cards for birthdays, holidays, graduation, and other occasions. 800-800-6647.

GUM BALL MACHINES

Norm & Mary Johnson, County Home Rd., Bowling Green, OH 43402: Free information with long SASE ❖ Slot machines, old arcade games, peanut and gumball machines, mechanical and still banks, and other coin-operated machines. 419-352-3041.

KAPS Vending, 593 Lavina Ct., Helmet, CA 92544: Free price list with long SASE ❖ Antique gumball machines, globes, parts, decals, gumballs, candy, and toys. 909-658-4620.

GUNS & AMMUNITION

Air Guns & Supplies

Armsport Inc., 3950 NW 49th St., Miami, FL 33142: Free information ❖ Air rifles and pistols, scopes, pellets and bb ammunition, and targets. 305-635-7850.

Beeman Precision Arms Inc., 5454 Argosy Dr., Huntington Beach, CA 92649: Catalog $2 ❖ Air rifles and pistols, scopes, pellets and bb ammunition, and targets. 714-890-4800.

Benjamin/Sheridan Company, Rt. 5 & 20, East Bloomfield, NY 14443: Free catalog ❖ Single shot and repeater air rifles, pistols, scopes, pellets and bb ammunition, and targets. 716-657-6161.

Century International Arms, 48 Lower Newton St., St. Albans, VT 05478: Free information ❖ Air rifles and pistols. 802-527-1252.

Compasseco Inc., Bardstown, KY 40004: Free information ❖ Air rifles and ammunition. 800-726-1696.

Crosman Air Guns, Rt. 5 & 20, East Bloomfield, NY 14443: Free information ❖ Air rifles and pistols, scopes, pellets and bb ammunition, and targets. 800-7AIR-GUN.

Daisy Manufacturing Company Inc., P.O. Box 220, Rogers, AR 72757: Free information ❖ Air rifles and pistols, pellets and bb ammunition, scopes, and targets. 501-636-1200.

Dixie Gun Works Inc., P.O. Box 130, Union City, TN 38261: Catalog $5 ❖ Air rifles and pistols. 800-238-6785.

Mandall Shooting Supplies, 3616 N. Scottsdale Rd., Scottsdale, AZ 85251: Free information ❖ Air guns, scopes, other equipment, and ammunition. 602-945-2553.

Ammunition & Ammunition-Loading Equipment

Accurate Arms Company, Rt. 1, Box 167, McEwen, TN 37101: Free information ❖ Black powder cartridges.

ACTIV Industries Inc., 1000 Zigor Rd., P.O. Box 339, Kearneysville, WV 25430: Free brochure ❖ Shotgun shells in a reloadable all-plastic hull. 304-725-0451.

Alpine Range Supply, 5482 Shelby, Fort Worth, TX 76140: Free information ❖ Reloading equipment. 817-572-1242.

Badger Shooter's Supply Inc., 202 N. Harding, Owen, WI 54460: Free catalog ❖ Sporting firearms and ammunition. 800-424-9069.

Ballistic Products Inc., 20015 75th Ave. North, Corcoran, MN 55340: Catalog $1 ❖ Ammunition supplies. 612-494-9237.

Blount Inc., 605 Oro Dam Blvd., Oroville, CA 95965: Free information ❖ Big game hunting bullets and ammunition for rifles and handguns. 800-627-3640.

Buffalo Bullet Company, 12637 Los Nietos Rd., Unit A, Santa Fe Springs, CA 90670: Free brochure ❖ Bullets for muzzle-loaders and other ammunition. 310-944-0322.

Century International Arms, 48 Lower Newton St., St. Albans, VT 05478: Free information ❖ Ammunition supplies. 802-527-1252.

Cheap Shot, Ammo Discount Warehouse, 1797 Rt. 980, Canonsburg, PA 15317: Free catalog ❖ Ammunition. 412-745-2658.

Colorado Shooter's Supply, P.O. Box 132, Fruita, CO 81521: Catalog $2 ❖ Bullet molds. 303-858-9191.

Cook Bullets, 1846 Rosemeade Pkwy., Carrollton, TX 75007: Free information ❖ Ammunition supplies. 214-394-8725.

Dillon Precision Products Inc., 8009 E. Dillon's Way, Scottsdale, AZ 85260: Free catalog ❖ Reloading equipment. 800-223-4570; 602-948-8009 (in AZ).

Federal Cartridge Company, 900 Ehlen Dr., Anoka, MN 55303: Free information ❖ Ammunition supplies. 612-422-2840.

Gander Mountain Inc., P.O. Box 248, Gander Mountain, Wilmot, WI 53192: Free catalog ❖ Reloading supplies. 800-558-9410.

Graf & Sons, Rt. 3, Hwy. 54 South, Mexico, MO 65265: Free information ❖ Hunting accessories, scopes, and reloading equipment. 800-531-2666.

Art Green, 485 S. Robertson Blvd., Beverly Hills, CA 90211: Catalog $2 ❖ Bullet casting metals.

Robert W. Hart & Son Inc., 401 Montgomery St., Nescopeck, PA 18635: Free information ❖ Ammunition supplies. 717-752-3655.

Hercules Incorporated, Hercules Plaza, Wilmington, DE 19894: Free information ❖ Propellants for handguns, rifles, and shotguns.

HKS Products Inc., 7841 Foundation Dr., Florence, KY 41042: Free information ❖ Revolver and magazine speed loaders.

Hogdon Powder Company Inc., 6231 Robinson, Shawnee Mission, KS 66202: Free information ❖ Powder for muzzle-loaders, propellants for rifles and pistols, and shotgun ammunition. 913-362-9455.

Hornady Manufacturing Company, P.O. Box 1848, Grand Island, NE 68802: Catalog $2 ❖ Ammunition supplies. 308-382-1390.

K & T Company, Division T & S Industries Inc., 1027 Skyview Dr., West Carrollton, OH 45449: Free information ❖ Shell reloading equipment and supplies. 513-859-8414.

Lawrence Leather Company, P.O. Box 1479, Lillington, NC 27546: Free information ❖ Ammunition supplies. 910-893-2071.

Lee Precision Inc., 4275 Hwy. U, Hartford, CT 53027: Catalog $1 ❖ Reloading equipment and supplies. 414-673-3075.

Mayville Engineering Company Inc., 715 South St., Mayville, WI 53050: Free brochure ❖ Shotgun shell reloading equipment. 414-387-4500.

Michaels of Oregon Company, P.O. Box 13010, Portland, OR 97213: Free information ❖ Ammunition supplies. 503-255-6890.

Muzzleload Magnum Products, RR 6, Box 384, Harrison, AR 72601: Free list ❖ Bullets for black powder rifles. 501-741-5019.

Nosler Bullets Inc., P.O. Box 671, Bend, OR 97709: Free catalog ❖ Hunting bullets. 800-285-3701.

Ponsness/Warren, P.O. Box 8, Rathdrum, ID 83858: Free catalog ❖ Reloading equipment and supplies. 208-687-2231.

Precision Reloading Inc., P.O. Box 122, Stafford Springs, CT 06076: Free information ❖ Reloading components and accessories. 860-684-5680.

Rapine Bullet Manufacturing Company, 9501 Landis Ln., East Greenville, PA 18041: Catalog $2 ❖ Bullet molds. 215-679-5413.

Remington Arms Company Inc., 1007 Market St., Wilmington, DE 19898: Free information ❖ Ammunition supplies. 302-773-5291.

Speer Products, Blount Sporting Equipment Division, 2299 Snake River Ave., Lewiston, ID 83501: Free information ❖ Hunting bullets and other ammunition. 208-746-2351.

Widener's Reloading & Shooting Supply Inc., P.O. Box 3009, Johnson City, TN 37602: Free catalog ❖ Reloading supplies. 615-282-6786.

❖ GUNS & AMMUNITION ❖

Antique, Muzzle Loading & Replica Guns

Antique Arms Company, 1110 Cleveland, Monett, MO 65708: Free information ❖ Antique muzzle-loading guns. 417-235-6501.

Armoury Inc., Rt. 202, Box 2340, New Preston, CT 06777: Free information ❖ Black powder handguns and rifles, black powder, kits, and replica guns. 203-868-0001.

Armsport Inc., 3950 NW 49th St., Miami, FL 33142: Free information ❖ Antique handguns, rifles, and kits. 305-635-7850.

BSI Sporting Goods, P.O. Box 5010, Vienna, WV 26105: Free catalog ❖ Firearm and muzzle-loading supplies, optics, clothing, and archery, fishing, and hunting equipment. 304-295-8511.

Buffalo Arms Company, 3355 Upper Gold Creek, Sandpoint, ID 83864: Catalog $2 ❖ Black powder cartridge rifles, target barrels and sights, lead and tin, and other supplies. 208-263-6953.

Douglas R. Carlson, Antique American Firearms, P.O. Box 71035, Des Moines, IA 50325: Catalog $20 (annual subscription) ❖ Antique firearms. 515-224-6552.

Cash Manufacturing Company Inc., P.O. Box 130, Waunakee, WI 53507: Free catalog ❖ Muzzle-loading equipment. 608-849-5664.

Cimarron, P.O. Box 906, Fredericksburg, TX 78624: Free information ❖ Replica cowboy guns. 210-997-9090.

Collector's Armoury, 800 Slaters Ln., P.O. Box 59, Alexandria, VA 22313: Free catalog ❖ Replica and antique guns. 800-544-3456.

Connecticut Valley Arms Inc., 5988 Peachtree Corners East, Norcross, GA 30071: Catalog $3 ❖ Reproductions of Sam Colt's mid-1880 handguns, black powder handguns, rifles, and kits. 800-251-9412.

Daisy Manufacturing Company Inc., P.O. Box 220, Rogers, AR 72757: Free information ❖ Replica guns. 501-636-1200.

Dixie Gun Works Inc., P.O. Box 130, Union City, TN 38261: Catalog $5 ❖ Antique and replica black powder handguns and rifles. Also black powder. 800-238-6785.

EMF Company, 1900 E. Warner Ave., Santa Ana, CA 92705: Catalog $1 ❖ Replica United States Cavalry and artillery revolvers. 714-261-6611.

Euroarms of America Inc., 208 E. Piccadilly St., P.O. Box 3277, Winchester, VA 22601: Catalog $3 ❖ Black powder rifles and handguns, replica guns, and kits. 540-662-1863.

N. Flayderman & Company Inc., P.O. Box 2446, Fort Lauderdale, FL 33303: Catalog $10 ❖ Antique guns, swords, knives, and western, nautical, and military collectibles. 305-761-8855.

Golden Age Arms Company, 115 E. High St., Box 366, Ashley, OH 43003: Catalog $4 ❖ Muzzle-loading guns, parts, and books. 614-747-2488.

Hansen Cartridge Company, 244 Old Post Rd., Southport, CT 06490: Free information ❖ Replica and antique guns. 203-259-5424.

House of Muskets Inc., P.O. Box 4640, Pagosa Springs, CO 81157: Free list of retail sources ❖ Replica and antique guns. 303-731-2295.

Kahnke Gunworks, 206 W. 11th St., Redwood Falls, MN 56283: Free information ❖ Muzzle-loading handguns. 507-637-2901.

Log Cabin Shop, Box 275, Lodi, OH 44254: Catalog $5 ❖ Antique and replica guns and muzzle-loading supplies. 216-948-1082.

Lyman Products Corporation, Rt. 147, P.O. Box 453, Middlefield, CT 06455: Catalog $2 ❖ Black powder rifles and handguns. Also kits. 800-22-LYMAN.

Mountain State Muzzleloading Supplies Inc., Rt. 2, Box 154-1, Williamstown, WV 26187: Catalog $4 ❖ Black powder rifles, handguns. Also kits. 304-375-7842.

Mowrey Gun Works, P.O. Box 246, Waldron, IN 46182: Catalog $2 ❖ Handmade rifles, shotguns, and muzzle-loaders. 317-525-6181.

Muzzle Loaders Etcetera Inc., 9901 Lyndale Ave. South, Bloomington, MN 55420: Free information ❖ Black powder and muzzle-loading supplies. 612-884-1161.

Navy Arms Company, 689 Bergen Blvd., Ridgefield, NJ 07657: Catalog $2 ❖ Black powder rifles and handguns, replica guns, kits, and black powder. 201-945-2500.

October Country, P.O. Box 969, Hayden Lake, ID 83835: Catalog $3 (refundable) ❖ Muzzle-loading equipment. 208-772-2068.

Ogan Antiques Ltd., P.O. Box 14831, North Palm Beach, FL 33408: Catalog $10 ❖ Antique arms. 407-844-2434.

S & S Firearms, 74-11 Myrtle Ave., Glendale, NY 11385: Free information ❖ Antique guns. 212-497-1100.

Shiloh Rifle Manufacturing Company Inc., P.O. Box 279, Big Timber, MT 59011: Free information ❖ Black powder and muzzle-loading guns. 406-932-4454.

Simmons Gun Specialties Inc., 20241 W. 207th, Spring Hill, KS 66083: Free information ❖ Black powder rifles and handguns, kits, and black powder. 800-444-0220.

South Bend Replicas Inc., 61650 Oak Rd., South Bend, IN 46614: Catalog $7 ❖ Replica and antique guns. 219-289-4500.

Springfield Sporters Inc., RD 1, Penn Ruth, PA 15765: Catalog $2 ❖ Replica and antique guns. 412-254-2626.

Jim Supica, Old Town Station Ltd., P.O. Box 15351, Lenexa, KS 66285: Catalog $20 (4 issues) ❖ Antique guns. 913-492-3000.

Taylor's & Company Inc., 304 Lenoir Dr., Winchester, VA 22603: Catalog $3 ❖ Black powder guns and accessories.

Tennessee Valley Manufacturing, P.O. Box 1175, Corinth, MS 38834: Catalog $3 ❖ Custom rifles. 601-286-5014.

Thompson/Center Arms Company, P.O. Box 5002, Rochester, NH 03866: Free catalog ❖ Muzzle-loading rifles, handguns, kits, and black powder. 603-332-2394.

Traditions Inc., 500 Main St., P.O. Box 235, Deep River, CT 06417: Free information ❖ Black powder rifles and handguns, kits, and replica guns. 203-526-9555.

Uncle Mike's Muzzleloading, P.O. Box 13010, Portland, OR 97213: Catalog $2 ❖ Muzzle-loading accessories.

Warren Muzzle Loading Company Inc., Hwy. 21, P.O. Box 100, Ozone, AR 72854: Catalog $2 ❖ Pistol and rifle bullets and muzzle-loading supplies. 800-874-3810.

The Winchester Sutler Inc., 270 Shadow Brook Ln., Winchester, VA 22603: Catalog $4 ❖ Reproduction Civil War muskets and carbines. 703-888-3595.

Racks, Cases & Holsters

Bob Allen Sportswear, Box 477, Des Moines, IA 50302: Free catalog ❖ Carrying cases, holsters, and racks. 515-283-2191.

American Import Company, 1453 Mission St., San Francisco, CA 94103: Free information ❖ Gun racks, soft cases, and slings. 415-863-1506.

American Sales & Manufacturing, Box 677, Laredo, TX 78042: Catalog $3 ❖ Handcrafted gun belts and holsters. 512-723-6893.

American Security Products Company, 11925 Pacific Ave., Fontana, CA 92335: Free information ❖ Gun and other safes for home and office security. 800-421-6142.

Americase, Box 271, Waxahachie, TX 75165: Free information ❖ Carrying cases. 800-880-3629.

API Outdoors Inc., P.O. Box 1432, Tallulah, LA 71282: Free information ❖ Gun racks. 800-228-4846.

Beeman Precision Arms Inc., 5454 Argosy Dr., Huntington Beach, CA 92649: Catalog $2 ❖ Holsters, slings, and soft cases. 714-890-4800.

Bowhunter Supply Inc., 1158 46th St., P.O. Box 5010, Vienna, WV 26105: Free information ❖ Hard and soft cases and stands for gun storage. 800-289-2211; 304-295-8511 (in WV).

❖ GUNS & AMMUNITION ❖

Brauer Brothers Manufacturing Company, 2020 Delmar Blvd., St. Louis, MO 63112: Free information ❖ Soft cases, cabinets, slings, and holsters. 314-231-2864.

Browning Company, Dept. C006, One Browning Pl., Morgan, UT 84050: Catalog $2 ❖ Hard and soft cases, holsters, and slings. 800-333-3288.

Coronado Leather, 120 C Ave., Coronado, CA 92118: Free information ❖ Dual-ply leather holsters. 800-283-9509.

Vee Dennis Manufacturing Company, 620 Park Rd., Cherry Hill, NJ 08034: Free brochure ❖ Gun rests. 609-428-7676.

DeSantis Holster & Leather Company, P.O. Box 2039, New Hyde Park, NY 11040: Free information ❖ Gun holsters. 516-354-8000.

A.G. English Inc., 708 S. 12th St., Broken Arrow, OK 74012: Free information ❖ Gun safes. 800-222-7233.

Fort Knox Security Products, 1051 N. Industrial Park Rd., Orem, UT 84057: Free information ❖ Burglar-proof gun safes. 800-821-5216.

Hilsport by Hilco Inc., 2102 Fair Park Blvd., Harlingen, TX 78550: Free brochure ❖ Luggage and gun cases. 210-423-1885.

Don Hume Leathergoods, Box 351, Miami, OK 74355: Catalog $1 ❖ Holsters. 800-331-2686; 918-542-6604 (in OK).

Hunter Company Inc., 3300 W. 71st Ave., P.O. Box 467, Westminster, CO 80030: Catalog $1 ❖ Holsters, slings, scabbards, and other leather goods. 800-676-HUNT.

Liberty Safe, 1060 N. Spring Creek Place, Springville, UT 84663: Free brochure ❖ Gun safes. 800-247-5625.

Mosler Specialty Products, 2423 Rudolph Ave., Erie, PA 16502: Brochure $1 ❖ Engraved handgun cases with optional velvet lining and security locks. 814-454-2349.

National Security Safe Company, P.O. Box 39, American Fork, UT 84003: Free brochure ❖ Gun safes with double steel walls. 800-544-3829.

Penguin Industries Inc., Airport Industrial Mall, Coatesville, PA 19320: Free information ❖ Gun cases and cabinets. 215-384-6000.

Quality Arms Inc., Box 19477, Houston, TX 77224: Free information ❖ Gun cases. 713-870-8377.

Rhino Gun Cases Inc., 4960 SW 52nd St., Ste. 408, Davie, FL 33314: Free information ❖ Aluminum gun cases and ported chokes. 800-226-3613; 305-797-0600 (in FL).

Safariland Leather Products, 3120 E. Mission Blvd., P.O. Box 51478, Ontario, CA 91761: Free information ❖ Gun holsters. 800-347-1200.

Shooting Systems, 1075 Headquarters Park, Fenton, MO 63026: Free information ❖ Canvas carrying and gun storage cases, holsters, and slings. 800-325-3049; 314-343-3575 (in MO).

Southern Security Safes, 1700 Oak Hills Dr., Kingston, TN 37763: Free information ❖ Gun safes with protective bolt-locking systems. 800-251-9992.

Sun Welding Safe Company, 290 Easy St., Ste. 3, Simi Valley, CA 93065: Free brochure ❖ Gun safes. 800-776-1908.

Treadlok, 1764 Granby St. NE, Roanoke, VA 24012: Free catalog ❖ Safes for guns and valuables. 800-729-8732.

Versatile Rack Company, 5761 Anderson St., Vernon, CA 90058: Free brochure ❖ Portable gun racks and accessories. 213-588-0137.

Wild Bills Leather, P.O. Box 13037, Burton, WA 98013: Brochure $3 ❖ Authentic reproduction holsters, gun belts, and accessories. 206-463-5738.

Wilson Case Company, P.O. Box 1106, Hastings, NE 68902: Free information ❖ Gun cases. 800-322-5493.

Winchester Gun Safes, Melink Safe Company, 111 Security Pkwy., New Albany, IN 47150: Free catalog ❖ Gun safes. 800-505-7575.

Wolf Ears Equipment, 702 S. Pine St., Laramie, WY 82070: Catalog $2 ❖ Cartridge belts and boxes, United States prairie belts, and 1800s-style holsters. 307-745-7135.

Scopes, Mounts & Sights

Aimpoint, 580 Herndon Pkwy., Herndon, VA 22070: Free brochure ❖ Electronic red-dot sight with an optional 3x scope attachment. 703-471-6828.

American Import Company, 1453 Mission St., San Francisco, CA 94103: Free information ❖ Scopes, mounts, and storage racks. 415-863-1506.

B-Square Company, P.O. Box 11281, Fort Worth, TX 76110: Free catalog ❖ Scope mounts for handguns, rifles, and shotguns. 800-433-2909.

Ball Photo Supply Company, 85 Tunnel Rd., Asheville, NC 28805: Free information ❖ Telescopes, spotting scopes, camera equipment, binoculars, eyepieces, and accessories. 704-252-2443.

Bausch & Lomb, 9200 Cody, Overland Park, KS 66214: Free list of retail sources ❖ Spotting scopes, night vision viewers, and mounts. 800-423-3537.

Maynard P. Buehler, 17 Orinda Way, Orinda, CA 94563: Free catalog ❖ Mounting bases and rings for rifle and handgun scopes. 510-254-3201.

Burris Company Inc., P.O. Box 1747, Greeley, CO 80632: Free catalog ❖ Mounts and spotting scopes. 303-356-1670.

Camera Bug Ltd., 1799 Briarcliff Rd., Atlanta, GA 3030: Free information ❖ Telescopes, binoculars, spotting scopes, and accessories. 404-873-4513.

Conetrol Scope Mounts, 10225 Hwy. 123 South, Sequin, TX 78155: Free information ❖ Scope mounting systems. 800-CONETROL.

Decker Enterprises, P.O. Box 310, Thurston, OR 97482: Free brochure ❖ Night vision rifle scope. 503-942-5649.

Europtik Ltd., P.O. Box 319, Dunmore, PA 18509: Free information ❖ Binoculars and rifle scopes. 717-347-6049.

Keng's Firearms Specialty Inc., 875 Wharton Dr. SW, Atlanta, GA 30336: Free information ❖ Scope mounts. 800-848-4671.

Kowa Optimed Inc., 20001 S. Vermont Ave., Torrance, CA 90502: Free information ❖ Spotting scopes. 800-966-5692.

Leupold & Stevens Inc., P.O. Box 688, Beaverton, OR 97075: Free list of retail sources ❖ Low-light rifle scope with variable power settings. 503-526-1491.

Millett Industries, 16131 Gothard St., Huntington Beach, CA 92647: Catalog $1 ❖ Gun sights. 800-645-5388.

Redfield Company, 5800 E. Jewell Ave., Denver, CO 80224: Catalog $2 ❖ Rifle scopes. 303-757-6411.

Simmons Outdoor Company, 2120 Killearney Way, Tallahassee, FL 32308: Catalog $2 ❖ Rifle scopes. 904-878-5100.

Tasco Sales Inc., P.O. Box 520080, Miami, FL 33152: Free information ❖ Gun scopes. 305-591-3670.

Visiontek, 1200 Industrial Rd., #17, San Carlos, CA 94070: Free catalog ❖ Gun scopes, monoculars, binoculars, and other optics. 800-780-7022; 415-508-4460 (in CA).

Warne Manufacturing Company, 9039 SE Jannsen Rd., Clackamas, OR 97015: Free information ❖ Easy-to-install detachable rifle scope mounts. 503-657-5590.

Williams Gun Sight Company, 7389 Lapeer Rd., P.O. Box 329, Davison, MI 48423: Free information ❖ Scope mounts for rifles, shotguns, and black powder guns. 800-530-9028.

Sportshooting Rifles, Handguns & Shotguns

American Derringer Corporation, 127 N. Lacy Dr., Waco, TX 76705: Free information ❖ Sport-shooting automatic pistols, derringers, and revolvers.

GUNS & AMMUNITION

Armoury Inc., Rt. 202, Box 2340, New Preston, CT 06777: Free information ❖ Guns for sport-shooting. 203-868-0001.

Badger Shooter's Supply Inc., 202 N. Harding, Owen, WI 54460: Free catalog ❖ Sporting firearms and ammunition. 800-424-9069.

Beretta U.S.A., 17601 Beretta Dr., Accokeek, MD 20607: Free information ❖ Shotguns and other guns. 800-528-7453.

Billingsley & Brownell Rifle Metalsmith, Box 25, Dayton, WY 82836: Brochure $2 ❖ Rifle accessories. 307-655-9344.

Brownells Inc., 200 S. Front St., Montezuma, IA 50171: Free catalog ❖ Gunsmithing supplies and tools. 515-623-5401.

Browning Company, Dept. C006, One Browning Pl., Morgan, UT 84050: Catalog $2 ❖ Bolt-and-lever action guns, semi-automatics and single shot rifles, and over and under, side-by-side, and single barrel shotguns. 800-333-3288.

Century International Arms, 48 Lower Newton St., St. Albans, VT 05478: Free information ❖ Bolt-and-lever action guns, semi-automatic rifles, and single shot rifles. 802-527-1252.

Clark Custom Guns Inc., 11462 Keatchie Rd., P.O. Box 530, Keithville, LA 71047: Catalog $1 ❖ Handguns. 318-925-0836.

Douglas Barrels Inc., 5504 Big Tyler Rd., Charleston, WV 25313: Free information ❖ Rifle barrels. 304-776-1341.

Dunns, P.O. Box 449, Grand Junction, TN 38039: Free catalog ❖ Camouflage and insulated clothing, outerwear, shoes and boots, hunting equipment, day packs and belt packs, gun care kits, sunglasses, game calls, decoys, and supplies. 800-223-8667.

Eagle Arms Inc., 128 E. 23rd Ave., Coal Valley, IL 61240: Free information ❖ Parts and complete rifles. 309-799-5619.

EMF Company, 1900 E. Warner Ave., Santa Ana, CA 92705: Catalog $1 ❖ United States and foreign revolvers, rifles, pistols, and shotguns. 714-261-6611.

Frank's Center Inc., P.O. Box 530, Nevada, MO 64772: Catalog $2 ❖ Sportshooting guns and backpacking, camping, and rescue/rappelling equipment. 417-667-9190.

Gun Parts Corporation, Williams Ln., West Hurley, NY 12491: Catalog $7.95 ❖ Commercial, military, antique, and foreign gun parts. 914-679-2417.

Gil Hebard Guns, 125-129 Public Square, Knoxville, IL 61448: Free catalog ❖ Pistols. 309-289-2700.

Hi-Grade Shooter's Supply, Box 448, Jacktown, Irwin, PA 15642: Free information ❖ Guns and accessories. 800-245-6824; 412-863-8200 (in AK & HI).

Interarms, 10 Prince St., Alexandria, VA 22314: Catalog $2 ❖ Bolt-and-lever action, target, semi-automatic, and single shot rifles. 703-548-1400.

Harry Lawson Company, 3328 N. Richey Blvd., Tucson, AZ 85716: Catalog $1 ❖ Rifles. 520-326-1117.

Liberty Mountain Sports, 9325 SW Barber St., Wilsonville, OR 97070: Free information ❖ Automatic and blank pistols, derringers, revolvers and auto-loading, automatic, over and under, semi-automatic, side-by-side, and single barrel shotguns. 503-685-9600.

Marlin Firearms Company, P.O. Box 248, North Haven CT 06473: Catalog $1 ❖ Semi-automatic, single shot, and bolt-and-lever action rifles. 203-239-5621.

Midway Arms Inc., 5875 W. Van Horn Tavern Rd., Columbia, MO 65203: Free catalog ❖ Handguns, rifles, and ammunition. 800-243-3220.

O.F. Mossberg & Sons Inc., 7 Grasso Ave., North Haven, CT 06473: Free information ❖ Shotguns. 203-288-6491.

Mowrey Gun Works, P.O. Box 246, Waldron, IN 46182: Catalog $2 ❖ Handmade rifles, shotguns, and muzzle-loaders. 317-525-6181.

Murray's Gunshop Inc., 14720 NE Sandy Blvd., Portland, OR 97230: Free information ❖ Custom gun stocks and gun smithing and blueing supplies. 800-459-3503.

Navy Arms Company, 689 Bergen Blvd., Ridgefield, NJ 07657: Catalog $2 ❖ Automatic pistols, blank guns, revolvers, and target, bolt-and-lever action, semi-automatic, and single shot rifles. 201-945-2500.

Pachmayr Ltd., 831 N. Rosemead Blvd., South El Monte, CA 91733: Free catalog ❖ Shooting and hunting accessories, other guns, clay-target shooting equipment, and supplies. 800-350-7408.

Perazzi USA Inc., 1207 S. Shamrock Ave., Monrovia, CA 91016: Free information ❖ Combination, single, sporting, skeet, and trap shotguns. 818-303-0068.

Precision Sales International, Box 1776, Westfield, MA 01086: Free information ❖ Firearms. 413-562-5055.

Remington Arms Company Inc., 1007 Market St., Wilmington, DE 19898: Free information ❖ Auto-loading, automatic, over and under, and semi-automatic shotguns. 302-773-5291.

Rig Products, 87 Coney Island Dr., Sparks, NV 89431: Free catalog ❖ Rifle and shotgun kits and supplies. 702-331-5666.

Savage Arms, 100 Springdale Rd., Westfield, MA 01085: Free information ❖ Sporting firearms for deer hunting. 413-568-7001.

Sherwood, 14830 Alondra Blvd., La Mirada, CA 90638: Free information ❖ Parts for guns. 800-962-3203.

Shooters Emporium, 606 SE 162nd, Portland, OR 97233: Free information ❖ Custom stocks. 800-323-7940.

Simmons Gun Specialties Inc., 20241 W. 207th, Spring Hill, KS 66083: Free information ❖ Automatic pistols, revolvers, derringers, and target, bolt-and-lever action, semi-automatic, and single shot rifles. 800-444-0220.

Smith & Wesson, 2100 Roosevelt Ave., Springfield, MA 01102: Free information ❖ Firearms. 413-781-8300.

Southwest Shooter's Supply, P.O. Box 9987, Phoenix, AZ 85068: Free information ❖ Guns and accessories. 602-943-8595.

Springfield Armory, 420 W. Main St., Geneseo, IL 61254: Catalog $3 ❖ Pistols, handguns, and rifles. 309-944-5631.

Sturm, Ruger & Company Inc., 198 Lacey Pl., Southport, CT 06490: Free catalog ❖ Semi-automatic and single shot, bolt-and-lever action, and target rifles. 203-259-7843.

Tar-Hunt Rifles Inc., RR 3, Box 572, Bloomsburg, PA 17815: Free information ❖ Left and right-handed sport-shooting slug guns. 717-784-6368.

Ultra Light Arms Inc., P.O. Box 1270, Granville, WV 26534: Free information ❖ Sporting firearms for deer hunting. 304-599-5687.

U.S. Repeating Arms Company, 275 Winchester Ave., New Haven, CT 06511: Free information ❖ Firearms. 203-789-5000.

Weatherby Inc., 3100 El Camino Real, Atascadero, CA 93422: Free information ❖ Sporting firearms.

Targets & Range Supplies

Beeman Precision Arms Inc., 5454 Argosy Dr., Huntington Beach, CA 92649: Catalog $2 ❖ Targets and range equipment. 714-890-4800.

Birchwood Laboratories Inc., 7900 Fuller Rd., Eden Prairie, MN 55344: Free catalog ❖ Spinning, swinging, and action targets. 800-328-6156.

Caswell International Corporation, 1221 Marshall St. NE, Minneapolis, MN 55413: Free information ❖ Range supplies and target carriers. 612-379-2000.

Crosman Air Guns, Rt. 5 & 20, East Bloomfield, NY 14443: Free information ❖ Targets and range equipment. 800-7AIR-GUN.

Daisy Manufacturing Company Inc., P.O. Box 220, Rogers, AR 72757: Free information ❖ Targets and range equipment. 501-636-1200.

Marksman Products, 5482 Argosy Dr., Huntington Beach, CA 92649: Free information ❖ Targets and range equipment. 714-898-7535.

National Target Company, 4690 Wyaconda Rd., Rockville, MD 20852: Free information ❖ Targets and range equipment. 301-770-7060.

NRA Sales Department, P.O. Box 5000, Kearneysville, WV 25430: Free information ❖ Life-size game targets.

Outers Laboratories Inc., Division Blount Inc., Rt. 2, Onalaska, WI 54650: Free information ❖ Targets and range equipment. 608-781-5800.

Peterson Instant Targets Inc., 147 West St., Middlefield, CT 06801: Free information ❖ Targets. 203-349-3421.

Trap & Clay Target Shooting

Ballistic Products Inc., 20015 75th Ave. North, Corcoran, MN 55340: Catalog $1 ❖ Targets and traps. 612-494-9237.

Beeman Precision Arms Inc., 5454 Argosy Dr., Huntington Beach, CA 92649: Catalog $2 ❖ Targets and traps. 714-890-4800.

Briley, 1230 Lumpkin, Houston, TX 77043: Free information ❖ Replacement chokes. 800-331-5718; 713-932-6995 (in TX).

Gamaliel Shooting Supply Inc., 1525 Ft. Run Rd., P.O. Box 156, Gamaliel, KY 42140: Free information ❖ Shooting supplies. 502-457-2825.

The Hunters Pointe, 14264 SW 50th St., Benton, KS 67017: Free information ❖ Manual and automatic traps for clay targets. 316-778-1122.

Ibis Target Products, 8267 N. Revere, Kansas City, MO 64151: Free information ❖ Clay target traps. 816-587-9540.

Kolar, 1925 Roosevelt Ave., Racine, WI 53406: Free information ❖ Small gauge sporting clays and shooting supplies. 414-554-0800.

Midwest Sales, 16036 East O Ave., Climax, MI 49034: Free information ❖ Automatic trap machines. 616-746-4868.

Monterey Sporting Clays, 2726 134th St., Hopkins, MI 49328: Free information ❖ Lightweight hand-manageable sporting clays. 616-793-7400.

Omark Industries, Blount Sporting Equipment Division, 2299 Snake River Ave., Lewiston, ID 83501: Free information ❖ Launchers, traps, and targets. 208-746-2351.

Rhino Gun Cases Inc., 4960 SW 52nd St., Ste. 408, Davie, FL 33314: Free information ❖ Aluminum gun cases and ported chokes. 800-226-3613; 305-797-0600 (in FL).

Shydas Shoe & Clothing Barn, 1535 S. Lincoln Ave., Lebanon, PA 17042: Free catalog ❖ Clay pigeon traps and trap shooting equipment. 717-274-2551.

Simmons Gun Specialties Inc., 20241 W. 207th, Spring Hill, KS 66083: Free information ❖ Traps, launchers, and targets. 800-444-0220.

Trius Inc., P.O. Box 25, Cleves, OH 45002: Free catalog ❖ Portable traps and range equipment. 513-941-5682.

Wings & Clays, P.O. Box 410, Birmingham, MI 48012: Free information ❖ Shotguns, clothing, and accessories.

GYMNASTICS

Ballet Etc., 106 W. Main St., Mechanicsburg, PA 17055: Free information ❖ Dance and gymnastic wear, shoes, and clothing for ice skaters. 800-DANCE-25.

Flaghouse, 150 N. MacQuesten Pkwy., Mt. Vernon, NY 10550: Free catalog ❖ Gymnastics equipment. 800-793-7900.

Miquelito's Dancewear, 7315 San Pedro Ave., San Antonio, TX 78216: Free information ❖ Ballet shoes, flamenco boots, and gymnastic wear. 210-349-2573.

J.C. Penney Company Inc., Catalog Division, Atlanta, GA 30390: Free information ❖ Athletic clothing and gymnastic equipment. 800-222-6161.

HAMMOCKS & SWINGS

Adirondack Store & Gallery, 109 Saranac Ave., Lake Placid, NY 12946: Free information ❖ Oak and maple porch swings, lawn furniture, and picnic table sets. 518-523-2646.

Brushy Mountain Bee Farm, Rt. 1, P.O. Box 135, Moravian Falls, NC 28654: Free catalog ❖ Porch swings, birdhouses and feeders, and beekeeping supplies. 800-BEESWAX.

Country Casual, 17317 Germantown Rd., Germantown, MD 20874: Catalog $3 ❖ Porch swings and classic British-style solid teak garden seats. 301-540-0040.

Denyll Enterprises, P.O. Box 199, Pembina, ND 58271: Information $2 ❖ Old-fashioned cedar garden swings, porch and platform glider swings, and indoor/outdoor glider chairs. 800-255-7119.

Gardner's Farm & Wood Products, HCR 01, Box 1193, Eagle Rock, MO 65641: Free information ❖ Country-style rockers, tables, swings, and other furniture. 417-271-3999.

Gazebo & Porchworks, 728 9th Ave. SW, Puyallup, WA 98371: Catalog $2 ❖ Outdoor swings and backyard play structures. 206-848-0502.

Grand ERA Reproductions, P.O. Box 1026, Lapeer, MI 48446: Catalog $2 ❖ Porch swings. 810-664-1756.

Green Enterprises, 43 S. Rogers St., Hamilton, VA 22068: Brochure $1 ❖ Swings, gliders, tables, and benches. 703-338-3606.

Hammock Etc., 1458 Ocean Shore Blvd., Ormond Beach, FL 32176: Free brochure ❖ Hammocks. 904-441-4832.

Hangouts Handwoven Hammocks, 1328 Pearl St., Boulder, CO 80302: Free brochure ❖ Hand-woven hammocks. 800-426-4688.

Lazy Day Hammocks, 6832 Countrywood Ln., Wendell, NC 27591: Free brochure ❖ Hand-woven cotton rope hammocks, chairs, and swings. 919-266-2819.

Mast General Store, Hwy. 194, Valle Crucis, NC 28691: Free information ❖ Hammocks and porch swings, housewares, boots, and clothing. 704-963-6511.

Mel-Nor Industries, 303 Gulf Bank, Houston, TX 77037: Information $1 ❖ Hanging lawn and porch swings, park benches, and old-time lamp posts. 713-445-3485.

O'Connor's Cypress Woodworks, 1259 Lions Club Rd., Scott, LA 70583: Brochure $2 ❖ Porch swings. 800-786-1051.

Quality Swings Inc., P.O. Box 813, State College, PA 16801: Free information ❖ Easy-to-assemble wooden swing kits. 800-952-6713.

Sun Designs, 173 E. Wisconsin Ave., Oconomowoc, WI 53066: Plan book $9.95 plus $3.95 postage ❖ Plans for gazebos, bridges, doghouses, arbors, lawn furniture, swings, outdoor play structures, and birdhouses. 414-567-4255.

Thaxted Cottage, Gardener, 121 Driscoll Way, Gaithersburg, MD 20878: Catalog $2 ❖ Redwood cottage with trellis sides and built-in seat, Amish-style wheelbarrows, and porch swings. 301-330-6211.

Marion Travis, P.O. Box 1041, Statesville, NC 28677: Catalog $1 ❖ Wooden porch swings. 704-528-4424.

Twin Oaks Hammocks, 138 Twin Oaks Rd., Louisa, VA 23093: Free catalog ❖ Hammocks and handcrafted hanging and standing chairs in oak and rope, plus hammock accessories. 800-688-8946.

Unique Simplicities, 93 Anderson Rd., Gardiner, NY 12525: Free catalog ❖ Easy-to-install hammocks. 800-845-1119.

Walpole Woodworkers, 767 East St., Walpole, MA 02081: Catalog $6 ❖ Porch and covered swings, swing sets for children, chairs, tables, and picnic table sets. 800-343-6948.

HANDBALL

Adidas USA, 5675 N. Blackstock Rd., Spartanburg, SC 29303: Free list of retail sources ❖ Balls. 800-423-4327.

Baden Sports Inc., 34114 21st Ave. South, Federal Way, WA 98003: Free information ❖ Balls. 800-544-2998; 206-925-0500 (in WA).

Canstar Sports, 50 Jonergin Dr., Swanton, VT 05448: Free list of retail sources ❖ Balls and eye guards. 800-362-3146; 802-868-2711 (in VT).

Ektelon, Prince Sports Group, 1 Sportsystem Plaza, Bordentown, NJ 08505: Free information ❖ Eye guards and gloves. 800-283-2635.

Professional Gym Inc., P.O. Box 188, Marshall, MO 65340: Free brochure ❖ Eye guards. 800-821-7665.

Spalding Sports Worldwide, 425 Meadow St., P.O. Box 901, Chicopee, MA 01021: Free list of retail sources ❖ Balls. 800-225-6601.

Unique Sports Products Inc., 840 McFarland Rd., Alpharetta, GA 30201: Free information ❖ Eye guards and gloves. 800-554-3707; 404-442-1977 (in GA).

Wa-Mac Inc., Highskore Products Inc., P.O. Box 128, Carlstadt, NJ 07410: Free information ❖ Balls and gloves. 800-447-5673; 201-438-7200 (in NJ).

HARDWARE

A & H Brass & Supply, 126 W. Main St., Johnson City, TN 37604: Catalog $1 ❖ Restoration furniture hardware. 800-638-4252; 615-928-8220 (in TN).

Acorn Manufacturing Company Inc., 457 School St., P.O. Box 31, Mansfield, MA 02048: Catalog $6 (request list of retail sources) ❖ Reproduction colonial hardware, sconces, hurricane lamps, fireplace tools, and bathroom accessories. 800-835-0121; 508-339-4500 (in MA).

American Home Supply, 191 Lost Lake Ln., Campbell, CA 95009: Catalog $2 ❖ Victorian and contemporary-style knobs, cabinet hardware and locks, faucets and bathroom hardware, grills and registers, and restoration items. 408-246-1962.

Antique Brass Works, 290 Port Richmond Ave., Staten Island, NY 10302: Free brochure ❖ Restored brass, hardware, and other metal fixtures. 718-273-6030.

Antique Hardware & Home, 7930 Easton Rd., Rt. 6121, Kintnersville, PA 18930: Free catalog ❖ Old-style hardware. 800-422-9982.

Antique Hardware Store, 1 Matthews Ct., Hilton Head Island, SC 29926: Catalog $3 ❖ Antique hardware, pedestal sinks, faucets, high tank toilets, cabinet hardware, weather vanes, brass bar rails, and tin and wooden chandeliers. 800-422-9982.

Antique Trunk Supply Company, 3706 W. 169th St., Cleveland, OH 44111: Catalog $1 ❖ Trunk repair parts. 216-941-8618.

Architectural Products by Outwater, 52 Passaic St., P.O. Box 347, Wood Ridge, NJ 07075: Free catalog ❖ Hardware, columns, millwork, moldings, and other decorative materials. 800-835-4403.

Armor Products, P.O. Box 445, East Northport, NY 11731: Free catalog ❖ Hardware, lamp parts, wood turnings and parts for toys and crafts, and replacement movements for mantel, banjo, and grandfather clocks. 800-292-8296.

Baldwin Hardware Corporation, P.O. Box 15048, Reading, PA 19612: Bathroom accessories brochure 75¢, lighting fixtures brochure $3, door hardware brochure 75¢, hardware brochure 75¢ ❖ Brass dead bolts and door hardware, bathroom accessories, and lighting fixtures. 800-346-5128.

Ball & Ball, 463 W. Lincoln Hwy., Exton, PA 19341: Catalog $7 (refundable) ❖ Brass and wrought-iron reproductions of American hardware, from 1680 to 1900. 610-363-7330.

Bathroom Machineries, 495 Main St., P.O. Box 1020, Murphys, CA 95247: Catalog $3 ❖ Solid brass reproduction Victorian door and cabinet hardware. 209-728-2031.

Beech River Mill Company, Old Rt. 16, Box 236, Centre Ossipee, NH 03814: Brochure $5 ❖ Custom-louvered and paneled products. Also period shutter and blind hardware. 603-539-2636.

Blaine Hardware International, 17319 Blaine Dr., Hagerstown, MD 21740: Free catalog ❖ Grab bars and other assistive aids for people with disabilities. Also replacement hardware for doors, screens, and windows. 800-678-1919.

Bona Decorative Hardware, 3073 Madison Rd., Cincinnati, OH 45209: Price list $2 ❖ Solid brass hardware for bathrooms, doors, cabinets, furniture, kitchens, and fireplaces. 513-321-7877.

Brass Menagerie, 524 St. Louis St., New Orleans, LA 70130: Free information with long SASE (specify items wanted) ❖ Hardware, fixtures, and plumbing. 504-524-0921.

The Broadway Collection, 1010 W. Santa Fe, Olathe, KS 66061: Free list of retail sources ❖ Plumbing fittings, brass bowls and bar sinks, grab bars, switch plates, and cabinet hardware. 800-766-1966.

By-Gone Days Antiques Inc., 3100 South Blvd., Charlotte, NC 28209: Free information ❖ Mantels, restored door hardware, and architectural antiques. 704-527-8717.

Camelot Enterprises, Box 65, Bristol, WI 53104: Catalog $2 (refundable) ❖ Bolts, screws, and tools. 414-857-2695.

A Carolina Craftsman, 975 S. Avacado St., Anaheim, CA 92805: Catalog $5 (refundable) ❖ Antique solid brass replacement hardware for houses and furniture. 714-776-7877.

Cirecast Inc., 380 7th St., San Francisco, CA 94103: Brochure $2.50 ❖ Reproduction and custom decorative and functional hardware. 415-863-8319.

Clement Hardware, 500 Ritchie Hwy., Severna Park, MD 21146: Free information ❖ Designer hardware. 410-647-4511.

The Coldren Company, 100 Race St., P.O. Box 668, North East, MD 21901: Catalog $3 ❖ Reproduction 18th and 19th-century hardware. 410-287-2082.

Colonial Bronze Company, P.O. Box 207, Torrington, CT 06790: Free list of retail sources ❖ Brass hardware. 203-489-9233.

Constantine, 2050 Eastchester Rd., Bronx, NY 10461: Catalog $1 ❖ Cabinet and furniture wood, hardware, veneers, plans and how-to books, carving tools and chisels, and inlay designs. 800-223-8087; 718-792-1600 (in NY).

Craftsmen in Wood, 5441 W. Hadley St., Phoenix, AZ 85043: Catalog $8 ❖ Door pulls, levers, knobs, and cabinet hardware. 602-278-8054.

Crown City Hardware, 1047 N. Allen Ave., Pasadena, CA 91104: Catalog $6.50 ❖ Restoration and decorative hardware. 818-794-1188.

Designer's HardWarehouse, P.O. Box 484, Wickliffe, OH 44092: Free brochure ❖ Door, cabinet, and bathroom hardware. Also solid brass faucets. 216-944-8800.

Dimestore Cowboys, 614 2nd St. SW, Albuquerque, NM 87102: Catalog $7 ❖ Door sets, cabinet pulls, shutters, bathroom accessories, curtain rods and rings, and handcrafted hardware. 505-244-1493.

Ed Donaldson Hardware Reproductions, P.O. Box 38, Boiling Springs, PA 17077: Catalog $3 ❖ Restoration hardware. 717-249-3624.

Downing Hardware, 103 N. Texas, DeLeon, TX 76444: Catalog $3 ❖ Antique hardware reproductions. 817-893-3863.

18th Century Hardware Company, 131 E. 3rd St., Derry, PA 15627: Catalog $3 ❖ Early American and Victorian-style hardware in black iron, porcelain, and brass. 412-694-2708.

Equiparts, 817 Main St., Pittsburgh, PA 15215: Free information ❖ Vintage plumbing, heating, and electrical parts. 800-442-6622.

Eugenia's Place, 5370-5272 Peachtree Rd., Chamblee, GA 30341: Catalog $1 ❖ Hard-to-find antique hardware. 800-337-1677; 770-458-1677 (in GA).

Faneuil Furniture Hardware Company Inc., 163 Main St., Salem, NH 03079: Catalog $5 ❖ Reproduction brass hardware for cabinets and furniture. 603-898-7733.

Charolette Ford Trunks, P.O. Box 536, Spearman, TX 79081: Catalog $3.50 ❖ Supplies and tools for restoring trunks. 806-659-3027.

GRANTCO, 349 Peel St., New Hamburg, Ontario, Canada N0B 2G0: Free brochure ❖ Reproduction Victorian window and door hardware. 519-662-2892.

Hardware Plus, 701 E. Kingsley Rd., Garland, TX 75041: Catalog $5 ❖ Period and restoration colonial, Victorian, nouveau, and decorative hardware. 800-522-7336.

Horton Brasses, Nooks Hill Rd., P.O. Box 120, Cromwell, CT 06416: Catalog $4 ❖ Reproduction Chippendale, Queen Anne, Hepplewhite, Sheraton, Victorian, and early 1900s knobs, drawer pulls, and hardware. 203-635-4400.

Kayne & Son Custom Hardware, 100 Daniel Ridge Rd., Candler, NC 28715: Catalog $4.50 ❖ Fireplace tools and hand-forged hardware. 704-667-8868.

Phyllis Kennedy Restoration Hardware, 9256 Holyoke Ct., Indianapolis, IN 46268: Catalog $3 ❖ Antique trunk hardware and supplies. 317-872-6366.

Klockit, P.O. Box 636, Lake Geneva, WI 53147: Free catalog ❖ Hardware, Swiss music box movements, clock-building components, and music box and clock kits. 800-556-2548.

Liz's Antique Hardware, 453 S. La Brea, Los Angeles, CA 90036: Catalog $5 ❖ Vintage and contemporary hardware. 800-939-9003.

Meisel Hardware Specialties, P.O. Box 70, Mound, MN 55364: Catalog $2 ❖ Hardware, wooden parts, and plans for musical door harps. 800-441-9870.

Merit Metal Products Corporation, 240 Valley Rd., Warrington, PA 18976: Catalog $10 ❖ Brass locks, hinges, and other hardware for doors, furniture, and cabinets. 215-343-2500.

Nexton Industries Inc., 51 S. 1st St., Brooklyn, NY 11211: Free information ❖ Brass hardware and bath accessories. 718-599-3837.

Old Smithy Shop, 195 Rt. 13, Brookline, NH 03055: Catalog $3 ❖ Hand-forged reproduction Colonial hardware and fireplace accessories. 603-672-4113.

Omnia, Box 330, Cedar Grove, NJ 07009: Free list of retail sources ❖ Lock sets and architectural hardware. 201-239-7272.

Paxton Hardware Ltd., P.O. Box 256, Upper Falls, MD 21156: Catalog $4 ❖ Cabinet hardware and hinges. 410-592-8505.

Remodelers & Renovators Supplies, P.O. Box 45478, Boise, ID 83711: Catalog $3 ❖ Vintage hardware and plumbing fixtures. 800-456-2135.

The Renovator's Supply, P.O. Box 2515, Conway, NH 03818: Free catalog ❖ Old-style hardware, plumbing, fixtures, and accessories. 800-659-0203.

The Restoration Place, 305 20th St., Rock Island, IL 61201: Free brochure ❖ Plumbing, hardware, architectural accessories, and fixtures. 309-786-0004.

Restoration Works Inc., P.O. Box 486, Buffalo, NY 14205: Catalog $3 ❖ Hardware, ceiling medallions and trims, plumbing fixtures, and bathroom accessories. 716-856-6400.

Wm. J. Rigby Company, 73 Elm St., Cooperstown, NY 13326: Catalog $7 ❖ Antique hardware. 607-547-1900.

Schlage Locks, Residential Marketing, 2401 Bayshore Blvd., San Francisco, CA 94134: Free information ❖ Door locks. 415-330-5600.

Southwest Door Company, 219 N. 3rd Ave., Tucson, AZ 85705: Free list of retail sources ❖ Traditional, contemporary, and country-style doors, windows, hardware, cabinets, and flooring. 602-624-1434.

Stock Drive Products, 2101 Jeritho Tnpk., New Hyde Park, NY 11042: Catalog $5.95 ❖ Hardware in inches and metric sizes. 516-328-0200.

Garrett Wade Company, 161 6th Ave., New York, NY 10013: Catalog $4 ❖ English-made solid brass hardware with many patterns similar to those of 100 years ago. 800-221-2942.

Wayne's Woods Inc., 39 N. Plains Industrial Rd., Wallingford, CT 06492: Catalog $2 (refundable) ❖ Refinishing supplies and brass and wooden reproduction hardware. 800-793-6208.

Williamsburg Blacksmiths Inc., P.O. Box 1776, Williamsburg, MA 01096: Catalog $5 ❖ Reproduction Early American hardware and wrought-iron furniture. 800-248-1776.

Windy Hill Forge, 3824 Schroeder Ave., Perry Hall, MD 21128: Catalog $3 (refundable) ❖ Custom-made and restored hardware. 410-256-5890.

Wise Company, 6503 St. Claude Ave., P.O. Box 118, Arabi, LA 70032: Catalog $4 ❖ Antique restoration materials, hardware, and furniture refinishing supplies. 504-277-7551.

Woodbury Blacksmith & Forge Company, P.O. Box 268, Woodbury, CT 06798: Catalog $3 ❖ Hand-forged Early American wrought-iron hardware. 203-263-5737.

Woodworker's Emporium, 4320 W. Bell Dr., Las Vegas, NV 89118: Catalog $3 ❖ Polished iron and brass pull knobs and keyholes. 800-779-7458.

Woodworker's Hardware, P.O. Box 180, Sauk Rapids, MN 56379: Catalog $3 ❖ Cabinet and furniture hardware. 800-383-0130.

The Woodworkers' Store, 21801 Industrial Blvd., Rogers, MN 55374: Free catalog ❖ Hardware and woodworking supplies. 800-403-9736.

HARMONICAS

Harmonica Music Publishing, P.O. Box 2101, Huntington Beach, CA 92647: Free information ❖ Harmonicas, books, videos, audio cassettes, and instructional tapes. 800-950-7664.

Kevins Harps, 210 Farnsworth Ave., Bordentown, NJ 08505: Catalog $2 ❖ Harmonicas and how-to video and cassette tape lessons. 800-274-2776; 609-298-2202 (in NJ).

Klutz Press, 2121 Staunton Ct., Palo Alto, CA 94306: Free information ❖ Harmonicas and how-to books. 415-424-0739.

Lee Oskar Harmonicas, P.O. Box 93155, Pasadena, CA 91109: Free information ❖ Harmonicas. 818-441-8874.

HATS

Az-Tex Hat Company, 15044 N. Cave Creek Rd., Phoenix, AZ 85032: Free brochure ❖ Traditionally styled hats with an American southwest style. 800-972-2095.

Back at the Ranch, 235 Don Gaspar, Santa Fe, NM 87501: Free information ❖ Vintage western clothing, boots, and hats. 505-989-8110.

BC Hats, P.O. Box 602, St. Augustine, FL 32085: Free information ❖ Western-style leather hats from Australia. Also straw, canvas, felt, and oilskin hats. 800-922-4288; 904-794-2008 (in FL).

Caledonia Hats, 300 Chestnut Hill Rd., Stevens, PA 17578: Free information ❖ Western-style hats. 800-338-2410.

Custom Cowboy Shop, 321 N. Main, Sheridan, WY 82801: Free information ❖ Cowboy hats. 800-487-2692.

D Bar J Hat Company, 3873 Spring Mt. Rd., Las Vegas, NV 89102: Free information ❖ Handmade hats. 800-654-1137; 702-362-4287 (in NV).

D.L. Designs, P.O. Box 27034, Los Angeles, CA 90027: Free catalog ❖ Men and women's hat patterns for costumes from the past. Also bridal headpieces and contemporary fashions.

The Hat Store, 5587 Richmond, Houston, TX 77056: Catalog $2 ❖ Western-style hats. 713-780-2480.

❖ HEALTH CARE SUPPLIES & AIDS ❖

Luskey/Ryan's Western Stores Inc., 2601 N. Main, Fort Worth, TX 76106: Free catalog ❖ Hats and boots in a western tradition for the entire family. 800-725-7966.

Mackey Custom Hats, 1485 Ward Rd., Bozeman, MT 59715: Free brochure ❖ Handcrafted western hats. 406-586-4993.

David Morgan, 11812 Northcreek Pkwy., Ste. 103, Bothell, WA 98011: Free catalog ❖ Hand-braided belts, fur hats, and wool and sheepskin clothing. 800-324-4934.

Rands Custom Hats, 2205 1st Ave. North, Billings, MT 59101: Catalog $3 ❖ Custom western hats. 800-346-9815; 406-259-4886 (in MT).

Andrew Thompson Company, 843 Arden Way, Signal Mountain, TN 37377: Free information ❖ Multi-sizing airflow and dermatologist-recommended sun hats. 615-886-5189.

Tonto Rim Trading Company, 2650 E. Tipton St., Seymour, IN 47274: Free catalog ❖ Western boots and hats. 800-242-4287.

Weather Hat Company of Wyoming, 1384 Coffeen Ave., Sheridan, WY 82801: Brochure $1 ❖ Cowboy-style hats. 307-674-6675.

Whipp Trading Company, RR 1, Arrasmith Trail, Ames, IA 50010: Free catalog ❖ Sheepskin rugs, slippers, mittens, and hats. 800-533-9447.

Wheeling Western Wear, 642 S. Milwaukee Ave., Wheeling, IL 60090: Free information ❖ Handmade western hats. 800-850-0383.

HEALTH CARE SUPPLIES & AIDS

Supplies & Aids

AARP Pharmacy Service Center Catalog, P.O. Box 1367, Richmond, VA 23225: Free catalog for American Association Retired Persons members ❖ Over-the-counter medications, cosmetics, vitamins, dental needs, sick room and other health care supplies, and personal care items. 800-456-2277.

Adventure Medical Kits, P.O. Box 43309, Oakland, CA 94624: Free catalog ❖ Compact sport-specific medical kits. 800-324-3517.

Allergy Control Products, 96 Danbury Rd., Ridgefield, CT 06877: Free catalog ❖ Air filters, mattress and pillow covers, face masks, dehumidifiers, and books. 800-422-3878; 203-438-9580 (in CT).

Allergy Resources Inc., P.O. Box 444, Guffey, CO 80820: Free catalog ❖ Cosmetics, bedding, skin and body resources, pet products, lawn and garden accessories, environment shields, cleaning products, and aids for allergy-prone individuals. 800-873-3529; 719-689-2969 (in CO).

American Ostomy Supplies, P.O. Box 13396, Milwaukee, WI 53213: Free catalog ❖ Urological, diabetic, and incontinence supplies. Also blood pressure monitor, wound care products, and aids for assisted living. 800-958-5858.

Atwater-Carey Ltd., 5505 Central Ave., Boulder, CO 80301: Free information ❖ First aid kits. 800-359-1646.

B & B Company Inc., 2417 Bank Dr., P.O. Box 5731, Boise, ID 83705: Free information ❖ Mastectomy breast forms. 800-262-2789.

BackSaver, 53 Jeffrey Ave., Holliston, MA 01746: Free catalog ❖ Aids for prevention and relief of pain to the back, neck, shoulders, wrists, and arms. 800-251-2225.

BCB Survival Equipment Inc., 7907 NW 53rd, Ste. 310, Miami, FL 33166: Free list of retail sources ❖ Emergency medical and first aid equipment and survival kits. 305-599-4929.

Biodex Medical Systems, Brookhaven R & D Plaza, 20 Ramsay Rd., Box 702, Shirley, NY 11967: Free catalog ❖ Nuclear medicine supplies and accessories. 800-224-6339; 516-924-9000 (in NY).

Bioenergy Nutrients, 6565 Odell Pl., Boulder, CO 80301: Catalog $1 ❖ Nutritional supplements, homeopathic medicines, antioxidants, and all-natural skin care products. 800-627-7775.

Bruce Medical Supply, 411 Waverly Oaks Rd., P.O. Box 9166, Waltham, MA 02154: Free catalog ❖ Health care supplies for ostomy patients, diabetics, sick rooms, post hospital care, and first aid. 800-225-8446.

Chinook Medical Gear Inc., P.O. Box 3300, Eagle, CO 81631: Catalog $1 (refundable) ❖ Emergency medical and first aid equipment and survival kits. 800-766-1365.

Dr. Clayton's Herbs, Division American Herbal Science Inc., 2717 7th Ave. South, Birmingham, AL 35233: Free catalog ❖ All-natural health care products. 800-633-6286.

Creative Solutions, P.O. Box 400821, Des Moines, IA 50347: Free information ❖ Easy-to-use finger blood pressure and pulse monitor. 800-666-6421.

Dyna-Med, 6300 Yarrow Dr., Carlsbad, CA 92009: Free catalog ❖ Emergency care products. 800-334-8211.

East Earth Trade Winds, P.O. Box 493151, 1620 E. Cypress Ave., Ste. 8, Redding, CA 96049: Free catalog ❖ Chinese herbs and herb products. 800-258-6878.

Emergency Medical Products, 9434 Chesapeake Dr., Ste. 1208, San Diego, CA 92123: Free information ❖ First aid kits. 800-228-1538.

Enrichments, P.O. Box 5050, Bolingbrook, IL 60440: Free information ❖ Health care products, personal care needs, and dressing and comfort aids. 800-323-5547.

ETAC USA, 2325 Parklawn Dr., Ste. J, Waukesha, WI 53186: Free brochure ❖ Walking aids, bath safety equipment, and wheelchairs. 800-678-3822.

Express Medical Supply Inc., P.O. Box 1164, Fenton, MO 63026: Free catalog ❖ Urological, ostomy, incontinence, and skin care products. 800-633-2139.

Fashion Ease, Division M & M Health Care, 1541 60th St., Brooklyn, NY 11219: Free catalog ❖ Clothing with Velcro closures, wheelchair accessories, and incontinence supplies. 800-221-8929; 718-853-6376 (in NY).

The Feelgood Store & Catalog, 14 Inverness Dr. East, Building F, Ste. 160, Englewood, CO 80112: Free catalog ❖ Pain-relief accessories for backs, knee pain, wrist and elbow tendinitis, weak ankles, shoulder pain, and sore muscles. 800-997-6789; 303-790-7249 (in CO).

Frohock-Stewart Inc., P.O. Box 330, Northborough, MA 01532: Free information ❖ Clamp-on bathtub bench and grip for bathing comfort and safety. 800-343-6059.

Gaia Garden Herbal Apothecary, 2672 W. Broadway, Vancouver, British Columbia, Canada V6K 2G3: Catalog $2 ❖ Herbal, aromatherapy, and related products. 604-734-4372.

Guardian Products Inc., 4175 Guardian St., Simi Valley, CA 93063: Free catalog ❖ One-piece, assembly-not-required, height-adjustable shower and commode chair. 800-255-5022.

Health Center for Better Living, 1414 Rosemary Ln., Naples, FL 33940: Free catalog ❖ Herbal health care products. 800-544-4225.

Healthhouse USA, Box 9036, Jericho, NY 11753: Free catalog ❖ Emergency medical and first aid equipment. 516-334-2099.

Healthy Living, 6836 Engle Rd., P.O. Box 94512, Cleveland, OH 44101: Free catalog ❖ Aids, appliances, and supplies for health and comfort. 800-800-0100.

Herbalist, P.O. Box 5, Hammond, IN 46325: Free catalog ❖ Herbal remedies.

Home Health Products, 949 Seahawk Circle, Virginia Beach, VA 23452: Free catalog ❖ Natural health care products and supplies, skin care preparations, and herbal medications. 800-284-9123.

House Calls, P.O. Box 331148, Fort Worth, TX 76163: Free catalog ❖ Health care supplies and equipment for the home. 800-460-7282.

HEALTH CARE SUPPLIES & AIDS

Hyland's Standard Homeopathic Company, 154 W. 131st St., Los Angeles, CA 90061: Free information ❖ Homeopathic medicines. 800-624-9659; 213-321-4284 (in CA).

Independent Living Aids/Can-Do Products, 27 East Mall, Plainview, NY 11803: Free catalog ❖ Health care supplies. 800-537-2118; 516-752-8080 (in NY).

Intimate Appeal, Palo Verde at 34th, P.O. Box 27800, Tucson, AZ 85726: Free catalog ❖ Intimate clothing for women who have had mastectomies. 520-748-8600.

Just My Size, P.O. Box 748, Rural Hall, NC 27098: Free catalog ❖ Aids for better living, elastic supports, foot care items, and home health care products. 800-522-9567.

Miles Kimball Company, 41 W. 8th Ave., Oshkosh, WI 54906: Free catalog ❖ Bathroom and kitchen accessories, arthritis aids, clothing, canes, and personal care items for people with disabilities. 800-546-2255.

L & H Vitamins Inc., 32-33 47th Ave., Long Island City, NY 11101: Free catalog ❖ Vitamins and nutritional supplements, homeopathic medicines, aromatherapy products, and natural health care products. 800-221-1152; 618-937-7400 (in NY).

Lady Grace Stores, P.O. Box 128, Malden, MA 02148: Free catalog ❖ Intimate apparel for everyday wear, nursing and maternity, and post-breast surgery. 800-922-0504.

Dr. Leonard's Health Care Catalog, 42 Mayfield Ave., P.O. Box 7821, Edison, NJ 08818: Free catalog ❖ Health care supplies. 800-785-0880.

Mail Order Medical Supply (MOMS), 24700 Avenue Rockefeller, Valencia, CA 91355: Free catalog ❖ A wide range of home care supplies, including incontinence, urological, and aids-for-daily-living.

Masuen First Aid & Safety, P.O. Box 901, Tonawanda, NY 14151: Free catalog ❖ First aid remedies, kits, and health care and medical supplies. 800-831-0894.

Moms Catalog, 24700 Avenue Rockefeller, Valencia, CA 91355: Free catalog ❖ Medical supplies for incontinence, urological aids for daily living, ostomy, wound and skin care, and diabetes. 800-232-7443.

National Medical Consumables Inc., P.O. Box 102495, Denver, CO 80250: Free information ❖ Ostomy, diabetic, urological, wound care, and incontinence products. 800-797-7107.

Nitro-Pak Preparedness Center, 151 N. Main St., Heber City, UT 84032: Catalog $3 ❖ Survival equipment and supplies, freeze-dried and dehydrated foods, books, and videos. 800-866-4876.

Oregon Scientific, 18383 SW Boones Ferry Rd., Portland, OR 97224: Free brochure ❖ Digital blood pressure meter. 800-863-8883.

Out N Back, 1797 S. State St., Orem, UT 84058: Free catalog ❖ Survival equipment for outdoor recreational activities. 800-533-7415.

Outdoor Research, 2203 1st Ave., Seattle, WA 98134: Free information ❖ Outdoor first aid kits.

Pillows for Ease, P.O. Box 402113, Miami, FL 33140: Free brochure ❖ Special support pillows, body wedges, back rests, cradles, and pillow-type supports for chiropractic, orthopedic, and massage therapy-related conditions. 800-347-1486.

Planta Dei Medicinal Herb Farm, Millville, New Brunswick, Canada E0H 1M0: Catalog $2 (refundable) ❖ Biologically grown teas, medicinal herbs, healing tea mixtures, cosmetics, natural ointments, and massage oils. 506-463-8169.

PolyMedica Healthcare Inc., 581 Conference Pl., Golden, CO 80401: Free list of retail sources ❖ Self-adhesive and water resistant dressings for blisters and abrasions. 303-271-0300.

J.A. Preston Corporation, P.O. Box 89, Jackson, MI 49204: Free catalog ❖ Exercise equipment, walkers, crutches, mats, positioning aids, perceptual motor accessories, self-help aids, and professional equipment for the doctor's office. 800-631-7277.

Radio Shack, Division Tandy Corporation, One Tandy Center, Fort Worth, TX 76102: Free information ❖ Health care supplies. 817-390-3011.

Safe Care Medical Supply Inc., P.O. Box 1164, Fenton, MO 63026: Free catalog ❖ Urological and ostomy supplies. 800-633-2139.

St. Louis Medical Supply, 10821 Manchester Rd., Kirkwood, MO 63122: Free catalog ❖ Health care and medical supplies. 800-950-6020.

Sears Home Healthcare, 20 Presidential Dr., Roselle, IL 60172: Free catalog ❖ Products for health maintenance and rehabilitation. 800-326-1750; 800-733-7249 (for the hearing-impaired).

SelfCare Catalog, P.O. Box 182290, Chattanooga, TN 37422: Free catalog ❖ Health care supplies. 800-345-1848.

Shield Healthcare Centers, P.O. Box 916, Santa Clarita, CA 91380: Free catalog ❖ Ostomy, urological, skin care, and home diagnostic products.

Silos Products Inc., 2139 N. University Dr., Coral Springs, FL 33071: Free brochure ❖ Portable dental cleaning systems, air cleaners, water purifiers, massaging shower heads, and accessories. 800-762-3355.

Slide Zone, P.O. Box 781572, San Antonio, TX 78278: Free information ❖ First-aid kits for disinfecting and treating wounds, repelling insects, and relieving discomfitures. 800-754-3305.

Support Plus, Box 500, Medfield, MA 02052: Free catalog ❖ Support hosiery, personal hygiene and home health care aids, bath safety products, and walking shoes. 508-359-2910.

The Survival Center, P.O. Box 234, McKenna, WA 98558: Catalog $2 ❖ Survival equipment for outdoor activities. 206-458-6778.

The Vitamin Shoppe, 4700 Westside Ave., North Bergen, NJ 07047: Free catalog ❖ Vitamins, herbs, homeopathic medicines, and pure and natural cosmetics. 800-223-1216.

Walton Way Medical, 948 Walton Way, Augusta, GA 30901: Free catalog ❖ Health care supplies and rehabilitation equipment. 800-241-4636.

Wheelchair Warehouse, 100 E. Sierra, #3309, Fresno, CA 93710: Free information ❖ Ostomy appliances, incontinence supplies, mastectomy breast forms, skin care products, and health care aids. 800-829-0202; 800-621-5938 (in OH).

Worldwide Home Health Center Inc., 926 E. Tallmadge Ave., Akron, OH 44310: Free catalog ❖ Ostomy appliances, incontinence supplies, mastectomy breast forms, skin care products, and health care aids. 800-223-5938; 216-633-0366 (in OH).

Software

Applied Medical Informatics, 2681 Parley's Way, Ste. 204, Salt Lake City, UT 84109: Free information ❖ Medical care management software. 800-584-3060; 801-464-6200 (in UT).

Great Bear Technology/HealthSoft, 1100 Moraga Way, Ste. 200, Moraga, CA 94556: Free catalog ❖ Windows-based software for guide to prescription and non-prescription drugs and symptoms and illnesses. 510-631-6800.

IVI Publishing, 7500 Flying Cloud Dr., Minneapolis, MN 55344: Free information ❖ Windows-based and Macintosh Mayo Clinic family health and medication management software on CD-ROMs. 800-952-4773; 612-996-6000 (in MN).

Lifestyle Software Group, 63 Orange St., St. Augustine, FL 32084: Free information ❖ Information software for managing personal health care programs. 800-289-1157; 904-825-0220 (in FL).

LivingSoft Inc., P.O. Box 970, Jamesville, CA 96114: Free information ❖ DOS-based dieting software. 800-626-1262; 916-253-2700 (in CA).

HEALTH CARE SUPPLIES & AIDS FOR THE DISABLED

Pixel Perfect Software, P.O. Drawer 410129, Melbourne, FL 32941: Free information ❖ Windows-based medical advisor, drug management, and self-health software on CD-ROMs. 800-788-2099.

SoftKey International Inc., 1 Athenaeum St., Cambridge, MA 02142: Free information ❖ Windows-based drug information software on CD-ROM. 800-227-5609; 617-494-1200 (in MA).

StarPress Inc., 425 Market St., 5th Floor, San Francisco, CA 94105: Free information ❖ Windows-based symptoms, illness, and surgery information CD-ROM. 800-782-7944; 415-778-3100 (in CA).

HEALTH CARE SUPPLIES & AIDS FOR THE DISABLED

Access with Ease Inc., P.O. Box 1150, Chino Valley, AZ 86323: Catalog $1 (refundable) ❖ Self-help products for persons with physical challenges. 800-531-9479.

AccessAble, 111 Cedar St., 3rd Floor, New Rochelle, NY 10801: Free information ❖ Bathroom access aids. 800-285-2525.

adaptAbility, P.O. Box 515, Colchester, CT 06415: Free catalog ❖ Mobility, grooming, dressing, bathing, eating and cooking aids, exercise and therapy games, and adaptive home products for independent living. 800-288-9941.

The Adaptive Design Shop, 12847 Point Pleasant Dr., Fairfax, VA 22033: Free brochure ❖ Toilet supports and combination bath and shower chairs for children and adults. 800-351-2327.

American Foundation for the Blind Inc., Product Center, 3342 Melrose Ave., Roanoke, VA 24017: Free catalog ❖ Describes products available from the American Foundation for the Blind. 800-829-0500.

American Ostomy Supplies, P.O. Box 13396, Milwaukee, WI 53213: Free catalog ❖ Urological, diabetic, and incontinence supplies. Also blood pressure and wound care products and aids for assisted living. 800-958-5858.

American Printing House for the Blind, 1839 Frankfort Ave., P.O. Box 6085, Louisville, KY 40206: Free catalog ❖ Braille writing and embossing equipment, electronic devices, reading readiness products, and educational aids and accessories for people with visual handicaps. 800-223-1839; 502-895-2405 (in KY).

American Standard Assistive Aids, P.O. Box 2303, Chatsworth, CA 91311: Free information ❖ Assistive aids for use in the bathroom. 800-524-9797.

AMI Altimate Medical Inc., 913 S. Washington, Redwood Falls, MN 56283: Free brochure ❖ Standing support and mobility stands. 800-342-8968.

Attainment Company Inc., P.O. Box 930160, Verona, WI 53593: Free catalog ❖ Special needs equipment for children and adults. 800-327-4269.

Barrier Free Lifts Inc., P.O. Box 4163, Manassas, VA 22110: Free information ❖ Battery-operated multi-directional barrier-free ceiling lift. 800-582-8732; 703-361-6531 (in VA).

Bath-Mate, P.O. Box 80095, Ontario, CA 91758: Free information ❖ Water-powered bathtub lift that pivots outward for safe patient transfer. 800-282-4928.

The Braun Corporation, 1014 S. Monticello, P.O. Box 310, Winamac, IN 46996: Free information ❖ Van conversion and driving accessories and wheelchair lifts. 800-THE-LIFT; 219-946-6153 (in IN).

Bruno Independent Living Aids, 1780 Executive Dr., P.O. Box 84, Oconomowoc, WI 53066: Free information ❖ Wheelchair and scooter lifts. 800-882-8183.

Caring Products International Inc., 200 1st Ave. West, Ste. 200, Seattle, WA 98119: Free information ❖ Incontinence supplies and maternity and special-needs clothing. 800-333-5379; 206-282-6040 (in WA).

Clarke Health Care, 1003 International Dr., Oakdale, PA 15071: Free information ❖ Bathlifts for transfer in and out of bathtubs. 412-695-2122.

Columbia Medical Manufacturing Corporation, P.O. Box 633, Pacific Palisades, CA 90272: Free catalog ❖ Car seats, bath and toilet supports, commodes, exercise equipment, and rehabilitation products for handicapped children and adults. 800-454-6612.

Columbus McKinnon Corporation, Medical Products Division, 140 John James Audubon Pkwy., Amherst, NY 14228: Free information ❖ Easy-to-operate mobility and lift system. 800-888-0985.

Consumer Care Products Inc., P.O. Box 684, Sheboygan, WI 53082: Free catalog ❖ Wheelchair trays and positioning, communication, and mobility aids and supplies for exceptional persons. 414-459-8353.

Crestwood Company, 6625 N. Sidney Pl., Milwaukee, WI 53209: Free catalog ❖ Communication aids for children and adults. 414-352-5678.

Crow River Industries, 14800 28th Ave. North, Minneapolis, MN 55447: Free information ❖ Wheelchair lifts for recreational vehicles. 800-488-0359.

Danmar Products Inc., 221 Jackson Industrial Dr., Ann Arbor, MI 48103: Free catalog ❖ Easy-to-hold utensil handles and other assistive aids for people with arthritis. 800-783-1998; 313-761-1990 (in MI).

The Doorman, Parisi Enterprises Inc., 23 Southward Ave., Congers, NY 10920: Free information ❖ No-tools-required and easy-to-install sliding door opener. 914-268-5983.

Equipment Shop, P.O. Box 33, Bedford, MA 01730: Free catalog ❖ Adaptive equipment. 617-275-7681.

ETAC USA, 2325 Parklawn Dr., Ste. J, Waukesha, WI 53186: Free brochure ❖ Walking aids, bath safety equipment, and wheelchairs. 800-678-3822.

Flaghouse, 150 N. MacQuesten Pkwy., Mt. Vernon, NY 10550: Free catalog ❖ Physical education and recreation, sports and play, and rehabilitation equipment. 800-793-7900.

Grant Waterx Corporation, 986 Bedford St., Stamford, CT 06905: Free information ❖ Pivoting bathtub lift that operates with household water pressure. 800-243-5237.

Guardian Products Inc., 4175 Guardian St., Simi Valley, CA 93063: Free catalog ❖ Walkers, crutches, canes, home activity aids, beds, lifts, ramps, and assistive transport equipment. 800-255-5022.

Handi-Move, 982 Rt. 1, Pine Island, NY 10969: Free information ❖ Remote overhead track or free-standing movable lift. 800-724-5305.

Handi-Ramp Inc., 1414 Armour Blvd., P.O. Box 745, Mundelein, IL 60060: Free catalog ❖ Fixed-in-place and portable ramps for vans and homes. 800-876-RAMP.

T.F. Herceg Inc., 982 Rt. 1, Pine Island, NY 10969: Free information ❖ Remote hand-controlled overhead track and free-standing lifts. 800-724-5305.

HIG'S Aluminum Products, 10625 Maple Ln., Rogers, MN 55374: Free information ❖ Portable lightweight wheelchair and scooter ramps. 800-795-2392.

Homecare Products Inc., 15824 SE 296th St., Kent, WA 98042: Free information ❖ Portable wheelchair ramps. 800-451-1903; 206-631-4633 (in WA).

I-Tec, P.O. Box 6304, Garden Grove, CA 92645, CA 92649: Free information ❖ Ceiling mounted or free-standing electrical-mechanical system for in-the-home mobility.

Imaginart Communication Products, 307 Arizona St., Bisbee, AZ 85603: Free catalog ❖ Speech, language, and learning materials for special education, speech and language pathology, occupational therapy, geriatric rehabilitation, and early childhood education. 800-828-1376.

Independent Living Aids/Can-Do Products, 27 East Mall, Plainview, NY 11803: Free catalog ❖ Self-help products for individuals with vision impairment and physical disabilities. 800-537-2118; 516-752-8080 (in NY).

Independent Mobility Systems, 4100 W. Piedras, Farmington, NM 87401: Free information ❖ Automatic door ramp for automotive vehicles.

Miles Kimball Company, 41 W. 8th Ave., Oshkosh, WI 54906: Free catalog ❖ Bathroom and kitchen accessories, arthritis aids, clothing, canes, and personal care items for people with disabilities. 800-546-2255.

Kohler Company, 444 Highland Dr., Kohler, WI 53044: Catalog $3 ❖ Low threshold shower stalls for wheelchair accessibility. 800-220-2291.

Laureate Learning Systems, 110 E. Spring St., Winooski, VT 05404: Free information ❖ Talking software programs for children 6 months to 8 years of age. Includes language intervention, cognitive processing, reading, and instructional games. 802-655-4755.

Leckey Support Furniture, 360 Merrimac, Building 5, Lawrence, MA 01843: Free information ❖ Adjustable bath chair. 800-LECKEY-O.

Lifestand, P.O. Box 153, Folcroft, PA 19032: Free information ❖ Combination power-assisted standing aid and wheelchair. 800-782-6324.

Lindustries, P.O. Box 66295, Auburndale, MA 02166: Free information ❖ Lever convertible adapters for making doors easy to open. 617-237-8177.

Lubidet USA Inc., 1980 S. Quebec St., Ste. 4, Denver, CO 80231: Free information ❖ Personal cleansing accessory that attaches to most toilets.

Maxi-Aids, 42 Executive Blvd., Farmingdale, NY 11735: Free catalog ❖ Aids and appliances for people with visual, hearing, and physical impairments. 800-522-6294.

Mobilitis Corporation, 308 E. Pima St., Phoenix, AZ 85004: Free information ❖ Three-wheel multiple-speed control bicycle with a built-in seat. 800-266-2454.

Mobility Products & Design, 14800 28th Ave. North, Minneapolis, MN 55447: Free information ❖ Hand controls for automotive vehicles. 800-488-0359.

MPS Controls, 7948 Ronson Rd., San Diego, CA 92111: Free information ❖ Hand-operated driver controls for recreational vehicles and vans. 619-292-1423.

MTF Geriatrics, P.O. Box 320, Ellis, KS 67637: Free catalog ❖ Easy-on and easy-off clothing and accessories for the elderly and disabled. 913-726-4807.

Open Sesame, 1933 Davis St., #279, San Leandro, CA 94577: Free information ❖ Remote-controlled door systems that open and close automatically from wheelchairs. 800-673-6911.

Power Access Corporation, Bridge St., P.O. Box 235, Collinsville, CT 06022: Free brochure ❖ Easily attached remote or manually operated door opener. 800-344-0088; 693-0751 (in CT).

Relaxo-Back Inc., P.O. Box 48580, Fort Worth, TX 76148: Free information ❖ Form-fitting auxiliary seat that can be used to relieve lower back pain. 800-527-5496.

Rock N' Roll Marketing Inc., P.O. Box 1558, Levelland, TX 79336: Free information ❖ Single riders, tandems, and hand and foot-powered cycles with optional seat configurations and custom fitting for individual needs. 800-654-9664.

S & S Adaptability, 75 Mill St., P.O. Box 515, Colchester, CT 06415: Free catalog ❖ Products for rehabilitation and therapy. 800-266-8856.

SFH Products, 1801 E. Medlock, Phoenix, AZ 85016: Free information ❖ Platform and chair lifts for motor homes. 602-265-7370.

Silcraft Corporation, 528 Hughes Dr., Traverse City, MI 49686: Free information ❖ Barrier-free roll-in showers, shower and bath accessories, lifts, and transporters.

Sinties Scientific Inc., 5616A S. 122nd East Ave., Tulsa, OK 74146: Free information ❖ Folding and adjustable power trainer for arms or legs. 800-852-6869; 918-254-7395 (in OK).

Space Tables Inc., P.O. Box 32082, Minneapolis, MN 55432: Free catalog ❖ Adjustable tables for wheelchairs. 800-328-2580.

Special Clothes, P.O. Box 333, East Harwich, MA 02645: Free catalog ❖ Adaptive clothing for children with disabilities, size 2 toddler through young adult. 508-430-5172.

Special Designs Inc., P.O. Box 130, Gillette, NJ 07933: Free information ❖ Custom equipment and furniture for "special kids." 908-464-8825.

Stand-Aid of Iowa Inc., Box 386, Sheldon, IA 51201: Free information ❖ Standing aid for disabled persons. 800-831-8580; 712-324-2153 (in IA).

Talk-A-Phone, 5013 N. Kedzie Ave., Chicago, IL 60625: Free brochure ❖ Compliant emergency hand-free telephones. 312-539-1100.

Thoele Manufacturing, Rt. 1, Box 116, Montrose, IL 62445: Free information ❖ Pedal-in-place exerciser. 217-924-4553.

Toys for Special Children, 385 Warburton Ave., Hastings-on-Hudson, NY 10706: Free catalog ❖ Enabling and special devices for the handicapped. 914-478-0960.

Ultimate Home Care Company, 3250 E. 19th St., Long Beach, CA 90804: Free information ❖ Portable lightweight threshold and folding ramps. 800-475-8122.

Vantage Mini Vans, 5214 S. 30th St., Phoenix, AZ 85040: Free catalog ❖ Mini-van conversions for the physically challenged. 800-348-8267.

Walk Easy Inc., 2915 S. Congress Ave., Delray Beach, FL 33445: Free brochure ❖ Crutches, walkers, commode chairs, and canes, tripod canes, and quad canes. 800-441-2904.

Walton Way Medical, 948 Walton Way, Augusta, GA 30901: Free catalog ❖ Medical supplies and rehabilitation equipment. 800-241-4636.

Worthington Distribution, P.O. Box 306, 36 Gumbletown Rd., Paupack, PA 18451: Free catalog ❖ Home automation products for turning off and on lights, televisions, stereos, and more. 800-282-8864; 717-226-8864.

HEARING & COMMUNICATION AIDS

Assistive Listening Device Systems Inc., 2-11220 Voyageur Way, Richmond, British Columbia, Canada V6X 3E1: Free information ❖ Assistive listening device systems. 800-665-2537.

Audiological Engineering Corporation, 35 Medford St., Somerville, MA 02143: Free information ❖ Infrared and loop hearing systems and other assistive aids for the hearing-impaired. 800-283-4601.

General Technologies, 7415 Winding Way, Fair Oaks, CA 95628: Free catalog ❖ Assistive listening devices. 800-328-6684.

Harris Communications, 6541 City West Pkwy., Eden Prairie, MN 55344: Free catalog ❖ Closed caption and cable-ready decoder, TDDs, signalers, clocks, and devices for hearing-impaired persons. 800-825-6758 (voice); 800-825-9187 (TDD).

Hear You Are Inc., 4 Musconetcong Ave., Stanhope, NJ 07874: Free catalog ❖ Doorbell signal, telephone aids, visual and smoke alarms, and assistive listening devices for hearing-impaired persons. 201-347-7662 (voice/TTY).

Hello Direct, 5884 Eden Park Pl., San Jose, CA 95138: Free catalog ❖ Amplification aids, cellular and paging accessories, telephones and answering machines, and other telephone productivity tools. 800-444-3556.

Hitec Group International, 8160 Madison, Burr Ridge, IL 60521: Free catalog ❖ Assistive devices for the hearing impaired person. 708-654-9200.

Independent Living Aids Inc./Can-Do Products, 27 East Mall, Plainview, NY 11803: Free catalog ❖ Writing, low-vision, braille, and communication aids. 800-537-2118; 516-752-8080 (in NY).

Nationwide Flashing Signal Systems Inc., 8120 Fenton St., Silver Spring, MD 20910: Free catalog ❖ Visual alerting devices and TDDs for hearing-impaired persons. 301-589-6671.

Phone-TTY Inc., 202 Lexington Ave., Hackensack, NJ 07601: Free information ❖ Modems and software for using computers to talk with TDDs. 201-489-7889; 201-489-7890 (TDD).

Phonic Ear Inc., 3880 Cypress Dr., Petaluma, CA 94954: Free catalog ❖ Sound enhancers for group functions and phonic ear personal FM systems for hearing-impaired individuals. 800-227-0735; 800-772-3374 (in CA).

Potomac Technology, One Church St., Ste. 402, Rockville, MD 20850: Free information ❖ Special needs devices for hearing-impaired persons. 800-433-2838 (voice/TTY).

Radio Shack, Division Tandy Corporation, One Tandy Center, Fort Worth, TX 76102: Free catalog ❖ Special needs devices for hearing-impaired persons. 817-390-3011.

Science Products, Box 888, Southeastern, PA 19399: Free catalog ❖ Voice sensory aids and electronics for people with hearing or visual impairments. 800-888-7400; 215-296-2111 (in PA).

Sennheiser, 6 Vista Dr., P.O. Box 987, Old Lyme, CT 06371: Free information ❖ Easy-to-use transmitters and receivers with 16 selectable frequencies, infrared add-on systems, and assistive devices for the hearing impaired person. 203-434-9190 (voice/TDD).

Siemans Hearing Instruments Inc., 10 Corporate Pl. South, Corporate Park 287, Piscataway, NJ 08854: Free information ❖ Easy-to-install infrared in-home TV listening system. 800-641-4786.

Silent Call, P.O. Box 868, Clarkston, MI 48016: Free information ❖ Electronically activated wireless personal alert system.

Temasek Telephone Inc., 21 Airport Rd., South San Francisco, CA 94080: Free information ❖ Voice-activated telephones. 800-647-8887.

Ultratec, 450 Science Dr., Madison, WI 53711: Free catalog ❖ All-in-one phone for people with different hearing abilities. 800-482-2424 (voice/TTY).

Weitbrecht Communications Inc., 2656 29th St., Ste. 205, Santa Monica, CA 90405: Free catalog ❖ Assistive listening devices and portable TDDs. 800-233-9130 (voice/TTY).

HEAT EXCHANGERS

Gaylord Industries Inc., P.O. Box 1149, Tualatin, OR 97062: Free information ❖ Air-to-air heat exchangers. 800-547-9696.

HOCKEY, FIELD

Action Sport Systems Inc., P.O. Box 1442, Morgantown, NC 28680: Free information ❖ Uniforms, balls, nets, cages, and leg guards. 800-631-1091; 704-584-8000 (in NC).

American Sports Inc., P.O. Box 36662, Los Angeles, CA 90036: Free list of retail sources ❖ Uniforms, balls, nets, cages, leg guards, shoes, and sticks. 800-922-8939.

Austin Athletic Equipment Corporation, 705 Bedford Ave., Box 423, Bellmore, NY 11710: Free information ❖ Nets and cages. 516-785-0100.

Doss Shoes, Soccer Sport Supply Company, 1745 1st Ave., New York, NY 10128: Free information ❖ Uniforms, balls, nets, cages, leg guards, shoes, and sticks. 800-223-1010; 212-427-6050 (in NY).

Olympia Sports, 745 State Circle, Ann Arbor, MI 48106: Free information ❖ Balls, goal nets, cages, leg guards, and sticks. 800-521-2832.

Sportime, Customer Service, 1 Sportime Way, Atlanta, GA 30340: Free information ❖ Balls, goal nets, cages, leg guards, and sticks. 800-444-5700; 770-449-5700 (in GA).

TC Sports, 7251 Ford Hwy., Tecumseh, MI 49286: Free information ❖ Balls, goal nets, and cages. 800-523-1498; 517-451-5221 (in MI).

Wolvering Sports, 745 State Circle, Box 1941, Ann Arbor, MI 48106: Catalog $1 ❖ Baseball, basketball, field hockey, soccer, football, and other athletic and recreation equipment. 313-761-5691.

HOCKEY, ICE

Clothing

Austin Sportsgear, 621 Liberty St., Jackson, MI 49203: Free information ❖ Uniforms. 800-999-7543; 517-784-1120 (in MI).

Betlin Manufacturing, 1445 Marion Rd., Columbus, OH 43207: Free information ❖ Uniforms. 614-443-0248.

Cliff Keen Athletic, 1235 Rosewood, Ann Arbor, MI 48106: Free information ❖ Uniforms. 800-992-0799; 313-769-9555 (in MI).

Majestic Athletic Wear, 636 Pen Argyl St., Pen Argyl, PA 18072: Free information ❖ Uniforms and sportswear. 800-955-8555; 215-863-6161 (in PA).

Manny's Baseball, 3000 SW 42nd Ave., Palm City, FL 34990: Catalog $2 ❖ Clothing for hockey players. 800-PRO-TEAM.

Venus Knitting Mills Inc., 140 Spring St., Murray Hill, NJ 07974: Free information ❖ Uniforms, clothing for ice skaters, and sportswear. 800-955-4200; 908-464-2400 (in NJ).

Equipment

Bauer Precision In-Line Skates, Box 716, Swanton, VT 05478: Free information ❖ Gloves, goal nets, cages, protective gear, helmets, pucks, sticks, and skates. 800-622-2189; 802-868-2711 (in VT).

Canstar Sports, 50 Jonergin Dr., Swanton, VT 05448: Free information ❖ Figure and hockey ice skates and blade sharpeners. 800-362-3146; 802-868-2711 (in VT).

Cooper International Inc., 501 Alliance Ave., Toronto, Ontario, Canada M6N 2J3: Free information ❖ Guards and pads, helmets, masks, mouth guards, pucks, nets, cages, sticks, figure and hockey ice skates, and blade protectors. 416-763-3801.

Easton Sports, 577 Airport Blvd., Burlingame, CA 94010: Free information ❖ Gloves, goal nets, cages, protective gear, sticks, and skates. 800-347-3901; 415-347-4727 (in CA).

Irwin Sports, 43 Hanna Ave., Toronto, Ontario, Canada M6K 1X6: Free information ❖ Gloves, goal nets, cages, protective gear, pucks, and skates. 800-268-1732.

Lowry's Manufacturing Ltd., 19 Keith Rd., Winnipeg, Manitoba, Canada R3H 0H7: Free information ❖ Figure and hockey ice skates, replacement blades, and blade protectors. 204-633-6359.

Maska USA Inc., 529 Main St., Ste. 205, Boston, MA 02129: Free information ❖ Guards and pads, helmets, masks, pucks, and figure and hockey ice skates. 800-451-4600; 617-242-8600 (in MA).

National Sporting Goods Corporation, 25 Brighton Ave., Passaic, NJ 07055: Free information ❖ Figure and hockey ice skates, blade protectors, and sharpeners. 201-779-2323.

Ocean Hockey Supply Company, 197 Chambers Bridge Rd., Brick, NJ 08723: Free catalog ❖ Hockey equipment. 800-631-2159; 908-477-4411 (in NJ).

Riedell Shoes Inc., P.O. Box 21, Red Wing, MN 55066: Free information ❖ Blade sharpeners, protectors, and figure, racing, and hockey skates. 612-388-8251.

USA Skate Company, 7 Brayton Ct., Commack, NY 11725: Free information ❖ Guards and pads, nets, cages, sticks, and skates. 800-426-3334.

HOME BUILDING & IMPROVEMENT

Ceilings

AA Abbingdon Affiliates, 2149 Utica Ave., Brooklyn, NY 11234: Brochure $1 ❖ Tin ceiling cornice moldings. 718-258-8333.

Chelsea Decorative Metal Company, 9603 Moonlight Dr., Houston, TX 77096: Catalog $1 ❖ Pressed-tin for ceilings or backsplash. Victorian Art Deco designs, 6", 12", and 24" repeat patterns. 713-721-9200.

W.F. Norman Corporation, P.O. Box 323, Nevada, MO 64772: Catalog $3 ❖ Cornices and sheet metal ornaments for ceilings. Also wallcoverings and corner, border, and filler plates. 800-641-4038.

❖ **HOME BUILDING & IMPROVEMENT** ❖

Snelling's Thermo-Vac, P.O. Box 210, Blanchard, LA 71009: Free information ❖ Replica tin ceilings in high-impact plastic. 318-929-7398.

Cupolas

Accent Millworks, 285 N. Amboy Rd., Conneaut, OH 44030: Free information ❖ Easy-to-install cupolas. 216-593-6775.

C & R Inquiries, P.O. Box 1874, Stillwater, OK 74076: Free catalog ❖ Weather vanes, sundials, bird baths, and cupolas. 800-248-5445.

Cape Cod Cupola Co. Inc., 78 State Rd., N. Dartmouth, MA 02747: Catalog $2 (refundable) ❖ Cupolas and weathervanes. Specialize in custom work. 508-994-2119.

Colonial Cupolas, P.O. Box 38, 1816 Nemoke Trail, Haslett, MI 48840: Brochure $3 ❖ Wooden cupolas and aluminum or copper weathervanes. Includes build-it-yourself kits. 800-678-1965.

Coppersmiths, Custom Copper & Brass Works, P.O. Box 2675, Oakhurst, CA 93644: Free brochure ❖ Fireplace hoods, cupolas, mailboxes, and dormers. 209-658-8909.

Country Cupolas, P.O. Box 400, East Conway, NH 03813: Free information ❖ Country-style cupolas assembled or ready-to-build kits. 603-939-2698.

Crosswinds Gallery, 15 Francis St., Bristol, RI 02809: Free catalog ❖ Cupolas with copper roofs and weather vanes. 800-638-8263.

Denninger Cupolas & Weathervanes, RD 1, Box 447, Middletown, NY 10940: Catalog $4 ❖ Redwood cupolas with copper roofs and weather vanes. 914-343-2229.

The Outhouse, 2853 Lincoln Hwy. East, Ronks, PA 17572: Free catalog ❖ Cupolas and copper, iron, and aluminum weather vanes. 800-346-7678; 717-687-9850 (in PA).

Sun Designs, 173 E. Wisconsin Ave., Oconomowoc, WI 53066: Plan book $9.95 plus $3.95 postage ❖ Plans for gazebos, bridges, cupolas, and structures. 414-567-4255.

Door Chimes

Caradon Friedland, 255 Quaker Ln., Ste. 100, West Warwick, RI 02893: Free information ❖ Door chimes and push buttons. 800-767-1837.

Hear You Are Inc., 4 Musconetcong Ave., Stanhope, NJ 07874: Free catalog ❖ Doorbell signals, telephone aids, visual and smoke alarms, and assistive listening devices for hearing-impaired persons. 201-347-7662 (voice/TTY).

Oxford Chime Works, P.O. Box 665, Ridgecrest, CA 93555: Catalog $3 ❖ Handcrafted door bells, chimes, and annunciators. 619-446-1040.

Doors

Andersen Windows, P.O. Box 3900, Peoria, IL 61614: Free information ❖ Energy-efficient windows and patio doors. 800-426-4261.

Architectural Components, 26 N. Leverett Rd., Montague, MA 01351: Brochure $5 ❖ Reproduction doors from the 18th and 19th centuries, windows and window frames, and moldings. 413-367-9441.

Arctic Glass & Window Outlet, 565 County Rd. T, Hammond, WI 54015: Catalog $2 ❖ Windows, entryway and patio doors, skylights, and sun rooms. 800-428-9276.

Benchmark Doors, 12842 Pennridge Dr., Bridgeton, MO 63044: Free information ❖ Steel doors with a wood-grain finish. 800-467-2329.

Beveled Glass Works, 23852 Pacific Coast Hwy., Ste. 351, Malibu, CA 90265: Free information ❖ Wooden doors with sidelights and beveled glass. 800-421-0518.

The Bilco Company, P.O. Box 1203, New Haven, CT 06505: Free information ❖ All-steel outside basement doors. 203-934-6363.

Ciro Coppa Doors, 1231 Paraiso Ave., San Pedro, CA 90731: Free catalog ❖ Wooden screen doors and Adirondack chairs. 310-548-4142.

Combination Door Company, P.O. Box 1076, Fond du Lac, WI 54936: Free list of retail sources ❖ Wooden combination storm and screen doors and windows. 414-922-2050.

Craftsmen in Wood, 5441 W. Hadley St., Phoenix, AZ 85043: Catalog $8 ❖ Distinctive doors and hardware. 602-278-8054.

Creative Openings, P.O. Box 4204, Bellingham, WA 98227: Catalog $4 ❖ Historical and traditionally-styled screen and other doors. 206-671-6420.

Crestline, P.O. Box 8007, Wausau, WI 54402: Free information ❖ French doors with optional glass panels and transoms. 800-552-4111.

Art Di Rico, 4109 E. Parkway, Gatlinburg, TN 37738: Free information ❖ Custom-sculpted oak and mahogany wooden doors and mantels. 800-434-5427.

Driwood Ornamental Wood Moulding, P.O. Box 1729, Florence, SC 29503: Catalog $6 (refundable) ❖ Doors, embossed wooden molding, raised paneling, mantels, and curved stairs. 803-669-2478.

Entrances Inc., RFD 1, Box 246A, Poocham Rd., Westmoreland, NH 03467: Catalog $2 ❖ Interior and exterior insulated wooden doors with optional beveled and stained glass. 603-399-7723.

Entry Systems, 911 E. Jefferson, Pittsburgh, KS 66762: Free information ❖ Steel doors with a choice of transom designs. 800-835-0364.

Fineman Doors Inc., 16020 Valley Wood Rd., Sherman Oaks, CA 91403: Information $2 ❖ Handcrafted solid hardwood entry and interior doors. 818-990-3667.

Georgia-Pacific, P.O. Box 2808, Norcross, GA 30091: Free information ❖ Doors and windows. 800-447-2882.

Grand ERA Reproductions, P.O. Box 1026, Lapeer, MI 48446: Catalog $2 ❖ Easy-to-assemble screen and storm door kits. 810-664-1756.

Hendricks Woodworking, RD 2, Box 227, Kempton, PA 19529: Free brochure ❖ Authentically styled reproduction doors. 610-756-6187.

Hess Manufacturing Company, Box 127, Quincy, PA 17247: Free information ❖ Insulated aluminum doors and windows. 800-541-6666; 717-749-3141 (in PA).

Hurd Millwork Company, 575 S. Whelen Ave., Medford, WI 54451: Free information ❖ Windows and hinged, sliding wood, and insulated aluminum patio doors. 800-223-4873.

Iberia Millwork, P.O. Box 12139, New Iberia, LA 70562: Free information ❖ French doors, interior and exterior shutters, and cabinets. 318-365-8129.

International Wood Products, 7312 Convoy Ct., San Diego, CA 92111: Free information ❖ Single or double wooden doors with a choice of transom designs and sidelights. 800-468-3667.

Jeld-Wen, 3303 Lake Port Blvd., Klamath Falls, OR 97601: Free information ❖ Pre-finished or ready for finishing provincial and colonial-style bi-fold interior doors. 800-877-9482.

Jessup Door Company, 300 E. Railroad St., P.O. Box 240, Dowagiac, MI 49047: Free information ❖ Wooden doors for homes. 616-782-2183.

Joinery Company, P.O. Box 518, Tarboro, NC 27886: Catalog $5 ❖ Reproduction antique entryways and doors. 800-726-7463.

Kenmore Industries, One Thompson Square, Boston, MA 02129: Catalog $3 ❖ Federal, Georgian, and Revival-style carved historical entries. 617-242-1711.

Lamson-Taylor Custom Doors, 5 Tucker Rd., South Acworth, NH 03607: Catalog $2 ❖ Energy-efficient doors. 603-835-2992.

Mad River Woodworks, P.O. Box 1067, Blue Lake, CA 95525: Catalog $3 ❖ Reproduction doors from the mid-1800s ready for painting or staining. 800-446-8560; 707-668-5671 (in CA).

Marvin Windows, P.O. Box 100, Warroad, MN 56763: Free information ❖ Windows and doors with divided and insulated storm windows and transoms. 800-346-5128.

HOME BUILDING & IMPROVEMENT

Maurer & Shepherd Joyners Inc., 122 Naubuc Ave., Glastonbury, CT 06033: Brochure $2.25 ❖ Windows, doors, entryways, and authentic colonial woodworking. 203-633-2383.

Morgan Manufacturing, P.O. Box 2446, Oshkosh, WI 54903: Free information ❖ Paneled and carved wood, sliding glass, and hinged patio doors. 414-235-7170.

Old Wagon Factory, P.O. Box 1427, Clarksville, VA 23927: Catalog $2 ❖ Victorian and Chippendale-style storm screen doors and furniture. 804-374-5787.

Oregon Wooden Screen Door Company, 2767 Harris St., Eugene, OR 97405: Catalog $3 (refundable) ❖ Screen and energy-efficient storm doors. 503-485-0279.

Peachtree Windows & Doors, P.O. Box 5700, Norcross, GA 30091: Free information ❖ Steel, wood, glass, and aluminum doors and windows. 800-477-6544.

Pease Industries Inc., P.O. Box 14-8001, Fairfield, OH 45014: Information $1 ❖ Steel entryways and hinged patio doors. 800-543-1180.

Remodelers & Renovators Supplies, P.O. Box 45478, Boise, ID 83711: Catalog $3 ❖ Ready-to-stain screen doors. 800-456-2135.

Scherr's Cabinet & Doors, 5315 Burdick Expwy. East, RR 5, Box 12, Minot, ND 58701: Brochure $2 ❖ Raised panel doors for cabinets, drawer fronts, and dovetail drawers. 701-839-3384.

Cole Sewell Corporation, 2288 University Ave., St. Paul, MN 55114: Free information ❖ Reinforced wooden storm doors with optional security protection. 800-328-6596.

Sheppard Millwork Inc., 21020 70th Ave. West, Edmonds, WA 98020: Free catalog ❖ Sanded and unfinished doors with optional hardware. 206-771-4645.

Silverton Victorian Millworks, P.O. Box 2987, Durango, CO 81302: Catalog $4 ❖ Doors with stained glass or etched glass inserts. 303-259-5915.

Simpson Door Company, P.O. Box 210, McCleary, WA 98557: Free brochure ❖ Paneled, carved, and standard wooden doors. 800-952-4057; 206-495-3291 (in WA).

Southeastern Insulated Glass, 6477-B Peachtree Industrial Blvd., Atlanta, GA 30360: Free information ❖ Greenhouse and sun room kits. Also sliding glass doors, and skylights with optional tempered insulated glass. 800-841-9842; 404-455-8838 (in GA).

Southwest Door Company, 219 N. 3rd Ave., Tucson, AZ 85705: Free list of retail sources ❖ Traditional, contemporary, and country-style doors, windows, hardware, cabinets, and flooring. (602) 624-1434.

Specialty Woodworks, P.O. Box 1450, Hamilton, MT 59840: Catalog $7 ❖ Doors and cabinets. 406-363-6353.

Stanley Hardware, 600 Myrtle St., New Britain, CT 06050: Free information ❖ Kits for make-your-own sliding closet doors. 800-835-2453.

Taylor Brothers, P.O. Box 11198, Lynchburg, VA 24506: Catalog $2 ❖ Handcrafted storm screen doors. 800-288-6767.

Touchstone Woodworks, P.O. Box 112, Ravenna, OH 44266: Catalog $2 ❖ Authentic Victorian-style screen doors, moldings, porch parts, and ornamental trim. 216-297-1313.

Jack Wallis Door Emporium, Rt. 1, Box 22A, Murray, KY 42071: Catalog $4 ❖ Handcrafted doors with optional stained glass. 502-489-2613.

Weather Shield Mfg. Inc., c/o HYC, 330 E. Kilbourn Ave., Milwaukee, WI 53202: Free information ❖ Wooden windows, patio doors, and steel entryways. 800-477-6808.

Wing Industries, P.O. Box 38347, Dallas, TX 75238: Free information ❖ Bi-fold French doors for interiors. 800-341-8464.

The Wood Factory, 111 Railroad St., Navasota, TX 77868: Catalog $2 ❖ Ornamental trim, mantels, screen doors, and millwork. 409-825-7233.

Woodstone Company, Patch Rd., P.O. Box 223, Westminster, VT 05158: Information $3 ❖ Insulated solid wooden doors and single, double, or triple-glazed windows with palladians and straight and fanned transoms. 802-722-9217.

Flooring

Aged Woods, 2331 E. Market St., York, PA 17402: Free brochure ❖ Re-milled flooring from antique boards and beams. 800-233-9307; 717-840-0330 (in PA).

Albany Woodworks, P.O. Box 729, Albany, LA 70711: Free information ❖ Antique heart pine and American hardwood flooring. 504-567-1155.

Aspen Specialties, Rt. 2, Box 256A, Longview, TX 75605: Free information ❖ Paneling and decking for interiors. 800-723-4399; 903-663-4399 (in TX).

Authentic Pine Floors Inc., 4042 Hwy. 42, P.O. Box 206, Locust Grove, GA 30248: Free information ❖ Wide plank pine flooring. 800-283-6038.

Bre Lumber/Rare Earth Hardwoods, 6778 E. Traverse Hwy., Traverse City, MI 49684: Free information ❖ Hardwood, other lumber, flooring, and decking. 800-968-0074.

Carlisle Restoration Lumber, HCR 32, Box 556C, Stoddard, NH 03464: Free information ❖ Wide pine flooring and paneling. 603-446-3937.

Carpet Express, 915 Market St., Dalton, GA 30720: Free information ❖ Carpet, oriental rugs, vinyl, and hardwood flooring. 800-922-5582.

Goodwin Lumber, Rt. 2, Box 119, Micanopy, FL 32667: Free information ❖ Heart pine and red cypress flooring, paneling, and beams. 800-336-3116.

Granville Manufacturing Company Inc., P.O. Box 15, Rt. 100, Granville, VT 05747: Free brochure ❖ Quarter-sawn clapboard siding, wide pine and hardwood flooring, and building materials. 802-767-4747.

Hartco Flooring Company, P.O. Box 4009, Oneida, TN 37841: Catalog $1 (request list of retail sources) ❖ Oak flooring in parquet, combination, parallel, herringbone, and basket-weave patterns. 800-442-7826.

Historic Floors of Oshkosh Inc., P.O. Box 572, Oshkosh, WI 54902: Free list of retail sources ❖ Hardwood reproduction borders and patterned flooring. 414-582-9977.

Joinery Company, P.O. Box 518, Tarboro, NC 27886: Catalog $5 ❖ Antique heart pine tongue-and-groove flooring, paneling, and trim from authentic colonial buildings. 800-726-7463.

Kentucky Wood Floors, P.O. Box 33276, Louisville, KY 40232: Catalog $2 ❖ Walnut, oak, cherry, and ash borders ready for glue-down installation. 502-451-6024.

Launstein Hardwoods, 384 S. Every Rd., Mason, MI 48854: Free information ❖ Easy-to-install and finish pre-sanded hardwood flooring. 517-676-1133.

Lee's Carpet Showcase, 3068 N. Dug Gap Rd., Dalton, GA 30720: Free information ❖ Carpet and Oriental rugs, vinyl and wooden flooring, and accessories. 800-433-8479.

Memphis Hardwood Flooring Company, 1551 N. Thomas St., P.O. Box 38217, Memphis, TN 38107: Free information ❖ Unfinished and finished oak flooring. 800-346-3010.

Northfields Restorations, Rt. 1, Hampton Falls, NH 03844: Free brochure ❖ Antique flooring. 603-926-5383.

Piedmont Mantel & Millwork, 4320 Interstate Dr., Macon, GA 31210: Catalog $3 ❖ Salvaged heart pine flooring. Also colonial-style mantels in a choice of woods. 912-477-7536.

J.L. Powell & Company Inc., 600 S. Madison St., Whiteville, NC 28472: Free information ❖ Antique heart pine flooring. 800-227-2007; 910-642-8989 (in NC).

Quality Woods Ltd., 63 Flanders Bartley Rd., Flanders, NJ 07836: Free brochure ❖ Teak, plywood, and Asian rosewood parquet, tongue-and-groove planks, and strip flooring. 201-584-7554.

HOME BUILDING & IMPROVEMENT

Sheoga Hardwood Flooring & Paneling Inc., P.O. Box 510, Burton, OH 44021: Free list of retail sources ❖ Unfinished, pre-sanded, and milled tongue-and-groove flooring. 216-834-1710.

Southwest Door Company, 219 N. 3rd Ave., Tucson, AZ 85705: Free list of retail sources ❖ Traditional, contemporary, and country-style doors, windows, hardware, cabinets, and flooring. 602-624-1434.

Vintage Lumber Company, 1 Council Dr., Woodsboro, MD 21798: Free information ❖ Re-milled antique heart pine, oak, chestnut, cherry, walnut, and poplar flooring. 800-499-7859.

The Wood Mill Box, Box 146, East Livermore, ME 04228: Free information ❖ Cherry, oak, maple, ash, wide pine, walnut, and birch flooring. 207-897-5211.

Frames & Beams

Bear Creek Lumber, P.O. Box 669, Winthrop, WA 98862: Brochure $4 ❖ Western red cedar building supplies. 800-597-7191.

Blue Ridge Timber Frame, 2030 Redwood Dr., Christianburg, VA 24073: Brochure $8 ❖ Timber frames for home construction. 703-382-1102.

E.F. Bufton & Son, Builders Inc., P.O. Box 164, Princeton, MA 01541: Brochure $5 ❖ Oak post-and-beam frames. 508-464-5418.

Goodwin Lumber, Rt. 2, Box 119, Micanopy, FL 32667: Free information ❖ Heart pine lumber and red cypress flooring, paneling, and beams. 800-336-3118.

Vermont Frames, P.O. Box 100, Hinesburg, VT 05461: Free brochure ❖ Post-and-beam frames. 802-453-3727.

Paint & Refinishing Supplies

Burr Tavern, Rt. 1, Box 474, East Meredith, NY 13757: Free information ❖ Reproduction 18th and 19th-century paints, brushes, and materials. 800-664-6293.

Easy Time Wood Refinishing Products, 1208 Lisle Pl., Lisle, IL 60532: Free catalog ❖ Easy-to-use wood refinishing supplies. 708-515-1161.

Homestead Paint & Finishes, P.O. Box 1668, Lunenburg, MA 01462: Free information with long SASE ❖ Flat and textured finish milk paint in assorted colors. 508-582-0329.

Howard Products Inc., 560 Linne Rd., Paso Robles, CA 93446: Free information ❖ Restoration products. 800-266-9545.

Janovic/Plaza Inc., 3-35 Thomson Ave., Long Island City, NY 11101: Catalog $4.95 ❖ Hard-to-find tools and finishes for painting and dyeing. 718-786-4444.

Johnson Paint Company Inc., 355 Newbury St., Boston, MA 02115: Catalog $1 ❖ Painting supplies, brushes, and tools. 617-536-4838.

The Old Fashioned Milk Paint Company, P.O. Box 222, 436 Main St., Groton, MA 01450: Free information ❖ Authentic Colonial and Shaker milk paint in several colors. 508-448-6336.

Primrose Distributing, 54445 Rose Rd., South Bend, IN 46628: Information $3 ❖ Original oil base formula for authentic refinishing of 18th and 19th-century architecture. 800-222-3092.

Stulb Colour Craftsmen, P.O. Box 1030, Fort Washington, PA 19034: Information $1 ❖ Natural earth pigment paints for authentic color decoration, restoration, and preservation. 215-654-1770.

Target Enterprises, P.O. Box 1582, Rutherford, NJ 07070: Free information ❖ Water-based topcoat finishes and stains. 800-752-9922.

Paneling

AFCO Industries Inc., 615 E. 40th St., Holland, MI 49423: Free information ❖ Scratch-resistant waterproof hardwood panels. 800-253-4644.

Aspen Specialties, Rt. 2, Box 256A, Longview, TX 75605: Free information ❖ Paneling and decking for interiors. 800-723-4399; 903-663-4399 (in TX).

California Redwood Association, 405 Enfrente Dr., Ste. 200, Novato, CA 94949: Free information with long SASE ❖ Redwood paneling. 415-382-0662.

Driwood Ornamental Wood Moulding, P.O. Box 1729, Florence, SC 29503: Catalog $6 ❖ Embossed wooden molding and raised paneling, mantels, curved stairs, and doors. 803-669-2478.

Georgia-Pacific, P.O. Box 2808, Norcross, GA 30091: Free information ❖ Wall paneling and pre-hung wallpaper on plywood panels. 800-447-2882.

Goodwin Lumber, Rt. 2, Box 119, Micanopy, FL 32667: Free information ❖ Heart pine and red cypress flooring, paneling, and beams. 800-336-3118.

Griffis Lumber & Sawmill, 9333 NW 13th St., Gainesville, FL 32653: Free information ❖ Cypress shingles and custom kiln-dried cypress siding and paneling. 904-372-9965.

Maple Grove Restorations, P.O. Box 9194, Bolton, CT 06043: Brochure $2 ❖ Interior raised panel shutters and walls and wainscoting. 203-742-5432.

Masonite Corporation, 1 S. Wacker Dr., Chicago, IL 60606: Free information ❖ Hardboard paneling. 800-446-1649.

Simpson Timber, Box 1169, Arcata, CA 95521: Free information ❖ Redwood paneling. 800-637-7077; 707-822-0371 (in CA).

Restoration Materials & Equipment

A & H Brass & Supply, 126 W. Main St., Johnson City, TN 37604: Catalog $1 ❖ Wooden ornaments, moldings, and veneers. 800-638-4252; 615-928-8220 (in TN).

Abatron, 5501 95th Ave., Kenosha, WI 53144: Free information ❖ Concrete restoration materials. 800-445-1754; 414-653-2000 (in WI).

Adkins Architectural Antiques, 3515 Fannin, Houston, TX 77004: Free brochure ❖ Salvaged architectural antiques. 713-522-6547.

Architectural Antiquities, Harborside, ME 04642: Free brochure ❖ Victorian supplies from the 18th and 19th-century for home building and restoration. 207-326-4938.

Architectural Iron Company, P.O. Box 126, Milford, PA 18337: Catalog $4 ❖ Reproduction 18th and 19th-century castings and wrought-iron accessories. 800-442-4766.

The Bank Architectural Antiques, 1824 Felicity St., New Orleans, LA 70113: Free brochure ❖ Reproduction and repaired New Orleans-style shutters, doors, hardware, and architectural supplies. 800-274-8883.

Bendix Moldings Inc., 37 Ramland Rd. South, Orangeburg, NY 10962: Free catalog ❖ Decorative wooden moldings and ornaments. 800-526-0240; 914-365-1111 (in NY).

Campbellsville Industries Inc., P.O. Box 278, Campbellsville, KY 42718: Free catalog ❖ Aluminum cornices, louvers, cupolas, columns, balustrades, and shutters with an optional baked-on finish. 502-465-8135.

A Carolina Craftsman, 975 S. Avocado St., Anaheim, CA 92805: Catalog $5 (refundable) ❖ Hard-to-find antique replacement parts for houses and furniture. 714-776-7877.

Cathedral Stone Products Inc., 8332 Bristol Ct., Ste. 107, Jessup, MD 20749: Free information ❖ Acrylic and latex-free bonding agents and restoration mortars. 301-317-4658.

Chadsworth Incorporated, P.O. Box 53268, Atlanta, GA 30355: Catalog $5 (refundable) ❖ Columns and replacement components in wood and fiberglass. 800-265-8667; 910-763-7600 (in GA).

Donald Durham Company, Box 804, Des Moines, IA 50304: Free list of retail sources ❖ Self-hardening water putty for many kinds of repairs.

Epoxy Technology Inc., 14 Fortune Dr., Billerica, MA 01821: Free information ❖ Epoxy adhesives for artifact restoration. 800-227-2201; 508-667-3805 (in MA).

Hardware Plus, 701 E. Kingsley Rd., Garland, TX 75041: Catalog $5 ❖ Supplies for restoring old houses and furniture. 800-522-7336.

❖ HOME BUILDING & IMPROVEMENT ❖

Improvements, 4944 Commerce Pkwy., Cleveland, OH 44128: Free catalog ❖ Tools and accessories for home repair and improvements. 800-642-2112.

Kentucky Millwork, P.O. Box 33276, Louisville, KY 40232: Catalog $2 (refundable) ❖ Architectural supplies for restoring houses. 502-451-6024.

Park Place, 2251 Wisconsin Ave. NW, Washington, DC 20007: Catalog $2 ❖ Classic outdoor furnishings and architectural products. 202-342-6294.

A.F. Schwerd Manufacturing Company, 3215 McClure Ave., Pittsburgh, PA 15212: Free brochure ❖ Wooden columns in seasoned northern white pine with matching pilasters and aluminum bases. 412-766-6322.

Tremont Nail Company, P.O. Box 111, Wareham, MA 02571: Free catalog ❖ Old-fashioned cut nails. 800-842-0560.

Tuff-Kote Company Inc., 210 Seminary Ave., Woodstock, IL 60098: Free information ❖ Filler for wall and ceiling cracks.

The Wood Factory, 111 Railroad St., Navasota, TX 77868: Catalog $2 ❖ Victorian-style moldings, screen doors, porch parts, ornamental trim, and other woodwork. 409-825-7233.

Roofing Materials

C & H Roofing, P.O. Box 2105, Lake City, FL 32056: Free information ❖ Red cedar shingles with a thatched look and historical roofing restoration supplies. 800-327-8115.

Cedar Valley Shingle Systems, 943 San Felipe Rd., Hollister, CA 95023: Free brochure ❖ Cedar shingle panels in regular or rough-sawn textures. 800-521-9523.

Celadon, P.O. Box 860, Valley Forge, PA 19482: Free brochure ❖ Slate-looking fired ceramic roofing material. 800-CEL-SLATE.

CertainTeed, P.O. Box 860, Valley Forge, PA 19482: Free information ❖ Asphalt-based roof shingles that resemble wood shakes. 800-345-1145.

Conklin Metal Industries, P.O. Box 1858, Atlanta, GA 30301: Brochure $3 ❖ Roofing shingles in galvanized steel, copper, and other materials. 404-688-4510.

Georgia-Pacific, P.O. Box 2808, Norcross, GA 30091: Free information ❖ Easy-to-install shingles with a textured look of cedar. 800-447-2882.

Griffis Lumber & Sawmill, 9333 NW 13th St., Gainesville, FL 32653: Free information ❖ Cypress shingles and custom kiln-dried cypress siding and paneling. 904-372-9965.

Liberty Cedar, 535 Liberty Ln., West Kingston, RI 02892: Free information ❖ Wooden roofing. 800-88-CEDAR; 401-789-6626 (in RI).

Masonite Corporation, 1 S. Wacker Dr., Chicago, IL 60606: Free information ❖ Wood-fiber shingles with an authentic shake look. 800-446-1649.

The New England Slate Company, Burr Pond Rd., Sudbury, VT 05733: Free brochure ❖ New and salvaged roofing slate. 802-247-8809.

Preservation Products, 221 Brooke St., Media, PA 19063: Free brochure ❖ Acrylic roof-coating system. 800-553-0523.

Revere Copper Products Inc., P.O. Box 300, Rome, NY 13442: Free information ❖ Copper shingles. 800-490-1776.

ShakerTown Corporation, 1200 Kerron St., Winlock, WA 98596: Free catalog ❖ Cedar shingles. 800-426-8970.

Supradur Manufacturing Corporation, P.O. Box 908, Rye, NY 10580: Free information ❖ Fireproof roofing shingles with a natural stone look. 800-223-1948.

Tile Roofs Inc., P.O. Box 177, Mokena, IL 60448: Free brochure ❖ New and used slate and tile roofing materials. 708-479-4366.

Salvaged Building Materials

Aged Woods, 2331 E. Market St., York, PA 17402: Free brochure ❖ Re-milled flooring from antique boards and beams. 800-233-9307; 717-840-0330 (in PA).

Albany Woodworks, P.O. Box 729, Albany, LA 70711: Free information ❖ Reclaimed antique building materials. 504-567-1155.

Architectural Antique Warehouse, P.O. Box 3065, Station D, Ottawa, Ontario, Canada K1P 6H6: Free information ❖ Reproduction old house parts. 613-526-1818.

Architectural Antiques, 801 Washington Ave. North, Minneapolis, MN 55401: Free information ❖ Architectural elements and ecclesiastical artifacts. 612-332-8344.

Architectural Antiques Exchange, 715 N. 2nd St., Philadelphia, PA 19123: Free brochure ❖ Salvaged building components and trim. 215-922-3669.

Architectural Antiquities, Harborside, ME 04642: Free brochure ❖ Brass lighting fixtures and hardware, Victorian plumbing fixtures, fireplace mantels, doors, windows, stained glass, and architectural antiquities. 207-326-4938.

Architectural Artifacts Inc., 1306 W. Kennedy Blvd., Tampa, FL 33606: Free information ❖ Architectural salvage. 813-254-1168.

Architectural Salvage Warehouse, 212 Battery St., Burlington, VT 05401: Free information ❖ Hardware, doors, stained glass, woodwork, mantels, fixtures, columns, and architectural antiques. 802-658-5011.

The Bank Architectural Antiques, 1824 Felicity St., New Orleans, LA 70113: Free brochure ❖ Salvaged building components. 800-274-8883.

The Brass Knob, 2311 18th St. NW, Washington, DC 20009: Free information ❖ Hardware, garden ornaments, bathroom accessories, fireplace equipment, and antique lighting, from 1870 to 1930. 202-332-3370.

By-Gone Days Antiques Inc., 3100 South Blvd., Charlotte, NC 28209: Free information ❖ Mantels, restored door hardware, and architectural antiques. 704-527-8717.

Conner's Architectural Antiques, 701 P St., Lincoln, NE 68508: Free information ❖ Interior and exterior architectural antiques. 402-435-3338.

The Emporium, 1800 Westheimer, Houston, TX 77098: Catalog $3 ❖ Plumbing, furniture, garden accessories, mantels, and architectural antiques. 713-528-3808.

Great Gatsby's, 5070 Peachtree Industrial Blvd., Atlanta, GA 30341: Free brochure ❖ Architectural antiquities and ornamental trim. 800-428-7297.

Olde Theatre Architectural Salvage, 2045 Broadway, Kansas City, MO 64108: Free brochure ❖ Salvaged building components and accessories. 816-283-3051.

Omega Too, 2204 San Pablo Ave., Berkeley, CA 94702: Free information ❖ Architectural ornamentation for houses and gardens. 510-843-3636.

The Original Cast Lighting, 6120 Delmar Blvd., St. Louis, MO 63112: Catalog $2 ❖ Restored antique fixtures. 314-863-1895.

Salvage One, 1524 S. Sangamon St., Chicago, IL 60608: Free brochure ❖ Salvaged building components. 312-733-0098.

Salvaged Building Materials, 653 Main St., Lititz, PA 17543: Quarterly newsletter subscription $10 a year ❖ Salvaged 18th and 19th-century materials from houses, grist mills, and barns. 717-626-4520.

United House Wrecking Inc., 535 Hope St., Stamford, CT 06906: Free brochure ❖ Doors, mantels, beveled glass, Victorian gingerbread, paneling, fixtures, dividers, screens, and salvaged architectural building components and trim. 203-348-5371.

Urban Archaeology, 285 Lafayette St., New York, NY 10012: Free information ❖ Staircases, balconies, plaster moldings, windows and skylights, doors, entryways, and Victorian and architectural antiques and accessories. 212-431-6969.

Wooden Nickel Architectural Antiques, 1410 Central Pkwy., Cincinnati, OH 45210: Free information ❖ Salvaged building components and trims. 513-241-2985.

Shutters

Alside Corporation, P.O. Box 2010, Akron, OH 44309: Free list of retail sources ❖ Shutter sets. 216-929-1811.

Beech River Mill Company, Old Rt. 16, Box 236, Centre Ossipee, NH 03814: Brochure $5 ❖ Custom-louvered and paneled products. Also period shutter and blind hardware. 603-539-2636.

Historic Windows, P.O. Box 1172, Harrisonburg, VA 22801: Catalog $3 ❖ Handcrafted Victorian-style hardwood shutters. 540-434-5855.

Iberia Millwork, P.O. Box 12139, New Iberia, LA 70562: Free information ❖ Interior and exterior shutters, cabinets, and French doors. 318-365-8129.

Inter Trade Inc., 3175 Fujita St., Torrance, CA 90505: Free information ❖ Roll shutters that provide security and protection from heat, sun, cold, rain, and noise. 213-515-7177.

Kestrel Manufacturing, P.O. Box 12, Saint Peters, PA 19470: Information $2 ❖ Knock-down and ready-to-hang folding screens and interior and exterior shutters. 610-469-6444.

Maple Grove Restorations, P.O. Box 9194, Bolton, CT 06043: Brochure $2 ❖ Interior raised panel shutters, panel walls, and wainscoting. 203-742-5432.

Perkowitz Window Fashions Inc., 135 Green Bay Rd., Wilmette, IL 60091: Catalog $1 ❖ Interior shutters, window shades, and all types of blinds. 847-251-7700.

REM Industries, P.O. Box 504, Northborough, MA 01532: Catalog $2 ❖ Custom-made wooden shutters. 508-393-8424.

The Shutter Depot, Rt. 2, Box 157, Greenville, GA 30222: Free brochure ❖ Shutter kits and pre-finished and unfinished interior and exterior shutters. 706-672-1214.

Shutter Shop, P.O. Box 11882, Charlotte, NC 28220: Catalog $3 ❖ Interior and exterior shutters. 704-334-8031.

Shuttercraft, 282 Stepstone Hill Rd., Guilford, CT 06437: Free brochure ❖ Unfinished or primed and painted western white pine shutters with movable or fixed louvers. 203-453-1973.

Vixen Hill, Main St., P.O. Box 389, Elverson, PA 19520: Catalog $4 ❖ Wooden shutters. 800-423-2766.

Siding

California Redwood Association, 405 Enfrente Dr., Ste. 200, Novato, CA 94949: Free information with long SASE ❖ Redwood siding. 415-382-0662.

Cedar Valley Shingle Systems, 943 San Felipe Rd., Hollister, CA 95023: Free brochure ❖ Red cedar shingle panels. 800-521-9523.

Dryvit Systems Inc., 1 Energy Way, West Warwick, RI 02893: Free information ❖ Siding that looks like stucco. 401-822-4100.

Georgia-Pacific, P.O. Box 2808, Norcross, GA 30091: Free information ❖ Hardboard siding with a colonial wood-grain texture. 800-447-2882.

Granville Manufacturing Company Inc., P.O. Box 15, Rt. 100, Granville, VT 05747: Free brochure ❖ Quarter-sawn clapboard siding, wide pine and hardwood flooring, and other building materials. 802-767-4747.

Griffis Lumber & Sawmill, 9333 NW 13th St., Gainesville, FL 32653: Free information ❖ Cypress shingles and custom kiln-dried cypress siding and paneling. 904-372-9965.

Louisiana-Pacific Corporation, P.O. Box 10266, Portland, OR 97210: Free information ❖ Treated and weatherized wooden siding. 800-299-0028.

VIPCO, P.O. Box 1058, Columbus, OH 43216: Free information ❖ Solid-vinyl exterior siding with a look of carved wooden clapboard. 800-366-8472.

Ward Clapboard Mill Inc., P.O. Box 1030, Waitsfield, VT 05673: Free information ❖ Spruce quarter-sawn clapboard siding. 802-496-3581.

Stairways

A.J. Stairs Inc., 1095 Towbin Ave., Lakewood, NJ 08701: Brochure $1 ❖ Easy-to-assemble spiral and curved stairways. 800-425-7824.

American Ornamental Metal, 5013 Kelley St., P.O. Box 21548, Houston, TX 77026: Free catalog ❖ Iron and wooden spiral staircases. 800-231-3693.

BentWood Building, 241 Addison Square, Kalispell, MT 59901: Catalog $4 ❖ Log spiral stairways and furniture. 406-257-4161.

Curvoflite, 205 Spencer Ave., Chelsea, MA 02150: Free information ❖ Spiral and circular oak staircases, paneling, moldings, cabinets, and millwork. 617-889-0007.

Driwood Ornamental Wood Moulding, P.O. Box 1729, Florence, SC 29503: Catalog $6 ❖ Curved stairs, embossed wooden molding, raised paneling, mantels, and doors. 803-669-2478.

Duvinage Corporation, 60 W. Oakridge Dr., Hagerstown, MD 21740: Free catalog ❖ Spiral and circular stairways. 800-541-2645.

Goddard Manufacturing, Box 502, Logan, KS 67646: Free information ❖ Spiral staircases with optional wooden railings. 913-689-4341.

The Iron Shop, 400 Reed Rd., P.O. Box 547, Broomall, PA 19008: Free brochure ❖ Iron circular stairway kits. 800-523-7427.

The Maizefield Company, P.O. Box 336, Port Townsend, WA 98368: Free brochure ❖ Mantels, staircases, and moldings. 360-385-6789.

Mylen Industries, 650 Washington St., Peekskill, NY 10566: Free brochure ❖ Easy-to-install space-saving indoor and outdoor spiral stairs. 800-431-2155; 914-739-8486 (in NY).

Piedmont Home Products Inc., P.O. Box 269, Ruckersville, VA 22968: Free brochure ❖ Handcrafted spiral stairs, rails, balusters, and newel posts. 800-622-3399.

Salter Industries, P.O. Box 183, Eagleville, PA 19408: Free brochure ❖ Easy-to-install spiral stairs. 800-368-8280.

Spiral Manufacturing Inc., 17251 Jefferson Hwy., Baton Rouge, LA 70817: Free brochure ❖ Wooden spiral and curved stairway kits. 800-535-9956.

Spiral Stairs of America, 1700 Spiral Ct., Erie, PA 16510: Free brochure ❖ Stairways. 800-422-3700.

Stair Systems Inc., 1480 E. 6th St., Sandwich, IL 60548: Free information ❖ Easy-to-assemble staircases with factory pre-assembled sections. 800-962-4299.

Stairways Inc., 4166 Pinemont, Houston, TX 77018: Free brochure ❖ Wood and metal stairways. 800-231-0793.

Steptoe & Wife Antiques Ltd., 322 Geary Ave., Toronto, Ontario, Canada M6H 2C7: Catalog $3 ❖ Easy-to-assemble interior and exterior cast-iron spiral and straight staircases in Victorian design. 416-530-4200.

York Spiral Stairs, RR 1, Box 945, North Vassalboro, ME 04962: Free brochure ❖ Spiral stairs in red oak, Honduran mahogany, and hardwood. 207-872-5558.

Stucco, Bricks & Stones

Connecticut Stone Supplies, 311 Post Rd., Orange, CT 06477: Free information ❖ Cobblestone, granite pavers, fieldstone, and flagstone. 203-795-9767.

Keystone Retaining Wall Systems, 4444 W. 78th St., Minneapolis, MN 55435: Free information ❖ Modular retaining wall systems. 800-891-9791.

Old Carolina Brick Company, 475 Majolica Rd., Salisbury, NC 28147: Free brochure ❖ Authentic handmade brick. 704-636-8850.

Stone Company Inc., W4520 Lime Rd., Eden, WI 53019: Free information ❖ Natural building and landscape cobblers, granite boulders, wall stone, steppers, and flagstone. 414-477-2521.

Stone Legends, 301 Pleasant Dr., Dallas, TX 75217: Free information ❖ Manufactured stone. 214-398-1199.

HOME BUILDING & IMPROVEMENT

Stone Magic, 5400 Miller, Dallas, TX 75206: Free brochure ❖ Interior and exterior cast-stone. Also classic to contemporary cast-stone mantels. 214-826-3606.

Switch Plates

Agnathous Cupboard, 11516 Palm Springs Avenue NE, Albuquerque, NM 87111: Brochure $2 ❖ Western-image and Native American theme switch plates. 505-298-6558.

Classic Accents Inc., P.O. Box 1181, Southgate, MI 48195: Catalog $1.50 ❖ Switch cover plates, push-button lighting switches, and solid brass cover plates. 313-282-5525.

The Country Store, 28 James St., Geneva, IL 60134: Catalog $2 ❖ Pewter-finished, punched tin switch plate covers. 708-879-0098.

Derk's Switchplates, 4176 S. Luce Ave., Fremont, MI 49412: Free information ❖ Hand-carved wooden switch plates. 616-924-3382.

River Connection Crafts & Gifts, 7513 N. Highland, Gladstone, MO 64188: Free information with long SASE ❖ Country-style switch plates. 816-741-3100.

Tile & Linoleum

American Olean Tile Company, 1000 Cannon Ave., Lansdale, PA 19446: Free information ❖ Easy-to-install ceramic mosaic tiles. 215-393-2237.

Amsterdam Corporation, 150 E. 58th St., 9th Floor, New York, NY 10155: Catalog $3 ❖ Authentic Dutch hand-painted tiles. 212-644-1350.

Armstrong World Industries, P.O. Box 3001, Lancaster, PA 17604: Free information ❖ Tile, linoleum, and other floor coverings with an optional no-wax surface. 717-397-0611.

Laura Ashley, Mail Order, P.O. Box 18413, Memphis, TN 38181: Free information ❖ Floor tiles. 800-367-2000.

Carpet Express, 915 Market St., Dalton, GA 30720: Free information ❖ Carpet and vinyl. 800-922-5582.

Color Tile, P.O. Box 749, Fort Worth, TX 76101: Free information ❖ Ceramic tile for bathroom counter tops and walls. 817-870-9540.

Country Floors Inc., 15 E. 16th St., New York, NY 10003: Catalog $6 ❖ Hand-molded and painted ceramic tiles. 212-627-8300.

Designs in Tile, P.O. Box 358, Mt. Shasta, CA 96067: Brochure $3 ❖ Historic reproductions, contemporary and traditional patterns, and other ceramic tiles. Also murals, corner blocks, and coordinated borders. 916-926-2629.

Epro Tiles Inc., 156 E. Broadway, Westerville, OH 43081: Free information ❖ Sandstone collection of handmade tiles. 614-882-6990.

Interceramic USA, 2333 S. Jupiter Rd., Garland, TX 75041: Free list of retail sources ❖ Durable flooring tile. 800-496-TILE.

Italian Tile Center, 499 Park Ave., New York, NY 10022: Free information ❖ Italian tiles with flowers, fruit, and other patterns. 212-980-1500.

Sun House Tiles, 9986 Happy Acres West, Bozeman, MT 59715: Free information ❖ Handmade reproduction period tiles. 406-587-3651.

Terra Designs, Rt. 202 South, Far Hills, NJ 07931: Catalog $1 ❖ Decorator bathroom tiles. 201-539-2999.

Victorian Collectibles, 845 E. Glenbrook Rd., Milwaukee, WI 53217: Catalog $5 ❖ Tiles and matching wallpaper duplicated from 19th-century patterns. 414-352-6971.

Trim & Ornamental Woodwork

A & M Victorian Decorations, 2411 Chico Ave., South El Monte, CA 91733: Free brochure ❖ Custom architectural trim. 818-575-0693.

American Custom-Millwork Inc., 3904 Newton Rd., P.O. Box 3608, Albany, GA 31706: Catalog $5 ❖ Embossed and plain architectural moldings and millwork. 912-888-3303.

Anderson-McQuaid Company Inc., 170 Fawcett St., Cambridge, MA 02138: Free price list ❖ Custom and restored moldings, flooring, paneling, and hardwood lumber. 617-876-3250.

Anthony Wood Products Inc., P.O. Box 1081, Hillsboro, TX 76645: Catalog $3 ❖ Handcrafted Victorian gingerbread. 817-582-7225.

Architectural Components, 26 N. Leverett Rd., Montague, MA 01351: Brochure $5 ❖ Custom and reproduction 18th and 19th-century doors, windows and window frames, moldings, and French doors. 413-367-9441.

Architectural Products by Outwater, 52 Passaic St., P.O. Box 347, Wood Ridge, NJ 07075: Free catalog ❖ Hardware, columns, millwork, moldings, and decorative materials. 800-835-4403.

Architectural Sculpture Ltd., 242 Lafayette St., New York, NY 10012: Free information ❖ Turn-of-the-century plaster ornaments, plaques, sculptures, and building and remodeling accouterments. 212-431-5873.

Arvid's Woods, 2500 Hewitt Ave., Everett, WA 98201: Catalog $6 ❖ Interior and exterior historical moldings and accessories. 800-627-8437.

The Balmer Studios Inc., 9 Codeco Ct., Don Mills, Ontario, Canada M3A 1B6: Catalog $25 ❖ Interior plaster molding patterns. 416-449-2155.

Bendix Moldings Inc., 37 Ramland Rd. South, Orangeburg, NY 10962: Free catalog ❖ Wooden moldings and ornaments. 800-526-0240; 914-365-1111 (in NY).

Bomar Designs, 2026 St., Hwy. 265, Branson, MO 05616: Free catalog ❖ Crafted composition replicas of wood carvings. 417-338-5133.

Boston Turning Works, 42 Plympton St., Boston, MA 02118: Brochure $1 ❖ Finials for gates, fence posts, and balustrades. 617-482-9085.

Bryant Stove Inc., Box 2048, Thorndike, ME 04986: Free brochure ❖ Wooden mantels and ornamental trim. 207-568-3665.

Campbellsville Industries Inc., P.O. Box 278, Campbellsville, KY 42718: Free catalog ❖ Aluminum cornices, louvers, cupolas, columns, balustrades, and shutters. 502-465-8135.

Chadsworth Incorporated, P.O. Box 53268, Atlanta, GA 30355: Catalog $5 (refundable) ❖ Columns and replacement components in wood, fiberglass, and other materials. 800-265-8667; 910-763-7600 (in GA).

Cinder Whit & Company, 733 11th Ave. South, Wahpeton, ND 58075: Free brochure ❖ Custom wood turning. 701-642-9064.

Cross Vinyl Lattice, 3174 Marjan Dr., Atlanta, GA 30340: Free information ❖ Vinyl lattice panels with diagonal or rectangular patterns. 800-521-9878.

Cumberland Woodcraft Company Inc., P.O. Drawer 609, Carlisle, PA 17013: Catalog $5 ❖ Ceiling treatments, corbels, brackets, molding, grilles, and Victorian architectural millwork, carvings, and trims. 717-243-0063.

Custom Woodturnings, 4000 Telephone Rd., Houston, TX 77087: Catalog $3 ❖ Reproduction Victorian millwork. 713-641-6254.

Decorators Supply Corporation, 3610 S. Morgan St., Chicago, IL 60609: Free list of retail sources ❖ Wooden mantels, capitals, brackets, medallions, plaster cornices, wooden moldings, and composition and wood-fiber ornaments. 312-847-6300.

Design Toscano, 17 E. Campbell St., Arlington Heights, IL 60005: Catalog $5 ❖ Replica gargoyles and goddesses, classical columns, capitals, table bases, brackets, urns, wall friezes, and other decorative objects. 800-525-1733.

Driwood Ornamental Wood Moulding, P.O. Box 1729, Florence, SC 29503: Catalog $6 ❖ Embossed wooden molding, raised paneling, mantels, curved stairs, and doors. 803-669-2478.

HOME BUILDING & IMPROVEMENT

Drummond Woodworks, 327 Bay St. South, Hamilton, Ontario, Canada L8P 3J7: Free brochure ❖ Reproduction ornamental woodcarvings. 800-263-2543.

Empire Woodworks, P.O. Box 717, Blanco, TX 78606: Catalog $3 ❖ Country-style and Victorian trim. 512-833-2119.

Erb Lumber Company, 1210 Morse Ave., Royal Oak, MI 48067: Free brochure ❖ Architectural millwork. 810-543-9100.

Federal Cabinet Company Inc., 409 Highland Ave., Box 190, Middletown, NY 10940: Free list of retail sources ❖ Architectural wood turnings. 914-342-1511.

Felber Ornamental Plastering Corporation, 1000 W. Washington St., P.O. Box 57, Norristown, PA 19404: Catalog $3 ❖ Period-style and plaster cornices, medallions, sculptures, niches, capitals, brackets, and domes. 800-392-6896; 610-275-4713 (in PA).

Fischer & Jirouch Company, 4821 Superior Ave., Cleveland, OH 44103: Catalog $10 ❖ Handcrafted plaster ornaments. 216-361-3840.

Florida Wood Moulding & Trim, 10780 47th St. North, Clearwater, FL 34622: Catalog $5 ❖ Hardwood moldings. 813-572-1983.

Focal Point Inc., P.O. Box 93327, Atlanta, GA 30377: Free information ❖ Ceiling medallions, cornice moldings, niche caps, and doorway treatments. 800-662-5550.

Fox Woodcraft, P.O. Box 846, Sutter Creek, CA 95685: Catalog $2 ❖ Custom gingerbread decorative trim. 209-267-0774.

Gazebo & Porchworks, 728 9th Ave. SW, Puyallup, WA 98371: Catalog $2 ❖ Wooden trims, ornamental items, outdoor swings, and backyard play structures. 206-848-0502.

The Gingerbread Man, 4664 Park Hill Dr., Pleasant Valley, CA 95667: Catalog $2.50 ❖ Victorian-style trim and ornamental woodwork. 916-644-0440.

Gingerbread Man Woodworks, Factory Outlet Store, P.O. Box 59, Noel, MO 64854: Catalog $5 ❖ Gazebos, garden structures, and ornamental trim. 417-775-2553.

Hallidays America Inc., P.O. Box 731, Sparta, NJ 07871: Free information ❖ Fireplace accessories, hand-carved mantels, and wooden moldings. 201-729-8876.

Heritage Woodcraft, 1230 Oakland St., Hendersonville, NC 28739: Catalog $2 ❖ Corbels, brackets, finials, scrolls, headers, trim, sawn balusters, and turned balusters. 704-692-8542.

House of Moulding, 15202 Oxnard St., Van Nuys, CA 91411: Catalog $5 ❖ Wooden moldings and trim, ceiling medallions, fireplaces, and mantels. 818-781-5300.

J.S. Keller & Associates, P.O. Box 270359, St. Louis, MO 63127: Catalog $10 (refundable) ❖ Reproduction paneling, moldings, and trim. 314-843-1199.

Dimitrios Klitsas, Wood Sculptor, 705 Union St., West Springfield, MA 01089: Free information ❖ Wooden sculptures for decorating. 413-732-2661.

Chip La Pointe Cabinetmaker, 41 Gulf Rd., Pelhamn, MA 01002: Catalog $4.50 ❖ Reproduction Victorian trim. 413-256-1558.

Mad River Woodworks, P.O. Box 1067, Blue Lake, CA 95525: Catalog $3 ❖ Corbels, balusters, trims, brackets, spandrels, wood gutters, and railings. 800-446-8560; 707-668-5671 (in CA).

The Maizefield Company, P.O. Box 336, Port Townsend, WA 98368: Free brochure ❖ Mantels, turnings, staircases, and moldings. 360-385-6789.

Melkton Classics Inc., P.O. Box 465020, Lawrenceville, GA 30246: Free catalog ❖ Classic columns. 800-963-3060.

Old World Moulding & Finishing Inc., 115 Allen Blvd., Farmingdale, NY 11735: Catalog $3 ❖ Wooden moldings. 516-293-1789.

Omega Too, 2204 San Pablo Ave., Berkeley, CA 94702: Brochure $1 ❖ Architectural embellishments for houses and gardens. 510-843-3636.

Ornamental Mouldings, 3804 Comanche Rd., Archdale, NC 27263: Free brochure ❖ Hardwood molding and accessories. 910-431-9120.

Pagliacco Turning & Milling, P.O. Box 225, Woodacre, CA 94973: Catalog $6 ❖ Wood balusters, newel and porch posts, railings, columns, and custom-turning. 415-488-4333.

Perkins Architectural Millwork & Hardwood Mouldings, Rt 5, Box 264, Longview, TX 75605: Catalog $5 ❖ Moldings, staircases, interior and exterior doors, windows, shutters, mantels, and trim. 903-663-3036.

The Porch Factory, P.O. Box 231, White House, TN 37188: Catalog $2 ❖ Victorian country trim and other ornamental woodwork. 615-672-0998.

The Restoration Place, 305 20th St., Rock Island, IL 61201: Free brochure ❖ Fixtures and plumbing, hardware, architectural accents, and accessories. 309-786-0004.

Richards Studio, Rt. 3, Box 848, Spicewood, TX 78669: Catalog $2.50 ❖ Decorative architectural accessories. 512-264-2007.

River Bend Turnings, 3730 Vandermark Rd., Scio, NY 14880: Free brochure ❖ Porch turnings, table and chair legs, newel posts, balusters, and finials. 716-593-3495.

A.F. Schwerd Manufacturing Company, 3215 McClure Ave., Pittsburgh, PA 15212: Free brochure ❖ Standard and detailed wooden columns in seasoned northern white pine with matching pilasters and aluminum bases. 412-766-6322.

Sepp Leaf Products Inc., 381 Park Ave. South, New York, NY 10016: Free information ❖ Gold and palladium metal leaf, tools, and kits. 212-683-2840.

Silverton Victorian Millworks, P.O. Box 2987, Durango, CO 81302: Catalog $4 ❖ Castings, crowns, corner blocks, doors, bases, wainscot, architectural accoutrements, and Victorian moldings and millwork. 303-259-5915.

Style-Mark, 960 W. Barre Rd., Archbold, OH 43502: Free catalog ❖ Arches, brackets, trim, louvers, window heads, moldings, entryways, millwork, and architectural accents. 800-446-3040.

M. Swift & Sons Inc., 10 Love Ln., Hartford, CT 06141: Free information ❖ Gold, silver, palladium, aluminum, and composite leaf for decorating and restoring interiors and exteriors of buildings, domes, walls, ceilings, furniture, and works of art. 800-628-0380.

Uncle John's Gingerbread House Trim, 5229 Choupique Rd., Sulphur, LA 70663: Catalog $2 ❖ Brackets, pendants, and gables in matched sets. 318-527-9696.

Victorian Interiors, 575 Hayes St., San Francisco, CA 94102: Catalog $10 ❖ Victorian trim and ornamental woodwork. 415-431-7191.

Vintage Wood Works, Hwy. 34 South, Box R, Quinlan, TX 75474: Catalog $2 ❖ Spandrels and shelves, fans, porch posts, balusters, brackets, signs, corbels, headers, gazebos, and handcrafted Victorian gingerbread. 903-356-2158.

Vulcan Supply Corporation, P.O. Box 100, Westford, VT 05494: Catalog $3 (refundable) ❖ Copper roof ornaments.

Weaver Company, 941 Air Way, Glendale, CA 91201: Brochure $7 ❖ Ornaments for decorating mantels, doors, furniture, walls, and ceilings. 818-500-1740.

The Wood Factory, 111 Railroad St., Navasota, TX 77868: Catalog $2 ❖ Authentic Victorian-style moldings, screen doors, porch parts, ornamental trim, and custom woodwork. 409-825-7233.

The Woodworkers' Store, 21801 Industrial Blvd., Rogers, MN 55374: Free catalog ❖ Hardware, ornamentals, woodworking supplies, and tools. 800-403-9736.

Wallcoverings

American Blind, Wallpaper & Carpet Factory, 909 N. Sheldon Rd., Plymouth, MI 48170: Free information ❖ Wood, micro, mini, and vertical blinds. Also roller and pleated shades, wallpaper, and carpet. 800-889-2631 (for blinds and wallpaper); 800-346-0608 (for carpet).

❖ HOME BUILDING & IMPROVEMENT ❖

American Wallcovering Distributors, 2260 Rt. 22, Union, NJ 07083: Free information ❖ Wallpaper and fabrics. 800-843-6567.

Laura Ashley, Mail Order, P.O. Box 18413, Memphis, TN 38181: Free information ❖ Wallpaper reproductions of period patterns with complementing borders and coordinating fabrics. 800-367-2000.

Benington's, 1271 Manheim Pike, Lancaster, PA 17601: Catalog $5 ❖ Wallpaper and rugs. 800-252-5060.

Bentley Brothers, 2709 Southpark Rd., Louisville, KY 40219: Free information ❖ Embossed wallcoverings with an ornate look of detailed plasterwork. 800-824-4777.

Best Wallcoverings Inc., 2618 Avenue U, Brooklyn, NY 11229: Free information ❖ Wallpaper and rugs. 800-624-1224.

BMI Home Decorating, 5976 E. Slauson Ave., Commerce, CA 90040: Free information ❖ Decorator fabrics and wallcoverings. 800-537-4374.

Bradbury & Bradbury Wallpapers, P.O. Box 155, Benicia, CA 94510: Catalog $10 ❖ Victorian-style wallpapers, hand-printed borders, friezes, ceiling papers, and coordinated wall frills. 707-746-1900.

J.R. Burrows & Company, P.O. Box 522, Rockland, MA 02370: Catalog $5 ❖ Artistic wallpaper and fabrics. Also period carpet reproductions by special order. 800-347-1795.

Crown Corporation, 1801 Wynkoop St., Ste. 235, Denver, CO 80202: Catalog $2 ❖ Victorian-style wallcoverings and borders. 800-422-2099.

Designer Secrets, P.O. Box 529, Fremont, NE 68025: Catalog $2 (refundable) ❖ Wallcoverings, fabrics, bedspreads, furniture, and window treatments. 800-955-2559.

East Carolina Wallpaper Market, 1106 Pink Hill Rd., Kinston, NC 28501: Free information ❖ Wallpaper, fabrics, and borders. 800-848-7283.

Eisenhart Wallcoverings Company, 1649 Broadway, Hanover, PA 17331: Free list of retail sources ❖ Wallcoverings and coordinated fabrics. 800-726-3267.

Georgia-Pacific, P.O. Box 2808, Norcross, GA 30091: Free information ❖ Wall paneling and pre-hung wallpaper on plywood panels. 800-447-2882.

Hang-It-Now Wallpaper Stores, 10517 N. Main St., Archdale, NC 27263: Free information with long SASE ❖ Wallcoverings and decorator fabrics. 800-325-9494; 919-431-6341 (in NC).

Harmony Supply Company Inc., P.O. Box 313, Medford, MA 02155: Free information (specify book and manufacturer's name, pattern number or style and color number, and number of rolls wanted with exact measurements) ❖ Wallpaper and fabrics for coordinating wall and window treatments. 617-395-2600.

Interiors Guild, P.O. Box 99352, Cleveland, OH 44199: Free information ❖ Wallpaper, borders, fabrics, and accessories. 800-461-5665.

Marlene's Decorator Fabrics, 301 Beech St., Hackensack, NJ 07601: Free brochure with long SASE ❖ Decorator fabrics. 800-992-7325.

Carol Mead Wallpapers, 434 Deerfield Rd., Pomfret Center, CT 06259: Catalog $5 ❖ Turn-of-the-century historical wallpapers. 203-963-1927.

Motif Designs, 20 Jones St., New Rochelle, NY 10802: Free list of retail sources ❖ Wallcoverings and fabrics. 800-431-2424.

Mt. Diablo Handprints, 940 Tyler St., P.O. Box 726, Benicia, CA 94510: Free information ❖ Hand-printed reproduction historic wallpaper. 707-745-3388.

Nation Wide Outlet, P.O. Box 135, Flanders, NJ 07836: Free information ❖ Wallcoverings and blinds. 800-537-WALL.

Number One Wallpaper, 2914 Long Beach Rd., Oceanside, NY 11572: Free information ❖ Wallpaper. 800-423-0084; 516-678-4445 (in NY).

Peerless Wallpaper & Blind Depot, 39500 14 Mile Rd., Walled Lake, MI 48390: Free information ❖ Wallcoverings and blinds. 800-999-0898.

Robinson's Wallcoverings, 225 W. Spring St., Titusville, PA 16354: Catalog $2 (refundable) ❖ Wallcoverings and decorator fabrics. 800-458-2426.

Charles Rupert, The Shop, 2004 Oak Bay Ave., Victoria, British Columbia, Canada V8R 1E4: Information $5 ❖ Wallpapers, from the 1770s to 1920s. 604-592-4916.

Sanz International Inc., P.O. Box 1794, High Point, NC 27261: Free information with long SASE ❖ Wallcoverings, decorator fabrics, furniture, lamps, and carpeting. 910-886-7630.

Sharp's Penn Wallpapers, Bridgeton-Fairton Rd., P.O. Box 237, Bridgeton, NJ 08302: Free information ❖ Wallcoverings and borders. 609-455-0495.

Silver's Wholesale Club, 3001-15 Kensington Ave., Philadelphia, PA 19134: Free information ❖ Wallcoverings, blinds, and verticals. 800-426-6600.

Singer Wallcoverings, Box 300, Kings Island, OH 45034: Free information ❖ Vinyl wallcoverings. 800-543-0412; 800-582-1760 (in OH).

Smart Wallcoverings, P.O. Box 2206, Southfield, MI 48037: Free information ❖ Wallcoverings. 800-677-0200.

Southern Discount Wall Covering, 1583 N. Military Trail, West Palm Beach, FL 33409: Free information ❖ Wallcoverings. 800-699-WALL.

Richard E. Thibaut Inc., 480 Frelinghuysen Ave., Newark, NJ 07114: Brochure $1 (request list of retail sources) ❖ Fabrics and wallcoverings. 201-643-3777.

Victorian Collectibles, 845 E. Glenbrook Rd., Milwaukee, WI 53217: Catalog $5 ❖ Wallpaper in 19th-century patterns with matching tiles. 414-352-6971.

Wallpaper & Blinds Company, 333 Skokie Blvd., Northbrook, IL 60062: Free information ❖ Wallcoverings and blinds. 800-536-5527.

Wallpaper & Blinds Connection, P.O. Box 492, Budd Lake, NJ 07828: Free information ❖ Wallpaper, fabrics, and blinds. 800-488-WALL.

Wallpaper Outlet, 337 Rt. 46, Rockaway, NJ 07866: Free information with long SASE ❖ Wallpaper. 800-291-WALL.

Wallpaper Warehouse Inc., 179 Rt. 46, Rockaway, NJ 07866: Free information ❖ Wallcoverings. 800-523-3503.

The Warner Company, 108 S. Desplaines St., Chicago, IL 60661: Free list of retail sources ❖ Wallcoverings, fabrics, and borders. 800-685-8822.

Worldwide Wallcoverings & Blinds Inc., 333 Skokie Blvd., Northbrook, IL 60062: Free information with long SASE ❖ Wallcoverings and blinds. 800-322-5400.

Yankee Wallpaper & Blind Mart, 6689 Orchard Lake Rd., Ste. 314, West Bloomfield, MI 48322: Free information ❖ Wallpaper and blinds. 800-529-2663.

Yield House, P.O. Box 2525, Conway, NH 03818: Free catalog ❖ Wallcoverings. 800-258-0376.

Yorktowne Wallpaper, 135 Gehrhart St., Millersburg, PA 17061: Free information ❖ Wallcoverings. 800-659-0206.

Window Coverings & Screens

Phifer Wire Products Inc., P.O. Box 1700, Tuscaloosa, AL 35043: Free information ❖ Coverings for windows, doors, porches, and sun rooms. 800-874-3007.

Screen Tight Porch Screening System, 407 St. James St., Georgetown, SC 29440: Free information ❖ Easy-to-do porch-screening system. 800-768-7325.

Windows & Skylights

Allied Window Inc., 2724 W. McMicken Ave., Cincinnati, OH 45214: Free information ❖ Windows. 800-445-5411.

Alside Corporation, P.O. Box 2010, Akron, OH 44309: Free list of retail sources ❖ Outdoor windows with vinyl trim and insulating glass. 216-929-1811.

The Alternative Window Company, 11-D Herman Dr., Simsbury, CT 06070: Catalog $5 (refundable) ❖ Glass interior storm windows. 800-743-6207; 203-651-3951 (in CT).

Andersen Windows, P.O. Box 3900, Peoria, IL 61614: Free information ❖ Energy-efficient windows, roof windows, and patio doors. 800-426-4261.

Arctic Glass & Window Outlet, 565 County Rd. T, Hammond, WI 54015: Catalog $2 ❖ Windows, entryway and patio doors, skylights, and sun rooms. 800-428-9276.

Art Glass Studio, 543 Union St., Brooklyn, NY 11215: Free brochure ❖ Custom-made and restoration of leaded and stained glass windows. 718-596-4353.

Art Glass Unlimited Inc., 412 N. Euclid, St. Louis, MO 63108: Free information ❖ Stained and leaded glass windows. 314-361-0474.

Bristolite Skylights, 401 E. Goetz Ave., P.O. Box 2515, Santa Ana, CA 92707: Free catalog ❖ Fixed residential skylights or with electric and manual openers. 800-854-8618.

Combination Door Company, P.O. Box 1076, Fond du Lac, WI 54936: Free list of retail sources ❖ Wooden storm and screen doors and basement and garage windows. 414-922-2050.

Cox Studios, 1004 S. 9th St., P.O. Box 1464, Canon City, CO 81215: Catalog $2 (refundable) ❖ Custom windows, mirrors, and glass items. 719-275-7262.

DAB Studio, 31 N. Terrace, P.O. Box 96, Maplewood, NJ 07040: Free catalog ❖ Stained glass windows and accessories. 800-682-6151.

Fox Light, 8300 Dayton Rd., Fairborn, OH 45324: Free information ❖ Skylights that can be converted from closed to opening units. 800-233-FOXX.

Georgia-Pacific, P.O. Box 2808, Norcross, GA 30091: Free information ❖ Doors and windows. 800-447-2882.

Great Lakes Windows, P.O. Box 1896, Toledo, OH 43603: Free information ❖ Windows. 800-666-0000.

Hope's Landmark Products Inc., P.O. Box 580, Jamestown, NY 14702: Free information ❖ Metal casement windows and hardware. 716-665-5124.

Louisiana-Pacific Corporation, P.O. Box 10266, Portland, OR 97210: Free information ❖ Windows. 800-299-0028.

Marvin Windows, P.O. Box 100, Warroad, MN 56763: Free information ❖ Divided and insulated storm windows and transoms. 800-346-5128.

Maurer & Shepherd Joyners Inc., 122 Naubuc Ave., Glastonbury, CT 06033: Brochure $2.25 ❖ Windows, doors, entryways, and authentic colonial woodworking. 203-633-2383.

Midwest Architectural Wood Products, 1051 S. Rolff St., Davenport, IA 52802: Catalog $2.50 ❖ Divided insulated storm windows. 319-323-4757.

Pella Windows & Doors, 100 Main St., Pella, IA 50219: Free list of retail sources ❖ Custom windows. 800-524-3700.

Perkasie Industries Corporation, 50 E. Spruce St., Perkasie, PA 18944: Free information ❖ Storm window kits for the do-it-yourselfer. 800-523-6747.

Pozzi Wood Windows, P.O. Box 5249, Bend, OR 97708: Free information ❖ Divided-windows. 800-323-6474.

Rollamatic Roofs Incorporated, 1441 Yosemite Ave., San Francisco, CA 94124: Free brochure ❖ Electrically controlled retractable skylights. 800-345-7392; 415-822-5655 (in CA).

Southeastern Insulated Glass, 6477-B Peachtree Industrial Blvd., Atlanta, GA 30360: Free information ❖ Greenhouse and sun room kits and sliding glass doors and skylights with optional tempered insulated glass. 800-841-9842; 404-455-8838 (in GA).

Southwest Door Company, 219 N. 3rd Ave., Tucson, AZ 85705: Free list of retail sources ❖ Traditional, contemporary, and country-style doors, windows, hardware, cabinets, and flooring. 602-624-1434.

Sundance Supply, 1678 Shattuck Ave., Ste. 173, Berkeley, CA 94709: Catalog $2 ❖ Building components for greenhouses, sun roofs, pool enclosures, and skylights. 800-776-2534.

Thermo-Press/Norvell Corporation, 1735 Arlington Rd., Richmond, VA 23230: Information $1 ❖ Storm windows. 804-355-9147.

Velux-America Inc., P.O. Box 5001, Greenwood, SC 29648: Free brochure ❖ Weather-tight roof windows and skylights. 800-283-2831.

Walsh Screen & Window Inc., 555 E. 3rd St., Mount Vernon, NY 10553: Free information ❖ Screens, windows, storm windows, and doors. 914-668-7811.

Weather Shield Mfg. Inc., c/o HYC, 330 E. Kilbourn Ave., Milwaukee, WI 53202: Free information ❖ Wooden windows, patio doors, and steel entryways. 800-477-6808.

Wenco Windows, P.O. Box 1248, Mount Vernon, OH 43050: Free information ❖ Exterior windows with operable sides. 614-397-3403.

Window Creations, P.O. Box 127, Scott, OH 45886: Free brochure ❖ Stained glass window restoration. 419-622-3210.

Window Saver Company, 177 E. Riding Dr., Carlisle, MA 01741: Free information ❖ Storm window kits for do-it-yourselfers. 800-321-WARM.

Woodstone Company, Patch Rd., P.O. Box 223, Westminster, VT 05158: Information $3 ❖ Insulated solid wooden doors and single or triple-glazed windows, with palladians and straight and fanned transoms. 802-722-9217.

HOMES & PREFABS

Conventional & Solar Energy Homes

Classic Post & Beam, P.O. Box 546, York, ME 03909: Catalog $6 ❖ Post-and-beam homes. 800-872-2326.

Davis Frame Company, P.O. Box 1079, Claremount, NH 03743: Brochure $12 ❖ Timber frame homes. 603-543-0993.

Deck House, 930 Main St., Acton, MA 01720: Information $20 ❖ Post-and-beam homes. 800-727-3325.

Deltec Homes, 604 College St., Asheville, NC 28801: Planning portfolio $12 ❖ Pre-engineered panel kits for circular homes. 800-642-2508.

Green Mountain Precision Frames, P.O. Box 293, Windsor, VT 05089: Video preview $10 ❖ Complete house packages. 802-674-6145.

Habitat Post & Beam Homes, 21 Elm St., South Deerfield, MA 01373: Information $5 ❖ Timber frame homes. 800-992-0121.

Honest Abe Log Homes Inc., 3855 Clay County Hwy., Moss, TN 38575: Brochure $10 ❖ Log homes. 800-231-3695.

Lindal Cedar Homes, P.O. Box 24426, Seattle, WA 98178: Catalog $15 ❖ Plans for custom sizing or building a new home. 800-426-0536.

Linwood Homes, 7220 Pacific Hwy. East, Tacoma, WA 98424: Plan book $12 ❖ Post-and-beam and truss kits. 800-451-4888.

Miles Homes, P.O. Box 9495, Minneapolis, MN 55440: Catalog $3 ❖ Homes with pre-cut materials and step-by-step building instructions. 800-343-2884.

HOMES & PREFABS

New Dimension Homes Inc., RFD 3, Box 1452, Skowhegan, ME 94976: Free information ❖ Post and beam homes. 207-474-5376.

New England Timber Frames, 674 Middle Rd., Portsmouth, RI 02871: Free information ❖ Post and beam structures. 401-683-2541.

Pan Abode Inc., 4350 Lake Washington Blvd. North, Renton, WA 98056: Catalog $15 ❖ Cedar homes. 800-782-2633; 206-255-8260 (in WA).

The Post & Beam Design Company, P.O. Box 121, South Deerfield, MA 01373: Portfolio $10 ❖ Post and beam homes. 800-665-0141.

Riverbend Timber Framing Inc., P.O. Box 26, Blissfield, MI 49228: Catalog $20 ❖ Timber frame home plans. 517-486-4355.

Thistlewood Timber Frame Homes, RR 6, Markdale, Ontario, Canada N0C 1H0: Free brochure ❖ Timber frame homes. 519-986-3280.

Timberpeg, Box 1500, Claremont, NH 03743: Information $15 ❖ Post-and-beam single and multi-level homes. 603-542-7762.

Vermont Timber Frames, 130 Bowen Rd., P.O. Box 410, Bennington, VT 05201: Free information ❖ Timber frame homes. 802-447-8860.

Woodhouse Post & Beam Inc., P.O. Box 219, Mansfield, PA 16933: Catalog $10 ❖ Post-and-beam homes. 800-227-4311; 717-549-6232 (in PA).

Domes

American Ingenuity, 8777-E Holiday Springs Rd., Rockledge, FL 32955: Catalog $2 (refundable with $10 order) ❖ Easy-to-build concrete and steel geodesic dome from kit of pre-finished panels.

GeoDomes WoodWorks, Building C, Box 4141, Riverside, CA 92514: Catalog $15 ❖ Pre-cut ready-to-assemble dome kits. 909-787-8800.

Monolithic Constructors Inc., P.O. Box 479, Italy, TX 76651: Free brochure ❖ Concrete dome kit.

Oregon Dome Living Inc., 3215 Meadow Ln., Eugene, OR 97402: Catalog $12 ❖ Energy-efficient domes. 800-572-8943.

Shelter Systems, P.O. Box 1294, Capitola, CA 95010: Catalog $1 ❖ Easy-to-setup portable domes and greenhouses. 415-323-6202.

Timberline Geodesics, 2015 Blake St., Berkeley, CA 94704: Catalog $12 ❖ Easy-to-assemble pre-cut geodesic dome homes. 800-DOME-HOME.

Log Homes

The Air-Lock Log Company, P.O. Box 2506, South Frontage Rd., Las Vegas, NM 87701: Catalog of plans $7 ❖ Log homes. 800-786-0525; 505-425-8888 (in NM).

Alpine Log Homes, Box 85, Victor, MT 59875: Catalog $15 ❖ Log homes. 406-642-3451.

Alta Industries Ltd., Rt. 30, Box 88, Halcottsville, NY 12438: Planning package $7 (request list of retail sources) ❖ Log homes. 800-926-2582.

L.C. Andrew Maine Cedar Log Homes, 35 Main St., Windham, ME 04062: Catalog $5 ❖ Log homes. 800-427-5647; 207-892-8561 (in ME).

Appalachian Log Homes, 11312 Station West, Knoxville, TN 37922: Catalog $8 ❖ Log homes in chinked and log-on-log styles. 615-966-6440.

Appalachian Log Structures, P.O. Box 614, Riley, WV 25271: Catalog $10 ❖ Log homes, garages, and other structures. 800-458-9990; 304-372-6410 (in Southeast).

Asperline Log Homes, RD 1, Box 240, Lock Haven, PA 17745: Planning guide $9.95 ❖ Easy-to-construct log homes. 800-428-4663.

Jim Barna Log Systems, P.O. Box 4529, Oneida, TN 37841: Catalog $7 ❖ Log homes. 800-962-4734.

Beaver Log Homes, P.O. Box 236, Beloit, WI 53512: Catalog $6 ❖ Pre-cut log home kits. 608-365-6833.

Conestoga Log Cabins, 987 Valley View Rd., New Holland, PA 17557: Free catalog ❖ One and two-room log cabin kits. 800-914-4606.

Confederation Log Homes, 14200 El Camino Ln., Lenoir City, TN 37771: Catalog $10 ❖ Log homes. 800-298-1867.

Country Log Homes, P.O. Box 158, Ashley Falls, MA 01222: Catalog $10 ❖ Log homes. 413-229-8084.

Fireside Log Homes, 200 River St., Ellijay, GA 30540: Catalog $8 ❖ Log homes. 800-521-5647.

Four Seasons Log Homes, P.O. Box 631, Parry Sound, Ontario, Canada P2Z 2Z1: Catalog $10 ❖ Log homes. 705-342-5211.

Garland Homes, 2172 Hwy. 93 North, Victor, MT 59875: Catalog $15 ❖ Log homes. 800-642-3837.

Gastineau Log Homes Inc., Box 248, New Bloomfield, MO 65063: Planning kit $8 ❖ Log homes. 800-654-9253; 314-896-5122 (in MO).

Great Northern Log Homes, 7580 Nash Rd., Bozeman, MT 59715: Catalog $7 ❖ Log homes. 406-585-9065.

Greatwood Log Homes, P.O. Box 707, Elkhart, WI 53020: Planning guide $9.50 ❖ Log homes. 800-242-1021; 800-558-5812 (in WI).

Hearthstone Log Homes, 1630 East Hwy., Dandrige, TN 37725: Plan book $15 ❖ Log homes. 800-247-4442.

Heritage Log Homes, P.O. Box 610, Gatlinburg, TN 37738: Catalog $12 ❖ Log homes. 800-456-4663.

Hiawatha Log Homes, P.O. Box 8, Munising, MI 49862: Plan book $6 ❖ Log homes. 800-876-8100.

Holland Log Homes, 13352 Van Buren, Holland, MI 49424: Plan book $8.95 ❖ Pre-cut log homes. 800-968-7564.

Homestead Log Homes, 6301 Crater Lake Hwy., Medford, OR 97502: Catalog $10 ❖ Pre-cut kits or on-site factory built log homes. 503-826-6888.

Honest Abe Log Homes Inc., 3855 Clay County Hwy., Moss, TN 38575: Brochure $10 ❖ Log homes. 800-231-3695.

Honka Log Homes, Honka Southeast, 448 N. Cedar Bluff Rd., P.O. Box 353, Knoxville, TN 37923: Free brochure ❖ Log homes. 800-656-LOGS.

Katahdin Forest Products, P.O. Box 145, Oakfield, ME 04763: Video catalog $15 ❖ Log homes. 207-757-8278.

Kuhns Brothers Log Homes, RD 2, Box 406A, Lewisburg, PA 17837: Catalog $10 ❖ Log homes. 800-346-7903.

Log & Timber Homes Inc., P.O. Box 448, St. Ignatius, MT 59865: Information packet $7 ❖ Log homes. 406-745-3482.

Lok-N-Logs, P.O. Box 677, Sherburne, NY 13460: Catalog $7.50 ❖ Log homes. 800-343-8928; 607-674-4447 (in NY).

Majestic Log Homes, P.O. Box 772, Fort Collins, CO 80522: Free brochure ❖ Log homes. 303-224-4857.

Maple Island Log Homes, Traverse City Office, 5046 S. West Bayshore Dr., Ste. A, Suttons Bay, MI 49682: Plan packet $12 ❖ Log homes. 616-271-4042.

Montana Log Homes, 3212 Hwy. 93 South, Kalispell, MT 59901: Plan guide $7 ❖ Log homes. 406-752-2992.

Mountaineer Log Homes Inc., P.O. Box 248, Morgantown, PA 19543: Catalog $8 ❖ Log homes. 215-286-2005.

National Log Homes, P.O. Box 69, Thompson Falls, MT 59873: Plan book $7 ❖ Log homes. 800-707-LOGS; 406-827-3521 (in MT).

Neville Log Homes, 2036 Hwy. 93, Victor, MT 59875: Catalog $10 ❖ Log homes. 406-642-3091.

Northeastern Log Homes, P.O. Box 7966, Louisville, KY 40257: Brochure $5 ❖ Log homes. 800-451-2724.

The Original Lincoln Logs, Riverside Dr., Box 135, Chestertown, NY 12817: Plans portfolio $12.50 (request list of retail sources) ❖ Log homes. 800-833-2461.

Original Log Homes, P.O. Box 1301, 100 Mile House, British Columbia, Canada V0K 2E0: Plan book $5 ❖ Log homes. 604-395-3868.

Otsego Cedar Log Homes, P.O. Box 127, Waters, MI 49797: Catalog $6 ❖ Post-and-beam log homes. 517-732-6268.

Pacific Log Homes Ltd., P.O. Box 80868, Vancouver, British Columbia, Canada V5H 3Y1: Free brochure ❖ Log homes. 800-663-1577.

Pioneer Log Systems Inc., P.O. Box 226, Kingston Springs, TN 37082: Catalog $10 ❖ Log and post-and-beam homes. 615-952-5647.

Precision Craft Log Structures, 711 E. Broadway Ave., Meridian, ID 843642: Planning package $14.95 ❖ Log homes. 208-887-1020.

Rapid River Rustic Inc., P.O. Box 10, Rapid River, MI 49878: Planning guide $10 ❖ Log homes. 800-422-3327.

Real Log Homes, P.O. Box 202, Hartland, VT 05048: Catalog $15 ❖ Log homes with optional full basements, garages, slabs, crawl spaces, and piers. 800-732-5564.

Rocky Mountain Log Homes, 1883 Hwy. 93 South, Hamilton, MT 59840: Catalog $14 ❖ Log homes. 406-363-5680.

Satterwhite Log Homes, Rt. 2, Box 256, Longview, TX 75605: Planning guide $5 ❖ Log homes. 800-777-7288.

South Eastern Log Home Manufacturing Inc., 110 S. Main St., P.O. Box 456, Fountain Inn, SC 29644: Free information ❖ Log homes. 800-847-5647.

Southern Cypress Log Homes Inc., U.S. Hwy. 19 South, P.O. Box 209, Crystal River, FL 32629: Plan book $4.95 ❖ Log homes. 904-795-0777.

Southland Log Homes, 7521 Broad River Rd., P.O. Box 1668, Irmo, SC 29063: Planning guide $7.50 ❖ Log homes. 800-845-3555.

Stonemill Log Homes, 7015 Stonemill Rd., Knoxville, TN 37919: Catalog $6 ❖ Log homes. 800-438-8274; 423-693-4833 (in TN).

Tennessee Log Homes, P.O. Box 865, Athens, TN 37371: Planning guide $8 ❖ Log homes. 800-251-9218.

Timber Log Building Systems, 639 Old Hartford Rd., Colchester, CT 06415: Planning portfolio $10 ❖ Log homes. 800-533-5906.

Tomahawk Log & Country Homes Inc., 2285 Bus. 51 Cty L, Tomahawk, WI 54487: Floor plans $13 ❖ Log homes. 800-544-0636; 715-453-3265 (in WI).

Town & Country Cedar Homes, 4772 US 131 South, Petoskey, MI 49770: Plan book $6 ❖ Log homes. 800-968-3178; 616-347-4360 (in MI).

Traverse Bay Log Homes, 6446 M-72 West, Traverse City, MI 49684: Planning kit $6 ❖ Log homes. 616-947-1881.

Ward Log Homes, P.O. Box 72, Houlton, ME 04730: Planning guide $8 ❖ Log homes. 800-341-1566.

Wilderness Log Homes, P.O. Box 902, Plymouth, WI 53073: Planning guide $12 ❖ Log homes. 800-237-8564.

Wisconsin Log Homes Inc., P.O. Box 11005, Green Bay, WI 54307: Catalog $14.95 ❖ Log homes. 800-678-9107.

HORSE & STABLE EQUIPMENT
Health Care & Stable Supplies

Rohn Agri Products, P.O. Box 2000, Peoria, IL 61656: Free information ❖ Heavy-duty horse stalls. 800-447-2264; 309-697-4400 (in IL).

Bargain Corral, P.O. Box 856, Allan, TX 75002: Free information with long SASE ❖ Saddles, stirrups and straps, blankets, spurs, halters, pads, bits, bridles and breast collars, boots, dusters, rain slickers, and supplies. 800-955-5616.

Chick's Harness & Supply, P.O. Box 59, Harrington, DE 19952: Free catalog ❖ Horse equipment. 800-444-2441; 302-398-4630 (in DE).

Colorado Saddlery Company, 1631 15th Street, Denver, CO 80202: Free catalog ❖ Grooming supplies. 800-521-2465; 303-572-8350 (in CO).

Econo-Vet Groom & Health, 8687 Blumenstein Rd., P.O. Box 1191, Minocqua, WI 54548: Free catalog ❖ Health care and grooming products for horses. 800-451-4162; 715-369-5591 (in WI).

Eisers, 360 Kiwanis Blvd., P.O. Box T, Hazleton, PA 18201: Free list of retail sources ❖ Health care supplies, saddles, tack, stable needs, books, and clothing. Also clothing for men and women. 800-526-6987.

Farnam Companies Inc., Horse Products Division, P.O. Box 34820, Phoenix, AZ 85013: Free list of retail sources ❖ Equine health care products. 800-234-2269.

Drs. Foster & Smith Inc., 2253 Air Park Rd., P.O. Box 100, Rhinelander, WI 54501: Free catalog ❖ Pet and equine products and health care supplies. 800-826-7206.

Happy Jack Inc., Box 475, Snow Hill, NC 28580: Free catalog ❖ Animal health care products. 800-326-5225.

Horsemen's General Store, 345 W. Leffel Ln., Springfield, OH 45506: Catalog $3 ❖ Everything for horse owners, trainers, breeders, riders, and horses. 800-343-0167; 513-323-0874 (in OH).

KV Vet Supply, P.O. Box 245, David City, NE 68632: Free catalog ❖ Veterinary supplies and tack. 402-367-6047.

Pony Express Horsemen's Supply, P.O. Box 505, Santa Ynez, CA 93460: Free information ❖ Grooming supplies. 805-688-3624.

Red River Portable Arenas, P.O. Box 549, Carbon, TX 76435: Free list of retail sources ❖ Portable enclosures for roping, riding and training, and team penning. 800-343-1026.

Joe Roberts Welding, P.O. Box 777, Ringling, OK 73456: Free information ❖ Portable roping arenas. 800-654-4584; 405-662-2071 (in OK).

Texas Outfitters Supply Inc., Rt. 6, Box 25, Sulphur Springs, TX 75482: Catalog $2 (refundable) ❖ Wall tents, folding stoves, panning equipment, saddles, team and driving harnesses, and pack equipment for horses and mules. 800-551-3534.

Valley Vet Supply, P.O. Box 504, Marysville, KS 66508: Free catalog ❖ Equine health products, roping gear, pack equipment, horse blankets, and English, Western, and Arabian tack. 800-468-0059.

Wholesale Vet Supply, P.O. Box 7086, Omaha, NE 68107: Free catalog ❖ Supplies for dogs, cats, rabbits, other household pets, horses, and cattle.

Wiese Equine Supply, 117 S. Oak., P.O. Box 197, Eldon, MO 65026: Free catalog ❖ Equine equipment, health care products, accessories, and clothing. 800-869-4373.

Horse Trailers

Charmac Trailers, Box 205, Twin Falls, ID 83301: Free information ❖ Horse trailers. 208-733-5241.

Circle J Trailers, 200 N. Kit Ave., Caldwell, ID 83605: Free information ❖ Horse trailers. 800-247-2535; 208-459-0842 (in ID).

Diamond D Trailer Manufacturing, 1000 N. Hwy. 48, Box 339, Shenandoah, IA 51601: Free information ❖ Horse trailers. 712-246-5375.

Exxiss Aluminum Trailers, 2613 Hwy 30, Box 634, Soda Springs, ID 83276: Free information ❖ Horse trailers. 800-733-0322.

Featherlite Manufacturing Inc., P.O. Box 320, Cresco, IA 52136: Free list of retail sources ❖ Horse trailers. 800-800-1230.

❖ HORSE & STABLE EQUIPMENT ❖

4-Star Trailers Inc., 10000 Northwest 10th, Oklahoma City, OK 73128: Free information ❖ Horse trailers. 405-324-7827.

Hillsboro Industries Inc., 220 Industrial Rd., Hillsboro, KS 67063: Free information ❖ Horse trailers. 800-835-0209; 316-947-3127 (in KS).

Kiefer Built, Box 88, Kanawha, IA 50447: Free information ❖ Horse trailers. 515-762-3201.

Logan Coach, 290 S. 400 West, Logan, UT 84321: Free information ❖ Horse trailers. 800-742-7047.

Pierce Sales, Rt. 1, Box 3A, Henrietta, TX 76365: Catalog $1 ❖ Cargo carriers, runabouts, horse trailers, and truck beds. 817-538-5646.

S & H Trailer Manufacturing Company, 800 Industrial Dr., Madill, OK 73446: Free information ❖ Recreational vehicles and horse, cargo, equipment, stock, RV, utility, and carryall trailers with optional features. 405-795-5577.

Sundowner Trailer Inc., HC 61, Box 27, Coleman, OK 73432: Free information ❖ Horse trailers. 800-438-4294.

Trails West Manufacturing of Idaho Inc., Box 67, Preston, ID 83263: Free information ❖ Horse trailers. 208-852-2200.

Turnbow Trailers Inc., P.O. Box 300, Oilton, OK 74052: Free information ❖ Horse trailers. 918-862-3233.

W-W Trailer, Box 807, Hwy. 177 West, Madill, OK 73446: Free information ❖ Horse trailers. 405-795-5571.

Saddles & Tack

The Australian Stock Saddle Company, P.O. Box 987, Malibu, CA 90265: Catalog $6 ❖ Leather saddles. 818-889-6988.

Bargain Corral, P.O. Box 856, Allan, TX 75002: Free information with long SASE ❖ Saddles, stirrups and straps, blankets, spurs, halters, pads, bits, bridles and breast collars, boots, dusters, rain slickers, and supplies. 800-955-5616.

Bona Allen Saddle Company, 6 Union Dr., Olney, IL 62450: Free catalog ❖ Saddles. (618) 392-3858.

Bridger Creek Outfitters, P.O. Box 126, Alder, MT 59710: Catalog $3 ❖ Western gear for people and horses. 406-842-5044.

J.M. Capriola Company, 500 Commercial St., Elko, NV 89801: Catalog $5 (refundable with first $50 order) ❖ Authentic western equipment and tack. 702-738-5816.

Circle R Boot & Saddle, Jess Ray Orndorff, 101 E. Main, Holdenville, OK 74848: Free information ❖ Custom boots and saddles. 800-540-5795.

Colorado Saddlery Company, 1631 15th Street, Denver, CO 80202: Free catalog ❖ Tents and accessories, sleeping bags, stoves, tack and pack equipment, and supplies. 800-521-2465; 303-572-8350 (in CO).

Country Supply, 1305 E. Mary St., Ottumwa, IA 52501: Free catalog ❖ Saddles, pads, harnesses, books and videos, and tack. 800-637-6721.

Courbette Saddlery Company, 585 Industrial Pkwy., P.O. Box 2131, Heath, OH 43056: Free information ❖ Handmade saddles with anatomically shaped front and thigh rolls. 614-522-1555.

Crooked Pine Saddle Shop, 662 Dry Gulch Rd., Stevensville, MT 59870: Catalog $4 (refundable) ❖ Custom saddles and pack equipment. 406-777-3108.

Down Under Saddle Supply, 5470 E. Evans Ave., Denver, CO 80222: Catalog $4 ❖ Australian saddles and tack. 303-753-6737.

Eisers, 360 Kiwanis Blvd., P.O. Box T, Hazleton, PA 18201: Free list of retail sources ❖ Health care supplies, saddles, tack, stable needs, books, and clothing. Also clothing for men and women. 800-526-6987.

John M. Fallis Custom Saddles, 38620 County Rd. 29, Elizabeth, CO 80107: Catalog $4 ❖ Saddles. 303-646-4125.

Hitching Post Supply, 10312 210th St. SE, Snohomish, WA 98290: Free catalog ❖ Handmade saddles and horseback riding accessories. 360-668-2349.

The Horse of Course, 6395 Gunpark Dr., Boulder, CO 80301: Free catalog ❖ Saddle packing gear and horse blankets. 800-569-1880.

Horseman's Corral, 906 N. Carpenter Rd., Modesto, CA 95351: Free information ❖ Saddles.

Horsemen's General Store, 345 W. Leffel Ln., Springfield, OH 45506: Catalog $3 ❖ Everything for horse owners, trainers, breeders, riders, and horses. 800-343-4987; 513-323-0874 (in OH).

K & B Saddlery, Rt. 1, Box 21, Council Bluffs, IA 51501: Catalog $1 ❖ Western saddles. 712-366-1026.

Kates Saddle Supply, 3551 S. Monaco Pkwy., Denver, CO 80237: Free information ❖ General purpose and Australian-style saddles. 800-395-TACK.

Kauffman International Ltd., Lenox Hill Station, Box 1672, New York, NY 10021: Catalog $5 ❖ Horseback riding equipment and clothing. 212-838-1080.

KV Vet Supply, P.O. Box 245, David City, NE 68632: Free catalog ❖ Veterinary supplies and tack. 402-367-6047.

Libertyville Saddle Shop Inc., P.O. Box M, Libertyville, IL 60048: Catalog $3 ❖ Saddles and clothing. 800-872-3353.

Mary's Tack & Feed, 3675 Via De La Valle, Del Mar, CA 92014: Free catalog ❖ Saddles and pads, bridles, books, and tack. 800-551-MARY.

Outback Ranch, 9698 Carmel Valley Rd., Carmel, CA 93923: Free information ❖ Saddles with optional fittings. 408-625-1417.

Rod's Western Palace, 3099 Silver Dr., Columbus, OH 43224: Free catalog ❖ Western wear and tack. 800-325-8508.

RoughOut, Box 2667, Missoula, MT 59806: Free catalog ❖ Riding equipment, clothing, and gifts. 800-428-1098.

Ryon's Saddle & Ranch Supplies, 2601 N. Main, Fort Worth, TX 76106: Free catalog ❖ Saddles, tack, and Western-style clothing and boots for men, women, and children. 800-725-7966.

Saddle Slicker, P.O. Box 58714, Houston, TX 77258: Free information ❖ Saddle covers. 800-332-1101.

Sawtooth Saddle Company, 14340 W. Dry Fork Canyon, Vernal, UT 84078: Brochure $4 ❖ Custom saddles and gear in a 1900 and modern style. 801-789-5400.

S.S. Schneiders, 8255 E. Washington St., Chagrin Falls, OH 44023: Free information ❖ Saddle, grooming, and tack storage systems. 800-365-1311.

Sherer Custom Saddles Inc., P.O. Box 385, Franktown, CO 80116: Catalog $5 (refundable) ❖ Handmade saddles.

State Line Tack Inc., P.O. Box 1217, Plaistow, NH 03865: Free catalog ❖ English and western riding tack and clothing. 800-228-9208.

Stelzig's Western Store, P.O. Box 727, Houston, TX 77001: Free catalog ❖ Saddles and other leather goods for horsemen. 713-988-6304.

Thornhill Enterprises, P.O. Box 3539, Wilmington, DE 19807: Free information ❖ Saddles and tack. 610-444-3998.

Chris Tornow, P.O. Box 984, Monroe, WA 98272: Catalog $3 (refundable) ❖ Pack equipment. 206-794-5959.

Valley Vet Supply, P.O. Box 504, Marysville, KS 66508: Free catalog ❖ Equine health products, roping gear, pack equipment, horse blankets, and English, Western, and Arabian tack. 800-468-0059.

Wiese Equine Supply, 117 S. Oak., P.O. Box 197, Eldon, MO 65026: Free catalog ❖ Equine equipment, health care products, accessories, and clothing. 800-869-4373.

HORSESHOES

Franklin Sports Industries Inc., 17 Campanelli Pkwy., P.O. Box 508, Stoughton, MA 02072: Free information ❖ Horseshoes. 800-426-7700.

General Sportcraft Company, 140 Woodbine Rd., Bergenfield, NJ 07621: Free information ❖ Horseshoes. 201-384-4242.

NC Tool Company, 6568 Hunt Rd., Pleasant Garden, NC 27313: Free information ❖ Horseshoeing supplies. 800-446-6498.

Spalding Sports Worldwide, 425 Meadow St., P.O. Box 901, Chicopee, MA 01021: Free list of retail sources ❖ Horseshoes. 800-225-6601.

Sport Fun Inc., 4621 Sperry St., Los Angeles, CA 90039: Free information ❖ Horseshoes. 800-423-2597; 818-240-6700 (in CA).

Wagon Mound Ranch Supply, P.O. Box 218, Wagon Mound, NM 87752: Free catalog ❖ Horseshoeing supplies. 800-526-0482.

HOT TUBS, WHIRLPOOLS & SAUNAS

Almost Heaven Ltd., Rt. 250, Renick, WV 24966: Free catalog ❖ Hot tubs, spas, saunas, and whirlpools. 304-497-3163.

Amerec Sauna & Steam, P.O. Box 40569, Bellevue, WA 98004: Free information ❖ Pre-assembled and easy-to-install free-standing modular sauna. 800-331-0349; 206-643-7500 (in WA).

AquaGlass Corporation, P.O. Box 412, Industrial Park, Adamsville, TN 38310: Free information ❖ Whirlpool baths, combination steam showers, lavatories, wall surrounds, and shower floors. 800-238-3940; 901-632-0911 (in TN).

Automatic Steam Products, 43-20 34th St., Long Island City, NY 11101: Free information ❖ Equipment to convert shower stalls into steam rooms. 800-238-3535.

T.E. Brown Hot Tub, 14361 Chapman Rd., San Leandro, CA 94578: Free information ❖ Redwood hot tubs. 800-675-8827.

Bruce Manufacturing Inc., 5203 North US 45, Bruce Crossing, MI 49912: Free brochure ❖ Sauna heaters and accessories. 906-827-3906.

Coleman Spas Inc., 25605 S. Arizona, Chandler, AZ 85248: Free information ❖ Spas and hot tubs. 800-926-5362.

Grohe America Inc., 241 Covington Dr., Bloomingdale, IL 60108: Information $3 ❖ Thermostat water valves. 708-582-7711.

Jacuzzi Whirlpool Bath, P.O. Drawer J, Walnut Creek, CA 94596: Free catalog ❖ Whirlpool spas, baths, and towers with hydro-massage control. 800-678-6889.

Lyons Industries, P.O. Box 88, Dowagiac, MI 49047: Free information ❖ Whirlpools for space-saving corner installation with optional walls and shatter-proof folding shower stall doors. 800-458-9036.

Plastic Creations, 1023 S. Hamilton St., Dalton, GA 30720: Free brochure ❖ Acrylic whirlpool baths. 800-868-0254.

Southland Spa, Box 638, Ray Farm Rd., Haleyville, AL 35565: Free information ❖ Spas, whirlpool baths, and saunas. 205-486-7919.

Universal Rundle, 303 North St., P.O. Box 29, New Castle, PA 16103: Free information ❖ Portable spa that operates by plugging into a standard grounded outlet. 412-658-6631.

Watkins Manufacturing Spas, 1280 Park Center Dr., Vista, CA 92083: Free information ❖ Spas. 800-999-4688.

HOT WATER HEATERS

BSAR Solar, 980 Santa Estella, Solana Beach, CA 92075: Free information ❖ Solar system for making hot and distilled water. 714-993-5890.

Controlled Energy Corporation, Fiddler's Green, Waitsfield, VT 05673: Free information ❖ Direct vent room heaters. Also tankless and mini storage tank instantaneous electric water heaters. 802-496-4436.

Kansas Wind Power, 13569 214th Rd., Holton, KS 66436: Catalog $4 ❖ Sun ovens, wind generators, composting toilets, tank-free water heaters, air cooler, and other solar energy equipment. 913-364-4407.

Myson, McNeely-Yuill Corporation, 9911 Horn Rd., Ste. 100-A, Sacramento, CA 95827: Free brochure ❖ Tank-free gas hot water heater. 800-456-3761.

Refrigeration Research Inc., P.O. Box 869, Brighton, MI 48116: Free information ❖ Solar water heating systems for homes. 810-227-1151.

Solar Depot, 61 Paul Dr., San Rafael, CA 94903: Catalog $6.50 ❖ Solar electric power systems, water heaters, electric and thermal systems, and other equipment. 415-499-1333.

Sunelco, P.O. Box 1499, Hamilton, MT 59840: Catalog $4.95 ❖ Solar modules, controllers, batteries, inverters, water pumps, propane-operated appliances, and power and heating systems for recreational vehicles and cabins. 800-338-6844.

Thermo Dynamics Ltd., 81 Thornhill Dr., Darmouth, Nova Scotia, Canada B3B 1R9: Free information ❖ Solar hot water system. 902-468-1001.

HOUSEWARES

Brookstone Company, Order Processing Center, 1655 Bassford Dr., Mexico, MO 65265: Free catalog ❖ Housewares and tools. 800-926-7000.

Chef's Catalog, 3215 Commercial Ave., Northbrook, IL 60062: Free catalog ❖ Professional restaurant equipment for the home chef. 800-338-3232.

Colonial Garden Kitchens, Hanover Direct Pennsylvania Inc., Hanover, PA 17333-0001: Free catalog ❖ Housewares, storage and bathroom accessories, cleaning and cooking needs, furniture, and laundry room aids. 717-633-3333.

Joan Cook, 119 Foster St., P.O. Box 6008, Peabody, MA 01961: Free catalog ❖ Housewares for cooking and home care. 800-935-0971.

Hold Everything, Mail Order Dept., P.O. Box 7807, San Francisco, CA 94120: Free catalog ❖ Clothing and closet organizers, garment protectors, kitchen and laundry aids, bathroom space makers, and bedroom furnishings. 800-421-2285.

Lakeside Products Company, 6646 N. Western Ave., Chicago, IL 60645: Catalog $1 (refundable) ❖ Housewares, novelties, and gifts. 312-761-5495.

HOVERCRAFT

Arrowprop, Box 610, Meeker, OK 74855: Catalog $5 ❖ Hovercraft supplies.

Neoteric Hovercraft, 1649 Tippecanoe St., Terre Haute, IN 47807: Information package $11 (refundable) ❖ Hovercraft. 812-234-1120.

SEVTEC, P.O. Box 846, Monrow, WA 98272: Information $8 ❖ Quick-build hovercraft.

Universal Hovercraft, 1204 3rd St. South, Box 281, Cordova, IL 61242: Free catalog ❖ Plans for easy-to-build hovercraft.

HUMIDIFIERS

Broan Manufacturing Company, 926 W. State St., Hartford, WI 53027: Free information ❖ Humidifiers. 414-673-4340.

Carrier Corporation, 7310 W. Morris, Indianapolis, IN 46231: Free information ❖ Humidifiers. 317-243-0851.

Hunter Fan Company, 2500 Fisco Ave., Memphis, TN 38114: Catalog $1 ❖ Electronically programmable thermostats. 901-745-9222.

Nortec Industries, Box 698, Ogdensburg, NY 13669: Free information ❖ Humidifiers. 315-425-1255.

Whirlpool Corporation, 2000 M63 North, Benton Harbor, MI 49022: Free information ❖ Humidifiers. 800-253-1301.

HUNTING

Clothing & Equipment

Advantage Camouflage, 1390 Box Circle, Columbus, GA 21907: Free information ❖ Camouflage patterns.

Amacker/Brell Mar Products, 5701 Hwy. 80 West, Jackson, MS 39209: Free information ❖ Tree stands. 800-262-2537.

Ambusher, 2007 W. 7th St., Texarkana, TX 75501: Free information ❖ Portable climbing ladders. 800-332-HUNT.

API Outdoors Inc., P.O. Box 1432, Tallulah, LA 71282: Free information ❖ Tree stands. 800-228-4846.

Avid Outdoor, 1120 W. 149th St., P.O. Box 578, Olathe, KS 66051: Free list of retail sources ❖ Camouflage patterned clothing. 913-780-AVID.

Barrie Archery, P.O. Box 482, Waseca, MN 56093: Free information ❖ Penetrating arrows.

L.L. Bean Inc., Freeport, ME 04033: Free catalog ❖ Outdoor clothing. 800-483-2326.

Bear River Industries Inc., 3110 Ranchview Ln., Minneapolis, MN 55447: Free information ❖ Portable tree stands and hunting supplies. 800-536-3337; 612-559-1092 (in MN).

Big Buck Treestands, 855 Chicago Rd., Quincy, MI 49082: Free information ❖ Tree stands. 517-639-3815.

Big Man Tree Stands, P.O. Box 605, Harrisonburg, LA 71340: Free information ❖ Tree stands. 800-682-1256.

Bowhunters Discount Warehouse Inc., 1045 Zeigler Rd., Wellsville, PA 17365: Free catalog ❖ Rifles, game calls, targets, camouflage clothing, and equipment for hunting, bow hunting, archery, and camping. 800-735-BOWS.

Broward Shooter's Exchange, 250 S. 60th Ave., Hollywood, FL 33023: Catalog $8 ❖ Shooting, reloading, muzzle loading, hunting, and archery equipment. 800-554-9002.

Browning Company, Dept. C006, One Browning Pl., Morgan, UT 84050: Catalog $2 ❖ Camouflage clothing. 800-333-3288.

BSI Sporting Goods, P.O. Box 5010, Vienna, WV 26105: Free catalog ❖ Firearm accessories, muzzle-loading supplies, optics, clothing, and archery, fishing, and hunting equipment. 304-295-8511.

BuckShot Treestands, P.O. Box 7127, Wilmington, NC 28406: Free information ❖ Lightweight and portable adjustable tree stand. 910-341-7900.

Bushy Ridge Products, Teledyne Brown Engineering, P.O. Box 897, Jackson, AL 36545: Free information ❖ Camouflage patterns. 334-246-1791.

Cabela's, 812 13th Ave., Sidney, NE 69162: Free catalog ❖ Hunting, fishing, and outdoor equipment. 800-588-7512.

Cougar Claw, 9559 Hickory St. South, Foley, AL 36535: Free information ❖ Tree stands.

Delta Decoys, 117 E. Kenwood St., Reinbeck, IA 50669: Free information ❖ Life-size ultra-light and collapsible deer decoys. 319-345-6476.

Double/Triple Trading, P.O. Box 5425, Buena Park, CA 90022: Free information ❖ Hunting accessories. 800-949-8546.

Dunns, P.O. Box 449, Grand Junction, TN 38039: Free catalog ❖ Camouflage and insulated clothing, outerwear, shoes and boots, hunting equipment, day and belt packs, gun care kits, sunglasses, game calls, decoys, and supplies. 800-223-8667.

Fieldline, 1919 Vineburn Ave., Los Angeles, CA 90032: Free brochure ❖ Fleece packs, pouches, and gaiters for hunters. 213-226-0830.

Flambeau Products Corporation, 15981 Valplast Rd., Middlefield, OH 44062: Free information ❖ Realistic deer decoys. 800-232-3474.

Flint River Outdoor Wear Inc., 5731 Miller Ct., Columbus, GA 31909: Free catalog ❖ Hunting apparel in cotton fabrics with concealment patterns. 706-562-0005.

Four Rivers, 244 Mid Rivers Center, Ste. 230, St. Peters, MO 63376: Catalog $3 ❖ Outdoor gear for campers, hunters, and fishermen.

Gander Mountain Inc., P.O. Box 248, Gander Mountain, Wilmot, WI 53192: Free catalog ❖ Camping equipment, boats, archery supplies, knives, rifle scopes, and hunting videos. 800-558-9410.

Graf & Sons, Rt. 3, Hwy. 54 South, Mexico, MO 65265: Free information ❖ Hunting accessories, scopes, and reloading equipment. 800-531-2666.

Haas Outdoors Inc., P.O. Box 757, West Point, MS 39773: Free information ❖ Camouflage supplies. 800-331-5624.

Invader, P.O. Box 624, Como, MS 38619: Free information ❖ Climbing stands.

Kobuk, 1305 S. Lyon St., Santa Ana, CA 92705: Free catalog ❖ Neoprene hunting outerwear. 800-KOBUK-99.

Leafy Wear, 1710 Dutch Fork Rd., Irmo, SC 29063: Free information ❖ Camouflage patterns.

Loc-On Company, 6903 International Dr., Greensboro, NC 27409: Free information ❖ Portable and semi-permanent climbing ladders. 910-668-3113.

Loggy Bayou Tree Stands, 10397 Rt. 1, Shrevesport, LA 71115: Free information ❖ Climbing and hang-on tree stands. 800-544-8733.

Lone Wolf Tree Stands, 3314 Grange Ave., Cudahy, WI 53110: Free information ❖ Tree stands. 414-744-4984.

Mill Creek Outfitters Inc., P.O. Box 110165, Nashville, TN 37222: Free catalog ❖ Tree stands, archery equipment, and outdoor clothing. 800-742-0656.

Natgear, 4209 S. Shackleford Rd., Ste. D, Little Rock, AR 72204: Free list of retail sources ❖ Camouflage accessories.

Nature's Edge Camouflage, P.O. Box 194, Columbus, GA 31902: Free information ❖ Camouflage patterns.

Nelson Weather-Rite Clothing, 14760 Santa Fe Trail Dr., Lenexa, KS 66215: Free list of retail sources ❖ Camouflage clothing and backpacks. 800-315-2267.

Nite Lite Company, P.O. Box 8210, Little Rock, AR 72221: Free catalog ❖ Kennel, training, and hunting supplies for dogs. Clothing and accessories for the hunter. 800-648-5483.

Norland Trading Company, Box 10, Norland, Ontario, Canada K0M 2L0: Video catalog $5 (refundable) ❖ Hunting, fishing, and outdoor products. 800-318-0717.

Portable Blinds Inc., 251 Quail Ridge Circle, Littleton, CO 80126: Free information ❖ Lightweight portable one, two, or three-person expandable hunting blinds.

Predator Camouflage, 2605 Coulee Ave., La Crosse, WI 54601: Free information ❖ Camouflage clothing.

RealBark Hunting Systems, P.O. Box 2078, Henderson, TX 75653: Free brochure ❖ Blinds, seat tripods, platforms, and game feeders. 800-256-4465.

Realtree Camouflage, 1390 Box Circle, Columbus, GA 21907: Free information ❖ Camouflage patterns.

Redhead, 1935 S. Campbell, Springfield, MO 65898: Free catalog ❖ Equipment and clothing for hunters. 800-227-7776.

Rivers Edge, P.O. Box 903, Monticello, MN 55362: Free list of retail sources ❖ Tree stands. 800-450-EDGE.

Scotts Inc., P.O. Box 189, Jay, FL 32565: Free information ❖ Scopes, bows, arrows, and hunting accessories. 800-289-4953.

Screaming Eagle, P.O. Box 4507, Missoula, MT 59806: Free catalog ❖ Self-climbing tree stands. 800-458-2017.

Senco Inc., 520 8th St., Gwinn, MI 49841: Free information ❖ Recreational shelters, portable hunting blinds, ice fishing houses, and greenhouses. 906-346-4116.

Shydas Shoe & Clothing Barn, 1535 S. Lincoln Ave., Lebanon, PA 17042: Free catalog ❖ Hunting and outerwear clothing. 717-274-2551.

HUNTING

Skyline, 184 Ellicott Rd., West Falls, NY 14170: Free brochure ❖ Camouflage supplies. 716-655-0230.

Spider Oak Outfitters, P.O. Box 551695, Dallas, TX 75355: Free information ❖ Camouflage patterns.

Sport Climbers, 2926 75th St., Kenosha, WI 53143: Free catalog ❖ Tree-climbing spikes. 800-877-7025.

Sport Shop of Grifton, Rt. 3, Box 187, Ayden, NC 28513: Free catalog ❖ Archery equipment, accessories, cases and racks, lures and cover scents, ladder stands, and targets. 800-334-5778.

Staghorn Treestands, 410 W. Lincoln Ave., Goshen, IN 46526: Free information ❖ Tree stands. 219-534-2234.

Sticks 'n Limbs Camouflage, 17250 S. Oak Park, Tinley Park, IL 60477: Free information ❖ Camouflage patterns.

Summit Specialties Inc., P.O. Box 786, Decatur, AL 35602: Brochure $1 ❖ Climbing tree stands. 205-353-0634.

Trailhawk Treestands, 2605 Coulce Ave., La Crosse, WI 54601: Free information ❖ Tree stands. 608-787-0500.

Trautman Outdoor Creations Inc., 378 Harlan Creek Rd., Hamilton, MT 59840: Free information ❖ Tree stand kits. 800-462-9639.

Trax America, Box 898, Forrest City, AR 72335: Free information ❖ Tree stands. 800-232-2327.

Trebark Camouflage, 3434 Buck Mountain Rd., Roanoke, VA 24014: Free catalog ❖ Camouflage gear for hunters. 800-843-2266; 540-774-9248 (in VA).

Treevanish Camouflage, 2169 Greenville Rd., LaGrange, GA 30240: Free information ❖ Camouflage patterns.

Trophy Whitetail Products, 329 E. Shockley Rd., Anderson, SC 29624: Free information ❖ Tree stands.

Warren & Sweat Manufacturing Company, Box 350440, Grand Island, FL 32735: Free information ❖ Portable and semi-permanent ladders. 904-669-3166.

Whitewater Outdoors Inc., W4118 Church St., Highdam, WI 53031: Free information ❖ Camouflage clothing.

Wilderness Tree Stands Inc., 3645 Whitehouse Spencer Rd., Swanton, OH 43558: Free information ❖ Compact lightweight tree stands. 419-877-0872.

Wiley Outdoor Sports, 1808 Sportsman Ln., Huntsville, AL 35816: Catalog $3 (refundable) ❖ Hunting equipment. 205-837-3920.

Woodstream Corporation, P.O. Box 327, Lititz, PA 17543: Free catalog ❖ Hunting and shooting equipment. 800-800-1819; 717-626-2125 (in PA).

Woolrich, Woolrich, PA 17779: Free information ❖ Camouflage clothing. 800-995-1299.

Game Calls, Lures & Scents

Abe & Son Natural Elk Sounds, 2273 N. Bayshore Dr., Coos Bay, OR 97420: Free information ❖ Game calls. 800-426-2417.

Ambush, P.O. Box 337, Shakopee, MN 55379: Free information ❖ Deer scents.

Antler Connection, 122 Beahm Crest Ln., Evans City, PA 16033: Free information ❖ Animal scents.

Rod Benson's Game Calls, 1050 Mart St., Muskegon, MI 49440: Free list of retail sources ❖ Adjustable deer calls. 616-726-3661.

Big River Game Calls, P.O. Box 388, Dunlap, IL 61525: Free information ❖ Game calls.

Bowhunter Supply Inc., 1158 46th St., P.O. Box 5010, Vienna, WV 26105: Free information ❖ Game calls, decoys, lures, and scents. 800-289-2211; 304-295-8511 (in WV).

Buck Stop Lure Company Inc., P.O. Box 636, Stanton, MI 48888: Free information ❖ Scents and lures. 800-477-2368; 517-762-5091 (in MI).

Cedar Hill Game Call Company, P.O. Box 550, Farmersville, LA 71241: Free information ❖ Game calls.

Cover Up Products, Rt. 1, Box 66C, Hill City, KS 67642: Free information ❖ Deer scents.

Deer Run Products Inc., 261 Ridgeview Terrace, Goshen, NY 10924: Free information ❖ Scents and lures. 914-294-9646.

Dunns, P.O. Box 449, Grand Junction, TN 38039: Free catalog ❖ Camouflage and insulated clothing, outerwear, shoes and boots, hunting equipment, day and belt packs, gun care kits, sunglasses, game calls, decoys, and supplies. 800-223-8667.

Faulk's Game Call Company, 616 18th St., Lake Charles, LA 70601: Free information ❖ Game calls.

Golden Eagle Archery, 1111 Corporate Dr., Farmington, NY 14425: Free information ❖ Game calls, lures, and scents. 716-924-1880.

Hancock's Advanced Outdoor Products, Rt. 2, Box 246A, Walla Walla, WA 99362: Free information ❖ All-in-one game call. 509-522-0964.

Haydel's Game Calls Inc., 5018 Hazel Jones Rd., Bossier City, LA 71111: Free information ❖ Game calls. 318-746-3586.

Hulme, P.O. Box 670, Hwy. 641 South, Paris, TN 38242: Free catalog ❖ Game calls and scents. 901-642-6400.

Hunter's Specialties Inc., 6000 Huntington Ct. NE, Cedar Rapids, IA 52402: Free list of retail sources ❖ Game calls, decoys, lures, and scents. 319-395-0321.

Jackie's Deer Lures, 2271 Plantation Trail, Bellbrook, OH 45305: Free information ❖ Deer scents.

James Valley Scents, HCR 1, Box 47, Mellette, SD 57461: Free catalog ❖ Gel and liquid animal scents. 605-887-3125.

Knight & Hale Game Calls, 5732 Canton Rd., Cadiz, KY 42211: Free information ❖ Turkey calls. 502-924-1755.

Lenartz, 5052 Mildred Ave., Kentwood, MI 49508: Free information ❖ Game calls.

Lohman Manufacturing Company, 4500 Doniphan Dr., Neosho, MO 64850: Free information ❖ Game calls. 417-451-4438.

Northern Whitetail, All Natural Hunting Lures, 1930 Ridgewood, White Bear Lake, MN 55110: Free information ❖ Deer scents.

P.S. Olt, 12662 5th St., Perkin, IL 61555: Free information ❖ Game calls.

Preston Pittman Game Calls, P.O. Box 12785, Jackson, MS 39236: Free information ❖ Game calls.

Primos Inc., Box 12785, Jackson, MS 39236: Information $2 ❖ Turkey, deer, elk, waterfowl, and other calls. 800-523-2395.

Quaker Boy Inc., 5455 Webster Rd., Orchard Park, NY 14127: Free information ❖ Turkey calls. 800-544-1600; 716-662-3979 (in NY).

Pete Rickard Inc., RD 1, Box 292, Cobleskill, NY 12043: Free information ❖ Animal scents for deer. 800-282-5663.

Robinson Laboratories, 293 Commercial St., St. Paul, MN 55106: Free information ❖ Deer lure gel. 800-397-1927; 512-224-1927 (in MN).

Simmons Gun Specialties Inc., 20241 W. 207th, Spring Hill, KS 66083: Free information ❖ Game calls, decoys, lures, and scents. 800-444-0220.

Southland Callers, 2031 Horns Lake Rd., Orchard Park, NY 14127: Free information ❖ Game calls.

Sport Shop of Grifton, Rt. 3, Box 187, Ayden, NC 28513: Free catalog ❖ Archery equipment, accessories, cases and racks, lures and cover scents, ladder stands, and targets. 800-334-5778.

Johnny Stewart Wild Life Calls Inc., 5100 Fort Ave., Waco, TX 76714: Free information ❖ Game calls. 800-537-0652; 817-772-3261 (in TX).

ICE-CREAM MACHINES

Sure-Shot Game Calls Inc., Box 816, Groves, TX 77619: Free information ❖ Game calls. 409-962-1636.

Tink's Safariland Hunting Corporation, P.O. Box 244, Madison, GA 30650: Free information ❖ Game calls, decoys, lures, and scents. 800-221-5054; 706-342-1916 (in GA).

Weaver's Scents, 2006 Snow Hill Rd., West Harrison, IN 47060: Free information ❖ Deer scents.

Wellington Outdoors, P.O. Box 244, Madison, GA 30650: Free information ❖ Game calls.

Wilderness Sound Productions Ltd., 4015 Main St., Springfield, OR 97478: Free brochure ❖ Game calls. 800-437-0006.

Wildlife Research Center, 4345 157th Ave. NW, Anoka, MN 55304: Free catalog ❖ Scent elimination spray. 800-655-7898; 612-427-3350 (in MN).

Woods Wise Callmasters, P.O. Box 681552, Franklin, TN 37068: Free catalog ❖ Deer, elk, squirrel, and waterfowl game calls. 800-735-8182.

ICE-CREAM MACHINES

Chef's Catalog, 3215 Commercial Ave., Northbrook, IL 60062: Free catalog ❖ Manual and electric-operated self-chilling ice-cream makers. 800-338-3232.

Lello Appliances Corporation, 355 Murray Hill Pkwy., East Rutherford, NJ 07073: Free information ❖ Electric-powered ice-cream maker. 800-527-4336.

Sun Appliances, 4554 E. Princess Anne Rd., Norfolk, VA 23502: Free information ❖ Electric-operated salt-and-ice ice-cream maker. 800-347-4197.

White Mountain Freezer Inc., 217 E. 16th St., Sedalia, MO 65301: Free information ❖ Old-fashioned rock salt and ice electric-operated ice-cream maker. 800-343-0065.

Williams-Sonoma, Mail Order Department, P.O. Box 7456, San Francisco, CA 94120: Free catalog ❖ Hand-cranked ice-cream machine. 800-541-1262.

Zabar's & Company, 2245 Broadway, New York, NY 10024: Free catalog ❖ Hand-cranked ice-cream maker. 212-787-2000.

ICE SKATING

Cal Pac Corporation, Triad Bicycles, 5250 Claremont Ave., Stockton, CA 95207: Free information ❖ Skates. 800-477-4734; 209-472-3451 (in CA).

Canstar Sports, 50 Jonergin Dr., Swanton, VT 05448: Free information ❖ Figure and hockey skates and blade sharpeners. 800-362-3146; 802-868-2711 (in VT).

Chisco Sports Accessories, 2424 S. 2570 West, Salt Lake City, UT 84119: Free information ❖ Skates. 800-825-4555.

Cooper International Inc., 501 Alliance Ave., Toronto, Ontario, Canada M6N 2J3: Free information ❖ Figure and hockey skates and blade protectors. 416-763-3801.

First Team Sports, 2274 Woodale Dr., Mounds View, MN 55112: Free information ❖ Skates. 800-528-5872.

Lowry's Manufacturing Ltd., 19 Keith Rd., Winnipeg, Manitoba, Canada R3H 0H7: Free information ❖ Figure and hockey skates, replacement blades, and blade protectors. 204-633-6359.

Maska USA Inc., 529 Main St., Ste. 205, Boston, MA 02129: Free information ❖ Figure and hockey skates. 800-451-4600; 617-242-8600 (in MA).

National Sporting Goods Corporation, 25 Brighton Ave., Passaic, NJ 07055: Free information ❖ Figure and hockey skates, blade protectors, and sharpeners. 201-779-2323.

Oberhamer USA, 4775 Dakota St. SE, Prior Lake, MN 55371: Free catalog ❖ Skating attire and skates for men and women. 800-207-OBER.

Riedell Shoes Inc., P.O. Box 21, Red Wing, MN 55066: Free information ❖ Blade protectors, sharpeners, and figure, racing, and hockey skates. 612-388-8251.

Roller Derby Skate Company, Box 930, Litchfield, IL 62056: Free information ❖ Skates. 217-324-3961.

Seneca Sports Inc., 75 Fortune Blvd., P.O. Box 719, Milford, MA 01757: Free information ❖ Skates and blade protectors. 800-861-7867; 508-634-3616 (in MA).

INCENSE

Angel's Earth, 1633 Scheffer Ave., St. Paul, MN 55116: Catalog $2 ❖ Soaps, candles, cosmetics, incense, skin care preparations, essential oils, and other aromatherapy items. 612-698-3601.

Cambridge Zen Center, 199 Auburn St., Cambridge, MA 02139: Catalog $2 ❖ Pants, mats, incense, Buddha figurines, malas, benches, and books. 617-492-4793.

Dharma Crafts, 405 Waltham St., Ste. 234, Lexington, MA 02173: Catalog $2 ❖ Statues, cushions, ritual objects, benches, books, incense, and meditation supplies. 617-862-9211.

The Essential Oil Company, P.O. Box 206, Lake Oswego, OR 97034: Free catalog ❖ Aromatherapy supplies and essential oils, soap molds and supplies, potpourri and fragrance oils, and incense materials. 800-729-5912.

The Excelsior Incense Works, 1413 Van Dyke, San Francisco, CA 94124: Catalog $1 ❖ How-to books and incense-making supplies. Also incense sticks, cones, and coils. 415-822-9124.

Green Cedar Needle Sachets, Box 551, State Rd. 165, Placitas, NM 87043: Free brochure ❖ Sachets, incense cones, and other fragrance products. 800-557-3463.

Legacy Herbs, Sue Lukens Herbalist/Potter, Box 442, Mountain View, AR 72560: Catalog 50¢ ❖ Herbs, wildflowers, perennial plants, soaps, bath and body care products, oils and fragrance, incense, potpourri, herbal food products, and other scented items. 501-269-4051.

INCONTINENCE SUPPLIES

AC Medical Supplies, P.O. Box 29011, Westmount Mall, London, Ontario, Canada N6K 1M0: Free catalog ❖ Hygienic waterproof pants for disabled adults. 519-471-8049.

Access Medical Supply, 2300 Edison Blvd., Twinsburg, OH 44087: Free catalog ❖ Incontinence shields, pads, undergarments, and other supplies for men and women. 800-242-2460.

American Ostomy Supplies, P.O. Box 13396, Milwaukee, WI 53213: Free catalog ❖ Urological, diabetic, and incontinence supplies, blood pressure and wound care products, and aids for assisted living. 800-958-5858.

Bruce Medical Supply, 411 Waverly Oaks Rd., P.O. Box 9166, Waltham, MA 02254: Free catalog ❖ Health equipment for disabled and incontinent persons. 800-225-8446.

Caring Products International Inc., 200 1st Ave. West, Ste. 200, Seattle, WA 98119: Free information ❖ Incontinence supplies and maternity and special-needs clothing. 800-333-5379; 206-282-6040 (in WA).

Comco Inc., P.O. Box 9039, North St. Paul, MN 55109: Free information ❖ Reusable incontinence products. 800-348-8375.

Duraline Medical Products, 324 Werner St., P.O. Box 67, Leipsic, OH 45856: Free catalog ❖ Re-usable and disposable health care items for children and adults. 800-654-3376.

Express Medical Supply Inc., P.O. Box 1164, Fenton, MO 63026: Free catalog ❖ Urological, ostomy, incontinence, and skin care products. 800-633-2139.

Fashion Ease, Division M and M Health Care, 1541 60th St., Brooklyn, NY 11219: Free catalog ❖ Incontinence supplies, wheelchair accessories, health care aids, and clothing with Velcro closures for arthritic, elderly, and handicapped persons. 800-221-8929; 718-853-6376 (in NY).

Home Delivery Incontinent Supplies Company, 1215 Dielman Industrial Ct., St. Louis, MO 63132: Free catalog ❖ Briefs, undergarments, shields, underpads, catheters, and skin care products. 800-269-4663.

Hygienics Direct Company, P.O. Box 414050, Kansas City, MO 64108: Free catalog ❖ Incontinence products. 888-463-7337.

LDB Medical Inc., 2909 Langford Rd., Ste. 500-B, Norcross, GA 30071: Free catalog ❖ Ostomy and incontinence supplies, urological products, and skin care items. 800-243-2554.

Moms Catalog, 24700 Avenue Rockefeller, Valencia, CA 91355: Free catalog ❖ Medical supplies for incontinence, urological, aids for daily living, ostomy, wound and skin care, and diabetes. 800-232-7443.

National Medical Consumables Inc., P.O. Box 102495, Denver, CO 80250: Free information ❖ Ostomy, diabetic, urological, wound care, and incontinence products. 800-797-7107.

Shield Healthcare Centers, P.O. Box 916, Santa Clarita, CA 91380: Free catalog ❖ Ostomy, urological, skin care, and home diagnostic products.

TMI Healthcare Products, 307 Bacon Rd., Rougement, NC 27572: Free information ❖ Reusable washable underwear for men, women, and children. 800-550-4666.

Woodbury Products Inc., 4410 Austin Blvd., Island Park, NY 11558: Free information ❖ Disposable diapers. 800-777-1111.

INDIAN (NATIVE AMERICAN) ARTS & CRAFTS

Alabama

American Indian Books & Relics, P.O. Box 16175, Huntsville, AL 35802: List $3 (10 issues) ❖ American Indian relics. 205-881-6727.

Alaska

Chilkat Valley Arts, Box 145, Haines, AK 99827: Free price list with long SASE ❖ Northwest Coast Tlingit Native American silver jewelry. 907-766-2990.

Mardina Dolls, P.O. Box 611, Wrangell, AK 99929: Free information with long SASE ❖ Eskimo dolls in ceremonial robes. 907-874-3854.

Musk Ox Producers Cooperative, 604 H St., Anchorage, AK 99501: Free information with long SASE ❖ Hand-knitted Qiviut scarves, caps, tunics, and clothing. 907-272-9225.

Nana Museum of the Arctic Craft Shop, P.O. Box 49, Kotzebue, AK 99752: Free information with long SASE ❖ Eskimo dolls, masks, birch bark baskets, ivory and whalebone carvings, and jewelry. 907-442-3304.

St. Lawrence Island Original Ivory Cooperative, P.O. Box 189, Gambell, AK 99742: Free price list with long SASE ❖ Bracelets, cribbage boards, baleen boats, etchings, and ivory carvings of Arctic animals. 907-985-5112.

Savoonga Native Store, P.O. Box 100, Savoonga, AK 99769: Free price list with long SASE ❖ Figurines, scrimshaw, ivory carvings, jewelry, and other crafts.

Taheta Arts & Cultural Group, 605 A St., Anchorage, AK 99501: Catalog $1 ❖ Ivory, stone, wood, and bone carvings; grass, birch bark, and baleen baskets; bead, porcupine, quill, silver, ivory, and baleen jewelry; and Eskimo dance fans, parkas, masks, etchings, and prints. 907-272-5829.

Amos Wallace, P.O. Box 478, Juneau, AK 99802: Free information with long SASE ❖ Carved silver and gold bracelets and earrings. 907-586-9000.

Arizona

Dawa's Hopi Arts & Crafts, P.O. Box 127, Second Mesa, AZ 86043: Free information with long SASE ❖ Hopi overlay silver jewelry. 602-734-2430.

Hatathli Gallery, Navajo Community College Development Foundation, Tsaile, AZ 86556: Free information with long SASE ❖ Jewelry, rugs, sand paintings, and beadwork. 602-724-3311.

Honani Crafts, Hopi Cultural Center, Shop #4, P.O. Box 317, Second Mesa, AZ 86043: Free information with long SASE ❖ Honani silver jewelry, pottery, paintings, and baskets. Also Navajo rugs, and Zuni, Navajo, and Santa Domingo jewelry. 602-734-2238.

Hopi Arts & Crafts, Silvercraft Cooperative Guild, P.O. Box 37, Second Mesa, AZ 86043: Catalog $2.50 ❖ Hopi overlay jewelry, coiled and wicker baskets, pottery, and paintings. 602-734-2463.

Hopi Kiva, P.O. Box 96, Oraibi, AZ 86039: Free information with long SASE ❖ Hopi silver and gold overlay jewelry. 602-734-2423.

Jay's of Tucson Inc., 6637 S. 12th Ave., Tucson, AZ 85706: Catalog $5 (refundable) ❖ Navajo, Hopi, & Zuni jewelry. Also southwestern gifts, Navajo rugs, Taos Moccasins and drums, sand paintings, and Czech seed, pony, Peruvian, and other beads and findings. 602-294-3397.

Percharo Jewelry, 313 Pima Ln., Laveen, AZ 85339: Free information with long SASE ❖ Silver and gold jewelry. 602-237-4249.

San Juan Southern Paiute Yingup Weavers Association, P.O. Box 1336, Tuba City, AZ 86045: Free information with long SASE ❖ Paiute baskets. 602-526-7143.

Phillip Titla Studio, P.O. Box 497, San Carlos, AZ 85550: Free brochure with long SASE ❖ Wood oil and watercolor paintings, etchings, serigraphs, and sculptures in bronze and other metals. 602-475-2361.

Arkansas

Caddo Trading, Box 669, Murfreesboro, AR 71958: Free list ❖ Native American artifacts, minerals, and fossils.

Bill & Mary Horn, Rt. 9, Box 227, Pine Bluff, AR 71603: Free information with long SASE ❖ Pottery, baskets, cornhusk dolls, beadwork, wood necklaces, and silver, turquoise, and mother-of-pearl jewelry. 501-879-1066.

California

De Luna Jewelers, 521 2nd St., Davis, CA 95616: Free information with long SASE ❖ Pottery, Navajo rugs, jewelry, baskets, paintings, carvings, and beadwork. 916-753-3351.

Going-to-the-Sun Studio, 1063 Hillendale Ct., Walnut Creek, CA 94596: Free information with long SASE ❖ Paintings, bas relief sculptures, tapestries, block-printed fabrics, drums, parfleche containers, dolls, beadwork, ribbon shirts, and shawls. 510-939-8803.

Indian Arts Gift Shop, NCIDC Inc., 241 F St., Eureka, CA 95501: Free information with long SASE ❖ Baskets, silver and shell jewelry, beadwork, paintings, and carvings. 707-445-8451.

Ophelia Johnson's Indian Variety Shop, 10256 Central Ave., Montclair, CA 91763: Free information with long SASE ❖ Silver jewelry, baskets, beadwork, pottery, and dolls. 714-625-2611.

Karok Originals by Vit, P.O. Box 3317, Eureka, CA 95502: Free information with long SASE ❖ Jewelry and wall hangings. 707-442-8800.

Chief George Pierre Trading Post, P.O. Box 3202, Torrance, CA 90510: Free information with long SASE ❖ Rugs, silver and turquoise jewelry, kachina dolls, and beadwork. 213-372-1048.

Tatewin-Petaki American Indian Arts & Crafts, P.O. Box 549, Big Bear City, CA 92314: Free information with long SASE ❖ Beadwork, stitchery items, beaded tapestries, decorated pipes, dolls, and leather work. 714-585-1435.

Colorado

alter-NATIVE VOICES/Morning Flower Press, P.O. Box 11443, Denver, CO 80211: Free price list with long SASE ❖ Books, music, and crafts by and about Native Americans. 303-477-8442.

B & J Indian Relics, P.O. Box 272464, Fort Collins, CO 80527: List $1 ❖ Native American artifacts, beadwork, and pottery.

Steve Eagles, Native American Regalia, P.O. Box 88142, Colorado Springs, CO 80908: Catalog $3 ❖ Native American souvenirs, gifts, clothing, jewelry, musical instruments, and other items. 719-495-0798.

❖ INDIAN (NATIVE AMERICAN) ARTS & CRAFTS ❖

Navajo Manufacturing Company, 5801 Logan St., Denver, CO 80216: Catalog $2 ❖ Handmade Navajo and Zuni jewelry. 303-292-3090.

Ben Nighthorse, P.O. Box 639, Ignacio, CO 81137: Free information with long SASE ❖ Contemporary silver, gold, and silver jewelry inlaid with copper, brass, and German silver. 303-563-4623.

Connecticut

The Raven's Den, P.O. Box 178, East Windsor, CT 06088: Catalog $2 ❖ Native American relics, points and spearheads, rare pipes, tomahawks, rare medals and tokens, and other collectibles.

District of Columbia

Naica Collectibles, 5223 Wisconsin Ave. NW, Ste. 138, Washington, DC 20015: Free information with long SASE ❖ Carvings, pottery, beadwork, and sterling silver, turquoise, and gold jewelry. 202-561-1354.

Florida

Me'shiwi, 433 Harrell Dr., Orlando, FL 32828: Free brochure with long SASE ❖ Men and women's gold and sterling silver jewelry inlaid with natural stones and shell, Zuni pottery, kachina dolls, and paintings. 407-568-5162.

This N' That, 204 Brevard Ave., Cocoa Village, FL 32922: Free information with long SASE ❖ Beadwork, jewelry, pottery, carvings, fetishes, baskets, moccasins, dolls, and Navajo rugs.

Idaho

Kamiakin Krafts, P.O. Box 358, Fort Hall, ID 83203: Free price list with long SASE ❖ Beadwork belts, buckles, watch bands, earrings, coin purses, medallion necklaces, moccasins and slippers, men and women's clothing, cedar and raffia baskets, native tanned hides, and crafts. 208-785-2546.

Trading Post Clothes Horse, P.O. Box 368, Fort Hall, ID 83203: Free brochure with long SASE ❖ Belt buckles, coin purses, earrings, barrettes, bolo ties, gloves, moccasins, dresses, vests, drums, and beaded and tanned buckskin items. 208-237-8433.

Kansas

Laurie Houseman-Whitehawk, RR 3, Box 155-B, Lawrence, KS 66044: Free information with long SASE ❖ Original paintings in gouache. 913-842-1948.

Louisiana

Native American Arts of the South, P.O. Box 217, Elton, LA 70532: Free price list with long SASE ❖ Pottery and swamp cane, white oak, and long-leaf pine needle baskets. 318-584-5130.

Maine

Basket Bank, Aroostook Micmac Council Inc., 8 Church St., Presque Isle, ME 04769: Free brochure with long SASE ❖ Potato, pack, clothes, fishing, decorative, shopping, cradle, and sewing baskets. 207-764-1972.

Longacre Enterprises Inc., Old Eastport Rd., P.O. Box 196, Perry, ME 04667: Free price list with long SASE ❖ Bow and arrow racks, incense burners, driftwood lamps, crafts, and Passamaquoddy birch bark, ash, and sweet grass baskets. 207-853-2762.

Nowetah's Indian Store & Museum, Rt. 27, Box 40, New Portland, ME 04954: Free brochure with long SASE ❖ Rugs and wall hangings, beadwork, leather work, moccasins, porcupine quill boxes, birch bark baskets, pottery, leather work, drums, dolls, masks, Navajo sand paintings, headdresses, peace pipes, and silver and turquoise jewelry. 207-628-4981.

Chief Poolaw Tepee Trading Post, 88 Main St., Old Town, ME 04468: Free information with long SASE ❖ Penobscot sweet grass and Passamaquoddy baskets, other baskets, pottery, moccasins, beadwork, wood carvings, dolls, war clubs, rugs, and jewelry. 207-827-8674.

Wabanaki Arts, P.O. Box 453, Old Town, ME 04468: Free price list with long SASE ❖ Carved Penobscot canes, war clubs, totem poles, stone tomahawks, baskets, beadwork, and quill work. 207-827-3447.

Maryland

Jewelry by Avery, 5134 Chalk Point Rd., West River, MD 20778: Free information with long SASE ❖ Kachinas, Native American art, precious and semi-precious gemstones, mineral specimens, and handcrafted Zuni, Navajo, and Hopi turquoise jewelry. 410-867-4752.

Massachusetts

Bluebird Indian Crafts, 130 Glenview St., Upton, MA 01568: Free information with long SASE ❖ Porcupine quill work, beadwork, clothing, and Native American crafts. 508-473-3708.

Silver Star, Wampanoag Crafts, c/o Anita G. Nielsen, 190 Wood St., P.O. Box 402, Middleboro, MA 02346: Free information with long SASE ❖ Moccasins, beadwork, leather crafts, baskets, quill work, wall plaques, and crafts. 617-947-4159.

Michigan

Indian Hills Trading Company & Indian Art Gallery, 1681 Harbor Rd., Petoskey, MI 49770: Free information with long SASE ❖ Porcupine quill boxes and pendants, drums, beadwork, buckskin baby moccasins, Navajo rugs, Southwestern silver and turquoise jewelry, Pueblo pottery, Eskimo art, and original Native American paintings. 616-347-3789.

Moon Bear Pottery, c/o Shirley M. Brauker, 6135 E. Broadway, #7, Mt. Pleasant, MI 48858: Free brochure with long SASE ❖ Pottery, wall hangings, sculptures, oil paintings and drawings, and dolls. 517-773-2510.

Native American Arts & Crafts Council, Indian Arts & Crafts Store, Goose Creek Rd., P.O. Box 1049, Grayling, MI 49738: Free information with long SASE ❖ Porcupine quill boxes, black ash splint and sweet grass baskets, beadwork, birch bark crafts, paintings and drawings, and leather work. 517-348-3190.

Minnesota

Amber Woods Studio, 26570 140th St., Zimmerman, MN 55398: Free information with long SASE ❖ Sculptures, wooden relief wall hangings, pipestone and marble carvings, graphics, walking sticks, and paintings. 612-856-2328.

Ikwe Marketing, White Earth Indian Reservation, Rt. 1, Osage, MN 56570: Free brochure with long SASE ❖ Birch bark baskets, Ojibway beadwork, star quilts, braided rugs, and quill work. 218-573-3411.

Lady Slipper Designs, RR 3, Box 556, Bemidji, MN 56601: Free information with long SASE ❖ Beaded charms, moccasins, birch bark birdhouses, crafts, and birch bark, willow, and black ash baskets. 800-950-5903.

Pipestone Indian Shrine Association, c/o Pipestone National Monument, Box 727, Pipestone, MN 56164: Free brochure with long SASE ❖ Pipes, jewelry, war clubs, arrowheads, buffalo and turtle effigies, and carvings. 507-825-5463.

Mississippi

Choctaw Museum of the Southern Indian Gift Shop, Rt. 7, Box 21, Philadelphia, MS 39350: Free price list with long SASE ❖ Baskets, beadwork jewelry, moccasins and Choctaw dresses and shirts by special order, dolls, quilts, pottery, stick ball rackets and balls, blowguns, and rabbit sticks. 601-656-5251.

Missouri

Turner Art Works, 14323 Spring Dr., De Soto, MO 63020: Catalog $25 ❖ Acrylic paintings and handmade traditional and contemporary necklaces, earrings, amulets, and chokers in shell, bone, and crayfish pinchers. 314-586-4105.

Montana

Blackfeet Trading Post, P.O. Box 626, Browning, MT 59417: Free information with long SASE ❖ Moccasins, beadwork, baskets, pottery, shawls, and paintings. 406-338-2050.

Coup Marks, Box 532, Ronan, MT 59864: Free information with long SASE ❖ Paintings, sculptures, ribbon shirts, moccasins, beadwork, dolls, shawls, drums, stick games, wing dresses, and cradle boards. 406-246-3216.

Flathead Indian Museum Trading Post & Art Gallery, P.O. Box 464, St. Ignatius, MT 59865: Free information with long SASE ❖ Moccasins, beaded buckles, medallions, hair ties, silver and turquoise jewelry, earrings, dance costumes, and Native American paintings. 406-745-2951.

Neeney, Box 84, Joplin, MT 59531: Free information with long SASE ❖ Beadwork, gemstone necklaces and rings, sacred red rock pipes and fetishes, and native-tanned hides. 406-292-3890.

Northern Plains Indian Crafts Association, P.O. Box E, Browning, MT 59417: Free price list with long SASE ❖ Buckskin vests, gloves, handbags, moccasins, beadwork jewelry and belts, dolls, decorated rawhide items, porcupine hair roaches, and native-tanned hides. 406-338-5661.

The Tipi Gift Shop, Rt. 62, Box 3110E, Livingston, MT 59047: Free information with long SASE ❖ Original paintings, pen and ink sketches, knives, shields, star quilts, and crafts. 406-222-8575.

Wolf Chief Graphics, 907 C Ave. NW, Great Falls, MT 59404: Free price list with long SASE ❖ Watercolor paintings, alabaster and bronze sculptures, and bone chokers. 406-452-4449.

Nevada

Arnold Aragon Sculpture & Illustration, Box 64, Schurz, NV 89427: Free information with long SASE ❖ Stone sculptures, drawings, and paintings. 702-773-2542.

Maggi Houten, P.O. Box 265, Nixon, NV 89424: Free information with long SASE ❖ Beadwork hair ties, necklaces, bolo ties, watch bands, belt buckles, belts, moccasins, baby baskets, and coin purses. 702-476-0205.

Malotte Studio, South Fork Reservation, Star Rt., Lee, NV 89829: Free information with long SASE ❖ Original drawings. 702-744-4305.

Winter Moon Trading Company, P.O. Box 189, Schurz, NV 89427: Free information with long SASE ❖ Beaded and silver jewelry, horsehair baskets, pottery, original artwork, and Native American crafts. 702-773-2510.

New Jersey

Lone Bear Indian Craft Company, 300 Main St., Orange, NJ 07050: Free price list with long SASE ❖ Woodland Native American beadwork, costumes, war bonnets, headdresses, and Native American collectibles.

New Mexico

Carolyn Bobelu, P.O. Box 443, Zuni, NM 87327: Free information with long SASE ❖ Jewelry with faceted and multi-levels of silver, turquoise, coral, and shell. 505-782-2773.

Chi Nah Bah, P.O. Box 122, Brimhall, NM 87310: Information $1 ❖ Jewelry, Navajo rugs, sand paintings, kachina dolls, leather belts, pottery, baskets, paintings, and crafts.

Indian Pueblo Cultural Center Inc., 2401 12th St. NW, Albuquerque, NM 87102: Free information with long SASE ❖ Pueblo pottery, baskets, wood carvings, fabrics, stone sculptures, silver and turquoise jewelry, drums, and crafts. 505-843-7270.

Jicarilla Arts & Crafts Shop/Museum, P.O. Box 507, Dulce, NM 87528: Free brochure ❖ Beadwork, baskets, leather work, and paintings. 505-759-3515.

Lilly's Gallery, P.O. Box 342, Acoma Pueblo, NM 87034: Free information with long SASE ❖ Handcrafted Acoma pottery and figurines. 505-552-9501.

Carol G. Lucero, P.O. Box 319, Jemez Pueblo, NM 87024: Free information with long SASE ❖ Pueblo pottery, baskets, cedar flutes, kachinas, drums, sculptures, Navajo dolls, sand paintings, and crafts. 505-843-9337.

Mary Laura's, 3636 San Mateo Blvd. NE, Albuquerque, NM 87110: Catalog $2 ❖ Native American jewelry from the Zuni Pueblo. 800-662-4848.

Ted Miller Custom Knives, P.O. Box 6328, Santa Fe, NM 87502: Free price list with long SASE ❖ Wood and horn carvings, deer horn pipes, elk horn belt buckles, bolos, and knives with hand-tooled steel blades in elk, stag horn, or bone handles. 505-984-0338.

Teresita Naranjo, Santa Clara Pueblo, Rt. 1, Box 455, Espanola, NM 87532: Free information with long SASE ❖ Santa Clara black and red pottery. 505-753-9655.

Native USA, P.O. Box 80690, Albuquerque, NM 87198: Free information ❖ Solid sterling silver and turquoise jewelry. 800-532-4718.

Navajo Gallery, P.O. Box 1756, Taos, NM 87571: Free information with long SASE ❖ Paintings, sculptures, lithographs, and drawings. 505-758-3250.

Oke Oweenge Arts & Crafts, P.O. Box 1095, San Juan Pueblo, NM 87566: Catalog $3 ❖ Wall hangings, pillows, pottery, dolls, beadwork, silver jewelry, baskets, paintings, and ceremonial mantas, shirts, sashes, vests, and blouses. 505-852-2372.

Pueblo of Zuni Arts & Crafts, P.O. Box 425, Zuni, NM 87327: Free information with long SASE ❖ Pottery, fetishes, contemporary art, and Zuni turquoise, shell, coral, jet, and silver jewelry. 505-782-4481.

Ramona Sakiestewa Ltd., P.O. Box 2472, Santa Fe, NM 87504: Free brochure with long SASE ❖ Handwoven limited edition fabrics, rugs, blankets, and tapestries. 505-982-8282.

Scripsit, c/o Billy, 3089 Plaza Blanca, Santa Fe, NM 87505: Free information with long SASE ❖ Paper and leather calligraphy crafts. 505-471-1516.

Silver Nugget, 416 Juan Tabo NE, Albuquerque, NM 87123: Catalog $2 ❖ American Native jewelry. 505-293-6861.

Southwest Indian Foundation, P.O. Box 86, Gallup, NM 87302: Free catalog ❖ Native American (Navajo, Zuni, and Laguna) handcrafts. 505-863-4037.

Carol Vigil, P.O. Box 443, Jemez Pueblo, NM 87024: Free information with long SASE ❖ Carved and painted Jemez pottery.

Zuni Craftsmen Cooperative Association, P.O. Box 426, Zuni, NM 87327: Information $2 with long SASE ❖ Zuni silver and turquoise jewelry, beadwork, fetishes, pottery, and paintings. 505-782-4425.

New York

Black Bear Trading Post, Rt 9W, P.O. Box 47, Esopus, NY 12429: Free information with long SASE ❖ Baskets, pottery, beadwork, kachina dolls, peace pipes, war clubs, soapstone and wood carvings, moccasins, cradle boards, paintings, and sterling silver and turquoise jewelry. 914-384-6786.

Chrisjohn Family Arts & Crafts, RD 2, Box 315, Red Hook, NY 12571: Free information with long SASE ❖ Masks and wood carvings, bone jewelry, silver items, cornhusk dolls, and pipes. 914-758-8238.

Peter B. Jones, Box 174, Versailles, NY 14168: Free information with long SASE ❖ Original works in clay, one-of-a-kind ceramic sculptures, and wall hangings. 716-532-5993.

Little Feather Trading Post, P.O. Box 3165, Jamaica, NY 11431: Free information with long SASE ❖ Beadwork and silver jewelry and leather work. 212-658-0576.

Mohawk Impressions, Box 20, Mohawk Station, Hogansburg, NY 13655: Free information with long SASE ❖ Dolls, beadwork, baskets, Mohawk paintings, and crafts. 518-358-2467.

Seneca-Iroquois National Museum Gift Shop, Broad St. Extension, P.O. Box 442, Salamanca, NY 14779: Free price list with long SASE ❖ Iroquois beadwork, baskets, false face masks, cornhusk masks and dolls, rattles, wampum and scrimshaw jewelry, leather crafts, ribbon shirts, and pottery. 716-945-1738.

Sweetgrass Gift Shop, Akwesasne Museum, Rt. 37, Hogansburg, NY 13655: Free brochure with long SASE ❖ Beadwork, quill work, cradle boards, and black ash splint and sweet grass baskets. 518-358-2240.

Tuskewe Krafts, 2089 Upper Mountain Rd., Sanborn, NY 14132: Free brochure with long SASE ❖ Women and men's field and box lacrosse sticks. 716-297-1821.

North Carolina

Haliwa-Saponi Tribal Pottery & Arts, P.O. Box 99, Hollister, NC 27844: Free price list with long SASE ❖ Pottery, quilts, beadwork, woodwork, and stonework. 919-586-4017.

Lumbee Indian Arts & Crafts, Rt. 1, Box 310 AA, Rowland, NC 28383: Free information with long SASE ❖ Baskets, beadwork, and leather work. 910-521-9494.

❖ INDIAN (NATIVE AMERICAN) ARTS & CRAFTS ❖

Qualla Arts & Crafts Mutual Inc., P.O. Box 277, Cherokee, NC 28719: Free brochure with long SASE ❖ Animal figurines, wood carvings, masks, beadwork, pottery, dolls, metalwork, and river cane, oak splint, and honeysuckle baskets. 704-497-3103.

Sacred Hoop Trading Post, 2701 Homestead Rd., #508, Chapel Hill, NC 27516: Free information with long SASE ❖ Eastern Cherokee baskets, pottery, wood and stone carvings, Lumbee paintings, and Native American crafts. 919-933-7595.

Tuscarora Indian Handcraft Shop, Rt. 4, Box 172, Maxton, NC 28364: Free price list with long SASE ❖ Leather boots, moccasins, shirts, hats, vests, handbags, pouches, headbands, belts, necklaces, costumes, sterling silver and brass jewelry, and copper bracelets. 910-844-3352.

Wayah'sti Indian Traditions, P.O. Box 130, Hollister, NC 27844: Free price list with long SASE ❖ Beadwork, leather crafts, stone pipes, sculptures, and pottery. 919-586-4519.

Robert D. Waynee, P.O. Box 5232, New Bern, NC 28560: Free information with long SASE ❖ Native American wooden sculptures. 919-637-2546.

Ohio

American Silver from the Southwest, 5700 Frederick Rd., Dayton, OH 45414: Free information ❖ Native American and contemporary jewelry, pottery, and kachinas. 513-890-0138.

Oklahoma

Adams Studios, Rt. 3, Box 615A, Ponca City, OK 74601: Free price list with long SASE ❖ Watercolors, lithographs, serigraphy, etchings, beadwork key chains, barrettes, and silver and brass buckles, bracelets, and rings decorated with turquoise and semi-precious stones. 405-765-5086.

American Indian Handicrafts, P.O. Box 533, Meeker, OK 74855: Free brochure with long SASE ❖ Ribbon work blankets, shirts, shawls, beadwork, and feather crafts. 405-279-3343.

Buffalo Sun, 605 E. Central, Box 1556, Miami, OK 74355: Free information with long SASE ❖ Native American blouses, skirts, ribbon shirts, dresses, jackets, vests, coats, moccasins, belts, shawls, and jewelry. 918-542-8870.

Cherokee National Museum Gift Shop, P.O. Box 515, TSA-LA-GI, Tahlequah, OK 74464: Free price list with long SASE ❖ Baskets, weapons, paintings, prints, and sculptures. 918-456-6007.

Crying Wind Gallery & Framing Company, 400 N. Indiana, Oklahoma City, OK 73106: Free information with long SASE ❖ Seminole patchwork, dolls, and watercolor portraits, landscapes, still lives, and other subjects. 405-235-9991.

The Dancing Rabbit, Designs by Patta LT, 814 N. Jones, Norman, OK 73069: Free information with long SASE ❖ Contemporary jewelry and bead-weaving. 405-360-0512.

Five Civilized Tribes Museum Trading Post, Agency Hill, Honor Heights Dr., Muskogee, OK 74401: Free brochure with long SASE ❖ Beaded medallion necklaces, key rings, combs, hair ties, rings, baskets, sculptures, and paintings. 918-683-1701.

Jack Gregory, Rt. 1, Box 79, Watts, OK 74964: Free information with long SASE ❖ Contemporary handmade wooden candle holders, bowls, lamps, jewelry, bowls, plates, and other crafts. 918-723-5408.

Kelley Haney Art Gallery, Haney Inc., P.O. Box 3817, Shawnee, OK 74802: Free brochure with long SASE ❖ Original paintings and prints, sculpture, jewelry, baskets, and pottery. 405-275-2270.

Mister Indian's Cowboy Store, 1000 S. Main, Sapulpa, OK 74066: Free information with long SASE ❖ Moccasins, fans, shawls, beadwork, ribbon shirts, rugs, pottery, purses, cradle boards, drums, dolls, silver and turquoise jewelry, and paintings. 918-224-6511.

Monkapeme, P.O. Box 457, Perkins, OK 74059: Free information with long SASE ❖ Native American contemporary fashions, traditional costumes, moccasins, shawls, headbands, medallions, belts, hair ties, buckskin dresses, leggings, and shirts. 405-547-2948.

Oklahoma Indian Arts & Crafts Cooperative, P.O. Box 966, Anadarko, OK 73005: Free price list with long SASE ❖ Beaded moccasins, belts, ties, pins, dance costume accessories, suede handbags, war dance bustle ensembles, nickel-silver jewelry, hand-sewn and decorated shirts, dolls, and paintings by Southern Plains Native Americans. 405-247-3486.

Connie Seabourn Studio, P.O. Box 23795, Oklahoma City, OK 73132: Free information with long SASE ❖ Original paintings, drawings, and hand-pulled prints. 405-728-3903.

Seabourn Studio, 6105 Covington Ln., Oklahoma City, OK 73132: Free information with long SASE ❖ Lithographs, serigraphs, and etchings. 405-722-1631.

Snake Creek Workshop, P.O. Box 147, Rose, OK 74364: Free brochure with long SASE ❖ Mussel shell gorget necklaces. 918-479-8867.

Supernaw's Oklahoma Indian Supply, P.O. Box 216, Skiatook, OK 74070: Catalog $1 ❖ Feather work, nickel-silver jewelry, beadwork, roaches, women's accessories, and crafts. 918-396-1713.

Tah-Mels, P.O. Box 1123, Tahlequah, OK 74465: Free information with long SASE ❖ Dolls, beadwork, baskets, quilts, Oochelata pink mussel shell and silver and gold jewelry, oil and watercolor paintings, and wood carvings. 918-456-5461.

Tiger Art Gallery, 2110 E. Shawnee St., Muskogee, OK 74403: Free information with long SASE ❖ Paintings and sculptures. 918-687-7006.

Touching Leaves Indian Crafts, 927 Portland Ave., Dewey, OK 74029: Catalog $1 ❖ Beadwork, German silver jewelry, and leather crafts. 918-534-2859.

Zadoka Pottery, 12515 E. 37th St., Tulsa, OK 74146: Free information with long SASE ❖ Earthenware storage vessels, vases, and bowls. 918-663-9455.

Oregon

Ed's House of Gems, 7712 NE Sandy Blvd., Portland, OR 97211: Free information with long SASE ❖ Clocks, clock-making parts, minerals, gemstones, lapidary equipment, mountings, shells, jewelry, and Native American relics. 503-284-8990.

Klahowya, American Indian Gift Shop, 947 S. 1st St., Coos Bay, OR 97420: Free information with long SASE ❖ Beadwork, dolls, earrings, drums, and feather hair ties from various tribes. 503-269-7349.

Quintana's Gallery of Indian & Western Art, 139 NW 2nd Ave., Portland, OR 97209: Free information with long SASE ❖ Northwest Coast art, contemporary western paintings, bronze sculptures, and antique and contemporary Native American art from over 300 tribes. 503-223-1729.

Red Bear Creations, 358 N. Lexington Ave., Brandon, OR 97411: Free information with long SASE ❖ Star quilts, star drum covers, and padded jackets. 503-347-9772.

Spotted Horse Tribal Gifts, Diane McAlister, P.O. Box 869, Oakridge, OR 97463: Catalog $2 ❖ Native American craft-making kits, tools, patterns, cassette tapes, books, and crafts.

Nadine Van Mechelen, Rt. 1, Box 270, Pendleton, OR 97801: Free information with long SASE ❖ Handmade dolls in authentic Native American costumes. 503-276-2566.

Rhode Island

The Turquoise, Rockland Rd., North Scituate, RI 02857: Free information with long SASE ❖ Southwest Native American jewelry, pottery, baskets, rugs, paintings, moccasins, and clothing. 401-647-2579.

South Carolina

Sara Ayers, 1182 Brookwood Circle, West Columbia, SC 29169: Free price list with long SASE ❖ Pottery pipes, vases, pitchers, canoes, candlesticks, bowls, jardinieres, cups, bookends, and other crafts. 803-794-5436.

South Dakota

Featherstone Productions, P.O. Box 487, Brookings, SD 57006: Free information with long SASE ❖ Sculptures and original paintings. 605-693-3183.

Jackson Originals, Box 1049, Mission, SD 57555: Catalog $2 ❖ Indian artistry and Western style buckskin clothing. Also custom-made vests, jackets, and other clothing with beadwork. 605-856-2541.

Lakota Jewelry Visions, 909 E. St. Patrick, Ste. 16, Rapid City, SD 57701: Free information with long SASE ❖ Jewelry and dance accessories. 605-343-0603.

Oyate Kin Cultural Cooperative, c/o Wesley Hare, Marty, SD 57361: Free information with long SASE ❖ Beadwork, feather and leather accessories for dance outfits, Native American star quilts, ribbon shirts, and leather crafts.

Prairie Edge, P.O. Box 8303, Rapid City, SD 57709: Catalog $5 ❖ Native American artifacts and collectibles.

Rings 'N' Things, P.O. Box 360, Mission, SD 57555: Free information with long SASE ❖ Silver gifts, quill work, and beadwork. 605-856-4548.

St. Joseph's Lakota Development Council, St. Joseph's Indian School, Chamberlain, SD 57326: Free brochure with long SASE ❖ Dot drawings, jewelry, kachina dolls, leather work, beadwork, patchwork quilts, and tote bags. 605-734-6021.

Sioux Trading Post Inc., 415 6th St., Rapid City, SD 57701: Catalog $2 ❖ Craft supplies, beads and beadwork, quill work, T-shirts and sweatshirts, books, tapes and CDs, botanicals, moccasins, and crafts. 800-456-3394.

Starboy Enterprises, P.O. Box 33, Rosebud Sioux Reservation, Okreek, SD 57563: Free brochure with long SASE ❖ Star quilts. 605-856-4517.

The Tipi Shop Inc., Box 1542, Rapid City, SD 57709: Catalog $2 ❖ Beaded buckskin moccasins, dance costume accessories, pottery, billfolds, coin purses, beadwork jewelry, quill work, dolls, parfleche boxes, willow baskets, and paintings by Sioux artists. 605-343-7851.

Texas

Annesley Studio, P.O. Box 3, Missouri City, TX 77459: Free information ❖ Limited edition bronze sculptures, original 24K gold and silver point drawings, paintings, and pastels. 713-729-8960.

Crazy Crow Trading Post, 107 N. Fannin, P.O. Box 314, Denison, TX 75020: Catalog $2 ❖ Silver items, moccasins, beadwork, and reproduction eagle feather war bonnets. 903-463-1366.

Eagle Dancer, 159 Gulf Freeway South, League City, TX 77573: Free information with long SASE ❖ Leather work, paintings, wood carvings, sculptures, jewelry, pottery, rugs, dolls, and other crafts. 713-332-6028.

Mystic Canyon Gallery, Rt. 3, P.O. Box 720, Rockwall, TX 75087: Brochure $5 ❖ Reproduction authentic Native American weapons and ceremonial items. 214-771-2546.

Naranjo's World of American Indian Art, P.O. Box 7973, Houston, TX 77270: Free price list with long SASE ❖ Jewelry, beadwork, leather work, pottery, baskets, rugs, dolls, and kachinas. 713-660-9690.

Tribal Enterprise, Alabama-Coushatta Indian Reservation, Rt. 3, Box 640, Livingston, TX 77351: Free information with long SASE ❖ Large and small coiled pine needle and grass baskets, animal effigies, beadwork, pottery, vests, and ribbon shirts. 713-563-4391.

Whitewolf Photography, P.O. Box 297, Redwater, TX 75573: Free information with long SASE ❖ Original photographs with Native American and western themes.

Utah

Eagle Feather Trading Post, 168 W. 12th St., Ogden, UT 84404: Catalog $3.50 ❖ Beading and Native American craft supplies, beads and bead-stringing kits, and how-to beading and craft books.

Virginia

The Silver Phoenix Inc., 2946-D Chain Bridge Rd., Oakton, VA 22124: Free information with long SASE ❖ Jewelry, sand paintings, pottery, kachinas, rugs, moccasins, and beadwork. 703-255-3393.

Washington

Bead Lady/Cherokee Rainbows, 315-B Roosevelt, Wenatchee, WA 98801: Free information with long SASE ❖ Beadwork, women and children's moccasins, dance costumes and clothing, and crafts.

Fran & Bill James, Lummi Indian Craftsmen, 4339 Lummi Rd., Ferndale, WA 98248: Free information with long SASE ❖ Northwest Coast Salish wool blankets and cedar bark baskets. 206-384-5292.

Makah Cultural Research Center, P.O. Box 95, Neah Bay, WA 98357: Free price list with long SASE ❖ Woven baskets, replicas of archaeological artifacts, carved wooden masks, totem poles, rattles and bowls, shell jewelry, engraved silver bracelets, miniature basket earrings, painted drums, beadwork, and original serigraphs. 206-645-2711.

Suquamish Museum, P.O. Box 498, Suquamish, WA 98392: Free information with long SASE ❖ Suquamish/Puget Sound Salish clam baskets, dolls, whistles, museum replicas, wooden bowls, spoons, canoe bailers, and wood carvings. 206-598-3311.

Templeton Tribal Art, P.O. Box 17941, Seattle, WA 98107: Catalog $3 ❖ Navajo rugs.

Tin-Na-Tit Kin-Ne-Ki Indian Arts & Gifts, P.O. Box 1057, Republic, WA 99166: Free information with long SASE ❖ Jewelry, masks, stone carvings, kachina dolls, baskets, pottery, quill work, beaded items, sand paintings, and other crafts. 509-775-3077.

Wisconsin

Wa-Swa-Gon Arts & Crafts, P.O. Box 477, Lac du Flambeau, WI 54538: Free information with long SASE ❖ Beadwork, birch bark items, moccasins, finger weavings, traditional and ceremonial clothes, and carvings. 715-588-7636.

Winnebago Public Indian Museum, P.O. Box 441, Wisconsin Dells, WI 53965: Price list $1 ❖ Winnebago baskets, beadwork, deerskin products, pottery, Navajo rugs, and silver items. 608-254-2268.

Wyoming

Fort Washakie Trading Company, 53 N. Fork Rd., P.O. Box 428, Fort Washakie, WY 82514: Free brochure with long SASE ❖ Beaded and quill jewelry, rawhide and smoked skin accessories, dolls, cradle boards, Navajo rugs, southwestern silver and turquoise jewelry, Papago baskets, and Pueblo pottery. 307-332-3557.

La Ray Turquoise Company, P.O. Box 83, Cody, WY 82414: Free information with long SASE ❖ Navajo rugs, Ojibwa beadwork, and Navajo, Zuni, Chippewa, and Hopi silver items. 307-587-9564.

INTERCOMS

Doorking, 120 Glasgow Ave., Inglewood, CA 90301: Free information ❖ Telephone entry and access control systems. 800-826-7493.

Interactive Technologies Inc., 2266 N. 2nd St., St. Paul, MN 55109: Free information ❖ Telephone-based home security systems. 612-777-2690.

Ja Mar Distributing/Su-Mar Enterprises, 1292 Montclair Dr., Pasadena, CA 91104: Free catalog ❖ Remote control equipment, personal assistance systems, alarms, and motion detectors. 410-437-4181.

JDS Technologies, 16750 W. Bernardo Dr., San Diego, CA 92127: Free information ❖ Telephone-based home security systems and remote controls for computers, lights, and other devices. 800-983-5537; 619-487-8787 (in CA).

M & S Systems Inc., 2861 Congressman Ln., Dallas, TX 75220: Free information ❖ Intercom with door chimes and release. 800-877-6631.

NuTone Inc., P.O. Box 1580, Cincinnati, OH 45201: Catalog $3 ❖ Video door-answering system with voice transmission over telephones and a wireless security system that can be zone programmed. 800-543-8687.

Paladin Electronics, 19425 Soledad Cyn Rd., Ste. 333, Canyon Country, CA 91351: Free information ❖ Talking security systems. 805-251-8725.

Siedle Communication System of America, 750 Parkway, Broomall, PA 19008: Free information ❖ Video intercoms. 800-874-3353.

JET SKIS (PERSONAL WATERCRAFT)

Talk-A-Phone Company, 5013 N. Kedzie Ave., Chicago, IL 60625: Free information ❖ Intercoms for two-way conversation with optional integration with master system. 312-539-1100.

JET SKIS (PERSONAL WATERCRAFT)

Arizona Jet Ski Center, 2430 E. Danbury, Phoenix, AZ 85032: Free information ❖ Jet skis. 800-245-3875.

Bert's, 900 W. Foothill Blvd., Azusa, CA 91702: Free catalog ❖ Personal watercraft accessories. 800-367-9464; 800-237-8159 (in CA).

Butch's Jet Ski, 3614 S. Division, Grand Rapids, MI 49508: Free information ❖ Jet skis. 800-54-BUTCH.

Castaic Ski and Sport, 32203 Castaic Rd., Castaic, CA 91384: Free catalog ❖ Personal watercraft and accessories. 805-257-3033.

Coki Manufacturing Company, 9525 Cozycroft Ave., Unit F, Chatsworth, CA 91311: Free information ❖ Personal watercraft accessories. 818-998-2426.

Competition Accessories Inc., 345 W. Lettrel Ln., Springfield, OH 45506: Catalog $5 ❖ Personal watercraft accessories. 800-543-4709.

Davit Master, 5560 Ulmerton Rd., Clearwater, FL 34620: Free information ❖ Personal watercraft lift systems. 800-878-5560.

DCT Sports, 4060 Palm, Ste. 602, Fullerton, CA 92635: Free information with long SASE ❖ Personal watercraft. 714-526-8415.

DG Performance Specialties Inc., 1220 La Loma Circle, Anaheim, CA 92806: Free catalog ❖ Performance parts and accessories for all-terrain vehicles and personal watercraft. 800-854-9134; 714-630-5471 (in CA).

Follansbee Dock Systems, P.O. Box 640, Follansbee, WV 26037: Free information ❖ Personal watercraft lifts in easy-to-assemble kits. 800-223-3444.

Intraser Inc., 3580 Wilshire Blvd., Los Angeles, CA 90010: Free information ❖ New and pre-owned motorcycles, ATVs, snowmobiles, trailers, personal water vehicles, and small boats. 213-365-6030.

Jet-Dolly Inc., 4208 Gravois Ave., St. Louis, MO 63116: Free information ❖ Dollies for personal watercraft. 800-564-2929.

Jet Express, 6355 Corte Del Abeto, Carlsbad, CA 92009: Free catalog ❖ Personal watercraft accessories. 800-538-3977.

Jetinetics Jet Ski Racing Products, 357 S. Acacia Ave., Fullerton, CA 92631: Free catalog ❖ Personal watercraft, parts, and tools. 714-525-9930.

Kawasaki Motors Corporation, P.O. Box 25252, Santa Ana, CA 92799: Free information ❖ One- and two-person jet skis. 714-770-0400.

KG Industries, 140 Pacific Dr., Quakertown, PA 18951: Free information ❖ Personal watercraft. 800-531-4252.

Dennis Kirk, 955 Southfield Ave., Rush City, MN 55069: Free catalog ❖ Personal watercraft. 800-328-9280.

Lake Cities Polaris, 6060 S. Stemmons Freeway, Lake Dallas, TX 75065: Free information ❖ Personal watercraft and accessories. 800-619-6729.

Norson Industries Inc., 242 Dudala Ln., Loudon, TN 37774: Free information ❖ Personal watercraft hoist. 219-842-3375.

Nyman Dock Shuttle, 1495 NW Gilman Blvd., Issaquah, WA 98027: Free information ❖ Personal watercraft hoist. 800-929-0468; 206-391-1101 (in WA).

Polaris Industries, 1225 Hwy. 169 North, Minneapolis, MN 55441: Free list of retail sources ❖ Personal watercraft and wetsuits. 800-POLARIS; 612-542-0500 (in MN).

Porta Dock Inc., 175 3rd St., P.O. Box 409, Dassel, MN 55325: Information $1 ❖ Easy-to-assemble single and double personal watercraft and boat lifts. 612-275-3312.

PSI Performance, P.O. Box 72, Hwy. 22, Wild Rose, WI 54984: Catalog $4 ❖ Personal watercraft engines, specialty kits, and sand painting accessories. 414-622-4555.

Recreation Unlimited, 1021 W. Taft Ave., Orange, CA 92665: Free information ❖ Personal watercraft accessories. 800-472-3754.

Riva-Yamaha, 3801 N. Dixie Hwy., Pompano Beach, FL 33064: Free catalog ❖ Yamaha watercraft and parts. 800-241-4544.

Rossier Engineering, 1340 Okray Ave., Plover, WI 54467: Free information ❖ Personal watercraft and accessories. 715-341-9919.

Sano Sports International, P.O. Box 141758, Austin, TX 78714: Free brochure ❖ Personal watercraft and accessories. 512-836-6685.

Sea-Doo, 1340 Okray Ave., Plover, WI 54467: Free information ❖ Personal watercraft. 715-341-9919.

Shorelander, Division Midwest Industries Inc., Hwy. 59 & 175, Ida Grove, IA 51445: Free information ❖ Personal watercraft trailers. 712-364-3365.

Solas USA Inc., 522 NW 165th St., Miami, FL 33014: Free information ❖ Personal watercraft. 305-625-4389.

Sunburst Performance, 1617 Industrial Blvd., Lake Havasu City, AZ 86403: Catalog $5 ❖ Personal watercraft accessories. 520-855-1354.

Tigershark Watercraft, South Brooks Ave., Thief River Falls, MN 56701: Free information ❖ Personal watercraft and wetsuits. 218-681-4999.

Top Gun Racing, Rt. 122 South, P.O. Box 429, Wirtz, VA 24184: Free information ❖ Jet ski parts. 703-721-4900.

Ultrac Performance Systems, 1971 W. McNab Rd., Pompano Beach, FL 33069: Free information ❖ Personal watercraft accessories. 305-974-4269.

VM Boat Trailers, 5200 S. Peach, Fresno, CA 93725: Free information ❖ Jet ski trailers. 209-486-0410.

Warner's Dock Inc., 928 N. Knowles Ave., New Richmond, WI 54017: Free information ❖ Personal watercraft gear and parts. 800-292-1760.

WetJet International Ltd., 100 Cherokee Cove, Venore, TN 37885: Free information ❖ Personal watercraft and clothing. 800-2-WETJET.

White Brothers, 24845 Corbit Pl., Yorba Linda, CA 92687: Catalog $4 ❖ Personal watercraft. 714-692-3404.

Yamaha Motor Corporation, P.O. Box 6555, Cypress, CA 90630: Free list of retail sources ❖ One- and two-person jet skis. 800-526-6650.

JEWELRY

A.R.C. Traders Inc., Box 3429, Scottsdale, AZ 85257: Free information ❖ Findings, chains, earrings, jewelry, and sterling silver, gold-filled, and 14K gold beads. 800-528-2374; 602-945-0769 (in AZ).

Alpha Omega Fine Watches, 57 JFK St., Harvard Square, Cambridge, MA 02138: Free information ❖ Watches. 800-447-4367; 617-864-1227 (in MA).

American Pearl and Diamond, 25 W. 47th St., New York, NY 10036: Free catalog ❖ Imported South Sea, akoya, and freshwater pearls for necklaces, earrings, and more at wholesale prices. 800-84-PEARL; 212-221-3045 (in NY).

American Silver from the Southwest, 5700 Frederick Rd., Dayton, OH 45414: Free information ❖ Native American and contemporary jewelry, pottery, and kachinas. 513-890-0138.

Arizona Traders, P.O. Box 2000, El Paso, TX 79950: Free price list ❖ Native American mandellas and handmade turquoise and silver jewelry. 800-351-1674; 915-544-7204 (in AZ).

Arrow Gems & Minerals Inc., 9827 Cave Creek Rd., Phoenix, AZ 85020: Free catalog ❖ Pewter figurines, pendants, buckles, beads and findings, mineral specimens, and faceted gemstones. 602-997-6373.

❖ JEWELRY ❖

Arch Avery Originals, Arch Avery Jr., Rt. 2, Box 233, Hayesville, NC 28904: Brochure $2 (refundable) ❖ Hand-finished solid sterling silver wildlife-style jewelry. 704-389-3209.

James Avery Craftsman, P.O. Box 1367, Kerrville, TX 78029: Free catalog ❖ Men and women's handcrafted gold and silver jewelry. 800-283-1770.

Maurice Badler Jewelry, 578 5th Ave., New York, NY 10036: Catalog $3 ❖ Men and women's jewelry. 800-M-BADLER; 212-575-9632 (in NY).

Marilyn Barnes Jewelry, 3512 S. Fort, Springfield, MO 65807: Brochure $1 ❖ Original Victorian-style jewelry. 417-887-1608.

Beaded Fashions by Shayla Arrasmith, P.O. Box 7996, Riverside, CA 92513: Brochure $2 ❖ Handmade earrings and necklaces. 909-359-7119.

Beauty by Spector Inc., McKeesport, PA 15134: Free catalog ❖ Women's wigs and hairpieces, men's toupees, jewelry, and exotic lingerie. 412-673-3259.

J.H. Breakell & Company, 132 Spring St., Newport, RI 02840: Catalog $2 ❖ Handcrafted sterling silver and gold jewelry. 800-767-6411.

Broadway Jewelry Ent., 287 Broadway, Brooklyn, NY 11211: Free brochure ❖ Women's high-fashion jewelry. 800-933-6465; 718-782-7088 (in NY).

Caribone Designs, Box 2128, Schefferville, P.Q., Canada G0G 2T0: Catalog $3 ❖ Nature-inspired handcrafted caribou bone jewelry. 418-585-3808.

Comstock Heritage Collection, 2300 Lockheed Way, Carson City, NV 89706: Free information (request list of retail sources) ❖ Silver belt buckles, pins, and other accessories. 702-246-3835.

Cross Jewelers, 570 Congress St., Portland, ME 04101: Free catalog ❖ Original jewelry. 800-433-2988.

Des Handmade Crafts, 112 Randy Rd., Madison, TN 37115: Free brochure ❖ Handcrafted clay jewelry. 615-868-5279.

Diamond Essence Company, 6 Saddle Rd., Cedar Knolls, NJ 07927: Free catalog ❖ Men and women's jewelry with simulated diamonds. 201-267-7370.

Christian Dior, 417 5th Ave., New York, NY 10016: Free catalog ❖ Fashionable jewelry for most occasions. 800-456-9444.

Discoveries, 526 N. Fayette St., Alexandria, VA 22314: Free information ❖ Handmade pendants, rings, bracelets, earrings, and personalized cartouche jewelry. 800-237-3358.

DoPaso Jewelry, P.O. Box 35430, Albuquerque, NM 87176: Catalog $7 ❖ Southwestern-style turquoise and sterling silver pins. 800-992-5234.

Earrings & Things, 114 5th Ave., New York, NY 10011: Free catalog ❖ Earrings, necklaces, chains, pins, and high fashion jewelry. 800-445-0057.

Ed's House of Gems, 7712 NE Sandy Blvd., Portland, OR 97211: Free information with long SASE ❖ Clocks, clock-making parts, minerals, gemstones, lapidary equipment, mountings, shells, jewelry, and Native American relics. 503-284-8990.

The Ellickson Collection, 3175 Middle Sattre Rd., Decorah, IA 52101: Brochure $3 (refundable) ❖ Sterling silver jewelry. 319-382-2295.

Fortunoff Fine Jewelry, P.O. Box 1550, Westbury, NY 11590: Free catalog ❖ Fine jewelry for men and women. 800-937-4376.

Goldware, P.O. Box 22335, San Diego, CA 92192: Free brochure ❖ Medical identification jewelry in 14K gold and sterling silver. 800-669-7311.

Grafstein & Company, Division Capetown Diamonds, 3340 Peachtree Rd. NE, Atlanta, GA 30326: Free brochure ❖ Fine jewelry and watches. 800-442-7866; 404-365-9503 (in GA).

Gray & Sons, 2998 McFarlane Rd., Coconut Grove, FL 33133: Catalog $10 ❖ Pre-owned and restored fine watches. 800-654-0756.

H & A Enterprises Inc., 14-21 150th St., P.O. Box 570489, Whitestone, NY 11357: Free catalog ❖ Women's jewelry. 800-327-3427.

Hand & Hammer Silversmiths, 2610 Morse Ln., Woodbridge, VA 22192: Free information ❖ Handcrafted sterling silver and vermeil jewelry. Also Christmas ornaments. 800-SILVERY.

Harmon's Agate & Silver Shop, Box 94, Crane, MT 59217: Catalog $3 ❖ Montana moss agate, sapphires, and handmade silver and gold jewelry. 406-482-2534.

Hay Charlie, 541 Historic Main St., Park City, UT 84060: Free information ❖ Handcrafted western-style boots, buckles and belts, hats, jewelry, and clothing.

Gayle Hayman Beverly Hills, 750 Lexington Ave., 16th Floor, New York, NY 10026: Free catalog ❖ Jewelry and cosmetics. 800-682-9932.

Heraldica Imports, 21 W. 46th St., New York, NY 10036: Free brochure ❖ Engraved family crest rings and jewelry. 212-719-4204.

Horsemen's General Store, 345 W. Leffel Ln., Springfield, OH 45506: Catalog $3 ❖ Western-style jewelry. 800-343-4987; 513-323-0874 (in OH).

Jaeger-LeCoultre, P.O. Box 1608, Winchester, VA 22604: Free catalog (request list of retail sources) ❖ Jaeger-LeCoultre watches. 800-JLC-TIME.

Jewelry by Avery, 5134 Chalk Point Rd., West River, MD 20778: Free information with long SASE ❖ Kachinas, Native American art, precious and semi-precious gemstones, mineral specimens, and handcrafted Zuni, Navajo, and Hopi turquoise jewelry. 410-867-4752.

Jewelry Company, P.O. Box 1020, Apache Junction, AZ 85217: Free brochure ❖ Military rings in yellow or white 10k or 14K solid gold. Also birthstones and gemstone and diamond rings. 800-544-9706; 602-982-2273 (in AZ).

Jewelry Values, Palo Verde at 34th St., P.O. Box 28807, Tucson, AZ 85726: Free catalog ❖ Women and men's jewelry. 602-747-5000.

Sharon E. Johnson Jewelry, P.O. Box 288, Rockville Centre, NY 11571: Free brochure ❖ Wire-wrapped gold and gemstone jewelry. 800-304-1282.

Kemp Designs, P.O. Box 10476, Bainbridge Is., WA 98110: Brochure $2 ❖ Miniature paintings decoupage on antiqued copper pins or pendants.

The Kenya Gem Company, 6509 Ventnor Ave., Ventnor, NJ 08406: Catalog $5 ❖ Men and women's jewelry with simulated diamonds. 800-523-0158.

Richard L. Kollinger Company Inc., 5952 Royal Ln., Ste. 103, Dallas, TX 75230: Free catalog ❖ Polished girdle diamond-cut cubic zirconia jewelry with 14K gold mountings. 214-361-1411.

Lenox Jewelers, 2379 Black Rock Tnpk., Fairfield, CT 06430: Free catalog ❖ Watches, figurines, jewelry, porcelain, china, and crystal. 800-243-4473; 203-374-6157 (in CT).

Lewis & Roberts, 6400 E. Rogers Circle, Boca Raton, FL 33499: Free catalog ❖ Men and women's watches, jewelry, and gifts. 800-767-5614.

Lonnie's Inc., 7155 E. Main St., Mesa, AZ 85207: Free findings catalog; tool catalog $5; jewelry catalog $5 ❖ Supplies for jewelers, casters, silversmiths, and lapidarists. Also silver jewelry. 602-832-2641.

Lovell Designs, P.O. Box 7130, Portland, ME 04112: Free catalog ❖ Pendants, pins, earrings, and jewelry in pewter, sterling silver, and gold plate. 800-533-9685.

Alan Marcus & Company, 815 Connecticut Ave. NW, Washington, DC 20006: Free catalog ❖ Jewelry and Rolex, Patek, Phillippe, Audemars Piguet, Baume Mercier, and Cartier watches. 800-654-7184; 202-331-0671 (in DC).

❖ JEWELRY MAKING ❖

Mary Laura's, 3636 San Mateo Blvd. NE, Albuquerque, NM 87110: Catalog $2 ❖ Native American jewelry from the Zuni Pueblo. 800-662-4848.

Melanie Collection, 12105 Bermuda NE, Albuquerque, NM 87111: Charm catalog $6; button catalog $2 ❖ Replicas of old, new, ancient, and ethnic artifacts in silver and bronze. 505-298-7036.

Merlite Industries Inc., 114 5th Ave., New York, NY 10011: Free catalog ❖ Contemporary and classic jewelry for men and women. 212-924-6440.

Museum of Jewelry, 3000 Larkin St., San Francisco, CA 94109: Free catalog ❖ Handcrafted reproductions of historic jewelry originals. 800-258-0888.

National Watch Exchange, 107 S. 8th St., Philadelphia, PA 19106: Free information ❖ Pre-owned vintage watches.

Nature's Jewelry, 222 Mill Rd., Chelmsford, MA 01824: Free catalog ❖ Leaves, shells, and other natural objects transformed into jewelry by preservation in precious metals. 800-333-3235.

Navajo Manufacturing Company, 5801 Logan St., Denver, CO 80216: Catalog $2 ❖ Turquoise and sterling silver jewelry, novelties, and sunglasses. 303-292-3090.

Nigro's Western Store, 3320 Merriam Ln., Kansas City, KS 66106: Free information ❖ Western-style jewelry. 800-521-3330; 913-262-7600 (in KS).

Olympia Gold, 11540 Wiles Rd., Coral Springs, FL 33076: Free catalog ❖ Necklaces, bracelets, diamond charms, filigree rings, and Austrian crystal chain. 800-395-7774.

Oriental Crest Inc., 6161 Savoy Dr., Houston, TX 77036: Free information ❖ Semi-precious gemstone and other jewelry, bead-stringing supplies, pendant carvings, and earring jackets. 800-367-3954; 713-780-2425 (in TX).

Palancar Jewelers, 1156 E. Alosta Ave., Glendora, CA 91741: Free catalog ❖ Diver's jewelry in 14K gold and sterling. 800-467-9067.

Palm Beach International, 6400 E. Rogers Circle, Boca Raton, FL 33499: Free catalog ❖ Earrings and jewelry. 800-633-9803.

S.A. Peck & Company, 55 E. Washington St., Chicago, IL 60602: Free catalog ❖ Diamonds and fine jewelry. 800-922-0090.

Barbra Pehrson Jewelry, 1435 Quebec St., Denver, CO 80220: Free information ❖ Custom-designed costume jewelry. 303-230-2522.

Q-C Turquoise, 3340 E. Washington, Phoenix, AZ 85034: Free information ❖ Turquoise nugget jewelry, nuggets by the strand or pound, and cutting material or blocks. 602-267-1164.

Rings & Things, 114 5th Ave., New York, NY 10011: Free catalog ❖ Discontinued jewelry. 212-807-9141.

Martin Rochelle Jewelry, 194 Barton St., Pawtucket, RI 02860: Catalog $2 ❖ Designer jewelry from around the world. 800-552-0699.

Rolex Watch U.S.A. Inc., Rolex Building, 665 5th Ave., New York, NY 10022: Free brochure ❖ Rolex watches.

Ross-Simons Jewelers, 9 Ross Simons Dr., Cranston, RI 02920: Free catalog ❖ China, crystal, flatware, silver, watches, figurines, and diamond, gold, pearl, and gemstone jewelry. 800-556-7376; 800-553-7370 (in RI).

Roussels, P.O. Box 476, Arlington, MA 02174: Catalog $1 ❖ Jewelry-making supplies and ready-to-wear jewelry. 508-443-8888.

Sadigh Gallery of Ancient Art, 303 5th Ave., Ste. 1603, New York, NY 10016: Free catalog ❖ Authentic ancient art and jewelry. 800-426-2007; 212-725-7537 (in NY).

S.E.A.T. Publication, P.O. Box 2593, Longmont, CO 80502: Information $4 ❖ Mineral specimens, jewelry, and beads. 303-678-9930.

Second Look, c/o Silver Works Inc., 3234-B Kirkwood Hwy., Wilmington, DE 19808: Free catalog ❖ Silver and turquoise earrings, bracelets, necklaces, watch bands, and jewelry by Southwest artisans. 800-544-8200.

Silver Eagle Creations, Rt. 2, Box 361, Franklin, TX 77856: Free catalog ❖ Silver and gold-plated United States and world coin jewelry. 409-828-3116.

Silver Nugget, 416 Juan Tabo NE, Albuquerque, NM 87123: Catalog $2 ❖ Native American jewelry. 505-293-6861.

Simcha Designs, P.O. Box 6562, Fresh Meadows Station, 192-04 Horace Harding Expwy., Flushing, NY 11365: Free catalog ❖ Judaich artware and jewelry. 718-776-6688.

Simply Diamonds, P.O. Box 682, Ardsley, NY 10502: Free catalog ❖ Diamond jewelry in 14K solid gold mountings. 800-55-CARAT.

Simply Whispers, 33 Riverside Dr., Pembroke, MA 02359: Free catalog ❖ Hypo-allergenic earrings and jewelry. 800-451-5700.

❖ **BODY JEWELRY** ❖

Huck Spaulding Enterprises Inc., Rt. 85, New Scotland Rd., Voorheesville, NY 12186: Free information ❖ Exotic body jewelry, professional body piercing kit, full line of body piercing supplies. 518-768-2070.

Tener's Western Outfitters, 4320 W. Reno Ave., Oklahoma City, OK 73107: Free catalog ❖ Western-style jewelry. 800-654-6715; 405-946-5500 (in OK).

Tiffany & Company, Customer Service, 801 Jefferson Rd., Parsippany, NJ 07054: Catalog $1 ❖ Jewelry, silver, china, crystal, watches and clocks, and other gifts. 800-452-9146.

Tourneau, 488 Madison Ave., New York, NY 10022: Free information ❖ Reconditioned pre-owned Rolex, Patek, Piaget, and other watches. 800-542-2389; 212-758-3671 (in NY).

Vanity Fair, S.A. Peck & Company, 55 E. Washington St., Chicago, IL 60602: Free catalog ❖ Diamond jewelry. 800-922-0090.

Wayfarer Trading Company, 2094 343rd St., Vail, IA 51465: Free brochure ❖ Sterling silver and 18k gold Egyptian cartouche pendants and jewelry. 800-432-1892.

Kate Webster Company, 83 Granite St., Rockport, MA 01966: Catalog $3 ❖ Doll costuming supplies and jewelry. 508-546-6462.

What on Earth Naturally, 6250 Busch Blvd., Columbus, OH 43229: Free information ❖ Minerals, fossils, jewelry, gemstones, and shells. 614-436-1458.

Williamsburg Merchants, 223 Parkway Dr., Williamsburg, VA 23185: Catalog $2 ❖ Sterling silver jewelry. 800-545-4556.

Windsor Collection, 6836 Engle Rd., P.O. Box 94549, Cleveland, OH 44101: Free catalog ❖ Men and women's fashion watches and jewelry. 216-826-1712.

JEWELRY MAKING

A & A Jewelry Tools & Findings, 319 W. 6th St., Los Angeles, CA 90014: Free catalog ❖ Jewelry-making tools and accessories. 213-627-8004.

A & B Jewels & Tools, 350 W. Grand River, Williamston, MI 48895: Catalog $2 ❖ Jewelry-making tools and supplies. 517-655-4664.

A & D Jewelry, P.O. Box 951, West Sacramento, CA 95691: Free catalog ❖ Supplies for making gold jewelry. 800-466-4453.

A.R.C. Traders Inc., Box 3429, Scottsdale, AZ 85257: Free information ❖ Findings, chains, earrings, jewelry, and sterling silver, gold-filled, and 14K gold beads. 800-528-2374; 602-945-0769 (in AZ).

A.R.E. Supply Co., 636 11th Ave., Minneapolis, MN 55343: Catalog $4 ❖ Tools, supplies, and equipment for technicians and craftsmen; craft metals and findings.

Abeada Corporation, 1205 N. Main St., Royal Oak, MI 48067: Free information ❖ Semi-precious gemstone and glass beads, freshwater and cultured pearls, and gold and silver findings. 800-521-6326; 313-399-6642 (in MI).

❖ JEWELRY MAKING ❖

Ackley's Rocks & Stamps, 3230 N. Stone Ave., Colorado Springs, CO 80907: Catalog $1 (refundable) ❖ Lapidary and silversmithing supplies, mountings, and findings. 719-633-1153.

Aleta's Rock Shop, 1515 Plainfield NE, Grand Rapids, MI 49505: Catalog $1.50 ❖ Jewelry-making supplies, tumblers, lapidary equipment, findings, silicon carbide grits, diamond material, and rocks for cutting, tumbling, and polishing. 616-363-5394.

Allcraft Tool & Supply Company, 666 Pacific St., Brooklyn, NY 11207: Catalog $5 ❖ Lapidary tools and supplies. 800-645-7124; 718-789-2800 (in NY).

Alpha Supply, P.O. Box 2133, Bremerton, WA 98310: Catalog $7 ❖ Casting and faceting equipment, jewelry-making tools, silver rings, wax models, lapidary tools, and clock movements and parts. 800-257-4211.

Amazon Imports, P.O. Box 58, Williston Park, NY 11596: Free price list ❖ Amethyst, aquamarine, emerald, garnet, kunzite, blue topaz, imperial topaz, and tourmaline from Brazil. 800-888-GEMS; 516-621-7481 (in NY).

Ambassador, Palo Verde at 34th St., P.O. Box 28807, Tucson, AZ 85726: Free catalog ❖ Cloisonne, turquoise, sterling silver, 14K gold, and onyx, ruby, emerald, pearl, jade, opal, zirconia, and other semi-precious gemstone settings. 520-748-8600.

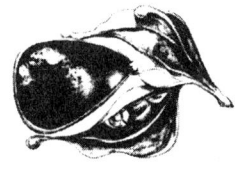

Amber Treasure, P.O. Box 99103, Emeryville, CA 94662: Catalog $2 ❖ Calibrated and free-form cabochons, amber spheres and beads, polished amber stones, Baltic amber rough, and finished jewelry. 510-547-8660.

Ambush - Wholesale Beads and Findings, P.O. Box 144, Worcester, MA 01613: Catalog $5 ❖ Beads: glass, semi-precious, clay, findings, African trade. 508-756-2802.

APL Trader, P.O. Box 1900, New York, NY 10185: Catalog $1 ❖ Precious and semi-precious gemstones, cabochons, carvings, and beads. 718-454-2954.

B. Rush Apple Company, 3855 W. Kennedy Blvd., Tampa, FL 33609: Free price list ❖ Jeweler's tools and supplies, casting equipment, and findings. 813-870-3180.

Arizona Gems & Minerals Inc., 22025 N. Black Canyon Hwy., Phoenix, AZ 85027: Catalog $4 ❖ Chip beads, other beads and findings, silversmithing and lapidary tools, jewelry-making supplies, and mineral specimens. 602-772-6443.

Arrow Gems & Minerals Inc., P.O. Box 9068, Phoenix, AZ 85068: Free catalog ❖ Unusual beads, findings, arrowheads, embedded scorpions, minerals, and faceted gemstones. 602-997-6373.

Art to Wear, 5 Crescent Pl., St. Petersburg, FL 33711: Catalog $1 ❖ Bead-stringing supplies, tools, and jewelry-making kits. 813-867-3711.

B & J Rock Shop, 14744 Manchester Rd., Ballwin, MO 63011: Catalog $3 ❖ Jewelry-making supplies, beads and bead-stringing supplies, quartz clock movements, clock-building kits, and quartz crystals, amethyst crystal clusters, Brazilian agate nodules, geodes, and imported and domestic gemstones. 314-394-4567.

Baubanbea Enterprises, P.O. Box 1205, Smithtown, NY 11787: Catalog $1 ❖ Rhinestones, sequins, beads, and gemstones. 516-724-4661.

Bead Bazaar, 1001 Harris Ave., Bellingham, WA 98225: Catalog $2.50 ❖ Jewelry-making supplies. 800-671-5655.

Bead Boppers, 11224 Meridian, East Puyallup, WA 98373: Catalog $2.50 (refundable) ❖ Beads and findings, tools, charms, seed beads, leather, supplies, and books. 206-848-3880.

Beada Beada, 4262 N. Woodward Ave., Royal Oak, MI 48073: Free catalog ❖ Semi-precious beads, cabochons, cultured and freshwater pearls, and 14K gold, gold-filled, and sterling findings. 810-549-1005.

Beadbox Inc., 10135 E. Via Linda, Scottsdale, AZ 85258: Catalog $5 ❖ Ready-to-assemble jewelry kits and beads from worldwide sources. 800-232-3269.

Beadworks, 149 Water St., Norwalk, CT 06854: Catalog $7.95 ❖ Thousands of beads. 800-232-3761.

Big Stone Beads & Findings Inc., 6200 Savoy, Ste. 308, Houston, TX 77036: Free information ❖ Beads, cabochons, and findings. 800-733-1313; 713-783-1855 (in TX).

Bourget Bros., 1636 11th St., Santa Monica, CA 90404: Catalog $5 ❖ Jewelry-making and lapidary tools, gemstones, cabochons, wax patterns, beads, bead-stringing supplies, and sterling silver and gold-filled chains. 310-450-6556.

Libby Brink, RR 1, Box 165B, Hunlock Creek, PA 18621: Catalog $3 ❖ Beaded jewelry-making kits.

Brown Brothers Lapidary, 2248 S. 1st Ave., Safford, AZ 85546: Catalog $1 (refundable) ❖ Gemstones. 602-428-6433.

Bucks County Classic, 73 Coventry Lane, Langhorne, PA 19047: Catalog $2 ❖ Fresh water pearls, Chinese cloisonne, cabochons, findings, and gemstone, handmade, metal, Austrian crystal, and stone accent beads. 800-942-4367.

C & R Enterprises Inc., 4833 East Park, Springfield, MO 65809: Free catalog ❖ Sterling silver and 14K gold mountings, lapidary supplies, mineral specimens, belt buckles, beads and beading supplies, and cut stones. 417-866-4843.

California Bolas, 3055 Palm St., San Diego, CA 92104: Free information ❖ Findings. 619-282-8701.

Carat Patch, College Station, TX 77841: Free price list ❖ Faceted semi-precious and rare gems. 800-881-0048.

CGM Inc., 19562 Ventura Blvd., Tarzana, CA 91356: Free catalog ❖ Precious and semi-precious gemstones and 14K gold, gold-filled, and sterling silver findings. 818-609-7088.

Charlie's Rock Shop, P.O. Box 399, Penrose, CO 81240: Free catalog ❖ Clocks, clock movements and parts, beads, jewelry-making supplies, and faceted gemstones. 719-372-0117.

Comstock Creations, P.O. Box 2715, Durango, CO 81302: Free information ❖ Cut and polished Brazilian agate and geodes. 800-844-9000; 303-247-3836 (in CO).

Constantine Gem World, 1270 E. Garvey Ave. North, Ste. 130, Covina, CA 91724: Free information ❖ Imported gemstones and custom jewelry.

Contempo Lapidary, 12257 Foothill Blvd., Sylmar, CA 91342: Catalog $3 ❖ Lapidary equipment and supplies. 818-899-1973.

Covington Engineering Corporation, P.O. Box 35, Redlands, CA 92373: Free catalog ❖ Lapidary equipment. 909-793-6636.

Craft Harbor, 2128 Main St., Dunedin, FL 34698: Free catalog ❖ Jewelry-making supplies. 813-736-6187.

Creative Beginnings, 475 Morro Bay Blvd., Morro Bay, CA 93442: Free brochure ❖ Kits, findings, books, and brass-plated and silver charms and ornaments for jewelry-making. 800-367-1739.

Creative Castle, 2321 Michael Dr., Newbury Park, CA 91320: Free catalog ❖ Bead-making jewelry kits. 805-499-1377.

Cridge Inc., Box 210, Morrisville, PA 19067: Catalog $2 ❖ Jewelry findings and supplies. 215-295-3667.

Cupboard Distributing, P.O. Box 148, Urbana, OH 43078: Catalog $2 ❖ Unfinished wooden parts for jewelry-making, miniatures, toys, tole and decorative painting, and woodworking crafts. 513-652-3338.

Diamond Pacific Tool Corporation, 2620 W. Main St., Barstow, CA 92311: Free catalog ❖ Lapidary, rockhounding, and jewelry-making supplies. 800-253-2954.

Dikra Gem Inc., 56 W. 45th St., Ste. 1005, New York, NY 10036: Free information ❖ Semi-precious gemstones. 800-873-4572.

JEWELRY MAKING

Discount Agate House, 3401 N. Dodge Blvd., Tucson, AZ 85716: Free information ❖ Rocks and minerals from around the world, lapidary equipment, sterling silver and metalsmithing supplies, and findings. 520-323-0781.

Discount Bead House, P.O. Box 186, The Plains, OH 45780: Catalog $5 ❖ Seed beads, findings, and tools. 800-793-7592.

Dremel Moto-Tool, P.O. Box 468, Racine, WI 53406: Free information ❖ Tools for grinding, sawing, drilling, carving, shaping, and polishing gemstones. 414-554-1390.

Dyer's Jewelers' Tools & Supplies, 4525 Guadelupe St., Austin, TX 78751: Tool catalog $4; findings catalog $3; wax pattern catalog $4 ❖ Tools, findings, wax and wax patterns, gemstones and rocks, rubber molds, and other supplies. 800-683-1631.

E & W Imports Inc., P.O. Box 15703, Tampa, FL 33684: Price list $1 ❖ Gemstone, cloisonne, and Austrian crystal beads and 14K findings. 813-885-1138.

Eastern Findings Corporation, 19 W. 34th St., New York, NY 10001: Free information ❖ Findings. 800-EFC-6640; 212-695-6640 (in NY).

Ebersole Lapidary Supply Inc., 11417 West Hwy. 54, Wichita, KS 67209: Catalog $2 ❖ Tools, findings, mountings, cabochons and rocks, jewelry-making kits, petrified wood, clocks and clock-making parts, beads, and bead-stringing supplies. 316-722-4771.

Ed's House of Gems, 7712 NE Sandy Blvd., Portland, OR 97213: Free information with long SASE ❖ Clocks, clock-making parts, minerals, gemstones, lapidary equipment, mountings, shells, jewelry, and Native American relics. 503-284-8990.

Eloxite Corporation, Dept. 51, P.O. Box 729, Wheatland, WY 82201: Catalog $1 ❖ Clock-making supplies, tools, gemstones, belt buckles, jewelry mountings, and rockhounding and jewelry do-it-yourself equipment. 307-322-3050.

Embellishments for Designing People, 4793 Telegraph Ave., Oakland, CA 94609: Catalog $2 ❖ Charms, stampings, books, tools, and findings. 510-436-6415.

Enterprise Art, P.O. Box 2918, Largo, FL 33771: Free catalog ❖ Beads from around the world, bead and jewelry-making kits, and supplies. 800-366-2218.

Evening Star Designs, 69 Coolidge Ave., Haverhill, MA 01832: Catalog $3 ❖ Craft and jewelry-making supplies. 800-666-3562.

David H. Fell & Company Inc., 6009 Bandini Blvd., City of Commerce, CA 90040: Free information ❖ Precious metals for crafting and brushes, buffers, rouges, findings, waxes, frames, and burs. 800-822-1996; 213-722-9992 (in CA).

Fire Mountain Gems, 28195 Redwood Hwy., Cave Junction, OR 97523: Catalog $3 ❖ Beads, gems, jewelry-making supplies, Japanese seed beads. 800-423-2319.

Foredom Electric Company, 16 Stony Hill Rd., Bethel, CT 06801: Free information ❖ Tools for grinding, sawing, drilling, carving, shaping, and polishing gemstones. 203-792-8622.

Gem Center U.S.A. Inc., 4100 Alameda Ave., El Paso, TX 79905: Free price list ❖ Geodes and nodules. 915-533-7153.

Gem-Fare, P.O. Box 213, Pittstown, NJ 08867: Price list 50¢ ❖ Rare and unusual gemstones and crystals. 908-806-3339.

Gem-O-Rama Inc., 150 Recreation Park Dr., Hingham, MA 02043: Free catalog ❖ Gemstones, beading supplies, and 14K gold, gold-filled, and sterling silver beads. 617-749-8250.

Gemstone Equipment Manufacturing Company, 750 Easy St., Simi Valley, CA 93065: Free information ❖ Vibratory tumblers and lapidary equipment. 800-235-3375; 805-527-6990 In CA).

Gilman's Lapidary Supply, Durham St., P.O. Box M, Hellertown, PA 18055: Free information ❖ Lapidary equipment, findings and mountings, silver and gold metal crafting supplies, and genuine and synthetic gemstones. 215-838-8767.

Kenneth Glasser, P.O. Box 441, Monsey, NY 10952: Catalog $10 ❖ All types, sizes, and qualities of diamonds. 914-426-1241.

Goodnow's, 3415 S. Hayden St., Amarillo, TX 79109: Free list with long SASE ❖ Gem roughs for faceting, cabbing, and tumbling. 806-352-0725.

Graves Company, 1800 Andrew Ave., Pompano Beach, FL 33069: Free catalog ❖ Lapidary equipment. 800-327-9103.

Grieger's, P.O. Box 93070, Pasadena, CA 91109: Free catalog ❖ Gemstones, lapidary equipment, jewelry-making supplies, mountings, and findings. 800-423-4181.

Griffith Distributors, Box 662, Louisville, CO 80027: Free information ❖ Jewelry-making chemicals. 303-442-8284.

T.B. Hagstoz & Son Inc., 709 Sansom St., Philadelphia, PA 19106: Catalog $5 (refundable with $25 order) ❖ Metal findings, jeweler's tools, casting equipment, gold and silver solders, and gold, silver, gold-filled, copper, bronze, brass-nickel, silver, and pewter metals. 800-922-1006; 215-922-1627 (in PA).

Hanneman Gemological Instruments, P.O. Box 942, Poulsbo, WA 98370: Catalog $2 (refundable) ❖ Gemological instruments and tools.

Hardies, P.O. Box 1920, Quartzsite, AZ 85346: Free catalog ❖ Beads, findings, buckles, bolas, Native American jewelry, gems, rocks, and books. 800-962-2775; 602-927-6381 (in AZ).

Harmon's Agate & Silver Shop, Box 94, Crane, MT 59217: Catalog $3 ❖ Montana moss agate, sapphires, and handmade silver and gold jewelry. 406-482-2534.

HHH Enterprises, P.O. Box 390, Abilene, TX 79604: Catalog $2 ❖ Jewelry components and make-your-own jewelry kits. 800-777-0218.

Hong Kong Lapidary Supplies, 2801 University Dr., Coral Springs, FL 33065: Catalog $3 ❖ Semi-precious gemstones and beads. 305-755-8777.

House of India, World Trade Center, P.O. Box 58316, Dallas, TX 75258: Free information ❖ Accessories and supplies for making designer watches. 800-527-7139; 214-741-6133 (in TX).

House of Onyx, The AARON Building, Greenville, KY 42345: Free catalog ❖ Jewelry, gemstones, and jewelry-making supplies. 800-844-3100.

Indian Jewelers Supply Company, 601 E. Coal Ave., Gallup, NM 87301: Catalog $6 ❖ Precious and base metals, findings, metalsmithing and lapidary equipment, semi-precious gemstones, shells, and coral. 505-722-4451.

International Gem Merchants Inc., 4168 Oxford Ave., Jacksonville, FL 32210: Free information ❖ Gemstones, pearls, and synthetic gemstones. 800-633-3653; 904-388-5130 (in FL).

Jarvi Tool Company, 780 E. Debra Ln., Anaheim, CA 92805: Free information ❖ Lapidary equipment, faceting machines, and tools. 714-774-9104.

Kikico Beads, P.O. Box 8353, Scottsdale, AZ 85252: Catalog $2 ❖ Beads for jewelry designing. 800-484-9565.

Kingsley North Inc., 910 Brown St., Norway, MI 49870: Free catalog ❖ Jewelry-making tools and supplies, metal casting and lapidary equipment, and rough, cut, and calibrated opals. 800-338-9280.

❖ JEWELRY MAKING ❖

Krona Gem Merchants, Box 9968, Colorado Springs, CO 80932: Free price list ❖ Faceted and rare gemstones. 719-597-8779.

L.R.S. Enameling, 1277 Pearl Wood Rd., Albany, OH 45710: Catalog $3 ❖ Handcrafted enamel earrings, pendants, and pins for use in beading and jewelry-making.

Lapcraft Company Inc., 195 W. Olentangy St., P.O. Box 389, Powell, OH 43065: Free information ❖ Lapidary equipment. 614-764-8993.

Lee Lapidaries Inc., 3425 W. 117th St., Cleveland, OH 44111: Free information ❖ Faceting equipment. 216-941-7458.

K.H. Lee Tool Supply, 9078 Artesia Blvd., Bellflower, CA 90706: Catalog $3 ❖ Tools for jewelers, crafters, and hobbyists. 310-920-3834.

Lentz Lapidary Inc., 11760 S. Oliver, Rt. 2, Box 134, Mulvane, KS 67110: Catalog $2 ❖ Jewelry, mountings, clocks and parts, rough rock specimens and cabochons, and rockhounding and lapidary equipment. 316-777-1372.

Victor H. Levy Inc., 1355 S. Flower St., Los Angeles, CA 90015: Catalog $5 ❖ Findings, rhinestones, gemstones, braids, and jewelry-making supplies. 800-421-8021; 213-749-8247 (in CA).

Lochs, P.O. Box 58, Emmaus, PA 18049: Catalog $3 ❖ Faceted and polished gemstones, 14K gold findings, and biron-created emeralds. 215-965-7833.

Lonnie's Inc., 7155 E. Main St., Mesa, AZ 85207: Free findings catalog; tool catalog $5; jewelry catalog $5 ❖ Supplies for jewelers, casters, silversmiths, and lapidarists. Also silver jewelry. 602-832-2641.

Lortone Inc., 2856 NW Market St., Seattle, WA 98107: Free catalog with long SASE ❖ Lapidary equipment. 206-789-3100.

Maxant Industries Inc., P.O. Box 454, Ayer, MA 01432: Catalog $1 ❖ Lapidary equipment. 508-772-0576.

MDR Manufacturing Inc., P.O. Box 6951, Kingwood, TX 77325: Free price list ❖ Faceting equipment. 713-358-3027.

Melanie Collection, 12105 Bermuda NE, Albuquerque, NM 87111: Charm catalog $6; button catalog $2 ❖ Silver and bronze replicas of old, new, ancient, and ethnic artifacts. 505-298-7036.

Meloon Enterprises Inc., 419 Commerce Ln., Berlin, NJ 08009: Free brochure ❖ Sterling silver for jewelry-making. 800-969-3331; 609-768-5707 (in NJ).

Metalliferous, 34 W. 46th St., New York, NY 10036: Catalog $5 ❖ Metals, tools, and supplies for jewelry-making and metal crafting. 212-944-0909.

Minnesota Lapidary Supply Corporation, 2825 Dupont Ave. South, Minneapolis, MN 55408: Free catalog ❖ Lapidary equipment. 612-872-7211.

✓ **Nasco,** 901 Janesville Ave., Fort Atkinson, WI 53538: Free catalog ❖ Jewelry-making supplies and tools. 800-558-9595.

New England International Gems Inc., 188 Pollard St., Billerica, MA 01862: Free catalog ❖ Brazilian quartz, rocks from India, beads, jewelry-making supplies, tools, and findings. 617-863-8331.

Neycraft, Division of Ney, Ney Industrial Park, Bloomfield, CT 06002: Free information ❖ Benchtop furnaces, ultrasonic cleaners, centrifugal casting machine, and air-driven and electric tools for jewelry-making. 800-538-4593.

The NgraveR Company, 67 Wawecus Hill Rd., Bozrah, CT 06334: Catalog $1 (refundable) ❖ Easy-to-use engraving tools and jewelry-making equipment. 203-823-1533.

Nonferrous Metals, P.O. Box 2595, Waterbury, CT 06723: Catalog $3 (refundable) ❖ Plain and ornamental brass, copper, bronze, and nickel-silver wire. 203-274-7255.

M. Nowotny & Company, 8823 Callahan Rd., San Antonio, TX 78230: Free information ❖ Gemstones and fossils from worldwide sources, jewelry, pewter figurines, key chains, scarabs, obsidian eggs, and peacock feathers. 800-950-8276; 210-342-2512 (in TX).

H. Obodda Mineral Specimens, P.O. Box 51, Short Hills, NJ 07078: Free list ❖ Rare and semi-precious gemstones. 201-467-0212.

Optional Extras, P.O. Box 8550, Burlington, VT 05402: Catalog $2 ❖ Jewelry findings and beads from worldwide sources. 800-736-0781.

Oriental Crest Inc., 6161 Savoy Dr., Houston, TX 77036: Free information ❖ Semi-precious gemstone jewelry, gemstones and findings, bead-stringing supplies, pendant carvings, and earring jackets. 800-367-3954; 713-780-2425 (in TX).

Ornamental Resources Inc., P.O. Box 3010, Idaho Springs, CO 80452: Catalog $15 ❖ Beads, pendants, charms, brass stampings, feathers, chains, rhinestones, antique tassels and trims, and findings. 800-876-6762.

Out On A Whim, 121 E. Cotan Ave., Cotati, CA 94931: Free information ❖ Glass beads, semi-precious stones, jewelry findings and supplies, and beading accessories. 707-664-8343.

✓ **Pikes Peak Rock Shop,** 451 Forest Edge Rd., Woodland Park, CO 80863: Free catalog ❖ Fossils, crystals, tumbled stones, beads, and strands. 800-347-6257.

Pioneer Gem Corporation, P.O. Box 1513, Auburn, WA 98071: Catalog $5 ❖ Cut and polished gemstones. 206-833-2760.

Poly-Metric, Spokane St., Box 400, Clayton, WA 99110: Free information ❖ Faceting instruments. 509-276-5565.

Prospectors Pouch Inc., P.O. Box 112, Kennesaw, GA 30144: Free information ❖ Rocks, gemstones, and jewelry making supplies. 404-427-6481.

Q-C Turquoise, 3340 E. Washington, Phoenix, AZ 85034: Free information ❖ Turquoise nugget jewelry, nuggets by the strand or pound, and cutting material or blocks. 602-267-1164.

Raytech, 147 West St., P.O. Box 449, Middlefield, CT 06455: Free information ❖ Lapidary and ultraviolet lighting equipment. 203-349-3421.

Richardson's Recreational Ranch Ltd., Gateway Route Box 440, Madras, OR 97741: Free information ❖ Rocks and gemstones from worldwide locations, lapidary equipment, and clocks, clock movements, and parts. 503-475-2680.

Rio Grande, 6901 Washington NE, Albuquerque, NM 87109: Free information ❖ Jewelry findings. 800-545-6566.

The Rock Barrell, 13650 Floyd Rd., Ste. 209, Dallas, TX 75243: Free catalog ❖ Findings and settings for jewelry design. 214-231-4809.

The Rock Peddler, 58 Wedgewood Rd., Franklin, NC 28734: Catalog $2 (refundable) ❖ Lapidary equipment. 704-524-6042.

Elvee Rosenberg, 21 W. 38th St., New York, NY 10018: Free catalog ❖ Beads, acrylic gemstones, pearls, and high-fashion jewelry. 212-575-0767.

Ross Metals, 54 W. 47th St., New York, NY 10036: Free information ❖ Findings, gold and silver wire, and spooled chains. 800-654-ROSS; 212-869-1407 (in NY).

Roussels, P.O. Box 476, Arlington, MA 02174: Catalog $1 ❖ Jewelry-making supplies and ready-to-wear jewelry. 508-443-8888.

Running T Trading Company, 1201 Iron Springs Rd., Ste. 11, Prescott, AZ 86301: Catalog $3 (refundable) ❖ Pre-notched mounts, beads, diamonds, gemstones, chains, safety clasps, and jewelry-making supplies. 602-778-2739.

Russell's Rock Shop, 27911 North St., North Liberty, IN 46554: Free information ❖ Gem trees and supplies, bookends, agate slabs, amethyst, cabs, findings, and lucite stands. 219-289-7446.

Marvin Schwab, 2740 Garfield Ave., Silver Spring, MD 20910: Catalog $3.50 (refundable) ❖ Beads and gems, jewelry findings, and supplies. 301-565-0487.

❖ JOKES & NOVELTIES ❖   301

Simara's Bead World, 215 1st St., Liverpool, NY 13088: Catalog $3.95 (refundable) ❖ Beads from worldwide sources, beaded jewelry kits, beading supplies, and books. 315-451-3784.

South Pacific Wholesale Company, Rt. 2, P.O. Box 249, East Montpelier, VT 05651: Free price list ❖ Beads, findings, semi-precious gemstone settings, gold and silver bracelets, necklaces, and earrings. 800-338-2162.

Southwest Rock & Gem Company, Rt. 3, Box 10, Hico, TX 76457: Free price list with long SASE ❖ Lapidary supplies. 817-796-4907.

Stardust Gallery, 2501 Jericho Tnpk., Centereach, NY 11720: Catalog $1 ❖ Pearls, Austrian crystals, sequins, findings, appliques, buttons, rhinestones, studs, and other supplies. 718-416-2702.

Stone Age Industries Inc., P.O. Box 383, Powell, WY 82435: Catalog $1.50 ❖ Rough gemstones, slabs, cutting and polishing equipment, and lapidary supplies. 307-754-4681.

Swest Inc., Catalog Dept., 11090 N. Stemmons Freeway, Dallas, TX 75229: Free information ❖ Jeweler's tools, wax patterns, findings, gemstones, and supplies. 800-527-5057.

Tagit, P.O. Box 1534, San Juan Capistrano, CA 92675: Free list of retail sources ❖ Jewelry finishing and lapidary equipment and supplies. 310-949-8380.

TECHNIQdesign, 1132 Meridian Circle, Santa Rosa, CA 95401: Catalog $2 ❖ Hang tags, labels and accessories, and jewelry cards.

Tierracast, 3177 Guerneville Rd., Santa Rosa, CA 95401: Free catalog ❖ Jewelry-making findings. 800-222-9939; 707-545-5787 (in CA).

Myron Toback Inc., 25 W. 47th St., New York, NY 10036: Free information ❖ Tools for jewelry-making and silver smithing. 800-223-7550; 212-398-8300 (in NY).

Tripp's Manufacturing, P.O. Box 1369, Socorro, NM 87801: Free catalog ❖ Pre-notched mounts. 800-545-7962; 505-835-2461 (in NM).

Tru-Square Metal Products, P.O. Box 585, Auburn, WA 98071: Free brochure ❖ Tumblers and other rock polishing equipment. 800-225-1017.

TSI Jewelry Supply, 101 Nickerson St., Seattle, WA 98109: Free catalog ❖ Jewelry-making tools and supplies, beads, findings, and gemstones. 800-426-9984.

Tumblecraft, 5401 James Ave., Minneapolis, MN 55430: Free catalog ❖ Cabochons, findings, opals, and supplies. 612-560-0736.

Ultra Tec, 1025 E. Chestnut, Santa Ana, CA 92701: Free brochure ❖ Lapidary equipment. 714-542-0608.

Veon Creations, 3565 State Rd. V, DeSoto, MO 63020: Catalog $4 ❖ Beads, gemstones, pearls, findings, and jewelry-making supplies. 314-586-5377.

Vibra-Tek Company, 1844 Arroya Rd., Colorado Springs, CO 80906: Free information ❖ Rock polishers. 800-634-8611.

Westbrook Bead Company, 16641 Spring Gulch Dr., Anderson, CA 96007: Catalog $2 ❖ Gemstone, faceted glass, cobalt blue, old trade, and other beads. Also bead-stringing supplies and jewelry components. 916-357-3143.

JOKES & NOVELTIES

Best Magic Gags & Costumes, 625 S. Magnolia Ave., Anaheim, CA 92804: Free information ❖ Magic, juggling equipment, costumes, gags, gifts, dancewear, and clown items. 714-827-MGIC.

Chazpro Magic Company, 603 E. 13th, Eugene, OR 97401: Catalog $3 ❖ Clown props, books, juggling equipment, jokes, and novelties. 503-345-0032.

Global Shakeup Snowdomes, 2265 Westwood Blvd., Ste. 618, Los Angeles, CA 90064: Catalog $2 (refundable) ❖ Unusual and hard-to-find plastic and glass snowdomes, snowdome books, and more. 213-259-8988.

Klutz Press, 2121 Staunton Ct., Palo Alto, CA 94306: Free information ❖ Novelty and fun merchandise, juggling equipment, and books. 415-424-0739.

Lighter Side Company, 4514 19th St. Court East, P.O. Box 25600, Bradenton, FL 34206: Free catalog ❖ Jokes and novelties, tricks, science and sports equipment, and hobby supplies. 813-747-2356.

Archie McPhee & Company, Box 30852, Seattle, WA 98103: Free catalog ❖ Voodoo dolls to fashion items, party supplies to flamingos, science things, footwear, T-shirts, outdoor lawn art, exotica, clocks, and exclusive gifts. 206-745-0711.

Things You Never Knew Existed, c/o Johnson Smith Company, 4514 19th St. Court East, Bradenton, FL 34203: Free catalog ❖ Novelties, tricks, hobby supplies, and other unusual things. 813-747-2356.

JUGGLING

Abracadabra Magic Shop, 125 Lincoln Blvd., Middlesex, NJ 08846: Catalog $5 ❖ Close-up and stage magic, clown props, juggling equipment, balloons, costumes, and theatrical make-up. 908-805-0200.

Aunt Clowney's Warehouse, P.O. Box 1444, Corona, CA 91718: Free catalog ❖ Books on juggling and clowning.

Best Magic Gags & Costumes, 625 S. Magnolia Ave., Anaheim, CA 92804: Free information ❖ Magic, juggling equipment, costumes, gags, gifts, dancewear, and clown items. 714-827-MGIC.

Chazpro Magic Company, 603 E. 13th, Eugene, OR 97401: Catalog $3 ❖ Juggling and clown supplies, books, jokes, and novelties. 503-345-0032.

Steve Dawson's Magic Touch Catalog, 144 N. Milpitas Blvd., Milpitas, CA 95035: Catalog $3 ❖ Magic effects, books, videos, accessories, clown and juggling supplies, and make-up. 408-263-9404.

Brian Dube Inc., 520 Broadway, 3rd Floor, New York, NY 10012: Free catalog ❖ Juggling equipment and books. 212-941-0060.

Juggling Arts, 5535 N. 11th St., Phoenix, AZ 85014: Catalog $1 ❖ Juggling props. 602-266-4391.

Klutz Press, 2121 Staunton Ct., Palo Alto, CA 94306: Free information ❖ Novelty and fun merchandise, juggling equipment, and books. 415-424-0739.

La Rock's Fun & Magic Outlet, 3847 Rosehaven Dr., Charlotte, NC 28205: Catalog $3 ❖ Clown and balloon how-to books, balloons, balloon sculpture kits, juggling supplies, and magic equipment. 704-563-9300.

Mecca Magic Inc., 49 Dodd St., Bloomfield, NJ 07003: Catalog $10 ❖ Juggling equipment, theatrical make-up, clown props, balloons, magic, costumes and wigs, puppets, and ventriloquism equipment. 201-429-7597.

Sparkle's Entertainment Express, Jan Lovell, 152 N. Water St., Gallatin, TN 37066: Product list $1 ❖ Make-up, costumes and clown shoes, balloons, juggling and magic equipment, puppets, books, and supplies. 615-452-9755.

Under the Big Top, P.O. Box 807, Placentia, CA 92670: Catalog $4 ❖ Juggling equipment, clown props, costumes, make-up, balloons, and party supplies. 800-995-7727.

JUKEBOXES

Antique Slot Machine Part Company, 140 N. Western Ave., Carpentersville, IL 60110: Free catalog ❖ Books and manuals, slot stands and pads, and parts for slot machines, jukeboxes, and pinballs. 847-428-8476.

Ken Arnold, 640 Devonshire Blvd., Longwood, FL 32750: Free information ❖ Jukeboxes and coin-operated machines. 407-332-6133.

Back Pages Antiques, 125 Greene St., New York, NY 10012: Free information ❖ Collector jukeboxes. 212-460-5998.

Coin Machine Trader, P.O. Box 602, Huron, SD 57350: Information $4 ❖ Manuals for most jukeboxes and slot machines. 605-352-7590.

Durfee Coin Op, 57 S. Main St., Orange, MA 01364: Free information with long SASE (specify items wanted) ❖ Original and used jukebox parts. 508-544-3800.

Home Arcade Corporation, 1108 Front St., Kisle, IL 60532: Catalog $3 ❖ Jukeboxes, coin-operated machines, and parts. 708-964-2555.

Illinois Antique Slot Machine Company, P.O. Box 542, Westmont, IL 60559: Free information ❖ Antique Wurlitzer jukeboxes, nickelodeons, music boxes, slot and other coin-operated machines. 708-985-2742.

Jukebox City, 1950 1st Ave. South, Seattle, WA 98134: Free photos with long SASE ❖ Jukeboxes and coin-operated machines. 206-625-1950.

Jukebox Classics & Vintage Slot Machines Inc., 6742 5th Ave., Brooklyn, NY 11220: Free information ❖ Antique jukeboxes and coin-operated machines. 718-833-8455.

Jukebox Junction, P.O. Box 1081, Des Moines, IA 50311: Catalog $2.50 ❖ Antique jukeboxes. 515-981-4019.

National Jukebox Exchange, 121 Lakeside Dr., Mayfield, NY 12117: Free catalog ❖ Antique jukeboxes, slot and other arcade machines, and parts. 888-321-PAPA.

New England Jukebox, 77 Tolland Tnpk., Manchester, CT 06040: Free list with long SASE and two 1st class stamps ❖ Jukeboxes and accessories. 203-646-7278.

Nostalgic Music Company, 58 Union Ave., New Providence, NJ 07974: Free information ❖ Restored jukeboxes, from the 1940s and 1950s. 908-464-5538.

Remember When Collectibles Inc., 6570 Memorial Dr., Stone Mountain, GA 30083: Free brochure ❖ Vintage Coca-Cola machines and jukeboxes. 404-879-7878.

Row/AMI Jukeboxes, 75 Troy Hills Rd., Whippany, NJ 07981: Free list of retail sources ❖ Jukeboxes. 201-887-0400.

Zygmunt & Associates, P.O. Box 542, Westmont, IL 60559: Free brochure ❖ Jukeboxes and slot machines. 708-985-2742.

KALEIDOSCOPES

Atlas Art & Stained Glass, P.O. Box 76084, Oklahoma City, OK 73147: Catalog $3 ❖ Kaleidoscopes, frames, lamp bases, and art and craft, stained glass, jewelry-making, and foil-crafting supplies. 405-946-1230.

Gemini Kaleidoscopes, 128 McCarrell Ln., Zelienople, PA 16063: Free information ❖ Handcrafted kaleidoscopes. 412-452-8700.

Kaleidoscopes by Laughing Coyote, Claudia & Ron Lee, 25 Upper Butcher Rd., Ellington, CT 06029: Free brochure ❖ Kaleidoscopes for one and two persons. 203-875-5098.

Karadimos Kaleidoscopes, 27325 Ridge Rd., Damascus, MD 20872: Free brochure ❖ Fused and slumped glass kaleidoscopes. 301-253-5789.

Van Cort Instruments Inc., 29 Industrial Dr., Northampton, MA 01060: Free list of retail sources ❖ Kaleidoscopes and optical equipment. 413-586-9800.

Whippoorwill Crafts, North Market Building, 6 Fanueil Hall Marketplace, Boston, MA 02109: Free information ❖ Kaleidoscopes, wooden boxes and chests, instrumentalist chimes, toys and games, clocks, and other crafts. 800-487-5937; 617-248-0671 (in MA).

KITCHEN UTENSILS & COOKWARE

Alsto Company, P.O. Box 1267, Galesburg, IL 61401: Catalog $1 ❖ Tools, pet products, and kitchen aids. 800-447-0048.

American Harvest, 4064 Peavey Rd., Chaska, MN 55318: Free information ❖ Food dehydrator and bread machine. 800-288-4545.

B-WEST Outdoor Specialties, 2425 N. Huachuca, Tucson, AZ 85745: Free information ❖ Outdoor cookware. 800-293-7855; 520-628-1990 (in AZ).

The Baker's Catalogue, P.O. Box 876, Norwich, VT 05055: Free catalog ❖ Baking equipment and recipe ingredients. 800-827-6836.

Bourgeat Cookware, Au Service De La Grande Cuisine, 20 Fernwood Rd., Boston, MA 02132: Catalog $1 ❖ Copper, aluminum, and stainless-steel kitchen accessories. 617-469-0189.

Bridge Kitchenware Corporation, 214 E. 52nd St., New York, NY 10022: Catalog $3 ❖ Imported cooking utensils. 212-838-6746.

Brookstone Company, Order Processing Center, 1655 Bassford Dr., Mexico, MO 65265: Free catalog ❖ Professional restaurant equipment for home chefs. 800-926-7000.

Chef's Catalog, 3215 Commercial Ave., Northbrook, IL 60062: Free catalog ❖ Calphalon cookware, Cuisinart accessories, Henckels cutlery, and professional restaurant equipment for the home chef. 800-338-3232.

Chef Revival, 12 Dyatt Pl., Hackensack, NJ 07601: Free information ❖ Professional clothing and equipment for chefs. 800-352-2433.

Colonial Garden Kitchens, Hanover Direct Pennsylvania Inc., Hanover, PA 17333-0001: Free catalog ❖ Cookware and accessories. 717-633-3333.

Commercial Aluminum Cookware Company, P.O. Box 583, Toledo, OH 43697: Free information ❖ Calphalon cookware.

A Cook's Wares, 211 37th St., Beaver's Falls, PA 15010: Catalog $2 ❖ Cookware, cutlery, bakeware, French copper pans, and food processors. 412-846-9490.

Country Manor, Mail Order Department, Rt. 211, P.O. Box 520, Sperryville, VA 22740: Catalog $3 ❖ Kitchen utensils, rugs, carpets, and decorative accessories. 800-344-8354.

Crate & Barrel, P.O. Box 9059, Wheeling, IL 60090: Free catalog ❖ Gourmet cooking equipment and appliances. 800-323-5461.

CUTCO/VECTOR, P.O. Box 1230, Olean, NY 14760: Catalog $1 ❖ Cutlery, knives, and kitchen accessories. 800-828-0448.

Dansk, 108 Corporate Park Dr., White Plains, NY 10604: Free list of retail sources ❖ Dinnerware, stemware, flatware, kitchenware, and serving pieces. 800-293-2675; 914-697-6400 (in NY).

EdgeCraft Corporation, 825 Southwood Rd., Avondale, PA 19311: Free list of retail sources ❖ Professional style food slicer for the home. 800-342-3255.

Enclume Design Products Inc., P.O. Box 700, Port Hadlock, WA 98339: Free list of retail sources ❖ Cookware racks and accessories. 206-385-6100.

The Faith Mountain Company, P.O. Box 199, Sperryville, VA 22740: Free catalog ❖ Kitchen utensils, country-style gifts, folk art reproductions, toys and dolls, handmade Appalachian baskets, and Christmas decorations. 800-822-7238.

Food Service Inc., Watson Division, 3712 Hagger Way, Dallas, TX 75209: Free catalog ❖ Professional quality appliances, cookware, bakeware, cutlery, and kitchen accessories. 800-229-2090.

Gatherings, Kaiser Crow, Inc., 3545 South Platte River Dr., Englewood, CO 80110: Free catalog ❖ Accessories for entertaining and gracious living. 800-469-2769.

Good Catalog Company, 5456 SE International Way, Portland, OR 97222: Free catalog ❖ Kitchen gadgets, and dining, gardening, and decorative accessories. 800-225-3870.

Iron Craft, Old Rt. 28, P.O. Box 351, Ossipee, NH 03864: Catalog $2 ❖ Kettles and grates, enameled cookware, butcher aprons, bellows, heating systems for fireplaces, weather vanes, signs, gifts, and cast-iron items. 603-539-2807.

King Arthur Flour Baker's Catalog, P.O. Box 876, Norwich, VT 05055: Free catalog ❖ Baking, bread-making, and pasta equipment. 800-827-6836.

Kitchen & Home, P.O. Box 72, Hanover, PA 17333: Free catalog ❖ Culinary tools, appliances, and gadgets. 717-646-5522.

Kitchen Etc., 32 Industrial Dr., Exeter, NH 03833: Catalog $2 ❖ Cookware, cutlery, flatware, crystal, and dinnerware. 800-232-4070.

Lamalle Kitchenware, 36 W. 25th St., New York, NY 10010: Free catalog ❖ Kitchenware and gadgets. 212-242-0750.

Lehman Hardware & Appliances Inc., P.O. Box 41, Kidron, OH 44636: Catalog $2 ❖ Kitchen accessories, housewares, stoves for heating and cooking, farming and homesteading items, non-electric appliances, woodworking and log-smithing tools, and other old-time general store items. 216-857-5757.

Nancy's Specialty Market, P.O. Box 530, Newmarket, NH 03857: Free catalog ❖ Wild mushroom caviar, exotic Mexican spices, pasta, extracts and flavorings, international specialties, books, and kitchen tools. 800-688-2433.

Pannikin Mail Order, 1205 J St., San Diego, CA 92101: Free brochure ❖ Gourmet spices, tea, hot chocolate, espresso machines, and coffee makers. 800-232-6482.

Pepperidge Farm, P.O. Box 917, Clinton, CT 06413: Free catalog ❖ Specialty and microwave cookware, tools, kitchen gadgets, glassware, silverware, cookbooks, and gourmet foods. 800-243-9314.

Product Innovations Inc., 277 Fairfield Rd., Ste. 337, Fairfield, NJ 07004: Free brochure ❖ Terra-cotta flower pots and saucers for baking and serving. 800-401-2529.

Professional Cutlery Direct, 170 Boston Post Rd., Ste. 135, Madison, CT 06443: Free catalog ❖ Easy-to-read cooking thermometers with an LCD display. Also professional cutlery and kitchen tools. 800-859-6994.

Sur La Table, Catalog Division, 410 Terry Ave. North, Seattle, WA 98109: Free information ❖ Hand-carved thistle-pattern wooden shortbread molds and cooking and baking equipment. 800-243-0852.

21st Century Quality Cookware, 20006 44th St., North Berghen, NJ 07047: Free catalog ❖ Imported cookware, cutlery, and kitchen accessories. 800-405-0334.

Vermont Country Store, Mail Order Office, P.O. Box 3000, Manchester Center, VT 05255: Free catalog ❖ Cookware and home accessories. 802-362-2400.

Lillian Vernon Kitchen, Virginia Beach, VA 23479: Free catalog ❖ Kitchen accessories, serving pieces, dinnerware, and outdoor cooking aids. 800-285-5555.

Williams-Sonoma, Mail Order Department, P.O. Box 7456, San Francisco, CA 94120: Free catalog ❖ Cookware for home chefs, serving pieces, household accessories, books, and gourmet foods. 800-541-1262.

Wilton Enterprise Inc., 2240 W. 75th St., Woodridge, IL 60517: Catalog $6 (refundable) ❖ Supplies for making cookies, cakes, and candy. 708-963-7100.

Winterthur Museum & Gardens, Catalog Division, 100 Enterprise Pl., Dover, DE 19901: Free catalog ❖ Cookware. 800-767-0500.

Wooden Spoon, P.O. Box 931, Clinton, CT 06413: Free catalog ❖ Cooking utensils, kitchen tools, and gifts. 800-431-2207.

Zabar's & Company, 2245 Broadway, New York, NY 10024: Free catalog ❖ Cookware, food processors, microwave ovens, kitchen tools, coffee makers, and gourmet foods. 212-787-2000.

KITES

Aerie Kiteworks, 200 Prairie St., Rockford, IL 61107: Free information ❖ Competition kites. 815-962-9680.

Aerodrome Sport Kites, 399 Church St., Wood River Junction, RI 02894: Free information ❖ Self-adjusting sail kites. 401-364-8989.

Banner Fabric, Kite Studio, 5555 Hamilton Blvd., Wescosville, PA 18106: Catalog $1 ❖ Fabrics, notions, and hardware for kites, flags, banners, and windsocks. 610-395-3560.

Caribbean Kite Company, 1099 NE 45th St., Fort Lauderdale, FL 33334: Free catalog ❖ Stunt, delta, sport, and quad kites. 954-776-5433.

Catch the Wind, 266 SE Hwy. 101, Lincoln City, OR 97367: Free information ❖ Kites. 800-227-7878.

Central Coast Creations, P.O. Box 3643, San Luis Obispo, CA 93403: Catalog $1 ❖ Patterns for banners and windsocks.

Chicago Kite Company, 6 S. Brockway, Palatine, IL 60067: Free information ❖ Sport and single-line kites and accessories. 708-359-2556.

Coast Kites Inc., 15953 Minnesota Ave., Paramount, CA 90723: Free information ❖ Kites. 310-634-3630.

Colores International Inc., 3860 148th Ave. NE, Redmond, WA 98052: Free information ❖ Custom windsocks and banners. 206-885-6323.

The Crystal Kite Company, 1320 Lakeview Dr., La Habra, CA 90631: Free information ❖ Competition stunt kites. 714-870-4546.

Delta Breeze Kites, 304 Marble Dr., Antioch, CA 94509: Free information ❖ Soft quad kite systems. 510-754-3091.

DJ Sport Kites, Dodd Gross, RD 2, Box 70, Windsor, PA 17366: Free catalog ❖ Stunt kites. 800-296-KITE.

Dyna-Kite Corporation, P.O. Box 24, Three Rivers, MA 01080: Free information ❖ Kites. 413-283-2555.

Eye's Up Kites, 3578 Birdland Ave., Akron, OH 44319: Catalog $1 ❖ Sport and single-line kites. 330-644-8200.

Force 10 Foils, 10920 N. Port Washington Rd., Mequon, WI 53092: Free list of retail sources ❖ Easy-to-fly foil kites. 414-241-8862.

Great Winds Kites, 402 Occidental Ave. South, Seattle, WA 98104: Free catalog ❖ Kites. 206-624-6886.

Grizzly Peak Kiteworks, 1305 Alvarado Rd., Berkeley, CA 94705: Free catalog ❖ Kites and kite-making materials. 510-644-2981.

Hang-Em High Fabrics, 1420 Yale Ave., Richmond, VA 23224: Free information ❖ Kite-making supplies. 804-233-6155.

Hearth Song, Mail Processing Center, 6519 N. Galena Rd., P.O. Box 1773, Peoria, IL 61656: Free catalog ❖ Kites, books, dollhouse miniatures, dolls, and art supplies. 800-325-2502.

Hyperkites, 720 Gateway Center Dr., San Diego, CA 92102: Free catalog ❖ High-performance kites. 619-262-4712.

Bob Ingraham Kites, 315 N. Bayard St., Silver City, NM 88061: Free information ❖ Easy-to-assemble and easy-to-fly delta kites. 505-538-9083.

International Connections, 835 Weldon Rd., Santa Barbara, CA 93109: Free information ❖ Kites, banners, and windsocks. 805-963-2964.

Into the Wind/Kites, 1408 Pearl St., Boulder, CO 80302: Free catalog ❖ Kites. 800-541-0314.

J.C. Kites, P.O. Box 245, Ingleside, IL 60041: Free catalog ❖ Stunt kites. 847-587-9918.

Kite Studio, 5555 Hamilton Blvd., Wescosville, PA 18106: Catalog $2 ❖ Kite-building supplies. 610-395-3560.

KiteCo, Division North Cloth/North Sails, 189 Pepe's Farm Rd., Milford, CT 06460: Free price list ❖ Ripstop fabric for kites and sails. 203-877-7638.

Kites & Fun Things, 1049 S. Main, Plymouth, MI 48170: Free information ❖ Kite-building supplies. 313-454-3760.

Klig's Kites, 811 Seaboard St., Myrtle Beach, SC 29577: Free catalog ❖ Stunt kites, single-line kites, windsocks, banners, and flags. 800-333-5944.

KNITTING

Krazy Kites, 8445 International Dr., Orlando, FL 32819: Free catalog ❖ Stunt and single-line kites, windsocks, and banners. 800-982-2635.

M.L.D. Associates, 1 Cedar Circle, Townsend, MA 01469: Free list of retail sources ❖ Nylon cordura kite bags. 508-597-6700.

MacKinaw Kite Company, 116 Washington St., Grand Haven, MI 49417: Free catalog ❖ Stunt kites. 800-622-4655.

NewTech Sports, 7208 McNeil Dr., Ste. 207, Austin, TX 78729: Free information ❖ Stunt and high-flying kites. 800-325-4768.

Ocean Kites, P.O. Box 1287, Long Beach, WA 98631: Free catalog ❖ Kites and accessories, windsocks, and flags. 360-642-2299.

Premier Kites Inc., 8673 Cherry Ln., Laurel, MD 20707: Free catalog ❖ Kites, windsocks, and air toys. 301-604-1881.

Revolution Enterprises, 6335 Nancy Ridge Dr., San Diego, CA 92121: Free information ❖ Easy-to-maneuver precision team-flying and ready-to-fly kites. 800-382-5132; 619-554-1106 (in CA).

Sky Burner, 47600 Hanford, Canton, MI 48187: Free information ❖ High-performance sport kites. 313-454-3760.

Sky Delight Kites, 503 Willow St., Austin, TX 78701: Free information ❖ Single-line stunt kites that collapse for portability. 512-476-1758.

Skynasaur Corporation, 7070 W. 117th Ave., Broomfield, CO 80020: Free information ❖ Kites. 303-466-4499.

Spectra Sport Kites, 350 E. 18th St., Yuma, AZ 85364: Free information ❖ Competition kites. 602-782-2541.

Trlby Kites, 65 New Litchfield St., Torrington, CT 06790: Free information ❖ Stunt kites. 800-328-7529.

What's Up Kites, 4500 Chagrin River Rd., Chagrin Falls, OH 44022: Free list of retail sources ❖ Ultra-light, stunt, and airfoil kites. 216-247-4222.

Wind Related Inc., P.O. Box 1431, Hamilton, MT 59840: Free information ❖ Handcrafted windsocks. 800-735-1885.

Windborne Kites, 585 Cannery Row, Ste. 113, Monterey, CA 93940: Free catalog ❖ Kites and accessories, windsocks, and flags. 408-373-7422.

KNITTING

Knitting Machines

All Brand Sew Knit Distributors, 9789 Florida Blvd., Baton Rouge, LA 70815: Free brochure (specify type of machine) ❖ Knitting, serger, and sewing machines and accessories. 800-289-5648.

Brother International Corporation, 200 Cottontail Ln., Somerset, NJ 08875: Free information ❖ Knitting machines. 908-356-8880.

Fiber Studio, 9 Foster Hill Rd., Box 637, Heniker, NH 03242: Spinning fibers catalog $1; yarn samples $4; equipment catalog $1 ❖ Spinning, weaving, and knitting equipment. Also cotton, mohair, wool, alpaca, silk, linen yarn, and spinning fibers. 603-428-7830.

Knitpicky Knitting Machines, 1505 Mayfair, Champaign, IL 61821: Free information ❖ New and used knitting machines and computer interface programs. 217-355-5400.

Krh Knits, P.O. Box 1587, Avon, CT 06001: Catalog $5 ❖ Knitting machines, accessories, how-to information, yarn winders, yarns, fabric paints, finishing tools, crochet accessories, elastic thread, patterns, and notions. 800-248-KNIT.

Mary Lue's Knitting World, 101 W. Broadway, St. Peter, MN 56082: Free information ❖ Refurbished and used Brother knitting machines. 819-362-2408.

Passap, 6690 Roswell Rd., Ste. 310-350, Atlanta, GA 30328: Free information ❖ Easy-to-use computerized knitting machines.

Sew-Knit Distributors, 9789 Florida Blvd., Baton Rouge, LA 70815: Free catalog ❖ Sewing and knitting machines. 800-289-5648.

Shannock Tapestry Looms, 10402 NW 11th Ave., Vancouver, WA 98685: Free information ❖ Heavy-duty, professional tapestry looms with roller beams and weaving accessories. 206-573-7264.

Studio Knitting Machines by White, 11760 Berea Rd., Cleveland, OH 44111: Free information ❖ Easy-to-operate knitting machines. 800-446-2333.

Threads Etc., 61568 Eastlake Dr., Bend, OR 97702: Catalog $2 (refundable) ❖ Knitting machines and accessories, yarns, books, patterns, and kits. 800-208-2046; 503-388-2046 (in OR).

The Weaver's Loft, 308 S. Pennsylvania Ave., Centre Hall, PA 16828: Free information ❖ Knitting, weaving, and spinning yarns. 814-364-1433.

Weaving Works, 4717 Brooklyn Ave. NE, Seattle, WA 98105: Catalog $4.50 ❖ Looms, spinning wheels, hand and machine knitting supplies, traditional and fashion yarns, and books. 206-524-1221.

Yarn-It-All, 2223 Rebecca Dr., Hatfield, PA 19440: Free information ❖ Knitting machines and yarn. 215-822-2989.

Patterns & Accessories

Aura Yarns, Box 602, Derby Line, VT 05830: Free information ❖ Icelandic wool sweater kits and alpaca, cashmere, mohair, merino, shetland, silk, and cotton yarns. 819-876-2998.

Anny Blatt Boutique, 6728 Lowell Ave., McLean, VA 22101: Catalog $2 ❖ Kits, how-to knitting books, and accessories. 800-767-4036.

Bette Bornside Company, 2733 Dauphine St., New Orleans, LA 70117: Catalog $4 ❖ Yarns, patterns, books, and needles. 800-221-9276.

Cotton Clouds, 5175 S. 14th Ave., Safford, AZ 85546: Catalog $6.50 ❖ Cotton yarns, spinning fibers, tools, books, looms, kits, and patterns. 800-322-7888.

Martha Hall, Natural Fibre Yarns, 20 Bartol Island Rd., Freeport, ME 04032: Catalog $2 ❖ Easy-to-knit wool sweater kits and hand-dyed silk, mohair, linen, cotton, cashmere, and alpaca yarn. 800-643-4566.

Herrschners Inc., 2800 Hoover Rd., Stevens Point, WI 54492: Free catalog ❖ Yarns, knitting accessories, and needle craft, crochet, and hooking kits. 800-441-0838.

Carolin Lowy Needlecraft, 630 Sun Meadows Dr., Kernersville, NC 27284: Price list $2 ❖ Needlepoint, knitting, embroidery, and counted cross-stitching patterns. 910-784-7576.

Mary Maxim Inc., 2001 Holland Ave., P.O. Box 5019, Port Huron, MI 48061: Free catalog ❖ Needle craft kits, yarn, and other supplies. 800-962-9504.

Moonrise, 2804 Fretz Valley Rd., Perkasie, PA 18944: Free catalog ❖ Books, yarn, thread, and lace-knitting supplies. 215-795-0345.

Orb Weaver, 4793 Telegraph Ave., Oakland, CA 94609: Catalog $2 ❖ Charms, books, stampings, findings, and other ornaments, and how-to decorate weavings. 510-658-0452.

Patternworks, P.O. Box 1690, Poughkeepsie, NY 12601: Catalog $3 ❖ Knitting supplies and accessories. 800-438-5464; 914-462-8000 (in NY).

Silver Creek Classics, P.O. Box 4026, Bellingham, WA 98227: Free list of retail sources with long SASE ❖ Easy-to-follow classic knitting designs. 360-733-7443.

Stitches East, 55 E. 52nd St., New York, NY 10022: Free information ❖ Knitting and needlepoint supplies, yarns, patterns, needles, and canvases. 212-421-0112.

The Stonebrier, 7900 E. Princess Ave., Scottsdale, AZ 85255: Price list $3 ❖ Designer yarns and accessories. 602-502-0800.

Thumbelina Needlework Shop, P.O. Box 1065, Solvang, CA 93464: Information $1.75 ❖ Books, fabrics, threads, yarns, kits, and other supplies. 800-789-4136.

The Weaver's Loft, 308 S. Pennsylvania Ave., Centre Hall, PA 16828: Free information ❖ Knitting, weaving, and spinning supplies. Also yarns and equipment. 814-364-1433.

Web-sters Handspinners, Weavers & Knitters, 11 N. Main St., Ashland, OR 97520: Free catalog ❖ Designer yarns, books, and tools. 800-482-9801.

Software

Cochenille Design Studio, P.O. Box 4276, Ecinas, CA 92023: Free information ❖ Knitting design software for PCs, Macintosh, and Amiga computers. 619-259-1698.

Impresario Software, 2055 Dahlia, Denver, CO 80207: Free information ❖ Hand-knitting software for PCs and machine-knitting software for PCs and the Macintosh. 303-333-3871.

M & R Technologies Inc., P.O. Box 9403, Wright Brothers Branch, Dayton, OH 45409: Free information ❖ Windows-based PC software for cross-stitch pattern design. 800-800-8517.

Oxford Craft Software, P.O. Box 208, Bonsall, CA 92003: Free information with long SASE ❖ Cross-stitch designer software for Macintosh and Amiga computers and DOS and Windows-based PCs. 800-995-0420.

Penelope Craft Programs Inc., P.O. Box 1204, Maywood, NJ 07607: Free information ❖ PC and Macintosh software for knitters. 201-368-8379.

KNIVES & KNIFE MAKING

Knives

Admiral Steel L.P., 4152 W. 123rd St., Chicago, IL 60658: Free catalog ❖ Specialty steel for knife blades.

Anza Knives, P.O. Box 710806, Santee, CA 92072: Free information ❖ High-carbon file knives. Also hunting, utility, kitchen, and fillet knives. 619-561-9445.

Arizona Custom Knives, 10721 E. Terra Dr., Scottsdale, AZ 85258: Price list $3 ❖ Handmade knives. 602-661-2142.

Atlanta Cutlery, Box 839, Conyers, GA 30207: Catalog $1 ❖ Knife-making supplies. 800-241-3595.

Hugh E. Bartrug, 505 Rhodes St., Elizabeth, PA 15037: Free information ❖ Knives and folders. 412-384-3476.

L.L. Bean, Freeport, ME 04033: Free catalog ❖ Knives for hunters, fishermen, and campers. 800-483-2326.

Beck's Cutlery Specialties, 748 E. Chatham St., Cary, NC 27511: Price list $2 ❖ Custom knives. 919-460-0203.

Benchmade Knife Company Inc., 15875-G SE 114th St., Clackamas, OR 97015: Brochure $2 ❖ Folding knives. 503-655-6004.

Beretta U.S.A., 17601 Beretta Dr., Accokeek, MD 20607: Free information ❖ Lightweight, standard, serrated, and other knives. 800-528-7453.

Berkshire Mountain Trading, 92 Bridges Rd., Williamstown, MA 01267: Catalog $2 (refundable) ❖ Knives and cutlery. 413-458-8669.

Blackjack Knives Ltd., 1307 W. Wabash, Effingham, IL 62401: Free information ❖ Knives. 217-347-7700.

Steve Brooks, Box 105, Big Timber, MT 59011: Catalog $2 ❖ Custom hand-forged, hunting, utility, and one-of-a-kind collectible knives. 406-932-5114.

W.R. Case & Sons Cutlery Company, Owens Way, Bradford, PA 16701: Catalog $2 ❖ Handcrafted knives.

Chef's Catalog, 3215 Commercial Ave., Northbrook, IL 60062: Free catalog ❖ Professional kitchen knives by Henckels and Sabatier. 800-338-3232.

Cold Steel, 2128 Knoll Dr., Ventura, CA 93003: Free catalog ❖ Limited edition, specialty, and closeout knives. 800-255-4716.

Cutlery Shoppe, 5461 Kendall St., Boise, ID 83706: Free catalog ❖ Knives and sheaths. 800-231-1272.

Dixie Gun Works Inc., P.O. Box 130, Union City, TN 38261: Catalog $5 ❖ Knife-making supplies. 800-238-6785.

The Edge Company, P.O. Box 826, Brattleboro, VT 05302: Free catalog ❖ Knives and tools. 800-732-9976.

Allen Elishewitz, 306 Mill St., San Marcos, TX 78666: Free information ❖ Knives. 512-754-8658.

Emerson Knives, 4142 W. 173rd St., Torrance, CA 90504: Catalog $2 ❖ Knives.

Ray W. Ennis, 509 S. 3rd St., Grand Forks, ND 58201: Brochure $2 ❖ Knives. 800-410-7603.

Fiskars Knives, Gerber Legendary Blades Division, Customer Service, P.O. Box 23088, Portland, OR 97281: Free catalog ❖ Outdoor recreational products, knives, sheaths, pocket tools, and accessories. 503-639-6161.

Foxwood Forge, Keith Kilby, 402 Jackson Trail Rd., Jefferson, GA 30549: Brochure $3 ❖ Damascus, cable, and carbon steel hand-forged knives. 706-367-9997.

Frost Cutlery, P.O. Box 22636, Chattanooga, TN 37422: Free information ❖ Knives. 800-251-7768; 615-894-6079 (in TN).

Gaston Knives, 330 Gaston Dr., Woodruff, SC 29388: Catalog $2 ❖ Knives. 803-433-0807.

B. Goers Knives, 3423 Royal Court South, Lakeland, FL 33813: Brochure $1 ❖ Knives. 800-392-7496.

Golden Edge Cutlery, P.O. Box 1279, Golden, CO 80402: Free catalog ❖ Knives and natural and man-made sharpening stones. 800-828-1925.

Dan Hockensmith, P.O. Box E, Drake, CO 80515: Brochure $3 ❖ Hand-forged Damascus, wire, and carbon steel knives. 303-669-5404.

International Marketing Group, 206 Kossuth Ave., Box 379, Utica, NY 13501: Free information ❖ Etching supplies and equipment. 800-775-3824.

Ken Jantz Supply, P.O. Box 584, Davis, OK 73030: Catalog $4 ❖ Knife-making supplies. 405-369-2316.

Bob Karp Knives, P.O. Box 47304, Phoenix, AZ 85068: Free information ❖ Throwing knives. 800-843-2523.

Katz Knives Inc., P.O. Box 730, Chandler, AZ 85224: Catalog $2.50 ❖ Knives and belt buckles. 602-786-9334.

Knife & Cutlery Products Inc., 4122 N. Troost Ave., Kansas City, MO 64116: Catalog $2 ❖ Knife-making supplies. 800-659-2712.

Knife & Gun Finishing Supplies, P.O. Box 458, Lakeside, AZ 85929: Catalog $3 ❖ Metal-finishing supplies for making knives. 602-537-8877.

Kopromed USA, 1701 Broadway, Ste. 282, Vancouver, WA 98663: Free information ❖ Hunting knives.

Koval Knives, P.O. Box 492, New Albany, OH 43054: Catalog $4 ❖ Knife-making supplies and equipment. 614-855-0777.

Jarrell Lambert, Rt. 1, Box 67, Ganado, TX 77962: Free information ❖ Knives. 512-771-3744.

Lansky Sharpeners, P.O. Box 800, Buffalo, NY 14231: Free catalog ❖ Knife sharpeners.

Lile Handmade Knives, 2721 S. Arkansas Ave., Russellville, AR 72801: Free information ❖ Handmade knives. 501-968-2011.

Masecraft Supply Company, 170 Research Pkwy., P.O. Box 423, Meriden, CT 06450: Free information ❖ Stag, pearl, horn, bone, mammoth ivory, and other knife handle materials. 800-682-5489.

Natural Products Company, 266 W. 37th St., New York, NY 10018: Free information ❖ India stag, buffalo horn, smooth bone, pearl and wood for knife handles and gun grips. 800-789-STAG; 212-564-3530.

Bud Neally, 822 Thomas St., Stroudsberg, PA 18360: Free brochure ❖ Knives. 717-421-4040.

Nordic Knives, 1634 Copenhagen Dr., Solvang, CA 93463: Catalog $4 ❖ Custom and Randall knives. 805-688-3612.

Northwest Knife Supply, 621 Fawn Ridge Dr., Oakland, OR 97462: Catalog $2 ❖ Knife-making supplies. 503-459-2216.

Ontario Knife Company, 26 Empire St., Franklinville, NY 14737: Free information ❖ Folding and fixed blade knives. 800-222-5233; 716-676-5527 (in NY).

Parkers' Knife Collector Service, 6715 Heritage Business Ct., P.O. Box 23522, Chattanooga, TN 37422: Free catalog ❖ Knives. 800-247-0599; 615-892-0448 (in TN).

Randall-Made Knives, P.O. Box 1988, Orlando, FL 32802: Catalog $2 ❖ Knives. 407-855-8075.

Jim Ray, 756 Camp Branch Rd., Waynesville, NC 28786: Free information ❖ Custom and production knives. 704-926-1626 (daytime); 704-452-4158 (evening).

Chris Reeve Knives, 6147 Corporal Ln., Boise, ID 83704: Brochure $2 ❖ Hand-ground knives in 16 blade styles. 208-375-0367.

Rio Cutlery & Luggage Inc., 10 W. 46th St., New York, NY 10036: Catalog $5 ❖ Custom and antique pocket knives. 212-819-0304.

A.G. Russell Knife Company, 1705 Hwy. 71 B North, Springdale, AR 72764: Free catalog ❖ Knives and cutlery. 800-255-9034.

Sheffield Knifemakers Supply, P.O. Box 741107, Orange City, FL 32724: Catalog $5 ❖ Knife-making supplies. 904-775-6453.

Cleston R. Sinyard, Nimo Forge, 27522 Burkhardt Dr., Elberta, AL 36530: Free information ❖ Damascus blade knives. 205-986-7984.

Jim Siska Knives, 6 Highland Ave., Westfield, MA 01085: Free brochure ❖ Knives. 413-568-9787.

Skylands Cutlery, P.O. Box 87, Ringwood, NJ 07456: Catalog $1 ❖ Factory and custom knives. 201-962-6143.

Smoky Mountain Knife Works, P.O. Box 4430, Sevierville, TN 37864: Free catalog ❖ Hunting, work, and survival knives. 800-251-9306.

SOG Specialty Knives & Tools Inc., P.O. Box 1024, Edmonds, WA 98020: Free brochure ❖ Pocket tool knives. 206-771-6230.

Southeast Knife Brokers, Rt. 1, Box 1070, Sautee-Nacoochee, GA 30571: Price list $2 ❖ Old, new, factory-made, and other knives. 706-878-3325.

Special Projects, Customer Service, 2128 Knoll Dr., Unit D, Ventura, CA 93003: Free catalog ❖ Limited edition and new knives. 800-258-1655.

Sportsman's Accessory Manufacturing, 615 Reed St., P.O. Box 18091, Philadelphia, PA 19147: Free information ❖ Knife cases. 215-336-6464.

Spyderco Inc., P.O. Box 800, Golden, CO 80402: Free information ❖ Mountain-climbing knives. 800-525-7770.

Star Sales Company Inc., 1803 N. Central St., P.O. Box 1503, Knoxville, TN 37901: Catalog $2 ❖ Knives. 615-524-0771.

Sutherland Knives, P.O. Box 23516, Flagstaff, AZ 86002: Brochure $2 (refundable) ❖ Knives. 602-774-6050.

Swiss Armory, 2838 Juniper St., San Diego, CA 92104: Free catalog ❖ Swiss army knives. 800-437-5423.

Texas Knifemakers Supply, P.O. Box 79402, Houston, TX 77279: Catalog $2 ❖ Knife-making supplies. 713-461-8632.

U.S. Cavalry, 2855 Centennial Ave., Radcliff, KY 40160: Free catalog ❖ Survival, military, and pocket-size knives. 800-908-9455.

United Cutlery, 1425 United Blvd., Sevierville, TN 37876: Free list of retail sources ❖ Knives. 800-548-0835.

Sharpeners

Golden Edge Cutlery, P.O. Box 1279, Golden, CO 80402: Free catalog ❖ Knives and natural and man-made sharpening stones. 800-828-1925.

The Great American Tool Company, P.O. Box 600, Getzville, NY 14066: Free information ❖ Easy-to-use sharpening tools. 800-LIV-SHARP.

L.S. Lansky Sharpeners, P.O. Box 800, Buffalo, NY 14231: Free catalog ❖ Knife sharpeners.

Norton, One New Bond St., P.O. Box 15008, Worcester, MA 01615: Free information ❖ Water-lubricated sharpening stones.

Razor Edge Systems Inc., 303 N. 17th St., Ely, MN 55731: Free catalog ❖ Sharpening equipment. 800-541-1458.

LABORATORY & SCIENCE EQUIPMENT

Advance Scientific, 2345 SW 34th St., Fort Lauderdale, FL 33312: Catalog $3 ❖ Laboratory chemicals, glassware, instrumentation, and supplies. 305-327-0900.

American Science & Surplus, 3605 Howard St., Skokie, IL 60076: Catalog $1 ❖ Surplus science, electrical-mechanical supplies, and equipment, and kits. 708-982-0870.

Analytical Scientific, 11049 Bandera, San Antonio, TX 78250: Catalog $3 (refundable) ❖ Laboratory glassware, chemicals, equipment, books, and charts. 210-684-7373.

Anatomical Chart Company, 8221 N. Kimball, Skokie, IL 60076: Catalog $2 ❖ Educational anatomical products on health, human anatomy, and other sciences. 800-621-7500; 708-679-4700 (in IL).

ASC Scientific, 2075 Corte del Nogal, Carlsbad, CA 92009: Free catalog ❖ Pocket transit for geologists, hand-held satellite navigator, and earth science equipment. 800-272-4327.

Bunting Magnetics Company, P.O. Box 468, Newton, KS 67144: Free catalog ❖ Magnets. 800-835-2526; 316-284-2020 (in KS).

Chem-Lab, 1060 Ortega Way, Placentia, CA 92670: Catalog $5 ❖ Chemicals, glassware, scales, microscopes, and other equipment. 714-630-7902.

Dino Productions, P.O. Box 3004, Englewood, CO 80155: Catalog $2 (refundable) ❖ Fossils, rocks and minerals, ecology and oceanography equipment, and chemistry, general science, astronomy, and biology supplies. 303-741-1587.

Edlie Electronics, 2700 Hempstead Tnpk., Levittown, NY 11756: Free catalog ❖ Electronics kits. 516-735-3330.

Edmund Scientific Company, Edscorp Building, Barrington, NJ 08007: Free catalog ❖ Microscopes, magnifiers, weather forecasting instruments, magnets, telescopes, binoculars and other optical, laser, and science equipment. 609-573-6260.

The Electronic Goldmine, P.O. Box 5408, Scottsdale, AZ 85261: Free catalog ❖ Science kits. 602-451-7454.

Hagenow Laboratories, 1302 Washington, Manitowoc, WI 54220: Catalog $2 ❖ Chemicals, glassware, and laboratory supplies. 414-683-3339.

J.L. Hammett Company, P.O. Box 9057, Braintree, MA 02184: Free catalog ❖ Science kits, microscopes, laboratory apparatus, rock collections, magnets, astronomy charts, and anatomical models. 617-848-1000.

Hubbard Scientific Company, 3101 Iris Ave., Boulder, CO 80301: Free catalog ❖ Science equipment for life, earth, physical science, energy, health and physiology, and topography experiments. 800-323-8368.

Magnet Sales & Manufacturing Company, 11248 Playa Ct., Culver City, CA 90230: Free brochure ❖ Flexible strip, flex-dot, button, and bar magnets. 800-421-6692; 310-391-7213 (in CA).

Merrell Scientific/World of Science, 1665 Buffalo Rd., Rochester, NY 14624: Catalog $2 ❖ Chemicals, glassware, and equipment for biology, nature, physical and earth science, rocket, and astronomy experiments. 716-426-1540.

Nasco, 901 Janesville Ave., Fort Atkinson, WI 53538: Free catalog ❖ Science and ultraviolet lighting equipment, kits, microscopes and dissection kits, rock collections, magnets, electric motors, astronomy charts and star maps, anatomical models, and other supplies. 800-558-9595.

The Nature Company, Catalog Division, P.O. Box 188, Florence, KY 41022: Free catalog ❖ Science supplies, kits, books, toys, novelties, and gifts. 800-227-1114.

Omni Resources, 1004 S. Mebane St., P.O. Box 2096, Burlington, NC 27216: Free catalog ❖ Earth science and laboratory equipment. 800-742-2677.

Pyrotek, P.O. Box 1, Catasauqua, PA 18032: Catalog $2 ❖ Laboratory chemicals, glassware, books and manuals, and supplies. 717-256-3087.

Schoolmasters Science, 745 State Circle, Box 1941, Ann Arbor, MI 48106: Catalog $2 ❖ Laboratory science equipment. 800-521-2832.

Southern Oregon Scientific, 1000 SE M St., Unit A, Grants Pass, OR 97526: Catalog $2 ❖ Laboratory glassware and chemicals.

Unitron Inc., 170 Wilbur Pl., P.O. Box 469, Bohemia, NY 11716: Free catalog ❖ Stereo microscopes and optical and scientific equipment. 516-589-6666.

Ward's Natural Science, P.O. Box 92912, 5100 W. Henrietta Rd., Rochester, NY 14692: Earth science catalog $10; biology catalog $15; middle school catalog $10 ❖ Science equipment and supplies. 800-962-2660.

Whatman LabSales, P.O. Box 1359, Hillsboro, OR 97123: Free catalog ❖ Laboratory science equipment. 800-Whatman.

LACROSSE

Athletes Wear Company, 145 Market Ave., Winnipeg, Manitoba, Canada R3B 1C5: Free catalog ❖ Clothing for lacrosse players. 204-949-1885.

Brine Inc., 47 Sumner St., Milford, MA 01757: Free information ❖ Balls, gloves, goals, protective equipment, sticks, and uniforms. 800-227-2722; 508-478-3250 (in MA).

Wm. T. Burnett & Company Inc., 1500 Bush St., Baltimore, MD 21230: Free information ❖ Balls and gloves, goals, protective gear, and sticks. 800-368-2250.

Jayfro Corporation, Unified Sports Inc., 976 Hartford Tnpk., P.O. Box 400, Waterford, CT 06385: Free catalog ❖ Lacrosse and field hockey goals, nets, and other equipment. 860-447-3001.

Olympia Sports, 745 State Cir., Ann Arbor, MI 48106: Free information ❖ Goal nets, balls, and sticks. 800-521-2832.

Reda Sports Express, 44 N. 2nd St., P.O. Box 68, Easton, PA 18044: Free information ❖ Balls, protective gear, helmets, and sticks. 800-444-REDA; 215-258-5271 (in PA).

Riddell Inc., 3670 N. Milwaukee Ave., Chicago, IL 60641: Free information ❖ Helmets. 800-445-7344; 312-794-1994 (in IL).

Sauk Valley Sports Resort, 10750 Prospect Hill, Brooklyn, MI 49230: Free information ❖ Balls, gloves, goals, helmets, protective equipment, and sticks. 800-252-SAUK; 517-467-2061 (in MI).

Seneca Sports Inc., 75 Fortune Blvd., P.O. Box 719 Milford, MA 01757: Free information ❖ Sticks and balls. 800-861-7867; 508-634-3616 (in MA).

STX Inc., 1500 Bush St., Baltimore, MD 21230: Free information ❖ Goal nets, protective gear, gloves, balls, and sticks. 800-368-2250; 410-837-2022 (in MD).

Tuskewe Krafts, 2089 Upper Mountain Rd., Sanborn, NY 14132: Free brochure with long SASE ❖ Women and men's field and box lacrosse sticks. 717-297-1821.

LADDERS

Jomy Safety Ladder Company, 1728 16th St., Ste. 201, Boulder, CO 80302: Free information ❖ Collapsible fire escape ladder. 800-255-2591.

Walter Kidde, Division Kidde Inc, 1394 S. 3rd, Mebane, NC 27302: Free information ❖ Escape ladders. 800-654-9677.

Ladder Man Inc., 3025 Silver Dr., Columbus, OH 43224: Free catalog ❖ Safety equipment, attic and fire escape equipment, and specialty, articulating, stairway, and stairwell ladders. 800-783-8887.

Lynn Ladder & Scaffolding & Company, 220 S. Common St., Lynn, MA 01905: Free list of retail sources ❖ Wood, aluminum, and fiberglass ladders. 800-225-2510.

The New Rebel Workshop, Robert & Sandy Little, P.O. Box 658, Franklin, TX 77856: Brochure $2 ❖ Chair step that converts to a stepladder. Also other craft items. 409-828-3849.

Putnam Rolling Ladder Company Inc., 32 Howard St., New York, NY 10013: Catalog $1 ❖ Ladders, library carts, and furniture. 212-226-5147.

LAMPS & LIGHTING

Chandeliers

A.J.P. Coppersmith & Company, 20 Industrial Pkwy., Woburn, MA 01801: Catalog $3 ❖ Chandeliers, sconces, cupolas, weather vanes, and handcrafted copper, tin, and brass reproduction colonial lanterns. 800-545-1776.

Ala Lite, 380 E. 1700 South, Salt Lake City, UT 84115: Free information ❖ Restored and reproduction antique lamps, shades, chandeliers, and parts. 800-388-5456.

American Light Source, 5211D W. Market St., Ste. 803, Greensboro, NC 27265: Free catalog ❖ Chandeliers. 800-741-0571.

Antique Hardware Store, 1 Matthews Ct., Hilton Head Island, SC 29926: Catalog $3 ❖ Antique chandeliers, indoor and outdoor lighting fixtures, pedestal sinks, faucets, high-tank toilets, cabinet hardware, and weather vanes. 800-422-9982.

Antler Designs for Sale, Jim & Goldie Mason, 15 Curtis Hill Rd., West Paris, ME 04289: Free information ❖ Antlers crafted into chandeliers, sconces, coffee tables, chairs, and novelties. 207-674-2655 (no Friday night or Saturday calls).

Antler Furnishings by Jay "Bird" Jones, 520 Pine Oaks Rd., #4, Colorado Springs, CO 80926: Catalog $10 ❖ Antler-crafted chairs, lamps, chandeliers, and carvings. 719-527-1845.

Art De Mexico, 5356 Riverton Rd., North Hollywood, CA 91601: Free catalog ❖ Hand-assembled furniture and lighting from naturally shed antlers. 818-508-0993.

V. Michael Ashford, 6543 Alpine Dr. SW, Olympia, WA 98512: Catalog $8 ❖ Hand-hammered copper and mica table. Also floor lamps, sconces, and chandeliers. 360-352-0694.

Authentic Designs, The Mill Rd., West Rupert, VT 05776: Catalog $3 ❖ Handcrafted reproduction 18th-century early American lighting fixtures and chandeliers in brass, copper, and tin. 802-394-7713.

Ball & Ball, 463 W. Lincoln Hwy., Exton, PA 19341: Catalog $7 (refundable) ❖ Reproduction antique lighting fixtures and chandeliers. 610-363-7330.

Brass Light Gallery, 131 S. 1st St., Milwaukee, WI 53204: Catalog $5 ❖ Solid brass chandeliers with glass shades, from the early 1900s. 800-243-9595.

Brass Reproductions, 9711 Canoga Ave., Chatsworth, CA 91311: Catalog $8 ❖ Solid brass Victorian and traditional chandeliers, floor and table lamps, and sconces. 818-709-7844.

Classic Illumination, 2743 9th St., Berkeley, CA 94710: Free information ❖ Chandeliers and wall sconces. 510-849-1842.

The Coppersmith, Rt. 20, P.O. Box 755, Sturbridge, MA 01566: Catalog $3 ❖ Handcrafted reproduction chandeliers, lanterns, and sconces. 508-347-7038.

Roc Corbett Custom Lighting, P.O. Box 339, Bigfork, MT 59911: Catalog $10 (refundable) ❖ Elk, deer, moose, and caribou antler-crafted wagon wheel chandeliers. 406-837-5823.

The Country Store, 28 James St., Geneva, IL 60134: Catalog $2 ❖ Punched tin and turned wooden chandeliers, ceiling lights, outlet covers, country-style decorative accessories, and braided rugs. 708-879-0098.

Dutch Creel Colonial Lighting, Box 103, Danville, AR 72833: Brochure $2 ❖ Early American chandeliers with a turned wood base. 501-495-2044.

❖ **LAMPS & LIGHTING** ❖

Gaslight Time, 5 Plaza St. West, Brooklyn, NY 11217: Catalog $4 ❖ Restored antique gas, combination, and early electric chandeliers and wall sconces, from 1850 to 1925. 718-789-7185.

Georgia Lighting Supply Company Inc., 530 14th St. NW, Atlanta, GA 30318: Catalog $12 ❖ Lighting fixtures in iron, brass, and bronze from European and American artisans. 800-282-0220.

Golden Valley Lighting, 274 Eastchester Dr., Ste. 117A, High Point, NC 27262: Catalog $5 ❖ Lighting fixtures and lamps. 800-735-3377; 919-882-7330 (in NC).

Graber's Crafted Lighting, Rt. 2, Box 140, Mammoth Spring, AR 72554: Catalog $4 ❖ Western-style chandeliers. 501-966-4996.

Greene's Lighting Fixtures, 1059 3rd Ave., New York, NY 10021: Catalog $10 (refundable) ❖ Custom-made chandeliers. 212-753-2507.

Hammerworks, 6 Fremont St., Worcester, MA 01603: Catalog $3 ❖ Handmade reproductions of copper, brass, iron, and tin colonial post and wall lanterns, chandeliers, and sconces. 508-755-3434.

Howard's Antique Lighting, Rt. 23 West, P.O. Box 472, South Edgemont, MA 01258: Free information ❖ Floor lamps, sconces, and electric, gas, and kerosene chandeliers. 413-528-1232.

Hubbardton Forge & Wood Corporation, Vermont Industries, P.O. Box 301, Rt. 103, Cuttingsville, VT 05738: Catalog $3 ❖ Wrought-iron and brass chandeliers, other hand-forged lighting accessories, hanging pan racks, bathroom and home accessories, plant hangers, and table, wall, and candlestick lamps. 800-639-1715; 802-492-3451 (in VT).

Hurley Patentee Lighting, 464 Old Rt. 209, Hurley, NY 12443: Catalog $3 ❖ Handcrafted replicas of Early American chandeliers, sconces, lanterns, and other lamps. 914-331-5414.

Iron Apple Forge, P.O. Box 724, Buckingham, PA 18912: Catalog $4 ❖ Traditional wrought-iron chandeliers. 215-794-7351.

Irvin's, RD 1, Box 73, Mt. Pleasant Mills, PA 17853: Free catalog ❖ Handcrafted colonial tinware and lighting fixtures. 717-539-8200.

King's Chandelier Company, P.O. Box 667, Eden, NC 27289: Catalog $3.75 ❖ Chandeliers, candelabras, and crystal sconces. 910-623-6188.

Lamp Warehouse, 1073 39th St., Brooklyn, NY 11219: Free information with long SASE ❖ Ceiling fans and lighting fixtures. 800-52-LITES; 718-436-8500 (in NY).

Little Big Horn Replica Company, P.O. Box 415, Crow Agency, MT 59022: Brochure $2 ❖ Wagon wheel clocks and chandeliers. 406-638-4458.

Luigi Crystal, 7332 Frankford Ave., Philadelphia, PA 19136: Catalog $2 ❖ Cut crystal accessories, decorative table lamps, crystal chandeliers, hurricane lamps, and sconces. 215-338-2978.

Marlborough Country Barn, N. Main St., Marlborough, CT 06447: Catalog $3 ❖ Reproduction lighting for log homes. 203-295-8231.

Nowell's Inc., 490 Gate 5 Rd., P.O. Box 295, Sausalito, CA 94966: Catalog $5 ❖ Reproduction and restored antique chandeliers and other lighting fixtures. 415-332-4933.

The Original Cast Lighting, 6120 Delmar Blvd., St. Louis, MO 63112: Catalog $2 ❖ Lighting fixtures and reproduction and restored antique units. 314-863-1895.

Period Lighting Fixtures, 167 River Rd., Clarksburg, MA 01247: Catalog $6.50 ❖ Early American lighting fixtures, chandeliers, lanterns, and sconces. 800-828-6990.

Ragged Mountain Antler Chandeliers, 897 Bourne Ln., Victor, MT 59875: Free brochure ❖ Chandeliers made from deer antlers. 406-961-2400.

The Renovator's Supply, P.O. Box 2515, Conway, NH 03818: Free catalog ❖ Solid brass chandeliers. 800-659-0303.

Roy Electric Company, 1054 Coney Island Ave., Brooklyn, NY 11230: Catalog $6 ❖ Victorian-style and turn-of-the-century chandeliers, sconces, and lighting fixtures. 800-366-3347; 718-434-7002 (in NY).

Saltbox Inc., 3004 Columbia Ave., Lancaster, PA 17603: Catalog $2.50 ❖ Handcrafted brass, copper, and tin colonial-style chandeliers, post lights, lanterns, and foyer lights. 717-392-5649.

Stanley Galleries, 2118 N. Clark St., Chicago, IL 60614: Free information ❖ Antique American chandeliers and light fixtures. 312-281-1614.

Star Antler Designs, P.O. Box 3093, Lake Isabella, CA 93240: Catalog $5 ❖ Deer antler chandeliers, lamps, furniture, mirrors, and decorative accessories. 619-379-5777.

Studio Steel, 159 New Milford Tnpk., New Preston, CT 06777: Catalog $2 ❖ Lamps, chandeliers, sconces, mirrors, and hand-wrought metalwork. 800-800-5217; 860-868-7305 (in CT).

Tin Bin, 20 Valley Rd., Neffsville, PA 17601: Catalog $2.50 ❖ Handcrafted antique copper and brass country-style chandeliers. 717-569-6210.

The Tinhorn, 1852 Forest Ln., Crown Point, IN 46307: Catalog $3 ❖ Pewter-like and antique-copper punched-heart scalloped chandeliers, sconces and other items. 219-988-3332.

Vermont Industries, P.O. Box 301, Rt. 103, Cuttingsville, VT 05738: Catalog $3 ❖ Wrought-iron and solid brass chandeliers, floor and table lamps, and wall fixtures. 800-639-1715; 802-492-3451 (in VT).

Victorian Lighting Works, 251 S. Pennsylvania Ave., P.O. Box 469, Centre Hall, PA 16328: Catalog $5 (refundable) ❖ Victorian-style wall sconces and chandeliers. 814-364-9577.

Village Lantern, 598 Union St., North Marshfield, MA 02059: Brochure 50¢ ❖ Handcrafted colonial-style chandeliers and lanterns. 617-834-8121.

Lt. Moses Willard Inc., 1156 US 50, Milford, OH 45150: Catalog $8.50 (request list of retail sources) ❖ Reproduction chandeliers, wall sconces, exterior lighting units, candle holders, lanterns, and wall and table lamps, from the 1700s. 513-248-5500.

Workshops of David T. Smith, 3600 Shawhan Rd., Morrow, OH 45152: Catalog $5 ❖ Reproduction furniture, pottery, lamps, and chandeliers. 513-932-2472.

Dome Lighting

Decolite, 11720 US 19, Port Richey, FL 34668: Free catalog ❖ Do-it-yourself dome lighting systems. 800-766-1058.

Lamps & Fixtures

A.J.P. Coppersmith & Company, 20 Industrial Pkwy., Woburn, MA 01801: Catalog $3 ❖ Handcrafted copper, tin, and brass reproduction colonial lanterns, chandeliers, sconces, cupolas, and weather vanes. 800-545-1776.

Ala Lite, 380 E. 1700 South, Salt Lake City, UT 84115: Free information ❖ Restored and reproduction antique lamps, shades, chandeliers, and parts. 800-388-5456.

Aladdin Industries Inc., Lamp Division, P.O. Box 100255, Nashville, TN 37224: Free catalog ❖ Lamps, lamp shades, and replacement parts. 800-456-1233.

American Home Supply, 191 Lost Lake Ln., Campbell, CA 95009: Catalog $2 ❖ Reproduction heritage lighting fixtures. 408-246-1962.

American Period Showcase, 3004 Columbia Ave., Lancaster, PA 17603: Catalog $2.50 ❖ Handcrafted lanterns, table lamps, chandeliers, and post lamps. 717-392-5649.

Antique Hardware Store, 1 Matthews Ct., Hilton Head Island, SC 29926: Catalog $3 ❖ Antique-style indoor and outdoor lamps and lighting fixtures, pedestal sinks, faucets, high tank toilets, cabinet hardware, weather vanes, and tin and wooden chandeliers. 800-422-9982.

Antique Lamp Parts & Service, Aladdin & Fenton, 218 N. Foley Ave., Freeport, IL 61032: Free information with long SASE (specify items wanted) ❖ Parts for old and new kerosene, electric, and gas lamps. 815-232-8968.

❖ LAMPS & LIGHTING ❖ 309

Antler Designs for Sale, Jim & Goldie Mason, 15 Curtis Hill Rd., West Paris, ME 04289: Free information ❖ Antlers crafted into chandeliers, sconces, coffee tables, chairs, and novelties. 207-674-2655 (No Friday night or Saturday calls).

Antler Furnishings by Jay "Bird" Jones, 520 Pine Oaks Rd., #4, Colorado Springs, CO 80926: Catalog $10 ❖ Antler chairs, lamps, chandeliers, and carvings. 719-527-1845.

Arroyo Craftsman, 4509 Little John St., Baldwin Park, CA 91706: Catalog $5 ❖ Original indoor and outdoor brass lighting fixtures. 818-960-9411.

V. Michael Ashford, 6543 Alpine Dr. SW, Olympia, WA 98512: Catalog $8 ❖ Hand-hammered copper and mica table. Also floor lamps, sconces, and chandeliers. 360-352-0694.

Aunt Sylvia's Victorian Lamps, P.O. Box 67364, Chestnut Hill, MA 02157: Catalog $3 ❖ Traditional and reproduction Victorian-style lamps. 800-231-6644.

Authentic Designs, The Mill Rd., West Rupert, VT 05776: Catalog $3 ❖ Handcrafted reproduction of early 18th-century brass, copper, and tin American lighting fixtures and chandeliers. 802-394-7713.

Baldwin Hardware Corporation, P.O. Box 15048, Reading, PA 19612: Bathroom accessories brochure 75¢, lighting fixtures brochure $3, door hardware brochure 75¢, decorative hardware brochure 75¢ ❖ Brass dead bolts and door hardware, bathroom accessories, and lighting fixtures. 800-346-5128.

Ball & Ball, 463 W. Lincoln Hwy., Exton, PA 19341: Catalog $7 (refundable) ❖ Reproduction lighting fixtures and chandeliers. 610-363-7330.

Barap Specialties, 835 Bellows Ave., Frankfort, MI 49635: Catalog $1 ❖ Lamp parts, chair caning, craft supplies, tools, and turned wooden parts. 800-3-BARAP-3.

Barton-Sharpe Ltd., 119 Spring St., New York, NY 10012: Free information ❖ Reproduction 18th and 19th-century furniture, lighting, bedding, stoneware, and decorative items. 212-925-9562.

Dennis & CeCe Bork, 715 Genesee St., Delafield, WI 53018: Catalog $5 ❖ Custom furniture, folk art, period lighting, Colonial Williamsburg reproductions, Windsor chairs and settees, and decorative items. 414-646-4911.

Brandon Industries, 1601 W. Wilmeth Rd., McKinney, TX 75069: Free catalog ❖ Wall sconces, aluminum lamp posts, planters, and mailboxes. 214-542-3000.

The Brass Knob, 2311 18th St. NW, Washington, DC 20009: Free information ❖ Antique lighting fixtures, from 1870 to 1930. 202-332-3370.

The Brass Lion, 5935 S. Broadway, Tyler, TX 75703: Catalog $5 ❖ Reproduction 17th and 18th-century lighting fixtures and wall sconces. 903-561-1111.

Brass Menagerie, 524 St. Louis St., New Orleans, LA 70130: Free information with long SASE (specify items wanted) ❖ Lighting fixtures, plumbing, and hardware. 504-524-0921.

Brass Reproductions, 9711 Canoga Ave., Chatsworth, CA 91311: Catalog $8 ❖ Solid brass Victorian and traditional chandeliers, floor and table lamps, and sconces. 818-709-7844.

Brass Works Lighting, 292 Main St., Nyack, NY 10960: Catalog $5 ❖ Ceiling, wall, and table lighting in antique and polished brass, chrome, pewter, and combinations. 800-358-5843.

Brubaker Metalcrafts, 209 N. Franklin St., Eaton, OH 45320: Catalog $2 ❖ Reproduction 18th-century tin and brass chandeliers, wall sconces, Paul Revere lanterns, and other fixtures. 513-456-5834.

Matthew Burak Furniture, Box 279, Rt. 2, Danville, VT 05828: Catalog $5 ❖ Reproduction 18th and 19th-century furniture, lighting, and folk art. 802-684-2156.

Century Studio, 200 3rd Ave. North, Minneapolis, MN 55401: Brochure $10 (refundable) ❖ Reproduction Tiffany lamps. 612-339-0239.

Chapman, 481 W. Main St., Avon, MA 02322: Brochure $4 (request list of retail sources) ❖ Lighting, furniture, and accessories.

City Lights, 2226 Massachusetts Ave., Cambridge, MA 02140: Free information (specify items wanted) ❖ Restored one-of-a-kind antique lighting fixtures. 617-547-1490.

David L. Claggett, Artistry in Tin, P.O. Box 41, Weston, VT 05161: Catalog $3 ❖ Reproduction lighting fixtures. 802-824-3194.

Classic Illumination, 2743 9th St., Berkeley, CA 94710: Free information ❖ Chandeliers and wall sconces. 510-849-1842.

Conant Custom Brass, 270 Pine St., Burlington, VT 05401: Free catalog ❖ Restored antique lighting. 802-658-4482.

The Coppersmith, Rt. 20, P.O. Box 755, Sturbridge, MA 01566: Catalog $3 ❖ Handcrafted reproduction colonial lanterns, sconces, and chandeliers. 508-347-7038.

Early American Lighting, 10 Mabel, Queensbury, NY 12804: Catalog $3 ❖ Reproduction electric or cordless early American lighting fixtures. 518-745-1334.

Elcanco Ltd., P.O. Box 682, Westford, MA 01886: Brochure $1 ❖ Handcrafted electric wax candles with flame-like bulbs. 508-392-0830.

Everything Ewenique, RR 1, Box 73, Mt. Pleasant Mills, PA 17853: Free catalog ❖ Tinware interior and exterior lighting, sconces, table lamps, potpourri tart warmers, and other units. 800-800-4TIN.

Fabby, 450 S. La Brea Ave., Los Angeles, CA 90036: Catalog $3 ❖ Ceramic wall sconces and handmade indoor and outdoor lighting fixtures. 213-939-1388.

Faire Harbour Ltd., 44 Captain Pierce Rd., Scituate, MA 02066: Catalog $2 ❖ One-of-a-kind antique lamps, parts, and oil, early gas, electric, and kerosene lamps. 617-545-2465.

David & Martha Fletcher, Blue Mist Morgan Farm, 68 Liberty St., Haverhill, MA 01830: Catalog $3 ❖ Handcrafted copper lanterns and weather vanes. 508-374-8783.

Gaslight Time, 823 President St., Brooklyn, NY 11215: Catalog $4 ❖ Restored antique gas, combination, and early electric chandeliers and wall sconces, from 1850 to 1925. 718-789-7185.

Genie House, P.O. Box 2478, Vincentown, NJ 08088: Catalog $5 ❖ Handcrafted copper, tin, and brass 17th and 18th-century reproduction lighting fixtures. 800-634-3643.

Georgia Lighting Supply Company Inc., 530 14th St. NW, Atlanta, GA 30318: Catalog $12 ❖ Lighting fixtures in iron, brass, and bronze from European and American artisans. 800-282-0220.

Hammerworks, 6 Fremont St., Worcester, MA 01603: Catalog $3 ❖ Handmade reproductions of copper, brass, iron, and tin colonial post and wall lanterns, chandeliers, and sconces. 508-755-3434.

Heirloom Reproductions, 1834 W. 5th St., Montgomery, AL 36106: Catalog $3 ❖ Reproduction French and Victorian lamps and furniture. 800-288-1513.

Historic Lighting Restoration, 10341 Jewell Lake Ct., Fenton, MI 48430: Free brochure with long SASE ❖ Electric-operated reproduction kerosene chandeliers. 313-629-4934.

Home Decorators Collection, 2025 Concourse Dr., St. Louis, MO 63146: Free catalog ❖ Lamp shades and contemporary, traditional, floor, table, halogen lamps, and lighting fixtures for the bathroom, ceiling, wall, and outdoors. 800-240-6047; 314-993-6045 (in MO).

Howard's Antique Lighting, Rt. 23 West, P.O. Box 472, South Edgemont, MA 01258: Free information ❖ Floor lamps, sconces, and electric, gas, and kerosene chandeliers. 413-528-1232.

Hurley Patentee Lighting, 464 Old Rt. 209, Hurley, NY 12443: Catalog $3 ❖ Handcrafted replica Early American chandeliers, sconces, lanterns, and other lamps. 914-331-5414.

LAMPS & LIGHTING

Independence Forge, Rt. 1, Box 1, Whitakers, NC 27891: Brochure $1 ❖ Handcrafted country-style iron furniture, chandeliers, and floor, table, and wall lamps. 919-437-1452.

Irvin's, RD 1, Box 73, Mt. Pleasant Mills, PA 17853: Free catalog ❖ Handcrafted colonial tinware and lighting. 717-539-8200.

Daniel Joseph Historic Styled Lighting, 31921 Camino Capistrano, #347, San Juan Capistrano, CA 92675: Free brochure ❖ Historic-styled lighting fixtures. 800-548-6984; 714-841-6200 (in CA).

Juno Lighting Inc., P.O. Box 5065, Des Plaines, IL 60017: Free information ❖ Indoor and outdoor lighting fixtures. 708-827-9880.

Lamps by Lynne, P.O. Box 190, Pipersville, PA 18947: Free information ❖ Lamps and lampshades. 215-766-7615.

Levenger, P.O. Box 1256, Delray Beach, FL 33447: Free catalog ❖ Reproduction brass-shade desk lamps. 800-545-0242.

Leviton Manufacturing Company, 59-25 Little Neck Pkwy., Little Neck, NY 11362: Free information ❖ Indoor and outdoor lighting fixtures. 800-323-8920.

Lighting by Gregory, 158 Bowery, New York, NY 10012: Free catalog ❖ Fixtures and accessories that enable design of lighting to accommodate individual desires and activities. 800-796-1965; 212-226-1276 (in NY).

Lighting Elegance, 147 W. Badillo St., Covina, CA 91723: Catalog $5 ❖ Reproduction 19th-century gas lighting fixtures. 818-339-7278.

Lightolier, 7151 Columbia Gateway Dr., Ste. A, Columbia, MD 21046: Free information ❖ Indoor and outdoor lighting fixtures. 410-995-6395.

Lucid Lighting, 287 S. Main St., Lamberville, NJ 08530: Catalog $5 ❖ Custom-made historic-style lighting fixtures. 609-397-9581.

Luigi Crystal, 7332 Frankford Ave., Philadelphia, PA 19136: Catalog $2 ❖ Table lamps, cut crystal chandeliers, hurricane lamps, and sconces. 215-338-2978.

Marlborough Country Barn, N. Main St., Marlborough, CT 06447: Catalog $3 ❖ Reproduction lighting for log homes. 203-295-8231.

Meyda Tiffany, 55 Oriskany Blvd., Yorkville, NY 13495: Catalog $5 ❖ Victorian light fixtures. Also beaded and Tiffany lamps. 800-222-4009.

Mica Lamp Company, 517 State St., Glendale, CA 91203: Free brochure ❖ Handcrafted copper turn-of-the-century lighting fixtures. 800-90-LAMPS.

Gates Moore Lighting, 2 River Rd., Silvermine, Norwalk, CT 06850: Catalog $2 ❖ Early American chandeliers, copper lanterns, and wall sconces. 203-847-3231.

Moultrie Manufacturing, P.O. Box 1179, Moultrie, GA 31776: Catalog $3 ❖ Colonial lanterns and "Old South" reproductions for the home. 800-841-8674.

C. Neri Antiques, 313 South St., Philadelphia, PA 19147: Catalog $5 ❖ Antique lighting fixtures. 215-923-6669.

New England Stained Glass, 5 Center St., West Stockbridge, MA 01266: Brochure $5 (refundable) ❖ Tiffany reproductions. 413-232-7181.

Newstamp Lighting Company, 227 Bay Rd., P.O. Box 189, North Easton, MA 02356: Catalog $2 ❖ Handmade replica Early American lamps for indoors and outdoors, sconces, chandeliers, and other lighting fixtures. 508-238-7071.

The Original Cast Lighting, 6120 Delmar Blvd., St. Louis, MO 63112: Catalog $2 ❖ Lighting fixtures and reproduction and restored antique units. 314-863-1895.

Period Lighting Fixtures, 167 River Rd., Clarksburg, MA 01247: Catalog $6.50 ❖ Early American lighting fixtures, chandeliers, lanterns, and sconces. 800-828-6990.

Rejuvenation Lamp & Fixture Company, 1100 SE Grand Ave., Portland, OR 97217: Free catalog ❖ Reproduction solid brass early 20th-century chandeliers, sconces, and lamps. 503-231-1900.

The Renovator's Supply, P.O. Box 2515, Conway, NH 03818: Free catalog ❖ Ceiling lighting fixtures and hanging, table and floor, and wall lamps. Also replacement glass shades. 800-659-0203.

The Restoration Place, 305 20th St., Rock Island, IL 61201: Free brochure ❖ Plumbing, hardware, architectural and decorative accessories, and lighting fixtures. 309-786-0004.

Roy Electric Company, 1054 Coney Island Ave., Brooklyn, NY 11230: Catalog $6 ❖ Art deco lighting fixtures. 800-366-3347; 718-434-7002 (in NY).

St. Louis Antique Lighting Company Inc., 801 N. Skinker, St. Louis, MO 63130: Catalog $3 ❖ Handcrafted antique brass reproduction ceiling fixtures, lamps, and sconces. 314-863-1414.

Saltbox Inc., 3004 Columbia Ave., Lancaster, PA 17603: Catalog $2.50 ❖ Handcrafted brass, copper, and tin colonial-style post lights, chandeliers, lanterns, and foyer lights. 717-392-5649.

George Scatchard Lamps, P.O. Box 71, Underhill, VT 05489: Free brochure ❖ Ready and custom-made floor and table lamps. 800-643-5267; 802-899-2181 (in VT).

Somers Stained Glass Company, 108 Brook Ave., Deer Park, NY 11729: Catalog $3 ❖ Replica Tiffany and other stained glass lamps. 516-667-0202.

Stanley Galleries, 2118 N. Clark St., Chicago, IL 60614: Free information ❖ Antique American chandeliers and light fixtures. 312-281-1614.

Star Antler Designs, P.O. Box 3093, Lake Isabella, CA 93240: Catalog $5 ❖ Deer antler chandeliers, lamps, furniture, mirrors, and decorative accessories. 619-379-5777.

Studio Steel, 159 New Milford Tnpk., New Preston, CT 06777: Catalog $2 ❖ Lamps, chandeliers, sconces, mirrors, and hand-wrought metalwork. 800-800-5217; 860-868-7305 (in CT).

Task Lighting Corporation, P.O. Box 1090, Kearney, NE 68848: Free information ❖ Indoor lighting fixtures. 800-445-6404.

The Tin Knocker, P.O. Box 164, Essex, CT 06426: Catalog $2 ❖ Reproduction 18th-century indoor and outdoor lighting fixtures.

The Tinhorn, 1852 Forest Ln., Crown Point, IN 46307: Catalog $3 ❖ Pewter-like, copper or antiqued copper, and punched-heart scalloped chandeliers, sconces, and other items. 219-988-3332.

Urban Archaeology, 285 Lafayette St., New York, NY 10012: Free information ❖ Antique lighting. 212-431-6969.

Vermont Industries, P.O. Box 301, Rt. 103, Cuttingsville, VT 05738: Catalog $3 ❖ Wrought-iron and solid brass chandeliers, floor and table lamps, and wall fixtures. 800-639-1715; 802-492-3451 (in VT).

Victorian Lampshades by Nadja Rider, 3440 Essex Ct., Craig, CO 81625: Catalog $4 (refundable) ❖ Handcrafted Victorian lamps. 970-824-9333.

Victorian Lightcrafters Ltd., P.O. Box 350, Slate Hill, NY 10973: Catalog $3 (refundable) ❖ Handcrafted Victorian-style lighting fixtures. 914-355-1300.

Victorian Lighting Works, 251 S. Pennsylvania Ave., P.O. Box 469, Centre Hall, PA 16828: Catalog $5 (refundable) ❖ Victorian-style lighting fixtures. 814-364-9577.

Village Lantern, 598 Union St., North Marshfield, MA 02059: Brochure 50¢ ❖ Handcrafted colonial-style chandeliers and lanterns. 617-834-8121.

Washington Copper Works, 49 South St., Washington, CT 06793: Catalog $3 (refundable) ❖ Handcrafted copper lanterns and wall fixtures. 203-868-7527.

Lt. Moses Willard Inc., 1156 US 50, Milford, OH 45150: Catalog $8.50 (request list of retail sources) ❖ Chandeliers, wall sconces, exterior lighting units, candle holders and lanterns, wall lamps, table lamps, and reproduction lighting fixtures from styles of the 1700s. 513-248-5500.

❖ LAMPS & LIGHTING ❖

Workshops of David T. Smith, 3600 Shawhan Rd., Morrow, OH 45152: Catalog $5 ❖ Reproduction lamps and chandeliers, furniture, and pottery. 513-932-2472.

Lamp Shades

Ala Lite, 380 E. 1700 South, Salt Lake City, UT 84115: Free information ❖ Restored and reproduction antique lamps, shades, chandeliers, and parts. 800-388-5456.

Aladdin Industries Inc., Lamp Division, P.O. Box 100255, Nashville, TN 37224: Free catalog ❖ Lamps, lamp shades, and replacement parts. 800-456-1233.

Art Wire Works Company, 5401 W. 65th St., Chicago, IL 60638: Free catalog ❖ Lampshade components. 800-336-0097; 708-458-3993 (in IL).

Birds of Paradise Lampshades, 114 Sherbourne St., Toronto, Ontario, Canada M5A 2R2: Free information ❖ Custom silk, parchment, and mica lampshades. 416-366-4067.

Brass Light Gallery, 131 S. 1st St., Milwaukee, WI 53204: Catalog $5 ❖ Replacement glass shades and lamps. 800-243-9595.

Burdoch Victorian Lamp Company, 757 N. Twin Oaks Valley Rd., San Marcos, CA 92069: Catalog $5 ❖ Lamp bases and long-fringed lamp shades in satinized polyester. 800-783-8738.

Fantasy Lighting, 7126 Melrose Ave., Los Angeles, CA 90046: Brochure $4 ❖ Victorian shades and lamp bases. 213-933-7244.

Garber's Crafted Lighting, Rt. 2, Box 140, Mammoth Spring, AR 72554: Catalog $4 ❖ Punched pewter-tin Tiffany shades. 501-966-4996.

Heart Enterprise, 101 Sharon Way, Roseville, CA 95678: Catalog $3 ❖ Victorian-style lamp shade kits and supplies. 916-783-4802.

Indulgence Lampshade Supplies, P.O. Box 8180, Bend, OR 97701: Free catalog ❖ Frames, beaded fringes, lace, bases, and lamp supplies. 541-317-1900.

Kiti Inc., P.O. Box 368, Woodstock, IL 60098: Catalog $4 ❖ Easy-to-follow patterns for one-of-a-kind hand-sewn Victorian lamp shades.

Lamp Glass, P.O. Box 791, Cambridge, MA 02140: Catalog $1 ❖ Replacement glass lamp shades and parts. 617-497-0770.

Lamp Shop, P.O. Box 3606, Concord, NH 03302: Catalog $2 ❖ Lampshade crafting supplies and kits. 603-224-1603.

Lamps by Lynne, P.O. Box 190, Pipersville, PA 18947: Free information ❖ Lamps and lamp shades. 215-766-7615.

Lampshades of Antique, P.O. Box 2, Medford, OR 97501: Catalog $4 ❖ Antique-style lamp shades. 503-826-9737.

Mainly Shades, One Hundred Gray Rd., Falmouth, ME 04105: Catalog $3 ❖ Lampshade crafting supplies and how-to books. 207-797-7568.

Oriental Lamp Shade Company, 816 Lexington Ave., New York, NY 10021: Free information ❖ In-stock silk and custom hand-sewn lampshades. 212-832-8190.

The Renovator's Supply, P.O. Box 2515, Conway, NH 03818: Free catalog ❖ Replacement glass shades, ceiling fixtures, and hanging, table, floor, and wall lamps. 800-659-0203.

Shades of Olde, 6040 Sherry Lane, Dallas, TX 75225: Catalog $2 ❖ Handmade lamp shades. 214-363-7510.

Shades of the Past, P.O. Box 206, Fairfax, CA 94930: Catalog $4 ❖ Fringed and beaded lamp shades. 415-459-6999.

Shady Lady, 5020 W. Eisenhower, Loveland, CO 80537: Catalog $3.50 ❖ Lamp shades. 303-669-1080.

Timeless Traditions, 5087 E. Taft Rd., St. Johns, MI 48879: Free information ❖ Reproduction Victorian lampshades. 517-834-2527.

Turn of the Century Lampshades, P.O. Box 6599, Bend, OR 97708: Brochure $5 ❖ Victorian-style lampshades. 503-382-1802.

Victorian Classics Lampshades, 4116 NE Sandy Blvd., Portland, OR 97212: Catalog $2 ❖ Handcrafted Victorian-style lampshades. 503-282-7055.

Victorian Lampshades, Nadja Rider, 3440 Essex Ct., Craig, CO 81625: Catalog $4 (refundable) ❖ Victorian-style fabric lampshades and bases. 970-824-9333.

Yestershades, 4327 SE Hawthorne, Portland, OR 97215: Catalog $3.50 ❖ Handcrafted Victorian silk lamp shades with lamp bases to match. 503-235-5645.

Outdoor Lighting

AK Exteriors, 298 Leisure Ln., Clint, TX 79836: Catalog $4 ❖ Cast-aluminum furniture, lighting fixtures, and mail boxes. 915-851-2594.

Ameron Pole Products Division, 1020 B St., Fillmore, CA 93015: Free information ❖ Traditional light poles that complement period and modern architectural styles. 800-552-6376.

Authentic Designs, The Mill Rd., West Rupert, VT 05776: Catalog $3 ❖ Outdoor post lighting units and handcrafted reproduction 18th-century Early American lighting fixtures in brass, copper, or tin. 802-394-7713.

Brandon Industries, 1601 W. Wilmeth Rd., McKinney, TX 75069: Free catalog ❖ Cast-aluminum street lamps and old-fashioned pedestal mail boxes with solid brass letter slot and cylinder key lock. 214-542-3000.

Cast Aluminum Reproductions, P.O. Box 1060, San Elizario, TX 79849: Catalog $2 ❖ Cast-aluminum and brass furniture, street lights, outdoor furniture, fountains, mail boxes, and plant stands. 915-764-3793.

Classic Lamp Posts, 3645 NW 67th St., Miami, FL 33147: Free catalog ❖ Colonial and Victorian-style lamp posts with single or multiple plastic globes. 800-654-5852.

Copper Craft Lighting Inc., 5100 Clayton Rd., Ste. 291, Concord, CA 94521: Free information ❖ Handmade copper landscape lights. 510-672-4337.

Copper House, RFD 1, Box 4, Epsom, NH 03234: Catalog $3 ❖ Indoor and outdoor lighting fixtures and hand-hammered copper weather vanes. 603-736-9798.

Josiah R. Coppersmythe, 80 Stiles Rd., Boylston, MA 01505: Catalog $3 ❖ Handcrafted brass or copper Early American indoor and outdoor lighting fixtures. 508-869-2769.

Doner Design Inc., 2175 Beaver Valley Pike, New Providence, PA 17560: Free brochure ❖ Copper landscape lights. 717-786-8891.

Escort Lighting, 201 Sweitzer Rd., Sinking Spring, PA 19608: Free information ❖ Lighting for garden ponds and landscape arrangements.

Genie House, P.O. Box 2478, Vincentown, NJ 08088: Catalog $5 ❖ Indoor and outdoor reproduction lighting fixtures. 800-634-3643.

Great Plains Polymers, 3385 N. 88th Plaza, Omaha, NE 68134: Free brochure ❖ Steel light poles for residential and courtyard lighting. 800-677-1131.

Hanover Lantern, 470 High St., Hanover, PA 17331: Free information ❖ Heavy duty cast-aluminum landscape lighting fixtures. 717-632-6464.

Heathkit Educational Systems, P.O. Box 1288, Benton Harbor, MI 49023: Free catalog ❖ Automatic turn-on and turn-off lighting controls. 800-253-0570.

Heritage Lanterns, 70-A Main St., Yarmouth, ME 04096: Catalog $3 ❖ Colonial-style outdoor lighting fixtures. 800-544-6070.

Herwig Lighting, P.O. Box 768, Russellville, AR 72801: Free brochure ❖ Lighting fixtures, bollards, street furniture, antique fence posts, street clocks, and post lanterns. 501-968-2621.

Honeywell Inc., Customer Assistance Center, 27-2164, Honeywell Plaza, P.O. Box 524, Minneapolis, MN 55440: Free information ❖ Motion activated lighting controls. 800-345-6770.

Hubbell Lighting, 2000 Electric Way, Christiansburg, VA 24073: Catalog $5 ❖ Low-voltage outdoor lighting systems. 703-382-6111.

Intermatic Lighting Inc., Intermatic Plaza, Spring Grove, IL 60081: Free information ❖ Low-voltage outdoor lighting systems. 815-675-2321.

Juno Lighting Inc., P.O. Box 5065, Des Plaines, IL 60017: Free information ❖ Indoor and outdoor lighting fixtures. 708-827-9880.

KIM Lighting, 16555 E. Gale Ave., P.O. Box 1275, City of Industry, CA 91749: Free information ❖ Landscape lighting equipment. 818-968-5666.

Lamplighter Corner Inc., P.O. Box 235, Edgartown, MA 02539: Free brochure ❖ Handmade solid brass and copper lanterns. 508-627-4656.

Legendary Lighting by Copper Sculptures, 1016 N. Flowood Dr., Jackson, MS 39208: Free brochure ❖ Handcrafted gas lanterns and architectural accent pieces. 601-936-4200.

Leviton Manufacturing Company, 59-25 Little Neck Pkwy., Little Neck, NY 11362: Free information ❖ Indoor and outdoor lighting fixtures. 800-323-8920.

Lightolier, 7151 Columbia Gateway Dr., Ste. A, Columbia, MD 21046: Free information ❖ Indoor and outdoor lighting fixtures. 410-995-6395.

Liteform Designs, P.O. Box 3316, Portland, OR 97208: Free information ❖ Low-voltage, incandescent, and fluorescent garden, driveway, post, and wall-mounted lighting units. 800-458-2505.

Mel-Nor Industries, 303 Gulf Bank, Houston, TX 77037: Information $1 ❖ Park benches, old-time lamp posts, and lawn and hanging porch swings. 713-445-3485.

Moultrie Manufacturing, P.O. Box 1179, Moultrie, GA 31776: Catalog $3 ❖ Cast-aluminum indoor and outdoor lighting fixtures, tables, chairs, settees, planters, urns, fountains, and chaises. 800-841-8674.

Sentry Electric Corporation, 185 Buffalo Ave., Freeport, NY 11520: Free information ❖ Colonial and early 1900s-style cast-aluminum lamp posts, area lighting fixtures, and accessories. 516-379-4660.

Spring City Electrical Manufacturing Company, P.O. Box 19, Spring City, PA 19475: Free catalog ❖ Heavy-duty cast-iron ornamental lamp posts. 215-948-4000.

Sternberg, 5801 N. Tripp Ave., Chicago, IL 60646: Free catalog ❖ Vintage lighting fixtures and ornamental poles. 312-478-4777.

Task Lighting Corporation, P.O. Box 1090, Kearney, NE 68848: Free information ❖ Indoor lighting fixtures. 800-445-6404.

Toro Company, 8111 Lyndale Ave., Bloomington, MN 55420: Free information ❖ Outdoor lighting units for landscape and security settings with optional power packs and photo sensors. 800-321-8676.

Tower Lighting Center, P.O. Box 1043, North Adams, MA 01247: Catalog $3 ❖ Hand-wrought copper lanterns. 413-663-7681.

U.S. Gaslight Company, 4658 S. Old Peachtree Rd., Norcross, GA 30071: Free information ❖ Lighting standards. 800-241-4317.

Urban Farmer Store, 2833 Vicente St., San Francisco, CA 94116: Catalog $1 ❖ Low-voltage outdoor lighting. 800-753-3747; 415-661-2204 (in CA).

Ultraviolet Light

Alpha Supply, P.O. Box 2133, Bremerton, WA 98310: Catalog $3 ❖ Ultraviolet lighting, jewelry-making, prospecting, and rockhounding equipment. 360-373-3302.

Bourget Bros., 1636 11th St., Santa Monica, CA 90404: Catalog $3 ❖ Ultraviolet lighting and rock-polishing equipment, jewelry-making tools, and supplies. 310-450-6556.

Cal-Gold, 2569 E. Colorado Blvd., Pasadena, CA 91107: Free catalog ❖ Ultraviolet lighting equipment, metal detectors, supplies for miners and geologists, maps, and books. 818-792-6161.

Diamond Pacific Tool Corporation, 2620 W. Main St., Barstow, CA 92311: Free catalog ❖ Ultraviolet lighting equipment. 800-253-2954.

Ebersole Lapidary Supply Inc., 11417 West Hwy. 54, Wichita, KS 67209: Catalog $2 ❖ Ultraviolet lighting equipment and jewelry-making, rockhounding, and bead-stringing supplies. 316-722-4771.

Gemstone Equipment Manufacturing Company, 750 Easy St., Simi Valley, CA 93065: Free information ❖ Ultraviolet lighting and lapidary equipment. 800-235-3375; 805-527-6990 (in CA).

Graves Company, 1800 Andrews Ave., Pompano Beach, FL 33069: Free catalog ❖ Ultraviolet lighting, rockhounding, and lapidary equipment. 800-327-9103.

Jeanne's Rock & Jewelry, 5420 Bissonet, Bellaire, TX 77401: Price list $1 ❖ Ultraviolet lighting equipment. 713-664-2988.

Raytech, 147 West St., P.O. Box 449, Middlefield, CT 06455: Free information ❖ Cabochon machines, trim and slab saws, faceting machines, and ultraviolet lighting and other equipment. 203-349-3421.

Riviera Lapidary Supply, 30595 Mesquite, Riviera, TX 78379: Catalog $3 ❖ Ultraviolet lighting equipment. 512-296-3958.

Taiclet Enterprises, Margie Taiclet, 440 Los Encinos Ave., San Jose, CA 95134: Free information ❖ Portable longwave ultraviolet blacklight. 408-954-8556.

UVP Inc., 2066 W. 11th St., Upland, CA 91786: Free information ❖ Short-wave, long-wave, and short/long-wave ultraviolet lighting equipment. 800-452-6788.

Wright's Rock Shop, 3612 Albert Pike, Hot Springs, AR 71913: Catalog $3 ❖ Ultraviolet lighting equipment. 501-767-4800.

LANGUAGE TRANSLATORS

Bengold Associates Inc., P.O. Box 3608, Cherry Hill, NJ 08034: Free information ❖ Portable, light-weight electronic English-Hebrew and Hewbrew-English dictionary. Optional installable extension cards for medical, legal, technical/professional, and business/office terminology available. 800-783-7417; 609-779-7841 (in NJ).

LEATHER CRAFTS

Bead Boppers, 11224 Meridian, East Puyallup, WA 98373: Catalog $2.50 (refundable) ❖ Beads and findings, tools, charms, seed beads, leather, supplies, and books. 206-848-3880.

Berman Leathercraft, 25 Melcher St., Boston, MA 02210: Catalog $3 (refundable) ❖ Chamois, suede, and leather for crafting. 617-426-0870.

Leather Unlimited, 7155 Cty. Hwy. B, P.O. Box 1, Belgium, WI 53004: Catalog $2 (refundable) ❖ Leather-crafting supplies and kits. 414-999-9464.

Muir & McDonald Company, Tanners, P.O. Box 136, Dallas, OR 97338: Free brochure ❖ Vegetable tanned leather. 800-547-1299.

Nasco, 901 Janesville Ave., Fort Atkinson, WI 53538: Free catalog ❖ Leather-crafting supplies, tools, and kits. 800-558-9595.

Tandy Leather Company, P.O. Box 791, Fort Worth, TX 76101: Catalog $3 (refundable) ❖ Leather-crafting kits, tools, books, patterns, sewing notions, and how-to videos.

Veteran Leather Company Inc., 204 25th St., Brooklyn, NY 11232: Free information ❖ Leather-crafting supplies, tools, and kits. 800-221-7565; 718-768-0300 (in NY).

LEFT-HANDED MERCHANDISE

Assenheimer Bows, 1005 River Rd., Bucyrus, OH 44820: Free brochure ❖ Handmade bows for right or left-handed persons with a choice of optional lengths. 419-562-7253.

Bob Charles, 1972 Williston Rd., South Burlington, VT 05403: Free price list ❖ Golf equipment for lefties. 800-533-8437.

Left Hand Center, 210 W. Grant, Unit 215, Minneapolis, MN 55403: Catalog $2 ❖ Gifts for left-handed persons. 612-375-0319.

Lefthanders International, P.O. Box 8249, Topeka, KS 66608: Catalog $2 ❖ Items for lefties. 913-234-2177.

Lefties Only, 1972 Williston Rd., South Burlington, VT 05403: Free price list ❖ Golf equipment for left-handed persons. 800-533-8437.

Odyssey Golf, 1945 Camino Vida Roble, Ste. J, Carlsbad, CA 92008: Free brochure ❖ Bags, hats, shirts, and left-handed putters. 800-487-5664.

The Southpaw Shoppe, Catalog Dept., P.O. Box 2870, San Diego, CA 92112: Free catalog ❖ Products for the left-handed person. 619-239-1731.

LOG SPLITTERS

Bailey's, P.O. Box 550, Laytonville, CA 95454: Free catalog ❖ Chain saws, bars, files, protective gear, forestry supplies, log splitters, books, other woodsman supplies, and gifts. 707-984-6133.

Mainline of North America, P.O. Box 526, London, OH 43140: Free information ❖ All-gear driven tiller with optional sickle bar and no belts or chains. Also hydraulic log splitter, carts, and snow throwers. 800-837-2097.

Mobile Manufacturing Company, P.O. Box 250, Troutdale, OR 97060: Free brochure ❖ Portable electric or gasoline-powered saw for cutting logs. 503-666-5593.

Northern Hydraulics, P.O. Box 1499, Burnsville, MN 55337: Free catalog ❖ Log splitters, gas engines, trailer parts, and tools. 800-533-5545.

Timberking Inc., 1431 N. Topping, Kansas City, MO 64120: Free information ❖ Portable one-man saw mill. 800-942-4406.

Wood-Mizer, 8180 W. 10th St., Indianapolis, IN 46214: Catalog $2 ❖ Portable sawmills and tools. 800-553-0219.

LUGGAGE, LUGGAGE-CARRIERS & BRIEFCASES

A to Z Luggage, 4627 New Utrecht Ave., Brooklyn, NY 11219: Free catalog ❖ Luggage and small leather goods. 800-342-5011; 718-435-2880 (in NY).

Ace Leather Products, 2211 Avenue U, Brooklyn, NY 11229: Free catalog ❖ Desk sets, leather attaché cases, luggage, wallets, handbags, and other gifts. 800-342-5223.

Al's Luggage, 2134 Larimer St., Denver, CO 80205: Catalog $2 (refundable) ❖ Luggage carts and luggage. 303-295-9009.

Altman Luggage, 135 Orchard St., New York, NY 10001: Free information ❖ Luggage, leather goods, and pens and pencils. 800-372-3377.

American Executive, Kittery Business Center, 72 Dow Hwy., Kittery, ME 03904: Catalog $2 ❖ Writing portfolios, travel cases and packs, day planners, wallets, briefcases and backpacks, and other leather essentials. 800-804-0825.

Asics Tiger Corporation, 10540 Talbert Ave., West Building, Fountain Valley, CA 92708: Free information ❖ Carryalls, tote bags, duffles, and shoulder bags. 800-678-9435.

Bally of Switzerland for Ladies, 689 Madison Ave., New York, NY 10021: Free information ❖ Women's shoes, clothing, luggage, and small leather goods. 212-751-2163.

Bally of Switzerland for Men, 711 5th Ave., New York, NY 10022: Free information ❖ Men's shoes, clothing, luggage, and small leather goods. 212-751-9082.

Bondy Export Corporation, 40 Canal St., New York, NY 10002: Free information with long SASE ❖ Luggage and accessories, appliances, typewriters, cameras, TVs, and video equipment. 212-925-7785.

Border Leather, 3800 Main St., Chula Vista, CA 91911: Free catalog ❖ Leather and textile goods. 800-732-6936.

Bottega Veneta, 635 Madison Ave., New York, NY 10022: Free catalog ❖ Wallets, purses and handbags, luggage, and small leather goods. 212-371-5511.

Coach Leatherware Company, 410 Commerce Blvd., Carlstadt, NJ 07072: Free catalog ❖ Leather handbags, gloves, belts, wallets, and briefcases. 201-460-4716.

The Complete Traveler of Overland Park, 7321 W. 80th St., Overland Park, KS 66204: Free catalog ❖ Maps, travel books, travel accessories, and luggage. 888-862-0888.

Copper Star Cattle & Trading Company, 2000 W. 3rd St., Amarillo, TX 79106: Catalog $2 ❖ Cowhide purses, wallets, satchels and bags, and accessories. 800-828-0442.

Creative House, 100 Business Pkwy., Richardson, TX 75081: Free catalog ❖ Luggage, briefcases, attaché cases, handbags, and wallets. 800-527-5940; 214-231-3463 (in TX).

Crouch & Fitzgerald, 400 Madison Ave., New York, NY 10017: Free information ❖ Leather goods with optional monogramming. 800-6-CROUCH; 212-755-5888 (in NY).

Lucy De Fave, Mason Woods Village Mall, 13476 Clayton Rd., St. Louis, MO 63131: Catalog $3 ❖ Quilted handbags, luggage, clothing, and accessories. 314-576-4717.

Dooney & Bourke Inc., 759 Madison Ave., New York, NY 10021: Free catalog ❖ Leather goods and accessories. 800-226-9046.

Double L Leatherworks, P.O. Box 1271, Taylor, TX 76574: Catalog $1 ❖ Hand-tooled leather purses, tote bags, wallets, and other western-style items. 512-352-6640.

Dunns, P.O. Box 449, Grand Junction, TN 38039: Free catalog ❖ Camouflage and insulated clothing, outerwear, shoes and boots, hunting equipment, day and belt packs, gun care kits, sunglasses, game calls, decoys, and supplies. 800-223-8667.

Eagle Creek, 1740 La Costa Meadows Dr., San Marcos, CA 92069: Free list of retail sources ❖ Luggage. 800-874-9925.

Charolette Ford Trunks, P.O. Box 536, Spearman, TX 79081: Catalog $3.50 ❖ Supplies and tools for restoring trunks. 806-659-3027.

Georgetown Leather Design/Tannery West, 400 S. Hwy. 169, Ste. 600, Minneapolis, MN 55426: Free list of retail sources ❖ Outerwear for men and women, purses, brief cases, and accessories.

Hilsport by Hilco Inc., 2102 Fair Park Blvd., Harlingen, TX 78550: Free brochure ❖ Luggage and gun cases. 210-423-1885.

Innovation Luggage, 20 Enterprise Ave., Secaucus, NJ 07094: Free list of retail sources ❖ Luggage, briefcases, portfolios, attaché cases, and handbags. 800-722-1800.

Kart-A-Bag, 510 Manhattan Rd., Joliet, IL 60433: Free list of retail sources ❖ Telescoping easy-to-store luggage transporter. 800-423-9328.

Kelty Packs Inc., 1224 Fern Ridge Pkwy., St. Louis, MO 63141: Free list of retail sources ❖ Cordura nylon backpacks that convert to luggage. 314-576-8069.

Lodis Corporation, 2261 S. Carme Lina Ave., Los Angeles, CA 90064: Free catalog ❖ Leather luggage, shaving and toilet kits, briefcases, note pads, wallets, and management systems. 800-421-8674; 310-207-6841 (in CA).

The Luggage Center, 960 Remillard St., San Jose, CA 95122: Free information with long SASE ❖ Luggage and accessories. 800-626-6789.

Madden Mountaineering, 2400 Central Ave., Boulder, CO 80301: Free catalog ❖ Carryalls, tote bags, duffles, and shoulder bags. 303-442-5828.

Mascot Metropolitan Inc., 380 Swift Ave., Unit 18, South San Francisco, CA 94080: Free brochure ❖ Luggage and computer equipment carriers. 415-873-0254.

Charles Miller Designs, 521 Truett Dr., Tallahassee, FL 32303: Free brochure ❖ Soft leather bags for carrying or wearing on the back. 800-624-4443.

Mont-Bell, Catalog Customer Service, 940 1st Ave., Santa Cruz, CA 95062: Free catalog ❖ Tri-fold garment bags. 800-683-2002.

North Beach Leather, 1335 Columbus Ave., San Francisco, CA 94133: Catalog $3 ❖ Men and women's leather clothing. 415-346-1113.

North Face, 999 Harrison St., Berkeley, CA 94710: Free list of retail sources ❖ Carryalls, tote bags, duffles, and shoulder bags. 800-447-2333.

Orvis Travel, 1711 Blue Hills Dr., P.O. Box 12000, Roanoke, VA 24022: Free catalog ❖ Luggage, travel accessories, and men and women's clothing. 800-541-3541.

Port Canvas Inc., P.O. Box H, Kennebunkport, ME 04046: Free brochure ❖ Canvas duffels, handbags, briefcases, general luggage and accessories, totes, and stroller and sports bags. 800-333-6788.

Tavros Leather, 217 Newbury St., Boston, MA 02116: Free brochure ❖ European styled saddle bags, briefcases, pouches, and other leather items. 800-8-TAVROS.

Hugh & Jennie Vaughn Luggage, 1613 Water St., Kerrville, TX 78028: Free information ❖ Italian tapestry handbags, luggage, and travel accessories. 800-626-8657; 210-896-7828 (in TX).

LUMBER

A & M Wood Specialty Inc., 358 Eagle St. North, Box 3204, Cambridge, Ontario, Canada N3H 5M2: Free catalog ❖ Hardwoods and veneers. 519-653-9322.

Adams Wood Products Inc., 974 Forest Dr., Morristown, TN 37814: Free catalog ❖ Kiln-dried oak, Honduras mahogany, walnut, cherry, maple, pine turning squares, and carving blanks. 615-587-2942.

Albany Woodworks, P.O. Box 729, Albany, LA 70711: Free information ❖ Antique lumber. 504-567-1155.

Anderson-McQuaid Company Inc., 170 Fawcett St., Cambridge, MA 02138: Free price list ❖ Custom and restoration molding, flooring, and paneling. 617-876-3250.

Architectural Timber & Millwork, 35 Mount Warner Rd., P.O. Box 719, Hadley, MA 01035: Free information ❖ Antique flooring, new wide plank flooring, and antique and reproduction beams and timber frames. 413-586-3045.

Barber Lumber Sales Inc., P.O. Box 263, Alachua, FL 32615: Free information ❖ Heart cypress, pine, and other softwood. 904-462-3772.

Berea Hardwoods Company, 6367 Eastland Rd., Brookpark, OH 44142: Free information ❖ Exotic hardwoods, figured woods, other lumber, and squares, planks, and burls. 216-243-4452.

❖ **LUMBER** ❖

Blue Ox Lumber, 2050 Elmwood Ave., Buffalo, NY 14207: Free information ❖ Optional wide and thick hardwoods. 800-758-0950.

Boulter Plywood Corporation, 24 Broadway, Somerville, MA 02145: Free catalog ❖ Domestic and exotic hardwood, other lumber, and marine plywood. 617-666-1340.

Bre Lumber/Rare Earth Hardwoods, 6778 E. Traverse Hwy., Traverse City, MI 49684: Free information ❖ Hardwood, other lumber, flooring, and decking. 800-968-0074.

Bristol Valley Hardwoods, 4054 Rt. 64 at Rt. 20A, Canandaigua, NY 14424: Catalog $1 ❖ Cherry, poplar, red oak, and hard maple. 800-724-0132.

Broad-Axe Beam Company, RD 2, Box 417, West Brattleboro, VT 05301: Price list $2 ❖ Wide pine flooring and beaded edge paneling. 802-257-0064.

Certainly Wood, 11753 Big Tree Rd., East Aurora, NY 14052: Free catalog ❖ Veneers and plywood. 716-655-0206.

Cirtain Plywood Inc., 677 Galloway Ave., Memphis, TN 38105: Free information ❖ Exotic and domestic premium hardwoods. Also plywood, abrasives, glues, and veneer. 800-593-3304.

Colonial Hardwoods Inc., 7953 Cameron Brown Ct., Springfield, VA 22158: Free information ❖ Hardwood and moldings. 800-466-5451; 703-451-9217 (in VA).

Maurice L. Condon Company, 252 Ferris Ave., White Plains, NY 10603: Catalog $2 ❖ Exotic woods and plywood. 914-946-4111.

Constantine, 2050 Eastchester Rd., Bronx, NY 10461: Catalog $1 ❖ Cabinet and furniture wood, veneers, plans, hardware, how-to books, carving tools and chisels, inlay designs, and supplies. 800-223-8087; 718-792-1600 (in NY).

Craftsman Lumber Company, 436 Main St., Groton, MA 01450: Information $2 ❖ Oak and pine flooring and paneling in widths up to 30 inches. 508-448-5621.

Craftsman Wood Service, 1735 W. Cortland Ct., Addison, IL 60101: Catalog $2 ❖ Kiln-dried and imported rare woods, veneers, hand and power tools, hardware, finishing materials, and clock movements and kits. 708-629-3100.

CraftWoods, 2101 Greenspring Dr., Timonium, MD 21093: Free catalog ❖ Kiln-dried domestic and exotic woods, and woodworking, wood carving, and power tools. 800-468-7070.

DJ Hardwoods, 317 Nebraska Ave., Columbia, MO 65201: Free brochure ❖ Hardwoods. 800-514-3449.

Donnell's Clapboard Mill, Country Rd., RR Box 1560, Sedgwick, ME 04676: Free information ❖ Quarter-sawn clapboard. 207-359-2036.

Downes & Reader Hardwood Company Inc., Box 456, Evans Dr., Stoughton, MA 02072: Free information ❖ Hardwoods, softwoods, and plywood. 800-788-5568; 617-442-8050 (in MA).

Duluth Timber Company, P.O. Box 16717, Duluth, MN 55816: Free information ❖ Beams, millwork, paneling, and flooring from recycled old-growth timbers from bridges and buildings. 218-727-2145.

Gilmer Wood Company, 2211 NW St. Helens Rd., Portland, OR 97210: Free information ❖ Exotic wooden logs, planks, and squares. 503-274-1271.

Good Hope Hardwoods, 1627 New London Rd., Landenburg, PA 19350: Free information ❖ Exotic and domestic hardwoods. 610-274-8841.

Granville Manufacturing Company Inc., P.O. Box 15, Rt. 100, Granville, VT 05747: Free brochure ❖ Quarter-sawn clapboard siding. 802-767-4747.

Groff & Hearne Lumber, 858 Scotland Rd., Quarryville, PA 17566: Free information ❖ Walnut, cherry, and other woods. 800-342-0001; 717-284-0001 (in PA).

The Harbor Sales Company Inc., 1401 Russell St., Baltimore, MD 21230: Information $1 ❖ Exotic woods. 800-345-1712.

The Hardwood Store, 1695 Dalton Dr., New Carlisle, OH 45344: Free catalog ❖ Lumber, plywood, and veneers. 800-849-9174.

Joinery Company, P.O. Box 518, Tarboro, NC 27886: Catalog $5 ❖ Reproduction flooring, millwork, cabinets, furniture, and timber frames in antique heart pine. 800-726-7463.

Mountain Lumber, P.O. Box 289, Ruckersville, VA 22968: Free information ❖ Recycled antique heart pine from pre-1900 buildings and antique American oak from century-old Appalachian barns. 800-445-2671.

Niagara Lumber & Wood Products Inc., 47 Elm St., East Aurora, NY 14052: Free information ❖ Northern Appalachian hardwood. 800-274-0397.

Sandy Pond Hardwoods, 921-A Lancaster Pike, Quarryville, PA 17566: Free information ❖ Exotic and domestic hardwoods. 800-934-4873; 209-532-1260 (in PA).

Pioneer Millworks, 1755 Pioneer Rd., Shortsville, NY 14548: Free information ❖ Reproduction period flooring from reclaimed timbers. Also trim, lumber, and board stock. 716-289-3090.

Randle Woods, P.O. Box 96, Randle, WA 98377: Free information ❖ Custom-cut wood from the northwest. 800-845-8042.

Specialty Lumber Inc., 6412 Yelton Rd., Appling, GA 30802: Free information ❖ Antique heart pine and lumber. 706-541-9231.

Superior Hardwoods & Millwork Inc., P.O. Box 4731, Missoula, MN 59806: Information $3 ❖ New and antique flooring, paneling, and molding. 800-572-9601.

Talarico Hardwoods, RD 3, Box 3268, Mohnton, PA 19540: Free catalog ❖ Quarter-sawn white oak, red oak, and figured lumber. 610-775-0400.

Mitch Talcove, Tropical Exotic Hardwoods, P.O. Box 1806, Carlsbad, CA 92018: Free price list ❖ Exotic hardwoods. 619-434-3030.

Tradewinds, HCR Box 64, Grafton, VT 05146: Free information ❖ Hardwoods. 802-843-2594.

Tropical Exotic Hardwoods, Box 1806, Carlsbad, CA 92018: Free information with long SASE ❖ Ebony, cocobolo, satinwood, and other exotic species. 619-434-3030.

Steve Wall Lumber Company, Box 287, Mayodan, NC 27027: Catalog $1 ❖ Hardwoods and woodworking machinery. 800-633-4062; 910-427-0637 (in NC).

Wood-Ply Lumber Corporation, 100 Bennington Ave., Freeport, NY 11520: Free price list ❖ Domestic and exotic hardwoods. 516-378-2612.

Woodhouse Antique Flooring, P.O. Box 7336, Rocky Mount, NC 27804: Free brochure; sample kit $15 ❖ Antique flooring, molding, stairparts, and new wood. 919-977-7336.

The Woods Company, 2357 Boteler Rd., Brownsville, MD 21715: Free information ❖ Antique lumber, custom flooring, and interior millwork. 301-432-8419.

Woodworker's Dream, Division Martin Guitar Company, 510 Sycamore St., Nazareth, PA 18064: Free information ❖ Exotic and domestic hardwoods and musical instrument woods. 800-345-3103.

Woodworkers' Paradise, 121 W. Nyack Rd., Unit 5, Nanuet, NY 10954: Free information ❖ Exotic and domestic hardwoods. Also carving and turning supplies. 914-624-1100.

Woodworkers Source, 5402 S. 40th St., Phoenix, AZ 85040: Free information ❖ Exotic and domestic lumber, plywood, veneers, turning squares, and blanks. 800-423-2450.

MACRAME

Al Con Enterprises, P.O. Box 429, Hickory, NC 28603: Free catalog ❖ Macrame, chair-weaving, and crochet supplies. 800-523-4371.

Craft King Mail Order Dept., P.O. Box 90637, Lakeland, FL 33804: Catalog $2 ❖ Craft, needlework, and macrame supplies. 888-CRAFTY-1.

Frederick J. Fawcett Inc., 1338 Ross St., Petaluma, CA 94954: Free information ❖ Looms, linen embroidery fabrics, macrame supplies, linen/cotton and wool yarns, and fibers. 800-289-9276.

Kings Kountry, Macrame Wholesale Warehouse, 17021 Stephens, Eastpointe, MI 48021: Free catalog ❖ Macrame supplies and easy-to-follow project designs. 810-779-1441.

H.H. Perkins Company, 10 S. Bradley Rd., Woodbridge, CT 06525: Free catalog ❖ Seat weaving and basket-making supplies, macrame supplies, and how-to books. 800-462-6660.

Western Products, Box 103, Poway, CA 92074: Free information ❖ Macrame supplies. 800-680-1328.

MAGIC TRICKS & VENTRILOQUISM

Abbott's Magic Company, 124 St. Joseph, Colon, MI 49040: Catalog $12.50 ❖ Props and close-up and stage magic for amateur and professional magicians. 616-432-3235.

Abracadabra Magic Shop, 125 Lincoln Blvd., Middlesex, NJ 08846: Catalog $5 ❖ Magician's props, close-up and stage magic, juggling equipment, balloons, clown accessories, costumes, and make-up. 908-805-0200.

Ron Allesi, Quality Used & Rare Magic, P.O. Box 54922, Cincinnati, OH 45254: Catalog $5 ❖ Used, rare, and antique magic apparatus. Also early magic sets, books, posters, and magic memorabilia. 513-753-5281.

An Amazing Shaners Castle & Magic Museum, 29 Brown & 6th St., Dayton, OH 45402: Free catalog ❖ Books, equipment, props, and accessories for magicians. 513-222-7853.

Axtell Expressions, 230 Glencrest Circle, Ventura, CA 93003: Catalog $2 ❖ Magic for amateur and professional magicians. 805-642-7282.

Balloon & Magic Store Inc., 88 Ryders Ln., Stratford, CT 06497: Free catalog ❖ Innovative new magic effects. 203-380-1445.

Best Magic Gags & Costumes, 625 S. Magnolia Ave., Anaheim, CA 92804: Free information ❖ Magic, juggling equipment, costumes, gags and gifts, dancewear, and clown items. 714-827-MGIC.

Aunt Clowney's Warehouse, P.O. Box 1444, Corona, CA 91718: Free catalog with two 1st class stamps ❖ Books and novelties for clowns, magicians, puppeteers, face painters, and balloon artists.

Mike Bornstein Clowns, 319 W. 48th St., New York, NY 10036: Free information with long SASE ❖ Magic for amateur and professional magicians.

Brad Burt's Magic Shop, 4690 Convoy St., San Diego, CA 92111: Free information ❖ Magic for amateur and professional magicians. 619-571-4749.

Captain Dick's Dummy Depot, 2631 NW 95th St., Seattle, WA 98117: Information $3 with long SASE ❖ New and used ventriloquist figures and books. 206-784-0883.

Chazpro Magic Company, 603 E. 13th, Eugene, OR 97401: Catalog $3 ❖ Magic for amateur and professional magicians. 503-345-0032.

Cosmar Magic, 6765 El Banquero Pl., San Diego, CA 92119: Catalog $15 ❖ Close-up and stage magic and clown supplies. 619-287-3706.

Steve Dawson's Magic Touch Catalog, 144 N. Milpitas Blvd., Milpitas, CA 95035: Catalog $3 ❖ Magic effects, books, videos, accessories, clown and juggling supplies, and make-up. 408-263-9404.

Daytona Magic, Harry Allen & Irv Cook, 136 S. Beach St., Daytona, FL 32114: Catalog $10 ❖ Props and close-up and stage magic for amateur and professional magicians. 904-252-6767.

Eddie's Trick Shop, 70 S. Park Square, Marietta, GA 30060: Free information ❖ Magic and clown supplies. 800-429-4314.

Alan Ende, 40 Morrow Ave., Scarsdale, NY 10583: List $3 ❖ Ventriloquist figures, accessories, and vintage magic books.

Flora & Company Productions, P.O. Box 8263, Albuquerque, NM 87198: Free catalog ❖ Multi-media equipment and illusions for magicians. 505-255-9988.

David Ginn Magic, 4387 St. Michaels Dr., Lilburn, GA 30247: Catalog $10 ❖ Props, books, and how-to-do magic on video tapes for magicians and clowns.

Jesters Magic Workshop, 1070 Bank St., Painesville, OH 44077: Free information ❖ Magic and props for amateur and professional magicians. 216-354-8749.

Klamm Magic, 1412 Appleton, Independence, MO 64052: Small props catalog $2; illusions catalog $3 ❖ Magic equipment for amateur and professional magicians. 816-461-4595.

La Rock's Fun & Magic Outlet, 3847 Rosehaven Dr., Charlotte, NC 28205: Catalog $3 ❖ Clown and balloon how-to books, balloons, balloon sculpture kits, juggling supplies, and magic equipment. 704-563-9300.

Laflin's Magic & Silks, P.O. Box 228, Sterling, CO 80751: Free information ❖ Entertaining and educational magic on video tapes for clowns and magicians. 303-522-2589.

Hank Lee's Magic Factory, Mail Order Division, P.O. Box 789, Medford, MA 02155: Catalog $4.50 ❖ Magic tricks and illusions, books, props, jokes, and novelties. 617-482-8749.

Magic World of Chatsworth, 10122 Topanga Cyn Blvd., Chatsworth, CA 91311: Free catalog ❖ Magic and juggling supplies for amateur and professional magicians. 818-700-8100.

Maher Studios, P.O. Box 420, Littleton, CO 80160: Catalog $2 ❖ Ventriloquist dummies, scripts and dialogues, puppets, and how-to books. 303-798-6830.

Mastercraft Puppets, P.O. Box 39, Branson, MO 65615: Catalog $2 ❖ Puppets and ventriloquist dummies. 417-561-8100.

Mecca Magic Inc., 49 Dodd St., Bloomfield, NJ 07003: Catalog $10 ❖ Magic and ventriloquism accessories, juggling supplies, make-up, clown equipment, balloons, costumes and wigs, puppets, and props. 201-429-7597.

Steven Meltzer, 670 San Juan, Venice, CA 90291: Free list with long SASE ❖ Marionettes, puppets, and ventriloquist dummies. 310-396-6007.

Meyerbooks Publisher, P.O. Box 427, Glenwood, IL 60425: Free catalog ❖ Books on the history of stage magic, herbs, health, cooking, and Americana. 708-757-4950.

More than Balloons Inc., 2409 Ravendale Ct., Kissimmee, FL 34758: Free information ❖ Regular balloons and accessories, balloons for making sculptures, how-to books, and magic. 800-BALUNES.

Morris Costumes, 3108 Monroe Rd., Charlotte, NC 28205: Catalog $20 ❖ Magic tricks and special effects, costumes, clown props, masks, jokes, novelties, balloons, and books. 704-332-3304.

Norm Nielsen, P.O. Box 34300, Las Vegas, NV 89133: Catalog $1 ❖ Magic for amateur and professional magicians. 702-656-7674.

Christopher A. Reesman, P.O. Box 187, St. Clair Shores, MI 48080: Free information ❖ Magic for amateur and professional magicians. 810-773-1787.

Matthew Roddy, 3283 Belvedere, Riverside, CA 92507: Free catalog ❖ Magic for amateur and professional magicians. 909-369-9704.

Ronjo's Magic & Costumes Inc., 4600 Nesconset Hwy., Unit 4, Port Jefferson Station, NY 11776: Catalog $2.50 ❖ Magic for amateur and professional magicians, costumes, and make-up and theatrical effects. 516-928-5005.

Sasco Magic Inc., 11609 Proctor Rd., Philadelphia, PA 19116: Free catalog ❖ Coin and other magic tricks. 215-364-7717.

Show-Biz Services, 1735 E. 26th St., Brooklyn, NY 11229: Free list ❖ Books for magicians. 718-336-0605.

Sparkle's Entertainment Express, Jan Lovell, 152 N. Water St., Gallatin, TN 37066: Product list $1 ❖ Make-up, costumes and clown shoes, balloons, juggling and magic equipment, puppets, books, and supplies. 615-452-9755.

Stevens Magic Emporium, 3238 E. Douglas, Wichita, KS 67208: Catalog $7.50 ❖ Professional magic and books. 316-683-9582.

Tannen's Magic, 24 W. 25th St., New York, NY 10010: Catalog $15 ❖ Close-up and parlor magic, illusions, books, and props for amateurs and professionals. 212-929-4500.

Douglas L. Tilford, P.O. Box 650, Experiment, GA 30212: Catalog $7 ❖ Magic for amateur and professional magicians. 800-537-5381; 404-227-7634 (in GA).

U.S. Toy Company Inc., 1227 E. 119th St., Grandview, MO 64030: Catalog $3 ❖ Parlor magic, professional illusions, and props for magicians. 800-448-7830; 816-761-5900 (in MO).

Windsor Magic, P.O. Box 46067, Chicago, IL 60646: Catalog $3 ❖ Magic for amateur and professional magicians. 312-631-09606.

Meir Yedid Magic, P.O. Box 2566, Fair Lawn, NJ 07410: Catalog $2 ❖ Magic equipment for amateur and professional magicians.

MAGNETS

Bunting Magnetics Company, P.O. Box 468, Newton, KS 67144: Free catalog ❖ Magnets. 800-835-2526; 316-284-2020 (in KS).

Desert Darlings, 4780 W. Plute Ave., Glendale, AZ 85308: Brochure $3 ❖ Magnets for refrigerators and other metal surfaces. Also magnetic picture frames. 602-492-0901.

Edmund Scientific Company, Edscorp Building, Barrington, NJ 08007: Free catalog ❖ Magnets, binoculars, telescopes, and educational and science equipment. 609-573-6260.

Magnet Sales & Manufacturing Company, 11248 Playa Ct., Culver City, CA 90230: Free brochure ❖ Flexible strip, flex-dot, button, and bar magnets. 800-421-6692; 310-391-7213 (in CA).

Nasco, 901 Janesville Ave., Fort Atkinson, WI 53538: Free catalog ❖ Magnets, microscopes, rock collections, astronomy charts and star maps, anatomical models, and other science equipment. 800-558-9595.

S & S Arts & Crafts, 75 Mill St., Dept. 2000, Colchester, CT 06415: Free catalog ❖ Magnets, educational games, puzzles, and arts and crafts projects and supplies. 800-243-9232.

MAGNIFYING GLASSES

Walter Drake & Sons, Drake Building, Colorado Springs, CO 80940: Free catalog ❖ Magnifying glasses. 800-525-9291.

Edmund Scientific Company, Edscorp Building, Barrington, NJ 08007: Free catalog ❖ Magnifying glasses, binoculars, telescopes, and educational and science equipment. 609-573-6260.

Precision Optical, 507 2nd Ave., Rochelle, IL 61068: Catalog $1 ❖ Magnifiers and magnifying and regular sunglasses. 815-562-2174.

Winthrop Coin Company, P.O. Box 519, New York, NY 10024: Free information ❖ Hand-held, pocket, and binocular head magnifiers. 212-245-0371.

MAILBOXES

Acorn Manufacturing Company Inc., 457 School St., P.O. Box 31, Mansfield, MA 02048: Catalog $6 (request list of retail sources) ❖ Locking forged iron mailboxes in vertical and horizontal styles. 800-835-0121; 508-339-4500 (in MA).

AK Exteriors, 298 Leisure Ln., Clint, TX 79836: Catalog $4 ❖ Cast-aluminum furniture, lighting fixtures, and mail boxes. 915-851-2594.

Brandon Industries, 1601 W. Wilmeth Rd., McKinney, TX 75069: Free catalog ❖ Old-fashioned cast-aluminum pedestal mailboxes with solid brass letter slots and cylinder key locks. 214-542-3000.

Cast Aluminum Reproductions, P.O. Box 1060, San Elizario, TX 79849: Catalog $2 ❖ Cast-aluminum and brass street lights, outdoor furniture, fountains, mail boxes, and plant stands. 915-764-3793.

Coppersmiths, Custom Copper & Brass Works, P.O. Box 2675, Oakhurst, CA 93644: Free brochure ❖ Fireplace hoods, cupolas, mailboxes, and dormers. 209-658-8909.

The Edisonville Woodshop, 1916 Edisonville Rd., Strasburg, PA 17579: Brochure $1 ❖ Handcrafted all-wood mailboxes. 717-687-0116.

Frank's Country Store, 162 Washington Ave., North Haven, CT 96473: Free brochure ❖ Handcrafted mailboxes with cedar shingle roofs. 800-875-1960.

Home Decorators Collection, 2025 Concourse Dr., St. Louis, MO 63146: Free catalog ❖ Mailboxes in contemporary and other styles. 800-240-6047; 314-993-6045 (in MO).

Mel-Nor Industries, 303 Gulf Bank, Houston, TX 77037: Information $1 ❖ Mailboxes, park benches, swings, lights, and landscaping items. 713-445-3485.

Redwood Unlimited, P.O. Box 2344, Valley Center, CA 92082: Brochure $2 ❖ Wall and post-mounted mail boxes and weather vanes. 800-283-1717.

Reed Brothers, 5000 Turner Rd., Sebastopol, CA 95472: Catalog $10 ❖ Mail boxes. 707-795-6261.

❖ MAILING LISTS ❖

The Renovator's Supply, P.O. Box 2515, Conway, NH 03818: Free catalog ❖ Victorian-style solid brass mailboxes, decorative accessories, and gifts. 800-659-0203.

MAILING LISTS

Advon, Drawer B, Shelley, ID 83274: Free information ❖ Mixed states mailing lists with adhesive labels. 800-992-3866.

American List Counsel Inc., 88 Orchard Rd., CN 5219, Princeton, NJ 08543: Free catalog ❖ Mailing and telemarketing lists and special high interest databases. 800-ALC-LIST.

Cahners Direct Mail Services, 245 W. 17th St., New York, NY 10011: Free information ❖ Mailing lists. 800-537-7930; 212-337-7167 (in NY).

Direct Response Leads, 1903 Walnut St., #145, Philadelphia, PA 19103: Free information ❖ Mailing lists. 800-465-9173.

C. Felix, I.S.I. Company, 41 Watchung Plaza, Ste. 175, Montclair, NJ 07042: Free information ❖ Mailing lists.

Irwin Hertzsprung Mailing Lists, 1706 Front St., Lynden, WA 98264: Free information ❖ Mailing lists.

List Associates, 116 Kellogg Ave., Ames, IA 50010: Free information ❖ Zip-code sorted mailing lists on self-adhesive labels, magnetic tape, or disk. 800-359-2621.

List-Masters, Box 425, Mt. Sinai, NY 11766: Free information ❖ Mailing lists on adhesive labels. 800-356-8664.

Mascor Lists, Box 8308, Silver Spring, MD 20907: Free information ❖ Mailing lists. 800-568-6127.

Progressive Business Associates, 8223 W. 113th Terrace, Overland Park, KS 66210: Free price list ❖ Mailing lists on self-sticking labels. 913-451-4905.

Quality Lists, P.O. Box 6060, Miller Place, NY 11764: Free information ❖ Computer-generated mailing lists on peel-and-stick labels in zip-code order. 516-744-7289.

Sellmore Lists, P.O. Box 290126, Brooklyn, NY 11229: Free information ❖ Mailing lists on self-adhesive labels, magnetic tape, or disk. 718-645-4111.

Success Lists, P.O. Box 4106, Rocky Point, NY 11778: Free information ❖ Mailing addresses on adhesive labels. 800-382-6815.

MAPS & INFORMATION NAVIGATORS

Access Maps & Gear, 321 S. Guadalupe, Santa Fe, NM 87501: Free catalog ❖ Worldwide maps and geographic gear. 505-982-3330.

Adventure Cycling Association, P.O. Box 8308, 150 E. Pine St., Missoula, MT 59807: Free information ❖ Bicycling maps. 406-721-1776.

Adventurous Traveler Bookstore, P.O. Box 577, Hinesburg, VT 05461: Free catalog ❖ Books and maps for hiking, climbing, kayaking, diving, and travel. 800-282-3963.

American Map Corporation, 46-35 54th Rd., Maspeth, NY 11378: Free information ❖ Maps, travel guides, and atlases. 718-784-0055.

Appalachian Mountain Club Books, 5 Joy Street, Boston, MA 02108: Free catalog ❖ Hiking, river, and recreation guides and maps. 617-523-0636.

W. Graham Arader Maps & Prints, 1000 Boxwood Ct., King of Prussia, PA 19406: Free catalog ❖ Rare maps and prints. 215-825-6570.

Big Ten Inc., P.O. Box 321231, Cocoa Beach, FL 32932: Free information ❖ Geological maps that locate gold-mining sites in California, Alabama, Virginia, and the Carolinas. 407-783-4595.

Bikecentennial, P.O. Box 8308, 150 E. Pine St., Missoula, MT 59807: Free information ❖ Bicycling maps. 406-721-1776.

The Complete Traveler of Overland Park, 7321 W. 80th St., Overland Park, KS 66204: Free catalog ❖ Maps, travel books, travel accessories, and luggage. 888-862-0888.

George F. Cram Company Inc., 301 S. LaSalle St., Indianapolis, IN 46201: Free catalog ❖ Maps, atlases, globes, and charts. 800-227-4199; 317-635-5564 (in IN).

First State Map & Globe, 12 Mary Ella Dr., Wilmington, DE 19805: Free information ❖ USA and world wall maps. 800-327-7992.

Richard Fitch Maps, 2324 Calle Halcon, Santa Fe, NM 87505: Catalog $6 ❖ Antiquarian maps and prints from North America, 16th to 19th-centuries. 505-982-2939.

Forsythe Travel Library Inc., P.O. Box 2975, Shawnee Mission, KS 66201: Free brochure ❖ Travel books, maps, and other publications. 800-367-7984; 913-384-3440 (in KS).

Grace Galleries Inc., Box 2488, Brunswick, ME 04011: Free information (specify items wanted) ❖ Original antique maps, prints, sea charts, and cartographic books. 207-729-1329.

Hammond Incorporated, 515 Valley St., Maplewood, NJ 07040: Free information ❖ Maps and prints, travel guides, road atlases, adult and juvenile references, and books on business. 201-763-6000.

Hays Electronics, P.O. Box 26848, Prescott Valley, AZ 86312: Free catalog ❖ Metal detectors, maps, electronic prospecting tools and accessories, and books on prospecting, mining, and relic hunting. 800-699-2624.

High-Grade Publications, P.O. Box 20904, Cheyenne, WY 82003: Catalog $1 ❖ Books and maps on treasure hunting, gold locations, lost mines, ghost towns, gems and minerals, and geology. 307-634-8835.

Historical Ink, RR1 Secret Lake, Phillipston, MA 01331: Catalog $2 ❖ Old maps of New England towns reproduced on parchment.

Hubbard Maps, P.O. Box 2121, Fort Collins, CO 80522: Free catalog ❖ Framed or unframed United States, world, and national park maps. 800-323-8368.

Map Express, P.O. Box 280445, Lakewood, CO 80228: Free catalog ❖ Maps and photographs from the United States Geological Service. 800-MAP-0039; 303-989-0003 (in CO).

MapLink, 25 E. Mason St., Santa Barbara, CA 93101: Free catalog ❖ Topographic, regional, county, state, city, country, world, and trail maps. 805-965-4402.

The Maritime Store, 2905 Hyde St. Pier, San Francisco, CA 94109: Free catalog ❖ Maritime maps, greeting cards, boat models, children's and maritime books, and gifts. 415-775-BOOK

MidAtlantic Antiques, P.O. Box 691, Mt. Laurel, NJ 08054: Catalog $1 (3 issues) ❖ Antiques and paper collectibles, historical military maps, autographs, and other memorabilia. 609-234-2651.

David Morgan, 11812 Northcreek Pkwy., Ste. 103, Bothell, WA 98011: Free catalog ❖ Maps of Great Britain for travel or genealogy research. 800-324-4934.

National Geographic Society, 1145 17th St. NW, Washington, DC 20036: Free catalog ❖ Books, games, videos, maps and globes, travel aids, and magazine subscriptions. 800-447-0647.

Kenneth Nebenzahl Inc., Glencove, IL 60022: Catalog $3 ❖ Rare old maps from around the world.

Nicholson's Trading Post, P.O. Box 291, Burley, WA 98322: Free catalog ❖ Maps and books on prospecting and mining. 206-876-0716.

Northern Map Company, Box 129, Dunnellon, FL 34430: Catalog $5 ❖ Maps from the Civil War, Canadian maps, map kits, and old state, city, railroad, and county maps, from 70 to 120 years old. 800-314-2474.

The Old Print Gallery, 1220 31st St. NW, Washington, DC 20007: Catalog $3 ❖ Prints and maps from the 18th and 19th-century. 202-965-1818.

Omni Resources, 1004 S. Mebane St., P.O. Box 2096, Burlington, NC 27216: Free catalog ❖ Fossils, rocks, hiking and topography maps, and globes. 800-742-2677.

Philadelphia Print Shop Ltd., 8441 Germantown Ave., Philadelphia, PA 19118: Catalog $4 ❖ Antique maps, prints, and books. 215-242-4750.

Rand McNally & Company, Catalog Operations Center, 2515 E. 43rd St., P.O. Box 182257, Chattanooga, TN 37422: Free catalog ❖ Gifts for sports enthusiasts, health and exercise equipment, maps, world globes, books, videos, clocks, prints, travel aids, and watches. 800-234-0679.

Raven Maps & Images, Box 850, Medford, OR 97501: Free catalog ❖ Mounted and framed maps. 800-237-0798.

Slocum Books, Box 10998, Austin, TX 78766: Free catalog ❖ Old city, county, state, and military maps. 800-521-4451.

Trails Illustrated, P.O. Box 4357, Evergreen, CO 80439: Free information ❖ Maps of the National Parks and other areas in the United States. 800-962-1643.

Travelers Bookstore, 22 W. 52nd St., New York, NY 10019: Catalog $2 ❖ Maps and books on travel. 800-755-8728; 212-664-0995 (in NY).

United Nations Publications, Room DC2-853, New York, NY 10017: Free information ❖ Maps and United Nations publications. 212-963-8323.

Universal Map, 201 Tech Dr., Sanford, FL 32771: Free catalog ❖ United States state and city maps. 800-359-6277; 407-324-4401 (in FL).

Wennawoods Publishing, RR 2, Box 529C, Lewisburg, PA 17837: Free catalog ❖ Reprints of books and maps on 17th and 18th-century Eastern Frontier Indian history. 717-524-4820.

Wilderness Press, 2440 Bancroft Way, Berkeley, CA 94704: Free catalog ❖ Outdoor books and maps. 800-443-7227.

MARBLES

Essof's, P.O. Box 176, Sisterville, WV 26175: Free information with long SASE. ❖ Toy, Chinese checker, and decorative marbles.

Heartbreak Ridge, 108 Public Square, Lebanon, TN 37087: Free information ❖ One-of-a-kind contemporary marbles. 615-449-5993.

Spice Island Traders, 21546 Golden Triangle Rd., Saugus, CA 91350: Free list with long SASE ❖ Marbles and related items.

MARTIAL ARTS

Academy of Karate Martial Arts Supply, 405 Black Horse Pike, Haddon Heights, NJ 08035: Free catalog ❖ Martial arts equipment and clothing. 609-547-5445.

Artistic Video, 87 Tyler Ave., Sound Beach, NY 11789: Free brochure ❖ Martial arts training videos. 516-744-5999.

Asian World of Martial Arts, 11601 Caroline Rd., Philadelphia, PA 19154: Catalog $5 ❖ Training and protective equipment, weapons, uniforms, belts, books, and videos. 800-345-2962.

Best Martial Arts Supply, 16630 Bellflower Blvd., Bellflower, CA 90706: Free information ❖ Clothing, shoes, bags, protectors, mats, and training equipment. 310-866-5378.

Black Belt Products Inc., 665 Haddon Ave., Collingswood, NJ 08108: Catalog $2 ❖ Martial arts weapons and accessories. 800-I-KICK-IT.

BLT Supplies Inc., Mail Order Dept., 35-01 Queens Blvd., Long Island City, NY 11101: Free information ❖ Asian martial arts films. 800-322-2860.

The Brute Group, 2126 Spring St., P.O. Box 2788, Reading, PA 19609: Free information ❖ Training equipment. 800-486-2788; 610-678-4050 (in PA).

Century Martial Art Supply Inc., 1705 National Blvd., Midwest City, OK 73110: Free information ❖ Sparring gear, belts, and clothing. 800-626-2787.

Close Range Combat Academy, 5826 N. Wayne, Chicago, IL 60660: Free information ❖ Small, medium, large, extra-large, and extra-extra-large T-shirts, sweatshirts, sweatpants, and satin jackets.

Co-Mart International, P.O. Box 16194, San Francisco, CA 94116: Catalog $1 ❖ Training equipment, weapons, uniforms, and shoes. 415-759-8640.

Crown Trophy, 1 Odell Plaza, Yonkers, NY 10701: Free information ❖ Martial arts awards. 800-227-1557; 914-963-0005 (in NY).

Dolan's Sports Inc., 26 Hwy. 547, P.O. Box 26, Farmingdale, NJ 07727: Free catalog ❖ Training and safety equipment, uniforms, shoes, Samurai swords, and books. 201-938-6656.

Dragon International Inc., 12310 Hwy. 99 South, Unit 106, Everett, WA 98204: Catalog $2 ❖ Martial arts equipment. 206-745-5176.

ESPYY-TV, 611 Broadway, New York, NY 10012: Free information ❖ Martial arts training videos. 800-735-6521.

Extreme Sport Karate, P.O. Box 14171, Lenexa, KS 66285: Free catalog ❖ Martial arts equipment and clothing. 800-KARATE-1; 913-888-1719 (in KS).

Fairtex Martial Arts Equipment, 100 Weber Dr., Chandler, AZ 85226: Free list of retail sources ❖ Martial arts equipment. 602-940-0042.

Genesport Industries Ltd., Hokkaido Karate Equipment Manufacturing Company, 150 King St., Montreal, Quebec, Canada H3C 2P3: Free information ❖ Belts, clothing, and equipment. 514-861-1856.

High View Publications, P.O. Box 51967, Pacific Grove, CA 93950: Free catalog ❖ Chinese martial arts books and videos. 408-655-2990.

Honda Martial Arts Supply, 61 W. 23rd St., New York, NY 10010: Free information ❖ Clothing, protective and safety equipment, shoes, books, and training gear. 212-620-4050.

Carson Hurley Enterprises Inc., 2945 Orange Ave. NE, P.O. Box 12783, Roanoke, VA 24028: Free information ❖ Stretching racks. 540-342-7550.

I & I Sports, 1524 W. 178th St., Gardena, CA 90248: Free information ❖ Martial arts equipment. 310-715-6800.

K.D. Sportswear, P.O. Box 85810, Seattle, WA 98145: Free information ❖ Clothing for training or casual dress. 206-646-1143.

K.P. Sporting Goods, 4141 Business Center Dr., Fremont, CA 94538: Free information ❖ Chop gloves, protective equipment, and kicking targets. 800-227-0500.

Kens Trading Company Inc., 13832 Magnolia Ave., Chino, CA 91710: Free information ❖ Martial arts equipment. 800-331-KENS.

Kim Pacific Trading Corporation Inc., 4141 Business Center Dr., Fremont, CA 94538: Free information ❖ Uniforms, shoes, and protective gear. 510-490-0300.

Kwon Martial Arts, 3755 Broadmoor, Grand Rapids, MI 49512: Free catalog ❖ Martial arts equipment.

Macho Products Inc., 10045 102nd Terrace, Sebastian, FL 32958: Free catalog ❖ Training equipment, belts, and clothing. 800-327-6812; 407-388-9892 (in FL).

The Martial Artist, 9 Franklin Blvd., Philadelphia, PA 19154: Free information ❖ Martial arts equipment. 800-726-0438.

Martial Athleisure Corporation, 27584 Commerce Center Dr., Temecula, CA 92590: Free information ❖ Martial art shoes. 800-622-4897; 909-693-0703 (in CA).

MC Martial Art Supply, 1467 McKinley St., Eugene, OR 97402: Free information ❖ Martial arts equipment.

9-90 Variety Inc., 5290 Kuhl Rd., Erie, PA 16510: Free information ❖ Sparring gear. 800-891-5220.

Ohara Publications Inc., P.O. Box 918, Santa Clarita, CA 91380: Free information ❖ Books on martial arts. 805-257-4066.

Otomix, 3691 Lenawee Ave., Los Angeles, CA 90016: Free information ❖ Fitness shoes and martial arts equipment. 800-597-5425.

Panther Productions, 1010 Calle Negocio, San Clemente, CA 92672: Free catalog ❖ Training videos for beginners and advanced students. 800-332-4442.

MASSAGE, SALON & SPA EQUIPMENT

PFS Video Inc., P.O. Box 50, Oley, PA 19547: Free information ❖ Martial arts videos on defense techniques. 610-689-5871.

RheeMax, 9000 Mendenhall Ct., Columbia, MD 21045: Free catalog ❖ Uniforms, competition equipment, protective gear, and exercisers. 410-381-2900.

Royal Martial Art Supplies, 2605 Peach St., Erie, PA 16508: Catalog $1 ❖ Martial arts supplies. 814-454-2774.

Ryukyu Imports Inc., P.O. Box 535, Olathe, KS 66051: Free price list ❖ Books on martial arts. 913-782-3920.

TKD Enterprises Inc., 1423 18th St., Bettendorf, IA 52722: Free information ❖ Martial arts books, videos, and shoes. 800-388-5966.

Turtle Press, 403 Silas Deane Hwy., P.O. Box 290206, Wethersfield, CT 06129: Free catalog ❖ Books on martial arts. 800-778-8785.

Unique Publications, 4201 W. Vanowen Pl., Burbank, CA 91505: Free information ❖ Martial arts videos. 800-332-3330.

Wandix International Inc., 88 Portland Ave., Bergenfield, NJ 07621: Free brochure ❖ Portable and water-proof interlockable sports mat. 800-385-6855; 201-385-6855 (in NJ).

YMAA Publication Center, 38 Hyde Park Ave., Jamaica Plain, MA 02130: Free catalog ❖ Martial arts books, videos, clothing, and music. 800-669-8892.

MASSAGE, SALON & SPA EQUIPMENT

New Life Systems, 2853 Hedberg Dr., Minneapolis, MN 55305: Free catalog ❖ Health and wellness products, including massage tables, Panasonic massages, loungers, and air purifiers. 800-852-3082.

Planta Dei Medicinal Herb Farm, Millville, New Brunswick, Canada E0H 1M0: Catalog $2 (refundable) ❖ Biologically grown teas, medicinal herbs, healing tea mixtures, cosmetics, natural ointments, and massage oils. 506-463-8169.

Sharper Image SPA, 650 Davis St., San Francisco, CA 94120: Free catalog ❖ Aerobic non-impact fitness machines, treadmills, massagers, and equipment. 800-344-5555.

MATCHBOOK COVERS

William Mankins, P.O. Box 736, Meadows of Dan, VA 24120: Free information (send want list) ❖ Pin-up and military matchbook covers and postcards. 540-776-9701.

Remember These, P.O. Box 736, Meadows of Dan, VA 24120: Free information with long SASE ❖ Postcards and matchbook covers.

Writewell Company, P.O. Box 68186, Indianapolis, IN 46268: Free catalog ❖ Loose-leaf matchbook cover albums with padded covers of leather-grained vinyl. 800-968-5850.

MEMORABILIA & COLLECTIBLES (MISCELLANEOUS)

Amusementica Americana, 414 N. Prospect Manor Ave., Mt. Prospect, IL 60056: Free list with seven 1st class stamps ❖ Old saloon artifacts, coin-operated machines, advertising collectibles, paper memorabilia, and other antique artifacts. 847-253-0791.

Celebrity Gallery, 1840 N. Federal Hwy., Boynton Beach, FL 33435: Catalog $5 ❖ Autographs and vintage sports memorabilia. 800-344-9103; 407-364-0453 (in FL).

Dance Mart, P.O. Box 994, Teaneck, NJ 07666: Free catalog with long SASE ❖ Rare books, prints, music, autographs, and dance collectibles. 201-833-4176.

4 x 1 Imports Inc., 5873 Day Rd., Cincinnati, OH 45251: Catalog $4 ❖ Nostalgic tin advertising signs and other collectibles. 513-385-8185.

H & L Collectibles, 4908 Poplar Dr., Alexandria, VA 22310: Free price list with long SASE ❖ Star Trek memorabilia. 703-971-6041.

The Limited of Michigan Ltd., 10861 Paw Paw Dr., Holland, MI 49424: Free catalog ❖ Hard-to-find Disney wood carvings and collectibles. 800-355-6363.

Movie Gallery, 1435 Thompson Blvd., Sedalia, MO 65301: Catalog $5 ❖ Star Wars collectibles. 816-826-3834.

The Opera Box, Box 994, Teaneck, NJ 07666: Free catalog ❖ Rare books, magazines, autograph material, and other opera collectibles. 201-833-4176.

Photo Antiquities, 531 E. Ohio St., Pittsburgh, PA 15212: Free information ❖ Vintage photography collectibles. 800-474-6862.

Robbie Music, Scherzer Rare Records Inc., P.O. Box 222, Pueblo, CO 81002: Free catalog ❖ Magazines, books, radio surveys, and memorabilia. 719-543-6858.

Rockabilia Inc., P.O. Box 4206, Hopkins, MN 55343: Free catalog ❖ T-shirts, backstage passes, promotional glossy photographs, imported rare posters from around the world, and other concert collectibles and investibles. 612-942-7895.

Rockin' Robin, 1800 S. Robertson Blvd., Los Angeles, CA 90035: Catalog $3.50 ❖ Magazines, books, posters, stickers, buttons, photos, and collectibles.

S.A.M. Inc., P.O. Box 77, Palo Alto, CA 94301: Free catalog ❖ Collectible memorabilia and limited edition sports figurines and bobbing heads. 415-369-0190.

Philip Sears Disney Collectibles, 24592 Via Carissa, Laguna Niguel, CA 92677: Free catalog ❖ Walt Disney autographs, animation art, and memorabilia. 714-543-1477.

Soda Mart-Can World, 1055 Ridgecrest Dr., Millersville, TN 37072: Free catalog ❖ Beer and soda cans, signs, trays, glasses, steins, bottle caps, and other nostalgic and reproduction collectibles. 615-859-5236.

Sports Heroes, 550 Kinderkamack Rd., Oradell, NJ 07649: Free information with long SASE ❖ Vintage and unique sports memorabilia. 800-233-4000; 201-262-8020 (in NJ).

SR Collectibles, P.O. Box 340658, Brooklyn, NY 11234: Free catalog ❖ Disney, Beatles, movie stars, tobacco, postcards, premiums, and other collectibles. 718-951-3629.

Stellar Toys, 253 Osborne Rd., Loudonville, NY 12211: Catalog $4 ❖ Science fiction and character toys, memorabilia, videos, and models. 518-482-0522.

Trendco Inc., 4723 W. Atlantic Ave., Delray Beach, FL 33445: Free catalog ❖ Figurines, plates, bobbing heads, and hand-signed memorabilia. 800-881-0181.

METAL CRAFTING & SILVERSMITHING

Ackley's Rock & Stamps, 3230 N. Stone Ave., Colorado Springs, CO 80907: Catalog $1 (refundable) ❖ Silversmithing supplies. 719-633-1153.

Allcraft Tool & Supply Company, 666 Pacific St., Brooklyn, NY 11207: Catalog $5 ❖ Tools and supplies for jewelry-making, metal-crafting and casting, and silversmithing. 800-645-7124; 718-789-2800 (in NY).

American Art Clay Company Inc., 4717 W. 16th St., Indianapolis, IN 46222: Free catalog ❖ Ceramic and metal enameling supplies, pottery-making equipment, tools, kilns, and coloring materials. 800-374-1600; 317-244-6871 (in IN).

ARE Inc., Rt. 16, Box 8, Greensboro Bend, VT 05842: Catalog $3 ❖ Silver, gold, pewter, base metals, tools, findings, chains, and semi-precious stones. 800-736-4273.

Automatic Tubing Corporation, 888 Lorimer St., Brooklyn, NY 11222: Free information ❖ Custom brass tubing. 800-527-3091; 718-383-0100 (in NY).

Bourget Bros., 1636 11th St., Santa Monica, CA 90404: Catalog $3 ❖ Silversmithing supplies and copper, gold, and silver wire and sheet. 310-450-6556.

Campbell Tools Company, 2100 Selma Rd., Springfield, OH 45505: Catalog $2 ❖ Tools, supplies, and brass, aluminum, steel, and other metals. 513-322-8562.

Cardinal Engineering Inc., RR 1, Box 163-1, Cameron, IL 61423: Catalog $2 ❖ Brass, aluminum, stainless, and tool steel. Also tools and shop supplies.

Country Accents, P.O. Box 437, Montoursville, PA 17754: Catalog $5 ❖ Handcrafted metal panels, pierced metal kits, patterns, and tools. 717-478-4127.

East West DyeCom, P.O. Box 12294, Roanoke, VA 24024: Catalog $5 (refundable) ❖ Pre-anodized aluminum sheets and colored tubing, dyes, kits, books, and other supplies. 540-345-1489.

Eastman Corporation, P.O. Box 247, Roselle, NJ 07203: Free information ❖ Stains for metal, glass, shells, bone, plastic, ceramics, and leather. 908-232-1212.

Ebersole Lapidary Supply Inc., 11417 West Hwy. 54, Wichita, KS 67209: Catalog $2 ❖ Gold and silver sheet and wire and silversmithing supplies. 316-722-4771.

Enco Manufacturing Company, 5000 W. Bloomingdale Ave., Chicago, IL 60639: Free catalog ❖ Metal-working tools, machinery, and accessories. 800-860-3200.

T.B. Hagstoz & Son Inc., 709 Sansom St., Philadelphia, PA 19106: Catalog $5 (refundable with $25 order) ❖ Metal findings, jeweler's tools, casting equipment, gold and silver solders, and gold, silver, gold-filled metals, copper, bronze, brass nickel, silver, and pewter. 800-922-1006; 215-922-1627 (in PA).

Indian Jewelers Supply Company, 601 E. Coal Ave., Gallup, NM 87301: Catalog $6 ❖ Copper and silver wire and sheet, silversmithing supplies, precious and base metal findings, tools and supplies, and semi-precious stones, shells, and coral. 505-722-4451.

K & S Engineering, 6917 W. 59th St., Chicago, IL 60638: Catalog $1 ❖ Aluminum and other metal tubing, rods, and sheets. 312-586-8503.

Kingsley North Inc., 910 Brown St., Norway, MI 49870: Free catalog ❖ Silversmithing supplies, tools, and casting, lapidary, and glass polishing equipment. 800-338-9280.

Lonnie's Inc., 7155 E. Apache Trail, Mesa, AZ 85207: Free findings catalog; tool catalog $5; jewelry catalog $5 ❖ Tools, equipment, and supplies for jewelers, casters, silversmiths, and lapidarists. 602-832-2641.

MBM Sales Ltd., N. 15th West, 2218 Watertown Rd., Unit 3, Waukesha, WI 53186: Catalog $2 ❖ Hard-to-find metals and fasteners in small quantities. 800-657-0721.

Metal Buyers Mart, N15 W22218, Watertown Rd., Waukesha, WI 53186: Free information ❖ Specializes in metals in small quantities. 800-657-0721; 414-547-3606 (in WI).

Metalliferous, 34 W. 46th St., New York, NY 10036: Catalog $5 ❖ Metals, tools, and supplies for jewelry-making and metal crafting. 212-944-0909.

The NgraveR Company, 67 Wawecus Hill Rd., Bozrah, CT 06334: Catalog $1 (refundable) ❖ Easy-to-use engraving tools and jewelry-making equipment. 203-823-1533.

Nolan Supply Corporation, P.O. Box 6289, 111-115 Leo Ave., Syracuse, NY 13217: Free catalog ❖ Metals and mill supplies. 800-736-2204; 315-463-6241 (in NY).

Nonferrous Metals, P.O. Box 2595, Waterbury, CT 06723: Catalog $3 (refundable) ❖ Plain and ornamental brass, copper, bronze, and nickel-silver wire. 203-274-7255.

Red & Green Minerals Inc., 7595 W. Florida Ave., Lakewood, CO 80226: Free information ❖ Silversmithing supplies. 303-985-5559.

Shapiro Supply Company, 5617 Natural Bridge Rd., St. Louis, MO 63120: Catalog $2 ❖ Aluminum, brass, and stainless supplies. 314-727-5588.

Myron Toback Inc., 25 W. 47th St., New York, NY 10036: Free information ❖ Tools for metal crafting and silversmithing. 800-223-7550; 212-398-8300 (in NY).

Unique Tool, P.O. Box 34, Miami, NM 87729: Catalog $3 ❖ Silversmithing stamps and tools. 505-483-2940.

METAL DETECTORS

Adventure Detectors, 2102 Roosevelt Dr., Arlington, TX 76013: Free list ❖ Pre-owned, demonstration, and blemished detectors. 817-461-FIND.

Alpha Supply, Box 2133, Bremerton, WA 98310: Catalog $1 (refundable with $15 order) ❖ Metal detectors, prospecting and gem-finishing equipment, and jewelry-making tools. 360-373-3302.

American Detector Distributors, 626 Grapevine Hwy., Hurst, TX 76054: Free information ❖ Metal detecting equipment and accessories. 800-933-BUYS; 817-498-7100 (in TX).

Arizona Al's Discount, 4238 W. Northern Ave., Phoenix, AZ 85051: Free information ❖ Metal detectors and prospecting equipment. 602-930-1755.

Armadillo Mining Shop, 2041 NW Vine, Grants Pass, OR 97526: Free information ❖ Metal detectors and mining supplies. 503-476-6316.

Barnes Enterprises, 9618 Edison St. NE, Alliance, OH 44601: Free information ❖ Metal detectors. 800-559-5449.

Brook's Detectors, P.O. Box 250382, Montgomery, AL 36125: Free catalog ❖ Metal detectors and accessories. 334-281-1806.

C & C Detectors, 2524 E. US Hwy. 14, Janesville, WI 53545: Free catalog ❖ Metal detectors. 800-356-6636.

Cal-Gold, 2569 E. Colorado Blvd., Pasadena, CA 91107: Free catalog ❖ Metal detectors, supplies for miners and geologists, maps, and books. 818-792-6161.

Clevenger Detector Sales, 8206 N. Oak, Kansas City, MO 64118: Free information ❖ New and used detectors. 800-999-9147.

Cochran & Associates Inc., P.O. Box 20148, Bowling Green, KY 42102: Catalog $10 ❖ Long-range treasure locating equipment. 502-843-0706.

D & K Detector Sales, 13809 Southeast Division, Portland, OR 97236: Catalog $2 ❖ Metal detectors and prospecting equipment. 800-542-GOLD; 503-761-1521 (in OR).

Detector Distribution Center, 11900 Montana Ave., El Paso, TX 79936: Free list of retail sources ❖ Metal detectors. 915-855-4206.

Detector Electronics Corporation, 419 Worcester Rd., P.O. Box 2132, Framingham, MA 01701: Free brochure ❖ Metal detectors. 800-446-0244.

The Detector Warehouse, P.O. Box 6055, Buffalo Grove, IL 60089: Free catalog ❖ Metal detectors, books, tapes, audio tapes, headphones, dredges, and digging tools. 800-828-1455.

Discovery Electronics Inc., 1115 Long St., Sweet Home, OR 97386: Free information ❖ Metal detectors. 800-337-4815; 503-367-2585 (in OR).

Down Under Treasures, P.O. Box 92080, Henderson, NV 89009: Free list of retail sources ❖ Metal detectors. 702-565-1353.

East Coast Prospecting & Mining Supplies, Rt. 3, Box 321J, Ellijay, GA 30540: Catalog $3 ❖ Metal detectors and accessories. 706-276-4433.

Falcon Prospecting Equipment, 6529 E. Fairbrook St., Mesa, AZ 85205: Free information ❖ Placer gold probe for prospecting. 602-854-0324.

Fisher Research Laboratory, 200 W. Wilmott Rd., Los Banos, CA 93635: Free information ❖ Metal detectors. 209-826-3292.

JW Fishers Manufacturing Inc., 65 Anthony St., Berkeley, MA 02779: Free information ❖ Underwater metal detectors. 800-822-4744; 508-822-7330 (in MA).

49'er Metal Detectors, 14093 Irishtown Rd., Pine Grove, CA 95665: Free information ❖ Metal detectors. 800-538-7501; 209-296-3544 (in CA).

MICROSCOPES

Garrett Metal Detectors, 1881 W. State St., Garland, TX 75042: Free buyer's guide ❖ Metal detectors. 214-278-6151.

Gettysburg Electronics, 24 Chambersburg St., Gettysburg, PA 17325: Free information ❖ Metal detectors. 717-334-8634.

The Golddigger, 253 N. Main, Moab, UT 84532: Catalog $3 ❖ Metal detectors. 801-259-5150.

Hays Electronics, 9234 E. Valley Rd., Prescott Valley, AZ 86314: Free catalog ❖ Metal detectors, maps, electronic prospecting tools and accessories, and books on prospecting, mining, and relic hunting. 800-699-2624.

House of Treasure Hunters, 5714 El Cajon Blvd., San Diego, CA 92115: Free information ❖ Metal detectors and gold prospecting equipment. 619-286-2600.

Kansas/Texas Detector Sales, P.O. Box 17015, Fort Worth, TX 76102: Free information ❖ Metal detectors and prospecting equipment. 800-876-3463; 817-498-2228 (in TX).

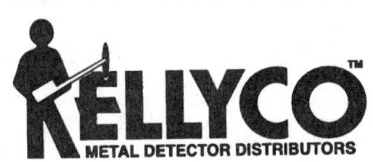

Kellyco Detector Distributors, 1085 Belle Ave., Winter Springs, FL 32708: Free catalog ❖ Coin and treasure metal detectors for finding valuables. Easy to use. Hundreds to choose from. 407-699-8700.

Metal Detectors of Minneapolis, 3746 Cedar Ave. South, Minneapolis, MN 55407: Free information ❖ Metal detectors, maps, books, accessories, and recovery tools. 800-876-8377; 612-721-1901 (in MN).

Mid-West Metal Detectors, 8338 Pillsbury Ave. South, Bloomington, MN 55420: Free information ❖ Metal detectors and books. 612-881-5254.

Northwest Treasure Supply, P.O. Box 52802, Bellevue, WA 98015: Free information ❖ Metal detectors. 800-845-5258.

Pedersen's Metal Detectors, 2521-A N. Grand Ave., Santa Ana, CA 92705: Free information ❖ Walk-through and hand-held detectors. Also gold and treasure-finding supplies. 800-953-3832.

Pioneer Mining Supplies, 943 Lincoln Way, Auburn, CA 95603: Free information ❖ Mining equipment and metal detectors. 916-885-1801.

Pot of Gold, 2616 Griffin Rd., Fort Lauderdale, FL 33312: Free catalog ❖ Metal detectors, books, and prospecting equipment. 954-987-2888.

Simmons Scientific Inc., P.O. Box 10057, Wilmington, NC 28405: Free brochure ❖ Directional locating equipment.

Tesoro Electronics, 715 White Spar Rd., Prescott, AZ 86303: Free information ❖ Easy-to-use lightweight metal detectors with high gain sensitivity. 800-528-3352.

Thomas Electroscopes, P.O. Box 5058, South Williamsport, PA 17701: Free catalog ❖ Long-range induction metal detectors for treasure hunting and prospecting.

White's Electronics, 1011 Pleasant Valley Rd., Sweet Home, OR 97386: Free list of retail sources ❖ Metal detectors. 800-547-6911.

MICROSCOPES

Chem-Lab, 1060 Ortega Way, Placentia, CA 92670: Catalog $5 ❖ Chemicals, glassware, scales, microscopes, and equipment. 714-630-7902.

Collector's Optics & Supplies, P.O. Box 281, Elk Grove Village, IL 60009: Free information ❖ Stereo microscopes. 708-439-8266.

Cosmos Ltd., 9215 Waukegan Rd., Morton Grove, IL 60053: Free catalog ❖ Ultra-wide field and equatorial telescopes. Also binoculars and microscopes. 708-827-4846.

Edmund Scientific Company, Edscorp Building, Barrington, NJ 08007: Free catalog ❖ Microscopes, magnifiers, weather forecasting instruments, magnets, telescopes, binoculars, lasers, and other science equipment. 609-573-6260.

J.L. Hammett Company, P.O. Box 9057, Braintree, MA 02184: Free catalog ❖ Science kits, microscopes, laboratory apparatus, rock collections, magnets, astronomy charts, and anatomical models. 617-848-1000.

Lire La Nature Inc., 1699 Chemin Chandly, Longueuil, Quebec, Canada J4J 3X7: Free price list ❖ Telescopes, microscopes, and accessories. 514-463-5072.

Mineralogical Research Company, 15840 E. Alta Vista Way, San Jose, CA 95127: Free list with long SASE and two 1st class stamps ❖ Microscopes, rare mineral specimens, meteorites, micro-mounts, specimen boxes, and other science equipment. 408-923-6800.

Nurnberg Scientific, 6310 SW Virginia Ave., Portland, OR 97201: Free information ❖ Microscopes. 503-246-8297.

Unitron Inc., 170 Wilbur Pl., P.O. Box 469, Bohemia, NY 11716: Free catalog ❖ Stereo microscopes and optical and scientific equipment. 516-589-6666.

MILITARY MEMORABILIA

General Memorabilia

Dale C. Anderson Company, 4 W. Confederate Ave., Gettysburg, PA 17325: Catalog (6 issues) $12 ❖ Civil War, Indian War, and other militaria.

Arms & Armor, 1101 Stinson Blvd. NE, Minneapolis, MN 55413: Catalog $2 ❖ Reproduction weapons and armor. 612-331-6473.

BattleZone Ltd., P.O. Box 266, Towsco, NJ 07082: Free information ❖ Military memorabilia.

Blacksword Armoury Inc., 11717 SW 99th Ave., Gainesville, FL 32608: Catalog $5 ❖ Antique and replica ancient, medieval, renaissance, Napoleonic, and American Civil War weapons and armor.

British Collectibles Ltd., 1727 Wilshire Blvd., Santa Monica, CA 90403: Catalog $15 ❖ British military collectibles, from the 1800s to World War II. 310-453-3322.

British Regalia Imports, P.O. Box 50473, Nashville, TN 37205: Catalog $6 ❖ British armed forces insignia. 615-341-5407.

The Bushwacker, Militaria, P.O. Box 966, Black Mountain, NC 28711: Price list $3 ❖ Military antiques and collectibles. 704-669-4603.

C & D Jarnagin Company, Historical Supply, P.O. Box 1860, Corinth, MS 38834: Civil War catalog $3, 18th-century (1750 to 1815) catalog $3 ❖ Military and historical memorabilia. 601-287-4977.

Collector's Armoury, 800 Slaters Ln., P.O. Box 59, Alexandria, VA 22313: Free catalog ❖ Replica model guns, medals, armor, swords, helmets, and other military collectibles. 800-544-3456.

Colors, Box 5403, Towson, MD 21204: Catalog $2 ❖ Full-size and miniature medals, insignia and badges, awards cases, and custom mounting.

Dixie Leather Works, P.O. Box 8221, Paducah, KY 42002: Catalog $6 ❖ Museum-quality military and civilian reproductions, from 1833 to 1872. 502-442-1058.

N. Flayderman & Company Inc., P.O. Box 2446, Fort Lauderdale, FL 33303: Catalog $10 ❖ Antique guns, swords, knives, and nautical, western, and military collectibles from the Civil War through World War II. 305-761-8855.

James E. Garcia, 1404 Luthy NE, Albuquerque, NM 87112: Catalog $3 ❖ Vintage aviation collectibles. 505-296-8765.

Hutchinson House, Box 41021, Chicago, IL 60641: Catalog $2 ❖ Full-size, made from the originals, World War I and Civil War reproduction war mementos and medals.

MILITARY MEMORABILIA

Jacques Noel Jacobsen, 60 Manor Rd., Ste. 300, Staten Island, NY 10310: Catalog $10 ❖ Antiques and military collectibles, insignia, weapons, photos and paintings, band instruments, and Native American and Western items. 718-981-0973.

Kel's Memorabilia, Box 125, Woburn, MA 01801: Catalog $2 ❖ German Nazi and World War II memorabilia, uniform accessories, insignia, flags, and other collectibles. 617-935-3389.

Lancer Militaria, P.O. Box 886, Mt. Ida, AR 71957: Catalog $2 ❖ Military and police insignia. 501-867-2232.

Legendary Arms Inc., P.O. Box 479, Three Bridges, NJ 08887: Free information ❖ Reproduction military period knives and swords. 800-528-2767; 908-788-9743 (in NJ).

Lodgewood Mfg., William H. Osborne, P.O. Box 611, Whitewater, WI 53190: Catalog $5 ❖ Civil War guns and parts and United States martial arms, from 1780 to 1898. 414-473-5444.

Manion's, P.O. Box 12214, Kansas City, KS 66112: Free catalog ❖ Militaria, toys, antiques, and memorabilia. 913-299-6692.

McGrogan's Military Patches, P.O. Box 502, Orofino, ID 83544: Free information ❖ Military patches. 800-861-9398.

Mess Dress, 1301 Bumps River Rd., Centerville, MA 02632: Catalog $5 ❖ British militaria. 508-775-2215.

Mid-Missouri Surplus, Russ Hinnard, 165 W. North St., Marshall, MO 65340: Free catalog ❖ Soviet military collectibles. 816-886-3585.

Midwest Military, 1823 Adamas, Quincy, IL 62301: Price list $1 (refundable) ❖ Military relics and memorabilia. 217-223-8095.

Military Art China Company Inc., 8 Park Dr., P.O. Box 406, Westford, MA 01886: Catalog $3 ❖ Handcrafted coffee mugs and steins with military crests. 508-392-0751.

The Military Collection, P.O. Box 830970, Miami, FL 33283: Catalog $8 ❖ Aviation and war relics. 305-271-5690.

Igor Moiseyev, Atlantic Crossroad Inc., P.O. Box 290715, Brooklyn, NY 11229: Catalog $1 ❖ Russian medals and militaria, from 1918 to the 1980s. 718-332-5889.

Museum Replicas Limited, P.O. Box 840, Conyers, GA 30207: Catalog $1 (refundable) ❖ Authentic museum quality historical replicas of weapons and period battle wear.

The Noble Collection, P.O. Box 3444, Merrifield, VA 22116: Free catalog ❖ Swords, armor, shields, helmets, sidearms, miniatures, and military collectibles. 800-806-6253.

Pieces of History, P.O. Box 4470, Cave Creek, AZ 85331: Catalog $2 ❖ Medals from around the world. 602-488-1377.

Jerry Price, 8086 Nashua Dr., Palm Beach Gardens, FL 33418: Catalog $3 (refundable with $30 purchase) ❖ Japanese military collectibles.

Red Lancer, P.O. Box 8056, Mesa, AZ 85214: Catalog $12 ❖ Original 19th-century military art, rare books, campaign medals, helmets, and toy soldiers. 602-964-9667.

Rocky Mountain Rarities, P.O. Box 303, Bountiful, UT 84011: Free list ❖ World War II collectibles. 801-296-6276.

The Russian Trade House, P.O. Box 20229, Alexandria, VA 22320: Catalog $1 ❖ Soviet military collectibles. 703-519-5769.

Treasure Trove at the Ahwatukee Commons, 4902 E. Warner Rd., Ste. 13, Phoenix, AZ 85044: Catalog $1 (refundable) ❖ Historical antiques, military memorabilia, books, medals, coins, and other collectibles. 602-496-0057.

Frederick J. Tyson Military Models, 701 W. Beaver Ave., State College, PA 16801: Free catalog ❖ Handcrafted military display models. 814-238-1951.

United States Marine Corps Collectables, James A. Johnson, 25 Northwood Dr., Laredo, TX 78041: Free information ❖ United States marine corps collectibles. 210-717-0166.

Woodhaven Army Surplus & Military Collectibles, 6295 S. Harrison Dr., Las Vegas, NV 89120: Catalog $2 ❖ United States, British, and French surplus from World War II to the present. 702-454-9111.

Civil War Collectibles

Dale C. Anderson Company, 4 W. Confederate Ave., Gettysburg, PA 17325: Catalog (6 issues) $12 ❖ Civil War, Indian War, and other militaria.

Armchair General's Merchantile, 1008 Adams, Bay City, MI 48708: Catalog $2 (refundable) ❖ Games, miniatures, and books for Civil War enthusiasts. 517-892-6177.

Broadfoot Publishing Company, 1907 Buena Vista Circle, Wilmington, NC 28405: Free catalog ❖ Old and new books about the Civil War. 919-686-4816.

C & D Jarnagin Company, Historical Supply, P.O. Box 1860, Corinth, MS 38834: Catalog $3 ❖ Civil War memorabilia, from 1833 to 1865. 601-287-4977.

Cedar Creek Relic Shop, P.O. Box 232, Middletown, VA 22645: Catalog $6 ❖ Civil War relics, weapons and firearms, and collectibles. 540-869-5207.

Civil War Antiques, P.O. Box 87, Sylvania, OH 43560: Catalog subscription $8 ❖ Civil War antiques. 419-882-5547.

Collector's Armoury, 800 Slaters Ln., P.O. Box 59, Alexandria, VA 22313: Free catalog ❖ Civil War memorabilia, World War II medals, Samurai swords, flags, and replica model guns. 800-544-3456.

Der Dienst, P.O. Box 221, Lowell, MI 49331: Catalog $5 (refundable) ❖ Full-sized replica Civil War medals, military badges, and United States and foreign insignia.

Fair Oaks Sutler Inc., 9905 Kershaw Ct., Spotsylvania, VA 22553: Free catalog with two 1st class stamps ❖ Reproduction Civil War military collectibles. 703-972-7744.

Farnsworth Military Gallery, 401 Baltimore St., Gettysburg, PA 17325: Free information ❖ Art prints and new, used, and rare books on the Civil War. 717-334-8838.

Fields of Glory, 55 York St., Gettysburg, PA 17325: Catalog $10 (12 issues) ❖ Civil War memorabilia. 800-517-3382.

Will Gorges Civil War Antiques, 2100 Trent Blvd., New Bern, NC 28560: Catalog $10 ❖ Authentic Civil War uniforms, weapons, and photographs. Also pre-1964 comic books. 919-636-3039.

The Horse Soldier, P.O. Box 184, Cashtown, PA 17310: Catalog $10 (annual subscription) ❖ Confederate and Union Civil War artifacts, paper items, photographs, edged weapons, artillery pieces, and battlefield relics. 717-334-0347.

Murray Hudson, 109 S. Church St., P.O. Box 163, Halls, TN 38840: Catalog $10 (refundable) ❖ Antique maps, books with maps, world globes, and historical prints. 800-748-9946; 901-836-9057 (in TN).

Indian Hollow Antiques, 298 W. Old Cross Rd., New Market, VA 22844: Free information with long SASE ❖ Weapons, uniforms, documents, buttons, and Civil War militaria. 703-740-3959.

Lawrence of Dalton, 4773 Tammy Dr. NE, Dalton, GA 30721: List $4 ❖ Civil War relics. 800-336-8894; 706-226-8894 (in GA).

Bill Mason Books, 104 N. 7th St., Morehead City, NC 28557: Free catalog ❖ Rare, new, and used books. Also prints, and Civil War, Western Americana, military, and nautical collectibles. 919-247-6161.

Northern Map Company, Box 129, Dunnellon, FL 34430: Catalog $5 ❖ Maps from the Civil War, Canadian maps, map kits, and old state, city, railroad, and county maps, from 70 to 120 years old. 800-314-2474.

Old Sutler John, P.O. Box 174, Westview Station, Binghamton, NY 13905: Catalog $3 ❖ Reproduction Civil War guns, bayonets, swords, uniforms, leather items, and other collectibles. 607-775-4434.

Olde Soldier Books Inc., 18779 N. Frederick Ave., Gaithersburg, MD 20879: Free information ❖ Civil War books, documents, autographs, prints, and Americana. 301-963-2929.

Panther, P.O. Box 32, Normantown, WV 25267: Catalog $2 (refundable) ❖ Historical re-enactment Civil War items. 304-462-7718.

Charles T. Phillips, 3863 Old Shell Rd., Mobile, AL 36608: Free catalog ❖ Reproductions of Civil War photographs.

Rapine Bullet Manufacturing Company, 9503 Landis Ln., East Greenville, PA 18041: Catalog $2 ❖ Civil War bullet molds. 215-679-5413.

Reb Acres, Bill & Sue Coleman, Rt. 2, Box 314, Raphine, VA 24472: Free catalog with three 1st class stamps ❖ Civil War memorabilia. 703-377-2057.

The Regimental Quartermaster, P.O. Box 553, Hatboro, PA 19040: Catalog $2 ❖ Civil War reproductions. 215-672-6891.

Len Rosa Military Collectibles, P.O. Box 3965, Gettysburg, PA 17325: Catalog subscription $10 ❖ Union and Confederate Civil War memorabilia and artifacts. 717-337-2853.

Steen Cannons, 10730 Midland Trail Rd., Cannonsburg, KY 41102: Catalog $5 ❖ Authentic and full scale reproduction cannons. 606-329-2477.

Dave Taylor Civil War Antiques, Box 87, Sylvania, OH 43560: Catalog $8 ❖ Guns, swords, uniforms, insignia, flags, drums, photographs, letters, diaries, autographs, and other antique memorabilia. 419-878-8355.

James Townsend & Son Inc., 133 N. 1st St., P.O. Box 415, Perceton, IN 46562: Catalog $2 ❖ Historical clothing, hats, lanterns, tomahawks, knives, tents, guns, and blankets. 800-338-1665.

Upper Mississippi Valley Mercantile Company, 1607 Washington St., Davenport, IA 52804: Catalog $3 ❖ Reproduction Civil War memorabilia. 319-322-0896.

The Winchester Sutler Inc., 270 Shadow Brook Ln., Winchester, VA 22603: Catalog $4 ❖ Civil War reproductions. 703-888-3595.

War Medals & Souvenirs

Collector's Armoury, 800 Slaters Ln., P.O. Box 59, Alexandria, VA 22313: Free catalog ❖ Collectible World War II medals, Samurai swords, flags, Civil War memorabilia, and replica model guns. 800-544-3456.

Der Dienst, P.O. Box 221, Lowell, MI 49331: Catalog $5 (refundable) ❖ Full-sized replica Civil War medals, military badges, and United States and foreign insignia.

R. Andrew Fuller Company, Box 2071, Pawtucket, RI 02861: Free catalog ❖ Medals, ribbons, and display cases.

Historical Americana, Peter Hlinka, P.O. Box 310, New York, NY 10028: Catalog 35¢ ❖ Military and civilian decorations and medals from the United States and foreign countries, military award certificates, insignias, books, militaria, and war relics. 718-409-6407.

Hoover's Manufacturing Company, 4015 Progress Blvd., Peru, IL 61354: Free catalog ❖ Dog tag key rings, beer and coffee mugs, belt buckles, patches, flags, pins, patches, and Vietnam, Korea, and World War II hat pins. 815-223-1159.

H.J. Saunders, P.O. Box 3133, Naples, FL 33939: Catalog $3 ❖ Collectibles United States military insignia, books, and other reference material. 813-775-2100.

Sydney B. Vernon, Box 890280, Temecula, CA 92589: Catalog $8 (10 issues) ❖ Military medals and related collectibles. 909-698-1646.

MIRRORS

Atlantic Glass & Mirror Works, 437 N. 63rd St., Philadelphia, PA 19151: Free information ❖ Antique mirrors and restoration of antique frames. 215-747-6866.

Bombay Company, P.O. Box 161009, Fort Worth, TX 76161: Free catalog ❖ Antique furniture reproductions, mirrors, prints, lamps, and decorative accents. 800-829-7789.

Cox Studios, 1004 S. 9th St., P.O. Box 1464, Canon City, CO 81215: Catalog $2 (refundable) ❖ Custom windows, mirrors, and glass items. 719-275-7262.

Custom Mirror Gallery, P.O. Box 508-702, Somersville, CT 06072: Catalog $1 ❖ Mirrors and wooden moldings. 203-749-2281.

Hansgrohe Inc., 1465 Ventura Dr., Cumming, GA 30130: Catalog $3 ❖ Faucets, massaging and hand-held showers, make-up and shaving mirrors, and other accessories.

La Barge Mirrors, P.O. Box 1769, Holland, MI 49422: Catalog $7 ❖ Handcrafted mirrors with optional decorative complements. 616-392-1473.

The Masters Collection, Drawer D-1025, Somersville, CT 06072: Catalog $5 ❖ Custom mirrors and oil reproductions on canvas. 800-222-6827.

Mirrorculous Designs, 6846 Pasatiempo Circle, El Paso, TX 79912: Free catalog ❖ Handcrafted decorative vanity and hand-held mirrors. 800-644-4411.

Robern Inc., 1648 Winchester Rd., Bensalem, PA 19020: Free list of retail sources ❖ Bathroom mirrors and cabinets. 215-245-6550.

Studio Steel, 159 New Milford Tnpk., New Preston, CT 06777: Catalog $2 ❖ Lamps, chandeliers, sconces, mirrors, and hand-wrought metalwork. 800-800-5217; 203-868-7305 (in CT).

MODELS & MODEL BUILDING

Aircraft Models

Ace R/C, 116 W. 19th St., P.O. Box 472, Higginsville, MO 64037: Catalog $2 ❖ R/C gliders. 816-584-7121.

Aeroloft Designs, 130 W. Hampton, Ste. 20, Mesa, AZ 85210: Free information ❖ Ducted fan-jet airplane models and accessories. 602-649-8662.

Aerotech Inc., 1955 S. Palm St., Ste. 15, Las Vegas, NV 89104: Free information ❖ Rocket launched R/C acrobatic glider. 702-641-2301.

The Airplane Factory Inc., 1135 Florida, Mandeville, LA 70448: Free information ❖ Quick-building R/C sport-flying airplanes. 504-626-7840.

The Airplane Shop, 18 Passaic Ave., Unit #6, Fairfield, NJ 07004: Free catalog ❖ America's largest distributor of aviation models and collectibles. 800-752-6346.

Airtronics Inc., 11 Autry, Irvine, CA 92718: Free information ❖ Electric sailplane with folding propeller and removable plug-in wing tips. 714-830-8769.

Altech Marketing, P.O. Box 391, Edison, NJ 08818: Free information ❖ Ready-to-fly models. 908-248-8738.

America's Hobby Center Inc., 146 W. 22nd St., New York, NY 10011: Catalog $3 ❖ Model airplanes, R/C equipment, and tools. 212-675-8922.

Anderson Enterprises, 405 Osage, Derby, KS 67037: Free information ❖ Hand-carved solid mahogany aircraft models. 800-732-6875.

Aristo-Craft, Polk's Model Craft Hobbies Inc., 346 Bergen Ave., Jersey City, NJ 07304: Catalog $2 ❖ R/C models. 201-332-8100.

Astro Flight Inc., 13311 Beach Ave., Marina Del Ray, CA 90292: Free information ❖ Electric-powered airplanes and engines. 310-821-6242.

Bob's Hobby Center, 7333 Lake Underhill Rd., Orlando, FL 32822: Free information ❖ R/C airplanes, helicopters, boats, and cars. 407-277-1248.

Bridi Aircraft Designs Inc., 23625 Pineforest Ln., Harbor City, CA 90710: Free information ❖ R/C model airplane kits and gliders. 213-549-8264.

Brodak's, 100 Park Ave., Carmichaels, PA 15320: Catalog $3 ❖ Control-line airplanes. 416-966-2726.

MODELS & MODEL BUILDING

Bruckner Hobbies Inc., 2920 Bruckner Blvd., Bronx, NY 10465: Free information ❖ Airplane and automobile kits, R/C equipment, and building supplies. 718-863-3434.

Byron Originals Inc., P.O. Box 279, Ida Grove, IA 51445: Catalog $4 ❖ Easy-to-assemble model airplanes and jet engines. 712-364-3165.

Century Helicopter Products, 521 Sinclair Frontage Rd., Milpitas, CA 95035: Free information ❖ R/C helicopters. 408-942-9525.

Century Jet Models Inc., 11216 Bluegrass Pkwy., Louisville, KY 40299: Catalog $3 ❖ R/C model jet airplane kits, large scale models, precision retracts, and accessories. 502-266-9234.

Cermark Electronic & Model Supply, 107 Edward Ave., Fullerton, CA 92633: Free information ❖ Ready-to-fly R/C airplanes. 714-680-5888.

Cleveland Model & Supply Company, 9800 Detroit Ave., Cleveland, OH 44102: Catalog $2 ❖ Airplane models. 216-961-3600.

Colpar Hobbies, 804 S. Havana St., Aurora, CO 80012: Free newsletter with long SASE ❖ Airplanes, armor, automobiles, ships, R/C equipment, parts, and accessories. 303-341-0414.

Combat Models Inc., 8535 Arjons Dr., San Diego, CA 92126: Free information ❖ R/C gliders and almost ready-to-fly R/C model airplanes. 619-536-9922.

Coverite, 420 Babylon Rd., Horsham, PA 19044: Free information ❖ R/C model airplane kits, building materials, and tools. 215-672-6720.

Cox Hobbies Inc., 350 W. Rincon St., Corona, CA 91720: Free list of retail sources ❖ R/C model airplanes and cars. 714-278-2551.

CS Flight Systems, 31 Perry St., Middleboro, MA 02346: Catalog $7 ❖ Electric flight systems and accessories. 508-947-2805.

Daniell's R/C Specialists, 3141 Ambrose Ave., Nashville, TN 37207: Catalog $1 ❖ R/C airplanes and helicopters and supplies. 615-228-0867.

Dean's Hobby Shop, 131 E. Main St., Flushing, MI 48433: Free list (specify cars, planes, or military models) with long SASE ❖ Old and collectible model kits. 810-659-2137.

Discount Hobby Center, P.O. Box 370, Utica, NY 13503: Catalog $5 ❖ Military and aircraft models. 315-733-3741.

Dodgson Designs, 21230 Damson Rd., Bothell, WA 98021: Free catalog with two 1st class stamps ❖ Easy-to-assemble competition gliders. 206-776-8067.

Don's Hobby Shop Inc., 1819 S. Broadway, Salina, KS 67401: Free information ❖ Scale and large aircraft models, engines, and supplies. 913-827-3222.

Dynaflite, P.O. Box 1011, San Marcos, CA 92079: Free information ❖ R/C airplane models, sailplanes, launching systems, and accessories. 619-744-7923.

Easy Built Models, Box 425, Lockport, NY 14095: Free catalog with long SASE ❖ Easy-to-build airplane kits. 716-438-0545.

Evers Toy Store, 204 1st Ave. East, Dyersville, IA 52040: Free information with long SASE ❖ Airplane models and miniature die-cast automobiles. 800-962-9481.

Florio Flyer Corporation, 837 Johnsonburg Rd., Saint Marys, PA 15857: Free information ❖ R/C airplane models. 814-885-8360.

G & P Sales, 410 College Ave., Angwin, CA 94508: Information $3 ❖ R/C model airplane kits. 707-965-3866.

Global Hobby Distributors, 10725 Ellis Ave., Fountain Valley, CA 92728: Free information ❖ R/C model airplane kits and gliders. 714-963-0133.

Great Planes, P.O. Box 9021, Champaign, IL 61826: Free list of retail sources ❖ R/C model airplanes.

Helicopter World Inc., 521 Sinclair Frontage Rd., Milpitas, CA 95035: Catalog $5 ❖ Helicopter models, accessories, parts, and R/C equipment. 488-942-9521.

Helicopters Unlimited, P.O. Box 726, Avon, CT 06001: Free information ❖ Helicopters, accessories, R/C equipment, and tools. 203-677-7278.

Herr Engineering Corporation, 1431 Chaffee Dr., Ste. 3, Titusville, FL 32780: Catalog $2 ❖ Rubber-powered model airplane kits. 407-264-2488.

Hobby Barn, P.O. Box 17856, Tucson, AZ 85731: Free catalog ❖ Airplane and boat models. 520-747-3792.

Hobby Lobby International Inc., 5614 Franklin Pike Circle, Brentwood, TN 37027: Catalog $2.50 ❖ Airplane models. 615-373-1444.

Hobby Shack, 18480 Bandilier Circle, Fountain Valley, CA 92728: Free catalog ❖ R/C systems and ready-to-assemble airplanes and automobiles. 800-854-8471.

Hobby Surplus Sales, P.O. Box 2170, New Britain, CT 06050: Catalog $4 ❖ Model railroading, plastic models, rockets, radio control, slot racing, and more. 860-223-0600.

Hobby World Ltd. of Montreal, 5450 Sherbrooke St. West, Montreal, Quebec, Canada H4A 1V9: Catalog $5 ❖ Airplanes, helicopters, cars and trucks, ships, military vehicles, and science models. 514-481-5434.

Hobbycraft Canada, 140 Applewood Crescent, Concord, Ontario, Canada L4K 4E2: Free information ❖ Scale models from the first World War to the Gulf War. 905-738-6556.

Bob Holman Plans, P.O. Box 741, San Bernardino, CA 92402: Catalog $5 ❖ R/C model airplane kits. 714-885-3959.

Ikon N'wst, P.O. Box 306, Post Falls, ID 83854: Catalog $4 ❖ Giant scale and R/C model airplane kits. 208-773-9001.

Indoor Model Supply, Box 5311, Salem, OR 97304: Catalog $2 ❖ Rubber-powered models for indoors and building supplies.

Indy R/C Sales Inc., 10620 N. College Ave., Indianapolis, IN 46280: Free information ❖ Pre-assembled airplane kits. 800-338-4639.

International Hobby Corporation, 413 E. Allegheny Ave., Philadelphia, PA 19134: Catalog $4.98 ❖ Battery-powered tools, model airplanes, railroad accessories, and military miniatures. 800-875-1600.

J'Tec, 164 School St., Daly City, CA 94014: Free catalog with long SASE ❖ Model engine mounts, mufflers, engine test stands, and power sticks. 415-756-3400.

J-Bar Hobbies, 117 E. Chicago, Tecumseh, MI 49286: Free information ❖ Plastic models. 517-423-3684.

JHModels, 73 Franklin St., Elmwood Park, NJ 07407: Free catalog ❖ Easy-to-assemble R/C airplanes. 201-791-8705.

K & B Manufacturing Inc., 2100 College Dr., Lake Havasu City, AZ 86403: Free information ❖ Airplane and marine engines.

Kress Jets Inc., 500 Ulster Landing Rd., Saugerties, NY 12477: Free information ❖ Jet engine and prop propulsion systems. 914-336-8149.

Lanier RC, P.O. Box 458, Oakwood, GA 30566: Free catalog with long SASE ❖ R/C model airplane kits, almost ready-to-fly models, and free-flight and R/C gliders. 404-532-6401.

Major Hobby, 1520 Corona Dr., Lake Havasu City, AZ 86403: Free information ❖ R/C sailplanes and other aircraft. Also engines, radio systems, accessories, and building components. 520-855-7901.

Matney's Models, 11325 Harold Dr., Luna Pier, MI 48157: Free information ❖ Kits for gliders, R/C models, and other aircraft. 313-848-8195.

Micro-X Incorporated, P.O. Box 1063, Lorain, OH 44055: Catalog $2 ❖ Rubber-powered indoor duration and R/C models. 216-282-8354.

Midwest Products Company Inc., 400 S. Indiana St., P.O. Box 564, Hobart, IN 46342: Free list of retail sources ❖ Giant scale model airplanes. 800-348-3497.

❖ MODELS & MODEL BUILDING ❖

Minimax Enterprise, P.O. Box 2374, Chelan Falls, WA 98816: Free information ❖ R/C gliders. 509-683-1288.

Model Expo Inc., P.O. Box 1000, Mt. Pocono, PA 18344: Catalog $5 (refundable) ❖ Airplane models, tools, automobile and boat kits, and trains. 800-222-3876.

Model Railway Post Office, Box 426, Hewitt, NJ 07421: Free price list ❖ Trains, kits, and accessories. 201-728-7595.

More than Models, P.O. Box 4001, Simi Valley, CA 93093: Catalog $3 ❖ Aircraft, armor, ships, books, and accessories. 805-527-8455.

MRC Models, Model Rectifier Corporation, 200 Carter Dr., Edison, NJ 08817: Free information ❖ Helicopter kits, airplanes, and automobiles. 908-248-0400.

OmniModels, P.O. Box 708, Mahomet, IL 61853: Free information ❖ Airplane models and R/C equipment, engines, accessories, and building supplies. 800-342-6464; 217-398-7738 (in IL).

Pacific Aircraft, 14255 N. 79th St., Scottsdale Airpark, AZ 85260: Free catalog ❖ Hand-carved solid mahogany model airplanes. 800-950-9944.

Peck-Polymers, Box 710399, Santee, CA 92072: Catalog $4 ❖ Rubber-powered flying model kits and plans. 619-448-1818.

Phoenix Model Company, P.O. Box 15390, Brookville, FL 34609: Catalog $3 ❖ Aircraft, motorcycles, automobiles, boats, and other models. 904-754-8522.

Pierce Aero Company, 9626 Jellico Ave., Northridge, CA 91325: Free information ❖ R/C sailplanes. 818-349-4758.

Pirate Models, 13907 Hirschfield, Unit L, Tomball, TX 77375: Free information ❖ Giant scale and jig-built ready-to-assemble kits. 713-351-6617.

Polk's Model-Craft Hobbies Inc., 346 Bergen Ave., Jersey City, NJ 07304: Catalog $2 ❖ Tools, R/C equipment, building supplies, and airplane, car, and boat models. 201-332-8100.

Proctor Enterprises, 25450 NE Eilers Rd., Aurora, OR 97002: Catalog $5 (refundable) ❖ R/C model airplane kits and hardware. 503-678-1300.

Reid's Quality Model Products, 16 Main St., Phelps, NY 14532: Catalog $1 ❖ Scale R/C model airplane kits and accessories. Also giant scale kits and plans for classic and sport aircraft. 315-548-3779.

Replicas by Tyson, P.O. Box 129, Covington, OH 45318: Free catalog ❖ Miniature aircraft, ships, rockets, vehicles, and figurines. 513-473-5726.

Rosemont Hobby Shop, 7720 Main St., Ste. 5, Fogelsville, PA 18051: Free information with long SASE ❖ Scale aircraft models. 610-398-0210.

Scande Research Inc., P.O. Box 133, Villa Park, IL 60181: Free information ❖ Rubber band-powered helicopter.

Sheldon's Hobbies, 2135 Old Oakland Rd., San Jose, CA 95131: Free catalog ❖ Airplane models and R/C equipment, engines, accessories, and building supplies. 800-822-1688.

Showcase Model Company, P.O. Box 129, Covington, OH 45318: Free catalog ❖ Aviation and space craft pre-built display models. 513-473-5725.

SIG Manufacturing Company Inc., 401 S. Front St., Montezuma, IA 50171: Catalog $3 ❖ R/C, control line, and rubber band-powered model planes. 515-623-5154.

Squadron Mail Order, 1115 Crowley Dr., Carrollton, TX 75011: Catalog $4.50 ❖ Aircraft, ships, and military models. 214-242-8663.

Standard Hobby Supply, P.O. Box 801, Mahwah, NJ 07430: Catalog $2 ❖ Ready-to-fly airplanes, off-road buggies, racing cars, other models, and parts. 201-825-2211.

Technopower II Inc., 610 North St., Chagrin Falls, OH 44022: Catalog $3 ❖ Radial gas engines. 216-564-9787.

Tower Hobbies, P.O. Box 9078, Champaign, IL 61826: Catalog $3 ❖ Model airplanes, cars, boats, R/C equipment, engines, and building supplies. 800-637-6050.

Vailly Aviation, 18 Oakdale Ave., Farmingville, NY 11738: Catalog $1 ❖ R/C model airplane kits. 516-732-4715.

VLS Mail Order, Lone Star Industrial Park, 811 Lone Star Dr., O'Fallon, MO 63366: Catalog $6 ❖ Aircraft and car models. Also other models and military miniatures. 314-281-5700.

Windward R/C, 20 Hudson Harbour Dr., Poughkeepsie, NY 12601: Free brochure ❖ R/C ultralights. 914-485-8346.

Wing Manufacturing, 306 E. Simmons, Galesburg, IL 61401: Free information ❖ R/C model airplane kits and building materials. 309-342-3009.

Armor & Military Models

Collectors Brass, P.O. Box 27191, Fresno, CA 93729: Free list with long SASE ❖ Scale miniature machine gun models, kits, mounts, and ammunition boxes.

Colpar Hobbies, 804 S. Havana St., Aurora, CO 80012: Free newsletter with long SASE ❖ Airplanes, armor, automobiles, ships, R/C equipment, parts, and accessories. 303-341-0414.

Dean's Hobby Shop, 131 E. Main St., Flushing, MI 48433: Free list (specify cars, planes, or military models) with long SASE ❖ Old and collectible model kits. 810-659-2137.

Discount Hobby Center, P.O. Box 370, Utica, NY 13503: Catalog $5 ❖ Military models and aircraft. 315-733-3741.

Kit Bunker, 2905 Spring Park Rd., Jacksonville, FL 32207: Catalog $1 with long SASE and three 1st class stamps ❖ Out-of-production and current military model kits. 904-399-1911.

More than Models, P.O. Box 4001, Simi Valley, CA 93093: Catalog $3 ❖ Aircraft, armor, ships, books, and accessories. 805-527-8455.

Pearl Harbor Hobbies, 7147 Jonesboro Rd., Morrow, GA 30260: Catalog $1 ❖ Military models. 404-961-9057.

South Replicas Inc., 61650 Oak Rd., South Bend, IN 46614: Catalog $7 ❖ Antique artillery reproductions for ship and fort restorations, museums, monuments, and other settings. 219-289-4500.

Squadron Mail Order, 1115 Crowley Dr., Carrollton, TX 75011: Catalog $4.50 ❖ Aircraft, ships, and military models. 214-242-8663.

Stuempfle's Military Miniatures, 13190 Scott Rd., Waynesboro, PA 17268: Catalog $3 ❖ Military miniatures. 717-762-0825.

VLS Mail Order, Lone Star Industrial Park, 811 Lone Star Dr., O'Fallon, MO 63366: Catalog $6 ❖ Military and aircraft models and miniature military figures. 314-281-5700.

West Hobbies, P.O. Box 7299, Loma Linda, CA 92354: Aircraft catalog $3; armor catalog $1; ship catalog $1 ❖ Military kits from around the world.

Automobile Models

Accent Models Inc., P.O. Box 295, Denville, NJ 07834: Catalog $2 ❖ Collectible car models. 201-887-8403.

America's Hobby Center Inc., 146 W. 22nd St., New York, NY 10011: Catalog $3 ❖ Car model kits. 212-675-8922.

American Classics Unlimited, Frank Groll-Karen Groll, P.O. Box 192, Oak Lawn, IL 60454: Free information ❖ Promotional model cars and banks, collectible automobilia, and other cars and kits. 708-424-9223.

Asheville Diecast, 1412 Brevard Rd., Asheville, NC 28806: Free information ❖ Die-cast model cars and trucks. 800-343-4685.

Astro Models, 13856 Roxanne Rd., Sterling Heights, MI 48312: Catalog $1 ❖ Model car parts and accessories. 810-268-3479.

Auto Motif Inc., 2968 Atlanta Rd., Smyrna, GA 30080: Catalog $3 ❖ Car models, gifts and collectibles with an automotive theme, books, prints, puzzles, office accessories, lamps, original art, and posters. 800-367-1161.

MODELS & MODEL BUILDING

Auto Toys, P.O. Box 81385, Bakersfield, CA 93380: Free price list with long SASE ❖ Die-cast racing collectibles, scale car models, and automobilia. 805-588-2277.

Autofanatics Ltd., P.O. Box 55158, Sherman Oaks, CA 91413: List $2 ❖ Scale model automobiles in kits or assembled. 818-787-3660.

Automobilia, Division Lustron Industries, 18 Windgate Dr., New City, NY 10956: Catalog $3 ❖ Die-cast and pewter automotive miniatures, car badges, cruise ship models, and toy cars of the 1950s. 914-639-6806.

Benjy's Trains & Toys, P.O. Box 16491, Temple Terrace, FL 33687: Free price list with long SASE ❖ Slot cars and accessories, trains, and toys. 813-980-3790.

Bill & Sharon's Collectables, 110 S. Main St., Randleman, NC 27317: Free price list with long SASE ❖ Die-cast models. 910-498-8244.

Bob's Hobby & Collector's Shop, 115 N. Main St., P.O. Box 796, Watervliet, MI 49098: Catalog $2 (refundable) ❖ Model kits. 616-463-7452.

Bob's Hobby Center, 7333 Lake Underhill Rd., Orlando, FL 32822: Free information ❖ R/C airplanes, helicopters, boats, and cars. 407-277-1248.

Bruckner Hobbies Inc., 2920 Bruckner Blvd., Bronx, NY 10465: Free information ❖ Automobile and airplane kits, R/C equipment, and building supplies. 718-863-3434.

C & D Collectible Diecasts, P.O. Box 66008, Mobile, AL 36660: Free list with long SASE ❖ Collectible die-cast cars. 800-333-3866.

Can-Am Marketing, 7900 Plaza Blvd., Unit 105, Mentor, OH 44060: Free information ❖ Die-cast replicas. 800-563-7223.

Cars & Parts Collectibles, 911 Vandemark Rd., P.O. Box 482, Sidney, OH 45365: Free information ❖ Precision scale car models. 800-448-3611; 800-327-1259 (in OH).

Coker Tires, 1317 Chestnut St., Chattanooga, TN 37402: Free information ❖ Collectible toy trucks. 800-251-6336; 615-265-6368 (in TN).

Collectibles by Hamilton, 2609 Parklawn Dr., Louisville, KY 40217: Free list with long SASE and three 1st class stamps ❖ Die-cast models. 502-634-9982.

Colpar Hobbies, 804 S. Havana St., Aurora, CO 80012: Free newsletter with long SASE ❖ Airplanes, armor, automobiles, ships, R/C equipment, parts, and accessories. 303-341-0414.

Cox Hobbies Inc., 350 W. Rincon St., Corona, CA 91720: Free list of retail sources ❖ R/C model airplanes and cars. 714-278-2551.

Dahm's Automobiles, P.O. Box 360, Cotati, CA 94931: Catalog $4 ❖ Racing bodies for R/C cars and trucks. 707-792-1316.

Dean's Hobby Shop, 131 E. Main St., Flushing, MI 48433: Free list (specify cars, planes, or military models) with long SASE ❖ Old and collectible model kits. 810-659-2137.

Direct Hobby Supply Center, P.O. Box 743, Nashville, NC 27856: Catalog $3 ❖ Plastic automobile kits, airbrushes, resin bodies, tools, decals, and supplies. 919-446-2291.

Dominion Models, P.O. Box 515, Salem, VA 24153: Free brochure ❖ Die-cast and white metal American car models. 540-375-3750.

Downtown Hobby, P.O. Box 848368, Hollywood, FL 33024: Free information ❖ R/C model cars. 305-964-0701.

Eastwood Automobilia, 580 Lancaster Ave., P.O. Box 3014, Malvern, PA 19355: Free catalog ❖ Transportation collectibles. 800-345-1178.

Evers Toy Store, 204 1st Ave. East, Dyersville, IA 52040: Free information with long SASE ❖ Model cars and airplanes. 800-962-9481.

EWA & Miniature Cars USA, 369 Springfield Ave., Berkeley Heights, NJ 07922: Free catalog ❖ Die-cast models, metal and plastic kits, and other model cars. 908-665-7811.

Exoticar Model Company, 2A New York Ave., Framingham, MA 01701: Free catalog ❖ Die-cast model cars. 800-348-9159.

Hobby Heaven, P.O. Box 3229, Grand Rapids, MI 49501: Free catalog with long SASE and two 1st class stamps ❖ Ready-to-build model automobiles, from the 1950s, 1960s, and 1970s. 616-453-1094.

Hobby House Inc., 30992 Five Mile Rd., Livonia, MI 48154: Free information ❖ Model cars and supplies. 313-425-9720.

Hobby Shack, 18480 Bandilier Circle, Fountain Valley, CA 92728: Free catalog ❖ R/C equipment and ready-to-assemble airplanes and automobiles. 800-854-8471.

Hobby Surplus Sales, P.O. Box 2170, New Britain, CT 06050: Catalog $2 ❖ Planes, cars, ships, model trains, R/C models, and craft supplies. 800-233-0872.

Hobby Warehouse of Sacramento, 8950 Osage Ave., Sacramento, CA 95828: Free information ❖ R/C automobiles and kits. 916-381-7588.

Long Island Train & Hobby Center, 192 Jericho Tnpk., Mineola, NY 11501: Price list $3 ❖ Car models. 516-742-5621.

Merkel Model Car Company, 9564 W. Grand Ave., Franklin Park, IL 60131: Catalog $2.95 each (specify type of car model) ❖ Collectible and current car model kits, promotional and pre-assembled cars, die-cast models, and building supplies. 847-455-1495.

Miniatures of the World Inc., 104 May Dr., Harrison, OH 45030: Catalog $3 ❖ Trucks, motorcycles, fire trucks, farm and construction equipment, collectibles, and race, performance, exotic, and sports cars. 513-367-1746.

Model Cars & Trains Unlimited, 28 Arthur Ave., Blue Point, NY 11715: Catalog $4 (specify type of model) ❖ Model cars, trains, toy soldiers, and accessories. 516-363-2134.

Model Empire, 7116 W. Greenfield Ave., West Allis, WI 53214: Catalog $3 (refundable with $20 order) ❖ Cars, trucks, figures, racers, space and military models, boats, airplanes, and die-cast models. 414-453-4610.

Model Expo Inc., P.O. Box 1000, Mt. Pocono, PA 18344: Catalog $5 (refundable) ❖ Detailed scaled models of legendary automobiles in kits or assembled. 800-222-3876.

Model Motorcars Ltd., 111 Primrose Dr., Longwood, FL 32779: Catalog $10 ❖ Models of classic cars with automotive finishes, working accessories, genuine leather, wiring, and other renditions. 407-862-5168.

The Model Shop, P.O. Box 68, Onalaska, WI 54650: Catalog $3 ❖ Model cars, trucks, and hobby supplies. 608-781-1864.

Motorhead, 1917 Dumas Circle NE, Takoma, WA 98422: Catalog $5 ❖ Scale model cars and kits, art prints, and collectibles. 206-924-0776.

Mountain State Hobby Supply, P.O. Box 356, Teays, WV 25569: Free list with long SASE and two 1st class stamps ❖ Kits and supplies. 304-757-3242.

MRC Models, Model Rectifier Corporation, 200 Carter Dr., Edison, NJ 08817: Free information ❖ Helicopter kits, airplanes, and automobiles. 908-248-0400.

Munchkin Motors, P.O. Box 266, Eastford, CT 06242: Catalog $3 ❖ Collectible miniature cars. 203-974-2545.

North Coast Miniature Motors, 3724 W. 32nd St., Erie, PA 16506: Free information ❖ Antique, classic, racing, promotional models, and die-cast and hand-built automotive miniatures. 814-838-1921.

North Coast Racing, 7280 Noble Rd., Windsor, OH 44099: Free price list ❖ Die-cast models. 216-272-5786.

Novak Electronics Inc., 18910 Teller Ave., Irvine, CA 92715: Free list of retail sources ❖ One-touch set-up speed controls. 714-833-8873.

Past-Time Hobbies Inc., 3734 Prairie Ave., Brookfield, IL 60513: Free information with long SASE ❖ American model cars. 708-485-4544.

Performance Miniatures, 118 N. Black Horse Pike, Bellmawr, NJ 08031: Free catalog ❖ Die-cast cars. 800-931-1227.

MODELS & MODEL BUILDING

Phoenix Model Company, P.O. Box 15390, Brookville, FL 34609: Catalog $3 ❖ Aircraft, motorcycles, automobiles, boats, and other models. 904-754-8522.

Polk's Model-Craft Hobbies Inc., 346 Bergen Ave., Jersey City, NJ 07304: Catalog $2 ❖ Tools, R/C equipment, and airplane, car, and boat models. 201-332-8100.

Neal Pope Inc., 4474 Buford Hwy., Atlanta, GA 30341: Free information ❖ Die-cast model cars. 404-455-7673.

Ranch Pit Shop, 1655 E. Mission Blvd., Pomona, CA 91766: Free catalog ❖ Automobiles and accessories. 909-623-1506.

Replicarz, 99 State St., Rutland, VT 05701: Free catalog ❖ Die-cast and plastic scale models of racing and street cars. 802-747-7151.

Sentinel Miniatures, P.O. Box 735, Larchmont, NY 10538: Catalog $8.50 ❖ Military, historical, and fantasy figure kits. Also HO and N scale trains and die-cast cars. 914-682-3932.

Sheldon's Hobbies, 2135 Old Oakland Rd., San Jose, CA 95131: Free catalog ❖ Automobiles and accessories. 800-822-1688.

Sinclair's Auto Miniatures, P.O. Box 8403, Erie, PA 16505: Catalog $2 ❖ Die-cast and handcrafted miniature cars. 814-838-2274.

Specialty Diecast Company, 370 Miller Rd., Medford, NJ 08055: Free information ❖ Die-cast model cars. 800-432-1933.

Standard Hobby Supply, P.O. Box 801, Mahwah, NJ 07430: Catalog $2 ❖ Ready-to-fly airplanes, off-road buggies and cars, racing cars, and parts. 201-825-2211.

Stormer Racing, 23 High Speed Rd., P.O. Box 126, Glasgow, MT 59230: Free information ❖ Kits and parts for R/C automobiles. 800-255-7223.

T 'N' T Hobbies, P.O. Box 414, Stormville, NY 12582: Free price list $1 ❖ Current and discontinued race car kits, decals, and supplies. 914-878-4456.

Tower Hobbies, P.O. Box 9078, Champaign, IL 61826: Catalog $3 ❖ Model airplanes, cars, boats, R/C equipment, engines, and building supplies. 800-637-6050.

Valley Plaza Hobbies, 3633 Research Way, Unit 104, Carson City, NV 89706: Catalog $6 ❖ Miniature car models. 702-887-1131.

Dioramas

Fantasy Craft, 933 Carson Ln., Pomona, CA 91766: Catalog $5 (refundable with $50 order) ❖ Traditional, contemporary, and southwest-style dollhouse kits. Also diorama, room boxes, and furniture kits. 909-591-8252.

Hansa Systems, 8 Meadow Glen Rd., Kings Park, NY 11754: Catalog $5 (refundable) ❖ Scale building components. 516-269-9050.

Scale Equipment Ltd., P.O. Box 20715, Bradenton, FL 34203: Catalog $5 (refundable) ❖ Diorama-making supplies. 813-739-4999.

Scale Model Concepts Ltd., 1990 N. Alma School Rd., Ste. 304, Chandler, AZ 85224: Catalog $2 ❖ Diorama-building supplies. 602-545-0569.

Paper Airplanes

Fiddlers Green, 1960 W. Ray Rd., Chandler, AZ 85224: Free information ❖ Cardstock models of "N" scale buildings and historical aircraft.

Radio Control Equipment

Ace R/C, 116 W. 19th St., Box 472, Higginsville, MO 64037: Catalog $2 ❖ R/C model airplane equipment. 816-584-7121.

America's Hobby Center Inc., 146 W. 22nd St., New York, NY 10011: Catalog $3 ❖ Model airplanes, R/C equipment, and tools. 212-675-8922.

Bruckner Hobbies Inc., 2920 Bruckner Blvd., Bronx, NY 10465: Free information ❖ Airplane and automobile kits, R/C equipment, and building supplies. 718-863-3434.

Colpar Hobbies, 804 S. Havana St., Aurora, CO 80012: Free newsletter with long SASE ❖ Airplanes, armor, automobiles, ships, R/C equipment, parts, and accessories. 303-341-0414.

Custom Electronics, RR 1, Box 123B, Higginsville, MO 64037: Free information ❖ Electronic support equipment for R/C systems. 816-584-6284.

Dicky Bird Models, P.O. Box 1249, Westminster, CA 92684: Catalog $1 ❖ R/C electric powered airplanes. 714-775-4153.

Futaba Corporation of America, P.O. Box 19767, Irvine, CA 92713: Free information ❖ R/C systems for cars, trucks, and buggies. 714-455-9888.

Hitec, 10729 Wheatlands Ave., Santee, CA 92071: Free information ❖ R/C systems. 619-258-4940.

Hobby Shack, 18480 Bandilier Circle, Fountain Valley, CA 92708: Free catalog ❖ R/C equipment. 800-854-8471.

Horizon Hobby Distributors, 4105 Fieldstone Rd., Champaign, IL 61821: Free information ❖ R/C systems. 217-352-1913.

McDaniel R.C. Inc., 1654 Crofton Blvd., Ste. 4, Crofton, MD 21114: Free information ❖ Accessories for R/C systems. 410-721-6303.

Northeast Sailplane Products, 16 Kirby Ln., Williston, VT 05495: Catalog $7 ❖ R/C and electric flight sailplanes and accessories. 802-658-9482.

The Quarterdeck, 5622 Hwy. 153, Hixson, TN 37343: Catalog $3.50 ❖ Wooden ship kits and R/C accessories. 615-870-5327.

SR Batteries Inc., Box 287, Bellport, NY 11713: Information $3 ❖ Batteries. 516-286-0079.

Jim Walston, Retrieval Systems, 725 Cooper Lake Rd., South East Smyrna, GA 30082: Free catalog ❖ Retrieval systems. 800-657-4672; 404-434-4905 (in GA).

Rocket Models

Aerotech Inc., 1955 S. Palm St., Ste. 15, Las Vegas, NV 89104: Free information ❖ Rocket launched R/C acrobatic glider. 702-641-2301.

Belleville Wholesale Hobby, 1827 N. Charles St., Bellville, IL 62221: Catalog $3 ❖ Rocket kits and parts. 618-234-5989.

Countdown Hobbies, 3 P.T. Barnum Square, Bethel, CT 06801: Catalog $2.50 ❖ Rocket and space flight equipment. 203-790-9010.

Custom Model Rockets, P.O. Box 2086, Augusta, ME 04338: Free catalog ❖ Model rocket kits. 800-394-4114; 207-623-4114 (in ME).

Dynamic Composites Inc., P.O. Box 85, Boston, PA 15135: Catalog $1 ❖ Parts, accessories, and kits. 412-751-9515.

High Sierra Rocketry, P.O. Box 343, Orem, UT 84059: Catalog $2 ❖ Rocket kits, hardware, and accessories. 801-224-2276.

Impulse Aerospace, 22833 Bothell Way SE, Ste. 1148, Bothell, WA 98021: Catalog $2 ❖ Ignition systems. 800-568-2785.

Loc/Precision Inc., P.O. Box 221, Macedonia, OH 44056: Catalog $3 ❖ Rocket kits and components. 216-467-4514.

Magnum Industries, Model Rocketry, P.O. Box 124, Mechanicsburg, OH 43044: Catalog $2 ❖ Rocket kits and accessories. 513-834-3306.

Merrell Scientific/World of Science, 1665 Buffalo Rd., Rochester, NY 14624: Catalog $2 ❖ Rockets, engines, and igniters. Other items include chemicals, laboratory glassware, and equipment for biology, chemistry, physical and earth science, and astronomy experiments. 716-426-1540.

Public Missiles Ltd., 38300 Long, Harrison Twp, MI 48045: Catalog $3 ❖ Rocket kits, accessories, and modeling supplies. 810-468-3521.

Robby's Rockets, P.O. Box 171, Elkhart, IN 46515: Catalog $3 ❖ Flashbulb igniters, thermalite and supplies, and ejection charges. 219-679-4143.

Teleflite Corporation, 11620 Kitching St., Moreno Valley, CA 92387: Catalog $2 ❖ Rocket engine equipment and how-to information.

Vaughn Brothers Rocketry, 4575 Ross Dr., Paso Robles, CA 93446: Catalog $1 ❖ Rocket kits and accessories. 805-239-3818.

❖ MODELS & MODEL BUILDING ❖

Ship Models

AC Model Boats, P.O. Box 23041, Plaza 33 Postal Outlet, Kelowna, British Columbia, Canada V1X 7K7: Price list $2 ❖ Catamarans, hydrofoils, and tunnel and vee hulls. 604-765-7730.

America's Hobby Center Inc., 146 W. 22nd St., New York, NY 10011: Catalog $3 ❖ Ship building kits. 212-675-8922.

Bluejacket Ship Crafters, P.O. Box 425, Stockton Springs, ME 04981: Catalog $2 (refundable) ❖ Kits, fittings, supplies, and tools. 800-448-5567.

Bob's Hobby Center, 7333 Lake Underhill Rd., Orlando, FL 32822: Free information ❖ R/C airplanes, helicopters, boats, and cars. 407-277-1248.

Central Model Marketing, P.O. Box 772, Aurora, CO 80040: Free information ❖ Boat models, engines and accessories, and R/C equipment. 800-962-2010.

Classic Model Marine, Fred Diel Products, 1616 Sydney St., San Luisa Obispo, CA 93401: Free information ❖ Boat kits, custom-built boats, and accessories. 805-545-0712.

Colpar Hobbies, 804 S. Havana St., Aurora, CO 80012: Free newsletter with long SASE ❖ Airplanes, armor, automobiles, ships, R/C equipment, parts, and accessories. 303-341-0414.

DPI Leisure Sports, 15500 Wood-Red Rd. NE, Building C, Ste. 100, Woodinville, WA 98072: Free list of retail sources ❖ Easy-to-assemble high-performance boats. 206-481-2456.

Dumas Boats, 909 E. 17th St., Tucson, AZ 85719: Free catalog ❖ R/C boat models. 520-623-3742.

Freedom Song Boatworks, P.O. Box 41 North, Edgecomb, ME 04556: Brochure $2 ❖ Model boat kits. 207-882-7154.

Hobby Barn, P.O. Box 17856, Tucson, AZ 85731: Free catalog ❖ Boat and airplane models. 520-747-3792.

Hobby House Inc., 30992 Five Mile Rd., Livonia, MI 48154: Free information ❖ Model boats, fittings, supplies, and tools. 313-425-9720.

Hobby Surplus Sales, P.O. Box 2170, New Britain, CT 06050: Catalog $2 ❖ Planes, cars, ships, model trains, and R/C models. 800-233-0872.

Hobby World Ltd. of Montreal, 5450 Sherbrooke St. West, Montreal, Quebec, Canada H4A 1V9: Catalog $5 ❖ Airplanes, helicopters, cars and trucks, ships, military vehicles, and science models. 514-481-5434.

International Marine Exchange, 37 Addington Dr., Feasterville, PA 19053: Catalog $5 ❖ Model ships, fittings, and equipment. 215-322-4773.

K & B Manufacturing Inc., 2100 College Dr., Lake Havasu City, AZ 86403: Free information ❖ Airplane and marine engines.

The Maritime Store, 2905 Hyde St. Pier, San Francisco, CA 94109: Free catalog ❖ Maritime maps and books, greeting cards, boat models, children's books, and gifts. 415-775-BOOK.

Model Boats Unlimited, P.O. Box 1135, Haddonfield, NJ 08033: Catalog $11 ❖ R/C and other boats, electric and sailboat accessories, fittings, and supplies. 609-783-9163.

Model Expo Inc., P.O. Box 1000, Mt. Pocono, PA 18344: Catalog $5 (refundable) ❖ Airplane models, tools, automobile and boat kits, and trains. 800-222-3876.

More than Models, P.O. Box 4001, Simi Valley, CA 93093: Catalog $3 ❖ Aircraft, armor, ships, books, and accessories. 805-527-8455.

Octura Models Inc., 7351 N. Hamlin Ave., Skokie, IL 60076: Free information with long SASE ❖ R/C boats. 708-674-7351.

Phoenix Model Company, P.O. Box 15390, Brookville, FL 34609: Catalog $3 ❖ Aircraft, motorcycles, automobiles, boats, and other models. 904-754-8522.

Polk's Model-Craft Hobbies Inc., 346 Bergen Ave., Jersey City, NJ 07304: Catalog $2 ❖ Tools, R/C equipment, building supplies, and airplane, car, and boat models. 201-332-8100.

Prather Products Inc., 1660 Ravenna Ave., Wilmington, CA 90744: Catalog $2 ❖ High-performance epoxy glass boats. 310-835-4764.

Prentiss Court, P.O. Box 8662, Greenville, SC 29604: Catalog $1 ❖ Handcrafted model sailboats. 803-299-3929.

Preston's, Main Street Wharf, Greenport, NY 11944: Free catalog ❖ Ship models. 800-836-1165.

Bob Priep, P.O. Box 560822, Orlando, FL 32856: Free information ❖ Ready-to-race hydrofoil boat. 407-898-4485.

The Quarterdeck, 5622 Hwy. 153, Hixson, TN 37343: Catalog $3.50 ❖ Wooden ship kits and R/C accessories. 615-870-5327.

Rocky Mountain Mini Sports, 13365 Birch Circle, Thornton, CO 80241: Catalog $3 ❖ Boat-building supplies. 303-426-0110.

Seaworthy Small Ships, P.O. Box 2863, Prince Frederick, MD 20678: Catalog $1 ❖ Rubber powered wooden model boat kits with pre-cut and pre-drilled parts. 410-586-2700.

Ships N' Things, P.O. Box 605, Somerville, NJ 08876: Catalog $5 (refundable with $25 order) ❖ Competition boats and hardware. 908-722-0075.

Shoreline Design Racing Team, 6864 SW 114th Pl., Building F, Miami, FL 33173: Free brochure ❖ Easy-to-handle racing boats. 305-252-8414.

Squadron Mail Order, 1115 Crowley Dr., Carrollton, TX 75011: Catalog $4.50 ❖ Aircraft, ships, and military models. 214-242-8663.

Swampworks Mfg., 1810 N. Farm Rd. 197, Springfield, MO 65802: Video catalog $6 ❖ Warship kits, drive gear, bilge pumps, BB cannons, and carbon dioxide delivery systems for R/C models. 417-831-2309.

Tower Hobbies, P.O. Box 9078, Champaign, IL 61826: Catalog $3 ❖ Model airplanes, cars, boats, R/C equipment, engines, and building supplies. 800-637-6050.

Trinity Products Inc., 1901 E. Linden Ave., Linden, NJ 07036: Free catalog with long SASE ❖ Electric motors and cooling units for model boats. 908-862-1705.

Victor Model Products, 12260 Woodruff Ave., Downey, CA 90241: Free brochure with long SASE ❖ R/C sailing yachts. 310-803-1897.

Warehouse Hobbies, 1180 C.R. 621 East, Lake Placid, FL 33852: Catalog $1 ❖ Ready-to-run gasoline-powered model boats. 813-699-1231.

Steam-Operated Models & Engine Kits

Allen Models, 5994 Cuesta Verde, Goleta, CA 93117: Catalog $3 ❖ Steam-operated locomotives.

Coles' Power Models Inc., P.O. Box 788, 839 E. Front St., Ventura, CA 93001: Catalog $5 ❖ Steam and gas engine castings, steam fittings, tools, metals, books, and model engineering supplies. 805-643-7065.

Darby's Railroad Supply, P.O. Box 1816, Rancho Cucamonga, CA 91730: Catalog $10 ❖ Diesel and steam locomotives, rolling stock, accessories, and parts. 909-948-0773.

Diamond Enterprises, Box 537, Alexandria Bay, NY 13607: Catalog $6.95 (refundable) ❖ Kits or assembled live steam models. 800-481-1353.

Graham Industries, P.O. Box 15230, Rio Rancho, NM 87174: Free brochure ❖ Twin cylinder vertical reversing steam engine kit.

Jerry E. Howell, 3980 Becket Dr., Colorado Springs, CO 80906: Free information ❖ Plans and parts kits (requires minimal lathe-turning) for building engines.

J & J Trains, P.O. Box 1226, 5348 Vista Del Mar, Cypress, CA 90630: Free information ❖ Steam-operated locomotives. 714-828-1537.

Little Engines, 11609 Dumfries Rd., Manassas, VA 22111: Catalog $7.50 ❖ Old-time and modern steam engines, accessories, and rolling stock. 703-791-5322.

MODELS & MODEL BUILDING

M.T.H. Electric Trains, 9693 Gerwig Ln., Columbia, MD 21046: Free information ❖ Live steam ready-to-run trains and kits. 410-381-2580.

Superscale Locomotive Company, 367-A Beckett Pl., Grover Beach, CA 93433: Catalog $9 ❖ Accessories for steam models.

Tiny Power, Steam Engines & Supplies, P.O. Box 1605, Branson, MO 65615: Catalog $5 ❖ Steam engines and pumps. 417-334-2655.

Yesteryear Toys & Books Inc., Box 537, Alexandria Bay, NY 13607: Catalog $6.95 (refundable) ❖ Working steam models. Available assembled or as kits. 800-481-1353.

Supplies, Hardware & Plans

Balsa USA, P.O. Box 164, Marinette, WI 54143: Free information ❖ Balsa wood and tools. 800-BALSA-US.

Dave Brown Products, 4560 Layhigh Rd., Hamilton, OH 45013: Free information ❖ R/C airplane equipment and building materials. 513-738-1576.

Bruckner Hobbies Inc., 2920 Bruckner Blvd., Bronx, NY 10465: Free information ❖ Airplane and automobile kits, R/C equipment, and building supplies. 718-863-3434.

Chrome-Tech U.S.A., 2914 Ravenswood Rd., Madison, WI 53711: Free brochure with long SASE ❖ Chrome plating for model cars. 608-274-9811.

Coverite, 420 Babylon Rd., Horsham, PA 19044: Free information ❖ R/C model airplane kits, building materials, and tools. 215-672-6720.

Detail Resources, P.O. Box 76, Owosso, MI 48867: Catalog $1 with long SASE and two 1st class stamps ❖ Automotive parts for model building.

Direct Hobby Supply Center, P.O. Box 743, Nashville, NC 27856: Catalog $3 ❖ Plastic automobile kits, airbrushes, resin bodies, tools, decals, and supplies. 919-446-2291.

Du-Bro Products, 480 Bonner Rd., Wauconda, IL 60084: Free information ❖ Hardware, tools, and building supplies. 312-526-2136.

Fiberglass Specialties, 38624 Mt. Kisco Dr., Sterling Heights, MI 48310: Catalog $1 ❖ Fiberglass cowls, wheel parts, and other parts. 810-978-2512.

Gallant Models Inc., P.O. Box 2459, Capistrano Beach, CA 92624: Catalog $2 ❖ Model building plans.

Hobby Shack, 18480 Bandilier Circle, Fountain Valley, CA 92728: Free catalog ❖ Model-making supplies and tools. 800-854-8471.

K & S Engineering, 6917 W. 59th St., Chicago, IL 60638: Catalog $1 ❖ Aluminum and other metal tubes, rods, and sheets for model building. 312-586-8503.

Kress Jets Inc., 500 Ulster Landing Rd., Saugerties, NY 12477: Free information ❖ Scale model aircraft plans. 914-336-8149.

Eldon J. Lind Company, 3151 Caravelle Dr., Lake Havasu City, AZ 86406: Free catalog with long SASE ❖ Model building tools and accessories. 520-453-7970.

Lone Star Models, Rt. 9, Box 437, Lubbock, TX 79423: Free information ❖ Balsa wood, plywood, basswood, model airplanes, and accessoriers. 806-745-6394.

MCW Automotive Finishes, Box 518, Burlington, NC 27216: Information $1 with long SASE ❖ Authentic model paints for American cars, from the 1930s to the 1990s.

Miniatronics, 561 Acorn St., Deer Park, NY 11729: Free catalog with long SASE ❖ Miniature electric supplies for the hobbyist.

Model Electronics Corporation, 6500 6th Ave. NW, Seattle, WA 98117: Catalog $3 ❖ Electric-powered flight motors. 206-782-7458.

More than Models, P.O. Box 4001, Simi Valley, CA 93093: Catalog $3 ❖ Aircraft, armor, ships, books, and accessories. 805-527-8455.

Northeastern Scale Models Inc., P.O. Box 727, Methuen, MA 01844: Catalog $1 ❖ Basswood and supplies for building models and doll houses. 508-688-6019.

Preston's Car Parts, 7221 White Eagle Dr., Fort Wayne, IN 46815: Catalog $1 ❖ Scale model accessories. 219-493-2032.

Proctor Enterprises, 25450 NE Eilers Rd., Aurora, OR 97002: Catalog $5 (refundable) ❖ R/C model airplane kits and hardware. 503-678-1300.

Robart Manufacturing, P.O. Box 1247, St. Charles, IL 60174: Free catalog with long SASE ❖ Model airplane accessories and tools. 708-584-7616.

SIG Manufacturing Company Inc., 401 S. Front St., Montezuma, IA 50171: Catalog $3 ❖ Balsa wood. 515-623-5154.

Superior Aircraft Materials, 12020 Centralia, Hawaiian Gardens, CA 90716: Free catalog with long SASE ❖ Balsa wood, birch, plywood, and other building materials. 310-865-3220.

Tools

Badger Air-Brush Company, 9128 W. Belmont, Franklin Park, IL 60131: Brochure $1 ❖ Tools and supplies for building model airplanes. 800-247-2787.

Campbell Tools Company, 2100 Selma Rd., Springfield, OH 45505: Catalog $2 ❖ Lathes, mills, taps, dies, micrometers, cutting tools, miniature screws, and brass, aluminum, steel, and other supplies. 513-322-8562.

Coverite, 420 Babylon Rd., Horsham, PA 19044: Free information ❖ R/C model airplane kits, building materials, and tools. 215-672-6720.

Dremel Moto-Tool, P.O. Box 468, Racine, WI 53406: Free information ❖ Power tools for modelers. 414-554-1390.

Du-Bro Products, 480 Bonner Rd., Wauconda, IL 60084: Free information ❖ Hardware, tools, and building supplies. 312-526-2136.

Griffin Manufacturing Company Inc., 1656 Ridge Rd. East, P.O. Box 308, Webster, NY 14580: Free catalog ❖ Cutters, knives, blades, and tools. 716-265-1991.

Hobby Horse Products, P.O. Box 543, Kendallville, IN 46755: Catalog $2 ❖ Train repair tools for O, S, and standard gauge trains. 219-347-3958.

In Scale, P.O. Box 5267, Eureka, CA 95502: Catalog $1 ❖ Hobby supplies, kits, accessories, and miniature jewelers and scratch-building tools. 707-445-9435.

International Hobby Corporation, 413 E. Allegheny Ave., Philadelphia, PA 19134: Catalog $4.98 ❖ Battery-powered tools, model airplanes, railroading accessories, and military miniatures. 800-875-1600.

K & S Engineering, 6917 W. 59th St., Chicago, IL 60638: Catalog $1 ❖ Precision tools. 312-586-8503.

Micro-Mark, 340 Snyder Ave., Berkeley Heights, NJ 07922: Catalog $1 ❖ Miniature and standard size tools. 908-464-6764.

Model Expo Inc., P.O. Box 1000, Mt. Pocono, PA 18344: Catalog $5 (refundable) ❖ Modeling tools, train sets, airplane and automobile kits, and wood and plastic ship models. 800-222-3876.

Polk's Model-Craft Hobbies Inc., 346 Bergen Ave., Jersey City, NJ 07304: Catalog $2 ❖ Modeling tools and supplies, R/C equipment, and airplanes, cars, boats, and other craft models. 201-332-8100.

Robart Manufacturing, P.O. Box 1247, St. Charles, IL 60174: Free catalog with long SASE ❖ Model airplane accessories and tools. 708-584-7616.

Sherline Products Inc., 170 Navajo St., San Marcos, CA 92069: Free catalog ❖ Precision-made miniature power-operated tools. 800-541-0735.

Warehouse Hobbies, 1180 C.R. 621 East, Lake Placid, FL 33852: Catalog $1 ❖ Three-in-one mill, drill, and lathe machine shop for model builders. 813-699-1231.

Xuron Corporation, 60 Industrial Park Rd., Saco, ME 04072: Free catalog ❖ Precision cutting tools and construction aids. 207-283-1401.

MODELS & MODEL BUILDING

Train Models

All Aboard Train Shoppe, P.O. Box 451, Lincroft, NJ 07738: Free price list ❖ Original post-war Lionel trains. 800-54-TRAIN; 908-842-4744 (in NJ).

Allied Model Trains, 4411 S. Sepulveda Blvd., Culver City, CA 90230: Catalog $1 ❖ Brass HO and N equipment, detail parts, tools, and supplies. 310-313-9353.

America's Hobby Center Inc., 146 W. 22nd St., New York, NY 10011: Catalog $3 ❖ Kits and equipment for building train layouts. 212-675-8922.

AMI, P.O. Box 11861, Clayton, MO 83105: Free information with long SASE ❖ Instant roadbeds.

Amro Ltd., 121 Lincolnway West, New Oxford, PA 17350: Catalog $3 ❖ Foreign railway models. 717-624-8920.

Aristo-Craft, Polk's Model Craft Hobbies Inc., 346 Bergen Ave., Jersey City, NJ 07304: Catalog $2 ❖ True-to-scale and true-to-life buildings, trestle sets, water towers, and bridges. 201-332-8100.

Arttista Accessories, 1616 S. Franklin St., Philadelphia, PA 19148: Free information with long SASE ❖ O and O27-gauge metal figures and accessories. 215-467-2493.

Benjy's Trains & Toys, P.O. Box 16491, Temple Terrace, FL 33687: Free price list with long SASE ❖ Slot cars and accessories, trains, and toys. 813-980-3790.

Bookbinder's Trains Unlimited, 84-20 Midland Pkwy., Jamaica, NY 11432: Catalog $5 ❖ Lionel standard and O-gauge trains. 718-657-2224.

Caboose Hobbies, 500 S. Broadway, Denver, CO 80209: Free information ❖ Z and G scale model trains and books. 303-777-6766.

Champion Decal Company, P.O. Box 1178, Minot, ND 58702: Catalog $5 ❖ HO and O scale decals. Wet-slide type only. 701-852-4938.

Christmas Village Company, 4411 Sepulveda Blvd., Culver City, CA 90230: Free catalog ❖ Current and retired Department 56 Snow Village and Heritage buildings, accessories, and model trains. 800-433-7856.

Classic Model Trains, P.O. Box 179, Hartford, OH 44424: Catalog $2 ❖ Ready-to-run standard gauge trains. Also power packs and train enamel for old electric trains, American Flyer, Lionel, and Ives equipment. 216-772-5177.

Dallee Electronics, 10 Witmer Rd., Lancaster, PA 17602: Catalog $6.50 ❖ Electronic control equipment for model railroads. 717-392-1705.

Doug's Train World, c/o Valley Junction Train Station, 401 Railroad Pl., West Des Moines, IA 50265: Free price list ❖ Lionel and LGB trains, O-gauge straight and curved track, remote switches, and accessories. 800-247-5096; 515-274-4424 (in IA).

Anthony F. Dudynski Supply Company, 2036 Story Ave., Bronx, NY 10473: Free information with long SASE ❖ Trains and scenic accessories. 718-863-9422.

Express Station Hobbies Inc., 640 Strander Blvd., Tukwila, WA 98188: Free information ❖ HO rolling stock, books, and scenery for train layouts. 800-237-5139.

The Freight Yard, 945 N. Euclid St., Anaheim, CA 92801: Newsletter $1 (specify N or HO scale) ❖ N and HO scale trains. 714-956-1355.

GarGraves Trackage Corporation, 8967 Ridge Rd., North Rose, NY 14516: Free information ❖ Track for model railroad layouts. 315-483-6577.

Gene's Trains, 1905 State Hwy. 88 East, Brick, NJ 08724: Free list with long SASE ❖ Engines and sets, rolling stock, and accessories. 908-840-9728.

Grand Central Ltd., 6929 Seward Ave., P.O. Box 29109, Lincoln, NE 68507: Free information with long SASE ❖ Lionel classics and new equipment, and operating and layout accessories. Also other large gauge items. 402-467-3738.

Great Traditions Toy Trains, 11706 Bustleton Ave., Philadelphia, PA 19116: Free information ❖ Rolling stock, kits, parts, and accessories. 215-698-1993.

Joseph A. Grzyboski Jr., P.O. Box 3475, Scranton, PA 18505: Free information ❖ Limited edition and classic trains. 717-347-3315.

Hansel Hardware, 13320 W. Warren, Dearborn, MI 48126: Free information ❖ New and used trains. 800-LIONEL-1.

Hobby Surplus Sales, P.O. Box 2170, New Britain, CT 06050: Catalog $2 ❖ Tools, scenery, hobby and craft supplies, and Lionel, American Flyer, and HO and N-gauge accessories. 800-233-0872.

Hobbyland, 1810 E. 12th St., Mishawaka, IN 46544: Catalog $2 ❖ Trains and scenic accessories. 800-225-6509.

International Hobby Corporation, 413 E. Allegheny Ave., Philadelphia, PA 19134: Catalog $4.98 ❖ Trains and scenic accessories. 800-875-1600.

K-Line Electric Trains Inc., P.O. Box 2831, Chapel Hill, NC 27515: Catalog $5 ❖ K-Line electric trains. 800-866-9986.

Leventon's Hobby Supply, P.O. Box 1525, Chehalis, WA 98532: Free train list with long SASE, parts catalog $2 ❖ Standard, HO, S, and O-gauge parts and rolling stock. 206-748-3643.

Mainline Hobby Supply, 15066 Buchanan Trl. E., Blue Ridge Summit, PA 17214: Free newsletter with long SASE ❖ Books, videos, locomotives, rolling stock, structures, parts, tools, scenery, and other accessories. 717-794-2860.

Miami Valley Products Company, P.O. Box 144, Morrow, OH 45152: Free information with long SASE ❖ HO, O, and G-gauge bridge and trestle kits. 513-899-9904.

Mike's Train House, 9693 Gerwig Ln., Columbia, MD 21046: Catalog $2 ❖ Locomotives, cars, and Lionel and Williams rolling stock, and accessories. 410-381-2580.

Model Cars & Trains Unlimited, 28 Arthur Ave., Blue Point, NY 11715: Catalog $4 (specify type of model) ❖ Model cars, trains, toy soldiers, and accessories. 516-363-2134.

Model Expo Inc., P.O. Box 1000, Mt. Pocono, PA 18344: Catalog $5 (refundable) ❖ Airplane models, tools, automobile and boat kits, and trains. 800-222-3876.

Model Rectifier Corporation, 200 Carter Dr., Edison, NJ 08817: Free information ❖ Power control units. 908-248-0730.

Mountain Car Company, P.O. Box 1073, Salem, VA 24153: Free catalog ❖ Kits and partially assembled railroad rolling stock and accessories. 703-387-0124.

New England Car Shops, 241 Crescent St., Waltham, MA 02154: Free brochure with long SASE ❖ Ready-to-run scale or hi-rail rolling stock. 617-899-8382.

Owen Upp Railroader's Supply Company, 11300 W. Greenfield Ave., West Allis, WI 53214: Free list with 1st class stamp ❖ Lionel, K-Line and Williams equipment. Also Gargraves track, books, and videos. 414-771-2353.

P & P Lines, P.O. Box 102, Easton, CT 06612: Catalog $2 ❖ Scenic-making supplies. 203-268-3243.

Precision Scale Company, P.O. Box 288, Stevensville, MT 59870: Free list with long SASE ❖ Detailed parts. 406-777-5071.

Red Caboose, 23 W. 45th St. (basement), New York, NY 10036: Free information ❖ European scale, American Flyer, and Lionel trains, and HO, N, and O-gauge equipment. 212-354-7349.

Charles Ro Supply Company, 662 Cross St., P.O. Box 100, Malden, MA 02148: Catalog 50¢ ❖ Lionel and LGB trains, HO rolling stock, and other equipment. 617-321-0090.

Roundhouse South, 146 E. International Speedway Blvd., Daytona Beach, FL 32118: Free information with long SASE ❖ Lionel, LGB, and Weaver trains. 904-238-7391.

Pat Russo Trains, 51 Vanderbilt Ave., Floral Park, NY 11001: Free information ❖ Trains and engines, rolling stock, accessories, and track. 516-358-5548.

San Antonio Hobby Shop, 2550 W. El Camino, Mountain View, CA 94040: Free information ❖ Scratch-building and brass supplies, books, and Lionel, LGB, HO, N, O, Z, and other narrow gauge equipment. 415-941-1278.

Scenery Unlimited, 7236 W. Madison, Forest Park, IL 60130: Catalog $6.95 ❖ Locomotives and rolling stock, tools, and scenery supplies. 708-366-7763.

Sentinel Miniatures, P.O. Box 735, Larchmont, NY 10538: Catalog $8.50 ❖ Military, historical, and fantasy figure kits. Also HO and N scale trains and die-cast cars. 914-682-3932.

Charles Siegel's Train City, 3133 Zuck Rd., Erie, PA 16506: Price list $3 ❖ American Flyer, Lionel, MPC, Marx, and other trains. 814-833-8313.

Nicholas Smith Trains, 2343 W. Chester Pike, Broomall, PA 19008: Free information with long SASE ❖ Pola, LGB, and other equipment. 215-353-8585.

Standard Hobby Supply, P.O. Box 801, Mahwah, NJ 07430: Catalog $2 ❖ Model railroad equipment. 201-825-2211.

T-Reproductions, 227 W. Main St., Johnson City, TN 37603: Catalog $3 (refundable) ❖ Buddy "L" railroad reproductions. 800-825-4287.

Todd's Train Depot, 404 W. Wilson Ave., P.O. Box 849, Wendell, NC 27591: Free price list ❖ Trains, engines, accessories, and supplies. 919-365-5006.

Town & Country/Hobbies & Crafts, Craig Kobar, 28 Dewey Ave., Totowa Boro, NJ 07512: Free list with long SASE ❖ Lionel replacement parts. 201-942-5176.

A Toy Train Depot, 4244 Broadway, Oakland, CA 94611: Free information ❖ Trains, engines, accessories, and supplies. 510-653-6923.

Toy Trains of Yesteryear, 480 Bergen Blvd., Ridgefield, NJ 07657: Free information with long SASE ❖ Pre- and post-war trains and accessories. 201-945-0223.

Train Express, 4365 W. 96th St., Indianapolis, IN 46268: Free information with long SASE ❖ Lionel train sets, American Flyer equipment, rolling stock, operating cars and accessories, kits, and track. 800-428-6177.

The Train Station, 12 Romaine Rd., P.O. Box 381, Mountain Lakes, NJ 07046: Free information ❖ Classic trains and accessories. 201-263-1979.

Train Terrain Products, Box 1960, Burbank, CA 91507: Free brochure ❖ Molded plastic layout modules for assembling operating railroads.

The Train Works, 251 Hurricane Shoals Rd., Lawrenceville, GA 30245: Free information with long SASE ❖ N and HO-gauge, American Flyer, Lionel, and other trains. 800-282-9311; 404-339-7780 (in GA).

Train World, 751 McDonald Ave., Brooklyn, NY 11218: Free information ❖ Model railroad equipment. 718-436-7072.

Walthers, 5601 W. Florist Ave., Milwaukee, WI 53218: Free list of retail sources ❖ Realistic HO and N scale structures for model train layouts.

Warren's Model Trains, 20520 Lorain Rd., Fairview Park, OH 44126: Price list $2 ❖ Lionel parts. 216-331-2900.

Watts' Train Shop, 9180 Hunt Club Rd., Zionsville, IN 46077: Free information ❖ Trains and scenic accessories. 800-542-7652.

Williams Electric Trains, 8835-F Columbia 100 Pkwy., Columbia, MD 21045: Free information ❖ Railroad classics, track, and accessories. 410-997-7766.

Charles C. Wood, P.O. Box 179, Hartford, OH 44424: Catalog $2 ❖ Standard gauge electric trains. 216-772-5177.

Woodland Scenics, P.O. Box 98, Linn Creek, MO 65052: Catalog $1.50 ❖ Trees, turf, foliage, ballast, and other scenery supplies and kits. 314-346-5555.

MOTORCYCLES & MOTOR BIKES

Clothing & Helmets

AGV USA, 801 East St., Frederick, MD 21701: Catalog $3 ❖ Leather clothing and helmets. 800-950-9006.

Arai Helmets Ltd., P.O. Box 9485, Daytona, FL 32120: Brochure $3 ❖ Helmets. 800-766-ARAI.

Bates Leathers, 3700 N. Industry Ave., Ste. 102, Lakewood, CA 90712: Free information ❖ Leather riding suits. 310-426-8668.

BMW, 300 Chestnut Ridge Rd., P.O. Box 1227, Woodcliff Lake, NJ 07675: Free information ❖ Leather riding suits. 201-307-3790.

Brockton Cycle Center, 2020 Main St., Brockton, MA 02401: Free information ❖ Clothing and helmets. Also parts and accessories for Kawasaki and Yamaha motorcycles. 508-584-1451.

Chaparral, 555 S. H St., San Bernardino, CA 92410: Free catalog ❖ Clothing, boots, goggles, and soft luggage. 800-841-2960.

Fieldsheer Clothing, 27122 Paseo Espada, Ste. 921-A, San Juan Capistrano, CA 92675: Catalog $5 ❖ Leather clothing.

Helimot European Accessories, 1141 Old Bayshore Hwy., San Jose, CA 95112: Free information ❖ Leather riding suits. 408-298-9608.

Hiper Sports, 131 Heather Ln., Howard, CO 81233: Free information ❖ Clothing, helmets, boots. Also high-performance accessories. 800-524-4737.

Intersport Fashions West, 333 S. Anita Dr., Ste. 1025, Orange, CA 92668: Free information ❖ Leather riding suits andclothing. 800-416-8255; 714-978-7718 (in CA).

Langlitz Leathers, 2446 Southeast Division, Portland, OR 97202: Catalog $1 ❖ Leather clothing. 503-235-0959.

Lazer Helmets, P.O. Box 279, Bellevue, CO 80512: Free information ❖ Helmets.

Lockhart-Phillips, 151 Calle Negocio St., San Clemente, CA 92673: Catalog $4 ❖ Leather jackets in small to extra-large. 800-221-7291; 714-498-9090 (in CA).

Motoport USA, 6110 Yarrow Dr., Carlsbad, CA 92009: Free information ❖ Men and women's touring and biker clothing and accessories. 800-777-6499.

Motorace, P.O. Box 861, Wilbraham, MA 01095: Free information ❖ Boots, vests, gloves, leather sportswear, motorcycle accessories, and tires. 800-628-4040.

Rider Wearhouse, 8 S. 18th Ave., Duluth, MN 55805: Free catalog ❖ Weatherproof motorcycle clothing. 800-222-1994.

Shoei, 333 S. Hope St., Ste. 2550, Los Angeles, CA 90071: Free information ❖ Helmets with face shields. 213-628-0275.

Malcom Smith Products, 252 Granite St., Corona, CA 91719: Free information ❖ Motorcycle helmets. 800-854-4742; 909-340-3301 (in CA).

Specialty Sports Limited, 5905 Belding Rd. NE, Rockford, MI 49341: Free brochure ❖ Leather clothing, boots, and gloves. 616-866-3722 (East); 714-363-0836 (West).

StarCycle Motorcycle Accessories Inc., 7437 Van Nuys Blvd., Van Nuys, CA 91405: Catalog $2 ❖ Clothing, helmets, and parts. 818-782-7223.

Tour Master Riding Gear, 2360 Townsgate Rd., Westlake Village, CA 91361: Free catalog ❖ Sport, Spandex finger-less, knit and leather finger-less summer and gauntlet gloves. Also tail and tank bags, clothing, rain suits and boots, and dry-knit socks. 800-421-7247; 805-373-6868 (in CA).

Vanson Leathers Inc., 213 Turnpike St., Stoughton, MA 02072: Catalog $8 ❖ Leather clothing. 617-344-5444.

Z Custom Leathers, 15902 Manufacture Ln., Huntington Beach, CA 92649: Free information ❖ Leather clothing. 714-890-5721.

❖ MOTORCYCLES & MOTOR BIKES ❖

Parts & Accessories

A & J Cycle Salvage, 10 Industrial Hwy., Lester, PA 19113: Free information ❖ New and used parts for Japanese motorcycles. 610-521-6700.

A-1 Used Cycle Parts Inc., 106 E. Arlington, St. Paul, MN 55117: Free information ❖ Honda, Suzuki, Yamaha, and Kawasaki used parts. 800-522-7891.

AA Cycles, Brooklyn Park, MD 21225: Free information ❖ Used parts for Honda, Kawasaki, Yamaha, Suzuki, and street bikes. 800-278-7099.

American Jawa Ltd., 185 Express St., Plainview, Long Island, NY 11803: Free brochure ❖ Motorcycle side cars. 516-938-3210.

Antique Cycle Supply, P.O. Box 600, Rockford, MI 49341: Catalog $5 ❖ Motorcycle parts, accessories, and literature. 616-636-8200.

Aritronix Ltd., 6000 Cornell Rd., Cincinnati, OH 45242: Free information ❖ Easy-to-install motorcycle security alarms. 800-428-0440.

Ron Ayers Motorsports, 1918 N. Memorial Dr., Hwy. 11 North, Greenville, NC 27834: Free information ❖ Honda, Suzuki, and Kawasaki parts and accessories. 800-888-3084.

Baltimore Cycle Salvage Inc., 760 Eislen St., Baltimore, MD 21230: Free information ❖ Used parts for Japanese motorcycles. 410-962-1335.

Bartels' Performance Products, 3237 Carter Ave., Marina del Ray, CA 90292: Catalog $3 ❖ Harley-Davidson accessories. 310-578-9888.

Blue Moon Cycle, 20 Skin Alley, Norcross, GA 30071: Free catalog ❖ Sidecars and BMW parts. 404-447-6945.

Brickhouse Cycles, 7819 N. Military Hwy., Norfolk, VA 23518: Free information ❖ Used parts for late model Japanese bikes. 800-877-4804; 804-480-4800 (in VA).

Britalia Motors, 1027 Rosedale, Capitola, CA 95010: Catalog $8 ❖ Triumph, BSA, Norton, Matchless, Ducati, Cagiva, Moto Guzzi, and Italjet parts. 408-476-3663.

British Cycle Supply Company, P.O. Box 119, Wolfville, Nova Scotia, Canada B0P 1X0: Free information ❖ Parts and accessories for Triumph, BSA, and Norton motorcycles. 902-542-7478.

British Only Motorcycles & Parts Inc., 32451 Park Ln., Garden City, MI 48135: Free information ❖ Reproduction parts for British motorcycles. 800-278-6659.

Brockton Cycle Center, 2020 Main St., Brockton, MA 02401: Free information ❖ Clothing and helmets. Also parts and accessories for Kawasaki and Yamaha motorcycles. 508-584-1451.

California Side Car, 5641 Computer Ln., Huntington Beach, CA 92649: Free information ❖ Motorcycle side cars. 800-824-1523; 714-891-1033 (in CA).

Capital Eurosport, 21580 Beaumeade Circle, Ste. 170, Ashburn, VA 22011: Free information ❖ Luggage systems. 703-729-7900.

Chaparral, 555 S. H St., San Bernardino, CA 92410: Free catalog ❖ Clothing, boots, goggles, soft luggage, and Dunlop, Metzeler, Michelin, Continental, Bridgestone, Cheng Shin, and other tires. 800-841-2960.

Charleston Custom Cycle, 211 Washington, Charleston, IL 61920: Free information ❖ NOS parts for Harley-Davidson Lightweights and other motorcycles, from 1948 to 1978. 217-345-2577.

Clubman Racing Accessories, P.O. Box 59, Fairfield, CT 06430: Catalog $3 ❖ Standard parts and cafe and racing equipment for Norton, Triumph, Triton, and Ducati motorcycles. 203-256-1224.

Competition Accessories Inc., 345 W. Leffel Ln., Springfield, OH 45506: Catalog $5 ❖ BMW, Moto Guzzi, Triumph, Yamaha, and Ducati accessories. 800-543-4709.

Competition Werkes, P.O. Box 5233, Rosebud, OR 97470: Free brochure ❖ Motorcycle parts. 800-736-2114.

Cycle Re-Cycle, 2233 E. 10th St., Indianapolis, IN 46201: Free information ❖ Honda, Kawasaki, Suzuki, and Yamaha parts. 317-634-7550.

Cycle Recyclers, 1538 Park Ave., Chico, CA 95928: Free information ❖ Used motorcycle parts. 800-356-4735.

Cycle Salvage Fontana, 14550 Arrow, Fontana, CA 92335: Free information ❖ Used parts. 800-659-6524; 909-355-3427 (in CA).

D & M Sportbike, 2520 Cass St., Fort Wayne, IN 46808: Free information ❖ Used Honda, Yamaha, Kawasaki, and Suzuki parts. 219-483-6833.

Donelson Cycles Inc., 9851 St. Charles Rock Rd., St. Ann, MO 63074: Free information ❖ Clothing, helmets, boots, rain suits, saddlebags, and BMW, Triumph, Norton, and Yamaha parts. 800-325-4144.

Dow Canvas Products Inc., 4230 Clipper Dr., Manitowoc, WI 54220: Free list of retail sources ❖ Vented water-repellant motorcycle cover. 800-558-7755.

East Coast Warehouse, Rt 2, Box 64, Wytheville, VA 24382: Free information ❖ Honda, Suzuki, Yamaha, and Kawasaki parts. 800-544-4814.

Eric's Motorcycle Company, 1361 E. Walnut St., Pasadena, CA 91106: Free information ❖ Current and vintage dirt bike and motorcycle parts and accessories. 818-449-ERIC.

Exigent Inc., Box 157, Mt. Holly Springs, PA 17065: Free information ❖ Bike covers. 717-486-3238.

Fairing Screens Gustafson, P.O. Box 3567, St. Augustine, FL 32085: Free catalog ❖ Standard and customized motorcycle fairing screens. 904-824-2119.

Freedom Cycles, 12505 S. 71 Hwy., Grandview, MO 64030: Free information ❖ Kawasaki, Honda, Suzuki, Yamaha, KTM, Ducati, Cagiva, and parts for other motorcycles. 816-761-6621.

Gorilla Products, 2141 E. 51st St., Los Angeles, CA 90058: Free information ❖ Cycle alarm for protection against theft or tampering. 800-262-6267.

H & H Worldwide, 8820 Bright Star Rd., Douglasville, GA 30134: Free information ❖ KTM motorcycles and parts. 404-920-1371.

Harbor Vintage Motor Company, Rt. 2, Box 248, Jonesville, VT 05466: Catalog $2 ❖ Parts for 1916 to 1994 motorcycles. 802-434-4040.

Harper's MotoGuzzi, 32401 Stringtown Rd., Greenwood, MO 64034: Free information (specify parts wanted) ❖ New, used, and hard-to-find MotoGuzzi parts, bikes, and after-market accessories. 800-752-9735.

Hiper Sports, 131 Heather Ln., Howard, CO 81233: Free information ❖ Clothing, helmets, boots, and high performance accessories. 800-524-4737.

Honda-Suzuki of Greenville, 1918 N. Memorial Dr., Greenville, NC 27834: Free information ❖ Motorcycle parts. 800-888-3084.

Hymer Manufacturing, 315 N. Silver St., Lexington, NC 27292: Free information ❖ Easy-to-install automobile bike rider. 704-869-4998.

Indian Joe Martin's Antique Motorcycle Parts, P.O. Box 3156, Chattanooga, TN 37404: Catalog $5 ❖ Indian and Harley-Davidson parts. 615-698-1787.

Indian Motorcycle Supply Inc., P.O. Box 207, Sugar Grove, IL 60554: Free information ❖ New parts for Indian Chief, Four Sport Scout, Arrow, VT Scout, and Warrior motorcycles. 708-466-4601.

Innovation Specialties, 2625 Alcatraz, P.O. Box 5899, Berkeley, CA 94705: Free information ❖ Motorcycle communicators, alarms with pagers, intercoms, and accessories. 800-222-8228.

Intraser Inc., 3580 Wilshire Blvd., Los Angeles, CA 90010: Free information ❖ New and pre-owned motorcycles, ATVs, snowmobiles, trailers, personal water vehicles, and small boats. 213-365-6030.

Kart World, 1488 Mentor Ave., Painesville, OH 44077: Catalog $3 ❖ Parts, engines, and accessories for mini-cars and bikes. 216-357-5569.

❖ MOUNTAIN & ICE CLIMBING ❖ 333

Kawasaki of Pittsburgh, 611 Butler St., Pittsburgh, PA 15223: Free information ❖ Kawasaki parts. 800-448-8611; 412-781-8611 (in PA).

Kick-Start Motorcycle Parts, P.O. Box 9347, Wyoming, MI 49509: Catalog $3 ❖ Rebuilt and replacement parts. 616-245-8991.

Dennis Kirk, 955 Southfield Ave., Rush City, MN 55069: Free information ❖ Motorcycle tires and tubes, accessories, gloves, helmets, luggage racks, carryall bags, and boots. 800-328-9280.

Klempf's British Parts Warehouse, RR 1, Box 85, Dodge Center, MN 55927: Free catalog ❖ Triumph, BSA, and Norton parts, from the 1960s to the present. 507-374-2094.

KTM Sportmotorcycle, 635 E. Powell, Gresham, OR 97030: Free information ❖ Husqvarna dirt bikes, parts, and accessories. 503-667-3970.

Laurel Highlands Accessories Plus, 84 University Dr., Lemont Furnace, PA 15456: Free information ❖ Motorcycle accessories and clothing. 800-332-0670; 412-437-0670 (in PA).

Limelite Electric Arts Inc., P.O. Box 11183, Fort Wayne, IN 46856: Free catalog ❖ High-intensity neon lighting for motorcycles. 800-860-4950.

Lockhart-Phillips, 151 Calle Negocio St., San Clemente, CA 92673: Catalog $4 ❖ Motorcycle accessories and windscreens. 800-822-6005; 714-498-9090 (in CA).

Los Angeles Triumph, W. Hyde Park Blvd., Inglewood, CA 90302: Catalog $3 ❖ Triumph parts and accessories. 310-677-5800.

M.A.P. Cycle Enterprises, 7165 30th Ave. North, St. Petersburg, FL 33710: Catalog $3 ❖ New, used, stock, and NOS parts for BSA motorcycles. 813-381-1151.

MAI Motor Bike, Terratran Manufacturing, 1819 Timberlake Dr., Delaware, OH 43015: Free information ❖ Folding motor bikes. 614-548-5561.

Marbel Associates Inc., 1819 Timberlake Dr., Delaware, OH 43015: Free information ❖ Folding motor bikes. 614-548-5561.

Michelin Cycle Department, P.O. Box 19001, Greenville, SC 29602: Free list of retail sources ❖ Motorcycle tires. 803-458-6053.

Midwest Action Cycle, 1401 Elkhorn Rd., Lake Geneva, WI 53147: Free information ❖ Suzuki parts. 800-343-9065.

Mike's Cycle Parts, 3511 Boone Rd. SE, Salem, OR 97301: Free information ❖ Used Japanese motorcycle parts. 800-327-7304.

Moores Cycle Supply, 49 Custer St., West Hartford, CT 06110: Catalog $4 ❖ Triumph and BSA parts. 860-953-1689.

Moto Race, P.O. Box 861, Wilbraham, MA 01095: Free information ❖ Tires, brakes, accessories, and clothing. 800-628-4040.

Motofixx, 505 N. Main St., Port Chester, NY 10573: Free catalog ❖ Ducati parts. 800-8-DUCATI.

Motorcycle Accessory Warehouse, 925 E. Fillmore St., Colorado Springs, CO 80907: Free information ❖ Tires, helmets, batteries, seats, saddlebags, and sportswear. 800-241-2222.

Motorcycle Salvage Company Inc., 3008 W. Mercury Blvd., Hampton, VA 23666: Free information ❖ Parts for Japanese street bikes. 800-346-4424.

Motoxtra, 1624 Wilshire Blvd., Santa Monica, CA 90403: Free information ❖ Motorcycle covers. 800-221-9872.

MR Motorcycle, 996 Patton Ave., Asheville, NC 28806: Free information ❖ Honda, Kawasaki, and Yamaha parts. 800-359-0567.

Performance Accessories, 8268 Miramar Rd., San Diego, CA 92126: Free information ❖ Motorcycle accessories. 619-271-8364.

Performance Motorcycle Center, 8268 Miramar Rd., San Diego, CA 92126: Free information ❖ Motorcycle parts. 619-271-8364.

Recycled Cycles Inc., P.O. Box 970, Hayden Lake, ID 83835: Free information ❖ Used snowmobile and motorcycle parts. 800-365-9530.

Rifle Fairings, 3140 El Camino Real, Atascadero, CA 93422: Free information ❖ Rifle windshields for all popular sport bikes. 800-262-1237.

RKA Accessories, 2175 Bluebell Dr., Ste. B, San Rosa, CA 95403: Free information ❖ Soft luggage for motorcycles.

Sam's Motorcycles, 605 Silver, Houston, TX 77007: Free information ❖ Used parts for most motorcycles. 713-862-4026.

David Sarafan Inc., 374 2nd Crown Point Rd., Rochester, NH 03867: Free information ❖ Parts for Harley-Davidson civilian and military motorcycles. 603-332-4280.

Satellite Parts Locating System, 3511 Boone Rd. SE, Salem, OR 97301: Free information ❖ New and used Japanese motorcycle parts. 800-327-7304.

Sky Cycle Inc., Rt. 13, Lunenburg, MA 01462: Free information ❖ Used Honda, KAW, Suzuki, and Yamaha parts. 800-345-6115; 508-345-4647 (in MA).

Spec II, 9812 Glen Oaks, Sun Valley, CA 91352: Catalog $3 ❖ High-performance parts and fairings. 818-504-6364.

StarCycle Motorcycle Accessories Inc., 7437 Van Nuys Blvd., Van Nuys, CA 91405: Catalog $2 ❖ Clothing, helmets, and parts. 818-782-7223.

Steve's Cycle, Rt. 5, Box 109, Tifton, GA 31794: Free information ❖ Used parts. 912-386-8666.

Storz Performance, 239 S. Olive St., Ventura, CA 93001: Catalog $4 ❖ Performance motorcycle accessories. 805-641-9540.

Rich Suski, 7061 County Road 108, Town Creek, AL 35672: Free catalog ❖ Cushman parts for vintage motorbikes and scooters. 205-685-2510.

Suzuki Motorcycle Parts & Accessories, Rt. 1, Box 182, Wytheville, VA 24383: Free information ❖ Suzuki parts. 800-544-4814.

Targa Accessories Inc., 21 Journey, Aliso Viejo, CA 92656: Catalog $5 ❖ Motorcycles and parts. 800-521-7845.

Tracy Fairings, Box 5222, Janesville, WI 53547: Free information ❖ Motorcycle fairings.

Travelcade, 6325 Alondra Blvd., Paramount, CA 90723: Free brochure ❖ Touring and custom saddles. 800-397-7709.

Vance & Hines Motorcycle Center, 14010 Marquardt Ave., Santa Fe Springs, CA 90670: Catalog $3 ❖ Performance accessories. 310-921-7461.

Western Manufacturing Corporation, Box 130, Marshalltown, IA 50158: Free information ❖ Air-operated motorcycle lift. Available in an electric version. 800-247-7594.

White Brothers, 24845 Corbit Pl., Yorba Linda, CA 92687: Catalog $4 ❖ Performance accessories for all makes of motorcycles. 714-692-3404.

World of Cycles, 8070 Ohio River Blvd., Pittsburgh, PA 15202: Free information ❖ Yamaha parts. 800-860-0686.

Yamaha Parts Warehouse, 8070 Ohio River Blvd., Pittsburgh, PA 15202: Free information ❖ Yamaha parts. 800-860-0686.

MOUNTAIN & ICE CLIMBING

A.H.E./B.V.E. Gear & Services, P.O. Box 1337, Norton, OH 44203: Free catalog ❖ Mountaineering, rock climbing, and rescue equipment. 216-825-7722.

Adventure 16 Inc., 11161 W. Pico Blvd., West Los Angeles, CA 90064: Free information ❖ Clothing, packs, ropes, and equipment. 619-283-6314.

Adventure Wear Inc., 225 State St., Ste. 113, Schenectady, NY 12305: Free catalog ❖ Outdoor clothing. 800-975-3742.

Aquanetics Inc., Outdoor Pursuits, 144 E. Olentangy St., P.O. Box 924, Powell, OH 43065: Free catalog ❖ Climbing equipment and supplies. 614-848-6663.

As Adventures Inc., 1109 S. Plaza Way, #296, Flagstaff, AZ 86001: Free catalog ❖ Portaledges, haul bags, aiders, and gear slings. 602-779-5084.

Black Diamond Equipment, 2084 E. 3900 South, Salt Lake City, UT 84124: Free information ❖ Mountain boots and backpacks for climbers. 801-278-5533.

W. Born & Associates, 2438 Blacklick-Eastern Rd., Millersport, OH 43046: Free information with long SASE ❖ Equipment and supplies for mountain climbing and rescue activities. 614-467-2676.

Bumjo's, 1700 E. 18th St., Ste. 100, Tucson, AZ 85719: Free catalog ❖ Caving, climbing, backpacking, and mountaineering equipment. 800-649-0318.

Climb Axe Ltd., 301 W. Holly St., Bellingham, WA 98225: Free information ❖ Mountaineering ropes and equipment. 206-734-8433.

Climb High Inc., 60 Northside Dr., Shelburne, VT 05482: Free catalog ❖ Boots and clothing, carabiners, ropes, backpacks, and other equipment. 802-985-5056.

Franklin Climbing Equipment, Box 7465, Bend, OR 97708: Free information ❖ Climbing equipment. 503-317-5716.

Garuda Mountaineering, P.O. Box 24804, Seattle, WA 98124: Free catalog ❖ Tents for mountain climbers. 206-763-2989.

Gregory Mountain Products, 100 Calle Cortez, Temecula, CA 92590: Free catalog ❖ Back packs and equipment for mountain climbers. 909-676-5621.

LaSportiva, 3235 Prairie Ave., Boulder, CO 80301: Free list of retail sources ❖ Climbing footwear. 303-443-8710.

Lowe Alpine, P.O. Box 1449, Broomfield, CO 80038: Free list of retail sources ❖ Mountain climbing boots and clothing, backpacks, ropes, and other equipment. 303-465-0522.

Misty Mountain Threadworks, 718 Burma Rd., Banner Elk, NC 28604: Free information ❖ Harnesses. 704-963-6688.

Moab Adventure Outfitters, 550 N. Main, Moab, UT 84532: Free catalog ❖ Climbing equipment. 801-259-2725.

Mountain Dreams International Inc., 1121 Bower Hill Rd., Pittsburgh, PA 15243: Free information ❖ Rock climbing shoes. 412-276-8660.

Mountain Gear, 2002 N. Division, Spokane, WA 99207: Free information ❖ Mountaineering equipment, clothing, shoes and boots, and clothing. 800-829-2009.

Mountain Hardware, 950 Gilman St., Berkeley, CA 94710: Free information ❖ Fast-setting-up tent. 510-559-6700.

Mountain High Ltd., 123 Diamond Peak Ave., Ridgecrest, CA 93555: Free catalog ❖ Climbing gear. 619-375-2612.

Mountain Safety Research, P.O. Box 24547, Seattle, WA 98124: Free list of retail sources ❖ Mountaineering equipment. 800-877-9677; 206-624-8573 (in WA).

Mountain Sports, 821 Pearl St., Boulder, CO 80302: Free catalog ❖ Outdoor and climbing gear. 800-558-6770; 303-443-6770 (in CO).

Mountain Tools Catalog & Equipment Guide, P.O. Box 22788, Carmel, CA 93922: Catalog $3 ❖ Equipment and soft goods for mountain and ice climbing. 408-393-1000.

Naked Edge Mountaineering, P.O. Box D, Eldorado Springs, CO 80025: Free catalog ❖ Mountaineering and ice climbing equipment. 303-499-1185.

New England Ropes, 848 Airport Rd., Fall River, MA 02720: Free information ❖ Climbing ropes. 508-678-8200.

Northern Lights, P.O. Box 3413, Mammoth Lakes, CA 93546: Free information ❖ Outdoor clothing. 619-924-3833.

PMI Petzal Distributors Inc., P.O. Box 803, LaFayette, GA 30728: Free list of retail sources ❖ Belay devices, harnesses, and equipment. 800-282-7673.

Ragged Mountain Equipment, Box 130, Rt. 16-302, Intervale, NH 03845: Free price list ❖ Mountaineering equipment, shoes and boots, and clothing. 603-356-3042.

Rock & Ice Catalog Guide, P.O. Box 18418, Boulder, CO 80308: Free information ❖ Mountaineering equipment.

Rocky Mountain Outfitter, 135 Main St., Kalispell, MT 59901: Free information ❖ Mountaineering equipment. 406-752-2446.

Shoreline Mountain Products, 11 Navajo Ln., P.O. Box 127, Corte Madera, CA 94976: Free information ❖ Mountaineering equipment. 800-381-2733.

Sterling Rope Company, 181 Elliott St., Ste. 707, Beverly, MA 01915: Free information ❖ Climbing ropes. 508-921-5500.

Summit Canyon Mountaineering, 549 Main, Grand Junction, CO 81501: Free price list ❖ Mountaineering equipment. 800-254-6248.

Sunrise Mountain Sports, 490 Ygnacio Valley Rd., Walnut Creek, CA 94596: Free catalog ❖ Mountain climbing gear. 800-910-ROCK.

Swallow's Nest, 2308 6th Ave., Seattle, WA 98121: Free catalog ❖ Backpacking and mountaineering equipment. 800-676-4041; 206-441-4100 (in WA).

Tents & Trails, 21 Park Pl., New York, NY 10007: Free information ❖ Camping and mountaineering equipment and clothing. 800-237-1760; 212-227-1760 (in NY).

Terramar Sports Ltd., 10 Midland Ave., Port Chester, NY 10573: Free information ❖ Insulated outdoor clothing. 800-468-7455.

Trango USA, 4439 N. Broadway, Boulder, CO 80304: Free list of retail sources ❖ Crampons. 800-860-3653.

Troll Harnesses, 759 N. 3rd St., Laramie, WY 82070: Free information ❖ Climbing harnesses. 307-745-5893.

J.E. Weinel Inc., P.O. Box 213, Valencia, PA 16059: Free information with long SASE ❖ Equipment and supplies for caving, climbing, and rappelling. 800-346-7673; 412-898-2335 (in PA).

Wild Things, P.O. Box 400, North Conway, NH 03860: Free catalog ❖ Clothing and equipment. 603-356-6907.

MOVIE & THEATRICAL MEMORABILIA

Archival Photography, 14845 Anne St., Allen Park, MI 48101: Catalog $6 ❖ Classic movie poster and lobby card reproductions. 313-388-5452.

Artrock Posters, 1153 Mission St., San Francisco, CA 94103: Free catalog ❖ Original rock concert posters, T-shirts, books, and memorabilia. 415-255-7390.

Pamela Banner, 3409 Lake Montebello Dr., Baltimore, MD 21218: Catalog $3 ❖ Foreign and domestic posters, lobby cards, press books, and stills. 410-235-7427.

Captain Bijou, P.O. Box 87, Toney, AL 35773: Catalog $4 ❖ Original movie posters, from 1930 to the present. 205-852-0198.

Dean Chapman, 7111 Amundson Ave., Ste. 120, Edina, MN 55439: Free list ❖ Movie memorabilia, from the 1920s to the 1990s. 612-922-8289.

Cinema City, Box 1012, Muskegon, MI 49443: Catalog $3 ❖ Movie posters, photos, autographs, and scripts. 616-739-8303.

Cinema Collectors, 1507 Wilcox Ave., Hollywood, CA 90028: Free catalog ❖ Movie posters, star photos, and books. 213-461-6516.

Cinema Graphics, P.O. Box 16177, Denver, CO 80216: Catalog $5 ❖ Original movie posters and lobby cards, from 1918 to the 1980s. 303-292-6691.

Cinema Memories, P.O. Box 4517, Key West, FL 33041: Free information with long SASE ❖ Stills, movie posters, and lobby cards. 305-292-0038.

Cinema Visions, P.O. Box 536, Berkeley, CA 94701: Free catalog ❖ Original American lobby cards. 510-848-8803.

Cinemonde, 1932 Polk St., San Francisco, CA 94109: Free information ❖ Rare movie posters, lobby cards, and books. 415-776-9988.

MOVIE & THEATRICAL MEMORABILIA   335

Dwight Cleveland, P.O. Box 10922, Chicago, IL 60614: Free information ❖ Lobby cards, one-sheets, window cards, glass slides, motion picture heralds, exhibitor's books, and studio annuals. 312-266-9152.

Collectors Warehouse Inc., 5437 Pearl Rd., Cleveland, OH 44129: Catalog $2 ❖ Rare movie posters. 216-842-2896.

Carl J. DeMaio, Classic Movie Posters, 288 Heathcliff Pl., Brea, CA 92621: Catalog $3 ❖ Vintage movie posters. 714-990-2446.

Dick's Movie Graphics, Box 23709, Gainesville, FL 32602: Catalog $3 ❖ Movie posters and photographs. 904-373-7202.

Euro Posters, 531 Clayton, Denver, CO 80206: Catalog $1 ❖ A large selection of European posters and lobbies from foreign and U.S. films. 303-329-0707.

Fantasy Animation, P.O. Box 426, Marlboro, NJ 07746: Free catalog ❖ Fantasy and science fiction animation and artwork. 800-863-7775.

Film Favorites, P.O. Box 133, Canton, OH 73724: Free information with long SASE ❖ Movie stills of hard-to-find scenes from the silent movies through the classics of the 1980s. 405-886-3358.

Filmart's Cartoon World, 362 New York Ave., Huntington, Long Island, NY 11743: Free catalog ❖ Contemporary and vintage animation art from most major studios. 800-ART-CELS.

Gifted Images Gallery, P.O. Box 34, Baldwin, NY 11510: Free catalog ❖ Cels, drawings, backgrounds, and animation art. 800-726-6708; 516-536-6886 (in NY).

Gone Hollywood, 172 Bella Vista Ave., Belvedere, CA 94920: Free information ❖ Vintage movie posters. 415-435-1929.

Granada Posters, 1007 N. Federal Hwy., Ste. 78, Fort Lauderdale, FL 33304: Free information ❖ Movie posters, lobby cards, black and white stills, and press books. 305-452-9827.

GZ Foreign Movie Memorabilia, P.O. Box 696, Dania, FL 33004: Free list (specify interests) ❖ Posters, magazines, photos, records, and foreign movie memorabilia. 305-989-4846.

John Hazelton Posters, 235 Horton Hwy., Mineola, NY 11501: Catalog $3 ❖ Movie posters, from Hollywood classics to other eras.

Hollywood Collectibles, P.O. Box 4035, Sedona, AZ 96339: Catalog $2 ❖ Movie posters, lobby cards, and glossies. 520-204-1965.

Hollywood Legends, 6621 Hollywood Blvd., Hollywood, CA 90028: Free information ❖ Theatrical performers' memorabilia, press kits, Disney books, autographed photos, and other collectibles. 213-962-7411.

Hollywood North, 4510 Excelsior Blvd., #102, St. Louis Park, MN 55416: Free catalog ❖ Lobby cards, stills, pressbooks, movie sheet music, soundtracks, and miscellaneous movie collectibles. 612-925-8695.

Hummerdude's, P.O. Box 4348, Dunellan, NJ 08812: Catalog $4 ❖ Thousands of celebrity photos, autographs, and collectibles. Movie and TV stars, music artists, and more. 908-424-9367.

Intergalactic Trading Company, P.O. Box 521516, Longwood, FL 32752: Free catalog ❖ Movie posters and related material. 800-383-0747.

Jim's TV Collectibles, P.O. Box 4767, San Diego, CA 92164: Catalog $2 ❖ Television and theatrical collectibles, from the 1950s through 1990s.

John's Collectible Toys & Gifts, 57 Bay View Dr., Shrewsbury, MA 01545: Catalog $2 ❖ Character toys and movie and TV collectibles. 508-797-0023.

Richard Kohl, 1848 N. Federal Hwy., Boynton Beach, FL 33435: Free information ❖ Vintage movie posters. 800-344-9103.

La Belle Epoque, 11661 San Vincente Blvd., Ste. 211, Los Angeles, CA 90024: List $4 ❖ Rare United States and foreign posters. 310-442-0054.

Last Moving Picture Company, 2044 Euclid Ave., Cleveland, OH 44115: Free information with long SASE ❖ Window and lobby cards, inserts, one-sheets, stills, and posters. 216-781-1821.

Werner H. Lehmann, Euro Posters, 531 Clayton St., Denver, CO 80206: Catalog $1 ❖ European and United States movie posters and lobbies. 303-329-0707.

LeMay Movie Posters, P.O. Box 480879-CC, Los Angeles, CA 90048: Catalog $5 ❖ Movie posters and lobby cards. 800-565-3629.

Alan Levine Movie & Book Collectibles, P.O. Box 1577, Bloomfield, NJ 07003: Catalog $5 ❖ Movie magazines from 1915 to 1970, movie posters, lobby cards, and celebrity autographs. 201-743-5288.

Rick Lipp, 427 Broadway, Jackson, CA 95642: Free information with long SASE ❖ Stills, lobby sets, inserts, and press kits. 209-296-4754.

Memory Lane Records, 1321 Grand Ave., North Baldwin, NY 11510: Catalog $6 ❖ Records from the 1950s to the 1980s, photos, movie prints, and nostalgia. 516-623-2247.

Metropolis, 7 W. 18th St., New York, NY 10011: Free information ❖ Vintage comic books and movie posters. 800-229-6387; 212-627-9691 (in NY).

Mile High Comics, 2151 W. 56th Ave., Denver, CO 80221: Catalog $1 ❖ Original and re-issued movie posters.

Miscellaneous Man, George Theofiles, Box 1776, New Freedom, PA 17349: Catalog $5 ❖ Rare and unusual American and European pre-1965 posters. 717-235-4766.

Moe's Movie Madness, 3526 N. Main, P.O. Box 246, Tomsbrook, VA 22660: Free information ❖ Movie posters and memorabilia. 800-382-2501; 703-436-9181 (in VA).

Motion Picture Arts Gallery, 133 E. 58th St., New York, NY 10022: Free information ❖ Vintage movie posters. 212-223-1009.

Movie Market, P.O. Box 3900, Dana Point, CA 92629: Catalog $5 ❖ Movie, TV, and rock star photos. 714-488-8444.

Movie Poster Place Inc., P.O. Box 128, Lansdowne, PA 19050: Catalog $1 (refundable) ❖ Movie posters, stills, press books, and trailers. 610-622-6062.

Movie Poster Shop, 1314 S. Grand Blvd., Ste. 2-156, Spokane, WA 99202: Free catalog ❖ Posters and lobby cards, from 1930 to the present. 403-250-7588.

Movie Star News, 134 W. 18th St., New York, NY 10011: Brochure $5 ❖ Movie photos and posters. 212-620-8160.

Odyssey Auctions Inc., 510-A S. Corona Mall, Corona, CA 91719: Catalog $20 ❖ Movie memorabilia and autographed letters, manuscripts, photographs, and documents from the arts and sciences to politics and entertainment. 909-371-7137.

Jerry Ohlinger's Movie Material Store Inc., 242 W. 14th St., New York, NY 10011: Free catalog ❖ Stills, movie posters, star photos, magazines, and books. 212-989-0869.

On Main, 2817 Main St., Santa Monica, CA 90405: Catalog $3 ❖ Original motion picture and television wardrobes and props. 310-399-0224.

One Shubert Alley, 346 W. 44th St., New York, NY 10036: Free information ❖ T-shirts, posters, mugs, jewelry from old and new Broadway shows, and other theatrical memorabilia. 800-223-1320; 212-586-7610 (in NY).

Paper Chase, 2056 Weems Rd., Tucker, GA 30084: Free information ❖ Movie posters, used videos, baseball cards, and comics. 404-270-1239.

Paper Collectors' Mart, 134 Main St., Suncook, NH 03275: Free information with long SASE. ❖ Lobby cards, posters, movie magazines, books, paperbacks, and other memorabilia. 603-485-5856.

Tom Peper, 32 Shelter Cove Lane, #109, Hilton Head Island, SC 29928: Price list $1 ❖ Autographs, lobby cards and posters, animation art and cels, and original comic art. 800-628-7497.

Posteritati, Sam Sarowitz, 23 E. 10th St., New York, NY 10003: Free information ❖ Vintage movie posters and lobby cards. 212-477-2499.

Quest-Eridon Books, Loraine Burdick, 413 10th Ave. NE, Puyallup, WA 98372: Price list $1 with long SASE ❖ Books, movie magazines, and movie and theatrical memorabilia.

Reel Memories, 3101 N. Rock Rd., Ste. 120, Wichita, KS 67226: Catalog $5 ❖ Original movie posters. Also reprints and custom framing. 316-636-5340.

Deke Richards, 648 W. Lake Samish Dr., Bellingham, WA 98226: Catalog $5 ❖ Foreign and American movie posters. 206-671-4490.

Rick's Movie Posters, P.O. Box 23709, Gainesville, FL 32602: Catalog $3 ❖ Original movie posters and photos, from the 1950s to the present. Includes many classic reproductions from earlier years. 904-373-7202.

Robbie Music, Scherzer Rare Records Inc., P.O. Box 222, Pueblo, CO 81002: Free catalog ❖ Black and white photo reprints. 719-543-6858.

Rockabilia Inc., P.O. Box 4206, Hopkins, MN 55343: Free catalog ❖ T-shirts, backstage passes, promotional glossy photographs, imported rare posters from around the world, and other concert collectibles and investibles. 612-942-7895.

Rogofsky Movie Collectibles, Box 107, Glen Oaks, NY 11004: Catalog $3 ❖ TV and movie magazines, photos, and collectibles. 718-723-0954 (after 6 pm).

S & P Parker's Movie Market, P.O. Box 3900, Dana Point, CA 92629: Catalog $5 ❖ Movie, TV, and rock star photos. 714-488-8444.

Salzer's, 5801 Valentine Rd., Ventura, CA 93003: Free information ❖ Vintage concert posters.

Eric D. Sanchez Photo Classics, P.O. Box 14410, Phoenix, AZ 85063: Free catalog ❖ Color and black-and-white photo stills of classic and contemporary movie stars.

Noel Dean Schiff, 6975 N. Sheridan, Chicago, IL 60626: Free information ❖ Vintage movie posters and lobby cards. 312-262-6011.

Philip Sears Disney Collectibles, 24592 Via Carissa, Laguna Niguel, CA 92677: Free catalog ❖ Walt Disney autographs, animation art, and memorabilia. 714-543-1477.

Soitenly Stooges, P.O. Box 63, Highland Park, IL 60035: Catalog $2 ❖ Three Stooges-related T-shirts, hats, videos, books, watches, and other collectibles. 847-432-9270.

Starland Collector's Gallery, P.O. Box 622, Los Olivos, CA 93441: Catalog $2.50 ❖ Sports cards, movie posters, comic art, and hard-to-find movies. 805-686-5122.

Murray A. Summers, 10670 Cliff Mills Dr., Marshall, VA 22115: Catalog $3 (refundable) ❖ Movie posters, memorabilia, and scarce movie magazines from the 1920s to the 1970s.

Theatre Poster Exchange, P.O. Box 752302, Memphis, TN 38175: Catalog $8 ❖ Original movie posters, lobby cards, and stills, from the 1920s through the present. 901-795-6383.

Toy Scouts Inc., 137 Casterton Ave., Akron, OH 44303: Catalog $3 ❖ Movie posters, Disney collectibles, and movie memorabilia. 216-836-0668.

Triton Gallery, 323 W. 45th St., New York, NY 10036: Catalog 50¢ ❖ Current and rare theatrical posters with optional frames. 212-765-2472.

S. Wallach, 335 Lesmill Rd., Don Mills, Ontario, Canada M3B 2V1: Catalog $2 ❖ Movie posters, lobbies, stills, and trailers. 416-391-0133.

Wex Rex Records & Collectibles, 280 Worcester Rd., Framingham, MA 01701: Catalog $3 ❖ Movie and theatrical memorabilia, movie and TV show character toys, and other collectibles. 508-620-6181.

Yesterday, 1143 W. Addison St., Chicago, IL 60613: Free information with long SASE ❖ Original stills, lobby cards, posters, press books, magazines, and newspapers. 312-248-8087.

MOVIE & TV SCRIPTS

Book City of Burbank, 308 N. San Fernando, Burbank, CA 91502: Catalog $2.50 ❖ Movie and TV scripts. 818-848-4417.

Cinema City, Box 1012, Muskegon, MI 49443: Catalog $3 ❖ Movie scripts, posters, photos, and autographs. 616-739-8303.

Script City, 8033 Sunset Blvd., Ste. 1500, Hollywood, CA 90046: Free catalog ❖ Movie scripts, TV scripts, film and media books, photos, and posters. 213-871-0707.

MOVIE & VIDEO PROJECTION EQUIPMENT

A & I Camera Classics Ltd., 2 World Financial Center, New York, NY 10281: Free information ❖ Photographic and movie equipment. 212-786-4695.

Chambless Cine Equipment, Rt. 1, Box 1595, Hwy. 2, Ellijay, GA 30540: Free information ❖ New and used professional motion picture equipment. 706-636-5210.

DA-LITE Screen Company, 3100 N. Detroit St., P.O. Box 137, Warsaw, IN 46581: Free information ❖ Movie projection screens. 800-622-3737; 219-267-8101 (in IN).

International Cinema Equipment Company, 100 NE 39th St., Miami, FL 33137: Free information ❖ Audiovisual and cinema sound equipment, cameras, sound projectors, and film editing equipment. 305-573-7339.

NVIEW Corporation, 860 Omni Blvd., Newport News, VA 23606: Free information ❖ LCD video projection equipment. 800-775-7575.

Polaroid Imaging Systems, P.O. Box 100, Penfield, NY 14526: Free information ❖ Electronic imaging systems. 800-816-2611.

Stewart Filmscreen Corporation, 1161 W. Sepulveda Blvd., Torrance, CA 90502: Free list of retail sources ❖ Movie projection screens. 310-326-1422.

MOVIES (FILMS)

Belle & Blade, 124 Penn Ave., Dover, NJ 07801: Catalog $3 ❖ Classic hard-to-get video action, romance, and adventure movies. Includes out-of-print and discontinued titles.

Bradley's Movies, 2222 Foothill Blvd., Ste. 107, La Canada, CA 91011: Catalog $2 ❖ Western movies.

Canyon Cinema, 2325 3rd St., Ste. 338, San Francisco, CA 94107: Catalog $20 ❖ Slides and documentary movies. 415-626-2255.

Classic Cinema, P.O. Box 18932, Encino, CA 91416: Catalog $5 ❖ Westerns, mysteries, comedies, and drama on video cassettes. 800-94-MOVIE.

Euro Posters, 531 Clayton, Denver, CO 80206: Catalog $1 ❖ Foreign films. 303-329-0707.

Festival Films, 6115 Chestnut Terrace, Shorewood, MN 55331: Free catalog ❖ United States and foreign films on video cassettes. Includes the silent era, early feature films, and other classics. 612-470-2172.

Foothill Video, P.O. Box 547, Tujunga, CA 91043: Free information ❖ Westerns, feature films, serials, and foreign classics on video cassettes. 818-353-8591.

Home Film Festival, P.O. Box 2032, Scranton, PA 18501: Catalog $5 ❖ Hard-to-find films on video cassettes. 800-258-3456.

Kino Video, 333 W. 39th St., Ste. 503, New York, NY 10018: Free catalog ❖ International and classic movies from Hollywood's golden era on video cassettes. 800-562-3330; 212-629-6880 (in NY).

MUSIC BOOKS & SHEET MUSIC

Meridian Video Corporation, 1575 Westwood Blvd., Ste. 305, Los Angeles, CA 90024: Free catalog ❖ Foreign films. 800-529-2300.

National Cinema Service, 12022 Laurel Terrace Dr., Studio City, CA 91604: Free list ❖ New and used 16mm full-length features, shorts, and cartoons. 818-753-9770.

National Gallery of Art, Extension Program, Washington, DC 20565: Free catalog ❖ Lends art appreciation films to individuals, schools, and community groups. 202-646-6466.

Pyramid Film & Video, P.O. Box 1048, Santa Monica, CA 90406: Free information ❖ Educational and entertainment films and videos. 800-421-2304.

Anthony Ross, P.O. Box 240322, Charlotte, NC 28224: List $1 ❖ "B" movies, westerns, and serials.

Richard Semowich, 56 John Smith Rd., Binghamton, NY 13901: Free information ❖ 16mm films. 607-648-4025.

Ed Shea, P.O. Box 860089, Ridgewood, NY 11386: Free catalog with four 1st class stamps ❖ Hard-to-find horror, science fiction, fantasy, and rare TV classics.

Sinister Cinema, P.O. Box 4369, Medford, OR 97501: Free information ❖ Science fiction, horror, mystery, suspense, fantasy, and other films on video cassettes. 503-773-6860.

Starland Collector's Gallery, P.O. Box 622, Los Olivos, CA 93441: Catalog $2.50 ❖ Sports cards, movie posters, comic art, and hard-to-find movies. 805-686-5122.

Thornhill Entertainment, 2143-E Statesville Blvd., Ste. 168, Salisbury, NC 28144: Catalog $5 ❖ 16mm films. 704-636-1116.

The Video Finder, Box 25066, Portland, OR 97298: Catalog $2 ❖ Hard-to-find and rare TV shows and serials on video. Also old radio shows.

Video Specialists International, 182-V Jackson St., Dallas, PA 18612: Catalog $3 ❖ Rare and hard-to-find movies, from 1903 to the 1970s. 717-675-0227.

Vintage Video, P.O. Box 53, Leeds Point, NJ 08220: Free information ❖ Saturday matinee and Golden Age Hollywood movies. 609-748-0368.

MUSIC BOOKS & SHEET MUSIC

Alcazar Music, P.O. Box 429, Waterbury, VT 05676: Free information ❖ Children's, folk, Celtic, blues, Cajun, bluegrass, world music, and other hard-to-find music. 800-541-9904.

Andy's Front Hall, P.O. Box 307, Voorheesville, NY 12186: Free catalog ❖ Books and music for and about folk, traditional, and acoustic arrangements. 800-759-1775; 518-765-4193 (in NY).

Augsburg Fortress Publishers, 426 S. 5th St., Box 1209, Minneapolis, MN 55440: Free catalog ❖ Books, curriculum materials, music, gifts, audiovisuals, and ecclesiastical arts items. 800-328-4648; 612-330-3300 (in MN).

Boston Music Company, 172 Tremont St., Boston, MA 02116: Free catalog ❖ Sheet music. 617-426-5100.

Chinaberry Book Service, 2780 Via Orange Way, Ste. B, Spring Valley, CA 91978: Free catalog ❖ Books and music for children and adults. 800-776-2242.

Fun Publishing Company, 2121 Alpine Pl., Cincinnati, OH 45206: Free information ❖ Teach-yourself books for the portable keyboard, piano, and xylophone. 513-533-3636.

Hollywood Sheet Music, Beverly A. Hamer, Box 75, East Derry, NH 03041: Free information with long SASE ❖ Collectible movie sheet music. 603-432-3528.

Indian House, P.O. Box 472, Taos, NM 87571: Free catalog ❖ Traditional Native American music. 505-776-2953.

Mainly Music, 32 Main St., Brattleboro, VT 05301: Catalog $3 ❖ New, used, and rare records, CDs, and tapes. Also vintage sheet music and collectibles. 802-257-0881.

Melton Book Company, P.O. Box 140990, Nashville, TN 37214: Free catalog ❖ Christian books, bibles, audio and video recordings, and music. 800-441-0511.

Mountain Musicrafts, Jeanalee Schilling Inc., 267 South Hwy. 32, P.O. Box 8, Cosby, TN 37722: Free catalog ❖ Hammered dulcimer playing instructions, building books, and songs. 615-487-5543.

Patti Music Company, 414 State St., Madison, WI 53703: Free catalog ❖ Music books, sheet music, metronomes, and teaching aids. 800-777-2884.

Player Piano Company, 704 E. Douglas, Wichita, KS 67202: Free catalog ❖ Player piano music rolls, piano parts, and accessories. 316-263-3241.

Samra Promotions, P.O. Box 2221, Redondo Beach, CA 90278: Catalog $3 ❖ Imported CDs, sheet music, music books, and videos. 310-318-3949.

Shar Products Company, P.O. Box 1411, Ann Arbor, MI 48106: Free catalog ❖ Music for violins, violas, and cellos. 800-248-7427; 313-665-3711 (in MI).

Willis Music Company, P.O. Box 548, Florence, KY 41022: Free catalog ❖ Sheet music, educational audio cassettes, and accessories. 800-354-9799.

World Around Songs Inc., 20 Colberts Creek Rd., Burnsville, NC 28714: Free catalog ❖ American and international folk, country, party, and religious music song books. 704-675-5343.

MUSIC BOXES

Bornand Music Box Company, 139 4th Ave., Pelham, NY 10803: Free information ❖ Antique music boxes. 914-738-1506.

Christmastime Traditions, Rt 2, Box 574, Pounding Mill, VA 24637: Free catalog ❖ Mini ornaments, fabric mache figures, music boxes, stocking hangers, ribbons and bows, door posters, and Christmas decorations. 540-964-5479.

Klockit, P.O. Box 636, Lake Geneva, WI 53147: Free catalog ❖ Clock-building parts, music box kits, and Swiss music box movements in 144, 72, 50, 36, and 18-notes. 800-556-2548.

Music Box Melodies, Panchronia Antiquities, P.O. Box 210, Whitehall, NY 12887: Catalog $1 ❖ Popular, classical, waltz, marches, and show tunes, from the 1850s to 1990s. Includes carousel band organs, calliopes, street organs, European fair organs, orchestrions, street pianos, disk and cylinder musical boxes, and monkey organs. 518-282-9770.

Music Box World, P.O. Box 814, Hendersonville, NC 28793: Catalog $2 ❖ Music boxes and movements.

Rocking B Mfg., The West Coast Music Box Company, 3924 Camphor Ave., Newbury Park, CA 91320: Free catalog ❖ Children's, Christmas, and popular tunes for music boxes. 805-499-9336.

San Francisco Music Box Company, Mail Order Dept., P.O. Box 7817, San Francisco, CA 94120: Free catalog ❖ Reproduction antique and other music boxes. 800-227-2190.

Shaker Shops West, P.O. Box 487, Inverness, CA 94937: Catalog $3 ❖ Reproduction Shaker music boxes and country crafts. 415-669-7256.

Smocking Bonnet, P.O. Box 53, Lisbon, MD 21765: Catalog $3 ❖ Music box movements. 800-524-1678.

Unicorn Studios, Box 370, Seymour, TN 37865: Catalog $1 ❖ Windup and electronic music box movements, winking light units, and voice boxes for talking dolls and bears. 615-984-0145.

MUSICAL INSTRUMENTS

Altenburg Piano House Inc., 1150 E. Jersey St., Elizabeth, NJ 07201: Free catalog ❖ Organs (including church organs) and pianos. 800-526-6979.

American Musical Supply, 600 Industrial Ave., Paramus, NJ 07652: Free catalog ❖ Musical instruments. 800-458-4076.

Anyone Can Whistle, P.O. Box 4407, Kingston, NY 12401: Free catalog ❖ Musical instruments, music boxes, wind chimes, whistles, and musical-sounding toys. 800-435-8863.

MUSICAL INSTRUMENTS

Aquarian Accessories, 1140 N. Tustin Ave., Anaheim, CA 92807: Free information ❖ Drumheads and accessories. 800-473-0231.

Ash Music Corporation, 401 Old Country Rd., Carle Place, NY 11514: Free information with long SASE ❖ Musical instruments. 800-4-SAMASH; 516-333-8700 (in NY).

Bell Brass Guitars, 2901 N. Monroe, Spokane, WA 99205: Free information ❖ Resonator guitars. 509-448-7777.

Bernunzio Vintage Instruments, 2001 Five Mile Line Rd., Penfield, NY 14526: Free catalog ❖ Banjos, mandolins, ukeleles, and guitars. 716-385-1800.

Bob Brozman, P.O. Box 1181, Ben Lomond, CA 95005: Free information ❖ Resonator guitars. 408-336-8307.

R.E. Bruné, Luthier, 800 Greenwood St., Evanston, IL 60201: Free catalog ❖ Handmade harpsichords, lutes, and classical and baroque guitars. 847-864-7730.

Calton Cases of Canada, Bay 3, 4215 Brandon St. SE, Calgary, Alberta, Canada T2G 4A7: Free information ❖ Cases for most stringed instruments. 403-243-4099.

Carmel Music Company, P.O. Box 2296, Carmel-by-the-Sea, CA 93921: Free information ❖ Vintage and handmade guitars, mandolins, and banjos. 408-624-8078.

Caruso Music, 20 Bank St., New London, CT 06320: Free information ❖ Keyboard and recording equipment for guitarists. 203-442-9600.

Carvin, 12340 World Trade Dr., San Diego, CA 92128: Free catalog ❖ Guitars, amplifiers, recording mixers, equalizers, crossovers, speakers, microphones, and other equipment. 800-854-2235.

Castiglione Accordion, 13300 E. 11 Mile, Warren, MI 48089: Catalog $5 ❖ New and used accordions, concertinas, and button boxes. 800-325-1832.

Celestial Wind, Rt. 3, Box 48-A, Hawthorne, FL 32640: Free brochure ❖ Handcrafted harps. 904-481-5856.

Charley's Guitar Shop, 11389 Harry Hines Blvd., Dallas, TX 75229: Free information ❖ New, used, and vintage guitars. 214-243-4187.

Daddy's Junky Music, Used Gear by Mail, P.O. Box 1018, Salem, NH 03079: Free catalog ❖ Used and new guitars, amplifiers and professional audio equipment, drums, keyboards, other instruments and accessories, and special effects. 603-894-6492.

Discount Music Supply, 41 Vreeland Ave., Totowa, NJ 07512: Free catalog ❖ Guitars and electronic equipment. 201-942-9411.

Discount Reed Company, 24307 Magic Mountain Pkwy., Ste. 181, Valencia, CA 91355: Free catalog ❖ Reeds for clarinets, saxophones, bassoons, oboes, and other instruments. 800-428-5993.

Dorogi Dulcimers, 5779 Ellicott Rd., Brockton, NY 14716: Free catalog ❖ Plucked and hammered dulcimers. 716-792-9012.

Elderly Instruments, 1100 N. Washington, Lansing, MI 48906: Free catalog ❖ Musical instruments, strings, straps, pickups, records, and books. 517-372-7890.

Fishbite Recordings, Box 280632, San Francisco, CA 94128: Free catalog ❖ Hammered and mountain dulcimer, Celtic, old-time, and other recordings. Also dulcimers and how-to information.

Fitch Brothers Guitars, 8532 151st St., Jamaica, NY 11432: Free list with long SASE ❖ Vintage and rare guitars. 718-297-5123.

Folkcraft Instruments, P.O. Box 807, Winsted, CT 06098: Catalog $1 ❖ Mountain and hammered dulcimers, folk harps, psalteries, books, and recordings. 203-379-9857.

Fork's Drum Closet, 2707 12th Ave. South, Nashville, TN 37204: Free information ❖ Drum sets, cymbals, drumsticks, drumheads, and hardware. 800-55-FORKS.

Freeport Music, 41 Shore Dr., Huntington Bay, NY 11743: Free catalog ❖ Musical instruments and electronics. 800-624-5141; 516-549-4108 (in NY).

Fretware Guitars, 4523 N. Main, Dayton, OH 45405: Free information ❖ Used guitars. 513-275-7771.

Giardinelli Band Instrument Company Inc., 7845 Maltlage Dr., Liverpool, NY 13090: Free catalog ❖ Brass and woodwind instruments. 800-288-2334.

Gibson Guitar Corporation, 641 Massman Dr., Nashville, TN 37210: Free catalog ❖ Gibson guitars. 800-4-GIBSON.

Gruhn Guitars Inc., 400 Broadway, Nashville, TN 37203: Free list ❖ Vintage, used, and new electric and acoustic guitars, banjos, mandolins, and violins. 615-256-2033.

Guitar Emporium, 1610 Bardstown Rd., Louisville, KY 40205: Free list ❖ Vintage, new, and used guitars. 502-459-4153.

Guitarmaker's Connection, Martin Guitar Company, 510 Sycamore, Nazareth, PA 18064: Catalog $2 ❖ Guitar kits, parts, and exotic and domestic hardwoods. 800-345-3103.

Gulfcoast Guitars, 1927 Beach Rd., Englewood, FL 34223: Free list ❖ Vintage and rare guitars. 941-474-1214.

Highlander Musical Audio Products, 305 Glenwood Ave., Ventura, CA 93003: Free information ❖ Integrated pickup and pre-amp for acoustic guitars and bass. 805-658-1819.

HQ Percussion Products, P.O. Box 430065, St. Louis, MO 63143: Free information ❖ Cymbals, hi-hats, drum set silencers, and percussion accessories. 314-647-9009.

Hughes Dulcimer Company, 4419 W. Colfax, Denver, CO 80204: Free catalog ❖ Kits for Appalachian and hammered dulcimers, banjos, mandolins, harps, and harpsichords. 303-572-3753.

Intermountain Guitar & Banjo, 712 E. 100 South, Salt Lake City, UT 84102: Free information ❖ New, used, and vintage banjos, mandolins, and guitars. 801-322-4682.

International Luthiers Supply, Box 580397, Tulsa, OK 74158: Catalog $1 ❖ Violin, banjo, and mandolin-making supplies and books.

International Musical Suppliers, P.O. Box 357, Mount Prospect, IL 60056: Free information ❖ Clarinets and saxophones. 800-762-1116.

International Violin Company, 1421 Clarkview Rd., Ste. 118, Baltimore, MD 21209: Free catalog ❖ European violins and bows, strings, imported tone wood, tools, varnishes, and parts. 800-542-3538.

Interstate Music Supply, P.O. Box 315, New Berlin, WI 53151: Free catalog ❖ Musical instruments. 800-982-BAND.

Ithaca Guitar Works, 215 N. Cayuga St., Ithaca, NY 14850: Free information ❖ Handcrafted acoustic-electric guitars and new and vintage instruments. 607-272-2602.

J.K. Lutherie Guitars, 11115 Sand Run, Harrison, OH 45030: Free catalog ❖ Vintage guitar parts, new and vintage accessories, catalogs and literature, guitar magazines, and out-of-print guitar books. 800-344-8880; 513-353-3320 (in OH).

Robert James Products, P.O. Box 2514, 1320 Grand Ave., Ste. 19, San Marcosa, CA 92079: Free information ❖ Instrument support stands. 800-345-8923.

Johnson Music Company, P.O. Box 615, Mt. Airy, NC 27030: Brochure $2 ❖ Antique pump organ parts. 919-320-2212.

Kennelly Keys Music Inc., 20505 Hwy. 99, Lynnwood, WA 98036: Free catalog ❖ Musical instruments.

Keyboard Outlet, 14235 Inwood, Dallas, TX 75244: Free information with long SASE ❖ New and used keyboards. 214-490-5397.

Korg USA, 89 Frost St., Westbury, NY 11590: Free information ❖ Keyboards and accessories.

Lark in the Morning, P.O. Box 1176, Mendocino, CA 95460: Catalog $3 ❖ Hard-to-find musical instruments, books about music, CDs and cassettes, and videos. 707-964-5569.

Lark Street Music, 227 Lark St., Albany, NY 12210: Free list ❖ Rare and vintage guitars. 518-463-6033.

MUSICAL INSTRUMENTS

Latch Lake Music Products, 3115 Mike Collins Dr., St. Paul, MN 55121: Free information ❖ Guitar slides. 800-528-2437; 612-688-7502 (in MN).

H.G. Leach Guitars, P.O. Box 1315, Cedar Ridge, CA 95924: Free information ❖ Handmade flattop, archtop, and acoustic bass guitars. 916-477-2938.

Ledford's Musical Instruments, 125 Sunset Heights, Winchester, KY 40391: Free information ❖ Handmade dulcimers. 606-744-3974.

Bernard E. Lehmann Stringed Instruments, 34 Elton St., Rochester, NY 14607: Free information ❖ Handmade and vintage guitars, basses, banjos, mandolins, and violins. 716-461-2117.

Victor Litz Music Center, 305 N. Frederick Ave., Gaithersburg, MD 20877: Free catalog ❖ Musical instruments. 301-948-7478.

Local Music, 774 E. 800 South, Salt Lake City, UT 84102: Free information ❖ Handcrafted guitars.

Lone Star Percussion, 10611 Control Pl., Dallas, TX 75238: Free catalog ❖ Percussion instruments. 214-340-0835.

Luthier Music Corporation, 341 W. 44th St., New York, NY 10036: Free information ❖ Classical and flamenco guitars and sheet music, CDs, videos, nylon strings, and accessories. 212-397-6038.

Luthiers Mercantile, P.O. Box 774, Healdsburg, CA 95448: Catalog $10 ❖ Banjo and guitar kits. 800-477-4437; 707-433-1823 (in CA).

M.H. Guitar & Fiddle Shop, 300 Main St., P.O. Box 644, East Brookfield, MA 01515: Free information ❖ Stringed instruments. 800-750-4946.

---

mandolin bros. Ltd.

629 FOREST AVENUE
STATEN ISLAND, NY 10310-2576
(718) 981-3226

Mandolin Bros. Ltd., 629 Forest Ave., Staten Island, NY 10310: Free catalog ❖ Fine guitars, banjos, and mandolins--Martin, Gibson, Dobro, National, Ramirez. Archtop, flattop, electric. Also books, tapes, and accessories. 718-981-3226.

Manny's Musical Instruments & Accessories Inc., 156 W. 48th St., New York, NY 10036: Free catalog ❖ Musical instruments. 212-869-5172.

Metropolitan Music Store, P.O. Box 1415, Mountain Rd., Stowe, VT 05672: Catalog $1.25 ❖ Violins, violas, cellos, luthier supplies, tools, and wood. 802-253-4814.

Montans & Lace Vintage Musical Instruments, 15182 Bolsa Chica Rd., Huntington Beach, CA 92649: Free catalog ❖ Vintage guitars, mandolins, and ukuleles. 714-898-2453.

Mountain Musicrafts, Jeanalee Schilling Inc., 267 South Hwy. 32, P.O. Box 8, Cosby, TN 37722: Free catalog ❖ Ready-to-use dulcimers, building supplies, kits, and accessories. 615-487-5543.

Musicmaker Kits, P.O. Box 2117, Stillwater, MN 55082: Catalog $1 ❖ Build-them-yourself musical instrument kits. 800-432-5487; 612-439-9120 (in MN).

Nadine's Music, 6251 Santa Monica Blvd., Hollywood, CA 90028: Free information ❖ New and used keyboards, guitars, amplifiers, and recording equipment. 800-525-5149.

National Educational Music Company Inc., 1181 Rt. 22, Box 130, Mountainside, NJ 07092: Free catalog ❖ Musical instruments, recorders, and accessories. 800-526-4593.

National Music Supply, P.O. Box 14421, St. Petersburg, FL 33733: Free catalog ❖ Musical instruments, accessories, and audio equipment. 813-823-6666.

National Resophonic Guitars, 871 C Via Esteban, San Luisa Obispo, CA 93401: Free information ❖ Resonator guitars. 805-546-8442.

Noteworthy Woodworking, Jeffrey Gaynor, P.O. Box 46, Rootstown, OH 44272: Free brochure ❖ Handcrafted lap and hammered dulcimers, banjos, Celtic harps, and bowed psalteries. 330-325-1542.

Ovation Instruments, P.O. Box 507, Bloomfield, CT 06002: Free information ❖ Finger-style guitars.

Planetary Percussion, 710 Grand Ave., #5, Glenwood Springs, CO 81601: Free catalog ❖ Middle Eastern, African, Native American, Brazilian and Latin American, North American, and Far Eastern percussion instruments and accessories. 800-385-8729; 970-928-7215 (in CO).

Player Piano Company, 704 E. Douglas, Wichita, KS 67202: Free catalog ❖ Player piano restoration supplies and music rolls. 316-263-3241.

Pro-Mark Corporation, 10707 Craighead Dr., Houston, TX 77025: Free information ❖ Drumsticks and percussion accessories. 800-233-5250.

Pro-Sing Karaoke, 7457 S. Sayre Ave., Bedford Park, IL 60638: Free information ❖ Karaoke hardware, software, and K-Tel and classical music. 708-594-1155.

Ragtime, 4218 Jessup Rd., Ceres, CA 95307: Catalog $10 ❖ Calliopes, band organs, nickelodeons, player pianos, other Victorian musical instruments, and kits to convert regular pianos to player-pianos. 209-667-5525.

Rayburn Musical Instrument Company, 263 Huntington Ave., Boston, MA 02115: Free information ❖ Mouthpieces, reeds, woodwind and brass instruments, and audio equipment. 617-859-7476.

Rhythm Band Instruments, P.O. Box 126, Fort Worth, TX 76101: Free catalog ❖ Musical instruments and accessories for children and adults. 800-424-4724; 817-335-2561 (in TX).

Rhythm City, 1485 NE Expressway, Atlanta, GA 30329: Free information ❖ Music equipment for beginners to professionals. 404-320-7253.

Ribbecke, P.O. Box 1581, Santa Rosa, CA 95402: Free information ❖ Handcrafted acoustic archtops and flattop guitars. 707-433-3778.

Rich Music, 1007 Avenue C, Denton, TX 76201: Free information ❖ Keyboards, recording equipment, synthesizers, drum machines, mixers and amplifiers, special effects, software, and accessories. 800-795-8493.

Rizzetta Music, P.O. Box 510, Inwood, WV 25428: Free brochure ❖ Standard, compact standard, and extended range dulcimers. Also tapes and compact discs.

Robinson's Harp Shop, P.O. Box 161, 33908 Mount Laguna Dr., Mount Laguna, CA 91948: Free catalog ❖ Harp-making parts, plans, strings, hardware, and books. (619) 473-8556.

Joe Sax, 55 Roxbury Rd., Dumont, NJ 07628: Free information ❖ Saxophones, clarinets, and flutes. 800-876-8771; 201-384-0833 (in NJ and New York City).

The Saxophone Shop, 2834 Central St., Evanston, IL 60201: Free information ❖ New and used saxophones, reeds, and mouthpieces. 847-328-5711.

Schilke Music Inc., 4520 James Ave., Melrose Park, IL 60160: Free list of retail sources (specify instruments or mouthpieces) ❖ Trumpets and mouthpieces. 708-343-8858.

Shar Products Company, P.O. Box 1411, Ann Arbor, MI 48106: Free catalog ❖ Violins, violas, cellos, and music for string instruments. 800-248-7427; 313-665-7711 (in MI).

Smith Family Music, 9175 Butte Rd., Sweet, ID 83670: Free information ❖ Enhancers for any style acoustic guitar. 800-942-6509.

Speir Music, 1207 S. Buckner, Dallas, TX 75217: Free information ❖ New and used keyboards, other instruments, and accessories. 800-219-3281.

Stewart-MacDonalds Guitar Shop Supply, P.O. Box 900, Athens, OH 45701: Free catalog ❖ Parts, tools, and supplies for building and repairing guitars, violins, banjos, dulcimers, and mandolins. 800-848-2273; 614-592-3021 (in OH).

Stringed Instrument Division, 123 W. Alder, Missoula, MT 59802: Catalog $15 (annual subscription) ❖ New and vintage banjos, mandolins, acoustic guitars, and electric instruments. 406-549-1502.

Gary Sugal Mouthpieces Inc., 99 South St., Providence, RI 02903: Free information ❖ Saxophone mouthpieces. 800-334-7299; 401-751-2501 (in RI).

Sweetwater Sound Inc., 5335 Bass Rd., Fort Wayne, IN 46808: Free information ❖ Keyboards, audio equipment and accessories, consoles, stands, monitors, mixers, and other equipment. 219-432-8176.

Synthony Music, 3939 E. Campbell, Phoenix, AZ 85018: Free information ❖ Electronic music instruments, midi peripherals, and other equipment. 800-221-KEYS; 602-955-3590 (in AZ).

Thoroughbred Music, 5511 Pioneer Park Blvd., Tampa, FL 33634: Free information ❖ Keyboards, electronics, drum machines, guitars, and accessories. 800-800-4654.

Used Gear by Mail, Division Daddy's Junky Music Stores Inc., P.O. Box 1018, Salem, NH 03079: Free catalog ❖ Vintage, rare, and collectible used musical equipment. 603-894-6492.

Vintage Drum Center, 2243 Ivory Dr., Libertyville, IA 52567: Free catalog ❖ Vintage drum sets and singles. 800-729-3111.

Waddell's Drum Center, 1104 S. Leechburg Hill, Leechburg, PA 15656: Free catalog ❖ Drums. 412-845-DRUM.

Frederic H. Weiner, 1325 2nd Ave., New Hyde Park, NY 11040: Free catalog ❖ Musical instruments. 800-622-CORK.

Weinkrantz Musical Supply Company, 870 Market St., Ste. 1265, San Francisco, CA 94102: Free catalog ❖ Violins, violas, and cellos. 800-736-8742.

West Manor Music, 831 E. Gun Hill Rd., Bronx, NY 10467: Free price list ❖ Brass, woodwind, string, and percussion instruments. 212-655-5400.

Whippoorwill Crafts, North Market Building, 6 Fanueil Hall Marketplace, Boston, MA 02109: Free information ❖ Kaleidoscopes, wooden boxes and chests, instrumentalist chimes, toys and games, clocks, and imaginative crafts. 800-487-5937; 617-248-0671 (in MA).

Wichita Band Instrument Company, 2525 E. Douglas, Wichita, KS 67211: Free catalog ❖ Used, vintage, and new musical instruments. 800-835-3006; 316-684-0291 (in KS).

The Willis Music Company, 7380 Industrial Rd., Florence, KY 41022: Free catalog ❖ Keyboard, guitar, instrumental music, and accessories. 606-283-2050.

Sylvia Woods Harp Center, P.O. Box 816, Montrose, CA 91021: Free catalog ❖ Harps, recordings, books, jewelry, and gifts. 818-956-1363.

The Woodwind & the Brasswind, 19880 State Line Rd., South Bend, IN 46637: Free catalog (specify woodwind or brasswind) ❖ Musical instruments.

Workshop Records, Box 49507, Austin, TX 78765: Free catalog ❖ Instruments, recorders, amplifiers, videos, cassettes, and books. 800-543-6125.

Yamaha Corporation of America, Band & Orchestral Division, 3445 E. Paris Ave. SE, P.O. Box 899, Grand Rapids, MI 49512: Free information ❖ Woodwinds, brass winds, student percussion kits, and band instrument accessories.

Yamaha Music Corporation, P.O. Box 6600, Buena Park, CA 90622: Free list of retail sources ❖ Handcrafted guitars, keyboards, and audio equipment. 714-522-9011.

J.R. Zeidler, 1441 S. Broad St., Philadelphia, PA 19147: Brochure $5 ❖ Concert guitars and mandolins. 215-271-6858.

Zeta Music, 2230 Livingston Ave., Oakland, CA 94606: Catalog $5 ❖ Electronic guitars, violins, and controllers. 800-622-6434.

NAMEPLATES

Country Punchin', 14757 Glenn Dr., Whittier, CA 90604: Brochure $1 ❖ Hand-punched tarnish-proof name signs and plaques in solid copper or pewter-like metal. 310-944-1038.

John Hinds & Company, 81 Greenridge Dr. West, Elmira, NY 14905: Free brochure ❖ Cast plaques and nameplates for homes, offices, buildings, parks, historic areas, and other uses. 607-733-6712.

Newman Brothers Inc., P.O. Box 16067, Cincinnati, OH 45216: Free information ❖ Hand-tooled bronze and aluminum plaques. 513-242-0011.

Smith-Cornell Inc., 1545 Holland Rd., Maumee, OH 43537: Free brochure ❖ Brass and aluminum historic markers. 800-325-0248; 419-891-4335 (in OH).

NEEDLECRAFTS

Abbey Yarns N' Kits, 1512 Myers Rd., Marion, OH 44302: Catalog $3 (refundable) ❖ Yarns and kits. 614-389-1461.

Al Con Enterprises, P.O. Box 429, Hickory, NC 28603: Free catalog ❖ Macrame, chair-weaving, and crochet supplies. 800-523-4371.

American Needlewomen, 2946 SE Loop 820, Fort Worth, TX 76140: Catalog $1 ❖ Needlecraft kits and supplies from Europe and the United States. 800-433-2231.

Anderson Handcrafted Products Ltd., Star Rt. Box 87A, Leonardtown, MD 20650: Free information ❖ Portable lap and floor stand frames. 301-994-2262.

Annie's Attic, 1 Annie Ln., Big Sandy, TX 75755: Catalog $2 ❖ Sewing and needlecraft patterns. 800-282-6643.

Artisan Design, 2208 S. Elder Circle, Broken Arrow, OK 74012: Free information ❖ Floor stand, ultra-compact tabletop or lap stand, and scroll frame for needle-crafting. 800-747-8263.

Barkim Ltd., 47 W. Polk St., Ste. 100, Chicago, IL 60605: Catalog and yarn samples $4 ❖ Sweater kits and yarns. 312-548-2211.

Anny Blatt Boutique, 6728 Lowell Ave., McLean, VA 22101: Catalog $2 ❖ Kits, how-to knitting books, and accessories. 800-767-4036.

Braid-Aid, 466 Washington St., Pembroke, MA 02359: Catalog $4 ❖ Braided rug kits and braiding accessories, wool by the pound or yard, and hooking, basket-making, shirret, spinning, and weaving supplies. 617-826-2560.

California Stitchery, 6015 Sunnyslope Ave., Van Nuys, CA 91401: Free catalog ❖ Judaic design needlepoint, embroidery, and latch-hook kits. 800-345-3332.

Camus International, 222 Gulf Rd., St. 822, Lansing, NY 14882: Price list $2 ❖ Tartan point pillow, cross-stitch, and needlepoint kits. 800-38-CAMUS.

Charles Craft, P.O. Box 1049, Laurinburg, NC 28353: Catalog $3 ❖ Cross-stitch kits.

Chris' Craft Supplies, Rt. 4, Box 458, Carthage, MO 64836: Catalog $1 (refundable) ❖ Cross-stitch and framing supplies. 417-358-1900.

Cottage Creek Cross-stitch, 13327 187th Ct. NE, Woodinville, WA 98072: Free information ❖ Counted needlework patterns made from personal photographs. 800-963-3357.

The Cotton Patch, 1025 Brown Ave., Lafayette, CA 94549: Catalog $8 ($5 refundable) ❖ Quilting books, fabric swatches, silk wire ribbon, hand-dyed fabrics, knitting needles, and other supplies. 510-284-1177.

Craft Gallery Ltd., P.O. Box 145, Swampscott, MA 01907: Catalog $2 ❖ Threads, fibers, books, fabrics, and accessories for stitchery, crochet, and needle crafts. 508-744-2334.

❖ NEEDLECRAFTS ❖

Craft King Mail Order Dept., P.O. Box 90637, Lakeland, FL 33804: Catalog $2 ❖ Needlecraft, art and craft, and macrame supplies. 888-CRAFTY-1.

Craft Resources Inc., P.O. Box 828, Fairfield, CT 06430: Catalog $1 ❖ Latch-hooking, needlepoint, crewel, cross-stitching kits, and supplies for string art, basket-making, metal and wood crafts, stained glass, and other crafts. 800-243-2874; 203-254-7702 (in CT).

Crafts by Donna, P.O. Box 1456, Costa Mesa, CA 92626: Catalog $2 ❖ Threads, craft supplies, and how-to books for Brazilian embroidery. 714-545-8567.

Crafty Lady, 15401 Hall Rd., Macomb, MI 48044: Free information ❖ Exotic and natural fibers, counted cross-stitch and needlepoint supplies, and knit-wear kits. 800-455-YARN.

Creative Keepsakes, P.O. Box 7651, Monroe, LA 71203: Free catalog ❖ Samplers and counted cross-stitch kits. 800-227-7996. ✓

Cross Stitch 'N Such, 1441 W. Schaumberg Rd., Schaumberg, IL 60194: Catalog $4 (refundable) ❖ Counted cross-stitch and embroidery kits and supplies. 708-894-6664.

The DMC Corporation, P.O. Box 8027, Clinton, IA 52736: Free information with long SASE ❖ Embroidery yarn.

Dyed in the Wool, P.O. Box 498, Crowley, LA 70527: Free list of retail sources with long SASE ❖ Needlecraft kits and yarns. 800-426-3393.

Ehrman Needlepoint, 5 Northern Blvd., Amherst, NH 03031: Catalog $5 (refundable) ❖ Needlepoint kits with gardening and floral themes. 800-433-7899.

Embroidery Studio, P.O. Box 5729, Greensboro, NC 27435: Brochure $1 ❖ Totes, T-shirts, sweatshirts, turtlenecks, and needlecraft items with embroidered botanical designs. 910-273-8941.

Enchanted Cottage, Brazilian Embroidery Studio, 112 E. Cheyenne Rd., Colorado Springs, CO 80906: Catalog $2 (refundable) ❖ Brazilian rayon threads, books, kits, and designs. 719-475-9244.

Ernel Yarns, 1419 Burlingame, Burlingame, CA 94010: Free information ❖ Yarns and kits. 800-343-4874.

Fingerlakes Yarns, 1193 Stewarts Corners Rd., Genoa, NY 13071: Yarn samples $3 (request list of retail sources) ❖ Sweater kits and merino, angora, and silk yarns. 800-441-9665.

The Fine Arts Heritage Society, 5950 17th Ave. SW, Seattle, WA 98106: Free brochure ❖ Renaissance and impressionist masters in cross-stitch or needlepoint patterns. 800-741-3175.

Karen L. Ford, Ecclesiastical Designs in Needlework, P.O. Box 15178, Phoenix, AZ 85060: Catalog $1 ❖ Christian-theme needlecraft kits. _AMY?_

The Golden Needle, 509 E. Park Ave., Libertyville, IL 60048: Free price list ❖ Needlepoint and counted cross-stitch supplies. 708-549-7579.

Gruber's Market, 1 Main St., Genola, MN 56364: Free information ❖ Lap quilting frame. 612-468-6435.

Halcyon Yarn, 12 School St., Bath, ME 04530: Free information ❖ Yarn and knitting accessories. 800-341-0282.

Han Dids Needleart, 54 N. Main, Winchester, IL 62694: Catalog $2 ❖ Cross-stitch and easy-to-stitch primitive embroidery. 217-742-3660.

Hannah's House, P.O. Box 158, St. Marys, WV 16170: Brochure $2 ❖ Counted needlecraft kits.

Martha Hall, Natural Fibre Yarns, 20 Bartol Island Rd., Freeport, ME 04032: Catalog $2 ❖ Easy-to-knit wool sweater kits and hand-dyed silk, mohair, linen, cotton, cashmere, and alpaca yarn. 800-643-4566.

Hedgehog Handworks, P.O. Box 45384, Westchester, CA 90045: Catalog $5 (refundable with $30 order) ❖ Semi-precious beads and attachments, sewing notions, gold and silver threads, needlecraft and embroidery supplies, and accessories. 310-670-6040.

Herr's & Bernat, 70 Eastgate Dr., P.O. Box 630, Danville, IL 61834: Free information ❖ Latch-hook kits. 217-442-4121.

Herrschners Inc., 2800 Hoover Rd., Stevens Point, WI 54492: Free catalog ❖ Needlecraft supplies, kits, and yarns. 800-441-0838. ✓

HH Designs, Box 183, Eastchester, NY 10709: Catalog $2 ❖ Needlecraft candlewick pillow kits.

The Hill Knittery, 10720 Yonge St., Richmond Hill, Ontario, Canada L4C 3C9: Catalog and yarn samples $7 (refundable) ❖ Yarns, kits, books, and how-to videos. 800-551-KNIT.

Sue Hillis Designs, P.O. Box 784, Dumfries, VA 22026: Free information ❖ Counted cross-stitch kits. 800-622-5353.

Homestead Needle Arts, 12235 S. Saginaw St., Grand Blanc, MI 48439: Catalog $3 (refundable) ❖ Threads, charts, hand-painted canvases, books, and accessories. 800-365-1462.

Imagiknit Ltd., 2586 Yonge St., Toronto, Ontario, Canada M4P 2J3: Catalog $4.50 ❖ Yarns, how-to books, and kits. 800-318-9426. ✓

Just CrossStitch, 405 Riverhills Business Park, Birmingham, AL 35242: Free information ❖ Counted cross-stitch kits. 800-768-5878.

Just Needlin', 611 NE Woods Chapel Rd., Lee's Summit, MO 64064: Catalog $3 (refundable) ❖ Cross-stitch kits and supplies. 816-246-5102.

Sasha Kagan, 1301 NW Glisan St., Portland, OR 97209: Free catalog ❖ Knitting kits. 800-509-0462. ✓

Keepsake Quilting, Rt. 25B, Centre Harbor, NH 03226: Free catalog ❖ Quilting books and accessories, patterns, notions, fabrics, scrap bags, and batting. 800-865-9458. ✓

Koigu Wool Designs, RR 1, Williamsford, Ontario, Canada N0H 2V0: Catalog $5 ❖ Virgin wool, other yarns, hand-knit sweaters, and kits. 519-794-3066.

Carolin Lowy Needlecraft, 630 Sun Meadows Dr., Kernersville, NC 27284: Price list $2 ❖ Needlepoint, knitting, embroidery, and counted cross-stitch patterns. 910-784-7576.

Maggie Company, 309 Chestnut St., San Francisco, CA 94133: Free brochure ❖ Contemporary and whimsical needlepoint designs.

The Magic Needle, RR 2, Box 172, Kimerick, ME 04048: Catalog $2 ❖ Needlework supplies.

Marnie's Crewel Studio Inc., 6442 E. Otero Pl., Englewood, CO 80112: Free price list with long SASE ❖ Needlepoint kits and supplies. 303-740-9649.

Mary Maxim Inc., 2001 Holland Ave., P.O. Box 5019, Port Huron, MI 48061: Free catalog ❖ Needlecraft kits, yarn, and accessories. 800-962-9504. ✓

McIntosh Samplers, 64669 Orchard Dr., Goshen, IN 46526: Catalog $4 ❖ English-style samplers, Shaker sewing boxes, and accessories. 219-534-0455.

Mimi's Fabrications, 502 Balsam Rd., Hazelwood, NC 28738: Catalog $3 ❖ Silk ribbon and embroidery supplies. 704-452-3455.

Moss Yarns Needlearts, 225 Pinewood, Hot Springs National Park, AR 71913: Catalog $3 ❖ Needlecraft supplies and imported and domestic yarns. 501-623-5106.

Claire Murray Inc., P.O. Box 390, Ascutney, VT 05030: Catalog $5 (refundable) ❖ Hand-hooked rugs and kits. 800-252-4733.

My Silk Garde, Linda Smock, 10123 England St., Huntington Beach, CA 92648: Catalog $3 ❖ Silk ribbon embroidery patterns and kits. 800-448-9468.

Nasco, 901 Janesville Ave., Fort Atkinson, WI 53538: Free catalog ❖ Weaving supplies, looms, tools, yarn, and needlecraft accessories. 800-558-9595. ✓

The Needlecraft Shop, 23 Old Pecan Rd., Big Sandy, TX 75755: Free catalog ❖ Plastic canvas supplies and patterns. 903-636-4000.

Needlecraft Shop, 23 Old Pecan Rd., Big Sandy, TX 75755: Free catalog ❖ Needlecraft kits and supplies. 903-636-4000.

NeedleMagic Inc., 2815 Orchard Rd., Dandridge, TN 37725: Free brochure ❖ Cross-stitch kits. 615-397-9423.

Nordic Needle, 1314 Gateway Dr., Fargo, ND 58103: Free catalog ❖ Needlework projects, supplies, and books. 800-433-4321.

Norselander, P.O. Box 1263, Gualala, CA 95445: Brochure $3 (refundable) ❖ Sweater kits and needlecraft pattern books.

Pattern Warehouse, P.O. Box 3135, Chicago, IL 60654: Catalog $3 ❖ Cross-stitch and soft craft patterns. 312-828-9634.

Patterncrafts, Box 25639, Colorado Springs, CO 80936: Catalog $2 ❖ Quilt patterns and hoops, counted cross-stitch and sewing projects, stencils, country crafts, wall hangings, needlecrafts, dolls, and stuffed animals. 800-414-3888.

Patternworks, P.O. Box 1690, Poughkeepsie, NY 12601: Catalog $3 ❖ Knitting supplies and kits. 800-438-5464; 914-462-8000 (in NY).

Peacock Alley Needlepoint Crafts, 650 Croswell SE, Grand Rapids, MI 49506: Catalog $2 ❖ Needlecraft kits, supplies, and canvasses. 616-454-9898.

Shay Pendray's Needle Arts Inc., 2211 Monroe, Dearborn, MI 48124: Catalog $2 ❖ Japanese embroidery supplies. 800-813-3103; 313-278-6266 (in MI).

Personal Threads Boutique, 8025 W. Dodge Rd., Omaha, NE 68114: Free information ❖ Yarns and needlecraft supplies. 800-306-7733.

Anne Powell Ltd.

P.O. Box 3060
Stuart, Florida 34995

Anne Powell Ltd., P.O. Box 3060, Stuart, FL 34995: Catalog $5 ❖ Finest needlework, accessories, gifts, sterling silver thimbles, needlecases, chatelaines—antique and new. 561-287-3007.

Pretty Punch, P.O. Box 430, Edgewater, FL 32132: Free catalog ❖ Punch embroidery supplies. 800-486-1234.

Ragtime Crochet, 12105 W. Center Rd., Ste. 286, Omaha, NE 68144: Catalog $2 (refundable) ❖ Rag crochet fabric and supplies. 800-228-6633.

Catherine Reurs Needlepoint, 50 Marion Rd., Watertown, MA 02172: Catalog $1 ❖ Needlepoint kits. 800-743-0675.

Eva Rosenstand, P.O. Box 185, Clovis, CA 93613: Catalog $5 ❖ Counted cross-stitch kits, embroidery supplies, and needlecraft accessories. 209-292-2241.

Sage Artworks Inc., 2940 N. Deer Track Rd., Tucson, AZ 85749: Free catalog ❖ Judaic needlepoint kits. 800-5154-0073.

The Scarlet Letter, P.O. Box 397, Sullivan, WI 53178: Catalog $3 ❖ Museum reproduction counted thread sampler kits, hand-woven linens and silks, sewing notions, books, and frames. 414-593-8470.

Schoolhouse Press, 6899 Cary Bluff, Pittsville, WI 54466: Catalog $3 ❖ Knitting books, kits, and supplies. 715-884-2799.

Shillcraft, 8899 Kelso Dr., Baltimore, MD 21221: Catalog $2 ❖ Needlecraft supplies and latch-hook kits for rugs, wall hangings, and other crafts. 410-682-3060.

The Spinning Wheel, Martha Hauschka, 2 Ridge St., Dover, NH 03820: Free information ❖ Needlecraft supplies, yarns, and natural fibers. Also cross-stitch, crewel, candle-wicking, and other needlecrafts. 603-749-4246.

A Stitch in Time, P.O. Box 507, Spring Lake, MI 49456: Free information ❖ Counted needlework patterns made from personal photographs. 616-847-0063.

The Stitchery, 120 N. Meadows Rd., Medfield, MA 02052: Free catalog ❖ Needlecraft kits. 800-388-9662.

Stitches East, 55 E. 52nd St., New York, NY 10022: Free information ❖ Knitting and needlecraft supplies. 212-421-0112.

Things Japanese, 9805 NE 116th St., Ste. 7160, Kirkland, WA 98034: Catalog $1 ❖ Brocade threads and yarns, silk-blend and metallic threads, needlework kits, silk ribbons, and embroidery and other supplies. 206-821-2287.

Three Kittens Yarn Shoppe, 805 Sibley Memorial Hwy., St. Paul, MN 55118: Information $2 ❖ Needlecraft supplies. 800-489-4969; 612-457-4969 (in MN).

Thumbelina Needlework Shop, P.O. Box 1065, Solvang, CA 93464: Information $1.75 ❖ Books, fabrics, threads, yarns, and kits. 800-789-4136.

Susan Vale Enterprises, 820 S. Monaco Pkwy., Ste. 174, Denver, CO 80224: Free information ❖ Mohair sweaters and jackets in knit-yourself kits.

The Weaver, Box 80, Smicksburg, PA 16256: Free information ❖ Yarns, needles, books, looms, and spinning wheels. 814-257-8891.

The Weaver's Loft, 308 S. Pennsylvania Ave., Centre Hall, PA 16828: Free information ❖ Knitting, weaving, and spinning supplies and yarn. 814-364-1433.

The Weaver's Place, 75 Mellor Ave., Baltimore, MD 21228: Free information ❖ Japanese braiding equipment and books. 410-788-7262.

Web of Thread, 1410 Broadway, Paducah, KY 42001, Paducah, KY 42003: Catalog $3 ❖ Supplies for serging and embroidery crafts and metallic, rayon, and silk threads for hand and machine embroidery. 502-575-9700.

The Woolery, RD 1, Genoa, NY 13071: Catalog $2 ❖ Books and spinning, weaving, and knitting supplies. 315-497-1542.

Woolgathering, 750 Calico Ct., Waukesha, WI 53186: Free price list ❖ Rowan yarns, needlepoint kits, buttons, books, magazines, and sewing notions. 800-248-3225.

Wooly Knits, 6728 Lowell Ave., McLean, VA 22101: Catalog $5 (12 issues) ❖ Designer yarns, unusual buttons, and needlework supplies. 703-448-9665.

Yarn Shop, 304 City View Ave., West Springfield, MA 01089: Free brochure ❖ Fashion kits for children and adults. Also supplies.

NEWSPAPERS & MAGAZINES

American Family Publishers, P.O. Box 62000, Tampa, FL 33662: Free information ❖ Magazine subscriptions. 800-237-2400.

Phil Barber Newspapers, Box 8694, Boston, MA 02114: Catalog $1 ❖ Historic newspapers.

Below Wholesale Magazines, 1909 Prosperity St., Reno, NV 89502: Free catalog ❖ Magazine subscriptions. 800-800-0062.

Box Seat Collectibles, P.O. Box 2013, Halesite, NY 11743: Catalog $5 ❖ Sports and historical newspapers and memorabilia. 516-423-1025.

Historic Newspaper Archives, 1582 Hart St., Rahway, NJ 07065: Free catalog ❖ Newspapers for the day on which you were born. 800-221-3221; 908-381-2332 (in NJ).

Hughes Newspapers, Box 3636, Williamsport, PA 17701: Catalog $1 ❖ Rare and historic newspapers, from the 1600s through the 1880s. 717-326-1045.

Timothy Hughes Newspapers, P.O. Box 3636, Williamsport, PA 17701: Free catalog ❖ Rare and early newspapers. 717-326-1045.

Alan Levine Movie & Book Collectibles, P.O. Box 1577, Bloomfield, NJ 07003: Catalog $5 ❖ Books on collecting, old-time movie posters and lobby cards, and radio, television, and movie magazines. 201-743-5288.

J.K. Lutherie Guitars, 11115 Sand Run, Harrison, OH 45030: Free catalog ❖ Vintage and new guitar parts, catalogs and other literature, guitar magazines, and out-of-print guitar books. 800-344-8880; 513-353-3320 (in OH).

Jim Lyons, 970 Terra Bella Ave., Mountain View, CA 94043: Free information ❖ Historic newspapers, from the 1600s to the 1970s. 415-969-6612.

OFFICE & BUSINESS SUPPLIES

Robert A. Madle, 4406 Bestor Dr., Rockville, MD 20853: Catalog $3 ❖ Science fiction and fantasy magazines and books, from 1900 to present. 301-460-4712.

MultiNewspapers, Box 866, Dana Point, CA 92629: Free brochure ❖ English language magazines and newspapers from over 60 countries. 714-499-6207.

The Opera Box, Box 994, Teaneck, NJ 07666: Free catalog ❖ Rare books, magazines, autograph material, and other opera collectibles. 201-833-4176.

The Overlook Connection, P.O. Box 526, Woodstock, GA 30188: Catalog $1 ❖ Books, audio cassettes, and magazines on horror, science fiction, fantasy, and mystery. 770-926-1762.

Paper Collectors' Mart, 134 Main St., Suncook, NH 03275: Free information with long SASE ❖ Lobby cards, posters, movie magazines, books, paperbacks, and other memorabilia. 603-485-5856.

Steven S. Raab, 2033 Walnut St., Philadelphia, PA 19102: Free catalog ❖ Autographs, signed books and photos, historic newspapers, World War I posters, and other memorabilia. 610-446-6193.

Rogofsky Movie Collectibles, Box 107, Glen Oaks, NY 11004: Catalog $3 ❖ TV and movie magazines, photos, and collectibles. 718-723-0954 (after 6 pm).

Murray A. Summers, 10670 Cliff Mills Dr., Marshall, VA 22115: Catalog $3 (refundable) ❖ Movie magazines from the 1920s to the 1970s, movie posters, and other memorabilia.

Vintage Newspapers, P.O. Box 48621, Los Angeles, CA 90048: Free catalog ❖ Authentic newspapers and magazines, from 1880 to the present. 800-235-1919.

Yesterday, 1143 W. Addison St., Chicago, IL 60613: Free information with long SASE ❖ Original stills, lobbies, posters, press books, magazines, and newspapers. 312-248-8087.

OFFICE & BUSINESS SUPPLIES

Business Forms & Booklets

Adams Business Forms, P.O. Box 91, Topeka, KS 66601: Free information ❖ Manifold books, guest checks, and forms. 800-444-3508.

Business Forms by Carlson Craft, 1750 Tower Blvd., North Mankato, MN 56002: Free information ❖ Business forms. 800-292-9207.

Caprock Business Forms Inc., 1211 Ave. F, Lubbock, TX 79401: Free information ❖ Continuous computer forms, letterheads and envelopes, snap-apart sets, manifold books, and scratch pads. 800-666-3322.

CFO Forms, 2205 Forsyth Rd., Unit L, Orlando, FL 32807: Free price list ❖ Carbonless business forms. 800-451-3676.

Champion Industries Inc., 2450 1st Ave., P.O. Box 2968, Huntington, WV 25728: Free information ❖ Continuous and snap-out forms. 800-624-3431; 304-528-2791 (in WV).

Champion Printing Company, 3250 Spring Grove Ave., Cincinnati, OH 45225: Free information ❖ Self-mailers and bind-ins. 800-543-1957.

Colonial Business Forms Inc., 355 Sackett Point Rd., North Haven, CT 06473: Free price list ❖ Snap-out forms. 800-562-4790.

Columbus Bookbinders & Printers Inc., P.O. Box 8193, 1326 10th Ave., Columbus, GA 31908: Free information ❖ Brochures, newsletters, and printed and bound books. 706-323-9313.

Economy Printing Company, 5067 W. 12th St., Jacksonville, FL 32205: Free information ❖ Business forms and booklets. 800-423-1475; 904-786-4070 (in FL).

Grand Forms & Systems Inc., 211 S. Arlington Heights, Arlington Heights, IL 60005: Free information ❖ Business forms. 800-682-1924; 708-259-4600 (in IL).

Greater American Business Products, 9321 Kirby, Houston, TX 77054: Free catalog ❖ Business forms, stationery, and signs. 800-231-0329; 713-790-1926 (in TX).

HG Professional Forms Company, 2020 California St., Omaha, NE 68102: Free catalog ❖ Pre-printed forms, accounting supplies, computer paper, record-keeping systems, binders, report covers, and envelopes. 800-228-1493.

Mattick Business Forms Inc., 333 W. Hintz Rd., Wheeling, IL 60090: Free catalog ❖ Stationery, office and business forms, and labels. 708-541-7345.

Moore Business Products, Catalog Division, P.O. Box 5000, Vernon Hills, IL 60061: Free catalog ❖ Business forms, typewriter and printer ribbons, print wheels, copier supplies, laser printer paper and toner cartridges, fax paper, computer accessories, and supplies. 800-323-6230.

Morgan Printing Company, 2365 Wyandotte Rd., Willow Grove, PA 19090: Free information ❖ Continuous letterheads, labels, and business forms. 800-435-3892.

NEBS Inc., 500 Main St., Groton, MA 01471: Free catalog ❖ Business forms, stationery, labels, checks, business cards, and supplies.

Professional Press, P.O. Box 4371, Chapel Hill, NC 27515: Free information ❖ Booklets. 800-277-8960.

Rapidforms Inc., 301 Grove Rd., Thorofare, NJ 08086: Free catalog ❖ Business forms and labels. 800-257-8354.

Shipman Printing Industries, P.O. Box 157, Niagara Falls, NY 14302: Free information ❖ Business forms, letterheads, padded forms, and window-style and other envelopes. 800-462-2114.

Stationery House, 1000 Florida Ave., Hagerstown, MD 21740: Free catalog ❖ Business stationery and forms, supplies, and gifts. 301-739-4487.

Trade Carbonless, P.O. Box 989, Elfers, FL 34680: Free price list ❖ Edge-glued carbonless forms. 800-704-7222.

Triangle Printing Company, 325 Hill Ave., Nashville, TN 37210: Free information ❖ Booklets. 800-843-9529.

General Office Supplies

Accountants Supply House, 3012 Grove Rd., Thorofare, NJ 08086: Free catalog ❖ Stationery and envelopes, forms and labels, adding machines, shipping materials, disk storage cabinets, typewriter and data processing ribbons, furniture, and supplies. 800-342-5274.

Ad Lib Advertising, P.O. Box 531, North Bellmore, NY 11710: Free information ❖ Custom Post-It Notes. 800-622-3542.

Alfax Wholesale Furniture, 370 7th Ave., Ste. 1101, New York, NY 10001: Free catalog ❖ General office equipment, furniture, and supplies. 800-221-5710; 212-947-9560 (in NY).

American Loose Leaf Business Products, 4015 Papin, St. Louis, MO 63110: Free catalog ❖ Binders, folders, and indexes. 800-467-7000.

American Thermoplastic Company, 106 Gamma Dr., Pittsburgh, PA 15238: Free catalog ❖ Binders, index sets, sheet protectors, clipboards, report and presentation folders, data processing and catalog binders, and cassette albums. 800-245-6600.

Arrow Star, 3-1 Park Plaza, Dept. 15, Glen Head, NY 11546: Free catalog ❖ Office equipment and supplies. 800-645-2833; 516-484-3100 (in NY).

Artgrafix Warehouse, 15 Tech Circle, Natick, MA 01760: Free catalog ❖ Office supplies. 800-443-4421.

Artistic Greetings Catalog, The Personal Touch, P.O. Box 1623, Elmira, NY 14902: Free catalog ❖ Business cards, memo and informal note cards, and personalized stationery. 800-733-6313.

Bangor Cork Company Inc., William & D Streets, Pen Argyl, PA 18072: Free catalog ❖ Cork bulletin, marker, and chalkboards. 215-863-9041.

Browncor International, 400 S. 5th St., Milwaukee, WI 53204: Free catalog ❖ Mailing and shipping supplies. 800-327-2278.

The Business Book, P.O. Box 8465, Mankato, MN 56002: Free catalog ❖ Pressure sensitive labels, stampers, personalized business envelopes and stationery, speed letters, memo pads, business cards and forms, greeting cards, books, and office supplies. 800-558-0220.

343

❖ OFFICE & BUSINESS SUPPLIES ❖

Carlson Craft, 1625 Roe Crest Dr., P.O. Box 8625, North Mankato, MN 56002: Free information ❖ Custom Post-It notes. 800-292-9207.

Chenesko Products Inc., 2221 5th Ave., Ste. 4, Ronkonkoma, NY 11779: Free catalog ❖ Recharge kits for laser printer and copier toner cartridges. 800-221-3516; 516-467-3205 (in NY).

Colwell Systems, P.O. Box 9024, Champaign, IL 61826: Free catalog ❖ Office supplies. 800-637-1140.

Day-Timers, One Day-Timer Plaza, Allentown, PA 18195: Free catalog ❖ Stationery and business cards. 800-225-5005.

Frank Eastern Company, 599 Broadway, New York, NY 10012: Catalog $1 ❖ Office equipment and supplies, furniture, and shipping materials. 800-221-4914; 212-219-0007 (in NY).

Fidelity Direct, 5601 International Pkwy., P.O. Box 155, Minneapolis, MN 55440: Free catalog ❖ Office equipment and supplies. 800-328-3034; 612-526-6500 (in MN).

Grayarc, P.O. Box 2944, Hartford, CT 06104: Free catalog ❖ Office equipment and supplies. 800-562-5468.

HG Professional Forms Company, 2020 California St., Omaha, NE 68102: Free catalog ❖ Pre-printed forms, computer paper, record-keeping systems, binders, report covers, and envelopes. 800-228-1493.

Robert James Company Inc., P.O. Box 520, Moody, AL 35004: Free information with long SASE ❖ Office supplies. 800-633-8296; 205-640-7081 (in AL).

Memindex Inc., 149 Carter St., P.O. Box 20566, Rochester, NY 14602: Free catalog ❖ Organizational tools for scheduling, planning, and controlling time. 716-342-7740.

Moore Business Products, Catalog Division, P.O. Box 5000, Vernon Hills, IL 60061: Free catalog ❖ Business forms, typewriter and printer ribbons, print wheels, copier supplies, laser printer paper and toner cartridges, fax and computer paper, and binders. 800-323-6230.

Newman Enterprises, P.O. Box 16, Martin, SC 29836: Free catalog ❖ Computer systems and office equipment. 312-604-1608.

Office Depot Inc., 2200 Old Germantown Rd., Delray Beach, FL 33445: Free catalog ❖ Office supplies and equipment. 800-685-8800.

The Office Mates, P.O. Box 306, W227 N6370 Sussex Rd., Sussex, WI 53089: Free brochure ❖ Vinyl envelopes and related products. 800-238-3957.

Paper Direct Inc., 100 Plaza Dr., Secaucus, NJ 07094: Free catalog ❖ Pre-designed papers and supplies. 800-A-PAPERS.

Paper Showcase, P.O. Box 8465, Mankato, MN 56002: Free catalog ❖ Laser-compatible papers. 800-287-8163.

Quill Office Supplies, 100 Schelter Rd., Lincolnshire, IL 60197: Free catalog ❖ Office supplies. 800-789-8965.

Science of Business Inc., 8245 Nieman, Ste. 108, Lenexa, KS 66214: Free information ❖ Custom Post-It Notes. 800-POST-ITS.

Staples Inc., Attention: Marketing Services, P.O. Box 1020, Westboro, MA 01581: Free catalog ❖ Office supplies, furniture, computer supplies and paper, drafting equipment, fax machines, and typewriters. 800-333-3330.

The Staplex Company, 777 5th Ave., Brooklyn, NY 11232: Free catalog ❖ Electric staplers. 800-221-0822.

Viking Office Products, 13809 S. Figueroa St., P.O. Box 61144, Los Angeles, CA 90061: Free catalog ❖ Office supplies. 800-421-1222.

Visible, Subsidiary Wallace Computer Services Inc., 1750 Wallace Ave., St. Charles, IL 60174: Free catalog ❖ Computer and office supplies. 800-323-0628.

Vulcan Binder & Cover, 1 Looseleaf Ln., Vincent, AL 35178: Free catalog ❖ Ring binders. 800-633-4526.

Labels & Tags

A-1 Labels Inc., P.O. Box 131694, Staten Island, NY 10313: Free catalog ❖ Laser, continuous card, and mini printer labels. 800-321-2011.

Computer Label Company, P.O. Box 3419, Mesquite, NV 89024: Free catalog ❖ Computer labels, continuous post cards, and index and rotary file cards. 800-332-4223.

Continental Data Forms, 69 Veronica Ave., Somerset, NJ 08873: Free information ❖ Pinfeed pressure-sensitive labels. 800-947-8020.

Data Label Inc., 1000 Spruce St., Terre Haute, IN 47807: Free information ❖ Labels. 800-457-0676.

Ennis Express Label Service, Tag & Label Division, P.O. Box D, Wolfe City, TX 75496: Free information ❖ Labels. 800-527-1008; 903-496-2244 (in TX).

C.J. Fox Company, P.O. Box 6186, Providence, RI 02940: Free information ❖ Labels. 800-556-6868.

GraphComm Services, P.O. Box 220, Freeland, WA 98249: Free catalog ❖ Labels. 800-488-7436.

Graphic Impressions, 8538 W. Grand Ave., River Grove, IL 60171: Free information ❖ Pressure-sensitive labels. 800-451-6658.

Grayarc, P.O. Box 2944, Hartford, CT 06104: Free catalog ❖ Stationery, business cards, forms, labels, envelopes, and supplies. 800-562-5468.

Hawks Tag Service, 3959 Fulton Grove, Cincinnati, OH 45245: Free price list ❖ Tags in short run orders. 800-752-5765.

Jet Labels, 3875 S. Blue Star Dr., Traverse City, MI 49684: Free catalog ❖ Labels. 800-622-3883.

Kay Toledo Tag, P.O. Box 5038, Toledo, OH 43611: Free brochure ❖ Tags in fluorescent, cloth, vinyl, and other materials. 800-822-8247.

Label Works, 100 Garfield Ave., P.O. Box 8100, North Mankato, MN 56002: Free catalog ❖ Labels. 800-522-3558.

Lancer Label, 301 S. 74th St., Omaha, NE 68114: Free catalog ❖ Bumper stickers and labels in rolls, sheets, and pinfeed. 800-228-7074.

Lixx Labelsz, 2619 14th St. S.W., P.O. Box 32055CC4, Calgary, Alberta, Canada T2T 5X0: Catalog $4 ❖ Labels and bookmarks that combine wildlife designs, calligraphy, eco-action, and recycling. 403-245-2331.

Morgan Printing Company, 2365 Wyandotte Rd., Willow Grove, PA 19090: Free information ❖ Continuous letterheads, labels, and business forms. 800-435-3892.

NEBS Inc., 500 Main St., Groton, MA 01471: Free catalog ❖ Business forms and cards, stationery, labels, checks, and paper and office supplies.

New York Label, 50 Oval Dr., Isoandia, NY 11722: Free catalog ❖ Self-adhesive labels in singles, rolls, or sheets. 800-257-2300.

PrintProd Inc., 419 Bainbridge St., Dayton, OH 45410: Free information ❖ Multi-color tags. 800-322-TAGS; 513-228-2181 (in OH).

Seton Name Plate Company, 20 Thompson Rd., P.O. Box 3L-819, Branford, CT 06405: Free information ❖ Heavy duty paper tags, write-on and bar code labels, and other identification supplies. 800-243-6624.

Short Run Labels, 1681 Industrial Rd., San Carlos, CA 94070: Free catalog ❖ Self-adhesive labels in small orders. 800-522-3583; 415-592-7683 (in CA).

Superfast Label Service, 300 E. 4th St., Safford, AZ 85546: Free information ❖ Labels. 800-767-8566.

U.S. Tag & Label Corporation, 2217 Robb St., Baltimore, MD 21218: Free catalog ❖ Tags and labels. 800-638-1018; 410-467-2633 (in MD).

Writewell Company Inc., P.O. Box 68186, Indianapolis, IN 46268: Free catalog ❖ Stationery and envelopes, note cards, memo pads, and labels. 800-968-5850.

Receipt Books

Cook Receipt Book Manufacturing Company, Box 2005, Dothan, AL 36302: Free catalog ❖ Receipt books. 800-842-0444.

ORIGAMI (PAPER FOLDING)

Herald Multiforms Inc., P.O. Box 1288, Dillon, SC 29536: Free information ❖ Continuous form, check, and snap-out receipt books. 800-845-5050; 803-774-9051 (in SC).

Rapidforms Inc., 301 Grove Rd., Thorofare, NJ 08086: Free catalog ❖ Labels and business forms. 800-257-8354.

Rush Receipt Book Company, 457 Houston South, Mobile, AL 36606: Free price list ❖ Receipt books. 800-654-4237.

Superior Receipt Book Company, 215 S. Clark St., P.O. Box 326, Centreville, MI 49032: Free information ❖ Receipt books. 800-624-2887; 616-467-8265 (in MI).

Shipping Supplies

Chiswick Trading Inc., 33 Union Ave., Sudbury, MA 01776: Free catalog ❖ Shipping and packaging supplies. 800-225-8708.

Consolidated Plastics Company, 8181 Darrow Rd., Twinsburg, OH 44087: Free catalog ❖ Bags, packaging, and shipping supplies. 800-362-1000.

Cornell Paper & Box Company Inc., 162 Van Dyke St., Brooklyn, NY 11231: Free catalog ❖ Packaging supplies. 718-875-3202.

Fidelity Direct, 5601 International Pkwy., P.O. Box 155, Minneapolis, MN 55440: Free catalog ❖ Office equipment and supplies. 800-328-3034; 612-526-6500 (in MN).

Kole Industries, P.O. Box 020152, Miami, FL 33102: Free catalog ❖ Shipping, storing, and organizing supplies. 800-327-6085.

National Bag Company Inc., 2233 Old Mill Rd., Hudson, OH 44236: Free catalog ❖ Bags and wrapping, packing, and shipping supplies. 800-247-6000.

U.S. Box Corporation, 1296 McCarter Hwy., Newark, NJ 07104: Catalog $3 ❖ Boxes and other containers. 201-481-2000.

Volk Corporation, 23936 Industrial Park Dr., Farmington Hills, MI 48024: Free information ❖ Marking devices, packaging supplies, and shipping room equipment. 800-521-6799; 810-477-6700 (in MI).

YAZOO Mills Inc., P.O. Box 369, New Oxford, PA 17350: Free information ❖ Mailing tubes. 800-242-5216.

ORIGAMI (PAPER FOLDING)

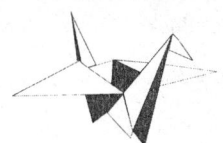

Fascinating Folds, P.O. Box 2820-235, Torrance, CA 90509: Catalog $1 ❖ Origami supplies, kits, and how-to books and videos. 801-968-2418.

Origami USA, 15 W. 77th St., New York, NY 10024: Free information with long SASE and two 1st class stamps ❖ Books, origami paper, and supplies. 212-769-5635.

OSTOMY SUPPLIES

A-Z Ostomy Supply, 321 W. Main, Marshall, MN 56258: Free catalog ❖ Ostomy supplies. 800-345-7850; 507-532-5754 (in MN).

AARP Ostomy Care Center, 5050 E. Belknap, Fort Worth, TX 76117: Free catalog ❖ Ostomy supplies. 800-284-4788.

American Ostomy Supplies, P.O. Box 13396, Milwaukee, WI 53213: Free catalog ❖ Urological and diabetic supplies, incontinent aids, blood pressure and wound care products, and aids for assistive living. 800-958-5858.

B & K Prescriptions, 601 E. Iron, Salina, KS 67104: Free information ❖ Ostomy supplies. 800-831-5219.

Blanchard Ostomy Products, 1510 Raymond Ave., Glendale, CA 91201: Free information ❖ Products for ileostomies, urostomies, and wet colostomies. 818-242-6789.

Bruce Medical Supply, 411 Waverly Oaks Rd., P.O. Box 9166, Waltham, MA 02154: Free catalog ❖ Ostomy supplies. 800-225-8446.

Coloplast Inc., 1955 W. Oak Circle, Marietta, GA 30062: Free information ❖ Conseal Colostomy System. 800-237-4555.

CompCare, 5534 Cortez Rd. West, Bradenton, FL 34210: Free information ❖ Ostomy supplies. 800-877-7317.

Convatec, Bristol-Myers Squibb Company, P.O. Box 5254, Princeton, NJ 08543: Free information ❖ Convatec appliance for ostomates. 800-422-8811.

Doubek Pharmacy Inc., 3846 W. 63rd St., Chicago, IL 60629: Free information ❖ Ostomy supplies. 800-DOUBLERS; 312-581-1122 (in IL).

Edgepark Surgical Inc., 2300 Edison Blvd., Twinsburg, OH 44087: Free catalog ❖ Ostomy supplies. 800-321-0591.

Express Medical Supply Inc., P.O. Box 1164, Fenton, MO 63026: Free catalog ❖ Urological, ostomy, incontinence, and skin care products. 800-633-2139.

Fairs' OPS Inc., Ostomy Prosthesis Support, P.O. Box 5760, Greenway Station, Glendale, AZ 85306: Free information ❖ Undergarments designed by ostomates for ostomates. 602-978-4435.

Georgetown Health Care Center, 9338 W. 75th St., Shawnee Mission, KS 66204: Free information ❖ Ostomy supplies. 800-279-3026; 913-262-0313 (in KS).

Hammer Medical Supply, 523 E. Grand Ave., Des Moines, IA 50309: Free information ❖ Ostomy supplies. 800-388-1187; 515-243-2886 (in IA).

Hollister, 2000 Hollister Dr., Libertyville, IL 60048: Free information ❖ Men and women's ostomy pouches. 800-323-4060.

Home Health Express, 8400 Baymeadows Way, Ste. 3, Jacksonville, FL 32256: Free information ❖ Ostomy supplies. 800-828-7123.

Home Medical Center Hospital Supplies, 7173 W. Cermack, Irwin, IL 60402: Free information ❖ Ostomy supplies. 800-323-2828.

Hospital Drug Store, 200 Loyola, New Orleans, LA 70112: Free information ❖ Ostomy supplies. 800-256-2007; 504-524-2254 (in LA).

King Ostomy Products, 431 W. 13th Ave., Ste. 4, Eugene, OR 97401: Free information ❖ Ostomy health care products. 503-345-0391.

LDB Medical Inc., 2909 Langford Rd., Ste. 500-B, Norcross, GA 30071: Free catalog ❖ Ostomy, incontinence, urological, and skin care supplies. 800-243-2554.

Mail Order Medical Supply, P.O. Box 916, Santa Clarita, CA 91380: Free catalog ❖ Urological, ostomy, skin and wound care, daily living, and home diagnostic aids. 800-232-7443.

Marc Medical Pharmacy, 6200 Wilshire Blvd., Los Angeles, CA 90048: Free information ❖ Ostomy supplies. 213-938-7131.

Marlen Manufacturing & Development Company, 5150 Richmond Rd., Bedford, OH 44146: Free information ❖ Protective adhesive skin barriers for ileostomies, colostomies, and urostomies. 216-292-7060.

Mason Laboratories Inc., P.O. Box 334, Horsham, PA 19044: Free information ❖ Ostomy pouches, pouch odor deodorant, and supplies. 800-523-2302; 215-675-6044 (in PA).

Medic Pharmacy & Surgical, 5100 W. Commercial Blvd., Fort Lauderdale, FL 33319: Free information ❖ Ostomy and medical supplies. 800-888-9417.

Medical Care Products, 4943 Beach Blvd., Jacksonville, FL 32207: Free information ❖ Ostomy supplies. 800-741-0110.

Moms Catalog, 24700 Avenue Rockefeller, Valencia, CA 91355: Free catalog ❖ Medical supplies for incontinence, urological, aids for daily living, ostomy, wound and skin care, and diabetes. 800-232-7443.

National Medical Consumables Inc., P.O. Box 102495, Denver, CO 80250: Free information ❖ Ostomy, diabetic, urological, wound care, and incontinence supplies. 800-797-7107.

Nihan & Martin Pharmacy, 1417 Myott Ave., Rockford, IL 60619: Free catalog ❖ Ostomy appliances. 815-963-8594.

Nu-Hope Laboratories Inc., P.O. Box 331150, Pacoima, CA 91333: Free information ❖ Urostomy pouches. 818-899-7711.

Osto-Covers, 405 El Camino Real, Ste. 419, Menlo Park, CA 94025: Free information ❖ Appliance covers. 800-833-OSTO.

Ostomed Healthcare, 3116 S. Oak Park Ave., Berwyn, IL 60402: Free information ❖ Ostomy supplies. 800-323-1353; 708-795-7701 (in IL).

Ostomy Discount of America, 3600 Laketon Rd., Pittsburgh, PA 15235: Free catalog ❖ Ostomy supplies. 800-443-7828.

Ostomy Supply & Care Center Inc., 510 6th Ave., Fargo, ND 58102: Free information ❖ Ostomy supplies. 701-293-0277.

Palisades Pharmaceuticals Inc., 64 N. Summit St., Tenafly, NJ 07670: Free information ❖ Internal deodorant for patients with colostomies, ileostomies, and incontinence. 800-237-9083.

Penny Saver Medical Supply, 1851 W. 52nd Ave., Denver, CO 80221: Free catalog ❖ Ostomy supplies. 800-748-1909.

The Perma-Type Company Inc., 83 Northwest Dr., Plainville, CT 06062: Free catalog ❖ Ileostomy, colostomy, wet colostomy, ileal bladder, and ureterostomy appliances. 800-243-4234; 203-677-7388 (in CT).

Safe Care Medical Supply Inc., P.O. Box 1164, Fenton, MO 63026: Free catalog ❖ Urological and ostomy supplies. 800-633-2139.

Salk Company Inc., 119 Braintree St., P.O. Box 452, Boston, MA 02134: Free information ❖ Natural-looking undergarments for active ostomates. 800-343-4497; 617-782-4030 (in MA).

Schilling & Morris Marketing Ltd., 30 Corporate Woods, #120, Rochester, NY 14623: Free information ❖ Deodorizers and skin cleansers. 716-436-1100.

Sender Care, P.O. Box 25-1679, Los Angeles, CA 90025: Free information ❖ Non-binding machine-washable fabric cover-ups.

Shield Healthcare Centers, P.O. Box 916, Santa Clarita, CA 91380: Free catalog ❖ Ostomy, urological, skin care, and home diagnostic products.

Tennessee Home Medical, 2005-A Memorial Blvd., Springfield, TN 37172: Free information ❖ Ostomy supplies. 800-966-6093; 615-384-6093 (in TN).

Torbot Group Inc., Ostomy Specialists, 1185 Jefferson Blvd., Warwick, RI 02886: Free brochure ❖ Ostomy appliances. 800-545-4254.

Undercover Cover Company, HC 79, 104 BB, Melba, ID 83641: Free information ❖ Appliance undercovers. 208-896-4716.

United Division of Pfizer, 11775 Starkey Rd., Largo, FL 33540: Free catalog ❖ Ostomy supplies. 813-392-1261.

VPI, A Cook Group Company, 127 S. Main St., P.O. Box 266, Spencer, IN 47460: Free information ❖ Non-adhesive systems for colostomy, urostomy, and ileostomy patients. 800-843-4851; 812-829-4891 (in IN).

Worldwide Home Health Center Inc., 926 E. Tallmadge Ave., Akron, OH 44310: Free catalog ❖ Ostomy and incontinence supplies, mastectomy breast forms, and clothing. 800-223-5938; 216-633-0366 (in OH).

Yentl's Secrets, 4415 Mockingbird Ln., Toledo, OH 43623: Free brochure ❖ Pouch covers. 419-841-1752.

PADDLEBALL

Adventure 16 Inc., 11161 W. Pico Blvd., West Los Angeles, CA 90064: Free information ❖ Paddles and balls. 619-283-6314.

Cannon Sports, P.O. Box 797, Greenland, NH 03840: Free list of retail sources ❖ Paddles and balls. 800-362-3146.

Century Sports Inc., Lakewood Industrial Park, 1995 Rutgers University Blvd., Box 2035, Lakewood, NJ 08701: Free information ❖ Balls and paddles. 800-526-7548; 908-905-4422 (in NJ).

Spalding Sports Worldwide, 425 Meadow St., P.O. Box 901, Chicopee, MA 01021: Free list of retail sources ❖ Paddles and balls. 800-225-6601.

Sportime, Customer Service, 1 Sportime Way, Atlanta, GA 30340: Free information ❖ Balls and paddles. 800-444-5700; 770-449-5700 (in GA).

Wa-Mac Inc., Highskore Products Inc., P.O. Box 128, Carlstadt, NJ 07410: Free information ❖ Paddles and balls. 800-447-5673; 201-438-7200 (in NJ).

PAGERS

Hello Direct, 5884 Eden Park Pl., San Jose, CA 95138: Free catalog ❖ Amplification aids, cellular and paging accessories, telephones and answering machines, and other telephone productivity tools. 800-444-3556.

Socket Communications, 6500 Kaiser Dr., Fremont, CA 94555: Free information ❖ Wireless Windows-based message system for use with computers and as a stand-alone pager. 510-744-2700.

PAPER COLLECTIBLES

Amusementica Americana, 414 N. Prospect Manor Ave., Mt. Prospect, IL 60056: Free list with seven 1st class stamps ❖ Old saloon artifacts, coin-operated machines, advertising collectibles, paper memorabilia, and other antique artifacts. 847-253-0791.

Barbara's Papertiques, P.O. Box 317, Port Jervis, NY 12771: Free information with long SASE ❖ Postcards and paper collectibles. 914-856-8572.

Box Seat Collectibles, P.O. Box 2013, Halesite, NY 11743: Catalog $5 ❖ Sports collectibles, historical newspapers, and memorabilia. 516-423-1025.

Buck Hill Associates, P.O. Box 4736, Queensbury, NY 12804: Free catalog ❖ Posters, handbills, historical documents and Americana from America's past, and other paper collectibles.

Cal National Coin Exchange, P.O. Box 1334, Roseville, CA 95678: Free information (specify items wanted) ❖ Americana and paper collectibles. 916-781-2991.

The Cartophilians, 430 Highland Ave., Cheshire, CT 06410: Free information with long SASE ❖ Collectible postcards, trading cards, and paper memorabilia. 203-272-1143.

Clinton Hollins, Box 112, Springfield, VA 22150: Free list with long SASE: Free information ❖ Old stock certificates.

The Evergreen Press, 3380 Vincent Rd., Pleasant Hill, CA 94523: Free information with long SASE ❖ Adult and children's books, greeting cards, book marks and bookplates, wedding certificates, calendars, ornaments, paper dolls, postcards, and 19th and early 20th-century paper memorabilia. 510-933-9700.

Hi-De-Ho Collectibles, P.O. Box 2841, Gaithersburg, MD 20886: Catalog $2.50 ❖ Antique movie posters and lobby cards, cartoon memorabilia, TV toys, games, puzzles, and dolls, advertising collectibles, and nostalgia. 301-926-4438.

Richard T. Hoober Jr., P.O. Box 3116, Key Largo, FL 33037: Free list with long SASE ❖ Bank and other financial paper collectibles.

MidAtlantic Antiques, P.O. Box 691, Mt. Laurel, NJ 08054: Catalog $1 (3 issues) ❖ Antiques, paper collectibles, historical military maps, autographs, and other memorabilia. 609-234-2651.

The Old Print Gallery, 1220 31st St. NW, Washington, DC 20007: Catalog $3 ❖ Paper collectibles. 202-965-1818.

Old Print Shop, 150 Lexington Ave., New York, NY 10016: Free information ❖ Paper collectibles. 212-683-3950.

Olde Soldier Books Inc., 18779 N. Frederick Ave., Gaithersburg, MD 20879: Free information ❖ Civil War books, documents, autographs, prints, manuscripts, photographs, and Americana. 301-963-2929.

Original Paper Collectibles, 700 Clipper Gap Rd., Auburn, CA 95603: Free brochure with long SASE ❖ Paper labels and used stock certificates. 916-878-0296.

❖ PAPER CRAFTING & SCULPTING ❖

Tom Peper, 32 Shelter Cove Lane, #109, Hilton Head Island, SC 29928: Price list $1 ❖ Autographs, lobby cards and posters, original comic art, animation art and cels, and collectibles. 800-628-7497.

Lee Poleske, Box 871, Seward, AK 99664: Free list with long SASE ❖ Bank and other financial paper collectibles.

Steven S. Raab, 2033 Walnut St., Philadelphia, PA 19102: Free catalog ❖ Autographs, signed books and photos, historic newspapers, World War I posters, and other historic paper memorabilia. 610-446-6193.

R.M. Smythe, 26 Broadway, New York, NY 10004: Catalog $15 ❖ Obsolete stocks and bonds, bank notes, and autographs. 800-622-1880; 212-943-1880 (in NY).

The Sports Alley, 15545 E. Whittier Blvd., Whittier, CA 90603: Free information with long SASE ❖ Hard-to-find sports cards, canceled checks by sports greats, autographed pictures, world series programs, photographs, and other memorabilia. 310-947-7383.

JoAnn Van Scotter Postcards, 208 E. Lincoln St., Mt. Morris, IL 61054: Free information with long SASE ❖ Paper collectibles. 815-734-6971.

Mark Vardakis Autographs, Box 1430, Coventry, RI 02816: Catalog $2 ❖ Autographs, paper Americana, other collectibles, and financial memorabilia that includes pre-1900 stocks, bonds, and checks. 401-823-8440.

Yesterday's Paper & Thimbleberry Antiques, P.O. Box 819, Concrete, WA 98237: Price list 75¢ (specify subject area) ❖ Financial, territorial, and western paper collectibles. Also documents and memorabilia, from 1700 and later. 206-853-8228.

PAPER CRAFTING & SCULPTING

Aiko's Art Materials Import, 3347 N. Clark St., Chicago, IL 60657: Catalog $1.50 ❖ Japanese handmade paper, Oriental and art supplies, and fabric dyes. 312-404-5600.

American Art Clay Company Inc., 4717 W. 16th St., Indianapolis, IN 46222: Free catalog ❖ Modeling and self-hardening clay, paper mache, casting compounds, mold-making materials, acrylics, fabric dyes, fillers and patching compounds, wood stains, and metallic finishes. 800-374-1600; 317-244-6871 (in IN).

Aves Products, P.O. Box 344, River Falls, WI 54022: Free information ❖ Self-hardening clays, paper mache, other modeling products, and sculpting materials. 715-386-9097.

Gerlachs of Lecha, P.O. Box 213, Emmaus, PA 18049: Catalog $2.25 ❖ Paper-sculpting kits. 215-965-9181.

Gold's Artworks Inc., 2100 N. Pine St., Lumberton, NC 28358: Free catalog with long SASE ❖ Paper-making pigments and chemicals, pulp materials, kits, and supplies. 800-356-2306; 910-739-9605 (in NC).

Holcraft Collection, 211 El Cajon Ave., P.O. Box 792, Davis, CA 95616: Catalog $2 ❖ Molds for paper mache and craft supplies. 916-756-3023.

Lake City Crafts, 1209 Eaglecrest St., P.O. Box 2009, Nixa, MO 65714: Catalog $2 ❖ Supplies for paper-quilling, crafting, and filigree projects. 417-725-8444.

Little Goodies, P.O. Box 1004, Lewisville, TX 75067: Catalog $2 ❖ Pre-cut paper flower kits.

Magnolia Paper Making, 2527 Magnolia St., Oakland, CA 94607: Free catalog ❖ Paper-making supplies, handmade paper, and books. 510-839-5268.

Nasco, 901 Janesville Ave., Fort Atkinson, WI 53538: Free catalog ❖ Paper-making and sculpting supplies. 800-558-9595.

Papercuttings by Alison, P.O. Box 2771, Sarasota, FL 34236: Catalog $2.50 ❖ Paper-cutting patterns and supplies. 813-957-0328.

The Pulpers, 1101 N. Highcross Rd., Urbana, IL 61801: Free information ❖ Prepared pulps for making paper and casting. 217-328-0118.

Quill-It, P.O. Box 1304, Elmhurst, IL 60126: Catalog $1 (refundable) ❖ Quilling papers, paper-snipping supplies, kits, books, tools, plaques, frames, and fringes.

Tree Toys, 2248 Obispo Ave., Ste. 206, Signal Hill, CA 90806: Catalog $1 with long SASE (refundable) ❖ Silhouette paper-snipping designs on antique parchment or black paper, iron-on fabrics, quilling supplies, and books. 708-323-6505.

Twinrocker Papermaking Supplies, P.O. Box 413, Brookston, IN 47923: Free catalog ❖ Paper-making supplies and ready-to-use handmade paper. (317) 563-3119.

PAPERWEIGHTS

A.V. Imports, Bill Sheehan, P.O. Box 716, Palmdale, CA 93590: Free information ❖ Aviation-theme paperweights. 805-943-8483.

Alberene Crystal, 435 5th Ave., New York, NY 10016: Free information ❖ Perthshire paperweights and Thomas Webb and Edinburgh crystal. Includes discontinued items. 800-843-9078.

Brielle Galleries, P.O. Box 475, Brielle, NJ 08730: Free catalog ❖ Watches, jewelry, paperweights, and crystal, silver, bronze, pewter, and porcelain items. 800-542-7435.

L.H. Selman Ltd., 761 Chestnut St., Santa Cruz, CA 95060: Free catalog ❖ Antique, modern, and contemporary paperweights. 800-538-0766; 408-427-1177 (in CA).

PARTY DECORATIONS

Allen-Lewis Manufacturing Company, Division TCC Industries Inc., P.O. Box 16546, 5601 Logan, Denver, CO 80216: Free catalog ❖ Souvenirs, carnival and party supplies, fund-raising merchandise, toys, games, T-shirts, sweatshirts, and craft supplies. 303-295-0196.

Anderson's, 4875 White Bear Pkwy., White Bear Lake, MN 55110: Free catalog ❖ Party and prom decorations and supplies. 800-328-9640; 612-426-1667 (in MN).

The Cracker Box, Solebury, PA 18963: Catalog $4.50 ❖ Ornament kits. 215-862-2100.

Hearth Song, Mail Processing Center, 6519 N. Galena Rd., P.O. Box 1773, Peoria, IL 61656: Free catalog ❖ Party decorations, children's books, dollhouse miniatures, art supplies, kites, and games. 800-325-2502.

Novelties Unlimited, 410 W. 21st St., Norfolk, VA 23517: Catalog $5 ❖ Magic, balloons, make-up, party decorations, and clown supplies, props, and gags. 804-622-0344.

B. Palmer Sales Company Inc., 3510 Hwy. 80 East, P.O. Box 850247, Mesquite, TX 75185: Free catalog ❖ Carnival, fund-raising, and party supplies. 800-888-3087; 214-288-1026 (in TX).

Paradise Products, P.O. Box 568, El Cerrito, CA 94530: Catalog $2 ❖ Theme party decorations and supplies. 510-524-8300.

Surprises & Jewelry, P.O. Box 1052, Orange, CT 06477: Price list $1 ❖ Party surprise bags for children. 203-934-8886.

U.S. Toy Company Inc., 1227 E. 119th St., Grandview, MO 64030: Catalog $3 ❖ Magic equipment and novelties, carnival supplies, and decorations and supplies for holidays, parties, and other celebrations. 800-448-7830; 816-761-5900 (in MO).

Under the Big Top, P.O. Box 807, Placentia, CA 92670: Catalog $4 ❖ Party supplies, costumes, clown props, and balloons. 800-995-7727.

PATIOS & WALKWAYS

Stone Company Inc., W4520 Lime Rd., Eden, WI 53019: Free information ❖ Natural building and landscape cobblers, granite boulders, wall stone, steppers, and flagstone. 414-477-2521.

PENS, PENCILS & DESK SETS

Ace Leather Products, 2211 Avenue U, Brooklyn, NY 11229: Free catalog ❖ Desk sets, leather attache cases, luggage, wallets, handbags, and gifts. 800-342-5223.

Altman Luggage, 135 Orchard St., New York, NY 10001: Free information ❖ Writing instruments, luggage, and leather goods. 800-372-3377.

PERFUMERY SUPPLIES

Bertram's Inkwell, 11301 Rockville Pike, Kensington, MD 20895: Free catalog ❖ Pens and pencils, desk sets, and gifts. 800-782-7680; 301-468-6939 (in MD).

Arthur Brown & Bros. Inc., 2 W. 46th St., New York, NY 10036: Free catalog ❖ New and contemporary-style fine writing instruments. 800-772-7367.

Chiasso, 303 W. Madison St., Chicago, IL 60606: Free catalog ❖ Desk sets and office gifts. 800-654-3570.

Gabriel Da Silva & Ariel Crespo, 1212 Forest Rd., New Haven, CT 06515: Free information ❖ Handcrafted sculptured pens. 203-387-9701.

Fahrney Pens Inc., 8329 Old Marlboro Pike, Upper Marlboro, MD 20772: Catalog $2 ❖ Writing instruments. 800-336-4775.

Fountain Pen Hospital, 10 Warren St., New York, NY 10007: Free information ❖ Fountain pens, pencils, and other writing accessories. 800-253-PENS; 212-964-0580 (in NY).

The Fountain Pen Shop, 510 W. 6th St., Ste. 1032, Los Angeles, CA 90014: Catalog $4 ❖ Pens, pencils, desk sets, and other writing accessories. 213-891-1581.

Hunt Manufacturing Company, 2005 Market St., Philadelphia, PA 19103: Free information ❖ Calligraphy papers, markers, kits and supplies, fountain pens, pen sets, nibs, inks, acrylics, oil paints, and water colors. 800-765-5669.

Levenger, P.O. Box 1256, Delray Beach, FL 33447: Free catalog ❖ Books, furniture, pens, briefcases, and gifts for serious readers. 800-545-0242.

Menash Signatures Inc., 213 W. 79th St., New York, NY 10024: Free catalog ❖ Writing instruments and refills. 800-PEN-SHOP.

Office Depot Inc., 2200 Old Germantown Rd., Delray Beach, FL 33445: Free catalog ❖ Pens, pencils, desk sets, and office supplies and equipment. 800-685-8800.

Staples Inc., Attention: Marketing Services, P.O. Box 9328, Framingham, MA 01701: Free catalog ❖ Pens, pencils, desk sets, and office supplies and equipment. 800-333-3330.

Viking Office Products, 13809 S. Figueroa St., P.O. Box 61144, Los Angeles, CA 90061: Free catalog ❖ Pens, pencils, desk sets, and office supplies and equipment. 800-421-1222.

PERFUMERY SUPPLIES

Angel's Earth, 1633 Scheffer Ave., St. Paul, MN 55116: Catalog $2 ❖ Soaps, candles, cosmetics, incense, skin care preparations, essential oils, and other aromatherapy items. 612-698-3601.

Aphrodesia Products, 264 Bleeker St., New York, NY 10014: Catalog $3 ❖ Herbs, essential oils, and perfumery supplies. 800-221-6898; 212-989-6440 (in NY).

AromaTherapy International, 300 N. 5th Ave., Ste. 210, Ann Arbor, MI 48104: Free information ❖ Essential oils. 313-741-1617.

Black Pearl Gardens, Herbal General Store, 220 Maple St., Franklin, OH 45005: Catalog $1 ❖ Herb plants, aromatherapy products, potpourri and supplies, culinary and medicinal herbs, herbal bath and body products, and dried florals. 800-891-0142.

Candlechem Products, 32 Thayer Circle, P.O. Box 705, Randolph, MA 02368: Catalog $1 ❖ Essential oils, dyes, and scenting materials for use in making candles and perfumes. 508-586-0844.

Caswell-Massey Company Ltd., Catalog Division, 100 Enterprise Pl., Dover, DE 19901: Catalog $1 ❖ Herbs, essential oils, and perfumery supplies. 800-326-0500.

Common Scents, 3920 A-24th St., San Francisco, CA 94114: Free catalog ❖ Bath and skin care products and essential oils. 800-850-6519.

Dabney Herbs, P.O. Box 22061, Louisville, KY 40222: Catalog $2 ❖ Natural health and beauty items, aromatherapy products, and oils. 502-893-5198.

East End Import Company, Essex St., Box 107, Montauk, NY 11954: Free brochure with long SASE ❖ Essential oils, absolutes, concretes, creams, lotions, and floral waters. 516-668-4158.

Essential Aromatics, 205 N. Signal St., Ojai, CA 93023: Catalog $3 ❖ Premium-quality pure essential oils, carriers, blends, diffusers, supplies, and books. 800-211-1313; 805-640-1300 (in CA).

The Essential Oil Company, P.O. Box 206, Lake Oswego, OR 97034: Free catalog ❖ Essential oils, soap-making molds and supplies, incense materials, potpourri, and aromatherapy items. 800-729-5912.

The Faith Mountain Company, P.O. Box 199, Sperryville, VA 22740: Free catalog ❖ Herbs, essential oils, and perfumery supplies. 800-588-2548.

Frontier Cooperative Herbs, 3021 78th St., P.O. Box 299, Norway, IA 52318: Free information ❖ Essential and fragrance oils and herbal extracts. 319-227-7991.

Gabrieana's Herbal & Organic Products, P.O. Box 215322, Sacramento, CA 95821: Free catalog ❖ Skin care and bath care items, essential oils, dried herbs, and organic products. 800-684-4372.

Gaia Garden Herbal Apothecary, 2672 W. Broadway, Vancouver, British Columbia, Canada V6K 2G3: Catalog $2 ❖ Herbal, aromatherapy, and perfumery products. 604-734-4372.

The Ginger Tree, 245 Lee Rd., Opelika, AL 36801: Catalog $1 (refundable) ❖ Potpourri, aromatherapy supplies, and essential and fragrance oils. 205-745-4864.

Good Hollow Greenhouse & Herbarium, 50 Slaterock Mill Rd., Taft, TN 38488: Catalog $1 ❖ Herb plants and dried herbs, perennials, wildflowers, scented geraniums, essential oils and potpourris, teas, and spices. 615-433-7640.

Grandma's Spice Shop, HC 62, Box 65D, Upper Tract, WV 26866: Free catalog ❖ Essential oils and herbal potpourris. 304-358-2346.

Hartman's Herb Farm, 1026 Old Dana Rd., Barre, MA 01005: Catalog $2 ❖ Herbs and herb products, potpourris, and essential oils. 508-355-2015.

Harvest Health Inc., 1944 Eastern Ave. SE, Grand Rapids, MI 49507: Free catalog ❖ Herbs, spices, and essential and perfume oils. 616-245-6268.

The Herb Lady, P.O. Box 2129, Shepherdstown, WV 25443: Free catalog ❖ Essential oils, potpourris, sachets, and aromatic blends to simmer on the stove top. 800-537-1846.

Herb Products Company, P.O. Box 898, 11012 Magnolia Blvd., North Hollywood, CA 91601: Free price list ❖ Botanicals, oils and fragrances, extracts, tinctures, and books. 818-984-3141.

Herbal Accents, P.O. Box 12303, El Cajon, CA 92022: Catalog $1 ❖ Aromatherapy skin care products. 619-440-4380. P.O. Box 12303, El Cajon, CA 92022: Catalog $1 ❖ Aromatherapy skin care products. 619-440-4380.

Indiana Botanic Gardens, 3401 W. 317th Ave., Hammond, IN 46325: Free catalog ❖ Herbs, fragrances, and essential oils.

Joint Adventure, Aromatherapy Catalog, P.O. Box 824, Rogers, AR 72757: Free catalog ❖ Essential oils and aromatherapy supplies. 800-898-PURE.

Lavender Lane, 7337 #1 Roseville Rd., Sacramento, CA 95842: Catalog $2 ❖ Essential and alcohol-free perfume oils, perfumery supplies, and equipment. 916-334-4400.

Legacy Herbs, Sue Lukens Herbalist/Potter, Box 442, Mountain View, AR 72560: Catalog 50¢ ❖ Herbs, wildflowers, perennial plants, soaps, bath and body care products, oils and fragrance, incense, potpourri, herbal food products, and other scented iems. 501-269-4051.

Sue Lukens Herbalist/Potter, Box 442, Mountain View, AR 72560: Catalog 50¢ ❖ Herbs, wildflowers, perennial plants, soaps, bath and body care products, oils and fragrances, incense, potpourri, herbal food products, and other scented items. 501-269-4051.

Meadowbrook Herb Gardens, 93 Kingstown Rd., Wyoming, RI 02898: Catalog $1 ❖ Herbs, essential oils, fragrances, and perfumery supplies. 401-539-7603.

❖ PERSONALIZED & PROMOTIONAL PRODUCTS ❖ 349

Meg's Garden, P.O. Box 161, Buffalo, NY 14205: Brochure $1 ❖ Potpourris and perfume oils. 716-883-7564.

Nature's Finest, P.O. Box 10311, Burke, VA 22009: Catalog $2.50 (refundable) ❖ Dried flowers, herbs, spices, oils, fixatives, bottles, books, and potpourri supplies. 703-978-3925.

Nature's Herb Company, 1010 46th St., Emeryville, CA 94608: Catalog $1 ❖ Herbs, spices, essential oils, perfumery supplies, and supplies for potpourris and sachets. 510-601-0700.

OlFactorium, 401 Euclid Ave., Ste. 155, Cleveland, OH 44114: Free information ❖ Botanical essential and carrier oils. 216-566-8234.

Penn Herb Company, 603 N. 2nd St., Philadelphia, PA 19123: Catalog $1 ❖ Herbs, essential oils, and perfumery supplies. 800-523-9971; 215-925-3336 (in PA).

The Rosemary House, 120 S. Market St., Mechanicsburg, PA 17055: Catalog $2 ❖ Herbs, oils, and spices. Also candles, soaps, teas, books, and potpourris. 717-697-5111.

Soap Opera, 319 State St., Madison, WI 55703: Free price list ❖ Essential and rare oils, designer fragrances, herbs, perfume base, and cosmetics and toiletries. 800-251-SOAP.

Spice Discounters, P.O. Box 6061, Aberdeen, SD 57401: Free catalog ❖ Herbs, spices, oils, extracts, and vitamins. 800-610-5950.

Tom Thumb Workshops, Rt. 13, P.O. Box 357, Mappsville, VA 23407: Catalog $1 ❖ Potpourri, herbs and spices, essential oils, and dried flowers. 804-824-3507.

The Uncommon Herb, P.O. Box 2908, Seal Beach, CA 90740: Catalog $1 ❖ Aromatherapy products and guide to essential oils. Diffusers and earth-friendly natural products. 800-308-6284.

PERSONALIZED & PROMOTIONAL PRODUCTS

AD-CAP Line, 1400 Goldmine Rd., Monroe, NC 28110: Free catalog ❖ T-shirts, banners, bandannas, head bands, tote bags, aprons, and other promotional items. 800-868-7111.

Advertising Ideas Company, 3281 Barber Rd., Barberton, OH 44203: Free catalog ❖ Luggage, desk accessories, caps, T-shirts, badges and holders, toys, and other advertising and promotional novelties. 800-323-6359.

Amsterdam Printing & Litho Corporation, 55 Wallins Corners Rd., Amsterdam, NY 12010: Free catalog ❖ Advertising novelties. 800-543-6882.

Atlas Pen & Pencil Corporation, 3040 N. 9th Ave., Hollywood, FL 33022: Free catalog ❖ Advertising specialties. 800-327-3232.

Balloon Printing Company, P.O. Box 150, Rankin, PA 15104: Free information ❖ Imprinted balloons. 800-533-5221.

Best Impressions Company, P.O. Box 802, LaSalle, IL 61301: Free catalog ❖ Advertising specialties for promotional incentive, and gift-giving programs. 800-635-2378.

CHS Inc., 5055 NE 13th Ave., Fort Lauderdale FL 33334: Free information ❖ Advertising specialties. 800-872-5329.

Enterprise Publishing Inc., 445 S. Figueroa St., Ste. 2600, Los Angeles, CA 90071: Free brochure ❖ Personalized promotional products. 213-612-7742.

Fancy Fortune Cookies, 6265 Coffman Rd., Indianapolis, IN 46268: Free information ❖ Individually wrapped fortune cookies in twelve flavors and brilliant colors. Enclosed messages can be customized for the promotional event. 317-299-8900.

Namark Cap & Emblem Company, 6325 Harrison Dr., Las Vegas, NV 89120: Free information ❖ Specialty caps, T-shirts, jackets, and screen-printed emblems. 800-634-6271.

Prestige Promotions, 4875 White Bear Pkwy., White Bear Lake, MN 55110: Free information ❖ Pens, coffee mugs, calendars, and bumper stickers. 800-328-9351.

Royal Graphics Inc., 3117 N. Front St., Philadelphia, PA 19133: Free information ❖ Posters, show cards, and bumper stickers. 215-739-8282.

Sac's & Boxes, 258 Cross Keys Mall, St. Louis, MO 63033: Free information ❖ Printed paper and plastic bags. 800-677-8214.

Sales Guides Inc., 4937 Otter Lake Rd., St. Paul, MN 55110: Free catalog ❖ Pens and pencils, key fobs, memo cubes, desk items, food and candy, games, and gifts. 800-654-6666.

Scratch-It Promotions Inc., 1763 Barnum Ave., Bridgeport, CT 06610: Free information ❖ Scratch-off, pull tabs, and fragrance promotional products. 800-966-9467; 203-367-5377 (in CT).

Shazzam Advertising Specialties, 14792 Alder Creek Rd., Truckee, CA 96161: Free information ❖ Promotional advertising specialties. 800-999-8907.

N.G. Slater Corporation, 220 W. 19th St., New York, NY 10011: Free catalog ❖ T-shirts, tote bags, pins, bumper stickers, jewelry, button-making supplies, and other advertising novelties. 212-924-3133.

J.T. Townes Inc., P.O. Box 760, Danville, VA 24543: Free information ❖ Scratch pads. 800-437-PADS; 804-792-3711 (in VA).

Tratter Graphics, P.O. Box 338, Syracuse, IN 46567: Free catalog ❖ Personalized promotional products. 219-834-2626.

Your Logo Inc., 3255 N. Milwaukee Ave., Chicago, IL 60618: Free catalog ❖ Personalized promotional products. 312-545-8299.

PEST CONTROL

Nixalite of America, 1025 16th Ave., P.O. Box 727, East Moline, IL 61244: Free information ❖ Humane bird control products. 800-624-1189.

Sutton AG Enterprises Inc., 746 Vertin Ave., Salinas, CA 93901: Free brochure ❖ Bird control products, seed planters, measuring devices, and field supplies. 408-422-9693.

PETS

Bird Supplies

Arbico, P.O. Box 4247, Tucson, AZ 85738: Free catalog ❖ Live and dried feeder insects. 800-827-2847.

Audubon Workshop, 1501 Paddock Dr., Northbrook, IL 60062: Free catalog ❖ Bird supplies. 800-325-9464.

Avian Outfitters, P.O. Box 876, Newport Richey, FL 34656: Free information ❖ All-natural products for exotic birds. 800-821-8808.

AVP/Animal Veterinary Products, Division U.S. Pet Inc., 500 Kehoe Blvd., Carol Stream, IL 60188: Free catalog ❖ Bird supplies.

Bassetts Cricket Ranch Inc., 535 N. Lovers Ln., Visalia, CA 93292: Free information ❖ Crickets and king meal worms for reptiles, birds, fish, hamsters, and other animals. 800-634-2445.

C & R Inquiries, P.O. Box 1874, Stillwater, OK 74076: Free catalog ❖ Weather vanes, sundials, bird baths, and cupolas. 800-248-5445.

C & S Products Company Inc., Box 848, Fort Dodge, IA 50501: Free catalog ❖ Wild bird suet products and suet-related feeders. 515-955-5605.

Bill Chandler Farms, RR 2, Box 105, Noble, IL 62868: Free price list ❖ Wild bird food. 800-752-2473.

Dakota Quality Bird Food, Box 3084, Fargo, ND 58108: Free catalog ❖ Niger thistle, small sunflower seeds, royal finch mix, safflower seed, and wild birdseed mixes. 800-356-9220.

Dancing Squirrel, P.O. Box 8000, Buffalo, NY 14267: Free information ❖ All-natural bird seed that squirrels avoid. 800-450-7631.

Duncraft, 102 Fisherville Rd., Concord, NH 03303: Free catalog ❖ Wild bird supplies, squirrel-proof feeders, birdhouses, bird baths, and books. 800-763-7878.

Feather Fantasy, 705 Soscol Ave., Ste. A, Napa, CA 94559: Catalog $2 (refundable) ❖ Bird supplies. 707-257-8815.

Hyde Bird Feeder Company, 56 Felton St., P.O. Box 168, Waltham, MA 02254: Free catalog ❖ Bird feeders and wild bird food. 617-893-6780.

Morton Jones Company, P.O. Box 123, Ramona, CA 92065: Free information ❖ Bird supplies. 800-443-5769.

Kester's Birdseed Inc., P.O. Box 516, Omro, WI 54963: Catalog $3 ❖ Seed mixes for cockatiels, lovebirds, parakeets, parrots, canaries, and finches. 800-558-8815; 414-685-2929 (in WI).

L/M Animal Farms, Pleasant Plain, OH 45162: Free information ❖ Bird food and treats. 800-332-5623; 513-877-2131 (in OH).

Lafeber Company, 24981 N. 1400 East Rd., Cornell, IL 61319: Free information ❖ Nutritional products for birds. 800-842-6445.

Lake's Minnesota Macaws Inc., 161 Winifred St. West, St. Paul, MN 55107: Free information ❖ Hand-rearing formulas, feeding syringes, and nutritionally balanced bird food for adult macaws, cockatoos, parakeets, conures, lories, cockatiels, and lovebirds. 800-634-2473; 612-290-0606 (in MN).

Lixit Animal Care Products, P.O. Box 2580, Napa, CA 94558: Free information ❖ Bird watering accessories.

Majestic Cocka2s, 8338 Terra Grande Ave., Springfield, VA 22153: Free information ❖ Bird supplies.

Master Animal Care, 12 Maplewood Dr., Hazleton, PA 18201: Free catalog ❖ Dog and cat grooming and health care supplies, bird supplies, professional care pet products, toys, books, and gifts. 800-346-0749.

Mellinger's Inc., 2310 W. South Range Rd., North Lima, OH 44452: Free catalog ❖ Thistle, safflower, finch mix, and sunflower birdseed. 216-549-9861.

Pennington Pet Products, Rt. 1, Box 3731, Mountain City, TN 37683: Free information ❖ Cuttlebone holders. 615-727-0123.

Pet Bird Express, 357 Sunnyslope Dr., Fremont, CA 94536: Free information ❖ Bird supplies. 800-729-7734.

Pet Warehouse, P.O. Box 310, Xenia, OH 45385: Free catalog ❖ Bird, tropical fish, dog, and cat supplies. 800-443-1160.

Saltwater Farms, P.O. Box 740, South Freeport, ME 04078: Free information ❖ Kelp meal for birds. 800-293-KELP.

Scooter's Pet Products, 4200 Park Blvd., Oakland, CA 94602: Free catalog ❖ Toys. 415-206-2003.

Seed Factory Inc., P.O. Box 245, Ceres, CA 95307: Free price list ❖ Custom-blended bird seed mixes. 800-635-9359.

Star Pet Supply, 1500 New Horizons Blvd., Amityville, NY 11701: Free catalog ❖ Supplies and grooming aids for dogs, cats, birds, and other pets. 800-274-6400.

UPCO, P.O. Box 969, St. Joseph, MO 64502: Free catalog ❖ Cages, birdseed, supplies, books, toys, and remedies for birds. 800-444-8651.

Volkman Bird Seed, 1040 22nd Ave., Oakland, CA 94606: Free information ❖ Premium birdseed and cuttlebone. 510-261-7780.

Wild Bird Supplies, 4815 Oak St., Crystal Lake IL 60012: Free catalog ❖ Feeders, bird houses, bird baths, birdseed mixes, and books on bird care. 815-455-4020.

Wildlife Nurseries, P.O. Box 2724, Oshkosh, WI 54903: Catalog $3 ❖ Upland game birdseed combinations and gardening supplies. 414-231-3780.

Dog & Cat Supplies

Abeta Products, 5021 Tara Tea Dr., Tega Cay, SC 29715: Catalog $1 ❖ Solid wooden furniture for cats. 803-548-1019.

Alsto Company, P.O. Box 1267, Galesburg, IL 61401: Catalog $1 ❖ Tools, pet products, kitchen aids, and convenience items. 800-447-0048.

AVP/Animal Veterinary Products, Division U.S. Pet Inc., 500 Kehoe Blvd., Carol Stream, IL 60188: Free catalog ❖ Health care supplies for dog and cat breeders, groomers, and kennels.

Care-A-Lot, 1617 Diamond Springs Rd., Virginia Beach, VA 23455: Free catalog ❖ Dog and cat supplies. 804-460-9771.

Cat Claws, 1004 W. Broadway, P.O. Box 1001, Morrilton, AR 72110: Free catalog ❖ Gifts for cats. 800-783-0977.

The Dog's Outfitter, Division Humboldt Industries Inc., Humboldt Industrial Park, 1 Maplewood Dr., Hazleton, PA 18201: Free catalog ❖ Dog grooming, training, and general pet care accessories. 800-FOR-DOGS.

Dog-Master Systems, Division Environmental Research Labs, Box 902347, Palmdale, CA 93590: Free catalog ❖ Supplies for raising and training puppies and dogs.

John Dromgoode's Natural Gardener's Catalog, 8648 Old Bee Caves Rd., Austin, TX 78735: Free catalog ❖ Organic fertilizers, growth stimulants, compost equipment, books on organic gardening, tools, pest controls, and pet products. 800-320-0724.

Drs. Foster & Smith Inc., 2253 Air Park Rd., P.O. Box 100, Rhinelander, WI 54501: Free catalog ❖ Pet and equine products and health care supplies. 800-826-7206.

Famous Fido's, 1533 W. Devon Ave, Chicago, IL 60660: Free information ❖ Preservative, meat, and meat biproducts-free dog snacks. 800-231-3436; 312-973-FIDO.

Flexi-Mat Corporation, 2244 South Western Ave., Chicago, IL 60608: Free list of retail sources ❖ Combination window perch cat bed. 312-376-5500.

Hudson Valley Beef Rawhide, P.O. Box 3537, Wallingford, CT 06494: Free brochure ❖ Pure beef rawhide products for dogs. 800-836-2333.

Hulme, P.O. Box 670, Hwy. 641 South, Paris, TN 38242: Free catalog ❖ Pet supplies, medications, flea control products, and training aids. 901-642-6400.

J-B Wholesale Pet Supplies, 5 Raritan Rd., Oakland, NJ 07435: Free catalog ❖ Supplies for cats and dogs. 800-JEFFERS.

Jeffers Vet Supply, P.O. Box 100, Dothan, AL 36302: Free catalog ❖ Books, medications, and pet supplies. 800-533-3377.

Kennel Vet Corporation, P.O. Box 4092, Farmingdale, NY 11735: Catalog $1 (refundable) ❖ Dog and cat supplies. 800-782-0627.

KV Vet Supply, P.O. Box 245, David City, NE 68632: Free catalog ❖ Pet supplies. 402-367-6047.

Leather Brothers Inc., P.O. Box 700, Conway, AR 72033: Free catalog ❖ Leather and nylon collars and leads, wire muzzles, dog harnesses, name tags, and training leads. 800-442-5522.

Leatherrite Manufacturing Inc., 261 2nd St. SW, Carmel, IN 46032: Free catalog ❖ Leather, nylon, and vinyl leads, collars, and harnesses. 800-722-5222; 317-844-7241 (in IN).

Leonine Products, P.O. Box 657, Springfield, VT 05156: Free catalog ❖ Handcrafted furniture for cats. 802-885-3888.

Master Animal Care, 12 Maplewood Dr., Hazleton, PA 18201: Free catalog ❖ Dog and cat grooming and health care supplies, bird supplies, professional care pet products, toys, books, and gifts. 800-346-0749.

The Natural Pet Care Company, 2713 E. Madison, Seattle, WA 98112: Free catalog ❖ Natural pet care products. 800-962-8266; 206-329-1417 (in WA).

Nite Lite Company, P.O. Box 8210, Little Rock, AR 72221: Free catalog ❖ Kennel, training, and hunting supplies for dogs. Also clothing and accessories for the hunter. 800-648-5483.

Nitron Industries Inc., P.O. Box 1447, Fayetteville, AR 72702: Free catalog ❖ Organic fertilizers, enzyme soil conditioners, natural pest controls, and pet care products. 800-835-0123.

Omaha Vaccine Company Inc., 3030 L St., P.O. Box 7228, Omaha, NE 68107: Free catalog ❖ Health, grooming, and training supplies for dogs, cats, other house pets, and horses. 800-367-4444.

The Path to Wellness, 22 W. Ridge Dr., Colchester, CT 06415: Free catalog ❖ Natural and holistic pet care products. 800-658-2225.

❖ PETS ❖

Pedigrees Pet Catalog, P.O. Box 905, Brockport, NY 14559: Free catalog ❖ Pet clothing, name tags, collars, leads, feeders, carriers, toys, and books. Also T-shirts for owners. 800-548-4786.

Pet USA, P.O. Box 325, Topsfield, MA 01983: Free catalog ❖ Crates and cages, training aids, stain and odor aids, and other pet supplies. 800-4-PET-USA.

Pet Warehouse, P.O. Box 310, Xenia, OH 45385: Free catalog ❖ Dog, cat, bird, and tropical fish supplies. 800-443-1160.

Pooch! Emporium for Dogs & Cats, 2817 E. 3rd Ave., Denver, CO 80206: Free catalog ❖ Whimsical and practical products for dogs and cats. 800-95-POOCH.

Sir Maxwell's, 7979 La Mirada Dr., Boca Raton, FL 33433: Free brochure ❖ Homemade dog cookies. 800-4-SIRMAX; 407-394-8814 (in FL).

Star Pet Supply, 1500 New Horizons Blvd., Amityville, NY 11701: Free catalog ❖ Supplies and grooming aids for dogs, cats, birds, and other pets. 800-274-6400.

R.C. Steele Dog Equipment, 1989 Transit Way, Box 910, Brockport, NY 14420: Free catalog ❖ Dog and kennel supplies. 800-872-3773.

Tierisch Exclusiv, P.O. Box 2834, Rohnert Park, CA 94928: Free information ❖ Leather collars, leashes, and harnesses. 707-795-7575.

TopTack Inc., 802 Hillman Rd., Yakima, WA 98908: Free information ❖ Dog leashes and collars. 800-419-1392.

Trainer's Choice, 221 Morrison Rd., Columbus, OH 43213: Free catalog ❖ Training accessories, toys, beds, and pet supplies.

United Pharmacal Company Inc., P.O. Box 969, St. Joseph, MO 64502: Free catalog ❖ Health and medical supplies for dogs, cats, and horses. 816-233-8800.

UPCO, P.O. Box 969, St. Joseph, MO 64502: Free catalog ❖ Dog and cat supplies. 800-444-8651.

Wahl Clipper Corporation, 2900 Locust St., Sterling, IL 61081: Free list of retail sources ❖ Animal grooming accessories. 800-435-7748.

Wow - Bow Distributors Ltd., 13 Lucon Dr., Deer Park, NY 11729: Free catalog ❖ Health food for pets. 800-326-0230; 516-254-6064 (in NY).

Tropical Fish Supplies

Anchor Bay Aquarium Inc., 36457 Alfred St., New Baltimore, MI 48047: Catalog $2 ❖ Rare cichlids, catfish, exotic tropical fish, books, supplies, and live plants. 313-725-1383.

Aquarium Instruments Inc., 18 Huntington Circle, Shelton, CT 06484: Catalog $2 ❖ Aquarium monitoring products. 203-925-9139.

The Aquarium Mail Order, P.O. Box 104, Charcona, FL 32710: Free information ❖ Tropical fish and reptile supplies. 800-258-8444.

Aquarium Masters, P.O. Box 396, Bel Air, MD 21014: Free catalog ❖ Aquarium supplies. 800-49-MARINE.

Aquarium Products, 180 Penrod Ct., Glen Burnie, MD 21061: Free information ❖ Medications and water conditioners for tropical fish. 410-761-2100.

Aquarium Systems, 8141 Tyler Blvd., Mentor, OH 44060: Free information ❖ Saltwater aquarium test kits. 800-822-1100; 216-255-1997 (in OH).

Aquarium Warehouse, 1401 Floyd Rd., Richardson, TX 75081: Free information ❖ Light systems, free-standing and built-in aquariums, fish, corals, invertebrates, and cured rock. 214-480-9779.

Aquatic Life, 7319 Rokeby Dr., Manassas, VA 22110: Free information ❖ Softeners, pH neutralizers, water purifiers, and water testing and treatment systems. 703-369-7124.

Aquatic Specialists, P.O. Box 918, Knoxville, TN 37940: Catalog $5 (refundable) ❖ Net-caught marine fish, marine invertebrates, macro algae, and cured live rock. 615-573-3474.

Aquatic Supply House, 42 Hayes St., Elmsford, NY 10523: Free catalog ❖ Tropical fish supplies, foods and automatic feeding devices, medications, heaters, air pumps, filters, sterilizers, water changers, and books. 800-777-PETS.

Aquatics of the Sea, 4234 47th St., Sarasota, FL 34235: Free price list ❖ Live rock and sand. 941-359-8887.

Bassetts Cricket Ranch Inc., 535 N. Lovers Ln., Visalia, CA 93292: Free information ❖ Crickets and king meal worms for reptiles, birds, fish, hamsters, and other animals. 800-634-2445.

Buckaroo Marine, 1319 N. Main, Tucson, AZ 85705: Free brochure ❖ Saltwater fish and invertebrates. 800-927-1050.

J.P. Burleson Inc., P.O. Box 32, Frederick, MD 21701: Catalog $3 ❖ Aquarium testing kits, cleansing solutions, water stabilization products, filter media, water conditioners, and conductivity meters. 301-846-4800.

By-Rite Pet Supplies, 23450 Kidder St., Hayward, CA 94545: Catalog $2 ❖ Aquarium supplies. 800-321-3448.

C & B Distributors, P.O. Box 913, Islamorada, FL 33036: Free information ❖ Atlantic and Caribbean tropical fish and live rock. 305-664-4588.

California Aquarium Supply Company, Attention: Catalog Department, 17719 Valley View St., Cerritos, CA 90701: Catalog $5 ❖ Acrylic aquariums, filters, and accessories. 714-522-8373.

California Reef Specialists, 740 Tioga Ave., Sand City, CA 93955: Catalog $5 (refundable) ❖ Cold water reef fish and invertebrates, aquarium chiller units, wet/dry filters, acrylic aquariums, protein skimmers, and pumps. 408-394-7271.

Caribbean Creatures, 112 Peace Ave., Tavernier, FL 33070: Free information ❖ Hand-caught Caribbean tropical fish, shrimp, snails, crabs, scallops, and plants. 305-852-3991.

Champion Supply Company, 570 Bethlehem Pike, Fort Washington, PA 19034: Free information ❖ Automatic water changing and evaporation control pumps. 800-673-7822; 215-283-9400 (in PA).

Clever Aquarium Accessories, P.O. Box 32112, Aurora, CO 80041: Video catalog $5 (deposit) ❖ Accessories for salt water reef aquariums. 888-888-SALT.

Coral Reef Aquatics, 102900 Overseas Hwy., Key Largo, FL 33037: Free price list with long SASE ❖ Aquarium equipment and supplies. 305-453-0033.

Daleco Master Breeder Products, 3556 N. 400 East, Warsaw, IN 46580: Catalog $6 ❖ Tropical fish supplies, live food cultures, power filters, purification equipment, medications, lighting and temperature controls, fresh and salt water support systems, and aquariums. 219-268-6300.

Debron Aquatics, 1800 W. Oxford Ave., Englewood, CO 80110: Free catalog ❖ Tropical fish equipment and supplies. 800-249-4375.

Delaware Aquatic Imports, 18 Anderson Rd., Newark, DE 19713: Free price list ❖ Water-grown aquatic plants. 302-738-4042.

Ecological Live Rock Inc., 840 NE 143rd St., North Miami, FL 33161: Free information ❖ Live rock. 305-797-1431.

Exotic Aquaria Inc., 1672 NE 205th Terrace, North Miami Beach, FL 33179: Free information ❖ Tropical fish, algae, and corals. 305-654-1171.

Exotic Fish, 406 Northside Dr., Valdosta, GA 31602: Catalog $3 ❖ Tropical fish supplies and aquarium accessories. 800-736-0473.

Filtronics, P.O. Box 2457, Oxnard, CA 93033: Free information ❖ Semi-submersible aquarium testers. 805-486-5319.

Gwynnbrook Farm, Discus & Angle Fish Hatchery, 125 Gywnnbrook Ave., Owings Mills, MD 21117: Free information ❖ Tank-raised discus fish. 410-356-7557.

Hamilton Technology Corporation, 14902 S. Figueroa St., Gardena, CA 90248: Free catalog ❖ Reef tank lights, digital electronic pH meter, and other aquarium equipment. 800-447-9797.

Hawaiian Marine Imports Inc., 10801 Kempwood, Ste. 2, Houston, TX 77043: Free information ❖ Filters and hoses. 713-460-0236.

Hikari Sales USA Inc., 2804 McCone Ave., Hayward, CA 94545: Free information ❖ Algae wafers, micro pellets, sinking wafers, food sticks, and other tropical fish food. 800-621-5619.

Innerspace Aquatics, 935 E. 79th St., Cleveland, OH 44103: Free information ❖ Aquarium supplies. 216-391-0010.

Dale Jordan, 76 Tanya Crescent, Winnipeg, Manitoba, Canada R2G 2Z8: Free information ❖ Tropical fish. 204-668-9780.

Kent Marine, 1377 Barclay Circle, Marietta, GA 30060: Free information ❖ Saltwater aquarium supplies. 404-427-8870.

Kordon, Division Novalek Inc., 2242 Davis Ct., Hayward, CA 94545: Free information ❖ Live and frozen brine shrimp and brine shrimp eggs, food, and a salt water mix. 510-782-4058.

Leisure Time Pet Center, 43041 W. Seven Mile Rd., Northville, MI 48167: Free price list ❖ Aquatic plants and supplies.

Lifereef Filter Systems, 4628 S. Ward Way, Morrison, CO 80465: Free catalog ❖ Aquarium filter systems, skimmers, controllers, air dryers, lighting fixtures, chillers, and water pumps. 303-978-0940.

Mac's Discus, 20103 174th Ave. NE, Woodinville, WA 98072: Free information ❖ Discus fish. 206-483-3729.

Mail Order Pet Shop, 1338 N. Market Blvd., Sacramento, CA 95834: Free catalog ❖ Filters, heaters, medications, marine supplies, plastic plants, air pumps, water conditioners for tropical fish, and supplies for dogs, cats, birds, and hamsters. 800-366-7387.

Majestic Pet Supply, 1550 N. Northwest Hwy., Park Ridge, IL 60068: Catalog $2.50 ❖ Tropical fish supplies. 847-635-7711.

Natural Aquarium & Terrarium, 2906 Ossenfort Rd., Glencoe, MO 63038: Free catalog ❖ Potted live aquarium plants. 800-423-4717.

Nature's Way, 4411 Bee Ridge Rd., Ste. 195, Sarasota, FL 34233: Free information ❖ Aquarium filters, pumps, and water purification equipment. 800-780-2320.

Neptune Imports, 5830 NE 21st Rd., Fort Lauderdale, FL 33308: Free information ❖ Net-caught tropical fish and hard-to-find species. 305-784-7770.

Nippon Pet Food, 1327 Post Ave., Torrance, CA 90501: Free information ❖ Tropical fish food for cichlids, goldfish, and koi. 310-787-8706.

O.S.I. Marine Lab Inc., 3550 Arden Rd., Hayward, CA 94545: Free information ❖ Tropical fish food. 510-670-0888.

Ocean In Your Home, 5001 Roscrea St., San Diego, CA 92117: Free information ❖ Baby clams. 619-576-1636.

Oregon Desert Brine Shrimp, 9360 NW Harbor Blvd., Portland, OR 97231: Free information ❖ Brine shrimp and Daphnia.

Pet Warehouse, P.O. Box 310, Xenia, OH 45385: Free catalog ❖ Tropical fish, bird, dog, and cat supplies. 800-443-1160.

Pet Xpress, 10520 Branchton Church Rd., Thonotosassa, FL 33592: Catalog $1 ❖ Tropical and marine fish, aquatic and marine plants, and supplies.

Pisces Coral & Fish, P.O. Box 208, Cotati, CA 94931: Free brochure ❖ Multi-colored corallines and macro algaes for living reef aquariums. 800-822-5333.

Reef Concepts, 1965 Lake Dr., Winston-Salem, NC 27127: Free information ❖ Ozone generators, pH controllers, trace elements, and tropical fish aids. 910-788-3017.

Reef Displays, 10925 Overseas Hwy., Marathon, FL 33050: Free catalog ❖ Net-caught Atlantic fish and invertebrates, macro algae, algae snails, Caribbean live rock, and fresh and cured reef rock. 305-743-0070.

Reef Life Inc., 5925 Ravenswood Rd., Fort Lauderdale, FL 33312: Free information ❖ Live rock and sand. 800-903-3474.

Reef Tech, 4550 Wadsworth, Ste. 179, Wheatridge, CO 80033: Free information ❖ Aquariums, filters, canopies, and stands. 303-422-3882.

San Francisco Bay Brand Inc., 8239 Enterprise Dr., Newark, CA 94560: Free brochure ❖ Frozen and packaged tropical fish foods. 510-792-7200.

Sanders Brine Shrimp Company, 3850 S. 540 West, Ogden, UT 84405: Free price list ❖ Brine shrimp eggs. 801-393-5027.

Sea-Aquatic International, 1631 S. Dixie Hwy., Pompano Beach, FL 33060: Free price list ❖ Tropical fish, invertebrates, live rock, and supplies. 305-784-9278.

Spectacular Sea Systems, 600 NE 42nd St., Pompano Beach, FL 33064: Free information ❖ Aquarium systems. 305-941-3792.

SpectraPure, 738 S. Perry Ln., Tempe, AZ 85281: Free information ❖ Aquarium water purification systems. 800-685-2783.

R.C. Steele Tropical Fish, 1989 Transit Way, Brockport, NY 14420: Free information ❖ Aquarium supplies. 800-872-3773.

Tenera Fish Food, P.O. Box 47596, St. Petersburg, FL 33743: Free brochure ❖ Sun-dried natural algae food.

That Fish Place, 237 Centerville Rd., Lancaster, PA 17603: Free catalog ❖ Aquarium supplies. 800-733-3829.

The Ultimate Aquarium, 686 Old Dixie Hwy., Vero Beach, FL 32962: Free information ❖ Tropical fish, live rock, and corals. 407-778-3007.

Village Wholesale, 704 New Loudon Rd., Latham, NY 12110: Free catalog ❖ Tropical fish and supplies. 518-783-6878.

World of Aquatics, 525 Jubilee St., Emmaus, PA 18049: Catalog $2 ❖ Live rock and sand, corals, saltwater fish, and invertebrates. 610-967-1456.

Carriers

Bali-MAC, P.O. Box 448, Port Bolivar, TX 77650: Free information ❖ Wearable pet carrier with optional handle or leash. 409-684-6312.

DAFCO, 2411 Grear St., Salem, OR 97301: Free brochure ❖ Lightweight collapsible dog carrier. 800-458-1562.

Kennels & Enclosures

Animal Environments, 2201 Camino Vida Roble, Ste. I, Carlsbad, CA 92009: Free information ❖ Animal cages.

Cal-Formed Plastics Company, 2050 E. 48th St., Los Angeles, CA 90058: Free information ❖ Easy-to-clean interlocking two-piece dog house with 5-way flow-through ventilation. 800-772-7723.

Central Metal Products Inc., State Rd. 213, North Edge, Windfall, IN 46076: Free catalog ❖ Wire cages for dogs. 800-874-3647; 317-945-7677 (in IN).

Comtrad Industries, 2820 Waterford Lake Dr., Ste. 106, Midlothian, VA 23113: Free information ❖ Electric invisible pet containment systems. 800-704-1211.

Horst Company, 101 E. 18th St., Greely, CO 80631: Free catalog ❖ Kennel framework for custom design of single to multiple runs and pet enclosures. 303-353-7724.

Innotek Pet Products Inc., One Innoway Dr., Garrett, IN 46738: Free list of retail sources ❖ Pet containment system and products for behavior problem solutions. 800-826-5527.

Invisible Fence Company Inc., 355 Phoenixville Pike, Malvern, PA 19355: Free information ❖ Invisible electronic pet containment fence. 800-538-DOGS.

Keipper Cooping Company, P.O. Box 249, W224 S8475 Industrial Dr., Big Bend, WI 53103: Free information ❖ All-wire collapsible coops. 414-662-2290.

Kennel-Aire Manufacturing Company, 6651 Hwy. 7, St. Louis Park, MN 55426: Free catalog ❖ Wire animal enclosures. 800-346-0134.

❖ PETS ❖

Mason Company, 260 Depot St., Box 365, Leesburg, OH 45135: Free catalog ❖ Kennels and cages for dogs. 800-543-5567.

Pet Castle, P.O. Box 1059, Brownwood, TX 76801: Free information ❖ One-piece molded dog house for indoors and outside. 800-351-1363; 915-643-2517 (in TX).

Radio Fence, 230 E. Russell St., Fayetteville, NC 28301: Free information ❖ Easy-to-install electronic invisible pet containment systems. 800-775-8404.

Ranger Portable Kennels, P.O. Box AA, Fayetteville, AR 72702: Free brochure ❖ Portable and fixed kennels. 501-443-2041.

West Virginia Fence Corporation, US Rt. 219, Lindside, WV 24951: Free catalog ❖ Permanent and portable electric pet containment fences. 800-356-5458; 304-753-4387 (in WV).

Pet Doors

Borwick Innovations Inc., P.O. Box 30345, Santa Barbara, CA 93130: Free information ❖ Easy-to-install screen door that snaps into any screen without screws or bolts. 800-365-5657.

Hale Security Pet Door, 5622 N. 52nd Ave., Glendale, AZ 85301: Free information ❖ Pet doors for walls and wooden doors. 800-888-8914.

Patio Pacific Inc., 1931 N. Gaffey St., San Pedro, CA 90731: Free catalog ❖ Pet door panels for sliding glass doors. 800-826-2871.

Pet Doors U.S.A., 4523 30th St. West, Bradenton, FL 34207: Free brochure ❖ Pet doors for walls, windows, doors, and patio doors, plus electronic door problem-solving pet products. 800-749-9609.

Pet-Eze, 862 Southhampton Rd., Benicia, CA 94510: Free brochure ❖ Doors with energy-conserving glass and aluminum insert panel with flexible flap for any size sliding door. 800-331-6702; 707-745-5026 (in CA).

Solo Inc., 970 W. 25th, Upland, CA 91784: Free catalog ❖ Self-opening and closing motorized pet door. 909-989-9999.

Reptiles & Amphibians

The Aquarium Mail Order, P.O. Box 104, Charcona, FL 32710: Free information ❖ Tropical fish and reptile supplies. 800-258-8444.

Armstrong's Cricket Farm, P.O. Box 125, West Monroe, LA 71294: Free information ❖ Crickets. 800-345-8778.

Bassetts Cricket Ranch Inc., 365 S. Mariposa, Visalia, CA 93292: Free information ❖ Crickets and king meal worms for reptiles, birds, fish, hamsters, and other animals. 800-634-2445.

The Bean Farm, 32514 NE 77th St., Carnation, WA 98014: Free catalog ❖ Herpetological and small animal supplies. 206-861-7964.

Bibliomania, 195 W. 200 North, Logan, UT 84321: Free price list ❖ Herpetological books, cage and field supplies, and collectibles.

Big Apple Herpetological, 33 Main St., Port Washington, NY 11050: Free catalog ❖ Reptile and amphibian supplies. 800-666-6672; 516-944-3432 (in NY).

Black Jungle Terrarium Supply, P.O. Box 93895, Las Vegas, NV 89195: Catalog $1 (refundable) ❖ Terrarium supplies. 800-268-1813.

Bush Herpetological Supply, P.O. Box 539, Neodesha, KS 66757: Free information ❖ Custom and standard cages and herpetological supplies. 800-451-6178.

Bushmaster Reptiles Inc., P.O. Box 19096, Boulder, CO 80308: Free information ❖ Imported rare and unusual reptiles. 303-530-2252.

Central Florida Reptile Farm, 4800 Kumquat St., Cocoa, FL 32926: Free information ❖ Captive-born turtles and tortoises. 407-639-3325.

Bob Clark, 12316 Val Verde Dr., Oklahoma City, OK 73142: Free information ❖ Micro-climate thermostats for herpetology. 405-722-5017.

Critter Corner Inc., 316 W. Mission, #117, Escondido, CA 92025: Free catalog ❖ Lighting and heating equipment, housing, and nutritional supplies for reptiles and amphibians. 619-746-5422.

Tom Crutchfield's Reptile Enterprises Inc., P.O. Box 1145, Bushnell, FL 33513: Free catalog ❖ Crocodiles, venomous reptiles, pythons, and other reptiles. 904-568-1830.

Danie's Neonates Inc., P.O. Box 735, Hollidaysburg, PA 16648: Free list with long SASE ❖ Captive-bred animals, imports, and supplies. 814-941-0997.

EastCoast Reptiles, 2320 N. Tryon St., Charlotte, NC 28206: Free catalog ❖ Captive-born and imported reptiles and supplies. Also live and frozen feeder rats and mice. 800-600-4113.

Ghann's Cricket Farm Inc., P.O. Box 211840, Augusta, GA 30917: Free information ❖ Live crickets and mealworms for reptiles and amphibians. 800-476-2248.

Glades Herp Inc., P.O. Box 50911, Fort Myers, FL 33905: Free information ❖ Captive-bred herps. 813-693-1077.

Dick Goergen Reptiles, P.O. Box 225, Alden, NY 14004: Price list $3 ❖ Pythons, boas, tortoises, and other reptiles. 716-681-4518.

Grubco, Box 15001, Hamilton, OH 45015: Free brochure ❖ Mealworms, fly larvae, wax worms, superworms, and crickets. 513-874-5881.

Hiss & Hers Reptiles, Jim & Debbie Rouse, 358 Spanish Oak Dr., Canyon Lake, TX 78133: Free price list ❖ Specializes in captive propagation of pythons.

Peter Kahl Reptiles, P.O. Box 150, Long Green, MD 21092: Free price list ❖ Specializes in captive-bred boas and pythons. 410-592-9675.

L/M Animal Farms, Pleasant Plain, OH 45162: Free information ❖ Reptile food and supplements. 800-332-5623; 513-877-2131 (in OH).

Lam Distributing Company, P.O. Box 407, Rusk, TX 75785: Free information ❖ Frozen natural food for snakes. 903-683-5212.

Sophia & John Lis, Box 206C, RD 2, Oley, PA 19547: Free price list with long SASE ❖ Frozen and live rodents. 610-689-4770.

Lorio Reptile Supplies Inc., P.O. Box 892, Langhorne, PA 19047: Free price list ❖ Herpetological products and rare captive-bred snakes. 215-757-8315.

Lyon Electric Company, 2765 Main St., Chula Vista, CA 91911: Free information ❖ Reptile incubation system. 619-585-9900.

Mail Order Pet Shop, 1338 N. Market Blvd., Sacramento, CA 95834: Free catalog ❖ Supplies for herpetoculturists. 800-366-7387.

Maryland Reptile Farm, 109 W. Cherry Hill Rd., Reisterstown, MD 21136: Free catalog with long SASE ❖ Books and related herp supplies. 410-526-4184.

Mice Unlimited, P.O. Box 71142, Project City, CA 96079: Free information ❖ Live and frozen feeder mice. 800-MICE-4-YOU.

The Mouse Factory, Ray Queen, P.O. Box 85, Alpine, TX 79831: Free information ❖ Frozen mice for reptiles. 915-837-7100.

Nekton USA Inc., 14405 60th St. North, Clearwater, FL 34620: Free information ❖ Food supplements for reptiles and amphibians. 813-530-3500.

Neodesha Plastics Inc., Twin Rivers Industrial Park, P.O. Box 371, Neodesha, KS 66757: Free information ❖ Reptile cages. 316-325-3096.

North County Exotics, P.O. Box 4856, Salinas, CA 93912: Free information ❖ Superworms for insect-eating herps, fish, and insectivorous animals. 408-663-0566.

Pet Food Warehouse, 777 N. Quentin Rd., Palatine, IL 60067: Free stock list ❖ Reptiles, amphibians, arachnids, and supplies. 708-705-7880.

Python Products Inc., 7000 W. Marcia Rd., Milwaukee, WI 53223: Free information ❖ Aquarium maintenance systems for aquatic turtles and herps. 414-355-7000.

Jamie Quick Reptiles, RD 3, Box 566, Middleton, NY 10940: Free price list with long SASE ❖ Pythons. 914-361-4206.

Rainbow Mealworms & Crickets, 126 E. Spruce St., P.O. Box 4907, Compton, CA 90224: Free information ❖ Mealworms and crickets for reptiles and amphibians. 800-777-9676.

Ray's Reptiles, P.O. Box 4732, Lincoln, NE 68504: Free information ❖ Feeder insects and captive-born lizards. 402-477-1975.

Rep-Cal Research Labs., P.O. Box 727, Los Gatos, CA 95031: Free information ❖ Calcium supplement for reptiles and amphibians. 408-356-4289.

Reptile Solutions, 3933 E. Pima, Ste. 109, Tucson, AZ 85712: Free list ❖ Captive-bred, rare, and unusual specimens from worldwide sources. 602-323-REPS.

Reptile Specialties, 7473 Foothill Blvd., P.O. Box 31, Tujunga, CA 91042: Free information ❖ Farm-raised imports and captive-bred chameleons. Also custom cages and terrariums. 818-352-1796.

Reptile World Imports of Tucson, 2727 E. Grant Rd., Tucson, AZ 85716: Free information ❖ Captive-bred and wild-caught exotic reptiles from worldwide sources. 602-325-2340.

Reptiles & Beyond, Jct. Rt. 12 & 20, Auburn, MA 01501: Free information ❖ Reptiles and live and frozen rodents. 508-832-5113.

Charles D. Dwayne Richard, 4533 W. Ave. K-12, Quartz Hill, CA 93536: Price list $4 ❖ Albino ball pythons and albino ruthveni. 805-943-1548.

San Diego Reptile Breeders, P.O. Box 556, Campo, CA 91906: Information $3 with long SASE ❖ Captive-bred boas, pythons, and other snakes. 619-478-5794.

SAS, 273 Hover Ave., Germantown, NY 12526: Free information ❖ Fresh-frozen and live rodents. 518-537-2000.

Serpent City Inc., P.O. Box 657, Island Lake, IL 60042: Catalog $1 ❖ Captive-bred snakes and herp supplies. 815-363-0290.

Southeast Reptile Exchange Inc., 4805 N. Westshore Blvd., Tampa, FL 33614: Free price list ❖ Captive-born and hand-picked imported reptiles from around the world. 800-881-3126.

Suwannee Mouse Farm, P.O. Box 14, Suwannee, FL 32692: Free price list with long SASE ❖ Frozen mice and rats. 904-542-2247.

Tarantula Ranch, 10222 Hammerly, #162, Houston, TX 77043: Free list with long SASE ❖ Captive-bred tarantulas.

Tetra Terrafauna, 3001 Commerce St., Blacksburg, VA 24060: Free information ❖ Iguana and tortoise food.

Top Hat Cricket Farm Inc., 1919 Forest Dr., Kalamazoo, MI 49002: Free information ❖ Live crickets. 800-638-2555.

Triple Cities Reptile, 1136 Upper Front St., Binghamton, NY 13905: Free price list ❖ Reptiles, food, and related products. 607-771-1056.

Uhn Inc., 6886 NW 82 Terrace, Parkland, FL 33067: Free list ❖ Captive-born and acclimated wild herps from over 10 countries. 305-753-2869.

V.P.I. Reptiles, P.O. Box 300, Boerne, TX 78006: Price list $2 ❖ Captive-hatched pythons. 210-537-5000.

Valentine Inc., 4259 S. Western Blvd., Chicago, IL 60609: Free catalog ❖ Supplies for the care and breeding of reptiles and amphibians. 800-GET-STUF.

Weis Reptiles, Rt. 4, Box 468, Tallahassee, FL 32304: Free price list with long SASE ❖ Captive-born lizards. 904-574-1037.

West Coast Chameleon Farms, P.O. Box 585, Aptos, CA 95001: Free information ❖ Parasite-free and captive-bred imported animals. 408-685-8136.

Zeigler Brothers Inc., P.O. Box 387, Hebron, IL 60034: Free price list with long SASE ❖ Reptile food. 800-724-7370.

PHONE CARDS

Buffalo Bill Telecard Gallery, 1980 Cliff Dr., Ste. 130, Santa Barbara, CA 93109: Free catalog ❖ McDonald's cards. 805-965-1454.

Freedman Collectibles Inc., P.O. Box 125, Newtonville, MA 02160: Free price list ❖ United States telecards. 617-965-7635.

Global Telecard Company, 1133 Dobbs Ferry Rd., White Plains, NY 10607: Free list with long SASE ❖ Disney, McDonald's, Coke, and other collectible phone cards. 914-674-0408.

International Phone Card Exchange, 41 Watchung Plaza, Montclair, NJ 07042: Free price list ❖ United States and international phone cards. 201-857-2121.

PATCO, P.O. Box 7702, Phoenix, AZ 85011: Free catalog ❖ Comic, fantasy, and science fiction phone cards. 800-408-3445.

N. Robillard, P.O. Box 160, Sheldonville, MA 02070: Free list with long SASE ❖ Telephone cards.

Sears Phone Card Department, 27001 US Hwy. 19 North, Clearwater, FL 34621: Free list ❖ United States and topical foreign phone cards. 813-791-7535.

The Shadow Group, 1187 Anderson Ave., Ste. 2C, Bronx, NY 10452: Free price list ❖ Worldwide phone cards. 718-681-8876.

United America Cards, P.O. Box 966, Menomonee Falls, WI 53052: Free catalog ❖ Phone cards. 414-353-3024 (evenings only).

PHONOGRAPHS

John Andolina Jr., The Early Sound Man, 28 Glen Oaks Dr., Rochester, NY 14624: Free information ❖ Antique phonographs. 716-247-3056.

Benedikt & Salmon Record Rarities, 3020 Meade Ave., San Diego, CA 92116: Free catalogs: indicate choice of (1) autographs and rare books, (2) classical, (3) jazz, big bands, and blues, and (4) personalities, soundtracks, and country music ❖ Early phonographs and cylinders, autographed memorabilia and rare books in music and the performing arts, and hard-to-find phonograph recordings from 1890 to date. 619-281-3345.

Hoctor Products, P.O. Box 38, Waldwick, NJ 07463: Free catalog ❖ Costumes, records, dance routines, videos, cassettes, phonographs and cassette players, and video recorders. 800-HOCTOR-9.

PHOTOGRAPHY

Albums & Photo Mounts

Albums Inc., P.O. Box 81757, Cleveland, OH 44181: Free catalog ❖ Wedding albums, photo mounts, plaques, and frames. 800-662-1000.

Camille Company Inc., 828 Bergen St., Brooklyn, NY 11238: Free list of retail sources ❖ Photo albums. 718-789-0100.

Clear-File (USA) Inc., 7549 Brokerage Dr., Orlando, FL 32809: Free brochure ❖ Presentation and storage supplies. 407-851-5966.

Creative Video Products, P.O. Box 7032, Endicott, NY 13761: Free information ❖ Video cassette albums. 607-754-6767.

Crown Products, 2178 Superior Ave., Cleveland, OH 44114: Free information ❖ Albums, folios, and photo mounts. 800-827-0363.

Exposures, 1 Memory Ln., P.O. Box 3615, Oshkosh, WI 54903: Free catalog ❖ Photo mounting supplies, albums, and frames. 800-572-5750.

Memories Inc., 1801 St. Albums Dr., Raleigh, NC 27609: Free information ❖ Handmade wedding books and albums. 800-462-5069.

Michel Company, 4664 N. Pulaski, Chicago, IL 60630: Free catalog ❖ Albums, photo mounts, and frames. 800-621-6649.

Penn Photomounts, Concord & Tryens Rd., Ashton, PA 19014: Free catalog ❖ Photo mounts, albums, and folios. 800-228-7366; 800-227-7366 (in PA).

Pierce Company, 9801 Nicollet, Minneapolis, MN 55420: Catalog $1 (refundable) ❖ Hand-painted backgrounds for portrait photography, mounts, albums, drapes, and printed forms. 612-884-1991.

❖ PHOTOGRAPHY ❖

Reel 3-D Enterprises Inc., P.O. Box 2368, Culver City, CA 90231: Free information ❖ Stereo and cardboard slip-in slide mounts and 3-D supplies. 310-837-2368.

Dave Sirken Distributors Inc., 1550 Wentzel St., Rochester, IN 46975: Free information ❖ Frames, folders, and albums. 800-348-2510.

Backgrounds

Backdrop Outlet, 1524 S. Peoria, Chicago, IL 60608: Free catalog ❖ Hand-painted backgrounds. 312-733-7703.

James Bright Backgrounds, 460 Elder Ave., Sand City, CA 93955: Free information ❖ Fine art backgrounds and motorized roller systems. 800-821-5796; 408-899-5011 (in CA).

Britten-Grant Event Design, 44632 Guilford Dr., Ashburn, VA 22011: Free information ❖ Scenic backdrops. 703-729-5937.

Calumet Photographic, 890 Supreme Dr., Bensenville, IL 60106: Free list of retail sources ❖ Translucent backgrounds. 800-225-8638.

Denny Manufacturing Company Inc., P.O. Box 7200, Mobile, AL 36670: Free catalog ❖ Background scenes and professional backdrops. 800-844-5616.

Steve Kaeser, 1333 Tower Square, Ste. 4, Ventura, CA 93003: Free information ❖ Backgrounds and accessories. 800-495-8148.

Photek Backgrounds, 549 Howe Rd., Shelton, CT 06484: Free information ❖ Featherlite, reversible, and washable backgrounds and support systems. 800-648-8868.

Photo-Tech Inc., P.O. Box 9326, North St. Paul, MN 55109: Free information ❖ Easy-to-use background system. 612-771-4438.

Photographers Specialized Services, 650 Amour Rd., P.O. Box 46, Oconomowoc, WI 53066: Catalog $8 ❖ Free-standing and folding background screens. Also professional and amateur accessories. 800-558-0114.

Photographic Products, 460 Elder Ave., Sand City, CA 93955: Free brochure ❖ Hand-painted backgrounds, motorized roller systems, stools and tables, umbrellas, cases and stands, strobe lights, and Victorian-style chairs. 800-821-5796; 310-973-8488 (in CA).

Pierce Company, 9801 Nicollet, Minneapolis, MN 55420: Catalog $1 (refundable) ❖ Hand-painted backgrounds for portrait photography, photo supplies, mounts, albums, drapes, and printed forms. 612-884-1991.

Superior Specialties Inc., 3013 Gilroy St., Los Angeles, CA 90039: Free list of retail sources ❖ Seamless background papers. 800-354-3049; 213-662-3031 (in CA).

F.J. Westcott Company, P.O. Box 1596, Toledo, OH 43603: Free information ❖ Reflectors and backgrounds. 419-243-7311.

Bags & Camera Cases

Charles Beseler Company, 1600 Lower Rd., Linden, NJ 07036: Free brochure ❖ Bags for cameras, video equipment, and camcorders. 908-862-7999.

The Camjacket Company, 2610 Adams Ave., San Diego, CA 92116: Free catalog ❖ All-weather cases for cameras and lenses. 800-338-8759.

Coast Manufacturing Company, 200 Corporate Blvd. South, Yonkers, NY 10701: Free information ❖ Camera bags. 800-333-6282; 914-376-1500 (in NY).

Domke, Division Saunders Group, 21 Jet View Dr., Rochester, NY 14624: Free information ❖ Camera bags and photo equipment. 716-328-7800.

GMI/Division Omega Arkay, 191 Shaeffer Ave., Westminster, MD 21158: Free information ❖ Camera bags and equipment cases. 800-777-6634.

Leica USA Inc., 156 Ludlow Ave., Northvale, NJ 07647: Free information ❖ Handcrafted bags for cameras, lenses, binoculars, and accessories. 201-767-7500.

Lightware, 1329 W. Byers Pl., Denver, CO 80223: Free catalog ❖ Camera cases. Includes lightweight airline shippable cases.

London Imports Ltd., 1344 Broadway, Ste. 210, Hewlett, NY 11557: Free information ❖ Handcrafted camera bags for small to large-format equipment. 516-295-3903.

LowePro, 2194 Northpoint Pkwy., Santa Rosa, CA 95407: Free information ❖ Camera bags. 707-575-4363.

Pelican Products Inc., 2255 Jefferson St., Torrance, CA 90501: Free information ❖ Watertight and unbreakable corrosion-proof cases. 310-328-9910.

Photoflex, 333 Encinal St., Santa Cruz, CA 95060: Free information ❖ Camera bags, studio lights, and accessories. 800-486-2674.

Porter Case Inc., 3718 W. Western Ave., South Bend, IN 46619: Free information ❖ Wheeled carry-on case with a built-in carrying cart. 800-356-8348.

Seal-Tight Photo/Video Cases, Camera Guard by Doskocil, P.O. Box 1246, Arlington, TX 76004: Free information ❖ Almost indestructible camera cases.

SunDog, 6700 S. Glacier St., Seattle, WA 98188: Free catalog ❖ Packs, bags, and cases for sports, travel, and photography equipment. 800-634-0005.

Tamrac, 9240 Jordan Ave., Chatsworth, CA 91311: Free catalog ❖ Camera and video bags. 800-662-0717.

TENBA Quality Cases Ltd., 503 Broadway, New York, NY 10012: Free information ❖ Camera equipment bags. 800-328-3622; 212-966-1013 (in NY).

Tocad America Inc., 300 Webro Rd., Parsippany, NJ 07054: Free information ❖ Protective camera cases. 201-428-9800.

Tundra Camjacket, Satter Inc., 4100 Dahlia St., Denver, CO 80207: Free information ❖ Camera bags. 303-831-7458.

Books

Harry N. Abrams Inc., 100 5th Ave., New York, NY 10011: Free information ❖ Books on photography. 212-206-7715.

Aperture, 20 E. 23rd St., New York, NY 10010: Free information ❖ Fine art photography books. 800-929-2323.

John S. Craig, 111 Edward Ave., P.O. Box 1637, Torrington, CT 06790: Free information ❖ Hard-to-find instruction books for photography equipment. Also other photographic literature. 203-496-9791.

Eastman Kodak Company, Information Center, 343 State St., Rochester, NY 14650: Free information ❖ Books and other publications on photography. 800-462-6495.

Focal Press, 313 Washington St., Newton, MA 02158: Free catalog ❖ Books on photography. 617-928-2500.

Hudson Hills Press, 230 5th Ave., Ste. 1308, New York, NY 10001: Free information ❖ Books on photography and art. 212-889-3090.

International Center of Photography, 1133 Avenue of Americas, New York, NY 10036: Free catalog ❖ Photography books. 800-688-8171.

Light Impressions, 439 Monroe Ave., P.O. Box 940, Rochester, NY 14607: Free catalog ❖ Books on photography and supplies for archival storage of negatives and prints. 800-828-6216.

Literature, P.O. Box 136, Bayville, NY 11709: Free information with long SASE ❖ Original and reproduction instruction manuals for photographic equipment.

Panorama Camera, P.O. Box 463, Williston Park, NY 11596: Free list with long SASE ❖ Photo copies of instruction manuals.

A Photographer's Place, P.O. Box 274, Prince St., New York, NY 10012: Free information ❖ Books on photography. 212-431-9358.

Leonard Rue Enterprises, 138 Millbrook Rd., Blairstown, NJ 07825: Free catalog ❖ How-to photography books. 908-362-6616.

Shutterbug Store, 5211 S. Washington Ave., Titusville, FL 32780: Free information ❖ Books on photography. 800-677-5212.

355

❖ PHOTOGRAPHY ❖

Camera Manufacturers

Ansco PhotoOptical, 1801 Touhy Ave., Elk Grove Village, IL 60007: Free information. 800-323-6697.

Bronica, GMI/Division Omega Arkay, 191 Shaeffer Ave., Westminster, MD 21158: Free information. 800-777-6634.

Calumet Photographic, 890 Supreme Dr., Bensenville, IL 60106: Free list of retail sources. 800-225-8638.

Camerama Corporation, 131 Newton St., Weston, MA 02193: Free information ❖ Panoramic cameras. 800-274-5722.

Canon, One Canon Plaza, Lake Success, NY 11042: Free information. 516-488-6700.

Chinon America Inc., 1065 Bristol Rd., Mountainside, NJ 07092: Free information. 908-654-0404.

Contax, 100 Randolph Rd., Box 6802, Somerset, NJ 08875: Free information. 800-526-0266.

Eastman Kodak Company, Information Center, 343 State St., Rochester, NY 14650: Free information. 800-462-6495.

Fuji Photo Film USA Inc., 555 Taxter Rd., Elmsford, NY 10523: Free information. 914-789-8100.

Peter Gowland Cameras, 609 Hightree Rd., Santa Monica, CA 90402: Free information. 310-454-7867.

Victor Hasselblad Inc., 10 Madison Rd., Fairfield, NJ 07004: Free brochure. 800-338-6477.

Konica USA Inc., 440 Sylvan Ave., Englewood Cliffs, NJ 07632: Free information. 201-568-3100.

Leica USA Inc., 156 Ludlow Ave., Northvale, NJ 07647: Free information. 201-767-7500.

Mamiya America Corporation, 8 Westchester Plaza, Elmsford, NY 10523: Free information. 914-347-3300.

Minolta, 101 Williams Dr., Ramsey, NJ 07446: Free information. 201-825-4000.

Nikon, Customer Relations, 19601 Hamilton Ave., Torrance, CA 90502: Free brochure. 800-645-6687.

Nikonos Cameras, Customer Relations, 19601 Hamilton Ave., Torrance, CA 90502: Free brochure. 800-645-6687.

Noblex U.S.A., 17851 Sky Park Cir., Ste. C, Irvine, CA 92714: Free information ❖ Panoramic cameras. 800-732-6361.

Olympus Corporation, 145 Crossways Park, Woodbury, NY 11797: Free information. 800-221-3000.

Pentax Corporation, 35 Inverness Dr. East, Englewood, CO 80112: Free brochure. 303-799-8000.

Polaroid Corporation, 201 Burlington Rd., Bedford, MA 01730: Free information. 617-386-2000.

Ricoh Consumer Products Group, 475 Lillard, Sparks, NV 89434: Free brochure. 800-225-1899.

Ritz Cameras, 6711 Ritzway, Beltsville, MD 20705: Free catalog. 301-419-0000.

Rollei Cameras, HP Marketing, 16 Chapin Rd., Pine Brook, NJ 07470: Free brochure. 201-808-9010.

Samsung Optical America Inc., 40 Seaview Dr., Secaucus, NJ 07094: Free information. 201-902-0347.

Sigma Corporation of America, 15 Fleetwood Ct., Ronkonkoma, NY 11779: Brochure $1. 516-585-1144.

Tamron Industries Inc., P.O. Box 388, Port Washington, NY 11050: Free brochure. 800-827-8880.

Tokina Optical Corporation, 1512 Kona Dr., Compton, CA 90220: Free information. 310-537-9380.

Vivitar Corporation, 1280 Rancho Conejo Blvd., P.O. Box 2559, Newbury Park, CA 91319: Free brochure. 805-498-7008.

Wisner Large Format Cameras, Wisner Classic Manufacturing Company Inc., P.O. Box 21, Marion, MA 02738: Free information. 800-848-0448.

WISTA Large Format Cameras, Foto-Care Ltd., 132 W. 21st St., New York, NY 10011: Free information.

Yashica Inc., 100 Randolph Rd., P.O. Box 6802, Somerset, NJ 08875: Free information. 908-560-0060.

Darkroom Equipment & Supplies

Alta Photographic Inc., 1421 International Dr., Bartlesville, OK 74006: Free information ❖ Darkroom chemicals. 800-688-8688.

Artcraft Chemicals Inc., P.O. Box 583, Schenectady, NY 12301: Free information ❖ Bulk chemicals, pre-packaged kits, and miscellaneous supplies. 518-355-8700.

Bencher Inc., 831 N. Central Ave., Wood Dale, IL 60191: Free information ❖ Enlargers, copystands, and darkroom equipment. 708-238-1183.

Berg Color Tone, 72 Ward Rd., Lancaster, NY 14086: Free information ❖ Color toners and retouching supplies. 716-684-0511.

Bogen Photo Corporation, 565 E. Crescent Ave., P.O. Box 506, Ramsey, NJ 07446: Free information ❖ Dry-mount presses. 201-818-9500.

Bostick & Sullivan, P.O. Box 16639, Santa Fe, NM 87506: Free information ❖ Chemicals and paper for platinum and palladian printing. 505-474-0890.

Bryant Laboratory Inc., 1101 5th St., Berkeley, CA 94710: Free information ❖ Chemicals. 800-367-3141; 510-526-3141 (in CA).

California Stainless Manufacturing, 32 N. Wood Rd., Camarillo, CA 93010: Free catalog ❖ Stainless sinks, film dryers, and accessories. 805-484-1038.

Darkroom Aids Company, 3449 N. Lincoln Ave., Chicago, IL 60657: Free information ❖ Used darkroom equipment. 312-248-4301.

Daylab, 400 E. Main, Ontario, CA 94545: Free catalog ❖ All-in-one, self-contained color enlarger with exposure meter, timer, and developing system. 800-678-3669.

Delta 1, CPM Inc., 10830 Sanden Dr., Dallas, TX 75238: Free catalog ❖ Temperature-regulated sinks and darkroom equipment. 800-947-0233.

Dimco-Gray, 8200 S. Suburban Rd., Centerville, OH 45459: Free brochure ❖ Darkroom timers. 513-433-7600.

Doran Enterprises, 2779 S. 34th St., Milwaukee, WI 53215: Free catalog ❖ Color print processors. 414-645-0109.

Durst, 10 County Line Rd., Ste. 29, Branchburg, NJ 08876: Free information ❖ Easy-to-operate continuous paper processor and enlarger system. 800-GO-DURST.

Freestyle, 5124 Sunset Blvd., Los Angeles, CA 90027: Free information ❖ Darkroom supplies and equipment. 800-292-6137.

GMI/Division Omega Arkay, 191 Shaeffer Ave., Westminster, MD 21158: Free information ❖ Darkroom chemicals and enlarging papers. 800-777-6634.

Helix, 310 S. Racine Ave., Chicago, IL 60607: Free catalog ❖ Cameras and accessories, darkroom equipment and supplies, and video and underwater photo equipment. 800-33-HELIX; 312-421-6000 (in IL).

Jobo Fototechnic Inc., P.O. Box 3721, Ann Arbor, MI 48106: Free information ❖ Photo processing chemicals, color retouching dyes for color and black-and-white photography, and processing equipment. 313-995-4192.

KingConcept, Division Amega/Arkay, 191 Shaeffer Ave., Westminster, MD 21157: Free information ❖ Automatic rotary tube film and print processor. 800-777-6634.

Leedal Inc., 1918 S. Prairie Ave., Chicago, IL 60616: Free brochure ❖ Stainless steel darkroom sinks with plumbing and back splash, stands, and shelves. 800-441-6663.

The Maine Photographic Resource, 2 Central St., Rockport, ME 04856: Free catalog ❖ Photography and dark room equipment. 800-227-1541; 207-236-4788 (in ME).

❖ PHOTOGRAPHY ❖

Omega/Arkay, 191 Schaeffer Ave., Westminster, MD 21157: Free information ❖ Darkroom equipment and enlargers. 410-857-6353.

The Palladio Company, P.O. Box 28, Cambridge, MA 02140: Free information ❖ Platinum and palladium printing papers. 617-393-0814.

Photo-Therm, 110 Sewell Ave., Trenton, NJ 08610: Free catalog ❖ Automatic film processor/dryer for slides, black-and-white, and color negatives. 609-396-1456.

Photographers Formulary, P.O. Box 950, Condon, MT 59826: Free catalog ❖ Photographic chemicals. 800-922-5255. ✓

Porter's Camera Store Inc., Box 628, Cedar Falls, Iowa 50613: Free catalog ❖ Picture-taking equipment, darkroom supplies, and photography novelties and accessories. 800-553-2001. ✓

Seal Products, 550 Spring St., Naugatuck, CT 06770: Free information ❖ Mounting, laminating, and texturizing products. 203-729-5201.

Solar Cine Products Inc., 4247 S. Kedzie Ave., Chicago, IL 60632: Free catalog ❖ Darkroom and other photographic equipment and supplies. 800-621-8796; 312-254-8310 (in IL). ✓

Zone VI Studios Inc., 22 High St., 4th Floor, Brattleboro, VT 05301: Free catalog ❖ Picture-taking equipment and darkroom equipment. 802-257-5161.

Enlargers

Bencher Inc., 831 N. Central Ave., Wood Dale, IL 60191: Free information ❖ Enlargers and darkroom equipment. 708-238-1183.

Charles Beseler Company, 1600 Lower Rd., Linden, NJ 07036: Free brochure ❖ Enlargers, color heads and electronic controls, modular units for color or black-and-white enlarging, and other equipment. 908-862-7999.

Doran Enterprises, 2779 S. 34th St., Milwaukee, WI 53215: Free catalog ❖ Color print processors. 414-645-0109.

Durst, 10 County Line Rd., Ste. 29, Branchburg, NJ 08876: Free information ❖ Easy-to-operate continuous paper processor and enlarger system. 800-GO-DURST.

Omega/Arkay, 191 Schaeffer Ave., Westminster, MD 21157: Free information ❖ Darkroom accessories and enlargers. 410-857-6353.

Paterson, Division Saunders Group, 21 Jet View Dr., Rochester, NY 14624: Free catalog ❖ Darkroom equipment and enlargers. 716-328-7800.

The Saunders Group, 21 Jet View Dr., Rochester, NY 14624: Free catalog ❖ Exposure and flash meters, medium format dichroic enlargers and equipment, strobe brackets, tripods, and other equipment. 716-328-7800.

Testrite Instrument Company Inc., 135 Monroe St., Newark, NJ 07105: Free catalog ❖ Enlargers and other equipment. 201-589-6767.

Exposure Meters & Guides

Bogen Photo Corporation, 565 E. Crescent Ave., Ramsey, NJ 07446: Free information ❖ Multi-purpose exposure meters, tripods, enlargers, and other equipment. 201-818-9500.

Harris Photoguides, 83 Rock Beach Rd., Rochester, NY 14617: Free information ❖ Easy-to-use hand-held exposure calculators. 716-342-3691.

Minolta, 101 Williams Dr., Ramsey, NJ 07446: Free brochure ❖ Exposure meters. 201-825-4000.

Pentax Corporation, 35 Inverness Dr. East, Englewood, CO 80112: Free brochure ❖ Exposure meters. 303-799-8000.

R.T.S. Inc./Sekonic, 40-11 Burt Dr., Deer Park, NY 11729: Free information ❖ Exposure meters, flash guns, and tripod studio ball heads. 516-242-6808.

The Saunders Group, 21 Jet View Dr., Rochester, NY 14624: Free catalog ❖ Exposure and flash meters, medium format dichroic enlargers, strobe brackets, tripods, and other equipment. 716-328-7800.

Shepherd Meters, Division Saunders Group, 21 Jet View Dr., Rochester, NY 14624: Free catalog ❖ Exposure meters. 716-328-7800.

Sinar Bron, 17 Progress St., Edison, NJ 08820: Free information ❖ Three-in-one meter that measures color temperature for flash, continuous light sources and flash-duration, and lux. 908-754-5800.

Smith-Victor, 301 N. Colfax St., Griffith, IN 46319: Free information ❖ Light meters and lighting equipment. 800-348-9862.

Film Manufacturers & Distributors

Agfa/Miles Inc., 100 Challenger Rd., Ridgefield Park, NJ 07660: Free information ❖ Color slide, color print, and black-and-white film. 201-440-2500.

Eastman Kodak Company, Information Center, 343 State St., Rochester, NY 14650: Free information ❖ Color slide, color print, black-and-white, infrared, and special process films. 800-462-6495.

Forte Film, GMI/Division Omega Arkay, 191 Shaeffer Ave, Westminster, MD 21158: Free information ❖ Black-and-white film. 800-777-6634.

Freestyle, 5124 Sunset Blvd., Los Angeles, CA 90027: Free information ❖ Film and paper. 800-292-6137.

Fuji Photo Film USA Inc., 555 Taxter Rd., Elmsford, NY 10523: Free information ❖ Color slide, color print, and black-and-white film. 914-789-8100.

Ilford Photo Corporation, W. 70 Century Rd., Paramus, NJ 07653: Free information ❖ Chromogenic black-and-white film. 800-631-2522.

Konica USA Inc., 440 Sylvan Ave., Englewood Cliffs, NJ 07632: Free information ❖ Color slide and print film. 201-568-3100.

Polaroid Corporation, 201 Burlington Rd., Bedford, MA 01730: Free information ❖ Color slide, black-and-white slide, and color print and black-and-white film packs. 617-386-2000.

3M Photo Color Systems Division, 3M Center, Building 223-2S-05, St. Paul, MN 55144: Free information ❖ Color slide and print film. 800-695-FILM.

Universal Distributors Corporation, 677 8th St., Lakewood, NJ 08701: Free information ❖ Fuji, Kodak, Polaroid, Agfa, and Konica film. Also Kodak and Fuji disposable cameras. 800-872-FILM; 908-364-0802 (in NJ).

Filters

Cambridge Camera Exchange, 7th Ave. & 13th St., New York, NY 10011: Free information ❖ Cambron filters. 212-675-8600.

Cokin Creative Filter System, Minolta Corporation, 101 Williams Dr., Ramsey, NJ 07446: Free information ❖ Filters. 201-825-4000.

Eastman Kodak Company, Information Center, 343 State St., Rochester, NY 14650: Free information ❖ Wratten filters. 800-462-6495.

Pro4 Imaging Inc., 21 Spragg Cir., Markham, Ontario, Canada L3P 5W1: Free information ❖ Filter systems for 35mm and medium and large-format cameras. 800-636-0844.

Schneider Corporation, 400 Crossways Park Dr., Woodbury, NY 11797: Free information ❖ Filters for black-and-white photography, neutral density filters, star and diffraction filters, lens shades, masks for matte boxes, lens reversal rings, tele-converters, and auto-extension tubes. 516-496-8500.

Singh-Ray Corporation, 153 Progress Circle, Venice, FL 34292: Free information ❖ Neutral density graduated filters. 800-486-5501.

THK Photo Products Inc., 1512 Kona Dr., Compton, CA 90220: Free information ❖ Tokina, Hoya, and Kenko filters. 310-537-9380.

Tiffen Manufacturing, 90 Oser Ave., Hauppage, NY 11788: Free information ❖ Filters. 800-645-2522.

Flash Units & Lighting

American Photographic Instrument Company Inc., P.O. Box 322, 12 Lincoln Blvd., Emerson, NJ 07630: Free information ❖ Light stands. 800-600-1147.

PHOTOGRAPHY

Bogen Photo Corporation, 565 E. Crescent Ave., Ramsey, NJ 07446: Free information ❖ Compact studio electronic flash systems and Metz Mecablitz flash units with a choice of power sources and system accessories. 201-818-9500.

Britek Inc., 12704 Marquardt Ave., Santa Fe Springs, CA 90670: Free information ❖ Professional studio flash and lighting equipment. 800-925-6258.

Brown Line, 310 S. Racine Ave., Chicago, IL 60607: Free catalog ❖ Lighting systems. 312-421-4050.

Paul C. Buff Inc., 2725 Bransford Ave., Nashville, TN 37204: Free information ❖ Compact lightweight studio flash equipment. 800-443-5542; 615-383-3982 (in TN).

Canon, One Canon Plaza, Lake Success, NY 11042: Free information ❖ Flash units for the Canon cameras. 516-488-6700.

✓ **Chimera,** 1812 Valtec Ln., Boulder, CO 80301: Free catalog ❖ Portable lighting units and accessories. 800-424-4075.

Courtenay Solaflash, Division Saunders Group, 21 Jet View Dr., Rochester, NY 14624: Free catalog ❖ Professional studio lighting equipment. 716-328-7800.

Creative Light Works, 4633 Mill Rd., Red Wing, MN 55066: Free information ❖ Adjustable light booms and flexible lighting systems. 612-388-5444.

✓ **Delta-1,** CPM Inc., 10830 Sanden Dr., Dallas, TX 75238: Free catalog ❖ Studio lighting and special effects equipment. 800-947-0233.

Dyna-Lite, 311-319 Long Ave., Hillside, NJ 07205: Free information ❖ Professional studio flash and lighting equipment. 908-687-8800.

Jones Photo Equipment, 10816 Burbank Blvd., North Hollywood, CA 91601: Free information ❖ Fixed and rotating over-the-lens flash brackets. 818-766-7189.

Konica USA Inc., 440 Sylvan Ave., Englewood Cliffs, NJ 07632: Free brochure ❖ Konica flash equipment and accessories. 201-568-3100.

Larson Enterprises Inc., 365 S. Mountainway Dr., P.O. Box 2150, Orem, UT 84058: Free information ❖ Compact lighting equipment and soft box systems. 800-227-5533.

Lowel-Light Manufacturing Inc., 140 58th St., Brooklyn, NY 11220: Free information ❖ Quick and easy-to-setup lighting equipment. 718-921-0600.

LPA Design, 1350 Shelburne Rd., Ste. 265, South Burlington, VT 05403: Free information ❖ Electronic slave flash system. 800-695-2696.

Lumedyne Lighting, 6010 Wall St., Port Richey, FL 34668: Free information ❖ Lighting systems. 813-847-5394.

Lumiquest, 140 Heimer, Ste. 775, San Antonio, TX 78232: Free information ❖ Tabletop lighting accessories and reflectors. 210-490-1400.

Minolta, 101 Williams Dr., Ramsey, NJ 07446: Free information ❖ Flash systems for Minolta cameras. 201-825-4000.

Multiblitz Lighting Company, HP Marketing Corporation, 16 Chapin Rd., Pine Brook, NJ 07058: Free information ❖ Studio electronic flash equipment for amateurs and professionals. 201-808-9010.

Nikon, Customer Relations, 19601 Hamilton Ave., Torrance, CA 90502: Free brochure ❖ Flash units and accessories. 800-645-6687.

Nikonos Cameras, Customer Relations, 19601 Hamilton Ave., Torrance, CA 90502: Free brochure ❖ Electronic flash systems for general and under water use. 800-645-6687.

✓ **Novatron of Dallas Inc.,** 8230 Moberly Ln., Dallas, TX 75227: Free catalog ❖ Studio flash equipment. 800-527-1595.

Olympus Corporation, 145 Crossways Park, Woodbury, NY 11797: Free information ❖ Flash systems for use with Olympus cameras. 800-221-3000.

Pentax Corporation, 35 Inverness Dr. East, Englewood, CO 80112: Free brochure ❖ Electronic flash units for Pentax cameras. 303-799-8000.

Photoflex, 333 Encinal St., Santa Cruz, CA 95060: Free information ❖ Camera bags, studio lights, and accessories. 800-486-2674.

Photogenic Machine Company, P.O. Box 3365, Youngstown, OH 44513: Free brochure ❖ Soft lighting equipment for use with studio or small battery-operated strobes. 800-682-7668.

Photographer's Warehouse, P.O. Box 3365, Boardman, OH 44513: Free information ❖ Electronic flash systems. 800-521-4311.

Quantum Instruments Inc., 1075 Stewart Ave., Garden City, NY 11530: Free information ❖ Portable studio-style flash units. 516-222-0611.

R.T.S. Inc./Sekonic, P.O. Box 604, Lindenhurst, NJ 11757: Free information ❖ Exposure meters, flash guns, and tripod studio ball heads. 516-242-6801.

Red Wing Light Boom, 4633 Mill Rd., Red Wing, MN 55066: Free information ❖ Compact light boom with finger-touch adjustment. 612-388-5444.

Ricoh Consumer Products Group, 475 Lillard Dr., Sparks, NV 89434: Free brochure ❖ Flash equipment for Ricoh cameras. 800-225-1899.

Satter Distributing, 4100 Dahlia, Denver, CO 80207: Free information ❖ Electronic flash systems. 303-831-7458.

The Saunders Group, 21 Jet View Dr., Rochester, NY 14624: Free catalog ❖ Bounce lighting equipment. 716-328-7800.

Sinar Bron, 17 Progress St., Edison, NJ 08820: Free information ❖ Three-in-one meter that measures color temperature for flash, continuous light sources and flash-duration, and lux. 908-754-5800.

Smith-Victor, 301 N. Colfax St., Griffith, IN 46319: Free information ❖ Light meters and lighting equipment. 800-348-9862.

Sonic Research, P.O. Box 850, Bonsall, CA 92003: Free information ❖ Underwater and high-powered strobe lights. 619-724-4540.

Speedotron Corporation, 310 S. Racine Ave., Chicago, IL 60607: Free information ❖ Electronic flash equipment. 312-421-4050.

Studiomate, 12704 Marquardt Ave., Santa Fe Springs, CA 90670: Free information ❖ Studio lighting equipment. 800-283-8346.

Sunpak Division of ToCAD America, 300 Webrow Rd., Parsippany, NJ 07054: Free information ❖ Electronic flash equipment. 201-428-9800.

Testrite Instrument Company Inc., 135 Monroe St., Newark, NJ 07105: Free catalog ❖ Portable light box systems, lightweight aluminum and chrome easels, opaque projectors, and darkroom equipment. 201-589-6767.

✓ **TriStar Photo Industrial Inc.,** 9960 Indiana Ave., Riverside, CA 92503: Free catalog ❖ Studio lighting equipment, backgrounds, light stands, brackets and holders, soft boxes, umbrellas, video camera supports, and other equipment. 800-424-8801.

Vivitar Corporation, 1280 Rancho Conejo Blvd., P.O. Box 2559, Newbury Park, CA 91319: Free brochure ❖ Electronic flash equipment, cameras, and lenses. 805-498-7008.

Wein Products Inc., The Saunders Group, 21 Jet View Dr., Rochester, NY 14624: Free information ❖ Sound and light-operated wireless meter and switches. 716-328-7800.

Woods Electronics Inc., 14781 Pomerado Rd., Poway, CA 92064: Free information ❖ Sound and infrared-operated remote flash triggering devices. 619-486-0806.

Zone VI Studios Inc., 22 High St., 4th Floor, Brattleboro, VT 05301: Free catalog ❖ Lighting and darkroom equipment. 802-257-5161.

Photo Processing

Associated Photo Company, Box 817, Florence, KY 41022: Free information ❖ Photo Christmas cards with name imprint. 606-282-0011.

C & C Photo Lab, 11 Farmingdale Rd., Rt. 109, West Babylon, NY 11704: Free information ❖ Custom enlargements. 800-647-5850.

❖ PHOTOGRAPHY ❖

Custom Photo, 550 Millcreek Mall, Erie, PA 16509: Free information ❖ Enlargements and photo T-shirts and mugs. 800-313-7454.

Dale Laboratories, 2960 Simms St., Hollywood, FL 33020: Free information ❖ Processes slides, prints, and negatives from Kodacolor film. 800-327-1776.

J.R. Degruttola, 425 Lafayette St., Newark, NJ 07105: Free information ❖ Custom hand-printed Ciba Chrome enlargements. 800-589-3360.

EMCAX Photo-finishing, P.O. Box 7383, Madison, WI 53707: Free information ❖ Hand-printed Ilfochrome enlargements. 800-497-6544; 608-244-4176 (in WI).

The Enlargement Works Inc., 316 N. Milwaukee St., Ste. 406, Milwaukee, WI 53202: Free information ❖ Handmade color enlargements from slides or negatives. 414-278-1210.

Flair Pro Color Lab, P.O. Box 140240, Gainesville, FL 32614: Free price list ❖ Fuji photo processing. 800-741-6004.

Fuji Anaheim Color Labs, 2665 Woodland Dr., Anaheim, CA 92802: Free information ❖ Fuji color slide and print processing. 800-634-2960.

G-B Color Lab, P.O. Box 562, Hawthorne, NJ 07507: Free brochure ❖ Ilfochrome color prints from slides. 201-427-0460.

General Color Corporation, 604 Brevard Ave., P.O. Box 70, Cocoa, FL 32923: Free brochure ❖ Photo and print processing with enlargements up to 24 x 30 inches. 800-321-1602.

Holland Photo, 1221 S. Lamar, Austin, TX 78704: Free information ❖ Ilfochrome prints from slides or transparencies. 800-477-4024.

Images Photo Processing, P.O. Box 32590, Tucson, AZ 85751: Free information ❖ Black-and-white photo processing. 800-337-5631.

Imagination Station, 730 NW 2nd St., Grants Pass, OR 97526: Free information ❖ Color, black-and-white, and sepia antique photo reproductions on paper and fabric. 800-338-3857.

International Foto, 472 Main St., Buffalo, NY 14202: Free information ❖ Poster prints, enlargements, and slide processing. 800-743-1969.

Kelly Color, Box 576, Morgantown, NC 28680: Free information ❖ Proofing, candid and portrait photos, package assortments, copy and restoration services, montages and composites, and display transparencies for light boxes. 704-433-0934.

LaserColor Laboratories, P.O. Box 24614, West Palm Beach, FL 33416: Free information ❖ Laser and computer-made color prints. 800-848-2018; 407-848-2000 (in FL).

Lightworks Custom B & W Lab, P.O. Box 37, Goose Creek, SC 29445: Free catalog ❖ Black-and-white enlargements and archival film processing. 803-797-5760.

Minox Processing Laboratories, P.O. Box 1041, New Hyde Park, NY 11040: Free information ❖ Sub-miniature film processing. 800-645-8172; 516-437-5750 (in NY).

Modernage Photographic Services, 1150 Avenue of Americas, New York, NY 10036: Free information with long SASE ❖ Photo restoration, custom color and black-and-white processing, exhibition prints, stills from black-and-white movies, and other services. 800-997-2510.

Moments in Time Ltd., 5145 Golden Foothill Pkwy., Ste. 140, El Dorado Hills, CA 95762: Free information ❖ High-resolution color printing. 916-939-9300.

Mystic Color Lab, P.O. Box 144, Mystic, CT 06355: Free information ❖ Processes black-and-white and color print film, Kodachrome and Ektachrome slide and movie film, and Kodacolor 35mm, 110, 126, and disc film. 800-367-6061.

National Color Labs, 306 W. 1st Ave., Roselle, NJ 07203: Free information ❖ Copy, restoration and retouching, custom processing and finishing services. Also albums, special effects, and business, holiday, and thank-you cards. 800-284-1947; 241-1010 (in 201 area code).

Owl Photo Corporation, 701 E. Main St., Weatherford, OK 73096: Free information ❖ Film processing and print-making services. 405-772-3353.

PFS Inc., 1124 Norwood St., Radford, VA 24141: Free information with long SASE ❖ Custom photo finishing. 540-639-6911.

Photosmith, 263 Central Ave., Dover, NH 03820: Free information ❖ Processes photographs on business cards, refrigerator art, T-shirts, steins, and gifts. 603-742-6659.

Phototech, 109 18th St., Richmond, VA 23223: Free information ❖ Archival printing and reproduction services. 804-648-2012.

PML Film Processing, P.O. Box 75981, St. Paul, MN 55175: Free price list ❖ Professional black-and-white film processing. 800-995-9431.

Pro Photo Labs, 213-219 S. Tyler Ave., P.O. Drawer 777, Lakeland, FL 33802: Free information ❖ Film developing, enlarging, and other services. 800-237-6429.

Reliable Photo Inc., P.O. Box 25553, Chicago, IL 60625: Free information ❖ Photo restoration and processing services. 312-907-0933.

Seattle Filmworks, Elliott Bay at Pier 89, P.O. Box 34056, Seattle, WA 98124: Free information ❖ Color or black-and-white prints, prints and slides (from same roll), slides (from 35mm color film), and pictures on disk. 206-283-9074.

Shore Color Lab, 9378 Calumet Ave., Munster, IN 46321: Free information ❖ Custom package printing services. 800-422-2575.

Silver Image Photographics, 3102 Vestal Pkwy. East, Vestal, NY 13850: Free information ❖ Custom photo cards, color business cards, enlargements and poster prints. 607-797-8795.

Skrudland Photo, 5311 Fleming Ct., Austin, TX 78744: Free information ❖ Film and slide processing, print-making, photo greeting cards, and special services. 512-444-0958.

Skyline Color Lab, 9016 Prince William St., Manassas, VA 22110: Free information ❖ Full-service color and black-and-white photo processing laboratory. 703-369-1906.

Specialty Photographic Laboratories, 132 Garden St., Santa Barbara, CA 93101: Free information ❖ Black-and-white photo processing. 805-962-6765.

UCL Photo, 812 S. La Brea Ave., Los Angeles, CA 90036: Free information ❖ Custom processing, slide duplication, and prints from slides. 800-933-2977.

Westside Processing Inc., 1523 26th St., Santa Monica, CA 90404: Free information ❖ Film processing. 310-4828-6850.

Photo Restoration

Artex Studio, 6 Forest Ave., Glen Cove, NY 11542: Free information ❖ Black-and-white and color photo restoration. Also conversion of black-and-white photographs to color. 516-676-0376.

Elbinger Laboratories Inc., 1136 N. Washington, East Lansing, MI 48906: Free information ❖ Archival reproduction of photographs in sepia, oil coloring, and black-and-white. 800-332-0302.

Kelly Color, Box 576, Morgantown, NC 28655: Free information ❖ Restoration and copy services, proofing, portraits and machine-processed candid photos, package assortments, montages and composites, and display transparencies for light boxes. 704-433-0934.

Modernage Photographic Services, 1150 Avenue of Americas, New York, NY 10036: Free information with long SASE ❖ Photo restoration services. 800-997-2510.

Ron's Gallery Supply, 159 Duane St., New York, NY 10013: Free information ❖ Photo restoration. 800-735-7667.

Retail Suppliers

A & I Camera Classics Ltd., 2 World Financial Center, New York, NY 10281: Free information ❖ Photographic and movie equipment. 212-786-4696.

AAA Camera Exchange Inc., 43 7th Ave., New York, NY 10011: Free catalog ❖ Cameras and darkroom equipment. 800-221-9521; 212-242-5800 (in NY).

❖ PHOTOGRAPHY ❖

Abbey Camera Inc., 1417-25 Melon St., Philadelphia, PA 19130: Free information ❖ Photographic and studio equipment and darkroom supplies. 215-236-1200.

Abe's of Maine Camera & Electronics, 1957 Coney Island Ave., Brooklyn, NY 11223: Free information ❖ Photography equipment. 800-531-2237.

Accessory Source, 1864 48th St., Brooklyn, NY 11204: Free information ❖ Photographic accessories. 718-435-0343.

Adorama, 42 W. 18th St., New York, NY 10011: Catalog $3 ❖ Photography, darkroom, and underwater photo equipment. 212-741-0466.

Alt Camera Exchange, 69 Queen St. East, Toronto, Ontario, Canada M5C 1R8: Free information ❖ New and used photographic equipment. 800-387-9891.

Stan Amarkin & Company, 198 Amity Rd., Woodbridge, CT 06525: Free information ❖ New and used equipment and photographic accessories. 800-289-5342; 203-397-7766 (in CT).

B & H Photo-Video, 119 W. 17th St., New York, NY 10011: Catalog $3.95 ❖ Photo and video equipment. 800-947-9905; 212-444-6605 (in NY).

Ball Photo Supply Company, 85 Tunnel Rd., Asheville, NC 28805: Free information ❖ Telescopes, spotting scopes, camera equipment, binoculars, eyepieces, and accessories. 704-252-2443.

Beach Camera of Maine, 203 Rt. 22 East, Greenbrook, NJ 08812: Free information ❖ Photography equipment, binoculars, radar detectors, and video equipment. 908-424-1103.

Beach Photo & Video Inc., 604 Main St., Daytona Beach, FL 32118: Free information ❖ Photography equipment and supplies. 904-252-0577.

Bel Air Camera & Video, 1025 Westwood Blvd., Los Angeles, CA 90024: Free information ❖ Photographic equipment and video cameras. 800-200-4999.

Bergen County Camera, 270 Westwood Ave., Westwood, NJ 07675: Free information ❖ Photography equipment. 201-664-4113.

Berger Brothers Camera Exchange, 209 Broadway, Amityville, NY 11701: Free information ❖ Photography equipment, camcorders, and accessories. 800-262-4160.

Bi-Rite Photo & Electronics, 20 E. 39th St., New York, NY 10016: Free information ❖ Cameras, underwater photography, and darkroom equipment. Also binoculars and telescopes. 800-223-1970; 212-685-2130 (in NY).

Dan Black, Box 2072, Bala Cynwyd, PA 19004: Free information ❖ Leica equipment. 610-664-7345.

Bromwell Marketing, 3 Alleghany Center, Pittsburgh, PA 15212: Free catalog ❖ Large-format view cameras, lenses, and tripods. 412-321-4118.

Brooklyn Camera Exchange, 488 Sunrise Hwy., Rockville Centre, NY 11570: Free information ❖ New and used cameras and supplies. 516-678-5333.

Cambridge Camera Exchange, 7th Ave. & 13th St., New York, NY 10011: Free information ❖ Photography equipment. 212-675-8600.

Camera Care, 906 Arch St., Philadelphia, PA 19107: Free information ❖ Photography equipment. 215-925-7805.

Camera City Inc., 342 Kings Hwy., Brooklyn, NY 11223: Free information ❖ Photographic equipment and accessories. 718-627-4224.

Camera Corner of Iowa, 3523 Eastern Ave., Davenport, IA 52807: Free information ❖ Camera equipment and binoculars. 319-391-6851.

Camera One of Sarasota Inc., 1301 Main St., Sarasota, FL 34236: Free information ❖ Photographic equipment. 941-955-1799.

Camera Sound of Pennsylvania, 1104 Chestnut St., Philadelphia, PA 19107: Free information ❖ Cameras and accessories, camcorders, laser disk players, and portable audio and high-fidelity equipment. 800-477-1003.

Camera Traders Ltd., 44 W. 17th St., New York, NY 10011: Free information ❖ Cameras, lenses, filters, enlargers and projectors, slide duplicators, tripods, copy equipment, flash and lighting equipment, cases, and books. 212-463-0097.

Camera World, 1809 Commonwealth Ave., Charlotte, NC 28205: Catalog $1 ❖ Darkroom and equipment for still, movie, video, and underwater photography. 704-375-8453.

Cameras & Electronics of New Jersey & Maine, 982 River Rd., Edgewater, NJ 07020: Free information ❖ Photography equipment. 201-886-7400.

Central Camera Company, 230 S. Wabash Ave., Chicago, IL 60604: Free information ❖ Photography equipment. 800-421-1899; 312-427-5580 (in IL).

Charlotte Camera Brokers Inc., 2400 Park Rd., Charlotte, NC 28203: Free information ❖ Photography equipment. 704-339-0084.

Don Chatterton of Seattle, P.O. Box 15150, Seattle, WA 98115: Free information ❖ Photographic equipment. 206-525-1100.

Coast to Coast, 2570 86th St., Brooklyn, NY 11214: Free information ❖ Cameras and audio and video equipment. 718-265-1723.

Columbus Camera Group Inc., 55 E. Blake, Columbus, OH 43202: Free information ❖ Photography equipment. 614-267-0686.

Custom Photo Manufacturing, 10830 Sanden Dr., Dallas, TX 75238: Free catalog ❖ Darkroom and studio equipment for amateurs, professionals, and industrial use. 800-627-0252.

Del's Camera, 923 Olive St., 2nd Floor, Santa Barbara, CA 93101: Free information ❖ Photographic equipment. 805-962-7557.

Dury's, 720 6th Ave. South, Nashville, TN 37203: Free information ❖ Photography equipment. 615-255-3456.

Electronic Mailbox, 10-12 Charles St., Glen Cove, NY 11542: Free information ❖ Home theater systems, photography accessories, video editing equipment, and electronics. 800-325-2325.

Executive Photo & Electronics, 120 W. 31st St., New York, NY 10001: Free information ❖ Photography and video equipment and electronics. 800-882-2802.

The F Stops Here, 1725 State St., Santa Barbara, CA 93101: Free information ❖ Large-format cameras and accessories. 800-894-8439.

Focus Camera, 4419 13th Ave., Brooklyn, NY 11219: Free information ❖ Cameras and darkroom equipment. 718-436-6262.

47th Street Photo, Mail Order Department, 455 Smith St., Brooklyn, NY 11231: Catalog $2 ❖ Photography and video equipment. 718-722-4750.

Foto Electric Supply Company, 31 Essex St., New York, NY 10002: Free information ❖ Cameras, lenses, and darkroom equipment. 212-673-5222.

Frank's Highland Park Camera, 5715 N. Figueroa St., Los Angeles, CA 90042: Catalog $3 ❖ Cameras, underwater photography and video, darkroom equipment, and books. 800-421-8230; 213-255-0123 (in CA).

Freestyle, 5124 Sunset Blvd., Los Angeles, CA 90027: Free information ❖ Photography and darkroom equipment. 800-292-6137.

Garden State Camera, 101 Kuller Rd., Clifton, NJ 07015: Free information ❖ Photographic equipment, camcorders, video and audio accessories, binoculars, and other optical equipment. 201-742-5777.

Genesis Camera Inc., 814 W. Lancaster Ave., Bryn Mawr, PA 19010: Free information ❖ Audio, video, and photographic equipment. 800-575-9977; 610-527-5261 (in PA).

Ghitelman Cameras Inc., 166 5th Ave., New York, NY 10010: Free information ❖ Photographic equipment and video cameras. 212-924-3020.

Ken Hansen Photographic, 625 N. Flagler Dr., #504, West Palm Beach, FL 33401: Free information ❖ New and used photographic equipment. 407-832-4844.

❖ PHOTOGRAPHY ❖

Helix, 310 S. Racine Ave., Chicago, IL 60607: Free catalog ❖ Cameras and accessories, darkroom equipment and supplies, and video and underwater photo equipment. 800-33-HELIX; 312-421-6000 (in IL).

W.B. Hunt Company Inc., 100 Main St., Melrose, MA 02176: Free catalog ❖ Cameras, optical accessories, and darkroom and studio equipment. 617-662-6685.

KEH Camera Brokers, 188 14th St., Atlanta, GA 30318: Free catalog ❖ Used cameras and accessories. 404-892-5522.

Ken-Mar Camera & Video, 27 Great Neck Rd., Great Neck, NY 11021: Free information ❖ Camera equipment, binoculars, and video equipment. 516-482-1025.

KOH'S Camera Sales & Service Inc., 2 Heitz Pl., Hicksville, NY 11801: Free information ❖ Cameras, studio accessories, and optical equipment. 516-933-9790.

Jim Kuehl & Company, 8527 University Blvd., Des Moines, IA 50325: Free information ❖ Leica cameras and photographic and optical equipment. 515-225-0110.

Lauderdale Camera, South Harbor Plaza, 1316 SE 17th St., Fort Lauderdale, FL 33316: Free information ❖ Photographic equipment. 800-749-4990; 305-524-9447 (in FL).

Le Camera, 4040 Quaker Bridge Rd., Mercerville, NJ 08619: Free information ❖ Camera equipment. 800-786-3686.

Lincoln Camera & Video Store, 2001 Delaware Ave., Wilmington, DE 19806: Free information ❖ New and used photographic equipment. 302-654-6241.

Lindahl Specialties Inc., 800 W. Beardsley Ave., Elkhart, IN 46514: Free information ❖ Photographic equipment for special effects. 219-296-7823.

M & M Photo Source Limited, 1135 37th St., Brooklyn, NY 11218: Free information ❖ Cameras, lenses, film, darkroom supplies, lighting and digital imaging equipment, and other accessories. 800-606-6746.

Midwest Photo Exchange, 3313 N. High St., Columbus, OH 43202: Free information ❖ Camera equipment, darkroom supplies, and lighting accessories. 614-261-1264.

Milford Camera Shop, 9 River St., Milford, CT 06460: Free information ❖ Photographic equipment. 203-878-0156; 800-562-5048 (in CT).

Negri's Camera Shop, 287 Main St., Farmingdale, NY 11735: Free information ❖ Used equipment. 516-249-1305.

Olden Camera & Lens Company Inc., 1265 Broadway, New York, NY 10001: Free information ❖ Photography and video equipment, darkroom supplies, computers, and electronics. 212-725-1234.

Peach State Photo, 1706 Chantilly Dr., Atlanta, GA 30324: Free information ❖ Camera and video equipment. 800-766-9653.

Photographic Systems, 412 Central SE, Albuquerque, NM 87102: Free catalog ❖ Used equipment. 505-247-9780.

Porter's Camera Store Inc., Box 628, Cedar Falls, Iowa 50613: Free catalog ❖ Photography equipment and darkroom supplies. 800-553-2001.

Profoto, 128 W. 31st St., New York, NY 10001: Free information ❖ Photographic equipment. 212-239-8689.

Reimers Photo Materials Company, 300 E. Bay St., Milwaukee, WI 53207: Free information ❖ Used and new cameras. 800-236-5435; 414-744-4471 (in WI).

Roberts, 255 S. Meridian St., Indianapolis, IN 46225: Free information ❖ Used photographic equipment. 800-726-5544; 636-5544 (in Indianapolis).

Leonard Rue Enterprises, 138 Millbrook Rd., Blairstown, NJ 07825: Free catalog ❖ Books, video tapes, equipment, and gifts for photographers and outdoor enthusiasts. 908-362-6616.

Samy's Camera, 200 S. La Brea, Los Angeles, CA 90036: Free information ❖ Photographic equipment, flash accessories, and new and used cameras. 800-321-4SAM.

SBI Sales, 259 A St., Boston, MA 02210: Free information ❖ Used and demonstration equipment and darkroom supplies. 800-234-5724.

Service Photo, 2225 N. Charles St., Baltimore, MD 21218: Free information ❖ Photographic equipment and darkroom supplies. 800-344-3PRO; 410-235-6200 (in MD).

Silvio's Photoworks, 3854 Sepulveda Blvd., Torrance, CA 90505: Free information ❖ New and used equipment and photographic accessories. 310-791-7100.

Smile Photo, 29 W. 35th St., New York, NY 10001: Free information ❖ Photography and video equipment and supplies. 212-967-5900.

Solar Cine Products Inc., 4247 S. Kedzie Ave., Chicago, IL 60632: Free catalog ❖ Darkroom and photographic equipment and supplies. 800-621-8796; 312-254-8310 (in IL).

Su's Cameras, 1161 Rt. 27, Highland Park, NJ 08904: Free information ❖ New and used photographic equipment. 908-572-5709.

Supreme Camera & Video, 1562 Coney Island Ave., Brooklyn, NY 11234: Free information ❖ Cameras and accessories. 800-332-2661; 718-692-4110 (in NY).

Tamarkin & Company, 198 Amity Rd., Woodbridge, CT 06525: Free price list ❖ Photographic equipment, new and used cameras, and flash accessories. 800-289-5342; 203-397-7766 (in CT).

Testrite Instrument Company Inc., 135 Monroe St., Newark, NJ 07105: Free catalog ❖ Photography equipment for the darkroom and studio. 201-589-6767.

Tri-State Camera, 650 6th Ave., New York, NY 10011: Free information ❖ Photography equipment. 800-221-1926; 212-633-2290 (in NY).

Unique Photo, 451 S. Jefferson St., Orange, NJ 07050: Free information ❖ Paper, chemistry, accessories, and supplies. 800-769-1200; 201-673-0100 (in NJ).

Vistek, 496 Queen St. East, Toronto, Canada M5A 4G8: Free information ❖ New and used photographic equipment. 800-561-1777.

The Wall Street Camera, 82 Wall St., New York, NY 10005: Catalog $2.95 (refundable with $50 purchase) ❖ Photography equipment. 212-344-0011.

Westbury Camera, 301 Rt. 110, Huntington Station, NY 11746: Free information ❖ Camera equipment and accessories. 516-271-0220.

Woodmere Camera Inc., 337 Merrick Rd., Lynbrook, NY 11563: Free information with long SASE ❖ Photography equipment. 516-599-6013.

Zone VI Studios Inc., 22 High St., 4th Floor, Brattleboro, VT 05301: Free catalog ❖ Photography and lighting equipment and darkroom supplies. 802-257-5161.

Slides

The Astronomical Society of the Pacific, 390 Ashton Ave., San Francisco, CA 94112: Free catalog ❖ Slide sets of the solar system and universe. 800-335-2624.

Cornell Laboratory of Ornithology, 159 Sapsucker Woods Rd., Ithaca, NY 14850: Free brochure ❖ Slides of North American birds. 607-254-2450.

MMI Corporation, P.O. Box 19907, Baltimore, MD 21211: Catalog $2 ❖ Astronomy 35mm slides. 410-366-1222.

The Planetary Society, 65 N. Catalina Ave., Pasadena, CA 91106: Free brochure ❖ Astronomy books, videos, and slide sets. 818-793-1675.

Visuals, 440 NW 130th St., Miami, FL 33168: Free list ❖ Domestic and foreign travel slides. 305-681-5379.

Worldwide Slides, 7427 Washburn, Minneapolis, MN 55423: Catalog $1 ❖ Travel slides about the United States, foreign countries, historic and scenic sites, and nature settings. 612-869-6482.

Storage & Filing Systems

Clear-File (USA) Inc., 7549 Brokerage Dr., Orlando, FL 32809: Free brochure ❖ Presentation and storage supplies. 407-851-5966.

Light Impressions, 439 Monroe Ave., P.O. Box 940, Rochester, NY 14607: Free catalog ❖ Books on photography and supplies for archival storage of negatives and prints. 800-828-6216.

Tropich Software Inc., 529 Central Ave., Scarsdale, NY 10583: Free information ❖ Windows-based filing system for photographs. 914-472-0278.

20th Century Plastics Inc., P.O. Box 2393, Brea, CA 92622: Free catalog ❖ Plastic pages to protect, organize, and display slides, prints, and negatives. 800-767-0777.

Tripods & Monopods

Benbo Tripods, Division Saunders Group, 21 Jet View Dr., Rochester, NY 14624: Free catalog ❖ Adjustable tripods. 716-328-7800.

Bogen Photo Corporation, 565 E. Crescent Ave., Ramsey, NJ 07446: Free information ❖ Gitzo tripods. 201-818-9500.

Cascade Designs Inc., 4000 1st Ave. South, Seattle, WA 98134: Free information ❖ Walking stick equipped with a universal camera mount that converts to a monopod. 800-531-9531.

Coast Manufacturing Company, 200 Corporate Blvd. South, Yonkers, NY 10701: Free information ❖ Photo and video luggage and tripods. 800-333-6282; 914-376-1500 (in NY).

GMI/Division Omega Arkay, 191 Shaeffer Ave., Westminster, MD 21158: Free brochure ❖ Cullman tripods. 800-777-6634.

Karl Heitz Inc., P.O. Box 427, Woodside, NY 11377: Free information ❖ Monopods. 718-565-0004.

KB Systems, 10407 62nd Pl. West., Mukilteo, WA 98275: Free information ❖ Wooden tripods. 206-355-8740.

Photographica, 45-1548 Richmond N., London, Ontario, Canada N6G 4W7: Free information ❖ Monopods. 519-858-0443.

R.T.S. Inc./Sekonic, P.O. Box 604, Lindenhurst, NJ 11757: Free information ❖ Exposure meters, flash guns, and tripod studio ball heads. 516-242-6801.

Raven Tripods, 334 E. Lake St., Petoskey, MI 49770: Free information ❖ Easy-to-use and quick-to-setup tripods. 616-347-0526.

The Saunders Group, 21 Jet View Dr., Rochester, NY 14624: Free catalog ❖ Tripods, exposure and flash meters, enlargers, strobe brackets, and other equipment. 716-328-7800.

ToCad America, SLIK Tripods, 300 Webrow Rd., Parsippany, NJ 07054: Free catalog ❖ Adjustable tripods. 201-428-9800.

Tracks Walking Staffs, 4000 1st Ave. South, Seattle, WA 98134: Free information ❖ Telescoping sectioned walking staffs that convert to a camera monopod. 800-527-1527.

Velbon, 2433 Moreton St., Torrance, CA 90505: Free information ❖ Tripods. 213-530-5446.

Underwater Photography Equipment

Adorama, 42 W. 18th St., New York, NY 10011: Catalog $3 ❖ Underwater and photography equipment. 212-741-0466.

Amphibico Inc., 9563 Cote de Liesse, Dorval, Quebec, Canada H9P 1A3: Free information ❖ Underwater housings and lights for Sony cameras. 514-636-9910.

B & H Photo-Video, 119 W. 17th St., New York, NY 10011: Free information ❖ Underwater photography equipment. 800-947-9905; 212-444-6605 (in NY).

Berry Scuba Company, 6674 Northwest Hwy., Chicago, IL 60631: Free catalog ❖ Skin diving, scuba equipment, and underwater camera equipment. Also diving lights. 800-621-6019; 312-763-1626 (in IL).

Bi-Rite Photo & Electronics, 20 E. 39th St., New York, NY 10016: Free information ❖ Underwater and general photography equipment. 800-223-1970; 212-685-2130 (in NY).

Camera World, 1809 Commonwealth Ave., Charlotte, NC 28205: Catalog $1 ❖ Equipment and supplies for still, movie, video, and underwater photography. 800-868-3686; 704-375-8453 (in NC).

Frank's Highland Park Camera, 5715 N. Figueroa St., Los Angeles, CA 90042: Catalog $3 ❖ Cameras, darkroom accessories, and underwater photography equipment. 800-421-8230; 213-255-0123 (in CA).

Fuji Photo Film USA Inc., 555 Taxter Rd., Elmsford, NY 10523: Free information ❖ Underwater camera equipment. 914-789-8100.

GMI/Division Omega Arkay, 191 Shaeffer Ave., Westminster, MD 21158: Free information ❖ Underwater cameras with electronic flash, close-up lenses, automatic film winding and re-winding, and built-in film coding. 800-777-6634.

Helix, 310 S. Racine Ave., Chicago, IL 60607: Free catalog ❖ Cameras, underwater photography equipment, darkroom supplies, and video equipment. 800-33-HELIX; 312-421-6000 (in IL).

Ikelite Underwater Systems, 50 W. 33rd St., Indianapolis, IN 46208: Catalog $1 ❖ Underwater housings for most cameras. 317-923-4523.

Merald Vision & Sound, 127 W. 24th St., New York, NY 10011: Free information ❖ Underwater video and single lens reflex housings, video and other cameras, and accessories. 800-980-2929; 212-463-7143 (in NY).

Minolta, 101 Williams Dr., Ramsey, NJ 07446: Free information ❖ Underwater camera equipment. 201-825-4000.

Nikon, Customer Relations, 19601 Hamilton Ave., Torrance, CA 90502: Free brochure ❖ Underwater camera equipment and lenses. 800-645-6687.

Nikonos Cameras, Customer Relations, 19601 Hamilton Ave., Torrance, CA 90502: Free brochure ❖ Underwater camera equipment and lenses. 800-645-6687.

Pioneer Research Inc., 216 Haddon Ave., Westmont, NJ 08108: Free information ❖ Underwater housings for cameras and video equipment. 800-257-7742; 609-854-2424 (in NJ).

Quest International, P.O. Box 175, Corona Del Mar, CA 92625: Free information ❖ Underwater video systems.

Sonic Research, P.O. Box 850, Bonsall, CA 92003: Free information ❖ Underwater strobe lights. 619-724-4540.

Vivitar Corporation, 1280 Rancho Conejo Blvd., P.O. Box 2559, Newbury Park, CA 91319: Free brochure ❖ Underwater camera equipment. 805-498-7008.

PINATAS

La Piñata, Number 2 Patio Market, Old Town, Albuquerque, NM 87104: Brochure $1 (refundable) ❖ Pinatas. 800-657-6208; 505-242-2400 (in NM).

PINE CONES

Creative Craft House, Box 2567, Bullhead City, AZ 86430: Catalog $2 (refundable) ❖ Sea shells, pine cones, and craft supplies.

Mountain Farms Inc., 307 Number 9 Rd., Fairview, NC 28730: Free catalog ❖ Pods, small and large cones, and foliage supplies. 704-628-4709.

Nature's Bounty, P.O. Box 1646, Flagstaff, AZ 86002: Information $1 ❖ Pine cones. 520-779-6982.

Nature Crafts, 164 Hillside Ave., Livingston, NJ 07039: Catalog $2 (refundable) ❖ Pine cone crafting supplies.

J. Page Basketry, 820 Albee Rd. West, Nokomis, FL 34275: Catalog $2 (refundable) ❖ Pine needle-crafting and wheat-weaving supplies, dried and preserved flowers and herbs, basket-making and craft materials, tools, and books. 813-485-6730.

PINS & PINBACK BUTTONS

A.T. Patch Company, Littleton, NH 03561: Free catalog ❖ Embroidered emblems, decals, and enameled pins. 603-444-3423.

Adhatters, Box 667, Effingham, IL 62401: Free information ❖ Patches, pins, and decals. 800-225-7642.

❖ **PLASTICS** ❖

Bale Company, 222 Public St., Box 6400, Providence, RI 02940: Free catalog ❖ Athletic, academic, and scholastic medals and pins. Also class and club school rings, novelties, charms, and awards. 800-822-5350.

Eastern Emblem, Box 828, Union City, NJ 07087: Free catalog ❖ Patches, cloisonne pins, decals, stickers, T-shirts, caps, and jackets. 800-344-5112.

Hoover's Manufacturing Company, 4015 Progress Blvd., Peru, IL 61354: Free catalog ❖ Dog tag key rings, beer and coffee mugs, belt buckles, patches, flags, and Vietnam, Korea, and World War II hat pins. 815-223-1159.

Frosty Little, 222 E. 8th St., Burley, ID 83318: Free information ❖ Sweatshirts, T-shirts, pins, and patches with clown graphics. 208-678-0005.

Stadri Emblems, 71 Tinker, Woodstock, NY 12498: Free catalog ❖ Embroidered emblems, pins, and decals. 914-679-6600.

William Tell, P.O. Box 4, Coopersburg, PA 18036: Catalog $5 ❖ Pinback buttons. 800-809-TELL.

PLASTICS

Castcraft, Box 17000, Memphis, TN 38187: Free information ❖ How-to information, rubber and plastic materials, and other mold-making and casting supplies.

Castolite, 4915 Dean, Woodstock, IL 60098: Catalog $3 ❖ Casting resins, mold-making supplies, and how-to books. 815-338-4670.

Magic Systems Inc., P.O. Box 23888, Tampa, FL 33623: Free information ❖ Easy-to-use mold-making kits, coloring materials, and plastic embedding supplies. 813-886-5495.

Synair Corporation, P.O. Box 5269, Chattanooga, TN 37406: Free information ❖ Urethane casting resin and molding systems. 800-251-7642; 615-698-8801 (in TN).

PLATES, COLLECTIBLE

Aftosa, 1034 Ohio Ave., Richmond, CA 94804: Free catalog ❖ Clear acrylic plate stands and bowl holders. 800-231-0397.

Anheuser-Busch Inc., 2700 S. Broadway, St. Louis, MO 63150: Free catalog ❖ Heirloom Budweiser and other collectible plates and steins. 800-PICK-BUD.

Jody Bergsma Galleries Inc., 1344 King St., Bellingham, WA 98226: Catalog $4 ❖ Statuary and figurines, plates, dolls, porcelain collectibles, and gifts. 800-237-4762; 360-733-1101 (in WA).

Biggs Limited Editions, 5517 Lakeside Ave., Richmond, VA 23228: Free information with long SASE ❖ Statuary and figurines, plates, dolls, other porcelain collectibles, and gifts. 800-637-0704.

Churchills, Twelve Oaks Mall, Novi, MI 48377: Free information ❖ Collectible plates. 800-388-1141.

Dexter & Company, 53 W. 49th St., New York, NY 10020: Free information ❖ Collectible plates. 800-BUY-DEXT; 212-245-7460 (in NY).

Gallery 247, 814 Merrick Rd., Baldwin, NY 11510: Free brochure ❖ Collectible plates and prints. 516-868-4800.

House of Tyrol, P.O. Box 909, Alpenland Center, Helen Highway/75 North, Cleveland, GA 30528: Free catalog ❖ Musical cuckoo clocks, steins, crystal, porcelain, lamps, music boxes, pillows, knitted items, decor accessories, bar equipment, collector plates, pewter, tapestries, cards, Alpine hat pins, Christmas decorations, and folk music videos. 800-241-5404.

Kaymon Arts & Design, RR 2, Box 41, Blueback Nanoose Bay, British Columbia, Canada V0R 2R0: Free information ❖ Limited edition china collector plates. 403-986-9891.

The Limited of Michigan Ltd., 10861 Paw Paw Dr., Holland, MI 49424: Free price list ❖ Old, new, club, dated, rare, back-issue plates and bells and other hard-to-find collectibles. 800-355-6363.

Quality Collectables, 71 S. Mast St., Goffstown, NH 03045: Free information ❖ Limited edition figurines and statues, signed plates, lithographs, and sports art. 800-422-6514.

Red Cross Gifts, 122 Walnut St., Spooner, WI 54801: Free information ❖ Collectible plates, Ashton-Drake dolls, and gifts, and collectibles. 800-344-9958.

Trendco Inc., 4723 W. Atlantic Ave., Delray Beach, FL 33445: Free catalog ❖ Figurines, plates, bobbing heads, and signed memorabilia. 800-881-0181.

Unicef, P.O. Box 182233, Chattanooga, TN 37422: Free catalog ❖ Stationery, postcards, gifts, and limited edition plates. 800-553-1200.

The Village Plate Collector, P.O. Box 1118, Cocoa, FL 32923: Free information ❖ Limited edition plates. 800-752-8371; 407-636-6914 (in FL).

White's Collectables & Fine China, P.O. Box 680, Newborg, OR 97132: Free information ❖ Collectible plates and new and discontinued china patterns. 800-618-2782.

Zaslow's Fine Collectibles, Strathmore Shopping Center, Rt. 34, Matawan, NJ 07747: Free information ❖ Plates, figurines, and collectibles. 800-526-2355; 908-583-1499 (in NJ).

PLATFORM TENNIS

Century Sports Inc., Lakewood Industrial Park, 1995 Rutgers University Blvd., Box 2035, Lakewood, NJ 08701: Free information ❖ Balls and paddles. 800-526-7548; 908-905-4422 (in NJ).

Sportime, Customer Service, 1 Sportime Way, Atlanta, GA 30340: Free information ❖ Balls and paddles. 800-444-5700; 770-449-5700 (in GA).

PLAYGROUND EQUIPMENT

BigToys, 7717 New Market, Olympia, WA 98501: Free information ❖ Playground equipment. 800-426-9788.

Cedar Works, P.O. Box 990, Rockport, ME 04856: Free catalog ❖ Wooden playsets for backyards and playgrounds. 800-461-3327.

ChildLife®

ChildLife Inc., 55 Whitney St., Holliston, MA 01746: Free catalog ❖ Back-yard wooden play systems since 1945. Slides, treehouses, swings, jungle gyms, and more. 800-462-4445.

Florida Playground & Steel Company, 4701 S. 50th St., Tampa, FL 33619: Free brochure ❖ Swings and equipment for backyards and playgrounds. 800-444-2655; 813-247-2812 (in FL).

Fun 'N' Play Inc., 607 Industrial Park Dr., Unit KK, Newport News, VA 23602: Free information ❖ Swing and gym set plans. 800-840-7529.

GameTime, P.O. Box 121, Fort Payne, AL 35967: Free information ❖ Playground/backyard play systems and outdoor fitness equipment. 800-235-2440.

Gazebo & Porchworks, 728 9th Ave. SW, Puyallup, WA 98371: Catalog $2 ❖ Swings and backyard play structures. 206-848-0502.

GYM-N-I Playgrounds Inc., 1980 IH 35 North, Laurel Bend, TX 78130: Free information ❖ Modular playground structures, swing sets, and other equipment. 800-294-9664.

PCA Industries Inc., 5642 Natural Bridge, St. Louis, MO 63120: Free information ❖ Aluminum playground equipment. 800-727-8180.

Playworld Systems, P.O. Box 505, New Berlin, PA 17855: Free information ❖ Wooden and metal play equipment. 800-233-8404; 717-966-1015 (in PA).

Victor Stanley Inc., P.O. Box 330, Dunkirk, MD 20754: Free information ❖ Playground equipment and outdoor furniture. 800-368-2573; 301-855-8300 (in MD).

Sun Designs, P.O. Box 6, Oconomowoc, WI 53066: Plan book $9.95 plus $3.95 postage ❖ Backyard structures. 414-567-4255.

Ultra Play Systems Inc., 425 Sycamore St., Anderson, IN 46016: Free information ❖ Outdoor gym equipment. 800-458-5872.

Woodenplay, P.O. Box 27904, Raleigh, NC 27611: Free catalog ❖ Redwood backyard play sets. 800-966-3752.

Woodset Inc., 4460 Printers Ct., White Plains, MD 20695: Free information ❖ Backyard and playground structures. 800-638-9663.

POLITICAL MEMORABILIA

Bold Concepts, 1501 Broadway, Ste. 1808, New York, NY 10036: Free catalog ❖ Political buttons. 212-764-6330.

Political Americana, Mail Order Department, 1456 G St. NW, Washington, DC 20005: Free catalog ❖ Political collectibles. 800-333-4555.

The Political Gallery, 5335 N. Tacoma Ave., Ste. 24, Indianapolis, IN 46220: Free information ❖ Political campaigns and sports memorabilia. 317-257-0863.

Presidential Coin & Antique Company, 6550 Little River Tnpk., Alexandria, VA 22312: Free catalog ❖ Political memorabilia, medals, and tokens. Also antiques, coins, and Americana. 703-354-5454.

Rex Stark-Americana, Box 1029, Gardner, MA 02019: Catalog $5 ❖ Political memorabilia, posters, flags, needlework, textiles, china, needlework, folk art, toys, and paintings. 508-630-3237.

PORCELAIN COLLECTIBLES & FIGURINES

All God's Children Collectors Club, P.O. Box 5038, Glencoe, AL 35905: Free list of retail sources ❖ Miss Martha original porcelain dolls. 205-492-0221.

Jody Bergsma Galleries Inc., 1344 King St., Bellingham, WA 98226: Catalog $4 ❖ Statuary and figurines, plates, dolls, other porcelain collectibles, and gifts. 800-237-4762; 360-733-1101 (in WA).

Biggs Limited Editions, 5517 Lakeside Ave., Richmond, VA 23228: Free information with long SASE ❖ Statuary and figurines, plates, dolls, other porcelain collectibles, and gifts. 800-266-7744.

Callahan's Calabash Nautical City, Hwy. 179, 9937 Beach Rd., Calabash, NC 28467: Free information ❖ Statuary and figurines, dolls, other porcelain collectibles, and gifts. 800-344-3816.

Department 56 Showroom, 4411 Sepulveda Blvd., Culver City, CA 90230: Catalog $5 ❖ Dickens' Village and Department 56 Snow Village and Heritage Village buildings and accessories. 800-433-7856.

European Imports & Gifts, Oak Mill Mall, 7900 N. Milwaukee Ave., Niles, IL 60648: Free information ❖ Art and porcelain collectibles, Christmas ornaments, and pewter. 708-967-5253.

Green Gable Gifts, Box 2525, Winnipeg, Manitoba, Canada R3C 4A7: Free information ❖ Figurines, certified and authorized by descendants of Lucy Maud Montgomery. 800-667-4957.

Jan Hagara Collectors Club, 40114 Industrial Park North, Georgetown, TX 78626: Free information ❖ Jan Hagara porcelain dolls. 512-863-9499.

Hawthorne, 9210 N. Maryland Ave., Niles, IL 60714: Free catalog ❖ Collectible cottages and sculptures. 800-772-4277.

Intrigue Gift Shop, 112 E. Elkhorn Ave., P.O. Box 2147, Estes Park, CO 80517: Free information ❖ Statuary and figurines, plates, dolls, other porcelain collectibles, and gifts. 800-735-GIFT.

Just Animals, 15525 Fitzgerald, Livonia, MI 48154: Free brochure with long SASE ❖ Detailed and hand-painted pottery animal collectibles. 313-464-8493.

Lenox Collections, P.O. Box 3020, Langhorne, PA 19047: Free catalog ❖ Porcelain sculptures, china, and crystal. 800-225-1779.

The Limited Edition, 2170 Sunrise Hwy., Merrick, NY 11566: Free information ❖ Precious Moments porcelain dolls and statuary. 800-645-2864; 516-623-4400 (in NY).

The Limited of Michigan Ltd., 10861 Paw Paw Dr., Holland, MI 49424: Free price list ❖ Old, new, club, dated, rare, back-issue plates and bells, and hard-to-find collectibles. 800-355-6363.

Lladró Society, 43 W. 57th St., New York, NY 10019: Free list of retail sources ❖ Porcelain collectibles. 800-634-9088.

Martin's Herend Imports Inc., P.O. Box 1178, Sterling, VA 20167: Free list of retail sources ❖ Hand-painted porcelain decorative pieces and dinner service. 800-643-7363; 703-450-1601 (in VA).

Quality Collectables, 71 S. Mast St., Goffstown, NH 03045: Free information ❖ Limited edition figurines and statues, signed plates, lithographs, and sports art. 800-422-6514.

The Red Cardinal, 1121 Horsham Rd., Ambler, PA 19002: Free information ❖ Statuary and figurines, plates, dolls, porcelain collectibles, and gifts. 800-568-2524; 215-628-2524 (in PA).

Red Cross Gifts, 122 Walnut St., Spooner, WI 54801: Free information ❖ Collectible plates, Ashton-Drake dolls, and gifts, and collectibles. 800-344-9958.

Royal Copenhagen Porcelain, Madison Ave. at 61st St., New York, NY 10021: Free brochure ❖ Danish porcelain statuary, fine china, and crystal. 212-759-6457.

S.A.M. Inc., P.O. Box 77, Palo Alto, CA 94301: Free catalog ❖ Collectible memorabilia and limited edition sports figurines and bobbing heads. 415-369-0190.

Trendco Inc., 4723 W. Atlantic Ave., Delray Beach, FL 33445: Free catalog ❖ Figurines, plates, bobbing heads, and signed memorabilia. 800-881-0181.

Windy Meadows Pottery Ltd., 1036 Valley Rd., Knoxville, MD 21758: Free brochure ❖ Hand-built cottages with optional special treatments and personalization. 800-527-6274.

The Windsor Shoppe, 117 Washington Ave., North Haven, CT 06473: Free information ❖ Department 56 collectibles. 800-676-4644; 203-239-4644 (in CT).

Zaslow's Fine Collectibles, Strathmore Shopping Center, Rt. 34, Matawan, NJ 07747: Free information ❖ Plates, figurines, and gifts. 800-526-2355; 908-583-1499 (in NJ).

Zucker's Fine Gifts, 151 W. 26th St., New York, NY 10001: Free catalog ❖ Hummel, Swarovski silver and crystal, Waterford crystal, Lladro porcelain, and gifts. 212-989-1450.

POSTCARDS

Abbott's Postcards, 1393 S. Woodward Ave., Birmingham, MI 48009: Free information with long SASE (enclose want list) ❖ Postcards, coins, stamps, and collectibles. 810-644-8565.

Alpenglow Collectibles, P.O. Box 211, Brookeville, MD 20833: Free information with long SASE ❖ Postcards. 301-774-7637.

Atlantis Rising Antique, 545 Warren St., Hudson, NY 12534: Free information with long SASE ❖ Postcards. 518-822-0438.

J.C. Ballentine Postcards, P.O. Box 761, Waycross, GA 31502: Free information with long SASE ❖ Postcards. 912-283-2221.

Barbara's Papertiques, P.O. Box 317, Port Jervis, NY 12771: Free information with long SASE ❖ Postcards and paper collectibles. 914-856-8572.

Barry's Postcards, P.O. Box 1865, Anderson, IN 46013: Free information with long SASE ❖ Postcards. 317-643-6465.

Ellen Budd Postcards, 6910 Tenderfoot Ln., Cincinnati, OH 45249: Free information with long SASE ❖ Postcards. 513-489-0518.

❖ POSTCARDS ❖

The Cartophilians, 430 Highland Ave., Cheshire, CT 06410: Free information with long SASE ❖ Collectible postcards, trading cards, and paper memorabilia. 203-272-1143.

Agnes Cavalari, Old Windsor, 89 Bethlehem Rd., New Windsor, NY 12553: Free information with long SASE ❖ State views, glamour, topicals, foreign, greetings, and other postcards. 914-564-6775.

Mrs. Coby De Boer, 2 Aviles St., St. Augustine, FL 32084: Free information with long SASE ❖ Postcards.

The Dekle's, Tod & Aileen Dekle, 2640 Cannon Farm Rd., China Grove, NC 28023: Free information with long SASE ❖ Postcards. 704-932-8511.

S. Dobres Postcards, P.O. Box 1855, Baltimore, MD 21203: Price list $1.25 ❖ Postcards. 800-342-5983.

Glimpse of Time, Doug Walberg, P.O. Box 589, Bandon, OR 97411: Free information with long SASE ❖ Postcards.

Gordie's Used Cards, 1235 Vista Superba, Glendale, CA 91205: Free information with long SASE ❖ Automobile-related postcards. 818-246-6686.

Clay Griffin Postcards, 4169 Tomahawk Trace, Akron, OH 44321: Free information with long SASE ❖ Postcards. 216-665-4878.

John H. Henel, 79 Fruehauf Ave., Snyder, NY 14226: Free information with long SASE ❖ Postcards from worldwide locations. 716-839-4174.

Herzog Postcards, P.O. Box 545, Vauxhall, NJ 07088: Free information (enclose want list) with long SASE ❖ Most major topics, state views, and other postcards. 201-379-1700.

Hey Enterprises, 2100 Hwy. 35, Old Mill Plaza, Sea Girt, NJ 08750: Free catalog ❖ Postcards, rare books, and collectibles. 908-974-8855.

Hobby House Distributors, P.O. Box 18025, Indianapolis, IN 46218: Free information ❖ Archival protection sleeves. 800-544-6229; 317-547-1372 (in IN).

Frank E. Howard Postcards, 856 Charlotte St., Macon, GA 34236: Free information with long SASE ❖ Postcards. 912-788-1514.

JAM Graphics Group, Barry L. Schack, 4 Heron Ct., Voorhees, NJ 08043: Free information with long SASE ❖ Postcards. 609-424-0499.

Judnick Postcards, P.O. Box 12248, Columbus, OH 43212: Free information with long SASE and $1 ❖ Postcards. 614-278-9399.

Fred N. Kahn Postcards, 258 Stratford Rd., Asheville, NC 28804: Free information with long SASE ❖ Postcards. 704-252-6507.

Robert J. Karrer Postcards, P.O. Box 6094, Alexandria, VA 22306: Free information with long SASE ❖ Panama Canal and Canal Zone postcards. 703-360-5105.

Dick & Sue Lightle Postcards, 5850 Park Circle, Shawnee, KS 66216: Free information with long SASE ❖ Postcards. 913-962-7531.

Hal Lutsky Postcards, 298 4th Ave., Ste. 475, San Francisco, CA 94118: Free information with long SASE ❖ Postcards. 415-668-1636.

Malcom Postcards, P.O. Box 453, Monroe, GA 30655: Free information with long SASE ❖ Postcards. 404-267-6897.

William Mankins, P.O. Box 736, Meadows of Dan, VA 24120: Free information (send want list) ❖ Pin-up and military matchbook covers and postcards.

Mary Jayne's Railroad Specialties Inc., 1905 Dressler Dr., Covington, VA 24426: Free information with long SASE ❖ Postcards. 703-962-6698.

Mary Martin Postcards, 4899 Pulaski Hwy., Rt. 40, Perryville, MD 21903: Free brochure with long SASE ❖ New, old, and hard-to-find United States views, topicals, greetings, foreign cards, rarities, and other postcards. 410-575-7768.

MDI Inc., 2058 Wright Ave., La Verne, CA 91750: Free information ❖ Postcard protectors. 909-596-2389.

Memory Lane Postcards, P.O. Box 66, Keymar, MD 21757: Free information with long SASE ❖ Postcards and collecting supplies, magazines, comics, sheet music, sports cards, and old newspapers. 410-775-0188.

Merry's Collectibles, Box 281, Carleton, MI 48117: Free information with long SASE ❖ Collectible postcards.

The Morgan Company, 5301 Highbanks Rd., Mascoutah, IL 62258: Free price list ❖ Postcard archival supplies. 800-422-4510.

Alison & Richard Moulton, 138 Linden Ave., Victoria, British Columbia, Canada V8V 4E1: Free information (enclose want list) ❖ Postcards from worldwide locations. 604-381-6198.

National Postcard Exchange, 225 3rd St., P.O. Box 886, Macon, GA 31202: Free information with long SASE ❖ Foreign postcards, topicals, and postcards from the early 1900s to the present. 912-743-8951.

NuAce Company, 131 Main St., Reading, MA 01867: Free information ❖ Albums for postcards and first day covers.

Terry & Noreen Pavey Postcards, P.O. Box 10614, Glendale, AZ 85318: Free information with long SASE ❖ Postcards. 602-439-2156.

Postcard News & Sales, Diane Allmen, P.O. Box 248, Cohoctah, MI 48816: Free information with long SASE ❖ Postcards.

Postcards Etc., P.O. Box 4318, Thousand Oaks, CA 91359: Free information with long SASE ❖ Postcards. 805-497-1725.

Postcards from Paradise, P.O. Box 265, Goodlettsville, TN 37070: Free information with long SASE ❖ Postcards. 615-859-7499.

Postcards International, P.O. Box 5398, 2321 Whitney Ave., Ste. 102, Hamden, CT 06518: Free information ❖ Postcards. 203-248-6621.

Potlatch Traders, Kent & Sandy Renshaw, P.O. Box 1349, Freeland, WA 98249: Free information with long SASE ❖ Old topical and rare postcards and Victorian collectibles. 360-331-0729.

Michael G. Price Postcards, P.O. Box 1384, Jackson, MI 49204: Free information with long SASE ❖ Postcards. 517-764-4517.

Arlene L. Raskin Postcards, 2580 Ocean Pkwy., Apt. 2L, Brooklyn, NY 11235: Free information with long SASE ❖ Postcards. 718-998-1910.

Mike E. Rasmussen Postcards, P.O. Box 726, Marina, CA 93933: Free information with long SASE ❖ Postcards. 408-759-0259.

Remember These, P.O. Box 736, Meadows of Dan, VA 24120: Free information with long SASE ❖ Postcards and matchbook covers.

RNProducts, 39 Monmouth St., Red Bank, NJ 07701: Free catalog with long SASE ❖ Archival supplies for postcards. 908-741-0626.

Ruggiero's Postcards, 359 Silver Sands Rd., East Haven, CT 06512: Free information with long SASE (specify items wanted) ❖ Postcards and stamps. 203-469-7083.

The Salty Professor Antiques, Bob & Myra Siegel, 4-1/2 Milk St., Portland, ME 04101: Free information with long SASE ❖ Postcards. 207-772-4640.

Scene Again, P.O. Box 395, Vienna, VA 22183: Catalog $1 ❖ Postcards. 703-255-1467.

Shiloh Postcards, P.O. Box 728, Clayton, GA 30525: Catalog $1 ❖ Postcards, collecting supplies, and books. 706-782-4100.

Hobart E. Smith, 10813 Main St., Lot 10, Thonotosassa, FL 33592: Free information with long SASE ❖ Postcards. 813-986-4541.

Richard Spedding Postcards, 22 Tanglewood Rd., Sterling, MA 01564: Free information with long SASE ❖ Topicals, views, and other postcards. 508-422-8480.

Mrs. Esther K. Springston, 1610 Park Ave. West, Mansfield, OH 44906: Free information with long SASE ❖ Postcards. 419-529-3667.

Tippett Postcards Inc., Ste. E, 6625 Gateway Ave., Sarasota, FL 34231: Free information with long SASE ❖ Postcards. 813-925-3772.

Mary Twyce Antiques & Books, 601 E. 5th St., Winona, MN 55987: Free information with long SASE ❖ Postcards. 507-454-4412.

JoAnn Van Scotter Postcards, 208 E. Lincoln St., Mt. Morris, IL 61054: Free information with long SASE ❖ Postcards. 815-734-6971.

Michael B. Wasserberg Postcards, 1025 Country Club Dr., Margate, FL 33063: Free information with long SASE ❖ Postcards. 305-972-3789.

✓ **Writewell Company,** P.O. Box 68186, Indianapolis, IN 46268: Free catalog ❖ Loose-leaf postcard albums with leather-grained vinyl padded covers and optional personalization. 800-968-5850.

POTPOURRI

Angel's Earth, 1633 Scheffer Ave., St. Paul, MN 55116: Catalog $2 ❖ Essential and fragrance oils, potpourri supplies, and perfume-making kits. 612-698-3601.

Black Pearl Gardens, Herbal General Store, 220 Maple St., Franklin, OH 45005: Catalog $1 ❖ Herb plants, aromatherapy products, potpourri and supplies, culinary and medicinal herbs, herbal bath and body products, and dried florals. 800-891-0142.

The Candle Factory, 4411 South IH 35, Georgetown, TX 78626: Free catalog ❖ Wax potpourri chips, hand-dipped tapers, dinner and novelty candles, and machine-made and molded decorative pillars. 512-863-6025.

Caswell-Massey Company Ltd., Catalog Division, 100 Enterprise Pl., Dover, DE 19901: Catalog $1 ❖ Potpourri and pomander mixes, dried flowers, and herb plants. 800-326-0500.

✓ **The Essential Oil Company,** P.O. Box 206, Lake Oswego, OR 97034: Free catalog ❖ Essential oils, soap-making molds and supplies, incense materials, potpourri, and aromatherapy items. 800-729-5912.

✓ **The Florist Shop,** 703 Madison Ave., New York, NY 10021: Free catalog ❖ Hand-milled soaps, bath oils, body milk, talc, room fragrances, and potpourri. 800-J-FLORIS.

Gardens Past, P.O. Box 1846, Estes Park, CO 80517: Catalog $1 ❖ Soaps and soap making supplies, potpourri, dried flowers, herbs, candles, and aromatherapy items. 303-823-5565.

The Gathered Herb & Greenhouse, 12114 N. State Rd., Otisville, MI 48463: Catalog $2 ❖ Potpourri supplies, herbs and herb teas, perennials, and dried flowers. 810-631-6572.

Good Hollow Greenhouse & Herbarium, 50 Slaterock Mill Rd., Taft, TN 38488: Catalog $1 ❖ Herb plants and dried herbs, perennials, wildflowers, scented geraniums, essential oils and potpourris, teas, and spices. 615-433-7640.

Grandma's Spice Shop, HC 62, Box 65D, Upper Tract, WV 26866: Free catalog ❖ Essential oils and herbal potpourris. 304-358-2346.

Hartman's Herb Farm, 1026 Old Dana Rd., Barre, MA 01005: Catalog $2 ❖ Potpourris, sachets, bath herbs and oils, herbal pillows, dried flowers, spices, teas, essential oils, and pomander balls. 508-355-2015.

✓ **Herb & Spice Collection,** P.O. Box 299, Norway, IA 52318: Free catalog ❖ Potpourris, culinary herbs and spices, and natural herbal body care products. 800-786-1388.

✓ **The Herb Lady,** P.O. Box 2129, Shepherdstown, WV 25443: Free catalog ❖ Essential oils and potpourris. 800-537-1846.

Herbs-Liscious, 1702 S. 6th St., Marshalltown, IA 50158: Catalog $2 (refundable) ❖ Dried flowers, herbs and spices, oils and fragrances, and potpourri.

JoLar Enterprises, 58052 Ox Bow Dr., Elkhart, IN 46516: Brochure $3 ❖ Oak refillable potpourri holders. 219-875-8369.

Legacy Herbs, Sue Lukens Herbalist/Potter, Box 442, Mountain View, AR 72560: Catalog 50¢ ❖ Herbs, wildflowers, perennial plants, soaps, bath and body care products, oils and fragrance, incense, potpourri, herbal food products, and other scented items. 501-269-4051.

Meadow Everlastings, 16464 Shabbona Rd., Malta, IL 60150: Catalog $2 (refundable) ❖ Dried flowers, wreath kits, and potpourri supplies.

Meg's Garden, P.O. Box 161, Buffalo, NY 14205: Brochure $1 ❖ Potpourris and perfume oils. 716-883-7564.

Mountain Farms Inc., 307 Number 9 Rd., Fletcher, NC 28732: Free catalog ❖ Dried floral products and herbs for potpourri arrangements. 704-628-4709.

Nature's Finest, P.O. Box 10311, Burke, VA 22009: Catalog $2.50 (refundable) ❖ Dried flowers, herbs, spices, oils, fixatives, bottles, books, equipment, and potpourri supplies. 703-978-3925.

✓ **San Francisco Herb Company,** 250 14th St., San Francisco, CA 94103: Free catalog ❖ Potpourri supplies and spices and herbs for cooking. 800-227-4530; 800-622-0768 (in CA).

Teasel, 46 Main St., Middlebury, VT 05753: Free information ❖ Lingerie, fine soaps and toiletries, potpourri, and candles. 800-300-1204.

Tussie Mussies, 16001 Water Gap Rd., Williams, OR 97544: Free brochure ❖ Hand-blended potpourris, colognes, and lotions. 800-445-5563.

Tom Thumb Workshops, Rt. 13, P.O. Box 357, Mappsville, VA 23407: Catalog $1 ❖ Potpourris, herbs and spices, essential oils, dried flowers, and craft supplies. 804-824-3507.

Village Herb Shop Catalogue, 152 S. Main St., Chagrin Falls, OH 44022: Catalog and herbal handbook $4 ❖ Books, potpourri, soaps, cosmetics, oils, herbal food products, and other items.

Well-Sweep Herb Farm, 205 Mt. Bethel Rd., Port Murray, NJ 07865: Catalog $2 ❖ Potpourri and pomander mixes, dried flowers, and herb plants. 908-852-5390.

A World of Plenty, P.O. Box 1153, Hermantown, MN 55810: Catalog $1 ❖ Potpourri and sachet-making supplies. 218-729-6761.

PRINTING PRESSES

Acme/Star, 2221 N. Lister, Chicago, IL 60614: Catalog $2 (refundable) ❖ Letterpress supplies and rubber stamps.

Barco, Box 1011, Bensonville, IL 60106: Catalog $2 (refundable) ❖ Letterpress supplies and rubber stamps.

Dickerson Press Company, P.O. Box 8, South Haven, MI 49090: Free information ❖ Printing presses for etching, lithography, and intaglio stone and plate reproductions. 616-637-4251.

Graphic Chemical & Ink Company, P.O. Box 27, Villa Park, IL 60181: Free catalog ❖ Printing supplies. 708-832-6004.

Quaker City Type., RD 3, Box 134, Honeybrook, PA 19344: Catalog $2 (refundable) ❖ Type for printing presses and stamps.

Think Ink, 7526 Olympic View Dr., Edmonds, WA 98026: Catalog $2 ❖ Easy-to-use multiple color machine for printing greeting cards, stationery, ribbons, and T-shirts. 800-778-1935; 206-778-1935 (in WA).

Turnbaugh Printers Supply, 104 S. Sporting Hill Rd., Mechanicsburg, PA 17055: Catalog $1 ❖ Type fonts, printing presses, and supplies. 717-737-5637.

PROSPECTING & ROCKHOUNDING

A & B Prospectors' Supply, 3929 E. Main, Mesa, AZ 85206: Free information ❖ Prospecting and metal assay equipment. 602-832-4524.

PROSPECTING & ROCKHOUNDING

Alpha Supply, P.O. Box 2133, Bremerton, WA 98310: Catalog $3 ❖ Prospecting and rockhounding equipment, jewelry-making tools, gem finishing equipment, and metal detectors. 360-373-3302.

Arizona Al's Discount, 4238 W. Northern Ave., Phoenix, AZ 85051: Free information ❖ Metal detectors and prospecting equipment. 602-930-1755.

Arizona Gems & Crystals, 1705 W. 14th Dr., Safford, AZ 85546: Free catalog ❖ Gold mining and rockhounding equipment. 520-428-5164.

Armadillo Mining Shop, 2041 NW Vine, Grants Pass, OR 97526: Free information ❖ Metal detectors and mining supplies. 503-476-6316.

B & J Rock Shop, 14744 Manchester Rd., Ballwin, MO 63011: Catalog $3 ❖ Rockhounding equipment, quartz crystals, amethyst crystal clusters, Brazilian agate nodules, and imported and domestic stones. 314-394-4567.

Bourget Bros., 1636 11th St., Santa Monica, CA 90404: Catalog $3 ❖ Gemstones and cabochons, wax patterns, beads and bead-stringing supplies, lapidary equipment, and rockhounding, treasure hunting, and prospecting equipment. 310-450-6556.

Cal-Gold, 2569 E. Colorado Blvd., Pasadena, CA 91107: Free catalog ❖ Metal detectors, mining and geology equipment, maps, books, and ultraviolet lighting accessories. 818-792-6161.

Century Products, 3502 C St. NE, Auburn, WA 98002: Free information ❖ Easy-to-operate automatic gold recovery equipment. 800-458-8889; 206-804-6880 (in WA).

Colorado Gold Resources, 7811 W. Mississippi Ave., Lakewood, CO 80226: Free catalog ❖ Metal detecting and prospecting equipment. 800-980-8463; 303-980-8430 (in CO).

Covington Engineering Corporation, P.O. Box 35, Redlands, CA 92373: Free catalog ❖ Gold mining and rockhounding equipment. 909-793-6636.

D.J.M. Corporation, P.O. Box 8614, Missoula, MT 59807: Free information ❖ Used mining equipment. 406-825-3120.

D & K Detector Sales, 13809 Southeast Division, Portland, OR 97236: Catalog $2 ❖ Prospecting equipment and metal detectors. 800-542-GOLD; 503-761-1521 (in OR).

The Detector Warehouse, P.O. Box 6055, Buffalo Grove, IL 60089: Free information ❖ Metal detectors, books, maps, digging tools, and other equipment. 800-828-1455.

East Coast Prospecting & Mining Supplies, Rt. 3, Box 321J, Ellijay, GA 30540: Catalog $3 ❖ Mining and prospecting equipment and supplies. 706-276-4433.

Ebersole Lapidary Supply Inc., 11417 West Hwy. 54, Wichita, KS 67209: Catalog $2 ❖ Rockhounding equipment, lapidary and jewelry-making tools, findings, mountings, cabochons, and gemstones and rocks. 316-722-4771.

Eloxite Corporation, Dept. 51, P.O. Box 729, Wheatland, WY 82201: Catalog $1 ❖ Clock-making supplies, gemstones, beads, cabochons, jewelry mountings, and equipment for rockhounding and jewelry do-it-yourself crafters. 307-322-3050.

Estwing Manufacturing Company, 2647 8th St., Rockford, IL 61109: Free information ❖ Equipment for geologists and rockhounds. 815-397-8665.

Falcon Prospecting Equipment, 6529 E. Fairbrook St., Mesa, AZ 85205: Free information ❖ Placer gold probe for prospecting. 602-854-0324.

Fisher Research Laboratory, 200 W. Wilmott Rd., Los Banos, CA 93635: Free information ❖ Metal detectors. 209-826-3292.

49'er Metal Detectors, 14093 Irishtown Rd., Pine Grove, CA 95665: Free information ❖ Prospecting supplies, tools, books, and videos. 800-538-7501; 209-296-3544 (in CA).

Fortyniner Mining Supply, 16238 Lakewood Blvd., Bellflower, CA 90706: Free information ❖ Mining and treasure hunting equipment, metal detectors, magazines, and books. 310-925-2271.

Gold Mine Engineering, 2640 Corey Pl., San Ramon, CA 94583: Free information with long SASE ❖ Gold recovery separator. 510-828-2667.

The Golddigger, 253 N. Main, Moab, UT 84532: Free information ❖ Prospecting supplies and equipment. 801-259-5150.

Graves Company, 1800 Andrews Ave., Pompano Beach, FL 33069: Free catalog ❖ Rockhounding and ultraviolet lighting equipment. 800-327-9103.

Hays Electronics, P.O. Box 26848, Prescott Valley, AZ 86312: Free catalog ❖ Metal detectors, electronic prospecting tools and accessories, and books. 800-699-2624.

Herkimer Diamond Mines, P.O. Box 510, Herkimer, NY 13350: Free information ❖ Petrified wood products, rockhounding equipment, minerals and rocks, and quartz crystals. 315-891-7355.

House of Treasure Hunters, 5714 El Cajon Blvd., San Diego, CA 92115: Free information ❖ Gold prospecting equipment and metal detectors. 619-286-2600.

International Resource Development, 5001 Convair Dr., Carson City, NV 89706: Free information ❖ New and used mining equipment. 702-882-5025.

Jeanne's Rock & Jewelry, 5420 Bissonet, Bellaire, TX 77401: Price list $1 ❖ Rockhounding equipment, shells, petrified wood products, beads, and bead-stringing supplies. 713-664-2988.

Kansas/Texas Detector Sales, P.O. Box 17015, Fort Worth, TX 76102: Free information ❖ Metal detectors and prospecting equipment. 800-876-3463; 817-498-2228 (in TX).

Kingsley North Inc., P.O. Box 216, Norway, MI 49870: Free catalog ❖ Rockhounding and metal-casting equipment, jewelry-making tools, tumblers, and opals. 800-338-9280.

Lentz Lapidary Inc., 11760 S. Oliver, Rt. 2, Box 134, Mulvane, KS 67110: Catalog $2 ❖ Jewelry, mountings, clocks and motors, rough rock specimens, cabochons, and rockhounding and lapidary equipment. 316-777-1372.

Miners Inc., P.O. Box 1301, Riggins, ID 83549: Free catalog ❖ Sample bags, instruments, hand tools, leather cases, and books for geologists and prospectors. 800-824-7452; 208-628-3247 (in ID).

Pedersen's Metal Detectors, 2521-A N. Grand Ave.: Free information ❖ Walk-through and hand-held detectors and gold and treasure finding supplies. 800-953-3832.

Pioneer Mining Supplies, 943 Lincoln Way., Auburn, CA 95603: Free information ❖ Mining equipment and metal detectors. 916-885-1801.

Placer Equipment Mfg. Inc., 427 1st St., Buckeye, AZ 85326: Catalog $3 (refundable) ❖ Dredges, dry washers, sluice boxes, gold pans, equipment, and beginners' prospecting kits. 602-386-7006.

Pot of Gold, 2616 Griffin Rd., Fort Lauderdale, FL 33312: Free catalog ❖ Metal detectors, books, and prospecting equipment. 954-987-2888.

Pro-Mack Mining Supplies, P.O. Box 47, Happy Camp, CA 96039: Free information ❖ Mining and treasure hunting equipment. 800-722-6463.

Pro-Mack South, 940 W. Apache Trail, Apache Junction, AZ 85220: Catalog $3 ❖ Prospecting supplies and tools. 800-722-6463.

Pyramid Industries, 24307 Magic Mountain Pkwy., Santa Clarita, CA 91355: Free information ❖ Prospecting and assay equipment. 805-255-5323.

Roberts Construction, P.O. Box 545, Kenwood, CA 95452: Free brochure with long SASE ❖ Back-packable gold-detection and mining equipment. 707-538-9541.

Jimmy Sierra Products, 3096 Kerner Blvd., Ste. H, San Rafael, CA 94901: Free information ❖ Treasure hunting and prospecting accessories. 415-456-0891.

Tru-Square Metal Products, P.O. Box 585, Auburn, WA 98071: Free brochure ❖ Tumblers and rock polishing equipment. 800-225-1017.

Watts & Franklin Placer Mining Equipment Inc., 1504 SE Harris, Richland, WA 99352: Free information ❖ Easy-to-operate gold recovery separator with pump and motor combination options. 509-627-0673.

PUPPETS & MARIONETTES

Audubon Naturalist, 8940 Jones Mill Rd., Silver Spring, MD 20815: Free information with long SASE ❖ Birdhouses, feeders, baths, handcrafted jewelry, binoculars, puppets, and gifts. 800-699-BIRD; 301-652-3606 (in MD).

Aunt Clowney's Warehouse, P.O. Box 1444, Corona, CA 91718: Free catalog with two 1st class stamps ❖ Books and novelties for puppeteers, clowns, magicians, face painters, and balloon artists.

Axtell Expressions Inc., 230 Glencrest Circle, Ventura, CA 93003: Catalog $2 ❖ Puppets for professionals. 805-642-7282.

Cherri-Oats & Company, Cheri Venturi, P.O. Box 723, North Olmsted, OH 44070: Free information ❖ Wigs and accessories, stickers, puppets, and face painting supplies. 216-979-9971.

Clown Heaven, 4792 Old State Rd. 37 South, Martinsville, IN 46152: Catalog $3 ❖ Balloons, make-up, puppets, wigs, ministry and gospel items, novelties, magic, clown props, and books. 317-342-6888.

Farm Family Puppets, P.O. Box 603, Wellington, CO 80549: Brochure $2 ❖ Puppets.

Freckles Clown Supplies, 5509 Roosevelt Blvd., Jacksonville, FL 32244: Catalog $6 ❖ Puppets, make-up, clown supplies, costumes, how-to books on clowning and ballooning, and theatrical supplies. 904-388-5541.

Maher Studios, P.O. Box 420, Littleton, CO 80160: Catalog $2 ❖ Ventriloquist dummies, scripts and dialogues, puppets, and how-to books. 303-798-6830.

Mastercraft Puppets, P.O. Box 39, Branson, MO 65615: Catalog $2 ❖ Puppets and ventriloquist dummies. 417-561-8100.

Mecca Magic Inc., 49 Dodd St., Bloomfield, NJ 07003: Catalog $10 ❖ Puppets, juggling supplies, theatrical make-up, clown equipment, balloons, and magic tricks. 201-429-7597.

Steven Meltzer, 670 San Juan, Venice, CA 90291: Free list with long SASE ❖ Marionettes, puppets, and ventriloquist figures. 310-396-6007.

Pelham Marionettes, Doris & Jerry Barrows, 5128 Ridge Rd., Lockport, NY 14094: Free list with long SASE ❖ Marionettes, from the 1960s to 1970s. 716-433-4329.

Sonrise Soft Crafts, P.O. Box 5091, Salem, OR 97304: Brochure 50¢ ❖ Patterns and kits for lifelike stuffed animals, puppets, shirt appliques, and wall hangings. 503-362-0027.

Sparkle's Entertainment Express, Jan Lovell, 152 N. Water St., Gallatin, TN 37066: Product list $1 ❖ Make-up, costumes and clown shoes, balloons, juggling and magic equipment, puppets, books, and other supplies. 615-452-9755.

PURSES & WALLETS

Ace Leather Products, 2211 Avenue U, Brooklyn, NY 11229: Free catalog ❖ Desk sets, leather attache cases, luggage, wallets, handbags, and gifts. 800-342-5223.

American Executive, Kittery Business Center, 72 Dow Hwy., Kittery, ME 03904: Catalog $2 ❖ Writing portfolios, travel cases and packs, day planners, wallets, briefcases and backpacks, and other leather essentials. 800-804-0825.

Bally of Switzerland for Ladies, 689 Madison Ave., New York, NY 10021: Free information ❖ Women's shoes, clothing, luggage, and small leather goods. 212-751-2163.

Bally of Switzerland for Men, 711 5th Ave., New York, NY 10022: Free information ❖ Men's shoes, clothing, luggage, and small leather goods. 212-751-9082.

Bottega Veneta, 635 Madison Ave., New York, NY 10022: Free catalog ❖ Wallets, purses and handbags, luggage, and other small leather goods. 212-371-5511.

Burberry's Limited, 9 E. 57th St., New York, NY 10022: Free list of retail sources ❖ Clothing, handbags, luggage, silk scarves and shawls, belts, hats, shoes, tennis accessories, sports bags, and toiletries. 212-371-5010.

Coach Leatherware Company, 410 Commerce Blvd., Carlstadt, NJ 07072: Free catalog ❖ Leather handbags, gloves, belts, wallets, briefcases, and accessories. 201-460-4716.

Copper Star Cattle & Trading Company, 2000 W. 3rd St., Amarillo, TX 79106: Catalog $2 ❖ Cowhide purses, wallets, satchels and bags, and accessories. 800-828-0442.

Creative House, 100 Business Pkwy., Richardson, TX 75081: Free catalog ❖ Luggage, briefcases and attache cases, handbags, wallets, and accessories. 800-527-5940; 214-231-3463 (in TX).

Lucy De Fave, Mason Woods Village Mall, 13476 Clayton Rd., St. Louis, MO 63131: Catalog $3 ❖ Quilted handbags, luggage, clothing, and accessories. 314-576-4717.

Deerskin Place, 283 Akron Rd., Ephrata, PA 17522: Catalog $1 ❖ Cowhide, sheepskin, and deerskin clothing and accessories. 717-733-7624.

Double L Leatherworks, P.O. Box 1271, Taylor, TX 76574: Catalog $1 ❖ Hand-tooled leather purses, tote bags, wallets, and items with a western style. 512-352-6640.

Georgetown Leather Design/Tannery West, 400 S. Hwy. 169, Ste. 600, Minneapolis, MN 55426: Free list of retail sources ❖ Outerwear for men and women, purses, brief cases, and accessories.

Mid Western Sport Togs, 227 N. Washington, Berlin, WI 54923: Free catalog ❖ Deerskin gloves, jackets and coats for men and women, footwear, handbags, and accessories. 414-361-5050.

Naples Creek Leather, 188 S. Main St., Naples, NY 14512: Free catalog ❖ Leather moccasins, slippers, belts, gloves, casual footwear, and deerskin handbags. 800-836-0616.

National Luggage Dealers Association, 245 5th Ave., New York, NY 10018: Free catalog ❖ Small leather goods and handbags. 212-684-1610.

Ravenworks Studio, P.O. Box 6, Mount Victory, OH 43340: Free brochure ❖ Handcrafted deerskin bags and accessories. 513-354-5151.

PUZZLES

Bits & Pieces, Stevens Point, WI 54481-7199: Free catalog ❖ Jigsaw puzzles, books, games, and gifts for adults and children. 800-884-2637.

CalAutoArt, 1520 S. Lyon St., Santa Ana, CA 92705: Free catalog ❖ Automotive-theme jigsaw puzzles. 714-835-9512.

Kadon Enterprises Inc., 1227 Lorene Dr., Ste. 16, Pasadena, MD 21122: Free brochure ❖ Puzzles, challenging and historical games, and abstract strategies. 410-437-2163.

Lucretia's Pieces, RFD 1, Box 501, Windsor, VT 05089: Free information ❖ Challenging puzzles designed with special shapes and unexpected surprises. 802-436-3006.

Mindware, 6142 Olson Memorial Hwy., Golden Valley, MN 55422: Free catalog ❖ Challenging puzzles and games. 800-999-0398.

The Old Game Store, Rt. 11/30, Manchester, VT 05254: Free information with long SASE ❖ Games, puzzles, collectible teddy bears, and toys. 802-362-2756.

Out of the Woodwork, 437 Robert E. Lee Dr., Wilmington, NC 28412: Free brochure ❖ Educational puzzles for children. 910-792-6882.

Puzzling, 8227 Hunter's Tr., Roanoke, VA 24019: Free information ❖ Wood puzzles for children. 540-563-8922.

Rainy Lake Puzzles, 4255 Garfield Ave. South, Minneapolis, MN 55409: Free catalog ❖ Intricately hand-cut wooden jigsaw puzzles. 612-827-5757.

❖ QUILTS & QUILTING ❖

Stave Puzzles, Box 329, Norwich, VT 05055: Free catalog ❖ Hand-cut jigsaw puzzles. 802-295-5200.

Toys from Times Past, 4299 E. Shearer Rd., Rhodes, MI 48652: Free brochure ❖ Action and skill toys, other toys, tricks, and puzzles. 517-689-4663.

White Mountain Puzzles, Jackson Falls Marketplace, P.O. Box 818, Jackson, NH 03846: Free catalog ❖ Fun and educational puzzles. 603-383-4346.

QUILTS & QUILTING

AK Sew & Serge, 1602 6th St. SE, Winter Haven, FL 33880: Catalog $5 ❖ Supplies for heirloom, fashion sewing, and quilting. 800-299-8096; 813-299-3080 (in FL).

Choices, 1000 Lake St., Oak Park, IL 60301: Brochure $2 ❖ Hand quilted 100 percent cotton yarn quilts with bonded cotton batting. Also quilted tote bags and pillow shams. 708-386-6555.

CMH Quiltworks, 809 Adams Ct., Monticello, IL 61856: Free information with long SASE ❖ Quilting fabrics.

The Cotton Patch, 1025 Brown Ave., Lafayette, CA 94549: Catalog $8 ($5 refundable) ❖ Fabrics, quilting books, and supplies. 510-284-1177.

The Cotton Shoppe of Key Largo, P.O. Box 3168, Key Largo, FL 33037: Sample swatches $7 ❖ Quilting fabrics. 305-453-0789.

The Creative Needle, 6905 S. Broadway, Ste. 113, Littleton, CO 80122: Catalog $1 ❖ Heirloom sewing, smocking, stitchery, and quilting supplies. 303-794-7312.

Gammill Quilting Machine Company, 1452 W. Gibson St., West Plains, MO 65775: Free information ❖ Quilting machines. 800-748-8105; 417-256-5919 (in MO).

Ginger's Needleworks, P.O. Box 92047, Lafayette, LA 70509: Catalog $2 ❖ Quilting fabrics. 318-232-7847.

Hancock Fabrics, 3841 Hinkleville Rd., Paducah, KY 42001: Free information ❖ Quilting supplies, fabrics, and sewing notions. 800-845-8723.

Hinterberg Design Inc., 2805 E. Progress Dr., West Bend, WI 53095: Free information ❖ Quilting frame with adjustable height and tilt, ratchet wheel tensioning, and optional extension or shorter poles. 800-443-5800.

House of White Birches, 306 E. Parr Rd., Berne, IN 46711: Free catalog ❖ Quilt patterns, kits, and supplies. 800-347-9887.

Keepsake Quilting, Rt. 25B, P.O. Box 1618, Centre Harbor, NH 03226: Free catalog ❖ Quilting books and accessories, patterns, notions, fabrics, scrap bags, and batting. 800-865-9458.

Kimi's Fabrications, 502 Balsam Rd., Hazelwood, NC 28738: Catalog $5 ❖ Quilting supplies. 704-452-3455.

Missouri Breaks Industries, Quilt Brochure, HCR 64, Box 52, Timber Lake, SD 57656: Free brochure ❖ Original Sioux Native American star quilt patterns. 605-865-3418.

Claire Murray Inc., P.O. Box 390, Ascutney, VT 05030: Catalog $5 (refundable) ❖ Quilts, hand-painted ceramics, and hand-hooked rugs. 800-252-4733.

Noltings, Rt. 3, Box 147, Hwy. 52 East, Stover, MO 65078: Free information ❖ Quilting and sewing machines. 573-377-2713.

Nustyle Quilting Frame Company, Box 61-294, Stover, MO 65078: Free information with 1st class stamp ❖ Supplies and long-arm machine for outline quilting. 800-648-2240; 314-377-2244 (in MO).

Omnigrid Inc., 1560 Port Dr., Burlington, WA 98233: Free brochure ❖ Rulers, rotary cutting mats, and accessories. 360-757-4743.

Pleasant Mountain Woodworks, P.O. Box 2294, Mt. Pleasant, TX 75456: Free information ❖ Adjustable quilting frames. 903-572-4109.

Salt Box Plaids, 23030 St. Rd. 37, Grabill, IN 46741: Brochure $3.75 ❖ Miniature quilt kits, patterns, and books. 800-44-PLAID.

Speed Stitch, 3113 Broadpoint Dr., Harbor Heights, FL 33983: Free catalog ❖ Machine arts and quilting supplies. 800-874-4115.

The Stencil Company, P.O. Box 1218, Williamsville, NY 14221: Catalog $1 ❖ Quilting designs.

Terran Fabrics, P.O. Box 11122, College Station, TX 77845: Brochure $3 with long SASE ❖ Tools, supplies, and imported cotton fabrics for sewing and quilting.

That Patchwork Place Inc., P.O. Box 118, Bothell, WA 95041: Free information ❖ Quilting books and supplies. 800-426-3126.

RACQUETBALL & SQUASH

Clothing

Alchester Mills Company Inc., 1160 Wright Ave., Camden, NJ 08103: Free information ❖ Gloves, socks, sweatbands, and eye guards. 609-964-9700.

Athletes Wear Company, 145 Market Ave., Winnipeg, Manitoba, Canada R3B 1C5: Free catalog ❖ Clothing for baseball players. 204-949-1885.

Dorson Sports Inc., 1 Roebling Ct., Ronkonkoma, NY 51779: Free information ❖ Gloves. 800-645-7215; 516-585-5440 (in NY).

Ektelon, Prince Sports Group, 1 Sportsystem Plaza, Bordentown, NJ 08505: Free information ❖ Clothing and gloves, socks, sweatbands, bags and balls, racquets, and eye guards. 800-283-2635.

Franklin Sports Industries Inc., 17 Campanelli Parkway, P.O. Box 508, Stoughton, MA 02072: Free information ❖ Gloves. 800-426-7700.

Head Sports, 4801 N. 63rd St., Boulder, CO 80301: Free information ❖ Gloves, shoes, sweatbands, bags, balls, and racquets. 800-874-3234; 303-530-2000 (in CO).

Holabird Sports Discounters, 9220 Pulaski Hwy., Baltimore, MD 21220: Free catalog ❖ Clothing and equipment. 410-687-6400.

Hunt-Wilde, 2835 Overpass Rd., Tampa, FL 33619: Free information ❖ Gloves. 800-248-1232.

Olympia Sports, 745 State Circle, Ann Arbor, MI 48106: Free information ❖ Gloves. 800-521-2832.

Pony USA Inc., 2801 Red Dot Ln., Knoxville, TN 37914: Free information ❖ Shoes, socks, and sweatbands.

Puma USA Inc., 147 Centre St., Brockton, MA 02403: Free information with long SASE ❖ Clothing, shoes, socks, and balls. 508-583-9100.

Reebok International Ltd., 100 Technology Center Dr., Stoughton, MA 02072: Free list of retail sources ❖ Clothing, shoes, and socks. 800-843-4444.

Spalding Sports Worldwide, 425 Meadow St., P.O. Box 901, Chicopee, MA 01021: Free list of retail sources ❖ Clothing, gloves, shoes, socks, sweatbands, bags, balls, and racquets. 800-225-6601.

Wa-Mac Inc., Highskore Products Inc., P.O. Box 128, Carlstadt, NJ 07410: Free information ❖ Gloves, socks, sweatbands, balls, bags, eye guards, and racquets. 800-447-5673; 201-438-7200 (in NJ).

Equipment

Alchester Mills Company Inc., 1160 Wright Ave., Camden, NJ 08103: Free information ❖ Eye guards, gloves, socks, sweatbands, and grips. 609-964-9700.

Allsop, P.O. Box 23, Bellingham, WA 98227: Free information ❖ Racquetball equipment. 800-426-4303; 206-734-9090 (in WA).

Austad's, 4500 E. 10th St., P.O. Box 5428, Sioux Falls, SD 57196: Free catalog ❖ Racquetball and other sports equipment. 800-444-1234.

Brine Inc., 47 Sumner St., Milford, MA 01757: Free information ❖ Bags, balls, and grips. 800-227-2722; 508-478-3250 (in MA).

H.D. Brown Enterprise Ltd., 23 Beverly St. East, St. George, Ontario, Canada N0E 1N0: Free information ❖ Gloves, racquets, and other equipment. 519-448-1381.

Cannon Sports, P.O. Box 797, Greenland, NH 03840: Free list of retail sources ❖ Balls, racquets, and eye guards. 800-362-3146.

Century Sports Inc., Lakewood Industrial Park, 1995 Rutgers University Blvd., Box 2035, Lakewood, NJ 08701: Free information ❖ Gloves, racquets, and other equipment. 800-526-7548; 908-905-4422 (in NJ).

Ektelon, Prince Sports Group, 1 Sportsystem Plaza, Bordentown, NJ 08505: Free information ❖ Bags and balls, racquets, eye guards, thongs, clothing and gloves, socks, and sweatbands. 800-283-2635.

Faber Brothers, 4141 S. Pulaski Rd., Chicago, IL 60632: Free information ❖ Balls, bags, and racquets. 312-376-9300.

Grid Inc., NDL Products Inc., 4031 NE 12th Terrace, Oakland Park, FL 33334: Free information ❖ Racquetball equipment. 800-843-3021.

Head Sports, 4801 N. 63rd St., Boulder, CO 80301: Free information ❖ Bags and balls, racquets, gloves, shoes, and sweatbands. 800-874-3234; 303-530-2000 (in CO).

Holabird Sports Discounters, 9220 Pulaski Hwy., Baltimore, MD 21220: Free catalog ❖ Equipment and clothing for basketball, tennis, running, and jogging, golf, exercising, racquetball, and other sports. 410-687-6400.

M.W. Kasch Company, 5401 W. Donges Bay Rd., Mequon, WI 53092: Free information ❖ Bags, balls, and racquets. 414-242-5000.

Las Vegas Discount Golf & Tennis, 5325 S. Valley View Blvd., Ste. 10, Las Vegas, NV 89118: Free catalog ❖ Equipment, shoes, and clothing for tennis, racquetball, golf, running, and jogging. 702-798-7777.

Leisure Marketing Inc., 2204 Morris Ave., Ste. 202, Union, NJ 07083: Free information ❖ Bags and racquets. 908-851-9494.

Markwort Sporting Goods, 4300 Forest Park Ave., St. Louis, MO 63108: Catalog $8 (request list of retail sources) ❖ Gloves, racquets, and other equipment. 800-669-6626; 314-652-3757 (in MO).

Penn Racquet Sports, 306 S. 45th Ave., Phoenix, AZ 85043: Free information ❖ Gloves, racquets, and other equipment. 800-289-7366; 602-269-1492 (in AZ).

Prince Racquet Sports, 1 Sport Systems Plaza, Bordentown, NJ 08505: Free information ❖ Gloves, racquets, and other equipment. 800-2-TENNIS; 609-291-5900 (in NJ).

Professional Golf & Tennis Suppliers, 7825 Hollywood Blvd., Pembroke Pines, FL 33024: Free catalog with long SASE ❖ Racquetball equipment. 305-981-7283.

Puma USA Inc., 147 Centre St., Brockton, MA 02403: Free information with long SASE ❖ Balls and bags. 508-583-9100.

Spalding Sports Worldwide, 425 Meadow St., P.O. Box 901, Chicopee, MA 01021: Free list of retail sources ❖ Bags, balls, and racquets. 800-225-6601.

Sportime, Customer Service, 1 Sportime Way, Atlanta, GA 30340: Free information ❖ Racquets and other equipment. 800-444-5700; 770-449-5700 (in GA).

Wa-Mac Inc., Highskore Products Inc., P.O. Box 128, Carlstadt, NJ 07410: Free information ❖ Balls, bags, eye guards, and racquets. 800-447-5673; 201-438-7200 (in NJ).

Wilson Sporting Goods, 8700 W. Bryn Mawr, Chicago, IL 60631: Free information ❖ Bags, balls, and racquets. 800-443-0011.

RADIATOR ENCLOSURES & REGISTERS

All American Wood Register Company, 239 E. Main St., Cary, IL 60013: Free brochure with long SASE ❖ Solid oak registers with adjustable dampers. 708-639-0393.

Arsco Manufacturing Company Inc., 3564 Blue Rock Rd., Cincinnati, OH 45247: Free information ❖ Steel radiator enclosures. 800-543-7040; 513-385-0555 (in OH).

Barker Metalcraft, 1701 W. Belmont, Chicago, IL 60657: Free catalog ❖ Drop-in and flat grills, grills with borders, convector grills, and other radiator covers and registers. 800-397-0129.

Grate Vents, 9502 Linder Ave., Crystal Lake, IL 60014: Catalog $2 ❖ Unfinished and finished wood floor and baseboard grates. 815-459-4306.

Hinges & Handles, 100 Lincolnway East, Osceola, IN 46561: Free catalog ❖ Solid brass registers. 800-533-4782.

Monarch Radiator Enclosures, 2744 Arkansas Dr., Brooklyn, NY 11234: Brochure $1 (refundable) ❖ Easy-to-assemble all-steel radiator enclosures. 201-796-4117.

Walter Norman & Company, P.O. Box 148037, Chicago, IL 60614: Free information ❖ Ready-to-assemble Prairie and Shaker-style radiator cabinets. 312-281-1088.

The Reggio Register, P.O. Box 511, Ayer, MA 01432: Catalog $1 ❖ Solid brass and cast-iron registers and grills. 508-772-3493.

A Touch of Brass, 9052 Chevrolet Dr., Ellicott City, MD 21042: Catalog $3 ❖ Polished, stamped, and cast-brass registers. 410-461-8585.

RADIOS

Amateur Radio Equipment

A.S.A./Antenna Sales & Accessories, P.O. Box 3461, Myrtle Beach, SC 29578: Free information ❖ Antennas. 800-722-2681; 803-293-7888 (in SC).

Ack Radio Supply Company, 3101 4th Ave., South Birmingham, AL 35233: Free information ❖ Amateur radio equipment. 800-338-4218; 205-322-0588 (in AL).

Advanced Specialties, 114 Essex St., Lodi, NJ 07644: Free information ❖ Amateur radio equipment, books, and accessories. 201-VHF-2067.

Alpha Delta Communications Inc., P.O. Box 620, Manchester, KY 40962: Free information ❖ Antennas. 606-598-2029.

Aluma Tower Company, P.O. Box 2806, Vero Beach, FL 32961: Free catalog ❖ Telescoping crank-up, guyed stack-up, tilt-over, roof-top, and mobile antenna towers. 407-567-3423.

Amateur & Advanced Communications, 3208 Concord Pike, Rt. 202, Wilmington, DE 19803: Free information with long SASE ❖ Amateur radio equipment. 302-478-2757.

Amateur Communications Etc., 263 Mink, San Antonio, TX 78213: Free information ❖ Amateur radio equipment. 210-733-0334.

Amateur Electronic Supply, 5710 W. Good Hope Rd., Milwaukee, WI 53223: Free information ❖ Amateur radio equipment. 800-558-0411; 414-358-0333 (in WI).

American Antenna Corporation, 1500 Executive Dr., Elgin, IL 60123: Free information ❖ HF and VHF mobile antennas. 800-323-6768; 708-888-7200 (in IL).

American Radio Relay League, 225 Main St., Newington, CT 06111: Free information ❖ Books on how to become a HAM radio operator, get a license, learn Morse code, organize equipment, set up a station, and other information. 800-326-3942.

Antenna Supermarket, P.O. Box 563, Palatine, IL 60078: Free information ❖ Antennas and accessories. 708-359-7092.

Arnold Company, P.O. Box 512, Commerce, TX 75428: Free information ❖ Amateur radio equipment. 903-395-2922.

Astron Corporation, 9 Autry, Irvine, CA 92718: Free information ❖ Power supplies. 714-458-7277.

Austin Amateur Radio Supply, 5325 North I-35, Austin, TX 78723: Free information ❖ Amateur radio equipment. 800-423-2604; 512-454-2994 (in TX).

Barker & Williamson, 10 Canal St., Bristol, PA 19007: Free information ❖ Easy-to-install portable antennas. 215-788-5581.

❖ RADIOS ❖

Barry Electronics Corporation, 540 Broadway, New York, NY 10012: Free information ❖ Amateur, professional, and commercial electronics equipment. 212-925-7000.

Base Station Inc., 1839 East St., Concord, CA 94520: Free information ❖ Amateur radio equipment. 510-685-7388.

Bilal Company, 137 Manchester Dr., Florissant, CO 80816: Free catalog ❖ Antennas. 719-687-0650.

Burghardt Amateur Center, 182 N. Maple, P.O. Box 73, Watertown, SD 57201: Free information ❖ Amateur radio equipment. 800-927-4261; 605-886-7314 (in SD).

Burk Electronics, 35 N. Kensington, LaGrange, IL 60525: Free information ❖ Amateur radio equipment. 708-482-9310.

Butternut Electronics, P.O. Box 1234, Olmito, TX 78575: Free catalog ❖ Vertical and compact two-element beam butterfly antennas. 210-350-5711.

Byers Chassis Kits, 5120 Harmony Grove Rd., Dover, PA 17315: Free catalog ❖ Chassis and cabinets, rack shelves, other equipment enclosures, and sheet aluminum and brass. 717-292-4901.

Wayne Carroll, W4MPY, 682 Mt. Pleasant Rd., Monetta, SC 29105: Free information ❖ QSL cards. 803-685-7117.

Comm-Pute Inc., 7946 S. State St., Midvale, UT 84047: Free information ❖ Amateur radio equipment. 800-942-8873; 801-567-9944 (in UT).

Communication Headquarters Inc., 3830 Oleander Dr., Wilmington, NC 28403: Free information ❖ Equipment and accessories. 800-688-0073.

Communications Data Corporation, 1051 Main St., St. Joseph, MI 49085: Free information ❖ Amateur radio and computer equipment. 800-382-2562; 616-982-0404 (in MI).

Communications Electronics Inc., P.O. Box 1045, Ann Arbor, MI 48106: Free information ❖ Equipment for shortwave, amateur, and scanner enthusiasts. 313-996-8888.

Connect Systems Inc., 2259 Portola Rd., Ventura, CA 93003: Free brochure ❖ Automatic phone patch equipment for base station radios. 800-545-1349; 805-642-7184 (in CA).

Copper Electronics Inc., 3315 Gilmore Industrial Blvd., Louisville, KY 40213: Free information ❖ Amateur radio equipment. 502-968-8500.

C. Crane Company, 558 10th St., Fortuna, CA 95540: Free catalog ❖ Short and long wave radio equipment, scanners, books, weather equipment, and other accessories. 800-522-8863.

Crystek Corporation, 2371 Crystal Dr., Fort Myers, FL 33907: Free information ❖ Crystals for radio operation and electronics experimenters. 813-936-2109.

Cushcraft, P.O. Box 4680, 48 Perimeter Rd., Manchester, NH 03108: Free list of retail sources ❖ Antennas. 603-627-7877.

Dentronics, 6102 Deland Rd., Flushing, MI 48433: Free information ❖ Amateur radio equipment. 810-659-1776.

Down East Microwave, 954 Rt. 519, Frenchtown, NJ 08825: Free catalog ❖ Microwave antennas and other equipment. 908-996-3584.

R.L. Drake Company, P.O. Box 3006, Miamisburg, OH 45343: Free information ❖ World band communications receivers and other shortwave equipment. 800-937-2530.

Electronic Distributors, 325 Mill St. NE, Vienna, VA 22180: Catalog $2 ❖ Antennas, roof towers, rotators, and other accessories. 703-938-8105.

Electronic Equipment Bank, 323 Mill St. NE, Vienna, VA 22180: Free information ❖ Equipment for shortwave broadcast listeners. 800-368-3270; 703-938-3350 (in VA).

EUR-AM Electronics, P.O. Box 990, Meredith, NH 03253: Catalog $2 ❖ Antennas for amateur radio, CB, cellular phones. 603-279-5113.

GAP Antenna Products, 6010 Building B, N. Old Dixie Hwy., Vero Beach, FL 32967: Free information ❖ Antennas for limited space. 407-778-3728.

Gateway Electronics, 8123 Page Blvd., St. Louis, MO 63130: Free information ❖ New and surplus electronics equipment. 314-427-6116.

Gilfer Shortwave, 52 Park Ave., Park Ridge, NJ 07656: Free information ❖ Shortwave radio equipment. 800-GILFER-1; 201-391-7887 (in NJ).

Grove Enterprises Inc., 300 S. Hwy. 64 West, P.O. Box 98, Brasstown, NC 28902: Free information ❖ Receiving equipment and publications. 800-438-8155.

Jo Gunn Enterprises, Hwy. 82, Box 32-C, Ethelsville, AL 35461: Catalog $2 ❖ Mobile antennas and other electronics equipment. 205-658-2229.

H.R. Electronics, 722-24 Evanston Ave., Muskegon, MI 49442: Free information ❖ Amateur radio equipment. 616-722-2246.

Ham Radio Outlet Inc., 933 N. Euclid St., Anaheim, CA 92801: Catalog $1 ❖ Radio amateur transceivers, receivers, mobile equipment, mini hand-held units, antennas, and rotators. 800-854-6046; 714-533-7373 (in CA).

Ham Radio Toy Store, 117 W. Wesley St., Wheaton, IL 60187: Free information ❖ Amateur radio equipment. 708-668-9577.

Ham Station, 220 N. Fulton Ave., Evansville, IN 47719: Free information with long SASE ❖ New and used amateur radio equipment. 800-729-4373; 812-422-0231 (in IN).

The Ham Store, 5730 Mobud, San Antonio, TX 78238: Free information ❖ Ham radio equipment. 800-344-3144.

Hamtronics/Trevose, 4033 Brownsville Rd., Trevose, PA 19053: Catalog $1 ❖ Amateur radio equipment. 800-426-2820; 215-357-1400 (in PA).

Hardin Electronics, 5635 E. Rosedale St., Fort Worth, TX 76112: Free information ❖ Amateur radio equipment. 800-433-3203; 817-429-9761 (in TX).

Hatry Electronics, 500 Ledyard St., Hartford, CT 06114: Free information ❖ Amateur radio equipment. 203-296-1881.

Hialeah Communications, 801 Hialeah Dr., Hialeah, FL 33010: Free information ❖ Amateur radio equipment. 305-885-9929.

High Sierra Antennas, Box 2389, Nevada City, CA 95959: Free information ❖ HF antennas. 916-273-3415.

ICOM America, 2380 116th Ave. NE, Bellevue, WA 98004: Free list of retail sources ❖ Amateur radio and single-side-band equipment. 800-999-9877.

Jun's Electronics, 5563 Sepulveda Blvd., Culver City, CA 90230: Free information ❖ Scanners, amateur and marine radio equipment, and cellular mobile phones. 800-882-1343; 213-390-8003 (in CA).

Kantronics, 1202 E. 23rd St., Lawrence, KS 66046: Free information ❖ Amateur and professional radio equipment. 913-842-7745.

Kenwood, P.O. Box 22745, Long Beach, CA 90801: Free information ❖ Amateur radio equipment. 800-536-9663.

KLM Antennas Inc., 14792 172nd Dr. SE, #1, Monroe, WA 98272: Free catalog ❖ Amateur antennas and accessories. 360-794-2923.

Larsen Antennas, 3611 NE 112th Ave., P.O. Box 1799, Vancouver, WA 98668: Free catalog ❖ Antennas. 800-426-1656; 206-944-7551 (in WA).

LaRue Electronics, 1112 Grandview St., Scranton, PA 18509: Free information ❖ Amateur radio equipment. 717-343-2124.

Lentini Communications Inc., 21 Garfield St., Newington, CT 06111: Free information ❖ Shortwave radios, scanners, and other equipment. 800-445-7717.

❖ RADIOS ❖

M2 Enterprises, 7560 N. Del Mar Ave., Fresno, CA 93711: Free information ❖ Antennas, accessories, and rotators. 209-432-3059.

Madison Electronics Supply, 12310 Zavalla St., Houston, TX 77085: Free information ❖ Hard-to-find parts and other equipment for amateur radio operation and electronics hobbyists. 800-231-3057; 713-729-7300 (in TX).

Maggiore Electronic Lab, 600 Westtown Rd., West Chester, PA 19382: Free catalog ❖ Amateur and professional radio equipment. 610-436-6051.

Maldol Antennas, 4711 NE 50th St., Seattle, WA 98105: Free information ❖ Mobile antennas.

Maryland Radio Center, 8576 Laureldale Dr., Laurel, MD 20707: Free information ❖ Amateur radio equipment. 301-725-1212.

Memphis Amateur Electronics, 1465 Wells Station Rd., Memphis, TN 38108: Free information ❖ Amateur radio equipment. 800-238-6168; 901-683-9125 (in TN).

Michigan Radio, 23040 Schoenherr, Warren, MI 48089: Free information ❖ Amateur radio base station and other equipment. 800-878-4266; 313-771-4711 (in MI).

Micro Control Specialties, 23 Elm Park, Groveland, MA 01834: Free information ❖ Receivers, transmitters, controllers, and other equipment. 508-372-3442.

Mobile Mark Inc., 3900 River Rd., Schiller Park, IL 60176: Free information ❖ Easy-to-mount mobile and window antennas. 708-671-6690.

Mosley Electronics, 10812 Ambassador Blvd., St. Louis, MO 63132: Free information ❖ HF, VHF, and UHF beam antennas, dipoles, and mobiles. 800-966-7539; 314-994-7872 (in MO).

Oklahoma Comm Center, 13424 Railway Dr., Oklahoma City, OK 73114: Free information ❖ Amateur radio equipment. 800-765-4267; 405-748-2866 (in OK).

Omni Electronics, 1007 San Dario, Laredo, TX 78040: Free information ❖ Amateur radio equipment and antennas. 210-725-OMNI.

Portland Radio Supply, 234 SE Grand Ave., Portland, OR 97214: Free information ❖ New and used amateur radio equipment. 503-233-4904.

R & L Electronics, 1315 Maple Ave., Hamilton, OH 45011: Free catalog ❖ Amateur radio equipment and antennas. 800-221-7735; 513-868-6399 (in OH).

Radio Adventures Inc., Main St., Seneca, PA 16346: Free information ❖ HF receiver and transmitter kits, test equipment kits, and radio accessories. 814-677-7221.

RF Parts, 435 S. Pacific St., San Marcos, CA 92069: Free information ❖ Antennas and power transistors and parts for amateur, marine, and commercial radio operation. 619-744-0900.

Rivendell Electronics, 8 Londonberry Rd., Derry, NH 03038: Free information ❖ Amateur radio equipment. 603-434-5371.

Standard Amateur Radio Products Inc., P.O. Box 48480, Niles, IL 60714: Free information ❖ Equipment for amateur radio operators. 312-763-0081.

Surplus Sales of Nebraska, 102 Jones St., Omaha, NE 68102: Catalog $2 ❖ Amateur radio equipment. 402-346-4750.

Telex/Hy-Gain Communications Inc., 8601 E. Cornhusker Hwy., Lincoln, NE 68505: Free information ❖ Antennas and rotators. 402-467-5321.

Texas Towers, 1108 Summit Ave., Ste. 4, Plano, TX 75074: Free information ❖ Antennas, towers, rotators, and other equipment.

Tri-Ex Tower Corporation, 7182 Rasmussen Ave., Visalia, CA 93291: Free information ❖ Antenna towers for amateur radio operation. 209-651-7850.

Tucker Electronics, 1717 Reserve St., Garland, TX 75042: Free information ❖ Short wave receivers, scanners, antennas, and other electronic equipment. 800-527-4642; 214-348-8800 (in TX).

Universal Radio Inc., 6830 Americana Pkwy., Reynoldsburg, OH 43068: Free catalog ❖ Equipment for amateur radio operators, shortwave listeners, and scanner enthusiasts. 800-431-3939; 614-866-4267 (in OH).

US Tower Corporation, 1220 Marcin St., Visalia, CA 93291: Free catalog ❖ Antenna towers. 209-733-2438.

W & W Associates, 800 S. Broadway, Hicksville, NY 11801: Free information ❖ Batteries. 800-221-0732; 516-942-0011 (in NY).

Wilson Antenna Inc., 1181 Grier Dr., Ste. A, Las Vegas, NV 89119: Free information ❖ CB and mobile antennas. 800-541-6116.

Yaesu USA, 17210 Edwards Rd., Cerritos, CA 90701: Free information ❖ Amateur radio base station equipment. 310-404-2700.

E.H. Yost & Company, 2211-D Parview Rd., Middleton, WI 53562: Free catalog ❖ Batteries for radios, computers, and other equipment. 608-631-3443.

Antique Radios & Repairs

Alltronics, 2300 Zanker Rd., San Jose, CA 95131: Free catalog ❖ Tubes and other components. 408-943-9773.

Antique Electronic Supply, 6221 S. Maple St., Tempe, AZ 85238: Catalog $2 ❖ Hard-to-find tubes, parts, and literature for antique radio restoration and repair. 602-820-5411.

Antique Radio Components, 1065 Faith Dr., Meadow Vista, CA 95722: Free information ❖ Antique radio tubes and components. 800-649-6550.

Antique Radio Hardware, Guy Frederick, 1121 Powers NW, Grand Rapids, MI 49504: Catalog $3 (refundable) ❖ Antique radio hardware. 616-456-9378.

The Antique Radio Store, 8376 La Mesa Blvd., La Mesa, CA 91941: Free list with long SASE ❖ Tubes. 619-668-5653.

ARS Electronics, 7110 Decelis Pl., Van Nuys, CA 91406: Catalog $2.50 ❖ Electronics equipment and tubes. 800-422-4250.

Don Diers, 4276 N. 50th St., Milwaukee, WI 53216: Catalog $3 ❖ Tubes and parts.

Electron Tube Enterprises, Box 8311, Essex, VT 05451: Free catalog ❖ Tubes. 802-879-1844.

Electronics Emporium Inc., 107 Trumbull St., Elizabeth, NJ 07206: Free information ❖ Tubes. 800-653-8823.

The Olde Tyme Radio Company, 2445 Lyttonsville Rd., Ste. 317, Silver Spring, MD 20910: Free information with long SASE and two 1st class stamps ❖ Antique radios, parts, tubes, and schematics. 301-587-5280.

PTI Antique Radios, 7925 Mabelvale Cutoff, Mabelvale, AR 72103: Free information ❖ Antique radio restoration parts. 501-568-1995.

Radio Electric Supply, Box 2790, RR 2, Melrose, FL 32666: Free price list ❖ Receiving and special purpose tubes. 904-475-1950.

A.G. Tannenbaum, P.O. Box 386, Ambler, PA 19002: Free catalog ❖ Repair parts. 215-540-8055.

Citizen Band Equipment & Transceivers

Alinco Electronics Inc., 438 Amapola Ave., Torrance, CA 90501: Free information ❖ Hand-held transceivers. 310-618-8616.

CBC International Inc., P.O. Box 31500, Phoenix, AZ 85046: Catalog $3 ❖ Parts for CB radios, 10-meter and FM conversion kits, books, and plans.

Cobra, 6500 W. Cortland St., Chicago, IL 60635: Free information ❖ Fixed-installation and portable citizen band radios. 800-COBRA-22.

Copper Electronics Inc., 3315 Gilmore Industrial Blvd., Louisville, KY 40213: Free catalog ❖ CB radios and accessories. 502-968-8500.

RADON TESTING

Firestik, 2614 E. Adams, Phoenix, AZ 85034: Free catalog ❖ CB antennas and accessories. 602-273-7151.

Furuno USA, P.O. Box 2343, South San Francisco, CA 94083: Free information ❖ Transceivers. 415-873-9393.

Ham Radio Outlet Inc., 933 N. Euclid St., Anaheim, CA 92801: Catalog $1 ❖ Radio amateur transceivers, receivers, mobile equipment, mini hand-held units, antennas, and rotators. 800-854-6046; 714-533-7373 (in CA).

ICOM America, 2380 116th Ave. NE, Bellevue, WA 98004: Free list of retail sources ❖ Hand-held transceivers. 206-450-6088.

Japan Radio Company Ltd., 430 Park Ave., 2nd Floor, New York, NY 10022: Free information ❖ Transceivers. 212-355-1180.

K-40 Electronics, 1500 Executive Dr., Elgin, IL 60123: Free brochure ❖ CB radios and antennas. 800-323-5608.

Nady Systems, 6701 Bay St., Emeryville, CA 94608: Free information ❖ UHF and VHF hand-held transceivers. 510-652-2411.

PageCom, 11545 Pagemill Rd., Dallas, TX 75243: Free information ❖ Portable outdoor two-way radio. 800-527-1670.

Radio Shack, Division Tandy Corporation, One Tandy Center, Fort Worth, TX 76102: Free information ❖ Portable and fixed installation citizen band radios, electronics components, science kits, computers and accessories, stereo equipment, and toys and games. 817-390-3011.

Transcrypt International Inc., 4800 NW 1st St., Lincoln, NE 68521: Free information ❖ Portable and hand-held two-way radios. 800-228-0226.

Wilson Antenna Inc., 1181 Grier Dr., Ste. A, Las Vegas, NV 89119: Free information ❖ CB and mobile antennas. 800-541-6116.

RADON TESTING

First Alert, 780 McClure Rd., Aurora, IL 60404: Free information ❖ Radon detectors. 800-323-9005.

RAFTING & WHITEWATER RUNNING

Cascade Outfitters, 145 Pioneer Pkwy. East, P.O. Box 209, Springfield, OR 97477: Free catalog ❖ Whitewater river running equipment. 800-223-7238.

Colorado Kayak, P.O. Box 3059, Buena Vista, CO 81211: Free catalog ❖ Paddles and sports clothing. 800-535-3565.

Easy Rider Canoe & Kayak Company, P.O. Box 88108, Seattle, WA 98138: Catalog $5 ❖ Whitewater and sea cruising paddles, single and double-seat kayaks and canoes, and rowing trainers. 206-228-3633.

Hyside Inflatables, P.O. Box Z, Kernville, CA 93238: Free information ❖ River running inflatable rafts, self-bailing kayaks, and other equipment. 619-376-3723.

Mitchell Paddles Inc., RD 2, P.O. Box 922, Canaan, NH 03741: Free information ❖ Canoe and kayak paddles, boats, and dry suits. 603-523-7004.

Nantahala Outdoor Center, 13077 Hwy. 19 West, Bryson City, NC 28713: Free catalog ❖ Equipment for whitewater paddling. 800-367-3521.

Northwest River Supplies Inc., 2009 S. Main, Moscow, ID 83843: Free catalog ❖ Rafts, waterproof bags, paddles, boats, and supplies. 800-635-5202.

Wyoming River Raiders, P.O. Box 50490, Casper, WY 82605: Free catalog ❖ Outdoor clothing, camping and river expedition equipment, fishing gear, hiking equipment, books, and other supplies. 800-247-6068.

RECYCLED & ENVIRONMENTALLY SAFE PRODUCTS

Atlantic Recycled Paper Company, 21 Winters Ln., Catonsville, MD 21228: Free catalog ❖ Office and restroom paper supplies. 800-323-2811; 410-747-7314 (in MD).

Basically Natural, 109 East G St., Brunswick, MD 21716: Free information ❖ Household cleaners, cosmetics, and pet and personal care products. 800-352-7099.

Clothcrafters Inc., P.O. Box 176, Elkhart Lake, WI 53020: Free catalog ❖ Reusable kitchen supplies and cotton bags, 100 percent cotton diapers, and other environmentally sensitive products. 800-876-2009; 414-876-2112 (in WI).

Conservatree Paper Company, 10 Lombard St., Ste. 200, San Francisco, CA 94111: Free information ❖ Recycled paper products. 415-433-1000.

Earth Care, 555 Leslie St., Ukiah, CA 95482: Free catalog ❖ Recycled paper products, environmental gifts, and household goods. 800-992-7747.

Energy Savers, Solar Components Corporation, 121 Valley St., Manchester, NH 03103: Catalog $2 ❖ Energy-saving products. 603-668-8186.

Environmentally Sound Products, 8845 Orchard Tree Ln., Towson, MD 21286: Free information ❖ Stains, paints, cleaning aids, and other products. 800-886-5432.

Idea Art, P.O. Box 291505, Nashville, TN 37229: Free catalog ❖ Laser/copier/offset recycled paper with preprinted designs. 800-433-2278.

Natural Resources, 6680 Harvard Dr., Sebastopol, CA 95472: Free information ❖ Natural cleansing products. 800-747-0390; 707-823-4340 (in CA).

Real Goods, 555 Leslie St., Ukiah, CA 95482: Free catalog ❖ Solar-operated tank-less water heater, water-saving appliances, composting toilets, gas appliances, and recycled paper products. 800-762-7325.

Seventh Generation, 49 Hercules Dr., Colchester, VT 05446: Free catalog ❖ Household products and decorative accessories for the environmental enthusiast. 800-456-1177.

Simmons Handcrafts, 42295 Hwy. 36, Bridgeville, CA 95526: Catalog $1 ❖ Natural products for home and personal care. 707-777-1920.

ROCKS, MINERALS & FOSSILS

Display Cases & Lights

Cabinets by Vector, 25736 Schrader Rd., Sturgis, MI 49091: Free catalog ❖ Specimen storage cabinets. 616-651-3823.

Collector Case Company, 194 Woodlark Rd., Versailles, KY 40383: Free catalog ❖ Display cases. 800-553-5294; 606-873-3569 (in KY).

Lustig International, P.O. Box 2051, San Leandro, CA 94577: Free information ❖ Display stands. 800-221-4456.

National Showcase Company Inc., 7462 Balto-Annapolis Blvd., Glen Burnie, MD 21061: Free catalog ❖ Showcases. 800-628-2352.

O'Brien Manufacturing, 2081 Knowles Rd., Medford, OR 97501: Free information ❖ Oak show cases with tempered glass, built-in plunger locks, halogen lighting, and roller bearing doors. 503-773-2410.

Sylmar Display Stands, P.O. Box 362, Youngtown, AZ 85363: Free catalog ❖ Display stands. 602-933-7301.

Fossils

Ackley's Rock & Stamps, 3230 N. Stone Ave., Colorado Springs, CO 80907: Catalog $1 (refundable) ❖ Fossils, lapidary and silversmithing supplies, jewelry boxes and trays, mountings, and findings. 719-633-1153.

Art By God, 3705 Biscayne Blvd., Miami, FL 33137: Free information ❖ Rocks, minerals, and fossils. 800-940-4449.

Hal Bach's Rock Shop, 137 Marne Rd., Cheektowage, NY 14215: Free information ❖ Fossils, minerals, and rock specimens. 800-568-6888.

Bitner's, 42 W. Hatcher, Phoenix, AZ 85021: Free information ❖ Rocks, minerals, and fossils. 602-870-0075.

Black Hills Institute of Geological Research Inc., 217 Main St., P.O. Box 643, Hill City, SD 57745: Free information ❖ Cretaceous ammonites, eocene fishes, oligocene mammals, dinosaurs, and other fossils. 605-574-4289.

❖ ROCKS, MINERALS & FOSSILS ❖

Bourget Bros., 1636 11th St., Santa Monica, CA 90404: Catalog $3 ❖ Fossils, gemstones, cabochons, wax patterns, beads, and bead-stringing and jewelry-making supplies. 310-450-6556.

Caddo Trading, Box 669, Murfreesboro, AR 71958: Free list ❖ Native American artifacts, minerals, and fossils.

L.A. Cave, 360 N. Palm Canyon Dr., Palm Springs, CA 92262: Free information ❖ Minerals, gems, fossils, books, gifts, and soapstone for carving. 619-320-1672.

Dino Productions, P.O. Box 3004, Englewood, CO 80155: Catalog $2 (refundable) ❖ Fossils, rocks and minerals, ecology and oceanography equipment, and supplies for chemistry, general science, astronomy, and biology. 303-741-1587.

Discount Agate House, 3401 N. Dodge, Tucson, AZ 85716: Free information ❖ Rocks, minerals, and fossils. 520-323-0781.

Ebersole Lapidary Supply Inc., 11417 West Hwy. 54, Wichita, KS 67209: Catalog $2 ❖ Fossils, petrified wood and rock specimens, tools, jewelry findings and kits, mountings, and cabochons. 316-722-4771.

Extinctions, P.O. Box 7, Clarita, OK 74535: Free catalog ❖ Trilobites, crinoids, vertebrates, ferns, and other museum and collector fossils. 405-428-3220.

Fossils & Amber, c/o IJB Marketing Inc., P.O. Box 5568, Woodridge, IL 60517: Free catalog ❖ Fossils and amber specimens. 800-AMBER-44.

Geo-Impressions, P.O. Box 989, Pelham, NH 03076: Catalog $1 ❖ Common to rare vertebrates and invertebrates, rocks, and minerals. 603-635-7923.

J & S Fossils, 17 Jeff Rd., Largo, FL 34644: Free information ❖ Collector and museum-quality specimens. 813-595-2661.

Jeanne's Rock & Jewelry, 5420 Bissonet, Bellaire, TX 77401: Price list $1 ❖ Petrified wood products, fossils, seashells, lapidary supplies, and gifts. 713-664-2988.

Lou-Bon Gems & Rocks, Lake Barcroft Plaza, 6341 Columbia Pike, Bailey's Crossroads, VA 22041: Free information ❖ Carvings, beads, mineral specimens, fossils, shells, and lapidary and jewelry equipment. 703-256-1084.

Minerals Unlimited, P.O. Box 877, Ridgecrest, CA 93556: Catalog $2 ❖ Rocks, minerals, and fossils. 619-375-5279.

Missing Link Fossils, 833 Poplar Way, Qualicum Beach, British Columbia, Canada V9K 1X8: Catalog $2 (refundable) ❖ Fossils and mineral specimens. 604-752-3979.

Nature's Treasures, 1163 E. Ogden Ave., Naperville, IL 60563: Free information ❖ Insects in Baltic amber. 708-983-5504.

Omni Resources, 1004 S. Mebane St., P.O. Box 2096, Burlington, NC 27216: Free catalog ❖ Fossils, rocks, hiking and topography maps, and globes. 800-742-2677.

PaleoSearch Inc., P.O. Box 621, Hays, KS 67601: Catalog $3 ❖ Fossils, educational posters, and rare reproductions. 913-625-2240.

Parsons' Minerals & Fossils, 2808 Eden Ln., Rapid City, SD 57701: Video catalog $13.50 ❖ Minerals and fossils from worldwide sources. 605-348-0937.

Phoenix Fossils, 6401 E. Camino De Los Ranchos, Scottsdale, AZ 85254: Catalog $5 ❖ Fossil specimens. Includes some one-of-a-kind items. 602-991-5246.

Pikes Peak Rock Shop, 451 Forest Edge Rd., Woodland Park, CO 80863: Free catalog ❖ Fossils, crystals, tumbled stones, agate products, amethyst, chips, beads, and display stands. 800-347-6257.

Potomac Museum Group, P.O. Box 27470, Golden Valley, MN 55427: Free catalog ❖ Rare specimen reproductions. 800-576-8662.

Prehistoric Journeys, P.O. Box 3376, Santa Barbara, CA 93130: Catalog $3 ❖ Rare vertebrate fossils and dinosaur bones. 805-563-2404.

J.F. Ray, RR 1, Box 213, Olar, SC 29845: Catalog $3 (refundable) ❖ Shark teeth jewelry, fossils, seashells, beach-combing treasures, and amber with inclusions.

Schooler's Minerals & Fossils, P.O. Box 1032, Blue Springs, MO 64013: Free information ❖ Mineral and fossil specimens.

Skullduggery, 624 South B St., Tustin, CA 92680: Free information ❖ Fossil replicas and hands-on educational kits. 800-336-7745.

Southeastern Fossil Supply Company, P.O. Box 12151, Knoxville, TN 37912: Free catalog ❖ Fossils, mineral collections, and teaching aids. 615-947-2950.

The Stone Company Science Specimens, Charlie & Florence Magovern, Box 18814, Boulder, CO 80308: Free information ❖ Museum-quality fossils and other science specimens. 303-581-0670.

STRATAGRAPHICS, 5565 E. Henrietta Rd., Rush, NY 14543: Catalog $1 ❖ Fish, mammals, reptiles, other vertebrates, and petrified wood and plant specimens.

Taylor Studios, P.O. Box 1063, Mahomet, IL 61853: Catalog $3 ❖ Museum-quality cast reproductions of fossils. 217-586-2047.

Two Guys Fossils & Minerals, 1 Lynnes Way, East Bridgewater, MA 02333: Catalog $2 ❖ Rocks, minerals, and fossils. Also fossil reproductions. 508-3478-7081.

Warfield Fossil Quarries, 2072 Muddy String Rd., Thayne, WY 83127: Catalog $2 ❖ Fish, leaves, turtles, reptiles, trilobites, ammonites, and other fossils. 307-883-2445.

What on Earth Naturally, 6250 Busch Blvd., Columbus, OH 43229: Free information ❖ Minerals, fossils, jewelry, gemstones, and shells. 614-436-1458.

Woods of the World & Fossils, P.O. Box 47, Somis, CA 93066: Free price list ❖ Petrified woods and fossil plants.

Meteorites

Bethany Sciences, P.O. Box 3726, New Haven, CT 06525: Catalog $2 ❖ Stony-iron meteorites, display stands, jewelry, and books. 203-393-3395.

Excalibur-Cureton Company, Division Excalibur Mineral Company, 1000 N. Division St., Peekskill, NY 10566: Catalog $1 ❖ Meteorites and mineral specimens. 914-739-1134.

Robert Haag Meteorites, P.O. Box 27527, Tucson, AZ 85726: Catalog $5 ❖ Meteorites. 520-882-8804.

Mineralogical Research Company, 15840 E. Alta Vista Way, San Jose, CA 95127: Free list with long SASE and two 1st class stamps ❖ Meteorites, rare mineral specimens, microscopes, micro mounts, and specimen boxes. 408-923-6800.

New England Meteoritical Services, P.O. Box 440, Mendon, MA 01756: Free list ❖ Meteorites. 508-478-4020.

Blaine Reed, 907 County Rd., Durango, CO 81301: Free price list ❖ Meteorites.

Ward's Natural Science, P.O. Box 92912, 5100 W. Henrietta Rd., Rochester, NY 14692: Earth science catalog $10; biology catalog $15; middle school catalog $10 ❖ Meteorites, telescopes, audio-visual aids, books, and other equipment. 800-962-2660.

Miscellaneous Varieties & Equipment

Aleta's Rock Shop, 1515 Plainfield NE, Grand Rapids, MI 49505: Catalog $1.50 ❖ Mineral specimens, rocks for cutting and tumbling, lapidary equipment, and silversmithing supplies. 616-363-5394.

Allen's Rocks & Gifts, 26513 Center Ridge Rd., Cleveland, OH 44145: Free information ❖ Minerals, findings, silversmithing supplies, casting and lapidary equipment, and tools. 216-871-6522.

Arizona Gems & Minerals Inc., 22025 N. Black Canyon Hwy., Phoenix, AZ 85027: Catalog $4 ❖ Geodes, silversmithing and lapidary tools, jewelry-making supplies, and mineral sets. 602-772-6443.

Arrow Gems & Minerals Inc., 9827 Cave Creek Rd., Phoenix, AZ 85020: Free catalog ❖ Pewter figurines, pendants, buckles, and bolas, beads, and findings. Also mineral specimens and faceted stones. 602-997-6373.

Art by God, 3705 Biscayne Blvd., Miami, FL 33137: Free information ❖ Rocks, minerals, and fossils. 800-940-4449.

ROCKS, MINERALS & FOSSILS

Aurora Mineral Corporation, 16 Niagara Ave., Freeport, NY 11520: Free information ❖ Amethyst, geodes, fossil fishes, quartz crystals, and mineral specimens from around the world. 516-623-3800.

Bitner's, 42 W. Hatcher, Phoenix, AZ 85021: Free information ❖ Rocks, minerals, and fossils. 602-870-0075.

C & N Minerals, P.O. Box 7484, Worcester, MA 01605: Free catalog ❖ Portable pocket-size and battery-operated Geiger counter, mineral specimens, and other items. 508-757-6607.

C & R Enterprises Inc., 4833 East Park, Springfield, MO 65809: Free catalog ❖ Sterling silver and 14K gold jewelry mountings, lapidary supplies, mineral specimens, belt buckles, beads and beading supplies, and cut stones. 417-866-4843.

Caddo Trading, Box 669, Murfreesboro, AR 71958: Free list ❖ Native American artifacts, minerals, and fossils.

Carousel Gem & Minerals, 1202 Perion Dr., Belen, NM 87002: Price list $1 ❖ Minerals from worldwide locations. 505-864-2145.

L.A. Cave, 360 N. Palm Canyon Dr., Palm Springs, CA 92262: Free information ❖ Minerals, gems, fossils, books, gifts, and soapstone for carving. 619-320-1672.

Charlie's Rock Shop, P.O. Box 399, Penrose, CO 81240: Free catalog ❖ Mineral specimens, jewelry supplies and findings, tools, and beads. 719-372-0117.

Dino Productions, P.O. Box 3004, Englewood, CO 80155: Catalog $2 (refundable) ❖ Fossils, rocks and minerals, ecology and oceanography equipment, and supplies for chemistry, general science, astronomy, and biology. 303-741-1587.

Discount Agate House, 3401 N. Dodge, Tucson, AZ 85716: Free information ❖ Rocks, minerals, and fossils. 520-323-0781.

Excalibur-Cureton Company, Division Excalibur Mineral Company, 1000 N. Division St., Peekskill, NY 10566: Catalog $1 ❖ Meteorites and mineral specimens. 914-739-1134.

Gemco International, P.O. Box 833, Fayston, VT 05673: Free price list ❖ Faceted rough gemstones and small cut stones. Includes some that are slightly or moderately flawed. 802-496-2770.

Geo-Impressions, P.O. Box 989, Pelham, NH 03076: Catalog $1 ❖ Common to rare vertebrates and invertebrates, rocks, and minerals. 603-635-7923.

Kenneth Glasser, P.O. Box 441, Monsey, NY 10952: Catalog $10 ❖ All types, sizes, and qualities of diamonds. 914-426-1241.

Grieger's, P.O. Box 93070, Pasadena, CA 91109: Free catalog ❖ Minerals and rare stones from around the world, lapidary equipment, jewelry supplies and findings, and mountings. 800-423-4181.

Herkimer Diamond Mines, P.O. Box 510, Herkimer, NY 13350: Free information ❖ Petrified wood products, rockhounding equipment, minerals and rocks, and quartz crystals. 315-891-7355.

Jewelry by Avery, 5134 Chalk Point Rd., West River, MD 20778: Free information with long SASE ❖ Handcrafted Zuni, Navajo, and Hopi turquoise jewelry, kachinas, Native American art, precious and semi-precious gemstones, and mineral specimens. 410-867-4752.

Lentz Lapidary Inc., 11760 S. Oliver, Rt. 2, Box 134, Mulvane, KS 67110: Catalog $2 ❖ Jewelry, mountings, clocks and motors, rough rock specimens, cabochons, and rockhounding and lapidary equipment. 316-777-1372.

Lou-Bon Gems & Rocks, Lake Barcroft Plaza, 6341 Columbia Pike, Bailey's Crossroads, VA 22041: Free information ❖ Carvings, beads, mineral specimens, fossils, shells, and lapidary and jeweler's equipment. 703-256-1084.

Mineralogical Research Company, 15840 E. Alta Vista Way, San Jose, CA 95127: Free list with long SASE and two 1st class stamps ❖ Mineral specimens and meteorites, microscopes, micro-mounts, specimen boxes, and supplies. 408-923-6800.

Minerals Unlimited, P.O. Box 877, Ridgecrest, CA 93556: Catalog $2 ❖ Rocks, minerals, and fossils. 619-375-5279.

Miners Inc., P.O. Box 1301, Riggins, ID 83549: Free catalog ❖ Sample bags, instruments, hand tools, leather cases, and books for geologists and prospectors. 800-824-7452; 208-628-3247 (in ID).

Missing Link Fossils, 833 Poplar Way, Qualicum Beach, British Columbia, Canada V9K 1X8: Catalog $2 (refundable) ❖ Fossils and mineral specimens. 604-752-3979.

Mountain Minerals International, P.O. Box 302, Louisville, CO 80027: Free information ❖ Gem crystals and rare and unusual gemstones from worldwide sources. 303-665-0672.

New England International Gems Inc., 188 Pollard St., Billerica, MA 01862: Free catalog ❖ Brazilian quartz, rocks from India, beads, jewelry-making supplies, tools, and findings. 617-863-8331.

H. Obodda Mineral Specimens, P.O. Box 51, Short Hills, NJ 07078: Free list ❖ Afghan and Pakistani pegmatite minerals. 201-467-0212.

Omni Resources, 1004 S. Mebane St., P.O. Box 2096, Burlington, NC 27216: Free catalog ❖ Fossils, rocks, hiking and topography maps, and globes. 800-742-2677.

The Outcrop, P.O. Box 9375, Springfield, IL 62791: Free information with long SASE ❖ Thumbnail to small cabinet size mineral specimens from around the world.

Pickens Minerals, 610 N. Martin Ave., Waukegan, IL 60085: Free list with 1st class stamp ❖ Mineral specimens. 708-623-2823.

Mark E. Rogers Minerals, P.O. Box 806, Minden, NV 89423: Free information ❖ Minerals and rare, used, and new books.

Roth International, One NE 1st St., Ste. 33, Miami, FL 33132: Free information ❖ Single and multiple crystal clusters from Brazilian mines. 305-372-0630.

Russell's Rock Shop, 27911 North St., North Liberty, IN 46554: Free information ❖ Gem trees and supplies, bookends, agate slabs, amethyst, cabs, findings, slabs, and lucite stands. 219-289-7446.

Rusty's Rock Shop, 4106 Buckingham Dr., Decatur, IL 62526: Free price list ❖ Fluorite octahedrons, pyrite suns, and other mineral specimens. 217-877-7122.

S.E.A.T. Publication, P.O. Box 2593, Longmont, CO 80502: Information $4 ❖ Mineral specimens, jewelry, and beads. 303-678-9930.

Salt Minerals, 540 Beaverbrook St., Winnipeg, Manitoba, Canada R3N 1N4: Free catalog ❖ Specimens from worldwide locations.

Schooler's Minerals & Fossils, P.O. Box 1032, Blue Springs, MO 64013: Free information ❖ Mineral and fossil specimens.

Southeastern Fossil Supply Company, P.O. Box 12151, Knoxville, TN 37912: Free catalog ❖ Fossils, mineral collections, and teaching aids. 615-947-2950.

TOPAZ-Mineral Exploration, 1605 Hillcrest, Grand Haven, MI 49417: Catalog $1 ❖ Pseudomorphs, rare and unusual specimens, and books on minerals. 616-842-3506.

Two Guys Fossils & Minerals, 1 Lynnes Way, East Bridgewater, MA 02333: Catalog $2 ❖ Rocks, minerals, and fossils. Also fossil reproductions. 508-3478-7081.

Rod & Helen Tyson, 10549 133rd St., Edmonton, Alberta, Canada T5N 2A4: Free information ❖ Mineral specimens. 403-452-5357.

V-Rock Shop, 7061 Sunset Strip Ave., North Canton, OH 44720: Free information ❖ Cabochons, beads, pearls, faceted stones, display stands, pyramids, enhydros, citrine, Brazilian agate, amethyst geodes and plates, and quartz specimens. 216-494-1759.

Charles B. Ward Minerals, 37 Deerwood Manor, Norwalk, CT 06851: Free catalog with long SASE and two 1st class stamps ❖ Fluorescent minerals. 203-849-3366.

Western Minerals, Gene & Jackie Schlepp, P.O. Box 43603, Tucson, AZ 85733: Free information ❖ Mineral collections, mining and mineralogical books, microscopes, goniometers, and alidades. 520-325-4534.

What on Earth Naturally, 6250 Busch Blvd., Columbus, OH 43229: Free information ❖ Minerals, fossils, jewelry, gemstones, and shells. 614-436-1458.

Stuart & Donna Wilensky, P.O. Box 386, 203 Sullivan St., Wurtsboro, NY 12790: Video catalog $7.50 ❖ Mineral specimens. 914-888-4411.

Wright's Rock Shop, 3612 Albert Pike, Hot Springs, AR 71913: Catalog $3 ❖ Quartz, tourmaline, healing crystals, marcasite, other minerals and fossils, and lapidary equipment. 501-767-4800.

Petrified Wood

Burnett Petrified Wood Inc., 37420 Sodaville Cutoff Dr., Lebanon, OR 97355: Free information ❖ Petrified wood. 503-258-3320.

Ebersole Lapidary Supply Inc., 11417 West Hwy. 54, Wichita, KS 67209: Catalog $2 ❖ Tools, findings, mountings, cabochons, rocks, and petrified wood. 316-722-4771.

Herkimer Diamond Mines, P.O. Box 510, Herkimer, NY 13350: Free information ❖ Petrified wood, mineral and rock specimens, quartz crystals, and gifts. 315-891-7355.

Jeanne's Rock & Jewelry, 5420 Bissonet, Bellaire, TX 77401: Price list $1 ❖ Petrified wood, seashells, lapidary supplies, and gifts. 713-664-2988.

Red & Green Minerals Inc., 7595 W. Florida Ave., Lakewood, CO 80226: Free information ❖ Petrified wood, faceting rough, crystals, books, and magazines. 303-985-5559.

Riviera Lapidary Supply, 70796 Mesquite, Box 40, Riviera, TX 78379: Catalog $3 ❖ Petrified wood, cabochons, slabs, cabbing rough, gemstones, crystals, beads, and bead-stringing supplies. 512-296-3958.

STRATAGRAPHICS, 5565 E. Henrietta Rd., Rush, NY 14543: Catalog $1 ❖ Fish, mammals, reptiles, other vertebrates, and petrified wood and plant specimens.

Woods of the World & Fossils, P.O. Box 47, Somis, CA 93066: Free price list ❖ Petrified wood and fossil plants.

RODEO EQUIPMENT

Barstow Pro Rodeo Equipment, P.O. Box 1516, Corsicana, TX 75151: Catalog $2 ❖ Rodeo riding equipment. 903-874-3995.

Bob Blackwood Equipment, P.O. Box 351, Farmersville, TX 75442: Free information ❖ Rodeo equipment. 800-959-1245; 214-782-6624 (in TX).

Grant Lariat Rope Company, 9486 Dub Grant Rd., Benton, AR 72015: Free information ❖ Rodeo equipment. 800-223-8478; 501-794-1912 (in AR).

Jim White Saddlery & Rodeo Equipment, HC 69, Box 55, Belle Fourche, SD 57717: Free brochure ❖ Saddles and other rodeo equipment. 605-692-4482.

ROLLER & IN-LINE SKATES

CCM Maska, 9 Vose Farm Rd., Peterborough, NH 03458: Free information ❖ Protective gear and skates. 800-451-4600.

Dominion Skate Company Ltd., 45 Railroad St., Brampton, Ontario, Canada L6X 1G4: Free information ❖ Roller skates and scooters. 416-453-9860.

Fast Forward Skate Shop, 4649 Verona Rd., Madison, WI 53711: Free catalog ❖ Skates for speed, hockey, stunts, distance, or recreation. 608-271-1211.

Grind Zone Skates, P.O. Box 524, Albertville, AL 35950: Free catalog ❖ In-line skates. 800-322-3851.

The House, 300 S. Owasso Blvd., St. Paul, MN 55117: Free catalog ❖ In-line skates and other gear. 800-992-7245.

Hyper Wheels, 15241 Transistor Ln., Huntington Beach, CA 92649: Free information ❖ Roller blade skates. 714-373-3300.

Kerjean Skate Line, 2501 NW 72nd Ave., Miami, FL 33122: Free information ❖ In-line skates. 305-499-9952.

Kryptonics Inc., 740 S. Pierce Ave., Louisville, CO 80027: Free information ❖ Roller skates and skateboards. 800-766-9146; 303-665-5353 (in CO).

Labeda Wheels, Precision Sports Inc., 18650 Collier Ave., Unit A, Lake Elsinore, CA 92530: Free information ❖ Inline wheels and frames. 909-674-1665.

National Sporting Goods Corporation, 25 Brighton Ave., Passaic, NJ 07055: Free information ❖ Roller skates, scooters, skateboards, and protective gear. 201-779-2323.

Ocean Hockey Supply Company, 197 Chambers Bridge Rd., Brick, NJ 08723: Free catalog ❖ Inline skates and hockey equipment. 800-631-2159; 908-477-4411 (in NJ).

Rainbow Sports Shop, 4836 N. Clark St., Chicago, IL 60640: Free catalog ❖ Skates, clothing, and gifts. 312-275-5500.

Ramptech Design & Construction, 7015 Westmoreland Rd., Falls Church, VA 22042: Magazine $2 ❖ Ramp blueprints. 703-573-RAMP.

Riedell Shoes Inc. P.O. Box 21, Red Wing, MN 55066: Free information ❖ Protective gear, skates, and wheels. 612-388-8251.

Rocky Mountain Deals on Wheels, P.O. Box 460302, Aurora, CO 80046: Free catalog ❖ Hockey, racing, and recreational skates. 800-660-2SK8; 303-617-0975 (in CO).

Roller Derby Skate Company, Box 930, Litchfield, IL 62056: Free information ❖ Roller and in-line skates, scooters, and skateboards. 217-324-3961.

Roller Warehouse, 7236 Owensmouth Ave., Building A, Canoga Park, CA 91303: Free catalog ❖ Inline skates, replacement wheels, and protective gear. 800-772-2502; 818-348-3282 (in CA).

Rollerblade Inc., 5101 Shady Oak Rd., Minnetonka, MN 55343: Free list of retail sources ❖ Protective gear, skates, and wheels. 800-232-7655.

Saucony/Hyde, 13 Centennial Dr., Peabody, MA 01961: Free list of retail sources ❖ Roller skates, scooters, and skateboards. 800-365-7282.

Seneca Sports Inc., 75 Fortune Blvd., P.O. Box 719, Milford, MA 01757: Free information ❖ Inline skates. 800-861-7867; 508-634-3616 (in MA).

Sportime, Customer Service, 1 Sportime Way, Atlanta, GA 30340: Free information ❖ Protective gear and skates. 800-444-5700; 770-449-5700 (in GA).

Team Karim, 2800 Telegraph Ave., Berkeley, CA 94705: Free information ❖ Speed skates. 510-841-2181.

Team Paradise, 16321 Gothard St., Unit D, Huntington Beach, CA 92647: Free catalog ❖ Inline skates. 800-756-5629.

Tour Hockey Skates, 311 W. Edwards St., Litchfield, IL 62056: Free information ❖ Hockey skates and protective equipment. 217-324-3961.

UFO Sports Inc., 18533 Roscoe Blvd., Ste. 323, Northridge, CA 91324: Catalog $3 ❖ Inline replacement wheels. 818-701-1521.

Variflex Inc., 5152 N. Commerce Ave., Moorpark, CA 93021: Free information ❖ Roller skates and skateboards. 805-523-0322.

RUBBER STAMPS & EMBOSSING SUPPLIES

Acme/Star, 2221 N. Lister, Chicago, IL 60614: Catalog $2 (refundable) ❖ Letterpress supplies and rubber stamps.

Alextamping, 21023 Lynn Ln., Sonora, CA 95370: Catalog $4.50 ❖ Rubber stamps.

Arben Stamp Company, P.O. Box 353, Evansville, IN 47703: Catalog $2.50 ❖ Rubber stamps. 800-223-3086; 812-423-4269 (in IN).

Auntie Amy Stamps, 6500 Streeter Ave., Riverside, CA 92504: Catalog $3 ❖ Original rubber stamps and supplies. 909-689-2530.

❖ RUBBER STAMPS & EMBOSSING SUPPLIES ❖

Barco, Box 1011, Bensonville, IL 60106: Catalog $2 (refundable) ❖ Letterpress supplies and rubber stamps.

Bartholomew's Ink, P.O. Box 359, Warner, NH 03278: Catalog $3 ❖ Murder and mystery rubber stamps.

Bizzaro Rubber Stamps, P.O. Box 292, Greenville, RI 02828: Catalog $3 ❖ Artistic rubber stamps and supplies. 401-231-8777.

Blue Tulip Rubber Stamps, 2632 Georgia, Kingman, AZ 86401: Catalog $1.50 ❖ Fun stamps.

Brooks Rubber Stamps, 3881 Belle Vista, St. Petersburg, FL 33706: Catalog $1 ❖ Humorous rubber stamps.

Ken Brown Stamps, P.O. Box 474, Saxtons River, VT 05154: Catalog $2.50 ❖ Rubber stamps and supplies. 802-869-2262.

Burpo Duh Clown, P.O. Box 160190, Cupertino, CA 95016: Free information ❖ Face-painting rubber stamps and supplies. 408-446-9314.

Carousel Collections, 6-25 Industrial Dr., Elmira, Ontario, Canada N3B 3K3: Catalog $2 (refundable) ❖ Rubber stamps. 800-265-6269.

Circustamps, Box 250, Bolinas, CA 94924: Free catalog ❖ Circus-theme rubber stamps. 415-868-1470.

Comotion Rubber Stamps Inc., 2711 E. Elvira Rd., Tucson, AZ 85706: Free catalog ❖ Decorative rubber stamps and accessories. 800-257-1288.

Country Impressions, P.O. Box 502, Layton, UT 84041: Catalog $3.50 ❖ Rubber stamps. 801-543-0206.

Crazy Folks Rubber Stamps, 855 Jefferson Ave., Livermore, CA 94550: Catalog $2 (refundable) ❖ Rubber stamps. 510-449-NUTS.

Design Impressions, c/o Andersonville Books, 5035 Pacific St., Rocklin, CA 95677: Free brochure ❖ Rubber stamps. 916-652-8918.

Detailed Rubber Stamps, 178-A Lincoln Pl., Brooklyn, NY 11217: Catalog $2 (refundable) ❖ Rubber stamps. 718-230-5326.

Dream Stamper, P.O. Box 59323, Chicago, IL 60659: Catalog $2 (refundable) ❖ Original rubber stamps.

DreamInk, P.O. Box 8028, Woodland, CA 95776: Catalog $2 (refundable with first $10 order) ❖ Rubber stamps.

Ecletibles, P.O. Box 9423, Fort Worth, TX 76147: Free catalog with three 1st class stamps ❖ Original rubber stamps and accessories. 817-732-3608.

Embossing Arts Company, P.O. Box 626, Sweet Home, OR 97386: Catalog $3 (specify retail) ❖ Rubber stamps and card-making and embossing supplies. 503-367-3279.

Enchanted Creations, 347 Fawn Lake Forest, Hawley, PA 18428: Rubber stamps catalog $4.75, accessories catalog $4.75 ❖ Mounted and unmounted rubber stamps and accessories. 717-685-7013.

GBLA Art Stamps, 17029 Devonshire Ave., Northridge, CA 91325: Catalog $5 ❖ Rubber stamps. 800-GBLA-ART.

Good Impressions Rubber Stamps, P.O. Box 33, Shirley, WV 26434: Catalog $2 ❖ Victorian and Edwardian-style rubber stamps. Also accessories. 800-846-6606.

Graphic Rubber Stamp Company, 11250 Magnolia Blvd., North Hollywood, CA 91601: Catalog $4 ❖ Rubber stamps. 818-782-9443.

Graven Images, 4211 Seneca, Chattanooga, TN 37409: Catalog $2 ❖ Rubber stamps. 423-821-7473.

Hippo Heart Rubber Stamps, 28 Second Ave., San Mateo, CA 94401: Catalog $2 (refundable with $20 purchase) ❖ Rubber stamps.

Darcie Hunter Publications, P.O. Box 1627, Grants Pass, OR 97526: Catalog $3 ❖ Rubber stamps. 800-453-1527.

ImaginAir Designs, 1007 Woodland NW, Albuquerque, NM 87107: Catalog $2 ❖ Aviation stamps and other designs. 505-345-2308.

Impress Me Rubber Stamps, 382 E. 520 North, American Fork, UT 84003: Catalog $3 ❖ Rubber stamps, storage cases, and accessories. 801-756-5447.

Imprints Graphic Studio Inc., 200 Vicery Rd., Apt. 10, Concord, Ontario, Canada L4K 3N6: Catalog $3 ❖ Rubber stamps and accessories.

Jackson Marketing Products, Brownsville Rd., Mt. Vernon, IL 62864: Free information ❖ Supplies and equipment for making regular and pre-inked rubber stamps. 800-STAMP-CALL.

Kidstamps, P.O. Box 18699, Cleveland Heights, OH 44118: Free catalog ❖ Rubber stamps. 800-727-5437.

Judi Kins, 17832 S. Hobart Blvd., Gardena, CA 90248: Catalog $5 ❖ Rubber stamps, paper, and accessories. 310-515-1115.

L.A. Stampworks, P.O. Box 2329, North Hollywood, CA 91610: Catalog $5 ❖ Rubber stamps. 818-761-8757.

Loving Little Rubber Stamps, 1 Federal St., Newburyport, MA 01950: Free catalog ❖ Mounted and unmounted rubber stamps.

Luv 'n Stuff, P.O. Box 85, Poway, CA 92074: Catalog $2 ❖ Rubber stamps. 619-748-8060.

Merry Mary-Anne's Rubber Art Stamps, Winterwood Pavilion, 2208 S. Nellis Blvd., Las Vegas, NV 89104: Catalog $2 (refundable) ❖ Rubber stamps.

Museum of Modern Rubber, 3015 Glendale Blvd., Ste. 100C, Los Angeles, CA 90039: Catalog $3 ❖ Rubber stamps. 213-662-1133.

National Stampagraphic, P.O. Box 370985, Las Vegas, NV 89137: Single issue $5 ❖ Published quarterly, includes articles and information of interest to rubber stamp users, and advertisements from rubber stamp hobbyists, manufacturers, and distributors. 702-233-4757.

100 Proof Press, RR 1, Box 136, Eaton, NY 13334: Catalog $4 (refundable with first $15 order) ❖ Rubber stamps on wood blocks, mounted only on self-sticking cushion, or unmounted and untrimmed. 315-684-3547.

Outstamping, 320 S. Archer St., Anaheim, CA 92804: Catalog $4 ❖ Rubber stamps. 714-535-1593.

Paper Angel, P.O. Box 1336, Santa Cruz, CA 95061: Brochure $2 ❖ Personalized rubber stamps, kits, and ink pads. 408-423-5115.

Penguin Stamps, 8716 176th St. SE, Snohomish, WA 98290: Catalog $2 ❖ Wacky words and other rubber stamps.

Pepperell Stamp Works, 548 High St., Bradford, PA 16701: Free information ❖ Civil War and other rubber stamps. 800-752-4656.

Personal Stamp Exchange, 360 Sutton Pl., Santa Rosa, CA 95407: Catalog $4 ❖ Rubber stamps. 800-782-6748; 800-782-6779 (in CA).

Purple Wave Stamp Designs, P.O. Box 5340, Ventura, CA 93005: Catalog $2.50 ❖ Mounted and unmounted rubber stamps.

Raindrops on Roses Rubber Stamp Company, 4808 Winterwood Dr., Raleigh, NC 27613: Catalog $3 ❖ Country stamp sets, brush markers, and supplies. 800-245-8617; 919-846-8617 (in NC).

Rubber Anarchy, P.O. Box 2559, Fontana, CA 92334: Catalog $3 ❖ Rubber stamps.

Rubber Poet Rubber Stamps, Box 218, Rockville, UT 84763: Catalog $2.50 (refundable) ❖ Rubber stamps.

Rubbernecker Stamp Company, 932 Laroda Ct., Ontario, CA 91762: Catalog $2 ❖ Original rubber stamps. Unmounted stamps available. 909-391-6388.

The Rubberstampler, 1945 Wealthy SE, Grand Rapids, MI 49506: Catalog $2 (refundable) ❖ Rubber stamps. 800-800-0424; 616-454-0424 (in MI).

Rural Route Mail Order Company, P.O. Box 6, Comstock, MI 49041: Catalog $3 ❖ Rubber stamps.

SonLight Impressions, 170 N. Maple St., Ste. 110, Corona, CA 91720: Catalog $3 ❖ Rubber stamps. 909-278-5656.

Stamp Affair, P.O. Box 7614, Round Lake, IL 60073: Catalog $5 ❖ Rubber stamps and accessories. 708-740-0967.

Stamp Francisco Rubber Stamps, 466 8th St., San Francisco, CA 04103: Catalog $5 ❖ Rubber stamps and accessories. 415-252-5975.

Stamp in the Hand Company, General Office, 20630 S. Leapwoods Ave., Ste. B, Carson, CA 90746: Catalog $3.75 ❖ Rubber stamps. 310-329-8555.

STAMPberry Farms, P.O. Box 370985, Las Vegas, NV 89137: Catalog $2 (refundable) ❖ Rubber stamps.

Stampendous Inc., 1357 S. Lewis St., Anaheim, CA 92805: Catalog $3 ❖ Rubber stamps, ink pads, brush markers, and glitter glue. 800-869-0474.

Stampinks, Unlimited Graphic Rubber Stamps, P.O. Box 97, Shortsville, NY 14548: Catalog $2.50 ❖ Rubber stamps.

Stardancer Stamp Company, 31 Green St., Medfield, MA 02052: Catalog $1 (refundable) ❖ Rubber stamps. 508-359-6705.

Jim Stephan's Rubber Art Ink, 1635 Notre Dame Ave., Belmont, CA 94002: Catalog $2 (refundable) ❖ Rubber stamps and accessories.

Stewart-Superior Corporation, 1800 W. Larchmont Ave., Chicago, IL 60613: Free information ❖ Rubber stamps, inks and ink pads, rollers, cleaners, sponge rubber, cements, and rubber stamp gum. 800-621-1205; 312-935-6025 (in IL).

Stubby Stampers, P.O. Box 1127, Brookhaven, MS 39601: Catalog $4 ❖ Rubber stamps. Available unmounted. 601-835-1835.

Synergistics Rubber Stamps, 6159 Manzanillo Dr., Goleta, CA 93117: Catalog $2 (refundable) ❖ Rubber stamps.

Under the Rubber Tree, P.O. Box 24291, Christiansted, St. Croix, Virgin Islands 00824: Catalog $2 (refundable) ❖ Rubber stamps that illustrate the life and styles of Caribbean people.

Visual Image, 1215 N. Grove St., Anaheim, CA 92806: Catalog $3 ❖ Rubber art stamps.

Viva Las Vegastamps, 330 S. Decatur Blvd., Ste. 226, Las Vegas, NV 89107: Catalog $4 ❖ Rubber stamps.

Wood Cellar Graphics, 87170 563rd Ave., Coleridge, NE 68727: Catalog $3 (refundable) ❖ Rubber stamps, ink pads, embossing supplies, and markers. 402-283-4725.

RUGBY

Mitre Sports, Genesco Park, Room 564, Nashville, TN 37202: Free information ❖ Balls and boots. 800-826-7650; 615-367-74754 (in TN).

Rugby & Soccer Supply, P.O. Box 565, Merrifield, VA 22116: Free catalog ❖ Balls, boots, jerseys, and shorts. 800-872-7842.

Rugby Imports Ltd., 885 Warren Ave., East Providence, RI 02914: Free catalog ❖ Clothing and shoes, balls, and other equipment. 800-431-4514; 401-438-2727 (in RI).

RUG MAKING

Braid-Aid, 466 Washington St., Pembroke, MA 02359: Catalog $4 ❖ Braided rug kits, braiding accessories, wool by the pound or yard, and latch-hooking, weaving, basket-making, shirret, and spinning supplies. 617-826-2560.

The Dorr Mill Store, P.O. Box 88, Guild, NH 03754: Free list ❖ Fine wools, fabrics, and hooking supplies. 800-846-DORR; 603-863-1197 (in NH).

Edgemont Yarn Services, P.O. Box 205, Washington, KY 41086: Free brochure ❖ Weaving and rug-making supplies. 800-446-5977.

Filature Lemieux Inc., Box 250, 125 Rt. 108, St. Ephrem, Quebec, Canada G0M 1R0: Free catalog ❖ Yarn for knitting, weaving, and making carpets and rugs. 418-484-2169.

Harry M. Fraser Company, 433 Duggins Rd., Stoneville, NC 27048: Catalog $6 ❖ Rug-hooking and braiding supplies. 910-573-9830.

Fredericksburg Rugs, P.O. Box 649, Fredericksburg, TX 78624: Catalog $4 ❖ Hooking and braiding rug-making supplies and rug-hooking kits. 210-997-6083.

Great Northern Weaving, P.O. Box 462, Kalamazoo, MI 49004: Catalog $1 ❖ Cotton and wool rags, warp, loopers, fillers, and braiding equipment. 616-341-9752.

Hooked on Rugs, 44492 Midway Dr., Novi, MI 48375: Brochure $3 ❖ Hand-dyed hooked rug kits. 810-344-4367.

I.W. Designs, 248 Outlook Dr., Pittsburgh, PA 15228: Free information ❖ Rug-hooking frame. 412-344-1257.

Jacqueline Designs, 237 Pine Point Rd., Scarborough, ME 04074: Catalog $7 ❖ Patterns, kits, and supplies.

Miller Rug Hooking, Nancy Miller, 2251 Ralston Rd., Sacramento, CA 95821: Information $4 ❖ Rug-hooking supplies and kits. 916-925-8017.

Claire Murray Inc., P.O. Box 390, Ascutney, VT 05030: Catalog $5 (refundable) ❖ Ready-made hand-hooked rugs or kits. 800-252-4733.

Oriental Rug Company, P.O. Box 205, Washington, KY 41086: Free information ❖ Rug-weaving wool and other supplies. 606-759-7614.

Penny Rugs & Runners, P.O. Box 1095345, Jefferson City, MO 65110: Brochure $2 with long SASE ❖ Kits for 18th-century designs and custom-dyed wool felts.

Red Clover Rugs, 2 Mill St., Middlebury, VT 05753: Catalog $3 ❖ Punch needle supplies. 800-858-YARN.

The Ruggery, 565 Cedar Swamp Rd., Glen Head, NY 11545: Catalog $2 ❖ Yarns, other rug-making supplies, patterns, and kits. 516-676-2056.

The Rugging Room, P.O. Box 824, Westford, MA 01886: Catalog $4.50 ❖ Rug-hooking supplies and publications. 800-822-2957; 508-692-8600 (in MA).

Sea Holly Hooked Rugs, 1906 N. Bayview Dr., Kill Devil Hills, NC 27948: Free information with long SASE ❖ Supplies, equipment, kits, patterns, and hand-dyed wools. 919-441-8961.

Shillcraft, 8899 Kelso Dr., Baltimore, MD 21221: Catalog $2 ❖ Latch-hook kits and supplies for rugs and wall hangings. 410-682-3060.

Sweet Briar Studio, Janet Dobson, 866 Main St., Hope Valley, RI 02832: Free catalog ❖ Traditional and primitive rug hooking supplies. 401-539-1009.

The White House, 653 E. Russell Lake Dr., Zionsville, IN 46077: Information $3 ❖ Primitive hooked rugs and kits.

RUG & CARPET RESTORATION

Restoration by Costikyan Ltd., 38-10 29th St., Long Island City, NY 11101: Free information ❖ Carpet re-weaving and restoration services. 800-247-RUGS.

RUGS & CARPETS

Access Carpet, P.O. Box 1007, Dalton, GA 30722: Free information ❖ Rugs and carpets. 800-848-7747.

American Blind, Wallpaper & Carpet Factory, 909 N. Sheldon Rd., Plymouth, MI 48170: Free information ❖ Wood, micro, mini, and vertical blinds. Also roller and pleated shades, wallpaper, and carpet. 800-889-2631 (for blinds and wallpaper); 800-346-0608 (for carpet).

American Southern Rug, 4422 Central Ave., St. Petersburg, FL 33711: Catalog $2 ❖ Authentic American handcrafted braided rugs. 800-541-7847.

Armstrong World Industries, P.O. Box 3001, Lancaster, PA 17604: Free information ❖ Carpet and rugs. 717-397-0611.

The Barn, Market St., Lehman, PA 18627: Free brochure ❖ Custom-woven rag, hand-stenciled rugs, and hand-woven throw rugs. Also stair carpeting and runners. 717-675-4232.

❖ RUGS & CARPETS ❖

Bearden Brothers Carpet, 4109 S. Dixie Hwy., Dalton, GA 30721: Catalog $3 ❖ Carpet and other floor coverings. 800-433-0074.

Best Wallcoverings Inc., 2618 Avenue U, Brooklyn, NY 11229: Free information ❖ Wallpaper and rugs. 800-624-1224.

Kimberly Black Rugs & Accessories, P.O. Box 472927, Charlotte, NC 28247: Catalog $3 ❖ Flat-braid and woven flat weave rugs. 800-296-6099.

Betsy Bourdon, Weaver, Scribner Hill, Wolcott, VT 05680: Catalog $3 ❖ Rugs, linens, and hand-woven blankets. 802-472-6508.

Bucklers Carpet Inc., P.O. Box 9, Dayton, GA 30722: Free information ❖ Rugs and carpets. 800-232-5537.

J.R. Burrows & Company, P.O. Box 522, Rockland, MA 02370: Catalog $5 ❖ Period carpet reproductions by special order and wallpaper and fabrics. 800-347-1795.

Carousel Carpet Mills Inc., One Carousel Ln., Ukiah, CA 95482: Catalog $10 ❖ Natural fiber custom carpets and rugs in cotton, jute, wool, and silk. 707-485-0333.

Carpet Express, 915 Market St., Dayton, GA 30720: Free information ❖ Carpet and vinyl. 800-922-5582.

Carpet Outlet, Box 417, Miles City, MT 59301: Free information ❖ Carpet and area rugs. 800-225-4351; 800-233-0208 (in MT).

Casa Dos Tapetes De Arraiolos Inc., D & D Building, 9793rd Ave., New York, NY 10022: Free brochure ❖ Portuguese needlepoint rugs. 212-688-9330.

Country Braid House, 462 Main St., Tilton, NH 03276: Free brochure ❖ Braided wool rugs, kits, and supplies. 603-286-4511.

Country Manor, Mail Order Department, Rt. 211, P.O. Box 520, Sperryville, VA 22740: Catalog $3 ❖ Hand-woven cotton rugs, kitchen utensils, and other country crafts. 800-344-8354.

Cyrus Carpets, 319 5th Ave., New York, NY 10016: Free information ❖ Persian and Oriental rugs. 212-213-8400.

Dalton Paradise Carpets, P.O. Box 1819, Rocky Face, GA 30740: Free information ❖ Carpets, rugs, and other floor coverings. 800-338-7811.

Elkes Carpet Outlet Inc., 1585 Bethel Dr., High Point, NC 27260: Free information with long SASE ❖ First-quality, irregulars, close-outs, and discontinued carpet. 800-727-3553.

Factory Direct Carpet Outlet, P.O. Box 417, Miles City, MT 59301: Free brochure ❖ Rugs and carpets. 800-225-4351; 800-233-0208 (in MT).

Family Heirloom Weavers, 775 Meadowview Dr., Red Lion, PA 17356: Catalog $4 ❖ All-wool carpets with historic patterns, from the late 18th-century to the early 1920s. 717-246-2431.

Gazebo of New York, 127 E. 57th St., New York, NY 10022: Catalog $6 ❖ Handmade braided rugs and quilted pillows. 212-832-7077.

Heirloom Rugs, 28 Harlem St., Rumford, RI 02916: Catalog $3.50 ❖ Hand-hooked rugs. 401-438-5672.

Heritage Rugs, Box 195, 4241 Sunny Side Dr., Buckingham, PA 18912: Catalog $1 ❖ Custom hand-woven rag wool rugs. 215-794-3465.

Home Etc., Palo Verde at 34th St., P.O. Box 28806, Tucson, AZ 85726: Free catalog ❖ Bedding ensembles, curtains, bedspreads and comforters, rugs, linens and pillows, and towels. 800-362-8415.

Charles W. Jacobsen Inc., 401 N. Salina St., Syracuse, NY 13203: Free brochure ❖ Hand-woven Oriental rugs. 315-422-7832.

Johnson's Carpets, 3239 S. Dixie Hwy., Dalton, GA 30720: Free information ❖ Carpets and rugs. 800-235-1079; 707-277-2775 (in GA).

Lee's Carpet Showcase, 3068 N. Dug Gap Rd., Dayton, GA 30720: Free information ❖ Carpet and Oriental rugs, vinyl and wood flooring, and accessories. 800-433-8479.

Lizzie & Charlie's Rag Rugs, 210 E. Bullion Ave., Marysvale, UT 84750: Free brochure ❖ Handmade rag rugs. 801-326-4213.

Long's Carpet Inc., 2625 S. Dixie Hwy., Dalton, GA 30720: Free information ❖ Carpets. 800-545-5664.

Luv Those Rugs, 103 N. Main St., Box 236, Elkton, KY 42220: Free brochure ❖ Country-style braided rugs and furniture. 502-265-5550.

M.C. Ltd., P.O. Box 17696, Whitefish Bay, WI 53217: Free information ❖ Pillows and steerhide rugs. 800-236-5224; 414-263-5422 (in WI).

MDC Direct Inc., P.O. Box 569, Marietta, GA 30061: Free information ❖ Wood blinds, cellular shades, and area rugs. 800-892-2083.

Michigan Custom Area Rugs, 1508 Rockwell Dr., Midland, MI 48640: Free brochure ❖ Custom area rugs in any size or shape. 517-839-8230.

Mills River Industries, 713 Old Orchard Rd., Hendersonville, NC 28739: Catalog $1 ❖ Flat-braided oval and round rugs. 704-687-9778.

Abraham Moheban & Son, 139 E. 57th St., 3rd Floor, New York, NY 10022: Free information ❖ Antique European and Oriental carpets. 212-758-3900.

Fred Moheban Gallery, 730 5th Ave., New York, NY 10019: Free information ❖ Rare and unusual decorative Oriental and European carpets and rugs. 212-397-9060.

Claire Murray Inc., P.O. Box 390, Ascutney, VT 05030: Catalog $5 ❖ Hand-hooked rugs and hand-sewn quilts. Available in kits. 800-252-4733.

Network Floor Covering, Division Parkers Carpet, 3200 Dug Gap Rd., Dalton, GA 30720: Free brochure ❖ Stain-protected carpets. 800-442-2013.

Paradise Mills Inc., P.O. Box 2488, Dalton, GA 30722: Free information ❖ Rugs and carpets. 800-338-7811.

Peerless Imported Rugs, 3033 Lincoln Ave., Chicago, IL 60657: Catalog $1 ❖ Hand and machine-woven Oriental rugs, rag rugs, Navajo rugs, colonial braids, grass rugs, and tapestries from Europe. 800-621-6573.

Quality Discount Carpet, 1207 W. Walnut Ave., Dalton, GA 30720: Free brochure ❖ Carpets. 800-233-0993.

Rave Carpets, 2875 Cleveland Rd., Dalton, GA 30721: Free information ❖ Residential and commercial carpets. 800-942-6969; 706-259-4864 (in GA).

The Rug Store, 2201 Crownpoint Executive Dr., Charlotte, NC 28227: Catalog $5 (refundable) ❖ Area rugs. 800-257-5078; 704-845-8591 (in NC).

S & S Carpet Mills, 200 Howell Dr., P.O. Box 1568, Dalton, GA 30722: Free brochure ❖ Carpet. 800-363-9034.

Santa Fe Interiors, 214 Old Santa Fe Trail, Santa Fe, NM 87501: Portfolio $5 ❖ Handmade 100-percent traditional and contemporary southwestern wool rugs. 505-988-2227.

Southern Rug, 2325 Anderson Rd., Crescent Springs, KY 41017: Catalog $5 ❖ Handcrafted flat-braided rugs in blended wool yarns. 800-541-RUGS.

Stylmark Carpet Mills Inc., 3358 Carpet Capitol Dr., Dalton, GA 30720: Free information ❖ Residential and commercial carpet. 800-532-2257.

Warehouse Carpets Inc., P.O. Box 3233, Dalton, GA 30721: Free information ❖ Rugs and carpets. 707-226-2229.

Whipp Trading Company, RR 1, Arrasmith Trail, Ames, IA 50010: Free catalog ❖ Sheepskin rugs, slippers, mittens, and hats. 800-533-9447.

Thomas K. Woodard American Antiques & Quilts, 506 E. 74th St., 5th Floor, New York, NY 10021: Catalog $6 ❖ Classic American-style room size area rugs and runners. 800-332-7847; 212-988-2906 (in NY).

Yankee Pride, 29 Parkside Circle, Braintree, MA 02184: Catalog $3 (refundable) ❖ Handcrafted quilts, Dhurries, comforters and bedspreads, and hand-braided, hooked, and rag rugs. 617-848-7610.

York Interiors Inc., 2821 E. Prospect Rd., York, PA 17402: Free brochure ❖ Oriental rugs. 800-723-7029.

Zaki Oriental Rugs, 1634 N. Main St., High Point, NC 27262: Free information ❖ Oriental rugs. 910-884-4407.

RUNNING, JOGGING & WALKING

Clothing & Shoes

Adidas USA, 5675 N. Blackstock Rd., Spartanburg, SC 29303: Free list of retail sources ❖ Shoes, shorts, singlets, socks, sweatbands, and warm-up suits. 800-423-4327.

Alchester Mills Company Inc., 1160 Wright Ave., Camden, NJ 08103: Free information ❖ Socks, sweatbands, and safety vests. 609-964-9700.

Alpha Shirt Company, 401 E. Hunting Park Ave., Philadelphia, PA 19124: Free information ❖ Shirts and tops. 800-523-4585; 215-291-0300 (in PA).

Asics Tiger Corporation, 10540 Talbert Ave., West Building, Fountain Valley, CA 92708: Free information ❖ Shoes, shorts, rainsuits, singlets, and warm-up suits. 800-678-9435.

Augusta Sportswear, Box 14939, Augusta, GA 30919: Free information ❖ Shirts and tops. 800-237-6695; 706-860-4633 (in GA).

California Best, 970 Broadway, Ste. 104, Chula Vista, CA 91911: Free catalog ❖ Shoes and clothing. 800-438-9327.

Champion Products Inc., 475 Corporate Square Dr., Winston Salem, NC 27105: Free information ❖ Shorts, singlets, socks, and warm-up suits.

Converse Inc., 1 Fordham Rd., North Reading, MA 01864: Free information ❖ Shoes, shorts, singlets, socks, sweatbands, and warm-up suits. 800-428-2667; 508-664-1100 (in MA).

Dolfin International Corporation, P.O. Box 98, Shillington, PA 19607: Free information ❖ Shorts, rainsuits, singlets, and warm-up suits. 800-441-0818; 215-775-5500 (in PA).

Eastbay Running Store Inc., 427 3rd St., Wausau, WI 54403: Free information ❖ Shoes and clothing. 800-826-2205.

Empire Sporting Goods Manufacturing Company, 443 Broadway, New York, NY 10013: Free information ❖ Rainsuits. 800-221-3455; 212-966-0880 (in NY).

Faber Brothers, 4141 S. Pulaski Rd., Chicago, IL 60632: Free information ❖ Pedometers, rainsuits, and safety vests. 312-376-9300.

Gold's Gym, 360 Hampton Dr., Venice, CA 90291: Free information ❖ Shirts and tops. 800-457-5375; 213-392-3005 (in CA).

Las Vegas Discount Golf & Tennis, 5325 S. Valley View Blvd., Ste. 10, Las Vegas, NV 89118: Free catalog ❖ Shoes and clothing. 702-798-7777.

Leisure Unlimited, P.O. Box 308, Cedarburg, WI 53012: Free information ❖ Pedometers and rainsuits. 800-323-5118; 414-377-7454 (in WI).

Movin USA, 7411 W. Boston, Ste. 1, Chandler, AZ 85225: Free information ❖ Shirts and tops. 800-445-6684.

New Balance Athletic Shoe Inc., 38 Everett St., Boston, MA 02134: Free list of retail sources ❖ Shoes, shorts, singlets, raincoats, sweatbands, and warm-up suits. 800-253-7463.

North Face, 999 Harrison St., Berkeley, CA 94710: Free list of retail sources ❖ Rainsuits. 800-447-2333.

Okun Brothers Shoes, Attention: Mail Order Department, 356 E. South St., Kalamazoo, MI 49007: Free catalog ❖ Shoes for men, women, and children. 800-433-6344.

Pearl Izumi, 2300 Central Ave., Boulder, CO 80301: Free information ❖ Shirts and tops. 800-328-8488; 303-938-1700 (in CO).

Puma USA Inc., 147 Centre St., Brockton, MA 02403: Free information with long SASE ❖ Shoes, shorts, singlets, rainsuits, socks, and warm-up suits. 508-583-9100.

Road Runner Sports, 6310 Nancy Ridge Rd., Ste. 101, San Diego, CA 92121: Free price list ❖ Shoes, other walking accessories, and fitness apparel. 800-551-5558.

Safesport Manufacturing Company, 5151 Bannock St., Denver, CO 80216: Free information ❖ Pedometers, rainsuits, and safety vests. 800-433-6506.

Shaffer Sportswear, 224 N. Washington, Neosho, MO 64850: Free information ❖ Shirts and tops. 417-451-9444.

Spalding Sports Worldwide, 425 Meadow St., P.O. Box 901, Chicopee, MA 01021: Free list of retail sources ❖ Shoes, shorts, singlets, sweatbands, and warm-up suits. 800-225-6601.

Spiegel, P.O. Box 182563, Columbus, OH 43218: Free information ❖ Men and women's walking shoes. 800-345-4500.

Tennis Gear & Running Center, P.O. Box 1486, Cumberland, MD 21502: Free price list ❖ Clothing and shoes. 301-729-0896.

Terramar Sports Ltd., 10 Midland Ave., Port Chester, NY 10573: Free information ❖ Insulated outdoor clothing. 800-468-7455.

Venus Knitting Mills Inc., 140 Spring St., Murray Hill, NJ 07974: Free information ❖ Shorts, singlets, sweatbands, and warm-up suits. 800-955-4200; 908-464-2400 (in NJ).

Pedometers & Stopwatches

Accusplit, 2290-A Ringwood Ave., San Jose, CA 95131: Free information ❖ Pedometers and sports watches. 800-538-9750; 408-432-8228 (in CA).

ACT USA, P.O. Box 5490, Evanston, IL 60204: Free list of retail sources ❖ Miniature computerized display for speed, distance, heart rate, and other functions. 800-804-7777.

Aristo Import Company Inc., 15 Hunt Rd., Orangeburg, NY 10962: Free information ❖ Pedometers for step counting, walking, or jogging. 800-352-6304; 914-359-0720 (in NY).

Compass Industries Inc., 104 E. 25th St., New York, NY 10010: Free information ❖ Pedometers. 800-221-9904.

Creative Health Products, 1000 Saddle Ridge Rd., Plymouth, MI 48170: Free catalog ❖ Pedometers and pulse monitors. 800-742-4478.

Dynamic Classics Ltd., 58 2nd Ave., Brooklyn, NY 11215: Free information ❖ Pedometers. 718-369-4160.

Faber Brothers, 4141 S. Pulaski Rd., Chicago, IL 60632: Free information ❖ Pedometers, rainsuits, and safety vests. 312-376-9300.

General Sportcraft Company, 140 Woodbine Rd., Bergenfield, NJ 07621: Free information ❖ Pedometers. 201-384-4242.

Innovative Time Corporation, 5858 Edison Pl., Carlsbad, CA 92008: Free information ❖ Pedometers. 800-765-0595; 619-438-0595 (in CA).

KNR Associates, 1307 Hickory St., Onalaska, WI 54650: Brochure $1 ❖ Pedometers. 800-234-1770.

Leisure Unlimited, P.O. Box 308, Cedarburg, WI 53012: Free information ❖ Pedometers and rainsuits. 800-323-5118; 414-377-7454 (in WI).

Precise International, 15 Corporate Dr., Orangeburg, NY 10962: Free information ❖ Walking and walking/jogging pedometers. 800-431-2996; 914-365-3500 (in NY).

Safesport Manufacturing Company, 5151 Bannock St., Denver, CO 80216: Free information ❖ Pedometers, rainsuits, and safety vests. 800-433-6506.

Silva Compass, P.O. Box 966, Binghamton, NY 13902: Free information ❖ Pedometers. 800-847-1460.

Sportline, 847 McGlincey Ln., Campbell, CA 95008: Free information ❖ Pedometers. 408-377-8900.

SAFES

American Security Products Company, 11925 Pacific Ave., Fontana, CA 92335: Free information ❖ Gun and other safes for homes and offices. 800-421-6142.

Kingsbery Safes, Kingsbery Mfg. Corporation, Crystal City, TX 78839: Free brochure ❖ Safes for collectibles and security. 800-445-0763.

Safe Specialties Inc., 10932 Murdock & Lovell Rd., Knoxville, TN 37932: Catalog $2 ❖ Office and home safes. 800-695-2815.

Treadlok, 1764 Granby St. NE, Roanoke, VA 24012: Free catalog ❖ Safes for guns and valuables. 800-729-8732.

Value-Tique Inc., P.O. Box 67, Leonia, NJ 07605: Free information ❖ Safes. 201-461-6500.

SAFETY & EMERGENCY EQUIPMENT

The Alan Company, 7909 Walerga Rd., Antelope, CA 95843: Free information ❖ Pepper sprays.

Champion America Inc., 1333 Highland Rd., Macedonia, OH 44056: Free catalog ❖ Safety-related products and identification, caution, warning signs, and markers. 800-521-7000.

Conney Safety Products, 3202 Latham Dr., Madison, WI 53713: Free catalog ❖ First aid supplies, survival equipment, and safety devices. 800-356-9100.

Direct Safety Company, 7815 S. 46th St., Phoenix, AZ 85044: Free catalog ❖ Safety equipment. 800-528-7405.

Enviro-Safety Products, 21344 Ave. 322, Woodlake, CA 93286: Free information ❖ Dust protection helmets. 800-637-6606.

Lab Safety Supply Inc., P.O. Box 1368, Janesville, WI 53547: Free information ❖ Dust protection masks. 800-356-0783.

Moore Medical Corporation, 389 John Downey Dr., P.O. Box 2740, New Britain, CT 06050: Free catalog ❖ Occupational safety and health accessories. 800-234-1464.

Nitro-Pak Preparedness Center, 151 N. Main St., Heber City, UT 84032: Catalog $3 ❖ Survival equipment and supplies, freeze-dried and dehydrated foods, books, and videos. 800-866-4876.

Northern Safety Company Inc., P.O. Box 4250, Utica, NY 13504: Free information ❖ Dust protection masks. 800-631-1246.

Out N Back, 1797 S. State St., Orem, UT 84058: Free catalog ❖ Survival equipment and supplies for outdoor recreational activities. 800-533-7415.

Perfectly Safe, 7245 Whipple Ave. NW, North Canton, OH 44720: Free catalog ❖ Safety items for children age 3 to 6. 216-494-2323.

The Safety Zone, P.O. Box 0019, Hanover, PA 17333: Free catalog ❖ Safety and security products. 800-999-3030.

Seton Identification Products, 20 Thompson Rd., Branford, CT 06405: Free catalog ❖ Identification and safety-related products. 800-243-6624; 203-488-8059 (in CT).

The Survival Center, P.O. Box 234, McKenna, WA 98558: Catalog $2 ❖ Survival equipment for outdoor activities. 206-458-6778.

United States Survival Society, 1223 Wilshire Blvd., #492, Santa Monica, CA 90403: Free catalog ❖ Emergency foods, water, solar radios, and survival and emergency equipment. 800-2-SURVIVE; 310-652-4777 (in CA).

WorkAbles for Women, Deborah Evans Crawford, Oak Valley, Clinton, PA 15026: Free catalog ❖ Gloves, hats, T-shirts, socks, outdoor clothing, rain gear, and personal safety items for women. 800-862-9317.

Worldwide Outfitters, 117 Benedict St., Waterbury, CT 06722: Free catalog ❖ Gloves, aprons, safety glasses, hearing protection, disposable clothing, and shoes and boots. 800-243-3570; 800-243-3571 (in CT).

SAILBOARDS

Skip Hutchison, Rastaboards-Surf-Sail-Snowboards, 4748 NE 11th Ave., Fort Lauderdale, FL 33334: Free information with long SASE ❖ Sailboards, surfboards, and snowboards. 954-491-7992.

Murrays WaterSports, P.O. Box 490, Carpinteria, CA 93014: Free information ❖ Catamaran and windsurfing accessories. 800-788-8964.

Sailboard Warehouse Inc., 300 S. Owasso, St. Paul, MN 55117: Catalog $1.50 ❖ Sailboards, sails and masts, wet suits, roof racks, harnesses, books, and videos. 800-992-7245; 612-482-9995 (in MN).

Windsurfing Warehouse, 428 S. Airport Blvd., South San Francisco, CA 94080: Free catalog ❖ Sailboards. 800-628-4599; 415-588-1714 (in CA).

SCIENCE KITS & PROJECTS

Advanced Sciences, 255 N. El Cielo Rd., Palm Springs, CA 92262: Catalog $4 ❖ Kits and other science products. 619-327-7355.

American Science & Surplus, 3605 Howard St., Skokie, IL 60076: Catalog $1 ❖ Surplus science and electro-mechanical supplies, equipment, and kits. 708-982-0870.

Edlie Electronics, 2700 Hempstead Tnpk., Levittown, NY 11756: Free catalog ❖ Electronics kits, parts, and supplies. 516-735-3330.

Edmund Scientific Company, Edscorp Building, Barrington, NJ 08007: Free catalog ❖ Microscopes, magnifiers, weather forecasting instruments, magnets, telescopes, lasers, and other optical, scientific, and educational items. 609-573-6260.

The Electronic Goldmine, P.O. Box 5408, Scottsdale, AZ 85261: Free catalog ❖ Science kits and supplies. 602-451-7454.

Gardens for Growing People, P.O. Box 630, Point Reyes Station, CA 94956: Free catalog ❖ Gardening supplies, kits, and resources for garden-based education. 415-663-9433.

J.L. Hammett Company, P.O. Box 9057, Braintree, MA 02184: Free catalog ❖ Science kits and projects, microscopes, laboratory apparatus, rock collections, magnets, astronomy charts, and anatomical models. 617-848-1000.

Heathkit Educational Systems, P.O. Box 1288, Benton Harbor, MI 49023: Free catalog ❖ Computers and robotic projects, TVs, home accessories, and educational and electronic kits. 800-253-0570.

Hobby World Ltd. of Montreal, 5450 Sherbrooke St. West, Montreal, Quebec, Canada H4A 1V9: Catalog $5 ❖ Airplanes, helicopters, cars and trucks, ships, military vehicles, and science models. 514-481-5434.

Hubbard Scientific Company, 3101 Iris Ave., Boulder, CO 80301: Free catalog ❖ Science equipment and supplies for life and earth science, introductory physical science, and energy, health and physiology, and topography projects. 800-323-8368.

Information Unlimited, P.O. Box 716, Amherst, NH 03031: Catalog $1 ❖ Lasers, communication equipment, Tesla coils and experiments, mini radios, rocket equipment, flying saucers, and other kits. 603-673-4730.

Merrell Scientific/World of Science, 1665 Buffalo Rd., Rochester, NY 14624: Catalog $2 ❖ Chemicals, glassware, and laboratory equipment. Also biology, nature, physical and earth science, astronomy, and model rocketry supplies and equipment. 716-426-1540.

Nasco, 901 Janesville Ave., Fort Atkinson, WI 53538: Free catalog ❖ Science supplies and kits, microscopes and dissection instruments, rock collections, magnets, electric motors, ultraviolet lighting equipment, astronomy charts and star maps, and anatomical models. 800-558-9595.

The Nature Company, Catalog Division, P.O. Box 188, Florence, KY 41022: Free catalog ❖ Science supplies, kits, books, toys, novelties, and gifts. 800-227-1114.

Radio Shack, Division Tandy Corporation, One Tandy Center, Fort Worth, TX 76102: Free information ❖ Electronic science projects, kits, electronics equipment, and supplies. 817-390-3011.

Rockville Creative Learning Inc., 785F Rockville Pike, Ste. 515, Rockville, MD 20852: Free catalog ❖ Children's educational science kits and workbooks. 800-588-9880.

Silicon Valley Surplus, 1273 Industrial Pkwy., Ste. 460, P.O. Box 55125, Hayward, CA 94544: Free information ❖ Light and motion projects, laser applications, computer interface equipment, and other kits. 510-582-6602.

Uptown Sales Inc., 33 N. Main St., Chambersburg, PA 17201: Catalog $1 ❖ Science kits for amateur scientists. 800-548-9941.

Wooley Bugger Entomology Company, P.O. Box 7571, Boulder, CO 80306: Free brochure ❖ Tools for the collection, preservation, and display of aquatic and terrestrial insects.

SCOOTERS

Dominion Skate Company Ltd., 45 Railroad St., Brampton, Ontario, Canada L6X 1G4: Free information ❖ Roller skates and scooters. 416-453-9860.

Motoboard International, P.O. Box 2224, Los Banos, CA 93635: Information $2 ❖ Motorized scooters. 209-827-1600.

National Sporting Goods Corporation, 25 Brighton Ave., Passaic, NJ 07055: Free information ❖ Roller skates, scooters, skateboards, and protective gear. 201-779-2323.

Roller Derby Skate Company, Box 930, Litchfield, IL 62056: Free information ❖ Skateboards, roller and in-line skates, and scooters. 217-324-3961.

Ron's Rad Toys, 4610 S. 133rd, Ste. 104, Omaha, NE 68137: Free information ❖ Fold-down motorized scooters and accessories. 800-841-3625; 402-333-6950 (in NE).

Roller Derby Skate Company, Box 930, Litchfield, IL 62056: Free information ❖ Roller skates, scooters, and skateboards. 217-324-3961.

Saucony/Hyde, 13 Centennial Dr., Peabody, MA 01961: Free information ❖ Roller skates, scooters, and skateboards. 800-365-7282.

Scooterworks USA, 5709 N. Ravenswood, Chicago, IL 60660: Free information ❖ Scooters, parts, and accessories. 312-338-4242.

L. Scot Enterprises, Box 1798, Sulsun City, CA 94585: Free brochure with long SASE ❖ Motorized scooters. 707-422-6755.

Rich Suski, 7061 County Road 108, Town Creek, AL 35672: Free catalog ❖ Cushman parts for vintage motorbikes and scooters. 205-685-2510.

SCOUTING

Boy Scouts of America, P.O. Box 909, Pineville, NC 28134: Free catalog ❖ Uniforms and insignia, camping equipment, sportswear, books, and scouting equipment and supplies. 800-323-0732.

Girl Scout Catalog, 420 5th Ave., New York, NY 10018: Free catalog ❖ Uniforms and insignia, camping equipment, sportswear, books, jewelry, and gifts. 212-852-8000.

J.C. Penney Company Inc., Catalog Division, Atlanta, GA 30390: Free information ❖ Boy and girl scout equipment and supplies. 800-222-6161.

SEASHELLS

Benjane Arts, P.O. Box 298, West Hempstead, NY 11552: Catalog $5 ❖ Seashells. 516-483-1330.

Bourget Bros., 1636 11th St., Santa Monica, CA 90404: Catalog $3 ❖ Seashells, jewelry-making tools and supplies, gemstones, beads, and bead-stringing supplies. 310-450-6556.

Creative Craft House, Box 2567, Bullhead City, AZ 86430: Catalog $2 (refundable) ❖ Seashells, pine cones, and craft supplies.

Ebersole Lapidary Supply Inc., 11417 West Hwy. 54, Wichita, KS 67209: Catalog $2 ❖ Shark teeth, cameo shells, murex or fox shells, tiger cowries, mushroom corals, seashells from worldwide sources, and lapidary equipment. 316-722-4771.

Ed's House of Gems, 7712 NE Sandy Blvd., Portland, OR 97211: Free information with long SASE ❖ Seashells, crystals, minerals, gemstones, lapidary equipment, mountings, and Native American relics. 503-284-8990.

Herkimer Diamond Mines, P.O. Box 510, Herkimer, NY 13350: Free information ❖ Petrified wood products, seashells, craft supplies, minerals and rocks, quartz crystals, and gifts. 315-891-7355.

Indian Jewelers Supply Company, 601 E. Coal Ave., Gallup, NM 87301: Catalog $6 ❖ Precious and base metals, findings, metalsmithing and lapidary tools and supplies, semi-precious stones, seashells, and coral. 505-722-4451.

Jeanne's Rock & Jewelry, 5420 Bissonet, Bellaire, TX 77401: Price list $1 ❖ Seashells, petrified wood products, lapidary supplies, and gifts. 713-664-2988.

Nature's Jewelry, 222 Mill Rd., Chelmsford, MA 01824: Free catalog ❖ Leaves, seashells, and other natural objects transformed into jewelry by preservation in precious metals. 800-333-3235.

J.F. Ray, RR 1, Box 213, Olar, SC 29845: Catalog $3 (refundable) ❖ Shark teeth jewelry, fossils, seashells, beach-combing treasures, and amber with inclusions.

Riviera Lapidary Supply, 30595 Mesquite, Riviera, TX 78379: Catalog $3 ❖ Seashells, beads, cabochons, slabs, cabbing rough gems, and crystals. 512-296-3958.

Shell-A-Rama, Box 291327, Fort Lauderdale, FL 33329: Catalog $2 ❖ Seashells for crafts, decorations, and collections. 954-434-2818.

U.S. Shell Inc., P.O. Box 1033, Port Isabel, TX 78578: Free catalog ❖ Shells for crafting and seashell novelties. 210-943-1709.

What on Earth Naturally, 6250 Busch Blvd., Columbus, OH 43229: Free information ❖ Minerals, fossils, jewelry, gemstones, and shells. 614-436-1458.

SEPTIC TANKS

Big K Inc., P.O. Box 568144, Atlanta, GA 31156: Free information ❖ Additive for septic tank maintenance. 800-533-2445.

Krane Products, P.O. Box 521, Larchmont, NY 10538: Free information ❖ Septic tank maintenance products. 800-544-4074.

SEWING

Dress Forms

Bonfit America Inc., 5959 Triumph St., Commerce, CA 90040: Free information ❖ No-paper pattern-maker that adjusts to different sizes and styles. 800-342-9555.

CSZ Enterprises Inc., 1288 W. 11th St., Ste. 200, Tracy, CA 95376: Free information ❖ Custom-made or make-them-yourself kits for dress and pants forms. 209-832-4324.

Dress Rite Forms, 3817 N. Pulaski, Chicago, IL 60641: Free information ❖ Dress-forms in all sizes and shapes. 312-588-5761.

Notions & Supplies

A.C.S., 447 W. 36th St., New York, NY 10018: Free catalog ❖ Notions, thread, lining, patterns, cutting tools, fasteners, and sewing machines. 800-SEW-TRUE.

AK Sew & Serge, 1602 6th St. SE, Winter Haven, FL 33880: Catalog $5 ❖ Heirloom and fashion sewing and quilting supplies. 800-299-8096; 813-299-3080 (in FL).

Atlanta Thread & Supply, 695 Red Oak Rd., Stockbridge, GA 30281: Catalog $1 ❖ Notions and machines. 800-847-1001.

Baer Fabrics, 515 E. Market St., Louisville, KY 40202: Catalog $3 ❖ Sewing notions and trim. 800-769-7776.

Banasch, 2810 Highland Ave., Cincinnati, OH 45212: Free catalog ❖ Beads, pearls, notions, and buttons. 800-543-0355; 513-731-2040 (in OH).

Baubanbea Enterprises, P.O. Box 1205, Smithtown, NY 11787: Catalog $1 ❖ Rhinestones, sequins, beads, jewels, lace, appliques, fringes, trim, feathers, imported and domestic fabrics, and silk flowers. 516-724-4661.

❖ SEWING ❖

Bay Area Tailoring Supply, 8000 Capwell Dr., Oakland, CA 94621: Free information ❖ Tailoring supplies. 800-359-0400; 510-635-1100 (in CA).

Bee Lee Company, Box 36108, Dallas, TX 75235: Free catalog ❖ Notions, belt buckles and snaps, trims, zippers, interfacings, threads, and notions. 800-527-5271.

Bridal by The Yard, P.O. Box 2492, Springfield, OH 45501: Free information ❖ Re-embroidered Alencon, Schiffli lace, imported Chantilly and Venice lace, satins, taffeta, organza, millinery supplies, trims, and notions. 513-325-2847.

Britex, 146 Geary St., San Francisco, CA 94108: Free information ❖ Cordings and braids. 415-392-2910.

BUTTON SHOP

SPECIALIZING IN SEWING SERVICES

The Button Shop, P.O. Box 1065, Oak Park, IL 60304: Free catalog ❖ Discount sewing supplies, hard-to-find sewing machine parts, and zippers cut to your need. 708-795-1234.

Buttons Unlimited, 205 E. Casino Rd., Everett, WA 98204: Catalog $2 (refundable) ❖ Classic to unique buttons.

Clotilde, 2 Sew Smart Way, B8031, Stevens Point, WI 54481: Free catalog ❖ Notions, books, patterns, and videos. 800-772-2891.

Coastal Button Supply, P.O. Box 160, Mt. Airy, MD 21771: Free catalog ❖ Buttons. 301-829-0201.

Craft Gallery Ltd., P.O. Box 145, Swampscott, MA 01907: Catalog $2 ❖ Threads, fibers, books, fabrics, and supplies for sewing, crochet, and stitchery crafts. 508-744-2334.

The Creative Needle, 6905 S. Broadway, Ste. 113, Littleton, CO 80122: Catalog $1 ❖ Heirloom sewing, smocking, stitchery, and quilting supplies. 303-794-7312.

Delectable Mountain Cloth, 125 Main St., Brattleboro, VT 05301: Brochure $1 with long SASE ❖ Buttons and natural fabrics from worldwide sources.

DK Sports, Division Daisy Kingdom, 3720 NW Yeon Ave., Portland, OR 97210: Free information ❖ Rainwear, outerwear fabrics, and notions. 800-234-6688.

Dogwood Lane Buttons, Box 145, Dugger, IN 47848: Catalog $2.50 (refundable) ❖ Handmade porcelain buttons. 800-648-2213.

Dritz Corporation, P.O. Box 5028, Spartanburg, SC 29304: Free information ❖ Marking pens, awls, cutting mats, cutters, scissors, needles, straight and safety pins, zipper glides, craft tape, glue sticks, tape measures, and other notions. 800-845-4948.

Fashion Touches, 170 Elm St., P.O. Box 804, Bridgeport, CT 06604: Catalog $1 ❖ Covered belts and buttons. 203-333-7738.

Fiskars Scissors, P.O. Box 8027, Wausau, WI 54402: Free information ❖ Scissors, safety scissors for children, and sharpeners.

Garden Fairies Trading Company, 309 S. Main St., Sebastopol, CA 95472: Catalog $4 ❖ Handmade collar and smocking patterns, French and Battenberg lace, Swiss embroideries, soft toy patterns, books, designer fabrics, and cotton fabrics. 800-925-9919.

Green Pepper, 1285 River Rd., Eugene, OR 97404: Catalog $2 ❖ Buckles, Velcro and fasteners, zippers, buttons, notions, and kits for coats and jackets, ski wear, water-repellent clothing, and duffel bags.

Greenberg & Hammer Inc., 24 W. 57th St., New York, NY 10019: Free catalog ❖ Tailoring supplies and notions. 800-955-5135.

Hancock Fabrics, 3841 Hinkleville Rd., Paducah, KY 42001: Free information ❖ Quilting supplies, fabrics, and notions. 800-845-8723.

Handcrafted Wood Products, 11280 US Hwy. 90, Daphne, AL 36526: Free information ❖ Wood-crafted spool and bobbin organizer and wall rack for serger cones. 334-633-4570.

Harper House, P.O. Box 39, Williamstown, PA 17098: Catalog $6 ❖ Historic and ethnic garment patterns, sewing notions, and books. 717-647-7807.

Hedgehog Handworks, P.O. Box 45384, Westchester, CA 90045: Catalog $5 (refundable with $30 order) ❖ Semi-precious beads, sewing notions, gold and silver threads, and needlecraft and embroidery supplies. 310-670-6040.

Home-Sew Inc., P.O. Box 4099, Bethlehem, PA 18018: Catalog $1 ❖ Sewing supplies, notions, and craft items. 610-867-3833.

Kagan Trim Center, 750 Towne Ave., Los Angeles, CA 90021: Catalog $14 (refundable) ❖ Trims, laces, braids, cords, and general apparel supplies. 800-437-8746.

Kreinik Manufacturing Company, 1708 Gihon Rd., P.O. Box 1966, Parkersburg, WV 26102: Free information with long SASE (request list of retail sources) ❖ Metallic and decorative threads. 800-311-8061.

Lace Heaven, P.O. Box 50150, Mobile, AL 36605: Catalog $3 (refundable) ❖ Lingerie fabrics, ribbons and trim, stretch lace, elastic, and notions. 205-478-5644.

Ledgewood Studio, 6000 Ledgewood Dr., Forest Park, GA 30050: Catalog $2 with long SASE and three 1st class stamps ❖ Dress patterns for antique dolls, supplies for authentic period costumes, notions, and braids, French lace, silk ribbons, silk taffeta, China silk, Swiss batiste, and trim. 404-361-6098.

Donna Lee's Sewing Center, 25234 Pacific Hwy. South, Kent, WA 98032: Catalog $4 ❖ Swiss batiste, imperial batiste, China silk, silk charmeuse, French val lace, English lace, Swiss embroidery, trim and yardage fabrics, and silk and embroidered ribbons. 206-941-9466.

Linda's Silver Needle, P.O. Box 2167, Naperville, IL 60567: Free information ❖ Sewing and smocking supplies. 800-SMOCK-IT.

Madeira USA Ltd., P.O. Box 6068, Laconia, NH 03246: Free information ❖ Gold and silver metallic thread. 800-225-3001.

Mary Jo's Needles & Pins, Village Shoppes at Martin Downs, 3063 SW Martin Downs Blvd., Palm City, FL 34990: Free information ❖ Heirloom sewing and smocking supplies. 407-220-9198.

Manny's Millinery Supply Center, 26 W. 38th St., New York, NY 10018: Catalog $3 ❖ Millinery supplies and accessories. 212-840-2235.

Meissner's Sewing, 2417 Cormorant Way, Sacramento, CA 95815: Free information ❖ Sewing machines and notions. 800-521-2332.

Nancy's Notions, P.O. Box 683, Beaver Dam, WI 53916: Free catalog ❖ Notions, threads, books, patterns, and interlock knits, fleece, gabardines, sweater knits, challis, and other fabrics. 800-833-0690.

National Thread & Supply, 695 Red Oak Rd., Stockbridge, GA 30281: Free catalog ❖ Cone threads and sewing notions. 800-331-7600.

Newark Dressmaker Supply, 6473 Ruch Rd., P.O. Box 20730, Lehigh Valley, PA 18002: Free catalog ❖ Supplies for sewing, crafts, and needlework. 800-736-6783.

Newman Enterprises, P.O. Box 16, Martin, SC 29836: Free information ❖ Automatic needle threader. 312-604-1608.

Oppenheim's, P.O. Box 52, North Manchester, IN 46962: Catalog $1 ❖ Sewing notions, fabrics, and craft supplies. 800-461-6728.

Oregon Tailor Supplies, 2123 SE Division St., Portland, OR 97242: Free information ❖ Sewing notions. 800-678-2457.

Ornamental Resources Inc., P.O. Box 3010, Idaho Springs, CO 80452: Catalog $15 ❖ Sewing notions. 800-876-6762.

Outdoor Wilderness Fabrics, 16195 Latah Dr., Nampa, ID 83651: Free price list ❖ Coated and uncoated nylon fabrics, fleece and blends in coat weights, waterproof fabrics, hardware, webbing, zippers, patterns, and other notions. 208-466-1602.

❖ SEWING ❖

Quest Outfitters, 2590 17th St., Sarasota, FL 34234: Free catalog ❖ Clothing, outdoor fabrics, patterns, fasteners, and zippers. 813-378-1620.

Rainshed Outdoor Fabrics, 707 NW 11th, Corvallis, OR 97330: Catalog $1 ❖ Rainwear and outerwear fabrics, notions, webbing, and patterns. 541-753-8900.

Renaissance Buttons, P.O. Box 130, Oregon House, CA 95962: Free catalog ❖ High-fashion custom buttons. 916-692-1663.

River Gems & Findings, 6901 Washington NE, Albuquerque, NM 87109: Free catalog ❖ Beads, beading supplies, sewing notions, and craft accessories. 800-396-9895.

Debra J. Rutherford Designs, P.O. Box 100, Essex, MA 01929: Free information ❖ Handcrafted ceramic buttons and jewelry pieces. 508-927-7012.

Seattle Fabrics, 8702 Aurora Ave. North, Seattle, WA 98103: Price list $3 (refundable) ❖ Notions and patterns. 206-525-0670.

Sew Fine, 18399 Ventura Blvd., Tarzana, CA 91356: Free information with long SASE ❖ Smocking and sewing supplies, French and English lace, buttons, ribbons, and Swiss embroideries. 818-886-1108.

Sewin' in Vermont, 84 Concord Ave., St. Johnsbury, VT 05819: Free information ❖ Sewing machines, sergers, and notions. 800-451-5124; 802-748-3803 (in VT).

Signal Thread Company, 521 Airport Rd., Chattanooga, TN 37421: Catalog $5 ❖ Spun polyester thread in mini cones. 800-THREADS.

Ben Silver, 149 King St., Charleston, SC 29401: Free catalog ❖ College crests, monograms, and blazer buttons. 800-BEN-SILVER.

Singer Sewing Center, 1667 Texas Ave., College Station, TX 77840: Free information with long SASE ❖ Sewing notions and sewing machine serger attachments. 800-338-5672.

Something Pretty, Rt 1, Box 93, Big Sandy, TN 38221: Brochure $2.50 ❖ Hand-cut and hand-painted ceramic buttons. 901-593-3807.

SouthStar Supply Corporation, P.O. Box 90147, Nashville, TN 37209: Free information ❖ Sewing notions and supplies. 800-288-6739.

Specialties, Pat Timms, 4425 Cotton Hanlon Rd., Montour Falls, NY 14865: Catalog $2 ❖ Lingerie fabrics, notions, and patterns. 607-594-2021.

Speed Stitch, 3113 Broadpoint Dr., Harbor Heights, FL 33983: Free catalog ❖ Machine quilting supplies. 800-874-4115.

Stonemountain & Daughter Fabrics, 2518 Shattuck Ave., Berkeley, CA 94704: Free information ❖ Cordings and braids. 510-845-6106.

Stretch & Sew, 8697 La Mesa Blvd., La Mesa, CA 91941: Catalog $3 ❖ Fabrics, patterns, and notions. 619-589-8880.

Tandy Leather Company, P.O. Box 791, Fort Worth, TX 76101: Catalog $3 (refundable) ❖ Leather crafting kits, tools, books, patterns, sewing notions, and how-to videos.

Taylor's Cutaways & Stuff, 2802 E. Washington St., Urbana, IL 61801: Brochure $1 ❖ Satins, lace, velvet, cottons, felt, calico, trims, polyester squares, sewing notions, craft supplies, books, and soft toy and crochet patterns.

Things Japanese, 9805 NE 116th St., Ste. 7160, Kirkland, WA 98034: Catalog $1 ❖ Silk filament sewing thread. 206-821-2287.

Thread Discount Sales, 10222 Paramount Blvd., Downey, CA 90241: Free information ❖ Embroidery and polyester thread, polyester cone thread for sergers and sewing machines, and wool-nylon, cotton, and silk thread. 310-928-4029.

Three Kittens Yarn Shoppe, 805 Sibley Memorial Hwy., St. Paul, MN 55118: Information $2 ❖ Hand-painted porcelain buttons. 800-489-4969; 612-457-4969 (in MN).

Treasures & Keepsakes, P.O. Box 331825, Fort Worth, TX 76163: Catalog $2 (refundable) ❖ Smocking and heirloom sewing supplies. 817-263-8535.

Ultramouse Ltd., 3433 Bennington Ct., Bloomfield Hills, MI 48301: Catalog $2 ❖ Notions, ultrasuede, and fabric scraps. 800-225-1887.

Utex Trading, 710 9th St., Ste. 5, Niagara Falls, NY 14301: Free brochure with long SASE ❖ Sewing supplies and imported silk fabrics. 416-596-7565.

Victorian Treasures, 12148 Madison St. NE, Blaine, MN 55434: Catalog $3.50 (refundable) ❖ Imported lace, fabrics, Swiss embroideries, notions, and sewing supplies. 612-755-6302.

Wawak Corporation, 2235 Hammond Dr., Schaumberg, IL 60173: Catalog $2.50 ❖ Tailoring and sewing supplies. 800-654-2235.

Web of Thread, 1410 Broadway, Paducah, KY 42001: Catalog $3 ❖ Supplies for serger and embroidery crafts and metallic, rayon, and silk thread for hand and machine embroidery. 502-575-9700.

Woolgathering, 750 Calico Ct., Waukesha, WI 53186: Free price list ❖ Rowan yarns, needle point kits, buttons, books and magazines, and sewing notions. 800-248-3225.

Wooly Knits, 6728 Lowell Ave., McLean, VA 22101: Catalog $5 (12 issues) ❖ Designer yarns, unusual buttons, and needlework supplies. 703-448-9665.

Patterns & Kits

A.C.S., 447 W. 36th St., New York, NY 10018: Free catalog ❖ Notions, thread, lining, patterns and cutting tools, fasteners, and sewing machines. 800-SEW-TRUE.

Amazon Drygoods, 2218 E. 11th St., Davenport, IA 52803: Catalog $7 ❖ Victorian and Edwardian clothing patterns, from the 1920s and 1930s. 800-798-7979.

Annie's Attic, 1 Annie Ln., Big Sandy, TX 75755: Catalog $2 ❖ Sewing and needlecraft patterns and supplies. 800-282-6643.

Buckaroo Bobbins, 377 S. 6300 West, Cedar City, UT 84720: Catalog $1 ❖ Authentic vintage western clothing sewing patterns. 801-865-7922.

Butterick Pattern Company, Consumer Services, 161 6th Ave., New York, NY 10013: Free information ❖ Patterns for clothing. 800-766-2670.

D.L. Designs, P.O. Box 27034, Los Angeles, CA 90027: Free catalog ❖ Men and women's hat patterns for costume pieces from the past. Also bridal headpieces and contemporary fashions.

Daisy Kingdom, 3720 NW Yeon Ave., Portland, OR 97210: Catalog $2 ❖ Nursery ensembles and children's ready-made fashions or kits. 800-234-6688.

Lois Ericson, Box 5222, Salem, OR 97304: Free information with long SASE ❖ Design and sew patterns for coats, jackets, vests, and blouses.

Fabricraft, P.O. Box 962, Cardiff, CA 92007: Catalog $2 ❖ Clothing patterns.

Forever Timeless, 81 Lakeshore Rd. East, P.O. Box 145, Port Credit, Ontario, Canada L5G 1C9: Catalog $3 ❖ Folk wear, historical, period impressions, and other patterns. 905-274-EVER.

Friends Patterns, 1006 Elm St., Rolfe, IA 50581: Catalog $1 ❖ Amish and modest clothing patterns for men, women, and children.

Frostline Kits, 2525 River Rd., Grand Junction, CO 81505: Catalog $2 ❖ Ready-to-sew kits for jackets, vests, comforters, luggage, camping gear, and ski wear. 800-548-7872.

Green Pepper, 1285 River Rd., Eugene, OR 97404: Catalog $2 ❖ Buckles, Velcro fasteners, zippers, buttons, and notions, and kits for coats and jackets, ski wear, water-repellent clothing for cold weather, and duffel bags.

Harper House, P.O. Box 39, Williamstown, PA 17098: Catalog $6 ❖ Historic and ethnic garment patterns, sewing notions, books, and supplies. 717-647-7807.

Kwik-Sew Pattern Company Inc., 3000 Washington Ave. North, Minneapolis, MN 55411: Catalog $5 ❖ Patterns and sewing instruction books. 612-521-7651.

❖ SEWING ❖

Little Memories, P.O. Box 170145, Arlington, TX 76003: Brochure $2.50 ❖ Smocking plates, duplicate stitch designs, and patterns. 817-860-2681.

Heidi Marsh Patterns, 3494 N. Valley Rd., Greenville, CA 95947: Catalog $3 ❖ Clothing patterns, from 1855 to 1865.

Park Bench Pattern Company, 5181 Baltimore Dr., La Mesa, CA 91942: Catalog $3 ❖ Clothing patterns. 619-464-6092.

Past Patterns, P.O. Box 7587, Grand Rapids, MI 49510: Catalog $4 ❖ Patterns for historically authentic clothing for men, women, and children. 616-245-9456.

Pattern Warehouse, P.O. Box 3135, Chicago, IL 60654: Catalog $3 ❖ Cross-stitch and soft craft patterns. 312-828-9634.

Patterns from Simpler Times, P.O. Box 145, 81 Lakeshore Rd. East, Port Credit, Ontario, Canada L5G 1C9: Catalog $3 ❖ Patterns. 905-274-EVER.

Rainshed Outdoor Fabrics, 707 NW 11th, Corvallis, OR 97330: Catalog $1 ❖ Rainwear and outerwear fabrics, notions, webbing, and patterns. 541-753-8900.

The Ready Wear Company, 391 3rd Ave., Troy, NY 12181: Free catalog ❖ One-size fits-all women's blouses, jogging suits, jackets, and skirts. 800-342-2400; 518-235-1700 (in NY).

Seattle Fabrics, 8702 Aurora Ave. North, Seattle, WA 98103: Price list $3 (refundable) ❖ Notions and patterns. 206-525-0670.

Sew/Fit Company, 5310 W. 66th St., Unit A, Bedford Park, IL 60638: Free catalog ❖ Patterns, books, notions, and supplies. 708-458-5600.

Sew Special, 777 E. Vista Way, Ste. 20, Vista, CA 92084: Catalog $2 ❖ Smocking and heirloom sewing supplies. 619-940-0363.

The Sewing Centipede, P.O. Box 218, Midway City, CA 92655: Catalog $2 ❖ Sewing patterns for craft projects.

Specialties, Pat Timms, 4425 Cotton Hanlon Rd., Montour Falls, NY 14865: Catalog $2 ❖ Lingerie fabrics, notions, and patterns. 607-594-2021.

Stretch & Sew, 8697 La Mesa Blvd., La Mesa, CA 91941: Catalog $3 ❖ Fabrics, patterns, and notions. 619-589-8880.

Sewing Machines, Pleaters & Sergers

A.C.S., 447 W. 36th St., New York, NY 10018: Free catalog ❖ Notions, thread, lining, patterns and cutting tools, fasteners, sewing machines, and serging accessories. 800-SEW-TRUE.

All Brand Sew Knit Distributors, 9789 Florida Blvd., Baton Rouge, LA 70815: Free brochure (specify type of machine) ❖ Knitting, serger, and sewing machines and accessories. 800-289-5648.

Atlanta Thread & Supply, 695 Red Oak Rd., Stockbridge, GA 30281: Catalog $1 ❖ Notions and sewing machines. 800-847-1001.

Bernina, 3500 Thayer Ct., Aurora, IL 60504: Free information ❖ Sewing machines and sergers. 708-978-2500.

Derry's Sewing Center, 925 Lindsay Ln., Florissant, MO 63031: Brochure $1 with long SASE ❖ Sewing machines, vacuum cleaners, and parts. 314-837-6103.

Ferdco Sewing Machines, P.O. Box 261, Harrison, ID 83833: Free information ❖ Heavy-duty sewing machines. 800-645-0197.

Juki America Inc., 5 Haul Rd., Wayne, NJ 07470: Free information ❖ Serging machines. 201-633-7200.

Meissner's Sewing, 2417 Cormorant Way, Sacramento, CA 95815: Free information ❖ Sewing machines and notions. 800-521-2332.

The New Home Sewing Machine Company, 10 Industrial St., Mahwah, NJ 07430: Free information ❖ Computerized sewing machines. 800-631-0183.

Noltings, Rt. 3, Box 147, Hwy. 52 East, Stover, MO 65078: Free information ❖ Quilting and sewing machines. 573-377-2713.

Pfaff American Sales Corporation, 610 Winters Ave., Paramus, NJ 07653: Free list of retail sources ❖ Sewing machines. 800-99-PFAFF.

SCS USA, 9631 NE Colfax, Portland, OR 97220: Free catalog ❖ Embellishment sewing machines. 800-542-4727.

Sew & Serg Company, 9789 Florida Blvd., Baton Rouge, LA 70815: Free information ❖ Sewing equipment. 800-739-7374.

Sew-Knit Distributors, 9789 Florida Blvd., Baton Rouge, LA 70815: Free catalog ❖ Sewing and knitting machines and supplies. 800-289-5648.

Sew Vac City, 1667 Texas Ave., College Station, TX 77840: Brochure $3 ❖ Sewing machines and vacuum cleaners. 800-338-5672.

Sewin' in Vermont, 84 Concord Ave., St. Johnsbury, VT 05819: Free information ❖ Sewing machines, sergers, and notions. 800-451-5124; 802-748-3803 (in VT).

Sewing Machine Service & Supply, 2217 Locust St., St. Louis, MO 63103: Free information ❖ Sewing machines and accessories. 314-241-9006.

Singer Sewing Center, 1667 Texas Ave., College Station, TX 77840: Free information with long SASE ❖ Sewing machines and serger attachments. 800-338-5672.

Tippman Industrial Products Inc., 3518 Adams Center Rd., Fort Wayne, IN 46806: Free information ❖ Leather sewing and cutting equipment. 800-533-4831.

Tosca Company, 13503 Tosca Ln., Ste. 250, Houston, TX 77079: Free information ❖ Pleating machines. 800-290-8327.

Stuffing & Fill

Air-Lite Synthetics Manufacturing, 342 Irwin St., Pontiac, MI 48053: Free information ❖ Batting, fiberfill, and pillow forms. 800-521-1267.

Brewer Sewing Supplies, 3800 W. 42nd St., Chicago, IL 60632: Free information ❖ Sewing machines, quilting supplies, batting and stuffing, and notions. 800-621-2501.

Buffalo Batt & Felt Corporation, Craft Product Division, 3307 Walden Ave., Depew, NY 14043: Information $1 ❖ Stuffing, polyester fiberfill, and patterns. 716-683-4100.

Oriental Rug Company, P.O. Box 205, Washington, KY 41086: Free information ❖ Polyester fiberfill, polyester quilt batting, and pillow inserts. 606-759-7614.

Royal Processing Company Inc., 3445 N. Spencer St., Charlotte, NC 28204: Free information ❖ Kapok and polyester fill for pillows, quilts, and stuffed toys. 704-376-5641.

Tags & Labels

Alpha Impressions Inc., P.O. Box 3156, Los Angeles, CA 90051: Free brochure ❖ Woven labels and hang tags. 800-834-8221.

Charm Woven Labels, Box 30027, Portland, OR 97294: Free brochure ❖ Silk, linen, wool, polyester, and cotton labels. 503-252-5542.

E & S Creations, P.O. Box 68, Rexburg, ID 83440: Catalog $1 ❖ Imaginative folk, country, and Victorian-style tags.

General Label Manufacturing, P.O. Box 640371, Miami, FL 33164: Free information ❖ Printed fabric labels. 800-944-4696.

Heirloom Woven Labels, P.O. Box 428, Moorestown, NJ 08057: Free information ❖ Woven labels. 609-722-1618.

IDENT-IFY Label Corporation, P.O. Box 140204, Brooklyn, NY 11214: Sample kit $1 ❖ Sew-on labels and name tapes. 718-436-3126.

Kimmeric Studio, P.O. Box 3586, Napa, CA 94558: Catalog $2 ❖ Craft hang tags. 707-255-8734.

Name Maker Inc., P.O. Box 43821, Atlanta, GA 30378: Free information ❖ Nylon, taffeta, or satin labels and name tapes with signature, logo, or custom artwork. 800-845-6575; 404-691-2237 (in GA).

Northwest Tag & Label Inc., 110 Foothills Rd., Ste. 237, Lake Oswego, OR 97034: Brochure $1 ❖ Nylon, satin, and woven edge iron-on and washable printed fabric tags and labels. 503-636-6456.

Sterling Name Tape Company, P.O. Box 939, Winsted, CT 06098: Samples $1 ❖ Printed custom labels. 800-654-5210.

TECHNIQdesign, 1132 Meridian Circle, Santa Rosa, CA 95401: Catalog $2 ❖ Hang tags, labels, and jewelry cards.

SHEDS, BARNS & OTHER BUILDINGS

Barnmaster Inc., 559 Floyd Smith Dr., El Cajon, CA 92020: Free list of retail sources ❖ Modular barns for horses. 800-262-BARN; 619-441-9400 (in CA).

Colonial Dependencies, Box 474B, Bowling Green, VA 22427: Catalog $6 ❖ Plans for guest quarters, offices, sea retreats, garages, gazebos, tool houses, and other buildings.

Country Designs, P.O. Box 774, Essex, CT 06426: Catalog $6 ❖ Plans for barns, sheds, and garages. 203-767-1046.

Gardensheds, 651 Millcross Rd., Lancaster, PA 17601: Information $4 ❖ Potting sheds, wood boxes, and storage units. 717-397-5430.

Hammond Barns, P.O. Box 584, New Castle, IN 47362: Brochure $2 ❖ Plans for storage and tool sheds, workshops, and other structures. 317-529-7822.

Handy Home Products, 6400 E. 11 Mile Rd., Warren, MI 48091: Free information ❖ Easy-to-assemble cedar barns with optional cupola and weather vane accents. 800-221-1849.

Heritage Garden Houses, City Visions Inc., 311 Seymour, Lansing, MI 48933: Catalog $3 ❖ Pool houses, potting sheds, tool storage, hot tub enclosures, colonnades, seats, cabinets, gazebos, and classical, Victorian, Japanese, and other garden retreats. 517-372-3385.

Homestead Design Inc., P.O. Box 1058, Bellingham, WA 98227: Plan book $5 ❖ Plans for barns, stables, workshops, garages, and garden sheds.

Kwik-Bilt Inc., 3114 Benton St., Garland, TX 75042: Free information ❖ Easy-to-assemble galvanized steel buildings. 214-494-1164.

New England Outbuildings, P.O. Box 621, Westbrook, CT 06498: Free information ❖ Kits for New England farm structures and outbuildings. 860-669-1776.

Pitcairn-Ferguson & Associates Inc., RD 2, Box 15-1A, Kempton, PA 19529: Free brochure ❖ Antique Pennsylvania bank barn kits. 610-756-6602.

Porta-Fab Corporation, P.O. Box 1084, Chesterfield, MO 63006: Free information ❖ Modular buildings for easy expansion. 800-325-3781.

Red Ball Consumer Products, 9300 Shelbyville Rd., Ste. 300, Louisville, KY 40222: Free information ❖ Waders. 800-451-1806.

Senco Inc., 520 8th St., Gwinn, MI 49841: Free information ❖ Recreational shelters, portable hunting blinds, ice fishing houses, and greenhouses. 906-346-4116.

Woodwright Design Company, P.O. Box 13216, Wauwatosa, WI 53213: Catalog $12 ❖ Construction plans for traditional to contemporary historically-inspired houses, carriage barns, outbuildings, and cupolas.

SHOES & BOOTS

Men & Women's Shoes & Boots

Active Soles, 20 Wapping Rd., Kingston, MA 02364: Free brochure ❖ Wide and extra-wide athletic shoes for women, sizes 5 to 13. 800-881-4322.

Allen-Edmonds Shoe Corporation, 201 East Seven Hills Road, P.O. Box 998, Port Washington, WI 53074: Free catalog ❖ Men's business, dress, and casual shoes. Also shoe care supplies. 414-284-7158.

Aussie Connection, 135 NE Broadway, Hillsboro, OR 97124: Free catalog ❖ Washable Australian sheepskin slippers and boots. 800-950-2668.

Bally of Switzerland for Ladies, 689 Madison Ave., New York, NY 10021: Free information ❖ Women's shoes, clothing, luggage, and small leather goods. 212-751-2163.

Bally of Switzerland for Men, 711 5th Ave., New York, NY 10022: Free information ❖ Men's shoes, clothing, luggage, and small leather goods. 212-751-9082.

Barnum Shoe, 1434 Barnum Ave., Stratford, CT 06497: Catalog $1 ❖ Medium to extra-wide men and women's clogs. 800-582-7995.

L.L. Bean Inc., Freeport, ME 04033: Free catalog ❖ Outdoor footwear for tall men. 800-483-2326.

Arthur Beren Shoes, 111 Maiden Ln., Ste. 402, San Francisco, CA 94108: Free catalog ❖ Women's shoes. 800-886-9797.

Birkenstock Express, 301 SW Madison Ave., Corvallis, OR 97333: Free catalog ❖ Waterproof clogs in sizes 4 to 11 for women and 5 to 13 for men. 800-231-6740.

Birkenstock Shoes, 3900 Cross Creek Rd., Malibu, CA 90265: Free information ❖ Birkenstock shoes. 800-217-5778.

Sue Brett, P.O. Box 8384, Indianapolis, IN 46283: Free catalog ❖ Women's leather and suede shoes and boots. 800-784-8001.

Lane Bryant, P.O. Box 8301, Indianapolis, IN 46283: Free catalog ❖ Women's shoes, size 7 to 12. 800-777-7030.

Church's English Shoes, 428 Madison Ave., New York, NY 10017: Free brochure ❖ Handcrafted all-leather shoes, sizes 6 to 14, AA-EEE. 800-221-4540; 212-755-4313 (in NY).

Classic Pumps, 1320 2nd St., DeKalb, IL 60115: Brochure $1 ❖ Leather pumps with optional heel sizes. 815-748-5507.

The Comfort Corner, P.O. Box 649, Nashua, NH 03061: Free catalog ❖ Men and women's dress and walking shoes, casuals, sandals, and other styles. 800-442-8730.

The Cordwainer Shop, Wild Orchard Farms, Deerfield, NH 03037: Catalog $3 ❖ Handmade custom footwear. 603-463-7742.

Coward Shoes, Palo Verde at 34th, P.O. Box 27800, Tucson, AZ 85726: Free catalog ❖ Leather shoes for men and women, sizes 5 to 12, AA to EEE. 520-748-8600.

Tanino Crisci, 795 Madison Ave., New York, NY 10314: Free catalog ❖ Men's shoes. 212-535-1014.

Deerskin Place, 283 Akron Rd., Ephrata, PA 17522: Catalog $1 ❖ Leather moccasins for men, women, and children. 717-733-7624.

Dunns, P.O. Box 449, Grand Junction, TN 38039: Free catalog ❖ Camouflage and insulated clothing, outerwear, shoes and boots, hunting equipment, day and belt packs, gun care kits, sunglasses, game calls, decoys, and supplies. 800-223-8667.

Esprit Outlet, 499 Illinois St., San Francisco, CA 94107: Free catalog ❖ Leather boots, oxfords, and loafers. 415-957-2540.

Executive Shoes, 141 Longwater Dr., Norwell, MA 02061: Free catalog ❖ Handcrafted athletic and walking shoes in hard-to-fit sizes. 800-934-1022.

Fabiano Shoe Company, 850 Summer St., South Boston, MA 02127: Free information with long SASE ❖ Thinsulate insulated Telemark boots. 617-268-5625.

Fashion Footnotes, Lester Square, Americus, GA 31710: Free catalog ❖ Women's shoes. 800-262-8888.

Footprints, The Birkenstock Store, 1339 Massachusetts, Lawrence KS 66044: Free catalog ❖ Birkenstock sandals and shoes for tall women. 800-827-1339.

Peter Fox Bridal Shoes, 806 Madison Ave., New York, NY 10021: Catalog $3 ❖ Bridal boots and shoes. 800-338-3430.

Haband for Men, 100 Fairview Ave., Prospect Park, NJ 07530: Free information ❖ Men's outdoor insulated boots and wash-and-wear clothing. 800-742-2263.

Hanover Shoe Company, 440 N. Madison St., Hanover, PA 17331: Free catalog ❖ Men's shoes, sizes 6 to 15, AA to EEE. 800-426-3708; 717-632-7575 (in PA).

❖ SHOES & BOOTS ❖

Hitchcock Shoes Inc., Hingham, MA 02043: Free catalog ❖ Men's shoes, sizes 5 to 13, EE to EEEEEE. 800-992-WIDE.

Johansen Bros. Shoe Company, 1915 W. Main, Corning, AR 72422: Free catalog ❖ Women's fashion shoes. 800-624-9079.

Johnston & Murphy, Mail Order Shop, 1415 Murfreesboro Rd., Ste. 190, Nashville, TN 37217: Free catalog ❖ Men's shoes, socks, belts, and accessories. 800-424-2854.

King Size Company, P.O. Box 9115, Hingham, MA 02043: Free catalog ❖ Shoes for tall men, sizes 12 to 16. 800-846-1600.

Knapp Shoes Inc., One Knapp Centre, Brockton, MA 02401: Free catalog ❖ Work shoes. 800-869-9955.

Koson's, P.O. Box 3663, St. Augustine, FL 32085: Free brochure ❖ Swedish clogs for men, women, and children. 800-654-0010.

Little Max's Shoes, 1536 W. Chicago Ave., Chicago, IL 60622: Free brochure ❖ Women's shoes and boots in sizes up to 14 wide and WW widths. 312-421-8435.

Martial Athleisure Corporation, 27584 Commerce Center Dr., Temecula, CA 92590: Free information ❖ Martial art shoes. 800-622-4897; 909-693-0703 (in CA).

Maryland Square, 1350 Williams St., Chippewa Falls, WI 54729: Free catalog ❖ Women's footwear in full and half sizes. 800-727-3895.

B.A. Mason Footwear, 1251 1st Ave., Chippewa Falls, WI 54774: Free catalog ❖ Men and women's shoes in regular and large sizes, moccasins, and shoe care supplies. 800-422-1000.

Masseys, Direct Footwear Merchants, 601 12th St., Lynchburg, VA 24504: Free catalog ❖ Casual, dress, and athletic shoes. Also boots and slippers. 800-462-7739.

Stuart McGuire, 425 Well St., Chippewa Falls, WI 54729: Free catalog ❖ Casual shoes and other styles for men. 800-678-4601.

Mid Western Sport Togs, 227 N. Washington, Berlin, WI 54923: Free catalog ❖ Deerskin gloves, footwear, handbags, accessories, and jackets and coats for men and women. 414-361-5050.

Minnetonka by Mail, P.O. Box 444, Bronx, NY 10458: Catalog $2 ❖ Leather moccasins for men, women, and children with soft, crepe, and polyurethane soles. Also shoes and boots for casual wear. 718-364-6266.

Moonwalker/Sierra Boot Company, 2001 Chester, Bakersfield, CA 93301: Free catalog ❖ Handmade boots and shoes. 800-93-BOOTS; 805-322-8505 (in CA).

Moose River Moccasin Company, 32 Main St., Freeport, ME 04032: Free catalog ❖ Hand-sewn moccasins. 800-851-4449.

Nancy's Choice, 34th & Palo Verde, P.O. Box 27800, Tucson, AZ 85726: Free catalog ❖ Shoes in hard-to-find sizes, from 9 to 13, widths N to WW, plus some slims. 520-748-8600.

Naples Creek Leather, 188 S. Main St., Naples, NY 14512: Free catalog ❖ Leather moccasins, slippers, belts, gloves, casual footwear, and deerskin handbags. 800-836-0616.

Okun Brothers Shoes, Attention: Mail Order Department, 356 E. South St., Kalamazoo, MI 49007: Free catalog ❖ Shoes and boots for men, women, and children. 800-433-6344.

Old Pueblo Traders, Palo Verde at 34th, P.O. Box 27800, Tucson, AZ 85726: Free catalog ❖ Shoes and boots for women. 520-748-8600.

Ortho-Vent Inc., 11851 30th Ct. North, St. Petersburg, FL 33716: Free catalog ❖ Men's casual and dress leather footwear. 813-573-3730.

Regalia, Palo Verde at 34th, P.O. Box 27800, Tucson, AZ 85726: Free catalog ❖ Fashions and intimate apparel in large sizes. Also shoes in hard-to-find sizes and narrow to wide-wide widths. 520-747-5000.

Reyers, Sharon City Centre, Sharon, PA 16146: Free information ❖ Shoes, from size 2-1/2 to 14, in widths AAAAAA to EE. 800-245-1550.

Richlee Shoe Company, P.O. Box 3566, Frederick, MD 21701: Free catalog ❖ Elevator shoes for men, sizes 5 to 11, B to EEE. 800-343-3810.

Sheepskin Imports, P.O. Box 4114, Dana Point, CA 92629: Free catalog ❖ Aussie Dog boots, shoes, and slippers. 800-237-0464.

Shoe Express, P.O. Box 31537, Lafayette, LA 70593: Free catalog ❖ Ladies large and wide shoes in sizes 9 to 15, AAAAA to WW and 6 to 15, wide and WW. 800-874-0469.

Shoecraft Corporation, 1395 NW 17th Ave., Ste. 102, Delray Beach, FL 33445: Free information ❖ Dress shoes, sandals, sport shoes, and flats, sizes 10 to 13. 800-225-5848.

Standard Shoes, 48 Main St., Bangor, ME 04401: Free catalog ❖ Arch-supporting shoes for women, sizes 2A to 3A; 6 to 12, A and B; 5 to 12, C and D; 5 to 12, E and EE; and some half sizes. 800-284-8366.

Swedish Clogs Inc., 320 State Rd. 16, St. Augustine, FL 32095: Free price list ❖ Women's clogs. 800-443-8167; 904-824-8844 (in FL).

Talbots, 175 Beal St., Hingham, MA 02043: Free catalog ❖ Women's shoes in regular, petite, and other sizes. 800-992-9010.

Norm Thompson, P.O. Box 3999, Portland, OR 97208: Free catalog ❖ Wood Ducks and casual shoes. 800-821-1287.

Tog Shop, Lester Square, Americus, GA 31710: Free catalog ❖ Women's footwear in full and half sizes and slim (AAA), narrow (AA), or medium (B) widths. 800-342-6789.

Vasque Boots, 314 Main St., Red Wing, MN 55066: Free list of retail sources ❖ Hiking boots for men and women. 612-388-8211.

Wissota Trader, 1313 1st Ave., Chippewa Falls, WI 54729: Free catalog ❖ Regular and hard-to-find shoes and clothes for men and women. 800-962-0160.

Wolverine Boots & Shoes, 9341 Courtland Dr., Rockford, MI 49351: Free list of retail sources ❖ Footwear for men and women. 800-543-2668.

World Traders, Bar Harbor Rd., Box 158, Brewer, ME 04412: Free catalog ❖ Hand-sewn moccasins. 800-603-0003.

Western Boots

America's Western Stores, P.O. Box 9200, Springfield, MO 65801: Free catalog ❖ Western-style clothing, shoes and boots, and gifts. 800-284-8191.

Ariat International, P.O. Box 593, San Carlos, CA 94070: Free information ❖ Boots with optional waterproof sock liner and Thinsulate insulation.

Austin-Hall Boot Company, 230 Chelsea St., El Paso, TX 79905: Free information ❖ Handmade boots. 915-771-6113.

Back at the Ranch, 235 Don Gaspar, Santa Fe, NM 87501: Free information ❖ Vintage western clothing, boots, and hats. 505-989-8110.

Boot Town, 10838 N. Central Expwy., Dallas, TX 75231: Free catalog ❖ Western boots. 800-222-6687.

Cavalry Regimental Supply, Box 64394, Lubbock, TX 79464: Catalog $2 with long SASE (refundable) ❖ Custom-made reproduction historic-style boots.

Champion Boot Company, 505 S. Cotton, El Paso, TX 79901: Catalog $1 ❖ Leather cowboy-style boots. 915-534-7783.

The Cowhand, P.O. Box 743, Woodland Park, CO 80866: Free information ❖ Gloves, spurs, bits, belts, buckles, and western-style boots for men, women, and children. 800-748-3837.

Drysdales Catalog, 3220 S. Memorial Dr., Tulsa, OK 74145: Free catalog ❖ Men's Justin Ropers in sizes 6-12, 13, and 14, A, B, D, E, and EE widths (full and half sizes) and women's sizes 4 to 9, A, B, and C widths. 800-444-6481.

Just Justin, 1505 Wycliff Ave., Dallas, TX 75207: Free catalog ❖ Shoes and boots for men and women, with a choice of many leathers. 800-292-2668.

Lucchese Boots, 6601 Montana, El Paso, TX 79925: Free list of retail sources ❖ Handmade boots and shoes.

Luskey/Ryan's Western Stores Inc., 2601 N. Main, Fort Worth, TX 76106: Free catalog ❖ Western-style clothing, boots, and hats for men, women, and children. Also saddles and tack. 800-725-7966.

Moonwalker/Sierra Boot Company, 2001 Chester, Bakersfield, CA 93301: Free catalog ❖ Handmade boots and shoes. 800-93-BOOTS; 805-322-8505 (in CA).

The Territory Ahead, PFI Western Stores, P.O. Box 9200, Springfield, MO 65801: Free catalog ❖ Men and women's western-style clothing. 800-284-8191.

Tonto Rim Trading Company, 2650 E. Tipton St., Seymour, IN 47274: Free catalog ❖ Western boots and hats. 800-242-4287.

West Coast Shoe Company, P.O. Box 607, Scappoose, OR 97056: Free catalog ❖ Custom boots. 800-326-2711.

Wilson Boot Company, 110 E. Callender St., Livingston, MT 59047: Brochure $1 ❖ Handmade leather boots. 406-222-3842.

SHUFFLEBOARD

Allen R. Shuffleboard Company Inc., 6585 Seminole Blvd., Seminole, FL 34642: Free information ❖ Cues, disks, and sets. 813-397-0421.

General Sportcraft Company, 140 Woodbine Rd., Bergenfield, NJ 07621: Free information ❖ Cues, disks, and sets. 201-384-4242.

International Billiards Inc., 2311 Washington Ave., Houston, TX 77007: Free information ❖ Cues, disks, and sets. 800-255-6386; 713-869-3237 (in TX).

Dick Martin Sports Inc., 181 E. Union Ave., P.O. Box 7384, East Rutherford, NJ 07073: Free information ❖ Cues, disks, and sets. 800-221-1993; 201-438-5255 (in NJ).

Playfair Shuffleboard Company Inc., 7021 Bluffton Rd., Fort Wayne, IN 46809: Free information ❖ Shuffleboards and accessories. 800-541-3743.

Saunier-Wilhem Company, 3216 5th Ave., Pittsburgh, PA 15213: Free catalog ❖ Equipment and accessories for bowling, billiards, darts, table tennis, shuffleboard, and board games. 412-621-4350.

SGD Company Inc., P.O. Box 8410, Akron, OH 44320: Free information ❖ Cues, disks, and sets. 216-239-2828.

Ultra Play Systems Inc., 425 Sycamore St., Anderson, IN 46016: Free information ❖ Cues, disks, and sets. 800-458-5872.

SIGNS & SIGN-MAKING

Americraft Corporation, 904 4th St. West, Palmetto, FL 34221: Free catalog ❖ Injection molded and formed letters. 800-237-3984; 813-722-6631 (in FL).

Battenberg Wood Products, 553 St. Mary's Rd., Villa Ridge, MO 63089: Free information ❖ Personalized signs. 314-742-3411.

Dick Blick Company, P.O. Box 1267, Galesburg, IL 61402: Catalog $1 ❖ Sign-making supplies and equipment. 800-447-8192.

BronceX Ltd., La Haye Division, P.O. Box 2319, Corona, CA 91718: Free brochure ❖ Solid cast-bronze signs. 800-523-9544.

Cambridge Metalsmiths, Box 1400, Lynden, Ontario, Canada L0R 1T0: Free brochure ❖ Hand-enameled metal signs on heavy metal relief with a choice of over 250 emblems. 519-647-3326.

Colores International Inc., 3860 148th Ave. NE, Redmond, WA 98052: Free information ❖ Custom windsocks and banners. 206-885-6323.

Country Junction, 9121 Old Hartford Rd., Utica, KY 42376: Brochure $2 ❖ Hand-painted country-style wood signs. 800-772-3289.

English Country Signs, 36 Newport Dr., Wayne, PA 19087: Free information ❖ Custom designed hand-cast and painted house signs. 610-296-2839.

Erie Landmark Company, 4449 Brookfield Corporate Dr., Chantilly, VA 22021: Free brochure ❖ Outdoor and indoor bronze or redwood markers and signs. 800-874-7848.

Farmhouse Originals, 1021 Sonya Ln., Brandon, FL 33511: Free information ❖ Framed and matted name signs. 813-685-1426.

4x1 Imports Inc., 5873 Day Rd., Cincinnati, OH 45251: Catalog $4 ❖ Nostalgic tin advertising signs. 513-385-8185.

Gold Leaf & Metallic Powders, 74 Trinity Pl., Ste. 1200, New York, NY 10006: Free information ❖ Genuine and composition leaf in rolls, sheets, books, and boxes. 800-322-0323; 212-267-4900 (in NY).

John Hinds & Company, 81 Greenridge Dr. West, Elmira, NY 14905: Free brochure ❖ Cast plaques and nameplates. 607-733-6712.

Hodgins Engraving, P.O. Box 597, Batavia, NY 14020: Free information ❖ Engraved plastic signs. 800-666-8950.

Just Country, P.O. Box 16024, Boise, ID 83709: Brochure $2 ❖ Hand-cut and carved indoor and outdoor solid-pine interchangeable welcome signs. 208-362-6214.

Lake Shore Industries, P.O. Box 59, Erie, PA 16512: Free information ❖ Cast-aluminum and bronze signs and plaques. 800-458-0463.

Lazer Images, 90 Amwell Rd., Flemington, NJ 08822: Free catalog ❖ Easy-to-use sign and banner-making equipment. 908-788-5731.

Leftover Design Company Inc., P.O. Box 397, Neenah, WI 54956: Catalog $3 ❖ Antique American-made heavy steel with porcelain and other signs. 414-725-1669.

Letters Unlimited, 32 W. Streamwood Blvd., Streamwood, IL 60103: Free catalog ❖ Vinyl letters. 800-422-4231.

Mayfair Signs, P.O. Box 2955, Sumas, WA 98295: Free information ❖ Hand-painted cast-aluminum signs. 604-823-4141.

Meierjohan-Wengler Inc., 10330 Wayne Ave., Cincinnati, OH 45215: Free catalog ❖ Bronze tablets and historic markers. 513-771-6074.

Earl Mich Company, 806 N. Peoria St., Chicago, IL 60622: Free information ❖ Vinyl and reflecting letters. 800-MICH-USA; 312-829-1552 (in IL).

Mossburg's Foam Products, 369 Whitley Rd., Spartanburg, SC 29303: Free information ❖ Easy-to-install foam, plastic, and vinyl letters. 800-845-6140.

Mountain Meadows Pottery, P.O. Box 163, South Ryegate, VT 05069: Free catalog ❖ Stoneware and humorous and sentimental plaques. 800-639-6790.

Nasco, 901 Janesville Ave., Fort Atkinson, WI 53538: Free catalog ❖ Sign-making supplies. 800-558-9595.

National Banner Company Inc., 11938 Harry Hines Blvd., Dallas, TX 75234: Free information ❖ Blank banners hemmed, roped, or grommeted with heavy duty rope sewn on the top and bottom. 800-527-0860.

Newman Brothers Inc., P.O. Box 16067, Cincinnati, OH 45216: Free information ❖ Hand-tooled bronze and aluminum plaques. 513-242-0011.

Northroad & Company, Wood Sign Products, P.O. Box 976, Groton, MA 01450: Catalog $2 (refundable) ❖ Historical markers, house numbers, and residential and small business signs carved in wood. 800-448-6420.

NUDO Products, 1500 Taylor Ave., Springfield, IL 62703: Free information ❖ Sign-painting boards. 800-826-4132.

Out of the Woods Sign Makers, 3 Pine Bluff Trail, Ormond Beach, FL 32174: Free information ❖ Personalized handcrafted wooden signs. 800-554-9315.

Rayco Paint Company, 6100 N. Pulaski Rd., Chicago, IL 60646: Free information ❖ Supplies and equipment for sign painters. 800-421-2327.

Redfeather Arts & Crafts, P.O. Box 341, Pennville, IN 47369: Brochure $2 ❖ Personalized message signs. 219-731-7562.

❖ SILK-SCREENING ❖

Reich Supply Company Inc., 811 Broad St., Utica, NY 13501: Free information ❖ Sign-making and screen-printing materials and equipment. 800-338-3322.

Royal Graphics Inc., 3117 N. Front St., Philadelphia, PA 19133: Free information ❖ Posters, show-cards, and bumper stickers. 215-739-8282.

Ryther-Purdy Lumber Company Inc., 174 Elm St., P.O. Box 622, Old Saybrook, CT 06475: Free information ❖ Handcrafted wooden signs. 203-388-4405.

SCT Signs, P.O. Box 1377, Lancaster, CA 93584: Catalog $2 ❖ Reproduction turn-of-the-century porcelain-enameled signs. 805-948-9093.

Sepp Leaf Products Inc., 381 Park Ave. South, New York, NY 10016: Free information ❖ Gold and palladium leaf, rolled gold, tools, and kits. 212-683-2840.

Sign-Mart, 410 W. Fletcher Ave., Orange, CA 92665: Free information ❖ Hemmed banners with grommets. 800-533-9099.

Signage, 1545 Saratoga Ave., San Jose, CA 951290: Free information ❖ Banners and magnetic signs. 800-541-SIGN.

Signs of all Kinds, 200 W. Main St., Vernon, CT 06066: Free catalog ❖ Hand-cut, sanded, and painted slate signs. Also steel and aluminum signs. 800-214-4449.

Smith-Cornell Inc., 1545 Holland Rd., Maumee, OH 43537: Free brochure ❖ Brass and aluminum historic markers. 800-325-0248; 419-891-4335 (in OH).

Southern Sign Supply Inc., 7601 Brandonwoods Blvd., Baltimore, MD 21226: Free information ❖ Supplies and equipment for sign painters. 800-638-5008.

Joseph Struhl Company Inc., 195 Atlantic Ave., P.O. Box N, Garden City Park, NY 11040: Free information ❖ Ready-made window signs for retail stores. 800-552-0023.

Wensco Sign Supplies, P.O. Box 1728, Grand Rapids, MI 49501: Catalog $5 ❖ Supplies and equipment for sign painters. 800-253-1569; 800-632-4629 (in MI).

The Whisperwood Collection, Box 164, Oxford, MI 48371: Free information ❖ Personalized signs. 800-545-1559.

SILK-SCREENING

The Art Store, 935 Erie Blvd. East, Syracuse, NY 13210: Price list $3 ❖ Supplies for fabric-dyeing, screen-printing, marbling, and art decor. 800-669-2787.

Chaselle Inc., 9645 Gerwig Ln., Columbia, MD 21046: Catalog $4 ❖ Art software and books, brushes and paints, tempera colors, acrylics, pastels, ceramic molds and kilns, sculpture equipment, and silk-screening supplies. 800-242-7355.

Crown Art Products, 90 Dayton Ave., Passaic, NJ 07055: Free catalog ❖ Silk-screening supplies and section frames. 201-777-6010.

Decart Inc., P.O. Box 309, Morrisville, VT 05661: Free list of retail sources ❖ Water-based enamels and paints for transfer techniques, glass-crafting, and silk-screening. 802-888-4217.

Guildcraft Company, 100 Firetower Dr., Tonawanda, NY 14150: Free catalog ❖ Supplies for silk-screening, batik, tie-dying, stenciling, block-printing, and foil crafts. 716-743-8336.

Ivy Crafts Imports, 12213 Distribution Way, Beltsville, MD 20705: Catalog $3.95 ❖ Paints, resists, applicators, and supplies. 301-595-0550.

Nasco, 901 Janesville Ave., Fort Atkinson, WI 53538: Free catalog ❖ Silk-screening and printing supplies. 800-558-9595.

Naz-Dar Company, 1087 N. North Branch St., Chicago, IL 60622: Free catalog ❖ Silk-screening and graphic arts equipment and supplies. 312-943-8215.

Reich Supply Company Inc., 811 Broad St., Utica, NY 13501: Free information ❖ Sign-making and screen-printing supplies. 800-338-3322.

Southern Emblem, P.O. Box 8, Toast, NC 27049: Free catalog ❖ Embroidered emblems, emblematic jewelry, badges, flags, and screen-printing supplies. 910-789-3348.

Technical Papers Corporation, P.O. Box 546, Dedham, MA 02027: Free catalog ❖ Sheets and rolls of handmade rice paper in prints and solid and multi-colors for all types of artistic printing, including block printing, etching, lithography, and silk-screening. 617-461-1111.

Welsh Products Inc., P.O. Box 845, Benicia, CA 94510: Free catalog ❖ Easy-to-use screen-printing kits. 800-745-3255; 707-645-3252 (in CA).

SILVER & FLATWARE

Aaron's, 576 5th Ave., New York, NY 10036: Free information ❖ Active, inactive, and obsolete silverware and flatware. 800-447-5868.

Alice's Past & Presents Replacements, P.O. Box 465, Merrick, NY 11566: Free information ❖ Replacement crystal, china, and flatware. 516-379-1352.

William Ashley, 50 Boor St. West, Toronto, Ontario, Canada M4W 3L8: Free information ❖ China, crystal, and silver. 800-268-1122.

Barrons, P.O. Box 994, Novi, MI 48376: Free information ❖ China, crystal, and silver. 800-538-6340.

Beverly Bremer Silver Shop, 3164 Peachtree Rd. NE, Atlanta, GA 30305: Free information ❖ New, used, discontinued, and hard-to-find patterns. 404-261-4009.

Buschemeyer's Silver Exchange, 515 4th Ave., Louisville, KY 40202: Free information ❖ New and used silver patterns and sterling. 800-626-4555.

Cattle Company Cowboy Exchange, P.O. Box 27, Elfrida, AZ 85610: Catalog $2 ❖ Western-style decorated china and stainless steel flatware. 520-824-3540.

China, Crystal & Flatware Replacements, P.O. Box 508, High Ridge, MO 63049: Free information ❖ China, crystal, and flatware. 800-562-2655.

China Cabinet Inc., 24 Washington St., Tenafly, NJ 07670: Free information with long SASE ❖ China, crystal, flatware, and gifts. 201-567-2711.

The China Warehouse, Box 21797, Cleveland, OH 44121: Free information ❖ China, crystal, and flatware. 800-321-3212.

Classic China, 870 N. Coit Rd., Richardson, TX 75080: Free information with long SASE ❖ China, flatware, and table setting accessories.

Clintsman International, 20855 Watertown Rd., Waukesha, WI 53186: Free information ❖ Discontinued china, crystal, and flatware. 800-781-8900.

Coinways Antiques, 475 Central Ave., Cedarhurst, NY 11516: Free information with long SASE ❖ Used and new sterling silver flatware. 800-645-2102; 516-374-1970 (in NY).

Dansk, 108 Corporate Park Dr., White Plains, NY 10604: Free list of retail sources ❖ Dinnerware, stemware, flatware, kitchenware, and serving pieces. 914-697-6400.

Walter Drake Silver Exchange, Drake Building, Colorado Springs, CO 80940: Free pattern directory ❖ Active, inactive, and obsolete sterling and silver plate patterns. 800-525-9291.

Felissimo, 10 W. 56th S., New York, NY 10019: Free catalog ❖ Porcelain dinnerware and handcrafted silver serving pieces. 800-565-6785.

Fortunoff Fine Jewelry, P.O. Box 1550, Westbury, NY 11590: Free catalog ❖ Sterling flatware, silver plate and stainless steel serving pieces, and china. 800-937-4376.

Gorham, 100 Lenox Dr., Lawrenceville, NJ 08648: Free list of retail sources ❖ Fine china dinnerware, crystal gifts, and silver. 800-635-3669.

Hagan's Sterling & Silverplate, P.O. Box 25487, Tempe, AZ 85282: Free information ❖ Discontinued and current sterling and silver plate. 800-528-7425.

Kaiser Crow Inc., 3545 S. Platte River Dr., Englewood, CO 80110: Free brochure ❖ Stainless, silver flatware, and other silver patterns. 800-468-2769.

Kinnzie's, Box 522, Turlock, CA 95381: Free information ❖ Silverplate and sterling matching service. 209-634-4880.

Kitchen Etc., 32 Industrial Dr., Exeter, NH 03833: Catalog $2 ❖ Cookware, cutlery, flatware, crystal, and dinnerware. 800-232-4070.

Lanac Sales, 73 Canal St., New York, NY 10002: Free catalog ❖ China, crystal, sterling, and gifts. 212-925-6422.

Helen Lawler, 5400 E. Country Rd., Blytheville, AR 72315: Free information ❖ Discontinued silver patterns. 314-720-8502.

Lenox Brands, 100 Lenox Dr., Lawrenceville, NJ 08648: Free list of retail sources ❖ Stainless steel flatware. 800-635-3669.

Littman's Sterling, 151 Granby St., Norfolk, VA 23510: Free information ❖ Individual sterling pieces and place settings. 800-368-6348.

Locators Inc., 908 Rock St., Little Rock, AR 72202: Free information ❖ Discontinued china, crystal, and silver. 800-367-9690.

Marks China, Crystal & Silverware, 315 Franklin Ave., Wyckoff, NJ 07481: Free information ❖ China, stainless, crystal, and silverware. 800-862-7578.

Michele's Silver Matching Service, 805 Crystal Mountain Dr., Austin, TX 78733: Free information ❖ Inactive and active silver patterns. 800-332-4693.

Midas China & Silver, 4315 Walney Rd., Chantilly, VA 22021: Free catalog ❖ Silverware, table settings, china, and gifts. 800-368-3153.

Mikasa, One Mikasa Dr., P.O. Box 1549, Secaucus, NJ 07096: Free catalog ❖ Designer china, stoneware, crystal, and flatware. 800-833-4681; 201-392-2501 (in NJ).

H.G. Robertson Fine Silver, 3263 Roswell Rd. NE, Atlanta, GA 30305: Free information ❖ Sterling flatware and holloware. 800-938-1330; 404-266-1330 (in GA).

Rogers & Rosenthal, 22 W. 48th St., Room 1102, New York, NY 10036: Free information with long SASE ❖ Sterling, silverplate, and stainless steel flatware. 212-827-0115.

Ross-Simons Jewelers, 9 Ross Simons Dr., Cranston, RI 02920: Free information ❖ Sterling and china. 800-556-7376, 800-553-7370 (in RI).

Wilma Saxton Inc., 37 Clementon Rd., Box 395, Berlin, NJ 08009: Free price list ❖ Sterling silver, silverplate, and stainless matching service. 800-267-8029.

Nat Schwartz & Company, 549 Broadway, Bayonne, NJ 07002: Free catalog ❖ Crystal, sterling, and china. 800-526-1440; 201-437-4443 (in NJ).

Silver Lane, P.O. Box 322, San Leandro, CA 94577: Free information ❖ Discontinued crystal and china patterns, current and obsolete silver, and serving pieces. 510-483-0632.

The Silver Queen, 730 N. Indian Rocks Rd., Bellair Bluffs, FL 34640: Free catalog ❖ New sterling silver and discontinued patterns. Also estate items. 800-262-3134; 813-581-6827 (in FL).

Silverladies & Nick, 5650 W. Central Ave., Toledo, OH 43615: Free information ❖ Sterling and silver plate in old, inactive, and obsolete patterns. 800-423-4390.

Sterling & Collectables Inc., P.O. Box 1665, Mansfield, OH 44901: Free list ❖ Current and obsolete sterling silver patterns, sterling Christmas ornaments, stainless, and serving pieces. 419-756-8817.

The Sterling Shop, P.O. Box 595, Silverton, OR 97381: Free list with long SASE ❖ Inactive and obsolete American-made sterling and discontinued silverplate patterns. 503-873-6315.

Thurber's, 2256 Dabney Rd., Richmond, VA 23230: Free information ❖ Sterling and china. 800-848-7237.

Treadwell's Western Mercantile, 201 W. Main, Stroud, OK 74079: Free brochure ❖ Western-style flatware, enamelware, and dinnerware. 918-587-5526.

Wallace International Silversmiths, 340 Quinnipiac St., Wallingford, CT 06492: Free information ❖ Silverplated and stainless steel flatware, silverplated hollowware, sterling silver place settings, and accessories. 203-269-4401.

Zucker's Fine Gifts, 151 W. 26th St., New York, NY 10001: Free catalog ❖ Hummel, Swarovski silver and crystal, Waterford crystal, Lladro porcelain, and gifts. 212-989-1450.

SKATEBOARDS

Attitude Skateboards, 13623 Annapolis Rd., Bowie, MD 20715: Free catalog ❖ Skateboards. 800-786-4973.

Beer City Skateboards, P.O. Box 26035, Milwaukee, WI 53226: Free information ❖ Skateboards. 414-257-1511.

Big Brand Products, P.O. Box 461, Escondido, CA 92046: Free information ❖ Skateboards and accessories. 619-742-2321.

Cali4nia Skate Express, 4629 N. Blythe, Fresno, CA 93722: Free information ❖ Skateboards, T-shirts, stickers, and shoes. 800-447-8989.

CCS Skateboards, 2701 McMillan Ave., San Luis Obispo, CA 93401: Free catalog ❖ T-shirts, shoes, stickers, skateboards and parts, and safety gear. 800-477-9283.

The Deluxe Store, 1831 Market St., San Francisco, CA 94103: Free information ❖ Skateboards. 800-275-3359.

FTC Skateboarding Shop, 622 Shrader St., San Francisco, CA 94117: Free catalog ❖ Skateboards and parts, snowboards, T-shirts, and clothing. 415-386-6693.

Intensity Skates, 11890 Old Baltimore Pike, Beltsville, MD 20705: Free catalog ❖ Skateboards, clothing, and hightops. 301-937-1349.

Kryptonics Inc., 740 S. Pierce Ave., Louisville, CO 80027: Free information ❖ Skateboards and roller skates. 800-766-9146; 303-665-5353 (in CO).

National Sporting Goods Corporation, 25 Brighton Ave., Passaic, NJ 07055: Free information ❖ Skateboards, roller skates, and scooters. 201-779-2323.

Rat City Sports, 3803 W. Magnolia Blvd., Burbank, CA 91505: Catalog $1 ❖ Skateboards, parts, and clothing. 800-245-2489.

Roller Derby Skate Company, Box 930, Litchfield, IL 62056: Free information ❖ Skateboards, roller and in-line skates, and scooters. 217-324-3961.

Saucony/Hyde, 13 Centennial Dr., Peabody, MA 01961: Free list of retail sources ❖ Skateboards, roller skates, and scooters. 800-365-7282.

60/40 Skateboards, P.O. Box 2067, Freedom, CA 95019: Free information ❖ Skateboards. 408-728-5382.

Skates on Haight, 384 Oyster Point Blvd., San Francisco, CA 94080: Free catalog ❖ Skateboards, wheels, shoes, T-shirts, and sweatshirts. 415-244-9800.

Smoothill Sports Distributors, 3060 Kerner Blvd., San Rafael, CA 94901: Free information ❖ Skateboards. 415-453-1170.

UFO Sports Inc., 18533 Roscoe Blvd., Ste. 323, Northridge, CA 91324: Catalog $3 ❖ Skateboards, wheels, decks, and stickers. 818-701-1521.

V.K. Sports, 775 W. 17th St., Unit O, Costa Mesa, CA 92627: Free information ❖ Skateboards and accessories. 714-722-8411.

Variflex Inc., 5152 N. Commerce Ave., Moorpark, CA 93021: Free information ❖ Skateboards and roller skates. 805-523-0322.

Z Products, P.O. Box 5397, Santa Monica, CA 90409: Free information ❖ Skateboards, trucks, and wheels. 310-476-4857.

SKIING

Clothing

Eddie Bauer, P.O. Box 3700, Seattle, WA 98124: Free catalog ❖ Men and women's ski clothing, natural fiber sportswear, down outerwear, footwear, and luggage. 800-426-8020.

❖ SKIING ❖

L.L. Bean Inc., Freeport, ME 04033: Free catalog ❖ Camping and workout gear, and men and women's clothing for skiing, back country travel, and snowshoeing. 800-483-2326.

Big Dog Sportswear, Mail Order, 121 Gray Ave., Santa Barbara, CA 93101: Free catalog ❖ Insulated outerwear and accessories. 800-642-3647.

Bogner of America, Bogner Dr., Newport, VT 05855: Free information ❖ Gloves and mittens, hats, parkas, jackets, pants, suits, separates, sweaters, wind shirts, and vests. 800-451-4417; 802-334-6507 (in VT).

Columbia Sportswear Company, 6600 N. Baltimore, Portland, OR 97203: Free list of retail sources ❖ Men, women, and children's hats, gloves, mittens, jackets, pants, suits, parkas, underwear, vests, and wind shirts. 800-MA-BOYLE.

Dynastar, Box 25, Hercules Dr., Colchester, VT 95446: Free catalog ❖ Boots and competition skis. 800-245-9001.

Eagle River Nordic, P.O. Box 936, Eagle River, WI 54521: Free catalog ❖ High-performance and cross-country racing ski equipment and clothing. 800-423-9730.

Early Winters, P.O. Box 4333, Portland, OR 97208: Free catalog ❖ Men and women's ski clothing, leisure separates for men and women, gifts, and equipment. 800-458-4438.

Gart Brothers Denver Sportscastle, 1000 Broadway, Denver, CO 80203: Free information ❖ Skis, boots, and men and women's clothing. 800-426-1399; 303-861-1122 (in CO).

Gorsuch Ltd., 263 E. Gore Creek Dr., Vail, Colorado 81657: Free catalog ❖ Clothing for men, women, and children. 800-525-9808.

Kid Sport, 122 E. Meadow Dr., Vail, CO 81657: Free catalog ❖ Winterwear and skiwear for children, from newborn through young adult. 800-833-1729.

Ladylike Ski Shop, 104 N. Ballard, Wylie, TX 75098: Free information ❖ Ski clothing for men, women, and children. 214-442-5842.

Marker Ltd., P.O. Box 26548, Salt Lake City, UT 84119: Free brochure ❖ Men and women's ski clothing. 800-462 7537; 801-972-0404 (in UT).

Marmot Mountain Works, 827 Bellevue Way NE, Bellevue, WA 98004: Free catalog ❖ Men and women's ski clothing. 800-254-6246.

Mont-Bell, Catalog Customer Service, 940 1st Ave., Santa Cruz, CA 95062: Free catalog ❖ All-weather shells, long underwear, ski wear, clothing and accessories for outdoors and travel. 800-683-2002.

Nordica, 139 Harvest Ln., P.O. Box 800, Williston, VT 05495: Free information ❖ Caps, gloves, jackets, boots, and pants. 800-343-7800; 802-879-4644 (in VT).

North Face, 999 Harrison St., Berkeley, CA 94710: Free list of retail sources ❖ Hats, mittens and gloves, jackets, parkas and suits, underwear, sweaters, vests, and wind shirts. 800-447-2333.

Northern Outfitters, 14072 Pony Express Rd., Draper, UT 84020: Free information ❖ Clothing.

Pearl Izumi, 2300 Central Ave., Boulder, CO 80301: Free information ❖ Caps, jackets, and pants. 800-328-8488; 303-938-1700 (in CO).

Rossignol Ski Company, Industrial Ave., P.O. Box 298, Williston, VT 05495: Free information ❖ Alpine skis and bindings, cross-country skis, and alpine boots. 802-863-2511.

Scandinavian Ski & Sport Shop, 40 W. 57th St., New York, NY 10019: Free information ❖ Men and women's ski clothing and equipment. 800-722-6754.

Sporthill, 1690 S. Bertelsen Rd., Eugene, OR 97402: Free information ❖ Caps, jackets, and pants. 800-622-8444; 503-345-9623 (in OR).

Yellow Turtle, Mt. Road, Stowe, VT 05672: Free catalog ❖ Children's clothing, ski wear, and accessories. 800-439-4435; 802-253-4434 (in VT).

Equipment & Accessories

Akers Ski Inc., One Akers Way, Andover, ME 04216: Free catalog ❖ Cross-country ski equipment. 207-392-4582.

Allsop, P.O. Box 23, Bellingham, WA 98227: Free information ❖ Nordic skis and poles, boot trees, and carriers. 800-426-4303; 206-734-9090 (in WA).

Alpina Sports Corporation, P.O. Box 23, Hanover, NH 03755: Free list of retail sources ❖ Boot bags, alpine and nordic boots, and nordic bindings and skis. 603-448-3101.

APPEND Multi-Sport Racks, MascoTech Accessories, 1418 N. Market Blvd., Ste. 500, Sacramento, CA 95834: Free brochure ❖ Bicycle, ski, snowboard, and surf and sailboard carriers for automobiles. 800-527-7363.

Black Diamond Equipment, 2084 E. 3900 South, Salt Lake City, UT 84124: Free catalog ❖ Skis. 801-278-5533.

Chisco Sports Accessories, 2424 S. 2570 West, Salt Lake City, UT 84119: Free information ❖ Alpine skis. 800-825-4555.

Climb High Inc., 60 Northside Dr., Shelburne, VT 05482: Free catalog ❖ Nordic boots. 802-985-5056.

Collins Ski Products Inc., P.O. Box 11, Bergenfield, NJ 07621: Free brochure ❖ Ski carriers, goggles, ski poles, and locks. 800-526-0369; 201-384-6060 (in NJ).

Daleboot USA, 2150 S. 3rd West, Salt Lake City, UT 84115: Free information ❖ Alpine ski poles, boots, and boot bags. 801-487-3649.

Dynastar, Box 25, Hercules Dr., Colchester, VT 95446: Free catalog ❖ Boots and competition skis. 800-245-9001.

Eagle River Nordic, P.O. Box 936, Eagle River, WI 54521: Free catalog ❖ Ski equipment, clothing, boots, gloves, hats, and videos. 800-423-9730.

Elan-Monark, 208 Flynn Ave., P.O. Box 4279, Burlington, VT 05401: Free information ❖ Boot and ski bags, alpine ski poles, bindings, boots, and alpine and nordic skis. 802-863-5593.

Excel Marketing Inc., One 2nd St., Peabody, MA 01960: Free list of retail sources ❖ Cross-country skis, boots, and poles. 800-521-2011.

Fabiano Shoe Company, 850 Summer St., South Boston, MA 02127: Free information with long SASE ❖ Nordic boots and bindings and apres ski boots. 617-268-5625.

Head Sports, 4801 N. 63rd St., Boulder, CO 80301: Free information ❖ Alpine skis, boots, poles, and bindings. 800-874-3234; 303-530-2000 (in CO).

Hunt-Wilde, 2835 Overpass Rd., Tampa, FL 33619: Free information ❖ Nordic ski poles. 800-248-1232.

Igloo Viksi Inc., P.O. Box 180, St. Agathe Des Monts, Quebec, Canada J8C 3A3: Free information ❖ Boot and ski bags, alpine and nordic ski poles, and nordic skis, boots, and bindings. 819-326-1662.

Karhu USA Inc., P.O. Box 4249, Burlington, VT 05406: Free list of retail sources ❖ Skis and boots. 800-869-3348.

Marmot Mountain Works, 827 Bellevue Way NE, Bellevue, WA 98004: Free catalog ❖ Skis, boots, bindings, poles, and accessories. 800-254-6246.

Maska USA Inc., 529 Main St., Ste. 205, Boston, MA 02129: Free information ❖ Nordic skis, poles, and boots. 800-451-4600; 617-242-8600 (in MA).

Nordica, 139 Harvest Ln., P.O. Box 800, Williston, VT 05495: Free information ❖ Alpine and cross-country skis. 800-343-7800; 802-879-4644 (in VT).

Raichle Molitor USA, Geneva Rd., Brewster, NY 10509: Free list of retail sources ❖ Alpine and cross-country skis, boots, and poles. 914-279-5121.

REI Recreational Equipment Company, Sumner, WA 98352: Free catalog ❖ Exercise and walking shoes, Gore-Tex rain gear, day packs that convert to tents, ski equipment, gifts, knives and utensils, sunglasses, and camping foods. 800-426-4840.

Reliable Racing Supply Inc., 643 Upper Glen St., Queensbury, NY 12804: Free catalog ❖ Ski equipment. 800-223-4448.

Rossignol Ski Company, Industrial Ave., P.O. Box 298, Williston, VT 05495: Free information ❖ Alpine skis and bindings, cross-country skis, and alpine boots. 802-863-2511.

Salomon/North America, 400 E. Main St., Georgetown, MA 01833: Free list of retail sources ❖ Alpine and nordic bindings and boots. 800-225-6850.

Skis Dynastar Inc., Hercules Dr., P.O. Box 25, Colchester, VT 05446: Free information ❖ Alpine and nordic skis, alpine boots, and boot and ski bags. 802-655-2400.

Spalding Sports Worldwide, 425 Meadow St., P.O. Box 901, Chicopee, MA 01021: Free list of retail sources ❖ Nordic and alpine skis and poles. 800-225-6601.

Swix Sport USA Inc., 261 Ballardvale St., Wilmington, MA 01887: Free information ❖ Boot and ski bags, goggles, alpine and nordic ski poles, and nordic bindings and boots. 508-657-4820.

Yamaha Sporting Goods Division, 6600 Orangethorpe Ave., Buena Park, CA 90622: Free information ❖ Alpine skis. 800-851-6514; 714-522-9011 (in CA).

Goggles

Bolle America, 3890 Elm St., Denver, CO 80207: Free information ❖ Ski goggles. 800-554-6686; 303-321-4300 (in CO).

Brigade Quartermasters Inc., 1025 Cobb International Blvd., Kenesaw, GA 30144: Free catalog ❖ Ski goggles. 404-428-1234.

Collins Ski Products Inc., P.O. Box 11, Bergenfield, NJ 07621: Free brochure ❖ Ski carriers, goggles, and ski poles and locks. 800-526-0369; 201-384-6060 (in NJ).

Gargoyles Performance Eyewear, 5866 S. 194th St., Kent, WA 98032: Free catalog ❖ Sunglasses and ski goggles. 206-872-6100.

Martin Sunglasses, Jack Martin Company Inc., 9830 Baldwin Pl., El Monte, CA 91731: Free information ❖ Ski goggles. 800-767-8555; 213-686-1100 (in CA).

Raichle Molitor USA, Geneva Rd., Brewster, NY 10509: Free list of retail sources ❖ Goggles. 914-279-5121.

Suunto USA, 2151 Las Palmas Dr., Carlsbad, CA 92009: Free list of retail sources ❖ Ski goggles. 619-931-6788.

Swix Sport USA Inc., 261 Ballardvale St., Wilmington, MA 01887: Free information ❖ Boot and ski bags, goggles, alpine and nordic ski poles, and nordic bindings and boots. 508-657-4820.

SKIN DIVING & SCUBA EQUIPMENT

Ador-Aqua, 42 W. 18th St., New York, NY 10011: Free information ❖ Skin diving equipment. 800-223-2500.

Apollo, 44 Montgomery St., Ste. 3065, San Francisco, CA 94104: Free information ❖ Skin diving equipment and accessories. 800-231-0909; 415-392-9143 (in CA).

Aquarius, 51 Lake St., Nashua, NH 03060: Free information ❖ Skin diving equipment. 800-435-8974; 603-889-4346 (in NH).

Atlantic Edge Scuba, 213 Muddy Branch Rd., Gaithersburg, MD 20878: Free list of retail sources ❖ Skin diving equipment. 800-325-8439.

Bare Sportswear Corporation, Box 8110-577, Blaine, WA 98230: Free information ❖ Wet suits and clothing. 604-533-7848.

Berry Scuba Company, 6674 N. Northwest Hwy., Chicago, IL 60631: Free catalog ❖ Skin diving and scuba equipment, inflatable boats, and underwater camera equipment. 800-621-6019; 312-763-1626 (in IL).

Body Glove International Inc., 530 6th St., Hermosa Beach, CA 90254: Free information ❖ Wet and skin diving suits and equipment. 800-678-7873; 310-374-4074 (in CA).

Brownie's Third Lung, 940 NW 1st St., Fort Lauderdale, FL 33311: Free information ❖ Surface air and tank-filling compressors. 800-327-0412.

Central Skin Divers, 160-09 Jamaica Ave., Jamaica, NY 11432: Free information ❖ Skin diving equipment and clothing. 718-739-5772.

Citizen Watch Company of America, 8506 Osage Ave., Los Angeles, CA 90056: Free information ❖ Professional diving watches and sports, flight, yachting, and windsurfer chronographs.

Competitive Aquatic Supply Inc., 15131 Triton Ln., Ste. 110, Huntington Beach, CA 92649: Free information ❖ Skin diving equipment and waterproof watches. 800-421-5192; 310-633-3333 (in CA).

Dacor Corporation, 161 Northfield Rd., Northfield, IL 60093: Free information ❖ Scuba equipment. 708-446-9555.

Divers Supply, 5208 Mercer University Dr., Macon, GA 31210: Free catalog ❖ Skin diving equipment and clothing. 800-999-3483.

Diving Unlimited International, 1148 Delevan Dr., San Diego, CA 92102: Free list of retail sources ❖ Dry suits, skin diving equipment, and accessories. 800-325-8439.

Innovative Designs Inc., 3785 Alt. 19 North, Ste. C, Palm Harbor, FL 34683: Free information ❖ Compact lightweight air supply equipment. 813-934-4619.

KME Diving Suits Inc., 3420 C St. NE, Auburn, WA 98002: Free information ❖ Wet suits. 800-800-8KME.

Leisure Pro, 42 W. 18th St., 3rd Floor, New York, NY 10011: Free information ❖ Scuba and skin diving equipment and clothing. Also tennis and backpacking equipment. 212-645-1234.

M & E Marine Supply Company, P.O. Box 601, Camden, NJ 08101: Catalog $2 ❖ Skin diving equipment. 800-541-6501.

Murrays WaterSports, P.O. Box 490, Carpinteria, CA 93014: Free information ❖ Wet suits. 800-788-8964.

Nautica International, 6135 NW 167th St., Miami, FL 33015: Free information ❖ Compressors. 305-556-5554.

Ocean Ray Wet Suits, 6731-3 Amsterdam Way, Wilmington, NC 28405: Free brochure ❖ Wet suits and skin diving equipment. 800-645-5554.

O'Neill, 1071 41st Ave., P.O. Box 6300, Santa Cruz, CA 95062: Free information ❖ Wet suits. 408-475-7500.

Performance Diver, P.O. Box 2741, Chapel Hill, NC 27514: Free catalog ❖ Wetsuits, buoyancy control devices, tank holders, boots, gloves, skin diving equipment, goggles, video cameras, and accessories. 800-933-2299.

Sea Quest, 2151 Las Palmas Dr., Carlsbad, CA 92009: Free information ❖ Scuba equipment. 619-438-1101.

Skin Diver Wet Suits, 1632 S. 250th St., Des Moines, WA 98032: Free information ❖ Wet suits. 206-878-1613.

Sport Europa, 7871 NW 15th St., Miami, FL 33126: Free catalog ❖ Wet suits for men, women, and children. 800-695-7000.

Sports Merchandizers, 1690 Cobb Pkwy. SE, Box 1262, Marietta, GA 30061: Free catalog ❖ Skin diving equipment. 800-241-1856; 404-952-3259 (in GA).

Submersible Systems, 18072 Gothard St., Huntington Beach, CA 92648: Free information ❖ Breathing systems. 714-842-6566.

Sunshine Sports, 5104 12th Ave., Brooklyn, NY 11219: Free information ❖ Skin diving and scuba equipment. 800-290-5622; 718-437-4257 (in NY).

Tackle Shack, 7801 66th St. North, Pinellas Park, FL 34665: Free catalog ❖ Skin diving equipment. 813-546-5080.

Tanks D'Art Inc., 330 Easy St., Simi Valley, CA 93065: Free information ❖ Diving tanks. 800-635-5815.

Tektite, P.O. Box 4209, Trenton, NJ 08610: Free information ❖ Scuba equipment. 609-581-2116.

3 Little Devils, S. 5780 A Hwy. 123, Baraboo, WI 53913: Free catalog ❖ Scuba equipment. 800-356-9016.

Tilos Products, 3202 Factory Dr., Pomona, CA 91768: Free list of retail sources ❖ Wet suits, gloves, carry-all bags, and accessories. 800-475-5703; 909-594-6809 (in CA).

U.S. Wet Suits, P.O. Box 428, 11475 Commercial Ave., Richmond, IL 60071: Free brochure ❖ Wet suits. 800-852-6049.

Curt Walker, Optician, 3434 4th Ave., Ste. 120, San Diego, CA 92103: Free information ❖ Optically corrected dive masks. 800-538-2878; 619-299-2878 (in CA).

Wenoka Sea Style, c/o Sea Quest Inc., 2151 Las Palmas Dr., Carlsbad, CA 19009: Catalog $4 ❖ Skin diving equipment. 800-327-7662; 619-438-1101 (in CA).

SLEDS, SNOWBOARDS & TOBOGGANS

APPEND Multi-Sport Racks, MascoTech Accessories, 1418 N. Market Blvd., Ste. 500, Sacramento, CA 95834: Free brochure ❖ Bicycle, ski and snowboard, and surf and sailboard carriers for automobiles. 800-527-7363.

Dorfman-Pacific, P.O. Box 213005, Stockton, CA 95213: Free information ❖ Sleds, snowmobile boots, and clothing. 800-367-3626; 209-982-1400 (in CA).

Faber Brothers, 4141 S. Pulaski Rd., Chicago, IL 60632: Free information ❖ Sleds. 312-376-9300.

Flexible Flyer Company, P.O. Box 1296, West Point, MS 39773: Free information ❖ Sleds. 800-521-6233.

FTC Ski & Sports, 1586 Bush St., San Francisco, CA 94109: Free catalog ❖ Skateboards and parts, snowboards, T-shirts, and clothing. (415) 673-8363.

Skip Hutchison, Rastaboards-Surf-Sail-Snowboards, 4748 NE 11th Ave., Fort Lauderdale, FL 33334: Free information with long SASE ❖ Sailboards, surfboards, and snowboards. 954-491-7992.

M.W. Kasch Company, 5401 W. Donges Bay Rd., Mequon, WI 53092: Free information ❖ Sleds and snowboards. 414-242-5000.

Murrays WaterSports, P.O. Box 490, Carpinteria, CA 93014: Free information ❖ Snowboards. 800-788-8964.

Paris Company Inc., Box 250, South Paris, ME 04281: Free information ❖ Sleds. 207-539-8221.

Sevylor USA, 6651 E. 26th St., Los Angeles, CA 90040: Free information ❖ Sleds. 213-727-6013.

SFO Snowboard Shop, 618 Shrader St., San Francisco, CA 94117: Free information ❖ Snowboards. 415-386-1666.

ZIFFCO, 18111-B S. Santa Fe Ave., Rancho Dominguez, CA 90221: Free information ❖ Toboggans. 800-532-2242.

SLIPCOVERS & UPHOLSTERY

Fabric Shop, 120 N. Seneca St., Shippensburg, PA 17257: Free information with long SASE ❖ Antique satins, custom draperies, and drapery, slipcover, and upholstery fabrics. 800-233-7012; 717-532-4150 (in PA).

Fabrics by Phone, P.O. Box 234, Walnut Bottom, PA 17266: Brochure and samples $3 ❖ Antique satins, custom draperies, and drapery, slipcover, and upholstery fabrics. 800-233-7012; 717-532-4150 (in PA).

Home Fabric Mills Inc., 882 S. Main St., Cheshire, CT 06410: Free brochure ❖ Velvets, upholstery, drapery, and thermal fabrics. Also velvets, prints, sheers, and antique satins. 203-272-3529.

Slipcovers of America, 58 W. 40th St., New York, NY 10018: Free catalog ❖ Slipcovers, matching draperies, and fabrics.

Tioga Mill Outlet, 200 S. Hartman St., York, PA 17403: Free brochure ❖ Upholstery and drapery fabrics. 717-843-5139.

SNOW BLOWERS

Ariens Company, 655 W. Ryan St., P.O. Box 157, Brillion, WI 54110: Free information ❖ Power-operated snow blowers. 414-756-2141.

SNOWMOBILES

Arctco Sales Inc., P.O. Box 810, 600 S. Brooks Ave., Thief River Falls, MN 56701: Free list of retail sources ❖ Arctic Cat snowmobiles. 218-681-8558.

Central Snowmobile Salvage, P.O. Box 13188, Green Bay, WI 54307: Free catalog ❖ Snowmobile parts and accessories. 800-558-6778.

F & R Sales & Service, 2048 N. Lewis Ave., Waukegan, IL 60087: Free catalog ❖ Polaris snowmobile clothing and accessories. 800-287-9975; 708-662-4243 (in IL).

Hunt-Wilde, 2835 Overpass Rd., Tampa, FL 33619: Free information ❖ Snowmobiles. 800-248-1232.

Intraser Inc., 3580 Wilshire Blvd., Los Angeles, CA 90010: Free information ❖ New and pre-owned motorcycles, ATVs, snowmobiles, trailers, personal water vehicles, and small boats. 213-365-6030.

Dennis Kirk Inc., 955 Southfield Ave., Rush City, MN 55069: Free information ❖ Snowmobiles and parts. 800-328-9280.

Polaris Industries, 1225 Hwy. 169 North, Minneapolis, MN 55441: Free list of retail sources ❖ Snowmobiles, clothing, and accessories. 800-POLARIS; 612-542-0500 (in MN).

Recycled Cycles Inc., P.O. Box 970, Hayden Lake, ID 83835: Free information ❖ Used snowmobile and motorcycle parts. 800-365-9530.

Starting Line Products Inc., 743 Iona Rd., Idaho Falls, ID 83401: Free catalog ❖ Snowmobile performance parts and accessories. (208) 529-0244.

SNOWSHOES

Atlas Snow-Shoe Company, 81 Lafayette St., San Francisco, CA 94103: Free information ❖ Snowshoes. 800-645-SHOE.

Buckeye Sports Supply, John's Sporting Goods, 2655 Harrison Ave. SW, Canton, OH 44706: Free information ❖ Snowshoes. 800-533-8691.

Croakies, P.O. Box 2913, Jackson, WY 83001: Free information ❖ Snowshoes. 800-443-8620; 307-733-2266 (in WY).

Havlick Snowshoe Company, 2513 State Hwy. 30, Drawer QQ, Mayfield, NY 12117: Free brochure with long SASE ❖ Aluminum and wood-framed snowshoes. 800-TOP-SHOE.

Iverson Snowshoe Company, Maple St., P.O. Box 85, Shingleton, MI 49884: Free information ❖ Snowshoes and bindings. 906-452-6370.

Liberty Mountain Sports, 9325 SW Barber St., Wilsonville, OR 97070: Free information ❖ Snowshoes and insulated clothing. 503-685-9600.

Longwood Equipment Company Ltd., 1940 Ellesmere Rd., Unit 8, Scarborough, Ontario, Canada M1H 2V7: Free information ❖ Snowshoes. 416-438-3710.

Northern Lites Performance Snowshoes, 1300 Cleveland, Wausau, WI 54401: Free list of retail sources ❖ Snowshoes. 800-360-LITE.

Safesport Manufacturing Company, 5151 Bannock St., Denver, CO 80216: Free information ❖ Snowshoes and bindings. 800-433-6506.

SOAP MAKING

The Essential Oil Company, P.O. Box 206, Lake Oswego, OR 97034: Free catalog ❖ Essential oils, soap-making molds and supplies, incense materials, potpourri, and aromatherapy items. 800-729-5912.

Gardens Past, P.O. Box 1846, Estes Park, CO 80517: Catalog $1 ❖ Soaps and soap-making supplies, potpourri, dried flowers, herbs, candles, and aromatherapy items. 303-823-5565.

Pourette Manufacturing, P.O. Box 17056, Seattle, WA 98107: Catalog $2 ❖ Candles and soap and candle-making supplies.

Soap Saloon, 7309 Sage Oak Ct., Citrus Heights, CA 95621: Catalog $2 ❖ Soap and candle-making supplies. 916-723-6859.

Summers Past Farm, 15602 Old Hwy. 80, Flinn Springs, CA 92021: Free catalog ❖ Soap-making kit. 800-390-9969.

Sun Feather Handcrafted Herbal Soap Company, 1551 State Hwy. 72, Potsdam, NY 13676: Catalog $2 ❖ Soap-making kits, supplies, and books. 800-771-7627.

Valley Hills Press, 1864 Ridgeland Ct., Starkville, MS 39759: Free information ❖ Soap-making and books about soap. 800-323-7102.

SOCCER

Clothing

Action & Leisure Inc., 45 E. 30th St., New York, NY 10016: Free information ❖ Shoes, uniforms, gloves, shorts, shirts, shin guards, and socks. 800-523-8508; 212-684-4470 (in NY).

Action Sport Systems Inc., P.O. Box 1442, Morgantown, NC 28680: Free information ❖ Uniforms, shirts, shorts, gloves, and socks. 800-631-1091; 704-584-8000 (in NC).

Adidas USA, 5675 N. Blackstock Rd., Spartanburg, SC 29303: Free list of retail sources ❖ Uniforms, shoes, socks, shirts, shorts, and shin guards. 800-423-4327.

American Soccer Company Inc., 726 E. Anaheim St., Wilmington, CA 90744: Free information ❖ Shorts, warm-up clothing, and uniforms. 800-626-7774; 310-830-6161 (in CA).

Asics Tiger Corporation, 10540 Talbert Ave., West Building, Fountain Valley, CA 92708: Free information ❖ Shoes, socks, shorts, and shin guards. 800-678-9435.

Betlin Manufacturing, 1445 Marion Rd., Columbus, OH 43207: Free information ❖ Shorts, warm-up clothing, and uniforms. 614-443-0248.

Bike Athletic Company, P.O. Box 666, Knoxville, TN 37901: Free information ❖ Shinguards, shirts, shorts, and uniforms. 800-251-9230.

Bomark Sportswear, P.O. Box 2068, Belair, TX 77402: Free information ❖ Uniforms. 800-231-3351.

Champion Products Inc., 475 Corporate Square Dr., Winston-Salem, NC 27105: Free information ❖ Uniforms, shoes, socks, and shirts.

Continental Sports Supply Inc., P.O. Box 1251, Englewood, CO 80150: Free information ❖ Gloves, shinguards, shirts, shorts, and uniforms. 303-934-5657.

Doss Shoes, Soccer Sport Supply Company, 1745 1st Ave., New York, NY 10128: Free information ❖ Gloves, shinguards, shirts, shorts, and uniforms. 800-223-1010; 212-427-6050 (in NY).

Empire Sporting Goods Manufacturing Company, 443 Broadway, New York, NY 10013: Free information ❖ Shorts and uniforms. 800-221-3455; 212-966-0880 (in NY).

Genesport Industries Ltd., Hokkaido Karate Equipment Manufacturing Company, 150 King St., Montreal, Quebec, Canada H3C 2P3: Free information ❖ Gloves, shinguards, shirts, and shorts. 514-861-1856.

Holabird Sports Discounters, 9220 Pulaski Hwy., Baltimore, MD 21220: Free catalog ❖ Soccer and sports equipment and clothing. 410-687-6400.

Lotto Sports, 1900 Surveyor Blvd., Carrollton, TX 75006: Free information ❖ Soccer shoes. 800-527-5126; 214-416-4003 (in TX).

Markwort Sporting Goods, 4300 Forest Park Ave., St. Louis, MO 63108: Catalog $8 (request list of retail sources) ❖ Shorts, warm-up clothing, and uniforms. 800-669-6626; 314-652-3757 (in MO).

Puma USA Inc., 147 Centre St., Brockton, MA 02403: Free information with long SASE ❖ Uniforms, gloves, shorts and shirts, socks, shoes, and shin guards. 508-583-9100.

Soccer International Inc., P.O. Box 7222, Arlington, VA 22207: Catalog $2 ❖ Soccer equipment, uniforms, balls, gifts, T-shirts, and books. 703-524-4333.

Soccer Kick, 2130 Henderson Mill Rd., Atlanta, GA 30345: Free catalog ❖ Soccer equipment and gifts. 800-533-KICK; 404-939-6355 (in GA).

Soccer Madness International, 5369 Hiatus Rd., Sunrise, FL 33351: Free catalog ❖ Clothing, shoes, and equipment. 800-447-8333.

Union Jacks, 3525 Roanoke Rd., Kansas City, MO 64111: Free information ❖ Uniforms, shin guards, shirts, shorts, shoes, and socks. 800-288-5550; 816-561-5550 (in MO).

Equipment

Action & Leisure Inc., 45 E. 30th St., New York, NY 10016: Free information ❖ Soccer balls, cleats, and wrenches. 800-523-8508; 212-684-4470 (in NY).

Action Sport Systems Inc., P.O. Box 1442, Morgantown, NC 28680: Free information ❖ Soccer balls. 800-631-1091; 704-584-8000 (in NC).

Adidas USA, 5675 N. Blackstock Rd., Spartanburg, SC 29303: Free list of retail sources ❖ Soccer balls, cleats, and equipment. 800-423-4327.

American Soccer Company Inc., 726 E. Anaheim St., Wilmington, CA 90744: ❖ Balls, goalie gloves, nets, and protective gear. 800-626-7774; 310-830-6161 (in CA).

The Athletic Connection, 1901 Diplomat, Dallas, TX 75234: Free information ❖ Balls and nets. 800-527-0871; 214-243-1446 (in TX).

Brine Inc., 47 Sumner St., Milford, MA 01757: Free information ❖ Balls, goalie gloves, nets, and protective gear. 800-227-2722; 508-478-3250 (in MA).

Buckeye Sports Supply, John's Sporting Goods, 2655 Harrison Ave. SW, Canton, OH 44706: Free information ❖ Goals, nets, and soccer balls. 800-533-8691.

Clarke Distributing Company, 9233 Bryant St., Houston, TX 77075: Catalog $2 ❖ Tennis, golf, soccer equipment, novelties, and gifts. 800-777-3444.

Continental Sports Supply Inc., P.O. Box 1251, Englewood, CO 80150: Free information ❖ German Bundesliga soccer balls. 303-934-5657.

Doss Shoes, Soccer Sport Supply Company, 1745 1st Ave., New York, NY 10128: Free information ❖ Goals, nets, and soccer balls. 800-223-1010; 212-427-6050 (in NY).

General Sportcraft Company, 140 Woodbine Rd., Bergenfield, NJ 07621: Free information ❖ Soccer balls, goals, and nets. 201-384-4242.

Holabird Sports Discounters, 9220 Pulaski Hwy., Baltimore, MD 21220: Free catalog ❖ Soccer equipment and clothing. 410-687-6400.

Irwin Sports, 43 Hanna Ave., Toronto, Ontario, Canada M6K 1X6: Free information ❖ Soccer balls, goals, and nets. 800-268-1732.

Jayfro Corporation, Unified Sports Inc., 976 Hartford Tnpk., P.O. Box 400, Waterford, CT 06385: Free catalog ❖ Portable goals, nets, and practice equipment. 860-447-3001.

Kwik Goal, 140 Pacific Dr., Quakertown, PA 18951: Free information ❖ Soccer balls, goals, nets, wrenches and cleats, training equipment, referee supplies, and video cassettes. 800-531-4252; 215-536-2200 (in PA).

Markwort Sporting Goods, 4300 Forest Park Ave., St. Louis, MO 63108: Catalog $8 (request list of retail sources) ❖ Soccer balls, goals, and nets. 800-669-6626; 314-652-3757 (in MO).

Pennray Billiard & Recreational Products, 6400 W. Gross Point Rd., Niles, IL 60714: Free catalog ❖ Darts, billiards, and soccer equipment. 800-523-8934.

Soccer International Inc., P.O. Box 7222, Arlington, VA 22207: Catalog $2 ❖ Soccer balls, uniforms, gifts, T-shirts, and books. 703-524-4333.

SOLAR & WIND ENERGY

Soccer Kick, 2130 Henderson Mill Rd., Atlanta, GA 30345: Free catalog ❖ Soccer equipment, clothing, and shoes. 800-533-KICK; 404-939-6355 (in GA).

Soccer Madness International, 5369 Hiatus Rd., Sunrise, FL 33351: Free catalog ❖ Clothing, shoes, and equipment. 800-447-8333.

Spalding Sports Worldwide, 425 Meadow St., P.O. Box 901, Chicopee, MA 01021: Free list of retail sources ❖ Soccer balls. 800-225-6601.

Sportime, Customer Service, 1 Sportime Way, Atlanta, GA 30340: Free information ❖ Balls and nets. 800-444-5700; 770-449-5700 (in GA).

Sportline of Hilton Head Ltd., 816 Friendly Center Rd., Greensboro, NC 27408: Free information ❖ Soccer balls. 800-438-6021.

Wolvering Sports, 745 State Circle, Box 1941, Ann Arbor, MI 48106: Catalog $1 ❖ Baseball, basketball, field hockey, soccer, football, and athletic and recreation equipment. 313-761-5691.

SOLAR & WIND ENERGY

Advance Solar Hydro Wind Power Company, 6291 N. State St., P.O. Box 23, Calpella, CA 95418: Information $1 ❖ Solar, hydro-electric, and wind energy power systems. 707-485-0588.

Alternative Energy Engineering, P.O. Box 339, Redway, CA 05560: Catalog $1 ❖ Solar energy equipment. 800-777-6609.

American Energy Technologies Inc., P.O. Box 1865, Green Cove Springs, FL 32043: Free information ❖ Solar energy thermal collectors, absorbers, and systems. 800-874-2190.

Array Technologies, 3402 Stanford NE, Albuquerque, NM 87107: Free information ❖ Solar trackers for photovoltaic arrays. 505-881-7567.

Ascension Technology, P.O. Box 314, Lincoln Center, MA 01773: Free information ❖ Photovoltaic power systems and monitoring and evaluation equipment. 617-890-8844.

Atlantic Solar Products, 9351 Philadelphia Rd., P.O. Box 70060, Baltimore, MD 21237: Free catalog ❖ Solar energy power systems for the home. 410-686-2500.

Backwoods Solar Electric, 8530 Rapid Lightning Creek, Sandpoint, ID 83864: Catalog $3 ❖ Solar electric-powered appliances and electricity-generating equipment. 208-263-4290.

Balmar, 902 NW Ballard Way, Seattle, WA 98107: Free information ❖ Wind-driven alternator. 206-789-4970.

Bergey Windpower Company Inc., 2001 Priestly Ave., Norman, OK 73069: Free information ❖ Wind turbines. 405-364-4212.

BSAR Solar, 980 Santa Estella, Solana Beach, CA 92075: Free information ❖ Solar system for heating water. 714-993-5890.

Dempster Industries Inc., P.O. Box 848, Beatrice, NE 68310: Free information ❖ Hand and windmill pumps and parts. 800-234-3367.

Environmental Solar Systems, 119 West St., Methuen, MA 01844: Free information ❖ Solar food dryers. 800-934-3848.

Fanta-Sea Pools, 10151 Main St., Clarence, NY 14031: Free information ❖ Solar energy heated swimming pools. 800-845-5500.

Fowler Solar Electric Inc., 226 Huntington Rd., P.O. Box 435, Worthington, MA 01098: Catalog $3 ❖ Solar energy systems and equipment for homes. 413-238-5345.

Kansas Wind Power, 13569 214th Rd., Holton, KS 66436: Catalog $4 ❖ Sun ovens, wind generators, composting toilets, tankless water heaters, air cooler, and solar energy equipment and parts. 913-364-4407.

Kipp & Zonen, Division Enraf-Nonius Company, 390 Central Ave., Bohemia, NY 11716: Free information ❖ Solar radiation measurement instrumentation to determine application needs. 800-645-1025.

Midway Labs Inc., 1818 E. 71st St., Chicago, IL 60649: Free information ❖ Solar energy electricity-generating components. 312-667-7863.

Offline Independent Energy Systems, P.O. Box 231, North Fork, CA 93643: Catalog $3 ❖ Independent energy systems. 209-877-7080.

Photocomm Inc., Distribution Division, 7681 E. Gray Rd., Scottsdale, AZ 85260: Catalog $5 ❖ Solar energy modules for homes, recreational vehicles, boats, and cabins. 800-544-6466; 602-951-6330 (in AZ).

Quad Energy, P.O. Box 690073, Houston, TX 77269: Catalog $4 ❖ Solar enereqy components. 713-259-0393.

Real Goods, 555 Leslie St., Ukiah, CA 95482: Free catalog ❖ Solar energy components, solar educational toys, environmental books and games, and alternative energy products. 800-762-7325.

Refrigeration Research Inc., P.O. Box 869, Brighton, MI 48116: Free information ❖ Do-it-yourself solar water heating systems for homes. 810-227-1151.

Self-Reliance Company Inc., P.O. Box 306, Florissant, MO 63032: Catalog $7.95 ❖ Solar, wind, and hydro-electric energy systems. 314-839-9292.

Siemens Solar Industries, P.O. Box 6032, Camarillo, CA 93010: Free information ❖ Solar panels for energy systems. 800-272-6765.

Sierra Solar Systems, 109 Argall Way, Nevada City, CA 95959: Catalog $5 (refundable) ❖ Solar electric energy systems and appliances. 800-51-SOLAR.

Solar Components Corporation, 121 Valley St., Manchester, NH 03103: Brochure $1 ❖ Lean-to and free-standing build-it-yourself greenhouse kits and solar energy equipment. 603-668-8186.

Solar Depot, 61 Paul Dr., San Rafael, CA 94903: Catalog $6.50 ❖ Solar electric power systems, water heaters, electric and thermal systems, and other equipment. 415-499-1333.

Solar Electric Inc., 555 Santa Fe St., #J, San Diego, CA 92109: Free information ❖ Solar panels and equipment. 800-842-5678.

Solarex Corporation, 630 Solarex Ct., Frederick, MD 21701: Free catalog ❖ Solar panels, battery chargers, and other photovoltaic equipment. 301-698-4200.

Specialty Concepts Inc., 8954 Mason Ave., Chatsworth, CA 91311: Free brochure ❖ Photovoltaic controls. 818-998-5238.

The Sun Electric Company, P.O. Box 1499, Hamilton, MT 59840: Free catalog ❖ Solar energy equipment for recreational vehicles, cabins, or homes. 800-338-6844.

Sun-Porch Structures, P.O. Box 1353, Stamford, CT 06904: Catalog $2 ❖ Solar greenhouses. 203-324-0010.

Sunelco, P.O. Box 1499, Hamilton, MT 59840: Catalog $4.95 ❖ Solar modules, controllers, batteries, inverters, water pumps, propane-operated appliances, home power systems, and heating systems for recreational vehicles and cabins. 800-338-6844.

Sunglo Solar Greenhouses, 4441 26th Ave. West, Seattle, WA 98199: Free brochure ❖ Solar greenhouses and solariums. 800-647-0606; 206-284-8900 (in WA).

Sunlight Energy Corporation, 4411 W. Echo Ln., Glendale, AZ 85302: Free information ❖ Solar battery chargers. 800-338-1781.

Sunnyside Solar, RD 4, Box 808, Green River Rd., Brattleboro, VT 05301: Free information ❖ Photovoltaic (solar electric) equipment, design, and installation. 802-257-1482.

Sunquest Inc., 1555 Rankin Ave., Newton, NC 28658: Free information ❖ Solar energy and radiant floor heating systems. 704-465-6805.

Thermo Dynamics Ltd., 81 Thornhill Dr., Dartmouth, Nova Scotia, Canada B3B 1R9: Free information ❖ Solar hot water system. 902-468-1001.

United Solar Systems Corporation, 5278 Eastgate Mall, San Diego, CA 92121: Free brochure ❖ Solar electric utility power modules and battery chargers. 619-625-2080.

Vanner Incorporated, 4282 Reynolds Dr., Hilliard, OH 43026: Free information ❖ High-powered system for alternative energy power needs. 800-989-2718.

World Power Technologies Inc., 19 N. Lake Ave., Duluth, MN 55802: Free brochure ❖ Easy-to-install wind-operated electric generators and solar equipment. 218-722-1492.

Yankee Environmental Systems Inc., P.O. Box 746, Turners Falls, MA 01376: Free information ❖ Solar radiation measurement systems. 413-863-0200.

Zomeworks Corporation, P.O. Box 25805, Albuquerque, NM 87125: Free information ❖ Passive solar trackers and fixed racks for top-of-pole, side-of-pole, or roof/ground/wall mounts. 800-279-6342.

SOLARIUMS & SUNROOMS

Arctic Glass & Window Outlet, 565 County Rd. T, Hammond, WI 54015: Catalog $2 ❖ Sunrooms, windows, entryway and patio doors, and skylights. 800-428-9276.

Creative Structures, 1765 Walnut Ln., Quakerstown, PA 18951: Catalog $1 ❖ Sunroom and greenhouse kits. 215-538-2426.

Florian Greenhouses Inc., 64 Airport Rd., West Milford, NJ 07480: Catalog $5 ❖ Easy-to-build solariums for do-it-yourselfers. 800-FLORIAN.

Four Seasons Solar Products, 5005 Veterans Memorial Hwy., Holbrook, NY 11741: Free information ❖ Modular solarium kits. 800-368-7732.

Glasswalls Porch Enclosures, Mon-Ray Windows, 8824 Olson Memorial Hwy., Minneapolis, MN 55427: Free information ❖ Supplies for converting a screened porch or enclosing a patio into an all-season room. 800-544-3646.

Habitat Solar Rooms, 21 Elm St., South Deerfield, MA 01373: Information $10 ❖ All-cedar kits for solar rooms. 800-992-0121.

International Screen Corporation, 3110 SE Slater St., Stuart, FL 34997: Free information ❖ Assemble-it-yourself Florida-style screen enclosures. 800-688-2943.

Janco Greenhouses, 9390 Davis Ave., Laurel, MD 20707: Brochure $5 ❖ Solariums with optional variable pitch roofs. 800-323-6933.

Lindal Cedar Homes, P.O. Box 24426, Seattle, WA 98124: Catalog $15 ❖ Sunrooms. 800-426-0536.

Machin Designs by Amdega, P.O. Box 7, Glenview, IL 60025: Catalog $10 ❖ English-style conservatories constructed in either western red cedar or aluminum. 800-922-0110.

North Country Creative Structures, Rt. 197, RD 1, Box 1060B, Argyle, NY 12809: Catalog $5 ❖ Do-it-yourself kits and components for add-on solar rooms and pool enclosures. 800-833-2300.

Progressive Building Products, 1678 Shattuck Ave., Ste. 173, Berkeley, CA 94709: Catalog $5.95 ❖ Greenhouse and solarium components. 800-776-2534.

Skytech Systems, P.O. Box 763, Bloomsburg, PA 17815: Catalog $3 ❖ Free-standing and window greenhouses, solariums, and sunrooms. 717-752-1111.

Solarium Systems International, 333 N. Mead, Wichita, KS 67219: Free information ❖ Solariums with optional variable pitch roofs. 800-225-6423.

Southeastern Insulated Glass, 6477-B Peachtree Industrial Blvd., Atlanta, GA 30360: Free information ❖ Greenhouse and sunroom kits, sliding glass doors, and skylights. 800-841-9842; 404-455-8838 (in GA).

Sturdi-Built Manufacturing Company, 11304 SW Boones Ferry Rd., Portland, OR 97219: Free catalog ❖ Greenhouses, cold frames, and sunrooms. 503-244-4100.

Sun Room Company, 354 N. Marshall St., Lancaster, PA 17602: Free information ❖ Sunrooms, window box greenhouses, skylights, window walls, and windows. 800-426-2737.

Sunbilt Solar Products by Sussman Inc., 109-10 180th St., Jamaica, NY 11433: Free information ❖ Easy-to-build sunrooms. 718-297-6040.

Sundance Supply, 1678 Shattuck Ave., Ste. 173, Berkeley, CA 94709: Catalog $2 ❖ Building components for greenhouses, sun rooms, pool enclosures, and skylights. 800-776-2534.

Sunspot Inc., 5030 40th Ave., Hudsonville, MI 49426: Free information ❖ Solariums, greenhouses, and conservatories. 800-635-4786.

Under Glass Manufacturing Corporation, P.O. Box 323, Wappingers Falls, NY 12590: Catalog $3 ❖ Greenhouses and solariums. 914-298-0645.

Vegetable Factory Inc., Sun-Porch Division, P.O. Box 1353, Stamford, CT 06904: Information $2 ❖ Insulated winter sun room that converts to a summer screen enclosure.

Window Quilt, P.O. Box 975, Brattleboro, VT 05362: Information $1 ❖ Sunrooms. 800-257-4501.

SOUVENIRS

Allen-Lewis Manufacturing Company, Division TCC Industries Inc., P.O. Box 16546, 5601 Logan, Denver, CO 80216: Free catalog ❖ Souvenirs, carnival and party supplies, fund-raising merchandise, toys and games, T-shirts and sweat shirts, and craft supplies. 303-295-0196.

Steve Eagles, Native American Regalia, P.O. Box 88142, Colorado Springs, CO 80908: Catalog $3 ❖ Native American souvenirs, gifts, clothing, jewelry, musical instruments, and items. 719-495-0798.

SPELEOLOGY (CAVE EXPLORATION)

W. Born & Associates, 2438 Blacklick-Eastern Rd., Millersport, OH 43046: Free information with long SASE ❖ Equipment and supplies for cavers. 614-467-2676.

Bumjo's, 1700 E. 18th St., Ste. 100, Tucson, AZ 85719: Free catalog ❖ Caving, climbing, backpacking, and mountaineering equipment. 800-649-0318.

Inner Mountain Outfitters, 102 Travis Circle, Seaford, VA 23696: Free catalog ❖ Equipment and supplies for cavers. 757-898-2809.

Pigeon Mountain Industries, P.O. Box 803, Lafayette, GA 30728: Free information ❖ Gear and supplies for cavers. 800-282-7673; 404-764-1437 (in GA).

PMI Petzal Distribution Inc., P.O. Box 803, LaFayette, GA 30728: Free list of retail sources ❖ Headlamps. 800-282-7673.

Speleoshoppe, P.O. Box 297, Fairdale, KY 40118: Free information ❖ Equipment and supplies for cavers. 800-626-5877.

J.E. Weinel Inc., P.O. Box 213, Valencia, PA 16059: Free information with long SASE ❖ Equipment and supplies for caving, climbing, and rappelling. 412-898-2335.

SPINNING WHEELS, LOOMS & CARDERS

AVL Looms, 601 Orange St., Chico, CA 95928: Catalog $2 ❖ Looms and supplies. 800-626-9615; 916-893-4915 (in CA).

Bountiful, Lois & Bud Scarbrough, P.O. Box 1727, Estes Park, CO 80517: Catalog $5 ❖ Spinning wheels, tapestry looms, books, videos, yarns, parts, and accessories. 970-586-9332.

Braid-Aid, 466 Washington St., Pembroke, MA 02359: Catalog $4 ❖ Braided rug kits, braiding supplies, spinning and weaving accessories, and wool by the pound or yard. 617-826-2560.

Clemes & Clemes Inc., 650 San Pablo Ave., Pinole, CA 94564: Free catalog ❖ Spinning wheels, drum carders, wool and cotton carders, drop spindles, and natural and dyed wool. 510-742-2036.

Country Spun Studio, RR 1, Box 269, Rochester Mills, PA 15771: Brochure $3 ❖ Hand-painted and hand-spun yarns, spinning wheels, books and videos, and accessories. 412-286-3255.

Crystal Palace Yarns, 3006 San Pablo Ave., Berkeley, CA 94702: Free list of retail sources ❖ Yarns, natural fibers, and spinning wheels. 510-548-9988.

The Designery, P.O. Box 308, Center Sandwich, NH 03227: Catalog $1 ❖ Spinning and weaving supplies, hand-dyed wool, mohair, and yarns. 603-284-6915.

Dundas Loom Company, P.O. Box 7522, Missoula, MT 59807: Free information ❖ Harness looms and treadle stands. 406-728-3050.

Earthsong Fibers, 5115 Excelsior Blvd., #428, Minneapolis, MN 55416: Catalog $2 ❖ Fibers, yarns, spinning wheels, looms, and accessories. 800-473-5350; 612-926-3451 (in MN).

Edgemont Yarn Services, P.O. Box 205, Washington, KY 41096: Free brochure ❖ Weaving supplies, 2 and 4-harness looms, tabletop looms, loom parts, and rug-making supplies. 800-446-5977.

Fiber Studio, 9 Foster Hill Rd., Box 637, Henniker, NH 03242: Spinning fibers catalog $1, yarn samples $4, equipment catalog $1 ❖ Spinning, weaving, and knitting equipment and spinning fibers. Also cotton, mohair, wool, alpaca, silk, and linen yarns. 603-428-7830.

Fireside Fiberarts, P.O. Box 1195, Port Townsend, WA 98368: Brochure $3 ❖ Portable cantilever tapestry looms and accessories. 206-385-7505.

Gilmore Looms, 1032 N. Broadway, Stockton, CA 95205: Free catalog ❖ Looms and accessories. 209-463-1545.

Glimakra Looms & Yarns Inc., 1338 Ross St., Petaluma, CA 94954: Catalog $2.50 ❖ Weaving equipment, looms, yarns, and lace-making equipment. 800-289-9276; 707-762-3362 (in CA).

Good Wood Ltd., Rt. 2, Box 447A, Bethel, VT 05032: Catalog $2 ❖ Frame and slant looms and accessories. 802-234-5534.

Patrick Green Carders, 48793 Chilliwack Lake Rd., Chilliwack, British Columbia, Canada V4Z 1A6: Free information ❖ Carders with optional motor units. 604-858-6020.

Harrisville Designs, Center Village, Box 806, Harrisville, NH 03450: Yarn catalog $6; free loom catalog ❖ Yarns and looms. 800-338-9415.

Heritage Looms, Rt. 6, Box 731-E, Alvin, TX 77511: Catalog $1.50 ❖ Table looms and weaving supplies. 409-925-4161.

J-Made Looms, P.O. Box 452, Oregon City, OR 97045: Catalog $3 ❖ Looms in 45, 60, and 72-inch models. 503-631-3973.

K's Creations, P.O. Box 161446, Austin, TX 78746: Free information ❖ Adjustable interchangeable lap frames, canvasses, and accessories. 800-727-3769.

Kokovoko Breeding Farm, Rt. 3, Box 134, Corinth, KY 41010: Free information ❖ Spinning wheels, accessories, how-to videos, and books. 800-804-5541.

Lacis, 3163 Adeline St., Berkeley, CA 94703: Catalog $4 ❖ Hairpin lace looms. 510-843-7178.

Leesburg Looms & Supply, 201 N. Cherry St., Van Wert, OH 45891: Free catalog ❖ Easy-to-operate 2 and 4-harness looms. 419-238-2738.

Gord Lendrum, RR 4, Odessa, Ontario, Canada K0H 2H0: Free information ❖ Folding spinning wheels, drum carders, and hand cards. 613-386-7151.

Louët Sales, P.O. Box 267, Ogdensburg, NY 13669: Catalog $2 ❖ Books, dyestuffs, yarns and fibers, and spinning, weaving, carding, felting, and lace-making equipment. 613-925-4502.

Macomber Looms, P.O. Box 186, York, ME 03909: Catalog $3 ❖ Looms. 207-363-2808.

Mannings Creative Crafts, P.O. Box 687, East Berlin, PA 17316: Catalog $1 ❖ Spinning wheels and looms, yarns and spinning fibers, books, and dyes and mordants. 717-624-2223.

Mary Lue's Knitting World, 101 W. Broadway, St. Peter, MN 56082: Free information ❖ Spinning wheels, looms, and accessories. Also yarns and how-to videos. 819-362-2408.

Mountain Loom Company, P.O. Box 1107, Castle Rock, WA 98611: Free brochure ❖ Sampler, table, pique, tapestry, and floor looms. 800-238-0296; 360-295-3856 (in WA).

Nasco, 901 Janesville Ave., Fort Atkinson, WI 53538: Free catalog ❖ Weaving supplies, looms, tools, yarns, and needlecraft accessories. 800-558-9595.

Nelson Light Looms, 1170 Brook Rd., Goshen, NH 03752: Free catalog ❖ Light looms (less than ½ pound).

Norsk Fjord Fiber, P.O. Box 271, Lexington, GA 30648: Catalog $3 ❖ Tapestry looms. 404-743-5120.

Norwood Looms, P.O. Box 167, Freemont, MI 49412: Catalog $2 ❖ Looms, quilting hoops, and frames. 616-924-3901.

Pendleton Shop, Jordan Rd., P.O. Box 233, Sedona, AZ 86336: Catalog $1 ❖ Looms and weaving supplies. 602-282-3671.

Rio Grande Weaver's Supply, 216 Pueblo Norte, Taos, NM 87571: Catalog $1 ❖ Spinning wheels, looms, and loom kits. Also hand-dyed yarns and dyes, fleece, books, and videos. 505-758-0433.

River Farm, Rt. 1, P.O. Box 471, Fulks Run, VA 22830: Catalog $1 ❖ Spinning wheels, looms, and American fleece for spinning. 800-USA-WOOL.

Schacht Spindle Company Inc., 6101 Ben Pl., Boulder, CO 80301: Catalog $2.50 ❖ Looms and accessories. 800-228-2553.

School Products Company Inc., 1201 Broadway, New York, NY 10001: Free information ❖ Spinning wheels, looms, yarns, and accessories. 800-847-4127; 212-679-3516 (in NY).

Shannock Tapestry Looms, 10402 NW 11th Ave., Vancouver, WA 98685: Free information ❖ Weaving supplies and tapestry looms with roller beams. 206-573-7264.

Bonnie Triola, 343 E. Gore Rd., Erie, PA 16509: Information $10 ❖ Natural fibers, synthetics, blends, discontinued designer yarns, and cone and stock yarns. 814-825-7821.

The Weaver's Loft, 308 S. Pennsylvania Ave., Centre Hall, PA 16828: Free information ❖ Knitting, weaving, and spinning supplies and yarns. 814-364-1433.

Weavers' Store, 11 S. 9th St., Columbia, MO 65201: Catalog $2 ❖ Looms, spinning wheels, yarns, and mill ends. 314-442-5413.

Weaving Works, 4717 Brooklyn Ave. NE, Seattle, WA 98105: Catalog $4.50 ❖ Looms, spinning wheels, hand and machine-knitting supplies, yarns, and books. 206-524-1221.

Woodland Woolworks, 262 S. Maple St., P.O. Box 400, Yamhill, OR 97148: Free catalog ❖ Spinning wheels and hand-spinning supplies. 800-547-3725.

Wool Room, Joe's Hill Rd., Brewster, NY 10509, Brewster, NY 10509: Brochure $1 ❖ Spinning fibers, weaving yarns, and equipment. 914-279-7627.

The Woolery, RD 1, Genoa, NY 13071: Catalog $2 ❖ Spinning, weaving, knitting, dye supplies, and books. 315-497-1542.

Yarn Barn, 918 Massachusetts, Lawrence, KS 66044: Free catalog ❖ Spinning wheels and looms, parts and accessories, and supplies. 800-468-0035.

SPORTS & NON-SPORTS CARDS

Non-Sports Cards

Johnny Adams Jr., P.O. Box 8491, Green Bay, WI 54308: Free information with long SASE ❖ Non-sports and sports cards. 414-465-9101.

Barrington Square Cards, 2332 W. Higgins Rd., Hoffman Estates, IL 60195: Free information ❖ Non-sports cards, coins, and comics. 847-882-7080.

Champion Sports Collectables Inc., 150 E. Santa Clara, Arcadia, CA 91006: Free information ❖ Autographed sports memorabilia, sports and non-sports cards, and supplies. 800-LA-CHAMP; 818-574-5500 (in CA).

Chattanooga Coin Company, P.O. Box 80158, Chattanooga, TN 37414: Free information ❖ Non-sports cards. 800-444-2646.

Clinton Dean's Figures & Collectibles, P.O. Box 383, Milford, NH 03055: Free catalog ❖ Character toys and figures, trading cards, toys, and collectibles. 603-673-3290.

Georgetown Card Exchange, P.O. Box 11572, Philadelphia, PA 19116: Free price list ❖ Non-sports comic cards and football, hockey, baseball, basketball, and sports cards. 215-698-0366.

Henri LaBelle, 1162 Lesage St., P.O. Box 561, Prevost, Quebec, Canada J0R 1T0: Free information with long SASE ❖ Non-sports cards collectibles. 514-224-2813.

Mile High Comics, 2151 W. 56th Ave., Denver, CO 80221: Catalog $1 ❖ Movie and TV-related trading cards.

Paul & Judy's Coins & Cards, P.O. Box 409, Arthur, IL 61911: Free information ❖ Trading cards and supplies for collectors of all ages, including sports, non-sports, adult, gaming, and magic. 217-543-3366.

T.J.'s Comics & Cards & Supplies, Lloyds Shopping Center, 330 Rt. 211 East, Middletown, NY 10940: Free information ❖ Comic books, sports and non-sports cards, and hobby supplies. 800-848-1482.

Unique Dist., 110 Denton Ave., New Hyde Park, NY 11040: Free information ❖ Sports and non-sports cards and comics. 800-294-5901; 516-294-5900 (in NY).

Wex Rex Records & Collectibles, 280 Worcester Rd., Framingham, MA 01701: Catalog $3 ❖ Non-sports cards, movie and TV show character toys, and collectibles. 508-620-6181.

Sports Cards

A.K.A. Sports Cards, 3701 Church Rd., Mt. Laurel, NJ 08054: Free information ❖ Collectible baseball, basketball, hockey, and sports cards. 609-778-0020.

A.S.E. Cards, P.O. Box 178, Tujunga, CA 91043: Free information with long SASE ❖ Sets, boxes, and single cards. 818-355-5426.

Johnny Adams Jr., P.O. Box 8491, Green Bay, WI 54308: Free information with long SASE ❖ Sports and non-sports cards. 414-465-9101.

B & E Collectibles Inc., 950 Broadway, Thornwood, NY 10594: Free information ❖ Hard-to-find sports card singles. 914-769-1304.

B & O Wholesale, 2880 N. Dayton-Lakeview Rd., New Carlisle, OH 45344: Free information ❖ Archival and storage supplies. 513-845-3372.

Ball Four Cards, 4732 N. Royal Atlanta Dr., Tucker, GA 30084: Free information ❖ Archival and storage supplies. 404-621-0377.

Barnetts Sports Cards, P.O. Box 964, Hartville, OH 44632: Free information with long SASE ❖ Hard-to-find sports card singles and sets. 216-877-4270.

Baseball Barons Sportscards, 1295 Boardman Canfield Rd., Boardman, OH 44512: Free information ❖ Basketball, baseball, and hockey sports cards. 800-437-7814.

Baseball Card Kingdom, 323 Jersey St., Harrison, NJ 07029: Free information ❖ Baseball card sets, minor league sets, sports impression figurines, Star Company platinum and gold edition sets, and memorabilia. 201-481-9630.

Baseball Card World, P.O. Box 970, Anderson, IN 46015: Free information with long SASE ❖ Sports card hobby supplies. 800-433-4229.

Best Comics Distribution Center, 252-01 Northern Blvd., Little Neck, NY 11362: Free information ❖ Comic books, original comic art, action figures, collector supplies, and trading cards. 800-966-2099; 718-279-2099 (in NY).

Bill's Cards & Supplies, 25 N. Colonial Dr., Hagerstown, MD 21742: Free information with long SASE ❖ Sports cards and hobby supplies. 301-797-2992.

Boca Cards & Investments, Doug Koval, 5030 Champion Blvd., Boca Raton, FL 33496: Free information ❖ Vintage collectible sports cards. 407-241-8316.

Louis Bollman Cards, 607 Redbud Ln., Columbia, MO 65203: Free information ❖ Vintage collectible sports cards. 314-874-9644.

Brewart Coins & Stamps, 1015 N. Euclid St., Anaheim, CA 92801: Free information with long SASE ❖ Rare and hard-to-find sports card singles and sets.

Brigandi Coin Company, 60 W. 44th St., New York, NY 10036: Free information with long SASE ❖ Sports cards. 800-221-2128.

Broadway Rick's Strike Zone, 1840 N. Federal Hwy., Boynton Beach, FL 33435: Free information with long SASE ❖ Autographed sports memorabilia, sports cards, and collectibles. 800-344-9103; 407-364-0453 (in FL).

Can-Am Card Company, P.O. Box 345, Ganges, British Columbia, Canada V0S 1E0: Free information with long SASE ❖ Vintage sports cards. 604-537-9460.

Card Collectors Company, 105 W. 77th St., New York, NY 10024: Catalog $2 ❖ Sports cards and collectibles. 212-873-6999.

Cardboard Gold Inc., 1855 Weinig St., Statesville, NC 28677: Free catalog ❖ Sports cards collecting supplies. 704-871-8000.

Cee-Jay Sports Card Company, Sunset Industrial Park, 52 20th St., Brooklyn, NY 11232: Free information with long SASE ❖ Hard-to-find football, basketball, hockey, golf, and tennis sports card singles and sets. 718-832-5296.

Champion Sports, 702 W. Las Tunas, San Gabriel, CA 91776: Free information ❖ Sports card hobby supplies. 818-570-1106.

Champion Sports Collectables Inc., 150 E. Santa Clara, Arcadia, CA 91006: Free information ❖ Autographed sports memorabilia, sports and non-sports cards, and supplies. 800-LA-CHAMP; 818-574-5500 (in CA).

Chicago Sports Cards Ltd., P.O. Box 448, Chelsea, MI 48118: Free information with long SASE ❖ Sports cards.

Dolloff, P.O. Box 719, Portsmouth, NH 03802: Free information with long SASE ❖ Basketball, boxing, football, swimming, track and field, and wrestling sports cards.

Doubleheaders, 1204 Lehigh Rd., Pittsburgh, PA 15205: Free catalog with six 1st class stamps ❖ Sports cards.

Durta Enterprises, 500 E. Ridge Rd., Unit E, Griffith, IN 46319: Free information with long SASE ❖ Archival and storage supplies and ball cubes and holders. 800-451-0096; 219-838-5510 (in IN).

Empire State Sports Memorabilia & Collectibles Inc., 331 Cochran Pl., Valley Stream, NY 11581: Free information ❖ Baseball and sports cards, autographs, and memorabilia. 516-791-9091.

Flip Cards & Supplies, 165 E. Union Ave., East Rutherford, NJ 07073: Free information ❖ Sports card collecting supplies. 201-933-7070.

Four Base Hits, P.O. Box 137, Centereach, NY 11720: Free information with long SASE ❖ Sports cards. 516-981-3286.

Georgetown Card Exchange, P.O. Box 11572, Philadelphia, PA 19116: Free price list ❖ Non-sports comic cards and football, hockey, baseball, basketball, and sports cards. 215-698-0366.

Gerry Guenther, W7521 Patchin Rd., Pardeeville, WI 53954: Free information ❖ Superstar sports cards. 608-742-2201.

Hall's Nostalgia, 9 Mystic St., P.O. Box 408, Arlington, MA 02174: Free information ❖ Sports cards. 800-367-4255; 617-646-7757 (in MA).

Bruce Harris Sportscards, 1291 Steeple Run Dr., Lawrenceville, GA 30243: Free information ❖ Sports cards. 404-822-0988.

Bill Henderson's Cards, 2320 Ruger Ave., Janesville, WI 53545: Free information with long SASE ❖ Rare and hard-to-find sports card singles and sets. 608-755-0922.

SQUARE DANCING

Hobby Supplies, P.O. Box 372, Marlboro, NJ 07746: Free information with long SASE ❖ Sports card collecting supplies. 908-780-3689.

Neil Hoppenworth's Cards, 3511 Lafayette Rd., P.O. Box 3117, Evansdale, IA 50707: Free information ❖ Vintage sports cards. 319-232-6011.

Hot Card USA, 1215 Harrison Ave., Kearny, NJ 07032: Free information with long SASE ❖ Hard-to-find sports cards. 201-998-1062.

Howard's Sports Collectibles, 128 E. Main St., P.O. Box 84, Leipsic, OH 45856: Catalog $5 ❖ Baseball and football cards in sets or singles. 800-457-9974.

Jake's House of Cards, 40 Freeway Dr., Cranston, RI 02920: Free information with long SASE ❖ Baseball cards, from 1948 to 1979. Also other sports cards. 800-892-0024.

Klassy Kollectibles Inc., 137 White Horse Pike, Berlin, NJ 08009: Free information with long SASE ❖ Sports cards singles and sets. 609-767-0250.

Koinz & Kardz-Madison, 1101 Stewart St., Madison, WI 53713: Free information with long SASE ❖ Rare and hard-to-find sports card singles and sets. 608-274-5275.

Mid-Atlantic Sports Cards, 22 S. Morton Ave., Morton, PA 19070: Catalog $1 ❖ Posters and hard-to-find sports card singles and sets. 610-544-2171.

The Minnesota Connection, 17773 Kenwood Trail, Lakeville, MN 55044: Free information with long SASE ❖ Baseball, football, basketball, and hockey sports cards. 612-892-0406.

Mark Murphy, 73 Harbor Dr., Ste. 415, Stamford, CT 06902: Free information ❖ Hard-to-find baseball, football, hockey, and basketball cards. 203-348-5050.

Paul & Judy's Coins & Cards, P.O. Box 409, Arthur, IL 61911: Free information ❖ Hard-to-find non-sports and sports cards. 217-543-3366.

Perfect Image Sports Cards, 11608 Reistertown Rd., Reistertown, MD 21136: Free information ❖ Baseball, boxing, basketball, football, golf, and hockey sports cards. 410-998-9500.

Quality Baseball Cards Inc., 106 Despatch Dr., East Rochester, NY 14445: Free information ❖ Hard-to-find sports card singles and sets. 800-HOBBY-88; 716-248-3510 (in NY).

Rotman Collectibles, 4 Brussels St., Worcester, MA 01610: Free information ❖ Sports cards and storage supplies. 508-791-6710.

St. Louis Baseball Cards, 5456 Chatfield, St. Louis, MO 63129: Free information ❖ Sports card sets, uniforms, press pins, autographs, advertising pieces, and baseball memorabilia. 314-892-4737.

San Diego Sports Collectibles, 659 Fashion Valley, San Diego, CA 92108: Catalog $2 ❖ Hard-to-find sports card singles, sets, and limited editions. 800-227-0483.

Kevin Savage Cards, c/o Mid-America Sports, 3509 Briarfield Blvd., Maumee, OH 43537: Free information ❖ Collectible sports cards. 419-861-2330.

The Score Board Inc., 1951 Old Cuthbert Rd., Cherry Hill, NJ 08034: Free information ❖ Sports card sets, star cards prior to 1970, commemorative cards prior to 1942, and sports memorabilia. 800-327-4145; 609-354-8011 (in NJ).

The Sports Alley, 15545 E. Whittier Blvd., Whittier, CA 90603: Free information with long SASE ❖ Hard-to-find sports cards, canceled checks by sports greats, autographed pictures, world series programs, photographs, and memorabilia. 310-947-7383.

Sports Collectibles Inc., P.O. Box 11171, Chattanooga, TN 37401: Catalog $1 ❖ Sports cards, autographed baseballs, bats, and color photos. 615-265-9366.

Sportscards, P.O. Box 707, Plumsteadville, PA 18949: Free information ❖ Sports cards and display cases. 215-249-0976.

SportsCards Plus, 28221 Crown Valley Pkwy., Laguna Niguel, CA 92677: Catalog $1 ❖ Sports cards, autographs, and sports memorabilia. 800-350-2273.

Starland Collector's Gallery, P.O. Box 622, Los Olivos, CA 93441: Catalog $2.50 ❖ Sports cards, movie posters, original comic art, and hard-to-find movies. 805-686-5122.

T.C. Card Company, 18 Via Aurelia, Palm Beach Gardens, FL 33418: Free information with long SASE ❖ Sports card singles, sets, and hard-to-find items. 407-624-1909.

T.J.'s Comics & Cards & Supplies, Lloyds Shopping Center, 330 Rt. 211 East, Middletown, NY 10940: Free information ❖ Comic books, sports and non-sports cards, and hobby supplies. 800-848-1482.

Texas Sportcard Company, 2816 Center St., Deer Park, TX 77536: Free information with long SASE ❖ Hard-to-find sports card singles and sets. 713-476-9964.

U.S. Gerslyn Ltd., 1100 Port Washington Blvd., Port Washington, NY 11050: Free brochure ❖ Sports card hobby supplies. 516-944-3553.

Unique Dist., 110 Denton Ave., New Hyde Park, NY 11040: Free information ❖ Sports and non-sports cards and comics. 800-294-5901; 516-294-5900 (in NY).

Brian Wallos & Company, 95 Newfield Ave., Edison, NJ 08837: Free information with long SASE ❖ Hard-to-find sports card singles and sets. 908-417-9757.

Gary Walter Baseball Cards, 561 River Terrace, Toms River, NJ 08755: Free information with long SASE ❖ Baseball cards. 908-286-9007.

West Coast Sports Cards Inc., 1808 S. 320th, Federal Way, WA 98003: Free information with long SASE ❖ Rare and hard-to-find sports card singles and sets. 206-941-1986.

Kit Young Sportscards, 11535 Sorrento Valley Rd., Ste. 403, San Diego, CA 92121: Catalog $2 ❖ Hard-to-find sports card singles and sets. 619-259-1300.

SQUARE DANCING

Amplifiers & Microphones

Ashton Electronics, 222 Stonegate Circle, San Jose, CA 95110: Free information ❖ Sound equipment. 408-995-6544.

Hilton Audio Products, 1033-E Shary Circle, Concord, CA 94518: Free information ❖ Sound equipment and cue cards for callers. 510-682-8390.

Merrbach Record Service, 323 W. 14th St., Houston, TX 77008: Free information ❖ Records, tape recorders, tapes, wireless microphones, cassette decks, and sound equipment. 713-862-7077.

Random Sound Inc., 7317 Harriet Ave. South, Minneapolis, MN 55423: Free catalog ❖ Sound equipment. 512-869-9501.

Supreme Audio Inc., P.O. Box 50, Marlborough, NH 03455: Free information ❖ Square dancing records and audio equipment. 800-445-7398.

Badges & Buckles

H & R Badge & Stamp Company, 2585 Mock Rd., Columbus, OH 43219: Free catalog ❖ In-stock and custom badges and rubber stamps. 614-471-3735.

KA-MO Engravers, P.O. Box 30337, Albuquerque, NM 87190: Free catalog ❖ Badges for square and round dancers. 800-352-5266; 505-883-4963 (in NM).

J.R. Kush & Company, 7623 Hesperia St., Reseda, CA 91335: Free information ❖ Handcrafted belt buckles for round dancers and square dancers. 818-344-9671.

Micro Plastics, Box 847, Rifle, CO 81650: Free information ❖ Club badges. 303-625-1718.

Books & Videos

Gold Star Video Productions, P.O. Box 1057, Sisters, OR 97759: Free information ❖ Video tapes on how to square or round dance. 800-87-HINGE; 503-549-4302 (in OR).

Clothing & Shoes

Andes S/D & Western Apparel, 2109 Liberty Rd., Eldersburg, MD 21784: Catalog $4 (refundable) ❖ Petticoats, pettipants, dresses, skirts, blouses, matching men's shirts, and scarf ties. 410-795-0808.

California Ranchwear Inc., 14600 S. Main St., Gardena, CA 90248: Free list of retail sources ❖ Square dance clothing and accessories. 310-532-8980.

The Catchall, 2310 Brookhollow, Wichita Falls, TX 76308: Free catalog ❖ Lace-trimmed petticoats and clothing. 817-692-8814.

Coast Shoes Inc., 13401 Saticoy, North Hollywood, CA 91605: Free list of retail sources ❖ Square dance shoes. 800-262-7851.

Doris Crystal Magic Petticoats, 8331 Pinecrest Dr., Redwood Valley, CA 95470: Free information ❖ Petticoats for square and round dancers. 800-468-6423; 707-485-7448 (in CA).

Dorothy's Square Dance Shop Inc., 3300 Strong Ave., P.O. Box 6004, Kansas City, KS 66106: Free catalog ❖ Clothing for square dancers. 913-262-4240.

Fabian's Western Wear, 18th & Jefferson, Lewisburg, PA 17837: Free information ❖ Men's clothing and women's petticoats. Will special order women's dresses. 717-523-6280.

Fashion Magic by Fendler, 702 Gashey Dr., Havre de Grace, MD 21078: Free list of retail sources ❖ Square dance clothing and accessories. 410-939-1149.

Grand Travel Square Dance Shop, Drawer 151, Holdenville, OK 74848: Free catalog ❖ Custom-crafted square dance apparel. 405-379-3872.

H Bar C Ranchwear, 14600 S. Main St., Gardena, CA 90248: Free list of retail sources ❖ Square dance clothing and accessories. 310-532-8980.

Honky Tonk Country Western Dance Wear, 4143 Aveinida De La Plata, Ocean Side, CA 92054: Free information ❖ Square dance clothing and accessories. 800-824-4222; 619-631-0080 (in CA).

Main-ly Country Western Wear, 166 Yarmouth Rd., Gray, ME 04039: Catalog $1 (refundable) ❖ Clothing for square dancers. 207-657-3412.

Oxbow Square Dance Shop, 8650 49th St. North, Pinellas Park, FL 34666: Free information ❖ Clothing for square dancers. 813-541-5700.

Palomino Square Dance Service, 2905 Scenic Dr., Marion, OH 43302: Free information ❖ Clothing for square dancers.

Shirley's S/D Shoppe, Rt. 9-D, Box 423, Hughsonville, NY 12537: Catalog $1 ❖ Patterns and petticoats and clothing for square dancers. 914-297-8504.

Meg Simkins, 119 Allen St., Hampden, MA 01036: Catalog $1 (refundable) ❖ Clothing for square dancers. 413-566-3349.

Square Dance & Western Wear Fashions Inc., 637 E. 47th St., Wichita, KS 67216: Free information ❖ Clothing and shoes. 316-522-6670.

Square Dance Attire, 7215 W. Irving Park Rd., Chicago, IL 60634: Free information ❖ Clothing for square dancers. 312-589-9220.

Steppin Out, P.O. Box 398, Humble, TX 77347: Free information ❖ Square and round dancing petticoats and dresses. 713-540-3557.

Stevens Worldwide Inc., Stevens Stompers, P.O. Box 112, Mercer, PA 16137: Free catalog ❖ Clogging shoes and supplies. 800-722-8040.

Tic-Tac-Toes, P.O. Box 953, Gloversville, NY 12078: Free information ❖ Square dance clothing and accessories. 518-773-8187.

Western Squares, 6820 Gravois, St. Louis, MO 63116: Catalog $2 ❖ Men and women's clothing for square dancing. 314-353-7230.

Records & CDs

A & S Record Shop, P.O. Box 6777, Warner Robins, GA 31095: Free information ❖ Square dancing records. 912-922-7510.

Chaparral Records Inc., 1425 Oakhill Dr., Plano, TX 75075: Free catalog ❖ Square dancing records. 614-383-5319.

Fort Brooke Quartermaster, Brandon B. Barszcz, P.O. Box 1628, Brandon, FL 33509: Catalog $2 ❖ Native American and square dancing cassettes and CDs. Also Celtic folk, Civil War, and Native American music. 813-621-7256.

Four BAR B Records Inc., Box 7-11, Macks Creek, MO 65786: Free list ❖ Square dancing records. 314-363-5432.

Hanhurst's Record Service, P.O. Box 50, Marlborough, NH 03455: Free information ❖ Square dancing records. 800-445-7398.

Hi Hat Dance Records, 3925 N. Tollhouse, Fresno, CA 93726: Free catalog ❖ Square dancing records. 209-227-2764.

Merrbach Record Service, 323 W. 14th St., Houston, TX 77008: Free information ❖ Records, tape recorders, tapes, wireless microphones, cassette decks, and sound equipment. 713-862-7077.

Palomino Square Dance Service, 2905 Scenic Dr., Marion, OH 43302: Free information ❖ Records for square, round, and folk dancing, and solo dancing and clogging.

Reeves Records Inc., 1835 S. Buckner Blvd., P.O. Box 17668, Dallas, TX 75217: Free information ❖ Record cases, books and manuals, plastic record jackets, sound equipment, and square, round, and clogging dancing records. 214-398-7508.

Silver Sounds Recordings, P.O. Box 229, Glastonbury, CT 06033: Free information ❖ Records for square dancing. 203-633-0370.

Square Dancetime Records, P.O. Box 3055, Yuba City, CA 95992: Free information ❖ Records for square dancing. 916-673-1120.

Supreme Audio Inc., P.O. Box 50, Marlborough, NH 03455: Free information ❖ Square dancing records and audio equipment. 800-445-7398.

TNT Records, RFD 2, Rt. 7, Box 227, St. Albans, VT 05478: Free information ❖ Square dance caller and instructor western-style and traditional records. 802-524-9424.

Wagon Wheel Records & Books, 17191 Cornina Ln., #203, Huntington Beach, CA 92649: Free catalog ❖ Square dancing records and books. 714-846-8169.

STAINED GLASS CRAFTING

AmeriGlas, P.O. Box 27668, Omaha, NE 68127: Free catalog ❖ Pre-cut kits, books and videos, tools, and supplies. 800-927-7877.

"Your Total Discount Supplier"

Anything in Stained Glass, 1060 Rt. 47 South, P.O. Box 444, Rio Grande, NJ 08242: Catalog $3.50 ❖ Discount art glass and supplies. Foil, solder, came, bevels, and books. 609-886-0416.

Art Glass House Inc., 3445 N. Hwy. 1, Cocoa, FL 32926: Free catalog ❖ Stained glass supplies. 800-525-8009; 407-631-4477 (in FL).

Atlas Art & Stained Glass, P.O. Box 76084, Oklahoma City, OK 73147: Catalog $3 ❖ Kaleidoscopes, frames, lamp bases, and art and craft, stained glass, jewelry-making, and foil-crafting supplies. 405-946-1230.

Big M Stained Glass, 3201 4th Ave., Seattle, WA 98134: Catalog $5 ❖ Stained glass supplies. 800-426-8307; 206-624-3962 (in WA).

Cline Glass Inc., 1135 SE Grand Ave., Portland, OR 97214: Catalog $5 ❖ Stained glass supplies. 800-547-8417.

Coran-Sholes, 509 E. 2nd St., South Boston, MA 02127: Catalog $3 ❖ Stained glass supplies. 617-268-3780.

STAIRLIFTS & ELEVATORS

DAB Studio, 31 N. Terrace, P.O. Box 96, Maplewood, NJ 07040: Free catalog ❖ Stained glass windows and decorative accessories. 800-682-6151.

Delphi Stained Glass, 2116 E. Michigan Ave., Lansing, MI 48912: Catalog $5 ❖ Stained glass supplies, tools, kits, and books. 800-248-2048.

Eastern Art Glass, P.O. Box 341, Wyckoff, NJ 07481: Catalog $2 (refundable) ❖ Stained glass kits and glass etching, engraving, and crafting supplies. 201-847-0001.

Franklin Art Glass, 222 E. Sycamore St., Columbus, OH 43206: Free brochure ❖ Stained glass tools and supplies. 800-848-7683.

Gemstone Equipment Manufacturing Company, 750 Easy St., Simi Valley, CA 93065: Free information ❖ Stained glass and lapidary supplies. 800-235-3375; 805-527-6990 (in CA).

Glass Crafters, 398 Interstate Ct., Sarasota, FL 34240: Catalog $3 ❖ Stained glass crafting supplies, tools, accessories, and books. 800-422-4552.

Houston Stained Glass Supply, 2002 Britmoore, Houston, TX 77043: Free information ❖ Stained glass supplies and beveled glass. 800-231-0148.

Hudson Glass, 219 N. Division St., Peekskill, NY 10566: Catalog $3 (refundable) ❖ Stained glass supplies, books, and patterns. 800-431-2964.

Kingsley North Inc., P.O. Box 216, Norway, MI 49870: Free catalog ❖ Stained glass and jewelry-making supplies and tools. 800-338-9280.

Nasco, 901 Janesville Ave., Fort Atkinson, WI 53538: Free catalog ❖ Stained glass supplies. 800-558-9595.

Sunshine Glassworks, 111 Industrial Pkwy., Buffalo, NY 14227: Catalog $3 ❖ Stained glass supplies and tools. 800-828-7159; 716-668-2918 (in NY).

Unique Colors, P.O. Drawer 20, Logansport, LA 71049: Free information ❖ Opaque colors for glass crafting. Also kits, pattern books, and tools. 318-697-4401.

United Art Glass, 1032 E. Ogden Ave., #128, Naperville, IL 60563: Free catalog ❖ Stained glass supplies. 800-323-9760; 708-369-8168 (in IL).

Wale Apparatus Company Inc., 400 Front St., P.O. Box D, Hellertown, PA 18055: Catalog $5 ❖ Bead-making and glass-working equipment and supplies. 800-334-WALE; 610-838-7047 (in PA).

Warner-Crivellaro, 1855 Weaversville Rd., Allentown, PA 18103: Free information ❖ Stained glass supplies and how-to books. 800-523-4242; 610-264-1100 (in PA).

Whittemore Glass, Box 2065, Hanover, MA 02339: Catalog $2 ❖ Stained glass kits, tools, patterns, etching, and engraving supplies. 617-871-1790.

H.L. Worden Company, P.O. Box 519, 118 Main St., Granger, WA 98932: Free catalog ❖ Forms, patterns, and accessories for making stained glass lampshades. 800-541-1103; 509-854-1557 (in WA).

STAIRLIFTS & ELEVATORS

Econol Lift Corporation, 2513 Center St., Box 854, Cedar Falls, IA 50613: Free information ❖ Wheelchair and stair-riding lifts, residential elevators, dumbwaiters, and vertical lifts. 319-277-4777.

Graventa, P.O. Box 1769, Blaine, WA 98231: Free information ❖ Easy-to-operate portable wheelchair lift for stairs. 800-663-6556.

Inclinator Company of America, P.O. Box 1557, Harrisburg, PA 17105: Free information ❖ Elevators and stairlifts for homes. 717-234-8065.

The National Wheel-O-Vator Company Inc., P.O. Box 348, Roanoke, IL 61561: Free information ❖ Wheelchair and side-riding stair lifts. 800-551-9095.

Whitakers, 1 Odell Plaza, Yonkers, NY 10703: Free catalog ❖ Motorized stairlifts for homes. 800-44-LIFTS; 800-924-LIFT (in NY).

STATIONERY & ENVELOPES

Accountants Supply House, 3012 Grove Rd., Thorofare, NJ 08086: Free catalog ❖ Stationery and envelopes, forms and labels, shipping materials, disk storage cabinets, furniture, office equipment, and supplies. 800-342-5274.

American Stationery Company, 100 Park Ave., Peru, IN 46970: Free catalog ❖ Regular and calligraphy stationery, wedding invitations, note cards and personal memos, envelopes, and postcards. 800-822-2577.

The American Wedding Album, American Stationery Company Inc., 300 Park Ave., Peru, IN 46970: Free catalog ❖ Wedding invitations, stationery, and gifts. 800-822-2577.

Bookmark, P.O. Box 335, Delafield, WI 53018: Catalog $1 ❖ Fine art calendars and boxed note cards. 414-646-4499.

The Business Book, P.O. Box 8465, Mankato, MN 56002: Free catalog ❖ Pressure sensitive labels, stampers, personalized business envelopes and stationery, speed letters, memo pads, business cards and forms, greeting cards, books, and office supplies. 800-558-0220.

Business Envelope Manufacturers, 900 Grand Blvd., Deer Park, NY 11729: Free catalog ❖ Envelopes, stationery, forms, labels, business cards, and office supplies. 516-667-8500.

Business Envelopes, Mid Atlantic Industrial Park, P.O. Box 517, Thorofare, NJ 08086: Free catalog ❖ Business envelopes, checks, pens, and other office supplies. 800-275-4400.

Caprock Business Forms Inc., 1211 Ave. F, Lubbock, TX 79401: Free information ❖ Continuous computer forms, letterheads and envelopes, snap-apart sets, manifold books, and scratch pads. 800-666-3322.

Creations by Elaine, 6253 W. 74th St., Box 2001, Bedford Park, IL 60499: Free catalog ❖ Wedding invitations and stationery, cake knives and servers, reception and ceremony accessories, and jewelry. 800-323-2717.

Current Inc., Express Processing Center, Colorado Springs, CO 80941: Free catalog ❖ Greeting cards, stationery, and gift wrapping. 800-848-2848.

Day-Timers, One Day-Timer Plaza, Allentown, PA 18195: Free catalog ❖ Stationery and business cards. 800-225-5005.

Kristin Elliott Inc., 6 Opportunity Way, Newburyport, MA 01950: Free catalog ❖ Boxed notes, gift enclosures, Christmas and greeting cards, memo pads, postcards, correspondence cards, and gift wrapping. 800-922-1899; 508-465-1899 (in MA).

Fine Stationery by Sonya Nussbaum, P.O. Box 328, Hollywood, SC 29449: Free catalog ❖ Stationery and envelopes. 803-889-3463.

Fingerhut, P.O. Box 800, St. Cloud, MN 56395: Free catalog ❖ Greeting cards, gift wraps, stationery, holiday decorations, organizers, and gifts. 800-322-2226.

Forever & Always Company, P.O. Box 1605, Syracuse, NY 13201: Free information ❖ Notepads and cards for special occasions. 800-404-4025.

Goes Lithographing Company, 42 W. 61st St., Chicago, IL 60621: Free information ❖ Stationery, envelopes, calendars, calendar pads, certificates, and printed items. 800-348-6700.

Grayarc, P.O. Box 2944, Hartford, CT 06104: Free catalog ❖ Stationery, business cards, forms, labels, envelopes, and office supplies. 800-562-5468.

Heirloom Editions, Box 520-B, Rt. 4, Carthage, MO 64836: Catalog $4 ❖ Lithographs, greeting cards, stickers, miniatures, stationery, framed prints, and turn-of-the-century art and paper collectibles. 800-725-0725.

Home Trends, 1450 Lyell Ave., Rochester, NY 14606: Free catalog ❖ Personalized stationery, toys, household items, clothing, and decorative and office accessories. 716-254-6520.

Hudson Envelope Corporation, 111 3rd Ave., New York, NY 10003: Free information ❖ Colored envelopes and paper. 212-473-6666.

Robert James Company Inc., P.O. Box 520, Moody, AL 35004: Free information with long SASE ❖ Stationery, furniture, and office supplies. 800-633-8296; 205-640-7081 (in AL).

✓ **Just Between Us,** 41 W. 8th Ave., Oshkosh, WI 54906: Free catalog ❖ Stationery with optional personalization. 800-258-3750.

Kimmeric Studio, P.O. Box 3586, Napa, CA 94558: Catalog $2 ❖ Postcards, envelopes, and stationery. 707-255-8734.

✓ **Jamie Lee Stationery,** P.O. Box 5343, Glendale, AZ 85312: Free catalog ❖ Wedding stationery for brides. 800-288-5800.

L & D Press, Box 641, 78 Randall St., Rockville Center, NY 11570: Free price list ❖ Business cards, letterheads, and envelopes. 516-593-5058.

Literary Calligraphy, Rt. 1, Box 56A, Moneta, VA 24121: Catalog $2 ❖ Framed art and stationery. 800-261-6325.

Main Street Press, P.O. Box 126, Delafield, WI 53018: Catalog $1 ❖ Wall calendars, boxed greeting cards, note cards and pads, and stationery. 414-646-8511.

Mattick Business Forms Inc., 333 W. Hintz Rd., Wheeling, IL 60090: Free catalog ❖ Stationery, office and business forms, and labels. 708-541-7345.

✓ **Merrimade Inc.,** 27 S. Canal St., Lawrence, MA 01843: Free catalog ❖ Stationery and printed items. 800-344-4256.

Morgan Printing Company, 2365 Wyandotte Rd., Willow Grove, PA 19090: Free information ❖ Continuous letterheads, labels, and business forms. 800-435-3892.

NEBS Inc., 500 Main St., Groton, MA 01471: Free catalog ❖ Business forms, stationery, labels, checks, business cards, and supplies.

New Century Envelope, Malott Industrial Park, P.O. Box 55530, Indianapolis, IN 46205: Free information ❖ Envelopes. 800-234-0666.

Peak Publishing, P.O. Box V, Flagstaff, AZ 86002: Catalog $2 ❖ Note cards with southwestern scenes. 800-299-4789.

Pendleton Cowgirl Company, P.O. Box 30142, Eugene, OR 97403: Catalog $2 ❖ Classic western theme T-shirts, lithographs, note cards, and calendars. 503-484-9194.

The Personal Touch Stationery, One Artistic Plaza, P.O. Box 1623, Elmira, NY 14902: Catalog $2 ❖ Personalized stationery and gifts. 800-733-6313.

Posh Papers, 532 Elmgrove Ave., Providence, RI 02906: Brochure $1 (refundable) ❖ Note cards with envelopes. 401-331-9873.

Prolitho Inc., 630 New Ludlow St., South Hadley, MA 01075: Free information ❖ Business cards, stationery, and envelopes with flat and raised printing. 413-532-9473.

✓ **Rexcraft,** Rexburg, ID 83441: Free catalog ❖ Invitations and stationery, bridal and reception accessories, and thank you cards. 800-635-4653.

Shipman Printing Industries, P.O. Box 157, Niagara Falls, NY 14302: Free information ❖ Forms, letterheads, envelopes, and printed items. 800-462-2114.

✓ **Stationery House,** 1000 Florida Ave., Hagerstown, MD 21740: Free catalog ❖ Business stationery and forms, office supplies, and executive gifts. 301-739-4487.

Sugar 'n Spice Invitations, P.O. Box 299, Sugar City, ID 83448: Free catalog ❖ Invitations and stationery, bridal and reception accessories, and thank you cards. 800-635-1433.

Traditional Papercutting, Faye & Bernie DuPlessis, 101 Blue Rock Rd., Wilmington, DE 19809: Catalog $2 ❖ Note cards and framed or unframed cuttings. 302-762-8896.

Triangle Envelope Company, 325 Hill Ave., Nashville, TN 37210: Free information ❖ Envelopes and stationery. 800-843-9529.

Wholesale Envelopes Inc., 2410 Rice St., Lubbock, TX 79415: Free information ❖ Matching envelopes and letterheads. 800-692-4676.

✓ **Willow Tree Lane,** One Willow Center, Sugarloaf, PA 18249: Free catalog ❖ Fine stationery and accessories. 800-593-9064.

✓ **The Write Touch,** The Rytex Company, 5850 W. 80th St., P.O. Box 68188, Indianapolis, IN 46268: Free catalog ❖ Stationery, writing aids, and gifts. 800-288-6824.

✓ **Writewell Company Inc.,** P.O. Box 68186, Indianapolis, IN: 46268: Free catalog ❖ Stationery and envelopes, note cards, memo pads, and labels. 800-968-5850.

STENCILS

Art-2-Go, 7859 Schenck Rd., Perry, NY 14530: Catalog $3 ❖ Nature and herbal stencils. 716-237-5330.

Adele Bishop, P.O. Box 3349, Kingston, NC 28501: Catalog $4 ❖ Decorative, historic, contemporary, traditional, Native American, and children's stencils. 919-527-4186.

Daydreams Stencil Company, P.O. Box 65, Oregon, WI 53575: Catalog $3 ❖ Folk art stencils. 608-873-3399.

✓ **Decorcal Inc.,** 165 Marine St., Farmingdale, NY 11735: Free catalog ❖ Decorative decals, letter and number stencils, and graphic accessories. 800-645-9868; 516-752-0076 (in NY).

Dee-signs Ltd., Box 490, Rushland, PA 18956: Catalog $5 ❖ Laser-cut stencils. 215-598-3330.

Dreamweaver Stencils, 910 Hardt St., Loma Linda, CA 92354: Catalog $2 ❖ Miniature brass stencils for embossing and stenciling. 909-796-5002.

Jan Dressler Stencils, 11030 173rd Ave. SE, Renton, WA 98059: Catalog $5 ❖ Garden scenes, birds, and nature-theme stencils. 206-226-0306.

Epoch Designs, P.O. Box 4033, Elwyn, PA 19063: Catalog $4.50 ❖ Pre-cut Victorian-style stencils. 610-565-9180.

Helen Foster Stencils, 71 Main St., Sanford, ME 04073: Catalog $4 ❖ Pre-cut laser stencils for decorating. 207-490-2625.

Great Tracers, 3 Schoenbeck Rd., Prospect Heights, IL 60070: Brochure $1 (refundable) ❖ Lettering stencils. 847-255-0436.

Gail Grisi Stenciling Inc., P.O. Box 1263, Haddonfield, NJ 08033: Catalog $2.50 (refundable) ❖ Pre-cut plastic stencils, kits, sponges, acrylic paints, and how-to instructions. 609-354-1757.

The Itinerant Stenciler, 11030 173rd Ave. SE, Renton, WA 98059: Catalog $5 ❖ Laser-cut stencils. 206-226-0306.

MB Historic Decor, P.O. Box 880, Norwich, VT 05055: Catalog $10 ❖ Vermont border stencils. Includes the Moses Eaton collection and floor patterns of New England. 802-649-1790.

Pricille's Stencils, P.O. Box 633, North Chelmsford, MA 01863: Catalog $6 ❖ Miniature stencils for use on dollhouse furniture and miniatures. Also stencils and accessories. 508-667-8760.

StenArt Inc., 24 Jefferson Ave., P.O. Box 114, Pitman, NJ 08071: Catalog $4.95 ❖ Pre-cut stencils. 609-589-9857.

The Stencil Collector, 1723 Tilghman St., Allentown, PA 18104: Catalog $10 ❖ English period design stencils. Also stenciling supplies. 610-433-2105.

Stencil House of N.H., P.O. Box 16109, Hooksett, NH 03306: Brochure $2.50 ❖ Cut and uncut mylar stencils, brushes, paints, stencil adhesive, and brush cleaner. 603-635-1716.

The Stencil Outlet, P.O. Box 80, West Nottingham, NH 03291: Catalog $5 ❖ Brass and laser cut stencils. 800-2-STENCIL.

The Stencil Shoppe, 3634 Silverside Rd., Wilmington, DE 19810: Catalog $3.95 ❖ Designer stencils. 800-822-STEN.

Stencil World, 350 Main St., Ste. 871, New Rochelle, NY 10801: Catalog $5 (refundable) ❖ Stencils, books, and paints. 800-274-7997.

Stencils & Stuff, 5198 TR 123, Millersburg, OH 44654: Catalog $3 (refundable) ❖ Florals, borders, other stencils, and paints. 216-893-2499.

Your Stencil Source, P.O. Box 220, Standard, CA 95373: Catalog $2.50 (refundable) ❖ Stencils for wall murals, home decoration, crafts, quilting, and other uses.

Yowler & Shepp Stencils, 3529 Main St., Conestoga, PA 17516: Catalog $4 (refundable) ❖ Ribbons and stencils. 717-872-2820.

STEREOS & CD PLAYERS

Headphones

Aiwa America Inc., 800 Corporate Dr., Mahwah, NJ 07430: Free information ❖ CD players, sound processors, and headphones. 800-289-2492.

Azden Corporation, 147 New Hyde Park Rd., Franklin Square, NY 11016: Free information ❖ Camcorders and headphones. 516-328-7500.

Denon America, 222 New Rd., Parsippany, NJ 07054: Free information ❖ Headphones, CD players, receivers, amplifiers, and sound processors. 201-575-7810.

JVC, 41 Slater Dr., Elmwood Park, NJ 07407: Free information ❖ Headphones, CD players, receivers, and amplifiers. 201-794-3900.

Nady Systems, 6701 Bay St., Emeryville, CA 94608: Free information ❖ Headphones and speakers. 510-652-2411.

Onkyo, 200 Williams Dr., Ramsey, NJ 07446: Free information ❖ CD players, receivers, amplifiers, universal remotes, and headphones. 201-825-7950.

Panasonic, Panasonic Way, Secaucus, NJ 07094: Free list of retail sources ❖ Headphones, receivers, and CD players. 201-348-7000.

Pioneer New Media Technologies, 2265 E. 220th St., Long Beach, CA 90810: Free information ❖ Headphones, speakers, CD players, sound processors, receivers, amplifiers, and decoders. 800-444-OPTI.

Recoton, 2950 Lake Emma Rd., Lake Mary, FL 32746: Free information ❖ Headphones, speakers, video and audio processors, and decoders. 800-223-6009.

Sony Consumer Products, 1 Sony Dr., Park Ridge, NJ 07656: Free information ❖ Headphones, speakers, CD players, camcorders, receivers, amplifiers, sound processors, decoders, universal remotes, and electronics. 201-930-1000.

Teac, 7733 Telegraph Rd., Montebello, CA 90640: Free information ❖ CD players, sound processors, and headphones. 213-726-0303.

Technics, One Panasonic Way, Secaucus, NJ 07094: Free list of retail sources ❖ Speakers, CD players, headphones, receivers, amplifiers, and sound processors. 201-348-7000.

Yamaha, P.O. Box 6660, Buena Park, CA 90620: Free information ❖ Headphones, speakers, audio and video systems, CD players, and sound processors. 800-492-6242.

Home-Theater & Surround Sound Systems

Atlantic Technology, 343 Vanderbilt Ave., Norwood, MA 02062: Free list of retail sources ❖ Home theater systems and components. 617-762-6300.

Chase Technologies, 111 2nd Ave. NE, St. Petersburg, FL 33701: Free information ❖ Add-on equipment to transform existing stereo and TV sets into a home theater system. 800-531-0631.

Denon America, 222 New Rd., Parsippany, NJ 07054: Free information ❖ Surround sound systems. 201-575-7810.

Electronic Mailbox, 10-12 Charles St., Glen Cove, NY 11542: Free information ❖ Home theater systems, photography accessories, video editing equipment, and electronics. 800-325-2325.

Home Theatre Systems, 44 Rt. 23 North, Little Falls, NJ 07424: Free information ❖ Home theater systems. 800-978-7768.

Klipsch, Customer Service, 8900 Keystone Crossing, Ste. 1220, Indianapolis, IN 46240: Free list of retail sources ❖ Home theater systems and components. 800-KLIPSCH.

Legacy Audio, 3021 Sangamon Ave., Springfield, IL 62702: Free catalog ❖ Home theater systems and audio equipment. 800-283-4644; 217-544-5252 (in IL).

Marine Park Camera & Video Inc., 3126 Avenue U, Brooklyn, NY 11229: Free information ❖ Video equipment, home theater systems, VCRs, and camcorders. 800-448-8811; 718-891-1878 (in NY).

NBO Satellite TV, 5670-A El Camino Real, Carlsbad, CA 92008: Free catalog ❖ Satellite and big-screen TV systems, surround sound equipment, and accessories. 800-604-2222.

New England Audio Resource, 12 Foss Rd., Lewiston, ME 04240: Free list of retail sources ❖ Home theater systems. 207-795-0609.

NuReality, 2907 Daimler St., Santa Ana, CA 92705: Free list of retail sources ❖ Surround sound in 3D for home theater systems. 714-442-1080.

Parasound Products Inc., 950 Battery St., San Francisco, CA 94111: Free information ❖ Home theater systems. 415-397-7100.

Pioneer Electronics, 2265 E. 220th St., Long Beach, CA 90810: Free information ❖ Surround sound systems. 213-PIONEER.

Runco, 2463 Tripaldi Way, Hayward, CA 94545: Free list of retail sources ❖ Home theater video systems. 510-293-9154.

Samman's Electronics, 1166 Hamburg Tnpk., Wayne, NJ 07470: Free information ❖ Video equipment and home theater systems. 800-AUDIO-93.

USA Direct, 600 Cape May St., Harrison, NJ 07029: Free information ❖ Home theater systems. 800-959-HIFI.

Manufacturers

a/d/s, 1 Progress Way, Wilmington, MA 01887: Free information ❖ CD players, speakers, receivers, and amplifiers. 800-522-4434.

Acoustic Research, 535 Getty Ct., Bldg. A, Benicia, CA 94510: Free information ❖ Amplifiers and speakers. 800-969-AR4U.

Adcom, 11 Elkins Rd., East Brunswick, NJ 08816: Free information ❖ Amplifiers, CD players, and tuners. 800-477-3257.

Aiwa America Inc., 800 Corporate Dr., Mahwah, NJ 07430: Free information ❖ CD players, sound processors, and headphones. 800-289-2492.

AudioSource, 1327 N. Carolan Ave., Burlingame, CA 94010: Free information ❖ Sound processors and audio controllers. 800-227-5087.

B & K Components Ltd., 2100 Old Union Rd., Buffalo, NY 14227: Free list of retail sources ❖ Audio and video control centers, amplifiers, and pre-amplifiers. 800-543-5252.

Cambridge Soundworks, 154 California St., Newton, MA 02158: Free catalog ❖ Speakers and audio systems. 800-367-4434.

Canon, One Canon Plaza, Lake Success, NY 11042: Free information ❖ CD players, camcorders, sound processors, and electronics. 516-488-6700.

Carver Corporation, P.O. Box 1237, Lynnwood, WA 98046: Free information ❖ Receivers, amplifiers, CD players, tuners, and speakers. 206-775-1202.

Denon America, 222 New Rd., Parsippany, NJ 07054: Free information ❖ CD players, receivers, amplifiers, sound processors, and headphones. 201-575-7810.

Emerson Radio Corporation, 9 Entin Rd., Parsippany, NJ 07054: Free information ❖ Camcorders, CD and cassette players, and TVs. 201-884-5800.

Fisher, 21350 Lassen St., Chatsworth, CA 91311: Free information ❖ Speakers, CD and cassette players, sound processors, receivers, amplifiers, camcorders, TVs, and universal remotes. 818-998-7322.

Goldstar, 1000 Sylvan Ave., Englewood, NJ 07632: Free information ❖ CD and cassette players and TVs. 201-816-2200.

Harmon/Kardon, 80 Crossways Park West, Woodbury, NY 11797: Free information ❖ CD and cassette players, receivers, amplifiers, and projection equipment. 800-422-8027.

Hitachi Sales Corporation, Customer Service, 675 Old Peachtree Rd., Suwanee, GA 30174: Free information ❖ CD and cassette players, receivers, amplifiers, and TVs. 800-241-6558.

❖ STEREOS & CD PLAYERS ❖

JVC, 41 Slater Dr., Elmwood Park, NJ 07407: Free information ❖ Audio and video systems, CD and cassette players, camcorders, receivers, amplifiers, TVs, and headphones. 201-794-3900.

Kenwood, P.O. Box 22745, Long Beach, CA 90801: Free information ❖ CD and cassette players, TVs, receivers, amplifiers, and sound processors. 800-536-9663.

Marantz America Inc., 440 Medinah Rd., Roselle, IL 60172: Free information ❖ Audio and video systems, speakers, CD and cassette players, sound processors, and electronics. 708-307-3100.

McIntosh, 2 Chambers St., Binghamton, NY 13903: Free information ❖ CD players. 607-723-3512.

Mitsubishi Electronics, 5665 Plaza Dr., Cypress, CA 90630: Free information ❖ Audio and video systems, CD and cassette players, camcorders, and TVs. 800-843-2515.

NAD, 200 Williams Dr., Ramsey, NJ 07446: Free information ❖ Receivers, amplifiers, CD players, and speakers. 201-825-7950.

Nakamichi, 955 Francisco St., Torrance, CA 90502: Free information ❖ Receivers, amplifiers, and CD players. 310-538-8150.

NEC Home Electronics, 1255 Michael Dr., Wood Dale, IL 60191: Free information ❖ Speakers, CD and cassette players, receivers, amplifiers, TVs, camcorders, sound processors, and electronics. 708-860-9500.

Onkyo, 200 Williams Dr., Ramsey, NJ 07446: Free information ❖ CD players, receivers, amplifiers, universal remotes, and headphones. 201-825-7950.

Panasonic, Panasonic Way, Secaucus, NJ 07094: Free list of retail sources ❖ Audio and video systems, CD and cassette players, TVs, camcorders, headphones, and electronics. 201-348-7000.

Pioneer New Media Technologies, 2265 E. 220th St., Long Beach, CA 90810: Free information ❖ Speakers, receivers, amplifiers, TVs, sound processors, headphones, and cassette, laser disk, and CD players. 800-444-OPTI.

Proton Corporation, 13855 Struikman Rd., Cerritos, CA 90703: Free information ❖ Speakers, CD players, receivers, amplifiers, TVs, and electronics. 310-404-2222.

Quasar, One Panasonic Way, Secaucus, NJ 07094: Free list of retail sources ❖ Audio and video systems, CD and cassette players, camcorders, TVs, and electronics. 201-348-7000.

Radio Shack, Division Tandy Corporation, One Tandy Center, Fort Worth, TX 76102: Free information ❖ Cassette and CD players, camcorders, universal remotes, computers, and electronics. 817-390-3011.

RCA Sales Corporation, Thomson Consumer Electronics, P.O. Box 1976, Indianapolis, IN 46206: Free information ❖ Audio and video systems, cassette and CD players, TVs, camcorders, sound processors, and electronics. 800-336-1900.

Recoton, 2950 Lake Emma Rd., Lake Mary, FL 32746: Free information ❖ Speakers, decoders, audio and video processors, and headphones. 800-223-6009.

Rotel, P.O. Box 8, North Reading, MA 01864: Free information ❖ Receivers, amplifiers, CD players, and speakers. 800-370-3740.

Sansui USA, 210 Clay Ave. West, P.O. Box 625, Lyndhurst, NJ 07071: Free information ❖ Speakers, cassette and CD players, camcorders, receivers, amplifiers, TVs, and sound processors. 201-460-9710.

Sanyo, 21350 Lassen St., Chatsworth, CA 91311: Free information ❖ CD and cassette players, camcorders, TVs, sound processors, universal remotes, and electronics. 818-998-7322.

Sharp Electronics, Sharp Plaza, Mahwah, NJ 07430: Free information ❖ Cassette and CD players, camcorders, TVs, receivers, amplifiers, and electronics. 800-BE-SHARP.

Sherwood, 14830 Alondra Blvd., La Mirada, CA 90638: Free information ❖ CD players, receivers, amplifiers, and sound processors. 800-962-3203.

Shure Brothers Inc., 222 Hartrey Ave., Evanston, IL 60202: Free information ❖ CD players, sound processors, and electronics. 800-447-4873.

Sony Consumer Products, 1 Sony Dr., Park Ridge, NJ 07656: Free information ❖ Speakers, cassette and CD players, camcorders, receivers, amplifiers, TVs, sound processors, universal remotes, headphones, and electronics. 201-930-1000.

Teac, 7733 Telegraph Rd., Montebello, CA 90640: Free information ❖ Sound processors, headphones, electronics, and cassette, CD, and laser disk players. 213-726-0303.

Technics, One Panasonic Way, Secaucus, NJ 07094: Free list of retail sources ❖ Speakers, CD players, sound processors, receivers, amplifiers, and headphones. 201-348-7000.

Toshiba, 82 Totowa Rd., Wayne, NJ 07470: Free information ❖ Cassette and CD players, camcorders, sound processors, and TVs. 201-628-8000.

Vector Research, 1230 Calle Suerte, Camarillo, CA 93012: Free information ❖ Cassette and CD players, receivers, speakers, and amplifiers. 805-987-1312.

Yamaha, P.O. Box 6660, Buena Park, CA 90620: Free information ❖ Speakers, receivers, amplifiers, sound processors, headphones, and CD, cassette, and laser disk players. 800-492-6242.

Retailers

AV Distributors, 10765 Kingspoint, Houston, TX 77075: Free information ❖ Audio, video, and stereo equipment and TVs. 800-843-3697.

Coast to Coast, 2570 86th St., Brooklyn, NY 11214: Free information ❖ Camcorders, video editing equipment, receivers, CD players, cassette decks, and equipment. 718-265-1723.

Computability Consumer Electronics, P.O. Box 17882, Milwaukee, WI 53217: Free catalog ❖ TVs, fax machines, copiers, computers, and audio, video, and stereo equipment. 800-554-9949.

Crutchfield, 1 Crutchfield Park, Charlottesville, VA 22906: Free catalog ❖ TVs and video, audio, and stereo equipment. 800-955-9009.

Data Vision, 445 5th Ave., New York, NY 10016: Free information ❖ Everything in electronics. 800-482-7466; 212-689-1111 (in NY).

Electronic Wholesalers, 1166 Hamburg Tnpk., Wayne, NJ 07470: Free information ❖ Receivers, cassette decks, TVs, telephones, laser disk and CD players, and camcorders. 201-696-6531.

Factory Direct, 35 W. 35th St., New York, NY 10001: Free information ❖ TVs and audio, video, and stereo equipment. 212-564-4399.

Focus Electronics, 4523 13th Ave., Brooklyn, NY 11219: Free catalog ❖ Appliances, photographic equipment, and audio, stereo, and video equipment. 718-436-4646.

Haven Industries, 2950 Lake Emma Rd., Lake Mary, FL 32746: Free information ❖ Computers, cellular telephones, audio and video equipment, and electronic accessories. 800-231-0031.

J & R Music World, 59-50 Queens-Midtown Expwy., Maspeth, NY 11378: Free catalog ❖ Audio equipment, car and portable stereos, video recorders, telephones, computers, and video and audio tapes. 800-221-8180.

Mission Service Supply Inc., 4565 Cypress St., West Monroe, LA 71291: Free catalog ❖ TVs and audio, video, stereo equipment, and accessories. 800-352-7222; 318-397-2755 (in LA).

New West Electronics, 4120 Meridian, Bellingham, WA 98226: Free information ❖ TVs, projection equipment, and audio, video, and stereo equipment. 800-488-8877.

Olden Video, 1265 Broadway, New York, NY 10001: Free information ❖ Video equipment, TVs, cassette players, and electronics. 212-725-1234.

Percy's Inc., 19 Glennie St., Worcester, MA 01605: Free information ❖ Appliances and electronics. 508-755-5334.

Planet Electronics, 8418 Lilley, Canton, MI 48187: Free catalog ❖ TVs, video recorders, telephones, tapes, cassettes, and CDs. 800-247-4663; 313-453-4750 (in MI).

PowerVideo, 6808 Hornwood Dr., Houston, TX 77074: Free information ❖ TVs and audio, video, and stereo equipment. 713-772-4400.

S & S Sound City, 58 W. 45th St., New York, NY 10036: Free information ❖ Audio and video equipment, telephones, office machines, and electronics. 212-575-0210.

S.B.H. Enterprises, 1678 53rd St., Brooklyn, NY 11204: Free information ❖ Audio and video equipment and radar detectors. 800-451-5851; 718-438-1027 (in NY).

Tri-State Camera, 650 6th Ave., New York, NY 10011: Free information ❖ Audio and video equipment, camcorders, copiers, fax machines, and electronics. 800-221-1926; 212-633-2290 (in NY).

Uncle's Stereo, 581 Broadway, New York, NY 10012: Free information ❖ Everything in electronics. 212-343-9111.

Wisconsin Discount Stereo, 2417 W. Badger Rd., Madison, WI 53713: Free information ❖ Video and audio equipment and TVs. 800-356-9514.

Speakers

a/d/s, 1 Progress Way, Wilmington, MA 01887: Free information ❖ CD players, speakers, receivers, and amplifiers. 800-522-4434.

Altec-Lansing, P.O. Box 277, Milford, PA 18337: Free information ❖ Speakers. 800-548-0620.

B & W Loudspeakers of America, 54 Concord St., North Reading, MA 01864: Free brochure ❖ Speakers. 800-370-3740.

Bose Express Music, The Mountain, Framingham, MA 01701: Catalog $6 (refundable) ❖ Speakers. 800-845-BOSE.

Boston Acoustics, 70 Broadway, Lynnfield, MA 01940: Free information ❖ Speakers. 617-592-9000.

Energy Loudspeakers, 3641 NcNicoll Ave., Scarborough, Ontario, Canada M1X 1G5: Free information ❖ Home theater sound system. 416-321-1800.

Fisher, 21350 Lassen St., Chatsworth, CA 91311: Free information ❖ Speakers, CD and cassette players, sound processors, receivers, amplifiers, and camcorders. 818-998-7322.

Infinity Systems, 10630 Nordhoff St., Chatsworth, CA 91311: Free information ❖ Speakers and TVs. 818-407-0228.

Marantz America Inc., 440 Medinah Rd., Roselle, IL 60172: Free information ❖ Audio and video systems, speakers, CD and cassette players, sound processors, and electronics. 708-307-3100.

Mirage Speakers, 3641 McNicoll Ave., Scarborough, Ontario, Canada M1X 1G5: Free list of retail sources ❖ Speakers. 416-321-1800.

Nady Systems, 6701 Bay St., Emeryville, CA 94608: Free information ❖ Speakers and headphones. 510-652-2411.

NEC Home Electronics, 1255 Michael Dr., Wood Dale, IL 60191: Free information ❖ Speakers, CD and cassette players, receivers, amplifiers, sound processors, and electronics. 708-860-9500.

Pioneer New Media Technologies, 2265 E. 220th St., Long Beach, CA 90810: Free information ❖ Speakers, CD players, sound processors, receivers, amplifiers, and headphones. 800-444-OPTI.

Polk Audio, 5601 Metro Dr., Baltimore, MD 21230: Free list of retail sources ❖ Speakers. 800-638-7276.

Proton Corporation, 16826 Edwards Rd., Cerritos, CA 90701: Free information ❖ Speakers, CD players, receivers, and amplifiers. 310-404-2222.

Recoton, 2950 Lake Emma Rd., Lake Mary, FL 32746: Free information ❖ Speakers, audio and video processors, video processors, and headphones. 800-223-6009.

Sansui USA, 210 Clay Ave. West, P.O. Box 625, Lyndhurst, NJ 07071: Free information ❖ Speakers, cassette and CD players, receivers, amplifiers, and sound processors. 201-460-9710.

Sony Consumer Products, 1 Sony Dr., Park Ridge, NJ 07656: Free information ❖ Speakers, audio and video systems, CD players, camcorders, sound processors, and headphones. 201-930-1000.

Speakerlab Factory, 6220 Roosevelt Way NE, Seattle, WA 98115: Free information ❖ Speakers and kits, tape decks, receivers, and electronics. 206-523-2269.

Technics, One Panasonic Way, Secaucus, NJ 07094: Free list of retail sources ❖ Speakers, CD players, headphones, receivers, amplifiers, and sound processors. 201-348-7000.

Vandersteen Audio, 116 W. 4th St., Hanford, CA 93230: Free list of retail sources ❖ Speaker systems. 209-582-0324.

Yamaha, P.O. Box 6660, Buena Park, CA 90620: Free information ❖ Speakers, CD and laser disk players, receivers, amplifiers, sound processors, and headphones. 800-492-6242.

Storage Cabinets & Racks

AGM Woodworking, 870 Capitolio Way, San Luis Obispo, CA 93401: Free brochure ❖ Audio and video component storage cabinets. 800-858-9005.

STICKERS

Cats, Box 735, Acton, MA 01720: Free information ❖ Self-sticking cat shaped stickers.

Cherri-Oats & Company, Cheri Venturi, P.O. Box 723, North Olmsted, OH 44070: Free information ❖ Wigs and accessories, stickers, puppets, and face painting supplies. 216-979-9971.

Eastern Emblem, Box 828, Union City, NJ 07087: Free catalog ❖ T-shirts, jackets, patches, cloisonne pins, decals, and stickers. 800-344-5112.

Heirloom Editions, Box 520-B, Rt. 4, Carthage, MO 64836: Catalog $4 ❖ Lithographs, greeting cards, stickers, miniatures, stationery, framed prints, and turn-of-the-century art and paper collectibles. 800-725-0725.

Holly Sales, 9926 Beach Blvd., Ste. 114, Jacksonville, FL 32246: Free information ❖ Clown stickers. 904-223-5828.

House-Mouse Designs, P.O. Box 48, Williston, VT 05495: Free catalog ❖ Christmas cards, note and recipe cards, stickers, and magnets. 800-242-6423.

Stick-Em Up, P.O. Box 3111, Livermore, CA 94551: Catalog $2 ❖ Stickers. 510-426-1040.

Turtles, Box 735, Acton, MA 01720: Free information ❖ Custom-printed stickers.

STOCK CAR RACING (NASCAR)

Brickel's Racing Collectibles, Rt. 61, Schoolside Plaza, P.O. Box 205, Leesport, PA 19533: Free catalog ❖ Racing collectibles. 610-926-6719.

Diversified Electronics Inc., 309 Agnew Dr., Ste. C, Forest Park, GA 30050: Free information ❖ Racing radios complete with NiCad battery pack, charger, and antenna. 800-669-1522; 404-366-3796 (in GA).

Frequency Fan Club, P.O. Box 610, Milledgeville, GA 31061: Free information ❖ Race scanners, headsets, and accessories. 800-722-3326.

Stewart Lehman, 19. W. Main St., P.O. Box 509, Apple Creek, OH 44606: Free information ❖ Cards, racing memorabilia, die-cast models, and collectibles. 216-698-1900.

Motor-Sport Products, P.O. Box 7667, Naples, FL 33941: Free information ❖ Select gifts for NASCAR racers and involved persons. 800-833-0696.

Ole Chevy Store, 2509 S. Cannon Blvd., Kannapolis, NC 28083: Free list ❖ Banks and automotive collectibles. 704-938-2923.

Redline Racing Collectibles, 10250 Cedarwood Dr., Union, KY 41091: Free information with long SASE ❖ Racing collectibles. 606-384-3854.

STONE SCULPTING & CARVING

Ebersole Lapidary Supply Inc., 11417 West Hwy. 54, Wichita, KS 67209: Catalog $2 ❖ Carving materials, beads and bead-stringing supplies, tools, findings, mountings, cabochons and rocks, and jewelry kits. 316-722-4771.

Gems by Jak, 113 Sherman St., Ihlen, MN 56140: Free catalog ❖ Indian gifts and catinite for carving. 507-348-8716.

Montoya/MAS International Inc., 435 Southern Blvd., West Palm Beach, FL 33405: Catalog $3 ❖ Carving stone and sculpture tools. 800-682-8665.

Richardson's Recreational Ranch Ltd., Gateway Route Box 440, Madras, OR 97741: Free information ❖ Rock and mineral specimens from all over the world, carving materials, and lapidary equipment. 503-475-2680.

Riviera Lapidary Supply, 30393 Mesquite, Riviera, TX 78379: Catalog $3 ❖ Carving materials, petrified wood, cabochons, slabs, cabbing rough, gemstones, crystals, beads, and bead-stringing supplies and kits. 512-296-3958.

Steatite of Southern Oregon Inc., 2891 Elk Ln., Grants Pass, OR 97527: Free information ❖ Soapstone for sculpturing and carving. 541-479-3646.

STOVES & OVENS

Aladdin Steel Products Inc., 401 N. Wynne St., Colville, WA 99114: Free list of retail sources ❖ Wood, pellet, and gas-burning stoves. Also fireplace inserts. 509-684-3745.

Barnstable Stove Shop, Rt. 149, Box 472, West Barnstable, MA 02668: Price list $1 ❖ Restored antique stoves and parts. 508-362-9913.

Blaze King Industries, 400 W. Whitman Dr., P.O. Box 367, College Place, WA 99324: Free list of retail sources ❖ Pellet-burning stoves. 509-522-2730.

Brunelle Enterprises Inc., 203 Union Rd., Wales, MA 01081: Catalog $2 ❖ Antique stoves, kitchen ranges, and parts. 413-245-7396.

Bryant Stove Inc., Box 2048, Thorndike, ME 04986: Free brochure ❖ Antique stoves for coal, gas, wood, wood and gas combination, and electricity. 207-568-3665.

Charmaster Products Inc., 2307 Hwy. 2 West, Grand Rapids, MN 55744: Free brochure ❖ Fireplaces and wood-burning, wood-gas, and wood-oil furnaces and conversion units. 218-326-6786.

Dynamic Cooking Systems, 10850 Portal Dr., Los Alamitos, CA 90720: Free catalog ❖ Outdoor gas grills and professional gas ranges for commercial settings. 714-220-9505.

Earthstone Wood-Fire Ovens, 1233 N. Highland Ave., Los Angeles, CA 90038: Free brochure ❖ Wood-fired ovens and fireplaces. 800-840-4915.

Elmira Stove Works, 595 Colby Dr., Waterloo, Ontario, Canada N2V 1A2: Catalog $5 ❖ Antique-style kitchen appliances.

FiveStar, P.O. Box 2490, Cleveland, TN 37320: Free brochure ❖ Commercial ranges, cooktops, and range hoods for the home. 800-251-7485.

Garland Commercial Industries, 185 East South St., Freeland, PA 18224: Free catalog ❖ Kitchen ventilation systems, professional-style ranges and cooktops for the home, and rack systems for pots and utensils.

Good Time Stove Company, Rt. 112, P.O. Box 306, Goshen, MA 01032: Free information ❖ Restored ready-to-use antique cooking and heating stoves. 413-268-3677.

HearthStone, P.O. Box 1069, Morrisville, VT 05661: Catalog $12 ❖ Automatic clean-burning wood stoves. 802-827-8683.

Heartland Appliances, 5 Hoffman St., Kitchener, Ontario, Canada N2M 3M5: Catalog $2 ❖ Classic cookstoves with state-of-the-art features. 519-743-8111.

Heatilator Inc., 1915 W. Saunders St., Mt. Pleasant, IA 52641: Free information ❖ Wood-burning stoves and fireplace inserts. 800-843-2848.

Heating Alternatives, 1926 Rt. 212, Pleasant Valley, Quakertown, PA 18951: Free catalog ❖ Coal and wood-burning stoves. 800-444-4328; 215-346-7896 (in PA).

The House of Webster, P.O. Box 1988, Rogers, AR 72757: Catalog $2 ❖ Electric stoves that resemble old-fashioned wood-burning stoves. 501-636-4640.

Hutch Manufacturing Company, 200 Commerce Ave., P.O. Box 350, Loudon, TN 37774: Free information ❖ Catalytic stoves. 800-251-9232.

Iron Craft, Old Rt. 28, P.O. Box 351, Ossipee, NH 03864: Catalog $2 ❖ Kettles and grates, enameled cookware, cookstoves, and coal and wood-heating stoves. 603-539-2807.

J.E.S. Enterprises, P.O. Box 65, Ventura, CA 93002: Free catalog ❖ Restored electric, gas, coal and wood-burning antique stoves and used, new, and restored parts. 805-643-3532.

Johnny's Appliances & Classic Ranges, 17549 Sonoma Hwy., P.O. Box 1407, Sonoma, CA 95476: Free information with long SASE ❖ Cooking ranges, from 1900 to 1960. 707-996-9730.

Jotul USA, P.O. Box 1157, Portland, ME 04104: Free list of retail sources ❖ Stoves and fireplaces. 800-797-5912.

Keokuk Stove Works, 1201 High St., Keokuk, IA 52632: Free information ❖ Original and restored antique stoves. 319-524-6202.

Macy's Texas Stove Works, 5515 Almeda Rd., Houston, TX 77004: Catalog $3.50 ❖ Vintage ranges and parts. 713-528-1297.

New Buck Corporation, 1265 Bakersville Hwy., Spruce Pine, NC 28777: Free information ❖ Gas and catalytic wood stoves. Also gas heaters and logs and wood stove to gas conversion kits. 704-765-6144.

Nu-Tec Incorporated, P.O. Box 908, East Greenwich, RI 02818: Free brochure ❖ Wood-burning stoves and fireplace inserts. 800-822-0600.

Otis Home Center Inc., 312 Armstrong Rd., Rogersville, TN 37857: Catalog $5 ❖ Wood, gas, or electric country-style heating and cooking stoves. 800-743-8133.

Russo Products Inc., 61 Pleasant St., Randolph, MA 02368: Free brochure ❖ Wood-burning stoves with optional brass trim, air deflectors, brass doors, and etched glass. 617-963-1182.

Stanley Iron Works, 64 Taylor St., Nashua, NH 03060: Free information ❖ Antique parlor stoves, gas and wood-gas combination stoves, and coal, gas, and electric conversions of antique stoves. 603-881-8335.

Tulikivi U.S. Inc., 225 Ridge McIntire Rd., Charlottesville, VA 22902: Planning guide $4.95 ❖ Baking ovens, cookstoves, and natural stone fireplaces. 804-977-5500.

The Ultimate Cooker, 803 W. Fairbanks, Winter Park, FL 32789: Free information ❖ Combination grilling and smoking cooker. 407-644-6680.

Vogelzang Corporation, 400 W. 17th St., Holland, MI 49423: Free information ❖ Wood-burning stove conversion kits. 800-222-6950.

Waterford Irish Stoves Inc., 16 Airport Park Rd., Ste. 3, West Lebanon, NH 03784: Free information ❖ Non-catalytic stoves. 603-298-5030.

Woodstock Soapstone Company Inc., 66 Airpark Rd., West Lebanon, NH 03784: Free brochure ❖ Traditional and contemporary-style woodburning stoves. 800-866-4344.

SUNDIALS

Armchair Shopper, P.O. Box 419464, Kansas City, MO 64141: Free catalog ❖ Old-world-style sundials, wind chimes, and lawn ornaments. 816-767-3200.

Betsy's Place, 323 Arch St., Philadelphia, PA 19106: Brochure $4.50 ❖ Sundials and stands, brass reproduction door knockers, and trivets. 800-452-3524; 215-922-3536 (in PA).

❖ SUNGLASSES & EYE WEAR ❖

407

Flora Fauna, P.O. Box 578, Gualala, CA 95445: Free information ❖ Hand-cast solid brass sundials and garden decor. 800-358-9120.

Kenneth Lynch & Sons, 84 Danbury Rd., Wilton, CT 06897: Catalog $4 ❖ Sundials. 203-762-8363.

Tom Outhouse, 2853 Lincoln Hwy. East, Ronks, PA 17572: Free catalog ❖ Antique and polished copper weather vanes with solid brass directional indicators and sundials. 800-346-7678.

Replogle Globes Inc., 2801 S. 25th Ave., Broadview, IL 60153: Free catalog ❖ Sundials. 708-343-0900.

Wind & Weather, P.O. Box 2320, Mendocino, CA 95460: Free catalog ❖ Sundials, weather vanes, and weather forecasting instruments. 707-964-1284.

SUNGLASSES & EYE WEAR

Action Optics, Division Smith Sport Optics Inc., Box 2999, Ketchum, ID 83340: Free brochure ❖ Polarized sunglasses. 800-654-6428.

Anarchy Eyewear, 2095 New Hwy., Farmingdale, NY 11735: Free information ❖ Sport sunglasses. 516-752-8900.

BluBlocker Corporation, 3350 Palms Centre Dr., Las Vegas, NV 89103: Free brochure ❖ Sunglasses. 800-508-5005.

Brigade Quartermasters Inc., 1025 Cobb International Blvd., Kenesaw, GA 30144: Free catalog ❖ Ski goggles and eyewear. 404-428-1234.

Gatorz Sport Optics, 5384 Linda Vista Rd., Ste. 104, San Diego, CA 92119: Free information ❖ Sport sunglasses and goggles. 619-293-7925.

Hidalgo Inc., 45 La Buena Vista, Wimberley, TX 78676: Free catalog ❖ Designer sunglasses. 512-847-5571.

Hobie Sunglasses, 1030 Calle Sombra, San Clemente, CA 92672: Free information ❖ Polarized sunglasses. 800-554-4335.

House of Eyes, 2222 Patterson St., Greensboro, NC 27407: Free information ❖ Designer eye wear. 800-331-4701; 910-852-7107 (in NC).

JT USA, 515 Otay Valley Rd., Chula Vista, CA 91911: Free information ❖ Sport sunglasses. 619-421-2660.

E.P. Levine Inc., 23 Dry Dock Ave., Boston, MA 02210: Free information ❖ Nikon sunglasses. 800-875-3055.

Martin Sunglasses, Jack Martin Company Inc., 9830 Baldwin Pl., El Monte, CA 91731: Free information ❖ Ski goggles and eyewear. 800-767-8555; 213-686-1100 (in CA).

Oakley Sunglasses, 10 Holland, Irvine, CA 92718: Free information ❖ Eye wear that provides ultraviolet light and injury-causing blue light protection. 800-733-6255.

Olympic Optical Company, P.O. Box 752377, Memphis, TN 38175: Free information ❖ Sunglasses that protect the eyes from ultraviolet light. 800-992-1255.

Optek Sunglass Corporation, 30 N. Gould St., Sheridan, WY 82801: Free information ❖ Sports sunglasses. 307-672-0875.

Penhall Eyewear, 711 W. 17th St., Ste. G-9, Costa Mesa, CA 94043: Free information ❖ Sport sunglasses and goggles. 714-574-5911.

Precision Optical, 507 2nd Ave., Rochelle, IL 61068: Catalog $1 ❖ Magnifiers and magnifying and regular sunglasses. 815-562-2174.

Revo Sunglass Inc., 455 E. Middlefield Rd., Mountain View, CA 94043: Free information ❖ Sport sunglasses. 415-962-0906.

Serengeti Eyewear, 1480 Colonial Dr., Horseheads, NY 14845: Free information ❖ Designer sunglasses. 800-525-4001.

Smith Sport Optics Inc., P.O. Box 2999, Ketchum, ID 83340: Free information ❖ Sport sunglasses and goggles. 208-726-4477.

Spex Amphibious Eye Wear, P.O. Box 2537, Costa Mesa, CA 92628: Free information ❖ Polarized eyewear with ultraviolet light protection. 714-548-1235.

Sunglass America, P.O. Box 147, Hewlett, NY 11557: Catalog $2 (refundable) ❖ Designer sunglasses. 800-424-LENS; 516-791-3400 (in NY).

Sunglass Hut International, P.O. Box 146, Boulder, CO 80306: Free catalog ❖ Eye-protection sunglasses. 800-786-4527.

Sunglasses U.S.A., 469 Sunrise Hwy., Lynbrook, NY 11563: Free catalog ❖ Ray-Ban sunglasses. 800-USA-RAYS.

SunRay Optical, 2038 Massachusetts Ave., Cambridge, MA 02140: Free catalog ❖ Custom-made fishing and sunglasses. 800-323-2932.

Terra Soar Inc., P.O. Box 1977, Harvey, LA 70059: Free catalog ❖ Ray Ban and Serengeti sunglasses. 800-949-4SUN.

Torelli Imports, 1181 Calle Suerte, Camarillo, CA 93012: Free list of retail sources ❖ Sunglasses with interchangeable lenses and temple and nose pieces. 805-484-8705.

SURFBOARDS & WINDSURFING

Adventure Sport Inc., 1607 NW 84th Ave., Miami, FL 33126: Free information ❖ Windsurfing boards. 305-591-3922.

American Athletic Inc., 200 American Ave., Jefferson, IA 50129: Free information ❖ Surfboards and swim rings. 800-247-3978; 515-386-3125 (in IA).

Body Glove International Inc., 530 6th St., Hermosa Beach, CA 90254: Free information ❖ Surfboards. 800-678-7873; 310-374-4074 (in CA).

Skip Hutchison, Rastaboards Surf-Sail-Snowboards, 4748 NE 11th Ave., Fort Lauderdale, FL 33334: Free information with long SASE ❖ Sailboards, surfboards, and snowboards. 954-491-7992.

Mistral Sports Inc., P.O. Box 1849, White Salmon, WA 98672: Free information ❖ Windsurfing boards and wet suits.

Recreonics Corporation, 4200 Schmitt Ave., Louisville KY 40213: Free information ❖ Surfboards, swim rings, and diving boards. 800-428-3254.

Rothhammer/Sprint, P.O. Box 3840, San Luis Obispo, CA 93403: Free information ❖ Surfboards, swim rings, and equipment for divers. 800-235-2156.

Sailworld-Hatteras, P.O. Box 628, Rt. 12, Avon, NC 97031: Free information ❖ Sails for windsurfing boards. 919-995-5441.

Tackle Shack, 7801 66th St. North, Pinellas Park, FL 34665: Free catalog ❖ Windsurfing equipment and clothing. 813-546-5080.

Windsurfing Express, 6043 NW 167th St., Miami, FL 33015: Free brochure ❖ Surfboards, windsurfing equipment, wetsuits, car-carrying racks, books, and accessories. 800-843-7873.

Windsurfing Warehouse, 128 S. Airport Blvd., South San Francisco, CA 94080: Free catalog ❖ Sailboards. 800-628-4599; 415-588-1714 (in CA).

SURPLUS & LIQUIDATION MERCHANDISE

American Science & Surplus, 3605 Howard St., Skokie, IL 60076: Catalog $1 ❖ Surplus science and electrical-mechanical equipment. 708-982-0870.

Barnes Surplus & John, Rt. 2, Box 136B, Tupelo, MS 38801: Free price list ❖ Surplus merchandise. 601-840-9244.

Burden's Surplus Center, P.O. Box 82209, Lincoln, NE 68501: Free catalog ❖ Liquidation merchandise. 800-488-3407.

COMB Authorized Liquidator, P.O. Box 29902, Minneapolis, MN 55440: Free catalog ❖ Liquidation merchandise. 800-328-0609.

Damark International Inc., 7101 Winnetka Ave. North, P.O. Box 0437, Minneapolis, MN 55429: Free information ❖ Liquidation of over-production, discontinued, or merchandise obtained through special arrangements with vendors. 800-729-9000.

SURVEILLANCE & PERSONAL PROTECTION EQUIPMENT

ET Supply, 5055 Exposition Blvd., P.O. Box 78190, Los Angeles, CA 90016: Free catalog ❖ Tools and electro-mechanical and other surplus items. 213-734-2430.

Fair Radio Sales Company Inc., P.O. Box 1105, Lima, OH 45802: Free information ❖ Industrial and military surplus electronic parts. 419-227-6573.

Falkner Enterprises, P.O. Box 1378, Ottumwa, IA 52501: Free catalog ❖ Electronic surplus liquidation. 515-683-7621.

H & R Company, P.O. Box 122, Bristol, PA 19007: Free catalog ❖ Surplus electro-mechanical and optical equipment. 800-848-8001.

Harbor Freight Salvage, 3491 Mission Oaks Blvd., Camarillo, CA 93011: Free catalog ❖ Hardware, tools, and surplus merchandise. 800-423-2567.

Massachusetts Army & Navy Store, 15 Fordham Rd., Boston, MA 02134: Free catalog ❖ Army and navy surplus from around the world. 800-343-7749; 617-783-1250 (in MA).

Mid-Missouri Surplus, Russ Hinnard, 165 W. North St., Marshall, MO 65340: Free catalog ❖ New and used military and outdoor gear. 816-886-3585.

Ruvel & Company Inc., 4128 W. Belmont Ave., Chicago, IL 60641: Catalog $2 ❖ Army-navy surplus. 312-286-9494.

Strand Surplus Center, 2202 Strand, Galveston, TX 77550: Brochure $1 ❖ All types of equipment that includes many hard-to-find items. 409-762-7397.

Surplus Center, P.O. Box 82209, Lincoln, NE 68501: Free catalog ❖ Hydraulics, motors, air compressors, spraying equipment, pumps, and surplus merchandise. 800-488-3407.

Woodhaven Army Surplus & Military Collectibles, 6295 S. Harrison Dr., Las Vegas, NV 89120: Catalog $2 ❖ U.S., British, and French surplus from World War II to the present. 702-454-9111.

SURVEILLANCE & PERSONAL PROTECTION EQUIPMENT

A & D Electronics, P.O. Box 601, Monsey, NY 10952: Catalog $6 ❖ Professional surveillance equipment. 914-356-7541.

A.M.C. Sales Inc., 193 Vaquero Dr., Boulder, CO 80303: Free information ❖ Telephone recording adapters, bugging detectors, telephone scramblers, voice changers, and equipment. 800-926-2488.

Action, P.O. Box 830760, Miami, FL 33283: Free catalog ❖ Active lifestye clothing and security accessories. 800-472-2388.

CME Inc., P.O. Box 4477, Englewood, CO 80155: Free catalog ❖ CCD surveillance cameras, transmitter and receiver systems, and accessories. 303-771-1288.

The Counter Spy Shop, 444 Madison Ave., New York, NY 10022: Free brochure ❖ Surveillance and personal protection aids. 212-688-8500.

Creative Micro Electronics Inc., P.O. Box 4477, Englewood, CO 80155: Free catalog ❖ Miniature black and white and color video camera modules and equipment. 303-771-1288.

Deco Industries, Box 607, Bedford Hills, NY 10507: Free information ❖ Easy-to-assemble programmable scanner and VHF surveillance receiver. 914-232-3878.

EMCOM, 10 Howard St., Buffalo, NY 14206: Catalog $5 ❖ Surveillance and counter-surveillance equipment. 716-852-3711.

Executive Protection Products Inc., 1325 Imola Ave. West, Ste. 504 N-10, Napa, CA 94559: Free catalog ❖ Electronic surveillance and counter measures equipment. 707-253-7142.

Great Southern Security, 513 Bankhead Hwy., Carrolton, GA 30117: Free information ❖ Electronic protection devices. 800-732-5000.

Guardian Personal Security Products, 22444 N. 19th Ave., Phoenix, AZ 85027: Free information ❖ Pepper spray, stun guns, locksmithing tools, and accessories. 800-527-4434.

International Logistics Systems Inc., Defense Assistance Research Corporation, 234 McLean Blvd., Paterson, NJ 07504: Free brochure ❖ Equipment for personal protection, telephone counter measure, law enforcement, intelligence operations, and night vision. 201-881-0001.

Polaris Electronics Industries, 141 W. Wieuca Rd., Atlanta, GA 30342: Free information ❖ Micro-size CCD cameras and wireless monitoring systems. 404-252-3340.

Protector Enterprises, P.O. Box 520294, Salt Lake City, UT 84152: Catalog $5 ❖ Spy, counterspy, and protection equipment. All at guaranteed lowest prices. 801-487-3823.

Seymor-Radix Inc., Box 166055, Irving, TX 75016: Free information ❖ Surveillance and recording devices. 214-255-7490.

Spy Outlet, 2468 Niagara Falls Blvd., Tonawanda, NY 14150: Catalog $5 ❖ Voice changers and scramblers, telephone recorders, bug detectors, and surveillance and counter-surveillance electronic devices. 716-695-8660.

SPY Supply, 1212 Boylston St., Ste. 120, Chestnut Hill, MA 02167: Catalog $5 ❖ Electronic lock pick, locksmith tools, and unusual gadgets. 617-327-7272.

Street Smart Security, 7147 University Ave., La Mesa, CA 91941: Free information ❖ Three-channel ultra-small remote security receiver. 619-462-1167.

Super Circuits, 13552 Research Blvd., #B, Austin, TX 78750: Free catalog ❖ Wireless micro-video CCD camera system, security and surveillance equipment, and mini products. 512-335-9777.

SWIMMING POOLS & EQUIPMENT

Aqua Products Inc., 25 Rutgers Ave., Cedar Grove, NJ 07009: Free information ❖ Above-ground water pressure-operated pool cleaner. 800-221-1750.

Aquasol Controllers Inc., 2918 Dupree, Houston, TX 77054: Free information ❖ Electronic pool sanitizer and pH monitoring and control equipment. 800-444-0675.

Chemtrol, 5375 Overpass Rd., Santa Barbara, CA 93111: Free information ❖ Electronic pool sanitizer and pH monitoring and control equipment. 800-621-2279.

Cover-Pools Inc., 66 E. 3335 South, Salt Lake City, UT 84115: Free information ❖ Swimming pool covers. 800-447-2838.

Endless Pools Inc., 200 E. Duttons Mill Rd., Aston, PA 19014: Free brochure ❖ Lap pool for swimming in place against a smooth, adjustable current. 800-732-8660.

Fanta-Sea Pools, 10151 Main St., Clarence, NY 14031: Free information ❖ Solar energy-heated swimming pools. 800-845-5500.

Guardex Pool & Spa Products, Biolab Inc., P.O. Box 67, Decatur, GA 30031: Free information ❖ 4-in-1 swimming pool testing kit. 800-959-7946.

Kreepy Krauly USA Inc., 13801 NW 4th St., Sunrise, FL 33325: Free information ❖ Pool vacuums. 800-222-6841.

Meyco Products Inc., 225 Park Ave., Hicksville, NY 11801: Free brochure ❖ Swimming pool covers. 800-446-3926; 516-935-0900 (in NY).

Pool Fence Company, 1791-907 Blount Rd., Pompano Beach, FL 33069: Free brochure ❖ Swimming pool security fences. 800-992-2206.

❖ TABLE TENNIS ❖

Recreonics Corporation, 4200 Schmitt Ave., Louisville KY 40213: Free information ❖ Swimming pools and supplies. 800-428-3254.

Sundance Supply, 1678 Shattuck Ave., Ste. 173, Berkeley, CA 94709: Catalog $2 ❖ Building components for greenhouses, sun rooms, pool enclosures, and skylights. 800-776-2534.

Swimex, P.O. Box 328, Warren, RI 02885: Free brochure ❖ Compact lap pool for swimming in place, with controls for adjusting water flow. 800-877-7946.

Water Warehouse, 801 W. Lunt Ave., Elk Grove Village, IL 60007: Free catalog ❖ Swimming pool supplies and maintenance equipment. 800-574-7946.

TABLE TENNIS

The Athletic Connection, 1901 Diplomat, Dallas, TX 75234: Free information ❖ Balls, nets, paddles, and tables. 800-527-0871; 214-243-1446 (in TX).

Cannon Sports, P.O. Box 797, Greenland, NH 03840: Free list of retail sources ❖ Paddles, balls, nets, brackets, and sets. 800-362-3146.

Escalade Sports, P.O. Box 889, Evansville, IN 47706: Free catalog ❖ Tables, paddles, balls, nets, and sets. 800-457-3373; 812-467-1200 (in IN).

Indian Industries Inc., P.O. Box 889, Evansville, IN 47706: Free catalog ❖ Sets. 800-457-3373; 812-467-1200 (in IN).

Markwort Sporting Goods, 4300 Forest Park Ave., St. Louis, MO 63108: Catalog $8 (request list of retail sources) ❖ Balls, nets, paddles, and tables. 800-669-6626; 314-652-3757 (in MO).

Olympia Sports, 745 State Circle, Ann Arbor, MI 48106: Free information ❖ Balls, nets, paddles, and tables. 800-521-2832.

Papa's Gameroom, 121 Lakeside Dr., Mayfield, NY 12117: Free catalog ❖ Everything for your home gameroom. Darts, billiards, foosball, table tennis, jukeboxes, home casino equipment, and gifts. 888-321-PAPA.

Saunier-Wilhem Company, 3216 5th Ave., Pittsburgh, PA 15213: Free catalog ❖ Equipment and accessories for bowling, billiards, darts, table tennis, shuffleboard, and board games. 412-621-4350.

Spalding Sports Worldwide, 425 Meadow St., P.O. Box 901, Chicopee, MA 01021: Free list of retail sources ❖ Paddles, balls, nets, brackets, and sets. 800-225-6601.

Sportime, Customer Service, 1 Sportime Way, Atlanta, GA 30340: Free information ❖ Balls, nets, paddles, and tables. 800-444-5700; 770-449-5700 (in GA).

Sporty's Preferred Living Catalog, Clermont Airport, Batavia, OH 45103: Free catalog ❖ Folding outdoor table tennis tables. 800-543-8633.

Tide-Rider Inc., P.O. Box 429, Oakdale, CA 95361: Free information ❖ Balls, nets, and paddles. 209-848-4420.

Wa-Mac Inc., Highskore Products Inc., 178 Commerce Rd., P.O. Box 128, Carlstadt, NJ 07072: Free information ❖ Paddles, balls, nets, brackets, and sets. 800-447-5673; 201-438-7200 (in NJ).

World of Leisure Manufacturing Company, 13504 Phantom St., Victorville, CA 92394: Free list of retail sources ❖ Paddles, balls, nets, brackets, and sets. 619-246-3790.

TABLECLOTHS, PADS & OTHER LINENS

Best Value Table Pad Company, 1170 Stella St., St. Paul, MN 55108: Free information ❖ Table pads. 800-345-9795; 612-646-6630 (in MN).

Brown's Country Creations, 838 E. 385 Rd., Dunnegan, MO 65640: Catalog $2.50 ❖ Place mats, napkins, runners, and other items. 417-326-4880.

Bucks Trading Post, 930 Old Bethlehem Pike, Sellersville, PA 18960: Catalog $2 ❖ European lace curtains, matching tablecloths, and doilies. 800-242-0738; 610-453-0623 (in PA).

Chambers, Mail Order Department, P.O. Box 7841, San Francisco, CA 94120: Free catalog ❖ Bed and bath furnishings. 800-334-1254.

Curtains & Home, 1600 Old Country Rd., Plainview, NY 11803: Free catalog ❖ Curtains, window treatments, bedspreads, quilts, table cloths, bathroom ensembles, and rugs. 800-228-7824.

Domestications, P.O. Box 40, Hanover, PA 17333: Free catalog ❖ Bedding and bath ensembles. 717-633-3333.

Eldridge Textile Company, 277 Grand St., New York, NY 10002: Catalog $3 (refundable) ❖ Bed, bath, and table linens. 212-925-1523.

Factory Direct Table Pad Company, 1501 W. Market St., Indianapolis, IN 46222: Free information ❖ Table pads. 800-737-3148.

Guardian Custom Products, P.O. Box A, LaGrange, IN 46761: Free information ❖ Table pads. 800-444-0778.

Home Etc., Palo Verde at 34th St., P.O. Box 28806, Tucson, AZ 85726: Free catalog ❖ Bedding ensembles, curtains, bedspreads and comforters, rugs, linens and pillows, and towels. 800-362-8415.

Horchow Fine Linen Collection, P.O. Box 620048, Dallas, TX 75262: Free catalog ❖ Comforters, sheets, pillows, blankets, bedspreads, throws, and tablecloths. 800-456-7000.

Harris Levy, 278 Grand St., New York, NY 10002: Free catalog ❖ Table, bed, and bath linens. 800-221-7750; 212-226-3102 (in NY).

Palmetto Linen Company, 50 Palmetto Bay Rd., Hilton Head, SC 29928: Free information ❖ Sheets, dust ruffles, bath towels, blankets, comforters, pillows, tablecloths, place mats, shower curtains, kitchen towels, and oven gloves. 800-972-7442.

Pioneer Table Pad Company, 6520 Carnegie Ave., Gates Mills, OH 44103: Free information ❖ Table pads. 800-541-0271.

Rue de France, 28 Jacome Way, Middletown, RI 02842: Catalog $3 ❖ Pillows, tablecloths, runners, and lace curtains. 800-777-0998.

Sentry Table Pad Company, 1170 Stella St., St. Paul, MN 55108: Free information ❖ Table pads. 800-328-7237.

A Touch of Country, P.O. Box 653, Palos Heights, IL 60463: Catalog $2 ❖ Table lace. 708-361-0142.

TAPESTRIES & WALL HANGINGS

Delights Of A Queen, 34 S. Main St., South Deerfield, MA 01373: Free price list ❖ Tapestries. 413-665-3511.

Heirloom European Tapestries, Box 539, Dobbins, CA 95935: Catalog $4 ❖ Reproduction museum classic tapestry wall hangings. 800-699-6836.

Lancaster Towne Quilts, 600 Olde Hickory Rd., Ste. 100, Strasburg, PA 17601: Catalog $5 ❖ Custom-made quilts and wall hangings. 717-581-9100.

Peerless Imported Rugs, 3033 Lincoln Ave., Chicago, IL 60657: Catalog $1 ❖ Hand and machine-woven Oriental rugs, colonial braids, tapestries from Europe, and rag, Navajo, and grass rugs. 800-621-6573.

Sonrise Soft Crafts, P.O. Box 5091, Salem, OR 97304: Brochure 50¢ ❖ Patterns and kits for lifelike stuffed animals, puppets, shirt appliques, and wall hangings. 503-362-0027.

A Touch of Country, P.O. Box 653, Palos Heights, IL 60463: Catalog $2 ❖ Tapestry runners. 708-361-0142.

TATTOOING SUPPLIES & BODY JEWELRY

American Tattoo Supply Inc., P.O. Box 3215, South Farmingdale, NY 11735: Free information ❖ Tattooing equipment. 516-293-4247.

Creative Alternatives, 2904 S. Barnes, Springfield, MO 65804: Brochure $4 ❖ Easy-to-remove waterproof temporary tattoos and face and body painting products. 417-887-8961

Latora Tattoo Products, P.O. Box 1569, Orting, WA 98360: Catalog $3 ❖ Tattooing equipment. 206-845-8503.

Papillon Studio Supply & Manufacturing, 118 Pearl St., Enfield, CT 06082: Free information ❖ Tattooing equipment. 860-745-9270.

Pleasurable Piercings Inc., 417 Lafayette Ave., Hawthorne, NJ 07506: Catalog $3 (refundable) ❖ Piercing equipment and body jewelry in surgical steel, niobium, and 14K or white gold. 201-238-0305.

Professional Tattoo Kits, Box 17326, Phoenix, AZ 85009: Free information ❖ Tattoo kits.

❖ TATTOO SUPPLIES ❖

Spaulding & Rogers Manufacturing, Rt. 85, New Scotland Rd., Voorheesville, NY 12186: Free catalog ❖ Tattoo machines, books, flash and videos, and equipment. 518-768-2070.

Superior Tattoo Equipment, 3334 W. Wilshire Dr., Ste. 30, Phoenix, AZ 85009: Catalog $2 ❖ Tattooing equipment and kits. 602-278-4444.

TAXIDERMY

Jim Allred Taxidermy, 216 Sugar Loaf Rd., Hendersonville, NC 28792: Free information ❖ Taxidermy supplies. 800-624-7507.

Aves Products, P.O. Box 344, River Falls, WI 54022: Free information ❖ Self-hardening clays, paper mache, and other sculpting materials. 715-386-9097.

Blue Ribbon Bases, 24 Dewey St., Sayville, NY 11782: Free catalog ❖ Walnut and hardwood bases and plaques for mounting projects. 516-589-0707.

Chandler's Taxidermy Supply Inc., 1637 Westhaven Blvd., Jackson, MS 39209: Free information ❖ Taxidermy supplies. 800-748-8765.

Dan Chase Taxidermy Supply, 13599 Blackwater Rd., Baker, LA 70714: Free catalog ❖ Taxidermy supplies and how-to videos. 800-535-8220.

Dixieland Taxidermy Supply, 9605 Hwy. 64, Somerville, TN 38068: Free catalog ❖ Taxidermy supplies. 800-465-2922.

J.W. Elwood Company, Elwood Building, Omaha, NE 68103: Free catalog ❖ Taxidermy supplies. 800-228-2291.

Foster Taxidermy Supply, 5124 Troy Hwy., Montgomery, AL 36116: Free catalog ❖ Taxidermy supplies. 800-848-5602.

Jameson Company Ltd., 2200 Terminal Rd., Niles, MI 49120: Free information ❖ Polyurethane molding foam. 616-684-4451.

David McBride Taxidermy Supply Company, 23901 Hwy. 59 North, Kingwood, TX 77339: Free catalog ❖ Taxidermy supplies. 713-358-1762.

McKenzie Taxidermy Supply, Box 480, Granite Quarry, NC 28072: Free catalog ❖ Taxidermy supplies. 800-279-7985.

O.H. Mullen Sales Inc., RR 2, Oakwood, OH 45873: Free information ❖ Taxidermy supplies. 800-258-6625.

Panels by Paith, Don C. & Greta S. Paith, 2728 Allensville Rd., Roxboro, NC 27573: Free catalog ❖ Plaques, bases, and accessories. 800-677-2484; 910-599-3437 (in NC).

Archie Phillips Taxidermy, 200 52nd St., Fairfield, AL 35064: Catalog $2 ❖ Taxidermy supplies. 800-423-8601.

Qesearch Mannikins Inc., P.O. Box 315, Lebanon, OR 97355: Free catalog ❖ Taxidermy forms and supplies. 800-826-0654.

John Rinehart Taxidermy Supply Company, 3032 McCormick Dr., P.O. Box 5010, Janesville, WI 53547: Free information ❖ Taxidermy supplies. 800-367-3337.

Touchstone Taxidermy Supply, 5011 E. Texas, Bossier City, LA 71111: Free catalog ❖ Taxidermy supplies. 800-256-4800.

Tru-Form Taxidermy Supplies Inc., Mike & Debbie Pere, 4070 Rt. 14 North, Lyons, NY 14489: Free catalog ❖ Taxidermy supplies. 315-946-3012.

VanDyke's, Box 278, Woonsocket, SD 57385: Catalog $1 ❖ Taxidermy supplies. 800-843-3320.

Wildlife Artist Supply Company, 1306 W. Spring, P.O. Box 967, Monroe, GA 30655: Free catalog ❖ Taxidermy supplies. 404-267-8970.

TELEPHONES & ANSWERING MACHINES

Antique Phones

Billard's Telephones, 21710 Regnart Rd., Cupertino, CA 95014: Brochure $1 ❖ Antique telephones and parts. 408-252-2104.

Chicago Old Telephone Company, P.O. Box 189, Lemon Springs, NC 28355: Free catalog ❖ Restored telephones that can be plugged into modern systems. 800-843-1320.

Mahantango Manor, Box 170, Dalmatia, PA 17017: Catalog $3 ❖ Working replicas of telephones from the 1900s. 800-642-3966.

Phone Wizard, P.O. Box 70, Leesburg, VA 22078: Catalog $3 ❖ Restored antique telephones and parts. 703-777-0000.

Phoneco Inc., P.O. Box 70, 19812 E. Mill Rd., Galesville, WI 54630: Catalog $3 ❖ Restored antique, novelty, art deco, character, and other telephones. Also parts. 608-582-4124.

Prosser Telephone Company, P.O. Box 14, Turtle Lake, WI 54889: Catalog $1 ❖ Antique hand-crank telephones and parts. 715-986-4414.

20th Century Classic American Telephones, 2780 Northbrook Pl., Boulder, CO 80304: Free information ❖ Restored telephones, from 1910 to 1937.

Cellular Telephones

AT&T Consumer Products, 5 Wood Hollow Rd., Parsippany, NJ 07054: Free information ❖ Portable cellular telephones. 800-232-5179.

Audiovox, 185 Oser Ave., Hauppage, NY 11788: Free information ❖ Portable and installation cellular phones. 516-233-3300.

Blaupunkt, 2800 S. 25th Ave., Broadview, IL 60153: Free information ❖ Portable and installation cellular phones. 708-865-5200.

CellStar Corporation, 1730 Briercroft Ct., Carrollton, TX 75006: Free information ❖ Cellular phone accessories. 800-766-8283.

Cellular Phone & Accessory Warehouse, 11741 Valley View St., Ste. I, Cypress, CA 90630: Free catalog ❖ Cellular phones. 800-342-2336.

Cellular World, Corporate Headquarters, 5025 Arapaho Rd., Ste. 330, Dallas, TX 75248: Free information ❖ Cellular telephones and fax machines for homes, offices, or cars. 800-825-5669.

Cincinnati Microwave, One Microwave Plaza, Cincinnati, OH 45249: Free information ❖ Portable cellular phones. 800-543-1608.

Clarion Corporation of America, 661 W. Redondo Beach Blvd., Gardena, CA 90247: Free information ❖ Installation cellular phones. 800-487-9007.

Ericsson GE Mobile Communications, 1 Triangle Dr., Research Triangle Park, NC 27709: Free information ❖ Cellular phones. 800-227-3663.

Fujitsu America, 2801 Telecom Pkwy., Richardson, TX 75082: Free information ❖ Portable cellular phones. 800-955-9926.

Haven Industries, 2950 Lake Emma Rd., Lake Mary, FL 32746: Free information ❖ Computers, cellular telephones, audio and video equipment, and other electronics. 800-231-0031.

Mitsubishi Electronics, 5665 Plaza Dr., Cypress, CA 90630: Free information ❖ Portable and installation cellular phones. 800-843-2515.

Mitsubishi International, 1500 Michael Dr., Ste. B, Wood Dale, IL 60191: Free information ❖ Portable cellular phones. 708-860-4200.

Motorola Cellular Subscriber Group, 600 N. US Hwy. 45, Libertyville, IL 60048: Free information ❖ Portable cellular telephones. 800-331-6456.

❖ TENNIS ❖

NEC America, 1555 W. Walnut Hill Ln., Irving, TX 75038: Free information ❖ Portable and installation cellular phones. 800-421-2141.

Newtech Video & Computers, 350 7th Ave., New York, NY 10001: Free information ❖ Video equipment, computers and peripherals, software, cellular phones, fax machines, and office equipment. 800-554-9747.

Nokia Mobile Phones Inc., 6200 Courtney Campbell Causeway, Ste. 900, P.O. Box 30730, Tampa, FL 33630: Free information ❖ Portable cellular telephones.

Oki Telecom, 437 Old Peachtree Rd., Suwanee, GA 30174: Free information ❖ Portable, briefcase, and installation cellular phones. 800-554-3112.

Panasonic, Panasonic Way, Secaucus, NJ 07094: Free list of retail sources ❖ Portable and installation cellular phones. 201-348-7000.

Qualcomm Inc., 6455 Lusk Blvd., San Diego, CA 92121: Free information ❖ Portable cellular telephones. 800-266-CDMA.

Radio Shack, Division Tandy Corporation, 1500 One Tandy Center, Fort Worth, TX 76102: Free information ❖ Installation and portable cellular phones. 817-390-3700.

Shure Brothers Inc., 222 Hartrey Ave., Evanston, IL 60202: Free information ❖ Hands-free cellular phones. 800-447-4873.

Uniden, 4700 Amon Carter Blvd., Fort Worth, TX 76155: Free information ❖ Portable cellular telephones. 800-297-1023.

Telephones & Answering Machines

Bernie's Discount Center Inc., 821 6th Ave., New York, NY 10001: Catalog $1 (refundable) ❖ Telephones and answering machines, audio and video equipment, large and small kitchen appliances, and personal care appliances. 212-564-8758.

Bi-Rite Photo & Electronics, 20 E. 39th St., New York, NY 10016: Free information ❖ Telephones, cameras, typewriters, calculators, video equipment, and other electronics. 800-223-1970; 212-685-2130 (in NY).

Crutchfield, 1 Crutchfield Park, Charlottesville, VA 22906: Free catalog ❖ Fax machines, telephones and answering machines, word processors, copiers, computers, and software. 800-955-9009.

East 33rd Street Electronics & Typewriters, 42 E. 33rd St., New York, NY 10016: Free information with long SASE ❖ Telephones and answering machines, typewriters, calculators, computers, software, TVs, video equipment, and other electronics. 212-686-0930.

Electronic Wholesalers, 1166 Hamburg Tnpk., Wayne, NJ 07470: Free information ❖ Telephones, camcorders, TVs, cassette and disk players, audio equipment, and other electronics. 201-696-6531.

Hello Direct, 5884 Eden Park Pl., San Jose, CA 95138: Free catalog ❖ Amplification aids, cellular and paging accessories, telephones and answering machines, and other telephone productivity tools. 800-444-3556.

J & R Music World, 59-50 Queens-Midtown Expwy., Maspeth, NY 11378: Free catalog ❖ Telephones, audio equipment, car and portable stereos, video recorders, computers, and other electronics. 800-221-8180.

Motorola AMSD, 5401 N. Beech St., Fort Worth, TX 76137: Free list of retail sources ❖ Hand-held miniature answering machine. 800-520-PAGE.

Olden Video, 1265 Broadway, New York, NY 10001: Free information ❖ Telephones, copiers, and photographic equipment. 212-725-1234.

Planet Electronics, 8418 Lilley, Canton, MI 48187: Free catalog ❖ Telephones, audio and video equipment, TVs, car and portable stereos, cassette players, and video tapes, cassettes, and disks. 800-247-4663; 313-453-4750 (in MI).

S & S Sound City, 58 W. 45th St., New York, NY 10036: Free information ❖ Audio and video equipment, telephones, office machines, and other electronics. 212-575-0210.

Sound City, Meadtown Shopping Center, Rt. 23, Kinnelon, NJ 07405: Free information ❖ Audio and video equipment, cassette and CD players, camcorders, TVs, processors, fax machines, telephones, and other electronics. 800-542-7283.

Talk-A-Phone, 5013 N. Kedzie Ave., Chicago, IL 60625: Free brochure ❖ Compliant emergency hand-free telephones. 312-539-1100.

Teleconcepts Inc., 11711 NW 39th St., Coral Springs, FL 33065: Free information ❖ Decorative telephones.

Telephone Engineering Company, P.O. Box 72, 786 Main St., Simpson, PA 18407: Free catalog ❖ Rotary and push-button phones, parts, two-line and novelty phones, business telephone systems, and sonic alert telephone ringing signalers. 717-282-5100.

Temasek Telephone Inc., 21 Airport Rd., South San Francisco, CA 94080: Free information ❖ Voice-activated telephones. 800-647-8887.

Trendware Phone Systems, 4448 W. El Segundo Blvd., Ste. 165, Hawthorne, CA 90250: Free information ❖ Telephone answering machine that works with pagers and cellular phones. 800-644-3014.

TENNIS

Clothing

Adidas USA, 5675 N. Blackstock Rd., Spartanburg, SC 29303: Free list of retail sources ❖ Dresses, sweaters, jackets, caps and sun visors, shirts and tops, shoes and socks, shorts, and warm-up suits. 800-423-4327.

Alchester Mills Company Inc., 1160 Wright Ave., Camden, NJ 08103: Free information ❖ Caps and sun visors, gloves, sweatband, and socks. 609-964-9700.

Asics Tiger Corporation, 10540 Talbert Ave., West Building, Fountain Valley, CA 92708: Free information ❖ Dresses, jackets, shirts and tops, shoes and socks, and warm-up suits. 800-678-9435.

Associated Tennis Suppliers, 200 Waterfront Dr., Pittsburgh, PA 15222: Free catalog ❖ Tennis racquets, supplies, easy-to-use stringing machines, and clothing. 800-866-7071.

Ball Hopper Products Inc., 200 Waterfront Dr., Pittsburgh, PA 15222: Free information ❖ Caps and sun visors, gloves, dresses, jackets, shirts and tops, socks, sweatbands, underwear, and warm-up suits. 800-323-5417; 412-323-9633 (in PA).

Betlin Manufacturing, 1445 Marion Rd., Columbus OH 43207: Free information ❖ Tennis jackets, shorts, and warm-up suits. 614-443-0248.

Converse Inc., 1 Fordham Rd., North Reading, MA 01864: Free information ❖ Caps and sun visors, jackets, shirts and tops, socks, sweatbands, and warm-up suits. 800-428-2667; 508-664-1100 (in MA).

Holabird Sports Discounters, 9220 Pulaski Hwy., Baltimore, MD 21220: Free catalog ❖ Tennis racquets, shoes, clothes, balls, and bags. 410-687-6400.

Las Vegas Discount Golf & Tennis, 5325 S. Valley View Blvd., Ste. 10, Las Vegas, NV 89109: Free catalog ❖ Equipment, shoes, and clothing for tennis, racquetball, golf, and running and jogging. 702-798-7777.

Lily's, 4910-B W. Rosecrans Ave., Hawthorne, CA 90250: Free information ❖ Dresses, jackets, caps and sun visors, shirts and tops, shorts, sweatbands, and warm-up suits. 800-421-4474.

Nike Footwear Inc., One Bowerman Dr., Beaverton, OR 97005: Free list of retail sources ❖ Jackets, shirts and tops, shoes and socks, shorts, and sweatbands. 800-344-6453.

Prince Racquet Sports, 1 Sport Systems Plaza, Bordentown, NJ 08505: Free information ❖ Caps and sun visors, dresses, jackets, shirts and tops, shoes and socks, sweatbands, underwear, and warm-up suits. 800-2-TENNIS; 609-291-5900 (in NJ).

Professional Golf & Tennis Suppliers, 7825 Hollywood Blvd., Pembroke Pines, FL 33024: Free catalog with long SASE ❖ Tennis racquets, clothing, shoes, and racquetball equipment. 305-981-7283.

Puma USA Inc., 147 Centre St., Brockton, MA 02403: Free information with long SASE ❖ Dresses, jackets, shirts and tops, socks, sweatbands, sweaters, and warm-up suits. 508-583-9100.

TENNIS

RayCo Tennis, 1434 University Ave., San Diego, CA 92103: Free price list ❖ Strings, shoes, grips, and stringing machines. 800-836-6476; 619-295-0325 (in CA).

Samuels Tennisport, 7796 Montgomery Rd., Cincinnati, OH 45236: Free information ❖ Tennis, squash, and racquetball racquets and shoes. 513-791-4636.

Spalding Sports Worldwide, 425 Meadow St., P.O. Box 901, Chicopee, MA 01021: Free list of retail sources ❖ Caps and sun visors, gloves, dresses, jackets, shirts and tops, shorts, shoes and socks, sweatbands, underwear, and warm-up suits. 800-225-6601.

Sport Casuals, Box 402337, Miami Beach, FL 33140: Free information ❖ Jackets, shirts and tops, shoes and socks, shorts, sweaters, and warm-up suits. 800-776-7803; 305-674-0001 (in FL).

Sporting Life, 1100 S. Powerline Rd., Deerfield Beach, FL 33442: Free catalog ❖ Shorts, socks, headbands, wristbands, hats, tennis shoes, boat shoes, beach sandals, sport bags, tennis outfits for men and ladies, sweat shirts, and sweat suits. 800-782-5373.

The Sporting Look, 1116 S. Powerline Rd., Deerfield Beach, FL 33442: Catalog $2 ❖ Tennis clothing. 800-782-5373.

Sportline of Hilton Head Ltd., 816 Friendly Center Rd., Greensboro, NC 27408: Free information ❖ Tennis racquets, shoes, bags, and clothing. 800-438-6021.

Sports Express, 5050 F.M. 1960 West, Houston, TX 77069: Free information ❖ Tennis racquets, court equipment, grips and wraps, shoes, bags, and clothing. 800-533-6321.

Sullivan Sports, P.O. Box 690906, Houston, TX 77269: Free information ❖ Tennis racquets, shoes, bags, and clothing. 800-543-0926.

Total Sports, 200 Waterfront Dr., Pittsburgh, PA 15222: Free catalog ❖ Tennis racquet strings, clothing, bags, and court supplies. 800-245-0208.

Equipment

Adidas USA, 5675 N. Blackstock Rd., Spartanburg, SC 29303: Free list of retail sources ❖ Composite graphite tennis racquets. 800-423-4327.

American Playground Corporation, 1801 S. Jackson, P.O. Box 2599, Anderson, IN 46011: Free information ❖ Posts, nets, and other court equipment. 800-541-1602.

American Tennis Mart, P.O. Box 690906, Houston, TX 77269: Free information ❖ Tennis racquets, shoes, bags, and clothing. 800-344-7707.

Associated Tennis Suppliers, 200 Waterfront Dr., Pittsburgh, PA 15222: Free catalog ❖ Tennis racquets, supplies, easy-to-use stringing machines, and clothing. 800-866-7071.

Atlantic Racquet Sports, 14891 64th Way North, Palm Beach Gardens, FL 33418: Free price list ❖ Strings and grips. 800-223-1540.

Austad's, 4500 E. 10th St., P.O. Box 5428, Sioux Falls, SD 57196: Free catalog ❖ Equipment for tennis and other sports. 800-444-1234.

Ball Hopper Products Inc., 200 Waterfront Dr., Pittsburgh, PA 15222: Free information ❖ Ball retrievers and balls, posts and nets, practice and stringing machines, strings, and aluminum, boron composite, graphite composite, ceramic, graphite, and wooden racquets. 800-323-5417; 412-323-9633 (in PA).

Cannon Sports, P.O. Box 11179, Burbank, CA 91510: Free list of retail sources ❖ Posts, nets, balls, ball retrievers, and other court equipment. 800-362-3146.

Carron Net Company, 1623 17th St., P.O. Box 177, Two Rivers, WI 54241: Free information ❖ Posts, nets, ball retrievers, practice machines, and other court equipment. 800-558-7768; 414-793-2217 (in WI).

Century Sports Inc., Lakewood Industrial Park, 1995 Rutgers University Blvd., Box 2035, Lakewood, NJ 08701: Free information ❖ Balls, nets, racquet covers, and racquets. 800-526-7548; 908-905-4422 (in NJ).

Clarke Distributing Company, 9233 Bryant St., Houston, TX 77075: Catalog $2 ❖ Tennis, golf, soccer equipment, novelties, and gifts. 800-777-3444.

Croquet International Ltd., 7100-42 Fairway Dr., Palm Beach Gardens, FL 33418: Free catalog ❖ Croquet and tennis sets. 800-533-9061; 407-627-4009 (in FL).

Dunlop, 728 N. Pleasantburg Dr., Greenville, SC 29607: Free list of retail sources ❖ Tennis racquets. 803-241-2200.

Easton, 5040 W. Harold Gatty Dr., Salt Lake City, UT 84116: Free list of retail sources ❖ Aluminum, ceramic, graphite, and graphite composite tennis racquets. 801-539-1400.

Estus, 1582 Parkway Loop, Tustin, CA 92680: Free list of retail sources ❖ Tennis racquets. 800-295-0938.

FEMCO Corporation, 235 Arcadia St., Richmond, VA 23225: Free information ❖ Ball retrievers, nets, posts, practice machines, balls, and stringing supplies. 800-476-5432.

Fischer Tennis, 2412 Logan Rd., Owings Mills, MD 21117: Free information ❖ Balls, racquet covers, and racquets. 410-356-0196.

Gamma Sports, 200 Waterfront Dr., Pittsburgh, PA 15222: Free information ❖ Tennis racquets. 800-333-0337.

Gared Sports Inc., 1107 Mullanphy St., St. Louis, MO 63106: Free information ❖ Tennis equipment. 800-325-2682.

Golden Shine Inc., 4075 E. La Palma Ave., Ste. O, Anaheim, CA 92807: Free information ❖ Portable easy-to-assemble tennis rebound net. 800-852-8525.

Guterman International Inc., 71 Pullman St., Worcester, MA 01606: Free information ❖ Portable stringers. 800-343-6096; 508-852-8206 (in MA).

Holabird Sports Discounters, 9220 Pulaski Hwy., Baltimore, MD 21220: Free catalog ❖ Tennis racquets, shoes, clothes, balls, bags, and other sports equipment. 410-687-6400.

Jayfro Corporation, Unified Sports Inc., 976 Hartford Tnpk., P.O. Box 400, Waterford, CT 06385: Free catalog ❖ Tennis net posts, nets, portable units, windscreens, court dividers, and practice tennis standards. 860-447-3001.

Charlie Johnson's Tennis & Squash Shop, 2648 Erie Ave., Cincinnati, OH 45208: Free information ❖ Racquets, shoes, strings, and grips. 800-222-1143.

Klipspringer USA Inc., 780 Church Rd., Elgin, IL 60123: Free brochure ❖ Stringing machines, hand tools, and strings. 800-522-5547; 708-742-1300 (in IL).

Las Vegas Discount Golf & Tennis, 5325 S. Valley View Blvd., Ste. 10, Las Vegas, NV 89109: Free catalog ❖ Equipment, shoes, and clothing. 702-798-7777.

Leisure Marketing Inc., 2204 Morris Ave., Ste. 202, Union, NJ 07083: Free information ❖ Aluminum, boron composite, ceramic, graphite, and graphite composite tennis racquets. 908-851-9494.

Leisure Pro, 42 W. 18th St., 3rd Floor, New York, NY 10011: Free information ❖ Racquets, strings, grips, footwear, ball hoppers, and balls. Also backpacking and scuba equipment. 212-645-1234.

Lob-Ster Inc., 1112 North Ave., Plainfield, NJ 07060: Free brochure ❖ Racquets, ball machines, balls, and other equipment. 800-526-4041.

Markwort Sporting Goods Company, 4300 Forest Park Ave., St. Louis, MO 63108: Catalog $8 (request list of retail sources) ❖ Balls, nets, racquet covers, and racquets. 800-669-6626; 314-652-3757 (in MO).

Master Corporation, P.O. Box 585, Auburn, IN 46706: Free information ❖ Portable tennis serving machine. 219-357-3337.

Midwest Sports & Tennis Supply, 8740 Montgomery Rd., Cincinnati, OH 45236: Free information ❖ Tennis racquets, shoes for men and women, tennis bags, strings, and court equipment. 800-334-4580.

New Tech Tennis, P.O. Box 201896, Austin, TX 78720: Free catalog ❖ Tennis ball and stringing machines. 800-577-1916.

❖ TERM PAPERS ❖

NRC Sports, P.O. Box 331, West Boylston, MA 01583: Free information ❖ Portable stringers and natural gut, synthetic, and nylon strings. 800-243-5033; 508-852-8987 (in MA).

Olympia Sports, 745 State Circle, Ann Arbor, MI 48106: Free information ❖ Nets, posts, and balls. 800-521-2832.

Powers Court, 40 S. Main St., New City, NY 10956: Free catalog ❖ Racquet stringers, strings, and other equipment. 800-431-2838; 914-634-6969 (in NY).

Prince Racquet Sports, 1 Sport Systems Plaza, Bordentown, NJ 08505: Free information ❖ Stringing machines, nylon and synthetic strings, and aluminum, boron composite, ceramic, graphite, graphite composite, and wooden tennis racquets. 800-2-TENNIS; 609-291-5900 (in NJ).

Prince Tennis Ball Machine, Master Corporation, P.O. Box 585, Auburn, IN 46706: Free information ❖ Two-hundred ball capacity tennis ball serving machine. 219-357-3337.

Pro-Kennex, 9606 Kearny Villa Rd., San Diego, CA 92126: Free information ❖ Tennis racquets. 800-854-1908; 619-271-8390 (in CA).

Professional Golf & Tennis Suppliers, 7825 Hollywood Blvd., Pembroke Pines, FL 33024: Free catalog with long SASE ❖ Tennis rackets, clothing and shoes, and racquetball equipment. 305-981-7283.

RayCo Tennis, 1434 University Ave., San Diego, CA 92103: Free price list ❖ Strings, shoes, grips, and stringing machines. 800-836-6476; 619-295-0325 (in CA).

ReSports, P.O. Box 679, Patton, CA 92369: Free information ❖ Tennis ball retrieval system. 909-864-7068.

Samuels Tennisport, 7796 Montgomery Rd., Cincinnati, OH 45236: Free information ❖ Tennis, squash, and racquetball racquets, equipment, and shoes. 513-791-4636.

Spalding Sports Worldwide, 425 Meadow St., P.O. Box 901, Chicopee, MA 01021: Free list of retail sources ❖ Tennis balls, composite tennis racquets, and nylon, synthetic, and gut strings. 800-225-6601.

Sport Casuals, Box 402337, Miami Beach, FL 33140: Free information ❖ Boron composite, ceramic, graphite, and graphite composite tennis racquets. 800-776-7803; 305-674-0001 (in FL).

Sportline of Hilton Head Ltd., 816 Friendly Center Rd., Greensboro, NC 27408: Free information ❖ Tennis racquets, shoes, bags, and clothing. 800-438-6021.

Sports Express, 5050 F.M. 1960 West, Houston, TX 77069: Free information ❖ Tennis racquets, court equipment, grips and wraps, shoes, bags, and clothing. 800-533-6321.

Sports Tutor, 2612 W. Burbank Blvd., Burbank, CA 91505: Free brochure ❖ Portable tennis ball machine. 800-448-8867.

Stringmeter, 8725 Burchell Rd., Gilroy, CA 95020: Free information ❖ Tension monitor for tennis strings. 800-860-1742.

Sullivan Sports, P.O. Box 690906, Houston, TX 77269: Free information ❖ Tennis racquets and bags, court and training equipment, strings, grips and wraps, and shoes and clothing for men and women. 800-543-0926.

Tennis Gear & Running Center, P.O. Box 1486, Cumberland, MD 21502: Free price list ❖ Tennis equipment. 301-729-0896.

Tennis Partner of Chicago, P.O. Box 59727, Chicago, IL 60659: Free information ❖ Tennis practice play board. 312-736-9772.

Total Sports, 200 Waterfront Dr., Pittsburgh, PA 15222: Free catalog ❖ Tennis racquet strings, clothing, bags, and court supplies. 800-245-0208.

Wa-Mac Inc., Highskore Products Inc., 178 Commerce Rd., P.O. Box 128, Carlstadt, NJ 07072: Free information ❖ Tennis balls and aluminum, boron composite, ceramic, graphite, graphite composite, and wooden tennis racquets. 800-447-5673; 201-438-7200 (in NJ).

Wilson Sporting Goods, 8700 W. Bryn Mawr, Chicago, IL 60631: Free information ❖ Stringing machines and strings, balls, nets, and aluminum, boron composite, ceramic, graphite, graphite composite, and wooden tennis racquets. 800-443-0011.

Yamaha Sporting Goods Division, 6600 Orangethorpe Ave., Buena Park, CA 90620: Free information ❖ Strings and boron composite, ceramic, graphite, and graphite composite tennis racquets. 800-851-6514; 714-522-9011 (in CA).

Yonex Corporation, 350 Challenger St., Torrance, CA 90503: Free list of retail sources ❖ Tennis racquets. 800-44-YONEX.

Zebest Racquet & Golf Sports, 12790 Hopewell Rd., Alpharetta, GA 30201: Free information ❖ Balls, racquet covers, and racquets. 800-272-7279.

TERM PAPERS

Academic Research Inc., 240 Park Ave., Rutherford, NJ 02070: Free catalog ❖ Over 20,000 reports and term papers. 201-939-0252.

Research Assistance, 11322 Idaho Ave., Los Angeles, CA 90025: Catalog $2 ❖ Over 10,000 term papers. 800-351-0222.

TETHERBALL

American Playground Corporation, 1801 S. Jackson, P.O. Box 2599, Anderson, IN 46011: Free information ❖ Balls, poles, and posts. 800-541-1602.

Franklin Sports Industries Inc., 17 Campanelli Parkway, P.O. Box 508, Stoughton, MA 02072: Free information ❖ Balls and sets. 800-426-7700.

General Sportcraft Company, 140 Woodbine Rd., Bergenfield, NJ 07621: Free information ❖ Balls, poles, posts, and sets. 201-384-4242.

Indian Industries Inc., P.O. Box 889, Evansville, IN 47706: Free catalog ❖ Sets. 800-457-3373; 812-467-1200 (in IN).

Dick Martin Sports Inc., 181 E. Union Ave., P.O. Box 7384, East Rutherford, NJ 07073: Free information ❖ Balls, poles, posts, and sets. 800-221-1993; 201-438-5255 (in NJ).

Venus Knitting Mills Inc., 140 Spring St., Murray Hill, NJ 07974: Free information ❖ Balls, paddles, poles, posts, and sets. 800-955-4200; 908-464-2400 (in NJ).

THEATRICAL SUPPLIES

Make-Up

Abracadabra Magic Shop, 125 Lincoln Blvd., Middlesex, NJ 08846: Catalog $5 ❖ Costumes, theatrical make-up, and supplies for magicians and clowns. 908-805-0200.

Apples & Company, 414 Conant Ave., Union, NJ 07083: Free information ❖ Clown-white make-up. 908-353-2193.

Burpo Duh Clown, P.O. Box 160190, Cupertino, CA 95016: Free information ❖ Face-painting rubber stamps and supplies. 408-446-9314.

Cherri-Oats & Company, Cheri Venturi, P.O. Box 723, North Olmsted, OH 44070: Free information ❖ Wigs, stickers, puppets, and face painting supplies. 216-979-9971.

Clown Heaven, 4792 Old State Rd. 37 South, Martinsville, IN 46152: Catalog $3 ❖ Balloons, make-up, puppets, wigs, ministry and gospel items, novelties, magic, clown props, and books. 317-342-6888.

Costumes by Betty, 2181 Edgerton St., St. Paul, MN 55117: Catalog $5 (refundable) ❖ Clown costumes, make-up, wigs, and shoes. 612-771-8734.

Steve Dawson's Magic Touch Catalog, 144 N. Milpitas Blvd., Milpitas, CA 95035: Catalog $3 ❖ Magic effects, books, videos, accessories, clown and juggling supplies, and make-up. 408-263-9404.

Eastern Costume Company, 510 N. Elm St., Greensboro, NC 27401: Free information ❖ Make-up and theatrical and masquerade costumes. 800-968-8461; 919-379-1026 (in NC).

Freckles Clown Supplies, 5509 Roosevelt Blvd., Jacksonville, FL 32244: Catalog $6 ❖ Make-up, costumes, clown supplies, puppets, how-to books on clowning and ballooning, and theatrical supplies. 904-388-5541.

Graftobian Ltd., 510 Tasman St., Madison, WI 53714: Free information ❖ Face-painting supplies. 800-255-0584.

Bob Kelly Cosmetics Inc., 151 W. 46th St., New York, NY 10036: Free catalog ❖ Make-up kits. 212-819-0030.

Lynch's Clown Supplies, 939 Howard, Dearborn, MI 48124: Catalog $5 ❖ Make-up, costume accessories, and clown equipment. 313-565-3425.

Mecca Magic Inc., 49 Dodd St., Bloomfield, NJ 07003: Catalog $10 ❖ Make-up, costumes and wigs, puppets, clown props, magic tricks, and juggling equipment. 201-429-7597.

Novelties Unlimited, 410 W. 21st St., Norfolk, VA 23517: Catalog $5 ❖ Make-up, clown props and gags, magic, balloons, and party decorations. 804-622-0344.

Ben Nye Makeup, 5935 Bowcroft St., Los Angeles, CA 90016: Catalog $2.50 ❖ Theatrical make-up. 310-839-1984.

Potsy & Blimpo Clown Supplies, P.O. Box 2075, Huntington Beach, CA 92647: Free catalog ❖ Clown make-up, wigs, and props. 800-897-0749; 714-897-0749 (in CA).

Ronjo's Magic & Costumes Inc., 4600 Nesconset Hwy., Unit 4, Port Jefferson Station, NY 11776: Catalog $2.50 ❖ Magic for amateur and professional magicians, costumes, and make-up and theatrical effects. 516-928-5005.

Rubie's Costume Company, National Sales Office, 999 Gould St., New Hyde Park, NY 11040: Free information ❖ Costumes, make-up, hair goods, and special effects. 516-326-1500.

Theatrical Lighting Systems Inc., 909 Meridian St., P.O. Box 2646, Huntsville, AL 35804: Free information ❖ Make-up, dimming and lighting control systems, follow spots, and stage equipment. 205-533-7025.

Under the Big Top, P.O. Box 807, Placentia, CA 92670: Catalog $4 ❖ Costumes, clown props, make-up, juggling equipment, and party supplies. 800-995-7727.

Up, Up & Away, P.O. Box 159, Beallsville, PA 15313: Catalog $3 ❖ Make-up, props, and clown equipment. 412-769-5447.

Victoria's Dance-Theatrical Supply, 1331 Lincoln Ave., San Jose, CA 95125: Catalog $2 ❖ Costume accessories. 800-626-9258.

Plays

Samuel French Catalog, 45 W. 25th St., New York, NY 10010: Catalog $4.50 ❖ Scripts for plays and theatrical productions. 212-206-8990.

Samuel French Trade, 7623 Sunset Blvd., Hollywood, CA 90046: Free catalog ❖ Over 2500 plays. Includes classics made into movies. 213-876-0570.

Stage Equipment

Alcone Company Inc., Paramount Theatrical Supplies, 5-49 49th Ave., Long Island City, NY 11101: Catalog $5 ❖ Fabrics, make-up, hardware and rigging, lighting and theatrical equipment, paint, and scenery supplies. 718-361-8373.

Altman Stage Lighting Company, 57 Alexander St., Yonkers, NY 10701: Free list of retail sources ❖ Stage lighting equipment. 914-476-7987.

BMI Supply, 28 Logan Ave., Glens Falls, NY 12801: Free information ❖ Theatrical supplies and equipment. 800-836-0524.

Bulbman, P.O. Box 12280, Reno, NV 89510: Free information ❖ Replacement bulbs for theatrical lighting equipment. 800-648-1163.

Florida Magic Company, P.O. Box 290781, Fort Lauderdale, FL 33329: Free information ❖ Portable AC or battery-operated public address system. 305-473-1902.

Four Star Lighting, Jupiter Scenic Inc., 603 Commerce Way West, Jupiter, FL 33458: Free information ❖ Scenery drapes and lighting equipment. 407-743-7367.

Gothic Scenic & Theatrical Paints, Long Island Paint Company, Box 189, Continental Hill, Glen Cove, NY 11542: Free information ❖ Scenic and theatrical paints and supplies. 516-676-6600.

The Great American Market, 826 N. Cole Ave., Hollywood, CA 90038: Free catalog ❖ Theatrical stage equipment and supplies. 213-461-0200.

Jupiter Scenic Inc., 603 Commerce Way West, Jupiter, FL 33458: Free information ❖ Scenery drapes and lighting equipment. 407-743-7367.

Kee Industrial Products Inc., P.O. Box 207, Buffalo, NY 14225: Free information ❖ Hardware for stage platforms, multi-level sets, and backgrounds. 716-896-4949.

Olesen, Division Entertainment Resources Inc., 1535 N. Ivar Ave., Hollywood, CA 90028: Free information ❖ Lighting and production supplies. 800-821-1656.

Peavey Electronics Corporation, 711 A St., P.O. Box 2898, Meridian, MS 39302: Free information ❖ Lighting equipment. 601-483-5365.

Pro Sound & Stage Lighting, Catalog Center, 11711 Monarch St., Garden Grove, CA 92641: Free catalog ❖ Stage, sound, lighting, and video systems. 800-945-9300.

Rose Brand Fabrics, 517 W. 35th St., New York, NY 10001: Free catalog ❖ Theatrical fabrics. 800-223-1624; 212-594-7424 (in NY).

Schacht Lighting, 5214 Burleson Rd., Austin, TX 78744: Free brochure ❖ Track lighting, replacement bulbs, and craft show lights. 800-256-7114.

Sitler's Supplies Inc., 702 E. Washington, P.O. Box 10, Washington, IA 52353: Free information ❖ Stage, studio, and projector lamps. 800-426-3938.

StageRight Corporation, 495 Holley Dr., Clare, MI 48617: Free information ❖ Portable units and extensions for stage assemblies. 800-438-4499.

Charles H. Stewart & Company, P.O. Box 440187, Somerville, MA 02144: Free information ❖ Scenery backdrops, curtains, scrims, and stage equipment. 617-625-2407.

Syracuse Scenery & Stage Lighting Company Inc., 101 Monarch Dr., Liverpool, NY 13088: Free information ❖ Curtains and other stage fabrics. 315-453-8096.

Theatrical Lighting Systems Inc., 909 Meridian St., P.O. Box 2646, Huntsville, AL 35804: Free information ❖ Dimming and lighting control systems, follow spots, other lighting equipment, and make-up. 205-533-7025.

Tobins Lake Studios, 7030 Old US 23, Brighton, MI 48116: Free catalog ❖ Drapes, drops, lighting equipment, and scenery paint. 810-229-6666.

Tri-Ess Sciences Inc., 1020 W. Chestnut St., Burbank, CA 91506: Catalog $3 ❖ Special effects equipment. 800-274-6910.

Westgate Enterprises, 2118 Wilshire Blvd., Ste. 612, Santa Monica, CA 90403: Free catalog ❖ Full spectrum color-corrected light bulbs, flood and spot lights, and tubes. 310-477-5891.

THERMOMETERS

Abbeon Cal Inc., 123 Gray Ave., Santa Barbara, CA 93101: Free catalog ❖ Thermometers, hygrometers, moisture meters, and humidity indicators. 805-966-0810.

THIMBLES

Gimbel & Sons Country Store, 36 Commercial St., P.O. Box 57, Boothbay Harbor, ME 04538: Free catalog ❖ Thimbles, collectibles, and gifts. 207-633-5088.

TICKETS

All Points Tag & Ticket Company, 1330 Lloyd Rd., Wickliffe, OH 44092: Free price list ❖ Raffle tickets. 800-342-2102.

Carter Printing, Box 289, Farmersville, IL 62533: Free information ❖ Raffle tickets. 217-227-4464.

LMN Printing, 118 N. Ridgewood Ave., Edgewater, FL 32132: Free price list ❖ Raffle books, tickets, and coupon books. 800-741-5668.

Quick Tickets, 3030 W. Pasadena, Flint, MI 48504: Free information ❖ Tickets. 800-521-1142; 313-732-0770 (in MI).

TOBACCO, PIPES & CIGARS

Rapid Raffles, P.O. Box 862, Marshalls Creek, PA 18335: Free information ❖ Chance books and raffle tickets. 800-972-3353.

Ready-Tickets, Box 227, Lyons, PA 19536: Free information ❖ Pre-numbered perforated tickets. 800-552-1400.

Ticket Craft, 1925 Bellmore Ave., Bellmore, NY 11710: Free catalog ❖ Theater tickets. 800-645-4944; 516-826-1500 (in NY).

TOBACCO, PIPES & CIGARS

Davidoff of Geneva Inc., 550 West Ave., Stamford, CT 06902: Free catalog ❖ Cigars and tobacco products. 800-328-4365.

Erie Tobacco Company, 1828 Euclid, Cleveland, OH 44115: Free catalog ❖ Cigars, pipes, and tobacco.

Famous Smoke Shop Inc., 55 W. 39th St., New York, NY 10018: Free catalog ❖ Pipe tobaccos and premium hand-rolled and generic cigars. 800-672-5544.

Georgetown Tobacco, 3144 M St. NW, Washington, DC 20007: Catalog $1 ❖ Private tobacco mixtures, pipes, imported and domestic cigars, lighters, and gifts. 202-338-5100.

Holt's Cigar Company, 114 S. 16th St., Philadelphia, PA 19102: Free information ❖ Premium cigars. 800-523-1641; 215-563-0763 (in PA).

J-R Tobacco, 301 Rt. 10, Whippany, NJ 07981: Free catalog ❖ Imported cigars and pipe tobaccos. 800-JRC-IGAR.

Marks Cigars, 8th & Central Ave., Ocean City, NJ 08226: Free brochure ❖ Cigars handcrafted with aged Jamaican tobaccos individually blended with Dominican long-filler leaf, rolled with clear Cuban seed and Mexican natural leaf binder, and finished with a shade grown Connecticut wrapper. 800-257-8645.

Mike's Cigars Inc., 1030 Kane Concourse, Bay Harbor, FL 33154: Free information ❖ Premium cigars. 800-962-4427.

Old Chicago Smoke Shop, Mail Order Division, 3300 W. Devon, Lincolnwood, IL 60659: Free catalog ❖ Premium cigars and humidors. 800-621-1453.

Iwan Ries & Company, 19 S. Wabash, 2nd Floor, Chicago, IL 60603: Free catalog ❖ Imported pipes, cigars and tobacco, and accessories. 312-372-1306.

Nat Sherman Company, 500 5th Ave., New York, NY 10110: Free catalog ❖ Cigars, pipes, domestic and imported cigarettes, tobaccos, and gifts. 800-221-1690.

Fred Stoker & Sons Inc., P.O. Box 707, Dresden, TN 38225: Catalog $1 ❖ Supplies for smokers, chewing tobaccos, and gifts. 800-243-9377.

Thompson Cigar Company, 5401 Hangar Ct., P.O. Box 30303, Tampa, FL 33630: Free catalog ❖ Cigars, pipes, and tobaccos. 800-237-2559.

TOLE & DECORATIVE PAINTING

Adventures in Ceramics Inc., 1421 Ellis St., Waukesha, WI 53186: Catalog $4 ❖ Ready-to-paint ceramic bisque pieces.

Bridgewater Scrollworks, P.O. Box 585, Osage, MN 56570: Catalog $5 (refundable) ❖ Wooden cutouts for tole decoration and crafts.

Stan Brown's Arts & Crafts Inc., 13435 NE Whitaker Way, Portland, OR 97230: Catalog $3.50 ❖ Tole and decorative painting supplies. 800-547-5531; 503-252-0559 (in OR).

Cabin Craft Southwest, 1500 Westpack Way, Euless, TX 76040: Catalog $4 ❖ Tole and decorative painting supplies. 800-877-1515.

Cabin Crafters, 1225 W. 1st St., Nevada, IA 50201: Catalog $4 ❖ Tole and decorative painting supplies. 800-669-3920; 515-382-5406 (in IA).

Capri Arts & Crafts, 866 S. McGlincey Ln., Campbell, CA 95008: Free catalog ❖ Books on decorative and fabric painting. 800-826-7777.

Char-Lee Originals, P.O. Box 606, Somonauk, IL 60552: Catalog $5 ❖ Unpainted resin figures and other ready-to-finish items. 800-242-7533.

Chatham Art Distributors, P.O. Box 3851, Frederick, MD 21705: Free information ❖ Acrylics, brushes, canvasses, oils, milk paint, tin supplies, books, and wooden items for decorating. 800-822-4747.

Chroma, 205 Bucky Dr., Lititz, PA 17543: Free information ❖ Acrylic polymer emulsion-based gessos for fine, decorative, and wildfowl art. 800-257-8278; 717-626-8866 (in PA).

Crafts Just for You, 2030 Clinton Ave., Alameda, CA 94501: Catalog $5 ❖ Tole painting supplies and kits. 800-272-3848.

Cridge Inc., Box 210, Morrisville, PA 19067: Catalog $2 ❖ Glazed porcelain pieces and ready-to-be-decorated bisque. 215-295-3667.

Cupboard Distributing, P.O. Box 148, Urbana, OH 43078: Catalog $2 ❖ Unfinished wooden parts for tole and decorative painting, crafts, miniatures, toys, jewelry-making, and woodworking. 513-652-3338.

Custom Wood Cut-Out's Unlimited, P.O. Box 518, Massilon, OH 44648: Catalog $2 (refundable) ❖ Sanded ready-to-finish wood items. 330-832-2919.

DecoArt, P.O. Box 370, Stanford, KY 40484: Information $1 with long SASE ❖ Decorative paints.

Finishing Touches Crafts, 5673 E. Shields Ave., Fresno, CA 93727: Free information ❖ Paint products and how-to information for transforming ordinary objects of plaster, wood, paper-mache, and metal into works of art. 800-4-DUNCAN.

Hofcraft, P.O. Box 72, Grand Haven, MI 49416: Catalog $4 ❖ How-to books and supplies for tole and decorative painting. 800-828-0359.

Hollins Enterprises Inc., P.O. Box 148, Alpha, OH 45301: Catalog $1 ❖ Tole and decorative painting supplies. 513-426-3503.

HomeCraft Express, P.O. Box 24890, San Jose, CA 95154: Free catalog ❖ Decorative paints, supplies, and books. 800-301-7377.

Homestead Designs Crafts, 2826 Old Street Rd. 67, West Martinsville, IN 46151: Free information ❖ Gourds for decorating and making into projects. 317-342-8097.

Homestead Handcrafts, N. 1301 Pines Rd., Spokane, WA 99206: Catalog $5 ($3 refundable) ❖ Tole and decorative painting supplies. 509-928-1986.

Darcie Hunter Publications, P.O. Box 1627, Grants Pass, OR 97526: Catalog $3 ❖ Painting supplies, books, and wooden items for finishing. 800-453-1527.

J.W. etc., 2205 1st St., Simi Valley, CA 93065: Free information ❖ Varnish, wood sealer and filler, stains, brush cleanser, and supplies. 805-526-5066.

Johnson Paint Company Inc., 355 Newbury St., Boston, MA 02115: Catalog $1 ❖ Hard-to-find painting supplies, brushes, and tools. 617-536-4838.

Kerry Specialties, P.O. Box 5129, Deltona, FL 32728: Free information ❖ Brushes for tole and decorative painting. 407-574-6209.

Larson Wood Manufacturing, P.O. Box 672, Park Rapids, MN 56407: Catalog $2 (refundable) ❖ Country-style mini cutouts, kits and parts, hardware, and supplies. 218-732-9121.

Perfect Palette, 5910 N. Lilly Rd., Menenomee Falls, WI 53051: Catalog $1 ❖ Decorative painting videos for all skill levels. 800-839-0306.

Plaid Enterprises, P.O. Box 7600, Norcross, GA 30091: Free information ❖ Acrylic paints and supplies. 404-923-8200.

Positively Country, Fred & Mary O'Neil, P.O. Box 51746, New Berlin, WI 51746: Catalog $2 ❖ Unfinished wooden items, paints, brushes, and other supplies. 414-789-0777.

Quality Wood Products, 5221 Bennett Rd., Paradise, CA 95969: Free brochure ❖ Clocks, serving trays, door harps, and wood products for decorating and painting. 916-872-8456.

415

416 ❖ TOOLS ❖

Faith Rollins, 13010 W. 66th St., Shawnee, KS 66216: Catalog $2 ❖ & Books, packets, wood and resin items, and supplies. 913-631-9148.

S & G Inc., P.O. Box 805, Howell, MI 48844: Free information ❖ Pre-primed ready-to-paint metal wind chimes. 517-546-9240.

Sandeen's, 1315 White Bear Ave., St. Paul, MN 55106: Catalog $2 (refundable) ❖ Supplies for folk art crafting, rosemaling, dalmalning, and bauernmalere. Also (separate catalogs, $3 each) supplies for Norwegian stitchery, Danish cross-stitching, and Swedish stitchery. 800-235-1315.

Sharon & Gayle Publications, P.O. Box 15394, Covington, KY 41015: Catalog $2 (refundable) ❖ How-to books on decorative art and tole painting. Also pattern packets.

Tara Materials Inc., P.O. Box 646, Lawrenceville, GA 30246: Free information ❖ Plates for tole art decorating.

Traditional Norwegian Rosemaking, Pat Virch, 1506 Lynn Ave., Marquette, MI 49855: Catalog $2 ❖ Patterns, books, paints, woodenware, tinware, and supplies for wood and tin decorating. 906-226-3931.

Vesterheim Sales Shop, Vesterheim Norwegian-American Museum, 502 W. Water St., Decorah, IA 52101: Free catalog ❖ Books and pattern packets, woodenware, brushes, paints, paper, and supplies. 319-382-9682.

Viking Woodcrafts Inc., 1317 8th St. SE, Waseca, MN 56093: Catalog $10 (refundable) ❖ Ready-to-finish craft items, resin figures, and books. 507-835-8043.

Barb Watson's Brushworks, P.O. Box 1467, Moreno Valley, CA 92556: Free catalog ❖ Ready-to-paint plates and metalware. 909-653-5780.

Western Woodworks, 1142 Olive Branch Ln., San Jose, CA 95120: Free catalog ❖ Wooden surfaces for decorative finishing. 408-997-2356.

Weston Bowl Mill, P.O. Box 218, Weston, VT 05161: Catalog $1 ❖ Woodenware for tole and decorative painting. 800-824-6219.

White Pine Box Company, 3877 Christy Town Rd., Story City, IA 50248: Free catalog ❖ Handcrafted Shaker boxes for decorating. 515-733-5086.

Woodcraft, P.O. Box 336, Methuen, MA 01844: Catalog $2 (refundable) ❖ Wood cutouts and turnings for painters and crafters.

TOOLS
Clamps

Addkison Hardware Company Inc., 126 E. Amite St., P.O. Box 102, Jackson, MS 39205: Free information ❖ Power tools and clamps. 800-821-2750.

Adjustable Clamp Company, 444 N. Ashland Ave., Chicago, IL 60622: Catalog $1 ❖ Clamps and work-holding equipment. 312-666-0640.

Advanced Machinery Imports, P.O. Box 312, New Castle, DE 19720: Free information ❖ Workshop clamps. 800-648-4264; 302-322-2226 (in DE).

American Clamping Corporation, P.O. Box 399, Batavia, NY 14021: Free information ❖ Woodworking clamps. 800-928-1004.

American Tool Companies Inc., P.O. Box 337, Dewitt, NE 68341: Free information ❖ Clamps for woodworking projects.

Colt Clamp Company Inc., 33 Swan St., Batavia, NY 14020: Free catalog ❖ C and bar clamps in screw and eccentric styles. 800-536-8420; 716-343-8622 (in NY).

Gross Stabil Corporation, P.O. Box 368, Coldwater, MI 49036: Free list of retail sources ❖ Woodworking clamps. 800-671-0838; 517-278-6121 (in MI).

Hartford Clamp Company, 466 Park Ave., P.O. Box 8131, Hartford, CT 06108: Free catalog ❖ Hand screws and bar, double bar, and miter clamps.

Inlet Inc., 412 Redhill Ave., Ste. 8, San Anselmo, CA 94960: Free information ❖ Clamps for most workshop needs. 800-786-5665.

Universal Clamp Corporation, 15200 Stagg St., Van Nuys, CA 91405: Free information ❖ Lightweight clamps. 818-780-1015.

Wade Manufacturing Company, P.O. Box 23666, Portland, OR 97218: Free information ❖ Clamps for woodworking projects.

Wetzler Clamp, Rt. 611, P.O. Box 175, Mt. Bethel, PA 18343: Free information ❖ Woodworking clamps. 800-451-1852.

Hand & Power Tools

A & T Supply, 401 Radio City Dr., North Pekin, IL 61554: Free information ❖ Woodworking tools and accessories. 800-260-2647.

Abbey Tools, 1132 N. Magnolia, Anaheim, CA 92801: Free information ❖ Power tools. 800-225-6321.

Abest Woodworking Machinery, Division Rudolph Bass Inc., 45 Halliday St., Jersey City, NJ 07304: Free information ❖ Dust collection systems for workshops. 201-433-3800.

Acme Electric Tools, Box 14040, Grand Forks, ND 58208: Catalog $3 ❖ Power tools. 800-358-3096.

Addkison Hardware Company Inc., 126 E. Amite St., P.O. Box 102, Jackson, MS 39205: Free information ❖ Power tools and clamps. 800-821-2750.

Adventures with Tools, 435 Main St., Johnson City, NY 13790: Catalog $5 (refundable) ❖ Tools and accessories for wood and metal-working. 800-477-6512; 607-729-6512 (in NY).

Airy Sales Corporation, 14535 Valley View Ave., Santa Fe Springs, CA 90670: Free list of retail sources ❖ Power-operated nailers and staplers. 310-926-6192.

William Alden Company, 27 Stuart St., Boston, MA 92116: Free catalog ❖ Power tools and accessories for woodworkers, contractors, homeowners, and do-it-yourselfers. 800-249-8665.

Alley Supply Company, P.O. Box 848, Gardnerville, NV 89410: Catalog $2 ❖ Precision lathes, milling machines, cutter grinders, and other metal-working tools. 702-782-3800.

American International Tool Industries, 1116 Park Ave., Cranston, RI 02910: Free information ❖ Paint removal and sanding tools. 800-932-5872; 401-942-7855 (in RI).

American Machine & Tool Company, 4th Ave. & Spring, P.O. Box 70, Royersford, PA 19468: Free catalog ❖ Woodworking power tools. 800-435-8665.

Johnson Atelier, 50 Princeton-Hightstown Rd., Ste. L, Princeton Junction, NJ 08550: Free catalog ❖ Sculpture and casting supplies. Also carving tools for wood and stone. 800-732-7203.

Bailey's, P.O. Box 550, Laytonville, CA 95454: Free catalog ❖ World's largest mail order woodsman supplies company. Chain saws, files, protective gear, log splitters, books, and more. 800-322-4539.

Bethel Mills Lumber Inc., Main St., Bethel, VT 05032: Free information ❖ Building supplies and tools. 800-234-9951.

Better Built Corporation, 845 Woburn St., Wilmington, MA 01887: Free brochure ❖ One-man portable sawmills. 508-657-5636.

Blue Ridge Machinery & Tools Inc., P.O. Box 536, Hurricane, WV 25526: Catalog $1 ❖ Lathes, milling machines, and supplies. 304-562-3538.

Blume Supply Inc., 3316 South Blvd., Charlotte, NC 28209: Free information ❖ Woodworking power tools. 800-288-9200; 704-523-7811 (in NC).

❖ TOOLS ❖

BrandMark, 462 Carthage Dr., Beavercreek, OH 45434: Free information ❖ Electric branding irons. 800-323-2570.

Bridge City Tool Works, 1104 NE 28th Ave., Portland, OR 97232: Catalog $2 ❖ Professional hand tools. 800-253-3332.

Brookstone Company, Order Processing Center, 1655 Bassford Dr., Mexico, MO 65265: Free catalog ❖ Hand tools. 800-926-7000.

Campbell Hausfeld, 100 Production Dr., Harrison, OH 45030: Free information ❖ Air compressors, pneumatic tools, and paint sprayers. 800-543-8622; 513-367-4811 (in OH).

Cape Forge, Box 987, Burlington, VT 05402: Catalog $1 ❖ Draw-knives and chisels.

The Cayce Company, 221 Cockeysville Rd., Hunt Valley, MD 21030: Free information ❖ Used tools and equipment. 410-771-0213.

Chicago Pneumatic Company, Electric Tools Division, 2220 Bleecker St., Utica, NY 13501: Free information ❖ Woodworking power tools. 800-243-0870.

Colwood Electronics, 15 Meridian Rd., Eatontown, NJ 07724: Free brochure ❖ All-in-one work station that includes a woodburning and texturizing system and high speed grinding equipment. 908-544-1119.

Conestoga Wood Machinery, 987 Valley View Rd., New Holland, PA 17557: Free information ❖ Woodworking power tools. 800-288-8783.

Constantine, 2050 Eastchester Rd., Bronx, NY 10461: Catalog $1 ❖ Cabinet and furniture wood and veneers, hardware, how-to books, and carving tools and chisels. 800-223-8087; 718-792-1600 (in NY).

Craft Supplies USA, P.O. Box 50300, Provo, UT 84605: Catalog $2 ❖ Woodturning tools and accessories. 800-551-8876.

CraftWoods, 2101 Greenspring Dr., Timonium, MD 21093: Free catalog ❖ Woodworking and carving accessories, power tools, and kiln-dried domestic and exotic woods. 800-468-7070.

Credo Tools, P.O. Box 340, Lincolnton, NC 28093: Free information ❖ Power tool accessories. 704-735-7464.

The Cutting Edge, 7123 Southwest Fwy., Houston, TX 77074: Free catalog ❖ Wood-turning and carving supplies and tools. 713-981-9228.

Delta International Machinery Corporation, 246 Alpha Dr., Pittsburgh, PA 15238: Catalog $2 ❖ Woodworking power tools. 800-438-2486.

DeVilbiss, 213 Industrial Dr., Jackson, TN 38301: Free brochure ❖ Air compressors, air-operated tools, and accessories. 800-888-2468; 901-423-7000 (in TN).

Gregory D. Dorrance Company, 1063 Oak Hill Ave., Attleboro, MA 02703: Free information ❖ Decoy-making and art supplies, tools, and wood for carving. 508-222-6255.

Dremel Moto-Tool, P.O. Box 468, Racine, WI 53406: Free information ❖ Hand power tools for modelers and home craftsmen. 414-554-1390.

Eagle America, P.O. Box 1099, Chardon, OH 44024: Free catalog ❖ Router bits and shaper cutters. 800-872-2511.

Eastern Tool & Supply Company, 149 Grand St., New York, NY 10013: Free information ❖ Metal-working tools. 800-221-2679; 212-925-1006 (in NY).

Ebac Lumber Dryers, 106 John Jefferson Rd., Ste. 102, Williamsburg, VA 23185: Free information ❖ Easy-to-operate lumber dryers. 800-433-9011.

Echo Inc., 400 Oakwood Rd., Lake Zurich, IL 60047: Free catalog ❖ Trimmers, blowers, hedge clippers, sprayers, chain saws, and shredders. 800-432-3246.

EMCO-Maier Corporation, 2757 Scioto Pkwy., Columbus, OH 43221: Free catalog ❖ Woodworking power tools. 800-521-8289.

Enco Manufacturing Company, 5000 W. Bloomingdale Ave., Chicago, IL 60639: Free catalog ❖ Metal-working tools, machinery, and accessories. 800-860-3200.

P.C. English Inc., P.O. Box 380, Thornburg, VA 22565: Free catalog ❖ Tools, cutouts, patterns, paints, carving woods, and supplies. 800-221-9474.

Excalibur Machine & Tool Company, 210 8th St. South, Lewiston, NY 14092: Free information ❖ Woodworking power tools. 416-291-8190.

Falcon-Wood, Peter & Annette Habieht, 1985 S. Undermountain Rd., Sheffield, MA 01257: Free brochure ❖ Collectible tools. 413-229-7745.

Falls Run Woodcarving, 9395 Falls Rd., Girard, PA 16417: Free information ❖ Woodcarving tools. 800-524-9077.

Farris Machinery, 1206 Pavilion Dr., Grain Valley, MO 64029: Free information ❖ Woodworking equipment and supplies. 800-872-5489.

Florida Tool, 4632 N. Powerline Rd., Pompano Beach, FL 33073: Free information ❖ Woodworking power tools. 800-805-0075.

Foley-Belsaw Company, 6301 Equitable Rd., Kansas City, MO 64120: Free information ❖ Woodworking power tools. 800-487-2100.

Foredom Electric Company, 16 Stony Hill Rd., Bethel, CT 06801: Free information ❖ Tools for grinding, sawing, drilling, carving, shaping, and polishing. 203-792-8622.

Forrest Manufacturing Company Inc., 461 River Rd., Clifton, NJ 07014: Free information ❖ Table and radial saw blades. 800-733-7111; 201-473-5236 (in NJ).

Franklin Ace Hardware, 115 E. 2nd Ave., Franklin, VA 23851: Free information ❖ Woodworking power tools. 800-662-0004.

Freeborn Tool Company Inc., P.O. Box 6246, 6202 N. Freya St., Spokane, WA 99207: Free information ❖ Carbide-tipped shaper cutters. 800-523-8988.

Freud Power Tools, 218 Feld Ave., High Point, NC 27264: Free catalog ❖ Woodworking power tools. 800-472-7307.

Frog Tool Company, 2169 IL Rt. 26, Dixon, IL 61021: Catalog $5 ❖ Woodworking hand tools and books. 800-648-1270.

Gesswein, Woodworking Products Division, 255 Hancock Ave., Bridgeport, CT 06605: Free information ❖ Woodcarving tools. 800-544-2043.

Granberg International, P.O. Box 425, Richmond, CA 94807: Free information ❖ Portable chain saw lumber mill. 510-237-2099.

Grand Tool Supply Corporation, US Hwy. 46 & Huyler St., Teterboro, NJ 07608: Free catalog ❖ Tools, measuring instruments, and machine shop equipment. 201-342-6900.

Griffin Manufacturing Company Inc., 1656 Ridge Rd. East, P.O. Box 308, Webster, NY 14580: Free catalog ❖ Cutters, knives, blades, and specialty tools. 716-265-1991.

Grizzly Imports Inc., P.O. Box 2069, Bellingham, WA 98227: Free information ❖ Woodworking power tools. 800-541-5537 (west of the Mississippi); 800-523-4777 (east of the Mississippi).

Harbor Freight Tools, 3491 Mission Oaks Blvd., Camarillo, CA 93011: Free catalog ❖ Hardware, power and hand tools, and accessories. 800-423-2567.

Harris Tools, 145 Sherman Ave., Jersey City, NJ 07307: Catalog $1 (refundable) ❖ Lapping and sharpening systems. 800-449-7747.

Hartville Tool & Supply, 13163 Market Ave. North, Hartville, OH 44632: Free catalog ❖ Woodworking tools. 800-345-2396.

Hida Japanese Tool Inc., 1333 San Pablo Ave., Berkeley, CA 94702: Catalog $4 ❖ Hand-forged tools for delicate work. 800-443-5512.

Highland Hardware, 1045 N. Highland Ave. NE, Atlanta, GA 30306: Free catalog ❖ Tools for home craftsmen. 404-872-4466.

TOOLS

Hitachi Power Tools U.S.A. Ltd., 3950 Steve Reynolds Blvd., Norcross, GA 30093: Free information ❖ Hand-held power tools. 800-546-1666.

Home Lumber Company, P.O. Box 370, Whitewater, WI 53190: Free information ❖ Portable power tools. 800-262-5482.

HTC Products, 120 E. Hudson, P.O. Box 839, Royal Oak, MI 48068: Free catalog ❖ Mobile machine bases to put workshops on wheels. 800-624-2027.

Christian J. Hummul Company, 11001 York Rd., Hunt Valley, MD 21030: Free catalog ❖ Carving tools, artist supplies, and how-to books. 800-762-0235.

International Tool Corporation, 2590 Davie Rd., Davie, FL 33020: Free information ❖ Power tools. 800-338-3384.

Jamestown Distributors, P.O. Box 348, Jamestown, RI 02835: Free catalog ❖ Workshop tools. 800-423-0030.

The Japan Woodworker, 1731 Clement Ave., Alameda, CA 94501: Catalog $1.50 ❖ Japanese hand tools for craftsmen, carpenters, cabinet makers, and woodcarvers. 800-537-7820.

JDS Company, 800 Dutch Square Blvd., Ste. 200, Columbia, SC 29210: Free brochure ❖ Precision woodworking equipment. 800-382-2637; 803-798-1600 (in SC).

W.S. Jenks & Son, 1933 Montana Ave. NE, Washington, DC 20002: Free catalog ❖ Hand and power tools. 202-529-6020.

Jensen Tools Inc., 7815 S. 46th St., Phoenix, AZ 85044: Free catalog ❖ Tools, tool kits, and cases. 800-426-1194; 602-968-6231 (in AZ).

Kasco Woodworking Company Inc., 170 W. 600 North, Shelbyville, IN 46176: Free information ❖ Portable band saw mills. 317-398-7973.

Bob Kaune, 511 W. 11th, Port Angeles, WA 98362: Catalog $3.50 ❖ Antique and used hand tools for collectors and woodworkers. 206-452-2292.

The Keller Dovetail System, 1327 I St., Petaluma, CA 94952: Free information ❖ Easy-to-use jig for making angled and curved dovetails, classic and variable spacing, and box joints. 800-995-2456; 707-763-9336 (in CA).

Kitts Industrial Tools, 22384 Grand River Ave., Detroit, MI 48219: Free catalog ❖ Precision metalworking tools and supplies. 800-521-6579; 313-538-2585 (in MI).

Klockit, P.O. Box 636, Lake Geneva, WI 53147: Free catalog ❖ Woodworking tools, wood finishing supplies, and clock-building equipment. 800-556-2548.

Knotts Knives, 471 Buckhurst Dr., Kernersville, NC 27284: Free information ❖ Carving tools. 800-388-6759.

Laguna Tools, 2265 Laguna Canyon Rd., Laguna Beach, CA 92651: Free information ❖ Space-saving all-in-one shop that includes a table saw, joiner, planer, shaper, mortise, and sliding table. 800-234-1976; 714-494-7006 (in CA).

Leatherman Tool Group Inc., P.O. Box 20595, Portland, OR 07220: Free information ❖ Compact multi-purpose tools. 503-253-7826.

K.H. Lee Tool Supply, 9078 Artesia Blvd., Bellflower, CA 90706: Catalog $3 ❖ Tools for jewelers, crafters, and hobbyists. 310-920-3834.

Leichtung Workshops, 23297 Commerce Park, Beachwood, OH 44122: Free catalog ❖ Tools for craftsmen and gardeners. 800-321-6840.

Leigh Industries Inc., P.O. Box 357, Port Coquitlam, British Columbia, Canada V3C 4K6: Free catalog ❖ Dovetailing jigs, cutters, and attachments. 800-663-8932.

Leisure Time Products, 2650 Davisson St., River Grove, IL 60171: Free information ❖ Electronic burning systems and equipment for carvers, artists, and pyrographers. 708-452-5400.

LeNeave Machinery & Supply Company, 305 W. Morehead St., Charlotte, NC 28202: Free information ❖ Woodworking power tools. 800-442-2302; 704-376-7421 (in NC).

Lie-Nielsen Toolworks, P.O. Box 9, Warren, ME 04864: Free brochure ❖ Heirloom quality tools. 800-327-2520.

Lobo Power Tools, 9031 E. Stauson Ave., Pico Rivera, CA 90660: Free information ❖ Woodworking power tools. 310-949-3747.

MacBeath Hardwood Company, 930 Ashby Ave., Berkeley, CA 94710: Catalog $2 (refundable with $10 order) ❖ Woodworking tools and supplies. 510-843-4390.

Makita USA Inc., 14930 Northam St., La Mirada, CA 90638: Free information ❖ Woodworking power tools. 800-4-MAKITA.

Marling Lumber Company, P.O. Box 7668, 1801 E. Washington Ave., Madison, WI 53707: Free information ❖ Woodworking tools. 800-247-7178.

McFEELY'S SQUARE DRIVE SCREWS

McFeely's, P.O. Box 11169, Lynchburg, VA 24506: Catalog $2 ❖ Premium quality wood screws and essentials for professional and recreational woodworkers. 800-443-7937.

Micro-Mark, 340 Snyder Ave., Berkeley Heights, NJ 07922: Catalog $1 ❖ Miniature tools for hobby craftsmen. 908-464-6764.

Mighty Mite Sawmill, P.O. Box 20427, Portland, OR 97220: Free information ❖ Transportable sawmill. 503-288-5923.

Miller Woodworking Machinery Inc., 1110 E. Quilcene Rd., Quilcene, WA 98376: Free information ❖ Wide belt sanders for the small shop. 206-765-3806.

Milwaukee Electric Tool Corporation, 13135 W. Lisbon Rd., Brookfield, WI 53005: Free information ❖ Woodworking power tools. 414-783-8311.

Minitech Machinery, 430 10th St., Atlanta, GA 30318: Free information ❖ Desktop metalworking machine tools. 800-662-1760.

MLCS Tools Ltd., P.O. Box 4053, Rydal, PA 19046: Free catalog ❖ Carbide-tipped router bits. 800-533-9298.

Mobile Manufacturing Company, P.O. Box 250, Troutdale, OR 97060: Free brochure ❖ Portable gasoline or electric-powered saw for cutting logs any diameter and lengths up to 60 feet. 503-666-5593.

Mountain Heritage Crafters, 601 Quail Dr., Bluefield, VA 24605: Free catalog ❖ Carving tools and books. 540-322-5921.

Nasco, 901 Janesville Ave., Fort Atkinson, WI 53538: Free catalog ❖ Woodburning and carving tools, woodcraft supplies, and wood projects. 800-558-9595.

Navesink Electronics, 820 Nut Swamp Rd., Red Bank, NJ 07701: Free information ❖ Woodburning systems, dust collectors, and carving tools. 908-747-5023.

Nippon/4/Less, P.O. Box 854, Los Altos, CA 94023: Free catalog ❖ Japanese hand tools. 415-917-0706.

Norcraft Custom Brands, P.O. Box 277, South Easton, MA 02375: Free information ❖ Custom-made branding irons. 508-238-2163.

Northern Hydraulics, P.O. Box 1499, Burnsville, MN 55337: Free catalog ❖ Power tools. 800-533-5545.

Northland Woodworking Supply, 65 Wurz Ave., Utica, NY 13502: Free catalog ❖ Carving tools. 315-724-1299.

Old World Brush & Tool Company Inc., 3467 Beldeer Dr., St. Charles, MO 63303: Free brochure ❖ Specialty brushes, graining tools, how-to videos, and books. 800-821-3314; 314-447-3624 (in MO).

Packard Woodworks, P.O. Box 718, Tryon, NC 28782: Free catalog ❖ Wood turning tools and supplies. 704-859-6762.

Palmren, 8389 S. Chicago Ave., Chicago, IL 60617: Free catalog ❖ Metalworking tools. 800-621-6145; 312-721-8675 (in IL).

❖ TOOLS ❖

Panasonic Cordless Power Tools, Panasonic Way, Secaucus, NJ 07094: Free list of retail sources ❖ Hand-held cordless power tools. 201-392-6655.

Penn State Industries, 2850 Comly Rd., Philadelphia, PA 19154: Free information ❖ Woodworking machines and accessories. 800-377-7297.

Pfingst & Company Inc., 105 Snyder Rd., P.O. Box 377, South Plainfield, NJ 07080: Free catalog ❖ Precision detailing tools for carving. 908-561-6400.

Porta-Nails Inc., P.O. Box 1257, Wilmington, NC 28402: Free list of retail sources ❖ Woodworking machines. 800-634-9281; 910-762-6334 (in NC).

Porter-Cable, 4825 Hwy. 45 North, P.O. Box 2468, Jackson, TN 38302: Free list of retail sources ❖ Woodworking power tools. 800-487-8665.

Poulan, 5020 Flournoy-Lucas Rd., Shrevesport, LA 71129: Free information ❖ Electric and gas-operated chain saws. 318-683-3546.

Power Tool Specialists, 3 Craftsman Rd., East Windsor, CT 06088: Free information ❖ Hand-held nail gun and portable power tools. 800-243-5114.

Powermatic Inc., 607 Morrison Rd., McMinnville, TN 37110: Free information ❖ Woodworking power tools. 800-248-0144.

RBIndustries, 1801 Vine St., Harrisonville, MO 64071: Free catalog ❖ Woodworking power tools. 800-487-2623.

Red Hill Corporation, P.O. Box 4234, Gettysburg, PA 17325: Free catalog ❖ Hot melt glue sticks, glue guns, and sandpaper in belts, sheets, and discs. 800-822-4003.

Ridge Carbide Tool Corporation, 595 New York Ave., P.O. Box 497, Lyndhurst, NJ 07071: Catalog $3 ❖ Carbide tipped router bits, saw blades, knives, and shaper cutters. Also custom tool manufacturing. 800-443-0992.

Roean Industries Inc., 12970 Bradford, Pacoima, CA 91331: Free information ❖ Air-powered caulking gun. 800-447-6326; 818-767-7047 (in CA).

Ryobi America Corporation, P.O. Box 1207, Anderson, SC 29622: Free information ❖ Woodworking power tools. 800-525-2579.

S.B. Power Tools, 100 Bosch Blvd., New Bern, NC 28562: Free information ❖ Woodworking power tools. 800-334-5730.

Safranek Enterprises Inc., 4005 El Camino Real, Atascadero, CA 93422: Free information ❖ Panel routers and accessories, air-vac clamps, keyhole machines, carbide cutters, and router bits. 800-553-9344.

Santa Rosa Tool & Supply Inc., 1651 Piner Rd., Santa Rosa, CA 95043: Free information ❖ Woodworking power tools. 800-346-0387; 800-464-8665 (in CA).

Sarah Glove Company Inc., P.O. Box 1940, Waterbury, CT 06722: Catalog $1 ❖ Tools for home craftsmen. 203-574-4090.

Seven Corners Hardware Inc., 216 W. 7th St., St. Paul, MN 55102: Free catalog ❖ Hand and power tools and supplies. 800-328-0457.

Shop Outfitters, 605 S. Adams St., Laramie, WY 82070: Free information ❖ Metalworking tools. 307-745-5999.

Shop-Task, P.O. Box 186, Aberdeen, WA 98520: Free catalog ❖ All-in-one home machine shop with mill, lathe, and drill. 800-343-5775.

Shop-Vac Corporation, 2323 Reach Rd., Williamsport, PA 17701: Free information ❖ Self-contained portable vacuum cleaner for workshops. 717-326-0502.

Shopsmith Inc., 6530 Poe, Dayton, OH 45414: Free information ❖ Multipurpose all-in-one power-woodworking tools. 800-543-7586; 513-898-6070 (in OH).

Silvacraft Sawmills, 90 Curtwright Dr., Unit 3, Amherst, NY 14221: Free information ❖ Sawmills. 800-661-7746.

Skil-Bosch, 4300 W. Peterson Ave., Chicago, IL 60646: Free information ❖ Hand-held power tools. 312-286-7330.

Smithy, P.O. Box 1517, Ann Arbor, MI 48106: Free information ❖ Lathe, mill, and drill (3-in-1 powered machine shop). 800-345-6342.

Stanley Tools, 600 Myrtle St., New Britain, CT 06050: Free information ❖ Woodworking power tools. 203-225-5111.

John Stortz & Son Inc., 210 Vine St., Philadelphia, PA 19106: Catalog $4 ❖ Metal and slate roofing, specialized masonry, cooperage, and ship-building tools. 215-627-3855.

Sugino Corporation, 1700 Penny Ln., Schaumberg, IL 60173: Free information ❖ Lightweight hand-held electric woodcarving tool with optional specialized blades. 708-397-9401.

Sunhill Machinery, 500 Andover Park East, Seattle, WA 98188: Free information ❖ Heavy-duty power tools, dust collectors, and accessories. 800-929-4321.

TAIG Tools, 12419 E. Nightingale Ln., Chandler, AZ 85249: Free information ❖ Four-inch metal cutting lathe and accessories. 602-895-6978.

Tamarack Log Building Tools Inc., P.O. Box 120783, New Brighton, MN 55112: Free catalog ❖ Tools, books, and supplies for log building. 612-783-9773.

Tarheel Filing Company Inc., 3400 Lake Woodard Dr., Raleigh, NC 27514: Free information ❖ Power tools. 800-322-6641; 919-231-3323 (in NC).

Tashiro's Tools, P.O. Box 3409, Seattle, WA 98114: Free catalog ❖ Japanese tools. 206-621-0199.

Tepper Discount Tools, 107 W. Springfield, Champaign, IL 61820: Free information ❖ Professional woodworking tools for home craftsmen. 800-626-0566.

Terrco Inc., 222 1st Ave. NW, Watertown, SD 57201: Free catalog ❖ Woodcarving machines. 605-882-3888.

Timberking Inc., 1431 N. Topping, Kansas City, MO 64120: Free information ❖ Portable one-man saw mill. 800-942-4406.

The Tool Club, P.O. Box 6, Calumet, MI 49913: Free catalog ❖ Inlay cutter.

Tool Crib of the North, Box 14040, Grand Forks, ND 58208: Free catalog ❖ Hand and power tools. 800-358-3096.

Tool Factory Outlet, P.O. Box 461, Goshen, NY 10924: Free information ❖ Woodworking power tools and accessories. 914-294-7900.

Tooland Inc., 1662 Broadway, Redwood City, CA 94063: Free information ❖ Power tools and accessories. 415-365-8665.

Toolhauz Corporation, 455 N. Main St., West Bridgewater, MA 02379: Free information ❖ Hand and portable power tools. 800-533-6135.

Total Shop, P.O. Box 25429, Greenville, SC 29616: Free information ❖ Woodworking power tools. 800-845-9356.

Trend-Lines, 135 American Legion Hwy., Revere, MA 02151: Free catalog ❖ Power and hand tools and accessories. 800-877-7899.

Vermont American, Indian Creek Rd., Lincolnton, NC 28092: Free catalog ❖ Power tool accessories and hand tools. 704-735-7464.

Garrett Wade Company, 161 6th Ave., New York, NY 10013: Catalog $4 ❖ Hand and power tools for woodworking. 800-221-2942.

Wahl Clipper Corporation, 2900 N. Locust St., Sterling, IL 61081: Free list of retail sources ❖ Lightweight precision drill for fine detailing. 800-435-7748.

Steve Wall Lumber Company, Box 287, Mayodan, NC 27027: Catalog $1 ❖ Hardwoods and woodworking machinery. 800-633-4062; 910-427-0637 (in NC).

Walnut Creek Woodworkers Supply Company, 3601 W. Harry, Wichita, KS 67213: Free catalog ❖ Woodworking tools and accessories. 800-942-0553.

Warren Tool Company Inc., P.O. Box 249, Rhinebeck, NY 12572: Catalog $1 ❖ Whittling and woodcarving tools, woods, sharpening stones, supplies, and books. 914-876-7817.

Ivan Whillock Studio, 122 NE 1st Ave., Faribault, MN 55021: Free catalog ❖ Woodcarving tools, how-to books, and kits. 800-882-9379.

Whole Earth Access, 822 Anthony St., Berkeley, CA 94710: Free information ❖ Power tools. 800-829-6300.

Wholesale America Inc., 4777 Menard Dr., Eau Claire, WI 54703: Catalog $1 ❖ Power tools and hardware. 615-874-5000.

Wilke Machinery Company, 3230 Susquehanna Trail, York, PA 17402: Catalog $2 ❖ Woodworking power tools with optional dust collector. 717-764-5000.

Williams & Hussey Machine Company Inc., P.O. Box 1149, Wilton, NH 03086: Free information ❖ Molder-planer for straight, circular, or elliptical moldings. 800-258-1380; 603-654-6828 (in CT).

Wood-Mizer, 8180 W. 10th St., Indianapolis, IN 46214: Catalog $2 ❖ Portable sawmills and tools. 800-553-0219.

Woodcraft Supply, 210 Wood County Industrial Park, P.O. Box 1686, Parkersburg, WV 26102: Free catalog ❖ Woodworking tools, supplies, hardware, and books. 800-542-9115.

Woodcrafters, 212 NE 6th Ave., Portland, OR 97232: Free information ❖ Woodcarving tools, knives, power-carving and burning tools, books, carving woods, and supplies. 503-231-0226.

Woodhaven, 5323 W. Kimberly Rd., Davenport, IA 52806: Free catalog ❖ Woodworking tools. 800-344-6657.

Woodmaster Tools, 1431 N. Topping Ave., Kansas City, MO 64120: Free information ❖ Variable feed multi-duty planer, wide-belt sander, and tools. 800-821-6651.

The Woodworkers' Store, 21801 Industrial Blvd., Rogers, MN 55374: Free catalog ❖ Hardware and ornamental woodworking supplies, tools, and finishing supplies. 800-403-9736.

Paint Sprayers

Apollosprayers Inc., 1030 Joshua Way, Vista, CA 92083: Free information ❖ Easy-to-use low-air consumption paint sprayers. 619-727-8300.

Hydraflow Equipment Company, 8125 Brentwood Industrial Dr., St. Louis, MO 63144: Free information ❖ High-volume and low-pressure sprayers. 800-444-0423; 314-644-6677 (in MO).

Kace Tech. Inc., P.O. Box 513, Milltown, NJ 08850: Free information ❖ Spraying equipment. 800-966-5223.

Welding Equipment

Eastwood Company, 580 Lancaster Ave., Box 3014, Malvern, PA 19355: Free catalog ❖ Welding and sand blasting equipment, rust removers, body repair tools, pin-striping equipment, and buffing supplies. 800-345-1178.

The Lincoln Electric Company, 22801 St. Clair Ave., Cleveland, OH 44117: Free information ❖ Easy-to-use welding equipment.

TOWELS

Chambers, Mail Order Department, P.O. Box 7841, San Francisco, CA 94120: Free catalog ❖ Bed and bath linens and furnishings. 800-334-1254.

Leron, 750 Madison Ave., New York, NY 10021: Free catalog ❖ Linens, towels, pillows and covers, and imported handkerchiefs with optional monograms for men and women. 212-753-6700.

Palmetto Linen Company, 50 Palmetto Bay Rd., Hilton Head, SC 29928: Free information ❖ Sheets and matching dust ruffles, bath towels, blankets, comforters, pillows, tablecloths, place mats, shower curtains, kitchen towels, and oven gloves. 800-972-7442.

TOY MAKING

Angelitos, P.O. Box 1926, Fort Collins, CO 80522: Catalog $2 (refundable) ❖ Handcrafted soft fabric sculptures. 800-624-9379.

Animal Crackers Patterns, 5824 Isleta SW, Albuquerque, NM 87105: Catalog $2.50 ❖ Kits, supplies, and patterns for easy-to-make stuffed toys and animals. 505-873-2806.

Atlanta Puffections, P.O. Box 13524, Atlanta, GA 30324: Catalog $1.50 ❖ Easy-to-make stuffed animals. 404-262-7437.

Golden Fun, P.O. Box 3324, Danville, CA 94526: Catalog $1 ❖ Soft toy-making supplies.

Larson Wood Manufacturing, P.O. Box 672, Park Rapids, MN 56407: Catalog $2 (refundable) ❖ Country-style mini cutouts, kits and parts, hardware, and supplies. 218-732-9121.

Patterncrafts, Box 25639, Colorado Springs, CO 80936: Catalog $2 ❖ Patterns for dolls and stuffed animals. 800-414-3888.

Patterns by Diane, 1126 Ivon Ave., Endicott, NY 13760: Catalog $3 ❖ Soft toys, puppet kits, bear-making supplies, and patterns for bears, soft toys, and puppets. 607-754-0391.

Sonrise Soft Crafts, P.O. Box 5091, Salem, OR 97304: Brochure 50¢ ❖ Patterns and kits for lifelike stuffed animals, puppets, shirt appliques, and wall hangings. 503-362-0027.

TOY SOLDIERS & MINIATURE FIGURES

A to Z Hobby Center, 543 Bedford Ave., Ste. 163, Brooklyn, NY 11211: Free information ❖ Miniature military figures. 718-486-5390.

ANI Toy Soldiers, 628 S. Myrtle Ave., Monrovia, CA 91016: Catalog $5 ❖ Miniature toy soldiers. 818-303-3990.

Armchair General Ltd., 12977 N. Outer Forty Dr., St. Louis, MO 63141: Catalog $2 ❖ Military miniatures and toy soldiers.

Armies in Miniature, 1745 Tradewinds Ln., Newport Beach, CA 92660: List $2 ❖ Miniature military figures. 714-646-4471.

ATS Toys, P.O. Box 365, Chinchilla, PA 18410: Free list ❖ Toy soldiers and miniature figures. 717-586-6551.

Brunton's Barracks, 415 S. Montezuma St., Prescott, AZ 86303: Free information ❖ Military figures and other miniatures. 602-778-1915.

CIV Miniatures, 115 S. Hooker, Denver, CO 80219: Free information with long SASE ❖ Cast-resin historical figures.

Classic Toy Soldier Company, 11528 Canterbury Circle, Leawood, KS 66211: Free information ❖ Collectible toy soldiers. 913-451-9458.

The Colonial Connection, 226 Wareham's Point, Williamsburg, VA 23185: Catalog $2.50 ❖ Model soldiers and equipment. 804-229-4547.

Cynthia's Country Store, The Wellington Mall, 12794 W. Forest Hill Blvd., Ste. 15A, West Palm Beach, FL 33414: Catalog $15 ❖ British and other toy soldiers. 407-793-0554.

Dunken, Box 95, Calvert, TX 77837: Free catalog ❖ Civil War, World War I and World War II, Napoleonic, Germany military, and lead soldier molds. 409-364-2020.

Dutkins' Collectables, 1019 West Rt. 70, Cherry Hill, NJ 08002: Catalog $4 ❖ Hand-painted all-metal toy soldiers and mold kits. 609-428-9559.

Excalibur Hobbies Ltd., 63 Exchange St., Malden, MA 02148: Free information ❖ Old and new toy soldiers, war games, plastic kits, books, and military collectibles. 617-322-2959.

TOYS & GAMES

F.J. Authentics, 9514 Country Roads Ln., Manassas, VA 22111: Free catalog ❖ Custom hand-painted Civil War figures. 703-361-0925.

Farina Enterprises, P.O. Box 101, Arlington, MA 02174: Catalog $5 ❖ Civil War miniatures and kits. 617-497-1406.

Gettysburg Toy Soldier, 200 Steinwehr Ave., Gettysburg, PA 17325: Free information with long SASE ❖ American Civil War and British Colonial War miniatures. 717-337-3151.

Historical Miniatures, Box 195, Port Richey, FL 34673: Free catalog ❖ Hand-painted metal castings, Civil War generals, American and German soldiers from World War II, and other miniatures. 813-868-3150.

I/R Miniatures Inc., P.O. Box 89-L, Burnt Mills, NY 12077: Catalog $6 ❖ Historically detailed military miniatures and kits from American military history. 518-885-6054.

In Stock Hobby, P.O. Box 853, Newton, NJ 07860: Free information ❖ Military miniatures, toy soldiers, plastic and metal models, tools, and supplies. 800-656-5390.

International Hobby Corporation, 413 E. Allegheny Ave., Philadelphia, PA 19134: Catalog $4.98 ❖ Battery-powered tools, model airplanes, railroading accessories, and military miniatures. 800-875-1600.

Military Mites, Box 2324, Rockville, MD 20847: Catalog $6 ❖ Miniature military figures from the past to the present. 800-296-6483.

Miniatures, Box 195, Port Richey, FL 34673: Free list ❖ Hand-painted metal toy soldiers. 813-868-3150.

Model Cars & Trains Unlimited, 28 Arthur Ave., Blue Point, NY 11715: Catalog $4 (specify type of model) ❖ Model cars, trains, toy soldiers, and accessories. 516-363-2134.

Model Cellar Productions, P.O. Box 388, Horsham, PA 19044: Catalog $3 ❖ World War I military miniatures.

Musket Miniatures, P.O. Box 1976, Denver, CO 80038: Catalog $2 ❖ Civil War miniatures. 303-439-9336.

Red Lancer, P.O. Box 8056, Mesa, AZ 85214: Catalog $6 ❖ Original 19th-century military art, rare books, Victorian era campaign medals and helmets, old toy soldiers, and collectibles. 602-964-9667.

The Red Lancers Miniatures, 324 S. Front St., Milton, PA 17817: Catalog $8 ❖ Military miniatures. 717-742-3195.

Saratoga Soldier Shop & Military Bookstore, 831 Rt. 67, Ste. 40, Ballston Spa, NY 12020: Catalog $6 ❖ Miniatures from the Civil War and other eras. 518-885-1497.

Scotty's Scale Soldiers, 1008 Adams, Bay City, MI 48708: Catalog $10 each (specify scale) ❖ Miniatures, 6mm to 30mm and 54mm to 120mm. 517-892-6177.

Jack Scruby's Toy Soldiers, P.O. Box 1658, 789 Main St., Cambria, CA 93428: List $1 ❖ Painted and unpainted individual and boxed sets of toy soldiers. 805-927-3805.

Sentinel Miniatures, P.O. Box 735, Larchmont, NY 10538: Catalog $8.50 ❖ Military, historical, and fantasy figure kits. Also die-cast cars and HO and N scale trains. 914-682-3932.

Spitz Mountain Enterprises, 3013 S. Wolf Rd., Ste. 292, Westchester, IL 60154: Catalog $2.50 ❖ Handcrafted miniature wood toy soldiers. 708-786-8606.

Stad's Miniature Figures, 815 12th St., Allentown, PA 18102: Price list $2 ❖ Miniature plastic figures.

Stuempfle's Military Miniatures, 13190 Scott Rd., Waynesboro, PA 17268: Catalog $3 ❖ Military miniatures. 717-762-0825.

TNC Enterprises, 318 Churchill Ct., Elizabethtown, KY 42701: Catalog $5 ❖ Toy soldier sets and individual pieces from different historical periods. 502-765-5035.

Toy Soldier Company, 100 Riverside Dr., New York, NY 10024: Plastics catalog $4; lead catalog $7.50 ❖ United States, British, French, and German lead and plastic toy soldiers and miniatures from 1900 to the present. 201-433-2370.

Toy Soldier Gallery Inc., 24 Main St., Highland Falls, NY 12928: Catalog $5 ❖ Toy soldier sets and individual pieces from different historical periods. 800-777-9904.

Tradition USA Toy Soldiers, 12924 Viking Dr., Burnsville, MN 55337: Catalog $10 ❖ Toy soldiers. 612-890-1634.

VLS Mail Order, Lone Star Industrial Park, 811 Lone Star Dr., O'Fallon, MO 63366: Catalog $6 ❖ Military and aircraft models and miniature military figures. 314-281-5700.

Warwick Miniatures Ltd., P.O. Box 1498, Portsmouth, NH 03801: Catalog $4 ❖ Imperial toy soldiers from New Zealand and detailed miniatures from historical periods of the United States, England, France, and Germany. 603-431-7139.

Wiley House Toy Soldiers, 913 Sheridan Ave., Cody, WY 82414: Free information with long SASE ❖ Military figures and miniatures. 307-587-6030.

TOYS & GAMES
Character Toys

Action Images, 335 Washington St., Ste. 219, Woburn, MA 01801: Free information ❖ Character toys and memorabilia. 617-933-2914.

Amok Time Toys, Paul James Lazo, 400 Warwick Rd., East Meadow, NY 11554: Catalog $3 ❖ Character and science fiction toys. 516-826-4570.

Ancient Idols Collectible Toys, 223 S. Madison St., Allentown, PA 18102: Catalog $3 ❖ Collectible character and science fiction toys, model kits, puzzles, and games. 610-820-0805.

Baker's Art & Collectibles, P.O. Box 558, Oakdale, NY 11769: Catalog $20 (8 issues) ❖ Antique and collectible toys. 516-567-9295.

Benjy's Trains & Toys, P.O. Box 16491, Temple Terrace, FL 33687: Free price list with long SASE ❖ Slot cars, accessories, trains, and toys. 813-980-3790.

Collectorholics, 15006 Fuller, Grandview, MO 64030: Catalog $5 ❖ Character TV and movie-related toys and other collectibles. 816-322-0906.

Collectors Showcase, 820 Caron Circle NW, Atlanta, GA 30318: Free information ❖ Character toys and memorabilia. 404-792-2929.

Cotswold Collectibles Inc., P.O. Box 249, Clinton, WA 98236: Free list ❖ G.I. Joe figures, accessories, uniforms, and vehicles. 360-579-1223.

Clinton Dean's Figures & Collectibles, P.O. Box 383, Milford, NH 03055: Free catalog ❖ Character toys and figures, trading cards, and other collectibles. 603-673-3290.

John DiCicco, 57 Bay View Dr., Shrewsbury, MA 01545: Catalog $2 ❖ Character toys and memorabilia. 508-797-0023.

Figures Inc., P.O. Box 19842, Johnston, RI 02919: Catalog $2 ❖ TV, movie, action, character toy collectibles, and other toys. 401-946-5720.

Fun House Toy Company, P.O. Box 343, Bradforwoods, PA 15015: Free catalog with four 1st class stamps ❖ MARX figures, play sets, and other collectibles. 412-935-1392.

Barry Goodman, P.O. Box 218, Woodbury, NY 11797: Free information with long SASE ❖ Character toys and dolls. 516-338-2701.

The Hobby Lobby, P.O. Box 228, Kulpsville, PA 19443: Catalog $6 ❖ G.I. Joe memorabilia, action figures, and vintage cars and toys, from the 1960s and 1970s. 215-721-9749.

M.R. Huber, 931 Emerson St., 1000 Oaks, CA 91362: Catalog $3 ❖ Snoopy and Peanuts classic collectibles. 805-497-0119.

Jim's TV Collectibles, P.O. Box 4767, San Diego, CA 92164: Catalog $2 ❖ TV and theatrical collectibles, from the 1950s through 1990s.

John's Collectible Toys & Gifts, 57 Bay View Dr., Shrewsbury, MA 01545: Catalog $2 ❖ Character toys and movie and TV collectibles. 508-797-0023.

Just Kids Nostalgia, 310 New York Ave., Huntington, NY 11743: Catalog $5 ❖ Movie and TV character dolls, movie memorabilia, and board games. 516-423-8449.

Kadon Enterprises Inc., 1227 Lorene Dr., Ste. 16, Pasadena, MD 21122: Free brochure ❖ Puzzles, challenging and historical games, board games, and abstract challenging strategies. 410-437-2163.

Long Island Train & Hobby Center, 192 Jericho Tnpk., Mineola, NY 11501: Price list $3 ❖ Collectible toys and character dolls. 516-742-5621.

Jim Makowski, P.O. Box 102, Holtsville, NY 11742: Catalog $2 ❖ Character toys. 516-736-8697.

Monolith Toys, Kevin Walker, P.O. Box 220624, Newhall, CA 91322: Catalog $1 ❖ Science fiction character toys. 805-288-2268.

Oasis of Quality, 336 Shamrock Rd., St. Augustine, FL 32086: Free catalog with three 1st class stamps ❖ TV, movie, action, and character toy collectibles. 904-797-9745.

Outer Limits, 433 Piaget Ave., Clifton, NJ 07013: Catalog $2 ❖ Science fiction and character toys. 201-340-9393.

Bob Sellstedt, 9307 Hillingdon Rd., Woodbury, MN 55125: Price list $2 ❖ Character toys and collectibles. 612-738-1597.

Splash Page Comics & Toys, 1007 E. Patterson, Kirksville, MO 63501: Free information ❖ Character toys and memorabilia. 800-237-PAGE.

Stellar Toys, 253 Osborne Rd., Loudonville, NY 12211: Catalog $4 ❖ Science fiction and character toys, collectibles, videos, and models. 518-482-0522.

Toy Scouts Inc., 137 Casterton Ave., Akron, OH 44303: Catalog $3 ❖ Collectible TV cartoon and comic characters, from 1940 through 1970. 216-836-0668.

Toys from Times Past, 4299 E. Shearer Rd., Rhodes, MI 48652: Free brochure ❖ Action, skill, and animated toys. Also tricks and puzzles. 517-689-4663.

Toys-Toys-Toys, Jerry & Ellen Harnish, 110 Main St., Bellville, OH 44813: Catalog $2 ❖ Action figures, games, puzzles, dolls, and other toys.

Tripwire Toys, 702 Mangrove, Ste. 125, Chico, CA 95926: Free catalog with 9x12 envelope and 78¢ postage ❖ Vietnam War and modern uniforms and gear for G.I. Joes.

Wex Rex Records & Collectibles, 280 Worcester Rd., Framingham, MA 01701: Catalog $3 ❖ Movie and TV show character toys and collectibles. 508-620-6181.

Educational Toys & Games

Animal Town, P.O. Box 485, Healdsburg, CA 95448: Free catalog ❖ Toys, novelties, games, puzzles, books, and recordings for children. 800-445-8642.

Aristoplay Games, P.O. Box 7028, Ann Arbor, MI 48107: Free catalog ❖ Educational games for all ages. 800-634-7738.

Mary Arnold Toys, 962 Lexington Ave., New York, NY 10021: Free catalog ❖ Activity play toys for children. 212-744-8510.

Back to Basics Toys, 4315 Walney Rd., Chantilly, VA 22021: Free catalog ❖ Activity toys and games, backyard games, and sports and family-oriented items. 800-356-5360.

Barclay School Supplies, 166 Livingston St., Brooklyn, NY 11201: Catalog $4 ❖ Educational and school supplies and teaching aids. 718-875-2424.

Childcraft, 250 College Park, P.O. Box 1811, Peoria, IL 61656: Free catalog ❖ Educational toys and games for babies and young children. 800-631-5657.

Constructive Playthings, 1227 E. 119th St., Grandview, MO 64030: Free catalog ❖ How-to build-them-yourself toys. 800-448-7830; 816-761-5900 (in MO).

Discovery Toys Inc., 2530 Arnold Dr., Ste. 400, Martinez, CA 94553: Free catalog ❖ Toys for children that encourage physical, emotional, and intellectual growth. 800-426-4777.

Early Learning Centre, 135 Lexington Ave., New York, NY 10016: Free catalog ❖ Toys that stimulate young minds and help with their development.

Edmund Scientific Company, Edscorp Building, Barrington, NJ 08007: Free catalog ❖ Scientific educational items. 609-573-6260.

Educational Insights, 19560 Rancho Way, Dominguez Hills, CA 90220: Free catalog (specify pre-K to age 8 or 8 years and up) ❖ Learning games and toys.

Fun Publishing Company, 2121 Alpine Pl., Cincinnati, OH 45206: Free information ❖ Soft toys for children ages 1 to 3; books for children ages 2 to 4, 5 to 6, kindergarten and 1st grade, and ages 7 and 8; music items for children ages 3 to adults; and special books for teachers. 513-533-3636.

The Great Kids Company, P.O. Box 609, Lewisville, NC 27023: Free catalog ❖ Developmental learning materials for early childhood education. 800-582-1493.

Hand in Hand, Catalogue Center, 891 Main St., Oxford, ME 04270: Free catalog ❖ Books, toys and games, and products that help nurture, teach, and protect children. 800-872-9745.

Hearth Song, Mail Processing Center, 6519 N. Galena Rd., P.O. Box 1773, Peoria, IL 61656: Free catalog ❖ Toys and games that provide opportunity for creativity, challenge, discovery, and improving reading skills. 800-325-2502.

Kapable Kids, P.O. Box 250, Bohemia, NY 11716: Catalog $2 ❖ Toys for the developing child. 800-356-1564.

Miles Kimball Company, 41 W. 8th Ave., Oshkosh, WI 54906: Free catalog ❖ Children's toys and crafts. 800-546-2255.

Kimbo Educational, Dept. W, P.O. Box 477, Long Branch, NJ 07740: Free catalog ❖ Cassettes, CDs, records, videos, read-alongs, and film strips for children. 800-631-2187.

Lauri, P.O. Box F, Phillips-Avon, ME 04966: Free catalog ❖ Crepe rubber and wooden puzzles, lacing toys, games, and other educational activities. 800-451-0520.

Lilly's Kids, Lillian Vernon Corporation, Virginia Beach, VA 23479: Free catalog ❖ Games, science sets, art activities, backyard and outdoor toys, dolls, animal toys, and rainy day and traveling fun things. 800-285-5555.

Music for Little People, Dept. BHR, P.O. Box 1720, Lawndale, CA 90260: Free catalog ❖ Toy musical instruments, stuffed animals, videos, cassettes, and CDs. 800-727-2233.

The Natural Baby Company Inc., 816 Silvia St., Trenton, NJ 08628: Free information ❖ Toys for babies. 800-388-BABY.

One Step Ahead, P.O. Box 517, Lake Bluff, IL 60044: Free catalog ❖ Playthings for babies. 800-950-5120.

Out of the Woodwork, 437 Robert E. Lee Dr., Wilmington, NC 28412: Free brochure ❖ Educational puzzles for children. 910-792-6882.

Playfair Toys, 1690 28th St., Boulder, CO 80301: Catalog $2 ❖ Toys, games, and teaching aids for children. 303-440-7229.

Right Start Catalog, Right Start Plaza, 5334 Sterling Center Dr., Westlake Village, CA 91361: Catalog $2 ❖ Infant, toddler, and pre-school toys and games. 800-548-8531.

S & S Arts & Crafts, 75 Mill St., Dept. 2000, Colchester, CT 06415: Free catalog ❖ Educational games, puzzles, arts and crafts projects, and curriculum products. 800-243-9232.

Sensational Beginnings, 987 Stewart Rd., Monroe, MI 48162: Free catalog ❖ Toys and books for babies and children up to age 4. 800-444-2147.

Toys to Grow On, P.O. Box 17, Long Beach, CA 90801: Catalog $1 ❖ Games, backyard, educational, and children's toys. 800-874-4242.

Troll Learn & Play, 100 Corporate Dr., Mahwah, NJ 07430: Free catalog ❖ Children's educational toys, books, puzzles, and videos. 800-247-6106.

U.S. Toy Company Inc., 1227 E. 119th St., Grandview, MO 64030: Catalog $3 ❖ Educational toys and games. 800-448-7830; 816-761-5900 (in MO).

❖ TOYS & GAMES ❖

World Book Family Catalog, 2515 E. 43rd St., P.O. Box 182246, Chattanooga, TN 37422: Free catalog ❖ Learning games, books, toys, and recordings for children. 800-874-5885.

Worldwide Games, P.O. Box 517, Colchester, CT 06415: Free catalog ❖ Children's puzzles and games. 800-937-3482.

Electronic Toys & Games

Accolade Inc., 5300 Stevens Creek Blvd., San Jose, CA 95128: Free information ❖ Video game cassettes. 800-245-7744.

Atari Computer, 455 S. Mathilda Ave., Sunnyvale, CA 94088: Free catalog ❖ Video game cartridges. 408-328-0900.

BRE Software, 352 W. Bedford Ave., Ste. 104, Fresno, CA 93711: Free catalog ❖ Video games.

Electronic Arts, 1450 Fashion Island Blvd., San Mateo, CA 94404: Free information ❖ Video game cassettes. 800-245-4525.

Haven Industries, 2950 Lake Emma Rd., Lake Mary, FL 32746: Free information ❖ Camcorders and accessories, car audio equipment, video games, and other electronics. 800-231-0031.

Impressions Software, 222 3rd St., Ste. 0234, Cambridge, MA 92142: Free information ❖ Video game cartridges. 800-545-7677.

Interplay Productions, 17922 Fitch Ave., Irvine, CA 92714: Free information ❖ Video game cartridges. 800-969-4263.

MicroProse Software Inc., 180 Lakefront Dr., Hunt Valley, MD 21030: Free information ❖ Video game cartridges. 800-879-7529.

NEC Technologies Inc., 1414 Massachusetts Ave., Boxborough, MA 01719: Free information ❖ Video game cassettes. 800-374-8000.

Play It Again, Dept. 40, P.O. Box 656718, Flushing, NY 11365: List $1 ❖ Used video game cartridges. 718-229-1435.

Radio Shack, Division Tandy Corporation, 1500 One Tandy Center, Fort Worth, TX 76102: Free information ❖ Electronic teaching toys, musical instruments, chess games, strategy games, sports games, and radio controlled toys. 817-390-3700.

Sega of America, SOA/Parts & Order Dept., P.O. Box 8097, Redwood City, CA 94063: Free information ❖ Video game cassettes. 800-USA-SEGA.

Sir-Tech Software, P.O. Box 245, Ogdensburg, NY 13669: Free information ❖ Video game cassettes. 315-393-6633.

Spectrum Holobyte, 2490 Mariner Square Loop, Alameda, CA 94501: Free information ❖ Video game cassettes. 510-522-3584.

SSI, 675 Almanor Ave., Ste. 201, Sunnyvale, CA 94086: Free information ❖ Video game cartridges. 408-737-6800.

Strategic Simulations Inc., c/o Electronic Arts, P.O. Box 7530, San Mateo, CA 94403: Free information ❖ Video game cartridges. 800-245-4525.

Viacom New Media, 1515 Broadway, New York, NY 10036: Free information ❖ Video game cartridges. 800-469-2539.

Virgin Games, 18061 Fitch Ave., Irvine, CA 92714: Free information ❖ Video game cartridges. 714-833-1999.

General Toys & Games

All But Grown-Ups, P.O. Box 555, Berwick, ME 03901: Free brochure ❖ Challenging toys for adults and children. 800-448-1550.

Allen-Lewis Manufacturing Company, Division TCC Industries Inc., P.O. Box 16546, 5601 Logan, Denver, CO 80216: Free catalog ❖ Souvenirs, carnival and party supplies, fund-raising merchandise, toys and games, T-shirts and sweatshirts, and craft supplies. 303-295-0196.

Ancient Idols Collectible Toys, 223 S. Madison St., Allentown, PA 18102: Catalog $3 ❖ Collectible character and science fiction toys, model kits, puzzles, and games. 610-820-0805.

Aristoplay Games, P.O. Box 7028, Ann Arbor, MI 48107: Free catalog ❖ Educational games for all ages. 800-634-7738.

Armchair General's Merchantile, 1008 Adams, Bay City, MI 48708: Catalog $2 (refundable) ❖ Games, miniatures, and books for Civil War enthusiasts. 517-892-6177.

Back to Basics Toys, 4315 Walney Rd., Chantilly, VA 22021: Free catalog ❖ Raggedy Ann dolls, Lincoln log building sets, Lionel trains, Tinkertoy, Radio Flyer wagons, Disney classics, science sets, telescopes, Meccano construction sets, sports games, play-in doll houses, and other toys. 800-356-5360.

Brandine Woodcraft Company, 158 Allen Blvd., Farmingdale, NY 11735: Free information ❖ Educational and wooden toys. 5416-604-8987.

Christian Book Distributors, P.O. Box 7000, Peabody, MA 01961: Free catalog ❖ Religious games for children. 508-977-5000.

CNN Reproductions, 1341 Ashover Ct., Bloomfield Hills, MI 48304: Catalog $4 ❖ Pedal car and pedal plane parts and kits. 810-852-1998.

Constructive Playthings, 1227 E. 119th St., Grandview, MO 64030: Free catalog ❖ Toys, novelties, games, puzzles, books, furniture, and sports and fitness equipment. 800-448-7830; 816-761-5900 (in MO).

Current Inc., Express Processing Center, Colorado Springs, CO 80941: Free catalog ❖ Toys, greeting cards, stationery, gift wrapping and decorations, and calendars. 800-848-2848.

Enchanted Doll House, Rt. 7A, RR 1, Box 2535, Manchester Center, VT 05255: Catalog $2 ❖ Stuffed animals, dolls, books, toys and games, and miniatures. 802-362-1327.

52 Girls Collectibles, P.O. Box 36, Morral, OH 43337: Catalog $3 ❖ Hard-to-find collectible toys and games. 614-465-6062.

Game-Line Inc., 667 Central Ave., Highland Park, IL 60035: Free catalog ❖ Specialty toys from around the world. 800-610-6300.

Games People Played, P.O. Box 1540, Pinedale, WY 82941: Catalog $4 ❖ Antique replica game boards. 307-367-2502.

Gordy's, P.O. Box 201, Sharon Center, OH 44274: Catalog $3 ❖ Collectible toys and model kits. 330-239-1657.

Green Mountain Studios, Rt. 10 North, Box 158, Lyme, NH 03768: Catalog $2 ❖ Toys, novelties, and gifts.

Hand in Hand, Catalogue Center, 891 Main St., Oxford, ME 04270: Free catalog ❖ Books, toys, games, car seats, furniture, and bathroom accessories. 800-872-9745.

Happy Collecting, 255 Jones St., P.O. Box 58, Amston, CT 06231: Catalog $2 ❖ Cars, planes, trucks, and die-cast miniatures.

Heart of America Toys, 14106 W. 107th St., Lenexa, KS 65215: List $1 (specify interests) ❖ Toys. 913-451-7622.

Richard Johnson, P.O. Box 27093, Prescott Valley, AZ 86312: Catalog $2 ❖ Collectible hard-to-find toys. 602-775-4714.

Miles Kimball Company, 41 W. 8th Ave., Oshkosh, WI 54906: Free catalog ❖ Toys and games for children and adults. 800-546-2255.

Larson Wood Manufacturing, P.O. Box 672, Park Rapids, MN 56407: Catalog $2 (refundable) ❖ Kits, parts, and supplies for toy-making. 218-732-9121.

Lilly's Kids, Lillian Vernon Corporation, Virginia Beach, VA 23479: Free catalog ❖ Exclusive and imaginative toys for children. 800-285-5555.

Lunar Models, 106 Century Dr., Cleburne, TX 76031: Catalog $5 ❖ Science fiction models and figure kits. 817-556-0296.

McVays Limited, P.O. Box 553, Leslie, MI 49251: Brochure $2 ❖ Handmade game boards. 517-589-5312.

Mountain Craft Shop, American Ridge Rd., Rt. 1, New Martinsville, WV 26155: Free brochure ❖ American folk toys. 304-455-3570.

423

The Nature Company, Catalog Division, P.O. Box 188, Florence, KY 41022: Free catalog ❖ Science and nature-oriented items, toys, and novelties. 800-227-1114.

Noveltoys, US Hwy. 19, Canton, TX 75103: Catalog $3 (refundable) ❖ Handmade wooden toys for children. 800-342-5452.

The Old Game Store, Rt. 11/30, Manchester, VT 05254: Free information with long SASE ❖ Games, puzzles, collectible teddy bears, and toys. 802-362-2756.

Papa's Gameroom, 121 Lakeside Dr., Mayfield, NY 12117: Free catalog ❖ Table tennis, football games, air hockey, billiards, darts, records, CDs, collectibles from the 1950s, slot machine, and other gameroom accessories and decorator items. 888-321-PAPA.

Patterns by Diane, 1126 Ivon Ave., Endicott, NY 13760: Catalog $3 ❖ Puppets and soft toys. 607-754-0391.

Pecos Pine, 242 E. Main St., Ste. 8, Ashland, OR 97520: Catalog $1 ❖ Handcrafted natural wooden toys and puzzles. 503-535-6606.

Portell Restorations, P.O. Box 91, Hematite, MO 63047: Catalog $2 ❖ Pedal car parts. 314-937-8192.

Real Goods, 555 Leslie St., Ukiah, CA 95482: Free catalog ❖ Solar energy-operating models. 800-762-7325.

Saunier-Wilhem Company, 3216 5th Ave., Pittsburgh, PA 15213: Free catalog ❖ Equipment and accessories for bowling, billiards, darts, table tennis, shuffleboard, and board games. 412-621-4350.

Steve's Lost Land of Toys, 3572 Turner Ct., Fremont, CA 94536: Catalog $3 ❖ Collectible toys. 510-795-0598.

Toys to Grow On, P.O. Box 17, Long Beach, CA 90801: Catalog $1 ❖ Games, T-shirts, party supplies and backyard, educational, and children's toys. 800-874-4242.

Toys-Toys-Toys, Jerry & Ellen Harnish, 110 Main St., Bellville, OH 44813: Catalog $2 ❖ Action figures, games, puzzles, dolls, and other items.

Troll Learn & Play, 100 Corporate Dr., Mahwah, NJ 07430: Free catalog ❖ Children's educational toys, books, puzzles, playhouse toys, videos and other recordings, costumes, and T-shirts. 800-247-6106.

Turn off the TV, P.O. Box 4162, Bellevue, WA 98009: Free catalog ❖ Family games. 800-949-8688.

U.S. Games Systems Inc., 179 Ludlow St., Stanford, CT 06902: Catalog $2 ❖ Deluxe double bridge, tarot, cartomancy, historical, and specialty decks. Also regular cards. 800-344-2637.

Dan Wells Antique Toys, P.O. Box 6751, Louisville, KY 40206: Catalog (6 issues) $8 ❖ Antique toys.

Whippoorwill Crafts, North Market Building, 6 Fanueil Hall Marketplace, Boston, MA 02109: Free information ❖ Kaleidoscopes, wooden boxes and chests, instrumentalist chimes, toys and games, clocks, and imaginative crafts. 800-487-5937; 617-248-0671 (in MA).

Allen Wilson, 1709 St. Cecelia, Kingsville, TX 78363: Catalog $5 ❖ Pedal car parts. 512-595-1015.

Wisconsin Wagon Company, 507 Laurel Ave., Janesville, WI 53545: Free brochure ❖ Handcrafted Janesville replica solid oak coaster wagon and Janesville pine and hardwood toddler first riding 3-wheeler, circa 1900-1934. Also scooters, sleds, wheelbarrows, swings, and doll furniture. 608-754-0026.

Worldwide Games, P.O. Box 517, Colchester, CT 06415: Free catalog ❖ Casino games, puzzles, outdoor games, kites, and games from worldwide sources. 800-937-3482.

Special-Needs Toys & Games

Kapable Kids, P.O. Box 250, Bohemia, NY 11716: Free catalog ❖ Toys, games, and books for children with and without special needs.

S & S Arts & Crafts, 75 Mill St., Dept. 2000, Colchester, CT 06415: Free catalog ❖ Educational games, puzzles, arts and crafts projects, and curriculum products. 800-243-9232.

Toys for Special Children, 385 Warburton Ave., Hastings-on-Hudson, NY 10706: Free catalog ❖ Assistive communication devices, specially adapted and activity toys, capability switches, skill builder equipment, computer training devices, and special devices for handicapped children. 914-478-0960.

Woodset Inc., 4460 Printers Ct., White Plains, MD 20695: Free information ❖ Backyard wooden play equipment with standard designs coupled with creative solutions to mobility and positioning concerns. 800-638-9663.

Worldwide Games, P.O. Box 517, Colchester, CT 06415: Free catalog ❖ Hardwood board games, puzzles, strategy and skill games, outdoor activities, and games for all ages. 800-937-3482.

Water Toys

American Athletic Inc., 200 American Ave., Jefferson, IA 50129: Free information ❖ Surfboards and swim rings. 800-247-3978; 515-386-3125 (in IA).

Recreonics Corporation, 4200 Schmitt Ave., Louisville KY 40213: Free information ❖ Surfboards, swim rings, and diving boards. 800-428-3254.

Rothhammer/Sprint, P.O. Box 3840, San Luis Obispo, CA 93403: Free information ❖ Surfboards, swim rings, and equipment for divers. 800-235-2156.

Sevylor USA, 6651 E. 26th St., Los Angeles, CA 90040: Free information ❖ Inflatable boats, mattresses, tubes, lounges, balls, and sports recreational products. 213-727-6013.

TRACK & FIELD SPORTS

Clothing

Adidas USA, 5675 N. Blackstock Rd., Spartanburg, SC 29303: Free list of retail sources ❖ Shoes and clothing. 800-423-4327.

Asics Tiger Corporation, 10540 Talbert Ave., West Building, Fountain Valley, CA 92708: Free information ❖ Shoes and clothing. 800-678-9435.

Athletes Wear Company, 145 Market Ave., Winnipeg, Manitoba, Canada R3B 1C5: Free catalog ❖ Clothing for track and field sports. 204-949-1885.

The Athletic Connection, 1901 Diplomat, Dallas, TX 75234: Free information ❖ Crossbars, discuses, hurdles, landing pits, relay batons, starting blocks, shotputs, and poles. 800-527-0871; 214-243-1446 (in TX).

Betlin Manufacturing, 1445 Marion Rd., Columbus OH 43207: Free information ❖ Clothing. 614-443-0248.

Compass Industries, 104 E. 25th St., New York, NY 10010: Free information ❖ Starter pistols. 800-221-9904.

Converse Inc., 1 Fordham Rd., North Reading, MA 01864: Free information ❖ Shoes. 800-428-2667; 508-664-1100 (in MA).

Everlast Sports Manufacturing Corporation, 750 E. 132nd St., Bronx, NY 10454: Free information ❖ Landing pits. 800-221-8777; 718-993-0100 (in NY).

Fab Knit Manufacturing Company, Division Anderson Industries, 1415 N. 4th St., Waco, TX 76707: Free information ❖ Clothing. 800-333-4111; 817-752-2511 (in TX).

Ivanko Barbell Company, P.O. Box 1470, San Pedro, CA 90731: Free list of retail sources ❖ Shotputs. 800-247-9044; 310-514-1155 (in CA).

Markwort Sporting Goods, 4300 Forest Park Ave., St. Louis, MO 63108: Catalog $8 (request list of retail sources) ❖ Discuses, relay batons, starter pistols, and tape measures. 800-669-6626; 314-652-3757 (in MO).

New Balance Athletic Shoe Inc., 38 Everett St., Boston, MA 02134: Free list of retail sources ❖ Shoes and clothing. 800-253-7463.

Nike Footwear Inc., One Bowerman Dr., Beaverton, OR 97005: Free list of retail sources ❖ Shoes. 800-344-6453.

J.C. Penney Company Inc., Catalog Division, Atlanta, GA 30390: Free information ❖ Atlanta, GA 30390: Free information ❖ Clothing and accessories. 800-222-6161.

Puma USA Inc., 147 Centre St., Brockton, MA 02403: Free information with long SASE ❖ Shoes. 508-583-9100.

Reebok International Ltd., 100 Technology Center Dr., Stoughton, MA 02072: Free list of retail sources ❖ Shoes. 800-843-4444.

Richardson Sports Inc., 3490 W. 1st Ave., Eugene, OR 97402: Free information ❖ Discuses, relay batons, and tape measures. 800-545-8686; 503-687-1818 (in OR).

Venus Knitting Mills Inc., 140 Spring St., Murray Hill, NJ 07974: Free information ❖ Clothing. 800-955-4200; 908-464-2400 (in NJ).

Equipment

Blazer Manufacturing Company Inc., P.O. Box 667, Fremont, NE 68025: Free information ❖ Crossbars, hurdles, discuses, javelins, shotputs, relay batons, tape measures, and starting blocks. 800-322-2731; 402-721-2525 (in NE).

Cramer Products Inc., P.O. Box 1001, Gardner, KS 66030: Free information ❖ Crossbars, hurdles, discuses, javelins, relay batons, starting blocks, and lane markers. 800-345-2231; 913-884-7511 (in KS).

Olympia Sports, 745 State Circle, Ann Arbor, MI 48106: Free information ❖ Crossbars, hurdles, hammers, lane markers, relay batons, starter pistols, landing pits, and starting blocks. 800-521-2832.

TRAMPOLINES

American Athletic Inc., 200 American Ave., Jefferson, IA 50129: Free information ❖ Trampolines. 800-247-3978; 515-386-3125 (in IA).

The Athletic Connection, 1901 Diplomat, Dallas, TX 75234: Free information ❖ Trampolines. 800-527-0871; 214-243-1446 (in TX).

Austin Athletic Equipment Corporation, 705 Bedford Ave., Box 423, Bellmore, NY 11710: Free information ❖ Trampolines. 516-785-0100.

Bollinger Fitness Products, 222 W. Airport Freeway, Irving, TX 75062: Free information ❖ Home gymnasiums, trampolines, monitoring aids, and other weight training and body building equipment. 800-527-1166; 214-445-0386 (in TX).

Cannon Sports, P.O. Box 11179, Burbank, CA 91510: Free list of retail sources ❖ Fitness and exercise equipment, monitoring aids, home gymnasiums, weight-lifting equipment, and trampolines. 800-362-3146.

JumpKing Trampolines, 901 W. Miller Rd., Garland, TX 75041: Free catalog ❖ Trampolines. 800-322-2211.

Spalding Sports Worldwide, 425 Meadow St., P.O. Box 901, Chicopee, MA 01021: Free list of retail sources ❖ Home gymnasiums, trampolines, monitoring aids, and weight training, body building, and exercise equipment. 800-225-6601.

Trampoline World, P.O. Box 808, Fayetteville, GA 30214: Free catalog ❖ Trampolines. 404-461-9941.

TRUNK (STORAGE CHEST) REPAIR

Antique Trunk Supply Company, 3706 W. 169th St., Cleveland, OH 44111: Catalog $1 ❖ Trunk repair parts. 216-941-8618.

Charolette Ford Trunks, P.O. Box 536, Spearman, TX 79081: Catalog $3.50 ❖ Supplies and tools for restoring trunks. 806-659-3027.

Phyllis Kennedy Restoration Hardware, 9256 Holyoke Ct., Indianapolis, IN 46268: Catalog $3 ❖ Antique trunk hardware. 317-872-6366.

TVS & VCRS

Manufacturers

Brookline Technologies, 2035 Carriage Hill Rd., Allison Park, PA 15101: Free information ❖ Automatic stabilizer for home video volume control. 800-366-9290.

Canon, One Canon Plaza, Lake Success, NY 11042: Free information ❖ Cassette players, camcorders, sound processors, and other electronics. 516-488-6700.

Emerson Radio Corporation, 9 Entin Rd., Parsippany, NJ 07054: Free information ❖ Camcorders, cassette and CD players, and TVs. 201-884-5800.

Fisher, 21350 Lassen St., Chatsworth, CA 91311: Free information ❖ CD and cassette players, sound processors, camcorders, TVs, and universal remotes. 818-998-7322.

G.E. Appliances, General Electric Company, Appliance Park, Louisville, KY 40225: Free information ❖ Audio and video equipment, cassette players, camcorders, TVs, and universal remotes. 800-626-2000.

Goldstar, 1000 Sylvan Ave., Englewood, NJ 07632: Free information ❖ CD and cassette players and TVs. 201-816-2200.

Harmon/Kardon, 80 Crossways Park West, Woodbury, NY 11797: Free information ❖ Cassette and CD players, receivers, amplifiers, and TVs. 800-422-8027.

Hitachi Sales Corporation, Customer Service, 675 Old Peachtree Rd., Suwanee, GA 30174: Free information ❖ Audio and video equipment, CD and cassette players, camcorders, and TVs. 800-241-6558.

Infinity Systems, 10630 Nordhoff St., Chatsworth, CA 91311: Free information ❖ Speakers and TVs. 818-407-0228.

Instant Replay, 8290 NW 27th St., Ste. 605, Miami, FL 33122: Free information ❖ Camcorders and cassette players. 305-854-6777.

JVC, 41 Slater Dr., Elmwood Park, NJ 07407: Free information ❖ Audio and video equipment, CD and cassette players, camcorders, receivers, amplifiers, TVs, and headphones. 201-794-3900.

Kenwood, P.O. Box 22745, Long Beach, CA 90801: Free information ❖ Audio and video equipment, CD and cassette players, receivers, amplifiers, TVs, and sound processors. 800-536-9663.

Mitsubishi Electronics, 5665 Plaza Dr., Cypress, CA 90630: Free information ❖ Audio and video equipment, CD and cassette players, camcorders, and TVs. 800-843-2515.

NEC Home Electronics, 1255 Michael Dr., Wood Dale, IL 60191: Free information ❖ Audio and video equipment, CD and cassette players, receivers, amplifiers, TVs, camcorders, sound processors, and other electronics. 708-860-9500.

Onkyo, 200 Williams Dr., Ramsey, NJ 07446: Free information ❖ CD players, receivers, amplifiers, universal remotes, and headphones. 201-825-7950.

Panasonic, Panasonic Way, Secaucus, NJ 07094: Free list of retail sources ❖ Audio and video systems, CD and cassette players, TVs, camcorders, headphones, and other electronics. 201-348-7000.

Pentax Corporation, 35 Inverness Dr. East, Englewood, CO 80112: Free information ❖ Cassette players and camcorders. 303-799-8000.

Pioneer New Media Technologies, 2265 E. 220th St., Long Beach, CA 90810: Free information ❖ Receivers, amplifiers, TVs, sound processors, headphones, and CD, cassette, and laser disk players. 800-444-OPTI.

Proton Corporation, 13855 Struikman Rd., Cerritos, CA 90703: Free information ❖ Speakers, CD players, receivers, amplifiers, and TVs. 310-404-2222.

Quasar, One Panasonic Way, Secaucus, NJ 07094: Free list of retail sources ❖ Audio and video equipment, cassette and CD players, camcorders, and TVs. 201-348-7000.

Radio Shack, Division Tandy Corporation, One Tandy Center, Fort Worth, TX 76102: Free information ❖ Cassette and CD players, camcorders, universal remotes, computers, and other electronics. 817-390-3011.

TVS & VCRS

RCA Sales Corporation, Thomson Consumer Electronics, P.O. Box 1976, Indianapolis, IN 46206: Free information ❖ Audio and video systems, cassette and CD players, TVs, camcorders, sound processors, and other electronics. 800-336-1900.

Samsung, 105 Challenger Rd., Ridgefield Park, NJ 07662: Free information ❖ Cassette players and TVs. 800-446-0262; 201-229-4000 (in NJ).

Sansui USA, 210 Clay Ave. West, P.O. Box 625, Lyndhurst, NJ 07071: Free information ❖ CD and cassette players, camcorders, receivers, amplifiers, TVs, and sound processors. 201-460-9710.

Sanyo, 21350 Lassen St., Chatsworth, CA 91311: Free information ❖ Cassette and CD players, camcorders, TVs, sound processors, universal remotes, and other electronics. 818-998-7322.

Sharp Electronics, Sharp Plaza, Mahwah, NJ 07430: Free information ❖ Cassette and CD players, camcorders, TVs, receivers, amplifiers, and other electronics. 800-BE-SHARP.

Sony Consumer Products, 1 Sony Dr., Park Ridge, NJ 07656: Free information with long SASE ❖ Audio and video equipment, cassette and CD players, camcorders, TVs, sound processors, universal remotes, headphones, and other electronics. 201-930-1000.

Teac, 7733 Telegraph Rd., Montebello, CA 90640: Free information ❖ Sound processors, headphones, other electronics, and CD, cassette, and laser disk players. 213-726-0303.

Toshiba, 82 Totowa Rd., Wayne, NJ 07470: Free information ❖ CD and cassette players, camcorders, sound processors, and TVs. 201-628-8000.

Vector Research, 1230 Calle Suerte, Camarillo, CA 93012: Free information ❖ Cassette and CD players, receivers, and amplifiers. 805-987-1312.

Yamaha, P.O. Box 6660, Buena Park, CA 90620: Free information ❖ Audio and video equipment, speakers, receivers, amplifiers, sound processors, headphones, and cassette, CD, and laser disk players. 800-492-6242.

Zenith, 1000 Milwaukee Ave., Glenview, IL 60025: Free catalog ❖ Cassette players, camcorders, TVs, universal remotes, and other electronics. 708-391-8181.

Retailers

Abe's of Maine Camera & Electronics, 1957 Coney Island Ave., Brooklyn, NY 11223: Free information ❖ Video, camcorder, and photography accessories. 800-531-2237.

AV Distributors, 10765 Kingspoint, Houston, TX 77075: Free information ❖ TVs, fax machines, and audio, video, and stereo equipment. 800-843-3697.

Beach Photo & Video Inc., 604 Main St., Daytona Beach, FL 32118: Free information ❖ Video equipment and camcorders. 904-252-0577.

Bondy Export Corporation, 40 Canal St., New York, NY 10002: Free information with long SASE ❖ Household appliances, cameras, video and TV equipment, office machines, typewriters, and luggage. 212-925-7785.

Coast to Coast, 2570 86th St., Brooklyn, NY 11214: Free information ❖ Camcorders, video editing equipment, receivers, CD players, cassette decks, and other electronics. 718-265-1723.

Colonel Video & Audio, 16451 Space Center Blvd., Houston, TX 77058: Free information ❖ Video and audio editing equipment, camcorders, and accessories. 713-486-8866.

Computability Consumer Electronics, P.O. Box 17882, Milwaukee, WI 53217: Free catalog ❖ TVs, fax machines, copiers, computers, and audio, video, and stereo equipment. 800-554-9949.

Crutchfield, 1 Crutchfield Park, Charlottesville, VA 22906: Free catalog ❖ Video, audio and stereo equipment and TVs. 800-955-9009.

Data Vision, 445 5th Ave., New York, NY 10016: Free information ❖ Everything in electronics. 800-482-7466; 212-689-1111 (in NY).

Dial-A-Brand Inc., 57 S. Main St., Freeport, NY 11520: Free information with long SASE ❖ TVs, appliances, video equipment, and other electronics. 516-378-9694.

Electronic Mailbox, 10-12 Charles St., Glen Cove, NY 11542: Free information ❖ Home theater systems, photography accessories, video editing equipment, and other electronics. 800-325-2325.

Electronic Wholesalers, 1166 Hamburg Tnpk., Wayne, NJ 07470: Free information ❖ Camcorders, TVs, cassette players, 8mm and beta home decks, receivers, and other electronics. 201-696-6531.

Electronics Depot, 22 Rt. 22 West, Springfield, NJ 07081: Free information ❖ Video equipment, camcorders, and accessories. 800-500-1553.

Executive Photo & Electronics, 120 W. 31st St., New York, NY 10001: Free information ❖ Photography and video equipment, camcorders, and other electronics. 800-882-2802.

Factory Direct, 35 W. 35th St., New York, NY 10001: Free information ❖ TVs, fax machines, and audio, video, and stereo equipment. 212-564-4399.

Focus Electronics, 4523 13th Ave., Brooklyn, NY 11219: Free catalog ❖ Appliances, photographic equipment, other electronics, and audio, stereo, and video equipment. 718-436-4646.

Garden State Camera, 101 Kuller Rd., Clifton, NJ 07015: Photographic equipment, camcorders, video and audio accessories, binoculars, and optical equipment. 201-742-5777.

Genesis Camera Inc., 814 W. Lancaster Ave., Bryn Mawr, PA 19010: Free information ❖ Audio, video, and photographic equipment. 800-575-9977; 610-527-5261 (in PA).

Haven Industries, 2950 Lake Emma Rd., Lake Mary, FL 32746: Free information ❖ Computers, cellular telephones, audio and video equipment for homes and cars, and electronic accessories. 800-231-0031.

J & R Music World, 59-50 Queens-Midtown Expwy., Maspeth, NY 11378: Free catalog ❖ Audio and stereo equipment, video recorders and tapes, telephones, and computers. 800-221-8180.

Marine Park Camera & Video Inc., 3126 Avenue U, Brooklyn, NY 11229: Free information ❖ Video equipment, VCRs, and camcorders. 800-448-8811; 718-891-1878 (in NY).

Mission Service Supply, 4565 Cypress St., West Monroe, LA 71291: Free catalog ❖ Video systems and accessories. 800-352-7222; 318-397-2755 (in LA).

New West Electronics, 4120 Meridian, Bellingham, WA 98226: Free information ❖ Camcorders, cassette and disk players, TVs and monitors, audio components, and speakers. 800-488-8877.

Olden Video, 1265 Broadway, New York, NY 10001: Free information ❖ Audio and video equipment, TVs, cassette players, and other electronics. 212-725-1234.

J.C. Penney Company Inc., Catalog Division, Atlanta, GA 30390: Free information ❖ Cassette players, TVs, audio and video systems, and other electronics. 800-222-6161.

Percy's Inc., 19 Glennie St., Worcester, MA 01605: Free information ❖ Appliances and electronics. 508-755-5334.

Planet Electronics, 8418 Lilley, Canton, MI 48187: Free catalog ❖ TVs, stereo receivers, video recorders, tapes and cassettes, and compact disks. 800-247-4663; 313-453-4750 (in MI).

Porter's Camera Store Inc., Box 628, Cedar Falls, IA 50613: Free catalog ❖ Video equipment. 800-553-2001.

PowerVideo, 6808 Hornwood Dr., Houston, TX 77074: Free information ❖ TVs and audio, video, and stereo equipment. 713-772-4400.

S & S Sound City, 58 W. 45th St., New York, NY 10036: Free information ❖ Video recorders, CD players, TVs, telephones, and other electronics. 212-575-0210.

Smile Photo, 29 W. 35th St., New York, NY 10001: Free information ❖ Photography and video equipment. 212-967-5900.

Sound City, Meadtown Shopping Center, Rt. 23, Kinnelon, NJ 07405: Free information ❖ Audio and video equipment, cassette and CD players, camcorders, TVs, processors, fax machines, telephones, and other electronics. 800-542-7283.

Sunshine South, 2606 N. Kings Hwy., Myrtle Beach, SC 29577: Free information ❖ Video equipment. 800-845-0693; 803-448-8474 (in SC).

Tri-State Camera, 650 6th Ave., New York, NY 10011: Free information ❖ Audio and video equipment, camcorders, copiers, video cassettes, and fax machines. 800-221-1926; 212-633-2290 (in NY).

Uncle's Stereo, 581 Broadway, New York, NY 10012: Free information ❖ Everything in electronics. 212-343-9111.

Wisconsin Discount Stereo, 2417 W. Badger Rd., Madison, WI 53713: Free information ❖ Video and audio equipment and TVs. 800-356-9514.

Cable TV Equipment

Apple Electronics, 3389 Sheridan St., Ste. 257, Hollywood, FL 33021: Free catalog ❖ Cable TV descramblers. 800-233-9388.

B & B Cable Inc., 4030 Beau-D-Rue Dr., Egan, MN 55122: Free catalog ❖ Cable TV equipment. 800-826-7623.

Basic Electrical Supply & Warehousing Corporation, P.O. Box 8180, Bartlett, IL 60103: Free information ❖ Cable TV equipment. 800-577-8775.

Boss Distributors, P.O. Box 1282, Beloit, WI 53511: Free information ❖ Cable TV equipment. 800-228-2677.

Buyer's Associates, P.O. Box 336, Livingston, NJ 07039: Catalog $1 ❖ Converters, descramblers, and video accessories. Also other electronics for the home, car, and recreational vehicles. 800-899-5139.

Cable Box Wholesalers Inc., 460 W. Roger Rd., #106, Tucson, AZ 85705: Free catalog ❖ Cable converters and descramblers. 800-841-7835.

Cable Warehouse, 10117 W. Oakland Park Blvd., Ste. 515, Sunrise, FL 33351: Free information ❖ Cable TV descramblers. 800-284-8432.

CNC Concepts, P.O. Box 49503, Minneapolis, MN 55449: Free information ❖ Cable TV equipment. 800-535-1843.

Greenleaf Electronics, P.O. Box 538, Bensenville, IL 60106: Free information ❖ Cable TV equipment. 708-616-8050.

Highlander, 6325-9 Falls of the Neuse Rd., Raleigh, NC 27615: Free catalog ❖ Cable TV equipment. 800-854-7119.

JP Video, 1470 Old Country Rd., Plainview, NY 11803: Free catalog ❖ Cable TV descramblers. 800-950-9145.

K.D. Video Inc., P.O. Box 29538, Minneapolis, MN 55429: Free catalog ❖ Cable TV descramblers. 800-327-3407.

KDE Electronics Inc., P.O. Box 1494, Addison, IL 60101: Free information ❖ Converters and descramblers. 708-889-0281.

L & L Electronics Inc., 1430 Miner St., Ste. 522, Des Plaines, IL 60016: Free catalog ❖ Cable TV equipment. 800-542-9425.

M & G Electronics Inc., 2 Aborn St., Providence, RI 02903: Free information ❖ Cable TV descrambler kits. 800-258-1134.

MD Electronics, 875 S. 72nd St., Omaha, NE 68114: Free catalog ❖ Cable TV equipment. 800-624-1150.

Mega Electronics, 21 S. Main St., Winter Garden, FL 34787: Free catalog ❖ Cable TV descramblers and converters. 800-676-6342.

Midwest Electronics Inc., P.O. Box 5000, Carpentersville, IL 60110: Free catalog with long SASE and three 1st class stamps ❖ Cable TV equipment. 800-648-3030.

Modern Electronics, 2125 S. 156th Circle, Omaha, NE 68130: Free catalog ❖ Cable TV equipment. 800-906-6664.

National Cable Brokers, 1801 W. Jefferson St., Plymouth, IN 45563: Free information ❖ Cable converters and descramblers. 219-935-4128.

Mike Nelson's Movie View Sales Inc., P.O. Box 26, Wood Dale, IL 60191: Free information ❖ Cable TV equipment. 708-250-8690.

Northeast Electronics Inc., 6 Wilkins Dr., Plainview, MA 02762: Free information ❖ Cable TV equipment. 800-886-8699.

Novaplex, 8818 Bradley Ave., Sun Valley, CA 91352: Free catalog ❖ Cable converters, parts, tools, and accessories. 800-644-6682.

Nu-Tek Electronics, 3250 Hatch Rd., Cedarpark, TX 78613: Free catalog ❖ Cable TV equipment. 800-228-7404.

Show Time Cable, 643 N. 98th St., Ste. 260, Omaha, NE 68114: Free catalog ❖ Converters and descramblers. 800-643-4258.

Teleview Distributors, P.O. Box 71465, Las Vegas, NV 89170: Free information ❖ Cable TV equipment. 800-847-3773.

TKA Electronics, 7914 W. Dodge Rd., Omaha, NE 68114: Free catalog ❖ Cable TV descramblers and converters. 800-729-1776.

United Electronic Supply, P.O. Box 1206, Elgin, IL 60121: Free information ❖ Cable TV equipment. 708-697-0600.

Satellite Equipment

R.L. Drake Company, P.O. Box 3006, Miamisburg, OH 45343: Free information ❖ Satellite TV antennas and receivers with optional remote control. 800-937-2530.

Multi-Vision Electronics, 12105 W. Center Rd., Ste. 364, Omaha, NE 68144: Free catalog ❖ Cable TV descramblers. 800-835-2330.

Phillips-Tech Electronics, P.O. Box 8533, Scottsdale, AZ 85252: Free catalog ❖ Satellite TV antennas. 602-947-7700.

R.C. Distributing, P.O. Box 552, South Bend, IN 46624: Free information ❖ Portable satellite antenna. 219-236-5776.

Skyvision Inc., 1016 Frontier Dr., Fergus Falls, MN 56537: Free catalog ❖ Satellite TV equipment for do-it-yourself installation and system upgrading. 800-334-6455.

Timberville Electronics, P.O. Box 202, Timberville, VA 22853: Free information ❖ Satellite TV receivers. 800-825-4641.

Toshiba America, P.O. Box 19724, Irvine, CA 92713: Free information ❖ TV satellite receivers and equipment for system upgrading.

Universal Antenna Manufacturing, P.O. Box 338, Ward, AR 72176: Free information ❖ Satellite reflector-type antennas with optional motorized mounts. 800-843-6517; 501-843-6517 (in AR).

Universal Electronics, 4555 Grove Rd., Ste. 13, Columbus, OH 43232: Free information ❖ Satellite audio receivers. 614-866-4605.

Xandi Electronics, 1270 E. Broadway, Tempe, AZ 85282: Free catalog ❖ Satellite TV receivers, voice disguisers, FM bugs, telephone transmitters, phone snoops, and other easy-to-build kits. 800-336-7389.

TYPEWRITERS & WORD PROCESSORS

Bondy Export Corporation, 40 Canal St., New York, NY 10002: Free information with long SASE ❖ Household appliances, cameras, video equipment, TVs, office machines and typewriters, and luggage. 212-925-7785.

Crutchfield, 1 Crutchfield Park, Charlottesville, VA 22906: Free catalog ❖ Word processors, fax machines, telephones and answering machines, computers, and software. 800-955-9009.

East 33rd Street Electronics & Typewriters, 42 E. 33rd St., New York, NY 10016: Free information with long SASE ❖ Typewriters, computers, software, calculators, telephones and answering machines, video equipment, and TVs. 212-686-0930.

Reliable Home Office, P.O. Box 1501, Ottawa, IL 61350: Catalog $2 ❖ Word processors, calculators, computer supplies, telephones, and office furniture. 800-869-6000.

Staples Inc., 8 Technology Dr., P.O. Box 1020, Westborough, MA 01581: Free catalog ❖ Office supplies, furniture, computer supplies and paper, drafting equipment, fax machines, word processors, and typewriters. 800-333-9328.

UMBRELLAS

Essex Manufacturing, 330 5th Ave., New York, NY 10001: Free information ❖ Golf umbrellas. 800-648-6010; 212-239-0080 (in NY).

Lloyd/Flanders, 3010 10th St., P.O. Box 550, Menominee, MI 49858: Free information ❖ Aluminum outdoor furniture and umbrella sets. 906-863-4491.

MDT-Muller Design Inc., 971 Dogwood Trail, Tyrone, GA 30290: Catalog $2 ❖ Giant outdoor umbrellas. 404-631-9074.

The Umbrella Shop, 233 E. Wacker Dr., Apt. 1112, Chicago, IL 60601: Catalog $2 ❖ Umbrellas and walking sticks.

Uncle Sam Umbrella Shop, 161 W. 57th St., New York, NY 10019: Free catalog ❖ Umbrellas, canes, and walking sticks. 212-247-7163.

VACUUM CLEANERS

ABC Vacuum Cleaner Warehouse, 6720 Burnet Rd., Austin, TX 78757: Free information ❖ Vacuum cleaners. 800-285-8145; 512-459-7643 (in TX).

Broan Manufacturing Company, 926 W. State St., Hartford, WI 53027: Free information ❖ Vacuum cleaner systems. 414-673-4340.

Central Vac International, 200 Kalamath St., Denver, CO 80223: Free information ❖ Vacuum cleaner systems. 800-666-3133.

Derry's Sewing Center, 430 St. Ferdinand, Florissant, MO 63031: Brochure $1 with long SASE ❖ Sewing machines, vacuum cleaners, and parts. 314-837-6103.

Dust Boy Inc., 10002 N. Hogan Rd., Aurora, IN 47001: Free information ❖ Portable and stationary dust collectors. 800-232-3878.

M & S Systems Inc., 2861 Congressman Ln., Dallas, TX 75220: Free information ❖ Vacuum cleaner systems. 800-877-6631.

MidAmerica Vacuum Cleaner Supply Company, 666 University Ave., St. Paul, MN 55104: Catalog $5 ❖ Vacuum cleaners and parts, floor machines, and small kitchen appliances. 612-222-0763.

NuTone Inc., P.O. Box 1580, Cincinnati, OH 45201: Catalog $3 ❖ Vacuum cleaner systems. 800-543-8687.

Oreck Corporation, 100 Plantation Rd., New Orleans, LA 70123: Free catalog ❖ Vacuum cleaners. 800-989-4200.

Sew Vac City, 1667 Texas Ave., College Station, TX 77840: Brochure $3 ❖ Sewing machines and vacuum cleaners. 800-338-5672.

Sewin' in Vermont, 84 Concord Ave., St. Johnsbury, VT 05819: Free information ❖ Vacuum cleaners and attachments. 800-451-5124; 802-748-3803 (in VT).

Shop-Vac Corporation, 2323 Reach Rd., Williamsport, PA 17701: Free information ❖ Wet and dry vacuum cleaners. 717-326-0502.

Vacuflo, 512 W. Gorgas St., Louisville, OH 44641: Free list of retail sources ❖ Built-in central vacuum cleaner systems. 800-822-8356.

VIDEO CASSETTES, TAPES & DISCS

Ace Video & Music, 285 Caillavet St., P.O. Box 1934, Biloxi, MS 39533: Catalog $5 ❖ Pop and rock group LPs, pop and rock female vocal LPs, pop and rock male vocal LPs, soul-blues-R&B LPs, Jazz and instrumental LPs, movie and Broadway sound track LPs, country-western-folk LPs, comedy LPs, and New Orleans and South Louisiana 45s and CDs. 601-374-0777.

American Communications Network, 14 Ely St., Binghamton, NY 13904: Free catalog ❖ Art, children's learning, gardening, health, home improvement, pets, photography, sports, and other special interest videos and CD-ROMs. 607-724-3044.

Australian Catalogue Company, 7412 Wingfoot Dr., Raleigh, NC 27615: Free catalog ❖ Videos that take you around Australia. 919-878-8266.

BLT Supplies Inc., Mail Order Dept., 35-01 Queens Blvd., Long Island City, NY 11101: Free information ❖ Asian martial arts films. 800-322-2860.

Brooklyn Botanic Garden, Attention: Plants & Gardens, 1000 Washington Ave., Brooklyn, NY 11225: Free brochure ❖ Gardening books and videos. 718-622-4433.

Calibre Press Inc., 666 Dundee Rd., Ste. 1607, Northbrook, IL 60062: Free catalog ❖ Law enforcement and EMS videos, books, and survival equipment. 800-323-0037; 708-498-5680 (in IL).

Christian Book Distributors, P.O. Box 7000, Peabody, MA 01961: Free catalog ❖ Religious videos for children and adults. 508-977-5000.

Classic Cinema, P.O. Box 18932, Encino, CA 91416: Catalog $5 ❖ Westerns, mysteries, comedies, and drama on video cassettes. 800-94-MOVIE.

Collage Video Specialties Inc., 5390 Main St. NE, Minneapolis, MN 55421: Free catalog ❖ Video and audio exercise and workout cassettes. 800-433-6769.

Critics' Choice Video, P.O. Box 749, Itasca, IL 60143: Free catalog ❖ Classics, new releases, special interest, and other subjects on video cassettes. 800-544-9852.

Defender Industries Inc., 255 Main St., P.O. Box 820, New Rochelle, NY 10801: Free catalog ❖ Marine books and videos. 800-435-7180; 914-632-3001 (in NY).

Double-Time Jazz, Jamey & Julia Aebersold, P.O. Box 1244, New Albany, IN 47151: Free catalog ❖ Jazz records and videos.

Ergo Media, 668 Front St., P.O. Box 2037, Teaneck, NJ 07666: Free catalog ❖ Award-winning videos on all aspects of Jewish life. 800-695-3746.

Flora & Company Productions, P.O. Box 8263, Albuquerque, NM 87198: Free catalog ❖ Videos for performers and craftspeople. 505-255-9988.

Foothill Video, P.O. Box 547, Tujunga, CA 91043: Free information ❖ Westerns, serials, and other features on video cassettes. 818-353-8591.

Full Circle Records, 279 Road 41, Blackwood, NJ 08012: Free information ❖ New and used CDs, imported recordings, other records, and videos. 609-227-0662.

Fusion Video, 100 Fusion Way, Country Club Hills, IL 60478: Catalog $3.99 ❖ Science fiction videos.

P. Garofalo, P.O. Box 280-005, Brooklyn, NY 11228: Catalog $1 ❖ Rare videos.

Gingerbread Group, 1109 Rogeretta Dr., Atlanta, GA 30329: Free information ❖ Judaic holiday tales on video cassettes. 404-634-8866.

Gold Medal Hair Products, 1 Bennington Ave., Freeport, Long Island, NY 11520: Free catalog ❖ Action, comedy, vintage, drama, documentary, vintage and new releases, and other all Black American videos. 800-535-8101.

Great Christian Books, 229 S. Bridge St., P.O. Box 8000, Elkton, MD 21922: Free catalog ❖ Bible video games. 800-775-5422.

Good Music Record Company, P.O. Box 1935, Ridgely, MD 21681: Free catalog ❖ Compact discs, cassettes, and videos.

High View Publications, P.O. Box 51967, Pacific Grove, CA 93950: Free catalog ❖ Chinese martial arts books and videos. 408-655-2990.

❖ VIDEO CASSETTES, TAPES & DISCS ❖

Historic Aviation, 1401 Kings Wood Rd., Eagan, MN 55122: Free catalog ❖ Books and videos on the history of commercial airliners, famous men in aviation, nostalgic classics, humor, military action, and other aviation topics. 800-225-5575.

Home Film Festival, P.O. Box 2032, Scranton, PA 18501: Catalog $5 ❖ Hard-to-find films, limited release features, Hollywood classics, documentaries, and other videotapes. 800-258-3456.

The House of Music, 2057 W. 95th St., Chicago, IL 60643: Free information ❖ Hard-to-find records, tapes, CDs, and videos. 312-239-4114.

House of Tyrol, P.O. Box 909, Alpenland Center, Helen Highway/75 North, Cleveland, GA 30528: Free catalog ❖ Musical cuckoo clocks, crystal, porcelain, lamps, music boxes, other gifts, and travel, folk music from around the world, language, and educational videos. 800-241-5404.

International Historic Films Inc., Box 29035, Chicago, IL 60629: Catalog $2 ❖ Military, political, and historical documentary films on video cassettes. 312-927-2900.

Kimbo Educational, Dept. W, P.O. Box 477, Long Branch, NJ 07740: Free catalog ❖ Cassettes, CDs, records, videos, read-alongs, and film strips for children. 800-631-2187.

Kino Video, 333 W. 39th St., Ste. 503, New York, NY 10018: Free catalog ❖ International, foreign, and classic movies from Hollywood's golden era on video cassettes. 800-562-3330; 212-629-6880 (in NY).

Lark in the Morning, P.O. Box 1176, Mendocino, CA 95460: Free catalog ❖ Hard-to-find musical instruments, books about music, CDs and cassettes, and videos. 707-964-5569.

Lloyd's Special Interest Videos, 235 Oak St., Ste. 10, Brentwood, CA 94513: Free catalog ❖ How-to videos on academic studies, art and graphic design, business skills, children's learning, computers and electronics, cooking and entertaining, crafts and hobbies, exercise and fitness, gardening, home improvement, and other topics. 510-634-8751.

Melton Book Company, P.O. Box 140990, Nashville, TN 37214: Free catalog ❖ Christian books, bibles, audio and video recordings, and music. 800-441-0511.

Metropolitan Opera Guild, 835 Madison Ave., New York, NY 10021: Free catalog ❖ Books and classical, concert, operatic, and documentary videos, records, and compact disks. 212-634-8406.

Moviecraft Inc., P.O. Box 438, Orland Park, IL 60462: Catalog $1 ❖ Old TV shows, rare cartoons, classics, contemporary releases, war newsreels, propaganda subjects, special interest topics, and feature films. 708-460-9082.

Murrays Catamarans, P.O. Box 490, Carpinteria, CA 93014: Free list of retail sources ❖ Catamarans, factory parts, books, and videos. 800-788-8964.

Music Connection, 430 Market St., Elmwood Park, NJ 07407: Free information ❖ New and used CDs, imported recordings, and videos. 201-797-5212.

Music Dispatch, P.O. Box 13920, Milwaukee, WI 53213: Free catalog ❖ Books, cassettes, CDs, and videos for guitars and percussion and other instruments. 800-637-2852.

Music for Little People, P.O. Box 1720, Lawndale, CA 90260: Free catalog ❖ Famous stories, favorite songs, lullabies, nature stories, folk music, classical music, and other children's music cassettes and videos. 800-727-2233.

Music Hunter, 60 E. 42nd St., New York, NY 10165: Free information (specify items wanted) ❖ CDs, audio and video cassettes, laser discs, blank tapes, and accessories. 212-687-5039.

The Noontide Press, P.O. Box 2739, Newport Beach, CA 92659: Free catalog ❖ Books, audio tapes, and videos on social, political, economic, and historical taboos of the modern age. 714-631-1490.

Pacific Arts Publishing, 11858 La Grange Ave., Los Angeles, CA 90025: Free catalog ❖ Public television and other programs on video cassettes. 800-538-5856.

PBS Home Video, Catalog Fulfillment Center, P.O. Box 4030, Santa Monica, CA 90411: Free catalog ❖ Video cassettes. 800-645-4PBS.

PFS Video Inc., P.O. Box 50, Oley, PA 19547: Free information ❖ Martial arts videos on defense techniques. 610-689-5871.

The Planetary Society, 65 N. Catalina Ave., Pasadena, CA 91106: Free brochure ❖ Astronomy books, videos, and slide sets. 818-793-1675.

Precept Ministries, P.O. Box 182218, Chattanooga, TN 37422: Free catalog ❖ Religious books, audio cassettes, and videos. 615-894-3277.

Pyramid Film & Video, P.O. Box 1048, Santa Monica, CA 90404: Free information ❖ Films and videos for educational and entertainment programming. 800-421-2304.

Reader's Digest, P.O. Box 107, Pleasantville, NY 10571: Free catalog ❖ Videos on travel, nature, drama, movies, children's subjects, how-to-information, sports, and music. 914-241-7445.

Ridge Runner, 84 York Creek Dr., Driftwood, TX 78619: Catalog $1 ❖ Guitar instruction and entertainment videos.

Roots & Rhythm Inc., P.O. Box 837, El Cerrito, CA 94530: Catalog $5 (specify blues, country, or vintage rock and roll) ❖ Records, tapes, compact disks, music books, and videos. 510-525-1494.

Rose Records, 214 S. Wabash Ave., Chicago, IL 60604: Free catalog ❖ Classical and opera recordings on long-playing records, CDs, cassettes, and music videos. Includes imports, new releases, and overstocks. 800-955-ROSE.

SAIL Videos, P.O. Box 7820, Torrance, CA 90504: Free information ❖ Videos on how to sail boats better. 800-362-8433.

Ed Shea, P.O. Box 860089, Ridgewood, NY 11386: Free catalog with four 1st class stamps ❖ Hard-to-find horror, science-fiction, fantasy, and classic TV videos.

Shokus Video, P.O. Box 3125, Chatsworth, CA 91313: Catalog $3 (refundable) ❖ Classic TV shows. 818-704-0400.

Sinister Cinema, P.O. Box 4369, Medford, OR 97501: Free information ❖ Science fiction, horror, mystery, suspense, fantasy, and other films on video cassettes. 503-773-6860.

Sounds True Audio, 735 Walnut St., Boulder, CO 80302: Free catalog ❖ Audio and video recordings on personal discovery, relationships, sacred music of the world, homeopathy, psychology and the spirit, health and healing, and other life-related topics. 800-333-9185.

Stage Step, P.O. Box 328, Philadelphia, PA 19105: Free catalog ❖ Dance, theater, film, music, and fitness books, videos, and CDs. 800-523-0960.

Time Warner Viewer's Edge, P.O. Box 85098, Richmond, VA 23285: Free catalog ❖ One hundred years of movies on video cassettes, from 1895 to 1995. 800-305-1989.

TKD Enterprises Inc., 1423 18th St., Bettendorf, IA 52722: Free information: Free information ❖ Martial arts books, videos, and shoes. 800-388-5966.

Unique Publications, 4201 W. Vanowen Pl., Burbank, CA 91505: Free information ❖ Martial arts videos. 800-332-3330.

Video Alternative, D. Freifeld, 244 Madison Ave., Ste. 334, New York, NY 10016: List $3 ❖ Videos.

Video Opera House, P.O. Box 800, Concord, MA 01742: Free catalog ❖ Opera, ballet, and classical video recordings. 800-99-OPERA.

Walden Video for Kids, 201 High Ridge Rd., Stamford, CT 06904: Free catalog ❖ Children's video tapes. 203-352-2092.

Whole Person Associates, 210 W. Michigan, Duluth, MN 55802: Free catalog ❖ Self-improvement books and videos on wellness promotion, stress management, and relaxation. 800-247-6789.

Windsurfing Express, 6043 NW 167th St., Miami, FL 33015: Free brochure ❖ Books and videos on windsurfing. 800-843-7873.

Wolverine Sports, 745 State Circle, Box 1941, Ann Arbor, MI 48106: Catalog $1 ❖ Sports instructional videos. 313-761-5691.

Woodworkers' Discount Books & Videos, 1649 Turn Point Rd., Friday Harbor, WA 98250: Free catalog ❖ How-to books and videos on woodworking. 800-378-4060.

YMAA Publication Center, 38 Hyde Park Ave., Jamaica Plain, MA 02130: Free catalog ❖ Martial arts books, videos, clothing, and music. 800-669-8892.

VISION IMPAIRMENT AIDS

American Council of the Blind, 1155 15th St. NW, Washington, DC 20005: Free list ❖ Large-print list of low vision aids and large-print publications. 202-467-5081.

American Foundation for the Blind Inc., Product Center, 3342 Melrose Ave., Roanoke, VA 24017: Free catalog ❖ Describes products available from the American Foundation for the Blind. 800-829-0500.

American Printing House for the Blind, 1839 Frankfort Ave., P.O. Box 6085, Louisville, KY 40206: Free catalog ❖ Braille writing and embossing equipment, electronic devices, low-vision simulation materials, reading readiness products, and educational aids. 800-223-1839; 502-895-2405 (in KY).

G & R Publishing Company, 507 Industrial St., Waverly, IA 50677: Free information ❖ Sign language workbooks. 800-383-1679.

Independent Living Aids/Can-Do Products, 27 East Mall, Plainview, NY 11803: Free catalog ❖ Writing aids, low-vision and braille items, household items, home health care supplies, mobility equipment, and communication aids. 800-537-2118; 516-752-8080 (in NY).

LS & S Group Inc., P.O. Box 673, Northbrook, IL 60065: Free catalog ❖ Magnifiers, watches, braille computers, gifts, and other products for people with visual impairments. 800-468-4789; 708-498-9777 (in IL).

Maxi-Aids, 42 Executive Blvd., Farmingdale, NY 11735: Free catalog ❖ Aids and appliances for people with visual, physical, hearing, and other impairments. 800-522-6294.

On the Move Inc., 334 Franklin St., Mansfield, MA 02048: Free brochure ❖ Mobility aid for visually impaired persons, from age 2 to adults. 508-339-4027.

Science Products, Box 888, Southeastern, PA 19399: Free catalog ❖ Voice technology equipment and other sensory aids for hearing and visually impaired persons. 800-888-7400; 215-296-2111 (in PA).

VITAMINS & NUTRITIONAL SUPPLEMENTS

ASF Enterprises Inc., 1588 Cardinal Dr., St. Joseph, MI 49085: Free catalog ❖ Multiple vitamins, gourmet herbal teas, and health and nutritional supplements.

Barth Vitamins, 3890 Park Central Blvd. North, Pompano Beach, FL 33064: Free catalog ❖ Natural vitamin and mineral supplements, cosmetics, health foods, and home health aids. 800-645-2328.

Bioenergy Nutrients, 6565 Odell Pl., Boulder, CO 80301: Catalog $1 ❖ Nutritional supplements, homeopathic medicines, antioxidants, and all-natural skin care products. 800-627-7775.

Brownville Mills, Box 145, Brownville, NE 68321: Free price list ❖ Fresh natural foods and vitamins. 800-305-7990; 402-825-4131 (in NE).

Earth Science Inc., P.O. Box 1925, Corona, CA 91718: Free catalog ❖ Skin and hair care preparations, vitamins, and nutrients. 714-692-7190.

Freeda Vitamins, 36 E. 41st St., New York, NY 10017: Free catalog ❖ Vitamins and dietary food supplements. 800-777-3737; 212-685-4980 (in NY).

General Nutrition Catalog, Puritan's Pride, 105 Orville Dr., Bohemia, NY 11716: Free catalog ❖ Vitamins, health foods, natural cosmetics, books, and gifts. 800-645-1030.

Gluten-Free Pantry, P.O. Box 881, Glastonbury, CT 06033: Free information ❖ Gluten-free vitamins. 203-633-3826.

Health Center for Better Living, 1414 Rosemary Ln., Naples, FL 33940: Free catalog ❖ Vitamins and minerals and other herbal health care products. 800-544-4225.

Hillestad Corporation, AV 178 US Hwy. 51 North, Woodruff, WI 54568: Free catalog ❖ Natural vitamins. 800-535-7742; 715-358-2113 (in WI).

Indiana Botanic Gardens Inc., 3401 W. 317th Ave., Hammond, IN 46325: Free catalog ❖ Vitamins, herbs, spices, and personal care products.

L & H Vitamins Inc., 32-33 47th Ave., Long Island City, NY 11101: Free catalog ❖ Vitamins and nutritional supplements, homeopathic medicines, aromatherapy products, and natural health care products. 800-221-1152; 618-937-7400 (in NY).

Lee Nutrition, 290 Main St., Cambridge, MA 02142: Free information ❖ Vitamins and nutritional supplements.

Nutrition Headquarters, One Nutrition Plaza, Carbondale, IL 62901: Free catalog ❖ Vitamins and mineral supplements, health and beauty aids, and herbal formulas.

Nutrition Warehouse, 106 E. Jericho Tnpk., P.O. Box 311, Mineola, NY 11501: Free catalog ❖ Vitamins and nutritional supplements. 800-645-2929.

Oleda & Company Inc., 6467 Southwest Blvd., Fort Worth, TX 76132: Free catalog ❖ Nutrition, health, and beauty aids. 817-731-1147.

Ozark Herb & Spice Company, RR 2, Box 2409, Pineville, MO 64856: Free information ❖ Vitamins, herbs, and nutritional supplements. 417-226-4620.

Puritan's Pride, 1233 Montauk Hwy., P.O. Box 9001, Oakdale, NY 11769: Free catalog ❖ Natural vitamins and health and beauty aids. 800-645-1030.

Puritan's Pride/Stur-Dee Health Products, 1233 Montauk Hwy., P.O. Box 9001, Oakdale, NY 11769: Free catalog ❖ Vitamins and health food supplements. 800-645-1030.

SDV Vitamins, P.O. Box 9215, Delray Beach, FL 33482: Free information ❖ Nutritional supplements and vitamins. 800-738-8482.

Spice Discounters, P.O. Box 6061, Aberdeen, SD 57401: Free catalog ❖ Herbs, spices, oils, extracts, and vitamins. 800-610-5950.

Star Pharmaceuticals Inc., 1500 New Horizons Blvd., Amityville, NY 11701: Free catalog ❖ Generic vitamins, nutritional supplements, toiletries, health care products, and pet supplies. 800-274-6400.

Stony Mountain Natural Foods & Herbs, P.O. Box 27, 3062 SR 3, Loudonville, OH 44842: Free information ❖ Nutritional supplements, spices, teas, and herbs. 419-994-4857.

Sunburst Biorganics, 832 Merrick Rd., Baldwin, NY 11510: Free catalog ❖ Nutritional supplements and toiletries. 800-645-8448.

Swanson Health Products Inc., The Swanson Building, 1322 39th St., P.O. Box 2803, Fargo, ND 58108: Free information ❖ Vitamins and food supplements. 800-437-4148.

U.S. Health Club Inc., P.O. Box 293, Yonkers, NY 10702: Free catalog ❖ Vitamins, nutritional supplements, and health preparations. 800-431-2186; 914-478-2505 (in NY).

Vitamin Co-Op, 13208 W. Washington Blvd., Los Angeles, CA 90066: Free catalog ❖ Vitamins, nutritional supplements, skin care products, and herbs. 310-823-7773.

Vitamin Direct Inc., P.O. Box 1983, San Marcos, CA 92079: Free catalog ❖ Vitamins, minerals, and nutritional supplements. 800-468-4027; 619-738-4940 (in CA).

Vitamin Power of Texas, P.O. Box 365, Bulverde, TX 78163: Free information ❖ Skin care products, vitamins, and nutritional supplements.

VOLLEYBALL

The Vitamin Shoppe, 4700 Westside Ave., North Bergen, NJ 07047: Free catalog ❖ Vitamins, herbs, homeopathic medicines, and pure and natural cosmetics. 800-223-1216.

Vitamin Specialties Company, 11445 Cronhill Dr., Owings Mills, MD 21117: Free catalog ❖ Vitamin supplements. 800-365-8482.

VP Health Savings Center, 3890 Park Central Blvd., North Pompano Beach, FL 33064: Free catalog ❖ Vitamins, natural supplements, and cosmetics and beauty aids. 800-645-2978.

VOLLEYBALL

Clothing

Action Sport Systems Inc., P.O. Box 1442, Morgantown, NC 28680: Free information ❖ Uniforms. 800-631-1091; 704-584-8000 (in NC).

Adidas USA, 5675 N. Blackstock Rd., Spartanburg, SC 29303: Free list of retail sources ❖ Shoes. 800-423-4327.

Asics Tiger Corporation, 10540 Talbert Ave., West Building, Fountain Valley, CA 92708: Free information ❖ Shoes and uniforms. 800-678-9435.

Champion Products Inc., 475 Corporate Square Dr., Winston Salem, NC 27105: Free information ❖ Uniforms.

Converse Inc., 1 Fordham Rd., North Reading, MA 01864: Free information ❖ Shoes. 800-428-2667; 508-664-1100 (in MA).

Flaghouse, 150 N. MacQuesten Pkwy., Mt. Vernon, NY 10550: Free catalog ❖ Volleyball equipment. 800-793-7900.

Foot-Joy & Titleist Worldwide, P.O. Box 965, Fairhaven, MA 02719: Free list of retail sources ❖ Golf shoes. 508-979-2000.

Mizuno Corporation, 651 Gateway Blvd., Ste. 300, South San Francisco, CA 94080: Free information ❖ Uniforms and shoes. 800-966-1211.

Nike Footwear Inc., One Bowerman Dr., Beaverton, OR 97005: Free list of retail sources ❖ Shoes. 800-344-6453.

Puma USA Inc., 147 Centre St., Brockton, MA 02403: Free information with long SASE ❖ Shoes. 508-583-9100.

Spike Nashbar, 4111 Simion Rd., Youngstown, OH 44512: Free information ❖ Shoes and equipment. 800-774-5348.

Sport Fun Inc., 4621 Sperry St., Los Angeles, CA 90039: Free information ❖ Uniforms and shoes. 800-423-2597; 818-240-6700 (in CA).

Sportline of Hilton Head Ltd., 816 Friendly Center Rd., Greensboro, NC 27408: Free information ❖ Volleyballs. 800-438-6021.

Venus Knitting Mills Inc., 140 Spring St., Murray Hill, NJ 07974: Free information ❖ Uniforms. 800-955-4200; 908-464-2400 (in NJ).

Equipment

Action Sport Systems Inc., P.O. Box 1442, Morgantown, NC 28680: Free information ❖ Volleyball sets, nets, posts, and standards. 800-631-1091; 704-584-8000 (in NC).

American Athletic Inc., 200 American Ave., Jefferson, IA 50129: Free information ❖ Nets. 800-247-3978; 515-386-3125 (in IA).

Cannon Sports, P.O. Box 797, Greenland, NH 03840: Free list of retail sources ❖ Nets and balls. 800-362-3146.

Franklin Sports Industries Inc., 17 Campanelli Pkwy., P.O. Box 508, Stoughton, MA 02072: Free information ❖ Volleyball sets, balls, and nets. 800-426-7700.

Gared Sports Inc., 1107 Mullanphy St., St. Louis, MO 63106: Free information ❖ Nets, posts, standards, and balls. 800-325-2682.

General Sportcraft Company, 140 Woodbine Rd., Bergenfield, NJ 07621: Free information ❖ Nets, posts, standards, balls, and protective gear. 201-384-4242.

Indian Industries Inc., P.O. Box 889, Evansville, IN 47706: Free catalog ❖ Nets and sets. 800-457-3373; 812-467-1200 (in IN).

Jayfro Corporation, Unified Sports Inc., 976 Hartford Tnpk., P.O. Box 400, Waterford, CT 06385: Free catalog ❖ Nets, posts, referee stands, and equipment carriers. 860-447-3001.

Dick Martin Sports Inc., 181 E. Union Ave., P.O. Box 7384, East Rutherford, NJ 07073: Free information ❖ Nets, posts, balls, and protective gear. 800-221-1993; 201-453-5255 (in NJ).

Spalding Sports Worldwide, 425 Meadow St., P.O. Box 901, Chicopee, MA 01021: Free list of retail sources ❖ Nets, posts, standards, and balls. 800-225-6601.

Spike Nashbar, 4111 Simion Rd., Youngstown, OH 44512: Free information ❖ Shoes and equipment. 800-774-5348.

Volleyball One, 15392 Assembly Ln., Ste. A, Huntington Beach, CA 92649: Catalog $3 (refundable) ❖ Volleyball equipment. 800-950-8844.

Wilson Sporting Goods, 8700 W. Bryn Mawr, Chicago, IL 60631: Free information ❖ Balls. 800-443-0011.

WATER PURIFIERS

Action Filter Inc., 239 Schuyler Ave., Ste. 7, Kingston, PA 18704: Free information ❖ Easy-to-install water filtration system. 800-520-5121.

American Health Solutions, 801 West Fwy., Ste. 715, Grand Prairie, TX 75051: Free information ❖ Easy-to-install in-home water treatment system. 800-360-7417.

Aquathin Corporation, 950 S. Andrews Ave., Pompano Beach, FL 33069: Free information ❖ Portable water purifier. 800-462-7634.

Basic Designs Inc., 5815 Bennett Valley Rd., Santa Rosa, CA 95404: Free information ❖ High-flow and pocket-size water filters. 707-575-1220.

Climb High Inc., 1861 Shelburne Rd., Shelburne, VT 05482: Free catalog ❖ Water purifiers. 802-985-5056.

Creative Solutions, P.O. Box 400821, Des Moines, IA 50347: Free information ❖ Water filter systems. 800-666-6421.

Filtration Concepts, 2226 S. Fairview, Santa Ana, CA 92704: Free brochure ❖ Water recovery systems. 714-850-0123.

General Ecology Inc., 151 Sheree Blvd., Exton, PA 19341: Free list of retail sources ❖ Portable, base camp, and travel-type water purifiers. 800-441-8166.

Global Water Technology, Division Village Marine Tec., 2000 W. 135th St., Gardena, CA 90249: Free information ❖ Water purification systems for installation on boats and land. 310-516-9911.

HRO Systems, P.O. Box 2560, Gardena, CA 90247: Free brochure ❖ Modular and compact water desalination equipment for boats. 310-327-2600.

Katadyn, Geneva Rd., Brewster, NY 10509: Free list of retail sources ❖ Water purification equipment. 800-431-2204.

Matrix Desalination Inc., 3295 SW 11th Ave., Fort Lauderdale, FL 33315: Free information ❖ Desalinization equipment. 305-524-5120.

Mountain Safety Research, P.O. Box 24547, Seattle, WA 98124: Free list of retail sources ❖ Portable water purification equipment. 800-877-9677; 206-624-8573 (in WA).

National Offshore Marine Laboratories, 22994 El Toro Rd., Ste. 105, Lake Forest, CA 92630: Catalog $5.25 ❖ Water purification systems and equipment. 800-458-3365; 714-455-0711 (in CA).

PentaPure, WTC Industries Inc., 14405 21st Ave. North, Minneapolis, MN 55447: Free catalog ❖ Water treatment equipment. 800-637-1244.

PUR Water Purifiers, 2229 Edgewood Ave. South, Minneapolis, MN 55426: Free list of retail sources ❖ Self-cleaning water purifier. 800-845-PURE.

Qelags USA Inc., 1705 14th St., Boulder, CO 80302: Free catalog ❖ Water purification systems. 303-440-8047.

Recovery Engineering, 2229 Edgewood Ave. South, Minneapolis, MN 55426: Free information ❖ Lightweight water purification equipment. 800-548-0406.

Reverse Osmosis, 12301 SW 133rd Ct., Miami, FL 33186: Free brochure ❖ Water recovery systems. 305-255-8115.

Sea Recovery Corporation, P.O. Box 2560, Gardena, CA 90247: Free brochure ❖ Water recovery systems. 800-354-2000; 310-327-4000 (in CA).

Silos Products Inc., 2139 N. University Dr., Coral Springs, FL 33071: Free brochure ❖ Portable air cleaners, water filtration and dental hygienic cleaning systems, and accessories. 800-762-3355.

SpectraPure, 738 S. Perry Ln., Tempe, AZ 85281: Free information ❖ Water purification systems. 800-685-2783.

SweetWater Inc., 2505 Trade Centre Ave., Ste. D, Longmont, CO 80503: Free list of retail sources ❖ Water purification systems. 800-55-SWEET.

Universal Aqua Technologies, 10555 Norwalk Blvd., Santa Fe Springs, CA 90670: Free brochure ❖ Water recovery systems. 800-777-6939.

Village Marine Tec., 2000 W. 135th St., Gardena, CA 90249: Free brochure ❖ Reverse osmosis water purification systems. 800-421-4503; 310-516-9911 (in CA).

Water Makers Inc., 2233 S. Andrews Ave., Fort Lauderdale, FL 33316: Free brochure ❖ Water recovery systems. 305-467-8920.

WATER SKIING

Clothing

Barefoot International, 6160 N. 60th St., Milwaukee, WI 53218: Free information ❖ Wet, dry suits, and barefoot suits. Also ropes and handles. 800-932-0685; 414-466-3668 (in WI).

Bart's Water Ski Center, P.O. Box 294, North Webster, IN 46555: Free catalog ❖ Kneeboards, ropes and handles, gloves, water toys, ski boards, wet and dry suits, and T-shirts. 800-348-5016.

Body Glove International, 530 6th St., Hermosa Beach, CA 90254: Free information ❖ Wet and barefoot suits. 800-678-7873; 310-374-4074 (in CA).

Connelly Skis Inc., P.O. Box 716, Lynnwood, WA 98046: Free information ❖ Water skis, ropes, gloves, vests, trick harnesses, boat harnesses, ski racks, and videos. 206-775-5416.

Harvey's Skin Diving Suits Inc., 2505 S. 252nd St., Kent, WA 98032: Free information ❖ Wet and dry suits. 800-347-0054; 206-824-1114 (in WA).

Jobe Ski Corporation, 15320 NE 92nd St., Redmond, WA 98052: Free information ❖ Water skis, wet suits, gloves, handles and ropes, boat and trick harnesses, vests, ski racks, and videos. 206-882-1177.

O'Brien International, P.O. Box 97020, Redmond, WA 98073: Free information ❖ Water skis, ropes and handles, boat harnesses, vests, ski and kneeboard racks, tubes, and gloves. 206-881-5900.

Overton's Sports Center Inc., P.O. Box 8228, Greenville, NC 27835: Free catalog ❖ Water skis, wet and dry suits, ropes, and handles. 800-334-6541.

Ski Limited, 7825 South Ave., Youngstown, OH 44512: Free catalog ❖ Vests, ski ropes and handles, and wet, dry, and barefoot suits. 800-477-4040.

Ski Warm, P.O. Box 726, Lynnwood, WA 98046: Free list of retail sources ❖ Wet suits, flotation vests, and accessories. 800-444-7848.

Stearns Manufacturing, P.O. Box 1498, St. Cloud, MN 56302: Free information ❖ Flotation equipment and water skiing vests. 800-697-5801; 612-252-1642 (in MN).

Surfer House, P.O. Box 726, Lynwood, WA 98046: Free list of retail sources ❖ Wet and dry suits and clothing for other water sports. 800-444-7848.

Thunderwear Inc., 1060 E. Calle Negocio, San Clemente, CA 92672: Free information ❖ Gloves. 800-422-6565.

Wellington Leisure Products, P.O. Box 244, Madison, GA 30650: Free information ❖ Water skis, gloves, ropes and handles, kneeboards and ski boards, trick and boat harnesses, videos, and ski racks. 706-342-4915.

Yamaha Motor Corporation, P.O. Box 6555, Cypress, CA 90630: Free list of retail sources ❖ Wet suits. 800-526-6650.

Equipment

Aamstrand Corporation, 629 Grove, Manteno, IL 60950: Free information ❖ Water skiing equipment. 800-338-0557; 312-458-8550 (in IL).

Barefoot International, 6160 N. 60th St., Milwaukee, WI 53218: Free information ❖ Wet, dry suits, and barefoot suits. Also ropes and handles. 800-932-0685; 414-466-3668 (in WI).

Bart's Water Ski Center, P.O. Box 294, North Webster, IN 46555: Free catalog ❖ Kneeboards, ropes and handles, gloves, water toys, ski boards, wet and dry suits, and T-shirts. 800-348-5016.

L.S. Brown Company, Pawley Industries Corporation, 3610 Atlanta Industrial Dr. NW, Atlanta, GA 30331: Free information ❖ Water skiing and marine sport equipment. 404-691-8200.

Buckeye Sports Supply, John's Sporting Goods, 2655 Harrison Ave. SW, Canton, OH 44706: Free information ❖ Water skiing equipment. 800-533-8691.

Burbank Water Ski Company, 1861 Victory Pl., Burbank, CA 91504: Free catalog ❖ Water skis, wakeboards, tubes, and accessories. 800-352-0572; 818-848-8808 (in CA).

Connelly Skis Inc., P.O. Box 716, Lynnwood, WA 98046: Free information ❖ Water skis, ropes, gloves, vests, trick harnesses, boat harnesses, ski racks, and videos. 206-775-5416.

Jobe Ski Corporation, 15320 NE 92nd St., Redmond, WA 98052: Free information ❖ Water skis, wet suits, gloves, handles and ropes, boat and trick harnesses, vests, ski racks, and videos. 206-882-1177.

Kransco Manufacturing, 333 Continental Blvd., El Segundo, CA 90245: Free information ❖ Water skis and ski boards.

Lynton Manufacturing, 442 Higgins Ave., Winnipeg, Manitoba, Canada R3A 1S5: Free information ❖ Knee boards and ski boards. 204-942-1166.

Maherajah Water Skis, 1595 University Rd., Hopland, CA 95449: Free information ❖ Water skis. 707-744-1816.

O'Brien International, P.O. Box 97020, Redmond, WA 98073: Free information ❖ Water skis, ropes and handles, boat harnesses, vests, ski and kneeboard racks, tubes, and gloves. 206-881-5900.

Overton's Sports Center Inc., P.O. Box 8228, Greenville, NC 27835: Free catalog ❖ Water skis, wet and dry suits, ropes, and handles. 800-334-6541.

Power-Sail Corporation, 47 E. Main St., P.O. Box 856, Flemington, NJ 08822: Free brochure ❖ Ascending parachutes. 800-426-3316; 908-782-9344 (in NJ).

RM Water Skis USA, 267 Columbia Ave., Chapin, SC 29036: Free information ❖ Slalom skis and knee boards. 800-433-8313.

Ski Limited, 7825 South Ave., Youngstown, OH 44512: Free catalog ❖ Vests, ski ropes and handles, and wet, dry, and barefoot suits. 800-477-4040.

Ski Warm, P.O. Box 726, Lynnwood, WA 98046: Free list of retail sources ❖ Wet suits, flotation vests, and accessories. 800-444-7848.

Stearns Manufacturing, P.O. Box 1498, St. Cloud, MN 56302: Free information ❖ Flotation equipment and water skiing vests. 800-697-5801; 612-252-1642 (in MN).

Tackle Shack, 7801 66th St. North, Pinellas Park, FL 34665: Free catalog ❖ Water skiing equipment. (813) 546-5080.

❖ **WEATHER FORECASTING** ❖ 433

Wellington Leisure Products, P.O. Box 244, Madison, GA 30650: Free information ❖ Water skis, gloves, ropes and handles, kneeboards and ski boards, trick and boat harnesses, videos, and ski racks. 706-342-4915.

WEATHER FORECASTING

Abbeon Cal Inc., 123 Gray Ave., Santa Barbara, CA 93101: Free catalog ❖ Thermometers, hygrometers, moisture meters, and humidity indicators. 805-966-0810.

Accu-Weather Inc., 619 W. College Ave., State College, PA 16801: Free information ❖ IBM compatible/modem on-line weather data base information system. 800-341-1262.

Advanced Receiver Research, P.O. Box 1242, Burlington, CT 06013: Free information ❖ Weather satellite information-management equipment. 203-584-0776.

Alden Electronics, 40 Washington St., Westborough, MA 01581: Free information ❖ Weather radar equipment, weather graphics systems, and radio facsimile weather chart recorder kits. 800-876-1232.

American Weather Enterprises, P.O. Box 1383, Media, PA 19063: Free catalog ❖ Electronic weather stations that provide electronic readouts of barometric pressure, daily and cumulative rainfall, indoor and outdoor temperatures, and wind speed and direction. 800-293-2555.

Boltek Corporation, 2316 Delaware Ave., #254, Buffalo, NY 14216: Free information ❖ Storm-tracking software for PCs. 905-734-8045.

Communications Electronics Inc., P.O. Box 1045, Ann Arbor, MI 48106: Free information ❖ Weather forecasting equipment and scanners. 313-996-8888.

C. Crane Company, 558 10th St., Fortuna, CA 95540: Free catalog ❖ AM/FM radios, long and shortwave equipment, scanners, books, and weather equipment. 800-522-8863.

Davis Instruments, 3465 Diablo Ave., Hayward, CA 94545: Free information ❖ Professional weather station for home use. Also other state-of-the-art instruments. 800-678-3669.

Edmund Scientific Company, Edscorp Building, Barrington, NJ 08007: Free catalog ❖ Weather forecasting instruments, microscopes, magnifiers, magnets, telescopes, binoculars, and other science equipment. 609-573-6260.

Fascinating Electronics Inc., 31525 Canaan Rd., Deer Island, OR 97054: Free brochure ❖ Full-size weather-monitoring instruments. Available assembled or build-them-yourself kits. 800-683-5487.

Hinds Instruments Inc., 3175 NW Aloclek Dr., Hillsboro, OR 97124: Free information ❖ Electronic weather data display station that can be linked directly to a computer modem or printer to provide a visible or audible record. 800-688-4463; 503-690-2000 (in OR).

Innovation Clock-Making Specialties, 11869 Teale St., Culver City, CA 90230: Free catalog ❖ Clock-making components and weather instruments. 800-421-4445; 310-398-8116 (in CA).

Klockit, P.O. Box 636, Lake Geneva, WI 53147: Free catalog ❖ Instruments for building weather/time stations, Swiss music box movements, and clock-building parts and supplies. 800-556-2548.

Luctor Canada, Division Emergo Inc., P.O. Box 1330, Brantford, Ontario, Canada N3T 5T6: Free information ❖ Weather satellite image capture and processing system for Windows 3.1 and Windows Workgroups 3.11. 800-668-3224.

Maximum Inc., 30 Barnett Blvd., New Bedford, MA 02745: Free catalog ❖ Instruments for wind, weather, tide, and time measurement with optional digital and analog versions. 508-995-2200.

MultiFax, Rt. 1, Box 27, Peachland, NC 28133: Free information ❖ Weather imaging software for IBM compatible computers. 704-272-9028.

OFS WeatherFAX, 6404 Lakerest Ct., Raleigh, NC 27612: Free information ❖ PC-based weather satellite image capturing system. 919-847-4545.

Oregon Scientific, 18383 SW Boones Ferry Rd., Portland, OR 97224: Free brochure ❖ Weather forecasting and temperature monitoring equipment. 800-863-8883.

PC Weather Products Inc., P.O. Box 72723, Marietta, GA 30007: Free information ❖ Windows-based hurricane and storm-tracking software. 800-605-2230.

Peet Bros. Company, 1308 Doris Ave., Ocean, NJ 07712: Free brochure ❖ Home weather stations. 800-USA-PEET; 908-531-4615 (in NJ).

Sensor Instruments Company Inc., 41 Terrill Dr., Concord, NH 03301: Free information ❖ Weather instruments. 800-633-1033.

SensorMetrics, P.O. Box 1049, Lakeville, MA 02347: Free information ❖ Temperature, humidity, pressure, wind, solar, rainfall, and other environmental monitoring equipment for display of data on PCs. 508-946-4904.

Simerl Instruments, 528 Epping Forest Rd., Annapolis, MD 21401: Free brochure ❖ Weather forecasting instruments. 410-849-8667.

Spectrum International, P.O. Box 1084, Concord, MA 01742: Free information ❖ Weather satellite information-management equipment. 508-263-2145.

Swift Instruments Inc., 952 Dorchester Ave., Boston, MA 02125: Free list of retail sources ❖ Telescopes, weather instruments, binoculars, and other optics. 800-446-1115; 617-436-2960 (in MA).

Texas Weather Instruments Inc., 5942 Abrams Rd., Dallas, TX 75231: Free information ❖ Easy-to-operate weather station. 800-284-0245; 214-368-7116 (in TX).

Vanguard Electronics Labs, 196-23 Jamaica Ave., Hollis, NY 11423: Free information ❖ Weather satellite information-management equipment. 718-468-2720.

Vetus-Denouden Inc., P.O. Box 8712, Baltimore, MD 21230: Free information ❖ Wind and weather forecasting equipment for boats. 410-712-0740.

Weather Bureau, P.O. Box 1045, Ann Arbor, MI 48106: Free information ❖ Scanners, transceivers, emergency broadcast equipment, weather stations and monitoring equipment, and other electronics. 313-996-8888.

WeatherTrac, P.O. Box 122, Cedar Falls, IA 50613: Free catalog ❖ Weather forecasting instruments, weather vanes, and educational aids. 800-798-8724.

Robert E. White Instruments Inc., 34 Commercial Wharf, Boston, MA 02110: Free catalog ❖ Electronic equipment for measuring indoor and outdoor temperatures and time of occurrence. 800-992-3045.

Wind & Weather, P.O. Box 2320, Mendocino, CA 95460: Free catalog ❖ Barometers, thermometers, hygrometers, psychrometers, wind direction instruments, anemometers, weather vanes, sundials, rain gauges, cloud charts, and books. 707-964-1284.

YFX/Information by FAX, Alden Electronics, 40 Washington St., Westborough, MA 01581: Free information ❖ Weather information system by fax machine. 800-876-1232.

WEATHER VANES

A.J.P. Coppersmith & Company, 20 Industrial Pkwy., Woburn, MA 01801: Catalog $3 ❖ Handcrafted copper, tin, or brass reproduction colonial lanterns, chandeliers, sconces, cupolas, and weather vanes. 800-545-1776.

Antique Hardware Store, 1 Matthews Ct., Hilton Head Island, SC 29926: Catalog $3 ❖ Antique-style indoor and outdoor lamps and lighting fixtures, pedestal sinks, faucets, high tank toilets, cabinet hardware, weather vanes, and tin and wooden chandeliers. 800-422-9982.

Berry-Hill Limited, 75 Burwell Rd., St. Thomas, Ontario, Canada N5P 3R5: Catalog $2 ❖ Weather vanes, canning equipment, cider press, and garden tools. 519-631-0480.

Cape Cod Cupola Company Inc., 78 State Rd., North Dartmouth, MA 02747: Catalog $2 (refundable) ❖ Early American-style weather vanes and cupolas. 508-994-1956.

434 ❖ WEDDING INVITATIONS & ACCESSORIES ❖

Colonial Casting Company Inc., 68 Liberty St., Haverhill, MA 01832: Catalog $3 ❖ Handcrafted lead-free pewter miniature castings, handmade copper weather vanes, and lighting. 508-374-8783.

Colonial Cupolas, P.O. Box 38, 1816 Nemoke Trail, Haslett, MI 48840: Brochure $3 ❖ Wooden cupolas and aluminum or copper weathervanes. Includes build-it-yourself kits. 800-678-1965.

Copper House, RFD 1, Box 4, Epsom, NH 03234: Catalog $3 ❖ Hand-hammered copper weather vanes and indoor and outdoor lanterns. 603-736-9798.

Crosswinds Gallery, 15 Francis St., Bristol, RI 02809: Free catalog ❖ Cupolas and copper, gold leaf-decorated, aluminum, and wooden weather vanes. 800-638-8263.

Denninger Cupolas & Weathervanes, RD 1, Box 447, Middletown, NY 10940: Catalog $4 ❖ Weather vanes and redwood cupolas with copper roofs. 914-343-2229.

Fischer Artworks, 6530 S. Windmere, Littleton, CO 80120: Free catalog ❖ Copper and cast-bronze Victorian-style weather vanes. 303-798-4841.

David & Martha Fletcher, Blue Mist Morgan Farm, 68 Liberty St., Haverhill, MA 01830: Catalog $3 ❖ Handcrafted copper weather vanes and lanterns. 508-374-8783.

Iron Craft, Old Rt. 28, P.O. Box 351, Ossipee, NH 03864: Free catalog ❖ Kettles and grates, enameled cookware, butcher aprons, bellows, heating systems for fireplaces, weather vanes, signs, gifts, and cast-iron items. 603-539-2807.

Marian Ives Weathervanes, Box 101, RR 1, Charlemont, MA 01339: Free brochure ❖ One-of-a-kind custom-designed metal weather vanes. 413-339-8534.

Q.B. Logan, 270 Rt. 35, Dayton, ME 04005: Free information ❖ Hand-carved weather vanes finished in 24K gold leaf over solid mahogany. 207-499-2486.

Walter Massey, 108 W. Cotton Ave., Black Mountain, NC 28711: Free brochure ❖ Hand-sculptured copper weather vanes. 704-669-2162.

Barry Norling Weathervanes, Beech Hill Rd., RFD 1, Box 5190, Skowhegan, ME 04976: Free brochure ❖ Handcrafted copper weather vanes. 207-474-2738.

Tom Outhouse, 2853 Lincoln Hwy. East, Ronks, PA 17572: Free catalog ❖ Antique and polished copper weather vanes with solid brass directional indicators and stainless steel chimney caps. Also cupolas. 800-346-7678.

Redwood Unlimited, P.O. Box 2344, Valley Center, CA 92082: Brochure $2 ❖ Weather vanes and post-mounted California redwood, cedar, and pine mailboxes. 800-283-1717.

Salt & Chestnut, Box 41, West Barnstable, MA 02668: Catalog $2 (refundable) ❖ Handcrafted weather vanes.

Travis Tuck, Metal Sculptor, Box 1832, Martha's Vineyard, MA 02568: Brochure $1 ❖ Sculpted metal weather vanes. 508-693-3914.

Wagonmaster Antiques, 409 N. Stark, Bennington, KS 67422: Free information ❖ American eagle-decorated weather vanes. 913-488-2136.

The Weathervane, 108 E. Front St., Traverse City, MI 49684: Brochure $1 ❖ Polished copper and antiqued-green weather vanes. 800-332-2460.

West Coast Weathervanes, 417-C Ingalls St., Santa Cruz, CA 95060: Free information ❖ Handcrafted and limited edition copper weather vanes and finials. 408-425-5505.

Westwinds, 3540 76th St. SE, Caledonia, MI 49316: Free brochure ❖ Weather vanes, post and mailbox signs, and hitching posts. 800-635-5262.

Wind & Weather, P.O. Box 2320, Mendocino, CA 95460: Free catalog ❖ Sundials, weather vanes, and weather forecasting instruments. 707-964-1284.

Windleaves Weathervanes, 7560 Morningside Dr., Indianapolis, IN 46240: Free brochure ❖ Weather vanes. 317-251-1381.

WEDDING INVITATIONS & ACCESSORIES

The American Wedding Album, American Stationery Company Inc., 300 Park Ave., Peru, IN 46970: Free catalog ❖ Wedding invitations, stationery, and gifts. 800-822-2577.

Ann's Wedding Stationery, P.O. Box, Milan, IN 47031: Free catalog ❖ Wedding invitations and accessories. 800-557-2667.

Creations by Elaine, 6253 W. 74th St., Box 2001, Bedford Park, IL 60499: Free catalog ❖ Wedding invitations and stationery, cake knives and servers, reception and ceremony accessories, and jewelry. 800-323 2717.

Dawn Invitations, 681 Main St., P.O. Box 100, Lumberton, NJ 08048: Free catalog ❖ Wedding invitations and gifts for attendants. 800-528-6677.

Dewberry Engraving Company, P.O. Box 2311, Birmingham, AL 35201: Free catalog ❖ Wedding invitations and bridal accessories. 800-633-6050.

Elaine Wedding Stationery, 6253 W. 74th St., P.O. Box 2001, Bedford Park, IL 60499: Free catalog ❖ Wedding invitations and accessories. 800-452-5833.

Evangel Wedding Service, P.O. Box 202, Batesville, IN 47006: Free catalog ❖ Wedding invitations, announcements, programs, napkins, and accessories with a Christian theme. 800-342-4227.

Gille Import Ltd., P.O. Box 42047, San Francisco, CA 94142: Free catalog ❖ Bridal supplies. 800-448-9988.

Heart Thoughts Original Wedding Stationery, 6200 E. Central, Ste. 100, Wichita, KS 67208: Free catalog ❖ Contempory, Victorian, and custom wedding invitations. 800-670-4224.

Heritage Wedding, Attention: Latoya, P.O. Box 384, Lumberton, NJ 08048: Free catalog ❖ Wedding invitations and accessories for African-American brides and grooms. 800-892-4291.

Jamie Lee Stationery, P.O. Box 5343, Glendale, AZ 85312: Free catalog ❖ Wedding stationery for brides. 800-288-5800.

Memories Inc., 1801 St. Albums Dr., Raleigh, NC 27609: Free information ❖ Handmade wedding albums and picture frames, bridal garters, birdseed bags, ring bearer's pillows, and flower girl baskets. 800-462-5069.

Now & Forever, P.O. Box 820, Goshen, CA 92227: Free catalog ❖ Accessories for the wedding ceremony and reception, gifts for attendants, and invitations with dramatic, romantic, and contemporary designs. 800-451-8616.

The Precious Collection, Merchandise Mart, P.O. Box 3403, Chicago, IL 60654: Free catalog ❖ Coordinated wedding invitation ensembles with traditional or contemporary designs. Also wedding ceremony and reception accessories. 800-284-9080.

Rexcraft, Rexburg, ID 83441: Free catalog ❖ Invitations and stationery, bridal and reception accessories, and thank you cards. 800-635-4653.

Romantic Moments Wedding Invitations, P.O. Box 6729, Chicago, IL 60680: Free catalog ❖ Wedding invitations. 800-826-2704.

Sugar 'n Spice Invitations, P.O. Box 299, Sugar City, ID 83448: Free catalog ❖ Invitations and stationery, bridal and reception accessories, and thank you cards. 800-635-1433.

Things Remembered, Wedding Party Gift Catalog, P.O. Box 2957, Des Plaines, IL 60017: Free catalog ❖ Personalized wedding party gifts. 800-281-7367.

Treasured Memories, 11062 S. Military Trail, #431, Boynton Beach, FL 33436: Catalog $2 ❖ Glass, crystal, porcelain cake tops, and other wedding accessories.

Wedding Treasures, P.O. Box 6678, Rockford, IL 61125: Free catalog ❖ Wedding invitations. 800-851-5974.

Weddingware, P.O. Box 1466, Coshocton, OH 43812: Free catalog ❖ Wedding program covers and invitations. 800-622-4489.

Willow Tree Lane, One Willow Center, Sugarloaf, PA 18249: Free catalog ❖ Wedding invitations. 800-593-9064.

WELDING & FOUNDRY EQUIPMENT

Am-Fast Bolt, Nut & Screw Company, 406 W. Boylston St., Worcester, MA 01606: Free information ❖ Foundry equipment, welding tools, power machine tools, and machine shop supplies. 508-852-8778.

Brodhead-Garrett, 100 Paragon Pkwy., Mansfield, OH 44903: Free information ❖ General workshop supplies and equipment, drafting and design accessories, and graphic arts, wood and metal working, electricity and electronics, automotive, and other tools. 800-321-6730.

McKilligan, 435 Main St., Johnson City, NY 13790: Catalog $5 ❖ Foundry equipment, welding tools, power machine tools, hand and portable power tools, machine shop supplies, and measuring, drafting, and layout tools. 607-729-6512.

Pyramid Products Company, 85357 American Canal Rd., Niland, CA 92257: Information $1 ❖ Foundry equipment and supplies for home and professional metal casting. 619-354-4265.

WELLS

Baker Manufacturing Company, 133 Enterprise St., Evansville, WI 53536: Free information ❖ Hand pump systems for water wells. 608-882-5100.

Deeprock Manufacturing Company, 7439 Anderson Rd., Opelika, AL 36802: Free information ❖ Well-digging equipment. 800-333-7762.

WHEAT WEAVING

J. Page Basketry, 820 Albee Rd. West, Nokomis, FL 34275: Catalog $2 (refundable) ❖ Wheat-weaving and pine needle crafting supplies, dried and preserved flowers and herbs, basket-making supplies, and books. 813-485-6730.

WHEELCHAIRS, TRANSPORTERS & LIFTS

Access Industries Inc., 4001 E. 138th St., Grandview, MO 64030: Free information ❖ Easy-to-install wheelchair and stairway lifts. 800-925-3100.

Access Unlimited, 570 Hance Rd., Binghamton, NY 13903: Free information ❖ Personal transfer lift for automobiles and homes. 800-849-2143.

Amigo Mobility International Inc., 6693 Dixie Hwy., Bridgeport, MI 48722: Free information ❖ Lightweight take-apart scooter for storage and easy transport. 800-MY-AMIGO.

Aquatec Bathtub Lift, PHP-ICM Building, 1003 International Dr., Oakdale, PA 15071: Free information ❖ Water pressure-operated portable bathtub lift for the home. 412-695-2122.

Aquatic Access, 417 Dorsey Way, Louisville, KY 40223: Free information ❖ In and above-ground lifts for spas and pools.

Barrier Free Lifts Inc., P.O. Box 4163, Manassas, VA 22110: Free information ❖ Battery-operated multi-directional barrier-free ceiling lift. 800-582-8732; 703-361-6531 (in VA).

Bath-Mate, P.O. Box 80095, Ontario, CA 91758: Free information ❖ Water-powered bathtub lift that pivots outward for safe patient transfer. 800-282-4928.

The Braun Corporation, 1014 S. Monticello, P.O. Box 310, Winamac, IN 46996: Free information ❖ Van conversion and driving accessories, wheelchair lifts, and other equipment. 800-THE-LIFT; 219-946-6153 (in IN).

Bruce Medical Supply, 411 Waverly Oaks Rd., P.O. Box 9166, Waltham, MA 02254: Free catalog ❖ Mobility equipment, health equipment, and supplies for people with physical disabilities. 800-225-8446.

Bruno Independent Living Aids, 1780 Executive Dr., P.O. Box 84, Oconomowoc, WI 53066: Free information ❖ Rear-wheel drive and battery-powered scooters, battery-powered stairway elevator system, and wheelchair and scooter lifts for cars, vans, and trucks. 800-882-8183.

Burke Inc., 1800 Merriam Ln., Kansas City, KS 66106: Free information ❖ Portable easy-to-operate rear wheel-powered mobility vehicles. 800-255-4147.

Columbus McKinnon Corporation, Medical Products Division, 140 John James Audubon Pkwy., Amherst, NY 14228: Free information ❖ Easy-to-operate mobility and lift system. 800-888-0985.

Convaid Products Inc., P.O. Box 4209, Palos Verde, CA 90274: Free information ❖ Lightweight compact folding mobility aids for children and adults. 800-552-1020.

Crow River Industries, 14800 28th Ave. North, Minneapolis, MN 55447: Free information ❖ All-electric easy-to-operate wheelchair lifts. 800-488-0359.

Diestco Manufacturing Company, P.O. Box 6504, Chico, CA 95927: Free information ❖ Collapsible wheelchair canopy covers and other accessories. 800-795-2392.

Electric Mobility Corporation, 1 Mobility Plaza, P.O. Box 156, Sewell, NJ 08080: Free information ❖ Electric scooters, power chairs, water-powered lift for tubs, and other mobility accessories. 800-662-4548.

ETAC USA, 2325 Parklawn Dr., Ste. J, Waukesha, WI 53186: Free brochure ❖ Wheelchairs, walking aids, bath safety equipment, and other aids to make daily living easier. 800-678-3822.

Fashion Ease, Division M & M Health Care, 1541 60th St., Brooklyn, NY 11219: Free catalog ❖ Wheelchair accessories and clothing with Velcro closures. 800-221-8929; 718-853-6376 (in NY).

Freedom Designs Inc., 2261 Madera Rd., Simi Valley, CA 93065: Free information ❖ Tilting, tilting and reclining, and reclining transport chairs. 800-331-8551; 805-582-0077 (in CA).

Gadabout Wheelchairs, 1165 Portland Ave., Rochester, NY 14621: Free information ❖ Easy-to-store and transport folding wheelchair. 800-338-2110.

Grant Waterx Corporation, 986 Bedford St., Stamford, CT 06905: Free information ❖ Pivoting bathtub lift that operates with household water pressure. 800-243-5237.

Guardian Products Inc., 4175 Guardian St., Simi Valley, CA 93063: Free catalog ❖ Walkers, crutches, canes, home activity aids, beds, lifts, ramps, and transport assistive equipment. 800-255-5022.

Handi-Move, 982 Rt. 1, Pine Island, NY 10969: Free information ❖ Remote overhead track or free-standing movable lift. 800-724-5305.

Handicaps Inc., 4335 S. Santa Fe Dr., Englewood, CO 80110: Free brochure ❖ Wheelchair lift for vans and motor homes. 800-782-4335; 303-781-2062 (in CO).

Health Care Inc., 71 S. Main St., Pittston, PA 18640: Free list of retail sources ❖ Personal mobility vehicles. 800-600-5035.

T.F. Herceg Inc., 982 Rt. 1, Pine Island, NY 10969: Free information ❖ Remote hand-controlled overhead track and free-standing lifts. 800-724-5305.

Hoveround, 8135 25th Ct. East, Sarasota, FL 34243: Free information ❖ Personal mobility vehicles. 800-96-HOVER.

I-Tec, P.O. Box 6304, Garden Grove, CA 92645: Free information ❖ Ceiling mounted or free-standing electrical-mechanical system for in-the-home mobility.

Independent Living Aids/Can-Do Products, 27 East Mall, Plainview, NY 11803: Free catalog ❖ Self-help products for individuals with vision impairment and physical disabilities. 800-537-2118; 516-752-8080 (in NY).

Kid-EZ Chairs, 732 Cruiser Ln., Belgrade, MT 59714: Free information ❖ Easy-to-fold transfer-adjust transport chairs for infants to age 7. 800-388-5278.

Lark of America, P.O. Box 1647, Waukesha, WI 53187: Free information ❖ Easy-to-transport three-wheel electric scooter. 800-554-3536.

Lifestand, P.O. Box 153, Folcroft, PA 19032: Free information ❖ Combination power-assisted standing aid and wheelchair. 800-782-6324.

436 ❖ WIGS ❖

MAC's Lift Gate Inc., 2801 South St., Long Beach, CA 90805: Free information ❖ Easy-to-install weather-proof residential lift system. 800-795-6227.

M.D.F. Technologies Inc., P.O. Box 153, Folcroft, PA 19032: Free information ❖ Power-assisted lift for wheelchairs. 800-782-6324.

Mobilectrics, 4014 Bardstown Rd., Louisville, KY 40218: Free information ❖ Electric-operated 3-wheel scooters and replacement batteries. 800-876-6846.

Mobility-Plus Inc., 1601 Big Springs Pl., Virginia Beach, VA 23456: Free information ❖ Scooter lifts and ramps. 800-229-1317.

The National Wheel-O-Vator Company Inc., P.O. Box 348, Roanoke, IL 61561: Free information ❖ Wheelchair and side-riding stair lifts. 800-551-9095.

Natural Access, 2611 Ala Wai Blvd., Honolulu, HI 96815: Free information ❖ All-terrain wheelchair. 800-850-4109.

Open Sesame, 1933 Davis St., #279, San Leandro, CA 94577: Free information ❖ Remote-controlled door systems that open and close automatically from wheelchairs. 800-673-6911.

Palmer Industries, P.O. Box 5707, Endicott, NY 13760: Free brochure ❖ Electric one-hand operated with double and single seats and gear-driven 3-wheelers. 800-847-1304; 607-754-1954 (in NY).

Permobil, 6B Gill St., Woburn, MA 01801: Free information ❖ Standing seat for power based wheelchairs. 800-736-0925.

Pride Health Care Inc., 71 S. Main St., Pittston, PA 18640: Free list of retail sources ❖ Scooters. 800-600-5035.

Ranger All Season Corporation, Box 132, George, IA 51237: Free brochure ❖ Easy-to-disassemble power scooter for transporting in a car. 800-225-3811.

Redman Wheelchairs, 945 E. Ohio, Ste. 4, Tucson, AZ 85714: Free brochure ❖ Power-driven wheelchairs. 800-727-6684.

The Ricon Corporation, 12450 Montague St., Pacoima, CA 91331: Free information ❖ Wheelchair lifts. 800-322-2884.

Rock N' Roll Marketing Inc., P.O. Box 1558, Levelland, TX 79336: Free information ❖ Single riders, tandems, and hand and foot-powered cycles with optional seat configurations and custom-fitting for individual needs. 800-654-9664.

Silcraft Corporation, 528 Hughes Dr., Traverse City, MI 49686: Free information ❖ Barrier-free roll-in showers, shower and bath accessories, lifts, and transporters.

Stand-Aid of Iowa Inc., Box 386, Sheldon, IA 51201: Free information ❖ Power adapter for manual wheelchairs. 800-831-8580; 712-324-2153 (in IA).

Stow Away Inc., 247 W. 6th, Chelsea, OK 74016: Free information ❖ Lightweight scooter lift. 800-221-3433.

Struck Corporation, Box 307, Cedarburg, WI 53012: Free information ❖ Lightweight battery-operated scooter for indoor and outdoor use. 414-377-3300.

Ultimate Home Care Company, 3250 E. 19th St., Long Beach, CA 90804: Free information ❖ Lightweight folding travel chair that stores in luggage. 800-475-8122.

Versa-Lift, 570 Hance Rd., Binghamton, NY 13903: Free information ❖ Personal transfer lift for home and car. 607-669-4822.

Wheelchair Warehouse, 100 E. Sierra, #3309, Fresno, CA 93710: Free information ❖ Wheelchairs, accessories, and urological supplies. 800-829-0202; 800-621-5938 (in OH).

Worldwide Engineering Inc., 3240 N. Delaware St., Chandler, AZ 85225: Free information ❖ Automatic and semi-automatic fold-up wheelchair and scooter carrier for automotive vehicles. 800-848-3433.

WIGS

Afro World Hair Company, 7262 Natural Bridge, St. Louis, MO 63121: Free brochure with two 1st class stamps ❖ Toupees, hairpieces, and male wigs in curly, wavy, or Afro-American styles. 800-325-8067.

Beauty by Spector Inc., McKeesport, PA 15134: Free catalog ❖ Women's wigs and hairpieces, men's toupees, jewelry, and exotic lingerie. 412-673-3259.

Beauty Trends, 14110 NW 57th Ct., Miami Lakes, FL 33014: Free information ❖ Adolfo, Revlon, and Dolly Parton wigs and add-ons. 800-777-7772.

Carla Corcini, P.O. Box 1700, Brockton, MA 02403: Catalog $5 ❖ Exclusive wig styles for women. 800-229-1234.

Costumes by Betty, 2181 Edgerton St., St. Paul, MN 55117: Catalog $5 (refundable) ❖ Clown costumes, make-up, wigs, and shoes. 612-771-8734.

Louis Feder & Joseph Fleischer Wigs, 14 E. 38th St., New York, NY 10016: Women's catalog $10; men's color video $29.95 ❖ Handmade natural-looking hairpieces and wigs for men and women. 212-686-7701.

Gold Medal Hair Products Inc., 1 Bennington Ave., Freeport, Long Island, NY 11520: Free catalog ❖ Wigs for black men and women, hair and beauty preparations, hair styling supplies, eye glasses, and jewelry. 800-535-8101.

Jacquely Wigs, 15 W. 37th St., New York, NY 10018: Catalog $2.50 ❖ Human hair, human hair blends, and synthetic wigs. 800-272-2424.

Oradell International Corporation, 3 Harding Pl., Little Ferry, NJ 07643: Free catalog ❖ Women's wigs. 800-223-6588; 201-440-9150 (in NJ).

Salon Perfect, 200 Lexington Ave., Hackensack, NJ 07601: Free catalog ❖ Professionally styled women's wigs. 800-346-0226.

Wig America, 270 Oyster Point Blvd., South San Francisco, CA 94080: Catalog $2 ❖ Wigs and hairpieces for men and women. 800-338-7600.

The Wig Company, P.O. Box 12950, Pittsburgh, PA 15241: Free catalog ❖ Women's wigs. 800-456-1788.

Paula Young Wigs, P.O. Box 483, Brockton, MA 02403: Free catalog ❖ Wig care supplies and women's wigs. 800-472-4017.

WIND CHIMES

Anyone Can Whistle, P.O. Box 4407, Kingston, NY 12401: Free catalog ❖ Bird feeders, wind chimes, and other musical gifts. 800-435-8863.

Armchair Shopper, P.O. Box 419464, Kansas City, MO 64141: Free catalog ❖ Old world-style sundials, wind chimes, and lawn ornaments. 816-767-3200.

Catskill Mountain Chimes, P.O. Box 18, Mt. Tremper, NY 12457: Free catalog ❖ "The ultimate in precision tuned chimes." Specializing in the highest quality handcrafted chimes for over 25 years. 800-868-6964.

Colts Neck Wind Chimes Inc., P.O. Box 902, Colts Neck, NJ 07722: Brochure $2 ❖ Wind chimes, ready-to-hang or in kits.

Harmony Hollow, P.O. Box 1303, Ann Arbor, MI 48106: Free information ❖ Bronze wind bells, brass and aluminum wind chimes, and mobiles. 800-468-2355.

His Hand...Crafts, 59 W. Union St., Holley, NY 14470: Free brochure ❖ Cow motif wind chimes. 716-638-5283.

David Kay Inc., One Jenni Ln., Peoria, IL 61614: Free catalog ❖ Wind chimes, planters, bird houses, furniture, garden accessories, pool and backyard toys, fireplace tools, games, and sculptures. 800-535-9917.

Westminster Chimes, 408 Front St., Kaslo, British Columbia, Canada V0G 1M0: Free brochure ❖ Wind chimes. 800-667-1184.

WINE, BEER & VINEGAR MAKING

Anderson's Home Brewing, 430 East US Hwy 6, Valparaiso, IN 46383: Free information ❖ Home-brewing and wine-making ingredients and equipment. 800-673-2384.

Barley Hops Trading Company, 1217 E. Hanna Ave., Tampa, FL 33604: Free catalog ❖ Beer and wine-making kits and supplies. 800-810-HOPS.

Beer & Wine Hobby, 180 New Boston St., Woburn, MA 01801: Free catalog ❖ Home-brewing and wine-making supplies. 800-523-5423.

Beer, Beer & More Beer, P.O. Box 4538, Walnut Creek, CA 94596: Free catalog ❖ Home-brewing supplies. 800-600-0033.

Beer Gear, Box 25093, Lansing, MI 48909: Free catalog ❖ Beer and wine-making supplies. 800-ALL-MALT.

Bierhaus International Inc., 3723 W. 12th St., Erie, PA 16505: Free information ❖ Home beer-making equipment, supplies, and ingredients to craft micro-brew quality beers. 814-833-7747.

Brew & Grow, 1824 N. Besly Ct., Chicago, IL 60622: Free information ❖ Home brewing supplies for making beer. Also hydroponic gardening equipment. 312-395-1500.

Brew City Supplies, P.O. Box 27729, Milwaukee, WI 53227: Free catalog ❖ Beer-making supplies and kits. 414-425-8595.

Brew Masters Ltd., 12266 Wilkins Ave., Rockville, MD 20852: Free catalog ❖ Home-brewing supplies. 800-466-9557; 301-984-9557 (in MD).

The Brewer's Gourmet Inc., P.O. Box 6611, Holliston, MA 01746: Free catalog ❖ Beer-making supplies. 800-591-2739.

Brewers Resource, 409 Calle San Pablo, Ste. 104, Camarillo, CA 93012: Free catalog ❖ Home-brewing supplies. 800-827-3983.

Brewery, 1320 Quincy, Minneapolis, MN 55413: Free catalog ❖ Home-brewing supplies. 800-234-0685.

The Brewery Company, 11 Market St., Potsdam, NY 13676: Free catalog ❖ Beer-brewing kits, equipment, and ingredients. 800-762-2560.

The Cellar Homebrew, P.O. Box 33525, 14411 Greenwood Ave. North, Seattle, WA 98133: Free catalog ❖ Beer and wine-making supplies - soda pop - liqueur extracts. Fast mail order service for 25 years. 800-342-1871.

Defalco's Home Brew, 2415 Robinhood, Houston, TX 77005: Free catalog ❖ Supplies for making beer and wine. 800-216-2739.

Great Fermentations of Marin, 87 Larkspur, San Rafael, CA 94901: Free catalog ❖ Home-brewing and wine-making supplies. 800-570-2337.

Heartland HomeBrew, 888 E. Belvidere Rd., #215, Grayslake, IL 60030: Free catalog ❖ Home-brewing supplies and equipment. 800-354-4769.

Homebrew Supply of Dallas, 777 S. Central, Richardson, TX 75080: Free catalog ❖ Home-brewing supplies. 214-234-5922.

HopTech, 3015 Hopyard Rd., Ste. E, Pleasanton, CA 94588: Free catalog ❖ Malts and grains, dry and liquid malt extracts, hops, CO2 extracted hop oils and extracts, natural fruit flavors, and brewing equipment. 800-379-4677.

E.C. Kraus, P.O. Box 7850, 733 S. Northern Blvd., Independence, MO 64053: Free catalog ❖ Home-brewing and vinegar-making supplies. 816-254-0242.

Lake Superior Brewing Company, 7206 Rix St., Ada, MI 49301: Free catalog ❖ Beer and wine-making supplies. 800-745-CORK.

The Market Basket, 14835 W. Lisbon Rd., Brookfields, WI 53005: Free catalog ❖ Home-brewing ingredients and books. 800-824-5562.

A Microbrew Adventure without Leaving Home, 480 Scotland, Unit C, Lakemoor, IL 60050: Free brochure ❖ Home-brewing beer kits and supplies. 800-TRY-A-SIP; 815-363-4000 (in IL).

New York HomeBrew, 221 Old Country Rd., Carle Pl., NY 11514: Free catalog ❖ Supplies for brewing beers, ales, stouts, and lagers at home. 800-YOO-BREW; 516-294-1164 (in NY).

Niagara Tradition, 7703 Niagara Falls Blvd., Niagara Falls, NY 14304: Free information ❖ Home-brewing supplies and kits. 800-283-4418.

Northern Brewer Ltd., 1106 Grand Ave., St. Paul, MN 55105: Free catalog ❖ Home-brewing supplies. 800-681-BREW.

Oak Barrel Winecraft, 1443 San Pablo Ave., Berkeley, CA 94702: Free information ❖ Wine, beer, and vinegar-making supplies. 510-849-0400.

James Page Brewing Company, 1306 Quincy St. NE, Minneapolis, MN 55413: Free catalog ❖ Home-brewing equipment and ingredients. 800-234-0685.

SABCO Industries, 4511 South Ave., Toledo, OH 43615: Free information ❖ Pilot brewing systems, home-brew kettles and fermenters, and beverage containers. 419-531-5347.

Sebastian Brewers Supply, 7710 91st Ave., Vero Beach, FL 32967: Free catalog ❖ Home-brewing supplies. 800-780-7837.

Semplex, P.O. Box 11476, Minneapolis, MN 55411: Free catalog ❖ Home-brewing and wine-making supplies. 800-488-5444.

South Bay Homebrew Supply, P.O. Box 3798, Torrance, CA 90510: Free catalog ❖ Home-brewing supplies. 800-608-BREW; 310-517-1841 (in CA).

Southwest Cap & Cork, 3118 US 12 East, Niles, MI 49120: Free catalog ❖ Beer and wine extracts. 616-663-0035.

Third Fork, P.O. Box 11, Union Star, MO 64494: Free information ❖ Home-brewing supplies. 816-593-2357.

U-Brew, 1207 Hwy. 17 South, North Myrtle Beach, SC 29582: Free catalog ❖ Home-brewing supplies. 800-845-4441.

William's Brewing Company, P.O. Box 2195, San Leandro, CA 94577: Free catalog ❖ Home-brewing supplies. 800-759-6025.

Wine & Brew by You, E. 3811 Hwy. 3, Shelton, WA 98584: Free catalog ❖ Supplies for making beer, wine, cider, mead, and soda pop. 800-298-BREW.

Wine Art, 5890 N. Keystone Ave., Indianapolis, IN 46220: Free catalog ❖ Wine, beer, and vinegar-making supplies. 800-255-5090; 317-546-9940 (in IN).

WINE CELLARS & RACKS

Jack Brubaker Designs, 2900 Shepherd Rd., Nashville, IN 47448: Free catalog ❖ Forged metal candle holders and wine racks. 812-988-7830.

Gironde Bros. Inc., 3184 NE 12th Ave., Fort Lauderdale, FL 33334: Free brochure ❖ Free-standing wine cellars with automatic temperature and humidity controls. 888-888-0102; 954-564-0006 (in FL).

WINES

International Wine Accessories, 11020 Audelia Rd., Dallas, TX 75243: Free catalog ❖ Refrigerators, thermal doors, wine racks, temperature gauges, and other equipment for building wine cellars. 800-527-4072.

Kedco Wine Storage Systems, 564 Smith St., Farmingdale, NY 11735: Free brochure ❖ Credenzas, vaults, wine stewards, and wine storage racks. 800-654-9988; 516-454-7800 (in NY).

Lift Your Spirits, 3308 Brownes Creek Rd., Charlotte, NC 28269: Catalog $3 ❖ Wine and bar furnishings and accessories. 800-308-2247.

Nordicorp Inc., 937 E. San Carlos Ave., San Carlos, CA 94070: Free catalog ❖ Wine cellars. 415-592-1818.

Pacific Wine Cellar Consultants, 2010 Vellejo St., Ste. 5, San Francisco, CA 94123: Free catalog ❖ Wine cellars, racks, and cooling systems. 800-354-9463.

Vinotemp International, 17631 S. Susana Rd., Rancho Dominguez, CA 90221: Free catalog ❖ Cellars, walk-in vaults, and racking and cooling systems. 800-777-8466; 310-886-3332 (in CA).

Wine Appreciation Guild, 155 Connecticut St., San Francisco, CA 94107: Free information ❖ Wine cellars, racks, accessories, and books. 800-231-9463.

Wine Cellars USA, 17631 S. Susana Rd., Rancho Dominguez, CA 90221: Free information ❖ Wine cellars. 800-777-8466; 310-886-3332 (in CA).

Wine Enthusiast, P.O. Box 39, Pleasantville, NY 10570: Catalog $2 ❖ Crystal, gifts, cellars, vintage keepers, racks, corkscrews, and wine accessories. 800-356-8466.

WINES

Golden West International, 2616 Buchanan, San Francisco, CA 94115: Free price list ❖ Fine and rare wines including French and American vintages. 415-931-2300.

Marin Wine Cellar, 2138 4th St., San Rafael, CA 94901: Free catalog ❖ Fine and rare wines. 415-459-3823.

Sam's Wines & Liquors, 1000 W. North Ave., Chicago, IL 60622: Free information ❖ Wines. 312-664-4394.

Wine Cask, 813 Anacapa St., Santa Barbara, CA 93101: Free catalog ❖ Wines. 800-436-9463; 805-966-9463 (in CA).

The Wine Stop, 1300 Burlingame Ave., Burlingame, CA 94010: Free information ❖ California imported and rare wines. 415-342-5858.

WIRE CRAFTING

Arizona Gems & Crystals, 1705 W. 14th Dr., Safford, AZ 85546: Free catalog ❖ Gem tree and wire-crafting supplies, chip beads, other beads and findings, silversmithing and lapidary tools, jewelry-making supplies, and mineral sets. 520-428-5164.

Bourget Bros., 1636 11th St., Santa Monica, CA 90404: Catalog $3 ❖ Silversmithing supplies and copper, gold, and silver wire and sheet. 310-450-6556.

Ebersole Lapidary Supply Inc., 11417 West Hwy. 54, Wichita, KS 67209: Catalog $2 ❖ Gold and silver sheet and wire and silversmithing supplies. 316-722-4771.

Marjorie Helwig, P.O. Box 5306, Arlington, VA 22205: Free information ❖ Wire designing jig.

Herkimer Diamond Mines, Box 510, Herkimer, NY 13350: Free information ❖ Gem tree and wire crafting supplies, petrified wood, rockhounding equipment, and mineral and rock specimens. 315-891-7355.

Indian Jewelers Supply Company, P.O. Box 1774, Gallup, NM 87305: Catalog $6 ❖ Copper and silver wire and sheet, silversmithing supplies, precious and base metal findings, tools, semi-precious stones, shells, and coral. 505-722-4451.

Jeanne's Rock & Jewelry, 5420 Bissonet, Bellaire, TX 77401: Price list $1 ❖ Seashells, petrified wood, gem tree supplies, and rockhounding equipment. 713-664-2988.

Jems Inc., 2293 Aurora Rd., Melbourne, FL 32935: Free price list ❖ Gem trees and wire-crafting supplies, tumbled gemstones, figurines, and jewelry-making supplies. 407-254-5600.

The NgraveR Company, 67 Wawecus Hill Rd., Bozrah, CT 06334: Catalog $1 (refundable) ❖ Easy-to-use engraving tools and jewelry-making equipment. 203-823-1533.

Nonferrous Metals, P.O. Box 2595, Waterbury, CT 06723: Catalog $3 (refundable) ❖ Plain and ornamental brass, copper, bronze, and nickel-silver wire. 203-274-7255.

Ross Metals, 54 W. 47th St., New York, NY 10036: Free information ❖ Findings, gold and silver wire, and spooled chains. 800-654-ROSS; 212-869-1407 (in NY).

WOOD FINISHING & RESTORING

Artistry in Veneers Inc., 450 Oak Tree Ave., South Plainfield, NJ 07080: Catalog $1 ❖ Electric tools, veneers, furniture plans, marquetry patterns and kits, finishing products, glues, and other supplies. 908-668-1430.

Barap Specialties, 835 Bellows Ave., Frankfort, MI 49635: Catalog $1 ❖ Chair cane, wood supplies, lamp parts, tools, finishing materials, hardware, and plans. 800-3-BARAP-3.

Bartley Gel Finishes, 65 Engerman Ave., Denton, MD 21629: Free information ❖ Easy-to-use wipe-on and wipe-off wood finishes. 800-787-2800.

Formby's, c/o Thompson Company, 825 Crossover Ln., Ste. 240C, Memphis, TN 38117: Free information ❖ Furniture refinishing products. 800-FORMBYS.

Historic Paints Ltd., Burr Tavern, Rt. 1, Box 474, East Meredith, NY 13757: Free information ❖ Paints with 18th and 19th-century colors. 607-433-0229.

Hood Finishing Products Inc., 77 Milltown Rd., East Brunswick, NJ 08816: Free catalog ❖ Wood finishing and refinishing supplies. 800-229-0934.

Industrial Water-Based Finishes Inc., 123 S. Monroe St., Waterloo, WI 53594: Free list of retail sources ❖ Non-flammable water-based finishes. 800-733-1776.

Klean-Strip, P.O. Box 1879, Memphis, TN 38101: Free catalog ❖ Restoration supplies for wooden floors without stripping or sanding. 901-775-0100.

Klockit, P.O. Box 636, Lake Geneva, WI 53147: Free catalog ❖ Wood kits and parts, decorative wooden accessories, finishing supplies, hardware, and clock-making kits and parts. 800-556-2548.

Minwax Company Inc., 50 Chestnut Ridge Rd., Montvale, NJ 07645: Free information ❖ Describes a one-step staining and sealing process using Minwax products. 201-391-0253.

W-W Finishing Supplies, 39 Ontario St., Honeoye Falls, NY 14472: Free information ❖ Water-based and other finishing supplies. 800-836-8424; 716-624-7270 (in NY).

Waterlox Chemical & Coatings Corporation, 9808 Meech Ave., Cleveland, OH 44105: Free information ❖ Tung oil finishes. 800-321-0377; 216-641-4877 (in OH).

Wayne's Woods Inc., 39 N. Plains Industrial Rd., Wallingford, CT 06492: Catalog $2 (refundable) ❖ Refinishing supplies and brass and wooden reproduction hardware. 800-793-6208.

Wise Company, 6503 St. Claude Ave., P.O. Box 118, Arabi, LA 70032: Catalog $4 ❖ Period and miscellaneous hardware and refinishing products to restore and repair antique furniture. 504-277-7551.

The Woodworkers' Store, 21801 Industrial Blvd., Rogers, MN 55374: Free catalog ❖ Wood parts, hardwood, veneers, knock-down fittings, finishing supplies, hardware, kits, tools, books, and plans. 800-403-9736.

WOODWORKING & WOOK CARVING

WOODWORKING & WOOD CARVING

Parts, Kits & Supplies

Adams Wood Products Inc., 974 Forest Dr., Morristown, TN 37814: Free catalog ❖ Cherry, mahogany, maple, pine, cedar, and oak wood parts. 615-587-2942.

Anthony Wood Products Inc., P.O. Box 1081, Hillsboro, TX 76645: Catalog $3 ❖ Handcrafted Victorian gingerbread. 817-582-7225.

Armor Products, P.O. Box 445, East Northport, NY 11731: Free catalog ❖ Wood turnings and parts, hardware, lamp parts, electronic music boxes, plans for toys and children's furniture, and clock movements for restoring mantel, banjo, and grandfather clocks. 800-292-8296.

Artistry in Veneers Inc., 450 Oak Tree Ave., South Plainfield, NJ 07080: Catalog $1 ❖ Electric tools, veneers, furniture plans, marquet patterns and kits, finishing products, glues, and other supplies. 908-668-1430.

Barap Specialties, 835 Bellows Ave., Frankfort, MI 49635: Catalog $1 ❖ Chair cane, wood supplies, lamp parts, tools, finishing materials, hardware, and plans. 800-3-BARAP-3.

Beaver Dam Decoys, 3311 State Rt. 305, P.O. Box 40, Cortland, OH 44410: Catalog $2 ❖ Decoys, decoy blanks, and carving supplies. 216-637-4007.

Big Sky Carvers, P.O. Box 507, Manhattan, MT 59741: Free catalog ❖ Carved and sanded blanks that are ready for detailing and painting. 800-735-7982.

Birds in Wood, P.O. Box 2649, Meriden, CT 06450: Catalog $2 (refundable) ❖ Decoy carving kits and supplies.

Blue Ribbon Bases, 24 Dewey St., Sayville, NY 11782: Free catalog with long SASE ❖ Hardwoods for woodcarving. 516-589-0707.

Buck Run Carving Supplies, 781 Gully Rd., Aurora, NY 13026: Catalog $2 (refundable) ❖ Woodcarving supplies. 315-364-8414.

Cherry Tree Toys, P.O. Box 369, Belmont, OH 43718: Catalog $1 ❖ Plans, kits, and unfinished hardwood parts for toys. 800-848-4363.

Cirtain Plywood Inc., 677 Galloway Ave., Memphis, TN 38105: Free information ❖ Exotic and domestic premium hardwoods. Also plywood, abrasives, glues, and other supplies. 800-593-3304.

Classic Designs by Matthew Burak, P.O. Box 279, Danville, VT 05828: Free brochure ❖ Ready-to-finish mortised hardwood furniture legs. 802-748-9378.

Coxe Blocks, P.O. Box 505, Darlington, SC 29532: Free price list ❖ Carving woods. 803-395-6769.

Craftsman Wood Service, 1735 W. Cortland Ct., Addison, IL 60101: Catalog $2 ❖ Kiln-dried wood, imported rare woods, veneers, hand and power tools, hardware, finishing materials, clock movements and kits, and parts for lamps. 708-629-3100.

Cupboard Distributing, P.O. Box 148, Urbana, OH 43078: Catalog $2 ❖ Unfinished wood parts for crafts, miniatures, toys, jewelry-making, tole and decorative painting, and woodworking. 513-652-3338.

Custom Wood Cut-Out's Unlimited, Box 518, Massilon, OH 44648: Catalog $2 (refundable) ❖ Ready-to-finish wooden items. 216-832-2919.

Gregory D. Dorrance Company, 1063 Oak Hill Ave., Attleboro, MA 02703: Free information ❖ Decoy-making and art supplies, tools, and wood for carving. 508-222-6255.

The Duck Blind, 8709 Gull Rd., Richland, MI 49083: Free catalog ❖ Carving and art supplies, books, and wood. 800-852-7352.

Dupli-Tech, P.O. Box 51, Charleroi, PA 15022: Free brochure ❖ Carving blanks for wildfowl, waterfowl, birds of prey, and song and game birds. 412-483-8883.

Dux' Dekes Decoy Company, RD 2, Box 66, Greenwich, NY 12834: Free information ❖ White pine and basswood carving blanks. 800-553-4725; 518-692-7703 (in NY).

P.C. English Inc., P.O. Box 380, Thornburg, VA 22565: Free catalog ❖ Decoy, bird, and woodcarving tools, cutouts, patterns, paints, and supplies. 800-221-9474.

Excel Dowel & Woodcrafts Inc., 2211 N. Elston Ave., Chicago, IL 60614: Free brochure ❖ Wood dowels. 312-384-3544.

Forest Products, P.O. Box 12, Avon, OH 44011: Free catalog ❖ Basswood carving kits and supplies.

Geneva Specialties, Division Klockit, P.O. Box 636, Lake Geneva, WI 53147: Free catalog ❖ Woodcraft patterns and plans, turned wooden parts, and hardware. 800-556-2548.

Green Mountain Studios, Rt. 10 North, Box 158, Lyme, NH 03768: Catalog $2 ❖ Wood turnings and other patterns.

Jennings Decoy Company, 601 Franklin Ave. NE, St. Cloud, MN 56304: Free catalog ❖ Woodcarving cutouts and kits, tools, and supplies. 800-331-5613.

J.H. Kline Carving Shop, P.O. Box 445, Forge Hill Rd., Manchester, PA 17345: Catalog $1 (refundable) ❖ Woodcarving tools and supplies, wood for carving, and patterns for precut wood blanks. 717-266-3501.

Klockit, P.O. Box 636, Lake Geneva, WI 53147: Free catalog ❖ Wood kits and parts, decorative wood accessories, finishing supplies, hardware, and clock-making kits and parts. 800-556-2548.

Little Mountain Supply Inc., Rt. 2, Box 1329, Bowling Green Rd., Front Royal, VA 22630: Free catalog ❖ Hard-to-find carving supplies. 703-636-3125.

MacBeath Hardwood Company, 930 Ashby Ave., Berkeley, CA 94710: Catalog $2 (refundable with $10 order) ❖ Woodworking tools and supplies. 510-843-4390.

Manasquan Premium Fasteners, P.O. Box 669, Allenwood, NJ 08720: Free catalog ❖ Stainless steel screws, nails, joist and framing connectors, staples, and other fasteners. 800-542-1978.

MDI Woodcarvers Supply, 228 Main St., Bar Harbor, ME 04609: Free catalog ❖ Woodcarving supplies, books, and tools. 800-866-5728.

Meisel Hardware Specialties, P.O. Box 70, Spring Park, MN 55364: Catalog $2 ❖ Hardware, wood parts, and plans and parts for musical door harps. 800-441-9870.

Midwest Dowel Works Inc., 4631 Hutchinson Rd., Cincinnati, OH 45248: Free catalog ❖ Oak, walnut, hickory, maple, cherry, mahogany, and teak dowels, plugs, and pegs. 513-574-8488.

Mountain Woodcarvers Supplies, P.O. Box 3485, Estes Park, CO 80517: Catalog $2 ❖ Carving supplies, tools, and books. 800-292-6788.

Nasco, 901 Janesville Ave., Fort Atkinson, WI 53538: Free catalog ❖ Woodburning and carving tools, woodcraft supplies, and wood projects. 800-558-9595.

Osborne Wood Products, 8116 Hwy. 123 North, Toccoa, GA 30577: Free information ❖ Easy-to-assemble pencil-post beds. Also turned legs in different styles and wood types. 800-849-8876; 706-886-1065.

Rainbow Woods, 20 Andrews St., Newnan, GA 30263: Free catalog ❖ Hardwood turnings. 800-423-2762; 404-251-4195 (in GA).

Ritter Carvers Inc., 1559 Dillon Rd., Maple Glen, PA 19002: Free catalog ❖ Woodcarving supplies and tools. 215-646-4896 (call after 5 PM).

Scherr's Cabinet & Doors, 5315 Burdick Expwy. East, RR. 5, Box 12, Minot, ND 58701: Brochure $2 ❖ Raised panel doors for cabinets, drawer fronts, and dovetail drawers. 701-839-3384.

Sugar Pine Woodcarving Supplies, P.O. Box 859, Lebanon, OR 97355: Free information ❖ Woodcarving supplies. 800-452-2783.

Vintage Wood Works, Hwy. 34 South, Box R, Quinlan, TX 75474: Catalog $2 ❖ Victorian-style gingerbread decorative cutouts. 903-356-2158.

Warren Tool Company Inc., P.O. Box 249, Rhinebeck, NY 12572: Catalog $1 ❖ Whittling and woodcarving tools, books, woods, sharpening stones, and supplies. 914-876-7817.

Ivan Whillock Studio, 122 NE 1st Ave., Faribault, MN 55021: Free catalog ❖ Woodcarving tools, supplies, how-to books, and kits. 800-882-9379.

Wil-Cut Company, 7113 Spicer Dr., Citrus Heights, CA 95621: Free information ❖ Carving woods and machines, woodburning tools, knives, books, and other supplies. 916-961-5400.

Winfield Collection, 112 E. Ellen St., Fenton, MI 48430: Catalog $1 ❖ Country woodcraft patterns for folk art, shorebirds, country birds, home and decorative accessories, and toys. 800-WINFIELD.

Wood N' Things Inc., 601 E. 44th St., Boise, ID 83714: Free catalog ❖ Carving supplies, tools, woods, and books. 208-375-9663.

Woodcraft Supply, 210 Wood County Industrial Park, P.O. Box 1686, Parkersburg, WV 26102: Free catalog ❖ Carving tools, supplies, kits, and books. 800-542-9115.

Woodcrafters, 212 NE 6th Ave., Portland, OR 97232: Free information ❖ Woodcarving tools, knives, power carving and burning tools, carving woods, books, and supplies. 503-231-0226.

Woodcrafts & Supplies, 405 E. Indiana St., Oblong, IL 62449: Catalog $2 ❖ Shaker pegs, candle cups, hardware, and woodworking supplies. 800-592-4907.

Woodsmith, 2200 Grand Ave., Des Moines, IA 50312: Free catalog ❖ Woodworking kits and supplies. 800-444-7002.

Woodworker's Hardware, P.O. Box 180, Sauk Rapids, MN 56379: Catalog $3 ❖ Cabinet and furniture hardware. 800-383-0130.

The Woodworkers' Store, 21801 Industrial Blvd., Rogers, MN 55374: Free catalog ❖ Wood parts, hardwood, veneers, knock-down fittings, finishing supplies, hardware, kits, tools, books, and plans. 800-403-9736.

Plans

Accents in Pine, Box 7387, Gonic, NH 03839: Catalog $2 ❖ Woodcraft patterns for the yard, home, country projects, gifts, and toys. 603-332-4579.

Armor Products, P.O. Box 445, East Northport, NY 11731: Free catalog ❖ Plans for rocking and riding horses, realistic working automobiles and trucks, and other projects. 800-292-8296.

Barap Specialties, 835 Bellows Ave., Frankfort, MI 49635: Catalog $1 ❖ Chair cane, wood supplies, lamp parts, tools, finishing materials, hardware, and plans. 800-3-BARAP-3.

Cherry Tree Toys, P.O. Box 369, Belmont, OH 43718: Catalog $1 ❖ Plans for wooden toys and other projects. 800-848-4363.

Constantine, 2050 Eastchester Rd., Bronx, NY 10461: Catalog $1 ❖ Cabinet and furniture wood, veneers, plans, hardware, how-to books, carving tools and chisels, inlay designs, and supplies. 800-223-8087; 718-792-1600 (in NY).

Country Designs, P.O. Box 774, Essex, CT 06426: Catalog $6 ❖ Building plans for barns, sheds, and garages. 203-767-1046.

Furniture Designs Inc., 1827 Elmdale Ave., Glenview, IL 60025: Catalog $3 ❖ Easy-to-build furniture. 708-657-7692.

Geneva Specialties, Division Klockit, P.O. Box 636, Lake Geneva, WI 53147: Free catalog ❖ Woodworking plans for children's furniture, yard ornaments, gun cabinets, and other projects. 800-556-2548.

Hammond Barns, P.O. Box 584, New Castle, IN 47362: Brochure $2 ❖ Plans for storage and tool sheds, workshops, and other structures. 317-529-7822.

Homestead Design Inc., P.O. Box 1058, Bellingham, WA 98227: Plan book $5 ❖ Plans for small barns, studios, workshops, garden sheds, and country homes.

U-Bild, P.O. Box 2383, Van Nuys, CA 91409: Catalog $3.95 ❖ Plans with step-by-step traceable patterns for woodworking and other projects. 800-828-2453.

Western Wood Products Association, Yeon Building, 522 SW 5th Ave., Dept. PL, Portland, OR 97204: Free list ❖ Consumer and technical information oriented toward do-it-yourself projects and for builders, engineers, and architects. 503-224-3930.

Winfield Collection, 112 E. Ellen St., Fenton, MI 48430: Catalog $2 ❖ Country woodcraft patterns for folk art, shorebirds, country birds, home and decorative accessories, and toys. 800-WINFIELD.

Sandpaper

Econ-Abrasives, P.O. Box 1628, Frisco, TX 75034: Free catalog ❖ Belts, cabinet paper, finishing paper, wet/dry paper, no-load paper, adhesive discs, jumbo cleaning sticks, and other sandpaper supplies. 214-377-9779.

Industrial Abrasives Company, 642 N. 8th St., Reading, PA 19612: Free information ❖ Belts, cabinet paper, no load paper, sticky discs, stones, and other sanding materials. 800-428-2222.

Red Hill Corporation, P.O. Box 4234, Gettysburg, PA 17325: Free catalog ❖ Hot melt glue sticks, glue guns, and sandpaper in belts, sheets, and discs. 800-822-4003.

Sand-Rite Manufacturing Company, 321 N. Justine St., Chicago, IL 60607: Free information ❖ Graded sandpaper and abrasives in belts, rolls, and sleeves. 800-521-2318.

The Timber Lace Company, P.O. Box 2128, Gilroy, CA 95021: Catalog $1 ❖ Fretwork woodworking patterns.

Unabridged Woodworking Plans, P.O. Box 502068, Indianapolis, IN 46250: Free information ❖ Shaker and contemporary plans.

WRESTLING

Adidas USA, 5675 N. Blackstock Rd., Spartanburg, SC 29303: Free list of retail sources ❖ Shoes. 800-423-4327.

Alchester Mills Company Inc., 1160 Wright Ave., Camden, NJ 08103: Free information ❖ Knee pads and braces. 609-964-9700.

Asics Tiger Corporation, 10540 Talbert Ave., West Building, Fountain Valley, CA 92708: Free information ❖ Knee pads, shoes, tights and trunks, and warm-up suits. 800-678-9435.

Bike Athletic Company, P.O. Box 666, Knoxville, TN 37901: Free information ❖ Knee pads and braces, and supporters. 800-251-9230.

The Brute Group, 2126 Spring St., P.O. Box 2788, Reading, PA 19609: Free information ❖ Knee pads and braces, mats and mat covers, shoes, supporters, tights and trunks, uniforms, and warm-up suits. 800-486-2788; 610-678-4050 (in PA).

Cliff Keen Athletic, 1235 Rosewood, Ann Arbor, MI 48106: Free information ❖ Knee pads and braces, mat covers, mats, mouth and teeth protectors, shoes, supporters, tights and trunks, uniforms, and warm-up suits. 800-992-0799; 313-769-9555 (in MI).

Cougar Sports, 6667 W. Old Shakotee Rd., Wilmington, MN 55438: Free information ❖ Knee pads, mouth and teeth protectors, and supporters. 800-445-2664.

Cramer Products Inc., P.O. Box 1001, Gardner, KS 66030: Free information ❖ Knee braces and pads, mouth and teeth protectors, and other equipment. 800-345-2231; 913-884-7511 (in KS).

Genesport Industries Ltd., Hokkaido Karate Equipment Manufacturing Company, 150 King St., Montreal, Quebec, Canada H3C 2P3: Free information ❖ Knee pads, mouth and teeth protectors, supporters, tights and trunks, and mats. 514-861-1856.

Royal Textile Mills Inc., P.O. Box 250, Yanceyville, NC 27379: Free information ❖ Knee pads and braces, mouth and teeth protectors, and supporters. 800-334-9361; 910-694-4121 (in NC).

YARN & SPINNING FIBERS

Abbey Yarns N' Kits, 1512 Myers Rd., Marion, OH 44302: Catalog $3 (refundable) ❖ Yarns and kits. 614-389-1461.

Allegro Yarns, 3535 Pierce St. NE, Minneapolis, MN 55418: Information $5 ❖ Merino, silk, wool, kid mohair, and other yarns from New Zealand.

❖ YARN & SPINNING FIBERS ❖

Aura Yarns, Box 602, Derby Line, VT 05830: Free information ❖ Icelandic wool sweater kits, and alpaca, cashmere, mohair, merino, shetland, silk, and cotton yarns. 819-876-2998.

Aurora Silk, 5806 N. Vancouver Ave., Portland, OR 97217: Brochure and color chart $15 ❖ Naturally dyed silk fibers. 503-286-4149.

Ayotte's Designery, P.O. Box 287, Center Sandwich, NH 03227: Free information with two 1st class stamps ❖ Spinning and weaving supplies, hand-dyed wool, mohair, and other yarns. 603-284-6915.

Bare Hill Studios, P.O. Bldg., Rt. 111, Box 327, Harvard, MA 01451: Catalog $5 ❖ Alpaca, cotton, wool, mohair, and synthetic yarns. 508-456-8669.

Barkim Ltd., 47 W. Polk St., Ste. 100, Chicago, IL 60605: Catalog and yarn samples $4 ❖ Sweater kits and yarns. 312-548-2211.

Bartlett Yarns, P.O. Box 95, Harmony, ME 04942: Free brochure with long SASE ❖ Wool yarns for knitting and weaving. 207-683-2251.

Bendigo Woollen Mills, P.O. Box 27164, Columbus, OH 43227: Free shade card ❖ Australian cabled wool. 800-829-WOOL.

Black Sheep Wools, P.O. Box 9205, Lowell, MA 01853: Samples $3 ❖ Natural fiber yarns. 508-937-0320.

Braid-Aid, 466 Washington St., Pembroke, MA 02359: Catalog $4 ❖ Braided rug kits, braiding supplies, wool by the pound or yard, and hooking, basket-making, shirret, and spinning and weaving supplies. 617-826-2560.

Broadway Yarn Company, P.O. Box 1467, Sanford, NC 27331: Information $3 (refundable) ❖ Loom selvage, wool yarns and blends, polyester yarn, macrame cord, and polyester, cotton, and nylon warp.

Clemes & Clemes Inc., 650 San Pablo Ave., Pinole, CA 94564: Free catalog ❖ Spinning wheels, drum carders, wool and cotton carders, drop spindles, and natural and dyed wool. 510-742-2036.

Cotton Clouds, 5175 S. 14th Ave., Safford, AZ 85546: Catalog $6.50 ❖ Looms, spinning fibers, kits, books, and 100 percent cotton knitting, weaving, and crochet cone and skein yarns. 800-322-7888.

Country Spun Studio, RR 1, Box 269, Rochester Mills, PA 15771: Brochure $3 ❖ Hand-spun yarns, spinning wheels, books and videos, and accessories. 412-286-3255.

Craft Gallery Ltd., P.O. Box 145, Swampscott, MA 01907: Catalog $2 ❖ Threads, fibers, books, fabrics, and stitchery, crochet, and other needlecraft supplies. 508-744-2334.

Crystal Palace Yarns, 3006 San Pablo Ave., Berkeley, CA 94702: Free list of retail sources ❖ Yarns, natural fibers, and spinning wheels. 510-548-9988.

The DMC Corporation, P.O. Box 8027, Clinton, IA 52736: Free information with long SASE ❖ Embroidery yarn.

Earthsong Fibers, 5115 Excelsior Blvd., #428, Minneapolis, MN 55416: Catalog $2 ❖ Fibers, yarns, spinning wheels, looms, and accessories. 800-473-5350; 612-926-3451 (in MN).

Edgemont Yarn Services, P.O. Box 205, Washington, KY 41086: Free brochure ❖ Cones and skeins of wools in naturals, soft naturals, heavy weights, rug yarn, boucles, wool loops, and piles. 800-446-5977.

Elann Fiber Company, Box 257, Eureka, MT 59917: Catalog and samples $4 (refundable) ❖ Natural fiber hand-knitting yarns.

Erdal Yarns Ltd., 303 5th Ave., St. 1104, New York, NY 10016: Free information ❖ Solid and variegated colored yarns. 800-237-6594; 212-725-0162 (in NY).

Ernel Yarns, 1419 Burlingame, Burlingame, CA 94010: Free information ❖ Yarns and kits from Classic Elite, Tiber, and Ale of Norway. Also specialty yarns. 800-343-4874.

Euroflax Inc., P.O. Box 241, Rye, NY 10580: Sample color card $2 ❖ Machine-washable and dryable linen yarn. 800-395-5463.

Frederick J. Fawcett Inc., 1338 Ross St., Petaluma, CA 94954: Free information ❖ Looms, linen embroidery fabrics, macrame supplies, linen/cotton and wool yarns, and other fibers. 800-289-9276.

Featheridge Designs, 4 Green Hill Rd., P.O. Box 504, Washington Depot, CT 06794: Catalog $3 (refundable) ❖ Natural fiber yarns and Persian and specialty stitching fibers. 800-868-1933.

Fiber Loft, Rt. 111, P.O. Box 327, Harvard, MA 01451: Information $5.25 ❖ Yarns and mill ends for knitters, weavers, and machines. Also silk, angora, ribbon, cashmere, and other fibers.

Fiber Studio, 9 Foster Hill Rd., Box 637, Heniker, NH 03242: Spinning fibers catalog $1; yarn samples $4; equipment catalog $1 ❖ Spinning, weaving, and knitting equipment and fibers. Also cotton, mohair, wool, alpaca, silk, and linen yarns. 603-428-7830.

Filature Lemieux Inc., Box 250, 125 Rt. 108, St. Ephrem, Quebec, Canada G0M 1R0: Free catalog ❖ Yarn for knitting, weaving, and making carpets and rugs. 418-484-2169.

Fingerlakes Yarns, 1193 Stewarts Corner Rd., Genoa, NY 13071: Yarn samples $3 (request list of retail sources) ❖ Sweater kits and merino, angora, and silk yarns. 800-441-9665.

Glimakra Looms & Yarns Inc., 1338 Ross St., Petaluma, CA 94954: Catalog $2.50 ❖ Weaving equipment, looms, yarns, and lace-making equipment. 800-289-9276; 707-762-3362 (in CA).

Great Yarns, Ridgewood Shopping Center, 1208 Ridge Rd., Raleigh, NC 27607: Catalog $2.50 ❖ Yarns. 919-832-3599.

Martha Hall, Natural Fibre Yarns, 20 Bartol Island Rd., Freeport, ME 04032: Catalog $2 ❖ Easy-to-knit wool sweater kits and hand-dyed silk, mohair, linen, cotton, cashmere, and alpaca yarn. 800-643-4566.

Harrisville Designs, Center Village, Box 806, Harrisville, NH 03450: Yarn catalog $6; free loom catalog ❖ Yarns, looms, and accessories. 800-338-9415.

Herrschners Inc., 2800 Hoover Rd., Stevens Point, WI 54492: Free catalog ❖ Yarns, knitting accessories, and crochet and hooking needle crafts. 800-441-0838.

The Hill Knittery, 10720 Yonge St., Richmond Hill, Ontario, Canada L4C 3C9: Catalog and yarn samples $7 (refundable) ❖ Yarns, kits, books, and how-to videos. 800-551-KNIT.

Hunt Valley Cashmere, 6747 White Stone Rd., Baltimore, MD 21207: Free information ❖ Ready-to-spin cashmere fiber and yarn in skeins or cones. Also kits. 410-298-8244.

Halcyon Yarn, 12 School St., Bath, ME 04530: Free information ❖ Yarn and knitting accessories. 800-341-0282.

Imagiknit Ltd., 2586 Yonge St., Toronto, Ontario, Canada M4P 2J3: Catalog $4.50 ❖ Yarns, how-to books, and kits. 800-318-9426.

Krh Knits, P.O. Box 1587, Avon, CT 06001: Catalog $5 ❖ Knitting machines, how-to information, yarn winders, yarns, fabric paints, finishing tools, crochet accessories, elastic thread, patterns, and notions. 800-248-KNIT.

La Lana Wools, 136 Paseo Norte, Taos, NM 87571: Sample card $6 ❖ Plant-dyed and hand-spun knitting yarns. 505-758-9631.

Q.H. Lindsay Company, 16 Mather St., P.O. Box 218, Boston, MA 02124: Sample cards $3 ❖ Wool for handcrafting. 617-288-1155.

Lion Brand Yarn Company, 34 W. 15th St., New York, NY 10011: Free information ❖ Yarns. 800-258-YARN.

Louët Sales, P.O. Box 267, Ogdensburg, NY 13669: Catalog $2 ❖ Books, dyestuffs, yarns and fibers, and spinning, weaving, carding, felting, and lace-making equipment. 613-925-4502.

The Lyphon & Gryphon, 3779 Schindler Rd., Fallon, NV 89406: Catalog $4 (refundable) ❖ Hand-spun yarns. 702-867-4574.

Magic Cabin Dolls, P.O. Box 64, Iroqua, WI 54665: Free information ❖ Natural fiber yarns. 608-637-2735.

Mannings Creative Crafts, P.O. Box 687, East Berlin, PA 17316: Catalog $1 ❖ Yarns and spinning fibers, spinning wheels and looms, dyes and mordants, and books. 717-624-2223.

Marr Haven, 772 39th St., Allegan, MI 49010: Free brochure with long SASE ❖ Wool yarn in natural and dyed colors. 616-673-8800.

✓ **Mary Maxim Inc.,** 2001 Holland Ave., P.O. Box 5019, Port Huron, MI 48061: Free catalog ❖ Needlecraft kits, yarns, and other supplies. 800-962-9504.

Morehouse Farm, RD 2, Box 408, Red Hook, NY 12571: Information $1 with long SASE ❖ Merino wool in natural colors. 914-758-6493.

Moss Yarns Needlearts, 225 Pinewood, Hot Springs National Park, AR 71913: Catalog $3 ❖ Needlecraft supplies and imported and domestic yarns. 501-623-5106.

Nancy's Knitworks, 1650 W. Wabash, Springfield, IL 62704: Catalog $3 ❖ Yarns. 800-676-9813.

The Needlework Attic, 4706 Bethesda Ave., Bethesda, MD 20814: Free information ❖ Knitting yarns and books. 301-652-8688.

Newburgh Yarn Mills, P.O. Box G, Newburgh, NY 12551: Brochure $3 ❖ Cotton and wool yarns. 914-562-2698.

Norsk Fjord Fiber, P.O. Box 271, Lexington, GA 30648: Catalog $3 ❖ Swedish Gotland fleece, rovings, and yarns. 404-743-5120.

On the Inca Trail, P.O. Box 1861, Taos, NM 87571: Free information ❖ Alpaca yarn. 800-942-0224.

Paua Fibre Ltd., 2204 Marietta Ave., Lancaster, PA 17603: Free information ❖ Kashgora, kid mohair, silk, and angora yarns. 717-393-5146.

Pendleton Shop, Jordan Rd., P.O. Box 233, Sedona, AZ 86336: Catalog $1 ❖ Looms and weaving supplies. 602-282-3671.

Personal Threads Boutique, 8025 W. Dodge Rd., Omaha, NE 68114: Free information ❖ Yarns and needlecraft supplies. 800-306-7733.

Rio Grande Weaver's Supply, 216 Pueblo Norte, Taos, NM 87571: Catalog $1 ❖ Spinning wheels, looms, and loom kits. Also hand-dyed rug, tapestry, clothing, and other yarns and dyes, fleeces, books, and videos. 505-758-0433.

✓ **Sajama Alpaca,** P.O. Box 1209, Ashland, OR 97520: Free catalog ❖ Alpaca yarns. 800-736-0949.

Schoolhouse Press, 6899 Cary Bluff, Pittsville, WI 54466: Catalog $3 ❖ Lace knitting books, wool samples, how-to videos, kits, and knitting tools. 715-884-2799.

Silk City Fibers, 155 Oxford St., Paterson, NJ 07522: Information $5 ❖ Color-coordinated cone yarns. 201-942-1100.

Smiley's Yarns, 92-06 Jamaica Ave., Woodhaven, NY 11421: Catalog $2 ❖ Yarn, needles, hooks, books, tools, and other supplies. 718-847-2185.

Spinner's Hearth, 7512 Lackey Rd., Vaughn, WA 98394: Catalog and color cards $1.50 and two 1st class stamps ❖ Spinning fibers. 206-884-1500.

Stitches East, 55 E. 52nd St., New York, NY 10022: Free information ❖ Knitting and needlepoint supplies, yarns, patterns, needles, and canvases. 212-421-0112.

Straw into Gold, 3006 San Pablo Ave., Berkeley, CA 94702: Catalog $2 with long SASE and two 1st class stamps ❖ Ready-to-spin alpaca and books for spinners, weavers, and knitters. 510-548-5243.

Studio Limestone, 253 College St., Box 316, Toronto, Ontario, Canada M5T 1R5: Price list $2 ❖ Yarns, kits, and books. 416-864-0984.

Threads Etc., 61568 Eastlake Dr., Bend, OR 97702: Catalog $2 (refundable) ❖ Knitting machines and accessories, yarns, books, patterns, and kits. 800-208-2046; 503-388-2046 (in OR).

Thumbelina Needlework Shop, P.O. Box 1065, Solvang, CA 93464: Information $1.75 ❖ Books, fabrics, threads, yarns, and kits. 800-789-4136.

TLC Yarns, 32022 8th Ave. South, Roy, WA 98580: Free color card ❖ Wool yarns. 800-382-1820.

Bonnie Triola, 343 E. Gore Rd., Erie, PA 16509: Information $10 ❖ Natural fibers, synthetics, blends, and discontinued designer yarns. 814-825-7821.

Unitex Inc., 81 Martine St., P.O. Box 4300, Fall River, MA 02723: Free information ❖ Skein, yarn, and ball winders. 508-676-8250.

The Weaver's Knot Inc., 508 Inlet Dr., Seneca, SC 29672: Catalog $1 ❖ Yarns, spinning fibers, looms, and knitting, crochet, and weaving supplies. 800-680-7747; 803-882-1214 (in SC).

The Weaver's Loft, 308 S. Pennsylvania Ave., Centre Hall, PA 16828: Free information ❖ Knitting, weaving, and spinning supplies and yarns. 814-364-1433.

Weavers' Store, 11 S. 9th St., Columbia, MO 65201: Catalog $2 ❖ Looms, spinning wheels, yarns, and mill ends. 314-442-5413.

Weaving Works, 4717 Brooklyn Ave. NE, Seattle, WA 98105: Catalog $4.50 ❖ Looms, spinning wheels, hand and machine knitting supplies, and traditional and fashion yarns. 206-524-1221.

Web-sters Handspinners, Weavers & Knitters, 11 N. Main St., Ashland, OR 97520: Free catalog ❖ Designer yarns, books, and tools. 800-482-9801.

Webs Yarn, P.O. Box 147, Northampton, MA 01060: Price list $2 ❖ Yarns and weaving and spinning equipment. 413-584-2225.

Wilde Yarns, P.O. Box 4662, Philadelphia, PA 19127: Catalog $6 ❖ Wool yarns. 215-482-8800.

WoodsEdge Wools, P.O. Box 275, Stockton, NJ 08559: Catalog and samples $10 ❖ Raw fleeces, processed fiber, and soft yarns. 609-397-2212.

The Wool Connection, Rt. 10, Riverdale Farms, Avon, CT 06001: Catalog $3 ❖ Yarns. 203-678-1710.

Wool Room, Joe's Hill Rd., Brewster, NY 10509: Brochure $1 ❖ Spinning fibers, weaving yarns, and equipment. 914-279-7627.

Woolgathering, 750 Calico Ct., Waukesha, WI 53186: Free price list ❖ Rowan yarns, needle point kits, buttons, books, magazines, and sewing notions. 800-248-3225.

Wooly Knits, 6728 Lowell Ave., McLean, VA 22101: Catalog $5 (12 issues) ❖ Designer yarns, unusual buttons, and needlework supplies. 703-448-9665.

✓ **Yarn Barn,** 918 Massachusetts, Box 334, Lawrence, KS 66044: Free catalog ❖ Fiber books and yarns. 800-468-0035.

The Yarn Basket, 5114 Top Seed Ct., Charlotte, NC 28226: Sample cards $5 (refundable) ❖ Natural yarns for weaving and knitting. 704-542-8427.

Yarn Gallery, 1509 Burning Lantern Ln., Kannapolis, NC 28081: Catalog $4 ❖ Natural fiber yarns. 704-933-5559.

Yarn-It-All, 2223 Rebecca Dr., Hatfield, PA 19440: Free information ❖ Knitting machines and yarns. 215-822-2989.

YLI Corporation, 482 N. Freedom Blvd., Provo, UT 84601: Catalog $2.50 ❖ Serging thread in solid colors and variegated color combinations, metallic thread in wool/nylon or nylon mono-filament, and rayon. 800-854-1932; 801-377-3900 (in UT).

YOGA

Allied/VCA-Delphi Productions, P.O. Box 867, Elk Grove Village, IL 60009: Free information ❖ Yoga instruction videos. 800-548-8200.

Body Bridge by ARCH/EEZ, 1011 E. Ginter Rd., Tucson, AZ 85706: Free information ❖ Lightweight folding support for body relaxation and posture improvement. 800-326-2724.

Dharma Crafts, 405 Waltham St., Ste. 234, Lexington, MA 02173: Catalog $2 ❖ Statues, cushions, ritual objects, benches, books, incense, and meditation supplies. 617-862-9211.

Fish Crane Yoga Props, P.O. Box 791029, New Orleans, LA 70179: Free information ❖ Lightweight sticky mats. 800-959-6116.

❖ YOGA ❖

Gravity Plus, P.O. Box 2182, La Jolla, CA 92038: Free information ❖ Inversion equipment, books, tables, swings, and other equipment. 800-383-8056.

Harmony in Design, 2050 S. Dayton St., Denver, CO 80231: Free catalog ❖ Yoga back bench that provides for different postures to open, stretch, and relax the body. 303-337-7728.

Healing Arts, P.O. Box 2939, Venice, CA 90291: Free information ❖ Yoga videos on flexibility, strength, and relaxation. 800-722-7347.

H2B Company, 610 22nd St., Ste. 247, San Francisco, CA 94107: Free catalog ❖ Pillows for relaxation. 800-829-6580.

Hugger-Mugger Yoga Products, 31 W. Gregson Ave., Salt Lake City, UT 841154: Free catalog ❖ Blocks, Tapas mats, bolsters, and straps. 800-473-4888; 801-487-4888 (in CA).

Mano Creations, P.O. Box 182, Vernon, British Columbia, Canada V1T 6M2: Catalog $2 (refundable) ❖ Mats, sandbags, blocks, cotton bolsters, wedges, benches, multi-purpose furniture, and other yoga equipment. 604-542-7688.

Mystic River Video, P.O. Box 716, Cambridge, MA 02140: Free information ❖ Yoga video tapes. 617-483-YOGA.

Pisces Productions, P.O. Box 208, Cotati, CA 94931: Free brochure ❖ Posture tables and chairs. 800-822-5333.

Proprioception Inc., Box 7612, Ann Arbor, MI 48107: Free information ❖ Straps, slings, tables, wall and ceiling mounts, bars, and other equipment. 800-488-8414.

Quantum Quests International, P.O. Box 98, Oak View, CA 93022: Free catalog ❖ Audio programs on personal improvement and spiritual discovery. 800-772-0090.

Samadhi Cushions, Church St., Barnet, VT 05821: Free information ❖ Meditation cushions. 800-633-4440.

Shasta Abbey Buddhist Supplies, P.O. Box 199, Mt. Shasta, CA 96067: Catalog $2 ❖ Buddhist meditation supplies and other accessories. 800-653-3315.

Tools for Yoga, P.O. Box 99, Chatham, NJ 07928: Free information ❖ Yoga mats and other accessories. Also gifts and audio and video tapes. 201-966-5311.

White Lotus Foundation, 2500 San Marcos Pass, Santa Barbara, CA 93105: Free information ❖ Aerobic yoga workout videos. 800-544-3569; 805-964-1944 (in CA).

Yoga Mats, P.O. Box 885044, San Francisco, CA 94188: Free information with long SASE ❖ Handcrafted 100 percent lightweight cotton yoga mats. 800-720-YOGA.

Yoga Pro Products, Box 7612, Ann Arbor, MI 48107: Free information ❖ Yoga posture equipment. 800-488-8414.

Yoga Props, 3055 23rd St., San Francisco, CA 94110: Catalog $1 ❖ Wall ropes for strengthening and stretching poses. 415-285-YOGA.

Yoga Togs, 14 Brookwood Rd., Asheville, NC 28804: Free information ❖ Women's clothing for yoga practice. 800-366-4541.

Yoga Training Props, 1934 John Towers Ave., El Cajon, CA 92020: Free catalog ❖ Ready-to-assemble kits or fully assembled yoga training props. 619-449-9195.

Yogaware, 1509 Kearney, Ann Arbor, MI 48104: Free information ❖ Exercise wear and pre-shrunk knit shorts with reinforced leg bands. 313-663-6819.

Zen Home Stitchery, 2693 Riverside Dr., Costa Mesa, CA 92627: Free catalog ❖ Meditation clothing, cushions, and accessories. 714-631-5389.

CORPORATE INDEX

A

A & A Jewelry Tools & Findings, 297
A & A Plating, 43
A & B Industries Inc., 76
A & B Jewels & Tools, 297
A & B Milling Company Inc., 199
A & B Prospectors' Supply, 366
A & C Books, 81
A & D Electronics, 408
A & D Jewelry, 297
A & H Brass & Supply, 114, 267, 276
A & I Camera Classics Ltd., 336, 359
A & I Supply, 47
A & J Cycle Salvage, 332
A & K Historical Art, 12
A & M Soffseal Inc., 45
A & M Victorian Decorations, 279
A & M Wood Specialty Inc., 314
A & S Record Shop, 400
A & T Supply, 416
A to Z Hobby Center, 420
A to Z Luggage, 313
A-1 Auto Wrecking, 23, 25
A-1 Labels Inc., 344
A-1 Used Cycle Parts Inc., 332
A-Cover, 45
A-C's Emporium of Miniatures, 160
A-Z Ostomy Supply, 345
A.B. Emblem Corporation, 258
A.C.S., 382, 384, 385
A.D.I. Corporation, 177
A.H.E./B.V.E. Gear & Services, 333
A.J. Stairs Inc., 278
A.J.P. Coppersmith & Company, 308
A.K.A. Sports Cards, 398
A.K.'s Fly Tying Tools, 178
A.M.C. Sales Inc., 408
A.R.C. Books, 81
A.R.C. Traders Inc., 295, 297
A.R.E. Supply Co., 297
A.R.T. Studio Clay Company, 111
A.S.A./Antenna Sales & Accessories, 370
A.S.E. Cards, 398
A.T. Patch Company, 362
A.V. Imports, 347
A/d/s, 403, 405
AA Abbingdon Affiliates, 273
AA Cycles, 332
AAA Camera Exchange Inc., 359
Aabar's Cadillac & Lincoln Salvage, 27, 35
AABCO Printing, 51
Aamstrand Corporation, 76, 432
Aardvark Adventures, 58
Aardvark Clay & Supplies, 111
Aaron's, 389
AARP Ostomy Care Center, 345
AARP Pharmacy Service Center Catalog, 269
Aase Brothers Inc., 36, 40
Aatrix Software, 138
Abacus Software, 138
Abatron, 11, 276
Abbeon Cal Inc., 414, 433

Abbey Camera Inc., 360
Abbey Garden Nursery, 231
Abbey Press, 258
Abbey Tools, 416
Abbey Yarns N' Kits, 340, 440
Abbott Office Systems, 217
Abbott's Magic Company, 315
Abbott's Postcards, 364
Abby Precision Manufacturing, 178
ABC Auto Upholstery & Top Company, 49
ABC Decorative Fabrics, 171
ABC Vacuum Cleaner Warehouse, 428
Abe & Son Natural Elk Sounds, 288
Abeada Corporation, 58, 297
Abebros Company, 55
Abel Reels, 178
Abenaki Publishers, 81
Abe's of Maine Camera & Electronics, 99, 360, 426
Abest Woodworking Machinery, 416
Abeta Products, 350
Abex Display Systems Inc., 159
Ability Plus Software, 138
Abingdon Spares Ltd., 37
Abode Lumber Corporation, 175
Abra Software Inc., 138
Abracadabra Magic Shop, 129, 148, 301, 315, 413
Abracadata, 138, 225
Abrams (Harry N.) Inc. 81, 355
Abundant Life Seed Foundation, 240
AC Medical Supplies, 289
AC Model Boats, 328
AC Originals, 149, 212
Academic Press Inc., 81
Academic Research Inc., 413
Academy of Karate Martial Arts Supply, 318
Accent Millworks, 274
Accent Models Inc., 325
Accents in Pine, 440
Access 90's, 135
Access Carpet, 378
Access Industries Inc., 435
Access Inflatable Boats, 74
Access Maps & Gear, 317
Access Medical Supply, 289
Access Software Inc., 138
Access Unlimited, 435
Access with Ease Inc., 271
AccessAble, 271
Accessory Source, 360
Accolade Inc., 138, 423
Accord Electronic Systems Inc., 167
Accountants Supply House, 80, 343, 401
Accra 300, 8
Accu-Weather Inc., 433
Accudart, 156
Accuform Golf Clubs, 259
Accurate Arms Company, 262
Accusplit, 380
Ace Communications, 167
Ace Leather Products, 251, 313, 347, 368
Ace Pecan Company, 199, 210

Ace R/C, 323, 327
Ace Resin, 11
Ace Specialty Foods, 192
Ace Video & Music, 107, 428
Ace Wire Brush Company Inc., 96
Acecad, 135
Acer America Corporation, 134
Achilles Inflatable Craft, 74
Ack Radio Supply Company, 370
Ackley's Rock & Stamps, 319, 373
Ackley's Rocks & Stamps, 298
Acme Electric Tools, 416
Acme Premium Supply Corporation, 210
Acme Tackle Company, 178
Acme/Star, 366, 376
Acorn Manufacturing Company Inc., 267, 316
Acoustic Research, 403
Acoustic Sounds, 108
Acquisto Silver Company, 160
ACR Electronics, 71
ACS Publications Inc., 16
ACT USA, 380
Action, 408
Action & Leisure Inc., 394
Action Filter Inc., 431
Action Images, 421
Action Optics, 407
Action Sport Systems Inc., 273, 394, 431
ACTIV Industries Inc., 262
Activa Products, 151
Active Electronics, 5
Active Soles, 386
Activision, 138
Acu-Drip Water System, 227
Acucraft Inc., 176
Ad Lib Advertising, 343
AD-CAP Line, 349
AD-RX Pharmacy, 158
Adagent Acres, 236
Adam Custom Cues, 67
Adamas Publishers, 81
Adams (Stephen), Furnituremaker 212
Adams Business Forms, 343
Adams Company, 176
Adams Jr. (Johnny) 397, 398
Adams Reels, 178
Adams Studios, 293
Adams USA, 208
Adams Wood Products Inc., 212, 314, 439
AdaptAbility, 12, 271
Adaptive Design Shop, 56, 271
Adcom, 403
Addison-Wesley Publishing Company, 81
Addkison Hardware Company Inc., 416
Ademco, 5
Adept Computer Solutions Inc., 138
Adhatters, 156, 362
Adidas USA, 95, 100, 120, 267, 380, 394, 411, 412, 424, 431, 440
Adirondack Designs, 217
Adirondack Store & Gallery, 149, 217, 266
Adjustable Clamp Company, 416

CORPORATE INDEX

Adkins Architectural Antiques, 276
Adler (Kurt S.) Inc. 15
Adler (M.F.) Books 80
Adler's Antique Autos Inc., 28
Admiral Steel L.P., 305
Adobe Systems Inc., 138
Adobie Corporation, 138
Ador-Aqua, 392
Adorama, 17, 68, 360, 362
ADP Hollander Inc., 21
Adriance Furniture Makers, 212
Adsit Company Inc., 36
ADT Security Systems, 5
Advance Camera Corporation, 68
Advance Computer Source, 134
Advance Scientific, 306
Advance Solar Hydro Wind Power Company, 395
Advanced Computer Innovations Inc., 138
Advanced Logic Research Inc., 134
Advanced Machinery Imports, 416
Advanced Para-Systems Inc., 3
Advanced Products, 96
Advanced Receiver Research, 433
Advanced Sciences, 381
Advanced Security, 5
Advanced Soaring Concepts, 2
Advanced Specialties, 370
Advanced Vivarium Systems, 81
Advanstar Marketing Service, 81
Advantage Camouflage, 287
Advantage Instruments Corporation, 168
Adventure 16 Inc., 76, 333, 346
Adventure Air, 1
Adventure Cycling Association, 317
Adventure Detectors, 320
Adventure Foods, 105
Adventure in Ceramics, 111, 151
Adventure Medical Kits, 269
Adventure Sport Inc., 407
Adventure Wear Inc., 333
Adventures in Cassettes, 111
Adventures in Ceramics Inc., 415
Adventures in Crafts, 158
Adventures in Crime & Space Books, 81, 94
Adventures with Tools, 416
Adventurous Traveler Bookstore, 81, 317
Advertising Ideas Company, 349
Advocacy Press, 80
Advon, 317
Aebersold (Jamey) Jazz Inc. 81
AEC Software Inc., 138
Aegean Sponge Company Inc., 111
Aerie Kiteworks, 303
Aero Designs Inc., 1
Aero Dovron Inc., 2
Aero Store Corporation, 3
Aerocell, 57
Aerodrome Sport Kites, 303
Aerodyne Research, 3
Aeroform, 45
Aeroloft Designs, 323
Aeroplane Store, 4
Aerotech Inc., 323, 327
Aerox Oxygen Systems, 4
AFCO Industries Inc., 276
African Corner, 12
Africana Colors, 111
Afro World Hair Company, 436
After the Stork, 50, 119
Afterimages, 138
Aftosa, 111, 159, 363
AGA Cookers, 211
Agape Auto, 49
Aged Woods, 275, 277

Ager Portable Computers, 134
Agfa, 131, 138
Agfa/Miles Inc., 357
AGM Woodworking, 111, 405
Agnathous Cupboard, 279
Agrelo Engineering, 168
Agri (Rohn) Products 284
Agri-Fab Inc., 223
Agua Fria Nursery, 238
Agua Viva Seed Ranch, 240, 246
AGV USA, 331
AH! LASKA Products, 189
AH!LASKA Products, 206
Aidells Sausage Company, 196
Aiko's Art Materials Import, 9, 347
Aim Kiln, 111
Aimpoint, 8, 264
Air Age Mail Order Service, 81
Air Command International Inc., 2
Air-Lite Synthetics Manufacturing, 385
Air-Lock Log Company, 283
Aircraft Components Inc., 4
Aircraft Spruce & Specialty, 3, 4
Aircraft Tool & Supply, 4
Aire, 72, 74
Airplane Factory Inc., 323
Airplane Shop, 323
AirStar Sales, 3
Airtronics Inc., 323
Airwich Avionics Inc., 3
AirXchange Inc., 1
Airy Sales Corporation, 416
Aitken's Salmon Creek Garden, 237
Aiwa America Inc., 46, 403
Ajay Leisure Products Inc., 67, 95, 170
AK Exteriors, 217, 311, 316
AK Sew & Serge, 171, 369, 382
Akerman Old Cadillac Parts, 27
Akers Ski Inc., 391
Al Con Enterprises, 114, 315, 340
Ala Electronics, 168
Ala Lite, 307, 308, 311
Aladdin Industries Inc., 308, 311
Aladdin Steel Products Inc., 406
Aladdin/Collier Books, 80
Alan Company, 381
Alaska Herb Tea Company, 206
Alaskan Harvest Seafood, 201
Albany Woodworks, 275, 277, 314
Alberene Crystal, 152, 347
Albers Rolls-Royce, 40
Alberta's Molds Inc., 111
Alberts & Merkel Brothers Inc., 231, 237
Albright's (Wm.) Vintage Coach 34
Album Hunter, 107
Albums Inc., 354
Albuquerque Hydroponics & Lighting, 221
Alcan Pipe/Kroy Industries, 175
Alcazar Music, 337
Alchester Mills Company Inc., 54, 208, 369, 380, 411, 440
Alcone Company Inc., 414
Alcott Press, 81
Alden (K.S.) Books 80
Alden (William) Company 416
Alden Comfort Mills, 61
Alden Electronics, 433
Alden Ocean Shells Inc., 72
Alder Creek Boat Works, 72
Aldila, 259
Aldridge Company, 138
Alessandro (Danny) 176, 177
Aleta's Rock Shop, 298, 374
Alexander Aeroplane Company Inc., 4

Alexandra's Homespun Textile & Seraph Textile Colle, 171
Alextamping, 376
Alfa Casa Company, 203
Alfa Ricambi, 32, 35
Alfax Wholesale Furniture, 217, 343
Alfie's Autographs of Hollywood, 19
Alfonso (Don) Foods 189
Alfrey Seeds, 233, 240, 245
Algar Enterprises Inc., 25, 32, 36
Alice's Past & Presents Replacements, 115, 152, 389
Alice's Violet Room, 228
Alien Sport Inc., 259
Alinco Electronics Inc., 372
Aljo Dyes, 171
All Aboard Train Shoppe, 330
All About Dolls, 163
All American Wood Register Company, 370
All Auto Acres, 23
All Brand Sew Knit Distributors, 304, 385
All But Grown-Ups, 423
All Cadillacs of the 40's, 27
All Cajun Food Company, 189
All Chevy Auto Parts, 48
All Electronics Corporation, 167
All God's Children Collectors Club, 164, 364
All Points Tag & Ticket Company, 414
All Pro Exercise Products, 170
All Rite Products Inc., 8
All Star Graphite Rods Inc., 178
All Star Pro Golf Company Inc., 258, 260
All States Decorating Network, 153
Allchevy Auto Parts, 28
Allcraft Tool & Supply Company, 115, 298, 319
Allegro New Media, 133
Allegro Yarns, 440
Allen, 240
Allen (Bob) Sportswear 263
Allen (Wm. B) Supply Company 168
Allen Allen USA, 122
Allen Brothers, 197
Allen Models, 328
Allen Plant Company, 229
Allen Products Company, 111
Allen R. Shuffleboard Company Inc., 388
Allen-Edmonds Shoe Corporation, 386
Allen-Lewis Manufacturing Company, 107, 127, 151, 210, 347, 396, 423
Allen's Basketworks, 55
Allen's Book Shop, 80
Allen's Rocks & Gifts, 374
Alleon Design Company, 258
Allergy Control Products, 269
Allergy Resources Inc., 195, 269
Allesi (Ron) 315
Alleson (Don) Athletic 53, 54
Alley Auto Parts, 23, 48
Alley Supply Company, 416
Allied Electronics, 167
Allied Model Trains, 330
Allied Window Inc., 282
Allied/VCA-Delphi Productions, 442
AlliedSignal General Aviation Avionics, 3
Alligator Records, 108
AllMicro Inc., 138
Allred (Jim) Taxidermy 410
AllServe Inc., 192
Allsop, 22, 99, 369, 391
Alltech Electronics Company Inc., 131, 135
Alltrista Corporation, 106
Alltronics, 167, 168, 372
Almond Plaza, 199, 203

❖ CORPORATE INDEX ❖

Almost Heaven Ltd., 286
Aloha Tropicals, 231
Alos Software, 207
AlpenBooks, 81
Alpenglow Collectibles, 364
Alpha Delta Communications Inc., 370
Alpha Impressions Inc., 385
Alpha Marine Systems, 78
Alpha Omega Fine Watches, 295
Alpha Shirt Company, 53, 380
Alpha Software Corporation, 138
Alpha Supply,
    58, 118, 169, 298, 312, 320, 367
Alpharetta Auto Parts Inc., 25, 26, 34
Alpina Sports Corporation, 100, 391
Alpine Adventures, 100, 102
Alpine Archery Inc., 8
Alpine Electronics of America, 46
Alpine Log Homes, 283
Alpine Publications, 81
Alpine Range Supply, 262
AlpineAire, 105
Al's Luggage, 313
Alside Corporation, 278, 282
Alsto Company, 225, 302, 350
Alt Camera Exchange, 360
Alta Industries Ltd., 283
Alta Photographic Inc., 356
Altco Trading International, 74
Altec-Lansing, 405
Altech Energy Corporation, 1
Altech Marketing, 323
Altenburg Piano House Inc., 337
Alter-NATIVE VOICES/Morning Flower Press, 290
Alternative Energy Engineering, 395
Alternative Food Cooperative, 195, 203
Alternative Garden Supply Inc., 221, 222
Alternative Window Company, 282
Altima Systems Inc., 134
Altitude Concepts, 3
Altman (Richard) 19
Altman Luggage, 313, 347
Altman Stage Lighting Company, 414
Aluma Tower Company, 370
Alumacraft Boat Company, 72
Alumax, 56
Alvas Ballet Barres, 154
Alvin & Company, 166
Alvin & Company Inc., 9
Am-Fast Bolt, 435
Amacker/Brell Mar Products, 287
AMACO, 111
Amadeus Press, 82
Amana Meat Shop & Smokehouse, 197
Amana Refrigeration, 7
Amand (Jacques) 240
Amarkin (Stan) & Company 360
Amaryllis Inc., 240
Amateur & Advanced Communications, 370
Amateur Communications Etc., 370
Amateur Electronic Supply, 370
Amazing Concepts, 168
Amazing Shaners Castle & Magic Museum, 315
Amazon Drygoods, 251, 384
Amazon Gourmet Coffee, 206
Amazon Imports, 298
Ambassador, 251, 298
Amber Treasure, 298
Amber Woods Studio, 291
Ambergate Gardens, 233, 238
Amberway Gardens, 237
Ambiance Quilt Company, 61
Ambush, 288

Ambush - Wholesale Beads and Findings, 298
Ambusher, 287
Amenta (Michael J.) Autographs 19
Amerec Sauna & Steam, 286
America Online Inc., 138
American Agriculture, 221
American Angling Supplies, 178
American Antenna Corporation, 370
American Arborist Supplies Inc., 225
American Art Clay Company Inc.,
    111, 115, 319, 347
American Athletic Inc.,
    170, 407, 424, 425, 431
American Avionics Inc., 3
American Bible Sales, 93
American Blind, 153, 280, 378
American Botanical Council, 82
American Bronze Fine Art Foundry, 15
American Bronzing Company, 169
American Business Information, 138
American Butterfly Company, 97
American Candle Classics, 105
American China, 56
American Clamping Corporation, 416
American Classic Automotive, 28
American Classic Truck Parts Inc., 48
American Classics Unlimited, 52, 325
American Clock Maker, 118
American Coffee Company, 206
American Communications Network, 428
American Council for an Energy-Efficient Economy, 82
American Council of the Blind, 430
American Custom-Millwork Inc., 279
American Daylily & Perennials, 235, 237
American Derringer Corporation, 264
American Design Components, 167
American Detector Distributors, 320
American Diabetes Association, 82, 159
American Education Publishing, 138
American Electronics Inc., 167
American Energy Technologies Inc., 395
American Excelsior Company, 8
American Executive, 313, 368
American Family Publishers, 342
American Fencers Supply Company, 175
American Fiberbodies International, 44
American Fireworks News, 177
American Flag & Gift, 181
American Flagpoles & Flags, 181
American Foundation for the Blind Inc.,
    106, 271, 430
American Frame Corporation, 209
American Furniture Galleries, 212
American Ginseng Gardens, 233
American Harvest, 183, 302
American Health Food, 195
American Health Solutions, 431
American Historical Guild, 19
American Home Supply, 267, 308
American Homeowners Foundation, 82
American Honda Motor Company Inc., 5
American Horticultural Society, 240
American Hydroponics, 221
American Import Company, 263, 264
American Indian Books & Relics, 80, 82, 290
American Indian Handicrafts, 293
American Ingenuity, 283
American Institute of Architects Press, 82
American International Tool Industries, 416
American Jawa Ltd., 332
American Lawn Mower Company, 223
American Light Source, 307
American List Counsel Inc., 317
American Log Furniture Designs, 212

American Loose Leaf Business Products, 343
American Machine & Tool Company, 416
American Map Corporation, 82, 317
American Megatrends, 138
American Microsystems Inc., 138
American Musical Supply, 337
American National Parks, 251
American Needlewomen, 340
American Olean Tile Company, 279
American Originals, 251
American Ornamental Metal, 278
American Ostomy Supplies,
    159, 269, 271, 289, 345
American Parts Depot, 25, 35, 40
American Pearl and Diamond, 295
American Performance Products, 23
American Performance Products Inc., 25, 35
American Period Showcase, 308
American Photographic Instrument Company Inc., 357
American Pie Company, 70
American Playground Corporation, 412, 413
American Power Conversion, 131
American Print Gallery, 12
American Printing House for the Blind,
    93, 271, 430
American Psychiatric Press Inc., 82
American Radio Relay League, 82, 370
American Regional Cookbooks, 82
American Research Corporation, 134
American Ribbon Company, 145
American Sales & Manufacturing, 263
American Science & Surplus, 306, 381, 407
American Security Products Company,
    217, 263, 381
American Silver from the Southwest,
    293, 295
American Soccer Company Inc., 394
American Southern Rug, 378
American Spoon Foods, 195, 200
American Sports Inc., 152, 170, 273
American Stair-Glide Corporation, 216
American Standard Assistive Aids, 271
American Standard Inc., 56
American Starbuck, 211
American Stationery Company, 98, 401
American Stitches, 148
American Tattoo Supply Inc., 409
American Tennis Mart, 412
American Thermoplastic Company, 343
American Tool Companies Inc., 416
American Traders Classic Canoes, 72
American Training International, 138
American Walker Inc., 106
American Wallcovering Distributors, 281
American Weather Enterprises, 433
American Wedding Album, 401, 434
Americana Antiques, 107
Americana Carousel Collection, 107
America's Hobby Center Inc.,
    323, 325, 327, 328, 330
America's Western Stores, 128, 251, 387
Americase, 263
Americraft Corporation, 388
AmeriGlas, 400
Amerind MacKissic Inc., 219, 225
Ameron Pole Products Division, 311
Ames Lawn & Garden Tools, 219, 225
Ames Orchard & Nursery, 243
Ames Performance Engineering,
    32, 34, 35, 40, 43
AMI, 330
AMI Altimate Medical Inc., 271
AMI Corporation, 99
Amicon Technology, 131

❖ CORPORATE INDEX ❖

Amigo Mobility International Inc., 435
Amigos, 105
Amish Country Collection, 149, 157, 211, 212, 217
Amish Outlaw Shareware Company, 137
Amishman, 189
Amko Inc., 54
Amok Time Toys, 421
Ampac Enterprises Inc., 208
Amphibico Inc., 362
Amprobe Test Equipment, 168
Amrel Technology Inc., 134
Amro Ltd., 330
Amsterdam Corporation, 279
Amsterdam Printing & Litho Corporation, 349
Amusement Arts, 107
Amusementica Americana, 130, 319, 346
Anagram International Inc., 52
Analytical Scientific, 17, 306
Anarchy Eyewear, 407
Anatomical Chart Company, 306
Anchor Bay Aquarium Inc., 351
Anchorage, 75
Ancient Idols Collectible Toys, 421, 423
Anco Wood Specialties Inc., 9
Ande Inc., 127, 178
Andersen Windows, 274, 282
Anderson (Dale C.) Company 321, 322
Anderson (Hanna) 119
Anderson (Rhonda N.) 55
Anderson Design, 222
Anderson Enterprises, 323
Anderson Handcrafted Products Ltd., 340
Anderson Iris Gardens, 237
Anderson-McQuaid Company Inc., 279, 314
Anderson's, 347
Anderson's (George) Yellowstone Angler 178
Anderson's Home Brewing, 437
Andes S/D & Western Apparel, 400
Andolina Jr. (John) 354
Andover Corvette, 30
Andover Shop, 122
Andover Wood Products, 212
Andrew (L.C.) Maine Cedar Log Homes 283
Andrews (David C.) 229
Andromeda Software Inc., 16, 138
Andy's Art Supplies Inc., 9
Andy's Front Hall, 82, 108, 337
Andy's Record Supplies, 107
Angel Children, 160, 164
Angela's Miniature World, 160
Angelitos, 420
Angell & Phelps, 185
Angel's Attic, 163
Angel's Earth, 105, 146, 289, 348, 366
Angler's, 98
Anglers Art, 82
Angler's Workshop, 178
AngleTech Cycles, 64
Anglia Obsolete, 31
Anheuser-Busch Inc., 64, 251, 363
ANI Toy Soldiers, 420
Animal Crackers Patterns, 60, 420
Animal Environments, 70, 352
Animal Haus Ltd., 60
Animal Town, 422
Animation Art Resources, 12
Animation Celection, 12
Animation Company, 12
Anjo's Imports, 189
Annapolis Seafood Market, 201
Annesley Studio, 294
Annie's Attic, 340, 384
Ann's Doll Patterns, 163

Ann's Wedding Stationery, 434
Ansco PhotoOptical, 356
Antenna Supermarket, 370
Antheil Booksellers, 82
Anthony (Ray) Autograph Company 19
Anthony Wood Products Inc., 279, 439
Anthro Corporation, 134
Anticipations by Ross Simons, 251
Antiquarian Traders, 212
Antique & Art Restoration by Wiebold, 5
Antique & Collectible Autos Inc., 44, 45
Antique Arms Company, 263
Antique Auto Battery Manufacturing Company, 21
Antique Auto Parts, 23
Antique Auto Parts Cellar, 23
Antique Automotive Accessories, 47
Antique Baths & Kitchens, 56, 174
Antique Brass Works, 267
Antique Collectors Club, 82
Antique Cycle Supply, 66, 332
Antique Electronic Supply, 372
Antique Hardware & Home, 267
Antique Hardware Store, 56, 267, 307, 308, 433
Antique Imports Unlimited, 6
Antique Lamp Parts & Service, 308
Antique Mall & Crown Restaurant, 184, 192, 201
Antique Quilt Source, 61
Antique Radio Components, 372
Antique Radio Hardware, 372
Antique Radio Store, 372
Antique Rose Emporium, 240
Antique Slot Machine Part Company, 130, 301
Antique Trunk Supply Company, 267, 425
Antiques of Science & Technology, 6
Antiquity, 212
Antiquity Millworks, 177
Antler Connection, 288
Antler Designs for Sale, 157, 212, 307, 309
Antler Furnishings by Jay "Bird" Jones, 157, 212, 307, 309
Antonelli Brothers, 229
Anyone Can Whistle, 70, 251, 337, 436
Anything Car Covers Ltd., 45
Anything Goes Inc., 60, 164
Anything in Stained Glass, 400
Anza Knives, 305
Anzen Oriental Foods & Imports, 189
AP Circuits, 167
Apelco Marine Electronics, 78
Aperture, 82, 355
APEX Inflatable, 74
Aphrodesia Products, 234, 348
API Outdoors Inc., 263, 287
APL Trader, 298
Aplets & Cotlets Factory, 185
Aplus Computer Inc., 135
Apollo, 392
Apollo Books, 82
Apollo Diesel Generators, 166
Apollosprayers Inc., 420
Appal (June) Recordings 108
Appalachian Gardens, 235
Appalachian Log Homes, 283
Appalachian Log Structures, 283
Appalachian Mountain Club Books, 82, 317
Appalachian Mountain Supply, 102
Apparel Warehouse, 154
APPEND Multi-Sport Racks, 391, 393
Apple (B. Rush) Company 169, 298
Apple Archery, 8
Apple Computer Inc., 134, 135, 138

Apple Electronics, 427
Apple Valley Doll Works, 163
Applegate & Applegate, 21
Applejack Limited Editions, 12
Apples & Company, 129, 413
Appleseed's, 122
Applewood Cards Inc., 21, 261
Applewood Seed Company, 246
Applied Bionomics, 219
Applied Hydroponics, 221
Applied Medical Informatics, 270
Applied Optical Media Corporation, 138
Apricot Farm Inc., 191
APS Technologies, 135
Aqua Culture Inc., 221
Aqua Meter Instrument Corporation, 78
Aqua Products Inc., 408
Aqua-Bound Technology Ltd., 72
Aqua-Ponics International, 221
AquaGlass Corporation, 56, 286
Aquanetics Inc., 333
Aquarian Accessories, 338
Aquarium Instruments Inc., 351
Aquarium Mail Order, 351, 353
Aquarium Masters, 351
Aquarium Pharmaceuticals Inc., 227
Aquarium Products, 351
Aquarium Systems, 351
Aquarium Warehouse, 351
Aquarius, 392
Aquasol Controllers Inc., 408
Aquatec Bathtub Lift, 435
Aquaterra, 72
Aquathin Corporation, 431
Aquatic Access, 435
Aquatic Life, 351
Aquatic Specialists, 351
Aquatic Supply House, 351
Aquatics of the Sea, 351
ARA Imports, 58
ARACO, 2
Arader (W. Graham) Maps & Prints 317
Aragon (Arnold) Sculpture & Illustration 292
Arai Helmets Ltd., 331
Arawjo (Karen & Darryl) 55
Arben Stamp Company, 376
Arbico, 349
Arbico Inc., 219
Arbogast (Fred) Company 178
Arbor Vitae Farm Inc., 242, 243
Arborvillage Farm Nursery, 242, 243
ARC Science Simulations, 16
Arc Teryx Backpacks, 102
Archery Dynamics, 8
Archia's Floral & Plants, 63, 240
Archia's Seed Store, 240, 245
Architectural Antique Warehouse, 277
Architectural Antiques, 277
Architectural Antiques Exchange, 277
Architectural Antiquities, 276, 277
Architectural Artifacts Inc., 277
Architectural Brick Paving Ltd., 222
Architectural Components, 274, 279
Architectural Etcetera, 160
Architectural Iron Company, 175, 276
Architectural Paneling Inc., 177
Architectural Products by Outwater, 267, 279
Architectural Salvage Warehouse, 277
Architectural Sculpture Ltd., 279
Architectural Timber & Millwork, 314
Archival Photography, 334
Archive Arts, 138
Archives & History Division of West Virginia, 250

❖ CORPORATE INDEX ❖

Archives Division of Oregon, 249
Archway Import Auto Parts Inc., 45
Arctco Sales Inc., 393
Arctic Glass & Window Outlet, 274, 282, 396
Arden's Gardens, 203
ARE Inc., 319
Area Rule Engineering, 178
Arhoolie Records, 108
Ariat International, 387
Ariens Company, 223, 225, 227, 393
Ariola Foods Inc., 184
Arion Software, 207
Aristo Import Company Inc., 380
Aristo-Craft, 323, 330
Aristokraft, 97
Aristoplay Games, 422, 423
Aritronix Ltd., 332
Arizona Al's Discount, 320, 367
Arizona Archery Enterprises Inc., 8
Arizona Champagne Sauces, 203
Arizona Chrome Plastic, 43
Arizona Custom Knives, 305
Arizona Gems & Crystals, 367, 438
Arizona Gems & Minerals Inc., 58, 298, 374
Arizona Jet Ski Center, 295
Arizona Traders, 295
Arizona-Sun Products Inc., 146
Arkansas Blue Heron Farms, 185, 200
Arlington Computer Products Inc., 135
Armadillo Mining Shop, 320, 367
Armchair General Ltd., 420
Armchair General's Merchantile, 322, 423
Armchair Sailor Bookstore, 68, 78
Armchair Shopper, 222, 251, 406, 436
Armies in Miniature, 420
Armoire, 122
Armor Products, 118, 267, 439, 440
Armour (Tommy) Golf Company 258, 259
Armoury Inc., 263, 265
Arms & Armor, 321
Armsport Inc., 262, 263
Armstrong World Industries, 279, 378
Armstrong's Cricket Farm, 353
Army Jeep Parts, 35
Arnold (Ken) 130, 302
Arnold (Mary) Toys 67, 422
Arnold Company, 370
Arnold's Auto Parts, 23, 48
Aroma De Terra, 146
AromaTherapy International, 348
Around the Corner, 12
Array Technologies, 395
Arrow Fastener Company Inc., 151
Arrow Gems & Minerals Inc., 15, 295, 298, 374
Arrow Star, 217, 343
Arrowhead Retail Nursery, 243
Arrowhead Traditional Archery, 8
Arrowprop, 286
Arrows by Kelly, 8
Arroyo Craftsman, 309
ARS Electronics, 167, 372
Arsco Manufacturing Company Inc., 370
Art & Artifact, 251
Art & Frame Classics, 12
Art Book Services, 82
Art By God, 373
Art by God, 374
Art De Mexico, 212, 307
Art Decal Company, 111
Art Essential of New York Ltd., 10
Art Express, 10
Art Glass House Inc., 400
Art Glass Studio, 282

Art Glass Unlimited Inc., 282
Art Institute of Chicago, 251
Art Marble & Stone, 176
Art of Food, 192
Art Store, 10, 151, 171, 389
Art Supply Warehouse Express, 10
Art to Wear, 58, 298
Art Wire Works Company, 311
Art-2-Go, 402
Art-Wear, 127
Artcraft Chemicals Inc., 356
Artex Studio, 359
Artgems Exporters Inc., 58
Artgrafix Warehouse, 343
Artisan Design, 340
Artisan/Santa Fe Inc., 10
Artisan's Choice, 213
Artist Magazine Bookshelf, 82
Artistic Greetings Catalog, 96, 251, 343
Artistic Video, 318
Artistry in Veneers Inc., 438, 439
Artist's Collar Neckties, 122
Artists' Connection, 10
Artograph Inc., 10
Artrock Posters, 12, 334
Arts & Designs of Japan, 12
Arts By Alexander, 213
Arttista Accessories, 330
Arvid's Woods, 279
As Adventures Inc., 334
ASC Scientific, 306
Ascalon Studios, 13, 118
Ascension Technology, 395
Ascot Chang, 126
Aseltine (Arthur W.) 41
ASF Enterprises Inc., 430
Ash Enterprises Inc., 192
Ash Manufacturing Company Inc., 16
Ash Music Corporation, 338
Asheville Diecast, 325
Ashford (V. Michael) 213, 307, 309
Ashley (Laura) 279, 281
Ashley (William) 115, 389
Ashman Manufacturing & Distributing Company, 203
Ashton Electronics, 399
Ashton-Drake Galleries, 164
Ashwood Basket Corporation, 55
Asian World of Martial Arts, 82, 318
Asics Tiger Corporation, 114, 313, 380, 394, 411, 424, 431, 440
AskSam Systems, 138
Asolo Boots, 101
Aspen Computer Inc., 134
Aspen Specialties, 275, 276
Asperline Log Homes, 283
Assenheimer Bows, 8, 312
Assenmacher (Mike) Bikes 64
Assistive Listening Device Systems Inc., 272
Associated Book & Document Restoration Company, 80
Associated Photo Company, 261, 358
Associated Tennis Suppliers, 411, 412
Assouline & Ting Inc., 106, 188, 199, 201, 203, 206
Ast Best Place, 129
AST Research Inc., 134
Aston Martin of Cincinnati, 25
Astor Books, 81
Astor Chocolate Corporation, 186
Astragal Press, 82
Astro Artcraft Supply, 111
Astro Communications Services Inc., 16
Astro Flight Inc., 323
Astro Haven, 16

Astro Models, 325
Astron Corporation, 370
Astronomical League Sales, 82, 127
Astronomical Society of the Pacific, 13, 16, 17, 361
Astronomics, 17, 68
Astronomy Shoppe, 17
AstroSystems Inc., 17
ASW Express, 10
AT&T Capital Corporation, 134, 169
AT&T Consumer Products, 410
Atari Computer, 134, 423
ATD-American Company, 134, 217
ATEC, 53
Atelier (Johnson) 416
Atelier De Paris, 171
Athletes Wear Company, 53, 54, 208, 307, 369, 424
Athletic Connection, 53, 54, 208, 394, 409, 424, 425
Athletic Supply, 122, 251
Athnena Design, 138
Atkinson's Vidalia Onions, 191
Atlanta Coffee Roastery Inc., 206
Atlanta Cutlery, 305
Atlanta Puffections, 420
Atlanta Stuttgart Auto Parts, 36
Atlanta Thread & Supply, 382, 385
Atlantic British Parts, 40
Atlantic Edge Scuba, 392
Atlantic Glass & Mirror Works, 323
Atlantic Mold Corporation, 111
Atlantic Racquet Sports, 412
Atlantic Recycled Paper Company, 373
Atlantic Solar Products, 211, 395
Atlantic Technology, 403
Atlantis, 71, 122, 178
Atlantis Rising Antique, 364
Atlas Art & Stained Glass, 151, 182, 209, 302, 400
Atlas Pen & Pencil Corporation, 349
Atlas Roll-Lite Door, 218
Atlas Snow-Shoe Company, 393
Atlas Tee Company, 259
Atlee Burpee (W.) & Company 225
Atrium, 213
Atronics International Inc., 134
ATS Toys, 420
Attainment Company Inc., 271
Attitude Skateboards, 390
Attitudes, 57, 251
ATV Research Inc., 5
ATVM Automotive Parts, 36
Atwater-Carey Ltd., 159, 269
Atwood Mobile Products, 47, 76
Audel Library, 82
Audio Diversions, 94
Audio Editions, 94
Audio House Compact Disk Club, 108
Audio-Depot, 94
Audio-Forum, 82, 108
Audio-Therapy Innovations Inc., 50
Audiological Engineering Corporation, 272
AudioSource, 403
Audiovox, 43, 46, 410
Audubon Naturalist, 70, 82, 251, 368
Audubon Workshop, 349
Auger's Sugarmill Farm, 196
Augsburg Fortress Publishers, 93, 258, 337
August House Publishers Inc., 82
Augusta Sportswear, 380
Aunt Clowney's Warehouse, 82, 129, 315, 368
Aunt Leah's Fudge, 186
Aunt Sylvia's Victorian Lamps, 309

❖ CORPORATE INDEX ❖

Auntie Amy Stamps, 376
Aura Yarns, 304, 441
Aurelia's World of Dolls Inc., 164
Aurora Auto Wrecking Inc., 37, 42
Aurora Mineral Corporation, 375
Aurora Press, 16, 82
Aurora Silk, 171, 441
Aussie Connection, 127, 386
Austad's, 120, 260, 369, 412
Austin Amateur Radio Supply, 370
Austin Athletic Equipment Corporation, 170, 208, 273, 425
Austin Direct, 134
Austin Sportsgear, 53, 273
Austin Sportsgear Inc., 54
Austin-Hall Boot Company, 387
Australian Catalogue Company, 82, 192, 251, 428
Australian Connection, 122
Australian Stock Saddle Company, 285
Authentic Cinema Collectibles, 19
Authentic Designs, 307, 309, 311
Authentic Pine Floors Inc., 275
Auto Accessories of America, 30
Auto Body Specialties Inc., 21, 23, 48
Auto Cards Inc., 21, 261
Auto Custom Carpets Inc., 49
Auto Heaven, 27, 32
Auto Krafters Inc., 26, 30, 32, 33, 36, 37, 41, 42
Auto Literature Shoppe, 21
Auto Motif Inc., 21, 251, 325
Auto Page, 46
Auto Review, 21
Auto Stand Fine Motoring Gifts & Accessories, 45
Auto Toys, 326
Auto Works, 26
Auto World Books, 21
Autofanatics Ltd., 326
Autograph Collector, 82
Autograph Outlet, 19
Autohelm, 78
Automatic Steam Products, 56, 286
Automatic Tubing Corporation, 319
Automobilia, 326
Automobilia Collectibles, 21
Automotion, 40
Automotive Emporium, 21
Automotive Information Clearinghouse, 21
Autosaurus, 21
Autoshow, 31, 36
Autotech/Viktron Group, 134
Autumn Glade Botanical, 238, 240
AV Distributors, 146, 404, 426
Available Plastic Inc., 212
Avalan Technology Inc., 138
Avalon Comics, 131
Avery (Arch) Originals 296
Avery (James) Craftsman 296
Avery Enterprises, 4
Aves Products, 347, 410
Aves Studio, 12
AVIA Group International Inc., 54
Avian Accents, 70
Avian Outfitters, 349
Aviation Book Company, 4, 82, 251
Avid Aircraft, 1
Avid Gardener, 230, 233, 235
Avid Outdoor, 287
AVL Looms, 396
Avocet Inc., 66
Avon Beauty & Fashion by Mail, 146
Avon Marine, 64, 74
Avon Seagull Marine, 76

Avonlea Books, 80
AVP/Animal Veterinary Products, 349, 350
Award Company of America, 50
Axe Wound Records, 107, 108
Axelrod, 22
Axtell Expressions, 129, 315
Axtell Expressions Inc., 368
Ayers (Ron) Motorsports 332
Ayers (Sara) 293
Ayotte's Designery, 441
Az-Tex Hat Company, 268
Azar Nut Company, 199
Azden Corporation, 99, 403
Aztekakti Seeds, 231
Aztex Corporation, 21

B

B & B Cable Inc., 427
B & B Company Inc., 269
B & B Etching Products Inc., 169
B & B Honey Farm, 63, 82, 105, 146
B & B Used Auto Parts, 30, 33, 43
B & D Lilies, 237
B & E Collectibles Inc., 398
B & F Aircraft Supply Inc., 4
B & H Photo-Video, 99, 360, 362
B & J Collectibles, 19
B & J Indian Relics, 290
B & J Rock Shop, 58, 118, 298, 367
B & K Buttons, 51
B & K Components Ltd., 403
B & K Prescriptions, 345
B & L Specialty Foods Inc., 189
B & O Wholesale, 398
B & P Associates, 57
B & R Gallery, 13
B & T Truck Parts, 48
B & W Antique Auto, 25, 31, 32, 33, 36, 38, 41
B & W Loudspeakers of America, 405
B-Square Company, 264
B-WEST Outdoor Specialties, 52, 302
B-West Outdoor Specialties, 101, 102
B.C. Automotive Inc., 23
B.C. Electronics, 169
B.H. Miniatures, 160
B3R Country Meats Inc., 197
Baby Basics, 50
Baby Biz Products Inc., 50
Baby Bunz & Company, 50
Baby Clothes Wholesale, 119
Baby Face, 71
Baby Me, 164
Babygram Service Center, 71
Babyworks, 50
Baccarat, 115, 152
Baché (Ella) Beauty Products 146
Bachrach Clothing Catalog, 122
Bach's (Hal) Rock Shop 373
Back at the Ranch, 128, 268, 387
Back Pages Antiques, 302
Back to Basics Toys, 67, 422, 423
Backcountry Bookstore, 82
Backdrop Outlet, 355
BackSaver, 269
Backwoods Furnishings, 213
Backwoods Solar Electric, 395
Backyard Buddy Corporation, 44
Backyard Sanctuary Company, 70
Bacon & Associates, 76
Baden Sports Inc., 208, 267
Badge-A-Minit Ltd., 51
Badger Air-Brush Company, 10, 111, 171, 329

Badger Shooter's Supply Inc., 262, 265
Badler (Maurice) Jewelry 296
Baer Fabrics, 382
Bagelicious, 183
Bagley Baits, 178
Bags Unlimited Inc., 107, 131
Baidarka Boats, 72
Bailey Ceramic Supply, 111
Bailey Craftsman Supply, 82
Bailey's, 313, 416
Bailey's (Dan) Fly Shop 178
Bailey's Wholesale Floral Supply, 182
Bainbridge/Aquabatten, 76
Baker, 78
Baker Book House, 93
Baker Manufacturing Company, 435
Baker's Art & Collectibles, 421
Baker's Auto Inc., 35
Baker's Catalogue, 184, 302
Baker's International Antiques & Collectibles, 6
Balance Bicycles, 64
Balducci's, 183, 192
Baldwin (Charles) & Sons 203
Baldwin Boat Company, 72
Baldwin Hardware Corporation, 56, 157, 267, 309
Baldwin Hill Bakery, 183
Bale Company, 50, 210, 363
Baler Software Corporation, 138
Bali-MAC, 352
Ball & Ball, 267, 307, 309
Ball Four Cards, 398
Ball Hopper Products Inc., 411, 412
Ball Photo Supply Company, 17, 68, 264, 360
Ballard Designs, 15, 157, 222
Ballentine (J.C.) Postcards 364
Ballet Barres Inc., 154
Ballet Etc., 154, 266
Ballistic Products Inc., 262, 266
Balloon & Magic Store Inc., 315
Balloon Printing Company, 52, 349
Balloons For You, 52
Bally Bead Company, 58
Bally of Switzerland for Ladies, 313, 368, 386
Bally of Switzerland for Men, 313, 368, 386
Balmar, 395
Balmer Studios Inc., 279
Balsa USA, 329
Baltazor's, 172, 173
Baltimore Cycle Salvage Inc., 332
Bamboo & Rattan Works Inc., 55, 114, 175
Bamboo Fencer, 175
Bamboo Sourcery, 229
Banana Productions, 137
Banana Tree, 229, 231, 240
Banasch, 58, 382
Bandon Cheese Inc., 188
Bangkok Produce, 189, 191
Bangor Cork Company Inc., 96, 343
Bank Architectural Antiques, 276, 277
Bankhead (H.) Gourds 233
Banner (Pamela) 334
Banner Fabric, 181, 303
Banner Ideas, 181
Bantam Doubleday Dell Publishing Group Inc., 82
Bantam Doubleday Dell Travel Books, 82
Bantam Electronic Publishing, 82
Baranof Berry Patch, 200
Barap Specialties, 114, 151, 309, 438, 439, 440
Barbara's Papertiques, 346, 364

CORPORATE INDEX

Barbeau Fine Fabrics, 172
Barber (Phil) Newspapers 342
Barber Lumber Sales Inc., 314
Barber Nursery, 242, 243
Barclay School Supplies, 422
Barco, 366, 377
Bare Hill Studios, 441
Bare Sportswear Corporation, 392
Bare-Metal Foil Company, 12, 182
Barefoot International, 432
Barefoot Pottery, 115
Bargain Book Warehouse, 80
Bargain Corral, 284, 285
Bargain John's Antiques, 6, 213
Barker & Williamson, 370
Barker Enterprises Inc., 105
Barker Metalcraft, 370
Barkim Ltd., 340, 441
Barkley Sound Marine, 76
Barley Hops Trading Company, 437
Barlow Tyrie, 217
Barlow's Tackle Shop, 178
Barn, 378
Barn Again Furniture Company, 213
Barn Stream Natural Foods, 183, 195
Barna (Jim) Log Systems 283
Barner Books, 80
Barnes & Barnes Fine Furniture, 213
Barnes & Noble, 80, 108
Barnes (Marilyn) Jewelry 296
Barnes (Vernon) & Son Nursery 229, 242, 243, 246
Barnes Enterprises, 320
Barnes Surplus & John, 407
Barnett International, 8
Barnett Rotorcraft, 2
Barnett's Photo Inc., 135
Barnetts Sports Cards, 398
Barney's Ginseng Patch, 82, 233
Barnmaster Inc., 386
Barnstable Stove Shop, 406
Barnum Shoe, 386
Baron/Barclay Bridge Supplies, 96
Baronet Gourmet Coffee, 206
Barracuda, 64
Barretta (F.M.) Rowing Boats 76
Barrie Archery, 287
Barrier Free Lifts Inc., 271, 435
Barrington Square Cards, 397
Barrons, 115, 152, 389
Barron's Educational Series, 82, 138
Barry (Paul) 35, 48
Barry Electronics Corporation, 371
Barry's Custom Leather, 8
Barry's Postcards, 364
Barstow Pro Rodeo Equipment, 376
Bartels' Performance Products, 332
Barth Vitamins, 146, 430
Barthman (William) Jewelers 251
Bartholomew's Ink, 377
Bartlett (G.W.) Company 34, 49
Bartlett Yarns, 441
Bartley Collection Ltd., 211, 212
Bartley Gel Finishes, 438
Bartnik Sales & Service, 23, 48
Barton Paddle Company, 72
Barton-Sharpe Ltd., 61, 115, 213, 309
Bartrug (Hugh E.) 305
Bart's Water Ski Center, 432
Bascom Maple Farms Inc., 196
Base Station Inc., 371
Baseball Barons Sportscards, 398
Baseball Card Kingdom, 398
Baseball Card World, 398
Basic Books Inc., 82

Basic Designs, 76
Basic Designs Inc., 431
Basic Electrical Supply & Warehousing Corporation, 427
Basically Natural, 373
Basil & Jones Cabinetmakers, 217
Basket Bank, 291
Basket Beginnings, 55
Basket Hollow, 55
Basket Works, 55
Basketfull Inc., 251
Baskets Galore, 192
Basketville Inc., 55
Basquetrie, 55
Bass Pond, 178
Bass Pro Shops, 102, 178
Basse's Choice Plantation, 192, 197
Bassetts Cricket Ranch Inc., 349, 351, 353
Bassett's Jaguar Inc., 34
Bates Leathers, 331
Bates Nut Farm Inc., 199
Bath Indulgences, 146
Bath-Mate, 271, 435
Bathroom Machineries, 56, 267
Baths from the Past, 56
Battenberg Wood Products, 388
Battery Biz, 58
Battery Specialists, 58
Battery-Tech Inc., 58
BattleZone Ltd., 321
Baubanbea Enterprises, 58, 151, 174, 182, 298, 382
Baudelaire Fine Imported Cosmetics Inc., 146
Bauder-Pine Ltd., 160
Bauer (Eddie) 101, 122, 390
Bauer Precision In-Line Skates, 273
Baum (W. & E.) Bronze Tablet Corporation 50, 118
Baum's Inc., 154
Bausch & Lomb, 17, 68, 264
Bavarian Auto Service Inc., 26
Bay (Betsie) Kayak 73
Bay Archery Sales, 102
Bay Area Tailoring Supply, 383
Bayberry Farm Peddlers, 146
Baycliff Company Inc., 201
BayCraft Inc., 75
Bayless Inc., 32, 35
Bayou Country Store, 149
Bayou to Go Seafood Inc., 189
BayTech, 135
BB Brass, 209, 222
BB Doll Supplies, 163
BC Hats, 268
BCB Survival Equipment Inc., 269
BCS America, 219, 223, 225, 227
BEA Comics, 131
Beach Camera of Maine, 360
Beach Imports, 25, 36
Beach Manufacturing, 67
Beach Photo & Video Inc., 99, 360, 426
Beach Seafood Market, 201
Bead Bazaar, 298
Bead Boppers, 58, 298, 312
Bead Dreamer, 58
Bead Fairy, 58
Bead Lady/Cherokee Rainbows, 294
Bead Source, 58
Bead Tackle, 178
Bead Warehouse, 58
Bead World, 58
Beada Beada, 58, 298
Beadbox Inc., 58, 298
Beaded Fashions by Shayla Arrasmith, 296

Beadniks, 58
Beads Galore International Inc., 58
Beadtrader, 58
Beadworks, 58, 298
BeadZip, 58
Bean (Dave) Engineering Inc. 31, 35, 36
Bean (L.L.) 71, 73, 101, 102, 122, 127, 178, 305
Bean (L.L.) Inc. 287, 386, 391
Bean Appetit, 192
Bean Bag, 206
Bean Bag Mail Order Company, 192, 203
Bean Farm, 353
Bean House, 157
Bear Archery Inc., 8, 102
Bear Clawset, 60
Bear Creek Canoe, 72
Bear Creek Lumber, 276
Bear Creek Nursery, 229, 243
Bear Hugs, 60
Bear Hugs & Baby Dolls, 60
Bear In Mind Inc., 60
Bear Pawse, 60
Bear River Industries Inc., 287
Beardeaux Farm, 60
Bearden Brothers Carpet, 379
Bears' Den, 60
Bears in the Attic, 60
Bears 'N Things, 60
Bears 'n Wares, 60
Bears of Bruton Street, 60
Beason Engraving, 223
Beatrice Farms, 219
Beau Ties Ltd. of Vermont, 122
Beautiful Music Company, 109
Beautiful Visions, 146
Beauty Boutique, 146
Beauty by Spector Inc., 121, 296, 436
Beauty Trends, 436
Beauvais Castle, 160
Beaver Dam Decoys, 158, 439
Beaver Log Homes, 283
Bébé House of Dolls, 164
Beck (Anita) Collection 261
Beck Development, 44, 45
Becker Battery Sales, 21
Beckers Auto Salvage, 23, 31, 41
Beckett Corporation, 227
Beck's Cutlery Specialties, 305
Beck's Feeders, 70
Beckson Marine, 68, 76
Becksvoort (C.H.) 213
Becky's Country Meats Inc., 197
Bed Factory, 211
Bed Rizer, 61
Bedford Fair, 122
Bedlam Brass, 211
Bedroom Secrets, 62
Bee Lee Company, 383
Beech River Mill Company, 267, 278
Beechmont Volvo, 43
Beehive Botanicals Inc., 146
Beeman Precision Arms Inc., 262, 263, 265, 266
Beer, 437
Beer & Wine Hobby, 437
Beer City Skateboards, 390
Beer Gear, 437
Beggars' Lace, 174
Behrman House Publishers Inc., 93
Bekan Rustic Furniture, 213
Bel Air Camera & Video, 99, 360
Bel Bay Publications Inc., 82
Bel Canto Fancy Foods Ltd., 188
Belisle's Violet House, 235

Bell Brass Guitars, 338
Bell Canoe Works, 73
Bell Ceramics, 163
Bell Family Nursery, 236
Bell Sports Inc., 66
Belle & Blade, 251, 336
Bellerophon Books, 81
Belleville Wholesale Hobby, 327
Bellows (Gina C.) 163
Belmont Metals Inc., 12
Below Wholesale Magazines, 342
Bemidji Woolen Mills, 119, 122
Benbo Tripods, 362
Benbow Chemical Packaging Inc., 10
Bencher Inc., 356, 357
Benchmade Knife Company Inc., 305
Benchmark Doors, 274
BenchSmith, 217
Bendel (Henri) 126
Bendigo Woollen Mills, 441
Bending Branches Paddles, 73
Bendix Moldings Inc., 276, 279
Benedikt & Salmon Record Rarities, 6, 19, 94, 107, 354
Benford Design Group, 72
Bengold Associates Inc., 312
Benington's, 281
Benisek (Dee) Studio 164
Benjamin (Walter R.), Autographs 19
Benjamin River Marine Inc., 76
Benjamin/Sheridan Company, 262
Benjane Arts, 382
Benjy's Trains & Toys, 326, 330, 421
Benkin & Company, 21
Benner's Gardens, 175
Bennett Automotive, 44
Bennett Brothers Inc., 158, 251
Bennett's Pottery & Ceramic Supplies, 111
Bennington Potters, 115
Bensinger (Daryl) 35, 48
Benson's (Rod) Game Calls 288
Bentley Brothers, 281
BentWood Building, 278
Bentwood Building, 213
Berea Hardwoods Company, 314
Beren (Arthur) Shoes 386
Beretta U.S.A., 265, 305
Berg Color Tone, 356
Bergdorf Goodman, 158
Bergen County Camera, 360
Berger Brothers Camera Exchange, 17, 68, 99, 360
Bergey Windpower Company Inc., 395
Bergsma (Jody) Galleries Inc. 251, 363, 364
Berkeley Inc., 76, 178
Berkeley Systems, 138
Berkshire House Publishers, 82
Berkshire Mountain Trading, 305
Berkshire Record Outlet Inc., 109
Berlin Seeds, 240
Berman Leathercraft, 312
Bernbaum (Andy) Auto Parts 29, 31, 39, 48
Bernel Music Ltd., 109
Bernie's Discount Center Inc., 7, 411
Bernina, 385
Bernunzio Vintage Instruments, 338
Berres Brothers Coffee, 206
Berry Scuba Company, 74, 362, 392
Berry-Hill Limited, 106, 183, 433
Berten (Bertie) 130
Bertram's Inkwell, 348
Bert's, 295
Beseler (Charles) Company 355, 357
Besherse Brothers, 8
Bess' Beans, 191

Best American Duffel, 178
Best Blinds, 153
Best Comics Distribution Center, 131, 398
Best Deal Porsche, 40
Best Feeders Inc., 70
Best Impressions Company, 349
Best Magic Gags & Costumes, 129, 148, 154, 301, 315
Best Martial Arts Supply, 318
Best Moulding Frames, 10
Best of Everything, 164
Best Power Technology Inc., 131
Best Products Company Inc., 57, 67, 98, 158
Best Value Table Pad Company, 409
Best Wallcoverings Inc., 281, 379
Best Ware, 138
Bethany Sales Company, 177
Bethany Sciences, 374
Bethel Mills Lumber Inc., 416
Beth's Farm Kitchen, 200, 203
Beth's Fine Desserts, 184
Betlin Manufacturing, 53, 54, 95, 114, 208, 273, 394, 411, 424
Betsy's Place, 157, 406
Better Built Corporation, 416
Better Concepts Inc., 132, 144
Better Health Fitness, 170
Better Homes & Gardens Books, 82
Better Living, 251
Betterbee-Meadery Inc., 63
Betterway Books, 82
Bette's Oceanview Diner, 184
Beveled Glass Works, 274
Beverly Hills Coffee Company, 206
Beverly Hills Motoring Accessories, 45
Beyond Beadery, 58, 81
Bi-Rite Photo & Electronics, 360, 362, 411
Biamón (Atelier) 122
Bianchi USA, 64
Bible Research Systems, 93, 138
Bibler Tents, 102
BibleSoft, 93, 138
Bibliomania, 83, 353
Bickford Flavors, 203
Bicycle Books Inc., 83
Bicycle Corporation of America, 64
Bierhaus International Inc., 437
Big Apple Herpetological, 353
Big Ben's Used Cars & Salvage, 23
Big Brand Products, 390
Big Buck Treestands, 287
Big Dog Sportswear, 119, 122, 127, 251, 391
Big K Inc., 382
Big M Stained Glass, 400
Big Man Tree Stands, 287
Big Red Computer Club, 137, 138
Big River Game Calls, 288
Big Sky Carvers, 439
Big Sky Log Furniture, 213
Big Stone Beads & Findings Inc., 298
Big Ten Inc., 317
Big Tree Daylily Garden, 237
Bigfoot Stilt Company, 129
Biggs Limited Editions, 164, 251, 363, 364
Bighorn Sheepskin Company, 46
BigToys, 363
Bike Athletic Company, 53, 54, 208, 394, 440
Bike Empire, 64
Bike Nashbar, 64, 67
Bike Pro, 64, 66, 67
Bike Rack Inc., 64
Bike Source, 67

Bike Tight, 67
Bikecentennial, 67, 317
Bila of California, 122
Bilal Company, 371
Bilco Company, 274
Bilenky Cycle Works, 64
Bilgore Groves, 191
Bilingual Software Inc., 139
Bill & Sharon's Collectables, 326
Billard's Telephones, 410
Billiard Pro Shop, 67
Billingsley & Brownell Rifle Metalsmith, 265
Bill's Birds, 40
Bill's Cards & Supplies, 398
Bill's Speed Shop, 21
Biltmore Estate Direct Inc., 251
Bingham Projects Inc., 8
Binks Manufacturing Company, 10
Biobottoms, 50, 119
Biodex Medical Systems, 269
Bioenergy Nutrients, 147, 269, 430
Biolet Composting Toilet, 56
BioTech Corporation, 170
Birchwood Laboratories Inc., 265
Bird Watcher's Digest, 83
Birding Concepts, 70
Birds in Wood, 158, 439
Birds of Paradise Lampshades, 311
Birkenstock Express, 386
Birkenstock Shoes, 386
Birth-O-Gram Company, 71
Bishop (Adele) 402
Bishop (Norman) 203
BISME Computers Inc., 132
Bissinger's (Karl) French Confections 186
Bit Software Inc., 139
BitBrain Software, 139
Bitner's, 373, 375
Bits & Pieces, 251, 368
Bitstream Inc., 139
Bittersweet Pastries, 184
Bizzaro Rubber Stamps, 377
BJ's Dahlias, 232
Black & Decker, 7, 176
Black & Decker Garden Tools, 223, 225
Black (Dan) 360
Black (Kimberly) Rugs & Accessories 379
Black Bart Paddles, 73
Black Bear Trading Post, 292
Black Belt Products Inc., 318
Black Boar, 67
Black Copper Kits, 231
Black Diamond Equipment, 334, 391
Black Feather Electronics, 168
Black Hills Institute of Geological Research Inc., 373
Black Hound New York, 186
Black Jungle Terrarium Supply, 353
Black Magic Cleaners, 111
Black Market Art Materials, 10
Black Moon Company, 83
Black Pearl Gardens, 147, 182, 234, 348, 366
Black Sheep Wools, 441
Black Shield Inc., 192, 200
Black Widow Custom Bows, 8
Blackberry Patch, 200, 203
Blackfeet Trading Post, 291
Blackheart Enterprises Ltd., 28
Blackjack Knives Ltd., 305
Blackship Computer Systems Inc., 134
Blackstone Audio Books, 94
Blacksword Armoury Inc., 321
Blackwelder's, 213
Blackwood (Bob) Equipment 376

❖ CORPORATE INDEX ❖

Blade Fencing Equipment Inc., 175
Blaine Hardware International, 267
Blair, 122
Blake (Warren), Old Science Books 6, 83
Blake Industries, 213, 217
Blanchard & Blanchard Ltd., 203
Blanchard Ostomy Products, 345
Bland Farms, 191, 192
Blank (Arthur) & Company Inc. 96
Blarney Gift Catalogue, 251
Blaser's Auto, 38, 40
Blatt (Anny) Boutique 83, 304, 340
Blaupunkt, 46, 410
Blaze King Industries, 406
Blazer Manufacturing Company Inc., 425
Blenko Glass Company Inc., 258
Blick (Dick) Company 10, 166, 388
Blind Center USA, 153
Blind Pig Records, 109
Bliss (James) Marine Company 76, 77
Blitz Computer, 135
Block (Allan) 222
Block Financial Software, 139
Bloomingdales's by Mail Ltd., 158
Bloomington Wholesale Garden Supply, 83, 221
Blossom Farm, 246
Blount Inc., 262
BLT Supplies Inc., 318, 428
BluBlocker Corporation, 407
Blue Crab Bay Company, 203
Blue Diamond Kiln Company, 111
Blue Heron Farm, 195
Blue Heron Fruit Shippers, 191, 192, 201
Blue Moon Cycle, 332
Blue Ox Lumber, 314
Blue Ray G.T. Engineering, 44
Blue Ribbon Bases, 158, 410, 439
Blue Ribbon Flies, 178
Blue Ribbon Products Ltd., 30
Blue Ridge Log Works, 213
Blue Ridge Machinery & Tools Inc., 416
Blue Ridge Rod Company, 178
Blue Ridge Timber Frame, 276
Blue Star Inc., 102
Blue Tulip Rubber Stamps, 377
Blue Willow Branch, 251
Blueberry Hill, 229
Bluebird Indian Crafts, 291
Bluebird Manufacturing Inc., 111
Bluegrass Case Company, 159
Bluejacket Ship Crafters, 328
Bluemel (Kurt) Inc. 229, 232, 233, 238
Blueprint-Printables, 171
Bluestone Perennials, 233, 236, 238
Bluff City British Cars, 34, 41
Blümchen (D.) & Company Inc. 117
Blume Supply Inc., 416
Blumenthal (John) Autographs 19
Blystone's Books, 83
Blyth Software, 139
BMC Racing, 65
BMI Home Decorating, 281
BMI Supply, 414
BMP Design, 26
BMW, 331
B'n'M Pole Company, 178
Boardman Flyfisherman, 178
Boast Inc., 54
Boat Owners Association of the United States, 77
Boat Plans International, 72
Bob & Art's Auto Parts, 23, 40
Bobcor Motors, 25
Bobelu (Carolyn) 292

Bob's Antique Auto Parts, 37
Bob's Auto Parts, 23
Bob's Automobilia, 26
Bob's Electronic Service, 16
Bob's Hobby & Collector's Shop, 326
Bob's Hobby Center, 323, 326, 328
Bob's T-Birds, 41
Boca Bons Inc., 184, 186
Boca Cards & Investments, 398
Bock (Jeffrey) 65
Body & Soul, 147
Body Bridge by ARCH/EEZ, 442
Body Glove International, 208, 432
Body Glove International Inc., 392, 407
Body Masters Sports Industries Inc., 170
Body Shop Inc., 147
Body Sport USA, 3
Body Wrappers, 120
Bodzer's Collectibles, 164
Boehringer Mannheim Corporation, 159
Boese (Fredi W.), Master Artist 6
Boetje's Foods Inc., 203
Bogart (Joan) 6
Bogen Photo Corporation, 356, 357, 358, 362
Bogland Inc., 192
Bogner of America, 258, 391
Bohndell Sails, 76
Bohning Company Ltd., 8
Bolco Athletic Company, 53
Bold Concepts, 364
Bold Strummer Ltd., 83
Bolind (Bruce) 251
Bolle America, 392
Bollier (Andre) Ltd. 186
Bollinger Fitness Products, 170, 425
Bollman (Louis) Cards 398
Boltek Corporation, 433
Bomar Designs, 279
Bomark Sportswear, 53, 208, 394
Bombard, 74
Bombay Company, 213, 251, 323
Bona Allen Saddle Company, 285
Bona Decorative Hardware, 56, 176, 267
Bond (Stuart & Mel) 107
Bondy Export Corporation, 7, 313, 426, 427
Bonfit America Inc., 382
Bonita Furniture Galleries, 213
Bonnard (Henry) Bronze Company 15
Bonnie Brae Gardens, 232
Bonsai Associates Inc., 230
Bonsai Boy of N.Y., 230
Bonsai by the Monastery, 230
Bonsai Farm, 230
Bonsai of Brooklyn, 230
Bonsai Shop, 230
Boogie Music, 109
Book City of Burbank, 336
Book Corner, 83
Book Publishing Company, 83
Book Sales Inc., 83
Bookbinder's Trains Unlimited, 330
Bookbinder's Warehouse, 80
BookBound, 83
Bookcassette Sales, 94
Booker's Specialty Gifts, 251
BookMakers, 80
Bookmark, 98, 401
Bookplate Ink, 80
Books for Cooks, 83
Books on Tape Inc., 94
Books that Work, 225
Books-On-Disk, 207
Bookshelf, 83

Bookup Inc., 115
Bookworm & Silverfish, 83
Boomerang Man, 94
Boot Town, 387
Boothe Hill Wildflowers, 246
Boothe Mold Company, 111
Bootlegger & Buckaroo Foods, 203
Borbeleta Gardens, 237
Border Leather, 313
Bork (Dennis & Cece) 149, 157, 213, 309
Borland International, 139
Born (W.) & Associates 334, 396
Bornand Music Box Company, 337
Bornside (Bette) Company 304
Bornstein (Mike) Clowns 129, 315
Borup (Maude) 186
Borwick Innovations Inc., 353
Bose Express Music, 405
Bosom Buddies, 51, 122
Boss Distributors, 427
Bostick & Sullivan, 356
Boston & Winthrop, 212
Boston Acoustics, 405
Boston Coffee Cake Company, 184
Boston Mountain Nurseries, 229
Boston Music Company, 337
Boston Proper, 122
Boston Turning Works, 279
Botanicals Etc., 160
Bottega Veneta, 313, 368
Bottelsen Dart Company Inc., 156
Bottom Line Distribution, 136
Bouchard L'Escaut USA Inc., 186
Boucher Kayak Company, 72
Boudin Gifts, 183
Boulder Bikes, 65
Boulevard Motoring Accessories, 45
Boulter Plywood Corporation, 77, 314
Boundary Waters Catalog, 102
Bounsall Aircraft, 1
Bountiful, 396
Bountiful Gardens, 224, 234, 240
Bourdon (Betsy), Weaver 61, 62, 379
Bourgeat Cookware, 302
Bourget Bros., 58, 298, 312, 320, 367, 374, 382, 438
Bow Tie Club, 122
Bow Works, 8
BowBends, 222, 246
Bowhunter Supply Inc., 8, 101, 102, 263, 288
Bowhunters Discount Warehouse Inc., 8, 287
Bowling's Bookstore, 83, 95
BowMasters, 261
Box Seat Collectibles, 342, 346
Boy Scouts of America, 382
Boyd Coffee Company, 206
Boyd's (Cecil) Miniatures 160
Boyds Mill Press, 81
Boyle (Dave) 107
Boyle Meat Packing Company, 197
Boyne (Pjilips) Corporation 172
Bozeman Bio-Tech, 219, 220
Bracklyn Archery, 8
Bradbury & Bradbury Wallpapers, 281
Braden River Engineering, 44
Bradley Auto Inc., 23
Bradley Custom Mantels & Woodworking, 177
Bradley's, 52
Bradley's Movies, 336
Bragg Farm, 196
Braid Products Inc., 178
Braid-Aid, 55, 340, 378, 396, 441

453

CORPORATE INDEX

Brainstorm Concepts, 139
Brainstorms, 251
Branda Shelby & Mustang Parts, 38, 41
Brandi (Bob) Honey 63
Brandine Woodcraft Company, 423
BrandMark, 417
Brandon Industries, 309, 311, 316
Brandy Station Bookshelf, 83
Branford Bike, 66, 67
Brass Bed Shoppe, 211
Brass Beds Direct, 211
Brass Knob, 277, 309
Brass Ladle Products, 184
Brass Light Gallery, 307, 311
Brass Lion, 6, 309
Brass Menagerie, 56, 267, 309
Brass Reproductions, 307, 309
Brass Ring Graphics, 127
Brass Works Lighting, 309
Brassworks, 44
Bratton's Antique Ford Parts, 37
Brauer Brothers Manufacturing Company, 264
Braun Appliances, 7
Braun Corporation, 271, 435
Bravado Designs, 51, 122
Bre Lumber/Rare Earth Hardwoods, 275, 314
BRE Software, 423
Bread Alone, 183
Breakell (J.H.) & Company 296
Breck's Dutch Bulbs, 232, 240
Breedlove Enterprises, 13
Bregstone Associates Inc., 157
Bremer (Beverly) Silver Shop 389
Brentwood Manor Furnishings, 213
Brentwood Volvo, 43
Brett (Sue) 120, 121, 122, 125, 127, 386
Brew & Grow, 221, 437
Brew City Supplies, 437
Brew Masters Ltd., 437
Brew Pot, 83
Brewart Coins & Stamps, 398
Brewer Sewing Supplies, 385
Brewer's (Charlie) Slider Company 178
Brewer's Gourmet Inc., 437
Brewers Resource, 437
Brewery, 437
Brewery Company, 437
Brewster Birdhouse, 70
Brian's Crafts Unlimited, 151
Briarwood Gardens, 228
Brickel's Racing Collectibles, 405
Brickhouse Cycles, 332
Brickyard House of Ceramics, 112
Bridal By The Yard, 172
Bridal by The Yard, 383
Bridal Slips, 119
Bridals International, 172
Bridge City Tool Works, 417
Bridge Kitchenware Corporation, 302
Bridger Creek Outfitters, 285
Bridges Roses, 240
Bridgestone Golf Clubs, 259
Bridgewater Scrollworks, 415
Bridi Aircraft Designs Inc., 323
Brielle Galleries, 251, 347
Brier Run Farm, 188
Brigade Quartermasters Inc., 101, 392, 407
Brigandi Coin Company, 398
Brigar Electronics, 167
Briggs Industries, 56
Bright (James) Backgrounds 355
Bright-Life, 251
Brightwater, 178

Briley, 266
Brine Inc., 307, 369, 394
Brink (Libby) 58, 298
Brinton's (Gary) Antique Auto Parts 39
Bristol (Lee) 237
Bristol Valley Hardwoods, 314
Bristolite Skylights, 282
Britalia Motors, 332
Brite Sky, 17
Britek Inc., 358
Britex, 383
British Auto/USA, 34
British Car Specialists, 26
British Collectibles Ltd., 321
British Cycle Supply Company, 332
British Miles, 25, 26, 37, 42
British Northwest Land-Rover Company, 41
British Only Motorcycles & Parts Inc., 332
British Pacific Ltd., 41
British Parts International, 34
British Parts Northwest, 34, 41, 42
British Regalia Imports, 321
British Shoppe, 188, 192
British Vintages Inc., 34
Britten-Grant Event Design, 355
Brittigan's Specialty Soups, 192
Brittingham Plant Farms, 229
Broad-Axe Beam Company, 314
Broadbent's B & B Food Products, 197
Broadfoot Publishing Company, 83, 322
Broadleaf Venison USA, 197
Broadview Dolls, 163
Broadway Collection, 267
Broadway Computer & Video, 136
Broadway Jewelry Ent., 296
Broadway Press, 83
Broadway Rick's Strike Zone, 19, 398
Broadway Yarn Company, 441
Broan Manufacturing Company, 286, 428
Brock (Ken) Manufacturing 2
Brockton Cycle Center, 331, 332
Brodak's, 323
Broder Brothers, 258
Broderbund Software, 250
Broderbund Software Inc., 139
Brodhead-Garrett, 435
Brodnax Prints, 160
Broken Arrow Ranch, 197
Bromwell Marketing, 360
BronceX Ltd., 388
Bronco Parts, 26
Bronica, 356
Brooklin Boat Yard, 75
Brookline Technologies, 425
Brooklyn Botanic Garden, 83, 428
Brooklyn Camera Exchange, 360
Brooks (Steve) 305
Brooks Brothers, 122
Brook's Detectors, 320
Brooks Rubber Stamps, 377
Brookstone Company, 225, 251, 286, 302, 417
Brookwood Gardens Inc., 235, 237
Brother International Corporation, 132, 304
Brothers Coffee, 206
Brothers Truck Parts, 48
Broward Shooter's Exchange, 8, 287
Brown (Arthur) & Bros. Inc. 10, 348
Brown (Dave) Products 329
Brown (Fritz T.)-Books 80
Brown (H.D.) Enterprise Ltd. 208, 370
Brown (Ken) Stamps 377
Brown (Ken) Studio 98
Brown (L.S.) Company 77, 432
Brown (T.E.) Hot Tub 286

Brown Adobe, 189
Brown Brothers Lapidary, 298
Brown Company, 70, 97
Brown House Dolls, 163
Brown Line, 358
Brown-Jordan, 217
Browncor International, 343
Brownells Inc., 169, 265
Brownies on Tour, 184
Brownie's Third Lung, 392
Browning Company, 8, 101, 178, 264, 265, 287
Browning Golf Clubs, 259
Brown's (Stan) Arts & Crafts Inc. 10, 415
Brown's Country Creations, 149, 409
Brown's Edgewood Gardens, 97, 224, 234
Brownstone Studio, 122
Brownstone Woman, 121
Brownville Mills, 195, 430
Brozman (Bob) 338
BRS Parachutes, 3
Brubaker (Jack) Designs 105, 437
Brubaker Metalcrafts, 309
Bruce Manufacturing Inc., 286
Bruce Medical Supply, 159, 269, 289, 345, 435
Bruckner Hobbies Inc., 324, 326, 327, 329
Brudy (John) Exotics 240
Brudy's Exotics, 83, 97, 229, 231, 235
Brugger Brothers, 203
Brumback (Mildred) 115, 152
Bruné (R.E.), Luthier 338
Brunelle Enterprises Inc., 406
Bruno Independent Living Aids, 271, 435
Bruns Manufacturing Ltd., 67
Brunton, 102
Brunton's Barracks, 420
Brush Strokes, 13, 149
Brushy Mountain Bee Farm, 63, 70, 266
Brute Group, 318, 440
Bryant (Lane) 121, 122, 127, 386
Bryant Laboratory Inc., 356
Bryant Stove Inc., 177, 279, 406
Bryant's Auto Parts, 23
BSAR Solar, 286, 395
BSI Sporting Goods, 8, 178, 263, 287
BSIA Mustang Supply, 37, 38
Bubba's Clown Supplies, 129
Buchanan (Curtis), Windsor Chairmaker 213
Buchanan Aviation Art, 13
Buchanan Hollow Nut Company, 199
Buchingers, 22
Buck Hill Associates, 13, 346
Buck Knives, 102, 156
Buck Run Carving Supplies, 439
Buck Stop Lure Company Inc., 288
Buckaroo Bobbins, 128, 384
Buckaroo Marine, 351
Buckeye Powered Parachutes Inc., 3
Buckeye Sports Supply, 8, 51, 393, 394, 432
Buckhorn Ginseng, 233
Bucklers Carpet Inc., 379
Bucks County Classic, 58, 298
Bucks Trading Post, 154, 409
BuckShot Treestands, 287
Budd (Ellen) Postcards 364
Buehler (Maynard P.) 264
Buff (Paul C.) Inc. 358
Buffalo Arms Company, 263
Buffalo Batt & Felt Corporation, 385
Buffalo Bill Historical Center, 251
Buffalo Bill Telecard Gallery, 354
Buffalo Bullet Company, 262
Buffalo Products Inc., 136

CORPORATE INDEX

Buffalo Sun, 293
Buffalo Tipi Pole Company, 102
Bufftech Inc., 175
Bufton (E.F.) & Son, Builders Inc. 276
Bufton's Collectable Miniatures, 160
Buick Farm, 26
Buick Specialist, 26
Bulb Crate, 237
Bulbman, 414
Bulldog Computer Products, 136
Bullock & Jones, 122
Bumjo's, 102, 334, 396
Bundles of Bulbs, 240
Bunting Magnetics Company, 306, 316
Burak (Matthew) Furniture 13, 213, 309
Burbank Water Ski Company, 432
Burberry's Limited, 126, 192, 252, 368
Burchill Antique Auto Parts, 25
Burden's Surplus Center, 407
Burdines, 158
Burdoch Victorian Lamp Company, 311
Bureau of Electronic Publishing, 139
Burford Brothers, 243
Burgers' Ozark Country Cured Hams Inc., 197
Burghardt Amateur Center, 371
Burk Electronics, 371
Burke Flex-O Products, 178
Burke Inc., 435
Burleson (J.P.) Inc. 351
Burley Design Cooperative, 65, 67
Burlington Foreign Car Parts Inc., 23
Burnett (Wm. T.) & Company Inc. 307
Burnett Petrified Wood Inc., 376
Burns Binnert Plating Inc., 43
Burnt Cabins Grist Mill, 96, 183, 192
Burnt Ridge Nursery & Orchards, 236, 243
Burpee (W. Atlee) & Company 219, 229, 231, 233, 236, 240
Burpo Duh Clown, 129, 377, 413
Burr Tavern, 276
Burrell (D.V.) Seed Company 240
Burris Company Inc., 264
Burrows (J.R.) & Company 281, 379
Burt Associates, 229
Burt's (Brad) Magic Shop 315
Buschemeyer's Silver Exchange, 389
Bush Herpetological Supply, 353
Bushmaster Reptiles Inc., 353
Bushnell Corporation, 68
Bushwacker, 321
Bushy Ridge Products, 287
Business & Institutional Furniture Company, 96, 217
Business Book, 96, 343, 401
Business Envelope Manufacturers, 96, 401
Business Envelopes, 114, 401
Business Forms by Carlson Craft, 343
Business Reader, 83
Busse Gardens, 232, 237
Busy Bee Products, 105
Butch's Jet Ski, 295
Butler Parachute Systems Inc., 4
Butler Racing Inc., 44
Butler's Bowhunting, 8
Butterbrooke Farm, 240
Butterick Pattern Company, 384
Butternut Electronics, 371
Butternut Mountain Farm, 196
Button Shop, 383
Buttons Unlimited, 383
Butwin Sportswear Company, 95, 114
Buyer's Associates, 427
By-Gone Days Antiques Inc., 177, 267, 277
By-Rite Pet Supplies, 351

Byers Chassis Kits, 371
Byers Company, 17
Byrd Cookie Company, 184
Byrne Ceramic Supply Company Inc., 112
Byron Originals Inc., 324

C

C & B Distributors, 351
C & C Detectors, 320
C & C Photo Lab, 358
C & D Collectible Diecasts, 326
C & D Jarnagin Company, 321, 322
C & F Wholesale Ceramics, 112
C & G Early Ford Parts, 33
C & H Lures Custom Lures, 178
C & H Roofing, 277
C & H Sales Company, 169
C & J Gallery, 160
C & N Minerals, 375
C & P Chevy Parts, 28, 48
C & R Enterprises Inc., 298, 375
C & R Inquiries, 274, 349
C & S Products Company Inc., 70, 349
C & S Sales Inc., 169
C & T Publishing/Fox Hill Workshop, 83
C.A.R.S. Inc., 28
C.D.I. Imports, 107, 109
C.D.M., 51
CA Animation Galleries, 13
Caballo, 126
Cabela's, 102, 178, 287
Cabin Craft Southwest, 415
Cabin Crafters, 415
Cabinets by Vector, 159, 373
Cable Box Wholesalers Inc., 427
Cable Car Clothiers, 122
Cable Warehouse, 427
Caboose Hobbies, 83, 330
Cabot Annex, 188
Cabot Creamery, 188, 195
Cache Junction, 174
Cactus by Mueller, 231
Caddo Trading, 290, 374, 375
Cadillac King Inc., 27
Cadillac USA Parts Supply, 27
Cadman (T.) 83
Caere Corporation, 139
Cafe Beaujolais, 184, 186, 206
Cafe Companies Inc., 203
Café La Semeuse, 206
Caffeinds, 206
Cagle (Gretchen) Publications 83
Cahall's Brown Duck, 122
Cahners Direct Mail Services, 317
Cal National Coin Exchange, 346
Cal Pac Corporation, 289
Cal West Supply Inc., 168
Cal-Formed Plastics Company, 352
Cal-Gold, 312, 320, 367
Cal-June, 71
Caladium World, 241
CalAutoArt, 368
Calcera, 167
Calco Food Company Inc., 206
Caldera Spas, 247
Caldwell Craft Supply, 151
Caledonia Hats, 268
Caledonian Graphics, 127
Calef's Country Store, 188
Cali4nia Skate Express, 390
Calibre Press Inc., 83, 428
Calico House, 172
Calico Kitchen Press, 210
California Albums, 108

California Aquarium Supply Company, 351
California Best, 120, 380
California Bolas, 298
California Bridal Fabrics, 172
California Cage Company, 70
California Cageworks Corporation, 70
California Gym Equipment Company, 170
California Mustang, 38, 44
California Power Systems Inc., 4
California Ranchwear Inc., 400
California Redwood Association, 175, 247, 276, 278
California Reef Specialists, 351
California Side Car, 332
California Stainless Manufacturing, 356
California Stitchery, 258, 340
California Telescope Company, 17, 68
Callahan's Calabash Nautical City, 364
Callaway Gardens Country Store, 192
Callaway Golf Clubs, 259
Calligraphy Shoppe, 98
Calton Cases of Canada, 338
Calumet Photographic, 355, 356
Camaro Connection, 27
Camaro Specialties, 27, 32
CAMBER Universal Sportswear, 114
Cambri Enterprises, 164
Cambridge Camera Exchange, 357, 360
Cambridge Designs, 224, 227
Cambridge Metalsmiths, 388
Cambridge Soundworks, 403
Cambridge University Press, 83
Cambridge Zen Center, 289
Camel Outdoor Products, 102
Camellia & Main, 252
Camelot Enterprises, 267
Camera Bug Ltd., 17, 68, 264
Camera Care, 360
Camera City Inc., 360
Camera Corner of Iowa, 69, 360
Camera One of Sarasota Inc., 360
Camera Sound of Pennsylvania, 99, 360
Camera Traders Ltd., 360
Camera World, 99, 360, 362
Camera World of Oregon, 99
Camerama Corporation, 356
Cameras & Electronics of New Jersey & Maine, 360
Camille Company Inc., 354
Camjacket Company, 355
Camp (J.O.) 139
Camp (Michael) 213
Camp 7 Inc., 101, 102
Camp Canoe & Paddle Manufacturing, 73
Camp Trails/Johnson Worldwide Associates, 102
Campagna Distinctive Flavors, 203
Campbell Cabinets, 97
Campbell Hausfeld, 1, 417
Campbell Pump Company Inc., 112
Campbell Tools Company, 320, 329
Campbell's Collectibles, 60
Campbellsville Industries Inc., 276, 279
Camper's Choice, 47
Camper's Library, 83
Camping World, 102
Campmor, 101, 102
Camus International, 340
Can-Am Card Company, 398
Can-Am Marketing, 326
Canadian Herb & Spice Company, 203
Canadian Home Rotors Inc., 2
Canadian Mustang, 38
Canari Cycle Wear, 66, 122
Candle Factory, 105, 366

CORPORATE INDEX

Candlechem Products, 105, 348
Candlertown Chairworks, 213
Cane & Basket Supply Company, 55, 114
CaneFire Software, 139
Canfield Motors, 23
Caning Shop, 55, 114
Cannon Sports,
    53, 95, 152, 170, 208, 346, 370, 409, 412, 425, 431
Cannon Sports Inc., 51, 54
Cannondale Corporation, 65, 66
Canon, 99, 356, 358, 403, 425
Canon Binoculars, 69
Canon Computer Systems, 132, 134, 136
Canor Plarex, 77
Canstar Sports, 267, 273, 289
Canvas Crafts, 76
Canvas Shoppe Inc., 45
Canyon Cinema, 336
Canyon Creek Nursery, 238
Capability's Books, 83
Capco Sportswear Inc., 53
Cape Cod Cupola Co. Inc., 274
Cape Cod Cupola Company Inc., 433
Cape Cod Worm Farm, 219
Cape Forge, 417
Cape May Miniatures, 160
CapellaSoft, 16
Capital Electronics Inc., 167
Capital Eurosport, 332
Capri Arts & Crafts, 415
Caprice Farm Nursery, 235, 237
Caprilands Herb Farm, 234
Caprine Supply Company, 114
Capriola (J.M.) Company 285
Caprock Business Forms Inc., 343, 401
Capstan Distributing, 225
Capstone/Intracorp Inc., 139
Capt. Harry's Fishing Supplies, 178
Captain Bijou, 334
Captain Dick's Dummy Depot, 315
Captain's Choice, 202
Captain's Emporium, 50, 79
Car Books, 22
Car Collectables, 21, 261
Car Cover Pros, 45
Car Shop, 28
Car-Line Manufacturing & Distributor Inc., 37
Carabella Collection, 122
Caradon Friedland, 274
Caran d'Ache of Switzerland Inc., 10
Carat Patch, 298
Carbite Golf Company, 259
CarCovers USA, 45
Card Collectors Company, 398
Cardboard Gold Inc., 398
Cardinal Engineering Inc., 320
Cardinal Incorporated, 160, 164
Cards USA, 210
Care-A-Lot, 350
Carib-America Inc., 55
Caribbean Creatures, 351
Caribbean Kite Company, 303
Caribe Inflatable USA, 75
Caribone Designs, 296
Caribou Imports Inc., 32, 35, 36
Caribou Mountaineering, 102
Carina Software, 16
Caring Products International Inc.,
    50, 122, 271, 289
Carino Nurseries, 243
Carleybrook Gardens, 238
Carlisle Development Corporation, 139
Carlisle Paddles, 73
Carlisle Restoration Lumber, 275

Carlson (Douglas R.) 263
Carlson Craft, 344
Carlson's Gardens, 228
Carlton Rose Nurseries, 240
Carmel Music Company, 338
Carolan Craft Supplies, 151
Carolina Basketry, 55
Carolina Classics, 48
Carolina Craftsman, 267, 276
Carolina Exotic Gardens, 231, 243
Carolina Interiors, 213
Carolina Mills Factory Outlet, 172
Carolina Mountain, 202
Carolina Smoked Specialties Inc., 202
Caroline's Country Ruffles, 154
Carol's Heirloom Cookies, 146, 184
Carolyn's Pecans, 199
Carousel at Casino Pier, 107
Carousel Carpet Mills Inc., 379
Carousel Collections, 377
Carousel Gem & Minerals, 375
Carousel Lady, 107
Carousel Records, 108
Carousel Shopper, 107
Carousel Workshop, 107
Carp River Trading Company, 186, 200, 203
Carpenter (Dennis) Reproductions
    30, 32, 33, 41, 42, 45, 48
Carpenter's Brothers Furniture, 211, 213
Carpenter's Shop, 224
Carpet Express, 275, 279, 379
Carpet King, 49
Carpet Outlet, 379
Carradus Gifts, 160
Carriage House Motor Cars Ltd., 26, 40
Carriage Trade Publishing II Inc., 210
Carrier Corporation, 1, 211, 286
Carroll (Wayne) 371
Carroll Gardens, 235, 239
Carron Net Company, 54, 412
Carrot-Top Industries Inc., 181
Carrousel Magic, 107
Carrt-Lite Inc., 8
Carruth Studio Inc., 222
Cars & Parts, 37
Cars & Parts Collectibles, 326
Cars Inc., 26
CARSoft, 139
Carter & Holmes Inc., 237
Carter (Harriet) 252
Carter (Jim) Antique Truck Parts 48
Carter Canopies, 61
Carter Heirlooms, 225
Carter Printing, 414
Cartoon Art Unlimited, 13
Cartoon Colour, 10
Cartoon Company, 13
CarTop Tent, 102
Cartophilians, 346, 365
Carts Vermont, 219, 225
Carushka Inc., 154
Caruso (Laura) 60
Caruso Music, 338
Carver Corporation, 403
Carver's Eye Company, 60, 163
Carvin, 338
Casa Dos Tapetes De Arraiolos Inc., 379
Casablanca Fan Company, 174
Cascade Conserves Inc., 200
Cascade Daffodils, 232
Cascade Designs Inc., 106, 362
Cascade Greenhouse Supply, 220
Cascade Medical Inc., 159
Cascade Outfitters, 373
Cascadia Company, 83

Cascadian Farm, 195
Casco Bay Fine Woolens, 122
Case (W.R.) & Sons Cutlery Company 305
Cases Plus, 159
Cash Manufacturing Company Inc., 263
Cashmeres Etc., 122
Cash's of Ireland, 252
Casio, 99
Casita Travel Trailers, 47
Cassens & Plath of U.S. Inc., 78
Cast Aluminum Reproductions,
    209, 213, 224, 311, 316
Castaic Ski and Sport, 295
Castcraft, 12, 363
Castiglione Accordion, 338
Castle Metal Finishing, 43
Castolite, 12, 363
Castriota Collection, 252
Casual Collections, 252
Casual Living, 252
Casual Male Big & Tall, 127
Caswell Electroplating in Miniature, 169
Caswell International Corporation, 265
Caswell-Massey Company Ltd.,
    147, 182, 348, 366
Cat Claws, 252, 350
Catch the Wind, 303
Catchall, 400
Cathedral Stone Products Inc., 276
Cats, 252, 405
Catskill Mountain Chimes, 436
Cattle Company Cowboy Exchange,
    115, 389
Cattle Kate, 128, 148
Catworkz...and DOGS' too Inc., 160
Cavalari (Agnes) 365
Cavalry Regimental Supply, 148, 387
Cavanaugh (Marlene) Posters 21
Cavanaugh Lakeview Farms Ltd., 192, 197
Cave (L.A.) 374, 375
Caviar & Caviar, 188
Caviar House Inc., 202
Caviarteria Inc., 188
Caviness Woodworking Company, 73
Cayce Company, 417
CB Performance Parts, 45
CBC International Inc., 372
CCM Maska, 376
CCS Skateboards, 127, 390
CCSI Furniture, 213
CCTV Corporation, 5
CD Research, 109
CD Technology Inc., 132
CD Wherehouse, 108
CD-ROM Warehouse, 136
CDW Computer Centers Inc., 136
CE Software Inc., 139
CEB Metasystems, 16
Cedar Auto Parts, 23
Cedar Creek Relic Shop, 322
Cedar Heights Clay Company Inc., 112
Cedar Hill Game Call Company, 288
Cedar Rock Furniture, 213
Cedar Valley Shingle Systems, 277, 278
Cedar Works, 363
Cedco Publishing Company, 98
Cee Cee China, 115
Cee-Jay Sports Card Company, 398
Cel-ebration Animation Art Gallery, 13
Celadon, 277
Celebration Fantastic, 252
Celebrity Gallery, 19, 319
Celestaire, 78
Celestial, 157, 213
Celestial Silks, 62, 121

CORPORATE INDEX

Celestial Wind, 338
Celestron International, 17, 69
Celia's & Susan's Dolls & Collectibles, 164
Celia's Sweets Inc., 184
Celiberti Motors, 35, 36
Cellar Homebrew, 437
CellStar Corporation, 410
Cellular Phone & Accessory Warehouse, 410
Cellular World, 146, 410
Cementex Latex Corporation, 12
Centaur Fencing Systems Inc., 175
Centaur Forge Ltd., 71
Central Boiler Inc., 211
Central Coast Creations, 303
Central Corvette, 30
Central Discount Flag & Banner, 181
Central Fire Sprinkler Corporation, 176
Central Florida Reptile Farm, 353
Central Industries, 44
Central Metal Products Inc., 352
Central Model Marketing, 328
Central Skin Divers, 392
Central Snowmobile Salvage, 393
Central Tractor Farm & Family Center, 175
Central Vac International, 428
Century Fireplace Furnishings Inc., 176
Century Helicopter Products, 324
Century Import & Export Inc., 324
Century Instrument Corporation, 3
Century International Arms, 262, 265
Century Jet Models Inc., 324
Century Martial Art Supply Inc., 318
Century Products, 367
Century Sauce Kitchens, 203
Century Sports Inc.,
  51, 346, 363, 370, 412
Century Studio, 309
Cer Cal Decals Inc., 112
Cerami Corner, 112, 115
Ceramic Supply of NY/NJ, 112
Ceramichrome, 112
Ceravolo Optical Systems, 17
Cermark Electronic & Model Supply, 324
Certainly Wood, 314
CertainTeed, 277
Certified Prime, 197
C'est Croissant Inc., 183
CFO Forms, 343
CGM Inc., 298
Chachere's (Tony) Creole Foods 83, 189
Chadsworth Incorporated, 276, 279
Chadwick's of Boston, 122
Chalet Suzanne Country Inn & Restaurant, 192
Chalfrin (R.) 80
Chalmers-Gabrych Plantasia, 182
Chambers, 61, 409, 420
Chambers (Charles) Parts 38
Chambers (John) Vintage Chevrolet 28
Chambless Cine Equipment, 336
Champion America Inc., 381
Champion Boot Company, 387
Champion Decal Company, 330
Champion Industries Inc., 343
Champion Printing Company, 343
Champion Products Inc.,
  53, 54, 120, 380, 394, 431
Champion Sports, 398
Champion Sports Collectables Inc.,
  19, 397, 398
Champion Supply Company, 351
Chandler (Bill) Farms 349
Chandler (David) Software 16
Chandler's Taxidermy Supply Inc., 410
Chaparral, 331, 332

Chaparral Records Inc., 400
Chapin's Fudge & Chocolates, 186
Chapman, 213, 309
Chapman (Ann) 252
Chapman (Carol) 58
Chapman (Dean) 334
Char-Broil, 52
Char-Lee Originals, 415
Charles (Bob) 312
Charles (Michael) Cabinetmakers 213
Charles Craft, 340
Charlesbridge Publishing, 83
Charleston Battery Bench, 217
Charleston Cake Lady, 184
Charleston Custom Cycle, 332
Charleston Gardens, 217
Charley's Greenhouse Supply, 225
Charley's Guitar Shop, 338
Charlie's Rock Shop,
  58, 115, 118, 298, 375
Charlotte Camera Brokers Inc., 360
Charm Woven Labels, 385
Charmac Trailers, 284
Charmaster Products Inc., 176, 211, 406
Charrington House, 81
Chartroom, 69
Chase (Dan) Taxidermy Supply 410
Chase Technologies, 403
Chaselle Inc., 10, 12, 112, 115, 151, 389
Chatham Art Distributors, 10, 415
Chatila Dance & Gymnastic Fashions, 155
Chattanooga Coin Company, 398
Chatterton (Don) of Seattle 360
Chautauqua Inc., 83
Chavant Inc., 12
Chazpro Magic Company, 129, 301, 315
Cheap Joe's Art Stuff, 10
Cheap Shot, 262
Checks in the Mail, 114
Cheesecake Lady, 184
Cheesecake Royale, 184
Cheesemaking Supply Outlet, 114
Chef Revival, 128, 252, 302
Chef's Catalog, 130, 286, 289, 302, 305
Chelsea Decorative Metal Company, 273
Chem-Lab, 306, 321
Chemtrol, 408
Chenesko Products Inc., 145, 344
Cheri's Desert Harvest, 200
Cherokee National Museum Gift Shop,
  13, 15, 293
Cherri-Oats & Company,
  129, 368, 405, 413
Cherry Auto Parts, 23
Cherry Hill Furniture, 213
Cherry Pond Designs, 213
Cherry Tree Clothing, 119
Cherry Tree Toys, 439, 440
Cherrywood Fabrics Inc., 172
Chesapeake Bay Gourmet, 202
Chesapeake Express, 202
Chesapeake Light Craft, 72, 73
Cheshire Cat Children's Books, 81
Chess (Mary) Inc. 147
Chessler Books, 83
Chestnut Hill Furniture, 213
Chestnut Hill Nursery Inc., 243
Chevelle Classics, 28, 31
Chev's of the 40's, 28, 48
Chevy Duty Pickup Parts, 48
Chevy Parts Warehouse, 27
Chevyland, 27, 30, 31, 38, 48
Chewning's Auto Literature Ltd., 22
Cheyenne Outfitters, 128
Cheyenne Pick Up Parts, 48

Chi Nah Bah, 292
Chiasso, 252, 348
Chicago Corvette Supply, 30
Chicago Faucet Company, 174
Chicago Kite Company, 303
Chicago Muscle Car Parts, 27, 32, 35
Chicago Old Telephone Company, 410
Chicago Pneumatic Company, 417
Chicago Sports Cards Ltd., 398
Chicago Trophy & Awards Company, 50
Chick's Harness & Supply, 284
Chicory Farm, 188
Chief Aircraft Inc., 3
Chief Seattle Seafood, 202
Childcraft, 67, 119, 422
ChildLife Inc., 363
Children's Book Press, 81
Children's Wear Digest, 119
Chile Head-Mouthsurfing by Mail, 203
Chile La Isla, 189, 191, 203
Chilkat Valley Arts, 290
Chilton Book Company, 22, 83
Chimera, 358
China, 115, 152, 389
China & Crystal Cabinet Inc., 115
China & Crystal Closet, 115
China & Crystal Matchers Inc., 115
China Books & Periodicals Inc., 83
China Cabinet (South Carolina), 152
China Cabinet Inc., 389
China Connection, 115
China Decorator Library, 83
China Diesel Imports, 166
China Hutch, 115
China Marketing, 115, 152
China Replacements, 115, 152
China Warehouse, 115, 152, 389
Chinaberry Book Service, 81, 337
Chinese Porcelain Company, 6
Chinon America Inc., 69, 99, 136, 356
Chinook Medical Gear Inc., 269
Chinook Motorhomes, 47
Chip Factory, 132
Chips & Bits, 144
Chisco Sports Accessories, 289, 391
Chiswick Trading Inc., 345
Chock Catalog Corporation, 121
Choco-Logo, 186
Chocoholics Divine Desserts, 186
Chocolate Barn, 186
Chocolate Catalogue, 184, 186
Chocolate Lady Inc., 186
Chocolate Photos, 186
Choctaw Museum of the Southern Indian
  Gift Shop, 291
Choices, 62, 369
Chris' Craft Supplies, 209, 340
Chrisjohn Family Arts & Crafts, 292
Christian Book Distributors,
  13, 81, 93, 98, 127, 144, 423, 428
Christmas Treasures, 117
Christmas Village Company, 330
Christmastime Traditions, 117, 337
Christophers Ltd., 69
Christy's Bears, 60
Chriswill Forge, 149
Chroma, 10, 415
Chrome Brite Plating, 43
Chrome-Tech U.S.A., 329
Chronicle Books, 83
Chronicles Bookshop, 83
CHS Inc., 349
Chuck's Used Auto Parts, 23
Chukar Cherries, 186, 191, 193, 200, 203

Church of Jesus Christ of Latter-day Saints, 139, 250
Churchills, 15, 363
Church's English Shoes, 386
Ciadella, 29
Cimarron, 263
Cincinnati Art Museum, 13
Cincinnati Microwave, 43, 410
Cinder Whit & Company, 279
Cindy's Stitches, 174
Cinema City, 334, 336
Cinema Collectors, 334
Cinema Graphics, 334
Cinema Memories, 334
Cinema Visions, 334
Cinemonde, 334
Cir-Kit Concepts Inc., 160
Circa Antiques, 6
Circadian Clock Company, 118
Circle Craft Supply, 151
Circle J Trailers, 284
Circle R Boot & Saddle, 285
Circuit Specialists Inc., 167
Circus Clowns, 129, 148
Circustamps, 377
Cirecast Inc., 267
Ciro Coppa Doors, 274
Cirtain Plywood Inc., 314, 439
Citizen America Corporation, 132
Citizen Watch Company of America, 4, 78, 392
City Camera, 17, 69
City Lights, 309
City Spirit, 122
City Wrecking Company, 23
CIV Miniatures, 420
Civil War Antiques, 6, 322
Civil War Genealogy, 250
CJ Originals, 160
CJ Pony Parts Inc., 38
CJ's Dolls & Dreams, 165
Claggett (David L.) 309
Clairine's Tropica USA Inc., 200
Clambake Celebrations, 202
Clapper's, 217, 225
Clargreen Gardens, 237
Clarion Corporation of America, 46, 410
Clarion Martin House, 70
Claris Corporation, 139
Clark (Bob) 353
Clark (David) Company Inc. 3
Clark (Stan) Military Books 83
Clark Craft Boat Company, 72
Clark Custom Guns Inc., 265
Clarke Distributing Company, 260, 394, 412
Clarke Health Care, 271
Clarkpoint Croquet Company, 152
Clark's Corvair Parts Inc., 30
Clark's Greenhouse & Herbal Country, 232, 234
Class Act Multi-media, 133
Classic Accents Inc., 279
Classic American Fund Raisers, 210
Classic Auto Air Mfg. Company, 23, 26, 38, 40
Classic Auto Parts, 35, 39
Classic Auto Parts Inc. (Chevrolet), 29
Classic Auto Replicar, 45
Classic Auto Supply Company Inc., 41
Classic Automobiles, 34
Classic Buicks Inc., 26
Classic Canoes, 77
Classic Carolina Collection, 64
Classic Cars Unlimited, 35

Classic China, 115, 389
Classic Cinema, 336, 428
Classic Cloth, 172
Classic Country Rabbit Company, 197
Classic Designs by Matthew Burak, 439
Classic Enterprises, 41
Classic Factory, 44
Classic Groundcovers Inc., 233
Classic Illumination, 307, 309
Classic Industries, 27, 32, 38
Classic Lamp Posts, 311
Classic Medallics, 50
Classic Memorials Inc., 181
Classic Model Marine, 328
Classic Model Trains, 330
Classic Motoring Accessories, 45
Classic Mustang, 38
Classic Mustang Parts of Oklahoma, 38
Classic Outfitters, 123
Classic Post & Beam, 282
Classic Pumps, 386
Classic Rarities & Company, 19
Classic Recordings, 109
Classic Roadsters, 44, 45
Classic Steaks, 197
Classic Tires of America Inc., 47
Classic Toy Soldier Company, 420
Classic Tube, 23, 48
Classic Wood Manufacturing, 37
Classical Fruit, 243
Classical Numismatic Group Inc., 83
Classics by Simply Country, 149
Classique Cars Unlimited, 35, 41
Classique Perfumes Inc., 147
Clay Craftsman, 115
Clay Creations, 115
Clay Factory, 12
Clay in Motion Inc., 116
Clay Magic Ceramic Products Inc., 112
Claycraft, 224
Clear Lake Furniture, 213
Clear Software Inc., 139
Clear-File (USA) Inc., 354, 361
Clearbrook Farms, 186, 200
Clearbrook Woolen Shop, 172
Clemens (Dale) Custom Tackle 178
Clement Hardware, 267
Clements (William), Boat Builder 73, 75, 77
Clemes & Clemes Inc., 396, 441
Cleveland (Dwight) 335
Cleveland Model & Supply Company, 324
Clevenger Detector Sales, 320
Clever Aquarium Accessories, 351
Cliff Keen Athletic, 440
Clifford & Wills, 123
Cliff's Classic Chevrolet Parts Company, 29, 48
Cliff's Notes Inc., 83, 139
Clifty Farm, 197
Climb Axe Ltd., 334
Climb High Inc., 101, 102, 334, 391, 431
Cline Glass Inc., 400
Clinton Hollins, 346
Clintsman International, 116, 153, 389
Cloarec (Clinton) Custom Wooden Boats 75
Clock Repair Center, 118
Clocks Etc., 118, 252
Clopay Corporation, 218
Close Range Combat Academy, 127, 318
Closetmaid, 119
Clothcrafters Inc., 373
Clotilde, 383
Clown City, 52, 129
Clown Factory, 129
Clown Heaven, 52, 129, 148, 368, 413

Club Kidsoft, 145
ClubMac, 136
Clubman Racing Accessories, 332
CM Specialties, 252
CMC Company, 189
CME Inc., 408
CMH Quiltworks, 369
CMO Superstore, 136
CNC Concepts, 427
CNN Reproductions, 423
Co-Du-Co Computer Dust Covers, 133
Co-Mart International, 318
Co-Op Artists Materials, 10
Co-Op Artists' Materials, 166
Coach Dairy Goat Farm, 188
Coach Leatherware Company, 252, 313, 368
Coachmen Recreational Vehicle Company, 47
Coast Kites Inc., 303
Coast Manufacturing Company, 355, 362
Coast Shoes Inc., 400
Coast to Coast, 99, 360, 404, 426
Coastal Button Supply, 383
Coastal Express Food & Spirits, 193
Cobra, 43, 372
Cobra Golf Clubs, 259
Cobra Restorers, 30, 41
Coca-Cola Catalog, 252
Cochenille Design Studio, 139, 305
Cochran & Associates Inc., 320
Cockpit, 123
Cocoa Beach Coffee, 206
Cocoa-Mill Chocolate Company, 186
Coeur d'Alene Bed Outlet, 213
Coffee Caboodle, 206
Coffey Furniture Galleries, 213
Coghlan's, 102
Cohan (Michael Dennis) Bookseller 94
Cohan (Michael Dennis), Bookseller 80
Cohasset Colonials, 211, 212, 213
Cohen (Dave) & Associates Inc. 159
Coin Machine Trader, 109, 302
Coin World Books, 83
Coinways Antiques, 389
Coker Tires, 47, 326
Cokesbury, 93, 117, 118, 210, 252
Coki Manufacturing Company, 295
Cokin Creative Filter System, 357
Cold Hollow Cider Mill, 193, 252
Cold Spring Anglers, 178
Cold Steel, 305
Coldren Company, 267
Coldwater Creek, 252
Cole (Bill) Enterprises Inc. 131
Coleman Outdoor Products Inc., 75, 101, 102
Coleman Powermate Compressors, 1
Coleman Spas Inc., 286
Cole's Appliance & Furniture Company, 213
Coles' Power Models Inc., 328
Collage Video Specialties Inc., 428
Collectables Records, 108
Collectible Doll Company, 163
Collectible Outlet Inc., 116
Collectibles by Hamilton, 326
Collections, 123
Collector Books, 84
Collector Case Company, 159, 373
Collectorholics, 421
Collector's Armoury, 252, 263, 321, 322, 323
Collector's Book Source, 84
Collectors Brass, 325
Collectors' Choice Music, 109
Collector's Corner Bears, 60

❖ CORPORATE INDEX ❖

Collector's Guide Publishing Inc., 84
Collector's Optics & Supplies, 321
Collectors Showcase, 421
Collectors Warehouse Inc., 335
College Board, 84
Collin Street Bakery, 184
Collins (William H.) Gardens 84, 233
Collins Ski Products Inc., 22, 391, 392
Colonel Gerrish Boomerangs, 94
Colonel Video & Audio, 99, 100, 426
Colonial Bronze Company, 267
Colonial Business Forms Inc., 343
Colonial Casting Company Inc., 149, 252, 434
Colonial Collections of New England Inc., 149
Colonial Connection, 420
Colonial Cupolas, 274, 434
Colonial Dependencies, 386
Colonial Garden Kitchens, 286, 302
Colonial Hardwoods Inc., 314
Colonial Williamsburg, 193, 252
Colonial Williamsburg Furniture, 213
Colophon Book Arts Supply, 80
Coloplast Inc., 345
Color Guard Fence Company, 175
Color Tile, 279
Color Tree, 96
Colorad Boomerangs, 94
Colorado Cyclist, 65
Colorado Frame Manufacturing, 209
Colorado Gold Resources, 367
Colorado Kayak, 71, 373
Colorado Log Furniture Company, 213
Colorado Saddlery Company, 102, 284, 285
Colorado Shooter's Supply, 262
Colorado Spice Company, 203
Colorado Tent Company, 102
Colorel Blinds, 153
Colores International Inc., 303, 388
Colorfast, 96
Colorful Images, 252
Colors, 321
Colpar Hobbies, 324, 325, 326, 327, 328
Colt Clamp Company Inc., 416
Colts Neck Wind Chimes Inc., 436
Columbia Arts, 151
Columbia Cascade, 217
Columbia Gifts, 84, 252
Columbia Historical Society, 247
Columbia Medical Manufacturing Corporation, 271
Columbia Sportswear Company, 123, 391
Columbia Trading Company, 84
Columbia University Press, 84
Columbus Bookbinders & Printers Inc., 343
Columbus Camera Group Inc., 360
Columbus McKinnon Corporation, 271, 435
Columbus Show Case Company, 159
Colvos Creek Nursery, 229, 242, 243
Colwell Systems, 344
Colwood Electronics, 417
Comanche Acres Iris Gardens, 238
Comanche Clown Shoes Mfg., 129
COMB Authorized Liquidator, 407
Combat Models Inc., 324
COMBI, 50
Combination Door Company, 274, 282
Comco Inc., 289
Comeaux's Grocery & Market, 189
Comet Products, 21
Comfort Corner, 386
Comic Book College, 13
Comic Conservation Company, 131
Comic Heaven, 131

Comm-Pute Inc., 371
Commax Technologies, 134
Commercial Aluminum Cookware Company, 302
Commissariat Imports Inc., 204
Commodore Country, 132, 145
Commodore Uniform & Nautical Supplies, 71, 128
Common Scents, 147, 348
Commonwealth of Massachusetts Archives, 248
Communication Concepts Inc., 167
Communication Graphics, 96
Communication Headquarters Inc., 371
Communications Data Corporation, 132, 371
Communications Electronics Inc., 167, 371, 433
Community Kitchens, 130, 189, 193
Community Products Inc., 186, 195
Comotion Rubber Stamps Inc., 377
Companion Plants, 234
Company Store, 62
Compaq Computer Corporation, 134
Compass Computer Products Corporation, 134
Compass Industries, 69, 424
Compass Industries Inc., 380
Compasseco Inc., 262
CompCare, 345
Competition Accessories Inc., 295, 332
Competition Automotive Inc., 27, 33
Competition Werkes, 332
Competitive Aquatic Supply Inc., 392
Compleat Angler Inc., 178
Compleat Company Inc., 52
Compleat Garden Clematis Nursery, 235
Complete Traveler of Overland Park, 84, 313, 317
Components Plus, 259
Composite Companions Inc., 1
Comprehensive Identification Products Inc., 96
Compton (Robert) Ltd. 209, 222
Compton's NewMedia, 139
CompuScope, 16
CompuServe, 136, 137, 139
ComputAbility Consumer Electronics, 43, 136, 145
Computability Consumer Electronics, 146, 404, 426
Computer Associates International Inc., 139
Computer City Direct Catalog, 136, 145
Computer Express, 145
Computer Free America, 134
Computer Friends Inc., 136
Computer Furniture Direct, 134
Computer Label Company, 344
Computer Peripherals Inc., 132
Computer Products Corporation, 132
Computer Support Corporation, 139
Computerlane, 146
Computrol Inc., 181
Comstock, 234, 241
Comstock Creations, 298
Comstock Heritage Collection, 126, 296
Comtrad Industries, 102, 175, 352
Comtrade Electronics USA Inc., 134
Conant Custom Brass, 309
Concept II Inc., 170
Concord Nurseries Inc., 233
Concord Records Inc., 109
Concours Parts & Accessories, 33, 41, 48
Concrete Machinery Company, 12
Condon (Maurice L.) Company 77

Condon (Maurice) Company 314
Conestoga Log Cabins, 283
Conestoga Wood Machinery, 417
Conetrol Scope Mounts, 264
Conewago Junction, 149
Confederate Yankee, 148
Confederation Log Homes, 283
Congressional Quarterly Inc., 84
Conklin Metal Industries, 277
Connect Systems Inc., 371
Connecticut Cane & Reed Company, 114
Connecticut Curtain Company, 153
Connecticut State Archives, 247
Connecticut Stone Supplies, 278
Connecticut Valley Arms Inc., 263
Connectix Corporation, 139
ConnectSoft Inc., 139
Connell's, 232, 233
Connelly Billiard Manufacturing, 68
Connelly Skis Inc., 432
Conner's Architectural Antiques, 277
Conney Safety Products, 381
Conrad Furniture, 213
Conrad Industries, 156
Conrad Machine Company, 10
Conservatree Paper Company, 373
Consolidated Electronics Inc., 167
Consolidated Plastics Company, 345
Consolidated Plastics Company Inc., 119
Constantine, 267, 314, 417, 440
Constantine Gem World, 298
Constructive Playthings, 422, 423
Consumer Care Products Inc., 271
Consumer Information Center, 84, 250
Consumer Reports Books, 84
Consumertronics, 168
Contact East, 167, 169
Contax, 356
Contempo Lapidary, 298
Contemporary Classic Motor Car Company, 30, 44
Contemporary Corvette, 30
Contemporary Frame Company, 209
Continental Archery Inc., 8
Continental Bridge, 222
Continental Clay Company, 112
Continental Data Forms, 344
Continental Enterprises, 27, 29, 33, 35, 36, 40, 41
Continental Showcase Inc., 159
Continental Sports Supply, 53
Continental Sports Supply Inc., 394
Control Memory Factory, 136
Controlled Energy Corporation, 286
Convaid Products Inc., 435
Convatec, 345
Converse (Gordon S.) & Company 6, 118
Converse Inc., 95, 380, 411, 424, 431
Cook (Bob) Classic Auto Parts 30, 31, 32, 33, 35, 36, 37, 38, 41, 42
Cook (Joan) 123, 286
Cook Bullets, 262
Cook in the Kitchen, 193
Cook Receipt Book Manufacturing Company, 344
Cookbook Cellar, 84
Cookbook Publishers Inc., 210
Cookbooks by Morris Press, 210
Cookie Tree, 117
Cook's Consulting, 225
Cook's Garden, 241
Cook's Wares, 130, 183, 302
Cooley's Gardens, 238
Cooley's Strawberry Nursery, 229
Coon's Mill Farm, 186

CORPORATE INDEX

Cooper International Inc., 273, 289
Cooper's Garden, 238
Cooper's Vintage Auto Parts, 26, 27, 39
Copenhaver (Laura) Industries Inc. 62
Coppa Woodworking Inc., 217
Copper Craft Lighting Inc., 311
Copper Electronics Inc., 371, 372
Copper House, 311, 434
Copper Star Cattle & Trading Company, 313, 368
Copperhead Technologies Inc., 132
Coppersmith, 307, 309
Coppersmith (A.J.P.) & Company 433
Coppersmiths, 176, 274, 316
Coppersmythe (Josiah R.) 311
Coral Reef Aquatics, 351
Coran-Sholes, 400
Corbett (Roc) Custom Lighting 307
Corbett's Collectable Dolls, 165
Corcini (Carla) 436
Cordon Bleu Daylilies, 238
Cordwainer Shop, 386
Corel Corporation, 139
Corex Technologies, 139
Cornell Laboratory of Ornithology, 361
Cornell Paper & Box Company Inc., 345
Cornette Ribbon & Trophy Company, 50
Cornucopia, 213
Coronado Leather, 264
Coronet Books, 108, 109, 111
Corporate Systems Center, 132
Correct Craft, 47
Corson Motorcars Ltd., 44
Corti Brothers, 189
Cortland Line Company, 178
Corvair Underground, 30
Corvette Central, 30
Corvette Rubber Company, 30
Corvette Specialties of MD, 30
Cosby (Gerry) & Company 208
Cosmar Magic, 315
COSMI Corporation, 139
Cosmic Connection Telescopes, 17
Cosmic Connections Inc., 17, 69
Cosmic Patterns, 16
Cosmopolitan Motors Inc., 67
Cosmos Ltd., 17, 69, 321
Costume Connection, 148
Costume Gallery, 155
Costume Shop, 155
Costumes by Betty, 129, 148, 413, 436
Cotswold Collectibles Inc., 421
Cottage Creek Cross-stitch, 340
Cotten Concept, 127
Cotton Clouds, 304, 441
Cotton Express, 172
Cotton Gin Inc., 149
Cotton Patch, 84, 340, 369
Cotton Shoppe of Key Largo, 172, 369
Cotuit Oyster Company, 202
Cougar Claw, 287
Cougar Mountain Software, 139
Cougar Sports, 208, 440
Coulter Optical Company, 17
Countdown Hobbies, 327
Counter Spy Shop, 408
Countree Living, 213
Country Accents, 149, 320
Country Basket Weaving, 55
Country Bed Shop, 211, 213
Country Bouquet, 149
Country Braid House, 379
Country Casual, 217, 222, 266
Country Charm Inc., 105, 149, 157
Country Coffee Company Inc., 206

Country Cousins, 157
Country Craftmasters, 153
Country Cupolas, 274
Country Curtains, 154
Country Designs, 386, 440
Country Elegance, 119
Country Estate Pecans, 199
Country Floors Inc., 279
Country Herbs, 193, 201
Country Home Products, 223
Country Impressions, 377
Country Iron Foundry, 176
Country Junction, 388
Country Log Homes, 283
Country Manor, 149, 157, 302, 379
Country Manufacturing, 219
Country Music Hall of Fame, 109
Country Plumbing, 56
Country Punchin', 149, 340
Country Seat, 55, 114
Country Spun Studio, 396, 441
Country Store, 149, 279, 307
Country Store Crafts, 149
Country Store Gifts, 252
Country Supply, 285
Countryside Prints Inc., 13
Coup Marks, 291
Courbette Saddlery Company, 285
Courtenay Solaflash, 358
Cover Up Products, 288
Cover-Pools Inc., 408
Cover-Up Enterprises, 45
Coverite, 324, 329
Covey Island Boatworks, 75
Covington Engineering Corporation, 298, 367
Covington Fine Arts Gallery, 13
Coward Shoes, 386
Cowboy Country General Store, 157
Cowboy Cuisine, 84
Cowen Manufacturing Company, 63
Cowens, 96
Cowhand, 387
Cox Hobbies Inc., 324, 326
Cox Studios, 282, 323
Coxe Blocks, 439
Coyote Cafe General Store, 189
CPA Computers, 132
CPG Direct, 19
CQ Communications Inc., 84
Crabtree & Evelyn Limited, 147, 184, 200, 204
Cracker Box, 58, 117, 347
Craft Catalog, 151
Craft Cottage, 157
Craft Gallery Ltd., 340, 383, 441
Craft Harbor, 298
Craft Inc., 176
Craft King Mail Order Dept., 151, 315, 341
Craft Kits, 151
Craft Makers, 151
Craft Resources Inc., 151, 341
Craft Room, 13, 157
Craft Supplies USA, 417
Craft Time Catalog, 12, 151
Craft Village Inc., 149
Craftmatic Beds, 212
Crafts by Donna, 341
Crafts Just for You, 415
Crafts 'N Clutter, 150
Craftsman Lumber Company, 314
Craftsman Wood Service, 118, 314, 439
Craftsmen in Wood, 97, 267, 274
CraftWoods, 314, 417
Crafty Lady, 341

Crafty's Featherworks, 151, 174
Craig (Jan) Headcovers 259
Craig (John S.) 84, 355
Cram (George F.) Company Inc. 258, 317
Cramer Products Inc., 54, 208, 425, 440
Crane (C.) Company 371, 433
Crane's (Ken) 109
Crary Bear Cat, 219
Crate & Barrel, 252, 302
Crawford (Gregan T.) 150, 214
Crayton Cove Gourmet Shop Inc., 191
Crazy Bob's Software, 137
Crazy Cajun Enterprises Inc., 204
Crazy Creek Products Inc., 102
Crazy Crow Trading Post, 294
Crazy Folks Rubber Stamps, 377
CRDC Laser System Group, 8
Create-A-Bed, 211
Createx Colors, 10, 171
Creations by Cranford, 150
Creations by Elaine, 80, 401, 434
Creations in Leather, 128
Creative Alternatives, 409
Creative Beginnings, 298
Creative Cakes, 195
Creative Calligraphy, 98
Creative Castle, 58, 298
Creative Ceramics, 112, 116
Creative Computers' PC Mall, 136
Creative Craft House, 151, 362, 382
Creative Crafts, 150
Creative Dimensions, 209
Creative Enterprises Inc., 225
Creative Health Products, 380
Creative Health Products Inc., 170
Creative Hobbies, 112
Creative Homeowner Press, 84
Creative House, 313, 368
Creative House Frames, 209
Creative Imaginations, 258
Creative Inventions, 68
Creative Keepsakes, 341
Creative Labs Inc., 132
Creative Light Works, 358
Creative Micro Electronics Inc., 408
Creative Needle, 369, 383
Creative Openings, 274
Creative Paperclay Company, 12, 163
Creative Services, 10
Creative Solutions, 269, 431
Creative Stitches, 84
Creative Structures, 220, 396
Creative Uniques Inc., 8
Creative Video Products, 354
Creative Wonders, 139
Credo Tools, 417
Creme Lure Company, 178
Creole Delicacies, 189
Crescenze (Steve) 107
Cress Manufacturing Company Inc., 112
Crestline, 274
Crestone Peak Bikes, 65
Crestwood Company, 271
Crew (J.) Outfitters 123, 126
Cricket Gallery, 13
Cricket Hill Garden, 238
Cricket Paddles, 73
Cridge Inc., 112, 115, 298, 415
Crisci (Tanino) 386
Critchfield Meat, 197
Critics' Choice Video, 80, 109, 428
Critter Corner Inc., 353
Croakies, 393
Crockett Farms, 191
Crockett's Tropical Plants, 231, 235, 237

CORPORATE INDEX

Croning Angels, 119
Crook & Crook, 77
Crooked Pine Saddle Shop, 285
Cropking Inc., 220, 221
Croquet International Ltd., 152, 412
Crosman Air Guns, 262, 265
Cross (Mark) 123
Cross (Norman) Boat Plans 72
Cross Jewelers, 296
Cross Stitch 'N Such, 341
Cross Vinyl Lattice, 222, 279
Crossroads Auto Dismantling, 33, 35, 36
Crossroads Rustic Furniture, 214
Crosswinds Gallery, 274, 434
Crouch & Fitzgerald, 313
Crow River Industries, 271, 435
Crowley Cheese, 188
Crown Art Products, 10, 209, 389
Crown City Hardware, 267
Crown Corporation, 281
Crown Products, 354
Crown Trophy, 50, 318
CrownPoint Cabinetry, 97
Crownsville Nursery,
    228, 232, 233, 235, 238, 246
Crow's Nest Birding Shop, 252
CR's Crafts, 60, 163
Cruickshank's, 241
Cruising Equipment, 77
Crunch Time, 210
Crusader Kilns, 112
Crutchfield, 47, 146, 404, 411, 426, 427
Crutchfield's (Tom) Reptile Enterprises Inc. 353
Cryer Creek Kitchens, 184
Crying Wind Gallery & Framing Company, 293
Crysbi Crafts Inc., 151
Crystal Brook Gift & Miniature Shop, 160
Crystal Cabinet Works Inc., 97
Crystal d'Arques, 153
Crystal Kite Company, 303
Crystal Lalique, 116, 153
Crystal Palace Yarns, 397, 441
Crystal Sonics, 47
CrystalGraphics, 100
Crystek Corporation, 371
CS Flight Systems, 324
CSZ Enterprises Inc., 382
Cub Cadet Corporation, 227
Cubel (Chuck & Judy) 37
Cubic Balance Golf Technology, 259
Cuddledown of Maine, 62, 63
Cuetender Company, 68
Cuisine Perel, 189
Culinary Arts Ltd., 84
Cumberland General Store, 71, 252
Cumberland Valley Nurseries Inc., 243
Cumberland Woodcraft Company Inc.,
    247, 279
Cummins Garden, 228
Cunard Associates, 58
Cupboard Distributing, 298, 415, 439
Cupid's Bow, 209
Current Adventures, 73
Current Designs, 73
Current Inc., 114, 261, 401, 423
Curriculum Associates, 84
Curry (Gerald), Cabinetmaker 214
Curtain Call Costumes, 155
Curtains & Home, 62, 154, 409
Curtains Up, 154
Curtio Cycles, 65
Curvoflite, 278
Cushcraft, 371

Cushman's, 191
Custom Autosound, 47
Custom Business Cards, 97
Custom Chrome Inc., 43
Custom Chrome Plating, 43
Custom Country Wood Products, 150, 214
Custom Cowboy Shop, 268
Custom Electronics, 327
Custom Golf Clubs Inc., 260
Custom Ironwork Inc., 175
Custom Manufacturing Inc., 156
Custom Mirror Gallery, 323
Custom Model Rockets, 327
Custom Photo, 359
Custom Photo Manufacturing, 360
Custom Plating, 43
Custom Windows & Walls, 153
Custom Wood Cut-Out's Unlimited,
    415, 439
Custom Woodturnings, 279
Cutbill & Company, 71
CUTCO/VECTOR, 302
Cutlery Shoppe, 305
Cutting Edge, 417
CyberMedia, 139
Cycad Gardens, 232
Cycle Goods, 22
Cycle Products Company, 22
Cycle Re-Cycle, 332
Cycle Recyclers, 332
Cycle Salvage Fontana, 332
CyclePro, 67
Cygnus-Quasar Books, 84
Cynthia's Country Store, 60, 420
Cypress Street Center, 212, 217
Cyrus Carpets, 379
Czarnick Nursery, 233, 238, 246

D

D & D Corvette, 44
D & G Optical, 17
D & K Detector Sales, 320, 367
D & L Doll Supply, 163
D & M Sportbike, 332
D & R Classic Automotive, 28, 33, 38
D & R Industries, 22, 67, 68
D & R Molds, 112
D & R Replicars Inc., 45
D & T Enterprises, 178
D Bar J Hat Company, 268
D-Mail U.S.A. Inc., 252
D.B. Enterprises, 260
D.D. Catalog Corporation, 10
D.J.M. Corporation, 367
D.L. Designs, 268, 384
D.L.T. Designs, 3
D.O.A. Lures, 178
Da Capo Press, 84
Da Silva (Gabriel) & Ariel Crespo 348
Da Vinci Fine Chocolates Inc., 186
DA-LITE Screen Company, 336
DAB Studio, 209, 282, 401
Dabney (Q.M.) & Company 84
Dabney Herbs,
    147, 232, 233, 234, 246, 348
DacEasy Inc., 139
Dackloe (Frederick) & Bros. Inc. 214
Dacor Corporation, 392
Dadant & Sons Inc., 63
Daddy's Junky Music, 338
Daedalus Books Inc., 80
DAFCO, 352
Daffodil Mart, 232, 241
Dagger Canoe Company, 73

D'Agnillo (Laurel) 13
Dahm's Automobiles, 326
Dahon California, 65
Daily Planet, 252
Daisy Fields, 238
Daisy Kingdom, 384
Daisy Kingdom Inc., 250
Daisy Manufacturing Company Inc.,
    262, 263, 266
Daiwa Corporation, 178, 259
Dakin Farm, 193, 197
Dakota Alert Inc., 5
Dakota Quality Bird Food, 349
Dalbani Electronics, 167
Dalco Athletic, 53
Dale Laboratories, 359
Daleboot USA, 391
Daleco Master Breeder Products, 351
Dalee Imports, 259
Dallas Alice, 127
Dallas Bonsai Garden, 230
Dallas Mustang Parts, 38
Dallee Electronics, 330
Dalton Paradise Carpets, 379
Dalton Pavilions Inc., 247
Damark International Inc., 407
Damart, 101, 121
Dame (Leslie) Enterprises Ltd. 111
Dana Designs, 102
Danbar Sales Company, 169
Dance Mart, 19, 84, 319
Dance Shop, 155
Danchuk Manufacturing Inc., 28, 29, 31
Dancing Dragon, 252
Dancing Rabbit, 293
Dancing Squirrel, 349
Danforth's Sugarhouse, 196
Daniell's R/C Specialists, 324
Danie's Neonates Inc., 353
Danmar Products Inc., 12, 120, 126, 271
Danner Shoe Manufacturing Company, 101
Dan's Garden Shop, 241
Dansant Boutique, 155
Dansk, 116, 153, 302, 389
Danskin, 114, 120, 155
D'Anton Leathers, 172
Darby's Railroad Supply, 328
Darkroom Aids Company, 356
Darowood Farms, 150
Darrow Production Company, 84
Dart Mart Inc., 156
Dart World Inc., 156
D'Artagnan, 197
Dartington Crystal, 153
Dartmouth Bookstore, 84
Darton Archery, 8
Darts Unlimited, 156
Dasher Pecan Company, 199
Data Comm Warehouse, 136
Data General Corporation, 134
Data Label Inc., 344
Data Pro Accounting Software Inc., 139
Data Vision, 99, 136, 404, 426
DataCal Corporation, 136, 145
DATASTORM, 139
DataViz Inc., 139
Dat'l Do-It World Headquarters, 204
Datrex, 71
David (Helen) Miniatures 160
Davidoff of Geneva Inc., 415
Davidson & Associates, 139
Davidson (Marl) Dolls 165
Davidson Cycle, 65
Davidson-Wilson Greenhouses,
    229, 232, 234, 235

CORPORATE INDEX

Davilyn Corporation, 17, 169
Davis (Charles) 84
Davis (Lou) Doll Supply 163
Davis (Lou) Wholesale Ceramics & Crafts 151
Davis Anchors, 77
Davis Cabinet Company, 214
Davis Frame Company, 282
Davis Instruments, 78, 433
Davit Master, 295
Davka Corporation, 139
Daw Books Inc., 84
Dawa's Hopi Arts & Crafts, 290
Dawn Invitations, 434
Dawson's (Steve) Magic Touch Catalog 129, 301, 315, 413
Day-Timers, 97, 344, 401
Daydreams Stencil Company, 127, 402
Daylab, 356
Daylily Discounters, 238
Daylily Farms & Nursery, 235, 238
Daylily World, 238
DayStar Avionics, 3
Daystar Digital, 136
Daystar Filter Corporation, 17
Dayton Computer Supply, 145
Dayton Marine Products, 75
Dayton Wheel Products, 49
Daytona Magic, 315
Daytona Manufacturing, 47
DC Electronics, 168
DCT Sports, 295
DD's Dollhouse, 160
De Boer (Mrs. Coby) 365
De Fave (Lucy) 313, 368
De Jager (Peter) Bulb Company 241
De Luna Jewelers, 290
De Pêche (Atelier) 178
Dean & DeLuca Mail-Order, 183, 206
Dean Ultimate Bicycles, 65
Dean's (Clinton) Figures & Collectibles 398, 421
Dean's Hobby Shop, 324, 325, 326
Dearborn Classics, 32, 40, 42, 48
Debbie's Dollhouses, 160
Debco Electronics, 167
Debcor Inc., 112
Deborah's Country French Bread, 183
Debron Aquatics, 351
Decart Inc., 10, 171, 389
Decathlon Corporation, 139
Decent Exposures, 51, 121, 122
Deck House, 282
Decker Enterprises, 264
Deco Industries, 408
DecoArt, 171, 415
Decolite, 308
Decor Frame Company, 209
Decorá, 97
Decorators Supply Corporation, 177, 279
Decorcal Inc., 156, 402
Decosse (Cy) Incorporated 84
Decoy, 13, 158
Decoy Den Galleries, 158
Decoys, 158
Dee-signs Ltd., 402
Deena'd Li'l Country Nook, 157
Deep River Publishing Inc., 140
Deep River Trading Company, 214
Deeprock Manufacturing Company, 435
Deer Creek Furniture Company, 214
Deer Run Products Inc., 288
Deer Valley Farm, 195
Deerskin Place, 123, 368, 386
Dee's Place of Dolls, 163

Defalco's Home Brew, 437
Defender Defender Industries Inc., 84
Defender Industries Inc., 71, 178, 181, 428
DeGiorgi Seed Company Inc., 241
DeGrandchamp's Blueberry Farm, 229
Degroot Inc., 232
Degruttola (J.R.) 359
Dekle's, 365
Del-Car Auto Wrecking, 23
Delancey Dessert Company, 184, 189
Delaney (Eileen) Autographs 19
Delaware Aquatic Imports, 351
Delaware Historical Society, 247
Delaware State Genealogical Society, 247
Delectable Mountain Cloth, 172, 383
Delegeane Garlic Farms, 191, 193, 204, 245
Delftree Farm, 191
Delgard Fence, 175
Deli Direct, 193
Delights Of A Queen, 409
Dell Computer Corporation, 134, 145
DeLong, 53, 208
Delorean One, 31
DeLorme Mapping, 140
Delphi Stained Glass, 401
Delrina Corporation, 140
Del's Camera, 360
Delta 1, 356
Delta Breeze Kites, 303
Delta Decoys, 287
Delta Faucet Company, 174
Delta Industries, 8
Delta International Machinery Corporation, 417
Delta Motorsports Inc., 35
Delta Technical Coatings, 10
Delta-1, 358
DeltaPoint, 140
Deltec Homes, 282
Deltiologists of America, 84
Deltran Corporation, 21
Deluxe Store, 390
DeMaio (Carl J.) 335
Demos Publications, 84
Dempster Industries Inc., 395
Deneba Software, 140
Denham Fabrics, 172, 174
Denman & Company, 225
Denning Automotive, 49
Denninger Cupolas & Weathervanes, 274, 434
Dennis (Vee) Manufacturing Company 264
Denny Manufacturing Company Inc., 355
Denon America, 46, 403
Denouden (Vetus) Inc. 22
Dent (Dorothy) 84
Dentronics, 371
Denver Buffalo Company, 197
Denyll Enterprises, 266
Denzer's Food Products, 202
Department 56 Showroom, 364
Der Dienst, 322, 323
DERATA Corporation, 159
Derf Electronics, 167
Derk's Switchplates, 279
Dern Trophy Corporation, 50
Derry's Sewing Center, 385, 428
DeRus Fine Art, 13, 84
Des Handmade Crafts, 296
DeSantis Holster & Leather Company, 264
Desert Darlings, 316
Desert Glory, 191
Desert Nursery, 231
Desert Rose Foods Inc., 204

Design Energy Inc., 44
Design Impressions, 377
Design Originals, 84
Design Salt, 103
Design Toscano, 222, 279
Design-Cast Materials Division, 12
Designer Home Fabrics, 172
Designer of Smiles, 129
Designer Secrets, 62, 154, 214, 281
Designer's HardWarehouse, 267
Designery, 397
Designs in the Home, 116
Designs in Tile, 279
DesignTech Systems, 3
Detail Resources, 329
Detailed Rubber Stamps, 377
Detector Distribution Center, 320
Detector Electronics Corporation, 320
Detector Warehouse, 320, 367
Deutsch Inc., 218
DEVA Lifewear Inc., 123
Devenco Products Inc., 153
Devers (Vin) of Sylvania 29
DeVilbiss, 417
DeVilbiss Air Power, 1
Dewberry Engraving Company, 434
Dewey's Good News Balloons, 52, 129
Dexter & Company, 363
DFE Communications Corporation, 5
DFM Engineering Inc., 17
DG Performance Specialties Inc., 5, 295
Dharma Crafts, 289, 442
Dharma Publishing, 93
Dharma Trading Company, 171, 172
Di Rico (Art) 177, 274
Diabetes Supplies, 159
Diabetic Express, 159
Diabetic Promotions, 159
Dial-A-Brand Inc., 7, 426
Diamond Back Bicycles, 65
Diamond Brand Canvas Products, 103
Diamond D Trailer Manufacturing, 284
Diamond Enterprises, 328
Diamond Essence Company, 296
Diamond Lights, 221
Diamond M Brand Mold Company, 160
Diamond Multimedia Systems Inc., 132
Diamond Needle Enterprises, 109
Diamond Organics, 195
Diamond Pacific Tool Corporation, 298, 312
Diamond Sports Company, 53
Diamondback, 178
Dianthus Ltd., 154
Diaperaps, 50
DiCamillo Bakery, 183, 184
DiCicco (John) 421
Dickerson Press Company, 10, 366
Dick's Chevy Parts, 27, 28, 38
Dick's Movie Graphics, 335
Dicky Bird Models, 327
Diehl (Richard) 22
Diers (Don) 372
Diestco Manufacturing Company, 435
Digging Dog Nursery, 233, 238, 243
Digi-Key Corporation, 5, 167
DigiCore Inc., 136
Digital Communications Associates Inc., 140
Digital Directory Assistance, 140
Digital Distributors, 58
Digital Equipment Corporation, 132, 134
Digital Impact, 140
Digital Vision Inc., 136
Dikra Gem Inc., 298
Dillon (D.D.) 146, 150
Dillon Precision Products Inc., 262

CORPORATE INDEX

Dimco-Gray, 356
Dimestore Cowboys, 56, 154, 267
Dimmock Hill Golf Course, 260
Dinn Brothers Inc., 50
Dino Productions, 17, 306, 374, 375
Dion-Jones Ltd., 121
Dior (Christian) 296
Direct Book Service, 84
Direct Hobby Supply Center, 326, 329
Direct Response Leads, 317
Direct Safety Company, 381
DirectTech Systems Inc., 136
Dirt Cheap Drives, 132, 136
DISCollection, 109
Discount Agate House, 299, 374, 375
Discount Bead House, 58, 151, 299
Discount Comics, 131
Discount Framesource USA Inc., 209
Discount Garden Supply Inc., 221
Discount Hobby Center, 324, 325
Discount Music Supply, 338
Discount Pond Supplies, 227
Discount Reed Company, 338
Discoveries, 296
Discovery Electronics Inc., 320
Discovery Kitchen, 193
Discovery Products, 97
Discovery Toys Inc., 422
Discwasher, 99
Disetronic Medical Systems Inc., 159
Disk Technician Corporation, 140
Disney Catalog, 252
Disney Interactive, 140
Display Fixtures Company, 159
Distant Caravans, 64
District of Columbia Archives, 247
Divers Supply, 392
Diversified Electronics Inc., 405
Diversified Overseas Marketing, 217
Divine Delights Bakery & Cafe, 184
Divine Little Delights, 60
Diving Unlimited International, 392
Dixie Art Supplies, 10
Dixie Greenhouse Manufacturing Company, 220
Dixie Gun Works Inc., 262, 263, 305
Dixie Leather Works, 321
Dixieland Taxidermy Supply, 410
Dixon Industries Inc., 223
Dixondale Farms, 245
DJ Hardwoods, 314
DJ Sport Kites, 303
DK Sports, 172, 383
D'lights Candles & Scents, 105
DMC Corporation, 341, 441
Dobi Capri Catalog, 28
Dobi Datsun Catalog, 31
Dobi Honda Catalog, 34
Dobi Mazda Catalog, 36
Dobi MGB Catalog, 37
Dobi Toyota Catalog, 42
Dobres (S.) Postcards 365
Doc Holliday Molds Inc., 112
Doc's Auto Parts, 23
Documounts, 209
Dodger Industries, 114
Dodgson Designs, 324
Doering Company, 182
Dog-Master Systems, 350
Dog's Outfitter, 350
Dogwood Lane Buttons, 383
Dolan's Sports Inc., 318
Dolch Computer Systems, 134
Dolfin International Corporation, 380
Dolgoff (Gary) Comics 131

Doll Centre, 165
Doll City USA, 165
Doll Faire Miniatures, 160
Doll Gallery, 165
Doll Gallery Supplies, 163
Doll House, 60, 165
Doll Parlor, 165
Doll Showcase, 165
Doll Works Etc., 163
Dollhouse, 160
Dollhouse Factory, 160
Dollhouses & Miniatures of Myrtle Beach, 160
Dollmasters, 252
Dolloff, 398
Dolls Galore, 163
Dolls 'n bearland, 60
Dolls of Yesterday & Today, 165
Dolls Plus, 163
Dollspart Supply Company, 163
Dollsville Dolls & Bearsville Bears, 60, 165
Dolphin Inc., 227
Domark Software, 140
Domestications, 62, 63, 409
Dominion Models, 326
Dominion Skate Company Ltd., 376, 382
Domino Ent. Co., 52
Domke, 355
Don Records, 108
Dona Designs, 62, 63
Donahue (Greg) 34
Donaldson (Ed) Hardware Reproductions 267
Dona's Molds Inc., 112
Doneckers at Home, 123
Donelson Cycles Inc., 332
Doner Design Inc., 311
Donna Lee's Sewing Center, 173
Donna's Custom Canopies, 62
Donna's Dollhouses of Frankfort, 160
Donnell's Clapboard Mill, 314
Donnelly (Richard H.) Fine Chocolates 186
Donnux Shareware, 137
Don's Hobby Shop Inc., 324
Dooley Mum Gardens, 231
Dooney & Bourke Inc., 313
Door County Design & Woodworking, 111
Doorking, 5, 294
Doorman, 271
DoPaso Jewelry, 296
Dor L'Dor Software, 140
Doran Enterprises, 356, 357
Doremus (David E.) Books 94
Dorfman-Pacific, 101, 393
Doris Crystal Magic Petticoats, 400
Dornan Uniforms, 128
Dorogi Dulcimers, 338
Dorothy's Ruffled Originals Inc., 154
Dorothy's Square Dance Shop Inc., 400
Dorr (Erik L.) 19
Dorr Mill Store, 378
Dorrance (Gregory D.) Company 10, 417, 439
Dorson Sports Inc., 260, 369
Dos Tejedoras, 84
Doskocil Manufacturing Company, 8
Doss Shoes, 273, 394
Doubek Pharmacy Inc., 345
Double L Leatherworks, 313, 368
Double Trouble, 50
Double-Time Jazz, 109, 428
Double/Triple Trading, 287
Doubleheaders, 398
Douglas Barrels Inc., 265
Douglas Sport Nets & Equipment, 53

Douglas Sport Nets & Equipment Company, 51
Doug's Auto Parts, 29, 33
Doug's Train World, 330
Dove Brushes, 10, 112
Dover Cards & Comics, 131
Dover Publications Inc., 81, 84
Dovetail Antiques, 6, 218
Dovetail Wood Works, 214
Dow Canvas Products Inc., 332
Dow Jones & Company Inc., 140
Down East Books & Gifts, 98, 252
Down East Direct, 202
Down East Microwave, 371
Down Home Comforts, 62, 63
Down Home Factory Outlet, 62, 63
Down Memory Lane, 163
Down River Equipment Company, 73, 75
Down Under Saddle Supply, 285
Down Under Treasures, 320
Downeast Seafood Express, 202
Downes & Reader Hardwood Company Inc., 314
Downing Hardware, 267
Downtown Hobby, 326
DPI Leisure Sports, 328
DR Marketing Enterprises, 252
Dr. Clayton's Herbs, 269
Dragich Auto Literature, 22
Drago (Mike) Chevrolet Parts 29
Dragon International Inc., 318
Drake (Bob) Reproductions Inc. 33
Drake (R.L.) Company 371, 427
Drake (Walter) & Sons 80, 252, 261, 316
Drake (Walter) Silver Exchange 389
DrapeBoss, 153
Draper's & Damon's, 123, 125
Dream Maker Software, 140
Dream Stamper, 377
Dreambeds, 211
DreamInk, 377
Dreamweaver Stencils, 402
Dremel Moto-Tool, 299, 329, 417
Dress Fore the 9's, 123
Dress Rite Forms, 382
Dressler (Jan) Stencils 402
Dritz Corporation, 383
Driwood Ornamental Wood Moulding, 177, 274, 276, 278, 279
Droll Yankees Inc., 70
Dromgoode's (John) Natural Gardener's Catalog 84, 219, 220, 224, 225, 350
Drop Zone Gear Store, 3
Drs. Foster & Smith Inc., 350
Drummond Woodworks, 280
Dry Creek Herb Farm, 147, 207
Drysdales Catalog, 387
Dryvit Systems Inc., 278
DSR Software Inc., 140
Du-Bro Products, 329
Dube (Brian) Inc. 301
Dubl-Click Software Inc., 140
Dubrow Antiques, 6, 84, 214
Duck Blind, 10, 439
Ducktrap River Fish Farm Inc., 202
Dudley Sports Company, 53
Dudynski (Anthony F.) Supply Company 330
Dufferin Inc., 68
Duffix Golf Products, 259
Dufour Pastry Kitchens Inc., 193
Duluth Timber Company, 314
Dumas Boats, 328
DuMor Inc., 217
Dunbar's Gallery, 6
Duncan Enterprises, 10, 112, 171

463

Duncan Royale, 15
Duncraft, 70, 349
Dundas Loom Company, 397
Dundee Orchards, 191, 199
Dunken, 420
Dunlop, 412
Dunlop-Beaufort, 75
Dunns, 265, 287, 288, 313, 386
Duo Delights, 184
Dupli-Tech, 439
Dupre (Gaston) Inc. 189
Duraco Products, 225
Duraline Medical Products, 289
Durey-Libby Nuts Inc., 199
Durfee (Charles) Cabinetmaker 214
Durfee Coin Op, 302
Durham (Donald) Company 276
Durham Boat Company, 76, 77
Durst, 356, 357
Durta Enterprises, 398
Dury's, 360
Dust Boy Inc., 428
Dutch Creel Colonial Lighting, 307
Dutch Gardens Inc., 241
Dutch Gold Honey Inc., 200
DutchGuard, 106
Dutkins' Collectables, 420
Duvinage Corporation, 278
Dux' Dekes Decoy Company, 158, 439
Dwyer Aluminum Mast Company Inc., 76
Dwyer's Doll House, 160, 165
Dyed in the Wool, 341
Dyer's Jewelers' Tools & Supplies, 299
Dyke Blueberry Farm & Nursery Inc., 229
Dyna-Kite Corporation, 303
Dyna-Lite, 358
Dyna-Med, 269
Dynacraft, 259, 260
Dynaflite, 324
Dynamic Classics Ltd., 170, 380
Dynamic Composites Inc., 327
Dynamic Cooking Systems, 7, 406
Dynapoint Inc., 132
Dynastar, 391
Dyno Safety Gear, 66

E

E & B Discount Marine, 76, 77
E & J Used Auto & Truck Parts, 23, 48
E & S Creations, 385
E & W Imports Inc., 59, 299
E.L.B. Software, 16
E.P. Woodworks, 214
Eagel EMS Specialties, 156
Eagle Arms Inc., 265
Eagle Claw Fishing Tackle, 179
Eagle Coach Works Inc., 44
Eagle Creek, 103, 313
Eagle Dancer, 294
Eagle Electronics, 78
Eagle Electronics Inc., 181
Eagle Feather Trading, 151
Eagle Feather Trading Post, 59, 84, 294
Eagle Golf, 84, 260
Eagle Optics, 17, 69
Eagle Plating Inc., 43
Eagle River Fly Shop, 179
Eagle River Nordic, 391
Eagles (Steve) 290
Early American Lighting, 309
Early Ford Parts, 33
Early Learning Centre, 422
Early West, 252
Early Wheel Company, 49

Early Winters, 103, 123, 252, 391
Early's, 197
Earrings & Things, 296
Earth Care, 252, 373
Earth Guild, 151
Earth Science Inc., 147, 430
Earthmade Products, 252
Earthsong Fibers, 397, 441
Earthstone Wood-Fire Ovens, 406
Earwig Music Company Inc., 109
East 33rd Street Electronics & Typewriters, 411, 427
East Carolina Wallpaper Market, 281
East Coast Hydroponics, 221
East Coast Prospecting & Mining Supplies, 85, 320, 367
East Coast Warehouse, 332
East Earth Trade Winds, 85, 204, 269
East End Auto Parts, 23
East End Import Company, 147, 348
East Hampton Industries Inc., 207
East Knoll North, 116
East West DyeCom, 320
Eastbay Running Store Inc., 380
EastCoast Reptiles, 353
Eastern (Frank) Company 217, 344
Eastern Art Glass, 151, 169, 171, 401
Eastern Bowling/Hy-Line Inc., 95
Eastern Camera & Computer Company, 136
Eastern Costume Company, 148, 413
Eastern Emblem, 127, 156, 363, 405
Eastern Findings Corporation, 299
Eastern Mountain Sports Inc., 103
Eastern Nebraska Auto Recyclers, 23
Eastern Plant Specialties, 228, 243, 246
Eastern Tool & Supply Company, 417
Eastman Corporation, 151, 320
Eastman Kodak Company, 85, 99, 355, 356, 357
Easton, 8, 412
Easton Sports, 273
Easton Sports Inc., 53
Eastpak, 67, 103
Eastside Gifts & Dinnerware, 116, 252
Eastside Ultralight Aircraft Inc., 4
Eastwood Automobilia, 326
Eastwood Company, 47, 420
Easy Built Models, 324
Easy Jack & Sons Auto Parts, 23
Easy Rider Canoe & Kayak Company, 73, 373
Easy Time Wood Refinishing Products, 276
EASYUP, 3
Eatman Archery, 8
Eaton Detroit Spring, 23, 48
Ebac Lumber Dryers, 417
Ebersole Arts & Crafts Supply, 98
Ebersole Lapidary Supply, 10, 118
Ebersole Lapidary Supply Inc., 59, 299, 312, 320, 367, 374, 376, 382, 406, 438
Ebonite International Inc., 95
Eborn Books, 93
Echelon Golf, 259
Echo Inc., 223, 417
Eckler's, 30
Ecletibles, 377
Eclipse International, 132
Eco Enterprises, 221
Eco-Gardens, 243
Ecological Live Rock Inc., 351
Ecomarine Ocean Kayak Center, 73
Econ-Abrasives, 440
Econo-Vet Groom & Health, 284
Econol Lift Corporation, 166, 401
Economics Press Inc., 133

Economy Printing Company, 343
Ecotrek, 103
Eddie's Trick Shop, 129, 315
Eddyline Kayak Works, 73
Edelman (Igor) 6
Eden Foods, 195, 204
Edensaw Woods Ltd., 77
Edes Custom Meats Inc., 197
Edgar B Furniture, 214
Edge Company, 305
EdgeCraft Corporation, 302
Edgemont Yarn Services, 378, 397, 441
Edgepark Surgical Inc., 345
EdgeWater Fishing Products, 179
Edible Landscaping, 231, 243
Edinburgh Imports Inc., 60
Edisonville Woodshop, 70, 316
Editions, 94
Edlie Electronics, 168, 306, 381
Edmark Software, 140
Edmonds Old Car Parts, 29
Edmund Scientific Company, 17, 69, 131, 169, 306, 316, 321, 381, 422, 433
Edmunds Roses, 240
Ed's House of Gems, 118, 293, 296, 299, 382
Edson International, 77
Educational Insights, 422
Educational Resources, 136, 145
Educorp Computer Services, 137
Edwards (S. Wallace) & Sons Inc. 193, 197, 202
Edwards Crosley Parts, 30
Edwards Engineering Corporation, 211
Effective Learning Systems Inc., 85, 109
EFS Company, 169
Efstonscience Inc., 17
Egge Machine Company, 23, 25
Egger's, 179
Egghead Software, 145
Eggs by Byrd, 166
Egleston (Bill) Inc. 6
Ehrman Needlepoint, 341
EightParts, 42
Eilenberger's Bakery, 184
Eisenhart Wallcoverings Company, 281
Eisentraut (Albert) 65
Eisers, 85, 284, 285
Eisner Brothers, 95, 127
Ektelon, 267, 369, 370
El Paso Chile Company, 204
El Paso Chili Company, 189
Elaine Wedding Stationery, 434
Elan-Monark, 391
Elann Fiber Company, 441
Elbinger Laboratories Inc., 359
Elcanco Ltd., 309
Elderly Instruments, 338
Eldredge Brothers Fly Shop, 179
Eldreth Pottery, 116
Eldridge Textile Company, 62, 63, 409
Elect-a-Lite, 160
Electra Marine, 77
Electric Mobility Corporation, 212, 435
Electrim Corporation, 16
Electro Automotive, 22, 43
Electro Tool Inc., 169
Electrodyne Inc., 26
Electron Tube Enterprises, 372
Electronic Arts, 140, 423
Electronic Distributors, 371
Electronic Equipment Bank, 371
Electronic Goldmine, 167, 168, 306, 381
Electronic Mailbox, 99, 360, 403, 426

❖ CORPORATE INDEX ❖

Electronic Rainbow, 168
Electronic Technology Today Inc., 85
Electronic Wholesalers, 99, 404, 411, 426
Electronics Depot, 100, 426
Electronics Emporium Inc., 372
Electronics International Inc., 3
Elegant Motors Inc., 44
Elegant Sweets, 184, 186
Eleganza Ltd., 15
Elek-Tek, 98, 132
Elena's by Houlihan's, 189, 195
Elena's Dollhouses & Miniatures, 160
Elephant Balls Ltd., 68
Elephant Garlic Seeds, 245
Elfa Closet Storage Accessories, 119
Elishewitz (Allen) 305
Elite Aluminum Fence Products, 175
Elite Custom Cues Inc., 68
Elite Greenhouses Ltd., 220
Eljer Plumbingware, 56
Elkay Manufacturing Company, 174
Elkes Carpet Outlet Inc., 379
Elkhorn Rod Company, 179
Ellenburg's Furniture, 218
Ellickson Collection, 296
Elliott (A. Lovell) 19
Elliott (Kristin) Inc. 261, 401
Elmer's Nostalgia Inc., 19
Elmira Stove Works, 406
Eloxite Corporation, 118, 126, 299, 367
Elsie's Exquisiques, 174
Elster's (Barbara) Miniature Corner 165
Elwood (J.W.) Company 410
Embee Parts, 36
Embellishments for Designing People, 299
Emblem & Badge Inc., 50
Embossing Arts Company, 377
Embroidery Studio, 341
EMCAX Photo-finishing, 359
EMCO-Maier Corporation, 417
EMCOM, 408
Emerald Collection, 253
Emergency Medical Products, 269
Emerson Knives, 305
Emerson Radio Corporation, 99, 403, 425
Emerson Wood Works Inc., 159
EMF Company, 263, 265
Emlong Nurseries, 229, 243
Emperor Clock Company, 118, 212
Empire Publishing, 85
Empire Sporting Goods Manufacturing Company, 53, 54, 208, 380, 394
Empire State Sports Memorabilia & Collectibles Inc., 9 19, 398
Empire Woodworks, 280
Emporium, 277
Enchanted Cottage, 341
Enchanted Creations, 377
Enchanted Doll House, 60, 160, 165, 423
Enchanted Seeds, 245
Enclume Design Products Inc., 302
Enco Manufacturing Company, 320, 417
Encore Records, 108
Encyclopedia Britannica Inc., 140
Endangered Species, 229, 239
Ende (Alan) 85, 315
Endless Pools Inc., 408
Ener-G Foods, 201
Energetic Music, 100
Energy Loudspeakers, 405
Energy Savers, 373
Enerzone Systems Corporation, 211
Enesco Corporation, 15, 165, 253
Enfield Stationers, 97, 98, 261
Engels (R.) & Company 118

Engine Mart, 166
England Things, 161
Englehart Products Inc., 73
Engler (Harriet A.) 148
English (A.G.) Inc. 264
English (P.C.) Inc. 417, 439
English Angling Trappings, 179
English Arbor Company, 222
English Basketry Willows, 55
English Car Spares Ltd., 25, 34, 37, 42
English Country Signs, 388
Enlargement Works Inc., 359
Ennis (Ray W.) 305
Ennis Express Label Service, 344
Enoch's Berry Farm, 229
Enrichments, 269
Ensata Gardens, 238
Ensoniq, 132
Enterprise Art, 59, 151, 299
Enterprise Publishing Inc., 349
Enterprising Solutions, 85
Entertainers Supermarket, 52
Entrances Inc., 274
Entry Systems, 274
Enviro-Safety Products, 381
Envirogear Ltd., 103
Environmental Concepts, 225
Environmental R & D, 225
Environmental Solar Systems, 183, 395
Environmentally Sound Products, 373
Environtrol Corporation, 1
Envisions Solutions Technology Inc., 136
Eon Industries, 223
Eoriatti (Angela) 163
Epi World, 231, 237
Epicurean International, 189
Epicurean Traders, 106, 193, 195
Epoch Designs, 402
Epoch Instruments, 17
Epoxy Technology Inc., 276
Eppinger Manufacturing Company, 179
Epro Tiles Inc., 279
Epson Accessories Inc., 132, 134
Epson America Inc., 136
Equatorial Platforms, 17
Equiparts, 57, 267
Equipment Shop, 271
ERA Replica Automobiles, 44
Erb Lumber Company, 280
Erdal Yarns Ltd., 441
Ereminas Imports Inc., 25
Ergo Computing, 134
Ergo Media, 258, 428
Eric Manufacturing Inc., 75
Erica's Rugelach & Baking Company Inc., 184, 189
Erickson Cycles, 65
Eric's Motorcycle Company, 332
Ericson (Lois) 384
Ericson Manufacturing Company, 166
Ericsson GE Mobile Communications, 410
Erie Landmark Company, 388
Erie Tobacco Company, 415
Ernel Yarns, 341, 441
Ernie's Toyland, 60, 165
Erstwhile Radio, 111
Escalade Sports, 54, 68, 152, 156, 170, 409
Escort Detectors, 43
Escort Lighting, 311
ESD USA Inc., 140
ESF Computer Services Inc., 140
Especially Lace, 154
Esprit Outlet, 119, 386
ESPYY-TV, 318

Essence by Mail, 121, 123
Essential Aromatics, 348
Essential Learning Products, 81
Essential Oil Company, 289, 348, 366, 393
Essential Products Company Inc., 147
Essentially Chocolate, 184, 186, 193
Essex Industries, 73, 77
Essex Manufacturing, 260, 428
Essex Street Pickle Corporation, 204
Essof's, 318
Estee Corporation, 184, 186, 206
Estes-Simmons Silverplating Ltd., 6, 169
Estus, 412
Estwing Manufacturing Company, 367
ESV Lighting Inc., 159
ET Supply, 408
ETA Wood Concepts Inc., 212
ETAC USA, 106, 269, 271, 435
Ethel-M Chocolates Mail-order, 186
Etion Software, 16
Etlon Software, 16
Eugenia's Place, 268
EUR-AM Electronics, 168, 371
Eureka Tents, 103
Eureka! Daylily Reference Guide, 85
Euro Posters, 335, 336
Euro-Tire Inc., 47
Euro-Works, 45
Euroarms of America Inc., 263
Eurocobble, 222
Euroflax Inc., 441
Euromeister, 25, 26, 36, 40, 43
Europa Aviation, 1
Europa Foods Ltd., 184
European Artist Dolls & Bears, 60
European Automotive Specialists, 41
European Furniture Importers, 214
European Imports & Gifts, 15, 117, 253, 364
European Parts Specialists Ltd., 36
Europtik Ltd., 69, 264
Eurosign Metalwerke Inc., 22
Evangel Wedding Service, 434
Evans Creole Candy Company, 186
Evenheat Kiln Inc., 112, 115
Evening Star Designs, 151, 299
Eventide Avionics, 3
Everett-Morrison Motorcars, 44
Everex Systems Inc., 134
Evergreen Garden Plant Labels, 223
Evergreen Nursery, 233
Evergreen Press, 22, 81, 85, 346
Evergreen Y.H. Enterprises, 241, 245
EverHealth Inc., 170
Everitt Knitting Company, 53
Everlast Sports Manufacturing Corporation, 95, 170, 424
Evers Toy Store, 324, 326
Everything Ewenique, 150, 157, 309
Evidence Music Inc., 109
EWA & Miniature Cars USA, 326
Ewing (John) Orchids Inc. 237
Ex Officio Outdoor Sport, 101
Ex-Cel Inc., 112
Excalibur Bronze Sculpture Foundry, 15
Excalibur Dehydrator, 183
Excalibur Hobbies Ltd., 420
Excalibur Machine & Tool Company, 417
Excalibur-Cureton Company, 374, 375
Excel Bridge Manufacturer, 222
Excel Dowel & Woodcrafts Inc., 439
Excel Industries Inc., 223
Excel Marketing Inc., 391
Excel Sports Boulder, 65, 67
Excel-nt Software, 137

465

CORPORATE INDEX

Excelsior Incense Works, 289
Exclusive Appeal, 119, 123
Exclusively Bar-B-Q, 52
Executive Photo & Electronics, 44, 100, 360, 426
Executive Protection Products Inc., 408
Executive Shoes, 386
Exigent Inc., 332
Eximious, 253
Exotic Aquaria Inc., 351
Exotic Automotive Designs, 45
Exotic Car Parts, 34
Exotic Fish, 351
Exotic Illusions, 45
Exotic Silks, 172
Exotic Tires International, 47
Exotic/Thai Silk, 172
Exoticar Model Company, 326
Expert Software, 115, 225, 250
Expert Software Inc., 140
Exposures, 209, 354
Express Design Inc., 1
Express Direct, 136
Express Medical Supply Inc., 269, 289, 345
Express Station Hobbies Inc., 330
Express Trax Accompaniment Tapes, 109
Expressions from Potpourri, 253
Expressly Avanti, 25
EXQ Catalog, 103
Extinctions, 374
Extrasport Inc., 123
Extreme Sport Karate, 318
Exxiss Aluminum Trailers, 284
Eye-1 Optics, 69
Eye's Up Kites, 303

F

F & R Sales & Service, 393
F Stops Here, 360
F.E.N. Enterprises, 27
F.J. Authentics, 421
F/S Discount Arrows and Supplies, 8
Fab Knit Manufacturing, 53, 208
Fab Knit Manufacturing Company, 424
Fabby, 309
Faber Brothers, 95, 370, 380, 393
Fabiano Shoe Company, 101, 386, 391
Fabian's Western Wear, 400
Fabric Barn, 174
Fabric Center, 172
Fabric Creations, 165
Fabric Gallery, 172
Fabric Hutch, 157
Fabric Outlet, 172
Fabric Shop, 154, 172, 393
Fabricators & Manufacturers Association Internation, 85
Fabricraft, 384
Fabrics by Phone, 154, 172, 393
Fabrics First, 172
Fabrics Unlimited, 172
Factory Direct, 146, 404, 426
Factory Direct Carpet Outlet, 379
Factory Direct Craft Supplies, 151
Factory Direct Furniture, 134, 217
Factory Direct Table Pad Company, 409
Faded Rose, 261
Fahrney Pens Inc., 348
Fair Oaks Sutler Inc., 322
Fair Radio Sales Company Inc., 167, 408
Faire Game, 197
Faire Harbour Ltd., 309
Fairfield Processing Corporation, 67, 151
Fairgate Rule Company Inc., 10, 166

Fairing Screens Gustafson, 332
Fairs' OPS Inc., 345
Fairtex Martial Arts Equipment, 318
Fairweather Gardens, 244
Fairyland Begonia Garden, 229, 238
FairyTales Inc., 60
Faith Mountain Company, 117, 123, 150, 253, 302, 348
Falcon, 85, 253
Falcon Northwest Computer Systems, 134
Falcon Prospecting Equipment, 320, 367
Falcon-Wood, 417
Falconar AVIA, 1, 2
Falkner Enterprises, 408
Falling Cloud Farms, 127
Fallis (John M.) Custom Saddles 285
Falls Run Woodcarving, 417
Family Heirloom Weavers, 62, 379
Family Heritage Baskets, 55
Family History Library, 250
Family History Library of The Church of Jesus Christ, 249
Family Travel Guides Catalog, 85
Famous Fido's, 350
Famous Pacific Dessert Company, 184
Famous Smoke Shop Inc., 147, 415
Famous Trading Company, 174
Fan Fair, 174
Fan Man (Oklahoma City), 174
Fan Man Inc., 174
Fanci' Premium Tea Company, 207
Fancy Foods Gourmet Club, 193
Fancy Fortune Cookies, 184, 210, 349
Fancy Pants, 114
Fancy Plants Farms, 241
Faneuil Furniture Hardware Company Inc., 268
Fannaly's Auto Exchange, 26, 27, 35, 39
Fannie May Candies, 186
Fanta-Sea Pools, 395, 408
Fantasy Animation, 335
Fantasy Craft, 161, 327
Fantasy Den, 60
Fantasy Distribution Company, 131
Fantasy Lighting, 311
Far North Gardens, 241, 246
Farina Enterprises, 421
Farm Family Puppets, 368
Farm Wholesale Inc., 220
Farmer (Emily) 60
Farmer Seed & Nursery Company, 106, 219, 229, 241, 243, 244
Farmer's Books, 85
Farmhouse Furniture, 214
Farmhouse Originals, 388
Farnam Companies Inc., 284
Farnsworth Military Gallery, 85, 322
Farpoint Research, 16
Farr (Bruce) & Associates 72
Farrington Aircraft Corporation, 2
Farris Machinery, 417
Fascinating Electronics Inc., 433
Fascinating Folds, 85, 345
Fash-en-Hues, 112
Fashion Ease, 12, 126, 269, 289, 435
Fashion Footnotes, 386
Fashion Magic by Fendler, 400
Fashion Touches, 383
FASPEC British Parts, 26
Fast Electronic U.S. Inc., 100
Fast Forward Skate Shop, 376
Fat City Cycles, 65
Fatwise, 85, 195, 261
Faucet Factory, 57
Faulk's Game Call Company, 288

Favorite Things, 161
Fawcett (Frederick J.) Inc. 441
1 315
Fax City Inc., 146
Faxon Auto Literature, 22
Feather Canoes Inc., 72
Feather Fantasy, 349
Feather Fletcher, 8
Feather-Craft Fly-fishing, 179
Feathercraft Kayaks, 73
Feathered Friends Mail Order, 62, 63, 103
Featheridge Designs, 441
Featherlite Manufacturing Inc., 284
Featherstone Productions, 294
Fedco Seeds, 245
Feder (Louis) & Joseph Fleischer Wigs 436
Federal Cabinet Company Inc., 280
Federal Cartridge Company, 262
Federation of North Carolina Historical Society, 249
Federation of Oklahoma Genealogical Societies, 249
Feelgood Store & Catalog, 269
Felber Ornamental Plastering Corporation, 280
Felissimo, 116, 389
Felix (C.) 317
Fell (David H.) & Company Inc. 299
Felt People, 172
FEMCO Corporation, 412
Feminist Press, 85
Fennell's Orchid Company, 237
Fenwick Corporation, 179
Ferdco Sewing Machines, 385
Ferncliff Gardens, 232
Ferrara Foods & Confections Inc., 189
Ferrill's Auto Parts Inc., 23
Ferry-Morse Seed Company, 236
Festival Films, 336
Festival Flags, 181
Fiat Tubs, 57
Fib-Con Corporation, 217
Fiber Loft, 441
Fiber Studio, 304, 397, 441
Fiberglass & Wood Company, 29, 48
Fiberglass Coatings Inc., 77
Fiberglass Specialties, 329
Fiddler's Creek Farm, 197
Fiddlers Green, 327
Fiddler's Green Farm, 195
Fidelity Direct, 344, 345
Fidelity Products Company, 98
Field & Forest Products Inc., 236
Fielding Worldwide Inc., 85
Fieldline, 103, 287
Field's (Henry) Seed & Nursery 219, 229, 231, 236, 241, 243, 244
Fields of Glory, 322
Fieldsheer Clothing, 331
Fieldstone Cabinetry Inc., 97
Fieldstone Gardens Inc., 233, 238, 239
Fiero Conversions Inc., 44
Fiero Plus, 44
Fiero Store, 32
Fig Tree Nursery, 229, 231, 233
Figi's, 186, 188, 193
Figures Inc., 421
Filaree Farm, 245
Filature Lemieux Inc., 378, 441
Filene's, 158
Filling Station, 29
Film Favorites, 335
Filmart's Cartoon World, 13, 335
Filson, 123
Filtration Concepts, 431

CORPORATE INDEX

Filtronics, 351
Fin 'n Feather, 193
Finals, 66, 123
Finch Blueberry Nursery, 229
Finch's (Cliff) Zoo 227
Find (Michael C.) 116
Find-A-Part, 33, 35
Findlay (Wally) Galleries 13
Fine Art Impressions, 13
Fine Art Restoration, 6
Fine Arts Heritage Society, 341
Fine Design, 182
Fine Gold Leaf People, 10
Fine Stationery by Sonya Nussbaum, 401
Fine-Line Inc., 8
Fineman Doors Inc., 274
Fineware Systems, 140
Finger Lakes Basketry Supply, 55
Fingerhut, 117, 253, 261, 401
Fingerlakes Yarns, 341, 441
Finish-It Furniture, 214
Finishing Touches Crafts, 415
Fink (Howard J.) 130
Fire & Shadow Creations, 157
Fire Mountain Gems, 59, 299
Firebird/Trans Am America, 33, 42
Fireboy Halon Systems, 71, 176
Firefighters Bookstore, 85, 175
Firemountain Gems, 115
Fireside Classics, 85
Fireside Coffee Company, 207
Fireside Distributors Inc., 176
Fireside Fiberarts, 397
Fireside Log Homes, 283
Fireside Reproductions, 214
Firestik, 373
Fireworks by Grucci, 177
Fireworks of America, 177
First Alert, 176, 373
First Colony Coffee & Tea Company, 207
First State Map & Globe, 258, 317
First Team Sports, 289
Fischer & Jirouch Company, 280
Fischer Artworks, 434
Fischer Tennis, 51, 412
Fish Crane Yoga Props, 442
Fish Creek Rod Company, 179
Fishbite Recordings, 109, 338
Fisher, 99, 403, 405, 425
Fisher (Gary) 65
Fisher Aero Corporation, 1
Fisher Flying Products Inc., 1
Fisher Research Laboratory, 320, 367
Fishers (JW) Manufacturing Inc. 320
Fisher's Garden Store, 241, 245
Fisher's Popcorn, 200
Fishing Creek Outfitters, 179
Fishman's Fabrics, 172
Fiskars Corporation, 85
Fiskars Incorporated, 103
Fiskars Knives, 305
Fiskars Scissors, 383
Fitch (Richard) Maps 317
Fitch Brothers Guitars, 338
Fitness Master Inc., 170
Fitness To Go Inc., 170
Fitz & Floyd Consumer Relations, 116
Fitz Auto Parts, 23
Fitzgerald Fairfield Inc., 204
Five Civilized Tribes Museum Trading Post, 293
Five Seasons Corporation, 116
FiveStar, 406
Fixture Exchange, 174
Fixture Factory, 159

Flag America Company, 181
Flag Fables Inc., 181
Flaghouse, 54, 170, 208, 266, 271, 431
Flaghouse Camping Equipment, 103
Flaghouse Furniture Express, 96
Flags & Flagpoles, 181
Flair Pro Color Lab, 359
Flambeau Products Corporation, 287
Flanders Industries Inc., 217
Flash Collectables, 64
Flat Earth Clay Works Inc., 116
Flathead Indian Museum Trading Post & Art Gallery, 291
Flathead Salvage & Storage, 23
Flax Artist Materials, 10, 253
Flayderman (N.) & Company Inc. 6, 263, 321
Fleetfoot Industries, 45
Fleetline Automotive, 23, 29
Fleetwood Enterprises Inc., 47
Fletcher (David & Martha) 309, 434
Fletcher Boats Inc., 75
Fletcher-Barnhardt & White, 71
Fletcher-Jones Motor Cars, 36
Fletcher-Lee & Company, 10
Fletcher-Terry Company, 209
Flex-A-Bed, 212
Flexi-Mat Corporation, 350
Flexible Flyer Company, 393
Flibbertigibbet, 253
Flickingers' Nursery, 244
Flies Only, 179
Flight Products International Inc., 4
Flightcom, 3
Flightstar, 1
Flint River Outdoor Wear Inc., 287
Flip Cards & Supplies, 398
Flipside Records, 108
Flora & Company Productions, 315, 428
Flora Fauna, 222, 407
Flora Lan Nursery, 228
Floralight, 222
Florals of Fredericks, 228
Florentine Craftsmen, 209, 222
Florian Gardening Tools, 225
Florian Greenhouse, 220
Florian Greenhouses Inc., 396
Floribunda Palms, 229, 237
Florida Genealogical Society, 247
Florida Magic Company, 414
Florida Mustang Inc., 38
Florida Playground & Steel Company, 363
Florida Tool, 417
Florida Wood Moulding & Trim, 280
Florio Flyer Corporation, 324
Floris of London, 147
Florist Products Inc., 220, 222
Florist Shop, 147, 366
Flounder Bay Boatbuilding, 77
Flowerplace Plant Farm, 238
Flowers & Balloons Inc., 52
Flowertown Bonsai, 230
Flowery Branch, 234, 241
Flowtron Outdoor Products, 219
Fly & Field, 179
Fly Box, 85, 179
Fly Shop, 179
Fly-Rite Inc., 179
Flytec, 3
FMCI Hydroponics, 221
Focal Point Inc., 280
Focal Press, 85, 355
Focus Camera, 17, 69, 360
Focus Electronics, 7, 404, 426
Fodor's Travel Publications Inc., 85

FOES Racing, 65, 67
Fogarty (Kenneth) 32
Folbot Inc., 75
Foley-Belsaw Company, 417
Foliage Gardens, 232
Folio One, 13
Folk-Legacy Records Inc., 109
Folkcraft Instruments, 338
Folk's Folly Prime Cut Shoppe, 197
Follansbee Dock Systems, 295
Food Service Inc., 302
Foot-Joy & Titleist Worldwide, 431
Footed Shaft, 8
Foothill Hydroponics, 221
Foothill Video, 336, 428
Footprints, 386
For the People Bookstore, 85
Force 10 Foils, 303
Ford (Charolette) Trunks 268, 313, 425
Ford (Karen L.) 341
Ford New Holland Inc., 227
Ford Parts Specialists, 32, 37, 41
Ford Parts Store, 32, 33, 42
Foredom Electric Company, 299, 417
Foreign Autotech, 43
Foreign Motors West, 26, 40
Forespar, 76
Forest Products, 439
Forestfarm, 230, 244, 246
Forever & Always Company, 401
Forever Leather, 123
Forever Timeless, 384
Forever Young, 165
Fork's Drum Closet, 338
Formagg, 188
FormalSoft, 140
Formby's, 438
Forrest Manufacturing Company Inc., 417
Forsooth Travel Library Inc., 85
Forsythe Travel Library Inc., 317
Fort Auto Parts, 23
Fort Brooke Quartermaster, 109, 400
Fort Knox Security Products, 264
Fort Washakie Trading Company, 294
Forte Film, 357
Fortuna's Sausage Company, 188, 190, 193, 197
Fortunoff Fine Jewelry, 116, 296, 389
Fortyniner Mining Supply, 367
Forum Publishing Company, 85
Fossils & Amber, 374
Foster & Smith (Drs.) Inc. 284
Foster (Helen) Stencils 402
Foster Manufacturing Company, 10
Foster Taxidermy Supply, 410
Foto Electric Supply Company, 7, 360
Fotronic Corporation, 169
Founders Club, 259
Fountain Pen Hospital, 348
Fountain Pen Shop, 348
Four BAR B Records Inc., 109, 400
Four Base Hits, 398
Four Oaks Farm Inc., 184, 197, 200, 204
Four Rivers, 103, 179, 287
Four Seasons Log Homes, 283
Four Seasons Nursery, 225, 231, 241
Four Seasons Solar Products, 220, 396
Four Seasons Tentmasters, 103
Four Star Lighting, 414
Fowler Solar Electric Inc., 395
Fox (C.J.) Company 344
Fox (Peter) Bridal Shoes 119, 386
Fox Hollow Farm, 204
Fox Light, 282
Fox Music, 108, 109

❖ CORPORATE INDEX ❖

Fox Ridge Outfitters Inc., 253
Fox Woodcraft, 280
Fox's Fine Foods, 204
Foxwood Forge, 305
Frabill Inc., 77, 179
Fractal Design Corporation, 140
Fragrance International, 147
Fragrant Path, 241, 246
Fralinger's Inc., 184, 186
Frame Factory, 209
Frame Fit Company, 209
Frame Technology Corporation, 140
Framing Fox Art Gallery, 13
Francesca's Favorites, 202
Francisco (Don) Coffee Traders 207
Franken Frames, 209
Frankford Bicycle Company, 67
Franklin, 85
Franklin Ace Hardware, 417
Franklin Art Glass, 401
Franklin Climbing Equipment, 334
Franklin Fixtures Inc., 160
Franklin Mint, 253
Franklin Sports Industries Inc.,
  51, 55, 95, 156, 208, 286, 369, 413, 431
Frank's Cane & Rush Supply, 55, 114
Frank's Center Inc., 103, 265
Frank's Country Store, 316
Frank's Highland Park Camera, 360, 362
Frank's Magic Crops, 221
Fran's Basket House, 218
Fran's Chocolates, 186
Fran's Pecans, 199
Frantz Bead Company, 59
Fraser (Harry M.) Company 378
Freckles Clown Supplies,
  129, 148, 368, 413
Freda's Fancy, 161
Frederick & Sons Custom Wood Carving, 107
Frederick (Paul) Shirt Company 126
Frederick's of Hollywood, 121, 123
Fredericksburg Herb Farm, 147, 204
Fredericksburg Historical Prints, 13
Fredericksburg Rugs, 378
Fred's Dollhouse & Miniature Center, 161
Fred's Plant Farm, 245
Free Spirit Publishing Inc., 81
Freeborn Tool Company Inc., 417
Freed of London Inc., 120, 155
Freeda Vitamins, 430
Freedman Collectibles Inc., 354
Freedom Boatworks, 75
Freedom Cycles, 332
Freedom Design Wheels, 49
Freedom Designs Inc., 435
Freedom Quilting Bee, 62
Freedom Song Boatworks, 328
Freeman (W.H.) & Company 81, 85
Freeperson Press, 85
Freeport Music, 338
Freestyle, 356, 357, 360
Freight Yard, 330
French (Samuel) Catalog 85, 414
French (Samuel) Trade 85, 414
French Meadow Bakery, 183
Frenchtown Flags Inc., 181
FrenchWyres, 222, 227
Frequency Fan Club, 405
Fretware Guitars, 338
Freud Power Tools, 417
Freudenberg/Pellon, 151
Frieda's By Mail, 193
Frieda's by Mail, 190
Friedman (A.I.) Art Supplies 10
Friends, 117, 150

Friends Patterns, 384
Friesen Honey Farms Inc., 63
Frigidaire Company, 7
Frog Pond Nursery, 223
Frog Tool Company, 417
Frohock-Stewart Inc., 269
Fromagerie Belle Chèvre, 188
Frontgate, 57, 253
Frontier Anglers, 179
Frontier Cooperative Herbs, 147, 348
Frontier Flags, 181
Frontier Furniture, 214
Frost Cutlery, 305
Frostline Kits, 384
Frosty Little, 127, 156, 363
Fruit Ranch-West, 188, 191, 199
Frye's Measure Mill, 150
Frysville Farms, 244
FSA Plus Woman, 121
FTC Skateboarding Shop, 390
FTC Ski & Sports, 123, 127, 393
Fuji America, 65
Fuji Anaheim Color Labs, 359
Fuji Photo Film USA Inc., 356, 357, 362
Fujinon, 69
Fujitsu America, 46, 410
Fujitsu Networks Industry Inc., 140
Fujitsu Personal Systems, 134
Fulcrum Publishing, 85
Full Circle Foods Inc., 105
Full Circle Records, 109, 428
Fuller (R. Andrew) Company 323
Fuller Direct, 96
Fullington Corporation, 126
Fultron, 46
Fun House Toy Company, 421
Fun 'N' Play Inc., 363
Fun Publishing Company, 85, 337, 422
Fun Stuff, 163
Fun Technicians Inc., 129
Fun-Tronics Inc., 130
Function One, 145
Fundcraft, 210
Fungi Perfecti, 236
Fungus Foods Inc., 236
Funk's Antique Auto Parts, 37
Funny Feet Fashions, 129
Furman Lumber Inc., 175
Furniture Connection of Carolina, 214
Furniture Designs Inc., 440
Furniture Patch of Calabash Inc., 214
Furuno USA, 78, 181, 373
Fusick Automotive Products, 39
Fusion Software, 140
Fusion Video, 428
Fusz (Lou) Toyota 33, 42
Futaba Corporation of America, 327
Futura Surf Skis, 75
FutureTech Systems Inc., 134
FutureVideo, 100
Fyrnetics Inc., 5

G

G & B Orchid Laboratory & Nursery, 237
G & G Foods, 188
G & J Enterprises, 112, 151
G & J Toys & Clocks, 52
G & K Enterprises, 62, 63, 98, 261
G & P Sales, 324
G & R Publishing Company, 210, 253, 430
G & S Sporting Goods, 95
G Street Fabrics, 172
G-B Color Lab, 359
G-M Marketing, 209

G.E. Appliances, 1, 7, 211, 425
G.E.L. Products Inc., 161
G.I.M.M. Dry Yard, 191
Gabrieana's Herbal & Organic Products,
  147, 348
Gabriel Video & Camera, 100
Gadabout Wheelchairs, 435
Gagne (Bill) 107
Gaia Garden Herbal Apothecary, 269, 348
Gainor Medical U.S.A. Inc., 159
Galaxy Optics, 17
Gale (Jeffrey E.), Basketmaker 55
Gale, Basketmaker 55
Galerie Robin, 13, 258
Gallant Models Inc., 329
Gallaudet University Press, 85
Gallery 247, 13, 363
Gallery Lainzberg, 13
Gallery of Time, 118
Gallina Canyon Ranch, 190
Gamaliel Shooting Supply Inc., 266
Gambell & Hunter Sailmakers, 76
Gambler's Book Shop, 85, 109
Gamblin, 10, 169
Game Sales International, 197
Game Tracker, 8
Game-Line Inc., 423
GameRoom Antiques, 130
Gameroom Antiques, 84
Gamer's Gold, 145
Games People Played, 6, 423
GameTime, 170, 363
Gamma Productions Inc., 140
Gamma Sports, 412
Gammill Quilting Machine Company, 369
Ganakatsu, 179
Gander Mountain Inc.,
  8, 77, 103, 127, 179, 262, 287
GAP Antenna Products, 371
Garber's Crafted Lighting, 311
Garbe's, 157
Garcia (James E.) 321
Gard Woodworking, 150
Garden Accents, 222
Garden Architecture, 222
Garden Botanika, 147
Garden City Seeds, 220, 241
Garden Concepts Collection, 222
Garden Fairies Trading Company, 383
Garden Gate, 222
Garden Highlights, 222
Garden of Beadin', 59
Garden of Delights, 231
Garden Ornaments Stone, 209, 222
Garden Place, 238
Garden Scapes, 236
Garden Spot Distributor, 195
Garden State Camera, 69, 100, 360, 426
Garden Tools of Maine, 222
Garden Valley Dahlias, 232
Garden Way, 219, 224, 225, 227
Garden-Ville, 219, 220, 224
Gardeners' Choice, 235, 241
Gardener's Choice, 244
Gardeners Eden, 226
Gardener's Supply Company,
  106, 219, 220, 226
Gardens Alive, 219, 224
Gardens for Growing People, 381
Gardens of the Blue Ridge, 229, 232, 246
Gardens Past, 105, 182, 366, 393
Gardensheds, 386
Gardenside Ltd., 217
GardenStyles, 220
Gardner's Farm & Wood Products, 214, 266

❖ CORPORATE INDEX ❖

Gare Incorporated, 112
Gared Sports Inc., 54, 55, 208, 412, 431
Gargoyles Performance Eyewear, 392
GarGraves Trackage Corporation, 330
Garland Commercial Industries, 1, 7, 406
Garland Homes, 283
Garman (J.) 179
Garmin, 78
Garmont, 101, 103, 106
Garn (Steve) 65
Garnet Hill,
    62, 63, 120, 122, 123, 125, 126
Garofalo (P.) 428
Garrett Metal Detectors, 321
Garrettson (F.P.) Inc. 204, 207
Gart Brothers Denver Sportscastle, 391
Garton's Auto, 29, 33, 36
Garuda Mountaineering, 103, 334
GarWood Boat Company Inc., 75
Gas Logs Direct, 176
Gaslight Auto Parts Inc., 37
Gaslight Time, 308, 309
Gasoline Alley, 6
Gaspar's Sausage Company, 197
Gastineau Log Homes Inc., 283
Gaston Knives, 305
Gateway 2000 Computers, 134
Gateway Electronics, 371
Gateway Products Corporation, 167
Gateway Toys, 52
Gateways, 85
Gathered Herb & Greenhouse,
    182, 234, 366
Gathering Place, 70, 106
Gatherings, 253, 302
Gatorz Sport Optics, 407
Gaudette (Paul) Books 85
Gavilan's, 253
Gavora (Robert) Bookseller 85
Gayla Balloons, 52
Gaylord Industries Inc., 273
Gazebo & Porchworks, 266, 280, 363
Gazebo of New York, 62, 379
Gazebo Woodcrafters, 247
Gazebos Ltd., 247
Gazin's Cajun Creole Foods, 193
GBLA Art Stamps, 377
GCC Technologies, 136
GDT Softworks Inc., 140
Gearfitter Inc., 103
Geary's, 253
Gee Gee Studios Inc., 21
Geiger (E.C.) 226
Gem Center U.S.A. Inc., 299
GEM Edwards Inc., 159
Gem-Fare, 299
Gem-O-Rama Inc., 59, 299
Gemco International, 375
Gemini Kaleidoscopes, 302
Gemmary, 6, 85
Gems by Jak, 406
Gemstone Equipment Manufacturing
    Company, 299, 312, 401
Gemstone Press, 85
Genada Imports, 214
Genealogical & Historical Society
    of Louisiana, 248
Genealogical Forum of Oregon, 249
Genealogical Publishing Company, 85
Genealogical Publishing Company Inc., 250
Genealogical Research Library, 250
Genealogical Society of Mississippi, 248
Genealogical Society of Montana, 248
Genealogy Society of Vermont, 250
Genealogy Society of Wisconsin, 250

Generac Corporation, 166
General Color Corporation, 359
General Ecology Inc., 431
General Label Manufacturing, 385
General Nutrition Catalog, 147, 430
General Sportcraft Company,
    51, 152, 156, 286, 380, 388, 394, 413, 431
General Technologies, 272
General's Books, 85
Generation Software Corporation, 159
Gene's Can Shop, 64
Gene's Trains, 330
Genesis Camera Inc., 100, 360, 426
Genesport Industries Ltd.,
    95, 152, 175, 318, 394, 440
Geneva Specialties, 439, 440
Genevieve's Gift Wrap Sales, 210
Gengler (J.) Boat Design 72
Genie, 5
Genie House, 309, 311
Genie Products, 121
Genie's Kitchen, 96, 183
Genovation Inc., 132
Gentlemen's Store, 123
Gentry (Robert) 19, 86, 109
Genuine Canadian Food Products, 197
Geo-Impressions, 374, 375
Geoban Engineering Company, 140
GeoDomes WoodWorks, 283
Georgetown Card Exchange, 398
Georgetown Health Care Center, 345
Georgetown Leather Design/Tannery West,
    123, 313, 368
Georgetown Tobacco, 415
GeorGI-Sports, 54, 208
Georgia Department of Archives & History,
    247
Georgia Lighting Supply Company Inc.,
    308, 309
Georgia "Sweets" Brand Inc., 191
Georgia Tees Inc., 53
Georgia-Pacific,
    274, 276, 277, 278, 281, 282
Georgies Ceramic & Clay Company, 112
Gepetto's Dolls N' More, 165
Geppi's Comic World Inc., 131
Gerard & Dominique Seafood, 202
Gerhard's Sausage, 197
Gerlachs of Lecha, 12, 347
Gerry Sportswear, 123
Gertz Seating & Upholstery, 214
Gesswein, 417
Getreuer (Bob) 108
Gettinger Feather Corporation, 174
Gettysburg Electronics, 321
Gettysburg Toy Soldier, 421
Getz (Wm.) Corporation 114
Gevalia Kaffe, 207
GH Productions, 55
Ghann's Cricket Farm Inc., 353
Ghitelman Cameras Inc., 360
Giant Artichoke Company, 191
Giant Bicycle Company, 65
Giardinelli Band Instrument Company Inc.,
    338
Gibbon's (Bob) Fun Technicians Inc. 129
Gibbsville Cheese Sales, 188
Gibraltar Trade Center North Inc., 19
Gibson Guitar Corporation, 338
Gibson Research Corporation, 140
Gift & Wicker Import Inc., 157, 218, 224
Gift Ahoy, 253
Gift World, 60, 253
Gifted Images Gallery, 13, 335
Gifts for All Occasions, 253

GiGi's Dolls & Sherry's Teddy Bears Inc.,
    60, 165
Gilbert's Early Chevy Pickup Parts, 48
Gilette's Coffee, 207
Gilfer Shortwave, 371
Gill Mechanical Company, 10
Gille (Rolf) Import Ltd. 151
Gille Import Ltd., 434
Gillespie Paddles, 73
Gillies Canoes & Kayaks, 73
Gillies Coffee Company, 207
Gilman (Marty) Inc. 208
Gilman's Lapidary Supply, 299
Gilmer Wood Company, 314
Gilmore Looms, 397
Gil's Gourmet Gallery, 204
Gilson Gardens Inc., 232, 233, 238
Gilway Company Ltd., 207
Gimbel & Sons Country Store, 414
Ginger Tree, 348
Gingerbread Group, 428
Gingerbread Man, 280
Gingerbread Man Woodworks,
    222, 247, 280
Ginger's Needleworks, 369
Ginn (David) Magic 86, 129, 315
Gin's (Maggie) Inc. 193
Ginsburg Company, 161
Ginsco Trims, 174
Ginseng, 233
Girard Nurseries, 228, 230, 243, 244
Girl Scout Catalog, 382
Giro Sport Designs, 67
Gironde Bros. Inc., 437
Gita Sporting Goods, 65
Giuseppe, 68
Giuseppe's Original Sausage Company, 197
Givens Ocean Survival Systems, 71
Givens Ocean Survival Systems Company
    Inc., 75
GJ's Wild West, 128
Glades Herp Inc., 353
Gladiator Sports, 96
Glass (Bill) Studio 15
Glass Crafters, 86, 401
Glasser (Kenneth) 299, 375
Glasshouse Works Greenhouses,
    229, 231, 235
Glasswalls Porch Enclosures, 396
Glazier's Mustang Farm, 38
Gleason's (Don) Camping Supply Inc. 103
Gleckler Seedmen, 244
Glen-L Marine Designs, 72
Glen-L Trailers, 47
Glenn Apiaries, 63
Glenwood Marine, 77
Glimakra Looms & Yarns Inc., 174, 397, 441
Glimpse of Time, 365
Global Computer Supplies, 134, 136, 145
Global Dolls Corporation, 163
Global Fixtures Inc., 160
Global Flyfisher, 179
Global Golf, 260
Global Hobby Distributors, 324
Global Shakeup Snowdomes, 117, 301
Global Specialties, 169
Global Telecard Company, 354
Global Video, 100
Global Village Communications Inc., 140
Global Water Technology, 431
Globalink Inc., 140
Globe Pequot Press, 86
Gloria's Kitchen, 184
Glory Flag & Pole Company, 181
Glorybee Honey & Supplies, 63, 200

CORPORATE INDEX

Glowing Candle Factory, 105
Glucoware Company, 159
Gluten-Free Pantry,
 86, 96, 183, 184, 195, 430
Glyph Technologies Inc., 132
GM Muscle Car Parts Inc., 26, 29, 39, 40
GMI/Division Omega Arkay, 355, 356, 362
GNS Spices, 190, 204
Goddard Manufacturing, 278
Godfrey (Ted) 179
Godiva Direct, 184, 186
God's World Books, 93
Goebel Inc., 15
Goergen (Dick) Reptiles 353
Goers (B.) Knives 305
Goes Lithographing Company, 401
Gohn Brothers, 121, 123
Going Bananas, 229
Going-to-the-Sun Studio, 290
Gold Coast Greenhouse, 221
Gold Leaf & Metallic Powders, 10, 388
Gold Leaf Studios, 209
Gold Medal Hair Products, 428
Gold Medal Hair Products Inc., 147, 436
Gold Mine Engineering, 367
Gold Mine Natural Food Company, 195
Gold Star Video Productions, 400
Gold-Eck of Austria, 103
Goldbergs' Marine, 76, 77, 131
Golddigger, 321, 367
Golden (Marv) Discount Sales Inc. 4
Golden Age Arms Company, 263
Golden Angels Apiary, 195
Golden Eagle Archery, 9, 288
Golden Edge Cutlery, 305, 306
Golden Fun, 420
Golden Gallery, 109
Golden Hackle Fly Shop, 179
Golden Jr. (Charlie) 64
Golden Kernel Pecan Company Inc., 199
Golden Lake Greenhouses, 235, 236
Golden Needle, 341
Golden Oldies, 108
Golden Rule Bears, 60
Golden Sands Salvage, 23
Golden Shine Inc., 412
Golden State Autographs, 19
Golden State Pickup Parts, 48
Golden Trophy, 197
Golden Valley Lighting, 308
Golden Walnut Specialty Fooods,
 184, 186, 207
Golden West International, 438
Golden West Publishers, 86
Goldentouch Golf Inc., 259
Gold's Artworks Inc., 12, 347
Gold's Gym, 120, 170, 380
Goldstar, 134, 403, 425
GoldStar Precision, 169
Goldware, 296
Goldwin Golf Inc., 259
Golf Day, 260
Golf Haus, 260
Golf Sellers Direct, 260
Golfer's Image, 260
Golfsmith, 260
Golfstats, 140
Golfworks, 260
Gone Hollywood, 6, 335
Good As Any...Better 'n Some, 108, 109
Good Catalog Company,
 157, 222, 253, 302
Good Hollow Greenhouse & Herbarium,
 232, 234, 238, 246, 348, 366
Good Hope Hardwoods, 314

Good Idea, 253
Good Impressions Rubber Stamps, 377
Good Music Record Company, 109, 428
Good Time Charlie's, 131
Good Time Flags, 181
Good Time Stove Company, 406
Good Wives Inc., 193
Good Wood Ltd., 397
Goodies from Goodman, 193
Goodman (Barry) 421
Goodnow's, 299
Good's Nursery, 235
Goodwin (Virginia) 154
Goodwin Creek Gardens,
 182, 234, 243, 244
Goodwin Lumber, 275, 276
Goose & Gander Country Gift Shop, 127
Gordie's Used Cards, 365
Gordon (Bruce) Cycles 65
Gordy's, 423
Gorges (Will) Civil War Antiques 131, 322
Gorham, 116, 153, 389
Gorilla & Sons, 101, 103, 179
Gorilla Gardens, 204
Gorilla Products, 332
Gorlics' Trading Inc., 128
Gorsuch Ltd., 391
Gospel Advocate Bookstores, 93
Gossler Farms Nursery, 243, 244
Gotham Book Mart, 86
Gothic Arch Greenhouses, 220
Gothic Scenic & Theatrical Paints, 414
Gourm-E-Co Imports, 188
Gourmet Gardener, 234, 238, 245
Gourmet Mushrooms, 236
Gowland (Peter) Cameras 356
Graber, 22
Graber's Crafted Lighting, 308
Grace Galleries Inc., 6, 317
Grace Tea Company, 207
Graceland Gifts Mail Order, 253
Graceland Records, 108
Gracewood Fruit Company, 191
Gradus (Ari) 13
Grady (Orville J.) 86
Grady (P.J.) Delorean 31
Graf & Sons, 262, 287
Graffam Brothers, 202
Grafstein & Company, 296
Graftobian Ltd., 129, 414
Grafton Village Apple Company, 196
Grafton Village Cheese Company, 188
Graham Industries, 328
Gramma's Graphics Inc., 171
Granada Posters, 335
Granberg International, 417
Grand Central Ltd., 330
Grand ERA Reproductions, 266, 274
Grand Finale, 253
Grand Forms & Systems Inc., 343
Grand River Workshop, 212
Grand Tool Supply Corporation, 417
Grand Travel Square Dance Shop, 400
Grand-Craft, 75
Grandma's Attic, 165
Grandma's Fruit Cake, 184
Grandma's Recipe Rugelach, 184, 190
Grandma's Spice Shop,
 200, 204, 207, 348, 366
Grandpa's Crafts, 150, 157
Grandt Line Products, 161
Granite Lake Pottery Inc., 57, 116
Granny's Turntable, 108, 109
Grant Lariat Rope Company, 376
Grant Waterx Corporation, 271, 435

GRANTCO, 268
Granville Country Store, 188
Granville Manufacturing Company Inc.,
 275, 278, 314
Grapevine Graphics, 71
GraphComm Services, 344
Graphic Chemical & Ink Company,
 10, 71, 169, 366
Graphic Display Systems, 160
Graphic Encountering Inc., 13
Graphic Impressions, 344
Graphic Rubber Stamp Company, 377
Graphics Inc., 261
Graphik Dimensions Ltd., 209
Grasshopper Company, 224
Grate Fires, 176
Grate Vents, 370
Graven Images, 377
Graventa, 401
Graves Company, 299, 312, 367
Graves Plating Company, 43
Graves-Mountain Lodge, 200
Gravity Plus, 170, 443
Gray & Sons, 296
Grayarc, 344, 401
Graymark, 168
Grayson (Kelly), Woodcarving & Design 217
Grayson's (Jean) Brownstone Studio
 Collection 125
Graywolf Press, 86
Grayworks/Winterworks, 13, 261
Great American Log, 157, 214
Great American Market, 414
Great American Tool Company, 306
Great Bear Technology/HealthSoft, 140, 270
Great Canadian Canoe Company, 73
Great Chefs Television, 86
Great Christian Books, 86, 93, 145, 428
Great City Traders, 157
Great Fermentations of Marin, 437
Great Gadgets, 253
Great Gatsby's, 277
Great Kids Company, 422
Great Lakes Boat Building Company, 72
Great Lakes Dart Distributors Inc., 156
Great Lakes Technology, 132
Great Lakes Windows, 282
Great Meadows Joinery, 214
Great Northern Log Homes, 283
Great Northern Longbow Company, 9
Great Northern Trading Company, 202
Great Northern Weaving, 378
Great Plains Meats, 197
Great Plains Polymers, 311
Great Planes, 324
Great River Outfitters, 73
Great Southern Sauce Company, 204
Great Southern Security, 408
Great Tracers, 402
Great Traditions Toy Trains, 330
Great Valley Mills, 190, 193, 197
Great Winds Kites, 303
Great Yarns, 441
Greater American Business Products, 343
Greatest Scapes, 13
Greatwood Log Homes, 283
Green (Art) 262
Green (Brian & Maria) 19
Green (Patrick) Carders 397
Green (T.) Enterprises 44
Green (W.M.) & Company 253
Green (Wade) Advertising Inc. 127
Green Cedar Needle Sachets, 147, 289
Green Design Furniture Company, 214
Green Earth Organics, 224

❖ CORPORATE INDEX ❖

Green Enterprises, 217, 266
Green Escape, 237
Green Fire, 221
Green Gable Gifts, 364
Green Gardens, 221
Green Grower Supply, 221
Green Horizons, 86, 246
Green Mountain Chocolate Company, 186
Green Mountain Coffee Roasters, 207
Green Mountain Mercantile, 123
Green Mountain Precision Frames, 282
Green Mountain Studios, 150, 151, 423, 439
Green Mountain Sugar House, 196
Green Pepper, 172, 383, 384
Green Pond Company, 121
Green River Rodmakers, 179
Green Spot Ltd., 219
Green Thumb Collection, 128
Green Thumb Software Inc., 225
Green Turtle Cannery, 202
Greenberg & Hammer Inc., 383
Greenberg (William) Desserts Inc. 184
Greenberg Smoked Turkey Inc., 197
Greene (James) Archery Products 9
Greene (Jeffrey P.), Furniture Maker 214
Greene's Lighting Fixtures, 308
Greenfield Herb Garden, 234
Greenfield Imported Car Parts, 26
Greengrass (Barney) 193
Greenhouse Miniature Shop, 161
Greenjeans (Mrs.) Hydroponic & Garden Supplies 221
Greenleaf Electronics, 427
Greenlee Nursery, 234
Green's (Susan) California Cuisine 191, 193
GreenTech, 220
Greenwich Workshop Inc., 13
Greer Gardens, 228, 230, 243, 244
Gregory (Jack) 293
Gregory Mountain Products, 103, 334
Grey Owl Paddle Company, 73
Greystone Automotive, 37
Grid Inc., 55, 208, 370
Grieger's, 299, 375
Griffey Nursery, 228, 232, 236, 239, 243, 244, 246
Griffin (Clay) Postcards 365
Griffin Enterprises Inc., 179
Griffin Manufacturing Company Inc., 329, 417
Griffis Lumber & Sawmill, 276, 277, 278
Griffith Distributors, 299
Grigsby Cactus Gardens, 231
Grill Parts Distributors, 52
Grimo Nut Nursery, 244
Grind Zone Skates, 376
Griot's Garage, 47
Grisi (Gail) Stenciling Inc. 402
Grizzly Imports Inc., 417
Grizzly Peak Kiteworks, 303
Gro-Tek, 226
Groff & Hearne Lumber, 314
Grohe America Inc., 174, 286
Grolier Electronic Publishing Inc., 140
Gross (Ken) 107
Gross (Roger) Ltd. 19
Gross Stabil Corporation, 416
Grossman's Seafood Inc., 202
Group Genesis Inc., 2
Grove Boat-Lift, 47, 77
Grove Enterprises Inc., 371
Groves Quality Collectibles, 60
Grovhac Inc., 227
Grow-It Instant Greenhouses, 220

Growers Service Company, 232, 238, 239, 241
Growing Experience, 221
GRS Tools, 170
Grubco, 353
Gruber's Market, 341
Gruhn Guitars Inc., 338
Grunewald Folk Art, 13, 150
Gryphon House Books, 86
Grzyboski (Joseph A.) Jr. 330
GT Bicycles, 65
GT Interactive Software, 140
Guadelupe Pit Smoked Meats, 197
Guardex Pool & Spa Products, 408
Guardian Custom Products, 409
Guardian Personal Security Products, 408
Guardian Products Inc., 106, 269, 271, 435
Guarisco Gallery, 13
Gudebrod, 179
Guenther (Gerry) 398
Guerlain Boutique by Mail, 147
Guildcraft Company, 151, 183, 389
Guitar Emporium, 338
Guitarmaker's Connection, 338
Gukich (Mary) 165
Gulf Harvest Gourmet Inc., 202
Gulf Publishing Company, 86
Gulf-Coast Avionics Corporation, 3
Gulfcoast Guitars, 338
Gumps by Mail, 253
Gun Parts Corporation, 265
Gund Bears, 60
Gundula's & Peerless Rattan & Reed, 56, 114
Gunn (Jo) Enterprises 371
Gunpowder Foods, 204
Gunsmoke Bar-B-Que Foods, 204
Gurney Seed & Nursery Company, 106, 231, 241, 244
Gutcheon Patchworks Inc., 172
Guterman International Inc., 412
Gwynnbrook Farm, 351
GYM-N-I Playgrounds Inc., 363
GZ Foreign Movie Memorabilia, 335

H

H & A Enterprises Inc., 296
H & B Recordings, 109
H & F Announcements, 71
H & H Bagels, 183
H & H Classic Parts, 29
H & H Worldwide, 332
H & L Collectibles, 319
H & R Badge & Stamp Company, 51, 399
H & R Company, 167, 408
H & R Magic Books, 86
H Bar C Ranchwear, 400
H-S Medical Supplies, 159
H.R. Electronics, 371
H2B Company, 443
Haag (Robert) Meteorites 374
Haas Cabinet Company Inc., 97
Haas Outdoors Inc., 287
Haband for Her, 123
Haband for Men, 123, 386
Habersham Plantation, 214
Habitat Post & Beam Homes, 282
Habitat Solar Rooms, 396
Hacker Boat Company, 76
Haddonstone (USA) Ltd., 222
Hadley Fruit Orchards, 191, 200
Häfele America Company, 57
Haffner (Lance) Games 140
Hagan's Sterling & Silverplate, 389
Hagara (Jan) Collectors Club 165, 364

Hagelberg Farm, 196
Hagenow Laboratories, 306
Hagensborg Foods U.S.A. Inc., 193, 202
Hagstoz (T.B.) & Son Inc. 115, 299, 320
Haida (Johanna) Bears USA 61
Haitian Art Company, 253
Hake's Americana, 6
Halcyon Yarn, 341, 441
Hale House, 62, 193
Hale Indian River Groves, 210
Hale Security Pet Door, 353
Half Halt Press, 86
Halibar Company, 13
Halide of Oregon, 221
Halides America Inc., 176, 177
Haliwa-Saponi Tribal Pottery & Arts, 292
Hall (Carol) 204
Hall (Jacquelyn) 116, 153
Hall (Martha) 341, 441
Hall 304
Hall Mock Productions, 204
Hallidays America Inc., 280
Hallmark at Home Inc., 253
Hall's Nostalgia, 398
Halotech Inc., 71
Halted Electronic Supply, 167
Haltek Electronics, 167
Ham Radio Outlet Inc., 371, 373
Ham Radio Toy Store, 371
Ham Station, 371
Ham Store, 371
Hamakor Judaica Inc., 258
Hambrick's Fabrics, 172
Hamilton (Edward R.), Bookseller 80
Hamilton Books, 86
Hamilton Marine Inc., 77
Hamilton Technology Corporation, 221, 351
Hammacher Schlemmer, 253
Hammer Medical Supply, 345
Hammer's Wire & Wood, 70
Hammerworks, 308, 309
Hammett (J.L.) Company 11, 306, 321, 381
Hammock Etc., 266
Hammon (David) Dolls & Toys 165
Hammond Barns, 386, 440
Hammond Incorporated, 86, 317
Hampton Coach, 49
Hamtronics/Trevose, 371
Han Dids Needleart, 341
Hancock Fabrics, 172, 369, 383
Hancock's Advanced Outdoor Products, 288
Hand & Hammer Silversmiths, 117, 296
Hand Engravers Supply Company, 170
Hand in Hand, 50, 250, 422, 423
Hand Painted Clothing, 120
Hand-y Home Products, 247
Handcraft Designs Inc., 12, 161
Handcrafted Log Furnishings, 214
Handcrafted Wood Products, 150, 383
Handelsman (M.) Company 258
Handi-Move, 271, 435
Handi-Ramp Inc., 271
Handicaps Inc., 435
Handshake Greeting Cards, 261
Handsome Rewards, 253
Handy Home Products, 386
Handy Softshell Crawfish, 202
Handy Store Fixtures, 160
Hanes' (Mrs.) Moravian Cookies 184
Haney (Kelley) Art Gallery 15, 293
Hang-Em High Fabrics, 303
Hang-It-Now Wallpaper Stores, 281
Hangouts Handwoven Hammocks, 266
Hanhurst's Record Service, 400

❖ CORPORATE INDEX ❖

Hankinson (Ken) Associates 72, 77
Hannah's House, 341
Hanneman Gemological Instruments, 299
Hanover House, 253
Hanover Lantern, 311
Hanover Shoe Company, 386
Hansa Systems, 327
Hansel Hardware, 330
Hansen (Ken) Photographic 360
Hansen Cartridge Company, 263
Hansen Caviar Company, 188
Hansen Planetarium, 253
Hansgrohe Inc., 57, 323
Hanson Helmets, 3
Happiness Farms, 241
Happy & Pappy's Clown Bicycles & Handcrafted Shoes, 129
Happy Collecting, 423
Happy House Miniatures, 161
Happy Jack Inc., 284
Happy Valley Ranch, 183
Harbor Candy Shop, 186
Harbor Freight Salvage, 408
Harbor Freight Tools, 417
Harbor Sales Company Inc., 77, 314
Harbor Sweets Inc., 186
Harbor Vintage Motor Company, 332
Hard Times Cafe, 128, 193
Hard Times Chili, 190
Hard-to-Find Needlework Books, 80, 86
Hardee, 105
Hardeman Apiaries, 63
Harden Furniture, 214
Hardens Muscle Car World, 29, 31, 39
Hardies, 59, 299
Hardin Electronics, 371
Harding's Custom Sheers, 154
Hardscrabble Enterprises Inc., 236, 245
Hardware Plus, 268, 276
Hardwicke Gardens, 227
Hardwood Store, 314
Hardy Motors, 44
Hargrove Manufacturing Corporation, 176
Harlow's Sugar House, 188, 196, 200
Harman's Cheese & Country Store, 193
Harmening's High Flyers Inc., 3
Harmon/Kardon, 46, 403
Harmonic Vision, 141
Harmonica Music Publishing, 86, 268
Harmon's Agate & Silver Shop, 296, 299
Harmon's Inc., 27, 28, 29, 37, 38, 48
Harmony Computers, 136
Harmony Farm Supply & Nursery,
    219, 220, 224, 226, 227, 236, 244
Harmony Filling Station, 21
Harmony Hollow, 436
Harmony in Design, 443
Harmony Supply Company Inc., 281
Harney & Sons Tea Company, 207
Haro Designs Inc., 65
Harold's, 123
Harper General Store, 61
Harper House, 383, 384
HarperCollins, 86
Harper's MotoGuzzi, 332
Harrell & Sons Inc., 63
Harrington (Russell) Cutlery Inc. 11, 209
Harrington Ham Company, 193, 197
Harrington's of Vermont, 193, 197
Harris (Bruce) Sportscards 398
Harris Communications, 272
Harris International Inc., 260
Harris Photoguides, 357
Harris Seeds, 226, 241
Harris Seeds Inc., 229, 236

Harris Tools, 417
Harrison-Hoge Industries Inc., 179
Harrisville Designs, 397, 441
Harry & David, 185, 186, 191, 193, 200
Harry's Crestview Groves, 191
Harry's Discounts & Appliances Corporation, 7
Hart (Ari T.) 179
Hart (Robert W.) & Son Inc. 262
Hart Tackle Company Inc., 179
Hart-Bake Charcoal Ovens, 53
Hartco Flooring Company, 275
Hartford Clamp Company, 416
Hartmann's Plantation, 229
Hartman's Herb Farm, 182, 234, 348, 366
Hart's Crestview Groves, 191
Hartstone Inc., 116
Hartville Tool & Supply, 417
Harvest Direct Inc., 195
Harvest Gallery Inc., 13
Harvest Health Inc., 234, 348
Harvest House Furniture, 214
Harvest Moon Hydroponics Inc., 221
Harvey's Skin Diving Suits Inc., 432
Harwell Studios, 13
Haskell's Handcraft, 118, 163
Haslam's Doll Houses, 161
Hasselblad (Victor) Inc. 356
Hasty-Bake, 53, 193
Hat Store, 268
Hatathli Gallery, 290
Hatchers Manufacturing Inc., 114
Hatry Electronics, 371
Haug (George) Company Inc.
    26, 34, 37, 40, 42
Hauser (John M.) 131
Have Book, 86
Haven Electronics, 100
Haven Industries,
    47, 100, 136, 404, 410, 423, 426
Haverhills, 131
Havlick Snowshoe Company, 393
Hawaiian Marine Imports Inc., 352
Hawaiian Queen Company, 63
Hawaii's Jungle Jerky, 197
Hawks Tag Service, 344
Haworth Press Inc., 86
Hawthorne, 364
Hay Charlie, 126, 128, 296
Haydel's Game Calls Inc., 288
Hayes (Jim) 19
Hayes Microcomputer Products Inc., 141
Hayman (Gayle) Beverly Hills 147, 296
Hays Electronics, 86, 317, 321, 367
Hazelden Publishing Group, 86
Hazelmere Mantel Company, 177
Hazelton (John) Posters 335
Head Golf, 259
Head Sports, 369, 370, 391
Headlight Headquarters, 22
Headquarters Windows & Walls, 153
Headwaters, 73
Healing Arts, 443
Health Care Inc., 435
Health Center for Better Living, 269, 430
Healthhouse USA, 269
HealthMax, 170
Healthy Kitchen Mail Order Company, 195
Healthy Living, 269
Healthy Trader, 195
Hear You Are Inc., 272, 274
Hearlihy & Company, 11, 145, 166
Heart Enterprise, 311
Heart of America Toys, 423
Heart of the Woods Inc., 150

Heart Thoughts Cards, 71
Heart Thoughts Original Wedding Stationery, 434
Heart-Rate Inc., 170
Heartbreak Ridge, 318
Heartcraft Kids, 163
Hearth Realities, 176
Hearth Song, 161, 250, 303, 347, 422
HearthStone, 406
Hearthstone Log Homes, 283
Heartland America, 253
Heartland Appliances, 406
Heartland HomeBrew, 437
Heartland Hydroponics, 221
Heartland Music, 109
Hearty Mix Company, 206
HeartyMix Company, 96, 183, 185, 201
Heat-N-Glo, 176
Heath Sedgwick, 157
Heathkit Educational Systems,
    5, 168, 311, 381
Heaths & Heathers, 239
Heatilator Inc., 176, 406
Heating Alternatives, 406
Heatway Radiant Floors & Snowmelting, 211
Heaven's Garden, 204
Heavy Chevy Truck Parts, 48
Hebard (Gil) Guns 265
Hecht's, 158
Hedgehog Handworks, 59, 341, 383
Hegg & Hegg, 202
Heidt's, 45
Heimburger House Publishing Company, 86
Heirloom Creations, 172, 174
Heirloom Editions,
    13, 97, 98, 261, 401, 405
Heirloom European Tapestries, 409
Heirloom Gardens, 241
Heirloom Old Garden Roses, 240
Heirloom Reproductions, 214, 309
Heirloom Rugs, 379
Heirloom Seeds, 241
Heirloom Woven Labels, 385
Heitkam's Honey Bees, 63
Heitz (Karl) Inc. 362
Heizer Software, 141
Helen's Tropical Exotics, 204
Helicopter World Inc., 324
Helicopters Unlimited, 324
Helicraft Inc., 2
Helimot European Accessories, 331
Helix, 69, 356, 361, 362
Hellamarine, 71
Hello Again, 111
Hello Direct, 132, 272, 346, 411
Hello Dolly, 163
Heluva Good Cheese Inc., 188
Helwig (Marjorie) 438
Hemmings Bookshelf, 86
Hemphill's Healey Haven, 25
Hen-Feathers & Company Inc., 222
Henderson Camp Products Inc., 103
Henderson's (Bill) Cards 398
Henderson's Heritage Herbs, 204
Hendricks Furniture Inc., 214
Hendricks Woodworking, 274
Hendrix Farms, 191
Henel (John H.) 365
Hennessy House, 182
Henrietta's Nursery, 231
Henriksen (Ole) of Denmark 147
Herald Multiforms Inc., 345
Heraldica Imports, 296
Herb & Spice Collection, 147, 204, 366
Herb Lady, 348, 366

❖ CORPORATE INDEX ❖

Herb N' Ewe, 223
Herb 'n' Lore, 204
Herb Patch Ltd., 207
Herb Products Company, 86, 234, 348
Herb Shady Acres Farm, 182
Herbach & Rademan, 5
Herbal Accents, 147, 348
Herbalist, 269
Herban Garden, 234, 245
Herbfarm, 234
Herbs for Healthy Living, 147
Herb's Porcelain Doll Studio, 163
Herbs-Licious, 204
Herbs-Liscious, 182, 234, 366
Herceg (T.F.) Inc. 271, 435
Hercules Incorporated, 262
Here's My Heart, 157
Heritage Aviation Art, 13
Heritage Books Inc., 250
Heritage Brushes, 11, 112
Heritage Custom Kitchens, 97
Heritage Fence Company, 175
Heritage Garden Houses, 386
Heritage Graphics, 141
Heritage Home Canning, 106
Heritage Lace, 154
Heritage Lanterns, 311
Heritage Log Homes, 283
Heritage Looms, 397
Heritage Mantels Inc., 177
Heritage Miniatures, 161, 163, 174
Heritage Rose Gardens, 240
Heritage Rugs, 379
Heritage Seed Company, 245
Heritage Wedding, 434
Heritage Woodcraft, 280
Herkimer Diamond Mines,
    367, 375, 376, 382, 438
Hermes (J.) 161
Hermes of Paris Inc., 123
Hermitage Bakery, 185
Hermitage Gardens, 209
Heronswood Nursery, 239
Herr Engineering Corporation, 324
Herrington, 253
Herr's & Bernat, 341
Herrschners Inc., 304, 341, 441
Hershey's Mailorder, 186
Herter's, 158
Hertzsprung (Irwin) Mailing Lists 317
Herwig Lighting, 311
Herzinger & Company, 86
Herzog Postcards, 365
Hess Manufacturing Company, 274
Hewlett-Packard Company, 132, 134
Hey Enterprises, 86, 365
HG Professional Forms Company,
    80, 343, 344
HH Designs, 341
HH Racing Group, 65
HHH Enterprises, 299
Hi Hat Dance Records, 400
Hi-De-Ho Collectibles, 346
Hi-Grade Shooter's Supply, 265
Hi-Lo Trailer Company, 47
Hi-Tec Sports USA Inc., 101
Hi-Tech Expressions, 141
Hi-Tech Motorsports, 44, 45
Hialeah Communications, 371
Hiawatha Log Homes, 283
Hickin's Mountain Mowings Farm, 193
Hickory Dickory Dolls, 163, 165
Hickory Farms, 188, 193
Hickory Furniture Mart, 214
Hida Japanese Tool Inc., 417

Hidalgo Inc., 407
Hidden Garden Nursery Inc., 240
Hidden Valley Auto Parts, 23
Higginson Books, 86, 250
High Country Archery, 9
High Country Garden, 224, 239
High Country Roses, 240
High Performance Bulbs, 22
High Seas Foul Weather Gear, 71, 123
High Sierra, 103
High Sierra Antennas, 371
High Sierra Rocketry, 327
High View Publications, 86, 318, 428
High Water Recording Company, 109
High Zoot/ViaTech Inc., 65
High-Grade Publications, 86, 317
High-Lonesome Books, 86
High-Quality Comics, 131
Higher Planes Inc., 2
Higher Yield, 221
Highland Hardware, 417
Highland Succulents, 231
Highlander, 427
Highlander Musical Audio Products, 338
Highlander Nursery, 229
Highlands Ceramic Supply, 112
Highsmith Multicultural Bookstore, 86
HighText Publications Inc., 86
Highway Classics, 30, 32, 38, 40, 42
Highwood Bookshop, 86
HIG'S Aluminum Products, 271
Hikari Sales USA Inc., 352
Hike-A-Bike Inc., 22
Hiker's Hut, 101
Hild Sails, 76
Hile (Warren) Studio 214
Hill (Howard) Archery 9
Hill Decal Company, 112
Hill Knittery, 341, 441
Hillary's Garden, 234, 239
Hillerich & Bradsby Company Inc., 54, 259
Hillestad Corporation, 430
Hillis (Sue) Designs 341
Hill's Boat Yard, 75, 76
Hills Products Inc., 111
Hillsboro Industries Inc., 285
Hilsport by Hilco Inc., 264, 313
Hilton Audio Products, 399
Hilyard & Hilquist, 195
Himalayan International Institute of Yoga
    Science, 86
Hind Sportswear, 120
Hinds (John) & Company 340, 388
Hinds Instruments Inc., 433
Hinges & Handles, 370
Hinterberg Design Inc., 369
Hiper Sports, 331, 332
Hippo Heart Rubber Stamps, 377
Hipp's Superbird's Inc., 1
Hirsch (Bill) 23, 46, 49
Hirsch (Edwin) 17
Hirsh Company, 97, 119
His Hand...Crafts, 436
Hiss & Hers Reptiles, 353
Historic Aviation, 86, 429
Historic Charleston Reproductions, 214
Historic Floors of Oshkosh Inc., 275
Historic Housefitters Company, 157
Historic Lighting Restoration, 309
Historic Newspaper Archives, 342
Historic Paints Ltd., 438
Historic Windows, 278
Historical Americana, 323
Historical Association of Texas, 249
Historical Documents International Inc., 19

Historical Ink, 317
Historical Iowa State Society, 248
Historical Miniatures, 421
Historical Sculptures, 15
Historical Society of Maine, 248
Historical Society of Vermont, 250
Historical Society of Virginia, 250
History Makers Inc., 19
Hitachi Power Tools U.S.A. Ltd., 418
Hitachi Sales Corporation, 46, 99, 403, 425
Hitchcock Shoes Inc., 387
Hitching Post Supply, 253, 285
Hitec, 327
Hitec Group International, 272
HKS Products Inc., 262
HKS USA Inc., 25, 31, 34, 36, 37, 42
Hobby Barn, 324, 328
Hobby Builders Supply, 161
Hobby Craft, 161
Hobby Gallery Miniature Loft, 165
Hobby Game Distributors Inc., 11
Hobby Heaven, 326
Hobby Horse Clothing Company Inc., 128
Hobby Horse Products, 329
Hobby House Distributors, 365
Hobby House Inc., 326, 328
Hobby House Press Inc., 86
Hobby Lobby, 421
Hobby Lobby International Inc., 324
Hobby Shack, 324, 326, 327, 329
Hobby Supplies, 399
Hobby Surplus Sales, 324, 326, 328, 330
Hobby Warehouse of Sacramento, 326
Hobby World Ltd. of Montreal,
    324, 328, 381
Hobby World Miniatures, 161
Hobbycraft Canada, 324
Hobbyland, 330
Hobie Sunglasses, 407
Hockensmith (Dan) 305
Hoctor Products, 155, 354
Hodges Badge Company Inc., 50
Hodgins Engraving, 97, 388
Hodgson Hook Company, 179
Hofcraft, 11, 415
Hoffco, 225
Hoffman BMW Parts, 26
Hoffman's Quality Meats, 197
Hogdon Powder Company Inc., 262
Hoist Fitness Systems, 170
Holabird Sports Discounters,
    55, 170, 260, 369, 370, 394, 411, 412
Holbrook Wholesalers, 147
Holcombe (Ted M.) Cadillac Parts 27
Holcraft Collection, 347
Hold Everything, 286
Holiday Rambler Corporation, 47
Holiday Treasures Catalog, 117
Holladay Jungle, 235
Holland Boone Polished Pewter, 253
Holland Bulb Farms, 241
Holland Cycles, 65
Holland Log Homes, 283
Holland Mold Inc., 112
Holland Photo, 359
Hollingsworth Furniture, 211, 214
Hollins Enterprises Inc., 415
Hollister, 345
Holly Sales, 129, 405
Hollydale Nursery, 244
Hollywood Classic Motorcars Inc., 42
Hollywood Collectibles, 335
Hollywood Legends, 19, 335
Hollywood North, 335
Hollywood Sheet Music, 337

CORPORATE INDEX

Holman (Bob) Plans 324
Holmes (Peter M.) Books 86
Holton Furniture Company, 214
Holt's Cigar Company, 415
Holy Cross Abbey, 185
Holzman & Stephanie Perfumes Inc., 147
Homan (Holder) & Sons Apiaries 63
Homarus Inc., 202
Home Arcade Corporation, 130, 302
Home Automation Systems Inc., 5
Home Baked Group Inc., 185, 190
Home Buyer Publications Inc., 86
Home Canning Supply, 106
Home Control Concepts, 5
Home Decorators Collection, 57, 157, 309, 316
Home Delivery Incontinent Supplies Company, 290
Home Etc., 62, 379, 409
Home Fabric Mills Inc., 172, 393
Home Film Festival, 336, 429
Home Gardener Manufacturing Company, 226
Home Health Express, 345
Home Health Products, 269
Home Lumber Company, 418
Home Medical Center Hospital Supplies, 345
Home Planners Inc., 86
Home Shop Machinist Magazine, 87
Home Silvo Hardware Company, 253
Home Theatre Systems, 403
Home Trends, 253, 401
Home-Sew Inc., 383
Homebrew Supply of Dallas, 437
Homecare Products Inc., 271
HomeCraft Express, 415
Homecraft Services, 62
HomeCrest Corporation, 97
Homelite Sales, 224
Homespun Fabrics & Draperies, 172
Homespun Tapes, 109
Homespun Weavers, 172
Homestead, 233
Homestead Carts, 219
Homestead Collectibles, 52
Homestead Design Inc., 386, 440
Homestead Designs Crafts, 415
Homestead Designs Gourds, 151
Homestead Handcrafts, 415
Homestead Log Homes, 283
Homestead Needle Arts, 341
Homestead Paint & Finishes, 276
Homeway Furniture Company, 214
Honani Crafts, 290
Honda Martial Arts Supply, 87, 318
Honda-Suzuki of Greenville, 332
Honest Abe Log Homes Inc., 282, 283
Honest John's Caddy Corner, 27
Honey Acres, 200
Honeywell Inc., 1, 311
Hong Kong Lapidary Supplies, 299
Honka Log Homes, 283
Honky Tonk Country Western Dance Wear, 400
Hoober Jr. (Richard T.) 346
Hood Finishing Products Inc., 438
Hook & Hackle Company, 179
Hooked on Rugs, 378
Hoosier-Peddler, 6
Hoover's Manufacturing Company, 156, 323, 363
Hope's Landmark Products Inc., 282
Hopestar Enterprises, 161
Hopewood Farm, 218
Hopi Arts & Crafts, 290
Hopi Kiva, 290
Hopkins Fishing Tackle, 179
Hoppenworth's (Neil) Cards 399
HopTech, 437
Horchow Collection, 62, 63, 123, 125, 253
Horchow Fine Linen Collection, 409
Horizon Dart Supply, 156
Horizon Hobby Distributors, 327
Horizon Instruments Inc., 3
Horkey (Bruce) Cabinetry 48
Horn (Bill & Mary) 290
Hornady Manufacturing Company, 262
Horne (Jerry) 232, 237, 239
Horowitz (F.B.) Fine Art Ltd. 14
Horse of Course, 285
Horse Prints, 87
Horse Soldier, 322
Horseman's Corral, 285
Horsemen's General Store, 284, 285, 296
Horst Company, 352
Horticultural Enterprises, 245
Horton Brasses, 268
Horton Manufacturing Company, 9
Horton's Seafood, 202
Hosfelt Electronics Inc., 167
Hospital Center Pharmacy, 159
Hospital Drug Store, 345
Hot Card USA, 399
Houle Rare Books & Autographs, 19
Hound Dog Fashions, 128
House, 376
House Calls, 269
House Dressing Furniture, 214
House of 1776, 116
House of Almonds, 199
House of Canes, 106
House of Caron, 112, 161, 163
House of Ceramics Inc., 112
House of Eyes, 407
House of Fire, 190
House of Flags, 182
House of Fragrances, 147
House of Hubcaps, 49
House of India, 299
House of International Fragrances, 147
House of Laird, 172
House of Miniatures, 161
House of Moulding, 177, 280
House of Music, 109, 429
House of Muskets Inc., 263
House of Onyx, 299
House of Tees, 259
House of Treasure Hunters, 321, 367
House of Tyrol, 64, 118, 253, 363, 429
House of Webster, 193, 406
House of White Birches, 369
House-Mouse Designs, 261, 405
House-on-the-Hill, 146
Houseman-Whitehawk (Laurie) 291
Houseworks, 161
Houston (Joyce) Products 163
Houston Seafood Corporation, 202
Houston Stained Glass Supply, 401
Houston's Peanut Outlet, 199
Houten (Maggi) 292
Hoveround, 435
Howard (Frank E.) Postcards 365
Howard Products Inc., 276
Howard's (Dan) Maternity Factory Outlet 122
Howard's Antique Lighting, 308, 309
Howard's Corvettes, 30
Howard's Sports Collectibles, 399
Howell (David) & Company 80, 209
Howell (Jerry E.) 328
Howell Book House Inc., 87
Hoya Crystal Gallery, 153, 157
Hoyt (Jeanne) Autographs 19
Hoyt USA, 9
HP Marketing Group, 69
HQ Percussion Products, 338
HRO Systems, 431
HSU's Ginseng Enterprises Inc., 233
HTC Products, 418
HTP America Inc., 47
Hubbard Maps, 317
Hubbard Scientific Company, 306, 381
Hubbard's Impala, 34
Hubbardton Forge & Wood Corporation, 308
Hubbell Lighting, 312
Hubcap Mike, 49
Huber (M.R.) 421
Huckleberry Haven, 186, 201
Hudson (J.L.), Seedsman 233, 241
Hudson (Murray) 258, 322
Hudson Envelope Corporation, 401
Hudson Glass, 401
Hudson Hills Press, 87, 355
Hudson Marine Plywoods, 77
Hudson Valley Beef Rawhide, 350
Hudson Valley Flags & Banners, 182
Hudson's Discount Furniture, 214
Huebler Industries Inc., 68
Huff's Garden Mums, 231
Huffy Sports, 55
Hug A Bear, 61
Hugger-Mugger Yoga Products, 128, 443
Hughes (Timothy) Newspapers 342
Hughes Dulcimer Company, 338
Hughes Newspapers, 342
Hughes Nursery, 244
Hulme, 288, 350
Human Code Inc., 141
Human Kinetics, 87
Humanities Press International Inc., 87
Hume (Don) Leathergoods 264
Hummerdude's, 19, 335
Hummul (Christian J.) Company 11, 418
Hunt (W.B.) Company Inc. 361
Hunt Country Foods Inc., 185
Hunt Galleries Inc., 214
Hunt Manufacturing Company, 98, 348
Hunt Valley Cashmere, 441
Hunt-Wilde, 369, 391, 393
Hunter (Darcie) Publications 377, 415
Hunter Company Inc., 264
Hunter Douglas Window Fashions, 153
Hunter Fan Company, 1, 174, 211, 286
Hunter Irrigation Products, 227
Hunter Publishing Inc., 87
Hunter's Angling Supplies, 179
Hunters Pointe, 266
Hunter's Specialties Inc., 288
Huntington Clothiers, 123, 126
Huntley-Moore Farms, 199
Hunt's Photo & Video, 100
Hurd Millwork Company, 274
Hurley (Carson) Enterprises Inc. 318
Hurley Patentee Lighting, 308, 309
Huronview Nurseries, 237
Hurricane Sports Inc., 259
Husqvarna Power Products, 224, 225, 227
Hussey (Darren) 118
Huston Dolls, 163
Hutch Manufacturing Company, 406
Hutch Sports USA, 55, 208
Hutchinson House, 321
Hutchison (Skip) 381, 393, 407
Huy Fong Foods Inc., 204
HY-Q Enterprises, 111

CORPORATE INDEX

Hyde Bird Feeder Company, 70, 349
Hyde Drift Boats, 75
Hydr-Sil, 211
Hydraflow Equipment Company, 420
Hydrofarm, 221
Hygienics Direct Company, 290
Hyland's Standard Homeopathic Company, 270
Hymer Manufacturing, 332
Hyper Wheels, 376
HyperCompleat Angler, 141
HyperData, 134
HyperGlot Software Company, 141
Hyperkites, 303
Hyside Inflatables, 73, 373
Hyundai Electronics America, 134

I

I & I Sports, 318
I-Tec, 271, 435
I.F.G. Cars, 45
I.W. Designs, 378
I/R Miniatures Inc., 421
Iandola Mold Company, 112
Iberia Millwork, 97, 274, 278
Ibis Cycles, 65
Ibis Software Inc., 141
Ibis Target Products, 266
IBM Personal Computer Company, 135
ICD/Your Move, 115
ICOM America, 3, 78, 371, 373
Icon Health & Fitness Inc., 170
ICS Books Inc., 87
Ide Honda, 34
Idea Art, 145, 373
Idea Development Company, 77
Ideal Cheese Shop, 188
Ideal Sausage Company, 197
IDENT-IFY Label Corporation, 385
IDG Books Worldwide Inc., 87
Igloo Viksi Inc., 391
IIMorrow, 3
IKEA Catalog Department, 214
Ikelite Underwater Systems, 362
Ikon N'wst, 324
Ikwe Marketing, 291
Ilford Photo Corporation, 357
Illinois Antique Slot Machine Company, 130, 302
Illinois Foundation Seeds, 245
Illinois Theatrical, 155
Illusions of Grandeur, 119
Image Club Graphics Inc., 87, 141
Image Papers by DataCal, 145
Images Photo Processing, 359
Imagiknit Ltd., 87, 341, 441
ImaginAir Designs, 377
Imaginart Communication Products, 271
Imagination Station, 359
Imagine That, 15
IMC Products Corporation, 170
IMC Software, 141
Immaculata Bookstore, 93
Impact Parts, 42, 43
Impact Publishers, 87
Impala Bob's, 34
IMPCO Inc., 36
Imperia Foods, 188
Imperial Manufacturing, 15
Imperial Marine Equipment, 77
Imperial Picture Frames, 209
Impex International Inc., 73
Imported Dutch Bulbs, 241
Impresario Software, 141, 305

Impress Me Rubber Stamps, 377
Impression Bridal, 119
Impressions Software, 141, 423
Imprints Graphic Studio Inc., 377
Improvements, 277
Impulse Aerospace, 327
Imtra, 77
In One Ear Publications, 87
In Scale, 329
In Stock Hobby, 421
In the Company of Dogs, 253
In-Sink-Erator, 7
Inclinator Company of America, 166, 401
Independence Forge, 150, 310
Independent Living Aids Inc./Can-Do Products, 272
Independent Living Aids/Can-Do Products, 270, 271, 430, 435
Independent Mobility Systems, 272
Independent Publishers Group, 87
Indian Arts Gift Shop, 290
Indian Hill Farms, 185, 197, 202
Indian Hills Trading Company & Indian Art Gallery, 291
Indian Hollow Antiques, 322
Indian House, 337
Indian Industries Inc., 51, 55, 68, 152, 156, 409, 413, 431
Indian Jewelers Supply Company, 170, 299, 320, 382, 438
Indian Joe Martin's Antique Motorcycle Parts, 332
Indian Motorcycle Supply Inc., 332
Indian Pueblo Cultural Center Inc., 292
Indian River Groves, 191
Indian Wells Date Gardens & Chocolatier, 186
Indiana Botanic Gardens, 147, 234, 348
Indiana Botanic Gardens Inc., 430
Indiana Hobby Molds, 112
Individual Software Inc., 250
Indoor Gardening Supplies, 222, 226
Indoor Model Supply, 324
Indulgence Lampshade Supplies, 311
Industrial Abrasives Company, 440
Industrial Uniforms, 128
Industrial Water-Based Finishes Inc., 438
Indy R/C Sales Inc., 324
Infinity Records Ltd., 109
Infinity Systems, 405, 425
Info Products, 132
InfoCenter Inc., 78
Infogrip Inc., 132
Information Unlimited, 168, 381
Informix Software Inc., 141
Infostar Inc., 135
Ingersoll (Ian), Cabinetmakers 214
Inglebrook Forges, 70
Ingraham (Bob) Kites 303
Inlet Inc., 416
Inmac, 134, 145
Inman Wild Game, 198
Inner Mountain Outfitters, 396
Innerspace Aquatics, 352
Innotek Pet Products Inc., 175, 352
Innovation Advertising & Design, 141
Innovation Clock-Making Specialties, 118, 433
Innovation Engineering Inc., 1
Innovation Luggage, 313
Innovation Specialties, 332
Innovations in Fiberglass, 45
Innovative & Quaint, 87
Innovative Designs Inc., 392
Innovative Photography, 161

Innovative Products, 22
Innovative Time Corporation, 380
Insect Lore, 97
Inset Systems Inc., 141
Insight Computers, 136
Insight Software Solutions, 141
Instant Replay, 99, 425
Instek, 169
Instructor's Choice, 155
Instrument Services Inc., 22
Integral Designs, 101, 103
Integrated Technologies, 132
Intel Corporation, 87
InteliOptics, 69
Intense Cycles, 65
Intensity Skates, 390
Inter Trade Inc., 50, 278
Inter-Tribal Traders, 157
Interactive Image Technologies Inc., 141
Interactive Technologies Inc., 5, 294
Interarms, 265
Interbath Inc., 57
Intercal, 60
Interceramic USA, 279
Intergalactic Trading Company, 14, 335
Interior Furnishings Ltd., 214
Interiors, 157
Interiors Guild, 281
Intermatic Lighting Inc., 312
Intermountain Cactus, 231
Intermountain Guitar & Banjo, 338
International, 40
International Aeration Systems (Irrigo), 227
International Aeration Systems (Oxyflo), 227
International Auto Parts Inc., 32
International Autosport, 21, 25, 35, 36
International Bead Trader, 59
International Billiards Inc., 68, 388
International Center of Photography, 87, 355
International Chess Enterprises Inc., 115, 141
International Chromium Plating Company, 43
International Cinema Equipment Company, 336
International Connections, 303
International E-Z UP Inc., 50
International Fabric Collection, 87, 172
International Foto, 359
International Gem Merchants Inc., 299
International Historic Films Inc., 429
International Hobby Corporation, 324, 329, 330, 421
International Home Cooking, 198
International Logistics Systems Inc., 175, 408
International Luthiers Supply, 338
International Male, 123
International Marine, 79, 87
International Marine Exchange, 328
International Marketing Group, 305
International Microelectronics, 167
International Musical Suppliers, 338
International Phone Card Exchange, 354
International Resource Development, 367
International Ribbons, 145
International Screen Corporation, 396
International Technical Ceramics Inc., 112
International Tool Corporation, 418
International Universities Press Inc., 87
International Violin Company, 338
International Wine Accessories, 438
International Wood Products, 274
International Yogurt Company, 195
Internet, 141
Interphase Technologies Inc., 181

CORPORATE INDEX

Interplay Productions, 423
Intersport Fashions West, 331
Interstate Music Supply, 338
Interweave Press, 87
Intimate Appeal, 121, 270
Into the Wind/Kites, 94, 303
Intraser Inc., 5, 47, 75, 295, 332, 393
Intrigue Gift Shop, 364
Intuit, 141
Invader, 287
Invisible Fence Company Inc., 175, 352
InWall Creations, 57
Iomega Corporation, 132, 136
Iowa Glass, 22
IPC Technologies Inc., 132, 135
IPCO Inc., 36
IPM Laboratories, 219
Iranbooks Inc., 87
Irion Company Furniture Makers, 215
Iris Pond, 238
Iron Apple Forge, 308
Iron Craft, 176, 302, 406, 434
Iron Design Center, 211
Iron Horse Bicycles, 65
Iron Horse Gifts, 165
Iron Shop, 278
Irontiques, 222
Ironwood, 222
Irrigro, 227
Irvin (Marlene) 107
Irvin's, 254, 308, 310
Irwin Sports, 273, 394
Island Arbors, 223
Island Computer Supply, 145
Island Dreams, 254
Island Falls Canoe, 73
Island Tan, 147
Islander Reels, 179
Ison's Nursery, 229, 233, 244
Italian Art Store, 11
Italian Tile Center, 279
Ithaca Guitar Works, 338
Itinerant Stenciler, 402
It's A Zoo, 61
It's About Time, 118
It's George, 68
ITT Night Vision, 69
Itty Bitty Builder, 161
Iva Mae's Treasures, 254
Ivanko Barbell Company, 96, 170, 424
Iverson Snowshoe Company, 215, 393
Ives (Marian) Weathervanes 434
IVI Publishing, 141, 270
Ivy Crafts Imports, 171, 389
Ivydene Software, 141

J

J & B Auto Parts Inc., 23
J & J Surface, 132
J & J Tackle, 179
J & J Trains, 328
J & L Orchids, 237
J & M Auto Parts, 27, 28, 29, 38
J & M Carousel, 107
J & M Custom Cabinets & Millworks, 97
J & M Vintage Auto, 23
J & N Creations, 98
J & P Custom Plating, 43
J & R Music World, 109, 404, 411, 426
J & S Fossils, 374
J-B Wholesale Pet Supplies, 350
J-Bar Hobbies, 324
J-Made Looms, 397
J-R Tobacco, 415

J-S Sales Company Inc., 68, 95
J.B. Dough Company, 96, 183
J.B.'s Corvette Supplies, 30
J.C. Kites, 303
J.E.S. Enterprises, 406
J.H. Sherard, 199
J.K. Lutherie Guitars, 338
J.M.B. Inc., 17
J.P. Instruments, 3
J.R.'S Chevy Parts, 29
J.W. etc., 415
Ja Mar Distributing/Su-Mar Enterprises, 294
Jackie & Pat's Dollhouses Inc., 161
Jackie's Deer Lures, 288
Jackson & Perkins, 240, 241
Jackson (Victoria) Cosmetics Inc. 147
Jackson (William H.) Company 176, 177
Jackson Marketing Products, 97, 377
Jackson Originals, 129, 294
Jackson's Cabinet Shop, 215
Jacobs Greenhouse Manufacturing, 220
Jacobsen (Charles W.) Inc. 379
Jacobsen (Jacques Noel) 6, 322
Jacqueline Designs, 378
Jacquely Wigs, 436
Jacquelynn's China Matching Service, 116
Jacuzzi Whirlpool Bath, 286
Jaeger-LeCoultre, 296
Jaegers (A.) Optical Supply Company 17, 69
Jaffe Brothers Natural Foods, 191, 195
Jaffrey Manufacturing Company, 183
Jagoda (Don) Associates Inc. 152, 156
Jaguar & SAAB of Troy, 34, 41, 42
Jaguar Heaven, 34
Jaguar Motor Works, 34
Jake's House of Cards, 399
JAM Graphics Group, 365
Jamaican Style, 128
JAMAR Company, 160
Jamar Distributing, 228
James (Fran & Bill) 294
James (Jayna) Designs 250
James (Robert) Company Inc. 344, 402
James (Robert) Products 338
James Kits, 103
James River Traders, 123, 126
James Valley Scents, 288
Jameson Company Ltd., 410
Jamestown Distributors, 77, 418
Jamis Bicycles, 65
Jamison Farm, 198
Jan Crystals, 167
Jan Dolls, 165
Janco Greenhouses, 220, 396
JANICE Corporation, 62, 63, 125
Jann's Sportsman's Supplies, 179
Janovic/Plaza Inc., 276
Jan's Dollhouse, 161
JanSport Inc., 103
Jantz (Ken) Supply 170
Jantz Supply (Ken) 305
Janus Books, 87
Japan Radio Company Ltd., 373
Japan Woodworker, 418
Jardine's Texas Foods, 190
Jarvi Tool Company, 299
Jasper's Sugar Bush, 193, 196
Javanco, 167
Jay Design, 147
Jay Distributors, 109
Jay-Kay Molds, 112
Jayfro Corporation,
   170, 208, 260, 307, 394, 412, 431
Jayfro Corporation Inc., 54, 55
Jaygot Products, 112

Jay's of Tucson Inc., 59, 290
Jazzertogs, 120
JDR Microdevices, 167, 169
JDS Company, 418
JD's Off-Road & Performance, 35
JDS Technologies, 5, 294
Jean Seat International, 46
Jeanne's Rock & Jewelry,
   59, 312, 367, 374, 376, 382, 438
Jeepers Miniatures, 161
Jeffers Vet Supply, 350
Jefferson (Thomas) Memorial Foundation Inc.
   254
Jehlor Fantasy Fabrics, 8, 172
Jeld-Wen, 274
Jems Inc., 438
Jenkins (C.W.) Fly Rod 179
Jenks (W.S.) & Son 169, 418
Jenn-Air Company, 7
Jennell's Doll House, 163
Jennifer's Trunk Antiques & General Store,
   215, 254
Jennings Decoy Company, 158, 439
Jensen, 46
Jensen Tools Inc., 169, 418
Jepson Studios Inc., 116, 150
Jerboa-Redcap Books, 87
Jerith Manufacturing Company Inc., 175
Jerry's Artarama Inc., 11
Jerry's Tackle, 179
Jersey Paddler, 73
Jesser's Classic Keys, 22
Jessica's Biscuit, 87
Jessup Door Company, 274
Jesters Magic Workshop, 315
Jet Express, 295
Jet Labels, 344
Jet Trends, 120
Jet-Dolly Inc., 295
JetForm Corporation, 141
Jetinetics Jet Ski Racing Products, 295
Jewel & Company Inc., 53
Jewelry by Avery, 291, 296, 375
Jewelry Company, 296
Jewelry Values, 296
Jewish Publication Society, 93
JHModels, 324
Jicarilla Arts & Crafts Shop/Museum, 292
JIL Industries Inc., 50
Jim's Auto Sales, 41
Jim's Mobile Inc., 17
Jim's TV Collectibles, 335, 421
Jinil Au Chocolat, 186
Joannou Cycle, 65
Jobe Ski Corporation, 432
Joblot Automotive, 32, 33, 34, 38, 42
Joblot Automotive Inc., 23, 48
Jobo Fototechnic Inc., 356
Joe's Nursery, 231, 237, 239, 241
Johannsen Boat Works, 76
Johansen Bros. Shoe Company, 387
John-Michael Furniture, 215
Johnny Average Records, 109
Johnny's Appliances & Classic Ranges, 406
Johnny's Selected Seeds, 226, 230, 241
John's Collectible Toys & Gifts, 335, 421
John's Corvette Cars, 30, 45
Johns Hopkins University Press, 87
John's Mustang, 38
Johnsen Woolen Mills Inc.,
   63, 121, 123, 126
Johnson (Debra Paulson) 56
Johnson (Gregory)/Game Traders 131
Johnson (Norm & Mary) 262
Johnson (Norman) 130

CORPORATE INDEX

Johnson (Richard) 423
Johnson (Sharon E.) Jewelry 296
Johnson Daylily Garden, 238
Johnson Fishing Inc., 179
Johnson Music Company, 6, 338
Johnson Nursery, 230, 244
Johnson Orchards Mail Order, 201, 204
Johnson Paint Company Inc., 276, 415
Johnson Publishing Company Inc., 87
Johnson Sails Inc., 77
Johnson's (Bob) Auto Literature 22
Johnson's (Charlie) Tennis & Squash Shop 412
Johnson's (Ophelia) Indian Variety Shop 290
Johnson's Carpets, 379
Johnston & Murphy, 123, 126, 387
Joinery Company, 274, 275, 314
Joint Adventure, 348
JoLar Enterprises, 366
Jomac Dolls & Supplies, 163
Jomy Safety Ladder Company, 175, 307
Jona Originals, 61, 254
Jones (F.W.) & Son Ltd. 63
Jones (Johnny) Jr. Company 114
Jones (Marlin P.) & Associates 166, 167
Jones (Morton) Company 350
Jones (Peter B.) 292
Jones Barbecue Sauce Inc., 204
Jones Mold Company, 112, 163
Jones Photo Equipment, 358
Jope's Bonsai Nursery, 87, 230
Jordan (Dale) 352
Jordan (Ruth E.) 258
Jordan Wood Boats, 72
Jo's Dolls-N-Fine Porcelain, 163
JoS Violets, 228
Joseph (Daniel) Historic Styled Lighting 310
Joseph (Janna) 161, 163
Joseph Electronics, 167, 169
Josephson's Smokehouse, 202
Josey B. (U.S.A.) Corporation, 106
Jotul USA, 176, 406
Journeyman Products Ltd., 119
Joy Creek Nursery, 239
Joyce's Doll House, 164
JoyFul Art, 151
JP Video, 427
JPE Enterprises, 52
JSL, 17
JT USA, 407
J'Tec, 324
JTG of Nashville, 87
Juarez Chile Company, 204
Judaic Folk Art, 15, 258
Judaica Occasions, 258
Judi's Dolls, 164
Judnick Postcards, 365
Judy's Little Gems, 161
Judy's Violets, 228
Juggling Arts, 301
Jukebox City, 130, 302
Jukebox Classics & Vintage Slot Machines Inc., 130, 302
Jukebox Junction, 6, 302
Juki America Inc., 385
JumpKing Trampolines, 425
Jung (J.W.) Seed Company 236, 241
Jungle Zoo Furniture, 215
Juno Lighting Inc., 310, 312
Jun's Electronics, 371
Jupiter Scenic Inc., 414
Just America Inc., 147
Just Animals, 364
Just Between Us, 157, 254, 402
Just Country, 388

Just CrossStitch, 341
Just for You, 63
Just Horsin' A-Round, 157
Just Justin, 387
Just Kids Nostalgia, 421
Just My Size, 121, 270
Just Needlin', 341
Just Quackers, 157
Just Reels, 179
Just Right Clothing, 121
JVC, 46, 99, 403, 404, 425
JW Outfitters, 75

K

K & B Manufacturing Inc., 324, 328
K & B Saddlery, 285
K & F Electronics Inc., 167
K & G Manufacturing Inc., 226
K & J Miniature Metal Works, 161
K & K Electronics, 167
K & K Flyfishers' Supply, 179
K & L Cactus/Succulent Nursery, 231
K & L Candles, 105
K & S Engineering, 320, 329
K & S Tole & Craft Supply, 11
K & T Company, 262
K Kraft Furniture, 212
K-12 MicroMedia Publishing, 136
K-40 Electronics, 43, 373
K-Ceramic Imports, 112
K-Gap Automotive Parts, 31, 34
K-Line Electric Trains Inc., 330
K-Log Inc., 134, 217
K.D. Sportswear, 318
K.D. Video Inc., 427
K.P. Sporting Goods, 318
KA-MO Engravers, 51, 399
Kace Tech. Inc., 420
Kadon Enterprises Inc., 368, 422
Kaeser (Steve) 355
Kagan (Sasha) 341
Kagan Trim Center, 174, 383
Kahl (Peter) Reptiles 353
Kahn (Fred N.) Postcards 365
Kahnke Gunworks, 263
Kaiser Crow Inc., 389
Kaleidoscopes by Laughing Coyote, 302
Kalend's Auto Wrecking, 24
Kalish Brushes, 11
Kaller Historical Documents Inc., 20
Kalmia Farm, 245
Kamiakin Krafts, 291
Kamyan Software, 137
Kane Klassics, 179
Kangaroo Motorcaddies, 260
Kansas City Steak Company, 198
Kansas Industries for the Blind, 254
Kansas State Genealogical Society, 248
Kansas Wind Power, 286, 395
Kansas/Texas Detector Sales, 321, 367
Kanter Auto Parts, 22, 24, 26, 27, 28, 29, 30, 33, 39, 46
Kanter Auto Products, 49
Kantronics, 371
Kapable Kids, 422, 424
KAPS Vending, 262
Kar-Ben Copies Inc., 81, 98
Karadimos Kaleidoscopes, 302
Karella Corporation, 68
Karen's Kitchen, 196
Karen's Miniatures, 161
Karges Furniture Company Inc., 215
Karhu USA Inc., 391
Kari & Judy's Creations, 164

Kari Rubber Manufacturing, 45
Karlin Pottery, 116, 150
Karok Originals by Vit, 290
Karp Knives (Bob) 305
Karrer (Robert J.) Postcards 365
Kart World, 258, 332
Kart-A-Bag, 313
Kartuz Greenhouses, 228, 229, 231, 243
Kasch (M.W.) Company 55, 170, 370, 393
Kasco Woodworking Company Inc., 418
Kasey's Quilts, 161
Kasson Game Tables, 68
Kasten Inc., 119
Katadyn, 431
Katagiri & Company, 190
Katahdin Forest Products, 283
Katch Seafoods, 202
Kates Saddle Supply, 285
Katz Knives Inc., 305
Kauffman International Ltd., 285
Kaufman Supply, 87
Kaufmann's Streamborn, 179
Kaune (Bob) 418
Kawasaki Motors Corporation, 5, 295
Kawasaki of Pittsburgh, 333
Kay (David) Inc. 254, 436
Kay Toledo Tag, 344
Kaye's Holiday, 117
Kaymon Arts & Design, 363
Kayne & Son Custom Hardware, 176, 268
Kay's Greenhouses, 229
KB Systems, 362
KDE Electronics Inc., 427
KDI Specialty Foods Inc., 190
Keath (Charles) Ltd. 123, 254
Kedco Homebrew & Wine Supply, 87
Kedco Wine Storage Systems, 438
Kee Industrial Products Inc., 414
Keel Haulers Outfitters, 73
Keen (Cliff) Athletic 273
Keen Parts Inc., 30
Keeping Room, 105
Keepsake Quilting, 87, 341, 369
KEH Camera Brokers, 361
Keiper-Recaro Inc., 46
Keipper Cooping Company, 352
Kelchner's, 204
Keller (J.S.) & Associates 280
Keller Dovetail System, 418
Kelley (Walter T.) Company Inc. 63
Kelleygreen Rhododendron Nursery, 228
Kelly & Sons, 191
Kelly (Bob) Cosmetics Inc. 414
Kelly Color, 359
Kelly Nurseries, 230, 243, 244
Kellyco Detector Distributors, 321
Kelly's Camping, 103
Kelly's Ceramics Inc., 112
Kel's Memorabilia, 322
Kelsey (Kurt) 40
Kelsey Auto Salvage, 24
Kelsey Tire Inc., 47
Kelty Packs Inc., 103, 313
Kelvin Electronics, 167, 169
Kelvinator, 7
Kemp Designs, 296
Kemper Tools & Doll Supplies Inc., 112, 164
Ken-Mar Camera & Video, 361
Kenco, 152
Keng's Firearms Specialty Inc., 264
Kenmore Industries, 274
Kennebec Company, 97
Kennedy (Phyllis) Restoration Hardware 268, 425
Kennedy Galleries, 14

❖ CORPORATE INDEX ❖

Kennel Vet Corporation, 87, 350
Kennel-Aire Manufacturing Company, 352
Kennelly Keys Music Inc., 338
Kenosha Computer Center, 136
Kens Trading Company Inc., 318
Kensington Orchids, 237
Kent Marine, 352
Kentucky Historical Society, 248
Kentucky Millwork, 277
Kentucky Wood Floors, 275
Kenwood, 46, 371, 404, 425
Kenya Gem Company, 296
Keokuk Stove Works, 406
Kepich (John) 22
Kerjean Skate Line, 376
Kerry Specialties, 112, 415
Kester's Birdseed Inc., 228, 350
Kestrel, 65
Kestrel Manufacturing, 153, 215, 223, 278
Ketter Canoeing, 73
Keuthan Aircraft Corporation, 1
Kevins Harps, 268
Key West Aloe Inc., 147
Keyboard Outlet, 338
Keydata International, 135
Keystone Retaining Wall Systems, 278
KG Industries, 295
Khan Scope Center, 17, 69
KHS Bicycles, 65
Kick-Start Motorcycle Parts, 333
Kid Sport, 120, 391
Kid-EZ Chairs, 435
Kidde (Walter) 175, 176, 307
Kids West, 120, 129
KidsArt, 11, 81
Kidstamps, 377
Kiefer Built, 285
Kieffer's Lingerie, 172
Kikico Beads, 59, 299
Kilanowicz (Chester J.) 64
KIM Lighting, 312
Kim Pacific Trading Corporation Inc., 318
Kimball (Miles) Company
    12, 106, 254, 261, 270, 272, 423
    Kimball Company 422
Kimbo Educational, 109, 422, 429
Kimi's Fabrications, 369
Kimmeric Studio, 261, 385, 402
Kimple Mold Corporation, 112
Kim's Gourmet Products Inc., 204
Kindred Spirits, 116
King & Queen Mufflers, 22
King (Dale) Obsolete Parts Inc.
    30, 32, 33, 36, 38, 49
King Arthur Flour Baker's Catalog,
    96, 183, 303
King Boat Works, 72
King Louie International, 95, 258
King Motorsports, 25, 34
King Ostomy Products, 345
King Size Company, 127, 387
KingConcept, 356
Kingfisher Glads, 233
King's Bumper Company Inc., 43
King's Chandelier Company, 308
King's Chrysanthemums, 231
King's Cupboard, 186
Kings Kountry, 315
Kingsbery Safes, 381
Kingsfield Gardens, 191
Kingsley North Inc., 299, 320, 367, 401
Kingsley-Bate Ltd., 217, 224
Kinnzie's, 390
Kino Video, 336, 429
Kins (Judi) 377

Kinsman Company, 70, 219, 226, 227
Kipp & Zonen, 395
Kirby Kraft, 75
Kirchen Brothers, 152, 164
Kirk (Dennis) 295, 333
Kirk (Dennis) Inc. 393
Kirkland Custom Seafood, 202
Kirkpatrick (Will) Decoys 15, 158
Kishline's (Ruth) Country Clothes 123
Kisselburg (Paul E.) 87
Kit Bunker, 325
Kitazawa Seed Company, 241
Kitchen & Home, 303
Kitchen Etc., 116, 153, 303, 390
Kitchen Kompact Inc., 97
Kitchen Krafts, 106, 183
KitchenAid Inc., 7
Kite Studio, 303
KiteCo, 303
Kites & Fun Things, 303
Kiti Inc., 311
Kitts Industrial Tools, 418
Kitty Hawk Software Inc., 141
Kitty Korner Designs, 152
Kiwi Kayak Company, 73
Klahowya, 293
Klamm Magic, 315
Klassy Kollectibles Inc., 399
Klean-Strip, 438
Klehm Nursery, 235, 238, 239
Klein Bicycle Corporation, 65
Klein Design Inc., 215
Klement Sausage Company, 198
Klempf's British Parts Warehouse, 333
Klepper America, 73
Klig's Kites, 303
Kline (J.H.) Carving Shop 439
Kline (Jonathan) Black Ash Baskets 56
Kling's Theatrical Shoe Company, 155
Klipsch, 403
Klipspringer USA Inc., 412
Klitsas (Dimitrios) 280
KLM Antennas Inc., 371
Klockit,
    118, 268, 337, 418, 433, 438, 439
Klose Bar-B-Que Pits, 53
Kloter Farms Inc., 247
Klutz Press, 81, 268, 301
KME Diving Suits Inc., 392
Knape & Vogt, 119
Knapp Shoes Inc., 387
Kneipp Corporation of America, 147
Knife & Cutlery Products Inc., 305
Knife & Gun Finishing Supplies, 305
Knight & Hale Game Calls, 288
Knight Galleries, 215
Knights Ltd. Catalog, 123
Knitpicky Knitting Machines, 304
Knollwood Books, 87
Knott (John W.), Bookseller 94
Knott's Berry Farm, 193, 201
Knotts Knives, 418
Knowledge Adventure Inc., 141
KNR Associates, 380
Knudsen's Candy & Nut Company, 187
Kobricks Coffee Company, 207
Kobuk, 287
Koch (Dave) Sports 141
Koch (Joseph) 131
Kodansha America Inc., 87
Koehnen (C.F.) & Sons Inc. 63
Kohl (Richard) 335
Kohler Company, 57, 174, 272
Kohl's Celebrity Gallery, 20
KOH'S Camera Sales & Service Inc., 361

Koigu Wool Designs, 341
Koinonia Partners Inc., 185, 187
Koinz & Kardz-Madison, 399
Kokatat, 71
Kokovoko Breeding Farm, 397
Kolar, 266
Kolb Company Inc., 1
Kole Industries, 345
Koller Dodge, 31
Kollinger (Richard L.) Company Inc. 296
Kolpin Manufacturing Inc., 9
Kona Mountain Bikes, 65
Kona Queen Company, 63
Konica USA Inc., 356, 357, 358
Koos Inc., 224
Koppers Chocolate Specialty Company Inc.,
    187
Kopromed USA, 305
Kordon, 352
Korg USA, 338
Kosher Cornucopia, 190
Koson's, 387
Kota Bows, 9
Kourik Drip, 228
Koval Knives, 305
Kowa Optimed Inc., 264
Kozlowski Farms, 193, 201, 204
KR Industries Inc., 95
KraftMaid Cabinetry Inc., 97
Kramer Brothers, 217, 223
Krane Products, 382
Kransco Manufacturing, 432
Krasow (Joseph) 128
Kraus (E.C.) 437
Krause Publications, 87
Krazy Kites, 304
Kreepy Krauly USA Inc., 408
Kreinik Manufacturing Company, 383
Kress Jets Inc., 324, 329
Krex Computers, 132
Krh Knits, 304, 441
Krieger Publishing Company, 87
Kris Technologies Inc., 135
Krohne Plant Farms, 230
Krona Gem Merchants, 300
Krull-Smith Orchids, 237
Krum's Chocolatier, 210
Krylon, 11
Kryptonics Inc., 376, 390
K's Creations, 397
KTM Sportmotorcycle, 333
Kubik (Owen D.) Fine Books 87
Kubota Tractor Corporation, 224, 225, 227
Kucharik Bicycle Clothing, 66
Kuehl (Jim) & Company 361
Kuempel Chime, 118
Kuhns Brothers Log Homes, 283
KUMA Beads, 59
Kunin Felt, 172
Kush (J.R.) & Company 51, 399
Kustom King Arrows, 9
KV Vet Supply, 284, 285, 350
KVH Industries Inc., 78
Kwik Goal, 394
Kwik-Bilt Inc., 386
Kwik-Sew Pattern Company Inc., 384
Kwon Martial Arts, 318

L

L & D Press, 97, 402
L & H Vitamins Inc., 270, 430
L & L Electronics Inc., 427
L & L Kiln, 112
L & R Specialties, 113

CORPORATE INDEX

L.A. Cave, 12
L.A. Stampworks, 377
L.D.P. Foods, 105
L.H. Selman Ltd., 347
L.R.S. Enameling, 300
L/M Animal Farms, 350, 353
La Barge Mirrors, 323
La Belle Epoque, 335
LA Bookstore, 87
La Costa Products International, 123, 147
LA Exotics, 44
La Jolla Golf Club Company, 259
La Lana Wools, 441
La Maison de l'Astronomie, 17
La Maison du Chocolat, 187
La Piñata, 362
La Pointe (Chip) Cabinetmaker 280
La Pointe Cabinetmaker, 97
La Ray Turquoise Company, 294
La Rock's Fun & Magic Outlet, 52, 87, 130, 301, 315
La Sportiva USA, 101
Lab Safety Supply Inc., 381
Labeda Wheels, 376
Label Works, 344
LaBelle (Henri) 398
Lace Corner, 8, 174
Lace Heaven, 172, 174, 383
Lacey Costume Wig, 148
Lacis, 87, 174, 397
Ladder Man Inc., 175, 307
Lady Bug Company, 117
Lady Dianne Gourmet Desserts, 185
Lady Grace Stores, 51, 121, 122, 270
Lady Slipper Designs, 70, 291
LadyBug Art Center, 87
Ladylike Ski Shop, 391
Ladyslipper Inc., 109
Lafeber Company, 350
Laflin's Magic & Silks, 130, 315
Lafuma Camping Equipment, 103
Laguna Clay Company, 113
Laguna Tools, 418
Laidlacker Historical Garments, 148
Lake Champlain Chocolates, 187
Lake Cities Polaris, 295
Lake City Crafts, 347
Lake Forest Antiquarians, 6
Lake Shore Industries, 388
Lake Superior Brewing Company, 437
Lake's Minnesota Macaws Inc., 350
Lakeside Products Company, 254, 286
Lakeview Vintage Ford Parts, 33, 49
Lakota Collection, 62
Lakota Jewelry Visions, 294
Lam Distributing Company, 353
Lamalle Kitchenware, 303
LaMance Autoworks, 27, 31, 35, 38, 40
Lambert (Jarrell) 305
Lambs Farm, 150, 194
Laminations Inc., 119
Lammes Candy, 187
Lamp Glass, 311
Lamp Shop, 311
Lamp Specialties Inc., 113
Lamp Warehouse, 174, 308
Lamplighter Corner Inc., 312
Lamps by Lynne, 310, 311
Lampshades of Antique, 311
Lamson-Taylor Custom Doors, 274
Lanac Sales, 116, 153, 390
Lancaster Towne Quilts, 62, 409
Lancer Label, 96, 344
Lancer Militaria, 88, 322
Landau Woolen Company Inc., 172

Landau Woolens, 62, 123, 126
Landmark Research International Corporation, 141
Landreth (D.) Seed Company 241
Landscape Forms Inc., 218, 224
Lane Luggage, 254
Lane Pecans, 199
Lanes & Gifts, 61
Lane's Toyland & Gifts, 165
Lang Companies, 98, 261
Langenbach Fine Tool Company, 226
Langenscheidt Publishers, 88
Langlitz Leathers, 331
Lang's Old Car Parts, 37
Lanier Furniture Company, 215
Lanier RC, 324
Lansky (L.S.) Sharpeners 306
Lansky Sharpeners, 305
Lanvino, 190
Lapcraft Company Inc., 300
Lapidary Journal Book & Video Sellers, 88
LaPosta (Richard A.) 80
Lapp's Bee Supply Center, 63
Lark Books, 88, 152
Lark in the Morning, 88, 109, 338, 429
Lark of America, 435
Lark Street Music, 338
Laron Aviation Technologies, 1
LaRose (S.) Inc. 118
Larry's Records, 108
Larry's Thunderbird & Mustang Parts, 38, 42
Larsen Antennas, 371
Larson Enterprises Inc., 358
Larson Wood Manufacturing, 415, 420, 423
LaRue Electronics, 371
Las Pilitas Nursery, 246
Las Vegas Discount Golf & Tennis, 260, 370, 380, 411, 412
Las Vegas Insider, 88
LaserColor Laboratories, 359
Laserdisc Fan Club Inc., 109
Lasertown Video Discs, 110
LaSportiva, 334
Last Best Place, 254
Last Moving Picture Company, 335
Last Vestige Music Shop, 110
Latch Lake Music Products, 339
Latora Tattoo Products, 409
Lattice Inc., 141
Laube's Stretch & Sew Fabrics, 8
Lauderdale Camera, 361
Laughing Bear, 120, 128
Laughing Loon, 72
Launstein Hardwoods, 275
Lauratex Fabrics Inc., 173
Lauray of Salisbury, 228, 229, 231, 235, 237
Laureate Learning Systems, 141, 272
Laurel Highlands Accessories Plus, 333
Lauri, 422
Lautard (Guy) 88
Lavender Lane, 348
Lawbre Company, 161
Lawler (Helen) 390
Lawn-Boy, 224, 225, 227
Lawrence Leather Company, 262
Lawrence of Dalton, 322
Lawrence Productions, 141
Lawson (Harry) Company 265
Lawson's Nursery, 244
Layton Studios, 107
Lazer Helmets, 331
Lazer Images, 388
Lazy B Trailer Sales Inc., 47
Lazy Day Hammocks, 266

Lazy Hill Farm Designs, 70, 223
LDB Medical Inc., 290, 345
Le Allala's Doll Shop, 165
Le Camera, 361
Le Comité des Archives de la Louisiane, 248
Le Coq Sportif, 258
Le Fanion, 116
Le Jardin du Gourmet, 234, 241
Leach (H.G.) Guitars 339
Leading Edge Air Foils Inc., 1, 3, 4
Leading Edge Products Inc., 135
Leafy Wear, 287
Leal's Archery Sights, 9
Lean-2 Racks, 119
Learning Company, 141
Learning Technologies Inc., 16
LearnKey Inc., 133
Leather Brothers Inc., 350
Leather Interiors, 215
Leather Unlimited, 312
Leatherman Tool Group Inc., 103, 418
Leatherrite Manufacturing Inc., 350
LeBaron Bonney Company, 37, 42, 49
Lebo's of Charlotte Inc., 155
Leckey Support Furniture, 272
Ledden (Orol) & Sons 236, 241
Ledford's Musical Instruments, 339
Ledgewood Studio, 164, 173, 383
Lee (Jamie) Stationery 402, 434
Lee (K.H.) Tool Supply 300, 418
Lee Century Farms, 194
Lee House, 210
Lee Lapidaries Inc., 300
Lee Nutrition, 430
Lee Oskar Harmonicas, 268
Lee Precision Inc., 262
Lee Valley Tools Inc., 226
Lee-McClain Company Inc., 124
Leedal Inc., 356
Leeland's Ginseng, 233
Lee's (Donna) Sewing Center 383
Lee's (Hank) Magic Factory 315
Lee's Botanical Gardens, 231, 232, 237
Lee's Carpet Showcase, 275, 379
Lee's Ceramic Supply, 113
Lee's Collectibles, 165
Lee's Company Inc., 97
Lee's Value Right Inc., 73
Leesburg Looms & Supply, 397
Lefebvre (R.) & Son Smokehouse Meats 198
Left Hand Center, 313
Lefthanders International, 254, 313
Lefties Only, 261, 313
Leftover Design Company Inc., 6, 388
Legacy Audio, 403
Legacy Herbs, 147, 204, 289, 348, 366
Legal Sea Foods, 202
Legendary Arms Inc., 322
Legendary Auto Interiors Ltd., 49
Legendary Design Technologies Inc., 145
Legendary Lighting by Copper Sculptures, 223, 312
Legendary Motorworks, 45
Legends Footwear, 101
L'eggs Brands Inc., 121
LeGresley (Robert A.) 20
Lehman (Stewart) 405
Lehman Hardware & Appliances Inc., 97, 114, 254, 303
Lehman Manufacturing Company Inc., 113
Lehmann (Bernard E.) Stringed Instruments 339
Lehmann (Werner H.) 335
Lehrer (Samuel) & Company Inc. 173
Leica Navigation & Positioning Division, 78

Leica USA Inc., 69, 355, 356
Leichtung Workshops, 418
Leigh Industries Inc., 418
Leister Productions, 141, 250
Leisure Arts, 88
Leisure Living, 254
Leisure Marketing Inc., 208, 370, 412
Leisure Outlet, 101, 103
Leisure Pro, 103, 392, 412
Leisure Time Pet Center, 352
Leisure Time Products, 418
Leisure Unlimited, 101, 380
Leisure Woods Inc., 247
Leki Sport USA, 103, 106
Lello Appliances Corporation, 289
LeMay Movie Posters, 335
Lemee's Fireplace Equipment, 176
Lenartz, 288
Lendrum (Gord) 397
LeNeave Machinery & Supply Company, 418
Lenette Greenhouses, 237
Lenoir Furniture Market Inc., 215, 218
Lenox Brands, 390
Lenox Collections, 116, 153, 364
Lenox Jewelers, 296
Lentini Communications Inc., 371
Lentz Lapidary Inc., 300, 367, 375
Leo T-Shirts, 128
Leonard (A.M.) Inc. 226
Leonard (Jim) Antique Hardware 176
Leonard's (Dr.) Health Care Catalog 270
Leonard's (Stew) 194
Leonard's Antiques, 6, 212
Leonine Products, 350
Leo's Dancewear Inc., 120, 155
Lerner New York, 121, 124
Leron, 62, 63, 420
Les Trois Petits Cochons Company, 194
Letrell Sports, 54
Letters Unlimited, 388
Leupold & Stevens Inc., 69, 264
Leuthardt (Henry) Nurseries 244
Levenger, 215, 254, 310, 348
Leventon's Hobby Supply, 330
Levine (Alan) Movie & Book Collectibles 88, 335, 342
LeVine (Blake) Autographs 20
Levine (E.P.) Inc. 407
Leviton Manufacturing Company, 310, 312
Levy (Harris) 63, 409
Levy (Leslie) Fine Art 14, 15
Levy (Victor H.) Inc. 59, 164, 300
Lewis & Roberts, 296
Lewis' (Frank) Alamo Fruit 191, 198
Lewis Creek Company, 124
Lewis Strawberry Nursery Inc., 230
Lewis-Michaels Engineering, 16, 17
Lexacon Pet Products, 70
Lexin Inc., 61
Lexmark International, 132
LH Studio, 164
Liberty Cedar, 277
Liberty Forge, 176
Liberty Medical Supply, 159
Liberty Mountain Sports, 265, 393
Liberty Orchards Company Inc., 187
Liberty Richter, 207
Liberty Safe, 264
Liberty Seed Company, 241
Libertyville Saddle Shop Inc., 285
Library Binding Company, 80
Lie-Nielsen Toolworks, 418
Life Raft & Survival Equipment, 71
LifeFitness Inc., 170
Lifegear Inc., 170

Lifereef Filter Systems, 352
Lifestand, 272, 435
Lifestyle Fascination Gifts, 254
Lifestyle Software Group, 207, 270
Lifestyle Systems, 119
Lift Your Spirits, 438
Lifton Studio Inc., 51, 126, 254
Light Impressions, 88, 210, 355, 362
Light Manufacturing Company, 221
Light Miniature Aircraft, 1
Light Source, 221
Light Speed Telescopes Inc., 17
Lighter Side Company, 254, 301
Lighting by Gregory, 310
Lighting Elegance, 310
Lightle (Dick & Sue) Postcards 365
Lightning Bug Aircraft Corporation, 1
Lightning Paddles, 73
Lightolier, 310, 312
Lightware, 355
Lightworks Custom B & W Lab, 359
Lile Handmade Knives, 305
Lilliput Art, 161
Lilliput Land, 161
Lilly's (Bud) Trout Shop 179
Lilly's Gallery, 292
Lilly's Kids, 250, 422, 423
Lily Garden, 238
Lily of the Valley Herb Farm, 232, 234, 239
Lily Pond Products, 113
Lilypons Water Gardens, 227
Lily's, 258, 411
Limelite Electric Arts Inc., 333
Limerock Ornamental Grasses Inc., 232, 234, 239
Limited Edition, 364
Limited Edition Presents, 201
Limited of Michigan Ltd., 254, 319, 363, 364
Lincoln (Abraham) Book Shop 20
Lincoln Camera & Video Store, 361
Lincoln Electric Company, 420
Lincoln Land Inc., 35
Lincoln Parts International, 36, 42
Lind (Eldon J.) Company 329
Lindahl Specialties Inc., 361
Lindal Cedar Homes, 220, 282, 396
Linda's Best for the True Brownie Lover, 185
Linda's Silver Needle, 383
Linden Books, 88
Linden Publishing Company Inc., 88
Lindenberg Seeds Ltd., 241
Lindsay (Q.H.) Company 441
Lindsay Publications Inc., 88
Lindsy (B.J.) Flag & Banner Company 182
Lindustries, 272
Linehan (William) Autographs 20
Linen & Lace, 62, 154, 173
Linen Fabric World, 173
Linen Source, 62, 63
Linn's Fruit Bin, 185, 201
Lint (Bob) Motor Shop 22, 25
Linwood Homes, 282
Lion Brand Yarn Company, 441
Lion Coffee, 207
Lion Publishing, 93
Lionheart Press Inc., 141
Lioni Bufala Corporation, 190
Lion's Pride Catalog, 124, 126, 127
Lipp (Rick) 335
Lippy Bikes, 65
Lire La Nature Inc., 17, 321
Liros Gallery Inc., 14
Lis (Sophia) 353
List Associates, 317

List-Masters, 317
Listening Library Inc., 94
Litchfield Industries Inc., 247
Liteform Designs, 312
Literary Calligraphy, 98, 254, 261, 402
Literature, 355
Little Big Horn Replica Company, 118, 308
Little Colorado Inc., 212
Little Engines, 328
Little Feather Trading Post, 292
Little Fox Factory, 146
Little Goodies, 161, 347
Little House of Miniatures on Chelsea Lane, 161
Little Max's Shoes, 387
Little Memories, 385
Little Mountain Supply Inc., 439
Little River Marine, 76
Little Something for Everyone, 161
Littlethings, 61, 161
Littman's Sterling, 390
Liturgical Press, 93
Litz (Victor) Music Center 339
Live Steam Magazine, 88
Living Extreme, 65
Living Farms, 196
LivingSoft Inc., 270
Lixit Animal Care Products, 350
Lixx Labelsz, 80, 344
Liz's Antique Hardware, 268
Lizzie & Charlie's Rag Rugs, 379
LKB Enterprises, 46
Lladró Society, 364
Lloyd/Flanders, 218, 428
Lloyds Literature, 22
Lloyd's Special Interest Videos, 429
LMN Printing, 414
LNS Technologies, 168
Lo-Can Glass International, 22
Lob-Ster Inc., 412
Lobo Power Tools, 418
Loc-On Company, 287
Loc/Precision Inc., 327
Local Music, 339
Locators Inc., 116, 153, 390
Lochs, 300
Lockhart Seeds Inc., 245
Lockhart-Phillips, 331, 333
Lockwood Aircraft Corporation, 1
Locus Foods Inc., 190
Lodgewood Mfg., 322
Lodis Corporation, 313
Loehle Aviation Inc., 1
Loehman's Cactus, 231
Loew-Cornell Inc., 11
Loftin-Black Furniture Company, 215
Log & Timber Homes Inc., 283
Log Cabin Shop, 263
Log Homes Books, 88
Logan (Q.B.) 434
Logan Coach, 285
Logee's Greenhouses, 231, 235
Loggy Bayou Tree Stands, 287
Logos Software, 16
LogSat Software Corporation, 141
Lohman Manufacturing Company, 288
Lok-N-Logs, 283
Lollipop Tree Inc., 201
Lolly's, 161
London (Harry) Candies Inc. 187
London Imports Ltd., 355
London Lace, 154
London's (Mrs.) Confections 187
Lone Bear Indian Craft Company, 292
Lone Peak, 67

CORPORATE INDEX

Lone Star Autographs, 20
Lone Star Farms, 191
Lone Star Models, 329
Lone Star Percussion, 339
Lone Wolf Tree Stands, 287
Lonely Planet Publications, 88
Long Elegant Legs, 127
Long Island Corvette Supply Inc., 30
Long Island Train & Hobby Center, 326, 422
Longacre Enterprises Inc., 291
Longhorn Archery Systems, 9
Long's Carpet Inc., 379
Long's Gardens, 238
Longwood Equipment Company Ltd., 393
Lonnie's Inc., 296, 300, 320
Lookingglass Miniatures, 161
Loomis (G.) Company 179
Loon Outdoors, 180
Loose Screws, 67
Lopi International Ltd., 177
Lorann Oils, 106
Lord & Taylor, 158
Lorentz Design Inc., 111
Lorio Reptile Supplies Inc., 353
Loriva Supreme Foods, 204
Lortone Inc., 300
Los Angeles Audubon Society Bookstore, 70, 80, 88
Los Angeles Optical Company, 18
Los Angeles Triumph, 333
Loshin's Dancewear, 155
Lots of Hots & Fiery Foods, 204
Lotto Sports, 54, 394
Lotus Development Corporation, 141
Lou-Bon Gems & Rocks, 374, 375
Louët Sales, 397, 441
Louisiana Nursery, 229, 238, 244
Louisiana State University Press, 88
Louisiana-Pacific Corporation, 278, 282
LouveRail, 175
Lovell Designs, 296
Loving Little Rubber Stamps, 377
Lowe Alpine, 101, 103, 334
Lowel-Light Manufacturing Inc., 358
Lowell's Boat Shop, 75
LowePro, 355
Lowe's Own Root Roses, 240
Lowrance Electronics, 78, 181
Lowry's Manufacturing Ltd., 273, 289
Lowy (Carolin) Needlecraft 304, 341
LPA Design, 358
LS & S Group Inc., 430
LTD Commodities Inc., 157
Lubidet USA Inc., 272
Lucarelli (W.H.) 25
Lucas Automotive, 47
Lucas Group International, 45
Lucchese Boots, 388
Lucero (Carol G.) 292
Lucid Lighting, 310
Lucidity Institute, 88
Lucky Heart Cosmetics, 148
Lucretia's Pieces, 368
Luctor Canada, 433
Ludlow Boat Works, 76
Luft (Herbert A.) 88, 94
Luggage Center, 313
Luigi Crystal, 153, 308, 310
Lukens (Sue) Herbalist/Potter 348
Lumbee Indian Arts & Crafts, 292
Lumedyne Lighting, 358
Lumicon, 18, 69
Lumiquest, 358
Lunar Models, 423
Lure-Craft Industries Inc., 180

Luskey/Ryan's Western Stores Inc., 129, 269, 388
Lustig International, 373
Lutherie (J.K.) Guitars 88, 342
Luthier Music Corporation, 339
Luthiers Mercantile, 339
Lutron Lighting Controls, 5
Lutsky (Hal) Postcards 365
Luttys Chevys, 27, 28, 34, 39
Luv 'n Stuff, 152, 377
Luv Those Rugs, 215, 379
Lyben Computer Systems, 136
Lyco Computer, 132
Lyman Products Corporation, 263
Lynch (Kenneth) & Sons 218, 407
Lynchburg Hardware & General Store, 254
Lynch's Clown Supplies, 130, 148, 155, 414
Lynn Dairy Inc., 188
Lynn Ladder & Scaffolding & Company, 307
Lynn's Lil' Darlings, 165
Lynton Manufacturing, 432
Lynx Golf Clubs, 259
Lyon (Lyndon) Greenhouses Inc. 228, 235
Lyon (Maggie) Chocolatiers 187
Lyon Electric Company, 353
Lyon Metal Products Inc., 217
Lyons (Jim) 342
Lyons Industries, 57, 286
Lyphon & Gryphon, 146, 441
Lyric Choir Gown Company, 117
Lyriq International Corporation, 141

M

M & E Marine Supply Company, 76, 77, 392
M & G Electronics Inc., 427
M & G Vintage Auto, 37
M & M Distributors, 210
M & M Photo Source Limited, 361
M & R Durango Inc., 219
M & R Technologies Inc., 141, 305
M & S Systems Inc., 294, 428
M-USA Business Systems, 141
M.A.P. Cycle Enterprises, 333
M.A.T.S. Auto Parts, 24, 49
M.C. Ltd., 63, 379
M.D.F. Technologies Inc., 436
M.F. Geriatrics, 126
M.H. Guitar & Fiddle Shop, 339
M.L.D. Associates, 304
M.T.H. Electric Trains, 329
M2 Enterprises, 372
MAAS Rowing Shells, 76
Mac Bargains, 136
Mac Industries, 70
Mac Neil Automotive Products Ltd., 46
MAC the Antique Plumber, 57, 174
Mac Warehouse, 136, 145
Mac Zone, 145
MacBeath Hardwood Company, 418, 439
MacConnection, 136, 145
MacDirect, 136
MacDoc Designs, 161
MacGregor Golf Clubs, 258, 259
Machin Designs by Amdega, 223, 396
Macho Products Inc., 96, 318
Mack & Rodel Cabinet Makers, 215
Mack (Daniel) Rustic Furnishings 215
Mackenzie Limited, 188, 202
MacKenzie Nursery Supply Inc., 226
Mackey Custom Hats, 269
MacKinaw Kite Company, 304
Mackinlay Teas, 194, 207
MacMail Order Department, 136

MacMillan Computer Publishing, 88
MacMillan Publishing Company, 88
MacMillan-Bloedel, 218
Macomber Looms, 397
MacPherson Jr. (Maxwell) 180
Macronix Inc., 136
Mac's Antique Auto Parts, 33, 37
Mac's Auto Body, 44
Mac's Discus, 352
MAC's Lift Gate Inc., 436
Macy's, 158
Macy's Texas Stove Works, 406
Mad River Canoe Inc., 73
Mad River Imports, 232
Mad River Woodworks, 274, 280
Maddalena (Joseph M.) 20
Madden Mountaineering, 67, 103, 313
Made-Rite Auto Body Products Inc., 21
Madeira USA Ltd., 383
Madeleine Fashions Inc., 124
Madison Electronics Supply, 372
Madison River 18th Company, 180
Madle (Robert A.) 94, 343
Magellan Systems Corporation, 78, 181
Magellan's, 131, 136
Maggie Company, 341
Maggiore Electronic Lab, 372
Magic Cabin Dolls, 164, 441
Magic Chef, 7
Magic Needle, 341
Magic of Chef Paul Prudhomme, 185, 205
Magic Systems Inc., 96, 363
Magic World of Chatsworth, 316
Magnet Sales & Manufacturing Company, 306, 316
Magnetic Imaginations, 210
Magnolia Hall, 215
Magnolia Paper Making, 347
Magnum Industries, 327
Magram (Lew) 124
MAH Nursery, 221
Mahantango Manor, 410
Maher Studios, 316, 368
Maherajah Water Skis, 432
Mahogany Smoked Meats, 188, 198, 202, 205
MAI Motor Bike, 333
Mail Order Catalog, 88, 196
Mail Order Medical Supply, 345
Mail Order Medical Supply (MOMS), 270
Mail Order Pet Shop, 352, 353
Main Street Fine Books & Manuscripts, 20
Main Street Press, 98, 261, 402
Main-ly Country Western Wear, 129, 400
Maine Photographic Resource, 356
Maine State Archives, 248
Mainline Hobby Supply, 330
Mainline of North America, 224, 225, 226, 313
Mainly Music, 108, 110, 337
Mainly Shades, 88, 311
Maison des Maisons, 161
Maison Glass Delicacies, 194
Maizefield Company, 177, 278, 280
Majestic, 177
Majestic Athletic Wear, 53, 54, 273
Majestic Cocka2s, 350
Majestic Log Homes, 283
Majestic Pet Supply, 352
Major Hobby, 324
Makah Cultural Research Center, 294
Makita USA Inc., 5, 153, 418
Makowski (Jim) 422
Makser, 259
Malcom Postcards, 365

CORPORATE INDEX

Maldol Antennas, 372
Mali (Henry W.T.) & Company 68
Mallery Press, 88
Mallory (Lisa) 14
Mallory's Furniture, 215
Malotte Studio, 292
Maltby (Ralph) Enterprises Inc. 260
Mamiya America Corporation, 356
Man at Arms Bookshelf, 88
Manasquan Premium Fasteners, 439
Manchester (Orvis) 101, 124, 180
Manchester/Manchester, 108
Mandall Shooting Supplies, 262
Mandolin Brothers, 339
Manganaro Foods, 190
Mangum's Beads, 59
Manhattan Analytics Inc., 141
Manhattan Bagel Company, 183
Manhattan Farms, 245
Manion's, 322
Mankel Blacksmith Shop, 71
Mankins (William) 319, 365
Mann (Seymour) 165
Mann Lake Supply, 63, 105
Mannings Creative Crafts, 397, 441
Mannon's Foods, 205
Mann's Bait Company, 180
Manny's Baseball, 53, 208, 273
Manny's Millinery Supply Center, 383
Manny's Musical Instruments & Accessories Inc., 339
Manny's Woodworkers Place, 88
Mano Creations, 443
Manochio (Dennis C.), Curator 177
Mansfield (W.L. Wally) 24
Manshape, 121
Mantels of Yesteryear Inc., 177
Mantis Bicycle, 65
Mantis Manufacturing Company, 219, 225, 226
Map Express, 317
Maple Grove Farms of Vermont, 196
Maple Grove Restorations, 276, 278
Maple Island Log Homes, 283
Maples Fruit Farm, 191, 194, 199
Maplewood Crafts, 152, 254
MapLink, 317
Marantz America Inc., 46, 404, 405
Marbel Associates Inc., 333
Marble Arch, 157
Marble Associates Inc., 65
Marbury (Mary Orvis) 124
Marc Medical Pharmacy, 345
Marcel (Philippe) 124
March (Katherine) Ltd. 148
Marcia Originals, 259
Marco (J.) Galleries 254
Marco Specialties, 130
Marcus (Alan) & Company 296
Mardina Dolls, 290
Mardiron Optics, 18, 69
Margaret's Superior Desserts, 187
Mariani Nut Company, 191, 199
Marietta Gardens, 238
Marilyn's Mini Studio, 161
Marin French Cheese Company, 188
Marin Mountain Bikes, 65
Marin Wine Cellar, 438
Marine Electronics, 78
Marine Park Camera & Video Inc., 100, 403, 426
Marine Technologies International Inc., 73
Mariner Kayaks, 73
Marinetics Corporation, 77
Marinoni USA Inc., 65

Maris Multimedia Software, 16, 141
Marisystems Inc., 78
Maritime Store, 79, 81, 88, 254, 261, 317, 328
Maritime Wood Products Corporation, 77
Marj's Doll Sanctuary, 61, 165
Mark, 124
Mark One Distributors, 103
Mark V Electronics Inc., 168
Marker Ltd., 391
Markertek Video Supply, 100
Market Basket, 437
Marks China, 116, 153, 390
Marks Cigars, 415
Marks Sales Company, 215
Marksman Products, 156, 266
Markwort Sporting Goods, 53, 54, 95, 114, 208, 370, 394, 409, 424
Markwort Sporting Goods Company, 412
Marl & Barbie, 164, 165
Marlborough Country Barn, 308, 310
Marlen Manufacturing & Development Company, 345
Marlene's Decorator Fabrics, 173, 281
Marlin Firearms Company, 265
Marling Lumber Company, 418
Marmot Mountain Works, 103, 391
Marnie's Crewel Studio Inc., 341
Maroni's (Jody) Sausage Kingdom 198
Marr Haven, 442
Marra (Ben) Studios 14
Marriott's Fly Store, 180
Marrs Tree Farm, 230
Marsh (Heidi) Patterns 149, 385
Marshall (John) Inc. 36
Marshall Field, 158
Marshall Marine Corporation, 75
Marshall's Fudge Shops, 187
Marske Aircraft, 2
Martial Artist, 318
Martial Athleisure Corporation, 318, 387
Martin (Dick) Sports Inc. 51, 54, 114, 208, 388, 413, 431
Martin (Kevin) Boatbuilder 73, 75, 76
Martin (Mary) Postcards 365
Martin Archery, 9
Martin Archery Inc., 101
Martin Marine Company, 76
Martin Reel Company, 180
Martin Sunglasses, 392, 407
Martin Universal Design, 11
Martin's Flag Company, 182
Martin's Herend Imports Inc., 116, 364
Martin's Mercantile & Millinery, 149
Martz Classic Chevy Parts, 27, 28, 29, 39
Marvin Display, 182
Marvin Windows, 274, 282
Marx (Gilda) Industries 120
Marx Brush Manufacturing Company Inc., 11, 113
Mary D's Dolls & Bears & Such, 61, 165
Mary Elizabeth Miniatures, 161
Mary Ellen & Company, 149
Mary Jayne's Railroad Specialties Inc., 365
Mary Jo's Needles & Pins, 383
Mary Laura's, 292, 297
Mary Lue's Knitting World, 304, 397
Mary of Puddin Hill, 185, 187
Marydolls Molds, 161
Maryland Aquatic Nurseries, 227, 228, 234, 238
Maryland China Company, 115
Maryland Historical Society, 248
Maryland Nautical Sales Inc., 78, 79
Maryland Radio Center, 372

Maryland Reptile Farm, 88, 353
Maryland Square, 387
Maryland State Genealogy Society, 248
Mary's Tack & Feed, 285
Mascor Lists, 317
Mascot Metropolitan Inc., 313
Mascot Pecan Company, 210
Masecraft Supply Company, 305
Maserati Automobiles Inc., 36
Mashuga Nuts Inc., 199
Maska USA Inc., 273, 289, 391
Mason (B.A.) Footwear 387
Mason (Bill) Books 88, 322
Mason Company, 353
Mason Laboratories Inc., 345
Mason Tackle Company, 180
Masonite Corporation, 276, 277
Massachusetts Army & Navy Store, 408
Massachusetts Society of Genealogists, 248
Massey (Walter) 434
Masseys, 387
Mast General Store, 124, 266
Master Animal Care, 350
Master Bisgrove Designs (Flagmakers), 182
Master Corporation, 412
Master Industries Inc., 95
Mastercraft Puppets, 316, 368
Masters Collection, 323
Masters Gallery, 14
Masters Golf, 260
Masterworks, 218
Material Control Inc., 119
Maternity Blues, 122
Mather's Department Store, 154
Mathews Archery, 9
Mathews Wire, 254
Matney's Models, 324
Matrix Desalination Inc., 77, 431
Matrix Group Ltd., 53
Matteucci (Nedra) Galleries 14
Matthews, 20
Matthews 1812 House, 185, 187, 194
Mattick Business Forms Inc., 343, 402
Maturna, 51, 122
Maui Jelly Factory, 205
Mauna Loa Macadamia Nut Corporation, 199
Maurer & Shepherd Joyners Inc., 275, 282
Maurice's Flying Pig, 198
Maury Island Farm, 201
Maverick Fine Western Wear, 129
Maverick Sugarbush Inc., 196
MAX-CAST, 15
Maxant Industries Inc., 63, 300
Maxi-Aids, 272, 430
Maxim (Mary) Inc. 304, 341, 442
Maximillian Importing Company, 26
Maximum Inc., 79, 433
Maximum Whitewater Performance, 71, 73, 75
Maxis Software, 16, 142
Maxxon Corporation, 211
May (Earl) Seeds & Nursery Company 107, 230, 233, 236, 240, 241, 244
May Silk, 182, 254
Maybelle's Doll Works, 164
Mayco Molds, 113
Mayfair Signs, 388
Mayfield Leather, 215
Mayhaw Tree, 201, 205
Maynard House Antiques, 215
May's Candy Shop, 187
Maytag Dairy Farms Inc., 189
Mayville Engineering Company Inc., 262
Mazzoli Coffee Inc., 130
Mazzula's (Mrs.) Foods 190, 191

❖ CORPORATE INDEX ❖

MB Historic Decor, 402
MBM Sales Ltd., 320
MC Martial Art Supply, 318
McBride (David) Taxidermy Supply Company 410
McCann Precision Golf Inc., 260
McClintock (Jessica) Bridal 119
McClure & Zimmerman, 232, 241
McCoy's Arts & Crafts, 70
McCoy's Auto & Truck Wrecking, 24
McCullough's Automotive Products, 46, 49
McCutcheon Apple Products Inc., 201, 205
McDaniel R.C. Inc., 327
McDavid Sports Medical Products, 208
McFeely's, 418
McGee (Ken) Holdings Inc. 22
McGowan Book Company, 94
McGrogan's Military Patches, 322
McGuire (John E.) Basketry Supplies 56
McGuire (Stuart) 387
McHale & Company, 103
McIlhenny Company, 205
McIntosh, 404
McIntosh Samplers, 341
McKenzie Taxidermy Supply, 9, 410
McKilligan, 435
McLaughlin (Damian) Jr. Corporation 75
McLaughlin Jr. (Damian) Corporation 76
McLellan (Rod) Company 237
MCM Electronics, 167, 169
McMahon Racing Components, 65
McNultys Tea & Coffee Company, 207
McPhee (Archie) & Company 301
McPherson Archery, 9
McRon Ceramic Molds, 113
McVays Limited, 423
McVay's Limited, 150
McVey's, 27, 35
MCW Automotive Finishes, 329
MD Electronics, 168, 427
MDC Direct Inc., 153, 379
MDI Inc., 365
MDI Woodcarvers Supply, 439
MDR Manufacturing Inc., 300
MDS Designs, 72
MDT-Muller Design Inc., 428
Mead (Carol) Wallpapers 281
Meade Instruments Corporation, 18, 69
Meadow Everlastings, 182, 366
Meadow View Farms, 228, 234, 236, 239
Meadowbrook Herb Gardens, 234, 348
Meadowlark Manufacturing Ltd., 70
Meadow's Chocolate & Cake Supplies, 106
Meadows Direct, 182
MECC Software, 142
Mecca Magic Inc., 52, 130, 149, 301, 316, 368, 414
MECI, 167
Med-Mar Metals, 113
Media Cybernetics L.P., 142
Medic Pharmacy & Surgical, 345
Medical Arts Press, 80
Medical Care Products, 345
Medicine Bow Motors Inc., 33
Medicool Inc., 159
MediSense Inc., 159
Meehan Military Posters, 14
Mega Computer Systems, 135
Mega Electronics, 427
MegaHaus, 132
Meg's Garden, 349, 366
MEI/Micro Center, 145
Meichsner (F.C.) Company 18, 69
Meier Auto Salvage, 24
Meierjohan-Wengler Inc., 388

Meisel Hardware Specialties, 268, 439
Meissner's Sewing, 383, 385
Mel-Nor Industries, 218, 228, 266, 312, 316
Melanie Collection, 297, 300
Melkton Classics Inc., 280
Mellinger's, 219, 220, 226, 230, 231, 233, 236, 237, 238, 239, 241, 243, 244, 246
Mellinger's Inc., 107, 350
Meloon Enterprises Inc., 300
Melton Book Company, 93, 110, 337, 429
Melton's Antiques, 6, 165
Meltzer (Steven) 316, 368
Memindex Inc., 96, 344
Memorex, 99
Memories Inc., 354, 434
Memory Lane Collector Car Dismantlers, 24
Memory Lane Postcards, 365
Memory Lane Records, 335
Memory Plus Inc., 132
Memphis Amateur Electronics, 372
Memphis Hardwood Flooring Company, 275
Menash Signatures Inc., 348
Mendelson Electronics Company Inc., 167
Mendocino Mustard, 205
Menig's Memorabilia, 20
MentorPlus Software Inc., 142
Merald Vision & Sound, 362
Merchandising Incentives Corporation, 21
Merco Products, 180
Mercury Research Company, 36
Meredith Instruments, 168
Meridian Video Corporation, 337
Merillat Industries Inc., 97
Merit Adventures, 20
Merit Metal Products Corporation, 268
Merit Studios, 142
Merkel Model Car Company, 326
Merlin Aircraft Inc., 1
Merlite Industries Inc., 297
Merrbach Record Service, 399, 400
Merrell Footwear, 101
Merrell Scientific/World of Science, 306, 327, 381
Merriam-Webster Inc., 88
Merrimack Canoe Company, 73
Merrimade Inc., 402
Merritt's Antiques Inc., 118
Merry Gardens, 235
Merry Mary-Anne's Rubber Art Stamps, 377
Merry-Go-Art, 107
Merry-Go-Round Antiques, 107
Merryman Boats, 72
Merry's Collectibles, 365
Mesa Garden, 231
Me'shiwi, 291
Mess Dress, 322
Messelaar Bulb Company, 232
Metacom Inc., 81
Metal Buyers Mart, 320
Metal Detectors of Minneapolis, 321
Metalliferous, 300, 320
Metric Equipment Sales Inc., 169
Metro ImageBase Inc., 142
Metro Motors, 36
Metro Moulded Parts Inc., 45
Metro Music, 108, 110
Metropolis, 131, 335
Metropolitan Museum of Art, 14, 250, 254
Metropolitan Music Store, 339
Metropolitan Opera Guild, 110, 429
Mettle Company, 210
Metz (Richard) Golf Studio Inc. 260
Meyco Products Inc., 408

Meyda Tiffany, 310
Meyer (David) Magic Books 94
Meyerbooks Publisher, 88, 316
Miami Clay Company, 113
Miami Valley Outdoor Products, 9
Miami Valley Products Company, 330
MiBAC Music Software, 142
Mica Lamp Company, 310
Mice Unlimited, 353
Mich (Earl) Company 388
Michael's (J.) Catalog Company 157, 254
Michael's Bromeliads, 235
Michaels of Oregon Company, 262
Michel Company, 354
Michele's Silver Matching Service, 390
Michelin Cycle Department, 333
Michigan Bulb Company, 241
Michigan Cane Supply, 56, 114
Michigan Custom Area Rugs, 379
Michigan Genealogical Council, 248
Michigan Historical Society, 248
Michigan Radio, 372
Michigan State Archives, 248
Micro 2000 Inc., 142
Micro Control Specialties, 372
Micro Design International Inc., 132
Micro Express, 135
Micro Kits, 168
Micro Perfect Corporation, 142
Micro Plastics, 51, 399
Micro Professionals Inc., 135
Micro Sports Inc., 142
Micro Star, 137
Micro Vision Software Inc., 142
Micro-Mark, 329, 418
Micro-X Incorporated, 324
MicroBiz, 142
Microbrew Adventure without Leaving Home, 437
MicroCode Engineering, 142
Microflight Products Inc., 3
Microforum, 142
Micrologic, 79
MicroLogic Software, 142
Microlytics Inc., 142
MicroPrecision Software Inc., 142
MicroProse Software Inc., 142, 423
Microscale Industries Inc., 156
Microsoft Corporation, 142, 207
Microsoft Press, 88
MicroSolutions, 132
MicroStar Research & Trading Inc., 142
MicroSYSTEMS Warehouse, 137
Microtek Lab Inc., 132
Mid America Designs Inc., 30
Mid Western Sport Togs, 368, 387
Mid-Atlantic Sports Cards, 399
Mid-Continent Agrimarketing Inc., 64, 105
Mid-Missouri Surplus, 322, 408
Mid-South Auto Sales, 29, 31, 39
Mid-South Business Cards, 97
Mid-West Metal Detectors, 321
MidAmerica Furniture, 215
MidAmerica Vacuum Cleaner Supply Company, 428
Midas China & Silver, 116, 390
MidAtlantic Antiques, 6, 20, 317, 346
Middlesex Farm Food Products, 196, 205
Midern Computer Inc., 135
Midisoft, 142
Midland Automotive Products, 26, 30, 32, 33, 38, 42, 49
Midland Tackle Company, 180
Midnight Records, 110
MidStates Classic Cars, 44

CORPORATE INDEX

Midway Arms Inc., 265
Midway Labs Inc., 395
Midway Plantation, 201
Midwest Action Cycle, 333
Midwest Architectural Wood Products, 282
Midwest Dowel Works Inc., 439
Midwest Electronics Inc., 427
Midwest Laser Products, 168
Midwest Micro, 135
Midwest Military, 322
Midwest Pepper Trading Company, 205
Midwest Photo Exchange, 361
Midwest Products Company Inc., 324
Midwest Sales, 266
Midwest Sports & Tennis Supply, 412
Midwest Toys, 52
Midwest Trade Imports, 124, 173
Midwest Wildflowers, 246
Midwestern Motors & Dismantlers, 36
Midwestern Sport Togs, 124
Mighty Mac, 220, 225, 226
Mighty Mite Sawmill, 418
Mikasa, 116, 153, 390
Mikdash Foods Inc., 194
Mike's Auto Parts, 29, 31, 39
Mike's Ceramic Molds Inc., 113
Mike's Cigars Inc., 415
Mike's Cycle Parts, 333
Mikes Fly Desk, 180
Mike's Train House, 330
Miki's Crystal Registry, 153
Miksa Honey Farm, 64
Milaeger's Gardens, 239
Mile Appliance Inc., 7
Mile Hi Ceramics Inc., 113
Mile High Comics, 335, 398
Miles Homes, 282
Miles Inc., 159
Milford Camera Shop, 361
Military Art China Company Inc., 322
Military Bookman, 80, 88
Military Collection, 322
Military Mites, 421
Mill Creek Outfitters Inc., 287
Mill End Store, 173
Mill Supply, 21
Miller (Charles) Designs 313
Miller (Gus) 24
Miller (Howard) Clock Company 118
Miller (J.E.) Nurseries 230, 233, 234, 239, 244
Miller (Ted) Custom Knives 292
Miller (Walter) 22
Miller Import Company, 15
Miller Manufacturing Inc., 166
Miller Nurseries, 236
Miller Rug Hooking, 378
Miller Wood Products, 64
Miller Woodworking Machinery Inc., 418
Miller-Stockman Western Wear, 129
Miller's Incorporated, 36
Millett Industries, 264
Millicent's Preserves, 201
Millie's Pierogi, 190
Millry Bee Company, 64
Mills River Industries, 97, 157, 379
Milstein (Emanuel) 118
Milwaukee Electric Tool Corporation, 418
Mimi's Fabrications, 174, 341
Mind Path Technologies, 132
Mind's Eye, 81, 88, 254
Mindscape Inc., 142
Mindware, 368
Mineralogical Research Company, 321, 374, 375

Minerals Unlimited, 374, 375
Miners Inc., 367, 375
Mini Creations By Judy, 161
Mini Mania, 26
Mini Rose Garden, 240
Mini Splendid Things, 161
Mini Temptations, 162
Mini World Doll Supplies, 164
Mini-tiques, 162
Miniatronics, 329
Miniature Carousel Components, 107
Miniature Crafters, 162
Miniature Kingdom of River Row, 162
Miniature Makers' Workshop, 162
Miniature MINIATURES, 162
Miniature Plant Kingdom, 230, 240
Miniature Rugs by Adams, 162
Miniature Teddy Bear Kits, 60
Miniature Village, 162
Miniatures, 421
Miniatures In-Your-Mailbox, 162
Miniatures of the World Inc., 326
Miniatures Plus, 162
Minimax Enterprise, 325
MiniMed Technologies, 159
Minitech Machinery, 418
Minnesota Ceramic Supply, 113
Minnesota Clay USA, 88, 113
Minnesota Connection, 399
Minnesota Historical Society Research Center, 248
Minnesota Lapidary Supply Corporation, 300
Minnesota State Parks Nature Store, 254
Minnetonka by Mail, 387
Minnie's Doll House, 164
Minolta, 16, 69, 99, 356, 357, 358, 362
Minot Wrecking & Salvage Company, 24
Minox Processing Laboratories, 359
Mint Condition Comic Books & Baseball Cards Inc., 131
Minwax Company Inc., 438
Miquelito's Dancewear, 266
Miracle of Aloe, 148
Mirador Optical, 69
Mirage Speakers, 405
Miramar Systems, 133
Mirror Image Motorworks, 45
Mirrorculous Designs, 323
Miscellaneous Man, 14, 335
Missing Link Fossils, 374, 375
Mission Orchards, 191
Mission Service Supply, 100, 426
Mission Service Supply Inc., 404
Mississippi Archives & History Department, 248
Mississippi History and Genealogy Association, 248
Mississippi Product Sales Inc., 194
Missouri Breaks Industries, 62, 369
Missouri Dandy Pantry, 199
Missouri State Genealogical Association, 248
Mister Boardwalk, 223
Mister Indian's Cowboy Store, 293
Mister Twister Inc., 180
Mistral Sports Inc., 407
Misty Mountain Threadworks, 334
MIT Press, 88
Mitchell & Ness Nostalgia Company, 53
Mitchell Motor Parts Inc., 29, 31, 39
Mitchell Paddles Inc., 73, 373
Mito Corporation, 22
Mitra, 135
Mitre Sports, 378
Mitsch (Grant) Novelty Daffodils 232
Mitsuba Computers, 135

Mitsubishi Electronics, 46, 99, 404, 410, 425
Mitsubishi International, 410
Miya Shoji & Interiors Inc., 215
Mizuno Corporation, 259, 260, 431
MK Model Products, 58
MKS Inc., 142
MLCS Tools Ltd., 418
MMI Corporation, 18, 361
Mo Hotta-Mo Betta, 205
MO Trailers, 47
Moab Adventure Outfitters, 334
Mobile Manufacturing Company, 313, 418
Mobile Mark Inc., 372
Mobilectrics, 436
Mobilitis Corporation, 272
Mobility Products & Design, 272
Mobility-Plus Inc., 436
Moby Dick Marine Specialties, 79, 254
Model Boats Unlimited, 328
Model Cars & Trains Unlimited, 326, 330, 421
Model Cellar Productions, 421
Model Display & Fixture Company Inc., 160
Model Electronics Corporation, 329
Model Empire, 326
Model Expo Inc., 325, 326, 328, 329, 330
Model Motorcars Ltd., 326
Model Railway Post Office, 325
Model Rectifier Corporation, 330
Model Shop, 326
Modern Classics, 215
Modern Electronics, 427
Modern Farm, 254
Modern Homesteader, 107, 226
Modern Performance Classics, 29, 39
Modernage Photographic Services, 359
Moen Inc., 174
Moerer (Craig) Records 110
Moe's Movie Madness, 335
Moffit's (Dick) Chevy Parts 29
Mohawk Canoes, 73
Mohawk Impressions, 292
Moheban (Abraham) & Son 379
Moheban (Fred) Gallery 379
Mohns Nursery, 239
Moiseyev (Igor) 322
Moishe's Homemade Kosher Bakery, 183
Molten USA Inc., 208
Moments in Time Ltd., 359
Momentum, 106
Momentum Alfa-Romeo, 25
Mom's Apple Pie Company, 185
Moms Catalog, 159, 270, 290, 345
Monarch Collectibles, 165
Monarch Longbow Company Inc., 9
Monarch Radiator Enclosures, 370
Mondo-tronics, 168
Monfort Associates, 72
Mongoose Bicycles, 65, 170
Monique Trading Corporation, 164
Monkapeme, 293
Monolith Toys, 422
Monolithic Constructors Inc., 283
Mont-Bell, 101, 103, 121, 124, 314, 391
Montague Bicycle Company, 65
Montana Historical Society, 248
Montana Log Homes, 283
Montans & Lace Vintage Musical Instruments, 339
Monte (Ron) Inc. 43
Monterey Inc., 60
Monterey Outlet Store, 173
Monterey Sporting Clays, 266
Montgomery Ward Direct, 254

CORPORATE INDEX

Montoya/MAS International Inc., 12, 406
Montpelier Stove Works, 182
Moon Bear Pottery, 291
Moon Mountain Wildflowers, 241, 246
MoonAcre IronWorks, 105, 150, 224
Moondog's Comics, 131
Moonlight Lane Inc., 105
Moonrise, 304
MoonShine Trading Company, 187, 201
Moonstone Factory Store, 101, 103
Moonstruck Chocolatier, 187
Moonwalker/Sierra Boot Company, 387, 388
Moore (Gates) Lighting 310
Moore Bears, 61
Moore Business Products, 343, 344
Moore Jaguar, 34
Moore Medical Corporation, 381
Moore's Candies Inc., 187
Moores Cycle Supply, 333
Moose River Moccasin Company, 387
Mooseburger (Pricilla) Originals 130
Morad Electronics, 79
Morco Products, 226
More Than Balloons Inc., 52
More than Balloons Inc., 316
More than Models, 325, 328, 329
Morehouse Farm, 442
Morgan (David) 124, 126, 250, 269, 317
Morgan Auto Parts, 24
Morgan Company, 365
Morgan Manufacturing, 275
Morgan Printing Company, 343, 344, 402
Morgan's Cycle & Fitness, 65
Morgan's Mills, 196
Morisi's Pasta, 190
Morning Light Emporium, 59
Morningside Bookshop, 88
Morris (Jim) Environmental T-Shirts 128
Morris Costumes, 52, 130, 149, 316
Morris Farms, 205
Morrison (Art) Enterprises 24
Morrone Company, 53
Morse Farm, 196
Morss (W.K.) & Son 233
Mosaic Records, 110
Moser (Thos.) Cabinetmakers 215
Mosler Specialty Products, 264
Mosley Electronics, 372
Moss Motors Ltd., 25, 26, 34, 37, 41, 42
Moss Portfolio, 14
Moss Tents Inc., 103
Moss Yarns Needlearts, 341, 442
Mossberg (O.F.) & Sons Inc. 265
Mossburg's Foam Products, 388
Mostly Mustang's Inc., 38, 39, 41
Mother Earth News, 88
Mother Muck's Minis, 162
Mother Myrick's Confectionary, 185, 187
Mother-ease, 50
Motherboard Discount Center, 133
Mother's Place, 122
Mother's Wear Diapers, 50
Mothers Work, 122
Mothertime, 120, 122
Motherwear, 51, 122
Motif Designs, 281
Motion Picture Arts Gallery, 335
Moto Race, 333
Moto-Lita Inc., 45, 46
Motoboard International, 382
Motofixx, 333
Motoport USA, 331
Motor-Sport Products, 405
Motorace, 331
Motorbooks International, 22, 88

Motorcars Ltd., 34
Motorcycle Accessory Warehouse, 58, 333
Motorcycle Salvage Company Inc., 333
Motorhead, 14, 21, 326
Motoring Music, 110
Motorola AMSD, 411
Motorola Cellular Subscriber Group, 410
Motorola Modems, 133
Motorsport, 31
Motorsport Specialties Inc., 49
Motoxtra, 333
Mott Miniatures & Doll House Shop, 162
Moulton (Alison & Richard) 365
Moulton Gallery Inc., 14
Moultrie Manufacturing, 175, 209, 215, 218, 310, 312
Mount Horeb Mustard Museum, 205
Mountain Ark Trading Company, 196
Mountain Car Company, 330
Mountain Craft Shop, 423
Mountain Dreams International Inc., 334
Mountain Equipment Inc., 103
Mountain Farms Inc., 182, 362, 366
Mountain Gear, 334
Mountain Goat Cycles, 65
Mountain Hardware, 103, 334
Mountain Heritage Crafters, 418
Mountain High Equipment & Supply Company, 3
Mountain High Ltd., 334
Mountain Loom Company, 397
Mountain Lumber, 314
Mountain Maples, 230
Mountain Meadows Pottery, 116, 388
Mountain Minerals International, 375
Mountain Musicrafts, 88, 108, 337, 339
Mountain Press Publishing Company, 88
Mountain Rose Herbs, 148
Mountain Safety Research, 334, 431
Mountain Sales, 175
Mountain Sports, 334
Mountain State Hobby Supply, 326
Mountain State Muzzleloading Supplies Inc., 263
Mountain Tools Catalog & Equipment Guide, 334
Mountain West Alarm Supply Company, 5
Mountain Woodcarvers Supplies, 439
Mountaineer Archery Inc., 9
Mountaineer Log Homes Inc., 283
Mountaineers Books, 89
Mountainman Woodshop, 215, 226
Mountainsmith, 104
Mouse Factory, 353
Mouser Electronics, 5, 167
Movie Gallery, 319
Movie Market, 335
Movie Poster Place Inc., 335
Movie Poster Shop, 335
Movie Star News, 335
Moviecraft Inc., 429
Movin USA, 53, 380
Mowrey Gun Works, 263, 265
Mozzarella Company, 189
MPR Associates, 152
MPS Controls, 272
MR Motorcycle, 333
Mr. & Mrs. of Dallas, 113, 115
MRC (Mariner Resource), 71
MRC Models, 325, 326
MS China, 116
MSI Structures Inc., 47
MSO Parts, 25, 26, 34, 36
Mt. Diablo Handprints, 281
Mt. Eden Books & Bindery, 88

Mt. Nebo Gallery, 14
Mt. Si Bonsai, 230
Mt. Vernon Coffee & Tea Traders, 207
MTD Products Inc., 224
MTF Geriatrics, 272
MTS Power Products, 166
Muck Motor Sales, 42
Mueller (Charles H.) Company 241
Mueller Sporting Goods Inc., 68, 156
Mueller Sports Medicine Inc., 209
Mug Merchant, 113
Muir & McDonald Company, 312
Muirhead of Ringoes, 201, 205
Mullen (H.) Sales Inc. 101
Mullen (O.H.) Sales Inc. 9, 104, 410
Multi-com Publishing Inc., 208
Multi-Tech Systems Inc., 133
Multi-Vision Electronics, 427
Multiblitz Lighting Company, 358
Multicom Publishing Inc., 225
MultiFax, 433
Multimedia Artboard, 11
MultiNewspapers, 343
Multisheep, 46
Munchkin Motors, 326
Mundy (C.W.) Studio/Gallery 14
Munn (Abe) Picture Frames Inc. 210
Muns (J.B.), Bookseller 20
Munyon & Sons, 15
Munzinger (A.J.) & Company 157
Murphy (Mark) 399
Murphy Aircraft Manufacturing Ltd., 1
Murphy Bed Company Inc., 212
Murray (Claire) Inc. 254, 341, 369, 378, 379
Murrays Catamarans, 74, 89, 429
Murray's Gunshop Inc., 265
Murrays WaterSports, 381, 392, 393
Murrey & Sons Company Inc., 68
Murrow Furniture Galleries, 215
Muscle Factory, 28, 31
Museum Collections, 157, 254
Museum Editions of New York Ltd., 14
Museum of Fine Arts, 254
Museum of Jewelry, 297
Museum of Modern Art New York, 157, 254
Museum of Modern Rubber, 377
Museum Replicas Limited, 254, 322
Mushroom Man, 191, 205
MushroomPeople, 236
Music Box Melodies, 108, 337
Music Box World, 337
Music By Mail, 110
Music Connection, 110, 429
Music Dispatch, 89, 110, 429
Music for Little People, 81, 107, 422, 429
Music Hunter, 110, 429
Music Lovers Recording Society, 110
Music Stand, 50, 254
Musicmaker Kits, 339
Musk Ox Producers Cooperative, 290
Musket Miniatures, 421
Musser Forests, 243, 244
Mustad, 180
Mustang Corral, 38
Mustang Headquarters, 38
Mustang of Chicago, 38
Mustang Specialties, 38
Mustang Survival, 71
Mustangs & More, 38
Mustangs Unlimited, 30, 33, 36, 38, 41
Muzzle Loaders Etcetera Inc., 263
Muzzleload Magnum Products, 262
MWK Industries, 168
My Dollhouse, 162

CORPORATE INDEX

My Grandma's of New England Coffee Cake, 185
My Kind of Bear, 61
My Own Bookplate, 80
My Silk Garde, 341
My Sister's Shoppe Inc., 162
My Software Company, 142
Mycelium Fruits, 236
Myers (T.) Magic Inc. 52
Myers Gourmet Popcorn, 200
Myers Meats, 105, 198
Mylen Industries, 278
Myron Toback Inc., 320
Myson, 286
Mysteries by Mail, 89
Mystic Canyon Gallery, 294
Mystic Color Lab, 359
Mystic River Video, 443
Mystic Seaport Museum Stores, 14, 15, 79, 89, 255

N

NAD, 404
Nadine's Music, 339
Nady Systems, 373, 403, 405
Nagle Forge & Foundry, 210
Naica Collectibles, 291
Nakamichi, 404
Naked Edge Mountaineering, 334
Namark Cap & Emblem Company, 156, 349
Name Maker Inc., 385
Nana Museum of the Arctic Craft Shop, 290
Nanco, 185, 199
Nancy's Choice, 387
Nancy's Knitworks, 442
Nancy's Notions, 173, 383
Nancy's Specialty Market, 89, 194, 303
Nantahala Outdoor Center, 373
Nantucket Off-Shore Seasonings Inc., 205
Nantucket Wholesaler, 56
Napa Valley Art Store, 11
Napa Valley Kitchens, 205
Naples Creek Leather, 126, 368, 387
Napoleon Fireplaces, 177
Naranjo (Teresita), 116, 292
Naranjo's World of American Indian Art, 294
Narco Avionics, 3
Narragansett Reproductions, 36
Nasco, 11, 12, 51, 56, 98, 105, 113, 115, 152, 166, 171, 261, 300, 306, 312, 316, 341, 347, 381, 388, 389, 397, 401, 418, 439
Nash (Jeanne) Studio 14
Nash Auto Parts, 24
Nassau Investment Casting Company, 259
Nate's Autographs, 20
Natgear, 287
Nation Wide Outlet, 153, 281
National Arbor Day Foundation, 243, 244
National Archives & Records Administration, 14, 250
National Artcraft Company, 113, 115, 152
National Bag Company Inc., 345
National Banner Company Inc., 388
National Blind & Wallpaper Factory, 153
National Business Furniture Inc., 217
National Cable Brokers, 427
National Camera Exchange, 18, 69
National CD-ROM, 145
National Cinema Service, 337
National Color Labs, 359
National Diabetic Pharmacies, 159
National Educational Music Company Inc., 339
National Fire Protection Association, 5
National Gallery of Art, 337
National Geographic Society, 89, 255, 258, 317
National Greenhouse Company, 220
National Jukebox Exchange, 130, 302
National Locksmith, 5
National Log Homes, 283
National Luggage Dealers Association, 368
National Medical Consumables Inc., 159, 270, 290, 345
National Merchandise of Virginia, 68
National Museum of Women in the Arts, 255
National Music Supply, 339
National Offshore Marine Laboratories, 431
National Parachute Industries, 4
National Parts Depot, 27, 28, 38, 42
National Postcard Exchange, 365
National Resophonic Guitars, 339
National Rifle Association, 89
National Security Safe Company, 264
National Showcase Company Inc., 373
National Sporting Goods Corporation, 95, 273, 289, 376, 382, 390
National Stampagraphic, 377
National Target Company, 266
National Technical Information Service, 16
National Thread & Supply, 383
National Watch Exchange, 297
National Wheel-O-Vator Company Inc., 401, 436
National Wholesale Company Inc., 121, 124
National Wildlife Federation, 89, 261
Nationwide Flashing Signal Systems Inc., 272
Native American Arts & Crafts Council, 291
Native American Arts of the South, 291
Native Gardens, 246
Native Grains Inc., 96, 183
Native USA, 292
Natural Access, 436
Natural Aquarium & Terrarium, 352
Natural Baby Company, 120
Natural Baby Company Inc., 50, 422
Natural Balance, 104
Natural Bedroom, 50, 63
Natural Gardening Company, 219, 224, 226, 228, 246
Natural Pet Care Company, 350
Natural Products Company, 305
Natural Resources, 196, 373
Naturally Irish, 202
Nature Company, 128, 255, 307, 381, 424
Nature Crafts, 362
Nature's Backyard Inc., 226
Nature's Bounty, 362
Nature's Control, 219
Nature's Edge Camouflage, 287
Nature's Finest, 349, 366
Nature's Gifts Wreath Company, 157
Nature's Herb Company, 349
Nature's Jewelry, 297, 382
Nature's Nest, 70
Nature's Treasures, 374
Nature's Way, 352
Nautica International, 75, 77, 392
Nautical Book Catalog, 89
Nautical Software, 79, 142
Nauticode Inc., 79, 124, 255
Nautilus Direct, 170
Nauvoo Mill & Bakery, 194
Navajo Gallery, 292
Navajo Manufacturing Company, 291, 297
Naval Academy Gift Shop, 255
Naval Institute Press, 79, 89, 98
Navarro Canoe Company, 73
Navarro Studio, 15
Navesink Electronics, 418
Navico Inc., 79
Navy Arms Company, 263, 265
Naylor Furnituremakers, 215
Naz-Dar Company, 11, 389
NBO Satellite TV, 403
NC Tool Company, 71, 286
NDL Products Inc., 96
Neal (John), Bookseller 80, 89, 99
Neal (Lawrence P.) 215
Neally (Bud) 305
Nearing (Kathy) 61
Nebenzahl (Kenneth) Inc. 317
Nebraska Plastics Inc., 218, 223
Nebraska State Genealogical Society, 248
NEBS Inc., 114, 343, 344, 402
NEC America, 411
NEC Home Electronics, 99, 404, 405, 425
NEC Technologies, 133
NEC Technologies Inc., 135, 423
Necessary Trading Company, 219, 225
Necky Kayaks Ltd., 73
Needlecraft Shop, 341
NeedleMagic Inc., 342
Needlework Attic, 89, 442
Neeney, 292
Negri's Camera Shop, 361
Neico Aviation Inc., 1
Neill's Farm, 191
Neiman-Marcus, 158
Nekton USA Inc., 353
Nelson Candle & Beeswax Co., 105
Nelson Crab Inc., 202
Nelson Light Looms, 397
Nelson Weather-Rite Clothing, 104, 287
Nelson's (Bob) Gameroom Warehouse 130
Nelson's (Mike) Movie View Sales Inc. 427
Neodesha Plastics Inc., 353
Neon Clock, 6, 118
Neosoft Corporation, 142
Neoteric Hovercraft, 286
Neptune Fireworks Company Inc., 177
Neptune Imports, 352
Neri (C.) Antiques 310
Nerman's Books & Collectibles, 81
Nestle-Beich, 210
Netcraft Company, 79, 180
Netherland Bulb Company, 241
NETIS Technology Inc., 133
NETiS Technology Inc., 135
Network Express, 137
Network Floor Covering, 379
Neubert (Wil) Aircraft Supply 4
Neubert (Wil) Aircraft Supply, 4
Neuhaus USA Inc., 187
Neumann Press, 94
Neustadt Studios Collectables, 160
Neustadt Studios Collecttables, 215
Nevada Genealogical State Society, 249
Nevada Mineral & Book Company, 89
Nevers Oak Fireplace Mantels, 177
Neville Log Homes, 283
New Archery Products Corporation, 9
New Avionics, 4
New Balance Athletic Shoe Inc., 101, 120, 380, 424
New Braunfels Smokehouse, 198
New British Bonsai Magazine, 230
New Buck Corporation, 406
New Canaan Farms, 187, 201, 205
New Century Envelope, 402
New Dawn Outfitters, 9
New Dimension Homes Inc., 283
New Earth Inc., 221

CORPORATE INDEX

New England Audio Resource, 403
New England Auto Accessories Inc., 46
New England Bamboo Company, 229
New England Basket Company, 56
New England Bonsai, 230
New England Car Shops, 330
New England Card Company, 261
New England Cheesemaking Supply Company, 115
New England Circuit Sales, 167
New England Comics, 131
New England Fire-backs, 176
New England Garden Ornaments, 223
New England International Gems, 59, 169
New England International Gems Inc., 300, 375
New England Jukebox, 302
New England Maple Museum, 196
New England Meteoritical Services, 374
New England Mustang, 26
New England Outbuildings, 386
New England Ropes, 77, 334
New England Slate Company, 277
New England Stained Glass, 310
New England Timber Frames, 283
New England Wildflower Society, 89, 246
New Found Metals Inc., 77
New Hampshire Division of Records Management & Arch, 249
New Hampshire Historical Society, 249
New Hampshire Society of Genealogists, 249
New Harbinger Publications, 89
New Holland North America Inc., 225
New Home Sewing Machine Company, 385
New Jersey Genealogical Society, 249
New Jersey State Department of Archives, 249
New Jersey State Library, 249
New Life Systems, 148, 319
New Media Corporation, 133
New Mexico Archives & Records Center, 249
New Mexico Astronomical, 18
New Mexico Catalog, 255
New Mexico Historical Society, 249
New Mexico State Genealogical Society, 249
New MMI Corporation, 133, 137
New Moon Gardening Books, 89
New Orleans School of Cooking and Louisiana General, 89, 194
New Penny Farm, 192
New Rebel Workshop, 307
New Scotland Lace Company, 174
New Sense, 65
New Skete Farms, 198
New South Athletic Company Inc., 53, 209
New Tech Tennis, 412
New Wave Kayak Products, 74
New West Electronics, 100, 404, 426
New Wireless Pioneers, 89
New York Barbell, 170
New York Central Art Supply Company, 11
New York Dancewear Company, 155
New York Golf Center, 260
New York HomeBrew, 437
New York Label, 344
New York State Archives, 249
Newark Dressmaker Supply, 383
Newbern Groves Gift Shop, 192
Newburgh Yarn Mills, 442
Newfound Woodworks Inc., 72, 74
Newman & Altman Inc., 25, 41
Newman Brothers Inc., 340, 388
Newman Enterprises, 344, 383
Newport News Fashions, 121, 124, 127

Newsom's (Colonel Bill) Hams 198, 201, 205
Newstamp Lighting Company, 310
NewTech Sports, 304
Newtech Video & Computers, 100, 137, 145, 146, 411
Nexco, 104
Nexton Industries Inc., 57, 268
Nexus Marine Corporation, 75, 76
Neycraft, 170, 300
NgraveR Company, 300, 320, 438
Niagara Lumber & Wood Products Inc., 314
Niagara Tradition, 437
Niche Gardens, 239, 243, 244, 246
Nichols Garden Nursery, 230, 233, 234, 236, 241
Nicholson's Trading Post, 89, 317
Nicke (Walt) Company 226
Nicolas (Holly) Nursing Collection 122
Nielsen (Norm) 316
Nighthorse (Ben) 291
NightinGale Resources, 80
Nightsun Performance Lighting, 67
Nigro's Western Store, 297
Nihan & Martin Pharmacy, 346
Nike Footwear Inc., 95, 101, 411, 424, 431
Nikon, 356, 358, 362
Nikon Photo, 69
Nikonos Cameras, 356, 358, 362
Nimbus Paddles, 74
Nippon Pet Food, 352
Nippon/4/Less, 418
Nite Lite Company, 287, 350
Nitro-Pak Preparedness Center, 105, 270, 381
Nitron Industries Inc., 224, 350
Niwa Tool, 226
Nixalite of America, 349
No Compromise Communications, 79
No Nonsense Direct, 121
No-Salt-Salt, 205
Nobilette Cycles, 65
Noble Collection, 322
Noble Farms Inc., 198
NobleMotion Inc., 106
Noblex U.S.A., 356
Noël Pie Plate Company, 116
Nokia Mobile Phones Inc., 411
Nolan Supply Corporation, 320
Nola's Miniature Shop, 162
Nolin River Nut Tree Nursery, 244
Nolo Press, 89, 142
Noltings, 369, 385
Nomadic Instand, 160
Nonferrous Metals, 300, 320, 438
Noontide Press, 89, 110, 429
Norco Products USA Inc., 66
Norcraft Custom Brands, 418
Nordic Knives, 305
Nordic Needle, 342
Nordica, 391
Nordicorp Inc., 438
NordicTrack, 171
Nordstrom Mail Order, 158
Nor'East Miniature Roses Inc., 240
Noritake China Replacements, 116
Norland Trading Company, 104, 180, 287
Norlander Company, 180
Norling (Barry) Weathervanes 434
Norman (W.F.) Corporation 273
Norman (Walter) & Company 370
Normark, 180
Norselander, 342
Norsk Fjord Fiber, 397, 442
Norson Industries Inc., 295

Nortec Industries, 1, 286
North American Bear Company, 61
North American Sports Distributing Inc., 4
North Beach Leather, 124, 314
North Branch Trading Company, 215
North by Northeast, 101
North Carolina Discount Furniture, 215
North Carolina State Archives, 249
North Coast Miniature Motors, 326
North Coast Racing, 326
North Country Crafts, 105, 150, 215
North Country Creative Structures, 396
North Country Gardens, 162
North Country Smokehouse, 198
North County Exotics, 353
North Dakota State Historical Society, 249
North End Wrecking Inc., 24
North Face, 101, 104, 314, 380, 391
North Light Books, 89
North River Boatworks, 75
North Star Gardens, 89, 230
North Systems, 142
North West Mushroom Company Inc., 192
North Woods Chair Shop, 215
North Yale Auto Parts, 29, 33
Northeast Electronics Inc., 427
Northeast Sailplane Products, 327
Northeastern Log Homes, 283
Northeastern Scale Models Inc., 162, 329
Northern Brewer Ltd., 437
Northern Discovery Seafoods, 202
Northern Hydraulics, 313, 418
Northern Lakes Wild Rice Company, 194
Northern Lights, 334
Northern Lites Performance Snowshoes, 393
Northern Map Company, 317, 322
Northern Outfitters, 391
Northern Plains Indian Crafts Association, 292
Northern Safety Company Inc., 381
Northern Tire & Auto Sales, 24
Northern Whitetail, 288
Northfields Restorations, 275
Northland Gardens, 230
Northland Publishing, 89
Northland Woodworking Supply, 418
Northridge Gardens Nursery, 230, 231
Northroad & Company, 388
Northstar Avionics, 3
Northstyle Gifts, 255
Northwest Classic Falcons, 30, 32
Northwest Design Works Inc., 74
Northwest Import Parts, 37
Northwest Kayaks, 74
Northwest Knife Supply, 305
Northwest Outdoor Center, 71, 74
Northwest Passages, 255
Northwest Public Domain, 137
Northwest River Supplies Inc., 75, 104, 373
Northwest Specialty Baking Mixes, 185
Northwest Tag & Label Inc., 386
Northwest Traders Inc., 149
Northwest Treasure Supply, 321
Northwestern Coffee Mills, 207
Northwestern Exposure Furniture, 215
Northwoods Retail Nursery, 231, 243, 244
Northystyle, 255
Norton, 306
Norton Boat Works, 75
Norton Products, 166
Norton-Lambert Corporation, 133
Norway Industries, 219
Norwood Looms, 397
Nosler Bullets Inc., 262
Nostalgia Decorating Company, 14

CORPORATE INDEX

Nostalgia Unlimited, 21
Nostalgic Motor Cars, 25
Nostalgic Music Company, 302
Not Just Dolls, 165
Notebook Supply Warehouse, 133
Noteworthy Woodworking, 339
Nourse Farms, 230
Nova Astronomics, 16
Nova Color, 11
Nova Craft Canoe, 74
Novagraphics, 14, 261
Novak (Kenneth F.) & Company 18
Novak Electronics Inc., 326
Novaplex, 427
Novatron of Dallas Inc., 358
Novelties Unlimited, 52, 130, 347, 414
Noveltoys, 424
Novurania Inflatable Boats, 75
Now & Forever, 434
Nowell's Inc., 308
Nowell's Molds, 113
Nowetah's Indian Store & Museum, 291
Nowotny (M.) & Company 300
NowWhat Software, 142
NRA Sales Department, 266
NRC Sports, 413
Nu-Hope Laboratories Inc., 346
Nu-Tec Incorporated, 177, 406
Nu-Tek Electronics, 427
NuAce Company, 365
NUDO Products, 388
Nueske's Hillcrest Farm Meats, 198
Number One Wallpaper, 281
Numismatic Arts of Santa Fe, 89
Nunes Farms Almonds, 187, 199
NuReality, 403
Nurnberg Scientific, 18, 321
Nursery, 230, 233, 243, 244
Nursery & Water Garden Supply, 228
Nurtured Baby, 51
Nussbaum (Susi), Basketmaker 56
Nustyle Quilting Frame Company, 369
NuTone Inc., 5, 97, 294, 428
Nutrition Headquarters, 148, 430
Nutrition Warehouse, 430
Nuts D'Vine, 199
NVIEW Corporation, 336
Nye (Ben) Makeup 130, 414
Nyman Dock Shuttle, 295
Nytro Bicycles, 66

O

O-S Systems, 71
O.E.M. Parts Distributor,
    25, 26, 36, 40, 41, 43
O.K. Market, 198
O.S.I. Marine Lab Inc., 352
Oak Barrel Winecraft, 437
Oak Grove Smokehouse Inc., 198
Oak Hill Gardens, 235, 237
Oak Orchard Canoe, 74
Oak Tree Furniture Company, 62
Oakes Daylilies, 238
Oakley Sunglasses, 407
Oakridge Corporation, 162
Oakridge Nurseries, 232, 246
Oakridge Smokehouse Restaurant, 198
OAS Art Supplies, 11
Oasis Date Gardens, 192
Oasis of Quality, 422
Oberhamer USA, 289
Obodda (H.) Mineral Specimens 300, 375
O'Brien International, 432
O'Brien Manufacturing, 373

Observa-Dome Laboratories Inc., 16
Obsolete Chevrolet Parts Company,
    27, 28, 29, 49
Obsolete Ford Parts (Oklahoma City), 36
Obsolete Ford Parts Company,
    26, 32, 33, 38, 42, 49
Obsolete Ford Parts Inc. (Oklahoma City),
    26, 30, 32, 33, 34, 37, 42
Obsolete Jeep & Willys Parts, 35, 43
Ocean Hockey Supply Company, 273, 376
Ocean In Your Home, 352
Ocean Kayak Inc., 74
Ocean Kites, 304
Ocean Ray Wet Suits, 392
Ocean State Electronics, 167, 168, 169
Ochsner International, 66
Ockam Instruments, 79
O'Connor's Cypress Woodworks, 266
October Country, 263
Octura Models Inc., 328
O'Donnell Elegant Americana, 215
Odyssey Auctions Inc., 20, 335
Odyssey Computing, 208
Odyssey Development, 142
Odyssey Golf, 259, 261, 313
Off the Beaten Path, 146
Office Depot Inc.,
    96, 98, 166, 217, 344, 348
Office Mates, 344
Offline Independent Energy Systems, 395
Offshore Marine Products Inc., 77
OFS WeatherFAX, 433
Ogan Antiques Ltd., 263
Ogden (Alice) 56
O'Grady Presents, 255
Ohara Publications Inc., 89, 318
OH'Brines Pickling Inc., 194
Ohio Ceramic Supply Inc., 113
Ohio Earth Food, 220
Ohio Historical Society, 249
Ohlinger's (Jerry) Movie Material Store Inc.
    335
Oikos Tree Crops, 244
Oke Oweenge Arts & Crafts, 292
Oki Telecom, 411
Okidata, 133
Oklahoma Comm Center, 372
Oklahoma Department of Libraries, 249
Oklahoma Historical Society, 249
Oklahoma Indian Arts & Crafts Cooperative,
    293
Okun Brothers Shoes, 380, 387
Ol' 55 Chevy Parts, 29
OlCar Bearing Company, 25
Old Car City USA, 24
Old Car Parts, 28, 29, 34
Old Carolina Brick Company, 278
Old Chicago Smoke Shop, 415
Old Fashioned Milk Paint Company, 276
Old Friends Antiques, 6, 61
Old Frontier Clothing Company, 129, 149
Old Game Store, 61, 368, 424
Old Glory Gallery & Frame Shop, 14
Old Gold Cars & Parts, 24
Old Grange Graphics, 14
Old Hickory Bookshop Ltd., 94
Old Hickory Furniture Company, 218
Old House Gardens, 242
Old Print Gallery, 14, 317, 346
Old Print Shop, 346
Old Pueblo Traders, 121, 126, 127, 387
Old Smithy Shop, 268
Old Southwest Trading Company,
    190, 192, 205

Old Sturbridge Village Museum Gift Shop,
    242
Old Sutler John, 322
Old Tech-Books & Things, 89
Old Town Canoe Company, 74
Old Towne Doll Shoppe, 165
Old Tyme Picture Frames, 210
Old Wagon Factory, 215, 275
Old West Signs, 6
Old Wooden Boatworks, 72
Old World Brush & Tool Company Inc., 418
Old World Craftsmen Dollhouses Inc., 162
Old World Moulding & Finishing Inc., 280
Old World Restorations, 6
Old-Timers Antiques, 61
Olde Glory Marketing, 177
Olde Soldier Books Inc., 20, 89, 322, 346
Olde Theatre Architectural Salvage, 277
Olde Tyme Radio Company, 372
Olden Camera & Lens Company Inc., 361
Olden Video, 146, 404, 411, 426
Oldfield (Barney) Aircraft Company 1
Oldies Unlimited, 108
Olds (L.L.) Seed Company 226, 236, 242
Oldsmobile USA Parts Supply, 39
Ole Chevy Store, 27, 28, 29, 39, 49, 405
Ole Fashion Things, 57
Oleda & Company Inc., 148, 430
Olesen, 414
Olesky Enterprises, 166
OlFactorium, 349
Olive Company, 205
Olivetti North America Inc., 135, 137
Olsen's Mill Direct, 124
Olson (C.J.) Cherries 187
Olsson's Books & Records, 89
Olt (P.S.) 288
Olympia Gold, 297
Olympia Sports,
    51, 152, 171, 209, 273, 307, 369, 409, 413, 425
Olympic Enterprises, 113
Olympic Kilns, 113
Olympic Optical Company, 407
Olympus Corporation, 99, 356, 358
Olympus Cove Antiques, 116
Omaha Steaks International, 198
Omaha Vaccine Company Inc., 350
Omark Industries, 266
Omega Research, 142
Omega Too, 277, 280
Omega/Arkay, 357
Omni Electronics, 372
Omni Resources, 258, 307, 317, 374, 375
Omnia, 268
Omniarts of Colorado, 162
Omnifac Corporation, 48, 79
Omnigrid Inc., 369
OmniModels, 325
O'Mona International Tea Company, 207
On Main, 335
On the Fly, 180
On the Inca Trail, 442
On the Move Inc., 430
Once Upon A Time, 162
One 212, 124
One Cookie Place, 185
One Hanes Place, 121
One Shubert Alley, 335
One Sport Outdoor Footwear, 101
One Step Ahead, 51, 57, 67, 422
One-Off Titanium, 66
One-Up Health & Sport Inc., 259
Oneida Labs Inc., 9
O'Neill, 392
Onkyo, 403, 404, 425

CORPORATE INDEX

Online Press Inc., 89
Only the Lightest Camping Equipment, 101, 104
Ontario Knife Company, 306
Oomingmak Musk Ox Producers' Co-operative, 124
Opel GT Source, 39
Opels Unlimited, 39
Open Sesame, 272, 436
Open Systems Computing Corporation, 142
Opening Scene Replicas, 162
Opera Box, 20, 89, 319, 343
Oppenheim's, 152, 173, 383
Optec Inc., 18
Optek Sunglass Corporation, 407
Optional Extras, 59, 300
Options Auto Salon, 25, 31, 34, 36, 37, 42
Optron Systems, 18, 69
Oradell International Corporation, 436
Orange Cherry, 142
Orange Trading Company, 130
Orb Weaver, 304
Orbis Books, 94
Orbit Manufacturing Company, 211
Orchid Club, 237
Orchid Gardens, 232, 243, 244, 246
Orchid Thoroughbreds, 237
Orchids by Hauserman Inc., 237
Orchids etc!, 255
Orcon, 219
Oreck Corporation, 183, 428
Oregon Apiaries, 201
Oregon Desert Brine Shrimp, 352
Oregon Dome Living Inc., 283
Oregon Hill Farms Inc., 201
Oregon Historical Society, 249
Oregon Miniature Roses, 240
Oregon Scientific, 118, 270, 433
Oregon Software Outlet, 137
Oregon Tailor Supplies, 383
Oregon Territory Company, 194
Oregon Wooden Screen Door Company, 275
O'Reilly & Associates, 89
Orgel's Orchids, 231, 237
Oriental Crest Inc., 297, 300
Oriental Lamp Shade Company, 311
Oriental Pantry, 190
Oriental Rug Company, 378, 385
Oriental Trading Company Inc., 107, 210, 255
Origami USA, 345
Origin Systems Inc., 142
Original Appalachian Artworks Inc., 165
Original Auto Interiors, 49
Original Cast Lighting, 277, 308, 310
Original Lincoln Logs, 284
Original Log Homes, 284
Original Paper Collectibles, 346
Original Parts Group Inc., 28, 31, 34, 35, 37, 40, 41
Original Print Collectors Group Ltd., 14
Originals By Elaine Inc., 164, 165
Orion Motors Inc., 32, 43
Orion Telescope & Binocular Center, 18, 69
Orlando's Classic & Sports Car Specialists, 26, 40
Orleans Carpenters, 150, 215
Ornamental Mouldings, 280
Ornamental Resources Inc., 300, 383
Orrefors Kosta Boda USA, 153
Ortho Books, 89
Ortho-Kinetics, 216
Ortho-Vent Inc., 259, 387
Orton, 113
Orvis Manchester, 255

Orvis Travel, 124, 255, 314
Osaanyin Herb Cooperative, 196, 233
Osagian, 74
Osborne Wood Products, 212, 439
Oshkosh Direct, 120
OSI Direct, 104
Osprey Aircraft, 2
Osprey Packs, 104
Ostercraft Inc., 75
Osto-Covers, 346
Ostomed Healthcare, 346
Ostomy Discount of America, 346
Ostomy Supply & Care Center Inc., 346
Otis Home Center Inc., 406
Otomix, 95, 318
Otsego Cedar Log Homes, 284
Otsuka, 124
Ott's Art Supplies, 11, 99
Out & In Furnishings, 218
Out N Back, 270, 381
Out of Control Swimwear Inc., 124
Out of the Past Parts, 29, 31, 33, 35, 39, 40
Out of the Woods Sign Makers, 388
Out of the Woodwork, 250, 255, 368, 422
Out On A Whim, 59, 300
Out There Gear, 101
Outback Ranch, 285
Outbound Golf Inc., 260
Outbound Products, 104
Outcrop, 375
Outdoor Kitchen, 105
Outdoor Outlet, 104
Outdoor Publications, 89
Outdoor Research, 270
Outdoor Wilderness Fabrics, 173, 383
Outer Limits, 422
Outers Laboratories Inc., 266
OuterSpace Landscape Furnishings Inc., 175, 223
Outhouse, 255, 274
Outhouse (Tom) 407, 434
Outstamping, 377
Ovation Instruments, 339
Overhead Door, 218
Overland Equipment, 67, 104
Overlook Connection, 89, 343
Overton's Sports Center Inc., 77, 432
Owen (Richard) Nursery 236
Owen Upp Railroader's Supply Company, 330
Owl Darts, 68, 156
Owl Photo Corporation, 359
Owl Software Corporation, 142
Oxbow Square Dance Shop, 400
Oxfam Publishing, 89
Oxford Chime Works, 5, 274
Oxford Craft Software, 142, 305
Oxford Paperbacks, 89
Oxmoor House, 89, 152
Oyate Kin Cultural Cooperative, 294
Ozark Basketry Supply, 56, 114
Ozark Herb & Spice Company, 430
Ozark Mountain Smoke House Inc., 198

P

P & P Lines, 330
P.C. Mary's Inc., 119
P.J.'s Miniatures, 162
Paasche Airbrush Company, 11
Pace (Barrie) Ltd. 124
Pachart Publishing House, 89
Pachmayr Ltd., 101, 104, 265
Pacific Aircraft, 325

Pacific Arts Publishing, 429
Pacific Auto Accessories, 24
Pacific Coast Avionics, 4
Pacific Log Homes Ltd., 284
Pacific Motorbooks, 89
Pacific Tree Farms, 231, 244
Pacific Water Sports, 74
Pacific Wine Cellar Consultants, 438
Pack Central Inc., 108, 110
Packard Bell, 135
Packard Farm, 39, 41
Packard Woodworks, 418
Packo (Tony) Food Company 205
Paddle & Pack Outfitters Inc., 74, 104
Paddock Inc., 27, 28, 33, 34, 38
Page (J.) Basketry 56, 182, 362, 435
Page (James) Brewing Company 437
PageCom, 373
Pagliacco Turning & Milling, 280
Pakboats, 74, 75
Paladin Electronics, 5, 294
Paladin Press, 89
Palais du Chocolat, 187
Palancar Jewelers, 297
PaleoSearch Inc., 374
Palestine Orchids Inc., 237
Palisades Pharmaceuticals Inc., 346
Palladio Company, 357
Palm Beach International, 297
Palm City Metal Finishing, 43
Palmer (B.) Sales Company Inc. 107, 210, 347
Palmer Industries, 436
Palmer's Maple Syrup, 196
Palmetto Apiaries, 64
Palmetto Linen Company, 63, 409, 420
Palminteri (Fran) 80
Palmren, 418
Palomar Optical Supply, 18
Palomino Square Dance Service, 400
Palos Verdes Begonia Farm, 242
Pan Abode Inc., 283
Pan Handler Products Inc., 201
Panasonic, 7, 46, 99, 135, 137, 403, 404, 411, 425
Panasonic Bicycle Division, 66
Panasonic Cordless Power Tools, 419
Pandora's Box Mail Order, 255
Panelectric, 211
Panels by Paith, 410
Pangaea Scientific, 142
Pannikin Mail Order, 130, 207, 303
Panola Pepper Corporation, 205
Panorama Camera, 89, 355
Pant Warehouse, 124
Panther, 322
Panther Productions, 318
Papa's Gameroom, 68, 156, 409, 424
Paper & Ink Books, 89
Paper Access, 145
Paper Angel, 377
Paper Chase, 336
Paper Collectors' Mart, 336, 343
Paper Direct Inc., 145, 344
Paper Place & Doll Place, 61, 165
Paper Showcase, 344
Papercuttings by Alison, 347
Papillon, 124
Papillon Studio Supply & Manufacturing, 410
Papke Enterprises, 33, 36
Papyrus Design Group, 142
PAR Seating Specialists, 46, 217
Par-Porsche Specialists, 40
Para Systems Inc., 137
Para-Gear Equipment Company Inc., 3

CORPORATE INDEX

Para-Phernalia Inc., 3
Paradigm Foodworks, 106, 185, 187
Paradise Mills Inc., 379
Paradise Products, 347
Paradise Water Gardens, 227
ParaFURnalia Pet Products, 255
Paragon Gifts, 255
Paragon Industries, 113, 115
Paragon Products, 57
Paragon Reproductions Inc., 30
ParaPlane International, 4
Parascender Technologies Inc., 4
Parasound Products Inc., 403
Paris Company Inc., 393
Park & Sun Inc., 52
Park (Homer E.) 64
Park Avenue Record Planet, 108, 110
Park Bears, 61
Park Bench Pattern Company, 385
Park Place, 223, 277
Park Seed Company,
    226, 230, 234, 236, 242
Park Tool Brochure, 67
Parker (J.) 165
Parker's (Bob) Sports Collectibles 15
Parkers' Knife Collector Service, 306
Parks Optical Company, 18, 69
Parlor Bears, 61
Parmer Studebaker Sales, 41
Parrish's Cake Decorating, 106
Parsons' Minerals & Fossils, 374
Parsons Technology, 142, 250
Parts Express, 167
Parts Hotline, 25, 40, 41
Parts Place, 37, 39
Passap, 304
Passport International Ltd., 124
Past Gas, 21
Past Patterns, 385
Past Times, 255
Past-Time Hobbies Inc., 326
Pasta Fresca, 190
Pasta Mama's, 190
Pastille, 124
Patagonia, 101, 120
Patagonia Mail Order, 71
Patchworks, 173
PATCO, 354
Paterson, 357
Path to Wellness, 350
Patio, 218
Patio Garden Ponds, 227
Patio Pacific Inc., 353
Patrician Industries Inc., 39
Patrick's Fly Shop, 180
Patrick's Nursery, 230, 233, 239, 242, 244
Patriot Company, 220
Patriots Plus, 182
Pat's Miniatures, 162
Patsy's Italian Restaurant, 190
Pattern Warehouse, 342, 385
Patterncrafts, 342, 420
Patterns by Diane, 60, 420, 424
Patterns from Simpler Times, 385
Patternworks, 304, 342
Patti Music Company, 337
Patton Orphan Spares, 40
Paua Fibre Ltd., 442
Paul & Judy's Coins & Cards, 131, 398, 399
Paul (Les), Steinologist 64
Paul, Steinologist 64
Pauli's Wholesale Optics, 18, 69
Paul's Chrome Plating Inc., 43
Pavey (Terry & Noreen) Postcards 365
Paw Paw Everlast Label Company, 223

Paxton Hardware Ltd., 268
Paxtron, 133
PBS Home Video, 429
PC Brand Inc., 135
PC Connection, 145
PC Solutions, 137, 145
PC Weather Products Inc., 433
PC Zone, 134
PCA Industries Inc., 171, 363
PCBoards, 167
PCs Compleat, 137
PD Source Inc., 3
Peaceful Valley Farm Supply,
    219, 224, 230, 232, 244
Peach State Photo, 100, 361
Peachtree Software, 142
Peachtree Windows & Doors, 275
Peacock Alley Needlepoint Crafts, 342
Peacock Crate Factory, 56
Peak Publishing, 402
Peanut Patch Inc., 199
Peanut Shop of Williamsburg, 194, 199, 210
Pearl Harbor Hobbies, 325
Pearl Izumi, 66, 124, 380, 391
Pearl Paint, 11
Pearson's Auto Dismantling & Used Cars, 24
Pease Boatworks, 76
Pease Industries Inc., 50, 275
Peavey Electronics Corporation, 414
Pecan Producers International, 187, 199
Pecci (David) Carpentry 72
Peck (S.A.) & Company 297
Peck-Polymers, 325
PeCo Inc., 226
Peconic Paddler, 71, 74, 77
Pecos Pine, 424
Pedal Pusher Ski & Sport, 67
Pedersen's Metal Detectors, 321, 367
Pedigrees Pet Catalog, 128, 351
Peekskill Nurseries, 234
Peerless Imported Rugs, 379, 409
Peerless Reel Company, 180
Peerless Wallpaper & Blind Depot, 153, 281
Peet Bros. Company, 433
Peg's Dollhouse, 162
Pehrson (Barbra) Jewelry 297
Pelham Marionettes, 368
Pelham Prints, 21
Pelican Products Inc., 355
Pella Windows & Doors, 282
Pen Y Bryn, 228, 229, 231, 232, 237, 239
Pendell Apiaries, 64
Pendery's Inc., 190, 205
Pendle Company Inc., 146
Pendleton Cowgirl Company, 14, 128, 402
Pendleton Shop, 124, 126, 397, 442
Pendragon, 99
Pendragon Software Library, 137
Pendray's (Shay) Needle Arts Inc. 342
Penelope Craft Programs Inc., 142, 305
Penelope's of Evergreen Ltd., 201
Pengellys, 20
Penguin in Paradise Miniatures, 162
Penguin Industries Inc., 264
Penguin Stamps, 377
Penhall Eyewear, 407
Peninsula Bead & Supply, 59
Peninsula Import Auto Parts, 34, 37
Peninsula Imports, 42
Penn Auto Sales, 25
Penn Fishing Tackle, 180
Penn Herb Company, 349
Penn Photomounts, 354
Penn Racquet Sports, 370
Penn State Industries, 419

Penney (J.C.) Company Inc.
    51, 53, 54, 57, 119, 120, 121, 122, 124, 126,
    127, 128, 158, 171, 208, 266, 382, 425, 426
Pennington Pet Products, 350
Pennray Billiard & Recreational Products,
    68, 156, 394
Penn's Woods Products Inc., 158
Pennsylvania Heritage Society, 249
Pennsylvania Historical & Genealogy Society,
    249
Pennsylvania State Archives, 249
Penny Rugs & Runners, 378
Penny Saver Medical Supply, 159, 346
Pennylane Beads, 59
Pennysticks, 185
Pennzoni Wood Products, 160
Pense Nursery, 230
PentaPure, 431
Pentax Corporation,
    69, 99, 356, 357, 358, 425
Penthouse Gallery, 124
Penzey's Spice House, 205
Pepco Poms, 114
Peper (Tom) 20, 336, 347
Pepper Gal, 242
Pepper Plant, 205
Pepperell Stamp Works, 377
Pepperidge Farm, 194, 303
Per Madsen Design, 111
Perazzi USA Inc., 265
Perception, 74
Perceptor, 18, 69
Percharo Jewelry, 290
Percy's Inc., 8, 404, 426
Perego (Peg) U.S.A. Inc. 51
Perennial Pleasures Nursery, 234, 239
Pereya (Arnet) Aero Design 2
Perfect Image Sports Cards, 399
Perfect Palette, 415
Perfect Plastics Industries Inc., 26, 31, 32
Perfect Skin by Buddy Maurice, 148
Perfectly Safe, 51, 381
Performance Accessories, 333
Performance Automotive Warehouse, 24
Performance Bicycle Shop, 66, 67
Performance Corner, 24, 49
Performance Diver, 392
Performance Golf Company, 260
Performance Miniatures, 326
Performance Motorcycle Center, 333
Performance Products, 40
Performance Speedway, 258
Perfumes for Less, 148
Peri Lithon Books, 89
Period Lighting Fixtures, 308, 310
Peripherals Plus, 145
Perkasie Industries Corporation, 282
Perkins (H.H.) Company 56, 114, 315
Perkins Architectural Millwork & Hardwood
    Mouldings, 280
Perkowitz Window Fashions Inc., 278
Perma-Type Company Inc., 346
Permobil, 436
Perpetual Perennials, 239
Persona Farms Food Specialties, 202
Personal Creations, 255
Personal Flight Inc., 4
Personal Stamp Exchange, 377
Personal Threads Boutique, 342, 442
Personal Touch, 71
Personal Touch Stationery, 255, 402
Persson (M.E.) 130
Perugina Chocolates, 187
Peruvian Bead Company, 59
Peruvian Connection, 127

CORPORATE INDEX

Pet Bird Express, 350
Pet Bookshop, 90
Pet Castle, 353
Pet Doors U.S.A., 353
Pet Food Warehouse, 353
Pet USA, 351
Pet Warehouse, 350, 351, 352
Pet Xpress, 352
Pet-Eze, 353
Petals, 182, 255
Peter Pauls Nurseries, 231, 243
Peterman (J.) Company 124, 255
Peters Feeders, 70
Peterson (Robert H.) Company 176
Peterson Instant Targets Inc., 266
Petite Innovations, 162
Petite Ms, 126
Petra Foods International Inc., 190
Petro Classics, 21
Petrossian Shop, 188, 194, 202
Petry's Junk Yard Inc., 24
Pets Unlimited, 227
Pettersen Infant Products, 51
Petticoat Express, 121
Pettit (R.H.) 80
Pewter Classics, 165
Pezzini Farms, 192, 205
PF Engineering, 40
Pfaelzer Brothers, 194, 198
Pfaff American Sales Corporation, 385
Pfaltzgraff Factory Outlet, 116
Pfingst & Company Inc., 419
PFS Inc., 359
PFS Video Inc., 319, 429
PG Music Inc., 143
Phamous Phloyd's Inc., 205
Phantom Fireworks, 177
Phantom Sport Airplane, 2
Phat Tire, 67
Phifer Wire Products Inc., 281
Philadelphia Print Shop Ltd., 6, 318
Philbates Auto Wrecking Inc., 24
Philips Consumer Electronics, 135
Philips Home Products, 218
Philips Laser Magnetic Storage, 133
Phillips (Archie) Taxidermy 410
Phillips (Charles T.) 323
Phillips Exotic Mushrooms, 192
Phillips-Tech Electronics, 427
Philly's Camera, 100
Phipps Ranch, 192, 194
Phoenix Big & Tall, 127
Phoenix Fossils, 374
Phoenix Model Company, 325, 327, 328
Phone Flies, 180
Phone Wizard, 410
Phone-TTY Inc., 273
Phoneco Inc., 410
Phonic Ear Inc., 273
Photek Backgrounds, 355
Photo Antiquities, 319
Photo Card Specialists Inc., 97
Photo Images, 97
Photo-Tech Inc., 355
Photo-Therm, 357
Photocomm Inc., 395
Photoflex, 355, 358
Photogenic Machine Company, 358
Photographers Formulary, 171, 357
Photographer's Place, 90, 355
Photographers Specialized Services, 355
Photographer's Warehouse, 358
Photographic Products, 355
Photographic Systems, 361
Photographica, 362

Photon Instrument Ltd., 18
Photosmith, 359
Phototech, 359
Physical Fashions, 155
Pickens Minerals, 375
Pickering Anomalies, 16
PicoScience, 16
Pictures Plus Marketing Corporation, 97
PiDiDDLE's T-Shirt Factory, 128
Pieces of History, 90, 322
Piedmont Home Products Inc., 278
Piedmont Mantel & Millwork, 177, 275
Piedmont Plant Company, 245
Pierce Aero Company, 325
Pierce Company, 354, 355
Pierce Sales, 48, 285
Pierce Tools, 113, 164
Pierre (Chief George) Trading Post 290
Pig Out Publications, 90
Pigeon Mountain Industries, 396
Pikes Peak Nurseries, 244
Pikes Peak Rock Shop, 300, 374
Pikled Garlik Company, 205
Pillows for Ease, 270
Pilot Supplies, 4
Pin Breaker Inc., 95
Pine Garden Bonsai, 231
Pine Ridge Country Honey, 201
Pine River Salvage, 24
Pine Tree Molds, 113
Pinetree Garden Seeds, 226, 242
PING, 259
Pinnacle Micro, 137
Pinnacle Orchards, 192, 194
Pinnacle Publishing Inc., 143
Pinocchio's Miniatures, 162
Pinpoint Publishing, 208
Pinseeker Golf Clubs, 259
Pioneer Classic Auto Inc., 29, 49
Pioneer Electronics, 403
Pioneer Gem Corporation, 300
Pioneer Log Systems Inc., 284
Pioneer Millworks, 314
Pioneer Mining Supplies, 321, 367
Pioneer New Media Technologies, 46, 133, 403, 404, 405, 425
Pioneer Press, 90
Pioneer Research, 69
Pioneer Research Inc., 362
Pioneer Table Pad Company, 409
Pipestone Indian Shrine Association, 291
Piragis Northwoods Company, 74, 78, 105
Pirate Models, 325
PISA Corporation, 44, 45
Pisces Coral & Fish, 352
Pisces Productions, 443
Pitcairn-Ferguson & Associates Inc., 386
Pitt Petri, 255
Pittman & Davis, 185, 192, 198, 218
Pittman (Preston) Game Calls 288
Pixel Perfect Software, 271
PJ Distributors Inc., 162, 255
Placer Equipment Mfg. Inc., 367
Plaid Enterprises, 11, 210, 415
Plain Folk, 150
Plain 'n Fancy Kitchens, 97
Planet Electronics, 100, 405, 411, 426
Planetary Percussion, 339
Planetary Society, 90, 361, 429
Planetree Health Resource Center, 90
Plant (Bud) Comic Art 90, 131
Plant (Bud) Illustrated Books 94
Plant Collectibles, 222, 224
Plant Delights Nursery, 239
Planta Dei Medicinal Herb Farm,
 148, 234, 270, 319
Plantation Bee Company, 64
Plantation Bulb Company, 239, 242
Planters International, 224
Plants of the Southwest, 234, 246
Plastic Creations, 57, 286
Plastimo USA Inc., 79
Plath (C.) 78, 79
Plating Service, 43, 169
Play Incorporated, 133
Play It Again, 423
Play-Mor Trailers Inc., 48
Playboy, 255
Playclothes, 120
Player Piano Company, 337, 339
Playfair Shuffleboard Company Inc., 388
Playfair Toys, 422
Playhouse, 61, 165
Playworld Systems, 363
Plaza Furniture Inc., 215
Pleasant Company, 51, 120, 165
Pleasant Mountain Woodworks, 369
Pleasant Valley Glads, 242
Pleasurable Piercings Inc., 410
Pletzel Company, 183
Plexi-Craft Quality Products, 215
Plextor, 133
Plimoth Lollipop Company, 187
PLOP, 259
Plow & Hearth, 70, 176, 218, 226, 255
Plumeria People, 235, 239
Plummer-McCutcheon, 255
Plymouth Cheese Corporation, 189
Plymouth Reed & Cane, 56
PMI Petzal Distribution Inc., 396
PMI Petzal Distributors Inc., 334
PML Film Processing, 359
Pocket Songs, 110
Pocono Mountain Optics, 18, 69
Poestenkill Hiking Staff, 106
Poise N' Ivy, 70
Polar Golf, 260
Polaris Electronics Industries, 408
Polaris Industries, 295, 393
Polaroid Corporation, 356, 357
Polaroid Imaging Systems, 336
Poleske (Lee) 347
Political Americana, 364
Political Gallery, 364
Polk Audio, 405
Polk's Model-Craft Hobbies Inc., 325, 327, 328, 329
Pollard Company, 28
Polo Grounds, 20
Poly Fiber Aircraft Coatings, 4
Poly-Metric, 300
Polyform Products Company, 12
PolyMedica Healthcare Inc., 270
PolyPhaser Corporation, 167
Polywell Computers Inc., 135
Pomegranate Calendars & Books, 98
Pompeian Studios, 218, 223
Ponsness/Warren, 262
Pony Express Horsemen's Supply, 284
Pony USA Inc., 54, 95, 120, 369
Pooch! Emporium for Dogs & Cats, 351
Pool Fence Company, 175, 408
Poolaw (Chief) Tepee Trading Post 291
Pootatuck, 210
Pop Tent, 104
Popcorn Factory, 200
Popcorn World Inc., 200
Pope (Neal) Inc. 327
Popie's Brands Inc., 205
Popular Topics Publications, 90

❖ CORPORATE INDEX ❖

Porcelain by Marilyn, 164
Porch Factory, 280
Poriloff Caviar, 188
Port Canvas Inc., 314
Port Chatham Smoked Seafood, 202
Port Supply/Lifesling, 72
Porta Dock Inc., 295
Porta-Bote International, 75
Porta-Fab Corporation, 386
Porta-Nails Inc., 419
Portable Blinds Inc., 287
Portell Restorations, 424
Porter Athletic Equipment Company, 52, 55, 152
Porter Auto Repair & Salvage, 24
Porter Case Inc., 355
Porter Emporium, 165
Porter-Cable, 419
Porter's Camera Store Inc., 357, 361, 426
Porter's Pick-A-Dilly, 205
Portland Radio Supply, 372
Portland Willamette, 176
Portrayal Press, 22, 90
Posh Papers, 402
Positive Books, 81
Positively Country, 415
Post & Beam Design Company, 283
Post Fence Company, 175
Post Scripts from Joan Cook, 255
Postcard News & Sales, 365
Postcards Etc., 365
Postcards from Paradise, 365
Postcards International, 365
Poster Restoration Studio, 6
Posteritati, 336
Posters of Santa Fe, 14
Poston Enterprises, 27
Posty Cards, 98, 261
Posy Patch Originals, 162
Pot of Gold, 321, 367
Potlatch Traders, 365
Potomac Museum Group, 374
Potomac Technology, 273
Potpourri, 255
Potsy & Blimpo Clown Supplies, 130, 414
Potters Shop, 90
Potterton-Myson, 57
Pottery Barn, 255
Pottery Place, 116
Poulan, 224, 225, 226, 227, 419
Pourette Manufacturing, 105, 393
Powell, 180
Powell & Powell Supply Company, 220
Powell (Anne) Ltd. 342
Powell (J.L.) & Company Inc. 275
Powell (Joe) Golf Inc. 259
Powell Apiaries, 64
Power Access Corporation, 272
Power Tool Specialists, 419
Power Up Software, 143
Power-King, 227
Power-Sail Corporation, 432
Powermatic Inc., 419
Powers Court, 413
PowerVideo, 100, 405, 426
Pozzi Wood Windows, 282
Practical Peripherals, 133
Practitioners Publishing Company, 90
PRADCO, 180
Prairie Edge, 294
Prairie Moon Nursery, 246
Prairie Nursery, 246
Prairie Ridge Nursery, 246
Prairie State Commodities, 234
Prather Products Inc., 328

Prathers Custom Cue Parts Inc., 68
Pratt (Wallace D.), Bookseller 94
Precept Ministries, 94, 110, 429
Preceptor Aircraft, 2
Precious Collection, 434
Precious Little Things, 162
Precise International, 380
Precision Aerodynamics Inc., 3
Precision Craft Log Structures, 284
Precision Movements, 118
Precision Optical, 316, 407
Precision Reloading Inc., 262
Precision Sales International, 265
Precision Scale Company, 330
Precision Type, 145
Precor USA, 171
Predator Camouflage, 287
Predator Performance Inc., 44
Preferred Living, 255
Preferred Rx of Ohio, 159
Prehistoric Journeys, 374
Premier International Inc., 104
Premier Kites Inc., 304
Premium Image, 198
Prentiss Court, 328
Prentiss Court Ground Covers, 234
Presentations Gallery, 14, 118, 255
Preservation Products, 277
Presidential Coin & Antique Company, 364
Preso-Matic Keyless Locks, 5
Press-On-Products, 210
Pressley's, 255
Prestige Imports, 25, 35, 36
Prestige Promotions, 96, 349
Prestige Thunderbird Inc., 42
Preston (J.A.) Corporation 270
Preston's, 79, 328
Preston's Car Parts, 329
Pretty Punch, 342
Priba Furniture Sales & Interiors, 215
Price (Gary) Studio 223
Price (Jerry) 322
Price (Michael G.) Postcards 365
Price Toyota Newark, 42
Price-Music Sales, 110
Pricille's Stencils, 162, 402
Pride & Joy Announcements, 71
Pride Health Care Inc., 436
Priep (Bob) 328
Priester's Pecans, 199
Prima, 260
Primarily Pillows, 63
Primary Layer, 121
Primax Electronics, 133
Prime Access, 198
Prime Electronic Components Inc., 167
Prime Meat Express, 198
Prime Time Video & Cameras, 100
Primex of California, 22, 74
Primos Inc., 288
Primrose Distributing, 276
Primrose Path, 239, 246
Primus-Sievert Inc., 226
Prince Racquet Sports, 370, 411, 413
Prince Tennis Ball Machine, 413
Print Books, 90
Printery House, 261
PrintProd Inc., 344
Private Garden Greenhouses, 220
Privateer Sportswear, 128
PRO Antique Auto Parts, 25, 27, 29, 31, 33, 37, 39, 40
PRO Chemical & Dye Inc., 171
Pro Photo Labs, 359
Pro Shop World of Golf, 260

Pro Sound & Stage Lighting, 414
Pro-Form, 171
Pro-Kennex, 413
Pro-Mack Mining Supplies, 367
Pro-Mack South, 90, 367
Pro-Mark Corporation, 339
Pro-Sing Karaoke, 339
Pro4 Imaging Inc., 357
ProAm, 46
Proctor Enterprises, 325, 329
PRODIGY Service, 143
Product Innovations Inc., 303
Profeel Video, 100
Professional Cutlery Direct, 303
Professional Golf & Tennis Suppliers, 260, 370, 411, 413
Professional Golf Factory, 260
Professional Gym Inc., 171, 267
Professional Press, 343
Professional Tattoo Kits, 410
Professional Technologies, 135
Professional Video Warehouse, 100
Profiles in History, 20
Profit Potentials, 211
Profoto, 361
Programmer's Shop, 145
Progressive Aerodyne, 2
Progressive Building Products, 220, 396
Progressive Business Associates, 317
Project Pluto Software, 16
Prolitho Inc., 97, 402
Promenade Le Bead Shop, 59
Pronto Business Cards, 97
Proprioception Inc., 443
Proscenium Lighting, 414
Prospectors Pouch Inc., 300
Prosser Telephone Company, 410
Protector Enterprises, 408
Proton Corporation, 46, 404, 405, 425
Provincial Ceramic Products, 113
Prudent Publishing, 261
Pruett Publishing Company, 90
PS Engineering, 4
PSI Performance, 295
PTI Antique Radios, 372
Public Missiles Ltd., 327
Publications International Ltd., 90
Publisher's Toolbox, 145
Publishing Perfection, 137
Pueblo of Zuni Arts & Crafts, 292
Pueblo to People, 194, 199, 255
Pullen (Martha) Company Inc. 173
Pulpers, 347
Pulps, 131
Puma USA Inc., 53, 54, 66, 120, 369, 370, 380, 394, 411, 425, 431
PUR Water Purifiers, 431
Purcells Activewear, 54
Purchase for Less, 90
Purely American, 194
Puritan's Pride, 148, 430
Puritan's Pride/Stur-Dee Health Products, 430
Purple Wave Stamp Designs, 377
Purr-sonality Plus Kit Company, 152
Putnam Rolling Ladder Company Inc., 307
Putney Nursery Inc., 246
Putnum Distributors, 210
Putt (Charles) 150
Puzzling, 368
Pygmy Boat Company, 74, 76
Pyramid Film & Video, 337, 429
Pyramid Industries, 367
Pyramid Products Company, 435
Pyramid Cooking Equipment, 104

❖ CORPORATE INDEX ❖

Pyrotek, 307
Python Products Inc., 353

Q

Q-C Turquoise, 297, 300
Qelags USA Inc., 431
Qesearch Mannikins Inc., 410
QMS Inc., 133
Quad City Ultralight Aircraft, 2
Quad Energy, 395
Quadratec, 35
Quaker Boy Inc., 288
Quaker City Type., 366
Quaker Maid, 98
Qualcomm Inc., 411
Qualin International, 171, 173
Quality Arms Inc., 264
Quality Baseball Cards Inc., 399
Quality Collectables, 14, 363, 364
Quality Discount Carpet, 379
Quality Dutch Bulbs, 232, 238, 242
Quality Lists, 317
Quality Recharge Company, 146
Quality Sheepskin, 46
Quality Swings Inc., 266
Quality Wood Products, 415
Quality Woods Ltd., 275
Qualla Arts & Crafts Mutual Inc., 293
Quantum Creations, 18
Quantum Instruments Inc., 358
Quantum Quests International, 443
Quarterdeck, 327, 328
Quarterdeck Office Systems, 143
Quartermaster Shop, 149
Quasar, 99, 404, 425
Quasar Optics, 18, 69
Que Corporation (Books), 90
Queen's Shilling, 20, 90
Queensboro Shirt Company, 126
Quest for Rare Books, 90
Quest International, 362
Quest Outfitters, 101, 173, 384
Quest-Eridon Books, 336
Questair, 2
Questar, 18
Quester Gallery, 6
Quick (Jamie) Reptiles 354
Quick Tickets, 414
Quicksilver Enterprises, 2
Quicksilver Inflatable, 75
Quikkit, 2
Quill Computers, 137
Quill Office Supplies, 98, 344
Quill-It, 347
Quilted Treasures, 62
Quilts Unlimited, 62
Quimby's Paddle Designs, 74
Quintanar (Enrique) 162
Quintana's Gallery of Indian & Western Art, 293

R

R & A Cycles Inc., 66
R & J Slots, 130
R & L Electronics, 372
R & N Miniatures, 162
R & R Books, 90
R & R Enterprises, 20
R & S Surplus, 169
R-Molds, 113
R.A. Enterprises, 168
R.C. Distributing, 427
R.F. Nature Farm Foods Inc., 96, 183
R.J. Tackle Inc., 180
R.T.S. Inc./Sekonic, 357, 358, 362
R.V.R. Optical, 18
Raab (Steven S.) 14, 20, 343, 347
Rabbit Shadow Farm, 227, 232, 234, 240
Racer Walsh Company, 28, 31, 38, 39
Racing Strollers Inc., 51, 171
Rackets International, 52
Radar City, 44
Radar U.S.A., 43, 44
Radbill (Mary) Doll Supplies 164
Rader's Horse House, 107
Radiant Technology Inc., 211
Radiantec, 211
Radio Adventures Inc., 168, 372
Radio Bookstore, 90
Radio Electric Supply, 372
Radio Fence, 175, 353
Radio Library, 110, 111
Radio Shack, 5, 43, 46, 99, 137, 168, 176, 270, 273, 373, 381, 404, 411, 423, 425
Radio Showcase, 111
Radio-Holland Group, 79
Rafal Spice Company, 205, 207
Ragged Mountain Antler Chandeliers, 158, 308
Ragged Mountain Equipment, 334
Ragtime, 339
Ragtime Crochet, 342
Raichle Molitor USA, 101, 391, 392
Raima Corporation, 143
Raiments, 149
Rain Bird, 228
Rain Control, 228
Rain or Shine, 220
Rainbow Designs, 72
Rainbow Factory, 165
Rainbow Gardens Bookshop, 90, 231, 236
Rainbow Mealworms & Crickets, 354
Rainbow Sports Shop, 376
Rainbow Woods, 439
Rainbow Woodworks, 212
Raindrip Inc., 228
Raindrops on Roses Rubber Stamp Company, 150, 377
Rainshed Outdoor Fabrics, 101, 173, 384, 385
Raintree Nursery, 224, 230, 232, 244
Rainy Day Books, 90
Rainy Lake Puzzles, 368
Rainy's Flies & Supplies, 180
Raleigh Cycle Company of America, 66
Ram Golf Clubs, 259
Rambod (Max) Autographs 20
RAMCO Computer Supplies, 146
Ramptech Design & Construction, 376
Ramsey Electronics Inc., 168
Ramsey Irrigation Systems, 228
Ramsey Outdoor Store, 101, 104, 180
Ranch Pit Shop, 327
Ranco Deluxe Design Books, 90
Rand McNally & Company, 255, 258, 318
Rand McNally New Media, 143
Rand-Robinson Engineering Inc., 2
Randall-Made Knives, 306
Randle Woods, 314
Random House, 90
Random Inc., 135
Random Sound Inc., 399
Rands Custom Hats, 269
Ranger All Season Corporation, 436
Ranger Manufacturing Company Inc., 104
Ranger Portable Kennels, 353
Rans Company, 2
Rapazzini Winery, 205

Rapid Raffles, 415
Rapid River Rustic Inc., 284
Rapidforms Inc., 343, 345
Rapine Bullet Manufacturing Company, 262, 323
Raskas (Ann) Candies 187, 206
Raskas Candies 206
Raskin (Arlene L.) Postcards 365
Rasland Farm, 182, 232, 234
Rasmussen (Mike E.) Postcards 365
Rat City Sports, 390
Rau (M.S.) 7
Rau (Walter) & Company 51
Rave Carpets, 379
Raven Maps & Images, 318
Raven Tripods, 362
Raven's Den, 291
Ravenworks Studio, 368
Rawlings Sporting Goods Company, 54, 55, 209
Ray (J.F.) 374, 382
Ray (Jim) 306
Rayburn Musical Instrument Company, 339
Rayco Paint Company, 388
RayCo Tennis, 412, 413
Raynor Garage Doors, 218
Ray's (Steven) Bamboo Gardens 229
Ray's Reptiles, 354
Raytech, 300, 312
Raytheon Marine Company, 79
Razor & Tie Music, 110
Razor Edge Systems Inc., 306
RBIndustries, 419
RCA Sales Corporation, 99, 404, 426
RDS Company, 9
Reach Out, 110
Readco Corporation, 180
Reader's Digest, 90, 429
Ready Wear Company, 385
Ready-Tickets, 415
Readybuilt Products Company, 177
Real Cookies Inc., 185
Real Good Toys, 162
Real Goods, 255, 373, 395, 424
Real Log Homes, 284
RealBark Hunting Systems, 287
Realtree Camouflage, 287
Reasonable Solutions, 137
Reb Acres, 323
Recap Universal, 255
Recco Maid Embroidery Company, 156
Recorded Books Inc., 94
Recoton, 403, 404, 405
Recovery Engineering, 432
Recreation Unlimited, 295
Recreatives Industries Inc., 5
Recreonics Corporation, 114, 407, 409, 424
Recycled Cycles Inc., 333, 393
Red & Green Minerals Inc., 59, 118, 320, 376
Red Ball Consumer Products, 386
Red Barn Ceramics Inc., 113
Red Bear Creations, 293
Red Caboose, 330
Red Cardinal, 364
Red Clover Rugs, 378
Red Cooper, 192
Red Cross Gifts, 255, 363, 364
Red Feather Arts & Crafts, 150
Red Fox Fine Art, 14, 15
Red Hill Corporation, 152, 419, 440
Red Lancer, 14, 94, 322, 421
Red Lancers Miniatures, 421
Red Rhino, 211
Red River Frontier Outfitters, 129

Red River Portable Arenas, 284
Red Rose Collection, 125, 256, 258
Red Wing Light Boom, 358
Reda Sports Express, 209, 307
Redfeather Arts & Crafts, 388
Redfield Company, 264
Redhead, 287
Rediscover Music Catalogue, 108
Redlich Optical, 18, 69
Redline Racing Collectibles, 405
Redman Wheelchairs, 436
Redwood City Seed Company, 235, 245
Redwood Shop, 247
Redwood Unlimited, 150, 316, 434
Reebok International Ltd., 369, 425
Reed (Blaine) 374
Reed (Carroll) 124
Reed Books, 80
Reed Brothers, 158, 212, 218, 316
Reef Concepts, 352
Reef Displays, 352
Reef Life Inc., 352
Reef Tech, 352
Reel 3-D Enterprises Inc., 355
Reel Memories, 336
Reel World, 90
Reesman (Christopher A.) 316
Reeve (Chris) Knives 306
Reeves Records Inc., 400
Reflections of the Past, 149
Reflections Organic Inc., 124
Refrigeration Research Inc., 286, 395
Regal Engineering Inc., 180
Regalia, 121, 387
Regency Cap & Gown Company, 117
Regency VSA Appliances Ltd., 7
Reggio Register, 370
Regimental Quartermaster, 323
Rego Irish Records & Tapes Inc., 110
REI Recreational Equipment Company, 67, 101, 104, 105, 391
Reich Supply Company Inc., 389
Reid (Chris) Company Inc. 182
Reid's Quality Model Products, 325
Reimers Photo Materials Company, 361
Rejuvenation Lamp & Fixture Company, 310
Relaxo-Back Inc., 46, 272
Relay Technology Inc., 143
Reliable Automatic Sprinkler Company, 176
Reliable Home Office, 98, 146, 217, 428
Reliable Photo Inc., 359
Reliable Racing Supply Inc., 391
REM Industries, 278
Remember These, 319, 365
Remember When Collectibles Inc., 130, 302
Remington Arms Company Inc., 262, 265
Remington Outdoor Products, 104
Remodelers & Renovators Supplies, 57, 268, 275
Renaissance Buttons, 384
Renaissance Greeting Cards Inc., 261
Renaissance Marketing, 15, 258
Rendell (Kenneth W.) Inc. 20
Reno (Eugene & Ellen) 7
Renovator's Supply, 158, 174, 268, 308, 310, 311, 317
Rent Mother Nature, 203, 256
Renzetti Inc., 180
Reon Shower, 57
Rep-Cal Research Labs., 354
Repetto Dance Shoes, 155
Replacement Parts Company, 26, 40
Replacement Service, 116
Replacements Ltd., 117, 153
Replicarz, 327

Replicas by Tyson, 325
Replogle Globes Inc., 258, 407
Repp Big & Tall, 127
Reptile Solutions, 354
Reptile Specialties, 354
Reptile World Imports of Tucson, 354
Reptiles & Beyond, 354
Reptiles Products, 128
Republic of Tea, 207
Resch (Thelma) 164
Research Assistance, 413
Research Products, 57
Research Unlimited, 90
Resolution Mapping Inc., 79, 143
ReSports, 413
Restoration by Costikyan Ltd., 378
Restoration Place, 57, 268, 280, 310
Restoration Specialties & Supply Inc., 24
Restoration Works Inc., 57, 268
Reurs (Catherine) Needlepoint 342
Revere Company, 211
Revere Copper Products Inc., 277
Reverse Osmosis, 432
Revo Sunglass Inc., 407
Revolution Enterprises, 304
Revolution Helicopter Corporation, 2
Revolution Records, 110
Rex Pure Foods Inc., 205
Rex Stark-Americana, 364
Rexcraft, 402, 434
Reyers, 387
RF Parts, 168, 372
RGP Composites, 74
Rhapis Gardens, 237
Rhapis Palm Growers, 235, 237
RheeMax, 319
Rhino Crossbows, 9
Rhino Foods Inc., 185
Rhino Gun Cases Inc., 264, 266
RhinoRamps, 44, 47
Rhoades Car, 66
Rhode Island State Archives, 249
Rhode Island State Genealogical Society, 249
Rhoney Furniture House, 215
Rhythm Band Instruments, 339
Rhythm City, 339
Rhythm Recordings, 110
Ribbecke, 339
Ribbon Factory Outlet, 174
Rich Music, 339
Richard (Charles D. Dwayne) 354
Richards (Anthony) 124
Richards (Deke) 336
Richard's Auto Sales & Salvage, 24
Richards Studio, 280
Richardson Sports Inc., 425
Richardson's Recreational Ranch Ltd., 119, 300, 406
Richeson (Jack) & Company Inc. 11
Richland, 232
Richlee Shoe Company, 387
Richlund Sales, 8, 48
Richmond's Woodworks Inc., 215
Richmoor Corporation, 105
Richters, 242
Rickard (Pete) Inc. 288
Rick's First Generation, 27
Rick's Movie Posters, 336
Ricoh Consumer Products Group, 69, 99, 356, 358
Ricon Corporation, 436
Riddell Inc., 54, 55, 209, 307
Rider Wearhouse, 331
Ridge Carbide Tool Corporation, 419
Ridge Doors, 219

Ridge Runner, 429
Riedel Cycles, 66
Riedell Shoes Inc., 273, 289
Riedell Shoes Inc. P.O. Box 21, 376
Ries (Iwan) & Company 415
Rifle Fairings, 333
Rig Products, 265
Rigby (Wm. J.) Company 268
Rigging Company, 76
Rigging Innovations Inc., 3
Right Hemisphere, 108
Right Start Catalog, 51, 250, 422
Rik's Unlimited, 30
Rinaldi (John F.) Nautical Antiques 7, 79
Rincon-Vitova Insectaries Inc., 219
Rinehart (John) Taxidermy Supply Company 410
Ringer, 220, 226
Rings & Things, 297
Rings 'N' Things, 294
Ringside, 96
Rinnai, 211
Rio Cutlery & Luggage Inc., 306
Rio Grande, 300
Rio Grande Weaver's Supply, 397, 442
RIO Products, 180
Ritchey Design, 66
Ritchie Compasses, 79
Ritter Carvers Inc., 439
Ritz Cameras, 356
Riva-Yamaha, 295
Rivendell Electronics, 372
Rivendell Inc., 164
River Bend Country Store, 196
River Bend Turnings, 280
River Computer Inc., 137
River Connection Crafts & Gifts, 279
River Gems & Findings, 59, 384
Riverbend Timber Framing Inc., 283
Riverhead Perennials, 239
Rivers Antiques, 7
Rivers Edge, 287
Riverside Bonsai, 231
Riverside Gardens, 182
Riverside-World, 94
Rivertown Products, 223
Riverview Molds Inc., 113
Riverwood Creations, 162
Riviera Lapidary Supply, 59, 312, 376, 382, 406
Rizzetta Music, 110, 339
RJC Records, 110
RKA Accessories, 333
RM Water Skis USA, 432
RMS Technology Inc., 143
RNProducts, 365
Ro (Charles) Supply Company 330
Road Runner Sports, 380
Roadster Factory, 43
Roaman's, 121, 124
Roanoke's Record Room, 108
Rob 'N' Wood, 150
Robart Manufacturing, 329
Robbie Music, 110, 319, 336
Robby's Rockets, 327
Robern Inc., 57, 323
Robert (Samuel) Direct 124
Roberts, 361
Roberts (Bruce) Designs 72
Roberts (Joe) Welding 284
Roberts Construction, 367
Roberts Furniture, 218
Roberts Motor Parts, 30, 31, 40, 49
Roberts Rinehart Publishers, 90
Robertson (H.G.) Fine Silver 390

CORPORATE INDEX

Robes (Dana) Wood Craftsmen 215
Robichaud Reels, 180
Robillard (N.) 354
Robin (Clyde) Seed Catalog 246
Robinson Helicopter Company, 2
Robinson Iron Corporation, 218
Robinson Laboratories, 288
Robinson's Auto Sales, 27, 30
Robinson's Harp Shop, 90, 339
Robinson's Wallcoverings, 281
Roby's Intimates, 121
Rochelle (Martin) Jewelry 297
Rochester Big & Tall, 127
Rock & Ice Catalog Guide, 334
Rock Barrell, 90, 300
Rock Cheese Company, 189, 201, 205
Rock Classics, 108
Rock Creek Vinegar, 205
Rock Hill Bakehouse, 183
Rock Island, 108
Rock Lobster Cycles, 66
Rock N' Roll Marketing Inc., 66, 272, 436
Rock Peddler, 300
Rockabilia Inc., 14, 128, 319, 336
Rockin' Robin, 110, 319
Rocking B Mfg., 337
Rocking Horse Country Store, 150, 189, 196
Rockville Creative Learning Inc., 382
Rockware Inc., 143
Rockwell (Norman) Museum 14, 90
Rocky Meadow Nursery, 244
Rocky Mountain Bicycle Company, 66
Rocky Mountain Deals on Wheels, 376
Rocky Mountain Log Homes, 284
Rocky Mountain Mini Sports, 328
Rocky Mountain Motorworks, 43
Rocky Mountain Outfitter, 334
Rocky Mountain Rarities, 322
Rocky Mountain Tanners Inc., 62
Rocky Shoes & Boots Inc., 101
Rocky Top Farms, 201
RoCocoa's Faerie Queene Chocolates, 187
Rodale Books, 90
Rodco Products, 256
Roddy (Matthew) 316
Rodriguez (Mario) Cabinetmaker 216
Rod's Western Palace, 129, 285
Roean Industries Inc., 419
Roehl (Marion) Recordings 110
Roemers, 129
Rogers & Rosenthal, 117, 153, 390
Rogers (Charles P.) Beds 212
Rogers (Mark E.) Minerals 90, 375
Rogofsky Movie Collectibles, 336, 343
Rohr (Ed) Company 52
Rolex Watch U.S.A. Inc., 297
Rollamatic Roofs Incorporated, 282
Rollei Cameras, 356
Roller Derby Skate Company, 289, 376, 382, 390
Roller Warehouse, 376
Rollerblade Inc., 376
Rollins (Faith) 416
Rolls-Royce Obsolete Parts Inc., 26, 40
Roloff Manufacturing, 78
Romantic Moments Wedding Invitations, 434
Rombough (Lon J.) 233
Romerhaus Creations, 61
Romic Cycle Company, 66
Romick's (Jace) into the West Gallery 216
Ronin Gallery, 14
Ronjo's Magic & Costumes Inc., 149, 316, 414
Ronniger's Seed Potatoes, 245

Ron's Auto Salvage, 24
Ron's Collectibles, 20
Ron's Gallery Supply, 359
Ron's Rad Toys, 382
Room & Board, 212
Roos (Melvin S.) & Company Inc. 160
Roosevelt (A.) Bear Company 60
Root (A.I.) Company 64
Rootlieb Inc., 21, 37
Roots & Rhythm Inc., 110, 429
Roris Gardens, 238
Rosa (Len) Military Collectibles 323
Rose (Jennie) Creations 164
Rose Brand Fabrics, 414
Rose Electronics, 137
Rose Furniture Company, 216
Rose Records, 110, 429
Rosehill Farm, 240
Rosemary House, 205, 235, 256, 349
RoseMary's Gifts, 194, 196, 198, 203
Rosemont Hobby Shop, 325
Rosen (Jack) 36
Rosenbaum Fine Art, 14
Rosenberg (Elvee) 59, 300
Rosenstand (Eva) 342
Roses by Fred Edmunds, 240
Rose's Doll House Store, 61, 162, 165
Roses of Yesterday & Today, 240
Roslyn Nursery, 229
Ross (Anthony) 337
Ross Bicycles USA, 66, 171
Ross Metals, 300, 438
Ross-Simons Jewelers, 117, 297, 390
Ross-Smith Pecan Company Inc., 199
Rosser (Leon) Jeep/Eagle 35
Rossi Pasta, 190, 194
Rossier Engineering, 295
Rossignol Ski Company, 391, 392
Rossman Apiaries Inc., 64
Rostand Fine Jewelers, 15
Roswell Seed Company Inc., 245
Rotary Air Force Inc., 2
Rotel, 404
Roth International, 375
Rothhammer/Sprint, 407, 424
Rothman (Harry) Clothing 126
Rotman Collectibles, 399
Roto-Hoe, 225
RotorWay International, 2
RoughOut, 256, 285
Rounder Roundup Records, 110
Roundhouse South, 330
Roussels, 297, 300
Rovers West, 41
Roverworks, 41
Row/AMI Jukeboxes, 302
Rowe Pottery Works, 117
Rowena's, 185, 201, 205
Roy Electric Company, 308, 310
Roy Electric Company Inc., 57
Royal Bell Ltd., 130
Royal Copenhagen Porcelain, 364
Royal Elk Sewing, 9, 104
Royal Graphics Inc., 96, 349, 389
Royal Martial Art Supplies, 319
Royal Optics, 18, 69
Royal Processing Company Inc., 385
Royal Robbins Company, 101
Royal Textile Mills Inc., 120, 209, 440
Royal Worcester, 117, 153
Royall River Roses, 240
Royalwood Ltd., 56, 114
Royers' Round Top Cafe, 205
RP & Company, 52
RT Computer Graphics Inc., 143

Rubber Anarchy, 377
Rubber Poet Rubber Stamps, 377
Rubbermaid, 119
Rubbernecker Stamp Company, 377
Rubberstampler, 377
Rubens & Marble Inc., 51, 120
Rubie's Costume Company, 149, 414
Rubin & Green, 63
Rubschlager Baking Corporation, 183
Ruddles Mills Products, 160
Rudi's Pottery, 117, 153
Rue (Leonard) Enterprises 256, 355, 361
Rue de France, 63, 154, 409
Rüegg Fireplaces, 177
Rug Store, 379
Rugby & Soccer Supply, 378
Rugby Imports Ltd., 378
Ruggery, 378
Ruggiero's Postcards, 365
Rugging Room, 378
Rule Industries Inc., 78
Runco, 403
Running T Trading Company, 300
Rupert, 171
Rupert (Charles), The Shop 281
Rupp Technology Corporation, 143
Rural Route Mail Order Company, 377
Rush Industries Inc., 220
Rush Receipt Book Company, 345
Russell (A.G.) Knife Company 104, 306
Russell Corporation, 152
Russell's Rock Shop, 300, 375
Russian Collection, 256
Russian Trade House, 322
Russo (Pat) Trains 330
Russo Products Inc., 211, 406
Rusty's Rock Shop, 375
Rutabaga, 74
Rutherford (Debra J.) Designs 384
Rutt Custom Cabinetry, 98, 119
Ruvel & Company Inc., 408
Ryan Recumbent Cycles, 66
Rynne China Company, 115
Ryobi America Corporation, 180, 224, 419
Ryobi-Toski Golf Clubs, 259
Ryon's Saddle & Ranch Supplies, 90, 129, 285
Ryther-Purdy Lumber Company Inc., 389
Ryukyu Imports Inc., 90, 319

S

S & G Inc., 416
S & H Trailer Manufacturing Company, 48, 285
S & P Parker's Movie Market, 336
S & S Adaptability, 272
S & S Arts & Crafts, 316, 422, 424
S & S Carpet Mills, 379
S & S Firearms, 263
S & S Sound City, 405, 411, 426
S & S Woodworks, 212
S & W Framing Supplies Inc., 210
S.A.E. Historical Book Series, 90
S.A.M. Inc., 319, 364
S.A.N. Associates Inc., 226
S.B. Power Tools, 419
S.B.H. Enterprises, 44, 47, 405
S.E.A.T. Publication, 59, 297, 375
SABCO Industries, 437
Sachs (Richard) Cycles 66
Sachs Bicycle Components, 67
Sacramento Vintage Ford Parts Inc., 37
Sacred Hoop Trading Post, 293
Sac's & Boxes, 349

❖ CORPORATE INDEX ❖

Saddle Slicker, 285
Sadé Bodywear, 155
Sadigh Gallery of Ancient Art, 297
Sadu Blue Water Inc., 180
Safariland Leather Products, 264
Safco Products Company, 11
Safe Care Medical Supply Inc., 270, 346
Safe Harbor Computers, 143
Safe Specialties Inc., 217, 381
Safeguard Products Inc., 70
Safesport Manufacturing Company, 380, 393
Safesport Outdoor Gear, 104
Safety Flag Company of America, 72, 182
Safety Zone, 381
Safka & Bareis, 20
Safranek Enterprises Inc., 419
Sage Artworks Inc., 342
SAIL Videos, 429
Sailboard Warehouse Inc., 381
Sailor's Source, 72, 79
Sailrite Kits, 76
Sailworld-Hatteras, 407
Saint Laurie Ltd., 124
Sajama Alpaca, 442
Sakiestewa (Ramona) Ltd. 292
Saks Fifth Ave., 158
Salco Products Inc., 228
Salem Furnishings, 216
Sales Guides Inc., 349
Salis International Inc., 11
Salk Company Inc., 346
Salomon/North America, 102, 392
Salon Perfect, 436
Salsa Bicycles, 66
Salsa Express, 194
Salt & Chestnut, 434
Salt Box Plaids, 173, 369
Salt Lake Costume Company, 149
Salt Minerals, 375
Saltbox Inc., 308, 310
Salter Industries, 278
Saltwater Angler, 180
Saltwater Farms, 350
Salty Professor Antiques, 365
Salvage One, 277
Salvaged Building Materials, 277
Salyers' (Donna) Fabulous-Furs 173
Salzer's, 14, 336
Samadhi Cushions, 443
Samman's Electronics, 100, 403
Sampler Publications, 90
Samra Promotions, 110, 337
Sam's Motorcycles, 333
Sam's Steins & Collectables, 64
Sam's Wines & Liquors, 438
Samsung, 135, 426
Samsung Optical America Inc., 356
Samuels Tennisport, 412, 413
Samurai Antiques, 7, 166
Samy's Camera, 361
San Antonio Hobby Shop, 331
San Antonio River Mill, 194
San Diego Reptile Breeders, 354
San Diego Sports Collectibles, 399
San Francisco Bay Brand Inc., 352
San Francisco Herb Company, 205, 366
San Francisco Music Box Company, 337
San Francisco Mustard Company, 205
San Juan Southern Paiute Yingup Weavers Association, 290
San-Val Discount, 4
Sanchez (Eric D.) Photo Classics 336
Sanchez (H. Drew) 20
Sanctuary, 256
Sanctuary Design Corporation, 118

Sanctuary Much Inc., 190
Sand Buggy Supply Company, 5
Sand-Rite Manufacturing Company, 440
Sandcastle Creations, 164
Sandeen's, 416
Sanders (Wm.) Company of New England 24
Sanders Brine Shrimp Company, 352
Sandwich Islands Genealogy Society, 248
Sandy Mush Herb Nursery, 233, 235
Sandy Pond Hardwoods, 314
Sandy's Dolls & Collectables Inc., 166
Sano Sports International, 295
Sansui Electronics, 46
Sansui USA, 46, 404, 405, 426
Santa Barbara Greenhouses, 220
Santa Barbara Olive Company, 205
Santa Cruz Chili & Spice Company, 206
Santa Fe Cookie Company, 185, 199
Santa Fe Interiors, 379
Santa Fe Select, 194
Santa Rosa Tool & Supply Inc., 419
Santana Cycles Inc., 66
Santarelli (J.M.) 90
Santelli (George) 175
Sanyo, 1, 7, 46, 99, 404, 426
Sanyo Electric, 176
Sanz International Inc., 281
Sarabeth's Kitchen, 201
Sarafan (David) Inc. 333
Sarah Glove Company Inc., 124, 419
Sara's Bears & Gifts, 61
Sarasota Camera Exchange & Video Center, 18, 69
Saratoga Soldier Shop & Military Bookstore, 90, 421
Sargent Art Inc., 11
Sarnia Wooden Boats, 75
Sarris Candies, 187
SAS, 354
Sasco Magic Inc., 316
Sasse Golf Inc., 259
Satellite Parts Locating System, 333
Satter Distributing, 358
Satterwhite Log Homes, 284
Sauces & Salsas Ltd., 206
Saucony/Hyde, 53, 95, 376, 382, 390
Sauk Trail Archery, 9
Sauk Valley Sports Resort, 307
Saunders (H.J.) 323
Saunders Archery Company, 9
Saunders Group, 357, 358, 362
Saunier-Wilhem Company, 68, 95, 156, 388, 409, 424
Sausage Maker Inc., 198
Savage (Kevin) Cards 399
Savage Arms, 265
Savage Farms Nursery, 243
Savage Nursery Center, 230, 240, 244
Savoonga Native Store, 290
Savory's Gardens Inc., 235
Sawbill Canoe Outfitters, 74
Sawdust & Stitches, 210
Sawtooth Saddle Company, 285
Sawyer (David) 216
Sawyer Brook Fabrics, 173
Sawyer Paddles & Oars, 74, 78
Sax (Joe) 339
Sax Arts & Crafts, 152
Saxophone Shop, 339
Saxton (Wilma) Inc. 390
SBI Sales, 361
SBIG Astronomical Instruments, 16
SC Automotive, 29, 39
Scale Equipment Ltd., 327
Scale Model Concepts Ltd., 327

Scamp Eveland's Inc., 48
ScanCo, 134
Scande Research Inc., 325
Scandinavian Computer Furniture Inc., 134
Scandinavian Country Shop, 256
Scandinavian Ski & Sport Shop, 391
Scanner World USA, 168
Scarborough Faire, 21, 26, 37
Scarlet Letter, 342
Scatchard (George) Lamps 310
Scene 1 T-Shirts, 128
Scene Again, 365
Scenery Unlimited, 331
Schacht Lighting, 160, 414
Schacht Spindle Company Inc., 397
Schachter (J.) Corporation 62
Schafer's Wholesale, 113
Schaffer (Frank) 94
Schaller & Weber Inc., 190, 198
Scharff (Heinz) Brushes 11, 113
Scheele Fine Arts, 14
Scheepers (John) Inc. 242
Scheewe (Susan) Publications Inc. 90
Scherer (S.) & Sons 227, 228
Scherr's Cabinet & Doors, 275, 439
Schiff (Noel Dean) 336
Schiff European Automotive Literature Inc., 22
Schild Azalea Gardens & Nursery, 229
Schilke Music Inc., 339
Schilling & Morris Marketing Ltd., 346
Schiltz Goose Farm, 166, 198
Schipper & Company USA, 242
Schlage Locks, 268
Schmelke Manufacturing Company, 68
Schneider Corporation, 357
Schneiders (S.S.) 285
Scholar's Bookshelf, 90
Scholastic Software, 143
School Products Company Inc., 397
Schooler's Minerals & Fossils, 374, 375
Schoolhouse Press, 90, 342, 442
Schoolmasters Science, 307
Schrader's Railroad Catalog, 256
Schreiner's Gardens, 238
Schueler's (Dr.) Health Informatics Inc. 140
Schulte Corporation, 119
Schumacher (F.W.) Company 242
Schwab (Marvin) 59, 300
Schwartz (Nat) & Company 117, 390
Schweizer Aircraft Corporation, 4
Schwerd (A.F.) Manufacturing Company 277, 280
Schwinn Bicycle Company, 66, 67
Science of Business Inc., 344
Science Products, 273, 430
Scientific, 97
Scientific Anglers, 180
Scientific Models Inc., 162
Scintilla, 180
Scioto Ceramic Products Inc., 113
Scooter's Pet Products, 350
Scooterworks USA, 382
Scope City, 18, 69
Score Board Inc., 20, 399
Scorpio Bikes, 66
Scot (L.) Enterprises 382
Scotland by the Yard, 124, 127, 256
Scott Hams, 198
Scott Publications, 90, 113
Scott USA, 66
Scottish Crown Ltd., 203
Scottish Lion Import Shop, 256
Scott's Food Products, 206
Scotts Inc., 287

CORPORATE INDEX

Scotty's Gifts & Accessories, 256
Scotty's Scale Soldiers, 421
Scout Mountain Equipment Inc., 9
Scoville (Woody) 216
Scratch-It Promotions Inc., 349
Screaming Eagle, 9, 287
Screen Tight Porch Screening System, 281
Scripsit, 292
Script City, 336
Scruby's (Jack) Toy Soldiers 421
SCS USA, 385
SCT Signs, 389
Scully & Scully Inc., 256
Sculpture House, 12
Sculpture Placement Ltd., 223
SDV Vitamins, 430
Sea Eagle, 75
Sea Holly Hooked Rugs, 378
Sea Island Mercantile, 194, 203
Sea Mate Products, 78
Sea Quest, 392
Sea Recovery Corporation, 432
Sea Rhoades, 75
Sea-Aquatic International, 352
Sea-Doo, 295
SeaBear, 203
Seaborn (Connie) Studio 14
Seabourn (Connie) Studio 293
Seabourn Studio, 293
Seacraft Classics, 256
Seafood Direct, 203
Seagull Creations, 57
Seagull Pewter, 256
Seagulls Landing Orchids, 237
Seal Products, 357
Seal-Tight Photo/Video Cases, 355
Seanix Technology Inc., 135
Seaport Autographs, 20
Search Gear, 102, 104
Searle's Autographs, 20
Sears (Philip) Disney Collectibles 15, 20, 319, 336
Sears Home Healthcare, 270
Sears Phone Card Department, 354
Season Extenders, 219, 220, 222, 224, 226
Seasons, 256
Seattle Fabrics, 173, 384, 385
Seattle Filmworks, 359
Seavivor, 74
Seaworthy Small Ships, 328
Sebastian Brewers Supply, 437
Second Look, 297
Secret Garden, 194
Seda Products, 72, 74
Seed Factory Inc., 350
Seeds Blüm, 242, 245
Seeds of Change, 235, 242
Seedway Inc., 242, 245
Seeley's, 164
See's Candies, 187
Sega of America, 423
Seibert & Rice, 224
Seiko Instruments USA Inc., 137
Seiler Instrument, 16
Seitech Marine Products Inc., 78
Select Artificials Inc., 117, 182
Select Origins, 187, 206
Select Seeds, 242
Self-Help Warehouse, 90
Self-Reliance Company Inc., 395
SelfCare Catalog, 270
Sellek Industries Inc., 64
Sellmore Lists, 317
Sellstedt (Bob) 422
Selsi Binoculars, 69

Semowich (Richard) 337
Semplex, 198, 437
Senco Inc., 180, 220, 287, 386
Sender Care, 346
Seneca Sports Inc., 289, 307, 376
Seneca-Iroquois National Museum Gift Shop, 292
Senese (Fred) 20
Sennheiser, 273
Señor Murphy, 187, 206
Senor Pistachio, 199
Sensational Beginnings, 422
Sensor Instruments Company Inc., 433
SensorMetrics, 433
Sentimental Times Inc., 91
Sentinel Miniatures, 327, 331, 421
Sentinel Systems Inc., 5
Sentry Electric Corporation, 312
Sentry Table Pad Company, 409
Sepp Leaf Products Inc., 11, 280, 389
Sequel, 102
Sequoia Nursery/Moore Miniature Roses, 240
Seraph, 154, 173, 216
Serendipity, 124
Serendipity Gardens, 238
Serengeti, 124, 256
Serengeti Eyewear, 407
Serif Inc., 143
Seroogy's Chocolates, 187
Serpent City Inc., 354
Servant & Company, 149
Service Merchandise Catalog, 158, 256
Service Photo, 361
Sescom Inc., 168
Sespe Supplies, 180
Setnik's in Time Again, 7
Seton Identification Products, 381
Seton Name Plate Company, 344
Seven Corners Hardware Inc., 419
Seventh Generation, 373
SEVTEC, 286
Sevylor USA, 74, 75, 393, 424
Sew & Serg Company, 385
Sew Fine, 174, 384
Sew Sassy Lingerie, 173
Sew Special, 173, 174, 385
Sew Sweet Dolls, 164
Sew Vac City, 385, 428
Sew What, 162
Sew-Knit Distributors, 304, 385
Sew/Fit Company, 385
Seward Auto Salvage Inc., 24
Sewell (Cole) Corporation 275
Sewin' in Vermont, 384, 385, 428
Sewing Centipede, 385
Sewing Machine Service & Supply, 385
Seyco Fine Foods, 194
Seymor-Radix Inc., 408
Seymour Manufacturing Company Inc., 176
Seymour's Selected Seeds, 242
SFH Products, 272
SFO Snowboard Shop, 393
SFW Company, 212
SGD Company Inc., 260, 388
SGF Gifts & Furnishings Catalog, 256
Shades of Olde, 311
Shades of the Past, 311
Shadow Box, 15
Shadow Group, 354
Shady Acres Herb Farm, 182, 206, 235, 245, 246
Shady Lady, 311
Shady Oaks Nursery, 232, 235, 236, 239, 244, 246
Shaffer, 185

Shaffer Sportswear, 54, 95, 114, 208, 380
Shaker Shops West, 150, 337
Shaker Workshops, 162, 212, 216
ShakerTown Corporation, 277
Shakespeare Company, 180
Shama Imports, 173
Shank (Bill) Auto Parts 24
Shannock Tapestry Looms, 304, 397
Shannon, 117
Shannon Duty Free Mail Order, 256
Shannon's Fancy Hackle, 180
Shape Plastics Corporation, 226
Shapiro Supply Company, 320
Shar Products Company, 337, 339
Sharon & Gayle Publications, 91, 416
Sharp Electronics, 7, 46, 99, 135, 404, 426
Sharper Image, 256
Sharper Image SPA, 148, 171, 319
Sharp's Penn Wallpapers, 281
Shasta Abbey Buddhist Supplies, 258, 443
Shaw & Tenney, 74
Shaw (H.W.) Inc. 155
Shaw (Jackie) Studio Inc. 91
Shaw Furniture Galleries, 216
Shazzam Advertising Specialties, 349
Shea (Ed) 337, 429
Sheepskin Imports, 387
Sheffield Knifemakers Supply, 306
Sheffield Pottery Inc., 113
Shein's Cactus, 231
Sheldon's Hobbies, 325, 327
Sheldon's Inc., 180
Shell Valley Motors, 44
Shell-A-Rama, 382
Shelly's Dolls & Crafts, 158
Shelter Systems, 220, 283
Shelton Sports Cars, 32
Sheoga Hardwood Flooring & Paneling Inc., 276
Shepherd Meters, 357
Shepherd's Garden Seeds, 242
Sheplers, 127, 129
Sheppard Millwork Inc., 275
Sherer Custom Saddles Inc., 285
Sherline Products Inc., 329
Sherman & Associates Inc., 24, 49
Sherman (Nat) Company 415
Sherry Street, 62
Sherwood, 47, 265, 404
Sherwood Brands Inc., 183
Shield Healthcare Centers, 270, 290, 346
Shillcraft, 342, 378
Shiloh Postcards, 365
Shiloh Rifle Manufacturing Compar 263
Shimano American Corporation,
Ship to Shore Inc., 91
Shipman Printing Industries,
Ships Chandler, 250
Ship's Hatch, 79, 256
Ships N' Things, 328
Shipwreck Beads Inc.,
Shirley's Doll House,
Shirley's S/D Shopp
SHIVA Environme
Shoe Express, 38
Shoecraft Corp
Shoei, 331
Shokus Vide 91
Shooner (G
Shooters F
Shootin'Inc., 216
Shooti
Shop
Sho

CORPORATE INDEX

Shop-Task, 419
Shop-Vac Corporation, 419, 428
Shopsmith Inc., 419
Shore Color Lab., 359
Shorelander, 295
Shoreline Design Racing Team, 328
Shoreline Mountain Products, 334
Short Run Labels, 344
Short Shop, 126
Short Sizes Inc., 126
Show Time Cable, 427
Show-Biz Services, 91, 316
Showbest Fixture Corporation, 160
Showcase Custom Cues, 68
Showcase Model Company, 325
Showerlux, 57
Shreve Systems, 137
Shriver's Carving Kits, 107
Shrubsole (S.J.) 7
Shumans (Jerry) Apiaries 64
Shumway (R.H.) Seedsman 230, 236, 240, 242, 243, 245
Shure Brothers Inc., 404, 411
Shutan Camera & Video, 18, 69
Shutter Depot, 153, 278
Shutter Shop, 278
Shutterbug Store, 91, 355
Shuttercraft, 154, 278
Shydas Shoe & Clothing Barn, 266, 287
Si-Tex Marine Electronics, 79, 181
Sickafus Sheepskins, 125
SICO Room Makers, 119, 212, 216
Sidney's, 125
Siedle Communication System of America, 294
Siegel Display Products, 160
Siegel's (Charles) Train City 331
Siemans Hearing Instruments Inc., 273
SieMatic Corporation, 98
Siemens Solar Industries, 5, 104, 395
Sierra (Jimmy) Products 367
Sierra Books, 91
Sierra Club Books, 91
Sierra Designs, 104
Sierra Direct, 143
Sierra On-Line Inc., 208
Sierra Solar Systems, 395
Sierra Trading Post, 102, 104
SIG Manufacturing Company Inc., 325, 329
Sigma Corporation of America, 356
Sign-Mart, 389
Signal Thread Company, 384
Signals Catalog, 256
Signature Line Accessories, 36
Signatures, 256
Signet Marine, 79
Signs of all Kinds, 389
Silics, 4
Silicon Corporation, 272, 436
Sil 176, 273
Sil 121
Silander Games, 137
Sil Inc., 133
Silos plus, 168, 382
Sil's Fe 42
Silstar A 171
Silva Com 270
Silvacraft S 432
Silver (Ben) Inc., 24
Silver Burdett 180
Silver Creek Clas.

Silver Eagle Creations, 297
Silver Image Photographics, 359
Silver Lane, 117, 390
Silver Lining Seafood, 203
Silver Nugget, 292, 297
Silver Phoenix Inc., 294
Silver Queen, 390
Silver Sounds Recordings, 400
Silver Star, 291
Silvercat Publications, 91
SilverDisc Music Company, 110
Silver's Wholesale Club, 154, 281
Silverstate Cadillac Parts, 27
Silverton Victorian Millworks, 275, 280
Silvio's Photoworks, 361
Simara's Bead World, 59, 301
Simcha Designs, 256, 297
Simerl Instruments, 79, 433
Simkins (Meg) 400
Simmons Gun Specialties Inc., 263, 265, 266, 288
Simmons Handcrafts, 148, 373
Simmons Outdoor Company, 69, 264
Simmons Scientific Inc., 321
Simons (Syd) Cosmetics 148
Simplicity Manufacturing Inc., 224, 227
Simply Country Furniture, 119, 150, 216
Simply Diamonds, 297
Simply Divine-All Cotton Clothing, 120, 125
Simply Lovely Gift Shoppe, 166
Simply Shrimp, 203
Simply Tops, 125
Simply Whispers, 297
Simpson & Vail Inc., 194, 207
Simpson Door Company, 275
Simpson Strong-Tie Company Inc., 220
Simpson Timber, 276
Sims Stoves, 104
Sinai Kosher Foods Corporation, 190, 198
Sinar Bron, 357, 358
Sinclair's Auto Miniatures, 327
Singer Sewing Center, 384, 385
Singer Wallcoverings, 281
Singh-Ray Corporation, 357
Sinister Cinema, 337, 429
Sink Factory, 57
Sinnett (Doreen) 164
Sinties Scientific Inc., 272
Sinyard (Cleston R.) 306
Sioux Trading Post Inc., 59, 294
Sir Maxwell's, 351
Sir Thomas Thumb, 162
Sir-Tech Software, 143, 423
Sirken (Dave) Distributors Inc. 355
Siska (Jim) Knives 306
Siskiyou Rare Plant Nursery, 239
Sitler's Supplies Inc., 414
Six-Chuter Inc., 4
Sixth Avenue Electronics, 100
Sixties Ford Parts, 32, 33, 42
Skates on Haight, 390
Sketch 'n' Cel, 15
Ski Limited, 432
Ski Warm, 432
Skil-Bosch, 419
Skin Diver Wet Suits, 392
Skipjack Press Inc., 91
Skipper Marine Electronics Inc., 76, 79, 131, 181
Skis Dynastar Inc., 392
Skolaski's Glads & Flowers, 233, 238, 239
Skrudland Photo, 359
Skullduggery, 374
Skutt Ceramic Products, 113

Sky Burner, 304
Sky Cycle Inc., 333
Sky Delight Kites, 304
Sky Designs, 18
Sky Publishing Corporation, 91
Sky Scientific, 16, 18
Skycrest Ceramics, 162
Skydance Photography, 3
Skylands Cutlery, 306
Skyline, 288
Skyline Color Lab, 359
Skynasaur Corporation, 304
SkyPro Inc., 2
SkySports, 3
Skystar Aircraft Corporation, 2
Skytech Systems, 396
Skyvision Inc., 427
Slater (N.G.) Corporation 51, 96, 349
Sleepy Eye Salvage Company, 24
Slide Zone, 270
Slim Waist Foods, 185, 196
Slipcovers of America, 173, 393
Slocum Books, 318
Slocum Water Gardens, 227
Slumberjack Inc., 104
Small Houses, 162
Small Parts, 5
Small Press Distribution Inc., 91
Smallwoods Yachtwear, 72, 128
Smart Buy, 49
Smart Modular Technologies, 133
Smart Saver, 121
Smart Wallcoverings, 281
SMAutomatic, 153
Smile Photo, 361, 427
Smiley's Yarns, 442
Smith, 91
Smith & Hawken, 125, 148, 218, 226
Smith & Jones Antique Parts, 37
Smith & Wesson, 265
Smith (Daniel) Art Supplies 210
Smith (Daniel) Art Supplies Inc. 11, 166
Smith (George) Sofas & Chairs Inc. 216
Smith (Hobart E.) 365
Smith (Kenneth) Golf Clubs 259
Smith (Malcom) Products 67, 331
Smith (Nicholas) Trains 331
Smith (O.B.) Chevy Parts 49
Smith (Samuel Patrick) 91
Smith Family Music, 339
Smith Sport Optics Inc., 407
Smith-Cornell Inc., 340, 389
Smith-Victor, 357, 358
Smithfield Ham & Products Company, 198
Smith's Country Cheese, 189
Smithsonian Catalogue, 256
Smithy, 419
Smocking Bonnet, 173, 337
Smocking Etceteras, 173, 174
Smoky Mountain Knife Works, 306
Smooth-On, 12
Smoothill Sports Distributors, 390
SMR Technologies Inc., 72
SMS Auto Fabrics, 49
Smyth (Gale) Antique Auto 24
Smythe (R.M.) 20, 347
Snag Proof, 180
Snake Creek Workshop, 293
Snake Wear Apparel Company, 128
Snapper Power Equipment, 220, 224, 227
Snapvent Company, 56, 114
Snelling's Thermo-Vac, 274
SnoBird Aircraft Inc., 2
Snugglebundle, 51
Snyder (Tom) Productions 143

CORPORATE INDEX

Snyder's Antique Auto Parts, 37, 47
Soap Opera, 148, 349
Soap Saloon, 106, 394
Soar Corporation, 108
SOAR Inflatable, 74, 75
Sobol House of Furnishings, 216
Soccer International Inc., 256, 394
Soccer Kick, 394, 395
Soccer Madness International, 394, 395
Society 250
Society Hill Snacks, 187, 200
Society's Child, 166
Socket Communications, 346
Soda Creek Western Outfitters, 129
Soda Mart-Can World, 64, 319
SofNet Inc., 143
Softdisk Publishing, 143
SoftKey International Inc., 271
Softkey International Inc., 143
Software Bisque, 16
Software House International, 137, 145
Software Hut, 145
Software Labs, 137
SoftwareLabs, 137
SOG Specialty Knives & Tools Inc., 306
Sohn's Forest Mushrooms, 236
Soho Design, 128
Soho South, 59, 171, 173
Soitenly Stooges, 336
Sokolow Music, 91
Solar Cine Products Inc., 357, 361
Solar Components Corporation, 220, 395
Solar Depot, 286, 395
Solar Electric Inc., 395
Solar Works, 16
Solarex Corporation, 395
Solarium Systems International, 396
Solas USA Inc., 295
Solo Golf Company, 259
Solo Inc., 353
Solo Loader, 78
Solstice, 102
Solution Technology, 143
Solutions, 256
Somers Stained Glass Company, 310
Somerset Publishing Company Inc., 79
Something Pretty, 384
Something Special Enterprises, 107
Something's Blooming, 182
Somfy/Sunbrella, 50
Sonic Recollections, 110
Sonic Research, 358, 362
SonLight Impressions, 377
Sonnen Motors, 25, 43
Sonoma Antique Apple Nursery, 244
Sonoma Cheese Factory, 189
Sonoma Woodworks Inc., 57, 97
Sonrise Soft Crafts, 8, 368, 409, 420
Sony Consumer Products, 47, 99, 403, 404, 405, 426
Sophia's Heritage Collection, 166
Sophisticats Catalog, 256
Soricé, 111
Sormani Calendars Inc., 98
Sorrenti Family Farms, 190
Sound City, 146, 411, 427
Sound Delivery, 110
Sound Exchange, 110, 256
Soundmind, 110
Sounds True Audio, 94, 110, 429
Soundtrek, 143
Soundware Corporation, 143
Source for Everything Jewish, 118, 258
Source One Business Systems, 135
South Bay Homebrew Supply, 437

South Bend Replicas Inc., 263
South Bend Sporting Goods, 180
South Bound Millworks, 154
South Carolina Department of Archives & History, 249
South Carolina Historical Society, 249
South Creek Ltd., 180
South Dakota Archives, 249
South Dakota Genealogical Society, 249
South Eastern Log Home Manufacturing Inc., 284
South Pacific Wholesale Company, 59, 301
South Prairie Crafts, 150
South Replicas Inc., 325
South Side Pepper Company, 206
Southampton Antiques, 7, 216
Southeast Discount Golf, 260
Southeast Knife Brokers, 306
Southeast Reptile Exchange Inc., 354
Southeastern Fossil Supply Company, 374, 375
Southeastern Insulated Glass, 220, 275, 282, 396
Southeastern Wood Products Company, 175
Southerlands for Leisure Living, 218, 223
Southern Brown Rice, 196
Southern Cypress Log Homes Inc., 284
Southern Discount Wall Covering, 281
Southern Emblem, 156, 389
Southern Exposure Sea Kayaks, 74
Southern Exposure Seed Exchange, 242
Southern Oregon Organics, 242
Southern Oregon Pottery & Supply, 113, 115
Southern Oregon Scientific, 307
Southern Rug, 379
Southern Season, 194
Southern Security Safes, 264
Southern Seeds, 242
Southern Sign Supply Inc., 389
Southern Statuary & Stone, 223
Southland Athletic, 54, 208
Southland Callers, 288
Southland Log Homes, 284
Southland Spa, 286
Southmeadow Fruit Gardens, 245
Southpaw Shoppe, 313
SouthStar Supply Corporation, 384
Southwest Avanti, 26
Southwest Cap & Cork, 437
Southwest Door Company, 98, 268, 275, 276, 282
Southwest Indian Foundation, 292
Southwest Rock & Gem Company, 301
Southwest Shooter's Supply, 265
Southwestern Classics, 28, 29, 31, 39
Southwestern Ohio Hive Parts Company, 64
Soyco Foods, 189, 196
Space Tables Inc., 272
Spadaro (Dick) Early Ford Reproductions 33
Spalding Sports Worldwide, 52, 54, 55, 120, 152, 156, 171, 209, 259, 267, 286, 346, 369, 370, 380, 392, 395, 409, 412, 413, 425, 431
Spare Bear Parts, 60
Sparkle's Entertainment Express, 52, 130, 301, 316, 368
Spartan Motorcar Company, 45
Spaulding & Rogers Manufacturing, 410
Spaulding Enterprises Inc., 297
Speakerlab Factory, 405
Spear's Specialty Shoe Company, 130
Spec II, 333
Special Clothes, 120, 272
Special Designs Inc., 272

Special Interest Autos of St. Louis Inc., 41, 49
Special Interest Car Parts, 34, 37, 43
Special Projects, 306
Specialized Bicycle Components, 66, 67
Specialties, 173, 384, 385
Specialty Automotive, 31
Specialty Books Company, 91
Specialty Concepts Inc., 395
Specialty Diecast Company, 327
Specialty Lumber Inc., 315
Specialty Photographic Laboratories, 359
Specialty Sauces, 206
Specialty Sports Limited, 331
Specialty Woodworks, 97, 275
Spectacular Sea Systems, 352
Spectra Astronomy, 16, 18
Spectra Sport Kites, 304
Spectral Kinetics, 41
SpectraPure, 352, 432
Spectre Security Systems, 46
Spectrum Cycles, 66
Spectrum Garden Supply, 236
Spectrum Holobyte, 143, 423
Spectrum International, 433
Spedding (Richard) Postcards 365
Speed & Sport Chrome Plating, 43
Speed Stitch, 369, 384
Speedotron Corporation, 358
Speedway Automotive, 27
Speedway Motors, 24, 45
Speer Products, 262
Speir Music, 339
Speleoshoppe, 396
Spell Bee Company, 64
Spencer Amphibian Aircraft, 2
Spencer's Inc., 120
Spence's Targets, 9
Spent Grain Baking Company, 96, 183
Sperry Marine, 79
Spex Amphibious Eye Wear, 407
SPG Software, 143
Sphinx Date Ranch, 192
Spice Discounters, 235, 349, 430
Spice Island Traders, 318
Spice Merchant, 206
Spices Etc, 206
Spider Oak Outfitters, 288
Spiegel, 57, 120, 121, 126, 127, 158, 380
Spiewak (I.) & Sons Inc. 127
Spike Nashbar, 431
Spike Nashbar Outlet Store, 125
Spinnaker Software Corporation, 143
Spinner's Hearth, 442
Spinning Wheel, 342
Spiral Manufacturing Inc., 278
Spiral Stairs of America, 278
Spirit of America Fund Raisers, 211
Spirit of the West, 216
Spirit of the West Clothing, 129
Spirit of the Wood, 71
Spirited Steeds, 107
Spitz Mountain Enterprises, 7, 421
Splash Page Comics & Toys, 422
Splintworks, 56
Split Creek Farm, 189
Splurge Inc., 187, 194
Spode, 117
Spoken Arts, 91
Sport Casuals, 412, 413
Sport Climbers, 288
Sport Copter, 2
Sport Europa, 392
Sport Fun Inc., 52, 79, 286, 431
Sport Shop of Grifton, 9, 288

499

CORPORATE INDEX

Sporthill, 391
Sportif USA, 102
Sportime, 52, 54, 55, 114, 152, 156, 175, 273, 346, 363, 370, 376, 395, 409
Sporting Clays Books & Videos, 91
Sporting Life, 412
Sporting Look, 412
Sportiva, 102
Sportline, 380
Sportline of Hilton Head Ltd., 55, 395, 412, 413, 431
Sports & Classics, 25, 26, 35, 37, 43
Sports Alley, 347, 399
Sports Collectibles Inc., 399
Sports Express, 412, 413
Sports Heroes, 319
Sports Merchandizers, 392
Sports Software Inc., 143
Sports Technologies Inc., 95
Sports Tutor, 413
Sportscards, 399
SportsCards Plus, 20, 399
Sportsman's Accessory Manufacturing, 306
Sportsman's Guide, 104, 256
Sportsman's Kitchen Inc., 104
Sportsprint Inc., 53
Sporty's Pilot Shop, 4, 91
Sporty's Preferred Living Catalog, 68, 131, 256, 409
Spot Target Decoys, 9
Spotted Horse Tribal Gifts, 293
Spring City Electrical Manufacturing Company, 312
Spring Creek Outfitters Inc., 78
Spring Hill Nurseries, 231, 236, 239, 240
Spring Lace Two, 154
Spring Tree Corporation, 196
Spring Valley Nursery, 245
Springer-Verlag New York, 91
Springfield Armory, 265
Springfield Sporters Inc., 263
Springhouse Direct, 91
Springston (Mrs. Esther K.) 365
SPS Marine, 78
SPSS Software Inc., 143
Spy Outlet, 408
SPY Supply, 408
Spyder Lock, 46
Spyderco Inc., 306
Spyke's Grove, 192
Squadron Mail Order, 325, 328
Square Dance & Western Wear Fashions Inc., 400
Square Dance Attire, 400
Square Dancetime Records, 400
Square One Parachute Sales & Service, 3
Squaw Mountain Gardens, 232, 239
Squire's Choice, 194, 200
Squirrel's Nest Miniatures, 162
SR Batteries Inc., 58, 327
SR Collectibles, 319
SR Instruments, 79
SSI, 143, 423
SSI Boating Accessories, 78
SSK Sports, 54
St. Croix Rod, 180
St. Dalfour Conserves, 201
St. Joseph's Lakota Development Council, 294
St. Lawrence Island Original Ivory Cooperative, 290
St. Louis Antique Lighting Company Inc., 310
St. Louis Baseball Cards, 20, 399

St. Louis Medical Supply, 270
St. Louis Slot Machine Company, 130
Stackpole Books, 91
Stadri Emblems, 157, 363
Stad's Miniature Figures, 421
Stafford & Sons 256
Stafford (George) & Sons 125, 256
Stage Clothes U.S.A., 125
Stage Step, 91, 110, 429
StageRight Corporation, 414
Staghorn Treestands, 288
Stair Systems Inc., 278
StairMaster Sports/Medical Products Inc., 171
Stairways Inc., 278
Stakes' (Eddie) Planet Houston AMX 35
Stamford Peugeot, 39
Stamford Subaru, 41
Stamford Volvo, 43
Stamp Affair, 378
Stamp Francisco Rubber Stamps, 378
Stamp in the Hand Company, 378
STAMPberry Farms, 378
Stampede Investments, 20, 91
Stampendous Inc., 378
Stampinks, 378
Stand-Aid of Iowa Inc., 272, 436
Stand-Up Comics, 131
Stand-Up Desk Company, 217
Standard Amateur Radio Products Inc., 372
Standard Candy Company, 187, 194
Standard Doll Company, 164
Standard Hobby Supply, 325, 327, 331
Standard Shoes, 387
Stanley (Ralph W.) Inc. 76
Stanley (Victor) Inc. 218, 364
Stanley Door Systems, 5, 219
Stanley Galleries, 308, 310
Stanley Hardware, 275
Stanley Iron Works, 406
Stanley Sales & Service by Amsley, 41
Stanley Tools, 419
Stanley-Bostitch Inc., 1
Stano Components, 18, 69
Staples Inc., 96, 98, 146, 166, 217, 344, 348, 428
Staplex Company, 344
Star (M.) Antler Designs 216
Star Antler Designs, 308, 310
Star Aviation Inc., 2
Star Instruments, 18
Star Micronics America Inc., 133
Star Pet Supply, 350, 351
Star Pharmaceuticals Inc., 148, 430
Star Quality, 36
Star Sales Company Inc., 306
Star Shots, 20
Star Soundtracks, 111
Star Stilts, 113
Star Styled Dancewear, 149, 155
Star-Liner Company, 18
Starboard Software, 143
Starboy Enterprises, 294
Starbucks Coffee, 207
Starcrest of California, 256
StarCycle Motorcycle Accessories Inc., 331, 333
Stardancer Stamp Company, 378
Stardrive Systems, 18
Stardust Gallery, 301
Stark Brothers, 230, 236, 242, 243, 245
Starland Collector's Gallery, 15, 336, 337, 399
StarPress Inc., 271
Starr Autographs, 20

Starship Industries, 110
Starsplitter Telescopes, 18
Start Fresh Weight Control Program, 190
Starting Line Products Inc., 393
Stash Tea, 207
State Archives of Florida, 247
State Archives of Kentucky, 248
State Archives of Maryland, 248
State Genealogical Society of Ohio, 249
State Historical Society of Nebraska, 249
State House Press, 91
State Library of Connecticut, 247
State Library of Kansas, 248
State Library of Montana, 248
State Library of North Dakota, 249
State Library of Ohio, 249
State Line Tack Inc., 285
State of Alabama Archives & History, 247
State of Alabama Historical Association, 247
State of Connecticut Historical Society, 247
State of Connecticut Society of Genealogists, 247
State of Delaware Archives, 247
State of Florida Genealogical Society, 247
State of Florida Historical Society, 247
State of Georgia Genealogical Society, 248
State of Georgia Historical Society, 248
State of Hawaii Archives, 248
State of Hawaii Historical Society, 248
State of Idaho Genealogical Society, 248
State of Idaho Historical Society, 248
State of Illinois Archives Division, 248
State of Illinois Genealogical Society, 248
State of Illinois Historical Society, 248
State of Indiana Archives, 248
State of Indiana Genealogical Society, 248
State of Indiana Historical Society, 248
State of Indiana Library, 248
State of Iowa Archives, 248
State of Iowa Genealogical Society, 248
State of Kansas Historical Society, 248
State of Kentucky Genealogical Society, 248
State of Louisiana Archives & Records, 248
State of Maine Genealogical Society, 248
State of Massachusetts Historical Society, 248
State of Minnesota Genealogical Society, 248
State of Minnesota Historical Society, 248
State of Montana Archives, 248
State of Nevada Historical Society, 249
State of Nevada Library & Archives, 249
State of New York Genealogical & Biographical Society, 249
State of New York Historical Association, 249
State of North Carolina Genealogical Society, 249
State of Rhode Island Historical Society, 249
State of South Carolina Genealogy Society, 249
State of South Dakota Historical Society, 249
State of Texas Genealogy Society, 249
State of Vermont Archives, 250
State of Washington Historical Society, 250
State of West Virginia Genealogy Society, 250
Stationery House, 343, 402
StatSoft, 143
Stauter Boat Works, 75
Stave Puzzles, 369
STB Books Inc., 91
Stearns Manufacturing, 432
Steatite of Southern Oregon Inc., 406
Stebner Pottery, 117
Steebar, 119

CORPORATE INDEX

Steele (Lynn H.) Rubber Products, 24, 27, 45
Steele (R.C.) Dog Equipment 351
Steele (R.C.) Tropical Fish 352
Steele Plant Company, 245
Steele's Sports Company, 54
Steel's Sauces, 187
Steen Cannons, 323
Stegall's Stoneware, 117
Steiner Binoculars, 69
Stellar Dynamics Company, 18
Stellar Software, 16
Stellar Toys, 319, 422
Stelzig's Western Store, 285
StenArt Inc., 402
Stencil Collector, 402
Stencil Company, 369
Stencil House of N.H., 402
Stencil Outlet, 402
Stencil Shoppe, 402
Stencil World, 402
Stencils & Stuff, 402
Stephan's (Jim) Rubber Art Ink 378
Stephensons-Warmlite, 104
Steppin Out, 400
Steptoe & Wife Antiques Ltd., 278
Sterling & Collectables Inc., 117, 390
Sterling Mold Company, 164
Sterling Name Tape Company, 386
Sterling Plumbing Group, 57
Sterling Publishing Company Inc., 91
Sterling Rope Company, 334
Sterling Shop, 390
Sternberg, 312
Stern's (Bob) Short Sizes Inc. 126
Steuben Glass, 153
Steve Eagles, 396
Stevens Auto Wrecking, 24
Stevens Furniture, 216
Stevens Magic Emporium, 316
Stevens Worldwide Inc., 400
Steve's Cycle, 333
Steve's Lost Land of Toys, 424
Steve's Mom Inc., 185
Steve's Studebaker-Packard, 39, 41
Stewart (Charles H.) & Company, 414
Stewart (Johnny) Wild Life Calls Inc. 288
Stewart Filmscreen Corporation, 336
Stewart Iron Works Company, 175
Stewart Orchids, 237
Stewart Research Enterprises, 16
Stewart-MacDonalds Guitar Shop Supply, 340
Stewart-Superior Corporation, 378
Stewart's of California Inc., 113
Stick-Em Up, 405
Stickley Furniture, 216
Stickney's Garden Houses, 223
Sticks 'n Limbs Camouflage, 288
Stik-EES, 256
Stillbrook Horticultural Supplies, 226
Stillwater Archery, 9
Stilwell's Obsolete Car Parts, 38
Stimson Marine Inc., 72, 78
Stinger Inc., 44
Stinson (Jim) Sports Collectibles 20
Stitch in Time, 342
Stitchery, 342
Stitches East, 304, 342, 442
Stits Poly-Fiber Aircraft Coatings, 4
Stock Drive Products, 268
Stock Yards Packing Company, 198
Stoddard Imported Cars Inc., 40
Stoddard-Hamilton Aircraft Inc., 2
Stoecklein's Nursery, 234

Stoker (Fred) & Sons Inc. 415
Stokes Collection, 15
Stokes Seeds Inc., 226, 236, 242
Stolp Starduster Corporation, 2
Stolz (Mary) Doll Shop 166
Stone (Art) Dancewear 155
Stone Age Industries Inc., 301
Stone Company Inc. 222, 278, 347
Stone Company Science Specimens, 374
Stone Forest, 209, 223
Stone Legends, 278
Stone Magic, 177, 279
Stonebrier, 91, 304
Stonehill Farm, 194, 196, 206
Stonemill Log Homes, 284
Stonemountain & Daughter Fabrics, 384
Stonewall Chili Pepper Company, 206
Stony Mountain Natural Foods & Herbs, 206, 207, 430
Storey's How-To Books for Country Living, 91
Storm Manufacturing Company, 181
Stormer Racing, 327
Stortz (John) & Son Inc. 78, 419
Story House Herb Farm, 235
Storybook Heirlooms, 120, 251
Storz Performance, 333
Stoudt Auto Sales, 30
Stow Away Inc. 436
Stowe Canoe & Snowshoe Company, 74
Strachan Apiaries Inc., 64
Straight'N Arrow, 9
Strand Surplus Center, 408
Strassacker Bronze America Inc., 209, 223
Strassen Plating Company, 169
Strata Inc., 143
STRATAGRAPHICS, 374, 376
Strategic Gaming Designs, 143
Strategic Simulations Inc., 143, 423
Strauss (David) Designs Inc. 118
Straw Hill Chairs, 216
Straw into Gold, 91, 442
Street Level Supply, 211
Street Smart Security, 408
Streetwise Software, 143
Stren Fishing Lines, 181
Stretch & Sew, 173, 384, 385
Stringed Instrument Division, 340
Stringmeter, 413
Strong Enterprises, 4
Struck Corporation, 436
Struhl (Joseph) Company Inc. 389
Stu-Art Supplies, 210
Stuart (Paul) 125
Stuart-Townsend-Carr Furniture, 217
Stubby Stampers, 378
Stuckey Brothers Furniture, 216, 218
Studio Knitting Machines by White, 304
Studio Limestone, 91, 442
Studio Steel, 308, 310, 323
Studio Workshop, 57
Studio Workshop Inc., 150
Studiomate, 358
Stuempfle's Military Miniatures, 325, 421
Stuf'd 'N Stuff, 61
Stulb Colour Craftsmen, 276
Sturbridge Yankee Workshop, 256
Sturdi-Built Manufacturing Company, 221, 396
Sturm, 265
STX Inc., 307
Style-Mark, 280
Stylmark Carpet Mills Inc., 379
Submatic Irrigation Systems, 228
Submersible Systems, 392

Suburban Balloon & Helium, 52
Success Lists, 317
Successories Inc., 50
Succulenta, 231
Sugal (Gary) Mouthpieces Inc. 340
Sugar Creek Industries Inc., 113, 164
Sugar Hill, 256
Sugar 'n Spice Invitations, 402, 434
Sugar Pine Woodcarving Supplies, 439
Sugar Shack, 188, 189, 196, 256
Sugar Spoon All Natural Cheesecake, 185
Sugarbush Farm, 189, 196
Sugarmill Farm, 196
Sugino Corporation, 419
Sullivan Harbor Farms, 203
Sullivan Sports, 412, 413
Sullivan Victory Groves, 192
Sultan's Delight Inc., 190
Sumeria Inc., 143
Summer Place, 7
Summerfield Farm, 198, 203
Summers (Murray A.) 336, 343
Summers (Nicole) 121
Summers Past Farm, 394
Summit Canyon Mountaineering, 334
Summit Racing Equipment, 24
Summit Specialties Inc., 288
Sumner Boat, 76
Sun, 239
Sun Appliances, 289
Sun Burst Farms, 200
Sun Designs, 218, 247, 266, 274, 364
Sun Electric Company, 395
Sun Feather Handcrafted Herbal Soap Company, 148, 394
Sun Garden Specialties, 223
Sun House Tiles, 279
Sun 'N Rain Greenhouses, 221
Sun Ray, 44
Sun River Packing Company, 200
Sun Room Company, 396
Sun Source Inc., 223
Sun State Trophy Supply, 50
Sun Welding Safe Company, 264
Sun-Porch Structures, 221, 395
Sunbeam Specialties, 41
Sunberry Baking Company, 183
Sunbilt Solar Products by Sussman Inc., 396
Sunburst Biorganics, 148, 430
Sunburst Performance, 295
Suncoast Discount Arts & Crafts Warehouse, 152
Suncoast Pharmacy & Surgical Supplies, 159
Suncom Technologies Inc., 143
Suncor Marine & Industrial, 78
Sundance Catalog, 256
Sundance Supply, 221, 282, 396, 409
SunDog, 104, 355
Sundome Greenhouses, 221
Sundowner Trailer Inc., 285
Sunelco, 286, 395
Sunflower Showerhead Company, 57
Sunglass America, 407
Sunglass Hut International, 407
Sunglasses U.S.A., 407
Sunglo Solar Greenhouses, 221, 395
Sunhill Machinery, 419
Sunlight Energy Corporation, 395
Sunlight Gardens, 232, 239, 246
Sunnybrook Farms Nursery, 233, 235, 236, 239
Sunnybrook RV Inc., 48
Sunnyland Farms Inc., 194, 200
Sunnyside Solar, 395
Sunpak Division of ToCAD America, 358

CORPORATE INDEX

Sunquest Inc., 211, 395
SunRay Optical, 407
Sunrise Auto Sales & Salvage, 24
Sunrise Gourmet Foods & Gifts, 183
Sunrise Mountain Sports, 334
Sunrise Specialty Company, 57
Sunroom Company, 221
Sunset Catalog, 256
Sunsetter Awning, 50
Sunshine Computers, 58
Sunshine Factory, 3
Sunshine Glassworks, 401
Sunshine South, 427
Sunshine Sports, 392
Sunshine Video & Computers, 100, 137
Sunspot Inc., 221, 396
Sunswept Laboratories, 237
Super Circuits, 408
Super Dock Products, 78
Super Locomotion Inc., 256
Super Sport Restoration Parts Inc., 28, 29
Superfast Label Service, 344
Superfluity Aircraft Supplies, 4
Supergo Bike Shops, 66
Superior Aircraft Materials, 329
Superior Fireplace, 177
Superior Growers Supply, 222
Superior Hardwoods & Millwork Inc., 315
Superior Receipt Book Company, 345
Superior Seat Covers, 46
Superior Specialties Inc., 355
Superior Tattoo Equipment, 410
SuperLife, 171
Supernaw's Oklahoma Indian Supply, 293
Superscale Locomotive Company, 329
Supica (Jim) 263
Support Plus, 126, 270
Supra Corporation, 137
Supradur Manufacturing Corporation, 277
Supreme Audio Inc., 399, 400
Supreme Camera & Video, 100, 361
Supreme Cards Inc., 97
Suquamish Museum, 294
Sur La Table, 146, 303
Sure-Shot Game Calls Inc., 289
Surfer House, 432
Surma Egg Crafting, 166
Surplus Center, 408
Surplus Sales of Nebraska, 372
Surplus Software Inc., 145
Surprises & Jewelry, 347
Surry Gardens, 239
Survival Center, 270, 381
Survival Products Inc., 72
Survival Technologies Group, 72
Su's Cameras, 361
Suski (Rich) 333, 382
Sutherland Knives, 306
Sutter Creek Antiques, 150
Sutter Street Emporium, 166
Sutton AG Enterprises Inc., 220, 349
Sutton Place Gourmet, 194
Sutton Supply Company, 12
Sutton-Council Furniture, 216
Suunto USA, 392
Suwannee Mouse Farm, 354
Suzuki Motorcycle Parts & Accessories, 333
Swahaa Spices Inc., 190
Swallow's Nest, 104, 334
Swampworks Mfg., 328
Swan Corporation, 57
Swan Island Dahlias, 232
Swan Technologies, 135
Swan's Nest, 61
Swanson Health Products Inc., 430
Swanson's, 27
Swarovski Optik, 69
Swedish Classics, 43
Swedish Clogs Inc., 387
Sweet Antiques Galleries, 150
Sweet Briar Studio, 378
Sweet Energy, 192
Sweet Home Farm, 189
Sweet Water Ranch, 216
Sweetgrass Gift Shop, 292
SweetWater Inc., 432
Sweetwater Sound Inc., 340
Swest Inc., 301
SWFTE International Ltd., 143
Swift (M.) & Sons Inc. 11, 280
Swift Instruments Inc., 18, 70, 433
Swift Plus Reserve Inc., 3
Swimex, 409
Swiss Armory, 306
Swiss Colony, 189, 194
Swissco Foods, 195
Switlik Parachute, 72
Swix Sport USA Inc., 392
Swords Apiaries, 64
Sylmar Display Stands, 373
Sylvan Publications, 91
Symantec Corporation, 143
Symmetree Company, 150
Synair Corporation, 363
SynApps Software Inc., 143
Syndee's, 164
Synergistics Rubber Stamps, 378
Synthony Music, 340
Syracuse Scenery & Stage Lighting Company Inc., 414

T

T & M Enterprises Inc., 171
T 'N' T Hobbies, 327
T-Bird Connection, 42
T-Bird Nest, 33, 42
T-Bird Sanctuary, 42
T-BRRRs, 61
T-M Cowboy Classics, 216
T-Reproductions, 331
T-Shirt City, 259
T.C. Card Company, 399
T.C. Vintage Autographs, 20
T.F. Wear USA, 96
T.J.'s Comics & Cards & Supplies, 131, 398, 399
T/Maker Company, 143
Tab Books Inc., 91
Taber's Honey Bee Genetics, 64
Tackle Craft, 181
Tackle Shack, 392, 407, 432
Tafford Manufacturing Inc., 128
Taggart Galleries, 15
Tagit, 301
Tah-Mels, 293
Taheta Arts & Cultural Group, 290
Taiclet Enterprises, 312
TAIG Tools, 419
Talarico Hardwoods, 315
TALAS, 80
Talbots, 125, 126, 387
Talbots for Kids, 120
Talcove (Mitch) 315
Tale of Two Kitties, 256
Talk O'Texas, 206
Talk-A-Phone, 272, 411
Talk-A-Phone Company, 295
Tallclassics, 127
Tallina's Doll Supplies Inc., 164
Tallon Software, 137
Tamarack Log Building Tools Inc., 419
Tamarkin & Company, 361
Tampa Bay Mold Company, 113
Tamrac, 355
Tamraz's Parts Discount Warehouse, 28, 31, 39
Tamron Industries Inc., 70, 356
Tandems Limited, 66
Tandy Leather Company, 312, 384
Tane Alarm Products, 5
Tanks D'Art Inc., 392
Tannenbaum (A.G.) 372
Tannen's Magic, 316
Tanner Pecan Company, 200
Taos Mesa Gourmet, 190
Tapestry, 257
Tappan, 7
Tar-Hunt Rifles Inc., 265
Tara Materials Inc., 416
Tarantula Ranch, 354
Targa Accessories Inc., 333
Target Enterprises, 276
Target Software Group Inc., 144
Targus Inc., 133
Tarheel Filing Company Inc., 419
Tari Tan Ceramic & Craft Supply, 113
Tarm USA, 211
Tasco Sales Inc., 70, 264
Tashiro's Tools, 419
Task Lighting Corporation, 310, 312
Tatewin-Petaki American Indian Arts & Crafts, 290
Tatman (Greg) Wooden Boats, 76
Tatung Company of America Inc., 137
Taunton Press, 91
TAURUS Technologies, 16
Tavros Leather, 314
Taxidermy Today Magazine, 91
Taylor (Ann) 125
Taylor (Dave) Civil War Antiques 7, 323
Taylor (R.D.) Rodmakers 181
Taylor Brothers, 275
Taylor Gifts, 257
Taylor Made Golf Clubs, 259, 260
Taylor Manufacturing, 211
Taylor Studios, 374
Taylor's & Company Inc., 263
Taylor's Cutaways & Stuff, 152, 173, 384
TC Sports, 55, 273
Teac, 403, 404, 426
Team America, 133
TEAM Inc., 2
Team Karim, 376
Team Paradise, 376
Teas Nursery Company, 236, 237
Teasel, 106, 121, 148, 366
Tebb (Fred) & Sons Inc. 78
TEC Trees, 245
Tech-Systems, 169
Techni-Tool, 169
Technic Tool Corporation, 22, 226
Technical Analysis Inc., 91
Technical Innovations Inc., 16
Technical Papers Corporation, 11, 71, 170, 389
Technics, 47, 403, 404, 405
TECHNIQdesign, 301, 386
Technopower II Inc., 325
TechPool Studios, 144
Techsonic Industries Inc., 181
Tecnica USA, 102
Tectron Telescopes, 18
Ted E. Bear's Shoppe, 61
Teddies N' Tole, 60

CORPORATE INDEX

Teddy Bear Emporium, 61
Teddy Bear Ranch, 61
Teddy Tailor, 60
Teddys by Tracy, 60
Teddytown U.S.A., 61
Tee-Bird Products Inc., 33, 42
Tefteller (John) 108
Teitel Brothers, 190
Tejas Fountain Designs, 223
Tektite, 392
Tele Vue Optics, 18
Teleconcepts Inc., 411
Teleflite Corporation, 327
Telephone Engineering Company, 411
Telepro Golf Shops, 260
Telescope Casual Furniture, 218
Teletire, 47
Teleview Distributors, 427
Telex/Hy-Gain Communications Inc., 372
Tell (William) 363
Temasek Telephone Inc., 273, 411
TEMP-CAST Enviroheat Ltd., 211
Tempest Micro, 135
Templeton Tribal Art, 294
TENBA Quality Cases Ltd., 355
Tender Heart Treasures Ltd., 60, 164, 257
Tenera Fish Food, 352
Tener's Western Outfitters, 297
Tennant (Lee) Enterprises Inc. 131
Tennessee Genealogical Society, 249
Tennessee Historical Commission, 249
Tennessee Home Medical, 346
Tennessee Log Homes, 284
Tennessee Moulding & Frame Company, 210
Tennessee Sports Company, 54
Tennessee State Archives & Library, 249
Tennessee Valley Manufacturing, 263
Tennis Gear & Running Center, 380, 413
Tennis Partner of Chicago, 413
Tents & Trails, 104, 334
Tepper Discount Tools, 419
Teri's Mini Workshop, 162
Terra Avionics, 4
Terra Designs, 279
Terra Soar Inc., 407
TerraCast, 225
Terramar Sports Ltd., 334, 380
Terran Fabrics, 173, 369
Terrco Inc., 419
Terre Celeste, 59
Terrill Machine Inc., 27, 29, 30, 31, 39, 40
Territorial Seed Company, 219, 220, 242
Territory Ahead, 129, 388
Terry (Georgia), Autographs 21
Terry Clocks, 119
Terry Precision Bicycles, 66
Terry's Auto Parts, 27
Terry's Jaguar Parts, 34
Terry's Village, 257
Terumo Medical Corporation, 159
Tesoro Electronics, 321
Tesseract Early Scientific Instruments, 7
Testfabrics Inc., 173
Testrite Instrument Company Inc., 11, 357, 358, 361
Teton Homes, 48
Tetra Pond, 227
Tetra Terrafauna, 354
Teuscher Chocolates of Switzerland, 188
Texas Art Supply Company, 11
Texas Greenhouse Company, 221
Texas Instruments Inc., 133, 135
Texas Knifemakers Supply, 306
Texas Mustang Parts, 38
Texas Nautical Repair Company, 18

Texas Outfitters Supply Inc., 284
Texas Platers Supply, 169
Texas Sportcard Company, 399
Texas Standard Picket Company, 175
Texas State Library, 249
Texas Towers, 372
Texas Weather Instruments Inc., 433
Texas Wild Game Cooperative, 198
Texicolor Corporation, 171
Texsport, 104
Textile Museum Shop, 91
Thai Silks, 125
Thames (H.M.) Pecan Company 200
That Fish Place, 352
That Patchwork Place, 91
That Patchwork Place Inc., 369
That's A Wrap Inc., 261
Thaxted Cottage, 247, 266
Thayer & Chandler, 11
The Best Source Inc., 26
The Masters' Collection, 14
Theatre Poster Exchange, 336
Theatrical Lighting Systems Inc., 414
Theatrix Interactive, 144
Theriault's Doll, 164
Thermador/Waste King, 7
Thermo Dynamics Ltd., 286, 395
Thermo-Press/Norvell Corporation, 282
Thetford Chair Company, 218
Thibaut (Richard E.) Inc. 281
Things Japanese, 342, 384
Things of Good Taste, 185, 188, 200, 206
Things Remembered, 434
Things You Never Knew Existed, 301
Think Ink, 11, 366
Third Fork, 437
Third Hand, 67
This Blooming Island, 201
This N' That, 291
Thistlewood Timber Frame Homes, 283
THK Photo Products Inc., 357
Thoele Manufacturing, 272
Thomas & Thomas, 181
Thomas (Eldridge C.) 196
Thomas (William A.) Braille Bookstore 93
Thomas Electroscopes, 321
Thomas Industries Inc., 1
Thomasville Furniture, 212
Thompson & Morgan Inc., 230, 234, 236, 242
Thompson (Andrew) Company 269
Thompson (Ernest) 216
Thompson (Norm) 125, 257, 387
Thompson Cigar Company, 257, 415
Thompson/Center Arms Company, 263
Thorndike Press, 93
Thornhill Enterprises, 285
Thornhill Entertainment, 337
Thoroughbred Coach Builders, 36
Thoroughbred Music, 340
Thoroughbred Racing Catalog, 15, 98, 257
Thorpe (Ken) 47
Thousand Mile Outdoor Wear, 102, 125
Thousand Oaks Optical, 18
Thread Discount Sales, 384
Threads at Gingerbread Hill, 173
Threads Etc., 304, 442
Three Kittens Yarn Shoppe, 342, 384
Three Rivers Archery Supply, 9
Three Rivers Pottery Productions Inc., 150
Thrifty Distributors, 58, 100
Thule Car Rack Systems, 67
Thumbelina Needlework Shop, 304, 342, 442
Thunder Bay Gourmet Foods, 195

Thunderbird, 32, 42
Thunderbird Bar, 42
Thunderbird Center, 42
Thunderbird Headquarters, 42
Thunderbird Parts & Restoration, 42
Thunderbirds One, 42
Thunderbirds USA Parts Supply, 42
Thundering Herd Buffalo Products, 198
Thunderwear Inc., 432
Thur (L.P.) Fabrics 173
Thurber's, 117, 390
Thyme Garden, 233, 235
Tic-Tac-Toes, 400
Ticket Craft, 415
Tide-Mark Press Ltd., 98
Tide-Rider Inc., 61, 156, 166, 409
Tidewater Specialties, 257
Tidewater Workshop, 218
Tidy's Storehouse, 150
Tierisch Exclusiv, 351
Tierra Verde, 242
Tierracast, 301
Tiffany & Company, 257, 297
Tiffen Manufacturing, 357
Tiger Art Gallery, 293
Tiger Direct Inc., 145
Tigershark Watercraft, 295
Tile Roofs Inc., 277
Tilearts, 117
Tilford (Douglas L.) 316
Tillamook Cheese, 195
Tilley Endurables, 125, 126
Tilos Products, 393
Tilton Engineering, 45
Timber Crest Farms, 192, 196
Timber Lace Company, 440
Timber Log Building Systems, 284
Timber Press, 91
Timberking Inc., 313, 419
Timberline Archery Products, 9
Timberline Furniture, 216
Timberline Geodesics, 283
Timberpeg, 283
Timberville Electronics, 427
Time Capsule Comics, 131
Time Gallery, 119
Time Machine Music & Video, 108
Time Savers Inc./Timeworks International, 144
Time Warner Viewer's Edge, 111, 257, 429
Timeless Books, 91
Timeless Garden, 175
Timeless Traditions, 311
Timeline Inc., 133
Times Cycles Research, 16
Tin Bin, 150, 308
Tin Knocker, 310
Tin Lizzie Antique Auto Parts, 37
Tin-Na-Tit Kin-Ne-Ki Indian Arts & Gifts, 294
Tinari Greenhouses, 228
Tinhorn, 308, 310
Tink's Safariland Hunting Corporation, 289
Tinmouth Channel Farm, 235
Tiny Colonies, 162
Tiny Power, 329
Tioga Mill Outlet, 173, 393
Tip Tools & Equipment, 47
Tip Top Mobility, 22
Tipi Gift Shop, 292
Tipi Shop Inc., 294
Tippett Postcards Inc., 366
Tippman Industrial Products Inc., 385
Tire Rack, 47, 49
Tischler Peony Gardens, 238

CORPORATE INDEX

Titan Aircraft, 2
Titan Games, 145
Titla (Phillip) Studio 290
Titleist Golf Equipment, 260
TKA Electronics, 427
TKD Enterprises Inc., 91, 319, 429
TLC (Dr.) Greenthumb 227
TLC Yarns, 442
TM Ceramic Service, 164
TMI Healthcare Products, 290
TNC Enterprises, 421
TNT Records, 400
Toback (Myron) Inc. 301
Tobins Lake Studios, 414
ToCad America, 362
Tocad America Inc., 355
Todaro Brothers, 192, 195
Today's Treasures, 61, 166
Todd Uniform Inc., 128
Todd's Train Depot, 331
Tog Shop, 125, 387
Tokina Optical Corporation, 70, 356
Tollett Apiaries, 64
Tom Thumb Workshops, 182, 349, 366
Tomahawk Log & Country Homes Inc., 284
Tomato Growers Supply Company, 245
Tomato Seed Company Inc., 245
Tomorrow Is Yesterday, 131
Tom's Obsolete Chevy Parts, 28, 29, 34, 39
Tom's Q Stix, 68
Tom's Tiny Trees & Supplies, 231
Toner (Marie) Lighting Designs Inc. 162
Toneup Music, 111
Toni Ann's Doll House, 166
Toni's Victorian Creations, 158
Tonto Rim Trading Company, 269, 388
Tool Chest, 91
Tool Club, 419
Tool Crib of the North, 419
Tool Factory Outlet, 419
Tooland Inc., 419
Toole's Bend Nursery, 245
Toolhauz Corporation, 419
Tools for Exploration, 91
Tools for Yoga, 443
Top Gun Racing, 295
Top Hat Company, 188
Top Hat Cricket Farm Inc., 354
Top of the World Books, 91
TOPAZ-Mineral Exploration, 92, 375
Topiary Inc., 227
TopTack Inc., 351
Torah Educational Software, 94, 144
Torbot Group Inc., 346
Torelli Imports, 66, 407
Tornello Landscape Corporation, 229
Tornow (Chris) 285
Toro Company, 224, 312
Toro Irrigation Division, 228
Toronto Surplus & Scientific, 169
Torrefazione Italia Inc., 207
Torrens (Tom) Sculpture Design Inc. 223
Torrington Brush Works Inc., 11
Tortellini, 120
Tosca Company, 385
Toscano Design, 223
Toshiba, 47, 404, 426
Toshiba America, 135, 427
Tot Tenders Inc., 51
Total Shop, 419
Total Sports, 412, 413
Totally Tomatoes, 245
Totem Graphics Inc., 144
Totem Smokehouse, 203
Touch of Brass, 212, 370

Touch of Class Catalog, 57, 125, 158
Touch of Country, 150, 409
Touching Leaves Indian Crafts, 293
Touchstone, 257
Touchstone Taxidermy Supply, 410
Touchstone Woodworks, 275
Tough Traveler, 51, 104
Tour Hockey Skates, 376
Tour Master Riding Gear, 331
Tournament Tackle Inc., 181
Tourneau, 297
Tower Hobbies, 325, 327, 328
Tower Lighting Center, 312
Tower Records Mailorder, 111
Town & Country Cedar Homes, 284
Town & Country/Hobbies & Crafts, 331
Townes (J.T.) Inc. 349
Townsend (James) & Son Inc. 92, 149, 323
Toy Box, 162
Toy Scouts Inc., 336, 422
Toy Shoppe, 61, 166
Toy Soldier Company, 421
Toy Soldier Gallery Inc., 421
Toy Train Depot, 331
Toy Trains of Yesteryear, 331
Toy Village, 61, 166
Toys for Special Children, 272, 424
Toys from Times Past, 369, 422
Toys Plus, 52
Toys to Grow On, 422, 424
Toys-Toys-Toys, 422, 424
Tracks Walking Staffs, 106, 362
Tracy Fairings, 333
Trade Carbonless, 343
Trader Rose, 59
Tradewinds, 315
Tradewinds Bamboo Nursery, 229
Trading Post Clothes Horse, 291
Tradition USA Toy Soldiers, 421
Traditional Country Crafts, 106
Traditional Norwegian Rosemaking, 416
Traditional Papercutting, 402
Traditions Inc., 263
Trafalgar Square Publishing, 92
Trail Foods Company, 105
Trail Ridge Traders, 104
Trailer World, 48
Trailers of New England, 48
Trailex, 48
Trailhawk Treestands, 288
TrailPrints, 102
Trails Illustrated, 318
Trails West Manufacturing of Idaho Inc., 285
Train Express, 331
Train Station, 331
Train Terrain Products, 331
Train Works, 331
Train World, 331
Trainer's Choice, 351
Trampoline World, 425
Trango USA, 334
Tranquil Lake Nursery, 238
Trans-Pacific Nursery, 236
Transcrypt International Inc., 373
TransLanguage Inc., 144
Transpacific Health Products, 196
Transparent Language Inc., 144
Transparent Software Systems, 144
Traphagen Honey, 195, 201
Trappistine Creamy Caramels, 188
Trappistine Quality Candy, 188
Tratter Graphics, 349
Trautman Outdoor Creations Inc., 288
Travaco Labs/ITW Philadelphia Resins, 78
Travel Keys Books, 92

Travel Smith, 125
Travelcade, 333
Travelers Bookstore, 92, 318
Traveling Light, 104
Traverse Bay Log Homes, 284
Travis (Marion) 216, 266
Travis Violets, 228
Trax America, 288
Traxx Golf Company, 260
Treadle Yard Goods, 173
Treadlok, 264, 381
Treadwell Shirt Company, 126
Treadwell's Western Mercantile, 117, 390
Treasure Chest Fund Raising, 211
Treasure Chest Sales, 38
Treasure Trove at the Ahwatukee Commons, 322
Treasured Memories, 434
Treasures & Keepsakes, 384
Treasures by Paula K, 163
Trebark Camouflage, 288
Tree Toys, 347
Trees on the Move Inc., 245
Treevanish Camouflage, 288
Trek Bicycle Corporation, 66
Trellis Structures, 223
Tremont Nail Company, 277
Trend-Lines, 419
Trendco Inc., 319, 363, 364
Trendware Phone Systems, 411
Trenna Productions, 94
Trenton Mold Boutique, 113
Tri-Ess Sciences Inc., 414
Tri-Ex Tower Corporation, 372
Tri-R Technologies, 2
Tri-Star Computer Corporation, 135
Tri-Star Trimarans, 72
Tri-State Camera, 100, 146, 361, 405, 427
Tri-State Computer, 137
Triangle Automotive, 33, 34, 35
Triangle Envelope Company, 402
Triangle Pacific Corporation, 98
Triangle Printing Company, 343
Tribal Enterprise, 294
Tricker (William) Inc. 228
Trifles, 125, 257
Trigon, 104
Trillium International, 201
Trimax, 171
Trimble Navigation Limited, 79
Trinity Products Inc., 328
Triola (Bonnie) 397, 442
Triple Cities Reptile, 354
Triple Crown Fence, 175
Triple Fish Fishing Line, 181
Tripp Lite, 133
Trippensee Transparent Globes, 258
Tripple Brook Farm, 229, 232, 243, 245
Tripp's Manufacturing, 301
Tripwire Toys, 422
TriStar Photo Industrial Inc., 358
Triton Gallery, 336
Trius Inc., 266
TRIUS Software, 144
Trlby Kites, 304
Troll Family Gift Catalog, 257
Troll Harnesses, 334
Troll Learn & Play, 422, 424
Trophy Supply, 50
Trophy Whitetail Products, 288
Trophyland USA Inc., 50
Tropical Exotic Hardwoods, 315
Tropich Software Inc., 144, 362
Tropiflora, 231
Trove Software, 144

CORPORATE INDEX

Troy-Bilt Manufacturing Company, 221
Tru-Form Taxidermy Supplies Inc., 410
Tru-Glo Archery Products, 9
Tru-Square Metal Products, 301, 368
Truck Shop, 49
Truck Shop Parts, 49
True BASIC Inc., 144
True Connections, 28
True Engineering Inc., 219
True Fitness Technology Inc., 171
True Reproductions, 15
Truebite Inc., 113
Truly Victorian Mercantile, 117
Trumble Greetings, 158, 261
Trusty Enterprises Inc., 68
Tryson House, 190
TS Imported Automotive, 26
TSI Jewelry Supply, 59, 301
Tuck (Travis) 434
Tucker Electronics, 168, 372
Tucker-Barry, 111
Tucker's Auto Salvage, 41
Tuf-Wear USA, 95
Tuff-Kote Company Inc., 277
Tulikivi U.S. Inc., 177, 406
Tumblecraft, 301
Tundra Camjacket, 355
Turf Cheesecake Corporation, 185
Turn of the Century Lampshades, 311
Turn off the TV, 424
Turnbaugh Printers Supply, 366
Turnbow Trailers Inc., 285
Turncraft Clocks Inc., 119
Turner Art Works, 291
Turner Greenhouses, 221
Turner-Tolson Inc., 216
Turquoise, 293
Turtle Beach Systems, 133
Turtle Lightning Amiga Domain, 137
Turtle Press, 92, 319
Turtles, 405
Tuscarora Indian Handcraft Shop, 293
Tuskewe Krafts, 292, 307
Tussie Mussies, 366
Tuthill (Roger W.) Inc. 18, 70
Tutino's, 206
Tuttle Golf Collection, 125, 259
Tweeds, 125
Twelve Tone Systems, 144
Twilley (Otis) Seed Company 236, 242
Twilley Seed Company, 246
Twin Oaks Hammocks, 266
Twincerely Yours, 51, 120, 251
Twinhead Corporation, 135
Twinrocker Papermaking Supplies, 347
Twist (Ryan) Gallery 166
Two Guys Fossils & Minerals, 374, 375
Twombly Nursery, 239, 245
Twyce (Mary) Antiques & Books 366
TYROL International, 257
Tyson (Frederick J.) Military Models 322
Tyson (Rod & Helen) 375

U

U-Bild, 440
U-Brew, 437
U.S. Box Corporation, 345
U.S. Bronze Sign Company, 118
U.S. Cavalry, 104, 306
U.S. Chess Federation, 92, 115
U.S. Flag Service, 182
U.S. Games Systems Inc., 424
U.S. Gaslight Company, 312
U.S. Gerslyn Ltd., 399
U.S. Government Printing Office, 92
U.S. Health Club Inc., 430
U.S. Industrial Tool & Supply Company, 4
U.S. Pen Fund Raising Company, 211
U.S. Repeating Arms Company, 265
U.S. Robotics, 133
U.S. Shell Inc., 382
U.S. Tag & Label Corporation, 344
U.S. Toy Company Inc., 107, 316, 347, 422
U.S. Wet Suits, 393
UCL Photo, 359
UFO Sports Inc., 376, 390
Uhn Inc., 354
Ujena Company, 125
Ulead Systems, 144
Ulrich (Jack) 181
Ulster Scientific Inc., 159
Ultimage Image Inc., 146
Ultimate Aquarium, 352
Ultimate Bicycle Support, 67
Ultimate Cooker, 406
Ultimate Home Care Company, 212, 272, 436
Ultra Light Arms Inc., 265
Ultra Play Systems Inc., 364, 388
Ultra Tec, 301
Ultra-Comp Computers, 135
Ultrac Performance Systems, 295
UltraGuard Fence, 175
Ultramouse Ltd., 173, 384
Ultratec, 273
Ultravia Aero International Inc., 2
Umatilla Auto Salvage, 24
UMAX Technologies Inc., 133
Umbrella Shop, 106, 428
Umpqua Feather Merchants, 181
Unabridged Woodworking Plans, 440
Uncle Bernie's Warehouse Club, 257
Uncle John's Foods, 105
Uncle John's Gingerbread House Trim, 280
Uncle Mike's Muzzleloading, 263
Uncle Sam Umbrella Shop, 106, 428
Uncle's Stereo, 405, 427
Uncommon Herb, 148, 206, 207, 349
Under Glass Manufacturing Corporation, 221, 396
Under the Big Top, 130, 149, 301, 347, 414
Under the Rubber Tree, 378
Undercover Cover Company, 346
Undergear, 121, 125
Unicef, 257, 261, 363
Unicorn Books & Crafts Inc., 92, 94
Unicorn Electronics, 168
Unicorn Software Company, 144
Unicorn Studios, 60, 164, 337
Uniden, 411
Union Jacks, 394
Unique Colors, 401
Unique Dist., 131, 398, 399
Unique Insect Control, 219
Unique Motorcars Inc., 44
Unique Needle, 173
Unique Petite, 126
Unique Photo, 361
Unique Publications, 319, 429
Unique Record Club, 108
Unique Simplicities, 266
Unique Sports Products Inc., 267
Unique Tool, 320
Uniquity, 92
Unit Structures, 223
United America Cards, 354
United Art Glass, 401
United Art Supply Company, 11
United Communications, 15
United Cutlery, 306
United Division of Pfizer, 346
United Electronic Supply, 427
United House Wrecking Inc., 277
United Mfrs. Supplies Inc., 210
United Nations Publications, 318
United Ostomy Association, 92
United Pharmacal Company Inc., 351
United Solar Systems Corporation, 395
United States Gypsum Company, 12
United States Holocaust Memorial Museum Shop, 92
United States Marine Corps Collectables, 322
United States Purchasing Exchange, 257
United States Survival Society, 381
United Supply Company Inc., 152
United Synagogue Book Service, 92
Unitex Inc., 442
Unitrol Data Protection Systems Inc., 144
Unitron Inc., 18, 70, 307, 321
UNIVEGA, 66
Universal Antenna Manufacturing, 427
Universal Aqua Technologies, 432
Universal Bowling, 68, 95
Universal Clamp Corporation, 416
Universal Distributors Corporation, 357
Universal Electronics, 427
Universal Gym Equipment, 171
Universal Hovercraft, 286
Universal Map, 318
Universal Radio Inc., 372
Universal Rundle, 286
Universal Tire Company, 21, 47
Universal Trav-Ler, 95
Universal Video & Camera, 100
Universal Vise Corporation, 181
University Optics, 19, 70
University Publishing, 169
Up, 130, 414
UPCO, 71, 350, 351
Upper Mississippi Valley Mercantile Company, 323
Upstill Software, 144, 208
Upton Tea Imports, 207
Uptown Sales Inc., 382
Urban Angler, 181
Urban Archaeology, 277, 310
Urban Artifacts, 177
Urban Farmer Store, 228, 312
Urdl's Waterfall Creations Inc., 222, 227
US Aviation, 2
US Aviator, 128
US Tower Corporation, 372
USA Blind Factory, 154
USA Direct, 403
USA Flex Inc., 133, 135, 137
USA Skate Company, 273
USA SportWear, 128
USATCO Tools, 4
Used Gear by Mail, 340
Usinger's Famous Sausage, 198
UsrEZ Software Inc., 144
Uster (Albert) Imports Inc. 106, 185
UT Golf, 260
Utah Archives & Record Services, 249
Utah Genealogical Association, 249
Utah State Historical Society, 249
Utex Trading, 173, 384
Utrecht Art & Drafting Supply, 11
UVP Inc., 312
Uwchlan Farm, 158, 223

❖ CORPORATE INDEX ❖

V

V & B Manufacturing, 226
V-Rock Shop, 375
V.I. Reed & Cane, 56, 114
V.I.P. Molds Inc., 113
V.K. Sports, 390
V.P.I. Reptiles, 354
Vacations with Children, 92
Vacuflo, 428
Vacuum Form, 12
VAI Direct, 111
Vailly Aviation, 325
Vale (Susan) Enterprises 342
Valentine Inc., 354
Valhalla Products, 74
Valley Crafts & Collectibles, 52
Valley Ford Parts, 33, 38, 41
Valley Furniture Shop, 216
Valley Hills Press, 394
Valley Motors, 25, 36, 40
Valley Plaza Hobbies, 327
Valley Recreation Products Inc., 68, 156
Valley Vet Supply, 284, 285
Valley View Automotive Products, 28, 33, 34, 39
Value Carpets Inc., 78
Value-Tique Inc., 381
ValueExpre$$, 133
Van Bourgondien Bros., 238, 239, 242
Van Cort Instruments Inc., 302
Van Dam Wood Craft, 76
Van Dyck's Flower Farms, 232
Van Engelen Inc., 242
Van Mechelen (Nadine) 293
Van Ness China Company, 117
Van Ness Water Gardens, 227
Van Schaik (Mary Mattison) 242
Van Sciver Bobbin Lace, 174
Van Scotter (JoAnn) Postcards 347, 366
Vance & Hines Motorcycle Center, 333
Vandenberg, 239, 242
Vander Haag's Inc., 49
Vandersteen Audio, 405
VanDyke's, 6, 410
Vanguard Crafts Inc., 152
Vanguard Electronics Labs, 433
Vanity Fair, 297
Vanner Incorporated, 396
Van's Aircraft Inc., 2
Van's Auto Salvage, 24
Vanson Leathers Inc., 331
Vantage Communications Inc., 128
Vantage Mini Vans, 272
Vardakis (Mark) Autographs 21, 347
Varga's Nursery, 232
Variety International, 104
Variflex Inc., 376, 390
Vasque Boots, 102, 387
Vaughn (Hugh & Jennie) Luggage 314
Vaughn Brothers Rocketry, 327
Vaughn Display & Flag, 182
VCH Publishers Inc., 92
Vector Research, 404, 426
Vectra Fitness Inc., 171
Vegetable Factory Inc., 396
Vektron International Inc., 137
Velbon, 362
Veldheer Tulip Gardens, 232
Velo, 257
Velocity Aircraft, 2
Veltec Sports Inc., 66
Velux-America Inc., 282
Ven-Tel Inc., 133
Vent-A-Hood Company, 7
Venus Knitting Mills Inc., 53, 55, 79, 208, 209, 273, 380, 413, 425, 431
Veon Creations, 59, 301
Veri-Lite Inc., 48
Vermont American, 419
Vermont Bean Seed Company, 235, 242
Vermont Castings Inc., 177
Vermont Confectionary, 188
Vermont Country Maple Mixes, 183, 185, 196
Vermont Country Store, 125, 257, 303
Vermont Frames, 276
Vermont FurnitureWorks, 150, 216
Vermont Garden Shed, 226
Vermont Industries, 158, 176, 257, 308, 310
Vermont Nature Creations, 71, 225
Vermont Outdoor Furniture, 218
Vermont Teddy Bear Company, 61
Vermont Timber Frames, 283
Vermont Wildflower Farm, 246
Verne's Chrome Plating, 43
Vernon (Lillian) 257
Vernon (Lillian) Kitchen 303
Vernon (Sydney B.) 323
Vernon Pottery, 163
VERNONscope & Company, 19
Versa-Lift, 436
Versatile Rack Company, 264
Versitex of America Ltd., 181
Vertical Aviation Technologies Inc., 2
Vertisoft Systems, 144
Very Thing, 125
Vesey Seeds Ltd., 242
Vestal Press Ltd., 15, 92, 107
Vesterheim Sales Shop, 416
Veteran Leather Company Inc., 312
Veterans Caning Shop, 114
Vetta/Orleander USA, 67
Vetus-Denouden Inc., 78, 79, 433
Viacom New Media, 144, 423
Vibra-Tek Company, 301
Vicarage, 34
Vicki's Miniatures, 163
Victor Model Products, 328
Victoria (Lisa) Brass Beds 212
Victoria British Ltd., 26, 37, 41, 43
Victorian Classics Lampshades, 311
Victorian Collectibles, 279, 281
Victorian Craftsman Ltd., 163
Victorian Cupboard, 206
Victorian Interiors, 280
Victorian Lampshades, 311
Victorian Lampshades by Nadja Rider, 310
Victorian Lightcrafters Ltd., 310
Victorian Lighting Works, 308, 310
Victorian Papers, 262
Victorian Replicas, 216
Victorian Times Houses, 163
Victorian Treasures, 173, 384
Victoria's Dance-Theatrical Supply, 154, 155, 414
Victoria's Secret, 121, 125
Victoria's Vinegars, 206
Video Alternative, 429
Video Direct Distributors, 100
Video Discount Warehouse, 100
Video Finder, 111, 337
Video Innovators, 100
Video Necessities, 100
Video Opera House, 429
Video Specialists International, 337
Video Surveillance Corporation, 5
Videonics, 100
Vidicomp Inc., 100
Viette (Andre) Nurseries 235, 239
Viewer's Edge, 257
Vigeant (Jeffrey W.) 163
Vigil (Carol) 117, 292
Viking Aircraft Inc., 2
Viking Components, 133
Viking Design, 174
Viking Folk Art Publications Inc., 92
Viking Office Products, 98, 114, 344, 348
Viking Range Corporation, 7
Viking Woodcrafts Inc., 416
Villa Tatra Colorado, 203
Village Blacksmith, 225
Village Furniture House, 216
Village Herb Shop Catalogue, 148, 206, 366
Village Lantern, 308, 310
Village Marine Tec., 432
Village Plate Collector, 363
Village Weaver, 62
Village Wholesale, 352
Vinotemp International, 438
Vintage '45 Press, 92
Vintage Animation Gallery, 15
Vintage Automotive, 24
Vintage Drum Center, 340
Vintage Ford & Chevrolet Parts of AZ, 49
Vintage Garage, 40
Vintage Gardens, 240
Vintage Lumber Company, 276
Vintage Newspapers, 343
Vintage Radio Restorations, 23
Vintage Speedsters, 45
Vintage Tin Auto Parts, 27, 30, 31, 33, 34, 38, 39, 40
Vintage Tire, 47
Vintage Valances, 154
Vintage Video, 337
Vintage Wood Works, 247, 280, 439
Vinylmaniac, 111
Violet Express, 228
Violet House, 225
Violet Showcase, 228
Violets by Appointment, 228
VIPCO, 278
Virgin Games, 423
Virginia Classic Mustang Inc., 38
Virginia Diner, 198, 200, 201
Virginia Genealogical Society, 250
Virginia Hydroponics, 222
Virginia State Library & Archives, 250
Virtual Entertainment, 144
Virtual Reality Labs Inc., 16
Visible, 146, 344
Vision Microsystems Inc., 4
VisionSoft, 133
Visiontek, 264
Visitect Inc., 168
Vista Aviation Inc., 3
Vista Instrument Company, 19
VistaLite, 67
Vistek, 361
Visual Image, 378
Visual Systems Company Inc., 11
Visuals, 361
Vita-Mix Corporation, 183
Vitajet Corporation, 159
Vitamin Co-Op, 430
Vitamin Direct Inc., 430
Vitamin Power of Texas, 430
Vitamin Shoppe, 148, 270, 431
Vitamin Specialties Company, 431
Vitrex Ceramics Ltd., 113
VIVA Crafts, 182
Viva Las Vegastamps, 378

CORPORATE INDEX

VIVANDE'S Italian Pantry, 190
Vivitar Corporation, 70, 356, 358, 362
Vixen Hill, 247, 278
Vladimir Arts U.S.A. Inc., 15
VLS Mail Order, 325, 421
VM Boat Trailers, 295
Vogel Enterprises Inc., 19
Vogelzang Corporation, 406
Vogt's Inc., 24
Volcano Corporation, 104
Volk Corporation, 50, 345
Volkman Bird Seed, 350
Volkmann Bros. Greenhouses, 228
Volleyball One, 431
Volpi Foods, 190, 199
Volunteer State Obsolete Chevy Parts, 28, 29, 39
Voluparts, 43
Vorbeck (Tom) 192
Vortech Inc., 2
Voyager Company, 144
Voyageur, 78
VP Health Savings Center, 431
VPI, 346
Vulcan Binder & Cover, 344
Vulcan Supply Corporation, 280

W

W & W Associates, 58, 372
W-H Autopilots, 79
W-W Finishing Supplies, 438
W-W Trailer, 285
Wa-Mac Inc., 68, 95, 261, 267, 346, 369, 370, 409, 413
Wa-Swa-Gon Arts & Crafts, 294
Wabanaki Arts, 291
Waddell's Drum Center, 340
Wade (Garrett) Company 268, 419
Wade (Wallace W.) Wholesale Tires 47
Wade Manufacturing Company, 416
Wag-Aero Group of Aircraft Services, 4
Wagon Mound Ranch Supply, 286
Wagon Wheel Records & Books, 92, 111, 400
Wagonhill Dolls, 166
Wagonmaster Antiques, 434
Wahl Clipper Corporation, 351, 420
Walck's Four Wheel Dr., 35
Walden Video for Kids, 429
Wale Apparatus Company Inc., 59, 401
Walk Easy Inc., 106, 272
Walker (Curt), Optician 393
Walker Manufacturing Company, 224
Walkers Shortbread Ltd., 185
Wall (Steve) Lumber Company 315, 420
Wall Street Camera, 361
Walla Walla Gardener's Association, 192
Wallace (Amos) 290
Wallace (Ann) & Friends 154
Wallace International Silversmiths, 390
Wallach (S.) 336
Wallis (Jack) Door Emporium 275
Wallos (Brian) & Company 399
Wallpaper & Blinds Company, 281
Wallpaper & Blinds Connection, 154, 281
Wallpaper Outlet, 281
Wallpaper Warehouse Inc., 281
Walmer Dollhouses, 163
Walnut Acres Organic Farms, 196
Walnut Creek Software, 138, 144
Walnut Creek Woodworkers Supply Company, 420
Walnut Grove Auto Parts, 21
Walpole Woodworkers, 216, 218, 267

Walrus Inc., 104, 125
Walsh Screen & Window Inc., 282
Walston (Jim) 327
Walter (Gary) Baseball Cards 399
Walter's Cookbooks, 211
Walthers, 331
Walton Way Medical, 270, 272
Wanda's Nature Farm Foods, 96, 183, 196
Wanderings Inc., 127, 257
Wandix International Inc., 319
Wapsi Fly Inc., 181
War Eagle Mill, 196, 257
Ward (Charles B.) Minerals 375
Ward Clapboard Mill Inc., 278
Ward Log Homes, 284
Wardrobe Wagon, 126
Ward's Natural Science, 19, 70, 307, 374
Warehouse Carpets Inc., 379
Warehouse Hobbies, 328, 329
Warfield Fossil Quarries, 374
Waring Products, 7
Warling Miniatures, 163
Warlock Designs, 45
Warm Things, 62, 63
Warne Manufacturing Company, 264
Warner Brothers Catalog, 128
Warner Company, 281
Warner-Crivellaro, 92, 401
Warner's Dock Inc., 295
Warren & Sweat Manufacturing Company, 288
Warren Muzzle Loading Company Inc., 263
Warren Publishing House Inc., 81
Warren Tool Company Inc., 420, 439
Warren's Model Trains, 331
Warscokins, 152, 174
Warth Esq. (T.E.), Automotive Books 92
Warwick Miniatures Ltd., 421
Washington Copper Works, 310
Washington State Archives, 250
Washington State Genealogical Society, 250
Washington State University Creamery, 189
Wasserberg (Michael B.) Postcards 366
Wasserman Uniform Company, 128
Water Makers Inc., 432
Water Warehouse, 409
WaterColours, 15
Waterford Crystal Inc., 117, 153
Waterford Gardens, 227, 228
Waterford Irish Stoves Inc., 406
Waterford Nut Company, 200
Waterfront Living, 257
Waterloo Records & Video, 111
Waterlox Chemical & Coatings Corporation, 438
WaterRower Inc., 171
Wathne Corporation, 125
Watkins Manufacturing Spas, 286
Watson-Guptill Publications, 92
Watson's (Barb) Brushworks 416
Watts & Franklin Placer Mining Equipment Inc., 368
Watts (Edwin) Golf Shops 261
Watts' Train Shop, 331
Waushara Gardens, 233
Waveco, 133
Wawak Corporation, 384
Wax Orchards, 196
Wayah'sti Indian Traditions, 293
Wayfarer Trading Company, 297
Wayland Marine Ltd., 72
Wayne Frame Products Inc., 210
Wayne-Dalton Corporation, 219
Waynee (Robert D.) 293
Wayner (Gary) Books 92

Wayne's Auto Salvage, 33, 34, 35, 38, 41
Wayne's Woods Inc., 268, 438
Waynesboro Nurseries, 245
Wayside Gardens, 235, 238, 239, 242, 245
Wayward Bookman, 80
Wayzata Technology, 144
We-Du Nursery, 240, 246
We-No-Nah Canoes, 74
WearGuard Corporation, 125
Wearnes Technology Corporation, 133
Weather Bureau, 433
Weather Hat Company of Wyoming, 269
Weather Shield Mfg. Inc., 275, 282
Weatherby Inc., 265
WeatherTrac, 433
Weathervane, 434
Weathervane Seafood, 203
Weaver, 342
Weaver (Daniel) Company 199
Weaver (Howard) Apiaries Inc. 64
Weaver Company, 280
Weaver's Ceramic Mold Inc., 113
Weaver's Knot Inc., 442
Weaver's Loft, 304, 342, 397, 442
Weaver's Place, 92, 342
Weaver's Scents, 289
Weavers' Store, 397, 442
Weaving Works, 56, 152, 304, 397, 442
Web of Thread, 342, 384
Web-sters Handspinners, 92, 305, 442
Webb (Charles) 216
Webb's Classic Auto Parts, 35, 40
Weber-Stephen Products, 53
Weber's Nostalgia Supermarket, 21
Webs Yarn, 442
Webster (Kate) Company 164, 297
Wedding Treasures, 434
Weddingware, 434
Wedgwood, 117
Wee-Pak, 105
Weeder Technologies, 168
Weekend Warrior Company, 5
Wehrung & Billmeier Company, 11
Weidlich Ceramics Inc., 113
Wein Products Inc., 358
Weindling (Barbara) 92
Weinel (J.E.) Inc. 334, 396
Weiner (Frederic H.) 340
Weinkrantz Musical Supply Company, 340
Weis Reptiles, 354
Weiss (Mendell) Inc. 121
Weiss Brothers Nursery, 228, 239
Weissman's Designs for Dance, 155
Weitbrecht Communications Inc., 273
WEKA Publishing Inc., 133
Welch (Samuel) Sculpture Inc. 223
Well-Sweep Herb Farm, 182, 233, 235, 236, 366
Wellborn Cabinet Inc., 98
Wellington Leisure Products, 432, 433
Wellington Outdoors, 289
Wellington's Furniture, 216
Wells (Bob) Nursery 230, 233, 240, 245
Wells (Dan) Antique Toys 424
Wells (Tom) Golf Company 261
Wells Cargo Inc., 48
Wells Interiors, 154
Welsh Jaguar Enterprises Inc., 34
Welsh Products Inc., 389
Wenco Windows, 282
Wendell (Mark T.) 207
Wennawoods Publishing, 92, 318
Wenoka Sea Style, 393
Wensco Sign Supplies, 389
Wenzel, 105

❖ CORPORATE INDEX ❖

West (Ed) 35
West (Eddy) 216
West 29th Auto Inc., 24
West Bend, 7
West Coast Chameleon Farms, 354
West Coast Cobra, 44
West Coast Shoe Company, 388
West Coast Sports Cards Inc., 399
West Coast Weathervanes, 434
West Hobbies, 325
West Manor Music, 340
West Marine Products, 75, 76, 78
West Mountain Gourd Farm, 152, 233
West Rindge Baskets Inc., 56
West Virginia Fence Corporation, 175, 353
Westbank Anglers, 181
Westbrook Bead Company, 59, 301
Westbury Camera, 361
Westbury Collection, 257
Westcoast Discount Video, 100
Westcon Inc., 169
Westcott (F.J.) Company 355
Western Biologicals, 236
Western Canoeing Inc., 74
Western Corvette Supply, 30
Western Digital Corporation, 133
Western Horseman Books, 92
Western Maine Nurseries, 245
Western Manufacturing Corporation, 333
Western Minerals, 376
Western Products, 315
Western Publishing Company Inc., 92
Western Squares, 400
Western Test Systems, 169
Western Trading Post, 62
Western Wood Products Association, 440
Western Woodworks, 416
Westfield Comics, 131
Westfield Components Inc., 45
Westgate Enterprises, 414
Westminster Chimes, 437
Weston Bowl Mill, 257, 416
Westside Processing Inc., 359
Westwinds, 150, 434
Wetherbee (Martha) Basket Shop 56
WetJet International Ltd., 295
Wetzler Clamp, 416
Wex Rex Records & Collectibles, 21, 336, 398, 422
What on Earth, 125, 257
What on Earth Naturally, 297, 374, 376, 382
Whatman LabSales, 307
What's Up Kites, 95, 304
Wheel Repair Service Inc., 49
Wheel Vintiques, 49
Wheel World, 67
WheelAround Corporation, 219
Wheelchair Warehouse, 270, 436
Wheelcovers - Robinson's Auto Sales, 49
Wheeler (Eldred) 216
Wheeling Western Wear, 269
Whet Your Appetite, 195
Whillock (Ivan) Studio 92, 420, 440
Whipp Trading Company, 125, 269, 379
Whippoorwill Crafts, 50, 119, 302, 340, 424
Whirlpool Corporation, 7, 286
Whisperwood Collection, 389
Whistle Creek, 106
Whitakers, 216, 401
Whitco/Vincent Whitney Company, 166
White (Chris) Designs Inc. 76
White (Jim) Saddlery & Rodeo Equipment 376

White (Robert E.) Instruments Inc. 433
White Brothers, 295, 333
White Buffalo, 174
White Coffee Corporation, 207
White Flower Farm, 230, 238, 242
White Home Products, 119
White House, 378
White Industries Inc., 4
White Lotus Foundation, 443
White Mountain Freezer Inc., 289
White Mountain Puzzles, 369
White Oak Nursery, 235
White Outdoor Products Company, 220, 224, 225, 227
White Pine Box Company, 416
White Water Creek Trading Company, 149
Whitehall Reproductions, 76
Whitehorse Press, 92
White's Collectables & Fine China, 117, 363
White's Electronics, 321
Whitetail Fly Tieing Supplies, 181
Whitewater Outdoors Inc., 288
Whitewolf Photography, 294
Whitley's Peanut Factory, 195, 200
Whitney (J.C.) & Company 24, 46
Whittemore Glass, 401
Whole Earth Access, 158, 420
Whole Life Products, 257
Whole Mirth Catalog, 92
Whole Person Associates, 92, 429
Whole Work Catalog, 92
Wholesale America Inc., 420
Wholesale Envelopes Inc., 402
Wholesale Frame Service-USA, 210
Wholesale Optics Division, 19
Wholesale Verticals, 154
Wholesale Vet Supply, 284
Wholesalers Inc., 137
Wichita Band Instrument Company, 340
Wicker Warehouse Inc., 218
Wicker Works, 218
Wicker Works of High Point, 218
Wicklein's Aquatic Farm & Nursery Inc., 228
Wicklund Farms, 192
Wicks Aircraft Supply, 4
Wicwas Press, 92
Widener's Reloading & Shooting Supply Inc., 262
Wiegand & Company, 92
Wiese Auto Recycling Inc., 24
Wiese Equine Supply, 284, 285
Wig America, 436
Wig Company, 436
Wiggy's Inc., 105
Wil-Cut Company, 440
Wilbanks Apiaries, 64
Wilcox Cabinet Works, 216
Wild (Gilbert H.) & Son Inc. 238
Wild Bills Leather, 129, 264
Wild Bird Supplies, 71, 350
Wild Country USA, 105
Wild Game Inc., 195, 199
Wild Things, 105, 334
Wild Thyme Farm, 206
Wild Wings, 158, 257
Wilde Yarns, 442
Wilder Agriculture Products Company Inc., 222
Wilderness House, 74
Wilderness Log Homes, 284
Wilderness Press, 92, 318
Wilderness Sound Productions Ltd., 289
Wilderness Systems, 74
Wilderness Tree Stands Inc., 288
Wilderness Wanderer, 105

Wildflower Nursery, 232, 236, 239, 243, 245, 246
Wildlife Artist Supply Company, 410
Wildlife Nurseries, 350
Wildlife Research Center, 289
Wildseed Farms, 246
Wildwasser Sport USA Inc., 74
Wildwood Gardens, 231
Wilensky (Stuart & Donna) 376
Wileswood Country Store, 195
Wiley House Toy Soldiers, 421
Wiley Outdoor Sports, 288
Wilhite Collectible Bookstore, 80, 92
Wilke Machinery Company, 420
Wilkinson (R.S.) 216
Willard (Lt. Moses) Inc. 308, 310
Willhite Seed Company, 242
Williamette Valley Garden, 233, 239
Williams & Hussey Machine Company Inc., 420
Williams (Joe C.) 200
Williams (R.B.) Company Inc. 155
Williams (Ted) 28, 31, 39
William's Brewing Company, 437
Williams Electric Trains, 331
Williams Gun Sight Company, 264
Williams-Sonoma, 207, 257, 289, 303
Williamsburg Blacksmiths Inc., 268
Williamsburg Merchants, 297
Willies Antique Tires, 47
Willis Music Company, 337, 340
Willmann-Bell Inc., 16, 19, 92
Willoughby's Coffee, 207
Willow Creek & Company, 158
Willow Ridge, 125
Willow Tree Lane, 402, 434
Willsboro Wood Products, 216
Willy's Jeep Parts, 35
Wilson (Allen) 424
Wilson (Nathaniel S.), Sailmaker 76
Wilson Antenna Inc., 372, 373
Wilson Boot Company, 388
Wilson Case Company, 264
Wilson Sporting Goods, 53, 208, 209, 370, 413, 431
Wilson WindowWare Inc., 144
Wilsonart, 98
Wilton Enterprise Inc., 106, 146, 303
Wimmer's Meat Products, 199
Winakor (Leo) & Sons Inc. 25
WinBook Computer Corporation, 135
Winchester Gun Safes, 264
Winchester Sutler Inc., 263, 323
Wind & Power, 144
Wind & Weather, 223, 407, 433, 434
Wind in the Rigging, 79
Wind Related Inc., 304
Windborne Kites, 182, 304
Windjammer, 95, 125
Windleaves Weathervanes, 434
Windmill Gardens, 238
Windmill Publishing Company, 92
Window Creations, 282
Window Quilt, 154, 396
Window Saver Company, 282
Windrose, 243, 245
Windsor Collection, 297
Windsor Magic, 316
Windsor Shoppe, 364
Windspeed Designs, 74
Windstorm Archery, 9
Windsurfing Express, 92, 407, 430
Windsurfing Warehouse, 381, 407
Windward Designs, 72
Windward R/C, 325

CORPORATE INDEX

Windy Hill Auto Parts, 25
Windy Hill Forge, 268
Windy Meadows Pottery Ltd., 15, 364
Windy Oaks, 227
Wine & Brew by You, 437
Wine Appreciation Guild, 93, 438
Wine Art, 93, 437
Wine Cask, 438
Wine Cellars USA, 438
Wine Enthusiast, 438
Wine Stop, 438
Winfield Collection, 440
Wing Industries, 275
Wing Manufacturing, 325
Wings & Clays, 266
Wings of Wausau, 71
Wink's Woods, 151
Winnebago Public Indian Museum, 294
Winnicks Auto Sales & Parts, 25, 29, 33
Winross Restorations Upholstery Shop, 49
Winston (R.L.) Rod Company 181
Winter (Thelma) 15
Winter Moon Trading Company, 292
WinterSilks, 125, 127
Winterthur Museum & Gardens, 257, 303
Winthrop Coin Company, 316
WinWay Corporation, 144
Wireless, 128, 257
Wireless Music Source, 111
Wiremold Company, 166
Wisconsin Cheeseman, 189
Wisconsin Discount Stereo, 405, 427
Wisconsin Fibrecraft Inc., 12
Wisconsin Fishing Company, 203
Wisconsin Log Homes Inc., 284
Wisconsin Pottery, 117
Wisconsin State Historical Society, 250
Wisconsin Wagon Company, 424
Wise Company, 268, 438
Wise Screenprint Inc., 114
Wiseman's Auto Salvage, 25
Wishing Well, 114
Wisner Large Format Cameras, 356
Wissota Trader, 125, 387
WISTA Large Format Cameras, 356
Wittek Golf Supply Company Inc., 261
Wizard Games of Scotland Ltd., 144
Wizardware Ltd., 144
Wojcik (Ted) 66
Wolf (Donna) 163
Wolf Chief Graphics, 16, 292
Wolf Ears Equipment, 264
Wolfe Publishing Company, 93
Wolferman's, 183
Wolfe's Neck Farm, 199
Wolfskin (Jack) 102, 105
Woller Auto Parts Inc., 25
Wolo Manufacturing Corporation, 46
Wolsk's Gourmet Confections, 190, 195
Wolverine Boots & Shoes, 95, 387
Wolverine Sports, 430
Wolvering Sports, 54, 55, 209, 273, 395
Womack's Nursery Company, 240, 245
Women's Golf Catalog, 259, 261
Wonder Products Inc., 107
Wonder Works, 19
Wonderbed Manufacturing Company, 212
Wonderduck Decoys, 158
Wood (Charles C.) 331
Wood Carvings by Ted Nichols, 16
Wood Cellar Graphics, 378
Wood Classics, 212, 218
Wood Concepts, 151, 216
Wood Factory, 177, 275, 277, 280
Wood Mill Box, 276

Wood N' Things Inc., 440
Wood Prairie Farm, 246
Wood Wand Putters, 260
Wood-Armfield Furniture Company, 216
Wood-Hu Kitchens Inc., 98
Wood-Knot Crafts, 56
Wood-Mizer, 313, 420
Wood-Mode Cabinets, 98
Wood-N-Crafts Inc., 152
Wood-Ply Lumber Corporation, 315
Woodard (Thomas K.) American Antiques & Quilts 379
Woodbine House, 93
Woodbury Blacksmith & Forge Company, 268
Woodbury Pewterers Inc., 257
Woodbury Products Inc., 290
Woodcraft, 416
Woodcraft Supply, 420, 440
Woodcrafters, 420, 440
Woodcrafts & Supplies, 440
Woodcrest Ltd., 71
Wooden Boat Shop, 72, 78
Wooden Nickel Architectural Antiques, 277
Wooden Porch Books, 93
Wooden Soldier, 118, 120
Wooden Spoon, 303
WoodenBoat Books, 72, 79, 93
Woodenplay, 364
Woodhaven, 420
Woodhaven Army Surplus & Military Collectibles, 322, 408
Woodhouse Antique Flooring, 315
Woodhouse Post & Beam Inc., 283
Woodland Books, 93
Woodland Scenics, 331
Woodland Woolworks, 397
Woodlanders Inc., 246
Woodmaster Tools, 420
Woodmere Camera Inc., 361
Woods (Sylvia) Harp Center 93, 111, 340
Wood's Cider Mill, 196, 201
Woods Company, 315
Woods Electronics Inc., 358
Woods of the World & Fossils, 374, 376
Woods of the World Inc., 166
Woods of Windsor, 148
Woods Wise Callmasters, 289
WoodsEdge Wools, 442
Woodset Inc., 364, 424
Woodside Gardens, 235, 239
Woodsmith, 440
Woodstock Soapstone Company Inc., 406
Woodstone Company, 275, 282
Woodstream Corporation, 288
Woodwind & the Brasswind, 340
Woodworkers' Discount Books & Videos, 93, 430
Woodworker's Dream, 315
Woodworker's Emporium, 268
Woodworker's Hardware, 268, 440
Woodworkers' Paradise, 315
Woodworkers Source, 315
Woodworkers' Store, 268, 280, 420, 438, 440
Woodworks Unlimited, 151
Woodwright Design Company, 386
Wool Connection, 442
Wool Room, 397, 442
Woolery, 93, 342, 397
Wooley (Pamela) Bears 61
Wooley Bugger Entomology Company, 382
Woolgathering, 342, 384, 442
Woolrich, 288
Wooly Knits, 342, 384, 442
Worden (H.L.) Company 401

Worden Brothers, 144
WordPerfect, 144
WorkAbles for Women, 125, 128, 381
Workman Publishing Company Inc., 93
Workshop Records, 340
Workshops of David T. Smith, 117, 216, 308, 311
World Around Songs Inc., 337
World Book Educational Products, 144
World Book Family Catalog, 423
World of Aquatics, 352
World of Chantilly, 188, 191, 195
World of Cycles, 333
World of Golf, 261
World of Golf Equipment, 261
World of Leisure Manufacturing Company, 68, 409
World of Plenty, 366
World Power Technologies Inc., 396
World Software Corporation, 144
World Trade Video, 100
World Traders, 387
World Upholstery & Trim, 49
World Variety Produce Inc., 206
World Wildlife Fund Catalog, 80, 257
Worldly Bear Company, 61
Worldwide Aquatics, 125
Worldwide Collectibles & Gifts, 257
Worldwide Engineering Inc., 22, 436
Worldwide Games, 423, 424
Worldwide Home Health Center Inc., 126, 270, 346
Worldwide Outfitters, 381
Worldwide Slides, 361
Worldwide Thai-Forschner, 191
Worldwide Treasure Bureau, 7
Worldwide Wallcoverings & Blinds Inc., 154, 281
Worm's Way, 222
Worthington Distribution, 5, 272
Worthington Silks, 158
Wow - Bow Distributors Ltd., 351
Wright (Carol) Gifts 257
Wright-Line, 134, 145
Wright's Rock Shop, 312, 376
Write Stuff Syndicate Inc., 93, 98
Write Touch, 257, 402
WritePro, 144
Writer's Digest Books, 93
Writewell Company, 257, 319, 366
Writewell Company Inc., 344, 402
Wurlitzer Digital, 133
Wyatt-Quarles Seed Company, 242
Wyco Props, 52
Wynnewood Pharmacy, 148
Wyoming River Raiders, 102, 105, 181, 373
Wyoming State Archives, 250
Wyoming State Library, 250

X

Xandi Electronics, 168, 427
XANTÉ Corporation, 133
Xi Compound Bows & Accessories, 9
XK's Unlimited, 35
Xuron Corporation, 329

Y

Yaesu USA, 372
Yakima, 22
Yakima Bait Company, 181
Yamaha, 47, 403, 404, 405, 426
Yamaha Corporation of America, 340
Yamaha Motor Corporation, 5, 295, 432
Yamaha Music Corporation, 340

Yamaha Outdoor Power Equipment Division, 227
Yamaha Parts Warehouse, 333
Yamaha Sporting Goods Division, 260, 392, 413
Yankee Barn Catalog, 258
Yankee Catalog, 258
Yankee Environmental Systems Inc., 396
Yankee Ingenuity, 119
Yankee Pride, 62, 380
Yankee Wallpaper & Blind Mart, 154, 281
Yarn Barn, 93, 397, 442
Yarn Basket, 442
Yarn Gallery, 442
Yarn Shop, 342
Yarn-It-All, 304, 442
Yashica Inc., 356
Yasutomo & Company, 11
Yazaki-VDO, 79
Yazoo Manufacturing Company, 226
YAZOO Mills Inc., 345
Ye Olde Sweet Shoppe Bakery, 183, 185
Year One Inc., 25, 27, 28, 29, 31, 33, 34, 35, 37, 39, 40
Yedid (Meir) Magic 316
Yellow Turtle, 120, 391
Yentl's Secrets, 346
Yesterday, 336, 343
Yesterday's Paper & Thimbleberry Antiques, 347
Yestershades, 311
Yesteryear Toys & Books Inc., 329
YFX/Information by FAX, 433
Yield House, 158, 212, 281
YLI Corporation, 174, 442
YMAA Publication Center, 93, 319, 430
Yoders Country Market, 195
Yoga Journal's Book & Tape Source, 93
Yoga Mats, 443
Yoga Pro Products, 443
Yoga Props, 443
Yoga Togs, 128, 443
Yoga Training Props, 443
Yogaware, 443
Yonex Corporation, 52, 260, 413
York Archery, 9
York Bee Company, 64
York Interiors Inc., 380
York Leather Collection of Hickory, 216
York Spiral Stairs, 278
Yorktowne Wallpaper, 281
Yost (E.H.) & Company 58, 372
Young (Kit) Sportscards 399
Young (Paula) Wigs 436
Young Pecans, 188, 200
Your Exceptional Home, 258
Your Logo Inc., 349
Your Old Friends Doll Shop, 166
Your Stencil Source, 403
Yowler & Shepp Stencils, 403
Yozie Molds Inc., 114
YZ Enterprises Inc., 185, 191

Z

Z Custom Leathers, 331
Z Products, 390
Z-RAM, 137
Zabar's & Company, 130, 183, 195, 289, 303
Zachariasen Studio, 71, 209, 223
Zadoka Pottery, 293
Zagros Software, 168
Zaki Oriental Rugs, 380
Zaks Company, 51
Zambelli Internationale, 177
Zaskar Bicycles, 66
Zaslow's Fine Collectibles, 363, 364
Zebest Racquet & Golf Sports, 413
Zeb's Salvage, 25
Zed Books, 93
Zedcor Publishing, 144
Zeh (Stephen), Basketmaker 56
Zeidler (J.R.) 340
Zeigler Brothers Inc., 354
Zeiss Optical Inc., 70
Zembillas Sponge Company Inc., 114
Zen Home Stitchery, 443
Zenith, 426
Zenith Aircraft Company, 2
Zenith Books, 93, 98
Zenith Data Systems, 135
Zeos International Ltd., 135
Zephyr Press, 93
Zephyr Services, 17
Zeta Music, 340
Zeug's K-F Parts, 35
ZIA Cosmetics, 148
Zielbauer, 130
ZIFFCO, 393
Zimmerman Handcrafts, 97, 151, 158
Zim's, 152
Zingerman's Delicatessen, 195
ZIP Business Cards, 97
Zip Products, 30
Zipperware, 145
Zodiac of North America Inflatable Boats, 75
Zomeworks Corporation, 396
Zon International Publishing Company, 93, 107
Zondervan DirectSource, 94
Zone VI Studios Inc., 357, 358, 361
Zoysia Farm Nurseries, 234
Zucker's Fine Gifts, 153, 258, 364, 390
Zuni Craftsmen Cooperative Association, 292
Zygmunt & Associates, 130, 302
ZZ Corporation, 105
Zzip Designs, 67

SUBJECT INDEX

A

Aerobics. See Exercise clothing
African violets, 228
Air compressors, 1
Air conditioners, 1
Air purifiers, 1
Aircraft, 1-4
    avionics equipment, 3
    gyroplanes, 2
    hang gliders, 3-4
    helicopters, 2
    kits for making, 1-2
    model, 323-25
    parts and tools, 4
    pilot supplies, 4
    recovery systems, 3
Alarm systems, 5. See also Smoke detectors; Surveillance & personal protection equipment
Albums, photo, 354-55
All-terrain vehicles, 5
Ammunition, 262
Amplifiers. See Square dancing; Stereos
Answering machines, 411
Antennas. See Radios; Satellite TV equipment
Antiques and reproductions, 5-7. See also Memorabilia
Apple cider, 183
Appliances, 7-8. See also Coffee & espresso makers; Food processors; Ice-cream machines
Appliques, 8
Aquariums. See Tropical fish supplies
Aquatic plants, 228
Archery, 8-9
Archival supplies, 131, 361-62
Art supplies, 9-12. See also Block printing; Calligraphy; Craft supplies; China painting & metal enameling; Drafting supplies; Engraving & etching; Fabric painting; Rubber stamps; Silk-screening; Stencils; Tole & decorative painting
Arthritis aids, 12
Arts & crafts, Indian, 290-94
Artwork, 12-16. See also Wall hangings
Astrology, 16
Astronomy, 16-19. See also Meteorites
Astrophotography, 16
Attache cases, 313-14
Audio cassettes, 94, 107-11
Autographs, 19. See also Paper collectibles
Automobiles
    batteries and chargers, 21
    books about, 21-22
    carriers & racks, 22
    electricity conversion, 22
    exhaust systems & mufflers, 22
    glass for, 22
    headlights, 22
    license plates, 22
    locks & keys, 22
    model, 325-26
    parts for all makes, 23-25
    parts for specific makes, 25-43
    plating, 43
    radar detectors, 43-44
    radiators, 44
    radio repair, 23
    ramps & lifts, 44
    replica & conversion kits, 44-45
    rubber parts, 45
    seat & body covers, 45-46
    seats, 46
    security systems, 47
    steering wheels, 46
    stereos, 46-47
    tires, 47
    tools, 47
    upholstery & carpets, 49
    wheels, 49
Automotive art & gifts, 21
Avionics equipment, 3
Awards & trophies, 50
Awnings, 50
Azaleas, 228

B

Baby care, 50-51. See also Bears; Birth announcements; Clothing; Safety & emergency equipment; Toys
Backpacking, 100-05. See also Camping; Compasses
Badges, 51
Badminton, 51-52
Ballet barres, 154
Balloons, 52
Balls. See names of specific sports
Bamboo, 229
Banana plants, 229
Banks, 52
Banners. See Flags; Signs & sign-making
Barbecue grills, 52-53
Barometers. See Weather forecasting
Baseball & softball, 53-54
Baseball cards. See Sports cards
Basketball, 54-55
Baskets, 55. See also County crafts; Wheat weaving
Bathroom fixtures, 56-57. See also Cabinets; Hot tubs
Bathroom scales, 57
Batteries & chargers, 57-58
Bead crafting, 58-59
Bear making, 60
Bears, 60-61
Bedding, 61-63. See also Quilts
Beds, 211-12
Beekeeping, 63-64
Beer cans & steins, 64
Beer making, 437
Begonias, 229
Belly dancing, 64
Belts, 126
Berry plants, 229
Bible. See Books: religious
Bicycles & accessories, 64-67
Billiards, 67-68
Binding, book, 80
Binoculars, 68-70
Biodegradable products, 373
Bird feeders & houses, 70-71
Bird supplies, 349-50
Birth announcements, 71
Blacksmithing, 71
Blind, products for the, 430
Blinds & window shades, 153-54
Block printing, 71
Boats & boating. See also Hovercraft; Jet skis; Sail boards; Water skiing
    apparel, 71
    boat-building kits, 72
    books about, 79
    canoes & kayaks, 72-74
    general supplies & equipment, 76-78
    inflatable boats, 74-75
    instruments & electronics, 78-79
    miscellaneous boats, 75
    rowing boats, 76
    safety gear, 71
    sailboats, 76
Boccie, 79
Bonsai, 230
Book repair, 80
Book search services, 80
Bookkeeping supplies, 80
Bookmarks, 80
Bookplates, 80
Books. See also Autographs; Comic books
    automotive, 21-22
    bargain, 80
    children's, 80-81
    general, 81-93
    large-print & braille, 93
    music, 337
    nautical, 79
    on tape, 94
    photography, 355
    religious, 93-94
    used, 94
Boomerangs, 94-95
Boots. See Shoes & boots
Bow hunting, 8-9
Bowling, 95
Boxing, 95-96
Braille equipment. See Vision impairment aids
Bread making, 96
Breads & rolls, 183
Bridal fashions, 119
Bridge, 96
Briefcases, 313-14
Brushes, 96
Bulletin & Chalkboards, 96
Bumper stickers, 96
Burglar alarms. See Alarm systems
Business cards, 96-97
Business supplies. See Office & business supplies
Butterchurns, 97
Butterflies, 97
Buttons, 51. See also Pins; Political memorabilia; Sewing

❖ SUBJECT INDEX ❖

C

Cabinets, 97-98
Cable TV equipment, 427
Cacti, 231
Cake decorating, 106
Cakes & cookies, 184-85
Calculators, 98
Calendars, 98
Calligraphy, 98-99
Camcorders, 99-100
Cameras. See Photography; Camcorders
Camping, 100-05. See also Backpacking; Compasses; Safety & emergency equipment
Candles & candle making, 105-06
Candy, 185-88. See also Dietetic foods; Fundraising
Candy making, 106
Canes, 106
Canning & preserving, 106-07
Canoes, 72-74
Card cases, 96-97
Cards. See also Birth announcements
   business, 96-97
   collectible, 397-99
   greeting, 261-62
Carnival supplies, 107
Carnivorous plants, 231
Carousel figures & art, 107
Carpeting
   automobile, 49
   home, 378-80
Carriers,
   car-mounted, 22
   pet, 352
Carts, garden, 219
Carving, 439-40
Cassette players. See Stereos
Cassettes, 107-11. See also Books on tape
Cat care supplies, 350-51
Cave exploration, 396
Caviar, 188
CB radios, 372-73
CDs, 107-11, 400
Ceilings, 273
Ceramic supplies, 111-14
Chair caning, 114
Chandeliers, 307-08
Checks, 114
Cheerleading, 114
Cheese, 188-89
Cheese making, 114-15
Chess, 115
Children's products. See also Baby care; Bears; Dolls; Toys
   books, 80-81
   clothing, 119-20
   furniture, 212
   gifts, 250
   recordings, 107
China painting & metal enameling, 115
China, pottery & stoneware, 115-17
Chippers & shredders, 219-20
Chocolates. See Candy; Fundraising
Choir gowns, 117
Christmas decorations & ornaments, 117-18
Chrysanthemums, 231
Church supplies, 118
Cigar store indians, 118
Cigars, 415
Clamps, 17, 416
Clay, modeling, 11-12
Clocks & clock making, 118-19
Closets, 119

Clothing. See also Hats; Shoes & boots
   baseball & softball, 53
   basketball, 54
   bicycling, 66
   bowling, 95
   boxing, 95-96
   bridal fashions, 119
   camping and backpacking, 100-05
   cheerleading, 114
   children's, 119-20
   dancing, 154-55
   exercise, 120
   football, 208-09
   full-figured women's, 120-21
   golf, 258-59
   hockey, 273
   hunting, 287-88
   lingerie and underwear, 51, 120-21
   maternity, 51, 122
   men's & women's, 122-25
   natural fiber, 125
   petite fashions, 125-26
   racquetball & squash, 369
   running & walking, 380
   shirts, 126
   short men's, 126
   ski wear, 392
   soccer, 394
   special-needs, 126
   square dancing, 399-400
   suspenders, belts & buckles, 126
   T-shirts & sweatshirts, 127-28
   tall & big men's, 127
   tall women's, 127
   tennis, 411
   track & field sports, 424
   volleyball, 431
   western clothing, 128-29
   women's, 122-25
Clown supplies, 129-30
Coats. See Clothing
Coffee, 206-07
Coffee & espresso makers, 130
Coin-operated machines, 130
Comforters, 61-62
Comic books, 131
Compact disks, 107-11
Compasses, 131
Computers & accessories. See also Software
   components & peripherals, 131-33
   dust covers, 133
   education and training, 133
   furniture, 134
   manufacturers of, 134-35
   retailers of, 135-37
   supplies, 145-46
Construction materials. See Home building & improvement; Lumber
Cookie cutters, 146
Cookies, 184-85
Cookware, 302-03
Copiers, 146
Cosmetics & skin care, 146-48
Costumes & vintage clothing, 148-49
Country crafts, 149-51
Craft supplies, 151-52
Cribs. See Baby care; Furniture: children's
Cricket, 152
Croquet, 152
Cross-stitch. See Needle crafts
Crystal & glassware, 152-53
Cupolas, 274
Curtains, 153-54

D

Daffodils, 232
Dahlias, 232
Dancing, 154-56
Darkroom equipment, 356-57
Darts, 156
Daylilies, 237-38
Decals, 156
Decorative items, 157-58. See also Artwork; Arts & crafts: Indian; Carousel figures; Christmas decorations; Clocks; Country crafts; Figurines; Gifts
Decoupage, 158
Decoys. See Fishing
Department stores, 158. See also Gifts
Diabetic supplies, 158-59
Diapers. See Baby care
Dietetic foods, 206
Disabled, products for the
   canes & walkers, 106
   clothing, 126
   health care supplies, 271-72
   hearing & communication aids, 272-73
   incontinence supplies, 289-90
   lift chairs, 216
   stairlifts, 401
   toys & games, 424
   vision impairment aids, 430
   wheelchairs, 435-36
Discount merchandise. See Surplus merchandise
Dishwashers. See Appliances
Display fixtures, 159-60
Dog care supplies, 350-51
Doll making, 163-64
Dollhouses & miniatures, 160-63
Dolls, 164-66
Door chimes, 274
Doors, 274-75
Drafting supplies, 166
Drapes, 154
Dumbwaiters, 166
Dyes, 171

E

Easels. See Art supplies
Egg crafting, 166
Electric generators, 166
Electrical supplies, 166
Electronic toys & games, 423
Electronics equipment, 167
Electroplating, 169
Emblems, 156
Embroidery. See Needle crafts
Energy conservation. See Solar & wind energy
Engraving & etching, 169-70
Enlargers, photo, 357
Environmentally safe products, 373
Escape ladders, 175
Exercise clothing, 120
Exercise equipment, 170-71. See also Trampolines
Exposure meters, 357

F

Fabric painting, 171
Fabrics, 171-73
Fans, 174
Farm equipment, 220
Faucets & plumbing fixtures, 174
Fax machines, 146
Feathers, 174

❖ SUBJECT INDEX ❖

Fences, 175. See also Kennels
Fencing (sport), 175
Ferns, 232
Fertilizers, 220
Figurines. See Porcelain collectibles; Toys, character
Film, camera, 357
Films, 336-37. See also Video cassettes
Fire alarms. See Alarm systems; Smoke detectors; Sprinkler systems
Fire extinguishers, 176
Fire safety, 175-76
Firefighting, 175
Fireplaces, 176-77
Fireworks, 177
First aid, 381
Fish, tropical, 351-52
Fishing, 178-81
Flags & flag poles, 181-82
Flash units, 357-58
Flatware, 389-90
Flooring, 275-76. See also Tile & linoleum
Flower pots, 224
Flowers, dried & artificial, 182. See also Plants & seeds; Potpourri
Fly-tying, 178-81
Foil crafts, 182
Food processors, 183
Foods, 183-207. See also specific types of foods; Vitamins & nutritional supplements; Vinegar making
Football, 209-09
Fossils, 373-74
Fountains, 209
Frames, picture, 209-10
Frames & beams, 276
Freeze-dried food, 105
Fruits, 191-92
Fund-raising, 210. See also Personalized & promotional products; Tickets
Furnaces, 211
Furniture. See also Slipcovers & upholstery; Wood finishing & restoring
    beds, 211-12
    children's, 212
    computer, 134
    kits, 212
    home, 212-16
    lift chairs, 216
    office, 217
    outdoor, 217-18
    wicker, 218

G

Game calls, lures & scents, 289
Games. See Toys & games
Garage doors & openers, 218-19
Gardening equipment & supplies. See also Plants & seeds
    beneficial insects, 219
    carts, 219
    chippers & shredders, 219-20
    farm equipment, 220
    fertilizers, 220
    greenhouses, 220-21
    hydroponics, 221-22
    indoor gardening, 222
    landscaping stone, 222
    lawn ornaments & statues, 222-23
    markers, 223
    mowers, trimmers, blowers, 223
    organic, 224
    pots & planters, 224
    software, 225
    soil testing, 225
    tillers, 225
    tools & sprayers, 225-26
    topiary frames & supplies, 227
    tractors, 227
    water gardening, 227
    watering & irrigation, 227
Gates, 175
Gazebos, 246-47
Gems. See Jewelry making; Rocks & minerals
Genealogy, 247-50
General merchandise, 250-58
Geraniums, 232
Gift wrap. See Greeting cards; Stationery
Gifts. See also Decorative items
    children's, 250-51
    gourmet foods, 192-95
    miscellaneous, 251-58
    religious, 258
Gingerbread houses, 195
Ginseng, 233
Gladioli, 233
Glass collectibles, 258
Glassware, 152-53
Gliders. See Aircraft
Globes, 258
Go karts, 248
Goggles, 392
Golf, 258-61
Gourds, 233
Grapevines, 233
Grasses & ground covers, 233-34
Greenhouses, 220-21
Greeting cards, 261-62. See also Birth announcements
Grills, barbeque, 53-54
Guitars. See Musical instruments
Guns, 262-66
Gymnastics, 266
Gyroplanes, 2

H

Ham radios, 370-72
Hammocks, 266
Handbags. See Purses
Handball, 267
Handguns. See Guns
Handicapped. See Disabled
Hang gliders, 3-4
Hardware, 267
Harmonicas, 268
Hats, 268-70
Health care supplies & aids, 269-72. See also Diabetic supplies; Ostomy supplies
Health foods, 195-96
Hearing & communication aids, 272
Heat exchangers, 273
Heating systems, 211. See also Solar & wind energy
Helicopters. See Gyroplanes
Helmets
    bicycle, 64
    football, 208
    motorcycle, 331-32
    pilot's, 4
Herb plants, 234-35
Hiking sticks, 106
Hockey, field, 273
Hockey, ice, 273
Holsters, 263
Home building & improvement
    ceilings, 273
    cupolas, 274
    door chimes, 274
    doors, 274-75
    flooring, 275-76
    frames & beams, 276
    lamps & lighting, 307-12
    lumber, 314-15
    paint, 276
    paneling, 276
    radiator enclosures, 370
    restoration materials, 276-77
    roofing materials, 277
    salvaged building materials, 277
    shutters, 278
    siding, 278
    solariums, 396
    stairways, 278
    stucco, 278
    switch plates, 279
    tile & linoleum, 279
    trim & ornamental woodwork, 279-80
    wallcoverings, 280-81
    window coverings & screens, 281
    windows, 282
Home security systems. See Alarm systems
Homes & prefabs, 282-84
Honey, 200
Horse & stable equipment, 284-85. See also Rodeo equipment
Horseshoes, 286
Hosiery. See Clothing: lingerie & underwear
Hostas, 235
Hot tubs & saunas, 286
Hot water heaters, 286
Houseplants, 235-36
Housewares, 286. See also Country crafts; China; Cookware; Flatware
Hovercraft, 286
Hoyas, 236
Hubcaps, 49
Humidifiers, 286
Hunting, 287-89. See also Archery; Decoys; Guns & ammunition; Knives
Hydrangeas, 236
Hydroponics, 221-22

I

Ice climbing, 333-34. See also Camping; Safety & emergency equipment
Ice cream machines, 289
Ice skating, 289. See also Hockey, ice
Incense, 289
Incontinence supplies, 289-90
Ink pads. See Rubber stamps
In-line skates, 376
Insects, beneficial, 219
Intercoms, 294
Invitations. See Greeting cards; Wedding invitations
Irises, 237-38
Irrigation equipment, 227
Ivies, 236

J

Jacuzzis. See Hot tubs
Jams & jellies, 200
Jet skis, 295
Jewelry, 295-97
Jewelry making, 297-301. See also Bead crafting; Metal crafting; Rocks & minerals; Wire crafting
Jogging, 380
Jokes & novelties, 301
Judo. See Martial arts
Juggling, 301
Jukeboxes, 130, 301-02

K

Kaleidoscopes, 302
Karate. See Martial arts
Kayaks, 72-74
Kennels & enclosures, 352
Keyboards. See Computers; Musical instruments
Keys, automotive, 22
Kilns. See Ceramic supplies; China painting
Kitchen utensils & cookware, 302-03. See also Housewares
Kites, 303-04
Knapsacks. See Backpacking
Knickknacks. See Decorative items; Gifts
Knitting, 304-05. See also Yarn & spinning fiber
Knives, 305-06. See also Camping & backpacking

L

Laboratory equipment, 306-07
Lace, 173-74
Lacrosse, 307
Ladders, 175, 307
Lamp shades, 311
Lamps & lighting, 307-12. See also Stage equipment
Landscaping stone, 222
Language translators, 312
Lanterns. See Camping & backpacking
Latch hooking. See Needle crafts
Lawn care. See Fertilizers; Grasses & ground covers; Lawn mowers
Lawn mowers, 223
Lawn ornaments, 222-23
Leather crafts, 312
Left-handed merchandise, 261, 312-13
License plates, 22
Lift chairs, 216
Lifts, 44, 435
Lilacs, 236
Linens. See Bedding; Pillows; Tablecloths; Towels
Lingerie, 51, 120-21
Locks. See Alarm systems
Locks, automotive, 22
Log splitters, 313
Looms, 396-97
Lotions. See Cosmetics & skin care
Luggage, 313-14. See also Trunk repair
Lumber, 314-15

M

Macrame, 315
Magazines, 342-43. See also Comic books
Magic tricks, 315. See also Jokes & novelties
Magnets, 316
Magnifying glasses, 316
Mailboxes, 316
Mailing lists, 317
Make-up, theatrical, 412-14. See also Cosmetics
Mantels, 177
Maple syrup, 196
Maps, 317-18
Marbles, 318
Marigolds, 236
Marionettes, 368
Martial arts, 318-19
Masks, dust protection, 381
Massage, salon & spa equipment, 319
Matchbook covers, 319
Maternity clothing, 51, 122

Meats, 196-99
Memorabilia. See also Paper collectibles
    miscellaneous, 319
    military, 321-23
    movie & theatrical, 334-36
    political, 364
Men's clothing. See Clothing
Metal crafting, 319-20
Metal detectors, 320-21
Metal enameling, 115
Meteorites, 374
Meteorology. See Weather forecasting
Microscopes, 321
Microwave ovens. See Appliances
Military memorabilia, 321-23
Miniatures, 420-21
Mirrors, 323
Modeling supplies, 11-12
Models
    aircraft, 323-25
    armor & military, 325
    automobiles, 325-27
    dioramas, 327
    paper airplanes, 327
    radio control equipment, 327
    rockets, 327
    ships, 328
    steam-operated, 328
    supplies, hardware & plans, 329
    tools, 329
    trains, 330-31
Motorcycles & motor bikes, 331-33
Mountain & ice climbing, 333-34. See also Camping; Safety & emergency equipment
Movie & theatrical memorabilia, 334-36
Movie & TV scripts, 336
Movie projection equipment, 336
Movies (films), 336-37. See also Video cassettes
Mowers, 223
Mufflers, 22
Museum catalogs. See Gifts: miscellaneous
Mushrooms, 236
Music books & sheet music, 337
Music boxes, 337
Music, dance, 155
Musical instruments, 337-40. See also Harmonicas

N

Nameplates, 340
Native American arts & crafts, 290-94
Necklaces. See Jewelry
Needlecrafts, 340-42
Newspapers & magazines, 342-43
Notions, sewing, 382-84
Nurseries, plant, 236
Nursing supplies, 51
Nuts, 199-200

O

Observatories, 16
Office & business supplies. See also Bulletin & chalkboards; Calculators; Checks; Computers; Recycled products; Rubber stamps; Stationery
    business forms & booklets, 343
    general office supplies, 343-44
    labels & tags, 344
    receipt books, 344-45
    shipping supplies, 345
Orchids, 236-37

Organic gardening, 224
Origami, 345
Ornaments, Christmas, 117
Ostomy supplies, 345-46

P

Paddleball, 346
Pagers, 346
Paint, house, 276. See also Art supplies; Automobiles; Tole & decorative painting
Paintings, 12-15
Palms, 237
Paneling, 276
Paper. See Art supplies; Computers: supplies; Stationery
Paper collectibles, 346-47. See also Autographs; Movie & Theatrical Memorabilia; Postcards
Paper crafting & sculpting, 347
Paperweights, 347
Parachutes, 3
Party decorations, 347. See also Pinatas
Patio covers, 50
Patios & walkways, 347
Patterns. See Knitting; Sewing; Woodworking
Pedometers, 380
Pens & pencils, 347-48. See also Art supplies; Calligraphy
Peonies, 237-38
Perennials, 238-39
Perfume. See Cosmetics
Perfumery supplies, 338-49
Personal watercraft, 295
Personalized & promotional products, 349
Pest control, 349
Petrified wood, 376
Pets
    bird supplies, 349-50
    carriers, 352
    dog & cat supplies, 350-51
    kennels & enclosures, 352
    pet doors, 353
    reptiles, 353-54
    tropical fish supplies, 351-52
Phone cards, 354
Phonographs, 354
Photo processing, 358-59
Photo restoration, 359
Photography. See also Astrophotography; Frames, picture
    albums & photo mounts, 354-55
    backgrounds, 355
    bags & camera cases, 355
    books, 355
    camera manufacturers, 356
    darkroom equipment, 356-57
    enlargers, 357
    exposure meters, 357
    film, 357
    filters, 357
    flash units & lighting, 357-58
    photo processing, 358-59
    photo restoration, 359
    retail stores, 359-61
    slides, 361
    storage & filing systems, 361-62
    tripods, 362
    underwater photography, 362
Picture frames, 209-10
Pillows, 62-63
Pinatas, 362
Pinball machines. See Coin-operated machines
Pine cones, 362

❖ SUBJECT INDEX ❖

Ping pong. See Table tennis
Pins, 362-63. See also Buttons
Pipes, tobacco, 415
Pistols. See Guns
Planetariums, 16
Plants & seeds, 228-46. See also Specific types of plants
Plaques. See Awards; Nameplates; Signs & sign making
Plastics, 363
Plates. See China
Plates, collectible, 363
Platform tennis, 363
Playground equipment, 363
Plays, 414
Plumbing fixtures. See Bathroom fixtures; Faucets & plumbing fixtures
Political memorabilia, 364
Popcorn, 200
Porcelain collectibles, 364
Postcards, 364-66
Posters, 12-15. See also Movie & theatrical memorabilia
Potpourri, 366
Pots & planters, 224
Pottery, 115-17
Pottery supplies, 111-14
Preserves, fruit, 200-201
Printing presses, 366
Prospecting, 366-68. See also Metal detectors
Protection equipment, 408
Puppets & marionettes, 368
Purses, 368
Puzzles, 368-69

Q

Quilts & quilting, 369

R

Racks
    car-mounted, 22
    gun, 263-64
Racquetball, 369-70
Radar detectors, 43-44
Radiator enclosures, 370
Radio control equipment, 327
Radios. See also Appliances; Stereos
    amateur, 370-72
    antique, 372
    citizen band, 372-73
Radon testing, 373
Rafting, 373. See also Boats & boating
Ramps & lifts, 44, 435
Receipt books, 344-45
Recipe management software, 207
Records, cassettes & CDs, 107-11, 400. See also Books on tape
Recreational vehicles, 47
Recycled products, 373
Refrigerators. See Appliances
Religious gifts, 258
Remote control equipment, 5
Reptiles, 353-54
Restoration materials (home), 276-77
Restoration services
    antiques, 5-6
    photographs, 359
Ribbon, 173-74
Rifles. See Guns
Rock gardens, 239
Rock hounding, 366-68. See also Rocks & minerals
Rockets, model, 327

Rocks & minerals, 373-76. See also Rock hounding
Rodeo equipment, 376. See also Horse & stable equipment
Roller blades & skates, 376
Roofing materials, 277
Roses, 240
Rowing boats, 76
Rubber stamps, 376-78
Rug making, 378
Rugby, 378
Rugs & carpets, 378-80. See also Arts & crafts, Indian
Running, jogging & walking, 380

S

Saddles, 285
Safes, 381
Safety & emergency equipment, 381
Sailboards, 381
Sailboats, 76
Salt-free foods, 201
Salvaged building materials, 277
Sandpaper, 440
Satellite TV equipment, 427
Saunas, 286
Scales, bathroom, 57
Science kits & equipment, 381-82. See also Electronics equipment; Magnets; Microscopes; Telescopes; Weather forecasting
Scooters, 382
Scopes, gun, 264
Scouting, 382
Scripts, movie & TV, 336. See also Plays
Scuba, 392-93
Sculptures, 15-16
Seafood, 201-03
Seashells, 382
Seasonings, 203-06
Security systems. See Alarm systems
Seeds & bulbs, 240-42
Self-defense products, 381, 408
Septic tanks, 382
Sewing. See also Emblems; Fabrics; Lace
    dress forms, 382
    notions & supplies, 382-84
    patterns & kits, 384-85
    sewing machines & sergers, 385
    stuffing & fill, 385
    tags & labels, 385-86
Sheds, 386
Shipping supplies, 345
Ships, model, 328
Shirts, 126. See also T-shirts
Shoes and boots. See also Skiing; Snowshoes; Camping & backpacking
    dancing, 155-56
    men's & women's, 386-87
    running, jogging & walking, 380
    western, 387-88
Shrubs, 242-43
Shuffleboard, 388
Shutters, 278
Siding, 278
Sights, gun, 264
Signs & sign-making, 388-89
Silk-screening, 389
Silver & flatware, 389-90
Silversmithing, 319-20
Skateboards, 390
Skates. See Hockey, ice; Ice skating; Roller blades & skates
Skiing, 390-92

Skin care products, 146-48
Skin diving, 392-93
Skydiving equipment, 3
Sleds, snowboards & toboggans, 393
Sleeping bags. See Camping & backpacking
Slides. See Playground equipment
Slipcovers & upholstery, 393. See also Fabrics
Slot machines. See Coin-operated machines
Smoke detectors, 176
Snow blowers, 393
Snowboards, 393
Snowdomes, 301
Snowmobiles, 393
Snowshoes, 393
Soap. See Cosmetics
Soap making, 393-94
Soccer, 394-95
Software
    astronomy, 16
    cooking & recipe management, 207
    gardening, 225
    health management, 270
    knitting design, 305
    public domain & shareware, 137-38
    publishers of, 138-44
    religious, 93-94
    retailers of, 144-45
Soil testing, 225
Solar & wind energy, 395-96
Solariums & sun rooms, 396
Souvenirs, 396. See also Postcards
Spa equipment, 319
Speakers, 405
Special-needs clothing, 126
Special-needs toys, 424
Speleology, 396
Spices. See Seasonings
Spinning wheels & looms, 396-97
Sports cards, 398-99
Sports equipment & clothing. See Badminton; Baseball & softball; Basketball; Bicycling; Bowling; Boxing; Cricket; Croquet; Fencing; Football; Golf; Handball; Hockey; Lacrosse; Paddleball; Platform tennis; Racquetball; Rugby; Squash; Skateboards; Skiing; Soccer; Surfboards; Table tennis; Tennis; Tetherball; Track & field sports; Volleyball; Water skiing; Wrestling
Sprinkler systems, 176
Square dancing, 399-400
Squash (sport), 369-70
Stage equipment, 414
Stained glass crafting, 400-01
Stairlifts, 401
Stairways, 278
Stamps, rubber, 376-78
Stationery, 401-02. See also Office and business supplies
Statuary, 15, 222-23
Steam-operated models, 328
Stencils, 402
Stereos & CD players, 403-05
Stickers, 405
Stock car racing, 405
Stockings. See Clothing: lingerie & underwear
Stone sculpting & carving, 406
Stones, landscaping, 222
Stoneware, 115-17
Stopwatches, 380
Storage chest repair, 425
Storage systems, 111, 119, 361-62, 405
Stoves, 406. See also Appliances
Stucco, 278
Stuffed animals. See Bears; Toy making; Toys: general toys & games

SUBJECT INDEX

Stuffing & fill, 385
Sugar-free foods, 206
Sun rooms, 396
Sundials, 406-07
Sunglasses & eye wear, 407
Surfboards, 407
Surplus & liquidation merchandise, 407-08
Surveillance equipment, 408. See also Alarms
Survival equipment, 381
Suspenders, 126
Sweaters, 126-27
Sweatshirts, 127-28
Swimming pools, 408-09. See also Toys: water toys
Swings, 266. See also Playground equipment
Switch plates, 279
Synagogue supplies, 118

T

T-shirts, 127-28
Table tennis, 409
Tablecloths & pads, 409
Tapestries, 409
Targets, 265-66. See also Archery
Tattooing, 409-10
Taxidermy, 410
Tea, 206-07
Teddy bears. See Bears
Telephones, 410-11. See also Phone cards; Surveillance equipment
Telescopes, 17-19
Tennis, 411
Tennis, platform, 363
Tennis, table, 409
Tents. See Camping & backpacking
Term papers, 413
Terrariums, 243
Tetherball, 413
Theatrical supplies, 413-14. See also Scripts
Thermometers, 414. See also Weather forecasting
Thermostats, 1
Thimbles, 414
Tickets, 414-15. See also Fund-raising
Tile & linoleum, 279
Tillers, 225
Tires, 47
Tobacco, pipes & cigars, 415
Toboggans, 393
Toiletries. See Cosmetics & skin care
Tole & decorative painting, 415-16
Tools
    for aircraft, 4
    for automobiles, 47
    for electronics, 169
    for engraving & etching, 169-70
    for gardening, 225-26
    for model building, 329
    for woodworking, 439-40
    general purpose, 416-20
    sandpaper, 440
    welding & foundry, 420, 435
Topiary, 227
Toupees. See Wigs
Towels, 420
Toy making, 420. See also Bear making; Doll making; Doll houses
Toy soldiers, 420-21
Toys
    bears, 60-61
    character toys, 421-22
    chess, 115
    dollhouses, 160-63
    dolls, 164-66
    educational, 422-23
    electronic toys & games, 423
    general toys & games, 423-24
    kaleidoscopes, 302
    kites, 303-04
    marbles, 318
    models, 323-30
    puzzles, 368
    special-needs toys, 424
    water toys, 424
Track & field sports, 424-25
Tractors, 227
Trailers, 47, 284-85
Trains, model, 330-31
Trampolines, 425
Trap shooting, 266
Trees, 243-45
Tricycles, 67
Trim & ornamental woodwork, 279-80
Tripods, 362
Trophies, 50
Tropical fish supplies, 351-52
Truck parts, 48
Trunk repair, 425
TVs & VCRs, 425-27
Typewriters & word processors, 427-28

U

Ultraviolet light, 312
Umbrellas, 428
Underwear, 51, 120-21
Uniforms, 128. See also Military memorabilia
Uniforms, sports. See Clothing
Upholstery, 49, 393
Utensils. See Kitchen utensils; Silver & flatware

V

Vacuum cleaners, 428
VCRs, 425-27
Vegetable plants, 245
Vegetables, 191-92
Vending machines. See Coin-operated machines
Ventriloquism, 315
Video cameras. See Camcorders
Video cassettes, tapes & discs
    firefighting, 175
    miscellaneous, 428-30
    square dancing, 400
Video editing equipment, 100
Video games. See Electronic toys & games
Vinegar making, 437
Vines, 236
Vision impairment aids, 430
Vitamins & nutritional supplements, 430-31
Volleyball, 431

W

Walkers, 106
Walking, 380
Wall coverings, 280-81
Wall hangings, 409
Wallets, 368. See also Card cases
Washing machines. See Appliances
Watches. See Jewelry
Water gardening, 227. See also Aquatic plants
Water purifiers, 431-32
Water skiing, 432
Watering & irrigation, 227
Weather forecasting, 433
Weather vanes, 433-34
Wedding gowns, 119
Wedding invitations & accessories, 434
Weight training. See Exercise equipment
Welding & foundry equipment, 420, 435
Wells, 435
Western clothing, 128-29, 387-88
Wet suits. See Skin diving; Water skiing
Wheat weaving, 435
Wheelchairs, 435
Wheels, 49
Whitewater running, 373
Wigs, 436
Wildflowers, 246
Wind chimes, 436
Wind energy, 395-96
Window coverings, 281
Window shades, 153-54
Windows, 282
Wine & beer making, 437
Wine cellars & racks, 437-38
Wines, 438
Wire crafting, 438
Women's clothing. See Clothing
Wood finishing & restoring, 438
Woodworking, 439-40. See also Lumber
Word processors, 427-28. See also Computers
Wrestling, 440
Yard care. See Lawn care
Yarn & spinning fibers, 440-42

Y

Yoga, 442-43

Z

Zippers. See Sewing: notions

NOTES

NOTES